Webster's New World Thesaurus

prepared by
Charlton Laird

updated by
William D. Lutz

WEBSTER'S NEW WORLD
New York

WEBSTER'S NEW WORLD

Simon & Schuster, Inc.
Gulf+Western Building
One Gulf+Western Plaza
New York, NY 10023

Dictionary Editorial Offices:
New World Dictionaries
850 Euclid Avenue
Cleveland, Ohio 44114

DISTRIBUTED BY PRENTICE HALL TRADE

Manufactured in the United States of America

6 7 8 9 10

Library of Congress Cataloging in Publication Data

Laird, Charlton Grant, 1901–
Webster's New World thesaurus.

1. English language—Synonyms and antonyms.
I. Lutz, William. II. Title.
PE1591.L27 1985 423′.1 85–14286
ISBN 0–671–60437–6 (indexed)
ISBN 0–671–60738–3 (plain)
ISBN 0–13–947151–0 (leathercraft)

FOREWORD

This book is intended to help writers and speakers in search of a better way to say what they want to. Traditionally, such a need was to be served by supplying a synonym. Within limits, this is sound auctorial practice, to cultivate choice of words and to replace words hastily or ineptly chosen with words more precise, more vigorous, better suited to the tone of a composition, or in some other way appropriate, but as a comprehensive statement of what to do about words it can now be seen to be both misleading and inadequate.

Strictly speaking, there are no synonyms, since by definition synonyms are words having the same meaning. But no two words are identical or even so nearly identical that we could lose either without loss to the language. If we think of meaning as the total impact of a word upon a reader or hearer, every word can do something that no other word could do. *Gun,* as either a sound or a sequence of three letters, can do more and less than can *cannon, howitzer, rifle,* or *revolver,* all of which are likely to appear in a list of synonyms for *gun.* Words assumed to be synonyms can refer to different objects, make varying observations about these objects, and stir different sorts of pictures and emotions in users of the langauge. If some industrious person, for whom we might coin the genus *cartolexicographer,* were to make maps of the meanings of words, we should find that no two of these maps could be imposed one upon the other so that the lower would be completely concealed, while the upper did not project at any point. Thus, if this volume were only a book of synonyms, strictly speaking there would be nothing to put into it, and if one wished to be quite literal he could reduce it to unobtrusive pocket size by imitating the celebrated chapter of Giraldus Cambrensis on the nonexistent snakes of Ireland, and write, "SYNONYMS. Chapter One: There are no synonyms. THE END."

And if there are no synonyms, how can there be antonyms, although antonyms have traditionally found a place in books on words? If no two words can be entirely alike, we should scarcely expect to find a collection of words precisely opposite to other words. *Down* as a direction is roughly opposite to *up* as a direction, but in no sense is it an antonym to the value of *up* in phrases like *grow up* or *double up,* in *drink it up* as against *drink it down.* And many words by their very nature can have no antonym. If *gun* has no precise synonym, still less does it have an antonym; even *no-gun* would not be an exact antonym, if there were such a word. One recalls that charming line in one of Edwin Ford Piper's poems, "What is the opposite of unless?" Obviously, there is no opposite of *unless,* although the question has found its way into some crudely constructed true-false examinations.

But if there are neither synonyms nor antonyms, there are other ways of speaking and writing, better or worse ways of expressing oneself. And here we are at the core of using language. Of course language is not only vocabulary; it is also grammar, phonetics, and rhetoric, along with some other studies, but those subjects are at least partly out of the realm of this book. Nonetheless, although devices like grammar and vocabulary must be employed simultaneously in any use of the language, something can be gained by studying each in itself. Word books can be tools to aid this study and practice, and over the centuries several sorts of such volumes have been developed, although developing them has required more centuries and more inspired editors than most users of such books suppose.

The first were glossaries, followed some four hundred years ago by printed dictionaries of what were called hard words. By the eighteenth century, lexicographers like Nathaniel Bailey and Samuel Johnson were preparing relatively comprehensive dictionaries based on citations, and Thomas Sheridan was improving means of representing pronunciation. In the next century the editors of the *Oxford English Dictionary,* also called *A New English Dictionary on Historical Principles,* endeavored to reflect the whole history of a language, and now lexicographers are learning to utilize the findings of modern linguistics, making dictionaries descriptive rather than prescriptive, revealing usage through quotation, incorporating the findings of linguistic geography, and the like. Moreover, during the nineteenth century specialized word books were appearing, dictionaries of science and theology, of Americanisms, of slang, and works to discriminate synonyms, of which the most famous was that by George Crabb, *Dictionary of English Synonyms* (1816), now outmoded but long the standard work.

The history of the sort of book which has come to be called a thesaurus is both curious and revealing. *Thesaurus* is a Latin word meaning "treasury" or "storehouse of knowledge," and its specialization as the name of one sort of word book reflects the fancy of Peter Mark Roget (1779–1869), Swiss by ancestry and English by birth. He was a remarkable man, having a questing intellect which he employed with indefatigable devotion, and he lived to be ninety. By profession he was a surgeon and lecturer on medicine, the Fullerian Professor of Physiology at the Royal Institution. He was multifarious; at the request of the government he surveyed the water system of London and published a description; he wrote a two-volume study of phrenology, a standard work on electricity and galvanism, and another on *Animal and Vegetable Physiology.* He developed a slide rule, endeavored to perfect a mechanical calculator, devised the Roget spiral, useful in electrical experiments, and a pocket chessboard, presumably a boon to traveling intellectuals—he was an inveterate inventor of chess problems—and being an intellectual himself, as a lifetime hobby he tried to classify all actual and possible ideas, and to represent them in words. From this hobby, not from his multitudinous activities as surgeon, scientist, and inventor, the name *Roget* has become a household word on two continents.

If he did not actually start the project in jail, he probably used it to while away the hours when he was for a time a political prisoner in Geneva. He writes that by 1805, shortly after his return, he "had completed a classed catalogue of words on a small scale . . . conceiving that such a compilation might help to supply my own deficiencies." He continued his hobby, and late in life—he was then seventy-three—he published this personal treasure house of knowledge as *Thesaurus of English Words and Phrases Classified and Arranged so as to Facilitate the Expression of Ideas and Assist in Literary Composition* (1852). The volume was an immediate success, and was revised first by the author and later repeatedly by his son.

Actually, the book is difficult to use. For its purpose it must have been superb; endeavoring to discriminate synonyms can be a polisher of the mind and Roget's purpose was "to supply" what he modestly terms his own "deficiencies," and for that end his organization was excellent. The fact that he resolved the ideas of all mankind into an even thousand suggests, however, that he may have been intrigued by fancy more than ruled by objectivity. But for a practical aid in writing, his was obviously not the best of all possible organizations. Many a frustrated writer, seeking help in *Roget,* has found himself wandering in a maze where each turn of thought promises to produce the desired synonym, although none of them does. Doubtless various people endeavored to make *Roget* more usable, but the first to attract much attention in the United States was C. O. Sylvester Mawson, a fine scholar, an orientalist, who in 1911 enlarged the book and endeavored to recast it in dictionary form. Since then, others have attempted various sorts of reorganization, but the fact is that unless an editor abandons Roget, he still has an agglomeration of synonyms arranged for philosophical concepts, not for ready reference by a writer.

Had Roget set out to prepare a handy reference work, the history of thesaurus-writing would have been different. He had an extremely logical mind and a practical bent—he was a skillful writer of manuals and textbooks—and if he had undertaken to prepare a good reference work he would no doubt have done so, but it would have been a different sort of book. Roget was not trying to prepare a handbook for ready reference; he was publishing, as an aging intellectual, the results of his lifelong hobby of classifying ideas by assorting words in his "storehouse of knowledge," for that is what *thesaurus* meant when he adopted it and incidentally gave it a new use. Only after half a century, apparently, did it occur to him that his hobby might have utilitarian application, "to facilitate the expression of ideas." Seemingly, no one was more surprised than he that the result of his hobby ministered to a deeply felt need, and although he was doubtless pleased, one can scarcely blame him if, in the deep autumn of life, he was not moved to embark upon a great new work of a different nature. Meanwhile, such has been the reputation of *Roget* as a handbook that the volume has provided at least part of the pattern for almost any subsequent reference work intended to suggest a fugitive synonym; it tended to inhibit fresh thinking on the whole subject of synonymy.

One result has been that although many editors have asked themselves what a dictionary should be, few seem seriously to have raised the question of what a thesaurus should be, a thesaurus in the sense of a handbook for writing, which has long since become the dominant sense of the word. Most editors since Roget who have edited a thesaurus have been, like Mawson, editors of dictionaries before they became editors of synonym books. They apparently assumed that if a thesaurus is not like *Roget,* it is rather like a dictionary, and have not troubled themselves with fundamental questions about the genus of the work they were preparing, or if they did, the evidence does not appear in the resulting volumes.

Had Mawson asked himself objectively what a thesaurus should be, he would have arrived at an answer more revolutionary than the assumption he apparently accepted, that a thesaurus should be *Roget* reorganized to resemble a dictionary. First, he would have started with a different philosophy; he would have seen at once that in some ways a thesaurus, far from being like a dictionary, is essentially different. When a user turns to a dictionary he already has the word he wants, but he knows less about it than he wishes to know. The word may be new to him, and he needs to know its meaning in order to understand something he has read or heard. Or, if he knows the word, he is uncertain of its meaning, its connotations, its spelling, its pronunciation, its etymology, or something of the sort. When a user turns to a thesaurus, however, he has a word, but for some reason he does not want to use it. He expects to rely on this word he has rejected only as a means to finding the locution he wants to use, which presumably he will recognize once it is suggested to him. If he does not feel sufficiently familiar with the proposed substitute he will then turn back to his dictionary for more information,

information he will not expect to find in a thesaurus. A dictionary and a thesaurus are companion volumes because of their differences, not because of their similarities. The two sorts of books, then, are so fundamentally different that one can scarcely expect that the philosophy of one will provide adequate principles for the other.

If we are to have good reference books, however, we must ask fundamental questions, questions like the following: What is a thesaurus? Who uses it? What is it good for? How should it be made? If one asks such questions he is likely to get answers like the following:

1. A thesaurus is a practical book. It is not concerned with classifying words as though they were botanical specimens. It is intended to give a writer or speaker specific help which he feels he needs.

2. The user of the book is not concerned with synonyms as such. He has thought of a way to say something. For reasons of his own he does not wish to say it that way; he has used a word *ad nauseam* and he wants a different locution, or he has thought of a word which is too general, or inexact, in bad taste, even vulgar. He wants suggestions of other ways in which he can attempt to say what he means.

3. A thesaurus should be developed to satisfy the needs of the user, not to elucidate the nature of synonymy; it should rest upon the mental processes of the prospective user when he is a speaker or writer; it should not reflect the needs of the same person when he is a reader or hearer. Accordingly, the editor of such a work, faced with an entry, should ask himself, "When the speaker or writer rejects this word, what word or combination of words is he likely to want?"

These principles, put into practice, produce a book quite different from Roget's, and different, also, from books prepared in part as though they are dictionaries. Consider the word list. The entries in a large reference dictionary should approach a half million words, providing more than two million discriminated senses. A literate reader may encounter any of at least that many semantic senses in current and recent English. Most good desk dictionaries enter a hundred thousand to a hundred-fifty thousand, or somewhat more. Most of these will be borrowed words, some of them specialized words, *colloquium* rather than *talk, acculturation* rather than *learning.* But a thesaurus needs no such entries in its word list. A thesaurus needs to enter a locution only if it is the kind of word or phrase that people recall readily. Nobody is troubled because he can think of no synonym for *fanfaron* or *latitant.* Most people have never heard of these words, and if they can think of *fanfaron* they will have no trouble calling up *boaster, braggart, bully,* and a dozen others. If they know *latitant* they will surely know *dormant, quiet, in repose,* and many more. The words that come to people's minds, and send them to a thesaurus, are common words, the words that leap readily to the tongue, but are not always appropriate; they are familiar words, general words, even slang and vulgar expressions. Someone might think, "It was a swell joint all right, but I didn't dig the deal they were rapping about." This is vivid expression, and under some circumstances appropriate, but if the speaker or writer does not wish to use such diction on the occasion, he may be unable to think of the words he does want to use. Accordingly, a thesaurus should enter words like *swell, joint, dig, deal,* and *rap,* even in their slang uses, not *fanfaron* and *latitant*—even though these last may on occasion be useful as synonyms. That is, if possible, a thesaurus should be organized on the basis of the commonest words in the language, whatever their standing in respectability, the words that most readily occur to a user of the book.

This principle has not usually been recognized. It was enunciated in the introduction to the previous edition of the present volume, issued under the title *Laird's Promptory*

(New York, 1948); the observation may have been made before, but if so it had not been the guiding principle recognized in the preparation of thesaurus entry lists, and although it has been sometimes applied since then, it has not always been followed as it might be. Words like those mentioned above, *fanfaron, latitant,* and many others too rare to be useful, can still be found as entries in synonym books. A recently published volume, which treats *fanfaron* as a main entry, provides for the verb *take* a brief, undifferentiated list comprising two inches of type, no cross references, and no phrasal combinations. But *take* is one of the most common words; the editors of the present volume found they had to recognize twenty-eight uses of the word as verb, along with over ninety phrasal uses, leading to more than a hundred cross references and thousands of synonyms. The entry for *fanfaron* might well have been sacrificed for phrases like *take in, take on, take off,* and *take up,* for each of which the present volume recognizes five different senses. Another recent volume devotes more than a third of a column to *latitant,* a consumption of book paper and printing which would surely be a good candidate for the most nearly useless entry of all time, since nobody is ever likely to consult it naturally, and the book carries no cross references to it.

In preparing the entry list for the present volume, the editors asked themselves which bodies of synonymic expressions are sufficiently common so that they belong in a general reference work, and how these can best be organized. They concluded that there are about 50,000 such semantic areas in Modern English, and that with limited use of cross references these could be brought together under some 30,000 entries, which ideally would be the 30,000 most common words as English is used in the United States. Fortunately, during the editing, a new linguistic tool for checking word frequencies became available. A body of American writing known as the Standard Corpus of the Present-Day American English had been assembled at Brown University, comprising more than a million words. This corpus has been studied by computer and the results published in Henry Kučera and W. Nelson Francis, *Computational Analysis of Present-Day American English* (Providence, R. I., 1967). The book was invaluable for checking, especially when its results were combined with studies of dialectal and other non-standard English. Both in preparing the entry list and in developing synonymies, the editors have been aware that Roget and some of his followers have tended to neglect phrases, compounds, verb sets, and the like, although such phrases are characteristic of Modern American English. In the present volume phrasal constructions have been given particular attention.

Another principle, enunciated in the first edition of this book, recognizes that specific equivalents often provide better alternatives than do synonyms. Every good writer knows that often composition can be strengthened by replacing general words with concrete, specific terms. Many specific terms have few if any synonyms, and of course no antonyms. Roget must have understood this aspect of language, but since he was classifying synonyms, not much trying to help writers, he ignored such terms. He did not include the word *muscle,* for example, which has no synonym in its anatomical sense, and Mawson did not add it. The editors of a recent thesaurus were content to supply a dictionary definition of the word, but if there are no synonyms for *muscle,* there are many kinds and sorts of muscles, the biceps, the triceps, the intercostal muscles—even the heart and tongue are muscles. Similarly, although good synonyms for *ear* and *eye* in their anatomical senses are almost nonexistent, there are phrases, and sometimes a part can be used instead of the whole, *retina* or *pupil* for *eye.* These are only two of the many ways in which a thesaurus becomes a different sort of book if the editor, instead of asking, "What are the synonyms of this word?"

poses himself the problem, "What is the user of this book likely to want to know when he picks it up?"

Many editions of the vintage *Roget,* and some of its modern adaptations, carry a section titled something like "How to Use This Book." Presumably the present volume needs no set of special instructions, since it can be used like any other alphabetical reference work. Words are in strict alphabetical order, and uses are numbered under words. Much has been done to make the book fast to work with; usually the commonest of a set of synonyms carries the main entry; uses of a word are arranged roughly by frequency of use, from common to uncommon, and the same sequence is maintained within the synonymies. The reference *see also* is used to direct the reader to lists of synonyms that reflect related meanings for a given word. The *see also* reference thus suggests to the user additional meanings of the word which might warrant consideration in the search for a synonym. Phrases are difficult to delimit, but they have mostly been entered under the first word and under a headword within the phrase, if there is one. The less common words, treated mainly as cross references to a main entry, carry also three of the most common synonyms, on the theory that most users most of the time will not need to search further; if a user needs to use a cross reference, prefaced by *see,* he will presumably need only one, and it will carry him to the specific use designated by number, not merely to the entry word. Abbreviations are few and generally familiar; we have used *mod.* for both *adjective* and *adverb,* since the same form can appear in both adjectival and adverbial structures, and many locutions, especially phrases, cannot be readily distinguished, if at all.

A few observations may be useful. No effort has been made to define words adequately, since definition is the function of a dictionary, not of a thesaurus, and a set of synonyms and antonyms in themselves provides one of the best sorts of definition; the skeleton definitions are intended only to distinguish uses of words and phrases from one another. As has been suggested earlier, there are no synonyms in any exact sense; we have used the term—abbreviated *Syn.*—very loosely, not to suggest words having the same meaning, but words or phrases that can be used in a sentence in place of the entry word. To conserve space, antonyms have been greatly curtailed from the first edition, but in most instances at least the first antonym has been starred to suggest that it is a main entry, and hence can be used for a cross reference to many antonyms.

One convention, so far as we know unique with this book, may warrant explanation. All makers of wordbooks are plagued by the problem of usage and usage labels. Most users of such books want some help with usage, but usage, the relative respectability of a locution, is extremely complex, too subtle to be well-handled by usage labels. Designations like *slang, colloquial,* and *vulgar* are so loose that nobody can define them exactly, and even if we can agree that a word or phrase is slang, it may not long remain so. *Teenage* was formerly labeled slang in most dictionaries, whereas it is now commonly entered without reservation, but *teenager* is accepted in some dictionaries but not in others. *Man* is certainly standard English in most uses, but is probably not in "Man! Was he traveling!" although one can think of exclamatory uses which could scarcely be called into account. Thus, we have despaired of applying usage labels in a consistent and reliable way, and in any event, a thesaurus has no more business using its space to describe usage than to define meaning. Accordingly, we have used the symbol (D) rather freely, meaning by it that there may be a problem of *diction* involved, and that if the user is not aware of this danger, he had best consult a *dictionary,* preferably a dictionary of usage, or a general dictionary which provides quotations calculated to reveal usage or provides comments on non-standard usages.

Thus a prospective user of this book should be neither surprised nor perturbed if he finds it different from other synonym books with which he is familiar. Some aberrations will reflect lapses or downright error; no complex reference work has ever been brought to fruition without blunders, and an editor can only hope that his inadequacies have not been too numerous or too glaring, and solace himself with the ancient proverb that even Homer occasionally nodded. The main difference between this and other synonym books, however, will arise from the fact that it embodies principles and practices not so extensively represented in any other volume as yet in print.

It remains to thank my staff for their devotion during the years of preparation that have gone into the manuscript of this book. Special mention should be made of Professor William Lutz, Wisconsin State University, who brought a perceptive mind and broad background in language study to the discrimination of senses recognized in main entries, and of Mrs. Meredith A. Hoffman, whose editorial acumen has left its imprint throughout the book. I am grateful, also, to World Publishing for establishing a fellowship, at the University of Nevada, Reno Campus, which, while concerned with pure science, has provided background for the solving of practical editorial problems. I wish also to thank Mr. David Guralnik, editor of *Webster's New World Dictionary of the American Language,* Second College Edition, for making galleys of that work available to us during our editing; these galleys were useful in many ways, but especially to suggest recently developed uses of old words and phrases now growing in popularity.

Charlton Laird, University of Nevada
May, 1970.

This edition of WEBSTER'S NEW WORLD THESAURUS is an updating of the solid work originally edited by Charlton Laird. Every attempt has been made to correct whatever lapses inadvertently occurred during the preparation of the first edition, and to bring the book up to date by listing new words and new uses of old words which have come into being since the publication of the first edition of this book. The present work contains over 300,000 references, with approximately 7,000 of those being new additions. I hope that among those additions the reader will find no errors, but should the reader discover any lapses, I will claim them as my own.

William D. Lutz, Rutgers University
July, 1985.

A

a, *mod.* and *prep.* **1.** [The indefinite article; before vowels, written *an*]—*Syn.* some, one, any, each, some kind of, some particular, any (one) of, a certain.—*Ant.* the*, this, that.
2. [An indication of frequency]—*Syn.* per, in *or* on a, each, every, to *or* by the, at the rate of.

aback, *mod.* —*Syn.* behind, to the rear, rearward; see **back, backward.**

abandon, *n.* —*Syn.* unrestraint, spontaneity, freedom, impetuosity, exuberance, uninhibitedness, spirit, verve, enthusiasm, dash, vigor, animation, élan.

abandon, *v.* **1.** [To relinquish]—*Syn.* leave (go *or* off), quit, withdraw (from), discontinue, give over *or* up, throw over *or* off, let go, cease, deliver (up), cast off *or* away *or* aside, discard, vacate, give away, part with, evacuate, surrender, yield, desist, concede, disclaim, renounce, break (with *or* off), emigrate (from), apostasize, abdicate, lose hope of, despair of, go back on, secede (from), cede, waive, demit, quitclaim, part with, forgo, back down from, forswear, quit of, lay down *or* aside, desist (from), dispose of, have done with; *all* (D): throw in the towel, hang up the fiddle, break the pattern *or* habit, break one's chains *or* fetters.
2. [To leave someone or something in trouble] —*Syn.* desert, forsake, ostracize, back out on, break (up) with, run away, discard, defect, reject, disown, cast off, liquidate, maroon, have done with, depart from, give over, throw overboard, jettison, leave behind, slip away from; *all* (D): stand up, leave in the lurch, turn one's back upon, run *or* walk out (on), fink (out on), take a powder, duck out, bolt, walk *or* skip out, double-cross, lay down on, leave flat, welsh (on), welsh out on, break squares with, bid a long farewell, leave in the cold, bundle off, let down, drop.—*Ant.* cherish*, uphold, protect.

abandoned, *mod.* **1.** [Left uninhabited or unsupported]—*Syn.* deserted, desolate, destitute, desperate, surrendered, empty, given up, unused, vacated, left, voided, neglected, relinquished, lonely, forsaken, solitary, hopeless, cast away *or* aside *or* off, forgotten, repudiated, derelict, shunned, adrift, at the mercy of the elements, forlorn, at the mercy of one's enemies, mournful, avoided, outcast, rejected, helpless, unfortunate, alone, lorn, discarded, demitted, scorned, lost, doomed, friendless, wretched, in the hands of fate, grounded, eliminated; *all* (D): in the wastebasket, thrown overboard, given back to the Indians, out on a limb, waiting at the church, left kicking, left in the lurch, left in the cold, left holding the bag. —*Ant.* inhabited*, used, in use.
2. [Having lost one's self-respect]—*Syn.* immoral, debased, degraded; see **wicked** 1.

abasement, *n.* —*Syn.* dishonor, deterioration, shame; see **disgrace.**

abate, *v.* **1.** [To make less]—*Syn.* reduce, lower, lighten; see **decrease** 2.
2. [To grow less]—*Syn.* lessen, decline, diminish; see **decrease** 1.

abatement, *n.* —*Syn.* lessening, decrease, decline; see **reduction** 1.

abbé, *n.* —*Syn.* friar, father, clergyman; see **minister** 1, **priest.**

abbey, *n.* —*Syn.* monastery, priory, friary; see **cloister.**

abbot, *n.* —*Syn.* prior, rector, archabbot, abbot-general, regular abbot, titular abbot, mitered abbot, cardinal abbot; see also **minister** 1.

abbreviate, *v.* —*Syn.* shorten, cut, condense, abridge; see **decrease** 2.

abbreviation, *n.* **1.** [An abbreviated form]—*Syn.* contraction, abridgment, sketch, précis, brief, compendium, abstract, epitome, synopsis, curtailment, reduction, abstraction, condensation, digest, résumé, outline, summary, syllabus, conspectus, elision, short form, condensed form, abbreviated version, initial.—*Ant.* addition*, expansion, enlargement.
2. [The act of abbreviating]—*Syn.* reducing, shortening, truncating, condensing, lessening, cutting (off *or* out *or* down), keeping down, restriction, constriction, removing from, taking out, truncation, reshaping, pruning, lopping off, paring (down), trimming, retrenchment, compression, foreshortening. —*Ant.* addition*, augmenting, expanding.

abdicate, *v.* —*Syn.* relinquish, give up, withdraw; see **abandon** 1, **resign** 2.

abdomen, *n.* —*Syn.* stomach, midsection, belly, paunch, epigastrium, belly cavity, venter, visceral cavity, ventral region, bowels, intestines, viscera, epigastric *or* hypogastric *or* umbilical regions, entrails; *all* (D): insides, gut, guts, breadbasket, bay window, tummy, pot, pot belly, middle.

abdominal, *mod.* —*Syn.* ventral, visceral, alvine, uterine, coeliac, gastric, gastronomic, stomachic, duodenal, in the solar plexus; *both* (D): belly, inside.

abduct, *v.* —*Syn.* rape, seize, carry off; see **kidnap.**

Abe, *n.* —*Syn.* Lincoln, Abraham Lincoln, Honest Abe, the Great Emancipator, savior of his country, the greatest American, the log cabin President (D).

aberrant, *mod.* —*Syn.* erroneous, devious, strange; see **wrong** 2.

aberration, *n.* **1.** [Deviation]—*Syn.* irregularity, lapse, wandering; see **difference** 2.

2. [Abnormality]—*Syn.* strangeness, peculiarity, disorder; see **characteristic, irregularity** 2.

abet, *v.* **1.** [To help]—*Syn.* assist, befriend, encourage; see **help** 1.
2. [To excite]—*Syn.* inspire, encourage, entreat; see **urge** 2.

abhor, *v.*—*Syn.* detest, abominate, loathe; see **hate** 1.

abhorrence, *n.*—*Syn.* dislike, distaste, aversion; see **hatred** 1.

abhorrent, *mod.*—*Syn.* disgusting, shocking, revolting; see **offensive** 2.

abide, *v.* **1.** [To lodge]—*Syn.* stay (at), room, sojourn; see **dwell, lodge.**
2. [To reside]—*Syn.* tenant, inhabit, settle; see **dwell.**
3. [To remain]—*Syn.* continue, keep on, persevere; see **endure** 1.
4. [To wait for]—*Syn.* expect, anticipate, be in readiness (for); see **wait** 1.
5. [To submit to]—*Syn.* put up with, bear (with), withstand; see **endure** 2.

abide by, *v.* **1.** [To adhere to]—*Syn.* follow, observe, comply with; see **follow** 2.
2. [To accept]—*Syn.* submit *or* consent *or* defer (to), acknowledge, concede; see **agree to.**

abiding, *mod.*—*Syn.* enduring, lasting, tenacious; see **permanent** 2.

ability, *n.* **1.** [Capacity to act]—*Syn.* aptitude, intelligence, innate qualities, powers, potency, worth, talent, gift, genius, flair, mind for, ingenuity, bent, strength, understanding, faculty, comprehension; *all* (D): makings, sense, what it takes, the stuff, the right stuff, brains, knack, hang, head.—*Ant.* inability*, ineptitude, awkwardness.
2. [Power that results from capacity]—*Syn.* capability, eligibility, competence, proficiency, adeptness, qualification(s), knowledge, strength, sufficiency, self-sufficiency, efficacy, expertise, tact, finish, technique, craft, skill, artistry, cunning, expertness, skillfulness, aptness, dexterity, facility, finesse, mastery, quickness, cleverness, deftness, handiness, experience, readiness, adroitness, artifice, energy, background; *all* (D): know-how, savvy, touch, the goods.—*Ant.* ignorance*, incompetence, inexperience.

ablaze, *mod.* **1.** [Burning]—*Syn.* blazing, lighted, aflame; see **burning** 1.
2. [Excited]—*Syn.* intense, vehement, heated; see **excited.**

able, *mod.* **1.** [Fitted by innate capacity]—*Syn.* intelligent, ingenious, worthy, talented, gifted, equipped, fitted, capable, clever, suitable, smart, crafty, cunning, bright, knowing, apt, agile, adroit, dexterous, canny, endowed, deft, adept, handy, alert, adaptable, easy, effortless, smooth, facile, ready, versatile, equal to, suited (to), capacitated, well-rounded, mighty, athletic, physically qualified, powerful, strong, robust, sturdy, brawny, potent, stalwart, vigorous, courageous, at home in, nimble-fingered, fit for; *all* (D): sharp, cut out for, having an ear for.—*Ant.* stupid*, bungling, unadaptable.
2. [Fitted by proven capacity]—*Syn.* effective, capable, efficient, qualified, well-qualified, enterprising, masterly, masterful, accomplished, responsible, finished, clever, adequate, competent, artful, proficient, skillful, facile, trained, expert, ingenious, having the capability *or* capacity, workmanlike, inventive, determined, practiced, experienced, skilled, adept, dexterous, nimble-fingered, mature, conversant, *au fait* (French), versed, learned, prepared; *all* (D): smooth, all-around, slick, an old dog at, up on, cool, hot shot, up to snuff, on the ball, having an ear for, cut out for, equal to.—*Ant.* inexperienced*, inefficient, unskillful.

able-bodied, *mod.*—*Syn.* fit, powerful, sturdy; see **strong** 1.

abnormal, *mod.*—*Syn.* strange, irregular, unnatural; see **unusual** 2.

abnormality, *n.* **1.** [Irregularity]—*Syn.* peculiarity, singularity, malformation; see **irregularity** 2.
2. [Freak]—*Syn.* monstrosity, monster, rarity; see **freak** 2.

aboard, *mod.*—*Syn.* on board, on ship, shipped, loaded, on board ship, freight on board (F.O.B.), being shipped, en route, consigned, in the hold, in carriage, in transit, in the vessel, being transported, embarked, afloat, at sea, on deck, *en voyage* (French), traveling, at point of entry.—*Ant.* ashore*, disembarked, on land.

abode, *n.*—*Syn.* house, dwelling, residence; see **home** 1.

abolish, *v.*—*Syn.* suppress, eradicate, terminate, exterminate, obliterate, annul, remove, revoke, abrogate, end, finish, extirpate, nullify, set aside, annihilate, abate, supplant, repeal, subvert, reverse, rescind, prohibit, quash, extinguish, cancel, erase, disannul, root out, pull up, uproot, disestablish, demolish, invalidate, overturn, overthrow, make *or* declare null and void, do away with, stamp *or* crush out, undo, throw out, put an end to, supersede, rescind, deprive of force, vitiate, inhibit, make void, dispense with, set aside, vacate, repudiate, make an end of, ravage, cut out, batter down, raze, squelch, not leave one stone upon another (D); see also **destroy** 1.

abolition, *n.* **1.** [Annulment]—*Syn.* dissolution, rescinding, revocation; see **withdrawal.**
2. [Destruction]—*Syn.* annihilation, eradication, overthrow; see **destruction** 2.

A-bomb, *n.*—*Syn.* nuclear weapon, nuclear device, nuclear warhead; see **atom bomb.**

abominable, *mod.*—*Syn.* odious, loathsome, nauseating; see **offensive** 2.

abominate, *v.*—*Syn.* abhor, despise, loathe; see **hate** 1.

abomination, *n.* **1.** [Detestation]—*Syn.* aversion, loathing, repugnance; see **hatred.**
2. [Corruption]—*Syn.* contamination, decay, uncleanness; see **filth.**
3. [Wickedness]—*Syn.* wrong, crime, offense; see **wickedness.**
4. [Annoyance]—*Syn.* torment, bother, nuisance; see **difficulty** 1, **trouble** 2.

abort, *v.* **1.** [To fail]—*Syn.* miscarry, fall short, miss; see **fail** 1.
2. [To cancel]—*Syn.* nullify, annul, stop; see **cancel** 2.

abortion, *n.* **1.** [Expulsion of a fetus from the womb]—*Syn.* unnatural birth, arrested development, termination of pregnancy, miscarriage, premature

birth *or* labor *or* delivery, casting, aborting, untimely birth, forced birth.
2. [An aborted object]—*Syn.* abnormality, malformation, monstrosity; see **freak** 2.
3. [A failure]—*Syn.* fiasco, total loss, disaster; see **failure** 1.

abortive, *mod.* —*Syn.* vain, failing, fruitless; see **futile** 1.

abound, *v.* —*Syn.* overflow, swell, be plentiful; see **teem.**

abounding, *mod.* —*Syn.* teeming, flowing, overflowing; see **plentiful** 2.

about, *mod.* and *prep.* **1.** [Approximately]—*Syn.* roughly, nearly, in general; see **approximately.**
2. [Concerning]—*Syn.* regarding, anent, respecting, touching, of, on, in relation to, relative *or* relating to, as regards, in *or* with regard to, on *or* in which, with *or* in respect to, in the matter of, in *or* with reference to, referring to, as concerns, so far as (something) is concerned, in connection with, connected *or* concerned with, dealing with, thereunto, *in re* (Latin), thereby, hereof, wherein, touching upon, with a view toward, as to *or* for, concerning.
3. [Around]—*Syn.* surrounding, round about, on all sides; see **around** 1.
4. [Active]—*Syn.* astir, in motion, alert; see **active** 2.

about to (D), *mod.* and *prep.* —*Syn.* not quite, on the verge of, at the point of, just about, *circa* (Latin); see also **almost.**

above, *mod.* and *prep.* **1.** [High in position]—*Syn.* over, high, higher, superior, beyond, on high, raised, above one's head, in a higher place, aloft, into the firmament, overhead, in the celestial heights, in excelsis, toward the sky.—*Ant.* low, below*, beneath.
2. [Referring to something earlier]—*Syn.* before, foregoing, earlier; see **preceding.**
3. [Higher]—*Syn.* larger than, more advanced than, greater than; see **higher.**
4. [Directly over]—*Syn.* just over, overhead, up from; see **over** 1.

above, *n.* —*Syn.* firmament, sky, heights; see **heaven** 1.

above all, *mod.* —*Syn.* in the first place, chiefly, especially; see **principally.**

aboveboard, *mod.* **1.** [In a candid manner]—*Syn.* candidly, honestly, frankly; see **openly** 1.
2. [Characterized by being candid]—*Syn.* honest, open, straightforward; see **frank.**

above par, *mod.* —*Syn.* higher, more advanced, superior; see **excellent.**

above reproach, *mod.* —*Syn.* blameless, flawless, impeccable; see **innocent** 1, 4, **perfect** 2.

abrasive, *mod.* **1.** —*Syn.* grinding, sharpening, cutting; see **rough** 1.
2. —*Syn.* irritating, annoying, caustic; see **disturbing.**

abrasive, *n.* —*Syn.* sharpener, cutter, grinder, grindstone, scarifier, polisher, grater, rasp, file, quern, millstone, sander, sharpening stone, whetstone, brush.
Types of abrasives include the following—grindstone, stone, wheel, file, sandstone, whetstone, pumice, carborundum, corundum, emery, oil stone, scouring powder, chalk, French chalk, salt, sand, dust, sandpaper, emery cloth.

abreast, *mod.* —*Syn.* level, equal, side by side, abeam of, against, off, stem to stem, bow to bow, over against, on a line with, opposite, by the side of, alongside, beside, in one line, in alignment, shoulder to shoulder, in line, salt and pepper (D).

abridge, *v.* —*Syn.* digest, condense, compress, shorten; see **decrease** 2.

abridgment, *n.* **1.** [The act of reducing or shortening]—*Syn.* shortening, reducing, cutting; see **abbreviation** 2.
2. [A record which has been reduced]—*Syn.* digest, précis, abstract; see **summary.**

abroad, *mod.* —*Syn.* away, at large, adrift, wandering, elsewhere, overseas, traveling, touring, outside, at some remove, afar off, distant, in a foreign land, in foreign parts, far away, gone, out of the country, removed; *all* (D): over there, across the pond, on the Continent, beyond seas, on one's travels.—*Ant.* at home, here*, domestic.

abrogate, *v.* —*Syn.* revoke, repeal, annul; see **cancel** 2.

abrupt, *mod.* **1.** [*Said of things, usually landscape*] —*Syn.* steep, precipitate, sheer, precipitous, sudden, sharp, angular, craggy, unexpected, uneven, rough, rugged, irregular, jagged, perpendicular, straight up, straight down, without a break, vertical, headlong, zigzag, broken, uphill, downhill, falling, bluffy.—*Ant.* level*, flat, horizontal.
2. [*Said of people or acts of people*]—*Syn.* rough, blunt, short, terse, brusque, unceremonious, sudden, hasty, impetuous, uncivil, gruff, violent, impolite, curt, bluff, ungracious, rude, crude, uncomplaisant, downright, outspoken, direct, unexpected, to the point, matter-of-fact, discourteous, bold; *all* (D): hard, tough, hard-boiled.—*Ant.* polite*, ceremonious, gracious.

abscess, *n.* —*Syn.* ulcer, boil, canker; see **sore.**

abscond, *v.* —*Syn.* flee, steal off, slip away; see **escape.**

absence, *n.* **1.** [The state of being elsewhere] —*Syn.* truancy, anesthesia, nonattendance, nonappearance, nonresidence, inexistence, loss, vacancy; *all* (D): cut, hooky, sneak.—*Ant.* presence, appearance*, attendance.
2. [The state of lacking something]—*Syn.* deficiency, need, inadequacy; see **lack** 1.

absent, *mod.* —*Syn.* away, missing, elsewhere, otherwise, vanished, moved, removed, gone (out), flown, not at home, not present, out, wanting, lacking, nonattendant, abroad, lost, overseas, out of sight, nowhere to be found, on leave, astray, on vacation, *in absentia* (Latin), on tour, engaged elsewhere, taken; *all* (D): on French leave, AWOL, playing hooky, omitted, split.—*Ant.* here*, present, at home.

absentee, *mod.* —*Syn.* remote, absent, at a distance; see **away** 1.

absenteeism, *n.* —*Syn.* truancy, defection, sneaking out; see **desertion.**

absent-minded, *mod.* —*Syn.* preoccupied, abstracted, dreamy, napping, inadvertent, listless, lost, unmindful, absent, unheeding, heedless, thoughtless, oblivious, distrait, inattentive, daydreaming, unconscious, unaware, withdrawn, musing, removed, faraway, woolgathering, distracted, remote, forgetful; *all* (D): blank, nobody home, mooning, not all there, moony, in a brown study, (with one's head) in the clouds.—*Ant.* attentive, observant*, alert.

absolute, *mod.* **1.** [Without limitation]—*Syn.* total, complete, entire, infinite, unalloyed, fixed, settled, supreme, full, self-sufficing, unconditioned, unrestricted, unlimited, unconditional, unconstrained, unrestrained, unequivocal, independent, self-existent, unmixed, unqualified, without reserve, wholehearted, sheer, unstinted, unbounded, self-determined, pure, unmitigated, utter, unabridged, thorough, clean, outright, downright, thoroughgoing, ideal, inalienable, free, simple, perfect, full; *all* (D): hard and fast, blanket, all out, out-and-out; see also **comprehensive.**—*Ant.* restricted*, limited, qualified.

2. [Perfect]—*Syn.* pure, faultless, unblemished, untarnished; see **perfect** 2.

3. [Without limit in authority]—*Syn.* authoritarian, domineering, supreme, arbitrary, official, haughty, authoritative, suppressive, highhanded, autocratic, self-willed, tyrannous, tyrannical, fascist, fascistic, absolutistic, overbearing, czarist, nazi, totalitarian, communistic, inquisitorial, oppressive, undemocratic, antidemocratic, imperative, imperious, dogmatic, commanding, controlling, compelling, despotic, lordly, intimidating, fanatic, dictatorial, peremptory, arrogant, exacting, with an iron hand; *both* (D): like godalmighty, high and mighty. —*Ant.* lenient*, tolerant, temperate.

4. [Pure]—*Syn.* unadulterated, unmixed, unalloyed; see **pure** 1.

5. [Certain]—*Syn.* positive, unquestionable, undeniable; see **certain** 3.

absolutely, *mod.* **1.** [Completely]—*Syn.* utterly, unconditionally, thoroughly; see **completely.**

2. [Positively]—*Syn.* unquestionably, certainly, definitely; see **surely.**

absolve, *v.* —*Syn.* pardon, set free, clear; see **excuse.**

absorb, *v.* **1.** [To take in by absorption]—*Syn.* digest, suck *or* take *or* drink in *or* up, receive in, ingest, intercept, appropriate, ingurgitate, embody, use up, assimilate, osmose, blot, imbibe, swallow, consume, incorporate, sop *or* soak *or* sponge up, get by osmosis.—*Ant.* eject*, expel, discharge.

2. [To occupy completely]—*Syn.* engage, engross, employ; see **occupy** 3.

3. [To take in mentally]—*Syn.* grasp, learn, sense; see **understand** 1.

absorbed, *mod.* **1.** [Soaked up]—*Syn.* assimilated, taken in *or* up *or* into, swallowed up, consumed, lost, drunk, imbibed, dissolved, fused, united, vaporized, incorporated (into), amalgamated, interfused, impregnated into, digested. —*Ant.* removed*, unassimilated, unconsumed.

2. [Occupied mentally]—*Syn.* engrossed, intent, preoccupied; see **rapt** 2.

absorbent, *mod.* —*Syn.* porous, absorptive, spongy, permeable, dry, soft, pervious, pregnable, assimilative, imbibing, penetrable, receptive, retentive, spongiose, thirsty.—*Ant.* thick*, impervious, solid.

absorbing, *mod.* —*Syn.* engaging, exciting, enthralling; see **interesting.**

absorption, *n.* —*Syn.* assimilation, digestion, osmosis, saturation, conversion, impregnation, penetration, fusion, intake, union, engorgement, consumption, ingestion, blending, swallowing up, taking in, imbibing, reception, retention, incorporation, appropriation, merging, ingurgitation, engulfment, bibulation, drinking in, suction, sopping *or* soaking *or* drying *or* blotting *or* sponging up, inhalation. —*Ant.* removal*, ejection, discharge.

abstain, *v.* —*Syn.* abstain from, refrain, forbear, renounce, desist, withhold, avoid, stop, deny oneself (to), hold *or* keep aloof from, eschew, refuse, decline, spare, hold back, shun, evade, cease, dispense with, do without, fast, starve (oneself), teetotal, have nothing to do with, let (well enough) alone, do nothing, keep from, keep one's hands off, stay one's hand, refrain (voluntarily) from, withhold oneself from, restrain oneself, turn aside from, abjure; *all* (D): swear off, kick over, lay off, turn over a new leaf, have no hand in, look not upon the wine when it is red, take the pledge, get on the water wagon. —*Ant.* indulge, join*, gorge.

abstainer, *n.* —*Syn.* teetotaler, prohibitionist, abstinent, teetotalist, temperance advocate, puritan, blue-ribbonist, water-drinker, Calvinist, member of the WCTU; *all* (D): one who is on the wagon, bluenose, hydropot.

abstemious, *mod.* —*Syn.* abstinent, temperate, sober; see **moderate** 5.

abstemiousness, *n.* —*Syn.* sobriety, self-denial, abstinence; see **moderation** 1, **restraint** 1.

abstinence, *n.* —*Syn.* abstaining, abstention, abstemiousness, temperance, forbearance, denial, self-denial, self-control, self-restraint, continence, fasting, frugality, abnegation, renunciation, avoidance, sobriety, desistance, austerity, withholding, refraining, keeping aloof, nonindulgence, asceticism, moderation, soberness, chastity, Puritanism; *both* (D): blue-ribbonism, teetotalism.—*Ant.* indulgence*, over-indulgence, intemperance.

abstract, *mod.* **1.** [Theoretical]—*Syn.* general, intellectual, ideal; see **theoretical.**

2. [Abstruse]—*Syn.* complex, involved, obscure; see **difficult** 2.

abstract, *n.* **1.** [The essential portion]—*Syn.* synopsis, outline, résumé; see **summary.**

2. [A legal document]—*Syn.* brief, writ, deed, affidavit, summation, bill, claim, counterclaim, plea, declaration.

abstract, *v.* **1.** [To take away]—*Syn.* withdraw, separate, extract; see **remove** 1.

2. [To prepare an abstract]—*Syn.* digest, summarize, condense; see **decrease** 2.

abstracted, *mod.* **1.** [Removed]—*Syn.* apart, separated, disassociated; see **separated.**

2. [Absent-minded]—*Syn.* preoccupied, dreaming, absorbed; see **absent-minded.**

abstraction, *n.* **1.** [The state of being absorbed] —*Syn.* deliberation, absorption, preoccupation, speculation, absent-mindedness, musing, thinking, reflecting, rumination, reflection, self-communing, reverie, daydreaming, engrossment, cogitation, contemplation, brooding, brown study, cerebration, detachment, aloofness, distraction, consideration, pondering, remoteness, inattention.—*Ant.* alertness, awareness*, attention.

2. [A mental concept]—*Syn.* theory, idea, notion; see **thought** 2.

abstractive, *mod.* —*Syn.* epitomizing, condensing, summarizing, contracting.

abstruse, *mod.* —*Syn.* complex, involved, intricate; see **difficult** 2.

absurd, *mod.* **1.** [*Said of persons*]—*Syn.* old-fashioned, foolish, stupid; see **unusual** 2.

2. [*Said of ideas or human productions*]—*Syn.* preposterous, ridiculous, ludicrous; see **stupid** 1.

absurdity, *n.* —*Syn.* improbability, foolishness, senselessness; see **nonsense** 1, 2.

abundance, *n.* —*Syn.* bounty, copiousness, profusion; see **plenty.**

abundant, *mod.* **1.** [Copious]—*Syn.* sufficient, ample, copious; see **plentiful** 2.

2. [Plentiful]—*Syn.* abounding, prolific, lavish, fulsome; see **plentiful** 1.

abundantly, *mod.* —*Syn.* plentifully, lavishly, fulsomely, satisfactorily, richly, handsomely, in large measure, profusely, amply, sufficiently, copiously, generously, luxuriantly, affluently, inexhaustibly; *all* (D): many times over, to one's heart's content, on the fat of the land, so that one's cup runneth over.—*Ant.* meagerly, poorly*, meanly.

abuse, *n.* **1.** [Misuse]—*Syn.* perversion, misapplication, debasement, degradation, ill-usage, misemployment, desecration, misappropriation, profanation, mishandling, mismanagement, pollution, wrong *or* improper use, defilement, prostitution. —*Ant.* respect, care*, veneration.

2. [Insult]—*Syn.* offense, affront, outrage; see **insult.**

3. [Ill-treatment]—*Syn.* injury, mistreatment, damage, harm, hurt, maltreatment, ill-usage, outrage, impairment, wrong, injustice, violation, ignominy, malevolence.—*Ant.* help*, aid, benefit.

abuse, *v.* **1.** [To treat badly]—*Syn.* insult, injure, hurt, harm, damage, impair, aggrieve, offend, ill-treat, ill-use, misuse, misemploy, disparage, berate, maltreat, mistreat, wrong, persecute, molest, nag, victimize, oppress, ruin, mar, spoil, vulgarize, reproach, rail at, outrage, do wrong by *or* to, mishandle, pervert, profane, prostitute, desecrate, pollute, harass, manhandle, do an injustice to, overstrain, overwork, overtax, overdrive, overburden, violate, defile, impose upon, deprave, taint, debase, corrupt, squander, waste, dissipate, exhaust; *all* (D): do one's worst, do one an injustice, knock about. —*Ant.* defend*, protect, befriend.

2. [To hurt with words]—*Syn.* malign, libel, vilify; see **slander.**

abused, *mod.* —*Syn.* maltreated, hurt, reviled, wronged, injured, insulted, harmed, offended, ill-treated, ill-used, misused, disparaged, berated, persecuted, oppressed, exploited, mishandled, harassed, molested, victimized, manhandled, violated, debased.—*Ant.* praised*, admired, aided.

abusive, *mod.* —*Syn.* insolent, sarcastic, sharp-tongued; see **rude** 2.

abut, *v.* —*Syn.* border on, adjoin, be adjacent to; see **join** 3.

abysmal, *mod.* —*Syn.* profound, bottomless, unfathomable; see **deep** 1.

abyss, *n.* —*Syn.* gorge, pit, chasm; see **hole** 2.

academic, *mod.* **1.** [Referring to learned matters] —*Syn.* scholastic, erudite, scholarly; see **learned** 1, 2.

2. [Of philosophic interest, but having little practical importance]—*Syn.* formalistic, hypothetical, speculative; see **theoretical.**

academy, *n.* **1.** [A private institution, usually for secondary education]—*Syn.* preparatory school, boarding school, finishing school, private intermediate school, secondary school, military school *or* academy, Latin school, day school, seminary, institute, prep school (D).

2. [A learned society]—*Syn.* association, institute, league, fraternity, federation, alliance, foundation, council, society, institution, scientific body, association of literary men, circle, salon.

accede, *v.* —*Syn.* consent, comply, acquiesce; see **agree.**

accelerate, *v.* —*Syn.* quicken, stimulate, expedite; see **hasten** 2.

acceleration, *n.* —*Syn.* speeding up, hastening, increase of speed, dispatch, quickening, hurrying, expedition, stepping up, picking up speed.

accelerator, *n.* —*Syn.* atomic *or* particle accelerator, atom smasher.

Types of accelerators include the following—bevatron, cosmotron, cyclotron, electron accelerator, linear accelerator, positive-ion accelerator, synchrotron, synchrocyclotron.

accent, *n.* **1.** [Importance]—*Syn.* stress, weight, significance; see **importance** 1.

2. [Stress]—*Syn.* beat, stroke, emphasis, pitch, modulation, accentuation, inflection, intonation, rhythm, meter, cadence.

accent, *v.* —*Syn.* accentuate, stress, intensify; see **emphasize.**

accentuate, *v.* —*Syn.* stress, accent, strengthen; see **emphasize.**

accept, *v.* **1.** [To receive]—*Syn.* get, take, acquire; see **receive** 1.

2. [To assent]—*Syn.* admit, consent (to), acquiesce (in); see **agree to.**

3. [To believe]—*Syn.* hold, trust, affirm; see **believe.**

acceptable, *mod.* —*Syn.* satisfactory, agreeable, pleasing; see **pleasant** 2.

acceptance, *n.* **1.** [The act of accepting]—*Syn.* reception, taking, receiving; see **receipt** 1.

2. [An expression of acceptance]—*Syn.* recognition, assent, approval; see **agreement** 3.

accepted, *mod.* —*Syn.* taken, received, assumed, approved, adopted, recognized, endorsed, verified, acclaimed, welcomed, engaged, hired, claimed, delivered, used, employed, affirmed, upheld, authorized, preferred, acknowledged, accredited, allowed, settled, established, customary, sanctioned, unopposed, authentic, confirmed, time-honored, fashionable, favorably received, chosen, acceptable, popular, formally admitted, stereotyped, orthodox, standard, conventional, in vogue, current, taken for granted, credited, okayed (D).—*Ant.* refused*, denied, nullified.

access, *n.* **1.** [Admission]—*Syn.* admittance, entree, introduction; see **entrance** 1.

2. [A means of admission]—*Syn.* path, passage, way; see **entrance** 2.

accessibility, *n.* —*Syn.* approachability, receptiveness, openness; see **convenience** 1.

accessible, *mod.* —*Syn.* approachable, obtainable, attainable; see **available.**

accession, *n.* **1.** [An act of coming near or on] —*Syn.* advent, advance, arrival; see **approach** 3.
2. [Coming into office or power]—*Syn.* induction, investment, inauguration; see **installation** 1.
3. [Addition]—*Syn.* increase, enlargement, augmentation; see **increase** 1.
4. [Agreement]—*Syn.* assent, acceptance, consent; see **agreement** 1.

accessories, *n.* pl.—*Syn.* appurtenances, frills, ornaments, adornments, appliances, decorations, additions, attachments; *both* (D): gimmicks, doodads. For specific kinds of accessories; see also **bag, decoration** 2, **equipment, glove, hat, jewelry, muffler, necktie, shoe.**

accessory, *n.* —*Syn.* helper, aid, assistant; see **associate.**

accident, *n.* **1.** [An unexpected misfortune]—*Syn.* mishap, mischance, setback; see **disaster.**
2. [A chance happening]—*Syn.* luck, adventure, fortune, contingency, occurrence, conjecture, happening, circumstance, turn, unforeseen occurrence, fortuity, event, occasion, befalling; see also **chance** 1.

accidental, *mod.* **1.** [Fortuitous]—*Syn.* adventitious, chance, coincidental; see **fortunate** 1, **unfortunate** 2.
2. [Incidental]—*Syn.* minor, secondary, nonessential; see **subordinate, under** 3.

accidentally, *mod.* —*Syn.* unintentionally, involuntarily, unwittingly, unexpectedly, inadvertently, casually, fortuitously, by chance, haphazardly, incidentally, randomly, undesignedly, adventitiously, not purposely, by a fluke (D). —*Ant.* deliberately*, voluntarily, intentionally.

acclaim, *n.* —*Syn.* approval, recognition, plaudits; see **praise** 1.

acclaim, *v.* —*Syn.* laud, commend, celebrate; see **praise** 1.

acclamation, *n.* —*Syn.* applause, acclaim, jubilation; see **praise** 1.

acclimate, *v.* —*Syn.* adapt, accommodate, adjust; see **conform.**

accommodate, *v.* **1.** [To render a service]—*Syn.* help, aid, comfort, make comfortable, oblige, suit, serve, gratify, please, favor, arrange, settle, provide, convenience, benefit, tender (to), supply, furnish, assist, support, sustain, do a favor (for), profit, avail, indebt, indulge, humor, pamper, yield, bow, defer, submit, attend to the convenience of, accept, put oneself out for, do a service for, meet the wants of.—*Ant.* upset*, inconvenience, discommode.
2. [To suit one thing to another]—*Syn.* fit, harmonize, adapt, patch up, modify, attune, reconcile, settle, agree, accord, correspond, make suitable *or* correspond *or* conform, bring into consistency; see also **adjust** 1.—*Ant.* disrupt, confuse*, derange.
3. [To provide lodging]—*Syn.* house, quarter, rent, give lodging to, put at ease, serve as host, receive, take in, entertain, lodge, welcome, put (one) up, furnish room for, supply accommodations for, entertain comfortably, host (D).—*Ant.* bar*, turn out, refuse entrance.

accommodating, *mod.* —*Syn.* obliging, helpful, neighborly; see **kind** 1.

accommodation, *n.* **1.** [Adjustment]—*Syn.* compromise, reconciliation, settlement; see **agreement** 2, 3.
2. [Convenience]—*Syn.* ease, comfort, luxury; see **convenience** 2.
3. [Favor]—*Syn.* service, benevolence, aid; see **kindness** 2.

accommodations, *n.* pl.—*Syn.* quarters, rooms, lodging, maintenance, housing, apartment, hotel, room and board, bunk, bed, board, place (to stay), roof over one's head; *all* (D): joint, digs, diggings. For kinds of accommodations; see also **apartment, apartment house, dormitory, home** 1, **hotel, motel, room** 4.

accompanied, *mod.* —*Syn.* attended, escorted, squired, chaperoned, tended, led, shown (around *or* about), having company *or* companions, not alone *or* unaccompanied *or* neglected, not left in the lurch *or* stood up (D); see also **driven.**

accompaniment, *n.* **1.** [That which accompanies as a necessary part of another]—*Syn.* accessory, adjunct, concomitant, consequence, necessary circumstance, appurtenance, attribute, context, appendage, necessary link, attendant condition, attachment, attendant, complement, coexistence, supplement.
2. [Incidental music]—*Syn.* accompanying instrument, minor instrument, orchestral part, obbligato, piano part, instrumental music, chords, musical background, attendant music, minor harmony, subsidiary part, supplementary part, continuo; see also **music** 1.

accompany, *v.* **1.** [To go with]—*Syn.* escort, attend, be a companion to *or* for, tend, be with, follow, keep company (with), give company, guard, guide, usher, lead (in), show about *or* in *or* around, show the way, conduct, squire, walk out with, convoy, go along (with), come along, chaperon, consort *or* couple with, associate with, go hand in hand with, give safe conduct, look after; *all* (D): hang around with, hang out together, herd together, bear one company, join in action, go side by side with; act as guide, philosopher, and friend.
2. [To supplement]—*Syn.* add to, complete, fill up; see **supplement.**
3. [To occur with]—*Syn.* happen with, coexist (with), appear with, be connected (with), go hand in hand (with), go together with, take place with, go hand in glove (with), add, occur in association (with), append, characterize, co-occur.

accomplice, *n.* —*Syn.* confederate, helper, aid; see **associate.**

accomplish, *v.* —*Syn.* fulfill, perform, finish; see **achieve** 1, **succeed** 1.

accomplished, *mod.* **1.** [Done]—*Syn.* completed, consummated, concluded; see **finished** 1.
2. [Skilled]—*Syn.* proficient, expert, skillful; see **able** 2.
3. [Polished]—*Syn.* cultured, cultivated, finished; see **refined** 2.

accomplishment, *n.* **1.** [The act of accomplishing] —*Syn.* finishing, completion, conclusion; see **success** 1.

2. [A completed action]—*Syn.* execution, fulfillment, attainment; see **achievement** 2.

accord, *n.* —*Syn.* harmony, understanding, reconciliation; see **agreement** 2.

accord, *v.* **1.** [To grant]—*Syn.* allow, accede, acquiesce; see **admit** 3.
2. [To be in agreement]—*Syn.* assent, correspond, affirm; see **agree.**

accordingly, *mod.* —*Syn.* in consequence, consequently, equally, respectively, proportionately, duly, subsequently, in respect to, thus, hence, therefore, as a result, resultantly, as a consequence, as the case may be, on the ground, under the circumstances, as things go, to that end, in that event, as an outgrowth.

according to, *prep.* —*Syn.* in accordance with, as, to the degree that, in consonance with, conforming to, just as, in keeping with, in line with, in agreement with, in confirmation, at first hand, consistent *or* congruent with, pursuant to.

accost, *v.* **1.** [To greet]—*Syn.* address, welcome, salute; see **greet.**
2. [To solicit]—*Syn.* proposition (D), approach, entice; see **solicit** 3.

account, *n.* **1.** [A narrative]—*Syn.* tale, recital, chronicle; see **story.**
2. [A record]—*Syn.* bulletin, annual, report; see **record** 1.
call to account—*Syn.* demand an explanation of, reprimand, censure; see **accuse.**
give a good account of oneself—*Syn.* acquit oneself, do well, justify one's actions; see **boast** 1, **justify** 2.
on account—*Syn.* charged, in *or* on layaway (D), on call; see **unpaid** 1.
on account of—*Syn.* because of, by virtue of, since; see **because.**
on no account—*Syn.* for no reason, no way, under no circumstances; see **never.**
on someone's account—*Syn.* because of, for someone's sake, in someone's behalf *or* interest; see **because.**
take account of—*Syn.* judge, evaluate, investigate; see **examine** 1.
take into account—*Syn.* judge, allow for, weigh; see **consider** 1.
turn to account—*Syn.* utilize, exploit, profit by; see **profit** 2, **use** 1.

account, *v.* —*Syn.* value, judge, reckon; see **estimate** 1, 3.

accountability, *n.* —*Syn.* culpability, liability, answerability; see **responsibility** 2.

accountable, *mod.* —*Syn.* liable, culpable, answerable; see **responsible** 1.

accountant, *n.* —*Syn.* bookkeeper, auditor, actuary, cashier, teller, bookkeeping expert, examiner of business accounts, expert in accounts, clerk, inspector of accounts, comptroller, controller, calculator, reckoner, analyst, chartered accountant, (certified) public accountant *or* C.P.A. *or* CPA, inventory expert.

account for, *v.* —*Syn.* clarify, resolve, elucidate; see **explain.**

accredited, *mod.* —*Syn.* vouched for, supported, authorized; see **approved.**

accretion, *n.* —*Syn.* accumulation, growth, addition; see **increase** 1.

accrue, *v.* —*Syn.* increase, collect, gather; see **accumulate** 1.

accumulate, *v.* **1.** [To amass]—*Syn.* mass, hoard, get together, gather (into a mass), collect (a bulk of), heap, store, assemble, cache, collocate, muster, aggregate, cumulate, concentrate, compile, agglomerate, accrue, provide, pile (up), scrape *or* stack up *or* together, stockpile, store up, heap up *or* together, procure, acquire, gain, load up, attach, draw *or* bring together, rake up, lump together, amalgamate, unite, incorporate, add to, profit, make money, grow rich, build up, gain control; *all* (D): drag *or* haul *or* rake *or* roll in, take up, bank. —*Ant.* scatter*, squander, distribute.
2. [To increase]—*Syn.* swell, build up, expand; see **grow** 1.

accumulation, *n.* **1.** [The act of amassing]—*Syn.* accretion, aggregation, augmentation, inflation, aggrandizement, addition, enlargement, multiplication, intensification, accession, agglomeration, growth, collecting (together), amassing, gathering, hoarding, growth by addition, conglomeration. —*Ant.* deflation, loss*, diminution.
2. [A heap]—*Syn.* mass, pile, quantity; see **heap.**

accuracy, *n.* **1.** [The state of being without error] —*Syn.* exactness, exactitude, correctness; see **truth** 1.
2. [The quality of precision or deftness]—*Syn.* skill, efficiency, exactness, precision, preciseness, one-for-one targeting, correctness, skillfulness, sharpness, incisiveness, mastery, dependability, strictness, certainty, sureness, dotting the *i's* and crossing the *t's* (D).—*Ant.* inability*, sloppiness, incompetence.

accurate, *mod.* **1.** [Free from error]—*Syn.* exact, infallible, right, correct, precise, perfect, nice, faultless, flawless, errorless, just, factual, unquestionable, veracious, unquestioned, unerring, unimpeachable, authoritative, authentic, valid, undisputed, undeniable, unrefuted, irrefutable, conclusive, absolute, final, certain, unambiguous, straight, true, proper, strict, undeviating, not amiss, definite, actual, definitive, fundamental, clear-cut, genuine, official; *all* (D): O.K., checked and double-checked, dead right, (right) on the nose *or* the button, (right) down the pike *or* the middle of the road. —*Ant.* erroneous, false*, questionable.
2. [Characterized by precision]—*Syn.* deft, reliable, trustworthy, true, correct, exact, well-defined, specific, dependable, skillful, methodical, systematic, discriminative, nice, distinct, particular, well-drawn, realistic, authentic, genuine, careful, close, critical, detailed, factual, severe, rigorous, literal, rigid, scrupulous, strict, meticulous, punctilious, discriminating, faithful, punctual, scientific, objective, detached, unprejudiced, unbiased, disinterested, veracious, matter-of-fact, rational, unmistakable, reasonable, judicious, right, explicit, mathematically precise, ultraprecise, definite, mathematically exact, religiously exact, scrupulously exact, unerring, concrete, defined, sharp, like clockwork; *all* (D): (right) on the button, on the spot, on the head, solid, on the nose.—*Ant.* incompetent*, faulty, slipshod.

accurately, *mod.* —*Syn.* correctly, precisely, exactly, certainly, truly, truthfully, justly, rightly, carefully, perfectly, invariably, in detail, strictly, unerringly, unmistakenly, infallibly, rigorously, scrupulously, literally, verbatim, squarely, explicitly, word for word, to a nicety, just so, as is just, in all respects; *all* (D): to a hair, to a turn, on the button *or* on the nose, to *or* within an inch.

accursed, *mod.* **1.** [Detestable]—*Syn.* hateful, loathsome, abhorrent; see **offensive** 2.

2. [Doomed]—*Syn.* ill-fated, cursed, damned; see **doomed.**

accusation, *n.* **1.** [The act of accusing]—*Syn.* arraignment, indictment, prosecution; see **indictment** 1.

2. [A charge]—*Syn.* indictment, allegation, imputation, denunciation, slur, exposé, complaint, citation, censure, insinuation; *all* (D): rap, beef, smear, frame-up.

accuse, *v.* —*Syn.* blame, censure, charge, arraign, challenge, denounce, prefer charges, indict, file a claim, summon, incriminate, attack, brand, impute, stigmatize, involve, inculpate, charge with, litigate, recriminate, implicate, arrest, apprehend, sue, bring up on charges, prosecute, slander, libel, betray, tax, slur, blame, cite, reprove, reproach, impeach, haul *or* bring into court, have the law on, inform against, hold accountable, bring proceedings *or* charges against, appeal to law, bring to trial, serve with a summons, complain against, lodge a complaint, charge to, declaim against, fix the responsibility for, connect with; *all* (D): hang *or* pin something on, put the finger on, put the screws on, smear, mark up against, pin the blame on, hold against, point the finger at, fasten on *or* upon, raise one's voice against, place to one's account, cast blame upon, cast in one's teeth, bring home to, cry out against, hale to court.—*Ant.* vindicate*, exonerate, pardon.

accused, *mod.* —*Syn.* arraigned, indicted, incriminated, charged with, under suspicion, under indictment, supposedly guilty, alleged to be guilty, on the police blotter, apprehended, held for questioning, liable, involved, in danger, subject to accusation, under attack, under fire, on the docket, given the blame, taxed with; *all* (D): up for, cooking, stewing.—*Ant.* discharged*, acquitted, cleared.

accuser, *n.* —*Syn.* prosecutor, plaintiff, objector, complainant, libelant, informant, district attorney, court, law, judicial party, suitor, petitioner, litigant, delator, adversary, opposer, opponent, informer, informant, state, government *or* state witness; *all* (D): rat, stool pigeon, fink.—*Ant.* defendant*, accused, prisoner.

accustomed, *mod.* —*Syn.* usual, customary, habitual; see **conventional** 1.

accustomed to, *mod.* in the habit, used to, wont to; see **addicted to.**

ace, *n.* **1.** [A one-spot in a deck of cards]—*Syn.* ace of hearts *or* clubs *or* diamonds *or* spades.

2. [(D) A pilot who has shot down five planes or more]—*Syn.* veteran, combat *or* fighter pilot, expert, seasoned aviator, dogfighter (D).

3. [An expert in an activity]—*Syn.* expert, master, champion; see **specialist.**

ace (D), *mod.* —*Syn.* expert, first-rate, outstanding; see **distinguished** 2, **able** 2.

acerbity, *n.* **1.** [Sourness]—*Syn.* astringency, tartness, acidity; see **bitterness** 1.

2. [Harshness]—*Syn.* irritability, ill temper, rancor; see **rudeness.**

acetic, *mod.* —*Syn.* tart, acid, biting; see **sour** 1.

ache, *n.* —*Syn.* twinge, pang, spasm; see **pain** 2.

ache, *v.* —*Syn.* pain, throb, be sore; see **hurt** 4.

achievable, *mod.* —*Syn.* obtainable, attainable, feasible; see **available.**

achieve, *v.* **1.** [To finish an undertaking]—*Syn.* complete, end, terminate, conclude, finish (up *or* off), do, perform, execute, fulfill, consummate, perfect, cap, carry off *or* out *or* on *or* through, turn out, bring about *or* off, settle, effect, bring to an end *or* a conclusion, close, stop, encompass, produce, realize, effectuate, actualize, discharge, make work out, wind up, work out, adjust, resolve, solve, accomplish, dispose of, adjourn, recess, dispatch, make an end of, enact, manage, contrive, negotiate, sign, seal, bring to pass, just do, have effect, fall to, look on *or* to, see (it) through, get done, close up, put the lid on, carry to completion, follow through, take measures, lose oneself in, deliver; *all* (D): knock off, fill the bill, round out, come through, polish off, score, clean *or* mop up, put across, pull over *or* off, make short work of, do up brown, act up to, dispose of, come it, do one's stuff, put through, go whole hog, go all the way, go the limit, button up, do oneself proud, call it a day, put the finishing touch on.—*Ant.* abandon*, fail, give up.

2. [To reach a goal]—*Syn.* realize, obtain, accomplish; see **succeed** 1.

achievement, *n.* **1.** [The act of reaching a goal] —*Syn.* progress, victory, accomplishment; see **success** 1.

2. [A creditable action completed]—*Syn.* fulfillment, feat, exploit, effectuation, contrivance, encompassment, accomplishment, triumph, hit, success, realization, acquirement, creation, completion, consummation, execution, actualization, masterwork, masterpiece, performance, deed, act, enactment, victory, conquest, *chef d'oeuvre* (French), attainment, rendition, action; *all* (D): stunt, knockout, feather in one's cap.—*Ant.* failure*, blunder, collapse.

acid, *mod.* **1.** [Having the characteristics of an acid] —*Syn.* sharp, tart, biting; see **sour** 1.

2. [Having the properties of an acid]—*Syn.* corrosive, erosive, eroding, corroding, oxidizing, rusting, eating away, biting, disinfectant, disintegrative, dissolvent, bleaching, acidific, anti-alkaline.

3. [Cutting or sarcastic]—*Syn.* biting, sharp, offensive; see **sarcastic.**

acid, *n.* **1.** [A sour substance]—*Syn.* acidulous compound, corrosive, Lewis acid, hydrogen-ion concentration; see also **element** 2.

2. [(D) A drug]—*Syn.* D-lysergic acid diethylamide *or* LSD, di-methyl triptamine *or* DMT, mescaline; see **drug** 2.

Common acids include the following—vinegar, verjuice, lemon juice; citric, ascorbic, nicotinic, boric, acetic, sulfuric, hydrochloric, hydrosulfurous, hydrobromic, hydrofluoric, hydrocyanic, hydroferrocyanic, hydriodic, hyponitrous, sulfonic, phosphoric, carbolic, nitric, benzoic, amino, monobasic, dibasic, polybasic acid: *aqua regia* (Latin; compound of nitric and hydrochloric acids).

acidity, *n.*—*Syn.* sourness, bitterness, acridity, acidosis, acidulousness, hyperacidity, tartness, sharpness, acridness, pungency, fermentation, vinegariness, harshness, causticity, astringency, keenness.—*Ant.* sweetness*, alkalinity, sugariness.

acidulous, *mod.* **1.** [Acid]—*Syn.* bitter, piquant, sharp; see **sour** 1.
2. [Sarcastic]—*Syn.* satirical, ironical, mocking; see **sarcastic.**

acknowledge, *v.* **1.** [To admit]—*Syn.* concede, confess, declare; see **admit** 2, 3.
2. [To recognize the authority of]—*Syn.* endorse, certify, confirm, uphold, support, recognize, ratify, approve, defend, subscribe to, acquiesce in, accede to, make legal, attest to, take an oath by, have to hand it to, defer to.
3. [To answer]—*Syn.* remark, thank, respond *or* reply (to); see **answer** 1.

acknowledged, *mod.*—*Syn.* admitted, confessed, recognized, unquestioned, accepted, authorized, confirmed, received, sanctioned, accredited, approved, receipted, professed, out and out (D).

acknowledgment, *n.* **1.** [The act of acknowledging]—*Syn.* acceptance, declaration, compliance, affirmation, asseveration, corroboration, avowal, recognition, confession, admission, admitting, conceding, concession, concurrence, assent, confirmation, accession, profession, allowance, ratification, acquiescence, assertion, owning up (D).—*Ant.* denial*, confutation, refutation.
2. [Something intended to acknowledge]—*Syn.* greeting, reply, answer, response, nod, confession, statement, apology, guarantee, return, support, signature, receipt, letter, card, contract, acclamation, public opinion, unanimity, applause, bow, token, bestowal, gift, bouquet, vote of thanks, I.O.U. (D).

acme, *n.*—*Syn.* zenith, summit, highest point; see **top** 1.

acolyte, *n.*—*Syn.* helper, attendant, aid; see **assistance.**

acquaint, *v.*—*Syn.* tell, advise, inform; see **notify** 1.

acquaintance, *n.* **1.** [The state of being acquainted]—*Syn.* association, companionship, knowledge; see **friendship** 1.
2. [A person with whom one is acquainted]—*Syn.* colleague, bowing acquaintance, speaking acquaintance, escort, neighbor; see also **friend** 1.
3. [Knowledge gained through personal experience or study]—*Syn.* familiarity, conversance, awareness; see **awareness, experience** 3.

acquainted (with), *mod.*—*Syn.* introduced, on speaking terms, having some connections; see **familiar with.**

acquaint with, *v.*—*Syn.* introduce, make acquainted, present; see **introduce** 3.

acquiesce, *v.*—*Syn.* consent, comply, approve; see **agree.**

acquiescence, *n.*—*Syn.* passive consent, quiet submission, resignation; see **permission.**

acquire, *v.* **1.** [To obtain]—*Syn.* take, get, earn, procure; see **obtain** 1.
2. [To receive]—*Syn.* get, gain, take possession, collect; see **receive** 1.

acquired, *mod.* **1.** [Gained by personal exertion]—*Syn.* reached, attained, won, accomplished, learned, adopted, earned, collected, gathered, secured, procured, obtained, captured, drawn, harvested, regained, retrieved, realized; *all* (D): got by the sweat of one's brow, dug out, raked in, cornered, netted, salted away, grabbed.
2. [Gained without special exertion]—*Syn.* inherited, given, accrued, derived, granted, endowed, transmitted, adapted (to), conveyed to, handed down, bequeathed, ceded, allowed, awarded, passed on, willed to; see also **won.**—*Ant.* wasted*, deprived, lost.

acquisition, *n.* **1.** [The act of acquiring]—*Syn.* acquirement, acquiring, obtainment, attainment, procuring, procurement, procuration, purchase, recovery, retrieval, redemption, salvage, accretion, addition, inheriting, winning.
2. [Anything acquired]—*Syn.* inheritance, gift, donation, grant, wealth, riches, fortune, profit, gain, earnings, wages, salary, income, winnings, remuneration, emolument, return(s), proceeds, benefit, prize, reward, award, accomplishment, achievement, increment, premium, bonus, fee, commission, net (receipts), pension, annuity, allowance, assurance, guaranty, security, gain, benefaction, patrimony, dividend.—*Ant.* loss*, expenditure, penalty.

acquisitive, *mod.*—*Syn.* grasping, avaricious, rapacious; see **greedy** 1.

acquit, *v.* **1.** [To exonerate]—*Syn.* clear, absolve, vindicate; see **excuse** 1.
2. [To behave]—*Syn.* comport, conduct, bear, act; see **behave** 2.

acquittal, *n.*—*Syn.* absolution, acquitting, suspended sentence, clearance, quittance, exoneration, dismissal, dismissing, deliverance, amnesty, discharge, discharging, pardon, reprieve, exemption, liberation, release, releasing, freedom, vindication, exculpation, remission, relief from, letting off, springing (D).—*Ant.* punishment*, sentence, imprisonment.

acre, *n.*—*Syn.* plot, acreage, bit of land, estate; see **area** 2, **property** 2.

acreage, *n.*—*Syn.* land, grounds, real estate; see **area** 2, **property** 2.

acres, *n.* pl.—*Syn.* estate, land, grounds; see **property** 2.

acrid, *mod.*—*Syn.* pungent, biting, caustic; see **sour** 1.

acrimonious, *mod.*—*Syn.* sharp, acid, irascible; see **sarcastic.**

acrimony, *n.*—*Syn.* severity, unkindness, irascibility; see **rudeness.**

acrobat, *n.*—*Syn.* tumbler, clown, trampolinist, aerial artist, aerialist, equilibrist, trapeze artist, contortionist, performer, tightrope walker, high-vaulter, somersaulter, bar swinger, rope dancer, flying trapezist, circus athlete, aerosaltant, stunt man, figure skater, vaudeville performer, ballet dancer, aerial gymnast, funambulist, gymnast, balancer; *all* (D): trap man, dangler, stunter, mat worker, flier, tramper.

acrobatics, *n.* pl.—*Syn.* tumbling, calisthenics, aerobatics; see **gymnastics.**

across, *mod.* and *prep.*—*Syn.* crosswise, crossed, athwart, to the opposite side of, over (against), (directly) opposite, on the other side, from side to side of, from one side to another, in a crossing position, transversely, contrariwise, in front of, opposite (to), beyond.

across the board (D), *mod.*—*Syn.* impartially, fairly, equivalently; see **equally.**

act, *n.* **1.** [An action]—*Syn.* deed, performance, exploit; see **action** 2.
2. [An official or legal statement]—*Syn.* law, proposal, judgment, commitment, verdict, amendment, order, announcement, edict, ordinance, decree, statute, writ, bull, warrant, summons, subpoena, document, bill, code, clause, law of the land (D).
3. [A division of a play]—*Syn.* scene, curtain, prologue, epilogue, introduction; first act, second act, third act, etc; *all* (D): canto, turn, swan song, unit of dramatic action.
4. [(D) A pose]—*Syn.* falsification, feigning, affectation; see **pretense** 1.

act, *v.* **1.** [To perform an action]—*Syn.* do, execute, carry out *or* on, operate, transact, accomplish, achieve, consummate, carry into effect, perpetrate, persevere, persist, labor, work, officiate, function, preside, serve, go ahead *or* about, step into, walk on, take steps, play *or* take a part, begin, move in, enforce, maneuver, be in process, be in action, operate, create, practice, deal in, prosecute, develop, make progress, interfere, interpose, be active, take effect, intrude, commit, fight, combat, respond, keep going, answer, rebuff, pursue, put forth energy, chase, hunt; *all* (D): hustle, get going, pull, do one's stuff, get down to brass tacks.—*Ant.* wait*, await, rest.
2. [To conduct oneself]—*Syn.* behave, seem, appear, carry *or* acquit *or* comport *or* bear *or* betake *or* demean oneself, give the appearance of, represent oneself (as), take on, play one's part, impress one as; *both* (D): put on airs, cut a figure; see also **behave** 2.
3. [To take part in a play]—*Syn.* perform, impersonate, personate, represent, enact, act out, simulate, live over, pretend, mimic, burlesque, parody, feign, portray, render the role of, rehearse, take a part (in), dramatize, star, spout, rant, play *or* act the part of, make one's debut; *all* (D): tread the boards, strut one's stuff, ham, throw a performance, go it, make a production of, have a free play, double in brass.

act for, *v.*—*Syn.* do the work of, replace, fill in (D); see **substitute** 2.

acting, *mod.*—*Syn.* substituting, temporary, alternate, deputy, officiating, delegated, assistant, adjutant, surrogate, pro tem (D).—*Ant.* official*, confirmed, regular.

acting, *n.*—*Syn.* pretending, feigning, simulating, gesturing, ranting, spouting, orating, dramatizing, performing, behaving, playing, showing (off), enactment, impersonation, depiction, portrayal, pantomime, rendition, dramatics, histrionic art, stage playing, stagecraft, personation, simulation, theatricals, performance, dramatic action, mimicry, histrionics, mime, play acting (D).

action, *n.* **1.** [Any state opposed to rest and quiet] —*Syn.* activity, conflict, business, occupation, work, response, reaction, movement, industry, bustle, turmoil, stir, flurry, animation, vivacity, enterprise, energy, liveliness, alacrity, alertness, agility, sprightliness, nimbleness, readiness, quickness, keenness, vigor, life, dash, commotion, rush, motion, mobility, haste, speed; *all* (D): life, go, doings, snap.—*Ant.* rest*, quiet, inaction.
2. [An individual deed]—*Syn.* feat, exploit, performance, performing, execution, blow, stroke, maneuver, step, achievement, act, deed, thing, thrust, stratagem, something done, accomplishment, commission, effort, enterprise, manipulation, move, movement, doing, effect, transaction, exertion, operation, bout, handiwork, dealings, procedure, manufacture; *all* (D): solo act, stunt, trick, kick.
3. [A process at law]—*Syn.* suit, claim, litigation, lawsuit; see **trial** 2.
4. [Military activity]—*Syn.* sortie, engagement, contest; see **fight** 1.
5. [The plot or events in a creative work]—*Syn.* development, progress, unfolding; see **plot** 2.
bring action—*Syn.* accuse, start a lawsuit, take to court; see **sue.**
see action—*Syn.* do battle, engage in combat, conflict; see **fight** 2.
take action—*Syn.* become active, do, initiate activity; see **act** 1.

actions, *n.* pl.—*Syn.* deportment, conduct, manner(s); see **behavior** 1.

activate, *v.*—*Syn.* stimulate, initiate, arouse; see **animate** 1, **begin** 1.

active, *mod.* **1.** [Having motion]—*Syn.* mobile, rolling, speeding, speedy, hasty, going, motive, rapid, progressive, turning, exertive, pushing, astir, walking, traveling, movable, impelling, shifting, acting, bustling, humming, efficacious, efficient, functioning, working, moving, restless, streaming, serviceable, swarming, rustling, flowing, effectual, in process *or* effect *or* action *or* force *or* play, alive, simmering, overflowing, stirring, effective, at work, in a state of action, in actual progress, operative, rushing, operating, flooding, fluxional, agitated; *all* (D): hopping, ripsnorting, going *or* at full blast, in high gear, in full blast *or* gear.—*Ant.* quiet*, inactive, motionless.
2. [Notable for activity]—*Syn.* busy, eventful, brisk, lively, dynamic, energetic, industrious, persevering, enthusiastic, agile, quick, nimble, astir, rapid, dexterous, spry, fresh, frisky, sprightly, wiry, alert, alive, ready, sharp, keen, keen-minded, wide-awake, animated, enlivened, ardent, unfaltering, purposeful, resolute, pushing, aggressive, forceful, intense, forcible, determined, unwearied, diligent, hard-working, assiduous, enterprising, inventive, vigorous, strenuous, eager, zealous, bustling, dashing, bold, daring, high-spirited; *all* (D): chipper, snappy, full of pep, on the ball, full of life, on one's toes, peppy, with plenty of go, rarin' to go, up and coming, on the job, like sixty, hot, hyped up, turned on (to).—*Ant.* lazy*, lethargic, sluggish.

activity, *n.*—*Syn.* motion, movement, liveliness; see **action** 1.

act one's age, *v.*—*Syn.* act properly, comport oneself, be orderly; see **behave** 2.

actor, *n.*—*Syn.* player, performer, character, impersonator, star, comedian, member of the cast, Thespian, dramatis persona, leading man *or* woman, entertainer, ingénue, artist, television star, character actor, supporting actor, featured player, deuteragonist, tritagonist, villain, motion picture actor, soubrette, stage actor *or* player, amateur actor, histrio, professional actor, mimic, mime, clown, ventriloquist, pantomimist, character man, mummer, masker, heavy lead, theatrical performer, photoplayer, dramatic artist, headliner, histrionic performer, understudy, personator, tragedian, principal, protagonist; *all* (D): extra, bit player, walk on, ham, movie idol, parlor artist, hamfatter, farceur, heavy, variety performer, barnstormer, gallery player, scenestealer, punchinello, vaudevillan; see also **actress, cast** 2.

actress, *n.*—*Syn.* female performer, member of the cast, ingénue, comedienne, tragedienne, prima donna, leading lady, star, soubrette; *all* (D): cinemactress, glamour girl, starlet; see also **actor, cast** 2.

actual, *mod.* **1.** [True]—*Syn.* original, real, exact; see **genuine** 1.
2. [Existent]—*Syn.* concrete, present, tangible, substantive; see **real** 2.

actuality, *n.*—*Syn.* materiality, substance, substantiality; see **reality** 1.

actualize, *v.*—*Syn.* realize, perfect, make good; see **complete** 1.

actually, *mod.*—*Syn.* truly, in fact, as a matter of fact; see **really** 1.

act up, *v.*—*Syn.* carry on, be naughty, create a disturbance; see **misbehave.**

act upon *or* **on,** *v.* **1.** [To act in accordance with] —*Syn.* adjust, regulate, behave; see **act** 1, 2, **obey** 1.
2. [To influence]—*Syn.* affect, sway, impress; see **influence.**

acumen, *n.*—*Syn.* keenness, insight, penetration, perspicacity, percipience, discernment, sharpness, acuteness, astuteness, sagacity, cleverness, shrewdness, accuracy, intelligence, wisdom, longheadedness, understanding, comprehension, intuition, sensitivity, vision, grasp, perception, smartness, brilliance, farsightedness, keensightedness, awareness, cunning, guile, acuity, wit, quickness of perception, perspicuity, mental acuteness, mother wit, *esprit* (French), foresightedness, quick sense *or* intelligence, intellect, discrimination, judgment, good taste, refinement; *all* (D): brains, horse sense, know-how, high I.Q., the smarts.—*Ant.* stupidity*, dullness, obtuseness.

acute, *mod.* **1.** [Pointed]—*Syn.* sharp-pointed, spiked, keen; see **sharp** 2.
2. [Crucial]—*Syn.* decisive, critical, important, vital; see **crucial** 1.
3. [Shrewd]—*Syn.* clever, astute, penetrating; see **intelligent** 1.
4. [Sharp]—*Syn.* severe, keen, cutting; see **intense.**
5. [Discerning]—*Syn.* discriminating, penetrating, sensitive, perceptive, keen, sharp, astute, intense; see also **judicious, observant** 1.—*Ant.* dull*, slow*, shallow*.

acutely, *mod.*—*Syn.* keenly, sharply, severely; see **very.**

acuteness, *n.* **1.** [Intensity]—*Syn.* forcefulness, severity, fierceness; see **intensity** 1.
2. [Shrewdness]—*Syn.* cleverness, keenness, astuteness; see **acumen.**

A.D., abbr.—*Syn.* *anno Domini* (Latin), in the year of our Lord, after the birth of Christ, the Christian era, Christian times, modern times.

ad (D), *n.*—*Syn.* announcement, display, notice; see **advertisement** 1, 2.

adage, *n.*—*Syn.* aphorism, saying, maxim; see **proverb.**

Adam, *n.*—*Syn.* the first man, progenitor, father, father of the race, mankind, aboriginal man, the fallen; see also **man** 1.

adamant, *mod.*—*Syn.* fixed, set, settled; see **resolute** 2.

adapt, *v.* **1.** [To alter or adjust]—*Syn.* modify, revise, readjust; see **change** 1.
2. [To adapt oneself]—*Syn.* grow used to, accustom, acclimatize; see **change** 4, **conform.**

adaptability, *n.*—*Syn.* changeability, flexibility, versatility, adjustability, ambidexterity, manysidedness, tractability, conformability, ductility, accommodativeness, pliableness, pliancy, malleability, amenability, docility, compliancy, pliability, plasticity.

adaptable, *mod.*—*Syn.* pliant, tractable, pliable; see **docile, flexible** 1.

adaptation, *n.* **1.** [The state or process of being adapted]—*Syn.* conversion, adoption, reworking; see **change** 1.
2. [Condition resulting from adaptation, sense 1] —*Syn.* acclimatization, correspondence, compliance; see **agreement** 2.

adapted, *mod.*—*Syn.* suitable, becoming, fitting; see **fit** 1, 2.

add, *v.* **1.** [To bring together, usually by mathematics]—*Syn.* total, sum (up), figure (up), compute, calculate, do a sum, tally (with), count *or* foot *or* cipher *or* add *or* cast up, do simple addition, run over, enumerate, reckon, tell off, use an adding machine, hitch *or* clap on (D).—*Ant.* subtract, decrease*, take *or* take away.
2. [To make a further remark]—*Syn.* append, say further, continue, write further, annex, supplement, affix, tack on, add a postscript, reply.

adder, *n.*—*Syn.* viper, reptile, asp.
Adders include the following—European, spotted, puffing, milk, African puff; see also **snake.**

addict, *n.*—*Syn.* habitué, practitioner, special problem offender; *all* (D): fiend, hophead, customer, head, dope fiend, drug fiend, cokey, mainliner, junkie, snowbird, nut, regular, hard case, tripper, freak, crystal-freak, acidhead, speed freak.

addicted (to), *mod.*—*Syn.* given over, given *or* disposed to, inclined, habituated, prone, accustomed, attached, abandoned, wedded, devoted, predisposed, used to, imbued with, fanatic about, obsessed with, wont to, in the habit of, under the influence of, in favor of, hooked on (D).—*Ant.* unaccustomed*, disinclined, averse to.

addiction, *n.*—*Syn.* fixation, inclination, bent; see **habit** 1, **obsession.**

addition, *n.* **1.** [The process of adding]—*Syn.* reckoning, computing, totaling, summing up, summation, sum, enlarging, accruing, dilating, increasing, expanding, tabulating, counting, accretion.—*Ant.* subtraction, reduction*, lessening.

2. [That which has been added]—*Syn.* interest, raise, additive, adjunct, augmentation, *addendum* (Latin), profit *or* profits, dividend *or* dividends, bonus, commission, increment, supplement, gain, tip-in, accretion, accession, accrual, subordinate part, enhancement, aggrandizement, reinforcement, appendage, appendix, accessory, appurtenance, attachment, extension, increase, annex, affix; *all* (D): ante, raise, appreciation.—*Ant.* loss*, reduction*, shrinkage.
3. [A real estate development]—*Syn.* annex, annexation, subdivision, shopping center, development, enlargement, accession, extension, expansion, branch, construction.
4. [An architectural extension]—*Syn.* wing, ell, annex, spare room; see also **room** 2.

additional, *mod.*—*Syn.* supplementary, new, further; see **extra.**

addleheaded, *mod.*—*Syn.* confused, witless, idiotic; see **stupid** 1.

address, *n.* **1.** [A formal speech]—*Syn.* oration, lecture, sermon; see **speech** 3.
2. [Place at which one may be reached]—*Syn.* (legal) residence, home, (living) quarters, dwelling, headquarters, place of business *or* residence, box number; street, number, and zip code; see also **business** 4, **home** 1, **hotel.**
3. [Directions for delivery]—*Syn.* inscription, label, superscription; see **directions.**
4. [Behavior]—*Syn.* delivery, manner(s), bearing, habit(s), approach; see also **behavior** 1.
5. [Storage place in a computer]—*Syn.* source of output, position of input, data storage; see **place** 3, **position** 1.

address, *v.* **1.** [To provide directions for delivery]—*Syn.* inscribe, label, mark, prepare for mailing *or* the post, type a label for, superscribe, put through the addressing machine *or* Addressograph (trademark); see also **write** 2.
2. [To speak formally to an assemblage]—*Syn.* lecture (to), discourse (on *or* upon), discuss, give *or* deliver a talk *or* speech *or* address, take the floor, orate, pontificate, declaim, harangue, rant, expatiate (on *or* upon), sermonize; *all* (D): strut and fret their (*or* his) petty hour upon the stage, speechify, spout (off), spiel, take the stump *or* the soapbox *or* the platform, do a spellbinder.
3. [To communicate in a formal way]—*Syn.* petition (for *or* about), appeal (to), write (to), lay a matter before someone, plead, enter a plea (for), seek redress (for), make *or* enter a suit (for), prepare a petition *or* formal request *or* complaint; see also **ask** 1.

address (oneself) to, *v.*—*Syn.* devote, turn to, apply (oneself); see **try** 1.

add to, *v.*—*Syn.* augment, amplify, expand; see **increase** 1.

add up (D), *v.*—*Syn.* be plausible *or* probable *or* reasonable *or* logical, stand to reason, hold water (D); see **make sense.**

add up to, *v.*—*Syn.* indicate, signify, imply; see **mean** 1.

adept, *mod.*—*Syn.* skilled, skillful, proficient, capable; see **able** 1, 2.

adequacy, *n.*—*Syn.* capacity, sufficiency, enough; see **plenty.**

adequate, *mod.*—*Syn.* sufficient, equal to the need, satisfactory; see **enough** 1.

adequately, *mod.* **1.** [Enough]—*Syn.* sufficiently, appropriately, suitably, fittingly, satisfactorily, abundantly, copiously, capably, competently; see also **well** 1, 2.—*Ant.* inadequately*, badly, insufficiently.
2. [Passably]—*Syn.* acceptably, tolerably, decently, presentably, modestly, not (too) badly, fairly well, well enough, up to (a minimal) standard, in a manner up to *or* satisfying the code, not so badly as it might be, pleasantly enough, not disgracefully, to an acceptable degree, in an ordinary way *or* manner; see also **badly** 1, **well** 2, 3.—*Ant.* badly*, poorly, unsatisfactorily.

adherent, *n.*—*Syn.* partisan, disciple, backer; see **follower.**

adhere (to), *v.* **1.** [To serve]—*Syn.* follow, be devoted to, practice; see **obey** 2.
2. [To conform to]—*Syn.* observe, abide by, comply (with); see **follow** 2.
3. [To stick to]—*Syn.* attach, cling, hold fast; see **stick** 1.

adhesive, *mod.*—*Syn.* adhering, adherent, sticking, sticky, glutinous, resinous, gummy, viscid, viscous, gluey, gelatinous, waxy, gummed, pasty, clinging, agglutinant, tenacious, hugging, conformable, sticking fast, tending to adhere, emplastic, mucilaginous.—*Ant.* loose*, inadhesive, cohesive.

adhesive, *n.* Varieties include the following—adhesive tape, paste, glue, mucilage, cement, epoxy, rubber cement, acetone, library paste, gummed tape, gummed paper, sticky tape, gummed label, mending tape, mending tissue, Scotch tape (trademark), masking tape, draftsman's tape, adhesive bandage, adhesive plaster, sticking plaster, court plaster.

adieu, *n.*—*Syn.* farewell; *both* (D): so long, see you later; see **good-by.**

ad infinitum, *mod.*—*Syn.* endlessly, forever, ceaselessly; see **regularly** 2.

adjacent, *mod.*—*Syn.* beside, alongside, bordering; see **near** 1.

adjective, *n.*—*Syn.* modifier, article, determiner, attribute, attributive, qualifier, descriptive word *or* term, limiting word, dependent, adjectival construction, identifier, qualifying word *or* term, attributive name, adjunct, adnoun, accessory, addition, dependent.

adjoin, *v.* **1.** [To be close to]—*Syn.* abut, lie beside, be adjacent to; see **join** 3.
2. [To join]—*Syn.* unite, append, annex; see **join** 1.

adjoining, *mod.*—*Syn.* adjacent, neighboring, bordering on; see **near** 1.

adjourn, *v.*—*Syn.* prorogue, postpone, discontinue; see **suspend** 2.

adjournment, *n.* **1.** [Leaving]—*Syn.* intermission, pause, break; see **recess** 1.
2. [Delay]—*Syn.* postponement, putting off, deferment; see **delay** 1.

adjudicate, *v.*—*Syn.* mediate, settle, adjudge, arbitrate; see **decide** 1.

adjunct, *n.* **1.** [Something added]—*Syn.* supplement, subordinate part, minor detail; see **addition** 2.

2. [Assistant]—*Syn.* associate, partner, collaborator; see **assistant.**

adjust, *v.* **1.** [To bring to agreement]—*Syn.* settle, arrange, conclude, complete, accord, reconcile, clarify, conform, sort, allocate, grade, tally, regulate, organize, methodize, systematize, coordinate, straighten, standardize, clean up; *both* (D): put in A-1 condition, make jibe; see also **accommodate** 2. —*Ant.* botch*, mix, confuse.

2. [To settle a claim]—*Syn.* make an adjustment, make payment, arrange a settlement; see **settle** 9.

3. [To place or regulate parts]—*Syn.* put *or* arrange in order, fix, connect, square, balance, regulate, tighten, fit, repair, focus, fine-tune, readjust, rectify, correct, set, mend, improve, overhaul, grind, sharpen, renovate, polish, collate, bring into line, align, put in working order, make exact, bring to a proper state, calibrate, accommodate for, temper, service; *all* (D): do a repair job, trouble-shoot, rehaul, tweak, revamp.

adjustable, *mod.*—*Syn.* adaptable, stretchable, tractable; see **flexible** 1.

adjustment, *n.* **1.** [The act of adjusting]—*Syn.* fixing, mending, repairing, improvement, balancing, adaptation, acclimation, shaping, readjustment, organization, organizing, standardization, regimentation, conformance, alleviation, regulating, regulation, grading, sorting, classifying, arrangement, correcting, correction, tweak (D). —*Ant.* demolishing, destruction*, destroying.

2. [A payment against a claim]—*Syn.* settlement, arrangement, pay, remuneration, reimbursement, stipulation, compensation, compromise, reconciliation, agreement, apportionment, allotment, share, benefit, stake, making up, mutual understanding, freeing from differences.

adjutant, *n.*—*Syn.* helper, aide, auxiliary; see **assistant.**

ad-lib, *v.*—*Syn.* improvise, extemporize, make up; see **invent** 1.

administer, *v.* **1.** [To manage]—*Syn.* conduct, direct, control; see **command** 2, **manage** 1.

2. [To minister]—*Syn.* provide with, give, bring in, furnish, dispense, regulate, apply, authorize, determine, administer to, give *or* mete *or* serve *or* measure *or* deal out, supply, tender, offer, proffer, distribute, make application of, impose, contribute, disburse.

3. [To inflict]—*Syn.* deal out, strike, deliver; see **inflict** 1.

4. [To tender]—*Syn.* extend, proffer, give; see **offer** 1.

administration, *n.* **1.** [The direction of affairs] —*Syn.* management, government, supervision, command, superintendence, guidance, surveillance, conduct, conducting, directing, decision making, decision theory, oversight, organization, agency, authority, disposition, policing, treatment, handling, strategy, policy, ordering, legislation, jurisdiction, execution, regulation, performance, rule, order, enforcement, charge, control, power, husbandry, housekeeping, stewardship.

2. [Those who direct affairs]—*Syn.* directors, administrators, officers, supervisors, superintendents, advisers, command, headmen, stewards, executives, strategists, officials, committee, board, board of directors, board of governors, board of overseers, executive, executive office, executive branch, legislature, office of the president, president, presidency, chief executive, presidium, commissariat, cabinet, ministry, commander, chairman, general, admiral, commander in chief, central office, headquarters, the management, executive committee, bureau, consulate, consulate general, embassy, legation, department, Washington, chargé d'affaires, governmental power, party in power; *all* (D): brass, front office, the powers that be, the profitorial, (insider's) insider, the man.

3. [The period in which an administration, sense 2, is operative]—*Syn.* term, term of office, tenure, presidency, regime, reign, dynasty, incumbency, power, stay.

administrative, *mod.*—*Syn.* executive, controlling, deciding, jurisdictional, decisive, commanding, directing, directorial, presiding, official, central, governmental, gubernatorial, directive, skillful in administration, supervising, superintending, managing, managerial, magisterial, lawgiving, governing, legislative, ruling, authoritative, departmental, regulative, bureaucratic, determining, in control (of), in charge (of), policy-making (D).

administrator, *n.*—*Syn.* executive, president, vice-president, secretary, treasurer, executive secretary, head of the department, department head, chief executive, CEO (Chief Executive Officer), supervising director, chairman of the board of directors, director-general, vice-president in charge, person in authority, divisional supervisor, district manager, chairman, dean, registrar, bursar, manager, head, chief, man in charge, superintendent, supervisor, minister, bureaucrat, ambassador, leader, governor, controller, chief controller, consul, comptroller, commissar, premier, mayor, organizer, official, businessman, master, commander, captain, guardian, director, custodian, overseer, leader, inspector, impressario, producer, judge; *all* (D): pencil pusher, key man, the brains, boss, big shot, front office, stuffed shirt, brass collar, the guv'nor.

admirable, *mod.*—*Syn.* worthy, attractive, good; see **excellent.**

admiral, *n.*—*Syn.* commander of the fleet, fleet admiral, admiral of the fleet, commander in chief, naval officer, chief of naval operations, admiralty, office of the admiral, vice admiral, rear admiral.

admiration, *n.* **1.** [A high degree of respect] —*Syn.* praise, deference, approbation, approval, estimation, encomium, regard, fondness, esteem, respect, appreciation, favor, pleasurable contemplation, adoration, applause, glorification, idolization, idolatry, honor, recognition, prizing, valuing, liking, love, high regard, high opinion, reverence, veneration, homage, obeisance, kneeling.—*Ant.* objection*, disregard, distrust.

2. [Wondering delight]—*Syn.* wonderment, amazement, astonishment; see **wonder** 1.

admire, *v.* **1.** [To have regard for]—*Syn.* esteem, honor, applaud, praise, extol, respect, approve, revere, venerate, eulogize, panegyrize, laud, boost, glorify, reverence, hold dear, appreciate, credit, commend, repute, value, treasure, prize, look up to, rate highly, pay homage to, idolize, adore, hail,

put a high price on, regard with approbation, have a high opinion of, think wonderful, wonder at, think highly of, rate high, value *or* esteem highly, regard as fine, consider brilliant, contemplate pleasurably, hold in respect, think well of, show deference to; *all* (D): take great stock in, put on a pedestal, make an ado about.—*Ant.* censure*, deride, deprecate.
2. [To be fond of]—*Syn.* cherish, have a fondness for, feel warmly toward; see **like** 2.

admirer, *n.* **1.** [One who admires a person or thing] —*Syn.* supporter, believer, patron; see **follower.**
2. [A suitor]—*Syn.* wooer, adorer, sweetheart, swain; see **lover** 1.

admissible, *mod.*—*Syn.* proper, suitable, right, just, fair, allowed, allowable, passable, probable, possible, tolerable, fit, approvable, reasonable, permissible, permitted, justifiable, rational, logical, warranted, legal, lawful, licit, legitimate, not impossible, warrantable, considerable, concedable, not unlikely, worthy, free, unprohibited, relevant, appropriate, likely, applicable, pertinent, all right, in place, okay (D).—*Ant.* unfair, banned, inadmissible.

admission, *n.* **1.** [The act of entering]—*Syn.* admittance, ingress, access; see **entrance** 1.
2. [The act of granting entrance]—*Syn.* acceptance, admittance, permission, reception, recipience, welcome, recognition, acknowledgment, certification, confirmation, designation, selection, initiation, *entrée* (French).—*Ant.* removal*, rejection, expulsion.
3. [The entrance fee]—*Syn.* (cover) charge, fee, ticket, price, check, dues, charges, demand, toll, tax, minimum, donation; *all* (D): cover, gate, tariff.
4. [Something acknowledged]—*Syn.* statement, disclosure, confession, profession, avowal, acknowledgment, concession, allowance, divulgence, declaration, affirmation, confirmation, assertion, accession, testimony, attestation, testimonial, averment, allegation, deposition, affidavit.—*Ant.* denial*, disallowance, repudiation.
5. [The act of admitting]—*Syn.* affirmation, assent, assertion; see **acknowledgment** 1.

admit, *v.* **1.** [To grant entrance]—*Syn.* receive, give access to, allow entrance to; see **receive** 4.
2. [To confess]—*Syn.* acknowledge, own, indicate, disclose, bare, unveil, uncover, lay bare, expose, proclaim, declare, open up, unbosom oneself, bring to light, go over, go into details, confide to, tell, relate, narrate, enumerate, divulge, reveal, make a clean breast of, avow, communicate, make known, recite, number, tell the whole story; *all* (D): break down and confess, plead guilty, let slip, own up, talk, sing, cough up, come clean, spill the beans, spill, let on, come out into the open.—*Ant.* hide*, cover up, obscure.
3. [To acknowledge]—*Syn.* concede, allow, accord, grant, accept, agree, confess, realize, indicate, concur, avow, consent, accede, acquiesce, yield, tolerate, recognize, declare, profess, adopt, assent, confirm, affirm, approve, reciprocate, subscribe to, coincide, assume, make way for, credit, give credence to, fall in with.—*Ant.* deny*, differ, disagree.
4. [To permit]—*Syn.* let, allow, grant; see **allow** 1.

admonish, *v.* **1.** [To reprimand]—*Syn.* reprove, chide, rebuke; see **scold.**
2. [To exhort]—*Syn.* urge, advise, counsel; see **warn** 2.

admonition, *n.*—*Syn.* advice, notice, exhortation; see **warning.**

adolescence, *n.*—*Syn.* minority, puberty, teens (D); see **youth** 1.

adolescent, *mod.*—*Syn.* pubescent, juvenile, youthful; see **young** 1.

adolescent, *n.*—*Syn.* youngster, minor, teenager; see **youth** 3.

adopt, *v.* **1.** [To take as a son or daughter]—*Syn.* pick, choose, select, transfer, father, mother, name, take in, raise, take from an orphanage, sign adoption papers for, take into one's family, make one's heir, take as one's own (child), naturalize, foster. —*Ant.* discard*, disinherit, cast out.
2. [To take as one's own]—*Syn.* embrace, appropriate, seize, take up *or* over, choose, assume, use, take to oneself, utilize, imitate, borrow, adapt for use, make one's own, espouse, affiliate, mimic.—*Ant.* deny*, repudiate, reject.
3. [To vote acceptance]—*Syn.* affirm, assent (to), ratify; see **approve** 1.

adoption, *n.* **1.** [Selection]—*Syn.* choosing, appropriation, choice; see **selection** 1.
2. [Acceptance]—*Syn.* confirmation, enactment, approval; see **permission.**

adorable (D), *mod.*—*Syn.* delightful, lovable, cute; see **charming.**

adoration, *n.* **1.** [Worship]—*Syn.* devotion, homage, veneration; see **worship** 1.
2. [Love]—*Syn.* ardor, affection, devotion; see **love** 1.

adore, *v.* **1.** [To worship]—*Syn.* venerate, revere, glorify; see **worship** 2.
2. [To love]—*Syn.* cherish, treasure, prize; see **love** 1.

adorn, *v.*—*Syn.* beautify, embellish, ornament; see **decorate.**

adorned, *mod.*—*Syn.* trimmed, decked, garnished; see **ornate** 1.

adornment, *n.* **1.** [The act of decorating]—*Syn.* ornamentation, embellishment, gilding; see **decoration** 1.
2. [A decoration]—*Syn.* ornament, trimming, frill; see **decoration** 2.

adrift, *mod.*—*Syn.* loose, floating, drifting; see **afloat.**

adroit, *mod.*—*Syn.* clever, skillful, adept; see **able** 1, 2.

adroitness, *n.* **1.** [Cunning]—*Syn.* craftiness, cleverness, trickiness; see **acumen, dishonesty.**
2. [Ability]—*Syn.* deftness, dexterity, skill; see **ability** 2.

adulation, *n.*—*Syn.* applause, commendation, laudation; see **flattery, praise** 1, 2.

adult, *mod.*—*Syn.* of age, grown, developed; see **mature** 1.

adult, *n.*—*Syn.* mature person, grown-up, fully developed member of a species; see **man** 2, **woman** 1.

adulterate, *v.*—*Syn.* weaken, mix, intermix, alloy, amalgamate, dilute, infiltrate, infect, lessen, reduce, concoct, infuse, transfuse, mingle, commingle, blend, taint, pollute, debase, corrupt, contaminate, depreciate, cheapen, devalue, vitiate, muddle, impair, make lower in quality, mingle *or* mix with, thin out, defile, denature, degrade, deteriorate, dissolve, make impure, simplify, falsify; *all* (D): cut, water (down), doctor.—*Ant.* purify*, cleanse, maintain.

adulterated, *mod.*—*Syn.* diluted, mixed, contaminated; see **impure** 1.

adulteration, *n.*—*Syn.* corruption, deterioration, contamination; see **pollution.**

adulterous, *mod.*—*Syn.* illicit, unchaste, immoral; see **wicked** 1.

adultery, *n.*—*Syn.* unlicensed intercourse, infidelity, cuckoldry; see **fornication.**

advance, *n.* **1.** [The act of moving forward]—*Syn.* impetus, progression, motion; see **progress** 1.

2. [Promotion]—*Syn.* enrichment, betterment, increase; see **improvement** 1.

3. [Increase]—*Syn.* rise, progress, boost (D); see **increase** 1.

4. [Loan]—*Syn.* accommodation, allowance, credit; see **loan.**

5. [Suggestion; *usually plural*]—*Syn.* overture, approach, proposal; see **suggestion** 1.

advance, *v.* **1.** [To move forward physically]—*Syn.* progress, proceed, move on, forge ahead, press on, stride forward, push ahead, go on, go forth, gain ground, speed on, make headway, storm across, step forward, come to the front, conquer territory, march *or* get on, move onward, continue ahead, push *or* press on; *all* (D): eat up ground, tear ahead, mush.—*Ant.* halt*, stop, stand still.

2. [To cause to move forward]—*Syn.* launch, propel, drive; see **push** 2.

3. [To propose]—*Syn.* set forth, introduce, suggest; see **propose** 1.

4. [To promote]—*Syn.* further, encourage, urge; see **promote** 1.

5. [To promote in rank or station]—*Syn.* raise, graduate, elevate; see **promote** 2.

6. [To accelerate]—*Syn.* dispatch, speed *or* move up, quicken; see **hasten** 2.

7. [To raise]—*Syn.* add to, magnify, enlarge; see **raise** 1.

8. [To lend]—*Syn.* loan, provide with, furnish; see **lend** 1.

9. [To pay]—*Syn.* make payment, prepay, pay up; see **pay** 1.

10. [To improve]—*Syn.* develop, make progress, get better; see **improve** 2.

advanced, *mod.* **1.** [Superior]—*Syn.* precocious, first, exceptional; see **excellent.**

2. [Aged]—*Syn.* seasoned, venerable, time-honored; see **old** 1, 3.

3. [Progressive]—*Syn.* radical, unconventional, ahead of the times; see **liberal** 2.

4. [In front]—*Syn.* forward, in advance, first; see **ahead** 2.

advancement, *n.* **1.** [Promotion in rank]—*Syn.* preferment, elevation, raise; see **promotion** 1.

2. [Progress]—*Syn.* gain, headway, progression; see **progress** 1.

advantage, *n.* **1.** [Preferred condition or circumstance]—*Syn.* luck, favor, approval, help, aid, sanction, leeway, good, patronage, support, preference, choice, odds, protection, start, leg-up, helping hand, upper hand, leverage, best plight, purchase, hold, favoring circumstance, dominating position, favorable opportunity, superior situation, best estate, vantage ground, play; *all* (D): pull, edge, ace in the hole, whip hand, card up one's sleeve. —*Ant.* handicap, disadvantage*, drawback.

2. [The result of having an advantage, sense 1.] —*Syn.* dominance, superiority, supremacy, lead, influence, vantage, upper hand, power, resources, wealth, mastery, profit, gain, authority, prestige, recognition, position, eminence, pre-eminence, hold, sway, precedence, ascendancy, prevalence. —*Ant.* failure*, submission, impotence.

3. [Benefit]—*Syn.* good, gain, profit, welfare, avail, interest, expediency, improvement, return, behalf, account, sake, worth, comfort, gratification, convenience, help, utility, success, emolument, windfall, satisfaction, consolation, enjoyment, pleasure, solace, bounty, favor, boon, weal, blessing, service, compensation, prize.—*Ant.* misfortune*, calamity, catastrophe.

have the advantage of—*Syn.* be superior, have the opportunity, be privileged; see **succeed** 1.

take advantage of—*Syn.* exploit, profit by, opportunize; see **use** 1.

to advantage—*Syn.* successfully, advantageously, well; see **helpfully.**

advent, *n.*—*Syn.* approach, coming, appearance; see **arrival** 1.

adventure, *n.*—*Syn.* happening, experience, story; see **event** 1, 2.

adventurer, *n.* **1.** [One who seeks adventure] —*Syn.* explorer, pirate, globe-trotter, free lance, soldier of fortune, knight-errant, daredevil, madcap, hero, pioneer, mountain climber, wild game hunter, record breaker, stunt flyer, Don Quixote, Robin Hood, romantic, dragonslayer, entrepreneur; see also **pioneer** 2, **traveler.**

2. [One who lives by his wits]—*Syn.* charlatan, opportunist, rogue; see **rascal.**

adventurous, *mod.*—*Syn.* bold, adventuresome, courageous; see **brave** 1.

adverb, *n.*—*Syn.* qualifier, (adverbial) modifier, qualifying construction, limiting word.

adversary, *n.*—*Syn.* opponent, rival, foe; see **enemy** 1, 2.

adverse, *mod.* **1.** [Hostile]—*Syn.* antagonistic, conflicting, inimical; see **unfriendly** 1.

2. [Unfavorable]—*Syn.* unpropitious, inopportune, disadvantageous; see **unfavorable** 2.

adversely, *mod.*—*Syn.* unfavorably, negatively, with prejudice, skeptically, resentfully, with scarce *or* without sympathy, unsympathetically, coolly, with a jaundiced *or* cold eye; see also **unfavorably.**

adversity, *n.*—*Syn.* misfortune, reverse, trouble; see **difficulty** 1, 2.

advertise, *v.* **1.** [To make public]—*Syn.* publicize, proclaim, herald, announce, blazon, declare, notify, promulgate, warn, display, exhibit, show, reveal, expose, disclose, unmask, divulge, uncover, communicate, publish abroad, issue, broadcast, print, circulate, placard, show off, parade, vent, post, propagate, disseminate, inform, celebrate, propagandize, spread, put on display, unveil, air, acquaint, apprise, noise abroad, give information to the public concerning, make known by printed public notice, announce publicly, make a public announcement of, lay before the public, call public attention to, give public notice of, bruit *or* blaze abroad, make proclamation of, give out; *all* (D): press-agent, ballyhoo, plug, play up.—*Ant.* hide*, conceal, cover.

2. [To solicit business]—*Syn.* praise the good qualities of, cry up, vaunt, commend to the public, make conspicuous, describe, promote, display, exhibit, show, spread, splash, build up, publicize, circularize, advance, give samples, sponsor, endorse; *all* (D): ballyhoo, boost, push, plug.

advertised, *mod.* —*Syn.* announced, posted, noted, publicized, billed, published, printed, pasted up, made public, broadcast, emphasized, pointed up *or* out, told of, displayed, exhibited, shown, offered, presented, put on sale, flaunted; *all* (D): plugged, boosted, ballyhooed, built up, pushed.—*Ant.* covered*, unannounced, forgotten.

advertisement, *n.* **1.** [A public notice]—*Syn.* proclamation, notification, declaration, broadcast, propaganda sheet, communication, publication, display, bill, placard, poster, printed public notice; see also **announcement** 2.

2. [Anything intended to promote a sale]—*Syn.* announcement, notice, publicity, exhibit, exhibition, (window) display, circular, handbill, broadside, display advertisement, classified advertisement, sample, endorsement; *all* (D): (want) ad, build-up, plug, ballyhoo, blurb, trailer, throwaway, (color) spread; classified; page, half page, etc.; leader, flyer.

advertiser, *n.* —*Syn.* dealer, merchant, peddler; see **businessman.**

advertising, *n.* **1.** [Calling goods to public attention] —*Syn.* exhibiting, exhibition, exposition, promoting, promotion, circularization, billing, posting, placarding, proclamation, announcing, displaying, broadcasting; *all* (D): ballyhooing, plugging, pushing.

2. [Anything intended to advertise]—*Syn.* announcement, window display, exhibit; see **advertisement** 1, 2.

advice, *n.* —*Syn.* guidance, instruction(s), consultation(s), suggestion(s), preaching, information, admonition, exhortation, forewarning, warning, caution, a word to the wise, injunction, charge, lesson, directions, advocacy, opinion, counsel, recommendation regarding a course of action, opinion recommended, advisement, encouragement, persuasion, dissuasion, prescription, recommendation, proposition, proposal, view, help, aid, judgment, words (D).

advisability, *n.* —*Syn.* recommendability, suitability, fitness; see **propriety** 1.

advisable, *mod.* —*Syn.* fitting, prudent, expedient; see **judicious.**

advise, *v.* **1.** [To give counsel]—*Syn.* recommend, prescribe, guide, exhort, direct, admonish, warn, instruct, counsel, advocate, suggest, urge, prompt, show, tell, enjoin, inform, move, caution, charge, encourage, preach, dissuade, teach, persuade, offer an opinion to, give counsel *or* advice *or* suggestions to, forewarn, give a recommendation, prepare, point out, opine, seek to persuade; *all* (D): wise up, straighten out, give the facts.—*Ant.* deceive*, misdirect, lead astray.

2. [To give information]—*Syn.* report, inform, make known; see **notify** 1.

advised, *mod.* —*Syn.* thought out, prudent, considered; see **deliberate.**

advisedly, *mod.* **1.** [After due consideration] —*Syn.* consciously, thoughtfully, intentionally; see **deliberately** 2.

2. [Carefully]—*Syn.* discreetly, cautiously, prudently; see **carefully** 2.

adviser, *n.* —*Syn.* counselor, counsel, lawyer, attorney, solicitor, instructor, preceptor, tutor, teacher, admonitor, back-seat driver, Solon, Nestor, monitor, coach, consultant, doctor, judge, priest, confessor, informant, helper, partner, referee, guide, director, mentor, prompter, expert, authority, cabinet; *both* (D): right-hand man, girl *or* man Friday; see also **authority** 3, **friend** 1, **teacher** 1.

advisory, *mod.* **1.** [Giving advice]—*Syn.* consulting, consultive, consultative, consultating, consultatory, having power to advise, acting under advice, prudential.

2. [Not mandatory]—*Syn.* discretionary, noncompulsory, voluntary; see **optional.**

advocacy, *n.* —*Syn.* support, assistance, backing; see **aid** 1.

advocate, *v.* **1.** [To defend]—*Syn.* vindicate, plead for, uphold; see **defend** 3.

2. [To promote]—*Syn.* bolster, push, further, advance; see **promote** 1.

aerial, *mod.* —*Syn.* in the air, flying, aeronautical, birdlike, atmospheric, aeriform, air-minded, airy, ethereal, up above, lofty, high-flying, on the ether waves (D); see also **high** 2.—*Ant.* terrestrial, earthly*, on the ground.

aeronaut, *n.* —*Syn.* aerial navigator, balloonist, astronaut; see **pilot** 1.

aeronautics, *n.* pl.—*Syn.* aviation, air transportation, flight, flying, theory of flight, aerography, pneumatics, aerodynamics, aeromechanics, aerostatics, aerial navigation, airmanship, ballooning, aerodonetics, science of flight in aircraft, art of navigation in the air, violation, volitation, aerial studies, aerial maneuvers, avigation.

aeroplane, *n.* —*Syn.* airplane, flying machine, heavier-than-air machine; see **plane** 3.

aesthete, *n.* —*Syn.* connoisseur, man of good taste, gourmet; see **critic** 2, **specialist.**

aesthetic, *mod.* —*Syn.* creative, appreciative, inventive; see **artistic** 1, 3, **beautiful** 1.

afar, *mod.* —*Syn.* far off, remote, far away; see **distant** 1.

affable, *mod.* **1.** [Friendly]—*Syn.* sociable, courteous, approachable; see **friendly** 1.

2. [Benign]—*Syn.* mild, gentle, gracious; see **kind** 1.

affair, *n.* **1.** [Business; *often plural*]—*Syn.* concern, responsibility, matter, duty, topic, subject, case, circumstance, thing, question, office, function, private concern, personal business, calling, employment, occupation, profession, pursuit, avocation, obligation, job, province, realm, interest, mission, assignment, task.

2. [An illicit love affair]—*Syn.* liaison, rendezvous, intrigue, amour, affaire, intimacy, romance, relationship, affair of the heart, *affaire d'amour, affaire de coeur* (*both* French).

3. [Party]—*Syn.* entertainment, gathering, function; see **party** 1.

4. [A thing]—*Syn.* occurrence, matter, concern; see **thing** 8.

affect, *v.* **1.** [To have an effect upon]—*Syn.* impress, sway, induce; see **influence.**

2. [To pretend]—*Syn.* assume, take on, feign, put on; see **pretend** 1.

3. [To move emotionally]—*Syn.* touch, stir, sway; see **move** 3.

affectation, *n.*—*Syn.* pose, mannerism, simulation; see **pretense** 1, 2.

affected, *mod.* **1.** [Being subject to influence] —*Syn.* moved, touched, melted, influenced, sympathetic, stimulated, stirred, grieved, overwhelmed, moved to tears, hurt, injured, excited, wakened, struck, impressed, brought to a realization of, overwrought, imbued with, devoured by, acted *or* worked upon, concerned, reached, compassionate, tender, sorry, troubled, distressed. —*Ant.* indifferent*, unmoved, untouched.

2. [Assumed artificially]—*Syn.* insincere, pretentious, pedantic, melodramatic, self-conscious, starchy, unnatural, histrionic, stilted, overprecise, superficial, awkward, mannered, theatrical, stiff, strained, mincing, overdone, apish, ostentatious, exhibitionistic, hollow, shallow; *all* (D): highfalutin', showy, arty, too-too, stuck-up, put-on. —*Ant.* simple*, natural, genuine.

3. [Feigned]—*Syn.* simulated, imitated, faked, apish, unnatural, counterfeited, falsified, shammed.

affecting, *mod.*—*Syn.* moving, touching, pathetic; see **pitiful** 1.

affection, *n.*—*Syn.* love, friendship, liking, attachment, good will, predilection, heart, endearment, partiality, passion, ardor, zealous, attachment, friendliness, concern, regard, desire, closeness, kindness, devotion, tenderness, fondness, solicitude.—*Ant.* hatred*, dislike, enmity.

affectionate, *mod.*—*Syn.* kind, tender, fond, friendly; see **loving.**

affidavit, *n.*—*Syn.* testimony, sworn statement, affirmation; see **oath** 1.

affiliate, *n.*—*Syn.* assistant, colleague, co-worker; see **associate.**

affiliate to *or* **with,** *v.*—*Syn.* combine, associate, form a connection with; see **associate** 3, **unite** 1.

affinity, *n.* **1.** [Attraction based on affection]—*Syn.* fondness, liking, closeness; see **affection.**

2. [A family feeling]—*Syn.* kinship, relation, relationship, bond, tie, connection, consanguinity, alliance, blood tie, association, attachment, union, propinquity, relationship by marriage, interconnection, parentage, fraternity, strain, lineage, heritage, agnation, cognation, breed, stock, affiliation.

3. [Appetency]—*Syn.* attraction, magnetism, magnetization, ionization, combining power, instability, susceptibility, attractivity, elective affinity, chemical affinity, valence.

4. [Similarity]—*Syn.* likeness, resemblance, correspondence; see **similarity.**

affirm, *v.*—*Syn.* assert, repeat, insist; see **declare** 1.

affirmation, *n.* **1.** [An assertion]—*Syn.* statement, avowal, attestation; see **declaration** 1.

2. [A declaration]—*Syn.* testimony, affidavit, sworn statement; see **oath** 1.

3. [Ratification]—*Syn.* confirmation, sanction, acceptance; see **confirmation** 1.

affirmative, *mod.*—*Syn.* agreeing, affirming, affirmatory, consenting, concurring, approving, ratifying, assenting, supporting, complying, endorsing, acknowledging, acquiescent, establishing, corroborative, confirmatory, confirmative.—*Ant.* negative*, contradictory, noncommittal.

in the affirmative—*Syn.* favorable, in assent *or* agreement, with an affirmative answer; see **yes.**

affix, *v.*—*Syn.* fasten, attach, append; see **join** 1.

afflict, *v.*—*Syn.* try, torment, trouble; see **hurt** 1.

affliction, *n.*—*Syn.* trouble, trial, hardship, plight; see **difficulty** 1, 2.

affluent, *mod.* **1.** [Abundant]—*Syn.* copious, full, bountiful; see **plentiful** 2.

2. [Rich]—*Syn.* wealthy, opulent, well-to-do; see **rich** 1.

afford, *v.* **1.** [To produce]—*Syn.* provide, furnish, yield; see **produce** 1.

2. [To be in a position to buy]—*Syn.* have enough for, spare (the money for), make both ends meet, allow, be able to, be disposed to, have the means for, be financially able, well afford, have sufficient means for, sustain, bear, manage, support, stand, spare the price of, be able to meet the expense of, incur without detriment to financial condition, bear the expense of, be in the market for.—*Ant.* fail*, go bankrupt, be unable to afford.

affront, *n.*—*Syn.* insult, indignity, offense; see **insult.**

affront, *v.*—*Syn.* slander, provoke, taunt; see **insult.**

afire, *mod.*—*Syn.* aflame, burning, flaming, on fire, blazing, ablaze, ignited, going up in smoke (D), oxidizing, smoking, glowing, smoldering.—*Ant.* extinguished*, smothered, drenched.

afloat, *mod.*—*Syn.* adrift, drifting, floating, unfastened, loose, untied, unfixed, on the seas, at sea, on board ship, sailing, seaworthy, flooded, on the high seas, in service, commissioned.—*Ant.* ashore*, docked, beached.

afoot, *mod.* **1.** [Walking]—*Syn.* on foot, hiking, marching; *all* (D): on footback, by hobnail express, on the ankle, on shanks' mare *or* mares.—*Ant.* traveling*, by ship, by plane.

2. [In preparation]—*Syn.* in progress, stirring, going on, brewing, forthcoming, hatching, advancing, being prepared, in its first stages, being born, in embryo, astir, abroad, in action, getting ready; *both* (D): in the cards, cooking up.—*Ant.* finished*, completed, ended.

aforesaid, *mod.*—*Syn.* previous, above-mentioned, foregoing; see **preceding.**

afraid, *mod.* **1.** [Apprehensive of the future]—*Syn.* hesitant, anxious, apprehensive, disturbed, frightened, fearful, nervous, timorous, cautious, uneasy, timid, fidgety, alarmed, cowed, intimidated, cowardly, dismayed, abashed, daunted, disheartened, discouraged, perplexed, worried, perturbed, upset, distressed, fainthearted; *all* (D): jittery, jumpy, leery, chicken, shaky, shook-up.—*Ant.* confident*, self-assured, poised.

2. [Gripped by fear]—*Syn.* panic-stricken, in a fright, scared, terrified, terror-stricken, frightened, terrorized, shocked, frozen, aghast, nerves all shot, alarmed, startled, aroused, horrified, petrified,

stunned, rattled, struck dumb, blanched, trembling, in awe, in consternation, as though looking into an abyss; *all* (D): frightened to death, scared stiff, out of one's wits *or* senses, in a (blue) funk. —*Ant.* brave*, courageous, bold.

afresh, *mod.* —*Syn.* anew, newly, once more, over again; see **again.**

Africa, *n.* —*Syn.* the Dark Continent, land of the Niger, equatorial Africa, land of the Sahara, South of the Sahara, the veld, the high veld.
Countries in Africa include the following—Senegal, Chad, Republic of the Congo, Dahomey, Gabon, Benin, Ivory Coast, Madagascar, Seychelles, Rwanda, Togo, Upper Volta, Algeria, Libya, Mauritania, Mali, Guinea, Guinea-Bissau, Liberia, Nigeria, Niger, Egypt, Sudan, Ethiopia, Zambia, Mozambique, Kenya, Democratic Republic of Congo, Tanzania, Burundi, Angola, Rhodesia, Uganda, Central African Republic, Cameroon, Ghana, Zaire, Morocco, Tunisia, Gambia, Somalia, Zimbabwe, South Africa, Namibia, Sierra Leone, Equatorial Guinea, Malawi, Botswana, Lesotho, Swaziland, Djibouti.

African, *mod.* **1.** [Concerning a part of Africa] —*Syn.* North African, Moroccan, Egyptian, Libyan, Algerian, Saharan *or* Saharian, Sudanese *or* Sudanic, East African, Kenyan, Tanzanian, Ugandan, Ethiopian, Abyssinian, Eritrean, Ethiop, Somali, West African, Liberian, Ghanaian, Nigerian, Dahomian, Senegalese, Congolese, Angolan, Central African, Zambian, Rhodesian, South African.
2. [Concerning the inhabitants of Africa]—*Syn.* Negro, negroid, black, Bantu, Zulu, Swazi, Matabele, Hottentot, Bushman, Pygmy, Afrikaaner, Boer, Colored, Cape Colored, Yoruba, Ibo, Hausa, Ashanti, Masai, Kikuyu, Somali, Ethiopian, Egyptian, Arab, Moor, Moorish.

aft, *mod.* —*Syn.* abaft, rearward, behind; see **back.**

after, *mod.* and *prep.* **1.** [Behind in space]—*Syn.* back of, in the rear, behind; see **back.**
2. [Following]—*Syn.* next, later, subsequent; see **following.**

after all, *mod.* —*Syn.* at last, when all is said and done, in the end; see **finally** 2.

afterlife, *n.* —*Syn.* life after death, eternity, heaven; see **immortality** 2.

aftermath, *n.* —*Syn.* consequence, outcome, aftereffect; see **result.**

aftermost, *mod.* —*Syn.* hindmost, rearward, utmost; see **last** 1.

afternoon, *n.* —*Syn.* post meridian, P.M., early afternoon, late afternoon, mid-afternoon, teatime, cocktail hour, siesta hour, evening (D).

afterthought, *n.* —*Syn.* second thought, reconsideration, review; see **review** 1.

afterward, *mod.* —*Syn.* later, after, subsequently, in a while, a while later, afterwards, by and by, eventually, soon, on the next day, ultimately, in subsequent time, another time, in aftertime, thereon, thereafter, then, latterly, thereupon, posteriorly, in the sequel, ensuingly, at a later time.

again, *mod.* —*Syn.* anew, afresh, newly, once more, once again, repeatedly, over (and over), from the beginning, again and again, on and on, encore, another time, bis, over again, a second time, anon, freshly, *de novo* (Latin), *da capo* (Italian), reiteratively, recurrently; *both* (D): ditto, repeat.—*Ant.* once*, once only, at first.

as much again, —*Syn.* doubled, twice as much, multiplied; see **double.**

again and again, *mod.* —*Syn.* repeatedly, once again, continuously; see **again.**

against, *mod.* and *prep.* **1.** [Counter to]—*Syn.* in the face of, into, toward, opposite to, facing.
2. [In contact with]—*Syn.* on, upon, in collision with, in contact with; see also **next** 2.
3. [Contrary to]—*Syn.* in opposition to, opposed to, counter to, adverse to, in violation of, versus, in contrariety to, over against.
4. [Opposite]—*Syn.* facing, fronting, abreast, corresponding; see **opposite** 3.

age, *n.* **1.** [The period of one's existence]—*Syn.* span, lifetime, duration; see **life** 4.
2. [A particular point or time in one's life]—*Syn.* infancy, childhood, girlhood, boyhood, adolescence, adulthood, youth, late youth, middle age, old age, dotage, senility; *all* (D): sweet sixteen, flaming youth, anecdotage.
3. [A period of time]—*Syn.* epoch, era, period, time, century, decade, generation, interval, interim, term, movement, in the days *or* time of someone *or* something; see also **life** 4.

of age, —*Syn.* adult, twenty-one, having attained (one's) majority; see **mature** 1.

age, *v.* **1.** [To grow old]—*Syn.* grow feeble, decline, wane, advance in years, wrinkle, deteriorate, waste away, turn white, show one's years; *all* (D): have one foot in the grave, go downhill, go over the hill.
2. [To mature]—*Syn.* ripen, develop, mellow; see **grow** 2.

aged, *mod.* —*Syn.* gray, elderly, worn; see **old** 1, 2.

agency, *n.* **1.** [Place where business is transacted] —*Syn.* firm, bureau, company; see **office** 3, **business** 4.
2. [An instrumentality]—*Syn.* power, auspices, action; see **means** 1.

agenda, *n.* —*Syn.* list, plan, schedule; see **program** 2.

agent, *n.* **1.** [One who acts for another]—*Syn.* broker, promoter, operator, representative, salesman, assistant, emissary, appointee, servant, regent, intermediary, abettor, executor, attorney, lawyer, go-between, surrogate, labor leader, procurator, mediary, deputy, principal, factor, minister, envoy, canvasser, middleman, commissioner, vice-regent, consignee, delegate, commissary, syndic, proxy, substitute, factotum, steward, functionary, solicitor, negociant, ambassador, comprador, proctor, negotiator, advocate, coagent, *chargé d'affairs* (French), press agent, claim agent, employment agent, actor's agent; *all* (D): flesh peddler, booking agent, bookie, handler.
2. [An instrumentality]—*Syn.* medium, factor, agency; see **means**1.

aggrandize, *v.* **1.** [To exalt]—*Syn.* acclaim, applaud, commend; see **praise** 1.
2. [To increase]—*Syn.* enlarge, intensify, extend; see **increase** 1.

aggravate, *v.* **1.** [To irritate]—*Syn.* exasperate, annoy, provoke; see **bother** 2.
2. [To make worse]—*Syn.* worsen, augment, complicate; see **increase** 1.

aggravation, *n.* **1.** [Intensification]—*Syn.* heightening, worsening, sharpening, inflammation, deepening, strengthening, exaggeration.
2. [A cause of aggravation]—*Syn.* worry, affliction, distress; see **difficulty** 1, 2, **trouble** 2.
3. [(D) Annoyance]—*Syn.* irritation, provocation, exasperation; see **annoyance** 1.
aggregate, *n.*—*Syn.* sum, gross, total; see **all** 1, **whole.**
aggregation, *n.*—*Syn.* collection, aggregate, gathering; see **all** 1, **whole.**
aggression, *n.*—*Syn.* offensive, assault, invasion; see **attack** 1.
aggressive, *mod.* **1.** [*Said of an energetic individual*] —*Syn.* enterprising, domineering, pushing; see **active** 2.
2. [*Said of a combative individual or group*] —*Syn.* martial, belligerent, pugnacious, encroaching, warlike, attacking, bellicose, combative, threatening, advancing, offensive, antipathetic, disruptive, disturbing, hostile, intrusive, destructive, warmongering, hawkish, onrushing, contentious, intruding, battering, rapacious, invading, on the offensive, assailing, barbaric, guilty of aggression; *both* (D): up in arms, on the warpath.—*Ant.* peaceful*, peace-loving, dovish, pacific.
aggressor, *n.*—*Syn.* assailant, invader, offender; see **attacker.**
aghast,, *mod.*—*Syn.* horrified, terrified, alarmed; see **afraid** 2.
agile, *mod.*—*Syn.* nimble, quick, spry, deft, vigorous, frisky, spirited, lithe, sprightly, supple, dexterous, limber, athletic, easy-moving, rapid, prompt, tripping, active, ready, winged, swift-footed, alive, sportive, buoyant, energetic, stirring, brisk, lively, swift, alert, bustling, vivacious, fleet, sure-footed, light-footed, nimble-footed, mercurial, light-fingered, nimble-fingered.—*Ant.* awkward*, slow, clumsy.
agility, *n.*—*Syn.* nimbleness, dexterity, spryness, quickness, deftness, briskness, swiftness, sprightliness, friskiness, rapidity, readiness, liveliness, promptitude, alacrity, promptness, alertness, dispatch, expedition, litheness, activity, fleetness, suppleness, celerity, adroitness.—*Ant.* awkwardness*, slowness, clumsiness.
aging, *mod.*—*Syn.* declining, waning, falling, sinking, mellowing, getting on *or* along, maturing, senescent, developing, fermenting, wasting away, wearing out, growing old, lapsing, outworn, fading, crumbling, slumping; *all* (D): one foot in the grave, on the downgrade, stale.—*Ant.* growing*, flowering, ripening.
agitate, *v.*—*Syn.* stir, move, arouse; see **excite** 1, 2.
agitated, *mod.*—*Syn.* disturbed, moved, upset, aroused; see **excited.**
agitation, *n.*—*Syn.* stir, confusion, tumult; see **excitement.**
agitator, *n.*—*Syn.* reformer, revolutionary, radical, revisionist, anarchist, dogmatist, malcontent, disrupter, heretic, fighter, propagandist, ringleader, stormy petrel, zealous, advocate, firebrand, incendiary, leftist, soapbox orator, active supporter, (active) partisan, ardent champion, exciter of public debate, troublemaker, demagogue, agent, rabble rouser, *agent provocateur* (French), reactionary, organizer, sans-culotte, dissident, fifth columnist (D); see also **conservative, radical, rebel** 1.
agnostic, *n.*—*Syn.* freethinker, unbeliever, doubter; see **skeptic.**
ago, *mod.*—*Syn.* gone, since, past; see **before.**
agonize, *v.*—*Syn.* wince, struggle, writhe; see **suffer** 1.
agonizing, *mod.*—*Syn.* struggling, tormenting, extreme; see **disturbing, painful** 1.
agony, *n.*—*Syn.* suffering, torture, anguish; see **pain** 1, 2.
agree, *v.*—*Syn.* harmonize (with), coincide, get along (with), side with, concur, stand together, match (up), come to terms, parallel, go well with, go along with, fit in, tie up with, fall in with, tally, accord, attune, suit, say yes (to), conform, go hand in hand (with), equal, correspond (to), go together, be in harmony (with), synchronize, measure up (to), come round, attain to; *all* (D): square with, tone in with, jibe (with), be on, click, hit it off (with), be a go, hitch horses, blend in with, come over, call it a go, see eye to eye, make allowances.—*Ant.* differ*, disagree, debate.
agreeable, *mod.*—*Syn.* pleasing, satisfactory, acceptable; see **fair** 3, **kind** 1, **mild** 2, **pleasant** 1, 2.
agreeably, *mod.*—*Syn.* well, appropriately, happily, good-humoredly, good-naturedly, wonderfully, kindly, politely, graciously, pleasantly, pleasingly, satisfactorily, affably, charmingly, sympathetically, convivially, benevolently, frankly, affirmatively, obligingly, genially, amicably, amiably, welcomely, cheerfully, mutually, peacefully, favorably.—*Ant.* disagreeably*, negatively, antagonistically.
agree about, *v.*—*Syn.* come to terms, see eye to eye, settle; see **agree on.**
agreement, *n.* **1.** [The act of agreeing]—*Syn.* understanding, complying, compromise, assenting, accession, ratifying, authorizing, granting, adjustment, concessions, arbitration, mediation, bargaining, arrangement, acknowledging, verifying, approving, acceding, endorsing, finding a middle course *or* ground *or* common ground, ironing out the difficulties, supporting, concurring, dealing. —*Ant.* disagreeing*, disrupting, disputing.
2. [The state of being in accord]—*Syn.* conformity, friendship, accord, accordance, accommodation, congruity, concordance, correspondence, harmony, concord, unison, concert, common view, understanding, meeting of minds, amity, sympathy, brotherhood, reconciliation, affiliation, *détente, entente* (*both* French), alliance, intimacy, fellowship, companionship, goodwill, cooperation, satisfaction, concurrence, compliance, fraternity, brotherliness, affinity, closeness, balance, congruousness, equality, kinship, comity, peace, love, unity, uniformity, union, equanimity, unanimity, acclimation, conjunction, adjustment, consonance, tie.—*Ant.* disagreement*, enmity, disunity.
3. [An expression of agreement, sense 1.]—*Syn.* recognition, assent, approval, concurrence, avowal, confirmation, acknowledgment, adjustment, indenture, okay (D), equalization, reconciliation, compromise, treaty, pact, contract, bargain, compact, adjudication, covenant, cartel, arrangement, gentleman's agreement, note, writ, oath, affidavit,

settlement, stipulation, bond, negotiation, charter, protocol, convention, codicil, lease, transaction, interchange, exchange, (the) meeting of minds.

agree on, *v.* —*Syn.* come to terms, settle, make an arrangement, come to an understanding, arrange, close a deal, make *or* strike a bargain; see **eye to eye** (D).

agree to, *v.* —*Syn.* admit, consent (to), approve, endorse, accept, settle for, support, allow, ratify, comply (with), acquiesce (in), assent (to), confirm, abide by, affirm, acknowledge, defer to, concede, accede, verify, yield, permit, let, suffer, promise, submit to, give in, sanction, authorize; *all* (D): sign up, take (something) in one's stride, call it square, shake on, not mind, pull together, go along with, adjust oneself to, O.K.—*Ant.* argue*, dispute, dissent.

agree with, *v.* **1.** [To concur]—*Syn.* coincide, accord, harmonize; see **agree.**

2. [To suit]—*Syn.* be suitable *or* favorable *or* agreeable *or* healthful, be appropriate to, satisfy, be acceptable, please, fit, befit.

agricultural, *mod.* —*Syn.* rustic, gardening, floricultural, horticultural, arboricultural, agronomical; see also **rural.**

agriculture, *n.* —*Syn.* tillage, cultivation, horticulture; see **farming.**

agriculturist, *n.* —*Syn.* husbandman, rancher, farm expert; see **farmer.**

aground, *mod.* —*Syn.* on the ground, washed ashore, beached, foundered, grounded, stranded, swamped, shipwrecked, reefed, disabled, marooned, touching on the shore, resting on the bottom, on a rock, stuck in the mud, stuck (fast), not afloat, cast away, wrecked, shoaled, piled up (D).

ahead, *mod.* **1.** [Going forward]—*Syn.* advancing, progressing, leading; see **forward** 1.

2. [To the fore]—*Syn.* before, earlier (than), in advance (of), ahead of, advanced, preceding, precedent, antecedent, foremost, leading, in the lead, at the head of, in the foreground, in lee of, to the fore, in the van, first, in front of, a jump ahead of, in the front line, victorious, before one's path, in the direct line of one's course, triumphant, preliminary. —*Ant.* behind, back*, toward the end.

get ahead, —*Syn.* advance, prosper, progress; see **succeed** 1.

ahead of, *mod.* —*Syn.* in advance of, before, above; see **ahead** 2.

get ahead of, —*Syn.* outdo, excel, subordinate; see **surpass.**

aid, *n.* **1.** [Assistance]—*Syn.* comfort, help, benefit, favor, benevolence, patronage, cooperation, salvation, giving, gift, reward, bounty, compensation, allowance, charity, benefaction, succor, alleviation, mitigation, ministry, ministration, reinforcement, advocacy, promotion, subvention, encouragement, treatment, furtherance, support, advancement, backing, advice, guidance, service, sustenance, reinforcements, relief, honorarium, subsidy, endowment, rescue, deliverance, attention, care, first aid; *all* (D): lift, shoulder, (a) hand, plug, boost, clout.—*Ant.* hindrance, barrier*, obstacle.

2. [One appointed to give assistance]—*Syn.* aid, deputy, lieutenant; see **assistant.**

aid, *v.* —*Syn.* support, assist, serve; see **help** 1.

ailing, *mod.* —*Syn.* ill, sickly, feeble, weak; see **sick.**

ailment, *n.* —*Syn.* illness, sickness, infirmity, indisposition; see **disease** 1, 2, 3.

aim, *n.* —*Syn.* intention, object, plan; see **purpose** 1.

take aim—*Syn.* sight, level (at), train (on); see **aim** 2.

aim, *v.* **1.** [To direct one's effort]—*Syn.* endeavor, strive, propose; see **try** 1.

2. [To point a weapon]—*Syn.* train, steer, level (at), beam, direct, cock, set up, look through the gunsight, set the sights, sight, take aim, hold to a target, bracket; *both* (D): zero in on, draw a bead on.

aimed, *mod.* —*Syn.* proposed, marked, intended for, directed, designed, calculated, leveled, trained, steered, set, planned, anticipated.

aimless, *mod.* —*Syn.* purposeless, pointless, erratic, unavailing, thoughtless, careless, neglected, heedless, rambling, wandering, blind, random, indiscriminate, unsettled, flighty, capricious, wayward, dissolute, without aim *or* end, chance, haphazard, desultory, fortuitous, to no purpose, rudderless, drifting, stray, accidental, undirected, objectless, casual, indecisive, irresolute, fitful, fanciful, fickle, eccentric, unplanned, planless, helpless, unpredictable, shiftless, unfruitful, wanton.—*Ant.* purposeful, careful*, planned.

air, *n.* **1.** [The gaseous envelope of the earth] —*Syn.* atmosphere, stratosphere, troposphere, wind, breeze, draft, the open air, ozone, ether, sky, oxygen, the open, ventilation, the out of doors (D).

2. [The apparent quality]—*Syn.* look, mien, demeanor; see **appearance** 1.

3. [A tune]—*Syn.* theme, melody, strain; see **song.**

off the air—*Syn.* not being broadcast, closed, signed off (D); see **quiet** 2.

on the air—*Syn.* broadcasting, transmitting, reporting; see **on the air.**

up in the air—*Syn.* **1.** undecided, unsettled, unsure; see **uncertain** 2. **2.** angry, excited, annoyed; see **excited.**

walk on air—*Syn.* feel good *or* happy, be lively, enjoy; see **enjoy oneself.**

air, *v.* **1.** [To introduce air]—*Syn.* ventilate, open, freshen, aerate, air out, air-condition, circulate air, change air, expel *or* eject air, aerify, expose to air, change the air of, draw in air, fan, refresh, cool, purify, oxygenate, revivify.—*Ant.* close*, keep in, stifle.

2. [To expose to the air]—*Syn.* expose, hang out, sun, dry, spread (out).

3. [To speak publicly; *often derogatory*]—*Syn.* disclose, tell, speak; see **utter.**

aired, *mod.* **1.** [Exposed to the air]—*Syn.* ventilated, opened, freshened, purified, oxygenated, hung out, sunned, dried, spread (out).—*Ant.* closed*, stuffy, dark.

2. [Exposed to public attention]—*Syn.* exposed, disclosed, bruited (about), discussed, revealed, told, unveiled, publicized, brought to light, advertised, propagated, made known *or* public, published, divulged, bared, promulgated, spread abroad, disseminated.—*Ant.* secret*, undisclosed, concealed.

air force, *n.* —*Syn.* air fleet, flying force, flying corps, aviation service, air power, air cover, aerospace team, air arm, air service, U.S. Air Force, Strategic Air Command (SAC), Tactical Air Command (TAC), Navy Air Force, Marine Corps Air Force, Royal Air Force (R.A.F.), air cadets, Military Air Transport Service (MATS), *Luftwaffe* (German), *force de frappe* (French).

air lift, *n.* —*Syn.* transit, airdrop, air jump; see **transportation.**

air lift, *v.* —*Syn.* transport, convey, fly; see **carry** 1.

airline, *n.* —*Syn.* air carrier, commercial airline, air passenger carrier, air freight carrier; see **business** 4. Specific airlines include—American, Air France, British Airways, Continental, Delta, Eastern, Flying Tiger Line, Icelandic (Lofleider), Royal Dutch Airlines (KLM), Lufthansa German Airlines, Republic Airlines, Northwest Orient Airline, US Air, Pan American World Airways, Pacific, Qantas Empire Airways Ltd., Trans World Airlines (TWA), United.

airman, *n.* Types of airmen include the following—pilot, copilot, fighter pilot, bomber pilot, electronic countermeasures man, radar man, bombardier, radar operator, radio operator, flight engineer, navigator.

airplane, *n.* —*Syn.* aircraft, aeroplane, airliner, glider; see **plane** 3.

airport, *n.* —*Syn.* airfield, spaceport, airdrome, aerodrome, cosmodrome, flying field, landing field *or* airstrip, zone *or* strip, hangar, heliport, helipad, installations.

American International Airports include the following—Dulles International, Washington, D.C.; Friendship International, Baltimore, Md.; Honolulu International, Honolulu, Hawaii; J. F. Kennedy International, New York, New York; Los Angeles International, Los Angeles, California; Miami International, Miami, Florida; Newark International, Newark, New Jersey; O'Hare International, Chicago, Illinois; San Francisco International, San Francisco, California; Washington National, Washington, D.C.; Stapleton Field, Denver, Colorado; Dallas-Ft. Worth International, Dallas, Texas.

airs, *n.* pl.—*Syn.* affectation, affectedness, pretense, show; see **pretense** 2.

airship, *n.* —*Syn.* dirigible, zeppelin, lighter-than-air craft; see **balloon, plane** 3.

airtight, *mod.* **1.** [Not allowing air to enter]—*Syn.* impermeable to air, closed, shut (tight); see **tight** 2.

2. [Incontestable]—*Syn.* unassailable, indisputable, irrefutable; see **certain** 3.

airy, *mod.* **1.** [Open to the breeze]—*Syn.* windy, breezy, draughty, exposed, ventilated, open, spacious, lofty, well-ventilated, atmospheric, aerial, out-of-doors, pneumatic, climatic, outdoors, in the open, fluttering.—*Ant.* stifling, closed*, confined.

2. [Light and gay]—*Syn.* flippant, sprightly, whimsical; see **happy** 1.

3. [Immaterial]—*Syn.* unsubstantial, intangible, ethereal; see **immaterial** 2.

4. [Delicate]—*Syn.* fragile, frail, thin; see **dainty** 1.

aisle, *n.* —*Syn.* passageway, center aisle, left aisle, right aisle, opening, way, walk, path, course, artery, clearing, avenue, corridor, passage, gangway, alley, lane, ingress, egress.

ajar, *mod.* **1.** [Open]—*Syn.* unshut, unclosed, unlatched; see **open** 1, 2.

2. [Out of harmony]—*Syn.* discordant, grating, jarring; see **harsh** 1.

akin, *mod.* —*Syn.* cognate, kindred, affiliated; see **alike** 2, **related** 3.

alacrity, *n.* —*Syn.* alertness, quickness, liveliness; see **action** 1.

alarm, *n.* **1.** [Anything that gives a warning]—*Syn.* drum, siren, horn, tocsin, signal, fog horn, fire siren, call, bell, alarm clock, gong, buzzer, whistle, trumpet, distress signal(s), SOS, Mayday, red light, hoot, blast, shout, alarm bell, alarm gun, sound of trumpet, call *or* summons to arms, warning sound, beat of drum, war cry, hue and cry, danger signal, signal of distress, cry, squeal, yell, scream, air raid siren; *all* (D): escape button, chicken switch, panic button.

2. [Apprehension of danger]—*Syn.* dread, fright, trepidation; see **fear** 1, 2.

3. [A warning]—*Syn.* alert, notification, caution; see **warning.**

alarmed, *mod.* —*Syn.* frightened, fearful, aroused; see **afraid** 2.

alarming, *mod.* —*Syn.* frightening, foreboding, distressing; see **disturbing.**

alarmist, *n.* —*Syn.* scaremonger, fanatic, panicmonger; see **agitator.**

alas, *interj.* —*Syn.* dear, dear me, oh, lackaday, alack, woe, woe is me, horrible, too bad, my God; *all* (D): gracious me, gee, tsk-tsk, terrible.

Alaska, *n.* —*Syn.* the Klondike, the 49th state, the frozen North, the gold country, land of the sourdoughs; *all* (D): Seward's Folly, Uncle Sam's Attic, America's Ice Box.

albeit, *conj.* —*Syn.* even though, admitting, even if; see **although.**

Albion, *n.* —*Syn.* Great Britain, Britannia, British Isles; see **England.**

album, *n.* —*Syn.* collection, stamp book, register, registry, index, autograph book, visitor's book, memento, snapshots, scrapbook, notebook, photograph album, bride's book, portfolio, commonplace book, register for names, blank book for autographs, depository for photographs, visitor's register, memorandum book, memory book.

alcohol, *n.* —*Syn.* spirits, liquor, intoxicant, palliative, methanol, ethanol, wood alcohol, rubbing alcohol; ethyl alcohol, amyl alcohol, methyl alcohol, etc; *all* (D): alky, hard *or* straight stuff, white lightning; see also **drink** 2.

alcoholic, *mod.* —*Syn.* spirituous, fermented, distilled; see **strong** 8.

alcoholic, *n.* —*Syn.* addict, heavy drinker, dipsomaniac, sot; see **drunkard.**

alcoholism, *n.* —*Syn.* intoxication, insobriety, dipsomania; see **drunkenness.**

alcove, *n.* —*Syn.* niche, anteroom, study; see **room** 2.

alderman, *n.* —*Syn.* magistrate, ward officer, (district) representative, borough elector, municipal legislator, member of the board of aldermen, assemblyman; *both* (D): City Father, Solon.

ale, *n.* —*Syn.* malt, tap-fermented ale, brew; see **beer.**

alert, *mod.* **1.** [Watchful]—*Syn.* wary, on guard, wide-awake; see **observant** 2.

2. [Intelligent]—*Syn.* bright, clever, quick, sharp; see **intelligent** 1.

alert, *n.* —*Syn.* signal, alarm, admonition; see **warning.**

on the alert—*Syn.* watchful, aware, vigilant, on guard; see **observant** 1, 2.

alert, *v.* —*Syn.* inform, put on guard, signal; see **warn** 1.

alertness, *n.* —*Syn.* sharpness, readiness, vigilance; see **watchfulness.**

Alexandrian, *mod.* —*Syn.* Alexandrine, Hellenistic, Greek, neoclassic; see **classical** 2.

alfalfa, *n.* —*Syn.* fodder, feed, legume; see **hay.**

algae, *n.* pl.—*Syn.* seaweed, rockweed, scum, stonewort, dulse, sea lettuce, pond life, kelp, red kelp, green kelp.

alias, *n.* —*Syn.* pseudonym, false name, assumed name, nom de plume, nom de guerre, nickname, false title, phoney (moniker) (D).

alibi, *n.* **1.** [A legal defense]—*Syn.* proof of absence, plea, explanation, declaration, defense, statement, case, defense of being elsewhere, allegation, affirmation, avowal, assurance, profession, plea of being in another place, (plausible) excuse, assertion, justification, answer, reply, retort, pretext, vindication; *all* (D): puncture-proof *or* airtight alibi, stall, out, song and dance.

2. [(D) An excuse]—*Syn.* defense, account, reason; see **explanation** 2.

alien, *mod.* **1.** [Of foreign extraction]—*Syn.* exotic, strange, unknown; see **foreign** 1, 2.

2. [Unlike]—*Syn.* different, dissimilar, outlandish, queer; see **unusual** 2.

alien, *n.* —*Syn.* foreigner, stranger, refugee, displaced person *or* D.P., outsider, outlander, *uitlander* (Dutch), migrant, *émigré* (French), colonist, immigrant, guest, visitor, newcomer, space creature, barbarian, incomer, Ishmael, settler, tenderfoot, stateless person, intruder, squatter, interloper, invader, noncitizen, man without a country. —*Ant.* inhabitant*, native, citizen.

alienate, *v.* —*Syn.* estrange, turn away, set against, disaffect, withdraw the affections of, make unfriendly, come between, disunite, make inimical, separate, divide, part, wean away, make indifferent *or* averse, turn off (D).—*Ant.* unite*, reconcile, acclimate.

alienation, *n.* —*Syn.* deflection, variance, separation, disaffection, coolness, withdrawal, estrangement, breach, rupture, weaning away, division, diverting.

align, *v.* **1.** [To adjust]—*Syn.* arrange, straighten, regulate; see **adjust** 1, 3.

2. [To join]—*Syn.* associate with, enlist (with), follow; see **join** 2.

alignment, *n.* —*Syn.* adjustment, arrangement, sequence; see **order** 3.

out of alignment—*Syn.* misaligned, out of adjustment, twisted; see **crooked** 1, **wrong** 2.

alike, *mod.* **1.** [With the same qualities]—*Syn.* like, same, self-same, neither more nor less, without distinction or difference, twin, one, indistinguishable, copied, facsimile, duplicate, consubstantial, matched, mated, equal, matching, identical; *all* (D): chip off the old block, one and the same, all one, in the same boat, on all fours with, the very image of.—*Ant.* distinct, incongruous*, heterogeneous.

2. [With similar qualities]—*Syn.* analogous, akin, kindred, like, similar, much the same, comparable, homologous, parallel, correspondent, resembling, related, cognate, approximate, proximate, proportionate, equivalent, allied, associated, corresponding, of that kind, of a kind, in as many, congeneric, concurrent; *all* (D): of the same kidney, much the same, nearly the same, same but different, the same more or less.—*Ant.* different*, dissimilar, unlike.

3. [In like manner]—*Syn.* similarly, equally, likewise, in common, in the same manner, in the same degree, comparably, consonantly, answerable to, analogously, comparatively, in accordance with, correspondently, the same way.—*Ant.* differently*, dissimilarly, divergently.

alimentary, *n.* —*Syn.* alimental, wholesome, supplying sustenance, nutritious, salutary, nourishing, nutrient, sustaining, nutritive, sustentative, digestive, digestible, succulent, food taking, invigorating, food carrying, comestible, dietary, dietetic, providing maintenance, eutropic, esculent, absorptive, eupeptic, peptic.

alimony, *n.* —*Syn.* upkeep, maintenance, provision; see **support** 3.

alive, *mod.* **1.** [Having life]—*Syn.* live, animate, animated, living, breathing, in a living state, existing, existent, subsisting, vital, not dead, mortal, organic, extant, viable, growing, inspirited, in existence, quick, having life, vivified, conscious; *all* (D): alive and kicking, above ground, among the living. —*Ant.* dead*, lifeless, inanimate.

2. [Alert]—*Syn.* quick, sharp, ready; see **active** 2.

3. [Active]—*Syn.* swarming, bustling, stirring, lively; see **active** 1.

alkali, *n.* —*Syn.* salt, antacid, base, caustic soda. Varieties include the following—potassium hydrate, sodium hydrate, lithium hydrate, caesium hydrate, rubidium hydrate, ammonium hydrate, lime, magnesia, sodium carbonate, potassium carbonate.

alkaline, *mod.* —*Syn.* alkali, alkalescent, basic, caustic, metal oxide, salty, bitter, acrid, soluble, chemical, antacid, neutralizing.

all, *mod.* **1.** [Completely]—*Syn.* totally, wholly, entirely; see **completely.**

2. [Each]—*Syn.* every, any, each and every, any and every, every member of, for everybody *or* anybody *or* anyone *or* anything *or* everything, barring no one; *all* (D): bar none, one's all, beginning and end, the alpha and the omega, from A to Z. —*Ant.* no*, not any, none.

3. [Exclusively]—*Syn.* alone, nothing but, solely; see **only** 1.

4. [Whole]—*Syn.* complete, total, full; see **whole** 1.

all, *n.* **1.** [The whole number]—*Syn.* everything, everyone, every person, sum, sum total, aggregate, aggregation, collection, group, accumulation, ensemble, total, totality, quantity, unit, integer, entity; *all* (D): whole kit and caboodle, lock, stock, and barrel, the works, the whole schmear, the devil and all.—*Ant.* none*, nobody, nothing.

2. [The whole amount]—*Syn.* entirety, mass, totality; see **whole.**

after all—*Syn.* nevertheless, in spite of everything, despite; see **although.**

at all—*Syn.* to the slightest degree, in the least, none; see **never, not.**

for all—*Syn.* after all, nevertheless, despite; see **although.**

in all—*Syn.* all told, collectively, on the whole; see **altogether** 2.

allay, *v.* **1.** [To lessen]—*Syn.* reduce, abate, moderate; see **decrease** 2.

2. [To soothe]—*Syn.* mollify, pacify, ease; see **quiet** 1.

allegation, *n.*—*Syn.* assertion, statement, affirmation; see **declaration** 1.

allege, *v.*—*Syn.* state, testify, affirm; see **declare** 1.

allegedly, *mod.*—*Syn.* assertedly, by allegation *or* declaration, according to affirmation, professedly, according to the statement, as told *or* stated *or* said, by deposition, according to an affidavit, supposedly.

Allegheny, *mod.*—*Syn.* Appalachian, Pennsylvanian, in the anthracite area; see **eastern** 2.

allegiance, *n.*—*Syn.* fidelity, homage, fealty; see **loyalty.**

allegorical, *mod.*—*Syn.* figurative, symbolic, metaphorical; see **illustrative.**

allegory, *n.*—*Syn.* moral story, allegorical representation, parable; see **story.**

allergic to, *mod.*—*Syn.* sensitive to, affected by, subject *or* susceptible to, repelled by, oversensitive *or* hypersensitive *or* responsive to.—*Ant.* immune*, unaffected by, hardened to.

allergy, *n.*—*Syn.* hypersensitive bodily reaction, pathological hypersensitivity, antipathy to certain substances; see **disease** 3.

alleviate, *v.*—*Syn.* lighten, mitigate, ease; see **relieve** 2.

alley, *n.*—*Syn.* back street, lane, rear way; see **road** 1.

up *or* **down one's alley**—*Syn.* suited to one's abilities *or* tastes *or* interest(s), enjoyable, useful; see **fit** 1.

alliance, *n.* **1.** [The state of being allied]—*Syn.* connection, adherence, membership, affinity, concurrence, participation, co-operation, support, collusion, union, interrelation, concord, agreement, common understanding, marriage, matrimony, betrothal, kinship, relation, collaboration, fraternization, consanguinity, federation, communion, entente, engagement, friendship, partnership, coalition, association, affiliation, confederation, implication, bond, accord, congruity, mutuality, tie (D).—*Ant.* separation*, rupture, repudiation.

2. [The act of joining]—*Syn.* fusion, combination, coupling; see **union** 1.

3. [A union]—*Syn.* league, federation, company; see **organization** 3.

allied, *mod.* **1.** [United]—*Syn.* unified, confederated, associated; see **united** 2.

2. [Related]—*Syn.* associated, connected, linked; see **related** 2.

all-inclusive, *mod.*—*Syn.* encircling, complete, extensive; see **comprehensive.**

allot, *v.* **1.** [To distribute]—*Syn.* apportion, allocate, dole; see **distribute** 1.

2. [To assign]—*Syn.* allocate, appoint, earmark, designate; see **assign** 1.

allotment, *n.*—*Syn.* portion, lot, part; see **share.**

all-out, *mod.*—*Syn.* total, entire, complete; see **absolute** 1.

allow, *v.* **1.** [To permit an action]—*Syn.* permit, let, sanction, grant, consent to, grant *or* give permission to *or* for, tolerate, favor, be favorable to, yield, suffer, bear, allow for *or* to, leave, privilege, accord (to), approve (of), give leave, accredit, endorse, certify, commission, humor, suffer to occur, interpose no obstacles in the way of, gratify, have no objection, release, pass, indulge, be indulgent of, oblige, authorize, pass over, license, warrant, empower, put up with; *all* (D): give the green light *or* the go-ahead *or* the high sign, bear with, blink at, hold a loose rein, give the reins to, give free rein to, grin and bear it, leave the door open, hear to, give one one's head, lay in the lap of the gods, give one leeway, not blink (or bat) an eye, give carte blanche, give a free course to, let things take their course, give one line.—*Ant.* deny*, forbid, prohibit.

2. [To grant a request or assertion]—*Syn.* recognize, support, approve; see **admit** 3.

3. [To include in an estimate]—*Syn.* concede, subtract, deduct, make allowance, give an allowance for, give at lower rates, add to, raise assessment.—*Ant.* discard*, disallow, declare worthless.

allowable, *mod.*—*Syn.* permissible, proper, legal; see **admissible.**

allowance, *n.* **1.** [Portion]—*Syn.* quantity, quota, ration; see **share.**

2. [A periodic gratuity]—*Syn.* salary, wage, commission, fee, recompense, hire, quarterage, pittance, remittance, stipend, gift (travel) grant, pension, alimony, annuity stated maintenance, settled rate, endowment, scholarship, fellowship, prize, bounty, interest, subsidy, honorarium, pay, viaticum, stint, bequest, legacy, inheritance, grant for support, contribution, aid, subvention; *all* (D): dole, handout, pin money, pocket money.

3. [Discount]—*Syn.* reduction, deduction, cut; see **discount.**

make allowances (for)—*Syn.* weigh, excuse, rationalize; see **allow for, consider** 1, **justify** 2.

allow for, *v.*—*Syn.* take into account *or* consideration, provide for, consider, make allowance *or* concession *or* provision for, make up for, set apart.—*Ant.* neglect*, ignore, reject.

alloy, *n.*—*Syn.* amalgam, admixture, compound, mixture, intermixture, combination, debasement, adulteration, reduction; see also **metal.**

Common metal alloys include the following—ferromanganese, ferrosilicon, pewter, type metal, chromesteel, nichrome, vanadium-steel, tungsten-steel, ferro-magnetic manganese, chrome-vanadium-steel, titanium-steel, uranium-steel, austenitic steel, stainless steel, non-magnetic steel, case-hardening steel, chromium steel, chrome-nickel steel, high tensile steel, cobalt-steel, tungsten-chromium-iron carbides, tungsten-chromium-cobalt, carbide of tungsten-cobalt, Widia (trademark), Carboloy (trademark), finishing steel, high speed steel, high tungsten steel, low tungsten steel, structural steel, carbon steel, brass, bronze, Muntz metal, green gold, electrum, magnanin, iridium, Wood's metal, lead-tin-bismuth-cadmium, nickel-silver, magnalium, zinc-aluminum, aluminum-bronze, boron bronze, copper-aluminum, Duralumin (trademark), aluminum-manganese-copper, manganese-copper, tin-manganese, tin-copper, antimony, molybdenum-chromium-nickel, Monel metal (trademark), R-301.

alloy, *v.* **1.** [To mix metals]—*Syn.* mix, amalgamate, combine, compound, blend, adulterate, fuse.
Metals are alloyed to produce the following qualities—hardness, brittleness, resistance to heat *or* acids *or* wear *or* stain *or* rust, light weight, tensile strength, malleability, lack of magnetism, conductivity, etc.
2. [To devaluate]—*Syn.* debase, devalue, admix; see **adulterate.**

all right, *mod.* **1.** [Adequately]—*Syn.* tolerably, acceptably, passably; see **adequately** 2.
2. [Yes]—*Syn.* agreed, very well, of course; see **yes.**
3. [Certainly]—*Syn.* without a doubt, definitely, positively; see **surely.**
4. [Suitable]—*Syn.* proper, appropriate, fitting; see **fit** 1, 2.
5. [Adequate]—*Syn.* satisfactory, acceptable, satisfying; see **enough** 1.
6. [Uninjured]—*Syn.* safe, well, unhurt; see **whole** 2.
7. [Correct]—*Syn.* exact, precise, right; see **accurate** 1.
8. [(D) Reliable]—*Syn.* honest, dependable, trustworthy; see **reliable** 1.
9. [(D) Excellent]—*Syn.* first-class, great, good; see **excellent.**

all-time, *mod.* **1.** [Permanent]—*Syn.* enduring, constant, everlasting; see **perpetual** 1.
2. [Best]—*Syn.* champion, record-breaking, to the greatest extent; see **best** 1.

all told, *mod.*—*Syn.* in all, in toto, on the whole; see **altogether** 2.

allude to, *v.*—*Syn.* imply, suggest, insinuate; see **hint** 1, 2.

allusion, *n.*—*Syn.* reference, mention, hint, suggestion, inference, quotation, citation, remark, statement, connection, implication, indication, connotation, casual reference, denotation, intimation, insinuation, innuendo, implied indication, charge, imputation, figure of speech, play of fancy, play on words, incidental mention.—*Ant.* explanation*, delineation, specification.

ally, *n.*—*Syn.* confederate, partner, collaborator; see **associate.**

alma mater, *n.*—*Syn.* place of matriculation *or* graduation, academy, institution; see **college, school, university.**

almanac, *n.*—*Syn.* calendar, yearbook, annual, ephemeris, astronomical table, register, registry, Whitaker, farmer's almanac, world almanac, nautical almanac, statistical almanac, chronicle, journal, record, register of the year, *fasti* (Latin).

almighty, *mod.* **1.** [Omnipotent]—*Syn.* invincible, all-powerful, mighty; see **powerful.**
2. [Omnipresent]—*Syn.* infinite, eternal, godlike, all-knowing, all-seeing, omniscient, deathless, immortal, deific, celestial, divine, godly, heavenly, enduring, pervading, all-pervading, boundless, illimitable, uncircumscribed, everlasting.—*Ant.* mortal*, transient, finite.
3. [(D) Great]—*Syn.* intense, desperate, severe; see **extreme** 2.
4. [(D) Exceedingly]—*Syn.* extremely, greatly, acutely; see **very.**

almighty, *n.*—*Syn.* all-ruling, omnipotent, all-powerful; see **god.**

almond-eyed, *mod.*—*Syn.* slant-eyed, sloe-eyed, slit-eyed.
Types of almond-eyed people include the following—Japanese, Chinese, Mongolian, Eskimo.

almost, *mod.*—*Syn.* all but, (very) nearly, well-nigh, nigh, for the greatest part, approximately, roughly, for ordinary purposes, to all intents, near upon, as good as, near to, substantially, tantamount to, essentially, in effect, on the edge *or* brink *or* point *or* eve *or* verge of, relatively, for all practical purposes, in a general way, to that effect, not quite, about to, with some exceptions, in the vicinity of, bordering on, within sight of, with little tolerance, close upon, with small probability of error, in the neighborhood of; *all* (D): about, just about, not quite, most, around, pretty near, nigh unto, within a hair of, by a narrow squeak, within an ace of, at one's feet.

alms, *n.*—*Syn.* charity, relief, dole; see **gift** 1.

aloft, *mod.*—*Syn.* on high, overhead, up; see **over** 1.

alone, *mod.* **1.** [Separate from others]—*Syn.* lone, lonely, solitary, deserted, forlorn, lorn, abandoned, individual, forsaken, desolate, detached, companionless, friendless, unaccompanied, isolated, lonesome, apart, by oneself, under one's own power, single, widowed, unmarried, unattached, unconnected.—*Ant.* accompanied*, attended, escorted.
2. [Exclusive of others]—*Syn.* solely, singly, simply; see **only** 1.
3. [Unique]—*Syn.* unparalleled, unexampled, unequaled; see **unique** 1.
let alone—*Syn.* **1.** not to mention *or* speak of, also, in addition to; see **besides. 2.** ignore, isolate, refrain from disturbing; see **leave** 3, **neglect** 2.
let well enough alone—*Syn.* forget, ignore, let alone; see **neglect** 2.

along, *mod.* **1.** [Near]—*Syn.* by, at, adjacent; see **near** 1.
2. [Ahead]—*Syn.* on, onward, forward; see **ahead** 2.
3. [Together with]—*Syn.* with, accompanying, in addition to, in company with, as a companion, along with, side by side, by the side (of), along that (this) line, coupled with, at the same time, simultaneously.
all along—*Syn.* all the time, from the beginning, constantly; see **regularly** 2.
get along—*Syn.* **1.** prosper, get by, make ends meet; see **succeed** 1. **2.** progress, move on, push ahead; see **advance** 1. **3.** grow old, decline, decay; see **age** 1. **4.** accord, stand together, equal; see **agree.**

alongside, *mod.* and *prep.*—*Syn.* parallel to, close by, close at hand, by or at the side of, along the side, close to the side, side by side, equal with, in company with, apace with, on the same plane with, almost touching; *both* (D): shoulder to shoulder, neck and neck.—*Ant.* beyond*, ahead, behind.

aloof, *mod.*—*Syn.* remote, reserved, distant, secluded; see **indifferent** 1.

aloud, *mod.* —*Syn.* vociferously, audibly, lustily, noisily; see **loudly.**

alphabet, *n.* **1.** [Linguistic symbols]—*Syn.* letters, syllabary, rune, pictograph, ideograph, graphic representation, characters, symbols, signs, the letters of the language, system of characters, hieroglyphs, cryptograms, phonemes, morphemes, sounds; see also **letter** 1.
Important alphabets include the following—Greek, Arabic, Sanskrit *or* Devanagari, Latin *or* Roman, Russian *or* Cyrillic, Hebrew.
2. [Elements]—*Syn.* fundamentals, first principles, rudiments; see **elements.**

alphabetical, *mod.* —*Syn.* systematic, logical, consecutive, progressive, one after another, step by step, graded, planned, ordered, letter by letter, from A to Z, indexed, in order of cataloging.

alphabetize, *v.* —*Syn.* arrange alphabetically, index, systematize; see **order** 3.

alpine, *mod.* —*Syn.* mountainous, alp-like, high, lofty, snowcapped, rocky, in the clouds, high-reaching, soaring, rangy, snow-clad, heaven-kissing, cloud-capped, aerial, ice-peaked, elevated, breathlessly high, rarified, towering; see also **high** 1, 2.

Alps, *n.* —*Syn.* Swiss Alps, Italian Alps, Austrian Alps, Jurian Alps, southern European border, the Alps area, mountain wall or barrier; see also **mountain** 1.

already, *mod.* —*Syn.* previously, by now, now, even now, by this time, at present, but now, just now, by the time mentioned, in the past, up to now, by that time, then.

also, *mod.* —*Syn.* too, likewise, besides, as well (as), in addition (to), additionally, withal, similarly, in like manner (with), along with, more than that, conjointly, *au reste* (French), over and above, in conjunction with, therewithal, thereto, together with, ditto, more, moreover, further, furthermore, including, plus, to boot (D).—*Ant.* excluding, without*, otherwise.

altar, *n.* —*Syn.* altar table, communion table, shrine, chantry, tabernacle, baptismal font, reredos, sacrificial stone, place for sacrifice, elevation for offerings, retable, scroll box.

alter, *v.* **1.** [To change for a purpose]—*Syn.* remodel, renovate, reconstruct; see **change** 1.
2. [(D) To castrate]—*Syn.* geld, sterilize, asexualize, spay, emasculate, caponize, mutilate, fix (D).
3. [To become different]—*Syn.* convert, develop, decay; see **change** 4.

alteration, *n.* **1.** [The act of altering]—*Syn.* exchange, modification, revision; see **change** 1.
2. [A modification]—*Syn.* qualification, correction, adjustment; see **change** 2.

altercation, *n.* —*Syn.* wrangle, argument, squabble; see **dispute** 1.

altered, *mod.* **1.** [Changed]—*Syn.* modified, qualified, revised; see **changed** 2.
2. [Recut]—*Syn.* fitted, refitted, renovated, adjusted, remade, put in order, redone, remodeled, retailored, made fashionable, up-dated (D).

alternate, *mod.* —*Syn.* alternative, substitute, make-shift; see **temporary.**

alternate, *n.* —*Syn.* replacement, equivalent, double; see **substitute.**

alternate, *v.* **1.** [To take or do by turns]—*Syn.* substitute, follow in turn, follow successively, happen by turns, follow one another, do by turns, act reciprocally, do one then the other, act alternately, relieve, fill in for, exchange, take one's turn, interchange; *both* (D): spell, spell (off).
2. [To fluctuate]—*Syn.* vary, vacillate, oscillate, waver, seesaw, rise and fall, blow hot and cold, teeter, shift, sway, totter, come and go, ebb and flow, shuffle, go to and fro; *all* (D): ride and tie, back and fill, teeter-totter.

alternation, *n.* —*Syn.* variation, transposition, shift; see **interchange** 2.

alternative, *n.* **1.** [A choice]—*Syn.* option, discretion, opportunity; see **choice** 1.
2. [The thing chosen]—*Syn.* pick, selection, preference; see **choice** 3.

although, *conj.* —*Syn.* though, even though, despite, still, despite the fact that, even supposing, be it that, in spite of, in spite of the fact that, granting all this, even if, while, however that may be, for all that, admitting *or* granting *or* supposing *or* notwithstanding *or* albeit that.

altitude, *n.* —*Syn.* elevation, distance, loftiness, eminence; see **height** 1.

altogether, *mod.* **1.** [Completely]—*Syn.* entirely, wholly, fully; see **completely.**
2. [In all]—*Syn.* all told, collectively, on the whole, with everything included, in the aggregate, in sum total, bodily, everything being considered, all in all, all things considered, by and large, in a mass, in a body, all, conjointly, taking all things together, as a whole, for the most part; *en bloc, tout ensemble, en masse* (all French), in the lump (D).

altruistic, *mod.* —*Syn.* unselfish, considerate, benevolent; see **kind** 1.

alumni or **alumnae,** *n.* pl.—*Syn.* graduates, postgraduates, supporters, Class of . . .; *both* (D): old grads, post grads.

always, *mod.* **1.** [Constantly]—*Syn.* periodically, continually, ceaselessly; see **regularly** 2.
2. [Forever]—*Syn.* ever, perpetually, eternally, evermore; see **forever** 1.

A.M., abbr.—*Syn.* after midnight, morning, early hours, before noon, forenoon, antemeridian, dawn, early morning, late morning, sunup, matins, lauds, prime.—*Ant.* afternoon, P.M., night*.

amass, *v.* —*Syn.* gather, hoard, store up, garner; see **accumulate** 1.

amateur, *n.* —*Syn.* beginner, novice, learner, nonprofessional, dabbler, recruit, dilettante, probationer, aspirant, hopeful, tyro, abecedarian, neophyte, initiate, apprentice; *all* (D): freshman, tenderfoot, ham, rookie, greenhorn, green hand, cub, fumbler, bungler, clod.—*Ant.* veteran*, professional, expert.

amateurish, *mod.* —*Syn.* crude, unskilled, clumsy; see **incompetent.**

amatory, *mod.* —*Syn.* affectionate, ardent, fervent, tender, devoted, fond, Anacreontic, doting, lovesome, rapturous, loving, lovesick, languishing, amorous, erotic, passionate, romantic, impassioned, sentimental, wooing.

amaze, *v.* —*Syn.* bewilder, astonish, perplex, astound; see **surprise** 1.

amazement, *n.* —*Syn.* astonishment, awe, bewilderment; see **wonder** 1.

amazing, *mod.* —*Syn.* astonishing, astounding, marvelous; see **unusual** 1.

amazon, *n.* —*Syn.* female warrior, virago, giantess, woman athlete, termagant, shrew, vixen, tartar, Xanthippe.

ambassador, *n.* —*Syn.* representative, envoy, minister; see **diplomat** 1.

amber, *mod.* —*Syn.* amber-colored, yellowish, golden; see **brown, tan, yellow** 1.

ambiguity, *n.* —*Syn.* doubtfulness, incertitude, vagueness; see **uncertainty** 2.

ambiguous, *mod.* —*Syn.* equivocal, enigmatic, vague; see **obscure** 1.

ambition, *n.* **1.** [Eager desire]—*Syn.* hope, earnestness, appetite for fame, aspiration, yearning, eagerness, longing, hankering, craving, passion, lust, itch, hunger, thirst, appetite, avidity, energy, ardor, zeal, enthusiasm, spirit, vigor, desire for superiority, love of glory, eagerness for distinction, emulation, enterprise; *all* (D): umph, drive, get up and go, what it takes.—*Ant.* indifference*, apathy, laziness.

2. [The object of desire]—*Syn.* aim, goal, objective; see **purpose** 1.

ambitious, *mod.* **1.** [Characterized by ambition] —*Syn.* aspiring, vaulting, longing, hopeful, zealous, hungry, thirsty, designing, bent upon, high-reaching, earnest, enterprising, soaring, aggressive, eager for superiority, resourceful, pushing, emulous of fame, determined, industrious, anxious for power, goal-oriented, wide-awake, enthusiastic, inspired, energetic, avid, incandescent, sharp, intent, climbing, ardent, power-loving; *all* (D): up and coming, pushy, high-flying.—*Ant.* uninspired, indifferent*, lazy.

2. [Challenging]—*Syn.* severe, hard, formidable; see **difficult** 1.

amble, *v.* —*Syn.* saunter, stroll, wander; see **walk** 1.

ambrosia, *n.* —*Syn.* nectar, immortal food, food of the gods, milk and honey, amrita, delectable sustenance, heavenly food, immortality-giving food, savory fare.

ambulance, *n.* —*Syn.* hospital wagon, mobile hospital, Red Cross truck, rescue squad, field wagon, hospital plane, sick transport, meat wagon (D).

ambush, *n.* —*Syn.* hiding place, pitfall, snare, camouflage, ambuscade, deception; see also **trap 1, trick** 1.

ambush, *v.* —*Syn.* waylay, ensnare, ambuscade, lay for, set a trap, attack from a concealed position, keep out of sight, lie concealed, wait in ambuscade, bait the hook, decoy, entrap, be-net, hook in, skulk, lurk, lie in wait for, surround, hem in; see also **attack** 1.

amenable, *mod.* —*Syn.* tractable, manageable, pliable; see **docile.**

amend, *v.* —*Syn.* correct, mend, revise; see **improve** 1.

amendment, *n.* **1.** [The act of amending]—*Syn.* alteration, reformation, correction; see **improvement** 1.

2. [A proposal to amend]—*Syn.* bill, measure, act, clause, motion, revision, modification of the law, legislative addition, supplement, rider, committee suggestion, redefinition, supplement, substitute motion, codicil.

amends, *n.* pl.—*Syn.* indemnity, reparation, restitution; see **reparation** 2.

amenity, *n.* **1.** [Pleasantness]—*Syn.* agreeableness, mildness, charity; see **kindness** 1.

2. [Manners]—*Syn.* refinement, courtesy, gentility; see **behavior** 1.

America, *n.* **1.** [One or both of the continents of the western hemisphere]—*Syn.* North America, Latin America, South America, Central America, the New World, this side of the Atlantic, the western hemisphere, Pan-American Union.

2. [The United States of America]—*Syn.* U.S., leader of the free world, the fifty states; *all* (D): Land of the Free, Land of Liberty, the U.S. of A., Columbia, Uncle Sam, Zone of the Interior (ZI), the Melting Pot, God's Country, the States, stateside.

American, *mod.* **1.** [Related to the Western Hemisphere]—*Syn.* hemispheric, continental, independent, republican, democratic, North American, Latin American, South American, Central American, Pan-American, Inter-American.

In reference to specific countries of the Western Hemisphere, the following are used—Canadian, Mexican, Nicaraguan, Costa Rican, Guatemalan, Honduran, San Salvadorian, Panamanian, Cuban, Haitian, Puerto Rican, Colombian, Venezuelan, Guianan, Brazilian, Peruvian, Ecuadorian, Chilean, Argentinian, Uruguayan, Paraguayan, Bolivian, etc.; in reference to the native races of the Western Hemisphere, the following are used—Indian, Aztec, Mayan, Incan, Araucanian, etc.

2. [Related to the United States of America] —*Syn.* republican, constitutional, democratic, patriotic, freedom-loving, all-American.

American, *n.* —*Syn.* citizen of the United States, United States national, Yankee, Northerner, Southerner, Indian, pioneer; *both* (D): Yank, gringo.

Americana, *n.* —*Syn.* American history, local history, Indian tales, regional folk-lore, pioneer stories, American materials.

Americanism, *n.* **1.** [Attachment to America as a place or a way of life]—*Syn.* patriotism, nationalism, provincialism, isolationism, flag waving, clean living, fair play, friendly rivalry, America for Americans, free enterprise, America first, the competitive system, spirit of '76 (D).

2. [Anything characteristic of the United States] —*Syn.* mannerism, habit, custom, trick of speech, American slang.

Americanize, *v.* —*Syn.* naturalize, enfranchise, assimilate, level, melt, make into an American, introduce to American ways, indoctrinate.

amiable, *mod.* —*Syn.* pleasant, genial, charming; see **friendly** 1.

amicable, *mod.* —*Syn.* peaceable, kindly, genial; see **friendly** 1.

amid, *prep.* —*Syn.* between, in the midst of, in the middle of; see **among.**

amiss, *mod.* —*Syn.* erring, unlawful, unfair, foul; see **wrong** 2.

ammonia, *n.* —*Syn.* gas, vapor, alkali, ammonia water, spirits of hartshorn, smelling salts (D).

ammunition, *n.* Types of ammunition include the following—buckshot, gunpowder, cartridge, bul-

let, napalm, bomb, missile, projectile, charge, depth charge, grenade, hand grenade, fuse, shrapnel, torpedo, shell, ball, cannonball, shot, ammo (D); see also **bomb, bullet, mine** 2, **munitions, shell** 2, **shot** 2.
Materials used in ammunition include the following—dynamite, trotyl, trinitrotoluene (TNT); nitrocotton, melinite, gelignite, cordite, trinitrocresol, poison gas, tear gas, mustard gas, nitroglycerine, nitrate compound, gun cotton, lyddite; see also **explosive.**

among, *prep.* —*Syn.* between, in between, in the midst *or* middle of, (mingled) with, surrounded by, in connection *or* association with, betwixt, encompassed by, in dispersion through, amid, amongst, amidst, in the company of, betwixt and between. —*Ant.* beyond*, away from, outside of.

amorous, *mod.* —*Syn.* passionate, affectionate, loving; see **amatory.**

amount, *n.* **1.** [The total of several quantities] —*Syn.* sum, product, sum total; see **all** 1, **whole.**
2. [The combined effect]—*Syn.* substance, value, significance; see **result.**
3. [Price]—*Syn.* expense, output, outlay; see **price.**
4. [Quantity]—*Syn.* bulk, mass, number; see **quantity.**

amount to, *v.* —*Syn.* reach, extend *or* mount to, come to, effect, aggregate, be equal *or* equivalent *or* tantamount to, approximate, check with, be equal in quantity to, rise by accumulation to, total *or* sum *or* foot up to, be in all, be in the whole, total, tally with, add up to.

amour, *n.* —*Syn.* romance, liaison, relationship, love affair; see **affair** 2.

ample, *mod.* —*Syn.* sufficient, enough, adequate; see **enough** 1.

amplification, *n.* —*Syn.* addition, augmentation, elaboration,; see **increase** 1.

amplifier, *n.* —*Syn.* speaker, bullhorn, amplifying device *or* mechanism, microphone, high-fidelity speaker, stereo speaker, woofer, tweeter, loudspeaker, hearing aid, echo chamber, megaphone.

amplify, *v.* —*Syn.* expand, augment, magnify, elaborate; see **increase** 1.

amply, *mod.* —*Syn.* enough, sufficiently, copiously; see **adequately.**

amputate, *v.* —*Syn.* cut off, sever, operate on *or* upon, eliminate, cut away, separate, excise, dismember, remove.

amulet, *n.* —*Syn.* talisman, fetish, ornament; see **charm** 2.

amuse, *v.* —*Syn.* divert, cheer, enliven; see **entertain** 1.

amusement, *n.* —*Syn.* recreation, pastime, play; see **entertainment** 1, 2.

amusing, *mod.* **1.** [Entertaining]—*Syn.* engaging, diverting, enchanting; see **entertaining.**
2. [Pleasant]—*Syn.* agreeable, enjoyable, charming; see **pleasant** 1, 2.

anachronism, *n.* —*Syn.* misdate, antedate, postdate, prochronism, chronological error, misplacement in time, prolepsis, metachronism.

analogous, *mod.* —*Syn.* correspondent, like, similar; see **alike** 2.

analogy, *n.* —*Syn.* relationship, similarity, resemblance; see **similarity.**

analysis, *n.* **1.** [The process of logical division] —*Syn.* separation, partition, subdivision; see **division** 1.
2. [A statement employing analysis, sense 1] —*Syn.* outline, report, abridgment; see **summary.**
3. [Examination]—*Syn.* study, investigation, search; see **examination** 1.
4. [Psychoanalysis]—*Syn.* psychotherapy, depth psychiatry, dream analysis; see **psychoanalysis.**
in the last *or* **final analysis**—*Syn.* lastly, (with) everything considered, in conclusion; see **finally** 2.

analyst, *n.* **1.** [Examiner]—*Syn.* questioner, investigator, inquisitor; see **examiner.**
2. [Psychoanalyst]—*Syn.* psychiatrist, neuropsychiatrist, psychotherapist; see **psychoanalyst.**

analytical, *mod.* **1.** [*Said of persons*]—*Syn.* logical, perceptive, penetrating; see **judicious.**
2. [*Said of written or spoken work*]—*Syn.* systematic, well-organized, precise, scientific, reasonable, rational, well-grounded, valid, sound, solid, cogent, perspicuous, perceptive, penetrating, searching, thorough, conclusive.—*Ant.* false*, illogical, unreasonable.

analyze, *v.* **1.** [To subject to analysis]—*Syn.* dissect, examine, investigate, separate, decompose, break down *or* up, disintegrate, resolve into elements, determine the essential features of, decentralize, decompose into constituent parts, examine minutely, hydrolize, anatomize, cut up, lay bare, electrolyze, dissolve, decompound, parse, X-ray, put under the microscope.—*Ant.* synthesize, compound*, fuse.
2. [To study carefully]—*Syn.* probe, survey, scan; see **examine** 2.

anarchist, *n.* —*Syn.* insurgent, rebel, revolutionary; see **agitator.**

anarchy, *n.* **1.** [Disorder]—*Syn.* turmoil, chaos, mob rule; see **disorder** 2.
2. [Absence of government]—*Syn.* political nihilism, disregard for law, lawlessness, avowed hostility to government.

anatomize, *v.* —*Syn.* dissect, cut up, lay bare, examine; see **analyze** 1.

anatomy, *n.* **1.** [The study of living organisms, especially of the body]—*Syn.* medicine, biology, zoology, histology, cytology, embryology, comparative anatomy, morphology, osteopathy, physiology, zootomy, genetics, etiology, ontogeny morphography.
2. [A body or skeleton]—*Syn.* bone structure, frame, physique, form, figure, shape; *all* (D): carcass, bone house, body beautiful, chassis.
3. [The act of dividing or separating for examination]—*Syn.* dissection, division, diagnosis; see **division** 1.

ancestor, *n.* —*Syn.* progenitor, forebear, founder of the family; see **forefather.**

ancestral, *mod.* —*Syn.* paternal, maternal, genealogical, consanguine, born with, inborn, innate, inbred, congenital, running in the family (D), lineal, belonging to the family, tribal, totemic, consanguineous, affiliated, past, old, inherited, transmissible, in the family.

ancestry, *n.* —*Syn.* lineage, heritage, parentage, pedigree; see **family** 1.

anchor, *n.* **1.** [A device to keep a vessel from drifting]—*Syn.* stay, tie, cramp, killick, grapnel, kedge, bower, mooring, drag anchor, sea anchor, bow anchor, waist anchor, mushroom anchor, grappling iron.
2. [Anything which holds]—*Syn.* support, mainstay, ballast, safeguard, stay, security, protection, hold, tie, pillar, staff, fastener, grip, defense, protection, foothold, belay.
cast *or* **drop anchor**—*Syn.* stay, dock, stop (over); see **anchor** 1, **stop** 1.
weigh anchor—*Syn.* depart, embark, set out; see **leave** 3, **sail** 1.

anchor, *v.* **1.** [To drop an anchor]—*Syn.* make port, tie up, moor, berth, bring a ship in; *all* (D): heave the hook, lay anchor, cast anchor, foul the anchor, carry out the anchor.—*Ant.* sail*, weigh anchor, set out for sea.
2. [To make fast]—*Syn.* tie, secure, attach; see **fasten** 1.

anchorage, *n.*—*Syn.* roadstead, port, harbor, harborage, wharf, dock, jetty, pier, mooring, safety, resting place, berth, refuge, facilities, amphibious installation(s), haven, quay, embankment, landing place, breakwater, embarcadero.

ancient, *mod.* **1.** [Very old]—*Syn.* antique, antiquated, aged; see **old** 1, 2, 3.
2. [Belonging to the periods called Ancient History]—*Syn.* Roman, Greek, Sumerian, Akkadian, Hittite, Israelite, Egyptian, Chaldean, Etruscan, Carthaginian, Babylonian, Phoenician, Biblical, pre-Homeric, in ancient times; see also **classical** 2.

anciently, *mod.*—*Syn.* long ago, of old, in ancient times, in days of yore, since Adam (D).

and, *conj.*—*Syn.* in addition to, also, including, plus, together with, as well as, furthermore, moreover.

Andes, *n.*—*Syn.* cordilleras, South American mountains, Andean range, Andean chain, Ecuadorean Andes, Peruvian Andes, Bolivian Andes, Chilean Andes, land of the condor (D); see also **mountain** 1.

andiron, *n.*—*Syn.* firedog, metal hearth support, fireplace lift.

anecdote, *n.*—*Syn.* tale, incident, episode; see **story.**

anemic, *mod.* **1.** [Pale]—*Syn.* pallid, wan, sickly; see **pale** 1.
2. [Weak]—*Syn.* frail, feeble, infirm; see **weak** 1.

anesthesia, *n.*—*Syn.* insentience, unconsciousness, numbness; see **stupor.**

anesthetic, *n.*—*Syn.* hypnosis, inhalant, gas, soporific, hypodermic injection, drops, opiate.
Some specific anesthetics include—horocaine, ether, chloroform, cocaine, sodium pentothal (*also* (D): truth serum), chloral hydrate, nitrous oxide (*also* (D): laughing gas), morphine, procaine, alcohol, canadol, scopolamine; *all* (D): dope, Mickey Finn, knockout drops; see also **drug** 2.

anew, *mod.*—*Syn.* again, once more, from the beginning, *de novo* (Latin), once again, afresh, newly, in a new *or* different manner, over again, in a different way, as a new act (D).

angel, *n.* **1.** [A heavenly messenger]—*Syn.* seraph, supernatural being, God's messenger, Angel of Death, good angel, dark angel, archangel, guardian angel, spirit, sprite, cherub, ministering spirit, celestial spirit, winged being, glorified spirit, attendant of God, invisible helper, heavenly spirit, saint, host of heaven.—*Ant.* devil*, demon, satan.
2. [(D) A financial supporter]—*Syn.* benefactor, supporter, backer of theatrical performances; see **patron** 1.

angelic, *mod.*—*Syn.* saintly, beneficent, good, otherworldly, humble, heavenly, ethereal, spiritual, celestial, kind, radiant, beautiful, divine, holy, pure, lovely, rapturous, devout, archangelic, virtuous, above reproach, seraphic, righteous, self-sacrificing, cherubic.—*Ant.* wicked*, demonic, evil.

anger, *n.*—*Syn.* wrath, rage, fury, passion, choler, temper, bad *or* ill temper, emotion of displeasure, acrimony, animosity, indignation, hatred, resentment, ire, (re)vengeful passion, hot temper, irascibility, displeasure, chagrin, impatience, vexation, annoyance, feeling of antagonism, hot blood, provocation, violence, turbulence, excitement, frenzy, umbrage, disapprobation, tantrum, petulance, dudgeon, fretfulness, sharpness, rankling, peevishness, exasperation, spleen, huff, irritation, gall, pique, enmity; *all* (D): fit, slow burn, bile, dander, distemper.—*Ant.* patience*, mildness, calm.

anger, *v.* **1.** [To arouse (someone) to anger]—*Syn.* arouse, infuriate, madden, goad, annoy, get on one's nerves, irritate, acerbate, agitate, affront, bait, cross, put out of humor, incense, fret, rankle, put into a temper, exacerbate, drive into a rage, vex, gall, enrage, chafe, nettle, excite, work *or* bridle *or* burn up, arouse resentment, provoke *or* arouse ire, ruffle, exasperate, embitter, goad into a frenzy, craze, provoke, make angry, stir up, tempt, offend, inflame, pique, rile, enkindle; *all* (D): make all hot and bothered, kick up a row, get one's back up, get one's goat, get in one's hair, make the fur fly, get *or* put one's dander up, make bad blood, keep at the boiling point, stir up a hornet's nest, make sore, make one blow his top.—*Ant.* calm*, soothe, placate.
2. [To become angry]—lose one's temper, forget oneself, get mad; see **rage** 1.

angle, *n.* **1.** [Figure or plane formed at an intersection]—*Syn.* notch, flare, crotch, elbow, fork, cusp, incline, obliquity, decline, Y, V, right angle, acute angle, divergence, obtuse angle, difference of direction of two lines, point where two lines meet.—*Ant.* curve*, arc, oval.
2. [A projecting edge]—*Syn.* corner, end, point; see **edge** 1.
3. [(D) Point of view]—*Syn.* standpoint, outlook, perspective; see **viewpoint.**
4. [A development]—*Syn.* turn, shift, phase; see **event** 1.
5. [(D) Purpose]—*Syn.* intention, aim, plan; see **purpose** 1.

angle for, *v.*—*Syn.* plot *or* scheme *or* maneuver *or* intrigue *or* strive *or* hint *or* connive *or* plan *or* try *or* conspire for, try by artful means to get, try to attain by artifice; see **plan** 1.

angle iron, *n.*—*Syn.* L-section, brace, joint; see **bracket.**

angler, *n.*—*Syn.* fisher, Waltonian, sportsman; see **fisherman.**

Anglo-Saxon, *mod.* —*Syn.* Old English, A.S., early English *or* British, Germanic, Alfredian, Northumbrian, East Anglian, West Saxon, Anglian, heroic, Beowulfian, Anglo-Saxonic; see also **English.**

angrily, *mod.* —*Syn.* heatedly, indignantly, testily, irately, grouchily, crisply, sharply, infuriatedly, savagely, hotly, fiercely, tartly, bitterly, acidly, furiously, wildly, violently; *both* (D): frothing at the mouth, (all) aboil.—*Ant.* calmly*, softly, quietly.

angry, *mod.* —*Syn.* enraged, fierce, fiery, irate, raging, fuming, infuriated, convulsed, furious, wrathful, stormy, indignant, cross, vexed, resentful, irritated, bitter, ferocious, turbulent, nettled, incensed, piqued, offended, sullen, irascible, hateful, inflamed, annoyed, provoked, galled, chafed, exacerbated, displeased, riled, affronted, wroth, storming, impassioned, sulky, restless, splenetic, choleric, huffy, hostile, rabid, infuriate; *all* (D): in the tantrums, in a passion, flown off the handle, in a pet, in a (high) dudgeon, out of temper, mad, up in the air, hot under the collar, boiling, burned up, steamed up, at the boiling point, purple in the face, with one's back up, all worked up (about), seeing red, out of humor, het up, teed off, in the heat of passion, in bad humor, in a huff, foaming at the mouth, wrought up, up in arms.—*Ant.* calm*, quiet, restrained.

anguish, *n.* —*Syn.* wretchedness, pain, agony; see **pain** 1.

angular, *mod.* **1.** [Coming to an angle]—*Syn.* sharp-cornered, intersecting, crossing, oblique, divaricate, with corners V-shaped, Y-shaped, crotched, forked, bent, akimbo, bifurcate(d), crooked, pointed, triangular, rectangular, scraggy, jagged, staggered, zigzag.—*Ant.* round*, parallel, side-by-side.

2. [Tall and bony]—*Syn.* lank, lean, gaunt, rawboned, bony, awkward, ungainly, lanky, stiff, sharp, spare, gangling, gawky (D), scrawny, clumsy. —*Ant.* round*, plump, fat.

animal, *mod.* **1.** [Referring to characteristics of the animal kingdom]—*Syn.* bestial, beastly, swinish, brutish, wild, beastlike, feral, untamed, zoological, mammalian, bovine, canine, serpentine, equine, feline, leonine, lupine, piscatorial, ophidian, reptilian, snakelike.

2. [Referring to the bodily characteristics of man] —*Syn.* corporeal, physical, bodily, muscular, fleshly, sensual, carnal, earthy, earthly, natural. —*Ant.* spiritual*, intellectual, supernatural.

animal, *n.* **1.** [A mobile organism]—*Syn.* living thing, creature, human being, beast, being, fish, crustacean, amphibian, cetacean, vertebrate, invertebrate, reptile, insect, bird, wild animal, domestic animal, mammal, a representative of the fauna, animalcule; see also **bird** 1, **fish, insect, man** 1, **reptile.**

2. [A nonhuman creature]—*Syn.* beast (of burden), brute, lower animal, quadruped, beast of the field, creeping thing, varmint, pet, farm animal, dumb animal, wild thing, one of God's creatures, monster, critter.—*Ant.* man*, spirit, soul*.

3. [A brutish human]—*Syn.* brute, savage, monster; see **beast** 2.

animate, *v.* **1.** [To give life to]—*Syn.* activate, vitalize, inform, vivify, revivify, make alive, arouse, quicken, give life to, endow with life, energize, put life into, breathe new life into, impart life into, imbue with life, furnish with vital principle.

2. [To incite]—*Syn.* inspire, arouse, excite; see **urge** 2.

animated, *mod.* —*Syn.* spirited, gay, lively; see **happy** 1.

animosity, *n.* —*Syn.* dislike, enmity, displeasure; see **hatred** 1, 2.

ankle, *n.* —*Syn.* anklebone, joint, tarsus, astragalus, talus; see also **bone, foot** 2.

Ann, *n.* —Anne, Anna, Hannah, Annie, Nan, Nancy, Nina, Nannie, Annette.

annals, *n.* pl.—*Syn.* chronicle, records, archives; see **history** 2, **journal** 1.

anneal, *v.* —*Syn.* toughen, temper, subject to high heat; see **strengthen.**

annex, *n.* —*Syn.* addition, additional quarters, new wing; see **addition** 2, 3.

annex, *v.* —*Syn.* append, attach, affix; see **join** 1.

annexation, *n.* **1.** [The act of joining]—*Syn.* addition, incorporation, merger; see **increase** 1.

2. [That which has been added]—*Syn.* increment, attachment, increase; see **addition** 2, 3.

annihilate, *v.* —*Syn.* demolish, exterminate, obliterate; see **destroy** 1.

anniversary, *mod.* —*Syn.* yearly, recurrent, once a year; see **annual.**

anniversary, *n.* —*Syn.* holiday, saint's day, birth date, birthday, yearly recurrence of the date of a past event, yearly observance of an event, commemoration of a past event, yearly celebration, feastday, ceremony, memorable date, day of annual celebration, celebration of a date, natal day, annual meeting, centenary, biennial, triennial, quadrennial, quintennial, sextennial, septennial, octennial, novennial, decennial, silver anniversary, golden anniversary, diamond jubilee, yearly commemoration, jubilee, festival, fiesta, centenary, centennial, sesquicentennial, bicentenary, bicentennial, tercentenary, tricentennial, red-letter day (D).

annotate, *v.* —*Syn.* comment, expound, interpret; see **explain.**

annotation, *n.* —*Syn.* footnotes, glossary, comment; see **explanation** 2.

announce, *v.* —*Syn.* proclaim, publish, state; see **advertise** 1, **declare** 1.

announced, *mod.* —*Syn.* reported, given out, promulgated, told, broadcast(ed), issued, circulated, proclaimed, declared, published, disclosed, divulged, released, made known, disseminated, revealed, publicized, made public.—*Ant.* hidden*, unannounced, unrevealed.

announcement, *n.* **1.** [The act of announcing] —*Syn.* declaration, notification, prediction, proclamation, communication, communicating, publishing, publication, broadcasting, expression, exposition, narration, retailing, reporting, exposing, briefing, promulgation, dissemination, recitation. —*Ant.* ban, secret*, silence.

2. [The thing announced]—*Syn.* report, statement, advertisement, decision, news, tidings, returns, brief, bulletin, edict, white paper, message, notice, interim report, survey, advice, item, detail, communiqué, speech, release.

3. [A printed announcement]—*Syn.* handbill, poster, pamphlet, flier, circular, broadside, placard, billboard, brochure, form letter, telegram, wire cable, letter, prospectus, leaflet, fourth-class mail, junk mail (D).

announcer, *n.* —*Syn.* program announcer, broadcaster, television announcer, telecaster, commentator, sportscaster, weather announcer, newscaster, communicator, radio announcer, disc jockey *or* DJ (D).

annoy, *v.* **1.** [To molest]—*Syn.* pester, irritate, trouble; see **bother** 2.

2. [To be disturbing]—*Syn.* distress, upset, grieve; see **bother** 3.

annoyance, *n.* **1.** [A feeling of annoyance]—*Syn.* vexation, irritation, pique, uneasiness, disgust, displeasure, provocation, nervousness, irascibility, exasperation, ferment, indignation, sullenness, sulkiness, bad humor, touchiness, perturbation, moodiness, mortification, vexation, worry, distress, unhappiness, discontent, heartache, misery, aches and pains, dissatisfaction, impatience, peeve (D). —*Ant.* pleasure*, joy, delight.

2. [A source of annoyance]—*Syn.* worry, inconvenience, nuisance; see **difficulty** 1, 2, **trouble** 2.

annoying, *mod.* —*Syn.* irritating, bothersome, vexatious; see **disturbing.**

annual, *mod.* —*Syn.* yearly, each year, every year, once a year, year end, occurring every year, lasting a year, anniversary, twelvemonth, seasonal, recurring once a year, reckoned by the term of a year, living only one growing season, expiring each year, performed in a year, valid for use during one year.

annually, *mod.* —*Syn.* by the year, each year, per year, once a year, periodically, every year, seasonally, once every twelve months, yearly, *per annum* (Latin), year after year.—*Ant.* daily*, weekly, monthly.

annul, *v.* —*Syn.* invalidate, render void, repeal, revoke; see **cancel** 2.

annulment, *n.* —*Syn.* invalidation, nullification, dissolution; see **cancellation.**

anomalous, *mod.* —*Syn.* irregular, abnormal, exceptional; see **unusual** 2.

anomaly, *n.* —*Syn.* peculiarity, unconformity, exception; see **irregularity** 2.

anonymous, *mod.* —*Syn.* unsigned, nameless, unknown, unacknowledged, having no acknowledged name, pseudonymous, unnamed, authorless, unavowed, unclaimed, unidentified, secret, without the name of the author, not disclosing a name, of unknown authorship, without a name, bearing no name, incognito, pseudo (D).—*Ant.* named*, signed, acknowledged.

another, *mod.* **1.** [Additional]—*Syn.* one more, a further, added; see **extra.**

2. [Different]—*Syn.* a separate, a distinct, some other; see **different** 1.

another, *n.* —*Syn.* someone else, a different person, one more, addition, something else.—*Ant.* same, one*, each.

answer, *n.* **1.** [A reply]—*Syn.* response, return, statement, antiphon, retort, echo, reverberation, respondence, repartee, password, rebuttal, approval, replication, acknowledgment, sign, rejoinder, comeback (D).—*Ant.* question*, query, request.

2. [A solution]—*Syn.* discovery, find, disclosure, satisfaction, revelation, explanation, interpretation, clue, resolution, elucidation, key; *all* (D): the why and the wherefore, idea, the dope.

3. [A defense]—*Syn.* plea, counterclaim, retaliation; see **defense** 3.

answer, *v.* **1.** [To reply]—*Syn.* reply, respond, rejoin, retort, acknowledge, give answer, field questions, say, echo, return, remark; *all* (D): give, talk *or* answer *or* come *or* flash back.—*Ant.* question*, inquire, make inquiry.

2. [To be sufficient]—*Syn.* fill, satisfy, fulfill; see **satisfy** 3.

3. [To move in response]—*Syn.* return, refute, retaliate, react, deny, dispute, rebut, parry, argue, plead, defend, contest, rejoin, claim, quash, counterclaim; *all* (D): backfire, squelch, smash, squash, crush, strike back.—*Ant.* admit, agree, take.

4. [To provide a solution]—*Syn.* solve, elucidate, clarify; see **explain.**

answerable, *mod.* —*Syn.* responsible, liable, amendable; see **responsible** 1.

answer for (D), *v.* —*Syn.* be responsible (for), take (the) blame (for), be accountable (for), accept the responsibility (for), be liable (for), pay (for), take upon oneself, sponsor, do at one's own risk, take the rap (for) (D).

answer to (D), *v.* —*Syn.* be responsible to, be ruled by, respect the authority of; see **agree to, respect** 2.

ant, *n.* —*Syn.* emmet, pismire, insect.

Types of ants include the following—worker, neuter, replete, queen, male; antlike insects include the following—termite *or* white ant, Texas red ant, black ant, visiting ant, agricultural ant, slave ant, soldier ant, carpenter ant, mining ant, European ant.

antagonism, *n.* —*Syn.* enmity, hostility, opposition; see **hatred** 1, 2.

antagonist, *n.* —*Syn.* opponent, opposition, competitor; see **enemy** 1, 2.

antagonistic, *mod.* —*Syn.* opposing, hostile, inimical; see **unfriendly** 1.

Antarctica, *n.* —*Syn.* the South Pole, the Antarctic Circle, Little America.

ante-bellum, *mod.* —*Syn.* before the war, prewar, prior to the war, pre-Civil War.

antecedent, *mod.* —*Syn.* preliminary, previous, prior; see **preceding.**

antedate, *v.* —*Syn.* date back, predate, anachronize, misdate, overdate, date before the true date, date earlier than the fact, transfer to an earlier date, accelerate, cause to happen sooner.

antediluvian, *mod.* —*Syn.* before the Flood, antiquated, out-of-date; see **old-fashioned.**

antelope, *n.* —*Syn.* gazelle, eland, addax, dik-dik.

Animals commonly called antelopes include the following—American antelope *or* pronghorn, Indian antelope *or* sasin, algazel, duiker *or* impoon, tumogo *or* waterbuck, roodebok *or* redgazel, korin of Senegal, Indian gazelle, muscat, Persian gazelle; see also **deer.**

antenna, *n.* —*Syn.* aerial, wire, TV antenna, receiving wire, radiating wire, high-gain antenna, very high frequency *or* VHF antenna, ultra high frequency *or* UHF antenna, rotating antenna (*also* (D): rotor), rabbit ears (D).

anteroom, *n.* —*Syn.* waiting room, antechamber, outer office; see **room** 2.

anthem, *n.* —*Syn.* hymn, divine song, melody; see **song.**

anthology, *n.* —*Syn.* book, miscellany, treasury; see **collection** 2.

Anthony, *n.* —*Syn.* Antonio, Antonius, Antony, Tony (D).

anthracite, *n.* —*Syn.* hard coal, Pennsylvania coal, long burning coal, eastern coal; see **coal** 1.

anthropology, *n.* —*Syn.* science of man, science of culture. Branches of anthropology include the following—anthropometry, anthropography, anthropogeography, ethnography, ethnology, demography, sociology, prehistoric anthropology, linguistics, cultural anthropology, human paleontology, archaeology, folklore, eugenics, criminology, psychology; see also **science** 1, **sociology.**

antibiotic, *n.* —*Syn.* antitoxin, wonder drug, miracle drug; see **medicine** 2.
Common antibiotics include the following—chlortetracycline, mycomycin, neomycin, penicillin, tetracycline, streptomycin; *all* trademarks: Aureomycin, Chloromycetin, Tetramycin.

antibody, *n.* —*Syn.* immunizer, neutralizer, natural *or* preventive reaction; see **medicine** 2, **prevention.**

antic, *n.* —*Syn.* caper, frolic, trick; see **joke** 1.

anticipate, *v.* **1.** [To foresee]—*Syn.* expect, forecast, prophesy, prognosticate, predict, hope for, look forward to, look for *or* to *or* ahead *or* beyond, wait for, count *or* plan on, have a hunch, bargain for, hold in view, have in prospect, assume, suppose, divine, conjecture, promise oneself, lean upon, entertain the hope, await, surmise, have a presentiment of, reckon *or* count on; *all* (D): have a funny feeling, look into the future, feel it in one's bones, champ at the bit, hold one's breath, intuit. —*Ant.* fear*, be surprised, be caught unawares.
2. [To forestall]—*Syn.* prepare for, provide against, delay, hold back, preclude, hinder, intercept, apprehend, block (off), be early, precede, be one step ahead (of) (D).—*Ant.* neglect*, be caught, ignore.
3. [To foretaste]—*Syn.* experience beforehand, hope for, look forward to, have an introduction to, have foreknowledge of, take a vicarious pleasure in; *both* (D): thrill to, know what's coming.

anticipated, *mod.* —*Syn.* foreseen, predictable, prepared for; see **expected** 2, **likely** 1.

anticipation, *n.* **1.** [Foretaste]—*Syn.* expectancy, outlook, trust, confident expectation, looking forward, contemplation, promise, prospect, awaiting, joy, impatience, preoccupation, hope, high hopes (D).—*Ant.* fear*, dread, surprise.
2. [Forethought]—*Syn.* prevision, presentiment, intuition, foresight, inkling, premonition, apprehension, foreboding, foreseeing, awareness, experience beforehand, foretaste, antepast, forethought, forefeeling, preassurance, forecast, prior realization, obsession, fixation, preconception, preoccupation, a prior knowledge, realization in advance, instinctive prevision, prescience; *both* (D): hunch, a feeling in one's bones.—*Ant.* surprise*, shock, wonder.

anticlimax, *n.* —*Syn.* bathos, drop, descent, decline; *all* (D): letdown, comedown, slump.

antidote,, *n.* —*Syn.* antitoxin, counteractant, remedy; see **medicine** 2.

antipathetic, *mod.* —*Syn.* hostile, averse, antagonistic; see **unfriendly** 1.

antipathy, *n.* —*Syn.* hostility, abhorrence, aversion; see **hatred** 1.

antiquarian, *mod.* —*Syn.* archaic, ancient, antique; see **old** 3.

antiquarian, *n.* —*Syn.* antiquary, student of antiquity, collector, savant, Egyptologist, anthropologist, historian, archaeologist, paleologist, medievalist, classicist, archaist, paleographer, bibliophile, archive keeper, archivist, curator, professor of classics; see also **scientist.**

antiquated, *mod.* **1.** [Obsolete]—*Syn.* outmoded, out-of-date, obsolescent; see **old-fashioned.**
2. [Ancient]—*Syn.* primeval, archaic, prehistoric, antediluvian; see **old** 3.

antique, *mod.* **1.** [Old]—*Syn.* ancient, archaic, prehistoric; see **old** 3.
2. [Old-fashioned]—*Syn.* obsolete, obsolescent, out-of-date; see **old-fashioned.**

antique, *n.* —*Syn.* relic, artifact, heirloom, old *or* early *or* ancient *or* outmoded example *or* evidence *or* exemplar *or* representative, survival, rarity, monument, vestige, *objet d'art* (French), ruin, Rosetta stone; *used only in pl.:* antiquities, reliques; see also **art** 3, **furniture, manuscript.**

antiquity, *n.* **1.** [The quality of being old]—*Syn.* antiqueness, ancientness, oldness, elderliness, age, old age, great age, venerableness, hoariness, archaism, archaicism, obsolescence.—*Ant.* newness*, modernity, youthfulness.
2. [An object out of the past]—*Syn.* artifact, monument, antique; see **relic** 1.
3. [Ancient times]—*Syn.* remote times, ancient times, old days, former ages, the olden time, days of old, days of yore, classical times, Homeric age, Athens, Etruscan period, Egyptian period, Chow Dynasty, Chinese Middle Kingdom, Roman era, era before Christ, pagan times, Nineveh and Tyre, Babylon, Bible days, Alexandrian period, Dark Ages, early ages, the time before the Middle Ages. —*Ant.* present*, modern times, contemporary times.

antiseptic, *mod.* **1.** [Free of germs]—*Syn.* clean, germ-free, sterilized; see **pure** 2.
2. [Destructive of germs]—*Syn.* prophylactic, aseptic, purifying, hygienic, antibacterial, medicated, germ-destroying, germicidal, disinfectant, bactericidal, sterilizing, antibiotic.

antiseptic, *n.* —*Syn.* detergent, prophylactic, preservative, preventive, preventative, counterirritant, sterilizer, immunizing agent, germicide, insecticide, disinfectant, deodorant; see also **antitoxin, medicine** 2.
Antiseptics include the following—iodine, sulfanilamide, sulfathiazole, Mercurochrome (trademark), hydrogen peroxide, salt solution, carbolic acid *or* phenol, alcohol, boiling water, soap, boric *or* boracic acid, silver vitellin, corrosive sublimate, mycozol, merthiolate, penicillin, iodoform *or* triiodomethane; see also **sulfa drug.**

antithesis, *n.* **1.** [Opposition]—*Syn.* contradiction, contraposition, contrariety; see **contrast** 2.
2. [Opposite]—*Syn.* direct opposite, reverse, converse; see **opposite.**

antitoxin, *n.* —*Syn.* vaccine, antibody, immunizing agent, serum, antiserum, counteragent, antiseptic, antipoison, defensive proteid, preventive, toxin neutralizer, neutralizing agent, counteractant, counterpoison, countervenom, antibiotic substance, alexipharmic, alexiteric; see also **antibiotic, medicine** 2.

antlers, *n.* pl.—*Syn.* horns, tusks, excrescences. Prongs of an antler include the following—brow antler, bez *or* bay antler, royal antler, surroyal *or* crown antler; see also **horn** 2.

anvil, *n.* —*Syn.* block, forge, plate, cast stone, support, hollow, blacksmith's instrument.

anxiety, *n.* —*Syn.* concern, trouble, misgiving; see **care** 2.

anxious, *mod.* **1.** [Disturbed in mind]—*Syn.* apprehensive, concerned, dreading; see **troubled.**
2. [Eager]—*Syn.* desirous, zealous, eager, fervent; see **enthusiastic** 2.

any, *mod.* **1.** [Without discrimination]—*Syn.* either, whatever, any sort, any kind, any one, in general, each, each and every (D), all, one and all.—*Ant.* only, one*, single.
2. [Every]—*Syn.* all, several, unspecified; see **each** 1.
3. [Some]—*Syn.* a little, part of, a bit; see **some** 1.

anybody, pron.—*Syn.* anyone, everyone, everybody, all, the whole world, the public, the rabble, the masses, each and every one, any person, any of, the whole kit and caboodle (D).—*Ant.* nobody*, no one, somebody.

anyhow, *mod.* **1.** [In any event]—*Syn.* at any rate, nevertheless, at all, in spite of, however, in any case, regardless, and so, whatever happens; *both* (D): irregardless, somehow or other.
2. [In any manner]—*Syn.* anyway, in any way, in whatever way, however, under any circumstances, in one way or the other, in any respect, in either way; *both* (D): anywhichway, nohow.—*Ant.* exactly*, in one way, in a certain way.

anyone, pron.—*Syn.* a person, one, anyone at all; see **anybody.**

anyplace (D), *mod.* —*Syn.* everywhere, wherever, in any place; see **anywhere.**

anything, pron.—*Syn.* everything, all, anything at all, anyone, any one thing; *all* (D): whatever one wants, you name it, anything around.—*Ant.* nothing*, something, one thing.

any time, *mod.* —*Syn.* whenever, at your convenience, when you will, no matter when, any time when, at any moment, anytime (D).

anyway, *mod.* —*Syn.* in any event, however, in any manner; see **anyhow** 1, 2.

anywhere, *mod.* —*Syn.* wherever, in any place, all over, everywhere, in whatever place; *both* (D): wherever you go, anyplace.—*Ant.* nowhere*, in no place, somewhere.
get anywhere—*Syn.* prosper, thrive, advance; see **succeed** 1.

apart, *mod.* **1.** [Separated]—*Syn.* disconnected, distant, disassociated; see **separated.**
2. [Aside]—*Syn.* to one side, at one side, aloof; see **aside.**
3. [Distinct]—*Syn.* separate, special, alone, isolated; see **individual** 1.
4. [Separately]—*Syn.* freely, exclusively, alone; see **independently.**
take apart—*Syn.* dismember, dissect, reduce; see **analyze** 1, **divide** 1.
tell apart—*Syn.* characterize, discriminate, differentiate; see **distinguish** 1.

apartment, *n.* —*Syn.* rooms, quarters, flat, suite, co-operative apartment, penthouse, residence, home; *all* (D): duplex, efficiency suite, bachelor apartment, digs, bachelor pad, pad, walk-up.

apartment house, *n.* —*Syn.* tenement, hotel, apartment building, condominium, condo, remodeled dwelling, high-rise apartments, apartment hotel, court.—*Ant.* home*, private residence, cottage.

apathetic, *mod.* —*Syn.* unemotional, cold, unconcerned; see **indifferent** 1.

apathy, *n.* —*Syn.* dullness, insensitivity, unconcern; see **indifference** 1.

ape, *n.* —*Syn.* gorilla, orangutan, chimpanzee, baboon; see **monkey.**

ape, *v.* —*Syn.* copy, mimic, impersonate; see **imitate** 2.

aperture, *n.* —*Syn.* opening, fissure, gap; see **hole** 1, 2.

apiary, *n.* —*Syn.* bees, stands *or* hives *or* colonies of bees, beehouse, bee stand, house-apiary.

apiece, *mod.* —*Syn.* respectively, separately, individually; see **each** 2.

apocryphal, *mod.* —*Syn.* spurious, unauthentic, doubtful; see **false** 2.

apologetic, *mod.* —*Syn.* regretful, supplicating, retracting, self-effacing, self-reproachful, self-condemnatory, self-incriminating, explanatory, extenuating, atoning, expiatory, rueful, expressing regret for fault or failure, regretfully acknowledging, compunctious, penitential, propitiatory, contrite, remorseful, sorry, penitent, conciliatory, down on one's knees (D).—*Ant.* stubborn, obstinate*, unregenerate.

apologize, *v.* —*Syn.* beg *or* ask pardon, excuse oneself, offer an excuse, atone, ask forgiveness, make amends, make apology for, (express) regret, purge, give satisfaction, clear oneself, make up with, bow to, make reparations for, confess, offer compensation, admit one's guilt, retract, withdraw; *both* (D): eat crow, eat one's words.—*Ant.* insult*, offend, hurt.

apology, *n.* —*Syn.* excuse, plea, justification; see **explanation** 2.

apoplexy, *n.* —*Syn.* breaking a blood vessel, thrombosis, occlusion, circulatory trouble, stroke, seizure; see also **disease** 2, 3.

apostate, *n.* —*Syn.* renegade, one of little faith, backslider; see **deserter, traitor.**

apostle, *n.* —*Syn.* messenger, witness, companion; see **follower.**

apostrophe, *n.* **1.** [A punctuation mark]—*Syn.* pause, contraction mark, sign of omission, plural mark, sign of possession.
2. [An appeal]—*Syn.* invocation, address, supplication; see **appeal** 1.

apothecary, *n.*—*Syn.* pharmacist, chemist (British), knight of the pestle (D); see **druggist.**

apothegm, *n.*—*Syn.* adage, maxim, saying; see **proverb.**

Appalachian, *mod.*—*Syn.* Allegheny, coastal mountainous; see **eastern** 2.

appall, *v.*—*Syn.* amaze, horrify, dismay; see **shock** 2.

appalling, *mod.*—*Syn.* horrifying, shocking, dreadful; see **frightful** 1.

apparatus, *n.*—*Syn.* appliances, machinery, outfit; see **device** 1, **equipment.**

apparel, *n.*—*Syn.* clothes, attire, suit; see **dress** 1.

apparent, *mod.* **1.** [Open to view]—*Syn.* visible, clear, manifest; see **obvious** 1.

2. [Obvious]—*Syn.* self-evident, glaring, patent; see **obvious** 2.

3. [Seeming, but not actual]—*Syn.* probable, possible, plausible; see **likely** 1.

apparently, *mod.*—*Syn.* obviously, at first sight *or* view, in plain sight, unmistakably, at a glance, indubitably, expressly, transparently, perceptibly, plainly, patently, evidently, clearly, openly, supposedly, overtly, conspicuously, evident to the senses, palpably, tangibly, presumably, possibly, supposedly, manifestly, most likely, ostensibly, reasonably, intuitively, seemingly, assumably, reputedly, as if, as though, if one may judge, to all appearances, in almost every way, allegedly, as far as it is possible to assume, in all likelihood, as it seems *or* were; *all* (D): on the face of it, at the first blush, to the eye.—*Ant.* surely*, certainly, undoubtedly.

apparition, *n.*—*Syn.* phantom, specter, spirit; see **ghost** 1.

appeal, *n.* **1.** [A plea]—*Syn.* request, bid, claim, suit, submission, solicitation, petition, question, imploration, recourse, entreaty, prayer, invocation, supplication, address, demand, importunity, call, requisition, application, overture, proposition, proposal, call for aid, earnest request, adjuration. —*Ant.* denial*, refusal, renunciation.

2. [Action to carry a case to a higher court]—*Syn.* petition, motion, application, request for retrial *or* review.

3. [Attractiveness]—*Syn.* charm, glamour, interest, charmingness, seductiveness, engagingness; *all* (D): sex appeal, class, oomph, bounce.

appeal, *v.* **1.** [To ask another seriously]—*Syn.* urge, request, petition; see **beg** 1.

2. [To carry a case to a higher court]—*Syn.* apply for a retrial, retry, contest, bring new evidence, advance, reopen, refer to, review.

3. [To attract]—*Syn.* interest, engage, fascinate, tempt, tantalize, awaken response, invite, entice, allure, captivate, intrigue, attract one's interest, enchant, beguile, catch the eye (D); see also **fascinate.**

appear, *v.* **1.** [To become visible]—*Syn.* emerge, rise, come in view, come forth *or* out *or* forward, be within view, be in sight, present *or* show *or* expose *or* discover *or* betray *or* manifest (itself), arise, come into sight, surface, become plain, issue, loom, arrive, come to light, enter the picture, recur, materialize, become visible, loom up, break through *or* forth, show (up), crop out *or* up, burst *or* look forth, turn up, stand out, come onto the horizon; *all* (D): spring *or* bob *or* poke up, cut a figure, heave in sight, see the light (of day), peep out, meet *or* catch the eye, break cover.—*Ant.* depart, disappear*, vanish.

2. [To seem]—*Syn.* look, have the appearance, resemble; see **seem.**

3. [To present oneself publicly]—*Syn.* be in attendance, put in an appearance, make an appearance, answer a summons, present oneself, be present, submit oneself (to), arrive, stand before, obey an order, oblige, come into public notice, come before the public, be placed before the public, come upon the stage; *all* (D): turn up, be there, show one's face, show up, show one's mug.—*Ant.* be absent, leave*, be missing.

appearance, *n.* **1.** [Looks]—*Syn.* countenance, face, bearing, mien, aspect, mannerism, look, condition, presentation, demeanor, carriage, cast, air, fashion, attitude, mode, stamp, expression, feature(s), guise, dress, outline, contour, visage, form, shape, semblance, color, port, presence, posture, pose, figure, outward form, character; *all* (D): make-up, cut (of one's jib), front.—*Ant.* mind*, personality, soul.

2. [That which only seems to be real]—*Syn.* impression, idea, image, reflection, sound, mirage, vision, façade, dream, illusion, phenomenon, semblance, seeming, specter, spirit, ghost, apparition, shadow, wraith, aura; *both* (D): will o' the wisp, spook.—*Ant.* being, fact*, substance.

3. [The act of appearing]—*Syn.* arrival, advent, presentation, representation, exhibition, unveiling, display, emergence, rise, introduction, occurrence, manifestation, actualization, materialization, debut, entrance, budding (D).—*Ant.* departure*, going, vanishing.

keep up appearances—*Syn.* be outwardly proper *or* decorous, hide one's faults *or* failures, keep up with the Joneses (D); see **deceive.**

make *or* **put in an appearance**—*Syn.* appear publicly, be present, come; see **arrive** 1.

appease, *v.* **1.** [To satisfy]—*Syn.* do, be enough, serve; see **satisfy** 1, 3.

2. [To calm]—*Syn.* soothe, quiet, soften; see **quiet** 1.

appeasement, *n.*—*Syn.* moderation, satisfaction, peace offering, settlement, amends, accommodation, assuagement, submission, assuasion, adjustment, reparation, pacification, alleviation, mollification, conciliation, propitiation, reconciliation, restoration (of harmony), mitigation, compromise, grant, relaxation.—*Ant.* irritation*, excitation, fomentation.

append, *v.* **1.** [To add]—*Syn.* affix, supplement, annex; see **add** 2.

2. [To attach]—*Syn.* fasten, fix, conjoin; see **join** 1.

appendage, *n.* **1.** [An addition]—*Syn.* attachment, appendix, accessory; see **addition** 2.

2. [A bodily extension]—*Syn.* arm, leg, limb, external organ, feeler, tentacle, extremity, member; *all* (D): flapper, fin, shank, stem, dog.

appendicitis, *n.*—*Syn.* diseased appendix, ruptured appendix, inflamed appendix, case for an appendectomy; see also **disease** 3.

appendix, *n.*—*Syn.* addendum, supplement, codicil, excursus, attachment, bibliography, tables,

notes, index, samples, quotations, verification, proof, letters, documents; see also **addition** 2.
Anatomical appendices include the following—vermiform appendix *or appendix vermiformis or appendix caeci* (both Latin), *appendices epiploicae, appendix auriculae, appendix vesicae* (all Latin).

appetite, *n.* **1.** [A craving for food or drink]—*Syn.* hunger, thirst, craving, longing, dryness, need for liquid, starvation, empty stomach, thirstiness, ravenousness, desire.—*Ant.* indifference*, satiety, surfeit.
2. [Desire]—*Syn.* longing, craving, hankering; see **desire** 1.

appetizer, *n.* —*Syn.* aperitif, antipasto, canapé, delicacy, relish, hors d'oeuvre; see also **delicatessen** 1.

appetizing, *mod.* —*Syn.* savory, tasty, tantalizing, delicious, appealing, mouth-watering, tempting, inviting, luscious, delectable; see also **delicious** 1. —*Ant.* tasteless*, uninteresting, unappealing.

applaud, *v.* —*Syn.* cheer, clap, give an ovation to, acclaim; see **praise** 1.

applause, *n.* —*Syn.* ovation, cheers, hurrahs; see **praise** 2.

apple, *n.* **1.** Apples include the following—MacIntosh, Baldwin, red delicious, golden delicious, yellow delicious, russet, Northern spy, Snow, crab, Jonathan, Rome beauty, Albermarle pippin, Missouri pippin, Newtown pippin, yellow Newtown, Rhode Island greening, sheep's nose, Arkansas black, Wolf River, blue pearmain, fameuse, Gravenstein, transcendent, wealthy, Ben Davis, Granny Smith, Grimes Golden, Oldenburg, red Astrakhan, white Astrakhan, Russian Astrakhan, winesap, Stayman winesap, yellow transparent, York Imperial, gillyflower, Janet, king, Lawyer, maiden's blush, Shockley, twenty-ounce, Peck's pleasant, Pennock, willow twig, red June, early harvest, winter banana, early redbird, Cortland.
2. [Something suggesting an apple]—*Syn.* oak apple, gall (nut), nut-gall, *quercus lusitanica* (Latin), crab apple, fir apple, balsam apple, raspberry apple, May apple, love apple, egg apple, apple of Cain, hawthorn berry, Dead Sea apple, apple of Sodom, mad apple, rose apple, hip, haw.

apple of (one's) eye, *n.* —*Syn.* pet, idol, ideal; see **favorite.**

apple polisher (D), *n.* —*Syn.* flatterer, toady, flunkey; see **sycophant.**

appliance, *n.* —*Syn.* instrument, machine, apparatus; see **device** 1.
Common electric household appliances include—broiler, deep-fryer, broom, floor waxer and polisher, can opener, carving knife, coffee maker, food and drink blender, food processor, microwave oven, food and drink mixer, frypan, portable oven, facial sauna, hair dryer, manicurist, popcorn popper, toaster, toothbrush, waffle iron, griddle, warming tray, iron, sewing machine, knitting machine, vacuum cleaner, videotape recorder (VCR), tape recorder; see also **radio** 2, **record player, television.**
Common gas or electric household appliances include—dishwasher, rotisserie, disposal, clothes dryer, clothes washer, stove, oven, refrigerator, freezer, barbecue, water heater, air conditioner, air purifier.

applicable, *mod.* —*Syn.* suitable, appropriate, usable; see **fit** 1, 2.

applicant, *n.* —*Syn.* petitioner, claimant, appellant; see **candidate.**

application, *n.* **1.** [Putting to use]—*Syn.* employment, appliance, utilization; see **use** 1.
2. [The ability to apply oneself]—*Syn.* devotion, assiduousness, diligence; see **attention** 2.
3. [That which is applied]—*Syn.* lotion, balm, wash, ointment, salve, face cream, mud pack, ice bag, bandage, compress, splint, sling, tourniquet, alcohol, alcohol rub, stimulant, rubefacient, emollient, pomade, poultice, (talcum) powder, unguent, plaster, heating pad; see also **cosmetic, lotion, medicine** 2, **salve.**
4. [Putting one thing on another]—*Syn.* administering, administration, applying, relation, laying *or* piling on, cementing, oiling, dosing, rubbing, reinforcement, creaming, treatment, upholstering, massaging, act of applying, bringing into contact, juxtaposing, justaposition.
5. [A request]—*Syn.* petition, entreaty, demand; see **appeal** 1.
6. [The instrument by which a request is made]—*Syn.* petition, form, blank, paper, letter, credentials, certificate, statement, requisition, draft, check, bill, formal application, letter of application.

applied, *mod.* **1.** [Put to use]—*Syn.* used, related, correlated, enforced, practiced, utilized, brought to bear, adapted, shaped, exercised, devoted, tested, adjustable, adjusted, activated.
2. [*Said of theoretical knowledge which can be used*]—*Syn.* pragmatic, utilitarian, practicable; see **practical.**

apply, *v.* **1.** [To make a request]—*Syn.* petition, demand, appeal; see **beg** 1.
2. [To make use of]—*Syn.* utilize, employ, practice, exploit; see **use** 1.
3. [To place upon]—*Syn.* affix, stamp, administer, lay *or* place *or* put *or* touch on *or* upon, bestow, rub *or* massage in *or* into; see also **fasten** 1, **join** 1.
4. [To be relevant]—*Syn.* be pertinent, pertain, bear on *or* upon, have bearing on, relate to, be applicable *or* adapted *or* suitable to, allude (to), concern, touch (on *or* upon), involve, affect, regard, have reference (to), connect, refer, fit (the case), have some connection (with), suit, be in relationship; *both* (D): hold good *or* true, come into play.

apply (oneself), *v.* —*Syn.* attend to, dedicate oneself, address oneself, be occupied with, keep close to, keep one's mind on, direct oneself to, concentrate on, persevere *or* persist in, give oneself wholly to, be industrious, buckle down (to) (D).

appoint, *v.* —*Syn.* select, designate, elect; see **delegate** 1, 2.

appointed, *mod.* —*Syn.* selected, chosen, delegated; see **named** 2.

appointee, *n.* —*Syn.* nominee, deputy, representative; see **delegate.**

appointment, *n.* **1.** [The act of appointing]—*Syn.* designation, election, selection, nomination, approval, choice, promotion, placing in office, ordination, assignment, assigning, commissioning, authorization, installation, deputation, delegation, delegating, certification, empowering.

2. [An engagement]—*Syn.* interview, meeting, arrangement, rendezvous, assignment, invitation, errand, something to do, date (D).
3. [A position]—*Syn.* place, employment, work; see **job** 1, **profession** 1.

apportion, *v.* —*Syn.* allot, parcel out, allocate; see **distribute** 1.

apportionment, *n.* —*Syn.* partition, allotment, division; see **distribution** 1.

appraisal, *n.* —*Syn.* examination, evaluation, assessment; see **estimate** 1, **judgment** 2.

appraise, *v.* **1.** [To set a price on]—*Syn.* assess, price, assay; see **value** 2.
2. [To estimate]—*Syn.* calculate, evaluate, figure; see **estimate** 2, 3.

appreciable, *mod.* —*Syn.* recognizable, considerable, perceptible, discernible, sizable, goodly, good-sized, large, moderate, substantial, tangible, definite, estimable, ascertainable, visible, apparent, distinguishable, sensible, material, perceivable, evident, detectable, noticeable; *all* (D): fairish, healthy, not inconsiderable.—*Ant.* trivial*, slight, inconsiderable.

appreciate, *v.* **1.** [To be grateful]—*Syn.* welcome, enjoy, pay respects to, be *or* feel obliged, be indebted, feel *or* be obligated, acknowledge, never forget, give thanks, overflow with gratitude; see **thank.**—*Ant.* find fault with, minimize, complain*, object.
2. [To recognize worth]—*Syn.* esteem, honor, extol, praise, applaud, admire, look up to; see **admire** 1.
3. [To enjoy art]—*Syn.* be sensitive to, have a taste for, have the faculty for, derive pleasure from; see **like** 1.

appreciation, *n.* **1.** [Sense of gratitude]—*Syn.* thankfulness, recognition, gratefulness; see **gratitude.**
2. [Favorable opinion]—*Syn.* esteem, commendation, high regard; see **admiration** 1.
3. [Enjoyment of art]—*Syn.* aesthetic sense, appreciativeness, love, affection, sensitivity, relish, sensibility, sensitiveness, attraction.
4. [Realization]—*Syn.* recognition, grasp, visualization; see **judgment** 1.

appreciative, *mod.* —*Syn.* thankful, appreciatory, grateful, obliged, indebted, responsive, keen, alive, understanding, sympathetic, generous, cooperative, enlightened, aware, perceptive, favorable, satisfied, cordial, considerate, friendly, kindly, magnanimous, affectionate, entertained, gladdened, sensible *or* cognizant *or* conscious of, alive *or* sensitive to, capable of appreciating, under obligation, beholden, enthusiastic, receptive.—*Ant.* unfriendly*, cold, hostile.

apprehend, *v.* **1.** [To understand]—*Syn.* perceive, comprehend, grasp; see **understand** 1.
2. [To arrest]—*Syn.* seize, place under arrest, take into custody; see **arrest** 1.

apprehension, *n.* **1.** [Foreboding]—*Syn.* trepidation, dread, misgiving; see **fear** 2.
2. [Understanding]—*Syn.* comprehension, grasp, perspicacity; see **judgment** 1.
3. [Arrest]—*Syn.* capture, seizure, detention; see **arrest.**
4. [Estimate]—*Syn.* opinion, conclusion, belief; see **judgment** 3.

apprehensive, *mod.* —*Syn.* fearful, worried, uncertain; see **troubled.**

apprentice, *n.* —*Syn.* beginner, student, learner; see **amateur.**

approach, *n.* **1.** [A way]—*Syn.* path, way, gate; see **entrance** 2, **road** 1.
2. [Plan of action]—*Syn.* method, program, procedure; see **plan** 2.
3. [The act of coming near or on]—*Syn.* accession, advent, arrival, access, appearance, coming, oncoming, reaching, landing, approaching, nearing, advance, act of drawing near, coming nearer.
4. [Overture; *usually plural*]—*Syn.* proposal, offer, proposition; see **suggestion** 1.

approach, *v.* **1.** [To approach personally]—*Syn.* appeal *or* apply to, address, speak *or* talk to, propose, request, accost, direct oneself to, make advances *or* overtures to, take aside, talk to in private; *all* (D): buttonhole, corner, descend on *or* upon.—*Ant.* avoid*, shun, turn away.
2. [To come near in space]—*Syn.* drift *or* go *or* move toward, roll *or* step *or* come up (to), loom up, creep *or* drive up, near, verge upon, go *or* draw near, converge *or* advance *or* bear *or* gain (on *or* upon), come into sight, progress, close in, surround, come on *or* near *or* forward *or* up (to), bear down (on *or* upon), edge *or* ease up to, head into (D). —*Ant.* leave*, recede, depart.
3. [To come near in time]—*Syn.* be imminent *or* forthcoming, threaten, slip by, loom (up), await, near, draw near, impend, diminish, decrease, grow short, stare one in the face (D).—*Ant.* increase*, extend, stretch out.
4. [To approximate]—*Syn.* come near, take after, come close to; see **resemble.**

approachable, *mod.* **1.** [Accessible]—*Syn.* convenient, attainable, obtainable; see **available.**
2. [Sociable]—*Syn.* agreeable, receptive, congenial; see **friendly** 1.

approaching, *mod.* —*Syn.* nearing, advancing, convergent, impending, oncoming, impinging, touching, approximating, coming, looming up, drawing near, (next) to come, threatening, emergent, rising, moving closer, gaining.—*Ant.* passing*, receding, diminishing.

approbation, *n.* **1.** [Approval]—*Syn.* high regard, esteem, favor; see **admiration** 1.
2. [Sanction]—*Syn.* consent, support, endorsement; see **permission.**

appropriate, *mod.* —*Syn.* proper, suitable, suited, fitting; see **fit** 1, 2.

appropriate, *v.* **1.** [To seize]—*Syn.* secure, usurp, take (possession of); see **seize** 2.
2. [To provide money]—*Syn.* set aside *or* apart, allocate, assign (to a particular use), reserve, apportion, devote, appoint, allow (for), disburse, budget, allot.

appropriately, *mod.* —*Syn.* fittingly, obligingly, suitably, judiciously, justly, aptly, fitly, relevantly, decorously, rightly, properly, competently, agreeably, happily, fortunately.—*Ant.* badly*, inappropriately, improperly.

appropriateness, *n.* —*Syn.* aptness, propriety, suitability; see **fitness.**

appropriation, *n.* **1.** [The act of providing money] —*Syn.* allocation, allotment, donation, funding, sponsoring, sponsorship, grant, bestowal, giving, endowing, budgeting, provision, allowance, concession, apportionment, stipulation, shelling out (D).—*Ant.* reduction*, curtailment, stoppage.

2. [Money provided]—*Syn.* stipend, grant, fund, allotment, allowance, allocation, contribution, cash, budget, subscription, benefit, relief, remittance, gift, remuneration, donation, support, subvention, pay, the wherewithal (D).

approval, *n.* **1.** [Favorable opinion]—*Syn.* regard, esteem, favor; see **admiration** 1.

2. [Sanction]—*Syn.* endorsement, support, consent; see **permission.**

approve, *v.* **1.** [To give approval]—*Syn.* ratify, affirm, encourage, support, countenance, endorse, sign, countersign, seal, confirm, license, be in favor of, favor, consent *or* agree *or* assent to, sanction, empower, charter, validate, legalize, recognize, accredit, give one's blessing, recommend, adjust oneself to, make allowances for, bear out, make law, confirm officially, pronounce legal, authorize, second, subscribe to, homologate, make valid, sustain, concur in, allow, go along with, maintain, vote for, accede to, corroborate, advocate, acquiesce in, establish; *all* (D): pass, O.K., give the green light, rubber stamp, come around, hold with.—*Ant.* oppose*, reject, veto.

2. [To favor]—*Syn.* recommend, acclaim, applaud; see **praise** 1.

approved, *mod.* —*Syn.* certified, authorized, validated, passed, affirmed, legalized, ratified, sanctioned, permitted, endorsed, vouched for, praised, canonical, recognized, recommended, backed, supported, upheld, made official, agreed to, allowed, inspected, audited, proven, ordered, commanded, established, ordained, doing credit to, O.K.'d (D). —*Ant.* refused*, censured, disapproved.

approximate, *mod.* **1.** [Near]—*Syn.* close, adjacent, bordering; see **near** 1.

2. [Resembling]—*Syn.* like, proximate, similar, matching; see **alike** 2.

3. [Nearly exact]—*Syn.* rough, inexact, unprecise, uncertain, guessed, imprecise, proximate, imperfect, close, by rule of thumb, surmised, unscientific, by means of trial and error, almost, more or less, not quite, coming close, fair, nearly correct, comparative, nearly perfect.

approximately, *mod.* —*Syn.* nearly, closely, roughly, close *or* near to *or* upon, *circa* (Latin), almost, around, about, well-nigh, very near, coming, very close, proximately, in general, in round numbers, not quite, not far from, more or less, practically, just about, on the edge of, for all practical purposes, bordering on, generally, comparatively, *both* (D): pretty nearly, in the neighborhood of.

approximation, *n.* —*Syn.* (re)semblance, likeness, approach; see **similarity.**

April, *n.* —*Syn.* spring, springtime, planting time, fourth month, month of rain, the cruelest month (D).

apron, *n.* —*Syn.* cover, smock, bib, overskirt.

apt, *mod.* **1.** [Quick to learn]—*Syn.* adept, clever, bright; see **able** 1, **intelligent** 1.

2. [Inclined]—*Syn.* prone, tending, liable; see **likely** 5.

3. [Well suited]—*Syn.* appropriate, suitable, proper; see **fit** 1, 2.

aptitude, *n.* **1.** [Inclination]—*Syn.* bent, tendency, drift; see **inclination** 1.

2. [Intelligence]—*Syn.* capability, competence, ability; see **judgment** 1.

aqualung, *n.* —*Syn.* self-contained underwater breathing apparatus *or* scuba, diving lung, compressed air tank; see **skin diving.**

aquarium, *n.* —*Syn.* artificial pond, fishbowl, fish tank, aquatic museum, marine exhibit.

aquatic, *mod.* —*Syn.* swimming, amphibian, amphibious, natatory, oceanic, of the sea, watery, floating, maritime, marine, fishlike, sea, deep-sea.

aqueduct, *n.* —*Syn.* conduit, water system *or* passage, canal, duct, canal structure, artificial water channel, waterworks, water bridge, pipeline.

aquiline, *mod.* —*Syn.* hooked, beaklike, eaglelike, curved, beaked, Roman-nosed, angular, resembling an eagle, bent, curving, prominent.—*Ant.* straight*, snub-nosed, pug.

Arab, *n.* —*Syn.* Bedawi, Bedouin, Arabian, Ishmaelite, Mohammedan, Hadji, Syrian, Moor, Iraqi, nomad, desert tribesman.

Arabia, *n.* —*Syn.* Arabian peninsula, Arabistan, Saudi Arabia, Yemen, Oman, Arabia Deserta, Arabia Felix, United Arab Republic *or* UAR, Arabia Petraca, Araby (D).

Arabian, *mod.* —*Syn.* Arabic, Semitic, from Arabia, Syrian, Jordanian, Lebanese, Iraqi, Egyptian, Tunisian, Libyan, Algerian, Moroccan, Saudi Arabian, Mesopotamian, Middle-Eastern, near-Eastern, Moorish.

arbiter, *n.* —*Syn.* referee, mediator, arbitrator; see **judge** 2.

arbitrary, *mod.* **1.** [Capricious; *said of people*] —*Syn.* willful, self-assertive, frivolous, injudicious, wayward, offhand, erratic, inconsistent, crotchety, irresponsible, opinionated, supercilious, bumptious, unaccountable, self-willed, whimsical, unreasonable, unscientific, superficial, irrational; *both* (D): half-baked, toplofty.—*Ant.* reasonable*, consistent, rational.

2. [Without adequate determining principle: *said of actions or ideas*]—*Syn.* unsatisfactory, temporary, unpremeditated, irrational, generalized, deceptive, superficial, unscientific, unreasonable, whimsical, fanciful, determined by no principle, depending on the will alone, done at pleasure, optional, uncertain, approximate, inconsistent, discretionary, subject to individual will, halfway (D). —*Ant.* judicious*, scientific, considered.

3. [Despotic]—*Syn.* imperious, dictatorial, tyrannical; see **absolute** 3, **autocratic** 1.

arbitrate, *v.* —*Syn.* settle peacefully, adjust differences, smooth out, adjust, reconcile, employ diplomacy, bring before a referee, hear both sides, act as arbiter, interfere, parley, placate, bring to terms, decide between opposing parties, intervene, intercede, conciliate, step in, mediate, interpose, negotiate, come between, submit to arbitration, straighten out, meet *or* go halfway, come to terms, make an adjustment, pour oil on troubled waters (D); see also **decide.**

arbitration, *n.* —*Syn.* compromise, adjustment, mediation; see **agreement** 1.

arbitrator, *n.* —*Syn.* arbiter, referee, mediator; see **judge** 2.

arc, *n.* —*Syn.* arch, curve, segment of a circle; see **arch, curve** 1.

Arcadia, *n.* —*Syn.* paradise, utopia, Shangri-la, Erewhon, land of dreams, heaven, Elysium, Elysian Fields, Eden, seventh heaven, abode of the blessed, bliss, Acadia, Arkady.—*Ant.* hell*, purgatory, damnation.

arch, *n.* —*Syn.* arc, curve, vault, dome, cupola, ogive, span, bend, archibolt, squinch, architrave, arching, archway, curvature, bend, cove, camber. Arches include the following—round, horseshoe, lancet, ogee, trefoil, basket-handle, decorated, Tudor, Egyptian, Gothic, Ionian.

arch, *v.* —*Syn.* extend, round, stretch, camber, curve, bend, form, shape, hunch, cover, hump, hook, arch over.—*Ant.* straighten*, unbend, smooth.

archaeologist, *n.* —*Syn.* paleontologist, paleologist, excavator, prehistorian, classicist, Americanist, archaeologian, student of antiquity; see also **antiquarian, scientist.**

archaeology, *n.* —*Syn.* antiquarianism, prehistory, paleoethnology, paleology, paleontology, study of archaic cultures *or* antiquity, paleohistory, digging (D).

archaic, *mod.* —*Syn.* antiquated, old, obsolete; see **old-fashioned.**

archbishop, *n.* —*Syn.* chief bishop, prelate, head of an ecclesiastical province, church dignitary, primate, high churchman; see also **minister** 1, **priest.**

archer, *n.* —*Syn.* bowman, longbowman, sagittary, toxophilite, primitive soldier, member of an archery team, crossbowman, arbalester, Sagittarius, William Tell (D).

archetype, *n.* —*Syn.* prototype, ideal, pattern; see **model** 2.

architect, *n.* **1.** [One who designs buildings]—*Syn.* planner, designer, draftsman, artist, engineer, structural engineer, architectural engineer, builder, director of construction *or* building, planner of structures, master builder, environmental engineer, civil architect, landscape architect, designer of buildings.
2. [Author]—*Syn.* creator, originator, prime mover; see **author** 1.

architectural, *mod.* —*Syn.* structural, constructive, architectonic, building, compositional, lineal, developmental, engineered.

architecture, *n.* —*Syn.* construction, planning, designing, building, structure, architectonics, ecclesiology, house-building, shipbuilding, bridge-building, environmental engineering.
Styles of architecture include the following—*Classic*—Ionian, Doric, Corinthian, Alexandrian, Egyptian, Etruscan, Roman; *Romanesque*—Early Romanesque, Norman, Rhenish; *Gothic*—Transitional, Lancet, Decorated, Flamboyant, Perpendicular; *Renaissance*—Italian, Jacobean. Elizabethan, Châteaux, English Classic, German Late; *Pseudo-Classic*—Rococo, Baroque, Georgian, Wren, Louis XIV; *Recent*—Pseudo-Gothic, Empire, Victorian, Colonial, Factory, Modernistic, Functional, Bauhaus, setback, skyscraper, Frank Lloyd Wright, Le Corbusier, Mies van der Rohe, futuristic; *misc.*—Mayan, Malayan, Hindu, Chinese, Japanese, Byzantine, Saracenic, Moresque.

archives, *n.* pl. **1.** [Place where documents are stored]—*Syn.* repository, vault, treasury; see **museum.**
2. [Documents]—*Syn.* chronicles, annals, public papers; see **records.**

archivist, *n.* —*Syn.* annalist, biographer, chronicler; see **historian.**

archway, *n.* —*Syn.* entrance, passage, opening; see **entrance** 2.

arctic, *mod.* —*Syn.* polar, in the Arctic Circle, in the tundra areas, frozen, icy, under the Bear (D); see also **cold** 1.

ardent, *mod.* **1.** [Passionate]—*Syn.* fervent, impassioned, warm; see **passionate** 2.
2. [Eager]—*Syn.* zealous, fervent, fervid; see **enthusiastic** 2, 3.
3. [Devoted]—*Syn.* constant, loyal, true; see **faithful.**

ardor, *n.* —*Syn.* zest, fervor, passion, warmth; see **enthusiasm** 1.

arduous, *mod.* —*Syn.* hard, severe, strenuous, laborious; see **difficult** 1.

area, *n.* **1.** [An expanse]—*Syn.* stretch, distance, space; see **expanse.**
2. [A physical unit]—*Syn.* section, lot, neighborhood, plot, zone, sector, patch, square, quarter, block, precinct, ward, field, meridian, territory, district, ghetto, township, region, tract, enclosure, parcel, division, city, parish, diocese, principality, dominion, duchy, kingdom, empire, state; see also **measure** 1.
3. [Scope]—*Syn.* sphere, range, operation; see **field** 4.

arena, *n.* —*Syn.* field, pit, ground, park, coliseum, square, football field, gridiron, stadium, athletic field, playing field, baseball field, amphitheater, boxing ring, hippodrome, circus, bowl, stage, platform, course, gymnasium *or* gym (D).

argue, *v.* **1.** [To endeavor to convince]—*Syn.* plead, appeal, explain, justify, elucidate, present, show, support, reason (with), dispute, contend, wrangle, oppose, battle, demonstrate, establish; *all* (D): join issue, have it out, put up an argument, bicker (over), (have a) brush with.—*Ant.* neglect*, ignore, scorn.
2. [To discuss]—*Syn.* dispute, talk about, clarify; see sense 1, **discuss.**
3. [To quarrel]—*Syn.* dispute, contend, fight; see **quarrel.**

argument, *n.* **1.** [An effort to convince]—*Syn.* discussion, exchange, contention; see **discussion** 1, 2.
2. [Material intended to convince]—*Syn.* evidence, reasons, exhibits; see **proof** 1.
3. [Verbal disagreement]—*Syn.* debate, quarrel, row; see **dispute** 1.

argumentative, *mod.* **1.** [Controversial]—*Syn.* debatable, questionable, disputable; see **controversial.**
2. [Disputatious]—*Syn.* pugnacious, contentious, factious; see **quarrelsome** 1.

arid, *mod.* **1.** [Dry]—*Syn.* parched, desert, dried; see **dry** 1.

2. [Barren]—*Syn.* desolate, waste, desert; see **sterile** 2.
3. [Dull]—*Syn.* uninteresting, flat, dry; see **dull** 4.

arise, *v.* **1.** [To get up]—*Syn.* rise, stand (up), turn out, get out of bed, get out of a chair, get to one's feet, jump up; *both* (D): roll out, hit the deck. —*Ant.* fall*, sit*, lie*.
2. [To ascend]—*Syn.* mount, go up, climb; see **rise** 1.
3. [To result]—*Syn.* proceed, emanate, originate, issue; see **begin** 2.

aristocracy, *n.*—*Syn.* nobility, privileged class, peerage, patriciate, house of lords, superior group, ruling class, noblemen, the elite, gentry, high society, upper class(es), persons of rank, patricians, optimates, gentility, fashionable world, class of hereditary nobility, body of nobles, body of persons holding exceptional privileges, *beau monde, haut monde, pur sang, noblesse,* (all French); *all* (D): the Quality, the upper ten, high livers, the four hundred, the upper crust, the social register, the jet set, the blue book crowd,; see also **society** 3.—*Ant.* people*, working class, peasantry.

aristocrat, *n.*—*Syn.* nobleman, peer, lord, noble, baron, earl, prince, patrician, chevalier, ruler, polished gentleman, man of fashion, member of the ruling class, thoroughbred, optimate, grandee, don, hidalgo, hereditary noble, king, duke, viscount, count, emperor, empress, *Graf* (German), queen, princess, duchess, marchioness, viscountess, countess, baroness, knight, lady, marquis; *all* (D): blue blood, magnifico, silk-stocking; see also **king** 1, 2, **lady** 3, **lord** 2.—*Ant.* citizen*, commoner, proletarian.

aristocratic, *mod.* **1.** [Having high personal qualities]—*Syn.* noble, refined, well-bred; see **noble** 1, 2, 3.
2. [Socially exclusive]—*Syn.* disdainful, aloof, snobbish; see **egotistic** 2.

arithmetic, *n.*—*Syn.* computation, addition, subtraction, multiplication, division, calculation, 'rithmetic (D):; see also **mathematics.**

Arizona, *n.*—*Syn. all* (D): Apache State, Aztec State, Sunset Land, Valentine State.

Arkansas, *n.*—*Syn.* Ozark country; *all* (D): Bear State, Guinea Pig State, Razorback State, Toothpick State.

arm, *n.* **1.** [The upper human limb]—*Syn.* member, appendage, forelimb, forearm; *all* (D): fin, flapper, fluke, soupbone.
2. [Anything resembling an arm, sense 1]—*Syn.* bend, crook, projection, cylinder, projector, sofa-end, branch, limb, appendage, rod, assembly, bough, offshoot, wing, prong, stump, hook, handle, bow.
3. [A narrow stretch of water]—*Syn.* waterbend, tributary, subdivision, branch, stream, estuary, sound, creek, run, brook, rivulet; see also **bay.**
4. [A weapon]—*Syn.* implement of war, gun, firearm; see **arms** 1.
at arm's length—*Syn.* aloof, distant, haughty, remote; see **unfriendly** 2.
with open arms—*Syn.* warmly, affectionately, joyously; see **friendly** 1.

arm, *v.* **1.** [To equip]—*Syn.* supply, outfit, furnish; see **provide** 1.
2. [To equip with weapons]—*Syn.* furnish weapons, prepare for combat, load, give firearms, issue weapons, equip with arms, accouter, array, gird, outfit, fit out, supply with instruments of warfare, provide with weapons *or* arms.—*Ant.* disarm*, demilitarize, deactivate.

armada, *n.*—*Syn.* flotilla, task force, invasion force; see **fleet.**

armaments, *n.* pl.—*Syn.* combat equipment, deadly weapons, munitions; see **arms** 1.

armchair, *n.*—*Syn.* easy chair, wing chair, Morris chair, captain's chair, elbow chair, rocking chair, rocker, reclining chair, recliner, throne, *fauteuil* (French).

armed, *mod.*—*Syn.* equipped, outfitted, girded, in battle formation, under arms, loaded, provided with arms, accoutered, fortified, protected, fitted out, in arms, well-armed, heavily armed, furbished, armed to the teeth (D).—*Ant.* unarmed*, vulnerable, unprotected.

armistice, *n.*—*Syn.* treaty of peace, cease-fire, temporary peace; see **truce.**

armor, *n.* **1.** [An armored protection]—*Syn.* shield, protection, covering, armor plate, breastplate, protective covering, mail, steel sheet, helmet, heat sheath, reinforced helmet, cuirass, bulletproof vest, flack vest, tin hat, hard hat, sallet, armet, target, gauntlet, visor, morion, basinet, heaume, casquetel, casque, siege-cap, helm, steel helmet, headpiece, brigandine, jambeaux, greaves, defensive clothing *or* equipment, leg armor, corset, defensive arms for the body, chain mail, buckler, hauberk, coat of mail, panoply, habergeon, lorica, plastron, trench helmet.
2. [An armored force]—*Syn.* tanks, tank force, Panzer divisions, armored personnel carriers (APC's), armored column, gun carriers, armor divisions.

armored, *mod.*—*Syn.* heavily clad, steel-plated, bulletproof, ironclad, protected, shielded, invulnerable, bombproof, casemated.—*Ant.* unarmed*, unarmored, unprotected.

armory, *n.* **1.** [Place where arms are made]—*Syn.* munitions plant, arsenal, arms factory; see **factory.**
2. [Building for military purposes]—*Syn.* ordnance headquarters, training center, drilling place, depot, gymnasium, drill center, shooting range, National Guard building, reserve corps headquarters.

arms, *n.* pl. **1.** [Weapons]—*Syn.* armament, armor, ammunition, firearms, munitions, muniments, panoply, guns, small arms, weapons of small caliber operated by hand, accouterments, instruments of war, harness, deadly *or* lethal weapons, means of offense and defense, martial array, pistols, rifles, machine guns, submachine guns, equipment, supplies, ordnance, artillery, material; *both* (D): hardware, ammo; see also **munitions.**
Arms include the following—CAM (cybernetic anthropomorphic machine), MRV (multiple re-entry vehicle), MIRV (multiple independently targetable re-entry vehicle), ABM (anti-ballistic missile), ICBM (intercontinental ballistic missile), sword, broadsword, foil, dagger, stiletto, bayonet, cutlass, scimitar, machete, saber, brand, ax, halberd, partisan, bill, tomahawk, hatchet, spear, pike, javelin, lance, boomerang, arrow, cross-bow, shaft, missile,

club, truncheon, bludgeon, cudgel, mace, sling, longbow, catapult, musket, blunderbuss, matchlock, breechloader, carbine, harquebus, pistol, cannon, automatic rifle, BAR (Browning automatic rifle), machine gun, rifle, M1, carbine, bazooka, trench mortar, hand grenade, howitzer, antitank gun, hand-held nuclear weapon, antiaircraft gun, depth bomb, semi-automatic rifle, gun, revolver, shotgun, switchblade, blackjack, knife, Saturday night special (D).

2. [The design used by family, town, etc., as its sign] —*Syn.* ensign, crest, insignia, heraldic bearings *or* devices *or* emblems, armorial ensigns *or* bearings, shield, scutcheon, emblazonry, (em)blazonment, official insignia, escutcheon, signet, pennon, coat of arms.

bear arms—*Syn.* carry weapons, be armed, be militant; see **arm** 2.

take up arms—*Syn.* go to war, rebel, do battle; see **fight** 2.

under arms—*Syn.* outfitted, in battle formation, fortified; see **armed.**

up in arms—*Syn.* hostile, indignant, willing to fight; see **angry.**

army, *mod.* —*Syn.* military, regimental, combat, land, air, ground, commando, veteran, guerrilla, fighting, militant, belligerent, martial, regimented, under arms, concerning the armed forces, in the army, under orders, drafted, volunteered, in service, serving one's country.

army, *n.* **1.** [Military land forces]—*Syn.* armed force, standing army, regulars, soldiery, troops, men, cavalry, *force de frappe* (French), infantry, artillery, air corps, reserves; see also **air force, artillery** 2, **infantry.**

2. [A unit of an army, sense 1]—*Syn.* division, regiment, air mobile division, armored division, airborne division, infantry division, regiment, battalion, company, battery, corps, brigade, flight, wing, amphibious force, task force, detail, detachment, squad, troop, platoon, blocking force, patrol, unit, command, formation, point, tercio, maniple, cohort, decury, column, legion, platoon, outfit.

3. [Any large group]—*Syn.* host, throng, multitude; see **crowd** 1.

aroma, *n.* —*Syn.* fragrance, perfume, odor; see **smell** 1, 2.

aromatic, *mod.* —*Syn.* pungent, fragrant, sweet-smelling; see **odorous** 2.

around, *mod.* and *prep.* **1.** [Surrounding]—*Syn.* about, in this area, on all sides, on every side, in circumference, neighboring, in the vicinity (of), all round, circuitously, round (about), encompassing, in various directions, nearby, approximately, in a sphere, in a circle, in a course making a circle, along a circuit, all about, close to *or* about, nearly in a circle, on various sides; *both* (D): round and round, right and left.—*Ant.* distant*, remote, far-off.

2. [In size]—*Syn.* in circumference, in area, in extent, in measure, in dimension, in bigness.

3. [Approximately]—*Syn.* almost, about, close to; see **approximately.**

have been around—*Syn.* worldly, sophisticated, knowledgeable; see **experienced.**

arouse, *v.* —*Syn.* move, stir (up), stimulate; see **excite** 1, 2.

arraign, *v.* —*Syn.* summon, charge, indict; see **accuse.**

arrange, *v.* **1.** [To put in order]—*Syn.* order, regulate, systematize; see **order** 3.

2. [To make arrangements]—*Syn.* determine, plan, devise, contrive, prepare for, get *or* make ready, draft, scheme, design, project, concert, provide, make preparations, set the stage, prepare, put into shape, make plans for, line up, organize, adjust, adapt, manage, direct, establish, decide, resolve, lay by the heels (D).—*Ant.* bother*, disorganize, disturb.

arrangement, *n.* **1.** [The act of arranging]—*Syn.* ordering, grouping, classification; see **organization** 1.

2. [The result of arranging]—*Syn.* method, system, form; see **order** 3.

3. [An agreement]—*Syn.* settlement, adjustment, compromise; see **agreement** 3.

4. [A design]—*Syn.* pattern, composition, combination; see **design** 1.

arrangements, *n.* pl.—*Syn.* plans, preparations, preparatory measures, provisions, accommodations.

array, *n.* **1.** [Formal order]—*Syn.* design, pattern, arrangement; see **order** 3.

2. [Relatively formal dress]—*Syn.* full dress, fashion, evening dress, apparel, dress clothes, finery; see also **clothes, dress** 1.

3. [A considerable number]—*Syn.* throng, multitude, host; see **crowd** 1.

arrears, *n.* pl.—*Syn.* back payments, unpaid *or* outstanding debt(s), unfinished work, obligation(s), deficiency, unpaid bill(s), deficit, debit, claim, arrearage, liability, debt unpaid though due, that which is behind in payment, balance due.

arrest, *n.* **1.** [Legal restraint]—*Syn.* appropriation, imprisonment, apprehension, commitment, confinement, incarceration, capture, captivity, protective *or* preventive custody, restraining, taking by force, taking into custody, constraint, duress, seizure, detention; *all* (D): pinch, haul, pickup, bust.—*Ant.* freedom*, acquittal, release.

2. [Act of stopping]—*Syn.* check, checking, stay, staying, stoppage, interruption, hindrance, obstruction, restraining, cessation, prevention, suspension, suppression; *both* (D): holdup, letup; see also **delay** 1, **restraint** 2.—*Ant.* action*, continuation*, extension.

under arrest—*Syn.* arrested, in custody, apprehended; see **under arrest.**

arrest, *v.* **1.** [To seize legally]—*Syn.* apprehend, take charge *or* hold of, hold, place under arrest, take into (protective *or* preventive) custody, capture, seize by legal warrant, take by authority, imprison, jail, incarcerate, detain, secure, seize, get, catch, take (prisoner); *all* (D): lay by the heels, lay one's hands on, nab, collar, grab, run in, pick up, bust.—*Ant.* free*, liberate, parole.

2. [To stop]—*Syn.* restrain, restrict, check; see **prevent.**

arrested, *mod.* —*Syn.* seized, taken into custody, jailed; see **under arrest.**

arrival, *n.* **1.** [The act of arriving]—*Syn.* entrance, advent, coming, entry, appearance, landing, homecoming, debarkation, alighting, ingress, influx,

landfall, inflow, approach, appearance, accession, dismounting, reaching a place from a distance, return, reaching one's destination, meeting, disembarkation.—*Ant.* departure*, leaving, leave-taking.
2. [That which has arrived]—*Syn.* passenger, visitor, tourist, guest, newcomer, delegate, representative, long-expected relative, traveler, envoy, conferee, cargo, freight, mail, shipment, package, parcel, addition.

arrive, *v.* **1.** [To come to a place]—*Syn.* enter, land, report, disembark, alight, dismount, halt, come into *or* at *or* upon *or* in, put *or* drop *or* roll in, roll up, reach, get to *or* in, visit, make shore, cast *or* drop anchor, come to hand, reach home, appear, get to; *all* (D): hit, touch, blow in *or* into, breeze *or* check *or* pull in, bob up, hit town, fetch up at.—*Ant.* leave*, go, depart.
2. [(D) To obtain recognized success]—*Syn.* grow famous, accomplish, achieve success; see **succeed** 1.

arrogance, *n.*—*Syn.* presumption, *hauteur* (French), pride, disdain, hubris, vainglory, swagger, pomposity, contemptuousness, reserve, overbearance, insolence, priggishness, smugness, vanity, braggadocio, superciliousness, self-importance, audacity, haughtiness, aloofness, indifference, display, ostentation, vaingloriousness, egotism, ego, conceit, self-love, affection, airs, pretension, pretense, snobbishness; *all* (D): nerve, high-and-mightiness, cheek, stiff neck, snootiness, the lifted eyebrow. —*Ant.* modesty*, unobtrusiveness, shyness.

arrogant, *mod.*—*Syn.* domineering, autocratic, sneering; see **egotistic** 2.

arrogantly, *mod.*—*Syn.* proudly, haughtily, insolently, loftily; *both* (D): with arms akimbo, with one's nose in the air.

arrow, *n.*—*Syn.* shaft, bolt, dart, barb, missile, sign, butt shaft, indicator, directive, pointer.

arsenal, *n.*—*Syn.* arms plant, military warehouse, armory, munitions factory, ammunition depot, magazine, ammunition dump.

arson, *n.*—*Syn.* pyromania, firing, incendiarism, deliberate burning of property, criminal setting of fires, willful burning of one's own property when insured, set conflagration, malicious burning of other's property.

arsonist, *n.*—*Syn.* incendiary, arsonite, pyromaniac, firebug (D), one who sets fires illegally, torch (D), *petroleur* (French); see also **criminal.**

art, *n.* **1.** [Skill or creative power]—*Syn.* ingenuity, inventiveness, imagination; see **ability**1, 2.
2. [The study and creation of beauty]—*Syn.* representation, illustration, delineation, abstraction, imitation, modeling, description, portrayal, pictorialization, design, simulation, performance, personification, sketching, molding, shaping, painting, symbolization, characterization, creating, creativity, sculpting, carving.
3. [The product of art, sense 2]—*Syn.* masterpiece, *magnum opus* (Latin), *chef d'oeuvre, objet d'art* (both French); see also **architecture, dance** 1, **literature** 1, **music** 1, **painting** 1, **picture** 3, **sculpture, statue.**
4. [The study of humanities; *plural*]—*Syn.* philosophy, music, painting, history, literature, language; see also **history** 2, **language** 2, **literature** 1, **music** 1, **philosophy** 1, **science** 1.

artery, *n.* **1.** [Main channel of communication of travel]—*Syn.* highway, course, passage, thoroughfare, trunk line, supply route, track, pathway, corridor, conduit, duct, canal; see also **road** 1, **way** 2.
2. [Blood vessel]—*Syn.* tube, aorta, arterial passageway; see **vein** 4.
Important arteries include the following—aorta, pulmonary artery, axillary artery, brachial artery, coronary artery, nutrient artery, radial artery, intercostal artery, femoral artery, innominate artery, abdominal aorta, scapular artery.

artesian well, *n.*—*Syn.* fountain, drinking place, watering place; see **well** 1.

artful, *mod.* **1.** [Crafty]—*Syn.* shrewd, cunning, wily; see **intelligent** 1, **sly** 1.
2. [Skillful]—*Syn.* clever, adroit, ingenious; see **able** 1, 2.

arthritis, *n.*—*Syn.* inflammation of a joint, arthropathy, collagen disease; see **disease** 3.

article, *n.* **1.** [An individual thing]—*Syn.* object, substance, commodity; see **thing** 1.
2. [Nonfiction appearing in a periodical]—*Syn.* essay, editorial, commentary; see **exposition** 2.
3. [A division of a piece of writing]—*Syn.* portion, section, provision, item, clause, stipulation, chapter.

articulate, *v.* **1.** [To speak clearly]—*Syn.* enunciate, pronounce, verbalize; see **utter.**
2. [To join]—*Syn.* fit (together), combine, connect, link; see **join** 1.

articulation, *n.* **1.** [Pronunciation]—*Syn.* enunciation, utterance, vocalization; see **diction.**
2. [The act of joining]—*Syn.* unification, coupling, junction; see **union** 1.
3. [A joint]—*Syn.* union, connection, coupling; see **joint** 1.

artifice, *n.* **1.** [Maneuver]—*Syn.* stratagem, wile, ruse; see **trick** 1.
2. [Trickery]—*Syn.* guile, cunning, deceit; see **dishonesty.**
3. [Skill]—*Syn.* ability, know-how, facility; see **ability** 2.

artificial, *mod.* **1.** [*Said of objects*]—*Syn.* unreal, synthetic, counterfeit; see **false** 3.
2. [*Said of conduct*]—*Syn.* mannered, unnatural, feigned; see **affected** 2, 3.

artillery, *n.* **1.** [Heavy ordnance]—*Syn.* gunnery, arms, weapons; see **cannon, munitions.**
2. [The branch of the service which mans artillery, sense 1]—*Syn.* gun crew, field battery, field artillery, motorized units, antiaircraft units, armored force.

artist, *n.* **1.** [A creative worker in the fine arts] —*Syn.* master, creator, painter, composer, artiste, virtuoso, musician, poet, novelist, dramatist, essayist, actress, actor, playwright, writer, performing artist, limner, practitioner of the arts, art student, devotee of the arts, skilled hand, adept, portraitist, watercolorist, landscapist, muralist; still-life artist, portrait artist, etc; belletrist, cartoonist, tragedian, tragedienne, comedienne, comedian, mime, opera singer, prima donna, dancer, ballet performer, danseuse, ballerina, sculptor, etcher, engraver, interpreter, designer, architect, photographer.

2. [A highly skilled workman]—*Syn.* artificer, inventor, artisan, mechanic, craftsman, operator, contriver, workman, builder, specialist, handicraftsman, professional.
3. [A clever trickster]—*Syn.* sharper, crook, con man (D); see **rascal.**

artistic, *mod.* **1.** [Pertaining to the fine arts]—*Syn.* aesthetic, decorative, picturesque, musical, pictorial, rhythmical, poetic, dramatic, compositional, patterned, studied, belletristic.
2. [Pertaining to the styles or schools of art] —*Syn.* realist, naturalist, *genre* (French), abstract, representational, functional, organic, modernist(ic), futurist *or* futuristic, nonobjective, cubist(ic), surrealist(ic), dadaist, primitivist(ic), impressionist(ic), expressionist(ic), symbolist(ic), constructivist(ic), dynamic, vitalistic, op, pop, art nouveau, pre-Columbian, pre-Raphaelite, pre-Raphaelistic, Victorian, Greek, Japanese, classical, medieval, Renaissance, Restoration, grotesque, rococo, baroque, romantic.
3. [Showing taste and skill]—*Syn.* inventive, skillful, artful, crafty, imaginative, discriminating, creative, graceful, talented, accomplished, well-turned, well-proportioned, well-executed, well-wrought, pleasing, selective, sublime, judicious, ideal, well-balanced, cultured, tasteful, exquisite, sensitive, fine, elegant, harmonious, grand, stimulating, elevated, noble, beautiful.—*Ant.* tasteless*, flat, inept.

artistry, *n.* —*Syn.* workmanship, skill, proficiency; see **ability** 2.

artless, *mod.* —*Syn.* simple, guileless, natural; see **naive.**

artlessness, *n.* **1.** [Simplicity]—*Syn.* ingenuousness, naïveté, candor; see **innocence** 2.
2. [Unskillfulness]—*Syn.* ineptitude, crudeness, ignorance; see **awkwardness** 1.

arty (D), *mod.* —*Syn.* imitative, tasteless, pseudo, false, deceptive, flaunting, catchy, illusory, ephemeral, popular, popularized, without taste; see also **affected** 2.

Aryan, *mod.* —*Syn.* Indo-European, Proto-Indo-European, Indo-Hittite, Indo-Germanic, Japhetic.

as, *conj.*, mod., and*prep.* **1.** [While]—*Syn.* in the process of, in the act of, on the point of; see **while** 1.
2. [Because]—*Syn.* since, inasmuch as, for the reason that; see **because.**
3. [To a degree]—*Syn.* in the same way, in the same manner, equally, comparatively, similarly.
4. [For a given purpose, end, use, etc]—*Syn.* just as, *qua* (Latin), just for, serving as, functioning as, acting as, being, in and of itself, by its nature, essentially.

as a matter of course, *mod.* —*Syn.* ordinarily, commonly, customarily; see **regularly** 1.

as a matter of fact, *mod.* —*Syn.* truly, actually, indeed; see **really** 1.

as a rule, *mod.* —*Syn.* usually, commonly, ordinarily; see **regularly** 1.

as a whole, *mod.* —*Syn.* altogether, all told, all in all; see **altogether** 2.

ascend, *v.* **1.** [To rise]—*Syn.* go *or* move upward, sprout, soar; see **rise** 1.
2. [To climb]—*Syn.* mount, scale, work one's way up; see **climb** 2.

ascendancy, *n.* —*Syn.* authority, sway, power; see **command** 2.

ascension, *n.* —*Syn.* ascent, rising, climbing; see **rise** 1.

ascent, *n.* **1.** [Rising]—*Syn.* ascendance, climbing, ascension; see **rise** 1.
2. [Upgrade]—*Syn.* incline, slope, acclivity; see **grade** 1.

ascertain, *v.* —*Syn.* learn, find out, determine; see **discover** 1.

ascetic, *mod.* —*Syn.* austere, plain, rigorous; see **modest** 2, **severe** 2.

ascetic, *n.* —*Syn.* holy man, monk, religious devotee, anchorite, self-denier, nun, self-tormenter, hermit, stylite, eremite, fakir, penitent, puritan, yogi, flagellant, mortifier of the flesh, recluse.

as far as, *mod.* —*Syn.* to the extent that, to the degree that, up to the time that, insofar as.

as good as, *mod.* —*Syn.* the same as, equivalent to (being), tantamount, practically, of equal goodness with; see also **equal.**

ashamed, *mod.* —*Syn.* embarrassed, shamed, discomfited, regretful, meek, chagrined, repentant, penitent, apologetic, demeaned, debased, abashed, crestfallen, conscience-stricken, mortified, uncomfortable, discomforted, hesitant, perplexed, bewildered, shamefaced, dashed, bowed down, disconcerted, sputtering, stammering, stuttering, gasping, floundering, rattled, muddled, confused, blushing, flustered, distraught, submissive; *all* (D): spotted, feeling like a jackass, off balance, in a hole, taken down a peg, red in the face, out of face *or* countenance, looking silly *or* foolish, at a loss. —*Ant.* rude*, brazen, proud.

ashes, *n.* pl. **1.** [Powdery remains after a fire] —*Syn.* dust, powder, cinders, slag, embers, charcoal, volcanic ash, soot, remains of what is burned, scoriae, ruins from destruction by fire.
2. [Ruins]—*Syn.* remains, vestiges, remnants; see **destruction** 2.

ashore, *mod.* —*Syn.* on shore, on (dry) land, on terra firma, beached, aground; *both* (D): on the beach, on the pavements.—*Ant.* afloat*, at sea, on board (ship).

Asia, *n.* —*Syn.* the Orient, the East, the mysterious East.
Parts of Asia include the following—*Far East:* China, Taiwan, Japan, North Korea, South Korea, Mongolia, Tibet, Siberia, Vietnam, Laos, Kampuchea, Thailand, Burma, India, Bhutan, Sikkim, Nepal, Malaysia, Indonesia; *Near and Middle East:* Turkey, Syria, Iraq, Iran, Jordan, Israel, Lebanon, Saudi Arabia, Yemen, Aden, Muscat and Oman, Kuwait, Qatar, Afghanistan, Pakistan.

Asian, *mod.* **1.** [*Said of people*]—*Syn.* Oriental, Mongolian, almond-eyed, yellow-skinned, Chinese, Hindu, Japanese, Mongoloid.
2. [*Said of objects, culture, etc.*]—*Syn.* Oriental, Far Eastern, Mongolian, Near Eastern, Confucian, Levantine, Sinitic, Buddhist, Buddhistic, Japanese, Nipponese, Korean, Thai, Vietnamese, Hindu, Indian, Brahman, Aryan, Cambodian, Chinese, Tibetan.

aside, *mod.* —*Syn.* to the side, to *or* on *or* by one side, at rest, out, by oneself, away from some position, apart, by the side of, at one side, by itself, alone, alongside, out of the way, aloof, laterally, down, away, in isolation, afar, in safekeeping, in preservation, beside, sidewise, sideways, abreast, abeam, at a short distance, by.

aside from, *prep.* —*Syn.* beside, in addition to, excluding; see **besides.**

as if, *conj.* and *mod.* **1.** [As though]—*Syn.* just as (if), (just as) though, as it were, in such a way that, as if it were, supposing, quasi, so to speak, as would be if, as might be, (just) like (D).

2. [Seemingly]—*Syn.* manifestly, supposedly, presumably; see **apparently.**

asinine, *mod.* —*Syn.* silly, simple, foolish, idiotic; see **stupid** 1.

as is (D), *mod.* —*Syn.* as it stands, as usual, just the same, the same way, just as usual (D).

as it were, *mod.* —*Syn.* so to speak, figuratively speaking, in a way, as it seems, as it would seem, in some sort, in a manner, so to say; *all* (D): kind of, in a manner of speaking, sort of.

ask, *v.* **1.** [To inquire]—*Syn.* request, query, question, interrogate, examine, cross-examine, demand, pose *or* raise *or* put a question, inquire, call *or* apply *or* ask *or* angle *or* file *or* contend for, frame a question, seek an answer, catechize, make inquiry *or* application, apply to, order, command, put questions to, requisition, direct, institute an inquiry, enjoin, bid, charge, petition, call upon, invite, urge (to), challenge, pry into, scour, investigate, hunt for; *all* (D): quiz, grill, dun, put the screws on, turn the heat on, needle, put the bee on, beg leave, sound out, pump, put through the third degree, pray. —*Ant.* answer*, refute, rejoin.

2. [To solicit]—*Syn.* request, entreat, supplicate; see **beg** 1.

3. [To expect]—*Syn.* hope for, claim, await, foresee; see **anticipate** 1.

4. [To invite]—*Syn.* propose, suggest, urge; see **invite** 1, 2.

askew, *mod.* —*Syn.* awry, aslant, slanting; see **crooked** 1.

asleep, *mod.* —*Syn.* sleeping, dreaming, inert, quiet, resting, snoring, somnolent, in a state of sleep, in a sound sleep, fast *or* dead *or* sound asleep, comatose, in a torpor, slumbering, heavy with sleep, reposing, taking a siesta, in slumber *or* repose, hibernating, dozing, wakeless, napping, unconscious, abed; *all* (D): dead to the world, in the arms of Morpheus, in the Land of Nod, asnore, caulked off, anesthetized, snoozing, conked out, out like a light, assuming the horizontal, dormant, dreaming. —*Ant.* awake*, waking, alert.

as long as, *conj.* —*Syn.* since, during, whilst; see **while** 1.

aspect, *n.* **1.** [Looks]—*Syn.* countenance, face, features; see **appearance** 1.

2. [View]—*Syn.* perspective, regard, slant; see **viewpoint.**

asperity, *n.* **1.** [Roughness]—*Syn.* harshness, unevenness, ruggedness; see **roughness** 1.

2. [Hardship]—*Syn.* trouble, misfortune, impediment; see **difficulty** 1, 2.

3. [Acrimony]—*Syn.* bitterness, sharpness, ill temper; see **roughness** 2, **rudeness.**

aspersion, *n.* —*Syn.* detraction, defamation, calumny; see **lie** 1.

asphalt, *n.* —*Syn.* asphaltum, bitumen, pavement, roadbed, asphalt track, asphalt lane, asphalt highway, speedway; see also **pavement** 1, **road** 1.

aspirant, *n.* —*Syn.* competitor, suitor, contestant; see **candidate.**

aspiration, *n.* —*Syn.* yearning, eagerness, inclination; see **ambition** 1.

aspire, *v.* —*Syn.* strive, struggle, yearn; see **try** 1.

aspiring, *mod.* —*Syn.* zealous, hopeful, enthusiastic; see **ambitious** 1.

as regards, *mod.* and*prep.* —*Syn.* concerning, regarding, respecting; see **about** 2.

ass, *n.* **1.** [A stupid person]—*Syn.* dolt, dunce, blockhead; see **fool** 1.

2. [A donkey]—*Syn.* burro, jackass, jennet; see **donkey.**

assail, *v.* —*Syn.* assault, molest, throw oneself upon; see **attack** 2.

assailable, *mod.* —*Syn.* vulnerable, defenseless, exposed; see **weak** 5.

assailant, *n.* —*Syn.* antagonist, foe, enemy; see **attacker.**

assassin, *n.* —*Syn.* murderer, slayer, butcher; see **killer.**

assassinate, *v.* —*Syn.* slay, slaughter, put to death; see **kill** 1.

assassination, *n.* —*Syn.* killing, shooting, slaying; see **murder.**

assault, *n.* **1.** [An attack]—*Syn.* charge, advance, onslaught; see **attack** 1.

2. [A rape]—*Syn.* attack, abduction, violation; see **rape.**

assault, *v.* **1.** [To attack]—*Syn.* assail, advance, strike; see **attack** 1, 2.

2. [To rape]—*Syn.* attack, violate, ravish; see **rape.**

assay, *v.* —*Syn.* test, measure, run tests on; see **examine** 1.

assemblage, *n.* —*Syn.* assembly, collection, association; see **gathering.**

assemble, *v.* **1.** [To come together]—*Syn.* meet, convene, congregate; see **gather** 1.

2. [To bring together]—*Syn.* rally, call, convoke, muster, round *or* head up, group, convene, summon, mobilize, call together, accumulate, amass, reunite, form a whole, invite guests, gather, collect, hold a celebration, hold a meeting, unite, hold a convocation; *all* (D): pack them in, throw a party, herd together, rally round, gather around, gang around, go into a huddle, lump together, make up. —*Ant.* scatter*, break up, send away.

3. [To put together]—*Syn.* piece *or* fit together, set up, erect, construct, join, unite, solder, mold, weld, glue, model. —*Ant.* break*, disassemble, break down.

assembly, *n.* **1.** [A gathering of persons]—*Syn.* assemblage, meeting, association; see **gathering.**

2. [The process of bringing parts together]—*Syn.* construction, piecing together, fitting in, joining, modeling, assembling, attachment, adjustment, collection, welding, soldering, molding, fixing. —*Ant.* separation*, dismantling, wrecking.

3. [An assembled mechanism]—*Syn.* arrangement, parts, equipment; see **device** 1, **machine** 1.

assent, *n.* —*Syn.* approval, authorization, consent; see **permission.**

assert, *v.* **1.** [To say positively]—*Syn.* state, say, affirm; see **declare** 1.
2. [To maintain]—*Syn.* cite, allege, advance; see **support** 2.

assertion, *n.*—*Syn.* affirmation, statement, report; see **declaration** 1.

assertive, *mod.*—*Syn.* positive, absolute, confident; see **certain** 1.

assess, *v.* **1.** [To tax]—*Syn.* charge, exact tribute, exact from; see **tax** 1.
2. [To estimate]—*Syn.* judge, reckon, guess; see **estimate** 1.

assessment, *n.* **1.** [Valuation]—*Syn.* appraisal, evaluation, estimation; see **estimate** 1.
2. [Tax]—*Syn.* levy, charge, fee; see **tax** 1.

assets, *n.* pl.—*Syn.* holdings, possessions, capital; see **property** 1, **wealth** 1.

assiduous, *mod.* **1.** [Careful]—*Syn.* scrupulous, attentive, exacting; see **careful.**
2. [Industrious]—*Syn.* hard-working, diligent, busy; see **active** 2.

assign, *v.* **1.** [To delegate to a specific purpose]—*Syn.* commit, commission, authorize, hand over, earmark, allocate, detail, appoint, allot, prescribe, nominate, name, select, hold responsible, empower, entrust, allow, cast, deputize, attach, charge, accredit, hire, elect, ordain, enroll, relegate, draft.—*Ant.* maintain*, reserve, keep back.
2. [To distribute]—*Syn.* give out, consign, allot; see **distribute** 1.
3. [To designate]—*Syn.* specify, indicate, set apart; see **designate** 1.

assignation, *n.*—*Syn.* rendezvous, clandestine meeting, tryst; see **date** 2.

assignee, *n.*—*Syn.* guardian, appointee, administrator; see **trustee.**

assignment, *n.* **1.** [An appointment]—*Syn.* designation, authorization, nomination; see **appointment** 1.
2. [Something assigned]—*Syn.* job, responsibility, talk; see **duty** 2.

assimilate, *v.* **1.** [To absorb]—*Syn.* take up, digest, osmose; see **absorb** 1.
2. [To understand]—*Syn.* grasp, learn, sense; see **understand** 1.
3. [To adjust]—*Syn.* adapt, acclimatize, accustom; see **conform.**

assimilation, *n.* **1.** [Absorption]—*Syn.* digestion, inhalation, soaking up; see **absorption.**
2. [Adjustment]—*Syn.* adaptation, acclimatization, conformity; see **agreement** 2.

assist, *v.*—*Syn.* support, aid, serve; see **help** 1.

assistance, *n.*—*Syn.* comfort, support, compensation; see **aid** 1.

assistant, *n.*—*Syn.* aide, deputy, henchman, friend, follower, adherent, auxiliary, lieutenant, associate, companion, colleague, partner, helper, acolyte, representative, second in command, apprentice, fellow-worker, secretary, supporter, appointee, abettor, ancillary, helping hand, patron, backer, bodyguard, aide-de-camp, ally, accessory, clerk, adjunct, collaborator, confederate, subaltern, confrere, mate, helpmate, co-aid, adjutant, subordinate, cooperator, accomplice, copartner, coworker; *all* (D): flunky, wet nurse, man Friday, right arm, stooge, yes-man, sidekick, gofer, right-hand man, friend in need.—*Ant.* enemy*, rival, antagonist.

associate, *n.*—*Syn.* comrade, brother-in-arms, peer, compeer, colleague, partner, copartner, friend, ally, buddy, accomplice, abettor, assistant, aid, attendant, henchman, confederate, auxiliary, co-operator, co-worker, co-helper, helper, accessory, coadjutor, collaborator, confrere, fellow-worker; *all* (D): stooge, plant, ringer, helping hand, right-hand man, man Friday, teammate; see also **assistant.**—*Ant.* enemy*, foe, antagonist.

associate, *v.* **1.** [To keep company with]—*Syn.* have relations with, be intimate with, work with, fraternize with, join with, get along with, consort with, be friendly with, have an acquaintanceship with; *all* (D): run *or* hang around with, pick up with, mix with, take up with, mess around with, hook up with, keep in with, get around, gang up with, mix with; see also **join** 2.—*Ant.* leave*, break off relations with, sever a friendship.
2. [To relate]—*Syn.* correlate, link, connect, join; see **compare** 1.
3. [To form an organization]—*Syn.* incorporate, affiliate, ally, unite, federate, amalgamate, take out a charter; see also **organize** 2.—*Ant.* disband*, dissolve, break up.
4. [To combine]—*Syn.* unite, blend, connect; see **join** 1.

association, *n.* **1.** [The act of associating]—*Syn.* frequenting, fraternization, friendship, acquaintanceship, co-operation, assistance, relationship, affiliation, agreement, participation, companionship, intercourse, intimacy, fellowship, familiarity, friendliness, camaraderie, membership, acquaintance, mingling, union, community.—*Ant.* disagreement*, severance, rupture.
2. [The process of intellectual comparison]—*Syn.* connection, relation, mental connection, train of thought, connection of ideas in thought, recollection, impression, remembrance, suggestibility, combination.—*Ant.* separation*, division, segregation.
3. [An organization]—*Syn.* union, federation, corporation; see **organization** 3.
4. [Companionship]—*Syn.* brotherhood, fraternization, friendship; see **fellowship** 2.

assort, *v.*—*Syn.* sort, arrange, group; see **classify.**

assorted, *mod.*—*Syn.* varied, miscellaneous, mixed; see **different** 2.

assortment, *n.*—*Syn.* variety, combination, group; see **collection** 2.

assuage, *v.* **1.** [To alleviate]—*Syn.* mitigate, lessen, soothe; see **relieve** 2.
2. [To satisfy]—*Syn.* appease, fill, surfeit; see **satisfy** 1, 3.
3. [To calm]—*Syn.* pacify, still, mollify; see **quiet** 1.

as such, *mod.*—*Syn.* in itself, by itself, alone, intrinsically.

assume, *v.* **1.** [To take for granted]—*Syn.* suppose, presume, posit, understand, predicate, gather, find, collect, theorize, presuppose, ascertain, consider as true, draw the inference, judge at random, divine, get the idea, have an idea that, suspect, postulate, regard, consider, ween, imply, hypothesize, guess, take without proof, treat as conceded, conjecture, suppose as fact, deem, imagine, surmise, opine,

judge, estimate, speculate, fancy, take the liberty, be of the opinion, dare say, premise, deduce, count upon, infer, conclude, put two and two together, be inclined to think, hold the opinion; *all* (D): think, calculate, hope, feel, be afraid, believe, have faith, take (it), expect, allow, reckon.—*Ant.* doubt*, be surprised, be unaware that.
2. [To pretend]—*Syn.* feign, put on, affect; see **pretend** 1.
3. [To take]—*Syn.* seize, appropriate, arrogate; see **seize** 2.

assumed, *mod.* **1.** [Taken for granted]—*Syn.* presumed, understood, presupposed, counted on, inferred, postulated, given, granted, taken as known, conjectured, accepted, supposed, suppositional, hypothetical, hypothesized.
2. [Fictitious]—*Syn.* pretended, counterfeit, spurious; see **false** 2, 3.

assuming, *mod.*—*Syn.* arrogant, presumptuous, bold; see **egotistic** 2.

assumption, *n.* **1.** [The act of taking for granted] —*Syn.* supposition, presupposition, presumption, supposal, conjecture, assuming, accepting, suspicion, surmise, theorization, hypothesization. —*Ant.* proof*, demonstrating, establishing.
2. [Something assumed]—*Syn.* hypothesis, theory, postulate; see **opinion** 1.
3. [The act of becoming responsible for]—*Syn.* accepting, assuming, taking on *or* up, appropriation, usurpation, arrogation.

assurance, *n.* **1.** [A guaranty]—*Syn.* insurance, support, pledge; see **promise** 1.
2. [Confidence]—*Syn.* conviction, trust, certainty, certitude; see **faith** 1.
3. [Audacity]—*Syn.* boldness, insolence, effrontery; see **rudeness.**

assure, *v.* **1.** [To guarantee]—*Syn.* vouch for, aver, attest; see **guarantee** 1.
2. [To convince]—*Syn.* prove, persuade, induce; see **convince.**
3. [To promise]—*Syn.* pledge, affirm, swear; see **promise** 1.
4. [To encourage]—*Syn.* reassure, inspire, hearten; see **encourage** 2.

assured, *mod.* **1.** [Certain]—*Syn.* sure, undoubted, guaranteed; see **certain** 3.
2. [Confident]—*Syn.* self-possessed, bold, unhesitating; see **confident** 2.

assuredly,, *mod.*—*Syn.* positively, definitely, certainly; see **surely.**

astern, *mod.*—*Syn.* (to the) rear, abaft, rearward; see **backward** 1.

as though, *conj.* and *mod.* **1.** [As if]—*Syn.* just as, just as if, just as though; see **as if** 1.
2. [Seemingly]—*Syn.* evidently, supposedly, presumably; see **apparently.**

astonish, *v.*—*Syn.* shock, amaze, astound; see **surprise** 1.

astonishing, *mod.*—*Syn.* surprising, startling, extraordinary; see **unusual** 1.

astonishment, *n.*—*Syn.* surprise, amazement, bewilderment; see **wonder** 1.

astound, *v.*—*Syn.* amaze, shock, startle; see **surprise** 1.

astray, *mod.*—*Syn.* straying, roaming, adrift; see **wandering** 1.

astride, *mod.*—*Syn.* with one leg on each side of, on the back of, sitting on, astraddle, straddling, piggyback (D).

astrologer, *n.*—*Syn.* soothsayer, horoscopist, genethlialogist; see **prophet.**

astronaut, *n.*—*Syn.* space traveler, cosmonaut, spaceman, space pilot, rocket pilot, rocketeer, rocket man, space walker, explorer.

astronomer, *n.*—*Syn.* star-gazer, astrochemist, astrophysicist, astrophotographer, astrophotometrist, uranologist, uranographer; see also **scientist.**

astronomical, *mod.* **1.** [Pertaining to astronomy] —*Syn.* uranographical, uranological, astrophotometric, astrophotographic, astrophysical, astrochemical, heavenly, celestial, cosmic, planetary, planetoidal, astral, solar, telescopic, four-dimensional.
2. [Of a magnitude suggesting distances in astronomy]—*Syn.* gigantic, enormous, immeasurable, infinite, ungraspable; see **large** 1, **many.**

astronomy, *n.*—*Syn.* star-gazing, astrochemistry, astrophysics, earth-space science, selenology, astrophotography, astrophotometry, uranology, uranography, uranometry, celestial mechanics, astrography, astrogynosy, astrology; see also **science** 1.

astute, *mod.*—*Syn.* keen, shrewd, clever; see **intelligent** 1.

astuteness, *n.*—*Syn.* sagacity, keenness, shrewdness; see **acumen.**

asunder, *mod.* **1.** [In pieces]—*Syn.* apart, in two *or* half, to shreds, in *or* into (little) (bits and) pieces, dismantled, sundered, dissected, in two parts, divided, into separate parts, separated, divergent, disjoined, rent, carved, dismembered, torn *or* broken apart, split; see also **broken** 1.—*Ant.* whole*, together, sound.
2. [Apart]—*Syn.* divided, disconnected, distant; see **separated.**

as well as, *mod.*—*Syn.* together *or* along with, in addition to, plus; see **including.**

as yet, *mod.*—*Syn.* still, not yet, till now; see **yet** 2.

at, *prep.* **1.** [Position]—*Syn.* on, by, near to, about, occupying the precise position of, in the vicinity (of), placed *or* situated at, found in, in front of, appearing in; see also **in** 1, **near** 1.
2. [Direction]—*Syn.* toward, in the direction of, through; see **to** 1.

at all, *mod.*—*Syn.* anyhow, ever, in any way *or* wise, in any case *or* respect, under any condition *or* circumstances, anywise, in the least, in any manner *or* degree, to any extent, in the least degree, anyway(s) (D).

at all events, *mod.*—*Syn.* whatever (may be) the case, come *or* happen what may, regardless, at any rate, whatever happens, no matter what else, anyhow, in any event *or* case, in the worst case, be as it will, at least, be that as it were *or* may.

at a loss, *mod.*—*Syn.* in a quandary, perplexed, puzzled; see **doubtful** 2.

at arm's length, *mod.*—*Syn.* distant, afar, off, aloof; see **away** 1.

at ease, *mod.*—*Syn.* relaxed, untroubled, carefree; see **comfortable** 1.

at fault, *mod.* **1.** [Culpable]—*Syn.* in the wrong, in error, to blame; see **guilty** 2.
2. [At a loss]—*Syn.* perplexed, puzzled, confused; see **doubtful** 2.
at first, *mod.*—*Syn.* in the beginning, in the first place, at the outset *or* start *or* beginning *or* commencement, first off (D).
at hand, *mod.* **1.** [Near]—*Syn.* nearby, accessible, convenient; see **available.**
2. [Imminent]—*Syn.* approaching, coming, impending; see **imminent.**
at heart, *mod.*—*Syn.* radically, basically, fundamentally; see **essentially.**
atheism, *n.*—*Syn.* irreligion, heresy, agnosticism, ungodliness, impiety, unbelief, positivism, disregard *or* denial of God, nihilism, iconoclasm, disbelief in God, irreverence, pyrrhonism, rationalism, dogmatic *or* skeptical atheism, infidelity, antichristianism, materialism, skepticism, freethinking, disbelief; see also **doubt** 1.
atheist, *n.*—*Syn.* freethinker, nonbeliever, irreligionist; see **skeptic.**
atheistic, *mod.*—*Syn.* freethinking, agnostic, skeptic, disbelieving, heretical, antichristian, unchristian, unconverted, profane, impious, blasphemous, worldly, materialistic, godless, irreverent, ungodly. —*Ant.* religious*, god-fearing, devout.
Athenian, *mod.*—*Syn.* classic, Attic, Hellenic; see **classical** 2, **Greek.**
athlete, *n.*—*Syn.* acrobat, gymnast, player, contestant, champion, sportsman, amateur, professional, semi-professional, contender, challenger; *all* (D): Varsity man, letterman, muscle man, jock, Tarzan.
Athletes include the following—baseball player, football player, basketball player, soccer player, volleyball player, boxer, pugilist, wrestler, swimmer, golfer, tennis player, badminton player, jockey, trackman, marathoner, javelin thrower, high-jumper, discus thrower, shot putter, skier, ski jumper, slalom racer, runner, jogger, relay runner, long-jumper, pole vaulter, hurdler, bowler, billiard player, polo player, hockey player, skater, bicyclist, fencer, swordsman, saber man, marksman, cricket player; *all* (D): ball hawk, gridder, kicker, booter, hoop man, soccerist, cauliflower, grappler, matsman, bone-bender, tankster, pill dunker, divot digger, netman, racketeer, monkey, bangtail chauffeur, flyer, spike digger, fleet-foot, miler, barrier boy, rubber legs, bamboo topper, skyscraper, pinster, roller, cueist, pool shark, cow-pasture pool shark, mallet-swinger, puck chaser, stick handler, foilsman, saberman, dead-shot.
athletic, *mod.*—*Syn.* muscular, husky, heavy-set, wiry, springy, slim, fast, solid, strapping, hardy, robust, strong, vigorous, well-knit, powerful, brawny, sinewy, sturdy, manly, well-built, well-proportioned; *all* (D): Herculean, Amazonian, Titanic, built like an ox.—*Ant.* sick*, weak*, fat*.
athletics, *n.* pl.—*Syn.* gymnastics, acrobatics, games; see **sport** 3.
Atlantic, *mod.*—*Syn.* oceanic, transoceanic, transatlantic, eastern, coastal.
atlas, *n.*—*Syn.* book of maps, charts, tables; see **book** 1.
at last, *mod.*—*Syn.* ultimately, in conclusion, at the end; see **finally** 2.
at length, *mod.* **1.** [Finally]—*Syn.* after a while, at last, in the end; see **finally** 2.
2. [Fully]—*Syn.* unabridged, extensively, without omission; see **completely.**
atmosphere, *n.* **1.** [The air]—*Syn.* layer of air, gaseous envelope, air pressure; see **air** 1.
2. [A pervading quality]—*Syn.* sense, impression, taste; see **character** 1, **characteristic.**
atmospheric, *mod.*—*Syn.* airy, climatic, barometrical, baroscopic, aeroscopic, meteorological, in the atmosphere, aerial.
at odds, *mod.*—*Syn.* disagreeing, at variance, discordant; see **quarreling.**
atom, *n.* **1.** [Tiny particle]—*Syn.* fragment, mite, speck, particle, iota, mote, jot, grain, tittle; see also **bit** 1.
2. [Particle in atomic physics]—*Syn.* the smallest particle of an element, molecule (D), smallest quantity of a radical, basic *or* irreducible unit *or* constituent, atomic mass unit.
Parts and forms of atoms include the following—electron, proton, neutron, positron, neutrino, positive electron, neutral electron, quark, cathode ray, alpha ray, beta ray, gamma ray; see also **atomic power, element** 2.
atom bomb, *n.*—*Syn.* atomic bomb, nuclear device, nuclear bomb, nuclear weapon, thermonuclear device, thermonuclear weapon, neutron bomb, hydrogen bomb, A-bomb.
atomic, *mod.* **1.** [Minute]—*Syn.* microscopic, tiny, diminutive; see **minute** 1.
2. [Referring to atoms]—*Syn.* nuclear, thermonuclear, fissionable, atom-powered, nuclear-controlled.
atomic power, *n.*—*Syn.* natural power, energy from fission *or* fusion, atomic chain discharge, nuclear *or* thermonuclear power, power from the sun.
Possible sources of atomic power include the following—uranium and uranium ores, isotopes of uranium, uranium 235 *or* U-235, U-238, plutonium and plutonium ores, plutonium isotopes, plutonium 239 *or* Pu-239, Pu-240.
atom smasher, *n.*—*Syn.* cyclotron, linear accelerator, atomic *or* particle accelerator; see **accelerator.**
at once, *mod.* **1.** [Simultaneously]—*Syn.* at the same time, concurrently, contemporaneously; see **together** 2.
2. [Immediately]—*Syn.* directly, without delay, now; see **immediately.**
atone for, *v.*—*Syn.* compensate (for), do penance, make amends; see **pay for.**
atonement, *n.*—*Syn.* satisfaction, amends, expiation; see **reparation** 1, 2.
at one's disposal, *mod.*—*Syn.* ready, on call, accessible; see **available.**
at rest, *mod.*—*Syn.* relaxed, inactive, undisturbed; see **resting** 1.
atrocity, *n.* **1.** [Brutality]—*Syn.* inhumanity, wickedness, barbarity; see **cruelty.**
2. [A cruel deed]—*Syn.* crime, offense, outrage, atrocious deed, horror, iniquity, plunder, slaughter, wrong; see also **crime** 1, 2, **murder, rape.**
at stake, *mod.*—*Syn.* in danger, risked, involved, implicated, in jeopardy *or* question, hazarded, at

risk *or* hazard, concerned, endangered, at the caprice of fortune (D).

attach, *v.* **1.** [To join]—*Syn.* connect, append, add; see **join** 1.
2. [To seize; especially, to seize legally]—*Syn.* appropriate, take over, confiscate; see **seize** 2.
3. [To attribute]—*Syn.* associate, impute, ascribe; see **attribute.**
4. [To assign]—*Syn.* appoint, name, detail; see **assign** 1.

attachable, *mod.* —*Syn.* adjustable, appendable, annexable, connective, portable, movable, detachable, separable, in sections, prefabricated *or* prefab (D).—*Ant.* whole*, in one piece, inseparable.

attachment, *n.* **1.** [Affection]—*Syn.* fondness, liking, devotion; see **affection.**
2. [Something attached]—*Syn.* accessory, adjunct, annex; see **addition** 2.

attack, *n.* **1.** [Offensive tactical action]—*Syn.* assault, raid, onslaught, advance, charge, thrust, offense, drive, strike, aggression, onset, irruption, outbreak, offensive military operation, skirmish, storming, assailment, broadside, cannonade, encounter, volley, sally, *coup de main* (French), shooting, barrage, fusillade, siege, firing, trespass, blockade, boarding, cross fire, assailing, initiative, invasion, offensive, incursion, forced entrance, intrusion, intervention, increased presence, onrush, inroad, encroachment, incursion.
Types of military attack include—commando raid, air strike, air raid, blitzkrieg, sally, charge, sortie, foray, aggressive first strike, counterforce, second strike, siege, bombardment, bomb run, rally, invasion, infiltration, encirclement, wave, attack *or* reconnaissance in force, pincer movement, strafing, fire mission, firing pass, low-level attack, mast-level attack, kamikaze attack *or* dive, atomic bombing *or* A-bombing, armored thrust, torpedo attack, mechanized attack, sustained attack, around-the-clock bombing, high-level bombing, amphibious operation, attack with depth charges, shelling, curtain of fire, patrol action, suicide attack, assault *or* siege arc, banzai charge, landing operation, armed landing, mortar attack, hit-and-run attack, covering action, covering counterthrust; *all* (D): jab, burst, lunge, wargasm.—*Ant.* withdrawal, retreat*, retirement.
2. [Verbal attack]—*Syn.* libel, slander, denunciation; see **blame** 1.
3. [Illness]—*Syn.* seizure, breakdown, relapse; see **illness** 1.
4. [Rape]—*Syn.* assault, violation, defilement; see **rape.**

attack, *v.* **1.** [To fight offensively; *used of an army*] —*Syn.* assault, beset, besiege, invade, storm, beleaguer, advance, infiltrate, take offensive action, raid, assail, encircle, march against, take the initiative *or* offensive, go forward, thrust *or* fire *or* strike *or* run *or* shoot *or* snipe *or* come *or* fly at, shell, board, take by surprise, sally forth, make a push, bombard, bomb, go over the top, burst *or* fall upon, fire the first shot, fan *or* mushroom out, lift a hand against, lay siege to, open fire, lay into *or* at, crack *or* bear *or* swoop down on *or* upon, launch an attack, spring *or* advance *or* turn on *or* upon, strafe, ambush, waylay, aggress, engage, tilt against, set upon with force, torpedo, stone, fire on *or* upon, push, combat, attempt violence to, trespass against, make aggression on, begin hostilities against, charge, fusillade, strike the first blow, enfilade, bayonet, saber, stab; *all* (D): tackle, close with, cut and thrust, pepper, rake, light *or* sail into, go for, have at, put upon, open up (on), have a cut at.—*Ant.* retreat*, fall back, recoil.
2. [To assault; *used of an individual*]—*Syn.* assail, combat, knock down, seduce, rape, punch, kick, molest, beat, hit, overwhelm, kidnap, strike, club, stab, knock unconscious, throw oneself on *or* upon; *all* (D): lay *or* tear *or* pitch into. gang up on, lower the boom (on), go for the jugular, mug.—*Ant.* retaliate*, resist, fight back.
3. [To assail with words]—*Syn.* revile, refute, reprove; see **censure.**
4. [To proceed vigorously]—*Syn.* take up, deal with, set to work, start in on; *all* (D): come to grips with, set to, buckle down, tackle, plunge *or* dive *or* wade *or* tear into.

attacked, *mod.* —*Syn.* assaulted, bombed, bombarded, assailed, stoned, torpedoed, fired upon, stormed, under attack, strafed, invaded, besieged; see also **ruined** 3.

attacker, *n.* —*Syn.* aggressor, fighter, assailant, antagonist, invader, foe, enemy, criminal, plunderer, intruder, trespasser, violator, ravager, spoiler, felon.—*Ant.* victim*, prey, martyr.

attain, *v.* —*Syn.* win, achieve, accomplish; see **succeed** 1.

attainable, *mod.* —*Syn.* achievable, feasible, reachable; see **available.**

attainment, *n.* —*Syn.* accomplishment, fulfillment, feat; see **achievement** 2.

attempt, *n.* —*Syn.* trial, struggle, endeavor; see **effort** 1, 2.

attempt, *v.* **1.** [To try]—*Syn.* endeavor, strive, venture; see **try** 1.
2. [To attack]—*Syn.* assault, assail, combat; see **attack** 2.

attend, *v.* **1.** [To go with]—*Syn.* escort, convoy, chaperon; see **accompany** 1, 3.
2. [To go to]—*Syn.* be present at, frequent, sit in on, visit, be a guest, revisit, haunt, be a member, be an habitué, make an appearance.—*Ant.* leave*, be missing, absent oneself.

attendance, *n.* **1.** [The act of attending]—*Syn.* presence, participation, appearance, being present, putting in an appearance, being in evidence; *both* (D): turning *or* showing up.—*Ant.* absence*, nonappearance, nonattendance.
2. [The persons attending]—*Syn.* audience, spectators, witnesses, hearers, patrons, onlookers, public, listeners, observers, house guests, company, assembly, assemblage, gathering, congregation; *all* (D): turn-out, gate, mob, cash customers, suckers.

attendant, *n.* —*Syn.* aid, orderly, valet, nurse, usher, bell hop, servant, domestic, secretary, understudy, disciple, pupil, auditor, *valet de chambre* (French), steward, stewardess, maid; see **assistant.**

attend school, *v.* —*Syn.* undergo schooling, learn, go to school, be educated, receive instruction, matriculate, study, take courses, be a student, enroll; see also **join** 2, **register** 4.

attention, *n.* **1.** [The state of giving heed]—*Syn.* observation, observance, regard, vigilance, mindfulness, inspection, heed, heedfulness, watching, listening.—*Ant.* indifference*, abstraction, inattention.

2. [The power of giving heed]—*Syn.* consideration, intentness, study, alertness, thought, application, assiduousness, diligence, caution, preoccupation, thoroughness, recognition, observance, regard, vigilance, mindfulness, inspection, indifference*, inattentiveness, negligence.

3. [Courtesies; *usually plural*]—*Syn.* respects, civilities, gestures, mannerliness, attentiveness, deference, offerings, consideration, kindnesses, politeness, obeisance, genuflections.—*Ant.* rudeness*, off-handedness, crudeness.

attitude, *n.* **1.** [Posture]—*Syn.* pose, stance, stand; see **position** 5.

2. [Viewpoint]—*Syn.* point of view, standpoint, position; see **viewpoint.**

3. [State of mind]—*Syn.* mood, opinion, idea about, belief, air, demeanor, condition of mind, habitual mode of regarding anything, disposition of mind, state of feeling, mind set, manner with regard to, position, reaction, bias, set, leaning, proclivity, bent, inclination, propensity, cast, emotion, temper, temperament, sensibility, disposition, mental state, notion, philosophy, view, orientation to, nature, make-up, frame of mind, character.

strike an attitude—*Syn.* be theatrical, assume a posture *or* pose *or* position, be affected; see **pose** 2.

attorney, *n.*—*Syn.* attorney at law, barrister, counsel; see **lawyer.**

attract, *v.* **1.** [To draw]—*Syn.* pull, drag, bring; see **draw** 1.

2. [To allure]—*Syn.* entice, lure, charm; see **fascinate.**

attraction, *n.* **1.** [The act of drawing toward]—*Syn.* magnetism, drawing power, allurement, fascination, temptation, pull, gravitation, affinity, inclination, tendency, enticement; *both* (D): pull, draw.—*Ant.* ugliness*, revulsion, alienation.

2. [That which draws toward itself]—*Syn.* gravity, magnet, lure, bait, decoy, blind, charm, appeal, glamour, spectacle, display, demonstration, performance; *all* (D): drawing card, main event, sucker bait, sex appeal, plant.

attractive, *mod.*—*Syn.* good-looking, winning, engaging; see **beautiful** 1, 2, **charming, handsome** 2.

attribute, *n.*—*Syn.* peculiarity, quality, trait; see **characteristic.**

attribute, *v.*—*Syn.* ascribe, refer *or* trace *or* lay *or* apply to, impute, connect, assign, give credit, accredit, associate *or* connect with, fix upon, set down, account for, blame; *all* (D): saddle, bring home to, lay on one's doorstep; see also **accuse.**—*Ant.* deny*, take, falsify.

attrition, *n.*—*Syn.* wearing down *or* away, friction, rubbing, abrasion, weakening, grinding, erosion, depreciation, gradual disintegration; see also **reduction** 1.—*Ant.* increase*, appreciation, build-up.

attune, *v.* **1.** [To tune]—*Syn.* adjust the pitch, put in tune, tune up; see **tune.**

2. [To adjust]—*Syn.* bring into accord, make agree, harmonize; see **accommodate** 2, **adjust** 1.

attuned (to), *mod.*—*Syn.* receptive, perceptive, in harmony with; see **sensitive** 3, **sympathetic.**

auburn, *mod.*—*Syn.* reddish, coppery, reddish-brown, reddish-yellow, titian; see also **brown, red.**

au courant (French), *mod.*—*Syn.* up-to-date, well-informed, fully acquainted with; see **cultured.**

auction, *n.*—*Syn.* disposal, bargain, bankruptcy sale; see **sale** 2.

auction, *v.*—*Syn.* put on sale, sell at auction, put under the hammer (D); see **sell** 1.

auctioneer, *n.*—*Syn.* salesman, seller, vendor, barker, crier.

audacious, *mod.*—*Syn.* dauntless, courageous, fearless; see **brave** 1.

audacity, *n.* **1.** [Courage]—*Syn.* daring, boldness, valor; see **courage** 1.

2. [Impudence]—*Syn.* impertinence, brazenness, insolence; see **rudeness.**

audible, *mod.*—*Syn.* perceptible, discernible, auricular, distinct, actually heard, perceptible by the ear, loud enough to be heard, capable of being heard, within earshot, within hearing distance, hearable, sounding, resounding, loud, deafening, roaring, aloud, clear, plain, emphatic; see also **sensory** 2.

audience, *n.* **1.** [A group attending an event]—*Syn.* witnesses, spectators, patrons; see **attendance** 2.

2. [An interview]—*Syn.* hearing, discussion, conference; see **conversation.**

audit, *n.* **1.** [Examination]—*Syn.* checking, scrutiny, inspection; see **examination** 1.

2. [Settlement]—*Syn.* adjustment, arrangement, pact; see **agreement** 1.

3. [Statement]—*Syn.* record, account, report; see **statement** 3.

audit, *v.*—*Syn.* examine, check, inspect; see **examine** 1.

audition, *n.*—*Syn.* test, tryout (D), trial; see **hearing** 1.

auditor, *n.* **1.** [One who listens]—*Syn.* listener, hearer, witness, spectator, eavesdropper, public, audience, patron, confessor, adviser, critic, judge.—*Ant.* actor*, entertainer, storyteller.

2. [One who audits accounts]—*Syn.* bookkeeper, cashier, actuary; see **accountant.**

auditorium, *n.*—*Syn.* hall, lecture, room, theater, playhouse, movie house, reception hall, amphitheater, assembly hall, opera house, music hall, odeum, concert hall, chapel, assembly room, auditory.

Sections of an auditorium included the following—stage, proscenium, orchestra, parquet, stalls, boxes, pit, orchestra circle, dress circle, balcony, gallery, top gallery, tiers, box office.

auditory, *mod.*—*Syn.* hearing, auditive, auricular, acoustic, aural, otic, audible, audient; see also **sensory** 1.

auger, *n.*—*Syn.* bit, twist drill, screw auger; see **drill** 2.

augment, *v.* **1.** [To increase]—*Syn.* enlarge, expand, magnify; see **increase** 1.

2. [To grow]—*Syn.* rise, progress, develop; see **grow** 1.

augmentation, *n.* **1.** [The act of augmenting] —*Syn.* development, growth, enlargement; see **increase** 1.

2. [An addition]—*Syn.* increment, accretion, gain; see **addition** 2.

augur, *v.* —*Syn.* predict, forecast, prognosticate; see **anticipate** 1.

august, *mod.* **1.** [Noble]—*Syn.* eminent, venerable, princely; see **noble** 1.

2. [Stately]—*Syn.* imposing, grand, majestic; see **grand** 2, **noble** 3.

August, *n.* —*Syn.* eighth month, midsummer, harvest (time), vacation (time), hottest *or* driest season; height *or* worst of a long, hot summer (D).

aunt, *n.* —*Syn.* mother's sister, father's sister, uncle's wife, grandaunt, great-aunt, auntie (D), *tante* (German and French); see also **relative.**

auspices, *n.* pl.—*Syn.* protection, aegis, support; see **patronage** 1.

auspicious, *mod.* —*Syn.* promising, propitious, favorable; see **hopeful** 2.

austere, *mod.* —*Syn.* harsh, hard, ascetic; see **severe** 1, 2.

austerity, *n.* —*Syn.* sternness, severity, strictness, harshness, asperity, sharpness, hardness, grimness, stiffness, acerbity, seriousness, rigidity, formalness, gravity, rigor, asceticism, formality; see also **determination** 2, **difficulty** 1, **inflexibility** 1.—*Ant.* mercy*, levity, casualness.

authentic, *mod.* **1.** [Reliable]—*Syn.* trustworthy, authoritative, factual; see **official** 3.

2. [Genuine]—*Syn.* real, true, actual; see **genuine** 1.

authenticate, *v.* —*Syn.* verify, confirm, validate; see **prove.**

author, *n.* **1.** [One who originates]—*Syn.* inventor, originator, creator, builder, father, composer, artificer, discoverer, innovator, maker, planner, strategist, designer, projector, founder, organizer, prompter, producer, fabricator, artist, begetter, architect, prime mover, initiator, the brains (D).

2. [One who writes]—*Syn.* writer, journalist, columnist, dramatist, playwright, poet, poetess, novelist, short story writer, essayist, scribe, authoress, contributor, *littérateur* (French), script writer, scenario writer, scenarist, librettist, correspondent, reporter, copywriter, literary man, ghost writer, encyclopedist, lexicographer, scholar, publicist, advertisement writer, critic, annotator, hack writer, free lance; *all* (D): ad-man, ghost, scripter; see also **editor, writer.**—*Ant.* reader*, audience, publisher.

authoritative, *mod.* **1.** [Official]—*Syn.* well-supported, well-documented, authentic; see **official** 3.

2. [Authorized]—*Syn.* official, executive, imperial, administrative, supreme, *ex cathedra* (Latin), dominant, lawful, legal, mandatory, departmental, impressive, imposing, orthodox, in the ascendant, regnant, bureaucratic, gubernatorial, ruling, sovereign, having due authority, weighty, sound, having the weight of authority, entitled to obedience, decisive, worthy of acceptance, canonical, valid, standard; see also **approved.**—*Ant.* unauthorized, illegal*, questionable.

3. [Suggestive of authority]—*Syn.* dogmatic, officious, domineering; see **absolute** 3, **autocratic** 1.

authority, *n.* **1.** [Power based on right]—*Syn.* right, authorization, jurisdiction; see **power** 2.

2. [The appearance of having authority, sense 1] —*Syn.* prestige, political influence, esteem; see **influence** 2.

3. [A person or persons vested with authority, sense 1; *usually plural*]—*Syn.* officialdom, ecclesiastics, judges, court, police, office-holders, administration, cabinet, executive, duly constituted representatives; see also **bureaucracy** 1.

4. [One who knows]—*Syn.* expert, veteran, professional; see **specialist.**

authorization, *n.* —*Syn.* sanction, signature, support; see **permission.**

authorize, *v.* **1.** [To allow]—*Syn.* permit, tolerate, suffer; see **allow** 1.

2. [To approve]—*Syn.* sanction, ratify, affirm, endorse; see **approve** 1.

authorized, *mod.* —*Syn.* allowed, sanctioned, confirmed; see **approved.**

authorship, *n.* —*Syn.* initiation, invention, instigation, signature, creation, making, doing, personal construction.

auto (D), *n.* —*Syn.* car, vehicle, passenger car; see **automobile.**

autobiography, *n.* —*Syn.* memoirs, personal history, self-portrayal, confession, life, experiences, self-account, adventures, biography, life story, journal, letters, fortunes, non-fiction book.

autocracy, *n.* —*Syn.* (absolute) monarchy, dictatorship, totalitarian government, despotism, czarism, absolutism, communism, tyranny, nazism; see also **fascism, government** 2.

autocrat, *n.* —*Syn.* absolute ruler, despot, tyrant; see **dictator.**

autocratic, *mod.* **1.** [*Said of persons*]—*Syn.* bigoted, domineering, aggressive, loud, officious, strict, severe, dictatorial, dogmatic, inquisitorial, authoritative, overbearing, peremptory, arrogant, imperious, repressive, tyrannical, harsh, inflexible, oppressive, vicious, extreme, cruel, unrelenting, barbarous, iron-handed, megalomaniacal, monomaniacal, power-crazed, power-mad, petulant, willful; *all* (D): headstrong, highhanded, bossy, like godalmighty, holier-than-thou.—*Ant.* friendly*, kindly, affable.

2. [*Said of governments*]—*Syn.* despotic, dictatorial, absolutistic; see **absolute** 3.

autograph, *n.* —*Syn.* signature, writing, handwriting, seal, token, memento, John Hancock (D).

automated, *mod.* —*Syn.* mechanical, mechanized, motorized, computerized, automatic, electronic, mechano-electronic, programmed, cybernetic, untouched by human hands (D); see also **automatic** 1.

automatic, *mod.* **1.** [Mechanical]—*Syn.* self-starting, motorized, self-regulating, automated, mechanized, electric, under its own power *or* steam, having the power of self-motion, cybernetic, self-moving, self-acting, self-propelling, computerized, programmed, electronic, push-button (D).—*Ant.* manual*, hand-operated, by hand.

2. [Habitual]—*Syn.* involuntary, unthinking, mechanical, instinctive, spontaneous, reflex, intuitive, unintentional, unforced, unconscious, unwilling; see also **habitual** 1.—*Ant.* deliberate*, willed, premediated.

automation, *n.* —*Syn.* industrialization, motorization, mechanization, computerization, cybernetics, self-regulation.

automaton, *n.* —*Syn.* humanoid, mechanical man, android; see **robot.**

automobile, *n.* —*Syn.* motor car, car, vehicle, passenger car, machine, auto (D).

Types of automobiles include the following—passenger car, limousine, sedan, saloon (British), hardtop, compact, subcompact, hatchback, sports car, convertible, station wagon, taxicab, squad car, prowl car, staff car, bus, stretch bus, truck, lorry, motor lorry, motor bus; *all* (D): bus, jeep, crate, job, buggy, wreck, lemon, clunker, jalopy, boat, creampuff, heap.

Principal parts of an automobile include the following—wheels, tires, fenders, chassis, motor, radiator, engine, fan, cylinder, carburetor, exhaust, muffler, throttle, gear, gear shift, clutch, steering wheel, transmission, universal joint, brake drum, generator, distributor, magneto, self-starter, oil gauge, speedometer, spark plug, ammeter, axles, emergency brake *or* hand brake, accelerator, chains, shock absorber, radius rod, piston, intake and exhaust valves, fuel pump, gas tank, control panel, steering column.

Automobiles include the following—United States: (Buick) Le Sabre, Regal, Electra, Riviera, Skylark; (Cadillac) Calais, Coupe de Ville, Fleetwood, Fleetwood Brougham, Eldorado, 75 Limousine Town Sedan, Fleetwood Limousine Forma; (Oldsmobile) F85, Cutlass, Cutlass Supreme, Delta 88 and 98; (Custom) Toronado; (Pontiac) Catalina, Bonneville, Grand Prix, Firebird; (Chevrolet) Impala, Caprice, Chevy-II, Nova, Camaro, Corvette, Chevelle; (Chrysler) Newport, Le Baron, Imperial, New Yorker; (Dodge) Colt, Diplomat, Omni, Charger; (Plymouth) Fury, Valiant, VIP, Belvedere, Barracuda; (Lincoln) Continental, Continental Mark II; (Mercury) Cougar, Parklane, Colony Park, Monterey; (Ford) Escort, Futura, Fairlane, Galaxy, Mustang, Tempo, Thunderbird, Maverick; (American) Ambassador, Javelin, Jeep. Foreign: (England) Rolls-Royce, Bentley, MGB, Austin Mini, Jaguar, E-Type Jaguar, Morgan, Mini Cooper S, Triumph, Vauxhall, Rover, Land Rover, Ford Cortina; (Germany) Mercedes-Benz, Opel, BMW, Audi, Porsche, Volkswagen, (France) Citroën, Peugeot, Renault, Simca; (Japan) Nissan, Honda, Isuzu, Subaru, Toyota; (Italy) Fiat, Alfa-Romeo.

autonomous, *mod.* —*Syn.* self-governing, self-ruling, independent; see **free** 1.

autonomy, *n.* —*Syn.* liberty, independence, sovereignty; see **freedom** 1.

autopsy, *n.* —*Syn.* post-mortem examination, dissection, necropsy, pathological examination of the dead; see also **examination** 3.

autumn, *n.* —*Syn.* harvest time, Indian summer, fall, autumnal equinox, close of the year, one of the four seasons.

autumnal, *mod.* —*Syn.* fall, cool, brisk, windy, dry, sere, late, in the latter part of the year.

auxiliary, *mod.* **1.** [Helping]—*Syn.* aiding, assisting, supporting, collaborating, co-operating, sustaining, abetting, ancillary, serving, assistant, ministering.
2. [Subsidiary]—*Syn.* secondary, accessory, subservient; see **subordinate.**
3. [Supplementary]—*Syn.* reserve, supplemental, spare; see **extra.**

auxiliary, *n.* —*Syn.* helper, accessory, adjutant; see **assistant.**

available, *mod.* —*Syn.* accessible, usable, ready, convenient, serviceable, prepared, handy, on call, ready for use, open to, derivable from, obtainable, attainable, practicable, achievable, feasible, possible, procurable, realizable, reachable, within reach, at one's disposal, at one's beck and call, at hand, at one's elbow; *both* (D): on tap, on deck. —*Ant.* occupied*, unavailable, unobtainable.

avalanche, *n.* **1.** [A mass moving down a slope] —*Syn.* mudslide, snowslide, landslide, landslip, rockslide, large mass of falling snow, snowslip, icefall.
2. [Any overwhelming mass]—*Syn.* flood, deluge, torrent; see **plenty.**

avant-garde (French), *mod.* —*Syn.* new, progressive, radical; see **liberal** 2.

avant-garde (French), *n.* —*Syn.* vanguard, forerunner, advance guard; see **vanguard.**

avarice, *n.* —*Syn.* covetousness, cupidity, greediness; see **greed.**

avaricious, *mod.* —*Syn.* grasping, covetous, mercenary; see **greedy** 1.

avenge, *v.* —*Syn.* retaliate, requite, punish for; see **revenge.**

avenue, *n.* —*Syn.* street, boulevard, parkway, promenade; see **road** 1.

average, *mod.* —*Syn.* ordinary, medium, mediocre; see **common** 1.

average, *n.* **1.** [A mean]—*Syn.* midpoint, standard, center, median, norm, middle, normal individual, standard performance, typical kind, rule, average man.—*Ant.* extreme*, highest, lowest.
2. [A score]—*Syn.* proportion, percentage, tally, aggregate; see **score** 1.

average, *v.* **1.** [To compute an average]—*Syn.* strike a balance, reduce to a mean, split the difference, equate, pair off.
2. [To do, on an average]—*Syn.* earn, do, perform, take, make, work, measure, complete, take in, receive, reach, attain, score, net, do at the rate of.
average out—*Syn.* stabilize, balance, to arrive at an average; see **equalize.**
on the average—*Syn.* usually, commonly, ordinarily; see **regularly** 1.

aversion, *n.* —*Syn.* dislike, repugnance, abhorrence; see **hatred** 1.

avert, *v.* **1.** [To turn away]—*Syn.* turn aside, sidetrack, shove aside, shunt, turn away from, look away, break one's eyes away, cock the eye, look another way, cast one's eyes down.
2. [To prevent]—*Syn.* ward off, thwart, avoid; see **prevent.**

aviation, *n.* —*Syn.* flying, flight, aeronautics, theory of flight, aeronautical engineering *or* navigation, piloting, aeromechanics, pneumatics, aerography, aerostatics, aerodynamics, aerodonetics, airmanship, aerodromics.

aviator, *n.* —*Syn.* flier, navigator, observer, spotter, bombardier, aerial gunner; see also **pilot** 1.

avid, *mod.* —*Syn.* eager, keen, greedy, desirous; see **enthusiastic** 2.

avocation, *n.* —*Syn.* side interest, pastime, diversion; see **hobby.**

avoid, *v.* —*Syn.* keep away *or* abstain *or* flee *or* shrink *or* escape from, evade, shun, fall back, elude, malinger, dodge, give one the slip, draw back, hold *or* edge *or* go off, turn aside, recoil from, keep at arm's length, desist, withdraw, stay off *or* back *or* away *or* out of, shirk off *or* out of, let alone, keep out of the way, keep clear of, keep *or* hold (oneself) aloof (from), keep at a respectful distance, let well enough alone, avert the eyes, keep in the background, avoid one's gaze, keep one's distance, keep away from, refrain from; *all* (D): steer clear of, lay off, pass up, shake off, fight shy of.—*Ant.* face*, meet, undertake.

avoidance, *n.* —*Syn.* evasion, delay, elusion, escape, retreat, abstention, restraint, forbearance, passive resistance (against), desistance, evasive action, temperance, flight, recoil, recession, nonparticipation, escape mechanism; *all* (D): slip, go-by, brush, dodge, duck.—*Ant.* meeting*, encounter, participation.

avow, *v.* —*Syn.* profess, admit, assert; see **declare** 1.

await, *v.* —*Syn.* wait for, attend, anticipate, expect; see **anticipate.**

awake, *mod.* —*Syn.* attentive, vigilant, alert, observant; see **vigilant, observant** 1.

awake, *v.* 1. [To arouse from sleep]—*Syn.* open one's eyes, become aware, gain consciousness, see the light, stir, get up, come out of sleep, rub one's eyes, rise up, stretch one's limbs, show signs of life, arise, turn *or* roll out; *all* (D): hit the deck, pile out, rise and shine.—*Ant.* sleep*, doze off, slumber.

2. [To awaken another]—*Syn.* rouse, call, arouse; see **awaken** 1.

awaken, *v.* 1. [To arouse another]—*Syn.* awake, call, play reveille, arouse, rouse; *both* (D): roll someone out, turn someone out.

2. [To excite]—*Syn.* stir up, stimulate, arouse, animate; see **excite** 1, 2.

awakening, *n.* —*Syn.* rebirth, arousal, renewal; see **revival** 1.

award, *n.* —*Syn.* citation, honor, scholarship; see **prize.**

award, *v.* —*Syn.* grant, confer, bestow; see **give** 1.

aware, *mod.* —*Syn.* knowledgeable, cognizant, appraised; see **conscious** 1.

awareness, *n.* —*Syn.* sensibility, mindfulness, discernment, cognizance, consciousness, alertness, keenness, attentiveness, aliveness, acquaintanceship, recognition, comprehension, perception, information, apprehension, appreciation, experience; see also **knowledge** 1.

away, *mod.* 1.[Removed]—*Syn.* absent, not present, distant, at a distance, not here, far afield, at arm's length, remote, from home, out of, far off *or* apart, beyond, off.—*Ant.* here*, present, at hand.

2. [Continuously]—*Syn.* on (and on), without stopping, without rest *or* end *or* break, tirelessly, endlessly, forever.—*Ant.* briefly*, momentarily, for a while.

do away with—*Syn.* eliminate, get rid of, reject; see **discard, end** 1.

awe, *n.* —*Syn.* fright, wonder, reverential fear; see **fear** 2, **reverence** 1.

awe-inspiring, *mod.* —*Syn.* majestic, awesome, remarkable; see **grand** 2, **impressive** 1.

awesome, *mod.* —*Syn.* striking, moving, exalted; see **grand** 2, **impressive** 1.

awful, *mod.* 1. [Impressive]—*Syn.* lofty, exalted, majestic; see **grand** 2.

2. [Frightful]—*Syn.* horrible, terrible, dreadful; see **frightful** 1.

3. [(D) Shocking]—*Syn.* appalling, disgusting, repulsive; see **offensive** 2.

4. [Very great]—*Syn.* gigantic, colossal, stupendous; see **large** 1.

awfully, *mod.* 1. [(D) Badly]—*Syn.* poorly, incompletely, clumsily; see **badly** 1.

2. [Very]—*Syn.* very much, indeed, truly; see **very.**

awhile, *mod.* —*Syn.* for a *or* the moment, briefly, momentarily, for a short time, for a brief respite, for some time, not for long, temporarily, for a little while, for a spell (D).—*Ant.* forever*, permanently, for a long time.

awkward, *mod.* 1. [Unskillful]—*Syn.* clumsy, bungling, ungraceful, maladroit, gawky, floundering, stumbling, ungainly, unwieldy, slovenly, lacking dexterity, without skill, discommodious, inexpert, unskilled, inept, unfit, inexperienced, shuffling, uncouth, gauche, left-handed, incompetent, rusty, unused to, green, amateurish; *all* (D): awkward as a cow, butterfingered, messy, all thumbs, cloddy, clod-hoppish, botchy, with two left feet.—*Ant.* able*, dexterous, smooth.

2. [Embarrassing]—*Syn.* inconvenient, inopportune, delicate; see **embarrassing.**

3. [Inconvenient]—*Syn.* annoying, disagreeable, cramped; see **uncomfortable** 2.

awkwardly, *mod.* —*Syn.* clumsily, bunglingly, unskillfully, inadroitly, ineptly, maladroitly, undexterously, lumberingly, ponderously, gawkily, lubberly, uncouthly, gracelessly, inelegantly, incompetently, artlessly, amateurishly, ungracefully, stiffly, woodenly, rigidly, with difficulty, with embarrassment, in an ungainly manner, with unaccustomed fingers. —*Ant.* gracefully*, skillfully, adroitly.

awkwardness, *n.* 1. [Clumsiness]—*Syn.* inaptitude, ineptitude, ineptness, inability, incompetence, botchery, gawkiness, artlessness, crudeness, ignorance, heavy-handedness, unhandiness, ungainliness, ungracefulness, oafishness, gracelessness; *both* (D): butterfingers, handful of thumbs.—*Ant.* ability*, grace*, competence.

2. [Rudeness]—*Syn.* slovenliness, tactlessness, boorishness; see **rudeness.**

awl, *n.* —*Syn.* bit, drill, pick, borer, bradawl, drawbore, punch, fid, needle.

awning, *n.* —*Syn.* canvas covering, canopy, shelter, sunshade, tent, tester; see also **cover** 1.

awry, *mod.* **1.** [Wrong]—*Syn.* amiss, astray, untrue; see **wrong** 2, 3.
2. [Askew]—*Syn.* aslant, crooked, slanting; see **crooked** 2.

ax, *n.* —*Syn.* hatchet, adz, mattock, tomahawk, battle-ax, poleax, pickax, cleaver, broadax, hand ax, single-bitted ax, double-bitted ax.
get the ax—*Syn.* be fired *or* dismissed *or* discharged, be dropped from the payroll, get in(to) trouble; see **get it** 2.
have an ax to grind—*Syn.* talk, confer, have something to talk over; see **discuss.**

axiom, *n.* —*Syn.* maxim, saying, adage, aphorism; see **proverb.**

axiomatic, *mod.* —*Syn.* aphoristic, self-evident, proverbial; see **obvious** 2.

axis, *n.* —*Syn.* shaft, pivot, axle, pole, stem, support, dividing line, spindle, arbor, line of symmetry *or* rotation *or* revolution.

axle, *n.* —*Syn.* shaft, arbor, pivot, spindle, axis, pin, gudgeon; see also **axis.**

azure, *mod.* —*Syn.* cerulean, pale blue, sky blue; see **blue** 1.

B

babble, *n.*—*Syn.* jabber, chatter, twaddle; see **nonsense** 1.

babble, *v.*—*Syn.* talk incoherently *or* foolishly *or* nonsensically, rant, rave, drivel, mouth, gush, maunder, run on, gossip, murmur, chat, chatter, prattle, prate, twaddle, gabble, tattle, jabber, palaver, blurt, patter, clack; *all* (D): beat the gums, run off at the mouth, talk off the top of one's head, bat the breeze, rattle (on), gab, cackle, blab, burble, sputter, blather, gibber, blabber, clatter; see also **talk** 1.

baby, *mod.* **1.** [Infantile]—*Syn.* youthful, babyish, juvenile; see **childish** 1.
2. [Small]—*Syn.* diminutive, miniature, tiny; see **little** 1.

baby, *n.* **1.** [An infant]—*Syn.* nursling, suckling, babe (in arms), child, toddler, tot, youngling, brat, bairn, young one, little one, least one, papoose, *bambino* (Italian), *enfant* (French); *all* (D): chick, kid, cherub, little shaver, totsie, pledge of love, little stranger *or* newcomer, (little) accident, bundle from heaven, bundle of joy, another mouth to feed, chit, brat.—*Ant.* man*, adolescent, grown-up.
2. [The youngest or smallest of a group]—*Syn.* junior, youngest, the baby of the family (D); see **sense** 1.
3. [A beginner]—*Syn.* learner, novice, apprentice; see **amateur.**

baby, *v.*—*Syn.* pamper, coddle, pet, spoil, fondle, caress, dandle, nurse, cherish, foster, cuddle, make much of, cosset, humor, indulge, mollycoddle.

baby buggy, *n.*—*Syn.* (baby) carriage, (baby) walker, stroller, perambulator, pram.

babyhood, *n.*—*Syn.* infancy, babyism, diaper days (D); see **childhood.**

baby-sit, *v.*—*Syn.* watch, care for, sit (D); see **guard** 2.

bachelor, *n.*—*Syn.* unmarried *or* single man, celibate, misogamist, misogynist, virgin, woman-hater; *both* (D): bach, lone wolf.—*Ant.* married man, husband*, benedict.

back, *mod.*—*Syn.* rear, hinder, after, back of, in the wake of, backward, hindmost, behind, abaft, astern, hind, rearward, aback, aft, to *or* in the rear, dorsal, caudal, following, at the heels of, posterior, terminal, in the wake, in the background, final.—*Ant.* front*, forward, head.

back, *n.* **1.** [The rear part or side]—*Syn.* hinder part, posterior, stern, poop, aft, tailpiece; *both* (D): tail, back end.—*Ant.* front*, fore part, fore.
2. [The rear of the torso]—*Syn.* posterior, dorsal aspect, tergum, dorsum, notacum, tergal *or* spinal portion.—*Ant.* chest*, stomach, ventral aspect.
3. [One who plays behind the line, especially in football]—*Syn.* linebacker, fullback, halfback, quarterback, tailback, flankerback, wingback, running back, slot back, blocking back, cornerback, safety man, free safety, ball carrier, kicker, passer, pass receiver.
behind one's back—*Syn.* in secret, slyly, hidden; see **secretive.**
(flat) on one's back—*Syn.* ill, defeated, helpless; see **sick.**
get off one's back (D)—*Syn.* let alone, ignore, stop nagging; see **neglect** 2.
get one's back up—*Syn.* become angry, be stubborn, lose one's temper; see **rage** 1.
go back on—*Syn.* deceive, reject, turn against; see **betray.**
in back of—*Syn.* at the rear, behind, coming after; see **following.**
turn one's back on—*Syn.* reject, desert, fail; see **abandon** 1.
with one's back to the wall—*Syn.* desperate, cornered, stopped; see **sad** 1.

back, *v.* **1.** [To push backward]—*Syn.* drive back, repel, repulse; see **push** 1.
2. [To further]—*Syn.* uphold, stand behind, encourage; see **support** 2, 5.
3. [To equip with a back]—*Syn.* stiffen, cane, line; see **strengthen.**

back and forth, *mod.*—*Syn.* zigzag, in and out, from side to side; see **to and fro.**

backbiting, *n.*—*Syn.* slander, calumny, detraction; see **lie** 1.

backbone, *n.* **1.** [Line of bones in the back supporting the body]—*Syn.* spine, spinal column, vertebrae, chine.
2. [Determination]—*Syn.* firmness, fortitude, resolution; see **determination** 2.

back down, *v.*—*Syn.* withdraw, recoil, back out; see **retreat** 1.

backed, *mod.* **1.** [Propelled backward]—*Syn.* driven back, shoved, repelled, repulsed, pushed, retracted.—*Ant.* ahead*, moved forward, impelled.
2. [Supported]—*Syn.* upheld, encouraged, approved, heartened, aided, assisted, advanced, promoted, sustained, fostered, countenanced, favored, championed, advocated, supplied, maintained, asserted, established, helped, bolstered, propped, stayed, incited, furthered, seconded, prompted, served; *all* (D): pushed, boosted, primed.—*Ant.* discouraged, opposed*, obstructed.
3. [Supplied with a back, or backing]—*Syn.* stiffened, built up, strengthened; see **reinforced.**

backer, *n.* —*Syn.* benefactor, supporter, follower; see **patron** 1.

backfire, *v.* **1.** [To explode]—*Syn.* burst, erupt, detonate; see **explode** 1.

2. [To go awry]—*Syn.* boomerang, recoil, rebound, ricochet, bounce (back), strike *or* kick *or* fly *or* spring back; see also **fail** 1.

background, *n.* **1.** [Setting]—*Syn.* backdrop, framework, environment; see **setting.**

2. [The total of one's experiences]—*Syn.* education, qualifications, preparation, grounding, rearing, credentials, capacities, accomplishments, achievements, attainments, acquirements, deeds, actions; see also **experience** 3, **knowledge** 1.

backhanded, *mod.* —*Syn.* obscure, sarcastic, unfavorable; see **indirect.**

backhouse, *n.* —*Syn.* latrine, outdoor toilet, outhouse; see **privy, toilet** 2.

backing, *n.* **1.** [Assistance]—*Syn.* subsidy, encouragement, help; see **aid** 1.

2. [Support]—*Syn.* reinforcement, buttress, lining; see **support** 2.

backlash, *n.* **1.** [Tangle]—*Syn.* snarl, snag, knot; see **confusion** 2.

2. [Reaction]—*Syn.* response, repercussion, resentment; see **reaction** 1.

backlog, *n.* —*Syn.* reserve, supply, stock; see **reserve** 1, **quantity.**

back off, *v.* —*Syn.* fall back, withdraw, retire, recede; see **retreat** 1, 2.

back out of, *v.* —*Syn.* withdraw, shrink from, escape; see **retreat** 1, 2.

backslide, *v.* —*Syn.* apostatize, break faith, fall from grace; see **relapse.**

backstop, *n.* —*Syn.* screen, net, barrier; see **fence** 1.

back up, *v.* **1.** [To move backward]—*Syn.* fall back, withdraw, retrogress; see **retreat** 1.

2. [To support]—*Syn.* aid, assist, help; see **support** 2.

backward, *mod.* **1.** [To the rear]—*Syn.* rearward, astern, behind, aback, retro-, retrograde, regressive, reflex.—*Ant.* forward*, progressive, onward.

2. [Dull]—*Syn.* stupid, slow-witted, dense; see **dull** 3.

3. [Retiring]—*Syn.* bashful, reserved, shy; see **humble** 1.

4. [Reversed]—*Syn.* turned around, counterclockwise, inverted; see **reversed.**

5. [Behind in development]—*Syn.* underdeveloped, slow, slow to develop, retarded, delayed, arrested, checked, behindhand, late, undeveloped, underprivileged, underbred.

bend over backward (D)—*Syn.* try (hard) (to please), conciliate, be fair; see **try** 1.

backwash, *n.* —*Syn.* wake, aftermath, repercussion; see **result.**

backwoods, *mod.* —*Syn.* rustic, secluded, forsaken; see **isolated.**

backwoods, *n.* pl.—*Syn.* groves, woodlands, timberland; see **country** 1, **forest.**

back yard, *n.* —*Syn.* patio, terrace, enclosure, play area, garden spot, lawn, grass, court; see also **garden, yard** 1.

bacon, *n.* —*Syn.* flitch, gammon, side pork, beef bacon, Danish bacon, Canadian bacon, breakfast meat; *both* (D): side meat, sowbelly.

bring home the bacon—*Syn.* earn a living, prosper, get paid; see **succeed** 1.

bacteria, *n.* pl.—*Syn.* bacilli, microbes, organisms; see **germ** 3.

bad, *mod.* **1.** [Wicked]—*Syn.* vile, evil, wrong, corrupt; see **wicked** 1, 2.

2. [Spoiled]—*Syn.* rancid, decayed, putrid; see **rotten** 1, 2.

3. [Below standard]—*Syn.* defective, inferior, imperfect; see **faulty, poor** 2.

4. [In poor health]—*Syn.* ill, diseased, ailing; see **sick.**

5. [Injurious]—*Syn.* hurtful, damaging, detrimental; see **harmful.**

6. [(D) Very good]—*Syn.* stylish, effective, sharp; see **fashionable, excellent.**

in bad (D)—*Syn.* in difficulty, unwanted, unwelcome; see **in trouble** 1, **undesirable.**

not bad (D)—*Syn.* all right, (pretty) good, passable; see **excellent, fair** 2.

badge, *n.* **1.** [Outward evidence]—*Syn.* marker, symbol, identification; see **emblem, identification** 2.

2. [A device worn as evidence]—*Syn.* pin, insigne, (*plural:* insignia), cordon, shield, ribbon, device, medallion, escutcheon, brassard, brand, ensign, token of office, epaulet, cockade, motto, official star, marker, phylactery, feather, rosette, weeper, aiguillette, aglet, cuff band, clasp, button, emblem, signet, seal, sigil, crest, star, chevron, stripe, medal; see also **decoration** 3.

badger, *v.* —*Syn.* harass, annoy, pester; see **bother** 2.

badly, *mod.* **1.** [In an ineffectual or incompetent manner]—*Syn.* wrongly, imperfectly, ineffectively, inefficiently, poorly, unsatisfactorily, crudely, boorishly, unskillfully, defectively, weakly, haphazardly, clumsily, carelessly, negligently, incompetently, stupidly, blunderingly, mistakenly, bunglingly, awkwardly, maladroitly, unhandily, faultily, shiftlessly, abominably; *both* (D): awfully, terribly.—*Ant.* carefully*, competently, adequately.

2. [Not well]—*Syn.* unwell, poorly, feeble; see **sick.**

3. [To a marked degree]—*Syn.* severely, seriously, greatly; see **very.**

baffle, *v.* **1.** [To confuse]—*Syn.* perplex, puzzle, bewilder; see **confuse.**

2. [To hinder]—*Syn.* block, obstruct, impede; see **hinder.**

bag, *n.* **1.** [A container]—*Syn.* poke, purse, pocket, sac(k), pouch, grip, handbag, ditty bag, kit (bag), tote (bag), knapsack, haversack, rucksack, backpack, carpetbag, kit, satchel, saddlebag, gunny sack, grain sack, woolsack, saccule, suitcase, brief case, attaché case, *saccus, sacculus* (both Latin), bursa, *poche, pochette* (both French), duffel bag, pack, container, feedbag, quiver, portmanteau, packet, pocketbook, Gladstone, holster, vanity bag, valise, sabretache, case, wallet, reticule; *all* (D): holdall, carryall, bindle, tuckerbag.

2. [(D) A specialty]—*Syn.* preference, (favorite) activity, one's thing (D); see **specialty** 1.

in the bag—*Syn.* absolute, sure, definite; see **certain** 3.

left holding the bag—*Syn.* deceived, tricked, deserted; see **abandoned** 1, **deceived.**

bag, *v.* —*Syn.* trap, seize, get; see **catch** 1.
baggage, *n.* —*Syn.* luggage, impedimenta, dunnage, gear, bags, trunks, valises, suitcases, steamer trunks, overnight cases, parcels, paraphernalia, encumbrances, effects, equipment, accouterments; *all* (D): grips, traps, duffel, things, truck, pack(s), movables.
baggy, *mod.* —*Syn.* slack, unshapely, bulging; see **loose** 1.
bail, *n.* **1.** [A wire handle]—*Syn.* grip, lift, wire; see **handle** 1.
2. [Security to provide temporary release]—*Syn.* bond, surety, recognizance, pledge, pawn, hostage, warrant, guaranty, collateral.
bail, *v.* **1.** [To dip]—*Syn.* scoop, spoon out, dredge; see **dip** 2.
2. [To empty]—*Syn.* clear, drain, deplete; see **empty** 2.
bail out, *v.* **1.** [To post bond for]—*Syn.* release, give security for, post bail for, assure, underwrite, guarantee, warrant, insure, deliver; *both* (D): go bail for, spring.
2. [(D) To retreat]—*Syn.* withdraw, flee, escape; see **retreat** 1, 2.
bait, *n.* —*Syn.* lure, inducement, bribe; see **attraction** 2.
bait, *v.* **1.** [To provide with a lure]—*Syn.* set, furnish, cover, charge.
2. [To torment]—*Syn.* anger, nag, tease; see **bother** 2.
3. [To lure]—*Syn.* entice, attract, draw; see *catch* 1, **deceive, fascinate.**
bake, *v.* **1.** [To cook]—*Syn.* roast, toast, warm; see **cook.**
2. [To harden]—*Syn.* temper, anneal, fire; see **harden** 1, 3.
baked, *mod.* —*Syn.* parched, scorched, dried, toasted, warmed, heated, cooked, grilled, burned, charred, roasted, incinerated.
baker, *n.* —*Syn.* pastry cook, chef, confectioner; see **cook.**
bakery, *n.* —*Syn.* bake *or* pastry shop, pastry kitchen, patisserie, boulangerie, confectionery, cook shop, bread *or* cake *or* biscuit factory, bread bakery, cake bakery.
balance, *n.* **1.** [(D) Whatever remains]—*Syn.* excess, surplus, residue; see **remainder.**
2. [An equilibrium]—*Syn.* equipoise, poise, counterpoise, symmetry, antithesis, offset, equivalence, counterbalance, tension, equalization, equality of weight, parity.—*Ant.* imbalance*, lopsidedness, topheaviness.
3. [An excess of credits over debits]—*Syn.* credit balance, surplus, dividend, profit, cash on hand, break-even point (D).
4. [A balance scale]—*Syn.* steelyard, spring balance, scales; see **scale** 3.
5. [Judgment]—*Syn.* perspective, discretion, insight; see **judgment** 1.
in the balance—*Syn.* undetermined, undecided, critical; **uncertain** 2.
balance, *v.* **1.** [To offset]—*Syn.* equipoise, counterpoise, counterbalance; see **offset.**
2. [To place in balance]—*Syn.* poise, oppose, place in equilibrium, steady, stabilize, neutralize, set, level, equalize, support, equilibrate, even, weigh, counteract, make equal *or* level *or* steady, compensate, tie, adjust, square, nullify, parallel, cancel, coordinate, readjust, equate, trim, match, level *or* pair off, restore, attune, harmonize, tune, countervail, accord, correspond.—*Ant.* topple, upset*, turn over.
3. [To demonstrate that debits and credits are in balance]—*Syn.* estimate, compare, account (for), count, compute, prove, adjust, settle, make up, strike a balance, take a trial balance, tell, audit, calculate, enumerate, equate, square, rally, total, reckon, take stock, sum up; see also **check** 3.
balanced, *mod.* **1.** [Made even]—*Syn.* equalized, poised, offset, in equilibrium, evened, counterweighted, equivalent, stabilized, antithetic, symmetrical, counterpoised, counterbalanced, on an even keel (D).—*Ant.* topheavy*, unbalanced, unequal.
2. [Audited]—*Syn.* validated, confirmed, certified; see **approved.**
balance of power, *n.* —*Syn.* equilibrium, distribution, degree of power, apportionment; see also **balance** 2.
balance sheet, *n.* —*Syn.* annual report, budget, liability and asset sheet; see **statement** 3.
balcony, *n.* —*Syn.* gallery, catwalk, mezzanine, balustrade, loggia, veranda, terrace, stoop, piazza, portico, porch, platform, parapet, box.
bald, *mod.* **1.** [Without natural covering; usually, without hair]—*Syn.* hairless, depilated, tonsured, shaven *or* shaved, bare, featherless, treeless, glabrous, shiny, smooth; *both* (D): hairless as an egg, like a billiard ball; see also **naked** 1.—*Ant.* hairy*, covered, bearded.
2. [Not adorned or elaborated]—*Syn.* simple, forthright, unadorned; see **modest** 2.
balderdash, *n.* —*Syn.* senseless talk, gibberish, bombast; see **jargon** 1, **nonsense** 1.
baldness, *n.* —*Syn.* hairlessness, lack *or* absence of hair, sparseness, alopecia.
bale, *n.* —*Syn.* bundle, bunch, parcel; see **package** 1, 2.
baleful, *mod.* —*Syn.* deadly, noxious, injurious; see **harmful.**
balk, *v.* **1.** [To refuse]—*Syn.* turn down, demur, desist; see **refuse** 1.
2. [To frustrate]—*Syn.* thwart, hinder, check; see **prevent.**
balky, *mod.* —*Syn.* contrary, stubborn, perverse; see **obstinate** 1.
ball, *n.* **1.** [A spherical body]—*Syn.* globe, spheroid, sphere, balloon, orb, perisphere, globule, globular *or* rounded *or* spherical *or* orbicular object, radical sphere, twelve-point sphere, oblique sphere, direct sphere, drop, knot, marble, pellet, pill (D).
2. [A game played with a ball]—*Syn.* baseball, football, catch (D); see **sport** 3.
3. [In baseball, a pitch which is not a strike] —*Syn.* wild pitch, inside *or* outside pitch; *all* (D): wide one, high baby, duster, insider.
4. [Missile for a gun]—*Syn.* bullet, shell, lead; see **ammunition, shot** 2.
5. [A dance]—*Syn.* grand ball, promenade, reception; see **dance** 2, **party** 1.

carry the ball (D)—*Syn.* assume responsibility, take command *or* control, bear the burden; see **lead** 1.
get *or* **keep the ball rolling** (D)—*Syn.* initiate action, commence, start; see **begin** 1.
have something on the ball (D)—*Syn.* skilled, alert, efficient; see **able** 1, 2, **responsible** 2.

ballad, *n.* —*Syn.* carol, chant, primitive song; see **poetry, song, story.**

ballade, *n.* —*Syn.* art song, ballad, lyric; see **poetry, song.**

ballast, *n.* —*Syn.* sandbags, counterbalance, counterweight; see **weight** 2.

ballet, *n.* —*Syn.* toe dancing, choreography, tap dancing; see **dance** 1.

ballet dancer, *n.* —*Syn.* (prima) ballerina, ballet girl, danseuse, danseur, figurante, coryphée, member of the chorus, student dancer.

balloon, *n.* —*Syn.* dirigible, aircraft, airship, weather balloon, nondirigible aerostat, mongolfier, free balloon, captive balloon, kite balloon, lighter-than-air craft, toy balloon, zeppelin, antisubmarine patrol craft, observation balloon, barrage balloon, radar balloon; *all* (D): blimp, bag, sausage, gasbag, zep.

balloon, *v.* —*Syn.* bloat, swell up, expand; see **inflate** 2.

ballot, *n.* **1.** [A vote]—*Syn.* tally, ticket, poll; see **vote** 1.
2. [A list of candidates]—*Syn.* choice, slate, line-up (D); see **ticket** 2.

ballroom, *n.* —*Syn.* dance hall, assembly, reception; see **hall** 1.

ball up (D), *v.* —*Syn.* confound, jumble, tangle; see **confuse.**

balm, *n.* **1.** [Anything healing and soothing]—*Syn.* solace, consolation, comfort, relief, easement, alleviation, refreshment, mitigation, remedy, assuagement, cure.—*Ant.* irritation*, vexation, irritant.
2. [An ointment of resin]—*Syn.* salve, unguent, lotion, potion, poultice, plaster, application, dressing, preparation, formula, compound, prescription, emollient, sweet oil, demulcent; see also **medicine** 2.

balmy, *mod.* **1.** [Warm and moist; *said of weather*] —*Syn.* tropical, summerlike, gentle; see **mild** 2.
2. [(D) Mentally incompetent]—*Syn.* crazy, moronic, mentally deranged; see **insane** 1.

bamboozle, *v.* **1.** [To cheat]—*Syn.* swindle, trick, dupe; see **deceive.**
2. [To perplex]—*Syn.* puzzle, confound, baffle; see **confuse.**

ban, *n.* —*Syn.* interdiction, prohibition, limitation; see **refusal, taboo.**

ban, *v.* —*Syn.* outlaw, prevent, declare illegal; see **forbid, halt** 2, **prevent.**

banal, *mod.* —*Syn.* dull, trite, hackneyed; see **common** 1.

banality, *n.* —*Syn.* commonplace, platitude, trite phrase; see **cliché.**

band, *n.* **1.** [A beltlike strip]—*Syn.* ribbon, belt, line, strip, tape, fillet, sash, twine, finger, twist, riband, cingle, surcingle, girth, cincture, scarf, bandage, *cincha* (Spanish), circuit, meridian, latitude, circle, ring, orbit, stripe, girdle, zodiac, zonule, circumference, cordon, zone, withe, streak, thong, wristband, braid, ferrule, brace, strap, binding, hoop, waistband, baldric, collar, hatband; see also **stripe.**
2. [That which binds]—*Syn.* bond, tie, ligature, binding, binder, hoop, stay, truss, belt, shackle, cord, tendon, harness, copula, cable, rope, link, chain, line, hawser, string, guy (wire), painter, strap, trace, thong; see also **sense** 1, **dressing** 3, **rope, wire** 1.
3. [A company of people]—*Syn.* group, collection, association; see **gathering.**
4. [A group of musicians]—*Syn.* orchestra, company, ensemble, troupe; *all* (D): group, combo, menagerie.
Kinds of bands include the following—military, brass, street, skiffle, concert, parade, jazz, rock, electric, stage, dance, German, Dixieland, jug; *both* (D): swing, sweet.

bandage, *n.* —*Syn.* compress, cast, gauze; see **dressing** 3.

bandage, *v.* —*Syn.* tie, swathe, truss; see **bind** 1, **fasten** 1.

bandit, *n.* —*Syn.* highwayman, thief, brigand; see **robber.**

band together, *v.* —*Syn.* ally, join, gather together; see **unite** 1.

bang, *n.* **1.** [A loud report]—*Syn.* blast, roar, detonation; see **noise** 1.
2. [A blow]—*Syn.* hit, cuff, whack; see **blow** 1.
3. [(D) A thrill]—*Syn.* enjoyment, pleasant feeling, kick (D); see **thrill.**

bang, *v.* **1.** [To beat]—*Syn.* strike, slam, whack; see **hit** 1.
2. [To make a noise]—*Syn.* crash, clatter, rattle; see **sound** 1.

banish, *v.* **1.** [To condemn to exile]—*Syn.* expatriate, ostracize, rusticate, excommunicate, proscribe, deport, transport, cast out, outlaw, extradite, sequester, isolate, exile, relegate, expel, dismiss; *both* (D): send to Coventry, put a price on.—*Ant.* receive*, welcome, accept.
2. [To remove completely]—*Syn.* expel, evict, discharge; see **dismiss** 1, 2.

banishment, *n.* —*Syn.* expatriation, deportation, expulsion; see **exile** 1.

banister, *n.* —*Syn.* railing, baluster, balustrade; see **rail** 1.

bank, *n.* **1.** [A wall of earth]—*Syn.* levee, embankment, mound; see **ridge** 2.
2. [Ground rising above adjacent water]—*Syn.* ledge, cliff, edge; see **shore.**
3. [A financial establishment]—*Syn.* counting-house, investment firm, banking house, financial custodian, (Federal) credit union, (mutual) fund, trust company, treasury, exchequer, repository of funds, national bank, state bank, commercial bank, savings bank, co-operative bank, savings and loan association, thrift (institution), Federal Reserve Bank, private bank.
4. [A row of objects close together]—*Syn.* series, group, sequence; see **line** 1.
5. [The pitch in a turn]—*Syn.* slope, lean, incline; see **inclination** 5.
6. [A gambling establishment]—*Syn.* the house, cashier, club; see **casino.**

bank, *v.* **1.** [To deposit money]—*Syn.* save, put in the bank, enter an account; see **deposit** 2.

2. [To operate a bank]—*Syn.* lend money, practice usury, hold money in trust, speculate.

3. [To heap earth or similar material]—*Syn.* dike, pile, hill; see **heap** 1.

4. [To cover a fire for the night]—*Syn.* trim, build up, stoke, replenish, regulate, cover.

5. [To tilt on a curve]—*Syn.* lean, pitch, bend, slope; see **lean** 1.

banker, *n.* **1.** [One who owns or operates a bank] —*Syn.* steward, treasurer, teller, manager, officer of the bank, broker, financier, capitalist, investment banker, money-lender, usurer.

2. [The holder of funds in a gambling game] —*Syn.* croupier, house, bank; see **dealer.**

banking, *n.* —*Syn.* investment, trading, funding, moneylending, usury, brokerage, speculation; see also **business** 1.

bank on (D), *v.* —*Syn.* rely *or* depend on, believe in, be sure about; see **trust** 1.

bankrupt, *mod.* —*Syn.* failed, out of business, broke (D); see **insolvent, ruined** 4.

bankruptcy, *n.* —*Syn.* insolvency, failure, financial loss *or* failure *or* disaster *or* ruin, nonpayment, defaulting, repudiation, overdraft, defalcation, liquidation, chapter XI, economic death, pauperism, destitution, indigence, privation, distress, straitened circumstances, destituteness, beggary, impecuniosity, ruination, going to the wall (D). —*Ant.* solvency, prosperity*, soundness.

banner, *n.* —*Syn.* colors, pennant, standard; see **emblem, flag** 1.

banquet, *n.* —*Syn.* repast, fete, festivity; see **dinner, feast.**

bantam, *mod.* —*Syn.* small, diminutive, tiny; see **little** 1.

banter, *n.* —*Syn.* teasing, joking, play; see **fun.**

banter, *v.* —*Syn.* tease, jest (with), kid (D); see **joke.**

baptism, *n.* —*Syn.* immersion, dedication, confirmation, christening, ablution, initiation, lustration, ritual, rite, baptismal regeneration, communion, sprinkling, infant baptism; *both* (D): dunking, water cure; see also **sacrament.**

Baptist, *n.* —*Syn.* immersionist, baptizer, Anabaptist, Dunker (D).
Baptist sects include the following—Regular, Six-principle, Free Original, Southern, Freewill, Seventh Day, General, Separate, United.

baptize, *v.* **1.** [To cleanse sacramentally]—*Syn.* immerse, purify, regenerate, sprinkle, dip, asperse, administer baptism to, give the water cure (D).

2. [To give a name]—*Syn.* christen, denominate, dub (D); see **name** 1.

baptized, *mod.* —*Syn.* christened, purified, held at the font; see **named** 1.

bar, *n.* **1.** [A relatively long, narrow object]—*Syn.* strip, stake, stick, crossbar, boom, rib, jimmy, handspike, crosspiece, pole, spar, pry, rail, ingot, lever, rod, pinch *or* wrecking bar, crowbar, shaft, slab, pig.

2. [A counter serving refreshments, especially drinks, or the accompanying establishment] —*Syn.* saloon, public house, counter, bar room, tavern, hotel, hostel, inn, canteen, bistro, beer parlor, cocktail lounge, fern bar, cabaret, restaurant, cafeteria, grill room, speak-easy, road house, brass rail, snack bar, tap (room), beer garden, alehouse, rathskeller; *all* (D): watering hole, booze joint, dive, barrel house, gin shop, pub (British), grill.

3. [A court of law]—*Syn.* tribunal, judiciary, session; see **court** 2.

4. [The legal profession]—*Syn.* lawyers, advocates, counselors, barristers, judiciary, solicitors, jurists, body of lawyers, attorneys, the legal fraternity, bar association.

5. [An obstruction]—*Syn.* hindrance, obstacle, hurdle; see **barrier.**

6. [A relatively long, narrow area]—*Syn.* strip, stripe, ribbon; see **band** 1.

bar, *v.* **1.** [To raise a physical obstruction]—*Syn.* barricade, dam, dike, fence, wall, erect a barrier, brick up, blockade, trammel, clog, exclude, shut *or* block *or* lock (out), keep out, debar, bolt, cork, plug, seal, jam, caulk, stop, impede, (set up a) roadblock, raise the drawbridge (D).—*Ant.* open*, free, clear.

2. [To obstruct by refusal]—*Syn.* interdict, ban, forbid, disallow, deny, refuse, debar, repudiate, suspend, segregate, boycott, ostracize, prevent, preclude, shut *or* keep out, exclude, exile, reject, outlaw, condemn, discourage, discountenance, interfere with, restrain, stop, frustrate, circumvent, override, except, freeze out (D).—*Ant.* allow*, admit, welcome.

3. [To close]—*Syn.* shut, lock, seal; see **close.**

4. [To hinder]—*Syn.* obstruct, impede, interfere with; see **hinder.**

barb, *n.* —*Syn.* arrow, thorn, spike; see **point** 2.

barbarian, *mod.* **1.** [Savage]—*Syn.* vicious, brutal, merciless; see **cruel** 1.

2. [Uncivilized]—*Syn.* savage, coarse, rude; see **primitive** 3.

barbarian, *n.* **1.** [An uncivilized person]—*Syn.* savage, brute, Hun, cannibal, Goth, Yahoo, wild Indian, Philistine, troglodyte, clod (D).

2. [A brute]—*Syn.* rascal, ruffian, monster; see **beast** 2.

3. [A foreigner]—*Syn.* stranger, outsider, newcomer; see **alien.**

barbaric, *mod.* **1.** [Cruel]—*Syn.* inhuman, brutal, fierce; see **cruel** 1.

2. [Primitive]—*Syn.* uncivilized, coarse, rude; see **primitive** 3.

barbarism, *n.* —*Syn.* inhumanity, brutality, barbarity; see **cruelty.**

barbarity, *n.* **1.** [Savagery]—*Syn.* savageness, cruelty, brutality; see **cruelty.**

2. [Crudity]—*Syn.* boorishness, vulgarity, crudeness; see **rudeness.**

barbarous, *mod.* **1.** [Characterized by cruelty] —*Syn.* inhuman, brutal, fierce; see **cruel** 1.

2. [Uncivilized]—*Syn.* barbaric, rude, unsophisticated; see **primitive** 3.

barbecue, *n.* **1.** [A grill]—*Syn.* roaster, grill, griddle; see **applicance, broiler.**

2. [A picnic]—*Syn.* cookout, wiener roast, clambake; see **picnic** 1.

barbecue, *v.* —*Syn.* grill, sear, broil; see **cook.**

barbed, *mod.* —*Syn.* pointed, spiked, piercing; see **sharp** 2.

barbed wire, *n.* —*Syn.* fence wire, galvanized wire, fencing, wire fence; *both* (D): picket wire, barbwire; see also **fence** 1, 2.

barber, *n.* —*Syn.* hairdresser, shaver, coiffeur *or* coiffeuse, hair cutter; *all* (D): cosmetologist, tonsorial artist, beauty parlor operator, hair stylist.

barber shop, *n.* —*Syn.* tonsorium, tonsorial parlor, styling salon, beauty parlor *or* salon *or* shop.

bard, *n.* —*Syn.* troubadour, versifier, minstrel; see **poet.**

bare, *mod.* **1.** [Without covering]—*Syn.* uncovered, bald, stripped; see **naked** 1, **open** 4.
2. [Plain]—*Syn.* unadorned, simple, unornamented; see **modest** 2.
3. [Without content]—*Syn.* barren, void, unfurnished; see **empty** 1.
4. [Without surplus]—*Syn.* scant, meager, insufficient; see **inadequate** 1.

bare, *v.* —*Syn.* publish, divulge, disclose; see **reveal** 1.

barefaced, *mod.* **1.** [Open]—*Syn.* unconcealed, clear, apparent; see **obvious** 1, 2.
2. [Impudent]—*Syn.* shameless, audacious, bold; see **rude** 2.

barefoot, *mod.* —*Syn.* shoeless, barefooted, unshod.

barely, *mod.* —*Syn.* almost, scarcely, just; see **hardly.**

bareness, *n.* **1.** [Nakedness]—*Syn.* nudity, undress, déshabillé; see **nakedness.**
2. [Plainness]—*Syn.* unadornment, starkness, rusticity; see **simplicity** 2.

bargain, *n.* **1.** [An agreement]—*Syn.* pact, compact, contract; see **agreement** 3.
2. [An advantageous purchase]—*Syn.* good value *or* deal, discount, reduction, marked-down price; *all* (D): value, buy, steal, giveaway, markdown, deal.
into the bargain (D)—*Syn.* in addition, too, additionally; see **also.**

bargain, *v.* **1.** [To trade]—*Syn.* barter, do business, merchandise; see **buy** 1, **sell** 1.
2. [To negotiate]—*Syn.* make terms, arrange, confer; see **negotiate** 1.

bargain for (D), *v.* —*Syn.* expect, plan on, foresee; see **anticipate** 1.

bargaining, *n.* —*Syn.* trade, transaction, haggling; see **business** 1.

barge, *n.* —*Syn.* scow, flatboat, canal boat, raft, pleasure barge, freight barge; see also **boat, ship.**

bark, *n.* **1.** [An outer covering, especially of trees] —*Syn.* rind, skin, peel, shell, case, crust, peeling, cork, husk, cortex, hide, pelt, coat.
2. [A short, explosive sound]—*Syn.* yelp, yap, grunt; see **noise** 1.
3. [A ship]—*Syn.* vessel, sloop, brig; see **boat, ship.**

bark, *v.* **1.** [To emit a dog's characteristic sound] —*Syn.* yelp, yap, bay, howl, cry, growl, snarl, gnar, gnarl, yip; *both* (D): woof, arf.
2. [To speak as though barking]—*Syn.* snap, snarl, growl; see **yell.**

bark at, *v.* —*Syn.* shout at, scold, rebuke; see **censure.**

bark up the wrong tree (D), *v.* —*Syn.* miscalculate, mistake, misconstrue; see **misjudge** 2.

barley, *n.* —*Syn.* small grain, barleycorn, cereal; see **grain** 1.

barn, *n.* —*Syn.* outbuilding, shed, outhouse, shelter, lean-to.
Kinds of barns include the following—stable, chicken house, cow barn, coop, cote, hutch, sty, fold, pen, byre, kennel, mow; *all* (D): pad, bullock lodge, cow house.

barnstormer (D), *n.* —*Syn.* entertainer, performer, member of a traveling theater group; see **actor.**

barnyard, *n.* —*Syn.* feedyard, pen, corral, stableyard, lot, feed-lot, run.

barometer, *n.* —*Syn.* glass, weather *or* storm gauge, pressure indicator.

baron, *n.* —*Syn.* peer, nobleman, noble; see **lord** 2.

baroness, *n.* —*Syn.* peeress, gentlewoman, noblewoman; see **lady** 3.

baroque, *mod.* —*Syn.* elaborate, rococo, grotesque; see **ornate** 1.

barracks, *n.* pl.—*Syn.* encampment, shelters, military enclosure, tents, quarters, (field) headquarters, camp, bivouac, cantonment, garrison (Quonset) huts, dormitory, prefabs (D).

barrage, *n.* —*Syn.* bombardment, blast, gunfire; see **fire** 3.

barred, *mod.* **1.** [Equipped or marked with bars] —*Syn.* striped, banded, stripped, streaked, twilled, pleated, pied, parti-colored, variegated, motley, tortoise-shell, calico, mottled, dappled, veined, brindled, ribbed, crosshatched, ridged, marked, piped, lined.
2. [Prohibited]—*Syn.* banned, outlawed, unlawful; see **illegal.**

barrel, *n.* —*Syn.* cask, keg, hogshead, stoup, vat, tub, puncheon, firkin, butt, carboy, cylinder, tun, receptacle, pipe, container, vessel.

barren, *mod.* **1.** [Incapable of producing young] —*Syn.* impotent, infertile, childless; see **sterile** 1.
2. [Incapable of producing vegetation]—*Syn.* fallow, unproductive, fruitless; see **sterile** 2.
3. [Without intellectual interest]—*Syn.* insipid, dry, stupid; see **dull** 4.
4. [Unprofitable]—*Syn.* fruitless, unproductive, profitless; see **worthless** 1.

barrenness, *n.* —*Syn.* sterility, unproductiveness, infecundity, unfertility, infertility, childlessness, effeteness, impotence, unfertileness, desolateness, unfruitfulness, bleakness, aridness, aridity, agenesis, unfructuosity.—*Ant.* fertility*, fruitfulness, richness.

barricade, *n.* —*Syn.* obstacle, bar, obstruction; see **barrier.**

barricade, *v.* —*Syn.* obstruct, block, fortify; see **bar** 1.

barrier, *n.* —*Syn.* bar, obstruction, difficulty, hindrance, obstacle, hurdle, fortification, stumbling block, fence, sound *or* sonic *or* transonic barrier, restriction, limitation restraint, impediment, let, drawback, check, preventive, encumbrance, stop, stay, bulwark, barricade, rampart, wall, palisade, picket, earthwork, breastwork, outwork, embankment, parapet, blockade, moat, trench, barbed wire, entanglement, pale, dust curtain, curtain of air, bamboo curtain, iron curtain.—*Ant.* way*, path, trail.

barrister, *n.* —*Syn.* counselor, attorney, advocate; see **lawyer.**

barroom, *n.* —*Syn.* tavern, saloon, pub (D); see **bar** 2.

barrow, *n.* —*Syn.* wheelbarrow, pushcart, handbarrow, handtruck, carriage, dumpcart, rickshaw, jinrikisha, go-cart.

barter, *n.* —*Syn.* trade, exchange, traffic; see **business** 1.

barter, *v.* —*Syn.* trade, bargain, swap (D); see **exchange** 2.

base, *mod.* —*Syn.* low, foul, sordid; see **vulgar** 1.

base, *n.* **1.** [A point from which action is initiated] —*Syn.* camp, field, landing field, strip, airport, airfield, airstrip, hangar, port, headquarters, terminal, station, garrison, billet, base camp, home base, base of operations, center, depot, supply base, dock, harbor, anchorage, station, site.
2. [The principal or basic ingredient]—*Syn.* chief constituent, filler, primary element; see **essence** 1.
3. [The bottom, thought of as a support]—*Syn.* root, foot, footing; see **foundation** 2.
4. [Foundation of a belief or statement]—*Syn.* principle, authority, evidence; see **basis** 1.
5. [A goal, especially in baseball]—*Syn.* mark, bound, station, plate, post, goal; *all* (D): first base, second base, third base, home plate, corner.
offbase (D)—*Syn.* erring, mistaken, incorrect; see **wrong** 2.

baseball, *n.* —*Syn.* *all* (D): ball, little league, the national pastime.
The major league teams in the United States include the following—National League: Los Angeles Dodgers, San Francisco Giants, Pittsburgh Pirates, Philadelphia Phillies, Atlanta Braves, St. Louis Cardinals, San Diego Padres, Cincinnati Reds, Houston Astros, Montreal Expos, New York Mets, Chicago Cubs; American League: Baltimore Orioles, Minnesota Twins, Detroit Tigers, Chicago White Sox, Cleveland Indians, California Angels, Kansas City Royals, Oakland A's, Milwaukee Brewers, Texas Rangers, Boston Red Sox, Toronto Blue Jays, Seattle Mariners, New York Yankees.

based, *mod.* —*Syn.* confirmed, planted, founded; see **established** 2.

baseman, *n.* —*Syn.* first baseman, second baseman, third baseman, sacker (D).

basement, *n.* **1.** [Foundation]—*Syn.* wall, footing, heavy construction; see **foundation** 2.
2. [A story wholly or partly below ground]—*Syn.* cellar, excavation, storage room, root cellar, wine cellar, furnace room, vault, subterranean apartment, crypt.

baseness, *n.* —*Syn.* meanness, debasement, degeneracy; see **rudeness.**

base on, *v.* —*Syn.* place *or* ground *or* depend *or* stand *or* settle *or* form *or* hinge *or* place *or* bottom *or* fasten on, institute, found, build; see also **establish** 2, **organize** 2.

bashful, *mod.* —*Syn.* retiring, reserved, timid; see **humble** 1, **modest** 2.

bashfulness, *n.* —*Syn.* modesty, timidity, reserve; see **shyness.**

basic, *mod.* —*Syn.* essential, central, primary; see **fundamental** 1, **necessary** 1.

basically, *mod.* —*Syn.* fundamentally, primarily, radically; see **essentially.**

basin, *n.* —*Syn.* pan, ewer, bowl; see **container.**

basis, *n.* **1.** [An intellectual foundation]—*Syn.* support, foundation, justification, reason, explanation, *raison d'être* (French), background, source, authority, principle, groundwork, axiom, assumption, *point d'appui* (French), premise, postulate, antecedent, backing, sanction, proof, evidence, data, security, crux, nexus, nucleus, center.
2. [A physical foundation]—*Syn.* foot, footing, resting place; see **foundation** 2.

bask, *v.* —*Syn.* loll, lounge, relax, luxuriate, revel, take comfort, enjoy, relish, wallow, laze, swim in (D).

basket, *n.* **1.** [A container]—*Syn.* bushel, crate, hamper, pannier, creel, nacelle, bassinet, bin, box, cradle; see also **container.**
2. [The contents of a basket]—*Syn.* basketful, bushel, load; see **measure** 1.
3. [The goal in basketball]—*Syn.* net, hoop; *all* (D): bucket, pot, swisher.

basketball, *n.* —*Syn.* court game, round ball; *both* (D): cage meet, hoopfest; see **sport** 3.

bass, *mod.* —*Syn.* deep, grave, low, sonorous, low-pitched, resonant; see also **musical** 1.

bass, *n.* Varieties include the following—black, striped, sea, small-mouthed, large-mouthed, rock, red, calico, channel, white, brass; see also **fish.**

bastard, *mod.* **1.** [Born out of wedlock]—*Syn.* illegitimate, natural, false, mongrel, baseborn, misbegotten, of illicit union, unfathered, misborn, unlawfully begotten, born on the wrong side of the sheet (D).—*Ant.* legitimate*, well-born, true.
2. [Of dubious extraction]—*Syn.* mingled, mixed, spurious; see **false** 1, 3.

bastard, *n.* **1.** [An illegitimate child]—*Syn.* natural child, spurious issue, whoreson, love child; *all* (D); come-by-chance, woods colt, Sunday's child.
2. [A rascal]—*Syn.* scoundrel, ne'er-do-well, cheat; *all* (D): sonuvabitch *or* SOB, stinker, rat, fink, ratfink; see also **rascal.**

bastardize, *v.* —*Syn.* debase, pervert, degrade, adulterate; see **corrupt** 1.

bastardy, *n.* —*Syn.* illegitimateness, bastardism, illegitimation; see **illegitimacy.**

baste, *v.* **1.** [To sew temporarily]—*Syn.* stitch, catch, tack; see **sew.**
2. [To dress cooking meat with fat or sauce] —*Syn.* lard, moisten, grease, drip, season; see also **cook.**
3. [(D) To beat]—*Syn.* club, trounce, thrash; see **beat** 1.

bat, *n.* **1.** [A club, especially one used in sports] —*Syn.* ball bat, baseball bat, cricket bat, stick, club, racket, pole, mallet.
2. [(D) A blow]—*Syn.* hit, rap, knock; see **blow** 1.
3. [A turn at batting]—*Syn.* inning; *all* (D): round, trip to the plate, up, turn.
blind as a bat—*Syn.* sightless, unseeing, blinded; see **blind** 1.
go to bat for (D)—*Syn.* intervene for, support, back up; see **defend** 3.
have bats in one's belfry (D)—*Syn.* mad, eccentric, peculiar; see **insane** 1.
not bat an eye *or* **eyelash** (**D**)—*Syn.* not be surprised *or* shocked *or* amazed, ignore, remain unruffled; see **neglect** 1.

(right) off the bat—*Syn.* at once, without delay, instantly; see **immediately.**

bat, *v.* —*Syn.* strike, whack, sock; see **hit** 1.

bat around, *v.* **1.** [To travel]—*Syn.* journey, cruise, tour; see **travel** 2.

2. [To discuss]—*Syn.* talk over or about, consider, debate; see **discuss.**

batch, *n.* —*Syn.* bunch, group, shipment; see **lot** 2.

bath, *n.* **1.** [The act of cleansing the body]—*Syn.* laving, washing, sponge bath, shower, tub, bath, steam bath, sauna (bath), Russian bath, Turkish bath; *all* (D): soak, dip, soaking.

2. [A liquid prepared for immersion]—*Syn.* wash, douche, spray, suds, shampoo, eyewash, rinse, tub, bath water.

3. [An enclosure prepared for bathing]—*Syn.* bathroom, shower, washroom, powder room, lavatory, steam room, Turkish bath, sauna (bath), public baths, pumproom, sweat lodge, toilet, shower room, spa.

bathe, *v.* **1.** [To cleanse oneself with liquid]—*Syn.* soap, scour, scrub; see **wash** 1.

2. [To sink]—*Syn.* dip, submerge, dunk; see **immerse** 1.

bathing suit, *n.* —*Syn.* bathing dress, swimming suit, swim suit, trunks, bikini, monokini, bathing costume, beach costume, two-piece bathing suit, topless bathing suit; *both* (D): two-piece, topless.

bathos, *n.* —*Syn.* melodrama, maudlinness, triteness; see **sentimentality.**

bathrobe, *n.* —*Syn.* (lounging) robe, wrapper, housecoat, negligee, kimono, happi coat, peignoir, muu-muu, duster, smock, wrap-around, tunic, bed jacket, dressing gown; see also **clothes.**

bathroom, *n.* —*Syn.* shower, toilet, lavatory; see **bath** 3.

baton, *n.* —*Syn.* stick, rod, staff; see **club** 3, **wand.**

battalion, *n.* —*Syn.* unit, force, corps; see **army** 2.

batten, *v.* —*Syn.* board up, secure, tie; see **fasten** 1.

batter, *n.* **1.** [One who bats]—*Syn.* hitter, batsman, pinch-hitter, designated hitter, switch-hitter, player; *all* (D): man who is up *or* at the plate, clouter, slugger, socker, lead-off man, clean-up man, walloper.

2. [A semifluid mixture for baking]—*Syn.* dough, mix, paste, recipe, concoction, preparation, mush; see also **mixture** 1.

batter, *v.* **1.** [To strike]—*Syn.* beat, punish, maul; see **hit** 1.

2. [To damage]—*Syn.* wreck, smash, injure; see **damage** 1.

battery, *n.* **1.** [Cells which generate or store electricity]—*Syn.* dry *or* wet *or* storage cells, storage battery, flashlight battery, solar battery, atomic battery, electric cell.

2. [An organized unit of artillery]—*Syn.* gunnery unit, artillery corps, field guns, cannon, primary *or* main battery, secondary battery.

3. [(D) In baseball, a pitching team]—*Syn.* pitcher and catcher; *both* (D): mound team, pitching combination.

4. [The act of beating]—*Syn.* assault, mayhem, attack, thumping, beating, physical violence; *both* (D): mugging, slugging.

battle, *n.* **1.** [An armed encounter]—*Syn.* fight, engagement, significant contact; see **fight** 1. Famous battles include the following—Thermopylae, Syracuse, Plataea, Lake Trasimenus, Actium, Siege and Capture of Carthage, Hastings, St Albans, Bosworth Field, Blenheim, Marston Moor, Culloden Moor, Fontenoy, Waterloo, Trafalgar, Austerlitz, Solferino, Balaklava, Borodino, Sadowa, Plassey, Bunker Hill, Yorktown, New Orleans, First Bull Run, Gettysburg, Mukden, Jutland, First and Second Marne, First and Second Ypres, the Somme, Verdun, Chateau-Thierry, Saint-Mihiel, Meuse, Argonne, Battle of France, Battle of Britain, Siege of Leningrad, Stalingrad, Pearl Harbor, Midway, El Alamein, Normandy Breakout, West Wall, Battle of the Bulge, Battle of Germany, Okinawa, Battle of the Philippine Sea, Iwo Jima, Inchon, Seoul, Chosin Reservoir, Heartbreak Ridge, Pork Chop Hill, Tet Offensive.

2. [The progress of a battle, sense 1]—*Syn.* strife, contention, struggle, combat, bombing, fighting, bloodshed, clash, onslaught, exchange of blows, onset, barrage, conflict, affray, warfare, fray, assault, human sea, press, crusade, military campaign, pincer, hostilities, havoc, carnage, ravage, rage of battle, blitzkreig, retreat, tactical retreat, maneuver.

give *or* **do battle**—*Syn.* fight back, struggle, engage in a battle *or* encounter; see **attack** 1, 2, **fight** 2.

battle cry, *n.* —*Syn.* slogan, motto, war cry; see **motto.**

battlefield, *n.* —*Syn.* field of battle *or* war, battleground, the front, front line, place of slaughter, scene of carnage, theater of war, area between the lines, area of confrontation, scene of battle, theater of operations, disputed territory, salient, no man's land (D).

battlement, *n.* —*Syn.* parapet, tower, escarpment, bartisan, barbican, bastion, balcony; see also **fortification** 2.

battleship, *n.* —*Syn.* man o' war, floating fortress, battlewagon (D); see **warship.**

bauble, *n.* —*Syn.* plaything, toy, knickknack; see **trinket.**

bawd, *n.* —*Syn.* procuress, madam, pimp; see **prostitute.**

bawdy, *mod.* —*Syn.* ribald, lustful, libidinous; see **lewd** 1, 2.

bawdyhouse, *n.* —*Syn.* brothel, whorehouse, house of prostitution; see **brothel.**

bawl, *v.* **1.** [To make a bellowing sound]—*Syn.* roar, howl, shout; see **yell.**

2. [To cry]—*Syn.* weep, shed tears, sob; see **cry** 1.

bawl out, *v.* —*Syn.* chide, berate, admonish; see **scold.**

bay, *mod.* —*Syn.* reddish-brown, reddish, brownish-red, castaneous, chestnut, rufous, badious, ruddy; see **brown.**

bay, *n.* —*Syn.* inlet, gulf, bayou, loch, bight, sound, fiord, firth, frith, estuary, strait, narrows, road, arm of the sea, mouth, lagoon, cove, anchorage, harbor.

at bay—*Syn.* cornered, caught, captured; see **trapped.**

bring to bay—*Syn.* corner, trap, catch; see **ambush.**

bay, *v.* —*Syn.* bellow, howl, cry; see **bark** 1.

bayonet, *n.* —*Syn.* spike, lance, pike; see **knife.**

bayonet, *v.* —*Syn.* stab, spear, stick; see **penetrate** 1.
bay window, *n.* —*Syn.* picture *or* bow window, oriel, alcove; see **window** 1.
bazaar, *n.* —*Syn.* market-place, fair, exchange, mart; see **market** 1.
B.C., *mod.* —*Syn.* before Christ, ante-Christian, pre-Christian; see **ancient** 2.
be, *v.* **1.** [To have being]—*Syn.* live, stay, be alive, exist, remain, continue, rest, endure, go on, stand, subsist, breathe, last, prevail, abide, survive, obtain, move, act, do, hold, have place.—*Ant.* die*, disappear, stop.
2. [To happen]—*Syn.* come about, transpire (D), occur; see **happen** 2.
3. [To equal]—*Syn.* amount to, consist of, comprise; see **equal.**
4. [To mean]—*Syn.* signify, denote, imply; see **mean** 1.
beach, *n.* **1.** [The edge of the water]—*Syn.* margin, strand, shingle; see **shore.**
2. [A waterside resort]—*Syn.* bathing beach, boardwalk, shore, seaside, watering place, the sea, the ocean, the lake, the sand(s), the coast.
beachcomber, *n.* —*Syn.* Bohemian, wanderer, sundowner; see **loafer.**
beached, *mod.* —*Syn.* stranded, marooned, abandoned; see **aground.**
beacon, *n.* —*Syn.* flare, lantern, guide, pharos, signal fire *or* light *or* beam, lighthouse, lamp, rocket, heliograph, beam, radar, sonar, airline beacon, radio beacon, air control beacon.
bead, *n.* **1.** [A small globule]—*Syn.* drop, droplet, pellet, grain, particle, speck, dot, dab, pea, shot, pill, spherule, driblet; see also **bean** 1.
2. [A small ornament]—*Syn.* pearl, gem, stone; see **jewel** 1.
draw a bead (on)—*Syn.* train (on), sight, get in the sights; see **aim** 2.
beadle, *n.* —*Syn.* acolyte, verger, churchwarden; see **assistant.**
beads, *n.* pl.—*Syn.* necklace, pendant, pearls, string of jewels, necklet, rosary, chaplet, wampum or peag; see also **necklace.**
beak, *n.* —*Syn.* nose, prow, bill, nib, mandible, projection, proboscis, snout, nozzle, neb; *both* (D): snozzle, handle.
beaked, *mod.* —*Syn.* curved, hooked, angled; see **bent.**
beaker, *n.* —*Syn.* goblet, stein, tumbler; see **cup.**
beam, *n.* **1.** [A relatively long, stout bar]—*Syn.* timber, brace, scantling, rafter, stringer, stud, two-by-four, strut, bolster, axle, reach, girder, sleeper, stay, crosspiece, prop, support, trestle, spar, transverse, pole, lath, furring strip, pile, balk, crossbar, T-beam, I-beam, steel beam, boom, post, kingpost, column, pillar, piling, stanchion, flitches, hammer beam, bail, joist, lintel, sill, jamb, cantilever, shaft, scaffolding.
2. [A ray or rays]—*Syn.* dartle, emission, shaft, bar, sparkle, twinkle, flicker, streak, laser, pencil, glitter, glare, stream of light, shimmer, glint, glow, chink, gleam, glimmer, finger, beacon.
3. [Radio waves intended as a guide]—*Syn.* direction finder, unidirectional radio signal, radar; see **beacon.**
off the beam (D)—*Syn.* faulty, incorrect, inaccurate; see **wrong** 2.
on the beam (D)—*Syn.* alert, keen, efficient; see **able** 1, 2.
beam, *v.* **1.** [To emit]—*Syn.* transmit, broadcast, give out; see **send** 1.
2. [To shine]—*Syn.* radiate, glitter, glare; see **shine** 1.
3. [To smile]—*Syn.* grin, laugh, smirk; see **smile.**
beamed, *mod.* —*Syn.* transmitted, aimed, pointed, channeled, broadcast, radiated; see also **sent.**
beaming, *mod.* **1.** [Giving forth beams]—*Syn.* radiant, glowing, gleaming; see **bright** 1.
2. [In very genial humor]—*Syn.* grinning, animated, sunny; see **happy** 1.
bean, *n.* **1.** [A small hard pellet]—*Syn.* kernel, nugget, bullet, pill, grain, knot, node, nodule, nodosity.
2. [A leguminous plant]—Varieties include the following—kidney, navy, lima, soy, castor, black, pinto, string, black-eyed *or* black-eye, stringless, pole, bush, green, wax, butter, Egyptian, hyacinth, Calabar *or* ordeal; see **string bean.**
beans, *n.* pl.—*Syn.* baked beans, Boston baked beans, stewed beans, bean soup, pork and beans, black beans, red beans, bean-hole beans, green beans, chili con carne, chili (D).
full of beans (D)—*Syn.* **1.** lively, vital, energetic; see **active** 2. **2.** mistaken, erring, incorrect; see **wrong** 2.
spill the beans (D)—*Syn.* divulge information, tell secrets, talk; see **tell** 1.
bear, *n.* **1.** [A bruin]—*Syn.* ursus, cub; *both* (D): bar, brownie.
Varieties include the following—American black, cinnamon, grizzly, brown, polar, Syrian, sloth *or* honey, Russian, sun *or* bruang, Kodiak, Japanese, Himalayan, black
2. [(D) an irritable person]—*Syn.* grumbler, growler, sourpuss (D); see **grouch.**
be a bear for punishment (D)—*Syn.* rugged, tough, determined; see **strong** 2.
bear, *v.* **1.** [To carry]—*Syn.* transport, convey, transfer; see **carry** 1, 2.
2. [To support weight]—*Syn.* sustain, hold up, shoulder; see **support** 1.
3. [To give birth to]—*Syn.* be delivered of, bring to birth, bring forth; see **produce** 1.
4. [To suffer]—*Syn.* tolerate, support, undergo; see **endure** 2.
bring to bear (on *or* **upon)**—*Syn.* affect, pressure, have an effect (on); see **influence.**
bearable, *mod.* —*Syn.* endurable, tolerable, passable, admissible, supportable, sufferable.
bear a hand, *v.* —*Syn.* support, assist, aid; see **help** 1.
bear away, *v.* —*Syn.* sail against the wind, haul *or* bring *or* heave to, keep *or* change course; see **sail** 2, **tack** 2.
beard, *n.* —*Syn.* whiskers, brush, Van Dyke, chin whiskers, imperial, muttonchops, goatee, spade beard, forked beard, side whiskers.
bearded, *mod.* —*Syn.* bewhiskered, bushy, unshaven; see **hairy** 1.
beardless, *mod.* **1.** [Hariless]—*Syn.* clean-shaven, smooth-faced, smooth; see **hairless.**

2. [Inexperienced]—*Syn.* callow, fresh, immature; see **inexperienced.**

bear down on *or* **upon,** *v.* **1.** [To press]—*Syn.* squeeze, compress, push; see **press** 1.
2. [To try]—*Syn.* endeavor, strive, attempt; see **try** 1.
3. [To approach]—*Syn.* draw near, converge on, close in (on); see **approach** 2, 3.

bearer, *n.* **1.** [One who presents a draft for payment] —*Syn.* payee, consignee, beneficiary, remittance man, casher, collector.
2. [One who carries a burden]—*Syn.* porter, packman, carrier, transporter, conveyor, pallbearer, messenger, beast of burden, coolie.

bearing, *n.* **1.** [A point of support]—*Syn.* block, frame, journal box, pivot, fulcrum, babbitted bearing, ball bearing, roller bearing.
2. [Manner of carriage]—*Syn.* mien, deportment, manner; see **behavior** 1, **posture** 1.

bear oneself, *v.* —*Syn.* act, appear, conduct *or* deport oneself; see **behave** 2.

bear out, *v.* —*Syn.* confirm, substantiate, support; see **prove.**

bear up, *v.* —*Syn.* withstand, persevere, carry on; see **endure** 2.

bear upon, *v.* —*Syn.* pertain, refer to, relate to, regard; see **concern** 1.

bear with, *v.* —*Syn.* tolerate, be patient, suffer, put up with; see **endure** 2.

bear witness, *v.* —*Syn.* affirm, attest, give evidence; see **testify** 2.

beast, 1. **1.** [A large animal]—*Syn.* brute, creature, lower animal; see **animal** 2.
2. [A person of brutish nature]—*Syn.* monster, brute, degenerate, animal, fiend, swine, throwback, pervert, lout, hun, savage, barbarian, pig, satyr, goat, sensualist, seducer, libertine, hog, voluptuary, monstrosity, fornicator, glutton, whoremonger, adulterer, lecher, gargoyle, Bluebeard; see also **freak** 2.

beastlike, *mod.* —*Syn.* ferocious, barbaric, savage; see **fierce** 1.

beastly, *mod.* **1.** [Bestial]—*Syn.* brutal, savage, coarse, swinish, repulsive, gluttonous, obscene, unclean, piggish, hoggish, irrational, prurient, boorish, carnal, brutish, depraved, abominable, loathsome, vile, low, degraded, sensual, foul, base, disgusting, inhuman, gross, unclean, vulgar.—*Ant.* refined*, sweet, nice.
2. [(D) Unpleasant]—*Syn.* nasty, disagreeable, revolting; see **offensive** 2.

beat (D), *mod.* **1.** [Tired]—*Syn.* weary, fatigued, worn out; see **tired.**
2. [Unconventional]—*Syn.* psychedelic, unorthodox, nonconformist, punk, iconoclastic, Bohemian, off-beat, third-stream, individualistic; *all* (D): beatnik, hippie, way out, turned on, tuned in, dropped out, Left Bank; see also **unusual** 2.

beat, *n.* **1.** [A stroke]—*Syn.* gesture, thump, punch, strike, hit, lash, slap, swing, shake; see also **blow** 1.
2. [A throb]—*Syn.* pulsation, cadence, flow, vibration, oscillation, turn, ripple, pressure, impulse, undulation, quiver, shake, pound, thump, surge, swell, palpitation, quake, flutter, rhythm.
3. [A unit of music]—*Syn.* accent, vibration, division, stress, measure, rhythm.

beat, *v.* **1.** [To strike repeatedly]—*Syn.* batter, whack, hammer; see **hit** 1.
2. [To thrash]—*Syn.* punish, whip, pistol-whip, flog, castigate, drub, cudgel, trounce, smite, spank, scourge, switch, lash, slap, cuff, box, trim, strap, birch, cane, flagellate, horsewhip, buffet, pommel, give a thumping, lay on blows, tap, rap, strike, bump, pat, hit, knock, lambaste, ram, pound, club, punch, bastinado, bat, flail, batter, maul, maltreat, belabor, pommel, clout; *all* (D): smack, lace, bang, swat, thump, slug, beat black and blue, pound *or* beat to a jelly *or* a paste, give a workout, whale, belt, whack, beat *or* knock the tar *or* daylights *or* hell *or* stuffing out of, lick the pants off of, larrup, wallop, lick, paste, bash, whang, lay into, baste, work over, thwack.
3. [To pulsate]—*Syn.* pound, thump, strike, throb, ripple, flutter, undulate, ebb and flow, vibrate, swing, palpitate, tremble, quiver, shiver, shake, quake, thrill, heave, rise and fall, alternate, fluctuate, flicker, oscillate, pulse, roll, quaver, flap, pitch, pound, twitch, bounce, toss, writhe, agitate, jerk, sway, bob, jounce, reel, buffet, flourish; *all* (D): pit-a-pat, wobble, waggle, wiggle, wriggle.
4. [To worst]—*Syn.* overcome, surpass, conquer; see **defeat** 1, 2, 3.
5. [To win]—*Syn.* be victorious, gain the prize, triumph; see **win** 1.
6. [To mix]—*Syn.* stir, whip, knead; see **mix** 1.
7. [To perplex]—*Syn.* puzzle, baffle, befuddle; see **confuse.**
8. [(D) To swindle]—*Syn.* defraud, cheat, dupe; see **deceive.**

beat around the bush, *v.* —*Syn.* quibble, avoid the issue, hesitate; see **evade** 1.

beaten, *mod.* **1.** [Defeated]—*Syn.* worsted, humbled, cowed, thwarted, bested, disappointed, frustrated, balked, circumvented, baffled, conquered, overthrown, subjugated, ruined, mastered, trounced, surmounted, undone, vanquished, discomfited, routed, crushed, overwhelmed, overpowered; *all* (D): licked, done in *or* for, kayoed, mugged, skinned, trimmed, had it, washed up, thrown for a loss, sunk.—*Ant.* victorious, successful*, triumphant.
2. [Made firm and hard]—*Syn.* hammered, tramped, stamped, rolled, milled, forged, trodden, pounded, tramped down, tamped.—*Ant.* soft*, ductile, loose.
3. [Made light by beating]—*Syn.* whipped, frothy, foamy, mixed, aerated, churned, creamy, bubbly, meringued.
4. [Threshed]—*Syn.* pounded, battered, bruised; see **attacked, hit.**

beater, *n.* —*Syn.* whipper, mixer, egg-beater, electric beater, blender.

beatific, *mod.* —*Syn.* blissful, joyful, heavenly; see **divine** 1.

beatify, *v.* —*Syn.* glorify, sanctify, consecrate; see **bless** 3.

beating, *n.* —*Syn.* thrashing, whipping, drubbing; see **defeat** 2, 3.

beatitude, *n.* —*Syn.* bliss, delight, joy; see **happiness** 2.

beatnik, *n.* —*Syn.* Bohemian, hippie-type, protestor, maverick, radical, iconoclast, demonstrator, nonconformist; *all* (D): hippie, peacenik, beat, dropout, teeny-bopper, flower child, love child.

beau, *n.* —*Syn.* fiancé, escort, boyfriend; see **lover** 1.

beautiful, *mod.* **1.** [Having qualities of beauty] —*Syn.* lovely, attractive, appealing, comely, pleasing, pretty, fair, fine, nice, dainty, good-looking, delightful, charming, enticing, fascinating, admirable, rich, graceful, sightly, ideal, delicate, refined, elegant, symmetrical, well-formed, shapely, harmonious, well-made, splendid, gorgeous, brilliant, radiant, exquisite, dazzling, flowerlike, resplendent, magnificent, superb, ornamental, marvelous, wonderful, grand, awe-inspiring, imposing, majestic, august, high, wondrous, excellent, impressive, showy, conspicuous, posh (D).—*Ant.* ugly*, foul, unsightly.

2. [Applied especially to human beings]—*Syn.* lovely, pretty, attractive, comely, fair, handsome, graceful, ideal, exquisite, refined, delicate, superb, divine, blooming, rosy, bonny, beauteous, statuesque, Junoesque, pulchritudinous, well-favored, bewitching, personable, pleasing, taking, alluring, slender, svelte, lissome, lithe, bright-eyed, good-looking, radiant; *all* (D): classy, swell-looking, (well) stacked, easy on the eyes, long on looks, built, looking good; see also **handsome** 2.—*Ant.* deformed*, hideous, ill-favored.

3. [Applied especially to works of art]—*Syn.* tasteful, fine, elegant; see **artistic** 3.

beautifully, *mod.* **1.** [In a beautiful manner] —*Syn.* gracefully, exquisitely, charmingly, attractively, prettily, delightfully, appealingly, seductively, alluringly, elegantly, gorgeously, splendidly, magnificently, ideally, tastefully, sublimely, bewitchingly, entrancingly, celestially, handsomely, superbly, divinely; *all* (D): marvelously, swingingly, groovily, jazzily.—*Ant.* hideously, repulsively*, foully.

2. [(D) Very well]—*Syn.* splendidly, wonderfully, superbly; see **excellently.**

beautify, *v.* **1.** [To make beautiful]—*Syn.* ornament, adorn, embellish; see **decorate.**

2. [To improve the grounds]—*Syn.* landscape, plant, garden; see **improve** 1.

beauty, *n.* **1.** [A pleasing physical quality]—*Syn.* grace, comeliness, fairness, pulchritude, charm, delicacy, elegance, attraction, fascination, allurement, shapeliness, majesty, attractiveness, good looks, winsomeness, glamour, loveliness, bloom; *all* (D): class, spiff, tone.—*Ant.* ugliness*, homeliness, deformity.

2. [An exalted mental or moral quality]—*Syn.* value, merit, excellence; see **virtue** 1.

3. [Use or value]—*Syn.* excellence, worth, importance; see **advantage** 3.

4. [A beautiful thing, particularly a woman]—*Syn.* goddess, belle, ornament, attraction, *belle chose* (French), siren, Circe, enchantress, seductress, Venus, femme fatale; *both* (D): looker, charmer. —*Ant.* witch*, blemish*, fright.

becalm, *v.* —*Syn.* soothe, calm, pacify; see **quiet** 1.

because, *conj.* —*Syn.* on account of, in consequence *or* view of, by cause *or* reason of, for the reason that, for the sake of, in behalf of, on the grounds that, in the interest of, as a result of, as things go, by virtue of, in that, since, by the agency of; *all* (D): due to, being as how, owing to.

be certain, *v.* —*Syn.* be sure, make certain, have confidence; see **know** 1.

beckon, *v.* —*Syn.* signal, motion, sign; see **summon** 1.

becloud, *v.* —*Syn.* darken, obscure, cloud, overcast; see **confuse.**

become, *v.* **1.** [To come to be]—*Syn.* develop *or* change *or* resolve *or* turn *or* pass *or* grow into, be metamorphosed, eventually be, emerge as, turn out (to be), progress toward being, come to be, be translated, shift, assume the form *or* shape *or* state of, be reformed *or* remodeled, be transmuted *or* transfigured, be reduced *or* converted to, convert, mature, increasingly grow, shift toward, incline to, melt into (D); see also **grow** 2.

2. [To be suitable]—*Syn.* enhance, set off, display, agree *or* accord *or* harmonize *or* go with, make handsome, adorn, be appropriate, heighten, belong to, be consistent with, match, enrich, garnish, grace, befit, ornament, suit, fit, be fitting, behoove, flatter, embellish, put in the best light, reveal the charm of, augment the attraction of.—*Ant.* distort*, detract from, spoil.

becoming, *mod.* **1.** [Appropriate]—*Syn.* suitable, proper, fitting; see **fit** 1, 2.

2. [Pleasing]—*Syn.* attractive, agreeable, handsome, seemly, comely, tasteful, well-chosen, fair, trim, graceful, flattering, spruce, effective, symmetrical, excellent, acceptable, welcome, nice (D); see also **beautiful** 1, 2, **neat** 1.—*Ant.* ugly*, unattractive, unpleasing.

bed, *n.* **1.** [A place of rest]—*Syn.* pallet, couch, mattress, cot, bedstead, berth, chaise, bunk; *all* (D): flop, hay, sack, rack, feathers, roost.

Beds include the following—single *or* double bed, davenport, cot, tester bed, four-poster, canopy bed, trundle bed, twin bed, water bed, platform bed, fold-away bed, Chesterfield, hammock, feather bed, double-deck bed, stretcher, folding bed, bunk bed, litter, cradle, crib, bassinet, Murphy bed, French bed, Hollywood bed, king-size bed, queen-size bed, hospital bed, gurney, circular bed, day bed, truckle bed.

2. [A foundation]—*Syn.* base, bottom, groundwork; see **foundation** 2.

3. [A seed plot]—*Syn.* patch, strip, area, piece, row, planting, hotbed, (cold) frame; see also **garden.**

bed, *v.* —*Syn.* embed, fix, implant; see **fasten** 1.

bedaub, *v.* —*Syn.* smear, stain, soil; see **dirty.**

bedbug, *n.* —*Syn.* *Cimex lectularius* (Latin), bloodsucker, bug (British), kissing bug, conenose.

bedding, *n.* —*Syn.* bedclothes, (bed) linen, (thermal) blankets, covers, bedcovers, pillows, coverlets, sheets, quilts, spreads, comforters.

bed down, *v.* **1.** [To provide with accommodations] —*Syn.* put up, house, accommodate; see **entertain** 2, **quarter** 2.

2. [To go to bed]—*Syn.* turn in, retire, hit the hay (D); see **lie** 4, **sleep.**

bedeck, *v.* —*Syn.* adorn, festoon, ornament; see **decorate.**

bedew, *v.* —*Syn.* shower, wet, dampen; see **moisten.**

bedevil, *v.* —*Syn.* baffle, bewilder, worry; see **confuse.**

bedlam, *n.* **1.** [A lunatic asylum]—*Syn.* madhouse, hospital for the insane, sanatorium; see **hospital.**
2. [Uproar]—*Syn.* confusion, pandemonium, clamor; see **confusion** 2, **noise** 2.

bedraggled, *mod.* —*Syn.* wet, soiled, unkempt; see **dirty** 1.

bedridden, *mod.* —*Syn.* incapacitated, confined to bed, laid up (D); see **disabled.**

bedroom, *n.* —*Syn.* bedchamber, dormitory, sleeping room, guest room, master bedroom, bunk room.

bedspread, *n.* —*Syn.* coverlet, spread, cover, bedcover, quilt, comforter, blanket.

bedtime, *n.* —*Syn.* slumbertime, time to retire; *all* (D): sleepy time, time to hit the hay, sack time; see also **night.**

bee, *n.* **1.** [A stinging, honey-gathering insect]—Varieties include the following—domestic: Caucasian, Madagascar, three-banded, three-band golden, golden Caucasian, black, Italian, German, Carniolan; wild: bumblebee, sweat bee, killer bee, carpenter bee.
2. [A communal gathering]—*Syn.* social, harvest home, work party; see **party** 1.
have a bee in one's bonnet (D)—*Syn.* be obsessed with *or* fussy about, hound somebody *or* something, busy oneself with; see **pursue** 1.

beef, *n.* **1.** [Bovine flesh used as food]—*Syn.* ox meat, cow's flesh, steer beef, manteca-fed beef, corn-fed, corned beef, pastrami, red meat; see also **meat.**
2. [A grown animal of the genus *Bos*]—*Syn.* bovine, bull, steer; see **cow.**
3. [(D) Human flesh]—*Syn.* flesh, brawn, meat (D); see **muscle.**
4. [(D) A complaint]—*Syn.* dispute, protestation, gripe (D); see **objection** 2.

beef up (D), *v.* —*Syn.* intensify, augment, increase; see **strengthen.**

beefy, *mod.* —*Syn.* brawny, burly, muscular; see **strong** 1.

beehive, *n.* —*Syn.* hive of bees, stand, apiary, colony, hive, swarm (D).

beeline, *n.* —*Syn.* direct route, air line, straightaway, path as straight as the crow flies (D).

Beelzebub, *n.* —*Syn.* Satan, fallen angel, prince of darkness; see **devil** 1.

beer, *n.* —*Syn.* malt beverage, malt liquor, brew; *all* (D): suds, the amber brew, slops.
Varieties include the following—lager, bock beer, ale, stout, porter, light beer, heavy *or* dark beer, black *or* Danzig beer, small beer, Schenk *or* winter beer, Pilsener, bitter beer, Bavarian beer.

beetle, *n.* —*Syn.* bug, scarab, crawling thing; see **insect.**

befall, *v.* —*Syn.* occur, take place, come to pass; see **happen** 2.

befog, *v.* —*Syn.* obscure, blur, cloud; see **confuse.**

before, *mod.* **1.** [In time]—*Syn.* previously, earlier, (in the) past, since, gone (by), in old days, heretofore, former(ly), aforetime, anteriorly, antecedently, in days of yore, back, sooner, up to now, ahead, in front *or* advance, afore, ere, facing, B.P. *or* before present (D).—*Ant.* in the future, coming*, to come.
2. [In space]—*Syn.* ahead of, in advance (of), advanced; see **ahead** 2.

before, *prep.* —*Syn.* prior *or* previous to, in front *or* ahead of, ere, in the presence *or* sight of, anterior to, under jurisdiction of, antecedent to.—*Ant.* behind*, following, at the rear.

beforehand, *mod.* —*Syn.* previously, already, in anticipation; see **before** 1.

befriend, *v.* —*Syn.* encourage, advise, stand by; see **help** 1.

befuddle, *v.* —*Syn.* make drunk, inebriate, muddle; see **confuse, intoxicate** 1.

befuddled, *mod.* —*Syn.* confused, inebriated, intoxicated; see **doubtful** 2, **drunk.**

beg, *v.* **1.** [To ask earnestly or importunately] —*Syn.* entreat, implore, beseech, supplicate, crave, solicit, pray for, urge, plead, sue, importune, petition, apply to, request, press, call *or* appeal to, requisition, conjure, abjure, apostrophize, canvass; see also **ask** 1.—*Ant.* admit*, concede, accede.
2. [To ask alms]—*Syn.* clamor for, appeal to, call on *or* upon, seek alms, mendicate, live on charity, want, starve, solicit charity; *all* (D): cadge, mooch, fish, bum, sponge, chisel, panhandle, (make a) touch, go from door to door, live from hand to mouth.—*Ant.* give*, bestow, endow.
go begging—*Syn.* be unwanted *or* unwelcome *or* unpopular, find no takers, lose (out); see **fail** 1.

beget, *v.* —*Syn.* father, sire, generate; see **propagate** 1.

beggar, *n.* **1.** [One who begs]—*Syn.* mendicant, supplicant, lazzarone, cadger, lazar; *all* (D): panhandler, moocher, gimmy guy, touch artist, bummer, fisher; see also **tramp** 1.—*Ant.* prodigal, donor*, giver.
2. [An impoverished person]—*Syn.* pauper, poor man, indigent, poverty-stricken *or* destitute person, bag lady, street person, suppliant, dependent, ghetto-dweller, poor relation, ward of the state, bankrupt, starveling; *both* (D): down-and-outer, church mouse.—*Ant.* financier*, millionaire, landed proprietor.
3. [A rascal]—*Syn.* scamp, fellow, scoundrel; see **rascal.**

beggarly, *mod.* —*Syn.* destitute, poverty-stricken, mean; see **poor** 1.

begging, *mod.* —*Syn.* desirous, anxious, in need, imploring, supplicating.

begin, *v.* **1.** [To initiate]—*Syn.* start, cause, inaugurate, make, occasion, impel, produce, effect, set in motion, launch, mount, start in *or* on *or* up *or* off, induce, do, create, bring about, get *or* set going *or* about, institute, lead up to, undertake, enter on *or* upon, open, animate, motivate, go into *or* ahead, lead the way, give impulse to, bring in *or* on, bring to pass, activate, initiate, make active, act on, generate, drive, actualize, eventuate, introduce, originate, found, establish, set up, trigger, give birth to, raise, breed, work, necessitate, take the lead, plunge into, lay the foundation for, break ground; *all* (D): get on the ball *or* beam, open up, get off *or* to *or* up, get cracking, put one's shoulder to the wheel, open fire, fire away, scratch the surface, open the door (to), touch a match to, throw the first

stone, break the ice, be in on the ground floor, kick off, take the plunge, strike out, spark, blast off. —*Ant.* end*, finish, terminate.
2. [To come into being, or to start functioning] —*Syn.* commence, get under way, set *or* start (in *or* out), come out, set *or* fall to, enter *or* embark upon, arise, rise, proceed *or* result from, enter, dawn, sprout, originate, spring, spring *or* crop up, come to birth, come into the world, be born, emanate, come into existence, occur, burst *or* issue *or* come forth, bud, stem *or* spring *or* come *or* derive from, grow out of, flower, blossom, break out, start up, set to work, have origin; *all* (D): lead out *or* off, kick off, jump off, go to it, dig in, take up *or* off, get the bugs out, make (something *or* someone) tick, get the show on the road, hit the ball, dive in, see the light of day, strike up.—*Ant.* stop*, cease, subside.
beginner, *n.* —*Syn.* novice, freshman, apprentice; see **amateur.**
beginning, *n.* **1.** [The origin in point of time or place]—*Syn.* source, outset, root; see **origin** 2.
2. [The origin, thought of as the cause]—*Syn.* germ, heart, antecedent; see **origin** 3.
3. [The act of beginning]—*Syn.* starting, commencement, inception; see **origin** 1.
begrime, *v.* —*Syn.* soil, spatter, stain; see **dirty.**
begrudge, *v.* —*Syn.* grudge, resent, be stingy, be reluctant; see **envy.**
beg the question, *v.* —*Syn.* equivocate, dodge, hedge; see **evade** 1.
beguile, *v.* **1.** [To deceive]—*Syn.* mislead, trick, delude; see **deceive.**
2. [To charm]—*Syn.* delight, divert, amuse; see **entertain** 1.
begun, *mod.* —*Syn.* started, initiated, instituted, under way, in motion *or* progress, on foot, inaugurated, happening, proceeding, going, active, kinetic, existing, operational, operative, working, in force, advanced.—*Ant.* potential, latent*, prospective.
behalf, *n.* —*Syn.* interest, part, welfare, sake, side, benefit, advantage, place, account, service, stead, profit, concern, furtherance, recommendation, favor, encouragement, aid, help, assistance, representation, countenance, support.—*Ant.* opposition*, derogation, detraction.
behave, *v.* **1.** [To act]—*Syn.* perform, work, run; see **act** 1.
2. [To act properly]—*Syn.* act with decorum, observe the golden rule, do unto others as you would have others do unto you, be nice *or* good *or* civil, mind one's p's and q's, be orderly, play one's part, live up to, observe the law, reform, acquit oneself well, mind one's manners, comport *or* deport *or* manage *or* discipline *or* behave oneself, be on one's best behavior, act one's age, avoid offense; *all* (D): keep the peace, toe the mark, play fair; see also **act** 2.—*Ant.* misbehave*, be rude, offend.
behaving, *mod.* —*Syn.* acting, performing, moving, acquitting *or* conducting oneself, appearing, seeming, making a spectacle.
behavior, *n.* **1.** [Public manner(s)]—*Syn.* bearing, deportment, comportment, mien, demeanor, air, presence, carriage, conduct, manner(s), action(s), attitude(s), way of life, speech, talk, tone, morals, habit(s), tact, social graces, seemliness, correctness, decorum, form, convention, savoir-faire, propriety, taste, management, mode, routine, practice, delivery, formality, style, expression, performance, code, role, observance, course, guise, act, deed, ethics; *all* (D): way, what's done, front, dealings.
2. [The action of an organism under given circumstances]—*Syn.* counteraction, execution, function, act, adaptation, operation, adjustment, work, deed, compliance, conduct, response, reaction, (condition) reflex, typical reaction, performance.
behead, *v.* —*Syn.* decapitate, execute, guillotine; see **kill** 1.
behest, *n.* —*Syn.* direction, order, precept, injunction; see **command** 1.
behind, *mod.* and *prep.* **1.** [To the rear in space] —*Syn.* back of, following, after; see **back.**
2. [Late in time]—*Syn.* tardy, dilatory, behind time; see **late** 1, **slow** 2.
3. [Slow in progress]—*Syn.* sluggish, slow-moving, delayed, backward, underdeveloped, retarded, behind schedule, belated, laggard; see also **slow** 1. —*Ant.* fast*, rapid, ahead of schedule.
behindhand, *mod.* **1.** [Late]—*Syn.* tardy, slow, behind time; see **late** 1, **slow** 2.
2. [Backward]—*Syn.* undeveloped, late, retarded; see **backward, slow** 3.
behind (one's) back, *mod.* **1.** [Secretly]—*Syn.* covertly, furtively, surreptitiously; see **secretly.**
2. [Treacherously]—*Syn.* deceitfully, foully, faithlessly; see **falsely.**
behind the times, *mod.* —*Syn.* antiquated, out-of-date, obsolete; see **old-fashioned.**
behold, *v.* —*Syn.* observe, look at, view; see **see** 1.
beholden, *mod.* —*Syn.* responsible, obligated, obliged; see **indebted.**
beholder, *n.* —*Syn.* spectator, onlooker, bystander; see **observer** 1.
behoove, *v.* **1.** [To be necessary]—*Syn.* be incumbent upon, be required *or* expected *or* requisite *or* needful, be one's obligation, be right *or* proper, owe it to.
2. [To become]—*Syn.* suit, be fitting, be proper for; see **become** 2.
being, *n.* **1.** [Existence]—*Syn.* presence, actuality, animation; see **life** 1.
2. [The essential part]—*Syn.* nature, quintessence, marrow; see **essence** 1.
3. [A living thing]—*Syn.* creature, conscious agent, beast; see **animal** 1, 2.
for the time being—*Syn.* temporarily, tentatively, for now *or* the present; see **briefly, now.**
belated, *mod.* —*Syn.* remiss, tardy, overdue; see **late** 1, **slow** 3.
belfry, *n.* —*Syn.* steeple, cupola, (bell) tower, spire, turret, dome, carillon, campanile, clocher, minaret; see also **tower.**
belie, *v.* **1.** [Mislead]—*Syn.* give the lie to, misrepresent, deceive; see **mislead.**
2. [Contradict]—*Syn.* disagree, repudiate, gainsay; see **deny** 1, **oppose** 1.
belief, *n.* **1.** [Mental conviction]—*Syn.* credit, credence, acceptance, trust, avowal, conviction, confidence, profession, opinion, notion, persuasion, position, understanding, faith, assent, mindset, surmise, suspicion, thesis, knowledge, feeling, conclusion,

presumption, hypothesis, thinking, hope, intuition, assurance, expectation, axiom, deduction, judgment, certainty, mind, impression, assumption, conjecture, postulation, theorem, divination, fancy, presupposition, supposition, notion, apprehension, theory, view, guess, conception, reliance, idea, inference.

2. [That which is believed]—*Syn.* creed, credo, dogma; see **faith** 2.

believable, *mod.* —*Syn.* trustworthy, creditable, acceptable; see **convincing** 2.

believe, *v.* **1.** [To accept as true]—*Syn.* accept, hold, think, conclude, have faith, be convinced, be certain of, deem, understand, regard, take at one's word, consider, affirm, be of the opinion, postulate, opine, conceive, give credence to, have no doubt, rest assured, swear by, take one's word for, cherish a belief, keep the faith, be credulous, entertain *or* nurture a belief, attach some weight to; *all* (D): doubt not, reckon (on), repose in, come round to. —*Ant.* doubt, deny*, suspect.

2. [To assume]—*Syn.* suppose, guess, gather; see **assume** 1.

believe in, *v.* —*Syn.* swear by, look to, put *or* have faith in; see **trust** 1.

believer, *n.* —*Syn.* convert, devotee, canonist, dogmatist, accepter, adherent, apostle, disciple, prophet, confirmed believer, doctrinaire; see also **follower.**—*Ant.* skeptic*, doubter, agnostic.

believing, *mod.* —*Syn.* maintaining, trusting, presuming, assuming, regarding, holding, accepting, impressed with, under the impression.—*Ant.* doubtful*, mistrustful, rejecting.

belittle, *v.* —*Syn.* lower, disparage, decry; see **deprecate** 2.

bell, *n.* **1.** [Device for signaling audibly]—*Syn.* chime(s), siren, angelus, signal, gong, tintinnabulum, buzzer; both (D): ding-dong, ringer; see also **alarm** 1.

2. [Sound made by a bell]—*Syn.* toll, carillon, gong, pealing, tocsin, buzz, chime, tintinnabulation, ringing; see also **sound** 2.

bellboy, *n.* —*Syn.* messenger boy, steward, porter; both (D): boy, bellhop; see also **assistant.**

belle, *n.* —*Syn.* beauty, coquette, debutante; see **girl** 1, **woman** 1.

bellicose,, *mod.* —*Syn.* warlike, belligerent, hostile; see **aggressive** 2.

belligerent, *mod.* —*Syn.* warlike, pugnacious, hostile; see **aggressive** 2.

bellow, *n.* —*Syn.* howl, cry, roar; see **cry** 1.

bellow, *v.* —*Syn.* howl, call, shout; see **cry** 2, **yell.**

bell tower, *n.* —*Syn.* campanile, turret, carillon; see **belfry, tower.**

belly, *n.* —*Syn.* stomach, paunch, gut (D); see **abdomen.**

belly, *v.* —*Syn.* swell, bulge *or* curve out, unfold; see **fill** 2, **spread** 3.

bellyache (D), *v.* —*Syn.* whine, grumble, protest; see **complain** 1.

belong, *v.* **1.** [To be properly placed]—*Syn.* reside, normally exist, pertain, appertain, bear, apply, relate, inhere, bear upon, regard, correlate *or* go *or* have to do with, be associated *or* affiliated *or* linked with, merge with, have respect *or* relationship *or* applicability to, be a part *or* constituent of, be a component *or* attribute *or* adjunct of, permeate, touch, be linked *or* joined *or* allied to, be akin *or* related *or* bound to, refer, concern, associate, be relevant.—*Ant.* disturb*, intrude, be incongruous.

2. [(D) To be acceptable in a group; *said of persons*] —*Syn.* fit in, have (a) place, have (its) place, be born so, be a member, take one's place with, be one of, be classified *or* counted among, be included *or* contained in, owe allegiance *or* support to, be a part of, be one of the family (D).—*Ant.* differ*, fight*, not fit (in).

belongings, *n.* pl.—*Syn.* possessions, goods, things (D); see **property** 1.

belong to, *v.* **1.** [To be in possession of, or be classified under]—*Syn.* pertain *or* relate to, be held *or* occupied *or* enjoyed *or* owned by, be in the hands *or* possession of, be at the disposal of, be the property *or* right of, concern, come *or* go *or* be associated with, fall under.—*Ant.* escape*, be free, have no owner.

beloved, *mod.* —*Syn.* loved, adored, worshiped, cherished, dear, favorite, admired, highly regarded *or* valued, idolized, precious, prized, dearest, yearned for, hallowed, popular, revered, venerated, treasured, well-liked, cared for, respected, endeared, favored, esteemed, doted on, nearest to one's own heart, dearly beloved, pleasing, after one's own heart, darling, pet (D).—*Ant.* hated*, abhorred, disliked.

beloved, *n.* —*Syn.* fiancé, sweetheart, object of one's affection; see **lover** 1.

below, *mod.* and *prep.* **1.** [Lower in position] —*Syn.* beneath, underneath, down from; see **under** 1.

2. [Lower in rank or importance]—*Syn.* inferior, subject, lesser; see **subordinate, under** 2.

3. [*In written work,* farther along]—*Syn. infra, vide infra, v.i.* (all Latin), later, on a following page, in a statement to be made, hereinafter, subsequently.—*Ant.* earlier, above*, on a former page.

4. [*In a ship,* on *or* to a lower deck]—*Syn.* (in) steerage, between-decks, below-decks, in the hold, in the engine room, below the waterline.

5. [On earth]—*Syn.* in mundane existence, in this period of earthly probation, in this world, here below, under the sun, on the face of the earth, in this our life, here.

6. [In hell]—*Syn.* in the underworld, with the fallen angels, in Pluto's realm, damned, condemned, in Inferno; see also **damned** 1.

below the belt, *mod.* —*Syn.* unjust, foul, unsporting; see **unfair** 1.

below the horizon, *mod.* —*Syn.* removed, remote, far-off; see **distant** 1.

below par, *mod.* —*Syn.* inferior, below average, second-rate (D); see **poor** 2.

belt, *n.* **1.** [A long flexible strip]—*Syn.* girdle, ribbon, string; see **band** 1.

2. [A distinctly defined area]—*Syn.* tract, region, territory; see **area** 2.

below the belt—*Syn.* unsupporting, foul, unjust; see **unfair.**

tighten one's belt—*Syn.* endure hunger *or* privation, suffer, bear misfortune; see **endure** 2.

under one's belt—*Syn.* past, achieved, complete(d); see **done** 1, **finished** 2.

bemoan, *v.* —*Syn.* lament, weep (over), grieve, express sorrow (for; see **mourn** 1.

bemuse, *v.* —*Syn.* muddle, bewilder, daze; see **confuse.**

bench, *n.* **1.** [A long seat]—*Syn.* settee, pew, form, lawn-seat, settle, bank, stall; see also **chair** 1, **seat** 1.
2. [A long table]—*Syn.* workbench, desk, trestle, counter, board, shelf, ledge, easel; see also **table** 1.
3. [Those who administer justice]—*Syn.* (the) bar, judges, tribunal; see **court** 2.

bend, *n.* —*Syn.* crook, bow, arch; see **curve** 1.

bend, *v.* **1.** [To force out of a straight line]—*Syn.* twist, warp, curve, arch, round, crimp, flex, pervert, spiral, camber, coil, crinkle, detour, curl, buckle, crook, bow, wind, incline, contort, deflect, deform, double, loop, twine; see also **turn** 3. —*Ant.* straighten*, stiffen*, support*.
2. [To be forced out of a straight line]—*Syn.* stoop, lean, buckle, waver, zigzag, careen, reel, crumple, meander, circle, swerve, diverge, droop, angle off *or* away, wilt; see also **deviate, turn** 6, **veer.**—*Ant.* stand up, extend*, straighten.
3. [To influence]—*Syn.* direct, persuade, mould; see **change** 1, **influence.**

bending, *mod.* **1.** [Turning]—*Syn.* twisting, veering, curving, buckling, twining, spiraling, looping, doubling, drooping, leaning, inclining, bowing, arching, curling, warping, crooking, winding, stooping, crumpling, waving, wavering.
2. [Bowing]—*Syn.* stooping, curtseying, dipping; see **bowing.**

beneath, *mod.* and *prep.* **1.** [Under]—*Syn.* below, underneath, in a lower place; see **under** 1.
2. [Lower in rank or importance]—*Syn.* subject, inferior, lesser; see **subordinate, under** 2.

beneath contempt, *mod.* —*Syn.* offensive; contemptible, despicable; see **offensive** 2.

benediction, *n.* —*Syn.* sanctification, benison, laying on of hands; see **blessing** 1.

benefaction, *n.* **1.** [A gift]—*Syn.* donation, legacy, grant; see **gift** 1.
2. [A good deed]—*Syn.* favor, charity, good turn; see **kindness** 2.

benefactor, *n.* —*Syn.* helper, protector, angel (D); see **patron** 1.

beneficent, *mod.* —*Syn.* benign, salutary, benevolent; see **helpful** 1, **kind** 1.

beneficial, *mod.* —*Syn.* useful, propitious, salubrious; see **helpful** 1.

beneficiary, *n.* —*Syn.* recipient, receiver, payee, legatee, heir, heiress, inheritor, possessor, successor, assignee, donee, stipendiary, pensioner, almsman, grantee, devisee, charity case (D).—*Ant.* donor*, giver, testator.

benefit, *mod.* —*Syn.* (for) charity, for a good *or* worthy cause, in one's favor.

benefit, *n.* **1.** [Advantage]—*Syn.* gain, profit, good; see **advantage** 3.
2. [Charitable affair]—*Syn.* charity ball, performance, donor dinner (or lunch), dance, fair, bazaar, exhibit, exhibition, raffle, concert.

benefit, *v.* —*Syn.* serve, profit, avail; see **help** 1.

benevolence, *n.* —*Syn.* charity, altruism, good will; see **kindness** 1.

benevolent, *mod.* —*Syn.* generous, altruistic, helpful; see **kind** 1.

benign, *mod.* —*Syn.* good, gracious, favorable; see **kind** 1.

bent, *mod.* —*Syn.* curved, warped, hooked, beaked, looped, twined, crooked, sinuous, bowed, contorted, stooped, doubled over, limp, wilted, drooping, humped, slumped, hunched, humpbacked, lordotic, bowlegged, inclined; see also **twisted** 1. —*Ant.* rigid, straight*, erect.

bent, *n.* —*Syn.* leaning, tendency, propensity; see **inclination.**

benumb, *v.* **1.** [To stupefy]—*Syn.* daze, stun, confound; see **confuse.**
2. [To deaden]—*Syn.* make numb, paralyze, freeze; see **deaden** 1.

bequeath, *v.* —*Syn.* grant, hand down, pass on; see **give** 1.

bequest, *n.* —*Syn.* inheritance, estate, endowment; see **gift** 1.

berate, *v.* —*Syn.* chide, reprimand, rebuke; see **scold.**

bereavement, *n.* —*Syn.* deprivation, misfortune, affliction; see **death** 1, **loss** 1.

bereft, *mod.* —*Syn.* bereaved, deprived, cut off, dispossessed, disfurnished, divested, destitute, stripped, impoverished, beggared, left unprovided for, naked, left without, robbed, fleeced, straitened; see also **poor** 1.—*Ant.* rich*, possessed, in enjoyment.

berry, *n.* **1.** [A small pulpy fruit]—*Syn.* drupe, hip, drupelet, haw, pome.
Common berries include the following—raspberry, blackberry, blueberry, loganberry, boysenberry, cranberry, huckleberry, whortleberry, bilberry, gooseberry, currant, strawberry, checkerberry, dewberry, hagberry, dogberry, bayberry, serviceberry, mulberry.
2. [A dry fruit]—*Syn.* seed, grain, kernel; see **bean** 2.

berth, *n.* **1.** [A bed, especially in a conveyance] —*Syn.* bunk, deck, hammock, upper *or* lower *or* transom berth, bedroom, roomette, sleeping compartment, shakedown (D).
2. [(D) A position]—*Syn.* place, situation, employment; see **job** 1, **profession** 1.
give a wide berth—*Syn.* keep clear of, evade, stay away (from); see **avoid.**

beseech, *v.* —*Syn.* implore, importune, entreat; see **beg** 1.

beset, *v.* —*Syn.* invade, besiege, assail; see **attack** 1, 2.

beside, *mod.* and *prep.* —*Syn.* at *or* on the side *or* edge of, adjacent *or* contiguous *or* next *or* parallel *or* close (to), adjoining, alongside, near, but a step from, close at hand, by, with, abreast, side by side, at one's elbow, bordering *or* verging on *or* upon, neighboring, overlooking, next door to, to one side, in juxtaposition, nearby, connected with; *both* (D): cheek by jowl, close upon.

besides, *mod.* —*Syn.* in addition to, additionally, moreover, over and above, supplementary *or* added to, likewise, further, furthermore, beyond, exceeding, secondly, more than, apart from, extra, in distinction to, in excess of, plus, (and) also, in other respects, exclusive of, with the exception of, as well as, not counting, other than, too, in conjunction with, conjointly; *all* (D): to boot, on top of (all) that *or* this, together *or* along with, on the side, and all, aside from, into the bargain, else.

beside the point, *mod.* —*Syn.* extraneous, not pertaining to, not connected with; see **irrelevant.**

besiege, *v.* —*Syn.* lay siege to, blockade, assault; see **attack** 1, 2.

best, *mod.* **1.** [Generally excellent]—*Syn.* choicest, finest, highest, first, transcendent, prime, premium, supreme, optimum, incomparable, culminating, pre-eminent, crowning, *sans pareil* (French), paramount, matchless, nonpareil, unrivaled, unparalleled, second to none, nonesuch, unequaled, inimitable, beyond compare, superlative, foremost, peerless, greatest; *all* (D): boss, tough, cool, A-one, first-rate.—*Ant.* worst*, poorest, lowest.

2. [Applied especially to people]—*Syn.* of the elite, belonging to the upper classes, socially preferred, aristocratic, wealthy, titled, presentable, desirable; *both* (D): born to the purple; see also **cultured, noble** 3, **rich** 1.

3. [Applied especially to things]—*Syn.* choice, prime, premium; see **excellent.**

4. [Applied especially to actions]—*Syn.* noblest, sincerest, most magnanimous *or* creditable *or* illustrious *or* glorious *or* honorable *or* praiseworthy, greatest; see also sense 1.—*Ant.* worst*, meanest, lowest.

5. [Largest]—*Syn.* greatest, biggest, bulkiest; see **large** 1.

best, *n.* —*Syn.* first, favorite, choice, finest, top, pick, prime, flower, cream; *both* (D): salt of the earth, pick *or* cream of the crop.

all for the best—*Syn.* favorable, fortunate, advantageous; see **helpful** 1, **hopeful** 2.

as best one can—*Syn.* skillfully, ably, capably; see **able** 2.

at best—*Syn.* good, highest, most favorable; see **best** 1.

at one's best—*Syn.* well, in one's prime, capable; see **able** 2, **strong** 1.

get *or* have the best of—*Syn.* outdo, overcome, defeat; see **surpass.**

make the best of—*Syn.* suffer, tolerate, get by; see **endure** 2.

with the best—*Syn.* excellently, well, ably; see **able** 2.

best, *v.* —*Syn.* worst, get the better of, overcome; see **defeat** 1, 3.

bestial, *mod.* —*Syn.* brutal, savage, depraved; see **cruel** 1.

bestir, *v.* —*Syn.* stir up, rouse, agitate; see **excite** 1, 2.

bestow, *v.* —*Syn.* bequeath, present, offer; see **give** 1.

bestride, *v.* —*Syn.* ride, mount, sit; see **straddle.**

bet, *n.* —*Syn.* gamble, wager, venture, pot, ante, hazard, tossup, stake, speculation, betting, raffle, odds, pitch and toss, uncertainty, chance, random shot, lottery, fortune, lot, game of chance, sweepstake(s), risk; *all* (D): blind, flyer, long shot, shot in the dark, blind bargain, fall of the dice, plunge, pig in a poke.

bet, *v.* —*Syn.* wager, gamble, stake, toss up, bet on *or* against, venture, hazard, trust, play against, speculate, tempt fortune, play (for), put *or* lay money down *or* on, dice, risk, game, chance, ante, make a bet; *all* (D): take a flyer *or* a chance, declare oneself in, lay the dough, lay down, buy in on, fight *or* buck the tiger, plank down, post, double the blind, punt, play the ponies, pony up, lay odds, lay even money.

you bet—*Syn.* certainly, by all means; yes, indeed; see **surely, yes.**

betray, *v.* **1.** [To deliver into the hands of an enemy] —*Syn.* play false, break faith *or* trust, inform on *or* against, turn in, commit (high) treason, turn informer, delude, break one's promise, be false-hearted to, go over to the enemy, trick; *all* (D): sell down the river, let down, play Judas, give the Judas kiss to, double-cross, deliver up, sell out, stab in the back, bite the hand that is feeding you, blow the gaff, cross up, turn state's evidence; see also **deceive.**—*Ant.* believe*, adhere, stand firm.

2. [To seduce and abandon]—*Syn.* abase, debauch, prostitute; see **corrupt** 1.

3. [To reveal]—*Syn.* divulge, disclose, uncover, make known; see **reveal** 1.

betrayal, *n.* —*Syn.* treason, treachery, disloyalty; see **deception** 1, **dishonesty.**

betrayer, *n.* —*Syn.* renegade, deceiver, conspirator; see **traitor.**

betroth, *v.* —*Syn.* publish the banns, become engaged, bestow *or* give one's hand, contract, pledge, affy, promise, precontract, plight faith *or* troth, bind, engage, affiance, tie *or* commit oneself to, undertake to marry, espouse.

betrothal, *n.* —*Syn.* publishing the banns, espousal, betrothing; see **engagement** 2.

better, *mod.* **1.** [Superior]—*Syn.* greater, finer, preferred; see **excellent.**

2. [Thought of as somewhat exclusive]—*Syn.* more select *or* individual *or* reserved *or* refined *or* important *or* aloof *or* retiring *or* noteworthy *or* prominent *or* sophisticated, politer, better for, posher (D).—*Ant.* common*, vulgar, popular.

3. [Recovering health]—*Syn.* convalescent, improved in health, stronger, recovering, improving, on the road to recovery, mending, progressing, on the mend (D).—*Ant.* sick*, failing, wasting away.

4. [Larger]—*Syn.* bigger, preponderant, weightier; see **large** 1.

for the better—*Syn.* favorable, fortunate, advantageous; see **helpful** 2, **hopeful** 2.

get *or* have the better of—*Syn.* outdo, overcome, defeat; see **surpass.**

better, *v.* —*Syn.* ameliorate, revamp, refine; see **improve** 1.

betterment, *n.* —*Syn.* prosperity, upgrading, progress; see **improvement** 1, 2.

between, *prep.* —*Syn.* separating, within, enclosed *or* bound(ed) by, amidst, amid, among, in, in between, interpolated, mid, interjacent, intervening, inserted, in the midst of, in the middle, medially, centrally located, surrounded by, midway, halfway, betwixt; *all* (D): in the thick of, sandwichwise, betwixt and between; see also **among.**

between you and me, *mod.* —*Syn.* confidentially, privately, personally; see **secretly.**

bevel, *n.* —*Syn.* angle, slant, slope; see **inclination** 5.

beverage, *n.* —*Syn.* liquor, refreshment, draft; see **drink** 2, 3.

bevy, *n.* —*Syn.* flock, pack, group; see **gathering.**

bewilder, *v.* —*Syn.* confound, upset, disconcert, puzzle; see **confuse.**

bewildered, *mod.* —*Syn.* confused, amazed, benighted, misguided, lost, astonished, thunderstruck, shocked, muddled, upset, dazed, giddy, dizzy, reeling, vertiginous, puzzled, misled, addled, uncertain, surprised, baffled, disconcerted, appalled, aghast, put out of countenance, adrift, at sea, off the track, awed, stupefied, astounded, struck speechless, agog, agape, breathless, befuddled, startled, struck dumb, dumbfounded, dazzled, stunned, electrified, confounded, staggered, petrified, awe-struck; *all* (D): flabbergasted, flustered, all balled up, rattled, in a dither, lost in the fog, bowled over, euchred, fazed, (come) unstuck, at a loss, all hot and bothered, going around in circles, in a stew, up in the air, stumped, snafu, goofy, punchdrunk.—*Ant.* self-possessed, rational*, cool.

bewitch, *v.* **1.** [Fascinate]—*Syn.* enthrall, beguile, capture; see **fascinate.**
2. [Charm]—*Syn.* enchant, spell, control magically; see **charm** 3.

bewitched, *mod.* **1.** [Fascinated]—*Syn.* enraptured, entranced, captivated; see **fascinated.**
2. [Charmed]—*Syn.* enchanted, ensorcelled, controlled supernaturally; see **charmed** 1.

beyond, *mod.* and *prep.* —*Syn.* on the other *or* far side, over there, beyond the bounds, in advance of, over *or* above the mark, away, out of range, a good *or* great *or* long way off, over the border (of), yonder, past, free *or* clear of, farther back *or* off, ahead, behind, more remote; *both* (D): wide of the mark, out of touch with.—*Ant.* on this side, here*, nearer.
the great beyond—*Syn.* (the) afterlife, heaven and hell, purgatory; see **heaven** 2, **hell.**

biannual, *mod.* —*Syn.* semiannual, occurring twice a year, half-yearly.

bias, *n.* —*Syn.* bent, preference, leaning; see **inclination** 1.

bias, *v.* —*Syn.* influence, prejudice, sway; see **influence.**

bib, *n.* —*Syn.* napkin, tucker, face cloth, chin-wiper, collar, dickey; see also **apron.**

bible, *n.* **1.** [Ultimate authority]—*Syn.* handbook, text, guidebook, manual, creed, accepted statement, authority, guide, unquestioned doctrine, court of final appeal, scripture; *both* (D): the last word, Hoyle.
2. [Holy Scripture; *capitalized*]—*Syn.* the Good Book, God's word, the Word, the (Holy) Scriptures, the Torah, the Canon, the Testaments, Sacred History, the Writings of the Apostles and Prophets, Holy Writ, the Holy Bible, the Word of God, Testament.
Famous Bibles include the following—Vulgate, Douay, King James *or* Authorized Version (KJV), Tyndale, Coverdale, Wycliffe, Revised Standard Version (RSV), Luther's, Wenzel, Mazarin, Wujek's, Gutenberg, Geneva *or* Breeches, Vinegar, Cicked, American *or* Revised, New English Bible (NEB) Book of Mormon.
Non-Christian Bibles include the following—Koran, Veda, Masora, Alcoran, Tripitaka, the Eddas.

bibliography, *n.* —*Syn.* catalogue, compilation, list of books; see **list.**

bibliophile, *n.* —*Syn.* book lover, reader, bibliolater, antiquarian, bibliomaniac, book nut (D).

bicker, *v.* —*Syn.* wrangle, squabble, dispute, argue; see **quarrel.**

bicycle, *n.* —*Syn.* cycle, machine, velocipede, tandem *or* bicycle built for two; *both* (D): bike, two-wheeler; see also **tricycle.**

bid, *n.* **1.** [An offer]—*Syn.* proposal, proposition, declaration; see **suggestion** 1.
2. [(D) An invitation]—*Syn.* request, summons, proposal; see **invitation** 1, 2.

bid, *v.* **1.** [To propose a price for purchase]—*Syn.* offer, venture, proffer, tender, bid for, submit a bid.
2. [To offer a commitment at cards]—*Syn.* declare, name a trump, bid in, name a suit, open, respond.
3. [To order]—*Syn.* demand, charge, direct, instruct; see **command** 1.
4. [To invite]—*Syn.* request, ask, solicit; see **invite** 1, 2.

bidding, *n.* **1.** [Order]—*Syn.* direction, demand, charge; see **command** 1.
2. [Invitation]—*Syn.* summons, call, request; see **invitation** 1.
do the bidding of—*Syn.* be obedient, obey, follow orders; see **serve** 2.

bide (one's) time, *v.* —*Syn.* await, watch for, lie in wait; see **wait** 1.

bier, *n.* —*Syn.* coffin, pall, hearse, catafalque, casket, stretcher, barrow, litter, pyre, sarcophagus, pine box, roughbox (D); see also **grave** 1, **shroud.**

big, *mod.* **1.** [Of great size]—*Syn.* huge, great, mammoth; see **high** 1, **large** 1, **long** 1, 2.
2. [Grown, or partially grown]—*Syn.* grown-up, full-grown, adult; see **mature** 1.
3. [With child]—*Syn.* gravid, parturient, expecting (D); see **pregnant** 1.
4. [Loud]—*Syn.* roaring, deafening, heavy; see **loud** 1.
5. [Important]—*Syn.* prominent, significant, influential; see **important** 1, 2.
6. [Pompous]—*Syn.* presumptuous, pretentious, imperious; see **egotistic** 2.
7. [Generous]—*Syn.* magnanimous, liberal, unselfish; see **generous** 1, 2.
8. [(D) Pompously]—*Syn.* pretentiously, ostentatiously, flamboyantly; see **pompously.**

bigamy, *n.* —*Syn.* unlawful polygamy, plural marriage, real bigamy, interpretative bigamy; see also **crime** 1, 2, **sin.**

bigot, *n.* —*Syn.* dogmatist, doctrinaire, fanatic, monomaniac, fideist, opinionated person, puritan, partisan, enthusiast, extremist; *all* (D): diehard, mule, stickler, bitter-ender, crank, red-neck, Bilbo; see also **radical, zealot.**

bigoted, *mod.* —*Syn.* biased, dogmatic, opinionated; see **prejudiced.**

bigotry, *n.* —*Syn.* dogmatism, narrow-mindedness, injustice; see **fanaticism, intolerance** 2, **prejudice.**

big shot (D), *n.* —*Syn.* *all* (D): big wheel, bigwig, big man on campus *or* BMOC; see **administrator.**

bilateral, *mod.* —*Syn.* two-sided, respective, reciprocal; see **mutual** 1.

bill, *n.* **1.** [A statement of account]—*Syn.* itemized account, statement of indebtedness, request for payment; see **statement** 3.
2. [A piece of paper money]—*Syn.* bank note, Federal Reserve note, currency, gold *or* silver certificate; *all* (D): long green, greenback, folding money; see also **money** 1.
3. [A statement prepared for enactment into law] —*Syn.* draft, measure, proposal, (proposed) act, (piece of) legislation; see also **law** 3.
4. [A handbill]—*Syn.* poster, circular, folder; see **advertisement** 1, 2.
5. [A formal statement, usually legal]—*Syn.* charge, allegation, indictment; see **declaration** 2.
6. [A beak]—*Syn.* nib, mandible, projection; see **beak.**
fill the bill—*Syn.* meet requirements, be satisfactory, serve the purpose; see **satisfy** 3.

bill, *v.* **1.** [To request payment]—*Syn.* dun, solicit, render *or* send account of indebtedness, draw upon.
2. [To advertise, especially a coming attraction] —*Syn.* announce, book, give advance notice of; see **advertise** 1.

billboard, *n.* —*Syn.* bulletin board, display panel, poster board; see **advertisement** 1, 2, **announcement** 3.

billed, *mod.* —*Syn.* announced, publicized, published; see **advertised.**

billfold, *n.* —*Syn.* card case, pocketbook, purse; see **wallet.**

billow, *n.* —*Syn.* surge, crest, tide; see **wave** 1, 2.

billowy, *mod.* —*Syn.* surging, swelling, rising, waving, rolling, rising and falling, heaving, undulating, ebbing and flowing, rippled, rippling, wavy, bouncy, bouncing; see also **rough** 1, **turbulent.**

billy goat (D), *n.* —*Syn.* sire, he-goat, buck; see **goat.**

bin, *n.* —*Syn.* bunker, hopper, storeroom, crib, mow, granary, silo, dusthole, locker; see also **container.**

binary, *mod.* —*Syn.* double, twofold, paired; see **double.**

bind (D), *n.* —*Syn.* dilemma, tight situation, quandary; see **predicament.**

bind, *v.* **1.** [To constrain with bonds]—*Syn.* truss *or* tie up, shackle, fetter, pinion, cinch, clamp, chain, leash, constrict, manacle, enchain, enfetter, lace, pin, restrict, restrain, moor, handcuff, hamper, muzzle, hitch, secure, yoke, pin *or* peg down, fix, strap, tether, bind up, lash (down), hobble, trammel; *both* (D): clamp down on, hogtie.
2. [To hold together or in palce]—*Syn.* secure, attach, adhere; see **fasten** 1.
3. [To obligate]—*Syn.* oblige, necessitate, compel; see **force** 1.
4. [To dress]—*Syn.* treat, wrap, bandage; see **dress** 3.
5. [To join]—*Syn.* unite, put together, connect; see **join** 1.

binder, *n.* **1.** [A person who binds]—*Syn.* tier, shackler, hobbler, coupler, grappler, bookbinder.
2. [A machine which binds]—*Syn.* reaper, harvester, harvesting machine; see **machine** 1.
3. [Anything used to bind]—*Syn.* tie, adhesive, fastener; see **adhesive, band** 2, **rope, wire** 1.

binding, *mod.* **1.** [Tying]—*Syn.* restraining, confining, limiting; see **tying.**
2. [Obligatory]—*Syn.* requisite, essential, required; see **necessary** 1.

binding, *mod.* —*Syn.* obligatory, requisite, required; see **necessary** 1.

binding, *n.* **1.** [The act of joining]—*Syn.* merging, coupling, junction; see **union** 1.
2. [Anything used to bind]—*Syn.* tie, adhesive, fastener; see **adhesive, band** 2, **rope, wire** 1.
3. [A cover]—*Syn.* wrapper, jacket, book cover; see **cover** 2.

biochemistry, *n.* —*Syn.* biological chemistry, physiological chemistry, chemistry of plant and animal life; see **science** 1.

biography, *n.* —*Syn.* life story, saga, memoir, journal, experiences, autobiography, vita, life, adventures, personal record *or* account *or* narrative, life history, confessions, fortunes, personal anecdote, profile, sketch, picture, biographical account *or* sketch; see also **record** 1, 2, **story.**

biological, *mod.* —*Syn.* organic, life, living, zoological, botanical, concerning life, concerned with organisms *or* organic matter.

biology, *n.* —*Syn.* science of organisms, natural science *or* history, nature study, life science.
Divisions of biology include the following—morphology, genetics, embryology, ecology, ethnology, biomathematics, astrobiology, aerobiology, biochemistry, oceanography, marine botany; see also **botany, physiology, science** 1, **zoology.**

biplane, *n.* —*Syn.* airplane, light plane, aircraft; see **plane** 3.

birch, *n.* —*Syn.* Popular classifications of birch include the following—paper, white, aspen-leaved, yellow, black, weeping; see also **tree, wood** 2.

bird, *n.* **1.** [Any warm-blooded vertebrate with feathers and wings]—*Syn.* fowl, feathered creature, *Avis* (Latin).
Common birds include the following—sparrow, starling, robin, blue jay, crow, hawk, meadow lark, owl, vulture, buzzard, turkey buzzard, woodpecker, cardinal, oriole, bluebird, kingfisher, canary, parrot, chickadee, swallow, skylark, nightingale, nuthatch, whippoorwill, flycatcher, thrush, catbird, cuckoo, bobolink, titmouse, wren, gull, eagle, cormorant, osprey, cedarbird, ovenbird, blackbird, dove, duck, brambling, bullfinch, parakeet *or* parrakeet, chat, creeper, crane, shitepoke, heron, goshawk, goatsucker, mockingbird, ostrich, emu, kestrel, petrel, auk; see also **hawk, owl, sparrow, thrush, woodpecker.**
2. [A game bird]—*Syn.* wild fowl, game; see also **duck, goose** 1, **pheasant.**
3. [(D) A mildly derogatory term]—*Syn.* person, fellow; *all* (D): guy, coot, duck, duffer.
eat like a bird—*Syn.* diet, starve, restrain one's appetite; see **fast.**
for the birds—*Syn.* ridiculous, absurd, useless; see **stupid** 1, **worthless** 1.

bird dog, *n.* —*Syn.* pointer, setter, hunting dog; see **dog** 1.

birdhouse, *n.* —*Syn.* aviary, bird cage, dovecote, roost, perch, roosting place, pigeon house, columbary; see also **enclosure** 1.

birth, *n.* **1.** [The coming into life]—*Syn.* delivery, parturition, nativity, beginning; *all* (D): blessed event, visit from the stork, act of God.—*Ant.* death*, decease, demise.
2. [The origin]—*Syn.* commencement, source, start; see **origin** 1, 2, 3.
3. [One's nature or condition by reason of birth]—*Syn.* position, station, status; see **rank** 3.
4. [That which is born]—*Syn.* infant, offspring, child; see **baby** 1.
give birth to—*Syn.* bring forth, have a child, reproduce; **produce** 1.

birthday, *n.*—*Syn.* natal day, name day, celebration; see **anniversary.**

birthplace, *n.*—*Syn.* place of origin *or* nativity, (one's) country, home town, native home *or* land; see also **country** 3.

biscuit, *n.*—*Syn.* cracker, wafer, roll; see **bread.** Biscuits include the following types—beaten, soda, baking powder, cream, hot, sea, ship, Brussels, pilot, raised, rolled.

bisect, *v.*—*Syn.* cut in two, hemisect, halve; see **divide** 1.

bisexual, *mod.*—*Syn.* androgynous, hermaphroditic, gynandrous, epicene, monoclinous, intersexual; *both* (D): switch-hitting, AC-DC.

bishop, *n.*—*Syn.* father, archbishop, primate; see **minister** 1, **priest.**

bishopric, *n.*—*Syn.* diocese, see, episcopate, episcopacy, prelacy, archbishopric, primacy, prelature, prelateship, archiepiscopacy, pontificate, bishopdom.

bison, *n.*—*Syn.* European aurochs, wisent, guar, urus, gayal, American buffalo; see also **buffalo.**

bit, *n.* **1.** [A small quantity]—*Syn.* piece, fragment, crumb, dot, particle, jot, trifle, mite, iota, whit, tittle, scintilla, splinter, parcel, portion, droplet, trickle, driblet, sprinkling, modicum, morsel, dollop, pinch, snippet, snip, shred, atom, speck, molecule, shard, chip, fraction, sliver, segment, section, lump, slice, shaving, moiety, sample, specimen, scale, flake, collop, excerpt, scrap, part, division, share, trace, rasher, item, chunk, paring, taste, lick, mouthful, dose, stub, butt, stump; *all* (D): a drop in the bucket, peanuts, chicken feed, smithereen, gob, hunk, smidgin, niggle, flyspeck, snatch; see also **division** 2, 3, **part** 1.—*Ant.* quantity*, lot*, excess.
2. [A brief time]—*Syn.* second, instant, minute, jiffy; see **moment** 1.
3. [A small degree]—*Syn.* jot, minimum, inch, tittle, modicum, hairbreadth, trifle, iota, mite, fraction, tolerance, margin; *all* (D): whisker, wink, hair, skin of one's teeth *or* nose, eyelash.—*Ant.* infinitude, maximum, great deal.
4. [The mouthpiece of a bridle]—*Syn.* curb, snaffle, gag, Hanoverian bit, Baldwin bit, Chifney bit; see also **halter.**
5. [A boring or gouging implement]—*Syn.* rock drill, drift, auger; see also **drill** 2.
Varieties include the following—carpenter's, blacksmith's, drilling-machine, spiral, expanding, brace, expanding-center, German, half-round, plug-center, twisted, coal-boring, countersink.
do one's bit—*Syn.* participate, share, do one's share; see **join** 2.
every bit—*Syn.* wholly, altogether, entirely; see **completely.**

bite, *n.* **1.** [What one takes in the mouth at one time]—*Syn.* mouthful, cud, chew, taste, spoonful, forkful, nip, morsel, nibble, chaw (D).
2. [The result of being bitten]—*Syn.* wound, sting, laceration; see **injury** 1.
3. [A sharp sensation]—*Syn.* sting, prick, burn; see **pain** 2.
4. [A quick meal]—*Syn.* snack, nibble, brunch; see **food.**

bite, *v.* **1.** [To seize or sever with the teeth]—*Syn.* snap, gnaw, sink (one's) teeth in, nip, lacerate, nibble, chew (up), mouth, gulp, worry, taste, masticate, clamp, champ, munch, bite into, crunch, ruminate, mangle, chaw (D); see also **eat** 1, **taste** 1.
2. [To be given to biting]—*Syn.* snap, be vicious, bare the teeth; see **attack** 2, **hurt** 1.
3. [To cut or corrode]—*Syn.* burn, sting, slash, smart, etch, eat *or* wear away, sear, rot, rust, oxidize, erode, dissolve, deteriorate, decay, consume, decompose, engrave.
4. [To take bait]—*Syn.* rise to the bait, strike, nibble, get hooked; swallow hook, line, and sinker (D).
5. [(D) To take a chance]—*Syn.* volunteer, risk, be a victim; see **chance** 2.
put the bite on (D)—*Syn.* pressure, ask for a loan, touch (D); see **borrow** 1.

bite the dust (D), *v.*—*Syn.* be fatally wounded, fall, drop; see **die** 1.

biting, *mod.* **1.** [Acidulous]—*Syn.* sharp, keen, tangy; see **sour** 1.
2. [The act of biting]—*Syn.* seizing, wounding, abrading, piercing, puncturing, incising, lacerating, holding, tasting, masticating, mangling, nipping, nibbling, snapping, gnawing, munching, crunching, gripping, chewing, worrying, in the mouth, with teeth in, sinking teeth into, chawing (D).
3. [Sarcastic]—*Syn.* caustic, acrimonious, bitter; see **sarcastic.**

bitten, *mod.*—*Syn.* chewed, mouthed, torn, lacerated, slashed, gulped, gnawed, nibbled, tasted, devoured, eaten, masticated, worried, tossed, stung, pierced, mangled, punctured, cut, ripped, chawed (D); see also **hurt.**

bitter, *mod.* **1.** [Acrid]—*Syn.* astringent, acid, tart; see **sour** 1.
2. [Intense]—*Syn.* sharp, harsh, severe; see **intense.**
3. [Sarcastic]—*Syn.* acrimonious, caustic, biting; see **sarcastic.**
4. [Painful]—*Syn.* grievous, hurtful, stinging; see **painful** 1.

bitterness, *n.* **1.** [The quality of being bitter to the tongue]—*Syn.* tartness, piquancy, pungency, astringency, acidity, acerbity, sourness, acridity, brackishness, brininess.—*Ant.* sweetness*, blandness, delectability.
2. [The quality of being bitter to the mind]—*Syn.* pain, painfulness, virulence, anguish, agony, grievousness, mordancy, venom, harshness, acrimony; see also sense 1, **distress** 1.—*Ant.* solace, balm*, enjoyment.

bituminous coal, *n.*—*Syn.* soft coal, western coal, low-grade coal; see **coal** 1.

biweekly, *mod.* —*Syn.* semiweekly, twice monthly, once every two weeks, fortnightly.

bizarre, *mod.* —*Syn.* odd, fantastic, eccentric, grotesque; see **unusual** 2.

blab, *v.* **1.** [To reveal]—*Syn.* disclose, tell, divulge; see **reveal** 1.
2. [To chatter]—*Syn.* prattle, jabber, gab; see **babble.**

blabber, *n.* —*Syn.* prattle, jabber, drivel; see **nonsense** 1.

blabber, *v.* —*Syn.* chatter, prattle, gabble; see **babble.**

black, *mod.* **1.** [Opposite to white]—*Syn.* swart, dark, blackish, nigrous, nigrescent, raven, atramentous, coal-black, dusky, dingy, murky, inklike, livid, somber, swarthy, jet, inky, ebony, pitch-black, black as coal *or* pitch *or* jet, sooty, raven-hued, sable, sombre, gun-metal, flat black, jet black; *all* (D): black as the ace of spades, black as night, ebon-hued, black as a crow.—*Ant.* white*, colored, colorful.
2. [Without light]—*Syn.* gloomy, shadowy, clouded; see **dark** 1.
3. [Negroid]—*Syn.* colored, African, swarthy, Ethiopian, swart, Melanesian, dusky, black-skinned; see also **Negro.**—*Ant.* white, Caucasian, fair-skinned.
4. [Unpropitious]—*Syn.* threatening, foreboding, sinister; see **ominous.**
5. [Angry]—*Syn.* fierce, enraged, sour; see **angry.**
6. [Evil]—*Syn.* villainous, mean, diabolical; see **wicked** 1.
7. [Dirty]—*Syn.* soiled, stained, spotted; see **dirty** 1.

black, *n.* **1.** [A chromatic color least resembling white]—*Syn.* lampblack, carbon, darkest gray, jet, sable, ebony, blackness.—*Ant.* white*, blond, brightness.
2. [A Negro]—*Syn.* colored man *or* woman, Afro-American, black man or woman; see **Negro.**
in the black—*Syn.* successful, lucratively, gainfully; see **profitably.**

black, *v.* —*Syn.* darken, make black, blacken; see **shade** 2.

blackball, *v.* —*Syn.* ostracize, exclude, repudiate; see **bar** 2.

blackbird, *n.* —Popular equivalents include the following—(purple) grackle, (jack)daw, English thrush, red-winged blackbird, yellow-winged blackbird, rusty blackbird; see also **bird** 1.

blackboard, *n.* —*Syn.* slate, board, chalkboard, wall-slate, greenboard (D).

blacken, *v.* **1.** [To make black]—*Syn.* darken, nigrify, make black; see **shade** 2.
2. [To smirch]—*Syn.* sully, tarnish, attack; see **slander.**
3. [To become black]—*Syn.* grow black *or* dark *or* dim, nigrify, deepen; see **shade** 3.

blackguard, *n.* —*Syn.* villain, scoundrel, rogue; see **rascal.**

blackjack, *n.* —*Syn.* bat, stick, cudgel; see **club** 3.

blacklist, *v.* —*Syn.* bar, exclude, blackball; see **bar** 2.

black magic, *n.* —*Syn.* sorcery, witchcraft, necromancy; see **magic** 1, 2.

blackmail, *n.* —*Syn.* hush money, tribute, protection (D); see **bribe.**

blackmail, *v.* —*Syn.* extort, exact, coerce; see **bribe, force** 1.

blackness, *n.* —*Syn.* gloom, duskiness, murkiness; see **darkness** 1.

black out, *v.* **1.** [To delete]—*Syn.* rub out, eradicate, erase; see **cancel** 1.
2. [To faint]—*Syn.* pass out, lose consciousness, swoon; see **faint.**
3. [To darken]—*Syn.* put out the lights, make dark, batten; see **shade** 2.

black sheep, *n.* —*Syn.* outcast, prodigal, reprobate; see **rascal, refugee.**

blacksmith, *n.* —*Syn.* metalworker, forger, smithy; see **smith.**

blade, *n.* **1.** [A cutting instrument]—*Syn.* edge, brand, sword; see **knife.**
2. [A relatively long leaf]—*Syn.* frond, spear, flag, shoot; see also **leaf** 1.

blamable, *mod.* —*Syn.* reprehensible, culpable, blameworthy; see **guilty** 2.

blame, *n.* **1.** [Censure]—*Syn.* disapproval, condemnation, reprehension, castigation, remonstrance, denunciation, reprobation, disparagement, depreciation, animadversion, opposition, depreciation, abuse, disfavor, opprobium, contumely, objection, reproach, stricture, derogation, criticism, dispraise, disfavor, repudiation, disapprobation, reprimand, invective, slur, accusation, reproof, reproach, attack, chiding, rebuke, objurgation, impeachment, complaint, diatribe, tirade, charge, expostulation, indictment, recrimination, attribution, jeremiad, arraignment, implication, obloquy, imputation, exprobation, inculpation, incrimination, Philippic, reflection, discountenance, calumny, ascription, frowning upon (D).—*Ant.* praise*, commendation, appreciation.
2. [Responsibility]—*Syn.* culpability, answerability, liability; see **responsibility** 2.
be to blame—*Syn.* guilty, at fault, culpable; see **wrong** 2.

blame, *v.* **1.** [To censure]—*Syn.* condemn, rebuke, criticize; see **censure.**
2. [To hold responsible for]—*Syn.* charge, indict, impute; see **accuse.**

blameless, *mod.* —*Syn.* faultless, not guilty, inculpable; see **innocent** 1.

blameworthy, *mod.* —*Syn.* at fault, culpable, blamable; see **guilty** 2.

blanch, *v.* —*Syn.* whiten, etiolate, wash out; see **bleach.**

bland, *mod.* **1.** [Suave]—*Syn.* affable, agreeable, urbane; see **pleasant** 1.
2. [Mild]—*Syn.* soothing, soft, smooth; see **mild** 4.
3. [Temperate; *said especially of weather*]—*Syn.* calm, clear, balmy; see **mild** 2.
4. [Flavorless]—*Syn.* flat, dull, insipid; see **tasteless** 1.

blank, *mod.* **1.** [Without writing]—*Syn.* white, clear, virgin, fresh, unused, plain, empty, unmarked, untouched, pale, new, spotless; see also **clean** 1.—*Ant.* used*, inscribed, printed*.
2. [Without meaning or expression]—*Syn.* impassive, expressionless, vague, vacant, vacuous, dull, hollow, empty, meaningless, fruitless, noncommittal, uncommunicative, masklike, stiff, immobile, inscrutable.—*Ant.* excitedly*, expressive, nervous.
3. [Without content]—*Syn.* void, barren, vacant, vacuous; see **empty** 1.

4. [Bewildered]—*Syn.* disconcerted, confused, muddled; see **bewildered.**

5. [Complete]—*Syn.* utter, total, unconditional; see **absolute** 1.

blank, *n.* **1.** [An empty space]—*Syn.* void, hollow, hole, cavity, vacancy, womb, gulf, nothingness, hollowness, vacuity, abyss, opening, vacuum, *tabula rasa* (Latin), hiatus, gap, interval; see also **emptiness.**

2. [A form]—*Syn.* questionnaire, data sheet, information blank; see **form** 5.

draw a blank—*Syn.* fail *or* be unable to remember, lose one's memory, disremember; see **forget** 1.

blanket, *mod.* —*Syn.* all-inclusive, powerful, unconditional; see **absolute** 1, **comprehensive.**

blanket, *n.* **1.** [A covering in the form of a layer] —*Syn.* sheet, sheath, strip; see **cover** 2, **sheet** 2.

2. [Fabric used as a covering]—*Syn.* quilt, plaid, fleece, lap *or* carriage robe, comforter, puff, featherbed, throw, stadium blanket, rug, mat, cloak; see also **linen.**

blanket, *v.* —*Syn.* envelop, conceal, bury; see **cover** 1.

blank out, *v.* —*Syn.* delete, erase, cross out; see **cancel** 1.

blare, *v.* —*Syn.* boom, trumpet, blast; see **sound** 1, **yell.**

blarney, *n.* —*Syn.* cajolery, blandishment, adulation; see **flattery.**

blasé, *mod.* —*Syn.* unconcerned, uninterested, nonchalant; see **indifferent** 1.

blaspheme, *v.* —*Syn.* swear, revile, utter impieties; see **curse** 1.

blasphemous, *mod.* —*Syn.* irreverent, profane, irreligious; see **impious** 1.

blasphemy, *n.* —*Syn.* impiety, sacrilege, profanity, irreverence, obscenity, lewdness, swearing, cursing, reviling, scoffing, profanation, profaneness, desecration; see also **heresy, sin.**—*Ant.* worship, piety*, prayer.

blast, *n.* **1.** [An explosion]—*Syn.* burst, eruption, detonation; see **explosion** 1.

2. [A sudden force of wind]—*Syn.* gust, gale, draft; see **wind** 1.

3. [A loud sound]—*Syn.* roar, din, bang; see **noise** 1.

4. [An explosive charge]—*Syn.* gunpowder, TNT, dynamite; see **explosive.**

5. [(D) Fun]—*Syn.* excitement, amusement, good time; see **fun.**

(at) full blast (D)—*Syn.* at full speed *or* capacity, rapid, quick; see **fast** 1.

blast, *v.* **1.** [To shatter by explosion]—*Syn.* blow up, dynamite, detonate; see **explode** 1.

2. [To ruin]—*Syn.* blight, shatter, annihilate, wreck; see **destroy** 1.

blast off, *v.* **1.** [To ascend]—*Syn.* rocket, climb, soar up; see **rise** 1.

2. [(D) To begin]—*Syn.* start, initiate, originate, get going; see **begin** 1.

blatant, *mod.* **1.** [Loud]—*Syn.* noisy, clamorous, boisterous; see **loud** 2.

2. [Obvious]—*Syn.* obtrusive, plain, clear; see **obvious** 1, 2.

blaze, *n.* **1.** [Fire]—*Syn.* conflagration, combustion, burning; see **fire** 1.

2. [Sudden or strong light]—*Syn.* burst, gleam, beam; see **flash** 1.

blaze, *v.* —*Syn.* flame, flash, flare up; see **burn** 1.

blaze away, *v.* **1.** [To shoot]—*Syn.* fire, discharge, blast; see **shoot** 1.

2. [(D) To proceed)—*Syn.* go ahead, press on, go *or* move on; see **advance** 1.

bleach, *v.* —*Syn.* blanch, fade, wash out, whiten, etiolate, achromatize.—*Ant.* color*, dye, stain.

bleachers, *n.* pl.—*Syn.* grandstand, stands, seats, benches, boxes.

bleak, *mod.* **1.** [Applied to countryside or conditions]—*Syn.* dreary, desolate, bare, cheerless, wild, exposed, barren, blank, disheartening, weary, melancholy, lonely, flat, somber, distressing, depressing, comfortless, drear, joyless, uninviting, dull, sad, mournful, monotonous, waste, gloomy, dismal, unsheltered, frowning, blighted, blasted, unpopulated, desert, deserted, fog-hung, craggy, scorched, stony, burned (over), denuded, bombed, deforested, bulldozed, cleared, frozen.—*Ant.* verdant, green*, fruitful.

2. [Applied to atmospher]—*Syn.* chill, windy, stormy, boisterous, cold, piercing, cutting, wintry, keen, biting, icy, hiemal, shivery, boreal, bitter, rigorous, chilly, nipping, severe, brumous, raw, freezing, inclement, frosty, pinching, glacial, polar, arctic, sharp, dank, foul, murky, misty, foggy.—*Ant.* mild*, pleasant, sunny.

blear, *v.* —*Syn.* dim, blur, obscure; see **shade** 2.

bleary, *mod.* —*Syn.* dim, blurred, indistinct; see **obscure** 1.

bleed, *v.* **1.** [To lose blood]—*Syn.* shed blood, be bleeding, have unstaunched wounds, (have a) hemorrhage.

2. [To issue as blood]—*Syn.* fall drop by drop, gush, spurt; see **flow** 2.

3. [(D) To extort money]—*Syn.* impoverish, pauperize, exhaust one's resources, blackmail, confiscate; *all* (D): put the squeeze on, strong-arm, put the screws to; see also **bribe, steal.**

4. [To let blood]—*Syn.* cup, draw *or* take blood, open a vein, leech, phlebotomize.

5. [To suffer]—*Syn.* ache, agonize, be in pain; see **suffer** 1.

6. [To drain]—*Syn.* exhaust, reduce, get rid of; see **drain** 1, 2, 3.

blemish, *n.* —*Syn.* flaw, defect, stain, spot, smudge, imperfection, disfigurement, defacement, blot, blur, chip, taint, tarnish, smirch, stigma, brand, deformity, dent, daub, discoloration, mole, nevus, pock, blister, birthmark, wart, scar, impurity, speckle, maculation, bruise, freckle, pimple, cicatrix, patch, lump, nodule, lentigo; *all* (D): glitch, blotch, smutch, hickey; see also **lack** 2.—*Ant.* flawlessness, perfection*, purity.

blench, *v.* —*Syn.* flinch, quail, shrink back; see **wince.**

blend, *n.* —*Syn.* combination, compound, amalgam; see **mixture** 1.

blend, *v.* —*Syn.* combine, mingle, compound; see **mix** 1.

bless, *v.* **1.** [To give]—*Syn.* endow, bestow, provide, grant; see **give** 1.

2. [To call the blessing of God upon]—*Syn.* commend to God, offer *or* give a benediction, pray for,

make the sign of the cross, cross, sign, sprinkle with holy water, anoint with oil, invoke benefits upon, give a blessing.—*Ant.* curse*, anathematize, imprecate.
3. [To dedicate to God]—*Syn.* baptize, canonize, glorify, honor, dedicate, make *or* pronounce holy, exalt, give benediction, absolve, anoint, ordain, hallow, consecrate, beatify, sanctify, enshrine, offer, render acceptable to, sacrifice, commend, confirm. —*Ant.* sell to the devil, damn*, condemn.

blessed, *mod.* **1.** [Joyful]—*Syn.* joyous, glad, content; see **happy** 1.
2. [Marked by God's favor, especially in heaven] —*Syn.* saved, redeemed, glorified, translated, exalted, rewarded, resurrected, enthroned among the angels, sanctified, glorious, beatified, holy, spiritual, religious.—*Ant.* lost, doomed*, accursed.
3. [Consecrated]—*Syn.* sacred, dedicated, sanctified; see **divine** 2.
4. [(D) Damned]—*Syn.* *all* (D): blamed, blasted, darned; see **damned** 2.

blessing, *n.* **1.** [Benediction]—*Syn.* benison, benedicite, commendation, sanctification, laying on of hands, absolution, baptism, unction, consecration, Eucharist, divine approval *or* sanction *or* approbation.—*Ant.* damnation, curse*, anathema.
2. [Anything which is very welcome]—*Syn.* boon, benefit, good, advantage, help, asset, good fortune, stroke of luck, godsend, windfall, miracle, manna from heaven; *both* (D): the breaks, (lucky) break(s); see also **advantage** 3, **aid** 1.—*Ant.* obstacle*, disadvantage, nuisance.

blight, *n.*—*Syn.* disease, withering, mildew; see **decay** 2.

blight, *v.*—*Syn.* damage, spoil, ruin; see **decay.**

blind, *mod.* **1.** [Without sight]—*Syn.* sightless, unseeing, eyeless, blinded, visionless, in darkness, dim-sighted, groping (in the dark), deprived of sight, sun-blind, purblind, undiscerning; *all* (D): stone-blind, moon-blind, blind as a mole *or* bat. —*Ant.* observant*, perceptive, discerning.
2. [Without consideration]—*Syn.* heedless, inconsiderate, thoughtless; see **blindly** 2, **careless** 1.
3. [Without looking]—*Syn.* obtuse, unseeing, by guesswork *or* calculation, with instruments; see also **blindly** 1, **unaware.**—*Ant.* observant*, looking, intent.
4. [Without passage]—*Syn.* obstructed, blocked, without egress; see **tight** 2, 3.
5. [Concealed]—*Syn.* secluded, obscured, disguised; see **hidden** 2.
6. [Random]—*Syn.* chance, accidental, unplanned; see **incidental** 2.

blind, *n.* **1.** [An obstruction to light or sight]—*Syn.* blindfold, blinder, blinker; see **curtain, veil.**
2. [Something intended to deceive]—*Syn.* front, cover, trap; see **trick** 1.

blind, *v.* **1.** [To obscure]—*Syn.* darken, shadow, dim; see **shade** 1, 2.
2. [To deceive]—*Syn.* conceal, delude, mislead; see **deceive.**

blindly, *mod.* **1.** [Without direction]—*Syn.* at random, wildly, in all directions, frantically, instinctively, madly, purposelessly, aimlessly, confusedly, indiscriminately, pell-mell; see also **unaware.** —*Ant.* directly, purposefully, straightforwardly.
2. [Without consideration]—*Syn.* heedlessly, carelessly, recklessly, passionately, tumultuously, wildly, thoughtlessly, regardlessly, impulsively, inconsiderately, willfully, obtusely, purblindly, unreasonably, unreasoningly, without (rhyme or) reason, senselessly; see also **carelessly, foolishly.** —*Ant.* considerately, carefully*, prudently.

blindness, *n.* **1.** [Loss of vision]—*Syn.* sightlessness, stone blindness, purblindness, myopia, astigmatism, night *or* day *or* snow *or* moon *or* color blindness, presbyopia; see also **defect** 2.—*Ant.* sight*, vision*, seeing.
2. [Insensitivity]—*Syn.* obtuseness, apathy, inattention; see **carelessness, indifference, stupidity** 2.

blind spot, *n.*—*Syn.* obstruction, lack of perception, mote in one's eye, oversight, failing, unseen area; see also **fault** 2, **weakness** 2.

blink, *v.* **1.** [To wink rapidly]—*Syn.* flicker, bat one's eyes, flick *or* flutter one's eyelids; see **wink** 1.
2. [To squint]—*Syn.* screw up the eyes, peek, peep; see **squint.**
3. [To twinkle]—*Syn.* glimmer, sparkle, glitter, shimmer; see **shine** 1.

blink at, *v.*—*Syn.* ignore, condone, wink at; see **approve** 1, **neglect** 1.

bliss, *n.*—*Syn.* joy, rapture, ecstasy; see **happiness** 2.

blissful, *mod.*—*Syn.* joyful, delightful, ecstatic; see **happy** 1.

blister, *n.*—*Syn.* vesicle, bleb, sac, bulla, wheal, wale, weal, welt, blood blister, water blister, second-degree burn; see also **injury** 1, **sore.**

blister, *v.*—*Syn.* scald, irritate, mark; see **burn** 2, 6, **hurt** 1.

blithe, *mod.*—*Syn.* gay, joyful, cheerful; see **happy** 1.

blitz, *n.*—*Syn.* blitzkrieg, raid, lightning war *or* attack; see **attack** 1.

blitzkrieg, *n.*—*Syn.* raid, assault, (lightning) attack; see **attack** 1.

blizzard, *n.*—*Syn.* snowstorm, tempest, blast, gale; see **storm** 1.

bloc, *n.*—*Syn.* cabal, group, ring; see **faction** 1.

block, *n.* **1.** [A mass, usually with flat surfaces] —*Syn.* slab, chunk, piece, square, cake, cube, slice, segment, loaf, clod, bar, oblong, section, mill end, hunk (D); see also **brick, slab, stone.**
2. [The area between streets]—*Syn.* vicinity, square, lots; see **neighborhood.**
3. [The distance of the side of a block, sense 2] —*Syn.* street, city block, intersection; see **distance** 3.
4. [An obstruction]—*Syn.* hindrance, bar, obstacle; see **barrier.**
5. [In sports, an obstruction to a move or play] —*Syn.* charge, tackle, check, body-block, running block, cross-body block, downfield block, pick (in basketball).
6. [A massive object]—*Syn.* chunk, mass, impediment, solid, cylinder block, base; see also sense 1.
7. [A pulley]—*Syn.* sheave, wheel, hoist, rope-block, chain-block, lift.
8. [A chunk used for chopping]—*Syn.* chopping block, slab, breadboard, cheeseboard, table, butcher's block.

9. [Place of execution]—*Syn.* headsman's block, guillotine, scaffold, stake, tree, cross, gibbet; see also **gallows.**

knock someone's block off (D)—*Syn.* thrash, hit, beat up (on) (D); see **beat** 2.

block, *v.* **1.** [To impede]—*Syn.* interfere with, prevent, close off (D); see **hinder.**

2. [In sports, to impede a play]—*Syn.* throw a block, tackle, charge, check, block out, take out of play.

3. [To shape by blocking]—*Syn.* press, reshape, steam; see **form** 1.

blockade, *n.*—*Syn.* barricade, encirclement, bar; see **barrier.**

run the blockade—*Syn.* break through (a blockade), go past, overcome an obstacle; see **penetrate** 1.

blockhead, *n.*—*Syn.* nitwit, fool, imbecile; see **fool** 1.

blockhouse, *n.*—*Syn.* stockade, fort, outpost; see **fortification** 2.

block out, *v.* **1.** [To obscure]—*Syn.* conceal, screen, cover; see **hide** 1.

2. [To plan]—*Syn.* outline, sketch, chart; see **plan** 2.

block up, *v.*—*Syn.* obstruct, barricade, dam; see **bar** 1.

blond, *mod.*—*Syn.* fair, fair-skinned, pale, sallow, ash-blond, bleached, blanched, light-complexioned, washed-out, high in tone, light, pearly, platinum, gray-white, towheaded, snowy, ivory, creamy, whitish, milky, albino, lily-white, pallid, light-haired, golden-haired, fair-haired, yellow-haired, sandy-haired, faded, colorless, white-skinned; *all* (D): platinum-blond, strawberry-blond, bleached-blond, natural-blond, peroxide-blond.—*Ant.* dark*, brunet, swarthy.

blood, *n.* **1.** [Fluid in the mammalian circulatory system]—*Syn.* life's *or* heart's blood, vital fluid *or* juices, gore, sanguine fluid, hemoglobin.

2. [Lineage]—*Syn.* stock, ancestry, descent, line; see **family** 1.

bad blood—*Syn.* malice, rancor, feud; see **anger, hatred** 2.

have (someone's) blood on one's head—*Syn.* be blamable, culpable *or* responsible; see **guilty** 2.

in cold blood—*Syn.* cruelly, intentionally, indifferently; see **deliberately.**

make one's blood boil—*Syn.* disturb, infuriate, agitate; see **anger** 1.

make one's blood run cold—*Syn.* terrify, horrify, scare; see **frighten** 1.

blooded, *mod.*—*Syn.* thoroughbred, pedigreed, choice, pure-bred, fullblooded, legitimate, fancy, high-bred, aristocratic, patrician, of high rank, of good family, high-born, royal, registered, quality; see also **genuine** 1, **noble** 3.—*Ant.* bastard*, mongrel, scrub.

bloodless, *mod.* **1.** [Pale]—*Syn.* pallid, wan, anemic; see **pale** 1.

2. [Coldhearted]—*Syn.* unemotional, unfeeling, unkind; see **indifferent** 1.

3. [Listless]—*Syn.* indolent, sluggish, lazy; see **slow** 2.

bloodshed, *n.*—*Syn.* slaughter, butchery, gore; see **battle** 2, **carnage.**

bloodshot, *mod.*—*Syn.* bloody, streaked, red; see **inflamed** 2.

bloody, *mod.* **1.** [Showing blood]—*Syn.* bleeding, blood-stained, blood-spattered, gaping, unstaunched, grisly, crimson, open, wounded, dripping blood, hematic, raw, blood-soaked.—*Ant.* unhurt*, whole*, uninjured.

2. [Fiercely fought]—*Syn.* sanguinary, savage, heavy, hand-to-hand, murderous, decimating, expensive, Pyrrhic, suicidal; see also **cruel** 2, **ferocious, fierce** 1, **savage** 2.—*Ant.* easy*, light, desultory.

3. [*British* (D) Disapproved of]—*Syn.* rotten, vile, indecent; see **damned** 2.

4. [*British* (D) Very]—*Syn.* extremely, exceedingly, excessively.

bloom, *n.*—*Syn.* blossom, floweret, efflorescence; see **flower** 1.

bloom, *v.*—*Syn.* flower, effloresce, burst into bloom, open, bud, sprout, burgeon, prosper, grow, wax, bear fruit, thrive, germinate, flourish, be in health, fructify, tassel out, blossom, display petals, blow, come out in flower, put forth flowers, be in flower, be in the flowering stage.

bloomers, *n.* pl.—*Syn.* breaches, drawers, trunks; see **pants** 1, 2.

blooming, *mod.*—*Syn.* flowering, blossoming, in flower, opening, flourishing, sprouting, burgeoning, bearing fruit, germinating; see also **budding, growing.**

blossom, *n.*—*Syn.* bloom, floweret, bud; see **flower** 1.

blossom, *v.*—*Syn.* flower, blow, burst into blossom; see **bloom.**

blossoming, *n.*—*Syn.* blooming, flowering, flourishing, budding, fructification, waxing, thriving, sprouting, burgeoning, germination; see also **budding, growing.**

blot, *n.*—*Syn.* spot, stain, smudge; see **blemish.**

blot, *v.* **1.** [To stain]—*Syn.* smudge, blotch, soil; see **dirty.**

2. [To disgrace]—*Syn.* sully, smirch, tarnish; see **disgrace.**

blotch, *n.*—*Syn.* blot, stain, spot; see **blemish.**

blot out, *v.* **1.** [To mark out]—*Syn.* deface, cross *or* scratch out, delete; see **cancel** 1.

2. [To obscure]—*Syn.* darken, blur, shroud; see **shade** 2.

blotter, *n.*—*Syn.* blotting paper, (desk) pad, ink absorber, pen-wiper.

blouse, *n.*—*Syn.* (shirt)waist, pullover, turtleneck, shell, bodysuit, V-neck, man-styled blouse, overblouse, peasant blouse, slipover; see also **clothes, shirt, sweater.**

blow, *n.* **1.** [A heavy physical stroke]—*Syn.* hit, strike, buffet, swing, bump, wallop, rap, bang, whack, thwack, cuff, box, uppercut, dint, knock, clout, slam, bruise, swipe, thump, kick, stroke, buck, (rabbit) punch, jab, gouge, lunge, thrust, swat, poke, prod, slap; *all* (D): the old one-two, bat, biff, belt, cut, bop, lam, lick, haymaker, crack, smack, roundhouse, a knuckle sandwich, kayo *or* K.O., push in the kisser.

2. [A catastrophe]—*Syn.* setback, calamity, tragedy; see **disaster.**

3. [A heavy wind]—*Syn.* gale, typhoon, hurricane; see **wind** 1.

blow, *v.* **1.** [To send forth air rapidly]—*Syn.* puff, blast, pant, fan, whiff, whisk, whisper, puff away, exhale, waft, breathe, whistle.
2. [To move rapidly; *said of air*]—*Syn.* rush, whirl, stream; see **flow** 1.
3. [To carry on the wind]—*Syn.* waft, flutter, bear, whisk, drive, fling, whirl, flap, flip, wave, buffet, sweep.
4. [To play a wind instrument]—*Syn.* pipe, toot, mouth; see **play** 3.
5. [To sound when blown]—*Syn.* trumpet, vibrate, blare; see **sound** 1.
6. [To give form by inflation]—*Syn.* inflate, swell, puff *or* pump up; see **fill** 1.
7. [(D) To leave suddenly]—*Syn.* go, depart, leave town; see **leave** 1.
8. [(D) To boast]—*Syn.* brag, swagger, bluster; see **boast** 1.
9. [(D) To fail]—*Syn.* miss, flounder, miscarry; see **fail** 1.
10. [(D) To spend]—*Syn.* lay *or* pay out, waste, squander; see **spend** 1.

blow a fuse (D), *v.*—*Syn.* rant, have *or* throw a tantrum, become enraged *or* angry *or* irate; see **rage** 1.

blow in (D), *v.*—*Syn.* appear, reach, land; see **arrive** 1.

blowing, *mod.* **1.** [Agitating the air]—*Syn.* blasting, puffing, fanning, panting, whisking, breathing, gasping.
2. [Being agitated by the air]—*Syn.* fluttering, flapping, waving, streaming, whipping, drifting, tumbling, gliding, straining; see also **flying** 1.—*Ant.* standing still, falling*, hovering.

blown, *mod.*—*Syn.* buffeted, blasted, puffed, fluttered, flung, fanned, waved, flapped, whisked, whirled, flicked.—*Ant.* quiet*, still, sucked in.

blowout, *n.* **1.** [The act of exploding]—*Syn.* eruption, blast, detonation; see **explosion** 1.
2. [The result of an explosion]—*Syn.* tear, break, puncture, rupture, leak, gap, seam, flat tire, flat (D); see also **hole** 2.
3. [(D) A celebration or party]—*Syn.* riot, spree, binge (D); see **party** 1.

blow out, *v.* **1.** [To extinguish]—*Syn.* put out, dampen, snuff; see **extinguish** 1.
2. [To burst]—*Syn.* shatter, erupt, rupture; see **explode** 1.

blow up, *v.* **1.** [To fill]—*Syn.* pump *or* puff up, swell, inflate; see **fill** 1.
2. [To explode]—*Syn.* erupt, rupture, go *or* blow off; see **explode** 1.
3. [To arise]—*Syn.* start, commence, mount; see **begin** 2.
4. [To destroy with explosives]—*Syn.* bomb, dynamite, detonate; see **attack** 1, **destroy** 1.
5. [(D) To lose one's temper]—*Syn.* become angry *or* enraged, rave, lose self-control; see **rage** 1.

blubber, *n.*—*Syn.* suet, lard, tallow; see **fat.**

blue, *mod.* **1.** [One of the primary colors]—*Syn.* of the color of the sky, azure, cerulean, sky-blue.
Tints and shades of blue include the following—indigo, watchet, sapphire, sapphirine, turquoise, smalt, lapis lazuli, (Oriental) aquamarine, blue-black, blue-green; royal, Prussian, navy, Dumont's *or* king's *or* starch, powder, baby, Paris *or* cobalt, Antwerp *or* Haarlem *or* mineral, Parma, Napoleon, Chinese, robin's egg, pale, teal, sky, light, dark, deep, livid, electric, etc., blue.
2. [(D) Despondent]—*Syn.* depressed, moody, melancholy; see **sad** 1.
once in a blue moon—*Syn.* rarely, infrequently, once in a while; see **seldom** 1.
out of the blue—*Syn.* unpredicted, unforeseen, surprising; see **unexpected.**

blue, *n.* **1.** [One of the primary colors]—*Syn.* blueness, bluing, azure; see **blue, color** 1.
2. [Heavens]—*Syn.* (vault of) the sky, ether, the (wild) blue yonder (D); see **heaven** 1, **sky, space** 1.

bluebell, *n.*—*Syn.* harebell, bluebell of Scotland, campanula; see **flower** 2.

blue-blooded, *mod.*—*Syn.* pedigreed, thoroughbred, purebread; see **blooded, genuine** 1, **noble** 3.

bluejay, *n.*—*Syn.* jay, common jay, jaybird; see **bird** 1.

blues, *n.* pl. **1.** [A state of despondency; *often with* the]—*Syn.* depressed spirits, heaviness of heart, melancholy, dejection; see **gloom** 2.
2. [Rhythmic lamentation in a minor key]—*Syn.* dirge, lament, torch song (D); see **music** 1.

bluff, *mod.*—*Syn.* outspoken, crusty, hearty; see **abrupt** 2, **rude** 1, 2.

bluff, *n.* **1.** [A bank]—*Syn.* cliff, precipice, steep; see **hill, mountain** 1.
2. [A trick]—*Syn.* ruse, deception, delusion; see **trick** 1.

bluff, *v.*—*Syn.* fool, mislead, trick; see **deceive.**

bluing, *n.*—*Syn.* whitener, bleach, rinse; see **solution** 2.

bluish, *mod.*—*Syn.* somewhat blue, pale blue, blue-gray; see **blue** 1.

blunder, *n.*—*Syn.* mistake, lapse, oversight; see **error** 1.

blunderbuss, *n.* **1.** [Gun]—*Syn.* musket, firearm, weapon; see **gun** 2.
2. [Dunce]—*Syn.* dolt, simpleton, moron; see **fool** 1.

blunt, *mod.* **1.** [Dull]—*Syn.* unsharpened, unpointed, round; see **dull** 1.
2. [Abrupt]—*Syn.* brusque, curt, bluff; see **abrupt** 2.

blur, *v.* **1.** [To dim]—*Syn.* obscure, blur, blear; see **shade** 2.
2. [To stain]—*Syn.* blemish, smudge, blot; see **dirty.**

blurt out, *v.*—*Syn.* speak unthinkingly, jabber, gush; see **talk** 1, **utter.**

blush, *v.*—*Syn.* change color, flush, redden, turn red, mantle, glow, have rosy cheeks, have heightened color.

blushing, *mod.*—*Syn.* coloring, mantling, suffusing, dyeing, staining, reddening, turning red *or* scarlet, flushing, glowing, changing color, burning; *all* (D): red as fire, red as a rose, rosy-red, with burning cheeks; see also **ashamed.**

bluster, *v.*—*Syn.* rant, rave, brag, crow, gloat, swagger, swell, vapor, strut, roister, bully, brazen, brawl, hector, badger, bulldoze, talk big, give oneself airs; *all* (D): ride the high horse, shoot off one's mouth, show off, yap, blow off; see also **boast** 1.

boar, *n.* —*Syn.* male hog, sire, pig; see **hog** 1.

board, *n.* **1.** [A piece of thin lumber]—*Syn.* plank, lath, strip; see **lumber**.

2. [Meals]—*Syn.* food, mess, fare, provisions, keep, victuals, eats (D); see also **food, meal** 2.

3. [A body of men having specific responsibilities] —*Syn.* jury, council, cabinet; see **committee**.

across the board—*Syn.* general, universal, affecting everyone; see **common** 5.

go by the board—*Syn.* be lost, go, vanish; see **fail** 1.

on board—*Syn.* present, in transit, en route; see **aboard, shipped**.

board, *v.* **1.** [Cover]—*Syn.* plank, tile, paper; see **cover** 1.

2. [Go aboard]—*Syn.* mount, embark, embus, entrain, enplane, put to sea, cast off, go on board ship; see also **climb** 2, **leave** 1, **rise** 1.—*Ant.* leave*, disembark, go ashore.

3. [Take care of]—*Syn.* lodge, room, put up, harbor, bed, accommodate, board and room, care for, let crash (D); see also **feed.**—*Ant.* neglect*, reject, starve.

boarder, *n.* —*Syn.* (paying) guest, diner, patron, star boarder (D).

boast, *n.* —*Syn.* brag, vaunt, source of pride, gasconade, pretension, self-satisfaction, avowal, bravado.

boast, *v.* **1.** [To brag]—*Syn.* gloat, triumph, swagger, bully, exult, crow, show off, vaunt, swell, brag, strut, bluff, flaunt, bluster, swash, vapor, gasconade, flourish; *all* (D): blow, sound off, give a good account of oneself, crow, act up, hug *or* flatter *or* congratulate oneself, pat oneself on the back, puff, oneself up, blow one's own trumpet, make the eagle scream, attract attention, bunch the hits, draw the long bow, give oneself airs.—*Ant.* apologize*, humble oneself, admit defeat.

2. [To have to one's credit]—*Syn.* possess, have in keeping, claim; see **own** 1.

boastful, *mod.* —*Syn.* bragging, pretentious, bombastic; see **egotistic** 2.

boat, *n.* —*Syn.* bark, sailboat, yacht, steamboat, craft, bottom, hulk; see **ship**.

Types of small boats include the following—rowboat, shell, scull, kayak, dugout, canoe, scow, jolly boat, raft, pinnace, launch, cockboat, motorboat, shallop, dory, Johnboat, galiot, catboat, tartan, sharp, pulk, hydrofoil, speedboat, yawl, iceboat, sloop, cutter, ketch, schooner, gig, lifeboat, barge, cockleshell, wherry, punt, outrigger, dinghy, bateau, pirogue, racer, hydroplane, catamaran, skiff, umiak, gondola, proa, longboat, coracle, war canoe, clam boat, Baltimore buckeye, settee, bombard, flatboat, collapsible boat, sponson, sharpie, paper boat, river boat, canal boat.

in the same boat (D)—*Syn.* in unison, in the same *or* a similar situation *or* condition, concurrently; see **together** 2.

miss the boat (D)—*Syn.* miss, fall short, neglect; see **fail** 1.

rock the boat (D)—*Syn.* upset, disturb, distort; see **confuse**.

boating, *n.* —*Syn.* rowing, sculling, canoeing, paddling, drifting, trawling, yachting; see also **sailing** 1.

bob, *n.* **1.** [A jerky motion]—*Syn.* duck, nod, weave, bow, genuflection, quaver, wobble, twist, inclination, jerk, motion, gesture, dance, quiver, falter, sway, swing, fall.

2. [A style of haircut]—*Syn.* boyish *or* Dutch bob, feather cut, long bob; see **haircut**.

bobbed, *mod.* —*Syn.* clipped, shortened, curtailed, cut, coiffed.

bobcat, *n.* —*Syn.* wildcat, lynx, *Lynx rufus* (Latin), catamount, painter, mountain cat; see also **cat** 2.

bobsled, *n.* —*Syn.* sleigh, coaster, toboggan; see **sled** 1, 2.

bobwhite, *n.* —*Syn.* quail, partridge, *Colinus* (Latin); see **bird** 1.

bodiless, *mod.* —*Syn.* incorporeal, insubstantial, spiritual; see **immaterial** 2.

bodily, *mod.* **1.** [Concerning the body]—*Syn.* carnal, fleshly, corporeal, gross, somatic, hylic, solid, physical, unspiritual, tangible, material, substantial, human, natural, normal, organic; see also **biological, physical** 1, **real** 2.

2. [As a whole]—*Syn.* entirely, totally, absolutely; see **completely**.

body, *n.* **1.** [The human organism]—*Syn.* (corporeal) frame, physique, form, figure, shape, make, carcass, mortal part, build, make-up, tenement of clay (D).

2. [A corpse]—*Syn.* cadaver, *corpus delicti* (Latin), dust, clay, carcass, dead body, relics, the dead, the deceased, mummy, skeleton, ashes, carrion, organic remains, bones, remains; *all* (D): cold meat, stiff, goner.

3. [The torso]—*Syn.* trunk, figure, form, shape, build.

4. [The central portion of an object]—*Syn.* chassis, basis, groundwork, frame, fuselage, assembly, trunk, hull, bed, box, substructure, skeleton, scaffold, anatomy; *both* (D): bones, guts; see also **essence** 1, **foundation** 2.

5. [The central portion of a composition]—*Syn.* dissertation, discourse, thesis, treatise, argument, material, heart, evidence, demonstration, exposition, gist (D); see also **basis** 1, **essence** 1, **theory** 1. —*Ant.* introduction*, preface, preamble.

6. [Individuals having an organization]—*Syn.* society, group, party; see **organization** 3.

7. [A unified or organized mass]—*Syn.* reservoir, supply, variety; see **collection** 2.

keep body and soul together—*Syn.* stay alive, endure, earn a living; see **survive** 1.

bog, *n.* —*Syn.* marsh, lowland, peat bog; see **swamp.**

bogey, *n.* —*Syn.* goblin, spook, phantom; see **ghost** 1.

Bohemian, *mod.* —*Syn.* hippie, nonconformist, unorthodox; see **beat** 2, **unusual** 2.

Bohemian, *n.* —*Syn.* hippie, nonconformist, iconoclast; see **beatnik.**

boil, *v.* **1.** [To subject to boiling]—*Syn.* steep, seethe, stew; see **cook.**

2. [To continue at the boiling point]—*Syn.* bubble, simmer, steam, parboil, boil over, evaporate; see also **cook.**

3. [To seethe]—*Syn.* effervesce, gurgle, percolate, surge, tumble, burble; see also **bubble.**

4. [To be angry]—*Syn.* fume, sputter, quiver with rage; see **rage** 1.

boil away, *v.* —*Syn.* steam, vaporize, dissipate; see **evaporate** 1.

boil down, *v.* —*Syn.* condense, summarize, sum up; see **decrease** 2.

boiled, *mod.* —*Syn.* parboiled, stewed, steeped, sodden, cooked.

boiler, *n.* —*Syn.* double boiler, evaporator, hot-water cooker; see **pan, pot** 1.

boiling, *mod.* **1.** [Cooking]—*Syn.* stewing, steeping, percolating, steaming, bubbling, seething, simmering, evaporating, distilling, boiling over; see also **cooking** 1.
2. [Hot]—*Syn.* warm, scorching, torrid; see **hot** 1.
3. [Angry]—*Syn.* raging, fuming, infuriated; see **angry.**

boisterous, *mod.* —*Syn.* tumultuous, uproarious, noisy; see **loud** 2, **rude** 2.

bold, *mod.* **1.** [Courageous]—*Syn.* intrepid, fearless, daring; see **brave** 1.
2. [Impertinent]—*Syn.* brazen, audacious, presumptuous; see **rude** 2.
3. [Prominent]—*Syn.* strong, clear, plain; see **bright** 2, **definite** 2.

boldly, *mod.* **1.** [*Said of animate beings*]—*Syn.* impetuously, headlong, intrepidly, fearlessly, with hardihood, recklessly, courageously, dauntlessly, daringly, forwardly, venturesomely, valiantly, stoutly, resolutely, brazenly, audaciously, saucily, firmly.—*Ant.* cowardly*, fearfully, cravenly.
2. [*Said of inanimate objects*]—*Syn.* prominently, conspicuously, saliently, sharply, clearly, plainly, openly, abruptly, steeply, eminently, vividly, strongly, palpably, commandingly, compellingly, showily.—*Ant.* obscurely*, inconspicuously, unobtrusively.

boldness, *n.* —*Syn.* audacity, hardihood, self-reliance; see **courage** 1.

Bolshevik, *n.* **1.** [An adherent of the Bolsheviki] —*Syn.* Marxist, revolutionary, Soviet, Communist, Socialist, Marxian socialist, collectivist, Bolshevist, *both* (D): Commie, Red.
2. [A radical; *usually lower case*]—*Syn.* revolutionary, extremist, proletarian; see **radical, rebel** 1.

Bolshevism, *n.* —*Syn.* collectivism, socialism, Marxism; see **communism.**

bolster, *v.* —*Syn.* prop, hold up, reinforce, sustain; see **support** 1, 2.

bolt, *n.* **1.** [A rod used for fastening]—*Syn.* staple, brad, nut, skewer, peg, dowel, rivet, pin, spike, stud, coupling, kingbolt, key, lag screw, pin, pipe; see also **nail, screw.**
2. [A roll of goods or paper]—*Syn.* cylinder, package, spindle, curl, coil, spiral, twist.
3. [Lightning]—*Syn.* discharge, fulguration, stroke *or* sheet of lightning, thunderbolt, flash, stroke, shock.

bomb, *n.* —*Syn.* weapon, high explosive, charge; see **explosive, mine** 2, **shell** 2.
Types of bombs include the following—incendiary, magnesium, high explosive, demolition, glider, jet-propulsion, time, six-ton, chain detonation, smoke, delayed-action, cyanide, parachute, antipersonnel bomb; 50-ton bomb, 100-pound bomb, 500-pound bomb, etc.; atom(ic) bomb *or* A-bomb, cobalt bomb *or* C-bomb, hydrogen bomb *or* H-bomb, neutron bomb, rack of bombs, cluster bomb unit *or* CBU, salvo of bombs, torpedo, depth charge, cherry bomb, hand grenade; *all* (D): blockbuster, ash can, pineapple, potato masher, Molotov cocktail, stink bomb.

bomb, *v.* —*Syn.* shell, bombard, torpedo, napalm, blow up, wipe out, subject to bombing (runs), blast, attack from the air, zero in on (D), rain destruction, raid, dive-bomb, skip-bomb, mass-bomb, precision-bomb, lay an egg (D); see also **attack** 1, **destroy** 1.

bombard, *v.* —*Syn.* besiege, assault, blast; see **attack** 1, **bomb.**

bombardment, *n.* —*Syn.* assault, shelling, barrage; see **attack** 1, **fire** 3.

bombast, *n.* —*Syn.* rant, fustian, drivel; see **nonsense** 1.

bombastic, *mod.* —*Syn.* pompous, declamatory, ostentatious; see **oratorical.**

bomber, *n.* —*Syn.* bombing plane, heavy *or* medium *or* light bomber, aerial attack plane; see **plane** 3.

bombing, *n.* —*Syn.* bombardment, shelling, air attack; see **attack** 1.
Methods of bombing include—high-altitude bombing, precision bombing, saturation bombing, carpet bombing, wave bombing, dive bombing, skip bombing, low-level bombing, nuisance bombing, mass bombing, tactical bombing, pattern bombing, around-the-clock bombing, A-bombing *or* atomic bombing, napalming, H-bombing, hedgehopping (D).

bond, *n.* **1.** [A physical tie]—*Syn.* shackle, linkage, chain; see **band** 2, **link, rope, wire** 1.
2. [A mental or emotional tie]—*Syn.* attachment, link, union, obligation, connection, relation, affinity, affiliation, bond of union, restraint; see also **duty** 2, **friendship** 1, **marriage** 2, **relationship.**
3. [A secured debenture]—*Syn.* security, warranty, debenture, certificate, registered bond, coupon bond, zero coupon bond, gold bond, government bond, municipal bond, long *or* short term bond, junk bond (D).
4. [Bail]—*Syn.* surety, guaranty, warrant; see **bail** 2.

bondage, *n.* —*Syn.* servitude, thralldom, subjugation; see **slavery** 1.

bonded, *mod.* **1.** [*Said of persons*]—*Syn.* shackled, fettered, manacled, chained, bound, confined, restrained, articled, debentured.—*Ant.* free*, liberated, independent.
2. [*Said of stored goods or storehouses*]—*Syn.* insured, certified, warranted; see **guaranteed, protected.**

bone, *n.* —*Syn.* skeletal substance, osseous matter, bony process, bone cartilage *or* ossein.
Bones of the human body include the following —cranium *or* skull, frontal, temporal, parietal, occipital, zygomatic *or* cheekbone, sphenoid, ethmoid, vomer *or* nasal bones, mandible *or* jawbone, maxilla, stapes *or* stirrup bone, spinal column *or* vertebrae *or* backbone, atlas, axis, coccyx, costal *or* ribcage, clavicle *or* collarbone, scapula *or* shoulder blade, humerus, radius, ulna, carpal, metacarpal, phalanges, pelvis, ischium, ilium *or* hipbone, femur *or* thighbone, patella *or* kneecap, tibia *or* shinbone, fibula, talus, tarsal, metatarsal.
feel in one's bones—*Syn.* be convinced, sure *or* positive; see **certain** 1.

have a bone to pick—*Syn.* have a complaint *or* quarrel, be angry, express an objection; see **complain** 1.
make no bones—*Syn.* confess, reveal, expose; see **admit** 2.

bonfire, *n.*—*Syn.* campfire, blaze, signal fire; see **fire** 1, 2.

bonnet, *n.*—*Syn.* hood, sunbonnet, cap; see **hat.**

bonus, *n.*—*Syn.* gratuity, reward, special *or* additional compensation; see **gift** 1, **tip** 2.

bony, *mod.* **1.** [Skeletal]—*Syn.* anatomical, osseous, formative; see **fundamental** 1, **structural.**
2. [Thin]—*Syn.* emaciated, skinny, scrawny; see **thin** 2.

book, *n.* **1.** [A bound volume]—*Syn.* publication, work, volume, booklet, paperback, chapbook, tome, pamphlet, work, reprint, preprint, offprint, hardcover, softcover, text, edition, brochure, folio, copy, opuscule, *vade mecum, opus* (both Latin), monograph, writing, codex, scroll, incunabulum, periodical, octavo, magazine, quarto.
Kinds of books include the following—manual, handbook, enchiridion, children's *or* juvenile book, atlas, cookbook, guidebook, story book, song book, trade book, reference book, fiction, nonfiction, textbook, workbook, hymnbook, bible *or* Bible, treatise, libretto, tract, thesis, portfolio, album, dissertation.
2. [A division of a literary composition]—*Syn.* canto, chapter, part; see **division** 3.
3. [An account of transactions]—*Syn.* record, register, roster; see **list.**
bring to book—*Syn.* reprimand, call to account, test; see **examine** 2.
by the book—*Syn.* according to the rules, properly, correctly; see **accurately, well** 3.
in one's book—*Syn.* in one's opinion, for oneself, to one's mind; see **personally** 2.
in one's good book(s) (D)—*Syn.* liked, favored, approved; see **honored.**
in the book (D)—*Syn.* practiced, done, established, prevalent; see **known** 2.
know like a book—*Syn.* understand, comprehend, be aware of; see **know** 1.
make (a) book (D)—*Syn.* bet, risk, wager; see **gamble** 1.
one for the books (D)—*Syn.* source of amazement, shock, novelty; see **surprise** 2.
on the books—*Syn.* listed, noted, set down; see **recorded.**
throw the book at (D)—*Syn.* the maximum punishment, charge with every possible offense, be overzealous with; see **accuse.**

book, *v.*—*Syn.* charge, take into custody, prefer charges; see **accuse, arrest** 1.

bookcase, *n.*—*Syn.* bookshelf, cabinet, sectional bookcase, secretary; see also **furniture.**

booked, *mod.* **1.** [Scheduled]—*Syn.* engaged, contracted, due, obligated, billed, advertised; see also **proposed.**
2. [Arrested]—*Syn.* charged, taken into custody, jailed; see **accused, under arrest.**

bookish, *mod.*—*Syn.* scholarly, academic, erudite; see **learned** 1.

bookkeeper, *n.*—*Syn.* controller *or* comptroller, actuary, auditor; see **accountant** 2, **clerk.**

bookkeeping, *n.*—*Syn.* accountancy, auditing, recording, accounting.

book review, *n.*—*Syn.* critical review, notice, blurb (D); see **review** 2.

bookworm, *n.*—*Syn.* savant, book lover, bibliophile; see **scholar** 2.

boom, *n.* **1.** [A loud noise]—*Syn.* roar, blast, blare; see **noise** 1.
2. [Sudden increase, especially sudden prosperity]—*Syn.* rush, growth, inflation; see **increase** 1.

boom, *v.* **1.** [To make a loud sound]—*Syn.* roar, reverberate, thunder; see **sound** 1.
2. [To increase rapidly]—*Syn.* prosper, expand, swell; see **grow** 1.
lower the boom (on) (D)—*Syn.* take action *or* move (against), beat, overcome; see **act** 1, **attack** 2.

boon, *n.*—*Syn.* benefit, good fortune, help; see **blessing** 2.

boor, *n.*—*Syn.* peasant, yokel, (back) countryman, rustic, lout, clown, (country) bumpkin, churl, oaf, lubber, swain, bear, looby, vulgarian, plowman, lumpkin, chuff, gaffer, cad, hobnail; *all* (D): hick, rube, clodpole, hayseed, clod, clodhopper; see also **farmer, laborer.**

boorish, *mod.*—*Syn.* awkward, clumsy, churlish; see **rude** 1, 2.

boost, *n.* **1.** [Aid]—*Syn.* assistance, help, helping hand; see **aid** 1.
2. [An increase]—*Syn.* addition, advance, hike (D); see **increase** 1.

boost, *v.* **1.** [To raise]—*Syn.* shove, hoist, advance; see **raise** 1.
2. [To promote]—*Syn.* encourage, support, advertise; see **promote** 1, 2.
3. [To increase]—*Syn.* raise, heighten, expand; see **increase** 1.

booster (D), *n.*—*Syn.* supporter, promoter, sponsor; see **patron** 1.

boot, *n.* **1.** [*British.* A shoe]—*Syn.* oxford, leather shoe, footwear; see **shoe.**
2. [High footwear, often of rubber]—*Syn.* hip-boot, bootie, wader, galoshes, laced boot, high shoe, jackboot, hiking boot, cowboy boot, climbing boot, riding boot, ski boot, combat boot, mukluk.
3. [(D) A kick]—*Syn.* drive, shove, knock; see **kick** 1.
bet your boots (D)—*Syn.* be certain, rely on it, trust in it; see **depend on.**
die with one's boots on (D)—*Syn.* die in action *or* suddenly *or* unexpectedly, keep going, die fighting; see **die** 1.
lick the boots of (D)—*Syn.* do service for, fawn over, be a pawn *or* lackey for; see **obey** 1, **serve** 2.

booth, *n.*—*Syn.* stall, counter, nook, corner, carrel, pew, berth, cote, compartment, hutch, shed, manager, cubbyhole, coop, pen, hut, enclosure, stand, dispensary, cubicle, repository, box.

bootleg, *mod.*—*Syn.* illegal, unlawful, contraband; see **illegal.**

bootlegger, *n.*—*Syn.* illicit liquor dealer, racketeer, whiskey peddler, moonshiner, rumrunner (D).

booty, *n.*—*Syn.* plunder, spoil, winnings, stolen goods, prey, (ill-gotten) gains, seizure, prize, haul, pillage; *all* (D): swag, pickings, loot, boodle, takings, take, hot stuff.

booze (D), *n.* —*Syn.* liquor, alcohol, whiskey; see **drink** 2.

border, *n.* **1.** [Edge]—*Syn.* hem, end, trim; see **decoration** 2, **edge** 1, **fringe** 2, **rim, trimming** 1.
2. [Boundary]—*Syn.* frontier, outpost, perimeter; see **boundary, edge** 1.

border, *v.* —*Syn.* be adjacent to, adjoin, abut (on); see **join** 3.

bordering, *mod.* —*Syn.* rimming, bounding, neighboring, fringing, edging, lining, conjoining, verging, connecting, on the edge (of), on the confines (of); see **near** 1.

border on, *v.* —*Syn.* lie next to, abut, touch; see **join** 3.

bore, *n.* —*Syn.* nuisance, pest, tiresome *or* tedious person; see **trouble** 2.

bore, *v.* **1.** [To pierce by rotary motion]—*Syn.* drill, ream, perforate; see **penetrate** 1.
2. [To weary]—*Syn.* fatigue, tire, put to sleep; see **weary** 1.

bored, *mod.* —*Syn.* wearied, fatigued, jaded, dull, irked, annoyed, *ennuyé* (French); *all* (D): bored to death, in a rut, sick and tired, bored stiff *or* silly, fed up; see also **tired.**—*Ant.* exhilarated, excited*, thrilled.

boredom, *n.* —*Syn.* ennui, lack of interest, *taedium vitae* (Latin), tiresomeness, apathy, wearisomeness, doldrums, listlessness, irksomeness; see also **dullness** 1, **indifference** 1, **monotony** 1.

boring, *mod.* —*Syn.* tedious, stupid, monotonous; see **dull** 3, 4.

born, *mod.* —*Syn.* intrinsic, innate, inherent; see **natural** 1.

borough, *n.* —*Syn.* precinct, ward, district; see **area** 2, **division** 6, **government** 2.

borrow, *v.* **1.** [To receive temporarily]—*Syn.* accept the loan of, obtain the use of, negotiate a loan for, take a loan, go into debt, get temporary use of, use, pledge, rent, hire, acquire, obtain, give a note for; *all* (D): touch (for), sponge (on *or* off of), hit up *or* for, bum, beg, cadge, chisel, mooch, borrow from Peter to pay Paul.—*Ant.* lend*, loan, give back.
2. [To adopt]—*Syn.* appropriate, assume, make one's own; see **adopt** 2.

borrowed, *mod.* —*Syn.* appropriated, taken, acquired, assumed, adopted, hired, plagiarized, imported, cultivated, imitated; see also **rented, stolen.** —*Ant.* owned*, possessed, titular.

borrowing, *n.* —*Syn.* renting, hiring, accepting a loan of, assuming, taking, adopting, appropriating, imitating, plagiarizing, utilizing, importing; see also **using.**—*Ant.* loan*, loaning, pawning.

bosom, *n.* **1.** [The breast]—*Syn.* breasts, bust, teats; see **breast** 2.
2. [The chest]—*Syn.* ribs, rib cage, thorax; see **chest** 2.
3. [One's inner self]—*Syn.* feelings, thoughts, conscience; see **breast** 3, **mind** 1, **thought** 2.

boss, *n.* —*Syn.* supervisor, manager, man in charge; see **administrator, foreman.**

Boston, *n.* —*Syn.* capital of Massachusetts, Athens of America; *all* (D): the Hub, City of Baked Beans, the Bay Horse, City of Notions, Puritan City, home of the bean and the cod.

botanical, *mod.* —*Syn.* concerning plants, vegetable, floral, arboreal, herbaceous, morphological, cytological, phytogenetical, paleobotanical, taxonomical, phytogeographical, physiological, agricultural; see also **biological.**

botany, *n.* —*Syn.* phytology, natural history, study of flora *or* vegetation *or* plant life.
Divisions of botany include the following—morphology, anatomy, cytology, physiology, paleobotany, horticulture, ecology, taxonomy, phytogeography, pathology, (phyto-)genetics, applied *or* economic botany; see also **biology, science** 1.

botch, *v.* —*Syn.* bungle, spoil, mar, ruin, wreck, mutilate, fumble, distort, blunder, mishandle, do clumsily, muddle, make a mess *or* hash of, trip, flounder, err, fall down, be mistaken, misapply, misjudge, misconjecture, mismanage, miscalculate, misconstrue, misreckon, miscompute, misestimate, execute clumsily, do unskillfully, stumble; *all* (D): put one's foot in it, pull a boner, goof (up), butcher, screw *or* mess *or* trip up, muff, flub (one's lines), bosh, put out of whack; see also **destroy** 1, **fail** 1. —*Ant.* succeed*, fix*, do well.

both, *mod.* —*Syn.* the two, (both) together, the one and the other, the pair *or* couple, one as well as the other.—*Ant.* one*, either*, each (alone).

bother, *n.* **1.** [Worry]—*Syn.* vexation, distress, anxiety; see **care** 2.
2. [A cause of worry]—*Syn.* problem, concern, care; see **difficulty** 1, 2, **trouble** 2.

bother, *v.* **1.** [To take trouble]—*Syn.* put oneself out, fret, go out of one's way, make a fuss about, fuss (over), take pains, make an effort, exert *or* concern oneself, be concerned (about), worry (about); see also **try** 1, **worry** 2.
2. [To give trouble]—*Syn.* plague, vex, annoy, perplex, pester, molest, irritate, irk, provoke, spite, insult, harass, chagrin, heckle, exacerbate, aggravate, badger, cross, discommode, discompose, mortify, goad, intrude upon, disquiet, pursue, hinder, impede, carp at, nag, harry, scare, exasperate, bore, afflict, taunt, torment, torture, bedevil, browbeat, tease, tantalize; *all* (D): ride, rub the wrong way, pick on, nag, needle, drive one nuts, get one's goat, make one's blood boil, put one's nose out of joint, put one's fur up, kick up a row, bug, get on one's case, get under one's skin; see also sense 3, **disturb** 2.—*Ant.* help*, please, delight.
3. [To be disturbing]—*Syn.* disturb, distress, upset, hurt, disgust, embarrass, pain , grieve, displease, disconcert, be the matter, trouble, grate on, agitate, nibble *or* gnaw at, worry, carp, inconvenience, perturb; *all* (D): bug, get in one's hair, give one a pain, jangle the nerves, gripe, put out, go against one's grain, jar on, get on one's nerves; see also sense 2.

bothered, *mod.* —*Syn.* harassed, vexed, annoyed, troubled, irked, chagrined, agitated, disturbed, disconcerted, disquieted, bugged (D); see also **troubled** 1.

bothersome, *mod.* —*Syn.* vexatious, vexing, troublesome; see **disturbing.**

bottle, *n.* —*Syn.* flask, flagon, decanter, demijohn, cruet, jug, urn, canteen, cruse, jar, ewer, gourd, carafe, hip flask, vial *or* phial, caster, vacuum bottle, glass, dead soldier (empty liquor bottle) (D); see also **flask.**

hit the bottle—*Syn.* get drunk, imbibe, become an alcoholic; see **drink** 2.

bottle up, *v.*—*Syn.* contain, check, curb; see **include** 1, **restrain** 1, **restrict** 2.

bottom, *n.* **1.** [The lowest part]—*Syn.* underside, nether portion, base, nadir, foot, pediment, depths, bed, floor, lowest *or* deepest part, sole, ground. —*Ant.* top*, peak, pinnacle.

2. [The foundation]—*Syn.* base, basis, substructure; see **foundation** 2.

at bottom—*Syn.* fundamentally, basically, actually; see **really** 1.

be at the bottom—*Syn.* originate, be the reason for, activate; see **cause** 2.

bet one's bottom dollar (D)—*Syn.* bet, risk, wager; see **gamble** 1.

bottomless, *mod.*—*Syn.* deep, unfathomable, boundless; see **infinite** 1.

bottom line (D), *n.* **1.** [Profits or losses]—*Syn.* net income, net loss, net profits; see **income, profit** 2, **loss** 3.

2. [Final decision]—*Syn.* conclusion, determination, last word (D); see **end** 2.

bottoms, *n.* pl.—*Syn.* low land, marsh, bottomland; see **swamp.**

bough, *n.*—*Syn.* limb, arm, fork; see **branch** 2.

bought, *mod.*—*Syn.* purchased, procured, budgeted (for), requisitioned, paid for, on order, to be delivered, contracted for, included in the purchase; see also **acquired** 1, 2, **ordered** 1.—*Ant.* sold*, pawned, given away.

boulder, *n.*—*Syn.* (field)stone, slab, crag; see **rock** 2.

boulevard, *n.*—*Syn.* street, avenue, highway; see **road** 1.

bounce, *v.* **1.** [To rebound]—*Syn.* ricochet, recoil, carom, glance (off), spring (back), leap, hop, skip, bob, buck, jump, bound, jerk up and down, fly *or* bounce *or* snap *or* kick back, boomerang, backlash, jounce; see also **jump** 3.

2. [To move suddenly]—*Syn.* spring, hop, leap, bolt, vault, bound; see also **jump** 1.

3. [(D) To discharge from one's employ *or* presence *or* establishment]—*Syn.* eject, oust, fire (D); see **dismiss** 1, 2.

bound, *mod.* **1.** [Literally confined in bonds] —*Syn.* fettered, shackled, trussed up, manacled, enchained, handcuffed, hobbled, captive, trammeled, pinioned, pilloried, muzzled, in leash, tied (up), harnessed, bound hand and foot, lashed fast, swathed, pinned *or* pegged down, tethered, picketed, secured, roped, gagged; *both* (D): loaded with irons, (roped and) hogtied.—*Ant.* free*, unrestrained, loose.

2. [Figuratively constrained]—*Syn.* impelled, compelled, obliged, obligated, restrained, under compulsion, constrained, forced, coerced, driven, pressed, urged, necessitated, under necessity, made, having no alternative, required, bounden. —*Ant.* unconstrained, free*, independent.

bound, *v.* **1.** [To move in leaps]—*Syn.* jump, spring, vault; see **jump** 1.

2. [To rebound]—*Syn.* bounce, ricochet, recoil; see **bounce** 1, **jump** 3.

3. [To set limits]—*Syn.* restrict, confine, circumscribe; see **define** 1.

out of bounds—*Syn.* off limits, not permitted, restricted; see **illegal.**

boundary, *n.*—*Syn.* outline, border, verge, rim, beginning, end, terminal, confine, bounds, radius, terminus, landmark, march, extremity, fence, compass, side, purlieus, hem, frame, skirt, line of demarcation, termination, margin, line, barrier, frontier, outpost, perimeter, extent, circumference, horizon, periphery, fringe, pale, mark, confines, limit, borderland; see also **edge** 1.—*Ant.* surface, area*, interior.

bounded, *mod.*—*Syn.* limited, edged, enclosed, defined, delimited, circumscribed, rimmed, encircled, hedged *or* hemmed *or* ringed *or* fenced *or* walled in, bordered, confined, surrounded, brimmed, boundaried, enveloped, encompassed, compassed about, girdled, belted, girt, flanked, neighbored, adjacent, next (to), contiguous, skirted, fringed, encroached upon, clasped, restricted. —*Ant.* unlimited*, ill-defined, unbounded.

boundless, *mod.* **1.** [Immense]—*Syn.* great, tremendous, vast; see **large** 1.

2. [Infinite]—*Syn.* limitless, endless, unlimited, illimitable; see **infinite** 1.

bound to, *v.*—*Syn.* certain *or* sure *or* destined to; see **inevitable.**

bountiful, *mod.*—*Syn.* bounteous, abundant, lavish; see **plentiful** 1, 2.

bounty, *n.* **1.** [A recompense]—*Syn.* prize, premium, bonus; see **pay** 1, 2.

2. [Liberality]—*Syn.* openhandedness, freedom, hospitality; see **generosity** 1.

bouquet, *n.* **1.** [Flowers]—*Syn.* nosegay, bunch of flowers, boutonniere, garland, vase (of flowers), flower arrangement, boughpot, wreath, spray; see also **wreath.**

2. [Fragrance]—*Syn.* aroma, scent, odor; see **smell** 1.

bourgeois, *mod.*—*Syn.* middle-class, commonplace, conventional; see **common** 1.

bout, *n.*—*Syn.* match, set-to, round; see **fight** 1.

bovine, *mod.*—*Syn.* slow, stolid, dense; see **dull** 3.

bovine, *n.*—*Syn.* cow, bull, calf; see **cow.**

bow, *n.*—*Syn.* longbow, self-bow, union bow, crossbow, single-piece bow, back bow, stone-bow, arbalist *or* arbalester, arblast; see also **weapon** 1.

bow, *n.* **1.** [Front of a boat]—*Syn.* forepart, bowsprit, prow, head, stem, fore; see also **front** 1.

2. [A bend from the waist]—*Syn.* nod, bend, salaam, curtsey, obeisance, kowtow, bowing and scraping.

take a bow—*Syn.* accept praise, be congratulated, feel honored; see **bow** 1.

bow, *v.* **1.** [To bend]—*Syn.* curtsey, do obeisance, stoop, dip, drop, hunch (over), incline, debase (oneself), bob, duck, dip, cower, kowtow, salaam. —*Ant.* rise*, tower, become erect.

2. [To submit]—*Syn.* bend, surrender, acquiesce, capitulate; see **yield** 1.

bowels, *n.* pl.—*Syn.* viscera, entrails, guts (D); see **abdomen, insides.**

move one's bowels—*Syn.* defecate, go to the bathroom, secrete; see **excrete.**

bower, *n.* —*Syn.* nook, dingle, boscage, dell, grove, thicket, croft, copse, coppice, grotto, cell, summerhouse, seclusion, shady retreat *or* lair *or* den, arbor, chamber; see also **forest, garden, refuge** 1, **retreat** 2.

bowing, *mod.* —*Syn.* curtseying, bending, inclining, making *or* doing obeisance, stooping, genuflecting, dipping, honoring; *both* (D): kowtowing, dropping.

bowl, *n.* —*Syn.* vessel, tureen, stoup, pot, porringer, saucer, crock, jar, urn, pitcher, basin, casserole, boat; see also **china, container, dish.**

bowl, *v.* **1.** [To play at bowls]—*Syn.* play ninepins *or* tenpins *or* duckpins *or* candlepins, roll, play at bowling *or* with bowls.

2. [In cricket, to pitch]—*Syn.* hurl, throw, fling; *both* (D): slow-bowl, fast-bowl; see **throw** 1.

bowlegged, *mod.* —*Syn.* misshapen, bowleg, curved; see **bent.**

bowling, *n.* —*Syn.* bowls, duckpins, candlepins, ninepins, tenpins, bocce ball, skittles, American bowls, kegling (D).

bow out, *v.* —*Syn.* withdraw, resign, quit; see **abandon** 1.

box, *n.* —*Syn.* receptacle, crate, carton; see **case** 7.

in a box—*Syn.* disturbed, worried, in difficulty; see **in trouble** 1, **troubled** 1.

box, *v.* **1.** [To enclose in a box]—*Syn.* confine, package, crate; see **pack** 2.

2. [To fight for sport]—*Syn.* spar, punch, slug, hit; *all* (D): cross gloves, mix (punches), scrap, swap punches, duke.

boxcar, *n.* —*Syn.* freight *or* refrigerator *or* automobile car, caboose, freighter; see **car** 2.

boxer, *n.* —*Syn.* pugilist, fighter, fisticuffer; see **fighter** 2.

boxing, *n.* —*Syn.* pugilism, fisticuffs, the manly art, the fights, sparring; *both* (D): fight racket, glove game.

boy, *n.* —*Syn.* lad, youth, stripling, fellow, schoolboy, master, cadet, youngster, whippersnapper, male child, junior, little gentleman; *all* (D): little guy, small fry, puppy; see also **child.**

boycott, *v.* —*Syn.* withhold patronage, hold aloof from, ostracize; see **avoid, strike** 2.

boyfriend, *n.* —*Syn.* date, young man, beau, escort, companion, gentleman friend, steady, lover, inamorato, sweetheart, gentleman caller, suitor, flame, paramour, truelove, wooer; *both* (D): main man, old man.

boyhood, *n.* —*Syn.* schoolboy days, adolescent *or* growing years, plastic age, formative period, adolescence, juniority (D); see also **childhood, youth** 1. —*Ant.* maturity*, manhood, declining years.

boyish,, *mod.* —*Syn.* puerile, boylike, adolescent; see **childish, young** 1.

boy scout, *n.* —*Syn.* cub scout, explorer (scout), troop member; see **scout** 2.

brace, *n.* —*Syn.* prop, bolster, stay, support, lever, beam, truss, shore, girder, block, skid, rib, strut, buttress, splice, reinforcement, bearing, upholder, peg, bracket, strengthener, band, bracer, stave, guy, sustainer, stirrup, arm, splint, boom, bar, staff, plinth, stanchion, cantilever, rafter, round, mainstay, jack, crutch; see also **beam, support** 2.

brace, *v.* **1.** [To give support]—*Syn.* prop, bolster, hold up; see **support** 1.

2. [To encourage]—*Syn.* uphold, hearten, give new life; see **encourage** 1, 2, **support** 2.

bracelet, *n.* —*Syn.* arm band, manacle, ornament, trinket, armlet, circlet, bangle; see also **jewelry.**

bracing, *mod.* —*Syn.* invigorating, rousing, exhilarating; see **stimulating.**

bracket, *n.* —*Syn.* angle iron, brace, cantilever, console, corbel, strut, *cul-de-lampe* (French), modillion wall bracket, section, L joint, hanging bracket, shelf bracket; see also **brace.**

brackish, *mod.* —*Syn.* somewhat salt(y), saline, undrinkable; see **salty.**

brag, *v.* —*Syn.* swagger, exult, gloat; see **boast** 1.

braggart, *n.* —*Syn.* boaster, blowhard, windbag, trumpeter, big talker, swaggerer, fanfaron, gascon, braggadocio, strutter, swashbuckler, exhibitionist, egotist, rodomont, peacock, blusterer, bragger; *all* (D): blowhard, hot dog, know-it-all, bull peddler.

braid, *n.* —*Syn.* twine, plait, mesh, net, wreath, knot, chain, filigree, weave, reticulation; see also **rope.**

braid, *v.* —*Syn.* twine, plait, mesh; see **weave** 1.

brain, *n.* **1.** [The organ of intelligence]—*Syn.* cerebrum, cerebellum and medulla oblongata, center of the nervous system, gray matter, cerebral matter, cortical and medullary substances, brain cells.

2. [The intelligence]—*Syn.* intellect, genius, mentality; see **mind** 1.

3. [(D) A very intelligent person]—*Syn.* academician, scholar, egghead (D); see **intellectual.**

have on the brain—*Syn.* be obsessed *or* involved (with), fuss, stew; see **bother** 2.

brainwash, *v.* —*Syn.* indoctrinate, instill, catechize; see **convince, influence, teach** 1, 2.

brainwashing, *n.* —*Syn.* implantation, indoctrination, conditioning; see **education** 1, **persuasion** 1.

brake, *n.* —*Syn.* check, hamper, curb, deterrent, obstacle, damper, hurdle, discouragement, hindrance, retarding device, governor.

Types of brakes include the following—shoe, drum, band, catch, pawl, disk, friction, webbing, ratchet, contracting, expanding, hand, (compressed) air, automatic, four-wheel, hydraulic, power.

brakeman, *n.* —*Syn.* (railroad) trainman; *all* (D): brake, nipper, donicker.

bramble, *n.* —*Syn.* brier, thorn, prick, burr, gorse, furze, thistle sage, (stinging) nettle, prickly shrub, goose grass, thistle, catch weed, cleaver, shrub, bramble bush, hedge, spray.

branch, *n.* **1.** [A part, usually of secondary importance]—*Syn.* tributary, outpost, chapter, member, part, office, bureau, subdivision, section, derivative, dependency, portion, connection, subsidiary, classification, department, category, ramification, branch office, branch factory, etc.; see also **division** 2.

2. [A secondary shoot]—*Syn.* bough, limb, offshoot, sprig, twig, sucker, scion, bud, arm, fork, growth.

branch off, *v.* —*Syn.* diverge, separate, part; see **divide** 1.

branch out, *v.* —*Syn.* expand, extend, add to; see **grow** 1, **increase** 1.

brand, *n.* **1.** [A trademark]—*Syn.* seal, mark, watermark; see **kind** 2, **label, name** 1.

2. [A mark indicating ownership]—*Syn.* stigma, scar, sear, welt, cauterization, range brand, mark of the branding iron, earmark, wattle, owner's sign *or* mark; *all* (D): heraldry of the range, the rancher's coat of arms, mark of Cain.
Common branding terms include the following—circle, bar, cross, rocking, lazy, tumbling, swinging, flying, double; letters: A, J, X, etc.; numbers: 0, 1, 2, 3, etc.; types of brands include: fast, slow, dewlap, overslope, underslope, crop, half crop, upperbit, underbit, jingle-bob, wattle, and ear-mark.
3. [A burning stick]—*Syn.* ember, live coal, spark, torch; see **coal** 2.

brand, *v.* —*Syn.* blaze, stamp, imprint; see **mark** 1.

brandish, *v.* —*Syn.* shake, gesture, warn; see **flourish** 1, **threaten** 1.

brandy, *n.* —*Syn.* cognac, *Schnaps* (German), *aguardiente* (Spanish), *eau-de-vie* (French), *aqua vitae* (Latin), grande champagne, Napoleon, brandywine, slivovitz; see also **drink** 2.
Types of brandy include the following—apple, prune, peach, cherry, apricot, grape.

brass, *n.* 1. [An alloy of copper and zinc]—*Syn.* copper alloy, pinchbeck, Muntz's metal, orichalc, mosaic gold, yellow metal, prince's metal, brass foil *or* brass leaf *or* Dutch gold, brass powder; see also **alloy.**
2. [(D) High-ranking officials]—*Syn.* officers; *both* (D): front office, brass hats (D); see **officer** 3.
3. [(D) Impudence]—*Syn.* effrontery, impertinence, audacity; see **rudeness.**

brasses, *n.* pl.—*Syn.* trumpet, trombone, (French) horn, B-flat cornet, fluegelhorn, sousaphone, bass tuba, helicon, bombardon, euphonium, serpent, E-flat cornet; see also **musical instrument.**

brassy, *mod.* —*Syn.* brazen, saucy, flirtatious, impudent, bold, pert, forward, brash; see also **rude** 2.

brat (D), *n.* —*Syn.* impudent *or* unruly child, youngster, kid (D); see **boy, child, girl** 1.

bravado, *n.* —*Syn.* boasting, pomposity, braggartry, vaunting, bragging, gasconade, grandiosity, storming, raging, fanfaronade, bombast, rant, braggadocio, swelling, bullying, blowing, puffing, self-glorification, crowing, swaggering, fuming, railing, bluff, hot air (D).

brave, *mod.* 1. [Courageous]—*Syn.* fearless, daring, dauntless, valiant, intrepid, undaunted, undismayed, confident, unabashed, chivalrous, valorous, heroic, bold, imprudent, adventurous, reckless, foolhardy, dashing, venturesome, mettlesome, forward, audacious, gallant, resolute, militant, defiant, hardy, doughty, unafraid, stout, stout-hearted, lion-hearted, manful, manly, firm, plucky, high-spirited, unshrinking, herolike, unblenching, dreadless, spirited, strong, stalwart, unflinching, unyielding, indomitable, unconquerable, soldierly, unappalled; *all* (D): spunky, gritty, game, full of guts, nervy, gutsy, with heart of oak, iron-hearted.—*Ant.* cowardly*, timid, craven.
2. [Making a good showing]—*Syn.* brilliant, colorful, high-colored; see **bright** 1, 2.

brave, *v.* —*Syn.* confront, risk, court; see **face** 1.

bravely, *mod.* —*Syn.* courageously, fearlessly, valiantly, boldly, daringly, dauntlessly, intrepidly, heroically, gallantly, doughtily, hardily, stoutly, manfully, staunchly, pluckily, resolutely, valorously, spiritedly, firmly, audaciously, with fortitude, unabashedly, unflinchingly, chivalrously, indomitably; *all* (D): spunkily, with plenty of guts, like a man, gamely, gutsily.—*Ant.* cowardly*, fearfully, timidly.

bravery, *n.* —*Syn.* valor, intrepidity, fearlessness; see **courage** 1, **strength** 1.

brawl, *n.* —*Syn.* fuss, squabble, riot; see **fight** 1.

brawn, *n.* —*Syn.* vigor, power, energy; see **muscle, strength** 1.

brawny, *mod.* —*Syn.* powerful, muscular, sturdy; see **strong** 1.

bray, *v.* —*Syn.* bawl, whinny, neigh; see **sound** 1, **yell.**

brazen, *mod.* 1. [Made of brass]—*Syn.* brass, bronze, brassy, brass-plated, of brass, of brassy quality, brasslike; see also **metallic** 1.
2. [Impudent]—*Syn.* audacious, impertinent, forward; see **rude** 2.

breach, *n.* 1. [An opening, especially in fortifications]—*Syn.* break, gap, rupture; see **hole** 1.
2. [An infraction of law or custom]—*Syn.* violation, infringment, transgression; see **crime** 1, 2, **violation** 1.

bread, *n.* 1. [Grain product]—*Syn.* loaf, baked goods, the staff of life (D).
Types of bread include the following—whole wheat, graham, rye, leavened, unleavened, matzo, salt-rising, corn, sour-dough, raisin, pumpernickel, Vienna, French, Italian, white, black, dark brown, Boston brown, steamed, Swedish, potato, hardtack.
Breadlike foods include the following—Zweiback, spoon bread, cake, dumpling, turnover, rusk, gem, bun, cookie, English muffin, corn bread, bagel, scone, shortbread, hoecake, pone, johnnycake, Indian bread; see **biscuit, roll** 4.
2. [Food]—*Syn.* meal, sustenance, bed and board (D); see **food.**
3. [(D) Money]—*Syn.* coin, cash, dollars, dough (D); see **money** 1.
break bread—*Syn.* partake, have a meal, indulge; see **eat** 1.
cast one's bread upon the waters—*Syn.* grant, endow, be generous; see **give** 1, **help** 1.
know which side one's bread is buttered on (D) —*Syn.* be prudent *or* cautious *or* shrewd, save, look out for number one (D); see **prosper.**

breadth, *n.* 1. [Width]—*Syn.* wideness, broadness, distance across; see **diameter, width.**
2. [Scope]—*Syn.* largeness, extent, vastness, compass, magnitude, inclusiveness, greatness, extensiveness, comprehensiveness, amplitude; see also **size** 2.—*Ant.* smallness*, narrowness, littleness.

breadwinner, *n.* —*Syn.* wage-earner, producer, supporter, worker, laborer, provider, toiler; see also **husband, laborer.**

break, *n.* 1. [The act of breaking]—*Syn.* fracture, rift, split, schism, cleavage, dissevering, riving, breach, rupture, eruption, bursting, failure, collapse, disjunction; see also **division** 1, **parting** 2. —*Ant.* mending, repair*, maintenance.
2. [The effect of breaking]—*Syn.* crack, split, tear; see **division** 2, **hole** 1.
3. [A pause]—*Syn.* intermission, interim, lapse; see **pause** 1.

4. [Quarrel and separation]—*Syn.* trouble, difference (of opinion), altercation; see **disagreement** 1, **dispute** 1, **fight.**
5. [(D) Fortunate change or event: *often plural*] —*Syn.* good luck, accident, favorable circumstances; see **luck** 1.

break, *v.* **1.** [To start a rupture]—*Syn.* burst, split, crack, rend, rive, sunder, sever, fracture, tear, cleave, break into *or* through, force open, puncture, split, snap, slash, gash, dissect, slice, disjoin, separate; see **cut, divide** 1.
2. [To shatter]—*Syn.* smash, shiver, crash, break up, crush, break to atoms, splinter, smash to flinders, pull to pieces, break all to pieces; *both* (D): make a hash of, break all to smithrs *or* smithereens.
3. [To fall apart]—*Syn.* disintegrate, shiver, burst, shatter, fall to pieces, splinter, collapse, break down, come apart *or* off, get loose, fall off *or* down, cave in, dilapidate, go to wrack and ruin, get wrecked; *all* (D): bust *or* split up, put out of joint, go on the fritz, go haywire, fall to dust, fold up, come unstuck; see also **disintegrate** 1.
4. [To bring to ruin or to an end]—*Syn.* demolish, annihilate, eradicate; see **destroy** 1.
5. [To happen]—*Syn.* come to pass, occur, develop; see **happen** 2.
6. [To blow up]—*Syn.* erupt, burst, shatter; see **explode** 1.

breakable, *mod.*—*Syn.* fragile, delicate, frail; see **weak** 2.

breakage, *n.*—*Syn.* harm, wreckage, ruined goods; see **damage** 2.

breakdown, *n.*—*Syn.* stoppage, collapse, rupture, disruption; see **failure** 1.

break down, *v.* **1.** [To analyze]—*Syn.* examine, investigate, dissect; see **analyze** 1.
2. [To overcome]—*Syn.* surmount, overwhelm, conquer; see **defeat** 2.
3. [To malfunction]—*Syn.* fail, stop, falter, misfire, give out, go down, cease, backfire; *all* (D): conk *or* peter *or* fizzle out, collapse, go kaput, crack *or* curl *or* roll up, bomb, come unstuck *or* unglued, run out of gas.

break free, *v.*—*Syn.* get *or* break out, go, break the *or* one's bonds; see **escape, fly** 1, 4, **leave** 1.

breaker, *n.*—*Syn.* comber, roller, surge; see **wave** 1.

breakfast, *n.*—*Syn.* morning meal, first meal of the day, early meal, first breakfast, second breakfast, brunch, *déjeuner* (French), *déjeuner à la fourchette* (French), breaking the fast; see also **meal.**

breakfast food, *n.*—*Syn.* breakfast *or* hot *or* dry cereal, porridge.
Breakfast foods include the following—rolled oats *or* oatmeal, farina, corn flakes, shredded wheat, rice flakes, wheat flakes, puffed wheat, puffed rice, pearl barley, bran, wheat germ.

break in, *v.* **1.** [Train]—*Syn.* educate, instruct, prepare; see **teach** 1, 2.
2. [Intrude]—*Syn.* invade, burglarize, trespass; see **meddle** 2, **rob, steal.**

breaking, *mod.*—*Syn.* bursting, splitting, cracking, rending, riving, sundering, parting, severing, dissevering, exploding, erupting, shattering, splintering, fracturing, tearing, cleaving, snapping, separating, smashing, shivering, crashing, splintering, disintegrating, collapsing, caving in, falling, dispersing; *both* (D): busting, going to pot.—*Ant.* enduring, strong*, stable.

breaking, *n.* **1.** [A fracture]—*Syn.* cleavage, rupture, separating; see **division** 1, **fracture** 1.
2. [A violation]—*Syn.* transgressing, shattering, violating; see **violation** 1.

break in *or* **upon,** *v.*—*Syn.* cut in (on), intrude, intervene; see **interrupt** 2.

break off, *v.*—*Syn.* end, cease, discontinue; see **stop** 2.

break out, *v.* **1.** [To start]—*Syn.* begin, commence, occur; see **begin** 2.
2. [To escape]—*Syn.* burst out, flee, depart; see **leave** 1.
3. [To erupt]—*Syn.* acquire blemishes, have acned skin, become diseased, get pimples.

break the sound barrier, *v.*—*Syn.* cause a report *or* sonic boom *or* ground wave, exceed the speed of sound, break through; **fly** 1, **speed.**

breakthrough, *n.*—*Syn.* discovery, finding, invention; see **discovery** 2.

break through, *v.*—*Syn.* penetrate, force away, intrude; see **penetrate.**

break up, *v.* **1.** [To scatter]—*Syn.* disperse, disband, separate; see **divide** 1.
2. [To dismantle]—*Syn.* take apart, disassemble, break down; see **dismantle.**
3. [To stop]—*Syn.* put an end to, halt, terminate; see **stop** 2.
4. [(D) To distress]—*Syn.* hurt, sadden, wound; see **hurt** 3.
5. [(D) To end relations]—*Syn.* halt, break off, drop; see **end** 1.

breakwater, *n.*—*Syn.* pier, wharf, jetty; see **dock** 1.

break water, *v.*—*Syn.* submerge, dive, go under, plunge, go down, crash-dive; see also **submerge** 2.

breast, *n.* **1.** [The forepart of the body above the abdomen]—*Syn.* thorax, heart, bosom; see **chest** 2.
2. [A protuberant mammary gland]—*Syn.* bosom, dug, teat, mammilla, tit, nipple, bust, udder; *all* (D): titty, jug, boobie, boob.
3. [One's inner self]—*Syn.* mind, heart, bosom, thoughts, conscience, soul, feelings, psyche, spirit, essential nature, being, character; see also **mind** 1, **thought** 2.
beat one's breast—*Syn.* repent, humble oneself, be penitent *or* sorry *or* remorseful; see **apologize, regret.**
make a clean breast of—*Syn.* confess, reveal, expose; see **admit** 2.

breastpin, *n.*—*Syn.* bar pin, clasp, brooch; see **jewelry, pin** 1.

breath, *n.* **1.** [Respiration]—*Syn.* inspiration, expiration, inhalation, exhalation, breathing, gasp, sigh, pant, suspiration, wheeze.
2. [A very light wind]—*Syn.* whiff, flutter, puff; see **wind** 1.
below *or* **under one's breath**—*Syn.* quietly, subdued, murmuring; see **whispering.**
catch one's breath—*Syn.* rest, stop, slow down; see **pause.**
in the same breath—*Syn.* simultaneously, concurrently, at the same time; see **together** 2.
out of breath—*Syn.* gasping, choking, out of wind; see **breathless.**

save one's breath—*Syn.* be quiet, stop talking, never mind; see **shut up.**
take one's breath away—*Syn.* thrill, stimulate, invigorate; see **excite** 1.

breathe, *v.* **1.** [To draw breath]—*Syn.* respire, use one's lungs, inhale, exhale, draw in, breathe in *or* out, gasp, pant, wheeze, snort, sigh, take air into one's nostrils, scent, sniff, open the flood-gates (D).
2. [To live]—*Syn.* move, exist, be alive; see **be** 1.
3. [To blow gently]—*Syn.* puff, fan, exhale; see **blow** 1.
4. [To pause]—*Syn.* take (a) breath, recuperate, take a breather (D); see **pause, rest** 2.

breathing, *mod.*—*Syn.* respiring, inhaling, inspiring, smelling, sniffing, scenting, respiratory, sensitive, palpitant; see **alive** 1.

breathless, *mod.*—*Syn.* out of breath, winded, spent, exhausted, used up, gasping, choking, windless, wheezing, blown, short-winded, asthmatic, emphysematous, panting, puffing, short of breath, out of wind (D); see also **excited, tired.**—*Ant.* fresh*, breathing freely, long-winded.

bred, *mod.*—*Syn.* developed, cultivated, cultured, reared, refined, produced, propagated.

breeches, *n.* pl.—*Syn.* trousers, slacks, jeans; see **pants** 1.

breed, *n.*—*Syn.* strain, variety, kind; see **class** 1, **race** 1.

breed, *v.* **1.** [To produce]—*Syn.* give birth to, deliver, bring forth; see **produce** 1.
2. [To cause]—*Syn.* bring about, effect, occasion, produce; see **begin** 1.
3. [To procreate]—*Syn.* impregnate, beget, sire; see **propagate** 1.

breeder, *n.*—*Syn.* stock raiser, stockman, herdsman, drover, cattleman, sheepman, horse breeder, swine breeder; see also **farmer, rancher.**

breeze, *n.*—*Syn.* zephyr, flurry, blast; see **wind** 1.
in a breeze—*Syn.* effortlessly, readily, jauntily; see **easily** 1.
shoot (*or* **bat**) **the breeze**—*Syn.* converse, chat, chatter; see **talk** 1.

breezy, *mod.* **1.** [*Said of weather*]—*Syn.* stormy, gusty, blowing; see **windy** 1.
2. [*Said of people, music, etc.*]—*Syn.* gay, jaunty, sprightly; see **happy** 1.

brevity, *n.*—*Syn.* shortness, conciseness, concision, briefness, terseness, pointedness, pithiness, compression, succinctness, crispness, compactness, curtness, economy.

brew, *n.*—*Syn.* concoction, preparation, instillation, distillation, liquor, compound, blend, infusion, broth, beer, homebrew, ale, stout; see also **beer, drink** 1, 2.

brew, *v.*—*Syn.* concoct, ferment, mull; see **cook.**

brewery, *n.*—*Syn.* still, distillery, wine press, bottling works, winery; see also **factory.**

bribe, *n.*—*Syn.* fee, reward, hush money, sop, lure, gift, remuneration, graft, compensation, corrupt money, tribute, protection, perquisite, bait, tip, blackmail, boodle, price, present, gratuity, lagniappe, payola (D).

bribe, *v.*—*Syn.* corrupt, get at *or* to, influence by a gift, pervert, reward, tip, give a bribe *or* sop *or* price to, coax, lure, entice, tempt, influence, buy, square *or* seduce with money, suborn; *all* (D): buy back *or* off, butter, grease *or* cross one's palm, salve, soap, square, sugar, fix.

brick, *n.*—*Syn.* cube, Roman brick, pressed brick, cement *or* concrete *or* cinder block, glass brick, section, chunk; see also **block** 1, **slab, stone.**

bridal, *mod.*—*Syn.* nuptial, marriage, wedding, hymeneal, matrimonial, marital, conjugal, connubial, nubile, wedded, epithalamic, prothalamic.

bride, *n.*—*Syn.* spouse, partner, mate, helpmate, helpmeet, newly married woman; see also **wife.**

bridegroom, *n.*—*Syn.* groom, benedict, spouse; see **husband.**

bridge, *n.* **1.** [An elevated structure]—*Syn.* viaduct, platform, pontoon, catwalk, gangplank, drawbridge, trestle, scaffold, transit, tram.
Types of bridges include the following—arch, pier, gantry, leg, suspension, cantilever, bowstring, tubular, bascule, pontoon, swing, tubular-arch, turnpike, floating, steel arch, vertical lift, box-girder, lattice, hoist, induction, bottom-road, arched-truss, panel-truss, covered Bailey.
Famous bridges include the following—Alexander Hamilton, Bayonne, Bronx-Whitestone, Brooklyn, Carquinez Strait, Chesapeake Bay, Connecticut Turnpike, Corpus Christi, Eads, Firth of Forth, Floriano Polis, George Washington, Golden Gate, Henry Hudson, Iberville Memorial, Karlsbrücke, Kitchikas, Lake Pontchartrain, London, Mackinac, Oakland *or* Bay Bridge, Pont Neuf, Pont d'Avignon, Ponte Vecchio, Verrazano-Narrows, Bridge of Sighs, Bridge of St. Angelo.
2. [A game at cards]—*Syn.* whist, bridge-whist, contract bridge, auction bridge; *both* (D): duplicate bridge, honeymoon bridge; see also **game** 1.
3. [A link]—*Syn.* connection, bond, tie; see **joint** 1, **link.**
burn one's bridges (behind one)—*Syn.* commit oneself, be determined, go forward (resolutely *or* blindly, etc.); see **advance** 1.

bridge, *v.*—*Syn.* connect, span, link; see **join** 1.

bridle, *n.*—*Syn.* hackamore, headstall, leash; see **halter.**

bridle, *v.*—*Syn.* check, curb, control; see **restrain** 1.

brief, *mod.* **1.** [Short in space]—*Syn.* skimpy, slight, small; see **short** 1.
2. [Abrupt]—*Syn.* hasty, curt, bluff; see **abrupt** 2.
3. [Short in time]—*Syn.* short-term, curtailed, concise; see **fleeting, short** 2.

brief, *n.*—*Syn.* digest, abstract, outline; see **summary.**
in brief—*Syn.* in short, succinctly, in (a) few words; see **briefly.**

brief, *v.* **1.** [To summarize]—*Syn.* epitomize, recapitulate, abridge; see **decrease** 2.
2. [To inform]—*Syn.* prime, advise, instruct; see **prepare** 1.

briefcase, *n.*—*Syn.* dispatch *or* attaché *or* note case, folder, portfolio; see **bag, baggage.**

briefing, *n.*—*Syn.* instruction, preamble, discussion; see **introduction** 4, **preparation** 1.

briefly, *mod.*—*Syn.* shortly, curtly, abruptly, quickly, hastily, cursorily, hurriedly, fleetingly, momentarily, temporarily, in passing, casually, lightly, briskly, transiently, summarily, in capsule form, succinctly, suddenly, in brief *or* outline, in quick order, in a few words, in a capsule, in a nutshell (D). —*Ant.* at length, extensively, compendiously.

brigade, *n.* —*Syn.* unit, detachment, force; see **army** 2.

brigand, *n.* —*Syn.* highwayman, thief, bandit; see **robber.**

bright, *mod.* **1.** [Shining]—*Syn.* gleaming, shiny, glittering, luminous, lustrous, burnished, polished, sparkling, mirrorlike, limpid, glowing, flashing, scintillating, coruscating, shimmering, incandescent, effulgent, fulgent, twinkling, illumined, relucent, light, argent, golden, nitid, silvery, lambent, fulgid, illuminated, shining, refulgent, irradiated, glistening, radiant, auroral, burning, glaring, beaming, glimmering, splendid, resplendent, brilliant, dazzling, alight, aglow, lighted (up), full of light, ablaze, flamelike, moonlit, sunlit, lamplit, on fire, phosphorescent, blazing, glossy.—*Ant.* dull*, clouded, opaque.

2. [Vivid]—*Syn.* colored, colorful, tinted, gay, intense, deep, sharp, rich, brilliant, exotic, tinged, hued, touched with color, fresh, clear, florid, ruddy, bright- *or* full- *or* deep- *or* rich- *or* high-colored, psychedelic.

3. [Intelligent]—*Syn.* clever, quick, alert; see **intelligent** 1.

4. [Not rainy]—*Syn.* clear, sunny, mild; see **fair** 3.

5. [Cheerful]—*Syn.* lively, vivacious, gay; see **happy** 1.

6. [Splendid]—*Syn.* famous, illustrious, eminent; see **glorious** 1.

7. [Promising]—*Syn.* auspicious, favorable, propitious; see **hopeful** 2.

brighten, *v.* **1.** [To become brighter]—*Syn.* clear up, lighten, grow calm, improve, grow sunny, become gentle, glow, kindle.—*Ant.* shade*, grow dull, darken.

2. [To make brighter]—*Syn.* polish, burnish, lighten; see **intensify, shine** 3.

brightly, *mod.* —*Syn.* glitteringly, sparklingly, limpidly, flashingly, lustrously, shiningly, glowingly, incandescently, effulgently, glisteningly, shimmeringly, radiantly, coruscatingly, burningly, glaringly, gleamingly, beamingly, splendidly, resplendently, brilliantly, dazzlingly, blazingly, glossily, flamingly, lambently, shinily, scintillatingly, gaily, freshly, vividly, colorfully, cleverly, quickly, sunnily, phosphorescently.—*Ant.* dully*, dingily, darkly.

brightness, *n.* —*Syn.* shine, luster, illumination; see **light** 1.

brilliant, *mod.* **1.** [Shining]—*Syn.* dazzling, gleaming, sparkling; see **bright** 1.

2. [Showing remarkable ability]—*Syn.* ingenious, profound, penetrating; see **intelligent** 1.

3. [Illustrious]—*Syn.* splendid, excellent, eminent; see **glorious** 1.

brilliantly, *mod.* **1.** [Very brightly]—*Syn.* shiningly, radiantly, blazingly; see **brightly.**

2. [With superior intelligence]—*Syn.* cleverly, shrewdly, knowledgeably; see **intelligently.**

brim, *n.* —*Syn.* margin, rim, border; see **edge** 1.

brindled, *mod.* —*Syn.* streaked, spotted, mottled; see **speckled.**

brine, *n.* —*Syn.* salt water, saline solution, sea water, artificial brine, pickling solution, saturated solution of salt, brackish water; see also **ocean, vinegar.**

bring, *v.* **1.** [To transport]—*Syn.* convey, take along, bear; see **carry** 1, **pick up** 6.

2. [To be worth in sale]—*Syn.* sell for, command, fetch, produce, net, return, gross, earn, yield, afford, draw, bring in, take; see also **pay** 2.

3. [To initiate legal action]—*Syn.* institute, declare, prefer, take (to court), appeal, serve, cite, arraign, summon, indict.

4. [To cause]—*Syn.* produce, effect, make; see **begin** 1.

bring about, *v.* **1.** [To achieve]—*Syn.* do, accomplish, realize; see **achieve** 1, **succeed** 1.

2. [To cause]—*Syn.* produce, effect, do; see **begin** 1, **manage** 1.

bring around, *v.* **1.** [To convince]—*Syn.* persuade, prove, induce; see **convince.**

2. [To revive]—*Syn.* restore, refresh, resuscitate; see **revive** 1.

bring down, *v.* **1.** [To kill]—*Syn.* slay, murder, cut *or* mow down (D); see **kill** 1.

2. [To hurt]—*Syn.* damage, injure, wound; see **damage, hurt** 1.

bring forth, *v.* —*Syn.* deliver, bear, yield; see **produce** 1, 2.

bring forward, *v.* —*Syn.* present, give, introduce; see **contribute** 1, **display** 1, **offer** 1.

bring home the bacon (D), *v.* —*Syn.* provide for, triumph, achieve; see **earn** 2, **provide** 1, **succeed** 1, **support** 5.

bring home to (one), *v.* —*Syn.* make apparent, convince, make one realize; see **emphasize.**

bring in, *v.* **1.** [To import]—*Syn.* ship in, introduce, buy abroad; see **import** 1.

2. [To produce]—*Syn.* yield, bear, accrue; see **produce** 1.

bringing, *n.* —*Syn.* fetching, carrying, transporting, importing, accompanying, introducing, shipping, bearing, hauling, ushering *or* bringing in, conveying, procuring, getting, providing.—*Ant.* taking*, deporting, sending.

bring off (D), *v.* —*Syn.* accomplish, realize, execute; see **achieve** 1, **succeed** 1.

bring on, *v.* —*Syn.* cause, lead to, provoke; see **begin** 1.

bring out, *v.* **1.** [To excite]—*Syn.* elicit, arouse, evoke; see **excite** 2.

2. [To publish]—*Syn.* print, issue, put out; see **publish** 1.

3. [To produce a play]—*Syn.* present, put on the stage, exhibit; see **perform** 2.

4. [To intensify]—*Syn.* heighten, sharpen, magnify; see **emphasize, increase** 1, **intensify.**

bring to, *v.* —*Syn.* resuscitate, restore, reanimate, revivify; see **revive** 1.

bring to bear, *v.* —*Syn.* exert, pressure, concentrate; see **apply** 4, **exercise** 2, **influence, use** 1.

bring to one's senses, *v.* —*Syn.* restore, bring to reason, persuade; see **convince.**

bring up, *v.* **1.** [To rear]—*Syn.* educate, teach, train; see **raise** 2, **support** 5.

2. [To discuss]—*Syn.* tender, submit, advance; see **discuss, propose** 1.

bring up to code, *v.* —*Syn.* rebuild, fix, redo; see **improve** 1, **remodel, repair.**

bring with, *v.* —*Syn.* get, accompany, go with, stop for; see **pick up** 6.

brink, *n.* —*Syn.* limit, brim, rim; see **edge** 1.
brisk, *mod.* **1.** [Active]—*Syn.* lively, energetic, nimble; see **active** 2.
2. [Stimulating]—*Syn.* sharp, keen, invigorating; see **stimulating.**
briskly, *mod.* —*Syn.* energetically, quickly, brusquely, rapidly, impulsively, nimbly, agilely, dexterously, decisively, firmly, actively, promptly, readily, vigorously, incisively, in a brisk *or* lively manner; see also **emphatically.**—*Ant.* listlessly, slowly*, sluggishly.
bristle, *n.* —*Syn.* hair, fiber, quill; see **point** 2, **thorn.**
bristle, *v.* **1.** [To display in abundance]—*Syn.* swarm, be alive, abound, exuberate, be thick with, thrust out, crawl with (D); see also **gather** 1, **teem.**
2. [To show sudden anger]—*Syn.* ruffle, swell, bridle; see **rage** 1.
Britain, *n.* —*Syn.* Great Britain, United Kingdom, Albion; England, Scotland, Wales, and Northern Ireland; see **England** 1.
British, *mod.* **1.** [English]—*Syn.* English, Anglian; see **Anglo-Saxon.**
2. [Celtic]—*Syn.* Gaelic, Cymric, Hibernian; see **Irish, Scots, Welsh.**
brittle, *mod.* —*Syn.* fragile, crisp, inelastic; see **weak** 2.
broach, *v.* **1.** [To mention]—*Syn.* suggest, introduce, bring up; see **ask** 1, **hint** 1, **propose** 1.
2. [To penetrate]—*Syn.* tap, pierce, puncture; see **open** 3, **penetrate.**
broad, *mod.* **1.** [Physically wide]—*Syn.* extended, large, extensive, ample, spacious, deep, expansive, immense, wide, roomy, outspread, capacious, outstretched, thick, widespread, broad-gauged, full, latitudinous; see also **deep** 2, **extensive** 1, **large** 1. —*Ant.* narrow*, thin*, slender.
2. [Extensive]—*Syn.* ubiquitous, all-inclusive, far-flung; see **comprehensive, general** 1, **widespread.**
3. [Culturally wide]—*Syn.* cultivated, experienced, cosmopolitan; see **cultured.**
4. [Tolerant]—*Syn.* progressive, open-minded, unbiased; see **liberal** 2.
5. [Indelicate]—*Syn.* dirty, off-color, suggestive, smutty; see **lewd** 1.
6. [Clear]—*Syn.* unequivocal, explicit, apparent; see **obvious** 2.
7. [Unrestrained]—*Syn.* outspoken, candid, open; see **frank.**
broad (D), *n.* —*Syn. all* (D): bird, chick, dame; see **girl** 1, **woman** 1.
broadcast, *n.* —*Syn.* radio program, wireless transmission, radiocast, television *or* TV program, newscast, simulcast, telecast; see also **performance** 2, **show** 2.
broadcast, *v.* **1.** [To disperse]—*Syn.* spread, distribute, disseminate; see **scatter** 2.
2. [To transmit electronically]—*Syn.* announce, relay, telephone, radiograph, send out, telegraph, radio, cable, transmit, televise, telecast, simulcast, air, put on the air, go *or* be on the air; see also **send** 1.
3. [To announce]—*Syn.* publicize, blazon, proclaim; see **advertise** 1, **declare** 1.
broadcasting, *n.* —*Syn.* radio transmission, announcing, television, airing, putting on a radio program, auditioning, performing before a microphone, telecasting, community antenna television (CATV), newscasting, being broadcast, transmitting, reporting.
broaden, *v.* —*Syn.* widen, expand, increase; see **grow** 1, **increase** 1.
broadening, *mod.* —*Syn.* refining, improving, cultivating; see **cultural.**
broad hint, *n.* —*Syn.* thinly veiled request, strong suggestion, allusion; see **hint** 1.
broad-minded, *mod.* —*Syn.* tolerant, progressive, unprejudiced; see **liberal** 2.
brochure, *n.* —*Syn.* handout, circular, pamphlet; see **advertisement** 2, **folder** 1.
broil, *v.* —*Syn.* sear, bake, roast; see **cook.**
broiler, *n.* —*Syn.* appliance, oven, electric broiler, roaster-oven, charcoal broiler, grill, hibachi, griddle, portable oven, barbecue (D); see also **appliance.**
broke (D), *mod.* —*Syn.* bankrupt, out of money, indebted; see **insolvent, ruined** 4.
go for broke (D)—*Syn.* gamble, wager, risk everything; see **risk.**
go broke (D)—*Syn.* become penniless *or* bankrupt, lose everything; be reduced to poverty; see **fail** 4, **lose** 2.
broken, *mod.* **1.** [Fractured]—*Syn.* shattered, ruptured, burst, splintered, shivered, smashed, in pieces, collapsed, destroyed, gashed, pulverized, crumbled, mutilated, bruised, injured, lacerated, damaged, rent, split, riven, cracked, mangled, dismembered, fragmentary, defective, disintegrated, crippled, shredded, crushed, slivered; see also **destroyed, hurt.**—*Ant.* sound, whole*, intact.
2. [Not functioning properly]—*Syn.* defective, inoperable, in need of repair, in disrepair, out of (working) order; *all* (D): busted, gone to pot, screwed up, shot, (gone) haywire, on the fritz *or* blink, gone to pieces, fallen apart, (come) unstuck *or* unglued, out of joint *or* gear *or* fix commission *or* whack *or* kilter; see also **disabled, faulty, unsatisfactory.**—*Ant.* operable, usable*, working.
3. [Discontinuous]—*Syn.* spasmodic, erratic, intermittent; see **irregular** 1, 4.
4. [Not kept; *said especially of promises*]—*Syn.* violated, dishonored, traduced, forgotten, ignored, transgressed, retracted, disregard; see also **abandoned** 1.—*Ant.* done*, kept, performed.
5. [Incoherent; *said of speech*]—*Syn.* muttered, unintelligible, mumbled; see **incoherent** 2.
6. [Infirm]—*Syn.* decrepit, frail, tottering; see **weak** 1.
7. [Bankrupt]—*Syn.* indebted, insolvent, broke (D); see **insolvent, ruined** 4.
8. [Disheartened]—*Syn.* discouraged, depressed, heartsick; see **sad** 1, **troubled** 1.
broken down, *mod.* —*Syn.* shattered, dilapidated, battered; see **old** 2.
brokenhearted, *mod.* —*Syn.* despondent, crushed, grieved; see **sad** 1.
broker, *n.* —*Syn.* stockbroker, agent, middleman; see **businessman, financier, merchant.**
bronco, *n.* —*Syn.* mustang, cattle-pony, wild *or* range horse, fuzztail, broomtail; *both* (D): bronc, *cerrero* (Spanish); see also **horse** 1.

bronze, *mod.* **1.** [Made of bronze]—*Syn.* bell-metal, copper alloy, cast bronze, made of copper and tin; see also **metallic** 1.
2. [Having the color of bronze]—*Syn.* copper-colored, reddish-brown, burnished, russet, rust; see also **brown, gold** 2.
bronze, *n.* —*Syn.* an alloy of copper and tin, often with zinc. Varieties include the following—white, steel, phosphor, aluminum, manganese, malleable, Bavarian, chemical; see also **alloy, metal.**
brooch, *n.* —*Syn.* bar pin, breastpin, cluster; see **jewelry, pin** 1.
brood, *n.* —*Syn.* flock, offspring, young; see **family** 1, **herd** 1.
brood, *v.* **1.** [To hatch]—*Syn.* set, cover, incubate, warm, sit; see also **produce** 1.
2. [To nurse one's troubles]—*Syn.* gloom, repine, grieve, fret, sulk, cherish anxious thoughts, mope, ruminate, ponder, consider, muse, deliberate, dwell upon, speculate, daydream, reflect, dream, chafe inwardly, give oneself over to reflections; *all* (D): be in a brown study, eat one's heart out, mull over; see also **meditate** 1, **think** 1, **worry** 2.
brook, *n.* —*Syn.* creek, stream, streamlet; see **river** 1.
broom, *n.* —*Syn.* (carpet) sweeper, besom, whisk (broom), mop, feather duster, swab, (floor) brush, electric broom.
broth, *n.* —*Syn.* brew, distillation, concoction, decoction, soup, potage, consommé, purée, bouillon, borsch, vichyssoise, pottage, stock, chowder, gumbo, porridge, olio, *olla podrida* (Spanish), hodge-podge, potpourri; see also **food, soup.**
brothel, *n.* —*Syn.* whorehouse, bawdyhouse, house of ill-fame *or* ill-repute, bagnio, house of prostitution *or* harlotry *or* lewdness, bordello; *all* (D): stew, red-light house, house with red doors, cathouse, house.
brotherhood, *n.* **1.** [The quality or state of being brothers]—*Syn.* fellowship, consanguinity, fraternity, equality, kinship, intimacy, (blood) relationship, family connection, affiliation, association, society, common humanity, family, race, comradeship, cameraderie, friendship, amity, filiation, sibling rivalry.
2. [A fraternal organization]—*Syn.* fraternity, secret society, Greek letter society; see **organization** 3.
brotherly, *mod.* —*Syn.* fraternal, solicitous, charitable, kindly, selfless, compassionate, humane, sympathetic, personal, comprehending, tender, disinterested, Christ-like, forgiving, comradely; see also **faithful, friendly, generous** 1, **intimate** 1, **kind** 1, **loving.**—*Ant.* unfriendly*, hostile, aloof.
brow, *n.* —*Syn.* temples, front, face; see **forehead.**
browbeat, *v.* —*Syn.* bully, intimidate, frighten; see **threaten** 1.
brown, *mod.* —*Syn.* brownish, copper-colored, reddish-brown, rust(-colored), snuff-colored, liver-colored; see also **brown***n.*
brown, *n.* Shades and tints of brown include the following—tan, bay, chestnut, nutbrown, copper-colored, mahogany, bronze, russet, chocolate, cinnamon, hazel, reddish-brown, sorrel, sepia, tawny, ochre, rust, rust-colored, brownish, puce, terracotta, fawn, snuff-colored, liver-colored, beige, ecru, dust, drab, dun, henna, coffee, khaki, maroon, cocoa, umber, brick, ginger, light brown, dark brown, auburn, buff, Caledonia, Antwerp, burnt orange, burnt ochre, burnt russet; Vandyke, Rembrandt, Verona brown; see also **color** 1.
brown, *v.* —*Syn.* toast, scorch, sauté; see **cook, fry.**
brownie, *n.* **1.** [Fairy]—*Syn.* spirit, sprite, goblin, elf; see **fairy** 1.
2. [Girl scout]—*Syn.* explorer, tenderfoot, camper; see **scout** 3.
browse, *v.* —*Syn.* skim, peruse, scan, glance at, flip *or* look *or* run through, look *or* glance *or* check *or* run over, survey, inspect loosely, pass the eye over, read here and there, examine cursorily, go through carelessly *or* in a desultory manner; *both* (D): dip into, wander here and there; see also **read** 1, **scan.**
bruise, *n.* —*Syn.* abrasion, wound, swelling; see **blemish.**
bruise, *v.* —*Syn.* beat, injure, wound; see **damage** 1, **hurt** 1.
brunet, *mod.* —*Syn.* dark, dark-complexioned, tawny, dusky, brown, tanned, swarthy, dark-haired, dark-skinned, pigmented, Latin, Mediterranean, Sicilian.—*Ant.* fair*, light, light-complexioned.
brush, *n.* **1.** [A brushing instrument]—Varieties include the following—bristle, fiber, wire, nail, clothes, camel's hair, hydraulic, rotary, paint, tooth, scrubbing, floor, hair, bath, dust; see also **broom, mop.**
2. [A touch]—*Syn.* rub, tap, stroke; see **touch** 2.
3. [A light encounter]—*Syn.* skirmish, scrap, patrol action; see **fight** 1.
4. [Underbrush]—*Syn.* thicket, boscage, undergrowth, second growth, chaparral, cover, brushwood, shrubbery, canebrake, grove, hedge, fern, underwood, gorse, bracken, sedge, scrub, copse, coppice, spinney, dingle, brake; see also **bush** 1.
5. [(D) The act of ignoring]—*Syn.* cut, slight, discourtesy; see **insult, rudeness.**
brush, *v.* **1.** [To cleanse by brushing]—*Syn.* sweep, whisk, wipe; see **clean** 2.
2. [To touch lightly]—*Syn.* stroke, smooth, graze; see **touch** 1, 2, 3.
brush aside, *v.* —*Syn.* deny, contradict, disclaim; see **refuse** 2.
brushfire, *n.* —*Syn.* burning, conflagration, forest fire; see **fire** 1.
brush off (D), *v.* —*Syn.* reject, get rid of, send away; see **dismiss** 1.
brush up, *v.* **1.** [To study]—*Syn.* reread, look over, review; see **study** 1.
2. [To clean]—*Syn.* renovate, refurbish, clean up; see **clean.**
brusque, *mod.* —*Syn.* terse, blunt, curt; see **abrupt** 2.
brutal, *mod.* **1.** [Cruel]—*Syn.* pitiless, harsh, unmerciful; see **cruel** 1, 2.
2. [Crude]—*Syn.* coarse, unfeeling, rude; see **crude** 1.
brutality, *n.* —*Syn.* savageness, grossness, unfeelingness; see **cruelty.**
brutally, *mod.* —*Syn.* ruthlessly, cruelly, callously, relentlessly, mercilessly, heartlessly, grimly, viciously, meanly, inhumanly, inhumanely, brutishly, savagely, in a ruthless *or* cruel *or* heartless manner

or way, hellishly, pitilessly, barbarously, remorselessly, unkindly, unrelentingly, wildly, inexorably, fiercely, atrociously, hard-heartedly, murderously, ferociously, diabolically, ferally, barbarically, demoniacally, in cold blood, animalistically.—*Ant.* gently, kindly*, mercifully.

brute, *n.* **1.** [An animal]—*Syn.* mammal, beast, creature; see **animal** 2, **monster** 1.
2. [A person lacking human feelings]—*Syn.* degenerate, scamp, lout; see **beast** 2, **freak** 2.

bubble, *n.*—*Syn.* globule, sac, air bubble, balloon, foam, froth, spume, effervescence, lather, barm, *Meerschaum* (German).

bubble, *v.*—*Syn.* froth, foam, gurgle, gush, well, trickle, effervesce, boil, percolate, spume, simmer, seep, work, eddy, ferment, erupt, issue, fret, fester; *all* (D): blob, giggle, fizzle, burble; see also **sound** 1.

buccaneer, *n.*—*Syn.* pirate, marauder, freebooter; see **criminal, robber.**

buck, *n.* **1.** [The male of certain animals]—*Syn.* sir, stag, bull; see **animal** 2, **deer.**
2. [In football, a running attack against the line]—*Syn.* smash through the line; *all* (D): line buck, straight buck, power play, lunge, plunge, line play, straight football; see also **attack** 1, **below** 1.
pass the buck (D)—*Syn.* avoid responsibility, shirk, shift the blame; see **evade** 1.

bucket, *n.*—*Syn.* pail, canister, cask, scuttle, kettle, hod; see also **can** 1, **container, pot** 1.
kick the bucket (D)—*Syn.* expire, lose one's life, pass away; see **die** 1.

buckle, *n.*—*Syn.* clasp, clamp, harness, fastening; see **fastener.**

buckle down (D), *v.*—*Syn.* apply oneself, attend to, devote *or* consecrate oneself to, keep one's mind on, keep close to, be occupied with, dedicate oneself, give oneself over to; see also **concentrate** 2.

buck off, *v.*—*Syn.* unseat, unhorse, dislodge, throw off, eject, buck; see also **oust.**

buck up (D), *v.*—*Syn.* cheer, comfort, hearten; see **encourage** 2.

bud, *n.*—*Syn.* shoot, incipient flower, germ, embryo; see **flower.**
nip in the bud—*Syn.* check, halt, stop; see **prevent.**

budding, *mod.*—*Syn.* maturing, developing, incipient, about to bloom, fresh, shooting up, burgeoning, opening, blossoming, bursting (forth), putting forth shoots, vegetating, beginning to grow *or* blossom *or* bloom, flowering, blooming, promising, young, pubescent, sprouting, germinating, pullulating, immature, latent, embryonic, in bud; see also **growing.**

buddy, *n.* **1.** [(D) A close friend]—*Syn.* intimate, mate, fellow, peer, companion, confidant; *all* (D): chum, pal, sidekick, crony; see also **associate, friend** 1.—*Ant.* stranger, enemy*, alien.
2. [An informal address]—*Syn.* Sir, I beg your pardon; *all* (D): you there, boy, Mack, bud, Jack, hey (you).

budge, *v.*—*Syn.* stir, change position, inch; see **move** 1, **shift** 1, 2.

budget, *n.*—*Syn.* estimates, estimated expenses, allocations, budgetary figures, accounts, financial statement *or* plan, cost of operation, funds, spending plan, planned disbursement; see **statement** 3.

budget, *v.* **1.** [To estimate expenditures and income]—*Syn.* allocate expenditures, balance income and outgo, forecast, allow for, figure in *or* on, estimate necessary expenditures; see also **estimate** 3.
2. [To estimate time or rations or distance, etc.]—*Syn.* compute, predict, calculate; see **estimate** 1, 2.

buff, *mod.*—*Syn.* tan, ochre, tawny, light brown; see **brown, tan, yellow** 1.
in the buff (D)—*Syn.* nude, bare, unclothed; see **naked.**

buff, *v.*—*Syn.* polish, burnish, brush; see **shine** 3.

buffalo, *n.*—Beasts called buffalo include the following—common *or* water buffalo, Cape buffalo, American bison, wild ox, African antelope; see also **animal** 2.

buffer, *n.*—*Syn.* fender, guard, bumper; see **defense** 1, **shield.**

buffet, *n.*—*Syn.* cabinet, sideboard, shelf; see **cupboard, furniture.**

buffet, *v.*—*Syn.* slap, strike, flail; see **beat** 2, 3, **hit** 1, 3.

buffoon, *n.*—*Syn.* joker, jester, comedian; see **clown, fool** 1, 2.

bug, *n.* **1.** [An insect]—*Syn.* beetle, vermin, gnat; see **insect, pest** 1.
2. [(D) A microbe]—*Syn.* bacillus, disease germ, virus; see **germ** 3.
3. [(D) A defect]—*Syn.* flaw, fault, imperfection; see **blemish, defect** 2.
4. [(D) An enthusiast]—*Syn.* devotee, zealot, fanatic; see **enthusiast** 1.

bug, *v.* **1.** [(D) To annoy]—*Syn.* irritate, plague, pester; see **bother** 2, 3, **disturb** 2.
2. [To install hidden microphones]—*Syn.* spy, overhear, listen in on, wiretap *or* tap (D); see also **eavesdrop.**

bugbear, *n.*—*Syn.* horror, terror, dread, hate, *bête noire* (French), nightmare, ghost, phantom, specter, goblin, curse; *all* (D): bear, bogy, bugaboo; see also **care** 2, **difficulty** 1, 2, **fear** 2.

buggy, *n.*—*Syn.* top buggy, buckboard, surrey; see **carriage** 2.

bugle, *n.*—*Syn.* clarion, trumpet, cornet; see **horn** 1.

build, *v.* **1.** [To construct]—*Syn.* erect, frame, raise, rear, make, manufacture, put *or* fit together, fabricate, contrive, carpenter, assemble, put *or* set up, model, hammer together, pile stone on stone, sculpture, fashion, compose, evolve, compile, cast, reconstruct, chisel, hew, mould, produce, figure, forge, block out, bring about, devise, carve, weave; see also **create** 2, **form** 1.—*Ant.* destroy*, demolish, wreck.
2. [To increase]—*Syn.* mount, wax, swell; see **grow** 1, 2, **increase** 1.
3. [To found]—*Syn.* formulate, institute, constitute; see **establish** 2, **organize** 2.

builder, *n.* **1.** [Carpenter]—*Syn.* manufacturer, contractor, mason, fabricator, artisan, craftsman, producer; see also **architect** 1.—*Ant.* destroyer*, wrecker, consumer.
2. [Creator]—*Syn.* maker, originator, inventor, constructor; see **author** 1.

build in, *v.*—*Syn.* incorporate, add, insert; see **include** 2.

building, *n.* **1.** [A structure]—*Syn.* edifice, erection, construction, fabrication, fabric, house, compages, framework, superstructure, frame, structure, architectural construction, pile; see also **apartment house, architecture, barn, castle, church** 1, **factory, home** 1, **hotel, motel, skyscraper, temple.**
2. [The act of building]—*Syn.* erection, raising, fabricating; see **construction** 1.

build on, *v.* —*Syn.* extend, enlarge, add (on) to, develop; see **increase** 1.

build up, *v.* **1.** [To increase]—*Syn.* strengthen, add to, expand; see **increase** 1.
2. [To construct]—*Syn.* make, erect, establish, construct; see **build** 1.

built, *mod.* **1.** [Erected]—*Syn.* constructed, fabricated, manufactured, made, put together, produced, assembled, contrived, reared, raised, remodeled, completed, joined, perfected, finished, realized, created, made actual, brought to conclusion; *both* (D): actualized, finalized; see also **formed.**
2. [(D) Buxom]—*Syn.* well-proportioned, shapely, stacked (D); see **buxom** 2.

bulb, *n.* —*Syn.* globe, globule, ball, knob, nodule, corn, nub, tuber, protuberance, head, bunch, swelling, tumor, tube, corm.
Plant bulbs include the following—tulip, gladiolus, day lily, spring-flowering, onion, camas, (grape) hyacinth, *Lilium grandiflora* (Latin); butterfly, tiger, spider, mariposa lily; see also **flower** 2, **plant.**
Electric light bulbs include the following—high-intensity, three-way, soft-white, two-way, flash bulb; fluorescent, incandescent, ultraviolet, infrared, sun lamp; black light, strobe light *or* strobe (D); see also **light** 3, **lamp.**

bulge, *n.* —*Syn.* swelling, bunch, lump, protrusion, protuberance, hump, bump, convexity, intumescence, bulb, bunching, outgrowth, superfluity, tumefaction, nodule, sagging, tuberosity, nodulation, growth, dilation, prominence, salience, excess, bagginess, appendage, projection, excrescence, tumor, gibbosity, boss, distention, salient, egg, sac, knob, horn, ridge, flange, rib, wart, promontory, hummock; see also **growth** 3, **point** 2.

bulge, *v.* —*Syn.* puff out, distend, protrude; see **swell.**

bulk, *n.* **1.** [Size]—*Syn.* magnitude, mass, extent; see **quantity, size** 2.
2. [Major portion]—*Syn.* greater *or* better *or* main *or* principal *or* major *or* best *or* predominant part, most, majority, plurality, biggest share, greater number, nearly *or* almost all, body, more than half, best, gross, staple, preponderance, lion's share (D). —*Ant.* bit*, remnant, fraction.

bulky, *mod.* —*Syn.* massive, big, huge; see **high** 1, **large** 1, **long** 1.

bull, *n.* **1.** [The male of the bovine species]—*Syn.* *Bostaurus* (Latin), herd leader, bullock, steer, sire, ox; *all* (D): top cow, masculine, beast, seed ox, animal; see also **calf, cow.**
2. [One who endeavors to profit from a rising market]—*Syn.* buyer, margin purchaser, long seller (D); see **businessman, financier.**—*Ant.* seller; *both* (D): short seller, bear.
3. [(D) Nonsense]—*Syn.* balderdash, rubbish, trash; see **nonsense** 1.
4. [(D) A policeman]—*Syn.* *all* (D): fuzz, cop, dick; see **policeman.**

bullet, *n.* —*Syn.* shell, cartridge, ball, bolt, projectile, missile, trajectile, (piece of) ammunition, slug; steel-jacketed, soft-nosed *or* dum-dum bullet, machine-gun bullet; ammo (D); see also **shot** 2, **weapon** 1.

bulletin, *n.* **1.** [A brief notice]—*Syn.* release, notice, communiqué; see **announcement** 2.
2. [A published report]—*Syn.* summary, journal, digest; see **record** 1.

bully, *n.* —*Syn.* ruffian, rowdy, tough (D); see **rascal.**

bully, *v.* —*Syn.* tease, domineer, harass; see **threaten** 1.

bulwark, *n.* —*Syn.* buttress, outwork, rampart; see **barrier, defense** 2, **fortification** 2, **support** 2.

bum, *n.* —*Syn.* hobo, transient, vagrant; see **beggar** 1, 2, **tramp** 1.

bump, *n.* **1.** [A jarring collision]—*Syn.* knock, bang, bounce, jounce, jar, box, smash, pat, crack, jolt, crash, sideswipe, collision, punch, appulse, hit, clap, push, shove, thrust, boost, shock, clash, impact, stroke, rap, tap, slap, clout, jab, jerk, crash, punch, prod, jolt, slam, nudge, buffet; *all* (D): swat, bash, wallop, belt, bat, swipe, thump, whack, poke, clump, plump, clunk, thwack, sock, whop, lick, smack, cuff, slug; see also **blow** 1, **collision** 1.
2. [A swelling]—*Syn.* projection, protuberance, knob; see **bulge, lump.**

bump, *v.* **1.** [To collide with]—*Syn.* collide, run against, strike; see **crash** 4, **hit** 1, 3.
2. [To make a bumping sound]—*Syn.* thud, whack, pound, smack, thwack, rap, slap, punch, slam, plop, plunk, thump, clump, bang, knock, clatter, clap, crash, rattle, thunder, tramp.

bumper, *n.* —*Syn.* cover, guard, protector; see **defense** 2, **fender, shield.**

bumpkin, *n.* —*Syn.* rustic, yokel, peasant; see **boor.**

bump off (D), *v.* —*Syn.* slaughter, murder, slay; see **kill** 1.

bumptious, *mod.* —*Syn.* conceited, arrogant, vain; see **egotistic** 2.

bun, *n.* —*Syn.* muffin, scone, hot cross bun; see **bread, roll** 4, **pastry.**

bunch, *n.* **1.** [A cluster]—*Syn.* clump, group, batch, spray, sheaf, tuft, shock, stack, thicket, tussock, fascicle, group, gathering, host, galaxy, faggot, bundle, knot, collection, agglomeration; *all* (D): passel, mess, slug, caboodle, oodles, shootin'-match, shebang; see also **collection** 2.
2. [(D) A group]—*Syn.* pack, band, assemblage; see **gathering.**

bundle, *n.* —*Syn.* packet, parcel, bunch; see **package** 1, 2.

bundle up, *v.* —*Syn.* clothe, don, get dressed; see **dress** 1.

bungalow, *n.* —*Syn.* cottage, lodging, one-story dwelling; see **home** 1.

bungle, *v.* —*Syn.* blunder, fumble, mishandle; see **botch, fail** 1.

bungler, *n.* —*Syn.* fumbler, botcher, blunderer, flounderer, mismanager, muddler, numskull, featherbrain, dolt, scatterbrain, dunce, clod, ignoramus, idiot, duffer, addlebrain, gawk, donkey, lobby, marplot, butterfingers, lubber; *all* (D): bonehead, blockhead, screw up, spoiler, goof off, rattlehead, clumsy oaf, bull in a china shop, harebrain, butcher, schlemiel, blunderhead, klutz, giddyhead, addlehead, block, muffer; see also **fool** 1.

bungling, *mod.* —*Syn.* clumsy, unskillful, inept; see **awkward** 1, **incompetent.**

bunk, *n.* **1.** [A bed]—*Syn.* berth, cot, pallet; see **bed** 1.

2. [(D) Anything untrue, silly, or unreliable] —*Syn.* rubbish, rot, hogwash (D); see **nonsense** 1.

bunker, *n.* —*Syn.* locker, box, chest; see **bin, container.**

bunt, *v.* **1.** [To butt]—*Syn.* toss, gore, horn; see **butt** 1, **throw** 1, 2.

2. [In baseball, to meet the ball with a loosely held bat]—*Syn. all* (D): meet it, lay it down, lay it along the base line, sacrifice, bunt and run; see also **hit** 5.

buoy, *n.* —*Syn.* float, drift, floating marker; see **float** 1.

Types of buoys include the following—bell, can, life, nun, light, whistling.

buoy, *v.* —*Syn.* keep afloat, sustain, uphold; see **support** 2.

buoyancy, *n.* **1.** [Lightness]—*Syn.* levity, ethereality, buoyance, airiness, weightlessness, floatability; see also **lightness** 2.

2. [Cheerfulness]—*Syn.* gaiety, good humor, jollity; see **happiness** 1, 2.

buoyant, *mod.* **1.** [Light in weight]—*Syn.* floatable, weightless, unsinkable; see **floating, light** 5.

2. [Light in spirits]—*Syn.* gay, jovial, cheerful; see **happy** 1.

bur, *n.* **1.** [A prickly seedcase]—*Syn.* nut, grain, acorn, (seed) pod; see also **seed** 1.

2. [A threaded metal block]—*Syn.* bolt, lock nut, cap; see **nut** 2.

burden, *n.* **1.** [Something carried]—*Syn.* lading, freight, pack; see **load** 1.

2. [Anything hard to support or endure]—*Syn.* encumbrance, punishment, mishap, thorn in the flesh, onus, weary load; see also **difficulty** 2, **misfortune** 1.

burden, *v.* —*Syn.* weigh down, encumber, cumber, overwhelm, hinder, hamper, strain, load (with), saddle *or* task with, handicap, obligate, lade, tax, supercharge, overtask, afflict, vex, try, trouble, pile, overcharge, overlay, bear *or* bog down, crush, depress, impede, overload, oppress, make heavy, press down; see also **force** 1, **hinder, oppress.** —*Ant.* lighten*. relieve, unload.

burdensome, *mod.* —*Syn.* heavy, oppressive, troublesome; see **difficult** 1, 2, **disturbing, onerous** 1.

bureau, *n.* **1.** [Committee]—*Syn.* commission, authority, board; see **committee.**

2. [Chest of drawers]—*Syn.* highboy, dresser, chiffonier; see **chest** 1, **furniture.**

bureaucracy, *n.* **1.** [Government]—*Syn.* officialdom, the Establishment, the authorities, apparatchiki, the powers that be, city hall, they *or* them, the system (D); see **authority** 3, **government** 1, 2.

2. [Rigid routine]—*Syn.* official procedure, inflexible routine, strict procedure; *all* (D): red tape, officialism, bumbledom.

burglar, *n.* —*Syn.* thief, housebreaker, second-story man; see **criminal, robber.**

burglary, *n.* —*Syn.* housebreaking, stealing, robbery; see **crime** 2, **theft.**

burial, *n.* —*Syn.* last rites, interment, obsequies; see **funeral** 1.

burial ground, *n.* —*Syn.* necropolis, graveyard, memorial park; see **cemetery.**

burlesque, *n.* **1.** [Anything intending to mock] —*Syn.* travesty, caricature, cartoon; see **parody** 1, 2.

2. [A burlesque show]—*Syn.* show, theatrical entertainment, revue; *all* (D): burleyque, strip, burly, topless show, nudie, pantyskew, girlesque, pantymimic; see **entertainment** 2, **performance** 2, **show** 2.

burly, *mod.* —*Syn.* husky, stout, portly; see **fat** 1, **strong** 1.

burn, *n.* —*Syn.* scorch, wound, impairment; see **blister.**

burn, *v.* **1.** [To oxidize]—*Syn.* consume, burn up, burn down, incinerate, rage, blaze, flame, flash, burn fiercely, flare, blaze *or* flame *or* flare up, burst into flame, grow bright, reduce *or* turn to ashes.

2. [To subject to fire]—*Syn.* enkindle, cremate, relight, conflagrate, consume with flames, incinerate, rekindle, reduce to ashes, set a match to, set on fire, set ablaze *or* afire, torch, ignite, kindle, sear, singe, scorch, brand, char, cauterize, consign to the flame, fire, light, roast, toast, heat, brake; see also **cook.** —*Ant.* extinguish*, put out, quench.

3. [To feel emotion suggestive of fire]—*Syn.* tingle, lust, desire ,yearn, thirst, be excited *or* inflamed *or* aroused, be stirred up, burn with, breathe fire and fury (D); see also **rage** 1.

4. [(D) To anger]—*Syn.* enrage, infuriate, arouse; see **anger** 1.

5. [(D) To cheat]—*Syn.* swindle, defraud, trick; see **deceive.**

6. [To scorch]—*Syn.* char, sear, roast, toast, parch, bake, singe, scald, wither; see also sense 2.

burned, *mod.* **1.** [Marked by fire]—*Syn.* scorched, charred, seared, burnt, singed, branded, cauterized, marked, blistered, scaled.

2. [Consumed]—*Syn.* burned up, reduced to ashes, incinerated; see **destroyed.**

burned up (D), *mod.* —*Syn.* angered, enraged, infuriated; see **angry.**

burner, *n.* —*Syn.* torch, jet, (heat) unit, heater, warmer, cooker, gas burner, individual heat, lamp; see also **stove.**

burning, *mod.* **1.** [Flaming]—*Syn.* fiery, blazing, glowing, ablaze, afire, on fire, smoking, in flames, aflame, inflamed, kindled, enkindled, ignited, red, hot, scorching, incandescent, turning to ashes, aglow, searing, in a blaze, blistering, red-hot, white-hot, smouldering, oxidizing, being consumed. —*Ant.* cold*, frozen, out.

2. [Fervent]—*Syn.* intense, ardent, impassioned; see **passionate** 2.

3. [Eager]—*Syn.* zealous, fervid, rapt, glowing; see **enthusiastic** 2, 3.

4. [Caustic]—*Syn.* sharp, biting, stinging; see **sour** 1.

burnish, *v.* —*Syn.* polish, wax, put on a finish; see **shine** 3.

burnt, *mod.* —*Syn.* scorched, singed, charred; see **burned** 1.

burrow, *n.* —*Syn.* tunnel, den, lair; see **hole** 3, **retreat** 2.

bursar, *n.* —*Syn.* controller, purser, cashier; see **accountant, treasurer.**

burst, *n.* **1.** [An explosion]—*Syn.* blowout, blast, blowup; see **explosion** 1.
2. [A sudden spurt]—*Syn.* rush, outburst, spate; see **fit** 2.
3. [A volley]—*Syn.* salvo, round, discharge; see **fire** 3, **volley.**

burst, *v.* **1.** [To explode]—*Syn.* blow up, erupt, rupture; see **break** 2, 3, **disintegrate** 1, **explode** 1.
2. [To break]—*Syn.* crack, split, fracture; see **break** 1, **destroy** 1.
3. [To puncture]—*Syn.* pierce, prick, perforate; see **penetrate** 1.

burst in, *v.* —*Syn.* rush *or* break in, invade, intrude; see **enter** 1, **meddle** 1.

bursting, *mod.* —*Syn.* exploding, erupting, shattering; see **breaking.**

burst into tears, *v.* —*Syn.* weep, start crying, break into tears; see **cry** 1.

bury, *v.* **1.** [To inter]—*Syn.* inhume, lay in the grave, entomb, consign to dust, enshrine, ensepulcher, deposit in the earth, embalm, give burial to, hold funeral services for, hold (the) last rites for, lay out, mummify, plant (D).
2. [To cover]—*Syn.* conceal, secrete, stow away; see **hide** 1.
3. [To defeat]—*Syn.* overcome, win over, beat, conquer; see **defeat** 1, 2.
4. [To occupy]—*Syn.* engross, engage, interest, rivet; see **occupy** 3.
5. [To embed]—*Syn.* sink, implant, drive in; see **embed** 1, **fasten** 1.

bus, *n.* —*Syn.* autobus, passenger bus, transit vehicle, sightseeing bus, motor coach, charabanc, interurban, airline bus, limousine, common carrier, public conveyance; *all* (D): Greyhound (trademark), minibus, limo, stretch bus.

bus (D), *v.* —*Syn* transport, equalize *or* integrate (by busing), redistrict; see **ship.**

bush, *n.* **1.** [A shrub]—*Syn.* bramble, thicket, shrubbery, briar bush, rosebush; see also **hedge, plant.**
2. [A wild region]—*Syn.* hinterland, backcountry, backwoods; see **country** 1, **forest.**
beat around the bush—*Syn.* speak indirectly *or* evasively, avoid the subject, be deceptive; see **evade** 1.

bushy, *mod.* —*Syn.* fuzzy, disordered, thick, shaggy, rough, full, tufted, fringed, woolly, nappy, fluffy, furry, crinkly, stiff, wiry, rumpled, unkempt, prickly, feathery, leafy, bristly, unruly, spreading, heavy; see also **hairy** 1.—*Ant.* thin*, sleek, smooth.

busily, *mod.* —*Syn.* diligently, actively, energetically, strenuosly, eagerly, earnestly, seriously, intently, determinedly, rapidly, dexterously, industriously, assiduously, sedulously, carefully, intently, laboriously, painstakingly, unremittingly, studiously, perseveringly, hurriedly, briskly, vivaciously, animatedly, purposefully, ardently, arduously, fervently, spiritedly, nimbly, zealously, agilely, vigorously, drudgingly, indefatigably, restlessly, vigilantly, enthusiastically, speedily, hastily, persistently, expeditiously, unweariedly, with all dispatch, like hell *or* the dickens *or* the devil (D). —*Ant.* listlessly*, idly, perfunctorily.

business, *mod.* —*Syn.* financial, monetary, commercial; see **commercial** 1.

business, *n.* **1.** [Industry and trade]—*Syn.* commerce, exchange, trade, traffic, barter, commercial enterprise, gainful occupation, buying and selling, negotiation, production and distribution, dealings, affairs, sales, contracts, bargaining, trading, transaction, banking, marketing, custom, undertaking, speculation, haggling, market, mercantilism, wholesale and retail, capital and labor, *laissez-faire* (French), free enterprise; *both* (D): game, racket.
2. [Occupation]—*Syn.* trade, profession, vocation; see **job** 1.
3. [One's proper concerns]—*Syn.* affair, concern, interest; see **affair** 1.
4. [A commercial enterprise]—*Syn.* firm, factory, mill, store, company, shop, corporation, concern, combine, establishment, enterprise, partnership, institution, house, market, syndicate, cartel, trust, monopoly, holding company, mutual company, pool.
Some of the large well-known businesses are—American Telephone and Telegraph (AT&T), Boeing Corporation, Chrysler Corporation, Exxon, Ford Motor Company, General Dynamics, General Electric, General Motors, DuPont, International Business Machines (IBM), International Telephone and Telegraph (IT & T), Mobil Oil, Standard Oil of California, Texaco, Texas Instruments, U.S. Steel, Xerox.
5. [The business cycle]—*Syn.* prosperity, boom, inflation, recession, depression, slump, crash, deflation, hard times, good times, upward *or* downward trend.
do business with—*Syn.* deal *or* trade with, patronize, employ; see **buy** 1, **sell** 1, **treat** 1.
get the business (D)—*Syn.* be mistreated *or* abused, endure, tolerate; see **suffer** 1, 3.
give the business (D)—*Syn.* mistreat, bother, victimize; see **abuse** 1.
mean business—*Syn.* be serious, stress, impress; see **emphasize.**

businesslike, *mod.* —*Syn.* purposeful, methodical, systematic, intent, earnest, serious, sedulous, energetic, hardworking, brisk, diligent, painstaking, careful, organized, professional, vigorous, direct, orderly, undeviating, skillful, dexterous, practiced, accustomed, thorough, accomplished, expeditious, prompt, active, industrious, assiduous, attentive, concentrated, enterprising, resolute, careful, economical, disciplined, effective; see also **efficient** 1, **practical.**—*Ant.* aimless*, dilatory, inefficient.

businessman, *n.* —*Syn.* industrialist, capitalist, employer, tycoon, broker, organization man, man in the gray flannel suit, retailer, wholesaler, stockbroker, manager, buyer, operator, franchiser, manipulator, speculator, entrepreneur, purchasing agent, storekeeper, tradesman; see also **financier, manufacturer, merchant.**

bustle, *v.* —*Syn.* move quickly, hasten, hustle; see **hurry** 1, **run** 2.

bust, *n.* **1.** [Breast]—*Syn.* bosom, thorax, torso; see **breast** 2, **chest** 2.

2. [Figurehead]—*Syn.* carving, sculpture, model; see **image** 2, **statue.**

busy, *mod.* **1.** [Engaged]—*Syn.* occupied, diligent, working, in conference, in a meeting, in the field, in the laboratory, on an assignment; with a customer *or* client *or* patient, etc.; on duty, on the job, (hard) at work, busy with, on the move *or* run, on the road, hard-working; *all* (D): busy as a bee, hustling, up to one's ears, always on the jump, on the go, (hard) at it, buried in, having many irons in the fire, on a kick, on the hop, having other fish to fry; see also **employed.**—*Ant.* idle, unemployed*, unoccupied.

2. [Active]—*Syn.* bustling, energetic, lively; see **active** 2.

3. [In use]—*Syn.* employed, occupied, in someone else's possession, unavailable, (already) taken; see also **rented.**—*Ant.* not in use, available*, clear.

4. [Officious]—*Syn.* meddlesome, curious, forward, intrusive, obtrusive, meddling, prying, interfering; *all* (D): butting in, snoopy, nosy, pushy; see also **inquisitive.**—*Ant.* humble*, circumspect, self-absorbed.

busybody, *n.*—*Syn.* snoop, meddler, pry, chatterbox, tattletale, eavesdropper, fussbudget, intriguer, intruder, troublemaker; *all* (D): buttinsky, kibitzer, fink, yenta, rubberneck; see also **gossip** 2.

but, *conj.* or *prep.* **1.** [Indicating contrast]—*Syn.* however, on the other hand, in contrast, nevertheless, still, yet, though, on the contrary, but then, but as you see; see also **although.**

2. [Indicating an exception]—*Syn.* save, disregarding, without, not including, not taking into account, let alone, leaving out of consideration, aside from, with the exception of, not to mention, passing over, barring, setting aside, forgetting, omitting (to mention); see also **except.**

3. [Indicating a limitation]—*Syn.* only (just), merely, simply, barely, solely, purely, just, no more, exactly, no other than, without; see also **only** 2.

butcher, *n.* **1.** [A meat-dealer]—*Syn.* meat seller, slaughterer, processor, skinner, boner, cutter, proprietor of a meat market; *all* (D): meatmarket man, pig-sticker, meat man; see also **businessman, merchant.**

2. [A killer]—*Syn.* murderer, slayer, gunman; see **criminal, killer.**

butcher, *v.* **1.** [To slaughter for human consumption]—*Syn.* stick, pack, dress, clean, cure, smoke, salt, cut, put up.

2. [To kill inhumanly]—*Syn.* slaughter, slay, massacre; see **kill** 1.

3. [(D) To ruin]—*Syn.* mutilate, spoil, wreck; see **botch, destroy** 1.

butchery, *n.*—*Syn.* slaughter, killing, massacre; see **carnage, crime** 2, **murder.**

butler, *n.*—*Syn.* steward, head servant, house boy; see **servant.**

butt, *n.* **1.** [The butt end]—*Syn.* base, tail end, bottom, hilt, extremity, tail, tip, fundament, stump, stub, fag end (D); see also **foundation** 2.—*Ant.* pinnacle, point, peak.

2. [A laughing stock]—*Syn.* sap, dupe, sucker; see **fool** 2.

3. [(D) The buttocks]—*Syn.* bottom, seat, posterior; see **back** 1, **rump.**

butt, *v.* **1.** [To strike with the head]—*Syn.* ram, push headfirst, bump, batter, knock, collide with, run into, smack, buffet, strike, hook, gore, horn, buck, toss, crash into, collide; see also **crash** 4, **hit** 3.

2. [To abut]—*Syn.* adjoin, touch, bound; see **join** 3.

butter, *n.*—Varieties of butter include the following—dairy, creamery, sweet, bulk, cube, country, tub, buffalo, ghee, yak, vegetable, soy, cacao, shea.

butterfly, *n.*—Common American butterflies include the following—Falcate Orange-tip, Tiger Swallowtail, Mourning Cloak, Common Sulphur, American Copper, Cabbage, Colorado Parnassian, Great Spangled Fritillary, Tortoiseshell, Viceroy, Monarch, Zebra, Buckeye, Red Admiral, Cloudless Sulphur, Grayling, Spicebush, Swallowtail, Ursula, Silverspot, Thecla, Violet; see also **insect.**

button, *n.*—*Syn.* knob, catch, disk; see **fastener.**

on the button—*Syn.* correctly, precisely, accurately; see **exactly.**

button, *v.*—*Syn.* close, clasp, make firm; see **fasten** 1.

buttress, *v.*—*Syn.* prop (up), bolster, sustain; see **support** 1.

buxom, *mod.* **1.** [Hearty]—*Syn.* plump, robust, vigorous; see **healthy** 1, **fat** 1.

2. [(D) Large-breasted]—*Syn.* well-proportioned, shapely, well-made, comely; *all* (D): stacked, built, busty, bazoomy.

buy (D), *n.*—*Syn.* value; *both* (D): good deal, steal; see **bargain** 2.

buy, *v.* **1.** [To acquire by purchase]—*Syn.* purchase, get, bargain *or* barter for, procure, gain, secure for a consideration, contract *or* sign for, get in exchange, go marketing, buy and sell, order, invest in, make an investment, shop for, acquire ownership of, procure title to, pay (cash) for, cheapen, redeem, pay a price for; *all* (D): buy into, score, traffic in; see also **obtain** 1.—*Ant.* sell*, vend, auction.

2. [To bribe]—*Syn.* suborn, have in one's pay, grease one's palm (D); see **bribe.**

buyer, *n.*—*Syn.* purchasing agent, purchaser, customer, client, prospect, emptor, consumer, representative, patron, user, shopper, bull (D).—*Ant.* salesman*, vendor, dealer.

buyer's market, *n.*—*Syn.* depression, recession, bargain prices; see **bargain** 2, **opportunity** 1, **sale** 3.

buying, *n.*—*Syn.* purchasing, getting, obtaining, acquiring, paying, investing, exchange, bartering, bargaining, procuring, trafficking.—*Ant.* selling*, vending, auctioning.

buy off, *v.*—*Syn.* corrupt, influence, fix (D); see **bribe.**

buzz, *n.*—*Syn.* murmur, buzzing, hum; see **noise** 1.

buzz, *v.* drone, hum, whir; see **noise** 1, **sound** 1.

buzzard, *n.*—*Syn.* bird of prey, *Buteo* (Latin), carrion-eater; see **bird** 1.

buzzer, *n.*—*Syn.* siren, signal, electric bell; see **alarm** 1, **bell, sign** 1, **warning, whistle** 1, 2.

by, *prep.* **1.** [Near]—*Syn.* close *or* next to, by the side of, nigh; see **near** 1, **next** 2.

2. [By stated means]—*Syn.* over, with, through, by means of, by the agency *or* intermediacy of, in the name of, at the hand of, along with, through the medium of, with the assistance *or* aid of, on, supported by.

by common consent, *mod.* —*Syn.* in agreement *or* accord, co-operatively, in unison; see **unanimously, united** 2.

bygone, *mod.* —*Syn.* former, olden, of old; see **old** 3.

by-law, *n.* —*Syn.* ordinance, local law, municipal regulation; see **law** 3.

by-pass, *n.* —*Syn.* detour, temporary route, side road; see **road** 1.

bystander, *n.* —*Syn.* onlooker, watcher, spectator; see **observer** 1.

by the book, *mod.* —*Syn.* strictly, according to rule, authoritatively, formally, regularly, lawfully, rigidly, rigorously, stringently; see also **legally** 1, **officially** 1.

by the same token, *mod.* —*Syn.* similarly, likewise, furthermore; see **besides.**

by the way, *mod.* —*Syn.* casually, incidentally, offhand; see **accidentally.**

byword, *n.* —*Syn.* standing joke, axiom, gnomic saying; see **proverb.**

C

cab, *n.* —*Syn.* taxi, tourist car, hack (D); see **automobile, taxicab, vehicle** 1.

cabal, *n.* —*Syn.* plot, scheme, conspiracy; see **intrigue** 1, **plan** 2, **trick** 1.

cabaret, *n.* —*Syn.* café, tavern, night club; see **bar** 2, **restaurant.**

cabin, *n.* —*Syn.* log house, cottage, hut; see **home** 1, **shelter.**

cabinet, *n.* [An executive body]—*Syn.* (advisory) council, bureau, governing body, administrators, (group of) counselors, assembly, assistants, department heads, (body of) advisers, United States Cabinet, ministry; *both* (D): backstairs cabinet, brain trust; see also **authority** 3, **bureaucracy** 1, **committee, government** 2.

cable, *n.* —*Syn.* cord, preformed cable, wire twist; see **chain** 1, **wire** 1.

caboose, *n.* —*Syn.* trainmen's *or* rear *or* crew car, boxcar, cab (D); see **car** 2, **train** 2.

cache, *n.* —*Syn.* hoard, supplies, hidden reserve; see **reserve** 1, **treasure, wealth** 2.

cache, *v.* —*Syn.* conceal, store, lay away; see **accumulate** 1, **hide** 1, **maintain** 3, **save** 3, **store** 2.

cackle, *v.* —*Syn.* cluck, gabble, chortle, chuckle, titter, snicker, quack, giggle, snigger; see also **laugh** 1.

cacophonous, *mod.* —*Syn.* ill-sounding, dissonant, discordant; see **harsh** 1.

cacophony, *n.* —*Syn.* dissonance, discord, harshness; see **noise** 1, 2.

cactus, *n.* —*Syn.* one of the *Cactaceae* (Latin), polypetalous dicotyledonous plant, desert flora *or* vegetation, succulent; see also **plant.**
Cactuses include the following—*Mammillaria, Melocactus, Phyllocactus* (all Latin); giant, saguaro, barrel, choya, hedgehog, cochineal, nipple, prickly pear, night-blooming cereus, century plant, mescal, echinocactus.

cad, *n.* —*Syn.* rogue, scoundrel, rake; see **boor, rascal.**

cadaver, *n.* —*Syn.* corpse, carcass, (the) remains; see **body** 2.

cadaverous, *mod.* —*Syn.* ghostly, pallid, gaunt; see **dead** 1, **pale** 1, **sallow, sick.**

cadence, *n.* —*Syn.* rhythm, meter, flow; see **beat** 2, 3, **measure** 3.

cadre, *n.* —*Syn.* staff officers, force, personnel; see **officer** 3, **organization** 3, **staff** 2.

café, *n.* —*Syn.* cafeteria, lunchroom, coffee shop; see **restaurant.**

cage, *n.* —*Syn.* coop, mew, crate; see **enclosure** 1, **jail, pen** 1.

caitiff, *mod.* —*Syn.* low, ignoble, degraded; see **cowardly** 2, **vulgar** 1, **weak** 3.

cajole, *v.* —*Syn.* wheedle, coax, flatter; see **influence, tempt, urge** 2.

cake, *n.* **1.** [flattish, compact mass]—*Syn.* cube, bar, loaf; see **block** 1, 6, **brick, mass** 1, **slab.**
2. [Sweet baked goods]. Kinds of cake include the following—wedding, birthday, angel food, devil's-food, corn, sponge, fruit, burnt-sugar, caramel, German chocolate, upside-down, tube, Bundt, pound, Martha Washington, maple, orange, white lemon, citron, walnut, almond, layer, white mountain, spice, marble, Lady Baltimore, coffeecake; jellyroll, gingerbread, éclair, shortbread, *petit four* (French); see also **bread** 1, **pastry.**
take the cake (D)—*Syn.* excel, outdo, win the prize; see **surpass.**

cake, *v.* —*Syn.* crust, solidify, pack; see **freeze** 1, **harden** 1, 2, **thicken** 1.

calamitous, *mod.* —*Syn.* disastrous, unfortunate, adverse; see **harmful, unfavorable** 2.

calamity, *n.* —*Syn.* cataclysm, distress, trial; see **catastrophe, disaster, misfortune** 1, **tragedy** 2.

calculable, *mod.* —*Syn.* measurable, ascertainable, predictable, foreseeable, accountable, reckonable, discoverable, estimable, computable, countable.

calculate, *v.* **1.** [To reckon]—*Syn.* enumerate, determine, rate, forecast, weigh, gauge, cast, number, figure (up), account, compute, sum (up), ascertain mathematically, divide, multiply, subtract, add, work out, cipher, tally; *both* (D): lump off, dope out; see also **count, estimate** 3, **measure** 1, **reckon.**
2. [(D) To expect]—*Syn.* suppose, judge, think (likely); see **anticipate** 1, **assume** 1.
3. [To estimate]—*Syn.* figure, appraise, assay; see **estimate** 1, 2, **foretell, guess** 1, **reckon.**

calculating, *mod.* —*Syn.* scheming, crafty, shrewd; see **intelligent** 1, **sly** 1.

calculation, *n.* **1.** [The act of calculating]—*Syn.* computation, estimation, prediction, reckoning, adding, subtracting, dividing, multiplying, totaling, count; see also **estimate** 1, **guess.**
2. [A forecast]—*Syn.* prediction, prognosis, prognostication; see **divination, forecast.**
3. [Prudence]—*Syn.* forethought, consideration, caution; see **discretion** 1, **prudence, thought** 1.

calculus, *n.* —*Syn.* calculation, computation, analysis; see **mathematics.**

caldron, *n.* —*Syn.* kettle, boiler, vat; see **container, pan, pot** 1.

calendar, *n.* —*Syn.* timetable, schedule, annals, menology, journal, diary, daybook, chronology, log, logbook, table, register, almanac, agenda, docket, system of reckoning, time, tabular register of the year, perpetual calendar, record of yearly periods; see also **list, program** 2, **record** 1.

calf, *n.* —*Syn.* young cow *or* bull, yearling, freemartin, maverick, dogie (D).
Similar terms for other young animals include the following—colt, cub, kitten, filly, lionet, pup, puppy; see also **animal** 1, 2, **cow.**
kill the fatted calf—*Syn.* have a feast *or* a party *or* celebration, feast, dine; see **celebrate** 1, 3.

caliber, *n.* **1.** [A measurement]—*Syn.* weight, striking power, diameter; see **length** 1, **measurement** 2, **width.**
2. [Character]—*Syn.* constitution, nature, quality; see **character** 2, **characteristic, essence** 1.

California, *n.* **1.** [The region and culture]—*Syn.* Golden Bear State, State of the Big Trees, Gold Rush State, Golden Poppy State, Bear Flag State, Gold Coast, Grape State, Sunny California; *all* (D): Cal, Cali, Sunkist State, Sunny Cal.
2. [The university]—*Syn.* The University of California at Berkeley, Davis, Irvine, La Jolla, Los Angeles, Riverside, Santa Barbara, Santa Cruz, Hastings College of Law in San Francisco, San Francisco Medical Center; *all* (D): blue and gold, Cal, (Golden) Bears, U.C.L.A., Bruins.

calisthenics, *n.* —*Syn.* exercises, workout, slimnastics (D); see **exercise** 1, **gymnastics.**

call, *n.* **1.** [A shout]—*Syn.* yell, whoop, hail; see **alarm** 1, **cry** 1.
2. [Characteristic sound]—*Syn.* twitter, tweet, shriek; see **cry** 2.
3. [A visit]—*Syn.* visiting, a few words, afternoon call; see **visit.**
4. [Word of command]—*Syn.* bugle *or* trumpet call, bell, cry, battle cry, rallying cry, reveille, last post, sacring bell, Sanctus bell, angelus; see also **alarm** 1, **command** 1, **cry** 1, **summons.**
5. [An invitation]—*Syn.* bidding, solicitation, proposal; see **invitation** 1, **request, summons.**
on call—*Syn.* usable, ready, prepared; see **available.**
within call—*Syn.* close by, approximate, not far away; see **near** 1.

call, *v.* **1.** [To raise the voice]—*Syn.* shout, call out, exclaim; see **yell.**
2. [To bring a body of people together]—*Syn.* collect, convene, muster; see **assemble** 2.
3. [To address]—*Syn.* denominate, designate, term; see **name** 1.
4. [To invite]—*Syn.* summon, request, ask; see **invite** 1, 2.
5. [To demand]—*Syn.* charge, order, command; see **ask** 1, **summon** 1.
6. [To estimate]—*Syn.* guess, make a rough calculation, say it is; see **estimate** 1, 3.
7. [To invoke]—*Syn.* call upon, entreat, appeal *or* pray (to); see **beg** 1.
8. [To arouse]—*Syn.* stir, awaken, shake; see **wake** 1.

call a halt to, *v.* —*Syn.* suspend, check, stop; see **halt** 2.

call (at, on, *or* **upon),** *v.* —*Syn.* attend, make a visit, stay with; see **remain** 1, **visit** 2.

call attention to, *v.* —*Syn.* point out, indicate, note; see **designate** 1, **remind** 2, **warn** 1.

call back, *v.* —*Syn.* call to mind, recall, summon *or* order back; see **remember** 1, **revoke, summon** 1.

call down (D), *v.* —*Syn.* rebuke, chide, admonish; see **censure, scold.**

called, *mod.* **1.** [Named]—*Syn.* christened, termed, labeled; see **named** 1.
2. [Appointed]—*Syn.* chosen, selected, denominated; see **named** 2.

call for, *v.* **1.** [To ask]—*Syn.* inquire *or* ask for, request, make inquiry about; see **ask** 1.
2. [To need]—*Syn.* require, want, lack; see **need.**
3. [To come to get]—*Syn.* come *or* stop (for), collect, fetch; see **obtain** 1, **pick up** 6.

call in, *v.* **1.** [To collect]—*Syn.* revoke, remove, receive; see **collect** 4, **withdraw** 2.
2. [To invite]—*Syn.* ask for, request, solicit; see **beg** 1, **summon** 1.

calling, *n.* —*Syn.* occupation, vocation, work (D); see **job** 1, **profession** 1, **trade** 2.

call names, *v.* —*Syn.* defame, slander, attack; see **curse** 2, **insult.**

call off, *v.* —*Syn.* cancel, postpone, cease; see **halt** 1, **stop** 2.

call on, *v.* —*Syn.* stop in, have an appointment with, go to see; see **visit** 4.

callous, *mod.* —*Syn.* unfeeling, careless, inured (to), hardened, unsusceptible, uncaring, unaffected by, hard, insensible, stubborn, stiff, unbending, indurated, obdurate, insensitive, insentient, insensate, inflexible, cold, unresponsive, unconcerned, impassive, apathetic, heartless, impenitent, unsympathetic, soulless, spiritless, toughened, blind *or* deaf to, unimpressionable; *all* (D): tough, hard-boiled, horny, thick-skinned, case-hardened, cold-blooded, hardhearted; see also **cruel** 2, **indifferent** 1.—*Ant.* concerned, compassionate, sensitive.

callow, *mod.* —*Syn.* puerile, young, green; see **ignorant** 2, **immature, inexperienced, young** 2.

call to the colors, *v.* —*Syn.* draft, select, conscript; see **enlist** 1, **recruit** 1.

call to witness, *v.* —*Syn.* bring forward, put on the (witness) stand, administer an oath; see **swear in.**

call up, *v.* **1.** [To remember]—*Syn.* recollect, recall, summon up; see **remember** 1, **summon** 1.
2. [To summon]—*Syn.* send for, bid, order; see **invite** 1.
3. [To telephone]—*Syn.* phone, call, ring (up); see **telephone.**

calm, *mod.* **1.** [*Said especially of persons*]—*Syn.* cool, composed, collected, unmoved, level-headed, cool-headed, impassive, detached, aloof, unconcerned, disinterested, incurious, unaroused, unimpressed, neutral, listless, gentle, amicable, sedate, serene, unanxious, unexcited, contented, meek, satisfied, pleased, amiable, temperate, placid, inoffensive, civil, kind, moderate, self-reliant, confident, poised, self-possessed, restful, relaxed, dispassionate, imperturbable, mild, still, phlegmatic, philosophic(al), self-controlled, patient, untroubled; *all* (D): cool as a cucumber, with ice in one's veins, unflappable, without a nerve in one's body; see also **sense** 2, **dignified, reserved** 3, **tranquil** 1.—*Ant.* violent*, excited*, furious*.
2. [*Said often of things*]—*Syn.* quiet, undisturbed, unruffled, in order, soothing, at peace, placid, smooth, still, restful, harmonious, bland, peaceful, pacific, balmy, waveless, windless, serene, motionless, reposeful, stormless, halcyon, at a standstill,

pastoral, rural, low-key, slow; see also **sense** 1; see also **comfortable** 2, **moderate** 4, **motionless** 1, **rural.** —*Ant.* rough*, agitated, aroused.

calm, *n.* **1.** [Peace]—*Syn.* stillness, under control, quiet; see **peace** 2, **rest** 2, **silence** 1.
2. [Composure]—*Syn.* serenity, tranquillity, peace of mind; see **composure, patience** 1, **restraint** 1.

calm, *v.* —*Syn.* tranquilize, soothe, pacify; see **quiet** 1.

calm down, *v.* —*Syn.* compose *or* control *or* calm *or* restrain oneself, keep oneself under control, keep cool, take it easy, get organized, rest, get hold of oneself; *all* (D): cool it, don't get shook, cool off *or* down, simmer down, go easy, keep one's shirt on; see also **relax.**

calmly, *mod.* —*Syn.* quietly, unexcitedly, tranquilly, unconcernedly, serenely, confidently, sedately, collectedly, composedly, placidly, smoothly, reposefully, impassively, restfully, motionlessly, uninterruptedly, peacefully, naturally, comfortably, unconfoundedly, unhurried, unconfusedly, without anxiety *or* fuss, free from agitation, dully, phlegmatically, stolidly, without further ado, without fuss and feathers (D); see also **easily** 1, **evenly** 1. —*Ant.* excitedly*, agitatedly, disturbedly.

calmness, *n.* —*Syn.* quietness, tranquillity, calm; see **composure, patience** 1, **peace** 2.

calumny, *n.* —*Syn.* slander, defamation, detraction; see **lie** 1.

camaraderie, *n.* —*Syn.* intimacy, sociability, comradeship; see **brotherhood** 1, **fellowship** 1, **friendship** 1, 2.

camera, *n.* —*Syn.* cinematograph, kodak (D).
Kinds of cameras include the following—camera obscura, astrograph, camera lucida, cinecamera, X-ray machine, image orthicon, photochronograph, photogrammeter, iconoscope, microcamera, photographic telescope, photomicroscope, photopitometer, photospectroscope, phototheodolite, cinematograph, photostat, spectrograph, spectroheliograph, spectrohelioscope; motion-picture, television *or* TV, press, movie, flash, still, aerial reconnaissance, electron-diffraction, box, stereo, zoom-lens, photomicrographic, Polaroid (trademark), single-lens reflex, double-lens reflex, spectroscopic, three-dimensional *or* 3-D, telescopic camera.

camouflage, *n.* **1.** [A misleading cover]—*Syn.* dissimulation, masquerade, simulation, cloak, shade, shroud, veil, blackout, masking, paint, netting, blind, front, plain brown wrapper (D); see also **coat** 3, **cover** 2, **screen** 1.
2. [A disguise]—*Syn.* veil, faking, deceit; see **disguise, make-up** 1, **mask** 1.

camouflage, *v.* —*Syn.* cover, conceal, veil; see **deceive, disguise, hide** 1, 2.

camouflaged, *mod.* —*Syn.* masked, disguished, falsified; see **covered** 1, **hidden** 2, **wrapped.**

camp (D), *mod.* —*Syn.* contemporary, *avant-garde* (French), futuristic, daliesque, current; *all* (D): in, op, pop, with it, mod, far *or* way out, groovy, wild, cool; see also **modern** 1, **popular** 3.

camp, *n.* **1.** [A temporary living place]—*Syn.* camping ground, campground, campsite, encampment, caravansary, campfire(s), tents, tent city, wigwams, tepees, wickiups; see also **sense** 2.
2. [Prepared facilities for vacationing]—*Syn.* tent, lean-to, cottage, tilt, shack, hut, lodge, (log) cabin, chalet, shed, log house, summer home, cottages; see also **home** 1.
3. [A military establishment]—*Syn.* post, fort, encampment, quarters, caserne, grounds, installation, compound, reservation, cantonment, laager (South African), *dowar* (Oriental); see also **barracks, fortification** 2.
break camp—*Syn.* dismantle, depart, pack up; see **leave** 1.

camp, *v.* —*Syn.* bivouac, stop over, make camp, encamp, dwell, nest, locate, pitch camp, pitch a tent, tent, quarter, lodge, sleep out, outspan (South African), station, lodge temporarily, put up for the night; *all* (D): maroon, camp out, rough it, make a dry camp, sleep under the stars.—*Ant.* leave*, decamp, depart.

campaign, *n.* —*Syn.* operations, crusade, warfare; see **attack** 1, **fight** 2.

campaign, *v.* **1.** [To solicit votes]—*Syn.* crusade, electioneer, run (for), agitate, tour, contend for, contest, canvass (for), swing through the country, solicit (votes), lobby; *all* (D): barnstorm, mend fences, go to the grass roots, stump, go baby-kissing, beat the bushes, whistle-stop; see also **compete.**
2. [To fight]—*Syn.* battle, wage war, invade; see **fight** 2.

campus, *n.* —*Syn.* seat of learning, the Yard (Harvard), (buildings and) grounds, (physical) plant, faculties, alma mater, backs *or* courts (Cambridge, England), quad (British); see also **college, school** 1, **university.**

can, *n.* **1.** [A container]—*Syn.* tin (can), canister, receptacle, package, jar, bottle, quart can, bucket, gallon can, vessel; no. 1 can, no. 2 can, etc.; see also **container.**
2. [(D) jail]—*Syn.* prison, penitentiary, stir (D); see **jail.**
3. [(D) A toilet]—*Syn.* lavatory, restroom, washroom; see **toilet** 2.
4. [(D) The buttocks]—*Syn.* seat, backside, posterior; see **rump.**

can, *v.* **1.** [To preserve]—*Syn.* bottle, put up, keep; see **preserve** 3.
2. [(D) To record]—*Syn.* tape, document, register; see **record** 3.
3. [(D) To discharge]—*Syn.* fire, expel, let go; see **dismiss** 2.
4. [(D) To stop]—*Syn.* cease, halt, end; see **stop** 2.
5. [To be able]—*Syn.* could, may, be capable of *or* equal to *or* up to (D), lie in one's power, be within one's area *or* control, manage, can do, take care of; *all* (D): make it *or* the grade, come it, make out (to), cut the mustard, have it made.

canal, *n.* —*Syn.* waterway, trench, ditch; see **channel** 1, **water** 2.

cancel, *v.* **1.** [To mark out]—*Syn.* erase, eradicate, wipe *or* cross *or* rub *or* wash *or* scratch *or* strike out *or* off, blank *or* blot *or* sponge *or* rule out, write *or* cross *or* break off, efface, deface, delete, dele, destroy, undo, expunge, obliterate, omit, render invalid, stamp across; *both* (D): scrub, wipe the slate clean; see also **eliminate** 1, **remove** 1.—*Ant.* maintain*, sanction, renew.

2. [To annul]—*Syn.* recant, vacate, repudiate, nullify, neutralize, ignore, invalidate, suppress, countermand, call off, set aside, render *or* declare null and void, declare invalid, rule out, refute, rescind, remove, repeal, counteract, recall, retract, abrogate, discharge, (make or render) void, put an end to, abort, offset, counterpoise, revoke, render inert, deprive of force, overthrow; *all* (D): scratch, drop, quash; see also **abolish, discard, revoke.**—*Ant.* sustain*, approve*, uphold.

cancellation, *n.* —*Syn.* canceling, annulment, nullification, abrogation, dissolution, dissolving, invalidation, invalidating, revocation, revoking, repudiation, repeal, abolition, abolishing, retraction, retracting, reversing, reversal, annulling, voidance, voiding, rescinding, recall, recalling, overruling, undoing, withdrawing, abandonment, abandoning; see also **removal** 1, **retirement** 1.

cancer, *n.* —*Syn.* growth, tumor, malignancy; see **disease** 3, **growth** 3.

cancerous, *mod.* —*Syn.* carcinogenic, virulent, mortal; see **destructive** 2, **harmful, malignant** 1.

candelabrum, *n.* —*Syn.* pricket, menorah, candleholder; see **candlestick.**

candid, *mod.* **1.** [Frank]—*Syn.* straightforward, sincere, open; see **frank, honest** 1.

2. [Fair]—*Syn.* impartial, just, upright; see **fair** 1.

candidacy, *n.* —*Syn.* willingness, candidature, application, readiness, competition, preparedness, offer, tender, running for office, candidateship, availability.

candidate, *n.* —*Syn.* aspirant, possible choice, nominee, applicant, suitor, political contestant, office-seeker, successor, competitor, bidder, place-hunter, solicitor, petitioner, claimant; *all* (D): job-hunter, stumper, pothunter; see also **contestant.**

candidly, *mod.* —*Syn.* frankly, sincerely, honestly; see **openly** 1.

candle, *n.* —*Syn.* taper, rush, torch; see **light** 3.
Candles include the following—wax, tallow, beeswax, holiday, Christmas, Hanukkah, Sabbath, birthday, sacramental, ceremonial, bayberry, scented, mineral, rush, butane, electric, hurricane lamp.

burn the candle at both ends—*Syn.* squander, lavish, spend; see **waste** 2.

not hold a candle to—*Syn.* unequal to, subordinate, inferior; see **poor** 2.

candlestick, *n.* —*Syn.* pricket, candelabrum, candelabra, taper holder, flat candlestick, menorah, candleholder; double-branched, triple-branched, four-branched, etc., candlestick.

candor, *n.* **1.** [Frankness]—*Syn.* openness, veracity, candidness; see **honesty** 1, **sincerity.**

2. [Fairness]—*Syn.* impartiality, probity, uprightness; see **fairness, honesty** 1.

candy, *n.* —*Syn.* confection, confectionery, sweetmeat, bonbon, confit.
Varieties of candy include the following—chocolate, maple, coconut, fruit, etc., caramel; sugar, orange, molasses, etc., taffy; chocolate, vanilla, maple, etc., fudge; orange, lemon, walnut, etc., cream; lemon, peppermint, licorice, etc., drop; fondant, fruit glacé, nougat, peanut brittle, praline, panocha, pistachio paste, fruit roll, marshmallow, crystallized fruit, cinnamon imperial, coconut bar, Turkish delight, lollipop, halvah, marchpane, gum drop, divinity, sea foam, toffee, after-dinner mint, Life Saver (trademark), *marron glacé* (French), *torrone* (Italian); stick, seed, hard, spun-sugar, cactus candy; all-day sucker (D); see also **pastry.**

cane, *n.* —*Syn.* walking stick, staff, pole; see **stick.**

canker, *n.* —*Syn.* ulcer, boil, infection; see **injury** 1, **sore.**

canned, *mod.* **1.** [Preserved]—*Syn.* bottled, conserved, kept; see **preserved** 2.

2. [Recorded]—*Syn.* documented, prerecorded, taped; see **recorded.**

3. [(D) Drunk]—*Syn.* intoxicated, inebriated, tipsy; see **drunk.**

cannibal, *n.* —*Syn.* man-eater, head-hunter, savage, native, islander, primitive, aborigine, tribesman, bushman, eater of one's own kind, ogre, ogress, anthropophagus, anthrophagite, anthropophaginian; see also **savage.**

cannibalistic, *mod.* —*Syn.* man-eating, anthropophagous, thyestean; see **cruel** 1, 2, **primitive** 3, **savage** 2, 3.

cannibalize, *v.* —*Syn.* salvage, strip for repair, disassemble; see **dismantle.**

canning, *n.* —*Syn.* preserving, conserving, tinning, putting up, bottling, keeping, storing.

cannon, *n.* Types of cannon include the following—self-propelled, muzzle-loading *or* muzzle-loader, breech-loading *or* breechloader, demi, whole cannon, cannon of seven, cannon of eight *or* royal cannon, tank destroyer, turret, mountain, siege, coast defense, field, antiaircraft, railway, stratosphere, antitank, bazooka, knee mortar, bombardelle, serpentine, carronade, pompom, recoilless rifle; Howitzer, Bren, Woolwich *or* Fraser, Armstrong, Parrot, Quaker, Lyle *or* lifesaving gun.
Some famous cannons include the following—Bombard, Ribeaudequin, Basilica (14th century); English cannon (15th century); Rabinet, Falconet, Culverin Bastard, Cannon Royal (17th century); American Revolutionary cannon, Howitzer (18th century); Columbiad, Union, Army Mortar, French 75mm (19th century); Big Bertha or Krupp cannon, 75 mm and 105mm Howitzer, 155mm Howitzer, 8-inch Howitzer (20th century); see also **gun** 1.

cannonade, *n.* —*Syn.* barrage, curtain of fire, bombardment; see **attack** 1, **fire** 3.

canny, *mod.* **1.** [Prudent]—*Syn.* watchful, wary, cautious; see **careful, discreet.**

2. [Clever]—*Syn.* skillful, shrewd, sharp; see **able** 1, 2, **intelligent** 1.

canoe, *n.* —*Syn.* kayak, dugout, outrigger, piragua, war canoe, pirogue, birch-bark canoe, coracle; see also **boat.**

canon, *n.* —*Syn.* decree, rule, order; see **command** 1, **declaration** 2, **law** 3.

canonical, *mod.* —*Syn.* sanctioned, authoritative, statutory; see **approved, lawful** 1, **legal** 1, **official** 3.

canonize, *v.* —*Syn.* saint, besaint, sanctify, beatify, glorify, deify, apotheosize, idolize, idolatrize, consecrate, dedicate, make canonical, put on a pedestal (D); see also **bless** 3, **love** 1, **worship** 2.

canopy, *n.* —*Syn.* covering, sunshade, umbrella; see **awning, cover** 1.

cant, *n.* —*Syn.* deceit, show, pomposity; see **dishonesty, hypocrisy** 2, **pretense** 1.

cantaloupe, *n.* —*Syn.* muskmelon, winter melon, rock melon; see **fruit** 1, **melon.**

cantankerous, *mod.* —*Syn.* peevish, quarrelsome, grouchy; see **critical** 2, **irritable, obstinate** 1.

canteen, *n.* **1.** [Mobile kitchen]—*Syn.* portable kitchen, snack bar, chowmobile (D); see **dining room, kitchen, restaurant.**
2. [Water bottle]—*Syn.* flasket, *flacon* (French), bota (bag); see **bottle, container, flask, jug.**

canter, *v.* —*Syn.* jog, lope, pace; see **run** 2, **trot.**

canting, *mod.* —*Syn.* insincere, two-faced, bigoted; see **dishonest** 2, **false** 1, **hypocritical, prejudiced.**

canvas, *n.* **1.** [A coarse cloth]—*Syn.* tenting, awning cloth, sailcloth, duck, coarse cloth; 10-ounce canvas, 12-ounce canvas, etc.; see also **cloth.**
2. [Anything made of canvas]—*Syn.* sail, shade, waterproof, fly, tarpaulin *or* tarp (D); see also **awning, cover** 1, **tent.**
3. [A painting on canvas]—*Syn.* portrait, still life, oil; see **art** 3, **painting** 1.

canvass, *v.* **1.** [To seek votes]—*Syn.* agitate, apply, run; see **campaign** 1.
2. [To sell from door to door]—*Syn.* call upon, peddle, sell house-to-house; see **sell** 1.
3. [To pass rapidly in review]—*Syn.* consult, review, check; see **examine** 1, **survey** 2.

canvasser, *n.* —*Syn.* poll-taker, representative, peddler; see **agent** 1, **salesman** 2.

canyon, *n.* —*Syn.* gulch, gorge, gully; see **ravine, valley.**

cap, *n.* **1.** [Hat]—*Syn.* beret, pillbox, bonnet; see **hat.**
2. [(D) Capsule]—*Syn.* dose, pill, tablet; see **medicine** 2.
set one's cap for (D)—*Syn.* woo, flirt, try to win; see **court, try** 1.

capability, *n.* —*Syn.* capacity, skill, aptitude; see **ability** 2, **inclination** 1.

capable, *mod.* —*Syn.* proficient, competent, fitted; see **able** 1, 2, **intelligent** 1.

capacious, *mod.* —*Syn.* spacious, substantial, roomy; see **extensive** 1, **large** 1.

capaciousness, *n.* —*Syn.* adequacy, enormousness, bigness; see **immensity, size** 2.

capacity, *n.* **1.** [The limit of contents]—*Syn.* contents, limit, retention, space, room, size, volume, holding power, cubic(al) contents, volume, burden, amplitude, extent, compass, magnitude, spread, expanse, scope, latitude, bulk, dimensions, measure, range, quantity, size, reach, (containing) power, holding ability, sweep, proportions, mass, sufficiency.
2. [Ability]—*Syn.* competency, aptitude, capability; see **ability** 1, 2, **inclination** 1.

cape, *n.* **1.** [Land jutting into the water]—*Syn.* headland, foreland, point, promontory, jetty, jutty, naze, head, tongue, point *or* neck of land, chersonese, ness, mole, finger, arm; see also **land** 1, **peninsula.**
2. [An overgarment]—*Syn.* cloak, pelerine, bertha, Vandyke, talma, tippet, fichu, wrapper, mantilla, pelisse, paletot, mantle, shawl, cope, gabardine, wrap, overdress, tabard, mantelletta, cardinal, poncho, victorine; see also **coat** 1.

caper, *n.* —*Syn.* prank, trick, escapade; see **joke** 1.

caper, *v.* —*Syn.* frolic, gambol, cavort; see **play** 1, 2.

capillary, *mod.* —*Syn.* fine, slender, slim; see **thin** 2.

capital, *mod.* **1.** [Excellent]—*Syn.* splendid, choice, delightful; see **excellent, superior.**
2. [Principal]—*Syn.* primary, dominant, foremost; see **first** 1, **principal.**

capital, *n.* **1.** [A seat of government]—*Syn.* metropolis, principal city, the political front (D); see **capitol, center** 2, **city.**
2. [Money and property]—*Syn.* cash, assets, interests; see **business** 1, **estate** 2, **industry** 3, **property** 1, **wealth** 1.
3. [A letter usually used initially]—*Syn.* initial, upper case, majuscule; see **letter** 1.
make capital of—*Syn.* exploit, get advantage from, profit by; see **use** 1.

capitalism, *n.* —*Syn.* capitalistic system, free enterprise, laissez-faire government, private ownership *or* possessions, competitive system, free market, creeping capitalism (D); see also **democracy** 2, **economics, government** 2.

capitalist, *n.* —*Syn.* entrepreneur, investor, landowner; see **banker** 1, **businessman, financier.**

capitalize, *v.* —*Syn.* gain, benefit, realize; see **obtain** 1, **profit** 2.

capitol, *n.* —*Syn.* statehouse, legislative hall, Senate, House of Representatives, state capitol, national capitol, seat of government; all (D): the political front, political scene, capitol hill; see also **center** 2.

capitulate, *v.* —*Syn.* surrender, submit, give up; see **yield** 1.

capitulation, *n.* **1.** [Surrender]—*Syn.* yielding, giving up, submission; see **resignation** 2, **surrender.**
2. [Summary]—*Syn.* synopsis, outline, abstract; see **abbreviation** 1, **summary.**

caprice, *n.* —*Syn.* whim, vagary, notion; see **fancy** 3, **impulse** 2, **thought** 2.

capricious, *mod.* —*Syn.* whimsical, inconstant, fickle; see **careless** 1, **changeable** 1, 2.

capsize, *v.* —*Syn.* overturn, invert, tip over; see **turn** 2.

capsule, *n.* **1.** [A space vehicle]—*Syn.* satellite, reentry vehicle, spaceship; see **spacecraft.**
2. [Pharmaceutical preparation]—*Syn.* pill, tablet, dose; see **medicine** 2, **tablet** 3.
3. [Container]—*Syn.* receptacle, can, enclosure; see **container.**

captain, *n.* **1.** [A leader]—*Syn.* director, commander, authority; see **administrator, guide** 1, **leader** 2.
2. [The officer in charge of a company]—*Syn.* company commander, commanding officer, junior officer, staff officer; *all* (D): C.O., skipper, Sam Brown; see also **officer** 3.
3. [One in command of a ship]—*Syn.* skipper, commander, operator; *both* (D): cap, Old Man; see also **officer** 3, **pilot** 2.

caption, *n.* —*Syn.* inscription, legend, subtitle; see **heading, title** 1.

captious, *mod.* **1.** [Tricky]—*Syn.* wily, subtle, sophistical; see **confusing, sly** 1.
2. [Critical]—*Syn.* faultfinding, carping, caviling; see **critical** 2, **sarcastic, severe** 1.

captivate, *v.* —*Syn.* delight, charm, enthrall; see **entertain** 1, **fascinate.**

captive, *mod.* **1.** [Confined]—*Syn.* restrained, incarcerated, jailed; see **bound** 1, 2, **restricted.**
2. [Captivated]—*Syn.* delighted, enraptured, enchanted; see **fascinated.**

captive, *n.* —*Syn.* bondman, convict, con (D); see **hostage, prisoner.**

captivity, *n.* —*Syn.* imprisonment, bondage, subjecton, servitude, duress, detention, incarceration, interment, limbo, enslavement, slavery, impoundment, entombment, constraint, durance, committal, the guardhouse, custody, serfdom, thralldom, durance vile (D); see also **confinement** 1, **imprisonment** 1, **jail, pen** 1, **restraint** 2, **slavery** 1.—*Ant.* liberty, freedom*, independence.

capture, *n.* —*Syn.* capturing, seizing, taking, seizure, acquisition, acquirement, obtaining, securing, gaining, winning, occupation, appropriation, appropriating, ensnaring, abduction, laying hold of, grasping, catching, trapping, commandeering, rape, apprehending, annexation, snatching, confiscation, taking into custody *or* captivity, apprehension, fall; see also **arrest** 1, **recovery** 3.—*Ant.* liberation, freeing*, setting free.

capture, *v.* **1.** [To take into legal custody]—*Syn.* seize, take, apprehend; see **arrest** 1, **seize** 2.
2. [To seize with armed force]—*Syn.* occupy, conquer, overwhelm; see **defeat** 2, **seize** 2.
3. [To seize figuratively]—*Syn.* captivate, attract, charm; see **entertain** 1, **fascinate.**
4. [To win]—*Syn.* gain, carry, achieve; see **obtain** 1, **win** 1.

captured, *mod.* **1.** [Caught]—*Syn.* taken, seized, arrested, apprehended, detained, grasped, overtaken, clutched, grabbed, snatched, kidnapped, abducted, netted, hooked, secured; *all* (D): collared, nabbed, bagged; see also **under arrest.**—*Ant.* released, unbound, loosed.
2. [Occupied]—*Syn.* possessed, overcome, won, gained, pre-empted, confiscated, usurped, repossessed, taken (over), appropriated, mastered, in possession of; see also **held.**—*Ant.* liberated, free*, demilitarized.

car, *n.* **1.** [A wheeled vehicle]—*Syn.* conveyance, truck, auto; see **automobile, vehicle** 1, **wagon.**
2. [A railroad vehicle]. Kinds of cars include the following—Pullman, sleeper, smoker, diner, coach, boxcar, flatcar, goods wagon, caboose; mail, freight, baggage, coal, ore, lounge, automobile, refrigerated, fruit, piggyback, stock, cattle, horse car; see also **train** 2.
3. [A motorized passenger vehicle]—*Syn.* auto, motor car, gas buggy (D); see **automobile, vehicle** 1.

caravan, *n.* **1.** [A desert cavalcade]—*Syn.* troop, band, expedition, camels, procession, train, safari; see also **journey.**
2. [A portable house]—*Syn.* house trailer, camper, trailer house *or* cabin; see **trailer.**

carbohydrate, *n.* —*Syn.* starch, sugar, monosaccharide, disaccharide, polysaccharide, glucose, sucrose, dextrose, fructrose, lactose, galactose, maltose, cellulose, dextrin, glycogen; see also **sugar.**

carbon, *n.* —*Syn.* carbon copy, reproduction, duplicate; see **copy.**

carcass, *n.* —*Syn.* corpse, cadaver, remains; see **body** 2.

card, *n.* —*Syn.* cardboard, ticket, sheet, square, Bristol board, fiberboard.
Varieties of cards include the following—poster, window card, show card, ticket, fortune-telling *or* tarot cards, label, badge, tally, check, billet, voucher, pass; calling, playing, bridge, poker, pinochle, address, visiting, credit, greeting, registration *or* filing, recipe, index, check-cashing, police, social security, identification *or* I.D. (D) card; see also **paper** 1, 5.
in *or* **on the cards**—*Syn.* probable, predicted, possible; see **likely** 1.
put *or* **lay one's cards on the table**—*Syn.* reveal, tell the truth, expose; see **admit** 2.

cards, *n.* —*Syn.* deck of cards, card game, game at *or* of cards; see **deck** 2, **entertainment** 2, **game** 1.

care, *n.* **1.** [Careful conduct]—*Syn.* heed, concern, caution, consideration, regard, thoughtfulness, forethought, heedfulness, precaution, wariness, vigilance, watchfulness, watching, attending, solicitude, diligence, meticulousness, fastidiousness, nicety, pains, application, conscientiousness, thought, discrimination, carefulness, scrupulousness, exactness, particularity, circumspection, oversight, watch, concentration; see also **attention** 2, **prudence.**—*Ant.* carelessness*, neglect, negligence.
2. [Worry]—*Syn.* concern, solicitude, anxiety, interest, chagrin, distress, bother, perplexity, trouble, disturbance, unhappiness, aggravation, fretfulness, charge, incubus, stress, hindrance, handicap, impediment, tribulation, responsibility, strain, load, onus, encumbrance, pressure, nuisance, vexation, fear, oppression, uneasiness, exasperation, annoyance, misgiving, anguish, foreboding, apprehension, discomposure; *all* (D): pins and needles, stew, sweat, fret; see also **difficulty** 2.—*Ant.* calm, peace, indifference*.
3. [Custody]—*Syn.* supervision, guardianship, keeping; see **administration** 1, **custody** 1.
4. [A cause of worry]—*Syn.* problem, care, concern; see **sense** 2, **disaster, misfortune** 1, **trouble** 2.
have a care *or* **take care**—*Syn.* be careful *or* cautious, beware, heed; see **mind** 3, **watch out.**
take care of—*Syn.* protect, attend to, be responsible for; see **guard** 2.

care, *v.* **1.** [To be concerned]—*Syn.* attend, take pains, regard; see **consider** 1.
2. [To be careful]—*Syn.* be cautious, look out for, be on guard, watch out, be aware of, heed, take precautions; see also **mind** 3.

care about, *v.*—*Syn.* cherish, be fond of, hold dear; see **like** 2, **love** 1.

careen, *v.* —*Syn.* lean, sway, tilt; see **bend** 2.

career, *n.* —*Syn.* occupation, vocation, work; see **job** 1, **profession** 1.

care for, *v.* **1.** [To look after]—*Syn.* provide for, attend to, nurse; see **raise** 2, **support** 5.
2. [To like]—*Syn.* be fond of, hold dear, prize; see **like** 2, **love** 1.
3. [To want]—*Syn.* desire, yearn for, wish; see **need, want** 1.

carefree, *mod.* —*Syn.* lighthearted, cheerful, jovial; see **happy** 1, **calm** 1.

careful, *mod.* —*Syn.* solicitous, thorough, concerned, deliberate, provident, conservative, prudent, meticulous, particular, rigorous, fussy, finicky, prim, exacting, wary, sober, vigilant, watchful, suspicious, alert, wide-awake, scrupulous, assiduous, overexact, fastidious, religious, hard to please, discriminating, sure-footed, precise, painstaking, exact, heedful, on one's guard, on the alert, conscientious, taking measures, politic, attentive, calculating, sparing, regardful, solicitudinous, mindful, cautious, canny, guarded, considerate, shy, circumspect, discreet, noncommittal, self-possessed, self-disciplined, solid, cool, calm, farsighted, frugal, thrifty, punctilious, stealthy, observant, chary, on guard, apprehensive, judicious; *all* (D): leery, choosy, picky, feeling one's way *or* ground, seeing how the land lies, putting the right foot forward, keeping a nose to the wind, picking one's steps, making haste slowly, going to great lengths; see also **accurate** 2, **economical** 1, **thoughtful** 2.—*Ant.* heedless, careless*, haphazard.

carefully, *mod.* **1.** [Scrupulously]—*Syn.* punctiliously, conscientiously, exactly, rigidly, correctly, strictly, precisely, minutely, painstakingly, faithfully, trustily, fastidiously, uprightly, honorably, attentively, rigorously, providently, deliberately, fully, reliably, particularly, solicitously, concernedly, meticulously, laboriously, thoroughly, dependably, in detail, with completeness, nicely, with (every) care, in a thorough-going manner, to a hair (D); see also **accurately.**—*Ant.* neglectfully, haphazardly*, indifferently.

2. [Cautiously]—*Syn.* prudently, discreetly, warily, guardedly, circumspectly, providently, watchfully, vigilantly, sparingly, frugally, thoughtfully, heedfully, regardfully, mindfully, with care *or* caution *or* difficulty, gingerly, delicately, noncommittally, anxiously, with forethought *or* reservations.—*Ant.* imprudently, foolishly*, wastefully.

careless, *mod.* **1.** [Inattentive]—*Syn.* loose, lax, remiss, unguarded, incautious, forgetful, unthinking, unobservant, uncircumspect, reckless, unheeding, indiscreet, injudicious, inadvertent, unconcerned, improvident, wasteful, unapprehensive, regardless, imprudent, unconsidered, unwary, cursory, hasty, inconsiderate, indolent, insouciant, lackadaisical, heedless, mindless, untroubled, negligent, neglectful, thoughtless, unmindful, indifferent, casual, disregardful, not seeing the forest for the trees, oblivious, absent-minded, listless, abstracted, nonchalant, undiscerning, offhand, slack, blundering; see also **rash.**—*Ant.* attentive, thoughtful*, careful.

2. [Artless]—*Syn.* unstudied, simple, natural; see **modest** 2, **naive, natural** 3.

3. [Carefree]—*Syn.* untroubled, fun-loving, happy-go-lucky; see **calm** 1, **happy** 1.

carelessly, *mod.* —*Syn.* heedlessly, negligently, neglectfully, thoughtlessly, nonchalantly, offhandedly, rashly, unmindfully, unconcernedly, without counting the cost, at random, happen what may, incautiously, inprovidently, irresponsibly, wastefully, without caution *or* care, without concern, with no attention, like crazy (D).

carelessness, *n.* —*Syn.* unconcern, nonchalance, heedlessness, rashness, omission, slackness, neglectfulness, delinquency, indolence, procrastination, dereliction, neglect, negligence, disregard, imprudence, haphazardness; see also **indifference** 1. —*Ant.* care*, consideration, caution.

caress, *n.* —*Syn.* embrace, stroke, feel (D); see **hug, kiss, touch** 2.

caress, *v.* —*Syn.* embrace, pet, dandle, fondle, make love to, nuzzle, toy with, handle, graze, snuggle, nestle, rub, massage, brush, coddle, cosset, cuddle, treat fondly, stroke, chuck under the chin, pat, clasp; *all* (D): buss, neck, mug, mush, feel (up), play around; see also **hug, kiss, love** 2, **touch** 1.—*Ant.* avoid*, withdraw, repulse.

caretaker, *n.* —*Syn.* porter, keeper, janitor; see **custodian** 2, **watchman.**

care to, *v.* —*Syn.* prefer, desire, wish; see **like** 1, **want** 1.

careworn, *mod.* —*Syn.* anxious, worn out, haggard; see **sad** 1, **tired, troubled** 1.

cargo, *n.* —*Syn.* shipload, baggage, lading; see **freight** 1, **load** 1.

caricature, *n.* —*Syn.* burlesque, exaggeration, cartoon; see **parody** 1, 2, **ridicule.**

caricature, *v.* —*Syn.* distort, satirize, mimic; see **parody.**

carillon, *n.* —*Syn.* (set of) bells, chimes, gong, peal of bells, orchestral bells, tocsin, angelus, glockenspiel, lyra, tintinnabulation; see also **bell.**

carnage, *n.* —*Syn.* slaughter, massacre, slaying, butchery, (wholesale) killing, (mass) murder *or* homicide, butchering, manslaughter, gore, blood, bloodshed, shambles, extermination, havoc, holocaust, hecatomb, warfare, annihilation, rapine, pogrom, slaying, internecion, effusion *or* saturnalia of blood, blood and guts (D); see also **crime** 2, **destruction** 1, **murder.**

carnal, *mod.* **1.** [Sensual]—*Syn.* fleshly, bodily, sensuous; see **lewd** 1, 2, **sensual.**

2. [Sexual]—*Syn.* venereal, genital, wanton; see **sexual.**

have carnal knowledge of—*Syn.* be intimate with, have an affair (with), seduce; see **love** 2.

carnality, *n.* —*Syn.* sensuality, lust, eroticism; see **desire** 3, **lewdness.**

carnival, *n.* **1.** [A festival]—*Syn.* festivity, revelry, merry-making, jollification, carousal, masquerade, debauch, festival, feasting, fete, street fair, celebration, spree, carousing, bacchanal, frolic, gala, heyday, jubilee, Saturnalia, orgy, wassail, rout, conviviality, Mardi Gras, jamboree (D); see also **celebration** 2, **feast, holiday** 1.

2. [An outdoor amusement]—*Syn.* side show, exposition, amusement park; see **circus, entertainment** 2, **fair, show** 2.

carnivorous, *mod.* —*Syn.* flesh-eating, predatory, voracious; see **greedy** 2, **hungry, rapacious** 2.

carol, *n.* —*Syn.* madrigal, Christmas song, ballad; see **hymn, song.**

carousal, *n.* —*Syn.* carousing, spree, frolic; see **celebration** 2, **feast, holiday** 2, **merriment** 2.

carouse, *v.* —*Syn.* make merry, imbibe, revel; see **drink** 2, **play** 1.

carp, *v.* —*Syn.* find fault, criticize, nag; see **bother** 2, **censure, complain** 1.

carpenter, *n.* —*Syn.* mason, craftsman, artisan; see **builder** 1, **laborer, workman.**

carpet, *n.* —*Syn.* wall-to-wall carpet *or* WW carpet (D); Orlon (trade mark), Acrilan (trade mark),

nylon, etc. carpet; (indoor *or* outdoor) carpeting, floor covering, matting; see also **linoleum, rug.**
Varieties of carpets include the following—Axminster, Brussels, (Wilton) velvet, mohair, chenille, (hit-and-miss) rag, ingrain (Scottish), fiber, jute, hair, Oriental, Chinese, Persian, Turkish, Armenian, Indo-Persian, Anatolian, Damascus, Turkoman, Chinese-Turkestan, Indian, Moroccan, Spanish, Caucasian, Turkestan, English handwoven, Polish handwoven, Venetian, tapestry, Savonnerie.
(called) on the carpet—*Syn.* reprimanded, censured, interrogated; see **in trouble** 1.

carpet, *v.* —*Syn.* superimpose, lay over, put on; see **cover** 1.

carping, *mod.* —*Syn.* faultfinding, nagging, caviling; see **critical** 2, **sarcastic, severe** 2.

carriage, *n.* **1.** [The manner of carrying the body] —*Syn.* walk, mien, pace, step, attitude, aspect, presence, look, comportment, cast, gait, bearing, posture, stance, pose, port, deportment, demeanor, poise, air; see also **behavior** 1, **position** 5.
2. [A horse-drawn passenger vehicle]—*Syn.* buggy, surrey, coach, coach-and-four, buckboard, cart, conveyance, dog-cart, two-wheeler, dearborn, van, trap, gig, sulky, hansom, runabout, rockaway, tilbury, tumbrel, coupe, four-wheeler, stagecoach, chariot, chaise, shay, brougham, taxicab, equipage, victoria, landau, hack, hackney coach, phaeton, calash, cabriolet, droshky, *drogi* (Russian), barouche; see also **vehicle** 1, **wagon.**

carrier, *n.* —*Syn.* aircraft carrier, escort carrier, flattop (D); see **ship, warship.**

carrion, *n.* —*Syn.* decaying flesh, remains, corpse; see **body** 2, **decay** 2.

carry, *v.* **1.** [To transport]—*Syn.* convey, move, transplant, transfer, cart, truck, import, transmit, freight, remove, conduct, bear, take, bring, shift, displace, waft, portage, haul, ferry, change, convoy, relocate, relay; *all* (D): lug, tote, fetch, pack off; see also **send** 1, **ship.**
2. [To transmit]—*Syn.* pass on, transfer, communicate, conduct, bear, transport, convey, relay, give; see also **send** 4.
3. [To support weight]—*Syn.* bear, sustain, shoulder; see **support** 1.
4. [To give support]—*Syn.* corroborate, back up, confirm; see **approve** 1, **support** 2, **strengthen.**
5. [To capture]—*Syn.* abduct, overcome, occupy; see **kidnap, seize** 2.
6. [To win]—*Syn.* be victorious, prevail, succeed; see **defeat** 1, 2.
be *or* **get carried away**—*Syn.* zealous, aroused, exuberant; see **excited.**

carry away, *v.* —*Syn.* enchant, charm, enrapture; see **fascinate.**

carry off, *v.* **1.** [To win]—*Syn.* earn, gain, get; see **deserve, obtain** 1.
2. [To abduct]—*Syn.* shanghai, capture, make off with; see **kidnap, obtain** 1, **seize** 2.

carry on, *v.* **1.** [To continue]—*Syn.* keep going, proceed, persist; see **achieve** 1, **continue** 1, 2, **endure** 1.
2. [To manage]—*Syn.* conduct, engage in, administer; see **manage** 1.
3. [To behave badly]—*Syn.* blunder, be indecorous, raise Cain (D); see **misbehave.**

carry (oneself), *v.* —*Syn.* appear, seem, comport *or* conduct *or* bear oneself; see **act** 2, **behave** 2, **walk** 1.

carry out, *v.* —*Syn.* complete, accomplish, fulfill; see **achieve** 1, **complete** 1, **succeed** 1.

carry over, *n.* —*Syn.* holdover, vestige, remains; see **remainder, remnant** 1.

carry over, *v.* —*Syn.* continue, persist, survive; see **endure** 1, **influence.**

carry (something) off, —*Syn.* do, triumph, accomplish, handle, take care of, make it *or* good; see **achieve** 1, **succeed** 1.

cart, *n.* —*Syn.* truck, wheelbarrow, (hand)barrow, (little) wagon, curricle, tip cart, handcart, tumbrel, gig, dray, two-wheeler, tilbury, pushcart, gocart, gurney, two-wheeled cart, dumpcart, dogcart, dolly (D); see also **carriage** 2, **vehicle** 1, **wagon.**
put the cart before the horse (D)—*Syn.* reverse, be illogical, err; see **mistake.**

carte blanche, *n.* —*Syn.* full *or* unconditional *or* free *or* complete authority *or* power *or* right, free hand, license, power of attorney, (open) sanction, free rein, blank check (D); see also **freedom** 2, **permission, power** 2.

carton, *n.* —*Syn.* (cardboard) box, corrugated carton, package; see **case** 7, **container.**

cartoon, *n.* **1.** [A sketch]—*Syn.* representation, painting, drawing; see **picture** 3, **sketch** 1.
2. [A satire]—*Syn.* caricature, lampoon, joke; see **parody** 1, 2, **ridicule.**

cartoonist, *n.* —*Syn.* illustrator, caricaturist, social critic; see **artist** 1, **critic** 2.

carve, *v.* **1.** [To form by cutting]—*Syn.* hew, chisel, engrave, etch, sculpture, incise, mold, fashion, insculp, rough-hew, cut, shape, model, tool, stipple, grave, block out, scrape, pattern, trim, sculp (D); see also **create** 2, **engrave** 2, **form** 1.
2. [To cut]—*Syn.* slice, cleave, dissect; see **cut** 1.

carved, *mod.* —*Syn.* incised, graven, graved, cut, chiseled, chased, furrowed, hewn, hewed, etched, sculptured, sculptural, carven, intaglioed, scarified, scratched, sabered, slashed, diapered, done in relief, scrolled, grooved, sliced, scissored; see also **engraved, formed.**—*Ant.* plain*, cast, molded.

cascade, *n.* —*Syn.* watercourse, rapids, cataract; see **water** 2, **waterfall.**

case, *n.* **1.** [An example]—*Syn.* instance, illustration, sample; see **example** 1.
2. [Actual conditions]—*Syn.* incident, occurrence, fact; see **circumstance** 1, **event** 1, 2, **fact** 2, **state** 2.
3. [A legal action]—*Syn.* suit, litigation, lawsuit; see **claim, trial** 2.
4. [An organized argument]—*Syn.* argument, petition, evidence; see **claim, proof** 1.
5. [Condition]—*Syn.* situation, status, position; see **cause** 3, **circumstance** 1, **state** 2.
6. [Difficulty]—*Syn.* plight, quandary, problem; see **crisis, predicament.**
7. [A container or its contents]—*Syn.* carton, canister, crate, compact, crating, box, casing, chest, drawer, holder, tray, receptacle, coffer, crib, chamber, chassis, caisson, bin, bag, grip, cabinet, sheath, scabbard, wallet, caddy, safe, basket, casket; see also **bag, baggage, container, trunk** 1.

8. [(D) A difficult person]—*Syn.* problem, bother, crank; see **rascal, trouble** 2.
in any case—*Syn.* in any event, anyway, however; see **anyhow** 1.
in case (of)—*Syn.* in the event that, provided that, supposing; see **if.**
in no case—*Syn.* by no means, under no circumstances, not at all; see **never.**

casehardened, *mod.*—*Syn.* unfeeling, callous, unaffected; see **cruel** 2, **hardened** 2, **indifferent** 1.

casement, *n.*—*Syn.* movable pane, single-hung *or* hinged pane, bay window, picture window, oriel; see also **window** 1.

cash, *n.* **1.** [Currency]—*Syn.* note, hard cash, legal tender; see **money** 1.
2. [Assets]—*Syn.* money in hand, ready money *or* assets, principal, available means, working assets, funds, payment, capital, finances, fluid assets, remuneration, stock, (pecuniary) resources, wherewithal, supply (in hand), investments, savings, riches, reserve, treasure, moneys, reimbursement, refund, bail, pledge, security; see also **pay** 2, **wealth** 1, 2.

cash, *v.*—*Syn.* realize, cash in, change, redeem for money, realize in cash, liquidate assets, discharge, draw, honor a bill, acknowledge; see also **exchange** 2, **pay** 1, **redeem** 1.—*Ant.* stop payment, refuse*, decline.

cashier, *n.*—*Syn.* purser, clerk, receiver; see **accountant, teller, treasurer.**

cashier, *v.*—*Syn.* discharge, displace, remove; see **dismiss** 2.

cash on delivery, *mod.*—*Syn.* cash *or* money down, collect, C.O.D.; see **paid.**

casino, *n.*—*Syn.* club, clubhouse, betting house, bank, gambling establishment, dance hall, poolroom, roadhouse, honky-tonk, gambling den; *all* (D): gambling joint, Monte Carlo, dive; see also **bar** 2, **saloon** 3.

cask, *n.*—*Syn.* keg, firkin, butt; see **barrel, container.**

casket, *n.* **1.** [A coffin]—*Syn.* box, sarcophagus, funerary box; see **coffin.**
2. [A small box]—*Syn.* cassette, tin, canister; see **case** 7, **chest, container.**

casserole, *n.* **1.** [Dish]—*Syn.* baking dish, Pyrex (trade mark), saucepan; see **china, dish, plate** 4.
2. [Food]—*Syn.* goulash, stroganoff, meat pie; see also **hash** 1, **stew.**

cast, *n.* **1.** [A plaster reproduction]—*Syn.* facsimile, duplicate, replica; see **copy, mold** 2, **sculpture.**
2. [Those in a play]—*Syn.* persons in the play, list of characters, players, roles, parts, dramatis personae, company, troupe, producers, dramatic artists; see also **actor, actress, staff** 2.
3. [Aspect]—*Syn.* complexion, face, looks; see **appearance** 1.
4. [A surgical dressing]—*Syn.* plaster-of-Paris dressing, plaster cast, arm cast, leg cast, full leg cast, half leg cast, knee cast, bent leg cast, walking cast, body cast, splint(s); see also **dressing** 3.
5. [The act of throwing]—*Syn.* casting, hurling, shooting, thrusting, pitching, tossing, flinging, chucking, heaving, lobbing, pelting, slinging, launching.
6. [A toss]—*Syn.* throw, pitch, heave, lob, fling, thrust, hurl, sling, launching, projection, expulsion, ejection, propulsion, shooting; see also **shot** 1.
7. [Arrangement]—*Syn.* disposition, plan, method; see **order** 3, **system** 1.
8. [A tinge]—*Syn.* hue, tinct, blend; see **color** 1, **shade** 2, **tint, tone** 4.

cast, *v.* **1.** [To throw]—*Syn.* pitch, fling, hurl; see **throw** 1.
2. [To form in a mold]—*Syn.* shape, roughcast, wetcast; see also **form** 1.
3. [To compute]—*Syn.* number, reckon, figure; see also **add** 1, **calculate** 1, **count.**
4. [To select actors for a play]—*Syn.* appoint, designate, decide upon, determine, pick, give parts, detail, name; see also **assign** 1, **choose** 1, **delegate** 2.

cast aside, *v.*—*Syn.* reject, jettison, throw away; see **abandon** 1, **discard.**

cast away, *v.*—*Syn.* dispose of, reject, throw out; see **abandon** 1, **discard.**

cast down, *v.* **1.** [To overthrow]—*Syn.* raze, demolish, wipe out; see **defeat** 1, 2, **destroy** 1.
2. [To discourage]—*Syn.* dishearten, dispirit, dismay; see **discourage** 1, **depress** 2.

caste, *n.* **1.** [Class]—*Syn.* station, cultural level, social stratum; see **class** 2, **rank** 3.
2. [Status]—*Syn.* standing, position, station; see **degree** 2, **rank** 2.

castigate, *v.*—*Syn.* chastise, reprimand, rebuke; see **censure.**

casting, *n.*—*Syn.* molding, part, chilled *or* compressed casting, dry cast, fitting; see also **equipment, fixture** 1.

castle, *n.*—*Syn.* stronghold, manor, seat, villa, fortress, château, citadel, keep, donjon, fort, hold, fasthold, safehold, fastness, acropolis; see also **building** 1, **fortification** 2.

cast off, *v.*—*Syn.* reject, jettison, throw away; see **abandon** 1, **discard.**

cast out, *v.*—*Syn.* evict, ostracize, expel; see **banish** 1, **eject** 1.

castrate, *v.*—*Syn.* emasculate, sterilize, asexualize, mutilate, cut, spay, geld, unman, steer, caponize, effeminize, eunuchize, deprive of virility *or* manhood; *both* (D): cut, fix; see also **maim, weaken** 2.

castrated, *mod.*—*Syn.* crippled, unmanned, devitalized, weakened, emasculate *or* emasculated, fixed (D); see also **deformed, disabled, hurt, mutilated.**

castration, *n.*—*Syn.* emasculation, gelding, cutting, orchidotomy, altering, unmanning, effeminization; see also **injury** 1, **operation** 4.

casual, *mod.* **1.** [Accidental]—*Syn.* chance, unexpected, unplanned; see **incidental** 2, **spontaneous.**
2. [Occasional]—*Syn.* erratic, random, infrequent; see **irregular** 1.
3. [Offhand]—*Syn.* accidental, purposeless, unplanned; see **aimless, haphazard** 1, **incidental** 2.
4. [Nonchalant]—*Syn.* blasé, apathetic, unconcerned; see **careless** 1, **indifferent** 1.

casually, *mod.* **1.** [Accidentally]—*Syn.* unintentionally, by chance, inadvertently; see **accidentally, haphazardly.**
2. [Nonchalantly]—*Syn.* indifferently, unconcernedly, coolly, unemotionally, impassively, re-

servedly, offhandedly, diffidently, apathetically, lackadaisically; see also **carelessly, easily** 1.
3. [Incidentally]—*Syn.* aimlessly, inconstantly, randomly; see **incidentally, haphazardly.**
casualty, *n.* **1.** [A misfortune]—*Syn.* accident, mishap, calamity; see **catastrophe, disaster, misfortune** 1.
2. [A loss in personnel; *often plural*]—*Syn.* killed, wounded, and missing; fatalities, losses, death toll, the injured, dead.
casuistry, *n.* —*Syn.* sophistry, delusion, evasion; see **fallacy** 1, **lie** 1, **trick** 1.
cat, *n.* **1.** [A domestic animal]—*Syn.* tom(cat), kitten; *all* (D): kit, tabby, puss, pussy, grimalkin, mouser, kitty.
House cats include the following—Maltese *or* blue cat (D), Persian, Siamese, Manx, Burmese, Angora, tortoiseshell, alley, tiger, short-haired domestic, calico; see also **animal** 2.
2. [A member of the cat family]—*Syn.* lion, tiger, leopard, panther, liger, tiglon, puma, wildcat, cheetah, lynx, bobcat, mountain lion, ocelot, serval *or* bushcat, cougar, catamount, jaguar; see also **animal** 2.
3. [(D) A caterpillar vehicle]—*Syn.* (caterpillar) tractor, tank, bulldozer, half-track; *all* (D): mucker, hush-hush, kitty, landship; see also **tank** 2, **tractor, truck** 1.
let the cat out of the bag (D)—*Syn.* expose, tell a secret, let slip (D); see **reveal** 1.
cataclysm, *n.* —*Syn.* upheaval, disturbance, calamity; see also **catastrophe, disaster, misfortune** 1.
catalog, *n.* **1.** [A list]—*Syn.* register, directory, schedule, inventory, bulletin, syllabus, brief, enumeration, cartulary, slate, table, calendar, list, docket, archive, gazette, gazetteer, muster, classification, record, draft, specification, roll, timetable, table of contents, prospectus, program, rent roll, Domesday Book; see also **file** 2, **index** 2.
2. [A publication based on a catalog]—*Syn.* statistics, census, compendium, synopsis, descriptive catalog, analytical catalog; see also **description** 1, **dictionary, encyclopedia, index** 2.
catalog, *v.* —*Syn.* classify, record, index; see **list** 1.
catalyst, *n.* **1.** [That which permits or accelerates a (chemical) reaction]—*Syn.* enzyme, reactant, synergist, a substance that speeds up a chemical reaction, chemical reactor; see also **chemical, matter** 1.
2. [An agitator]—*Syn.* reactionary, iconoclast, incendiary; see **agitator, radical.**
catapult, *n.* —*Syn.* sling, slingshot, ballista, trebuchet, arbalest; see also **mortar** 2, **weapon** 1.
cataract, *n.* —*Syn.* rapids, torrent, deluge; see **flood** 1, **water** 2, **waterfall.**
catastrophe, *n.* —*Syn.* calamity, mishap, mischance, misadventure, misery, accident, trouble, casualty, misfortune, infliction, affliction, contretemps, stroke, alluvion, havoc, ravage, wreck, fatality, grief, crash, devastation, desolation, avalanche, hardship, blow, visitation, ruin, reverse, emergency, scourge, convulsion, debacle, tragedy, adversity, bad luck, upheaval, down (D); see also **disaster, misfortune** 1.—*Ant.* benefit, advantage*, good luck.
catcall, *n.* —*Syn.* hiss, jeer, heckling; see **cry** 1, **insult, ridicule, scorn.**
catch, *n.* **1.** [(D) A likely mate]—*Syn.* unmarried suitor, sweetheart, inamorata, betrothed, fiancé, eligible bachelor, rich man, playboy; *all* (D): score, fish, trick, john, action, number, piece, date, daytripper, playmate, make, pair of pants; see also **lover** 1.
2. [Something stolen]—*Syn.* capture, seizure, grasping, apprehension, taking into captivity, take; *all* (D): nab, cop, bag, scoop, pickup, grab, haul; see also **booty.**
3. [A catching]—*Syn.* treasure, prize, cache, disclosure, uncovering, bonanza; *all* (D): good thing, plum, find, jewel, pride and joy, discovery, gem, lucky strike.
4. [A trick]—*Syn.* catch question, puzzle, conundrum, hidden idea, trap, puzzler (D); see **joke** 1, 2.
5. [A hook]—*Syn.* clasp, clamp, snap; see **fastener.**
catch, *v.* **1.** [To seize hold of]—*Syn.* snatch, take, take hold (of), snag, grab, pick, pounce on, fasten upon, snare, pluck, hook, claw, clench, clasp, grasp, clutch, grip; *all* (D): nab, net, glom, glove, bag; see also **seize** 1.—*Ant.* free, miss*, unleash.
2. [To bring into captivity]—*Syn.* trap, apprehend, capture; see **arrest** 1, **seize** 2.
3. [To come to from behind]—*Syn.* overtake, overhaul, reach, go after, get, come upon, run down, ram; see also **pass** 1.—*Ant.* falter, fail*, lag behind.
4. [To contract a disease]—*Syn.* get, fall ill (with), become infected (with), incur, become subject *or* liable to, fall victim to, take, succumb to, break out (with), receive, come down with (D).—*Ant.* ward off, escape*, get over.
5. [To trick]—*Syn.* fool, hoax, trip up (D); see **deceive.**
6. [To reach in time to board]—*Syn.* climb on, make, take; *all* (D): hop on, grab, jump; see also **board.**
catching, *mod.* —*Syn.* contagious, communicable, infectious, epidemic, endemic, pestilential, transmittable, pestiferous, noxious, miasmatic, epizootic, pandemic; see also **dangerous** 2.
catch it (D), *v.* —*Syn.* be scolded *or* reprimanded *or* punished, suffer (the consequences), get caught; see **get it** 2.
catch on (D), *v.* **1.** [To understand]—*Syn.* grasp, comprehend, perceive; see **understand** 1.
2. [To become popular]—*Syn.* become fashionable *or* prevalent *or* common *or* widespread *or* acceptable, grow in popularity, find a market, find favor; see also **prosper.**
catch (on) fire, *v.* —*Syn.* inflame, ignite, burst into flame; see **burn** 1, 2.
catch one's breath, *v.* —*Syn.* rest, wait, stop; see **hesitate, pause.**
catch the eye, *v.* **1.** [To appear]—*Syn.* become visible, show, materialize; see **appear** 1.
2. [To attract]—*Syn.* attract notice, engage attention, interest; see **fascinate.**
catchup, *n.* —*Syn.* tomato sauce *or* pureé, relish, chili sauce; see **ketchup.**
catch up, *v.* **1.** [To absorb]—*Syn.* engage, engross, employ; see **fascinate, occupy** 3.
2. [To overtake]—*Syn.* catch, join, equal; see **reach** 1.
catch up with *or* **to,** *v.* —*Syn.* overtake, join, overcome; see **reach** 1.

catchword, *n.* —*Syn.* slogan, watchword, password; see **motto, word** 1.

catchy, *mod.* —*Syn.* tricky, popular, memorable; see **charming, funny** 1, **pleasant** 2.

catechize, *v.* **1.** [To instruct systematically]—*Syn.* instruct, train, educate; see **teach** 1, 2.
2. [To question]—*Syn.* interrogate, inquire, quiz; see **ask** 1, **question** 1.

categorical, *mod.* —*Syn.* unqualified, unconditional, unequivocal; see **absolute** 1, **certain** 3, **definite** 1.

category, *n.* —*Syn.* level, section, classification; see **class** 1, **division** 2, **kind** 2.

cater, *v.* —*Syn.* procure, supply, furnish; see **provide** 1.

caterwaul, *v.* —*Syn.* screech, scream, bawl; see **cry** 1, **yell.**

catharsis, *n.* —*Syn.* purgation, cleansing, ablution; see **cleaning, purification.**

cathartic, *mod.* —*Syn.* purging, cleansing, purifying; see **cleaning, detergent.**

cathedral, *n.* —*Syn.* church that houses a bishop's throne, temple, house of God, house of prayer, Holy place, minster, basilica; see also **church** 1, **temple.**
Parts of a cathedral include the following—altar, sanctuary, holy of holies, sacristy, sacrarium, holy table, baptistery, chancel, apse, choir, nave, aisle, transept, crypt, pew, seat, pulpit, confessional.
Famous cathedrals include the following—St. Peter's, Rome; St. Paul's, London; Notre Dame, Paris; St. John the Divine, New York; St. Patrick's, New York.
Famous cathedrals are also at: Rouen, Beauvais, Rheims, Milan, Pisa, Florence, Cologne, Canterbury, Lincoln, Wells, Nidaros, Madrid, Mexico City.

catholic, *mod.* **1.** [Concerning humanity]—*Syn.* worldwide, worldly, cosmopolitan; see **general** 1, **international, universal.**
2. [Liberal]—*Syn.* receptive, open-minded, unprejudiced; see **fair** 1, **intelligent** 1, **liberal** 2, **rational** 1, **reasonable** 1, 2.
3. [Pertaining to the Catholic Church; *usually capitalized*]—*Syn.* Roman, Romanish, Romanist, popish, papist, papistical, ultramontane; see also **papal.**

cattle, *n.* —*Syn.* stock, cows, steers, calves, herd, beef cattle, dairy cattle, beef on the hoof; see also **animal** 2, **bull** 1, **calf.**

caucus, *n.* —*Syn.* assembly, meeting, council; see **gathering.**

caught, *mod.* —*Syn.* taken, seized, arrested; see **captured** 1, **under arrest.**

cause, *n.* **1.** [An underlying principle]—*Syn.* motive, causation, object, purpose, explanation, inducement, incitement, prime mover, motive power, mainspring, ultimate cause, ground, matter, element, stimulation, instigation, foundation, (the why and) wherefore (D); see also **basis** 1, **reason** 2. —*Ant.* effect, result*, outcome.
3. [The origin or source, thought of as the cause] —*Syn.* antecedent, root, beginning; see **origin** 3.
4. [The immediate moving force]—*Syn.* antecedent, agent, condition, etiology, prompting, ground, problem, subject of dispute, matter, occasion, case, circumstance, precedent, situation, fault, straw that breaks the camel's back; see also **circumstance** 1, **circumstances** 2, **event** 1, 2.
5. [A person who brings about a result]—*Syn.* originator, agent, doer; see **author** 1.
6. [A belief]—*Syn.* principles, conviction, creed; see **belief** 1, **faith** 2.
7. [Aim]—*Syn.* object, goal, intention, objective; see **plan** 2, **purpose** 1.

cause, *v.* **1.** [To bring about]—*Syn.* produce, effect, make; see **begin** 1, **create** 2.
2. [To be the cause]—*Syn.* originate, provoke, generate, occasion, let, kindle, give rise to, spell, give origin *or* occasion to, lie at the root of, be at the bottom of, bring to pass *or* to effect, sow the seeds of; see also **begin** 1, 2.

causeway, *n.* —*Syn.* highway, paved road, access road; see **path** 1, **road** 1.

caustic, *mod.* **1.** [Corrosive]—*Syn.* burning, strongly alkaline, erosive; see **acid** 2, **alkaline.**
2. [Sarcastic]—*Syn.* biting, sharp, stinging; see **sarcastic.**

cauterize, *v.* —*Syn.* disinfect by burning, sear, singe; see **burn** 2, **clean.**

caution, *n.* **1.** [The quality of considering beforehand]—*Syn.* care, heed, discretion; see **attention** 2, **prudence.**
2. [A warning]—*Syn.* forewarning, premonition, admonition; see **hint** 1, **sign** 1, **warning.**

caution, *v.* —*Syn.* forewarn, alert, advise; see **warn.**

cautious, *mod.* —*Syn.* circumspect, watchful, wary; see **careful.**

cautiously, *mod.* —*Syn.* tentatively, with due precautions, slowly; see **carefully** 2.

cavalcade, *n.* —*Syn.* drill, procession, spectacle; see **march** 1, **parade** 1, **review** 4.

cavalier, *n.* **1.** [Horseman]—*Syn.* cavalryman, rider, man-at-arms; see **knight, sir** 1.
2. [Gentleman]—*Syn.* gallant, escort, man of honor; see **aristocrat, gentleman** 1.

cavalry, *n.* —*Syn.* hussars, dragoons, rangers, light cavalry, heavy cavalry, air cavalry, Cossacks, uhlans, lancers, cuirassiers, chasseurs, Parthians, mounted riflemen, motorized cavalry, cavalry division, mounted troops, horse soldiers, mounted men, squadrons; see also **army** 1, 2, **troops.**

cave, *n.* —*Syn.* rock shelter, cavern, grotto; see **hole** 3.

caveat, *n.* —*Syn.* alarm, admonition, caution; see **sign** 1.

cave man, *n.* —*Syn.* cave dweller, cliff dweller, troglodyte; see **hominid.**

cavern, *n.* —*Syn.* cave, hollow, grotto; see **hole** 3.

cavernous, *mod.* **1.** [Hollow]—*Syn.* curved (inward), sunken, concave; see **hollow** 2.
2. [Large]—*Syn.* deep, huge, wide; see **broad** 1, **large** 1.

cavil, *v.* —*Syn.* quibble, find fault, criticize; see **censure, discuss.**

cavity, *n.* **1.** [Sunken area]—*Syn.* pit, depression, basin; see **hole** 2.
2. [Hollow place in a tooth]—*Syn.* dental caries, distal pit, gingival pit; see **decay** 2.

cavort, *v.* —*Syn.* prance, caper, frisk; see **dance** 2, **play** 2.

cease, *v.* —*Syn.* desist, terminate, discontinue; see **halt** 2, **stop** 1, 2.

ceaseless, *mod.* —*Syn.* continual, endless, unending; see **constant** 1, **eternal** 1, 2.

ceiling, *n.* —*Syn.* groined, beamed, timbered, plaster, cove ceiling; fan vaulting, topside covering, covert, roof, dome, baldachin, canopy, *plafond, planchement* (both French).

hit the ceiling (D)—*Syn.* become angry, lose one's temper, fume; see **rage** 1.

ceiling price, *n.* —*Syn.* fixed *or* top *or* maximum *or* legal price, price ceiling; *both* (D): Wage Labor Board (WLB) price, Office of Price Administration (OPA) price; see also **price.**

celebrate, *v.* **1.** [To recognize an occasion]—*Syn.* keep, observe, consecrate, hallow, sanctify, dedicate, memorialize, commemorate, honor, proclaim, extol, solemnize, keep, signalize, ritualize, ceremonialize; *both* (D): live it up, mark with a red letter.—*Ant.* forget*, overlook, neglect.

2. [To honor]—*Syn.* do honor to, fete, lionize; see **admire** 1, **praise** 1.

3. [To indulge in celebration]—*Syn.* feast, give a party, carouse, rejoice, kill the fatted calf, revel, jubilate; *all* (D): go on a spree, make whoopee, blow *or* let off steam, have a party *or* a ball, kick up one's heels, let loose *or* go, blow out, live *or* whoop it up, paint the town red, make merry, fire a salute, go it, kick up a row, beat the drum.

celebrated, *mod.* —*Syn.* well-known, renowned, noted; see **famous, important** 2.

celebration, *n.* **1.** [The act of recognizing an occasion]—*Syn.* commemoration, commemorating, observance, observing, glorification, magnification, laudation, recognition, anniversary, jubilee, remembrance, ceremonial, solemnization, memorialization, solemnity, keeping, observance, fete, Mardi Gras, birthday, centenary, centennial, bicentennial, bicentenary, tercentenary, tricentennial, millennium; see also **holiday** 1.

2. [Activities that accompany a celebration]—*Syn.* inauguration, installation, coronation, presentation, carnival, bacchanal, revelry, conviviality, spree, wassail, Saturnalia, jubilation, jollification, festivity, festival, feast, jamboree, ovation, triumph, merrymaking, gaiety, frolic, hilarity, joviality, merriment, mirth; see also **ceremony** 2.—*Ant.* sadness, solemnity, sorrow.

3. [The celebration of the Mass]—*Syn.* reading, reciting, singing, conducting, performing, intoning, chanting, praising God; see also **worship** 1.

celebrity, *n.* **1.** [The quality of being widely known] —*Syn.* glory, renown, notoriety; see **fame** 1, **honor** 1.—*Ant.* disgrace*, discredit, obloquy.

2. [A widely known person]—*Syn.* famous man *or* woman, notable, magnate, dignitary, worthy, figure, personage, famous person, man of note, Maecenas; *all* (D): someone, somebody, V.I.P., luminary, lion, lioness, star, bigwig, big gun, big shot, ace; see also **hero** 1, **heroine** 1, **leader** 2.

celestial, *mod.* —*Syn.* heavenly, ethereal, hallowed; see **angelic, divine** 1, **holy** 1.

celibacy, *n.* —*Syn.* virginity, purity, continence; see **chastity.**

celibate, *mod.* —*Syn.* continent, virginal, virgin; see **chaste** 3, **single** 3.

cell, *n.* **1.** [Any small container]—*Syn.* apartment, cavity, receptacle; see **container, hole** 2.

2. [A unit of a living organism]—*Syn.* corpuscle, cellule, microorganism, utricle, vacuole, spore, plastid, organism, egg, ectoplasm, embryo, germ, haematid, follicle.

3. [A room]—*Syn.* vault, hold, pen, cage, tower, hole, coop, keep, bastille, chamber, den, recess, retreat, alcove, manager, crypt, crib, nook, burrow, stall, closet, booth, cloister, antechamber, compartment, number, lockup (D); see also **room** 2.

4. [A unit of an organization]—*Syn.* group, block, claque; see **organization** 3.

cellar, *n.* —*Syn.* half basement, underground room, basement apartment; see **basement** 2.

cement, *n.* —*Syn.* glue, lute, lime, putty, tar, gum, mortar, paste, solder, adhesive, rubber cement, size, birdlime, grout, epoxy (resin), white cement, waterproof cement, bond; both (D): butter, mud; see also **adhesive.**

cement, *v.* —*Syn.* mortar, plaster, connect; see **fasten** 1, **join** 1, **paste.**

cemetery, *n.* —*Syn.* burial ground, memorial park, funerary grounds, churchyard, necropolis, potter's field, catacomb, city of the dead, tomb, ossuary, vault, crypt, charnel house, sepulcher, graveyard, mortuary; *all* (D): (last) resting place, God's Acre, Golgotha, eternal home, garden, boneyard; see also **grave** 1.

censor, *n.* —*Syn.* inspector, judge, expurgator, guardian of morals; see **examiner.**

censor, *n.* —*Syn.* control, restrict, strike out, revile, forbid, suppress, ban, withhold, enforce censorship, control the flow of news, supervise communications, inspect, oversee, abridge, examine, expurgate, review, criticize, exert pressure, conceal, refuse transmission, prevent publication, blacklist, throttle the press, debase freedom of speech; *all* (D): blue-pencil, cut, drop the iron curtain, black out; see also **restrain** 1.

censorious, *mod.* —*Syn.* carping, faultfinding, complaining; see **critical** 2, **severe** 2.

censorship, *n.* —*Syn.* licensing, restriction, forbidding, controlling the press, infringing the right of freedom of speech *or* press, governmental control, security blackout, news blackout, thought control, iron curtain, the censor's blue pencil; *both* (D): nonsensorship, censcissorship; see also **restraint** 2.

censurable, *mod.* —*Syn.* blameworthy, culpable, reprehensible; see **guilty** 2, **wrong** 1.

censure, *n.* —*Syn.* criticism, reproof, admonition; see **blame** 1, **objection** 2.

censure, *v.* —*Syn.* criticize, judge, blame, reprove, reprimand, rebuff, rebuke, reproach, upbraid, scold, denounce, condemn, backbite, attack, admonish, denigrate, tear *or* pull *or* pick apart, cut up, get after, read out, dress down, snap *or* bark at, tell off, animadvert, disapprove, impugn, disparage, deprecate, reprehend, depreciate, lecture, take to task, berate, discipline, chastise, carp at, contemn, incriminate, asperse, cavil, remonstrate, find fault with, moralize *or* frown upon, look askance, chide, ostracize, castigate, comment upon, decry, charge to, declaim *or* exclaim *or* fulminate against, cast blame upon, cast a slur upon, bring into discredit, discountenance; *all* (D): blackball, shoot down, lower the boom on, bawl the hell out of, cuss out, call *or* cry down, slam, sit on, rip into, hit out at, knock, call on the carpet, rake *or* haul over the coals, rap on the knuckles, chew out, throw *or* cast the first stone, throw a stone at, give a good talking to, take a dim view of, not speak well of, not be able to say much for, come down on, tell a thing or two, tear into, give the devil *or* deuce, bark at, blow up, jump on, cut (one) down to size, give a piece of one's mind, jump down one's throat, bring to book, read the riot act.—*Ant.* praise*, laud, commend.

census, *n.* —*Syn.* statistics, enumeration, valuation, account, registration, listing, (census) returns, evaluation, demography, figures, statement, specification, numeration, numbering, capitation, registering, roll (call), tabulation, tally, poll, count, counting, nose count (D).

cent, *n.* —*Syn.* penny, Indian penny, 100th part of a dollar; see **money** 1.

centenary, *n.* —*Syn.* century, 100th anniversary, centennial (celebration); see **anniversary, celebration** 1, **hundred.**

center, *mod.* —*Syn.* mid, middle, inmost, inner, midway, medial, deepest, at the inmost, innermost, internal, interior, at the halfway point; see also **inside** 4.—*Ant.* outer, outside*, exterior.

center, *n.* **1.** [A central point]—*Syn.* point, middle, focus, nucleus, core, place, heart, nave, hotbed, hub, omphalos, navel, point of convergence *or* concentration, focal point, midst, middle point, focalization, radiant, centrality, marrow, centriole, cynosure, kernel, bull's-eye, pivot, axis, marrow, pith, dead center (D).—*Ant.* edge*, verge, rim.

2. [A point that attracts people]—*Syn.* city, town, metropolis, plaza, capital, shopping *or* trading center, concourse, station, hub, mart, market, crossroads, mall, social center, meeting place, club, market place.

3. [Essence]—*Syn.* core, gist, kernel; see **character** 1.

center, *v.* —*Syn.* concentrate, centralize, focus, intensify, unify, unite, combine, converge upon, concenter, join, meet, focalize, gather, close on, concentralize, consolidate, bring to a focus, center round *or* in, gather *or* flock together, collect, draw *or* bring together, focus attention, attract.—*Ant.* decentralize, spread*, branch off.

central, *mod.* **1.** [Situated at the center]—*Syn.* middle, midway, equidistant, medial, focal, nuclear, pivotal, axial, umbilical, midmost, mean, centric, inner, median, inmost, middlemost, centroidal, intermediate, interior, in the center of; see also **inside** 4.—*Ant.* peripheral, outer*, verging on.

2. [Fundamental]—*Syn.* prime, basic, primary; see **fundamental** 1, **necessary** 1.

centralization, *n.* —*Syn.* consolidation, systematization, unification; see **concentration** 1, **organization** 1, 2.

centralize, *v.* —*Syn.* concentrate, incorporate, unify; see **accumulate** 1, **assemble** 2, **gather** 1, **organize** 1.

centrally, *mod.* —*Syn.* in the middle, centric, focal, middle-most, centroidal, in the center, in the heart of; see also **central** 1.

centrifugal, *mod.* —*Syn.* eccentric, diverging, radiating, outward, radial, diffusive, divergent, deviating, efferent, deviating from the center; see also **spiral, spreading.**

century, *n.* —*Syn.* 100 years, centenary, era; see **age** 3, **hundred, time** 1.

ceramics, *n.* —*Syn.* earthenware, crockery, porcelain; see **pottery, sculpture.**

cereal, *n.* —*Syn.* corn, small grain, seed; see **breakfast food, grain** 1.

ceremonial, *mod.* —*Syn.* ritual, formal, stately; see **conventional** 3.

ceremonious, *mod.* —*Syn.* ceremonial, formal, dignified; see **conventional** 2.

ceremony, *n.* **1.** [A public event]—*Syn.* function, commemoration, services; see **celebration** 1, 2.

2. [A rite]—*Syn.* observance, ritual, rite, service, solemnity, formality, ceremonial, custom, tradition, liturgy, ordinance, sacrament, liturgical practice, conformity, etiquette, politeness, decorum, propriety, preciseness, strictness, nicety, formalism, conventionality, usage, prescription, incantation, mummery.

stand on ceremony—*Syn.* ritualize, follow *or* insist on formality *or* etiquette *or* protocol, be ceremonial; see **behave** 2.

certain, *mod.* **1.** [Confident]—*Syn.* assured, questionless, sure, positive, satisfied, self-confident, undoubting, undoubtful, believing, secure, untroubled, unconcerned, undisturbed, unperturbed, (fully) convinced, assertive, cocksure (d); see also **calm, confident** 2.

2. [Sure]—*Syn.* destined, determined, predestined; see **inevitable.**

3. [Beyond doubt]—*Syn.* indisputable, unquestionable, assured, positive, real, true, genuine, plain, clear, undoubted, indubitable, guaranteed, unmistakable, unassailable, sure, incontrovertible, undeniable, definite, supreme, unqualified, infallible, undisputed, unerring, indeniable, sound, reliable, trustworthy, evident, conclusive, unambiguous, authoritative, irrefutable, unconditional, incontestable, unerring, unquestioned, absolute, unequivocal, inescapable, conclusive; *all* (d): in the bag, on ice, done up, salted away; see also **accurate** 1.—*Ant.* doubtful, uncertain, dubious.

4. [Dependable]—*Syn.* trustworthy, safe, sound; see **reliable** 2.

5. [Fixed]—*Syn.* settled, concluded, set; see **definite** 1, **determined** 1.

6. [Specific but not named]—*Syn.* special, marked, specified, defined, one, some, a few, a couple, several, upwards of, regular, particular, singular, especial, precise, specific, express; see also **definite** 1, **individual** 1, **special** 1.

for certain—*Syn.* without doubt, absolutely, certainly; see **surely.**

certainly, *mod.* **1.** [Without doubt; *used to qualify statements*]—*Syn.* positively, absolutely, unquestionably; see **surely.**

2. [Without doubt; *used to express agreement*] —*Syn.* assuredly, of course, without fail; see **yes.**

certainty, *n.* **1.** [Firmness of belief]—*Syn.* certitude, assurance, conviction; see **faith** 1, **truth** 1.

2. [A result looked upon as certain]—*Syn.* consequence, foregone conclusion, inevitable result; see **end** 2, **result.**

certificate, *n.* —*Syn.* declaration, warrant, voucher, testimonial, credential(s), license, testament, endorsement, diploma, affidavit, certification, coupon, document, authentication, pass, ticket, warranty, guarantee, testimony, attestation, testification, receipt, affirmation, docket, record; see also **diploma.**

certify, *v.* **1.** [To give assurance]—*Syn.* assure, reassure, attest; see **guarantee** 1.
2. [To state formally]—*Syn.* swear, attest, state; see **declare** 1, **testify** 2.

cessation, *n.* —*Syn.* stop, rest, recess; see **end** 2, **pause** 1, 2.

chafe, *v.* **1.** [To rub]—*Syn.* abrade, grate, scrape; see **rub** 1.
2. [To annoy]—*Syn.* irritate, vex, harass; see **bother** 2, 3, **disturb** 2.

chaff, *n.* **1.** [Husk]—*Syn.* shard, crust, pod; see **shell** 1.
2. [Trash]—*Syn.* refuse, waste, debris; see **trash** 1, 3.

chagrin, *n.* —*Syn.* mortification, humiliation, dismay; see **disgrace** 1, **embarrassment** 1, **shame** 2.

chain, *n.* **1.** [A series of links]—*Syn.* series, train, set, string, connection, cable, link, (charm) bracelet, ring series, shackle, manacle.
2. [A sequence]—*Syn.* succession, progression, continuity; see **series.**

chain, *v.* **1.** [To fasten]—*Syn.* connect, attach, secure; see **fasten** 1, **hold** 1.
2. [To bind]—*Syn.* shackle, fetter, tie up; see **bind** 1, **hold** 1.

chains, *n.* —*Syn.* fetters, bonds, irons, shackles, ball and chain, gyves, manacles, leg irons, handcuffs; see also **captivity, imprisonment** 1.

chair, *n.* **1.** [A single seat]—*Syn.* seat, place, room, space, cathedra; see also **armchair, bench** 1, **furniture, seat** 1.
Chairs include the following—stool, taboret, throne, faldstool, footstool, rocker, wing chair, armchair, easy chair, wheel chair, highchair, roundabout; curule, bath, occasional, dining *or* dining-room, desk, kitchen, beach, deck, lawn, period, swivel, folding, bentwood, cane-seated, split-bottom chair; Duncan Phyfe, Hepplewhite, Cromwell, Windsor, Morris, Queen Anne, X-legged Barcelona, Eames, S-squared Tugend hat, S-curved Brno, etc., chair.
2. [A position of authority]—*Syn.* Papal See, throne, woolsack, headship, professorship, tutorage, instructorship, readership, professorate, fellowship, tutorship; see also **authority** 3, **influence** 2.
3. [A death sentence; *usually used with* the]—*Syn.* execution, electric chair, electrocution, death chair; *all* (D): hot seat *or* squat, a burning, Sing Sing siesta; see also **punishment.**
take the chair—*Syn.* chair, preside (over), act as chairman; see **lead** 1.

chairman, *n.* —*Syn.* president, director, presider, toastmaster, speaker, moderator, prolocutor, monitor, leader, principal, captain, master of ceremonies *or* M.C. *or* emcee (D); see also **administrator.**

chalice, *n.* —*Syn.* grail, goblet, vessel; see **cup.**

chalk up, *n.* —*Syn.* credit, enter, register; see **add** 1, **record** 1, **score** 1, 2.

chalky, *mod.* —*Syn.* blanched, milky, pale; see **dull** 2, **gray** 1, **white** 1.

challenge, *n.* —*Syn.* dare, provocation, threat; see **objection** 2.

challenge, *v.* **1.** [To invite to a contest]—*Syn.* defy, denounce, invite competition; see **dare** 2, **threaten** 1.
2. [To question]—*Syn.* dispute, inquire, search out; see **ask** 1, **doubt** 1, **question** 1.
3. [To claim]—*Syn.* reclaim, exact, ask for, claim as one's due, vindicate, assert, demand one's rights, impose, make a stand, insist upon, call upon one for, make a point of; see also **claim** 1, **require** 2. —*Ant.* abandon*, give up, put away.

chamber, *n.* **1.** [A room, especially a bedroom]—*Syn.* apartment, cubicle, antechamber; see **room** 2.
2. [A small compartment]—*Syn.* box, cell, chest; see **case** 7, **container.**
3. [An organized group]—*Syn.* representatives, organization, body; see **government** 2, **legislature.**

champ, *n.* —*Syn.* munch, chew, masticate; see **bite** 1, **eat** 1.

champaign, *n.* —*Syn.* steppe, prairie, moor; see **field** 1, **land** 1, **meadow, plain.**

champion, *n.* **1.** [A winner]—*Syn.* vanquisher, conqueror, victor; see **hero** 1, **heroine** 1, **winner.**
2. [A defender]—*Syn.* upholder, guardian, backer; see **protector, supporter.**

chance, *mod.* —*Syn.* accidental, unplanned, unintentional; see **aimless, incidental** 2.

chance, *n.* **1.** [The powers of uncertainty]—*Syn.* fate, fortune, fortuity, hazard, casualty, lot, accident, luck, good luck, bad luck, destiny, outcome, cast, lottery, gamble, hap, adventure, contingency, kismet, happening, future, doom, destination, occurrence; *all* (D): hit, Lady Luck, turn of the cards, the way the cookie crumbles, hazard of the dice, heads or tails (D).—*Ant.* aim, purpose*, design.
2. [A possibility]—*Syn.* opening, occasion, prospect; see **opportunity** 1, **possibility** 2.
3. [An uncertainty]—*Syn.* venture, gamble, speculation; see **risk** 2, **uncertainty** 3.
4. [Probability; *often plural*]—*Syn.* likelihood, odds, indications; see **probability.**
by chance—*Syn.* by accident, as it happens, unexpectedly; see **accidentally.**
on the (off) chance—*Syn.* in case, in the event that, supposing; see **if.**

chance, *v.* **1.** [To happen]—*Syn.* come to pass, befall, occur; see **happen** 2.
2. [To take a chance]—*Syn.* venture, stake, hazard, wager, risk, gamble, try, attempt, jeopardize, speculate, tempt fate *or* fortune; *all* (D): play with fire, take a shot *or* leap in the dark, buy a pig in a poke, go out on a limb, go it blind, chance one's luck, chance it, have *or* take a fling at, put all one's eggs in one basket, skate on thin ice, run the risk, put one's shirt on it; see also **gamble** 1, **risk.**

chandelier, *n.* —*Syn.* candelabrum, gasolier, luster, corona, electrolier, crown, candleholder; see also **light** 3.

change, *n.* **1.** [The act of altering]—*Syn.* alteration, variation, vicissitude, diversion, substitution, swerving, deviation, shuffling, difference, reconstruction, aberration, evolution, restyling, innovation, move, interchange, trade, switch, fluctuation, wavering, modulation, alternating, exchange, mutation, transformation, transmutation, modification, transition, metamorphism, transfiguration, transshaping, adoption, transference, reworking, transmogrification, metamorphosis, improvisation, revolution, conversion, regeneration, shifting, warping, remodeling, veering, transubstantiation, shift, reformation, revision, rearrangement, enlargement, renewal, removal, disguising, reversal, tampering, qualification, turning, metathesis, inflection, vaciliating, vacillation, resolution, metastasis, reorganization; see also **variety** 1.—*Ant.* constancy*, consistency, permanence.

2. [An alteration]—*Syn.* modification, correction, remodeling, switch, reformation, reconstruction, shift, reform, conversion, transformation, tempering, revolution, rearrangement, adjustment, readjustment, reorganization, reshaping, renovation, realigning, realignment, redirecting, redirection, reprogramming, variation, addition, refinement, advance, modulation, development, diversification, turn, turnover, enlargement, revision, qualification, distorting, distortion, compressing, compression, contracting, contraction, telescoping, widening, narrowing, lengthening, flattening, shortening, fitting, setting, adjusting, rounding, getting out of round, ovalization, squaring; *all* (D): getting out of whack, gone every which way, ups and downs.

3. [Substitution]—*Syn.* switch, replacement, swap; see **exchange** 3.

4. [Variety]—*Syn.* diversity, novelty, variance; see **difference** 1, **variety** 1.

5. [Small coins]—*Syn.* pocket *or* spending *or* pin money, silver, small change, (small) coins, pennies, nickels, dimes, quarters, half dollars, chicken feed (d); see also **money** 1.

change, *v.* **1.** [To make different]—*Syn.* vary, alter, turn, diminish, replace, mutate, transshape, render different, diversify, modulate, fluctuate, transmute, swerve, warp, merge into, alternate, evolve, resolve into, translate, denature, transubstantiate, inflect, regenerate, disguise, restyle, revolutionize, reduce, substitute, diverge, commute, reorganize, vacillate, increase, intensify, shade, make *or* do over, cloud, shape, shift, modify, transform, remake, recondition, convert, reconvert, remodel, tailor, reform, renovate, recast, revamp, remold, modernize, reconstruct, convert, moderate, temper, adjust, adapt, accommodate, naturalize, transpose, invert, switch around, reverse, diversify, readjust, revise, transfigure, redo, metamorphose, transmogrify, swerve, tack, shift, deflect, come about *or* around *or* round, break, graduate, grade, tamper with, revolutionize, make innovations, change *or* reverse the signals, give a color to, do something about, bring up *or* down to date. —*Ant.* set, fix*, establish.

2. [To put in place of another]—*Syn.* displace, supplant, transpose; see **exchange** 1, **replace** 1, **substitute** 2.

3. [To change clothing]—*Syn.* undress, disrobe, make one's toilet; see **dress** 1.

4. [To become different]—*Syn.* alter, vary, modify, metamorphose, evolve, be converted, turn into *or* from, resolve into, grow, ripen, mellow, mature, transform, backfire, reform, moderate, adapt, adjust; see also **become** 1.

changeable, *mod.* **1.** [*Said of persons*]—*Syn.* inconstant, unstable, fickle, irresolute, flighty, irresponsible, unreliable, purposeless, wayward, unsettled, motiveless, uncertain, spasmodic, fanciful, impulsive, quiet, wavering, uneasy, unsteady, changeful, undecided, uneven, vagrant, faddish, fidgety, roving, many-sided, vacillating, mutable, versatile, light, lightheaded, moody, irregular, capricious, indecisive, restless, erratic, uneasy, agitated, whimsical, volatile, shifty, skittish, mercurial, fitful. —*Ant.* steady, reliable*, constant.

2. [*Said of conditions*]—*Syn.* variable, varying, variant, uncertain, mutable, unsteady, unsettled, doubtful, plastic, kaleidoscopic, convertible, transformable, protean, permutable, commutative, reversible, inconstant, transitional, unstable, revocable, wavering, fluid, fluctuating, movable, mobile, unfixed, alterable, alternating, modifiable, ever-changing, transmutable; see also **irregular** 1. —*Ant.* immovable, permanent*, fixed.

changed, *mod.* **1.** [Exchanged]—*Syn.* substituted, surrogated, interchanged, replaced, commutated, reciprocated, transposed, transferred, shuffled, swapped, replaced, traded, bartered, returned, succeeded by, reversed, reverted, restored, recurred, retracted, alternated.—*Ant.* placed*, stored, kept.

2. [Altered]—*Syn.* qualified, reconditioned, modified, limited, reformed, shifted, veered, moved, mutated, permutated, deteriorated, aged, become run-down, restated, rewritten, conditioned, modernized, remodeled, reprogrammed, rescheduled, redone, done over, brought up *or* down to date, edited, moderated, modulated, inflected, innovated, deviated, diverted, fluctuated, tacked, chopped, swerved, warped, dodged, passed to; see also **altered** 2.—*Ant.* unchanged*, unvaried, unmodified.

3. [Transformed]—*Syn.* remade, recreated, converted, transfigured, metamorphosed, transmuted, transmogrified, transubstantiated, transanimated, transmigrated, suffered a sea change.—*Ant.* permanent*, stabilized, final.

change hands, *v.* —*Syn.* be sold, be bought *or* purchased, be *or* open under new management, undergo a change of management.

changeless, *mod.* —*Syn.* permanent, unchanging, enduring; see **constant** 1, **perpetual** 1, **regular** 3.

change one's mind, *v.* —*Syn.* decide against, recant, alter one's convictions, modify one's ideas; see also **change** 1, **choose** 1.

changing, *mod.* —*Syn.* changeful, mobile, dynamic, vibratory, alternative, modifying, unstable, inconstant, uncertain, mutable, fluid, mercurial, declining, deteriorating, unsteady, irresolute, degenerating, wavering, AC/DC (D); see also **changeable** 1, 2, **uncertain** 2.—*Ant.* stable, fixed*, unchanging.

changing, *n.* —*Syn.* becoming different, altering, developing; see **growing.**

channel, *n.* **1.** [A passageway for liquid]—*Syn.* conduit, tube, canal, duct, course, carrier, gutter, furrow, trough, tunnel, tideway, strait, sound, race, raceway, dig, sewer, main, artery, vein, runway,

ditch, aqueduct, airway, canyon, cesspipe, pipe, lateral path; see also **way** 2.—*Ant.* ridge*, crest, dam.
2. [The deeper portion of a river]—*Syn.* current, marked *or* buoyed *or* dredged channel, body of the river, flood, deep water; see also **flow, water** 2.
3. [A groove]—*Syn.* gouge, gutter, slit; see **sense** 1; see **groove.**

channel, *v.* —*Syn.* route, send, direct; see **send** 1.

chant, *n.* —*Syn.* religious song, chorus, incantation; see **hymn, song.**

chant, *v.* —*Syn.* intone, chorus, carol; see **sing.**

chaos, *n.* —*Syn.* turmoil, anarchy, discord; see **confusion** 2, **disorder** 2.

chaotic, *mod* —*Syn.* disorganized, disordered, uncontrolled; see **confused** 2.

chap, *v.* —*Syn.* chafe, crack open, roughen; see **rub** 1.

chapbook, *n.* —*Syn.* booklet, compilation, tract; see **book** 1, **pamphlet.**

chapel, *n.* —*Syn.* place of worship, tabernacle, God's house; see **church** 1.

chaperon, *n.* —*Syn.* escort, governess, duenna; see **companion** 3.

chaplain, *n.* —*Syn.* clergyman, pastor, cleric; see **minister** 1, **priest, rabbi.**

chapter, *n.* —*Syn.* part, section, book; see **division** 3.

char, *v.* —*Syn.* scorch, sear, singe; see **burn** 2.

character, *n.* **1.** [The dominant quality]—*Syn.* temper, temperament, nature, sense, complex, mystique, mood, streak, attribute, singularity, badge, turn, tone, style, aspect, complexion, specialty, spirit, genius, humor, frame, grain, vein; see also **attitude** 3, **characteristic, temperament.**
2. [The sum of a person's characteristics]—*Syn.* personality, disposition, nature, makeup, reputation, constitution, repute, individuality, estimation, record, caliber, standing, type, shape, quality, habit, appearance; see also **kind** 2.
3. [A symbol, especially in writing]—*Syn.* sign, figure, emblem; see **letter** 1, **mark, number** 2.
4. [A queer or striking person]—*Syn.* personality, figure, personage, original, eccentric; *all* (D): crank, nut, case, queer duck, oddball, weirdo, freak, psycho.
in character—*Syn.* consistent, usual, predictable; see **expected** 2.
out of character—*Syn.* inconsistent, unpredictable, unusual; see **unexpected.**

characteristic, *mod.* —*Syn.* innate, fixed, essential, distinctive, distinguishing, marked, discriminative, symbolic, individualizing, discriminating, representative, specific, personal, original, peculiar, emblematic, individualistic, differentiating, individual, idiosyncratic, unique, special, appropriate, particular, symptomatic, private, exclusive, inherent, inborn, inbred, ingrained, native, diagnostic, indicative, diacritical, inseparable, ineradicable, in the blood; see also **natural** 1, 2, **typical.**—*Ant.* erratic, irregular*, aberrant.

characteristic, *n.* —*Syn.* flavor, attribute, quality, savor, essential, faculty, peculiarity, idiosyncrasy, individuality, style, aspect, tone, tinge, feature, distinction, manner, bearing, inclination, nature, personality, temperament, frame, originality, singularity, qualification, virtue, mark, essence, point, turn, caliber, complexion, streak, stripe, particularity, idiosyncrasy, lineament, diagnostic, cast, trick, earmark, mannerism, trademark, badge, symptom, disposition, specialty, mood, character, endowment, bent, tendency, component; *both* (D): thing, bag.

characterize, *v.* **1.** [Describe]—*Syn.* delineate, designate, portray; see **define** 2, **describe.**
2. [Distinguish]—*Syn.* discriminate, mark, identify; see **distinguish** 1.

charade, *n.* —*Syn.* mimicry, trick, put-on (D); see **deception** 1, **fake, pantomime.**

charge, *n.* **1.** [A charged sale]—*Syn.* entry, debit, carrying charge, credit, sale on account; see also **price, sale** 2.
2. [An attack]—*Syn.* assault, invasion, outbreak; see **attack** 1.
3. [A load]—*Syn.* clip, round, blast; see **ammunition, explosive, load** 3.
4. [An address to the jury]—*Syn.* admonition, statement, adjuration; see **speech** 3.
in charge (of)—*Syn.* responsible (for), controlling, managing; see **responsible.**

charge, *v.* **1.** [To ask a price]—*Syn.* require, sell for, fix the price at; see **price.**
2. [To enter on a charge account]—*Syn.* debit, put to account, charge to, run up an account, take *or* receive credit, take on account, put on one's account, incur a debt, put down, credit, accredit, encumber, sell *or* buy on credit; *all* (D): book, score, chalk up, put on the books, carry, put on the cuff; see also **credit** 2, **sell** 1.—*Ant.* pay, cash down, buy for cash, sell cash and carry.
3. [To attack]—*Syn.* assail, assault, invade; see **attack** 1.
4. [To accuse]—*Syn.* indict, censure, impute; see **accuse, censure.**
5. [To load]—*Syn.* lade, heap, burden; see **fill** 1, **load** 1.
6. [To command]—*Syn.* instruct, direct, entrust; see **command** 1.
7. [To take charge of]—*Syn.* watch over, safeguard, look after; see **defend** 2, **guard** 2, **manage** 1.

chargeable, *mod.* —*Syn.* liable, answerable, imputable; see **responsible** 1.

charged, *mod.* **1.** [Bought but not paid for]—*Syn.* debited, placed on the account of, unpaid, on credit *or* account, on time, on layaway, owing, owed; *all* (D): on the cuff, à la cuff, on the tab *or* bill; see also **bought, due.**
2. [Loaded]—*Syn.* laden, filled, burdened; see **full** 1.
3. [Accused]—*Syn.* taxed, confronted with, arraigned; see **accused.**

charger, *n.* —*Syn.* war horse, steed, mount; see **animal** 2, **horse** 1.

charity, *mod.* —*Syn.* cautiously, frugally, sparingly; see **carefully** 2.

charitable, *mod* —*Syn.* beneficent, liberal, philanthropic; see **generous** 1, **kind** 1.

charity, *n.* **1.** [Kindness]—*Syn.* benevolence, magnanimity, compassion; see **kindness** 1, **tolerance** 1.
2. [An organization to aid the needy]—*Syn.* charitable institution, eleemosynary corporation *or* foundation; see **foundation** 3.
Organized charities include the following—American Cancer Society, American Foundation for the

Blind, American Heart Association, American Red Cross, CARE, Catholic Charities, Community Chest, Easter Seal Society, Heart and Lung Foundation, Jewish Welfare Fund, Leukemia Society Inc., March of Dimes, Medico, Multiple Sclerosis Research Foundation Corp., Muscular Dystrophy Association of America Inc., National Association for Retarded Children, National Association for Mental Health Inc., National Cystic Fibrosis Research Foundation, National Epilepsy League, National Foundation for Neuromuscular Diseases, National Hemophilia Foundation, National Kidney Disease Foundation Inc., National Paraplegia Foundation Inc., National Society for the Prevention of Blindness, National Tuberculosis Association, St. Vincent de Paul Society, Salvation Army, United Cerebral Palsy Association Inc., United Fund, United Health Foundation Inc., United Leukemia Fund Inc., United Way.

charlatan, *n.* —*Syn.* quack, pretender, fraud; see **cheat** 1, **impostor.**

charm, *n.* **1.** [An incantation]—*Syn.* bewitchery, enchantment, sorcery; see **magic** 1.

2. [An object thought to possess power]—*Syn.* amulet, talisman, fetish, mascot, good-luck piece, madstone; *both* (D): lucky piece, rabbit's foot. —*Ant.* hoodoo, curse*, bad genius.

3. [The quality of being charming]—*Syn.* grace, attractiveness, attraction; see **beauty** 1.

charm, *v.* **1.** [To bewitch]—*Syn.* enchant, captivate, voodoo, possess, enrapture, enthrall, transport, entrance, bewitch, vamp, mesmerize; see also **fascinate, hypnotize.**

2. [To entertain]—*Syn.* delight, please, beguile; see **entertain** 1.

charmed, *mod.* —*Syn.* enchanted, bewitched, enraptured, entranced, captivated, attracted, lured, tempted, enticed, bedazzled, hypnotized, mesmerized, under a spell, in a trace, spellbound, moonstruck, witch-charmed, hagridden, possessed, obsessed; *all* (D): psyched, out of it, high, stoned; see also **fascinated.**

charming, *mod.* —*Syn.* enchanting, bewitching, entrancing, captivating, cute, fascinating, delightful, lovable, sweet, winning, irresistible, attractive, amiable, appealing, alluring, charismatic, pleasing, choice, nice, graceful, winsome, magnetizing, rare, seducing, seductive, desirable, enticing, tempting, inviting, ravishing, enrapturing, glamorous, elegant, infatuating, dainty, delicate, *charmant* (French), absorbing, tantalizing, engrossing, titillating, engaging, enamoring, enthralling, rapturous, electrifying, lovely, intriguing, thrilling, fair, exquisite, catching, likeable, transporting, diverting, fetching, provocative, delectable; *all* (D): having sex appeal *or* S.A., sexy, sexotic, sharp, smooth, adorable; see also **beautiful** 2, **handsome** 2, **pleasant** 1.—*Ant.* disgusting, offensive, unpleasant.

chart, *n.* —*Syn.* graph, outline, diagram; see **map, plan** 1.

chart, *v.* —*Syn.* map, outline, draft; see **plan** 2.

charter, *n.* **1.** [A grant]—*Syn.* concession, endowment, allotment; see **gift** 1, **grant.**

2. [A treaty]—*Syn.* contract, settlement, pact; see **agreement** 3, **treaty.**

charter, *v.* **1.** [To license]—*Syn.* authorize, sanction, permit; see **allow** 1.

2. [To hire]—*Syn.* lease, contract, use; see **borrow** 1, **rent** 2.

chary, *mod.* **1.** [Careful]—*Syn.* cautious, fastidious, particular; see **careful.**

2. [Frugal]—*Syn.* stingy, sparing, miserly; see **economical** 1.

chase, *v.* —*Syn.* trail, track, seek; see **hunt** 1, **pursue** 1.

give chase—*Syn.* chase, trail, hunt; see **pursue** 1.

chasm, *n.* —*Syn.* abyss, gorge, gap; see **hole** 2, **ravine.**

chassis, *n.* —*Syn.* framework, skeleton, undercarriage; see **body** 4, **case** 7, **frame** 1.

chaste, *mod.* **1.** [Restrained]—*Syn.* classic, classical, pure, simple, modest, Spartan, academic, severe, prudish, subdued, honest, disciplined, inornate; see also **simple** 1.—*Ant.* ornate*, gaudy*, rococo.

2. [Incorruptible]—*Syn.* immaculate, unstained, clean, innocent, virginal, unblemished, unsullied, uncontaminated, spotless, infallible, strong; see also **innocent** 4, **pure** 2.—*Ant.* corruptible, weak*, frail.

3. [Continent]—*Syn.* virgin, celibate, platonic, controlled, virtuous, monogamous, frigid, impotent, never having had sexual intercourse, unmarried, unwed, spouseless, wifeless, husbandless; see also **inexperienced, prudish.**—*Ant.* lewd*, lascivious, lecherous.

4. [Virtuous]—*Syn.* moral, modest, proper; see **decent** 2, **righteous** 1.

chasten, *v.* **1.** [To punish]—*Syn.* humble, humiliate, subdue, chastise, castigate, afflict, discipline, restrain, reprove, berate, take to task, upbraid, chide, rap on the knuckles, reproach, reprehend, admonish, rebuke, fulminate against, reprimand, tongue-lash, exprobrate, objurgate, scourge, penalize, scold; *all* (D): call down, roast, haul over the coals, have on the carpet; see also **censure, punish.** —*Ant.* encourage*, uplift, benefit.

2. [To purify]—*Syn.* refine, correct, clarify; see **improve** 1, **purify.**

chastise, *v.* —*Syn.* scold, discipline, spank; see **punish.**

chastity, *n.* —*Syn.* innocence, purity, virtue, uprightness, honor, singleness, monogamy, celibacy, integrity, decency, loyalty, devotion, honesty, delicacy, cleanness, goodness, bachelorhood, unmarried state, demureness, temperance, moderation, abstinence, morality, chasteness, spinsterhood, abstemiousness, modesty, sinlessness, continence, immaculacy, coldness, restraint, virginity, immaculateness, spotlessness, seemliness, gentleness, shame; see also **purity** 1, **virtue** 1.—*Ant.* adultery, lewdness*, licentiousness.

chat, *v.* —*Syn.* converse, prattle, chatter; see **talk** 1.

château, *n.* —*Syn.* manor house, mansion, palace; see **building** 1, **castle, home** 1.

chattel, *n.* —*Syn.* belongings, goods, assets; see **property** 1, **wealth** 1.

chatter, *v.* —*Syn.* gossip, chat, prattle; see **babble.**

chatterer, *n.* —*Syn.* chatterbox, prattler, jabberer; see **gossip** 2.

chatty, *mod.* —*Syn.* intimate, spontaneous, familiar; see **friendly** 1, **informal** 1, **talkative.**

chauffeur, *n.* —*Syn.* licensed operator, domestic, cabdriver; see **driver, servant.**
chauvinism, *n.* —*Syn.* fanatical patriotism, extreme nationalism, bellicism; see **jingoism, patriotism.**
cheap, *mod* **1.** [Low in relative price]—*Syn.* inexpensive, low-priced, moderate, of small *or* little cost *or* price, family-size, economy-size, budget, utility (grade), depreciated, slashed, standard, cut-rate, on sale, competitive, lowered, thrifty, bargain, irregular, reduced, cut-priced, low-cost, at a bargain, at prime cost, reasonable, marked down, half-priced, popular-priced, worth the money; *all* (D): dime-a-dozen, dirt-cheap, peanuts, for a song, second, bargain-basement; see also **economical** 2. —*Ant.* expensive*, dear, costly.
2. [Low in quality]—*Syn.* inferior, ordinary, shoddy; see **common** 1, **poor** 2.
3. [Dishonest or base]—*Syn.* dirty, tawdry, low; see **dishonest** 2, **mean** 3, **vulgar** 1.
cheapen, *v.* —*Syn.* ruin, spoil, debase, mar, degrade, devalue, undervalue, reduce, diminish, demean, render worthless; see also **corrupt** 1, **damage** 1, **depreciate** 2.
cheaply, *mod.* —*Syn.* economically, inexpensively, advantageously, at a bargain *or* a good *or* a fair price; on sale, at cost, below cost, discounted, at a discount, from a discount house, reduced, at a reduced price, sacrificed, at a sacrifice (sale), luckily, fortuitously, *bon marché* (French), in the economy *or* family size; *all* (d): dirt cheap, given away, stolen; see also **easily, fortunately** 1.
cheat, *n.* **1.** [One who cheats]—*Syn.* rogue, cheater, confidence man, quack, shyster, charlatan, conniver, fraud, swindler, scammer, enticer, chiseler, decoy, beguiler, allurer, twister, masquerader, picaroon, fake, bluff, deceiver, inveigler, hypocrite, trickster, mountebank, pettifogger, pretender, knave, cozener, dodger, humbug, crook, dissembler, coney catcher (Obs.); *all* (D): bilk, diddler, wolf in sheep's clothing, sharper, blackleg, con man, shark, jockey *or* jock, fourflusher, shill; see also **criminal, impostor, rascal.**
2. [A trick]—*Syn.* sham, humbug, deceit; see **fake, trick** 1.
cheat, *v.* —*Syn.* defraud, swindle, beguile; see **deceive.**
cheated, *mod.* —*Syn.* defrauded, swindled, tricked, finessed (out of), deprived of, scammed, imposed upon, victimized, beguiled, trapped, dealt with dishonestly, foiled, lured; *all* (D): humbugged, taken in, bamboozled, hoodwinked; see also **deceived** 1.—*Ant.* helped*, treated fairly, not cheated.
cheating, *n.* —*Syn.* lying, defrauding, deceiving; see **deception** 1, **dishonesty.**
check, *n.* **1.** [An order on a bank]—*Syn.* money order, letter of credit, traveler's check, bank *or* teller's *or* cashier's check, counter check, note, remittance, deposition; see also **draft** 5, **money** 1.
2. [A control]—*Syn.* poll, roll call, rein; see **restraint** 2.
3. [An examination]—*Syn.* investigation, analysis, inquiry; see **examination** 1, 3.
4. [The symbol √]—*Syn.* cross, ex, sign, line, stroke, score, dot; see also **mark** 1.
5. [A pattern in squares]—*Syn.* tartan, patchwork, quilt, diaper, checkered design, checkerboard, over-all pattern of squares; see also **plaid.**
6. [A reversal]—*Syn.* rebuff, obstruction, trouble; see **defeat** 3, **impediment** 1.
in check—*Syn.* controlled, under control, checked; see **restrained.**
check, *v.* **1.** [To slacken the pace]—*Syn.* curb, hinder, impede, moderate, obstruct, reduce, slacken, stay, restrain, choke, (cause a) bottleneck, deadlock, slow down, block, withhold, weaken, lessen, brake, keep back, cog, anchor, rein in; see also **halt** 2, **hinder.**—*Ant.* speed, hasten*, urge on.
2. [To bring under control]—*Syn.* bridle, repress, inhibit, control, checkmate, counteract, discourage, repulse, neutralize, bar, squelch, rebuff, snub; see also **restrain** 1.—*Ant.* free, liberate*, loose.
3. [To determine accuracy]—*Syn.* review, monitor, balance accounts, balance the books, keep account of, correct, compare, find out, investigate, count, tell, call the roll, take (an) account of, take stock; *all* (D): go through, go over with a fine-toothed comb, case; see also **examine** 1.
4. [To halt]—*Syn.* hold, terminate, cut short; see **halt** 2, **stop** 1.
5. [To mark]—*Syn.* brand, sign, stamp; see **mark** 1, 2.
checker, *n.* —*Syn.* person at the check stand, check-out person *or* personnel, cashier, examiner, tallier, rechecker, controller, validate, checking department, department of weights and measures, checking staff, inspector, examining officer, tally man.
checkered, *mod.* —*Syn.* patterned, spotted, checky, motley, variegated, diversified, plaid, mutable; see also **irregular** 4.
check in, *v.* —*Syn.* appear, sign in, come; see **arrive** 1, **register** 4.
checkmate, *v.* —*Syn.* halt, thwart, counter; see **check** 2, **halt** 2.
check off, *v.* —*Syn.* mark off, notice, correct; see **mark** 2.
check out, *v.* —*Syn.* depart, pay one's bill, settle up; see **leave** 1, **pay** 1.
checkroom, *n.* —*Syn.* parcel room, cloakroom, locker; see also **room** 2.
check up on (D), *v.* —*Syn.* watch, investigate, control; see **examine** 1.
cheek, *n.* **1.** [Either side of the face]—*Syn.* jowl, gill, chop (D); see **face** 1.
2. [Insolence]—*Syn.* impertinence, impudence, disrespect; see **rudeness.**
cheep, *v.* —*Syn.* peep, chirp, tweet; see **sound** 1.
cheer, *n.* **1.** [A gay social time]—*Syn.* party, gaiety, festivity; see **merriment** 2.
2. [An agreeable mental state]—*Syn.* delight, mirth, glee; see **happiness** 1, **joy** 3.
3. [An encouraging shout]—*Syn.* roar, applause, hurrah, hurray, huzzah, (organized) cheering, college yell, approval, approbation; see also **cry** 1, **encouragement** 2, **yell** 1.
cheer, *v.* **1.** [To hearten]—*Syn.* console, inspirit, brighten; see **comfort** 1, **encourage** 2, **help** 1.
2. [To support with cheers]—*Syn.* applaud, shout, salute; see **support** 2, **yell.**

cheerful, *mod.* **1.** [*Said especially of persons*] —*Syn.* gay, merry, joyful; see **happy** 1.
2. [*Said especially of things*]—*Syn.* bright, sunny, sparkling; see **comfortable** 2, **pleasant** 2.

cheerfully, *mod.* —*Syn.* cheerily, gladly, willingly, readily, happily, merrily, joyfully, lightheartedly, blithely, brightly, vivaciously, airily, genially, jovially, sportively, elatedly, winsomely, pleasantly, gleefully, gaily, mirthfully, playfully, hopefully, optimistically, breezily, briskly, with good cheer; see also **happily** 2.—*Ant.* unwillingly, reluctantly*, sadly.

cheerfulness, *n.* —*Syn.* good humor, gaiety, geniality; see **happiness** 1, **humor** 3.

cheering, *mod.* —*Syn.* heartening, promising, bright; see **hopeful** 2.

cheerless, *mod.* —*Syn.* gloomy, sorrowful, bleak; see **dismal** 1, **sad** 1.

cheers, inter.—*Syn.* here's to you, to your health, *skoal* (Scandinavian); see **toast** 1.

cheer up, *v.* **1.** [To make cheerful]—*Syn.* make happy *or* gay *or* lively, etc; enliven, inspirit; see **encourage** 2.
2. [To become cheerful]—*Syn.* become happy *or* gay *or* lively, etc.; improve one's outlook *or* spirits *or* mood, etc; perk up; see **improve** 2.

cheery, *mod.* —*Syn.* gay, lively, cheerful; see **pleasant** 2.

cheese, *n.* —Varieties of cheese include the following—mild, American, appetitost, (aged) cheddar, Cheshire, Dutch, Tamales Bay, Wisconsin nippy, New York State nippy, Philadelphia cream cheese, creamed cottage, Edam (Cheddar), hand, jack, brick, Roquefort, Brie, Bleu d'Auvergne, mozzarella, provolone, Gorgonzola, Monterey Jack, Swiss, Camembert, Liederkranz, Neufchâtel, Gruyère, Emmenthaler, Wensleydale, Parmesan, Stilton, Gouda, (double) Gloucester, Limburger, Leyden, muenster, oka, Pecorino, Port du Salut, pot, ricotta, Romano, Schweizer, smearcase, bel paese, tilsit, jeta; see also **food.**

chef, *n.* —*Syn.* head cook, head of the kitchen, *chef de cuisine* (French); see **cook, servant.**

chemical, *mod.* —*Syn.* analytical, synthetic(al), alchemical, synthesized, petrochemical, actinic, artificial, made in the laboratory, ersatz.

chemical, *n.* —*Syn.* substance, synthetic, compound; see **drug** 2, **element** 2, **medicine** 2.

chemistry, *n.* —Branches of chemistry include the following—pure, quantitative, qualitative, organic, inorganic, theoretical, physical, physiological, pathological, metallurgical, mineralogical, geological, applied, agricultural, pharmaceutical, sanitary, industrial, technical, engineering chemistry; chemurgy, biochemistry, electrochemistry, zoochemistry, petrochemistry, phytochemistry; see also **medicine** 3, **science** 1.

cherish, *v.* **1.** [To hold dear]—*Syn.* treasure, value, cling to, esteem, honor, admire, prize, revere, worship, entertain, harbor, enshrine (in the memory), like, care for, fancy, have a fancy for, caress, pet, coddle, clasp, cosset, embrace, adore, dote on, idolize, fondle, hug; *both* (D): feed the flame, fan the fires; see also **love** 1, 2.—*Ant.* give up, abandon, ill-treat.
2. [To tend solicitously]—*Syn.* nurture, harbor, cheer; see **comfort** 1, 2, **defend** 2.

cherry, *mod.* —*Syn.* ruddy, reddish, rosy, cerise, claret, Harvard crimson, dark red, bright *or* light red, Turkey red, blushing, incarnadine, rubescent, rubicund, erubescent, cherry-colored, cherry-red, bright, blooming, rosy-cheeked, cherry-cheeked; see also **red.**

cherry, *n.* —Cherries include the following—Bing, Lambert, black Tartarian, Napoleon, Windsor, Royal Ann, Royal Duke, Surinam, Cornelian, Japanese flowering, Montmorency, English Morello, wild, pin, chokecherry, bird, black, yellow, red, brush, sour, sweet, coffee, maraschino, native, Barbados; see also **fruit** 1.

cherub, *n.* —*Syn.* seraph, cherubim, beautiful infant; see **angel** 1, **baby** 1, **child.**

chest, *n.* **1.** [A box-like container]—*Syn.* case, box, coffer, cabinet, commode, strongbox, receptacle, crate, locker, chiffonier, clothespress, bureau, coffin, casket, treasury, reliquary, caddie, pyxis; see also **container.**
2. [The ribbed portion of the body]—*Syn.* breast, thorax, bosom, rib cage, heart, upper trunk, pulmonary cavity, peritoneum, ribs.

chew, *v.* —*Syn.* bite, champ, munch, crunch, masticate, nibble (at), feast upon, gnaw, gulp, dispatch, grind, chew the cud, rend, manducate, scrunch, ruminate; see also **eat** 1.

Chicago, *n.* **1.** [An American city]—*Syn. all* (D): the Windy City, Fort Dearborn, City of the Lakes and Prairies, Chi; see also **city.**
2. [The University of Chicago]—*Syn. all* (D): Rockefeller's College, Institute on the Midway, Chi; see also **university.**

chicanery, *n.* —*Syn.* trickery, sophistry, cheating; see **deception** 1.

chicken, *n.* **1.** [A barnyard fowl]—*Syn.* chick, hen, rooster, pullet, cock, heeler, cockalorum, cockerel, capon; see also **fowl.**
Chickens include the following—Black Cochin, Buff Cochin, Partridge Cochin, White Cochin, Game, Indian Game, Houdan, Black Leghorn, White Leghorn, Minorca, Buff Orpington, White Orpington, Rhode Island Red, Barred Plymouth Rock *or* Barred Rock *or* Plymouth Rock, White Plymouth Rock *or* White Rock.
2. [Flesh of the chicken]. Parts of the chicken include the following—breast, back, thigh, leg, wing, neck, giblets, heart, liver, gizzard, dark meat, white meat, light meat; *both* (D): drumstick, part that goes over the fence last; see also **meat.**
3. [(D) A coward]—*Syn.* recreant, dastard, craven; see **coward.**
count one's chickens before they are hatched (D) —*Syn.* rely (on), depend on, put trust in; see **anticipate** 1.

chide, *v.* —*Syn.* rebuke, reprimand, criticize; see **censure, scold.**

chief, *mod.* —*Syn.* leading, main, foremost; see **first, principal.**

chief, *n.* **1.** [The outstanding person or thing] —*Syn.* principal, manager, overseer, governor, president, foreman, proprietor, supervisor, director, chairman, ringleader, general, master, dictator, superintendent, head, ruler, captain, commander;

all (D): brass hat, bigwig, high muck-a-muck, first fiddle, top sawyer, prima donna, boss, honcho, *Der Fuehrer* (German), *Il Duce* (Italian), triton among minnows, it, the only pebble on the beach, the biggest frog in the puddle; see also **administrator, leader** 2.—*Ant.* subordinate, servant*, retainer.

2. [A chieftain]—*Syn.* prince, master, sachem, sagamore, emperor, duke, majesty, monarch, overlord, suzerain, lord, potentate, sovereign, chieftain, *burra* (Hindi), Maharaja, sahib, Rajah, boyar, effendi, emir, sheik, pasha; see also **king** 1, 2, **ruler** 1.

chiefly, *mod.* —*Syn.* mainly, particularly, in the first place; see **principally.**

child, *n.* —*Syn.* newborn, infant, nestling, toddler, moppet, preteen, youth, adolescent, teen-ager, youngster, daughter, son, grandchild, stepchild, foster child, foster brother, foster sister, offspring, descendant, innocent, stripling, minor, youngling, mite, chick, juvenile, tad, tyke, cub, tot, cherub, chit, whippersnapper, pubescent; *all* (D): papoose, tot, teeny-bopper, nymphet, kid, kiddie, whelp, brat, imp, young *or* small fry, urchin, shaver; see also **baby** 1, **bastard, boy, girl.**—*Ant.* parent*, forefather, adult.

with child—*Syn.* bearing *or* carrying a child, going to have a baby, fertile; see **pregnant** 1.

childbirth, *n.* —*Syn.* delivery, childbearing, parturition, childbed, labor, nativity, delivering, accouchement, lying-in, confinement, travail, procreation, reproduction, propagation, giving birth, parturience, blessed event (D); see also **birth** 1, **pregnancy.**

childhood, *n.* —*Syn.* infancy, youth, minority, pupilage, juvenility, juniority, school days, adolescence, nonage, nursery days, babyhood, boyhood, girlhood, teens, puberty, immaturity, tender age, adolescency.—*Ant.* maturity*, age, senility.

childish, *mod.* **1.** [Having qualities of a child] —*Syn.* childlike, baby, infantile, juvenile, puerile, youthful, primitive, babyish, boyish, girlish, adolescent, green, soft, immature; see also **naive, simple** 1, **young** 2.—*Ant.* adult, mature*, grown.

2. [Silly or stupid]—*Syn.* foolish, imbecile, absurd; see **stupid** 1.

3. [Young]—*Syn.* youthful, early, former; see **young** 1.

4. [Childlike because of senility]—*Syn.* senile, in one's dotage, in one's second childhood; see **old** 1.

childlike, *mod.* —*Syn.* unaffected, innocent, childish; see **natural** 3, **spontaneous.**

chill, *mod.* **1.** [Cool]—*Syn.* brisk, frosty, wintry; see **cold** 1.

2. [Cold in manner]—*Syn.* formal, distant, aloof; see **indifferent** 1, **unfriendly** 1.

3. [Depressing]—*Syn.* discouraging, unhappy, dispiriting; see **dismal** 1, **sad** 2.

chill, *n.* **1.** [Chilliness]—*Syn.* rigor, crispness, coolness, coldness, frigidity, sharpness, iciness, gelidity; see also **cold** 1.

2. [An illness]—*Syn.* virus, head cold, cough; see **cold** 3, **disease** 2.

chill, *v.* **1.** [To reduce temperature]—*Syn.* frost, refrigerate, make cold; see **cool** 2, **freeze** 2.

2. [To check]—*Syn.* dispirit, dishearten, dampen; see **depress** 2, **discourage** 1.

chilly, *mod.* —*Syn.* brisk, fresh, crisp; see **cold** 1, **cool** 1.

chime, *v.* —*Syn.* tinkle, clang, toll; see **ring** 3, **sound** 1.

chimera, *n.* —*Syn.* figment, delusion, fabrication; see **fancy** 3, **illusion** 1.

chimney, *n.* —*Syn.* smokestack, fireplace, furnace, hearth, flue, vent, pipe, funnel, smokeshaft, stack, chimney pot *or* can *or* stack, *cheminée* (French).

chin, *n.* —*Syn.* mentum, mandible, jawbone; see **jaw** 1.

China, *n.* —*Syn.* an Asiatic country, Chung Kwoh, People's Republic of China, mainland China, Red China, the Celestial Kingdom, the Middle Kingdom, Chung Hwa Kwoh, Central Flowery Country, Chinese Empire, Manchu Empire, Sung Empire, Ming Empire, Han Empire, the East, the Orient, the Mysterious East, Home of Sinicism, Country of Taoism, Land of Buddhism; see also **Asia.**

china, *n.* —*Syn.* chinaware, earthenware, pottery, crockery, procelain, stoneware; see also **dish.** Varieties of china include the following—Bow, bone, Chelsea, Lowestoft, Royal Doulton, Spode, Crown Derby, Worcester, Derby, Plymouth, Swansea, Limoges, Haviland, Chantilly, Sèvres, Dresden, Delft, eggshell, Belleek, Imari, Hizen, Rose Medallion, Kouan-Ki Rose, Wedgwood.

Chinese, *mod.* —*Syn.* Sinic, Sinaic, Celestial, Sinitic; see **Asiatic** 1, 2.

chip, *n.* **1.** [A fragment]—*Syn.* fragment, slice, wedge; see **bit** 1, **flake, part** 1.

2. [A microcircuit]—*Syn.* integrated circuit, semiconductor, microprocessor, computer on a chip.

having a chip on one's shoulder—*Syn.* ready to fight, disturbed, agitated; see **angry.**

in the chips (D)—*Syn.* wealthy, having money, flush (D); see **rich** 2.

let the chips fall where they may—*Syn.* gamble, exploit, proceed without concern for the consequences; see **risk.**

when the chips are down—*Syn.* in a crisis, having trouble, in a difficult position; see **in trouble** 1.

chip, *v.* —*Syn.* slash, hew, hack, crumble, snip, fragment, incise, shape (bit by bit), cut fragments from, gobbet, whittle, crack off, splinter, gash, hackle, snick, notch, sliver, cut (off), chop, split, slice, chisel, clip, break, crack, flake, cut away, nick, shiver, reduce, shear, whack (D).—*Ant.* join*, unite, mend.

chip in, *v.* —*Syn.* contribute, pay; *all* (D): ante (in *or* up), pitch in, go Dutch.

chipper (D), *mod.* —*Syn.* in good spirits, lively, brisk; see **happy** 1.

chips, *n.* **1.** [Small slices]—*Syn.* slivers, leaves, scales; see **flake.**

2. [Parings]—*Syn.* cuttings, shavings, turnings; see **part** 1.

3. [Counters used in games]—*Syn.* tokens, poker chips, counters; see **piece** 2.

4. [(D) Money]—*Syn.* cash; *both* (D): coin(s), bread; see **money** 1.

chirography, *n.* —*Syn.* calligraphy, penmanship, script; see **handwriting.**

chirp, *v.* —*Syn.* chirrup, lilt, purl, quaver, trill, twitter, warble, cheep, pipe, roll; see also **sound** 1.

chisel, *n.* —*Syn.* gouge, blade, edge; see **knife, tool** 1.

chisel, *v.* **1.** [To work with a chisel]—*Syn.* carve, hew, incise; see **cut** 1.
2. [(D) To get by imposition]—*Syn.* impose upon, defraud, gyp; see **deceive, steal.**

chitchat, *n.* —*Syn.* informal talk, prattle, small talk; see **gossip** 1, **talk** 5.

chivalrous, *mod.* —*Syn.* courteous, gentlemanly, gentlemanlike, heroic, valiant, courageous, gallant, knightly, generous, spirited, high-minded, valorous, lofty, intrepid, noble-minded, sublime; see also **brave** 1, **noble** 1, 2, **polite** 1.—*Ant.* cowardly*, boorish, pusillanimous.

chivalry, *n.* —*Syn.* valor, gallantry, fairness; see **courtesy** 1, **nobility** 1.

chock-full, *mod.* —*Syn.* packed, crammed, stuffed; see **full** 1.

choice, *mod.* —*Syn.* superior, fine, exceptional; see **best** 1.

choice, *n.* **1.** [The power to choose]—*Syn.* option, co-optation, discretion, decision, determination, free will, opportunity, choosing, election, selection, vote, volition, distinction; see also **choosing.**
2. [The act of choosing]—*Syn.* preference, decision, expression of an opinion; see **judgment** 2, **selection** 1.
3. [That which is chosen]—*Syn.* selection, preference, alternative, election, substitute, favorite, pick, appointee, chosen one, successful candidate, a good bet *or* guess (D).

choke, *v.* **1.** [To deprive of air]—*Syn.* asphyxiate, strangle, strangulate, stifle, throttle, garrote, drown, overpower, noose, gibbet, smother, grab by the throat, wring the neck, stop the breath, kill by suffocation, cut off one's air supply, suffocate; see also **gag** 1, **kill** 1.
2. [To be deprived of air]—*Syn.* strangle, gag, gasp, suffocate, be out of air, drown, choke off, be choked, burn out, die out, smother, throttle, die by asphyxiation; see also **die** 1.

choke up, *v.* **1.** [To be overcome with emotion] —*Syn.* give way to one's feelings, weep, break down; see **cry** 1.
2. [To fail under pressure]—*Syn.* falter, become confused, perform poorly; see **fail** 1.

choleric, *mod.* —*Syn.* quick-tempered, peevish, irascible; see **irritable.**

choose, *v.* **1.** [To select]—*Syn.* decide (on), take, pick out, draw lots, cull, prefer, make a choice of, accept, weigh, judge, sort, appoint, cast, embrace, co-opt, will, call for, fancy, take up, excerpt, extract, separate, favor, exercise, determine, resolve, discriminate (between), make a decision, adopt, engage, collect, mark out for, cut out, arrange, keep, take up, make one's choice *or* selection, pick and choose, settle on, use one's discretion, determine upon, fix on *or* upon, place one's trust in *or* on, glean, single out, espouse, exercise one's choice *or* option, make up one's mind, set aside *or* apart, commit oneself; *all* (D): divide the sheep from the goats, separate the wheat from the tares *or* chaff, incline toward, opt (for), cast one's lot with, take for better or for worse, burn one's bridges, take to one's bosom; see also **decide.**—*Ant.* discard*, reject, refuse.
2. [To like]—*Syn.* wish, prefer, feel disposed to *or* toward; see **like** 4, **want** 1.

choosing, *n.* —*Syn.* selecting, picking, culling, separating, electing, making a choice *or* selection, selection, election, option, separation, making up one's mind, exercising judgment, segregating, segregation, eliminating the undesirables, choosing by elimination, natural selection, survival of the fittest; see also **choice** 1.

chop, *v.* —*Syn.* fell, cut with an ax, whack; see **cut** 1.

choppy, *mod.* —*Syn.* wavy, uneven, ripply; see **rough** 1.

chord, *n.* —*Syn.* two or more musical tones sounded simultaneously, harmonizing tones, triad, octave; second, third, fourth, fifth, sixth, seventh, ninth, etc., chord; diminished chord, augmented chord, inverted chord, broken chord; primary, secondary, tertiary chord; tetrachord, perfect fourth, arpeggio, first inversion, second inversion, common chord; see also **harmony** 1, **music** 1.

chore, *n.* —*Syn.* task, routine, errand; see **job** 2.

chortle, *v.* —*Syn.* chuckle, snort, cackle; see **laugh** 1.

chorus, *n.* **1.** [A body of singers]—*Syn.* choir, singing group, choristers, voices, glee club, singing society, church singers, male chorus, female chorus, mixed chorus, chorale; see also **music** 1.
2. [A refrain]—*Syn.* undersong, melody, bob, theme, motif, recurrent verse, strain, main section, chorale, tune; see also **music, song**

chosen, *mod.* —*Syn.* picked, conscript, preferred; see **named** 2.

Christ, *n.* —*Syn.* the Saviour, Jesus, Jesus of Nazareth, the Anointed, the Redeemer, Messiah, Messias, Immanuel, the Mediator, the Intercessor, the Advocate, the Judge, the Word, the Son, the Son of Man, the Son of God, God the Son, the Son of David, the Son of Mary, the Risen, the King of Glory, the Prince of Peace, the Good Shepherd, the King of the Jews, the Lamb of God, the OnlyBegotten, Fairest among Thousands, Lily of the Valley, King of Kings, Alpha and Omega, Lord of Lords, Christ Our Lord, the Way, the Door, the Truth, the Life, the Bread of Life, the Light of the World, the Vine, the True Vine, the Lord of our Righteousness, the Sun of Righteousness, the Incarnate Word, the Word made Flesh, Rose of Sharon; see also **God** 2.

christen, *v.* —*Syn.* immerse, sprinkle, dedicate (to God); see also **baptize** 1, **bless** 3, **name** 1.

Christendom, *n.* —*Syn.* Zion, Christology, the Church, Christians, Christian faith, Christian community; see also **Christianity** 1, 2, **church** 3.

Christian, *mod.* —*Syn.* evangelical, gentile, orthodox, pious, pietistic, reverent, devoted, charitable, faithful, believing, strict, scriptural; see also **humble** 1, **religious** 1, 2.—*Ant.* impious*, immoral, profane.

Christian, *n.* —*Syn.* Nazarene, professor, true believer, witness, one of the faithful, one of the flock, convert, gentile, probationer, Christian man *or* woman, Christian socialist, Christian soul; Methodist, Unitarian, Baptist, Presbyterian, Protestant, Catholic, etc.; see also **Christianity** 2, **church** 3, **saint** 1.

Christianity, *n.* **1.** [A religion based upon the divinity of Christ]—*Syn.* teachings of Christ, religion of Christ, divine revelation, the Gospel, the Faith, the faith once delivered to the saints; see also **faith** 2, **religion** 2.

2. [The body of Christian people]—*Syn.* Christendom, Christians, body of Christ, followers of Christ, Christian community, fellow *or* even Christians; see also **church** 3.
3. [An attitude associated with Christianity, senses 1 and 2]—*Syn.* Christlike temper, Christian mercy *or* spirit, loving spirit, loving-kindness, forgiving disposition, having God in one's heart; see also **kindness** 1, **tolerance** 1.

Christmas, *n.* —*Syn.* Christmastide, Xmas, Yuletide, Noel, Yule, Christmas night, Christmas Eve, Christmas Day, the Nativity, birth of the Christ Child; see **holiday** 1, **winter.**

chronic, *mod.* —*Syn.* inveterate, confirmed, settled, rooted, deep-seated, continuing, persistent, persisting, stubborn, uncured, incurable, lasting, unyielding, tenacious, enduring, lingering, deep-rooted, abiding, perennial, fixed, continual, incessant, long-standing, recurring, continuous, of long duration, long-lived, unabating, protracted, ceaseless, sustained, lifelong, prolonged, recurrent, unmitigated, returning at intervals, intermittent, continued, obstinate, unceasing, inborn, inbred, ingrained, ever-present; see also **constant** 1, **habitual** 1, **permanent** 2.—*Ant.* acute, temporary*, casual.

chronicle, *n.* —*Syn.* narrative, annals, account; see **history** 2, **record** 1.

chronicler, *n.* —*Syn.* reporter, annalist, recorder; see **antiquarian, historian.**

chronological, *mod.* —*Syn.* datal, temporal, chronologic, historical, tabulated, classificatory, classified, according to chronology, in the order of time, sequential, archival, chronoscopic, sequent, horometrical, consecutive, chronometrical, horological, properly dated, measured in time, in sequence, chronometric, progressive in time, horologic, chronographic, ordered, in order, in due time *or* course.

chubby, *mod.* —*Syn.* plump, round, pudgy; see **fat** 1.

chuck, *v.* **1.** [To caress]—*Syn.* pat, tap, squeeze; see **touch** 1.
2. [(D) To throw away]—*Syn.* relinquish, eject, reject; see **discard.**

chuckle, *n.* —*Syn.* giggle, smile, grin; see **laugh.**

chuckle, *v.* —*Syn.* giggle, smile, snigger; see **laugh** 1.

chum (D), *mod.* —*Syn.* companion, playmate, pal (D); see **associate, friend** 1.

chummy (D), *mod.* —*Syn.* affectionate, intimate, constant; see **friendly** 1.

chunk, *n.* —*Syn.* piece, mass, lump; see **part** 1.

chunky, *mod.* —*Syn.* stocky, thickset, stout; see **fat** 1.

church, *n.* **1.** [A building consecrated to worship] —*Syn.* house of God, Lord's house, temple, synagogue, mosque, masjid, oratory, girja, place *or* house of worship, meeting-house, chapel, minster, basilica, tabernacle, bethel, abbey, sanctuary, sacellum, chantry, house of prayer, pantheon, conventicle, collegiate church, mission, shrine, *duomo* (Italian), pagoda; see also **cathedral.**
2. [A divine service]—*Syn.* rite, ordinance, prayer(s), (prayer) meeting, Sunday school, (divine) worship, Mass, Holy Mass, Lord's Supper, sacrament, the holy sacrament, Angelus, matin, vespers, rosary, ritual, religious rite, morning service, evening service, evensong, camp meeting, congregational, worship, fellowship, devotion(s), office, duty, revival meeting, exercises, chapel service, liturgics, sermon, communion; see **ceremony** 2.
3. [An organized religious body]—*Syn.* congregation, denomination, sect, chapter, body, order, communion, faith, religion, religious society *or* order, schism, affiliation, persuasion, belief, faction, doctrine, creed, cult, ism (D); see also **gathering, temple.**
Christian churches include the following—Methodist, Presbyterian, Unitarian, Universalist, Episcopalian, Baptist, Christian Science, Latter-day Saint *or* Mormon (D), Congregational, Lutheran, (Roman) Catholic, (Greek) Orthodox, Russian, Armenian, Coptic, Pentecostal, Evangelical Reformed, Church of England, Church of the Nazarene, Disciples of Christ, Church of the Brethren *or* Dunkers (D), United Brethren, Society of Friends *or* Quakers (D).

churl, *n.* **1.** [Peasant]—*Syn.* rustic, yokel, provincial; see **boor, peasant.**
2. [Miser]—*Syn.* niggard, tightwad, skimper; see **miser** 2.

churlish, *mod.* —*Syn.* rustic, boorish, base; see **rude** 1, 2, **vulgar** 1.

churlishness, *n.* —*Syn.* coarseness, vulgarity, roughness; see **rudeness.**

churn, *v.* —*Syn.* stir, beat, agitate; see **mix** 1.

chute, *n.* —*Syn.* trough, rapid(s), watercourse; see **waterfall.**

cigarette, *n.* —*Syn.* *all* (D): fag, smoke, coffin nail; see **tobacco.**

cinder, *n.* —*Syn.* embers, hot coals, soot; see **ashes** 1, **coal** 2.

cinema, *n.* **1.** [Motion picture]—*Syn.* film, photoplay, the movies (D); see **movie.**
2. [Motion-picture theater]—*Syn.* movie house, playhouse, hall; see **auditorium, theater** 1.

cipher, *n.* —*Syn.* naught, blank, goose egg (D); see **zero** 1.

cipher, *v.* —*Syn.* compute, figure, estimate; see **add** 1, **calculate** 1, **count.**

circle, *n.* **1.** [A round closed plane figure]—*Syn.* ring, loop, wheel, sphere, globe, halo, orb, orbit, circlet, crown, corona, colure, zodiac, aureole, circus, bowl, stadium, vortex, cirque, hoop, horizon, perimeter, periphery, circumference, amphitheater, parallel of latitude, tire, wheel, full turn, circuit, disk, record, meridian, equator, ecliptic, cordon, cycle, bracelet, belt, wreath; see also **ball** 1, **curve** 1.
2. [An endless sequence of events]—*Syn.* cycle, round, course, succession, continuation, range, epicycle, cause and effect, systole and diastole; see also **progress** 1, **series, sequence** 1.
3. [A coterie]—*Syn.* set, surroundings, party; see **gathering.**
come full circle—*Syn.* go through a cycle *or* series, come around *or* back, revert; see **return** 1.

circle, *v.* —*Syn.* round, encircle, compass, girdle, loop, tour, circumnavigate, ring, belt, embrace, gird, encompass, wind about, revolve around, circumscribe, hedge in, curve around, circuit, enclose, ensphere, cincture, spiral, compass about, be circumjacent, coil, circulate, detour, wind, roll, wheel, swing past, go round about, evade, circumambulate; see also **surround** 1.—*Ant.* divide*, bisect, cut across.

circuit, *n.* —*Syn.* circumference, turning, periphery, line, course, round, circling, circle, turn, wind, tour, compass, ambit, circuity, lap, hookup, detour, winding, twist, circumnavigation, circumscription; see also **orbit** 1, **revolution** 1.

circuit, *v.* —*Syn.* move *or* go around, detour, encircle, compass, encompass, skirt, beat about (D); see also **circle.**

circuitous, *mod.* —*Syn.* complicated, roundabout, devious; see **indirect.**

circuits, *n.* —*Syn.* integrated circuits, microcircuitry, systems, solid-state circuits, connections; see also **electronics, wiring.**

circular, *mod.* —*Syn.* annular, orbicular, disklike; see **round** 1, 2.

circular, *n.* —*Syn.* handbill, broadside, leaflet; see **advertisement** 1, 2, **pamphlet.**

circulate, *v.* **1.** [To go about]—*Syn.* move *or* get around, get *or* fly *or* go about, wander; see also **travel** 2, **walk** 1.

2. [To send about]—*Syn.* diffuse, report, broadcast; see **distribute** 1.

circulating, *mod.* —*Syn.* current, circulative, ambient, diffusive, rotating, circling, in circulation, in motion, fluid; see also **moving** 1.—*Ant.* still, motionless*, stationary.

circulation, *n.* **1.** [Motion in a circle]—*Syn.* rotation, current, flowing; see **flow, revolution** 1.

2. [Number of copies distributed]—*Syn.* transmission, apportionment, dissemination; see **distribution** 1.

circumference, *n.* **1.** [Boundary]—*Syn.* bounds, outline, limit; see **boundary, edge** 1.

2. [Distance around]—*Syn.* perimeter, periphery, border; see **circuit.**

circumlocution, *n.* —*Syn.* periphrasis, verbal evasion, redundancy; see **wordiness.**

circumscribe, *v.* **1.** [To trace a line around]—*Syn.* encircle, encompass, girdle; see **surround** 1.

2. [Limit]—*Syn.* restrict, outline, confine; see **define** 1.

circumspect, *mod.* —*Syn.* watchful, cautious, wary; see **careful.**

circumspection, *n.* —*Syn.* heed, caution, wariness; see **care** 1, **prudence.**

circumstance, *n.* **1.** [An attendant condition] —*Syn.* situation, condition, contingency, phase, factor, detail, item, fact, case, place, time, cause, status, element, particular, feature, point, incident, proviso, article, stipulation, concern, matter, thing, event, adjunct, occurrence, juncture, exigency, intervention, supervention, crisis, fortuity, coincidence, concurrent event, happenstance (D); see also **state** 2.

2. [An occurrence]—*Syn.* episode, happening, incident; see **event** 1.

3. [Ceremony]—*Syn.* formality, ritual, solemnity; see **ceremony** 2.

circumstances, *n.* pl. **1.** [Condition in life]—*Syn.* material welfare, worldly goods, outlook, prospects, chances, means, assets, prosperity, financial status *or* condition, resources, standing, property, net worth, financial standing, credit rating, terms, estate, way of life, pecuniary standing, monetary condition, vicissitudes of fortune, rank, class, degree, capital, degree of wealth, position, command, financial responsibility, footing, dowry, precedence, income, sphere, substance, stock in trade, lot, prestige, what one is worth, place on the ladder, notch (D); see also **state** 2, **wealth** 1, 2.

2. [attendant conditions]—*Syn.* situation, environment, surroundings, facts, particulars, factors, features, motives, controlling *or* qualifying *or* governing factors, the times, occasion, basis, grounds, setting, background, needs, requirements, necessities, course of events, imposed terms, legal status, departmental provisions, governmental provisions, economic requirements, political exigencies, terms imposed, milieu, change, promptings, life, bearings, vicissitudes, fluctuation, phase, case, premise, condition, (governing) agents, (accompanying) events, state of affairs, modifying features, surrounding facts, order of the day; *all* (D); the score, the scene, the story, where it's at, how the land lies, the lay of the land, a tide in the affairs of men, current regime, ups and downs.

under no circumstances—*Syn.* under no conditions, by no means, absolutely not; see **never.**

under the circumstances—*Syn.* conditions being what they are, for this reason, because of; see **because.**

circumstantial, *mod.* **1.** [Detailed]—*Syn.* minute, environmental, precise; see **detailed.**

2. [Depending upon circumstances]—*Syn.* presumptive, inferential, inconclusive; see **uncertain** 2.

circumvent, *v.* **1.** [To go around]—*Syn.* encircle, encompass, entrap; see **surround** 1, 2.

2. [To gain an advantage over]—*Syn.* outwit, trick, dupe; see **deceive.**

3. [To avoid]—*Syn.* dodge, elude, shun; see **avoid, evade** 1.

circus, *n.* —*Syn.* hippodrome, spectacle, entertainment, bazaar, show, fair, festival, kermis, big top (D).

cistern, *n.* —*Syn.* reservoir, pond, tank; see **well** 1.

citadel, *n.* —*Syn.* fortress, stronghold, manor; see **castle, fortification** 2.

citation, *n.* **1.** [Summons]—*Syn.* bidding, charge, writ; see **command** 1, **summons.**

2. [Citing]—*Syn.* mention, reference, quoting; see **quotation** 1.

cite, *v.* **1.** [To summon]—*Syn.* call, arraign, order; see **summon** 1.

2. [To refer to as authority]—*Syn.* quote, mention, refer *or* allude *or* appeal to, repeat, point out *or* up, enumerate, tell, (cite an) instance, quote chapter and verse, number, recount, recite, rehearse, illustrate with, excerpt, indicate, give as example, extract, exemplify, call to witness, evidence; see also **mention, refer** 2.—*Ant.* ignore, neglect*, distrust.

citizen, *n.* —*Syn.* inhabitant, denizen, national, subject, burgher, burgess, cosmopolite, commoner, civilian, urbanite, taxpayer, member of the community, householder, house dweller, native, occupant, settler, aborigine, (registered) voter, dweller, immigrant, naturalized person, townsman, freeman, the man on the street, villager, member of the body politic, John Q. Public (D); see also **resident.**

city, *mod.* —*Syn.* metropolitan, civil, civic; see **municipal.**

city, *n.* —*Syn.* town, place, municipality, borough, burg, capital, megalopolis, metropolis, suburb, central city, provincial town, county town, county seat, (trading) center, inner city, downtown, shopping center *or* district, business *or* financial district, urban place, incorporated town, metropolitan area, township, port; see also **center** 2, **village.**

civic, *mod.* —*Syn.* civil, urban, municipal; see **public.**

civil, *mod.* **1.** [Civic]—*Syn.* local, civic, public; see **municipal.**

2. [Polite]—*Syn.* formal, courteous, refined; see **polite** 1.

civilian, *mod.* —*Syn.* unmilitary, nonmilitary, unmilitant, nonmilitant, noncombat, noncombative, noncombatant, unhostile, pacificist, not in the armed forces, in civilian life, in civies *or* mufti (D).

civilian, *n.* —*Syn.* (private) citizen, noncombatant, person not in the armed forces; see **commoner.**

civilization, *n.* **1.** [Culture]—*Syn.* cultivation, polish, enlightenment, refinement, civility, illumination, advancement of knowledge, elevation, edification, race *or* national culture, state of refinement, level of education, advancement, social well-being, degree of cultivation, material well-being, acculturation, *Kultur* (German), education, breeding; see also **culture** 2, 3, **progress** 1.—*Ant.* barbarism, savagery, degeneration.

2. [The civilized world]—*Syn.* civilized life, modern man, literate society; see **society** 2.

civilize, *v.* —*Syn.* enlighten, cultivate, enrich, reclaim, refine, render civil, acculturate, polish, spiritualize, humanize, edify, uplift, tame, foster, instruct, ethicize, reclaim from barbarism, promote, help forward, better (materially), make gentle, inform of civilized ways, acquaint with culture, indoctrinate, idealize, elevate, educate, advance, ennoble; see also **develop** 1, **improve** 1, **teach** 1.

civilized, *mod.* —*Syn.* enlightened, refined, humanized; see **cultured, educated** 1.

civil rights, *n.* pl.—*Syn.* civil liberties, equality, four freedoms; see **choice** 1, **freedom** 1, 2.

clack, *v.* **1.** [To talk heedlessly]—*Syn.* clatter, rattle, prate; see **babble.**

2. [To make a rattling noise]—*Syn.* clatter, rattle, clap; see **sound** 1.

claim, *n.* —*Syn.* demand, declaration, pretense, requisition, profession, entreaty, petition, suit, ultimatum, call, request, requirement, application, postulation, reclamation, case, pretension, assertion, plea, counterclaim, right, interest, title, part; see also **appeal** 1.—*Ant.* disclaimer, renunciation*, repudiation.

lay claim to—*Syn.* demand, challenge, stake out a claim (to) (D); see **require** 3.

claim, *v.* **1.** [To assert a claim to]—*Syn.* demand, lay claim to, stake out (a claim) (D); see **challenge** 3, **require** 3.—*Ant.* disclaim, renounce, resign.

2. [To assert]—*Syn.* insist, pronounce, pretend; see **believe** 1, **declare** 1.

claimant, *n.* —*Syn.* petitioner, applicant, claimer; see **candidate.**

clairvoyance, *n.* **1.** [Intuition]—*Syn.* premonition, foreknowledge, precognition; see **feeling** 4, **sign** 1.

2. [Discernment]—*Syn.* penetration, insight, perception; see **acumen.**

clairvoyant, *mod.* **1.** [Psychic]—*Syn.* telepathic, second-sighted, spiritualistic; see **mental** 2, **mysterious** 2.

2. [Discerning]—*Syn.* perceptive, penetrating, clear-sighted; see **judicious.**

clam, *n.* —*Syn.* bivalve, quahog, mollusk, mussel, shellfish, sea food; see also **fish.**

Clams include the following—round, soft, hard, long, marine, sea, fresh-water, surf, hen, thorny, giant, razor, geoduck.

clamber, *v.* —*Syn.* ascend, mount, scale; see **climb** 2.

clammy, *mod.* —*Syn.* moist, damp, soggy; see **cold** 2, **wet** 1.

clamor, *n.* **1.** [A loud outcry]—*Syn.* din, outcry, discord; see **noise** 2, **uproar**

2. [A protesting]—*Syn.* lament, complaint, remonstrance; see **objection** 2, **protest.**

clamorous, *mod.* —*Syn.* noisy, uproarious, vociferous; see **loud** 2.

clamp, *n.* —*Syn.* snap, clasp, catch; see **fastener, lock** 1.

clan, *n.* —*Syn.* group, clique, moiety; see **organization** 3, **race** 2.

clandestine, *mod.* —*Syn.* furtive, private, surreptitious; see **hidden** 2, **secret** 3.

clang, *n.* —*Syn.* clank, clatter, jangle; see **noise** 1.

clank, *n.* —*Syn.* clang, chink, clink; see **noise** 1.

clank, *v.* —*Syn.* clink, tinkle, chime; see **ring** 2, 3, **sound** 1.

clannish, *mod.* **1.** [Of a clan]—*Syn.* close, associative, akin; see **alike** 2, **like, related** 2.

2. [Unreceptive]—*Syn.* select, reserved, cliquish; see **exclusive.**

clap, *v.* **1.** [To applaud]—*Syn.* cheer, acclaim, approve; see **praise** 1.

2. [To strike]—*Syn.* bang, slap, slam; see **hit** 1.

clapper, *n.* —*Syn.* tongue of a bell, clack, noisemaker; see **tongue** 3.

clapping, *mod.* —*Syn.* cheering, applauding, acclaiming; see **enthusiastic** 1, 2.

claptrap, *mod.* —*Syn.* ostentatious, bombastic, theatrical; see **affected** 2.

claptrap, *n.* —*Syn.* empty talk, drivel, jargon; see **nonsense** 1.

clarification, *n.* —*Syn.* exposition, elucidation, description; see **definition** 2, **explanation** 1, 2, **interpretation** 1.

clarify, *v.* **1.** [Purify]—*Syn.* filter, refine, cleanse; see **clean, purify.**

2. [Explain]—*Syn.* interpret, define, elucidate; see **explain.**

clarion, *mod.* —*Syn.* clear, sharp, shrill; see **definite** 2.

clarity, *n.* —*Syn.* limpidness, limpidity, clearness, purity, brightness, precision, explicitness, exactness, decipherability, intelligibility, explicability, perceptibility, penetrability, unmistakability, distinctness, comprehensibility, cognizability, plain speech, legibility, openness, directness, perspicuity, evidence, prominence, manifestness, overtness, salience, precision, transparency, palpability, conspicuousness, certainty, ease, innocence, lucidity; see also **accuracy** 2, **simplicity** 1.—*Ant.* darkness*, haze*, obscurity*.

clash, *n.* **1.** [Collision]—*Syn.* crash, encounter, impact; see **collision** 1.

2. [Disagreement]—*Syn.* opposition, conflict, argument; see **disagreement** 1, **dispute** 1.

clash, *v.*—*Syn.* be dissimilar, mismatch, not go with; see **contrast** 1, **differ** 1.

clashing, *n.*—*Syn.* dissension, opposition, discord; see **disagreement** 1.

clasp, *n.*—*Syn.* buckle, pin, clamp; see **fastener.**

clasp, *v.*—*Syn.* clamp, pin, buckle; see **fasten** 1.

class, *n.* **1.** [A classification]—*Syn.* degree, order, rank, grade, standing, genus, division, distinction, breed, type, kingdom, subdivision, phylum, subphylum, superorder, family, cast, mold, sect, category, quality, rate, collection, denomination, department, sort, species, variety, branch, group, genre, range, brand, set, kind, estate, hierarchy, section, domain, nature, suit, color, origin, character, humor, frame, temperament, school, designation, temper, sphere, brood, spirit, vein, persuasion, head, province, heat, make, grain, feather, source, name, mood, habit, form, selection, stamp, stripe, status, range, streak, property, aspect, disposition, tone; see also **classification** 1, **state** 2.

2. [A division of society]—*Syn.* caste, clique, circle, clan, moiety, coterie, station, cultural level, intelligentsia, bourgeoisie, family, breed, sect, layer of society, social rank, standing, place, sphere, stock, nobility, high rank, pedigree, society, prestige, (social) stratum, income group, title, degree, position, status, connection, precedence, genealogy, power, company, derivation, source, descent, birth, ancestry, influence, hierarchy, state, lineage, condition, strain, tribe, estate, extraction, origin, club, quality; see also **sense** 1; see also **tribe.**

3. [A group organized for study]—*Syn.* form, lecture, recitation, section, subdivision, seminary, round table, quiz section, seminar, colloquium, meeting for study *or* lecture, grade, period, lesson, assembly, course, group, session, room, division, course of study.

in a class by itself—*Syn.* unusual, different, one of a kind; see **unique.**

class, *v.*—*Syn.* identify, rank, grade; see **classify, mark** 2.

classic, *n.*—*Syn.* *magnum opus* (Latin), masterwork, exemplar; see **masterpiece.**

classical, *mod.* **1.** [Of recognized importance]—*Syn.* standard, first-rate, established, ideal, flawless, distinguished, paramount, esthetic, ranking, superior, artistic, well-known; see also **excellent, famous, perfect** 2.—*Ant.* modern*, popular*, transitory.

2. [Concerning ancient Greece or Rome]—*Syn.* humanistic, canonical, canonic, correct, Attic, Hellenic, Ciceronian, academic, classicistic, classic, Latin, Homeric, Virgilian, Roman, Augustan; see also **ancient** 2.

classicism, *n.*—*Syn.* aesthetic principles, objectivity, dignity, balance, refinement, formality, simplicity, restraint, pure taste, nobility, formal style, classicalism, reverence for the ancients, observance of classic principles, lucidity, classical taste, the grand style, conventional formality, proportion, propriety, rhythm, symmetry, majesty, grandeur, polish, finish, clarity, rationalism, eloquence, Atticism, purity, neoclassicism, conformity to classical style, authority of the ancients, Ciceronianism, sobriety, high art, sublimity, excellence, severity, established forms, well-turned periods, Hellenism; see also **elegance** 2.

classification, *n.* **1.** [The act of putting into classes]—*Syn.* arrangement, assortment, grouping, ordering, allotment, allotting, organization, gradation, co-ordination, graduation, disposal, disposition, reducing to order, categorizing, apportionment, regulation by a system, tabulating, consignment, orderly arrangement, analysis, division, assignment, designation, taxonomy, collocation, sizing, assorting, ordination, distributing, distribution, allocation, systematization, codification, categorization; see also **order** 3.

2. [A division]—*Syn.* kind, order, group; see **class** 1.

classified, *mod.*—*Syn.* assorted, grouped, classed, indexed, filed, orderly, recorded, listed, registered, detailed, arranged, reduced, regulated, compiled, co-ordinated, characterized, ranked, distributed, catalogued, separated, allocated, labeled, numbered, systematized, tabulated, alphabetized, typed, on file, rated.—*Ant.* confused, mixed*, jumbled.

classify, *v.*—*Syn.* arrange, order, pigeonhole, tabulate, organize, distribute, categorize, systematize, co-ordinate, correlate, incorporate, codify, collocate, label, alphabetize, place in a category, range, form into classes, divide, docket, allocate, number, rate, ticket, class, dispose, rank, catalogue, segregate, distinguish, brand, digest, allot, analyze, regiment, name, group, tag, type, put in order, break down, embody, assort, sort, index, grade, match, size, reduce to order, introduce a system; see also **file** 1, **list** 1.—*Ant.* disorganize, disorder*, disarrange.

clatter, *n.*—*Syn.* clack, rattle, bang; see **noise** 1.

clatter, *v.*—*Syn.* rattle, clash, crash; see **sound** 1.

clause, *n.* **1.** [A provision]—*Syn.* condition, codicil, ultimatum; see **limitation** 2, **requirement** 1.

2. [A grammatical structure]. Clauses include the following—independent, dependent, relative, subordinate, substantive *or* noun, adjective *or* adjectival, adverb *or* adverbial; sentence modifiers, transform *or* transformations; see also **transformations** 2.

clavier, *n.*—*Syn.* claviature, keys, ivories (D); see **keyboard.**

claw, *n.*—*Syn.* talon, hook, tentacle, spur, fang, paw, grappling iron *or* hook, forked end, clutching hand, nipper, grapnel, crook, barb, retractile, pincers, clapperclaw, fingernail, cant hook, tack claw, nail claw, manus, ungula, unguis, nail.

claw, *v.*—*Syn.* tear, scratch, rip open; see **break** 1, **hurt** 1, **rip.**

clay, *n.*—*Syn.* loess, argil, loam, kaolin, clunch, earth, till, wacke, slip, bole, argillaceous earth, marl, potter's clay, clayware, green pottery, terra cotta, green brick, china clay, porcelain clay, adobe; see also **mud.**

having feet of clay—*Syn.* ignoble, overestimated, weak; see **inadequate.**

clean, *mod.* **1.** [Not soiled]—*Syn.* spotless, washed, stainless, laundered, untarnished, speckless, un-

stained, neat, tidy, clear, blank, white, dirtless, unblemished, unspotted, (newly) cleaned, snowy, well-kept, dustless, unsmirched, cleansed, immaculate, unsullied, unsoiled, unpolluted; *both* (D): spic and span, clean as a whistle.—*Ant.* soiled, dirty*, stained.
2. [Not contaminated]—*Syn.* unadulterated, wholesome, unsullied; see **pure** 2, **sanitary.**
3. [Having sharp outlines]—*Syn.* clear-cut, sharp, distinct; see **definite** 2.
4. [Legible; having few errors]—*Syn.* clear, plain, distinct, readable, precise, correct; see also **accurate** 1.—*Ant.* illegible*, confusing, vague.
5. [Trim]—*Syn.* orderly, tidy, regular; see **neat** 1.
6. [Sinless]—*Syn.* pure, wholesome, unsullied; see **innocent** 1, 4.
7. [Thorough]—*Syn.* complete, entire, total; see **absolute** 1, **whole** 1.
8. [Fair]—*Syn.* reliable, decent, lawful; see **fair** 1, **honest** 1.
9. [Well-proportioned]—*Syn.* shapely, slender, graceful; see **trim** 2.
10. [Free from radioactivity]—*Syn.* decontaminated, not dangerous, checked; see **safe** 4.
11. [(D) Highly salable]—*Syn.* like new, reconditioned, unused, little used, fixed up, repaired, painted, overhauled, superior, excellent, fashionable, smart, modish, modern, recent, good, reliable; *all* (D): clean as a whistle, O.K., smooth, not a scratch on it, sharp.
come clean (D)—*Syn.* confess, reveal, expose; see **admit** 2.

clean, *v.* —*Syn.* cleanse, clean *or* clear up *or* out, purge, purify, soak, shake out, wash down, scrub off, disinfect, tidy up, deodorize, expurgate, swab, absterge, polish, sterilize, lixiviate, scrape, sweep out, scour, launder, vacuum, scald, dust, mop, cauterize, rinse, sponge, brush, dress, comb, dredge, pick, blow, whisk, scrub, sweep, rout out, wipe (up), clarify, elutriate, winnow, rake, clean away, make clear, lave, hatchel, bathe, expunge, soap, hackle, rasp, erase, neaten, shampoo, edulcorate, refine, flush, depurate, defecate, blot, leach, rub up; *all* (D): do up, spruce up, slick up, clear the decks, deterge, neatify; see also **wash** 1, 2.—*Ant.* dirty*, soil, smear.

cleaner, *n.* —*Syn.* detergent, disinfectant, cleaning agent; see **cleanser, soap.**

cleaning, *mod.* —*Syn.* cleansing, purgative, detergent, abstergent, washing, delousing, dusting, sweeping, scouring, soaking, sterilizing, purificatory, laundering, vacuuming, scalding, purifying, cathartic, depurative, purging.—*Ant.* dirtying *or* corrosive*, corruptive.

cleaning, *n.* —*Syn.* cleansing, purge, purgation, scrubbing, scouring, purification, ablution, scrub, sweeping, brush, antisepsis, prophylaxis, rendering sterile, sterilizing, washing, brushing, purifying, deodorizing, making hygienic, applying antisepsis, catharsis; see also **sanitation.**

cleanliness, *n.* —*Syn.* cleanness, neatness, pureness, nattiness, tidiness, trimness, spruceness, immaculateness, spotlessness, dapperness, finicality, orderliness, niceness, whiteness, daintiness, disinfection, sanitation.—*Ant.* filth*, dirtiness, griminess.

cleanly, *mod.* —*Syn.* neat, tidy, spotless; see **clean** 1.

cleanse, *v.* **1.** [To remove dirt from the surface] —*Syn.* launder, wash, scrub; see **clean.**
2. [To remove impurities from within]—*Syn.* refine, disinfect, purge; see **clean, purify.**
3. [To free from sin or its effects]—*Syn.* absolve, purge, restore; see **excuse.**

cleanser, *n.* —*Syn.* cleansing *or* cleaning agent, abrasive, lather, solvent, purgative, deodorant, fumigant, soap flakes, polish, disinfectant, antiseptic, cathartic, purifier, cleaning *or* scouring powder, spray cleaner, cleaner, detergent, abstergent, soap powder, cleaning fluid, dry cleaner, suds (D); see also **soap.**
Cleansers include the following—water, soap and water, soap, washing powder, scouring powder, oven cleaner, naphtha, French chalk, washing soda, furniture polish, borax, lye, household ammonia, bleaching compound, solvent, cathartic soap, bluing, carbon tetrachloride, toiletbowl cleanser, chloride of lime, sal soda, baking soda, washing crystals, chlorine compound, wallpaper cleaner, silverpolish, kerosene, gasoline, benzine, vinegar, rug shampoo.

clear, *mod.* **1.** [Open to the sight or understanding] —*Syn.* explicit, plain, manifest; see **obvious** 1, 2.
2. [Offering little impediment to vision]—*Syn.* lucid, pure, transparent, apparent, pellucid, limpid, translucent, crystal, crystalline, thin, crystal clear. —*Ant.* opaque*, dark, muddy.
3. [Unclouded]—*Syn.* sunny, cloudless, bright, rainless; see **fair** 3.
4. [Discernible]—*Syn.* distinct, precise, sharp; see **definite** 2.
5. [Freed from legal charges]—*Syn.* free, guiltless, cleared, exonerated, blameless, innocent, uncensurable, sinless, exculpated, dismissed, discharged, absolved.—*Ant.* accused, charged*, blamed.
6. [Audible]—*Syn.* loud enough to be heard, distinct, definite; see **audible.**
in the clear—*Syn.* guiltless, not suspicious *or* suspected, cleared; see **free** 2, **innocent** 1.

clear, *v.* **1.** [To free from uncertainty]—*Syn.* clear up, relieve, clarify; see **explain.**
2. [To free from obstacles]—*Syn.* disentangle, rid, unloose; see **free** 2, **remove** 1.
3. [To free from contents]—*Syn.* clean, unload, unpack; see **empty** 1, 2.
4. [To free from guilt]—*Syn.* acquit, discharge, get off the hook (D); see **free** 1, **release.**
5. [To profit]—*Syn.* realize, net, make; see **receive** 1.

clearance, *n.* **1.** [Removal]—*Syn.* withdrawal, removing, clearing; see **removal** 1.
2. [Permission]—*Syn.* approval, consent, leave; see **permission.**

clear-cut, *mod.* —*Syn.* precise, plain, evident; see **obvious** 1, 2.

cleared, *mod.* **1.** [Emptied]—*Syn.* cleaned, unloaded, cleared away; see **empty** 1.
2. [Freed of charges]—*Syn.* vindicated, exculpated, set right; see also **discharged, free** 2.
3. [Made negotiable]—*Syn.* cashable, validated, certified; see **valid** 1.

clearheaded, *mod.*—*Syn.* sensible, perceptive, confident; see **composed** 2, **intelligent** 1, **judicious.**

clearing, *n.* **1.** [The act of clearing]—*Syn.* freeing, riddance, clearance, removing, elimination, eradication, defoliating, defoliation, clarification, opening up, freeing from obstruction, evacuation, deforestation, disposal, voidance, dispersal, FIDO (Fog Investigation and Dispersal Operations), sweeping out *or* away, clearing away, mopping up, emptying; see also **removal** 1.
2. [A cleared space]—*Syn.* (open *or* empty) space, assart, opening, clearance, defoliated area, margin; see also **area** 2, **court** 1, **expanse, yard** 1.

clearly, *mod.* **1.** [Distinctly; *said of sight*]—*Syn.* plainly, precisely, lucidly, purely, translucently, brightly, perceptibly, crystallike, unmistakably, in full view, transparently, in focus, discernibly, decidedly, starkly, incontestably, undoubtedly, indubitably, noticeably, admittedly, before one's eyes, beyond doubt, prominently, obviously, patently, openly, overtly, observably, certainly, apparently, manifestly, recognizably, conspicuously, in plain sight, definitely, markedly, surely, visibly, positively, seemingly, evidently; *all* (D): to the eye, at first blush *or* sight, to all appearances, on the face of.—*Ant.* dully, hazy*, cloudily.
2. [Distinctly; *said of sounds*]—*Syn.* sharply, acutely, ringingly, penetratingly, sonorously, audibly, bell-like, with absolute clarity, with good articulation.—*Ant.* indistinct*, mutteringly, unclearly.
3. [Obviously; *said of concepts*]—*Syn.* apparently, openly, unquestionably; see **surely.**

clearness, *n.*—*Syn.* brightness, distinctness, lucidity; see **clarity.**

clear out, *v.* **1.** [To remove]—*Syn.* clean out, dispose of, get rid of; see **eliminate** 1, **excrete.**
2. [(D) To leave]—*Syn.* depart, go, remove oneself; see **leave** 1.

clear-sighted, *mod.*—*Syn.* perceiving, understanding, discerning; see **conscious** 1, 2, **judicious, observant** 1.

clear up, *v.* **1.** [To become clear; *said especially of weather*]—*Syn.* blow over, stop raining *or* snowing *or* storming, run out, lapse, run its course, die *or* pass (away), die down, show improvement, pick up, lift, become fair, brighten, have fair *or* fine weather; see also **improve** 2.
2. [To make clear]—*Syn.* explain (away), clarify, make plausible *or* explicable *or* reasonable, etc.

cleat, *n.*—*Syn.* wedge, lug, brace; see **fastener, support** 2.

cleavage, *n.* **1.** [A cleaving]—*Syn.* dividing, splitting, separating; see also **division** 1.
2. [A fissure]—*Syn.* split, cleft, rift; see **hole** 2, **valley.**

cleave, *v.* **1.** [Split]—*Syn.* sever, hew, split; see **cut** 1, **divide** 1.
2. [Stick]—*Syn.* cling, adhere, attach; see **stick** 1.

cleaver, *n.*—*Syn.* butcher's knife, chopper, blade; see **ax.**

cleft, *mod.*—*Syn.* split, rent, parted; see **separated, torn.**

clemency, *n.* **1.** [Mildness of temper]—*Syn.* leniency, charity, compassion; see **kindness** 1, **mercy** 1.
2. [Mildness of weather]—*Syn.* mildness, calm, stillness; see **peace** 2.

clement, *mod.* **1.** [Merciful]—*Syn.* lenient, benevolent, compassionate; see **kind** 1, **merciful** 1.
2. [Mild; *said of weather*]—*Syn.* warm, clear, peaceful; see **calm** 2, **fair** 3, **mild** 2.

clench, *v.*—*Syn.* grip, grasp, double up (D); see **hold** 1.

clergy, *n.*—*Syn.* priesthood, prelacy, pastorate; see **ministry** 2.

clergyman, *n.*—*Syn.* pastor, parson, preacher; see **minister** 1, **priest, rabbi.**

clerical, *mod.* **1.** [Concerning clerks]—*Syn.* subordinate, stenographic, accounting, scribal, bookkeeping, secretarial, typing, written, assistant, on the sales force; see also **recorded.**
2. [Concerning the clergy]—*Syn.* ministerial, sacerdotal, priestly, parsonical, apostolic, monastic, theocratical, monkish, hierarchic, parsonish, pastoral, rabbinical, churchly, cleric, prelatic, papal, episcopal, canonical, pontifical, ecclesiastic, clerkly, sacred, holy, ecclesiastical, in God's service, devoted to the Lord, in the Lord's work; see also **divine** 2.—*Ant.* lay, worldly*, civilian.

clerk, *n.* **1.** [A person engaged in selling]—*Syn.* saleswoman, saleslady, shop assistant, salesclerk, salesman, salesperson, counterman, seller, shopman, counter jumper (D); see also **agent** 1.
2. [An office assistant]—*Syn.* auditor, bookkeeper, recorder, registrar, stenographer, office girl, office boy, timekeeper, cashier, teller, corresponder, scribe, office worker, notary, controller, copyist, amanuensis, law clerk, switchboard operator, steno (D); see also **accountant, secretary** 2, **typist.**

clever, *mod.* **1.** [Apt, particularly with one's hands]—*Syn.* skillful, expert, adroit; see **able** 1, 2.
2. [Mentally quick]—*Syn.* smart, bright, shrewd; see **intelligent** 1, **sly** 1.

cleverly, *mod.* **1.** [In an intelligent manner]—*Syn.* sensibly, judiciously, discerningly; see **intelligently.**
2. [In a dexterous manner]—*Syn.* adroitly, neatly, skillfully, diplomatically, tactfully, politically, dexterously, aptly, ingeniously, resourcefully, handily, deftly, nimbly, agilely, proficiently, expertly, smoothly, facilely, quickly, speedily, readily, with dispatch, in a practiced *or* polished *or* finished manner, without apparent effort, with consummate skill; see also **easily** 1.—*Ant.* awkwardly, clumsily, unskillfully.

cleverness, *n.*—*Syn.* skill, adroitness, ingenuity; see **ability** 2.

cliché, *n.*—*Syn.* commonplace, platitude, stereotype, proverb, saying, slogan, trite phrase *or* remark, saw, old saw, stereotyped saying, vapid expression, prosaism, triteness, rehashed story, threadbare phrase, banality, triviality, bromide, staleness, vapidity, hackneyed phrase *or* idea *or* expression; see also **motto.**

click, *n.*—*Syn.* tick, snap, bang; see **noise** 1.

click, *v.* **1.** [To make a clicking sound]—*Syn.* tick, snap, bang; see **sound** 1.
2. [(D) To be successful]—*Syn.* match, go off well, meet with approval; see **succeed** 1.

client, *n.*—*Syn.* customer, patient, patron, buyer, purchaser, disciple, follower, believer.

clientele, *n.* —*Syn.* dependents, clientry, body of customers, purchasers of goods *or* services, cortege, buyers, shoppers, constituency, clientage, customers, patrons; see also **following.**

cliff, *n.* —*Syn.* bluff, crag, steep rock; see **hill, mountain** 1, **wall** 1.

cliff dweller, *n.* —*Syn.* Pueblo, aborigine, cave dweller; see **Indian** 1.

climacteric, *n.* —*Syn.* trial, crucial period, crux; see **crisis, emergency.**

climate, *n.* —*Syn.* latitude, characteristic weather, meteorological character, atmospheric *or* meteorologic conditions, altitude, aridity, humidity, (weather) conditions; see also **cold** 1, **heat** 1, **weather.**

climax, *n.* —*Syn.* peak, apex, highest point, culmination, acme, pinnacle, meridian, intensification, crest, zenith, height, summit, apogee, extremity, limit, pitch, successive increase of effect, ascendancy, utmost extent, highest degree, point of highest development, turning *or* crowning point, turning of the tide, *ne plus ultra* (Latin); see also **maximum, top** 1.—*Ant.* anticlimax, depression*, nadir.

climax, *v.* **1.** [To come to a climax]—*Syn.* culminate, tower, end, top, conclude, rise to a crescendo, reach a peak, come to a head, reach the zenith, break the record; see also **achieve** 1.

2. [To bring to a climax]—*Syn.* finish, accomplish, fulfill; see **succeed** 1.

climb, *n.* **1.** [The act of climbing]—*Syn.* climbing, clamber, mounting; see **rise** 1.

2. [An ascending place]—*Syn.* slope, incline, dune; see **grade** 1, **hill.**

climb, *v.* **1.** [To ascend]—*Syn.* scale, go up, soar; see **rise** 1.

2. [To mount]—*Syn.* scale, work one's way up, ascend gradually, scramble *or* clamber *or* swarm up, start up, go up, ascend, go on board, labor *or* struggle up, get *or* climb on, progress upward, rise, lift, rise hand over hand, come up, creep up, strive up, escalate, surmount, soar up; *all* (D): shinny up, scrabble up, shoot up.

climb down, *v.* —*Syn.* step off, come down, dismount; see **descend** 1.

clinch, *v.* **1.** [To attach]—*Syn.* clamp, secure, grip; see **fasten** 1, **hold** 1.

2. [To lay hold of]—*Syn.* grab hold of, lay hands on, snatch; see **seize** 1.

cling, *v.* —*Syn.* adhere, clasp, hold fast; see **stick** 1.

clinic, *n.* —*Syn.* infirmary, dispensary, sick bay (D); see **hospital.**

clink, *n.* —*Syn.* ring, tinkle, jingle; see **noise** 1.

clink, *v.* —*Syn.* tinkle, jingle, clang; see **ring** 3, **sound** 1.

clinker, *n.* **1.** [Cinder]—*Syn.* fusion, fused materials, coal; see **ashes** 1.

2. [Building material]—*Syn.* cement slab, block, stone; see **brick.**

clip, *v.* —*Syn.* snip, crop, clip off; see **cut** 1, **decrease** 2.

clippers, *n.* —*Syn.* scissors, cutting instruments, barber's tools; see **shears.**

clipping, *n.* —*Syn.* excerpt, cutting, piece; see **part** 1.

clique, *n.* —*Syn.* coterie, clan, club; see **faction** 1, **organization** 3.

cloak, *n.* **1.** [An outer garment]—*Syn.* mantle, wrap, shawl; see **coat** 1.

2. [Something that covers or hides]—*Syn.* pretext, cover, mask; see **camouflage** 1, **coat** 3, **disguise.**

clock, *n.* —*Syn.* timekeeper, timepiece, timemarker, timer, ticker (D).

Kinds of clocks include the following—alarm, atomic, cuckoo, electric, grandfather, pendulum clock; hourglass, mission timer, stop watch, sundial, wrist watch, digital, chronometer, chronograph; see also **watch** 1.

around the clock—*Syn.* continuously, continually, twenty-four hours a day; see **regularly.**

clock, *v.* —*Syn.* time, measure time, register speed *or* distance; see **measure** 1, **time.**

clockwork, *n.* —*Syn.* perfect timing, precision, regularity; see **accuracy** 2.

like clockwork—*Syn.* precisely, smoothly, consistently; see **regularly.**

clod, *n.* **1.** [Lump of earth]—*Syn.* clay, soil, dirt; see **earth** 2.

2. [Stupid fellow]—*Syn.* dolt, simpleton, imbecile; see **boor, fool** 1.

clodhopper, *n.* —*Syn.* rustic, hick, yokel; see **boor, fool** 1.

clog, *v.* —*Syn.* stop up, seal, obstruct; see **close** 2, **hinder, plug.**

cloister, *n.* —*Syn.* monastery, convent, friary, Charterhouse, hermitage, chapter house, priory, nunnery, abbey, house, order, retreat, cell(s), *khancah* (Hindu), cenoby, retreat from the world, cloistered walls, religious community, religious house, lamasery, place of religious seclusion; see also **sanctuary** 2.

cloistered, *mod.* —*Syn.* secluded, sheltered, recluse; see **withdrawn.**

close, *mod.* **1.** [Nearby]—*Syn.* neighboring, across the street, around the corner; see **near** 1.

2. [Intimate]—*Syn.* confidential, related, familiar; see **intimate** 1, **private.**

3. [Compact]—*Syn.* dense, solid, compressed; see **thick** 1.

4. [Stingy]—*Syn.* narrow, parsimonious, niggardly; see **stingy.**

5. [Stifling]—*Syn.* sticky, stuffy, unventilated, moldy, heavy, motionless, fusty, uncomfortable, choky, stale-smelling, musty, stagnant. confined, suffocating, sultry, sweltering, sweltry, tight, stale, oppressive, breathless; see also **uncomfortable** 2. —*Ant.* fresh*, refreshing, brisk.

6. [Confining]—*Syn.* confined, cramped, restricted; see **confining, narrow** 1.

7. [Similar]—*Syn.* resembling, having common qualities, much the same; see **alike** 2, **like.**

close, *n.* —*Syn.* termination, adjournment, ending; see **end** 2.

close, *v.* **1.** [To put a stop to]—*Syn.* conclude, finish, terminate; see **end** 1.

2. [To put a stopper into]—*Syn.* shut, stop down, choke off, occlude, stuff, clog, calk, prevent passage, retard flow, shut *or* turn off, lock, block, bar, dam, cork, seal, button; see also **plug.**—*Ant.* open, uncork, unseal.

3. [To come together]—*Syn.* meet, unite, coalesce, chain, connect, tie, bind, inclose, put together, agree; see also **join** 1.—*Ant.* disconnect, separate*, untie.
4. [To shut]—*Syn.* slam, close *or* shut down *or* up, seal, fasten, bolt, clench, bar, shutter, clap, lock, bring to.

closed, *mod.* **1.** [Terminated]—*Syn.* ended, concluded, final; see **finished** 1.
2. [Not in operation]—*Syn.* shut (down), out of order, (temporarily) out of service, service suspended, bankrupt; *all* (D): closed up, padlocked, folded up; see also **broken** 2.
3. [Not open]—*Syn.* shut, fastened, sealed; see **tight** 2.

closed shop, *n.*—*Syn.* union house, union shop *or* establishment, organized trade union membership organization, preferential shop, completely unionized business *or* industry; see also **labor** 4.

closefisted, *mod.*—*Syn.* tight, miserly, niggardly; see **greedy** 1, **stingy.**

closefitting, *mod.*—*Syn.* skintight, snug, hugging; see **tight** 3.

closely, *mod.*—*Syn.* approximately, similarly, exactly, nearly, strictly, firmly, intimately, jointly, in conjunction with; see also **almost.**—*Ant.* separately, individually*, one by one.

closemouthed, *mod.*—*Syn.* silent, sedate, reticent; see **quiet** 2, **reserved** 3, **taciturn.**

closet, *n.*—*Syn.* cabinet, recess, cupboard, sideboard, buffet, locker, wardrobe, receptacle, safe, bin, drawer, chest of drawers, vault, cold storage, clothespress, clothes room, walk-in, ambry; see also **room** 2.

close with, *v.*—*Syn.* compromise, complete an agreement or deal, settle (something) with; see **agree, decide.**

closure, *n.*—*Syn.* conclusion, cessation, finish; see **end** 2.

clot, *n.*—*Syn.* lump, bulk, clotting, curdling, consolidation, coagulation, mass, clump, thrombus, embolus, grume, coagulum, thickness, coalescence, conglutination, coagulated protein, curd, precipitate.

clot, *v.*—*Syn.* coagulate, set, lump; see **thicken** 1.

cloth, *n.*—*Syn.* fabric, material, stuff, goods, dry goods, textiles, weave, tissue, twill, yard goods, synthetics.
Cloth includes the following—canvas, linen, piqué, broadcloth, percale, poplin, lawn, linen, chintz, gingham, muslin, cambric, calico, drill, cotton, terry, khaki, denim, permanent press denim, dimity, tweed, serge, homespun, cheviot, cashmere, worsted, wool, plaid, flannel, silk, mercerized cotton, taffeta, pongee, satin, crepe de Chine, damask, voile chiffon, alpaca, velvet, corduroy, plush, hopsacking, brocade, vicuña, angora, blanketing, bagging, bunting, carpeting, ramie, sacking, skirting, felt, oilcloth, burlap, tarpaulin, organza, organdy, sharkskin.
Man-made cloths include the following—nylon, rayon, acrylics, polyester, olefin, polyethelene, acetate; (all trademarks), Dacron, Orlon, Acrilon, Avril, Spandex, Saran, Terylene, Vinyon, Naugahyde.

clothe, *v.*—*Syn.* attire, dress up, costume, robe, put garments on, apparel, array, muffle up, breech, don, cloak, gown, caparison, mantle, jacket, accouter, vest, invest, garb, deck, drape, equip, guise, disguise, coat; *all* (D): rig, tog *or* fit *or* deck out *or* up, bundle up; see also **dress** 1.—*Ant.* unclothe, undress*, strip.

clothed, *mod.*—*Syn.* clad, invested, costumed, robed, shod, dressed, attired, decked, disguised, covered, draped, veiled; see also **dressed up.**—*Ant.* naked*, exposed, stripped.

clothes, *n.*—*Syn.* (wearing) apparel, raiment, clothing, garments, garb, vesture, vestments, attire, array, habiliments, casual *or* informal wear, evening clothes, work clothes, *tout ensemble* (French), suit of clothes, *tailleur* (French), costume, equipment, overwear, wardrobe, accouterment, trappings, caparison, harness, gear, livery, regalia, overclothes, underclothes; *all* (D): outfit, wearables, get-up, rags, tatters, rigging, toggery, togs, duds, things; see also **dress** 1.
Men's clothes include the following—business suit, jacket and slacks, trousers, double-breasted suit, shorts, breeches, knickerbockers *or* knickers (D); tuxedo *or* (*both* D) tux, tuck; dress suit, dinner jacket, tail coat, swallow-tailed coat, jungle coat, jungle jacket, uniform, shirt, guru suit *or* shirt, body shirt, hiphugger pants, continental suit, socks; long underwear *or* (*both* D) long johns, red flannels.
Women's clothes include the following—housecoat, negligee, morning dress, evening gown, kimono, shorts, wrapper, frock, blouse, jumper, slip, shirtwaist, robe, underwear *or* unmentionables (D); slacks, panties, brassiere *or* bra, girdle; nightgown *or* (*both* D) nightie, pajamas *or* P.J.'s; noon dress, street dress, spectator sports clothes, suit, pullover, slipover sweater, jerkin, golf dress, house dress, tennis dress, dickey, nylon stockings *or* nylons, A-line dress *or* skirt, mini-skirt, maxi-skirt, shift, muumuu, little girl's dress, paper dress, op-art suit, hiphugger slacks, gilet, vestee, guimpe, bolero, smock, skirt, coat, toreador pants, petticoat, hat, bonnet.
Clothes worn by both men and women include the following—blue jeans, denims, levis, turtleneck, sweat shirt, T-shirt kimono, slack suit, raincoat, tights, bell-bottom pants, sweater, cardigan, cutoff's (D). Children's clothes include the following—rompers, playsuit, coveralls, snow suit, sweater, leggings, dress. Work clothes include the following—overalls, windbreaker, blue jeans, coveralls, jumper, cords (D).
Clothing of foreign origin includes the following—rebozo, mantilla, poncho, serape, huipil (*all* Latin American); parka, mukluks, kapta (*all* Eskimo); sarafan (Russian); fez, bourka, tunic, chalwar, jube, fustenella (*all* southeastern European); burnoose, yashmak, tarboosh, djubbeh, chalwar, chader, caftan, aba, chargat (*all* Mohammedan); sarong, sari, dhoti, burka (*all* southeastern Asian); kimono, obi, juban, shitagi, dogi, hakama, haori, shitojuban, ymogi, kosh-imaki (*all* Japanese); mantilla, bolero, kilt, tartan (*all* western European); toga, jupon, kirtle, chlamys, jerkin, brachae (*all* historical); see also **coat, dress, hat, pants** 1, 2.

clothing, *n.*—*Syn.* attire, raiment, garb; see **clothes, dress** 1.

cloud, *n.* **1.** [Fog at a distance from the earth] —*Syn.* haze, mist, rack, fogginess, haziness, film, puff, billow, frost, nebulosity, smoke, veil, cloud cover, overcast, pea soup (D).
Types of clouds include the following—cirrus, cumulus, stratus, nimbus, cirro-cumulus, cirro-stratus; *all* (D): woolpack, scud, meteor, curl-cloud, mare's tail, colt's tail, cat's tail, mackerel sky, thunderhead, sheep
2. [Any nebulous mass]—*Syn.* smoke, vapor, dimness; see sense 1; see **fog** 1.
3. [Anything ominous]—*Syn.* spot, fault, blemish, dark spot, stain, shadow, flaw, blotch, obscurity, gloom; see also **warning.**
in the clouds—*Syn.* fanciful, fantastic, romantic; see **impractical.**
under a cloud—*Syn.* **1.** suspect, dubious, uncertain; see **suspicious** 2. **2.** depressed, worried, sad; see **troubled** 1.
cloudburst, *n.*—*Syn.* deluge, rain, torrent; see **storm** 1.
cloudless, *mod.*—*Syn.* clear, bright, sunny; see **fair** 3.
cloud seeding, *n.*—*Syn.* rainmaking, causing rain, seeding clouds, fertilizing clouds, supersaturation of clouds.
cloudy, *mod.* **1.** [Hazy]—*Syn.* overcast, foggy, sunless; see **dark** 1.
2. [Not clear]—*Syn.* dense, nontransparent, nontranslucent; see **opaque** 1.
3. [Obscure]—*Syn.* vague, indistinct, indefinite; see **obscure** 1.
clown, *n.*—*Syn.* buffoon, fool, mummer, droll, a joker, harlequin, merry-andrew, punch, punchinello, funnyman, humorist, pierrot, jester, wag, antic, comedian, comic, wit, zany, cut-up (D); see also **actor.**
clown (around), *v.*—*Syn.* fool around, kid around, cut up; see **joke.**
cloy, *v.*—*Syn.* satiate, surfeit, suffice; see **satisfy** 1.
club, *n.* **1.** [A social organization]—*Syn.* association, order, society; see **faction** 1, **organization** 3.
2. [A clubhouse]—*Syn.* center, base (of operations), meetinghouse; see **headquarters, room** 2.
3. [A cudgel]—*Syn.* stick, bat, bludgeon, baton, night stick, blackjack, shillelagh, staff, mace, crabstick, warclub, hammer, mallet, hickory, singlestick, quarterstaff, *lathee* (Hindu); *both* (D): swatter, billy club.
4. [A golf club]. Types include the following—driver, brassie, cleek, midiron, spoon, mashie, niblick, wedge, putter.
club, *v.*—*Syn.* batter, whack, pound; see **beat** 2, **hit** 1.
cluck, *v.*—*Syn.* call, cry, clack; see **sound** 1.
clue, *n.*—*Syn.* evidence, trace, mark; see **proof** 1, **sign** 1.
clue, *v.*—*Syn.* leave evidence, give information, leave tracks *or* traces; see **notify** 1.
clump, *n.* **1.** [A group]—*Syn.* cluster, bundle, knot; see **bunch** 1.
2. [A thump]—*Syn.* bump, clatter, thump; see **noise** 1.
clump, *v.*—*Syn.* thump, clatter, tramp; see **bump** 2.
clumsily, *mod.*—*Syn.* crudely, gawkily, stumblingly; see **awkwardly.**
clumsiness, *n.*—*Syn.* crudity, ineptitude, boorishness; see **awkwardness** 1.
clumsy, *mod.*—*Syn.* ungainly, gawky, inexpert; see **awkward** 1.
cluster, *n.* **1.** [A bunch]—*Syn.* group, batch, clump; see **bunch** 1.
2. [A gathering]—*Syn.* assemblage, group, pack; see **crowd.**
cluster, *v.*—*Syn.* collect, assemble, group; see **gather** 1.
clutch, *n.* **1.** [A mechanical device]—*Syn.* friction clutch, coupling, connection; see **link, part** 3.
2. [Grip]—*Syn.* grasp, clasp, hold; see **grip** 2.
clutch, *v.*—*Syn.* grab, grasp, grip; see **hold** 1, **seize** 1.
clutches, *n.*—*Syn.* control, grasp, keeping; see **power** 2.
clutter, *n.*—*Syn.* disarray, jumble, disorder; see **confusion** 2.
coach, *n.* **1.** [A carriage]—*Syn.* fourwheeler, chaise, victoria; see **carriage** 2, **vehicle** 1.
2. [An instructor]—*Syn.* mentor, drillmaster, physical education instructor; see **teacher** 1, **trainer.**
coach, *v.*—*Syn.* train, drill, instruct; see **teach** 1, 2.
coadjutor, *n.*—*Syn.* colleague, helper, coworker; see **assistant, associate.**
coagulate, *v.*—*Syn.* curdle, clot, congeal; see **thicken** 1.
coagulation, *n.*—*Syn.* clotting, curdling, thickening, caseation, jellification, agglomeration, incrassation, congelation, consolidation, gelatination, condensation, concretion, inspissation; see also **concentration** 1.
coal, *n.* **1.** [Mineral fuel]—*Syn.* sea coal, stone coal, mineral coal; see also **fuel.**
Coals include the following—hard coal, soft coal, charcoal, pit coal, lignite, cannel, anthracite, bituminous, coke, carbocoal, turf, peat, semianthracite *or* semibituminous coal. Grades of coal include the following—broken, lump, chunk, egg, stove, nut, pea, rice, buckwheat, briquette, slack *or* duff, flaxseed *or* mustard seed.
2. [An ember]—*Syn.* spark, live coal, brand; see **embers. haul** *or* **rake** *or* **drag over the coals** (D), —*Syn.* reprimand, criticize, castigate; see **censure.**
coalesce, *v.*—*Syn.* blend, fuse, combine; see **join** 1, **mix** 1.
coalition, *n.* **1.** [An allied group]—*Syn.* combination, alliance, confederacy; see **organization** 3.
2. [A faction]—*Syn.* compact, conspiracy, association; see **faction** 1.
coarse, *mod.* **1.** [Not fine]—*Syn.* rough, rude, unrefined; see **crude** 1.
2. [Of poor quality]—*Syn.* loose, mediocre, inferior; see **common** 1, **poor** 2.
3. [Vulgar]—*Syn.* low, common, base; see **rude** 1, **vulgar** 1.
coarsen, *v.*—*Syn.* roughen, callous, toughen; see **harden** 3.
coarseness, *n.* **1.** [Crudeness]—*Syn.* vulgarity, unrefinement, callousness; see **harshness, rudeness.**
2. [Roughness of texture]—*Syn.* stiffness, rawness, crudity; see **roughness** 1.
coast, *n.*—*Syn.* shoreline, beach, seaboard; see **shore.**

coast, *v.* —*Syn.* glide, float, ride on the current; see **drift, ride** 1, 3.

coastal, *mod.* —*Syn.* near *or* along a coast, bordering, seaside, marginal, skirting, riverine, littoral; see also **marshy.**

coat, *n.* **1.** [An outer garment]—*Syn.* topcoat, overcoat, cloak, suit coat, tuxedo, dinner jacket, sport coat, dress coat, ermine jacket, mink jacket, mink coat, fur coat, ski jacket, cutaway, mackintosh, greatcoat, raincoat, ulster, jacket, windbreaker, peacoat, three-quarter length coat, wrap, cocktail jacket, leather jacket; *all* (D): sou'wester, slicker, mac, tux, tails; see also **cape** 2, **clothes.**
2. [The covering of an animal]—*Syn.* integument, protective covering, pellicle, husk, shell, crust, scale, fell, fleece, epidermis, rind, scarfskin, ectoderm, pelt, peltry, membrane; see also **fur, hide** 1, **leather, skin.**
3. [An applied covering]—*Syn.* coating, layer, set, wash, glaze, priming, crust, painting, overlay, whitewashing, varnish, lacquer, gloss, tinge, finish, roughcast, prime coat, plaster, bark; see also **cover** 2.

coat, *v.* —*Syn.* surface, glaze, enamel; see **paint** 2, **varnish.**

coating, *n.* —*Syn.* crust, covering, layer; see **coat** 3, **cover** 2.

coat of arms, *n.* —*Syn.* ensign, crest, escutcheon, pennon, pennant, arms; see also **emblem.**

coat of mail, *n.* —*Syn.* suit of armor, metal garment, protection; see **armor** 1.

coax, *v.* —*Syn.* persuade, cajole, inveigle; see **influence, urge** 2.

coaxing, *mod.* —*Syn.* attractive, tempting, enticing; see **charming, persuasive.**

cobbler, *n.* —*Syn.* bootmaker, cordwainer, shoe repairman; see **shoemaker, workman.**

cobweb, *n.* **1.** [A spider's web]—*Syn.* filament, gossamer, extrusive threads; see **fiber, web** 1.
2. [A network]—*Syn.* snare, labyrinth, entanglement; see **net, web** 2.

cock, *n.* —*Syn.* rooster, capon, cockalorum; see **chicken** 1.

cockade, *n.* —*Syn.* rosette, spangle, ribbon; see **decoration** 2.

cocktail, *n.* Cocktails include the following—(dry) Manhattan, (dry) Martini, Gibson, old-fashioned, champagne, sidecar, horse's neck, Margarita, Bronx, pink lady, whisky sour, black Russian, orange blossom, piña colada, Rob Roy, Sazerac, blue blazer, old Hickory, Vieux Carré, green opal, jitters, Daiquiri, Bacardi, Kentucky whiskey, orange blossom, Roffignac, Alexander; see **drink** 2.

cocoon, *n.* —*Syn.* silky case, chrysalis, pupa; see **cover** 2.

coddle, *v.* **1.** [To cook gently]—*Syn.* simmer, brew, poach; see **cook.**
2. [To pamper]—*Syn.* caress, favor, baby; see **pamper.**

code, *n.* —*Syn.* codex, method, digest; see **law** 2, **system** 2.

codicil, *n.* —*Syn.* addendum, supplement, postscript; see **addition** 2, **appendix.**

codify, *v.* —*Syn.* systematize, classify, arrange; see **order** 3.

coequal, *mod.* —*Syn.* same, parallel, corresponding; see **alike** 1, 2, **equal, like.**

coerce, *v.* **1.** [To hold back]—*Syn.* restrict, repress, suppress; see **hinder, restrain** 1.
2. [Force]—*Syn.* impel, compel, constrain; see **force** 1.

coercion, *n.* —*Syn.* compulsion, persuasion, constraint; see **pressure** 2, **restraint** 2.

coeval, *mod.* —*Syn.* contemporary, of the same age, coincident; see **simultaneous.**

coexist, *v.* —*Syn.* exist together, synchronize, be contemporary; see **accompany** 3.

coexistence, *n.* **1.** [Contemporaneousness]—*Syn.* conjunction, coevality, concurrence; see **coincidence.**
2. [Harmony]—*Syn.* order, conformity, accord; see **peace** 1, 2.

coexistent, *mod.* —*Syn.* contemporary, concurrent, coexisting; see **simultaneous.**

coffee, *n.* —*Syn.* beverage, decoction, java (D); see **drink** 3.
Coffees include the following—Mocha, Sumatra, Java, Brazilian, Santos, Rio, Guatemalan, mild, decaffeinated, Maracaibo, Bogotá, Medellín, Colombian.
Prepared coffee includes the following—Turkish, Armenian, drip, percolated, vacuum, instant, French roast, coffee with cream, *demitasse, café noir, café au lait, café crème, filtré* (all French), *kaffee wien, kaffee mit schlag* (both German), *cappuccino, espresso* (both Italian), *turska kava* (Slavic), *turetskoe kofe* (Russian), camp coffee (D).

coffee break, *n.* —*Syn.* respite, break, rest period; see **rest** 1.

coffin, *n.* —*Syn.* box, casket, sarcophagus, stone *or* lead *or* wood coffin, catafalque, pall, burial *or* funerary urn *or* vase, funerary box, mummy case; see also **case** 7, **container.**

cog, *n.* —*Syn.* cogwheel, gear, pinion, rack, wheel, ratchet, transmission, differential.

cogent, *mod.* **1.** [Persuasive]—*Syn.* convincing, sound, forceful; see **persuasive.**
2. [Relevant]—*Syn.* fitting, apt, apposite, pertinent; see **relevant.**

cogitation, *n.* —*Syn.* reflection, consideration, contemplation; see **thought** 1.

cognate, *mod.* **1.** [Allied by blood]—*Syn.* akin, consanguine, kindred; see **related** 3.
2. [Allied in characteristics]—*Syn.* akin, consanguine, kindred; see **related** 3.
3. [Allied in characteristics]—*Syn.* same, comparable, similar; see **alike** 2, **like, related** 2.

cognition, *n.* —*Syn.* awareness, perception, insight; see **knowledge** 1, **thought** 1, 2.

cognizance, *n.* —*Syn.* awareness, perception, insight; see **knowledge** 1, **thought** 1, 2.
take cognizance of—*Syn.* notice, acknowledge, be aware of; see **recognize** 1.

cognizant, *mod.* —*Syn.* informed, aware, perceptive; see **conscious** 1, **judicious, observant** 1.

cognomen, *n.* —*Syn.* last name, surname, nickname; see **name** 1.

cohabit, *v.* —*Syn.* live *or* stay *or* lodge *or* room *or* abide together, share an address, take up housekeeping, have relations with someone, live illegally *or* without benefit of matrimony *or* clergy;

all (D): shack up (with), play house (with), be roommates (with); see also **live with.**

cohere, *v.* **1.** [To stick together]—*Syn.* cleave, adhere, cling; see **stick** 1.
2. [To be logically connected]—*Syn.* relate, harmonize, correspond; see **agree, make sense.**

coherence, *n.* **1.** [Cohesion]—*Syn.* stickiness, viscosity, gluishness, gumminess, cementation, congelation, soldering, coherency, adhesiveness, glutinousness, sticking together, agglutination, coagulation, viscidity, glutinosity, adherence, set, amalgamation, fusion, sticking, union, adhesion, conglutination, cohesiveness, consistency.
2. [Closely built relationship]—*Syn.* continuity, contiguity, union, adherence, attachment, connection, tenacity, solidarity, integrity, consonance, attachment, cementation, construction, inseparability, inseparableness; see also **unity** 1.—*Ant.* separation*, disunion, disjunction.

coherent, *mod.* **1.** [Closely integrated]—*Syn.* consistent, identified, combined; see **joined, unified.**
2. [Understandable]—*Syn.* comprehensible, sound, intelligible; see **logical** 1, **understandable.**

cohesion, *n.*—*Syn.* union, attachment, adherence; see **coherence** 2.

cohort, *n.* **1.** [Gathering]—*Syn.* band, company, group; see **following, gathering.**
2. [An accomplice]—*Syn.* partner, ally, companion; see **assistant, associate, friend** 1.

coiffure, *n.*—*Syn.* permanent, hairdo, haircut; see **hairstyle.**

coil, *n.*—*Syn.* turn, ring, wind, convolution, twine, twist, twirl, lap, loop, curlicue, bight, corkscrew, roll, spiral, helix, tendril, scroll; see also **circle** 1, **curl.**

coil, *v.*—*Syn.* scroll, wind, loop, twist, fold, twine, intertwine, entwine, convolute, make serpentine, intervolve, sinuate, lap, twirl, spire, wreathe; see also **curl, roll** 4—*Ant.* unfold*, unwind, ravel.

coin, *n.*—*Syn.* legal tender, gold *or* silver piece, copper coin; see **money** 1.

coin, *v.* **1.** [To mint money]—*Syn.* counterfeit, strike, stamp; see **manufacture, mint** 1.
2. [To invent a word, etc.]—*Syn.* mint, create a phrase, make up (D); see **invent** 1.

coinage, *n.* **1.** [The process of making money]—*Syn.* coining, making coins, minting; see **manufacturing, production** 1.
2. [Metal money]—*Syn.* silver, cash, coins; see **change** 5.

coincide, *v.* **1.** [Correspond]—*Syn.* accord, harmonize, match; see **agree.**
2. [Happen]—*Syn.* eventuate, come about, befall; see **happen** 2.

coincidence, *n.* **1.** [Agreement]—*Syn.* accord, accordance, consonance, unison, parallelism, conformity, correspondence, collaboration; see also **agreement** 2.
2. [An incidental occurrence]—*Syn.* incident, happening, eventuality; see **accident** 2, **chance** 1, **event** 1.

coincident, *mod.*—*Syn.* coinciding, contemporary, concurring; see **simultaneous.**

coincidental, *mod.* **1.** [Occurring simultaneously]—*Syn.* concurrent, concomitant, contemporaneous; see **simultaneous.**
2. [Apparently accidental]—*Syn.* chance, casual, unplanned; see **incidental** 2.

coitus, *n.*—*Syn.* sexual intercourse, coition, union; see **copulation.**

cold, *mod.* **1.** [*Said of the weather*]—*Syn.* crisp, cool, icy, rimy, freezing, frosty, frigid, wintry, bleak, nippy, brisk, keen, inclement, penetrating, snowy, frozen, sleety, blasting, cutting, brumal, snappy, algid, gelid, piercing, chill, bitter, numbing, severe, boreal, stinging, glacial, intense, Siberian, chilly, sharp, raw, nipping, arctic, polar, below zero, biting; see also **wintry.**—*Ant.* warm, hot*, heated.
2. [*Said of persons, animals, etc.*]—*Syn.* cold-blooded, frozen, clammy, stiff, chilled, frostbitten, shivering; *all* (D): blue from cold, refrigerated, in cold storage.—*Ant.* hot*, perspiring, thawed.
3. [*Said of temperament*]—*Syn.* unconcerned, apathetic, reticent; see **indifferent** 1, **reserved** 3.

cold, *n.* **1.** [Conditions having a low temperature]—*Syn.* coldness, frozenness, chilliness, frostiness, gelidity, draft, frostbite, congelation, absence of warmth, want of heat, chill, shivers, coolness, shivering, goose flesh, numbness, iciness, frigidity, freeze, glaciation, refrigeration; see also **weather.**—*Ant.* warmth, heat*, hot wave.
2. [The outdoors of a cold season]—*Syn.* frost, wintertime, snow; see **winter.**
3. [An aural or respiratory congestion]—*Syn.* rheum, cough, hack, catarrh, sore throat, cold in the head, sinus trouble, cold on one's chest, bronchial irritation, ague, common cold, laryngitis, hay fever, whooping cough, grippe, influenza *or* flu (D), rose fever, rose cold, asthma, bronchitis, pertussis, streptococcic throat, staphylococcic infection, palatal infection, bad throat; *all* (D): strep throat, strep, sniffles, frog in one's throat; see also **disease** 3.
catch *or* **take cold**—*Syn.* come down with a cold, become ill, get a cold; see **sicken** 1.
have *or* **get cold feet**—*Syn.* go back on one's word, back down, retreat; see **fear** 1.
(out) in the cold (D)—*Syn.* forgotten, ignored, rejected; see **neglected.**
throw cold water on (D)—*Syn.* dishearten, squelch, dampen; see **discourage** 1.

cold-blooded, *mod.*—*Syn.* relentless, pitiless, unfeeling; see **callous, cruel** 2.

coliseum, *n.*—*Syn.* stadium, open-air theater, amphitheater; see **arena, theater** 1.

collaborate, *v.*—*Syn.* work together, conspire, work with; see **co-operate** 1.

collaborator, *n.*—*Syn.* helper, co-worker, colleague; see **assistant, associate.**

collage, *n.*—*Syn.* photomontage, abstract composition, found art (D); see **picture** 3, **sculpture.**

collapse, *n.*—*Syn.* breakdown, downfall, destruction; see **failure** 1, **wreck** 1.

collapse, *v.*—*Syn.* drop, deflate, give way; see **fail** 1, **fall** 1, 2.

collar, *n.*—*Syn.* neckband, neckpiece, ruff, frill, jabot, dicky, Vandyke, Eton, fichu, bertha, attached collar, linen collar, celluloid collar, torque, *fraise* (French); see also **clothes.**

collar (D), *v.*—*Syn.* apprehend, capture, abduct; see **arrest** 1, **seize** 2.

collate, *v.* **1.** [Compare]—*Syn.* relate, match, analogize; see **compare** 2, **examine** 1.
2. [Check]—*Syn.* verify, group, assemble; see **order.**

collateral, *mod.* **1.** [Side by side]—*Syn.* lateral, coordinate, corresponding; see **parallel** 1.
2. [Accompanying]—*Syn.* concomitant, concurrent, coincident; see **simultaneous.**
3. [Secondary]—*Syn.* dependent, supporting, ancillary; see **subordinate.**

collateral, *n.*—*Syn.* security, guarantee, pledge, (financial) promise, endorsement, warrant; see also **insurance, money** 1, **wealth** 1.

collation, *n.*—*Syn.* resemblance, examination, relation; see **comparison** 2, **relationship.**

colleague, *n.*—*Syn.* partner, collaborator, coadjutor; see **associate.**

collect, *v.* **1.** [To bring into one place]—*Syn.* amass, consolidate, convoke; see **accumulate** 1, **assemble** 2, **concentrate** 1.
2. [To come together]—*Syn.* congregate, assemble, flock; see **gather** 1.
3. [To obtain funds]—*Syn.* solicit, raise, secure; see **obtain** 1.
4. [To arrange settlement of a debt]—*Syn.* settle, manage, handle, receive payment, draw upon for, receive; see also **negotiate** 1, **receive** 1.
5. [To obtain specimens]—*Syn.* get, assemble, make a collection; see **accumulate** 1.

collected, *mod.* **1.** [Composed]—*Syn.* poised, self-possessed, cool; see **calm** 1.
2. [Assembled]—*Syn.* accumulated, amassed, compiled; see **gathered.**

collection, *n.* **1.** [The act of collecting]—*Syn.* gathering, finding, making *or* completing a collection, collecting, compilation, recovering, bringing together, searching for, assembling, amassing, compiling, acquisition, obtaining, securing, discovering, accumulating, acquiring; see also **accumulation.**
2. [That which has been collected]—*Syn.* specimens, samples, examples, extracts, citations, gems, models, assortment, medley, accumulation, agglomeration, pile, stack, group, assemblage, compilation, mass, quantity, selection, garland, treasury, omnibus, anthology, miscellany, aggregation, combination, number, symposium, amassment, store, stock, digest, arrangement, concentration, discoveries, clone, finds, collation; *all* (D): batch, mess, lot, heap, bunch; see also **heap.**

collective, *mod.*—*Syn.* aggregated, massed, summed, accumulated, gathered, concentrated, consolidated, heaped, piled, stored, hoarded, grouped, assembled, compiled, collected, collated; see also **gathered.**

collective, *n.*—*Syn.* co-operative, collective unit, communistic project; see **gathering, organization** 3.

collectivism, *n.*—*Syn.* communalism, co-operation, communization; see **communism, sharing, socialism.**

collector, *n.* **1.** [One who collects accounts]—*Syn.* solicitor, representative, customs *or* tax official, tax gatherer, toll gatherer, office *or* officer of internal revenue, revenue office, income tax collector *or* officer, tax man; see also **agent** 1, **receiver.**
2. [One who collects specimens]—*Syn.* antiquary, authority, hobbyist, fancier, (serious *or* informed) amateur, gatherer, discoverer, compiler, finder, assembler, amasser, hoarder, anthologist, museologist, museographer, specialist in museology *or* museography, librarian; see also **antiquarian, curator, historian, scientist, specialist.**
Collectors include the following—*of books:* bibliophile, bibliopole, bibliotaph, bibliolater, bibliomaniac, bookworm (D); *of coins:* coin collector, numismatist, specialist in numismatics; *of eggs:* oölogist, egger, egg collector, specialist in oölogy, (bird's) egg fancier, devotee of egging, egg hound (D); *of human materials:* archaeologist, historiographer, biographer, local historian, ethnologist, ethnographer, ethnographic specialist, specialist in ethnography, ethnohistorian, ethnolinguist, folklorist, curator of folkloristic materials, ethnobotanist; *of insects:* entomologist, entomographist, lepidopterist, entomographer, specialist in *or* practitioner of entomology *or* entomography *or* lepidoptery, collector of bugs *or* insects *or* butterflies, etc.; *of rocks:* rock collector, historical geologist, geognosist, physical geologist, mineral geologist, mineralogist, geographer, rock hound (D); *of plants:* botanist, herbalist, ecologist, botanologer, paleobotanist, curator of a herbarium *or* of herbal collections, physiobotanist; *of stamps:* stamp collector, philatelist, philatelic dealer *or* specialist, expert *or* specialist in philately; *of zoological materials:* biologist, zoologist, taxonomist, ecologist, cytologist, student of *or* expert in birds *or* fish *or* reptiles *or* vertebrates, etc., (field) ornithologist, closet ornithologist, ichthyologist, cetologist, ecospherist, herpetologist *or* snake man, curator of a reptile house *or* reptilium *or* herpetological vivarium, anatomist, physiologist, biophysiologist, paleontologist, histologist, morphologist, embryologist, geneticist.

college, *n.*—*Syn.* institute, institution, professional school, organization, association, community college, liberal arts college, teachers college, junior college, state college, privately endowed college, denominational college, seminary, lyceum, hall, *lycée* (French), *Gymnasium* (German); see also **university.**

collide, *v.* **1.** [To come into violent contact]—*Syn.* hit, strike, smash; see **crash** 4.
2. [To come into conflict]—*Syn.* clash, conflict, disagree; see **oppose** 1.

colliery, *n.*—*Syn.* coal mine, shaft, industrial complex; see **mine** 1.

collision, *n.* **1.** [A violent meeting]—*Syn.* impact, contact, shock, accident, encounter, crash, colliding, bump, percussion, concussion, jar, jolt, sideswipe, strike, hit, slam, blow, thud, thump, knock, smash, foul, butt, rap, head-on crash; one-car, two-car, etc., accident *or* crash *or* collision; *both* (D): head-on, fender-bender; see also **disaster.**
2. [A conflict]—*Syn.* interference, discord, contention; see **disagreement** 1, **dispute** 1.

collocate, *v.*—*Syn.* compile, gather, collect; see **accumulate** 1, **assemble** 2.

colloquial, *mod.*—*Syn.* conversational, popular, everyday; see **common** 1, **familiar** 1, **informal** 1.

colloquialism, *n.*—*Syn.* idiom, commonness, informality; see **dialect, jargon** 1, **language.**

colloquy, *n.* —*Syn.* debate, dialogue, conference; see **conversation, discussion** 1.

collude, *v.* —*Syn.* conspire, intrigue, plot; see **plan** 1.

collusion, *n.* —*Syn.* conspiracy, intrigue, plot; see **trick** 1.

collusive, *mod.* —*Syn.* deceitful, conniving, tricky; see **dishonest** 1, 2, **false** 1, 2.

colonial, *mod.* **1.** [Concerning a colony]—*Syn.* pioneer, isolated, dependent, planted, transplanted, settled, provincial, frontier, imperial, pre-Revolutionary, Pilgrim, emigrant, immigrant, territorial, outland, pioneering, daughter, mandated, early American, overseas, protectoral, Puritan, dominion, Anglo-Irish, Anglo-Indian, established; see also **distant** 2, **remote** 1.
2. [Having qualities suggestive of colonial life] —*Syn.* pioneer, hard, raw, crude, harsh, wild, unsettled, limited, uncultured, new, unsophisticated; see also **primitive** 3, **severe** 2.—*Ant.* old, cultured*, decadent.

colonist, *n.* —*Syn.* settler, pilgrim, homesteader; see **pioneer** 2.

colonization, *n.* —*Syn.* immigration, pioneering, settling, (pioneer) settlement, transplanting, founding, expanding, peopling, (group) migration, clearing, expansion, establishment, forging a new home; see also **establishing** 1.

colonize, *v.* —*Syn.* plant, found, locate, people, migrate, immigrate, transplant, pioneer, open a country, go before; see also **establish** 2, **settle** 7.

colonnade, *n.* —*Syn.* columns, portico, corridor, pillar, arcade, mezzanine, peristyle, peripteros, columniation, series, covered way, cloisters, veranda, gallery, piazza, columnar building; see also **column** 1.

colony, *n.* **1.** [A colonial area]—*Syn.* settlement, dependency, subject state, colonial state, dominion, offshoot, (political) possession, mandate, province, group, new land, clearing, protectorate, hive, daughter country, satellite state *or* province, community, group migration, swarm, home in the wilderness (D); see also **nation** 1, **territory** 2.
2. [A colonial people or culture]—*Syn.* pioneers, forerunners, forefathers, antecedents, beginnings, early days, offshoot, daughter country; see also **forefather.**

color, *n.* **1.** [The quality of reflected light]—*Syn.* hue, tone, shade, tinge, chroma, tinct, luminosity, chromaticity, chromatism, chromism, undertone, value, iridescence, intensity, polychromasia, colorimetric quality, coloration, discoloration, pigmentation, coloring, cast, glow, blush, wash, tincture; see also **tint.**—*Ant.* blackness, gloom, blankness.
Colors include the following—*colors in the solar spectrum:* red, orange, yellow, green, blue, violet; *physiological primary colors:* red, green, blue; *psychological primary colors:* red, yellow, green, blue, black, white; *primary colors in painting:* red, blue, yellow; see also **black** 1, **blue** 1, **brown, gold** 1, **gray** 1, **green** 1, **orange, pink, purple, red, tan, yellow** 1.
2. [Vividness]—*Syn.* brilliance, intensity, piquancy, zest, freshness, liveliness, colorfulness, brightness, richness, glow; see also **light** 1.—*Ant.* drabness, dullness*, dimness.
3. [Semblance or pretense]—*Syn.* pretext, deception, guise; see **disguise, pretense** 1.
call to the colors—*Syn.* draft, conscript, enlist; see **recruit** 1.
change color—*Syn.* flush, redden, become red in the face; see **blush.**
lose color—*Syn.* become pale, blanch, faint; see **whiten** 1.
under color of—*Syn.* under the pretext of, pretending to be, disguised as; see **imitating.**

color, *v.* **1.** [To impart color to]—*Syn.* gloss, infuse, chalk, daub, gild, fresco, japan, enamel, lacquer, suffuse, stipple, variegate, pigment, distemper, glaze, tinge, tint, stain, tone, shade, dye, wash, crayon, chrome, enliven, embellish, give color to, adorn, imbue, emblazon, illuminate, rouge; see also **decorate, paint** 1, 2.—*Ant.* bleach, fade*, deaden.
2. [To take on color]—*Syn.* flush, redden, become rosy, turn red, bloom, glow; see also **blush.**—*Ant.* fade*, whiten, grow ashen.
3. [To misrepresent]—*Syn.* distort, pervert, disguise; see **corrupt** 2, **deceive.**

color blindness, *n.* —*Syn.* achromatism, dichromatism, monochromatism; see **blindness** 1, **defect** 2.

colored, *mod.* **1.** [Treated with color]—*Syn.* hued, tinted, tinged, shaded, flushed, reddened, glowing, stained, dyed, washed, rouged; see also **painted** 3.
2. [Belonging to a dark-skinned race]—*Syn.* brown, black, mulatto, red, bronze; see also **Indian** 1, 2, **Negro.**
3. [Falsified]—*Syn.* misrepresented, perverted, tampered with; see **false** 2, 3.

colorful, *mod.* —*Syn.* vivid, picturesque, realistic; see **bright** 1, 2.

colorless, *mod.* —*Syn.* achromic, pale, neutral; see **dull** 2, **transparent** 1.

colors, *n.* pl.—*Syn.* banner, standard, symbol; see **emblem, flag** 1.

colossal, *mod.* —*Syn.* huge, enormous, immense; see **large** 1.

colossus, *n.* —*Syn.* gigantic statute, Goliath, Hercules; see **giant** 1, 2.

colt, *n.* —*Syn.* foal, filly, yearling, two-year-old, young horse; see also **horse** 1.

coltish, *mod.* —*Syn.* frisky, playful, lively; see **active** 2, **jaunty.**

Columbia, *n.* **1.** [An American university]—*Syn.* King's College, Columbia College, Columbia University, Teachers College, Barnard College, T.C. (D); see also **university.**
2. [An allegorical representation of the United States]—*Syn.* (Miss) Liberty, U.S.A., Land of the Free; see **America** 2.

column, *n.* **1.** [A pillar]—*Syn.* support, prop, shaft, monument, totem, cylindrical body, pylon, obelisk, stele, standard, tower, minaret, cylinder, mast, caryatid, peristyle, monolith, upright, pedestal, pilaster; see also **post** 1.
Types of columns include the following—fluted, plain, round, square, Egyptian, Doric, Corinthian, Ionic, Roman, Romanesque, Gothic.
2. [Journalistic commentary]—*Syn.* comment, article, editorial; see **exposition** 2.
3. [A military formation]—*Syn.* single file, platoon, company; see **army** 2.

columnist, *n.—Syn.* newspaperman, journalist, correspondent; see **reporter, writer.**
coma, *n.—Syn.* unconsciousness, trance, insensibility; see **stupor.**
comatose, *mod.—Syn.* lethargic, insensible, torpid; see **indifferent** 1, **unconscious** 1.
comb, *n.* Combs include the following—hair comb, ivorycomb, currycomb, flax comb, carding knife, graining instrument; see also **brush** 1.
comb, *v.—Syn.* untangle, disentangle, adjust, cleanse, scrape, arrange, rasp, straighten, lay smooth, smooth, dress, hackle, hatchel, card; see also **rake** 1.
combat, *n.—Syn.* struggle, warfare, conflict; see **battle** 2, **fight** 1.
combat, *v.—Syn.* battle, oppose, resist; see **fight** 2.
combatant, *n.—Syn.* belligerent, warrior, serviceman; see **fighter** 1, **soldier.**
combination, *n.* **1.** [The act of combining]—*Syn.* uniting, joining, unification; see **union** 1.
2. [An association]—*Syn.* union, alliance, federation; see **organization** 3.
3. [Something formed by combining]—*Syn.* compound, aggregate, blend; see **mixture** 1.
4. [Symbols used as a key]—*Syn.* order, sequence, succession; see **key** 2.
combine, *v.* **1.** [To bring together]—*Syn.* connect, couple, link; see **join** 1.
2. [To become one]—*Syn.* fuse, merge, blend; see **mix** 1, **unite** 1.
combined, *mod.—Syn.* linked, mingled, connected; see **joined.**
combining, *mod.—Syn.* joining, linking, bringing together; see **connecting.**
combustible, *mod.* **1.** [Inflammable]—*Syn.* flammable, burnable, ignitable; see **inflammable.**
2. [Easily aroused]—*Syn.* passionate, fiery, volatile; see **excitable, irritable.**
combustion, *n.* **1.** [The state of being on fire]—*Syn.* flaming, kindling, oxidization; see **fire** 1.
2. [Violent disturbance]—*Syn.* tumult, agitation, turmoil; see **disturbance** 2, **excitement.**
come, *v.* **1.** [To move toward]—*Syn.* close in, advance, draw near; see **approach** 2.
2. [To arrive]—*Syn.* appear at, reach, attain; see **arrive** 1.
3. [To be available]—*Syn.* appear, be at one's disposal, be ready, be obtainable, be handy, be accessible, be able to be reached, show *or* turn up, be procurable, be convenient, appear on the market; see also **appear** 1, 3.
4. [To extend]—*Syn.* join, expand, spread; see **reach** 1, **stretch** 3.
5. [To become]—*Syn.* mature, develop, get; see **become** 1, **grow** 2.
6. [(D) To have an orgasm]—*Syn.* to reach sexual fulfillment, ejaculate; see **achieve, copulate.**
as good as they come—*Syn.* choice, superior, fine; see **best** 1, **excellent.**
how come? (D)—*Syn.* for what reason? how so? what is the cause of *or* the reason for that?; see **why.**
come about, *v.* **1.** [To happen]—*Syn.* occur, take place, result; see **happen** 2.
2. [To turn]—*Syn.* swing, tack, veer; see **turn** 6.
come across, *v.* **1.** [To find]—*Syn.* uncover, stumble upon, notice; see **discover** 1, **find** 1.
2. [(D) To do]—*Syn.* enact, fulfill, accomplish; see **achieve** 1, **perform** 1.
3. [(D) To give]—*Syn.* deliver, pay, part with, and over; see **give** 1.
come again, *v.* **1.** [To return]—*Syn.* come back, go again, go back; see **return** 1.
2. [(D) To repeat]—*Syn.* reiterate, retell, restate; see **repeat** 3.
3. [To happen again]—*Syn.* reoccur, recur, occur again; see **happen** 2, **repeat** 2.
come along, *v.* **1.** [To accompany]—*Syn.* accompany, go with, attend; see **arrive** 1, **advance** 1.
2. [To progress]—*Syn.* show improvement, do well, get on; see **improve** 2, **prosper.**
come and get it (D), *interj.—Syn.* grub's on, eat hearty *or* hardy, eat up, soup's on, chow down, dinner time.
come around, *v.* **1.** [To recover]—*Syn.* improve, recuperate, rally; see **recover** 3, **revive** 2.
2. [(D) To visit]—*Syn.* call on, stop by, drop in on (D); see **visit** 4.
3. [To turn]—*Syn.* veer, tack, change direction; see **turn** 6.
come at, *v.* **1.** [Reach]—*Syn.* come to, grasp, feel for; see **reach** 2, **touch** 2.
2. [To attain]—*Syn.* win, achieve, accomplish; see **succeed** 1.
3. [To attack]—*Syn.* invade, assault, assail; see **attack** 1, 2.
comeback (D), *n.—Syn.* improvement, triumph, winning; see **recovery** 1, **victory** 1, 2.
come back, *v.* **1.** [To return]—*Syn.* come again, reappear, re-enter; see **return** 1.
2. [(D) To reply]—*Syn.* retort, rejoin, respond; see **answer** 1.
3. [(D) To recover]—*Syn.* do better, triumph, gain; see **improve** 2, **win** 1.
comeback trail (D), *n.—Syn.* revival, progress, betterment; see **improvement** 1, **recovery** 1.
come between, *v.—Syn.* intervene, interpose, interrupt; see **happen** 2, **meddle** 1.
come by, *v.* **1.** [To pass]—*Syn.* go by, overtake, move past; see **pass** 1.
2. [To acquire]—*Syn.* get, win, procure; see **obtain** 1.
come clean (D), *v.—Syn.* confess, reveal, acknowledge; see **admit** 2, 3.
comedian, *n.—Syn.* comic, jester, entertainer; see **actor, clown.**
comedown, *n.—Syn.* reversal, blow, defeat; see **failure** 1.
come down, *v.—Syn.* worsen, decline, suffer; see **decrease** 1, **fail** 1.
come down on *or* **upon,** *v.—Syn.* rebuke, reprimand, land on (D); see **attack** 2, **scold.**
comedy, *n.—Syn.* comic drama, burlesque, light entertainment; see **comedy of manners, drama** 1, 2, **parody** 1, 2.
Types of comedies include the following—high comedy, low comedy, satirical comedy, comedy of manners, musical comedy, situation comedy, sitcom, farce, interlude, tragicomedy, play of wit, satire, travesty, burlesque; *all* (D): gag show, laugh sensation, slapstick, funnies.
comedy of manners, *n.—Syn.* light social satire, high comedy, play; see **drama** 1, **parody** 1, 2.

Famous comedies of manners include the following —*She Stoops to Conquer,* Goldsmith; *School for Scandal, The Rivals,* Sheridan; *The Relapse, The Provok'd Wife,* Vanbrugh; *The Recruiting Officer, The Beaux' Stratagem,* Farquhar; *Les précieuses ridicules, Le bourgeois gentilhomme, Les femmes savantes,* Molière; *The Way of the World, Love for Love,* Congreve.

come for, *v.* —*Syn.* call for, accompany, come *or* try to get *or* collect, etc.; see **pick up** 6.

come forward, *v.* —*Syn.* offer oneself, appear, make a proposal; see **volunteer.**

come in, *v.* **1.** [To enter]—*Syn.* pass in, set foot (in), intrude; see **enter** 1.
2. [To arrive]—*Syn.* reach, disembark, alight; see **land** 3.

come in for (D), *v.* —*Syn.* get, be eligible for, acquire; see **receive** 1.

come in handy (D), *v.* —*Syn.* be useful, have a use, aid; see **help** 1.

come into, *v.* **1.** [To inherit]—*Syn.* fall heir to, succeed (to), acquire; see **inherit, obtain** 1, **receive** 1.
2. [To join]—*Syn.* enter into, associate with, align; see **join** 2.

comely, *mod.* —*Syn.* pretty, pleasing, attractive; see **beautiful** 2, **handsome** 2.

come off, *v.* **1.** [To become separated]—*Syn.* be disconnected, be disengaged, be severed, be parted, be disjoined, be detached, be disunited; see also **cut** 1, **divide** 1.
2. [(D) To happen]—*Syn.* occur, befall, come about; see **happen** 2.

come on, *v.* **1.** [To meet]—*Syn.* encounter, come across, come upon; see **meet** 6.
2. [To progress]—*Syn.* proceed, increase, gain; see **advance** 1, **improve** 2.
3. [To enter]—*Syn.* pass in, set foot in, come into; see **enter** 1.

come out, *v.* **1.** [To be made public]—*Syn.* be published, be made known, be announced, be issued, be brought out, be promulgated, be reported, be revealed, be divulged, be disclosed, be exposed; see also **appear** 1.
2. [To result]—*Syn.* end, conclude, terminate; see **succeed** 1.

come out for, *v.* —*Syn.* announce, state, affirm; see **declare** 1, **support** 1.

come out with, *v.* —*Syn.* report, declare, announce; see **advertise** 1, **declare** 1, **publish** 1.

come over, *v.* —*Syn.* take possession of, befall, overcome; see **happen** 2, **seize** 1.

comestible, *n.* —*Syn.* *chef-d'oeuvre* (French), foodstuff, victual; see **delicacy** 2, **food.**

come through, *v.* **1.** [To be successful]—*Syn.* accomplish, score, triumph; see **achieve** 1, **succeed** 1.
2. [To survive]—*Syn.* live through, persist, withstand; see **endure** 2.
3. [To do]—*Syn.* accomplish, achieve, carry out; see **perform** 1.

come to, *v.* **1.** [To recover]—*Syn.* rally, come around, recuperate; see **recover** 3, **revive** 2.
2. [To result in]—*Syn.* end in, terminate (by), conclude; see **happen** 2, **result.**

come to life, *v.* —*Syn.* recover, regain consciousness, live; see **revive** 2.

come to pass, *v.* —*Syn.* result, befall, occur; see **happen** 2.

come to the point, *v.* —*Syn. all* (D): cut the matter short, make a long story short, descend to particulars, get down to brass tacks; see **define** 2.

come up, *v.* —*Syn.* appear, arise, move to a higher place; see **rise** 1.

come upon, *v.* —*Syn.* locate, identify, recognize; see **discover** 1, **find** 1.

come up to, *v.* **1.** [To equal]—*Syn.* match, resemble, rank with; see **equal, rival.**
2. [To reach]—*Syn.* extend (to), get *or* come to, near; see **approach** 1, 2, **arrive** 1, **reach** 1.

come up with (D), *v.* **1.** [To propose]—*Syn.* suggest, recommend, offer; see **propose** 1.
2. [To find]—*Syn.* uncover, detect, stumble on; see **discover** 1, **find** 1.
3. [To produce]—*Syn.* compose, bring forth, originate; see **create** 2, **invent** 1, **produce** 2.

comfort, *n.* **1.** [Physical ease]—*Syn.* rest, quiet, relaxation, repose, alleviation, relief, assuagement, poise, well-being, opulence, cheer, snugness, abundance, sufficiency, gratification, luxury, warmth, plenty, creature comforts, satisfaction of bodily wants, coziness, pleasure, happiness, contentment, restfulness, peacefulness, cheerfulness, exhilaration, complacency, bed of roses (D); see **ease** 1, **enjoyment** 2, **satisfaction** 2.—*Ant.* weakness*, discomfort, uneasiness.
2. [Consolidation]—*Syn.* solace, compassion, sympathy; see **pity** 1.
3. [Anything that brings comfort]—*Syn.* help, support, succor; see **aid** 1, **encouragement** 2.

comfort, *v.* **1.** [To console]—*Syn.* condole, solace, commiserate, grieve with, compassionate, share with, cheer, gladden, uphold, succor, hearten, pat on the back, put (someone) in a good humor, sustain, support, help, aid, confirm, reassure, refresh, inspirit, sit by (D); see also **encourage** 2, **pity** 1. —*Ant.* be indifferent, discourage*, depress*.
2. [To make easy physically]—*Syn.* alleviate, make comfortable, assuage, soothe, allay, mitigate, gladden, quiet one's fears, help one in need, lighten one's burden, grant respite, encourage, calm, revive, sustain, aid, assist, nourish, support, compose, reanimate, delight, divert, bolster up, salve, enhearten, invigorate, refresh, inspirit, disburden, put at ease, reassure, warm, ameliorate, lighten, soften, abate, remedy, release, restore, free, make well, revitalize, revivify; see also **help** 1, **relieve** 2, **strengthen**—*Ant.* make uneasy, weaken*, worsen.

comfortable, *mod.* **1.** [In physical ease]—*Syn.* contented, cheerful, easy, at rest, relaxed, at ease, untroubled, healthy, hale, hearty, rested, enjoying, pleased, complacent, soothed, relieved, strengthened, restored, in comfort, made well, at home (with), without care, snug as a bug in a rug (D); see also **happy** 1, **satisfied.**—*Ant.* ill, uneasy*, disturbed.
2. [Conducive to physical ease]—*Syn.* satisfactory, snug, cozy, commodious, warm, sheltered, convenient, protected, cared for, appropriate, useful, roomy, spacious, palatial, fit to live in, luxurious, rich, satisfying, restful, in comfort, well-off, well-to-do, cool, breezy, ventilated; see also **pleasant** 2. —*Ant.* poverty-stricken, shabby*, tumble-down.

3. [(D) Adequate]—*Syn.* sufficient, suitable, ample; see **enough** 1.

comfortably, *mod.* —*Syn.* luxuriously, in comfort, restfully, snugly, cozily, reposefully, pleasantly, warmly, conveniently, adequately, with ease, competently, amply; see also **easily** 1.—*Ant.* inadequate*, insufficiently, poorly.

comforter, *n.* **1.** [A person or thing that comforts] —*Syn.* consoler, pacifier, sympathizer; see **friend** 1.
2. [A quilted bed covering]—*Syn.* spread, bedcover, coverlet; see **bedspread, cover** 1, **quilt.**

comforting, *mod.* —*Syn.* cheering, encouraging, inspiriting, invigorating, health-giving, warming, solacing, consoling, sustaining, reassuring, refreshing, upholding, succoring, relieving, soothing, assuaging, lightening, mitigating, alleviating, allaying, abating, softening, remedying, analeptic, curing, restoring, releasing, freeing, revitalizing, revivifying, tranquilizing; see also **sympathetic.** —*Ant.* disturbing*, distressing, upsetting.

comfortless, *mod.* —*Syn.* forlorn, desolate, cold; see **dismal** 1.

comic, *mod.* —*Syn.* ridiculous, humorous, ironic; see **funny** 1.

comical, *mod.* —*Syn.* witty, amusing, humorous; see **funny** 1.

coming, *mod.* **1.** [Approaching]—*Syn.* advancing, drawing near, progressing, passing a check point, checking in, docking, nearing, in the offing, coming in *or* on, arriving, gaining upon, pursuing, running after, getting near, near *or* close at hand, almost on one, converging, immediate, future, in view, preparing, to come, instant, predestined, eventual, fated, written, hereafter, at hand, in store, due, about to happen, looked *or* hoped for, deserving, close, in prospect, prospective, ulterior, anticipated, subsequent, forthcoming, certain, ordained, impending, to be, expected, near, *en route* (French), pending, foreseen; *all* (D): at one's back, on the horizon, in the wind; see also **expected** 2, **imminent, likely** 1.—*Ant.* going, distant*, leaving.
2. [Having a promising future]—*Syn.* marked, full of promise, better off, on the way to fame *or* success, ongoing, promising, aspiring, progressing, improving one's place, advancing, likely, probable, giving grounds for expectations, excellent, brilliant, reassuring, hopeful, auspicious, encouraging, making strides (D); see also **able** 1, 2, **ambitious** 1. —*Ant.* unpromising, hopeless*, discouraging.
3. [Future]—*Syn.* lying ahead, pending, impending; see **expected** 2, **future.**

coming, *n.* —*Syn.* approach, landing, reception; see **arrival** 1.

comity, *n.* —*Syn.* civility, amenity, affability; see **courtesy** 1.

command, *n.* **1.** [An order]—*Syn.* injunction, direction, dictation, demand, decree, prohibition, interdiction, canon, rule, call, summons, imposition, precept, mandate, charge, behest, edict, proclamation, instruction, proscription, ban, adjuration, requirement, dictate, subpoena, commandment, dictum, word of command, writ, citation, imperative, notification, will, regulation, ordinance, act, fiat, bidding, word, requisition, ultimatum, exaction, enactment, order of the day, caveat, prescript, warrant; see also **law** 3, **request.**—*Ant.* countermand, revocation, revocal.
2. [The power to issue orders]—*Syn.* authority, control, leadership, mastery, sway, domination, dominion, sovereignty, rule, coercion, compulsion, constraint, restraint, hold, grasp, grip, prerogative, right, headship, warrant, authorization, supremacy, primacy, suzerainty, jurisdiction, absolutism, despotism, tyranny, royalty; see also **administration** 1, **power** 2.
3. [Those in a position to issue orders]—*Syn.* commander, potentate, ruler; see **administrator, administration** 2, **chief** 1, 2, **leader** 2.
4. [An area or group subject to orders]—*Syn.* unit, squad, group, company, batallion, regiment, division, army, post, fort, camp, garrison, brigade, platoon, corps, battery, administrative and tactical unit, sector, ascendency, supervision, predominance, government, rulership, superintendence, charge, lead, directorship, presidency, empire, lordship, field of command, vanguard, rear, center, left flank, right flank, area *or* station under a commander; see also **army** 2, 3, **organization** 1.

command, *v.* **1.** [To issue an order]—*Syn.* order, bid, charge, authorize, enjoin, dictate, decree, proscribe, prescribe, direct, instruct, tell, forbid, demand, restrain, check, prohibit, interdict, inhibit, ban, bar, rule (out), debar, call, summon, ordinate, cite, set, require, impose, exact, appoint, mark *or* lay out, give orders *or* directions, proclaim, issue a command, call to order, send for, beckon, send on a mission, force upon, call on *or* upon, take charge, take the lead, enact, ordain, order with authority, make a requisition, grant, task, inflict, compel, adjure, subpoena, warrant, call for, state authoritatively; *all* (D): lay down the law, call the signals, put one's foot down; see also **require** 2.—*Ant.* request, ask*, desire.
2. [To have control]—*Syn.* rule, dominate, overrule, have sway, direct, determine, override, control, master, conquer, guide, lead, have the ascendancy, compel, conduct, administer, supervise, superintend, run, reign, have authority over, overbear, coach, head, dictate, exact, restrain, check, manage, curb, stop, have at one's bidding *or* disposal, hold (back), force, wield, influence, carry authority, be head of, predominate, preside *or* reign over, oppress, tyrannize, repress, prevail, prescribe, exercise power over, domineer, lord (it), constrain, charge, hinder, subdue, prevail over, push, coerce, be master of, oppress, have superiority *or* dominion over, require, oblige, shepherd, train, limit, carry through, hold office, occupy a post, officiate, take possession of, have superiority over, impel, drive, move, regulate, have the deciding voice in, take *or* have charge of, take over; *all* (D): keep in hand, take *or* hold the reins, be the boss of, rule the roost, crack the whip, boss the show, be in the saddle, wrap around one's finger, have the upper whip *or* hand, call the signals; see also **govern, manage** 1.

commandeer, *v.* **1.** [Force into military service] —*Syn.* draft, conscript, activate; see **enlist** 1, **enslave, recruit** 1.
2. [To seize for public use]—*Syn.* appropriate, sequester, confiscate; see **seize** 2.

commander, *n.* —*Syn.* commandant, officer, head; see **administration** 2, **administrator, chief** 1, **leader** 2.

commanding, *mod.* —*Syn.* dominant, dictatorial, imperious; see **absolute** 3, **autocratic** 1, **powerful** 1.

commanding, *n.* —*Syn.* leading, directing, controlling, steering, guiding, determining, ordering, charging, ruling, enjoining, decreeing, instructing, dictating, forbidding, issuing, dominating, overruling, compelling, managing, checking, curbing, forcing, coercing, requiring, restraining, having dominion over, in command *or* authority, in charge, at the helm *or* head, regulating; see also **government** 1.—*Ant.* obeying, yielding*, submitting.

commeasurable, *mod.* —*Syn.* commensurate, coinciding, congruous; see **equal, regular** 3.

commeasure, *v.* —*Syn.* match, parallel, correspond; see **equal, resemble.**

commemorate, *v.* —*Syn.* solemnize, honor, memorialize; see **admire** 1, **celebrate** 1.

commemoration, *n.* —*Syn.* recognition, remembrance, observance; see **celebration** 1, **ceremony** 2, **custom** 2.

commemorative, *mod.* —*Syn.* dedicatory, in honor of, observing; see **memorial**

commence, *v.* —*Syn.* start, enter upon, originate; see **begin** 2.

commencement, *n.* **1.** [A beginning]—*Syn.* genesis, start, initiation; see **origin** 1.
2. [Graduation ceremony]—*Syn.* admission, services, convocation; see **celebration** 1, 2, **ceremony** 2, **graduation.**

commend, *v.* **1.** [To praise]—*Syn.* laud, support, acclaim; see **approve** 1, **praise** 1.
2. [To recommend]—*Syn.* accredit, sanction, advocate; see **approve** 1, **recommend** 1.
3. [To present with confidence]—*Syn.* entrust, consign, confer; see **assign** 1, **trust** 1.

commendable, *mod.* —*Syn.* praiseworthy, laudable, deserving; see **excellent.**

commendation, *n.* **1.** [Approbation]—*Syn.* tribute, approval, acclamation, approbation; see **honor** 1, **praise** 1, **tribute** 1.
2. [A tribute]—*Syn.* pay, honor, award; see **prize, tribute** 2.

commendatory, *mod.* —*Syn.* laudatory, praising, approving; see **complimentary.**

commensurate, *mod.* —*Syn.* comparable, equivalent, proportionate; see **equal.**

comment, *n.* **1.** [An explanation]—*Syn.* footnote, opinion, annotation; see **judgment** 3, **remark, review** 2.
2. [A remark]—*Syn.* report, commentary, editorial; see **discussion** 1, 2, **explanation** 1, 2, **remark.**

comment, *v.* **1.** [To make a remark]—*Syn.* observe, remark, criticize, notice, state, express, pronounce, assert, affirm, mention, interject, say, note, touch *or* remark upon, pass on, interpose, reflect, disclose, bring out, opine, point out, conclude; see also **gossip, talk** 1, **utter.**
2. [To annotate]—*Syn.* illustrate, elucidate, clarify; see **explain.**

commentary, *n.* **1.** [An exposition]—*Syn.* discourse, critique, consideration; see **exposition** 2, **review** 2.
2. [A comment]—*Syn.* criticism, analysis, explication; see **explanation** 2, **interpretation** 1.

commentator, *n.* —*Syn.* observer, analyst, pundit; see **author** 2, **critic** 2, **reporter, writer.**

commerce, *n.* —*Syn.* buying and selling, trading, marketing; see **business** 1, **economics.**

commercial, *mod.* **1.** [Concerning, commerce] —*Syn.* trading, business, financial, economic, commissary, mercantile, merchandising, bartering, exchange, pecuniary, fiscal, monetary, trade, market, jobbing, supplying, retail, retailing, wholesale, wholesaling, marketable, in the market, for sale, across the counter; see also **industrial.**
2. [Intended primarily for financial gain]—*Syn.* monetary, for profit, pecuniary, materialistic, investment, mundane, prosaic, profit-making, money-making, Wall Street; see also **practical, profitable.**

commercial, *n.* —*Syn.* message from the sponsor, commercial announcement, plug (D); see **advertisement** 2.

commercialize, *v.* **1.** [To adapt to business]—*Syn.* make marketable, market, make salable, make pay, make profitable, make bring returns, develop as a business; see also **advertise** 2, **profit** 2, **sell** 1.
2. [To cheapen]—*Syn.* lessen, degrade, lower the quality; see **cheapen, depreciate** 2.

commination, *n.* —*Syn.* ban, curse, malediction, tirade, condemnation, censure, challenge, imprecation, anathema, execration, diatribe, excommunication, threatening, obloquy, aspersion, malison, vituperation, threat of punishment, imprecation, damaging imputation, menace, proscription, intimidation, denunciation, denouncing as evil, objurgation.

commingle, *v.* —*Syn.* blend, unite, mingle; see **mix** 1.

commiserate, *v.* —*Syn.* share sorrow, condole, console; see **pity** 1, **sympathize.**

commiseration, *n.* —*Syn.* consolation, compassion, sympathy; see **pity** 1.

commissary, *n.* —*Syn.* deputy, representative, legate; see **agent** 1.

commission, *n.* **1.** [The act of committing]—*Syn.* sending, delegation, empowering, charging, deputing, deputizing, authorizing, assignment, entrusting, commitment, handing *or* making *or* passing over, authorization, engagement, employment, nomination, nominating, ordaining, ordainment, accrediting, command, investiture, constitution, inauguration, coronation.
2. [An authorization]—*Syn.* order, license, command; see **permission.**
3. [A duty]—*Syn.* work, function, obligation; see **duty** 2.
4. [A committee]—*Syn.* commissioners, representatives, board; see **committee.**
5. [A payment]—*Syn.* remuneration, royalty, salary, fee, stipend, indemnity, rake-off (D); see also **pay** 2, **payment** 1.
out of commission—*Syn.* damaged, not working *or* running, out of order; see **broken** 2.

commission, *v.* —*Syn.* send, delegate, appoint, authorize, charge, depute, empower, constitute, ordain, commit, entrust, give in charge, send out, dispatch, consign, deputize, assign, entrust with a mission, empower to act for another, charge with an errand, confide to, accredit, engage, employ, inaugurate, invest, name, nominate, hire, bespeak, enable, license, command, elect, select; see also **approve** 1.

commissioner, *n.* —*Syn.* spokesman, magistrate, government official; see **administrator.**

commit, *v.* **1.** [To perpetrate]—*Syn.* act, do, complete; see **perform** 1.

2. [To entrust]—*Syn.* confide, delegate, relegate (to), leave to, give to do, promise, consign, intrust, turn over to, put in the hands of, allot, charge, invest, allocate, apportion, rely upon, depend upon, confer a trust, give in charge, bind over, make responsible for, put an obligation upon, make another's duty, empower, employ, dispatch, send, vest in, invest with power, authorize, deputize, grant authority to, engage, commission, depute, convey; see also **assign** 1.—*Ant.* relieve of, dismiss*, discharge.

commitment, *n.* —*Syn.* engagement, responsibility, assurance; see **duty** 1, 2, **promise** 1.

commit suicide, *v.* —*Syn.* kill oneself, take an overdose (of any dangerous drug), slash one's writs, slit one's (own) throat, take one's own life; *all* (D): end it all, throw in the towel, blow one's brains out, give up the ship, jump ship, commit hara-kiri.

committee, *n.* —*Syn.* consultants, board, bureau, council, cabinet, investigators, trustees, appointed group, task force, board of inquiry, representatives, soviet panel, investigating committee, study group, executive committee, standing committee, planning board, crown commission, court commission, court committee board, *ad hoc* (Latin) *or* special committee, grand jury, referees, deliberative *or* advisory group, court, convocation, subcommittee, chamber, assignee; see also **delegate, jury, organization** 3, **representative** 2.

in committee—*Syn.* under consideration, being weighed *or* evaluated, not settled; see **considered.**

commix, *v.* —*Syn.* blend, unite, compound; see **mix** 1.

commode, *n.* **1.** [A chest of drawers]—*Syn.* high boy, cabinet, dresser, chiffonier, dressing table; see also **chest** 1, **furniture.**

2. [Toilet]—*Syn.* rest-room, bathroom, men's *or* women's room; see **toilet** 2.

commodious, *mod.* —*Syn.* ample, big, roomy; see **comfortable** 2, **enough** 1, **large** 1.

commodity, *n.* —*Syn.* goods, article(s), merchandise, wares, materials, possessions, property, chattel, assets, belongings, thing(s), specialty, stock(s), stock in trade, consumers' goods; *all* (D): line, what one handles, what one is showing.

common, *mod.* **1.** [Ordinary]—*Syn.* universal, familiar, natural, normal, everyday, accepted, commonplace, characteristic, customary, bourgeois, conventional, passable, general, informal, conformable, habitual, prevalent, probable, typical, prosaic, simple, current, prevailing, trite, nonliterary, banal, unvaried, homely, colloquial, trivial, stock, oft-repeated, indiscriminate, tedious, worn thin, worn-out, hackneyed, monotonous, stale, wearisome, casual, undistinguished, unassuming, Philistine, uneducated, artless, plebeian, workaday, provincial, unsophisticated, unrefined, untutored, plain, uncultured, vulgar, slangy, jargony, vernacular, koine, vulgate, of the folk, unadorned, ugly, platitudinous, truistic, obvious, average, quotidian, orthodox, mediocre, well-known, insipid, stereotyped, patent, moderate, middling, abiding, indifferent, pedestrian, tolerable, temperate, innocuous, undistinguished; *all* (D): run-of-the-mill, humdrum, run-of-the-mine, lower-level, garden variety, warmed-over, fair-to-middling, household, so-so, not too bad, second-rate, nothing to write home about; *comme ci, comme ça* (French); motheaten, below the salt; see also **conventional** 1, 3, **dull** 4, **fair** 2, **popular** 1, 3, **regular** 3, **traditional** 2. —*Ant.* unnatural, unique*, extraordinary.

2. [Of frequent occurrence]—*Syn.* customary, constant, usual; see **frequent** 1, **habitual** 1, **regular** 3.

3. [Generally known]—*Syn.* general, prevalent, well-known; see **familiar** 1, **traditional** 2.

4. [Low]—*Syn.* cheap, inferior, mean; see **poor** 2, **subordinate.**

5. [Held or enjoyed in common]—*Syn.* communal, commutual, equivalent, united, belonging equally to, identical, coincident, correspondent, congruous, shared, joint, mutual, socialistic, communistic, in common; see also **co-operative** 2, **public, universal** 3.—*Ant.* private*, individual, personal.

in common—*Syn.* shared, communal, mutually *or* commonly held; see **common** 5.

commoner, *n.* —*Syn.* plebeian, bourgeois(e), common man, civilian, citizen, peasant, noncombatant, little man, man in the street; see also **citizen.**

commonly, *mod.* —*Syn.* usually, ordinarily, generally; see **regularly** 1.

commonplace, *mod.* —*Syn.* usual, hackneyed, mundane; see **common** 1, **conventional** 1, 3.

commonplace, *n.* —*Syn.* truism, triteness, platitude; see **cliché, motto.**

commons, *n.* —*Syn.* dining hall, canteen, mess hall; see **dining room, restaurant.**

commonsense, *mod.* —*Syn.* sensible, sound, rational; see **judicious, practical, reasonable** 1.

common sense, *n.* —*Syn.* good sense, practicality, horse sense (D); see **sense** 2, **wisdom** 2.

commonwealth, *n.* **1.** [The body politic]—*Syn.* the people, commonality, polity; see **nation** 1.

2. [A republic]—*Syn.* federation, democracy, constitutional government; see **republic.**

commotion, *n.* **1.** [Social agitation]—*Syn.* riot, agitation, mutiny; see **disorder** 2, **revolution** 2.

2. [Physical disturbance]—*Syn.* violence, tumult, uproar; see **disturbance** 2, **fight** 1.

communal, *mod.* —*Syn.* shared, public, mutual; see **common** 5, **co-operative** 2.

commune, *n.* —*Syn.* community, village, municipality; see **city, co-operative, neighborhood** 1.

communicable, *mod.* —*Syn.* transferable, infectious, pandemic; see **catching, contagious.**

communicant, *n.* —*Syn.* informant, dispatcher, notifier; see **messenger, reporter.**

communicate, *v.* **1.** [To impart information] —*Syn.* give, pass *or* hand on, make known, impart, carry, inform, advise, acquaint, transfer, write, convey, send *or* leave word, bestow, promulgate, broadcast, telecast, announce, state, publish, print, publicize, advertise, divulge, disclose, reveal, enlighten, transmit, telephotograph, picture, telephone, phone, call in, telegraph, televise, radio, cable, comment, instill, deliver, enunciate, impart knowledge of, bring word, emit, dictate, say, assert, apprise (of), utter, describe, express, enlighten, articulate, narrate, remark, hint, demonstrate, relate, recite, proclaim, express, insinuate, mention, give one to understand, call attention to, impress upon the mind, lay before, put into one's head, instruct, point out, blurt *or* speak *or* pour out, acquaint with, shout, come out with, observe, allege, pronounce, set *or* put forth; *all* (D): tip, let fall, breathe, give voice to, wigwag, drop (a hint); see also **declare** 1, **notify** 1, **teach** 1, **tell** 1.—*Ant.* keep, censor*, keep secret.

2. [To be in communication]—*Syn.* correspond, be in touch, have access to, reach, hear from, be within reach, be in respondence with, be near, make advances, be close to, have the confidence of, associate with, commune with, be congenial with, establish contact (with), be in agreement with *or* about, confer, talk, converse, confabulate, chat, convey thoughts, discourse *or* speak together, deal with, commune, write to, telephone, call up, wire, cable, have interchange of thoughts, reply, answer; *both* (D): have a meeting of minds, find a common denominator; see also **agree.**—*Ant.* be out of reach, differ*, be removed from.

communication, *n.* **1.** [The act of transmitting information]—*Syn.* talk, utterance, announcing, revelation, telepathy, extrasensory perception *or* ESP, publication, writing, picturing, drawing, painting, radioing, broadcasting, televising, disseminating, flashing, giving, passing on, making known, imparting, informing, advisement, notifying, acquainting, disclosing, discovering, telling, submitting, delivery, notification, correspondence, disclosure, speaking, description, exposition, pronouncement, mention, announcement, conference, presentation, interchange, expression, narration, relation, declaration, assertion, allegation, articulation, elucidation, transfer, transmission, reception, reading, translating, interpreting, corresponding; see also **conversation, speech** 2.—*Ant.* concealment, censorship*, withholding.

2. [Transmitted information]—*Syn.* news, ideas, announcement, statement, disclosure, work, utterance, speech, language, warning, revelation, prophecy, communiqué, briefing, bulletin, excerpt, précis, summary, information, report, account, declaration, publicity, translation, printed work, advice, intelligence, tidings, conversation, converse; see also **communications.**

Means of communication include the following—book, letter, electronic mail, newspaper, magazine, radio, proclamation, broadcast, dispatch, radio report, telecast, telephone call, telegram, computer net, cable, radiogram, broadside, circular, notes, memorandum, (picture) post card, poster, billboard; see also **journal** 2, **news** 2, **report** 1, 2.

communications, *n.* Means and systems of promoting communication include the following—railroad, bus, airplane, ship, post office, telegraph, cable, wireless, mass media, communications satellite, COMSAT, Telstar, computer system, radar, airmail, long-distance telephone, wireless telephone, wireless telegraph, dictaphone, address system, loud-speaker, teletype, two-way radio; *all* (D): intercom, ship-to-shore, shore-to-ship, walkie-talkie; see **mail, radar, telephone, television, radio** 1, 2.

communicative, *mod.* —*Syn.* voluble, loquacious, enlightening; see **informative, talkative.**

communion, *n.* **1.** [Association]—*Syn.* fellowship, accord, union; see **agreement** 2, **association** 1.

2. [A Christian sacrament]—*Syn.* Lord's Supper, Holy Communion, Breaking of Bread, Eucharist; see also **sacrament.**

communiqué, *n.* —*Syn.* official communication, bulletin, dispatch, report; see **announcement** 2, **communication** 2.

communism, *n.* —*Syn.* state socialism, Marxism, Marxism-Leninism, dictatorship of the proletariat, collectivism, state ownership of production, equal distribution of wealth; see also **socialism.**

Terms for communist organizations include the following—Communist Party, The Party, Comintern, The Third International, Red International, Maoism, Castroism, Titoism.

communist, *n.* —*Syn.* card-carrying communist, (avowed) Party member, comrade, (fellow) traveler, member of the Communist Party, C.P. member, apparatchik, sympathizer, Marxist, Bolshevist, Viet Cong, Trotskyite, Leninist, Stalinist, Maoist, revisionist, believer in peaceful co-existence, *communista* (Spanish); *all* (D): commie, red, comsymp, pinko; see also **agitator, radical.**—*Ant.* fascist, conservative*, capitalist.

communistic, *mod.* —*Syn.* communist, Bolshevist, red (D); see **radical** 2, **revolutionary** 1.

community, *mod.* —*Syn.* joint, group, co-operative; see **common** 5, **public.**

community, *n.* **1.** [A town]—*Syn.* center, colony, hamlet; see **city, town** 1, **village.**

2. [Society]—*Syn.* the public, the people, the nation; see **society** 2, **town** 4.

3. [Similarity]—*Syn.* likeness, sameness, identity; see **similarity.**

commutation, *n.* —*Syn.* substitution, replacement, compensation; see **change** 1, 2, **exchange** 1, 3.

commute, *v.* **1.** [To exchange reciprocally for something else]—*Syn.* interchange, change, trade; see **exchange** 1, 2.

2. [To exchange for something less severe]—*Syn.* reduce, alleviate, mitigate; see **decrease** 2.

3. [Travel]—*Syn.* go back and forth, drive, take the subway *or* bus *or* train; see **travel** 2.

commuter, *n.* —*Syn.* suburbanite, city worker, daily traveler; see **driver, traveler.**

compact, *mod.* —*Syn.* compressed, close, impenetrable; see **full** 1, **thick** 1, 3.

compact, *n.* —*Syn.* vanity case, vanity box, vanity, make-up case, powder case, powder and rouge box; see also **case** 7, **container.**

companion, *n.* **1.** [A personal friend]—*Syn.* comrade, mate, fellow; see **friend** 1.

2. [An associate]—*Syn.* partner, colleague, co-worker; see **assistant, associate.**

3. [One who accompanies another]—*Syn.* attendant, escort, chaperon, (practical) nurse, governess, matron, safeguard, protector, guide, convoy.

companionable, *mod.* —*Syn.* cordial, sociable, amicable; see **friendly** 1, **social** 2.

companionship, *n.* —*Syn.* fraternity, rapport, association; see **brotherhood** 1, **fellowship** 1, **friendship** 1.

company, *n.* **1.** [Associates]—*Syn.* group, club, fellowship; see **organization** 3.
2. [A group of people]—*Syn.* assembly, throng, band; see **gathering.**
3. [People organized for business]—*Syn.* partnership, firm, corporation; see **business** 4.
4. [Social intercourse]—*Syn.* friendly intercourse, fraternity, companionship; see **association** 1, **fellowship** 1.
5. [A guest or guests]—*Syn.* visitor(s), caller(s), overnight guest(s), unexpected guest(s), boarder(s); see also **guest** 1.
keep (a person) company—*Syn.* stay with, visit, amuse; see **entertain** 1.
keep company—*Syn.* go together, be friends with, join company with; see **associate** 1.
part company—*Syn.* separate, part, stop associating with; see **leave** 1.

comparable, *mod.* **1.** [Worthy of comparison] —*Syn.* as good as, equivalent, tantamount; see **equal.**
2. [Capable of comparison]—*Syn.* similar, akin, relative; see **alike** 2, **like.**

comparative, *mod.* —*Syn.* comparable, relative, correlative, corresponding, connected, metaphorical, allusive, similar, analogous, parallel, contrastive, near, close to, approaching, in proportion, matching, rivaling, vying, not positive *or* absolute, with reservation, contingent, restricted, inconclusive, provisional, qualified; see also **conditional, like, related** 2.—*Ant.* unrelated, opposing*, dissimilar.

comparatively, *mod.* —*Syn.* relatively, similarly, analogously; see **approximately.**

compare, *v.* **1.** [To liken]—*Syn.* relate, connect, make like, notice the similarities, allege as similar, associate, link, balance against, distinguish between, bring near, put alongside, record correspondences, reduce to a common denominator, declare similar, equate, match, express by metaphor, show correspondence, allegorize, correlate, parallel, show to be similar *or* analogous, identify with, bring into meaningful relation with, draw a parallel between, represent as resembling; *all* (D): tie up, come up to, stack up with; see also **distinguish** 1.
2. [To examine on a comparative basis]—*Syn.* collate, contrast, balance, parallel, bring into comparison, estimate relatively, set over against, compare notes, exchange observations, weigh one thing against another, set side by side, correlate, weigh, oppose, divide, measure, separate, segregate, place in juxtaposition, confront, note the similarities and differences of, juxtapose; see also **analyze** 1, **examine** 1.
3. [To stand in relationship to another]—*Syn.* match, vie, rival; see **equal, match** 3.
beyond *or* **past** *or* **without compare**—*Syn.* incomparable, without equal, distinctive; see **unique** 1.

compared, *mod.* —*Syn.* distinguished, set side by side, in comparison, brought into comparison, correlated, as to, by comparison with; see also **related** 2.

compare favorably to *or* **with,** *v.* —*Syn.* be better than, improve on *or* upon, do well (in comparison with); see also **compare** 1, 2.

compare to *or* **with,** *v.* —*Syn.* put beside *or* side by side, relate to, equate; see **compare** 1.

comparison, *n.* **1.** [The act of comparing]—*Syn.* likening, collating, analyzing, relative estimation, comparative relation, testing by a criterion, testing by close scrutiny, distinguishing between, analogizing, corresponding, paralleling, contrasting, balancing, relating, collation, dividing, opposition, separation, segregation, bringing together, identification, measuring, weighing, justaposing, exemplification, observation, correlation, discrimination; see also **association** 2, **judgment** 2.
2. [A prepared comparison, sense 1]—*Syn.* metaphor, resemblance, analogy, illustration, correspondence, relation, collation, correlation, parable, allegory, similarity, likening, identification, equation, measurement, example, contrast, association, ratio, parallel, comparative estimate *or* statement, connection, critical judgment, estimate of likeness and difference; see also **estimate** 1, **simile.**

compartment, *n.* —*Syn.* section, portion, subdivision; see **part** 1.

compass, *n.* **1.** [Boundary]—*Syn.* circumference, range, extent; see **boundary, expanse.**
2. [Instrument]—*Syn.* mariner's compass, direction guide, surveyor's compass, earth inductor, sun compass, induction compass, gyrocompass, cardinal points, card (magnetic) compass, needle (D); see also **device** 1.

compassion, *n.* —*Syn.* sympathy, consideration, clemency; see **kindness** 1, **pity** 1.

compassionate, *mod.* —*Syn.* merciful, humane, sympathetic; see **merciful** 1.

compatibility, *n.* —*Syn.* harmony, unity, congeniality; see **adaptability, agreement** 2.

compatible, *mod.* —*Syn.* agreeable, congruous, co-operative; see **harmonious** 2.

compatriot, *n.* —*Syn.* fellow countryman, statesman, national; see **citizen, patriot.**

compeer, *n.* **1.** [A comrade]—*Syn.* companion, comrade, consort; see **associate, friend** 1.
2. [One of equal rank]—*Syn.* peer, match, colleague; see **equal.**

compel, *v.* —*Syn.* enforce, constrain, coerce; see **force** 1.

compendious, *mod.* —*Syn.* concise, inclusive, succinct; see **comprehensive, short** 2.

compendium, *n.* —*Syn.* abridgment, abstract, essence; see **summary.**

compensate, *v.* **1.** [To pay]—*Syn.* recompense, remunerate, requite; see **pay** 1, **repay** 1.
2. [To offset]—*Syn.* counterbalance, neutralize, counterpoise; see **offset.**

compensating, *mod.* —*Syn.* refunding, atoning, adjusting, reimbursing, repaying, settling, balancing, in compensation; see also **balanced** 1.

compensation, *n.* —*Syn.* remuneration, recompense, indemnity, satisfaction, requital, remittal, buyback, return for services, commission, gratuity, reimbursement, allowance, deserts, remittance, salary, stipend, wages, hire, earnings, settlement, honorarium, defrayal, coverage, consideration, meed, counterclaim, damages, repayment, recoupment, fee, quittance, reckoning, equivalent price, indemnification, bonus, premium, amends, reciprocity, reward, advantage, profit, benefit, gain; *both* (D): kickback, comeback; see also **pay** 2, **payment** 1, **return** 3, **tip** 2.—*Ant.* loss*, deprivation, confiscation.

compete, *v.*—*Syn.* enter competition, take part, race (with), strive, struggle, vie *or* cope with, be in the running, become a competitor, enter the rolls *or* lists, run for, participate (in), contend for a prize, take part in athletics, engage in a contest, oppose, wrestle, be rivals, tussle, joust, battle, seek the same prize, bandy with, spar, fence, employ stratagem, collide, tilt, bid, face, clash, encounter, match wits *or* strength (with), play, grapple; *all* (D): take on all comers, go in for, lock horns (with), carry one's colors, go out (for), break a lance with; see also **contest** 2, **fight** 1, 2.

competence, *n.* **1.** [Adequate income]—*Syn.* subsistence, provision, sufficient means; see **income, support** 3.
2. [Qualification]—*Syn.* capability, skill, fitness; see **ability** 1, 2.

competent, *mod.* **1.** [Capable]—*Syn.* fit, qualified, skilled; see **able** 1, 2.
2. [Adequate]—*Syn.* sufficient, complete, satisfactory; see **enough** 1.

competently, *mod.*—*Syn.* capably, skillfully, efficiently, proficiently, expertly, dexterously, with everything that is in one (D); see also **effectively.**

competition, *n.* **1.** [The act of competing]—*Syn.* rivalry, contention, contest, striving, (common) strife, struggle, controversy, coping with, opposition, pairing off, meeting, engagement, candidacy, racing, trial, athletic event, contest for prize *or* advantage, pitting of strength *or* wits, combat, fight, game, conflict, debate, tournament, attempt to outsell, rivalry for patronage, attempt at betterment, clash, counteraction, encounter, match, antagonism, joust; see also **sport** 1.—*Ant.* partnership, alliance*, co-operation.
2. [An instance of competition]—*Syn.* race, match, contest, meet, matchup, fight, tilt, bout, boxing match, game of skill, trial, sport, athletic event, wrestling; *both* (D): rumpus, tangle; see also **game** 1, **sport** 3.

competitive, *mod.*—*Syn.* competing, antagonistic, opposing; see **rival.**

competitor, *n.*—*Syn.* emulator, rival, antagonist; see **contestant, opponent** 1, 2.

compilation, *n.* **1.** [The action of compiling]—*Syn.* gathering (together), incorporating, drawing together, codifying, codification, collocating, collecting, aggregating, methodizing, systematizing, gleaning, accumulating, combining, assembling, organizing, coordinating, compiling, selecting, garnering, ordering, arranging, consolidating, joining, unifying, incorporating; see also **accumulation** 1, **collection** 1.
2. [Something compiled]—*Syn.* accumulation, anthology, garner; see **collection** 2.

compile, *v.*—*Syn.* collect, put *or* group *or* bring *or* draw *or* get together, gather, amass, arrange, edit, collate, recapitulate, abridge, concentrate, consolidate, compose, note down, anthologize, cull, glean, congregate, heap up, garner, assemble, collocate, unite, colligate, muster, compose; see also **accumulate** 1, **edit** 1, 2.—*Ant.* originate, scatter*, disperse.

complacency, *n.*—*Syn.* pleasure, contentment, smugness; see **comfort** 1, **satisfaction** 2.

complacent, *mod.*—*Syn.* self-satisfied, contented, self-righteous; see **egotistic** 1, **happy** 1, **satisfied, smug.**

complain, *v.* **1.** [To express an objection]—*Syn.* remonstrate, disapprove, accuse, deplore, criticize, denounce, differ, disagree, dissent, cavil, charge, report adversely (upon), reproach, oppose, contravene, grumble, whine, whimper, nag, fret, protest, fuss, moan, make a fuss (about), take exception to, object (to), deprecate, enter a demurrer, grieve, demur, defy, gainsay, expostulate, carp, impute, indict, lay, ascribe, attack, refute, countercharge; *all* (D): grouse, kick, bitch, grouch, croak, gripe, grunt, beef, bellyache, ace out, tattle, kick up a fuss, make noises about, take a dim view of, look askance, raise a howl *or* fuss, quarrel with one's bread and butter; see also **censure, oppose** 1.—*Ant.* sanction, approve*, countenance.
2. [To express grief]—*Syn.* lament, bemoan, bewail; see **cry** 1, **mourn** 1.

complaining, *mod.*—*Syn.* objecting, lamenting, murmuring, mourning, regretting, repining, bewailing, deploring, weeping, moaning, protesting, charging, accusing, disapproving, grumbling, fretting, whining, countercharging, indicting, laying to, imputing, resenting, dissenting, registering a protest, filing a complaint, making an adverse report, kicking (D).—*Ant.* enjoying*, appreciating, praising.

complaint, *n.* **1.** [An objection]—*Syn.* charge, criticism, reproach; see **accusation** 2, **objection** 1, 2.
2. [An illness]—*Syn.* ailment, malady, infirmity; see **disease** 2, 3, **illness** 1.

complaisance, *n.*—*Syn.* politeness, respect, friendliness; see **courtesy** 1, **kindness** 1.

complaisant, *mod.*—*Syn.* obliging, amiable, compliant; see **friendly** 1.

complement, *n.* **1.** [That which completes]—*Syn.* supplement, correlative, counterpart; see **addition** 2.
2. [Full amount]—*Syn.* totality, wholeness, entirety; see **whole.**
3. [That which completes the number of something]—*Syn.* balance, filler, rest; see **remainder.**

complementary, *mod.* **1.** [Forming a complement]—*Syn.* integral, equivalent, corresponding, reciprocal, parallel, commutual, correlative, correspondent, interrelated, interconnected, interdependent, companion, completing; see also **equal.**
2. [Matched]—*Syn.* paired, mated, corresponding; see **alike** 2, **matched.**

complete, *mod.* **1.** [Not lacking in any part]—*Syn.* total, replete, entire; see **full** 1, 3, **whole** 1.
2. [Finished]—*Syn.* concluded, terminated, ended; see **finished** 1.
3. [Perfect]—*Syn.* flawless, unblemished, impeccable; see **perfect** 2, **whole** 2.

complete, *v.* **1.** [To make entire]—*Syn.* execute, make excellent, consummate, perfect, accomplish, realize, perform, achieve, fill out, fulfill, supplement, effectuate, equip, actualize, furnish, make (up), elaborate, make good, bring to fullness *or*

completion *or* maturity *or* fruition, make complete, develop, fill in, refine, effect, carry out *or* off; *all* (D): crown, go through with, get through, cap, round out; see also **build** 1, **create** 2, **form** 1. —*Ant.* start, begin*, commence.
2. [To bring to an end]—*Syn.* finish, conclude, close; see **achieve** 1, **end** 1, **perform** 1.

completed, *mod.* —*Syn.* achieved, ended, concluded; see **built** 1, **done** 2, **finished** 1.

completely, *mod.* —*Syn.* entirely, fully, totally, utterly, wholly, undividedly, perfectly, exclusively, simply, effectively, competently, solidly, bodily, absolutely, unanimously, thoroughly, en masse, exhaustively, minutely, unabridged, painstakingly, extensively, conclusively, positively, unconditionally, finally, without omission, to the *or* one's utmost, ultimately, in toto, in entirety, determinedly, maturely, radically, altogether, quite, all the way, comprehensively, to the end, from beginning to end, on all counts, in all, in full measure, in the mass, to the limit *or* full, in full, to completion; *all* (D): to the nth degree, to a frazzle, downright, to the backbone, through thick and thin, down to the ground, through and through, in the altogether, hook, line, and sinker, rain or shine, in one lump, from A to Z, root and branch, from head to foot; see also **finally** 1.—*Ant.* somewhat, partly*, partially.

completion, *n.* —*Syn.* finish, conclusion, fulfillment; see **end** 2.

complex, *mod.* **1.** [Composed of several parts] —*Syn.* composite, heterogeneous, conglomerate, multiple, mingled, motley, mosaic, manifold, multiform, compound, complicated, aggregated, aggregate, mazed, involved, combined, compact, compounded, miscellaneous, multiplex, multifarious, variegated; see also **mixed** 1.—*Ant.* simplified*, single, homogeneous.
2. [Difficult to understand]—*Syn.* entangled, tangled, interlaced, circuitous, convoluted, puzzling, mixed, mingled, muddled, jumbled, impenetrable, inscrutable, unfathomable, undecipherable, bewildering, intricate, perplexing, abstruse, recondite, labyrinthine, complicated, involved, enigmatic, hidden, interwoven, knotted, meandering, winding, sinuous, tortuous, snarled, irreducible, rambling, paradoxical, excursive, Daedalian, Gordian, twisted, disordered, devious, Byzantine, discursive, cryptic, inextricable; *all* (D): knotty, mazy, roundabout, crabbed; see also **confused** 2, **difficult** 2, **obscure** 1.—*Ant.* understandable*, plain, apparent.

complex, *n.* **1.** [An obsession]—*Syn.* exaggerated reaction syndrome, phobia, mania, repressed emotions *or* fears *or* desires *or* hates, group of repressed associations, repressions centered around a particular emotion; see also **fear** 2, **insanity** 1, **neurosis.**
Types of mental complexes include the following —Cain, castration, Clerambaut-Kandinsky, Diana, Electra *or* father, Friedman's *or* Friedman's syndrome, inferiority, Narcissus, Oedipus *or* mother, sex, persecution, superiority.
2. [A composite]—*Syn.* conglomerate, syndrome, image, ecosystem, ecological complex, aggregation, association, group, entanglement, totality; see also **collection** 2, **system** 1.

complexion, *n.* **1.** [Appearance]—*Syn.* aspect, semblance, seeming; see **appearance** 2.
2. [Skin coloring]—*Syn.* tone, glow, color, coloration, general coloring, tinge, cast, flush, skin texture, tint, hue, pigmentation; see also **skin.**
Descriptions of complexions include the following —blond, fair, pale, pallid, sallow, sickly, dark, brunet, olive, bronze, sandy, rosy, red, ruddy, brown, yellow, black, blue-black, Negroid, Caucasian, Nordic, Aryan, Melanesian, Malaysian, mulatto, Oriental, Semitic, Amerindian, tan, (sun)-tanned, yellowish-brown, pinkish, sanguine, redheaded; *all* (D): peroxide *or* drugstore blond, strawberry (*or* peaches) and cream.

compliance, *n.* —*Syn.* yielding, acquiescence, assent; see **agreement** 2, **docility.**

compliant, *mod.* —*Syn.* obedient, pliant, acquiescent; see **docile.**

complicate, *v.* —*Syn.* combine, fold, infold, multiply, interfuse, twist, snarl (up), associate with, involve, convolute, embroil, obscure, make multiform *or* various *or* intricate *or* complex, confound, muddle, interrelate, elaborate, embarrass, implicate, tangle, conceal, mix up, impede, perplex, vex, hinder, hamper, encumber, hobble, bedevil, handicap, darken, render unintelligible; *all* (D): tie up with, jumble, fan the flames, clog, spike one's guns, ball up; see also **confuse, entangle.** —*Ant.* simplify*, clear up, unfold.

complicated, *mod.* —*Syn.* intricate, various, mixed; see **complex** 2, **confused** 2, **difficult** 2.

complication, *n.* —*Syn.* complexity, dilemma, development; see **confusion** 2, **difficulty** 1, 2.

complicity, *n.* —*Syn.* conspiracy, confederacy, complot; see **intrigue** 1, **partnership.**

compliment, *n.* —*Syn.* felicitation, tribute, encomium, approval, commendation, endorsement, confirmation, sanction, applause, an expression of praise, flattery, acclaim, acclamation, laudation, panegyric, eulogy, cajolery, adulation, notice, regards, honor, appreciation, respects, blessing, ovation, veneration, admiration, congratulation, homage, good word, sentiment; *all* (D): comp, trade-last *or* T.L., bouquet, pat on the back; see also **praise** 2. —*Ant.* censure*, abuse, disapproval.

compliment, *v.* **1.** [Congratulate]—*Syn.* felicitate, wish joy to, rejoice with, remember, commemorate, send a remembrance, pay one's respects, greet, honor, cheer, salute, hail, toast, applaud, panegyrize, extol, celebrate, pay tribute to, pat on the back, give a bouquet; see also **praise** 1.
2. [Flatter]—*Syn.* be in favor of, commend, endorse, sanction, confirm, acclaim, please, satisfy, pay a compliment to, sing the praises of, speak highly of, exalt, make much of, ingratiate oneself with, soothe, charm, applaud, worship, eulogize, glorify, magnify, cajole, fawn upon, toady *or* truckle to, laud, adulate; *all* (D): butter up, puff (someone) up, hand it to (someone); see also **praise** 1.—*Ant.* denounce*, disapprove of, censure.

complimentary, *mod.* —*Syn.* commendatory, flattering, laudatory, approving, encomiastic, encomiastical, eulogistic, adulatory, celebrating, honoring, plauditory, honeyed, fawning, respectful, sycophantic, unctuous, congratulatory, well-wishing, fair-spoken, panegyric, highly favorable, approbatory, approbative, praiseful, praising, abounding in praise, singing the praises of, with highest recommendations, with high praise; see also **appreciative, polite** 1.

comply with, *v.* —*Syn.* conform, agree to, acquiesce; see **agree, obey** 1, 2.

component, *mod.* —*Syn.* constituent, elemental, basic; see **fundamental** 1, **integral.**

component, *n.* —*Syn.* element, segment, ingredient; see **part** 1.

compose, *v.* **1.** [To be the parts or the ingredients] —*Syn.* constitute, comprise, be an adjunct, go into the making of, make up, enter *or* merge *or* go into *or* in, be a component *or* ingredient, be an element *or* portion of, belong to, consist of, be made *or* compounded of; see also **comprise, include** 1.

2. [To give form]—*Syn.* make, fashion, put together; see **form** 1.

3. [To create]—*Syn.* score, fabricate, write (music), orchestrate, forge, discover, design, conceive, imagine, make up, poetize, turn out, draw up; *both* (D): write on, fudge together; see also **create** 2, **invent** 1, 2, **produce** 2.—*Ant.* blot out, cancel*, erase.

4. [To prepare for printing]—*Syn.* set (up), set type, cast, make up; see also **form** 1.—*Ant.* pie, distribute*, melt.

composed, *mod.* **1.** [Made]—*Syn.* written, created, authored, made (up) of, comprising, consisting of, compounded, constituted, formed, fashioned, formulated; see also **formed, written** 1.

2. [Calm]—*Syn.* poised, confident, self-assured, self-possessed, clearheaded, sensible, sure of oneself, relaxed, untroubled, determined, soothed, quieted, calmed, cool (D); see also **calm** 1, **confident** 2.

compose oneself, *v.* —*Syn.* control *or* calm oneself, get organized, collect one's wits; see **calm down, quiet** 1.

composer, *n.* —*Syn.* arranger, song-writer, musical author; see **author** 2, **musician, poet, writer.**

Major composers include the following—Giovanni Palestrina, Claudio Monteverdi, Georg Telemann, Antonio Vivaldi, Johann Sebastian Bach, George Frederick Handel, Franz Joseph Haydn, Wolfgang Amadeus Mozart, Ludwig van Beethoven, Franz Schubert, Johannes Brahms, Felix Mendelssohn, Robert Schumann, Frédéric Chopin, Franz Liszt, Georges Bizet, Hector Berlioz, Peter Ilyich Tchaikovsky, Giuseppe Verdi, Richard Wagner, Antonin Dvořák, Gustav Mahler, Richard Strauss, Modest Mussorgsky, Nicolas Rimsky-Korsakov, Giacomo Puccini, Jean Sibelius, Claude Debussy, Arthur S. Sullivan, Maurice Ravel, Camille Saint-Saëns, Béla Bartók, Sergei Prokofiev, Dmitri Shostakovich, Ralph Vaughan Williams, George Gershwin, Igor Stravinsky, Arnold Schoenberg, Paul Hindemith, Aaron Copland, Benjamin Britten.

composition, *n.* **1.** [The act of arranging for effect] —*Syn.* combination, distribution, relation; see **organization** 1, 2.

2. [Arrangement]—*Syn.* symmetry, proportion, balance, harmony, style, concord, agreement, consonance, form, beauty, proportion of line and mass, spacing, placing, rhythm; see also **consistency** 1, **form** 1, **harmony** 1.

3. [The act of producing creative work]—*Syn.* creation, making, fashioning, formation, conception, presentation, forging, shaping, sculpturing, invention, designing, planning, bringing into existence; see also **discovery** 1, **production** 1, **writing** 1, 3.

4. [A written work]—*Syn.* romance, fiction, novel, tale, short story, essay, play, drama, verse, stanza, symphony, concerto, quartet, song, rhapsody, melody; see also **biography, creation** 3, **exposition** 2, **literature** 2, **music** 1, **poetry, writing** 2.

compositor, *n.* —*Syn.* printer, make-up man, typesetter, ad dispatcher, linotype operator; *all* (D): compo, galley slave, floorman; see also **printer.**

compost, *n.* **1.** [A fertilizing mixture]—*Syn.* manure, ordure, compost pit *or* pile; see **fertilizer.**

2. [A mixture]—*Syn.* compound, composition, blend; see **mixture** 1.

composure, *n.* —*Syn.* serenity, peace of mind, calm, calmness, placidity, collectedness, repose, self-possession, nonchalance, cool-headedness, control, self-control, balance, contentment, tranquility, stability, harmony, concord, assurance, self-assurance, imperturbability, poise, serene state of mind, inexcitability, dispassion, even temper, tranquil mind, equanimity, coolness, level-headedness, *sangfroid* (French), fortitude, moderation, self-command, gravity, sobriety, a cool head, presence of mind, equilibrium, aplomb, self-restraint, quiescence, imperturbation, ease, evenness, complacence, staidness, tolerance, content, quiet, quietude, command of one's faculties, stoicism, forbearance; *all* (D): cool, unflappability, the even tenor of one's ways; see also **dignity** 1, **patience** 1, **peace** 3, **restraint** 1.—*Ant.* exuberance, passion*, wildness.

compound, *mod.* —*Syn.* mixed, combined, complicated; see **complex** 1, **difficult** 2.

compound, *n.* —*Syn.* composite, union, aggregate; see **mixture** 1.

compound, *v.* **1.** [To blend]—*Syn.* combine, coalesce, unite; see **join** 1, **mix** 1.

2. [To complicate]—*Syn.* make complex *or* intricate, intensify, confound; see **complicate, confuse.**

comprehend, *v.* **1.** [To include]—*Syn.* contain, comprise, embrace; see **include** 1, **involve.**

2. [To understand]—*Syn.* grasp, discern, perceive; see **know** 1, **understand** 1.

comprehensible, *mod.* —*Syn.* intelligible, plain, explicit; see **understandable.**

comprehension, *n.* **1.** [Capacity to understand] —*Syn.* understanding, perception, cognizance; see **awareness, knowledge** 1.

2. [An including]—*Syn.* incorporation, circumscription, embodiment; see **inclusion.**

comprehensive, *mod.* —*Syn.* inclusive, extensive, wide, compendious, synoptic, sweeping, widespread, far-reaching, comprising, encircling, containing, all-embracing, all-inclusive, complete, discursive, encyclopedic, of great scope, expansive, over-all, blanket (D); see also **absolute** 1, **full** 3, **general** 1, **infinite** 1, **large** 1, **whole** 1.

compress, *v.* —*Syn.* condense, compact, press together, consolidate, squeeze (together), tighten, cramp, contract, crowd, force into a smaller space, constrict, abbreviate, shrivel, make brief, reduce, dehydrate, pack, shorten, shrink, narrow, abridge, restrict in area, make terse, bind tightly, reduce volume by pressure, wrap closely, coagulate, abstract, summarize, epitomize, wedge; *all* (D): boildown, ram, stuff, cram; see also **concentrate** 1, **decrease** 2, **press** 1, **tighten** 1.—*Ant.* spread*, stretch, expand.

compression, *n.*—*Syn.* condensation, squeezing, confining; see **concentration** 1.

comprise, *v.*—*Syn.* comprehend, contain, embrace, include, involve, enclose, embody, encircle, encompass, sum up, cover, consist of *or* in, be composed *or* made up of, constitute, incorporate, infold, span, compass, hold, engross, take into account *or* consideration, subsume, be resolvable into, be contained in; *all* (D): add up to, amount to take in; see also **compose** 1, **include** 1.—*Ant.* need*, lack, exclude.

compromise, *n.* **1.** [The act of compromising] —*Syn.* bargaining, granting concessions, finding a middle course; see **agreement** 1.
2. [An action involving compromise, sense 1] —*Syn.* covenant, bargain, give and take (D); see **agreement** 3.

compromise, *v.* **1.** [Make concession]—*Syn.* agree, conciliate, find a middle ground, take to arbitration; see **negotiate** 1.
2. [Damage one's honor]—*Syn.* jeopardize, hazard, imperil; see **endanger, yield** 1.

comptroller, *n.*—*Syn.* controller, cashier, business manager; see **accountant, administrator.**

compulsion, *n.* **1.** [Obligation]—*Syn.* urgency, pressure, demand; see **duty** 1.
2. [Force]—*Syn.* drive, necessity, need; see **requirement** 2.
3. [An obsession]—*Syn.* preoccupation, prepossession, engrossment; see **obsession, requirement** 2.

compulsive, *mod.* **1.** [Obligatory]—*Syn.* compelling, compulsory, urgent; see **necessary** 1.
2. [Obsessive]—*Syn.* driving, impelling, besetting; see **enthusiastic** 2, 3, **passionate** 2.

compulsorily, *mod.*—*Syn.* forcibly, imperatively, by *or* with force; see also **urgently** 1, 2.

compulsory, *mod.*—*Syn.* obligatory, required, requisite; see **necessary** 1.

compunction, *n.* **1.** [A sense of guilt or remorse] —*Syn.* remorse, contrition, shame; see **guilt, regret** 1.
2. [A feeling of regret or pity]—*Syn.* misgiving, sympathy, qualm; see **pity** 1, **regret** 1.

compunctious, *mod.*—*Syn.* remorseful, contrite, penitent; see **sorry** 1.

computable, *mod.*—*Syn.* estimable, measurable, determinable; see **calculable.**

computation, *n.* **1.** [A computing]—*Syn.* counting, data processing, reckoning; see **calculation** 1, **guess.**
2. [Result of computing]—*Syn.* total, sum, figure; see **estimate** 1, **result.**

compute, *v.*—*Syn.* reckon, figure, measure; see **calculate** 1, **count, estimate** 3.

computer, *n.*—*Syn.* electronic *or* electric brain, electrocomputer, thinking machine, IBM (trademark), microcomputer, minicomputer, mainframe, personal computer, calculator, master control, high-speed data processor, electronic circuit, number cruncher (D), cybernetic organism, analog computer, digital computer.
Some computers include the following—Apple, Commodore, Atari, Compaq, IBM 701, 705, 709, 7090, 1401, 1620; Univac 1105, ERMA, ENIAD, OARAC, IDP, BINAC, IDA, MARK 1, ENVIAL; see also **machine** 1.

computerized, *mod.*—*Syn.* scientifically worked out, mechanically *or* electronically planned and/or processed, programmed, computed; see also **prepared** 2.

computer language, *n.*—*Syn.* macroinstruction system, machine language, programming language, artificial language, computer-processed instructions.
Some computer languages include the following —FORTRAN (Formula translation), COBOL (Common Business Oriented Language), MAD (Michigan Algorithmic Decoder), Jovial (Jule's own version of the International Algebraic Language), BASIC, SEPOL, LISP, APL, LISA, PASCAL, ACE, ACOM, ADAPT, NL-1, PL-1, TABSOL, SLIP, ALGOL, SNOBOL, SIMSCRIPT; see also **language** 1.

comrade, *n.*—*Syn.* confidant, confidante, intimate; see **associate, friend** 1.

con, *mod.*—*Syn.* conversely, opposed to, in opposition; see **against** 3.

con (D), *n.*—*Syn.* deception, dupe, cheat, swindle, fraud mockery, bluff; *all* (D): gyp, doublecross, take in, graft, gold brick; see also **trick** 1.

con (D), *v.*—*Syn.* cheat, dupe, mislead; see **deceive.**

con man (D), *n.*—*Syn.* confidence man, swindler, scamp; see **cheat** 1, **rascal.**

concatenation, *n.* **1.** [A linking together in a series] —*Syn.* connecting, uniting, linking; see **order** 3.
2. [A series of interconnected events]—*Syn.* succession, continuity, connection; see **chain** 1, **link, sequence, series.**

concave, *mod.*—*Syn.* curved, sunken, cupped; see **round** 3.

concavity, *n.*—*Syn.* depression, indentation, impression; see **hole** 2.

conceal, *v.*—*Syn.* screen, secrete, cover; see **hide** 1, 2.

concealed, *mod.*—*Syn.* covered, obscured, unseen; see **hidden** 2.

concealment, *n.* **1.** [Act of concealing]—*Syn.* hiding, covering, camouflage; see **disguise.**
2. [Hiding place]—*Syn.* ambush, haven, shield; see **shelter.**

concede, *v.*—*Syn.* yield, grant, acknowledge; see **admit** 2, 3, **allow** 1.

conceit, *n.*—*Syn.* vanity, self-admiration, narcissism; see **arrogance.**

conceited, *mod.*—*Syn.* vain, arrogant, stuck up (D); see **egotistic** 2.

conceivable, *mod.*—*Syn.* understandable, credible, believable; see **convincing** 2, **imaginable, likely** 1.

conceive, *v.* **1.** [To form a concept or image of] —*Syn.* consider, formulate, speculate; see **imagine** 1, **think** 1.
2. [To understand]—*Syn.* grasp, comprehend, perceive; see **understand** 1.

3. [To become pregnant]—*Syn.* become with child, superfetate, be impregnated, get in the family way (D).

concentrate, *v.* **1.** [To bring *or* come together] —*Syn.* amass, mass, assemble, combine, consolidate, compact, condense, reduce, eliminate, coalesce, hoard, garner, centralize, store, salt down *or* away, bring into a small compass, bring toward a central point, embody, localize, strengthen, bring to bear on one point, direct toward one object, constrict, fix, bring *or* draw to a common center *or* point of union, cramp, agglomerate, focus, reduce, aggregate, intensify, crowd *or* draw *or* flock together, contract, muster, bunch, heap up, swarm, forgather, conglomerate, stow away, congest, focalize, narrow, compress, converge, center, collect, cluster, congregate, huddle; see also **accumulate** 1, **gather** 1, **pack** 2, **unite** 1.—*Ant.* separate*, widen, extend.

2. [To employ all one's mental powers]—*Syn.* intensify, bring to bear, think intensely, give attention to, meditate (upon), ponder, focus attention on, fasten on, direct attention to one object, muse (over), weigh, consider closely, scrutinize, attend minutely, regard carefully, contemplate, ruminate, study deeply, peruse carefully, examine closely, brood over, put one's mind to, be engrossed in, attend, think about with absorption, give exclusive attention to, occupy the mind *or* thoughts with, fix one's attention, apply the mind, give (*or* pay) heed, focus (one's thought), give the mind to, direct the mind upon, center, think hard; *all* (D): rack one's brains, get on the beam, keep one's eye on the ball, knuckle *or* buckle down, apply the seat of one's pants to the chair; see also **analyze** 1, **examine** 1, **think** 1.—*Ant.* be inattentive, drift*, ignore.

concentrated, *mod.* **1.** [Undiluted]—*Syn.* rich, undiffused, unmixed, unadulterated, real, unmingled, straight; see also **strong** 8, **thick** 1, 3.—*Ant.* weak*, diffused, diluted.

2. [Intense]—*Syn.* intensive, deep, hard; see **intense.**

concentration, *n.* **1.** [The act of bringing together] —*Syn.* assembly, consolidation, unity, combination, massing, amassing, compression, coalescing, narrowing, compacting, converging, congregation, flocking, huddling, clustering, fixing, centering, focusing, intensification; see also **collection** 1. —*Ant.* dispersal, separation*, scattering.

2. [Anything brought together]—*Syn.* company, concourse, audience, miscellany, collectanea, band, party, flock, herd, mass, group, array; see also **army** 2, **collection** 2, **mob** 1.

3. [Attention]—*Syn.* close attention, concern, application; see **thought** 1.

4. [Density]—*Syn.* solidity, consistency, frequency; see **congestion, density** 1.

concept, *n.*—*Syn.* idea, theory, notion; see **thought** 2.

conception, *n.* **1.** [The act of conceiving mentally] —*Syn.* apprehension, comprehension, imagining, speculating, meditation, communing, bethinking, dreaming, cogitating, deliberating, fancying, concentrating, meditating, philosophizing, realization, consideration, considering, musing, speculation, envisaging, understanding, cognition, perception, mental grasp, apperception, forming *or* formulation of an idea *or* principle *or* mental image; see also **thought** 1.

2. [The act of conceiving physically]—*Syn.* inception, impregnation, insemination; see **fertilization** 2.

3. [A mental image]—*Syn.* representation, impression, fancy; see **thought** 2.

4. [An interpretation]—*Syn.* version, explanation, exposition; see **interpretation** 2.

conceptualize, *v.*—*Syn.* form a concept of, develop a thought, visualize mentally; see **imagine** 1.

concern, *n.* **1.** [Affair]—*Syn.* business, matter, interest; see **affair** 1.

2. [Regard]—*Syn.* attention, interest, solicitude; see **care** 2.

3. [A business]—*Syn.* firm, company, business establishment; see **business** 4.

concern, *v.* **1.** [To have reference to]—*Syn.* refer *or* pertain *or* appertain *or* relate *or* be related *or* be pertinent *or* have relation to, have significance for, bear on *or* upon, regard, be concerned *or* connected with, be about, have to do with, be a matter of concern to, have a bearing on, have connections with, be applicable to, depend upon, be dependent upon, be interdependent with, stand in relationship to, have interrelationship with, answer to, deal with, belong to, have implications for, be well taken; *both* (D): touch upon, figure in; see also **influence, treat** 1, 2.

2. [Concern oneself]—*Syn.* be concerned, become involved, take pains; see **bother** 1, **care, worry** 2.

as concerns—*Syn.* regarding, concerning, with *or* in reference to; see **about** 2.

concerning, *mod.*—*Syn.* respecting, touching, regarding; see **about** 2.

concert, *n.* **1.** [Agreement]—*Syn.* harmony, accord, concord; see **agreement** 2, **unity** 3.

2. [Musical entertainment]—*Syn.* (musical) selections, musicale, recital; see **performance** 2, **show** 2.

concerted, *mod.*—*Syn.* combined, mutual, joint; see **united** 2.

concession, *n.* **1.** [A conceding]—*Syn.* granting, giving in, yielding; see **admission** 4.

2. [A privilege granted by a government]—*Syn.* permit, authorization, warrant; see **grant, permission.**

conciliate, *v.*—*Syn.* placate, appease, pacify; see **satisfy** 1, 3.

conciliatory, *mod.*—*Syn.* civil, agreeable, compatible; see **harmonious** 2.

concise, *mod.*—*Syn.* succinct, brief, condensed; see **short** 1.

conclave, *n.*—*Syn.* conference, parley, meeting; see **gathering.**

conclude, *v.* **1.** [To finish]—*Syn.* terminate, bring to an end, complete; see **achieve** 1.

2. [To come to an end]—*Syn.* cease, end, desist; see **stop** 2.

3. [To determine]—*Syn.* resolve, confirm, settle; see **decide.**

4. [To deduce]—*Syn.* presume, reason, gather; see **assume** 1, **infer** 1.

concluded, *mod.*—*Syn.* closed, terminated, ended; see **finished** 1.

conclusion, *n.* **1.** [An end]—*Syn.* finish, termination, completion; see **end** 2.
2. [A decision]—*Syn.* determination, resolve, resolution; see **judgment** 3.
in conclusion—*Syn.* lastly, in closing, in the end; see **finally** 1.

conclusive, *mod.* —*Syn.* final, decisive, deciding, definitive, unquestionable, unmistakable, convincing, demonstrative, resolving, indisputable, determinative, settling, unconditional, undeniable, unanswerable, irrevocable, absolute, determining, telling, revealing; see also **certain** 3.

concoct, *v.* **1.** [To make by combining ingredients] —*Syn.* compound, prepare, formulate; see **cook.**
2. [To make up]—*Syn.* devise, plan, create, scheme; see **invent** 1, **plan** 1.

concoction, *n.* **1.** [Mixture]—*Syn.* brew, blend, solution; see **mixture** 1.
2. [Plan]—*Syn.* scheme, intention, project; see **plan** 2.

concomitant, *mod.* —*Syn.* accompanying, attendant, connected, coactive, co-ordinate, associated with, coupled with, contemporaneous, joint, concurrent, conjoined with, fellow, collateral, coefficient, attending, conjoined, corollary, belonging, agreeing, coincident, synchronal, coterminous, accessory, concordant, synchronous, contemporary, coexistent, coetaneous, synergistic, in time, isochronous, twin, in tempo, constantaneous, synergetic, coeval, isochronal; see also **simultaneous.**

concord, *n.* **1.** [Unity of feeling]—*Syn.* harmony, consensus, accord; see **agreement** 2, **unity** 1.
2. [A treaty]—*Syn.* compact, contract, pact; see **agreement** 3, **treaty.**

concourse, *n.* **1.** [A crowd]—*Syn.* gang, assembly, throng; see **crowd** 1, **gathering, mob** 1.
2. [A thoroughfare]—*Syn.* highway, avenue, boulevard; see **path** 1, **road** 1.

concrete, *mod.* **1.** [Specific]—*Syn.* particular, solid, precise; see **accurate** 1, **definite** 1, **detailed, real** 2.
2. [Made of concrete]—*Syn.* cement, monolithic, poured, solid, strong, precast, concrete and steel, compact, unyielding; see also **firm** 2.

concrete, *n.* —*Syn.* concretion, ferroconcrete, reinforced concrete; see **cement, pavement** 1.

concretion, *n.* —*Syn.* crystallization, fusion, consolidation; see **coagulation, concentration** 1, **solidification** 1.

concubine, *n.* —*Syn.* harlot, courtesan, kept woman; see **mistress** 2, **prostitute.**

concupiscence, *n.* —*Syn.* lust, lechery, depravity; see **desire** 3.

concupiscent, *mod.* —*Syn.* desirous, lustful, carnal; see **sensual, voluptuous** 2.

concur, *v.* —*Syn.* accord, be consonant with, be in harmony (with); see **agree, approve** 1, **equal.**

concurrent, *mod.* **1.** [Occurring at the same time] —*Syn.* synchronal, parallel, coexisting; see **simultaneous.**
2. [Meeting at the same point]—*Syn.* converging, coinciding, coterminous, convergent, meeting, uniting, confluent, centrolineal; see also **joined.**
3. [Acting together]—*Syn.* co-operating, allied, mutual; see **alike** 2, **jointly, related** 2.
4. [In agreement]—*Syn.* unified, agreeing, concerted; see **co-operative** 2, **harmonious** 2, **unanimous.**

concussion, *n.* **1.** [A blow]—*Syn.* hit, punch, impact; see **blow** 1.
2. [The result of a blow]—*Syn.* rupture, gash, crack; see **fracture** 3, **injury** 1.

condemn, *v.* **1.** [To send to punishment]—*Syn.* doom, sentence, damn, adjudge, proscribe, pass sentence on, find guilty, utter judicial sentence against, seal the doom of, reprobate, pronounce, judgment, prescribe punishment; see also **convict, punish.**—*Ant.* acquit, excuse*, exonerate.
2. [To blame]—*Syn.* judge, rebuke, reprove; see **censure, denounce.**

condemnation, *n.* —*Syn.* denunciation, disapprobation, reproach; see **accusation** 2, **blame** 1, **objection** 2.

condemnatory, *mod.* —*Syn.* condemning, disapproving, censorious; see **critical** 2.

condensation, *n.* **1.** [The act of condensing]—*Syn.* compression, consolidation, crystallization; see **concentration** 1.
2. [A condensed state or form]—*Syn.* reduction, contraction, synopsis; see **abbreviation** 1, **essence** 1, **summary.**

condense, *v.* **1.** [To compress]—*Syn.* press together, constrict, consolidate; see **compress, contract** 1, 2, **decrease** 1, 2.
2. [To abridge]—*Syn.* abbreviate, summarize, digest; see **contract** 2, **decrease** 2.

condensed, *mod.* **1.** [Shortened]—*Syn.* concise, brief, succinct; see **short** 2, **terse.**
2. [Compressed]—*Syn.* hardened, dense, solidified; see **firm** 2, **thick** 1.
3. [Concentrated]—*Syn.* undiluted, rich, evaporated; see **concentrated** 1, **thick** 3.

condescend, *v.* —*Syn.* vouchsafe, stoop, lower oneself, agree, humble *or* degrade *or* demean oneself, submit with good grace, assume a patronizing air, lower one's tone, graciously stoop, accommodate oneself to an inferior, descend, waive a privilege, comply, oblige, acquiesce, favor, concede, grant, accord, deign, unbend, accommodate to; *all* (D): come down off one's high horse, come down a peg, yield the palm, sing small; see also **patronize** 2.

condescending, *mod.* —*Syn.* patronizing, complaisant, superior; see **egotistic** 2.

condescension, *n.* —*Syn.* deference, toleration, civility; see **patronage** 3.

condiment, *n.* —*Syn.* seasoning, vinegar, salt; see **flavoring, herb, pickle** 2, **relish** 1, **spice.**

condition, *n.* **1.** [A state]—*Syn.* situation, position, status; see **state** 2.
2. [A requisite]—*Syn.* stipulation, contingency, provision; see **requirement** 1.
3. [A limitation]—*Syn.* restriction, qualification, prohibition; see **limitation** 2, **restraint** 2.
4. [State of health]—*Syn.* physical state, fitness, lack of fitness, tone, form, trim, shape (D); see also **health.**
5. [(D) Illness]—*Syn.* ailment, infirmity, temper; see **disease** 1, 2.

condition, *v.* —*Syn.* adapt, modify, work out (D); see **practice** 1, **train** 3, 4.

conditional, *mod.*—*Syn.* provisional, provisory, conditioned, subject, modified by conditions, contingent, qualified, tentative, limited, restricted, relying on, subject to, restrictive, guarded, not absolute, granted on certain terms; see also **dependent** 3.

conditionally, *mod.*—*Syn.* provisory, provisionary, hypothetically, with the condition *or* stipulation (that), with reservations *or* limitations, tentatively, possibly; see also **temporarily.**

conditioned, *mod.*—*Syn.* altered, disciplined, modified; see **trained.**

conditions, *n.*—*Syn.* environment, surrounding(s), setting; see **circumstances** 2.

condole, *v.*—*Syn.* sympathize, console, soothe; see **comfort** 1, **pity** 1.

condolence, *n.*—*Syn.* sympathy, comfort, solace; see **pity** 1.

condominium, *n.* **1.** [Co-operative apartment dwelling]—*Syn.* commonly owned apartment house, jointly owned dwelling, *both* (D): condo, co-op; see also **apartment house, home** 1.
2. [Joint dominion]—*Syn.* common ownership, joint sovereignty, co-operative jurisdiction; see **administration** 1, **dominion** 1, **government** 1, **jurisdiction, ownership.**

condone, *v.*—*Syn.* pardon, excuse, overlook; see **approve** 1.

condoning, *mod.*—*Syn.* approving, tolerating, indulgent; see **humane** 1, **kind** 1, **lenient.**

conducive, *mod.*—*Syn.* accessory, contributive, useful; see **helpful** 1.

conduct, *n.* **1.** [Behavior]—*Syn.* deportment, demeanor, manner; see **behavior** 1.
2. [Management]—*Syn.* guidance, regulation, government, care, charge, direction, treatment, carrying on, transaction, superintendence, oversight, posture, control, handling, wielding, rule, manipulation, strategy, policy, execution, tactics, supervision, regimen, plan, organization; see also **administration** 1.

conduct, *v.* **1.** [To guide]—*Syn.* escort, convoy, attend; see **accompany** 1, **lead** 1.
2. [To manage]—*Syn.* administer, handle, carry on; see **manage** 1.
3. [To transmit]—*Syn.* convey, pass on, transfer; see **carry** 1, 2, **send** 1, 2, 4.

conduct (oneself), *v.*—*Syn.* comport oneself, act properly, acquit oneself well; see **behave** 2.

conductor, *n.* **1.** [That which conducts]—*Syn.* conduit, conveyor, transmitter; see **channel** 1, **wire** 1, **wiring** 2, 3.
2. [One who conducts]—*Syn.* orchestra leader, pilot, head; see **administrator, guide** 1, **leader** 3.
3. [One in charge of a car or train]—*Syn.* trainman, railroad man, ticket taker, brakeman, streetcar conductor, motorman, bus driver, guard (D); see also **driver, engineer** 2.

conduit, *n.*—*Syn.* flume, canal, pipe, tube, conductor, cable, flow area, culvert, lead-in, lead-out, aqueduct, pipe for conveying water, spout, trough, gully, gutter, sewer, watercourse, main, cloaca, race, drain, natural passage; see also **channel** 1.

cone, *mod.*—*Syn.* conoid, conoidal, tapering; see **conical.**

cone, *n.* **1.** [A conical object]—*Syn.* conoid, cone-shaped *or* conoidal area *or* surface, strobiloid; see **figure** 3.
Cones include the following—(right) circular, chief, stepped, supplemental, oblique, retinal, endostylic, pyrometric, crystalline; cone of spread *or* dispersion.
2. [A loudspeaker]—*Syn.* cone speaker, electrodynamic speaker, amplifier; see **loudspeaker.**
3. [A fruit- or flower-bearing cluster]—*Syn.* strobile, fruit of the Coniferae *or* Coniferales, raceme; see **flower** 1, **seed,** 1, 2.

confection, *n.*—*Syn.* sweet, jam, dainty; see **cake** 2, **candy, pastry.**

confectionery, *n.*—*Syn.* ice-cream parlor, candy store *or* shop, (carnival *or* midway) concession; see **store** 1.

Confederacy, *n.*—*Syn.* Confederate States of America, secessionists, rebel states, American Confederacy, Southern Confederacy, Southern aristocracy, the South; *both* (D): Dixie, the Rebs; see also **south** 2.

confederacy, *n.*—*Syn.* a loose union, confederation, federation; see **government** 1, 2, **organization** 3.

Confederate, *mod.*—*Syn.* secessionist, Rebel, Southern, slave, slaveholding, south of the Mason Dixon line.

Confederate, *n.*—*Syn.* Southerner, secessionist, one of the Gray, Johnny Reb (D); see also **rebel** 1.

confederate, *mod.*—*Syn.* federated, combined, confederated, federate, in alliance, incorporated, corporate, united in federal compact, federal, unionized, syndicated, amalgamated, leagued, allied, associated, organized, in league; see also **joined, united** 2.

confer, *v.* **1.** [To grant as a gift]—*Syn.* bestow, award, present; see **give** 1.
2. [To hold a conference]—*Syn.* converse, deliberate, parley; see **discuss.**

conference, *n.* **1.** [A meeting for discussion]—*Syn.* conversation, discussion, interchange; see **gathering.**
2. [A consultation]—*Syn.* interview, appointment, conferring; see **discussion** 1.
3. [An association of athletic teams]—*Syn.* league, circuit, ring; see **organization** 3.

conferring, *mod.*—*Syn.* holding a conference, discussing, deliberating, counseling, comparing opinions, conversing, in conference *or* conclave *or* consultation; see also **talking.**

confess, *v.* **1.** [To admit]—*Syn.* acknowledge, own, concede; see **admit** 3.
2. [To recount one's evil actions]—*Syn.* relate, narrate, level with (D); see **admit** 2.
3. [To participate in the sacrament of confession]—*Syn.* go to confession, be shriven, confess to the priest, receive absolution, humble oneself, go as a communicant, stand confessed as, make (a clean) confession; see also **admit** 2.—*Ant.* withhold, hide*, conceal.
4. [To profess]—*Syn.* announce, state, avow; see **declare** 1.

confession, *n.* **1.** [The act of confessing]—*Syn.* concession, allowance, assenting, owning to *or* up, revelation, revealing, disclosure, disclosing, divul-

gence, publication, affirmation, assertion, unbosoming, utterance, vent, declaration, telling, relation, avowal, exposure, revelation, recitation, narration, exposé, acknowledgment of guilt, avowal of error, admission (of fault), enumeration, proclamation, making public; see also **acknowledgment** 1.—*Ant.* concealment, denial*, disclaimer.
2. [That which has been confessed]—*Syn.* statement, disclosure, profession; see **admission 4, declaration** 1.
3. [A sacrament]—*Syn.* absolution, contrition, repentance; see **penance** 2, **sacrament.**

confessional, *n.*—*Syn.* confessionary, confession booth *or* chair, shriving pew; see also **booth.**

confessor, *n.* **1.** [A priest who hears confessions]—*Syn.* priest, spiritual judge, penitentiary; see **adviser, priest.**
2. [One who professes his faith in spite of persecution]—*Syn.* martyr, true believer, saint; see **believer, victim** 1.

confidant, *n.*—*Syn.* adherent, intimate associate, companion; see **adviser, friend** 1.

confide, *v.* **1.** [To reveal in trust]—*Syn.* disclose, admit, divulge; see **reveal** 1, **tell** 1.
2. [To commit to the charge of]—*Syn.* consign, charge, entrust; see **delegate** 1, 2, **trust** 3.

confidence, *n.* **1.** [Faith]—*Syn.* reliance, trust, assurance; see **faith** 1.
2. [Self-assurance]—*Syn.* self-confidence, self-reliance, morale, fearlessness, boldness, hardihood, resolution, firmness, stoutheartedness, intrepidity, sureness, faith in oneself, tenacity, mettle, fortitude, *élan* (French), aplomb, certainty, resoluteness, daring, spirit, reliance, manliness; *all* (D): pluck, dash, grit, cool, heart, sand, backbone, nerve, spunk; see also **courage** 1, **determination** 2.
3. [A secret]—*Syn.* private *or* personal matter, privileged communication, confidential information; see **secret.**

confidence man, *n.*—*Syn.* cheat, fraud, con man (D); see **impostor.**

confident, *mod.* **1.** [Certain]—*Syn.* positive, sure, convinced; see **certain** 3.
2. [Self-assured]—*Syn.* self-confident, self-reliant, assured, having no misgivings, being certain, fearless, having faith in, sure of oneself, dauntless, self-sufficient; see also **able** 1, 2, **certain** 1.
3. [Trusting]—*Syn.* bold, presumptuous, hopeful, presuming, expecting, expectant, depending *or* counting *or* relying on; see also **trusting** 2.

confidential, *mod.*—*Syn.* classified, intimate, privy; see **private, secret** 1, 3.

confidentially, *mod.*—*Syn.* privately, personally, in confidence; see **secretly.**

confidently, *mod.*—*Syn.* in an assured manner *or* way, with *or* having conviction, assuredly; see **boldly** 1, **positively** 1.

configuration, *n.*—*Syn.* contour, outline, shape; see **form** 1.

confine, *v.* **1.** [To restrain]—*Syn.* repress, hold back, keep within limits; see **hinder, restrain** 1.
2. [To imprison]—*Syn.* cage, incarcerate, shut up; see **enslave, imprison.**
3. [To restrict]—*Syn.* limit, shorten, circumscribe; see **hinder, restrict.**
4. [To set limits]—*Syn.* limit, bound, fix; see **define** 1.

confined, *mod.* **1.** [Restricted]—*Syn.* limited, hampered, compassed; see **bound** 1, 2, **restrained, restricted.**
2. [Bedridden]—*Syn.* indisposed, keeping to the house, bedfast, on one's back, invalided, ill; *both* (D): laid up, flattened out; see also **sick.**
3. [In prison]—*Syn.* behind bars, locked up, sealed up, in bonds *or* irons *or* chains, in jail, imprisoned, jailed, held in custody, cooped up, immured, incarcerated, detained, under lock and key, on ice (D).—*Ant.* free*, released, at liberty.

confinement, *n.* **1.** [The state of being confined]—*Syn.* restriction, limitation, circumscription, constraint, repression, control, coercion, keeping, safekeeping, custody, curb, bounding, bounds, trammels, check, closeness, bonds, detention, imprisonment, incarceration, immuration; see also **jail, restraint** 2.—*Ant.* freedom*, release, independence.
2. [The period that accompanies childbirth]—*Syn.* lying-in, accouchement, childbed, delivery, parturition, childbirth, travail, labor, (one's) time (D); see also **childbirth, delivery** 3.

confines, *n.* **1.** [Borders]—*Syn.* bounds, limits, periphery; see **boundary.**
2. [Scope]—*Syn.* proportions, range, dimension; see **size** 2.
3. [Territory]—*Syn.* region, country, terrain; see **land** 1, **territory** 2.

confining, *mod.*—*Syn.* limiting, restricting, bounding, circumscribing, compassing, prescribing, restraining, hampering, repressing, trammeling, checking, enclosing, imprisoning, immuring, incarcerating, detaining, keeping locked up, keeping behind bars.—*Ant.* delimiting, infinite*, boundless.

confining, *n.*—*Syn.* restricting, enclosing, restraining, bounding, detaining, imprisoning.

confirm, *v.* **1.** [To strengthen]—*Syn.* make firm, invigorate, fortify; see **strengthen.**
2. [To ratify]—*Syn.* sanction, affirm, settle; see **approve** 1, **endorse** 2.
3. [To prove]—*Syn.* verify, authenticate, validate; see **explain, prove.**

confirmation, *n.* **1.** [The act of confirming]—*Syn.* ratification, proving, authenticating, authentication, corroborating, corroboration, support, supporting, endorsement, sanction, sanctioning, authorizing, authorization, verifying, verification, substantiation, affirming, affirmation, accepting, acceptance, passing, passage, validating, validation, approval, attestation, assent, accord, avowal, admission, recognition, witness, visa, nod, consent, testimony, agreement, evidence, corroborative statement; see also **agreement** 1, 3, **proof** 1.—*Ant.* annulment, cancellation*, disapproval.
2. [A sacrament]—*Syn.* rite, consecration, liturgy; see **ceremony** 2, **sacrament.**

confirmatory, *mod.*—*Syn.* corroborative, agreeing, acquiescent; see **affirmative.**

confirmed, *mod.* **1.** [Firmly established]—*Syn.* proved, valid, accepted; see **certain** 3, **established** 3, **guaranteed.**
2. [Inveterate]—*Syn.* ingrained, seasoned, regular; see **chronic, habitual** 1.

confiscate, *v.* —*Syn.* appropriate, impound, usurp; see **seize** 2, **steal.**

conflagration, *n.* —*Syn.* blaze, bonfire, holocaust; see **fire** 1.

conflict, *n.* **1.** [A fight]—*Syn.* struggle, strife, engagement; see **battle** 1, 2, **fight** 1.
2. [Mutual animosity]—*Syn.* strife, contest, contention; see **disagreement** 1, **dispute** 1.

conflict, *v.* —*Syn.* clash, contrast, contend; see **differ** 1, **fight** 2, **oppose** 1, 2.

conflicting, *mod.* —*Syn.* clashing, contrary, opposing, contradictory, adverse, unfavorable; see also **unfavorable** 2.

confluence, *n.* **1.** [Flowing together]—*Syn.* junction, conflux, convergence; see **meeting** 1.
2. [A flocking together]—*Syn.* crowd, concourse, assembly; see **gathering.**

confluent, *mod.* —*Syn.* meeting, joining, flowing, mingling, concurrent, coalescent, growing *or* coming together, convergent; see also **concurrent** 2, **connecting.**

conform, *v.* —*Syn.* comply, accord, acquiesce, submit, accommodate, live up to, fit, suit, acclimate, conventionalize, accustom, be regular, acclimatize, harmonize, adapt (oneself), be guided by, fit the pattern, be in fashion *or* the mode, reconcile, settle (down), obey (rules), grow used to, reconcile with, do as others do, get in line, keep in countenance *or* formation, fall in with, go by, adhere *or* adjust *or* keep *or* assimilate to, keep up; *all* (D): get one's bearings, keep up with the Joneses, chime in with, join the parade, play the game, gear to, go according to Hoyle, follow the beaten path, toe the mark, follow suit, run with the pack, swim with the stream, follow the crowd, travel in a rut, do in Rome as Romans do; see also **agree, follow** 2, **obey** 2, **settle** 8.—*Ant.* conflict, differ*, disagree.

conformable, *mod.* **1.** [Alike]—*Syn.* resembling, similar, comparable; see **alike** 2, **like.**
2. [In agreement]—*Syn.* unified, consistent, suitable; see **harmonious** 2.
3. [Obedient]—*Syn.* amenable, submissive, agreeable; see **docile, obedient** 1.

conformation, *n.* **1.** [Agreement]—*Syn.* compliance, conformity, concord, unison, harmony, affinity, congruity, compatibility, synchronism, adaptation, accordance; see also **agreement** 1, 2.
2. [Shape]—*Syn.* structure, formation, symmetry; see also **form** 1.

conforming, *mod.* —*Syn.* agreeing, in line with, in agreement *or* conformity; see **harmonious** 2.

conformist, *mod.* —*Syn.* conforming, conventionalist, congruous; see **harmonious** 2.

conformist, *n.* —*Syn.* conformer, conventionalist, advocate; see **follower.**

conformity, *n.* **1.** [Similarity]—*Syn.* congruity, correspondence, resemblance; see **similarity.**
2. [Obedience]—*Syn.* willingness, submission, compliance; see **docility.**

conform to, *v.* —*Syn.* correspond, parallel, fit; see **agree, compare** 1.

confound, *v.* **1.** [To mix]—*Syn.* jumble, commingle, blend; see **entangle, mix** 1.
2. [To confuse]—*Syn.* puzzle, perplex, bewilder; see **confuse, confute.**

confounded, *mod.* —*Syn.* confused, bewildered, disconcerted; see **doubtful** 2.

confront, *v.* —*Syn.* brave, defy, repel; see **dare** 2, **face** 1.

confrontation, *n.* —*Syn.* meeting, battle, strife; see **dispute** 1, **fight** 1.

confronting, *mod.* —*Syn.* facing, face to face, meeting, encountering, in the teeth *or* face of (D); see also **opposing** 1, **rebellious** 1.

confuse, *v.* —*Syn.* disconcert, abash, confound, fluster, discompose, flurry, upset, befuddle, mislead, misinform, puzzle, perplex, bewilder, embarrass, daze, astonish, disarrange, disorder, jumble, blend, mix, mingle, cloud, becloud, fog, stir up, agitate, bedevil, amaze, worry, trouble, snarl, unsettle, muddle, clutter, darken, addle, discomfit, fuddle, nonplus, complicate, involve, rattle, derange, baffle, frustrate, perturb, dismay, distract, entangle, encumber, befog, obscure, obfuscate, mystify, addle the wits, embroil, render uncertain; *all* (D): make a harsh *or* mess of (it), throw off (the scent), fuss up, unhinge, cross *or* foul *or* mix *or* ball up, put at a loss, lead astray, faze, stump, rattle, make the fur fly, make one's head swim; see also **bother** 2, **confute, disturb** 2, **hide** 1, **tangle.**—*Ant.* clear*, clarify, untangle.

confused, *mod.* **1.** [Puzzled in mind]—*Syn.* disconcerted, abashed, perplexed; see **doubtful** 2.
2. [Not properly distinguished]—*Syn.* mistaken, jumbled, snarled, deranged, bewildered, out of order, embroiled, disarrayed, confounded, mixed (up), chaotic, disordered, muddled, fuddled, befuddled, miscellaneous, inextricable, slovenly, untidy, messy, addled, misapprehended, involved, miscalculated, misunderstood, blurred, mazy, mazed, obscured; *all* (D): topsy-turvy, higgledy-piggledy, balled *or* fouled *or* screwed up, in a mess, haywire, snafu; see also **obscure** 1, **tangled.**—*Ant.* discriminated, distinguished*, ordered.

confusing, *mod.* —*Syn.* disconcerting, abashing, confounding, baffling, discomposing, puzzling, disturbing, unsettling, upsetting, embarrassing, discomfiting, agitating, obscuring, blurring, fuddling, befuddling, addling, tangling, snarling, cluttering, muddling, disarranging; see also **difficult** 2, **obscure** 1.—*Ant.* reassuring, orderly*, clear.

confusion, *n.* **1.** [The act of confusing]—*Syn.* upsetting, disturbing, embarrassing, discomfiting, abashing, agitating, addling, fuddling, miscalculation, miscalculating, obscuring, befuddling, blurring, tangling, mixing, cluttering, disarranging, unsettling, dumbfounding, confounding, perplexing, demoralization, stirring up, snarling, embroiling, misconceiving.—*Ant.* straightening, order*, arranging.
2. [A confused state]—*Syn.* lack of clearness *or* distinction, disarray, dislocation, anarchy, complication, intricacy, mess, untidiness, complexity, labyrinth, wilderness, discomfiture, difficulty, mistake, stupefaction, bewilderment, turmoil, tumult, pandemonium, commotion, stir, ferment, imbroglio, convulsion, bustle, trouble, row, riot, uproar, fracas, distraction, abashment, agitation, discomposure, emotional upset, daze, astonishment, surprise, fog, haze, perturbation, mystification, consternation, racket, ado, perplexity, disarrangement, misman-

agement, befuddlement, excitement, hysteria, disharmony, chaos, turbulence, dismay, uncertainty, irregularity, maze, quandary, interruption, cessation, stoppage, clutter, entanglement, backlash, clog, break, breakdown, knot, obstruction, trauma, congestion, interference, nervousness, disorganization, melee, muddle, mass, Gordian knot, lump, derangement, snarl, snag, farrago; *all* (D): jungle, to-do, hurly-burly, hubbub, tie-up, blur, shutdown, jumble, bungle, botch, rumpus, scramble, shuffle, mess, hodgepodge, stew, going round and round, muss, jam, fix, pretty mess, pretty pickle, bull in a china shop; see also **disorder** 2, **disturbance** 2, **embarrassment** 1.—*Ant.* quiet*, calm, order.

covered with confusion—*Syn.* confused, embarrassed, bewildered; see **doubtful.**

confute, *v.* —*Syn.* disprove, confound, dismay, defeat, overwhelm, overcome, silence, expose, bring to naught, rebut, controvert, parry, negate, vanquish, demolish, invalidate, answer conclusively, overturn, prove to be wrong, set aside, overcome in debate, upset, subvert, quash, oppugn, contradict; *all* (D): show up, clinch an argument, get the better of, shut up, not leave a leg to stand on, cut the ground from under one's feet, put down; see also **deny** 1, **oppose** 1, **refute.**—*Ant.* prove, verify*, confirm.

congeal, *v.* **1.** [To solidify as by freezing or curdling] —*Syn.* set, refrigerate, solidify; see **freeze** 1, **harden** 1, 2.

2. [To clot]—*Syn.* solidify, gell, coagulate; see **harden** 1, 2, **thicken** 1.

congenial, *mod.* **1.** [Agreeable]—*Syn.* kindred, compatible, suitable; see **friendly, harmonious** 2.

2. [Favorable]—*Syn.* agreeable, delightful, genial; see **pleasant** 1, 2.

congenital, *mod.* —*Syn.* latent, innate, intrinsic; see **fundamental** 1, **inherent, natural** 1.

congeries, *n.* —*Syn.* pile, accumulation, mass; see **bunch** 1, **collection** 2, **heap.**

congestion, *n.* —*Syn.* profusion, crowdedness, slum housing *or* conditions, overpopulation, ghetto conditions, press, traffic (jam), overcrowding, overdevelopment, too many people *or* things, too much *or* many, excessive concentration, surplus; see also **excess** 1.

conglomerate, *mod.* —*Syn.* blended, variegated, heterogeneous; see **complex** 1, **different** 2, **mixed** 1.

congratulate, *v.* —*Syn.* felicitate, wish joy to, toast; see **compliment** 1, **praise** 2, **salute** 2.

congratulation, *n.* —*Syn.* salute, best wishes, well-wishing; see **compliment, praise** 2.

congratulations, *interj.* —*Syn.* best wishes, compliments, hail, good going, good work, bully for you; hear, hear; bless you; see also **compliment, toast** 1.

congratulatory, *mod.* —*Syn.* congratulant, flattering, laudatory; see **complimentary.**

congregate, *v.* —*Syn.* convene, meet, converge; see **gather** 1.

congregation, *n.* —*Syn.* meeting, group, assemblage; see **gathering**

congress, *n.* [*Often capital C*]—*Syn.* parliament, deliberative assembly, legislative body; see **committee, government** 2, **legislature.**

congruent, *mod.* —*Syn.* in agreement, harmonious, corresponding; see **harmonious** 2.

congruous, *mod.* —*Syn.* suitable, appropriate, fitting; see **harmonious** 2.

conical, *mod.* —*Syn.* cone-shaped, funnel-shaped, coned, tapering, tapered, conoid, conoidal, strobiloid, strobilate, pointed, pyramidal; see also **sharp** 2.

conjectural, *mod.* —*Syn.* theoretical, assumed, unresolved; see **doubtful** 2, **hypothetical** 2, **uncertain** 2.

conjecture, *n.* —*Syn.* inference, theory, guess; see **guess, hypothesis, opinion** 1.

conjecture, *v.* —*Syn.* suppose, speculate, surmise; see **guess** 1, **think** 1.

conjugal, *mod.* —*Syn.* nuptial, marital, connubial; see **matrimonial.**

conjunction, *n.* **1.** [Act of joining together]—*Syn.* combination, connection, association; see **union** 1.

2. [Concurrence]—*Syn.* congruency, concomitance, parallelism; see **agreement** 2, **coincidence.**

3. [A syntactic connecting word]. Conjunctions include the following—and, but, if, for, or, nor, so, yet, only, else, than, before, since, then, though, when, where, why, both, either, while, as, neither, although, because, unless, until.

conjure, *v.* **1.** [To practice magic]—*Syn.* enchant, exorcise, entrance; see **charm** 1.

2. [Appeal to]—*Syn.* entreat, implore, adjure; see **beg** 1, **urge** 2.

conjurer, *n.* —*Syn.* sorcerer, seer, magician; see **witch, wizard** 1.

conjure up, *v.* **1.** [To summon]—*Syn.* call, invoke, materialize; see **summon** 1, **urge** 2.

2. [To recollect]—*Syn.* recall, recognize, review; see **remember** 1.

connate, *mod.* **1.** [Born in one]—*Syn.* innate, congenital, original; see **inherent, natural** 1.

2. [Existing together]—*Syn.* allied, cognate, akin; see **alike** 1, **joined, related** 3.

connect, *v.* **1.** [To join]—*Syn.* combine, unite, attach; see **join** 1.

2. [To associate]—*Syn.* relate, equate, correlate; see **compare** 1.

connected, *mod.* **1.** [Joined together]—*Syn.* united, combined, coupled; see **joined.**

2. [Related]—*Syn.* associated, applicable, pertinent; see **related** 2, **relevant.**

3. [Joined in proper order]—*Syn.* coherent, associated, undivided; see **consecutive** 1, **constant** 1.

connecting, *mod.* —*Syn.* joining, linking (to), combining (with), uniting, associating, relating, tying *or* bringing *or* knitting *or* fusing *or* hooking together, clinching, fastening, mixing, mingling, fusing, welding, intertwining, interlacing, pairing, coupling, concatenating, making complementary, making interdependent, bringing into (close) relationship; see **joined.**

connection, *n.* **1.** [Relationship]—*Syn.* kinship, association, reciprocity; see **association** 2, **relationship.**

2. [A junction]—*Syn.* combination, juncture, consolidation; see **junction** 2, **union** 1.

3. [A link]—*Syn.* attachment, fastening, bond; see **link.**

4. [(D) An agent]—*Syn.* contact, go-between, intermediary; see **agent** 1, **messenger.**

in connection with—*Syn.* in conjunction with, associated with, together with; see **with.**

connoisseur, *n.* —*Syn.* judge, gourmet, expert; see **critic** 2, **specialist.**

connotation, *n.* —*Syn.* implication, intention, essence; see **meaning.**

connotative, *mod.* —*Syn.* connoting, meaning, implying, suggesting, suggestive of, hinting; see also **referring.**

connote, *v.* —*Syn.* imply, suggest, indicate; see **hint** 1, **mean** 1.

connubial, *mod.* —*Syn.* marital, nuptial, conjugal; see **matrimonial.**

conquer, *v.* **1.** [To win]—*Syn.* triumph, achieve, prevail; see **succeed** 1, **win** 1.
2. [To defeat]—*Syn.* subdue, overcome, crush; see **defeat** 2.

conquering, *mod.* —*Syn.* succeeding, winning, dominating; see **successful, triumphant.**

conqueror, *n.* —*Syn.* vanquisher, master, champion; see **hero** 1, **winner.**

conquest, *n.* —*Syn.* subjugation, success, conquering; see **triumph** 1, **victory** 1.

consanguinity, *n.* **1.** [Any close connection]—*Syn.* affiliation, connection, affinity; see **brotherhood** 1.
2. [Blood relationship]—*Syn.* kinship, lineage, strain; see **brotherhood** 1, **family** 1, **race** 2.

conscience, *n.* —*Syn.* moral sense, inner voice, the still small voice (D); see **duty** 1, **morals, shame** 2.
have on one's conscience—*Syn.* be culpable, blamable *or* responsible for; see **guilty** 2.
in (all) conscience—*Syn.* rightly, fairly, properly; see **justly** 1.

conscience-stricken, *mod.* —*Syn.* remorseful, repentant, chastened; see **sorry** 1.

conscientious, *mod.* **1.** [Pious]—*Syn.* honest, scrupulous, strict; see **pious** 3.
2. [Thorough]—*Syn.* fastidious, meticulous, complete; see **careful, reliable** 1.

conscientiousness, *n.* —*Syn.* scrupulousness, pains, exactitude, punctiliousness, dutifulness, faithfulness, mindfulness, steadfastness, veracity, uprightness, honor, meticulousness, incorruptibility; see also **care** 1, **duty** 1, **honesty** 1, **responsibility** 1.—*Ant.* negligence, indifference*, nonchalance.

conscientious objector, *n.* —*Syn.* war-hater, noncombatant, neutralist, non-violent person; *all* (D): conchie, C.O., draft-dodger.
Religious groups that object on conscientious grounds to warfare include the following—Quakers, Seventh Day Adventists, Jehovah's Witnesses, Plymouth Brethren, Jains.

conscious, *mod.* **1.** [Aware]—*Syn.* cognizant, informed, sure, certain, apprised, assured, inwardly sensible, discerning, percipient, endowed with consciousness, apperceptive, felt, known, sensible, sensitive, acquainted, attentive, watchful, mindful, vigilant, understanding, keen, alert, awake *or* alert *or* alive *or* sensitive to, on the qui vive, conscious *or* mindful *or* cognizant of; *all* (D): hep to, on to, with it; see also **intelligent** 1.—*Ant.* unaware*, insensitive, inattentive.
2. [In possession of one's senses]—*Syn.* awake, knowing, seeing, recognizing, able to recognize, in one's right mind; see also **active** 2, **alive** 1.—*Ant.* unconscious*, insensible, in a faint.

consciousness, *n.* —*Syn.* alertness, cognizance, mindfulness; see **awareness, knowledge** 1.

conscript, *n.* —*Syn.* recruit, draftee, infantryman; see **soldier.**

conscript, *v.* —*Syn.* draft, enroll, call up (D); see **enlist** 1, **recruit** 1.

conscription, *n.* —*Syn.* enrollment, induction, choice; see **draft** 6, **selection** 1.

consecrate, *v.* **1.** [To dedicate to God]—*Syn.* hallow, sanctify, anoint; see **bless** 3.
2. [To set apart]—*Syn.* ordain, devote, apply; see **dedicate** 2.

consecrated, *mod.* —*Syn.* blessed, sanctified, hallowed; see **divine** 2.

consecration, *n.* —*Syn.* santification, sanctifying, exalting, exaltation, glorification, glorifying, dedication, hallowing, canonization, canonizing, immortalization, immortalizing, apotheosis, enthronement, enthroning, making holy, celebrating; see also **celebration** 1.

consecutive, *mod.* **1.** [Successive]—*Syn.* continuous, serial, seriatim, in turn, progressive, connected, in order *or* sequence, sequential, going on, continuing, one after another *or* the other, serialized, numerical; see also **chronological, constant.**
2. [Characterized by logical sequence]—*Syn.* sequential, following, numerical; see **logical, understandable.**

consecutively, *mod.* —*Syn.* following, successively, continuously, serially, progressively, in file, Indian file (D); see also **gradually.**

consensus, *n.* —*Syn.* consent, unison, accord; see **agreement** 3.

consent, *n.* —*Syn.* assent, approval, acquiescence; see **permission.**

consent, *v.* —*Syn.* accede, assent, acquiesce; see **agree** 2, **allow** 1, **approve** 1.

consequence, *n.* **1.** [Effect]—*Syn.* outgrowth, end, outcome; see **result.**
2. [Importance]—*Syn.* moment, value, weight; see **importance** 1.
in consequence (of)—*Syn.* consequent (on), as a result (of), following; see **because.**
take the consequences—*Syn.* accept the results of one's actions, suffer, bear the burden of; see **endure** 2.

consequent, *mod.* **1.** [Following]—*Syn.* resulting, sequential, indirect; see **following.**
2. [Logical]—*Syn.* reasonable, consistent, inferable; see **logical, understandable.**

consequential, *mod.* —*Syn.* significant, eventful, considerable; see **important** 1.

conservation, *n.* —*Syn.* maintenance, sustentation, keeping, preservation, preserving, conserving, guarding, storage, protecting, saving, safekeeping, upkeep, husbandry, economy, keeping in trust *or* in a safe state; see also **protection** 2, **support** 3. —*Ant.* waste*, destruction, misuse.

conservatism, *n.* —*Syn.* opposition to change, inaction, preservation; see **stability** 1.

conservative, *mod.* —*Syn.* conserving, saving, holding to, keeping, preserving, preservative, unchanging, unchangeable, stable, constant, steady, traditional, reactionary, illiberal, conventional, moderate, unprogressive, firm, obstinate, inflexible, opposed to change, cautious, sober, Tory, not speculative, taking no chances, timid, fearful, not extreme, unimaginative, uncreative, undaring, disliking novelty; *both* (D): right-wing, in a rut *or* groove; see also **careful, moderate.**—*Ant.* radical*, risky, changing.

conservative, *n.* —*Syn.* reactionary, right-winger, preserver, die-hard, Whig, Federalist, conserver, champion of the status quo, opponent of change, classicist, traditionalist, Tory, unprogressive, obstructionist, conventionalist; *all* (D): John Bircher, Goldwaterite, Reaganite, mossback, old fogy, fossil, Neanderthal, silk-stocking.—*Ant.* radical*, progressive, liberal.

conservatory, *n.* **1.** [A greenhouse]—*Syn.* glasshouse, hothouse, nursery; see **greenhouse.**
2. [A school of music]—*Syn.* college of music, conservatoire, studio; see **academy** 1, **school** 1.

conserve, *n.* —*Syn.* fruit butter, jelly, marmalade; see **jam** 1, **jelly.**

consider, *v.* **1.** [To take into account]—*Syn.* allow *or* provide for, grant, take up, accede, concede, acknowledge, assent *or* subscribe to, recognize, favor, value, take under advisement, deal with, regard, make allowance for, take into consideration, keep in mind; *all* (D): reckon with, play around with, toss *or* throw *or* bat around, dream of, chew over, flirt with (an idea), see about; see also **admit** 3, **reconsider.**—*Ant.* deny, refuse*, reject.
2. [To regard]—*Syn.* look upon, count, analyze, hold, suppose, reflect, deem, judge, take (for), view, think of, set down, hold an opinion; see also **estimate** 2, **reckon, think** 1.

considerable, *mod.* **1.** [Important]—*Syn.* noteworthy, significant, essential; see **important** 1.
2. [Much]—*Syn.* abundant, lavish, bountiful; see **much** 2, **plentiful** 1.
3. [Large]—*Syn.* huge, great, big; see **large** 1.

considerate, *mod.* —*Syn.* charitable, kind, solicitous; see **polite** 1, **thoughtful** 2.

consideration, *n.* **1.** [The act of considering] —*Syn.* reflection, study, forethought; see **attention** 2, **thought** 1.
2. [The state of being considerate]—*Syn.* kindliness, thoughtfulness, attentiveness; see **courtesy** 1, **kindness** 1, **tolerance.**
3. [A considerate action]—*Syn.* philanthropy, benefaction, favor; see **courtesy** 2, **kindness** 2.
4. [Payment]—*Syn.* remuneration, salary, wage; see **payment** 1.
5. [Something to be considered]—*Syn.* situation, problem, judgment, notion, fancy, perplexity, puzzle, concern, point, factor, proposal, difficulty, incident, evidence, new development, occurrence, state, estate, pass, occasion, exigency, emergency, idea, thought, trouble, minutiae, plan, particulars, items, scope, extent, magnitude; see also **event** 1, **opinion** 1.
in consideration of—*Syn.* because of, on account of, for; see **considering.**
on no consideration—*Syn.* for no reason, on no account, by no means; see **never.**
take into consideration—*Syn.* take into account, weigh, keep in mind; see **consider** 1.
under consideration—*Syn.* thought over, discussed, evaluated; see **considered** 1.

considered, *mod.* **1.** [Thought through]—*Syn.* carefully thought about, treated, gone into, contemplated, weighed, mediated, investigated, examined; see also **determined** 1.
2. [Deliberate]—*Syn.* well chosen, given due consideration, (well) advised; see **deliberate** 1.

considering, *prep.* and *conj.* —*Syn.* in light *or* view *or* consideration of, pending, taking into account, everything being equal, inasmuch as, insomuch as, forasmuch as, with (something) in view, being as how (D).

consign, *v.* **1.** [To give over or deliver]—*Syn.* convey, dispatch, transfer; see **give** 1, **send** 1, **ship.**
2. [To put in the charge of]—*Syn.* appoint, entrust, authorize; see **assign** 1, **commission, delegate** 1.

consigned, *mod.* —*Syn.* shipped, directed (to), for delivery (to); see **sent.**

consignee, *n.* —*Syn.* representative, factor, proctor; see **agent** 1, **means** 1.

consigner, *n.* —*Syn.* sender, shipper, businessman; see **distributor, merchant.**

consistency, *n.* **1.** [Harmony]—*Syn.* congruity, union, correspondence, uniformity, accord, appropriateness, unity, cohesion, compatibility, concurrence, proportion, conformability; see also **agreement** 2, **symmetry.**—*Ant.* incongruity, disagreement*, inappropriateness.
2. [The degree of firmness or thickness]—*Syn.* hardness, softness, elasticity, pliability, firmness, flexibility, suppleness, limberness, plasticity, moldability, bendability, bendableness, viscosity, solidity, viscidity; see also **density** 1, **texture** 1.

consistent, *mod.* **1.** [Being in logical agreement] —*Syn.* compatible, equable, expected; see **logical** 1, **rational** 1, **regular** 3.
2. [Acting in accordance with one's beliefs]—*Syn.* according to, conforming with, matching; see **like.**

consist of, *v.* —*Syn.* embody, contain, involve; see **comprise, include** 1.

consolation, *n.* **1.** [Solace]—*Syn.* sympathy, compassion, fellow feeling; see **pity** 1.
2. [Something that consoles]—*Syn.* comfort, ease, support; see **encouragement** 1, **relief** 4.

consolation prize, *n.* —*Syn.* second-place honor, booby prize, red ribbon; see **prize.**

console, *v.* —*Syn.* cheer, sympathize with, gladden; see **comfort** 1, **encourage** 1.

consolidate, *v.* **1.** [To become united]—*Syn.* combine, solidify, condense; see **unite** 1.
2. [To cause to unite]—*Syn.* combine, render solid, mass, amass, bring *or* piece *or* put together, condense, compact, solidify, make firm, thicken, concentrate, fuse, blend, centralize, connect, mix, conjoin, incorporate, compound, hitch, bind, concatenate, unify; see also **compress, pack** 2. —*Ant.* sever, cut*, scatter.
3. [To develop as a defensible position]—*Syn.* fortify, add to, build up; see **strengthen.**

consolidation, *n.* **1.** [Union]—*Syn.* alliance, association, federation; see **incorporation** 2.
2. [Solidification]—*Syn.* compression, concentration, strengthening; see **solidification** 1.

consonant, *n.* Linguistic terms referring to consonant sounds include the following—voiceless, voiced; labial, bilabial, labiodental, apical, dental, alveolar, retroflex, frontal, alveopalatal, prepalatal, dorsal, palatal, velar, uvular, glottal, pharyngeal, interdental, labiovelar; stop, fricative *or* spirant, lenis, resonant, sibilant; aspirated, unaspirated, affricated, glottalized, preaspirated, prenasalized, implosive, plosive, nasal; click, glide, continuant, trill, flap. In spelling, English consonants are as follows —b, c, d, f, g, h, j, k, l, m, n, p, q, r, s, t, v, w, x, y, z; see also **letter, sound** 2, **vowel.**

consort, *n.* —*Syn.* companion, spouse, associate; see **friend** 1, **husband, wife.**

consort, *v.* **1.** [To join]—*Syn.* fraternize, befriend, associate; see **accompany** 1, **join** 2.
2. [To be in agreement]—*Syn.* harmonize, concur, coincide; see **agree, conform.**

conspectus, *n.* —*Syn.* précis, outline, synopsis; see **summary.**

conspicuous, *mod.* **1.** [Attracting attention]—*Syn.* outstanding, eminent, distinguished, celebrated, noted, notable, illustrious, prominent, commanding, well-known, salient, signal, arresting, remarkable, renowned, famed, notorious, flagrant, glaring, gross, rank, important, influential, far-famed, noticeable; *both* (D): the observed of all observers, standing out like a sore thumb; see also **famous, striking.**—*Ant.* unknown, inconspicuous*, unsung.
2. [Obvious]—*Syn.* apparent, evident, distinct; see **clear** 2, **obvious** 1, **plain.**

conspiracy, *n.* —*Syn.* intrigue, collusion, connivance; see **trick** 1, **trickery.**

conspirator, *n.* —*Syn.* betrayer, schemer, cabalist; see **traitor.**

conspire, *v.* **1.** [To plan secretly]—*Syn.* plot, scheme, contrive; see **plan** 1.
2. [To act together]—*Syn.* join, consort (with), unite; see **co-operate** 1, **join** 2.

constancy, *n.* **1.** [Faithfulness]—*Syn.* fidelity, attachment, adherence, fealty, allegiance, devotion, ardor, eagerness, zeal, passion, love, earnestness, steadfastness, permanence, staunchness, principle, integrity, honor, faith, honesty, truthfulness, devotedness, abidingness, endurance, dependability, trustworthiness, trustiness, unchangeableness, certainty, unfailingness, surety; see also **loyalty, reliability.**—*Ant.* faithlessness, disloyalty*, perfidy.
2. [Determination]—*Syn.* resolution, perseverance, doggedness; see **determination** 2.

constant, *mod.* **1.** [Showing little variation]—*Syn.* steady, uniform, unchanging, continual, equable, uninterrupted, unvarying, connected, even, incessant, unbroken, nonstop, monotonous, monochrome, monochromatic, monophonic, standardized, regularized; see also **perpetual** 1, **regular** 3.
2. [Faithful]—*Syn.* loyal, attached, devoted; see **faithful.**

constantly, *mod.* —*Syn.* uniformly, steadily, invariably; see **regularly** 2.

constellation, *n.* —*Syn.* group *or* configuration of stars, zodiac, sign of the zodiac, stars, planets. Some constellations include the following—Southern Cross, Orion, Cancer, Taurus, Big Dipper *or* Ursa Major *or* Great Bear, Little Dipper *or* Little Bear *or* Ursa Minor, Leo, Leo Minor, Draco, Pegasus, Aries, Gemini, Virgo, Aquarius, Libra, Scorpio, Capricorn, Sagittarius, Andromeda, Cassiopeia, Canis Major, Canis Minor, Cygnus, Pictor, Pisces; see also **star** 1, **zodiac.**

consternation, *n.* —*Syn.* alarm, terror, fright; see **fear** 1, **panic** 1.

constipated, *mod.* —*Syn.* bound, costive, obstructed; see **sick.**

constipation, *n.* —*Syn.* stasis of the lower bowel, alimentary stoppage, costiveness; see **illness** 1.

constituency, *n.* —*Syn.* (the) voters, electorate, body politic, electors, voting public, voting area, body of voters, balloters, the nation, the people; the district, the county, the ward, etc.; see also **voter.**

constituent, *mod.* **1.** [Composing]—*Syn.* constituting, forming, combining; see **fundamental** 1, **integral.**
2. [Voting]—*Syn.* electoral, electing, overruling; see **official** 2, **voting.**

constituent, *n.* —*Syn.* component, element, ingredient; see **part** 1.

constitute, *v.* **1.** [To found]—*Syn.* establish, develop, create; see **organize** 2.
2. [To empower]—*Syn.* commission, authorize, appoint; see **delegate** 1, 2.
3. [To enact]—*Syn.* order, draft, decree; see **enact** 1, **legislate** 1.
4. [To make up]—*Syn.* frame, compound, aggregate; see **compose** 1.

constitution, *n.* **1.** [Health]—*Syn.* vitality, physical nature, build; see **health, physique.**
2. [A basic political document]—*Syn.* custom, code, written law; see **law** 2.
3. [Make-up]—*Syn.* nature, disposition, structure; see **character** 2, **essence** 1, **organization** 1.

constitutional, *mod.* **1.** [Based upon a constitution] —*Syn.* representative, republican, safeguarding liberty; see **democratic** 1.
2. [In accordance with a constitution]—*Syn.* lawful, approved, ensured; see **legal** 1.
3. [Physical]—*Syn.* built-in, vital, inborn; see **inherent, natural** 1.

constrain, *v.* —*Syn.* necessitate, compel, stifle; see **force** 1, **urge** 2.

constraint, *n.* **1.** [The use of force]—*Syn.* coercion, force, compulsion; see **pressure** 2.
2. [Shyness]—*Syn.* bashfulness, restraint, timidity; see **humility, modesty** 1, **reserve** 2.
3. [Confinement]—*Syn.* captivity, detention, restriction; see **arrest** 1, **confinement** 1.

constrict, *v.* —*Syn.* contract, cramp, choke up; see **tighten** 1.

constriction, *n.* **1.** [The act of constricting]—*Syn.* narrowing, compression, reduction; see **contraction** 1.
2. [That which constricts]—*Syn.* choking, squeezing, binding; see **stricture** 2.

construct, *v.* **1.** [To build a physical structure] —*Syn.* make, erect, fabricate; see **build** 1, **create** 2.
2. [To erect mentally]—*Syn.* create, compose, envision; see **imagine** 1, **invent** 1.

construction, *n.* **1.** [The act of constructing] —*Syn.* creation, composition, origination, planning, invention, formation, conception, improvisation, making, erection, fabrication, manufacture, foundation, roadwork, building, elevation, erecting, fabricating, rearing, raising, putting up; see also **architecture, production** 1.
2. [A method of constructing]—*Syn.* structure, arrangement, organization, disposition, system, systematization, plan, development, steel and concrete, prefabrication, contour, format, mold, cast,

outline, type, shape, build, cut, fabric, formation, turn, framework, figuration, conformation, configuration, fitted stone, brick and mortar, ribbon development, prefab (D); see also **form** 1, **frame** 1.

constructive, *mod.* —*Syn.* useful, valuable, effective; see **helpful** 1, **valuable** 2.

construe, *v.* —*Syn.* define, infer, decipher; see **explain, interpret** 1.

consul, *n.* —*Syn.* legate, envoy, emissary; see **delegate, representative** 2.

consulate, *n.* —*Syn.* government *or* consular office, embassy, ministry; see **government** 2, **office** 3.

consult, *v.* —*Syn.* take counsel, deliberate, confer, parley, conspire *or* counsel *or* be closeted with, compare notes about, put heads together, confabulate, commune, treat, negotiate, debate, argue, talk over, call in, consider with, seek the opinion of, ask advice of, turn to, seek advice; see also **advise** 1, **ask** 1, **discuss, interview.**

consultation, *n.* —*Syn.* interview, conference, deliberation; see **discussion** 1.

consume, *v.* **1.** [To destroy]—*Syn.* exhaust, expend, devastate; see **destroy** 1, **waste** 1, 2.

2. [To use]—*Syn.* utilize, employ, apply, avail oneself of, make use of, turn to account, put to use, have recourse to, profit by; *all* (D): finish up, put away, run out of, use up, wear out; see also **spend** 1, **use** 1.—*Ant.* waste*, misapply, misspend.

3. [To eat or drink]—*Syn.* absorb, feed, devour; see **eat** 1.

consumer, *n.* —*Syn.* user, customer, purchaser; see **buyer, shopper.**

consuming, *mod.* —*Syn.* immoderate, exhausting, devastating; see **harmful, wasteful.**

consummate, *mod.* —*Syn.* perfect, total, utter; see **whole** 1.

consummate, *v.* —*Syn.* complete, perfect, finish; see **achieve** 1.

consummation, *n.* —*Syn.* fulfillment, completion, culmination; see **end** 2, **perfection** 1.

consumption, *n.* **1.** [The act of consuming]—*Syn.* using, decay, burning, expenditure, exhaustion, depletion, dissipation, dispersion, misuse, devastation, diminution, loss, damage, wear and tear, ruin, desolation; see also **destruction** 1, **use** 1, **waste** 1. —*Ant.* saving, conservation*, preservation.

2. [Tuberculosis]—*Syn.* phthisis, pulmonary consumption, lung disease; see **disease** 2, **tuberculosis.**

consumptive, *mod.* —*Syn.* destructive, immoderate, devastating; see **harmful, wasteful.**

contact, *n.* —*Syn.* touch, junction, connection; see **meeting** 1.

contact (D), *v.* —*Syn.* speak to, reach, make contact with (D); see **communicate** 2, **talk** 1.

contagion, *n.* **1.** [Communicable disease]—*Syn.* poison, virus, illness; see **disease** 1.

2. [Infection]—*Syn.* transmittal, transmission, communication; see **contamination, infection** 1.

contagious, *mod.* —*Syn.* communicable, infectious, transmittable, spreading, poisonous, epidemic, pestiferous, deadly, endemic, epizootic, taking, tending to spread, inoculable, impartible; see also **catching.**

contain, *v.* **1.** [Include]—*Syn.* comprehend, embrace, be composed of; see **include** 1.

2. [Restrict]—*Syn.* hold, keep back, stop; see **restrain** 1.

container, *n.* —*Syn.* receptacle, repository, cauldron, holder, vessel, alembic, capsule, package, packet, chest, purse, pod, silicle, pouch, casket, cask, sac, sack, bag, poke, pot, pottery, jug, ewer, bucket, bunker, canteen, crock, storage space, pit, box, carton, canister, crate, magnum, pail, kettle, chamber, boxlike object, jug-shaped container, pouchlike protuberance; see also **bag, basket** 1, **bin, bowl, can** 1, **case** 7, **dish, jar** 1, **tub, vase.**

contaminate, *v.* —*Syn.* pollute, infect, defile; see **corrupt** 1, **dirty.**

contamination, *n.* —*Syn.* impurity, corruption, defilement, foulness, rottenness, spoliation, disease, decay, epidemic, plague, pestilence, contagion, taint; see also **infection** 1, **pollution.**

contemplate, *v.* **1.** [To look at]—*Syn.* regard, view, scan, inspect, gaze at, notice, witness, pore over, peer, pry, behold, observe thoughtfully, view with continued attention, scrutinize, survey, observe, look over, audit, probe, penetrate, pierce; see also **examine** 1, **see** 1, **witness.**—*Ant.* neglect, disregard*, slight.

2. [To consider]—*Syn.* ponder, muse, speculate on; see **study** 1, **think** 1.

contemplation, *n.* **1.** [Intention]—*Syn.* design, intention, ambition; see **plan** 2, **purpose** 1.

2. [Meditation]—*Syn.* consideration, reflection, study; see **thought** 1.

contemplative, *mod.* —*Syn.* meditative, pensive, attentive; see **studious, thoughtful** 1.

contemporary, *mod.* **1.** [Occurring at the same time]—*Syn.* synchronal, coexistent, coincident; see **simultaneous.**

2. [Current]—*Syn.* present, fashionable, à la mode; see **modern** 1, 3.

contemporary, *n.* —*Syn.* peer, fellow, counterpart; see **equal.**

contempt, *n.* **1.** [A feeling of scorn]—*Syn.* scorn, derision, slight; see **hatred** 2, **malice.**

2. [A state of disgrace]—*Syn.* shame, dishonor, stigma; see **disgrace** 1.

contemptible, *mod.* —*Syn.* base, worthless, degenerate; see **mean** 3.

contemptuous, *mod.* —*Syn.* disdainful, derisive, disrespectful; see **scornful** 1.

contend, *v.* —*Syn.* contest, battle, dispute; see **fight** 2.

content, *mod.* —*Syn.* appeased, gratified, comfortable; see **happy** 1, **satisfied.**

contented, *mod.* —*Syn.* content, pleased, thankful; see **happy** 1, **satisfied.**

contention, *n.* **1.** [A quarrel]—*Syn.* struggle, belligerency, combat; see **battle** 2, **competition** 1, **dispute** 1, **fight** 1.

2. [An assertion supported by argument]—*Syn.* stand, ground, assertion, allegation, avowal, asseveration, explanation, predication, profession, deposition, advancement, discussion, charge, plea, demurrer; *both* (D): paper war, war of words; see also **attitude** 3, **declaration** 1.

contentious, *mod.* —*Syn.* quarrelsome, hostile, cross; see **unfriendly** 1.

contentment, *n.* —*Syn.* peace, pleasure, happiness; see **comfort** 1, **ease** 1, **satisfaction** 2.

contents, *n.* **1.** [Matter contained]—*Syn.* gist, essence, meaning, significance, intent, implication, connotation, text, subject matter, sum, substance, sum and substance, details, constituents; see also **ingredients, matter** 1, **subject** 1, **writing** 2.
2. [Capacity to contain]—*Syn.* volume, space, cubical contents; see **capacity** 1, **size** 2.

conterminous, *mod.* **1.** [Contained within the same limits]—*Syn.* commensurate, coterminous, coincident, coextensive, identical in limits, equivalent; see also **equal, like.**
2. [Having a common boundary line]—*Syn.* proximal, adjacent, bordering; see **contiguous, near** 1.

contest, *n.* **1.** [A competition]—*Syn.* trial, match, challenge; see **discussion** 1, **game** 1, **sport** 1.
2. [A conflict]—*Syn.* engagement, controversy, fray; see **battle** 2, **fight** 1.

contest, *v.* **1.** [To oppose]—*Syn.* debate, question, stand up for the other side; see **argue** 1, **oppose** 1.
2. [To fight]—*Syn.* contend, battle, defend, struggle, wrangle, altercate, conflict, quarrel, brawl, scuffle, feud, attack, strike, tilt; *all* (D): have a run-in with, take on (all comers), rumpus; see also **dare** 2, **fight** 2.—*Ant.* stop, rest*, shake hands.

contestant, *n.* —*Syn.* competitor, participant, rival, challenger, contester, disputant, antagonist, adversary, one who takes part in a contest, combatant, player, member of the field, team member; *all* (D): scrapper, warrior, battler; see also **opponent** 1, **player** 1.

context, *n.* —*Syn.* connection, text, substance; see **meaning.**

contiguous, *mod.* —*Syn.* adjacent, adjoining, meeting, coterminous, abutting, touching, contactual, next to, in contact; see also **near** 1.

continence, *n.* —*Syn.* purity, virtue, self-restraint; see **chastity, restraint** 1.

continent, *n.* —*Syn.* mainland, (continental) land mass, major earth division, body of land; see also **Africa, America, Asia, Australia, Europe, region** 1.

contingency, *n.* **1.** [Possibility]—*Syn.* likelihood, chance, odds; see **possibility** 2, **probability.**
2. [Accident]—*Syn.* predicament, incident, exigency; see **accident** 2.

contingent, *mod.* **1.** [Accidental]—*Syn.* chance, unforeseen, fortuitous; see **uncertain** 2, **unexpected.**
2. [Possible]—*Syn.* unpredictable, probable, conditional; see **likely** 1, **uncertain** 2.

contingent upon, *mod.* —*Syn.* dependent upon, conditional on, subject to; see **dependent** 3.

continual, *mod.* **1.** [Constant]—*Syn.* uninterrupted, unbroken, connected; see **consecutive** 1, **regular** 3.
2. [Perpetual]—*Syn.* ceaseless, unceasing, permanent; see **endless** 1, **perpetual** 1.

continually, *mod.* —*Syn.* steadily, continuously, constantly; see **frequently, regularly** 2.

continuance, *n.* —*Syn.* duration, extension, perpetuation; see **continuation** 1.

continuation, *n.* **1.** [The act of being continued] —*Syn.* prolongation, prolonging, continuance, continuing, propagation, succession, line, carrying on to a further point, extension in time *or* space, production, producing, increase, increasing, augmenting, protracting, protraction, going on, maintenance, maintaining, endurance, enduring, sustenance, sustaining, perpetuating, perpetuation, self-perpetuation, persisting, preserving, preservation, perseverance, persevering, ratifying, ratification, sanctioning, carry-over (D); see also **persistence, sequence** 1.—*Ant.* cessation, end*, termination.
2. [The act of being resumed]—*Syn.* return to, resumption, resuming, recommencement, reinitiation, recommencing, recurrence, recurring, restoring, reoccurrence, restoration, recapitulation, recapitulating, reorganizing, reorganization, reestablishment, reinstitution, reiteration, reiterating, iterating, iteration, duplication, reduplication, repeating, reinstating, reinstatement, new start; see also **renewal, repetition.**—*Ant.* pause*, wait, delay.
3. [Whatever serves to continue]—*Syn.* supplement, new chapter, correction, emendation, postscript, epilogue, peroration, wake, postlude, sequel, installment, appendix, revision, complement, succession, new version, translation, extension, augmentation; see also **addition** 2, **increase** 1.

continue, *interj.* —*Syn.* keep on, carry on, keep going, keep talking, keep reading, etc.; keep it up.

continue, *v.* **1.** [To persist]—*Syn.* persevere, carry forward, maintain, carry *or* roll *or* keep *or* go *or* run *or* push *or* live on, sustain, promote, progress, uphold, forge ahead, remain, press onward, make headway, move ahead, never cease; *all* (D): keep the ball rolling, leave no stone unturned, chip away at, hang in *or* on, hang on like grim death; see also **advance** 1, **endure** 1.—*Ant.* cease, end*, give up.
2. [To resume]—*Syn.* begin again, renew, recommence, begin *or* carry over, return to, recapitulate, take up again, begin where one left off, be reinstated *or* reinstituted *or* reestablished *or* restored; see also **resume.**—*Ant.* discontinue, halt*, postpone.
3. [To remain]—*Syn.* stay, linger, loiter; see **remain** 1.

continuing, *mod.* —*Syn.* ongoing, persisting, persevering, maintaining, carrying on, pursuing, advancing, progressing, enduring, sustaining; see also **progressive** 1.

continuity, *n.* **1.** [The state of being continuous] —*Syn.* continuousness, perpetuity, prolongation, constancy, continuance, flow, succession, uniting, unity, sequence, continuum, chain, linking, train, progression, dovetailing, protraction, extension; see also **continuation** 1.—*Ant.* intermittence, dissipation*, desultoriness.
2. [(D) Transitional matter, especially in a radio or television program]—*Syn.* action, preparation, script, dialogue, cue, announcement; *all* (D): cushion, drool, cut.

continuous, *mod.* —*Syn.* unfaltering, repeated, perpetual; see **consecutive** 1, **constant** 1, **regular** 3.

contort, *v.* —*Syn.* deform, misshape, twist; see **distort** 3.

contortion, *n.* **1.** [Something contorted]—*Syn.* deformity, distortion, grimace, *moue* (French), twist, mutilation, deformation, misproportion, ugliness, anamorphosis, pout, wryness, crookedness, misshapement, malformation, unsightliness; see also **knot** 2.

2. [The act of distorting]—*Syn.* distortion, deforming, dislocating; see **bending.**

contortionist, *n.*—*Syn.* clown, tumbler, juggler; see **acrobat.**

contour, *n.*—*Syn.* profile, silhouette, shape; see **form** 1.

contour, *v.*—*Syn.* shape, mold, carve; see **form** 1.

contoured, *mod.*—*Syn.* shaped, molded, modeled; see **formed.**

contraband, *mod.*—*Syn.* forbidden, unauthorized, unlawful; see **illegal.**

contraband, *n.* **1.** [Illegal trafficking]—*Syn.* smuggling, poaching, violation of trade laws, piracy, counterfeiting; *all* (D): bootlegging, moonshining, rumrunning, wetbacking; see also **crime** 2, **theft.**
2. [Illegal goods or trade]—*Syn.* smuggled *or* bootlegged *or* poached goods *or* traffic *or* commerce *or* trade, seized *or* confiscated goods, goods subject to confiscation *or* seizure, contraband of war, freed slaves, plunder; see also **booty.**

contraceptive, *mod.*—*Syn.* preventive, controlling conception, preventing birth *or* impregnation, prophylactic.

contraceptive, *n.*—*Syn.* prophylactic, birth-control device, preventative.
Contraceptives include the following—birth-control *or* hormone pill *or* the pill (D); condom *or* safety, rubber (*both* D); diaphragm, intrauterine device *or* IUD, loop, coil (*all* D); foam, spermicidal cream *or* jelly, vaginal suppositories, (vaginal) douche.

contract, *n.* **1.** [A legal agreement]—*Syn.* covenant, compact, stipulation, contractual statement *or* obligation, convention, understanding, promise, pledge, engagement, obligation, guarantee, liability, concordat, agreement, *entente cordiale* (French), settlement, gentleman's agreement, commitment, contractual budget *or* conbud (D), cartel, bargain, pact, indenture, mise, arrangement; *all* (D): the papers, get-together, deal; see also **treaty.**
2. [The document executed to bind a contract, sense 1]—*Syn.* deposition, paper, evidence; see **proof, record** 1.

contract, *v.* **1.** [To diminish]—*Syn.* draw in *or* back, shrivel, weaken, shrink, be reduced in compass, become smaller, be drawn together, decline, fall away, abate, subside, grow less, ebb, wane, wrinkle, knit, lessen, lose, dwindle, consume, recede, fall off, wither, waste, condense, constrict, deflate, evaporate; see also **decrease** 1.—*Ant.* stretch*, expand, strengthen.
2. [To cause to diminish]—*Syn.* abbreviate, abridge, epitomize, edit, omit, narrow, condense, confine; see also **compress, decrease** 2.
3. [To enter into an agreement by contract]—*Syn.* covenant, pact, pledge, undertake, come to terms, make terms, adjust, dicker, (make a) bargain, agree on, limit, bound, circumscribe, settle by covenant, establish by agreement, engage, stipulate, consent, enter into a contractual obligation, sign the papers, negotiate a contract, accept an offer, obligate oneself, work out the details, put something in writing, swear to, sign for, assent, give one's word; *all* (D): shake hands on it, initial, close; see also **negotiate** 1, **promise** 1.
4. [To catch; *said of diseases*]—*Syn.* get, incur, become infected with; see **catch** 4.
5. [To become obligated by; *said especially of debts*]—*Syn.* become indebted, take on, obligate oneself; see **owe.**

contract for, *v.*—*Syn.* acquire, order, purchase; see **buy** 1.

contraction, *n.* **1.** [The act of contracting]—*Syn.* dwindling, shrinking, receding, withdrawing, shriveling, lessening, recession, withdrawal, consumption, condensation, consuming, condensing, elision, omission, deflation, evaporation, constriction, abbreviating, decrease, shortening, abridging, compression, narrowing, confinement, curtailment, omitting, deflating, evaporating, decreasing, abridgment, reducing, confining, curtailing, diminishing, cutting down, drawing together, constricting, consolidating, consolidation, diminishment, lowering, lopping, epitomizing, editing; see also **abbreviation** 2, **reduction** 1, **shrinkage.**—*Ant.* expansion, increase*, extension.
2. [A contracted form]—*Syn.* colloquialism, compendium, abstract; see **abbreviation** 1.

contractor, *n.*—*Syn.* entrepreneur, jobber, constructor; see **architect** 1, **builder** 1.

contradict, *v.* **1.** [To oppose]—*Syn.* differ, call in question, confront; see **dare** 2, **oppose** 1.
2. [To deny]—*Syn.* disclaim, refuse to accept, repudiate; see **deny** 1.

contradiction, *n.* **1.** [Denial]—*Syn.* dissension, dispute, defiance; see **disagreement** 1.
2. [Discrepancy]—*Syn.* incongruity, inconsistency, opposition; see **difference** 1, **opposite.**

contradictory, *mod.*—*Syn.* opposite, inconsistent, incongruous; see **different** 1.

contrary, *mod.* **1.** [Opposed]—*Syn.* antagonistic to, hostile, counter; see **against** 3, **opposed.**
2. [Opposite in position]—*Syn.* facing, adverse, versus; see **opposite** 3.
3. [Unfavorable]—*Syn.* untimely, bad, unpropitious; see **unfavorable** 2.
4. [Obstinate]—*Syn.* perverse, contradictory, headstrong; see **obstinate** 1.

contrary, *n.*—*Syn.* converse, antithesis, just the opposite; see **contrast** 1, **opposite.**
on *or* **to the contrary**—*Syn.* conversely, contrary to, on the other hand; see **opposed.**

contrast, *n.* **1.** [The state of being sharply different]—*Syn.* divergence, incompatibility, disparity, variation, variance, dissimilarity, inequality, distinction, incongruousness, heterogeneity, oppositeness, contradiction, dissimilitude, diversity, unlikeness, disagreement, opposition; see also **difference** 1.—*Ant.* agreement*, similarity, uniformity.
2. [A contrasting effect]—*Syn.* contrariety, antithesis, contradiction, inconsistency, foil, reverse, contraposition, inverse, adverse, converse, opposition; see also **difference** 2, **opposite.**—*Ant.* equality*, unity, oneness.

contrast, *v.* **1.** [To provide a contrast]—*Syn.* contradict, disagree, conflict, set off, be contrary to, diverge *or* depart *or* deviate *or* differ from, mismatch, vary, show difference, stand out, be dissimilar *or* diverse *or* variable *or* unlike, be a foil

to; see also **differ** 1, **oppose** 1.—*Ant.* agree*, concur, be identical.
2. [To indicate a contrast]—*Syn.* separate, balance, weigh; see **compare** 2, **distinguish** 1.

contrasting, *mod.* —*Syn.* divergent, contradictory, dissimilar; see **different** 1.

contravene, *v.* —*Syn.* contradict, defy, interpose; see **hinder, oppose** 1, 2.

contravention, *n.* —*Syn.* contradiction, violation, infringement; see **disagreement** 1, **opposition** 1.

contretemps, *n.* —*Syn.* mishap, misfortune, calamity; see **catastrophe, disaster.**

contribute, *v.* **1.** [To give]—*Syn.* add, share, endow, supply, furnish, bestow, present, confer, bequest, commit, accord, dispense, settle upon, enrich, proffer, grant, afford, donate, dispense, assign, give away, subscribe, tender, devote, demise, will, dower, bequeath, subsidize, hand out, sacrifice; *all* (D); ante up, chip *or* kick in, have a hand in, get in the act, go Dutch, break no bones; see also **give** 1, **offer** 1, **provide** 1.—*Ant.* receive*, accept.
2. [To aid]—*Syn.* assist, advance, uphold; see **help** 1, **support** 5.

contributing, *mod.* —*Syn.* aiding, helpful, supporting, sharing, causative, providing a background, forming a part of, not to be overlooked, to be considered, providing a minor cause, coming into the picture (D); see also **helpful, secondary** 1, **subordinate, valuable** 2.

contributing, *n.* —*Syn.* sharing, supplying, aiding; see **giving.**

contribution, *n.* **1.** [Gift]—*Syn.* donation, present, bestowal; see **gift** 1, **grant.**
2. [A significant addition]—*Syn.* augmentation, improvement, supplement; see **addition** 2, **increase** 1.

contributor, *n.* —*Syn.* subscriber, giver, grantor; see **donor, patron** 1.

contrite, *mod.* —*Syn.* repentant, regretful, humbled; see **sorry** 1.

contrition, *n.* —*Syn.* penitence, remorse, sorrow; see **penance** 1, 2, **regret** 1, **repentance.**

contrivance, *n.* **1.** [A plan, especially an ingenious plan]—*Syn.* ruse, artifice, stratagem; see **plan** 2.
2. [A mechanical device]—*Syn.* appliance, mechanism, gadget, invention, apparatus, gear, implement, discovery, instrument, machine, engine, convenience, contraption, utensil, harness, material, tackle, equipment, creation; *all* (D): dojigger, thingamajig, thingamabob, gigamaree; see also **device** 1, **equipment, tool** 1.

contrive, *v.* **1.** [To invent]—*Syn.* make, improvise, devise; see **create** 2, **invent** 1.
2. [To succeed with difficulty]—*Syn.* manage, pass, compass, negotiate, afford, engineer, manipulate, shift, make shift, arrange, execute, carry out, effect, maneuver; *both* (D): swing, wrangle; see also **achieve** 1, **succeed** 1.

control, *n.* **1.** [The power to direct]—*Syn.* dominion, force, management; see **government** 1, **power** 2.
2. [The document executed to bind a contract, sense 1]—*Syn.* deposition, paper, evidence; see **proof, record** 1.
3. [Restraint]—*Syn.* qualification, limitation, restriction; see **restraint** 2.

control, *v.* **1.** [To hold in check]—*Syn.* constrain, master, repress; see **check** 2, **command** 2, **restrain** 1.
2. [To direct]—*Syn.* lead, instruct, guide; see **advise** 1, **manage** 1.
3. [To verify]—*Syn.* establish, test, experiment; see **check** 3, **examine** 1, **measure** 1, **verify.**

controlling, *mod.* —*Syn.* ruling, supervising, regulating; see **authoritative** 2, **governing.**

controversial, *mod.* —*Syn.* debatable, contestable, arguable, polemical, controvertible, open to question *or* discussion *or* doubt *or* debate, dubious, doubtful, dubitable, contentious, doubtable, subject to controversy, in question, suspect, in dispute, disputable, argumentative; see also **questionable** 1, **uncertain** 2.

controversialist, *n.* —*Syn.* debater, disputer, parliamentarian, logomacher, belligerent, dialectician, reasoner, casuist, polemist, polemicist, arguer, disputant, wrangler, discussant, litigant; see also **fighter** 1.

controversy, *n.* —*Syn.* contention, debate, quarrel; see **difference** 1, **discussion** 1.

controvert, *v.* **1.** [To argue against]—*Syn.* counter, contradict, refute; see **deny** 1, **oppose** 1.
2. [To argue about]—*Syn.* argue, dispute, contest; see **debate, discuss.**

contumacious, *mod.* —*Syn.* unyielding, intractable, inflexible; see **obstinate** 1.

contusion, *n.* —*Syn.* bruise, cut, wound; see **injury** 1.

conundrum, *n.* —*Syn.* enigma, riddle, problem; see **puzzle** 2.

convalescent, *mod.* —*Syn.* recovering, improving, recuperating, discharged, dismissed, released, ambulatory, getting well *or* better, out of the hospital, past the crisis, out of emergency care, getting over (something), mending, healing, gaining strength, strengthening, restored, rejuvenating, rejuvenated, on the mend (D); see also **well** 1.

convalescent, *n.* —*Syn.* (walking *or* ambulatory) patient, one recovering from a sickness *or* injury, convalescent *or* walking case; see **patient.**

convene, *v.* —*Syn.* unite, congregate, collect; see **assemble** 2, **gather** 1.

convenience, *n.* **1.** [The quality of being convenient]—*Syn.* fitness, availability, accessibility, suitability, suitableness, appropriateness, decency, handiness, agreeableness, acceptability, receptiveness, openness, accord, consonance, adaptability, approachability, usefulness, serviceableness; see also **utility** 1.—*Ant.* unfitness, trouble*, unsuitability.
2. [An aid to ease or comfort]—*Syn.* ease, comfort, accommodation, help, aid, assistance, means, support, luxury, succor, personal service, the comforts of home, relief, cooperation, promotion, advancement, satisfaction, ministry, ministration, service, benefit, avail, furtherance, contribution, forwarding, accessory, advantage, utility, labor *or* time saver, lift (D); see also **advantage** 3, **appliance.** —*Ant.* discomfort, awkwardness*, hindrance.
3. [Time and circumstances that are convenient] —*Syn.* occasion, chance, place, hour, freedom, liberty, a free hour, a minute at liberty, preference; see also **circumstances** 2. **at one's convenience**

—*Syn.* suitable, conveniently, when convenient; see **appropriately.**

convenient, *mod.* **1.** [Serving one's convenience] —*Syn.* ready, favorable, suitable, adapted, available, fitted, suited, adaptable, commodious, roomy, well-arranged, appropriate, well-planned, decent, agreeable, acceptable, useful, serviceable, assisting, aiding, contributive, beneficial, accommodating, advantageous, in the public interest, conducive, comfortable, opportune, timesaving, labor-saving; see also **fit** 1, 2, **helpful** 1.—*Ant.* disturbing*, unserviceable, disadvantageous.

2. [Near]—*Syn.* handy, ready to hand, close (by *or* in), near at hand, central, easy to reach, within reach, readily arrived at, nearby, nigh, adjacent, adjoining, next door, in the neighborhood, within walking distance, a short walk away, on hand, at one's elbow *or* fingertips (D); see also **contiguous, near** 1.—*Ant.* far, distant*, inaccessible.

convent, *n.* —*Syn.* religious community, monastery, nunnery; see **cloister, retreat** 2.

convention, *n.* **1.** [An occasion for which delegates assemble]—*Syn.* assembly, convocation, meeting; see **gathering.**

2. [Those assembled at a convention, sense 1] —*Syn.* delegates, representatives, members; see **organization.**

3. [Custom]—*Syn.* practice, habit, fashion; see **custom** 1, 2.

4. [An established mode of procedure]—*Syn.* canon, code, precept; see **custom** 2, **law** 2.

conventional, *mod.* **1.** [Established by convention] —*Syn.* accustomed, prevailing, accepted, customary, regular, standard, orthodox, wonted, normal, typical, expected, usual, routine, general, everyday, commonplace, ordinary, plain, current, popular, prevalent, predominant, expected, well-known, stereotyped, in established usage; see also sense 2; see also **common** 1, **familiar** 1, **habitual** 1. —*Ant.* atypical, unusual*, unpopular.

2. [In accordance with convention]—*Syn.* established, sanctioned, correct, confirmed, seemly, decorous, fitting, fixed, standard, permanent, set, conforming, conformable, fashionable, formal, ritual, ceremonious, processional, right, precise, ceremonial, not taboo, prearranged, undivergent, undeviating, orderly, arranged, stiff, rigid, stylish, modish, according to Hoyle (D); see also sense 1; see also **fit** 1, 2, **popular** 3.—*Ant.* relaxed, beat*, unconventional.

3. [Devoted to or bound by convention]—*Syn.* formal, stereotyped, orthodox, narrow, narrow-minded, illiberal, dogmatic, insular, isolationist, parochial, strict, rigid, puritanical, inflexible, hidebound, conservative, doctrinal, conforming, literal, believing, unheterodox, not heretical, canonical, evangelical, scriptural, literal, textual, bigoted, obstinate, straight-laced; see also **polite** 1, **prejudiced.**—*Ant.* liberal*, broad-minded, unconventional.

4. [Formalized; *said especially of artistic designs*] —*Syn.* conventionalized, disciplined, regularized; see **regular** 3.

converge, *v.* —*Syn.* meet, unite, focalize, concentrate; see **gather** 1.

convergence, *n.* —*Syn.* union, concurrence, concentration; see **concentration** 1, **meeting** 1.

convergent, *mod.* —*Syn.* converging, meeting, coming together; see **concurrent** 2, **confluent, connecting.**

conversant with, *mod.* —*Syn.* practiced, knowledgeable, well-informed; see **learned** 1.

conversation, *n.* —*Syn.* talk, discourse, discussion, communion, intercourse, consultation, hearing, conference, gossip, converse, chat, colloquy, parley, dialogue, causerie, expression of views, mutual exchange, *tête-à-tête* (French), questions and answers, traffic in ideas, getting to know one another, engaging in persiflage, exchange of witticisms, general conversation, questioning, oral examination, exchange of confidences, unburdening oneself, talking it out, heart-to-heart talk; *all* (D): grooming talk(ing), palaver, powwow, bull session, talkfest, chinfest, pillow talk, rap session, chitchat, tattle; see also **communication** 2, **speech** 3.

converse, *mod.* —*Syn.* reversed, contrary, opposite; see **different** 1.

converse, *n.* —*Syn.* inverse, antithesis, reverse; see **opposite.**

conversion, *n.* **1.** [The act of converting or the state of being converted]—*Syn.* growth, passage, metastasis, metabolism, turning point, alteration, transformation, exchange, translation, resolution, passing, transmigration, transfiguration, transmutation, resolving, progress, changeover, flux, transmogrification, reduction, metamorphosis; see also **change** 1, 2.—*Ant.* establishing*, settlement, fixation.

2. [A basic change in belief; especially, espousal of the Christian faith]—*Syn.* turn, spiritual change, regeneration, rebirth, accepting the true faith, turning to the church *or* God *or* Christ (*or* other deity), being born again, being baptized, accepting baptism, seeing the light, change from one religion to another, change in character *or* of heart, new birth; see also **reformation** 1, 2.—*Ant.* reversion, desertion*, fall from grace (D).

convert, *n.* —*Syn.* proselyte, neophyte, disciple; see **follower.**

convert, *v.* **1.** [To alter the form or use]—*Syn.* turn, transform, alter; see **change** 1, **revise.**

2. [To alter convictions]—*Syn.* turn, regenerate, save, bring *or* show the light to, bring to God, baptize, make a Christian *or* convert of, change into, bring over *or* to *or* around, make over, assimilate to, lead to believe, gain the confidence of, change the heart of, proselytize, create anew, cause to adopt a different religion; see also **reform** 1.

converted, *mod.* —*Syn.* convinced, indoctrinated, perverted; see **changed** 2, 3.

convertible, *mod.* —*Syn.* interchangeable, reciprocal, equivalent; see **changeable** 2.

convertible, *n.* —*Syn.* open car, sportscar, hardtop (D); see **automobile.**

convex, *mod.* —*Syn.* curved, arched, raised; see **bent.**

convey, *v.* **1.** [To transport]—*Syn.* bear, dispatch, move; see **carry** 1, **send** 1.

2. [To transmit]—*Syn.* pass on, communicate, conduct; see **carry** 2, **send** 4.

conveyance, *n.* **1.** [The act of conveying]—*Syn.* transfer, movement, transmission; see **communication** 1, **transportation.**
2. [Vehicle]—*Syn.* car, carriage, machine; see **automobile, bus, truck** 1, **vehicle** 1, **wagon.**

convict, *n.* —*Syn.* captive, malefactor, felon; see **criminal, prisoner.**

convict, *v.* —*Syn.* find *or* pronounce guilty, sentence, pass sentence on, adjudge, doom, declare guilty of an offense, bring to justice, seal one's doom; *all* (D): cook, send up, bring home to, rap, do for, put the screws to; see also **condemn** 1.—*Ant.* acquit, liberate*, find not guilty.

conviction, *n.* **1.** [Belief]—*Syn.* persuasion, confidence, reliance; see **belief** 1, **faith** 2.
2. [The state of finding guilty]—*Syn.* unfavorable verdict, determining guilt, condemnation, condemning; see also **blame** 1.

convince, *v.* —*Syn.* prove (to), persuade, induce, establish, refute, satisfy, assure, demonstrate, argue into, change, sway, effect, overcome, turn, put *or* bring *or* win *or* gain over, bring around *or* round, put across, bring to one's senses, bring to reason, gain the confidence of; *all* (D): have the ear of, cram *or* put into one's head, sell (a bill of goods), bring home to; see also **confute, prove, teach** 1.

convinced, *mod.* —*Syn.* converted, indoctrinated, talked into something; see also **changed** 2, 3.

convince oneself, *v.* —*Syn.* be convinced *or* converted, persuade oneself, make up one's (own) mind; see **believe** 1, **prove.**

convincing, *mod.* **1.** [Persuasive]—*Syn.* impressive, swaying, moving; see **persuasive.**
2. [Believable]—*Syn.* trustworthy, credible, acceptable, reasonable, creditable, plausible, probable, likely, presumable, possible, dependable, hopeful, worthy of confidence, to be depended on; see also **rational** 2, **reliable** 2.

convivial, *mod.* **1.** [Sociable]—*Syn.* genial, jovial, gay; see **friendly, pleasant** 1.
2. [Festive]—*Syn.* festal, holiday, entertaining; see **pleasant** 2.

conviviality, *n.* —*Syn.* festivity, gaiety, sociability; see **merriment** 2.

convocation, *n.* —*Syn.* assembly, meeting, conference; see **gathering.**

convoke, *v.* —*Syn.* convene, gather together, muster; see **assemble** 2.

convoy, *n.* —*Syn.* guard, attendance, protection; see **companion** 3, **escort.**

convoy, *v.* —*Syn.* escort, attend, watch; see **accompany** 1, **guard** 2.

convulse, *v.* —*Syn.* disturb, agitate, mix, stir, torment, irritate, torture; see also **bother** 2, **disturb** 2.

convulsion, *n.* **1.** [Spasm]—*Syn.* paroxysm, epilepsy, attack; see **fit** 1.
2. [Disturbance]—*Syn.* turbulence, agitation, commotion; see **disturbance** 2.

cook, *n.* —*Syn.* meat cook, pastry cook, short-order cook, chef, salad chef, pastry chef, mess sergeant, *chef de cuisine* (French), cook-general (British), head cook; see also **servant.**

cook, *v.* —*Syn.* prepare, fix, mull, warm (up *or* over), stew, simmer, sear, braise, decoct, scald, blanch, broil, parch, scorch, poach, toast, dry, chafe, fricassee, percolate, steam, pressure-cook, curry, devil, bake, sauté, griddle, brew, boil (down), parboil, coddle, seethe, barbecue, grill, roast, pan fry, pan broil, deep *or* French fry, brown, steep, imbue, reduce, inspissate, microwave, cook over a slow fire, broast (D); see also **fry, heat** 1, **toast** 2.

cooking, *mod.* **1.** [Being cooked]—*Syn.* simmering, heating, scalding, mulling, brewing, stewing, decocting, steeping, frying, broiling, griddling, grilling, browning, roasting, baking; see also **boiling.**
2. [(D) In preparation]—*Syn.* being made *or* prepared, going on, under way; see **happening.**

cooking, *n.* —*Syn.* cookery, dish, dainty; see **food.**

cookout, *n.* —*Syn.* festivity, barbecue, outdoor dinner; see **picnic** 2.

cook up (D), *v.* —*Syn.* make up, concoct, falsify; see **arrange** 2, **plan** 1, 2.

cooky, *n.* —*Syn.* small cake, sweet wafer, bun; see **bread** 1, **cake** 2, **pastry.**
Common varieties of cookies include the following—cream, lemon, Boston, seed, icebox, oatmeal, lace, vanilla, chocolate, sugar, eggless, ginger, molasses, etc., cooky; gingersnap, fig bar, raisin bar, chocolate chip, jumble, Scotch shortbread, Scotch cake, doughnut, macaroon, Mary Ann, tart, fruit bar, brownie, Marguerite, *petit beurre* (French), pinwheel, wafer.

cool, *mod.* **1.** [Having a low temperature]—*Syn.* cooling, frigid, frosty, wintry, somewhat *or* a little *or* moderately *or* rather cold, chilly, heat-repelling, shivery, chill, chilling, refrigerated, air-conditioned, snappy, nippy, nipping, biting; see also **cold** 1.—*Ant.* tepid, warm*, heated.
2. [Calm]—*Syn.* unruffled, imperturbable, composed; see **calm** 1.
3. [Somewhat angry or disapproving]—*Syn.* disapproving, annoyed, offended; see **angry, indifferent** 1.
4. [(D) Excellent]—*Syn.* *all* (D): neat, keen, groovy; see **excellent.**
play it cool—*Syn.* hold back, underplay, exercise restraint; see **restrain** 1.

cool, *v.* **1.** [To become cool]—*Syn.* lose heat, moderate, lessen, freeze, reduce, calm, chill, cool off, become cold, be chilled to the bone, become chilly; see also **freeze** 1, 2.—*Ant.* heat, thaw*, become warm.
2. [To cause to become cool]—*Syn.* temper, mitigate, chill, moderate, lessen, abate, allay, refrigerate, infrigidate, air-cool, air-condition, pre-cool, frost, reduce the temperature of, freeze, quick-freeze (D); see also **freeze** 2.—*Ant.* burn*, warm, defrost.

cool it (D), *v.* —*Syn.* quiet down, hold back, be sensible; see **restrain oneself.**

co-operate, *v.* **1.** [To work together]—*Syn.* unite, combine, concur, conspire, concert, pool, join forces, act in concert, stand *or* hold *or* stick together, show (a) willingness, comply with, join in, go along with, make common cause, unite efforts, share in, second, cast in one's lot with, take part, be a party to, act jointly, work in unison, participate, work side by side (with), side with, take sides with, join hands with, fraternize; *all* (D): level with, play along (with), play fair, throw *or* fall in with, be in cahoots, chip in, stand shoulder to shoulder, pull

together; see also **agree, join** 2.—*Ant.* act independently, differ*, diverge.
2. [To help]—*Syn.* contribute, second, espouse, uphold, befriend, succor, lend oneself to, share, lend a hand, go out of the way for, assist, relieve, reinforce, promote, further, forward, advance, sustain, back up, stand by, side with; see also **encourage** 1, **help, support** 2.—*Ant.* hamper, hinder*, harm.

co-operating, *mod.* —*Syn.* assisting, agreeing, collaborating; see **helpful** 1.

co-operation, *n.* **1.** [Mutual assistance]—*Syn.* collaboration, participation, combination, concert, confunction, union, concurrence, confederacy, confederation, conspiracy, alliance, society, company, partnership, coalition, fusion, federation, clanship, partisanship, unanimity, concord, harmony, gung hoism (D); see also **agreement** 2, **association** 1.—*Ant.* discord, disagreement*, separation.
2. [Aid]—*Syn.* help, assistance, service; see **aid** 1.

co-operative, *mod.* **1.** [Helpful]—*Syn.* sociable, companionable, useful; see **helpful** 1.
2. [Concerning co-operative organization]—*Syn.* co-operating, agreeing, joining, combining, collaborating, collegial, coactive, uniting, concurring, participating, symbiotic, in joint operation; see also **united.**—*Ant.* competitive, independent*, rival.

co-operative, *n.* —*Syn.* marketing co-operative, consumer's co-operative, communal society *or* business *or* enterprise *or* establishment, kibbutz, commune, collective farm, state farm, soviet; *kolkhoz, sovkhoz* (*both* Russian); collective, co-op (D); see also **association** 1, **organization** 3.

co-ordinate, *mod.* —*Syn.* coequal, same, alike; see **equal, like.**

co-ordinate, *v.* —*Syn.* harmonize, regulate, organize; see **adjust** 1, **agree.**

co-ordinates, *n.* —*Syn.* points of reference, latitude and longitude, specifications of the location of a point, set of variables, set of parameters, system of measurement of state *or* motion; see also **measure** 1, **position** 1.

co-ordinator, *n.* —*Syn.* superintendent, supervisor, organizer; see **administrator, adviser.**

cope with, *v.* —*Syn.* encounter, suffer, confront; see **endure** 2, **face** 1.

copied, *mod.* **1.** [Reproduced]—*Syn.* dittoed, duplicated, transcribed; see **printed, reproduced.**
2. [Imitated]—*Syn.* made in facsimile, mimicked, aped; see **imitated.**

copious, *mod.* **1.** [Abundant]—*Syn.* lavish, replete, extensive; see **plentiful** 2.
2. [Verbose]—*Syn.* profuse, prolix, wordy; see **verbose.**

copiousness, *n.* —*Syn.* abundance, richness, affluence; see **plenty.**

copper, *n.* **1.** [(D) A coin of small value]—*Syn.* cent, penny, farthing (British); see **money** 1.
2. [A metallic element]—*Syn.* Cu (chemical symbol), biological trace element, major element of the alloys bronze and brass; see **element** 2, **metal.**

copse, *n.* —*Syn.* thicket, brushwood, scrub; see **brush** 4, **hedge, plant, tree.**

copulate, *v.* —*Syn.* unite, couple, cover, serve, lie with, know, sleep with *or* together, (go to) bed, make love, have sex, mate, have relations, have sexual *or* marital *or* extramarital relations, be carnal, unite sexually, have (sexual) intercourse, breed, cohabit, have coition, fornicate, break the seventh commandment; *all* (D): lay, ball, fool around, screw, make out, have funny business, do *or* make it, get it on; see also **join** 1.—*Ant.* abstain*, be continent, be celibate.

copulation, *n.* —*Syn.* coitus, intercourse, sex, sex act, sexual union *or* congress, coupling, mating, coition, carnal knowledge, love, venereal act; see also **fornication, sex** 1.

copulative, *mod.* —*Syn.* joining, uniting, linking; see also **connecting.**

copy, *n.* —*Syn.* facsimile, photostat, likeness, print, similarity, mimeograph sheet, simulation, mirror, impersonation, offprint, Xerox (trademark), semblance, HC *or* hard copy, MC *or* microfiche, imitation of an original, forgery, counterfeit, reprint, rubbings, transcript, carbon, replica, typescript, transcription, cast, tracing, effigy, counterpart, likeness, portrait, model, reflection, representation, study, photograph, carbon, *or* examined *or* certified *or* exemplified *or* office *or* typed *or* pencil *or* fair copy, ditto (D); see also **duplicate** 1, **imitation** 2, **reproduction** 3.

copy, *v.* **1.** [To imitate]—*Syn.* follow the example of, mimic, ape; see **follow, imitate.**
2. [To reproduce]—*Syn.* represent, paraphrase, counterfeit, forge, cartoon, delineate, depict, portray, picture, limn, draw, sketch, paint, sculpture, mold, engrave, reduplicate; see also **reproduce** 1, 2.

copyist, *n.* **1.** [One who imitates]—*Syn.* mimic, copier, parrot; see **imitator.**
2. [One who makes copies]—*Syn.* clerk, copier, scrivener; see also **photographer, secretary** 2.

coquet, *v.* —*Syn.* tease, titillate, wink at; see **flirt with** 1.

coquette, *n.* —*Syn.* tease, trifler, gold-digger (D); see **flirt.**

cord, *n.* **1.** [Twine]—*Syn.* string, cordage, fiber; see **rope.**
2. [A tendon]—*Syn.* vinculum, sinew, ligament, thew, umbilical cord, connective tissue, tie; see also **muscle.**

cordial, *mod.* **1.** [Hearty]—*Syn.* genial, affable, warm-hearted; see **friendly** 1, **hearty** 1.
2. [Friendly and sincere]—*Syn.* amicable, neighborly, social; see **friendly** 1, **polite** 1.

cordiality, *n.* —*Syn.* affability, warmth, earnestness; see **sincerity.**

cordially, *mod.* —*Syn.* genially, warmly, hospitably; see **sincerely.**

core, *n.* **1.** [Essence]—*Syn.* gist, kernel, heart; see **essence** 1.
2. [Center]—*Syn.* hub. focus, pivot; see **center** 1.

corespondent, *n.* —*Syn.* third party, second man *or* woman, other man *or* woman, one corner of the triangle, joint respondent *or* defendant; see also **defendant, other.**

cork, *n.* —*Syn.* stopper, tap, spike; see **plug** 1.

cormorant, *n.* —*Syn.* gourmand, hog, greedy person; see **glutton.**

corn, *n.* —*Syn.* oats, millet, maize; see **food, grain** 1.

corn, *v.* —*Syn.* can, salt, pickle; see **preserve** 3.

corn bread, *n.* —*Syn.* hoe cake(s), corndodgers, corncakes, hot bread, johnnycake, journey cakes, hush puppies, corn pone, spoon bread; see also **bread, cake** 2.

corner, *n.* **1.** [A projecting edge]—*Syn.* ridge, sharp edge, projection; see **edge** 1, **rim.**
2. [A recess]—*Syn.* niche, nook, indentation; see **hole** 2.
3. [A sharp turn]—*Syn.* bend, veer, shift; see **curve** 1, **turn** 2.
4. [The angle made where ways intersect]—*Syn.* corners, fork, branch, V, Y, intersection, four corners, cloverleaf; see also **crossing** 1, **junction** 2.
5. [(D) Difficulty]—*Syn.* impediment, distress, knot; see **difficulty** 2.
around the corner—*Syn.* immediate, near, next; see **soon** 1.
cut corners—*Syn.* cut down *or* back, shorten, reduce; see **decrease** 2.
the (four) corners of the earth—*Syn.* all over the world, world-wide, universal; see **everywhere.**
turn the corner—*Syn.* survive, proceed, bear up; see **endure** 2.

corner, *v.* —*Syn.* trap, trick, fool; see **catch** 1, **deceive.**

cornerstone, *n.* —*Syn.* base, foundation stone, memorial stone, starting point; see also **foundation** 2.

cornerwise, *mod.* —*Syn.* cornerways, diagonally, cater-corner, cater-cornerways, obliquely, askew, slanting, aslant, from corner to corner, on the bias, angling, diagonalwise; *all* (D): slaunchwise, kitty-corner, catawampus.

corn on the cob, *n.* —*Syn.* green corn, sweet corn, field corn; see **food, grain** 1.

corny (D), *mod.* —*Syn.* stale, trite, stereotyped; see **dull** 4, **stupid** 1.

corollary, *n.* **1.** [An inference]—*Syn.* deduction, analogy, result; see **judgment** 3.
2. [A natural consequence]—*Syn.* culmination, conclusion, upshot; see **end** 2, **result.**

coronation, *n.* —*Syn.* accession, crowning, inauguration; see **installation** 1.

coronet, *n.* —*Syn.* headdress, tiara, diadem; see **crown** 2.

corporal punishment, *n.* —*Syn.* spanking, execution, torture; see **punishment.**

corporation, *n.* —*Syn.* partnership, enterprise, company; see **business** 4, **organization** 3.

corporeal, *mod.* —*Syn.* human, mortal, material; see **bodily** 1, **physical** 1.

corps, *n.* —*Syn.* troops, brigade, regiment; see **army** 2, **organization** 3.

corpse, *n.* —*Syn.* carcass, remains, cadaver; see **body** 2.

corpulence, *n.* —*Syn.* obesity, stoutness, plumpness; see **fatness.**

corpulent, *mod.* —*Syn.* overweight, fleshy, beefy; see **fat** 1.

correct, *mod.* **1.** [Accurate]—*Syn.* exact, true, right; see **accurate** 1.
2. [Proper]—*Syn.* suitable, becoming, fitting; see **fit** 1.

correct, *v.* **1.** [To make needed corrections]—*Syn.* better, help, ameliorate, remove the errors *or* faults of, emend, improve, remedy, alter, rectify, retouch, redress, reclaim, accommodate for, make right, mend, amend, fix (up), do over, reform, remodel, review, reconstruct, reorganize, edit, revise, make corrections, make improvements (in), set aright, make right, make compensation *or* reparation (for), put in order; *all* (D): doctor, touch up, polish; see also **adjust** 3, **change** 1, **improve** 1, **repair.**
2. [To administer correction]—*Syn.* admonish, chide, reprimand; see **punish.**

corrected, *mod.* —*Syn.* rectified, amended, reformed; see **changed** 2, **revised.**

correction, *n.* **1.** [The act of correcting]—*Syn.* revisal, revising, re-examination, rereading, remodeling, rectification, editing, removal, righting, redress, indemnification, reparation, amelioration, mending, fixing, amending, emendation, changing; see also **repair.**
2. [The result of correcting]—*Syn.* alteration, reconstruction, reorganization; see **review** 1, **revision.**

corrective, *mod.* —*Syn.* restorative, curative, healing; see **remedial.**

correctly, *mod.* —*Syn.* rightly, precisely, perfectly; see **accurately.**

correctness, *n.* **1.** [Accuracy]—*Syn.* precision, exactness, exactitude; see **accuracy** 2, **truth** 1.
2. [Propriety]—*Syn.* decency, decorum, rightness; see **fitness, propriety** 1.

correlate, *v.* **1.** [To relate]—*Syn.* connect, equate, associate; see **compare** 1.
2. [To interact]—*Syn.* correspond, reciprocate, relate mutually (with *or* to); see **alternate** 1, **exchange** 2.

correlation, *n.* —*Syn.* interdependence, alternation, equivalence; see **interchange** 2, **relationship.**

correspond, *v.* **1.** [To be alike]—*Syn.* compare, match, be similar *or* identical; see **resemble.**
2. [To communicate, usually by letter]—*Syn.* exchange letters, hear from, write to, correspond *or* communicate with, send word, send a letter (to), keep up a correspondence, epistolize, reply; *both* (D): drop a line, keep in touch, have a pen pal; see also **answer** 1, **communicate** 2.

correspondence, *n.* **1.** [The quality of being like]—*Syn.* conformity, equivalence, accord; see **agreement** 2, **similarity.**
2. [Communication, usually by letter]—*Syn.* messages, reports, exchange of letters; see **communication** 2.

correspondent, *n.* **1.** [One who sends or receives letters]—*Syn.* (letter) writer, friend, acquaintance, pen pal (D).
2. [One who writes for journals]—*Syn.* journalist, contributor, free-lancer (D); see **reporter, writer.**

corresponding, *mod.* —*Syn.* identical, similar, coterminous; see **like.**

correspond to, *v.* —*Syn.* accord, concur, harmonize; see **agree.**

corridor, *n.* —*Syn.* passage, foyer, lobby; see **hall** 2.

corroborate, *v.* —*Syn.* confirm, strengthen, establish; see **approve** 1, **prove.**

corroborative, *mod.* —*Syn.* assenting, affirmatory, agreeing; see **affirmative.**

corrode, *v.* **1.** [To destroy]—*Syn.* erode, gnaw, consume; see **destroy** 1.

2. [To deteriorate]—*Syn.* rot, degenerate, deteriorate; see **decay, rust.**

corrosive, *mod.* **1.** [Corroding]—*Syn.* eroding, strongly acid, caustic; see **destructive** 2.

2. [Sarcastic]—*Syn.* caustic, incisive, biting; see **sarcastic.**

corrugated, *mod.* —*Syn.* ridged, grooved, furrowed, folded, fluted, roughened, creased, flexed, crinkled, crumpled, puckered; see also **wrinkled.** —*Ant.* flat*, flattened, even.

corrugation, *n.* —*Syn.* groove, crease, channel; see **fold** 2, **ridge** 1.

corrupt, *mod.* **1.** [Tainted]—*Syn.* putrid, foul, noxious; see **rotten** 1.

2. [Depraved]—*Syn.* low, debased, evil; see **wicked** 1.

3. [Characterized by graft]—*Syn.* exploiting, underhanded, venal, mercenary, fraudulent, crooked, nefarious, iniquitous, profiteering, extortionate, unscrupulous; *all* (D): shady, on the pad, on the take, fixed, padded, crooked as a dog's hind leg; see **dishonest** 1, 2.

4. [Inaccurate]—*Syn.* fallacious, deceptive, misleading; see **wrong** 2.

corrupt, *v.* **1.** [To debase]—*Syn.* pervert, vitiate, degrade, demean, lower, pull down, reduce, abase, adulterate, depreciate, deprave, debauch, defile, demoralize, pollute, taint, contaminate, infect, stain, spoil, load, weight, alloy, blight, blemish, mark against, undermine, impair, mar, injure, harm, hurt, damage, deface, disfigure, deform, abuse, maltreat, ill-treat, outrage, mistreat, misuse, dishonor, disgrace, despoil, violate, waste, ravage, cause to degenerate, cause to deteriorate; *all* (D): dope up, heap dirt upon, engage in personalities; see also **rape, weaken** 2.—*Ant.* purify, clean*, restore.

2. [To render inaccurate]—*Syn.* falsify, misrepresent, misstate, belie, garble, disguise, color, gloss over, varnish, counterfeit, adulterate, fabricate, invent; *all* (D): tamper with, doctor, gerrymander, profiteer, buncomize, fix, pad, boodle; see also **disguise, forge.**

corrupted, *mod.* —*Syn.* debased, perverted, depraved; see **wicked** 1.

corrupter, *n.* —*Syn.* debaucher, sensualist, adulterer; see **criminal, lecher.**

corruption, *n.* **1.** [Decay]—*Syn.* rot, rottenness, noxiousness; see **decay** 2, **pollution.**

2. [Vice]—*Syn.* baseness, depravity, degradation; see **crime** 1, **evil** 1.

3. [Conduct involving graft]—*Syn.* extortion, exploitation, fraudulency, venality, misrepresentation, dishonesty, profiteering, neoptism, breach of trust, malfeasance, bribery, crookedness, shady deal, jobbery, shuffle, racket; see also **crime** 2. —*Ant.* reliability, trustworthiness, truthfulness.

corset, *n.* —*Syn.* corselet, maternity corset, foundation garment, abdominal belt, garter belt, bodice, support, whalebone stays, panty girdle, stomacher (D); see also **clothes, underwear.**

cosmetic, *mod.* —*Syn.* beautifying, corrective, restorative; see **improving, remedial.**

cosmetic, *n.* —*Syn.* makeup, beautifier, beautifying agent *or* application *or* preparation, beauty *or* cosmetic preparation; *all* (D): war paint, get-up, face; see also **makeup** 1.

Cosmetics include the following—hair, muscle, body, cuticle, lip, sunburn, sun tan, etc., oil; hair, vanishing, eye, cold, theatrical, cleansing, liquefying, night, wrinkle, hormone, complexion, skin, massage, lemon, dry-skin, hand, chap, etc., cream; astringent, after-shave, hand, sun tan, etc., lotion; talcum, face, bath, tooth, etc., powder; eyebrow pencil, (cake *or* cream *or* liquid) mascara, (powder *or* cream) eye shadow, eye liner (pencil), (cream *or* dry) rouge, blusher, toner, (lip *or* face) slicker, lipstick, lip rouge, pancake, nail polish, powder base, moisturizer, (cake *or* cream *or* liquid) foundation, (loose *or* pressed) powder, leg make up, body paint, solid perfume, liquid sachet, toilet water, (eau de) cologne, *friction pour le bain* (French), bath salts, bath oil, royal jelly, brilliantine, pomade, hair tonic, hair dye, hair bleach, mouthwash, liquid dentifrice, nail polish remover, moustache wax, facial pack, mud pack, tooth paste, dry shampoo, liquid shampoo, conditioner, rinse, shaving soap *or* cream *or* foam, depilatory, deodorant, antiperspirant; see also **lotion, perfume, powder, soap.**

cosmic, *mod.* —*Syn.* vast, empyrean, grandiose; see **universal** 1.

cosmopolitan, *mod.* —*Syn.* metropolitan, gregarious, catholic; see **international, public** 2, **universal** 3.

cosmopolite, *n.* —*Syn.* citizen of the world, humanist, internationalist, cosmopolitan, wanderer, globe-trotter, eclectic; see also **idealist, traveler.**

cosmos, *n.* **1.** [Order]—*Syn.* harmony, structure, organization; see **order** 3.

2. [The universe]—*Syn.* solar system, galaxy, star system; see **universe.**

cost, *n.* **1.** [Price]—*Syn.* payment, value, charge; see **price, value** 1.

2. [Damage]—*Syn.* hurt, detriment, deprivation; see **damage** 1, 2.

cost, *v.* **1.** [To require in money]—*Syn.* be asked *or* demanded *or* paid *or* given *or* received *or* needed, require, take, be priced *or* marked *or* valued (at), be worth, amount to, be for sale (at), command a price of, mount up to, bring in, sell for; *all* (D): set one back, nick, rap, stand in.

2. [To require in sacrifice]—*Syn.* expect, necessitate, obligate; see **require** 2.

costing, *mod.* —*Syn.* as much as, to the amount of, priced at, no less than, estimated (at), selling (for), on sale (at), reduced (to), a bargain *or* steal (at) (D).

costly, *mod.* —*Syn.* high-priced, dear, precious; see **expensive.**

costs, *n.* —*Syn.* price, outgo, living costs; see **expenses.**

at all costs—*Syn.* by any means, in spite of difficulties, without fail; see **regardless** 2.

costume, *n.* —*Syn.* attire, apparel, garb; see **clothes, dress** 1.

costume, *v.* —*Syn.* dress (up), outfit, fit out; see **clothe.**

cot, *n.* —*Syn.* folding bed, small bed, trundle bed; see **bed** 1, **furniture.**

Cots include the following—army cot, canvas cot, folding cot, iron cot, hospital cot, gurney, *charpoy* (Anglo-Indian).

coterie, *n.* —*Syn.* clique, circle, cadre; see **faction** 1.

cottage, *n.* —*Syn.* cot, cabin, small house; see **home** 1.

cotton, *n.* —*Syn.* *gossypium* (Latin); *both* (D): King Cotton, cotton shrub.
Varieties of cotton include the following—long-staple, short-staple, upland, Sea Island, *Barbadense* (Latin), Nankin, Peruvian, Brazil, Bahia, Egyptian, kidney.
Cotton cloth includes the following—lawn, batiste, chintz, organdy, dotted swiss, voile, cambric, calico, chambray, broadcloth, denim, ticking, net, muslin, crinoline, flannelette, gingham, jersey, piqué, eyelet batiste, lace, monkscloth, poplin, velveteen, gabardine, crepe, twill, canvas, percale, balloon cloth, toweling, terry cloth, sailcloth, cheesecloth, shirting, theatrical gauze; see also **cloth.**

couch, *n.* —*Syn.* sofa, lounge, resting place; see **bed, chair** 1, **davenport, furniture.**

cough, *n.* —*Syn.* hem, hack, frog in one's throat (D); see **cold** 3, **disease** 3.

cough, *v.* —*Syn.* hack, convulse, bark (D); see **choke** 2.

council, *n.* **1.** [A chosen group, usually advisory] —*Syn.* advisory board, cabinet, directorate; see **committee.**
2. [A deliberative meeting]—*Syn.* chamber, senate, congregation; see **gathering.**

counsel, *n.* **1.** [Advice]—*Syn.* guidance, instruction, information; see **advice, suggestion** 1.
2. [A lawyer]—*Syn.* attorney, legal adviser, barrister; see **adviser, lawyer.**
keep one's own counsel—*Syn.* be secretive, conceal oneself, keep quiet; see **hide** 2.
take counsel—*Syn.* listen to advice, confer, talk; see **discuss.**

counsel, *v.* —*Syn.* admonish, direct, inform; see **advise** 1, **teach** 1.

counselor, *n.* **1.** [An adviser]—*Syn.* guide, instructor, mentor; see **adviser, teacher** 1.
2. [An attorney at law]—*Syn.* counsel, advocate, solicitor; see **lawyer.**

count, *n.* **1.** [Man of rank]—*Syn.* nobleman, peer, grandee; see **lord** 2, **nobility** 1.
2. [Total]—*Syn.* number, sum, outcome; see **result, whole.**

count, *v.* —*Syn.* compute, reckon, enumerate, number, add up, sum, figure, cast up, count off *or* up, cipher; *all* (D): foot (up), count noses, score; see also **add** 1, **total** 1.

countdown, *n.* —*Syn.* preparation, launch procedure, hold; see **program** 2.

countenance, *n.* —*Syn.* look, aspect, visage; see **appearance** 1, **expression** 4.

countenance, *v.* —*Syn.* confirm, commend, endorse; see **approve** 1.

counter, *n.* —*Syn.* board, shelf, ledge; see **bench** 2, **table** 1.
under the counter—*Syn.* black-market, surreptitious, unofficial; see **illegal.**

counteract, *v.* —*Syn.* frustrate, neutralize, invalidate; see **check** 2, **halt** 2, **hinder, prevent.**

counteraction, *n.* **1.** [Opposition]—*Syn.* resistance, antagonism, contradiction; see **opposition** 1.
2. [An attack]—*Syn.* counterattack, blow, counterassault; see **attack** 1.

counteractive, *n.* —*Syn.* relief, cure, preventive; see **medicine** 2, **remedy** 2.

counteractively, *mod.* —*Syn.* nullifying, clashing, reacting, checking, countering, interfering, counter to; see also **opposite** 3.

counterbalance, *v.* —*Syn.* compensate, counteract, equalize; see **balance** 2, **offset.**

counterfeit, *mod.* **1.** [Not genuine]—*Syn.* sham, spurious, fictitious; see **false** 3.
2. [Pretended]—*Syn.* assumed, pretentious, put-on; see **affected** 2, **pretended.**

counterfeit, *v.* **1.** [To defraud by making copies of money, stamps, etc.]—*Syn.* print *or* copy money *or* stamps, make (counterfeit) money, imitate bills, coin, circulate bad money; see also **forge, mint** 1.
2. [To pretend]—*Syn.* simulate, cheat, delude; see **deceive, pretend** 1.

counterfeiter, *n.* —*Syn.* forger, pretender, plagiarist; see **criminal, impostor.**

counterfeiting, *n.* —*Syn.* copying, simulation, duplication; see **imitation** 1, **reproduction** 1.

countermand, *v.* —*Syn.* rescind, reverse, retract; see **revoke.**

counterpane, *n.* —*Syn.* eiderdown, comforter, coverlet; see **bedspread, cover** 2, **quilt.**

countersign, *n.* —*Syn.* watchword, slogan, catchword; see **motto, password.**

countess, *n.* —*Syn.* member of the peerage, great lady, wife *or* window of a count *or* earl; see **lady** 3, **nobility** 1.

countless, *mod.* —*Syn.* innumerable, incalculable, numberless; see **infinite** 1, **many.**

count off, *v.* —*Syn.* number, get numbers for, give numbers to; see **check** 3, **count, total** 1.

count on, *v.* —*Syn.* rely *or* depend on *or* upon, reckon *or* count *or* calculate *or* lean *or* build *or* rest upon, expect from, place a trust *or* confidence in, take on trust *or* for granted, believe *or* trust in, heed, swear by, place reliance on, make oneself easy about, stake on (D); see also **trust** 1.

count out, *v.* —*Syn.* remove, mark off, get rid of; see **eliminate** 1.

count over, *v.* —*Syn.* audit, tally, review; see **correct** 1, **examine** 1, **revise.**

countrified, *mod.* —*Syn.* provincial, agrarian, rural; see **rustic** 2.

country, *mod.* **1.** [Said of people]—*Syn.* countrified, unsophisticated, rural, homey, bucolic, georgic, unpolished, unrefined, uncouth, uncultured; see also **ignorant** 2, **rude** 1, 2, **rustic** 2.
2. [*Said of areas*]—*Syn.* rustic, agrarian, provincial; see **rural.**

country, *n.* **1.** [Rural areas]—*Syn.* farms, farmland, farming district, farm tracts, rural region *or* area, country district, back country, bush, forests, woodlands, backwoods, sparsely settled areas; *all* (D): sticks, the boondocks *or* boonies, the hinterland; see also **farm, forest, range** 4.—*Ant.* city*, borough, municipality.
2. [A nation]—*Syn.* government, a people, a sovereign state; see **nation** 1.
3. [Land and all that is associated with it]—*Syn.* homeland, native land, fatherland, *patria* (Latin), all we hold dear, *Vaterland* (German), *la patrie*

(French); all (D): Sweet Land of Liberty, the flag; mother and apple pie.

countryman, *n.* **1.** [A compatriot]—*Syn.* fellow citizen, national, kinsman; see **citizen.**
2. [A man living in the country]—*Syn.* rustic, bucolic, rancher, agriculturist, farm *or* rural laborer, farm help *or* hand, country person, farm vote; *all* (D) rube, hayseed, hick; see also **boor, farmer, peasant.**

countryside, *n.* —*Syn.* rural area *or* district, farmland, woods; see **country** 1.

count up, *v.* —*Syn.* compute, get a total for, bring together; see **add** 1, **total** 1.

county, *n.* —*Syn.* province, constituency, shire; see **division** 6.

coup, *n.* **1.** [Maneuver]—*Syn.* plot, stratagem, achievement; see **tactics.**
2. [Revolution]—*Syn.* upset, overthrow, *coup d'état* (French); see **revolution** 2.

coup de grâce (French), *n.* —*Syn.* deathblow, final stroke, quietus; see **blow** 1, **defeat** 2, 3.

coup d'etat (French), *n.* —*Syn.* revolt, rebellion, overthrow; see **revolution** 2.

couple, *n.* **1.** [A pair]—*Syn.* two, set, brace; see **pair.**
2. [(D) A few]—*Syn.* two, several, a handful; see **few.**

couple, *v.* —*Syn.* unite, come *or* bring together, link; see **copulate, join** 1.

coupon, *n.* —*Syn.* token, box top, order blank, detachable portion, separate ticket, redeemable part, redemption slip, (premium) certificate, (commuter) ticket, (ration) slip, evidence of purchase, credit *or* installment slip *or* check; see also **card, ticket** 1.

courage, *n.* **1.** [Readiness to dare]—*Syn.* bravery, *bravura* (Italian), valor, valorousness, boldness, intrepidity, fearlessness, spirit, audacity, audaciousness, temerity, manliness, dauntlessness, pluck, mettle, enterprise, stoutheartedness, firmness, self-reliance, hardihood, heroism, gallantry, daring, prowess, power, resolution, resoluteness, élan, doughtiness, adventuresomeness, adventurousness, venturesomeness, dash, recklessness, derring-do, pugnacity, pluckiness, gameness, rashness, defiance, the courage of one's convictions; *all* (D): spunk, grit, face, backbone, guts, what it takes, nerve, nerves of steel, intestinal fortitude; see also **strength** 1.—*Ant.* cowardice, fear*, timidity.
2. [Ability to endure]—*Syn.* sufferance, coolness, firmness; see **determination** 2, **endurance** 2.

courageous, *mod.* —*Syn.* daring, gallant, intrepid; see **brave** 1.

courier, *n.* —*Syn.* runner, dispatcher, herald; see **messenger.**

course, *n.* **1.** [A route]—*Syn.* passage, path, way; see **route** 1.
2. [A prepared way, especially for racing]—*Syn.* lap, cinder path, cinder track; see **road** 1, **track** 1.
3. [A plan of study]—*Syn.* subject, studies, curriculum, matriculation, program, specialty, professional *or* humanistic *or* scientific preparation; see also **education** 1.
4. [A series of lessons]—*Syn.* classes, class meetings, lectures, laboratories *or* laboratory periods, discussion group, seminar, conferences, sessions, colloquia, labs (D); see also **class** 3.
in due course—*Syn.* in due time, properly, conveniently; see **appropriately.**
in the course of—*Syn.* during, in the process of, when; see **while.**
of course—*Syn.* certainly, by all means, indeed; see **surely.**
off course—*Syn.* misdirected, erratic, going the wrong way; see **wrong** 2.
on course—*Syn.* on target, correct, going in the right direction; see **accurate** 1.

courser, *n.* —*Syn.* racer, racing dog, thoroughbred; see **dog.**

court, *n.* **1.** [An enclosed, roofless area]—*Syn.* square, courtyard, quadrangle, enclosure, street, forum, patio, quad (D); see also **yard** 1.
2. [An instrument for administering justice]—*Syn.* tribunal, forum (of justice), judicial forum, bench, magistrate, bar, session; see also **judge** 1.
Types of courts include the following—the Supreme Court of the United States, appellate court of the United States, Federal court, State supreme court, district court, county court, municipal court, probate court, traffic court, justice's court, magistrate's court, mayor's court, police court.
3. [The home of a court, sense 2]—*Syn.* courthouse, justice building, court building, hall of justice, courtroom, federal building, county courthouse, municipal building, city hall.
4. [A ruler and his surroundings]—*Syn.* prince, sovereign, king, retinue, lords and ladies, attendants, suite, royal persons, staff, train, royal residence, palace, castle, hall, royal household, entourage; see also **government** 2, **royalty, ruler** 1.
5. [An area for playing certain games]—*Syn.* rink, ring, lists, cockpit, circus, the hardwood (D); see also **arena, field** 2.
pay court to—*Syn.* woo, attract, solicit; see **court** 1.

court, *v.* **1.** [To woo]—*Syn.* invite, bid, attract, allure, solicit, beseech, entice, entreat, importune, sue for, pursue, follow, seek after, make suit, supplicate, plead, make love, pay court, make interest, pay attentions to, pay court to, seek the hand of, pay one's addresses to, philander, coquet, pay one's court, make overtures, go courting, propose, make a proposal, ask in marriage; *all* (D): set one's cap for, pop the question, chase, make time with, go steady, go together *or* with, make a play for; see also **accompany** 1, **date** 2, **praise** 3.
2. [To seek favor]—*Syn.* attend, flatter, please; see **grovel, praise** 1.

courteous, *mod.* —*Syn.* courtly, affiable, cultivated; see **polite** 1.

courteously, *mod.* —*Syn.* civilly, affably, obligingly; see **politely.**

courtesan, *n.* —*Syn.* mistress, concubine, whore; see **prostitute.**

courtesy, *n.* **1.** [Courteous conduct]—*Syn.* kindness, friendliness, courtliness, complaisance, affability, courteousness, gentleness, consideration, thoughtfulness, sympathy, geniality, cordiality, graciousness, solicitude, amiability, tact, good behavior *or* manners, amenities, politeness, *prévenance, bienséance* (*both* French), comity, culture, refinement, address, cultivation, chivalry, urbanity, gallantry, respect, indulgence, familiarity, favor, reverence, deference, elegance of manners, polished

manners, good *or* gentle breeding, suavity of manner, excellence of behavior; see also **generosity** 1.
2. [Courteous act]—*Syn.* compassion, service, favor, benevolence, unselfishness, loving-kindness, accommodation, liberality, generosity, charity, bounty; see also **kindness** 2.—*Ant.* selfishness, inhumanity, ruthlessness.

courtier, *n.* —*Syn.* valet, subject, squire; see **attendant, servant.**

courtliness, *n.* —*Syn.* gallantry, refinement, politeness; see **courtesy** 1, **elegance** 1.

courtly, *mod.* —*Syn.* elegant, dignified, refined; see **cultured, polite** 1.

courtship, *n.* —*Syn.* love-making, dating, wooing; see **love** 1.

courtyard, *n.* —*Syn.* court, patio, lawn; see **yard** 1.

cousin, *n.* —*Syn.* kin, an aunt's child, an uncle's child, father's *or* mother's sibling's child, first cousin, second cousin, distant cousin, kinsman, kinswoman; see also **relative.**

cove, *n.* **1.** [Bay]—*Syn.* inlet, sound, lagoon; see **bay.**
2. [Cave]—*Syn.* cavern, retreat, nook; see **hole** 3.

covenant, *n.* —*Syn.* bond, pact, promise; see **agreement** 3, **contract** 1, **treaty.**

covenant, *v.* —*Syn.* promise, concur, pledge; see **agree, contract** 3.

cover, *n.* **1.** [A covering object]—*Syn.* covering, ceiling, canopy, awning, tent, marquee, umbrella, parasol, thatch, coverlet, dome, stopper, lid, canvas, seal, tarpaulin, book cover, folder, wrapper, wrapping paper, jacket, case, spread, tarp (D); see also **blanket** 2, **envelope, folder** 2, **hood** 1, 2, **roof, sheath, sheet** 1.
2. [A covering substance]—*Syn.* overlay, binding, slate, paint, shingle, veneer, varnish, polish; see also **coat** 3, **sheet** 2.
3. [Shelter]—*Syn.* harbor, asylum, refuge; see **retreat** 2, **sanctuary** 2, **shelter.**
4. [Protection]—*Syn.* covert, hiding place, screen; see **camouflage** 1, **defense** 2, **shelter.**
take cover—*Syn.* conceal oneself, take shelter, go indoors; see **hide** 2.
under cover—*Syn.* secretive, hiding, concealed; see **hidden** 2.

cover, *v.* **1.** [To place as a covering]—*Syn.* carpet, set *or* put on, overlay, lay over, surface, board (up), superimpose, settle, back in *or* out; see also **spread** 4.
2. [To wrap]—*Syn.* envelop, enshroud, encase; see **wrap** 2.
3. [To protect]—*Syn.* shield, screen, house; see **defend** 1, 2, **shelter.**
4. [To hide]—*Syn.* screen, camouflage, mask; see **disguise, hide** 1.
5. [To include]—*Syn.* embrace, comprise, incorporate; see **include** 1.
6. [To suffice]—*Syn.* reach, be enough, meet; see **satisfy** 3.
7. [To copulate; *said of animals*]—*Syn.* couple, unite, mate; see **copulate, join** 1.
8. [To travel]—*Syn.* traverse, journey over, cross; see **travel** 2.
9. [To send down in plenty]—*Syn.* deluge, pour, rain, inundate, submerge, shower, drench, engulf, overcome, drown out, overflow, overspread, send down like manna from heaven (D); see also **flood.**
10. [(D) To report upon, especially for a newspaper] —*Syn.* recount, narrate, relate; see **broadcast** 2, **record** 3.

covered, *mod.* **1.** [Provided with a cover]—*Syn.* topped, overlaid, lidded, roofed, hooded, wrapped, enveloped, sheathed, veiled, bound, painted, varnished, coated, surfaced, camouflaged, sheltered, shielded, separated, disguised, masked, secreted, protected, concealed, socked in (D); see also **hidden** 2.—*Ant.* revealed, obvious*, exposed.
2. [Plentifully bestrewn]—*Syn.* scattered with, bejeweled, sprinkled over, spattered, spangled, dotted, strewn with, starred, starry with, flowery, flowered, spotted with, sown, dusted over, powdered, spread with.—*Ant.* bare, empty*, unfurnished.
3. [Attended to]—*Syn.* noted, taken note of, accounted for, recorded, written, included, marked, explored, regarded, scrutinized, examined, surveyed, investigated, observed, looked to, cared for; see also **recognized, reported.**—*Ant.* unheeded*, unnoticed, passed over.

covering, *n.* —*Syn.* concealment, top, tegument; see **cover** 1.

coverlet, *n.* —*Syn.* spread, cover, comforter; see **bedspread, quilt.**

covert, *n.* **1.** [A thicket]—*Syn.* copse, underwood, bushes; see **brush** 4, **bush.**
2. [A shelter or hiding place]—*Syn.* shield, asylum, harbor; see **refuge** 1, **retreat** 2, **sanctuary** 2, **shelter.**

cover up for, *v.* —*Syn.* front *or* lie for; *both* (D): take the rap for, be the goat; see also **defend** 1, 2, **shelter.**

covet, *v.* —*Syn.* desire, envy, wish for; see **want** 1.

covetous, *mod.* —*Syn.* avaricious, selfish, rapacious; see **greedy.**

covetousness, *n.* —*Syn.* avarice, cupidity, avariciousness; see **greed.**

covey, *n.* —*Syn.* group of birds, bunch, flock; see **bird** 1, **herd** 1.

cow, *n.* —*Syn.* heifer, milk cow, dairy cow, bovine; *both* (D): critter, bossy; see also **bull** 1, **calf.**
Breeds of cows include the following—*beef:* Aberdeen Angus, Hereford, Longhorn, Texas Longhorn, Durham, Sussex, Galloway, whiteface (D); *dairy:* Ayrshire, Guernsey, Jersey, Holstein-Friesian, Alderney, Brown Swiss, Dexter, Kerry, Simmenthal, Jutland, Red Danish; *dual-purpose:* Red Poll, Shorthorn, Devon, Dutch Belted, French Canadian.

coward, *n.* —*Syn.* poltroon, craven, recreant, dastard, caitiff, cur, wheyface, sneak, faintheart, mollycoddle, milksop, shirk, shirker, deserter, browbeater, bully, swaggerer, blusterer, weakling, panicmonger, scaramouch, alarmist, pessimist, base fellow, malingerer; *all* (D): funk, slacker, quitter, punk, chicken, lily-liver, scaredy-cat, chickenheart, fraidy-cat, rabbit, yellow-belly; see also **deserter.**

cowardice, *n.* —*Syn.* pusillanimity, cowardliness, cravenness, timorousness, timidity, effeminacy, faint-heartedness, baseness (abject) fear, weakness, quailing, shrinking, cowering, crouching, fawning, groveling, sniveling, abjectness, bullying, funk, funkiness, recreancy, dastardy, dastardliness, want of courage, poltroonery, apprehension, dread, browbeating, diffidence, apprehensiveness, fearfulness, suspicion; *all* (D): baby act, white feather, yellow streak, lack of guts, cold feet; see also **fear** 2, **shyness.**—*Ant.* bravery, valor*, fearlessness.

cowardly, *mod.* **1.** [Lacking courage]—*Syn.* timid, timorous, frightened, shrinking, afraid, fearful, shy, diffident, backward, retiring, cowering, apprehensive, nervous, anxious, full of dread, dismayed, faint-hearted, panicky, scared; *all* (D): scary, jittery, chicken, lacking *or* having no guts; see also **afraid** 1, **weak** 3.—*Ant.* fearless, brave*, intrepid.
2. [Suggestive of a coward]—*Syn.* pusillanimous, poltroonish, craven, dastardly, recreant, poor-spirited, mean-spirited, weak, bullying, soft, effeminate, unmanly, irresolute, pliant; *all* (D): chicken-livered, lily-livered, rabbit-hearted, yellow; see also **irresolute, vulgar** 1.—*Ant.* frank*, candid, open.
3. [In the manner of a coward]—*Syn.* skulking, sneaking, cringing, cowering, trembling, shaken, crouching, wincing, shaky, running, quaking, shaking like a leaf, pale with fear; *both* (D): in a funk, showing the white feather, shaking in one's boots.

cow barn, *n.*—*Syn.* shelter, stable, dairy barn; see **barn.**

cowboy, *n.* **1.** [Cattlehand]—*Syn.* cowhand, hand, wrangler, top hand, rider, herder, night herder, *vaquero, gaucho, illanero* (*all* Spanish), cattleherder, drover, herdsman; *all* (D): cowpuncher, cowpoke, puncher, broncobuster, buckaroo; see also **rancher.**
2. [Rustic]—*Syn.* lout, lumpkin, hick (D); see **boor.**

cower, *v.*—*Syn.* cringe, flinch, quail; see **wince.**

coy, *mod.*—*Syn.* bashful, shy, demure; see **humble** 1.

cozenage, *n.*—*Syn.* plot, swindle, treachery; see **deception** 1, **trick** 1.

cozy, *mod.*—*Syn.* secure, sheltered, snug; see **comfortable** 2, **safe** 1.

crab, *n.*—*Syn.* (short-tailed *or* soft-tailed) crustacean, seafood, podothalmian, *Anomura, Brachyura* (both Latin); see also **shellfish.**
Kinds of crabs include the following—softshell, hardshell, cancer, deep-sea, king, shore, rock, land, fiddler, Dungeness, Jonah, green, pea, box, porcelain, lady, swimming, paddle, shuttle, edible, hermit, purse.

crabbed (D), *mod.* **1.** [Sour-tempered]—*Syn.* grouchy, peevish, perverse; see **irritable.**
2. [Difficult to understand]—*Syn.* unreadable, intricate, sloppy; see **illegible.**

crack (D), *mod.*—*Syn.* first-rate, first-class, skilled; see **able** 1, 2, **excellent.**

crack, *n.* **1.** [An incomplete break]—*Syn.* chink, split, cut; see **hole** 1.
2. [A crevice]—*Syn.* cleft, fissure, rift; see **division** 3, **hole** 2.
3. [A cracking sound]—*Syn.* splintering, splitting, burst; see **noise** 1.
4. [A blow]—*Syn.* hit, thwack, stroke; see **blow** 1.
5. [(D) A witty or brazen comment]—*Syn.* return, witticism, jest; see **joke** 2, **remark.**

crack, *v.* **1.** [To become cracked]—*Syn.* cleave, burst, split; see **break** 3.
2. [To cause to crack]—*Syn.* cleave, split, sever; see **break** 1, 2.
3. [To damage]—*Syn.* injure, hurt, impair; see **damage** 1.
4. [To become mentally deranged]—*Syn.* become insane, go crazy, blow one's mind (D); see **crack up** 2.
5. [To solve]—*Syn.* figure out, answer, decode; see **solve.**
get cracking (D)—*Syn.* get going, go, start; see **begin** 2, **move** 1.

crack a book (D), *v.*—*Syn.* scrutinize, peruse, scan; see **examine** 1, **read** 1, **study** 1.

crack a bottle, *v.*—*Syn.* have a drink, tipple, open a bottle; see **drink** 2.

crack a joke, *v.*—*Syn.* quip, jest, jape; see **joke.**

cracked, *mod.*—*Syn.* fissured, split, fractured; see **broken** 1.

cracker, *n.*—*Syn.* wafer, soda cracker, oyster cracker, biscuit, saltine, cocktail cracker, hardtack, sea biscuit, *knäckebröd* (Swedish), wheat biscuit; see also **cookie.**

crack up, *v.* **1.** [(D) To crash a vehicle]—*Syn.* collide, be in an accident, smash *or* break up; see **crash** 4.
2. [To fail suddenly in health, mind, or strength]—*Syn.* go (all) to pieces, decline, fail, deteriorate, sicken, derange, collapse, become confused, go *or* become insane *or* crazy *or* demented, become psychotic, become a (mental) patient, be committed (to a hospital *or* an institution); *all* (D): freak out, blow one's mind, go out of one's mind, go off one's rocker, blow a fuse, go off the deep end; see also **weaken** 1.
3. [(D) To laugh]—*Syn.* roar, howl, roll in the aisles (D); see **laugh** 1.

cradle, *n.* **1.** [A baby's bed]—*Syn.* trundle bed, crib, basinet; see also **bed** 1, **furniture**
2. [A place of nurture]—*Syn.* spring, fountain, ultimate cause; see **foundation** 2, **origin** 2.

craft, *n.* **1.** [Skill]—*Syn.* proficiency, competence, adeptness; see **ability** 2.
2. [Guile]—*Syn.* cunning, duplicity, trickery; see **dishonesty.**
3. [Trade]—*Syn.* occupation, career, work; see **job** 1, **profession** 1.
4. [Ship]—*Syn.* vessel, air *or* water vehicle, airplane; see **boat, ship, spacecraft.**

craftsman, *n.*—*Syn.* artisan, skilled worker *or* tradesman *or* workman, journeyman, follower *or* practitioner of a trade, maker, wright, union man, technician, manufacturer, machinist, handcraftsman, mechanic, artificer; see also **artist** 2, **laborer, specialist.**

crafty, *mod.* **1.** [Sly]—*Syn.* wily, tricky, foxy; see **sly** 1.
2. [Shrewd]—*Syn.* clever, sharp, astute; see **intelligent** 1.

crag, *n.*—*Syn.* bluff, jutting rock, peak; see **mountain** 1, **rock** 2.

craggy, *mod.*—*Syn.* rough, jagged, rugged; see **rocky.**

cram, *v.* **1.** [To stuff]—*Syn.* crush, jam, compact; see **compress, pack** 2, **press** 1.
2. [(D) To eat greedily]—*Syn.* gorge, devour, satiate; see **eat** 1.
3. [To study hurriedly]—*Syn.* read, teach, review; see **study** 1.

cramp, *n.* **1.** [A pain]—*Syn.* spasm, crick, pang; see **pain** 2.
2. [An obstruction]—*Syn.* encumbrance, hindrance, restriction; see **impediment** 1.
cramp, *v.* **1.** [To restrain]—*Syn.* object, restrict, obstruct; see **hinder, restrain** 1.
2. [(D) To fasten]—*Syn.* clasp, clamp, grip; see **fasten** 1.
cramped, *mod.* **1.** [Restricted]—*Syn.* narrow, confined, restraining; see **restricted, uncomfortable** 1.
2. [Crowded]—*Syn.* packed, jammed in, overcrowded; see **jammed** 2.
cramp one's style (D), *v.*—*Syn.* obstruct, hamper, disrupt; see **hinder, restrain** 1.
crane, *n.*—*Syn.* lift, derrick, davit; see **elevator** 1.
cranium, *n.*—*Syn.* cerebrum, cerebellum, brain encasing, brainpan, skull (of a vertebrate), pericranium, bony covering, brain box (D); see also **brain** 1, **head** 1.
Parts of the cranium include the following—occipital, frontal, parietal, temporal and sphenoid bones, mastoid, superior maxillary, inferior maxillary.
crank, *n.* **1.** [A device for revolving a shaft]—*Syn.* brace, bracket, turning device, elbow, bend; see also **arm** 2, **handle** 1.
2. [A person with an obsession]—*Syn.* eccentric, fanatic, monomaniac; see **character** 4.
3. [(D) An ill-natured person]—*Syn.* eccentric, misanthrope, complainer; see **grouch.**
cranky, *mod.*—*Syn.* disagreeable, cross, perverse; see **irritable.**
cranny, *n.*—*Syn.* crevice, crack, break; see **hole** 2.
crash, *n.* **1.** [A crashing sound]—*Syn.* clatter, clash, din; see **noise** 1, **sound** 2.
2. [A collision]—*Syn.* wreck, accident, shock; see **collision** 1.
crash, *v.* **1.** [To fall with a crash]—*Syn.* overturn, upset, break down, dash to pieces, plunge, be hurled, pitch, smash, dive, hurtle, lurch, sprawl, tumble, fall headlong, fall flat, drop, slip, collapse, fall prostrate, precipitate oneself; *both* (D): come a cropper, spin in; see also **fall** 1.
2. [To break into pieces]—*Syn.* shatter, shiver, splinter; see **break** 2, **smash.**
3. [To make a crashing sound]—*Syn.* clatter, bang, smash; see **sound** 1.
4. [To have a collision]—*Syn.* collide (with), run together, run *or* smash *or* bump *or* nose *or* dash *or* bang into, meet, jostle, impinge, bump, rear-end, butt, knock, punch, jar, jolt, go aground, hurtle into, crack up (D); see also **hit** 1, 3.
5. [(D) To collapse]—*Syn.* fall asleep, pass out, become unconscious; see **faint, sleep**
6. [(D) To go uninvited]—*Syn.* disturb, invade, intrude; see **interrupt** 2, **meddle** 1.
crash program, *n.*—*Syn.* crash project, immediate undertaking, intensive *or* telescoped program, marathon, around-the-clock endeavor, all-out effort, intensification, revised plan, speed-up (D); see also **emergency.**
crass, *mod.*—*Syn.* gross, doltish, stupid; see **ignorant** 1, 2, **vulgar** 1.
crate, *n.*—*Syn.* carton, box, cage; see **case** 7, **container, package** 1.
crate, *v.*—*Syn.* box, enclose, case; see **pack** 1.
crater, *n.*—*Syn.* hollow, opening, abyss; see **hole** 2.
crave, *v.* **1.** [To long for]—*Syn.* require, desire, covet; see **need, want** 1.
2. [To beg]—*Syn.* entreat, ask, plead; see **beg** 2.
craven, *mod.*—*Syn.* fearful, weak, yellow (D); see **cowardly** 1, **timid** 1, 2.
craving, *n.*—*Syn.* need, longing, yearning; see **desire** 1.
craw, *n.*—*Syn.* gizzard, intestines, stomach; see **abdomen.**
crawfish, *n.*—*Syn.* crayfish, crustacean, crawdad (D); see **shellfish.**
crawl, *v.* **1.** [To move like an insect]—*Syn.* creep, worm along, wriggle, squirm, slither, move on hands and knees, writhe; *all* (D): go on all fours, worm one's way, go on one's belly; see also **grovel, sneak.**
2. [To move slowly]—*Syn.* plod, hang back, poke (D); see **lag** 1.
crawling, *mod.*—*Syn.* moving slowly, dragging, on hands and knees; see **creeping** 1.
crayon, *n.*—*Syn.* chalk, pastel, colored wax, crayon pencil, lithographic pencil, drawing medium, conté (crayon); see **pencil** 1.
craze, *n.*—*Syn.* fad, rage, fashion; see **fad.**
crazily, *mod.*—*Syn.* furiously, irrationally, hastily, madly, rashly, witlessly, insanely, psychotically, maniacally, as though out of one's mind, ravingly, rabidly; see also **violently** 1, 2, **wildly** 1.
crazy, *mod.*—*Syn.* crazed, demented, mad; see **insane** 1.
creak, *v.*—*Syn.* squeak, grate, rasp; see **sound** 1.
cream, *mod.*—*Syn.* beige, eggshell, ivory; see **tan, white** 1.
cream, *n.* **1.** [The fatty portion of milk]—*Syn.* rich milk, creamy milk, *crème* (French), coffee cream, whipping cream, ice cream, half-and-half, *Schlag* (German), butterfat, top of the bottle (D); see also **milk.**
2. [A creamy substance]—*Syn.* emulsion, demulcent, jelly; see **cosmetic, lotion, salve.**
3. [(D) The best part]—*Syn.* pick, finest, favorite; see **best.**
creamy, *mod.*—*Syn.* smooth, oily, buttery, luscious, lush, greasy, creamed; see also **rich** 2, **soft** 2.
crease, *n.*—*Syn.* tuck, overlap, pleat; see **fold** 2, **wrinkle.**
crease, *v.*—*Syn.* double, rumple, plait; see **fold** 2, **wrinkle** 1.
create, *v.* **1.** [To conceive in the mind]—*Syn.* formulate, devise, conceive; see **imagine** 1.
2. [To make]—*Syn.* produce, actualize, effect, invest, constitute, form, occasion, perform, cause (to exist), bring *or* call into being *or* existence, rear, erect, build, fashion, originate, beget, generate, construct, discover, shape, forge, design, plan, fabricate, author, contrive, cause to be, give birth to, bring to pass; see also **compose** 3, **invent** 1, **produce** 2.
creation, *n.* **1.** [The process of creating]—*Syn.* imagination, production, formulation; see **conception** 1, **making.**
2. [All that has been created]—*Syn.* cosmos, nature, totality; see **earth** 1, **universe.**

3. [A work of art]—*Syn.* creative *or* imaginative work, work of genius, (magnum) opus, *chef d'oeuvre* (French), piece; *both* (D): brain child, little thing; see also **production** 1, **work** 3.

creative, *mod.* —*Syn.* formative, inventive, productive; see **artistic** 3, **original** 2.

Creator, *n.* —*Syn.* First Cause, Deity, Maker; see **god** 2.

creator, *n.* —*Syn.* inventor, producer, originator; see **author** 1.

creature, *n.* —*Syn.* creation, being, beast; see **animal** 1.

credence, *n.* —*Syn.* confidence, belief, reliance; see **faith** 1.

credential, *n.* —*Syn.* declaration, warrant, voucher; see **certificate, record** 1.

credibility, *n.* —*Syn.* likelihood, prospect, chance; see **possibility** 2, **probability.**

credible, *mod.* **1.** [Likely]—*Syn.* probable, seeming, conceivable; see **likely** 1.

2. [Reliable]—*Syn.* trustworthy, dependable, sincere; see **reliable** 1.

credit, *n.* **1.** [Belief]—*Syn.* credence, reliance, confidence; see **faith** 1.

2. [Unencumbered funds]—*Syn.* assets, stocks, bonds, paper credit, (bank) account, mortgages, liens, securities, debentures, capital outlay, surplus cash; see also **balance** 3, **wealth** 1.

3. [Reputation]—*Syn.* prestige, repute, good name; see **honor** 1, **reputation** 1, 2.

4. [Permission to defer payment]—*Syn.* extension, respite, continuance, trust (in future payment), accounts carried on the books (D); see also **loan.**

do credit to—*Syn.* bring approval to, please, do honor to; see **satisfy** 1.

give credit to—*Syn.* believe in, rely on, have confidence in; see **trust** 1.

give one credit for—*Syn.* believe in, rely on, have confidence in; see **trust** 1.

on credit—*Syn.* on loan, delayed, postponed; see **unpaid** 1.

to one's credit—*Syn.* good, honorable, beneficial; see **worthwhile.**

credit, *v.* **1.** [Believe]—*Syn.* trust, have faith in, rely on; see **believe** 1.

2. [Accounting term]—*Syn.* put on the books, charge to an account, place to the credit of, accredit to, give credit to, place to one's credit *or* to one's account, defer payments; see also **charge** 2.

credit card, *n.* —*Syn.* plastic money, the card, charge card, funny money, smart card, plastic. Major credit cards include: American Express, Mastercharge, Visa, Diners Club, Carte Blanc.

creditable, *mod.* —*Syn.* decent, honorable, honest; see **excellent, respectable, worthy.**

creditor, *n.* —*Syn.* realtor, lessor, mortgager; see also **banker** 1, **lender.**

credulous, *mod.* —*Syn.* gullible, simple, unsophisticated; see **naive, trusting** 1.

creed, *n.* —*Syn.* belief, doctrine, dogma; see **faith** 2.

creek, *n.* —*Syn.* stream, spring, brook; see **river** 1.

up the creek (D)—*Syn.* in difficulty, desperate, lost; see **in trouble** 1.

creep, *v.* —*Syn.* slither, writhe, worm along; see **crawl** 1.

make one's flesh creep (D)—*Syn.* repel, frighten, terrorize; see **disgust, frighten** 1.

creeper, *n.* —*Syn.* runner, climber, clinging plant; see **plant, vine.**

creeping, *mod.* **1.** [In the act of creeping]—*Syn.* crawling, worming, squirming, writhing, wriggling, groveling, crouching, cowering, quailing, slinking, skulking, inching, dragging, lagging, shambling, limping, faltering, shuffling, hobbling, staggering, sneaking, moving slowly, barely moving; *both* (D): going at a snail's pace, worming along.

2. [Given to creeping]—*Syn.* reptant, reptilian, formicant, vermicular, serpentine, prostrate, clinging, dwarf, dwarfed, spreading, growing along the ground, horizontal, vinelike, recumbent, climging. —*Ant.* upright*, standing, vertical.

crescent, *n.* —*Syn.* new moon, old moon, increasing moon, sickle, horned moon, convex *or* concave figure, half-moon, demilune, meniscus, bow, lune; see also **curve** 1, **moon.**

crest, *n.* **1.** [Growth on the head of an animal] —*Syn.* plume, tuft, topknot; see **feather.**

2. [Apex]—*Syn.* peak, pinnacle, culmination; see **climax, top** 1.

crestfallen, *mod.* —*Syn.* discouraged, depressed, dejected; see **sad** 1.

crevasse, *n.* —*Syn.* precipice, abyss, chasm; see **gap** 3.

crevice, *n.* —*Syn.* chasm, cleft, slit; see **division** 3, **gap** 3.

crew, *n.* **1.** [Company of seamen]—*Syn.* seafarers, sailors, hands, (able) seamen, (ship's) complement, full complement, ship's company, mariners, sea dogs, *matelots* (French); *all* (D): gobs, Jacks, manjacks, shellbacks.

2. [A group of men organized to do a particular job] —*Syn.* company, troupe, squad; see **organization** 3, **team** 2.

crib, *n.* **1.** [A baby's bed]—*Syn.* trundle *or* truckle bed, cradle, bassinet; see **bed** 1.

2. [A storage space, especially for corn]—*Syn.* manager, stall, silo; see **bin, storehouse.**

crick, *n.* —*Syn.* spasm, cramp, ache; see **pain** 2.

crier, *n.* —*Syn.* herald, proclaimer, bellman; see **messenger.**

crime, *n.* **1.** [An outrageous act]—*Syn.* transgression, misdemeanor, vice, outrage, wickedness, immorality, misdeed, infringement, depravity, evil behavior, antisocial behavior, wrongdoing, abomination, misconduct, corruption, villainy, iniquity, delinquency, wrong, trespass, malefaction, dereliction, lawlessness, crime in the streets, atrocity, felony, capital crime, offense, scandal, infraction, violation, enormity, crime of passion, cold-blooded crime, mortal sin, deed without a name (D); see sense 2; see **evil** 1, 2, **sin.**

2. [A serious infraction of the law]—*Syn.* homicide, voluntary manslaughter, involuntary manslaughter, simple assault, aggravated assault, rape, battery, mayhem, larceny, robbery, burglary, holdup, kidnapping, swindling, arson, defrauding, embezzlement, white-collar crime, smuggling, extortion, bribery, malicious mischief, breach of the peace, libel, breaking prison, perjury, act injurious to the public welfare, aggravated misdemeanor, fornica-

tion, sodomy, crime in the streets, conspiracy, counterfeiting, inciting to revolt, sedition; see also **arson, corruption** 3, **murder, rape, theft, treason.**

criminal, *mod.* —*Syn.* unlawful, felonious, illegal; see **wicked** 1, 2.

criminal, *n.* —*Syn.* lawbreaker, convict, malefactor, felon, crook, hardened criminal, underworld character, blackmailer, black marketeer, evildoer, sinner, culprit; *all* (D): scofflaw, inside man, night-rider, pay-off man, hustler.
Criminals include the following—murderer, manslayer, assassin, killer, desperado, thug *or* gorilla (D), gangster, gang leader *or* the brains, big brains (*both* D), raider, burglar, safecracker, quitting-business promoter, swindler *or* clip artist, griffer (*both* D), confidence man *or* con man (D), thief, bandit, sneak thief *or* cat burglar, second-story man (*both* D), cattle thief *or* rustler (D), horse thief, automobile thief, pickpocket, grafter, arsonist, counterfeiter, forger *or* check artist (D), smuggler, buccaneer, extortionist, kidnapper, mugger, gunman *or* trigger man, torpedo plugger (*both* D), accomplice *or* ringer, stooge (*both* D), decoy *or* blind, come-on (*both* D), briber *or* fixer, greaser (*both* D), scouter *or* bird dog, fingerer (*both* D), informer *or* stool pigeon, bleater, squealer (*all* D), absconder, convict *or* con (D), dope peddler *or* pusher (D).

criminality, *n.* **1.** [Guilt]—*Syn.* culpability, guiltiness, censurability; see **guilt.**
2. [Misbehavior]—*Syn.* corruption, badness, depravity; see **crime** 1, **evil** 1, 2, **sin.**

crimp, *v.* **1.** [Fold]—*Syn.* pleat, crease, coil; see **fold** 2, **wrinkle** 1.
2. [Curl]—*Syn.* set, undulate, flow; see **curl, wave** 4.

crimson, *mod.* —*Syn.* blood-red, bright red, scarlet; see **color** 1, **red.**

cringe, *v.* —*Syn.* flinch, quail, recoil; see **wince.**

cringing, *mod.* —*Syn.* servile, crouching, submissive; see **cowardly** 1, 2, **docile.**

crinkle, *v.* —*Syn.* coil, wind, crease; see **fold** 2, **wrinkle** 1.

crinkly, *mod.* —*Syn.* wavy, sinuous, crimped; see **curly, wrinkled.**

cripple, *v.* —*Syn.* stifle, mangle, injure; see **hurt** 1, **maim.**

crippled, *mod.* **1.** [Physically defective]—*Syn.* maimed, mutilated, mangled; see **deformed, disabled.**
2. [Damaged]—*Syn.* harmed, impaired, marred; see **broken** 1, 2.

crisis, *n.* —*Syn.* straits, exigency, urgency, necessity, dilemma, puzzle, perplexity, pressure, embarrassment, pinch, juncture, pass, change, contingency, situation, condition, plight, imbroglio, impasse, deadlock, entanglement, predicament, corner, decisive turn, critical juncture *or* occasion *or* situation, trauma, quandary, extremity, trial, crux, moment of truth, turning point, critical situation, moment of change, hour of decision; *all* (D): pickle, stew, fix, mess, big trouble, hot potato, kettle of fish, hot water.—*Ant.* normality, stability*, regularity*.

crisp, *mod.* **1.** [Fresh and firm]—*Syn.* green, plump, firm; see **fresh** 1, **ripe** 1.
2. [Brisk]—*Syn.* fresh, invigorating, bracing; see **stimulating.**
3. [Curt]—*Syn.* brusque, brief, terse; see **abrupt** 2, **short** 2.

criterion, *n.* —*Syn.* basis, foundation, test, standard, rule, proof, exemplar, paradigm, scale, prototype, pattern, example, standard of judgment *or* criticism, point of comparison, archetype, norm, original, precedent, touchstone, fact, law, principle, opinion; see also **measure** 2, **model** 1, 2.

critic, *n.* **1.** [One who makes adverse comments] —*Syn.* faultfinder, carper, caviler, censor, censurer, quibbler, blamer, detractor, slanderer, maligner, complainer, complainant, doubter, disputer, nagger, fretter, scolder, worrier, disapprover, defamer, disparager; *all* (D): Monday morning quarterback, mud-slinger, knocker, panner.—*Ant.* praiser, believer*, supporter.
2. [One who endeavors to interpret and judge] —*Syn.* commentator, analyst, analyzer, connoisseur, reviewer, writer of reviews, contributor to a review, cartoonist, caricaturist, expert, diagnostic, annotator, master, evaluator; *all* (D): blurb writer, crick, drammer damner, pix crix, sharpshooter; see **examiner, scholar** 2.

critical, *mod.* **1.** [Capable of observing and judging] —*Syn.* penetrating, perceptive, discerning; see **judicious, observant** 1.
2. [Inclined to adverse criticism]—*Syn.* faultfinding, trenchant, inclined to judge with severity, derogatory, choleric, disapproving, Zoilean, withering, calumniatory, hypercritical, captious, demanding, carping, hairsplitting, satirical, cynical, caviling, nitpicking, nagging, scolding, condemning, censuring, censorious, reproachful, disapproving, disparaging, exacting, sharp, cutting, biting; see also **severe** 1, **sarcastic.**—*Ant.* praising, flattering, encouraging.
3. [Dangerous]—*Syn.* perilous, risky, hazardous; see **dangerous** 1.
4. [Crucial]—*Syn.* decisive, significant, deciding; see **important** 1.

criticism, *n.* **1.** [A serious estimate or interpretation] —*Syn.* study, analysis, critique; see **judgment** 2, **review** 2.
2. [An adverse comment]—*Syn.* caviling, carping, faultfinding; see **objection** 2.
3. [An example of criticism, sense 1]—*Syn.* critique; critical essay *or* piece *or* book, etc.; survey; see **exposition** 2, **review** 2.

criticize, *v.* **1.** [To make a considered criticism] —*Syn.* study, probe, scrutinize; see **analyze** 1, **examine** 1.
2. [To make adverse comments]—*Syn.* chastise, reprove, reprimand; see **censure.**

critique, *n.* —*Syn.* commentary, analysis, editorial; see **exposition** 2, **judgment** 2, **review** 2.

croak, *v.* **1.** [(D) To complain]—*Syn.* grumble, worry, fret; see **complain** 1.
2. [(D) To die]—*Syn.* expire, pass away, perish; see **die** 1.
3. [To give a hoarse call]—*Syn.* caw, quack, squawk; see **sound** 1.

crock, *n.* —*Syn.* vessel, pitcher, crockery; see **container, pot** 1.

crockery, *n.* —*Syn.* earthenware, ceramics, porcelain; see **pottery.**

crone, *n.* —*Syn.* witch, old woman, slattern; see **hag.**

crony, *n.* —*Syn.* comrade, buddy (D), accomplice; see **associate, friend** 1

crook, *n.* **1.** [Criminal]—*Syn.* swindler, thief, rogue; see **criminal.**
2. [A bend]—*Syn.* fork, V, notch; see **angle** 1.

crooked, *mod.* **1.** [Having a crook]—*Syn.* curved, curving, hooked, incurving, devious, winding, bowed, spiral, serpentine, not straight, zigzag, twisted, meandering, tortuous, anfractuous, sinuous; see also **angular** 1, **bent, oblique** 1.—*Ant.* unbent, straight*, direct.
2. [Dishonest]—*Syn.* iniquitous, corrupt, nefarious; see **dishonest** 1.

croon, *v.* —*Syn.* sing sentimentally, warble, purr; see **hum, sing** 1.

crop, *n.* —*Syn.* harvest, yield, product, crops, growing things, annual production, reaping, agricultural production, hay, fodder, grain(s), gathering, gleaning, vintage, fruits; see also **produce, vegetable.**

cross, *mod.* **1.** [Having an irritable nature]—*Syn.* jumpy, easily annoyed, pettish; see **critical** 2, **irritable.**
2. [Crossbred]—*Syn.* crossed, mixed, alloyed; see **hybrid.**

cross, *n.* **1.** [Religious symbol, especially of Christianity]—*Syn.* crucifix, cruciform, Greek cross, swastika, papal cross, Maltese cross, St. Andrew's cross, Celtic cross, Jerusalem cross, patriarchal cross, cross of Lorraine, Latin cross, Calvary cross.
2. [A tribulation]—*Syn.* affliction, trial, misfortune; see **difficulty** 2.
3. [A mixed offspring]—*Syn.* mongrel, crossbreed, half-breed; see **hybrid, mixture** 1.

cross, *v.* **1.** [To pass over]—*Syn.* traverse, move *or* go *or* pass across *or* over, pass, ford, cut across, overpass, span.
2. [To lie across]—*Syn.* intersect, lie athwart, rest across; see **divide** 1.
3. [To mix breeds]—*Syn.* mingle, interbreed, cross-pollinate, hybridize, cross-fertilize, crossbreed, intercross, blend; see also **mix** 1.

cross-country, *mod.* —*Syn.* across the fields, through field and wood, off the roads, as the crow flies, directly; see also **across, direct** 1.

cross-examine, *v.* —*Syn.* investigate, check, interrogate; see **examine** 2, **question** 1.

crossing, *n.* **1.** [A place to cross]—*Syn.* intersection, overpass, underpass, crossway, crosswalk, crossroad, interchange, cloverleaf, exchange, passage, traverse, loop (D); see also **bridge** 1, **junction** 2.
2. [A mixing of breeds]—*Syn.* hybridization, interbreeding, cross-fertilization, cross-pollination; see also **mixture** 1.

crossroad, *n.* —*Syn.* intersecting road, cross-country road, byroad, joining road, side road, secondary highway, service road, frontage road, driveway; see also **junction** 2, **road** 1.

crosswise, *mod.* —*Syn.* across, athwart, thwart, cross, contrariwise, perpendicular, transversely, vertically, horizontally, at right angles, awry, over, sideways, crisscross, askew, crossways; see also **angular** 1.

crotch, *n.* **1.** [Angle]—*Syn.* fork, corner, elbow; see **angle** 1, **curve** 1.
2. [Loins]—*Syn.* pubic area, groin, pelvic girdle; see **lap** 1.

crotchet, *n.* —*Syn.* whim, quirk, fad; see **fancy** 3, **notion** 2.

crotchety, *mod.* —*Syn.* eccentric, queer, odd; see **obstinate** 1, **unusual** 2.

crouch, *v.* **1.** [To stoop]—*Syn.* dip, duck, bend; see **bow** 1.
2. [To cower]—*Syn.* cringe, flinch, quail; see **grovel, wince.**

crow, *n.* —*Syn.* black bird, raven, *Corvus brachyrhynchos* (Latin); see also **bird** 1.

crow, *v.* **1.** [To boast]—*Syn.* cry, exult, brag; see **boast** 1.
2. [To make a crowing sound]—*Syn.* squawk, caw, cackle; see **cry** 3, **sound** 1.
as the crow flies—*Syn.* straight, straightway, in a straight line; see **direct** 1.
eat crow (D)—*Syn.* retract, confess an error, take back; see **admit** 2.

crowd, *n.* **1.** [Throng]—*Syn.* multitude, concourse, host, horde, flock, mob, company, confluence, swarm, press, crush, surge, stream, troop, conflux, legion, force, bevy, galaxy, rout, group, body, pack, army, posse, drove, array, party, flood, gaggle, throng, troupe, deluge, meet, muster, congregation, cluster, assembly, crew; *all* (D): jam, herd, bunch, gang, clutch, batch; see also **gathering.**
2. [The common people]—*Syn.* mob, rank and file, masses; see **people** 3.
3. [(D) A clique]—*Syn.* set, circle, coterie; see **faction** 1, **organization** 3.

crowd, *v.* —*Syn.* stuff, jam, squeeze; see **pack** 2, **press** 1, **push** 1.

crowded, *mod.* —*Syn.* packed, huddled, crushed; see **full** 1, **jammed** 2.

crown, *n.* **1.** [The top]—*Syn.* apex, crest, summit; see **top** 1.
2. [The symbol of royalty]—*Syn.* diadem, headdress, tiara, coronet, circlet.
3. [The possessor of sovereign power; *usually capital C*]—*Syn.* monarch, potentate, emperor; see **king** 1, **royalty.**
4. [The head]—*Syn.* cerebrum, skull, brain; see **cranium, head** 1.

crown, *v.* **1.** [To make complete or perfect]—*Syn.* round out, fulfill, consummate; see **complete** 1.
2. [To empower with a crown]—*Syn.* commission, authorize, invest, install, endow, enable, sanction, inaugurate, fix, arm, strengthen, dignify, coronate, enthrone, exalt, raise, heighten, erect, set up, ennoble, establish, determine, stabilize, settle; see also **delegate** 1, 2.—*Ant.* topple, abolish*, overthrow.
3. [(D) To hit]—*Syn.* knock, strike, smite; see **hit** 1.

crowning, *mod.* —*Syn.* supreme, ultimate, paramount; see **excellent, principal.**

crucial, *mod.* **1.** [Critical]—*Syn.* decisive, climatic, deciding; see **important** 1.
2. [Severe]—*Syn.* trying, taxing, hard; see **difficult** 1.

crucible, *n.* —*Syn.* retort, melting pot, cauldron; see **container, pot** 1.

crucifix, *n.* —*Syn.* Maltese cross, Christian emblem, Latin cross; see **cross** 1.

crucifixion, *n.* **1.** [Death by being nailed to a cross] —*Syn.* torture, suffering, martyrdom; see **execution** 2.
2. [The death of Jesus or the artistic representation of His death; *usually capitalized*]—*Syn.* the Passion, the execution of Christ, the Martyrdom, the Sacrifice on the Cross.

crucify, *v.* **1.** [To kill by crucifixion]—*Syn.* execute, hang, torture; see **kill** 1.
2. [To torment]—*Syn.* torture, bedevil, browbeat; see **bother** 2.

crude, *mod.* **1.** [Unrefined]—*Syn.* rude, rough, unpolished, in a raw state, unprocessed, homemade, homespun, thick, coarse, harsh, rudimentary, roughhewn, unfashioned, unformed, undeveloped, in the rough, raw, immature, sketchy; see also **savage** 1, **unfinished** 1.—*Ant.* finished, polished, refined.
2. [Lacking address or skill]—*Syn.* ungainly, clumsy, unskillful; see **awkward** 1.
3. [Lacking manners or taste]—*Syn.* uncouth, vulgar, coarse; see **rude** 1, 2.

crudely, *mod.* —*Syn.* clumsily, coarsely, impudently; see **rudely.**

cruel, *mod.* **1.** [Vicious]—*Syn.* malevolent, spiteful, depraved, wicked, sadistic, delighting in torture, vengeful, revengeful, evil, sinful, degenerate, sensual, disposed to inflict suffering, brutish, demoniac, rampant, outrageous, tyrannical, gross, swinish, demoralized, evil-minded, rancorous, vicious, brutal, rough, wild, bestial, ferocious, monstrous, barbarous, barbaric, maleficent, fell, ravening, fiendish, truculent, demoniacal, debased, destructive, harmful, malignant, virulent, evilly disposed, pernicious, mischievous; see also sense 2; see also **vulgar** 1. —*Ant.* kindly*, virtuous, high-minded.
2. [Pitiless]—*Syn.* callous, unnatural, merciless, sadistic, unpitying, unmerciful, unyielding, obdurate, cold-blooded, remorseless, pitiless, unfeeling, inflexible, inclement, bloodthirsty, indifferent to suffering, unrelenting, inexorable, relentless, revengeful, absolute, grim, grim-visaged, inhuman, atrocious, harsh, heartless, stony, unconcerned, iron-handed, without pity; *all* (D): knowing no mercy, giving no quarter, turning a deaf ear, hard as nails; see also **fierce** 1, **ruthless** 1, 2, **savage** 2. —*Ant.* merciful*, touched, compassionate.

cruelly, *mod.* —*Syn.* savagely, inhumanly, viciously; see **brutally.**

cruelty, *n.* —*Syn.* brutality, barbarity, masochism, savageness, unkindness, inhumanity, barbarism, mercilessness, barbarousness, unmercifulness, wickedness, coarseness, ruthlessness, severity, malignity, malice, rancor, venom, coldness, unfeelingness, insensibility, indifference, insensitiveness, fierceness, bestiality, animality, truculence, ferocity, savagery, brutishness, implacability, grimness, monstrousness, inflexibility, fiendishness, hardness of heart, bloodthirstiness, unnaturalness, relentlessness, torture, persecution, inquisition, despotism, harshness, outrage, heartlessness, atrocity; see also **evil** 1, **tyranny.**—*Ant.* benevolence, kindness*, humanity.

cruet, *n.* —*Syn.* receptacle, decanter, vessel; see **bottle, container, jar** 1.

cruise, *n.* —*Syn.* voyage, sail, jaunt; see **journey.**

cruise, *v.* —*Syn.* voyage, meander, coast; see **drift, navigate, sail** 2, **travel** 2.

cruiser, *n.* —*Syn.* cabin cruiser, boat, privateer; see also **ship, warship.**
Types of cruisers include the following—battle, light, armored, heavy, rocket cruiser; dreadnought, man-of-war, battlewagon, corvette, battleship, capital ship.

crumb, *n.* —*Syn.* particle, scrap, pinch; see **bit** 1.

crumble, *v.* —*Syn.* fall apart, disintegrate, break up; see **break** 3, **decay.**

crumbling, *mod.* —*Syn.* rotting, breaking up, wasting away; see **decaying.**

crumbly, *mod.* —*Syn.* breaking up *or* down, falling to pieces, decayed, degenerated, perishing, deteriorated, deteriorating, soft, corroded, rusted, rotted, oxidized, worn away, friable, fragile, brittle, frail, rotten, breakable, shivery, apt to crumble, frangible, eroded, disintegrated, impaired, damaged, spoiled, marred, blemished, disfigured, defaced, tumbling down; see also **decaying, gritty** 1.—*Ant.* sound, firm*, undecayed.

crumple, *v.* **1.** [To wrinkle]—*Syn.* rumple, crush, crease; see **fold** 2, **wrinkle** 1.
2. [To become wrinkled]—*Syn.* shrivel, fold, rumple; see **wrinkle** 2.

crunch (D), *n.* —*Syn.* test, emergency, trouble; see **difficulty** 1.

crunch, *v.* —*Syn.* munch, gnaw, masticate; see **bite** 1, **chew.**

crusade, *n.* —*Syn.* campaign, march, demonstration; see **movement** 2.

crusader, *n.* —*Syn.* reformer, protester, progressive; see **radical, rebel** 1.

crush, *v.* **1.** [To break into small pieces]—*Syn.* smash, pulverize, powder; see **grind** 1.
2. [To bruise severely]—*Syn.* press, mash, contuse; see **beat** 2, **break.**
3. [To defeat utterly]—*Syn.* overwhelm, beat *or* force down, annihilate; see **defeat** 2.

crust, *n.* **1.** [A crisp covering]—*Syn.* hull, rind, piecrust; see **shell** 1.
2. [The edge]—*Syn.* verge, border, band; see **edge** 1.

crustacean, *n.* —*Syn.* mollusk, sea creature, sea food; see **shellfish.**

crusty, *mod.* —*Syn.* cross, harsh, scornful; see **rude** 2, **sarcastic.**

cry, *n.* **1.** [A loud utterance]—*Syn.* outcry, exclamation, clamor, shout, call, battle cry, war cry, halloo, hurrah, hullabaloo, cheer, huzza, vociferation, scream, shriek, yell, whoop, yawp, squall, yammer, groan, bellow, howl, bawl, holler, uproar, acclamation, roar; see also sense 2; see also **noise** 2.—*Ant.* whisper, murmur, silence.
2. [A characteristic call]—*Syn.* howl, hoot, wail, bawl, grunt, screech, mewling, bark, squawk, squeak, yelp, meow, whinney, nicker, moo, chatter, bay, cluck, crow, whine, pipe, trill, quack, clack, cackle, caw, bellow, coo, whistle, gobble, hiss, growl; see also **yell** 1.

3. [A fit of weeping]—*Syn.* lamentation, lamenting, sobbing, bewailing, wailing, shedding tears, sorrowing, mourning, whimpering, the blues (D); see also **tears.**

a far cry (from)—*Syn.* unlike, dissimilar, opposed (to); see **different.**

cry, *v.* **1.** [To weep]—*Syn.* sob, wail, shed tears, snivel, squall, lament, bewail, bemoan, moan, howl, keen, whimper, whine, weep over, lift up the voice, complain, deplore, sorrow, grieve, fret, groan, caterwaul, burst into tears; *all* (D): choke up, cry one's eyes out, break down *or* up, boohoo, blubber, yammer, turn on the waterworks, fill the air, rip out, bawl; see also **mourn** 1, **regret, weep.**—*Ant.* rejoice, laugh*, exult.

2. [To raise the voice]—*Syn.* shout, scream, bellow; see **yell.**

3. [To call; *said of other than human creatures*] —*Syn.* howl, bark, hoot, scream, screech, squawk, squeak, yelp, grunt, roar, shriek, meow, whinney, nicker, moo, bawl, snarl, chatter, bay, cluck, crow, whine, pipe, trill, coo, whistle, caw, bellow, quack, clack, bay at the moon, gabble, hiss, growl, croak, cackle, twitter, tweet; see also **sound** 1, **yell.**

crying, *mod.*—*Syn.* blubbering, mourning, sorrowing; see **weeping.**

crying, *n.*—*Syn.* shrieking, sorrow, sobbing; see **cry** 3, **tears.**

for crying out loud (D)—*Syn.* for God's *or* heaven's sake; oh, no; for the love of Mike *or* Pete (D); see **curse, no.**

crypt, *n.*—*Syn.* vault, tomb, sepulcher; see **grave** 1.

cryptic, *mod.*—*Syn.* enigmatic, mystic, hidden; see **mysterious** 2, **obscure** 3, **secret** 1.

crystal, *mod.*—*Syn.* limpid, lucid, pellucid; see **clear** 2, **transparent** 1.

crystal, *n.*—*Syn.* symmetrically faceted substance, quartz, sparkling gem, brilliant, cut glass, gleaming *or* shining object; see also **gem** 1, **diamond** 1, **jewel** 1.

crystalize, *v.*—*Syn.* become settled *or* delineated *or* definite, take form *or* shape, assume a pattern, take on character, be outlined, form into crystals, assume crystalline structure; see also **form** 4.

cub, *n.*—*Syn.* young, offspring, whelp; see **bear** 1, **fox** 1, **wolf** 1.

cube, *n.*—*Syn.* six-sided solid, hexahedron, die; see **solid.**

cuddle, *v.* **1.** [Nestle]—*Syn.* snuggle, huddle, curl up; see **nestle.**

2. [Embrace]—*Syn.* kiss, enfold, fondle; see **caress, hold** 1, **hug, touch** 1.

cudgel, *n.*—*Syn.* stick, bat, cane; see **club** 3.

cudgel, *v.*—*Syn.* strike, pommel, thrash; see **beat** 2, **hit** 1.

cue, *n.* **1.** [Theatrical or musical warning]—*Syn.* prompt, preceding speech, warning signal, opening bar(s), immediately preceding words, tip-off (D); see also **sign.**

2. [Hint]—*Syn.* lead, innuendo, idea; see **hint** 1, 2, **suggestion** 1.

cuff, *n.* **1.** [Edge of a sleeve or pants leg]—*Syn.* French cuff, armband, wristband; see **band** 1, **hem.**

2. [A blow]—*Syn.* slap, punch, hit; see **blow** 1.

off the cuff (D)—*Syn.* extemporaneous, unofficial, offhand; see **informal** 1.

on the cuff (D)—*Syn.* on credit, charged, delayed; see **unpaid** 1.

cuff, *v.*—*Syn.* slap, punch, beat; see **hit** 1.

cuisine, *n.*—*Syn.* table, culinary department, bill of fare; see **food** 1, **kitchen, menu.**

cul-de-sac, *n.*—*Syn.* dead end, dead-end street, blind alley, impasse, blind, mew(s), enclosure; see also **road** 1, **trap** 1.

cull, *v.* **1.** [Choose]—*Syn.* select, elect, pick out; see **choose** 1.

2. [To gather]—*Syn.* collect, amass, round up; see **accumulate** 1.

culminate, *v.*—*Syn.* finish, close, end up (D); see **climax** 1, **end** 1.

culmination, *n.* **1.** [Acme]—*Syn.* peak, summit, zenith; see **climax, top** 1.

2. [Finish]—*Syn.* conclusion, finale, finish; see **end** 2.

culpability, *n.*—*Syn.* lapse, blame, fault; see **guilt.**

culpable, *mod.*—*Syn.* blameworthy, punishable, blamable; see **guilty** 2.

culprit, *n.*—*Syn.* offender, felon, fugitive; see **criminal.**

cult, *n.* **1.** [Ceremony]—*Syn.* liturgy, rite, ritual; see **ceremony** 2, **religion** 1, 2.

2. [Sect]—*Syn.* clique, clan, band; see **church** 3, **faction** 1, **religion** 1.

cultivate, *v.* **1.** [Plant]—*Syn.* till, garden, seed; see **farm** 1, **harvest, plant.**

2. [Educate]—*Syn.* nurture, refine, improve; see **teach** 1, 2.

3. [Encourage]—*Syn.* advance, further, bolster; see **encourage** 1, **promote** 1.

cultivation, *n.* **1.** [Farming]—*Syn.* horticulture, agriculture, gardening; see **farming.**

2. [Progress]—*Syn.* refinement, advancement, breeding; see **education** 1, **improvement** 2, **progress** 1.

cultural, *mod.*—*Syn.* educational, socializing, refining, refined, constructive, influential, nurturing, disciplining, enlightening, civilizing, advancing, instructive, humanizing, beneficial, learned, educative, polishing, enriching, promoting, elevating, uplifting, corrective, ennobling, raising, inspirational, regenerative, adorning, ornamenting, beautifying, dignifying, glorifying, liberalizing, broadening, expanding, widening, democratizing, catholicizing, developmental, imparting, open-minded, freeing from prejudice, stimulating though; see also **artistic** 1, 2, **helpful** 1.—*Ant.* primitive*, feral, insular.

culture, *n.* **1.** [The act of encouraging growth] —*Syn.* tending, raising, cultivation; see **farming** 1.

2. [Civilizing tradition]—*Syn.* folklore, folkways, instruction, education, study, law, society, family, convention, habit, inheritance, learning, arts, sciences, custom, mores, ethos, knowledge, letters, literature, poetry, painting, music, lore, ethnology, architecture, history, religion, humanism, the arts and the sciences; see also **civilization** 1, **humanities.** —*Ant.* barbarism, disorder*, chaos.

3. [Refinement and education]—*Syn.* breeding, gentility, cultivation, enlightenment, learning, capacity, ability, skill, proficiency, science, lore, practice, erudition, education, training, art, perception, discrimination, finish, taste, grace, dignity, politeness, savoir-faire, manners, urbanity, dress, fashion, address, tact, nobility, kindness, polish (D); see also **courtesy** 1, **elegance** 1, **experience** 3, **sophistication.** —*Ant.* ignorance*, crudeness, vulgarity.

cultured, *mod.* —*Syn.* cultivated, educated, informed, advanced, accomplished, enlightened, polished, well-bred, genteel, elegant, courteous, intellectual, sophisticated, sensitive, intelligent, *au courant* (French), able, well-read, up-to-date, well-informed, traveled, experienced, tolerant, understanding, appreciative, civilized, aesthetic, enjoying the arts, versed in the humanities, literary, savant, urbane, mannerly, gently bred, chivalrous, erudite, gallant, lettered; *all* (D): high-brow, bluestocking, high-class; see also **learned** 1, 2, **liberal** 2, **polite** 1, **refined** 2.—*Ant.* narrow, prejudiced*, backward.

culvert, *n.* —*Syn.* duct, canals, watercourse; see **channel** 1, **conduit, pipe** 1.

cumulative, *mod.* **1.** [Becoming more intense] —*Syn.* heightening, intensifying, advancing, snowballing; see **increasing** 2.

2. [Gained]—*Syn.* gathered, obtained, secured; see **acquired** 1.

cunning, *mod.* **1.** [Sly]—*Syn.* crafty, tricky, wily; see **sly** 1.

2. [Shrewd]—*Syn.* clever, skillful, ingenious; see **intelligent** 1.

cunning, *n.* —*Syn.* craft, art, shrewdness, subtlety, artifice, craftiness, deceit, intrigue, chicanery, finesse; see also **deception** 1.

cup, *n.* —*Syn.* vessel, bowl, goblet, mug, tumbler, noggin, pannikin, beaker, stein, bumper, taster, standard, jorum, porringer, cannikin, grail, chalice, *chark* (Russian), *tazza* (Italian), gourd, demitasse; see also **can** 1, **container.**

Varieties of cups include the following—tea, coffee, demitasse, soup, boullion, cream soup, ale, chocolate, measuring, mustache.

cupboard, *n.* —*Syn.* closet, locker, storeroom, sideboard, press, buffet; see also **furniture.**

Cupid, *n.* —*Syn.* Eros (Greek), Roman god of love, Amor, matchmaker, marriage arranger, matrimonial agent, lonely hearts expert, son of Venus, Hymen.

cupidity, *n.* —*Syn.* avarice, rapacity, avidity, possessiveness; see **greed.**

cupola, *n.* —*Syn.* bend, vault, mosque roof; see **arch, dome** 1, **roof.**

cur, *n.* —*Syn.* mongrel, hound, pop (D); see **dog** 1.

curable, *mod.* —*Syn.* improvable, reparative, corrigible, amenable *or* susceptible *or* subject to cure, not hopeless, correctable, capable of improvement, healable, restorable, mendable, not too bad (D); see also **temporary.**

curate, *n.* —*Syn.* chaplain, clergyman, pastor; see **minister** 1, **priest, rabbi.**

curative, *mod.* —*Syn.* therapeutic, healing, corrective; see **remedial.**

curator, *n.* —*Syn.* keeper, custodian, guardian, museum man *or* personnel *or* officer, officer in charge of a collection, museographer, museologist, specialist in museology *or* museography; see also **antiquarian, collector** 2, **scientist.**

curb, *n.* **1.** [Restraint]—*Syn.* hindrance, chain, check; see **barrier, restraint** 2.

2. [Edge]—*Syn.* border, ledge, lip; see **edge** 1, **rim.**

curb, *v.* —*Syn.* retard, impede, subdue; see **hinder, restrain** 1, **restrict** 2.

curdle, *v.* —*Syn.* coagulate, condense, clot; see **thicken** 1.

cure, *n.* —*Syn.* restorative, healing agent, antidote; see **medicine** 2.

cure, *v.* **1.** [To heal]—*Syn.* make healthy, restore, make whole; see **heal** 1.

2. [To preserve]—*Syn.* keep, salt, pickle; see **preserve** 3.

3. [To harden]—*Syn.* temper, fire, steel; see **harden** 1.

curfew, *n.* —*Syn.* late hour, (time) limit, check-in time, evening, midnight, lockout (D); see also **limitation** 1.

curiosity, *n.* **1.** [Investigation *or* interest]—*Syn.* concern, regard, inquiring mind, inquiringness, inquisitiveness, mental acquisitiveness, thirst for knowledge, a questing mind, questioning, searching, interest, desire to know, eagerness to find out, disposition to inquire, inclination to ask questions, interest in learning, scientific interest, healthy curiosity.

2. [A tendency to snoop]—*Syn.* meddlesomeness, intrusiveness, officiousness, meddling, prying; *all* (D): nosiness, long-nosiness, snoopiness.

3. [An unusual object]—*Syn.* exoticism, rarity, marvel; see **wonder** 2.

curious, *mod.* **1.** [Strange or odd]—*Syn.* rare, queer, unique; see **unusual** 2.

2. [Interested]—*Syn.* inquiring, analytical, questioning; see **inquisitive, interested** 1.

curl, *n.* —*Syn.* ringlet, coil, spiral, wave, tress of hair, love-lock, curlicue; see also **hair** 1, **lock** 2.

curl, *v.* **1.** [To twist]—*Syn.* curve, coil, bend, spiral, crinkle, wind, twine, loop, crimp, scallop, lap, fold, roll, indent, contort, form into a spiral *or* curved shape, wreathe, meander, ripple, buckle, loop, zigzag, entwine, wrinkle, undulate, twirl, crisp; see also **turn** 6, **wave** 4.—*Ant.* uncurl, straighten*, unbend.

2. [To set hair]—*Syn.* pin *or* roll (up), form into ringlets, put up (D); see **wave** 5.

curly, *mod.* **1.** [Rolled]—*Syn.* curled, kinky, wavy, waving, convoluted, coiled, crinkling, crinkly, frizzly, frizzy, spiraling, looping, looped, winding, wound; see also **rolled** 1.

2. [Naturally or artificially curled; *said of hair*] —*Syn.* kinky, wavy, given a permanent wave, naturally curly, waved, kinked.

currant, *n.* Varieties include the following—red, white, black, Missouri *or* buffalo, wild, flowering; see also **berry.**

currency, *n.* —*Syn.* coin, bank notes, government notes; see **money** 1.

current, *mod.* —*Syn.* prevailing, contemporary, in fashion; see **fashionable, modern** 1.

current, —*Syn.* drift, tidal motion, ebb and flow; see **flow, tide** 1.

curry, *v.* **1.** [Groom]—*Syn.* smooth, dress, brush; see **comb, groom.**

2. [Beat]—*Syn.* thrash, drub, cudgel; see **beat** 2.

curse, *n.* —*Syn.* oath, imprecation, malediction, malison, blasphemy, expletive, sacrilege, profanation, execration, anathema, ban, fulmination, cursing, profanity, profane swearing, blaspheming, denunciation, damning, commination, objuration, obscenity, vilification, obloquy, bane; *all* (D): blue word, cuss word, cussing, naughty words.

Common exclamations and curses include the following—plague on it, Lord, oh God, (the) Devil, bless my soul, bless me, by Jove, gracious, goodness, oh my, oh me, in Heaven's name, great Caesar's ghost, the deuce, did you ever; *all* (D): gee, gee whillikins, mercy, sakes alive, drat it all, good night, so what, dang, land of Goshen, darn, hang it all, bejaises, blast, blimy, by crickey, Chrisamighty, Keerist, damn it, damn, double-damn, by golly, Chrisake, damn-it-to-hell, for cripe's sake, for crying out loud, Gawd, Judas Priest, Jesus H. Christ, I swan the Deil, Lord-a-mercy, I'll be cow-kicked and hornswoggled, I'll be a lop-eared gazelle, God's teeth, hell's whiskers, hell's bells, ye gods (and little fishes), holy mackerel, cheese and crackers, holy bilge water, geez, jeepers creepers, *ach, Gott in Himmel, Gottlob, Donnerwetter* (German), *sacré bleu, mon Dieu, diable, cochon* (French), *diablo* (Spanish).

curse, *v.* **1.** [To swear]—*Syn.* utter, affirm, avow, blaspheme, profane, swear profanely, use foul language, be foul-mouthed, be obscene, take the Lord's name in vain, damn, turn the air blue (D).

2. [To swear at]—*Syn.* objurate, execrate, imprecate, vituperate, abuse, revile, swear at, insult, call down curses on the head of, bring a curse upon, invoke harm on, call down evil on, maledict, wish calamity on, blast, doom, fulminate, thunder against, destroy, blaspheme, use invective, denounce, blight, utter curses; *all* (D): take the hide off of, call names, cuss (out).

3. [To pronounce a religious curse]—*Syn.* ban, anathematize, read out of the church; see **damn** 1.

cursed, *mod.* **1.** [Damned]—*Syn.* blighted, doomed, confounded; see **damned** 1.

2. [Detestable]—*Syn.* hateful, odious, disgusting; see **offensive** 2.

be cursed with—*Syn.* suffer from, be afflicted with, bear; see **suffer** 1.

cursory, *mod.* —*Syn.* quick, slight, desultory; see **careless** 1, **superficial.**

curt, *mod.* —*Syn.* brief, concise, terse; see **abrupt** 2, **short** 2.

curtail, *v.* —*Syn.* shorten, cramp, diminish; see **decrease** 2, **halt** 2.

curtailment, *n.* —*Syn.* decrease, abbreviation, condensation; see **reduction** 1.

curtain, *n.* —*Syn.* hanging, screen, shade, drape, drapery, window covering, film, decoration, interior furnishing, blind; see also **veil.**

Kinds of curtains include the following—fiberglass curtain (trademark), jalousie, draw curtain, roller shade, shutter, portiere, arras, valance, lambrequin, ridel, *purdah* (East Indian), Venetian blind(s), perpendicular blind(s), Austrian drape(s).

draw (*or* **drop**) **the curtain**—*Syn.* finish, stop, halt; see **end** 1.

lift the curtain on—*Syn.* **1.** start, initiate, commence; see **begin** 1. **2.** expose, disclose, uncover; see **reveal** 1.

curtsey, *n.* —*Syn.* obeisance, salaam, kowtow; see **bow** 2.

curvature, *n.* —*Syn.* bend, shape, deflection; see **curve** 1.

curve, *n.* **1.** [A bend]—*Syn.* sweep, flexure, bow, arch, circuit, ambit, curvature, crook, catenary, trajectory, conic section, equation.

Types of curves including the following—bell *or* bell-shaped curve, hairpin curve, S-curve, sine curve, extrapolated curve, hyperbolic curve, parabolic curve, normal curve, asymptomatic curve, logarithmic curve, French curve, linear curve, parabola, hyperbola, circle, ellipse, ogee, arc, chord.

2. [In baseball, a pitch that curves]—*Syn.* incurve, outcurve, dropcurve; *all* (D): in, out, drop, outdrop, fade-away, upshoot, jumpball, straight drop, slant, slider, bender, curly one, breaker, hook, snake.

curve, *v.* **1.** [To bend]—*Syn.* bow, crook, twist; see **bend** 1.

2. [To be bent]—*Syn.* buckle, stoop, crumple; see **bend** 2.

curved, *mod.* —*Syn.* bowed, arched, rounded; see **bent.**

cushion, *n.* —*Syn.* mat, woolsack, seat, rest, bolster; see also **pillow.**

custodian, *n.* **1.** [Guardian]—*Syn.* governor, curator, overseer, manager, governess, babysitter, guard, warden, escort, bodyguard; see also **curator, guardian** 1.

2. [Janitor]—*Syn.* superintendent, porter, cleaner, cleaning man, attendant, janitress, cleaning woman, caretaker, building superintendent, doorkeeper, concierge, super, maintenance, keeper, gatekeeper, night watchman, member of the department of buildings and grounds; see also **watchman.**

custody, *n.* **1.** [Protection]—*Syn.* care, guardianship, supervision, keeping, safekeeping, charge, watch, trusteeship, superintendence, tutelage, wardship, auspices, aegis, safeguard, ward; see also **administration** 1.

2. [Detention]—*Syn.* jail, keeping, confinement; see **arrest** 1, **imprisonment** 1.

take into custody—*Syn.* capture, apprehend, seize; see **arrest** 1.

custom, *n.* **1.** [A habitual action]—*Syn.* habit, practice, usage, wont, fashion, routine, precedent, use, habitude, form, consuetude, addiction, rule, procedure, manner, observance, characteristic, second nature, matter of course; *both* (D): beaten path, rut; see also **method** 2, **system** 2.—*Ant.* irregularity, strangeness*, newness.

2. [A traditional action]—*Syn.* manner, way, mode, method, system, style, vogue, fashion, convention, habit, rule, practice, precedent, formality, form, mold, established way of doing things, pattern, design, type, taste, character, routine, ritual, rite, ceremony, attitude, immemorial usage, observance, social usage, mores, dictates of society, familiar way, unwritten law, etiquette, conventionality, second nature, conventionalism, matter of course; see also **tradition** 1.—*Ant.* deviation, departure*, shift.
3. [The whole body of tradition]—*Syn.* inheritance, folkways, mores; see **culture** 2.
4. [A tax]—*Syn.* duty, excise, revenue; see **tax** 1.

customarily, *mod.* —*Syn.* usually, commonly, traditionally, conventionally, naturally, generally, habitually, frequently, normally, ordinarily; see also **regularly** 1.

customary, *mod.* —*Syn.* usual, wonted, habitual; see **common** 1, **conventional** 1, 2.

customer, *n.* —*Syn.* clientele, patron, consumer; see **buyer, client.**

cut, *mod.* **1.** [Formed]—*Syn.* shaped, modeled, arranged; see **formed.**
2. [Reduced]—*Syn* lowered, debased, marked down; see **depleted, gone** 2, **reduced** 1, 2.
3. [Severed]—*Syn.* split, divided, sliced through; see **carved.**
4. [Slashed]—*Syn.* slit, scored, scratched; see **carved, hurt, wounded.**

cut, *n.* **1.** [The using of a sharp instrument]—*Syn.* slash, thrust, dig, prick, gouge, knifing, penetrating, dividing, cleaving, incising, separation, severance, hewing, felling, quarter, intersecting, slitting, hack, slice, carve, chop, stroke; see also **division** 1.
2. [The path left by a sharp instrument]—*Syn.* slash, prick, incision, cleavage, penetration, gash, cleft, mark, nick, notch, opening, passage, groove, kerf, furrow, intersection, slit, wound, fissure; see also **hole** 1, **injury** 1.
3. [A reduction]—*Syn.* decrease, diminution, lessening; see **reduction** 1.
4. [The shape]—*Syn.* fashion, figure, construction; see **form** 1.
5. [An illustration]—*Syn.* representation, likeness, interpretation; see **illustration** 2, **picture** 3.
6. [A section]—*Syn.* segment, slice, portion; see **part** 1, **piece** 1.
7. [A piece of butchered meat]—*Syn.* piece, slice, chunk; see **meat.**
8. [(D) An insult]—*Syn.* indignity, offense, abuse; see **insult.**
a cut above—*Syn.* superior, higher, more capable *or* competent *or* efficient, etc.; see **better** 2.

cut, *v.* **1.** [To sever]—*Syn.* separate, slice (through), cleave, fell, hew, mow, prune, reap, scythe, sickle, shear, dice, chop (down), slit, split, rive, sunder, cut apart *or* asunder, rip, saw through, chisel, cut away *or* through *or* off, snip, skive, sliver, chip, quarter, dissect, clip, truncate, behead, saber, scissor, facet, flitch, bite, shave, dissect, bisect, amputate; see also **carve** 1, **divide** 1.
2. [To cut into]—*Syn.* gash, incise, slash, slice, notch, nick, indent, score, carve into, mark, scratch, furrow, rake, wound, mar, scotch, gouge, scarify, lacerate; see also **carve** 1.
3. [To penetrate]—*Syn.* pierce, perforate, puncture; see **penetrate** 1.
4. [To cross]—*Syn.* intersect, pass, move across; see **cross** 1.
5. [To shorten]—*Syn.* curtail, delete, lessen; see **decrease** 2.
6. [To hit sharply]—*Syn.* strike, hew, chop; see **hit** 1.
7. [To divide]—*Syn.* split, sever, separate; see **divide** 1.
8. [To castrate]—*Syn.* alter, geld, emasculate; see **castrate.**
9. [(D) To ignore deliberately]—*Syn.* look the other way, slight, disregard; see **insult, neglect.**
10. [(D) To absent oneself]—*Syn.* shirk, evade, stay away, play truant *or* hooky, be absent without leave *or* AWOL; *all* (D): skip, duck, ditch, dump.
11. [To record electronically]—*Syn.* make a record, film, tape; see **record** 3.
12. [To weaken]—*Syn.* dilute, impair, undermine; see **weaken** 2.
13. [To shape]—*Syn.* fashion, cast, make; see **form** 1.

cut back, *v.* —*Syn.* reduce, curtail, shorten; see **decrease** 2.

cute (D), *mod.* —*Syn.* dainty, attractive, delightful; see **charming, pleasant** 1, 2.

cuticle, *n.* —*Syn.* dermis, epidermis, tegument; see **skin.**

cut in, *v.* **1.** [Interrupt]—*Syn.* butt in (D), interfere, move in; see **interrupt** 2.
2. [To include, especially in card games]—*Syn.* make room for, deal in, invite to join; see **include** 2, **invite** 1.

cut off, *v.* **1.** [To remove]—*Syn.* lift up, tear out, pull off; see **remove** 1.
2. [To interrupt]—*Syn.* intrude, break in, intervene; see **interrupt** 2.

cutout, *n.* —*Syn.* paper doll, sticker, newspaper article, article.

cut out, *v.* **1.** [Remove]—*Syn.* pull out, extract, carve; see **remove** 1.
2. [(D) To leave]—*Syn.* go away, depart, leave the scene (D); see **leave** 1.

cut out for, *mod.* —*Syn.* suitable, adequate, good for; see **fit** 1, 2.

cutpurse (D), *n.* —*Syn.* thief, pickpocket, bandit; see **criminal, robber.**

cut short, *v.* **1.** [Terminate]—*Syn.* finish, halt, quit; see **end** 1, **stop** 1, 2.
2. [Interrupt]—*Syn.* intercept, check, halt; see **hinder, interrupt** 2.
3. [Diminish]—*Syn.* abridge, abbreviate, shorten; see **decrease** 2.

cutthroat, *n.* —*Syn.* assassin, murderer, slayer; see **criminal, killer.**

cutting, *mod.* —*Syn.* biting, incisive, caustic; see **sarcastic.**

cut up, *v.* **1.** [To chop]—*Syn.* chop up, slice, dice; see **cut** 1, 2.
2. [To cavort]—*Syn.* show off, play jokes, fool around (D); see **joke, play** 2.

cybernetics, *n.* —*Syn.* science of computers, comparative study of complex electronic machines, artificial intelligence, AI, system to describe the nature of the brain, science employing thermostats and photoelectric sorters; see also **computer, science** 1.

cycle, *n.* —*Syn.* succession, revolution of time, period; see **age** 3, **circle** 2, **sequence** 1, **series.**

cyclone, *n.* —*Syn.* destructive wind, typhoon, twister (D); see **hurricane, storm** 1, **tornado, wind** 1.

cylinder, *n.* **1.** [An automobile part]—*Syn.* compression chamber, expansion chamber, machine *or* engine part; see **automobile.**

2. [A geometrical form]—*Syn.* circular solid, barrel, volumetric curve; see **solid.**

cylindrical, *mod.* —*Syn.* tubular, barrel-shaped, circular; see **round.**

cynic, *n.* —*Syn.* misanthrope, misogynist, misogamist, mocker, satirist, scoffer, pessimist, sarcastic person, caviler, sneerer, flouter, carper, unbeliever, egotist, egoist, manhater, skeptic, doubter, questioner, detractor, doubting Thomas (D); see also **critic** 1.—*Ant.* optimist, believer*, idealist.

cynical, *mod.* —*Syn.* sardonic, unbelieving, sneering; see **sarcastic.**

cynicism, *n.* —*Syn.* acrimony, asperity, acerbity; see **sarcasm.**

cyst, *n.* —*Syn.* sac, bag, pouch; see also **blister, injury** 1, **sore.**

czar, *n.* —*Syn.* emperor, autocrat, despot; see **king** 1, **leader** 2, **ruler** 1.

D

dab, *n.* —*Syn.* bit, pat, small quantity; see **bit** 1.
dab, *v.* —*Syn.* tap, peck, pat; see **touch** 1.
dabble, *v.* —*Syn.* trifle (with), have sport with, engage in superficially, amuse oneself with, dally, putter, fiddle *or* flirt with, toy with, be an amateur, have a dilettante's interest, idle away time, concern oneself with anything slightly, make slight efforts, work superficially, do something in a light manner; *all* (D): play the market, putter (around), diddle, fool with *or* around, dip into.—*Ant.* study*, work at, become an expert.
dabbler, *n.* —*Syn.* novice, beginner, dilettante; see **amateur, loafer.**
dad (D), *n.* —*Syn.* progenitor, male parent, sire; see **father** 1, **parent.**
daft, *mod.* **1.** [Silly]—*Syn.* foolish, ridiculous, asinine; see **silly, stupid** 1.
2. [Insane]—*Syn.* crazy, demented, deranged; see **insane** 1.
dagger, *n.* —*Syn.* stiletto, point, blade; see **knife.**
look daggers at—*Syn.* glower, look at with anger *or* hatred, scowl (at); see **dislike.**
daily, *mod.* —*Syn.* diurnal, quotidian, per diem, every day, occurring every day, issued every day, periodic, cyclic, recurring day after day, once daily, by day, once a day, during the day, day by day, from day to day; see also **regular** 3.
dainty, *mod.* **1.** [Notable for fineness *or* fragility] —*Syn.* delicate, fragile, petite, frail, thin, light, pretty, beautiful, lovely, comely, well-made, attractive, graceful, fine, neat, choice, elegant, exquisite, trim, pleasing, tasteful, precious, tasty, delicious, rare, soft, tender, feeble, airy, diaphanous, lacy,; *all* (D): nice, darling, cute, sweet; see also **charming, weak** 1, 3, 4.—*Ant.* coarse, rough*, gross.
2. [Having taste for dainty things]—*Syn.* refined, tasteful, ladylike; see **cultured, refined** 2.
dairy, *n.* —*Syn.* creamery, dairy farm, cow barn, processing plant, ice-cream plant, cheese factory, buttery, milk station, Babcock testing station, pasteurizing plant, co-operative, produce company; see also **farm.**
dairy products, *n.* —*Syn.* produce, cottage industry, farm products; see **butter, cheese, cream** 1, **milk, produce.**
dale, *n.* —*Syn.* lowland, vale, glen; see **valley.**
dalliance, *n.* **1.** [Flirting]—*Syn.* toying, petting, seduction; see **flirting.**
2. [Idling]—*Syn.* dawdling, loitering, loafing, puttering; see **trifling.**
dally, *v.* **1.** [To flirt]—*Syn.* toy, tease, play; see **flirt** 1.
2. [To trifle]—*Syn.* dawdle, idle, putter; see **dabble, trifle with** 1.
dam, *n.* **1.** [Structure to impound water]—*Syn.* dike, ditch, wall, bank, embankment, gate, weir, grade, levee, irrigation dam, diversion dam; see also **barrier.**
Famous dams include the following—United States: Gatun, Fort Peck, Kingsley, Glen Canyon, Grand Coulee, Bonneville, Shasta, Boulder, Hoover, Wilson, Bartlett, Bagnell, Conowingo, Tygart River; Russia: Dnepropetrovsk; France: Sautet, Chambon, Sarrans; Egypt: Aswan; India: Metur; South Africa: Vaalbank.
2. [Mother, usually of beasts]—*Syn.* progenitor, bitch, mare; see **mother** 1, **parent.**
dam, *v.* —*Syn.* hold (back), check, obstruct, bar, slow, retard, restrict, stop (up), close, clog, choke, block (up), impede, confine; see also **hinder, restrain** 1.—*Ant.* advance, release*, clear.
damage, *n.* **1.** [Injury]—*Syn.* harm, hurt, wound, bruise, bane, wrong, infliction, casualty, detriment, deprivation, suffering, illness, affliction, accident, catastrophe, adversity, outrage, hardship, disturbance, mutilation, impairment, mishap, mischance, evil, blow, devastation, mischief, stroke, disservice, reverse; *all* (D): crack-up, crash landing, cave-in, knockout; see also **disaster, injury** 1, **misfortune** 1. —*Ant.* blessing*, benefit, boon.
2. [Loss occasioned by injury]—*Syn.* ruin, breakage, ruined goods, wreckage, detriment, waste, spoliation, shrinkage, depreciation, deprivation, dry rot, pollution, corruption, blemish, contamination, spoil, ravage, atrophy, adulteration, defacement, vitiation, degeneration, canker, deterioration, havoc, erosion, disrepair, debasement, corrosion, discoloration; *both* (D): wear and tear, foul play; see also **destruction** 2, **loss** 1.—*Ant.* return*, profit, recompense.
damage, *v.* **1.** [To impair the value of]—*Syn.* ruin, wreck, bleach, fade, water-soak, tarnish, burn, scorch, drench, dirty, rot, smash, batter, discolor, mutilate, scratch, smudge, crack, torpedo, bang up, abuse, maltreat, mar, deface, disfigure, mangle, ravage, scathe, contaminate, crumple, dismantle, cheapen, blight, disintegrate, ghettoize, pollute, hamstring, sap, stain, tear, undermine, gnaw, corrode, break, split, stab, rend, crack, pierce, mildew, cripple, rust, warp, maim, mutilate, lacerate, wound, taint, despoil, incapacitate, pervert, bruise, spoil, wreak havoc on, wear away, abuse, defile, wrong, vitiate, corrupt, maltreat, infect; see also **break** 2, **destroy** 1.
2. [To debase]—*Syn.* pervert, vitiate, degrade; see **corrupt** 1.
3. [To slander]—*Syn.* malign, calumniate, disparage; see **slander.**

4. [To cause pain]—*Syn.* beat, kick, flog; see **hurt** 1.

damaged, *mod.* **1.** [Less valuable than formerly] —*Syn.* injured, in need of repair, in poor condition; see **broken** 1, 2.

2. [Reduced in value because of damage]—*Syn.* on sale, depreciated, dated, faded, secondhand, used, shopworn, out of season, out of style, outsized, left over, remaindered, reconditioned, repossessed, water-soaked, weathered, smoked, smoke-damaged, ghettoized, beat-up (D); see also **cheap** 1. —*Ant.* unused*, unhurt, prime.

3. [Harmed]—*Syn.* injured, marred, spoiled; see **hurt.**

damages, *n.* —*Syn.* reparations, costs, reimbursement; see **expense** 1, 2, **expenses.**

dame, *n.* —*Syn.* damsel, baroness, aristocrat; see **lady** 2, 3.

damn, *v.* **1.** [To consign to hell]—*Syn.* curse, accurse, confound, ban, doom, anathematize, proscribe, banish, read out of the church, excommunicate, fulminate *or* declaim against, excoriate, sentence, convict, cast into hell, consign to the lower regions, torment, condemn to hell *or* to eternal punishment, doom to perdition; *all* (D): curse with bell, book, and candle; thunder against, call down curses on the head of, send to the bad place, sent to a warm climate; see also **condemn** 1. —*Ant.* bless, forgive*, elevate.

2. [To swear at]—*Syn.* revile, imprecate, abuse; see **curse** 2.

3. [To disapprove strongly]—*Syn.* object to, complain of, attack; see **denounce.**

not give (*or* **care**) **a damn** (D)—*Syn.* not care, be indifferent, reject; see **neglect** 1.

not worth a damn (D)—*Syn.* useless, unproductive, valueless; see **worthless** 1.

damnable, *mod.* —*Syn.* outrageous, depraved, detestable; see **offensive** 2, **wicked** 1, 2.

damnation, *n.* —*Syn.* damning, condemnation, sending to hell, consigning to perdition, ban, anathema, excommunication, condemnation to punishment in the hereafter, proscription, doom, *damnatio* (Latin), *Verdammung* (German); *all* (D): thunders of the Vatican, giving a ticket to the bad place, sending to Old Nick; see also **blame** 1, **curse.**

damned, *mod.* **1.** [Consigned to hell]—*Syn.* cursed, condemned, accursed, unhappy, anathematized, lost, reprobate, infernal; *both* (D): hell-bound, gone to blazes; see also **unfortunate** 2.—*Ant.* saved, blessed*, on high.

2. [(D) Disapproved of]—*Syn.* bad, unwelcome; *all* (D): blamed, blankety-blanked, blithering, blessed, blasted, bloody, consarned, cussed, danged, darned, goldarned, goldast, doggoned, dashed, double-damned, dratted, lousy; see also **undesirable, wicked** 1, 2.—*Ant.* desirable, welcomed*, favorite.

do (*or* **try**) **one's damnedest** (D)—*Syn.* endeavor, do one's best, give one's all; see **try** 1.

damning, *mod.* —*Syn.* serious, ruinous, fatal; see **incriminating.**

damn with faint praise, *v.* —*Syn.* condemn, find fault with, reject; see **rebuff** 1.

damp, *mod.* **1.** [Somewhat wet]—*Syn.* moist, sodden, soggy; see **wet** 1.

2. [Rainy]—*Syn.* drizzly, cloudy, humid; see **wet** 2.

dampen, *v.* **1.** [To wet]—*Syn.* sprinkle, water, rinse; see **moisten.**

2. [To discourage]—*Syn.* humble, dispirit, dismay; see **depress** 2. **discourage** 1.

damper, *n.* —*Syn.* hindrance, depressant, bridle; see **restraint** 2.

damp off, *v.* —*Syn.* wilt, droop, shrivel; see **die** 1, 3.

damsel, *n.* —*Syn.* maiden, maid, nymph; see **girl** 1, **lady** 2, 3, **woman.**

dance, *n.* **1.** [Rhythmic movement]—*Syn.* hop, jig, skip, prance, shuffle, fling, swing, caper; *all* (D): rag, rock, hoedown.

Dances include the following—Social: fox trot, shimmy, polka, conga, rhumba, tango, samba, cha-cha, mambo, rock-and-roll, disco, jerk, frug, jitterbug, one-step, two-step, box-step, Charleston, bunny hug, twist; theatrical: ballet, Russian ballet, modern ballet, adagio, tap dance, soft-shoe, toe dance; traditional: cotillion, quadrille, pavane, galliard, branle, sarabande, courante, *bourrée* (French), loure, *passepied* (French), mazurka, polonaise, beguine, bolero, fandango, round dance, square dance, minuet, gavotte, schottische, *contredanse* (French), morris dance, (Virginia) reel, rigadoon, shuffle, gallopade, buck and wing, galop; folkloristic and primitive: sun dance, ghost dance, sword dance, snake dance, fertility dance, Highland fling, paso doble, flamenco, Irish jig, clog, tarantella, hora, hornpipe, bolero, czardas, hula; see also **waltz.**

2. [A dancing party]—*Syn.* promenade, (grand) ball, dress ball, reception; *all* (D): shindig, rat race, brawl, prom; see also **party** 1.

dance, *v.* **1.** [To move rhythmically]—*Syn.* waltz, step, trip, tread, jig, one-step, perform the steps of, execute the figures of, shuffle the feet, two-step, fox-trot, cha-cha, samba, mambo, tango, pirouette, polka, reel, quadrille; *all* (D): jitterbug, dance the soles off one's feet, hoof it, drag, hop, swing a mean leg, cut a rug, twist, rock, jerk, foot it; see also **move** 1.

2. [To move in a gay and sprightly manner] —*Syn.* hop, skip, jump, leap, bob, bobble, scamper, skitter, jiggle, jigger, caper, bounce, cavort, sway, swirl, sweep, swing, careen, curvet, cut capers (D); see also **jump** 1, 3, **play** 2.—*Ant.* sit*, perch, stand.

dance attendance on, *v.* —*Syn.* be subservient *or* subject to, serve abjectly, humble oneself (to); see **follow** 2, **serve** 2.

dancer, *n.* —*Syn.* terpsichorean, *danseur, danseuse* (*both* French), (prima) ballerina, chorus girl, dancing student; ballet, tap, toe, figure, hula, belly, taxi, go-go, cage, folk, square, modern, flamenco, geisha, classical ballroom, etc., dancer; *all* (D): hoofer, stripper, rock-and-roller; see also **actor, actress.**

dance to another tune, *v.* —*Syn.* revolt, act differently, refuse to conform *or* comply; see **differ** 1.

dander (D), *n.* —*Syn.* wrath, temper, animosity; see **anger.**

get one's dander up (D)—*Syn.* enrage, infuriate, annoy; see **anger** 1.

dandle, *v.* —*Syn.* fondle, pet, nuzzle; see **caress, touch** 1.

dandy, *n.* **1.** [Fop]—*Syn.* coxcomb, dude, cavalier; see **fop.**
2. [(D) Specimen]—*Syn.* criterion, standard, paragon; see **example** 1, **measure** 2, **model** 2.

danger, *n.* **1.** [The quality of being dangerous]—*Syn.* uncertainty, risk, peril, jeopardy, threat, hazard, insecurity, low probability, instability, exposure, venture, destabilizing factor, menace, precariousness, vulnerability, slipperiness; see also **chance** 1.—*Ant.* safety*, security, certainty.
2. [Something that is dangerous]—*Syn.* possibility, probability, exigency; see **chance** 1, **trouble** 2.

dangerous, *mod.* **1.** [Not safe]—*Syn.* perilous, unshielded, unsheltered, critical, serious, pressing, vital, urgent, vulnerable, exposed, involving *or* full of risk, threatening, alarming, portentous, hazardous, risky, causing danger, insecure, precarious, ticklish, delicate, speculative, unstable, touchy, treacherous, bad, fraught *or* beset with danger, thorny, jeopardous, breakneck; *all* (D): chancy, shaky, hairy, under fire, unhealthy, hot; see also **endangered, uncertain** 2, **unsafe.**—*Ant.* certain*, sure, secure.
2. [Involving an active threat]—*Syn.* menacing, threatening, serious, critical, impending, ugly, nasty, imminent, malignant, formidable, terrible, impregnable, armed, fatal, mortal, deadly; *all* (D): between the frying pan and the fire, between Scylla and Charybdis, on a collision course, tough; see also **ominous.**—*Ant.* helpful*, innocent, beneficial.

dangerously, *mod.*—*Syn.* desperately, precariously, severely; see **seriously** 1.

dangle, *v.*—*Syn.* droop, sway, suspend; see **hang** 1, 2.

dank, *mod.*—*Syn.* damp, humid, moist; see **close** 5, **wet** 1, 2.

dapper, *mod.*—*Syn.* trim, chic, spruce; see **neat** 1.

dare, *v.* **1.** [To be courageous]—*Syn.* take a chance, venture, adventure, undertake, stake, attempt, endeavor, try (one's hand), hazard, be not afraid, have the necessary boldness for, be bold enough to undertake, make bold, despite danger; *all* (D): pluck up, take heart, take the bull by the horns, shoot the works, go ahead, take *or* run a chance; see also **chance** 2, **risk, try** 1.—*Ant.* avoid*, dread, fear.
2. [to defy]—*Syn.* challenge, meet, confront, front, oppose, disregard, brave, cope, scorn, outdare, insult, resist, threaten, spurn, denounce, bully, mock, laugh at, offer defiance to, assume a fighting attitude (toward), square off, run the gauntlet, outbrazen, outbrave; *all* (D): double the fist (at), call out, snap one's fingers (at), show fight, go through fire and water, pluck by the beard, pluck up heart, nerve oneself, gather courage, look big, kick against, put one's feet down, have the nerve, bell the cat, put up a bold front, have the courage of one's convictions, beard the lion (in his den), face the music, measure swords with, look full in the face, muster courage, face up to, call one's bluff; see also **face** 1.—*Ant.* avoid*, shun, evade.

daredevil, *n.*—*Syn.* stunt man, madcap, gambler; see **adventurer** 1.

daring, *mod.* **1.** [Indifferent to danger]—*Syn.* bold, courageous, fearless; see **brave** 1.
2. [Lacking in modesty and discretion]—*Syn.* impudent, forward, obtrusive; see **rude** 1, 2.

dark, *mod.* **1.** [Lacking illumination]—*Syn.* unlighted, unlit, dim, shadowy, somber, cloudy, foggy, sunless, lightless, indistinct, dull, faint, vague, dusky, murky, gloomy, misty, darkish, obscure, nebulous, shady, shaded, clouded, darksome, darkened, overcast, Cimmerian, opaque, crepuscular, stygian, without light, tenebrous, obfuscous, bereft of light, ill-lighted, lurid; *all* (D): darkling, inky, pitchy; see also **black** 1, **hazy** 1.—*Ant.* bright*, lighted, illuminated.
2. [Lacking brightness]—*Syn.* grimy, drab, dingy; see **dull** 2.
3. [Not known]—*Syn.* cryptic, hidden, mysterious; see **obscure** 3, **secret** 1.
4. [Lacking light for the future]—*Syn.* sinister, foreboding, unpropitious; see **ominous.**
5. [Dark in complexion]—*Syn.* brunet, swarthy, tan, Negroid, dusky, sable, dark-complexioned, nonwhite, colored, Indian; see also **African** 2, **black** 3, **negro.**
6. [Ignorant]—*Syn.* unenlightened, unread, uncultivated; see **ignorant** 2.
7. [Evil]—*Syn.* bad, immoral, corrupt; see **wicked** 1.

dark, *n.* **1.** [Darkness]—*Syn.* gloom, murk, duskiness; see **darkness** 1.
2. [Night]—*Syn.* nighttime, nightfall, evening; see **night** 1.
3. [Secrecy]—*Syn.* concealment, inscrutability, seclusion; see **mystery** 1, **secrecy.**
4. [Ignorance]—*Syn.* denseness, crudeness, vulgarity; see **ignorance** 2.
in the dark—*Syn.* uninformed, unaware, naive; see **ignorant** 1.
keep dark—*Syn.* conceal, keep secret, obscure; see **hide** 1.

darken, *v.* **1.** [To grow darker]—*Syn.* cloud up *or* over, deepen, become dark; see **intensify, shade** 3.
2. [To make darker]—*Syn.* cloud, shadow, blacken; see **intensify, shade** 2.

darkling (D), *mod.*—*Syn.* dusky, dim, shadowy; see **dark** 1.

darkness, *n.* **1.** [Gloom]—*Syn.* dark, murk, dusk, murkiness, duskiness, dimness, blackness, shadiness, shade, tenebrosity, smokiness, blackness, lightlessness, pitch darkness, twilight, crepuscule, eclipse, nightfall, obscurity, cloudiness, opacity; *all* (D): Stygian darkness, Cimmerian shade, Egyptian blackness, shades of evening *or* night, palpable darkness; see also **night** 1.
2. [Ignorance]—*Syn.* denseness, crudeness, vulgarity; see **ignorance** 2.
3. [Evil]—*Syn.* wickedness, sin, corruption; see **evil** 1.
4. [Secrecy]—*Syn.* concealment, isolation, seclusion; see **privacy, secrecy.**

darling, *mod.*—*Syn.* dearest, dear, favorite; see **beloved.**

darling, *n.* **1.** [A beloved one]—*Syn.* love, dear one, beloved; see **dear, favorite, friend** 1, **lover** 1.
2. [Term of endearment]—*Syn.* lover, sweetheart, dear one, beloved, my own, (dear) heart, heart's desire, dearest; *all* (D): pet, sweet, angel, truelove, love, jewel, treasure, pearl, sweetie-pie, sugar,

honey, honey bun, honeybunch, precious, sweetie, princess, dearie, ducky, baby, sweet mama, sugarplum, (honey) lamb, hon, lambie pie, chéri baby, light of my life, lady love, heartsease, one and only.

darn, *v.* **1.** [*Variant of damn*]—*Syn.* abuse, blame, swear at; see **curse** 2.

2. [To repair]—*Syn.* mend, knit, embroider; see **repair.**

darned, *mod.* **1.** [Mended with thread]—*Syn.* patched, knitted up, stitched; see **repaired, sewn.**

2. [*Variant of damned*]—*Syn.* bad, awful, undesirable; see **damned** 2, **wicked** 1.

dart, *n.*—*Syn.* missile, barb, flechette; see **arrow, weapon** 1.

dart, *v.* **1.** [To move in the manner of a dart]—*Syn.* shoot (up *or* out), speed, plunge, launch, thrust, hurtle, fling, heave, pitch, cast, dash, spring (up), go like an arrow, spurt, scud, skim, fly; *all* (D): fire off, scoot, skitter, spearhead; see also **move** 1. —*Ant.* stop*, amble, loiter.

2. [To move quickly]—*Syn.* hasten, speed, rush; see **hurry** 1, **race** 1, **run** 2.

dash, *n.* **1.** [A sprint]. Common dashes include the following—50-yard, 100-yard *or* century (D), 220-yard, 50-meter, 100-meter, 200-meter; see also **race** 3, **sport** 3.

2. [A short, swift movement]—*Syn.* spurt, sortie, rush; see **run** 1.

3. [Punctuation marking a break in thought]—*Syn.* em, em dash, em quad, quad, quadrat, en, en quad, en dash, two-em quad, etc.; *both* (D): mutton quad, nut quad; see also **mark** 1, **punctuation.**

4. [A little of something]—*Syn.* little, a few drops, hint, sprinkle, scattering, seasoning, zest, touch, slight admixture, small quantity, grain, trace, suspicion, suggestion, squirt, taste, *soupçon* (French), infinitesimal amount, teentsy-weentsy bit (D); see also **bit** 1, **part** 1.—*Ant.* too much*, quantity, excess.

dash, *v.* **1.** [To strike violently]—*Syn.* hit, bludgeon, cudgel; see **beat** 2.

2. [To discourage]—*Syn.* dampen, dismay, dispirit; see **discourage** 1.

3. [To sprint]—*Syn.* race, speed, hurry; see **run** 2.

4. [To throw]—*Syn.* hurl, fling, cast; see **throw** 1.

5. [To break against]—*Syn.* splash, shatter, plunge; see **hit** 3.

dashing, *mod.* **1.** [Bold and lively]—*Syn.* daring, fearless, adventurous; see **brave** 1.

2. [Being dashed; *said especially of water*]—*Syn.* striking, splashing, beating, hurled *or* cast *or* blown against, shattering, breaking, crushing, flinging, tossing, rolling, storm-tossed, wind-blown; see also **high** 1, 2.

dash off, *v.*—*Syn.* rush, fail to take pains *or* prepare; hurry; see **hasten** 2.

dastardly, *mod.*—*Syn.* craven, timid, unmanly; see **afraid** 1, **cowardly** 1, **weak** 3.

data, *n.*—*Syn.* evidence, reports, details, results, notes, documents, abstracts, dossier, testimony, matters of direct observation, known facts, available figures, information base, raw materials, memorandums, statistics, figures, measurements, conclusions, compilations, information, circumstances, experiments; *both* (D): info, dope; see also **declaration** 2, **knowledge** 1, **proof** 1.

date, *n.* **1.** [A specified period of time]—*Syn.* epoch, period, era, particular point of time, generation, day, term, course, spell, semester, quarter, trimester, duration, span, moment, year, while, reign, hour, century; see also **age** 3, **time** 2, **year.**

2. [(D) An appointment]—*Syn.* tryst, assignation, rendezvous, engagement, interview, call, visit; see also **appointment** 2.

3. [Person with whom one has a date, sense 2]—*Syn.* sweetheart, companion, escort, partner; *all* (D): honey, girl *or* boy friend, sweetie, cutie, blind date, heavy (date), trick, steady; see also **friend** 1, **lover** 1.

4. [The fruit of the *Phoenix dactylifera*]—*Syn.* fresh dates, dried dates, stuffed dates; see **fruit** 1.

out of date—*Syn.* passé, old, obsolete; see **old-fashioned.**

to date—*Syn.* until now, as yet, so far; see **now** 1.

up to date—*Syn.* modern, contemporary, current; see **fashionable.**

date, *v.* **1.** [To indicate historical time]—*Syn.* appoint, determine, mark *or* ascertain the time of, assign a time to, measure, mark (with a date), fix the date of, affix a date to, get a carbon *or* silicon *or* potassium-argon *or* tree-ring date *or* dating (for), furnish with a date, fix the time of, carbon-date, chronicle, isolate, measure, indicate *or* arrange the sequence, put in its place; see also **define** 1, **measure** 1, **record** 1.

2. [(D) To court or be courted]—*Syn.* escort, attend, associate with, take out, keep company (with), consort with; *all* (D): go (out) with, go together, make a date, keep an engagement with, go steady; see also **accompany** 1.

daub, *v.*—*Syn.* smear, plaster, dab; see **paint** 2, **spread** 4, **varnish.**

daughter, *n.*—*Syn.* female child, girl, (female) dependent, offspring, descendant, stepdaughter, infant; *both* (D): her mother's daughter, apple of her father's eye; see **child, girl** 1.

dauntless, *mod.*—*Syn.* bold, daring, gallant; see **brave** 1.

davenport, *n.*—*Syn.* (studio) couch, settee, sectional, day bed, chesterfield, lounge, double chair, love seat, sofa, chaise longue *or* chaise lounge (D), divan, pallet; see also **furniture, seat** 1.

dawdle, *v.*—*Syn.* loaf, idle, lounge; see **loiter.**

dawn, *n.* **1.** [The coming of day]—*Syn.* dawning, sunrise, daybreak; see **morning** 1.

2. [The beginning]—*Syn.* source, start, fountainhead; see **origin** 2.

dawn, *v.*—*Syn.* start, appear, show itself; see **begin** 2.

day, *n.* **1.** [The period of the earth's revolution]—*Syn.* sidereal day, artificial day, time between sunrise and sunset, period from dawn to dark, nautical day, natural day, civil day, astronomical day, mean solar day, twenty-four hours, diurnal course (D).

2. [The time of light or work]—*Syn.* daylight, daytime, broad *or* full day, working day, daylight hours, broadcast day, eight-hour day, ten-hour day, union day; good, bad, hot, cold, damp, etc., day; *all* (D): sizzler, scorcher, good day for the races.

3. [A special day]—*Syn.* feast day, celebration, festival; see **holiday** 1.

4. [A period of time]—*Syn.* term, days, years; see **age** 3.
call it a day (D)—*Syn.* finish, quit working, end; see **stop** 1.
from day to day—*Syn.* without thought *or* plan for the future, sporadically, irresponsibly; see **irregularly.**

day after day, *mod.* —*Syn.* continually, day by day, steadily; see **regularly** 2.

daybreak, *n.* —*Syn.* dawn, sunrise, dayspring; see **morning** 1.

day by day, *mod.* —*Syn.* gradually, monotonously, persistently; see **regularly** 2.

daydream, *n.* —*Syn.* reverie, vision, fantasy; see **dream** 1.

day in and day out, *mod.* —*Syn.* consistently, steadily, every day; see **daily, regularly** 2.

daylight, *mod.* —*Syn.* by day *or* daylight, during the day, under sunlight; see **bright** 1.

daylight, *n.* —*Syn.* daytime, daylight hours, broad day; see **day** 2.
scare (*or* **beat** *or* **knock**) **the daylights out of** (D) —*Syn.* frighten, scare, beat; see **threaten** 1.

daze, *n.* —*Syn.* stupor, distraction, bewilderment; see **confusion** 2.

daze, *v.* —*Syn.* perplex, puzzle, amaze; see **confuse.**

dazed, *mod.* —*Syn.* confused, bewildered, perplexed; see **doubtful** 2.

dazzle, *v.* —*Syn.* impress, astonish, stupefy; see **surprise** 1.

deacon, *n.* —*Syn.* elder, vicar, church officer; see **minister** 1.

dead, *mod.* **1.** [Without life]—*Syn.* not existing, deceased, perished, expired, lifeless, not possessing life, inanimate, brain dead, late, defunct, cadaverous, breathless, mortified, no longer living, not endowed with life, devoid *or* destitute *or* deprived of life, departed, gone, clinically dead; *all* (D): cut off, bought the farm, dead as a doornail, no more, done for, gone the way of all flesh, gone to one's reward, gone west, gone to meet the Maker, liquidated, wasted, out of one's misery, snuffed out, blooey, gone to one's last rest, erased, gone home in a box, pushing up daisies, put to bed with a shovel, grounded for good, gathered to one's fathers, rubbed out, with the saints, beneath the sod, numbered with the dead, bereft of life, washed up, at rest with God, clay-cold, gone by the board, resting in peace; see also **extinct.**—*Ant.* alive*, animate, enduring.
2. [Without the appearance of life]—*Syn.* inert, still, stagnant; see **dull** 6.
3. [Numb]—*Syn.* insensible, deadened, anesthetized; see **numb, unconscious** 1.
4. [Extinct]—*Syn.* ended, extinguished, terminated; see **extinct.**
5. [(D) Exhausted]—*Syn.* wearied, worn, spent; see **tired.**
6. [(D) Complete]—*Syn.* final, total, unconditional; see **absolute.**

dead, *n.* [*Usually used with* the]—*Syn.* the departed, the deceased, ancestors; see **forefather.**

deadbeat, *n.* —*Syn.* vagrant, bum, bad debtor; see **tramp** 1.

deaden, *v.* **1.** [To reduce life or the evidence of life] —*Syn.* blunt, impair, dull, repress, slow, paralyze, etherize, chloroform, gas, freeze, anesthetize, put to sleep, numb, make unfit, knock out, benumb, incapacitate, depress, stupefy, smother, deprive, stifle, frustrate, devitalize, injure, exhaust, tire, retard, consume, destroy, make unfruitful, make unproductive; *all* (D): knock stiff, KO, lay out, dope, put out of order; see also **hurt** 1, **weaken** 2.—*Ant.* animate*, revitalize, invigorate.
2. [To soften]—*Syn.* tone down, dim, muffle; see **soften** 2.

deadlock, *n.* —*Syn.* standstill, stalemate, cessation; see **pause** 2.

deadly, *mod.* **1.** [Causing death]—*Syn.* fatal, lethal, murderous, mortal, deathly, homicidal, poisonous, bloody, noxious, destructive, venomous, deleterious, baleful, malignant, virulent, injurious, pestilential, pestiferous, death-dealing, carcinogenic, suicidal, bloodthirsty, cannibalistic, tending to cause death, baneful, pernicious, harmful, violent, inevitable; see also **dangerous** 1, 2.—*Ant.* healthful*, reviving, beneficial.
2. [Very tiresome]—*Syn.* boring, tedious, tiresome; see **dull** 3, 4.

deaf, *mod.* **1.** [Not able to hear]—*Syn.* earless, stone-deaf, dull of hearing, unable to distinguish sound, unable to hear, without hearing, deaf and dumb, lacking sense of hearing, stunned, deafened, hard of hearing; *both* (D): deaf as a post *or* a doorknob, with rubber ears.—*Ant.* auditory*, acute, clear.
2. [Not willing to hear]—*Syn.* unaware, stubborn, blind; see **oblivious, obstinate** 1.

deafen, *v.* —*Syn.* make deaf, cause or induce deafness, split the ears (D); see also **damage** 1, **hurt** 1.

deafening, *mod.* —*Syn.* thunderous, overpowering, shrieking; see **loud** 1, 2.

deal, *n.* **1.** [An agreement]—*Syn.* pledge, compromise, pact; see **agreement** 3, **bargain** 2, **contract** 1.
2. [(D) A secret or dishonest agreement]—*Syn.* swindle, robbery, extortion, graft, blackmail, smuggling, counterfeiting, prostitution, pimping, protection (D); see also **crime** 2, **theft.**
3. [A hand at cards; *often used figuratively*] —*Syn.* new deal, cut and shuffle, single round, appointment, distribution of cards, honest deal, opportunity, chance, fresh start, square deal.
4. [A lot]—*Syn.* plethora, abundance, superabundance; see **plenty.**
a good (*or* **great**) **deal**—*Syn.* a lot, quite a bit, a considerable amount; see **much.**
make a big deal out of (D)—*Syn.* expand, magnify, blow up; see **exaggerate.**

deal, *v.* **1.** [To distribute]—*Syn.* apportion, allot, disseminate; see **distribute** 1.
2. [To do business with]—*Syn.* trade, bargain, barter; see **buy** 1, **sell** 1.

dealer, *n.* **1.** [One engaged in buying or selling] —*Syn.* bursar, vendor, changer; see **businessman, merchant.**
2. [One who deals cards]—*Syn.* banker, (card)-player, croupier, shuffler, dispenser, divider; *all* (D): pit man, pit boss, the house, mechanic; see also **gambler.**

deal in, *v.* —*Syn.* handle, trade, specialize in; see **buy** 1, **sell** 1.

dealings, *n.* —*Syn.* business, trade, sale; see **transaction.**

deal with, *v.* **1.** [To deal with a person]—*Syn.* handle, manage, have to do with; see **treat** 1.
2. [To deal with a subject]—*Syn.* review, discuss, approach; see **concern** 1, **treat** 2.

dean, *n.* **1.** [A distinguished person]—*Syn.* legislator, innovator, authority; see **leader** 2.
2. [A high ecclesiastical official]—*Syn.* churchman, ecclesiastic, dignitary; see **minister** 1.
3. [A collegiate or administrative official]—*Syn.* Dean of Students, Dean of Men, Dean of Women *or* petticoat dean (D), Dean of the Faculties, Dean of the Graduate School, Dean of the College of Liberal Arts, of Engineering, Law, Education, Medicine, Dentistry, Pharmacy, Agriculture, etc.; Executive Dean, Junior Dean, Assistant Dean; see also **administrator.**

dear, *mod.* **1.** [High in one's affections]—*Syn.* precious, endeared, cherished; see **beloved.**
2. [High in price]—*Syn.* costly, prized, high-priced; see **expensive, valuable** 1.

dear, *n.* —*Syn.* loved one, sweetheart, love; see **darling** 2, **favorite, lover** 1.

dearly, *mod.* **1.** [In an affectionate manner]—*Syn.* fondly, affectionately, yearningly; see **lovingly.**
2. [To a great extent]—*Syn.* greatly, extremely, profoundly; see **very.**

dearth, *n.* —*Syn.* scarcity, deficiency, scantiness; see **lack** 1, **poverty** 2.

death, *n.* **1.** [The cessation of life]—*Syn.* decease, dying, demise, passing, expiration, failure of vital functions, loss of life, dissolution, departure, release, parting, quietus, end of life, extinction, oblivion, mortality, euthanasia, passing over, necrosis; *all* (D): exit, end, finish, finis, roll call, the way of all flesh, the Grim Reaper, debt to nature, the Great Divide, crossing the river, crossing the bar, the great adventure, eternal rest, last rest, the deep end, last roundup; see also **destruction** 1.—*Ant.* birth*, beginning, origin.
2. [The state after death, sense 1]—*Syn.* dissolution, repose, sleep, separation, darkness, afterlife, other world, grave, tomb, future home, heaven, paradise; *both* (D): Abraham's bosom, the big sleep; see also **hell** 1.—*Ant.* life*, living, existence.
at death's door—*Syn.* failing, wasting away, nearly dead; see **dying** 1, 2.
be death on (D)—*Syn.* ruinous, deadly, harmful; see **destructive** 2.
put to death—*Syn.* execute, cause to be killed, murder; see **kill** 1.
to death—*Syn.* very much, extremely, to the extreme; see **much** 1.
to the death—*Syn.* to the end, constantly, faithfully; see **loyally.**

deathless, *mod.* —*Syn.* undying, constant, everlasting; see **eternal** 1, 2, **immortal** 1.

deathlike, *mod.* —*Syn.* cadaverous, ghastly, gaunt; see **dead** 1, **dull** 6, **pale** 1.

debacle, *n.* —*Syn.* downfall, dissolution, collapse; see **disaster, failure** 1.

debar, *v.* **1.** [Exclude]—*Syn.* evict, suspend, shut out; see **bar** 1, **dismiss** 1, **eliminate** 1.
2. [Prevent]—*Syn.* restrict, prohibit, deny; see **bar** 2, **hinder, prevent.**

debase, *v.* —*Syn.* pervert, deprave, abase; see **corrupt** 1.

debased, *mod.* —*Syn.* depraved, degraded, base; see **wicked** 1.

debasement, *n.* —*Syn.* perversion, depravation, pollution; see **corruption** 3, **evil** 1.

debatable, *mod.* —*Syn.* disputable, unsettled, up for discussion; see **controversial, questionable** 1.

debate, *n.* —*Syn.* contest, match, argumentation; see **discussion** 1.

debate, *v.* —*Syn.* confute, refute, controvert, oppose, question, contend, contest, reason, wrangle, answer, ponder, weigh, differ, dispute, engage in oral controversy *or* discussion, argue the pros and cons of; *all* (D): hold a confab, jaw, chew the fat, cross verbal swords, moot, bandy; see also **argue** 1, **discuss.**—*Ant.* agree*, concur, concede.

debauch, *v.* —*Syn.* debase, deprave, defile; see **abuse** 1, **corrupt** 1.

debauched, *mod.* —*Syn.* corrupted, debased, depraved; see **wicked** 1.

debauchee, *n.* —*Syn.* sensualist, immoralist, carouser; see **rake** 1, **rascal.**

debaucher, *n.* —*Syn.* rapist, seducer, ravisher; see **lecher.**

debauchery, *n.* **1.** [Dissipation]—*Syn.* intemperance, carousal, revelry; see **indulgence** 3.
2. [Seduction]—*Syn.* lasciviousness, lust, lechery; see **desire** 3, **lewdness.**

debilitate, *v.* —*Syn.* enervate, injure, incapacitate; see **hurt** 1, **weaken** 2.

debility, *n.* —*Syn.* incapacity, feebleness, infirmity; see **weakness** 1.

debit, *n.* —*Syn.* entry, deficit, indebtedness, obligation, liability, arrears, account, accounts collectable, bills, amount due *or* payable, charge; see also **debt** 1.—*Ant.* credit*, tally, settlement.

debonair, *mod.* **1.** [Gay]—*Syn.* jaunty, buoyant, cheery; see **happy** 1, **pleasant** 1.
2. [Casual]—*Syn.* urbane, detached, unconcerned; see **indifferent** 1, **nonchalant** 1.

debrief, *v.* —*Syn.* quiz, interrogate, declassify; see **question** 1.

debris, *n.* —*Syn.* rubbish, ruins, wreckage; see **trash** 1.

debt, *n.* **1.** [That which is owed]—*Syn.* liability, obligation, chattel mortgage, debit, score, pecuniary due, duty, arrears, deficit, note, bill, accounts outstanding *or* collectable, debt of honor *or* nature, incumbrance, outstandings, claim, indebtedness, arrearage, deferred payment, national *or* contingent *or* floating *or* ancestral *or* funded *or* future debt, account; see also **lien, mortgage.**—*Ant.* credit*, asset, capital.
2. [Capital covered by funded obligations]—*Syn.* outstanding issues, mortgages, bonds, shares, stocks, notes, securities, checks, debentures, indentures; see also **money** 1.

debtor, *n.* —*Syn.* purchaser, borrower, defaulter, mortgagor; *all*(D): account, bankrupt, risk, lame duck, welsher, fly-by-night; see also **buyer**—*Ant.* creditor*, lender, mortgagee.

debunk (D), *v.* —*Syn.* expose, deflate, demystify; see **ridicule.**

debut, *n.* —*Syn.* coming out, presentation, entrance into (society), first public appearance, first step, graduating, graduation, appearance; see also **introduction** 1, 2.

decadence, *n.* —*Syn.* deterioration, decline, degeneration; see **decay** 1, **evil** 1.

decadent, *mod.* **1.** [Regressive]—*Syn.* declining, moribund, decaying; see **dying** 2.

2. [Corrupt]—*Syn.* immoral, dissolute, degenerate; see **wicked** 1.

decamp, *v.* —*Syn.* desert, move, evacuate; see **escape, leave** 1.

decant, *v.* —*Syn.* tap, pour out, draft; see **empty** 2, **spill.**

decapitate, *v.* —*Syn.* behead, guillotine, execute; see **kill** 1.

decapitation, *n.* —*Syn.* capital punishment, beheading, truncation; see **execution** 2.

decay, *n.* **1.** [A progressive worsening]—*Syn.* decline, decrease, consumption, decomposition, collapse, degeneracy, downfall, decadence, depreciation, corruption, spoilage, retrogradation, wasting away, retrogression, degeneration, gradual crumbling, disrepair, loss of health, dry rot, senescence, deterioration, failure of body, ruination, extinction, progressive decline, dilapidation, dissolution, disintegration, decrepitude, ruin, crumbling, waste, breakup, corrosion, impairment, discoloration, reduction, wear and tear, falling off, pejority; see also **sense** 2.—*Ant.* improvement*, increase, preservation.

2. [A breaking down]—*Syn.* decomposition, disintegration, putrefaction, corruption, adulteration, rottenness, breakup, spoliation, spoiling, carrion, putrescence, putridity, decrepitude, mold, rust, dry rot, black rot, caries, spur, atrophy, emaciation, blight, marasmus, gangrene, mildew, uncleanness; *all* (D): ravages of time, way of all flesh, crackup; see also **sense** 1.—*Ant.* birth*, growth, germination.

decay, *v.* —*Syn.* spoil, blight, run *or* go to seed, fade, be impaired, rot, wither, molder, crumble, turn, break up, curdle, discolor, mold, mildew, dry-rot, must, corrupt, corrode, putrefy, putresce, decompose, degenerate, become tainted *or* contaminated, collapse, shrivel, atrophy, pejorate, suppurate, decline, depreciate, degenerate, worsen, sink, go bad, fall off *or* apart *or* into decay *or* away *or* to pieces *or* toward dissolution, slump, fade away, get worse, lessen, fail, sicken, weaken, go from bad to worse, wear away, touch bottom, slow down, thin out; *all* (D): go to wrack and ruin, eat away, go to the dogs, hit the skids, go to pot, die on the vine, reach a new low, reach the depths, hit rock bottom, fall on evil days, nod to its fall; see also **die** 1, 2, 3.—*Ant.* clean*, refresh, purify.

decayed, *mod.* —*Syn.* decomposed, putrid, putrefied; see **rotten** 1, **spoiled.**

decaying, *mod.* —*Syn.* rotting, crumbling, spoiling, breaking down *or* up, wasting away, falling, deteriorating, oxidizing, wearing away, disintegrating, worsening, tumbling down; see also **rotten** 1, 3.

decease, *v.* —*Syn.* cease, perish, expire; see **die** 1.

deceased, *mod.* —*Syn.* late, former, defunct; see **dead** 1.

deceit, *n.* **1.** [Deceitfulness]—*Syn.* fraud, trickery, duplicity; see **deception** 1, **dishonesty.**

2. [Deceitful action]—*Syn.* sham, fraud, artifice; see **deception** 1, **trick** 1.

deceitful, *mod.* —*Syn.* tricky, cunning, insincere; see **dishonest** 1, 2.

deceive, *v.* —*Syn.* mislead, swindle, outwit, fool, delude, rob, defraud, not play fair, play a practical joke (on *or* upon), falsify accounts, victimize, hoax, betray, beguile, take advantage of, impose upon, entrap, ensnare, hoodwink, gull, cozen, dupe, fleece, humbug, circumvent; *all* (D): con, put on, scam, bamboozle, take for, get around, play one false, cross up, buffalo, nick, bilk, gouge, clip, skin, beat, fake, fluff, gyp, beat out of, put on, burn, sell (out), chisel, double-cross, hook, put over a fast one, play for a sucker, shake down, make a sucker out of, take to the cleaners, pull a quickie, sell a gold brick to, screw out of, drive to the wall, do out of, string along, take for a ride, snow, slip *or* put (one) over on, take in, sail under false colors, pull the wool over one's eyes, flimflam, murphy, give someone the run-around, dress up, trip up, bleed white, beguile out of, do in, pack the deal, do up brown, hit below the belt, come over, lead astray, higgle the market, get around, euchre out of, butter up, let in, play upon, make a monkey of, play with marked cards, stack the cards; see also **trick.**

deceived, *mod.* **1.** [Led astray]—*Syn.* turned aside, duped, gulled, fooled, humbugged, hoaxed, trifled with, culled, snared, trapped, decoyed, baited, played, hoodwinked, betrayed, circumvented, thwarted; *all* (D): bamboozled, sucked in, conned, hauled for a sucker.—*Ant.* trusted*, dealt with openly, informed.

2. [Led into an erroneous conclusion]—*Syn.* deluded, mistaken, misapprehending; see **confused** 2.

3. [Cheated]—*Syn.* defrauded, imposed upon, swindled; see **cheated.**

deceiver, *n.* —*Syn.* conniver, swindler, imposter; see **cheat** 1.

December, *n.* —*Syn.* winter month, Christmas season, (the) holidays, holiday season, last month of the year, first winter month; see also **Christmas, month.**

decency, *n.* —*Syn.* propriety, seemliness, respectability; see **honesty** 1, **righteousness** 2, **virtue** 1.

decent, *mod.* **1.** [In accordance with common standards]—*Syn.* seemly, standard, approved; see **conventional** 2.

2. [In accordance with the moral code]—*Syn.* nice, decorous, honorable, proper, seemly, chaste, modest, continent, pure, ethical, reserved, free from obscenity, spotless, respectable, prudent, *comme il faut* (French), mannerly, virtuous, immaculate, delicate, stainless, clean, trustworthy, upright, worthy, untarnished, unblemished, straight (D); see also **honest** 1, **moral** 1.

3. [Moderately good]—*Syn.* satisfactory, average, mediocre; see **common** 1, **fair** 2.

deception, *n.* **1.** [The practice of deceiving]—*Syn.* trickery, double-dealing, mendacity, untruth, dupery, insincerity, indirection, craftiness, circumvention, juggling, defraudation, treachery, treason, betrayal, pretense, disinformation, falsehood, trickiness, trumpery, beguilement, cozenage, humbug, flimflam, lying, sophism, deceitfulness, deceit, equivocation, prevarication, duplicity, cunning,

misleading by falsehood, act of deceiving, imposture, imposition; *all* (D): bamboozlement, fast one, snow job, hokum, boondoggle, skullduggery, flimflam, blarney; see also **dishonesty, hypocrisy** 2. —*Ant.* honesty*, frankness, naïvete.
2. [A deceptive act]—*Syn.* hoax, swindle, fraud; see **trick** 1.

deceptive, *mod.* **1.** [Misleading]—*Syn.* unreliable, ambiguous, illusory; see **false** 2, 3.
2. [Dishonest]—*Syn.* deceitful, tricky, lying; see **dishonest** 1, 2.

decide, *v.* —*Syn.* decide *or* fix *or* settle upon, settle, determine on, judge, conclude, adjudge, adjudicate, mediate, conciliate, arbitrate, compromise, award, choose, terminate, vote, poll, form a resolution, settle in one's mind, make a decision, come to a conclusion, form an opinion *or* judgment, make up one's mind, make a selection, select, pick, make one's choice, commit oneself, draw a conclusion, come to an agreement, arrive at a conclusion, cast the die, fix on, have the final word; see also **agree, resolve.**—*Ant.* delay*, hesitate, hedge.

decided, *mod.* **1.** [Determined]—*Syn.* settled, decided upon, arranged for; see **determined** 1.
2. [Certain]—*Syn.* emphatic, determined, clear; see **certain** 3, **definite** 1.

decidedly, *mod.* **1.** [In a decided manner]—*Syn.* strongly, determinedly, emphatically; see **firmly** 2, **vigorously.**
2. [Surely]—*Syn.* certainly, by all means, of course; see **surely.**

deciding, *mod.* —*Syn.* determining, crucial, conclusive; see **important** 1, **necessary** 1.

decipher, *v.* —*Syn.* make clear, interpret, read, translate from secret characters, spell, unravel, reveal, unfold, elucidate, bring out from a cipher, interpret by use of a key, disentangle, expound, render, cipher, construe, explain, decode; *all* (D): make out, figure out, make head *or* tail of, crack, dope out; see also **solve, translate** 1.—*Ant.* misunderstand*, fail to solve, misconstrue.

decision, *n.* **1.** [A conclusion]—*Syn.* determination, arrangement, settlement; see **end** 2.
2. [A statement involving a decision, sense 1] —*Syn.* resolution, result, declaration; see **judgment** 3, **opinion** 1.

decisive, *mod.* —*Syn.* final, definitive, absolute; see **certain** 3, **conclusive, definite** 1, **determined** 1.

deck, *n.* **1.** [The floor of a ship]—*Syn.* level, flight, story, layer, tier, forecastle; *both* (D): fo'c'sle, topside; see also **floor** 1, 2.
Specific decks include the following—upper, lower, hurricane, top, fore, after, poop, poop royal.
2. [Cards sufficient for a game]—*Syn.* pack, set, pinochle-deck, playing cards, tarots, the cards; *all* (D): devil's picture book, instrument of the devil, book of four kings; see also **card.**
on deck (D)—*Syn.* prepared, available, on hand; see **ready** 2.

deck, *v.* **1.** [To decorate]—*Syn.* ornament, adorn, garnish; see **decorate.**
2. [(D) To knock (someone) down]—*Syn.* beat, strike down, punch; see **hit** 1.

declaim, *v.* —*Syn.* proclaim, speak, harangue; see **declare** 1, **lecture.**

declamation, *n.* **1.** [Discourse]—*Syn.* lecture, address, oration; see **speech** 3.
2. [Ranting]—*Syn.* haranguing, spouting, tirade; see **repetition, wordiness.**

declamatory, *mod.* **1.** [Eloquent]—*Syn.* rhetorical, elocutionary, formal; see **fluent** 2, **oratorical.**
2. [Pompous]—*Syn.* bombastic, windy, stuffy; see **egotistic** 2, **verbose.**

declaration, *n.* **1.** [An assertion]—*Syn.* avowal, (positive) statement, formal assertion, (explicit) utterance, information, notification, affirmation, presentation, exposition, communication, disclosure, allegation, explanation, revelation, publication, answer, broadcast, advertisement, saying, report, testimony, deposition, oath, expression, profession, admission, enunciation, attestation, remark, protestation, acknowledgment; see also **announcement** 1.—*Ant.* denial*, negation, equivocation.
2. [A formal statement]—*Syn.* profession, affirmation, manifesto, public announcement, pronunciamento, document, bulletin, attestation, acclamation, denunciation, article, proclamation, promulgation, confirmation, ultimatum, notice, resolution, affidavit, testimony, charge, indictment, allegation, deposition, declaration of war, canon, bill of rights, constitution, plea, demurrer, creed, credo, article of faith, gospel, testament; see also **announcement** 2, **communication** 2.—*Ant.* retraction*, repudiation, recantation.
3. [The act of announcing]—*Syn.* notification, expression, proclamation; see **announcement** 1, **communication** 1.

declaratory, *mod.* —*Syn.* declarative, enunciatory, demonstrative; see **descriptive, explanatory.**

declare, *v.* **1.** [To speak formally and emphatically] —*Syn.* assert (oneself), announce, pronounce, claim, tell, state, render, affirm, maintain, aver, avow, attest *or* testify *or* certify to, repeat, insist, assert formally, contend, advance, allege, argue, demonstrate, propound, promulgate, issue a statement, put forward, set forth, stress, affirm explicitly, allegate, cite, inform, be positive, utter with conviction, advocate, bring forward, pass, vouch, state emphatically, proclaim, acknowledge, reaffirm, reassert, reassure, asseverate, enunciate, profess, maintain, divulge, reveal, give out, assure, certify, swear; see also **report** 1, **say.**—*Ant.* hide*, equivocate, withhold.
2. [To admit to one's possessions]—*Syn.* confess, reveal, swear, avow, manifest, disclose, impart, represent, convey, indicate, state, notify; see also **list** 1. —*Ant.* deny*, contradict, conceal.

declared, *mod.* —*Syn.* asserted, stated, affirmed; see **announced.**

declare oneself, *v.* —*Syn.* make an announcement *or* a pronouncement, take a stand, assert oneself; see **advertise** 1, **declare** 1.

declaring, *mod.* —*Syn.* noting, remarking, asserting; see **saying.**

decline, *n.* —*Syn.* deterioration, dissolution, lessening; see **decay** 1.

decline, *v.* **1.** [To refuse]—*Syn.* desist, beg to be excused, send regrets; see **refuse.**
2. [To decrease]—*Syn.* degenerate, deteriorate, backslide; see **decay, decrease** 1.

3. [To sink slowly]—*Syn.* sag, droop, settle; see **descend** 1, **sink** 1.
4. [To become weaker]—*Syn.* fail, sink, fade; see **weaken** 1.

declivity, *n.* —*Syn.* slope, declination, descent; see **inclination** 5.

decompose, *v.* —*Syn.* rot, crumble, break up; see **decay, disintegrate** 1.

decomposition, *n.* —*Syn.* dissolution, breakdown, disintegration; see **decay** 2, **dissipation** 1.

decontaminate, *v.* —*Syn.* disinfect, purify, sterilize; see **clean.**

decor, *n.* —*Syn.* decoration, ornamentation, adornment; see **decoration** 1.

decorate, *v.* —*Syn.* adorn, beautify, bedizen, ornament, bedeck, deck, paint, color, renovate, enrich, brighten, gild, burnish, enhance, festoon, embellish, illuminate, spangle, trick *or* dress out, emblazon, elaborate, furbish, enamel, bead, polish, varnish, chase, grace, garnish, finish, frill, tile, bejewel, encrust, emboss, embroider, beribbon, make more beautiful, redecorate, add the finishing touches, perfect, idealize, tool, put up decorations, dress up, fix up; *both* (D): deck out, pretty up; see also **trim** 2.

decorated, *mod.* **1.** [Notable for decoration]—*Syn.* adorned, ornamented, embellished; see **ornate** 1.
2. [An architectural style; *often capitalized*] —*Syn.* late Gothic, 15th-century (England), 14th-century (France), transitional Gothic, heavily mullioned; see also **architecture.**—*Ant.* modern*, pure Gothic, classical*.

decoration, *n.* **1.** [The act of decorating]—*Syn.* adornment, ornamentation, embellishment, enrichment, gilding, painting, patterning, embossing, beautifying, redecorating, redecoration, beautification, festooning, wreathing, trimming, designing, improvement, bedizenment, bedecking, garnishment, enhancement, decking out, bedizening, spangling, illumination, illustration.—*Ant.* destruction*, demolition, denuding.
2. [Something used for decorating]—*Syn.* tinsel, thread work, lace, ribbon, braid, gilt, color, frippery, curlicue, scroll, appliqué, wreath, festoon, glass, parquetry, flourish, tooling, inlay, figure work, cockade, spangle, sequin, garniture, finery, fretwork, filigree, arabesque, plaque, design, ornament, extravagance, fine writing, gingerbread (D); see also **embroidery** 1, **jewelry, paint** 1, **trimming** 1.—*Ant.* dullness*, plainness, severity.
3. [An insignia of honor]—*Syn.* citation, award, mention, medal, ribbon, badge, cross; see also **emblem.**
Decorations include the following—United States: Congressional Medal of Honor, Distinguished Service Medal, Bronze Star, Distinguished Service Cross, Navy Cross, Distinguished Flying Cross, Silver Star, Order of the Purple Heart; Great Britain: Military Cross, Distinguished Conduct Medal, Victoria Cross, Distinguished Service Order, Military Medal, Distinguished Flying Cross, Cross of St. George; France: Medal of French Recognition, Médaille Militaire, Croix de Guerre with Palm; Belgium: Croix de Guerre with Palms, Military Cross, Medal of King Albert; Italy: Medal for Valor, Cross of Merit; Germany: Iron Cross; Russia: Order of Lenin, Order of Suvarov; Japan: Order of the Golden Kite, Grand Cordon of the Rising Sun with Paulownia Flowers.

Decoration Day, *n.* —*Syn.* Memorial Day, May 30, Confederate Memorial Day(s); see **holiday** 1.

decorative, *mod.* —*Syn.* embellishing, beautifying, florid; see **ornamental** 1.

decorous, *mod.* —*Syn.* correct, becoming, proper; see **conventional** 1, 2.

decorum, *n.* —*Syn.* conduct, habits, demeanor; see **behavior** 1, **tact.**

decoy, *n.* —*Syn.* imitation, bait, fake; see **camouflage** 1, **trick** 1.

decoy, *v.* —*Syn.* lure, bait, trap; see **deceive, fascinate.**

decrease, *n.* —*Syn.* shrinkage, lessening, abatement; see **contraction** 1, **discount, reduction** 1.
on the decrease—*Syn.* decreasing, declining, waning; see **reduced** 1.

decrease, *v.* **1.** [To grow less]—*Syn.* lessen, diminish, decline, abate, modify, wane, deteriorate, degenerate, dwindle, be consumed, sink, settle, lighten, slacken, ebb, lower, melt away, moderate, subside, shrink, shrivel (up), depreciate, soften, quiet, narrow (down), droop, waste, fade (away), run low, weaken, crumble, let *or* dry up, slow *or* calm down, burn away *or* down, smooth (out), die away *or* down, lose its edge, wither (away), decay, drop *or* tail off, devaluate, evaporate, fall down *or* away *or* off, slack off, wear off *or* away *or* out *or* down; *both* (D): boil down, slump; see also **contract** 1.—*Ant.* grow*, increase, multiply.
2. [To make less]—*Syn.* reduce, check, curb, restrain, quell, tame, mollify, dampen, compose, hush, still, palliate, sober, pacify, allay, blunt, qualify, tranquilize, curtail, lessen, lower, subtract, render less, abridge, abbreviate, downsize, condense, shorten, minimize, diminish, slash, attenuate, dilute, retrench, shave, pare, prune, abate, mitigate, modify, make brief, digest, limit, level, deflate, compress, strip, thin, bleed, make smaller, devaluate, curtail, clip, abstract, summarize, epitomize, sum up, recapitulate, restate, lighten, trim, rake *or* level off, take from *or* off, roll back, hold *or* mark *or* step *or* scale *or* boil down, let up, cut off *or* down *or* short *or* back, strike off; *all* (D): minus, chisel, rev down, wind down, knock off; see also **compress, contract** 2.—*Ant.* increase*, expand, augment.

decree, *n.* —*Syn.* edict, pronouncement, proclamation; see **declaration** 2, **judgment** 3.

decree, *v.* —*Syn.* proclaim, announce, pronounce; see **declare** 1.

decrepit, *mod.* —*Syn.* infirm, senile, frail; see **old** 1, 2, **weak** 1, 2.

decrepitude, *n.* —*Syn.* feebleness, infirmity, senility; see **weakness** 1.

decry, *v.* —*Syn.* criticize, depreciate, discredit; see **censure.**

dedicate, *v.* **1.** [To consecrate]—*Syn.* sanctify, hallow, anoint; see **bless** 3.
2. [To set apart for special use]—*Syn.* devote, apply, give, appropriate, set aside, surrender, allot, consign, restrict, apportion, assign, give over to, donate.

dedication, *n.* —*Syn.* sanctification, devotion, glorification; see **celebration** 1, **consecration.**

deduce, *v.*—*Syn.* assume, conclude, reason; see **infer** 1, **understand** 1.

deducible, *mod.*—*Syn.* inferable, consequent, following; see **provable.**

deduct, *v.*—*Syn.* take away *or* from, diminish (by), subtract; see **decrease** 2.

deduction, *n.* **1.** [The act of deducing]—*Syn.* inferring, concluding, reasoning; see **thought** 1.
2. [A conclusion]—*Syn.* result, answer, inference; see **judgment** 3, **opinion** 1.
3. [A reduction]—*Syn.* subtraction, abatement, decrease; see **discount, reduction** 1.

deed, *n.* **1.** [An action]—*Syn.* act, commission, accomplishment; see **action** 2.
2. [Legal title to real property]—*Syn.* document, release, agreement, instrument, charter, (title) deed, record, certificate, voucher, indenture, warranty, lease; see also **proof, record** 1, **security** 2.
in deed—*Syn.* in fact *or* reality *or* actuality, actually, really; see **surely.**

deem, *v.*—*Syn.* judge, assume, consider; see **believe** 1, **think** 1.

deep, *mod.* **1.** [Situated or extending far down]—*Syn.* low, below, beneath, profound, bottomless, submerged, subterranean, submarine, inmost, deep-seated, rooted, abysmal, extending far downward, fathomless, sunk, subaqueous, immersed, dark, dim, unfathomed, impenetrable, buried, having a specified dimension, inward, underground, downreaching, of great depth, depthless, immeasurable, reaching backward, yawning; see also **under** 1.—*Ant.* shallow*, near the surface, surface.
2. [Extending laterally or vertically]—*Syn.* far, wide, yawning, penetrating, distant, thick, fat, spread out; *both* (D): to the bone, up to the hilt; see also **broad** 1, **extensive** 1, **long** 1.—*Ant.* narrow*, thin, shallow.
3. [Showing evidence of thought and understanding]—*Syn.* penetrating, acute, incisive; see **profound** 2.
4. [Having ways or purposes difficult to penetrate]—*Syn.* shrewd, cunning, designing; see **intelligent** 1, **judicious.**
go off the deep end (D)—*Syn.* **1.** go to extremes *or* too far, lose one's good sense, rant; see **exaggerate, rage. 2.** collapse, lose control (of oneself), become irresponsible *or* insane; see **break down, crack up.**
in deep water (D)—*Syn.* in difficulty, having trouble, suffering; see **in trouble** 1.

deepen, *v.* **1.** [To grow deeper]—*Syn.* intensify, expand, extend; see **develop** 1, **grow** 1, **increase** 1.
2. [To cause to grow deeper]—*Syn.* dig out *or* down, scrape out, hollow; see **dig** 2.

deeply, *mod.*—*Syn.* surely, profoundly, genuinely; see **sincerely, truly** 2.

deer, *n.*—*Syn.* doe, buck, fawn, roe, hind, pricket, stag, venison, *cervus* (Latin); see also **antelope.**
The *Cervidae,* or deer family, includes the following—American elk *or* wapiti, European elk *or* red deer *or* stag, moose *or* moose deer, western moose, caribou, reindeer, musk deer, roebuck, muntjac, fallow deer *or* dama.
Cervidae more popularly called deer include the following—mule, blacktail, Barbary, Japanese, spotted, Virginia, white-tailed, Pampas, Persian, Pudu, Philippine, axis, hog deer; Chinese water deer, African water deerlet.

deface, *v.*—*Syn.* disfigure, scratch, mutilate; see **destroy** 1.

defacement, *n.*—*Syn.* mutilation, impairment, injury; see **contortion** 1, **damage** 1, **destruction** 1, 2.

de facto **(Latin),** *mod.*—*Syn.* actual, tangible, existing; see **real** 2.

defamation, *n.*—*Syn.* slander, libel, scandal; see **lie** 1.

defamatory, *mod.*—*Syn.* slanderous, libelous, abusive; see **opprobrious** 1.

defame, *v.*—*Syn.* traduce, besmirch, malign; see **slander.**

default, *n.*—*Syn.* failure, lack, error, offense, failure to act, wrongdoing, transgression, imperfection, oversight, neglect, blemish, shortcoming, want, inadequacy, insufficiency, failure to appear *or* pay, lapse, fault, weakness, vice, blunder; see also **omission** 1.—*Ant.* perfection*, attention, completeness.
in default of—*Syn.* lacking, insufficient, failing; see **wanting.**

defaulter, *n.* **1.** [Embezzler]—*Syn.* defalcator, swindler, insolvent; see **criminal.**
2. [Delinquent]—*Syn.* offender, reprobate, derelict; see **delinquent.**

defeat, *n.* **1.** [A state of being worsted]—*Syn.* failure, downfall, disappointment; see sense 2; **destruction** 1, **loss** 1.
2. [Defeat in war]—*Syn.* repulse, reverse, rebuff, conquest, tour, overthrow, subjugation, destruction, breakdown, collapse, extermination, vanquishment, annihilation, break, check, trap, ambush, breakthrough, encirclement, withdrawal, pincer movement, setback, stalemate, ruin, blow, loss, butchery, massacre, Waterloo; see also sense 3; **loss** 1.—*Ant.* triumph*, victory*, conquest.
3. [Defeat in personal encounters and sport]—*Syn.* beating, whipping, thrashing, fall, count, drubbing, repulse, licking, comedown, upset; *all* (D): short end of the score, battering, pasting, walloping, whaling, thumping, scalping, trimming, cropper, black eye, dud, shellacking, slaughter, massacre, hiding, whitewashing, lacing, KO, no go, the old one-two; see also sense 2; **damage** 1.—*Ant.* triumph*, victory*, success*.

defeat, *v.* **1.** [To get the better of another]—*Syn.* master, baffle, surmount, worst, undo, block, thwart, disconcert, frustrate, balk, spoil, nullify, neutralize, quell, subdue, overpower, crush, subjugate, vanquish, get the best *or* better of, beat down, foil, outwit, puzzle, disappoint, contravene, circumvent, cross, checkmate, outargue, refute, outdo, overturn, rebut, expose, silence, overmatch, nonplus, counterplot, disprove, put an end to, invalidate, victimize, overturn, cast down, scatter to the winds, reduce to silence, show the fallacy of; *all* (D): take the wind out of (another's) sails, stump, have by the short hairs, lay by the heels, give a setback to, cook one's goose, put down, euchre; see also senses 2, 3; **confute, win** 1.—*Ant.* yield*, give up, concede.
2. [To worst in war]—*Syn.* overcome, vanquish, conquer, crush, rout, entrap, subdue, overrun, best, prevail over, overthrow, crush, smash, drive off,

discomfit, annihilate, overwhelm, scatter, repulse, halt, reduce, outflank, finish off, encircle, slaughter, butcher, outmaneuver, ambush, subjugate, repel, demolish, parry, sack, torpedo, sink, shipwreck, drown, swamp, countermine, put to flight *or* rout, split up, wipe out, decimate, obliterate, roll back; *all* (D): wipe out, mop up, outgeneral, chew up, mow down, roll in the dust, trample under foot, drive to the wall; see also senses 1, 3; **destroy** 1, **ravage.**—*Ant.* yield*, give up, relinquish.

3. [To worst in sport or in personal combat] —*Syn.* beat, overpower, outplay, trounce, win (from), knock out, throw, floor, pommel, pound, flog, outhit, outrun, outjump, thrash; *all* (D): edge, shade, lay low, blank, skin, drub, trim, lick, wallop, clean up on, beat up, take, KO, take the scalp of, run roughshod over, snooker, put down, take to the cleaners, outslick, knock the socks off of, beat the pants off of, pulverize, knock the spots off of, steam-roll, plow under, smear, get the bulge on, goose-egg, hang a win on; see also senses 1, 2; **beat** 2. —*Ant.* suffer*, be defeated, fail.

defeated, *mod.* —*Syn.* crushed, overcome, conquered; see **beaten** 1.

defecate, *v.* —*Syn.* move (one's) bowels, discharge, pass; see **excrete.**

defecation, *n.* —*Syn.* elimination, expurgation, passing off; see **excrement, excretion** 1.

defect, *n.* **1.** [A lack of quantity]—*Syn.* deficiency, shortage, scarcity; see **lack** 1, 2.

2. [A faulty part]—*Syn.* imperfection, flaw, drawback, shortcoming, fault, spot, stain, taint, speck, mark, weak point, break, rift, scratch, unsoundness, frailty, gap, twist, crack, check, discoloration, hole, knot, foible, vice, failing, sin, injury, birthmark, blot, scar, marring, deformity, demerit, blotch, weakness, error, patch, seam, mistake, rough spot, blindness, infirmity; *all* (D): bug, blind spot, cloven foot; see also **blemish, lack** 2.

defect, *v.* —*Syn.* fall away from, abscond, forsake; see **abandon** 2, **desert** 2, **leave** 1.

defection, *n.* **1.** [Failure]—*Syn.* failing, lack, deficiency; see **failure** 1.

2. [Desertion]—*Syn.* withdrawal, abandonment, apostasy; see **desertion, retreat** 1.

defective, *mod.* —*Syn.* imperfect, incomplete, inadequate; see **faulty, poor** 2, **unfinished** 1.

defend, *v.* **1.** [To keep off an enemy; *often used figuratively*]—*Syn.* protect, shield, shelter, screen, resist, beat off, avert, fight for, withstand, cover, retain, hold, repel danger from, ward off, contend for, keep *or* stave off from, keep *or* hold at bay, take evasive action, fend off, hedge, entrench, mine, resist invasion, stand on the defensive, provide air cover for, sustain a mortar *or* aerial *or* machine gun *or* other attack, garrison, convoy, escort, fence round, give an air umbrella (D); see also sense 2; **guard** 2.—*Ant.* yield*, surrender, give up.

2. [To provide general protection]—*Syn.* safeguard, secure, maintain, uphold, preserve, espouse, champion, insure, patronize, watch, sustain, apologize for, rally to, house, keep, second, provide sanctuary, take in, sustain, bolster, nourish, foster, care for, compass about, cherish, guard against, look after; see also sense 1; **raise** 2, **support** 5.—*Ant.* abandon*, leave, forsake.

3. [To support an accused person or thing]—*Syn.* plead, justify, bear one out, uphold, second, exonerate, back, vindicate, advocate, aid, espouse the cause of, befriend, say in defense, be a partisan of, guarantee, endorse, warrant, prove a case, exculpate, maintain, recommend, rationalize, plead one's cause, say a good word for, argue *or* speak *or* stand up *or* plead *or* put in a good word *or* apologize *or* take up for; *all* (D): go to bat for, cover (up) for, back up, stick up for; see also **support** 2. —*Ant.* convict*, accuse, charge.

defendant, *n.* —*Syn.* the accused, defense, respondent, litigant, appellant, offender, prisoner at the bar, party; see also **prisoner.**—*Ant.* accuser*, complainant, plaintiff.

defended, *mod.* —*Syn.* protected, guarded, safeguarded; see **safe** 1.

defender, *n.* —*Syn.* champion, patron, sponsor; see **guardian** 1, **protector.**

defense, *n.* **1.** [The act of defending]—*Syn.* resistance, protection, safeguard, aegis, preservation, security, custody, resistance against attack, buffer, stand, front, backing, advocacy, maintenance, guardianship, the defensive, precaution, antitoxin, inoculation, excusing, apologizing, explaining, justifying, exoneration, explanation; see also **justification.**—*Ant.* offense*, retaliation, aggression.

2. [A means or system for defending]—*Syn.* trench, Maginot line, Siegfried line, Mannerheim line, Hindenburg line, defense in depth, bulwark, palisade, dike, stockade, machine-gun nest, bastille, bastion, fortification, fort, breastworks, chemical and biological warfare (program) (CBW), earthworks, redoubt, barricade, garrison, picket, rampart, fence, wall, embankment, scarp, citadel, fortress, armor, Panzer, antiaircraft, Anti-ballistic Missile System (ABM), distant early warning (DEW) line, bumper, camouflage, (gas) mask, shield, screen, helmet, glove, barbed wire, stronghold, parapet, buttress, counterattack, counterblow, bolt position, blocking position, rolling defense, tank trap, strong point, defense arc, guard; see also **fortification** 2, **munitions, trench.**—*Ant.* attack*, siege, blitzkrieg*.

3. [In law, the reply of the accused]—*Syn.* denial, plea, pleading, rejoinder, answer, reply, retort, writ of mandamus, right of habeas corpus, alibi, bribe, testimony, vindication, surrejoinder, counterclaim, rebuttal, argument, assertion, case; see also **declaration** 2, **proof** 1, **statement** 1.

4. [An apology]—*Syn.* excuse, justification, argument; see **explanation** 2.

defenseless, *mod.* —*Syn.* open, indefensible, poor; see **weak** 1, 3, 6.

defensible, *mod.* —*Syn.* justifiable, proper, permissible; see **fit** 1, 2, **logical** 1.

defensive, *mod.* —*Syn.* protective, protecting, shielding, guarding, safeguarding, warding off, watchful, preventive, averting, forestalling, foiling, balking, arresting, checking, interrupting, frustrating, thwarting, opposing, resistive, withstanding, coping with, armored, on the defensive, in self-defense, in opposition; see also **armed, unfriendly** 1. —*Ant.* aggressive*, offensive, combative.

defensively, *mod.* —*Syn.* suspicious, on the defensive, at bay; see also **carefully** 2.

defer, *v.* **1.** [To postpone]—*Syn.* put off, delay, shelve; see **delay** 1, **suspend** 2.
2. [To yield]—*Syn.* submit, obey, accede, acquiesce, concede, comply; see **admit** 3, **agree.**
deference, *n.* **1.** [Honor]—*Syn.* veneration, acclaim, homage; see **reverence** 1, 2.
2. [Obedience]—*Syn.* submission, compliance, condescension; see **docility.**
deferential, *mod.*—*Syn.* obeisant, respectful, complaisant; see **obedient** 1, **polite** 1.
deferment, *n.*—*Syn.* postponement, suspension, putting off; see **delay** 1, **pause** 1, 2.
deferred, *mod.* **1.** [Put off to a later date]—*Syn.* delayed, protracted, prolonged, retarded, adjourned, held up, temporized, remanded, staved off, stalled off (D); see also **postponed.**
2. [To be paid in installments]—*Syn.* partial, indebted, assessed, funded, negotiated, renegotiated; see also **charged** 1.
defer to, *v.*—*Syn.* concede, submit, agree; see **admit** 3, **agree to, yield** 1.
defiance, *n.*—*Syn.* insubordination, rebellion, insurgence; see **disobedience.**
in defiance of—*Syn.* contemptuous (of), nevertheless, in spite of; see **regardless** 2.
defiant, *mod.*—*Syn.* resistant, obstinate, disobedient; see **rebellious** 2, 3.
deficiency, *n.* **1.** [The state of being lacking]—*Syn.* scarcity, insufficiency, paucity; see **lack** 1.
2. [A lack]—*Syn.* want, need, loss; see **lack** 2.
deficient, *mod.* **1.** [Inadequate]—*Syn.* insufficient, skimpy, meager; see **inadequate** 1.
2. [Incomplete]—*Syn.* imperfect, sketchy, unassembled; see **unfinished** 1.
deficit, *n.*—*Syn.* shortage, paucity, deficiency; see **lack** 2.
defile, *v.* **1.** [To corrupt]—*Syn.* debase, pollute, adulterate; see **corrupt.**
2. [To rape]—*Syn.* ravish, violate, molest; see **hurt** 1, **rape.**
defilement, *n.*—*Syn.* degradation, corruption, depravity; see **evil** 1.
definable, *mod.*—*Syn.* determinable, apparent, perceptible; see **definite** 2, **obvious** 1, 2.
define, *v.* **1.** [To set limits]—*Syn.* bound, confine, limit, outline, fix, settle, delimit, circumscribe, mark, set, distinguish, establish, compass, encompass, delineate, mark the limits of, determine the boundaries of, fix the limits of, demarcate, curb, edge, border, enclose, set bounds to, fence in, rim, encircle, hedge *or* wall in, mew up, envelop, girdle, gird, belt, flank, stake (out); see also **surround** 2.—*Ant.* confuse*, distort, mix*.
2. [To provide a name or description]—*Syn.* determine, entitle, ascertain, label, designate, individualize, formalize, characterize, elucidate, interpret, illustrate, decide, represent, render precise, individuate, find out, popularize, spell out, literalize, construe, denominate, denote, expound, translate, exemplify, specify, assign, prescribe, nickname, dub, hang a moniker on (D); see also **describe, explain, name** 1, 2.—*Ant.* misunderstand*, misconceive, mistitle.
definite, *mod.* **1.** [Determined with exactness]—*Syn.* fixed, exact, precise, positive, accurate, correct, decisive, absolute, clearly defined, well-defined, circumscribed, limited, bounded, strict, explicit, specific, settled, determinate, decided, prescribed, restricted, assigned, unequivocal, rigorous, special, express, conclusive, formal, categorical, particular, diplomatic, unerring, unimpeachable, to the point, substantially correct, beyond doubt, hard and fast (D); see also **certain** 3, **determined** 1.—*Ant.* obscure*, indefinite, inexact.
2. [Clear in detail]—*Syn.* sharp, visible, audible, tangible, distinct, vivid, minute, unmistakable in meaning, straightforward, obvious, marked, plain, not vague, well-drawn, clearly defined, well-marked, well-defined, clear-cut, explicit, unmistakable, distinguishable, silhouetted, palpable, well-grounded, undubitable, undistorted, crisp, bold, ringing, severe, graphic, downright, in focus *or* in relief, undisguised, in plain sight, clear as day, standing out like a sore thumb (D).—*Ant.* confused*, vague, hazy.
3. [Positive]—*Syn.* sure, beyond doubt, convinced; see **certain** 1.
definitely, *mod.*—*Syn.* clearly, unmistakably, unquestionably; see **surely.**
definition, *n.* **1.** [Expressed meaning of a term]—*Syn.* meaning, terminology, signification, denotation, diagnosis, analogue, synonym, exposition, elucidation, rendering, drift, interpretation, formalization, explication, clue, individuation, exemplification, annotation, gloss, cue, key, translation, comment, rendition, rationale, commentary, formal statement of meaning, explanation of meaning, representation, characterization, recursive definition, solution, answer, expounding; see also **description** 1, **explanation** 1.—*Ant.* nonsense*, absurdity, error.
2. [The process of making limits clear]—*Syn.* delineation, determination, demarcation, determining of the boundary, encompassment, circumscription, outline, outlining, surveying, certification; see also **boundary.**—*Ant.* confusion*, muddling, mixing.
definitive, *mod.* **1.** [Decisive]—*Syn.* final, ultimate, absolute; see **conclusive.**
2. [Limiting]—*Syn.* precise, absolute, plain; see **definite** 1.
deflate, *v.*—*Syn.* exhaust, flatten, void; see **empty** 1, 2.
deflect, *v.*—*Syn.* swerve, diverge, curve; see **turn** 3, 6, **veer.**
deflower, *v.*—*Syn.* ravish, molest, despoil; see **rape.**
deform, *v.*—*Syn.* disfigure, deface, injure; see **damage** 1.
deformed, *mod.*—*Syn.* distorted, misshapen, disfigured, crippled, misproportioned, malformed, bowed, cramped, ill-proportioned, disjointed, awry, unseemly, ill-favored, dwarfed, hunchbacked, warped, misconceived, humpbacked, writhing, mangled, splay-footed, crushed, unnatural in form, unshapely, clubfooted, curved, contorted, gnarled, askew, crooked, ill-made, grotesque, lame, irregular, ill-shaped; see also **damaged** 2, **twisted** 1, **ugly** 1.—*Ant.* regular*, shapely, well-formed.
deformity, *n.* **1.** [Deformation]—*Syn.* malformation, ugliness, unsightliness; see **contortion** 1, **damage** 1.

2. [Deviation]—*Syn.* depravity, irregularity, corruption; see **evil** 1.
defraud, *v.* —*Syn.* hoax, dupe, cheat; see **deceive.**
defray, *v.* —*Syn.* meet, clear, settle; see **pay** 1.
deft, *mod.* —*Syn.* skilled, expert, apt; see **able** 1, 2.
defunct, *mod.* —*Syn.* late, deceased, exanimate; see **dead** 1, **extinct.**
defy, *v.* —*Syn.* insult, resist, face; see **dare** 2, **oppose** 1, 2.
degeneracy, *n.* **1.** [Deterioration]—*Syn.* degeneration, decline, depravation; see **decay** 1.
2. [Abasement]—*Syn.* meanness, debasement, inferiority; see **inability** 1.
degenerate, *mod.* —*Syn.* depraved, immoral, corrupt; see **wicked** 1, 2.
degenerate, *v.* —*Syn.* worsen, lessen, fall off; see **decay, decrease** 1.
degradation, *n.* —*Syn.* depravity, corruption, degeneration; see **evil** 1.
degrade, *v.* **1.** [To humble]—*Syn.* demote, discredit, diminish; see **humble.**
2. [To corrupt]—*Syn.* deprave, degenerate, deteriorate; see **corrupt** 1.
degraded, *mod.* —*Syn.* disgraced, debased, depraved; see **wicked** 1.
degree, *n.* **1.** [One in a series used for measurement] —*Syn.* measure, grade, step, mark, interval, space, measurement, gradation, size, dimension, shade, point, line, plane, step in a series, gauge, rung, term, link, tier, stair, ratio, tenor, period, stint; see also **division** 2.
2. [An expression of relative excellence, attainment, or the like]—*Syn.* extent, station, order, quality, development, standard, height, expanse, length, potency, range, proportion, compass, quantity, amplitude, standing, strength, reach, intensity, scope, caliber, pitch, point, stage, sort, status, rate, primacy; see also **rank** 2, 3.
3. [Recognition of academic achievement]—*Syn.* distinction, testimony, testimonial, honor, qualification, approbation, dignity, eminence, credit, approval, credentials, dignification, baccalaureate, doctorate; *all* (D): sheepskin, kudos, oscar; see also **diploma, graduation.**
Academic degrees include the following—Bachelor of Arts (B.A., A.B.), Bachelor of Science (B.S.), Bachelor of Laws (LL.B.), Master of Arts (M.A., A.M.), Master of Science (M.S.), Master of Arts in Teaching (M.A.T.), Doctor of Philosophy (Ph.D.), Doctor of Medicine (M.D.), Doctor of Dental Surgery (D.D.S.), Doctor of Laws (LL.D.), Doctor of Divinity (D.D.), Doctor of Education (Ed.D.), Doctor of Jurisprudence (J.D.), Bachelor of Literature *or* Letters (B.Litt.), Doctor of Literature *or* Letters (D.Litt., D.Lit.).
by degrees—*Syn.* step by step, slowly (but surely), inch by inch; see **gradually.**
to a degree—*Syn.* somewhat, partially, to an extent; see **partly.**
dehydrate, *v.* —*Syn.* dessicate, parch, drain; see **dry** 1, 2.
deify, *v.* —*Syn.* adore, extol, consecrate; see **worship** 2.
deign, *v.* —*Syn.* vouchsafe, lower oneself, stoop; see **condescend, patronize** 2.
deity, *n.* —*Syn.* divinity, goddess, idol; see **god** 1, 2, 3.
dejected, *mod.* —*Syn.* depressed, dispirited, cast down; see **sad** 1.
dejection, *n.* —*Syn.* despondency, sorrow, melancholy; see **depression** 2, **grief** 1, **sadness.**
de jure **(Latin),** *mod.* —*Syn.* by right, rightfully, by law; see **legally** 1.
delay, *n.* **1.** [Postponement]—*Syn.* deferment, adjournment, putting off, demurral, procrastination, suspension, moratorium, surcease, reprieve, setback, retardation, remission, prorogation, stay, stop, discontinuation; *all* (D): cooling-off period, holdup, holding pattern; see also **pause** 1, 2, **respite.**
2. [Hindrance]—*Syn.* problem, obstacle, obstruction; see **impediment** 1.
delay, *v.* **1.** [To cause a delay]—*Syn.* postpone, defer, retard, hold up, deter, hamper, clog, choke, slacken, keep, hold, protract, keep back, impede, discourage, interfere with, detain, stay, stop, withhold, lay over, arrest, check, prevent, repress, curb, obstruct, gain time, inhibit, restrict, prolong, encumber, confine, remand, prorogue, procrastinate, adjourn, block, bar, filibuster, intermit, suspend, stave off, table, slow, put aside, lay aside *or* by, push aside, hang up *or* back, hold back *or* off *or* over, hold everything, be dilatory, bide one's time, arrest temporarily, impede the progress of, slow up, limit, slacken, stand off, stall, put off, restrain, coerce; *all* (D): leave a loose thread, put on ice, hold one's horses, shelve, pigeonhole; see also **hinder, interrupt** 2.—*Ant.* speed*, accelerate, encourage.
2. [To make a delay]—*Syn.* hesitate, hold back, slow down; see **pause.**
delayed, *mod.* —*Syn.* held up, slowed, put off; see **late** 1, **postponed.**
delectable, *mod.* —*Syn.* enjoyable, delightful, tasty; see **delicious** 1, **pleasant** 2.
delegate, *n.* —*Syn.* legate, emissary, proxy, deputy, substitute, envoy, regent, viceroy, consul, appointee, plenipotentiary, minister, surrogate, alternate, nominee, commissioner, ambassador, congressman, senator, member, duly elected representative; *all* (D): the people's choice, stand-in, sub, pinch hitter; see also **agent** 1, **representative** 2.
delegate, *v.* **1.** [To give authority to another] —*Syn.* authorize, commission, appoint, name, accredit, nominate, select, choose, assign, cast, constitute, license, empower, deputize, depute, swear in, send as a deputy, ordain, invest, place trust in, fix upon, assign power of attorney to, elect, warrant; *all* (D): give one the nod, give one the green light, give one the go-ahead; see also **approve** 1.—*Ant.* dismiss*, repudiate, reject.
2. [To give duties to another]—*Syn.* entrust, authorize, give to, hold responsible for, parcel out to *or* among, send on a mission *or* errand, transfer, relegate, shunt; *all* (D): shove off on, dump on, pass the buck; see also **assign** 1.—*Ant.* maintain*, retain, keep.
delegation, *n.* **1.** [The act of assigning to another] —*Syn.* assignment, giving over, nomination, trust, mandate, sending away, commissioning, ordination, authorization, charge, deputization, investiture, entrustment, investing with authority, deputation, referring, reference, apportioning,

submitting, submittal, transference, transferring, transferal, consignment, consigning, conveyance, conveying; see also **appointment** 1, **installation** 1. —*Ant.* retraction*, abrogation, revocation.

2. [A group with a specific mission]—*Syn.* deputation, commission, envoys; see **committee, gathering, organization** 3.

delete, *v.* —*Syn.* cross out, erase, destroy; see **cancel** 1, **eliminate** 1, **remove** 1.

deleterious, *mod.* —*Syn.* injurious, pernicious, bad; see **harmful.**

deliberate, *mod.* **1.** [Characterized by forethought; *said of an action*]—*Syn.* thought out, predetermined, outlined beforehand, conscious, advised, prearranged, fixed, with forethought, well-considered, cautious, studied, intentional, planned in advance, done on purpose, aforethought, willful, considered, thoughtful, purposed, purposive, planned, reasoned, pondered, judged, weighed, calculated, intended, purposeful, premeditated, voluntary, designed, cold-blooded, predeterminate, predesigned, resolved, cut-and-dried; see also **careful.** —*Ant.* incidental*, unintentional, accidental.

2. [Characterized by forethought; *said of persons*] —*Syn.* prudent, circumspect, sober; see **careful, judicious.**

3. [Slow in motion]—*Syn.* slow-moving, stolid, leisurely; see **slow** 1.

deliberate, *v.* —*Syn.* ponder, judge, weigh; see **consider** 2, **think** 1.

deliberately, *mod.* —*Syn.* resolutely, determinedly, emphatically, knowingly, meaningfully, voluntarily, consciously, on purpose, purposively, willfully, premeditatedly, in cold blood, with malice aforethought, advisedly, after mature consideration, freely, independently, without any qualms, by design, premeditatively, designed, wittingly, intentionally, purposely, advisedly, predeterminately, with intent *or* forethought, all things considered, studiously, with a view *or* an eye to, pointedly, to that end, with eyes wide open (D); see also **carefully** 2.

deliberation, *n.* —*Syn.* reflection, consideration, speculation; see **thought** 1.

delicacy, *n.* **1.** [Fineness of texture]—*Syn.* airiness, daintiness, etherealness, transparency, flimsiness, softness, smoothness, translucency, gossameriness, cobwebbiness, tenuity, diaphaneity, subtlety, tenderness, exquisiteness; see also **lightness** 2.

2. [A rare commodity, especially for the table] —*Syn.* tidbit, luxury, gourmet dish *or* food, dainty, dessert, sweet, rarity, delight, ambrosia, nectar, pleasure, party dish, sweetmeat, imported food, frozen food, food out of season, delicatessen, *bonne bouche* (French), chef's special (D); see also **food.**

3. [Lack of strength, usually to resist disease] —*Syn.* frailty, debility, tenderness; see **weakness** 1.

delicate, *mod.* **1.** [Sickly]—*Syn.* susceptible, in delicate health, feeble; see **sick, weak** 1.

2. [Having fine sensibilities]—*Syn.* gentle, alert, sensitive; see **cultured, refined** 2.

3. [Dainty]—*Syn.* fragile, frail, fine; see **dainty** 1.

delicately, *mod.* —*Syn.* deftly, skillfully, cautiously; see **carefully** 2.

delicatessen, *n.* **1.** [Ready-to-serve foods]. Varieties of delicatessen include the following—cold meats, luncheon meats, salad, dairy products, blintzes, salami, pastrami, bologna, wurst, kielbasa, smoked meats, sausage, frankfurters, olives, sauerkraut, *Sauerbraten, Hassenpfeffer* (*both* German), pickled peppers, pickled fish, pickled pigs' knuckles, dill pickles, sweet pickles, kosher pickles, gherkins, caviar, lox, knishes, pirogi, anchovies, liver paste, *pâté de foie gras* (French); see also **bread** 1, **cheese, dessert, fish, fruit** 1, **hors d'oeuvres, meat, sausage, roll** 4, **roast, wine.**

2. [A place that sells delicatessen, sense 1]—*Syn.* food store, butcher store, grocery; see **market** 1.

delicious, *mod.* **1.** [Excellent in taste]—*Syn.* tasty, savory, good, appetizing, choice, palatable, well-prepared, well-seasoned, well-done, spicy, sweet, tasteful, rich, toothsome, delectable, nice, exquisite, dainty, luscious, rare, distinctive, ambrosial, tempting, enticing, nectareous, piquant, titillating; *both* (D): fit for a king, flattering the palate; see also **rich** 4.—*Ant.* rotten*, flat, stale.

2. [Very pleasant or enjoyable]—*Syn.* delightful, gratifying, pleasing; see **pleasant** 2.

delight, *n.* —*Syn.* enjoyment, joy, pleasure; see **happiness** 2.

delight, *v.* **1.** [To give pleasure]—*Syn.* fascinate, amuse, please; see **entertain** 1.

2. [To take pleasure]—*Syn.* be content *or* pleased, amuse oneself, luxuriate in; see **like** 1.

delighted, *mod.* **1.** [Greatly pleased]—*Syn.* entranced, excited, pleasantly surprised; see **happy** 1.

2. [An expression of acceptance or pleasure] —*Syn.* thank you, by all means, to be sure, of course, certainly, splendid, excellent, overwhelmed, charmed, so glad.

delightful, *mod.* **1.** [*Said of occasions*]—*Syn.* charming, pleasing, refreshing; see **pleasant** 2.

2. [*Said of persons*]—*Syn.* charming, amusing, clever; see **pleasant** 1.

delineate, *v.* —*Syn.* picture, portray, describe; see **draw** 2.

delineation, *n.* **1.** [A drawing]—*Syn.* sketch, portrait, picture; see **drawing** 1.

2. [A description]—*Syn.* account, depiction, rendition; see **description** 1, **picture** 2, **representation.**

delinquency, *n.* —*Syn.* misdeed, wrongdoing, offense; see **crime** 1, 2, **default, fault** 2.

delinquent, *mod.* **1.** [Lax in duty]—*Syn.* slack, behind hand, tardy, procrastinating, criminal, neglectful, faulty, shabby, guilty of misdeed, failing in duty, neglectful of obligation, blameworthy, blamable, culpable, negligent, red-handed, censurable, derelict, remiss, offending, reprehensible; see also **careless** 1.—*Ant.* punctual*, punctilious, scrupulous.

2. [Not paid on time; *said especially of taxes*] —*Syn.* owed, back, overdue; see **due, unpaid** 1.

delinquent, *n.* —*Syn.* defaulter, tax evader, offender, reprobate, loafer, lounger, dawdler, derelict, bad debtor, poor risk, neglecter of duty, felon, miscreant, malefactor, lawbreaker, wrongdoer, sinner, juvenile offender *or* delinquent *or* JD (D), punk (D), hoodlum, blackguard, *âme damnée* (French), recreant, outlaw; *all* (D): jailbird, scamp, black sheep, fallen angel, welsher; see also **criminal.**

delirious, *mod.* —*Syn.* demented, crazy, irrational; see **insane** 1.

delirium, *n.*—*Syn.* madness, fever, hallucination; see **insanity** 1.

deliver, *v.* **1.** [To free]—*Syn.* set free, liberate, save; see **free** 1, **release.**
2. [To transfer]—*Syn.* pass, remit, hand over *or* in; see **give** 1.
3. [To speak formally]—*Syn.* present, read, give; see **address** 2.
4. [To bring to birth]—*Syn.* bring forth, be delivered of, accouch; see **produce** 2.
5. [To surrender]—*Syn.* give up, let go, resign; see **abandon** 1.
6. [To distribute]—*Syn.* allot, dispense, give out; see **distribute** 1.
7. [To throw]—*Syn.* pitch, hurl, fling; see **throw** 1.
8. [To carry]—*Syn.* transport, transfer, convey, cart; see **carry** 1.
be delivered of—*Syn.* reproduce, give birth to, bear; see **produce** 2.

deliverance, *n.*—*Syn.* ransom, release, forgiveness; see **pardon** 1, **rescue** 1.

delivered, *mod.*—*Syn.* brought, deposited, transported, checked in, forwarded, expressed, hand-delivered, mailed, dispatched, sent *or* dispatched by messenger *or* post *or* express *or* parcel delivery service (PDS) *or* courier, at the door, on the siding, in the yards, sent out by truck, trucked, laid down; *both* (D): dumped in your lap, pinpointed; see also **mailed, sent, shipped.**

delivery, *n.* **1.** [The act of freeing]—*Syn.* release, deliverance, liberation; see **freeing, pardon** 1, **rescue** 1.
2. [Bringing goods into another's possession] —*Syn.* consignment, carting, shipment, transfer, portage, freighting, transmission, dispatch, commitment, intrusting, conveyance, mailing, special delivery, parcel post, rendition, impartment, giving *or* handing over, transferral, cash on delivery (C.O.D.), free on board (F.O.B.); see also **transportation.**
3. [Delivery of a child]—*Syn.* birth, parturition, confinement, lying-in, childbirth, labor, travail, bringing forth, geniture, midwifery, obstetrics, accouchement, Caesarian operation *or* section; see also **birth** 1.
4. [The manner of a speaker]—*Syn.* articulation, enunciation, accent, utterance, pronunciation, emphasis, diction, elocution; see also **eloquence** 1, **speech** 2, 3.
5. [The manner in which a baseball pitcher throws] —*Syn.* control, performance, game, ball, arm; *all* (D): rendition, hurling, offering, tossing, elbowing, twirling, flinging, heaving, round-arm delivery, southpaw delivery, freak delivery, buggy-whip delivery.

delude, *v.*—*Syn.* trick, betray, fool; see **deceive.**

deluded, *mod.*—*Syn.* tricked, betrayed, fooled; see **deceived** 1.

delusion, *n.* **1.** [An illusion]—*Syn.* phantasm, hallucination, fancy; see **illusion** 1.
2. [A mistake]—*Syn.* blunder, lapse, oversight; see **error** 1.

deluxe, *mod.*—*Syn.* elegant, luxurious, grand; see **luxurious.**

delve, *v.*—*Syn.* investigate, search, probe; see **examine** 1.

demagogue, *n.*—*Syn.* fanatic, politician, revolutionary; see **radical, rebel** 1.

demand, *n.* **1.** [A peremptory communication] —*Syn.* order, call, charge; see **command** 1.
2. [Willingness to purchase]—*Syn.* trade, request, sale, bid, need, requirement, interest, vogue, call for, rush, pursuit, search, inquiry, desire to buy, earnest seeking; see also **desire** 1.—*Ant.* indifference*, lack of interest, sales resistance.
in demand—*Syn.* sought, needed, requested; see **wanted.**
on demand—*Syn.* ready, prepared, usable; see **available.**

demand, *v.* **1.** [To ask]—*Syn.* charge, direct, enjoin; see **ask** 1, **command** 1.
2. [To require]—*Syn.* oblige, command, necessitate; see **need, require** 2.

demanding, *mod.* **1.** [Difficult]—*Syn.* hard, bothersome, troublesome; see **difficult** 1.
2. [Querulous]—*Syn.* fussy, imperious, exacting; see **critical** 2.

demarcate, *v.*—*Syn.* differentiate, detach, mark off; see **divide** 1, **separate** 2.

demarcation, *n.* **1.** [Limit]—*Syn.* margin, confine, terminus; see **boundary.**
2. [Distinction]—*Syn.* split, differentiation, separation; see **distinction** 1, **division** 1.

demeanor, *n.*—*Syn.* conduct, disposition, deportment; see **attitude** 3, **behavior** 1.

demented, *mod.*—*Syn.* crazy, bemused, unbalanced; see **insane**

dementia, *n.*—*Syn.* mania, madness, craziness; see **insanity** 1.

demerit, *n.*—*Syn.* bad *or* low mark, loss of points *or* credit *or* distinction, poor grade; see **fault** 2, **punishment.**

demesne, *n.*—*Syn.* domain, realm, district; see **area** 2.

demilitarized zone, *n.*—*Syn.* neutral ground *or* strip *or* area *or* territory, buffer, buffer zone, no man's land, zone policed by the United Nations *or* an international control commission, DMZ (D).

demise, *n.*—*Syn.* dying, decease, passing; see **death** 1.

demobilize, *v.*—*Syn.* retire, disperse, withdraw; see **disarm** 1, **disband.**

democracy, *n.* **1.** [Government through representation]—*Syn.* popular government, republic, commonwealth; see **government** 1.
2. [A way of life providing extensive personal rights]—*Syn.* justice, the greatest good for the greatest number, equality before the law, popular suffrage, equalitarianism, egalitarianism, republicanism, social security, psephocracy, individual enterprise, capitalism, laissez faire, rugged individualism, freedom of religion, freedom of speech, freedom of the press, the right to work, private ownership, emancipation, free education, political equality, democratic spirit, social equality; *both* (D): the Four Freedoms, the American Way; see also **equality, freedom** 1.—*Ant.* autocracy*, dictatorship, feudalism.
3. [A democratic country]—*Syn.* democratic power, liberal government, part of the free world (D); see **nation** 1.

democrat, *n.* —*Syn.* republican, Social Democrat, evolutionist, state socialist, advocate of democracy, parliamentarian, constitutionalist, individualist, believer in civil liberties, latitudinarian; see also **liberal.**—*Ant.* dictator*, Nazi, autocrat.

Democrat, *n.* —*Syn.* Southern Democrat, constitutional Democrat, Jeffersonian Democrat; *all* (D): Dixiecrat, Fair Dealer, Great Society Democrat, New Dealer; see also **Republican.**—*Ant.* Republican*, Tory, Socialist.

democratic, *mod.* **1.** [Concerning government by the people]—*Syn.* popular, constitutional, orderly, just, representative, Jeffersonian, free, equal, advocating democracy, characterized by principles of political equality, common, bourgeois, individualistic, communal, laissez-faire; see also **Republican.** —*Ant.* autocratic*, aristocratic, oligarchic.

2. [Considerate of mankind]—*Syn.* friendly, common, human; see **thoughtful** 2.

demolish, *v.* —*Syn.* wreck, devastate, obliterate; see **destroy** 1, **raze.**

demolition, *n.* —*Syn.* extermination, annihilation, wrecking; see **destruction** 1, **explosion** 1.

demon, *n.* **1.** [Spirit]—*Syn.* imp, vampire, incubus; see **devil** 1.

2. [Villain]—*Syn.* fiend, brute, rogue; see **beast** 2, **rascal.**

demoniac, *mod.* **1.** [Devilish]—*Syn.* fiendish, diabolical, impious; see **wicked** 2.

2. [Frenzied]—*Syn.* furious, mad, aroused; see **insane** 1, **violent** 2.

demonstrable, *mod.* —*Syn.* deducible, inferable, ascertainable; see **conclusive, provable.**

demonstrate, *v.* **1.** [To prove]—*Syn.* show, make evident, confirm; see **prove.**

2. [To explain]—*Syn.* express, illustrate, make clear; see **describe, explain.**

3. [To present for effect]—*Syn.* exhibit, manifest, parade; see **display** 1.

demonstration, *n.* **1.** [An exhibition]—*Syn.* showing, presentation, exhibit; see **display** 2, **show** 1.

2. [The presentation of evidence]—*Syn.* illustration, proof, induction; see **explanation** 2, **proof** 1.

3. [A mass rally]—*Syn.* picket line, (peace) march, sit-in (D); see **protest.**

demonstrative, *mod.* **1.** [Conclusive]—*Syn.* decisive, specific, convincing; see **certain** 3, **conclusive, definite** 2.

2. [Communicative]—*Syn.* expressive, descriptive, illustrative; see **explanatory.**

demoralization, *n.* **1.** [Corruption]—*Syn.* debasement, depravity, evil; see **perversion** 2, **vice** 2.

2. [Confusion]—*Syn.* trepidation, agitation, discomfiture; see **confusion** 2.

demoralize, *v.* **1.** [To corrupt]—*Syn.* deprave, debase, pervert; see **corrupt** 1.

2. [To unnerve]—*Syn.* weaken, unman, enfeeble; see **discourage** 1.

demoralized, *mod.* **1.** [Wicked]—*Syn.* depraved, immoral, sinful; see **wicked** 1.

2. [Discouraged]—*Syn.* unnerved, weakened, depressed; see **sad** 1.

demote, *v.* —*Syn.* downgrade, lower, bust (D); see **decrease** 2, **dismiss** 2.

demur, *v.* —*Syn.* disagree, dispute, challenge; see **complain** 1.

demure, *mod.* —*Syn.* prim, coy, bashful; see **humble** 1.

demurrer, *n.* —*Syn.* challenge, demurral, protest; see **objection** 1, 2.

den, *n.* **1.** [The home of an animal]—*Syn.* cavern, lair, cave; see **hole** 3.

2. [A private or secluded room]—*Syn.* study, hideout, recreation *or* rec (D) room; see **retreat** 2, **room** 2.

denial, *n.* **1.** [Refusal to recognize a situation] —*Syn.* disavowal, forswearing, repudiation, repudiating, disclaiming, disclaimer, abnegation, rejection, refutation, rejecting, retraction, dismissal, renunciation, dismissing, refusing *or* refusal to recognize *or* acknowledge; *all* (D): the go-by, the cold shoulder, the brush-off; see also **opposition** 2. —*Ant.* acknowledgement*, avowal, confession.

2. [Refusal to give consent]—*Syn.* contradiction, dissent, disapproval; see **opposition** 2, **refusal.**

denizen, *n.* —*Syn.* inhabitant, occupant, native; see **citizen, resident.**

denominate, *v.* —*Syn.* designate, title, nickname; see **name** 1.

denomination, *n.* **1.** [A class]—*Syn.* category, classification, group; see **class** 1.

2. [A name]—*Syn.* title, identification, label; see **name** 1.

3. [A religious group]—*Syn.* belief, creed, sect; see **church** 3, **faith** 2.

denotation, *n.* —*Syn.* implication, signification, explanation; see **meaning.**

denote, *v.* —*Syn.* imply, signify, express; see **mean** 1.

denouement, *n.* —*Syn.* outcome, conclusion, climax; see **result.**

denounce, *v.* —*Syn.* condemn, threaten, charge, blame, indict, arraign, adjudicate, vituperate, cry down, implicate, incriminate, upbraid, impugn, vilify, prosecute, revile, stigmatize, ostracize, reproach, castigate, brand, boycott, rebuke, dress down, take to task, damn, impeach, scold, reprimand, reprehend, reprove, inveigh against, publicly accuse, condemn openly, assail with censure, charge with, blacklist, expose, derogate, call to account; *all* (D): knock, pitch *or* rip into, give away, blackball, show up, smear, hang something on; see also **accuse, censure.**—*Ant.* praise*, laud, commend.

de novo **(Latin),** *mod.* —*Syn.* once more, repeatedly, from the beginning; see **again, anew.**

dense, *mod.* **1.** [Close together]—*Syn.* solid, compact, impenetrable; see **thick** 1.

2. [Slow-witted]—*Syn.* stupid, half-witted, imbecilic; see **dull** 3, **ignorant** 2.

density, *n.* **1.** [The quality of being solid or heavy] —*Syn.* solidity, thickness, impenetrability, consistency, incompressibility, impermeability, massiveness, quantity, bulk, substantiality, heaviness, occurrence, frequency, body, compactness, concretion, denseness, crowdedness; see also **mass** 1, **weight** 1.—*Ant.* lightness*, rarity, thinness.

2. [The measure of an electrical charge]—*Syn.* current density, high frequency, relative frequency, kilowatt, kilocycle, ampere, erg; see also **frequency** 2.

3. [Stupidity]—*Syn.* dullness, ineptitude, stolidity; see **stupidity** 1.

dent, *n.* —*Syn.* indentation, depression, impression, dimple, dint, nick, notch, dip, cavity, dimple, cut, incision, sink, embrasure, scallop, crenel, pit, concavity, trough, furrow, scratch; see also **hole** 1.

dent, *v.* —*Syn.* hollow, depress, indent, gouge, sink, dig, press in, imprint, mark, dimple, pit, make concave, notch, scratch, nick, make a dent in, perforate, ridge, furrow.—*Ant.* straighten*, bulge, make protrude.

dentist, *n.* —*Syn.* D.D.S., dental practitioner, specialist; see **doctor** 1.
Dentists include the following—dental surgeon, oral surgeon, maxillofacial surgeon, extractionist, dental diagnostician, orthodontist, prosthodontist, periodontist, exodontist, endodontist, pedodontist, radiodontist, crown and bridge expert, ceramic specialist, specialist in radiology; *all* (D): tooth-yanker, jawsmith, ivory carpenter, bridge man.

denude, *v.* —*Syn.* strip, divest, defoliate; see **decay.**

denunciation, *n.* —*Syn.* indictment, charge, censure; see **accusation** 2, **blame** 1.

deny, *v.* —*Syn.* contradict, disagree (with), disprove, disallow, gainsay, disavow, disclaim, negate, repudiate, contravene, controvert, revoke, recant, rebut, abnegate, call one a liar, rebuff, withhold, reject, renounce, discard, not admit, take exception to, disbelieve, spurn, doubt, veto, discredit, nullify, abjure, assert the negative of, say "no" to, declare not to be true; *all* (D): not buy, deny flatly, give the lie to, give one the lie in his teeth, call on *or* out, spike; see also **confute, refuse.**—*Ant.* admit*, accept, affirm.

deodorant, *n.* —*Syn.* disinfectant, deodorizer, fumigator; see **cleanser, cosmetic.**

deodorize, *v.* —*Syn.* disinfect, fumigate, aerate; see **clean, purify.**

depart, *v.* **1.** [To go away]—*Syn.* go, quit, withdraw; see **leave** 1.
2. [To die]—*Syn.* perish, expire, pass on; see **die** 1.

departed, *mod.* **1.** [Dead]—*Syn.* defunct, expired, deceased; see **dead** 1.
2. [Gone away]—*Syn.* left, disappeared, quitted, moved; see **gone** 1.

department, *n.* **1.** [The field of one's activity] —*Syn.* jurisdiction, activity, interest, occupation, province, bureau, incumbency, business, capacity, dominion, administration, (appointed) sphere, sphere of duty, station, function, office, walk of life, avocation, vocation, specialty, field, duty, assignment; *all* (D): berth, spot, niche, bailiwick; see also **job** 1.
2. [An organized subdivision]—*Syn.* section, office, bureau, precinct, tract, range, quarter, area, arena, corps, agency, board, commission, administration, shire, circuit, territory, canton, parish, constituency, commune, ward, geographical division, regional authority, state office, district office, force, staff, beat (D); see also **authority** 3, **committee, division** 2, 6.

department store, *n.* —*Syn.* variety store, supermarket, shopping center, shopper's square, mall, notions store, dry-goods store, furnishings store, ready-to-wear, discount store, mail-order house, emporium, bazaar, fair, exchange, bargain store; see **market** 1.

departure, *n.* **1.** [Leaving for another place] —*Syn.* going, departing, withdrawing, separation, embarkation, taking leave, sailing, withdrawal, hegira, evacuation, passage, setting out *or* forth, parting, take-off, taking off, becoming airborne, starting, leaving, congé, removal from a place, recession, flight, abandonment, retirement, removal, exodus, exit; *all* (D): fade-out, walkout, getaway; see also **retreat** 1.—*Ant.* arrival*, landing, invasion.
2. [Difference from a norm]—*Syn.* deviation, variance, declination; see **difference** 2, **variation.**

depend (on *or* **upon),** *v.* **1.** [To be undecided] —*Syn.* be held up, be under advisement, be uncertain, be doubtful, hang in suspense, be awaiting the issue; *both* (D): hang in the balance, hang by a thread.
2. [To be contingent]—*Syn.* be determined by, rest with *or* on, be subordinate to, be dependent on, be based on, be subject to, hinge on, turn on *or* upon, be in control of, be in the power of, be conditioned, be connected with, revolve on, trust to, be at the mercy of.
3. [To rely upon]—*Syn.* put faith in, confide in, believe in; see **trust** 1.

dependable, *mod.* —*Syn.* trustworthy, steady, sure; see **reliable** 1, 2.

dependence, *n.* **1.** [The inability to provide for oneself]—*Syn.* need of, yoke, servility, inability to act independently, subordination to the direction of another, subjection to control, inability to work, subservience; see also **necessity** 3.
2. [Contingency]—*Syn.* sequence, connection, interdependence; see **relationship.**
3. [Reliance]—*Syn.* trust, belief, credence; see **faith** 1.

dependency, *n.* **1.** [The state of being dependent] —*Syn.* servility, need of, yoke; see **dependence** 1.
2. [A territory or state subject to the dominion of another state]—*Syn.* dominion, province, mandate; see **colony** 1, **territory** 2.

dependent, *mod.* **1.** [Subordinate]—*Syn.* inferior, secondary, lesser; see **subordinate.**
2. [Needing outside support]—*Syn.* helpless, poor, indigent, minor, immature, clinging, not able to sustain itself, on a string (D); see also **weak** 6.
3. [Contingent]—*Syn.* liable to, subject (to), incidental to, conditioned, under the control of something exterior, sustained by, unable to exist without, subordinate, ancillary, accessory to, subservient, provisory, controlled *or* regulated *or* determined by, on a string (D); see also **conditional.**

dependent, *n.* —*Syn.* retired person, old man *or* woman, orphan, minor, delinquent, protegé, hanger-on (D); see also **child, ward** 2.

depending (on), *mod.* —*Syn.* contingent upon, regulated *or* controlled *or* determined by, in the event of, on the condition that, subject to, providing, provided, incumbent on, secondary (to), springing *or* growing from; see also **conditional.**

depend on, *v.* —*Syn.* bank *or* count *or* build *or* fall back *or* rest *or* verge on, turn to, verge *or* build upon; see **trust** 1, 3.

depict, *v.* —*Syn.* picture, design, portray; see **draw** 2, **paint** 1, **represent** 2.

deplete, *v.* —*Syn.* use up, drain, exhaust; see **consume** 2, **spend** 1, **waste** 1, 2.

depleted, *mod.* —*Syn.* reduced, almost sold out, depreciated, emptied, exhausted, spent, used (up), consumed, wasted, collapsed, vacant, bare, drained, short *or* bereft *or* out *or* disposed *or* destitute *or* devoid *or* denuded of, slack, sucked out, worn, in want, without resources, pooped out (D); see also **empty** 1, **sold.**

depletion, *n.* —*Syn.* exhaustion, reduction, deficiency; see **consumption** 1, **emptiness.**

deplorable, *mod.* —*Syn.* grievous, regrettable, unfortunate; see **faulty, poor** 2, **unsatisfactory.**

deplore, *v.* —*Syn.* mourn, be against, object to; see **complain, hate** 2, **regret.**

deploy, *v.* —*Syn.* open, expand, display, unfold, dispose, extend, spread out in battle formation, form an extended front, put out patrols, fan out, take up assigned positions *or* battle stations, assign to positions *or* battle stations; see also **use** 1.

depopulate, *v.* —*Syn.* kill, massacre, slaughter, remove the inhabitants from, resettle, evict, oust, exile, ostracize, eradicate the population of, deprive of inhabitants, perpetrate genocide, eliminate, wipe out (D); see also **banish** 1, **kill** 1.

deport, *v.* —*Syn.* exile, ship out *or* away, expel (from a given place); see **banish** 1, **dismiss** 1.

deportation, *n.* —*Syn.* expulsion, eviction, banishment; see **exile** 1. **removal** 1.

deportment, *n.* —*Syn.* conduct, manners, actions; see **behavior** 1.

depose, *v.* —*Syn.* eliminate, impeach, demote; see **dismiss** 1, 2, **oust.**

deposit, *v.* **1.** [To lay down]—*Syn.* drop, locate, put; see **install, place** 1.

2. [To present money for safekeeping]—*Syn.* invest, amass, store, keep, stock up, bank, hoard, collect, garner, treasure, lay away, put in the bank, entrust, enter an account, commit, give in trust, transfer, deliver over, commit to custody, put for safekeeping; *all* (D): put aside for a rainy day, plump down, come down with, salt away; see also **accumulate** 1, **save** 3.—*Ant.* spend*, withdraw, pay out.

on deposit—*Syn.* hoarded, stored, saved; see **kept** 2.

deposition, *n.* **1.** [Legal attestation]—*Syn.* allegation, affirmation, announcement; see **declaration** 2.

2. [Discharge]—*Syn.* ousting, displacement, degradation; see **removal** 1.

depositor, *n.* —*Syn.* patron, creditor, contributor, donor, payee, investor, account, bank client; see also **client.**—*Ant.* treasurer*, receiver, bursar.

depository, *n.* —*Syn.* repository, safety-deposit *or* safe-deposit box *or* vault, museum, storehouse for safekeeping, place of deposit, repertory, cache, depot, warehouse, magazine, bunker, place of safety, tomb, art gallery, archives, collection, mint, savings bank; see also **bank** 3, **safe, treasury, vault** 2.

depot, *n.* **1.** [A warehouse]—*Syn.* annex, depository, magazine; see **storehouse.**

2. [A railway station]—*Syn.* station, base, lot, dump, freight *or* passenger *or* relay *or* railway *or* railroad *or* parking depot, way *or* railway station, railroad *or* switching *or* marshalling *or* loading *or* unloading yards, stockyards, sidetrack, loading track, ammunition dump, ticket office, waiting room, loft, junction, central station, airport, harbor, station house, haven, *gare* (French), *Bahnhof* (German), railway terminus, stopping-place, halting-place, destination; see also **terminal.**

deprave, *v.* —*Syn.* pervert, debase, degrade; see **corrupt** 1.

depraved, *mod.* —*Syn.* low, mean, base; see **wicked** 1.

depravity, *n.* —*Syn.* degradation, baseness, sensuality; see **evil** 1.

deprecate, *v.* —*Syn.* deplore, object, expostulate; see **censure, regret.**

depreciate, *v.* **1.** [To become less in value or quantity]—*Syn.* deteriorate, lessen, worsen; see **decay, decrease** 1.

2. [To lower in reputation]—*Syn.* belittle, lower, run down, decry, disparage, discredit, ridicule, condemn, contemn, denounce, dispraise, calumniate, denigrate, undervalue, underrate, traduce, asperse, attack, vilify, defame, malign, slander, sneer at, fault, lower in the sight of one's fellows, revile, deride, spurn, make slighting reference to, derogate, slight, detract, slur, clamor against, hold cheap, scoff *or* sneer at, find fault with; *all* (D): knock, smear, smack, put down, take down a peg, rap, slam, roast; see also **censure, disgrace, humble, humiliate.**—*Ant.* raise*, praise, extol.

depreciation, *n.* —*Syn.* harm, reduction, shrinkage; see **loss** 3.

depredation, *n.* —*Syn.* pillage, stealing, burglary; see **theft.**

depress, *v.* **1.** [To bring to a lower level]—*Syn.* press down, squash, settle; see **flatten** 2, **lower, press** 1.

2. [To bring to a lower state]—*Syn.* reduce, dispirit, dampen, dishearten, debase, degrade, abase, dismay, mortify, sadden, weary, mock, darken, desolate, scorn, reduce to tears, deject, cow, weigh *or* keep *or* cast *or* beat down, chill, dull, daunt, damp, oppress, give an inferiority complex (to), lower in spirits, cast gloom upon, make despondent; *all* (D): throw cold water on, bear down, keep under; see also **discourage, disgrace, humble, humiliate.** —*Ant.* urge*, animate, stimulate.

depressed, *mod.* —*Syn.* discouraged, pessimistic, cast down; see **sad** 1.

depressing, *mod.* —*Syn.* discouraging, disheartening, saddening; see **dismal** 1, **sad** 2.

depression, *n.* **1.** [Something lower than its surroundings]—*Syn.* cavity, dip, sink; see **hole** 2.

2. [Low spirits]—*Syn.* despair, despondency, sorrow, unhappiness, gloom, dejection, melancholy, abjectness, abjection, misery, trouble, mortification, worry, abasement, discouragement, dispiritedness, hopelessness, distress, desperation, desolation, dreariness, heaviness of spirit, dullness, disconsolation, downheartedness, woefulness, lugubriosity, vapors, cheerlessness, disconsolateness, melancholia, dolor, dolefulness, darkness, bleakness, oppression, low-spiritedness, spleen, lowness, gloominess, dole, melancholia, disheartenment, hypochondria, qualm; *all* (D): dumps, mulligrubs, blues, blue devils, doldrums, hangover, horrors, blue funk; see also **grief** 1, **sadness.**—*Ant.* joy*, cheer, satisfaction.

3. [Period of commercial stress]—*Syn.* decline, unemployment, slack times, hard *or* bad times, inflation, economic downturn, crisis, overproduction, retrenchment, economic decline *or* dislocation *or* paralysis *or* stagnation, financial storm, business inactivity, recession, period in which there is a decline in business, panic, slowness; *all* (D): crash, Black Friday, slump; see also **bankruptcy, failure** 1. —*Ant.* prosperity*, good times, boom (D).

deprivation, *n.* —*Syn.* removal, seizure, divestment; see **loss** 3.

deprive, *v.* —*Syn.* strip, bereave, despoil, divest; see **seize** 2.

depth, *n.* **1.** [Vertical or lateral distance]—*Syn.* lowness, measurement downward *or* upward, declination, pitch, distance backward, remoteness, extent down from a given point, downward *or* upward measure, perpendicular measurement from the surface *or* bottom; see also **expanse, measurement** 2.—*Ant.* height*, shallowness, flatness.
2. [Deepness]—*Syn.* profundity, intensity, abyss, pit, substratum, underground, base, lower register, bottom of the sea; see also **bottom** 1.
3. [Intellectual power]—*Syn.* profundity, weightiness, wisdom; see **acumen.**
in depth—*Syn.* extensive, broad, thorough; see **comprehensive.**

deputation, *n.* —*Syn.* commission, assignment, nomination; see **appointment** 1, **delegation** 1, **installation** 1.

deputy, *n.* —*Syn.* lieutenant, appointee, aide; see **assistant, delegate.**

derail, *v.* —*Syn.* run *or* go off the rails, be wrecked, fall off; see **crash** 1, **wreck** 1.

derange, *v.* **1.** [To disarrange]—*Syn.* disorder, muss (up), unsettle; see **confuse, misplace.**
2. [To upset]—*Syn.* disconcert, perplex, render *or* make insane, dement, madden, unsettle the reason of, craze, unbalance; *both* (D): addle the wits, send over the edge, unhinge; see also **confuse, disturb** 2.

deranged, *mod.* **1.** [Disordered]—*Syn.* displaced, misplaced, dislocated; see **disordered.**
2. [Insane]—*Syn.* demented, crazy, mad; see **insane** 1.

derangement, *n.* **1.** [Confusion]—*Syn.* disorder, muddle, jumble; see **confusion** 2.
2. [Insanity]—*Syn.* dementia, madness, lunacy; see **insanity** 1.

derelict, *mod.* **1.** [Abandoned]—*Syn.* forsaken, deserted, relinquished; see **abandoned** 1.
2. [Careless]—*Syn.* lax, remiss, negligent; see **careless** 1, **delinquent** 1.

derelict, *n.* **1.** [A social outcast]—*Syn.* renegade, pariah, bum (D); see **tramp** 1.
2. [One who neglects a duty]—*Syn.* loafer, lounger, dawdler; see **delinquent.**

dereliction, *n.* **1.** [Abandonment]—*Syn.* forsaking, desolation, relinquishment; see **desertion.**
2. [Delinquency]—*Syn.* negligence, evasion, nonperformance; see **carelessness, crime** 1, **neglect** 1.

deride, *v.* —*Syn.* scorn, jeer, mock; see **ridicule.**

derision, *n.* —*Syn.* scorn, mockery, disdain; see **ridicule.**

derisive, *mod.* —*Syn.* insulting, taunting, contemptuous; see **rude** 2, **sarcastic, scornful** 1, 2.

derivable, *mod.* —*Syn.* obtainable, resultant, determinable; see **available, likely** 1.

derivation, *n.* —*Syn.* root, source, beginning; see **origin** 3.

derivative, *mod.* —*Syn.* derived (from), caused, evolved, not original, plagiarized, not fundamental, not primitive, hereditary, inferential, inferred, coming from, obtained by transmission, transmitted, acquired, born from *or* of, from the same origin, cognate, connate; see also **ancestral, secondary** 1, **subordinate.**

derive, *v.* **1.** [To draw a conclusion]—*Syn.* determine, work out, conclude; see **assume** 1, **infer** 1.
2. [To receive payment]—*Syn.* acquire, obtain, procure; see **receive** 1.

derogate, *v.* —*Syn.* take away, disparage, discredit; see **detract, humiliate, insult, slander.**

derogatory, *mod.* —*Syn.* belittling, disparaging, slighting, dishonoring, deprecatory, reproachful, disdainful, fault-finding, uncomplimentary, pejorative, slanderous, censorious, unfavorable, unflattering, injurious, defamatory, detracting from value; see also **critical** 2, **opprobrious** 1, **sarcastic.**

descant, *n.* —*Syn.* discourse, comment, criticism; see **discussion** 1, **remark, review** 2.

descant, *v.* —*Syn.* remark, discourse, criticize; see **comment** 1, **discuss.**

descend, *v.* **1.** [To move lower]—*Syn.* slide, settle, stoop, gravitate, slip, dismount, topple, plunge, sink, dip, pass downward, pitch, slope, alight, light, disembark, detrain, deplane, tumble, move downward, come down on *or* upon, slump, pass from a higher to a lower place, trip, stumble, flutter down plummet, submerge, penetrate, step *or* climb *or* get *or* tumble *or* go *or* swoop down *or* off, swoop; *both* (D): plump, plop (down); see also **dive, drop** 1, **fall.**—*Ant.* climb*, ascend, mount.
2. [To descend figuratively]—*Syn.* decline, deteriorate, degenerate; see **decrease** 1.
3. [To condescend]—*Syn.* concede, stoop, humble oneself; see **condescend, patronize** 2.

descendants, *n.* —*Syn.* offspring, kin, children; see **family** 1.

descendent, *mod.* —*Syn.* descending, downward, moving directly downward, sloping, moving *or* coming *or* falling *or* going down, sinking, plunging, toppling, drooping, dipping, dropping, slipping, tumbling, plummeting; see also **down** 1, **falling.**

descend on, *v.* **1.** [To approach]—*Syn.* close in, converge *or* advance *or* gain upon, come near; see **approach** 2.
2. [To attack]—*Syn.* beset, invade, raid; see **attack** 1, **bomb.**

descent, *n.* **1.** [A downward incline]—*Syn.* declivity, fall, slide; see **hill, inclination** 5.
2. [The act of descending]—*Syn.* degradation, abasement, droop, cadence, debasement, slump, downfall, drop, lapse, subsiding, declination, falling, coming down, swoop, sinking, reduction, precipitation, landslide, tumble, decline; see also **fall** 1. —*Ant.* rise*, mounting, growth.
3. [Lineal relationship]—*Syn.* extraction, origin, lineage; see **family1, relationship.**
4. [An invasion]—*Syn.* advance, incursion, assault; see **attack** 1.

describe, *v.* —*Syn.* delineate, characterize, portray, depict, picture, illuminate, make clear *or* apparent *or* vivid, give the details of, convey a verbal image of, particularize, specify, give meaning to, elucidate, epitomize, report, draw, narrate, chronicle, paint, illustrate, detail, represent in words, make sense of, relate, recount, outline, express, narrate, label, name, call, term, catch; *all* (D): write up, pin down, give the dope on; see also **define, explain, represent** 2.

description, *n.* **1.** [A picture, usually in words] —*Syn.* narration, story, portrayal, word picture, account, report, delineation, sketch, specification(s), characterization, declaration, rehearsal, recitation, information, recital, (informal) definition, record, monograph, brief, summary, summarization, depiction, confession, explanation, writeup; see also **record** 1, **representation.**

2. [A sort or group]—*Syn.* order, genus, classification; see **kind** 2.

descriptive, *mod.* —*Syn.* designating, identifying, definitive, photographic, describing, narrative, expository, interpretive, anecdotic, characterizing, illuminating, illuminative, expressive, clear, true to life, illustrative, lifelike, vivid, portraitive, picturesque, circumstantial, eloquent, detailed, pictorial, classificatory, indicative, revealing, extended; see also **characteristic, explanatory, graphic** 1, 2. —*Ant.* dull*, analytical, expository.

desecrate, *v.* —*Syn.* despoil, commit sacrilege, befoul; see **profane.**

desecration, *n.* —*Syn.* sacrilege, profanation, irreverence; see **blasphemy.**

desert, *n.* **1.** [Appropriate reward]—*Syn.* due, compensation, recompense; see **payment** 1.

2. [Appropriate punishment]—*Syn.* penalty, retribution, chastisement; see **punishment, revenge** 1.

desert, *n.* —*Syn.* waste, sand, wastelands, sahara, barren plains, arid region, deserted region, sand dunes, lava beds, area deficient in moisture, uncultivated expanse, infertile area *or* region, salt *or* alkali flats, abandoned country *or* land; see also **wilderness.**

Famous deserts include the following—Sahara, Kalahari, Kara Kum, Great American, Death Valley, Mohave, Atakama, Negev, Arabian, Rub' al Khali *or* Great Sandy *or* Dahna, Persian *or* Samnan, Tarim *or* Sinkiang, Gobi *or* Shamo (Chinese), Great Victoria, Gidi, Libyan.

desert, *v.* **1.** [To abandon in time of trouble]—*Syn.* forsake, leave, quit; see **abandon** 1, 2.

2. [To leave armed forces without permission] —*Syn.* defect, be absent without leave, abandon one's post, sneak off, abscond, run away from duty *or* military service, violate one's oath, decamp, leave unlawfully; *all* (D): go AWOL, go over the hill, give leg bail, take French leave, play truant; see also **abandon** 2.—*Ant.* obey*, stay, do one's duty.

deserted, *mod.* —*Syn.* left, forsaken, relinquished; see **abandoned** 1, **empty** 1.

deserter, *n.* —*Syn.* runaway, fugitive, refugee, truant, defector, derelict, delinquent, apostate, lawbreaker, betrayer, traitor, renegade from military service, backslider, recreant, slacker, shirker, rat (D); see also **criminal, traitor.**

desertion, *n.* —*Syn.* abandonment, flight, escape, departing, departure, leaving, secession, defection, defecting, dereliction, renunciation, disavowing, disavowal, disaffection, apostasy, withdrawal, avoidance, evasion, elusion, truancy, repudiation, relinquishment, retirement, resignation, divorce, willful abandonment, abrogation, backsliding, recreancy, falling away, forsaking; *all* (D): running out on, going back on, runout; see also **retreat** 1. —*Ant.* loyalty*, co-operation, union.

deserve, *v.* —*Syn.* merit, be worthy of, earn, be deserving, earn as due compensation, lay claim to, have the right to, be given one's due, be entitled to, warrant; *both* (D): rate, have it coming.—*Ant.* fail*, be unworthy, usurp.

deserved, *mod.* —*Syn.* merited, earned, justified, meet, appropriate, suitable, equitable, right, rightful, proper, fitting, just, due, well-deserved; see also **fit** 1.—*Ant.* extreme*, excessive, inordinate.

deserving, *mod.* —*Syn.* needy, rightful, fitting; see **worthy.**

desiccate, *v.* **1.** [Dry]—*Syn.* exsiccate, drain, parch; see **dry** 2.

2. [Preserve]—*Syn.* dehydrate, anhydrate, evaporate; see **preserve** 3.

desideratum, *n.* —*Syn.* objective, aim, goal; see **purpose** 1, **requirement** 2.

design, *n.* **1.** [Arrangement for artistic effect] —*Syn.* pattern, layout, conception, diagram, drawing, (preliminary) sketch, rough representation, draft, blueprint, picture, tracing, commercial design, architectural design, outline, depiction, chart, map, plan, tracery, delineation, perspective, treatment, idea, study; see also **composition** 2, **form** 1. —*Ant.* confusion*, jumble, mess.

2. [An application of design, sense 1]—*Syn.* painting, sketch, portrait; see **illustration** 2, **picture** 3.

3. [Planned intention or procedure]—*Syn.* object, intention, scheme; see **plan** 2, **purpose** 1.

by design—*Syn.* on purpose, with intent, purposely; see **deliberately.**

design, *v.* **1.** [To plan in a preliminary way]—*Syn.* block out, outline, sketch; see **plan** 2.

2. [To conceive]—*Syn.* create, originate, make up; see **compose** 3, **create** 2, **invent** 1, **produce** 2.

3. [Intend]—*Syn.* mean, set apart, aim at; see **intend** 2, **prepare** 1.

designate, *v.* **1.** [To specify]—*Syn.* indicate, set apart, point *or* mark out, name, characterize, entitle, set aside, appoint, assign, prefer, favor, individualize; see also **choose** 1.

2. [To appoint]—*Syn.* select, authorize, charge; see **assign** 1.

designation, *n.* **1.** [The act of designating]—*Syn.* selection, indication, specification; see **appointment** 1.

2. [A mark that designates]—*Syn.* classification, key word, appellation; see **class** 1, **name** 1.

designedly, *mod.* —*Syn.* purposely, intentionally, on purpose; see **deliberately** 2.

designer, *n.* —*Syn.* planner, layout man, draftsman, delineator, carver, limner, caricaturist, sketcher, modeler; see also **architect** 1, **artist** 1, **sculptor.**

designing, *mod.* **1.** [Scheming]—*Syn.* tricky, artful, crafty; see **sly** 1.

2. [Heedful]—*Syn.* wide-awake, diligent, alert; see **observant** 1, 2.

designing, *n.* —*Syn.* conception, drafting, creating; see **drawing** 1, **plan** 2.

desirability, *n.* —*Syn.* worth, advantage, usefulness; see **value** 3.

desirable, *mod.* **1.** [Stimulating erotic desires] —*Syn.* seductive, fascinating, alluring; see **charming, sexual** 2.
2. [Generally advantageous]—*Syn.* useful, beneficial, expedient; see **helpful** 1, **profitable.**
3. [Having many good qualities]—*Syn.* good, welcome, acceptable; see **excellent.**

desire, *n.* **1.** [The wish to enjoy]—*Syn.* aspiration, wish, motive, will, urge, eagerness, ardor, solicitude, propensity, predilection, fancy, avidity, cupidity, covetousness, frenzy, craze, mania, urge, hunger, thirst, attraction, rapaciousness, longing, yearning, fondness, liking, inclination, proclivity, ravenousness, ardent impulse, craving, voracity, relish, grasping, monomania; *all* (D): hankering, itch, stomach, yen; see also **ambition** 1, **greed.** —*Ant.* indifference*, unconcern, apathy.
2. [Deep affection]—*Syn.* rapture, admiration, devotion; see **love** 1.
3. [Erotic wish to possess]—*Syn.* lust, concupiscence, passion, urge, hunger, appetite, fascination, doting, infatuation, fervor, excitement, satyriasis, nymphomania, sexual love, carnality, libido, lasciviousness, sensual appetite, pruriency, priapism, carnal passion, venery, salacity, lecherousness, eroticism, estrus, amorousness, biological urge; *all* (D): the hots, rut, heat.—*Ant.* abstinence*, coldness, frigidity.
4. [Wish]—*Syn.* request, hope, want; see **wish** 2.

desire, *v.* **1.** [To wish for]—*Syn.* long for, crave, covet; see **want** 1, **yearn.**
2. [To request]—*Syn.* ask for, seek, solicit; see **beg** 1.
3. [To want sexually]—*Syn.* lust after *or* for, long (for), hunger *or* wish for; *both* (D): have the hots for, be turned on by; see **want** 1.

desiring, *mod.* —*Syn.* impassioned, yearning, needing; see **enthusiastic** 2.

desirous, *mod.* —*Syn.* anxious, willing, lustful; see **enthusiastic** 2.

desist, *v.* —*Syn.* cease, halt, discontinue; see **stop** 2.

desk, *n.* **1.** [A piece of furniture]—*Syn.* secretary, bureau, box, lectern, frame, case, retable, ledge, pulpit; roll-top, flat-top, executive's, secretary's, walnut, steel, modern, etc., desk; see also **furniture, table** 1.
2. [A department of an editorial office]—*Syn.* jurisdiction, occupation, bureau; see also **department** 2. Newspaper desks include the following—city, telegraph, cable, state, copy, rewrite, financial, political, international, crime, art, sports, society, farm; *all* (D): ring, slot, horseshoe.

desolate, *mod.* **1.** [Left unused]—*Syn.* deserted, forsaken, uninhabited; see **abandoned** 1, **isolated.**
2. [Gloomy]—*Syn.* downcast, melancholy, dolorous; see **dismal** 1.

desolation, *n.* **1.** [The quality of being uninhabited] —*Syn.* bareness, barrenness, devastation, havoc, ruin, dissolution, wreck, demolition, annihilation, extinction; see also **desert, waste** 3.—*Ant.* fertility*, luxuriance, productivity.
2. [The quality of being hopeless]—*Syn.* wretchedness, misery, loneliness; see **gloom** 2.

despair, *n.* —*Syn.* hopelessness, depression, discouragement; see **desperation** 1, **gloom** 2.

despairing, *mod.* —*Syn.* hopeless, despondent, miserable; see **sad** 1.

despair of, *v.* —*Syn.* lose hope *or* faith *or* heart *or* courage, give up (hope), abandon (all) hope, give up (all) expectation, give way, give in to despair, have no hope, have a heavy heart, lose faith in, abandon oneself to fate; see also **abandon** 1.

desperado, *n.* —*Syn.* outlaw, bandit, ruffian; see **criminal.**

desperate, *mod.* **1.** [Hopeless]—*Syn.* despairing, despondent, downcast; see **hopeless** 2, **sad** 1.
2. [Reckless]—*Syn.* incautious, frenzied, wild; see **careless** 1, **rash.**
3. [Extreme]—*Syn.* great, drastic, acute; see **extreme** 2.

desperately, *mod.* **1.** [Dangerously]—*Syn.* severely, harmfully, perilously; see **carelessly, seriously** 1.
2. [Appallingly]—*Syn.* frightfully, shockingly, fearfully; see also **hopelessly** 1.

desperation, *n.* **1.** [Hopelessness]—*Syn.* despondency, despair, depression, discomfort, dejection, distraction, distress, desolation, disconsolateness, anxiety, anguish, agony, melancholy, grief, sorrow, worry, trouble, pain, hopelessness, torture, pang, heartache, concern, misery, unhappiness; see also **fear** 2, **gloom.**—*Ant.* hope*, hopefulness, confidence.
2. [Rashness]—*Syn.* frenzy, recklessness, foolhardiness; see **carelessness, trouble** 2.

despicable, *mod.* —*Syn.* contemptible, abject, base; see **mean** 3.

despise, *v.* —*Syn.* scorn, disdain, condemn; see **hate** 1.

despite, *mod.* and *prep.* —*Syn.* in spite of, in defiance of, even with; see **notwithstanding.**

despoil, *v.* —*Syn.* plunder, pillage, maraud; see **raid, ravage, rob.**

despoilment, *n.* —*Syn.* plunder, depredation, piracy; see **theft.**

despondency, *n.* —*Syn.* dejection, despair, sadness; see **desperation** 1, **gloom** 2, **grief** 1.

despondent, *mod.* —*Syn.* dejected, discouraged, depressed; see **sad** 1.

despot, *n.* —*Syn.* oppressor, autocrat, tyrant; see **dictator.**

despotic, *mod.* —*Syn.* absolutistic, oppressive, authoritarian; see **absolute** 3, **autocratic** 1, **tyrannical.**

despotism, *n.* **1.** [Autocracy]—*Syn.* absolutism, dictatorship, imperialism; see **autocracy, government** 2.
2. [Tyranny]—*Syn.* repression, coercion, domination; see **oppression** 1, **tyranny.**

dessert, *n.* —*Syn.* sweet, tart, cobbler, dumpling, trifle, jelly, custard, ice, sherbet, sorbet, sundae, compote, fruit salad, soufflé, mousse, crumble, ice cream; see also **cake** 2, **candy, cheese, delicacy** 2, **fruit** 1, **pastry, pie, pudding.**

destination, *n.* —*Syn.* objective, goal, aim; see **purpose** 1.

destine, *v.* **1.** [Predestine]—*Syn.* fate, decide, doom; see **predetermine.**
2. [Intend]—*Syn.* design, reserve, dedicate; see **intend** 2.

destined, *mod.* **1.** [Fixed by a higher power] —*Syn.* fated, compulsory, foreordained, menacing, near, forthcoming, instant, brewing, threatening, in prospect, ineluctable, predestined, predetermined, preordained, compelled, condemned, at hand, impending, looming, unborn, inexorable, that is to be, that will be, in store, to come, directed, ordained, settled, sealed, closed, predesigned; *all* (D): written in the book of fate, in the wind, in the lap of the gods, stated, in the cards; see also **doomed, imminent, inevitable.**—*Ant.* voluntary*, at will, by chance.

2. [Intended for a certain destination]—*Syn.* bound for, on the road to, headed, ordered to, consigned, assigned, specified, directed, delegated, appropriated, prepared, chosen, appointed, designated, determined, entrained, en route, bent upon (D); see also **intended.**—*Ant.* wandering*, derelict, unconsigned.

destiny, *n.* **1.** [Fate as a power]—*Syn.* predetermination, predestination, decree, finality, conclusion, foreordination, decrees of fate, course of events, inevitability, doom, certainty, condition, divine decree, book of fate, future, weird, the Fates, destined way, ordinance, kismet, fortune, luck, karma, inevitable necessity, God's will, Fortune; *all* (D): serendipity, happenstance, wheel of fortune, the stars, Dame Fortune, will of heaven, Sisters Three, Ides of March, Hobson's choice, the lap of the gods; see also **chance** 1.

2. [Fate as a personal future]—*Syn.* fortune, lot, end; see **doom** 1.

destitute, *mod.*—*Syn.* impoverished, poverty-stricken, penniless; see **poor** 1.

destitution, *n.*—*Syn.* indigence, want, privation; see **poverty** 1.

destroy, *v.* **1.** [To bring to nothing]—*Syn.* ruin, demolish, exterminate, raze, tear *or* throw down, plunder, ransack, pillage, eradicate, overthrow, cause the downfall of, devastate, swallow up, butcher, extirpate, consume, liquidate, break up, dissolve, blot out, cast *or* put down, quash, quell, level, abort, stamp out, suppress, squelch, scuttle, undo, annihilate, lay waste, spoliate, root up, overturn, annul, impair, damage, ravish, deface, maraud, dilapidate, expunge, efface, sweep over *or* away, shatter, split (up), crush, obliterate, burn to the ground, knock *or* break to pieces, abolish, crash, extinguish, desolate, dynamite, put a damper on, wrench *or* tear apart, wreck, dismantle, fell, upset, bomb, stave in, despoil, subvert, mutilate, smash, trample, overturn, maim, mar, vitiate, end, counteract, nullify, blast, neutralize, gut, snuff out, erase, sabotage, repeal, pull down *or* to pieces, terminate, conclude, finish, bring to ruin, stop, put a stop to, dissipate, dispel, wipe out; *all* (D): do in, do *or* make away with, finish off, make short work of, total (out), scorch, blitz, cream, foul up, destruct, self-destruct, ravage with fire and sword, make mincemeat of, put an end to, seal the doom of, bring to ashes, lay in ruins; see also **defeat 2, ravage.** —*Ant.* build*, construct, establish.

2. [To kill]—*Syn.* murder, butcher, slaughter; see **kill.**

destroyed, *mod.*—*Syn.* wrecked, annihilated, killed, lost, devastated, wasted, made away with, demolished, overturned, overwhelmed, upset, nullified, annulled, undone, put to an end, mown down, felled, shattered, smashed, scuttled, ravished, engulfed, submerged, overrun, desolated, extirpated, extinguished, eradicated, devoured, consumed, withered, disintegrated, burned up *or* down, incinerated, gone to pieces, razed, lying in ruins, sacked; *all* (D): reduced to ashes, gone by the board, totalled (out); see also **broken** 1, **dead** 1, **ruined** 1.—*Ant.* saved*, protected, restored.

destroyer, *n.* **1.** [A destructive agent]—*Syn.* iconoclast, nihilist, assassin, executioner, hangman, strangler, butcher, slayer, gunman, decapitator, guillotiner, slaughterer, cutthroat, lyncher, wrecker, anarchist, terrorist, firebrand, incendiary, pyromaniac, exterminator, desperado, scourge, annihilator, dealer of destruction, demolisher, electronic ground automatic destruct sequence (button) (EGADS), savage, plague, pestilence, rust, cancer, acid, bane, canker, wild beast, poison, virus, fungus; *all* (D): hatchet man, Goth, Hun, Nazi; see also **arsonist, criminal, killer, weapon** 1.—*Ant.* author*, restorer, creator.

2. [A swift armed surface vessel]—*Syn.* light unit, battleship, fighting vessel; see **ship, warship.**

destroying, *n.*—*Syn.* ruining, spoiling, wrecking; see **carnage, destruction** 1, **wreck** 1.

destruction, *n.* **1.** [The act of destroying]—*Syn.* demolition, demolishing, annihilating, annihilation, Holocaust, eradication, slaying, slaughter, liquidation, extirpation, overthrow, subversion, extermination, elimination, ravaging, raging, abolition, murder, assassination, killing, disruption, bombardment, subversion, disintegration, extinction, ravagement, wreckage, subjugation, despoiling, dissolution, butchery, sabotage, eradicating, liquidating, extirpating, murdering, assassinating, abolishing, disrupting, subverting, disintegrating, ravaging, subjugation, dissolving, invalidating, sacking, extinguishing, exterminating, overthrowing, eliminating, invalidation, crashing, falling, felling, sack, tearing down; *both* (D): crack of doom, wrack and ruin; see also **carnage, wreck** 1.—*Ant.* production*, formation, erection.

2. [The condition after destruction]—*Syn.* waste, ashes, wreck, annihilation, remnants, devastation, vestiges, desolation, ruins, overthrow, decay, disintegration, loss, bane, dilapidation, remains, havoc, prostration, injury, impairment, ravage, downfall, end, bankruptcy, starvation, plague, shipwreck, dissolution, removal, sacrifice, disorganization, immolation; see also **damage** 2.—*Ant.* restoration*, renovation, renewal.

destructive, *mod.* **1.** [Harmful]—*Syn.* hurtful, injurious, troublesome; see **harmful.**

2. [Ruinous]—*Syn.* noxious, baneful, pestiferous, noisome, cancerous, baleful, fatal, deleterious, pestilential, productive of serious evil, cataclysmal, eradicative, ruinous, fell, demolitionary, devastating, dire, lethal, extirpative, internecine, mortal, mischievous, detrimental, annihilative, hurtful, harmful, arsonistic, conflagrative, subversive, incendiary, murderous, disruptive, suicidal, evil, injurious, venomous, pernicious, toxic, disintegrative, disastrous; see also **deadly, poisonous, vicious** 1. —*Ant.* helpful*, curative, life-saving.

desultory, *mod.* —*Syn.* erratic, random, miscellaneous; see **aimless, variable.**

detach, *v.* —*Syn.* separate, withdraw, disengage; see **divide** 1.

detached, *mod.* **1.** [Cut off or removed]—*Syn.* loosened, divided, disjoined; see **separated.**
2. [Disinterested]—*Syn.* apathetic, uninvolved, unconcerned; see **indifferent** 1.

detachment, *n.* **1.** [Indifference]—*Syn.* coldness, dreaminess, unconcern; see **indifference** 1.
2. [A small body of troops]—*Syn.* patrol, task force, squad; see **army** 2, **organization** 3.

detail, *n.* **1.** [A part]—*Syn.* item, portion, particular, trait, specialty, feature, minute part, aspect, accessory, article, peculiarity, minutia, fraction, particularity, specification, article, technicality, singularity, circumstantiality; see also **circumstance** 1, **part** 1.—*Ant.* entirety*, whole, synthesis.
2. [A small military force having a specific duty] —*Syn.* detachment, squad, force; see **army** 2, **organization** 3.
in detail—*Syn.* item by item, thorough, detailed; see **comprehensive.**

detail, *v.* **1.** [To make clear in detail]—*Syn.* itemize, particularize, exhibit, show, report, relate, narrate, tell, designate, catalog, recite, spread, delineate, specialize, depict, portray, enumerate, specify the particulars of, mention, uncover, reveal, recount, recapitulate, communicate, analyze, set forth, produce, go into the particulars, get down to cases (D); see also **describe.**—*Ant.* dabble*, summarize, epitomize.
2. [To assign to a specific duty]—*Syn.* detach, appoint, allocate; see **assign** 1.

detailed, *mod.* —*Syn.* enumerated, specified, explicit, specific, particularlized, individual, individualized, individuated, developed, itemized, definite, minute, described, precise, full, narrow, complete, exact, fussy, particular, meticulous, point by point, circumstantial, nice, accurate, unfolded, disclosed, elaborated, complicated, all-inclusive, comprehensive, seriatim, one after another; *all* (D): at length, newsy, gone into; see also **elaborate** 2.—*Ant.* general*, brief, hazy.

details, *n.* —*Syn.* analysis, trivia, minutiae, particulars, prospectus, table, bill, (itemized) account, (distinct) parts, trivialities, fine points, items, niceties, minor circumstances, enumeration, amplification; see also **detail** 1.

detain, *v.* —*Syn.* hold, keep, inhibit; see **delay** 1, **restrain** 1.

detect, *v.* **1.** [To find out]—*Syn.* distinguish, recognize, identify; see **discover** 1.
2. [To identify a criminal]—*Syn.* disclose, expose, catch; see **reveal** 1.

detection, *n.* —*Syn.* apprehension, exposure, disclosure; see **discovery** 1, **exposure** 1.

detective, *n.* —*Syn.* policeman, agent, plainclothesman, private eye (D), narcotics agent, police sergeant *or* officer, Scotland Yard man, FBI man, wiretapper, polygraphist, investigator, criminologist, member of a crime detection squad *or* division, analyst, prosecutor, patrolman, sleuth, shadow (D), eavesdropper, obtainer of secret information, spy, reporter; *all* (D): shamus, newshound, slewfoot, minion of the law, bug artist, gumshoe, flatfoot, dick, bloodhound, hawkshaw, Sherlock, bull, G-man, copper, cop, fed, nark; see also **policeman.**

detector, *n.* —*Syn.* indicator, pointer, revealer, warner, locater, discoverer, director, distant early warning *or* DEW line, sonar, detectaphone, lie detector, (Keeler) polygraph, listening device, sound detector, spotter; see also **radar.**

détente, *n.* —*Syn.* precaution, passivity, relaxation of hostilities; see **pause** 1, 2, **peace** 1, **rest** 2.

detention, *n.* **1.** [Withholding]—*Syn.* retention, hindrance, detainment; see **delay** 1, **impediment** 1.
2. [Restraint]—*Syn.* custody, impediment, quarantine; see **arrest** 1, **confinement** 1, **restraint** 2.

deter, *v.* —*Syn.* caution, stop, dissuade; see **prevent, warn** 1.

detergent, *mod.* —*Syn.* purificatory, disinfectant, cathartic; see **cleaning.**

detergent, *n.* —*Syn.* cleansing agent, disinfectant, washing substance; see **cleanser, soap.**

deteriorate, *v.* —*Syn.* depreciate, lessen, degenerate; see **decay.**

deterioration, *n.* —*Syn.* decadence, rotting, degeneration; see **decay** 1.

determinable, *mod.* —*Syn.* definable, discoverable, judicable, ascertainable, subject *or* amenable to law *or* measurement *or* scientific *or* objective measurement(s) *or* procedure(s), fixable, capable of being determined, that may be accurately found out, admitting of decision, assayable, deductive, inductive, inferential.

determination, *n.* **1.** [The act of determining] —*Syn.* visualization, perception, measurement; see **judgment** 2.
2. [Firmness of mind]—*Syn.* resolution, certainty, dogmatism, resoluteness, persistence, stubbornness, obstinacy, resolve, certitude, decision, assurance, conviction, intrepidity, boldness, fixity of purpose, hardihood, tenacity, courage, independence, self-confidence, purposefulness, coolness, fortitude, constancy, steadfastness, self-assurance, firmness, dauntlessness, self-reliance, nerve, heart, bravery, fearlessness, valor, intransigence, will, firmness of purpose, energy, vigor, manliness, stamina, perseverance, strength of will, undauntedness, a brave *or* bold front, a stout heart, mettle, firm faith, enterprise, imperiousness; *all* (D): doggedness, guts, spunk, grit, pluck, a stiff upper lip; see also **confidence** 2, **faith** 1, **purpose** 1.—*Ant.* hesitation*, vacillation, irresolution.

determine, *v.* **1.** [To define]—*Syn.* limit, circumscribe, delimit; see **define** 1, **restrict** 2.
2. [To find out the facts]—*Syn.* ascertain, find out, learn; see **discover** 1.
3. [To decide the course of affairs]—*Syn.* devise, invent, plot; see **arrange** 2, **command** 2, **manage** 1, **plan** 1, **prepare** 1.
4. [To resolve]—*Syn.* fix upon, settle, conclude; see **decide** 1, **resolve.**

determined, *mod.* **1.** [Already fixed or settled] —*Syn.* decided, agreed, acted *or* agreed upon, concluded, compounded, contracted, set, ended, resolved, closed, terminated, consummated, achieved, finished, over, at an end, checked, measured, tested, budgeted, passed, given approval; *all* (D): given the green light *or* the go-ahead, over and done with, (all) washed up, smoothed over, case closed, set to rest; see also **approved.**—*Ant.* unfinished*, argued, suspended.

2. [Having a fixed attitude]—*Syn.* stubborn, firm strong-minded; see **resolute** 2.

determining, *mod.*—*Syn.* deciding, decisive, definitive; see **certain** 3, **conclusive.**

deterrent, *n.*—*Syn.* hindrance, impediment, obstacle; see **restraint** 2.

deterring, *mod.*—*Syn.* stopping, hampering, forbidding; see **blocking.**

detest, *v.*—*Syn.* abhor, loathe, despise; see **hate** 1.

detestable, *mod.*—*Syn.* hateful, disgusting, abhorrent; see **offensive** 2.

detestation, *n.*—*Syn.* dislike, aversion, revulsion; see **hatred** 1.

dethrone, *v.*—*Syn.* depose, oust, degrade; see **dismiss** 1.

detonate, *v.*—*Syn.* touch off, discharge, blast; see **explode** 1, **shoot** 1.

detonation, *n.*—*Syn.* implosion, blast, discharge; see **explosion** 1.

detour, *n.*—*Syn.* temporary *or* alternate *or* circuitous route, byway, bypath, back road, service road, alternate highway, secondary highway, bypass, indirect way, circuit, deviation from a direct course, temporary substitute for a main route, roundabout course; see also **road** 1.—*Ant.* highway*, pavement, main road.

detract, *v.*—*Syn.* decrease, take away a part, divert, subtract from, draw away, diminish, lessen, withdraw, derogate, depreciate, discredit; see also **lower, slander.**

detraction, *n.*—*Syn.* slander, derogation, defamation; see **lie** 1.

detractor, *n.*—*Syn.* derogator, defamer, censor; see **critic** 1.

detriment, *n.*—*Syn.* loss, harm, hurt; see **damage** 2, **injury** 1.

detrimental, *mod.*—*Syn.* damaging, disturbing, deleterious; see **harmful.**

detritus, *n.*—*Syn.* rubbish, waste, debris; see **trash** 1.

Detroit, *n.*—*Syn.* City of Straits, Detroit the Beautiful, Automobile City, Motor Capital of the World; *both* (D): Motown, Fordtown.

devalue, *v.*—*Syn.* revalue, depreciate, mark down, devaluate; see **decrease** 2.

devastate, *v.*—*Syn.* ravage, sack, pillage; see **destroy** 1, **raid.**

devastation, *n.*—*Syn.* destruction, defoliation, waste; see **desolation** 1, **ruin** 2.

develop, *v.* **1.** [To improve]—*Syn.* enlarge, expand, extend, promote, advance, exploit, magnify, build up, augment, refine, enrich, cultivate, beautify, elaborate, polish, finish, perfect, deepen, lengthen, heighten, widen, intensify, fix up, shape up (D); see also **grow** 1, **improve** 1, **strengthen.**—*Ant.* damage*, disfigure, spoil.

2. [To grow]—*Syn.* mature, evolve, advance; see **grow** 2.

3. [To reveal slowly]—*Syn.* unfold, disclose, exhibit, unravel, disentangle, uncover, make known, explain, unwind, unroll, explicate, produce, detail, tell, state, recount, unfurl, untwist, uncoil, untwine, account for, give account of; see also **narrate, reveal** 1.—*Ant.* hide*, conceal, blurt out.

4. [To work out]—*Syn.* enlarge upon, expatiate, elaborate (upon), fill out *or* in, amplify, evolve, explicate, expand upon, go into detail, build on (D); see also **explain, increase** 1.—*Ant.* decrease*, summarize, abridge.

5. [To begin]—*Syn.* start, originate, commence; see **begin** 2.

developed, *mod.*—*Syn.* grown, refined, advanced; see **matured, perfected.**

development, *n.* **1.** [Improvement]—*Syn.* gain, rise, advancement; see **improvement** 1, **progress** 1.

2. [The process of growth]—*Syn.* growth, unfolding, elaboration, maturing, progress toward a more perfect state, ripening, maturation, progress to maturity, enlargement, augmentation, addition, spread, (gradual) evolution, evolving, advancement, improvement, reinforcement, growing, increasing, elaborating, augmenting, spreading, developing, adding to, reinforcing, progressing, perfecting, making progress, advancing; see also **increase** 1.—*Ant.* reduction*, decrease, lessening.

deviate, *v.*—*Syn.* deflect, digress, swerve, shy, vary, wander, stray, turn aside, keep *or* stay aside, bear off, go out of control, divagate, depart from, break the pattern, go amiss, angle away *or* off, leave the beaten path, not conform, break bounds, get off the subject, edge off, go out of the way, veer; *all* (D): cut back *or* across, fly *or* go off on a tangent, go haywire, sing a different tune, swim against the stream; see also **differ** 1.—*Ant.* conform*, keep on, keep in line.

deviation, *n.*—*Syn.* change, deflection, alteration; see **difference** 2, **variation.**

device, *n.* **1.** [An instrument]—*Syn.* invention, contrivance, mechanism, gear, equipment, appliance, medium, contraption, arrangement, expedient, wherewithal, means, agent, tackle, rigging, harness, material, implement, utensil, construction, apparatus, outfit, article, accessory, makeshift, auxiliary, stopgap; *all* (D): gadget, thingumabob, whatnot, wrinkle, thing, dohickey, whatsit, whatchamacallit; see also **machine** 1, **tool** 1.

2. [A shrewd method]—*Syn.* artifice, scheme, design, trap, dodge, machination, trick, pattern, proposition, loophole, wile, craft, cunningness, stratagem, ruse, expedient, subterfuge, plan, project, plot, fake, chicanery, racket, game, craftiness, cabal, evasion, finesse, clever move; *all* (D): sucker trap, catch, joker; see also **discovery** 2, **method** 2, **trick** 1.

3. [A figure or scroll]—*Syn.* slogan, symbol, sign; see **emblem.**

devil, *n.* **1.** [The power opposed to God]—*Syn.* Satan, demon in human shape, fiend, adversary, evil principle, error, sin, god of this world, supreme spirit of evil, archenemy of God, powers of evil *or* of darkness, imp, mischiefmaker, Beelzebub, fallen angel, trickster, hellhound, Asmodeus, Mammon, Moloch, Diabolus, Azazel, Ahriman, Eblis, Belial, Baal, Samael, Hades, Abaddon, Apollyon, Lucifer, Set, Mephistopheles, diabolical *or* satanic force: *all* (D): the Deuce, the Old Boy, Harry, Old Nick, the Tempter, the Old One, the Wicked One, prince of darkness, author of evil, the Foul Fiend, the common enemy, shadow of shadows, Evil One, the

Adversary; see also **evil** 1, **witch.**—*Ant.* angel*, Christ, God.

2. [A vicious person]—*Syn.* villain, renegade, dastard; see **beast** 2, **rascal.**

between the devil and the deep (blue sea) (D) —*Syn.* desperate, stopped, in difficulty; see **in trouble** 1.

give the devil his due (D)—*Syn.* give one credit, give credit where credit is due, recognize; see **acknowledge** 2.

go to the devil (D)—*Syn.* **1.** degenerate, fall into bad habits, go to pot (D); see **decay, fail** 1. **2.** go to hell, damn you, be damned; see **curse.**

raise the devil (D)—*Syn.* cause trouble, riot, be boisterous *or* unruly; see **distrub** 2, **fight** 2.

devilish, *mod.* —*Syn.* fiendish, brutish, inhuman; see **wicked** 2.

devil-may-care, *mod.* —*Syn.* defiant, reckless, flippant; see **careless** 1, **rash.**

deviltry, *n.* —*Syn.* rascality, roguery, trouble; see **mischief** 3.

devious, *mod.* **1.** [Erring]—*Syn.* confounding, blundering, deviating; see **erring, mistaken** 1.

2. [Crafty]—*Syn.* foxy, insidious, shrewd; see **dishonest** 1, **sly** 1.

devoid, *mod.* —*Syn.* void, needed, lacking; see **empty** 1, **wanting.**

devote, *v.* —*Syn.* apply, consecrate, give; see **bless** 3, **dedicate** 2.

devoted, *mod.* —*Syn.* dutiful, loyal, constant; see **faithful.**

devotee, *n.* —*Syn.* zealot, adherent, believer; see **follower.**

devotion, *n.* —*Syn.* allegiance, service, consecration, devotedness, adoration, piety, zeal, ardor, earnestness, fealty, faithfulness, fidelity, constancy, deference, sincerity, devoutness, adherence, observance, intensity; see also **loyalty, worship** 1. —*Ant.* indifference*, apathy, carelessness.

devotional, *mod.* —*Syn.* devout, pious, reverential; see **divine** 2, **religious** 1, 2.

devotions, *n.* —*Syn.* religious worship, church services, prayers; see **church** 2, **worship** 1.

devour, *v.* —*Syn.* gulp, swallow, gorge; see **eat** 1.

devouring, *mod.* —*Syn.* overwhelming, powerful, excessive; see **intense.**

devout, *mod.* —*Syn.* devoted, pious, reverent; see **faithful, holy** 1, **religious** 2.

dexterity, *n.* —*Syn.* aptitude, facility, skill; see **ability** 2.

dexterous, *mod.* —*Syn.* artful, skillful, adroit; see **able** 1, 2.

diabolic, *mod.* —*Syn.* fiendish, devilish, impious; see **wicked** 2.

diadem, *n.* —*Syn.* headdress, tiara, coronet; see **crown** 2.

diagnosis, *n.* —*Syn.* analysis, determination, investigation; see **summary.**

diagnostic, *mod.* —*Syn.* demonstrative, distinguishing, peculiar; see **characteristic.**

diagonal, *mod.* —*Syn.* slanting, inclining, askew; see **oblique** 1.

diagonally, *mod.* —*Syn.* cornerways, slanting, askew; see **cornerwise.**

diagram, *n.* —*Syn.* sketch, layout, picture; see **description** 1, **design** 1, **plan** 1.

dial, *n.* —*Syn.* face, front, disk with figures, circle, numbers, control, indicator, device for showing time, meter, register, measuring device, horologe, compass; see also **gauge, index** 1.

dial, *v.* **1.** [To turn]—*Syn.* rotate, twist, wheel; see **turn** 1.

2. [To telephone]—*Syn.* ring (up), call (up), phone; see **telephone.**

dialect, *n.* —*Syn.* idiom, accent, vernacular, patois; see also **language** 1.

Accents and dialects of English include the following—United States: Standard American, stage, Northern, Midland, Southern, General American, Eastern New England, Boston, Down East, Upstate New York, New York City, Bronx, Brooklyn, Chelsea, Virginia Piedmont, Highland Southern, Southern Highlands, Southern Tidewater, Coastal Southern, Gulla, Southern Appalachian, Deep South, Texas, Cajun, Fort Worth, Houston, Texas Panhandle, Chicago, Mormon *or* Latter-day Saints, Western; British Isles: (British) (Received) Standard, BBC, public-school, Northern, Midland, Birmingham, Southern, cockney, Southeastern, Kentish, Gloucestershire, Devonshire, Cornish, Shropshire, Oxford, Lincolnshire, Norfolk, Yorkshire, Lancashire, Liverpool, Northumbrian, Lowland Scots, Glasgow, Highland Scots, Edinburgh, Inverness, Welsh, Irish, Dublin, Ulster, Belfast, Arran Islands, Western Irish; others: Australian, New Zealand, South African, Canadian, Maritime, Ontario, Western Canadian.

Accents and dialects of languages other than English include the following—French: *langue d'oc, langue d'oïl* (*both* French), Parisian, Norman, Anglo-Norman, Breton, Gascon, Provençal, French Canadian, Algerian; Spanish: Castilian, Catalan, Andalusian, South *and* Central American, Mexican, Puerto Rican, Cuban, Philippine; German: High German; Bavarian, Franconian, Swabian, Swiss German, Austrian German, Rhenish, Yiddish; Low German: Plattdeutsch, Prussian, Berlin, Hamburg, Saxon, Pennsylvania Dutch, Pennsylvania German; Italian: Tuscan, Piedmontese, Roman, Venetian, Neopolitan, Sicilian; Russian: Muscovite, Little Russian, Belorussian, White Russian, Georgian, Ukrainian, Siberian; Chinese: Mandarin, Fukien, Peking, Cantonese, Manchurian, Shansi.

dialectal, *mod.* —*Syn.* limited, dialectical, colloquial, vernacular, indigenous, restricted geographically *or* socially, nonstandard, not generally accepted *or* spoken *or* in use; see also **local** 1.

dialectic, *mod.* **1.** [Colloquial]—*Syn.* idiomatic, vernacular, rural; see **dialect, informal.**

2. [Argumentative]—*Syn.* rationalistic, analytic, persuasive; see **controversial.**

dialectic, *n.* —*Syn.* argumentation, persuasion, deduction; see **thought** 1.

dialogue, *n.* —*Syn.* talk, exchange, remarks; see **conversation.**

diameter, *n.* —*Syn.* bore, caliber, breadth, measurement across, broadness; see also **width.**

diametrical, *mod.* —*Syn.* contrary, adverse, facing; see **opposite** 3.

diamond, *n.* **1.** [A crystalline jewel]—*Syn.* (precious) stone, solitaire, engagement ring, brilliant, bort(s), diamond chips *or* flakes, crystal, ring, finger ring; *all* (D): stone, rock, sparkler, glass, ice; see also **jewel** 1.

Grades, sizes, and forms of diamonds include the following—green, blue, blue-green, yellow, canary, red, pink, brown, gray, smoky, black, rough, uncut, brilliant, double brilliant, half-brilliant, trap-brilliant *or* split-brilliant, old-mine, Kimberley, Brazilian, artificial; ½-carat, 1-carat, 2-carat, etc.; table, pear-shaped, marquise, baguette, emerald-cut, table-cut, flat-cut, square-cut, oval-cut; diamond of the first *or* second *or* third water; see also **gem** 1, **stone.**

Famous diamonds include the following—Jubilee, Orlof, Nassak, Pigott, Hope, Great Mogul, Shah of Persia, Florentine, Star of the South, Koh-i-noor, Regent *or* Pitt, Pascha of Egypt.

2. [An instrument using a diamond]—*Syn.* cutter, glass cutter, diamond point; see **tool** 1.

3. [Shape or figure]—*Syn.* lozenge, rhomb, rhombus; see **form** 1, **solid.**

4. [A baseball playing field, particularly the infield] —*Syn.* lot, ball park; *all* (D): sandlot, orchard, pasture, inner works, scalped field, ash heap; see also **field** 2, **park** 1.

diaphanous, *mod.* —*Syn.* translucent, sheer, pure; see **clear** 2, **thin** 1, **transparent** 1.

diary, *n.* —*Syn.* chronicle, record, log; see **journal** 1.

diatribe, *n.* —*Syn.* criticism, denunciation, tirade; see **objection** 2.

dice, *n.* —*Syn.* cubes, counters, pair of dice, misspotted dice; *all* (D): African dominoes, ivories, tombstones, galloping dominoes, rattling bones, shakers.

no dice (D)—*Syn.* never, nothing doing, no deal; see **no.**

dicker, *v.* —*Syn.* trade, barter, bargain; see **argue** 1, **buy** 1, **sell** 1.

dictate, *v.* **1.** [To speak for record]—*Syn.* speak, deliver, give forth, interview, communicate directly to an amanuensis, compose, formulate, verbalize, record, orate, emit, give an account, draft correspondence, prepare the first draft; see also **talk** 1.

2. [To give peremptory orders]—*Syn.* instruct, direct, regiment; see **command** 1, **manage** 1.—*Ant.* beg*, plead, petition.

dictation, *n.* —*Syn.* account, record, correspondence, dictated matter, verbal composition, typewriting, stenography, dictography, copy, transcription, material *or* message *or* utterance for transcription; see also **notes, shorthand.**

dictator, *n.* —*Syn.* autocrat, despot, tyrant, mogul, shah, rajah, sirdar, Grand Turk, tycoon, sultan, sheik, czar, fascist, absolute ruler, usurper, oppressor, absolutist, terrorist, oligarch, inquisitor, master, leader, *duce* (Italian), caesar, kaiser, ringleader, magnate, emir, khan, lama, lord, commander, chief, adviser, overlord, taskmaster, person with absolute control in a government, disciplinarian, headman, caliph, martinet, lord of the ascendant, sachem; *all* (D): wirepuller, cock of the walk, man at the wheel, *Führer* (German), Nazi, boss, robber baron, slave-driver; see also **leader** 2, **ruler** 1.

dictatorial, *mod.* **1.** [Overbearing]—*Syn.* haughty, pompous, arrogant; see **egotistic** 2.

2. [Autocratic]—*Syn.* despotic, authoritarian, arbitrary; see **absolute** 3, **autocratic** 1, **tyrannical.**

dictatorship, *n.* —*Syn.* despotism, unlimited rule, coercion; see **autocracy, fascism, government** 2, **tyranny.**

diction, *n.* —*Syn.* style, expression, wording, usage, choice of words, command of language, literary artistry, manner *or* turn of expression, literary power, locution, rhetoric, fluency, oratory, articulation, enunciation, vocabulary, phraseology, verbiage, language; *all* (D): lingo, line, gift of gab; see also **eloquence** 1, **enunciation** 1, **speech** 2.

dictionary, *n.* —*Syn.* word book, word list, lexicon, thesaurus, concordance, reference work, glossary, gazetteer, encyclopedia, cyclopedia, dictionary of synonyms, promptory, *promptorium* (Latin), lexicographical work; dictionary of religion and ethics, dictionary of airplane mechanics, dictionary of law, etc.; see also **reference** 3.

dictum, *n.* **1.** [Pronouncement]—*Syn.* dictate, affirmation, assertion; see **announcement** 2, **declaration** 1.

2. [Proverb]—*Syn.* maxim, adage, precept; see **motto, proverb.**

didactic, *mod.* —*Syn.* instructive, expository, academic; see **educational** 1.

die, *v.* **1.** [To cease living]—*Syn.* expire, pass away *or* on, depart, perish, succumb, go, commit suicide, suffocate, lose one's life, cease respiration, emit the last breath, relinquish life, suffer death, cease to exist, come to a violent end, come to naught *or* nothing, drown, hang, fall, meet one's death, be no more, end one's earthly career, be taken, drop dead; *all* (D): go to glory, go up *or* off, return to the earth, fall asleep, be done for, catch one's death, fade away, rest in peace, go belly up, be numbered with the dead, join the choir invisible, pay the supreme sacrifice, go to one's last home, cross the Styx, pass over to the great beyond, give up the ghost, go the way of all flesh, pay the debt of nature, shuffle off this mortal coil, slide into oblivion, become one with nature, awake to immortal life, join the majority, turn *or* return to dust, close one's eyes, hand in one's chips, cash in, go west, push up daisies, buy the farm, kick the bucket, shut up shop, answer the last call, bite the dust, lay down one's life, drop dead, breathe one's last, croak, bite the bullet, kick in, go to glory, keel over, conk out, go home feet first, check out, burn out, kick off, end one's days, go by the board.—*Ant.* live*, thrive, exist.

2. [To cease existing]—*Syn.* stop, extinguish, dissolve, disappear, go out, recede, vanish, evanesce, burn out, be heard of no more, come to nothing, evaporate, become extinct, be null and void, be no more, leave not a trace behind, discontinue, vanish; *both* (D): go blooey, go *pfft*; see also **stop** 2. —*Ant.* endure*, go on, continue*.

3. [To decline as though death were inevitable] —*Syn.* fade, wither, decline, wane, sink, wear away, ebb, droop, lapse, retrograde, lose active qualities, run low, rot, crumble, diminish, deteriorate, molder, rankle, dilapidate, die out *or* down, melt away, subside; *all* (D): go bad, totter to a fall, go downhill; see also **decay, weaken** 2.—*Ant.* grow*, increase, improve*.

die away, *v.*—*Syn.* decline, go away, sink; see **stop** 2.

die down, *v.*—*Syn.* decline, disappear, recede; see **die** 2, 3, **decrease** 1.

die-hard, *mod.*—*Syn.* immovable, convinced, extremist; see **firm** 1, 5.

die-hard, *n.*—*Syn.* zealot, reactionary, extremist; see **conservative.**

die off *or* **out,** *v.*—*Syn.* go, cease (to exist), vanish; see **disappear.**

diet, *n.* **1.** [What one eats]—*Syn.* victuals, fare, daily bread (D); see **food, menu.**

2. [Restricted intake of food]—*Syn.* weight-reduction plan, nutritional therapy, regimen, fast, abstinence from food, starvation, diet, bread and water (D).

diet, *v.*—*Syn.* go without, starve oneself, lose weight, slim down, go on a diet, reduce, abstain, watch one's weight, tighten one's belt (D).

dieter, *n.*—*Syn.* reducer, weight-loser, faster, abstainer from food *or* eating, health-food nut (D).

differ, *v.* **1.** [To be unlike]—*Syn.* vary, modify, not conform, digress, take exception, turn, reverse, qualify, alter, change, bear no resemblance, not look like, divaricate from, jar with, clash *or* conflict with, be distinguished from, diversify, lack resemblance, show contrast, stand apart, diverge *or* deviate *or* depart from, be unlike *or* dissimilar *or* distinct in nature; *all* (D): go off on a tangent, sing a different tune, leave the beaten path; see also **contrast** 1.—*Ant.* resemble*, parallel, take after.

2. [To oppose]—*Syn.* disagree, object, fight; see **oppose** 1.

difference, *n.* **1.** [The quality of being different] —*Syn.* disagreement, divergence, state of being different, nonconformity, contrariety, contrariness, deviation, opposition, antithesis, dissimilarity, inequality, diversity, unlikeness, departure, lack of identity *or* resemblance, variance, discrepancy, separation, differentiation, distinctness, separateness, heterogeneity, dissemblance, asymmetry, discongruity; see also **contrast** 1, **variety** 1.—*Ant.* agreement*, similarity, resemblance.

2. [That which is unlike in comparable things] —*Syn.* disparity, distinction, variance, deviation, departure, deflection, distinguishing characteristic, peculiarity, idiosyncrasy, exception, digression, contrast, unconformity, aberration, irregularity, anomaly, abnormality, contradistinction, interval; see also **variation.**—*Ant.* similarity*, likeness, common ground.

3. [Personal dissension]—*Syn.* discord, estrangement, dissent; see **dispute** 1.

make a difference—*Syn.* change, have an effect, affect; see **matter** 1.

split the difference (D)—*Syn.* compromise, go half way, come to an agreement; see **agree.**

what's the difference?—*Syn.* what does it matter? what difference does it make? so what? (D); see **why.**

different, *mod.* **1.** [Unlike in nature]—*Syn.* distinct, separate, not the same, nothing like, other than, in disagreement, divergent, contrasted, variant, dissonant, deviating, incongruous, varying, diverse, contradistinct, altered, incompatible, changed, modified, dissimilar, unlike, contrary, contradictory, contrasting, discordant, inharmonious, opposed, disagreeing, varied, clashing, antagonistic, unsuitable, diametric, reverse, deviative, unidentical, contrastive, ranging, to be contrasted, not identical, set apart, other than; *all* (D): out of line with, far from it, a bit on the off side, out of it, offbeat, at odds; see also **various.**—*Ant.* alike*, like, similar.

2. [Composed of unlike things]—*Syn.* diverse, manifold, divergent, diversified, inconsistent, incongruous, indiscriminate, dissonant, heterogeneous, variant, sundry, variegated, collected, anthologized, miscellaneous, unselected, unclassified, many, several, disparate, jarring, asymmetrical, varicolored, assorted; see also **complex** 1, **mixed** 1, **various.**—*Ant.* harmonious*, identical, uniform.

3. [Unusual]—*Syn.* unconventional, strange, startling; see **unusual** 1, 2.

differentiate, *v.* **1.** [Distinguish]—*Syn.* contrast, set apart, separate; see **distinguish** 1.

2. [Change]—*Syn.* modify, adapt, alter; see **change** 1.

differently, *mod.* **1.** [In various ways]—*Syn.* variously, divergently, individually, distinctively, creatively, uniquely, separately, each in his own way, severally, diversely, disparately, incongruously, heterogeneously, abnormally, not normally, contrastively, contrastingly, in differing ways *or* manners, uncomfortably, nonconformably, unusually, asymmetrically, in a different manner, with a difference, multiformly, otherwise.—*Ant.* evenly*, uniformly, invariably.

2. [In opposition]—*Syn.* adversely, discordantly, dissimilarly, oppositely, contradictorily, contrarily, conflictingly, antagonistically, imcompatibly, hostilely, antithetically, negatively, vice versa, on the contrary, on the other hand; *both* (D): poles apart, on the other side of the fence,; see also **against** 3. —*Ant.* similarly, unanimously*, identically.

difficult, *mod.* **1.** [Hard to achieve]—*Syn.* laborious, hard, hard-won, unyielding, beyond the ability, strenuous, exacting, stiff, heavy, arduous, painful, labored, trying, titanic, bothersome, troublesome, demanding, burdensome, backbreaking, not easy, wearisome, onerous, attended by obstacles, rigid, crucial, Herculean, requiring much effort, Gargantuan, uphill, Sisyphean, upstream, challenging, exacting, formidable, ambitious, intricate, irritating, immense; *all* (D): tough, heavy, man-sized, no picnic, stiff, galling; see also **severe** 1.—*Ant.* easy*, wieldy, light.

2. [Hard to understand]—*Syn.* intricate, involved, perplexing, abstruse, abstract, delicate, hard, knotty, thorny, nice, troublesome, ticklish, obstinate, puzzling, mysterious, mystifying, subtle, confusing, bewildering, dark, confounding, esoteric, unclear, mystical, tangled, hard to explain *or* solve, entangled, profound, vexing, baffling, enmeshed, rambling, loose, meandering, trackless, inexplicable, pathless, awkward, digressive, turgid, complex, complicated, deep, stubborn, labyrinthine, hidden, formidable, enigmatic, enigmatical, occult, paradoxical, incomprehensible, unintelligible, inscrutable, inexplicable, unanswerable, not understandable, unsolvable, unfathomable, concealed,

unaccountable, ambiguous, equivocal, metaphysical, inconceivable, recondite, unknown; *all* (D): steep, deep, over one's head, beyond one's depth, too deep (for), beyond one's comprehension, not making sense, Greek to, past comprehension; see also **obscure** 1, 3.—*Ant.* clear*, obvious, simple.
3. [Hard to manage socially]—*Syn.* impolite, perverse, boorish; see **irritable, rude** 1, 2.

difficulty, *n.* **1.** [Something in one's way]—*Syn.* obstacle, obstruction, stumbling block, complication, hardship, adversity, misfortune, distress, deadlock, dilemma, hard job, exigency, labyrinth, maze, arduousness, stone wall, barricade, impasse, prejudice, knot, opposition, quandary, struggle, Herculean task, frustration, quagmire, pass, quicksands, critical situation, crisis, trouble, intricacy, embarrassment, entanglement, thwart, cul-de-sac, mess, slough, paradox, muddle, swamp, bafflement, strait, financial embarrassment, poser, crux, emergency, matter, standstill, hindrance, perplexity, bar, trial, check, predicament; *all* (D): peck of troubles, hot water, hornet's nest, pickle, fix, stew, scrape, hard nut to crack, hard row to hoe, hazard, hitch, dead end, snag, hump, corner, rub, crimp, monkey wrench in the works, pinch, deep water, tough proposition, jam, horns of a dilemma, Gordian knot, the devil to pay, hang-up; see also sense 2, **barrier, impediment** 1.—*Ant.* aid*, assistance, help.
2. [Something mentally disturbing]—*Syn.* trouble, annoyance, to-do, ado, worry, weight, complication, distress, critical situation, oppression, depression, aggravation, perplexity, bafflement, anxiety, discouragement, touchy situation, embarrassment, burden, grievance, vicissitude, quandary, strait, exigency, irritation, strife, puzzle, responsibility, imbroglio, frustration, harassment, rigor, misery, predicament, setback, pressure, stress, strain, care, charge, millstone, struggle, maze; *all* (D): jam, hangup, mess, pickle, pinch, scrape, where the shoe pinches, goings-on; see also sense 1; **crisis, emergency.**—*Ant.* ease, comfort, happiness.
3. [Contention]—*Syn.* trouble, strife, misunderstanding; see **fight** 1.
with difficulty—*Syn.* in trouble, in the face of great odds, having a hard *or* bad time, under handicap(s), in spite of one's best efforts, being troubled *or* pestered *or* tormented, etc.; with embarrassment *or* reverses *or* opposition, etc.

diffidence, *n.* —*Syn.* timidity, reserve, constraint; see **restraint** 1, **shyness.**

diffident, *mod.* —*Syn.* shy, bashful, timid; see **humble** 1.

diffuse, *mod.* **1.** [Widely separated]—*Syn.* dispersed, thin, diluted; see **distributed, scattered.**
2. [Rambling and dull]—*Syn.* discursive, prolix, wordy; see **verbose.**

diffuse, *v.* —*Syn.* spread, expand, distribute; see **scatter** 1, 2.

diffusion, *n.* —*Syn.* dissemination, spread, dispersion; see **dissipation** 1, **distribution** 1.

dig, *n.* **1.** [Insult]—*Syn.* slur, innuendo, cut; see **insult.**
2. [Excavation]—*Syn.* digging, archaeological expedition, exploration; see **expedition** 2, **hole** 2.

dig, *v.* **1.** [To stir the earth]—*Syn.* delve, spade, mine, excavate, fork, elevate, channel, deepen, till, drive (a shaft), clean, undermine, burrow, dig out *or* down, depress, gouge, dredge, scoop *or* tunnel *or* hollow *or* clean out; *all* (D): muck, stope, grub, cat, bulldoze, put a whirler to work; see also **shovel.** —*Ant.* embed*, fill, bury.
2. [To remove by digging]—*Syn.* dig up, discover, uncover, bring to the surface, empty, exhume, unearth, turn up, produce, bring to light, excavate, investigate, sift; see also **harvest.**
3. [(D) To like]—*Syn.* enjoy, love, groove on (D); see **like** 1, 2.
4. [(D) To understand]—*Syn.* comprehend, recognize, follow; see **understand** 1.

digest, *n.* —*Syn.* epitome, précise, condensation; see **summary.**

digest, *v.* **1.** [To transform food]—*Syn.* chymify, consume, absorb; see **eat** 1.
2. [To understand by deliberation]—*Syn.* consider, analyze, think over; see **think** 1, **understand** 1.
3. [To summarize]—*Syn.* abstract, survey, abbreviate; see **decrease** 2.

digestible, *mod.* —*Syn.* edible, absorbable, good to eat; see **eatable.**

digestion, *n.* —*Syn.* digesting, eupepsy, separation, disintegration, conversion, reducing to an ingestible condition *or* state, conversion of food into chyme, separation of nutritions from waste elements of food, process by which food is digested, absorption, chymification.

dig in, *v.* **1.** [To begin]—*Syn.* commence, rise, spring; see **begin** 2.
2. [To entrench]—*Syn.* delve, burrow, undermine; see **dig** 1.
3. [(D) To eat]—*Syn.* chew, begin eating, consume; see **bite** 1, **eat** 1.

dig into, *v.* —*Syn.* investigate, research, probe; see **examine** 1.

digit, *n.* **1.** [A finger or toe]—*Syn.* phalange, extremity, thumb; see **finger, toe.**
2. [A number]—*Syn.* symbol, arabic notation, numeral; see **number** 2.

dignified, *mod.* —*Syn.* stately, somber, solemn, courtly, reserved, ornate, elegant, exalted, classical, classic, tall, quiet, lordly, aristocratic, princely, imperial, majestic, queenly, of consequence, formal, respected, ladylike, gentlemanly, noble, regal, superior, exquisite, chic, magnificent, grand, eminent, sublime, august, marked by dignity of manner, grave, distinguished, magisterial, imperious, imposing, portly, haughty, honorable, decorous, lofty, proud, *distingué* (French), glorious, gravely courteous; *all* (D): classy, snazzy, as one who has a ramrod down his back, sober as a judge, tops, highbrow, nifty, slick; see also **cultured, refined** 2. —*Ant.* rude*, undignified, boorish.

dignify, *v.* —*Syn.* exalt, elevate, prefer; see **praise** 1.

dignity, *n.* **1.** [A presence that commands respect] —*Syn.* nobility, self-respect, hauteur, nobility of manner, lofty bearing, elevated deportment, sublimity, dignified behavior, grand air, loftiness, quality, superior modesty, culture, distinction, stateliness, elevation, nobleness of mind, worthiness, worth, regard, character, importance, renown, splendor, majesty; *all* (D): that mysterious something, stuff, class, something on the ball, tone; see also **honor** 1, **pride** 1.—*Ant.* humility*, lowness, meekness.

2. [A station that commands respect]—*Syn.* rank, honor, significance; see **fame** 1, **importance** 1.

digress, *v.* —*Syn.* stray, diverge, maunder; see **ramble** 2.

digression, *n.* —*Syn.* deviation, diversion, excursus; see **difference** 2, **variation.**

dig up, *v.* —*Syn.* find, uncover, excavate; see **dig** 2, **discover** 1.

dike, *n.* —*Syn.* wall, grade, barrier; see **dam** 1.

dilapidated, *mod.* —*Syn.* decayed, fallen in, decaying; see **crumbly, old** 2.

dilapidation, *n.* —*Syn.* ruin, disintegration, remnants; see **destruction** 2.

dilate, *v.* —*Syn.* stretch, widen, broaden; see **increase** 1.

dilation, *n.* —*Syn.* distention, expansion, extension; see **increase** 1.

dilatory, *mod.* —*Syn.* tardy, procrastinating, lazy; see **late** 1, **slow** 2.

dilemma, *n.* —*Syn.* quandary, perplexity, predicament; see **difficulty** 1.

dilettante, *n.* —*Syn.* dabbler, trifler, aesthete; see **amateur.**

diligence, *n.* —*Syn.* assiduity, alertness, keenness, constancy, earnestness, briskness, quickness, perseverance, industry, vigor, persistent exertion, assiduousness, pertinacity, heed, carefulness, intent, intentness, intensity; see also **attention** 2, **care** 1. —*Ant.* carelessness*, sloth, laziness.

diligent, *mod.* —*Syn.* hardworking, pertinacious, occupied; see **busy** 1, **careful.**

dillydally, *v.* —*Syn.* hesitate, falter, waver; see **delay** 1.

dilute, *v.* —*Syn.* mix, reduce, thin; see **weaken** 2.

dim, *mod.* —*Syn.* faint, dusky, shadowy; see **dark** 1.

take a dim view of (D)—*Syn.* suspect, disapprove, be skeptical about; see **doubt** 2.

dime, *n.* —*Syn.* ten cents, thin dime, ten-cent piece; *all* (D): short bit, ten-center, thin one, hog; see also **money.**

dimensions, *n.* —*Syn.* size, measurements, extent; see **height** 1, **length** 1, 2, **width.**

diminish, *v.* **1.** [To grow less]—*Syn.* wane, abate, decline; see **decrease** 1.

2. [To make less]—*Syn.* lessen, reduce, abbreviate; see **decrease** 2, **depreciate** 2.

diminution, *n.* —*Syn.* lessening, decrease, alleviation; see **reduction** 1.

diminutive, *mod.* —*Syn.* small, tiny, mini (D); see **little** 1, **minute** 1.

din, *n.* —*Syn.* clamor, commotion, hubbub; see **confusion** 2, **noise** 2.

dine, *v.* —*Syn.* lunch, feast, sup; see **eat** 1.

diner, *n.* **1.** [One who eats]—*Syn.* patron, customer, guest, boarder, eater, gourmet, gourmand; *all* (D): chow, chucker, garbage hound, wallowing Willie.

2. [A dining room, especially on a train]—*Syn.* saloon, café, dining car *or* coach; see **dining room.**

dingy, *mod.* —*Syn.* grimy, muddy, soiled; see **dirty** 1.

dining room, *n.* Varieties include the following—dining hall, breakfast nook, dinette, tea room, tea shop, buffet, lunch counter, lunch room, cafeteria, café, ice-cream parlor, drug store, grill, coffee shop, inn, hotel, soda fountain, steak house, fish house, sandwich shop, fast-food outlet, pizza parlor, diner, mess hall, galley, confectionery, canteen, facility, rotisserie, refectory, cookshop, lunch wagon, automat, chuck wagon, *bistro, salle à manger* (both French), *Speisezimmer* (German), *sala da pranzo* (Italian), *comedor* (Spanish); *all* (D): dine-and-dance joint, hash house, dump, greasy spoon, hashery; see also **restaurant.**

dinner, *n.* —*Syn.* feast, banquet, principal *or* main meal, principal meal of the day, supper, refection, collation, repast, New England boiled dinner, Christmas dinner, course dinner, table d'hôte, *prix fixe* (French), *pranzo* (Italian), *comida principal* (Spanish); see also **meal** 2.

diocese, *n.* —*Syn.* episcopate, prelacy, benefice; see **jurisdiction, parish.**

dip, *n.* **1.** [The action of dipping]—*Syn.* plunge, immersion, soaking, ducking, douche, drenching, sinking; see also **bath** 1.

2. [Material into which something is dipped] —*Syn.* preparation, infusion, solution, suspension, dilution, suffusion, concoction, saturation, mixture; see also **bath** 2, **liquid.**

3. [A low place]—*Syn.* depression, slope, inclination; see **hole** 2.

4. [A drop]—*Syn.* sag, slip, decline; see **fall** 1.

5. [A swim]—*Syn.* plunge, bath, dive; see **swim.**

6. [Food to be eaten by dipping]—*Syn.* mixture, canapé, snack; see **delicatessen** 1.

Dips include the following—clam, cheese, Roquefort, blue cheese, cheddar, ham salad, egg salad, onion, chili, pickle, poi, sour cream.

dip, *v.* **1.** [To put into a liquid]—*Syn.* plunge, lower, wet, slosh, submerge, place in a fluid and withdraw again, irrigate, steep, drench, douse, souse, moisten, lower and raise quickly, immerse temporarily, splash, lave, slop, water, duck, bathe, rinse, baptize, dunk (D); see also **immerse** 1, **soak** 1, **wash** 1.

2. [To transfer by means of a vessel]—*Syn.* scoop, shovel, ladle, lade, bale, draft off, raise by a dipping action, take out with a ladle, spoon, lift by scooping, decant, handle, dredge, lift, draw, strain, dish, dip up *or* out, offer; see also **serve** 4.—*Ant.* empty*, pour, let stand.

3. [To fall]—*Syn.* slope, decline, incline, recede, tilt, swoop, slip, spiral, sink, plunge, bend, verge, veer, slant, settle, slump, slide, go down; see also **dive, drop** 2, **fall** 1.

dip into, *v.* —*Syn.* take, get, appropriate; see **catch** 1, **receive** 1, **seize** 1, 2.

diploma, *n.* —*Syn.* graduation certificate, credentials, honor, award, recognition, commission, charter, warrant, authority, voucher, confirmation, sheepskin (D); see also **degree** 3, **graduation.**

diplomacy, *n.* —*Syn.* artfulness, skill, discretion; see **tact.**

diplomat, *n.* **1.** [An accredited representative abroad]—*Syn.* ambassador, consul, minister, plenipotentiary, ambassadorial representative, consular representative, member of the diplomatic corps, legate, nuncio, emissary, envoy, attaché, agent, expert on *or* in international affairs, shuttle diplomat, cabinet member, chargé d'affaires; see also **representative** 2, **statesman.**

2. [A shrewd, suave person]—*Syn.* public speaker, orator, businessman, strategist, tactician, negotiator, Machiavelli, propagandist, bargainer, man of the world, cosmopolitan, artful dodger; *all* (D): apple polisher, shyster, smoothie; see also **lawyer, politician** 1, 3.—*Ant.* bungler*, fumbler, clod (D).

diplomatic, *mod.* —*Syn.* tactful, suave, gracious, calculating, shrewd, opportunistic, smooth, capable, conciliatory, conniving, sly, artful, wily, subtle, arch, crafty, sharp, cunning, contriving, scheming, discreet, deft, dexterous, adept, intriguing, politic, strategic, astute, clever; *all* (D): savvy, brainy, cagey; see also **polite** 1.—*Ant.* frank*, artless, bungling.

dipped, *mod.* —*Syn.* immersed, plunged, bathed, ducked, thrust, doused, plumped, drenched, soused, coated, covered, waxed; *both* (D): sozzled, dunked; see also **soaked, wet** 1.

dipper, *n.* —*Syn.* ladle, tablespoon, cup, basin, pail, pan, can, fork, pot, crock, bucket, bowl, glass, tumbler, spatula, mug, jug, pitcher, skimmer, gourd, calabash, (steam) shovel, spade, dredge, trowel, long-handled utensil, bailer, scoop; see also **container, silverware, spoon.**

dipsomania, *n.* —*Syn.* alcoholism, inebriety, insobriety; see **drunkenness.**

dipsomaniac, *n.* —*Syn.* alcoholic; *both* (D): boozer, sot; see **drunkard.**

dire, *mod.* —*Syn.* dreadful, terrible, horrible; see **frightful** 1.

direct, *mod.* **1.** [Without divergence]—*Syn.* in a straight line, straight ahead, undeviating, uninterrupted, right, unswerving, straightaway, shortest; *all* (D): nonstop, in a bee line, as the crow flies, straight as an arrow, point-blank; see also **straight** 1. —*Ant.* zigzag*, roundabout, crooked.

2. [Frank]—*Syn.* straightforward, outspoken, candid; see **frank, honest** 1.

3. [Immediate]—*Syn.* prompt, succeeding, resultant; see **immediate** 1.

direct, *v.* **1.** [To show the way]—*Syn.* conduct, show, guide; see **lead** 1.

2. [To decide the course of affairs]—*Syn.* regulate, govern, influence; see **command** 2, **manage** 1.

3. [To teach]—*Syn.* inform, instruct, give directions; see **advise** 1, **teach** 1.

4. [To address]—*Syn.* deliver, lecture, read; see **address** 2.

5. [To aim a weapon]—*Syn.* sight, train, level; see **aim** 2.

6. [To command]—*Syn.* order, bid, charge; see **command** 1.

7. [To direct one's effort]—*Syn.* strive, endeavor, aim; see **try** 1.

8. [To write directions on a letter or package] —*Syn.* inscribe, label, designate; see **address** 1, **mark** 1, 2.

directed, *mod.* —*Syn.* supervised, controlled, conducted, sponsored, under supervision, assisted, counseled, guided, serviced, managed, organized, orderly, modern, purposeful, functioning, under (one's) orders; see also **aimed, organized.**—*Ant.* wandering*, misdirected, vagrant.

direction, *n.* **1.** [A position]—*Syn.* point of the compass, objective, bearing, region, area, road, place, spot; see also **route** 2, **way** 2.

Points of the compass include the following—north (N), south (S), east (E), west (W), NE, NW, SE, SW, NNE, NNW, SSE, SSW, ENE, ESE, WNW, WSW, E by N, E by S, W by N, W by S, N by E, S by E, N by W, S by W, NE by E, NE by N, NW by N, NW by W, SE by E, SE by S, SW by W, SW by S.

2. [Supervision]—*Syn.* management, superintendence, control; see **administration** 1.

3. [An order]—*Syn.* charge, regulation, injunction; see **command** 1.

4. [A tendency]—*Syn.* bias, bent, proclivity; see **inclination** 1.

directions, *n.* —*Syn.* formal instructions, advice, advisement, notification, specification, indication, order(s), assignment, guidelines, recommendation(s), summons, directive, regulation, prescription, sealed orders, plans, word from the administration *or* the office *or* the boss *or* the higher-ups (D); *all* (D): the specs, the dope, the low-down.

directly, *mod.* —*Syn.* instantly, at once, quickly; see **immediately.**

director, *n.* **1.** [An executive officer]—*Syn.* manager, supervisor, executive; see **administrator, leader** 2.

2. [Person in charge of a theatrical production] —*Syn.* producer, stage director, play director, moving-picture director, television *or* TV director; see also **leader** 3.

directory, *n.* —*Syn.* list, syllabus, notice, register, record, almanac, roster, dictionary, gazetteer, telephone book, Red Book, Domesday book, Yellow Pages, city directory, Social Register, professional directory, office of information, student directory; *both* (D): Who's Who, blue book; see also **catalogue** 1, **index** 2.

dirge, *n.* —*Syn.* chant, lament, march; see **cry** 3, **hymn, song.**

dirigible, *n.* —*Syn.* blimp, lighter-than-air machine, zeppelin; see **balloon, plane** 3.

dirk, *n.* —*Syn.* dagger, stiletto, blade; see **knife.**

dirt, *n.* **1.** [Earth]—*Syn.* soil, loam, clay; see **earth** 2.

2. [Filth]—*Syn.* rottenness, filthiness, smut; see **filth.**

do one dirt (D)—*Syn.* harm, hurt, deceive, cheat; see **abuse.**

dirty, *mod.* **1.** [Containing dirt]—*Syn.* soiled, unclean, unsanitary, unhygienic, filthy, polluted, nasty, slovenly, dusty, undusted, messy, squalid, sloppy, lousy, disheveled, uncombed, unsightly, slatternly, bedraggled, untidy, disarrayed, dishabille, straggly, unwashed, unkempt, stained, tarnished, spotted, smudged, foul, fouled, grimy, greasy, spattered, smutty, smutted, flyspecked, muddy, mucky, sooty, smoked, slimy, rusty, murky, unlaundered, unswept, unsalable, unpolished; *all* (D): crummy, scrubby, icky, grubby, raunchy, scuzzy, yucky, scummy.—*Ant.* pure*, unspotted, sanitary.

2. [Obscene]—*Syn.* pornographic, smutty, lewd; see **lewd** 1, 2, **ribald, sensual.**

3. [Nasty]—*Syn.* mean, contemptible, disagreeable; see **mean** 3, **ruthless** 1.

dirty, *v.* —*Syn.* soil, sully, defile, pollute, foul, encrust, coat, tarnish, spot, smear, daub, blot, blur, make dusty, smudge, smutch, smitch, smoke, drabble, draggle, heap dirt upon, dabble, botch, bedaub, spoil, speck, sweat up, blotch, spatter, besmear, befoul, splash, stain, debase, corrupt, taint, contaminate, rot, decay, mold, make impure. —*Ant.* clean*, cleanse, rinse.

disability, *n.* **1.** [The state of lacking a necessary quality]—*Syn.* feebleness, unfitness, incapacity; see **inability** 1, **injury** 1, **weakness** 1.
2. [A specific lack]—*Syn.* impotence, disqualification, inexperience; see **lack** 2.

disable, *v.* —*Syn.* cripple, impair, put out of action; see **damage** 1, **weaken** 2.

disabled, *mod.* —*Syn.* crippled, helpless, useless, wrecked, stalled, maimed, hamstrung, wounded, mangled, lame, mutilated, silenced, run-down, worn-out, incapacitated, bedridden, weakened; confined to (one's) bed *or* (one's) home *or* a hospital *or* a rest home, etc.; impotent, castrated, halting, palsied, superannuated, paralyzed, paraplegic, handicapped, imbecile, senile, decrepit; *all* (D): laid on one's back, laid up, done up *or* for *or* in, cracked up, banged up, broken down, (put) out of action, done up brown, counted out; see also **hurt, useless** 1, **weak** 1.—*Ant.* healthy*, strong, capable.

disabuse, *v.* —*Syn.* undeceive, clarify, inform; see **correct** 1.

disadvantage, *v.* —*Syn.* undeceive, clarify, inform; see **correct** 1.

disadvantage, *n.* **1.** [Loss]—*Syn.* damage, harm, deprivation; see **loss** 3.
2. [A position involving difficulties]—*Syn.* bar, obstacle, handicap; see **impediment** 1, **restraint** 2.
3. [Unfavorable details or prospects; *often plural*] —*Syn.* disadvantageousness, weak, point, impediment, undesirableness, inconvenience, deprivation of advantage, stumbling block, discommodity, inexpedience, obstacle, handicap, drawbacks, limitations, bad *or* poor conditions, unsatisfactoriness, hindrances, objections, problems, failings, weaknesses, lacks, harmful *or* fatal *or* adverse *or* disadvantageous *or* unfortunate *or* damaging, etc., circumstances, ineffectiveness, faults, defects, deficiencies, imperfections, inadequacies; see also **weakness** 2.—*Ant.* advantage*, satisfactoriness, effectiveness.

disaffect, *v.* —*Syn.* estrange, antagonize, repel; see **alienate.**

disaffected, *mod.* —*Syn.* antagonistic, disloyal, estranged; see **indifferent** 1, **unfriendly** 1.

disaffection, *n.* —*Syn.* estrangement, aversion, resentment; see **hatred** 1, 2.

disagree, *v.* **1.** [To differ]—*Syn.* dissent, object, oppose; see **differ** 2.
2. [To have uncomfortable effect]—*Syn.* be disturbing *or* sickening *or* nauseating *or* unsuitable *or* distasteful, nauseate, hurt, injure, make ill, go against the grain, be hard on one's stomach (D); see also **bother** 3.

disagreeable, *mod.* **1.** [Having an unpleasant disposition]—*Syn.* difficult, obnoxious, offensive; see **irritable, rude** 2.
2. [Irritating; *said of things and conditions*] —*Syn.* bothersome, unpleasant, upsetting; see **disturbing, offensive** 2.

disagreeably, *mod.* —*Syn.* antagonistically, negatively, belligerently, adversely, contrarily, incompatibly, incongruously, inconsistently, opposingly.

disagreeing, *mod.* —*Syn.* differing, dissenting, at odds; see **quarreling.**

disagreeing, *n.* —*Syn.* disrupting, quarreling, disputing, disapproving, differing; see also **disagreement** 1, **dispute** 1.

disagreement, *n.* **1.** [Discord]—*Syn.* contention, strife, conflict, cross-purposes, controversy, wrangle, vendetta, dissension, atmospherics, animosity, ill feeling, ill will, misunderstanding, division, opposition, hostility, breach, discord, disunion, feud, clashing, antagonism, disunity, dissidence, dissent, bickering, squabble, divisiveness, lack of concord, tension, split, quarreling, jarring, falling out, break, rupture, quarrel, clash, opposition, altercation, variance, contest, friction; see also **battle** 2, **competition** 1, **fight** 1.
2. [Inconsistency]—*Syn.* discrepancy, dissimilarity, disparity; see **difference** 1.
3. [A quarrel]—*Syn.* fight, argument, feud; see **dispute** 1.

disallow, *v.* —*Syn.* ban, embargo, censor; see **forbid.**

disappear, *v.* —*Syn.* vanish, come to naught, retreat, cease, lose identity, fade, die, drop out of sight, become imperceptible, withdraw, dissolve, cease to appear, pass out of sight, recede from view, cease to be (seen), suffer *or* undergo eclipse, pass, go, leave no trace, pass out, retire (from sight), vanish from sight, be lost to view, sink, exit, go off the stage, pass on, leave, vacate, abscond, depart, dissolve, perish, die *or* fade out, abandon, escape, be gone, evanesce, be no more, cease to exist *or* be known, decamp, end gradually, dissipate, wane, be swallowed up, leave no trace, ebb, disperse, pass *or* fall *or* fade *or* go *or* die *or* melt away; *all* (D): vamoose, do a disappearing act, be done for, take French leave, take wing *or* flight, pass out of the picture; see also **escape, evaporate** 1.—*Ant.* appear*, emerge, materialize.

disappearance, *n.* —*Syn.* vanishing, dissolution, dispersal, fading, departure, ebbing away, recession *or* receding from view, removal, dissipation, vanishment, evanescence, ceasing to exist *or* appear, desertion, flight, retirement, escape, wane, exodus, vanishing point, going, wearing away, disintegration, exit, withdrawal, decline and fall, eclipse; see also **escape** 1, **evaporation.**

disappoint, *v.* —*Syn.* fail, delude, deceive, dissatisfy, disgruntle, disillusion, tantalize, harass, embitter, disconcert, chagrin, dumbfound, put out, come *or* fall short of, cast down, ruin one's prospects, dash one's hopes, frustrate, torment, tease, miscarry, abort, thwart, foil, disconcert, baffle, founder, disenchant, balk, bring to naught, fail to fulfill the expectations of, mislead, stand up, come to nothing *or* naught, come to grief, meet with disaster, run aground; *all* (D): fall down on, dish, bungle, let down, knock the props from under, end in smoke, flash in the pan, put one's nose out of joint, fall flat, leave in the lurch, fizzle out.

disappointed, *mod.* **1.** [Displeased]—*Syn.* dissatisfied, discouraged, unsatisfied, despondent, depressed, objecting, complaining, distressed, hope-

less, balked, disconcerted, aghast, disgruntled, disillusioned; *both* (D): laughing out of the wrong side of one's mouth, shot down; see also **sad** 1, 2. —*Ant.* satisfied*, pleased, content.
2. [Beaten]—*Syn.* vanquished, defeated, worsted; see **beaten** 1.

disappointing, *mod.* —*Syn.* unsatisfactory, ineffective, uninteresting, discouraging, unpleasant, inferior, unlooked for, lame, insufficient, failing, at fault, limited, second-rate, mediocre, ordinary, unexpected, unhappy, depressing, disconcerting, disagreeable, irritating, annoying, troublesome, disheartening, unlucky, uncomfortable, bitter, distasteful, disgusting, deplorable, short of expectations; see also **inadequate** 1.—*Ant.* pleasing*, encouraging, satisfactory.

disappointment, *n.* **1.** [The state of being disappointed]—*Syn.* dissatisfaction, unfulfillment, frustration, chagrin, thwarted expectation(s), miscarriage of plan(s), lack of success, despondency, displeasure, distress, hope deferred, discouragement, ill luck, disillusionment, foiling, nonsuccess, mortification, vain expectation, check, bafflement, disillusion, abortion, balk, setback, discontent, blighted hope, adverse fate, adversity, the knocks (D), hard fortune, ill hap; see also **defeat** 3, **failure** 1, **regret** 1.—*Ant.* success*, fulfillment, realization.
2. [A person *or* thing that disappoints]—*Syn.* balking, miscarriage, misfortune, mischance, calamity, blunder, inefficacy, setback, downfall, slip, defeat, impasse, mishap, error, mistake, discouragement, obstacle, slip 'twixt the cup and the lip, faux pas, cold comfort, labor in vain, miscalculation, shipwreck, fiasco, something that disappoints; *all* (D): no go, blind alley, fizzle, frost, washout, lemon, dud, flash in the pan, letdown, bust, bungle, false alarm; see also sense 1; **failure** 2.—*Ant.* achievement*, successful venture, success.

disapproval, *n.* **1.** [A disapproving attitude]—*Syn.* dissatisfaction, discontent, displeasure; see **objection** 1.
2. [An adverse expression]—*Syn.* criticism, censure, disparagement; see **objection** 2.

disapprove, *v.* **1.** [To condemn]—*Syn.* blame, chastise, reprove; see **censure, denounce.**
2. [To reject]—*Syn.* spurn, disallow, set aside; see **oppose** 1, **refuse.**

disapprove of, *v.* —*Syn.* object to, dislike, deplore; see **complain** 1, **oppose** 1.

disarm, *v.* **1.** [To deprive of weapons]—*Syn.* demobilize, disable, unarm, weaken, debilitate, render powerless, disqualify, incapacitate, invalidate, deaden, muzzle, deprive of weapons *or* means of defense, put out of combat, conciliate, subdue, bare, strip; *all* (D): tie the hands, draw the teeth of, clip the wings of, spike one's guns; see also **disband, defeat** 1, 3.—*Ant.* arm*, outfit, equip.
2. [To reduce national armaments]—*Syn.* deprive of power, demilitarize, render powerless, subjugate, occupy, deescalate, pacify, neutralize, internationalize, remove *or* prevent nuclear competence; see also **weaken** 2.—*Ant.* arm*, mobilize, prepare.
3. [To persuade]—*Syn.* win over, seduce, coax; see **convince, urge** 2.

disarmament, *n.* —*Syn.* reduction of the armaments of, demobilization, disablement, disabling, disqualification, disqualifying, crippling, unilateral *or* multilateral disarmament, incapacitating, rendering powerless, reduction to order, arms reduction, paralyzing, pacification, laying aside of arms, de-escalation, demilitarization, nuclear freeze, subjugation, occupation, conquest, neutralizing, beating swords into plowshares (D).—*Ant.* training*, armament, escalation.

disarming, *mod.* —*Syn.* convincing, seductive, inveigling; see **persuasive.**

disarray, *n.* —*Syn.* disorder, chaos, upset; see **confusion** 2.

disassemble, *v.* —*Syn.* take apart, knock down, strike (D); see **dismantle.**

disaster, *n.* —*Syn.* accident, calamity, mishap, debacle, casualty, mischance, emergency, adversity, harm, misadventure, collapse, slip, fall, collision, crash, hazard, crash landing, setback, defeat, sinking, flood, failure, holocaust, affliction, fell stroke, woe, trouble, scourge, depression, grief, bale, undoing, overthrow, ill luck, ruination, bane, fiasco, curse, tragedy, blight, visitation, contretemps, exigency, infliction, cataclysm, extremity, downfall, evil *or* rainy day, (crushing) reverse, great mishap, terrible accident, gathering clouds, sudden misfortune, adverse happening, bankruptcy, upset, blast, blow, blaze, wreck, bad luck; *all* (D): comedown, crack-up, sideswipe, roll-over, pile-up, smash-up, washout, flop, bust, hard luck, head-on; see also **catastrophe, misfortune** 1.

disastrous, *mod.* —*Syn.* calamitous, ruinous, unfortunate; see **harmful, unfavorable** 2.

disavow, *v.* —*Syn.* disclaim, disown, repudiate; see **deny** 1, **refuse** 1.

disband, *v.* —*Syn.* scatter, disperse, demobilize, disarm, break up, call off, dismiss, send home, go home, disorganize, muster out; see also **leave** 1.

disbelief, *n.* —*Syn.* unbelief, skepticism, mistrust; see **doubt** 1.

disbeliever, *n.* —*Syn.* doubter, questioner, agnostic; see **critic** 1, **skeptic.**

disburse, *v.* —*Syn.* expend, use, contribute; see **pay** 1, **spend** 1.

disbursement, *n.* —*Syn.* expenditure, spending, outlay; see **expense** 1, **payment** 1.

disbursements, *n.* —*Syn.* expenditures, outgoings, operating expenses; see **expense** 1.

discard, *v.* —*Syn.* reject, expel, repudiate, protest, cast aside *or* away *or* out *or* off, throw away *or* off *or* aside *or* overboard *or* out, lay *or* thrust off *or* away *or* aside, put by, get rid of, give up, shuffle off, slough, renounce, supersede, have done with, make away with, drop all idea of, dismantle, discharge, write off, banish, eject, divorce, dispossess, dispense with, toss aside *or* away *or* off *or* out *or* back, shake off, pass up, free oneself from, free of, root out, get quit of, deliver oneself from, give away, part with, file off, dispose of, do away with, dispense with, shed, dismiss from use, abjure, jettison, relinquish, repeal, thrust *or* cast *or* lay aside, dispatch, shovel out, sweep away, cancel, abandon, forsake, desert, lay on the shelf, cut, have nothing to do with, brush away, deal with; *all* (D): scotch, chuck, heave *or* toss overboard, drop, wash one's hands of, junk; see also **abandon** 1, **dismiss** 1.—*Ant.* save*, retain, preserve.

discarded, *mod.* —*Syn.* rejected, repudiated, cast off, thrown away, dismantled, dismissed, useless, damaged, outworn, worn out, done with, run down, not worth saving, superannuated, superseded, abandoned, obsolete, shelved, neglected, deserted, forsaken, outmoded, out of date, out of style *or* fashion, old-fashioned, archaic; *all* (D): junked, old hat, ancient.—*Ant.* kept*, worthwhile, modern.

discern, *v.* **1.** [To descry]—*Syn.* behold, make out, perceive; see **see** 1.
2. [To detect]—*Syn.* find out, determine, discriminate; see **discover** 1.

discernible, *mod.* —*Syn.* perceptible, perceivable, observable; see **audible, obvious** 1.

discerning, *mod.* —*Syn.* discriminating, perceptive, penetrating; see **judicious.**

discernment, *n.* —*Syn.* perception, judgment, insight; see **acumen.**

discharge, *v.* **1.** [To unload]—*Syn.* unpack, release, remove cargo; see **empty** 1, 2, **unload.**
2. [To remove]—*Syn.* take off, send, carry *or* take away; see **remove** 1.
3. [To emit]—*Syn.* send forth, give off, exude; see **emit** 1.
4. [To cause to fire]—*Syn.* blast, shoot off, fire; see **shoot** 1.
5. [To dismiss]—*Syn.* let go, replace, relieve; see **dismiss** 2.
6. [To release]—*Syn.* emancipate, liberate, let go; set **free** 1, **release.**
7. [To perform]—*Syn.* fulfill, execute, accomplish; see **achieve** 1, **perform** 1.
8. [To pay a debt]—*Syn.* liquidate, settle, satisfy; see **pay** 1.
9. [To annul]—*Syn.* cancel, invalidate, render void; see **cancel** 2.

discharged, *mod.* **1.** [Dismissed]—*Syn.* mustered out, sent home, dishonorably discharged, honorably released, recalled, freed, liberated, released, let go, sent away, delivered, emancipated, expelled, ejected, dismissed, laid-off, fired, ousted; *all* (D): canned, scrapped, sacked, axed, given the gate, given the old heave-ho; see also **free** 2, 3.
2. [Fulfilled]—*Syn.* achieved, performed, accomplished; see **done** 2, **fulfilled.**
3. [Fired]—*Syn.* exploded, set off, shot; see **fired** 1.

disciple, *n.* **1.** [A follower]—*Syn.* adherent, pupil, believer; see **follower.**
2. [A follower of Christ; *usually capitalized*] —*Syn.* apostle, witness, chosen witness, revealer; *both* (D): revelator, seer. Christ's disciples mentioned in the New Testament include—Matthew, Bartholomew *or* Nathaniel, John, Peter, James, Philip, Andrew, Thaddaeus, Thomas, Judas Iscariot, James the son of Alphaeus, Simon the Canaanean; other figures called Apostles include—Paul and Matthias.

disciplinarian, *n.* —*Syn.* trainer, sergeant, tyrant, despot, advocate of strict discipline, formalist, taskmaster, bully, stickler, hard master, enforcer (of discipline), drill sergeant, one who maintains discipline; see also **dictator, teacher** 1.

discipline, *n.* **1.** [Mental self-training]—*Syn.* preparation, development, exercise, drilling, inculcation, training, regulation, self-disciplining; see also **drill** 3, **education** 1.
2. [A system of obedience]—*Syn.* conduct, regulation, drill, orderliness, restraint, limitation, curb, subordination to rules of conduct, indoctrination, brainwashing; see also **training.**

discipline, *v.* **1.** [To regulate]—*Syn.* train, control, drill; see **teach** 2.
2. [To punish]—*Syn.* chastise, correct, limit; see **punish.**

disc jockey, *n.* —*Syn.* radio announcer, commentator, DJ (D); see **announcer, reporter.**

disclaim, *v.* **1.** [To deny]—*Syn.* repudiate, negate, contradict; see **deny, refuse** 1.
2. [To disown]—*Syn.* revoke, retract, reject; see **discard.**

disclose, *v.* **1.** [To expose]—*Syn.* lay bare, uncover, unveil; see **expose** 1.
2. [To divulge]—*Syn.* make known, confess, publish; see **reveal** 1.

disclosure, *n.* **1.** [The act or process of disclosing] —*Syn.* revealing, divulgence, enlightenment; see **exposure** 1.
2. [That which is disclosed]—*Syn.* exposé, acknowledgment, confession; see **admission** 4, **declaration** 1, **revelation** 1.

discolor, *v.* —*Syn.* stain, rust, tarnish; see **color** 1, **dirty.**

discoloration, *n.* —*Syn.* blot, blotch, splotch; see **blemish, stain.**

discomfit, *v.* **1.** [To defeat the plans of]—*Syn.* thwart, frustrate, foil; see **prevent.**
2. [To confuse]—*Syn.* disconcert, embarrass, perplex; see **confuse.**

discomfiture, *n.* **1.** [Frustration]—*Syn.* conquest, disappointment, beating; see **defeat** 3.
2. [Embarrassment]—*Syn.* chagrin, confusion, humiliation; see **embarrassment** 1.

discomfort, *n.* —*Syn.* trouble, displeasure, uneasiness; see **annoyance** 1, **embarrassment** 1.

discommode, *v.* —*Syn.* inconvenience, annoy, molest; see **disturb** 2.

discompose, *v.* —*Syn.* perturb, upset, ruffle; see **bother** 2, **embarrass** 1.

discomposure, *n.* —*Syn.* disturbance, agitation, annoyance; see **confusion** 2.

disconcert, *v.* —*Syn.* perturb, trouble, perplex; see **confuse, disturb** 2.

disconnect, *v.* —*Syn.* separate, detach, disengage; see **cut** 1, **divide** 1.

disconnected, *mod.* **1.** [Incoherent]—*Syn.* disjointed, loose, irregular; see **incongruous** 1.
2. [Separated]—*Syn.* broken off, detached, switched off; see **separated.**

disconnection, *n.* **1.** [Separation]—*Syn.* parting, disunion, cleavage; see **division** 1.
2. [Break]—*Syn.* intrusion, disruption, cessation; see **interference** 1, **interruption.**

disconsolate, *mod.* **1.** [Dejected]—*Syn.* inconsolable, hopeless, melancholy; see **sad** 1.
2. [Dismal]—*Syn.* cheerless, gloomy, dreary, dark; see **dismal** 1.

discontent, *n.* —*Syn.* envy, uneasiness, depression; see **dissatisfaction** 1, **regret** 1.

discontented, *mod.* —*Syn.* unhappy, disgruntled, malcontented; see **sad** 1.

discontinue, *v.* —*Syn.* finish, close, cease; see **end** 1, **stop** 2.

discontinued, *mod.* —*Syn.* ended, terminated, given up *or* over; see **abandoned** 1.

discontinuous, *mod.* —*Syn.* spasmodic, broken, disconnected; see **intermittent, irregular** 1.

discord, *n.* **1.** [Conflict]—*Syn.* strife, contention, dissension; see **disagreement** 1.

2. [Noise]—*Syn.* din, tumult, racket; see **noise** 2.

discordant, *mod.* **1.** [Inharmonious]—*Syn.* grating, dissonant, cacophonous; see **harsh** 1.

2. [Disagreeing]—*Syn.* clashing, at odds, out of accord; see **quarreling.**

discount, *n.* —*Syn.* deduction, allowance, rebate, decrease, markdown, abatement, concession, percentage, salvage, premium, diminution, subtraction, commission, exemption, modification, qualification, drawback, tare, tare and tret, depreciation; *all* (D): cut, something off, rake-off, payola, cut rate; see also **interest** 3, **reduction** 1.—*Ant.* increase*, markup, surcharge.

at a discount—*Syn.* discounted, cheap, depreciated; see **reduced** 2.

discount, *v.* **1.** [To deduct]—*Syn.* reduce, remove, redeem, diminish, depreciate, deduct from, lower, make allowance (for), allow, take from *or* off, charge *or* strike off, rebate, abate, modify, mark down, mark the tare of, anticipate, discredit, rake off (D); see also **decrease** 2.—*Ant.* raise*, mark up, advance.

2. [To disregard]—*Syn.* question, disbelieve, mistrust; see **disregard, doubt** 2.

discountenance, *v.* —*Syn.* dispute, reject, resist; see **discourage** 1, **oppose** 1.

discount rate, *n.* —*Syn.* (advance) interest, deduction, charge; see **interest** 3.

discourage, *v.* **1.** [To dishearten]—*Syn.* repress, appall, dispirit, intimidate, deprive of courage, lessen the self-confidence of, depress in spirits, break one's heart, deject, prostrate, unnerve, damp the courage, scare, confuse, dampen, dismay, daunt, overawe, bully, cast down, demoralize, unman; *all* (D): throw a wet blanket on, throw cold water on, beat off *or* down, cast gloom upon, dampen the spirits, dash one's hopes; see also **depress** 2, **frighten** 1.—*Ant.* encourage*, cheer, inspire.

2. [To warn]—*Syn.* dissuade, alarm, deprecate; see **warn** 1.

3. [To restrain]—*Syn.* obstruct, impede, check, quiet, interfere with, withhold, keep back, inhibit, dissuade, curb, deter, control, turn aside, hold back *or* off, repress; see also **restrain** 1.—*Ant.* help*, expedite, facilitate.

discouraged, *mod.* —*Syn.* downcast, pessimistic, depressed; see **sad** 1.

discouragement, *n.* **1.** [Dejection]—*Syn.* melancholy, despair, the blues (D); see **depression** 2, **sadness.**

2. [A restriction]—*Syn.* constraint, hindrance, deterrent; see **impediment** 1.

discouraging, *mod.* **1.** [Acting to discourage one] —*Syn.* depressing, disheartening, repressing; see **dismal** 1.

2. [Suggesting an unwelcome future]—*Syn.* inopportune, disadvantageous, dissuading; see **unfavorable** 2.

discourse, *n.* —*Syn.* dialogue, talk, chat; see **conversation, discussion** 1, **speech** 2.

discourse, *v.* —*Syn.* treat, converse, lecture; see **discuss, talk** 1.

discourteous, *mod.* —*Syn.* boorish, crude, impolite; see **rude** 2.

discourtesy, *n.* —*Syn.* impudence, impoliteness, vulgarity; see **rudeness.**

discover, *v.* **1.** [To find]—*Syn.* invent, find out, ascertain, detect, discern, descry, recognize, distinguish, determine, observe, contrive, explore, find out once and for all, hear of *or* about, open one's eyes, awake to, collect knowledge, bring to light, uncover, ferret *or* root *or* trace out, elicit, unearth, look up, come on *or* upon, run across, fall *or* strike *or* light upon, think of, perceive, glimpse, identify, devise, disinter, catch, spot, create, make out, dissect, evolve, sense, feel, sight, smell, hear, spy, bring out, find a clue, catch a glimpse of; *all* (D): get wise to, dig out *or* up, turn up, smell *or* sniff out, come up with, hit *or* happen upon, smell a rat, nose out, break through, fish up, smell something in the wind, get wind of, fall in with, get one's hands on, catch at *or* up, hit upon, nose out, lay one's fingers on, run down, put *or* lay one's hands on; see also **find** 1, **learn** 1.—*Ant.* miss*, pass by, omit.

2. [To make known]—*Syn.* disclose, expose, unearth; see **reveal** 1.

discovered, *mod.* —*Syn.* found, searched out, come on, happened on *or* upon, unearthed, ascertained, descried, unlocked, espied, detected, disinterred, revealed, disclosed, unveiled, observed, sighted, shown, exposed, traced out, elicited, made out, met with, come across, lighted *or* stumbled upon, recognized, identified, empirical, laid bare, opened, presented, spotted, perceived, learned; see also **observed** 1, **real** 2.—*Ant.* hidden*, unfound, lost.

discovery, *n.* **1.** [The act of finding the unknown] —*Syn.* invention, detection, uncovering, exploration, unearthing, identification, discernment, distinguishing, sensing, distinction, determination, calculation, experimentation, empiricism, feeling, hearing, sighting, spying, espial, descrial, strike, ascertainment, finding, hitting, learning, striking, disinterring; see also **examination** 1.

2. [Something discovered]—*Syn.* results, findings, formula, device, find, contrivance, design, machine, invention, process, breakthrough, data, principle, law, theorem, algorithm, innovation, conclusion, method, way; see also **result.**

3. [The act of making known]—*Syn.* disclosure, unfolding, showing; see **exposure** 1, **revelation** 1.

discredit, *n.* —*Syn.* censure, reproach, disrepute; see **blame** 1.

discredit, *v.* **1.** [To bring into disrepute]—*Syn.* disesteem, reproach, frown upon; see **censure.**

2. [To doubt]—*Syn.* question, disbelieve, distrust; see **doubt** 2.

discreet, *mod.* —*Syn.* cautious, prudent, discerning, discriminating, observant of decencies, not rash, wise in avoiding mistakes, strategic, noncommittal, precautious, sagacious, heedful, vigilant, civil, sensible, reserved, alert, awake, chary, wary, watchful, wise, circumspect, attentive, considerate, having foresight, intelligent, guarded, politic, diplomatic;

all (D): not born yesterday, tight-lipped, cagey, swift, worldly-wise; see also **careful, judicious, polite** 1, **thoughtful** 2.—*Ant.* rash*, indiscreet, imprudent.

discrepancy, *n.* **1.** [Inconsistency]—*Syn.* variance, contrariety, disparity; see **difference** 2.
2. [An error]—*Syn.* miscalculation, mistake, flaw; see **error** 1.

discretion, *n.* **1.** [Cautious or prudent conduct] —*Syn.* caution, foresight, mature responsibility *or* judgment, circumspection, carefulness, wariness, sound judgment, thoughtfulness, attention, heed, concern, consideration, considerateness, observation, watchfulness, precaution, good sense, providence, judiciousness, maturity, discernment, solicitude, forethought, calculation, deliberation, vigilance, discrimination, responsibility, sagacity, warning, presence of mind; see also **care** 1, **prudence, tact.**—*Ant.* carelessness*, thoughtlessness, rashness.
2. [Sagacity]—*Syn.* shrewdness, perspicacity, good sense; see **judgment** 1.
at one's discretion—*Syn.* as one wishes, whenever appropriate, discreetly; see **appropriately.**

discretionary, *mod.* —*Syn.* optional, left to discretion, discretional; see **changeable** 1, 2, **optional.**

discriminate, *v.* **1.** [To differentiate]—*Syn.* specify, separate, tell apart; see **distinguish** 1.
2. [To be (racially) prejudiced]—*Syn.* be a bigot, set apart, segregate; see also **hate** 1, **separate** 2.

discriminating, *mod.* **1.** [Discerning]—*Syn.* particular, astute, acute; see **judicious.**
2. [Differentiating]—*Syn.* distinctive, distinguishing, individualizing; see **characteristic.**
3. [Particular]—*Syn.* fastidious, finicky, fussy; see **careful.**

discrimination, *n.* **1.** [The power to make distinctions]—*Syn.* perception, acuteness, understanding; see **acumen.**
2. [The act of drawing a distinction]—*Syn.* separation, differentiation, difference; see **distinction** 1.
3. [Partiality]—*Syn.* unfairness, bias, bigotry; see **hatred** 2, **prejudice.**

discriminative, *mod.* —*Syn.* discriminating, discerning, distinguishing; see **judicious.**

discursive, *mod.* —*Syn.* rambling, desultory, digressive; see **verbose.**

discus, *n.* —*Syn.* plate, quoit, squail; see **circle** 1, **disk.**

discuss, *v.* —*Syn.* argue, debate, dispute, talk of *or* about, explain, contest, confer, deal *or* advise *or* reason with, exchange observations, come to a point, take up, look over, consider, talk over *or* out, take up in conference, engage in conversation, go into, think over, telephone about, have a conference on *or* upon, take into consideration *or* account, discourse on *or* with, reason *or* discourse about, contend, wrangle, argue for and against, canvass, consider, handle, present, review, recite, ventilate, examine by argument, plead, treat *or* speak of, converse, present varied opinions, parley, discourse, altercate, ratiocinate, take under advisement, interchange views, comment upon, have out, speak on; *all* (D): kick about *or* around, toss *or* bat around, have a bull session, chew the fat, jaw, air out, hold forth, confabulate, knock around, go into a huddle, put heads together, compare notes, chew the rag, rap; see also **talk** 1.—*Ant.* delay*, table, postpone.

discussed, *mod.* —*Syn.* talked over, debated, argued; see **considered** 1.

discussion, *n.* **1.** [The act of considering in words] —*Syn.* conversation, exchange, consultation, interview, deliberation, argumentation, contention, confabulation, (meaningful) dialogue, talk, excursus, conference, wrangling, argument(s), dialogue, disputation, (round-table) debate, panel discussion, forensics, summit meeting, dealing with the agenda, consideration, controversy, altercation, review, reasons, dialogism, critical argumentation, dispute, canvass, dissertation, symposium, quarrel, pros and cons, disquisition; *all* (D): powwow, gabfest, wrangle, bull (*or* rap) session, confab; see also **conversation, dispute** 1.—*Ant.* agreement*, decision, conclusion.
2. [A published consideration]—*Syn.* analysis, criticism, examination, forum, study, investigation, determination, inquiry, dissertation, treatment, proposal; see also **exposition** 2, **thesis** 2, **writing** 2.

disdain, *n.* —*Syn.* scorn, haughtiness, contempt; see **arrogance, hatred** 2.

disdain, *v.* —*Syn.* reject, scorn, ignore; see **hate** 1, **refuse.**

disdainful, *mod.* —*Syn.* aloof, proud, arrogant; see **egotistic** 2, **indifferent** 1.

disease, *n.* **1.** [A bodily infirmity]—*Syn.* sickness, malady, illness, indisposition, unhealthiness, disorder, ailment, spell, condition, complaint, distemper, unsoundness, affection, visitation, morbidity, pathological case, psychosomatic illness, epidemic, plague; see also **illness** 1.—*Ant.* health*, strength, vigor.
2. [Loosely used term for any ailment]—*Syn.* (patient's) condition, defect, infirmity, collapse, complaint, breakdown, (nervous *or* functional) disorder, temperature, fever, infection, attack, contusion, stroke, fit, seizure, convulsions, congestion, inflammation, fracture, lesion, adhesion, hemorrhage, flux, atrophy, cramps, ache, collapse; see also **pain** 1, 2.
Specific diseases include the following—diseases affecting various organs or the body generally: cancer, ulcer, shock, paresis, paralysis, focal infection, atrophy, psittacosis, streptococcal infection, staphyloccic infection, chicken pox, cholera, diphtheria, malaria, chills and fever, (German) measles, mumps, Rocky Mountain spotted fever, Legionnaires' disease, rabies, scarlet fever, scarlatina, smallpox, tuberculosis, toxic-shock syndrome, tularemia, typhoid fever, typhus, leprosy, yellow fever; venereal or social diseases: gonorrhea *or both* (D): clap, dose; herpes, AIDS, syphilis *or all* (D): French disease, *maladie anglaise* (French), English disease, pox; brain and nervous system: encephalitis *or* sleeping sickness, meningitis, aphasia, Alzheimer's disease, hemiplegia, Reye's syndrome, brain tumor, poliomyelitis *or* polio *or* infantile paralysis, sclerosis, multiple sclerosis *or* MS (D), delirium tremens *or* D.T.'s (D); diseases affecting the respiratory organs and passages: bronchitis, rhinitis *or* common cold *or* sniffles (D), cough, influenza *or* flu, Asian flu, laryngitis, pleurisy, (viral *or* pulmo-

nary) pneumonia, phthisis, tonsillitis, emphysema, streptococcal infection *or* strep (D), sinusitis, croup, tuberculosis *or* TB (D), whooping cough; diseases affecting the digestive system: acidosis, appendicitis, Bright's disease, colitis, diabetes, diarrhea, constipation, dysentery, anasarca *or* dropsy, gravel, jaundice; diseases affecting the circulatory system: angina pectoris, high blood pressure, cystic fibrosis, hemorrhage, hardening of the arteries, hypertension, (heart) murmur, palpitations, arteriosclerosis, leakage of the heart, coronary thrombosis; skin diseases: athlete's foot, boils, eczema, psoriasis, erysipelas, dermatitis, scabies, ringworm, trench foot, seven year itch, acne; diseases of the joints and muscles: arthritis, bends, cramp *or both* (D): charley horse, crick; rheumatism, lumbago, a sacroiliac strain; diseases of the eye: cataracts, glaucoma, pink eye, trachoma; allergies or psychosomatic diseases: migraine, hay fever, rose fever, asthma, hives; allergy to dust *or* wheat *or* feathers *or* pollen, etc.; glandular diseases: hyperthyroidism, hypothyroidism, progeria, hyperpituitarism, hypopituitarism, etc.; diseased membranes: rupture, hernia, adhesion; diseases common to animals and birds: anthrax, black leg, blind staggers, bloat, cholera, colic, distemper, encephalitis, hydrophobia *or* rabies, heaves, hoof and mouth disease, glanders, milk sickness, pneumonitis, roup, spavin, trichomoniasis; diseases common to plants: blight, rot, rust, scale, smut, wilt; see also **complex** 1, **insanity** 1.

diseased, *mod.* —*Syn.* unhealthy, unsound, ailing; see **sick.**

disembark, *v.* —*Syn.* arrive, debark, anchor; see **land** 3.

disembodied, *mod.* —*Syn.* incorporeal, bodiless, disincarnate; see **immaterial** 2.

disembowel, *v.* —*Syn.* eviscerate, gut, embowel; see **kill** 1.

disenchant, *v.* —*Syn.* disenthrall, embitter, disentrance; see **disillusion.**

disengage, *v.* —*Syn.* loose, undo, disentangle; see **free** 1, 2, **release.**

disengaged, *mod.* —*Syn.* detached, unattached, disjoined; see **separated.**

disengagement, *n.* **1.** [Rest]—*Syn.* pause, leisure, relaxation; see **ease** 1, **rest** 1.

2. [Detachment]—*Syn.* severance, withdrawal, partition; see **division** 1, **separation** 1.

disentangle, *v.* —*Syn.* disengage, untangle, untwist; see **free** 2.

disfavor, *n.* **1.** [Dissatisfaction]—*Syn.* displeasure, disapproval, disrespect; see **dissatisfaction** 1.

2. [Disgrace]—*Syn.* disrepute, disregard, dishonor; see **disgrace** 1.

disfigure, *v.* —*Syn.* deface, mar, mutilate; see **damage** 1, **distort** 3, **hurt** 1.

disgorge, *v.* —*Syn.* eject, throw up, spew; see **vomit.**

disgrace, *n.* **1.** [A shameful condition]—*Syn.* dishonor, humiliation, reproach, discredit, odium, degradation, opprobrium, disrepute, disfavor, scorn, derision, abuse, obloquy, abasement, infamy, ignominy, disrespect, corruption, meanness, contumely, venality, prostitution, ill repute, scandal, disesteem, humbling, ingloriousness, contempt, disbarment, unfrocking, dishonorable discharge; see also **shame** 2.—*Ant.* honor*, esteem, dignity.

2. [Whatever lowers one in the eyes of one's fellows]—*Syn.* scandal, shame, stain, slur, slight, stigma, brand, spot, slander, blur, culpability, dishonor, ignominy, infamy, reproach, disrepute, humiliation, degradation, turpitude, taint, tarnish, pollution; *all* (D): mark of Cain, scarlet A, scarlet letter; see also **insult** 1.—*Ant.* pride*, praise, credit.

disgrace, *v.* —*Syn.* debase, shame, degrade, abase, dishonor, disparage, discredit, deride, disregard, strip of honors, dismiss from favor, disrespect, mock, humble, depress, reduce, put to shame, throw dishonor upon, tarnish, stain, besmirch, blot, sully, taint, defile, expel, stigmatize, bring into discredit, cast a slur upon, brand, post; *all* (D): drag through the mire, tar and feather, condemn to the stocks, bring low, heap dirt upon, put down, snub, derogate, belittle, take down a peg; see also **humiliate, lower, ridicule, slander.**—*Ant.* praise*, honor, exalt.

disgraced, *mod.* —*Syn.* discredited, in disgrace, dishonored, degraded, demoted, shamed, overcome, downtrodden, humiliated, in disfavor, in disrepute, discharged, exposed, in bad repute, mocked, abject; *all* (D): down and out, shown up, in Dutch, fallen from one's high estate, tarred and feathered, put down, out on one's ear.—*Ant.* honored*, restored, in favor.

disgraceful, *mod.* —*Syn.* dishonorable, disreputable, shocking; see **offensive** 2, **shameful** 1, 2.

disgruntled, *mod.* —*Syn.* grumpy, discontented, displeased; see **disappointed** 1, **irritable, sad** 1.

disguise, *n.* —*Syn.* mask, deceptive covering, make-up, faking, (false) front, deception, (smoke) screen, blind, concealment, counterfeit, pseudonym, dress, guise, costume, masquerade, veil, cover, façade, pen name, nom de plume, put-on (D); see also **camouflage** 1.

disguise, *v.* —*Syn.* mask, conceal, dissemble, camouflage, pretend, screen, cloak, shroud, cover, veil, alter, obscure, feign, dissimulate, counterfeit, varnish, age, antique, redo, make up, simulate, muffle, alter the appearance of, make unrecognizable, employ plastic surgery; both (D): dress *or* touch *or* doctor *or* phoney up, run a band on; see also **change** 1, **deceive, hide** 1, 2.—*Ant.* reveal*, open, strip.

disguised, *mod.* —*Syn.* cloaked, masked, camouflaged; see **changed** 2, 3, **covered** 1, **hidden** 2.

disgust, *n.* —*Syn.* loathing, abhorrence, aversion; see **hatred** 1, **objection** 1.

disgust, *v.* —*Syn.* repel, revolt, offend, displease, nauseate, sicken, make one sick, fill with loathing, cause aversion, offend the morals of, be repulsive, cause nausea in, irk, pique, scandalize, shock, upset, pall, disenchant; *both* (D): turn one's stomach, give one a bellyful; see also **bother** 3, **disturb** 2, **insult.**

disgusted, *mod.* —*Syn.* overwrought, offended, sickened, displeased, repelled, unhappy, revolted, abhorred, appalled, outraged; *all* (D): had a bellyful, fed up, had it, had enough; see also **insulted, shocked.**

disgusted with (someone *or* something), *mod.* —*Syn.* displeased with, appalled by, unhappy with, repelled by; *all* (D): sick of, fed up with, had enough of, full up to here with; see also **insulted, shocked.**

disgusting, *mod.* —*Syn.* repugnant, revolting, sickening; see **offensive** 2.

dish, *n.* **1.** [Plate]—*Syn.* vessel, pottery, ceramic; see also **china, plate** 4.
Table dishes include the following—dinner plate, luncheon plate, salad plate, bread-and-butter plate, platter, casserole, cake plate, (breakfast) coffee cup, coffee mug, after-dinner coffee cup, espresso cup, demitasse, teacup, chocolate cup, egg cup, bouillon cup, custard cup, saucer, child's mug, Tom-and-Jerry mug, beer mug, cereal bowl, soup bowl *or* plate, gravy bowl *or* boat, vegetable dish, open dish, covered dish, olive dish, celery dish, conserve dish, relish tray, cruet, teapot, coffeepot, chocolate pot, cream pitcher, water pitcher, lemonade pitcher, sugar bowl, butter dish, salt cellar, pepper cellar, individual salt dish, *presentoir* (French); see also **bowl, container, cup, pottery.**
2. [Meal]—*Syn.* course, serving, helping; see **meal** 2.
3. [(D) A good-looking female]—*Syn.* beauty; *both* (D): doll, cutie; see **girl** 1, **woman** 1.

dishearten, *v.* —*Syn.* dampen, dismay, put down (D); see **depress** 2, **discourage** 1, **humble, humiliate.**

disheveled, *mod.* —*Syn.* rumpled, untidy, unkempt; see **dirty** 1, **disordered.**

dish of tea (D), *n.* —*Syn.* preference, customary *or* usual thing, selection; see **favorite, preference.**

dishonest, *mod.* **1.** [Knavish]—*Syn.* deceiving, fraudulent, double-dealing, backbiting, treacherous, deceitful, cunning, sneaky, tricky, wily, crooked, deceptive, misleading, bluffing, elusive, slippery, unctuous, shady, pettifogging, swindling, cheating, sneaking, recreant, roguish, traitorous, villainous, sinister, lying, mendacious, untruthful, perfidous, hoodwinking, underhanded; *all* (D): two-timing, two-faced, scrounging, double-crossing, on the shady side, gossipy; see also **corrupt** 3, **false** 1, **mean** 3.—*Ant.* fair*, just, reasonable.
2. [Lacking integrity]—*Syn.* unprincipled, shiftless, unscrupulous, undependable, disreputable, questionable, dishonorable, false-hearted, counterfeit, infamous, corrupt, immoral, discredited, ignoble, inglorious, unworthy, degraded, shabby, mean, low, venial, self-serving, contemptible, canting, corruptible; *all* (D): rotten, dirty, fishy, crooked, fork-tongued; see also sense 1; **false** 1, **hypocritical.** —*Ant.* honest*, irreproachable, scrupulous.

dishonesty, *n.* —*Syn.* infamy, infidelity, faithlessness, falsity, falsehood, deceit, trickery, craft, artifice, duplicity, wiliness, untrustworthiness, insidiousness, cunning, guile, perfidiousness, slyness, perfidy, double-dealing, craftiness, astuteness, trickiness, treachery, knavishness, knavery, cant, crookedness, corruption, mythomania, cheating, subtlety, stealing, lying, swindle, fraud, chicanery, rascality, mendacity, cleverness, artfulness, subtleness, fraudulence, embezzlement, counterfeit, forgery, perjury, treason, false pretension(s), false swearing; *all* (D): flimflam, hocus-pocus, hanky-panky, skulduggery, bunk, boondoggle; see also **deception** 1, **hypocrisy** 2, **lie** 1.—*Ant.* honesty*, virtue, integrity.

dishonor, *n.* **1.** [Disgrace]—*Syn.* shame, ignominy, abasement; see **disgrace** 2.
2. [Discredit]—*Syn.* insult, indignity, reproach; see **blame** 1, **insult.**

dishonorable, *mod.* —*Syn.* infamous, disgraceful, ignoble; see **offensive** 2, **shameful** 2.

dish out, *v.* —*Syn.* give *or* hand out, serve (up), deliver; see **distribute** 1, **give** 1.

dish towel, *n.* —*Syn.* tea towel, kitchen towel, drying towel; see **towel.**

disillusion, *v.* —*Syn.* disenchant, disenthrall, shatter one's illusions, free from illusion, disabuse, free of, embitter; *all* (D): let down easy, open one's eyes, take the ground from under, burst the bubble, knock the props from under, bring down to earth, bring down, let the air out of, send one's air castles tumbling, show the feet of clay; see also **disappoint.**

disinclination, *n.* —*Syn.* reluctance, repugnance, dislike; see **hatred** 1.

disinclined, *mod.* —*Syn.* unwilling, balking, hesitant; see **doubtful** 2, **reluctant, slow** 2.

disinfect, *v.* —*Syn.* purify, fumigate, use disinfectant upon; see **clean.**

disingenuous, *mod.* —*Syn.* insincere, artful, deceitful; see **dishonest** 1, **sly** 1.

disinherit, *v.* —*Syn.* exclude from inheritance, disown, cut off, exheridate, evict, deprive of hereditary succession, divest, disaffiliate, cut off without a penny, oust, prevent from coming into possession of any property, dispossess of hereditary right; see also **dismiss** 1, **neglect** 2.

disintegrate, *v.* **1.** [To break up]—*Syn.* break down, separate, atomize, divide, dismantle, break into pieces, disunite, disperse, crumble, disband, take apart, disorganize, detach, break *or* come *or* fall apart, sever, disconnect, wash out *or* away; *all* (D): fall to pieces, turn to dust, fade away, reduce to ashes; see also **dissolve** 1.—*Ant.* unite*, put together, combine.
2. [To decay]—*Syn.* crumble, rot, wither; see **decay, destroy** 1.

disinter, *v.* —*Syn.* unearth, dig up, disentomb; see **exhume, expose** 1.

disinterested, *mod.* —*Syn.* impartial, not involved, unconcerned; see **indifferent** 1.

disjoin, *v.* —*Syn.* separate, detach, disunite; see **divide** 1.

disjoint, *v.* —*Syn.* dismember, cut up, carve; see **cut** 1, **divide** 1, **separate** 2.

disjointed, *mod.* —*Syn.* disconnected, divided, unattached; see **separated.**

disk, *n.* —*Syn.* disc, plate, platter, discoid *or* discoidal *or* circular object *or* surface, dish, saucer, discus, quoit, flan, sabot, phonograph record, concave *or* convex disk, shell; see also **circle** 1.

dislike, *n.* —*Syn.* opposition, offense, distaste; see **blame** 1, **hate, hatred** 1, 2, **objection** 1.

dislike, *v.* —*Syn.* detest, condemn, deplore, regret, lose interest in, speak down to, have hard feelings toward, not take kindly to, not be able to say much for, not have the stomach *or* taste for, not speak well of, not have any part of, bear malice toward, not care for, owe *or* bear *or* carry a grudge, have nothing to do with, look coldly upon, keep one's distance, look askance at, not bear with, care nothing for, resent, not appreciate, not endure, hold cheap, not feel like, be averse to, abhor, antipathize, hate, abominate, disapprove, execrate, loathe, despise, eschew, object to, shun, shrink *or* recoil from, mind, shudder at, scorn, avoid, feel repugnance (toward), be displeased by, be disinclined, turn up the nose at, disesteem, contemn, consider obnoxious, hold as disagreeable, look on with aversion, not be able to stomach, regard with displeasure *or* disfavor, not like; *all* (D): have all one can take, make faces, take a dim view of, have it in for, keep the wound open, give a dirty look, not give a hoot for, not go for, have no relish for, be down on, look down one's nose, have a bone to pick with, have a bellyful; see also **hate** 1.

dislocate, *v.* **1.** [Displace]—*Syn.* disorder, upset, disturb; see **confuse.**

2. [Disconnect]—*Syn.* disjoint, disunite, disengage; see **break** 1, 3, **divide** 1, **separate** 2.

dislocation, *n.* **1.** [Displacement]—*Syn.* disorder, disruption, disturbance; see **confusion** 2.

2. [Disjointing, especially of a bone]—*Syn.* displacement, discontinuity, luxation; see **break** 1, **division** 1.

dislodge, *v.* —*Syn.* eject, evict, uproot; see **oust, remove** 1.

disloyal, *mod.* —*Syn.* perfidious, treacherous, traitorous; see **false** 1, **unfaithful** 1.

disloyalty, *n.* —*Syn.* infidelity, inconstancy, treachery, unfaithfulness, recreancy, apostasy, betrayal of trust, faithlessness, disaffection, subversion, sedition, deliberate breaking of faith, breach of trust, subversive activity, undutifulness, lack of fidelity *or* loyalty, double-dealing, wishing harm to one's country, perfidy, Iscariotism, bad faith, dereliction of allegiance, violation of allegiance to a government; see also **dishonesty, treason.**

dismal, *mod.* **1.** [Depressing]—*Syn.* gloomy, monotonous, dim, melancholy, desolate, doleful, dreary, dispiriting, dolorous, sorrowful, inauspicious, morbid, troublesome, horrid, shadowy, tenebrous, overcast, cloudy, unhappy, discouraging, hopeless, black, unfortunate, ghastly, horrible, boring, gruesome, frowning, lowering, tedious, mournful, dull, disheartening, afflictive, unwholesome, regrettable, cheerless, dusky, dingy, sepulchral, joyless, forlorn, funereal, comfortless, murky, wan, bleak, somber, woebegone, disagreeable; *all* (D): creepy, grisly, spooky, blue; see also **cold** 1, **dark** 1, **sad** 2.—*Ant.* happy*, joyful, cheerful.

2. [Sad]—*Syn.* miserable, depressed, sorrowful; see **sad** 1.

dismantle, *v.* —*Syn.* take apart, disassemble, break up *or* down, take *or* tear *or* pull *or* break *or* knock down, undo, dismount, demolish, remove the assemblage of, level, unbuild, ruin, unrig, subvert, raze, take to pieces, fell, take apart, strike (D); see also **destroy** 1.

dismay, *n.* —*Syn.* terror, dread, anxiety; see **fear** 2.

dismember, *v.* —*Syn.* dissect, disjoint, amputate; see **cut** 1, **divide** 1.

dismiss, *v.* **1.** [To send away]—*Syn.* discard, reject, decline, repel, repudiate, dispatch, disband, detach, send *or* lay *or* pack off, cast off *or* forth *or* out, relinquish, dispense with, disperse, dissolve, push *or* put back, remove, expel, abolish, relegate, supersede, push aside, shed, slough off, do without, have done with, dispose of, sweep away, clear, rid, rout, chase, bundle, chuck *or* chase *or* run *or* boot *or* drive *or* turn *or* show *or* force *or* lock *or* let out, ostracize, dispossess, dethrone, boycott, exile, expatriate, banish, outlaw, deport, excommunicate, get rid of; *all* (D): send packing, drop, brush off, give one his walking papers, kick out, blackball, blacklist, give the gate, write off, pitch overboard, give the hook *or* the air, read out of, send abroad, send to Coventry; see also **refuse.**—*Ant.* maintain*, retain, keep.

2. [To remove an employee]—*Syn.* discharge, give notice *or* warning, let go, lay off, displace, fire, terminate, shut out, pension, suspend, disemploy, recall, impeach, unseat, drop, disqualify; *all* (D): cashier, can, bounce, sack, ax, bust, boot out, send packing, put away; see also **oust.**—*Ant.* hire*, employ, engage.

dismissal, *n.* **1.** [Freedom]—*Syn.* release, liberation, dissolution; see **freeing.**

2. [Discharge]—*Syn.* deposition, displacement, expulsion; see **removal** 1.

dismissed, *mod.* —*Syn.* sent away, ousted, removed; see **discharged** 1, **free** 2, 3.

dismount, *v.* —*Syn.* get down *or* off, alight, light; see **descend** 1.

disobedience, *n.* —*Syn.* insubordination, defiance, insurgence, disregard, violation, lack of obedience, neglect, mutiny, revolt, nonobservance, strike, infringement, transgression, waywardness, stubbornness, noncompliance, refractoriness, recalcitrance, infraction, insubmission, intractableness, unruliness, derliction, sedition, rebellion, sabotage, riot; see also **revolution** 2.

disobedient, *mod.* —*Syn.* insubordinate, refractory, defiant; see **rebellious** 2, 3, **unruly.**

disobey, *v.* —*Syn.* balk, decline, neglect, set aside, desert, be remiss, ignore (the commands of), refuse (submission to), disagree, differ, refuse to support, evade, disregard (the authority of), break rules, object, defy, resist, revolt, strike, violate, infringe, transgress, shirk, misbehave, withstand, counteract, take the law into one's own hands; *all* (D): kick over the traces, not mind, pay no attention to, hurl defiance at, go counter to, slide *or* worm one's way out of, not heed, (run) riot, write one's own ticket, fly in the face of, answer to no man, not listen to; see also **dare** 2, **oppose** 1, **rebel** 1.—*Ant.* obey*, follow, fulfill.

disoblige, *v.* **1.** [Insult]—*Syn.* offend, affront, displease; see **insult.**

2. [Inconvenience]—*Syn.* annoy, discommode, upset; see **disturb** 2.

disobliging, *mod.* —*Syn.* uncivil, discourteous, ill-disposed; see **rude** 2.

disorder, *n.* **1.** [Physical confusion]—*Syn.* disarrangement, irregularity, derangement; see **confusion** 2.

2. [Social or mental confusion]—*Syn.* tumult, bustle, discord, misrule, turmoil, complication, chaos, mayhem, terrorism, rioting, mob rule, anarchy, anarchism, lawlessness, imbroglio, entanglement, commotion, agitation, insurrection, revolution, rebellion, strike, disorganization, riot, state of violence, reign of terror, uproar; *all* (D): mobocracy, tangled skein, tizzy, dither, ruckus, discombobula-

tion, static; see also **disturbance** 2, **trouble** 2. —*Ant.* order*, peace, tranquility.
3. [An illness]—*Syn.* sickness, indisposition, malady; see **disease** 1.

disorder, *v.* —*Syn.* disarrange, clutter, scatter; see **confuse, disorganize.**

disordered, *mod.* —*Syn.* displaced, misplaced, dislocated, mislaid, out of place, deranged, in disorder, out of kilter, out of hand, in confusion, in a mess, all over the place, in a muddle *or* jumble, upset, unsettled, disorganized, disarranged, moved, removed, shifted, meddled *or* tampered with, shuffled, tumbled, ruffled, rumpled, tousled, riffled, jumbled, molested, jarred, tossed, stirred (up), roiled, rolled, jolted, muddled, discombobulated (D); see also **confused** 2, **tangled.**—*Ant.* ordered*, arranged, settled.

disorderly, *mod.* **1.** [Lacking orderly arrangement] —*Syn.* indiscriminate, confused, tumultuous, jumbled, undisciplined, unrestrained, heterogeneous, scattered, dislocated, unsystematic, messy, slovenly, untidy, cluttered, unkempt, scrambled, uncombed, badly managed, in confusion, disorganized, untrained, out of control; *all* (D): topsy-turvy, out of whack *or* order *or* line, out of step, all over the place, mixed up, cockeyed, banged *or* messed up; see also **irregular** 1, 4.—*Ant.* regular*, neat, trim.
2. [Creating a disturbance]—*Syn.* intemperate, drunk, rowdy; see **unruly.**

disorganization, *n.* —*Syn.* disunion, dissolution, derangement; see **confusion** 2.

disorganize, *v.* —*Syn.* break up, disperse, destroy, scatter, litter, clutter, break down, deprive of organization, put out of order, disarrange, disorder, upset, disrupt, derange, dislocate, demobilize, disband, jumble, muddle, mislay, misplace, embroil, unsettle, disturb, perturb, shuffle, toss, throw into disorder, turn topsy-turvy, complicate, confound, overthrow, overturn, stampede, agitate, disarray, dishevel, scramble, get the cart before the horse (D); see also **confuse.**—*Ant.* systematize*, order, distribute.

disown, *v.* —*Syn.* repudiate, deny, retract; see **discard.**

disparage, *v.* —*Syn.* deprecate, discredit, defame; see **depreciate** 2, **lower.**

disparagement, *n.* **1.** [Detraction]—*Syn.* depreciation, debasement, degradation; see **lie** 1.
2. [Something that discredits]—*Syn.* slander, aspersion, censure; see **blame** 1, **ridicule.**

disparity, *n.* —*Syn.* inequality, difference, incongruity; see **difference** 2, **variation.**

dispassionate, *mod.* —*Syn.* impartial, judicial, just; see **fair** 1.

dispatch, *v.* **1.** [To send something on its way] —*Syn.* transmit, express, forward; see **send** 1.
2. [To kill deliberately]—*Syn.* destroy, murder, finish; see **kill** 1.
3. [To make an end]—*Syn.* finish, conclude, perform; see **achieve** 1.

dispel, *v.* **1.** [To scatter]—*Syn.* disperse, deploy, dissipate; see **distribute** 1, **scatter** 2.
2. [To drive off]—*Syn.* cancel, repel, beat off; see **dismiss** 1, 2, **oust.**

dispensable, *mod.* **1.** [Superflous]—*Syn.* removable, excessive, unnecessary; see **trivial, useless** 1.
2. [Pardonable]—*Syn.* condonable, not binding, venial; see **excusable.**

dispensation, *n.* **1.** [Distribution]—*Syn.* allocation, allotment, endowment; see **distribution** 1, 2.
2. [Management]—*Syn.* direction, regulation, supervision; see **administration** 1.

dispense, *v.* **1.** [Distribute]—*Syn.* apportion, assign, allocate; see **distribute** 1, **give** 1.
2. [Administer]—*Syn.* undertake, enforce, direct; see **command** 2, **manage** 1.

dispenser, *n.* **1.** [A distributor]—*Syn.* divider, allocater, dealer; see **businessman, merchant.**
2. [A device that dispenses something]—*Syn.* vendor, vending machine, spray can, aerosol spray, spray gun, paint gun, cigarette machine, Coke machine (trademark), soap dispenser, automat, squeeze bottle, tapper, beer keg; bubblegum, coffee, cold drink, etc., machine; see also **can** 1, **container, faucet.**

dispense with, *v.* —*Syn.* ignore, pass over, brush aside; see **disregard, neglect** 2.

disperse, *v.* —*Syn.* break up, separate, disband; see **scatter** 1.

dispersion, *n.* —*Syn.* dispersal, scattering, diffusion; see **distribution** 1.

dispirited, *mod.* —*Syn.* dejected, depressed, disheartened; see **sad** 1.

displace, *v.* **1.** [To remove]—*Syn.* replace, transpose, dislodge; see **remove** 1.
2. [To put in the wrong place]—*Syn.* mislay, lose, disarrange; see **misplace.**

display, *n.* **1.** [Pretentious show]—*Syn.* affectation, pretension, pedantry; see **ostentation** 2, **vanity** 1.
2. [A spectacle]—*Syn.* exhibition, exhibit, presentation, representation, exposition, arrangement, demonstration, performance, revelation, procession, parade, pageant, exposure, array, example, appearance, waxworks, fireworks, tinsel, carnival, fair, bravura, frippery, flaunt, pomp, splendor, unfolding; *all* (D): turnout, splash, splurge, chamber of horrors; see also **show** 1, 2.
3. [Matter presented to encourage sale]—*Syn.* sample, layout, spread; see **advertisement** 2.

display, *v.* **1.** [To present for effect]—*Syn.* show (off), exhibit, expand, uncover, open (up), unfold, spread, parade, manifest, unmask, present, represent, perform, flaunt, lay *or* put *or* set out, evidence, air, evince, disclose, visualize, unveil, arrange, lay bare, bring to view, make clear, reveal, impart, show forth, make known, promulgate; see also **expose** 1.—*Ant.* hide*, conceal, veil.
2. [To advertise]—*Syn.* illustrate, promote, publicize; see **advertise** 1, 2.

displayed, *mod.* —*Syn.* presented, laid *or* spread out, visible, on display, in the public view, dressed up; see also **advertised, shown** 1.—*Ant.* secret*, held back, unknown.

displease, *v.* **1.** [To leave a person dissatisfied] —*Syn.* worry, perplex, chagrin; see **bother** 2.
2. [To anger]—*Syn.* vex, provoke, enrage; see **anger** 1.

displeased, *mod.* —*Syn.* unhappy, vexed, annoyed; see **angry, disappointed** 1.

displeasure, *n.* —*Syn.* disapproval, annoyance, resentment; see **anger, dissatisfaction.**

disposal, *n.* **1.** [Getting rid of something]—*Syn.* riddance, dispatching, disposition, transference, transfer, discarding, demolition, dispensation, throwing away, transaction, sale, clearance (sale), selling, auctioning, trading, vending, bartering, conveyance, sacrifice, reducing to clear, clearing out, making way for new stock, relinquishment; see also **destruction** 1, **distribution** 1.—*Ant.* collection*, collecting, accumulation.

2. [The final treatment of a matter]—*Syn.* action, provision(s), determination, disposition, distribution, arrangement(s), conclusion, division, ordering, allocation, assortment, settlement, control, effectuation, winding up; see also **adjustment** 1, **administration** 1, **end** 2.—*Ant.* revision*, change, alteration.

at one's disposal—*Syn.* ready, prepared, usable; see **available.**

dispose, *v.* —*Syn.* settle, adapt, condition; see **adjust** 1, **prepare** 1.

disposed, *mod.* —*Syn.* inclined, prone, apt; see **likely** 5.

dispose of, *v.* **1.** [To eliminate]—*Syn.* relinquish, throw away, part with; see **discard, sell** 1.

2. [To kill]—*Syn.* murder, eliminate, slaughter, destroy; see **kill** 1.

disposition, *n.* **1.** [Arrangement]—*Syn.* decision, method, distribution; see **organization** 1, **plan** 2.

2. [Temperament]—*Syn.* character, nature, temper; see **mood** 1, **temperament.**

dispossess, *v.* **1.** [Take away from]—*Syn.* confiscate, divest, steal; see **seize** 2.

2. [Evict]—*Syn.* dislodge, drive out, expel; see **eject** 1, **oust.**

dispraise, *v.* —*Syn.* blame, criticize, reprove; see **censure.**

disproportion, *n.* —*Syn.* disparity, insufficiency, inadequacy; see **difference, imbalance.**

disproportionate, *mod.* —*Syn.* unsymmetrical, incommensurate, excessive; see **irregular** 4, **superflous.**

disprove, *v.* —*Syn.* prove false, throw out, set aside, find unfounded, find fault in, point out the weakness of *or* in, controvert, rebut, invalidate, weaken, overthrow, tear down, confound, expose; *all* (D): take *or* cut the ground from under, blow up, scrap, poke holes in; see also **deny, refute.**

disputable, *mod.* —*Syn.* debatable, doubtful, dubious; see **questionable** 1, **uncertain** 2.

disputant, *n.* —*Syn.* contender, arguer, discussant, antagonist, debater, opponent, adversary; see also **critic** 1, 2, **controversialist, enemy** 1, 2, **opponent** 2.

disputation, *n.* —*Syn.* dissension, debate, controversy; see **discussion** 1, **dispute** 1.

disputatious, *mod.* —*Syn.* contentious, argumentative, captious; see **controversial, quarrelsome** 1.

dispute, *n.* **1.** [A verbal disagreement]—*Syn.* argument, quarrel, debate, row, misunderstanding, verbal contention, conflict, strife, discussion, polemic, bickering, squabble, wrangle, broil, disturbance, feud, uproar, commotion, tiff, fracas, brouhaha, controversy, altercation, dissension, variance, squall, difference of opinion; *all* (D): rumpus, row, hubbub, flare-up, fuss, fireworks; see also **disagreement** 1.

2. [Physical violence]—*Syn.* controversy, quarrel, disagreement; see **fight** 1.

beyond dispute—*Syn.* settled, sure, not open to question; see **certain** 3.

in dispute—*Syn.* argued, unsettled, undetermined; see **uncertain** 2.

dispute, *v.* —*Syn.* debate, contradict, quarrel; see **argue** 1, **discuss.**

disqualification, *n.* **1.** [Disability]—*Syn.* inability, unfitness, incapacity; see **lack** 2.

2. [Incompetency]—*Syn.* unproficiency, clumsiness, ineptitude; see **awkwardness** 1.

disqualify, *v.* **1.** [Disable]—*Syn.* incapacitate, invalidate, paralyze; see **weaken** 2.

2. [Debar]—*Syn.* preclude, disentitle, disbar; see **bar** 2.

disquiet, *n.* —*Syn.* anxiety, restlessness, uneasiness; see **care** 2, **fear** 2.

disquieting, *mod.* —*Syn.* disturbing, troubling, disconcerting; see **disturbing.**

disquisition, *n.* —*Syn.* study, dissertation, commentary; see **thesis** 2.

disregard, *v.* —*Syn.* ignore, despise, pass over, let (it) go *or* pass, make light of, not heed, make allowances for, have no use for, laugh off, take no account of, brush aside; *all* (D): turn a deaf ear to, be blind to, shut one's eyes to, wink *or* blink at; see also **neglect** 1.

disrepair, *n.* —*Syn.* decrepitude, deterioration, dilapidation; see **decay** 2.

disreputable, *mod.* **1.** [In ill repute]—*Syn.* low, objectionable, discreditable; see **offensive** 2, **shameful** 1, 2.

2. [Suggestive of ill repute]—*Syn.* licentious, libidinous, dissolute; see **lewd** 2.

disrepute, *n.* —*Syn.* dishonor, disfavor, infamy; see **disgrace** 1.

disrespect, *n.* —*Syn.* discourtesy, coarseness, irreverence; see **rudeness.**

disrespectful, *mod.* —*Syn.* ill-bred, discourteous, impolite; see **rude** 2.

disrobe, *v.* —*Syn.* strip, divest, unclothe; see **undress.**

disrupt, *v.* **1.** [To break]—*Syn.* fracture, intrude, obstruct; see **break** 1, **interrupt** 2.

2. [To confuse]—*Syn.* upset, disturb, agitate; see **confuse.**

disruption, *n.* **1.** [Division]—*Syn.* splitting, severance, separation; see **division** 1, **separation** 1.

2. [Turmoil]—*Syn.* debacle, disturbance, agitation; see **confusion** 2.

dissatisfaction, *n.* **1.** [Lack of satisfaction]—*Syn.* discontent, disappointment, discontentment, uneasiness, disquiet, desolation, querulousness, hopelessness, boredom, weariness, anxiety, trouble, worry, oppression, discouragement; see also **grief** 1. —*Ant.* satisfaction*, contentment, relief.

2. [Active disapproval]—*Syn.* dislike, displeasure, disapproval; see **objection** 1, 2.

dissatisfied, *mod.* —*Syn.* displeased, discontented, ungratified, querulous, disgruntled, malcontent, offended, unsatisfied; *both* (D): fed up, put out; see also **disappointed** 1.

dissatisfy, *v.* —*Syn.* disturb, upset, perturb; see **anger** 1.

dissect, *v.* **1.** [Anatomize]—*Syn.* dismember, quarter, operate; see **cut** 1, **divide** 1.
2. [Examine]—*Syn.* scrutinize, investigate, inspect; see **analyze** 1, **examine** 1.

dissection, *n.* **1.** [Anatomization]—*Syn.* dismemberment, vivisection, autopsy; see also **operation** 4.
2. [Investigation]—*Syn.* study, inquest, analysis; see **examination** 1.

dissemble, *v.* **1.** [Disguise]—*Syn.* shroud, cover, camouflage; see **disguise, hide.**
2. [Pretend]—*Syn.* feign, sham, simulate; see **pretend** 1.

dissembler, *n.* —*Syn.* quack, charlatan, deceiver; see **impostor.**

disseminate, *v.* —*Syn.* sow, propagate, broadcast; see **distribute** 1.

dissemination, *n.* —*Syn.* propagation, distribution, diffusion; see **dissipation** 1.

dissension, *n.* —*Syn.* difference, quarrel, trouble; see **disagreement** 1, **dispute** 1.

dissent, *n.* —*Syn.* nonconformity, difference, heresy; see **disagreement** 1, **objection** 2, **protest.**

dissent, *v.* —*Syn.* disagree, refuse, contradict; see **differ** 1, **oppose** 1.

dissenter, *n.* **1.** [Heretic]—*Syn.* apostate, dissident, protestant; see **protestor, skeptic.**
2. [Objector]—*Syn.* disputant, dissentient, demonstrator; see **nonconformist, radical, rebel** 1.

dissertation, *n.* —*Syn.* discourse, treatise, commentary; see **exposition** 2, **thesis** 2.

disservice, *n.* —*Syn.* wrong, injury, outrage; see **damage** 1, **injustice** 2, **insult.**

dissidence, *n.* —*Syn.* feud, dissent, discordance; see **disagreement** 1.

dissimilar, *mod.* —*Syn.* disparate, divergent, unique; see **different** 1.

dissimilarity, *n.* —*Syn.* unlikeness, divergence, separation; see **contrast** 1, **difference** 1, **variation.**

dissimulation, *n.* —*Syn.* pretence, hypocrisy, wile; see **deception** 1, **dishonesty.**

dissipate, *v.* **1.** [To dispel]—*Syn.* spread, diffuse, disseminate; see **scatter** 2.
2. [To squander]—*Syn.* use up, consume, misuse; see **spend** 2, **waste** 2.
3. [To vanish]—*Syn.* evanesce, melt away, run dry; see **evaporate.**

dissipated, *mod.* **1.** [Scattered]—*Syn.* dispersed, strewn, disseminated; see **scattered.**
2. [Wasted]—*Syn.* squandered, destroyed, consumed; see **empty** 1, **spent** 2, **wasted.**
3. [Corrupt]—*Syn.* intemperate, dissolute, self-indulgent; see **wicked** 1.

dissipation, *n.* **1.** [Dispersion]—*Syn.* scattering, dissemination, dispersal, diffusion, spread, radiation, emission, disintegration, dissolution; see also **distribution** 1.
2. [Debauchery]—*Syn.* indulgence, intemperance, dissolution; see **evil** 1.

dissociate, *v.* **1.** [To separate]—*Syn.* disunite, disconnect, disjoin; see **divide** 1, **scatter** 2.
2. [To disperse]—*Syn.* break up, disrupt, quit; see **disband, scatter** 1.

dissociation, *n.* —*Syn.* severance, disunion, disengagement; see **division** 1, **separation** 1.

dissoluble, *mod.* —*Syn.* dissolvable, solvent, dispersible; see **soluble.**

dissolute, *mod.* —*Syn.* loose, licentious, evil; see **lewd** 2, **wicked** 1.

dissolution, *n.* **1.** [Disintegration]—*Syn.* resolution, destruction, decomposition; see **decay** 1.
2. [Termination]—*Syn.* ending, adjournment, dismissal; see **end** 2.
3. [Death]—*Syn.* release, demise, extinction; see **death** 1.

dissolve, *v.* **1.** [To pass from a solid to a liquid state] —*Syn.* liquefy, melt (away), thaw, soften, run, liquesce, fluidify, defrost, diffuse, waste away, flux, cause to become liquid *or* fluid; see also **evaporate** 1, **melt** 1.—*Ant.* harden*, freeze, solidify.
2. [To disintegrate]—*Syn.* break up, separate, break into pieces; see **disintegrate** 1.
3. [To destroy]—*Syn.* put an end to, eradicate, do away with; see **destroy** 1.
4. [To dismiss]—*Syn.* adjourn, postpone, discontinue; see **dismiss** 1.
5. [To annul]—*Syn.* repeal, invalidate, render void; see **cancel** 2.
6. [To fade away]—*Syn.* vanish, melt away, fade; see **disappear.**

dissonance, *n.* **1.** [Discord]—*Syn.* discordance, jangle, cacophony; see **noise** 2.
2. [Disagreement]—*Syn.* controversy, dissension, antagonism; see **disagreement** 1.

dissonant, *mod.* **1.** [Discordant]—*Syn.* strident, inharmonious, tuneless; see **harsh** 1.
2. [Inconsistent]—*Syn.* incompatible, irregular, anomalous; see **incongruous** 1.

dissuade, *v.* —*Syn.* deter, thwart, persuade not to; see **discourage** 1, **hinder, prevent.**

dissuasion, *n.* —*Syn.* discouragement, diversion, check; see **impediment** 1, **restraint** 2.

distance, *n.* **1.** [A degree or quantity of space] —*Syn.* reach, span, range; see **expanse, extent, length** 1, 2.
2. [A place or places far away]—*Syn.* background, horizon, as far as the eye can reach, sky, heavens, the blue, far lands, outpost, outskirts, foreign countries, new *or* other *or* different world(s), strange place(s), distant *or* strange *or* foreign *or* unknown terrain, objective, where one is *or* is not going, the country, beyond the horizon, the sticks (D).—*Ant.* neighborhood*, surroundings, neighbors.
3. [A measure of space]—*Syn.* statute mile, English mile, rod, yard, foot, inch, kilometer, meter, centimeter, millimeter, micrometer, league, fathom, ell, span, hand, cubit, furlong, block; *all* (D): a stone's throw, as the crow flies, down the road a piece, spitting distance, whoop and a holler; see also **inch** 1, **measure** 1, **mile.**
go the distance (D)—*Syn.* finish, bring to an end, see through; see **complete** 1.
keep at a distance—*Syn.* ignore, reject, shun; see **avoid.**
keep one's distance (D)—*Syn.* be aloof *or* indifferent, ignore, shun; see **avoid.**

distant, *mod.* **1.** [Removed in space from the speaker]—*Syn.* afar, far (back *or* off), abroad, not (at) home, faraway, yonder, backwoods, removed, abstracted, inaccessible, unapproachable, indirect, indistinct, out of the way, below *or* beyond the horizon, wide of, outlying, at arm's length, stretching to, Godforsaken, out of range *or* reach, telescopic, out of earshot, out of sight, in the background, in the distance; see also **remote** 1.—*Ant.* near*, adjacent, next.

2. [Separated by space]—*Syn.* separate, (wide) apart, farther, further, far away, at a distance, abroad, scattered, dispersed, diffuse, different, sparse, sparely sown, transatlantic, transpacific, transmarine, ultramarine, ultramontane, antipodal, excentric, asunder; see also **separated.**—*Ant.* close*, packed, jammed.

3. [Aloof in manner]—*Syn.* aloof, unconcerned, cold; see **indifferent** 1, **reserved** 3.

distaste, *n.* —*Syn.* aversion, dislike, abhorrence; see **hatred** 1, 2.

distasteful, *mod.* —*Syn.* disagreeable, repugnant, undesirable; see **offensive** 2.

distend, *v.* —*Syn.* enlarge, widen, inflate; see **distort** 3, **increase** 1, **stretch** 1, 2.

distention, *n.* —*Syn.* inflation, expansion, enlargement; see **increase** 1.

distill, *v.* —*Syn.* vaporize and condense, volatilize, draw out, steam, give forth in drops, precipitate, extract, infuse, purify, press; see also **concentrate** 1, **evaporate** 1.

distinct, *mod.* **1.** [Having sharp outlines]—*Syn.* lucid, plain, obvious; see **clear** 2, **definite** 2.

2. [Not connected with another]—*Syn.* discrete, separate, disunited; see **separated.**

3. [Clearly heard]—*Syn.* clear, sharp, enunciated; see **audible.**

distinction, *n.* **1.** [The act or quality of noticing differences]—*Syn.* differentiation, separation, discrimination, discretion, sharpness, discreteness, discernment, perception, sensitivity, penetration, acuteness, analysis, clearness, judgment, refinement, estimation, nicety, tact, diagnosis, marking out; see also **acumen, definition** 2.—*Ant.* dullness*, indifference, obtuseness.

2. [A difference used for distinction, sense 1] —*Syn.* distinctive feature, particular, qualification; see **characteristic, detail** 1.

3. [A mark of personal achievement]—*Syn.* repute, renown, prominence; see **fame** 1.

4. [Excellence]—*Syn.* flair, style, manner; see **perfection** 3.

distinctive, *mod.* —*Syn.* peculiar, unique, distinguishing; see **characteristic.**

distinctly, *mod.* —*Syn.* precisely, sharply, plainly; see **clearly** 1, 2, **surely.**

distinctness, *n.* **1.** [Discreteness]—*Syn.* detachment, dissociation, separation; see **division** 1, **isolation.**

2. [Clearness]—*Syn.* sharpness, lucidity, explicitness; see **clarity.**

distinguish, *v.* **1.** [To make distinctions]—*Syn.* discriminate (between), differentiate, classify, specify, identify, individualize, characterize, separate, recognize as separate, divide, collate, sort out *or* into, estimate, set apart, mark off, criticize, select, see, exercise discrimination, make a distinction, sift, draw the line, tell from, pick and choose; *both* (D): separate the wheat from the chaff, separate the sheep from the goats; see also **analyze** 1, **define** 2.

2. [To discern]—*Syn.* detect, discriminate, notice; see **discover** 1, **see** 1.

3. [To provide an identification]—*Syn.* identify, label, tag (D); see **mark** 2, **name** 1, 2.

4. [To bestow honor upon]—*Syn.* pay tribute to, signalize, celebrate; see **acknowledge** 2, **admire** 1, **praise** 1.

distinguishable, *mod.* —*Syn.* separable, perceptible, discernible; see **audible, obvious** 1, **tangible.**

distinguished, *mod.* **1.** [Made recognizable by markings]—*Syn.* characterized, labeled, marked, stamped, denoted, signed, signified, identified, made certain, obvious, set apart, branded, earmarked, separate, unique, differentiated, noted, observed, distinct, conspicuous, having distinguishing or unusual characteristics; see also **separated.** —*Ant.* typical*, unidentified, indistinct.

2. [Notable for excellence]—*Syn.* eminent, illustrious, venerable, renowned, honored, memorable, celebrated, well-known, noted, notable, noteworthy, highly regarded, esteemed, prominent, reputable, remarkable, distingué, peerless, superior, outstanding, especial, aristocratic, genteel, noble, brilliant, glorious, extraordinary, singular, great, imposing, special, striking, unforgettable, arresting, shining, salient, foremost, nonpareil, dignified, royal, stately, lordly, signal, radiant, transcendent, famed, talked of; *all* (D): first-rate, big-name, headline, bred to the purple, blue-blooded, nonesuch; see also **famous, important** 2. —*Ant.* obscure*, insignificant, unimportant.

distinguishing, *mod.* —*Syn.* distinctive, differentiating, different; see **characteristic.**

distort, *v.* **1.** [To change by pressure]—*Syn.* warp, crush, twist; see **bend** 1.

2. [To alter the meaning]—*Syn.* pervert, misinterpret, misconstrue; see **deceive.**

3. [To change shape]—*Syn.* contort, sag, twist, slump, knot, get out of shape, buckle, writhe, melt, warp, decline, deteriorate, deform, collapse, become misshapen, take on *or* assume another shape, deviate from the standard *or* normal form; see also **change** 1, 4.

distortion, *n.* **1.** [Deformity]—*Syn.* twist, malformation, mutilation; see **contortion** 1.

2. [Misrepresentation]—*Syn.* perversion, misinterpretation, misuse; see **lie** 1.

distract, *v.* **1.** [To divert someone's attention from] —*Syn.* detract, divert the mind *or* thoughts *or* attention, occupy, amuse, draw *or* lead away (from), beguile, call away, take *or* draw one's attention from, lead astray, attract from; see also **entertain** 1, **mislead.**

2. [To confuse]—*Syn.* bewilder, puzzle, perplex; see **confuse.**

distracted, *mod.* —*Syn.* distraught, panicked, frenzied; see **troubled** 1.

distraction, *n.* **1.** [Confusion]—*Syn.* perplexity, abstraction, complication; see **confusion** 2.

2. [Diversion]—*Syn.* amusement, pastime, drawing the mind in different directions, preoccupation, engrossment; see also **entertainment** 1, 2, **game** 1.

distraught, *mod.* —*Syn.* harassed, confused, distracted; see **bothered, troubled** 1.

distress, *n.* **1.** [Mental agony]—*Syn.* worry, anxiety, perplexity, misery, sorrow, wretchedness, pain, de-

jection, irritation, vexation, suffering, ache, heartache, dolor, ordeal, desolation, anguish, mortification, affliction, woe, torment, torture, shame, embarrassment, disappointment, tribulation, pang; see also **grief** 1, **trouble** 2.—*Ant.* joy*, happiness, jollity.
2. [Physical agony]—*Syn.* anguish, suffering, ache; see **pain** 2.
3. [Misfortune]—*Syn.* bad luck, calamity, adversity; see **catastrophe, disaster.**

distress, *v.* —*Syn.* irritate, disturb, upset; see **bother** 2, 3.

distribute, *v.* **1.** [To allot]—*Syn.* dispense, divide, share, deal, bestow, issue, endow, dispose, disperse, dole, mete *or* pass *or* parcel *or* dole *or* hand *or* pay out, administer, give away, assign, allocate, ration, apportion, consign, prorate, appropriate, pay dividends; *all* (D): dish out, divvy up, cut a melon; see also **give** 1.—*Ant.* hold*, keep, preserve.
2. [To scatter]—*Syn.* spread, sow, seed; see **scatter** 1, 2.
3. [To classify]—*Syn.* categorize, group, file; see **classify, order** 3.

distributed, *mod.* —*Syn.* delivered, scattered, shared, dealt, divided, apportioned, assigned, awarded, peddled from door to door, sowed, dispensed, dispersed, appropriated, budgeted, made individually available, equally divided, spread evenly, returned, rationed, given away, handed *or* parceled out, spread.—*Ant.* retained*, undistributed, reserved.

distribution, *n.* **1.** [The act of distributing]—*Syn.* dispersal, dispersion, dispersing, allotment, allotting, partitioning, partition, dividing, deal, dealing, circulating, circulation, disposal, disposing of, apportioning, apportionment, prorating, rationing, allowance, arrangement, arranging, scattering, diffusion, diffusing, disseminating, dissemination, administration, assessment, assessing, dissipating, dissipation, sorting, making generally available, assigning by lot, spreading, parceling *or* dealing *or* handing out, peddling, assorting; see also sense 2; **division** 1.—*Ant.* collection*, retention, storage.
2. [The result or measure of distributing]—*Syn.* frequency, arrangement, occurrence, occurring, disposition, ordering, pattern, combination, relationship(s), appearance, configuration, scarcity, number, plenty, saturation, population, spread, concentration; see also **division** 2, 3, **order** 3. —*Ant.* confusion*, tangle, puzzle.

distributor, *n.* **1.** [Dispenser]—*Syn.* seller, seeder, scatterer, sower, publisher; see also **dispenser** 2.
2. [One who handles goods]—*Syn.* wholesaler, jobber, merchant; see **businessman.**

district, *mod.* —*Syn.* divisional, immediate, ward, provincial, restricted, limited, community, rural, territorial, inferior, superior, higher, lower, state, federal, county; see also **local** 1.—*Ant.* unlimited*, unrestricted, international.

district, *n.* —*Syn.* neighborhood, community, vicinity; see **area** 2.

distrust, *v.* —*Syn.* mistrust, suspect, disbelieve; see **doubt** 2.

distrustful, *mod.* —*Syn.* distrusting, doubting, fearful; see **suspicious** 1.

disturb, *v.* **1.** [To upset physical relationship] —*Syn.* disorder, displace, distort; see **confuse.**
2. [To upset mental calm]—*Syn.* trouble, worry, agitate, perplex, rattle, startle, shake, amaze, unman, astound, give a turn to, unnerve, alarm, excite, arouse, affright, affect one's mind, badger, plague, fuss, perturb, vex, upset, outrage, molest, grieve, depress, distress, dishearten, irk, ail, tire, provoke, afflict, irritate, pain, make uneasy, harass, exasperate, pique, gall, make an ado, displease, complicate, embroil, involve, astonish, fluster, ruffle; *all* (D): burn (up), shake up, play the devil with, make the fur fly; see also **bother** 2, 3, **confuse.** —*Ant.* quiet*, calm, soothe.

disturbance, *n.* **1.** [Interpersonal disruption] —*Syn.* quarrel, brawl, fisticuffs; see **fight** 1.
2. [Physical disruption]—*Syn.* turmoil, rampage, tumult, clamor, violence, restlessness, uproar, race riot, disruption, agitation, turbulence, change, bother, stir, racket, ferment, unruliness, spasm, convulsion, tremor, shock, explosion, eruption, quake, earthquake, tidal wave, flood, shock wave, storm, whirlwind, tempest, gale, hurricane, tornado, twister, avalanche, whirlpool, blowing, flurry, whirl; *all* (D): blow, wind, hurly-burly, long hot summer; see also **trouble** 2.
3. [The result of disturbance]—*Syn.* disarrangement, irregularity, perplexity; see **confusion** 2.
4. [A political or social uprising]—*Syn.* revolt, insurrection, riot; see **revolution** 2.

disturbed, *mod.* **1.** [Disturbed physically]—*Syn.* upset, disorganized, confused; see **disordered.**
2. [Disturbed mentally]—*Syn.* agitated, disquieted, upset; see **troubled** 1.

disturbing, *mod.* —*Syn.* disquieting, upsetting, tiresome, perturbing, bothersome, irksome, unpleasant, provoking, annoying, alarming, painful, discomforting, nettling, inauspicious, foreboding, consequential, aggravating, disagreeable, troublesome, onerous, worrisome, burdensome, trying, vexatious, frightening, startling, perplexing, threatening, distressing, galling, laborious, difficult, severe, hard, toilsome, inconvenient, discouraging, pessimistic, gloomy, uncertain, disconcerting, depressing, irritating, harassing, unpropitious, unlikely, prophetic, impeding, discommoding, embarrassing, ruffling, agitating, wearisome, causing *or* leading to worry *or* anxiety, not propitious *or* encouraging, calculated to be disturbing, having unforeseen *or* discouraging qualities *or* characteristics *or* consequences; *all* (D): messed up, not (too) good, fouled up; see also **ominous.**

disunion, *n.* **1.** [Dissension]—*Syn.* dissidence, discord, alienation; see **disagreement** 1.
2. [Separation]—*Syn.* disconnection, partition, detachment; see **division** 1, **separation** 2.

disunite, *v.* **1.** [Disconnect]—*Syn.* dissociate, disjoin, separate; see **divide** 1.
2. [Alienate]—*Syn.* estrange, embroil, entangle; see **alienate.**

disuse, *n.* **1.** [The stoppage of use]—*Syn.* discontinuance, abolition, desuetude, nonobservance, inaction, discarding, cessation, intermission, interruption, abolishment, abrogation, forbearance, abstinence, relinquishment.—*Ant.* use*, continuance, continuation.

2. [The state of being unused]—*Syn.* decay, neglect, abandonment, unemployment, desertedness; see also **idleness** 1, **neglect** 1, **omission** 1. —*Ant.* production*, usefulness, employment.

ditch, *n.* —*Syn.* canal, moat, furrow; see **channel** 1, **trench** 1.

ditch, *v.* **1.** [To make a ditch]—*Syn.* furrow, trench, drain; see **dig** 1.
2. [(D) To run into a ditch]—*Syn.* skid, overturn, derail; see **crash** 1, 4, **wreck** 1.
3. [(D) To get rid of]—*Syn.* desert, forsake, leave; see **abandon** 2, **discard.**

ditto, *n.* —*Syn.* do., ditto mark ("), an identical item, *idem* (Latin), same, the (very) same, agreement, as is, an identity; see also **alike** 3.

diurnal, *mod.* —*Syn.* during the day, once a day, every day; see **daily, regular** 3.

divan, *n.* —*Syn.* couch, sofa, settee; see **chair** 1, **davenport, furniture.**

dive, *n.* **1.** [A sudden motion downward]—*Syn.* plunge, leap, spring, nosedive, headlong leap *or* jump, pitch, ducking, swim, swoop, dip; see also **fall** 1, **jump** 1.
2. [(D) An establishment offering accommodation]—*Syn.* saloon, pub, café, cabaret, hotel, motel *or* motor hotel, pizza parlor, tavern, inn, club, beer garden, pool parlor, pool hall, billiard parlor, bowling alley, night club, coffee shop, coffee house, ice-cream parlor, soda fountain, drugstore, dancehall; *all* (D): hamburger stand, chophouse, joint, dump, dine and dance, flophouse, stophouse, flea trap, hole; see also **bar** 2, **restaurant.**

dive, *v.* —*Syn.* plunge, spring, jump, vault, leap, go headfirst, plummet, sink, dip, duck, plumb, submerge, disappear, vanish, nose-dive; see also **fall** 1, **jump** 1.

dive-bomber, *n.* —*Syn.* fighter-bomber, slip bomber, *kamikaze* (Japanese); see **plane** 3.

diver, *n.* —*Syn.* high diver, fancy diver, submarine diver, deep-sea diver, aquanaut, pearl diver, sponge diver, skin diver, scuba diver, underwater reconnaissance specialist, swimmer, athlete, competitor, contestant; *all* (D): tanker, tankerette, frog man, rubber back; see also **athlete.**

diverge, *v.* **1.** [Move in different directions from the same source]—*Syn.* radiate, separate, swerve; see **deviate, veer.**
2. [Disagree]—*Syn.* dissent, disapprove, argue; see **differ** 1, **oppose** 1.

divergence, *n.* **1.** [Radiation]—*Syn.* deviation, ramification, separation; see **division** 1, **radiation** 1.
2. [Difference]—*Syn.* mutation, deviation, alteration; see **difference** 1, 2.

divergent, *mod.* —*Syn.* deviating, conflicting, variant; see **different** 2.

diverse, *mod.* —*Syn.* several, assorted, distinct; see **different** 1, 2, **various.**

diversify, *v.* —*Syn.* vary, expand, alter; see **change** 1, **increase** 1.

diversion, *n.* **1.** [The act of changing a course]—*Syn.* detour, alteration, deviation; see **change** 1.
2. [Entertainment]—*Syn.* amusement, recreation, play; see **distraction** 2, **entertainment** 1, 2, **sport** 1.

divert, *v.* **1.** [To deflect]—*Syn.* turn aside, redirect, avert; see **turn** 3, **veer.**
2. [To amuse]—*Syn.* relax, delight, beguile; see **entertain** 1.
3. [To distract]—*Syn.* attract the attention of, lead away from, disturb; see **distract** 1.

diverted, *mod.* —*Syn.* deflected, turned aside, redirected, perverted, averted, turned into other channels, rechanneled, appropriated to other uses *or* purposes, pre-empted, taken, wrested away, adopted, used, made use of, taken over, rebudgeted, reclassified; see also **changed** 2, 3.—*Ant.* untouched*, undiverted, left.

divest, *v.* **1.** [To undress]—*Syn.* strip, disrobe, uncover; see **undress.**
2. [To deprive]—*Syn.* dispossess, strip, take from; see **seize** 2.

divide, *v.* **1.** [To separate by parting]—*Syn.* part, cut up, fence off, disunite, disconnect, disjoin, detach, disengage, dissolve, sever, rupture, dissever, dismember, sunder, split, unravel, carve, cleave, section, intersect, cross, bisect, rend, tear, segment, undo, unbind, halve, quarter, dislocate, third, break down, demarcate, divorce, dissociate, insulate, isolate, loose, unchain, count off, pull away, disentangle, abscind, chop, hew, incise, slash, gash, carve, splinter, pull to pieces, tear *or* break apart, circumcise, segregate, fork, branch; *all* (D): tear limb from limb, throw out of gear *or* whack *or* kilter, split off *or* up, salt out; see also **break** 1, **cut** 1, **separate** 2.—*Ant.* unite*, combine, connect.
2. [To distribute]—*Syn.* deal, dole, apportion; see **distribute** 1.

dividend, *n.* —*Syn.* pay, check, coupon, proceeds, returns, quarterly *or* annual dividend, share, allotment, dispensation, appropriation, remittance, allowance; *all* (D): cut, rake-off, divvy; see also **interest** 3, **profit** 2.

divination, *n.* —*Syn.* augury, calculation, interpretation of omens, prediction, soothsaying, sorcery, foretelling, foreshadowing, palmistry, table-tipping, spirit-rapping, prognostics, prognostication, clairvoyance, prophecy, extrasensory perception (ESP), thaumaturgy, horoscopy, penetration, intimation, portent, insight, warning, fortunetelling, phrenology, astrology, graphology, tea-leaf reading, hieromancy, necromancy, hydromancy, ichthyomancy, myomancy, pyromancy, crystallomancy, sciomancy, ornithomancy, ophiomancy, dactyliomancy, Bibliomancy, anthropomancy, austromancy, alectryomancy, catoptromancy, psephomancy, capnomancy, sideromancy, alphitomancy, molybdomancy, lithomancy, onychomancy, oneiromancy, chiromancy, aeromancy, rhabdomancy, cleromancy, aleuromancy, axinomancy, belomancy, tephramancy, aruspicy, orniscopy, genethliacs, geloscopy, beltonism, estispicy; see also **forecast.**

divine, *mod.* **1.** [Having qualities of a god]—*Syn.* godlike, ambrosial, supernal, superhuman, celestial, almighty, unearthly, heavenly, deific, eternal, beatific, deiform, supreme, spiritual, godly, angelic, theistic, deistic, eternal, omnipotent, omniscient, omnipresent, all-powerful, ghostly, superphysical, supernatural, transcendent, hyperphysical, Elysian, Arcadian, Olympian, Jovian, Christlike, immaculate, paradisiacal, all-loving, beyond praise;

see also **perfect** 2.—*Ant.* human*, devilish, diabolical.
2. [Dedicated to the service of a god]—*Syn.* sacred, hallowed, devotional, spiritual, sacrificial, sacramental, ceremonial, ritualistic, reverent, consecrated, dedicated, devoted, venerable, pious, religious, anointed, sanctified, ordained, destined, sanctioned, set apart, sacrosanct, scriptural, blessed, worshiped, revered, venerated, mystical, worshipful, prayerful, adored, reverenced, solemn, faithful, fervid, ministerial, papistical; see also **holy** 1.—*Ant.* impious*, profane, blasphemous.
3. [Excellent]—*Syn.* supreme, superb, amazing; see **excellent, perfect** 2.

divine, *n.* —*Syn.* parson, theologian, clergyman; see **minister** 1, **priest, rabbi.**

divine, *v.* —*Syn.* predict, prophesy, prognosticate; see **foretell.**

diviner, *n.* —*Syn.* prophet, seer, sorcerer, witch; see **magician.**

divinity, *n.* —*Syn.* deity, godhead, higher power; see **god** 1.

divisible, *mod.* —*Syn.* separable, distinguishable, distinct, divided, fractional, fragmentary, partible, detachable, severable, dissolvable, dissoluble, apportionable; see also **separated.**—*Ant.* inseparable*, indivisible, fast.

division, *n.* **1.** [The act or result of dividing]—*Syn.* separation, separating, detachment, detaching, apportionment, apportioning, partition, parting, partitioning, distribution, distributing, severance, severing, cutting, disseverance, dissevering, carving, subdivision, subdividing, dismemberment, dismembering, disconnecting, disconnection, distinction, distinguishing, selection, selecting, segmenting, segmentation, disparting, partage, parceling, parcelment, analysis, diagnosis, autopsy, vivisection, reduction, breaking down *or* up, districting, rending, scissure, splitting, disuniting, breaking, breakdown, fracture, bisection, bipartition, lobation, lobotomy, demarcation, disjuncture, contrasting, departmentalizing, diglossia, schizogenesis, fission, schizogony, schizocephaly.—*Ant.* union*, joining, glueing.
2. [A part produced by dividing]—*Syn.* section, kind, sort, ramification, portion, compartment, share, split, member, subdivision, parcel, segment, fragment, sector, department, category, branch, fraction, dividend, lemma, degree, piece, slice, lump, wedge, cut, lobe, front, movement, column, book, chapter, decade, verse, canto, fit, phrase, clause, line, paragraph, apartment, cell, passage, class, moiety, totem, race, clan, tribe, caste, cut (D); see **department** 2, **part** 1.
3. [Discord or disunion]—*Syn.* trouble, words, difficulty; see **disagreement** 1, **dispute** 1.
4. [An organic military unit]—*Syn.* armored division, airborne division, infantry division; see **army** 2.
5. [An organized area]—*Syn.* province, country, state, government, dominion, shire, department, district, county, municipality, city, town, canton, village, commune, ward, township, residency, constituency, presidency, bishopric, prelacy, parish, range; see **nation** 1, **territory** 2.

divorce, *n.* —*Syn.* separation, partition, dissociation, breach, divorcement, bill of divorce *or* divorcement, annulment, separate maintenance, parting of the ways, decree nisi, dissolution, disparateness; *all* (D): split-up, busted event, holy deadlock, shattered seal, the cure; see **cancellation.** —*Ant.* marriage*, betrothal, wedding.

divorce, *v.* —*Syn.* separate, unmarry, annul, release from *or* put out of wedlock *or* matrimony, sunder, nullify, put away, split up (D); see **cancel** 2.

divorced, *mod.* —*Syn.* dissolved, parted, disunited, disjoined, discontinued, isolated, divided; *all* (D): Reno'd, split, washed up, unhitched, cured; see **separated.**—*Ant.* married*, joined, mated.

divulge, *v.* —*Syn.* disclose, impart, confess; see **admit** 3, **expose** 1.

dizzy, *mod.* **1.** [Temporarily without control of one's senses]—*Syn.* confused, lightheaded, giddy, bemused, staggering, upset, staggered, disturbed, dazzled, dazed, blind, blinded, dumb, faint, bleary-eyed, with spots before one's eyes, troubled with vertigo, unsteady, having a whirling *or* spinning sensation, dumbfounded, out of control, weak-kneed; *both* (D): tipsy, wobbly; see **unsteady** 1.
2. [Causing dizziness]—*Syn.* steep, lofty, vertiginous; see **abrupt** 1.
3. [(D) Lacking good sense]—*Syn.* flighty, unstable, crazy; see **abrupt** 2, **changeable** 1.

DNA, *n.* —*Syn.* genetic alphabet *or* codon, molecule containing chromosomal material *or* genes, double helix, template, hereditary information, deoxyribonucleic acid; see **genetic code.**

do, *v.* **1.** [To discharge one's responsibilities]—*Syn.* effect, execute, accomplish; see **achieve 1, perform** 1, **succeed** 1.
2. [To execute commands or instructions]—*Syn.* carry out, complete, fulfill; see **obey** 1.
3. [To bring to a close]—*Syn.* fulfill, finish, conclude; see **achieve** 1, **end** 1.
4. [To cause]—*Syn.* bring about, produce, effect; see **begin** 1, **cause** 2, **create** 2.
5. [To suffice]—*Syn.* serve, be sufficient, give satisfaction; see **satisfy** 3.
6. [To solve]—*Syn.* figure *or* work out, decipher, decode; see **solve.**
7. [To translate]—*Syn.* render, transpose, transliterate; see **interpret** 1, **translate** 1.
8. [To present a play, etc.]—*Syn.* give, put on, produce; see **perform** 2.
9. [To act]—*Syn.* perform, portray, render the role of; see **act** 3.
10. [To travel]—*Syn.* journey, explore, tour; see **travel** 2.
11. [To cheat]—*Syn.* swindle, defraud, trick; see **deceive.**
12. [To conduct oneself]—*Syn.* behave *or* comport *or* acquit oneself, seem, appear; see **behave** 2.
have to do with—*Syn.* related, connected, concerning; see **about** 2.
make do—*Syn.* get by *or* along, manage, survive; see **endure** 2.

do about, *v.* —*Syn.* assist, take care of, correct; see **help** 1, **improve** 1, **repair.**

do away with, *v.* **1.** [To eliminate]—*Syn.* get rid of, cancel, take away; see **eliminate 1, remove** 1.
2. [To kill]—*Syn.* slay, execute, put to death; see **kill** 1.

do badly by, *v.* —*Syn.* mistreat, harm, abuse; see **damage** 1, **hurt** 1.

do by, *v.* —*Syn.* handle, act toward, deal with; see **treat** 1.

docile, *mod.* —*Syn.* meek, mild, tractable, pliant, submissive, accommodating, complacent, acquiescent, adaptable, resigned, agreeable, willing, obliging, well-behaved, manageable, pliable, tame, compliant, yielding, teachable, easily influenced, easy, easygoing, young, usable, amenable, soft, governable, childlike; see **gentle** 3, **humble** 1, **obedient** 1. —*Ant.* fierce*, resolute, dogged.

docility, *n.* —*Syn.* tractability, obedience, submissiveness, compliance, meekness, mildness, gentleness, manageability, pliability, pliancy, acquiescence, willingness, flexibility, amenability, flexibleness, adaptability, tameness, subordination, bending the knee (D); see **humility, shyness.** —*Ant.* disobedience*, undutifulness, stubbornness.

dock, *n.* **1.** [A landing or mooring place]—*Syn.* landing pier, wharf, lock, (boat) landing, marina, (ferry) slip, dry dock, floating dock, repair dock, *embarcadero* (Spanish), embarkment, waterfront, quay; see also **harbor** 2.

2. [A weed]. Varieties include the following—sour dock, yellow dock, burdock, curled dock, smooth dock, fiddle dock, candock, hardock, patience dock, golden dock, water dock; see **plant, weed** 1.

dock, *v.* **1.** [To clip]—*Syn.* prune, crop, shorten; see **cut** 1.

2. [To diminish]—*Syn.* lessen, withhold, deduct; see **decrease** 2.

doctor, *n.* **1.** [A medical practitioner]—*Syn.* Doctor of Medicine (M.D.), physician, general practitioner (G.P.), surgeon, country doctor, medical attendant, consultant, specialist, interne, house physician, veterinarian, chiropractor, homeopath, osteopath, acupuncturist, Christian Science practitioner, (faith) healer, witch doctor, shaman, medicine man, quack, animal doctor; *all* (D): bones, doc, sawbones, fixemup, pill bag, medico, medicine-dropper, castor-oil artist.

Types of doctors include the following—heart specialist; eye, ear, nose, and throat specialist; respiratory specialist, family doctor, etc.; anesthetist, anesthesiologist, aurist, dentist, podiatrist, internist, pediatrician, gynecologist, oculist, obstetrician, psychiatrist, psychoanalyst, public health physician, industrial surgeon, orthopedist, gynecologist, radiologist, neurologist, cardiologist, pathologist, dermatologist, endocrinologist, opthamologist, laryngologist, urologist, neurologist, oncologist, gastroenterologist, allergist, proctologist, hematologist, diathermist, radiothermist; heart transplant surgeon, kidney transplant surgeon, etc.; orthopedic surgeon, cardiac *or* heart surgeon, etc.; *all* (D): bone man, heart man, eye man, etc.; see **dentist, medicine** 3.

2. [A holder of a doctoral degree]—*Syn.* expert, specialist, student; see **degree, professor, scholar, scientist.**

doctor, *v.* —*Syn.* attend, administer, supply professional services; see **treat.**

doctrinaire, *mod.* —*Syn.* opinionated, bigoted, one-sided; see **dogmatic** 2.

doctrinaire, *n.* —*Syn.* visionary, utopist, bigot; see **idealist.**

doctrine, *n.* **1.** [A tenet]—*Syn.* principle, proposition, precept, article, concept, conviction, opinion, convention, (established) position, attitude, statement (of position *or* belief), tradition, unwritten law, universal *or* natural *or* common law *or* principle, teachings, accepted belief, article of faith *or* belief, canon, regulation, rule, pronouncement, declaration, bull; see **law** 2, 4.

2. [Several tenets built into a faith]—*Syn.* dogma, creed, gospel; see **faith** 2.

document, *n.* —*Syn.* paper, diary, report; see **record** 1.

dodder, *v.* —*Syn.* tremble, totter, quaver; see **reel, shake** 1.

doddering, *mod.* —*Syn.* senile, trembling, decrepit; see **shaky** 2, **weak** 1.

dodge (D), *n.* —*Syn.* trick, strategy, scheme; see **method** 2, **plan** 1.

dodge, *v.* —*Syn.* duck, elude, evade; see **avoid.**

do dirt to (D), *v.* —*Syn.* hurt, mistreat, injure; see **abuse** 1, **slander.**

doer, *n.* —*Syn.* actor, performer, instrument; see **means** 1.

do for, *v.* **1.** [To help]—*Syn.* provide *or* care for, assist, look after; see **help** 1, **support** 5.

2. [(D) To kill]—*Syn.* murder, deprive of life, slaughter; see **destroy** 1, **kill** 1.

dog, *n.* **1.** [A domestic animal]—*Syn.* *canis familiaris* (Latin), hound, bitch, puppy, pup; *all* (D): mongrel, stray, canine, poodle, cur, pooch, parapooch, bow-wow, flea bag, fido, mutt.

Types and breeds of dogs include the following—hunting dog, field dog, racing dog, courser, boxer, water dog, shepherd dog, bloodhound, wolfhound, greyhound, whippet, St. Bernard, mastiff, Newfoundland, Great Dane, borzoi, German shepherd, Doberman (pinscher), Afghan (hound), Irish wolfhound, Labrador retriever, Chesapeake Bay retriever, malamute, husky, Samoyed, collie, Briard, Old English sheep dog, Gordon setter, English setter, Irish setter, pointer, springer, spaniel, cocker (spaniel), water spaniel, Brittany spaniel, foxhound, basset, beagle, dachshund, Dalmatian, English bulldog, spitz, chow, Pomeranian, poodle, toy poodle, standard poodle, barbet, French poodle, Pekingese, Chihuahua, Mexican hairless, Airedale, schnauzer, Sealyham, fox terrier, wirehaired terrier, Scottie, Kerry blue, black and tan, Bedlington terrier, Aberdeen, Irish terrier, Cairn terrier, bull terrier, Boston terrier, Manchester terrier, Cardigan, Corgi, Pembroke.

2. [Insulting term]—*Syn.* scamp, swine, blackguard; see **rascal.**

a dog's life (D)—*Syn.* wretched existence, bad luck, trouble; see **poverty** 1, 2.

every dog has his day (D)—*Syn.* have a chance, recover, do well; see **prosper, succeed** 1.

go to the dogs (D)—*Syn.* deteriorate, degenerate, weaken; see **decay.**

let sleeping dogs lie (D)—*Syn.* ignore, leave well enough alone, pass over; see **neglect** 1.

put on the dog (D)—*Syn.* show off, entertain lavishly, exhibit; see **display** 1.
teach an old dog new tricks (D)—*Syn.* influence, convince, change; see **persuade** 1.

dog eat dog, *mod.* —*Syn.* vicious, ferocious, brutal; see **cruel** 1, 2, **ruthless** 1, 2.

dogged, *mod.* —*Syn.* stubborn, tenacious, firm; see **obstinate** 1, **resolute** 2.

dogma, *n.* —*Syn.* belief, opinion, conviction; see **doctrine** 1, **faith** 2.

dogmatic, *mod.* **1.** [Based on an assumption of absolute truth]—*Syn.* unchangeable, inevitable, immovable, categorical, unqualified, eternal, positive, doctrinal, doctrinaire, authoritative, systematic, orthodox, formal, *ex cathedra* (Latin), canonical, positive, authoritarian, imperative, peremptory, pragmatic, prophetic, theoretical, axiomatic, unerring, by fiat, on faith, as a matter of course, by nature, by God's will, by natural law; see **absolute** 1.—*Ant.* irresolute*, uncertain, whimsical.
2. [Acting as though one possessed absolute truth] —*Syn.* dictatorial, stubborn, egotistical, bigoted, fanatical, intolerant, opinionated, overbearing, imperious, magisterial, arrogant, stupid, domineering, oracular, tyrannical, fascistic, despotic, obstinate, confident, downright, arbitrary, unequivocal, definite, formal, stubborn, determined, emphatic, tenacious, obdurate, narrow-minded, wrong-headed, one-sided, wedded to an opinion, hidebound; *all* (D): high and mighty, stiff-necked, hard-shelled, pigheaded, bullheaded, stubborn as a mule, far-right; see **absolute** 3, **autocratic** 1.—*Ant.* liberal*, tolerant, dubious.

dogmatism, *n.* —*Syn.* opinionatedness, peremptoriness, positiveness; see **belief** 1.

dog's life, *n.* —*Syn.* hard life, trouble, suffering; see **difficulty** 1, 2.

do in (D), *v.* —*Syn.* eliminate, slay, murder; see **destroy** 1, **kill** 1.

doing, *n.* —*Syn.* performing, accomplishing, achieving; see **performance** 1.

doings (D), *n.* —*Syn.* activities, conduct, dealings; see **action** 1.

do justice to, *v.* —*Syn.* esteem, pay tribute, honor; see **admire** 1, **consider** 1, **respect** 2.

dole, *n.* —*Syn.* charity, living wage, alms; see **subsistence** 1, 2.

doleful, *mod.* —*Syn.* sorrowful, mournful, wretched; see **sad** 1, 2.

dole (out), *v.* —*Syn.* share, assign, parcel; see **distribute** 1.

doll, *n.* —*Syn.* baby, moppet, figure, figurine, manikin, model, effigy; *both* (D): dolly, doll baby; see also **toy** 1.
Types of dolls include the following—puppet, marionette, rag doll, china doll, troll, Barbie doll (trademark); *both* (D): mamma doll, baby doll.

dollar, *n.* —*Syn.* coin, legal tender, dollar bill, silver dollar, currency, bank note, Federal Reserve note, silver certificate; *all* (D): greenback, folding money, buck, one-spot, shekel, peso, oner, iron smacker, iron man, ace; see also **money** 1.

dollar diplomacy, *n.* —*Syn.* (selfish) foreign policy, self-interest, commercially directed international affairs; see **economics, policy.**

dollop, *n.* —*Syn.* bit, touch, dash; see **dash** 4, **bit** 1.

doll up (D), *v.* —*Syn.* fix up, put on one's best clothes, primp; see **dress up.**

dolor, *n.* —*Syn.* sorrow, distress, anguish; see **grief** 1, **sadness.**

dolorous, *mod.* —*Syn.* mournful, distressed, grievous; see **sad** 1, 2.

dolt, *n.* —*Syn.* simpleton, nitwit, blockhead; see **fool** 1.

domain, *n.* —*Syn.* dominion, field, specialty; see **area** 2.

dome, *n.* **1.** [A semispherical roof]—*Syn.* cupola, top, bulge, mosque, roof, onion dome, vault, coving, church roof, bubble dome, goedesic dome, macrodome, clinodome, orthodome, brachydome; see also **arch, roof.**
2. [(D) The top of the head]—*Syn.* skull, cranium, noggin (D); see **head** 1.

domestic, *mod.* **1.** [Home-loving]—*Syn.* house-loving, devoted to one's family, having home interests, homely, homelike, domesticated, fond of home, addicted to family life, stay-at-home, household, family, devoted to the lares and penates, liking one's own fireside, quiet, sedentary, indoor, tame, settled; see also **calm** 1, 2, **tranquil** 1, 2.—*Ant.* upruly*, roving, restless.
2. [Home-grown]—*Syn.* indigenous, handcrafted, home-made; see **native** 2.

domesticate, *v.* —*Syn.* tame, breed, housebreak; see **teach** 2, **train** 4.

domesticated, *mod.* —*Syn.* tamed, trained, housebroken; see **tame** 1.

domicile, *n.* —*Syn.* residence, house, habitation; see **home** 1, 2.

dominant, *mod.* **1.** [Having effect or power]—*Syn.* ruling, prevailing, governing; see **predominant** 1.
2. [Inclined to use force]—*Syn.* commanding, imperious, imperative, authoritative, lordly, despotic, domineering, demonstrative, assertive, bossy (D); see also **aggressive** 2, **autocratic, powerful** 1. —*Ant.* humble*, retiring, meek.

dominate, *v.* —*Syn.* rule, manage, control, dictate (to), manage dictatorially, subject, subjugate, carry authority, tyrannize, keep subjugated, have one's (own) way, have influence over, domineer, carry authority; *all* (D): bend to one's will, play first fiddle, lead by the nose, boss, keep under one's thumb, rule the roost; see also **command** 2, **govern.**

domination, *n.* —*Syn.* rule, control, mastery; see **command** 2, **power** 2.

domineering, *mod.* —*Syn.* despotic, imperious, oppressive; see **autocratic, egotistic** 2, **tyrannical.**

dominion, *n.* **1.** [The acknowledged right to govern]—*Syn.* authority, seniority, jurisdiction, control, regiment, rule, sway, authorization, reign, ascendancy, sovereignty, supremacy, mastership, lordship, prerogative, privilege, regency, commission, empire; see also **administration** 1, **power** 2. —*Ant.* anarchy*, subjugation, bondage.
2. [Actual control]—*Syn.* management, control, regimentation; see **administration** 1, **government** 1.
3. [A semiautonomous governmental area]—*Syn.* region, district, state; see **area** 2, **nation** 1, **territory** 2.

don, *v.* —*Syn.* clothe, enrobe, put on; see **dress** 1, **wear** 1.

donate, *v.* —*Syn.* grant, bestow, bequeath; see **distribute** 1, **give** 1, **provide** 1.

donation, *n.* —*Syn.* benefaction, offering, present; see **gift** 1.

done, *mod.* **1.** [Accomplished]—*Syn.* over, through, completed, realized, consummated, effected, executed, wrought, performed, rendered, compassed, fulfilled, brought to pass, brought about, succeeded, perfected, *both* (D): roger, over and out; see also **finished** 1.—*Ant.* unfinished*, unrealized, failed.

2. [Cooked]—*Syn.* brewed, stewed, broiled, boiled, crisped, crusted, fried, browned, done to a turn; see also **baked.**—*Ant.* raw*, burned, uncooked.

3. [Agreed upon]—*Syn.* agreed, settled, compacted; see **approved, determined** 1.

done for (D), *mod.* —*Syn.* defeated, conquered, vanquished; see **beaten** 1.

done in (D), *mod.* —*Syn.* exhausted, worn out, weary; see **tired.**

done out of (D), *mod.* —*Syn.* defrauded, bilked, taken (D); see **cheated, deceived** 1.

done up (D), *mod.* —*Syn.* prepared, packaged, finished; see **wrapped.**

done with (D), *mod.* —*Syn.* finished with, dispatched, no longer needing *or* in need of; see **finished** 1.

Don Juan, *n.* —*Syn.* lothario, pursuer, Romeo; see **wolf** 2.

donkey, *n.* —*Syn.* burro, ass, jackass, jennet, beast of burden, Jerusalem pony, back burro; *all* (D): jack, jenny, Rocky Mountain canary, Missouri hummingbird, Arcadian nightingale, maud, donk, hee-haw; see also **horse** 1.

donor, *n.* —*Syn.* benefactor, contributor, patroness, benefactress, philanthropist, giver, donator, subscriber, grantor, public-spirited individual, altruist, savior, Good Samaritan; *all* (D): angel, the cash, the bank, fairy godmother; see also **patron** 1.

do-nothing, *mod.* —*Syn.* idle, indolent, passive; see **indifferent** 1, **lazy** 1.

do-nothing, *n.* —*Syn.* idler, shirker, sluggard, layabout; see **loafer.**

don'ts (D), *n.* —*Syn.* objections, veto(s), adverse reaction; see **objection** 2.

doom, *n.* **1.** [One's appointed end]—*Syn.* fate, lot, destination, predestination, foreordination, terrible ending, fixed future, evil condition, predetermination, fortune, kismet, annihilation, ruin, portion, conclusion, goal; *both* (D): the inescapable, fall of the curtain; see also **destiny** 1.

2. [A verdict]—*Syn.* opinion, decision, judgment; see **sentence** 1.

doomed, *mod.* —*Syn.* ruined, cursed, sentenced, lost, condemned, unredeemed, unfortunate, ill-fated, foreordained, predestined, reprobate, threatened, menaced, overthrown, overwhelmed, undone, cut down, thrown down, suppressed, wrecked, convicted; see also **destroyed.**

do one proud (D), *v.* —*Syn.* entertain lavishly *or* handsomely *or* sumptuously *or* well, feast, provide for; see **entertain** 2.

door, *n.* **1.** [Entrance]—*Syn.* entry, portal, bar, hatch, hatchway, postern, doorway, gateway, opening, aperture; see also **entrance** 2, **gate.**

Varieties of doors include the following—cellar, front, back, side, kitchen, barn, revolving, electric eye, automatic, secret, sliding, double, French, Dutch, trap.

2. [Approach]—*Syn.* gateway, opening, access; see **approach** 3, **opportunity** 1.

lay at the door of—*Syn.* censure, charge, blame; see **accuse.**

out of doors—*Syn.* outside, in the air, out; see **outdoors.**

show (someone) the door (D)—*Syn.* show out, ask to leave, eject; see **oust.**

doorkeeper, *n.* —*Syn.* porter, doorman, turnkey; see **watchman.**

do out of (D), *v.* —*Syn.* cheat, trick, beat out of (D); see **deceive, steal.**

do over, *v.* **1.** [To repeat]—*Syn.* redo, do again, rework; see **repeat** 1.

2. [(D) To redecorate]—*Syn.* refurbish, remodel, renew; see **redecorate.**

dope, *n.* **1.** [(D) A drug]—*Syn.* narcotic, stimulant, opiate; see **drug** 2.

2. [(D) Pertinent information]—*Syn.* details, account, developments; see **information, knowledge** 1, **news** 1.

3. [(D) A dull-witted person]—*Syn.* dunce, dolt, simpleton; see **fool** 1.

dope, *v.* **1.** [(D) To drug]—*Syn.* anesthetize, stupefy, put to sleep; see **deaden** 1, **drug.**

2. [(D) To include an additive]—*Syn.* doctor, impregnate, treat; see **include** 2, **soak** 1.

dope out (D), *v.* —*Syn.* figure out, comprehend, grasp; see **solve, understand** 1.

dormant, *mod.* **1.** [Sleeping]—*Syn.* torpid, comatose, lethargic; see **asleep.**

2. [Inactive]—*Syn.* passive, inoperative, inert; see **latent.**

dormitory, *n.* —*Syn.* (sleeping) quarters, barracks, room(s), apartment, hostel, men's dormitory, women's dormitory, residence, residence hall *or* house, dorm (D); see also **hotel.**

dos (D), *n.* —*Syn.* approval; *both* (D): (the) O.K.('s), the go-ahead; see **permission.**

dos and don'ts (D), *n.* —*Syn.* rules, regulations, instruction(s); see **advice, command** 1, **directions.**

dose, *n.* **1.** [The amount administered at one time]—*Syn.* dosage, treatment, measurement, measure, fill, spoonful, portion, lot, draught, application, shot, lethal *or* toxic dose, doctor's orders (D); see also **prescription, quantity, share.**

2. [(D) Venereal disease]—*Syn.* social disease, syphilis, gonorrhea; see **disease** 3.

dot, *n.* —*Syn.* point, period, spot, speck, pin-point, atom, particle, grain of sand, iota, droplet, mite, mote, dab, tittle, jot; see also **mark** 1.

on the dot—*Syn.* precisely, accurately, punctually; see **exactly.**

dotage, *n.* —*Syn.* feebleness, fatuity, imbecility; see **senility.**

dote, *v.* —*Syn.* adore, pet, admire; see **love** 1.

do time (D), *v.* —*Syn.* serve (out) a sentence, be incarcerated *or* in jail, pay one's debt to society; see **serve time.**

doting, *mod.* —*Syn.* lovesick, struck, foolish; see **fascinated, loving.**

double, *mod.* —*Syn.* twofold, two times, paired, coupled, binary, binate, geminate, doubled, redoubled, duplex, renewed, dual, both one and the other, repeated, second, increased, as much again, duplicated; see also **twice, twin.**—*Ant.* single*, alone, apart.
on (or at) the double—*Syn.* hastily, rapidly, hurriedly; see **quickly** 1.

double, *v.* **1.** [To make or become double]—*Syn.* make twice as much, duplicate, multiply; see **grow** 1, **increase** 1.
2. [(D) To replace]—*Syn.* substitute for, stand in, act for; see **substitute** 2.

double back, *v.* —*Syn.* backtrack, reverse, circle; see **return** 1, **turn** 2, 6.

double-cross, *v.* —*Syn.* cheat, defraud, trick; see **deceive.**

double-dealer, *n.* —*Syn.* deceiver, cheater, rogue; see **cheat** 1, **hypocrite, traitor.**

double-dealing, *mod.* —*Syn.* tricky, untrustworthy, deceitful; see **dishonest** 1, 2, **hypocritical.**

double-dealing, *n.* —*Syn.* deceit, cheating, mendacity; see **dishonesty, hypocrisy** 2.

double-entendre (French), *n.* —*Syn.* double meaning, ambiguity, pun; see **joke** 2.

double meaning, *n.* —*Syn.* *double-entendre* (French), ambiguity, play on words, innuendo, pun; see also **joke** 2.

doublet, *n.* —*Syn.* duplicate, couple, two; see **pair.**

double up, *v.* —*Syn.* combine, join, share; see **join** 1, 2, **unite** 1.

doubly, *mod.* —*Syn.* twofold, redoubled, increased; see **again, double, twice.**

doubt, *n.* **1.** [Questioning]—*Syn.* distrust, mistrust, disbelief, unbelief, suspicion, misgiving, skepticism, reluctance to believe, apprehension, dubiousness, doubtfulness, agnosticism, incredulity, faithlessness, lack *or* want of faith *or* confidence *or* certainty, jealousy, misdoubt, discredit, misbelief, diffidence, rejection; see also **uncertainty** 1.—*Ant.* faith*, trust, credence.
2. [Hesitation arising from uncertainty]—*Syn.* skepticism, scruple, misgiving, perplexity, indecision, irresolution, incertitude, hesitancy, suspense, lack of confidence *or* certainty, dubiety, undecidedness, faltering, vacillation, lack of conviction, ambiguity, dilemma, reluctance, difficulty, apprehension, wavering, demur, demurral, bewilderment, feeling of uncertainty, quandary, incredulity, dubiousness, unsettled opinion, timidity, bashfulness, feeling of inferiority, inferiority complex; see also **uncertainty** 2.—*Ant.* belief*, conviction, certainty.
beyond (*or* **without) doubt**—*Syn.* doubtless, sure, unquestionable; see **certain** 3.
no doubt—*Syn.* doubtless, in all likelihood, certainly; see **probably, surely.**

doubt, *v.* **1.** [To raise a question]—*Syn.* wonder, imagine, query, ponder, dispute, be dubious *or* uncertain *or* undetermined *or* curious *or* puzzled *or* doubtful, be in a quandary, refuse to believe, demur, hold in doubt, have doubts about, have one's doubts, stop to consider, have qualms, be uncertain in opinion, call in question, hesitate to accept as true, hold questionable, skepticize, doubt one's word, give no credit to, throw doubt upon, have no conception, not know which way to turn, not know what to make of, close one's mind, not admit, give no credence to, not believe, refuse to believe; *both* (D): not buy, make bones about; see also **ask** 1, **deny, question** 1.—*Ant.* believe, trust*, confide.
2. [To entertain doubt]—*Syn.* suspect, mistrust, distrust, lack confidence in, discredit, give no credence *or* credit to, disbelieve, hesitate, scruple, surmise, impugn, be apprehensive of, insinuate, misdoubt, misgive, read (somewhat) differently, misbelieve, challenge, harbor suspicions; *all* (D): smell a rat, not buy, take a dim view (of), set no store by, smell something in the wind.—*Ant.* support*, prove, demonstrate.

doubter, *n.* —*Syn.* questioner, unbeliever, agnostic; see **cynic, skeptic.**

doubtful, *mod.* **1.** [Ambiguous]—*Syn.* vague, indistinct, unclear; see **obscure** 1, **uncertain** 2.
2. [Uncertain in mind]—*Syn.* dubious, doubting, questioning, undecided, unsure, wavering, hesitating, undetermined, theoretical, uncertain, unsettled, confused, disturbed, lost, puzzled, disconcerted, perplexed, discomposed, flustered, flurried, baffled, faithless, hesitant, equivocal, distracted, faltering, unresolved, in a quandary, of two minds, unable to make up one's mind, wavering, indecisive, agnostic, like a doubting Thomas, troubled with doubt *or* uncertainty, having *or* of little faith, open to doubt, in question, without faith, not knowing what's what, under examination, having no idea, not following, in a dilemma; *all* (D): under a spell, in the clouds, up a tree, in a haze, not able to make head or tail of, from Missouri, going around in circles, out of focus, beat up, out of one's bearings, up in the air, wishy-washy, yes and no, iffy; see also **suspicious** 1.
3. [Of questionable character]—*Syn.* dubious, sneaky, disreputable; see **questionable** 2, **suspicious** 2.

doubting, *mod.* —*Syn.* questioning, dubious, skeptical; see **doubtful** 2, **suspicious** 1.

doubtless, *mod.* —*Syn.* positively, certainly, unquestionably; see **surely.**

dough, *n.* **1.** [A soft mixture]—*Syn.* paste (especially of flour), pulp, mash; see **batter, mixture** 1.
2. [(D) Money]—*Syn.* dollars, change, silver; see **money** 1, **wealth** 2.

doughnut, *n.* —*Syn.* friedcake, cruller; jelly doughnut, powdered doughnut, chocolate doughnut, etc; *all* (D): dunker, gasket, sinker, submarine; see also **cake** 2, **pastry.**

doughty, *mod.* —*Syn.* valiant, bold, strong; see **brave** 1, **resolute** 2.

do up (D), *v.* **1.** [To launder]—*Syn.* put through the laundry, wash and iron, finish; see **clean, wash** 2.
2. [To wrap up]—*Syn.* enclose, package, gift-wrap; see **wrap** 2.

dour, *mod.* —*Syn.* forbidding, gloomy, morose, dreary; see **dismal** 1.

douse, *v.* **1.** [To immerse in water]—*Syn.* submerge, splash, drench; see **immerse** 1, **soak** 1.
2. [To put out]—*Syn.* quench, drown *or* snuff out, splash; see **extinguish** 1.

dove, *n.* **1.** [A member of the Columbidae]—*Syn.* domesticated pigeon, turtledove *or* mourning dove, squab; see **pigeon.**

2. [(D) A promoter of peace]—*Syn.* peacemaker, peace lover, peaceman, activist for peace, pacifer, pacificator, conciliator, United Nations representative, reconciler, appeaser, peacemonger (D); see also **pacifist.**

dovetail, *v.*—*Syn.* link, interlock, fit together; see **join** 1.

dowager, *n.*—*Syn.* widow, matron, dame; see **lady** 2, **woman** 1.

dowdy, *mod.*—*Syn.* frumpy, tasteless, unfashionable, untidy, slovenly, frowzy, drab, tacky, shabby, homely, unseemly, plain, slatternly, unkempt, baggy; see also **dull** 2.

do well by, *v.*—*Syn.* aid, favor, treat well; see **help** 1.

do with, *v.*—*Syn.* get on, manage, get along with; see **endure** 2.

do without, *v.*—*Syn.* manage, get along without, forego; see **endure** 1, 2, **need.**

down, *prep.* and *mod.* **1.** [Having a downward motion]—*Syn.* forward, headlong, bottomward, downhill, downgrade, on a downward course, from higher to lower, to the bottom, downwardly, in a descending direction, to a lower position, declining, falling, descending, gravitating, slipping, sliding, cascading, sagging, precipitating, slumping, dropping, sinking, earthward, groundward, downward, hellward; see also **backward** 1.—*Ant.* up*, upward, rising.

2. [Physically lower]—*Syn.* below, depressed, underneath; see **under** 1.

3. [Figuratively lower]—*Syn.* inferior, lowly, below par; see **poor** 1, **sad** 1, **sick.**

down, *n.*—*Syn.* feathers, fluff, fur; see **hair** 1.

down, *v.*—*Syn.* put *or* throw *or* pull *or* knock down, throw, fell, subdue, tackle, trip, seize, conquer, overthrow, vanquish, overpower, upset, overturn, fling, trample in the dust; *all* (D): knock out, nail, bop; see also **defeat** 3, **hit** 1.—*Ant.* raise*, lift, elevate.

down and out, *mod.*—*Syn.* ruined, defeated, finished; see **beaten.**

downcast, *mod.*—*Syn.* discouraged, dejected, unhappy; see **sad** 1.

downfall, *n.* **1.** [Destruction]—*Syn.* drop, comedown, ruin; see **destruction** 2.

2. [Downpour]—*Syn.* rain, deluge, cloudburst; see **flood** 1, **storm** 1.

downgrade, *n.*—*Syn.* descent, decline, slope; see **hill, inclination** 5.

downgrade, *v.*—*Syn.* minimize, deprecate, lower; see **decrease** 2, **depreciate** 2.

downhearted, *mod.*—*Syn.* dejected, despondent, downcast; see **sad** 1.

down on (D), *mod.*—*Syn.* against, disillusioned (about), furious (with); see **opposed.**

downpour, *n.*—*Syn.* rain, deluge, flood, monsoon; see **storm** 1.

downright, *mod.* **1.** [Thorough]—*Syn.* total, complete, utter; see **absolute** 1, **whole** 1.

2. [Thoroughly]—*Syn.* absolutely, entirely, utterly; see **completely.**

downstairs, *mod.*—*Syn.* underneath, below decks, on the floor below; see **below** 4, **under** 1.

downstairs, *n.*—*Syn.* first floor, ground floor, cellar; see **basement** 2.

down-to-date, *mod.*—*Syn.* until now, up-to-date, recent; see **modern** 1, 3.

down-to-earth, *mod.*—*Syn.* sensible, mundane, practicable; see **common** 1, **practical, rational** 1.

downtown, *mod.*—*Syn.* city, central, inner-city, main, mid-city, midtown, in the business district, on the main street, metropolitan, business, shopping; see also **urban** 2.—*Ant.* suburban*, residential, rural.

downtown, *n.*—*Syn.* hub, crossroads, inner city; see **center** 2, **city.**

downtrodden, *mod.*—*Syn.* tyrannized, subjugated, overcome; see **oppressed.**

downward, *mod.*—*Syn.* earthward, descending, downwards; see **down** 1.

downy, *mod.*—*Syn.* woolly, fleecy, fuzzy, fluffy, covered with soft hair *or* feathers, plumose, feathery, velvety, pubescent, silky; see also **light** 5, **soft** 2.—*Ant.* rough*, hard, bald.

dowry, *n.*—*Syn.* dower, dot, (bride's *or* woman's) marriage portion, bride's share, bridal gift, jointure, tocher (Scottish); see also **money** 1, **property** 1.

doxology, *n.*—*Syn.* paean, hymn, gloria, glorification, psalm, hallelujah, hosanna, *Te Deum* (Latin); see also **song.**

doze, *v.*—*Syn.* nap, drowse, slumber; see **sleep.**

dozen, *mod.*—*Syn.* twelve, baker's dozen, long dozen, handful, pocketful.

drab, *mod.* **1.** [Dismal]—*Syn.* dingy, colorless, dreary; see **dull** 2, 4.

2. [Dun-colored]—*Syn.* yellowish brown, dull color, brownish, brownish yellow, dull brown *or* gray, grayish, yellowish gray, achromatic, murky, mouse-colored, slate-colored, leaden-hued; see also **brown, gray** 1.

draft, *n.* **1.** [A preliminary sketch]—*Syn.* plans, blueprint, sketch; see **design** 1.

2. [A drink]—*Syn.* swallow, glass, quaff; see **drink** 1.

3. [A breeze]—*Syn.* current of air, gust, puff; see **wind** 1.

4. [A contrivance for controlling the flow of air]—*Syn.* damper, check, control, flap, front draft, check draft, smoke draft; see also **valve.**

5. [An order for payment]—*Syn.* cashier's check, bank draft, (money) order, receipt, promissory note, warrant, coupon, bond, debenture, letter of credit, IOU (D); see **check** 1.

6. [The selection of troops]—*Syn.* conscription, induction, assignment, registration, allotment, recruiting, lottery, levy, selective service, call of duty, call to the colors, roll call, call-up (D); see also **selection** 1.

on draft—*Syn.* ready to be drawn (from the cask), bulk, unbottled; see **available, potable, ready** 2.

draft, *v.* **1.** [Make a rough plan]—*Syn.* outline, delineate, sketch; see **plan** 1, 2.

2. [Select for military service]—*Syn.* select, conscript, choose; see **enlist** 1, **recruit** 1.

draftsman, *n.*—*Syn.* sketcher, delineator, drawer; see **architect** 1, **artist** 1, **designer.**

drag, *n.* **1.** [Anything that is drawn]—*Syn.* harrow, scraper, bar, dragnet, seine, clog, brake, shoe, anchor, dragrope, floater; see also **net.**

2. [The influence of air on an airplane]—*Syn.* curb, pull, suction, friction, suck, tow, vacuum action; see also **resistance** 3.

3. [A restraint]—*Syn.* hindrance, burden, incumbrance; see **impediment** 1.
4. [(D) An annoying person, thing, or situation] —*Syn.* bother, annoyance, hang-up (D); see **nuisance** 3, **trouble** 2.

drag, *v.* **1.** [To go slowly; *said of animate beings*] —*Syn.* lag, straggle, dawdle; see **loiter, pause.**
2. [To go slowly; *said of an activity*—*Syn.* slow down, encounter difficulties, be delayed, fail to show progress, creep along, be unsatisfactory, stagnate, mark time, suffer from a slow-down, be off-season, be quiescent *or* quiet, show a poor progress report, crawl (D); see also **delay** 1.—*Ant.* improve*, progress, pick up.
3. [To pull an object]—*Syn.* haul, move, transport; see **draw** 1.
4. [To pulverize]—*Syn.* work, harrow, level; see **grind** 1.
5. [(D) To race]—*Syn.* compete in speed, run at top speed, hot-rod (D); see **race** 2.
6. [To smoke]—*Syn.* puff, inhale deeply, breathe in; see **smoke** 2.

dragging, *mod.* —*Syn.* monotonous, going slowly, boring; see **dull** 4.

dragline, *n.* —*Syn.* towline, cable, rope; see **chain** 1, **drag** 1, **wire** 2.

dragnet, *n.* **1.** [A net]—*Syn.* trawl, seine, trammel; see **drag** 1, **net** 1.
2. [A system for apprehending criminals or suspects]—*Syn.* police sweep *or* network, all-points bulletin, stakeout(s), *both* (D): roundup, the works; see also **arrest** 1, **trap** 1.

drag on, *v.* —*Syn.* go on slowly *or* badly, keep going, persist; see **continue** 1, **endure** 1.

dragon, *n.* —*Syn.* mythical beast, serpent, hydra; see **monster** 1, **snake.**

drag one's feet, *v.* —*Syn.* lag behind, obstruct, hold back; see **hesitate, hinder, pause, resist.**

dragoon, *n.* —*Syn.* mounted infantryman, trooper, cavalryman; see **soldier.**

drain, *n.* —*Syn.* duct, channel, sewer; see **conduit, pipe** 1.
down the drain (D)—*Syn.* wasted, ruined, gone; see **lost** 1.

drain, *v.* **1.** [To withdraw fluid]—*Syn.* divert, bleed, milk, tap, draw off, remove, evaporate, catheterize; see also **empty** 2.
2. [To withdraw strength]—*Syn.* exhaust, empty, consume, weary, tire (out), expend, sap, dissipate, waste, tax, deplete, get rid of, free from, bleed, debilitate, devitalize, reduce, filter off *or* away, remove, milk (D); see also **spend** 1, **weaken** 2. —*Ant.* revive*, refresh, replenish.
3. [To seep away]—*Syn.* run *or* flow *or* seep away *or* out *or* off, exude, trickle (out), filter (off), ooze, percolate, effuse, find an opening, osmose, decline, diminish, leave (something) dry; see also **flow** 1, 2.
4. [To empty]—*Syn.* pour, bail out, dump; see **empty** 2.

drainage, *n.* —*Syn.* seepage, waste, bilge, waste water, drain water, sewerage, that which is drained off, effluvium, effluent; see also **trash** 1.

dram, *n.* —*Syn.* measure, sip, drop; see **dose** 1.

drama, *n.* **1.** [A theatrical composition or production]—*Syn.* play, (theatrical) piece *or* production, dramatic representation *or* work, dramatization, (stage) show, (legitimate) stage, theatre, vehicle (D). Types of drama include the following—melodrama, tragicomedy, comedy of manners, social document, burlesque, pantomime, mime, opera, operetta, light opera, musical comedy, musical, mystery, murder mystery, farce, problem drama, classical drama, historical drama, expressionism, theater of the absurd, theater of cruelty, mixed media theater, epic, pageant, masque, miracle play, revival, serial (drama), radio play, television play *or* drama; *all* (D): thriller, high-brow stuff, whodunit, agitprop, melo; see also **comedy, tragedy** 3.
2. [Action having the qualities of drama]—*Syn.* farce, climax, emotion, tension, scene, histrionics, melodrama, tragedy, comedy; *all* (D): riot, sob stuff, tear-jerker, soap opera; see also **excitement.**

dramatic, *mod.* —*Syn.* tense, climactic, moving; see **exciting.**

dramatis personae, *n.* —*Syn.* players, actors, performers; see **actor, actress, cast** 2.

dramatist, *n.* —*Syn.* playwright, script writer, scenario writer; *all* (D): scenarist, scripter, the brains; see also **author** 2, **writer.**
Major dramatists include the following—Great Britain: Christopher Marlowe, Ben Jonson, William Shakespeare, William Congreve, Richard Brinsley Sheridan, Oliver Goldsmith, James Barrie, Oscar Wilde, George Bernard Shaw, Sean O'Casey, John Millington Synge, Tom Stoppard, Harold Pinter, John Osborne; United States: Thornton Wilder, Eugene O'Neill, Maxwell Anderson, William Inge, Tennessee Williams, Arthur Miller, Edward Albee; Greece: Aeschylus, Sophocles, Euripides, Aristophanes; France: Molière, Pierre Corneille, Jean Racine, Edmond Rostand, Jean Anouilh, Jean Giraudoux, Eugène Ionesco, Jean Genêt, Jean Cocteau, Jean-Paul Sartre; Germany: Wolfgang von Goethe, Friedrich Schiller, Bertolt Brecht, Gerhardt Hauptmann; other: Luigi Pirandello, Maxim Gorky, Anton Chekov, Henrik Ibsen, August Strindberg, Friedrich Dürrenmatt, Calderón, Lope de Vega, Federico Garcia Lorca, Samuel Beckett, Karel Čapek, Monzaemon Chikamatsu.

dramatize, *v.* **1.** [To present a performance] —*Syn.* enact, produce, execute; see **perform** 2.
2. [To exaggerate]—*Syn.* overstate, give color to, amplify; see **exaggerate.**

drape, *v.* —*Syn.* enclose, hang, dress, wrap, model, display, line, don; see also **clothe.**

drapes, *n.* —*Syn.* window covering, drapery, hanging; see **curtain.**

drastic, *mod.* —*Syn.* extravagant, exorbitant, radical; see **extreme** 2.

draw, *v.* **1.** [To move an object]—*Syn.* pull, drag, attract, move, bring, convey, tug, trail, lug, tow, take in tow, carry, jerk, wrench, yank, trawl, unsheathe, hook, siphon, haul, wind in, draw out, extract, magnetize, draw into.—*Ant.* repel*, repulse, reject.
2. [To make a likeness by drawing]—*Syn.* sketch, describe, draft, express, etch, crayon, pencil, outline, trace (out), make a picture of, limn, depict, model, form, portray, engrave, caricature, litho-

graph, profile, silhouette, chart, map, dash; see also **paint** 1.
3. [To lure]—*Syn.* allure, induce, entice; see **fascinate.**
beat to the draw (D)—*Syn.* be quicker than another, forestall, stop; see **anticipate** 2, **defeat** 1, **prevent.**
draw away, *v.* —*Syn.* pull away (from), gain on, increase a lead; see **advance** 1, **defeat** 1, **leave** 1.
drawback, *n.* **1.** [A shortcoming]—*Syn.* detriment, hindrance, check; see **disadvantage** 3, **lack** 2.
2. [A refund]—*Syn.* rebate, repayment, reduction; see **refund.**
draw back, *v.* —*Syn.* withdraw, recede, draw in; see **retreat** 1, 2.
drawing, *n.* **1.** [The practice or study of drawing] —*Syn.* sketching, designing, illustrating, tracing, limning, etching, design, illustration, commercial art, commercial designing; see also **art** 2.
Kinds of drawing include the following—life, line, figure, architectural, mechanical, isometric, scale, freehand, pen and ink, charcoal, red charcoal, pencil, black and white, chiaroscuro; see **picture** 3, **representation.**
2. [A work produced by drawing]—*Syn.* sketch, likeness, work of art; see **picture** 3, **representation.**
3. [A work produced by drawing]—*Syn.* sketch, likeness, work of art; see **picture** 3, **representation.**
drawing room, *n.* —*Syn.* reception room, living room, sitting room, apartment, stateroom, salon, best room, front room; see also **parlor, room** 2.
drawl, *v.* —*Syn.* lengthen, extend, pronounce slowly and lazily, protract in utterance, prolong syllables, speak monotonously, spin out; see also **utter.**
drawling, *mod.* —*Syn.* monotonous, languid, droning; see **dull** 4.
draw on, *v.* —*Syn.* take from, extract, employ; see **require** 2, **use** 1.
draw out, *v.* **1.** [To induce to talk]—*Syn.* make talk, lead on, extract; see **discover** 1, **obtain** 1.
2. [To pull]—*Syn.* drag, tug, attract; see **draw** 1.
draw up, *v.* —*Syn.* draft, execute, prepare (a statement); see **write** 1, **write up.**
draw upon, *v.* —*Syn.* rely upon, employ, make use of; see **use** 1.
dray, *n.* —*Syn.* hand truck, van, vehicle; see **cart, wagon.**
drayage, *n.* —*Syn.* truckage, cartage, haulage; see **freight** 1, **load** 1, **transportation.**
dread, *n.* —*Syn.* awe, horror, terror; see **fear** 2.
dreadful, *mod.* —*Syn.* hideous, fearful, shameful; see **frightful** 1.
dreadnought, *n.* —*Syn.* man-of-war, battleship, gunboat; see **ship, warship.**
dream, *n.* **1.** [Mental picture(s)]—*Syn.* nightmare, apparition, hallucination, wraith, specter, incubus, image, trance, idea, impression, reverie, emotion, romance, daydream, dream life, evidence of the unconscious; *all* (D): castle in the air, will-o'-the-wisp, castle in Spain, air castle, chimera; see **fantasy** 2, **illusion** 1, **thought** 2, **vision** 3, 4.—*Ant.* reality*, verity, truth.
2. [An unreliable interpretation]—*Syn.* imagination, mistake, deception; see **error** 1, **illusion** 1, **vision** 4.
3. [Unattainable idea]—*Syn.* wish, flight of fancy, pipe dream; see **fantasy** 2, **hope** 2.
dream, *v.* **1.** [To have visions, usually during sleep or fever]—*Syn.* be delirious, have nightmares, see in a vision, have flashes, hallucinate, fancy, visualize, envisage; see also **imagine** 1.
2. [To entertain or delude oneself with imagined things]—*Syn.* fancy, indulge in reveries *or* fancies, imagine, conceive, have notions, conjure up, create, picture, idealize, sublimate, daydream; *all* (D): be up in the clouds, be on cloud nine, build castles in the air *or* in Spain, be moonstruck, talk through one's hat, pipe-dream, go for a sleigh ride, blow bubbles, search for the rainbow's end, look for the pot of gold; see also **invent** 1, 2.
3. [To conceive mentally; *usually used in the negative*]—*Syn.* believe, credit, understand; see **assume** 1.
dreamer, *n.* —*Syn.* visionary, utopist, theorizer; see **idealist.**
dreaming, *mod.* —*Syn.* thinking, daydreaming, in a reverie; see also **rapt** 2, **thoughtful** 1.
dreamland, *n.* —*Syn.* cloudland, fairyland, slumber; see **sleep.**
dream up (D), *v.* —*Syn.* devise, contrive, concoct; see **imagine** 1.
dreamy, *mod.* **1.** [As if in a dream]—*Syn.* whimsical, fanciful, daydreaming, visionary, given to reverie, illusory, abstracted, musing, introspective, in a reverie, out of this world, introvertive, not of this world, otherworldly, idealistic, mythical, utopian, romantic, quixotic; see also **imaginary, impractical, legendary** 2.—*Ant.* practical*, active, real.
2. [Suggestive of a dream]—*Syn.* intangible, fantastical, nightmarish; see **impractical, unreal.**
dreary, *mod.* —*Syn.* damp, raw, windy; see **cold** 1, **dismal** 1.
dredge, *v.* —*Syn.* drag, net, fish; see **draw** 1.
dregs, *n.* **1.** [Sediment]—*Syn.* lees, grounds, slag; see **residue.**
2. [Debris]—*Syn.* scum, refuse, waste; see **trash** 1.
drench, *v.* —*Syn.* wet, saturate, flood; see **immerse** 1, **soak** 1.
dress, *n.* **1.** [Clothing]—*Syn.* ensemble, attire, garment(s), garb, apparel, array, costume, toilet, wardrobe, raiment, habiliments, accouterments, uniform, habit, livery, formal dress, evening clothes, informal dress; *all* (D): gear, trappings, weeds, things, guise, togs, rigging, get-up, front, harness, rags, glad rags, duds; see also **clothes, coat** 1, **pants** 1, **shirt, skirt, suit** 3, **sweater, underwear.**
2. [A woman's outer garment]—*Syn.* frock, gown, wedding dress, evening gown *or* formal (D), cocktail gown, suit, skirt, toga, muumuu, robe, sun dress, shift, strapless, wraparound, housedress, smock, housecoat; see also **clothes.**
dress, *v.* **1.** [To put on clothes]—*Syn.* don, wear, garb, clothe, change clothes, robe, attire, drape, array, cover; *all* (D): get *or* pile into, fit *or* deck out, throw *or* slip on, trick *or* fix *or* spruce *or* dress *or* muffle *or* spiff *or* doll *or* dud *or* bundle up, put on the dog; see also **wear** 1.
2. [To provide with clothes]—*Syn.* costume, outfit, fit out; see **clothe, support** 5.

3. [To make ready for show or use]—*Syn.* groom, ornament, make ready; see **decorate, prepare** 1, **trim** 2.
4. [To give medical treatment]—*Syn.* attend, treat, bandage, cleanse, sterilize, cauterize, give first aid, bind, apply a surgical dressing *or* dressings, apply antiseptics, plaster, sew up, remove stitches; see also **heal** 1.

dress down (D), *v.* —*Syn.* rebuke, scold, reprimand; see **censure.**

dressed up, *mod.* —*Syn.* dressed formally, in full dress, dolled *or* spruced up (D); see **fancy** 2, **fashionable, formal** 4, **ornate.**

dresser, *n.* —*Syn.* dressing table, chest of drawers, bureau; see **furniture, table** 1.

dressing, *n.* **1.** [A food mixture]—*Syn.* stuffing, filling, forcemeat.
Dressings include the following—bread, giblet, oyster, chestnut, potato, prune, plum, apple, duck, turkey, chicken, fish, clam, wild rice.
2. [A flavoring sauce]. Salad dressings include the following—mayonnaise, French, Russian, thousand island, green goddess, blue cheese, Roquefort, Italian, Caesar, boiled, oil and vinegar.
Other sauces include the following—Hollandaise, drawn butter, tartar, Worcestershire, mustard; see also **relish** 1, **sauce** 1.
3. [An external medical application]—*Syn.* bandage, plaster cast, adhesive tape, Bandaid (trademark), compress, strip, gauze, tourniquet, pack, wet dressing; see also **cast** 4.
4. [The act of clothing]—*Syn.* getting dressed, arraying, robing, appareling, making a toilette, adorning, decking.
5. [Fertilizer]—*Syn.* manure, humus, leaf mold; see **fertilizer.**

dressing gown, *n.* —*Syn.* robe, negligee, gown; see **clothes, nightgown.**

dressmaker, *n.* —*Syn.* seamstress, ladies' tailor, modiste, designer, draper, manufacturing tailor, sewing woman, (dress) fitter, operator; *all* (D): operative, needle pusher, shears, snips; see also **tailor.**

dress up, *v.* —*Syn.* primp, dress for dinner; *all* (D): spruce *or* doll *or* spiff *or* dud *or* bundle *or* fix *or* trick up, deck *or* fit out, put on the dog; see also **dress** 1.

dressy, *mod.* —*Syn.* dressed up, elegant, elaborate; see **fancy** 2, **fashionable, formal** 4, **ornate** 1.

dribble, *v.* —*Syn.* trickle, spout, squirt; see **drop** 1.

driblet, *n.* —*Syn.* mite, morsel. scrap; see **bit** 1, **drop** 1.

dried, *mod.* —*Syn.* drained, dehydrated, desiccated; see **dry** 1, **preserved** 2.

drift, *n.* **1.** [A tendency in movement]—*Syn.* bent, tenor, trend, tendency, end, effort, inclination, impulse, propulsion, aim, scope, tone, goal, push, bias, set, gravity, leaning, progress, conduct, propensity, disposition, bearing, proneness, line, tack, set, spirit; see also **direction** 1, **route** 2, **way** 2.—*Ant.* indifference*, aimlessness, inertia.
2. [The measure or character of movement] —*Syn.* wash, deviation, aberration, motion, leeway, flux, drift, current, stream, diversion, digression, swerving, sweep, warp, departure; see also **flow.**
3. [The tendency in ideas or discussion]—*Syn.* intention, object, end; see **meaning.**
4. [Something blown]—*Syn.* bank, mass, pile; see **heap.**
5. [A tunnel following a vein of ore]—*Syn.* adit, underground passage, subway; see **tunnel.**

drift, *v.* —*Syn.* float, ride, sail, cruise, wander at random, move with the current, gravitate, tend, be carried along (by the current), draw near, move toward, go with the tide, be caught in the current, move without effort, move slowly; see also **flow** 1, **move** 1.—*Ant.* steer*, push, pull.

drill, *n.* **1.** [Practice]—*Syn.* preparation, repetition, learning by doing; see **practice** 3.
2. [A tool for boring holes]—*Syn.* borer, wood bit, gimlet, countersink, steel drill, steam drill, diamond drill, compressed-air drill, turbo-corer, cylindrical borer, boring tool, well drill, tap-borer, auger, corkscrew, awl, wimble, trepan, trephine, riveter, jackhammer; see also **bit** 5.
3. [Exercise, especially in military formation] —*Syn.* training, maneuvers, marching, close-order drill, open-order drill, conditioning, survival training, guerilla training, paratroop *or* drop training; *all* (D): footslogging, monkey drill, push and pull; see also **parade** 1.
4. [Device for planting seed in holes]—*Syn.* planter, seeder, drill seeder, implement, dibble; see also **tool** 1.

drill, *v.* **1.** [To bore]—*Syn.* pierce, sink (in), puncture; see **dig** 1, **penetrate** 1.
2. [To train]—*Syn.* practice, rehearse, discipline; see **teach** 2.

drilling, *n.* —*Syn.* drill hole, opening, Project Mohole; see **hole** 2.

drink, *n.* **1.** [A draft]—*Syn.* gulp, sip, potion, libation, drop, bottle, glass, toast, refreshment, tall drink, long drink; *all* (D): dust-cutter, mouthwash, shot, double, boilermaker, stiff one, flip, slug, nip, drag, bracer, dram, swig, spot, short one, nightcap, one for the road, hair of the dog, three fingers, tonic, tonsil-bath.
2. [An alcoholic beverage]—*Syn.* rye, Bourbon, Scotch, Irish whiskey, gin, liqueur, ale, stout, grog, toddy, rum, arrack, absinthe, Pernod (trademark), tequila, pulque, slivovitz, mead, vodka; see also **brandy, beer, cocktail, gin, highball, whisky, wine.**
3. [A nonalcoholic beverage]—*Syn.* distilled water, mineral water, carbonated water, mixer, tonic, quinme, Apollinaris, Roland, Seltzer, Vichy, Perrier, cocoa, (hot) chocolate, chocolate milk, milkshake *or* frappé, lemonade, orangeade, punch, soft drink, soda (water), cola drink, ginger ale, ice-cream soda, fountain drink, bottled drink, orange *or* tomato *or* grapefruit, etc. juice; collins *or* Tom Collins *or* rum, etc. mix; *all* (D): pop, soda pop, chaser; see also **coffee, milk, tea** 1, **water** 1.

drink, *v.* **1.** [To swallow liquid]—*Syn.* gulp (down), take (in), take a draft, quaff, sip, suck (in), guzzle, slake (one's) thirst, imbibe; *all* (D): absorb, moisten the tonsils, wash down, gargle, irrigate, inhale; see also **swallow.**
2. [To consume alcoholic liquor]—*Syn.* tipple, swill, swig, guzzle, dissipate; *all* (D): take a drop *or* nip, wet one's whistle, down, grease the gills, soak, booze, likker up, hit the bottle, drain the cup, raise

or bend *or* exercise the elbow, go on a drunk *or* a binge, cheer the inner man, pledge, salute.

drinker, *n.*—*Syn.* tippler, guzzler, alcoholic, lush (D); see **drunkard.**

drinking bout, *n.*—*Syn.* debauch, spree, bacchanalia; see **entertainment** 1, **orgy.**

drink to, *v.*—*Syn.* honor, pledge, salute; see **praise** 1, **toast** 1.

drip, *v.*—*Syn.* dribble, trickle, plop; see **drop** 1.

drive, *n.* **1.** [A ride in a vehicle]—*Syn.* ride, trip, outing, ramble, airing, tour, expedition, excursion, jaunt, run; *all* (D): turn, spin, Sunday drive; see also **journey.**

2. [In baseball, a low, fast fly]—*Syn.* line drive, infield drive, home run; *all* (D): bleacher drive, grand tour, circuit; see also **hit** 3.

3. [A driveway]—*Syn.* approach, avenue, boulevard; see **driveway, road** 1.

4. [Impelling force]—*Syn.* energy, effort, impulse; see **force** 3.

drive, *v.* **1.** [To urge on]—*Syn.* impel, propel, instigate, incite, animate, hasten, egg *or* urge on, compel, coerce, induce, force, press, stimulate, hurry, actuate, frighten, constrain, provoke, arouse, make, put up to, inspire, prompt, call *or* spirit up, rouse, smoke *or* ferret out, operate upon, work on, act upon; see also sense 2; **encourage** 1, **push** 2. —*Ant.* stop*, hinder, drag.

2. [To cause to move; *usually said of domestic animals*]—*Syn.* chase, herd, prod, goad, worry, spur, hustle, hound, dog, hunt, kick, beat, rap, shove, hurry along, drive up; *all* (D): pound on the back, hit the trail with, ride herd on; see also **sense** 1;**push** 2.

3. [To manage a propelled vehicle]—*Syn.* direct, manage, handle, run, send, spin, wheel; bicycle *or both* (D): bike, cycle; advance, rush, transport, head for, float, raft, drift, dash, put in motion, give an impetus, start, turn, rattle, set going, speed, roll, slide, coast, get under way, keep going, vehiculate, pound, back in *or* up; *all* (D): bowl along, chariot, burn up the road, go like hell, go hellbent (for election), step on it, handle *or* hold the reins, crack the whip, open her up, give it the gun *or* the gas; see also **ride** 1, 2.—*Ant.* walk*, crawl, stay.

4. [To force with blows]—*Syn.* strike, knock, punch, hammer, ram, whack, maul, butt, smite, shoot, thwack, throw, thump, batter; *all* (D): wham, sock, soak, pop, tickle, jackhammer, give it to; see also **beat** 2, **hit** 1.

5. [To carry on offensive movement]—*Syn.* push forward, thrust, counterattack; see **attack** 1.

drive a bargain (D), *v.*—*Syn.* deal, close a deal, bargain; see **buy** 1, **sell** 1.

drive at, *v.* **1.** [To intend]—*Syn.* design, contemplate, propose; see **intend** 1.

2. [To imply]—*Syn.* allude, indicate, signify; see **mean** 1.

drive away, *v.*—*Syn.* drive off, disperse, banish; see **scatter** 2.

drive crazy, *v.*—*Syn.* anger, bemuse, infuriate; see **bother** 2.

drivel, *v.* **1.** [Drool]—*Syn.* slobber, drip, slaver; see **drool.**

2. [Ramble]—*Syn.* talk foolishly, prate, gabble; see **babble, ramble** 2.

drive mad, *v.*—*Syn.* anger, bemuse, infuriate; see **bother** 2.

driven, *mod.*—*Syn.* blown, drifted, herded, pushed, pounded, washed, guided, steered, directed, induced, urged (on), forced, shoved, sent, hard pressed, impelled, unable to help oneself, at the mercy of wind and wave; *all* (D): up tight, up against it, with (one's back (up) to the wall.

driver, *n.*—*Syn.* chauffeur, motorist, coachman, whip, (licensed) operator; bus driver, truck driver, cab driver, four-in-hand driver, etc.; horse trainer, handler, person in the driver's seat; *all* (D): autoist, (mule) skinner, bull whacker, hit-and-runner spinner, jitney jockey, cabbie, hack.

driveway, *n.*—*Syn.* drive, entrance, street, avenue, roadway, parkway, carriage way, boulevard, approach, lane, track, path, pavement, palms; palm drive, oak drive, etc.; see also **road** 1.

drizzle, *v.*—*Syn.* spray, shower, sprinkle; see **drop** 1, **rain.**

droll, *mod.*—*Syn.* comical, laughable, ridiculous; see **funny** 1.

drollery, *n.*—*Syn.* buffoonery, humor, pleasantry; see **joke** 1, 2.

drone, *n.* **1.** [A continuous sound]—*Syn.* hum, buzz, vibration; see **noise** 1.

2. [An idle person]—*Syn.* idler, loafer, parasite; see **loafer.**

drone, *v.* **1.** [To make a continuous sound]—*Syn.* hum, buzz, vibrate; see **noise** 1, **sound** 1.

2. [To loaf]—*Syn.* lounge, idle, kill time; see **loaf** 1.

drool, *v.* **1.** [To slobber]—*Syn.* drivel, drip, slaver, salivate, spit, water at the mouth, dribble, trickle, ooze, run (out); see also **drop** 1.

2. [To want]—*Syn.* drool over; *both* (D): mouthwater, lick one's chops; see **want.**

droop, *v.*—*Syn.* settle, sink, hang down; see **lean** 1.

drop, *n.* **1.** [Enough fluid to fall]—*Syn.* drip, trickle, droplet, globule, bead, tear(drop), dewdrop, raindrop; see also **tear.**

2. [A lowering or falling]—*Syn.* fall, tumble, reduction, decrease, slide, descent, slump, lapse, slip, decline, downfall, upset, precipitation, landslide (D); see also **fall** 1.

3. [A small quantity]—*Syn.* speck, dash, dab; see **bit** 1.

at the drop of a hat (D)—*Syn.* without warning, at the slightest provocation, quickly; see **immediately.**

get (or have) the drop on (D)—*Syn.* get or take advantage of, defeat, exploit; see **use** 1.

drop, *v.* **1.** [To fall in drops]—*Syn.* drip, fall, dribble, trickle, descend, leak, ooze, percolate, emanate, distill, precipitate (out), seep, drain, filter, sink, bleed, bead, splash, snow, purl, trill down, plash, plump, hail; see also **rain.**—*Ant.* rise*, spurt, squirt.

2. [To cause or to permit to fall]—*Syn.* let go, give up, release, shed, relinquish, abandon, loosen, lower, plump, floor, ground, shoot, knock (down), fell, unload, topple; see also **dump.**—*Ant.* raise*, elevate, send up.

3. [To tumble]—*Syn.* cave in, go to ruin, collapse; see **fall** 1.

4. [To discontinue]—*Syn.* give up, quit, leave; see **stop** 2.

5. [(D) To break off an acquaintance]—*Syn.* break (with), part from *or* with, cast off, forsake, end, interrupt, desert, leave, forget about, divorce, be alienated from, separate *or* withdraw (from), forego, fling aside, have done with; *all* (D): lose, ditch, write off, shake, throw over, dust off; see also **abandon** 2.—*Ant.* incite*, welcome, make friends with.

drop a hint, *v.*—*Syn.* suggest, intimate, imply; see **hint** 2, **propose** 1.

drop a letter, *v.*—*Syn.* post, dispatch, write; see **communicate** 2, **notify** 1.

drop a line, *v.*—*Syn.* write (to), post, communicate with; see **communicate** 2, **notify** 1.

drop an idea, *v.*—*Syn.* forgo, give up, quit; see **forget** 1, 2, **stop** 2.

drop back, *v.*—*Syn.* lag, fall back, retier; see **recede** 2, **retreat** 1.

drop behind, *v.*—*Syn.* slow down, worsen, decline; see **fail** 1, **lose** 3.

drop dead (D), *v.*—*Syn.* expire, collapse, succumb; see **die** 1.

drop in, *v.*—*Syn.* call, stop, look in on; see **visit** 4.

drop off, *v.* **1.** [To sleep]—*Syn.* fall asleep, doze, drowse; see **sleep.**
2. [To deliver]—*Syn.* leave, hand over, present; see **give** 1.

dropout (D), *n.*—*Syn.* failing student, truant, quitter; see **failure** 2.

drop out, *v.*—*Syn.* withdraw, cease, quit; see **abandon** 1, **retreat** 1.

dropped, *mod.*—*Syn.* discontinued, released, expelled; see **abandoned** 1.

dross, *n.*—*Syn.* rubbish, waste, garbage; see **trash** 1.

drought, *n.*—*Syn.* dry season, aridity, desiccation, dehydration, rainless period, dry spell; see also **dryness.**

drove, *n.*—*Syn.* flock, pack, rout; see **crown** 1, **herd** 1.

drown, *v.* **1.** [To cover with liquid]—*Syn.* swamp, inundate, overflow; see **flood.**
2. [To lower into a liquid]—*Syn.* dip, plunge, submerge; see **immerse** 1, **sink** 2.
3. [To kill *or* to die by drowning]—*Syn.* go down three times, suffocate, asphyxiate; see **die** 1, **kill** 1.

drowned, *mod.*—*Syn.* undergone death by drowning, suffocated, immersed, submerged, sunk, foundered; *all* (D): asleep in the deep, in a watery grave, under hatches; see also **dead** 1, **gone** 2.

drown out, *v.*—*Syn.* silence, overwhelm, muffle; see **hush** 1.

drowse off, *v.*—*Syn.* doze, nap, snooze; see **sleep.**

drowsy, *mod.* **1.** [Sleepy]—*Syn.* slumberous, dozing, somnolent; see **tired.**
2. [Lethargic]—*Syn.* sluggish, languid, indolent; see **lazy** 1.

drub, *v.*—*Syn.* cudgel, thrash, flog; see **beat** 2.

drudge, *n.*—*Syn.* hard worker, toiler, crammer, slave, menial, scullion, burner of midnight oil (D); see also **laborer, workman.**

drug, *n.* **1.** [Medicinal substance]—*Syn.* remedy, prescription, pill; see **medicine** 2.
2. [Any stimulant or depressant]—*Syn.* sedative, potion, essence, stupefacient, anodyne, fumes, smelling salts, powder, tonic, immunosuppressive, opiate, arouser; *all* (D): ups and downs, uppers, dolls, pills, downers.
Kinds of drugs include the following—general: caffeine, coffee, smelling salts, alcohol, quinine, tea, salts, adrenalin, angel dust (D), amphetamine, nicotine; hallucinogens: marijuana *or all* (D): pot, grass, dope, weed, killer weed, boo, maryjane, hemp; THC (synthetic marijuana), peyote *or both* (D): cactus, buttons; mescaline, psilocybin *or all* (D): mushrooms, magic mushroom, dots, purple dots; D-lysergic acid diethylamide *or* LSD *or all* (D): acid, hawk, the chief; di-menthyl triptamine *or* DMT *or* grandaddy (D), STP; stimulants: cocaine *or all* (D): coke, baby powder, snort, C, corinne, happy dust, snow; benzedrine *or both* (D): bennies, pep pills; Ibogaine, Harmine (telepathine), JB- 318, JB- 329 (Piperidyl Benzilate Esters); dexedrine *or all* (D): A, dex, mother's little helper, dexies; methedrine *or all* (D): A, meth, crank, crystal, speed; amyl nitrate *or* poppers (D): depressants: Nembutal (trademark) *or* yellowjackets (D), Seconal (trademark) *or* redbirds (D), Luminal (trademark) *or* purple *or* red hearts (D), Amytal (trademark) *or* blue heavens (D), Thorazine (trademark) *or* downers (D), Miltown (trademark); narcotics: opium; morphine *or both* (D): M, Miss Emma; heroine *or all* (D): H, horse, lady jane, junk, smack, sugar; codeine.

drug, *v.*—*Syn.* anesthetize, stupefy, desensitize, narcotize, numb, benumb, blunt; *both* (D): dose, dope; see also **deaden** 1.

drugged, *mod.*—*Syn.* comatose, doped, stupefied; see **unconscious** 1.

druggist, *n.*—*Syn.* apothecary, chemist (British), (registered *or* licensed) pharmacist, manufacturing pharmacist, proprietor, drugstore owner, merchant, knight of the pestle (D); see also **doctor.**

drum, *n.* Varieties include the following—bass drum, kettledrum, timpani, snare drum, side drum, native drum, tabor, water drum, flower drum, tom-tom, tabla, tambour, tambourine; *all* (D): boiler, thud-box, tub, hot skin, traps; see also **musical instrument.**
beat the drum for—*Syn.* expound, support, further; see **promote** 1.

drum up (D), *v.*—*Syn.* attract, provide, succeed in finding; see **discover** 1, **find** 1.

drunk, *mod.*—*Syn.* intoxicated, inebriated, befuddled, tipsy, groggy, given to drink, muddled, overcome, flushed, maudlin, sottish, drunken; *all* (D): annihilated, out cold, stoned, feeling no pain, fired up, in one's altitudes, out of it, seeing double, having a jag on, smashed, blotto, canned, gassed, plowed, under the table, tanked, wired, wasted, wiped out, soused, high, loop-legged, pickled, stewed, boozed up, in one's cups, mellow, schnockered, tight, sewed up, higher than a kite, three sheets to the wind, lit (up), squiffy; see also **dizzy.** —*Ant.* sober*, steady, temperate.

drunkard, *n.*—*Syn.* sot, dipsomaniac, inebriate, toper, souse, (heavy) drinker, tippler, carouser, (confirmed) alcoholic, drunken sot; *all* (D): revolving-door alcoholic, drunk, soak, sponge, boozer, barfly, hooch-hound, rum-pot, rummy, pub-crawler, lush, wino, rounder; see also **addict.**

drunkenness, *n.*—*Syn.* inebriety, intoxication, intemperance, insobriety, libations, dipsomania, alcoholism; *all* (D): pickle, glow, mellowness, jag, barrel fever, head full of bees.—*Ant.* abstinence*, sobriety, temperance.

dry, *mod.* **1.** [Having little or no moisture]—*Syn.* arid, parched, waterless, hard, dried (up), evaporated, desiccated, juiceless, barren, dehydrated, anhydrous, drained, rainless, not irrigated, bare, thirsty, waterproof, rainproof, baked, shriveled, desiccant, desert, dusty, sapless, unmoistened, dryish, sear, drinkless, depleted; *both* (D): dry as a bone, dry as hay; see also **sterile** 2.—*Ant.* wet*, moist, damp.

2. [Thirsty]—*Syn.* parched, dehydrated, athirst; see **thirsty.**

3. [Lacking in interest]—*Syn.* boring, uninteresting, tedious; see **dull** 4.

4. [Possessed of intellectual humor]—*Syn.* satirical, subtle, sarcastic, cynical, sly, arcane, salty, ironical, humorous, restrained, sardonic, biting, caustic; see also **funny** 1, **witty.**—*Ant.* raucous*, crude, gusty.

5. [Having restrictions on alcoholic liquors]—*Syn.* prohibited, temperate, abstemious, parched, restricted, having local option, having state monopoly; *all* (D): bone-dry, arid, on the water wagon, teetotaling.

not dry behind the ears—*Syn.* immature, young, naive; see **inexperienced.**

dry, *v.* **1.** [To become dry]—*Syn.* lose moisture, dry up *or* out, shrivel, wilt, undergo evaporation; see also **evaporate** 1, **wither.**

2. [To cause to become dry]—*Syn.* air dry, condense, concentrate, dehydrate, freeze dry, blot, sponge, desiccate, exsiccate, parch, scorch, dry up, exhaust, torrefy; see also **drain** 1, **empty** 2.

dryad, *n.* —*Syn.* goddess, nymph, sprite; see **fairy** 1.

dry goods, *n.* —*Syn.* cloth, clothes, yard goods, yardage, bolt goods, furnishings, textiles, fabrics, cloth materials.

Dry goods include the following— woolens, woven goods, knit goods, worsted, rayon, acetate, Orlon (trademark), jersey, nylon, artificial silk, synthetics, synthetic cloth; see also **cotton, linen, silk, wool** 2.

dryness, *n.* —*Syn.* aridity, lack of moisture, desiccation, exsiccation, parchedness; see also **drought, thirst.**

dry out *or* up, *v.* —*Syn.* desiccate, become arable, undergo evaporation; see **dry** 1, 2.

dual, *mod.* —*Syn.* binary, twofold, coupled; see **double, twin.**

dualism, *n.* —*Syn.* duality, doubleness, duplexity, twofoldness, biformity, polarity; see also **pair.**

dub, *v.* **1.** [To hit]—*Syn.* strike, poke, push; see **hit** 1.

2. [Entitle]—*Syn.* denominate, christen, call; see **name** 1.

dubiety, *n.* —*Syn.* doubtfulness, indecision, incertitude; see **doubt** 1, **uncertainty** 1.

dubious, *mod.* **1.** [Doubtful]—*Syn.* indecisive, perplexed, hesitant; see **doubtful** 2, **uncertain** 1.

2. [Vague]—*Syn.* ambiguous, indefinite, unclear; see **obscure** 1.

dubiously, *mod.* —*Syn.* doubtfully, doubtingly, indecisively; see **suspiciously.**

duck, *n.* Ducks include the following—fresh-water, sea, gadwall, garganey, shoveler, spoonbill, widgeon, baldpate, bufflehead, butterball, whistler, broad-bill, ruddy, old, squaw, harlequin, ringneck, black, wood, mandarin, musk, pintail, redhead, pochard, canvasback, mallard, Peking, eider, fulvous, tree, Mexican; cinnamon teal, green-winged teal, scoter, surf, scoter, coot, scaup, merganser, sheldrake; see also **bird** 1, 2.

like water off a duck's back (D)—*Syn.* ineffective, ineffectual, weak; see **useless** 1.

duck, *v.* **1.** [To immerse quickly]—*Syn.* plunge, submerge, drop; see **dip** 1, **immerse** 1.

2. [To avoid]—*Syn.* dodge, escape, elude; see **avoid, evade** 1.

duct, *n.* —*Syn.* tube, canal, channel; see **conduit, pipe** 1.

ductile, *mod.* —*Syn.* plastic, pliable, malleable; see **flexible** 1.

ductility, *n.* —*Syn.* malleability, elasticity, pliancy; see **flexibility** 1.

dud, *n.* —*Syn.* failure, flop, debacle; see **failure** 1.

dude, *n.* —*Syn.* dandy, beau, exquisite; see **fop.**

duds (D), *n.* —*Syn.* garb, garments, gear; see **clothes.**

due, *mod.* —*Syn.* payable, owed, owing, overdue, collectable, unsatisfied, unsettled, not met, matured, receivable, to be paid, chargeable, outstanding, in arrears, coming out (D); see also **unpaid** 1, 2.

become (*or* **fall) due**—*Syn.* be owing *or* owed, payable, reach maturity, remain unsettled *or* unsatisfied; see **mature** 1.

duel, *n.* —*Syn.* combat, engagement, contest; see **fight** 1.

duenna, *n.* —*Syn.* chaperone, governess, protector; see **companion** 3.

dues, *n.* —*Syn.* contribution, obligation, toll, duty, levy, collection, fee; annual dues, initiation dues, lodge dues, etc.; assessment, tax, rates; *all* (D): ante, kickback, protection; see also **pay** 1, **tax** 1.

due to, *conj.* and *mod.* —*Syn.* because *or* as a result of, resulting from, accordingly; see **because.**

dugout, *n.* —*Syn.* cave, cellar, burrow; see **hole** 3.

dulcet, *mod.* —*Syn.* melodious, sonorous, euphonious; see **harmonious** 1, **musical** 1.

dull, *mod.* **1.** [Without point or edge]—*Syn.* blunt, blunted, unsharpened, pointless, unpointed, round, square, flat, edgeless, turned, nicked, battered, used, broken, toothless, edentate.—*Ant.* sharp*, sharpened, keen.

2. [Lacking brightness or color]—*Syn.* gloomy, sober, somber, drab, mat, dismal, dark, dingy, dim, dusky, dun, colorless, plain, obscure, lackluster, tarnished, unglazed, lusterless, opaque, leaden, grave, grimy, pitchy, sooty, inky, dead, black, coal-black, unlighted, sordid, dirty, muddy, gray, ashen, wan, lifeless, rusty, flat; *both* (D): black as the ace of spades, without snap.—*Ant.* bright*, colorful, gleaming.

3. [Lacking intelligence; *said usually of living beings*]—*Syn.* stupid, tedious, stolid, sluggish, heavy, slow, retarded, witless, sleepy, backward, boresome, dense, daft, dullwitted, wearisome, petty, unintelligent, ignorant, unintellectual, vacuous, doltish, besotted, shallow-brained, scatterbrained, feeble-minded, half-witted, addled, addlepated, thick-witted, imbecilic, insensate, obtuse, dim, prosy, prosaic, fatuous, insensitive, unfeeling, numb, listless, apathetic, phlegmatic, not bright, torpid, spiritless, brainless, shallow, indolent, unentertaining, *non compos mentis* (Latin), simple-minded, moronic; *all* (D): thickskulled, dumb, lowbrow, stupid as an ox, blockheaded, muscle-bound, nitwitted, off one's trolley or rocker, balmy, batty, daffy, dimwitted, dead from the ears up, half-baked.—*Ant.* witty*, quick, smart.

4. [Lacking interest; *said usually of writing, speaking, or inanimate things*]—*Syn.* prosy, heavy, prosaic, trite, hackneyed, monotonous, humdrum, tedious, dreary, dismal, dry, arid, colorless, insipid, boring, vapid, flat, senseless, longwinded, stupid, commonplace, ordinary, common, usual, unenlivened, old, ancient, stale, prolix, moth-eaten, out of date, antediluvian, archaic, hoary, worn out, tiring, banal, tired, uninteresting, driveling, pointless, uninspiring, piddling, senile, platitudinous, proverbial, jejune, tame, routine, familiar, known, well-known, conventional, depressing, sluggish, repetitious, boresome, abused, repetitive, oft-repeated, well-used, fatiguing, wearisome, soporific, tiresome, producing ennui, lifeless, wearying, unexciting, flat, irksome, stereotyped, stereotypical, stock, the usual thing, the same old thing, the same thing day after day; *all* (D): slow, dry as a bone, dry as dust, cut and dried, without any kick, dead as a doornail.—*Ant.* exciting*, fascinating, exhilarating.

5. [Not loud or distinct]—*Syn.* low, soft, softened; see **faint** 3.

6. [Showing little activity]—*Syn.* slow, placid, languid, still, routine, sluggish, listless, regular, depressed, inactive, lifeless, unexciting, slothful, without incident, quiet, even, torpid, inert, bovine, cowlike, usual, accustomed, slack, monotonous, unresponsive, stagnant, boring, falling off, apathetic, stolid, flat; *all* (D): off, tight, sitting tight, lumpy, bearish.—*Ant.* stimulating*, lively, active.

7. [Gloomy]—*Syn.* cloudy, dim, unlit; see **dark** 1.

dullard, *n.* —*Syn.* nitwit, simpleton, idiot; see **fool** 1.

dullness, *n.* **1.** [Quality of being boring]—*Syn.* flatness, sameness, routine, levelness, evenness, uninterestingness, aridity, depression, dimness, tediousness, commonplaceness, mediocrity, tedium, meagerness, insipidity, vapidity, tameness, familiarity; see also **boredom, monotony** 1, **slowness** 1. —*Ant.* action*, liveliness, interest.

2. [Stupidity]—*Syn.* stupidness, insensibility, slow-wittedness; see **stupidity** 1.

dully, *mod.* —*Syn.* stupidly, densely, obtusely; see also **slowly.**

duly, *mod.* —*Syn.* rightfully, properly, decorously; see **justly** 1.

dumb, *mod.* **1.** [Unable to speak]—*Syn.* silent, inarticulate, impaired, deaf and dumb, voiceless, speechless, having a speech impediment *or* problem *or* difficulty; see also **mute** 1, **quiet** 2.

2. [Temporarily speechless]—*Syn.* speechless, tongue-tied, wordless; see **surprised.**

3. [Slow of wit]—*Syn.* simple-minded, feeble-minded, moronic; see **dull** 3, **stupid** 1.

dumbbell (D), *n.* —*Syn.* blockhead, fool, dunce; see **fool** 1.

dumbfound, *v.* —*Syn.* amaze, astonish, puzzle; see **surprise** 1.

dumbfounded, *mod.* —*Syn.* amazed, astonished, puzzled; see **surprised.**

dummy, *mod.* —*Syn.* counterfeit, faked, simulated; see **false** 3.

dummy, *n.* **1.** [Fool]—*Syn.* dolt, blockhead, oaf; see **fool** 1.

2. [Imitation]—*Syn.* sham, counterfeit, duplicate; see **copy, imitation** 2.

duo, *n.* —*Syn.* couple, twosome, mates; see **pair.**

dump, *n.* —*Syn.* refuse *or* ash heap, junk pile, garbage dump, city dump, dumping ground, swamp, cesspit, garbage lot, discard (D).

dump, *v.* —*Syn.* empty, unload, deposit, unpack, discharge, throw down in a mass, fling down, evacuate, drain, eject, exude, expel, throw out *or* over *or* overboard; see also **discard.**—*Ant.* load*, fill, pack.

dumps (D), *n.* —*Syn.* despondency, dejection, despair; see **desperation** 1, **gloom** 2.

dun, *mod.* —*Syn.* brownish, sallow, dull; see **brown, drab** 2.

dunce, *n.* —*Syn.* dolt, lout, moron; see **fool** 1.

dune, *n.* —*Syn.* rise, knoll, ridge; see **hill.**

dung, *n.* —*Syn.* offal, defecation, compost, manure, guano, fertilizer, excreta; horse dung, cow dung, etc.; chips, pellets, spoor, tracks, evidence, leavings, muck, ordure, feces, filth, garbage, sludge, slop, sewage; *all* (D): cowflop, pancakes, road apples, buttons; see also **excrement, fertilizer.**

dungeon, *n.* —*Syn.* stockade, vault, prison; see **cell** 3, **jail.**

dupe, *v.* —*Syn.* fool, trick, victimize; see **deceive.**

duplicate, *n.* **1.** [A second object like the first] —*Syn.* double, second, mate, facsimile, replica, carbon (copy), likeness, counterpart, counterfeit, analogue, second edition, parallel, correlate, counterscript, repetition, duplication, recurrence, germination, match, twin, Xerox (trademark), chip off the old block (D); see also **copy, imitation, reproduction** 2.—*Ant.* original*, pattern, prototype.

2. [An exact representation]—*Syn.* likeness, facsimile, similarity; see **copy.**

in duplicate—*Syn.* duplicated, doubled, copied; see **reproduced.**

duplicate, *v.* **1.** [To copy]—*Syn.* reproduce, counterfeit, make a replica of; see **copy** 2.

2. [To double]—*Syn.* make twofold, multiply, make twice as much; see **increase** 1.

3. [To repeat]—*Syn.* redo, remake, rework; see **repeat** 1.

duplicity, *n.* —*Syn.* double-dealing, deceit, dishonesty; see **deception** 1, **hypocrisy** 2.

durability, *n.* —*Syn.* durableness, stamina, persistence; see **endurance** 2.

durable, *mod.* —*Syn.* impervious, firm, enduring; see **permanent** 2.

duration, *n.* —*Syn.* span, continuation, continuance; see **term** 2.

duress, *n.* **1.** [Coercion]—*Syn.* compulsion, discipline, control; see **pressure** 2, **restraint** 2.

2. [Imprisonment]—*Syn.* bondage, confinement, detention; see **arrest** 1, **captivity, imprisonment** 1, **jail, slavery** 1.

during, *mod.* and *prep.* —*Syn.* as, at the time, at the same time as, the whole time, the time between, in the course of, in the middle of, when, all along, pending, throughout, in the meanwhile, in the interim, all the while, for the time being; see also **meanwhile, while** 1.

dusk, *n.* —*Syn.* gloom, twilight, dawn; see **night** 1.

dusky, *mod.* —*Syn.* gloomy, shady, murky; see **dark** 1, 5, **dull** 2.

dust, *n.* —*Syn.* dirt, lint, soil, sand, particles, flakes, granules, loess, ashes, cinders, grime, soot, grit, filings, sawdust; *all* (D): devil's snow, house moss, Mormon rain; see also **earth** 2, **filth, powder.**

bite the dust (D)—*Syn.* be killed, fall in battle, succumb; see **die** 1.

lick the dust—*Syn.* be servile, grovel, placate; see **serve** 2.

make the dust fly—*Syn.* move swiftly, work hard, be active *or* energetic; see **act** 1, **move** 1.

dust, *v.* —*Syn.* sprinkle, sift, powder; see **scatter** 2.

dusty, *mod.* —*Syn.* undusted, unused, untouched; see **dirty** 1.

dutiful, *mod.* —*Syn.* devoted, respectful, conscientious; see **faithful, obedient** 1.

duty, *n.* **1.** [A personal sense of what one should do] —*Syn.* (moral) obligation, conscience, liability, charge, accountability, faithfulness, pledge, burden, good faith, accountableness, devoir, honesty, integrity, sense of duty, call of duty, bounden duty; *all* (D); the hell within, inward monitor, still small voice; see also **responsibility** 1, 2.—*Ant.* dishonesty*, irresponsibility, disloyalty.

2. [Whatever one has to do]—*Syn.* work, office, task, occupation, function, business, province, part, calling, charge, service, mission, obligation, contract, station, trust, trouble, burden, undertaking, commission, engagement, assignment, routine, chore, pains, responsibility; see also **job** 2.—*Ant.* entertainment*, amusement, sport.

3. [A levy, especially on goods]—*Syn.* charge, revenue, custom; see **tax** 1.

off duty—*Syn.* not engaged, free, inactive; see **unemployed.**

on duty—*Syn.* employed, engaged, at work; see **busy** 1.

dwarf, *mod.* —*Syn.* dwarfed, low, diminutive; see **little** 1.

dwarf, *v.* **1.** [To keep small]—*Syn.* stunt, retard, hinder; see **restrain** 1.

2. [To cause to appear small]—*Syn.* minimize, overshadow, dominate, predominate over, tower over, detract from, belittle, rise over *or* above, look down upon.—*Ant.* intensify*, magnify, enhance.

dwarfish, *mod.* —*Syn.* diminutive, tiny, small, minute; see **little** 1.

dwell, *v.* —*Syn.* live, inhabit, stay, lodge, abide, sojourn, stop, settle, tarry, remain, live in *or* at, continue, go on living, rent, tenant, have a lease on, make one's home at, have one's address at, keep house, be at home; *all* (D): hang out, hang up one's hat, flop, room, bunk, quarter, tent, pitch tent, have digs *or* diggings (at); see also **reside.**

dweller, *n.* —*Syn.* tenant, inhabitant, occupant; see **resident.**

dwelling, *n.* —*Syn.* house, establishment, lodging; see **home** 1.

dwell on, *v.* —*Syn.* involve (oneself) in, tarry over, be engrossed in; see **consider** 1, **emphasize.**

dwindle, *v.* —*Syn.* wane, lessen, diminish; see **decrease** 1.

dye, *n.* —*Syn.* tinge, stain, tint; see **color** 1.

dye, *v.* —*Syn.* tint, stain, impregnate with color; see **color** 1.

dying, *mod.* **1.** [Losing life]—*Syn.* sickening, sinking, passing (away), fated, going, perishing, failing, *in extremis* (Latin), expiring, moribund, withering away; *all* (D): at death's door, paying the debt of nature, done for, booked, giving up the ghost, cashing in, on one's last legs, with one foot in the grave (and the other on a banana peel), near one's bed, hopping the twig; see also **weak** 2.—*Ant.* immortal*, living, lively.

2. [Becoming worse or less]—*Syn.* declining, going down, receding, retarding, decreasing, disappearing, dissolving, disintegrating, vanishing, failing, fading, ebbing, decaying, smoldering, recessive, overripe, decadent, passé, doomed, neglected, superannuated; *both* (D): done for, fizzling out; see also **sick, weak** 2.—*Ant.* growing*, eternal, rising.

dynamic, *mod.* —*Syn.* energetic, potent, compelling, forceful, changing, progressive, productive, vigorous, magnetic, electric, effective, influential; *all* (D): up-tempo, charismatic, high-powered, peppy, hopped *or* hyped up; see also **active** 2, **powerful** 1.—*Ant.* listless*, quiescent, static.

dynamite, *n.* —*Syn.* trinitrotoluene *or* TNT, detonator, blasing powder; see **explosive.**

dynamite, *v.* —*Syn.* blow up, explode, raze; see **destroy** 1.

dynamo, *n.* —*Syn.* source of power, generator, dynamo-electric machine.

Varieties include the following—AC, DC, shunt-wound *or* shunt, series-wound *or* series, compound.

dynasty, *n.* —*Syn.* sovereignty, empire, absolutism; see **nation** 1.

dysentery, *n.* —*Syn.* looseness, diarrhea, diarrheal *or* diarrheic *or* diarrhetic infection, amoebic dysentery, shigellosis, defecation; *all* (D): Montezuma's *or* Aztec revenge, the trots *or* runs, Malayan rumbles, collywobbles, African drizzles, GI's; see also **disease** 3.

E

each, *mod.* **1.** [Every]—*Syn.* all, any, one by one, separate, particular, specific, private, several, respective, various, piece by piece, individual, personal, without exception.
2. [For each time, person, or the like]—*Syn.* individually, proportionately, respectively, for one, per unit, singly, per capita, apiece, separately, every, without exception, by the; *all* (D): per, a whack, a throw, a shot.

each, *pron.* —*Syn.* each one, one, each for himself, each in his own way, every last one, one another, each other.

eager, *mod.* —*Syn.* anxious, keen, fervent; see **enthusiastic** 1, 2, 3.

eagerly, *mod.* —*Syn.* zealously, intently, anxiously, sincerely, anticipatorily, vigorously, readily, earnestly, willingly, heartily, strenuously, fiercely, cordially, rapidly, hungrily, thirstily, fervently, speedily, zestfully, actively, cravingly, with enthusiasm, longingly, gladly, lovingly, with zeal, with zest *or* a will, with heart in hand, with a good will, with open arms, keenly, with all the heart, with heart and soul, from the bottom of one's heart, with delight; *all* (D): with relish, with all the good will in the world, with might and main, raring to go, full tilt, with gusto, spoiling for.—*Ant.* unwillingly, slowly*, grudgingly.

eagerness, *n.* —*Syn.* zest, anticipation, excitement; see **enthusiasm** 1.

eagle, *n.* —*Syn.* aquila, *Aquilla* (Latin), hawk, bird of Jove, eaglet, falcon, griffin, erne, bird of prey.
Kinds of eagles include the following—American *or* bald, black, golden, harpy, imperial, sea, fish *or* osprey.

eagle-eyed, *mod.* —*Syn.* discerning, keen-sighted, clear-sighted; see **observant** 1.

ear, *n.* **1.** [The organ of hearing]—*Syn.* outer ear, middle ear, inner ear, auricle, eardrum, labyrinth, semicircular canal, hammer, anvil, stirrup, cochlea, concha, pinna, acoustic organ, lug, auditory apparatus, tympanum; *all* (D): flapper, listener, cauliflower ear.
2. [A projection]—*Syn.* lug, prong, projection; see **bulge.**
all ears (D)—*Syn.* attentive, hearing, paying attention; see **listening.**
bend someone's ear (D)—*Syn.* jabber, chatter, be discursive; see **talk** 1.
fall on deaf ears (D)—*Syn.* be ignored, fail to attract notice, be received with indifference; see **fail** 1, **wait** 1.
give (*or* **lend) ear**—*Syn.* give attention, heed, take notice; see **listen** 1.
have (*or* **keep) an ear to the ground** (D)—*Syn.* be aware (of) *or* attuned (to), observe, keep one's eyes open (D); see **listen** 1, **mind** 3.
in one ear and out the other (D)—*Syn.* ignored, forgotten, received with indifference; see **neglected.**
play by ear—*Syn.* improvise, recall, know by heart; see **remember** 1, 2.
play it by ear (D)—*Syn.* improvise, concoct, adlib (D); see **invent** 2.
set on its ear (D)—*Syn.* stir up, agitate, arouse; see **excite** 2.
turn a deaf ear (to) (D)—*Syn.* be heedless, ignore, shun; see **neglect** 2.

earache, *n.* —*Syn.* ache, otalgy, otalgia; see **pain** 2.

eared, *mod.* —*Syn.* aurate, spiked, auriculate, having earlike appendages, spicigerous, spicate.

earl, *n.* —*Syn.* nobleman, noble, count; see **lord** 2.

earlier, *mod.* —*Syn.* former, previous, prior; see **preceding.**

early, *mod.* **1.** [Near the beginning]—*Syn.* recent, primitive, prime, new, brand-new, fresh, budding, raw, hasty.—*Ant.* late*, old, superannuated.
2. [Sooner than might have been expected]—*Syn.* quick, premature, in advance, far ahead, in the bud, precocious, preceding, anticipatory, advanced, too much before the time, needlessly before the time, unanticipated, immediate, unexpected, precipitant, speedy, ahead of time, before the appointed time, direct, prompt, punctual, briefly, shortly, presently, unhatched, immature, unlooked-for, beforehand; *all* (D): on short notice, on the dot, pronto, with time to spare.—*Ant.* late, slow*, tardy.
3. [Maturing soon]—*Syn.* dwarf, bush, quick-maturing, early-maturing, early-flowering *or* blooming, perennial, hardy, short-stemmed, spring, summer, frostproof, northern.—*Ant.* late*, pale, climbing.

earmark, *n.* —*Syn.* characteristic, attribute, quality; see **characteristic.**

earmark, *v.* —*Syn.* reserve, set aside, keep back; see **maintain** 3.

earn, *v.* **1.** [To deserve as reward]—*Syn.* win, merit, gain; see **deserve.**
2. [To receive in payment]—*Syn.* obtain, attain, get, procure, realize, obtain a return, make money by, acquire, consummate, effect, perform, profit, net, clear, score, draw, gather, secure, derive, gain as due return, get as one's due, gain by labor *or* service, make money, bring home, bring in, turn a penny, collect, pick; *all* (D): pick up, get in, make a fast buck, coin money, make the pot boil, bring

grist to the mill, scrape together.—*Ant.* spend*, consume, exhaust.

earnest, *mod.* **1.** [Characterized by zeal]—*Syn.* ardent, zealous, warm; see **enthusiastic** 1, 2, 3.
2. [Of great importance]—*Syn.* serious, grave, sober; see **solemn** 1.

earnestly, *mod.*—*Syn.* solemnly, soberly, thoughtfully; see **seriously** 2.

earnestness, *n.* **1.** [Fervor]—*Syn.* ardor, intensity, zeal; see **enthusiasm** 1.
2. [Solemnity]—*Syn.* gravity, stress, sobriety; see **seriousness** 2.
3. [Determination]—*Syn.* resolution, persistence, tenacity; see **determination** 2.

earnings, *n.*—*Syn.* net proceeds, balance, receipts; see **pay** 2.

earring, *n.*—*Syn.* pendant, ornament, jewel; see **jewelry.**

earth, *n.* **1.** [The world]—*Syn.* globe, sphere, planet, *terra* (Latin), mundane world, creation, terrestrial sphere, orb, *mappemonde* (French), cosmos, universe, sublunary world, star.
2. [The earthly crust]—*Syn.* dirt, clean dirt, loam, humus, clay, gravel, sand, terra firma, land, dry land, terrain, mud, muck, soil, glebe, topsoil, ground, peat moss, fill, compost, topsoil, decomposed granite, turf, mold, alluvium, marl, terrane, surface, subsoil, shore, coast, littoral, deposit.
come back (*or* **down) to earth** (D)—*Syn.* be practical *or* sensible, return to one's senses, quit dreaming; see **calm down, work** 1.
down to earth—*Syn.* earthly, realistic, mundane; see **practical.**
on earth—*Syn.* of all things, of everything, what; see **whatever.**

earthborn, *mod.*—*Syn.* human, temporal, perishable; see **mortal** 2.

earthen, *mod.*—*Syn.* clay, stone, mud, dirt, rock, fictile, made of earth, made of baked *or* burnt clay.

earthenware, *n.*—*Syn.* crockery, ceramics, china; see **pottery.**

earthly, *mod.* **1.** [Terrestrial]—*Syn.* human, mortal, sublunary, terrene, terraqueous, tellurian, subastral, telluric, global, geotic, alluvial, mundane, worldly; *both* (D): under the sun, in all creation. —*Ant.* unearthly, superhuman, unnatural.
2. [Temporal]—*Syn.* unspiritual, secular, physical; see **worldly** 1.

earthquake, *n.*—*Syn.* tremor, temblor *or* tremblor *or* trembler, earthquake shock, shock, quake, fault, sudden undulation of the earth's crust, slip, movement of the earth's surface *or* crust, earth tremor, microseism, earthshaking quake, earth shock, world-girdling quake, an earthquake *or* a quake registering *or* reading one *or* two, etc., points on the Richter scale, secondary tremor, tertiary tremor, seismic upheaval, volcanic quake; *both* (D): shake, wiggler.

earthwork, *n.*—*Syn.* ditch, dugout, fortification; see **trench** 1.

earthworm, *n.*—*Syn.* annelid, angleworm, dew worm; see **worm** 1.

earthy, *mod.* **1.** [Characteristic of earth]—*Syn.* clayey, sandy, dusty, made of earth, of the nature of soil, terrene, earthlike, cloddy, muddy.
2. [Unrefined]—*Syn.* coarse, dull, unrefined; see **crude** 1.

ear trumpet, *n.*—*Syn.* hearing aid, otophone, sonifer, auricle, amplifier, sound intensifier, instrument to collect and concentrate sound.

ease, *n.* **1.** [Freedom from pain]—*Syn.* comfort, rest, quietness, peace, prosperity, relaxed physical condition, tranquil rest, state of being comfortable, leisure, repose, easiness, satisfaction, calm, calmness, restfulness, tranquillity, ataraxia, bed of roses, solace, consolation.—*Ant.* pain*, discomfort, unrest.
2. [Freedom from difficulty]—*Syn.* expertness, dispatch, facility, efficiency, knack, readiness, quickness, adroitness, skillfulness, dexterity, artfulness, cleverness, smoothness; *all* (D): child's play, clear sailing, snap, breeze, cinch, pipe, setup, duck soup, pushover.—*Ant.* difficulty, trouble, clumsiness.
3. [Freedom from affectation]—*Syn.* naturalness, familiarity, affability; see **informality** 2.
4. [Well-being]—*Syn.* gratification, prosperity, comfort; see **luxury** 1.
at ease—*Syn.* relaxed, collected, resting; see **calm** 1.
take one's ease—*Syn.* be calm, rest, be comfortable; see **relax.**

ease, *v.* **1.** [To relieve of pain]—*Syn.* alleviate, allay, mitigate, drug, keep under sedation *or* tranquilizers, tranquilize, sedate, administer an opiate *or* a sedative, anesthetize, render less painful, give relief, comfort, give an anesthetic, fit a splint, relieve pressure, cure, attend to, doctor, nurse, relieve, ameliorate, restore to health, palliate, soothe, poultice, set at ease, cheer.—*Ant.* hurt*, injure, pain.
2. [To lessen pressure or tension]—*Syn.* prop up, lift, bear, hold up, set at ease, make comfortable, raise, disburden, unburden, release, soften, give repose to, free from anxiety, relieve one's mind, assuage, lighten, let up on, give rest to, compress, abate, ameliorate, relax, quiet, calm, pacify, meliorate.—*Ant.* weight*, press, force.
3. [To move carefully]—*Syn.* induce, remove, extricate, disentangle, set right, right, insert, join, facilitate, slide, maneuver, handle, expedite.—*Ant.* rush, hurry*, blunder.
4. [To comfort]—*Syn.* soothe, calm, pacify; see **comfort** 1.

easily, *mod.* **1.** [Without difficulty]—*Syn.* readily, with ease, in an easy manner, effortlessly, facilely, simply, with no effort, without trouble, handily, evenly, regularly, steadily, efficiently, smoothly, plainly, quickly, comfortably, calmly, coolly, surely; *all* (D): just like that, hand over fist, hands down, with one hand tied behind one's back, like nothing, like walking on air.—*Ant.* laboriously, wearily, arduously.
2. [With caution]—*Syn.* cautiously, gently, lightly; see **carefully** 2.

easiness, *n.*—*Syn.* carelessness, nonchalance, facility; see **ability** 2.

east, *mod.* **1.** [Situated to the east]—*Syn.* eastward, in the east, on the east side of, toward the sunrise, east side, eastern, lying *or* situated toward the east, easterly, eastmost, easternmost.

2. [Going toward the east]—*Syn.* eastbound, eastward, to *or* toward the east, headed east, in an easterly direction.

3. [Coming from the east]—*Syn.* westbound, headed west, out of the east, westward, westerly, tending to *or* toward the west.

East, *n.* **1.** [The eastern part of the United States] —*Syn.* (the) eastern states, the Atlantic *or* Eastern seaboard, land east of the Alleghenies *or* Allegheny Mountains *or* Appalachians *or* Appalachian Mountains *or* the Mississippi valley, older sections of the country.

Areas in the East include the following—East Coast, Atlantic Coast, Boston to Washington megalopolis, Appalachia, Middle Atlantic States, Maine, New England, down East, the Thirteen Colonies; see also **Boston, New York, Washington.**

2. [The eastern part of Eurasia]—*Syn.* Asia, Asia Minor, Near East, Far East, Middle East, Siberia, Mongolia, southeast Asia, Arabia, Mesopotamia, Orient, Levant, Mohammedan peoples; for countries in the East; see **Asia.**

Easter, *n.* —*Syn.* commemoration of the Resurrection of Christ, *Pasqua* (Italian), *Pâques* (French), *Ostern* (German), Easter Sunday, Easter week, paschal festival.

eastern, *mod.* **1.** [Concerning the direction to the east]—*Syn.* easterly, eastward, on the east side of; see **east** 1.

2. [Concerning the eastern part of the United States]—*Syn.* East, Atlantic, Atlantic Seaboard, east of the Appalachian Mountains, Allegheny, Appalachian, New England, Middle Atlantic, South Atlantic, down-East.

3. [Concerning the Near East or Middle East] —*Syn.* Southwest Asian, Levantine, Egyptian, of the Holy Land, Arabic, Hellenic, Hebraic, Israeli, in Asia Minor.

4. [Concerning the Orient]—*Syn.* Far Eastern, East Asian, Asian; see **Asiatic** 1, 2.

easy, *mod.* **1.** [Free from constraint]—*Syn.* secure, at ease, prosperous, commodious, well-to-do, leisurely, unembarrassed, spontaneous, forthright, calm, peaceful, tranquil, careless, content(ed), carefree, untroubled, equable, moderate, hospitable; *all* (D): cushy, in clover, soft.—*Ant.* difficult*, impoverished, hard.

2. [Providing no difficulty]—*Syn.* simple, facile, obvious, apparent, yielding, easily done, not burdensome, requiring no effort, presenting few difficulties, smooth, manageable, accessible, wieldy, slight, mere, little, paltry, inconsiderable; *all* (D): nothing to it, plain sailing, simple as ABC, pushover, easy as pie, like taking candy from a baby, like shooting fish in a rain barrel.—*Ant.* difficult*, complicated, hard.

3. [Lax]—*Syn.* tractable, indulgent, easygoing; see **lenient.**

4. [Fluent]—*Syn.* flowing, unaffected, serene; see **fluent** 2.

on easy street—*Syn.* well-to-do, wealthy, prosperous; see **rich** 1.

take it easy—*Syn.* relax, rest, slow down; see **calm down.**

easygoing, *mod.* —*Syn.* tranquil, carefree, patient; see **calm** 1.

eat, *v.* **1.** [To take as food]—*Syn.* consume, bite, chew, devour, swallow, fatten *or* feast upon *or* on, dine out, do justice to, do oneself proud, dispose of, get away with, peck at, gorge, gobble up *or* down, eat up, digest, masticate, ruminate, feed on, breakfast, dine, eat out, sup, lunch, feed, dispatch, feast, banquet, batten, discuss, fare, bolt, snap, fall to, have for, break bread, live *or* feed on, take in, enjoy a meal; *all* (D): have a bite, absorb, cram, pack *or* put away, polish off, make short work of, attack, make a hog *or* pig of oneself, eat out of house and home, entertain the inner man, ply a good knife and fork, eat like a bird, put on the feed bag. —*Ant.* fast*, starve, vomit.

2. [To reduce gradually]—*Syn.* eat up *or* away, condense, liquefy, melt, disappear, vanish, waste, rust (away), spill, dissipate, squander, drain, spill, potter *or* fool away, run through.—*Ant.* increase*, swell, build.

3. [To bother]—*Syn.* worry, vex, disturb; see **bother** 2.

eatable, *mod.* —*Syn.* edible, digestible, dietary, nutritious, good, safe, delicious, succulent, palatable, appetizing, tempting, satisfying, fit to eat, good to eat, comestible, savory, piquant, warm, hot, tasty, nutritive, culinary, kosher; *all* (D): O.K., yummy, hot stuff, delish, scrumptious.—*Ant.* rotten*, uneatable, polluted.

eatables, *n.* —*Syn.* foodstuff, provender, victuals; see **food.**

eat humble pie, *v.* —*Syn.* be humiliated, ask *or* beg pardon, excuse oneself; see **apologize.**

eating, *n.* —*Syn.* consuming, consumption, devouring, feasting *or* gorging *or* feeding (on *or* upon), biting, chewing, masticating, dining, breakfasting, lunching, supping, banqueting, eating *or* dining out, eating up, having a coffee *or* lunch break, taking tea, partaking of food, having a bite *or* a snack, breaking bread, feeding the inner man, making a hog *or* a pig of oneself, enjoying *or* partaking of a meal *or* a repast *or* refreshment, collation, refection, bolting, swallowing, gulping (down), gobbling (up *or* down); *all* (D): putting on the feed bag, doing a meal full justice, hogging it, eating out of house and home; see also **digestion**

eating house, *n.* —*Syn.* café, tavern, cafeteria; see **restaurant.**

eat one's heart out, *v.* —*Syn.* fret, pine, grieve; see **worry** 2.

eat one's words, *v.* —*Syn.* retract (a statement), abjure, rescind; see **recant.**

eat out (D), *v.* —*Syn.* rebuke, reprove, admonish; see **censure.**

eat out of house and home, *v.* —*Syn.* devour, be ravenous, have a huge appetite; see **eat** 1.

eat out of one's hand, *v.* —*Syn.* be tame, submit, acquiesce; see **yield** 1.

eats (D), *n.* —*Syn.* food, victuals, meal; see **food.**

eau de Cologne, *n.* —*Syn.* cologne, scent, toilet water; see **perfume.**

eaves, *n.* —*Syn.* overhang, rim, balcony; see **roof.**

eavesdrop, *v.* —*Syn.* overhear, wiretap, listen, listen in (on), try to overhear, listen stealthily; *all* (D): bend an ear, bug, wire, tap, prick up one's ears.

eavesdropper, *n.* —*Syn.* listener, wiretapper, hearer, auditor of private conversation, sleuth, Peeping Tom.

ebb, *n.* —*Syn.* recession, decline, outward flow *or* sweep, shrinkage, wane, waste, reflux, reduction, lessening, ebb tide, diminution, abatement, regression, withdrawal, decrease, depreciation.—*Ant.* flow, increase*, rise.

ebb, *v.* —*Syn.* recede, subside, retire, flow back, sink, decline, decrease, drop off, melt, fall away, peter out, wane, languish, fall off, decay.—*Ant.* flow*, rise, increase.

ebony, *mod.* —*Syn.* jet, midnight, coal black; see **black** 1.

ebony, *n.* —*Syn.* hard wood, dark wood, durable wood, tropical wood.

ebullience, *n.* —*Syn.* exhilaration, agitation, ferment; see **enthusiasm** 1, **excitement.**

ebullient, *mod.* —*Syn.* agitated, effervescent, vivacious; see **enthusiastic** 3, **excited.**

ebullition, *n.* **1.** [Bubbling over]—*Syn.* seething, estuation, exestuation, decoction, boiling, effervescing, fermentation.

2. [Agitation]—*Syn.* vehemence, turbulence, commotion; see **enthusiasm** 1, **excitement.**

eccentric, *mod.* —*Syn.* odd, queer, strange; see **unusual** 2.

eccentricity, *n.* —*Syn.* peculiarity, abnormality, idiosyncrasy; see **irregularity** 2.

ecclesiastic, *n.* —*Syn.* clergyman, churchman, preacher; see **minister** 1.

ecclesiastical, *mod.* —*Syn.* ministerial, clerical, churchly; see **religious** 1.

echo, *n.* —*Syn.* repetition, imitation, reply; see **answer** 1.

echo, *v.* —*Syn.* repeat, mimic, impersonate; see **imitate** 2.

éclat, *n.* **1.** [Conspicuous success]—*Syn.* splendor, pomp, brilliance; see **ostentation** 2.

2. [Renown]—*Syn.* celebrity, notoriety, distinction; see **fame** 1.

eclectic, *mod.* —*Syn.* selective, catholic, diverse; see **general** 1, **universal** 3.

eclipse, *n.* —*Syn.* eclipse of the sun, solar eclipse, eclipse of the moon, lunar eclipse, total eclipse, partial eclipse, penumbra, obscuration, dimming, darkening, concealment, shroud, shadow, veil, extinguishment, obliteration.

eclogue, *n.* —*Syn.* georgic, idyll, lyric; see **poem, poetry.**

ecologist, *n.* —*Syn.* environmentalist, conservationist, naturalist, ecological engineer, oceanographer, student of environment *or* ecosystems, antipollutionist, biologist, botanist, specialist in aquabiology *or* marine biology *or* population control *or* smog control, etc.; see **engineer, scientist.**

ecology, *n.* —*Syn.* environmental science(s) *or* study *or* studies, ecological engineering, human environment, antipollution project(s), pollution control, survival studies, study of ecosystems, conservation (of natural resources), earthly livability; see also **biology, botany, science, zoology.**

economic, *mod.* —*Syn.* industrial, business, financial; see **commercial** 1.

economical, *mod.* **1.** [Careful of expenditures] —*Syn.* saving, sparing, careful, economizing, thrifty, prudent, frugal, provident, niggardly, meager, miserly, stingy, mean, close, shabby, avaricious, sordid, penurious, chary, watchful, circumspect, parsimonious; *all* (D): tight, closefisted, penny-pinching, curmudgeonly, cheeseparing. —*Ant.* liberal, generous*, wasteful.

2. [Advantageously priced]—*Syn.* cheap, sound, low, reasonable, fair, moderate, inexpensive, marked down, on sale.

3. [Making good use of materials]—*Syn.* practical, having high efficiency, methodical; see **efficient** 1.

economics, *n.* —*Syn.* commerce, finance, public economy, political economy, science of wealth, economic theory, method of developing public wealth, commercial theory, theory of business *or* finance, science of the distribution and consumption of goods and services, principles of business *or* finance *or* industry, study of industry, study of production and distribution, theory of trade, financial *or* economic principles; see also **law 4, science 1, social science.**

Terms relating to economic theories include the following—balance of trade, favorable balance of trade, Gresham's Law, bad money drives out good, economic laws of James Mill *or* John Stuart Mill, laissez faire, law of supply and demand, economic modeling, supply and demand regulate the price, theory of the marginal producer, Ricardian economics, Keynesian economics, Laffer Curve, Supply Side economics, trickle-down theory, doctrine of rents, sound money, cheap money, bimetallism, gold standard, fiat money, Henry George's single tax, protective tariff, tariff for revenue only, protection of infant industries, principle of tax structures, war economy, Thorstein Veblen's theory of the leisure class, production for use, right to work, business cycle, debtor's economy, creditor's economy, economy of scarcity, economy of abundance, guns or butter economics, controlled economy, collective bargaining, mass production, cooperative buying and marketing, Marxian economics, input-output model, microeconomics, macroeconomics, corporate state.

economist, *n.* —*Syn.* statistician, business analyst, efficiency expert, physiocrat, student of business, specialist in economics, plutologist, economic thinker, social planner, economic reformer *or* theorist, banker, professor, political scientist, brain truster (D); see also **scientist.**

economize, *v.* —*Syn.* husband, manage, stint, conserve, scrimp, retrench, skimp, be frugal *or* prudent, pinch, cut costs *or* corners, meet expenses, keep within one's means, cut down, meet a budget; *all* (D): run a tight ship, make both ends meet, tighten one's belt, save for a rainy day, pinch pennies; see also **accumulate** 1, **maintain** 3, **save** 3. —*Ant.* spend*, waste, splurge.

economy, *n.* **1.** [The supervision of affairs]—*Syn.* conduct, direction, supervision; see **administration** 1.

2. [Economical administration]—*Syn.* retrenchment, caution, prudence, regulation of finances, thriftiness, thrift, prudent use of resources, political economy, savng, stinginess, frugality, husbandry, care, parsimony, miserliness, scrimping (D).—*Ant.* carelessness*, lavishness, waste.

3. [An example of economy, sense 2]—*Syn.* curtailment, retrenching, retrenchment, cutback, rollback, business recession, reduction, deduction, abridgement, layoff, payroll shrinkage, wage decrease, cut in wages, volume ordering, moratorium, good gas mileage, good fuel consumption, excursion fare, low passenger-mile rate, lowered materials cost *or* contract price *or* piece rate, etc; see also **automation, depression** 3, **standardization.**—*Ant.* increase*, outlay, raise.

ecru, *mod.* —*Syn.* brownish, yellowish brown, tawny, flesh (colored), natural, pace, fawn, grayish yellow, old ivory, chamois; see also **tan.**

ecstasy, *n.* —*Syn.* joy, rapture, delight; see **happiness** 2.

ecstatic, *mod.* —*Syn.* rapturous, ravished, overjoyed; see **happy** 1.

eczema, *n.* —*Syn.* skin disease, psydracia, inflammation; see **disease** 3.

edacious, *mod.* —*Syn.* voracious, ravenous, gluttonous; see **greedy** 2.

eddy, *n.* —*Syn.* whirl, whirlpool, maelstrom, rapids, swirl, back current, countercurrent, backwash, backwater, gorge, vortex.

edge, *n.* **1.** [The outer portion]—*Syn.* border, frontier, extremity, portal, threshold, brink, boundary, end, term, limit, edging, molding, brim, rim, margin, ring, frame, side, corner, point, bend, crook, hook, split, peak, turn, crust, verge, bound, ledge, skirt, outskirt, lip, limb, hem, welt, seam, selvage, terminator, fringe, frill, flange, flounce, list, listing, trimming, mouth, shore, strand, dike, quay, bank, beach, wharf, dock, mole, curb, crest, deckle, berm, groin, arris, gunwale, periphery, circumference. —*Ant.* surface, center*, interior.

2. [Anything linear and sharp]—*Syn.* blade, cutting edge, razor edge; see **knife.**

3. [(D) Advantage]—*Syn.* upper hand, handicap, head start; see **advantage** 1, 2.

on edge—*Syn.* nervous, tense, uptight (D); see **irritable.**

set one's teeth on edge—*Syn.* irritate, annoy, provoke; see **bother** 2.

take the edge off—*Syn.* weaken, subdue, dull; see **soften** 2.

edge, *v.* **1.** [To trim]—*Syn.* border, fringe, bind; see **trim** 2, **decorate.**

2. [(D) To defeat narrowly]—*Syn.* nose out, slip by *or* past, squeeze by *or* past; see **defeat** 3.

edgy, *mod.* **1.** [Sharp-edged]—*Syn.* edgelike, angular, keen; see **sharp** 1.

2. [Nervous]—*Syn.* irritable, touchy, critical; see **excitable.**

edible,, *mod.* —*Syn.* palatable, nutritious, digestible; see **eatable.**

edict, *n.* —*Syn.* decree, proclamation, order; see **judgment** 3.

edification, *n.* —*Syn.* improvement, instruction, learning; see **education** 1, **knowledge** 1.

edifice, *n.* —*Syn.* structure, architectural monument, pile; see **building** 1.

edify, *v.* —*Syn.* instruct, improve, educate; see **teach** 1.

edit, *n.* **1.** [To prepare for publication]—*Syn.* revise, alter, excise, rewrite, make up, arrange, materials for publication, prepare for the press, compose, compile, select, adapt, assign, report, arrange, rearrange, set up, censor, amplify, polish, finish, choose, analyze, revise and correct, delete, condense, discard, strike out, write, prepare, copy, correct proof, proofread, correct galleys, write headlines, cut, trim, draft; *all* (D): blue-pencil, boil down, feature, kill, massacre, butcher, rehash, doctor up, chase commas.

2. [To supervise publication]—*Syn.* direct, publish, see through the press, formulate, dictate, style, draw up, prescribe, regulate, bring out, issue, distribute, disseminate.

edition, *n.* —*Syn.* printing, publication, issue of a literary work, published form of a literary work, impression, issue, number, imprint, version, reprint, release.

editor, *n.* —*Syn.* redactor, reviser, copyreader, supervisor, director, manager, editor-in-chief, annotator, proofreader, copyholder, reader, editorial writer; *all* (D): desk, desk man, newspaper man, bluepenciler, old man.

Editors include the following—managing, general, associate, assistant, night, newspaper, magazine, city, telegraph, sports, state, wire, women's, society, feature, Sunday, picture, art; see also **author** 2, **journalist, writer.**

editorial, *n.* —*Syn.* essay, article, column; see **exposition** 2.

educate, *v.* —*Syn.* tutor, instruct, train; see **teach** 1.

educated, *mod.* **1.** [Having a formal education] —*Syn.* trained, accomplished, skilled, well-taught, scientific, scholarly, intelligent, learned, well-informed, well-read, well-versed, well-grounded, erudite, fashioned, formed, disciplined, shaped, prepared, instructed, developed, civilized, fitted, versed in, informed in, acquainted with, nurtured, corrected, informed by education, enriched, professional, expert, polished, cultured, finished, initiated, enlightened, literate, lettered, tutored, schooled; *all* (D): savant, bluestocking(ed), highbrow, bookish, up on.—*Ant.* illiterate, ignorant*, unlettered*.

2. [Cultured]—*Syn.* cultivated, refined, polished; see **cultured.**

education, *n.* **1.** [The process of directing learning] —*Syn.* schooling, study, training, direction, instruction, guidance, teaching, tutelage, learning, reading, enlightenment, edification, inculcation, discipline, tuition, preparation, adult education, book learning, information, indoctrination, brainwashing, proselytism, propagandism, catechism, cultivation, background, rearing, apprenticeship; *all* (D): reading, writing, and 'rithmetic; the three R's, book larnin'.

2. [Knowledge acquired through education] —*Syn.* learning, wisdom, scholarship; see **knowledge** 1.

3. [The teaching profession]—*Syn.* teaching, tutoring, pedagogy, instruction, training, pedagogics, didactics, the field of education, the educational profession, progressive education, lecturing, professing (British).

4. [Refinement]—*Syn.* cultivation, finish, enlightenment; see **culture** 3.

educational, *mod.* **1.** [Academic]—*Syn.* scholastic, collegiate, pedagogical, didactic, institutional, school, tutorial, scholarly.
2. [Instructive]—*Syn.* enlightening, educative, enriching; see **cultural.**

educator, *n.*—*Syn.* pedagogue, instructor, tutor; see **teacher** 1, **professor.**

educe, *v.*—*Syn.* evoke, elicit, extract; see **obtain** 1.

eerie, *mod.* **1.** [Inspiring fear]—*Syn.* strange, ghostly, weird; see **frightful** 1.
2. [Superstititous]—*Syn.* fearful, uneasy, frightened; see **afraid** 2.

efface, *v.*—*Syn.* rub out, obliterate, erase; see **cancel** 1, **destroy** 1.

effect, *n.*—*Syn.* conclusion, consequence, outcome; see **result.**
give effect to—*Syn.* practice, employ, activate; see **use** 1.
in effect—*Syn.* as a result, in fact, actually; see **really** 1.
take effect—*Syn.* work, produce results, become operative; see **act** 1.
to the effect (that)—*Syn.* as a result, so that, therefore; see **for.**

effect, *v.* **1.** [To bring about]—*Syn.* produce, cause, make; see **begin** 1, **cause** 2.
2. [To achieve]—*Syn.* accomplish, conclude, fulfill; see **achieve** 1.

effective, *mod.*—*Syn.* efficient, serviceable, producing the expected result, useful, serving to effect the purpose, operative, efficacious, effectual, sufficient, adequate, productive, capable, competent, yielding, practical, valid, resultant.—*Ant.* inoperative, useless*, inefficient.

effectively, *mod.*—*Syn.* efficiently, completely, finally, expertly, conclusively, definitely, effectually, energetically, persuasively, to good purpose, with telling effect, dramatically, adequately, capably, forcibly, productively; see also **excellently.**

effects, *n.*—*Syn.* personal property, baggage, possessions; see **property** 1.

effectual, *mod.* **1.** [Effective]—*Syn.* adequate, efficient, qualified; see **effective.**
2. [Legally valid]—*Syn.* authoritative, binding, valid; see **legal** 1.

effeminacy, *n.*—*Syn.* unmanliness, delicacy, womanishness; see **weakness** 1.

effeminate, *mod.*—*Syn.* unmanly, womanish, emasculate; see **feminine** 2.

effervesce, *v.*—*Syn.* fizz, foam, froth; see **bubble.**

effervescence, *n.* **1.** [Foaming]—*Syn.* bubbling, fizzing, foaming; see **ebullition** 1.
2. [Vivacity]—*Syn.* liveliness, excitement, gaiety; see **action** 1.

effervescent, *mod.* **1.** [Foaming]—*Syn.* boiling, bubbling, fizzing; see **frothy** 1.
2. [Lively]—*Syn.* gay, vivacious, excited; see **happy** 1.

effete, *mod.* **1.** [Incapable of production]—*Syn.* unproductive, sterile, barren; see **sterile** 1, 2.
2. [Lacking vigor]—*Syn.* exhausted, obsolete, spent; see **weak** 1.

efficacious, *mod.*—*Syn.* effectual, efficient, productive; see **effective** 2.

efficacy, *n.*—*Syn.* effectiveness, potency, productiveness; see **efficiency** 2.

efficiency, *n.* **1.** [A high degree of effectiveness]—*Syn.* productivity, capability, capableness; see **ability** 2.
2. [The relation of results to expenditure]—*Syn.* power, potency, suitability, suitableness, adaptability, thoroughness, completeness, abundance, quantity, energy, effectualness, efficaciousness, adequacy, productiveness, powerfulness, efficacy, competency, proficiency, elasticity, conductivity, response, potential energy, faculty, talent, facility.

efficient, *mod.* **1.** [*Said of persons*]—*Syn.* competent, businesslike, good at, apt, adequate, fitted, able, capable, qualified, skillful, clever, talented, energetic, skilled, adapted, familiar with, deft, adept, expert, experienced, adequate in performance, having the requisite skill, workmanlike, having adequate energy, equal to, drilled, exercised, practiced, practical, proficient, accomplished, potent, active, productive, dynamic, decisive, tough, shrewd, highpowered (D); see also sense 2.—*Ant.* incompetent*, inefficient, incapable*.
2. [*Said of things*]—*Syn.* economical, fitting, suitable, suited, effectual, effective, efficacious, adequate, serviceable, useful, saving, profitable, valuable, expedient, handy, subsidiary, conducive, well-designed, streamlined, good for.—*Ant.* inadequate*, unsuitable, ineffectual.

effigy, *n.*—*Syn.* representation, likeness, puppet; see **image** 2.

effloresce, *v.*—*Syn.* flower, open, blossom; see **bloom.**

efflorescence, *n.*—*Syn.* sprouting, blooming, flowering; see **blossoming.**

effluence, *n.*—*Syn.* discharge, issue, emanation; see **flow.**

effluent, *mod.*—*Syn.* emanating, issuing forth, profluent; see **flowing.**

effluvium, *n.*—*Syn.* emanation, exhaust, odor; see **exhalation** 1, **vapor.**

effort, *n.* **1.** [The act of striving]—*Syn.* endeavor, industry, labor, pains, trouble, force, toil, work, travail, stress, strife, struggle, attempt, exertion, pull, spurt, stretch, push, strain, tension, tug; *all* (D): sweat, sweat of one's brow, toil and trouble, elbow grease.—*Ant.* carelessness*, sloth, ease.
2. [An instance of effort, sense 1]—*Syn.* attempt, enterprise, undertaking, application, struggle, battle, try, trial, work, essay, venture, aim, aspiration, purpose, intention, resolution, exercise, discipline, drill, training; *all* (D): crack, go, whirl, the old college try.

effortless, *mod.*—*Syn.* simple, offhand, smooth; see **easy** 2.

effrontery, *n.*—*Syn.* insolence, audacity, boldness; see **rudeness.**

effulgence, *n.*—*Syn.* radiance, blaze, luster; see **light** 1.

effulgent, *mod.*—*Syn.* luminous, glowing, brilliant; see **bright** 1.

effusion, *n.* **1.** [An outflow]—*Syn.* diffusion, stream, emanation; see **flow.**
2. [Verbosity]—*Syn.* oration, sermon, chatter; see **wordiness.**

effusive, *mod.*—*Syn.* unrestrained, profuse, talkative; see **verbose.**

egalitarian, *mod.* —*Syn.* impartial, equal, just; see **fair** 1.

egg, *n.* —*Syn.* ovum, seed, germ, spawn, roe, bud, embryo, nucleus, cell, food; *both* (D): berry, hen fruit.

Eggs used as food include the following—hen, duck, goose, turtle, fish, ostrich, guinea hen.

Sizes and grades of eggs include the following—fancy, select, farm, ranch, western, day-old, fresh, cold-storage, large pullet, medium, small, large, jumbo, white, brown; grade AA, A, B, etc.

Prepared eggs include the following—fried, scrambled, poached, deviled, coddled, hard boiled, soft boiled, creamed, shirred, stuffed, soufflé, raw, buttered, baked, on toast, dropped, goldenrod; egg salad, ham *or* bacon and eggs, eggs Benedict; *all* (D): over easy, sunnyside up, up, bull's eye, two shipwrecked on a raft.

lay an egg (D)—*Syn.* be unsuccessful, err, make a mistake; see **fail** 1.

put (*or* **have**) **all one's eggs in one basket** (D) —*Syn.* chance, gamble, bet; see **risk.**

egg on, *v.* —*Syn.* encourage, goad, incite; see **drive** 1, 2, **urge** 2, 3.

egg-shaped, *mod.* —*Syn.* rounded, oval, pear-shaped; see **oblong.**

ego, *n.* —*Syn.* personality, individuality, self; see **character** 1, 2.

egoism, *n.* —*Syn.* selfishness, vanity, pride; see **egotism.**

egoist, *n.* —*Syn.* self-seeker, egotist, boaster; see **braggart.**

egoistic, *mod.* —*Syn.* individualistic, introverted, self-centered; see **egotistic** 1, 2.

egotism, *n.* —*Syn.* egoism, conceit, vanity, pride, assurance, self-love, narcissism, self-confidence, self-consciousness, self-glorification, self-conceit, self-assertion, self-esteem, self-applause, elation, presumption, self-worship, arrogance, insolence, overconfidence, self-regard, haughtiness, ostentation, boastfulness, vainglory, misanthropy, self-concentration, preoccupation with one's ego.—*Ant.* humility, modesty*, meekness.

egotist, *n.* —*Syn.* coxcomb, boaster, egoist; see **braggart.**

egotistic, *mod.* **1.** [Centered in self]—*Syn.* personal, intimate, subjective, ingrained, intrinsic, implanted, ingrown, congenital, inherent, individualistic, independent, isolated, isolationist, idiosyncratic, inborn, inward, inner, instinctive, radical, inverted, obsessive, inner-directed.—*Ant.* social*, extrinsic, cosmopolitan.

2. [Having offensive concern for self]—*Syn.* conceited, vain, vainglorious, egoistic, boastful, inflated, pompous, arrogant, insolent, autocratic, swollen, puffed up, affected, narcissistic, self-centered, self-glorifying, self-magnifying, presumptuous, overweening, supercilious, blustering, prideful, showy, bumptious, boisterous, grandiose, high-flown, haughty, snobbish, high-handed, aristocratic, lordly, imperious, magisterial, scornful, contemptuous, disdainful, high-minded, proud, bullying, sneering, aloof, vaingloryinq, pretentious, assuming, ostentatious, consequential, cocky (D), brazen, impertinent, selfish, bombastic, bragging, insulting, flashy, theatrical, garish, gaudy, spectacular, flaunting, flamboyant, presuming, reckless, impudent, vaunting, inflated, stiff, overbearing, swaggering, dictatorial, domineering, bold, rash, overconfident, self-satisfied; *all* (D): proud as a peacock, like God Almighty, highfalutin', stuck up, too big for one's boots, looking down one's nose, high-hat, snooty, swanky, uppity, wrapped up in oneself, stuffed-shirted, on one's high horse, high and mighty, too big for one's breeches, in one's altitudes, taking merit to oneself, impressed with oneself, big as you please.—*Ant.* humble*, meek, modest.

egotistically, *mod.* —*Syn.* vainly, self-lovingly, boastfully, arrogantly, haughtily, with a flourish of trumpets, ostentatiously, pretentiously, airily, loftily.

egregious, *mod.* —*Syn.* flagrant, excessive, extreme; see **outrageous.**

egress, *n.* **1.** [A going out]—*Syn.* departure, emergence, escape; see **departure** 1.

2. [A place of exit]—*Syn.* doorway, passage, way out; see **exit** 1.

either, *conj.* and *mod.* —*Syn.* on the one hand, whether or not, unless, it could be that, it might be that.

either, *pron.* —*Syn.* one, one or the other, this one, either/or, each of two, as soon one as the other, one of two.

ejaculate, *v.* —*Syn.* howl, vociferate, call; see **yell.**

ejaculation, *n.* **1.** [A cry]—*Syn.* utterance, shout, exclamation; see **cry** 1.

2. [An orgasm]—*Syn.* climax, secretion, discharge, emission; see **copulation, excretion** 1.

eject, *v.* **1.** [To remove physically]—*Syn.* dislodge, discard, reject, emit, disgorge, bounce *or* run *or* kick *or* throw *or* heave *or* send *or* put *or* force *or* weed *or* cast *or* spit *or* turn *or* rout *or* blow *or* squeeze out, oust, do away with, evict, banish, throw off, pour forth, spout, vomit, expectorate, urinate, excrete, evacuate, dump, unloose, throw overboard, get rid of, eradicate, exterminate; *all* (D): send packing, show the gate to, bundle off, give the boot, ditch, bounce.

2. [To remove from a social or economic position] —*Syn.* expatriate, ostracize, excommunicate; see **dismiss** 1, 2.

ejection, *n.* —*Syn.* eviction, expulsion, dismissal; see **removal.**

eke out, *v.* —*Syn.* barely exist, live a makeshift existence, (just) get by (D); see **subsist.**

elaborate, *mod.* **1.** [Ornamented]—*Syn.* gaudy, decorated, garnished, showy, ostentatious, imposing, fussy, dressy, embellished, refined, beautified, festooned, spangled, flowery, bedecked, flashy, super-elegant (D); see also **ornate** 1.—*Ant.* common*, ordinary, unpolished.

2. [Detailed]—*Syn.* complicated, extensive, laborious, minute, widely developed, intricate, involved, highly organized, many-faceted, complex, a great many, prodigious, painstaking, studied.—*Ant.* general*, usual, unified.

elaborate, *v.* —*Syn.* embellish, bedeck, deck; see **decorate.**

elaborate upon, *v.* —*Syn.* expand, discuss, comment upon; see **explain.**

elaboration, *n.* —*Syn.* illustration, comment, discussion; see **explanation** 1, 2.

élan (French), *n.* —*Syn.* spirit, impetus, ardor; see **enthusiasm** 1.

elapse, *v.* —*Syn.* transpire, pass away, slip by; see **pass** 2.

elastic, *mod.* —*Syn.* plastic, tempered, pliant; see **flexible** 1.

elasticity, *n.* —*Syn.* resiliency, buoyancy, pliability; see **flexibility** 1.

elate, *v.* —*Syn.* inspire, cheer, stimulate; see **encourage** 2.

elated, *mod.* —*Syn.* exhilarated, exalted, aroused; see **excited.**

elation, *n.* —*Syn.* enthusiasm, delight, rapture; see **happiness** 1, 2.

elbow, *n.* —*Syn.* joint, bend, ulna, turn, half turn, crook, angle, curve, fork, crutch, funny bone (D).
rub elbows with (D)—*Syn.* mingle (with), join, be friends (with); see **associate** 1.
up to the elbows (in) (D)—*Syn.* engaged, employed, working at; see **busy** 1.

elbowroom, *n.* —*Syn.* sweep, range, margin; see **space** 2.

elder, *mod.* —*Syn.* earlier, more mature, senior; see **older.**

elder, *n.* **1.** [Old person]—*Syn.* veteran, old lady, old man, old woman, superior, old timer, senior, one of the old folk(s) *or* older generation, sexagenarian, octogenarian, ancestor, nonagenarian, centenarian; *all* (D): golden ager, senior citizen, older adult, Methuselah, graybeard, oldster, old fogey, little old lady *or* L.O.L.; see also **forefather.**
2. [A superior]—*Syn.* patriarch, chief, tribal head, dignitary, senator, counselor, presbyter, church dignitary, father, uncle, grandfather.

elderly, *mod.* —*Syn.* declining, retired, venerable; see **old** 1.

elect, *v.* —*Syn.* choose, name, select; see **choose** 1.

elected, *mod.* —*Syn.* chosen, duly elected, in on a landslide (D); see **named** 2.

election, *n.* **1.** [The act of choosing]—*Syn.* option, choice, preference; see **choice** 1, **selection** 1.
2. [The act of choosing by votes]—*Syn.* poll, polls, ballot, balloting, ticket, vote, voting, voice vote, vote-casting, primaries, hustings (British), suffrage, plebiscite, referendum, (elective) franchise, constitutional right, yea or nay (D).

electioneer, *v.* —*Syn.* canvass, barnstorm, stump (D); see **campaign** 1.

elective, *mod.* **1.** [Pertaining to the right to choose by vote]—*Syn.* constituent, voting, campaigning; see **electoral.**
2. [Subject to choice]—*Syn.* voluntary, selective, not compulsory; see **optional.**

elector, *n.* —*Syn.* suffragist, constituent, balloter; see **voter.**

electoral, *mod.* —*Syn.* discretional, elective, optional, by vote *or* (popular) election, electing, appointing, appointive, constituent.

electorate, *n.* —*Syn.* (registered) voters, those casting ballots, body politic; see **constituency, voter.**

electric, *mod.* —*Syn.* electrical, magnetic, voltaic, galvanic, electronic, power (driven), telegraphic, electrified, instantaneous, surcharged, pulsing, vibrating, dynamic, energetic.—*Ant.* old-fashioned*, manual, steam.

electric chair, *n.* —*Syn.* means *or* mode *or* instrument of execution, form of capital punishment; *all* (D): roaster, toaster, hot seat.

electrician, *n.* —*Syn.* electrical *or* electronic(s) technician *or* expert, repairman, lineman, maintenance man, tester; *all* (D): Alec, juicer, troubleshooter.

electricity, *n.* **1.** [Electricity as a public utility] —*Syn.* power, current, service, heat, light, ignition, spark, utilities, public utilities, alternating current (A.C.), direct current (D.C.), voltage, 110 volts, 220 volts, high voltage, high tension, kilowatts, kilowatt hours, kilocycles, megacycles; *all* (D): Reddy Kilowatt (trademark), juice, hot stuff, megs, kilos.
2. [Electricity as a form of matter]—*Syn.* magnetism, electromagnetism, radioactivity, electron, neutron, proton, positron, penetron, dynatron, barytron, X particle, heavy electron.
Kinds of electricity include the following—static, statical, dynamic, dynamical, current, positive, negative, natural, celestial, induced.

electrify, *v.* **1.** [To provide electricity]—*Syn.* wire, charge, power, heat, light, equip, lay wires *or* cables, electrize, provide service, magnetize, galvanize, faradize, energize, dynamize, apply electricity to, loop in, subject to electricity, pass an electric current through, give an electric shock to, render electric, charge with electricity.
2. [To affect deeply]—*Syn.* shock, stun, strike; see **disturb** 2, **excite** 1, 2.

electrocardiogram, *n.* —*Syn.* electrical heart recording, recording, EKG *or* ECG.

electrocute, *v.* —*Syn.* execute, put to death, kill by electric shock, execute by electricity, put in the electric chair; *all* (D): send to the hot seat, fry, burn, hot-chair, give a permanent, top off.

electrode, *n.* —*Syn.* terminal, plate, wire, inert anode, inert cathode, copper cathode, zinc anode, negative electrode, positive electrode.

electron, *n.* —*Syn.* (negative) particle, negatron, electrically charged element; see **atom.**

electronic, *mod.* —*Syn.* photoelectric, thermionic, cathodic, anodic, voltaic, photoelectronic, autoelectronic, computerized, automatic, automated; see also **electric.**

electronics, *n.* —*Syn.* radionics, electron physics, electron dynamics, electron optics, radiogoniometry, thermionics, spectrophotometry, radar, transistor, physics, infrared spectroscopy, X-ray photometry, photoelectronics, automatics, serioinstrumentation, electrical patterning, cybernetics, computer electronics; see also **physics, science.**

eleemosynary, *mod.* —*Syn.* charitable, tributary, gratuitous; see **generous** 1.

elegance, *n.* **1.** [Refinement]—*Syn.* culture, tastefulness, taste, cultivation, politeness, *politesse* (French), polish, style, grace, delicacy, class (D), gentility, breeding, splendor, beauty, magnificence, munificence, courtliness, hauteur, nobility, noblesse, charm, grace, sophistication, propriety, nicety, style.
2. [Proportion]—*Syn.* symmetry, balance, rhythm, clarity, purity, felicity, grace, gracefulness, dainti-

ness, exquisiteness, sumptuousness, luxuriousness, delicacy, finery, comeliness, poshness.

elegant, *mod.* **1.** [*Said of personal surroundings*] —*Syn.* rich, tasteful, classic; see **beautiful, dignified** 1.

2. [*Said of persons*]—*Syn.* well-bred, cultured, aristocratic; see **beautiful** 2, **dignified, refined** 2.

3. [*Referring opprobriously to a past style*]—*Syn.* Victorian, outmoded, *démodé* (French), outlived, super-refined, passé, gaudy, ostentatious, baroque, stuffy affected, overdone, turgid, anachronistic, moth-eaten.—*Ant.* restrained*, modernistic, classic.

4. [*Said of writing or speech*]—*Syn.* ornate, polished, perfected, elaborated, finished, ornamented, rhythmical, adorned, embellished, embroidered, chaste, balanced, well-turned, flowing, stylized, Ciceronian, artistic, grandiloquent, euphuistic, rhetorical, florid, fancy, rich, artistic, mellifluous, pure, fluent, neat.—*Ant.* dull*, ill-chosen, inarticulate.

elegiac, *mod.* —*Syn.* sorrowful, mournful, funeral; see **sad** 1, 2.

elegy, *n.* —*Syn.* funeral song *or* poem, requiem, ululation; see **poem, song.**

element, *n.* **1.** [A constitution]—*Syn.* portion, particle, detail; see **part.**

2. [A form of matter]—The older sciences determined the following elements—earth, air, fire, water; modern chemistry and physics identify the following elements—actinium (Ac), aluminum (Al), americium (Am), antimony (Sb), argon (Ar), arsenic (As), astatine (At), barium (Ba), berkelium (Bk), beryllium (Be), bismuth (Bi), boron (B), bromine (Br), cadmium (Cd), calcium (Ca), californium (Cf), carbon (C), cerium (Ce), cesium (Cs), chlorine (Cl), chromium (Cr), cobalt (Co), copper (Cu), curium (Cm), dysprosium (Dy), einsteinium (Es), erbium (Er), europium (Eu), fermium (Fm), fluorine (F), francium (Fr), gadolinium (Gd), gallium (Ga), germanium (Ge), gold (Au), hafnium (Hf), helium (He), holmium (Ho), hydrogen (H), indium (In), iodine (I), iridium (Ir), iron (Fe), krypton (Kr), lanthanum (La), lawrencium (Lr), lead (Pb), lithium (Li), lutetium (Lu), magnesium (Mg), manganese (Mn), mendelevium (Md), mercury (Hg), molybdenum (Mo), neodymium (Nd), neon (Ne), neptunium (Np), nickel (Ni), niobium (Nb), nitrogen (N), nobelium (No), osmium (Os), oxygen (O), palladium (Pd), phosphorus (P), platinum (Pt), plutonium (Pu), polonium (Po), potassium (K), praseodymium (Pr), promethium (Pm), protoactinium (Pa), radium (Ra), radon (Rn), rhenium (Re), rhodium (Rh), rubidium (Rb), ruthenium (Ru), samarium (Sm), scandium (Sc), selenium (Se), silicon (Si), silver (Ag), sodium (Na), strontium (Sr), sulphur (S), tantalum (Ta), technetium (Tc), tellurium (Te), terbium (Tb), thallium (Tl), thorium (Th), thulium (Tm), tin (Sn), titanium (Ti), tungsten (W), uranium (U), vanadium (V), xenon (Xe), ytterbium (Yb), ytrrium (Y), zinc (Zn), zirconium (Zr); see **atomic power.**

elementary, *mod.* **1.** [Suited to beginners]—*Syn.* primary, introductory, rudimentary; see **easy** 2.

2. [Fundamental]—*Syn.* foundational, essential, basic; see **fundamental** 1.

elements, *n.* —*Syn.* basic material, fundamentals, grammar, ABC's, initial stage, first principles, basis, beginning, first step, principles, basic work, rudiments, groundwork.

elephantine, *mod.* **1.** [Immense]—*Syn.* huge, monstrous, enormous; see **large** 1.

2. [Clumsy]—*Syn.* ungraceful, ungainly, clumsy; see **awkward** 1.

elevate, *v.* **1.** [To lift bodily]—*Syn.* hoist, heave, tilt; see **raise** 1.

2. [To promote]—*Syn.* advance, appoint, further; see **promote** 1.

3. [To exalt]—*Syn.* glorify, extol, dignify; see **praise** 1.

elevated, *mod.* **1.** [Raised]—*Syn.* aerial, towering, tall; see **high** 2, **raised** 1.

2. [Noble]—*Syn.* sublime, dignified, eminent; see **noble** 1.

elevation, *n.* —*Syn.* top, roof, platform; see **height** 1.

elevator, *n.* **1.** [Machine for lifting]—*Syn.* lift, escalator, conveyor, endless belt *or* chain, buckets, elevator stack, chair lift, aerial tramway, passenger elevator, freight elevator, automatic elevator, hoist, dumbwaiter, chute.

2. [A building handling grain]—*Syn.* bin, storage plant, shipping point, grain buyer, co-operative elevator, silo.

elf, *n.* —*Syn.* brownie, sprite, leprechaun; see **fairy** 1.

elfish, *mod.* —*Syn.* mischievous, prankish, fiendish; see **naughty.**

elicit, *v.* —*Syn.* extract, extort, derive; see **obtain** 1.

elide, *v.* **1.** [To delete]—*Syn.* curtail, nullify, erase; see **cancel** 1.

2. [To suppress]—*Syn.* omit, ignore, skip; see **neglect** 2.

eligibility, *n.* —*Syn.* fitness, acceptability, capability; see **ability** 2.

eligible, *mod.* —*Syn.* qualified, fit, suitable, suited, acceptable, seemly, equal to, worthy of being chosen, fit to be chosen, capable of, fitted for, satisfactory, trained, employable, usable, becoming, likely; *all* (D): in the running, in line for, up to.—*Ant.* unfit*, ineligible, disqualified.

eliminate, *v.* **1.** [To remove]—*Syn.* take *or* wipe *or* clean *or* throw *or* weed *or* stamp *or* blot *or* cut *or* crop *or* phase *or* drive *or* cast out, dispose *or* get rid of, dispense *or* do away with, put *or* set aside, exclude, eject, cast off, defeat, disqualify, oust, evict, shut the door upon, clear away, cancel, eradicate, erase, expel, discharge, dislodge, put out of doors, reduce, disentitle, forfeit, invalidate, abolish, repeal, abrogate, exterminate, annihilate, kill, murder, waive, throw overboard, be done with, relinquish, relegate, discard, dismiss, blot out, elide, obliterate, remove *or* eliminate from consideration *or* the competition, discount, exile, banish, deport, expatriate, maroon, blackball, ostracize, fire; *all* (D): dump, ditch, scrap, bounce, sack, root out, drop, eighty-six, clear the decks.—*Ant.* accept, include*, welcome.

2. [To remove waste matter]—*Syn.* discharge, throw off, pass; see **excrete.**

elimination, *n.* **1.** [The act of removing]—*Syn.* dismissal, expulsion, exclusion; see **removal** 1.

2. [The act of declining to consider]—*Syn.* rejection, repudiation, denial, disqualification, avoidance, rejecting, eliminating, repudiating, disqualifying, avoiding, denying.

elite, *n.* —*Syn.* society, nobility, celebrities; see **aristocracy.**

elixir, *n.* —*Syn.* balm, compound, tincture; see **potion.**

ell, *n.* —*Syn.* addition, annex, extension; see **wing** 2.

ellipse, *n.* —*Syn.* oval, conic section, curve; see **circle.**

elliptical, *mod.* —*Syn.* oval, ovoid, egg-shaped; see **oblong.**

elm, *n.* —Varieties include the following—American, white, red, slippery, English, Japanese, Siberian *or* Chinese, Grand Rapids oak (D); see also **tree, wood** 2.

elocution, *n.* **1.** [Speech training]—*Syn.* voice culture, dramatic reading, declamation, art of oral expression, oratory, rhetoric.
2. [Manner of speaking]—*Syn.* eloquence, locution, articulation; see **speech** 2.

elongate, *v.* —*Syn.* prolong, stretch, extend; see **lengthen** 1.

elope, *v.* —*Syn.* abscond, run away (with), escape with a lover, slip out, fly, flee, go secretly; *both* (D): skip, go to Gretna Green.

eloquence, *n.* **1.** [The quality of effective speech] —*Syn.* fluency, wit, wittiness, expression, expressiveness, appeal, ability, diction, articulation, delivery, power, force, vigor, mellifluousness, facility, vivacity, style, poise, expressiveness, flow, volubility, grandiloquence, loquacity, command of language, dramatic power, gift of gab (D).
2. [Formal and fluent speech]—*Syn.* oration, expression, rhetoric; see **speech** 3.

eloquent, *mod.* —*Syn.* vocal, articulate, outspoken; see **fluent** 2.

else, *mod.* —*Syn.* something different from *or* in addition to, different, additional; see **extra, other.**

elsewhere, *mod.* —*Syn.* gone, somewhere (else), not here, in another place, in *or* to some other place, otherwhere, away, absent, abroad, hence, removed, remote, outside, not under consideration, formerly, subsequently.—*Ant.* here*, at this point, in this spot.

elucidate, *v.* —*Syn.* interpret, illustrate, clarify; see **explain.**

elucidation, *n.* —*Syn.* illustration, commentary, definition; see **explanation** 1.

elude, *v.* —*Syn.* dodge, shun, escape; see **avoid.**

elusive, *mod.* **1.** [Evasive]—*Syn.* slippery, evanescent, fugitive; see **fleeting, temporary.**
2. [Mysterious]—*Syn.* occult, imponderable, equivocal; see **difficult** 2, **obscure** 1.

Elysium, *n.* —*Syn.* abode of the blessed, heaven, nirvana; see **paradise** 3.

em, *n.* —*Syn.* em quad, em dash, mutton quad (D); see **dash** 3.

emaciated, *mod.* —*Syn.* gaunt, famished, wasted; see **thin** 2.

emaciation, *n.* —*Syn.* malnutrition, starvation, undernourishment; see **hunger.**

emanate, *v.* **1.** [To emit]—*Syn.* exude, radiate, exhale; see **emit** 1.
2. [To begin]—*Syn.* arise, spring, originate; see **begin** 2.

emanation, *n.* **1.** [Emergence]—*Syn.* flowing, arising, issuing, emerging, springing, welling, issuance, escape, outflow, effusion, oozing, gush, outpour, effluence, beginning, origin, origination.—*Ant.* decay*, stagnation, stay.
2. [Emission]—*Syn.* effluvium, discharge, drainage, exhalation, leakage, efflux, vapor, steam, radiation, exudation, percolation, ejaculation.—*Ant.* stopping*, stoppage, withholding.

emancipate, *v.* —*Syn.* release, liberate, deliver; see **free** 1.

emancipation, *n.* —*Syn.* liberty, release, liberation; see **freedom** 1, **freeing.**

emancipator, *n.* —*Syn.* deliverer, rescuer, redeemer; see **liberator.**

emasculate, *v.* **1.** [To sterilize]—*Syn.* geld, unman, mutilate; see **castrate.**
2. [To weaken]—*Syn.* soften, enervate, cripple; see **weaken** 2.

emasculation, *n.* **1.** [Castration]—*Syn.* sterilization, mutilation, eunuchization; see **castration.**
2. [Weakness]—*Syn.* enervation, debilitation, unmanliness; see **weakness** 1.

embalm, *v.* —*Syn.* preserve, process, freeze, fill with formaldehyde, anoint, wrap, mummify, preserve from putrefaction, prepare for burial, lay out (D).

embankment, *n.* —*Syn.* dike, breakwater, pier; see **dam.**

embargo, *n.* —*Syn.* restriction, prohibition, impediment; see **restraint** 2.

embark, *v.* —*Syn.* set out, leave port, set sail; see **leave** 1.

embarrass, *v.* **1.** [To upset mentally]—*Syn.* perplex, annoy, puzzle, vex, distress, disconcert, agitate, bewilder, confuse, chagrin, confound, upset, bother, plague, tease, worry, trouble, distract, discomfort, disturb, discomfit, let down, perturb, flurry, mortify, fluster, discompose, discountenance, irk, dumbfound, abash, shame, stun; *all* (D): put in a hole, nonplus, rattle, put on the spot, put to the blush, discombobulate, make a monkey of, put out of face, faze.—*Ant.* encourage*, cheer, please.
2. [To hinder]—*Syn.* keep back, obstruct, hamper; see **hinder.**

embarrassed, *mod.* **1.** [In social difficulties]—*Syn.* abashed, perplexed, disconcerted; see **ashamed.**
2. [In financial difficulties]—*Syn.* bankrupt, impoverished, poor; see **insolvent.**

embarrassing, *mod.* —*Syn.* difficult, disturbing, confusing, distracting, bewildering, puzzling, rattling, perplexing, delicate, unbearable, distressing, disconcerting, upsetting, discomforting, ticklish, flustering, troubling, troublesome, worrisome, uncomfortable, awkward, disagreeable, inopportune, helpless, unseemly, impossible, uneasy, mortifying, shameful, annoying, equivocal, irksome, ambiguous, exasperating, unbalanced, unpropitious, inconvenient, unmanageable, sticky (D).—*Ant.* comfortable*, easy, agreeable.

embarrassment, *n.* **1.** [The condition of being embarrassed]—*Syn.* confusion, chagrin, mortification, discomfiture, shame, humiliation, disconcertion, shyness, timidity, inhibition, dilemma, puzzle, perplexity, tangle, strait, pinch, quandary; *all* (D): hot seat, hot water, pickle, stew.

2. [Anything that embarrasses]—*Syn.* mistake, blunder, faux pas, clumsiness, indebtedness, uncertainty, gaucherie, hindrance, poverty, impecuniosity, destitution, distress, difficulties, involvement, intricacy, obligation, crude *or* stupid action, indiscretion, default, deficit, debt, awkward situation, predicament, plight; *all* (D): pinch, fix, snag, hitch.

embassy, *n.* **1.** [Ambassadorial residence and offices] —*Syn.* government *or* consular *or* official office(s), ministry, consulate; see **government** 2, **office** 3.
2. [Ambassadorial legation]—*Syn.* commission, mission, delegation; see **committee, diplomat** 1.

embattle, *v.* —*Syn.* marshal, mobilize, array; see **arm** 2.

embed, *v.* **1.** [To put in]—*Syn.* imbed, stick *or* place *or* thrust *or* stuff *or* set *or* drive *or* press *or* ram *or* plunge *or* tuck *or* hammer in, insert, put into, root, plant, implant, install, fix, deposit, sink, bury, enclose, inlay, pierce, impact.
2. [To fix]—*Syn.* plant, implant, secure; see **fasten** 1.

embellish, *v.* —*Syn.* adorn, ornament, deck; see **decorate.**

embellishment, *n.* **1.** [Decoration]—*Syn.* ornament, adornment, frill; see **decoration** 1, 2.
2. [Exaggeration]—*Syn.* embroidery, hyperbole, elaboration; see **exaggeration** 1.

embers, *n.* —*Syn.* coals, cinders, ash, live coals, slag, smoking remnants, smoldering remains of a fire, clinkers (D).

embezzle, *v.* —*Syn.* thieve, forge, pilfer; see **steal.**

embezzlement, *n.* —*Syn.* fraud, misappropriation, stealing; see **theft.**

embezzler, *n.* —*Syn.* thief, robber, defaulter; see **criminal.**

embitter, *v.* **1.** [To sour]—*Syn.* make bitter, acidulate, sour; see **decay.**
2. [To anger]—*Syn.* irritate, aggravate, annoy; see **bother** 2.

emblazon, *v.* **1.** [To decorate]—*Syn.* embellish, ornament, beautify; see **decorate.**
2. [To proclaim]—*Syn.* herald, extol, glorify; see **celebrate** 1.

emblem, *n.* —*Syn.* symbol, figure, image, design, token, sign, attribute, insignia, banner, seal, colors, crest, coat of arms, memento, type, representation, effigy, reminder, marker, mark, identification, badge, souvenir, keepsake, medal, regalia, miniature, character, device, motto, impress, hallmark, monogram, colophon, flag, pennant, banner, standard, arms.

emblematic, *mod.* —*Syn.* typical, symbolical, indicative; see **symbolic.**

embodiment, *n.* **1.** [Personification]—*Syn.* incarnation, matter, structure; see **characteristic, essence** 1, **image** 2.
2. [Realization]—*Syn.* formation, manifestation, realization; see **awareness.**
3. [Incorporation]—*Syn.* comprisal, composition, materialization; see **inclusion.**

embody, *v.* **1.** [To actualize]—*Syn.* substantiate, personify, materialize; see **complete** 1.
2. [To organize]—*Syn.* incorporate, integrate, establish; see **organize** 2.

embolden, *v.* —*Syn.* inspirit, animate, impel; see **encourage** 1, 2.

emboss, *v.* —*Syn.* raise, design, enchase; see **decorate.**

embossment, *n.* —*Syn.* molding, tracery, adornment; see **decoration** 1.

embowel, *v.* **1.** [To bury]—*Syn.* embed, conceal, secrete; see **hide** 1.
2. [To kill]—*Syn.* gut, eviscerate, disembowel; see **kill** 1.

embrace, *v.* **1.** [To clasp]—*Syn.* enfold, squeeze, grip; see **hug.**
2. [To adopt]—*Syn.* espouse, welcome, take advantage of; see **adopt** 2.

embroider, *v.* **1.** [To add adornment]—*Syn.* stitch, knit, quilt, braid, weave, pattern, ornament, beautify, embellish, garnish, deck, bedeck, decorate, work, gild, pattern.
2. [(D) To exaggerate]—*Syn.* lie, falsify, enlarge; see **exaggerate.**

embroidery, *n.* **1.** [Stitchery]—*Syn.* needlework, sampler, arabesque, brocade, tracery, lacery, bargello, edging, decoration, patterning, adornment, fringing.
Kinds of embroidery include the following—cross-stitch, crewel, needlepoint, tapestry, appliqué, quilting.
2. [Exaggeration]—*Syn.* embellishment, fabrication, hyperbole; see **exaggeration** 1.

embroil, *v.* —*Syn.* disorder, derange, entangle; see **confuse.**

embryo, *n.* —*Syn.* fetus, incipient organism, nucleus; see **egg.**

embryonic, *mod.* —*Syn.* incipient, immature, undeveloped; see **early** 1.

emend, *v.* **1.** [To edit]—*Syn.* improve, redact, revise; see **edit** 1.
2. [To correct]—*Syn.* rectify, touch up, better; see **correct** 1.

emendation, *n.* **1.** [A revision]—*Syn.* editing, redaction, revisal; see **improvement** 2, **revision.**
2. [An improvement]—*Syn.* amendment, amelioration, betterment; see **correction** 1, **improvement** 1.

emerald, *mod.* —*Syn.* bright green, verdigris, malachite; see **green** 1.

emerald, *n.* —*Syn.* rare green beryl, valuable gem, precious stone; see **jewel** 1.

emerge, *v.* —*Syn.* rise, arrive, come out; see **appear** 1, 3.

emergence, *n.* **1.** [An output]—*Syn.* issue, outburst, discharge; see **emanation** 1, 2.
2. [An appearance]—*Syn.* rise, evolution, visibility; see **appearance** 3.

emergency, *n.* —*Syn.* accident, unforeseen occurrence, misadventure, strait, urgency, exigency, (pressing) necessity, pressure, tension, distress, depression, compulsion, turn of events, obligation, pass, crisis, predicament, turning point, impasse, dilemma, quandary; *all* (D): pretty pass, pinch, fix, hole; see also **difficulty** 1, 2.

emergent, *mod.* **1.** [Rising]—*Syn.* emanant, outgoing, efflorescent, issuing forth, emerging, emanating, rising.

2. [Urgent]—*Syn.* pressing, sudden, immediate; see **urgent** 1.

emeritus, *mod.* —*Syn.* retained on the rolls, reversed, respected; see **retired** 1.

emery, *n.* —*Syn.* grinder, wheel, sharpener, Carborundum (trademark), corundum, emery paper, emery board, sand paper, garnet paper.

emigrant, *n.* —*Syn.* *émigré* (French), exile, expatriate, colonist, migrant, migrator, displaced person (D.P.), traveler, foreigner, pilgrim, refugee, fugitive, wayfarer, peregrinator, wanderer, immigrant, alien, outcast, man without a country.

emigrate, *v.* —*Syn.* migrate, immigrate, quit; see **leave** 1.

emigration, *n.* —*Syn.* re-establishing, departure, removal, leaving, expatriation, displacement, moving (away), crossing, migrating, transplanting, uprooting, exodus, exile, trek, journey, movement, trend, march, travel, voyage, wayfaring, wandering, peregrination, migration, shift, settling, homesteading, *Volkswanderung* (German).—*Ant.* immigration*, arriving, remaining.

émigré, *n.* —*Syn.* exile, emigrant, refugee; see **refugee.**

eminence, *n.* **1.** [An elevation]—*Syn.* projection, peak, highland; see **height** 1, **hill.**

2. [Importance]—*Syn.* standing, prominence, distinction; see **fame** 1.

eminent, *mod.* **1.** [Physically lofty]—*Syn.* tall, elevated, raised; see **high** 1, 2.

2. [Distinguished]—*Syn.* renowned, celebrated, prominent; see **distinguished** 2, **important** 2.

eminently, *mod.* —*Syn.* notably, exceptionally, suitably; see **well** 2.

emissary, *n.* —*Syn.* intermediary, ambassador, consul; see **agent** 1.

emission, *n.* —*Syn.* ejection, effusion, eruption; see **emanation** 1, 2, **radiation.**

emit, *v.* **1.** [To discharge]—*Syn.* give *or* let off *or* out, send forth *or* out, cast *or* throw up *or* out, breathe *or* throw *or* spill *or* pour out, pour *or* give forth, eject, blow, hurl, gush, secrete, spurt, shoot, erupt, squirt, shed, expel, expend, vomit, belch, purge, excrete, issue, perspire, void, vent, evacuate, spew (forth), spit, expectorate, ooze, exude, slop (over), exhale, extrude, emanate, jet.

2. [To express]—*Syn.* voice, pronounce, speak; see **utter.**

emolument, *n.* —*Syn.* reward, payment, returns; see **pay** 2.

emotion, *n.* —*Syn.* perturbation, agitation, tremor, commotion, excitement, disturbance, sentiment, feeling(s), tumult, turmoil, sensation, excitability. Emotions include the following—love, passion, ecstasy, fire, warmth, affection, glow, vehemence, fervor, ardor, zeal, thrill, elation, flutter, palpitation, joy, satisfaction, happiness, inspiration, sympathy, empathy, tenderness, concern, grief, remorse, sorrow, sadness, melancholy, despondency, despair, depression, trepidation, worry, discomposure, disquiet, uneasiness, dread, fear, apprehension, hate, resentment, conflict, jealousy, greed, covetousness, cupidity, anger, rage, ire, shame, pride, prurience, concupiscence, sensuality, lust, desire, lechery, pathos, bathos.

emotional, *mod.* **1.** [Stirring one's emotions] —*Syn.* moving, fervent, ardent; see **passionate** 2.

2. [Given to emotion]—*Syn.* gushing, hysterical, demonstrative, fiery, warm, zealous, sensuous, fervent, ardent, enthusiastic, passionate, fanatical, excitable, impulsive, spontaneous, ecstatic, impetuous, nervous, disturbed, wrought-up, overwrought, temperamental, irrational, histrionic, sensitive, sentient, oversensitive, hypersensitive, sentimental, maudlin, overflowing, affectionate, loving, feminine, lachrymose, neurotic, fickle; *all* (D): sloppy about, gaga, drooling, icky, heart in hand, with *or* wearing one's heart on one's sleeve, high-strung, mushy.—*Ant.* rational, cold*, hard.

emotionalism, *n.* **1.** [Emotion]—*Syn.* hysteria, sentimentality, excitement; see **emotion.**

2. [Stimulation]—*Syn.* agitation, entrancement, provocation; see **incentive.**

empathy, *n.* —*Syn.* vicarious emotion, insight, understanding; see **pity** 1.

emperor, *n.* —*Syn.* monarch, sovereign, dictator; see **ruler** 1.

emphasis, *n.* —*Syn.* stress, accent, weight; see **importance** 1.

emphasize, *v.* —*Syn.* make clear *or* emphatic, underline, underscore, highlight, dramatize, pronounce, enunciate, articulate, accentuate, accent, stress, point up *or* out, strike, punctuate, play *or* speak up, call to the attention of, reiterate, repeat, insist, maintain, impress, affirm, enlarge, indicate, italicize, lay stress on; *all* (D): rub in, pound *or* drum into one's head, labor the point, make much of, make a fuss about.

emphatic, *mod.* **1.** [Having force and certainty] —*Syn.* assured, strong, determined, forceful, forcible, earnest, positive, energetic, cogent, potent, powerful, dynamic, stressed, solemn, sober, trenchant, pointed, flat, confident, definitive, categorical, dogmatic, insistent, express, explicit.—*Ant.* unemphatic, hesitant*, vacillating.

2. [Attracting attention by positive character] —*Syn.* notable, outstanding, spectacular; see **important** 2.

emphatically, *mod.* —*Syn.* definitely, certainly, of course, undoubtedly, decidedly, assuredly, with decision, decisively, absolutely, entirely, unequivocally, flatly, distinctly, with no ifs, ands, or buts about it (D).—*Ant.* slowly*, hesitantly, indistinctly.

empire, *n.* —*Syn.* union, people, federation; see **nation** 1.

empirical, *mod.* —*Syn.* experiential, provisional, speculative; see **hypothetical** 1.

empiricism, *n.* —*Syn.* induction, experimentation, experientialism; see **philosophy** 1.

employ, *v.* **1.** [To make use of]—*Syn.* operate, manipulate, apply; see **use** 1.

2. [To obtain services for pay]—*Syn.* engage, contract, procure; see **hire** 1.

employed, *mod.* —*Syn.* working, occupied, busy, laboring, gainfully employed, not out of work, not on the unemployed *or* relief rolls, not on the town *or* county, in collar, in one's employ, (hard) at it, on the job, hired, operating, selected, active, engaged, on duty; *all* (D): in harness, on the grind, plugging, in one's pay, on the payroll.—*Ant.* out of work*, unemployed, jobless.

employee, *n.* —*Syn.* worker, laborer, servant, domestic, agent, representative, (hired) hand, member, salesman, (hired) man, assistant, attendant, apprentice, operator, workman, laboring man, workingman, breadwinner, craftsman, wage earner; *all* (D): slave, hireling, punk, plug, lackey, flunky, cog.

employer, *n.* —*Syn.* patron, owner, manager, proprietor, management, head, director, executive, superintendent, supervisor, master, overseer, lord, president, chief, capitalist, businessman, entrepreneur, manufacturer, corporation, company; *all* (D): boss, front office, old man, kingpin, big shot.

employment, *n.* **1.** [The act of employing]—*Syn.* hiring, using, calling, commissioning, awarding, servicing, occupying, engaging, carrying.

2. [An occupation]—*Syn.* job, profession, vocation; see **business** 1, **trade** 2, **work** 2.

empower, *v.* —*Syn.* grant, authorize, permit; see **allow** 1.

empress, *n.* —*Syn.* female sovereign, maharani, czarina; see **ruler** 1.

emptiness, *n.* —*Syn.* void, vacuum, vacuity, vacancy, gap, chasm, blankness, blank, depletedness, inanition, exhaustion, hollowness.

empty, *mod.* **1.** [Without content]—*Syn.* hollow, bare, clear, blank, unfilled, unfurnished, unoccupied, vacated, vacant, void, vacuous, void of, devoid, lacking, wanting, barren, emptied, abandoned, exhausted, depleted, deserted, desert, stark, deprived of, *in vacuo* (Latin), despoiled, dry, destitute, negative, deflated, eviscerated, evacuated, unsatisfactory.—*Ant.* full*, filled, occupied.

2. [Without food]—*Syn.* starved, unfed, starving; see **hungry.**

3. [Without sense]—*Syn.* barren, fruitless, meaningless; see **blank** 2.

empty, *v.* **1.** [To become empty]—*Syn.* discharge, leave, pour, flow (out), ebb, become void, run (out), open into, converge, be discharged, void, purge, release, exhaust, vomit forth, leak, drain (off), rush out, escape.—*Ant.* flow in, enter*, absorb.

2. [To cause to become empty]—*Syn.* dump, dip, ladle, decant, tap, void, pour, spill *or* let out, deplete, exhaust, deflate, drain, lade, shed, pour forth, bail (out), clean *or* clear out, evacuate, eject, expel, make void, draw off *or* out, disgorge, suck dry, clear, drink.—*Ant.* pack, fill*, stuff.

empyrean, *n.* —*Syn.* cosmos, firmament, space; see **heaven** 1.

emulate, *v.* —*Syn.* challenge, contend, imitate; see **compete, follow** 2.

en, *n.* —*Syn.* en quad, en dash, nut quad; see **dash** 3.

enable, *v.* —*Syn.* make possible, sanction, give power *or* authority (to *or* for), invest, endow, authorize, empower, allow, let, permit, license, capacitate, set up; see also **approve** 1.

enact, *v.* **1.** [To legislate]—*Syn.* decree, sanction, ordain, order, dictate, make into law, legislate, pass, establish, ratify, vote in, proclaim, vote favorably, determine, transact, authorize, appoint, institute, railroad through, get the floor, put in force, make laws, put through, constitute, fix, set, formulate.

2. [To accomplish]—*Syn.* execute, do, perform; see **achieve** 1.

3. [To act]—*Syn.* personify, impersonate, act out; see **act** 3.

enactment, *n.* **1.** [Law]—*Syn.* edict, decree, statute; see **law** 3.

2. [An accomplishment]—*Syn.* performance, achievement, execution; see **success** 1.

3. [Acting]—*Syn.* personification, impersonation, playing; see **acting.**

enamel, *n.* —*Syn.* lacquer, coating, finish, polish, gloss, glossy surface, top coat, japan, varnish, paint, glaze, veneer, lead glaze, cloisonné, plique-à-jour, champlevé.

enamel, *v.* —*Syn.* lacquer, glaze, gloss, japan, paint, veneer, coat, varnish, finish, paint, give a finish; *both* (D): Duco (trademark), spray gun.

enamor, *v.* —*Syn.* please, entice, enthrall; see **fascinate.**

enamored, *mod.* —*Syn.* attracted, enchanted, in love; see **fascinated.**

encage, *v.* —*Syn.* cage, coop up, confine; see **imprison.**

encamp, *v.* —*Syn.* billet, quarter, settle; see **camp.**

encampment, *n.* —*Syn.* caravansary, campsite, bivouac; see **camp** 1, 3.

enceinte (French), *mod.* —*Syn.* with child, gestating, expecting; see **pregnant** 1.

enchain, *v.* **1.** [To confine]—*Syn.* pinion, handcuff, bind; see **fasten** 1.

2. [To attract]—*Syn.* captivate, hypnotize, mesmerize; see **fascinate.**

enchant, *v.* **1.** [To put under a spell]—*Syn.* charm, bewitch, enthrall; see **hypnotize.**

2. [To attract strongly]—*Syn.* entrance, entice, allure; see **fascinate.**

enchanted, *mod.* **1.** [Fascinated]—*Syn.* enraptured, entranced, captivated; see **fascinated.**

2. [Charmed]—*Syn.* bewitched, ensorcelled, controlled; see **charmed** 1.

enchanter, *n.* —*Syn.* wizard, conjurer, witch; see **magician. 1.** [Extreme attraction]—*Syn.* spell, allurement, fascination; see **attraction** 1.

enchantress, *n.* —*Syn.* witch, sorceress, siren; see **magician.**

enchase, *v.* —*Syn.* emboss, engrave, incise; see **carve** 1.

encircle, *v.* —*Syn.* encompass, circle, throw a cordon about; see **surround** 2.

enclose, *v.* **1.** [To shut up or shut in]—*Syn.* insert, imbue, intern, jail, picket, corral, impound, confine, blockade, imprison, block *or* fence off, set apart, induct, lock up *or* in, freeze over, implant, infuse, drive *or* stick *or* keep *or* build *or* box *or* close *or* hem *or* shut *or* rail *or* wall in, box off *or* up.—*Ant.* free*, liberate, open.

2. [To encircle]—*Syn.* encompass, circumscribe, circle; see **surround** 2.

enclosed, *mod.* **1.** [Placed within]—*Syn.* inserted, injected, stuffed, *or* locked *or* penned in, immured, jailed, enfolded, packed *or* wrapped *or* shut up, buried, encased, interred, imprisoned.

2. [Encircled]—*Syn.* girdled, encompassed, hemmed in; see **surrounded.**

enclosure, *n.* **1.** [A space enclosed]—*Syn.* pen, sty, yard, jail, garden, corral, cage, asylum, pound, park, fenced-in field, arena, zone, precinct, plot, court, patch, walk, region, aviary, mew(s), coop, cote, hutch, den, cell, dungeon, vault, crawl, kraal, paddock, stockade, warren, concentration camp, detention camp, pale, ghetto, prison, stadium, bowl, coliseum; see also **building** 1, **place** 2, **room** 2.

2. [Something inserted]—*Syn.* information, check, money, circular, copy, questionnaire, forms, documents, printed matter.

encomium, *n.* —*Syn.* approval, praise, acclaim; see **admiration** 1.

encompass, *v.* **1.** [To surround]—*Syn.* encircle, compass, gird; see **surround** 2.

2. [To include]—*Syn.* embrace, comprise, incorporate; see **include** 1.

encore, *n.* **1.** [Applause]—*Syn.* plaudits, acclamation, cheers; see **praise** 2.

2. [A performance in answer to applause]—*Syn.* repeat performance, number, response; see **performance** 1, **repetition.**

encounter, *n.* **1.** [A coming together]—*Syn.* interview, rendezvous, appointment; see **meeting** 1.

2. [Physical violence]—*Syn.* conflict, clash, collision; see **fight** 1.

encounter, *v.* **1.** [To meet unexpectedly]—*Syn.* meet, confront, come across; see **find** 1.

2. [To meet in conflict]—*Syn.* battle, attack, struggle; see **fight** 2.

encourage, *v.* **1.** [To give support]—*Syn.* solace, console, ease, relieve, help, aid, comfort, foster, sanction, approve, sustain, fortify, advocate, reassure, assist, abet, succor, befriend, uphold, reinforce, back, bolster, brace, further, forward, favor, strengthen, second, subscribe to, smile upon, side with, back up, pull for; *all* (D): lead *or* egg on, extend a helping hand, give a hand *or* foot up, root for, pat on the back.—*Ant.* restrain*, discourage, caution.

2. [To raise the spirits]—*Syn.* inspirit, embolden, elate, animate, cheer, incite, refresh, instigate, enliven, exhilarate, inspire, cheer up, brighten, applaud, sway, praise, goad, spur, rally, hearten, restore, give new promise *or* life, revitalize, give encouragement, gladden, fortify, revivify, promise *or* augur well, buoy up, bid fair; *all* (D): boost, prick, whet, give a shot in the arm, clap on the back, brighten up, buck up.—*Ant.* discourage*, depress, dispirit.

encouraged, *mod.* —*Syn.* inspired, animated, enlivened, renewed, aided, supported, prepared, determined, hopeful, confident, enthusiastic, certain, fearless, roused, cheered, inspirited, buoyed up; see also **helped.**—*Ant.* sad*, discouraged, disheartened.

encouragement, *n.* **1.** [The act of encouraging] —*Syn.* solacing, consoling, urging, reassuring, enlivening, refreshment, comfort, easement, softening, relieving, invigoration, supporting, helpfulness.

2. [That which encourages]—*Syn.* aid, faith, help, assistance, support, cheer, confidence, trust, advance, promotion, reward, reassurance, incentive, backing, animation, optimism, comfort, consolation, hope, relief, fortitude, firmness; *all* (D): pat on the back, lift, shot in the arm, good omen.

encouraging, *mod.* —*Syn.* bright, good, promising; see **hopeful** 1, 2.

encroach, *v.* —*Syn.* infringe, trespass, invade; see **meddle** 1.

encroachment, *n.* —*Syn.* infringement, aggression, invasion; see **attack** 1.

encumber, *v.* —*Syn.* burden, hamper, obstruct; see **hinder.**

encumbrance, *n.* —*Syn.* burden, hindrance, impediment; see **difficulty** 1.

encyclopedia, *n.* —*Syn.* book of facts, thesaurus, book of knowledge, compilation, concordance, general *or* encyclopedic reference work, cyclopedia.

encyclopedic, *mod.* —*Syn.* exhaustive, broad, all-encompassing; see **comprehensive, general** 1, **widespread.**

end, *n.* **1.** [Purpose]—*Syn.* aim, object, intention; see **purpose** 1.

2. [The close of an action]—*Syn.* expiration, completion, target date, termination, adjournment, final event, ending, close, denouement, finish, conclusion, arrangement, finis, finale, cessation, retirement, accomplishment, attainment, determination, achievement, fulfillment, pay-off, realization, period, consummation, concluding part, culmination, perfection, execution, performance, last line, perfecting, closing piece *or* scene, curtain, terminus, omega; *all* (D): last word, bottom line, wrap-up, windup, beginning of the end, *commencement de la fin* (French), cutoff, mopping up, end of the line.—*Ant.* beginning, start*, opening.

3. [A result]—*Syn.* conclusion, effect, outcome; see **result.**

4. [The extremity]—*Syn.* terminal, termination, terminus, boundary, limit, borderline, point, stub, stump, tail (end), edge, tip, top, head, butt end, nib, pole, dissolving *or* melting point, deadline.—*Ant.* center*, middle, hub.

5. [The close of life]—*Syn.* demise, passing, doom; see **death** 1.

end, *v.* **1.** [To bring to a halt]—*Syn.* stop, finish, quit, close, halt, shut (down), settle (up), leave *or* switch off, bring to an end, make an end of, break off *or* up, leave unfinished, relinquish, put an end to, discontinue, abort, postpone, delay, conclude, playout, interrupt, dispose of, drop; *all* (D): call it a day, pull the plug, cut short, put the lid on, wind up, get done, choke *or* call off, give up, ring down the curtain, wrap up.—*Ant.* begin*, initiate, start.

2. [To bring to a conclusion]—*Syn.* settle, conclude, terminate; see **achieve** 1.

3. [To come to an end]—*Syn.* desist, cease, die; see **stop** 2.

4. [To die]—*Syn.* expire, depart, pass away; see **die** 1.

keep one's end up (D)—*Syn.* do one's share, join, participate; see **share** 1.

make (both) ends meet (D)—*Syn.* manage, get along *or* by, survive; see **endure** 2.

no end (D)—*Syn.* very much, extremely, greatly; see **much** 1, **very.**

on end—*Syn.* **1.** ceaseless, without interruption, constant; see **endless** 1. **2.** straight, vertical, standing up; see **upright** 1.

put an end to—*Syn.* stop, finish, cease; see **end** 1.

endanger, *v.* —*Syn.* imperil, jeopardize, bring under suspicion, expose to danger, leave defenseless *or* unprotected, put *or* bring into danger *or* jeopardy, subject to loss, make liable to danger, bring into jeopardy, expose to hazard *or* peril, be careless with; *all* (D): fish in troubled waters, lay open, put on the spot, leave in the middle.—*Ant.* save*, protect, preserve.

endangered, *mod.* —*Syn.* exposed, imperiled, in a dilemma, in a predicament, jeopardized, overdue, in danger, (put) in jeopardy, fraught with danger; *all* (D): in the cannon's mouth, in a bad way, on thin ice, up the creek without a paddle, (caught) between Scylla and Charybdis, hanging by a thread, at the last extremity.

endear, *v.* —*Syn.* prize, treasure, value; see **cherish** 1.

endearment, *n.* —*Syn.* attachment, fondness, love; see **affection.**

endeavor, *n.* —*Syn.* effort, try, attempt; see **effort** 1.

endeavor, *v.* —*Syn.* attempt, aim, essay; see **try** 1.

ended, *mod.* —*Syn.* done, completed, concluded; see **finished** 1.

ending, *n.* —*Syn.* finish, closing, terminus; see **end** 2.

endless, *mod.* **1.** [Having no end in space]—*Syn.* infinite, measureless, interminable, indeterminable, untold, without end, being without bounds, unbounded, unlimited, immeasurable, unmeasured, limitless, unsurpassable, having no bounds, multitudinous, boundless, incalculable, illimitable, unfathomable.—*Ant.* fixed*, finite, bounded.
2. [Having no end in time]—*Syn.* enduring, perpetual, everlasting; see **eternal** 2.

endorse, *v.* **1.** [To inscribe one's name]—*Syn.* sign, put one's signature on, countersign, indorse, underwrite, sign one's name on, inscribe one's signature, subscribe, superscribe, notarize, add one's name to; *all* (D): put the seal to, say amen to, sign on the dotted line, autograph a check.
2. [To indicate one's active support of]—*Syn.* approve, confirm, sanction, ratify, guarantee, underwrite, support, lend one's name to, stand up for, stand *or* be behind, vouch for, uphold, recommend, commend, praise, defend, give one's word for; *all* (D): O.K., back up, go to bat for.—*Ant.* censure*, condemn, denounce.

endorsed, *mod.* —*Syn.* signed, notarized, legalized, ratified, sealed, affirmed, concluded, settled, attested, approved, upheld, supported, commended, recommended, sanctioned, advocated, blessed; *all* (D): backed, O.K.'d, boosted.—*Ant.* cancelled*, disapproved, vetoed.

endorsement, *n.* —*Syn.* support, sanction, permission; see **signature.**

endow, *v.* **1.** [To give to]—*Syn.* enrich, provide, supply; see **give** 1.
2. [To provide support for all times]—*Syn.* bequeath, found, establish in perpetuity; see **organize** 2.

endowment, *n.* **1.** [A gift]—*Syn.* donation, bounty, award; see **gift** 1.
2. [A human quality or special capacity]—*Syn.* talent, genius, qualification; see **ability** 1.
3. [That which supplies perpetual support]—*Syn.* benefit, provision, bequest, gratuity, grant, pension, stipend, legacy, inheritance, subsidy, revenue, trust, dispensation, bestowal, nest egg (D).
4. [The act of providing perpetual support]—*Syn.* funding, subsidizing, giving *or* providing an endowment (for), setting up, supporting, giving money to *or* for, establishing, granting in perpetuity; see also **giving.**

end up, *v.* —*Syn.* finish, cease, come to a close; see **end** 1, **stop** 2.

endurable, *mod.* —*Syn.* sustainable, tolerable, supportable; see **bearable.**

endurance, *n.* **1.** [An enduring state]—*Syn.* persistence, duration, continuance; see **continuation** 1.
2. [Ability to face difficulty]—*Syn.* sufferance, fortitude, submission, forebearance, long-suffering, capacity to endure, ability to suffer without succumbing, resignation, patience, tolerance, allowance, coolness, courage, perseverance, stamina, restraint, resistance, will; *all* (D): backbone, pluck, mettle, guts, spunk, grit.—*Ant.* weakness*, feebleness, infirmity.
3. [The suffering of troubles]—*Syn.* undergoing, bearing, suffering, continuing, holding up, withstanding torture, enduring, standing (D).—*Ant.* ease*, comfort, relaxation.

endure, *v.* **1.** [To continue]—*Syn.* persist, remain, last, continue, be long lived, exist, be, abide, bide, stay, prevail, wear, be timeless, sustain, survive, outlast, superannuate, be left, carry *or* stay *or* live *or* go *or* hold *or* hang *or* keep *or* run on, linger, outlive, have no end, hold out; *all* (D): be solid as a rock, never say die, wear on, stick to *or* at, ride out.—*Ant.* die*, cease, end.
2. [To sustain adversity]—*Syn.* suffer, tolerate, bear with *or* up, allow, permit, support, undergo, sit through, brook, take, withstand, bear up under, stand, accustom oneself to, abide, submit *or* be subject to, countenance, sustain, go *or* pass through, feel, experience, know, meet with, go far, encounter, be patient with, keep up, repress one's feelings, resign oneself, weather, brave, face; *all* (D): put up with, live through, stand for, swallow, live out, stomach, eat, pocket one's pride, bear the brunt, pass muster, never say die, not flag, grin and bear it, brace oneself, like it or lump it, ride out, carry through, hang on, do without, go hard with, pull through, make one's own bed and lie in it, take one's punishment, keep one's chin up.—*Ant.* avoid*, resist, refuse.

enduring, *mod.* —*Syn.* lasting, abiding, surviving; see **permanent** 2.

enema, *n.* —*Syn.* douche, purgative, clyster; see **medicine** 2.

enemy, *n.* **1.** [A national or public opponent] —*Syn.* foe, attacker, antagonist, opponent, adversary, public enemy, criminal, opposition, guerrilla(s), guerrilla force *or* army *or* band, fifth column, enemy within the gates, borer from within, saboteur, spy, foreign agent, parachutist, assassin, murderer, betrayer, traitor, terrorist, revolutionary, seditionist, rebel, invader; see also **army** 1, 2.—*Ant.* ally, assistant*, aid.

2. [A personal opponent]—*Syn.* rival, detractor, backbiter, prosecutor, inquisitor, informer, calumniator, falsifier, disputant, foe, antagonist, assailant, adversary, traducer, asperser, defiler, defamer, competitor, slanderer, backbiter, vilifer, villain, bad guy (D).—*Ant.* friend*, supporter, benefactor.

energetic, *mod.* —*Syn.* industrious, vigorous, forcible; see **active** 2.

energetically, *mod.* —*Syn.* actively, firmly, strenuously; see **vigorously.**

energize, *v.* —*Syn.* fortify, invigorate, stimulate; see **strengthen.**

energy, *n.* **1.** [One's internal powers]—*Syn.* force, power, virtility; see **strength** 1.

2. [Vigor in expression]—*Syn.* effectiveness, spontaneity, vehemence; see **force** 3.

3. [Power developed or released by a device] —*Syn.* horsepower, reaction, response, co-ordination, power, pressure, potential energy, kinetic energy, atomic energy, solar energy, high pressure, foot-pounds, magnetism, friction, voltage, kilowatts, kilowatt-hours, current, service, dynamism, electricity, gravity, heat, friction, conductivity, suction, elasticity, rays, radioactivity, potential, (1-second, 2-second, 3-second, etc.) burn, (highly) critical burn, power descent (PD), gas mileage, fuel consumption.

enervate, *v.* —*Syn.* debilitate, devitalize, enfeeble; see **weaken** 2.

enfeeble, *v.* —*Syn.* cripple, disable, exhaust; see **weaken** 2.

enfold, *v.* —*Syn.* envelope, encase, enclose; see **surround** 2, **wrap** 2.

enforce, *v.* **1.** [To add strength]—*Syn.* reinforce, fortify, support; see **strengthen.**

2. [To require compliance]—*Syn.* urge, compel, incite, exert, drive, demand, carry out vigorously, put in force, have executed, expect, dictate, exact, commandeer, require, strain, constrain, execute, coerce, oblige, insist (upon), emphasize, necessitate, press, impel, make, sanction, wrest, extort, force (upon), goad, stress, spur; *all* (D): egg on, hound, dragoon, whip, lash, put the screws on, crack down.—*Ant.* abandon*, neglect, evade.

enforced, *mod.* —*Syn.* prescribed, ordained, compelled, established, demanded, exacted, commandeered, required, constrained, executed, pressed, sanctioned, forced upon, kept, dictated, admonished, advocated, charged, enjoined, meted out, prevalent, cracked *or* slapped down (D).

enforcement, *n.* —*Syn.* requirement, enforcing, prescription, exaction, compulsion, constraint, coercion, pressure, duress, martial law, obligation, compelling necessity, necessitation, compulsory execution *or* action, impulsion, insistence, carrying out, fulfilling, translating into action; *all* (D): Hobson's choice, spur, whip, lash, prick.

enfranchise, *v.* **1.** [To liberate]—*Syn.* emancipate, release, manumit; see **free** 1.

2. [To empower]—*Syn.* license, authorize, sanction; see **allow** 1.

enfranchisement, *n.* **1.** [Liberation]—*Syn.* disimprisonment, emancipation, release; see **freeing.**

2. [Permission]—*Syn.* authorization, warranty, license; see **permission.**

engage, *v.* **1.** [To hire]—*Syn.* employ, contract, retain; see **hire** 1.

2. [To engross]—*Syn.* absorb, captivate, bewitch; see **fascinate.**

3. [To occupy]—*Syn.* keep busy, employ, interest; see **occupy** 3.

4. [To attack]—*Syn.* assault, strike, fall upon; see **attack** 1, **fight** 2.

5. [To enmesh, especially gears]—*Syn.* interlock, mesh, interlace; see **fasten** 1.

engaged, *mod.* **1.** [Promised in marriage]—*Syn.* bound, pledged, betrothed, plighted, affianced, matched; *both* (D): hooked, ringed.—*Ant.* free*, unpledged, unbetrothed.

2. [Not at liberty]—*Syn.* working, occupied, employed; see **busy** 1, 3.

3. [In a profession, business, or the like]—*Syn.* employed, practicing, performing, dealing in, doing, interested, absorbed in, pursuing, at work, involved *or* engaged with *or* in, working (at), connected with; see also **employed.**—*Ant.* unemployed*, out of a job, without connection.

engage in, *v.* —*Syn.* take part in, attack, undertake; see **perform** 1.

engagement, *n.* **1.** [A predetermined action] —*Syn.* meeting, rendezvous, errand; see **appointment** 2.

2. [The state of being betrothed]—*Syn.* compact, match, betrothal, espousal, betrothing, troth, publishing the banns, betrothment.

3. [A battle]—*Syn.* action, combat, skirmish; see **fight** 1.

engaging, *mod.* —*Syn.* pleasant, enticing, inviting; see **charming.**

engender, *v.* —*Syn.* induce, incite, cause; see **produce** 1.

engine, *n.* **1.** [A machine for transforming power] —*Syn.* motor, power plant, dynamo, generator, turbine, diesel engine, traction engine, plasma engine, ion engine, steam turbine, delta piston type motor, nuclear engine for rocket vehicle applications (NERVA), (step up) transformer, source of power; *both* (D): diesel, powerhouse.

2. [A locomotive]—*Syn.* steam engine, motor, traction engine; see **locomotive.**

engineer, *n.* **1.** [A professional engineer]—*Syn.* surveyor, designer, planner, builder; *all* (D): bridge monkey, sights, grease monkey with a slide rule for a brain.

Types of engineers include the following—mining, civil, metallurgical, geological, atomic, nuclear, architectural, chemical, construction, stationary, military, naval, flight, pneumatic, hydraulic, marine, electronic, communications, electrical, industrial, research, developmental, systems; see also **electronics, science** 1.

2. [The operator of a locomotive]—*Syn.* driver, motorman, brakeman, stoker, fireman, engineman; *all* (D): boilerhead, hog head, Casey Jones, lokey man, engine tamer.

engineer, *v.* —*Syn.* direct, superintend, mastermind; see **manage** 1.

engineering, *n.* **1.** [The act of turning material to use]—*Syn.* construction, manufacturing, organization, organizing, building, arranging, constructing,

implementing, authorizing, systematizing, systematization, handling; see **sense** 2.
2. [The science of applying power to use]—*Syn.* design, planning, blueprinting, structure *or* structures, surveying, metallurgy, architecture, heavy *or* light *or* industrial construction, shipbuilding, installations, stresses, communications; see sense 1. Branches of engineering include the following—aeronautical, agricultural, architectural, chemical, civil, contracting, designing, electrical, flight, heating, highway, human, industrial, irrigation, marine, mechanical, military, mining, naval, nuclear, radio, railroad, sanitary, stationary, steam, systems, traction, transportation, tunnel, utilities.

England, *n.*—*Syn.* Britain, Great Britain, British Isles, United Kingdom, Britannia, member of the British Commonwealth of Nations, "the tight little isle," Albion, the mother country, John Bull (D).

English, *mod.*—*Syn.* British, Britannic, Anglian, Anglican, Anglic, Anglo-, England's His *or* Her Majesty's, Commonwealth, non-Celtic, anglicized, insular, English-speaking, (insular) Saxon, Norman, Limey (D); see also **Anglo-Saxon.**

English, *n.*—*Syn.* British, Anglo-Saxons, islanders, Britons; *all* (D): John Bulls, Limeys, cockneys.

engrave, *v.* **1.** [To carve upon]—*Syn.* scratch, initial, enchase; see **carve** 1.
2. [To prepare a plate for printing]—*Syn.* etch, bite, stipple, lithograph, cut, burn, ornament with incised designs, intaglio, chase, incise, grave, chisel, mezzotint, crosshatch, hatch, diaper, impress upon.

engraved, *mod.*—*Syn.* carved, decorated, minted, chased, etched, scratched, bitten into, embossed, furrowed, incised, deepened, marked deeply, lithographed, rotographed.

engraver, *n.*—*Syn.* graver, etcher, sculptor, artist, cutter, carver, lithographer, lapidary.

engraving, *n.* **1.** [A process of reproduction]—*Syn.* photoengraving, etching, carving; see **reproduction** 1.
2. [A picture reproduced by engraving]—*Syn.* print, incised design, wood engraving, xylograph, etching, aquatint, dry point, graphotype, photogravure, steelplate, rotogravure, lithograph, chromolithograph, copperplate, mezzotint, cut, woodcut, linocut, intaglio, halftone, illustration, impression, copy, print, pull, proof, positive.

engross, *v.* **1.** [To occupy one's time]—*Syn.* absorb, busy, fill; see **occupy** 3.
2. [To occupy's one's mind]—*Syn.* attract, captivate, bewitch; see **fascinate.**

engrossment, *n.*—*Syn.* intentness, preoccupation, study; see **reflection** 1.

engulf, *v.*—*Syn.* swallow up, imbibe, inundate; see **submerge** 1.

enhance, *v.*—*Syn.* heighten, magnify, amplify; see **intensify.**

enhancement, *n.*—*Syn.* augmentation, enlargement, intensification; see **increase** 1.

enigma, *n.* **1.** [Puzzle]—*Syn.* problem, riddle, parable; see **puzzle** 3.
2. [Mystery]—*Syn.* anything *or* anyone inexplicable, sphinx, bewilderment; see **puzzle** 2, **secret.**

enigmatic, *mod.*—*Syn.* ambiguous, occult, mysterious; see **obscure** 1, **secret** 1.

enjoin, *v.*—*Syn.* order, ordain, appoint; see **require** 2.

enjoy, *v.* **1.** [To take pleasure in]—*Syn.* relish, luxuriate in, delight in; see **like** 1.
2. [To have the use of]—*Syn.* command, hold, process; see **use** 1.

enjoyable, *mod.*—*Syn.* agreeable, welcome, genial; see **pleasant** 1, 2.

enjoying, *mod.*—*Syn.* gratified, refreshed, experiencing, partaking of, tasting, savoring, feeling, sensing, sharing, undergoing, reveling *or* delighting *or* luxuriating *or* basking *or* swimming in, relishing, feasting on, making use of, exercising; *both* (D): getting a kick out of, having a ball.—*Ant.* suffering*, enduring, experiencing.

enjoyment, *n.* **1.** [The result of obtaining one's desire]—*Syn.* pleasure, delight, happiness; see **satisfaction** 2.
2. [The act of fulfilling one's desire]—*Syn.* satisfaction, gratification, triumph, loving, enjoying, rejoicing, delighting, spending, having, using, occupation, use, diversion, entertainment, amusement, luxury, sensuality, indulgence, self-indulgence, voluptuousness, hedonism.—*Ant.* abstinence*, refusal, rejection.

enjoy oneself, *v.*—*Syn.* take pleasure, celebrate, have a good time, revel *or* delight *or* luxuriate in, be pleased with; see also **play** 1.

enkindle, *v.* **1.** [To ignite]—*Syn.* fire, inflame, kindle; see **ignite.**
2. [To stimulate]—*Syn.* incite, evoke, arouse; see **excite** 2.

enlarge, *v.* **1.** [To increase]—*Syn.* expand, spread, swell; see **grow** 1.
2. [To cause to increase]—*Syn.* extend, augment, expand; see **increase** 1.

enlarged, *mod.*—*Syn.* increased, augmented, expanded, developed, exaggerated, caricatured, extended, amplified, spread, added to, aggrandized, lengthened, broadened, widened, thickened, magnified, filled out, inflated, stretched, distended, dilated, heightened, intensified, blownup (D).—*Ant.* declined, decreased*, declining.

enlargement, *n.* **1.** [Growth or extension]—*Syn.* augmentation, amplification, expansion; see **increase** 1.
2. [An enlarged photograph]—*Syn.* view, enlarged print, blow up (D); see **photograph, picture** 2.

enlighten, *v.* **1.** [To provide information or understanding]—*Syn.* inform, divulge, acquaint; see **teach** 1, **tell** 1.
2. [To bring supposed spiritual truth]—*Syn.* illumine, illuminate, persuade, reveal, inculcate, indoctrinate, inspirit, disclose, open up, elucidate, give faith, preach, save, catechize, convert; *all* (D): lead to the light, save a soul, bring out of the wilderness, raise up.

enlightened, *mod.*—*Syn.* instructed, learned, informed; see **educated** 1.

enlightenment, *n.*—*Syn.* wisdom, culture, education; see **knowledge** 1.

enlist, *v.* **1.** [To enroll others]—*Syn.* engage, hire, retain, reserve, incorporate, embody, call up, sign up, recruit, mobilize, induct, register, list, levy, record, initiate, inscribe, employ, place, admit, press

into service, draft, conscribe, muster, call to arms (D).—*Ant.* refuse*, neglect, turn away.
2. [To request assistance]—*Syn.* interest, attract, procure, induce, obtain, get, engage, oblige, appoint, assign, make available.—*Ant.* shun, avoid*, discourage.
3. [To enroll oneself]—*Syn.* enter, sign up, serve; see **join** 2, **register** 4.

enlisted, *mod.* —*Syn.* recruited, enrolled, commissioned, engaged, joined, registered, entered, volunteered; *both* (D): hooked, lined up.

enlistment, *n.* —*Syn.* conscription, levy, recruitment; see **draft** 6.

enliven, *v.* —*Syn.* cheer, vivify, quicken; see **excite** 1.

enlivenment, *n.* —*Syn.* cheerfulness, joy, liveliness; see **happiness** 1.

en masse, *mod.* —*Syn.* bodily, ensemble, together; see **jointly.**

enmesh, *v.* —*Syn.* trap, entrap, snare; see **catch** 1.

enmity, *n.* —*Syn.* animosity, malice, rancor; see **hatred** 1, 2.

ennoble, *v.* —*Syn.* honor, exalt, glorify; see **praise** 1.

ennoblement, *n.* —*Syn.* exaltation, promotion, dignity; see **fame** 1, **honor** 1.

ennui, *n.* —*Syn.* apathy, languor, tedium; see **boredom.**

enormity, *n.* **1.** [Vice]—*Syn.* atrocity, outrage, depravity; see **crime** 1, 2, **injustice** 2.
2. [Magnitude]—*Syn.* immensity, enormousness, bulk; see **size** 2.

enormous, *mod.* —*Syn.* monstrous, immense, huge; see **large** 1.

enough, *mod.* **1.** [Sufficient]—*Syn.* plenty, abundant, adequate, full, replete, plenteous, acceptable, copious, ample, satisfactory, complete, plentiful, satisfying, bounteous, lavish, unlimited, suitable. —*Ant.* inadequate*, deficient, insufficient.
2. [Sufficiently]—*Syn.* satisfactorily, amply, abundantly; see **adequately** 1.
3. [Fully]—*Syn.* quite, rather, just; see **very.**
4. [Just adequately]—*Syn.* tolerably, fairly, barely; see **adequately** 2.

enough, *n.* —*Syn.* abundance, sufficiency, adequacy; see **plenty.**

enquire, *v.* —*Syn.* inquire, question, query; see **ask** 1.

enrage, *v.* —*Syn.* incense, infuriate, madden; see **anger.**

enrapture, *v.* —*Syn.* enchant, allure, delight; see **fascinate.**

enrich, *v.* —*Syn.* adorn, better, ameliorate; see **decorate, improve** 1.

enriched, *mod.* —*Syn.* improved, ameliorated, embellished; see **improved** 1, **increased.**

enrichment, *n.* —*Syn.* advancement, promotion, endowment; see **improvement** 1.

enroll, *v.* **1.** [To obtain for service]—*Syn.* recruit, obtain, employ; see **hire** 1.
2. [To prepare a roll]—*Syn.* inventorize, schedule, register, catalogue, matriculate, place upon a list, engross, enter, poll, inscribe, mark, affix, enlist, fill out, bill, book, slate, file, index.—*Ant.* discard*, reject, omit.
3. [To register oneself]—*Syn.* enter, sign up, enlist; see **join** 2, **register** 4.

enrolled, *mod.* —*Syn.* joined, entered, inducted, registered, installed, settled, subscribed, ordained, pledged, enlisted, commissioned, employed, recruited, signed up (D).—*Ant.* separated*, mustered out, discharged.

enrollment, *n.* **1.** [The act of enrolling]—*Syn.* inducting, registering, recording, listing, record, enlistment, matriculation, the act of recording officially, rallying, rally, induction, entry, enlisting, mobilizing, selecting, registration, installing, reception.
2. [The persons enrolled]—*Syn.* group, students, student body, volunteers, an enrolled entry, number enrolled, response, registration, conscription, entrance, accession, subscription, influx.

en route, *mod.* —*Syn.* in transit, *en voyage* (French), on the way, flying, driving, entrained, traveling, midway, in passage, on the road (to), advancing, pressing on, making headway toward, bound, progressing *or* heading toward.—*Ant.* motionless*, delayed, stalled.

ensemble, *n.* **1.** [Entirety]—*Syn.* group, aggregate, composite; see **collection** 2, **gathering, organization** 3, **whole.**
2. [Costume]—*Syn.* coordinates, suit, garb; see **clothes.**
3. [Group of entertainers]—*Syn.* troupe, chamber musicians, jazz band; string *or* woodwind *or* brass *or* vocal trio, quartet, quintet, sextet, etc.

enshrine, *v.* —*Syn.* consecrate, hallow, sanctify; see **bless** 3.

enshroud, *v.* —*Syn.* cover, conceal, wrap; see **hide** 1.

ensign, *n.* **1.** [A symbolic standard]—*Syn.* banner, insignia, colors, jack, pennant, streamer, pennon, pendant, title; see also **flag** 1.
2. [The lowest commissioned naval officer]—*Syn.* subaltern, cadet, standard bearer; see **officer** 3.

enslave, *v.* —*Syn.* bind, imprison, incarcerate, shut in, enclose, confine, immure, put in irons, hold under, subjugate, restrain, oppress, restrict, enthrall, indenture, coerce, circumscribe, check, subdue, capture, suppress, reduce to slavery, make a slave of, hold in bondage, subjugate, compel, chain, fetter, hold, jail, hobble, yoke, deprive, tie, tether, secure, shackle; *all* (D): clap in irons, bend to the plow *or* the yoke.

enslavement, *n.* —*Syn.* thralldom, subjection, servitude; see **slavery** 1.

ensnare, *v.* **1.** [To capture]—*Syn.* entrap, trap, snare; see **catch** 1.
2. [To deceive]—*Syn.* mislead, cheat, trick; see **deceive.**

ensue, *v.* —*Syn.* result, occur, appear; see **succeed** 2.

ensure, *v.* —*Syn.* secure, assure, warrant; see **guarantee** 1.

entail, *v.* —*Syn.* occasion, necessitate, evoke; see **cause** 2, **require** 2.

entangle, *v.* —*Syn.* ensnare, entrap, trap, involve, complicate, implicate, snarl, corner, enmesh, catch, tangle, ravel, dishevel, unsettle, embroil; *all* (D): foul *or* mess up, muddle, goof.—*Ant.* liberate*, disentangle, extricate.

entanglement, *n.* —*Syn.* complexity, intricacy, complication; see **difficulty** 1, 2.

entente, *n.*—*Syn.* friendship, harmony, concert; see **agreement** 3.

enter, *v.* **1.** [To enter physically]—*Syn.* invade, set foot in, pass *or* come *or* drive *or* burst *or* rush *or* go *or* break *or* wriggle *or* get *or* go in *or* into, penetrate, intrude, make way into, gain entrée, reenter, make an entrance, wriggle, creep, crawl, slip, sneak, insinuate (oneself), infiltrate, insert; *all* (D): horn *or* butt *or* bust *or* pile *or* put *or* move *or* blow *or* hop *or* burst *or* edge *or* jump in, fall into, fall to one, breeze *or* barge *or* crowd *or* work *or* push in, worm oneself into.—*Ant.* leave*, depart, exit.
2. [To enter upon]—*Syn.* start, open, make a beginning; see **begin** 2.
3. [To join]—*Syn.* enroll, subscribe, take part in; see **join** 2.

entered, *mod.*—*Syn.* filed, listed, posted; see **recorded.**

enter into, *v.*—*Syn.* engage in, take part (in), become part of; see **join** 2.

enter on *or* **upon,** *v.*—*Syn.* start, take up, making a beginning; see **begin** 2.

enterprise, *n.* **1.** [A venture]—*Syn.* undertaking, work, endeavor, performance, scheme, engagement, adventure, affair, business, operation, project of importance, campaign, action, activity, project, cause, crusade, effort, striving, move, trade, buying and selling, risk, hazard, plan, try, task, attempt, pursuit, purpose, speculation, stake.
2. [A venturesome or industrious disposition] —*Syn.* pluck, foresight, industry; see **courage** 1, **force** 3.

enterprising, *mod.*—*Syn.* progressive, busy, eager; see **active** 2.

entertain, *v.* **1.** [To keep others amused]—*Syn.* amuse, cheer, please, interest, enliven, delight, divert, beguile, engross, enthrall, charm, captivate, disport, rejoice, inspire, inspirit, stimulate, gratify, satisfy, humor, distract, indulge, flatter, solace, relax, make merry, comfort, put in good humor, ecstasize, elate, gladden, tickle.—*Ant.* tire, bore*, weary.
2. [To act as host or hostess]—*Syn.* receive, invite, treat, regale, recreate, gratify, charm, occupy, rouse, exhilarate, feed, dine, wine, host, chaperone, give a party, be at home, see one's friends, keep open house, do the honors, welcome, give a warm reception (to), receive with open arms, kill the fatted calf.—*Ant.* bore*, keep aloof, neglect, ignore.
3. [To consider]—*Syn.* heed, deliberate, recognize; see **consider** 1, **think** 1.

entertained, *mod.* **1.** [Given hospitality]—*Syn.* harbored, sheltered, cherished, welcomed, regaled, honored, received, feasted, banqueted, picknicked, wined and dined, feted, treated.—*Ant.* neglected*, ignored, spurned.
2. [Mentally or socially diverted]—*Syn.* amused, diverted, pleased, beguiled, entranced, occupied, charmed, engrossed, enthralled, exhilarated, cheered, interested, relaxed, delighted, enjoying oneself, happy, in good humor, in good company, transported.—*Ant.* bored*, depressed, irritated.

entertainer, *n.*—*Syn.* performer, player, artist; see **actor, actress.**

entertaining, *mod.*—*Syn.* diverting, amusing, engaging, enchanting, sprightly, lively, witty, clever, interesting, gay, charming, edifying, enjoyable, delightful, funny, droll, pleasing, cheerful, relaxing, restorative, affecting, moving, inspiring, captivating, thrilling, entrancing, engrossing, enthralling, stirring, enticing, piquant, poignant, impressive, soul-stirring, stimulating, absorbing, striking, exciting, compelling, provocative, fascinating, ravishing, rousing, animating, zestful, delectable, satisfying, gratifying, winning, alluring, seductive, enlivening; see also **funny** 1.—*Ant.* boring*, irritating, dull.

entertainment, *n.* **1.** [The act of amusing]—*Syn.* amusement, enjoyment, merriment, bodily enjoyment, *divertissement* (French), fun, pleasure, delight, cheer, sport, play, recreation, frolic, pastime, diversion, recreation, revelry, relaxation, distraction, regalement.—*Ant.* tediousness, boredom*, ennui.
2. [Something intended to entertain]—*Syn.* play, feast, banquet, picnic, cards, play, show, television, moving picture, movie, the movies, sport, dance, concert, merrymaking, reception, treat, game, fete, surprise, party, lunch, tea, dinner, supper, hootenanny, coffee klatch, reflection, spree; see also **drama** 1, **performance** 2.
3. [Provision for a guest]—*Syn.* accommodation, reception, board and lodging; see **hospitality** 1.

enthrall, *v.* **1.** [To overcome]—*Syn.* subjugate, enslave, master; see **subject.**
2. [To charm]—*Syn.* captivate, bewitch, enchant; see **fascinate.**

enthrallment, *n.* **1.** [Captivity]—*Syn.* slavery, subjugation, imprisonment; see **captivity.**
2. [Attraction]—*Syn.* fascination, enchantment, charm; see **attraction** 1.

enthrone, *v.*—*Syn.* elevate, exalt, deify; see **praise** 1.

enthused, *mod.*—*Syn.* excited, approving, eager; see **enthusiastic** 1, 2.

enthusiasm, *n.* **1.** [Ardent zeal]—*Syn.* fanaticism, flame, fervor, ardor, vehemence, eagerness, zealousness, earnestness, frenzy, intensity, feeling, nerve, zest, keenness, vim, energy, activity, ardency, ecstasy, fad, vivacity, impetuosity, fever, fieriness, *élan* (French), excitement, vigor, verve, furor, spirit, flare, rapture, heat, passion, transport, joy, joyousness, joyfulness, emotion, warmth, exhilaration, hilarity, mirth, gaiety, glow, rage, conviction, devotion, fury, orgasm, fullness of heart; *all* (D): fire, life, go, snap, pep, zip, dash.—*Ant.* dullness*, weariness, ennui.
2. [Wholehearted co-operation]—*Syn.* participation, help, devotion; see **co-operation** 1.

enthusiast, *n.* **1.** [An impetuous, zealous person] —*Syn.* optimist, Pollyanna, Pangloss, zealot, fanatic, extremist, votary, fan, devotee, partisan, *aficionado* (Spanish), worshiper, believer, bigot, megalomaniac, eccentric, lover; *all* (D): crackpot, left-winger, right-winger, crank, bug, head.—*Ant.* cynic*, pessimist, detractor.
2. [One who has warm personal interest]—*Syn.* partisan, supporter, participant; see **follower.**

enthusiastic, *mod.* **1.** [Excited by something] —*Syn.* interested, fascinated, animated, willing, thrilled, fevered, flushed, concerned, pleased, excited, attracted, titillated, exhilarated, hilarious, gay, anxious, tantalized, athirst, ablaze, intent, eager, heated; *all* (D): agog, nuts about, all hepped up, wacky, gushy, keyed up, dying to.—*Ant.* indifferent*, detached, uninterested.

2. [Strongly in favor of something]—*Syn.* zealous, inflamed, tireless, absorbed, rapt, devoted, diligent, resolute, indefatigable, desirous, eager, steadfast, assiduous, sleepless, impassioned, ardent, fiery, rabid, partial, voracious, raging, keen, yearning, longing, desiring, sedulous, burning, glowing, spirited, zestful, fervent, ecstatic, transported, impatient, delighted, rapturous, enraptured, intent, vehement, avid; *all* (D): wild *or* crazy *or* mad about, gone *or* hot on, keen on *or* about, all worked up over, jumping at, nuts about, all hopped up over, hot for, gung-ho, ready and willing, champing at the bit, cracked on, aching for, aching to, hyped on. —*Ant.* opposed*, reluctant, apathetic.

3. [Inclined to enthusiasm]—*Syn.* excitable, warm, ardent, forward, passionate, importunate, earnest, impetuous, impatient, aspiring, spirited, vivacious, effervescent, willing, inclined, possessed, inspired, intense, hot, impulsive, sanguine, maniacal, ambitious, ebullient, mercurial, apt for, given to enthusiasm(s), not prudent *or* restrained.—*Ant.* dull*, lethargic, sluggish.

entice, *v.* —*Syn.* lure, allure, attract; see **fascinate.**

enticement, *n.* **1.** [The act of attraction]—*Syn.* allurement, charm, fascination; see **attraction** 1.

2. [That which attracts]—*Syn.* lure, bait, promise; see **attraction** 2.

entire, *mod.* —*Syn.* complete, untouched, undamaged; see **whole** 1, 2.

entirely, *mod.* **1.** [Completely]—*Syn.* totally, fully, wholly; see **completely.**

2. [Exclusively]—*Syn.* uniquely, solely, undividedly; see **only** 1.

entirety, *n.* **1.** [Wholeness]—*Syn.* completeness, totality, collectiveness, intactness, plentitude, entireness, allness, universality, integrality, wholeness, omnitude, ensemble.

2. [A whole]—*Syn.* total, aggregate, sum; see **whole.**

entitle, *v.* **1.** [To name]—*Syn.* call, designate, lable; see **name** 1.

2. [To permit]—*Syn.* authorize, empower, qualify; see **allow** 1.

entity, *n.* **1.** [Essence]—*Syn.* existence, substance, actuality; see **reality** 1.

2. [An object]—*Syn.* item, article, something; see **thing** 1.

entomb, *v.* **1.** [To bury the dead]—*Syn.* inurn, inter, inhume; see **bury** 1.

2. [To conceal]—*Syn.* cache, screen, cover; see **hide** 1.

3. [To imprison]—*Syn.* incarcerate, confine, immure; see **imprison.**

entombment, *n.* **1.** [Burial]—*Syn.* interment, inurnment, sepulture; see **funeral** 1.

2. [Imprisonment]—*Syn.* immuration, enclosement, incarceration; see **imprisonment** 1.

entourage, *n.* **1.** [Environment]—*Syn.* surroundings, milieu, locale; see **neighborhood.**

2. [Companions]—*Syn.* retinue, associates, followers; see **following.**

entrails, *n.* —*Syn.* viscera, guts, insides; see **intestines.**

entrain, *v.* —*Syn.* board, depart, take off; see **leave** 1.

entrance, *n.* **1.** [The act of coming in]—*Syn.* ingress, progress, incoming, ingoing, arrival, ingression, access, entry, passage, approach, induction, initiation, inception, baptism, adit, admission, admittance, accession, entree, appearance, import, importation, introduction, penetration, trespass, debut, enrollment, enlistment, registering, invasion, immigration.—*Ant.* escape*, exit, issue.

2. [The opening that permits ingress *or* entree] —*Syn.* gate, door, doorway, entry, inlet, gateway, portal, portico, opening, passage, vestibule, staircase, porch, hall, hallway, archway, ingress, path, way, entrance *or* passageway, threshold, lobby, corridor, approach, foregate, aperture, hole, gape, port, gorge, propylon.—*Ant.* exit*, mouth, outlet.

entrance, *v.* **1.** [To enchant]—*Syn.* charm, enrapture, captivate; see **fascinate.**

2. [To put into a trance]—*Syn.* hypnotize, mesmerize, anesthetize; see **hypnotize** 1.

entrant, *n.* **1.** [A suitor]—*Syn.* petitioner, solicitor, aspirant; see **candidate.**

2. [An opponent]—*Syn.* rival, participant, competitor; see **opponent** 1.

entrap, *v.* —*Syn.* catch, ensnare, decoy; see **catch** 1.

entrapment, *n.* —*Syn.* snare, ambush, ruse; see **trap.**

entreat, *v.* —*Syn.* beg, implore, supplicate, plead; see **beg** 1.

entreaty, *n.* —*Syn.* petition, supplication, plea; see **request.**

entree, *n.* **1.** [The act of entering]—*Syn.* admittance, induction, importation; see **entrance** 1, **introduction** 1.

2. [A dish served between the soup and the main course]—*Syn.* side dish, entremets, vegetable, savory, salad.

3. [The principal course of a meal]—*Syn.* main course, main dish, *pièce de résistance* (French); see **fish, food, game** 4, **meat.**

4. [An appetizer; *mistakenly*]—*Syn.* tidbit, soup, snack; see **delicatessen** 1.

entrench, *v.* **1.** [To surround]—*Syn.* fortify, fence, protect; see **surround** 2.

2. [To trespass]—*Syn.* encroach, infringe, invade; see **meddle** 1.

entrenched, *mod.* —*Syn.* fortified, barricaded, dug in; see **safe** 1.

entre nous (French), *mod.* —*Syn.* confidentially, intimately, privately; see **secretly.**

entrepreneur, *n.* —*Syn.* manager, contractor, producer; see **administrator.**

entrust, *v.* —*Syn.* deposit with, trust to, leave with; see **trust** 3.

entry, *n.* —*Syn.* approach, hall, lobby, foyer, door, gate; see also **entrance** 2.

entwine, *v.* —*Syn.* twine, lace, twist; see **weave** 2.

enumerate, *v.* —*Syn.* list, mention, identify; see **count.**

enumeration, *n.* —*Syn.* inventory, catalog, register; see **record** 1.

enunciate, *v.* **1.** [To state formally]—*Syn.* announce, proclaim, affirm; see **declare** 1.
2. [To pronounce distinctly]—*Syn.* voice, articulate, modulate, intone, vocalize, deliver, express; see also **utter.**

enunciation, *n.* **1.** [Clear speech]—*Syn.* inflexion, pronunciation, articulation; see **diction.**
2. [A formal statement]—*Syn.* pronouncement, remark, opinion; see **speech** 3.

envelop, *v.* —*Syn.* encompass, contain, hide; see **surround** 2, **wrap** 2.

envelope, *n.* —*Syn.* receptacle, pouch, pocket, bag, container, box, covering, case, hide, wrapper, wrapping, enclosure, vesicle, cover, sheath, casing.

envenom, *v.* **1.** [To poison]—*Syn.* infect, contaminate, pollute; see **poison.**
2. [To alienate]—*Syn.* embitter, estrange, anger; see **alienate.**

enviable, *mod.* —*Syn.* welcome, good, superior; see **excellent.**

envious, *mod.* **1.** [Having a jealous nature]—*Syn.* distrustful, suspicious, watchful; see **jealous.**
2. [Desiring a possession of another]—*Syn.* covetous, desirous, resentful, desiring, wishful, longing for, aspiring, greedy, grasping, craving, fain, hankering, begrudging; *all* (D): green-eyed, jaundice-eyed, green with envy.—*Ant.* generous*, trustful, charitable.

environment, *n.* —*Syn.* conditions, living conditions, circumstances, surroundings, ambiance, encompassment, entourage, scene, external conditions, milieu, background, setting, habitat, situation.

environs, *n.* —*Syn.* suburbs, vicinity, locality; see **neighborhood.**

envisage, *v.* **1.** [To confront]—*Syn.* dare, meet, confront; see **face** 1.
2. [To imagine]—*Syn.* visualize, realize, conceive; see **imagine** 1.

envoy, *n.* —*Syn.* emissary, medium, intermediary; see **agent** 1.

envy, *n.* —*Syn.* jealousy, ill-will, spite, rivalry, opposition, grudge, malice, prejudice, malevolence, the evil eye, enviousness, grudgingness, jealous competition, jaundiced eye, discontent at another's good fortune, backbiting, covetousness, cupidity, invidiousness, maliciousness, envy in one's heart, lack of Christian charity, one of the seven deadly sins, bad sportsmanship, lusting after another's goods, coveting another's wife, coveting one's neighbor's ass or his ox, *invidia* (Latin), the green-eyed monster (D).

envy, *v.* —*Syn.* grudge, begrudge, have hard feelings toward, covet, lust after, regard with envy, desire inordinately, crave, be envious of, feel ill toward, feel resentful toward, hunger and thirst after, have a grudge against, object to.

enwreathe, *v.* —*Syn.* encircle, garland, entwine, festoon, interweave, interlace, twine, twist, wreathe, plait, braid; see also **decorate.**

enzyme, *n.* —*Syn.* protein, ferment, barm, yeast, leaven, organic catalyst; see also **catalyst.**

eon, *n.* —*Syn.* eternity, cycle, time; see **age** 3.

epaulet, *n.* —*Syn.* badge, ornament, insignia; see **decoration** 3.

ephemeral, *mod.* —*Syn.* transient, evanescent, fleeting; see **temporary.**

epic, *mod.* —*Syn.* heroic, classic, grand, grandiose, narrative, Homeric, historic, momentous, significant, tremendous, huge, major, on a grand scale. —*Ant.* unimportant*, small, lyric.

epic, *n.* —*Syn.* narrative *or* heroic poem *or* story, saga, legend; see **poem, story.**

epicure, *n.* **1.** [A gourmet]—*Syn.* connoisseur, gourmand, gastronome; see **critic** 2,**specialist.**
2. [A sensualist]—*Syn.* hedonist, voluptuary, sybarite; see **glutton.**

epicurean, *n.* —*Syn.* hedonist, sensualist, sybarite; see **glutton.**

epicureanism, *n.* —*Syn.* hedonism, sensuality, lechery; see **greed, lewdness.**

epidemic, *n.* —*Syn.* plague, scourge, pestilence; see **disease** 1, 3.

epidermis, *n.* —*Syn.* cuticle, dermis, hide; see **skin.**

epigram, *n.* —*Syn.* witticism, quip, aphorism; see **joke** 2, **motto.**

epigrammatic, *mod.* —*Syn.* terse, laconic, concise; see **witty.**

episcopacy, *n.* —*Syn.* prelacy, pontificate, canonry; see **bishopric.**

episcopal, *mod.* —*Syn.* papal, pontifical, apostolic; see **clerical** 2.

Episcopalian, *n.* —*Syn.* believer in prelacy, Anglican, churchman; see **Protestant.**

episode, *n.* —*Syn.* happening, occurrence, interlude; see **event** 1, 2.

episodic, *mod.* —*Syn.* rambling, roundabout, discursive; see **incidental** 2.

epitaph, *n.* —*Syn.* inscription, commemoration, remembrance, memorial, sentiment, eulogy, elegy, monument, lines on a gravestone.

epithet, *n.* —*Syn.* designation, title, appellation; see **name** 3.

epitome, *n.* —*Syn.* brief, abridgment, abstract; see **characteristic, summary.**

epitomize, *v.* —*Syn.* outline, summarize, condense; see **decrease** 2.

epoch, *n.* —*Syn.* era, period, time; see **age** 3.

equal, *mod.* —*Syn.* even, regular, like, same, identical, similar, uniform, invariable, equable, unvarying, fair, just, impartial, unbiased, to the same degree, on a footing with, without distinction, answerable for, in as many as, equitable, selfsame, co-ordinate, identical in size *or* value *or* quantity, one and the same, of a piece, level, parallel, corresponding, correspondent, equivalent, commensurate, according, proportionate, coextensive, comparable, tantamount—*Ant.* irregular*, unequal, uneven.

equal, *n.* —*Syn.* parallel, match, counterpart, complement, peer, compeer, fellow, twin, double, likeness, opposite number, companion, copy, duplicate, rival, competitor.

equal, *v.* —*Syn.* match, equalize, make equal *or* alike, rank with, be the same in quantity *or* value *or* number *or* degree, rival, touch, equate, co-ordinate, approach, live *or* come up to, amount to, consist of, comprise, be made *or* composed of, measure up (to), give in kind, knot the score, check with, even off, break even, be the equivalent of, keep pace with, come to, compare, accord *or* square *or* tally with, agree, correspond, be tantamount to, be identical, be commensurate, meet, rise to (meet).

equality, *n.*—*Syn.* balance, parity, uniformity, sameness, likeness, identity, evenness, equalization, equilibrium, sameness, impartiality, fairness, fair play brotherhood, civil rights, state of being equal, identical value, equivalence, fellowship, lack of distinction, tolerance, democratic right; *all* (D): all for one and one for all, six of one and half a dozen of the other, a fair shake, even-steven.—*Ant.* injustice*, inequality, unfairness.

equalize, *v.*—*Syn.* make even *or* equal, balance, equate, match, bring to a common level, level, adjust, establish equilibrium, communize, democratize, socialize, even up (D).

equally, *mod.*—*Syn.* evenly, coequally, symmetrically, proportionately, co-ordinately, equivalently, on a level, both, either . . . or, impartially, justly, fairly, across the board, on even terms, dispassionately, to all intents and purposes, as well as, distinction without a difference, the same for one as for another, "with malice towards none."—*Ant.* unequally, unfairly*, unevenly.

equal to, *mod.*—*Syn.* adequate (for), capable, qualified; see **able** 1, 2.

equanimity, *n.*—*Syn.* serenity, poise, patience; see **composure.**

equate, *v.* **1.** [To equalize]—*Syn.* make equal, average, balance; see **equalize.**

2. [To compare]—*Syn.* liken, associate, relate; see **compare** 1.

equation, *n.*—*Syn.* mathematical statement, formal statement of equivalence, chemical statement. Kinds of equations include the following—linear, quadratic, conic, cubic.

equator, *n.*—*Syn.* middle, circumference of the earth, great circle; see **tropics.**

equatorial, *mod.*—*Syn.* tropical, mediterranean, central; see **tropic** 1.

equilibrium, *n.*—*Syn.* stability, center of gravity, equipoise; see **balance** 2.

equip, *v.* **1.** [To supply]—*Syn.* furnish, outfit, implement; see **provide** 1.

2. [To array]—*Syn.* adorn, deck, dress; see **decorate.**

equipage, *n.*—*Syn.* apparatus, outfit, gear; see **equipment.**

equipment, *n.*—*Syn.* material, materiel, tools, facilities, implements, utensils, apparatus, casting kit, furnishings, equipage, appliances, paraphernalia, belongings, armor, devices, outfit, accessories, appurtenances, attachments, extras, conveniences, accouterments, contraptions, articles, tackle, rig, machinery, fittings, trappings, contrivances, fixtures, movables, supplies, accompaniments, gear; *all* (D): shebang, fixings, stuff, gadgets, things; see also **machine** 1. **part** 3.

equipped, *mod.*—*Syn.* outfitted, furnished, supplied, rigged (up), fitted (out), arrayed, dressed, accoutered, assembled, readied, provided, implemented, decked, bedecked, appareled, appointed, completed, complemented, supplemented, set up, harnessed, armed, invested.—*Ant.* unfurnished*, stripped, bare.

equitable, *mod.*—*Syn.* impartial, just, moral; see **fair** 1.

equity, *n.*—*Syn.* investment, money, outlay; see **property** 1.

equivalence, *n.*—*Syn.* parity, identity, synonym; see **equality**

equivalent, *mod.*—*Syn.* commensurate, comparable, similar; see **equal.**

equivocal, *mod.*—*Syn.* ambiguous, dubious, puzzling; see **obscure** 1.

equivocate, *v.*—*Syn.* hedge, dodge, prevaricate; see **lie** 1.

equivocation, *n.*—*Syn.* quibbling, evasion, prevarication; see **lie** 1.

era, *n.*—*Syn.* epoch, period, date; see **age** 3, **time** 2.

eradicate, *v.*—*Syn.* extirpate, exterminate, annihilate; see **destroy** 1.

eradication, *n.*—*Syn.* extermination, annihilation, elimination; see **destruction** 1.

erase, *v.* **1.** [To obliterate]—*Syn.* expunge, efface, eradicate; see **cancel** 1.

2. [(D) To kill]—*Syn.* murder, slay, dispatch; see **kill** 1.

erasure, *n.*—*Syn.* cancellation, expunging, abrasion, cancelling, rubbing *or* blotting *or* sponging *or* scratching out, obliteration, deletion, effacing, deleting.

ere, *prep.* and *conj.*—*Syn.* prior to, aforetime, previously; see **before** 1.

erect, *mod.*—*Syn.* upright, vertical, perpendicular; see **straight** 1.

erect, *v.* **1.** [To build]—*Syn.* construct, raise, fabricate; see **build** 1.

2. [To assemble]—*Syn.* put *or* fit together, join, set up; see **assemble** 3.

3. [To raise]—*Syn.* lift *or* set up, plant, upraise; see **raise** 1.

4. [To establish]—*Syn.* found, institute, form; see **organize** 2.

erected, *mod.* **1.** [Stood on end]—*Syn.* implanted, reared, upraised, raised, reared, elevated, lifted, hoisted, set *or* stood up, uplifted, upreared, boosted (D).—*Ant.* lowered, degraded, leveled.

2. [Built]—*Syn.* constructed, completed, raised; see **built.**

erection, *n.*—*Syn.* building, erecting, constructing; see **construction** 1.

erelong, *mod.*—*Syn.* before long, shortly, presently; see **soon** 1.

eremite, *n.*—*Syn.* solitary, recluse, anchorite; see **hermit.**

ergo (Latin), *mod.*—*Syn.* hence, consequently, thus; see **therefore.**

erode, *v.*—*Syn.* disintegrate, corrode, consume; see **decay.**

erosion, *n.*—*Syn.* wearing away, decrease, land despoliation, desedimentation, carrying *or* eating away, washing (down); see also **destruction** 1, 2.

erotic, *mod.*—*Syn.* amorous, lecherous, carnal; see **lewd** 1, 2, **sensual.**

err, *v.*—*Syn.* misjudge, blunder, be mistaken; see **fail** 1.

errand, *n.*—*Syn.* mission, task, commission; see **duty** 2.

errand boy, *n.*—*Syn.* messenger, courier, runner, dispatch rider, office *or* delivery *or* copy *or* messenger boy, clerk, porter, shop assistant; *all* (D): bellhop, boots, boy, Western Union (trademark), kid, flunky, redcap, rider, punk.

errant, *mod.* —*Syn.* itinerant, rambling, shifting; see **wandering** 1.
erratic, *mod.* **1.** [Wandering]—*Syn.* nomadic, rambling, roving; see **wandering** 1.
2. [Strange]—*Syn.* eccentric, queer, irregular; see **unusual** 2.
3. [Variable]—*Syn.* inconsistent, unpredictable, inconstant; see **variable.**
erratically, *mod.* —*Syn.* intermittently, eccentrically, carelessly; see **irregularly.**
erratum, *n.* —*Syn.* misprint, mistake, blunder; see **error** 1.
erring, *mod.* —*Syn.* mistaken, blundering, fallible, straying, deviating, sinful, sinning, faulty, delinquent, culpable, criminal; see also **wrong** 1.
erroneous, *mod.* —*Syn.* untrue, inaccurate, incorrect; see **false** 2.
error, *n.* **1.** [A specific miscalculation]—*Syn.* blunder, mistake, fault, faux pas, oversight, inaccuracy, mismanagement, misdoing, omission, misjudgment, deviation, fall, slip, wrong, lapse, miss, failure, slight, absurdity, misbelief, misprint, misstep, misunderstanding, misreport, untruth, trip, stumble, flaw, erratum; *all* (D): howler, glitch, boner, boo-boo, bloomer, bungle, muff, bad job, bonehead, blooper, botch.—*Ant.* record*, precise statement, transcript.
2. [General misconception]—*Syn.* falsity, delusion, transgression; see **fallacy** 1.
ersatz, *mod.* —*Syn.* artificial, synthetic, imitation; see **false** 3, **manufactured.**
erstwhile, *mod.* —*Syn.* former, past, recent; see **preceding.**
erudite, *mod.* —*Syn.* well-read, scholarly, educated; see **learned** 1, 2.
erudition, *n.* —*Syn.* education, refinement, enlightenment; see **culture** 3, **knowledge** 1.
erupt, *v.* —*Syn.* eruct, eject, emit; see **explode** 1.
eruption, *n.* —*Syn.* burst, outburst, flow; see **explosion** 1.
escalate, *v.* —*Syn.* heighten, intensify, make worse; see **increase**
escalation, *n.* —*Syn.* intensification, growth, acceleration; see **increase** 1, **rise** 2.
escalator, *n.* —*Syn.* moving stair, *escalier* (French), incline; see **elevator** 1.
escapade, *n.* **1.** [A trick]—*Syn.* caper, vagary, prank; see **joke** 1.
2. [An impropriety]—*Syn.* indiscretion, folly, blunder; see **error** 1.
escape, *n.* **1.** [The act of escaping]—*Syn.* flight, retreat, disappearance, evasion, avoidance, leave, departure, withdrawal, hegira, elopement, desertion, abdication, liberation, deliverance, rescue, freedom, release, extrication; *all* (D): break, French leave, close call *or* shave, slip, A.W.O.L.—*Ant.* imprisonment*, retention, grasp.
2. [Place of escape]—*Syn.* exit, overflow, outflow, leakage, leak, fire escape, waste pipe, sewer, hatch, porthole, alleyway, floodgate, exhaust, draft, escape valve, vent.
escape, *v.* —*Syn.* flee, fly, leave, depart, elude, avoid, evade, shun, run off *or* away, make off, wriggle out, disappear, vanish, steal off *or* away, flow out, gush forth, emerge, get away (from), break out *or* away, desert, slip by *or* away, elope, run out (on), burst out, avoid danger, go scot-free, decamp, double; *all* (D): duck *or* cut out, take it on the lam, get clear of, leg it, get by *or* off, free oneself, get away with, take flight, come forth, break loose, cut and run, worm out (of), lock the door, fly to, go at liberty, show one's heels, lead one a merry chase, leak out, cut loose, play at hide and seek, break one's bonds, clear out, gain one's liberty, make oneself scarce, deliver oneself, play hooky, find a loophole, hook it, bail out, crawl out of, save one's bacon, save one's neck, scram, skidoo, take a powder, give one the slip, make a break, fly the coop.—*Ant.* return*, come back, remain.
escaped, *mod.* —*Syn.* out, at liberty, liberated; see **free** 2.
escapist, *n.* —*Syn.* dreamer, romanticist, evader; see **idealist.**
escarpment, *n.* —*Syn.* slope, cliff, ledge; see **hill, mountain** 1.
eschew, *v.* —*Syn.* shun, keep away from, abstain; see **avoid.**
escort, *n.* —*Syn.* guide, protection, bodyguard, attendant, henchman, safeguard, guard, consort, gentleman friend, cavalier, squire, guard of honor, retinue, entourage, train, convoy; see also **companion** 3.
escort, *v.* —*Syn.* go with, attend, take out (D); see **accompany** 1, **date** 2.
escutcheon, *n.* —*Syn.* shield, coat of arms, crest; see **decoration** 3.
a blot on one's escutcheon—*Syn.* stain, stigma, disgrace; see **scandal.**
esophagus, *n.*—*Syn.* jugular region, gullet; see **throat.**
esoteric, *mod.* —*Syn.* arcane, private, recondite; see **secret** 1.
especial, *mod.* —*Syn.* special, particular, individual; see **unusual** 1, 2.
especially, *mod.* **1.** [To an unusual degree]—*Syn.* particularly, unusually, abnormally, extraordinarily, uncommonly, peculiarly, pre-eminently, eminently, supremely, remarkably, wonderfully, oddly, queerly, strangely, curiously, notably, unaccountably, uniquely, uncustomarily, singularly, unfamiliarly, unexpectedly, observably, to a psecial *or* marked *or* unusual *or* notable degree, in particular, occasioning comment, never so, above all, above the mark.—*Ant.* usually*, commonly, normally.
2. [For one more than for others]—*Syn.* chiefly, mainly, primarily; see **principally.**
espionage, *n.* —*Syn.* undercover work, reconnaissance, watching; see **spying.**
espousal, *n.* **1.** [Marriage]—*Syn.* wedding, betrothal, matrimony; see **marriage** 2.
2. [Support]—*Syn.* adoption, advocacy, promotion; see **aid** 1.
espouse, *v.* **1.** [Marry]—*Syn.* marry, wed, betroth; see **marry** 1.
2. [To support]—*Syn.* advocate, adopt, uphold; see **support** 2.
esprit (French), *n.* —*Syn.* quickwittedness, intelligence, acumen; see **wit** 1.
esprit de corps (French), *n.* —*Syn.* morale, sociality, fellowship; see **co-operation** 1.
essay, *n.* **1.** [Expository writing]—*Syn.* dissertation, treatise, tract; see **exposition** 2.

2. [An effort]—*Syn.* trial, attempt, endeavor; see **effort** 1, 2.

essayist, *n.*—*Syn.* columnist, discussant, editorial writer; see **author** 2, **writer.**

essence, *n.* **1.** [Basic material]—*Syn.* pith, core, kernel, vein, gist, root, nature, basis, being, essential quality, spirit, sum and substance, reality, quintessence, constitution, substance, binder, filler, nucleus, vital part, base, chief constituent, primary element, germ, heart, marrow, backbone, caliber, soul, bottom, life, grain, structure, principle, character, fundamentals.
2. [Distinctive quality]—*Syn.* principle, nature, essential quality; see **characteristic.**
3. [A distilled spirit]—*Syn.* elixir, distillation, juice, spirit(s), tincture, effusion, liquor, alcohol, ammonia, potion, drug, drops, exhalation, perfume.

essential, *mod.* **1.** [Necessary]—*Syn.* imperative, required, indispensable; see **necessary** 1.
2. [Rooted in the basis or essence]—*Syn.* basic, primary, quintessential; see **fundamental** 1.

essentially, *mod.*—*Syn.* basically, fundamentally, radically, at bottom, at heart, centrally, originally, intimately, chiefly, indispensably, naturally, inherently, permanently, determinately, necessarily, primarily, significantly, importantly, at the heart of, in effect, in essence, at bottom, in the main, all the more, at first, characteristically, intrinsically, substantially, typically, vitally, approximately, quite, precisely, exactly, actually, truly, really, factually, materially, more or less so (D); see also **principally.**—*Ant.* apparently*, superficially, on the surface.

establish, *v.* **1.** [To set up in a formal manner]—*Syn.* institute, found, authorize; see **organize** 2.
2. [To work or settle in a permanent place]—*Syn.* build *or* set up, install, build, erect, entrench, set, plant, root, build, place, settle (in), lay the foundation (for *or* of), domiciliate, practice, live, ground, ensconce; *both* (D): set on its feet, land.—*Ant.* unsettle, leave*, break up.
3. [To determine]—*Syn.* ascertain, learn, find out; see **discover** 1.
4. [To prove]—*Syn.* verify, authenticate, confirm; see **prove.**
5. [To make secure]—*Syn.* fix, secure, stabilize; see **fasten** 1.

established, *mod.* **1.** [In a firm position]—*Syn.* secure, fixed, stable; see **permanent** 2.
2. [Set up to endure]—*Syn.* endowed, founded, organized, instituted, set up, realized, originated, chartered, incorporated, settled, inaugurated, codified, systematized, ratified, equipped, brought into existence, conceived, produced, begun, initiated, completed, finished; see also **finished** 1, **certain** 3.—*Ant.* temporary*, unsound, insolvent.
3. [Conclusively proved]—*Syn.* approved, verified, guaranteed, endorsed, demonstrated, determined, confirmed, substantiated, assured, concluded, closed, authenticated, corroborated, found out, achieved, upheld, certain, ascertained, valid, validated, identified, proved, undeniable, sure, objectified.—*Ant.* false*, invalidated, untrue.

establishing, *n.* **1.** [The act of founding]—*Syn.* organizing, starting, setting up, beginning, founding, inaugurating, instituting, originating, constituting, initiating, settling, endowing, fixing, subsidizing, implementing, stabilizing, building, regulating, setting on foot, laying the cornerstone.—*Ant.* ending, tearing down, dissolving.
2. [The act of proving]—*Syn.* verifying, substantiating, demonstrating, authenticating, corroborating, validating, confirming; see also **proof** 1.

establishment, *n.* **1.** [The act of setting up]—*Syn.* founding, endowment, institution; see **establishing** 1.
2. [A business, organization, or the like]—*Syn.* company, corporation, enterprise; see **business** 4.
3. [The act of proving]—*Syn.* verification, substantiation, demonstration; see **establishing** 2, **proof** 1.

estate, *n.* **1.** [An extensive residence]—*Syn.* holdings, land, property, manor, grounds, freehold, domain, farm, rural seat, country place *or* home, plantation, ranch, territory, fields, realty, dominion.
2. [Possessions left at one's death]—*Syn.* property, bequest, inheritance, fortune, endowment, wealth, legacy, heritage, patrimony, belongings, chattels, effects, earthly possessions, personal property, private property.
the fourth estate—*Syn.* the press, mass media, journalists; see **journalism, newspaper, radio** 1, **television.**

esteem, *n.*—*Syn.* regard, respect, appreciation; see **admiration** 1.

esteem, *v.* **1.** [Attach a high value to]—*Syn.* prize, respect, appreciate; see **admire** 1.
2. [To consider]—*Syn.* account, judge, deem; see **consider** 3.

esthetic, *mod.*—*Syn.* creative, appreciative, emotional; see **artistic** 1, 3, **beautiful** 1.

esthetics, *n.*—*Syn.* philosophy *or* principles *or* theory of art, science of the principles of art, theory of the fine arts, the study of beauty, the nature of beauty, the science of art, the philosophy of beauty, the philosophy of the fine arts, the philosophy of taste, the science of the beautiful.

estimable, *mod.* **1.** [Calculable]—*Syn.* appreciable, computable, appraisable; see **calculable.**
2. [Worthy]—*Syn.* deserving, admirable, venerable; see **worthy.**

estimate, *n.* **1.** [An appraisal on the value of something]—*Syn.* evaluation, assessment, appraisal, estimation, valuation, appraisement, calculation, gauging, rating, assay, survey, measure, mensuration, reckoning; see also **judgment** 2.
2. [Opinion]—*Syn.* valuation, appraisal, estimation; see **judgment** 3.
3. [A considered guess]—*Syn.* impression, conclusion, calculation; see **guess.**

estimate, *v.* **1.** [To make a rough guess]—*Syn.* rate, value, evaluate, count, number, reckon, guess, judge, figure, class, classify, tax, plan, scheme, outline, run over, rank, furnish an estimate, set a value on, appraise, assess, assay.—*Ant.* check, measure*, calculate.
2. [To make a considered prediction]—*Syn.* consider, reckon, suspect, predict, suppose, prophesy, reason, compute, think through, expect, regard, judge, look upon, surmise, determine, decide, size up (D).
3. [To calculate probable costs]—*Syn.* measure, calculate, appraise, evaluate, figure (costs), assess, account, compute, plan, look into, examine, extract

roots, prepare a budget *or* an estimate, set a figure, budget, enumerate, do the cost accounting, get figures for, appraise.

estimated, *mod.* —*Syn.* supposed, approximated, guessed at; see **likely** 1.

estimating, *n.* —*Syn.* judging, supposing, reckoning; see **guessing.**

estimation, *n.* **1.** [A personal estimate]—*Syn.* opinion, appraisal, valuation; see **judgment** 2.
2. [The act of making an estimate]—*Syn.* calculating, estimating, predicting; see **guess.**

estrange, *v.* **1.** [To alienate]—*Syn.* divert, sunder, disunite; see **alienate.**
2. [To withdraw]—*Syn.* separate, part, withhold; see **leave** 1.

estrangement, *n.* —*Syn.* disaffection, removal, withdrawal; see **alienation.**

estuary, *n.* —*Syn.* fiord, drowned river, tidewater, tidal river, river mouth, inlet, arm of the sea; see **bay, water** 2.

et cetera (etc.), *mod.* —*Syn.* and so forth, and so on, and others, et al., and the like, and, and on and on, and (all) the rest, *und so weiter* (German), along with others, and all, *both* (D): whatever, whatnot.

etch, *v.* **1.** [To remove metal with acid]—*Syn.* erode, cut, reduce; see **bite** 3.
2. [To use etching as an artistic medium]—*Syn.* compose, execute, use the burin; see also **engrave** 2, **paint** 1.

etching, *n.* **1.** [A process for producing printing plates]—*Syn.* biting, cutting, engraving, photoengraving, processing, transferring, treating with acid, preparing a plate, obtaining proper reproduction; see also **reproduction** 1.
2. [A work of art]—*Syn.* print, black and white, colored print, colored etching, old master, aquatint, mezzotint, *eau-forte* (French); the work of an etcher: Rembrandt, Whistler, Pennell, Goya, etc.; see **art** 2, 3.

eternal, *mod.* **1.** [Without pause]—*Syn.* endless, interminable, continual, unbroken, continuous, continued, unceasing, incessant, ceaseless, constant, unending, undying, enduring, persistent, always, relentless, uninterrupted.—*Ant.* changeable*, inconstant, fluctuating.
2. [Without end]—*Syn.* everlasting, unending, perpetual, never-ending, termless, indefinite, permanent, enduring, ageless, boundless, timeless, immortal, forever, indeterminable, dateless, immeasurable, unfading, indestructible, always, having no limit, enduring, imperishable, illimitable, indomitable, unconquerable, unyielding, eonian, to one's dying day; *all* (D): till doomsday, forever and a day, for ever and ever.—*Ant.* finite, temporary*, ending.

eternally, *mod.* —*Syn.* endlessly, continually, perpetually; see **regularly** 2.

eternity, *n.* **1.** [Time without end]—*Syn.* endlessness, forever, endless *or* infinite duration, timelessness, forever and a day, world without end, *saecula saeculorum* (Latin), the future, infinity, all eternity, for ever and ever (D).—*Ant.* moment, instant, second.
2. [Life after death]—*Syn.* other world, everlastingness, afterlife; see **immortality** 2.

ethereal, *mod.* **1.** [Celestial]—*Syn.* heavenly, supernal, empyreal; see **divine** 1.
2. [Delicate]—*Syn.* subtile, airy, fragile; see **light** 5.

ethical, *mod.* —*Syn.* humane, moral, respectable; see **decent** 2, **honest** 1, **noble** 1, 2.

ethics, *n.* —*Syn.* conduct, morality, mores, decency, integrity, moral conduct, social values, moral practice, principles, code of right and wrong, natural law, honesty, goodness, honor, social laws, human nature, categorical imperative, the Golden Rule, *bushido* (Japanese).

ethnology, *n.* —*Syn.* a branch of anthropology, study of mores *or* customs, science of races, science of man; see also **anthropology.**

etiquette, *n.* —*Syn.* conduct, manners, social graces; see **behavior** 1.

étude, *n.* —*Syn.* composition, exercise, piece; see **music** 1.

etymology, *n.* —*Syn.* derivation, a branch of linguistics, word origins, word history, growth of vocabulary, philology; see also **language** 2.

Eucharist, *n.* —*Syn.* sacrament, mass, oblation; see **communion** 2.

eugenics, *n.* —*Syn.* a branch of the biological sciences, genetics, race improvement; see **biology, zoology.**

eulogist, *n.* —*Syn.* praiser, apologist, flatterer; see **sycophant.**

eulogize, *v.* —*Syn.* laud, extol, applaud; see **praise** 1.

eulogy, *n.* —*Syn.* panegyric, glorification, commendation; see **praise** 2.

euphemism, *n.* —*Syn.* substitution, doublespeak, restraint, softened expression, mock modesty, prudishness, metaphorical speech, verbal extenuation, word in verbal good taste, over-delicacy of speech, (affected) refinement of language.

euphemistic, *mod.* —*Syn.* extenuative, metaphorical, mild, euphemious, soft, vague, figurative, affected, inoffensive, delicate; see also **refined** 2.

euphonious, *mod.* —*Syn.* mellifluous, musical, melodious; see **harmonious** 1.

euphony, *n.* —*Syn.* smoothness, ease of utterance, mellifluousness; see **harmony** 1.

euphoria, *n.* —*Syn.* relaxation, health, well-being; see **happiness** 2.

euphuism, *n.* —*Syn.* inflation, grandiloquence, floridness, ornateness of style, delicacy, purism, Gongorism, linguistic cultism, affected elegance of language, pomposity of speech; see also **pretense** 2.

Europe, *n.* —*Syn.* the Continent, continental Europe, part of Eurasia *or* the Eurasian landmass, ancient home of the Indo-Europeans, Cromagnons, Ligurians, Celts, etc. Terms associated with countries, areas, and political divisions in Europe include the following—western, northern, southern, central, eastern, etc. Europe; the West, the East, *Mittel-Europa* (German), (the) Mediterranean world, the Low Countries, Balkan states, Adriatic states, Baltic states, Slavic countries, Scandinavian peninsula, Holy Roman Empire, Hellenic *or* Balkan peninsula, Albania, Austria, Austria-Hungary, Bulgaria, Czechoslovakia, Denmark, Finland, France, *la belle France* (French), Gaul, Provence, Normandy, Brittany, Gascony, Château country, Côte d'Azur, the Midi, Germany, West Germany, East Germany, Greece, the Isles of Greece, Hungary, Land of the Magyars, Iceland, Republic of Ireland, Eire, Ulster, the Emerald Isle, Italy, Liechtenstein, Luxembourg, Malta, Monaco, (The) Netherlands, Holland, Norway, Spitsbergen, Poland, Portugal, Romania, San Marino, Spain, Andalusia, Catalonia, Castile, Navarre, Costa Brava, Galicia, Switzerland, Helvetia, Swiss Confederation, Turkey, Union of Soviet Socialist Republics, USSR, Russia, the Soviets, Red Russia, the Reds (D), The Russian Soviet Federal Socialist Republic, Karelo-Finnish Republic, Ukrainian Soviet Socialist Republic, the Ukraine, the breadbasket of Russia (D), Byelorussian Soviet Republic, White Russia, Lithuanian Soviet Socialist Republic, Lithuania, Estonia, Estonian Soviet Socialist Republic, Latvia, Latvian Soviet Socialist Republic, Georgia, Georgian Soviet Socialist Republic, United Kingdom of Great Britain and Northern Ireland, England, Britain, Scotland, Wales, the British Isles, Albion, State of Vatican City, the Vatican, Rome, the Holy See, the Papacy, Yugoslavia, Serbia, Croatia, Montenegro, Bosnia-Herzegovina; see also **England, France, Germany, Great Britain, Greece, Italy, Paris, Rome, Russia, Spain**

European, *mod.* —*Syn.* Continental, Old Country *or* World, Eurasiatic, Eurasian, Eurafrican, Caucasian, Europoid, Indo-European, Motherland, Western, West European, East European.

Terms associated with particular areas include the following—Anglo-Saxon, British, English, Irish, Anglo-Irish, Ulster, Scottish, Scots, Scotch, Welsh, Cornish, Kentish, French, Romanic, Romance, Breton, Norman, Corsican, Monacan, Gallic, Provençal, Gaulish, German, Germanic, Dutch, Netherlandish, Belgian, Flemish, Low German, Saxon, Bavarian, Prussian, Frank, Frankish, Burgundian, Allemanic, Gothic, Teutonic, Nordic, Scandinavian, Danish, Swedish, Norwegian, Icelandic, Swiss, Alpine, Greek, Hellenic, Athenian, Corinthian, Spartan, Peloponnesian, Mycenean, Cretan, Thracian, Illyrian, Ionian, Corinthian, Slovak(ian), Ruthenian, Rumanian, Bulgarian, Slav(ic), Macedonian, Aegean, Balkan, Adriatic, Yugoslavian, Serbian, Croatian, Serbo-Croat, Austro-Hungarian, Hungarian, Magyar, Czechoslovak(ian), Czech, Bohemian, Turk, Turkish, Ottoman, Musselman, Russian, Polish, Baltic, Estonian, Latvian, Lithuanian, Ukranian, Georgian, Moldavian, Muscovite, Uralic, Finnish, Lap, Lappish, Italian, Italic, Latin, Roman, Venetian, Etruscan, Lombard(ic), Tuscan, Florentine, Neapolitan, Sicilian, Maltese, Sardinian, Tyrolese, Savoyard, Apennine, Spanish, Hispanic, Iberian, Portuguese, Catalan, Basque, Majorcan, Castilian, Navarrese, Andalusian, Galician, Romany, Gipsy, Jewish, Yiddish; see also **Anglo-Saxon, classical** 2, **English, German, Greek, Irish, Italian, Roman, Russian, Scotch, Scandinavian, Slavic, Spanish.**

European, *n.* —*Syn.* Continental, person from the Old Country, immigrant, emigrant, white, Caucasian.

Terms associated with Europeans from particular areas include the following—Englishman, Briton; Scotsman, Scot, Highlander, Lowlander; Welshman; Irishman, Ulsterman, Son of Erin, person from the old sod *or* with the map of Ireland all over his face (D); Cornishman, Celt, Anglo-Saxon; Frenchman, Savoyard, Norman, Breton, Basque *or* Gascon; German, Teuton, Prussian, Bavarian, Saxon; Swiss; Dutchman, Netherlander, Hollander; Belgian, Fleming, Walloon; Scandinavian, Norseman, Viking, Norlander, Dane, Norwegian, Swede, Icelander, Finn, Lapp; Italian, Roman, Sicilian, Venetian, Florentine; Spaniard, Castilian, Catalan, Andalusian, Portuguese, Iberian; Austrian, Hungarian, Czechoslovak(ian), Czech, Bohemian, Slovak, Slav, Russian, Pole, Polander, Lithuanian, Latvian, Estonian, Ukrainian, White Russian, Yugoslav(ian), Bulgar, Rumanian, Balkan, Greek, Turk, Ottoman, Musselman, Jew, Gipsy; see also **European,***mod.* **French** 1, **German** 2, **Greek** 1, **Spaniard.**

euthanasia, *n.* —*Syn.* killing, mercy killing, painless death, vivisection, easy death; see also **death** 1, **murder.**

evacuate, *v.* **1.** [To empty]—*Syn.* void, exhaust, deplete; see **remove** 1.

2. [To abandon]—*Syn.* vacate, desert, leave; see **abandon** 1.

evacuation, *n.* **1.** [Removal]—*Syn.* draining, depletion, exhaustion; see **removal** 1.

2. [Withdrawal]—*Syn.* abandonment, removal, retreat; see **departure** 1.

evade, *v.* **1.** [To use trickery to avoid a sharp issue] —*Syn.* lie, prevaricate, dodge, shun, put off, shuffle, avoid, elude, trick, baffle, quibble, shift, subtilize, cavil, mystify, dissemble, cloak, cover, conceal, deceive, screen, veil, hide, drop the subject, pretend, confuse, pettifog; *all* (D): dodge the issue, beat around the bush, give (someone) the runaround, beg the question, beat about, throw off the scent, lead one a merry chase, pass up, put off, get around, evade an issue, lie out of.—*Ant.* explain*, make clear, elucidate.

2. [To avoid a meeting]—*Syn.* retire, slip out, sneak away from; see **escape.**

evaluate, *v.* —*Syn.* appraise, judge, assess; see **decide, estimate** 3.

evanesce, *v.* —*Syn.* dissipate, vanish, evaporate; see **disappear.**

evanescence, *n.* —*Syn.* dissipation, evaporation, vanishing; see **disappearance.**

evanescent, *mod.* —*Syn.* vanishing, transient, disappearing, passing (away), fading, shifting, fleeting, transitory, flitting, fugitive, ephemeral, short-lived; see **temporary.**

evangel, *n.* —*Syn.* revelation, writings, message; see **bible.**

evangelical, *mod.* **1.** [Sacred]—*Syn.* evangelistic, apostolic, orthodox; see **divine** 2.

2. [Devout]—*Syn.* pious, fervent, spiritual; see **religious** 2.

evangelist, *n.* —*Syn.* preacher, missionary, revivalist; see **minister** 1.

evangelize, *v.* —*Syn.* proselytize, instruct, convert; see **preach.**

evaporate, *v.* **1.** [To vaporize]—*Syn.* diffuse, dissipate, gasify, steam, steam *or* boil away, fume, burn off, distill, turn to steam, rise in a fog *or* mist.

2. [To dehydrate]—*Syn.* concentrate, dessicate, parch; see **dry** 1, 2.

3. [To disappear]—*Syn.* vanish, fade, dissolve; see **disappear.**

evaporation, *n.* —*Syn.* drying, dehydration, desiccation, evanescence, vanishing, vaporescence, steaming *or* boiling away, vaporization, gasification, volatilization, distillation, dissipation, disappearance; *both* (D): vanishing into thin air, escape. —*Ant.* solidification*, materialization, liquefaction.

evasion, *n.* —*Syn.* quibble, subterfuge, equivocation; see **lie** 1, **trick** 1.

evasive, *mod.* **1.** [Deceptive]—*Syn.* misleading, equivocating, deceitful; see **false** 1, 2.
2. [Elusive]—*Syn.* elusory, fugitive, shifty; see **sly** 1.

eve, *n.* —*Syn.* night *or* evening before, night preceding, evening; see **night** 1.

even, *mod.* **1.** [Lying in a smooth plane]—*Syn.* smooth, level, surfaced; see **flat** 1.
2. [Similar]—*Syn.* uniform, unbroken, homogeneous; see **alike** 2, **regular** 3.
3. [Equal]—*Syn.* commensurate, coterminous, equivalent; see **equal.**
4. [In addition]—*Syn.* also, too, as well, plus, still more, moreover, in spite of, despite, likewise, but also.
break even—*Syn.* make nothing, tie, neither win nor lose; see **balance** 3.

even-handed, *mod.* —*Syn.* impartial, equitable, just; see **fair** 1.

evening, *n.* —*Syn.* twilight, dusk, late afternoon; see **night** 1.

evening star, *n.* —*Syn.* morning star, the planet Venus, the moist planet, Vesper, Hesperus; see also **planet.**

evenly, *mod.* **1.** [On an even plane]—*Syn.* smoothly, regularly, without bumps *or* lumps, uniformly, placidly, unvaryingly, steadily, constantly, tranquilly, fluently, on an even keel, in a groove, without variation, neither up nor down.—*Ant.* irregularly*, unevenly, jaggedly.
2. [Equally proportioned or distributed]—*Syn.* exactly, justly, fairly, precisely, equally, impartially, identically, equitably, symmetrically, conformably, commensurably, proportionately, synonymously, analogously, correspondingly, tied, alike; *both* (D): fifty-fifty, squarely.—*Ant.* wrongly*, unjustly, unfairly.

evenness, *n.* —*Syn.* smoothness, similarity, likeness; see **regularity.**

evensong, *n.* —*Syn.* vespers, evening prayer, angelus; see **hymn, prayer** 2.

event, *n.* **1.** [Anything that happens]—*Syn.* occurrence, happening, episode, incident, circumstance, affair, phenomenon, development, function, transaction, experience, appearance, turn, tide, shift, phase, accident, chance, pass, ceremony, juncture, conjuncture, situation, proceeding, advent, story, case, matter, occasion.
2. [A notable happening]—*Syn.* accident, catastrophe, mishap, mischance, mistake, experience, parade, triumph, coincidence, miracle, adventure, holiday, wonder, marvel, celebration, crisis, predicament, exigency, misfortune, situation, calamity, emergency, something to write home about (D); see also **disaster, holiday** 1, **wonder** 2.
3. [A performance]—*Syn.* final *or* main *or* preliminary etc., event, attraction, contest, bout, joust, display, performance, happening, spectacle, play, drama, match, game, exhibition; *all* (D): tilt, scuffle, stanza, curtain raiser; see also **performance** 2.
4. [An outcome]—*Syn.* effect, issue, conclusion; see **result.**
in any event—*Syn.* anyway, no matter what happens, however; see **anyhow** 1.
in the event of (*or* **that**)—*Syn.* in case of, if it should happen that, if there should happen to be; see **if.**

eventful, *mod.* —*Syn.* momentous, memorable, signal; see **important** 1.

eventual, *mod.* **1.** [Final]—*Syn.* inevitable, ultimate, consequent; see **last** 1.
2. [Conditional]—*Syn.* contingent, possible, dependent; see **conditional.**

eventually, *mod.* —*Syn.* in the end, at last, ultimately; see **finally** 2.

eventuate, *v.* **1.** [To close]—*Syn.* result, end, terminate; see **stop** 2.
2. [To occur]—*Syn.* come about, take place, befall; see **happen** 2.

ever, *mod.* —*Syn.* eternally, always, at all times; see **regularly** 2.
for ever and a day (D)—*Syn.* always, for ever and ever, perpetually; see **forever** 1.

evergreen, *n.* —*Syn.* coniferous tree, ornamental shrub, fir; see **pine, tree.**

everlasting, *mod.* —*Syn.* permanent, unending, perpetual; see **eternal** 2.

evermore, *mod.* —*Syn.* always, eternally, ever; see **forever** 1.

every, *mod.* —*Syn.* each one, all, without exception; see **each** 1.

everybody, *n.* —*Syn.* each one, every one, all, the public, big and little, old and young; men, women, and children; the people, the populace, the voters; the buying *or* traveling *or* voting, etc., public; generality, anybody, all sorts, the masses; *all* (D): the man on *or* in the street, John (Q.) Smith, you and I, all and sundry, John Q. Public, the devil and all, hoi polloi; see **man** 1.—*Ant.* nobody*, no one, not a one.

everyday, *mod.* —*Syn.* commonplace, normal, plain; see **common** 1.

every day, *mod.* —*Syn.* always, all the time, frequently; see **regularly** 1.

every now and then *or* **every so often** (D), *mod.* —*Syn.* sometimes, occasionally, once in a while; see **frequently.**

everyone, *pron.* —*Syn.* all, each person, whoever; see **everybody.**

everything, *pron.* —*Syn.* all, all things, the universe, the whole complex, the whole, many things, all that; *all* (D): every little thing, the whole kit and kaboodle; lock, stock and barrel; the whole bit *or* shebang, the works, the lot.

everywhere, *mod.* —*Syn.* here and there, all over, at all points *or* places, wherever (one turns), at each point, without exception, ubiquitously, universally, at all times and places; here, there and everywhere; in every quarter *or* direction, on all hands, all over the place, throughout; *all* (D): from Dan to Beersheba, from pole to pole, to the four winds, in all creation, to hell and back, inside and out, to *or* from *or* in all four corners of the earth, from beginning to end, high and low, all around, the world over, in all quarters.

evict, *v.* —*Syn.* remove, expel, oust; see **dismiss** 1, 2.

eviction, *n.* —*Syn.* ouster, ejection, dispossession; see **removal** 1.

evidence, *n.* —*Syn.* testimony, data, confirmation; see **proof** 1.

in evidence—*Syn.* evident, visible, manifest; see **obvious** 1, 2.

evident, *mod.* **1.** [Open to view]—*Syn.* apparent, visible, manifest; see **obvious** 1.

2. [Clear to the understanding]—*Syn.* logical, indisputable, reasonable; see **obvious** 2.

evidently, *mod.* —*Syn.* seemingly, obviously, so far as one can see; see **apparently.**

evil, *mod.* **1.** [Morally bad]—*Syn.* immoral, sinful, corrupt; see **wicked** 1.

2. [Unpropitious]—*Syn.* destructive, calamitous, disastrous; see **harmful.**

evil, *n.* **1.** [The quality of being evil]—*Syn.* sin, wickedness, depravity, crime, sinfulness, corruption, vice, immorality, iniquity, knavery, perversity, badness, villainy, vileness, baseness, meanness, infamy, heinousness, criminality, malignity, impiety, malevolence, indecency, hatred, viciousness, wrong, debauchery, looseness, lewdness, licentiousness, dissoluteness, lasciviousness, wantonness, grossness, turpitude, wrongdoing, foulness, degradation, lustfulness, worm in the apple, the devil within one, obscenity, profligacy.—*Ant.* virtue*, good, goodness.

2. [A harmful or malicious action]—*Syn.* ill, harm, mischief, misfortune, scandal, calamity, pollution, contamination, catastrophe, blow, disaster, plague, outrage; *all* (D): foul play, ill wind, crying shame, machinations of the Devil, double cross, raw deal.

evildoer, *n.* —*Syn.* malefactor, sinner, wrongdoer; see **criminal.**

evil eye, *n.* —*Syn.* hex, injurious stare, magic look; see **magic** 1, 2.

evil-minded, *mod.* **1.** [Wicked]—*Syn.* malicious, depraved, malign; see **wicked** 1.

2. [Licentious]—*Syn.* salacious, prurient, lecherous; see **lewd** 2.

evil one, *n.* —*Syn.* Belial, Satan, Lucifer; see **Devil** 1.

evince, *v.* —*Syn.* manifest, reveal, show; see **prove.**

eviscerate, *v.* —*Syn.* disembowel, gut, viscerate; see **kill** 1.

evocation, *n.* —*Syn.* summoning, conjuration, calling; see **summons** 2.

evoke, *v.* **1.** [To call forth]—*Syn.* summon forth, call out, invoke; see **summon** 1.

2. [To arouse]—*Syn.* elicit, provoke, arouse; see **excite** 2.

evolution, *n.* —*Syn.* growth, unfolding, natural process; see **development** 2.

evolve, *v.* —*Syn.* result, unfold, emerge; see **develop** 3, **grow** 2.

ewe, *n.* —*Syn.* lamb, female sheep, animal; see **sheep.**

ewer, *n.* —*Syn.* jar, vessel, decanter; see **pitcher** 1.

exacerbate, *v.* **1.** [To irritate]—*Syn.* exasperate, annoy, provoke; see **bother** 2.

2. [To aggravate]—*Syn.* worsen, heighten, increase; see **intensify.**

exacerbation, *n.* **1.** [Irritation]—*Syn.* exasperation, irritation, provocation; see **annoyance** 1.

2. [Intensification]—*Syn.* heightening, worsening, increasing; see **aggravation** 1.

exact, *mod.* **1.** [Accurate]—*Syn.* precise, correct, perfect; see **accurate** 1, 2, **definite** 1.

2. [Clear]—*Syn.* sharp, distinct, clear-cut; see **definite** 2.

3. [Strict]—*Syn.* rigorous, scrupulous, demanding; see **severe** 1, 2.

exacting, *mod.* —*Syn.* precise, careful, critical; see **difficult** 1, 2.

exaction, *n.* **1.** [Extortion]—*Syn.* demand, oppression, expropriation; see **theft.**

2. [Something exacted]—*Syn.* toll, ransom, levy; see **bribe, tax** 1.

exactly, *mod.* —*Syn.* precisely, specifically, correctly; see **accurately.**

exactness, *n.* —*Syn.* precision, nicety, scrupulousness; see **accuracy** 2.

exaggerate, *v.* —*Syn.* overestimate, overdraw, overstate, misrepresent, falsify, magnify, expand, amplify, pile up, heighten, intensify, distort, enlarge (on), stretch, overdo, overcolor, misquote, misreport, hyperbolize, go to extremes, give color to, misjudge, elaborate, romance, embroider, embellish, color, make too much of, lie, fabricate, corrupt; *all* (D): shoot with a long bow, pull a hot one, pretty up, paint in glowing colors, sling the bull, carry too far, lay it on, make a mountain out of a molehill, cook up, build up, grasp at straws, make much of, make the most of, make the eagle scream, heap up.—*Ant.* underestimate*, tell the truth, minimize.

exaggerated, *mod.* —*Syn.* highly colored, magnified, overwrought, extravagant, hyperbolic, preposterous, impossible, fabulous, *outré* (French), sensational, spectacular, melodramatic, hyperbolic, out of proportion, fantastic, high-flown, farfetched, false, distorted, embroidered, fabricated, strained, artificial, abstract, glaring, pronounced, stylized, unrealistic; *all* (D): half-cocked, howling, whopping, a bit thick, too much.—*Ant.* accurate*, exact, precise.

exaggeration, *n.* **1.** [An excessive estimate]—*Syn.* overestimation, misrepresentation, misjudgment, extravagance, elaboration, coloring, flight, flight of fancy, embroidery, embellishment, hyperbole, fantasy, fancy, stretch of the imagination, figure of speech, yarn; *all* (D): tempest in a teapot, much ado about nothing, making a mountain out of a molehill, tall story, whopper, play-up.—*Ant.* truth*, accuracy, understatement.

2. [A deliberate falsification of fact]—*Syn.* falsehood, untruth, fabrication; see **lie** 1.

exalt, *v.* **1.** [To elevate]—*Syn.* erect, promote, magnify; see **raise** 1.

2. [To praise]—*Syn.* commend, glorify, laud; see **praise** 1.

exaltation, *n.* **1.** [Elevation]—*Syn.* glory, deification, worship; see **praise** 1, 2.

2. [Ecstasy]—*Syn.* rapture, elation, rhapsody; see **happiness** 2.

exalted, *mod.* **1.** [Noble]—*Syn.* illustrious, magnificent, imposing; see **noble** 1, 3.
2. [Rapturous]—*Syn.* inspired, rhapsodic, elated; see **happy** 1.

examination, *n.* **1.** [The act of seeking evidence] —*Syn.* search, research, survey, scrutiny, investigation, inquiry, inspection, observation, inquisition, checking, exploration, reconnaissance, raid, analysis, audit, study, questioning, inquiry into, testing program, quest, inquest, test, perusal, trial, cross-examination, polygraphy; *all* (D): third degree, the grill, the eye.
2. [A formal test]—*Syn.* experiment, review, questionnaire, battery, quiz; *all* (D): exam, make-up, midterm, final, tryout, blue book, prelims, orals, writtens, once-over; see **test.**
3. [A medical checkup]—*Syn.* postoperative *or* postop (D): checkup, autopsy, biopsy, (physical) examination; *all* (D): physical, medical, exam, checkup; see **test.**

examine, *v.* **1.** [To inspect with care]—*Syn.* inspect, analyze, criticize, scrutinize, investigate, go *or* inquire *or* delve into, scan, probe, sift, explore, reconnoiter, audit, take stock *or* note of, make an inventory of, consider, canvass, ransack, review, assay, check, check out, check up on, re-examine, go back over, concentrate on, give one's attention to, look at *or* into *or* over, conduct research on, fathom, thresh *or* search out, run checks on, put to the test, parse, winnow, sound *or* feel out, probe, subject to scrutiny, peer *or* look *or* pry into, hold up to the light, finger, turn over, pick over, look for flaws, sample, experiment with; *all* (D): case, give the once-over, pass over, size up, get the lay of, play around with, give a going over, run the eye over, run tests on, smell out *or* around, search into, see about *or* into, poke into, nose around, look up and down, peer at, go over with a fine-toothed comb, get the lay of the land, cast the eyes over, flip through the pages, dive into, see how the land lies, bury oneself, go behind, fool around with, sit on, track down, be memoried up, dig into, go deep into.
2. [To test]—*Syn.* question, query, catechise, cross-examine, interrogate, judge, measure, experiment, weigh, check, try, give an exam, try out, quiz (D).

examined, *mod.*—*Syn.* checked, tested, inspected; see **investigated.**

examiner, *n.*—*Syn.* tester, questioner, inquisitor, inquirer, district attorney, inspector, prosecutor, observer, investigator, quizmaster, scrutinizer, interrogator, explorer, assayer, appraiser, analyst, surveyor, catechist, censor, critic, prober, auditor, reviewer, accountant, interlocutor, doctor, teacher, psychoanalyst; *both* (D): D.A., quizzer; see also **checker.**

example, *n.* **1.** [A representative]—*Syn.* illustration, representation, part, warning, exemplar, exemplification, sample, citation, case in point, concrete example, pattern, model, object lesson, case, *exempli gratia* (Latin), prototype, archetype, stereotype, original, copy, symbol, instance, quotation, kind of thing (D).
2. [Something to be imitated]—*Syn.* standard, pattern, sample; see **model** 2.
set an example—*Syn.* instruct, behave as a model, set a pattern; see **teach** 1.
without example—*Syn.* unprecedented, novel, new and different; see **unique** 1.

exasperate, *v.*—*Syn.* disturb, upset, provoke; see **bother** 2.

ex cathedra, *mod.*—*Syn.* authoritative, formal, magisterial; see **official** 3.

excavate, *v.*—*Syn.* shovel, empty, hollow out; see **dig** 1, 2.

excavation, *n.* **1.** [The act of excavating]—*Syn.* unearthing, disinterring, mining, exhuming, scooping *or* digging out, scouring, shoveling, blasting, removal, digging a basement *or* foundation, using a back hoe *or* trencher, cut and fill, stoping, underhand *or* bottom stoping, overhand stoping, power *or* diesel shovel work; *all* (D): pick and shoveling, mucking out, digging.
2. [The result of excavating]—*Syn.* cavity, hollow, pit; see **hole** 3.

exceed, *v.*—*Syn.* excel, outdo, overdo, overtax, distance, outdistance, pass, overstep, outrun, outpace, beat, go by *or* beyond, exaggerate, surpass, transcend, surmount, outstrip, outvie, eclipse, rise above, pass over; *all* (D): run circles around, get *or* have the bulge *or* edge on, have it on, have a bent for, have a good head for, have an eye for, excel in, have it all over, pull a gun on, get the drop on, beat to the draw, break the record, carry all before one, get *or* have the better of, put one's nose out of joint, know all the tricks of the trade, have the best of, hold aces, have a card up one's sleeve, have the jump on, cut out, meet one at every turn, beat the wind out of, be ahead of the game, get *or* have the advantage, gain the ascendancy, gain the upper hand, rank out.—*Ant.* lag*, dally, fall short.

exceedingly, *mod.*—*Syn.* greatly, remarkably, in a marked degree; see **very.**

excel, *v.*—*Syn.* surpass, transcend, improve upon; see **exceed.**

excellence, *n.*—*Syn.* superiority, worth, distinction; see **perfection** 3.

excellent, *mod.*—*Syn.* first-class, premium, choice, first, choicest, prime, high, picked, the best obtainable, select, exquisite, high-grade, (very) fine, finest, good, desirable, admirable, distinctive, attractive, great, highest, superior, world-class, exceptional, superb, perfectly good, striking, capital, certified, accomplished, supreme, estimable, enticing, unique, custom made, incomparable, surprising, transcendent, priceless, rare, peerless, invaluable, highest priced, magnificent, wonderful, skillful, excelling, superlative, worthy, refined, well-done, cultivated, foremost, to be desired, exemplary, praiseworthy, masterful, masterly, competent, skilled, paramount, notable; *all* (D): bully, above par, first-rate, crackerjack, terrific, well and good, sensational, sharp, keen, neat, cool, groovy, real fine, all right, well turned out, ace-high, A-1, grade A, classy, top-notch, cream, tops, crack, frontline, out of this world, a jump ahead of, up to par, above par, up to the notch.—*Ant.* poor*, inferior, imperfect.

excellently, *mod.*—*Syn.* (very) well, perfectly, exquisitely, splendidly, distinctively, magnificently, wonderfully, admirably, incomparably, masterfully, ingeniously, supremely, superbly, notably, nobly, remarkably, flawlessly, in an excellent way *or* manner; *all* (D): famously, fine, swimmingly, sensationally, neatly.—*Ant.* poorly*, badly, awkwardly.

excelling, *mod.* —*Syn.* bearing the palm, surpassing, exceeding, outreaching, prevailing; see also **excellent.**

except, *prep.* —*Syn.* excepting, excluding, rejecting, omitting, barring, saving, save, but, with the exclusion *or* exception of, other than, if not, not for, without, outside of, aside from, lacking, leaving out, exempting; *both* (D): minus, short of.

except, *v.* —*Syn.* exclude, reject, leave out; see **omit** 1.

exception, *n.* **1.** [The act of excepting]—*Syn.* exclusion, omission, making an exception of *or* for, rejection, barring, reservation, leaving out, noninclusion, segregation, limitation, exemption, elimination, repudiation, expulsion, excusing.—*Ant.* approval, conformity, acceptance.

2. [That which is excepted]—*Syn.* irregularity, peculiarity, anomaly, difference, allowance, exemption, nonconformity, privilege, dispensation, deviation, eccentricity.—*Ant.* custom*, rule, convention.

3. [An adverse reaction]—*Syn.* offense, complaint, affront; see **objection** 2.

take exception (to)—*Syn.* **1.** object, disagree, demur; see **differ** 2. **2.** resent, be offended, take offense; see **dislike.**

exceptional, *mod.* —*Syn.* uncommon, extraordinary, rare; see **unusual** 1, 2.

exceptionally, *mod.* —*Syn.* unusually, particularly, abnormally; see **especially** 1.

excerpt, *n.* —*Syn.* selection, extract, citation; see **quotation** 1.

excerpt, *v.* —*Syn.* quote, select, extract; see **cite** 2.

excess, *n.* **1.** [More than is needed]—*Syn.* profusion, abundance, plethora, superabundance, surplus, remainder, superfluity, redundancy, redundance, undue amount, too much *or* many, fulsomeness, exuberance, inundation, overflow, exorbitance, surfeit, waste, wastefulness, luxuriance, lavishness, over-supply, plenty; *all* (D): snootful, bellyful, enough and then some, glut, drug on the market, too much of a good thing.—*Ant.* lack*, dearth, deficiency.

2. [Conduct that is not temperate]—*Syn.* prodigality, dissipation, intemperance; see **indulgence** 3.

3. [The portion that exceeds a minimum]—*Syn.* overweight, charge, valuation, overvaluation, balance, overload, chargeable *or* assessable part.

4. [The portion that remains]—*Syn.* balance, remainder, rest, surplus, residue, leavings, refuse, byproduct, waste, tailings, tare, leftovers.

in excess of—*Syn.* additional, surplus, more than; see **extra.**

to excess—*Syn.* too much, excessively, extravagantly; see **extreme** 2.

excessive, *mod.* —*Syn.* immoderate, extravagant, exorbitant; see **extreme** 2.

excessively, *mod.* —*Syn.* extravagantly, extremely, unreasonably; see **very.**

exchange, *n.* **1.** [The act of replacing one thing with another]—*Syn.* transfer, substitution, replacement, change, supplanting, rearrangement, shift, revision, resale, transposition, interchange, transposing, commutation, shuffle, shuffling, castling, sleight-of-hand,hocus-pocus(D).

2. [The act of giving and receiving reciprocally]—*Syn.* reciprocity, reciprocation, barter, correspondence, interrelation, interdependence, cross fire, buying and selling, negotiation, transaction, commerce, trade; *both* (D): tit for tat, give and take.

3. [A substitution]—*Syn.* change, shift, swap, trade, interchange, replacing, shuffle, reciprocation, supplanting, replacement, switch, supplantment, commutation.

4. [A place where exchanges take place]—*Syn.* shop, store, bazaar; see **market** 1.

exchange, *v.* **1.** [To replace one thing with another]—*Syn.* substitute, transfer, replace, go over to, invert, give in exchange, commute, remove, pass to, reverse, provide a substitute *or* replacement, transpose, shuffle, shift, revise, rearrange, change, interchange, castle, transact, transmute, bandy, reset, change hands; *all* (D): borrow from Peter to pay Paul, swap horses in the middle of the stream, swap.

2. [To give and receive reciprocally]—*Syn.* reciprocate, barter, alternate, interact, cash in (on), trade with, trade off, correspond, trade, buy and sell, return the compliment.

exchangeable, *mod.* —*Syn.* interchangeable, transmutable, convertible, returnable, commutable, substitutive, reciprocal, mutual, complementary, correlative, equivalent, correspondent, like.

exchanged, *mod.* —*Syn.* restored, traded, brought *or* sent back; see **returned.**

exchequer, *n.* —*Syn.* bursary, bank, almonry; see **treasury.**

excise, *v.* —*Syn.* cut off, extract, eradicate; see **remove** 1.

excision, *n.* —*Syn.* eradication, abscission, extermination; see **removal** 1.

excitable, *mod.* —*Syn.* sensitive, high-strung, mettlesome, high-mettled, neurotic, easily excited, peevish, irritable, impatient, intolerant, moody, irascible, resentful, vehement, demonstrative, restless, uneasy, unquiet, mercurial, galvanic, fidgety, fussy, hysterical, emotional, hotheaded, enthusiastic, overzealous, mercurial, turbulent, impressible, tempestuous, impulsive, impetuous, rash, hasty, quick, passionate, uncontrolled, heedless, reckless, fiery, violent, quick-tempered, temperamental, hot-tempered, short-tempered, easily angered, furious, fierce, wild, volcanic; *all* (D): touchy, flighty, (always) up in the air, likely to go off at half cock, have a short fuse, like a bundle of nerves.—*Ant.* quiet*, sedate, easy-going.

excite, *v.* **1.** [To stir one mentally]—*Syn.* stimulate, inflame, arouse, anger, delight, move, tease, worry, infuriate, madden, stir (up), fire (up), fire the blood, give one a turn, convulse, work up (to), goad, taunt, mock, provoke, incite, astound, amaze, fluster, annoy, jar, jolt, chill, feed the fire, fan the flames, blow *or* call *or* light up, carry away, make an ado, carry on over, arrest the thoughts, warm, irritate, offend, chafe, vex, bother.

2. [To activate]—*Syn.* irritate, charge, energize, stimulate, intensify, dilate, bring out *or* about, stir up, animate, move, start, induce, precipitate, instigate, convulse, elicit, kindle, foment, attract, fire, fuse, accelerate, impel, touch off (a response), turn on (D).

excited, *mod.* —*Syn.* aroused, stimulated, inflamed, agitated, hot, annoyed, seething, wrought up, frantic, flushed, overwrought, restless, feverish, stirred, apprehensive, roused, disturbed, perturbed, flustered, upset, angry, disconcerted, discomfited, disquieted, tense, discomposed, abashed, tumultuous, embarrassed, hurt, piqued, atingle, angered, distracted, distraught, edgy, furious, beside oneself, delighted, eager, enthusiastic, frenzied, concerned, troubled, ruffled, moved, avid, hysterical, passionate, glowing, provoked, quickened, inspired, wild, fired, nervous, overheated, animated, uneasy, galvanized, ill at ease; *all* (D): jumpy, jittery, on the ragged edge, keyed up, red hot, turned on, in a tailspin, all a twitter, boiling over, all hot and bothered, hyped up, in a quiver *or* dither, hopped up, worked up, feeling one's oats, on pins and needles, in a tizzy, haywire, up tight, in heaven, all nerves, flashing up, wringing one's hands, blue in the face, jumping at, het up, on the *qui vive,* on fire. —*Ant.* calm*, reserved, self-confident.

excitedly, *mod.* —*Syn.* tensely, apprehensively, hysterically, restlessly, frantically, uncontrolledly, uncontrollably, erratically, irresponsibly, tempestuously, passionately, unstably, with heart in mouth, in an excited *or* excitable manner *or* way, lacking calm *or* poise, without balance *or* restraint, under stress of emotion *or* excitement; see also **excited.**

excitement, *n.* —*Syn.* confusion, disturbance, tumult, enthusiasm, rage, ferment, trepidation, turmoil, stir, excitation, agitation, hurry, perturbation, excitedness, movement, feeling, exhilaration, emotion, stimulation, drama, melodrama, activity, provocation, commotion; *all* (D): fuss, hullabaloo, bother, dither, hubbub, fluster, flutter, flurry, bustle, to-do.—*Ant.* peace*, calm, quiet.

exciting, *mod.* —*Syn.* stimulating, moving, animating, provocative, arousing, rousing, arresting, impelling, stirring, thrilling, dangerous, breathtaking, overwhelming, interesting, zestful, new, unknown, mysterious, biting, overpowering, inspiring, impressive, soul-stirring, sensational, astonishing, electrifying, bracing, appealing; *all* (D): blood-curdling, racy, hair-raising, mind-blowing.—*Ant.* dull*, pacifying, tranquilizing.

exclaim, *v.* —*Syn.* cry *or* call out, ejaculate, blurt, burst out, assert, emit, shout, call aloud, say loudly, vociferate, speak vehemently, rend the air, rip out (D); see also **yell.**

exclamation, *n.* —*Syn.* ejaculation, clamor, vociferation; see **cry** 1.

exclude, *v.* **1.** [To bar]—*Syn.* shut out, reject, ban; see **bar** 1, 2.

2. [To expel]—*Syn.* banish, put out, force out; see **dismiss** 1.

exclusion, *n.* —*Syn.* keeping out, rejection, ejection, discharge, elimination, prohibition, cut, embargo, nonadmission, relegation, omission, segregation, isolation, interdiction, interdicting, preventing admission, erecting bars *or* regulations *or* provisions against, blockade, repudiation, separation, ousting, eviction, dismissal, suspension, excommunication, refusal, expulsion, debarring, barring.—*Ant.* welcome*, invitation, inclusion.

exclusive, *mod.* —*Syn.* restricted, restrictive, fashionable, aristocratic, socially correct, preferential, privileged, particular, circumscribed, licensed, select, private, segregated, prohibitive, cliquish, aloof, clannish, independent, sole; *all* (D): tony, upper crust, high-hat, ritzy, swank, swellish, country club, cliquy.—*Ant.* free*, inclusive, unrestricted.

exclusively, *mod.* —*Syn.* particularly, solely, completely; see **only** 1.

excommunicate, *v.* —*Syn.* expel, curse, oust; see **dismiss** 1.

excommunication, *n.* —*Syn.* expulsion, dismissal, suspension; see **removal** 1.

excoriate, *v.* **1.** [To remove strips of skin, bark, etc.] —*Syn.* abrade, chafe, flay; see **skin.**

2. [To denounce]—*Syn.* condemn, criticize, flay; see **censure, denounce.**

excrement, *n.* —*Syn.* excretion, ordure, stool, excreted matter, fecal matter, offal, droppings, evacuation, discharge, exudation, dung, chips, manure, urine, effluvium, feces, secrement, smegma, sweat, perspiration, egesta, excreta.

excrescence, *n.* **1.** [A growth on the skin]—*Syn.* swelling, lump, wart; see **bulge, growth** 3.

2. [An excess]—*Syn.* superfluity, redundancy, surplus; see **excess.**

excrete, *v.* —*Syn.* remove, eliminate, eject, defecate, urinate, discharge, secrete, void, expel from the tissues, throw off waste matter, go to (the) stool *or* the bathroom *or* the toilet *or* the (water) closet, answer a call of nature, evacute, pass, expel, exude, perspire, sweat, squeeze out, give off.

excretion, *n.* **1.** [The act of excreting]—*Syn.* eliminating, elimination, urinating, evacuating, evacuation, discharging, secreting, secretion, defecation, defecating, expelling, expulsion, ejecting, ejection, voiding, leaving, passing off.—*Ant.* accretion, eating, receiving.

2. [The product of excretion]—*Syn.* defecation, excreta, feces; see **excrement.**

excruciating, *mod.* —*Syn.* torturing, intense, agonizing; see **painful** 1.

exculpate, *v.* —*Syn.* absolve, exonerate, forgive; see **excuse.**

excursion, *n.* —*Syn.* jaunt, ramble, tour; see **journey.**

excursionist, *n.* —*Syn.* visitor, voyager, tourist; see **traveler.**

excursive, *mod.* —*Syn.* discursive, digressive, erratic; see **rambling** 1, 3, **wandering** 1.

excursus, *n.* **1.** [A supplemental discussion]—*Syn.* essay, dissertation, summary; see **discussion** 1, 2.

2. [A digression]—*Syn.* wandering, diversion, deviation; see **digression.**

excusable, *mod.* —*Syn.* pardonable, forgivable, understandable, justifiable, reasonable, defensible, permissible, trivial, passable, slight, vindicatory, exculpatory, warrantable, plausible, allowable, venial, reprieve, specious, explainable, not excessive *or* fatal *or* too bad *or* inexcusable *or* injurious, moderate, temperate, all right, fair; *all* (D): within limits, not beyond the pale, O.K.—*Ant.* inexcusable, unforgivable, culpable.

excuse, *n.* **1.** [An explanation]—*Syn.* apology, reason, defense; see **explanation** 2.

2. [A pretext]—*Syn.* semblance, subterfuge, trick; see **pretense** 2.

a poor excuse for—*Syn.* inferior, poor, unsatisfactory; see **inadequate** 1.

make one's excuses (for)—*Syn.* regret, apologize (for), offer an explanation (of); see **apologize, explain.**

excuse, *v.* —*Syn.* pardon, forgive, justify, discharge, vindicate, apologize (for), release (from), dispense with *or* for, free, set free, overlook, purge, exempt (from), mitigate, rationalize, acquit, condone, appease, reprieve, remit, absolve, exonerate, exculpate, clear (of), shrive, give absolution (to), pass over, give as an excuse, make excuses *or* allowances *or* apologies (for), dispense from, grant remission (to), remit a penalty of *or* for, grant amnesty (to), blot out one's sins, expunge the record (of), provide with an alibi (for), plead ignorance (of); *all* (D): whitewash, let off (easy), let go (scot free), wink at, wipe the slate clean, shrug off, take the rap for.

excused, *mod.* —*Syn.* exonerated, freed, permitted; see **pardoned.**

excuse me, *interj.* —*Syn.* pardon me, forgive me, *pardonnez-moi, pardon* (*both* French), *entschuldigen Sie (mich)* (German), I'm sorry, *izvenitye mne* (Russian).

execrable, *mod.* **1.** [Abominable]—*Syn.* detestable, confounded, vile; see **offensive** 2.

2. [Inferior]—*Syn.* bad, defective, wretched; see **poor** 2.

execrate, *v.* **1.** [To curse]—*Syn.* revile, accurse, denounce; see **curse** 2.

2. [To detest]—*Syn.* loathe, abhor, abominate; see **hate** 1.

execration, *n.* **1.** [Loathing]—*Syn.* detesting, abhorrence, abomination; see **hatred** 1.

2. [A denunciation]—*Syn.* malediction, anathema, condemnation; see **curse.**

execute, *v.* **1.** [To carry out instructions]—*Syn.* act, do, effect; see **perform** 1.

2. [To bring to fruition]—*Syn.* finish, accomplish, fulfill; see **achieve** 1.

3. [To put to death]—*Syn.* electrocute, hang, behead; see **kill** 1.

executed, *mod.* **1.** [Performed]—*Syn.* completed, done, carried out; see **finished** 1.

2. [Formally put to death]—*Syn.* killed, hanged, electrocuted, gassed, shot (at sunrise), sent before a firing squad, beheaded, guillotined, impaled, crucified, drawn and quartered, immured, murdered by decree; *all* (D): sent to the chair, scorched, stretched, sent up the river, hung up to dry, fried, cooked, sent to the showers.

execution, *n.* **1.** [The carrying out of instructions or plans]—*Syn.* fulfilling, accomplishment, doing; see **achievement** 2, **performance** 1.

2. [Death by official order]—*Syn.* punishment, capital punishment, killing, electrocution, hanging, gassing, lethal injection, beheading, decapitation, guillotining, strangulation, contract killing, strangling, crucifixion, martyrdom, impalement, shooting, ultimate penalty.

executioner, *n.* —*Syn.* hangman, lyncher, strangler, firing squad, one who puts to death, electrocutioner, headsman, garroter, killer, hired gun (D).

executive, *mod.* —*Syn.* managing, governing, ruling; see **administrative.**

executive, *n.* —*Syn.* businessman, official, manager; see **administrator.**

executor, *n.* —*Syn.* enforcer, administratrix *or* administratress, official; see **administrator.**

exegesis, *n.* —*Syn.* interpretation, exposition, critique; see **explanation** 2.

exegetical, *mod.* —*Syn.* expository, interpretive, explicatory; see **explanatory.**

exemplar, *n.* —*Syn.* pattern, prototype, copy; see **example** 1, **model** 1, 2.

exemplification, *n.* —*Syn.* embodiment, illustration, instance; see **example** 1.

exemplify, *v.* —*Syn.* illustrate, elucidate, embody; see **explain.**

exempt, *mod.* —*Syn.* free(d), clear(ed), liberated, privileged, excused, absolved, not subject to, released from, not responsible (to *or* for), void of, set apart, excluded, released, free(d), not liable, unrestrained, unbound, uncontrolled, untrammeled, unshackled, unchecked, unrestricted, free(d) from, not restricted by *or* to, outside.—*Ant.* responsible*, liable, subject.

exempt, *v.* —*Syn.* free, liberate, pass by; see **excuse.**

exemption, *n.* —*Syn.* exception, immunity, privilege; see **freedom** 2.

exercise, *n.* **1.** [Action, undertaken for training] —*Syn.* practice, exertion, drill, drilling, gymnastics, sports, jogging, calisthenics, toil; *both* (D): workout, daily dozen.

2. [The means by which training is promoted] —*Syn.* performance, act, action, activity, occupation, operation, study, theme, lesson, task, test, examination.

3. [Use]—*Syn.* application, employment, operation; see **use** 1.

exercise, *v.* **1.** [To move the body]—*Syn.* stretch, bend, pull, tug, hike, jog, work, promote muscle tone, labor, strain, move briskly, exert, loosen up, discipline, drill, execute, perform exercises, practice, maneuver, take a walk; *all* (D): work out, get in trim, pump iron, take a constitutional, do one's daily dozen, limber *or* warm up; see **train** 3.

2. [To use]—*Syn.* employ, practice, exert, apply, operate, execute, sharpen, handle, utilize, devote, put in practice; see **use** 1.

3. [To train]—*Syn.* drill, discipline, give training to; see **teach** 2, **train** 3.

exercises, *n.* —*Syn.* services, meeting, convocation, graduation, commencement.

exert, *v.* —*Syn.* put forth, bring to bear, exercise; see **use** 1.

exertion, *n.* —*Syn.* struggle, attempt, endeavor; see **effort** 1.

exert oneself, *v.* —*Syn.* strive, attempt, endeavor; see **try** 1.

exfoliate, *v.* —*Syn.* scale, drop, peel; see **shed.**

exfoliation, *n.* **1.** [Shedding]—*Syn.* molting, peeling, depilation; see **shedding.**

2. [That which is peeled]—*Syn.* hide, shell, husk; see **skin.**

exhalation, *n.* **1.** [Breathing]—*Syn.* exhaling, expiration, respiration, exhausting, exhaustion, emission of vapor, vaporization; see **removal** 1.

2. [That which is exhaled]—*Syn.* emanation, vapor, air; see **breath** 1.

exhaust, *v.* **1.** [To consume strength]—*Syn.* debilitate, tire, wear out *or* down; see **weaken** 1, 2, **weary** 1, 2.

2. [To use entirely]—*Syn.* use up, take the last of, deplete; see **consume** 2.

exhausted, *mod.* **1.** [Without further physical resources]—*Syn.* debilitated, wearied, worn; see **tired, weak** 1.

2. [Having nothing remaining]—*Syn.* all gone, consumed, used; see **empty** 1.

exhaustible, *mod.* —*Syn.* expendable, limited, modest; see **inadequate** 1.

exhaustion, *n.* —*Syn.* weariness, fatigue, depletion; see **lassitude.**

exhibit, *n.* —*Syn.* show, performance, presentation; see **display** 2.

exhibit, *v.* —*Syn.* show, present, manifest; see **display** 1.

exhibited, *mod.* —*Syn.* shown, presented, advertised; see **displayed.**

exhibition, *n.* **1.** [The act of presenting for examination]—*Syn.* presentation, advertisement, showing; see **display** 2.

2. [An elaborate performance]—*Syn.* exposition, fair, carnival; see **show** 1.

exhibitionist, *n.* —*Syn.* fop, show-off, nudist; see **extrovert, pervert.**

exhilarate, *v.* —*Syn.* enliven, stimulate, inspire; see **animate** 1.

exhilarating, *mod.* —*Syn.* enlivening, inspiring, invigorating; see **stimulating.**

exhilaration, *n.* —*Syn.* liveliness, animation, stimulation; see **action** 1.

exhort, *v.* —*Syn.* caution, admonish, warn; see **urge** 2.

exhortation, *n.* —*Syn.* persuasion, instigation, urging; see **appeal** 1.

exhume, *v.* —*Syn.* unearth, disclose, reveal, disinhume, disentomb, disinter, dig up, unbury.

exigency, *n.* **1.** [Pressure]—*Syn.* emergency, crisis, distress; see **difficulty** 2.

2. [Demand]—*Syn.* need, want, urgency; see **necessity** 1, 2, **requirement** 2.

exigent, *mod.* **1.** [Urgent]—*Syn.* pressing, critical, imperative; see **urgent** 1.

2. [Demanding]—*Syn.* exacting, severe, oppressive; see **difficult** 1.

exiguous, *mod.* —*Syn.* scanty, meager, petty; see **inadequate** 1.

exile, *n.* **1.** [Banishment]—*Syn.* expulsion, deportation, expatriation, ostracism, displacement, proscription, separation.

2. [An outcast]—*Syn.* fugitive, outlaw, man without a country (D); see **refugee.**

exile, *v.* —*Syn.* ostracize, outlaw, cast out; see **banish** 1.

exist, *v.* **1.** [To have being]—*Syn.* breathe, live, survive; see **be** 1.

2. [To carry on life]—*Syn.* be alive, endure, go on; see **subsist.**

existence, *n.* **1.** [The carrying on of life]—*Syn.* being, actuality, reality; see **life** 1.

2. [The state of being]—*Syn.* presence, actuality, permanence; see **reality** 1.

existing, *mod.* —*Syn.* for the time being, temporary, just now; see **present** 1.

exit, *n.* **1.** [A means of egress]—*Syn.* way *or* passage out, outlet, egress, opening, fire escape; see also **door, hole** 1, 2.

2. [The act of leaving]—*Syn.* going, farewell, exodus; see **departure** 1.

exodus, *n.* —*Syn.* migration, emigration, flight; see **departure** 1, **journey.**

ex officio, *mod.* —*Syn.* by virtue of office, sanctioned, authoritatively; see **approved, officially** 1.

exonerate, *v.* —*Syn.* absolve, vindicate, justify; see **excuse.**

exoneration, *n.* **1.** [Vindication]—*Syn.* absolution, exculpation, acquittal; see **pardon** 1.

2. [Liberation]—*Syn.* exemption, release, reprieve; see **freeing.**

exorbitance, *n.* —*Syn.* extravagance, costliness, excess; see **luxury** 1, 2.

exorbitant, *mod.* —*Syn.* excessive, extravagant, extreme; see **wasteful.**

exorcism, *n.* **1.** [Witchcraft]—*Syn.* sorcery, conjuring, enchantment; see **magic** 1, 2.

2. [A spell]—*Syn.* charm, incantation, cabala; see **magic** 1.

exotic, *mod.* **1.** [Foreign]—*Syn.* imported, not local *or* native, extrinsic; see **foreign** 1.

2. [Peculiar]—*Syn.* strange, fascinating, different; see **foreign** 2, **unusual** 2.

expand, *v.* —*Syn.* extend, augment, dilate; see **grow** 1.

expanse, *n.* —*Syn.* breadth, width, length, extent, extension, reach, stretch, distance, area, belt, space, field, territory, span, spread, room, fairness, scope, range, compass, sphere, margin, sweep, remoteness, latitude, radius, wilderness, region, wide extent of space, continuous area, uninterrupted space, expanded surface, amplitude, immensity.

expansion, *n.* —*Syn.* enlargement, augmentation, extension; see **increase** 1.

expansive, *mod.* —*Syn.* broad, widespread, comprehensive; see **extensive** 1.

ex parte, *mod.* —*Syn.* one-sided, partisan, biased; see **prejudiced.**

expatiate, *v.* —*Syn.* rant, elaborate, enlarge; see **ramble** 2.

expatriate, *n.* —*Syn.* exile, *émigré* (French), outcast; see **refugee.**

expatriate, *v.* —*Syn.* exile, ostracize, deport; see **banish** 1.

expect, *v.* **1.** [To anticipate]—*Syn.* await, wait for, hope for; see **anticipate** 1.

2. [To require]—*Syn.* demand, insist upon, exact; see **require** 2.

3. [(D) To assume]—*Syn.* presume, suppose, suspect; see **assume** 1.

expectancy, *mod.* —*Syn.* hope, prospect, likelihood; see **anticipation** 1.

expectant, *mod.* **1.** [Characterized by anticipation] —*Syn.* expecting, hoping, hopeful, waiting, awaiting, anticipative, in anticipation, watchful, vigilant, eager, ready, prepared, in suspense, gaping, wide-eyed; *all* (D): on tenterhooks, on edge, itching, raring, wild, with bated breath.—*Ant.* indifferent*, nonchalant, unprepared.

2. [Anticipating birth]—*Syn.* pregnant, parturient, *enceinte* (French); see **pregnant** 1.

expectation, *mod.* —*Syn.* hope, belief, prospect; see **anticipation** 1.

expected, *mod.* **1.** [Wonted]—*Syn.* normal, familiar, habitual; see **conventional** 1.

2. [Anticipated]—*Syn.* looked for, counted upon, contemplated, looked forward to, hoped for, relied upon, forseeable, foreseen, predictable, predetermined, foretold, prophesied, planned *or* prepared for, budgeted, (included) within (normal) expectations; *all* (D): in the works *or* the cards, coming up, in the bag; see also **likely** 1.

expecting, *mod.* —*Syn. enceinte* (French), due, about to become a mother; see **pregnant** 1.

expectorate, *v.* —*Syn.* cough up, slobber, spew; see **spit.**

expediency, *n.* **1.** [Appropriateness]—*Syn.* suitability, propriety, desirableness; see **fitness.**

2. [Usefulness]—*Syn.* advantageousness, efficiency, profitableness; see **usefulness.**

expedient, *mod.* **1.** [Appropriate]—*Syn.* desirable, advisable, fitting; see **fit** 1, 2.

2. [Advantageous]—*Syn.* profitable, useful, convenient; see **practical.**

expedite, *v.* —*Syn.* hurry, assist, promote; see **advance** 1, **hasten** 2.

expedition, *n.* **1.** [Travel undertaken]—*Syn.* excursion, voyage, campaign; see **journey**

2. [That which undertakes travel]—*Syn.* party, hunters, safari, explorers, pioneers, traders, soldiers, squadron, contingent, scouts, archaeologists, tourists, sightseers, cavalcade, patrol, caravan, posse, astronauts, cosmonauts, space travelers; see also **air force, army** 1, **crowd** 1, **fleet.**

expeditious, *mod.* —*Syn.* speedy, quick, prompt; see **fast** 1, **punctual.**

expel, *v.* **1.** [To eject]—*Syn.* get rid of, cast out, dislodge; see **eject** 1.

2. [To dismiss]—*Syn.* suspend, discharge, oust; see **dismiss** 1, 2.

expend, *v.* **1.** [To use]—*Syn.* exhaust, use up, employ; see **consume** 2.

2. [To spend]—*Syn.* pay (out), write checks for, lay out; see **spend** 1.

expenditure, *n.* —*Syn.* outgo, investment, payment; see **expense** 1.

expense, *n.* **1.** [Whatever is paid out]—*Syn.* expenditure, cost, price, outlay, charge, payment, outgo, disbursement, alimony, child support, value, worth, sum, amount, risk, capital, rate, custom, excise, tax, carrying charges, budgeted items, cost of materials, overhead, time, payroll, investment, interest (charges), operating expense, surcharge, deductible *or* nondeductible expense, duty, assessment, nut (D).—*Ant.* profit*, income, receipts.

2. [Whatever causes money to be paid out]—*Syn.* responsibility, obligation, loan, mortgage, lien, debt, liability, investment, insurance, upkeep, alimony, loss, enterprise, debit, account.—*Ant.* credit*, asset, accounts receivable.

at the expense of—*Syn.* paid by, at the cost of, charged to; see **spent** 2.

expenses, *n.* —*Syn.* expense, living, cost of living, per diem, reparations, damages, outlay, overhead, expense account, traveling expenses, living expenses, costs, lodging, room and board, incidentals, carrying charge, cash-out (D).

expensive, *mod.* —*Syn.* dear, precious, valuable, invaluable, rare, high-priced, costly, prized, choice, rich, priceless, high, too high, uneconomical, unreasonable, exorbitant, fancy, extravagant; *all* (D): worth a king's ransom, at a premium, out of sight, at great cost, sky-high, steep, stiff.—*Ant.* inexpensive, cheap*, low.

experience, *n.* **1.** [The act of living]—*Syn.* strife, struggle, combat, endurance, sacrifice, forbearance, action, actuality, reality, practice, activity, existence, continuance, school of hard knocks (D); see also **life** 1.

2. [What one lives through]—*Syn.* occurrences, happenings, adventures; see **life** 2.

3. [That which one gains from having lived] —*Syn.* background, skill, knowledge, perspicacity, wisdom, practice, maturity, seasoning, judgment, practical knowledge, sense, savoir-faire, patience, caution, know-how (D).

experience, *v.* —*Syn.* undergo, feel, live through; see **endure** 2, **feel** 2.

experienced, *mod.* —*Syn.* skilled, practiced, instructed, accomplished, versed, qualified, able, skillful, knowing, trained, wise, expert, veteran, matured, seasoned, mature, with a good background, mellowed, mastered, old, rounded; *all* (D): to hell and back, knowing the score *or* the ropes *or* all the answers, in the know, having been around *or* through the mill, broken in.—*Ant.* new*, apprentice, beginning.

experiment, *n.* **1.** [An operation to establish a principle or a truth]—*Syn.* analysis, essay, examination, trial, clinical trial, inspection, search, organized observation, research, scrutiny, speculation, check, proof, verification, sifting, dissection, operation, test, exercise, quiz, investigation.

2. [A trial arrangement]—*Syn.* undertaking, probation (trial), agreement, attempt, pilot project, testing program, dry run, rehearsal, trial and error method, practice, venture, enterprise, measure, try, tryout (D); see **sense** 1.

experiment, *v.* **1.** [To investigate scientifically] —*Syn.* analyze, investigate, probe, search, venture, explore, diagnose, prove, conduct an experiment, research, verify, speculate, study, examine, scrutinize, weigh, dissect, make inquiry, follow a clue; *all* (D): put to the test, hit and miss, play around with, fool with, cut and try.

2. [To put on trial]—*Syn.* test, rehearse, try out, try tentatively, sample, put on one's honor, hold under probation, subject to discipline, try by ordeal, give an opportunity, practice upon.

experimental, *mod.* —*Syn.* tentative, trial, temporary, test, probationary, experiential, provisional, empirical, preliminary, preparatory, under probation, on approval *or* trial, pending verification, rodential, momentary, primary, beginning, unconcluded, unproved, unformulated, laboratory, in its first stage, in the model stage.—*Ant.* permanent*, tried, tested.

experimentally, *mod.* —*Syn.* tentatively, temporarily, on trial, momentarily, for the moment, provisionally, on probation, analytically, step by step, empirically.

expert, *mod.* —*Syn.* skillful, practiced, proficient; see **able** 2.

expert, *n.* —*Syn.* graduate, master, trained personnel; see **specialist.**

expiate, *v.* —*Syn.* absolve, appease, compensate; see **excuse, forgive** 1.

expiation, *n.* **1.** [Atonement]—*Syn.* redemption, satisfaction, compensation; see **reparation** 1.
2. [Something done in atonement]—*Syn.* amends, penance, flagellation; see **reparation** 2.

expiration, *n.* **1.** [End]—*Syn.* close, closing, finish; see **end** 2.
2. [Death]—*Syn.* dying, demise, passing; see **death** 1.

expire, *v.* **1.** [To end]—*Syn.* stop, finish, quit; see **end** 1.
2. [To die]—*Syn.* pass on, depart, perish; see **die** 1.

explain, *v.* —*Syn.* interpret, explicate, account for, elucidate, illustrate, clarify, illuminate, make clear, describe, expound, teach, manifest, reveal, point up *or* out, demonstrate, tell, refine, read, translate, paraphrase, render, put in other words, decipher, assign a meaning to, construe, define, disentangle, justify, untangle, unravel, make plain, unfold, come to the point, put across, throw light upon, show by example, restate, rephrase, get to, annotate, comment *or* remark upon *or* on, make *or* prepare *or* offer an explanation *or* and exposition (of), resolve, clear up, get right, set right, put (someone) on the right track, unscramble, spell out, go into detail, get over, get to the bottom of, figure out, speak out, emphasize, cast light upon, get across *or* through, bring out, work out, solve, make oneself understood; *both* (D): hammer into one's head, put in plain English.—*Ant.* puzzle, confuse*, confound.

explainable, *mod.* —*Syn.* explicable, accountable, intelligible; see **understandable.**

explained, *mod.* —*Syn.* made clear, interpreted, elucidated; see **known** 2, **obvious** 2.

explanation, *n.* **1.** [The act of making clear] —*Syn.* elucidation, clarification, statement, interpretation, narration, recital, rendition, showing, display, exposition, explication, demonstration, specification, confession, telling, talking, writing, expression.
2. [Something intended to make clear]—*Syn.* information, answer, account, reason, illustration, description, comment, justification, narrative, story, tale, history, annotation, glossary, footnote, anecdote, example, apology, analysis, criticism, exegesis, résumé, gloss, key, commentary, note, summary, report, brief, the details, budget, breakdown, (documentary) evidence, the dope (D); see also **proof** 1, 2.

explanatory, *mod.* —*Syn.* expository, illustrative, informing, informative, allegorical, interpretive, hermeneutic, exegetical, annotative, instructive, guiding, declarative, descriptive, analytical, graphic, discursive, critical, summary, supplementary.

expletive, *n.* —*Syn.* exclamation, interjection, oath; see **curse**

explicable, *mod.* —*Syn.* explainable, solvable, intelligible; see **understandable.**

explicate, *v.* —*Syn.* clarify, illustrate, interpret; see **explain.**

explication, *n.* —*Syn.* clarification, exegesis, interpretation; see **explanation** 1.

explicit, *mod.* —*Syn.* express, sure, plain; see **definite** 1, **understandable.**

explode, *v.* **1.** [To burst]—*Syn.* blow up, blow out, blow a fuse, fly out, break out, erupt, go off, detonate, discharge, backfire, fly apart *or* into *or* off, shatter, rupture, fracture, split, convulse, collapse, thunder, blow off, blast, blow to smithereens (D).
2. [To discredit]—*Syn.* disprove, refute, confute; see **discard.**

exploit, *n.* —*Syn.* deed, venture, escapade; see **achievement** 2.

exploit, *v.* —*Syn.* utilize, take advantage of, employ; see **use** 1.

exploited, *mod.* —*Syn.* used, taken advantage of, utilized, worked, put to use *or* service, milked (D).

exploration, *n.* —*Syn.* investigation, research, search; see **examination** 1.

explore, *v.* —*Syn.* search, investigate, hunt, seek; see **examine** 1.

explorer, *n.* —*Syn.* adventurer, traveler, pioneer, wayfarer, pilgrim, voyager, space traveler, investigator, inventor, seafarer, mountaineer, mountain climber, scientist, globe-trotter, navigator, circumnavigator, spelunker, creator, founder, colonist, Conquistador.
Famous explorers include the following—Marco Polo, Christopher Columbus, Amerigo Vespucci, Magellan, Ponce de Leon, Balboa, Vasco da Gama, Sir Francis Drake, Henry Hudson, John Cabot, De Soto, Hernán Cortés, Father Marquette and Joliet, David Livingstone, Lewis and Clark, Robert E. Peary, Robert Scott, Vilhjalmur Stefanson, Roald Amundsen, Richard E. Byrd, Thor Heyerdahl, Sir Edmund Hillary, Maurice Herzog, John Glenn, Yuri Gagarin, Virgil Grissom, Alan Shephard, Edward White, Scott Carpenter, Neil Armstrong.

explosion, *n.* **1.** [The act of blowing up]—*Syn.* detonation, blast, burst, discharge, blowout, blowup, concussion, eruption, percussion, combustion, outburst, firing, ignition, backfire, fulmination, pop.
2. [A loud noise]—*Syn.* report, roar, blast; see **noise** 1.

explosive, *mod.* **1.** [Eruptive]—*Syn.* bursting, detonating, eruptive, dangerous, convulsive, fulminating, atomic, fulminant, fiery.—*Ant.* harmless*, burned out, quenched.
2. [Violent; *said of persons or events*]—*Syn.* stormy, ebullient, meteoric, forceful, raging, wild, violent, uncontrollable, consequential, vehement, gruff, sharp, impetuous, far-reaching, rampant, hysterical, frenzied, savage.—*Ant.* gentle*, mild, uneventful.

explosive, *n.* —*Syn.* mine, gunpowder, ammunition, high explosive, detonator, propellant, bomb, missile, grenade, charge, shell, Molotov cocktail (D); see also **ammunition, mine** 2, **munitions.**
Common explosives include the following—dynamite, nitroglycerine, TNT (Trinitrotoluene), salt-

peter, hexamine (hexamethylenetetramine), Ballistite *or* ballistite, gun cotton, nitrate compound, nitro cotton, cellulose nitrate, pyroxylin, melinite, gelignite, cordite, lyddite; *all* (D): nitro, peter, soup, vaseline, grease, powder, sawdust, bang juice; see also **atomic powder.**

exponent, *n.* **1.** [Explainer]—*Syn.* advocate, interpreter, expounder; see **supporter.**

2. [Index]—*Syn.* representative, type, specimen; see **index** 1.

export, *n.* —*Syn.* exportation, shipping, trading, foreign sale, overseas shipment, transoceanic cargo, commodity, merchant traffic, international trade, foreign trade.

export, *v.* —*Syn.* send out, sell *or* trade abroad, ship (across), transport, convey outside, act as a shipper *or* shipping representative, transship, consign, find a foreign market *or* an outlet, dump (D).

expose, *v.* **1.** [To uncover]—*Syn.* disclose, smoke out, show up, present, prove, reveal, air, exhibit, unmask, lay open *or* bare, bring to light, open, unearth, dig up, drag before the public, give away, bring into view, bare, unveil, unseal, unroll, unfold, unwrap, untie; *all* (D): let the cat out of the bag, drag through the mud, paint in its true color, put the finger on, muckrake.

2. [To endeavor to attract attention]—*Syn.* show, show off, bare; see **display** 1.

3. [To open to danger]—*Syn.* lay open to, subject to, imperil; see **endanger.**

4. [To betray]—*Syn.* show, evidence, manifest; see **betray** 1.

exposé, *n.* —*Syn.* revelation, confession, truth; see **exposure** 1.

exposed, *mod.* **1.** [In sight]—*Syn.* visible, apparent, clear; see **obvious** 1.

2. [Revealed in the true light]—*Syn.* disclosed, defined, revealed, divulged, unmasked, unveiled, bared, unsealed, made public, laid bare, pointed *or* ferreted out, dug up, brought to light *or* the light of day, brought to justice, solved, resolved, untied, unriddled, discovered, found out, seen through, debunked (D).—*Ant.* hidden*, concealed, disguised.

exposition, *n.* **1.** [The process of making clear] —*Syn.* elucidation, delineation, explication; see **explanation** 1.

2. [A specific piece of explanation]—*Syn.* dissertation, tract, treatise, paper, composition, disquisition, thesis, theme, article, monograph, editorial, comment, commentary, critique, study, report, text, essay, review, analysis, piece, annotation, position paper, data paper, white paper, enunciation, (the) details, (expository) statement, discourse, discussion, story, tale, review, history.

3. [A popular exhibition]—*Syn.* exhibit, showing, performance; see **display** 2.

expositor, *n.* —*Syn.* explainer, commentator, expounder; see **interpreter, professor, teacher** 1.

expository, *mod.* —*Syn.* informative, descriptive, illustrative; see **explanatory.**

ex post facto, *mod.* —*Syn.* subsequently, retroactively, retrospectively; see **finally** 2.

expostulate, *v.* —*Syn.* remonstrate, reason with, dissuade; see **oppose** 1.

expostulation, *n.* —*Syn.* protest, complaint, disapproval; see **objection** 2.

exposure, *n.* **1.** [The act of subjecting to outside influences]—*Syn.* disclosure, betrayal, introduction, unfolding, display, exhibition, laying open, unmasking, production, publication, showing, expression, manifestation, revelation, confession, unveiling, acknowledgment, exposé; *all* (D): giveaway, bombshell, stink, break, show-up.—*Ant.* protection*, concealment, secrecy.

2. [The result of an exposure, sense 1]—*Syn.* weathering, frostbite, heat prostration; see **illness** 1.

expound, *v.* **1.** [To interpret]—*Syn.* explicate, clarify, elucidate; see **explain.**

2. [To set forth in detail]—*Syn.* delineate, present, express; see **describe.**

express, *mod.* **1.** [Explicit]—*Syn.* definite, specific, exact; see **definite** 1.

2. [Nonstop]—*Syn.* fast, direct, high-speed; see **fast** 1.

express, *v.* **1.** [To give utterance]—*Syn.* declare, tell, signify; see **utter.**

2. [To send by rapid conveyor]—*Syn.* dispatch, forward, ship; see **send** 1.

expression, *n.* **1.** [Significant appearance]—*Syn.* look, cast, character; see **appearance** 1.

2. [Putting into understandable form]—*Syn.* representation, art product, articulation, utterance, symbolization, narration, exposition, formulation, argument, interpretation, invention, creation, declaration, materialization, commentary, diagnosis, definition, rendition, elucidation, explanation, illustration; see also **composition** 3, **writing** 1.

3. [A traditional form of speech]—*Syn.* locution, idiom, speech pattern; see **phrase, word** 1.

4. [Facial cast]—*Syn.* grimace, smile, smirk, mug, sneer, *moue* (French), pout, simper, grin, facial distortion *or* contortion, wry face; see also **smile.**

expressionless, *mod.* —*Syn.* wooden, dull, vacuous; see **blank** 2.

expressive, *mod.* —*Syn.* eloquent, demonstrative, revealing, indicative, representative, dramatic, stirring, sympathetic, articulate, touching, significant, meaningful, pathetic, spirited, emphatic, strong, forcible, energetic, lively, tender, understanding, passionate, self-assured, artistic, ingenious, warm, masterly, colorful, vivid, picturesque, brilliant, showy, stimulating.—*Ant.* indifferent*, impassive, dead.

express oneself, *v.* —*Syn.* communicate, declare, enunciate; see **utter.**

expressway, *n.* —*Syn.* superhighway, freeway, turnpike; see **road** 1.

expropriate, *v.* —*Syn.* confiscate, deprive of property, dispossess; see **seize** 2.

expropriation, *n.* —*Syn.* confiscation, depriving of property, dispossession; see **removal** 1.

expulsion, *n.* —*Syn.* ejection, suspension, purge; see **removal** 1.

expunge, *v.* —*Syn.* erase, delete, efface; see **cancel** 1.

expurgate, *v.* —*Syn.* purify, cleanse, bowdlerize; see **censor.**

exquisite, *mod.* —*Syn.* fine, scrupulous, precise; see **dainty** 1.

extant, *mod.* —*Syn.* surviving, living, existent, existing, undestroyed, in existence, not lost, in current use.

extemporaneous, *mod.* —*Syn.* spontaneous, unpremeditated, improvised, extempore, extemporary, impromptu, unprepared, ad lib (D), offhand, unstudied, informal, unrehearsed, *ad hoc* (Latin), at first sight *or* thought *or* glance, by ear, on impulse, without preparation, off the cuff *or* elbow (D); see also **automatic** 1, 2, **immediate** 1, **immediately.**—*Ant.* prepared*, studied, premeditated.

extemporaneously, *mod.* —*Syn.* without preparation, spontaneously, on the spur of the moment (D); see **freely** 1, 2.

extempore, *mod.* —*Syn.* offhand, impromptu, unexpectedly; see **extemporaneous.**

extemporize, *v.* —*Syn.* improvise, ad lib, devise; see **invent** 1.

extend, *v.* **1.** [To make larger]—*Syn.* lengthen, enlarge, prolong; see **increase** 1.
2. [To occupy space to a given point]—*Syn.* continue, go as far as, spread; see **reach** 1.

extended, *mod.* **1.** [Outspread]—*Syn.* spread, widespread, expansive; see **outspread.**
2. [Very long]—*Syn.* elongated, drawn out, lengthened; see **long** 1.

extending, *mod.* —*Syn.* reaching, continuing, continuous, continual, perpetual, radiating, ranging, stretching, approaching, spreading, spanning, going on, running to, drawn out (to), lengthening; see also **endless** 1.

extension, *n.* **1.** [The action of continuing]—*Syn.* augmentation, enlargement, expansion; see **increase.**
2. [The quality of extending]—*Syn.* distance, width, size; see **length** 2.
3. [Something added]—*Syn.* section, branch, additional *or* second telephone; see **addition** 2.

extensive, *mod.* **1.** [Large in area]—*Syn.* wide, broad, long, great, huge, capacious, extended, protracted, expanded; see also **large** 1.
2. [Widespread]—*Syn.* general, unrestricted, boundless; see **widespread.**
3. [Comprehensive]—*Syn.* inclusive, comprising, unexclusive; see **comprehensive.**

extensively, *mod.* —*Syn.* widely, broadly, greatly; see **largely** 2.

extent, *n.* —*Syn.* degree, limit, span, space, area, measure, size, proportions, bulk, length, compass, scope, reach, sweep, amplitude, spaciousness, capaciousness, wideness, width, range, amount, expanse, magnitude, intensity; see also **breadth** 1, 2.

extenuate, *v.* —*Syn.* reduce, lessen, diminish, palliate, mitigate, qualify, apologize for; see also **decrease** 1, **excuse.**

extenuating circumstances, *n.* —*Syn.* extenuation, mitigation, uncontrollable situation, palliation, excuse.

extenuation, *n.* **1.** [An excuse]—*Syn.* apology, vindication, justification; see **explanation** 2.
2. [Reduction]—*Syn.* diminution, abatement, mitigation; see **reduction** 1.

exterior, *mod.* —*Syn.* outer, outlying, outermost; see **outside.**

exterior, *n.* —*Syn.* surface, covering, visible portion; see **outside** 1.

exterminate, *v.* —*Syn.* annihilate, eradicate, abolish; see **destroy** 1.

external, *mod.* —*Syn.* surface, visible, open to the air; see **obvious** 1.

externals, *n.* pl.—*Syn.* visible forms, façade, exterior; see **outside** 1.

extinct, *mod.* —*Syn.* dead, ended, terminated, exterminated, deceased, lost, without a survivor, vanquished, gone out, unknown, no longer known.

extinction, *n.* **1.** [Extinguishment]—*Syn.* quenching, drowning, putting *or* blotting out, darkening, snuffing, turning out *or* off.
2. [Annihilation]—*Syn.* abolition, extermination, extirpation; see **destruction** 1, **murder.**

extinguish, *v.* **1.** [To put out]—*Syn.* smother, choke, quench, douse, trample *or* put *or* blot *or* snuff *or* drown *or* blow out, stifle, switch *or* turn off, suffocate, put down.
2. [To destroy]—*Syn.* wipe out, annihilate, exterminate; see **destroy** 1.

extirpate, *v.* —*Syn.* exterminate, annihilate, abolish; see **destroy** 1.

extirpation, *n.* —*Syn.* extermination, extinction, annihilation; see **destruction** 1.

extol, *v.* —*Syn.* laud, exalt, acclaim, eulogize; see **praise** 1, **worship** 2.

extort, *v.* —*Syn.* extract, wrench, force; see **steal.**

extortion, *n.* —*Syn.* exaction, stealing, blackmail; see **theft.**

extortionate, *mod.* **1.** [Oppressive]—*Syn.* exacting, avaricious, rapacious; see **severe** 1, 2.
2. [Excessive]—*Syn.* exorbitant, extravagant, unreasonable; see **wasteful.**

extortionist, *n.* —*Syn.* thief, blackmailer, oppressor; see **criminal.**

extra, *mod.* —*Syn.* additional, in addition, other, one more, spare, reserve, surplus, supplemental, increased, another, new, fresh, auxiliary, added, besides, also, further, more, beyond, over and above, plus, supplementary, extraordinary, accessory, special, unused.—*Ant.* less*, short, subtracted.

extract, *n.* **1.** [An excerpt]—*Syn.* passage, citation, selection; see **quotation** 1.
2. [Essence]—*Syn.* distillation, infusion, decoction; see **essence** 3.

extract, *v.* **1.** [To remove]—*Syn.* extort, extricate, eradicate; see **remove** 1.
2. [To elicit]—*Syn.* evoke, derive, secure; see **obtain** 1.
3. [To cite]—*Syn.* excerpt, quote, select; see **cite** 2.

extraction, *n.* **1.** [One's personal or racial origin] —*Syn.* ancestry, parentage, race; see **family** 1.
2. [The pulling of a tooth]—*Syn.* elevation, toothdrawing, uprooting, removal, wrenching.

extradite, *v.* **1.** [To deliver by extradition]—*Syn.* release, surrender, give up; see **abandon** 1.
2. [To acquire by extradition]—*Syn.* obtain, apprehend, bring to justice *or* to trial; see **arrest** 1.

extraneous, *mod.* **1.** [Foreign]—*Syn.* extrinsic, external, exotic; see **foreign** 1.
2. [Irrelevant]—*Syn.* unessential, inappropriate, incidental; see **irrelevant.**

extraordinarily, *mod.* —*Syn.* remarkably, notably, peculiarly; see **very.**

extraordinary, *mod.* —*Syn.* remarkable, curious, amazing; see **unusual** 1.—*Ant.* usual, normal, ordinary.

extravagance, *n.* —*Syn.* lavishness, expenditures, improvidence; see **indulgence** 3, **waste** 1.

extravagant, *mod.* **1.** [Excessive]—*Syn.* inordinate, exaggerated, absurd; see **extreme** 2.
2. [Wasteful]—*Syn.* lavish, prodigal, immoderate; see **wasteful.**

extravagantly, *mod.* —*Syn.* expensively, beyond one's means, without restraint; see **rashly, wastefully.**

extravaganza, *n.* —*Syn.* caricature, divertissement, fantasy; see **parody** 1, 2, **show** 2.

extreme, *mod.* **1.** [The most remote]—*Syn.* utmost, final, ultimate; see **last** 1.
2. [Going beyond moderation and reason]—*Syn.* radical, intemperate, immoderate, imprudent, excessive, inordinate, immeasurable, profuse, extravagant, exorbitant, overkill, flagrant, outrageous, unreasonable, irrational, improper, fabulous, preposterous, abysmal, greatest, thorough, far, gross, out of proportion, absolute, fanatical, rabid, overzealous, desperate, severe, intense, strict, drastic, sheer, total, advanced, violent, sharp, acute, unseemly, beyond control, fantastic, to the extreme, nonsensical, unqualified, absurd, foolish, monstrous, unmitigated, hyperbolic, exaggerated; *all* (D): large, gonzo, almighty, tall, stiff, steep, out of bounds, at its height.—*Ant.* cautious, restrained*, moderate.

extreme, *n.* —*Syn.* height, apogee, apex; see **end** 4, **limit** 2.
go to extremes—*Syn.* be excessive *or* immoderate *or* careless, act rashly, fly apart; see **exceed.**
in the extreme—*Syn.* extremely, to the highest degree, inordinately; see **much** 1.

extremely, *mod.* —*Syn.* greatly, remarkably, notably; see **much** 1.

extremist, *mod.* —*Syn.* excessive, extreme, severe; see **radical** 2.

extremist, *n.* —*Syn.* zealot, fanatic, die-hard; see **agitator, radical.**

extremity, *n.* **1.** [The end]—*Syn.* the last, outside, most remote; see **end** 4, **limit** 2.
2. [A remote part of the body]—*Syn.* posterior, hand, foot, finger, toe, limb, end, backside; *all* (D): bottom, behind, hind end, fanny, dog, flipper, mitt, derrière, butt, can.

extricate, *v.* —*Syn.* disentangle, deliver, liberate; see **free** 1.

extrinsic, *mod.* —*Syn.* extraneous, external, outward; see **foreign** 1.

extrovert, *n.* —*Syn.* exhibitionist, show-off, other-directed individual, gregarious person, life of the party (D).

extrude, *v.* —*Syn.* force out, expel, project; see **eject** 1.

exuberance, *n.* **1.** [Plenty]—*Syn.* abundance, affluence, profusion; see **plenty.**
2. [Excessive ardor]—*Syn.* fervor, eagerness, exhilaration; see **enthusiasm** 1.

exuberant, *mod.* **1.** [Plentiful]—*Syn.* abundant, affluent, profuse; see **plentiful** 1, 2.
2. [Enthusiastic]—*Syn.* ardent, vivacious, passionate; see **enthusiastic** 3.

exude, *v.* —*Syn.* secrete, discharge, sweat; see **excrete.**

exult, *n.* **1.** [To give expression to satisfaction] —*Syn.* rejoice, make merry, cheer; see **celebrate** 1, 3.
2. [To boast triumphantly]—*Syn.* brag, bluster, bully; see **boast** 1.

exultant, *mod.* —*Syn.* exulting, elated, jubilant; see **triumphant.**

exultation, *n.* —*Syn.* rejoicing, triumph, elation; see **celebration** 1.

eye, *n.* **1.** [The organ of sight]—*Syn.* instrument of vision, eye speck, compound eye *or oculus* (Latin), simple eye *or ocellus* (Latin), naked eye, optic; *all* (D): orb, peeper, lamp.
Parts of the eye include the following—eyeball *or* ball, conjunctiva, pupil, retina, iris, cornea, ciliary body, eye muscles, optic nerve, aqueous humor, fovea, sclera, vitreous body, choroid, white, lens, optic nerve.
2. [Appreciation]—*Syn.* perception, taste, discrimination; see **appreciation** 3.
3. [A center]—*Syn.* focus, core, heart, kernel, nub; see **center** 1.
private eye (D)—*Syn.* detective, investigator, gumshoe (D); see **policeman.**
all eyes (D)—*Syn.* attentive, aware, perceptive; see **observant** 2.
an eye for an eye—*Syn.* punishment, retaliation, vengeance; see **revenge** 1.
catch one's eye—*Syn.* attract one's attention, cause notice, stand out; see **fascinate.**
easy on the eyes (D)—*Syn.* attractive, appealing, pleasant to look at; see **beautiful** 1.
feast one's eyes on (D)—*Syn.* look at with pleasure, be attracted to, watch with delight; see **watch** 1.
give a person the eye (D)—*Syn.* attract, charm, invite; see **seduce.**
have an eye for—*Syn.* appreciate, be interested in, desire; see **want** 1.
have an eye to—*Syn.* watch (out) for, be mindful of, attend to; see **watch out** 1.
have eyes for—*Syn.* appreciate, be interested in, desire; see **want** 1.
in a pig's eye (D)—*Syn.* under no circumstances, impossible, no way; see **never.**
in the public eye—*Syn.* well-known, renowned, celebrated; see **famous.**
keep an eye on—*Syn.* look after, watch over, protect; see **guard** 2.
keep an eye out for (D)—*Syn.* watch for, be mindful of, attend to; see **watch out** 1.
keep one's eyes open (*or* **peeled** *or* **skinned**) (D) —*Syn.* be aware, regard, look out; see **watch** 1.
lay eyes on (D)—*Syn.* look at, stare, survey; see **see** 1.
make eyes at—*Syn.* attract, charm, invite; see **seduce.**
my eye! (D)—*Syn.* the hell! (D), ridiculous, impossible; see **never, no.**
open one's eyes—*Syn.* make aware, inform, apprise; see **tell** 1.
run one's eyes over (D)—*Syn.* scan, skim, glance at; see **see** 1.

see with half an eye (D)—*Syn.* comprehend, perceive, see; see **understand** 1.

shut one's eyes to—*Syn.* refuse, reject, ignore; see **shun.**

with an eye to—*Syn.* considering, mindful of, aware of; see **observant** 1, 2.

eye doctor, *n.*—*Syn.* optometrist, oculist, ophthalmologist; see **doctor** 1.

eyeless, *mod.*—*Syn.* unseeing, sightless, blinded; see **blind** 1.

eyelet, *n.*—*Syn.* opening, aperture, perforation; see **hole** 1.

eye of a needle, *n.*—*Syn.* opening, aperture, orifice; see **hole** 1.

eyesight, *n.*—*Syn.* vision, sense of seeing, visual perception; see **sight** 1.

eyesore, *n.*—*Syn.* ugly thing, distortion, deformity; see **ugliness.**

eyewitness, *n.*—*Syn.* onlooker, passer-by, observer; see **witness.**

F

Fabian, *mod.* —*Syn.* procrastinating, deliberating, delaying; see **slow** 2.
fable, *n.* —*Syn.* allegory, tale, parable; see **story.**
fabled, *mod.* —*Syn.* mythical, fanciful, legendary, unreal, mythological; see **legendary** 1.
fabric, *n.* **1.** [Material]—*Syn.* textile, stuff, material; see **cloth**
2. [Structure or framework]—*Syn.* structure, framework, substance; see **frame** 1, **material** 2.
fabricate, *v.* **1.** [To construct]—*Syn.* erect, make, form; see **build** 1, **manufacture** 1.
2. [To misrepresent]—*Syn.* make up, contrive, prevaricate; see **invent** 2.
3. [To assemble]—*Syn.* put *or* fit *or* piece together, compose, join; see **assemble** 3.
fabrication, *n.* —*Syn.* invention, untruth, fib; see **lie** 1.
fabulous, *mod.* **1.** [Suggestive of a fable]—*Syn.* false, apocryphal, mythical; see **legendary** 2.
2. [Unbelievable]—*Syn.* remarkable, amazing, immense; see **unusual** 1.
façade, *n.* —*Syn.* face, appearance, look; see **front** 4.
face, *n.* **1.** [The front of the head]—*Syn.* visage, countenance, appearance, feature, lineaments, silhouette, profile, physiognomy, front; *all* (D): map, mug, pan, puss.
2. [Bold or inconsiderate conduct]—*Syn.* effrontery, impudence, impertinence; see **rudeness.**
3. [A plane surface]—*Syn.* front, surface, finish; see **plane** 1.
4. [Prestige]—*Syn.* status, standing, social position; see **reputation** 2.
5. [Appearance]—*Syn.* light, aspect, presentation; see **appearance** 1.
fly in the face of—*Syn.* defy, rebel against, disobey; see **dare** 2.
make a face—*Syn.* distort one's face, grimace, scowl; see **frown.**
on the face of it—*Syn.* to all appearances, seemingly, according to the evidence; see **apparently.**
pull (or wear) a long face (D)—*Syn.* look sad, scowl, pout; see **frown.**
set one's face against—*Syn.* oppose, be determined, set oneself against; see **fight** 1, 2, **resist** 1.
show one's face—*Syn.* be seen, show up, come; see **appear** 1, 3.
to one's face—*Syn.* candidly, openly, frankly; see **boldly** 1.
face, *v.* **1.** [To confront conflict or trouble]—*Syn.* confront, oppose, defy, meet, dare, brave, challenge, withstand, beard, court, encounter, risk, put *or* set before, buck (up), tolerate, endure, sustain, suffer, bear, throw *or* cast in one's teeth, tell to one's face, show a bold front, make a stand, meet face to face, grapple with, stand at bay, cope with, brook, allow, stand, submit, abide, countenance; *all* (D): go up against, swallow, stomach, take (it), bell the cat.—*Ant.* evade*, elude, shun.
2. [To put a face on a building]—*Syn.* refinish, front, decorate, put a surface on, dress, smooth the surface of, polish, level, redecorate, remodel, brick over, cover, shingle, plaster, veneer.
3. [To put facing on goods]—*Syn.* bind, trim, hem, back, pipe, tuck, overlay, fold, bias.
4. [To look out on]—*Syn.* front (toward), border, be turned toward, lie with the front toward.
faced, *mod.* —*Syn.* plated, covered, filmed; see **finished** 2.
face lifting, *n.* —*Syn.* plastic surgery, facial, lift, face-lift.
facet, *n.* —*Syn.* aspect, face, side; see **phase, plane** 1.
facetious, *mod.* —*Syn.* jocular, jocose, humorous, jocund, waggish, jesting, sportive, sprightly, gay, witty, merry, pleasant, comical, droll, laughable, clever, ludicrous, farcical, whimsical, fanciful, foolish, smart, bantering, pert, light, irreverent, quippish, joking, playful, quizzical, conceited, dry, wry, salty, sarcastic, ironic, satirical, quibbling, trifling, punning, epigrammatic, capering, indecorous, ridiculous, jolly, flippant; *all* (D): flip, kidding, joshing, wisecracking, pulling one's leg, putting one on; see also **funny** 1.
face to face, *mod.* —*Syn.* eye to eye, cheek by jowl, facing; see **confronting.**
facial (D), *n.* —*Syn.* (facial) massage, facial treatment, beauty treatment, mud pack, oatmeal mask, face mask.
facile, *mod.* **1.** [Easy]—*Syn.* simple, obvious, apparent; see **easy** 2.
2. [Skillful]—*Syn.* skilled, practiced, accomplished; see **able** 1, 2.
facilitate, *v.* —*Syn.* promote, aid, make easy, simplify; see **help** 1.
facility, *n.* **1.** [Easy skillfulness]—*Syn.* dexterity, adroitness, ease; see **ability** 2.
2. [Material; *usually plural*]—*Syn.* tools, plant, buildings; see **equipment.**
3. [Agency; *usually plural*]—*Syn.* department, bureau, company; see **office** 3.
facing, *n.* **1.** [An architectural finish]—*Syn.* surface, revetment, covering, front, false front.
Facings include the following—concrete, stucco, brick, tile, glass, stone, plaster, whitewash, shingle, veneer, shiplap, marble.
2. [Finish for dress goods]—*Syn.* appliqué, backing, embroidery, hem, piping, tucks, braid, folds, bias, overlay, trim, binding.

facsimile, *n.* —*Syn.* duplicate, reproduction, mirror; see **copy.**

fact, *n.* **1.** [A reliable generality]—*Syn.* certainty, truth, substantiality; appearance, palpability, experience, matter, the very thing, not an illusion, *fait accompli* (French), what has really happened, something concrete, what is the case, anything strictly true, matter of fact, real existence, intelligence, hard evidence, actuality, *nuda veritas* (Latin), verity, naked truth, gospel, certitude, scripture, reality, law, solidity, permanence, stability, basis, physical reality, (corporeal) existence, state of being; *all* (D): dope, low-down, what's what, hard facts, straight dope, scene, the case.—*Ant.* fancy*, fiction, imagination.

2. [An individual reality]—*Syn.* circumstance, detail, factor, case, consideration, datum, evidence, event, action, deed, happening, occurrence, creation, conception, manifestation, being, entity, experience, affair, act, episode, performance, proceeding, phenomenon, incident, thing done, adventure, transaction, organism, construction, truism, plain fact, accomplishment, accomplished fact, *fait accompli* (French).—*Ant.* error*, illusion, untruth.

as a matter of fact—*Syn.* in reality, in fact, actually; see **really** 1.

in point of fact—*Syn.* actually, factually, in reality; see **really** 1.

faction, *n.* **1.** [An organized group]—*Syn.* cabal, combine, party, conspiracy, plot, gang, crew, wing, block, claque, junta, clique, conclave, intrigue, splinter party, design, set, clan, club, lobby, camp, inner circle, sect, coterie, partnership, cell, unit, mob, Mafia, side, camarilla, machine, tong, band, pressure group, team, machine, ring, knot, circle, concern, guild, Black Hand, Camorra, schism, entente; *all* (D): outfit, crowd, in group, bunch.

2. [Tendency to break into warring groups]—*Syn.* dissension, quarrelsomeness, disunity; see **disagreement** 1.

factious, *mod.* —*Syn.* dissident, seditious, hostile; see **opposing** 1.

factitious, *mod.* —*Syn.* unnatural, false, artificial; see **affected** 2.

factor, *n.* **1.** [A component part]—*Syn.* portion, constituent, determinant; see **part** 1, 3.

2. [A manager]—*Syn.* agent, steward, representative; see **administrator.**

factory, *n.* —*Syn.* manufactory, plant, branch, shop, industry, workshop, machine shop, mill, laboratory, assembly plant, manufacturing plant *or* establishment, foundry, forge, loom, mint, carpenter shop, brewery, sawmill, supply house, warehouse, sweatshop, guild, co-operative, processing plant, works, workroom, firm, packing plant, outfitters, equipment makers, layout (D).

factotum, *n.* —*Syn.* jack-of-all-trades, eager beaver (D), handy man; see **man-of-all-work.**

facts, *n.* —*Syn.* reality, certainty, actuality, data, information; *both* (D): the score, the low-down.

factual, *mod.* —*Syn.* exact, specific, descriptive; see **accurate** 1.

faculty, *n.* **1.** [A peculiar aptitude]—*Syn.* peculiarity, strength, forte; see **ability** 1.

2. [A group of specialists, usually engaged in instruction or research]—*Syn.* staff, trained people, teachers, research workers, personnel, instructors, employees, university, college, institute, department, teaching *or* instructional *or* research staff *or* personnel, teaching assistants, body of professors, professorate, clinic, society, body, organization, literati, corps, instructional corps, mentors, professors, assistant professors, associate professors, docents, tutors, functionaries, foundation, department, advocates, pedagogues, lecturers, monitors, advisers, masters, scholars, proficients, adepts, dons, fellows; *all* (D): TA's, ABD's, profs, spielers.

fad, *n.* —*Syn.* affectation, fancy, sport, caprice, whim, style, freak, craze, hobby, cry, innovation, custom, amusement, fashion, humor, vagary, fit, *dernier cri* (French), crotchet, prank, maggot, quirk, kink, flimflam, escapade, eccentricity, temporary fashion, popular innovation, vogue, prevailing taste, frivolity, fantasy, whimsy, passing fancy; *all* (D): latest word, (all the) rage, the (latest) thing, the in thing, the last word, the new look, the go, in joke, fluke, wheeze, fool notion.—*Ant.* custom*, convention, practice.

fade, *v.* **1.** [To lose color or light]—*Syn.* bleach, tone down, wash out, decolorize, become colorless, blanch, tarnish, dim, discolor, pale, grow dim, flicker, neutralize, become dull, lose brightness *or* luster *or* color, achromatize, etiolate.—*Ant.* color, brighten, glow.

2. [To diminish in sound]—*Syn.* hush, quiet, sink; see **decrease** 1.

3. [To lose character]—*Syn.* evaporate, dissolve, disperse; see **disappear.**

faded, *mod.* —*Syn.* used, bleached, shopworn; see **dull** 2.

fading, *mod.* —*Syn.* declining, paling, growing dimmer; see **evanescent, hazy** 1, **obscure** 1, **temporary.**

fail, *v.* **1.** [To be unsuccessful]—*Syn.* miscarry, fall short, miss, back out, abandon, desert, funk, leave, neglect, slip, make nothing of, lose one's labor, lose ground, come to naught *or* nothing, falter, flounder, blunder, break down, run aground, founder, come to grief, get into trouble, abort, fault, backslide, come down, be demoted, lose status, play into, fall flat *or* through, go amiss, be all over with, go astray, fall down *or* away, get left, be heading for a fall, let onself go, be found lacking, go down, go under, go up, hit a slump, not hold a candle to, fall to the ground, miss an opportunity, fold up, go on the rocks, not have it in one, miss the boat, not measure up (to expectation), lose out, give out, break one's word, come *or* fall short of, not make the grade, miss the mark, lose control, fall down on the job, go wrong; *all* (D): fall from one's high estate, bite *or* lick the dust, be out of it, blow the chance, kick the beam, flat out, fizzle out, go belly up, bite the hand that feeds you, hit rock bottom, buffet the waves, crap out, go down the tubes, go down swinging, back the wrong horse, bark up the wrong tree, end or go up in smoke, bomb, not get to first base, touch bottom, get hung up *or* bogged down, flunk, flop, lay an egg, get left, come a cropper, conk out, peter out.—*Ant.* succeed, win*, triumph.

2. [To prove unsatisfactory]—*Syn.* lose out, come short of, displease; see **disappoint.**

3. [To grow less]—*Syn.* lessen, worsen, sink; see **decay.**

4. [To become insolvent]—*Syn.* go bankrupt, default, defalcate, dishonor, repudiate, be in arrears, overdraw, go out of business, default on payment; *all* (D): go to the wall, throw in the sponge, be unable to make both ends meet, go under, drown in red ink, crash, go broke, go belly up, go down the tubes, lose one's shirt.—*Ant.* prosper*, gain, thrive.

5. [To dismiss for failure]—*Syn.* send home, dismiss, suspend, probate, put on (academic or social) probation; *both* (D): flunk, send down.

without fail—*Syn.* constantly, dependably, reliably; see **regularly.**

failing, *mod.*—*Syn.* declining, feeble, faint; see **weak** 1.

fail-safe (D), *mod.*—*Syn.* safety, emergency, safeguarding; see **protective.**

fail-safe design, *n.*—*Syn.* (built-in) emergency *or* protective *or* safety provisions *or* equipment *or* devices *or* features, last resort.

fail-safe device, *n.*—*Syn.* (automatic) safety *or* emergency equipment *or* device *or* provision, last resort; see also **device.**

failure, *n.* **1.** [An unsuccessful attempt]—*Syn.* fiasco, misadventure, nonperformance, abortion, bankruptcy, nonsuccess, dead failure, miscarriage, labor in vain, frustration, misstep, faux pas, breakdown, checkmate, stoppage, collapse, rupture, defeat, overthrow, downfall, implosion, breakdown in communication, total loss, stalemate; *all* (D): no go, flop, turkey, clinker, loser, bust, dud, washout, dog, bomb, bummer, lead balloon, lemon, flash in the pan, slip 'twixt the cup and the lip, botch, bungle, false step, losing game, rout, sinking ship, sleeveless errand, louse-up, mess.—*Ant.* success*, accomplishment, triumph.

2. [An unsuccessful person]—*Syn.* no-good, incompetent, defaulter, nonperformer, underachiever, ne'er-do-well, scapegrace, prodigal, bankrupt, derelict, castaway, beachcomber, ski bum; *all* (D): flunker, born loser, turkey, dead duck, fizzle, has-been, also-ran, lemon, flop, bum, dud. —*Ant.* success*, veteran, star.

faint, *mod.* **1.** [Having little physical strength] —*Syn.* faltering, enervated, dizzy; see **weak** 1.

2. [Having little light or color]—*Syn.* vague, thin, hazy; see **dull** 2.

3. [Having little volume of sound]—*Syn.* whispered, breathless, murmuring, inaudible, indistinct, low, stifled, dull, muted, hoarse, muttering, soft, soothing, bated, heard in the distance, quiet, low-pitched, low-toned, muffled, hushed, padded, distant, subdued, gentle, softened, from afar, moderate, grave, deep, deadened, rumbling, heavy, far-off, flat, faint and far, aside, between the teeth, floating on the air, dulcet, imperceptible, out of earshot.—*Ant.* loud*, audible, raucous.

faint, *n.*—*Syn.* unconsciousness, coma, insensibility; see **stupor.**

faint, *v.*—*Syn.* lose consciousness, become unconscious, be overcome, swoon, fall, go into a coma, have a stroke, suffer syncope, faint away, drop, collapse, succumb, suffer sunstroke; *all* (D): pass out, go out like a light, keel over, black out, freak out. —*Ant.* recover*, awaken, come to.

fainthearted, *mod.*—*Syn.* irresolute, halfhearted, weak; see **weak** 3, **cowardly.**

fair, *mod.* **1.** [Just]—*Syn.* forthright, impartial, plain, scrupulous, upright, amiable, candid, generous, frank, open, sincere, manly, straightforward, honest, lawful, clean, legitimate, decent, honorable, virtuous, righteous, temperate, pious, godly, unbiased, reasonable, civil, courteous, blameless, sterling, uncorrupted, square, equitable, fair-minded, dispassionate, uncolored, objective, unprejudiced, evenhanded, good, handsome, principled, dutiful, moderate, beneficial, praiseworthy, respectable, benevolent, above-board, tried, trustworthy, meet, due, fit, appropriate, regular, orderly; *all* (D): on the level, on the up-and-up, fair and square, straight, leaning over backward, giving the devil his due.—*Ant.* unfair*, unjust, biased.

2. [Moderately satisfactory]—*Syn.* average, pretty good, not bad, up to standard, ordinary, mediocre, medium, unsual, common, all right, commonplace; *all* (D): fairish, betwixt and between, fair to middling, so-so, O.K., medium good, just fair; see also **common** 1.—*Ant.* poor*, bad, unsatisfactory.

3. [Not stormy or likely to storm]—*Syn.* clear, pleasant, sunny, bright, unclouded, calm, placid, tranquil, unthreatening, favorable, balmy, mild, smiling.—*Ant.* stormy*, threatening, overcast.

4. [Of light complexion]—*Syn.* blond, light colored *or* complexioned, pallid, pale, sallow, white, bleached, white-skinned, milky, flaxen, fair-haired, argent, snow-white, snowy, chalky, silvery, whitish, pearly, blanched, light, lily-white, ivory-white, faded, neutral, colorless; *all* (D): platinum blonde, peroxide blonde, bleached blonde, whey-faced, pale-faced, white as a sheet *or* as the driven snow. —*Ant.* dark*, brunet, black.

5. [Personally attractive]—*Syn.* lovely, charming, beauteous; see **beautiful** 2.

fair, *n.*—*Syn.* exposition, county *or* state *or* world fair, carnival, bazaar, exhibition, mart, display, festival, market, bourse, staple, exchange, spectacle, centennial, observance, celebration, occasion, Donnybrook Fair.

fairground, *n.*—*Syn.* enclosure, coliseum, race track, racecourse, exhibition place, fairway, concourse, place, rink, booth, stall, midway, exposition, show ring.

fairly, *mod.* **1.** [In a just manner]—*Syn.* honestly, reasonably, honorably; see **justly** 1.

2. [A qualifying word]—*Syn.* somewhat, moderately, reasonably; see **adequately** 2.

fairness, *n.*—*Syn.* decency, honesty, probity, rectitude, uprightness, truth, integrity, charity, charitableness, impartiality, justice, veracity, tolerance, right, candor, honor, moderation, civility, consideration, good faith, decorum, propriety, courtesy, reasonableness, rationality, humanity, rightness, equity, equitableness, righteousness, justness, goodness, seemliness, full measure, measure for measure, suitability, give and take, even-handedness, disinterestedness, fair-mindedness, open-mindedness, just dealing, good sense, fair treatment, even-handed justice, due, accuracy, scrupulousness, exactitude, merit, rationality, detachment, correctness, punctilio, virtue, benignity, benevolence, duty, dutifulness, seeing justice done, legitimacy, legality, rightfulness, lawfulness, straightforwardness, blamelessness, respectability, praiseworthiness, niceness, plain dealing, right doing; *all* (D): giving the devil his due, square deal, fair play, fair shake, square dealing, straight shooting, doing right by, a fair field and no favor, the handsome thing.—*Ant.* injustice*, unfairness, partiality.

fair-spoken, *mod.* —*Syn.* civil, courteous, well-spoken; see **refined** 2.

fairy, *n.* —*Syn.* spirit, sprite, fay, good fairy, elf, goblin, hobgoblin, dryad, hamadryad, oread, maenad, nymph, bacchante, naiad, pixy, mermaid, nereid, nixie, kelpie, sylph, siren, bogie, genie, jinni, puck, imp, enchantress, witch, warlock, banshee, werewolf, ogre, ogress, Ariel, Robin Goodfellow, demon, daemon, daeva, succubus, devil, vampire, *lamia* (Greek), ghoul, harpy, Lorelei, siren, Circe, demiurge, familiar, brownie, flibbertigibbet, poltergeist, troll, gnome, coltpixie, leprechaun, kobold, ouphe, will-o'-the-wisp, visitant, afrit, barghest, peri, satyr, faun, fiend, White Lady, Norn, Fate, Weird Sister; see also **ghost** 1.

fairyland, *n.* —*Syn.* land of fay, dreamland, cloudland, happy valley, castles in the air, Utopia, Shangri-La, Atlantis, Land of Prester John, Kingdom of Micomicon, land of make-believe, daydream, East o' the Sun and West o' the Moon, the valley of the moon, Avalon, elfland, faerie.

fairy tale, *n.* —*Syn.* folk tale, children's story, romance; see **story.**

faith, *n.* **1.** [Complete trust]—*Syn.* confidence, trust, credence, credit, assurance, acceptance, troth, dependence, conviction, sureness, fidelity, loyalty, certainty, surety, allegiance, assent, credulity, certitude, reliance.—*Ant.* doubt*, suspicion, distrust.

2. [A formal system of beliefs]—*Syn.* creed, doctrine, dogma, tenet, revelation, credo, gospel, profession, confession, conviction, canon, principle, piety, church, orthodoxy, worship, theism, teaching, theology, doxy, decalogue, denomination, cult, sect. For specific faiths; see **church** 3, **religion** 2.

bad faith—*Syn.* insincerity, duplicity, infidelity; see **dishonest.**

break faith—*Syn.* be disloyal, abandon, fail; see **betray.**

good faith—*Syn.* sincerity, honor, trustworthiness; see **honesty** 1.

in faith—*Syn.* indeed, in fact, in reality; see **really** 1.

keep faith—*Syn.* be loyal, adhere, follow; see **support** 2.

faithful, *mod.* —*Syn.* loyal, trusting, confiding, constant, devoted (to), true, patriotic, trusty, dutiful, trustworthy, reliable, genuine, dependable, incorruptible, firm in adherence, straight, honest, upright, honorable, scrupulous, firm, circumspect, sure, unswerving, conscientious, unwavering, enduring, unchanging, steady, staunch, attached, obedient, steadfast, sincere, veracious, resolute; *all* (D): hard-core, true as steel, on the level, tried and true, at the feet of.—*Ant.* fickle*, false*, faithless.

faithful, *n.* —*Syn.* adherents of a faith, loyal members of a church, believers, true believers, belonging to "the Faith", the saved, the believing, the children of God.

faithfully, *mod.* **1.** [Loyally]—*Syn.* trustingly, conscientiously, truly; see **loyally.**

2. [Always]—*Syn.* patiently, constantly, forever; see **regular** 3.

faithfulness, *n.* —*Syn.* trustworthiness, care, duty; see **devotion.**

faithless, *mod.* **1.** [Perfidious]—*Syn.* disloyal, deceitful, unreliable; see **dishonest** 1, 2.

2. [Unbelieving]—*Syn.* agnostic, skeptical, dubious; see **atheistic.**

faithlessness, *n.* **1.** [Doubt]—*Syn.* skepticism, disbelief, agnosticism; see **doubt** 1.

2. [Disloyalty]—*Syn.* perfidy, fraud, treachery; see **dishonesty, treason.**

fake (D), *mod.* —*Syn.* pretended, fraudulent, bogus; see **false** 3.

fake, *n.* —*Syn.* deception, counterfeit, sham, copy, cheat, imitation, charlatan, fraud, make-believe, pretense, fabrication, forgery, cheat, imposition, humbug, sleight, trick, swindle, stratagem; *all* (D): phony, gyp, spoof, plant, suck-in hocum, bunk, gold brick, put-on, scam, flimflam.—*Ant.* fact*, original, reality.

fake, *v.* —*Syn.* feign, simulate, disguise; see **pretend** 1.

fakir, *n.* —*Syn.* holy beggar, yogi, mendicant; see **ascetic.**

fall, *n.* **1.** [The act of falling]—*Syn.* drop, decline, lapse, collapse, breakdown, tumble, spill, downfall, abasement, overthrow, diminution, defeat, degradation, humiliation, descent, plunge, slump, subsidence, recession, ebb, abatement; *both* (D): slip, flop.—*Ant.* rise*, elevation, ascent.

2. [Capture]—*Syn.* capitulation, loss, ruin; see **destruction** 2.

3. [A mishap]—*Syn.* tumble, drop, roll; see **disaster.**

4. [That which falls]—*Syn.* rainfall, snowfall, precipitation, snow, rain, hail, sleet, blanket, carpet, covering, one *or* two *or* three, etc., inches of snow *or* rain.

5. [The season after summer]—*Syn.* autumn, the sere and yellow leaf, the fall of the year, harvest, September, October, November, harvest time, "when the frost is on the punkin' and the fodder's in the shock."

6. [A waterfall]—*Syn.* cascade, force, cataract; see **waterfall.**

fall, *n.* [*With* the]—*Syn.* original sin, transgression, error; see **sin.**

ride for a fall (D)—*Syn.* endanger oneself, take risks *or* chances, act indiscreetly; see **risk** 1.

fall, *v.* **1.** [To pass quickly downward]—*Syn.* sink, topple, drop, settle, droop, stumble, trip, plunge, tumble, descend, lower, totter, break down, cave in, make a forced landing, decline, subside, collapse, buckle, regress, lapse, drop down, pitch, gravitate, come down suddenly, be precipitated, fall down *or* flat, fall in, descend upon, fold up, keel over, tip over, slope, slip, recede, relapse, abate, ebb, diminish; *all* (D): spin in, backslide, flop, take a spill, buffet the waves.—*Syn.* rise*, ascend, climb.

2. [To be overthrown]—*Syn.* submit, yield, surrender, succumb, be destroyed, be taken, pass into enemy hands, bend, defer to, obey, lie down, resign, capitulate; *all* (D): back down, eat gravel, get one's come-uppance, fall to pieces, break up. —*Ant.* prevail, endure*, resist.
3. [To die in battle]—*Syn.* go down, slump, drop; see **die** 1.
4. [To occur]—*Syn.* arrive, take place, befall; see **happen** 2.
fall in love (with), *v.* —*Syn.* become enamored (of), lose one's heart (to), take a fancy *or* liking to, have eyes for, become attached to *or* fond of, fancy, favor; see also **love** 1.

fallacious, *mod.* —*Syn.* deceptive, misleading, fradulent; see **false** 2.

fallacy, *n.* **1.** [An error in reasoning]—*Syn.* inconsistency, sophism, sophistry, casuistry, quibble, quibbling, evasion, deceit, deception, delusion, equivocation, subterfuge, Jesuitry, misinterpretation, erroneousness, inexactness, deviation from truth, perversion, bias, prejudice, preconception, *non sequitur* (Latin), deceptive belief, deceptiveness, aberration, false *or* misleading appearance *or* notion, illusion, speciousness, equivoke, artifice, ambiguity, solecism, paradox, miscalculation, quirk, flaw, cavil, illogicality, irrelevancy, erratum, invalidity, heresy, heterodoxy.—*Ant.* theory*, logic*, reason*, law*.
2. [An ignorant misconception]—*Syn.* delusion, deceit; see **error** 1.

fall asleep, *v.* —*Syn.* go to sleep, doze, drop off (D); see **sleep.**

fall away, *v.* —*Syn.* pine, die, decline; see **decay.**

fall back, *v.* —*Syn.* yield, recede, surrender; see **retreat** 2.

fallen, *mod.* —*Syn.* sinful, shamed, shameless; see **disgraced.**

fall for (D), *v.* —*Syn.* become infatuated, desire, flip over (D); see **love** 1.

fall foul of, *v.* —*Syn.* encounter, differ with, have trouble with; see **flight** 1, 2.

fallibility, *n.* —*Syn.* imperfection, misjudgment, frailty; see **uncertainty** 2.

fallible, *mod.* —*Syn.* deceptive, frail, imperfect, ignorant, uncertain, erring, unpredictable, unreliable, in question, liable to be erroneous, liable to mistake, prone to be inaccurate, prone to error, human, untrustworthy, questionable; see also **human.**

fall in, *v.* —*Syn.* get into line, form ranks, take a place; see **line up.**

falling, *mod.* —*Syn.* dropping, sinking, descending, plunging, slipping, sliding, declining, lowering, settling, toppling, tumbling, tottering, diminishing, weakening, decreasing, abating, ebbing, subsiding, collapsing, crumbling, perishing, dying.—*Ant.* increasing*, improving, mounting.

fall in love, *v.* —*Syn.* become enamoured, lose one's heart, take a fancy to, have eyes for, take a liking to, become attached to, become fond of (someone), fancy.

fall off, *v.* —*Syn.* decline, lessen, wane; see **decrease** 1.

fall on, *v.* **1.** [To attack]—*Syn.* assault, battle, descend upon; see **attack** 1, 2.
2. [(D) To discover]—*Syn.* meet, find, recognize; see **discover** 1.

fallout, *n.* —*Syn.* radioactivity, radioactive dust *or* debris *or* waste, byproduct of atomic *or* thermonuclear explosion.

fall out, *v.* **1.** [To quarrel]—*Syn.* argue, disagree, fight; see **quarrel.**
2. [To happen]—*Syn.* result, befall, occur; see **happen** 2.

fallow, *mod.* **1.** [Uncultivated]—*Syn.* untilled, unsowed, neglected, unplowed, unseeded, unplanted, unsowed, unproductive; see also **unused** 1.
2. [Idle]—*Syn.* inert, inactive, dormant; see **idle** 1.

fall short, *v.* —*Syn.* fail, be deficient, be lacking; see **need.**

fall to, *v.* —*Syn.* set about, start, undertake; see **begin** 2.

false, *mod.* **1.** [*Said of persons*]—*Syn.* perfidious, villainous, treasonable, faithless, treacherous, unfaithful, disloyal, dishonest, lying, base, foul, hypocritical, double-dealing, knavish, roguish, malevolent, rascally, scoundrelly, mean, malicious, venal, deceitful, underhanded, corrupt, forsworn, wicked, unscrupulous, untrustworthy, falsehearted, dishonorable, canting, two-faced (D); see senses 2, 3. —*Ant.* faithful*, true, honorable.
2. [*Said of statements or supposed facts*]—*Syn.* untrue, spurious, apocryphal, fanciful, lying, mendacious, untruthful, fictitious, deceptive, concocted, fallacious, incorrect, sophistical, casuistic, Jesuitical, misleading, delusive, imaginary, illusive, erroneous, invalid, inaccurate, deceiving, misrepresentative, fraudulent, trumped up; *both* (D): fishy, cooked-up; see senses 1, 3.—*Ant.* accurate*, correct, established.
3. [*Said of things*]—*Syn.* sham, counterfeit, fabricated, manufactured, synthetic, factitious, bogus, spurious, make-believe, assumed, unreal, copied, forged, pretended, faked, made-up, simulated, lifeless, pseudo, hollow, mock, feigned, bastard, base, alloyed, artificial, contrived, colored, disguised, deceptive, adulterated, plated, so-called, meretricious; *all* (D): fake, ersatz, phony, gyp, catchpenny, bum, shoddy, snide, false-colored, queer, not what it's cracked up to be; see senses 1, 2. —*Ant.* real*, genuine, authentic.
play (a person) false—*Syn.* cheat, trick, betray; see **deceive.**
put in a false position—*Syn.* misrepresent, embarrass, misquote; see **betray, mistake.**

falsehood, *n.* —*Syn.* equivocation, prevarication, story; see **lie** 1.

falsely, *mod.* —*Syn.* traitorously, treacherously, deceitfully, foully, faithlessly, falseheartedly, behind one's back, disloyally, underhandedly, basely, maliciously, malevolently, unfaithfully, perfidiously, dishonestly, unscrupulously, roguishly, knavishly, under the garb of, dishonorably, crookedly (D). —*Ant.* truly*, justly*, honorably.

falsetto, *n.* —*Syn.* artificially high-pitched voice, *voce di testa* (Italian), unnatural register, shrillness, affection; see also **pretense** 2.

falsify, *v.* —*Syn.* adulterate, counterfeit, misrepresent; see **deceive.**

falter, *v.* —*Syn.* waver, fluctuate, be undecided; see **hesitate.**

fame, *n.* **1.** [Illustrious and widespread reputation] —*Syn.* renown, glory, distinction, eminence, honor, celebrity, esteem, name, estimation, public esteem, *aura popularis* (Latin), credit, note, greatness, dignity, rank, account, luster, splendor, position, standing, pre-eminence, one's hour in the sun, superiority, exaltation, regard, laurels, elevation, character, nobility, majesty, station, place, degree, popularity, public favor; *both* (D): kudos, rep. —*Ant.* oblivion*, obscurity, contempt.
2. [Report]—*Syn.* reputation, rumor, repute, notoriety, hearsay, talk, common knowledge, opinion, bruit.

familiar, *mod.* **1.** [Commonly known]—*Syn.* everyday, well-known, customary, frequent, homely, humble, usual, intimate, habitual, accustomed, common, ordinary, informal, unceremonious, plain, simple, matter-of-fact, workaday, prosaic, commonplace, homespun, natural, native, unsophisticated, unvarnished; *both* (D): old hat, garden variety.—*Ant.* unusual*, exotic, strange.
2. [Intimate]—*Syn.* gracious, courteous, easy; see **intimate** 1.

familiarity, *n.* **1.** [Acquaintance with people] —*Syn.* friendliness, acquaintanceship, fellowship; see **friendship** 1, 2.
2. [Acquaintance with things]—*Syn.* sense of use, the feel of, being at home with, thorough knowledge, cognition, comprehension; see also **awareness, experience** 3.

familiarize (oneself with), *v.* —*Syn.* acquaint, accustom, habituate, enlighten, become adept in, make the acquaintance of, get acquainted (with), gain the friendship of, make friends (with), awaken to, inure, come to know, become aware of, get in (D).

familiar with, *mod.* —*Syn.* well-acquainted with, acquainted with, aware of, introduced, informed of, on speaking terms (with), having some connections, cognizant of, attuned to.—*Ant.* unacquainted, unaware*, unknown.

family, *mod.* —*Syn.* kindred, common, tribal; see **group.**

family, *n.* **1.** [Blood relatives]—*Syn.* kin, folk, clan, relationship, relations, tribe, dynasty, breed, house, kith and kin, blood, blood tie, progeny, offspring, descendants, antecedents, forebears, heirs and assigns, brethren, generations, race, ancestry, progenitors, pedigree, genealogy, descent, parentage, extraction, patrimony, paternity, inheritance, former generations, kinsmen, kinship, lineage, line, one's own flesh and blood, strain, siblings, clone; *all* (D): in-laws, the whole tribe, homefolks, whole famdamily, people.
2. [Several of one kind]—*Syn.* order, class, genus, species, subdivision; see also **collection** 2.
in a family way (D)—*Syn.* with child, (about) to give birth, going to have a baby; see **pregnant** 1.

famine, *n.* —*Syn.* starvation, want, misery; see **hunger.**

famish, *v.* **1.** [To kill]—*Syn.* starve, stint, withhold; see **kill** 1.
2. [To die]—*Syn.* starve to death, perish from hunger, die from lack of food; see **die** 1.

famished, *mod.* —*Syn.* starving, hungering, starved; see **hungry.**

famous, *mod.* —*Syn.* eminent, brilliant, splendid, foremost, famed, pre-eminent, acclaimed, illustrious, celebrated, noted, conspicuous, far-famed, prominent, honored, reputable, renowned, recognized, notable, important, well-known, of note, of mark, notorious, exalted, remarkable, extraordinary, great, powerful, noble, august, grand, mighty, applauded, universally recognized, peerless, imposing, towering, storied, influential, leading, noteworthy, talked of, outstanding, distinguished, excellent, memorable, elevated; *all* (D): in the spotlight, on top of the heap, making noise in the world, in the limelight.—*Ant.* unknown*, obscure, humble.

fan, *n.* **1.** [An instrument for creating currents of air] —*Syn.* winnowing machine, ventilator, thermantidote, agitator, palm leaf, blower, forced draft, winnower, vane, flabellum, *punkah* (India), air conditioner, propeller, electric fan, Japanese fan, windmill, wind charger (D).
2. [Anything having the shape of a fan]—*Syn.* vane, fin, wing, plane, blade, sector, section, face, pyramid, triangle, delta.
3. [(D) Supporter]—*Syn.* follower, amateur, rooter (D); see **enthusiastic** 1.

fanatic, *n.* —*Syn.* devotee, bigot, enthusiast; see **zealot.**

fanatical, *mod.* —*Syn.* obsessed, impassioned, passionate, bigoted, devoted, feverish, prejudiced, biased, zealous, radical, immoderate, partisan, domineering, impulsive, erratic, obstinate, headstrong, burning, fiery, fervent, rabid, frenzied, willful, excessively enthusiastic, raving, of the lunatic fringe, made, wild, superstitious, credulous, unfair, partial, stubborn, singleminded, one-ideaed, monomaniacal, infatuated, possessed, opinionated, narrow-minded, dogmatic, arbitrary, positive, contumacious, cross-grained, incorrigible, tenacious, unruly, violent, extreme.—*Ant.* moderate*, reasonable, impartial.

fanaticism, *n.* —*Syn.* bigotry, faction, intolerance, obsession, predjudice, hatred, superstition, narrowmindedness, monomania, injustice, obstinacy, stubbornness, bias, unreasonableness, unreasoning zeal, excessive enthusiasm, zealotry, illiberality, unfairness, partiality, devotion, warmth, partisanship, violence, immoderation, zeal, wild and extravagant notions, singlemindedness, willfulness, infatuation, dogma, arbitrariness, contumacy, unruliness, incorrigibility, tenacity, enthusiasm, abandonment, frenzy, passion, rage, transport.—*Ant.* tolerance, indifference*, moderation*.

fanciful, *mod.* **1.** [Characterized by use of the fancy] —*Syn.* fantastical, ideal, whimsical, capricious, imaginative, chimerical, visionary, dreamlike; see also **imaginary.**
2. [Not based upon good sense]—*Syn.* unreal, incredible, notional; see **fantastic.**

fancy, *mod.* **1.** [Distinctive]—*Syn.* special, custom, deluxe; see **unusual** 1, 2.
2. [Ornamental]—*Syn.* elegant, embellished, rich, adorned, ostentatious, gaudy, showy, florid, intricate, rococo, baroque, gingerbread, resplendent, sumptuous, lavish; see also **elaborate** 1, **ornate** 1.

fancy, *n.* **1.** [Artistic creative power]—*Syn.* conception, visualization, creation; see **imagination** 1.

2. [The mind at play]—*Syn.* whimsy, frolic, caprice, banter, sport, diversion, reverie, romancing, badinage, give-and-take, wit, raillery, chaff, jollification, piquancy, point, *esprit* (French), buffoonery, fooling, waggery, drollery, facetiousness, jocularity, persiflage, farce, merriment, levity, humor.
3. [The product of a playful mind]—*Syn.* vagary, conceit, jest, whim, witticism, capricious creation, freak, freak of humor, notion, quip, quirk, maggot, prank, mot, riposte, pleasantry, repartee, retort, sally, impulse, *jeu d'esprit* (French), pun, frolic, harlequinade.
4. [Inclination]—*Syn.* wishes, will, preference; see **desire** 1.

fanfare, *n.*—*Syn.* alarum, parade, demonstration; see **display** 2, **show** 2.

fang, *n.*—*Syn.* tusk, prong, duct; see **tooth.**

fantasia, *n.*—*Syn.* rhapsody, musical fantasy, capriccio, roulade, fantastical air, capricious composition.

fantastic, *mod.*—*Syn.* whimsical, capricious, extravagant, freakish, strange, odd, queer, quaint, singular, peculiar, outlandish, farfetched, erratic, wonderful, comical, humorous, foreign, exotic, extreme, ludicrous, ridiculous, preposterous, implausible, grotesque, chimerical, crotchety, frenzied, absurd, vague, illusive, hallucinatory, high-flown, affected, mannered, artificial, Italianate; *all* (D): newfangled, out of sight, fandangled, ultra-ultra.—*Ant.* conventional, routine, common.

fantasy, *n.* **1.** [Whimsical imagination]—*Syn.* reverie, daydream, flight of fancy; see **fancy** 2.
2. [Whimsical or fantastic artistic creation]—*Syn.* vision, appearance, vagary, air castle, extravaganza, phantasm, illusion, castle in Spain, flight, figment, fiction, romance, conceit, chimera, illusion, mirage, will-o'-the-wisp, *ignis fatuus* (Latin), bugbear, nightmare, fantasia, Utopia, Atlantis, fairyland.

far, *mod.* **1.** [Distant from the speaker]—*Syn.* removed, faraway, remote; see **distant** 1.
2. [To a considerable degree]—*Syn.* extremely, incomparably, notably; see **very.**
by far—*Syn.* very much, considerably, to a great degree; see **much** 1. **very.**
few and far between—*Syn.* scarce, sparse, in short supply; see **rare** 2.
(in) so far as—*Syn.* to the extent that, in spite of, within limits; see **considering.**
so far—*Syn.* thus far, until now, (up) to this point; see **now** 1.
so far, so good (D)—*Syn.* all right, favorable, going well; see **successful.**

farce, *n.* **1.** [Anything light and humorous]—*Syn.* travesty, burlesque, horseplay; see **fun** 1.
2. [A trivial comedy]—*Syn.* play, skit, interlude; see **comedy, drama** 1.

farcical, *mod.*—*Syn.* absurd, ludicrous, ridiculous; see **stupid** 1.

fare, *n.* **1.** [A fee paid, usually for transportation]—*Syn.* ticket, charge, passage, passage money, toll, book, tariff, expense(s), transportation, slug, check, token.
2. [One who pays a fare]—*Syn.* passenger, patron, occupant; see **buyer.**
3. [Served food]—*Syn.* menu, rations, meals; see **food.**

fare, *v.*—*Syn.* prosper, prove, turn out; see **happen** 2.

farewell, *n.*—*Syn.* adieu, valediction, parting; see **departure** 1.

farfetched, *mod.*—*Syn.* forced, strained, recondite; see **fantastic.**

farina, *n.*—*Syn.* starch, cereal, flour; see **meal** 1.

farinaceous, *mod.*—*Syn.* granular, starchy, mealy; see **gritty.**

farm, *n.*—*Syn.* plantation, ranch, homestead, claim, holding, field, kibbutz, pasture, meadow, grassland, truck farm, estate, farmstead, enclosure, land, improved farm, acres, freehold, leasehold, cropland, soil, acreage, garden, patch, vegetable garden, orchard, nursery, vineyard, demense, hacienda, experiment station, *potrero, estancia* (both Spanish American).

farm, *v.* **1.** [To do farm work]—*Syn.* cultivate land, engage in agronomy, produce crops, cultivate, till, garden, work, operate, lease, run, ranch, crop, graze, homestead, run cattle *or* sheep; keep cattle *or* pigs *or* chickens, etc.; husband, produce, enclose, pasture, break the soil, till the soil, take up a claim, dress the ground, hop clods (D); see also **farming.**
2. [To manage farm property]—*Syn.* direct, superintend, look after; see **manage**1.

farmer, *n.*—*Syn.* planter, grower, (livestock) breeder, stockman, feeder, agriculturist, agriculturalist, agronomist, rancher, dirt farmer, tenter, tenant, tacksman, lessee, villein, homesteader, husbandman, producer, tiller of the soil, cultivator, peasant, peon, herdsman, plowman, sharecropper, operator, hired man, gentleman farmer, cropper, grazer, cattleman, sheepman, harvester, son of the soil, hind, truck gardener, gleaner, gardener, nurseryman, orchardist, horticulturist, hydroponist, pomologist, settler; *all* (D): sodbuster, farm hand, hired hand, help; see also **cowboy.**

farming, *n.*—*Syn.* agriculture, tillage, cultivation, husbandry, farm management, soil culture, ranching, share-cropping, homesteading, plantation, horticulture, business of operating a farm, geoponics, agronomics, soil culture, agronomy, pomology, apiculture, grazing, livestock raising, renting, leasing, operating, taking up a claim, hydroponics, tank farming, tray agriculture, tenancy, growing, crop-raising.
Farming operations include the following—dressing the ground, fertilizing, manuring, plowing, disking, listing, harrowing, seeding, sowing, planting, drilling, cultivating, cultipacking, weeding, hoeing, transplanting, harvesting, reaping, gleaning, threshing, winnowing, haying, raking, tedding, binding, combining, stacking, breaking, shocking, husking, digging, picking, curing, strip farming, rotating crops, irrigating *or* irrigation, contour farming, milking, breeding, grazing, pasturing, herding, feeding, stocking, fattening, marketing, spraying, disinfecting, picking, selecting, grading, clipping, shearing.

farm out (D), *v.*—*Syn.* lease, rent, allot; see **distribute** 1, **rent** 1.

farmyard, *n.* —*Syn.* barnyard, yard, enclosure, farmstead, barns, ranchyard, corral, farm buildings, buildings, grange, hacienda toft, garth, messuage, the place (D).

far-off, *mod.* —*Syn.* far, remote, strange; see **distant** 1.

farrago, *n.* —*Syn.* medley, hodgepodge, jumble; see **mixture** 1.

farrier, *n.* —*Syn.* veterinarian, animal doctor, vet (D); see **doctor** 1.

farsighted, *mod.* **1.** [Farseeing]—*Syn.* hypermetropic, presbyopic, long-sighted, seeing to a great distance.

2. [Sagacious]—*Syn.* provident, perceptive, sagacious; see **judicious.**

farther, *mod.* —*Syn.* at a greater distance, more distant, beyond, further, more remote, remoter, longer.

farthest, *mod.* —*Syn.* remotest, ultimate, last; see **furthest.**

farthingale, *n.* —*Syn.* crinoline, hoop (skirt), skirt framework; see **skirt.**

fascia, *n.* —*Syn.* belt, fillet, sash; see **band** 1.

fascicle, *n.* —*Syn.* group, bundle, cluster; see **bunch** 1, **collection** 2.

fascinate, *v.* —*Syn.* charm, entrance, captivate, enchant, bewitch, ravish, enrapture, beguile, delight, overpower, subdue, enslave, please, attract, compel, lure, allure, seduce, entice, tempt, ensnare, draw, attach, invite, engage, excite, titillate, stimulate, overwhelm, provoke, animate, arouse, intoxicate, thrill, fire, stir, kindle, absorb, pique, tantalize, transport, gladden, rejoice, win, interest, enthrall, influence, gain ascendancy over, capture, coax, tease; *all* (D): make one's mouth water, lead on, make a hit, knock dead, raise to fever heat, cast a spell over, catch one's eye, inflame with love, carry away, put a curse on, bait the hook, cast out all devils, beggar all description, engage the thoughts, invite attention.—*Ant.* disgust*, repel, horrify.

fascinated, *mod.* —*Syn.* enraptured, enchanted, bewitched, dazzled, entranced, captivated, beguiled, attracted, seduced, enticed, charmed, enamored, transported, mesmerized, hypnotized, delighted, infatuated, excited, aroused, intoxicated, thrilled, transported, enthralled, tantalized, titillated, spellbound, transfixed, overpowered; *all* (D): hipped on, mashed *or* gone *or* sweet *or* stuck on, badly smitten, fond of, in love with, wild *or* keen about.—*Ant.* disgusted,* repelled, disenchanted.

fascinating, *mod.* —*Syn.* engaging, attractive, delightful; see **charming.**

fascination, *n.* —*Syn.* charm, power, enchantment; see **attraction** 1.

fascism, *n.* —*Syn.* dictatorship, bureaucracy, party government, one-party system, autocracy, regimentation, racism, totalitarianism, National Socialism *or* Nazism, Hitlerism, Third Reich, despotism, absolutism, demagogy; see also **government** 2. —*Ant.* democracy*, self-government, socialism.

fascist, *mod.* —*Syn.* Nazi *or* nazi, dictatorial, authoritarian; see **absolute** 3.

fascist, *n.* —*Syn.* reactionary, Nazi *or* nazi, rightist; see **agitator, radical.**

fashion, *n.* **1.** [The kind]—*Syn.* sort, make, type, brand; see **kind** 2.

2. [The manner of behavior]—*Syn.* way, custom, convention, style, vogue, etiquette, mode, tendency, trend, form, formality, formula, procedure, practice, precedent, prevalence, device, sort, usage, observance, wont, order, usual run of things, prescription, guise, new look, *modus operandi* (Latin), custom of the country, mores.

3. [Whatever is temporarily in vogue]—*Syn.* craze, rage, cry; see **fad.**

after (*or* **in**) **a fashion**—*Syn.* somewhat, to some extent, in a way; see **moderately.**

fashion, *v.* **1.** [To mold]—*Syn.* model, shape, form; see **create** 2.

2. [To adapt]—*Syn.* adjust, accommodate, fit; see **conform.**

fashionable, *mod.* —*Syn.* in fashion *or* style *or* vogue, being done, well-liked, favored, *à la mode* (French), all the rage, contemporary, rakish, smart, modish, stylish, popular, current, French, Parisian, Hollywood, imported, chic; *all* (D): hot, in, trendy, upscale; yuppie, mod, going like wild fire, up to the minute, with-it, the cat's pajamas, jamming them in, in the latest mode.

fashioned, *mod.* —*Syn.* molded, shaped, intended; see **formed.**

fast, *mod.* **1.** [Rapid]—*Syn.* swift, fleet, quick, speedy, brisk, flying, expeditious, accelerated, hasty, nimble, winged, mercurial, lightninglike, flashing, swift-footed, hypersonic, active, electric, agile, ready, dashing, swift as an arrow, quick as lightning, like a flash, quick as thought, racing, fleeting; *all* (D): up-tempo, like a bat out of hell, lickety-split, like hell's afire *or* a house afire. —*Ant.* slow*, sluggish, tardy.

2. [Firmly fixed]—*Syn.* adherent, attached, immovable; see **firm** 1.

3. [Gay, often to the point of easy virtue]—*Syn.* flirtatious, frivolous, sportive; see **lewd** 2.

4. [Permanent in color]—*Syn.* fadeproof, colorfast, durable, lasting, washable, vat-dyed, indelible, waterproof, fade-resistant.

play fast and loose (with) (D)—*Syn.* behave recklessly, run wild, be careless; see **misbehave.**

fast, *n.* —*Syn.* abstinence (especially from food), day of fasting, Lent, Ramadan, Yom Kippur, banyan day, xerophagy.

fast, *v.* —*Syn.* abstain from food, forbear eating, not eat, go hungry, starve, observe a fast, diet (D).

fasten, *v.* **1.** [To make something secure]—*Syn.* lock, fix, tie, lace, close, bind, adhere, batten, tie back, tighten, make firm, attach, secure, anchor, strengthen, grip, zip (up), shutter, grapple, hold, screw up, screw down, clasp, clamp, clutch, pin, nail, tack, bolt, rivet, screw, solder, set, weld, cement, glue, wedge, jam, mortise, twist, fix firmly in a given position, hold immovable, hold fixed *or* fast, make secure *or* fast, entangle, stick, cinch, cement, bed, embed, catch, buckle, bolt, bar, grasp, seal up, have an anchor to windward (D).—*Ant.* release*, loosen, unfasten.

2. [To join two or more things]—*Syn.* cement, combine, connect; see **join** 1.

fastened, *mod.* —*Syn.* locked, fixed, tied; see **tight** 2.

fastener, *n.* —*Syn.* buckle, hook, hasp, lock, turnbuckle, clamp, tie, stud, vise, mortise, grip, grappling iron, clasp, snap, bolt, bar, lace, lacing, Velcro (trademark), cinch, wedge, grip, pin, safety pin, nail, rivet, tack, thumbtack, screw, dowel, hook, brake, binder, binding, weld, button, padlock, catch, bond, band, mooring, rope, cable, guy wire, hawser, anchor, chain, harness, strap, thong, girdle, latch, staple, skewer, lug, tag, hook and eye, pawl, zipper, latchet.

fastening, *n.* —*Syn.* catch, clasp, hook; see **fastener.**

fastidious, *mod.* —*Syn.* squeamish, overnice, meticulous; see **careful.**

fastness, *n.* —*Syn.* swiftness, haste, rapidity; see **speed.**

fat, *mod.* **1.** [Having excess flesh]—*Syn.* portly, stout, obese, corpulent, fleshy, potbellied, beefy, gargantuan, brawny, abdominous, solid, plumpish, plump, rotund, burly, bulky, unwieldy, heavy, husky, puffy, weighty, on the heavy *or* plump, etc., side, in need of dieting *or* reducing, pursy, porcine, swollen, tumid, hypertrophied, inflated, ponderous, lumpish, fat as a pig, dilated, distended, tubby (D).—*Ant.* thin*, lean, skinny.

2. [Having a large cross section]—*Syn.* large, plump, big; see **deep** 2, **thick.**

3. [Productive]—*Syn.* good, black, rich; see **fertile** 1.

4. [Oily]—*Syn.* greasy, unctuous, oleaginous; see **oily** 1.

chew the fat (D)—*Syn.* chat, gossip, confer; see **talk** 1.

fat, *n.* —*Syn.* blubber, grease, adipose tissue, hydrogenated vegetable fats, tallow, suet, lard, shortening, oil.

Edible fats include the following—butter, butterfat, oleomargarine, lard, cottonseed, oil, olive oil, corn oil, wormwood oil, soybean oil, safflower oil, cod-liver oil, halibut oil, peanut oil.

Chemically, common fats include the following—glycerine, stearine, oleagine, elaine, palmitin, ethal, spermaceti.

fatal, *mod.* —*Syn.* inevitable, mortal, lethal; see **deadly.**

fatalism, *n.* —*Syn.* predestinarianism, passivity, inexorable necessity, acceptance, determinism, necessarianism, destinism, predestination, doctrine that all things are subject to fate, necessitarianism.

fatality, *n.* **1.** [Mortality]—*Syn.* deadliness, virulence, lethality, poisonousness, destructiveness, inevitability, necrosis; see also **death** 1.

2. [A death]—*Syn.* casualty, dying, accident; see **body** 2.

fate, *n.* **1.** [The predetermined course of events] —*Syn.* fortune, destination, luck; see **destiny** 1.

2. [A personal destiny]—*Syn.* destined lot, end, predetermination; see **doom** 1.

Fate, *n.* —*Syn.* destiny, Nemesis, the Fates, the Weird Sisters, Parcae, the Norns, the three sisters; Clotho, Lachesis, and Atropos.

fated, *mod.* —*Syn.* lost, destined, elected; see **doomed.**

fateful, *mod.* **1.** [Momentous]—*Syn.* portentous, critical, decisive; see **crucial** 1.

2. [Fatal]—*Syn.* destructive, ruinous, lethal; see **deadly.**

Fates, *n.* —*Syn.* the three goddesses, Destinies, Weird Sisters; see **fate.**

fat-headed, *mod.* —*Syn.* dull, asinine, thick-witted; see **stupid** 1.

father, *n.* **1.** [A male parent]—*Syn.* sire, progenitor, procreator, forebear, begetter, ancestor, head of the house(hold); *all* (D): papa, dad, daddy, pa, the governor, the old man, pappy, pater, pop.

2. [An originator]—*Syn.* founder, inventor, sponsor, promoter, publisher, introducer, supporter, encourager, promulgator, author.

3. [A civic or tribal elder]—*Syn.* patriarch, city father, dean, Solon; see also **administrator.**

4. [A priest, especially a Catholic priest]—*Syn.* pastor, ecclesiastic, parson; see **priest.**

5. [An important early Christian]—*Syn.* hermit, commentator, a Gregory, prophet, martyr, patriarch, Doctor of the Church, apostolic father, anti-Nicene father.

Father, *n.* —*Syn.* Supreme Being, Creator, Author; see **God** 1.

fatherhood, *n.* —*Syn.* paternity, parentage, fathership, progenitorship, paternal headship.

father-in-law, *n.* —*Syn.* father, spouse's father, parent, connection by marriage, relative; *both* (D): shirt-tail relation, in-law.

fatherland, *n.* —*Syn.* mother country, homeland, native land; see **country** 3.

fatherless, *mod.* —*Syn.* orphan, orphaned, homeless; see **abandoned** 1.

fatherly, *mod.* —*Syn.* paternal, patriarchal, benevolent; see **kind** 1.

fathom, *v.* —*Syn.* interpret, comprehend, penetrate; see **understand** 1.

fatigue, *n.* —*Syn.* weariness, lassitude, exhaustion, languor, enervation, debilitation, weariness from exertion, fatigation, weakness, feebleness, faintness, anoxia, pilot fatigue, battle fatigue, nervous exhaustion, dullness, heaviness, listlessness, tiredness, ennui.—*Ant.* vigor*, briskness, liveliness.

fatness, *n.* —*Syn.* plumpness, obesity, weight, flesh, heaviness, portliness, grossness, corpulence, bulkiness, girth, breadth, largeness, protuberance, inflation, tumidity, distention, hypertrophy, fleshiness, dilation, *embonpoint* (French); *all* (D): stoutness, "this too, too solid [*or* 'sullied'] flesh," heftiness, slobbiness.

fatten, *v.* **1.** [To grow fat]—*Syn.* expand, swell, increase; see **grow** 1.

2. [To make fat]—*Syn.* feed, stuff, prepare for market, plump, cram, fill, round one out, augment. —*Ant.* starve*, reduce, constrict.

fatty, *mod.* —*Syn.* greasy, blubbery, containing fat, oleaginous, unctuous, lardaceous, adipose, suety; see also **oily** 1.

fatuity, *n.* —*Syn.* folly, asininity, idiocy; see **stupidity** 1, 2.

fatuous, *mod.* —*Syn.* inane, foolish, mad (D); see **stupid** 1.

faucet, *n.* —*Syn.* tap, fixture, petcock, cock, drain, spigot, plumbing, stopcock, hot-water faucet, cold-water faucet; *both* (D): hot, cold.

fault, *n.* **1.** [An imperfection]—*Syn.* flaw, defect, lack; see **blemish.**

2. [A moral delinquency]—*Syn.* misdemeanor, solecism, weakness, offense, wrongdoing, transgression, crime, sin, impropriety, moral shortcoming, evil doing, delinquency, trespass, fall from vir-

tue *or* grace, loss of innocence, misconduct, dereliction, malpractice, malefaction, malfeasance, failing, peccancy, sins of omission and commission.
3. [An error]—*Syn.* blunder, mistake, misdeed; see **error** 1.
4. [Responsibility]—*Syn.* liability, accountability, blame; see **responsibility** 2.
at *or* **in fault**—*Syn.* culpable, blamable, in the wrong; see **guilty** 2.
find fault (with)—*Syn.* complain (about), carp (at), criticize; see **censure.**
to a fault—*Syn.* too much, excessively, to excess; see **very.**
fault, *v.* **1.** [To fail]—*Syn.* bungle, err, blunder; see **fail** 1.
2. [To censure]—*Syn.* blame, charge, accuse; see **censure.**
faulted, *mod.*—*Syn.* found at fault, blamed, attacked; see **accused.**
faultfinding, *mod.*—*Syn.* censorious, sarcastic, derogatory; see **critical** 2.
faultless, *mod.*—*Syn.* ideal, supreme, impeccable; see **perfect** 2.
faulty, *mod.*—*Syn.* imperfect, flawed, blemished, deficient, malformed, distorted, weak, tainted, debased, adulterated, leaky, seamed, defective, damaged, incomplete, awry, unsound, spotted, cracked, warped, lame, maimed, crazy, sprung, injured, broken, wounded, hurt, impaired, worn, battered, frail, crude, botched, insufficient, inadequate, incomplete, found wanting, out of order, below par, incorrect, unfit, blamable; see also **unsatisfactory.**—*Ant.* whole*, perfect, complete.
faun, *n.*—*Syn.* woodland deity, satyr, man and goat; see **fairy** 1.
faux pas (French), *n.*—*Syn.* blunder, misconduct, mistake; see **error** 1.
favor, *n.* **1.** [Preference]—*Syn.* help, support, encouragement; see **preference.**
2. [Kindness]—*Syn.* service, courtesy, boon; see **kindness** 2.
3. [A token]—*Syn.* compliment, present, tribute; see **gift** 1.
find favor—*Syn.* please, suit, become welcome; see **satisfy.**
in favor—*Syn.* liked, esteemed, wanted; see **favorite.**
in favor of—*Syn.* approving, endorsing, condoning; see **supporting.**
in one's favor—*Syn.* to one's advantage *or* credit, on one's side, creditable; see **favorable** 3.
out of favor—*Syn.* disliked, not favored, detested; see **hated.**
favor, *v.* **1.** [To have a preference]—*Syn.* prefer, like, approve, sanction, praise, regard with favor, be in favor of, pick, choose, lean toward, incline toward, opt for, honor (before), value, prize, esteem, think well of, set great store by, look up to, eulogize; *all* (D): think the world of, stick up for, be sweet on, have in one's good books *or* graces.—*Ant.* dislike*, misprize, disesteem.
2. [To treat with favoritism]—*Syn.* be partial to, oblige, grant favors to, further, promote, treat with partiality, deal with gently, play favorites, show consideration for, spare, make an exception for, treat as a special character, use one's influence for, pull strings for (D); see also **promote** 1.—*Ant.* abuse*, bear a grudge against, mistreat.
favorable, *mod.* **1.** [Friendly]—*Syn.* well-disposed, kind, well-intentioned; see **friendly** 1.
2. [Displaying suitable or promising qualities]—*Syn.* propitious, convenient, beneficial; see **hopeful** 2.
3. [Commendatory]—*Syn.* approving, commending, approbative, approbatory, assenting, recommendatory, complimentary, acclamatory, well-disposed, in favor of, agreeable, in one's favor.
4. [Advantageous]—*Syn.* propitious, beneficial, useful; see **helpful** 1.
favorably, *mod.* **1.** [In an encouraging fashion]—*Syn.* approvingly, agreeably, kindly, helpfully, usefully, fairly, willingly, heartily, cordially, genially, generously, amiably, graciously, courteously, receptively, with favor *or* approval *or* approbation, in an approving *or* encouraging *or* cordial, etc., manner, positively, included in the budget, without prejudice.—*Ant.* unfavorably*, adversely, discouragingly.
2. [At a propitious time]—*Syn.* opportunely, conveniently, auspiciously; see **fortunately.**
favorite, *mod.*—*Syn.* liked, beloved, childhood favorite, especial, personal, favored, intimate, to one's heart, especially liked, to one's taste *or* liking, choice, pet, desired, wished-for, preferred, adored.—*Ant.* unpopular*, unwanted, unwelcome.
favorite, *n.*—*Syn.* darling, pet, idol, ideal, favored *or* adored *or* beloved one, mistress, love, minion, wanton, paramour, pampered darling, favorite son, *enfant gâté* (French), favorite child, one in a favored *or* preferred position *or* situation, one having the odds in his favor; *all* (D): white *or* fair-haired boy, a favorite two to one *or* three to one, etc., teacher's pet, odds-on favorite, apple of one's eye, boss's son.
favoritism, *n.*—*Syn.* bias, partiality, inequity; see **inclination** 1.
fawn, *v.*—*Syn.* cringe, court, grovel, crouch, bow, stoop, kneel, creep, fall on one's knees, curry favor, toady, truckle; see also **flatter.**
fawn, *n.*—*Syn.* baby deer, baby doe, baby buck; see **deer.**
fawner, *n.*—*Syn.* parasite, sponge, toady; see **sycophant.**
fawning, *mod.*—*Syn.* sniveling, adulatory, flattering; see **obsequious.**
fay, *n.*—*Syn.* elf, brownie, pixie; see **fairy** 1.
faze, *v.*—*Syn.* bother, intimidate, worry; see **disturb** 2.
FBI, *n.*—*Syn.* Federal Bureau of Investigation, federal law enforcement agency, feds (D); see **police.**
fealty, *n.*—*Syn.* homage, allegiance, fidelity; see **loyalty.**
fear, *n.* **1.** [Alarm occasioned by immediate danger]—*Syn.* fright, affright, terror, horror, panic, consternation, dread, dismay, awe, scare, abhorrence, revulsion, aversion, tremor, bodily fear, mortal terror; *all* (D): funk, cold feet, cold sweat; see also sense 2.—*Ant.* courage*, intrepidity, dash.
2. [General apprehension]—*Syn.* cowardice, trepidation, dread, timidity, misgiving, trembling, fear and trembling, disquietude, anxiety, perturbation, phobia, bugbear, irresolution, fearfulness, forebod-

ing, despair, agitation, hesitation, pusillanimity, worry, concern, suspicion, doubt, qualm, presentment, cravenness, recreancy, timorousness, abject fear; see also sense 1.—*Ant.* courage*, bravery, boldness.

for fear of—*Syn.* avoiding, lest, in order to prevent; see **or.**

fear, *v.* **1.** [To anticipate immediate personal danger]—*Syn.* be afraid, shun, avoid, falter, lose courage, stand in awe of, be alarmed *or* frightened *or* scared, stand aghast, live in terror, dare not, have qualms, cower, take fright *or* alarm, quaver, flinch, shrink, quail, quake, cringe, turn pale, blanch, start, tremble, shy, break out in a sweat (D).—*Ant.* outface, withstand, dare.

2. [To be apprehensive]—*Syn.* apprehend, dread, fret; see **worry** 2.

fearful, *mod.* **1.** [Inclined to fear]—*Syn.* timid, shy, apprehensive; see **cowardly** 1.

2. [Astounding]—*Syn.* shocking, amazing, strange; see **frightful** 1.

fearfully, *mod.* **1.** —*Syn.* timorously, diffidently, apprehensively, shyly, with fear and trembling, for fear of, with heart in mouth, in fear *or* terror *or* fright *or* trepidation.

2. [Very much]—*Syn.* awfully, frightfully, excessively; see **very.**

fearless, *mod.*—*Syn.* bold, daring, courageous, dashing; see **brave** 1.

feasibility, *n.*—*Syn.* practicability, utility, expediency; see **usefulness.**

feasible, *mod.* **1.** [Practicable]—*Syn.* achievable, attainable, workable; see **available.**

2. [Suitable]—*Syn.* fit, expedient, worthwhile; see **convenient** 1.

3. [Likely]—*Syn.* probable, practicable, attainable; see **likely** 1.

feast, *n.*—*Syn.* banquet, entertainment, festivity, festival, treat, repast, refreshment, carousal, wassail, merrymaking, carnival, fiesta, jollification, barbecue, carouse, picnic; see also **dinner.**

feat, *n.*—*Syn.* act, effort, deed; see **achievement** 2.

feather, *n.*—*Syn.* quill, plume, plumage, shaft, down, fin, wing, calamus, tuft, crest, fringe, plumule, spike, pompon. Feathers include the following—wing feather, powder-down feather *or* dust feather *or* pulviplume, tail feather, rudder feather *or* rectrix, covert feather *or* tail covert, flight feather *or* rowing feather *or* remex, half-feather *or* semi-plume, metallic feather *or* metallic scale, down feather, duck feather, contour feather, pin-feather *or* ungrown feather, auricular feather.

in fine or high or good feather—*Syn.* gay, well, in good humor *or* health; see **happy** 1.

feathery, *mod.*—*Syn.* plumed, fluffy, downy; see **light** 5.

feature, *n.* **1.** [(D) Anything calculated to attract interest]—*Syn.* innovation, main item, highlight, prominent part, drawing card, main bout, specialty, special *or* featured attraction, peculiarity.

2. [(D) Matter other than news published in a newspaper]—*Syn.* article, comment, story, editorial, letters to the editor, humor, cartoon, comics, opinion, feature story, column, biography, fiction, serial, short story, background; *all* (D): art, human interest, woman's page stuff, pix, gossip.

3. [A salient quality]—*Syn.* point, pecularity, notability; see **characteristic.**

featured (D), *mod.*—*Syn.* promoted, recommended, in the public eye; see **popular** 1.

features, *n.*—*Syn.* lineaments, looks, appearance; see **face** 1.

featuring (D), *mod.*—*Syn.* presenting, showing, recommending, calling attention to, giving prominence to, emphasizing, making much of, pointing up, drawing attention to, giving prominence *or* a prominent position (to), turning the spotlight on, giving the center of the stage to, centering attention on *or* upon, giving elaborate treatment to; *both* (D): starring, pushing.

febrile, *mod.*—*Syn.* hysterical, delirious, feverish; see **hot** 1.

February, *n.*—*Syn.* winter (month), second month of the year, basketball season, first month of the second semester, shortest month (of the year), month of leap year; see also **month, winter.**

feces, *n.*—*Syn.* excretion, waste, dung; see **excrement.**

fecund, *mod.*—*Syn.* prolific, productive, fruitful; see **fertile** 2.

fecundity, *n.*—*Syn.* productivity, fruitfulness, abundancy; see **fertility** 1.

federal, *mod.*—*Syn.* general, central, governmental; see **national** 1.

federate, *v.*—*Syn.* combine, unify, confederate; see **unite** 1.

federation, *n.*—*Syn.* confederacy, alliance, combination; see **organization** 3.

fee, *n.*—*Syn.* remuneration, salary, charge; see **pay** 2.

feeble, *mod.* **1.** [Lacking strength]—*Syn.* fragile, puny, strengthless; see **weak** 1, 2.

2. [Lacking effectiveness]—*Syn.* impotent, ineffectual, insufficient; see **ineffective.**

feeble-minded, *mod.*—*Syn.* foolish, fatuous, senile; see **weak** 1.

feebleness, *n.*—*Syn.* infirmity, inability, senility; see **weakness** 1.

feed, *n.*—*Syn.* provisions, supplies, fodder, food for animals, pasture, forage, provender, feeding stuff, pasturage, roughage.

Common feeds include the following—grain, small grain, corn, oats, barley, rye, wheat, peanuts, pulse, hay, clover, timothy, alsike, sweet clover, alfalfa, vetch, cowpeas, sorghum, rape, kale, soybeans, beets, ensilage, silage, molasses, oil meal, bean meal, tankage, bone meal, straw, bran, maize, Kaffir corn, grass, pasture.

feed, *v.*—*Syn.* feast, regale, give food to, satisfy hunger of, nourish, supply, support, state, satisfy, fill, stuff, cram, gorge, banquet, dine, nurse, give suck to, maintain, augment, fatten, provide, provision, victual, cater to, stock, furnish, nurture, sustain, foster, keep alive, encourage, pasture, graze, gratify, serve, minister to, wait upon.—*Ant.* starve*, deprive, quench.

feed on, *v.*—*Syn.* batten on *or* upon, live off of, sponge, feast upon, prey on *or* upon.

feel, *n.*—*Syn.* touch, quality, air; see **feeling** 2.

feel, *v.* **1.** [To examine by touch]—*Syn.* finger, explore, stroke, palm, caress, handle, manipulate, press, squeeze, fondle, tickle, paw, feel for, fumble,

grope, grasp, grapple, grip, clutch, clasp, run the fingers over, pinch, poke, twiddle; *both* (D): contact, fiddle with.
2. [To experience]—*Syn.* sense, perceive, receive, be aware of, observe, be moved by, respond, be sensible of, welcome, know, acknowledge, appreciate, accept, be affected *or* impressed *or* excited by, have the experience of, take to heart.—*Ant.* ignore*, be insensitive to, be unaware of.
3. [To believe]—*Syn.* consider, hold, sense, know; see **think** 1.
4. [To give an impression through touch]—*Syn.* appear, exhibit, suggest; see **seem.**

feeler, *n.* **1.** [Anything that investigates by touch] —*Syn.* tentacle, antenna, finger, claw, hand, tactile organ, vibrissa, exploratory arm *or* member.
2. [(D) An effort to discover opinion]—*Syn.* exploratory representation, hint, essay, tentative proposal, prospectus, intimation, trial balloon.

feeling, *n.* **1.** [The sense of touch]—*Syn.* tactile sensation, tactility, digital sensibility, power of perceiving by touch, tangibility.
2. [State of the body, or of a part of it]—*Syn.* sense, sensation, sensibility, feel, sensitiveness, sensory response, perception, perceptiveness, perceptivity, susceptibility, consciousness, receptivity, responsiveness, excitability, excitement, awareness, motility, activity, impressibility, titillation, enjoyment, sensuality, voluptuousness, pain, pleasure, reaction, shrinking, motor response, synesthesia, galvanism, reflex, contractibility, innervation, excitation, intellection.—*Ant.* indifference*, apathy, numbness.
3. [A personal reaction]—*Syn.* opinion, thought, outlook; see **attitude** 3.
4. [Sensitivity]—*Syn.* taste, emotion, passion, tenderness, discrimination, delicacy, discernment, sentiment, sentimentality, refinement, culture, cultivation, capacity, faculty, judgment, affection, sympathy, empathy, imagination, intelligence, intuition, keenness, sharpness, spirit, *esprit* (French), soul, pathos, aesthetic sense, appreciation, response.—*Ant.* rudeness*, crudeness, coldness.

feign, *v.* —*Syn.* simulate, imagine, fabricate; see **invent** 2, **pretend** 1.

feigned, *mod.* **1.** [Made up]—*Syn.* imagined, fictitious, simulated; see **imaginary.**
2. [Meant to deceive]—*Syn.* counterfeit, sham, false; see **pretended.**

feint, *n.* —*Syn.* pretense, bait, snare; see **deception** 1, **trick** 1.

felicitate, *v.* —*Syn.* congratulate, praise, salute; see **compliment** 1.

felicitation, *n.* —*Syn.* congratulation, good wishes, salutation; see **compliment.**

felicitious, *mod.* —*Syn.* appropriate, apt, well-chosen; see fit 1, 2.

feline, *mod.* —*Syn.* catlike, subtle, cunning; see **sly** 1.

fell, *mod.* —*Syn.* barbarous, vicious, inhuman; see **cruel** 1.

fell, *v.* —*Syn.* chop *or* hew *or* mow *or* fling *or* pull *or* blow *or* fetch *or* knock *or* dash *or* hurl *or* bring down, cause to fall, ground, knock *or* blow *or* bowl over.

fellow, *n.* **1.** [A young man]—*Syn.* youth, lad, boy, person, stripling, novice, cadet, *señor* (Spanish), *Herr* (German), *garçon* (French), apprentice, adolescent, pubescent, whippersnapper, master, chap, beau, juvenile, younker, youngster, scion; *all* (D): guy, duffer, kid, cat, teen-ager, squirt, sprig.
2. [An associate]—*Syn.* peer, associate, colleague; see **friend** 1.
3. [A term of opprobrium]—*Syn.* lout, churl, knave; see **rascal.**
4. [An academic or scholarly appointee]—*Syn.* assistant, pensioner, associate, graduate, scholar, licentiate, academician, tutor, master, gownsman, don, instructor, professor, lecturer, assistant professor, associate professor, docent, teaching assistant *or* TA (D), research assistant *or* RA (D), wrangler, drudge, *agrége* (French), bachelor, clerk, candidate, doctor, holder of a fellowship.

fellow feeling, *n.* —*Syn.* understanding, compassion, sympathy; see **pity** 1.

fellowship, *n.* **1.** [Congenial social feeling]—*Syn.* comradeship, companionability, conviviality, sociality, sociability, intimacy, acquaintance, approachability, friendliness, familiarity, good-fellowship, amity, affability, camaraderie, fraternity, togetherness (D).—*Ant.* rudeness*, unsociability, surliness.
2. [Congenial social activity]—*Syn.* brotherhood, society, companionship, comradeship, association, fraternization, communion, familiar intercourse, alliance.—*Ant.* withdrawal*, retirement, aloofness.
3. [An association of people]—*Syn.* corporation, club, gang; see **organization** 3.
4. [Subsistence payment to encourage study] —*Syn.* stipend, grant, scholarship, honorarium, subsidy, foreign fellowship, teaching fellowship, Rockefeller fellowship, Woodrow Wilson fellowship, Rhodes fellowship, Guggenheim fellowship, assistantship.

felon, *n.* —*Syn.* outlaw, delinquent, convict; see **criminal.**

felonious, *mod.* —*Syn.* unlawful, nefarious, corrupt; see **wicked** 1, 2.

felony, *n.* —*Syn.* misconduct, offense, transgression; see **crime** 2.

female, *mod.* **1.** [Feminine]—*Syn.* womanly, womanlike, ladylike; see **feminine** 2.
2. [Belonging to the female sex]—*Syn.* oviparous, reproductive, fertile, child-bearing, pistillate, pistil-bearing, producing pistillate flowers, of the female gender, "more deadly than the male."—*Ant.* masculine, male*, staminate.

feminine, *mod.* **1.** [Belonging to the feminine sex] —*Syn.* womanly, womanlike, pistillate; see **female** 2.
2. [Having qualities stereotypically associated with women]—*Syn.* soft, womanly, delicate, gentle, ladylike, female, matronly, maidenly, sensitive, tender, womanish, graceful, changeable, fair, fluttering, shy, vixenish; see also **dainty** 1, **refined** 2, **womanly.**—*Ant.* male*, masculine, virile.

femininity, *n.* **1.** [The quality of being female] —*Syn.* womanhood, femaleness, feminineness, feminality, femineity, muliebrity, womanliness, softness; see **docility, gentleness** 2, **kindness** 1.

2. [Effeminacy]—*Syn.* womanishness, unmanliness, effeminateness; see **weakness** 1.

fen, *n.* —*Syn.* bog, morass, marsh; see **swamp.**

fence, *n.* 1. [That which surrounds an enclosure] —*Syn.* picket fence, wire fence, board fence, electric *or* electrified fence, barbed-wire fence, snake fence, Cyclone fence (trademark), rail fence, chain fence, iron fence, hedge, paling, balustrade, backstop, rail, railing, barricade, net, barrier, wall, dike.
2. [Material to make an enclosure]—*Syn.* barbed wire, chicken wire, pickets, woven wire, palings, (grape) stakes, posts, rails.
3. [A receiver of stolen goods]—*Syn.* accomplice; *all* (D): front (man), drop, dump, family man, uncle, swagman.
mend one's fences (D)—*Syn.* renew contacts, look after one's political interests, solicit votes; see **campaign.**
on the fence (D)—*Syn.* uncertain, uncommitted, indifferent; see **undecided.**

fencing, *n.* —*Syn.* foils, foil work, fencing match, épée, saber, play, contest, fight; see also **sport** 3.

fend, *v.* —*Syn.* parry, repel, resist; see **defend** 1, **oppose** 2.

fender, *n.* —*Syn.* guard, mudguard, shield, apron, buffer, mask, cover, frame, ward, cushion, protector, splashboard, bumper, cowcatcher, screen, fireguard, curb.

fend for oneself, *v.* —*Syn.* take care of oneself, stay alive, eke out an existence; see **subsist, survive.**

fend off, *v.* —*Syn.* keep off, ward away, repel; see **defend** 1.

feral, *mod.* 1. [Not tame]—*Syn.* wild, untamed, not domesticated; see **primitive** 3.
2. [Savage]—*Syn.* fierce, bestial, vicious; see **cruel** 1, **ferocious.**

ferment, *n.* —*Syn.* stir, excitement, fermentation; see **disturbance** 2.

ferment, *v.* —*Syn.* effervesce, sour, foam, froth, bubble, seethe, fizz, sparkle, boil, acidify, work, ripen, dissolve, overflow, evaporate, rise.

fermentation, *n.* —*Syn.* effervescence, ebullition, turbulence, souring, agitation, foaming, frothing, seething, bubbling, evaporation, volatilization, dissolving, overflowing.

fern, *n.* —*Syn.* greenery, bracken, lacy plant, pteridophyte, Venus's hair, maidenhair, brake, polypody.

ferocious, *mod.* —*Syn.* fierce, savage, wild, feral, barbarous, untamed, fell, brutal, cruel, sanguinary, ravenous, vehement, violent, unrestrained, bloodthirsty, murderous, brutish, pitiless, merciless, unmerciful, fearsome, frightful.—*Ant.* gentle*, meek, mild.

ferocity, *n.* —*Syn.* fierceness, brutality, barbarity; see **cruelty.**

ferret, *v.* —*Syn.* ferret out, seek, search; see **hunt** 2.

ferret out, *v.* —*Syn.* unearth, search out, track down; see **hunt** 2.

ferry, *n.* —*Syn.* passage boat, barge, packet; see **boat.**

ferry, *v.* —*Syn.* carry over, move across, ship; see **carry** 1, **send** 1.

fertile, *mod.* 1. [*Said of land*[—*Syn.* fruitful, rich, productive, fat, teeming, yielding, plenteous, black, arable, flowering, flowing with milk and honey.—*Ant.* sterile*, barren, desert.
2. [*Said of women*]—*Syn.* teeming, fecund, prolific, generative, bearing, bringing forth, breeding, pregnant, gravid, with child.—*Ant.* sterile*, impotent, barren.
3. [*Said of ideas, minds, and the like*]—*Syn.* inventive, resourceful, imaginative; see **original** 2.

fertility, *n.* 1. [Reproductive capacity]—*Syn.* fecundity, richness, fruitfulness, prolificity, potency, virility, pregnancy, gravidity, productiveness, productivity, generative capacity.—*Ant.* barrenness*, sterility, infecundity.
2. [Ingenuity]—*Syn.* resourcefulness, imagination, inventiveness; see **ability** 1, 2.

fertilization, *n.* 1. [The enrichment of land]—*Syn.* manuring, dressing, preparation, covering, liming, mulching, spreading.
2. [Impregnation of the ovum]—*Syn.* insemination, impregnation, pollination, implantation, breeding, fecundation, propagation, generation, procreation, conjugation, begetting.

fertilize, *v.* 1. [To enrich land]—*Syn.* manure, dress, spread, lime, prepare, mulch, cover, treat.
2. [To impregnate]—*Syn.* breed, make pregnant, fecundate, generate, germinate, pollinate, inseminate, propagate, procreate, get with child, beget, knock up (D).

fertilizer, *n.* —*Syn.* manure, top dressing, commercial *or* chemical fertilizer, plant food, compost, humus, mulch.
Common fertilizers include the following—barnyard manure, guano, sphagnum, peat moss, phosphorus, phosphate, dung, litter, crushed limestone, bone dust, kelp, bone meal, nitrogen, nitric nitrogen, ammonic nitrogen, ammonium sulphate, legumes, potash.

fervent, *mod.* —*Syn.* zealous, eager, ardent; see **enthusiastic** 1, 2, 3.

fervor, *n.* 1. [Great warmth]—*Syn.* fervency, ardor, zeal; see **enthusiasm** 1.
2. [Warmth]—*Syn.* heat, glow, fire; see **warmth.**

festal, *mod.* —*Syn.* festive, gala, social; see **happy** 1.

fester, *v.* —*Syn.* rankle, putrefy, rot; see **decay.**

festival, *n.* —*Syn.* festivity, feast, competition; see **celebration** 2.

festive, *mod.* —*Syn.* merry, gay, joyful; see **happy** 1.

festivity, *n.* —*Syn.* revelry, pleasure, amusement; see **entertainment** 1, 2.

festoon, *n.* —*Syn.* lei, garland, chaplet; see **wreath.**

festoon, *v.* —*Syn.* trim, array, hang; see **decorate.**

fetch, *v.* 1. [To draw forth]—*Syn.* elicit, go after, call for; see **obtain** 1.
2. [To get and bring back]—*Syn.* bring to, get, retrieve; see **carry** 1.

fetching, *mod.* —*Syn.* attractive, pleasing, captivating; see **charming.**

fete, *n.* —*Syn.* party, banquet, ball; see **party** 1.

fete, *v.* —*Syn.* feast, festival, holiday; see **celebration** 1, 2.

fetid, *mod.* —*Syn.* rank, foul, stinking; see **offensive** 2.

fetish, *n.* 1. [Obsession]—*Syn.* fixation, craze, mania; see **obsession.**
2. [The object of an obsession]—*Syn.* amulet, talisman, object of superstition; see **charm** 2.

fetter, *v.* **1.** [To bind]—*Syn.* shackle, tie up, chain; see **bind** 1.
2. [To confine]—*Syn.* hamper, check, repress; see **restrain** 1.

fetters, *n.*—*Syn.* manacles, shackles, bonds; see **chains.**

fetus, *n.*—*Syn.* young germ, organism, embryo, the young of an animal in the womb, unborn *or* unhatched vertebrate.

feud, *n.*—*Syn.* quarrel, strife, bickering; see **fight** 1.

fever, *n.*—*Syn.* abnormal temperature and pulse, febrile disease, pyrexia; see **illness** 1.

feverish, *mod.*—*Syn.* burning, above normal, running a temperature; see **hot** 1.

few, *mod.*—*Syn.* not many, minority, scarcely any *or* anything, less, sparse, scant, scanty, thin, scattering, straggling, widely spaced, inconsiderable, negligible, infrequent, not too many, a few, some, any, scarce, rare, seldom, middling, few and far between.—*Ant.* many*, numerous, innumerable.

few, *pron.*—*Syn.* not many, a small number, a handful, scarcely any, not so many as one might expect, not too many, several, a scattering, a number that can be counted on one's fingers, three or four, a sprinkling.—*Ant.* many*, a multitude, a great many.
quite a few—*Syn.* several, some, a large number; see **many.**

fey, *mod.*—*Syn.* eccentric, crazy, peculiar; see **unusual** 2.

fiancé, *n.*—*Syn.* intended, betrothed, engaged person, person engaged to be married, affianced person.

fiasco, *n.*—*Syn.* breakdown, blunder, farce; see **error** 1, **failure** 1.

fiat, *n.*—*Syn.* authorization, decree, proclamation; see **command** 1, **declaration** 2.

fib, *n.*—*Syn.* prevarication, fabrication, misrepresentation; see **lie** 1.

fiber, *n.* **1.** [A threadlike structure]—*Syn.* thread, cord, string, rootlet, strand, staple, pile, tissue, filament, vein, hair, tendril, strip, shred.
Some common fibers include the following—vegetable fiber, animal fiber, natural fiber, synthetic fiber, silk, linen, hemp, cotton, wool, jute, rayon, nylon, orlon, Fiberglas, Banlon (both trademarks), acetate.
2. [Quality]—*Syn.* grain, tissue, nap, grit, tooth, feel, hand, surface, warp and woof; see also **character** 1, **texture** 1.

fibrous, *mod.*—*Syn.* stringy, woody, pulpy, veined, hairy, coarse, stalky, threadlike, ropy, tissued, fibroid.

fibula, *n.*—*Syn.* brooch, clasp, buckle; see **pin** 1.

fickle, *mod.* **1.** [Not to be relied upon]—*Syn.* capricious, whimsical, mercurial; see **changeable** 1, 2.
2. [Unfaithful in love]—*Syn.* faithless, inconstant, coquettish, frivolous, untrue; see also **lewd** 1, 2.—*Ant.* faithful*, loving, true.

fiction, *n.* **1.** [Falsehood]—*Syn.* fabrication, untruth, invention; see **lie** 1.
2. [Imaginative prose narrative]—*Syn.* novel, tale, romance; see **story.**

fictitious, *mod.*—*Syn.* made-up, untrue, counterfeit; see **false** 1, 2.

fiddle (D), *n.*—*Syn.* violin, stringed instrument, cornstalk fiddle (D); see **musical instrument.**
fit as a fiddle (D)—*Syn.* healthy, strong, sound; see **well** 1.

fidelity, *n.* **1.** [Faithfulness in allegiance]—*Syn.* fealty, loyalty, devotion; see **constancy** 1.
2. [Conformity to a standard]—*Syn.* closeness, scrupulousness, faithfulness; see **care** 1.

fidget, *v.*—*Syn.* stir, twitch, toss, wiggle, jiggle, joggle, hitch, fret, chafe, worry.

fidgety, *mod.*—*Syn.* nervous, uneasy, apprehensive; see **restless** 1.

fiduciary, *n.*—*Syn.* trustee, depositary, curator; see **guardian** 1.

field, *mod.*—*Syn.* farm, stock, meadow, outdoor, agricultural, rural, land, soil, earth, earthen, agrarian, bucolic, pastoral.

field, *n.* **1.** [Open land]—*Syn.* grainfield, hayfield, meadow, pasture, range, acreage, plot, patch, garden, enclosure, land under cultivation, mead, glebe, tract of land for pasture, cultivated ground, grassland, green, ranchland(s), arable land, plowed *or* cultivated land, cleared land, moor, moorland(s), lea, cropland, tract, vineyard.
2. [An area devoted to sport]—*Syn.* diamond, gridiron, track, rink, court, course, racecourse, golf course, race track, circus, arena, lists, stadium, theater, amphitheater, playground, park, turf, green, hippodrome, fairground.
3. [An area devoted to a specialized activity]—*Syn.* airfield, airport, flying field, playing field, terminal, battle, battlefield, battleground, terrain, no man's land, scene of conflict, theater of war, field of battle, field of honor, parade ground, range, parking lot.
4. [An area which can be comprehended in a given way]—*Syn.* field of vision, field of investigation, field of operations, territory, province, domain, bailiwick, purview, sphere, reach, range, area, scope, jurisdiction, field of interest, field of study.
5. [Competitors or available candidates]—*Syn.* entries, entrants, participants, contestants, applicants, nominees, possibilities, suitable applicants *or* candidates, properly trained *or* capable men.
play the field—*Syn.* experiment, explore, look elsewhere; see **discover, examine** 1, **try** 1.

field, *v.*—*Syn.* handle, cover, play, hold, occupy, patrol the pasture (D).

field day, *n.*—*Syn.* success, holiday, triumph; see **victory** 2.

fielder, *n.*—*Syn.* ball chaser; *all* (D): fly chaser, fly hawk, gardener, shagger.
Fielders include the following—infielder, outfielder, right fielder, left fielder, center fielder; *all* (D): right *or* center *or* left gardener.

field gun, *n.*—*Syn.* piece, field piece, light artillery; see **cannon.**

fiend, *n.* **1.** [A devil]—*Syn.* demon, Satan, evil spirit; see **devil** 1.
2. [A wicked or cruel person]—*Syn.* monster, barbarian, brute; see **beast** 2.
3. [(D) An addict]—*Syn.* fan, aficionado, monomaniac; see **addict, enthusiast** 1.

fiendish, *mod.*—*Syn.* diabolical, demoniac, infernal; see **wicked** 2.

fierce, *mod.* **1.** [*Said expecially of men and animals*]—*Syn.* ferocious, wild, furious, enraged, raging, impetuous, untamed, angry, passionate, savage, primitive, brutish, feral, animal, raving, outrageous, terrible, vehement, frightening, awful, horrible, venomous, bold, malevolent, malign, brutal, bloodthirsty, truculent, monstrous, hysterical, severe, rough, rude, clamorous, vicious, dangerous, frenzied, mad, insane, desperate, ravening, frantic, wrathful, irate, rabid, virulent, fanatical, bestial; *all* (D): hard, tough, hard-boiled; see **sense** 2.—*Ant.* gentle*, reasonable, peaceful*.
2. [*Said especially of actions and the weather*] —*Syn.* boisterous, violent, threatening, stormy, thunderous, howling, inclement, tumultous, turbulent, uncontrolled, raging, storming, blustering, cyclonic, blizzard, blizzardous, torrential, of hurricane force *or* strength, frightful, fearful, lowering, devastating, hellish, rip-roaring (D); see **sense** 1. —*Ant.* mild*, moderate, calm.
3. [Intense]—*Syn.* ardent, fervent, deep; see **intense.**

fiercely, *mod.*—*Syn.* ferociously, violently, wildly, terribly, vehemently, angrily, threateningly, frighteningly, awfully, horribly, venomously, mightily, passionately, impetuously, boldly, irresistibly, furiously, riotously, malevolently, maleficently, malignly, brutally, monstrous, forcibly, forcefully, convulsively, hysterically, severely, roughly, rudely, viciously, dangerously, madly, tumultuously, raveningly, insanely, desperately, outrageously, savagely, frantically, wrathfully, irately, virulently, rabidly, relentlessly, truculently, turbulently, overpoweringly, strongly, deliriously, fanatically, with rage, in a frenzy, tooth and nail (D).—*Ant.* mildly*, reasonably, peacefully.

fiery, *mod.*—*Syn.* fierce, passionate, unrestrained; see **enthusiastic** 3.

fiesta, *n.*—*Syn.* festival, holiday, feast; see **celebration** 1, 2.

fifth columnist, *n.*—*Syn.* quisling, saboteur, secret agent; see **traitor.**

fifty, *mod.*—*Syn.* half a hundred, half a century, two score and ten, many, a considerable number.

fight, *n.* **1.** [A violent physical struggle]—*Syn.* strife, contention, feud, quarrel, contest, encounter, row, dispute, disagreement, battle, battle royal, confrontation, controversy, brawl, affray, affair, fray, bout, match, fisticuffs, boxing match, round, broil, fracas, difficulty, altercation, bickering, wrangling, riot, argument, dissension, debate, competition, sparring match, a coming to blows, rivalry, conflict, skirmish, scrimmage, clash, scuffle, collision, brush, action, engagement, melee, passage of arms, sortie, pitched battle, tilt, joust, combat, blow, exchange of blows, wrestling match, squabble, game, discord, estrangement; *all* (D): fuss, mix-up, tussle, scrap, free-for-all, ruckus, mix, run-in, tiff, flare-up, go, row, rumpus, donnybrook, set-to, shake-up, hubbub, difference of opinion.
2. [Willingness or eagerness to fight]—*Syn.* mettle, hardihood, boldness; see **courage** 1.

fight, *v.* **1.** [To struggle for an end]—*Syn.* carry on, persevere, persist, maintain, further, continue, push forward, support, uphold, endure, exert oneself, effect, force, travail, hammer away, toil on, take pains, put forth strength, spare no effort, buckle down (D).—*Ant.* stop*, give up, quit.
2. [To engage in an encounter]—*Syn.* strive, war, struggle, resist, assert oneself, challenge, meet, contend, attack, carry on war, withstand, give blow for blow, do battle, war against, cross swords, draw the sword, engage in hostilities, go to war, exchange shots *or* blows, ply one's weapons, exchange fisticuffs, encounter, oppose, bear arms against, bandy with, tussle, grapple, brush with, flare up, engage with, combat, close with, wrestle, box, spar, fight to the last man *or* ditch, fight the good fight, fight one's way, measure swords with, skirmish, wrangle, quarrel, bicker, dispute, have it out, joust, tilt; *all* (D): pitch into, squabble, take on all comers, swim against the stream, come to grips with, enter the lists, take up the gauntlet, rag, row, pick a bone with, take the field, light *or* tear at *or* into, scrap, mix it up with.—*Ant.* retreat*, submit, yield.

fight back, *v.*—*Syn.* defend oneself, resist, retaliate; see **oppose** 2.

fighter, *n.* **1.** [One who fights]—*Syn.* contestant, disputant, contender, party to a quarrel, warrior, soldier, combatant, belligerent, assailant, aggressor, antagonist, rival, opponent, champion, swashbuckler, fire-eater, swordsman, duelist, bully, gladiator, janissary, feudist, competitor, controversialist, quarrelsome fellow, scrapper (D).
2. [A professional pugilist]—*Syn.* boxer, prize fighter, fisticuffer; *all* (D): battler, pug, chump, bruiser.
3. [An airplane built to fight]—*Syn.* combat plane, interceptor, pursuit plane; see **plane** 3.

fighting, *mod.*—*Syn.* combative, battling, brawling, determined, unbeatable, resolute, contentious, disputatious, under arms, argumentative, angry, ferocious, quarrelsome, ready to fight, ripe for a fight, bellicose, belligerent, boxing, wrestling, sparring, fencing, jousting, skirmishing, tilting, pugnacious, warlike, contending, in the thick of the fray; *all* (D): like cats and dogs, at the point of the bayonet, in the cannon's mouth, up in arms.—*Ant.* peaceful*, peaceable, meek.

fighting, *n.*—*Syn.* combat, struggle, strife; see **fight** 1.

fight off, *v.*—*Syn.* defend from, hold back, resist; see **defend** 1.

fight shy of (D), *v.*—*Syn.* keep away *or* out, shun, elude; see **avoid.**

figment, *n.*—*Syn.* fabrication, invention, falsehood; see **lie** 1.

figurative, *mod.*—*Syn.* not literal, metaphorical, allegorical; see **illustrative.**

figure, *n.* **1.** [A form]—*Syn.* shape, mass, structure; see **form** 1.
2. [The human torso]—*Syn.* body, frame, torso, shape, form, development, configuration, build, appearance, outline, posture, attitude, pose, carriage; *both* (D): chassis, bod.
3. [An arrangement of lines, masses, and the like] —*Syn.* sketch, composition, pattern; see **design** 1, **mold** 1, 2, **statue.**
4. [A representation of quantity]—*Syn.* sum, total, symbol; see **number** 2.
5. [(D) price]—*Syn.* value, worth, terms; see **price.**

figure, *v.* **1.** [To compute]—*Syn.* reckon, number, count; see **calculate** 1.
2. [To estimate]—*Syn.* set a figure, guess, fix a price; see **estimate** 3.
3. [(D) to come to a conclusion]—*Syn.* suppose, think, opine; see **decide, infer** 1.
4. [Figure out]—*Syn.* comprehend, master, reason; see **discover** 1.

figured, *mod.*—*Syn.* scrolled, flowered, geometric; see **ornate** 1.

figurehead, *n.*—*Syn.* titular head, nonentity, cipher; see **nothing.**

figure of speech, *n.* Varieties include the following—image, comparison, metaphor, simile, metonymy, synecdoche, trope, epic simile, Homeric simile, personification, apostrophe, oxymoron, hysteron proteron, litotes, hyperbole, allegory, parable, allusion, euphemism, euphuism, analogue, adumbration, parallel, irony, satire, understatement, paradox.

figurine, *n.*—*Syn.* puppet, manikin, statuette, small figure, ornamental model, doll, small-scale sculptural representation, marionette.

filament, *n.*—*Syn.* wire, tendril, thread; see **fiber** 1.

filch, *n.*—*Syn.* rob, pilfer, purloin; see **steal.**

file, *n.* [Receptacle for the orderly preservation of papers]—*Syn.* filing cabinet, letter file, card file, letter case, pigeon hole, repository. **1.** [An orderly collection of papers]—*Syn.* card index, card file, portfolio, record, classified index, list, ready reference list, register, dossier, notebook, docket, census, Domesday book.
2. [Steel abrasive]—*Syn.* rasp, steel, sharpener. Types of files include the following—flat, round *or* rat-tail, triangular *or* saw, fingernail, wood, 10-inch, 12-inch, etc.
3. [A line]—*Syn.* rank, row, column; see **line** 1.
on file—*Syn.* filed, cataloged, registered; see **recorded.**

file, *v.* **1.** [To arrange in order]—*Syn.* classify, index, deposit, categorize, catalog, record, register, list, arrange, pigeonhole, docket.
2. [To use an abrasive]—*Syn.* abrade, rasp, scrape, smooth, rub down, level off, finish, sharpen, grind.

file clerk, *n.*—*Syn.* secretary, office girl, assistant; see **clerk** 2.

filial, *mod.*—*Syn.* dutiful, affectionate, respectful; see **obedient** 1.

filibuster, *n.* **1.** [Legislative delaying tactic]—*Syn.* hindrance, postponement, interference, opposition, procrastination, delay in legislation, obstruction to congressional action, stonewalling, getting *or* holding the floor.
2. [A pirate]—*Syn.* freebooter, robber, buccaneer; see **pirate.**

filiform, *mod.*—*Syn.* threadlike, stringy, ropy; see **fibrous.**

filigree, *n.*—*Syn.* lacework, tracery, wirework; see **lace** 1.

fill, *n.*—*Syn.* enough, capacity, satiety; see **plenty.**

fill, *v.* **1.** [To pour to the capacity of the container]—*Syn.* pack, stuff, lade, replenish, furnish, supply, satisfy, sate, ram, blow *or* fill *or* pump *or* puff up, fill to capacity, fill to overflowing, brim over, swell, charge, inflate, cram *or* ram in.—*Ant.* empty, exhaust, drain*.
2. [To occupy available space]—*Syn.* take up, pervade, overflow, stretch, bulge *or* curve out, distend, brim over, overspread, stretch, swell, blow up, belly, run over at the top, permeate, take over.
3. [To supply with an occupant]—*Syn.* elect, name, appoint; see **choose** 1.

fill an order, *v.*—*Syn.* put up, dispatch, pack; see **distribute** 1.

fill a prescription, *v.*—*Syn.* compound, fix, blend; see **mix** 1.

filled, *mod.*—*Syn.* finished, completed, done; see **full** 1.

filler, *n.* **1.** [Waste material]—*Syn.* padding, packing, calking; see **stuffing** 1.
2. [A replaceable portion]—*Syn.* refill, cartridge, pad, pack, cylinder, liner, bushing, shim.
3. [In journalism, matter used to fill a column]—*Syn.* features; *all* (D): time copy, locals, (wire) shorts.

fill in, *v.* **1.** [To insert]—*Syn.* write in, answer, sign; see **fill out** 2.
2. [To substitute]—*Syn.* replace, act for, represent; see **substitute** 2.

filling, *n.*—*Syn.* stuffing, dressing, custard, contents, mixture, center, layer, filler, fill, sauce, insides, lining, wadding, padding, bushing, cement; *both* (D): innards, guts.

fillip, *v.* **1.** [To rap sharply]—*Syn.* tap, slap, pat; see **hit** 1.
2. [To stimulate]—*Syn.* spur, arouse, goad; see **excite** 1.

fill out, *v.* **1.** [To enlarge]—*Syn.* swell out, expand, overgrow; see **grow** 1.
2. [To insert]—*Syn.* write *or* fill in, sign, write information on the blanks, answer, apply, put one's signature on, fill in the blanks.

fill up, *v.*—*Syn.* saturate, pack, stuff; see **fill** 1.

filly, *n.*—*Syn.* young mare, female colt, jade; see **horse** 1.

film, *n.* **1.** [Thin, membranous matter]—*Syn.* gauze, tissue, fabric, sheet, membrane, integument, layer, transparency, foil, fold, partition, skin, onionskin, coat, coating, scum, pellicle, veil, cobweb, web, mist, cloud, nebula, obscuration.
2. [A preparation containing a light-sensitive emulsion]—*Syn.* negative, positive, Kodachrome (trademark), microfilm, panchromatic film, panatomic film, color film, infrared film.
3. [A moving picture film]—*Syn.* motion picture, cinema, photoplay; see **movie.**

film, *v.*—*Syn.* record, take, shoot (D):; see **photograph.**

filmy, *mod.* **1.** [Composed of or like film]—*Syn.* gauzy, flimsy, diaphanous; see **sheer** 2.
2. [Covered with a film]—*Syn.* misty, cloudy, dim; see **hazy** 1.

filter, *v.* **1.** [To soak slowly]—*Syn.* seep, osmose, soak through, penetrate, permeate, distill, percolate, exude, ooze, drain, metastasize, infiltrate, trickle.
2. [To clean by filtering]—*Syn.* strain, purify, sift, sieve, refine, filtrate, clarify, clean, separate.

filth, *n.*—*Syn.* dirt, ordure, dung, feces, contamination, corruption, pollution, uncleanness, foul matter, excreta, sewage, muck, coprolite, guano, manure, slop, squalor, trash, grime, mud, smudge, silt, mire, offal, spawn, garbage, carrion, slush, slime, sludge, foulness, nastiness, filthiness, excrement, alvine discharge, pus, dregs, lees, sediment, putridity, putrescence, putrefaction, rottenness, impurity.—*Ant.* cleanliness*, purity, spotlessness.

filthy, *mod.*—*Syn.* foul, squalid, nasty; see **dirty** 1.

fin, *n.*—*Syn.* membrane, paddle, propeller, balance, guide, blade, ridge, organ, spine, pectoral fin, ventral fin, pelvic fin, dorsal fin, caudal fin, anal fin, flipper, spline, fishtail.

final, *mod.* **1.** [Last]—*Syn.* terminal, concluding, ultimate; see **last** 1.
2. [Conclusive]—*Syn.* decisive, definitive, irrevocable; see **conclusive.**

finale, *n.*—*Syn.* close, denouement, finish; see **end** 2.

finality, *n.*—*Syn.* decisiveness, conclusiveness, totality, completeness, intactness, entirety, wholeness, integrity, perfection, final character, terminality, definiteness, finish.

finalized, *mod.*—*Syn.* concluded, decided, completed; see **finished** 1.

finally, *mod.* **1.** [As though a matter were settled] —*Syn.* with finality *or* conviction, settled, in a final manner, certainly, irrevocably, decisively, definitely, beyond recall, past regret, permanently, for all time, determinately, conclusively, enduringly, assuredly; *all* (D): done with, once and for all, for good, beyond the shadow of a doubt.—*Ant.* temporarily*, momentarily, for the time being.
2. [After a long period]—*Syn.* at length, at last, in *or* at the end, subsequently, in conclusion, lastly, after all, after a time *or* a while, as a sequel, eventually, as it may be, despite delay, ultimately, at long last, at the final point, at the last moment, at the end, tardily, belatedly; *all* (D): when all is said and done, late in the day, in the crunch, as the world goes, as things go, at the eleventh hour, in spite of all.

finance, *n.*—*Syn.* business, commerce, financial affairs; see **economics.**

finance, *v.*—*Syn.* fund, pay for, provide funds (for); see **underwrite** 3.

finances, *n.*—*Syn.* revenue, capital, funds; see **wealth** 1.

financial, *mod.*—*Syn.* economic, business, monetary; see **commercial** 1.

financier, *n.*—*Syn.* capitalist, moneylender, banker, merchant, rich man, broker, operator, manipulator, speculator, backer, money-changer, entrepreneur, stockbroker, usurer; *both* (D): Shylock, moneybags; see also **businessman.**

financing, *n.*—*Syn.* matching funds, expenditures, payment; see **expense** 1.

find, *n.*—*Syn.* (fortunate) discovery, findings, acquisition, bonanza; see **discovery** 2.

find, *v.* **1.** [To happen upon]—*Syn.* descry, espy, discover, detect, notice, observe, perceive, arrive at, discern, hit upon, encounter, uncover, recover, expose; *all* (D): stumble *or* happen *or* come on *or* upon *or* across, track down, light *or* hit *or* strike upon, dig *or* turn *or* scare up, smell *or* make out, run across *or* into, trip (up) on, meet up with, lay one's finger *or* hand on, bump *or* knock into, bring to light, spot; see also **see** 1.—*Ant.* lose*, mislay, miss.
2. [To achieve]—*Syn.* attain, win, get; see **obtain** 1.
3. [To discover]—*Syn.* ascertain, unearth, recover; see **discover** 1.
4. [To reach a legal decision]—*Syn.* announce, determine, affirm; see **decide.**

finder, *n.* **1.** [One who discovers a thing]—*Syn.* acquirer, discoverer, appropriator, claimant, lucky searcher, search party.—*Ant.* loser*, owner, stray.
2. [A locating device]—*Syn.* sight, telescopic *or* bomb *or* gun sight, electronic finder *or* homing device, synchronic radar detector, radar reflector, view-finder, range-finder, periscope, glass, radar, sonar, supersonic mechanism, sonabuoy (D).

find fault, *v.*—*Syn.* blame, criticize, condemn; see **censure.**

find favor, *v.*—*Syn.* be appreciated, win praise, gain credit; see **rank** 3.

find in, *v.*—*Syn.* find, perceive, realize; see **discover** 1.

finding, *n.*—*Syn.* verdict, decision, sentence; see **judgment** 3.

findings, *n.*—*Syn.* data, discoveries, conclusions; see **summary.**

find out, *v.*—*Syn.* recognize, learn, identify; see **discover** 1.

fine, *mod.* **1.** [Not coarse]—*Syn.* light, powdery, granular; see **little** 1, **minute** 1.
2. [Of superior quality]—*Syn.* well-made, supreme, fashionable; see **excellent.**
3. [Refined or exquisite]—*Syn.* rare, subtle, expensive; see **dainty** 1.
4. [Exact]—*Syn.* precise, distinct, strict; see **accurate** 2, **definite** 2.

fine, *n.*—*Syn.* penalty, damage, forfeit; see **punishment.**

fine, *v.*—*Syn.* penalize, mulct, exact, amerce, tax, confiscate, levy, sequestrate, seize, extort, alienate, sconce, make pay; see also **punish.**

finery, *n.*—*Syn.* apparel, suit, trimmings; see **clothes.**

finespun, *mod.*—*Syn.* slim, slight, subtle; see **dainty** 1.

finesse, *n.*—*Syn.* discernment, guile, craftiness; see **acumen, cunning.**

finger, *n.*—*Syn.* digit, organ of touch, tactile member, forefinger, thumb, index finger, extremity, pointer, feeler, antenna, tentacle, pinky (D).
have a finger in the pie (D)—*Syn.* participate, join, be a part of; see **share** 2.
have (or keep) one's fingers crossed (D)—*Syn.* wish, aspire to, pray for; see **hope.**
lift a finger—*Syn.* make an effort, attempt, endeavor; see **try** 1.
put one's finger on (D)—*Syn.* indicate, ascertain, detect; see **discover** 1.
put the finger on (D)—*Syn.* inform on, turn in, spy on; see **betray** 1.

finger, *v.* **1.** [To feel]—*Syn.* handle, touch, manipulate; see **feel** 1.
2. [(D) To choose or specify]—*Syn.* appoint, point out, name; see **designate** 1.

fingernail, *n.*—*Syn.* nail, claw, talon, matrix, hook (D).

finial, *n.*—*Syn.* pinnacle, peak, terminal; see **decoration** 2.

finis, *n.* —*Syn.* close, finale, conclusion; see **end** 2.
finish, *n.* **1.** [The end]—*Syn.* close, termination, ending; see **end** 2.
2. [An applied surface]—*Syn.* shine, polish, burnish, glaze, surface.
Finishes include the following—shellac *or* shellack, oil, turpentine, lacquer, size, stain, varnish, polish, wall paper, wash, whitewash, alabastine, calcimine, paint, casein paint, flat paint, cold-water paint, Bakelite enamel (trademark), tung-oil, enamel, gold leaf, aluminum paint, anticorrosion paint, wax, veneer, japan, cement, stucco, megilp, luster.
finish, *v.* **1.** [To bring to an end]—*Syn.* complete, end, perfect; see **achieve** 1.
2. [To develop a surface]—*Syn.* polish, wax, stain; see **face** 3.
3. [(D) To defeat]—*Syn.* annihilate, best, worst; see **defeat** 2.
4. [To come to an end]—*Syn.* cease, close, end; see **stop** 2.
finished, *mod.* **1.** [Completed]—*Syn.* done, accomplished, perfected, achieved, ended, performed, executed, dispatched, concluded, complete, through, fulfilled, closed, over, decided, consummated, effected, effectuated, brought about, ceased, stopped, lapsed, terminated, resolved, settled, compassed, elaborated, made, worked out, rounded out, discharged, satisfied, disposed of, broken up, realized, finalized, effected, put into effect, all over with, attained, shut, turned *or* shut off, done with, come to an end, made an end of, brought to a conclusion *or* a close; *all* (D): done for, said and done, sewed up, wound up, to the last extremity, all over but the shooting *or* the burying. —*Ant.* unfinished*, imperfect, incomplete.
2. [Given a finish]—*Syn.* polished, rubbed, sanded, planed, beaten, burnished, etched, smoothed, coated, washed, dusted, brushed, lacquered, shellacked, varnished, painted, waxed, oiled, sized, stained, calcimined, blacked.
finite, *mod.* —*Syn.* limited, terminable, restricted; see **restricted.**
fiord, *n.* —*Syn.* inlet, gulf, cove; see **bay, water** 2.
fire, *n.* **1.** [Visible oxidation]—*Syn.* flame, conflagration, burning, blaze, signal fire, campfire, pyre, incandescence, devouring element, sparks, heat, glow, warmth, luminosity, scintillation, phlogiston, combustion.
2. [Fuel in process of burning]—*Syn.* coals, flame and smoke, blazing fire, hearth, burning coals, tinder, bonfire, radiant hearth, bed of coals, embers, source of heat.
3. [The discharge of ordnance]—*Syn.* artillery attack, cannonading, bombarding, bombardment, rounds, barrage, explosions, bombings, curtain (of fire), volley, fusillade, sniping, mortar attack, salvos, shells, pattern of fire, fire superiority, drum fire, rolling barrage, creeping barrage, barrage in depth, artillery preparation, softening up, cross fire, enfilading fire, machine-gun *or* automatic fire, rifle *or* small-arms fire, antiaircraft fire; *both* (D): flak, ack-ack; see also **attack.**
4. [Fiery temperament]—*Syn.* dash, sparkle, verve; see **enthusiasm** 1.
catch (on) fire—*Syn.* begin burning, ignite, flare up; see **burn** 1.
go through fire and water (D)—*Syn.* undergo difficulty *or* danger, survive, suffer; see **endure** 2.
on fire 1. —*Syn.* flaming, fiery, hot; see **burning** 1.
2. full of ardor, enthusiastic, zealous; see **excited.**
open fire—*Syn.* start shooting, shoot (at), attack; see **shoot** 1.
play with fire (D)—*Syn.* gamble, endanger oneself *or* one's interests, do something dangerous; see **risk.**
set fire to—*Syn.* ignite, oxidize, make burn; see **burn** 1.
set the world on fire (D)—*Syn.* achieve, become famous, excel; see **succeed** 1.
strike fire—*Syn.* ignite, oxidize, make burn; see **burn** 1.
take fire—*Syn.* begin burning, ignite, flame up; see **burn** 1.
under fire—*Syn.* criticized, censured, under attack; see **questionable** 1, 2, **suspicion** 2.
fire, *v.* **1.** [To set on fire]—*Syn.* kindle, enkindle, ignite, inflame, light, burn, set fire to, put a match to, apply a hot coal, start a fire, set burning, touch off, rekindle, relight.—*Ant.* extinguish*, smother, quench.
2. [To shoot]—*Syn.* discharge, shoot *or* set off, hurl; see **shoot** 1.
3. [(D) To dismiss]—*Syn.* discharge, let go, eject; see **dismiss** 2.
4. [To animate]—*Syn.* inspirit, enliven, inflame; see **excite** 2.
firearm, *n.* —*Syn.* side arm, pistol, revolver; see **cannon, gun** 2.
firebrand, *n.* **1.** [A burning stick]—*Syn.* torch, flame, spill; see **coal.**
2. [An inflammatory person]—*Syn.* incendiary, mischiefmaker, marplot; see **agitator.**
firecracker, *n.* —*Syn.* cherry-bomb, cannon-cracker, cracker (D); see **fireworks.**
fired, *mod.* **1.** [Subjected to fire]—*Syn.* set on fire, burned, baked, ablaze, afire, on fire, aflame, burning, incandescent, scorched, glowing, kindled, enkindled, kindling, alight, smoking, smoldering, unquenched, heated.
2. [(D) Discharged]—*Syn.* dropped, let out, given one's walking papers (D); see **discharged** 1.
fire-eater, *n.* —*Syn.* brawler, rowdy, bully, devil-maker; see **rascal.**
fire escape, *n.* —*Syn.* ladder, chute, rope ladder, net, stair, fire exit, fire door.
fireman, *n.* **1.** [One who extinguishes fires]—*Syn.* firefighter, engineman, ladderman, fire chief.
2. [One who fuels engines or furnaces]—*Syn.* stoker, engineer's helper, railroad man, trainman, attendant, oil feeder; *all* (D): cinder monkey, hell-holer, boy in the hot spot.
fireplace, *n.* —*Syn.* hearth, chimney, ingle, inglenook, ingleside, hob, settle, hearthside, stove, furnace, blaze, bed of coals, grate.
fireproof, *mod.* —*Syn.* noninflammable, noncombustible, nonflammable, fire-resistant, incombustible, noncandescent, concrete and steel, asbestos. —*Ant.* flammable, combustible, incandescent.
fireside, *n.* —*Syn.* hearth, nook, camp; see **fireplace.**
firewood, *n.* —*Syn.* cordwood, kindling, stove-lengths; see **fuel.**

fireworks, *n.* pl.—*Syn.* pyrotechnics, rockets, Roman candles, sparklers, Catherine wheels, illuminations.

firkin, *n.*—*Syn.* tub, keg, cask; see **barrel.**

firm, *mod.* **1.** [Stable]—*Syn.* fixed, solid, rooted, immovable, fastened, motionless, secured, steady, substantial, durable, rigid, bolted, welded, riveted, soldered, imbedded, nailed, tightened, screwed, spiked, fast, secure, sound, immobile, unmovable, mounted, unmoving, stationary, set, petrified, settled.—*Ant.* loose*, movable, mobile.
2. [Firm in texture]—*Syn.* solid, dense, compact, hard, stiff, impenetrable, close-grained, fine-grained, impervious, rigid, inelastic, hardened, inflexible, congealed, unyielding, thick, compressed, substantial, heavy, nonporous, close, condensed, thickset, impermeable, refractory.—*Ant.* soft*, porous, flabby.
3. [Settled in purpose]—*Syn.* determined, steadfast, constant; see **resolute** 2.
4. [Definite]—*Syn.* specific, exact, explicit; see **definite** 1.
5. [Indicating firmness]—*Syn.* strong, vigorous, steady, determined, adamant, hard, cold, sound, stout, sturdy, staunch.—*Ant.* weak*, irresolute, unsteady.
stand *or* **hold firm**—*Syn.* be steadfast, endure, maintain one's resolution; see **fight** 1, **resolve.**

firmament, *n.*—*Syn.* the welkin, atmosphere, heaven; see **sky.**

firmly, *mod.* **1.** [Not easily moved]—*Syn.* immovably, solidly, rigidly, stably, fixedly, durably, enduringly, substantially, securely, heavily, stiffly, inflexibly, unshakeably, soundly, strongly, thoroughly; *all* (D): like a stone wall, solid as Gibraltar, there for all time.—*Ant.* lightly*, tenuously, insecurely.
2. [Showing determination]—*Syn.* resolutely, steadfastly, doggedly, stolidly, tenaciously, determinedly, staunchly, adamantly, constantly, intently, purposefully, obdurately, persistently, obstinately, stubbornly, perseveringly, pertinaciously, unwaveringly, unchangeably, indefeasibly, with a heavy hand, through thick and thin (D).—*Ant.* temporarily*, weakly, feebly.

firmness, *n.* **1.** [Firmness of position]—*Syn.* solidity, durability, substantiality; see **stability** 1.
2. [Firmness of material]—*Syn.* stiffness, impliability, hardness, toughness, solidity, impenetrability, durability, imperviousness, temper, impermeability, tensile strength, inflexibility.—*Ant.* penetrability, flexibility*, fluidity.
3. [Firmness of mind]—*Syn.* resolution, steadfastness, obstinacy; see **determination** 2.

first, *mod.* **1.** [Foremost in order]—*Syn.* beginning, original, primary, prime, primal, antecedent, anterior, initial, virgin, earliest, opening, introductory, inceptive, incipient, inaugural, primeval, aboriginal, leading, in the beginning, front, head, rudimentary.—*Ant.* last*, ultimate, final.
2. [Foremost in importance]—*Syn.* chief, greatest, prime; see **principal.**
in the first place—*Syn.* firstly, initially, to begin with; see **first** 1.

first aid, *n.*—*Syn.* emergency medical aid, Red Cross, emergency relief, roadside treatment, field dressing.

first-class, *mod.*—*Syn.* superior, supreme, choice; see **excellent.**

first-rate, *mod.*—*Syn.* prime, very good, choice; see **excellent.**

fiscal, *mod.*—*Syn.* monetary, economic, financial; see **commercial** 1.

fish, *n.*—*Syn.* *piscis* (Latin), seafood, panfish, denizen of the deep, finny prey, one of the finny tribe. Types of fish include the following—catfish, pickerel, pike, perch, trout, flounder, sucker, sunfish, bass, crappy, bream, sole, turbot, mackerel, cod, horse mackerel, salmon, carp, minnow, eel, bullhead, hogfish, blenny, blindfish, herring, shad, barracuda, swordfish, goldfish, gar, bowfin, flatfish, devilfish, octopus, dogfish, goby, flying fish, blackfish, whitefish, tuna, roughy, grampus, pompano, haddock, hake, halibut, mullet, loach, muskellunge, prawn, bluefish, sardine, smelt; see also **bass, clam, lobster, oyster, shrimp, trout, turtle, whale** 1.
drink like a fish (D)—*Syn.* imbibe, get drunk, become inebriated; see **drink** 2.
like a fish out of water (D)—*Syn.* out of place, alien, displaced; see **unfamiliar** 1.
neither fish, flesh, nor fowl.—*Syn.* unrecognizable, indefinite, unknown; see **strange** 1.

fish, *v.*—*Syn.* go fishing, troll (for), seine, net, bob (for), shrimp, cast one's hook, bait the hook, whale, trawl, angle, cast one's net, bait up (for) (D).

fisherman, *n.*—*Syn.* angler, fisher, Waltonian, piscator, harpooner, sailor, seaman, trawler, caster, whaler, seiner, cod-fisher, fish catcher.

fishery, *n.*—*Syn.* fish hatchery, spawning place, fishing banks, fishtrap, weir, fish cannery, aquarium, tank, piscary, processing plant.

fish for, *v.*—*Syn.* hint at, elicit, try to evoke; see **hint** 1, 2.

fishing, *n.*—*Syn.* angling, casting, trawling, seining, netting, spearing, harpooning, the piscatorial sport.

fishing rod, *n.*—*Syn.* fishpole, bamboo, casting rod, jointed rod, pole.

fish market, *n.*—*Syn.* dock, seafood market, *Embarcadero* (Spanish), Fisherman's Wharf, fish mart, salesroom.

fishy, *mod.*—*Syn.* improbable, dubious, implausible; see **unlikely.**

fission, *n.*—*Syn.* splitting, cleavage, parting; see **division** 1.

fissure, *n.*—*Syn.* gap, cleft, crevice; see **division** 2, 3.

fist, *n.*—*Syn.* clenched hand, clenched fist, hand, clutch, clasp, grasp, grip, gripe, hold, vise; *all* (D): mitt, duke, paw.

fistic, *mod.*—*Syn.* pugilistic, contentious, combative; see **unfriendly** 1.

fisticuffs, *n.*—*Syn.* fist fight, combat, encounter; see **fight** 1.

fistulous, *mod.*—*Syn.* tubelike, pipe-shaped, hollow; see **tubular.**

fit, *mod.* **1.** [Appropriate by nature]—*Syn.* suitable, meet, proper, fitting, fit, likely, expedient, apt, adapted, appropriate, apposite, convenient, timely, opportune, feasible, practicable, wise, advantageous, favorable, preferable, beneficial, desirable, *comme il faut* (French), adequate, conformable, seemly, comely, tasteful, becoming, correspondent, agreeable, seasonable, befitting, due, rightful, equitable, legimate, decent, decorous, congruous, harmonious, pertinent, concordant, according, accordant, consonant, relevant, in keeping, consistent, congenial, applicable, compatible, admissible, concurrent, pat, felicitous, to the point *or* purpose, answerable *or* agreeable *or* adapted to, right, auspicious, happy, lucky, timely, cut out for (D).—*Ant.* unfit*, unseemly, inappropriate.

2. [Appropriate by adaption]—*Syn.* fitted, adapted, suited, well-contrived, calculated, prepared, qualified, competent, matched, ready-made, accommodated, tailor-made; see also **sense** 1.—*Ant.* spoiled*, ill-contrived, mismatched.

3. [In good physical condition]—*Syn.* trim, competent, robust; see **healthy** 1.

fit, *n.* **1.** [Sudden attack of disease]—*Syn.* (muscular) convulsion, rage, convulsive disease, spasm, spasmodic twitching, seizure, stroke, epileptic attack, apoplectic attack, attack of St Vitus dance *or* chorea, paroxysm; *all* (D): spell, jumps, staggers, twister; see also **illness** 1.

2. [Transitory spell of action or feeling]—*Syn.* impulsive action, caprice, burst, rush, spate, outbreak, torrent, tantrum, capricious action *or* movement, mood, fit of love *or* anger *or* hate, etc.; irregular action, passing humor, transitory mood, outburst, sudden motion, whimsy, huff, miff, rage, spell.

by fits and starts—*Syn.* periodic, uneven, episodic; see **irregular** 1.

have (or throw) a fit (D)—*Syn.* become angry *or* excited, lose one's temper, give vent to emotion; see **rage** 1, 3.

fit, *v.* **1.** [To be suitable in character]—*Syn.* agree, suit, accord, harmonize, apply, belong, conform, consist, fit (right) in, be in keeping, be consonant, be apposite, parallel, relate, concur, match, tally, correspond, be apt, befit, respond, have its place, answer the purpose, meet, chime, comport with, click (D)—*Ant.* disagree, oppose*, clash.

2. [To be suitable in size and shape]—*Syn.* be comfortable, conform to the body, hang, drape, give support, permit free movement.

3. [To make suitable]—*Syn.* arrange, alter, adapt; see **adjust** 1, 3.

4. [To equip]—*Syn.* outfit, furnish, implement; see **provide** 1.

fit for, *mod.*—*Syn.* adequate, suitable, appropriate; see **fit** 1, 2, **helpful** 1.

fitful, *mod.*—*Syn.* erratic, shifting, capricious; see **changeable** 1.

fitfully, *mod.*—*Syn.* intermittently, variably, erratically; see **irregularly.**

fitness, *n.*—*Syn.* appropriateness, suitability, propriety, expediency, aptness, aptitude, convenience, adequacy, seemliness, correspondence, agreeableness, seasonableness, decency, decorum, congruousness, harmony, pertinence, accordance, consonance, relevancy, keeping, consistency, congeniality, applicability, compatibility, admissibility, concurrency, patness, rightness, timeliness, auspiciousness, adaptation, qualification, accommodation, assimilation, competence.—*Ant.* trouble*, unfitness, ineptitude.

fit out, *v.*—*Syn.* supply, equip, outfit; see **provide** 1.

fitted, *mod.* **1.** [Appropriate]—*Syn.* suited, proper, adapted; see **fit** 1, 2.

2. [Having proper equipment]—*Syn.* furnished, outfitted, implemented; see **equipped.**

fitting, *mod.*—*Syn.* suitable, appropriate, due; see **fit** 1, 2.

fitting, *n.*—*Syn.* connection, instrument, attachment; see **fixture.**

fix, *v.* **1.** [To make firm]—*Syn.* plant, implant, secure; see **fasten** 1.

2. [To prepare a meal]—*Syn.* prepare, heat, get ready; see **cook** 1.

3. [To put in order]—*Syn.* correct, mend, adjust; see **repair** 1.

4. [(D) To prearrange]—*Syn.* precontrive, predesign, preorder, preplan; *all* (D): stack the deck, frame, set or put up, pin down, rig.

5. [(D) To get even with]—*Syn.* punish for, pay back, get (D); see **revenge.**

6. [To decide]—*Syn.* determine, settle, conclude; see **decide** 1.

7. [To harden]—*Syn.* solidify, set, thicken; see **harden** 3.

fixation, *n.*—*Syn.* preoccupation, mania, fetish; see **obsession.**

fixed, *mod.* **1.** [Firm]—*Syn.* solid, rigid, immovable; see **firm** 1.

2. [Repaired]—*Syn.* rebuilt, in order, in working order; see **repaired.**

3. [(D) Prearranged]—*Syn.* precontrived, planned, predesigned, preordered; *all* (D): rigged, packed, put-up, set-up, in the bag, framed.—*Ant.* unexpected*, surprising, unplanned.

fixing, *n.* **1.** [The act of putting into order or repair]—*Syn.* mending, adjusting, ordering, arranging, adapting, fixing up (D).

2. [(D) Anything useful]—*Syn.* instrument, material, equipment, gear, apparatus.

fixings, *n.* **1.**—*Syn.* parts, components, constituents; see **ingredients.**

fixity, *n.*—*Syn.* permanence, persistency, endurance; see stability 1, 2.

fixture, *n.* **1.** [A fitting]—*Syn.* attachment, electric *or* gas *or* plumbing fixture, castings, faucet, bibcock, inlet, outlet, switch, connection, plug, tap, head.

2. [Household appliance]—*Syn.* convenience, gas *or* electric appliance *or* fixture *or* machine *or* devices *or* equipment; see **appliance.**

fix up (D), *v.*—*Syn.* fix, mend, rehabilitate; see **repair** 1.

fizz, *n.* **1.** [A hissing sound]—*Syn.* hissing, sputtering, bubbling; see **noise** 1.

2. [A drink]—*Syn.* soda, cocktail, pop (D); see **drink** 1, 2.

fizzle (D), *n.*—*Syn.* disappointment, fiasco, defeat; see **failure** 1.

flabbergast, *v.*—*Syn.* confound, amaze, astound; see **surprise** 1.

flabbiness, *n.*—*Syn.* softness, obesity, roundness; see **fatness.**

flabby, *mod.*—*Syn.* limp, tender, soft; see **fat** 1.

flaccid, *mod.*—*Syn.* soft, flabby, weak; see **limp** 1.

flaccidity, *n.*—*Syn.* limpness, flabbiness, softness; see **fatness.**

flag, *n.* **1.** [A symbol, especially of a nation, usually on cloth]—*Syn.* banner, standard, pennant, pennon, streamer, colors; see also **emblem.**

2. [Lilylike plant or flower]—*Syn.* blue flag, iris, fleur-de-lis, sweet flag.

3. [A flagstone]—*Syn.* block, paving block, stone; see **pavement** 1.

strike the flag—*Syn.* surrender, quit, give up; see **yield** 1.

flag, *v.* —*Syn.* signal, wave, give a sign to; see **signal.**

flagellate, *v.* —*Syn.* whip, flog, thrash; see **beat** 2.

flagon, *n.* —*Syn.* canteen, jug, decanter; see **pitcher** 1.

flagrant, *mod.* —*Syn.* notorious, disgraceful, infamous; see **outrageous.**

flagstone, *n.* —*Syn.* rock, stone, flat paving stone; see **pavement** 1.

flair, *n.* —*Syn.* talent, aptitude, gift; see **ability** 1, 2.

flak (D), *n.* —*Syn.* antiaircraft fire, shells, shrapnel; see **fire** 3.

flake, *n.* —*Syn.* scale, cell, sheet, wafer, peel, skin, slice, sliver, membrane, lamina, layer, sheet, leaf, shaving, pellicle, foil, plate, lamella, drop, section, scab.

flake, *v.* —*Syn.* scale, peel, sliver, shed, drop, chip, scab, slice, pare, trim, wear away, desquamate.

flambeau, *n.* —*Syn.* torch, candle, brand; see **light** 3.

flamboyant, *mod.* **1.** [Showy]—*Syn.* baroque, bombastic, ostentatious; see **ornate** 1.

2. [Brilliant in color]—*Syn.* flaming, flashy, resplendent; see **bright** 2.

flame, *n.* —*Syn.* blaze, flare, flash; see **fire** 1.

flame, *v.* —*Syn.* blaze, oxidize, flare up; see **burn** 1.

flaming, *mod.* **1.** [In flames]—*Syn.* blazing, ablaze, fiery; see **burning** 1.

2. [Flamelike]—*Syn.* brilliant, scintillating, vivid; see **bright** 1, 2.

flange, *n.* —*Syn.* rib, spine, shield; see **rim.**

flank, *n.* —*Syn.* loin, thigh, pleuron, hand, haunch.

flannel, *n.* —*Syn.* woolen, cotton flannel, flannelette; see **cloth.**

flap, *n.* —*Syn.* fold, ply, tab, lapel, fly, cover, adjunct, hanging, pendant, drop, tippet, tail, lobe, lappet, appendage, tag, accessory, apron, skirt, strip, queue, wing, pendulosity.

flap, *v.* —*Syn.* flutter, flash, swing; see **wave** 1.

flapjack, *n.* —*Syn.* griddlecake, johnnycake *or* journeycake, hotcake; see **pancake.**

flare, *n.* —*Syn.* glare, brief blaze, spark; see **flash** 1.

flare, *v.* **1.** [To flash]—*Syn.* blaze, glow, burn; see **flash** 1.

2. [To erupt]—*Syn.* go off, burst, blow up; see **explode** 1.

flare out, *v.* **1.** [To spread out]—*Syn.* widen out, spread out; splay; see **grow** 1.

2. [To happen]—*Syn.* happen suddenly, break out, occur; see **happen** 2.

flare up, *v.* **1.** [*Said of persons*]—*Syn.* lose one's temper, rant, seethe; see **rage** 1. **2.** [*Said of fire*] —*Syn.* glow, burst into flame, blaze; see **burn** 1.

flash, *n.* **1.** [Sudden, brief light]—*Syn.* glimmer, sparkle, glitter, glisten, scintillation, gleam, beam, coruscation, blaze, flicker, flame, glare, burst, impulse, vision, imprint, dazzle, shimmer, shine, glow, twinkle, twinkling, phosphorescence, glister, reflection, bedazzlement, radiation, ray, luster, spark, streak, pencil, stream, illumination, incandescence; see **image** 2.

2. [Brief, important news]—*Syn.* bulletin, dispatch, report; see **news** 1, 2.

flash, *v.* **1.** [To give forth a light by flashing]—*Syn.* glimmer, sparkle, glitter, glisten, scintillate, gleam, beam, coruscate, blaze, flame, glare, dazzle, shimmer, shine, glow, twinkle, phosphoresce, reflect, bedazzle, radiate, shoot out beams, shed luster, flicker; see **shine** 1, 2.

2. [To move with the speed of a flash]—*Syn.* speed, flit, shoot; see **fly** 1, **run** 2.

flash card, *n.* —*Syn.* card, drill card, spelling card, vocabulary card, teaching device.

flash in the pan, *n.* —*Syn.* fiasco, disappointment, unsuccessful person *or* attempt; see **failure** 1, 2.

flashlight, *n.* —*Syn.* pocket flash, electric lantern, electric lamp, flash lamp, spotlight, torch.

flashy, *mod.* —*Syn.* gaudy, showy, ostentatious; see **ornate** 1.

flask, *n.* —*Syn.* bottle, decanter, flagon, demijohn, container, jar, jug, crystal, glass, ewer, cruse, carafe, crock, canteen, leather bottle, boda bag, flasket, noggin, vial, phial, cruet, caster, gourd, urn, chalice, tumbler, goblet, beaker, horn, alembic, retort, *fiasco* (Italian), hip flask, pocket flask.

flat, *mod.* **1.** [Lying in a smooth plane]—*Syn.* level, even, smooth, spread out, extended, prostrate, horizontal, low, on a level, fallen, debased, depressed, level with the ground, prone, supine, flat as a billiard table.—*Ant.* rough*, raised, uneven.

2. [Lacking savor]—*Syn.* unseasoned, insipid, flavorless; see **tasteless** 1.

flatboat, *n.* —*Syn.* barge, ferry, clam boat; see **boat.**

flat-footed, *mod.* **1.** [Standing solidly]—*Syn.* intransigent, unwavering, firm; see **resolute** 2.

2. [(D) Unprepared]—*Syn.* not ready, not prepared, surprised; see **unprepared.**

flatiron, *n.* —*Syn.* iron, sadiron, electric iron; see **iron** 3.

flatten, *v.* **1.** [To grow flat]—*Syn.* level (off), even out, smooth (off), grow smooth *or* level *or* even.

2. [To make flat]—*Syn.* spread out, depress, squash, smash, raze, level, even, debase, prostrate, knock *or* wear *or* beat down, fell, floor, ground, smooth, abrade, roll out, straighten, deflate.—*Ant.* raise*, elevate, inflate.

flattened, *mod.* —*Syn.* leveled, depressed, planed, smoothed; see **flat** 1.

flatter, *v.* **1.** [To praise unduly]—*Syn.* overpraise, adulate, glorify; see **praise** 1.

2. [To fawn upon]—*Syn.* kowtow to, cater to, toady to; see **grovel.**

3. [To be becoming to a wearer]—*Syn.* enhance, suit (one), beautify, grace, embellish, enrich, adorn, go with; see also **become** 2.

flattered, *mod.* —*Syn.* praised, lauded, exalted, deceived, lulled.

flatterer, *n.* —*Syn.* flunky, toady, truckler; see **sycophant.**

flattering, *mod.* —*Syn.* laudatory, favorable, unduly favorable; see **complimentary.**

flattery, *n.* —*Syn.* adulation, blandishment, compliments, flattering, remarks, gallantry, honeyed words, unctuousness, sycophancy, (fulsome) praise, excessive compliment, plaudits, applause, eulogy, approbation, insincere commendation, false praise, commendation, tribute, encomium, cajolery, gratification, pretty speeches, soft words, fawning, toadying, wheedling, sweet speech, blarney; *all* (D): applesauce, apple polishing, banana oil, soft soap, eyewash, hokum, oil, lip salve, mush.—*Ant.* criticism*, censure, derision.

flatulence, *n.* —*Syn.* boastfulness, pomposity, bombast, empty talk, boasting, twaddle, babble, idle words, mere words, fustian, claptrap, hot air (D).

flatulent, *mod.* —*Syn.* pretentious, bombastic, pompous; see **oratorical.**

flaunt, *v.* —*Syn.* vaunt, display, brandish; see **boast** 1.

flaunting, *mod.* —*Syn.* gaudy, ostentatious, pretentious; see **ornate** 1.

flavor, *n.* **1.** [That which pleases the palate]—*Syn.* taste, savor, tang, relish, smack, sapidity, twang, gusto, piquancy; *all* (D): vim, wallop, zing.
Individual flavors include the following—tartness, sweetness, acidity, saltiness, spiciness, pungency, piquancy, astringency, bitterness, sourness, pepperiness, hotness, gaminess, greasiness, fishy taste.
2. [Essential nature]—*Syn.* character, quality, feeling; see **characteristic.**

flavor, *v.* —*Syn.* season, salt, pepper, spice (up), give a tang to, make tasty, impart a flavor to, bring out a flavor in, put in flavoring; *both* (D); pep up, give a zip to.

flavoring, *n.* —*Syn.* essence, extract, seasoning, spice, distillation, quintessence, additive, condiment, sauce, relish, pepper-upper (D); see also **herb, pickle.**
Flavorings include the following—vanilla, lemon, chocolate, cinnamon, almond, pistachio, nutmeg, raspberry, strawberry, banana, licorice, caramel, burnt sugar, orange, peach, sarsaparilla, coconut, rum, onion, garlic, clove, pimento, turmeric, purslane, parsley, celery, aloes, marjoram, rosemary, basil, tarragon, oregano, sage, summer savory, saffron, rose.

flavorless, *mod.* —*Syn.* insipid, vapid, mawkish; see **tasteless** 1.

flavorous, *mod.* —*Syn.* tasty, savory, flavorsome; see **delicious** 1.

flaw, *n.* —*Syn.* defect, imperfection, stain; see **blemish.**

flawless, *mod.* —*Syn.* faultless, sound, impeccable; see **perfect** 2.

flaxen, *mod.* —*Syn.* straw-colored, golden, yellowish; see **yellow.**

flay, *v.* **1.** [To remove skin, bark, hide, etc.]—*Syn.* peel, scalp, excoriate; see **skin.**
2. [To criticize]—*Syn.* reprove, castigate, rebuke; see **censure.**

flea, *n.* —*Syn.* hopper, skipper, jumper, dog flea, human flea, sand flea, leaper, flea louse, flea hopper, flea beetle.

fleck, *n.* **1.** [A tiny bit]—*Syn.* mite, speck, dot; see **bit** 1.
2. [A spot]—*Syn.* streak, patch, stripe; see **dot.**

flecked, *mod.* —*Syn.* streaked, spotted, mottled; see **multicolored.**

flee, *v.* —*Syn.* desert, escape, run; see **retreat** 1.

fleece, *n.* —*Syn.* fell, hide, pelt; see **wool** 1.

fleece, *mod.* —*Syn.* fuzzy, fluffy, woolly; see **downy.**

fleer, *v.* —*Syn.* deride, mock, scoff; see **ridicule, sneer.**

fleet, *mod.* —*Syn.* swift, rapid, speedy; see **fast** 1.

fleet, *n.* —*Syn.* armada, flotilla, naval force, argosy, invasion force, task force, squadron, formation, line; see also **navy.**

fleeting, *mod.* —*Syn.* transient, transitory, brief, ephemeral, evanescent, short, flitting, flying, fugitive, passing, swift, meteoric, sudden, cursory, short-lived, fading, temporary, vanishing, momentary.—*Ant.* enduring, constant*, lasting.

fleetness, *n.* —*Syn.* quickness, velocity, rapidity; see **speed.**

flesh, *mod.* —*Syn.* flesh-colored, cream, creamy; see **tan.**

flesh, *n.* **1.** [Soft parts of an animal]—*Syn.* meat, fat, muscle, brawn, tissue, cells, flesh and blood, protoplasm, plasm, plasma, corpuscles, body parts.
2. [Soft parts of a fruit, root, or the like]—*Syn.* meat, tissue, cortex, edible portion, pulp, bulb, heart, insides (D).
one's (own) flesh and blood—*Syn.* family, kindred, kin; see **relative.**

fleshiness, *n.* —*Syn.* corpulence, obesity, plumpness; see **fatness.**

fleshly, *mod.* **1.** [Pertaining to the body]—*Syn.* human, corporeal, mundane; see **bodily** 1.
2. [Sensuous]—*Syn.* carnal, lascivious, lecherous; see **lewd** 2.

fleshy, *mod.* —*Syn.* obese, plump, corpulent; see **fat** 1.

flexibility, *n.* **1.** [Pliability]—*Syn.* pliancy, plasticity, flexibleness, pliableness, suppleness, elasticity, flaccidity, extensibility, limberness, litheness.
2. [Tractability]—*Syn.* compliance, affability, complaisance; see **docility.**

flexible, *mod.* **1.** [Pliant]—*Syn.* limber, lithe, supple, willowy, plastic, elastic, bending, springy, malleable, ductile, pliable, soft, extensile, extensible, spongy, marshy, tractable, moldable, yielding, tractile, flexile, formable, bendable, formative, impressionable, like putty *or* wax, adjustable, stretchable.—*Ant.* stiff*, hard, rigid.
2. [Tractable]—*Syn.* compliant, manageable, amendable; see **docile.**

flicker, *v.* **1.** [To shine]—*Syn.* sparkle, twinkle, glitter; see **flash** 1, **shine** 1.
2. [To quiver]—*Syn.* flutter, waver, vibrate; see **wave** 1, 3.

flight, *n.* **1.** [Act of remaining aloft]—*Syn.* soaring, winging, gliding, volitation, flying, journey by air, avigation.
2. [Travel by air]—*Syn.* aerial navigation, aeronautics, flying, space flight, air transport, aviation, stratospheric travel, (moon *or* lunar *or* Mars, etc.) probe, ballooning, hedgehopping (D).
3. [Flight conceived figuratively]—*Syn.* effort, inspiration, sublime conception; see **imagination** 1.
4. [Act of fleeing]—*Syn.* fleeing, running away, retreating; see **retreat** 1.
5. [Stairs]—*Syn.* steps, staircase, ascent; see **stairs.**
put to flight—*Syn.* chase away, scare (off), frighten off; see **defeat** 1, 2, **pursue** 1.
take (to) flight—*Syn.* flee, run away, leave; see **escape, retreat** 1.

flightiness, *n.* —*Syn.* levity, giddiness, fickleness, inconstancy, changeability, volatility, mercurialness, frivolity, flippancy, capriciousness, whimsicalness, whimsicality, crotchetiness, eccentricity, variability.

flighty, *mod.* —*Syn.* capricious, fickle, whimsical; see **changeable** 1, 2.

flimflam, *n.* **1.** [Nonsense]—*Syn.* trifling, drivel, foolishness; see **nonsense** 1.
2. [Deception]—*Syn.* trickery, deception, craft; see **trick** 1.

flimsy, *mod.* **1.** [*Said of physical things*]—*Syn.* slight, infirm, frail, weak, gauzy, sleazy, unsubstantial, inadequate, defective, wobbly, rickety, fragile, makeshift, decrepit; see also **poor** 2.
2. [*Said of arguments, reasons, and the like*] —*Syn.* trifling, inept, superficial, inane, without plausibility *or* reason, not carefully thought out, puerile, fallacious, false, assailable, controvertible, contemptible, wishful; see also **sense** 1, **illogical.** —*Ant.* cogent, logical*, unanswerable.

flinch, *v.* —*Syn.* start, shrink back, blench; see **wince.**

fling (D), *n.* —*Syn.* indulgence, party, good time; see **celebration** 2.

fling, *v.* —*Syn.* toss, sling, dump; see **throw** 1.

flint, *n.* —*Syn.* quartz, adamant, silica; see **mineral, rock** 1, **stone.**

flinty, *mod.* —*Syn.* hard, unmerciful, obdurate; see **cruel** 2.

flippancy, *n.* —*Syn.* impertinence, impudence, sauciness; see **rudeness.**

flippant, *mod.* —*Syn.* impudent, saucy, smart; see **rude** 2.

flirt, *n.* —*Syn.* coquette, tease, hoyden, siren, mischief, wanton, trifler, frivolous person, philanderer, inconstant, seducer, vamp, vixen, flibbertigibbet (D).

flirt, *v.* **1.** [To coquet]—*Syn.* wink at, play *or* toy *or* sport *or* trifle *or* dally *or* banter with, make advances, philander, tease, display one's charms freely; *all* (D): ogle, make eyes at, linger with, fidget with, look sweetly upon, cast sheep's eyes at.
2. [To play with]—*Syn.* toy with, expose oneself carelessly to, monkey with (D); see **trifle with** 1.

flirtation, *n.* —*Syn.* dalliance, coquetry, courting; see **flirting.**

flirtatious, *mod.* —*Syn.* philandering, flirty, coquettish, spoony, dallying, wolfish, libidinous, nymphomaniac.

flirting, *n.* —*Syn.* coquetry, flirtation, wantonness, trifling, dalliance, amorous dalliance, toying, frolic, banter, sport, ogling, frivolity, coaxing, seduction, blandishment, beguilement.

flit, *v.* —*Syn.* flutter, flash, pass; see **dance** 2.

flitting, *mod.* —*Syn.* transitory, ephemeral, evanescent; see **temporary.**

float, *n.* **1.** [A watertight vessel used for buoyancy] —*Syn.* buoy, air cell, air cushion, lifesaver, pontoon, outrigger, cell, bobber, cork, quill, raft, diving platform, life preserver.
2. [A vehicle used for display]—*Syn.* exhibit, entry, car, chariot, platform.

float, *v.* —*Syn.* waft, stay afloat, swim; see **drift.**

floating, *mod.* —*Syn.* buoyant, hollow, unsinkable, nonsubmersible, lighter-than-water, light, swimming, inflated, sailing, soaring, volatile, loose, free, unsubstantial, hovering, unattached, vagrant. —*Ant.* heavy*, submerged, sunk*.

flocculent, *mod.* —*Syn.* hairy, woolly, fluffy; see **downy.**

flock, *n.* **1.** [Herd]—*Syn.* group, pack, litter; see **herd** 1.
2. [Gathering]—*Syn.* assembly, throng, congregation; see **crowd** 1, **gathering.**

flock, *v.* —*Syn.* throng, congregate, crowd; see **gather** 1.

floe, *n.* —*Syn.* berg, ice mass, icefield; see **iceberg.**

flog, *v.* —*Syn.* strike, thrash, whip; see **beat** 2.

flogging, *n.* —*Syn.* lashing, beating, whipping, thrashing, giving *or* administering lashes, using the cat o' nine tails; see also **defeat** 3, **punishment.**

flood, *n.* **1.** [A great flow of water]—*Syn.* deluge, surge, tide, high tide, freshet, overflow, torrent, alluvion, wave, bore, flood tide, eagre, tidal flood *or* flow, inundation.
2. [An overwhelming quantity]—*Syn.* abundance, bounty, superabundance; see **sense** 1, **plenty.**

flood, *v.* —*Syn.* inundate, swamp, overflow, deluge, submerge, immerse, brim over, rush upon.

floodgate, *n.* —*Syn.* sluice gate, spout, conduit; see **gate.**

floor, *n.* **1.** [The lower limit of a room]—*Syn.* floorboards, deck, flagstones, tiles, planking, parterre, ground, carpet, rug, linoleum.
2. [The space in a building between two floors] —*Syn.* story, stage, landing, level, flat, basement, cellar, ground floor *or* story, lower story, first floor, mezzanine, upper story, downstairs, upstairs, loft, attic, garret, penthouse.

floor-covering, *n.* —*Syn.* linoleum, tile, rug, carpet; see **flooring.**

flooring, *n.* —*Syn.* floors, woodwork, oak flooring, hardwood flooring, parquet, tile, flagstones, boards, earthen floor, cement, floor covering, linoleum, inlaid linoleum, planks, mosaic, tesselation; see also **tile.**

flop, *v.* **1.** [To move with little control]—*Syn.* wobble, teeter, stagger, flounder, wriggle, squirm, stumble, tumble, totter, flounce, toss, shake, shuffle, quiver, flap, whisk, churn, wiggle, wamble, spin, turn topsy-turvy, jitter, jerk.
2. [To fall without restraint]—*Syn.* tumble, slump, drop; see **fall** 1.
3. [To be limp]—*Syn.* flap, droop, dangle; see **hang** 1.
4. [(D) To be a complete failure]—*Syn.* miscarry, founder, fall short; see **fail** 1.

flora, *n.* —*Syn.* vegetable life, verdure, plants; see **vegetation.**

floral, *mod.* —*Syn.* flowery, flowering, made of flowers, botanic, sylvan, blossoming, herbaceous, dendritic, blooming, efflorescent, verdant, decorative.

florescence, *n.* **1.** [The state or process of blossoming]—*Syn.* flowering, blossoming, flourishing; see **blooming.**
2. [Prosperity]—*Syn.* outgrowth, production, development; see **prosperity.**

floriculture, *n.* —*Syn.* horticulture, arboriculture, cultivation; see **gardening.**

florid, *mod.* —*Syn.* ornate, flowery, decorative; see **ornamental** 1.

florist, *n.* —*Syn.* floriculturist, flower dealer, professional gardener.

flotsam, *n.* —*Syn.* debris, floating wreckage, refuse; see **trash** 1.

flounce, *n.* **1.** [Jump]—*Syn.* spring, leap, jerk; see **jump** 1.

2. [Frill]—*Syn.* ruffle, furbelow, trimming; see **decoration** 2.

flounce, *v.* —*Syn.* fling, jerk, toss; see **flop** 1.

flounder, *v.* —*Syn.* struggle, wallow, blunder; see **flop** 1, **toss** 2.

flour, *n.* —*Syn.* meal, pulp, powder, grit, bran, farina, breadstuff, gluten, starch, bleached, unbleached, wheat germ, patent flour, middlings, shorts, white flour, (whole) wheat flour, rye flour, graham flour, potato flour, barley meal, corn meal, oatmeal, rolled oats, cake flour, pancake flour, soybean *or* soybean *or* soyflour.

flourish, *v.* **1.** [To wave triumphantly]—*Syn.* brandish, twirl, shake, flaunt, gesture, wave, swing.

2. [To prosper]—*Syn.* thrive, increase, wax; see **prosper.**

flourishing, *mod.* —*Syn.* thriving, doing well, growing; see **rich** 1, **successful.**

flout, *v.* —*Syn.* mock, outrage, affront; see **insult, ridicule, sneer.**

flow, *n.* —*Syn.* current, movement, progress, stream, tide, run, river, flood, ebb, gush, spurt, spout, leakage, dribble, oozing, flux, outpourings, overflow, emanation, issue, discharge, outflow, drift, course, draft, down-draft, up-current, draw, wind, breeze, indraft, slipstream, propeller race.

flow, *v.* **1.** [To move in one direction]—*Syn.* stream, course, slide, slip, glide, move, progress, run, pass, float, sweep, rush, whirl, flow in, flow from, surge, roll, tumble, march, continue, swell, ebb.

2. [To issue forth]—*Syn.* pour out, spurt, squirt, flood, jet, spout, rush, gush, emerge, well, out, drop, drip, sweep, emanate, trickle, overflow, spill, run, sputter, spew, stream, brim, cascade, swell, gurgle, surge, leak, exudate, run out, ooze, regurgitate, splash, distill, dribble, percolate, exude, pour forth, bubble.

3. [To keep up a circular motion]—*Syn.* swirl, eddy, ripple, circle, circulate, percolate, whirl, slosh.

flower, *n.* **1.** [A bloom]—*Syn.* blossom, bud, pompon, efflorescence, spike, spray, cluster, head, floweret, floret, shoot, inflorescence, cone.

2. [A plant valued for its bloom]—*Syn.* floweret, posy, herb, vine, annual, perennial, flowering shrub, potted plant.

Common flowers include the following—daisy, violet, cowslip, jack-in-the-pulpit, goldenrod, orchid, primrose, bluebell, salvia, geranium, begonia, pansy, calendula, forsythia, daffodil, jonquil, crocus, dahlia, cosmos, zinnia, tulip, iris, lily, petunia, gladiolus, aster, rose, peony, nasturtium, cyclamen, chrysanthemum, four-o'clock, gaillardia, poppy, morning-glory, lily-of-the-valley, clematis, buttercup, bougainvillaea, dandelion, fuchsia, bridal wreath, lilac, stock, sweet William, bachelor's button, tuberose, bleeding heart, phlox; see also **fruit** 1.

flower, *v.* —*Syn.* open, blossom, blow; see **bloom.**

flowerpot, *n.* —*Syn.* jardiniere, vase, stand, plant stand, window box, tub, pot, vessel, receptacle.

flowery, *mod.* **1.** [Ornate]—*Syn.* elaborate, ornamented, rococo; see **ornate** 1.

2. [*Said of writing or speech*]—*Syn.* florid, fancy, ornate; see **elegant** 4.

flowing, *mod.* —*Syn.* sweeping, sinuous, spouting, running, gushing, pouring out, emitting, rippling, smooth, issuing, fluid, tidal, liquid.

fluctuate, *v.* **1.** [To oscillate]—*Syn.* undulate, vibrate, flutter; see **wave** 3.

2. [To hesitate]—*Syn.* vacillate, waver, falter; see **hesitate.**

fluctuation, *n.* —*Syn.* vacillation, variation, inconstancy; see **change** 1.

flue, *n.* —*Syn.* pipe, vent, exhaust; see **chimney.**

fluency, *n.* —*Syn.* facility of speech, volubility, multiloquence; see **eloquence** 1.

fluent, *mod.* **1.** [Capable of flowing]—*Syn.* molten, liquid, influx; see **flowing.**

2. [Capable of speaking easily]—*Syn.* eloquent, voluble, loquacious, glib, facile, wordy, smooth, copious, talkative, mellifluent, mellifluous, able to speak readily, smooth-spoken, ready in speech, garrulous, effusive, declamatory, verbose, chatty, disputatious, argumentative, articulate, vocal, clamorous, cogent, persuasive, honeyed; *all* (D): blarneying, silver-tongued *or* -throated, blabbery, having *or* with the gift of gab.—*Ant.* dumb*, tongue-tied, stammering.

fluff, *n.* —*Syn.* foam, bubbles, down; see **froth, fur.**

fluffy, *mod.* —*Syn.* fleecy, fuzzy, lacy; see **downy.**

fluid, *mod.* —*Syn.* liquid, fluent, flowing, running, aqueous, watery, molten, liquefied, juicy, serous, lymphatic, uncongealed, in solution.—*Ant.* stiff*, solid, frozen.

fluid, *n.* —*Syn.* liquor, vapor, solution; see **liquid.**

flunk (D), *v.* —*Syn.* miss, drop, have to repeat; see **fail** 1.

flush, *mod.* —*Syn.* tight, close, full; see **flat** 1.

flute, *n.* —*Syn.* pipe, piccolo, whistle, flue, woodwind, wind instrument, fife, tube, shawm, Panpipe, recorder *or* fipple flute *or Blokflöte* (German), flageolet, transverse flute, direct flute *or flûte-à-bec* (French), German flute; see also **musical instrument.**

flutter, *v.* —*Syn.* flap, ripple, wiggle; see **wave** 1, 3.

fly, *n.* **1.** [An insect]—*Syn.* housefly, bluebottle, bug, winged insect, gnat, horsefly, fruit fly, tsetse fly.

2. [A ball batted into the air]—*Syn.* infield, fly, high fly, fly ball; *all* (D): fungo, aerial, boost, second-story work, pop fly, hoist.

3. [A hook baited artificially]—*Syn.* lure, weed, fish lure, dry fly, wet fly, spinner, trout fly, bass fly, minnow.

fly, *v.* **1.** [To pass through the air]—*Syn.* wing, soar, float, glide, remain aloft, take to the air, take flight, fly aloft, fly about, float in the air, take wing, hover, sail, swoop, dart, plummet, drift, flutter, circle.

2. [To move swiftly]—*Syn.* rush, dart, flee away; see **speed.**

3. [To flee from danger]—*Syn.* retreat, hide, withdraw; see **escape.**

4. [To manage a plane in the air]—*Syn.* pilot, navigate, control, aviate, jet, take off, operate, glide, climb, dive, manipulate, maneuver, zoom (D).

5. [To pass over by flying]—*Syn.* cross, circumnavigate, reach; see **travel** 2.

fly at, *v.* —*Syn.* assail, assault, rush (upon); see **attack** 1, 2.

flyer, *n.* **1.** [One who flies]—*Syn.* aviator, navigator, airman; see **pilot** 1.
2. [(D) A venture, especially in stocks]—*Syn.* purchase, investment, plunge (D); see **venture.**

flying, *mod.* **1.** [In flight]—*Syn.* floating, making flight, passing through the air, moving freely in the air, on the wing, soaring, gliding, winging, swooping, darting, plummeting, drifting, blowing, volant, rising, fleeting, swift, air-borne, in mid-air, zooming (D).
2. [In the habit of flying]—*Syn.* winged, avian, mercurial, plumed, air-minded, fond of air travel, Icarian.—*Ant.* earthbound, pedestrian, old-fashioned.

flying boat, *n.* —*Syn.* amphibian, patrol bomber, Catalina; see **plane** 3.

flying column, *n.* —*Syn.* task force, spearhead, pincer; see **army** 2.

flying machine, *n.* —*Syn.* airplane, hydroplane, glider; see **plane** 3.

fly leaf, *n.* —*Syn.* end paper, page, title page, end sheet.

foal, *n.* —*Syn.* filly, pony, colt; see **horse** 1.

foam, *n.* —*Syn.* fluff, bubbles, lather; see **froth.**

foam, *mod.* —*Syn.* bubbly, creamy, lathery; see **frothy** 1.

focus, *n.* —*Syn.* focal point, locus, point of convergence; see **center** 1.
in focus—*Syn.* distinct, obvious, sharply defined; see **clear** 2.
out of focus—*Syn.* indistinct, unclear, blurred; see **obscure** 1.

focus, *v.* **1.** [To draw toward a center]—*Syn.* attract, converge, convene; see **center.**
2. [To make an image clear]—*Syn.* adjust, bring out, get detail; see **sharpen** 2.

fodder, *n.* —*Syn.* food, hay, grain; see **feed.**

foe, *n.* —*Syn.* opponent, antagonist, adversary; see **enemy** 1, 2.

fog, *n.* **1.** [Vapor near the earth]—*Syn.* mist, exhalation, haze, Thule fog, murk, cloud, nebula, film, steam, wisp, effluvium, brume, smoke, London fog; *all* (D): grease, soup, pea soup, smog.
2. [Mental obscurity]—*Syn.* stupor, confusion, daze; see **uncertainty** 1, 2.

foggy, *mod.* —*Syn.* dull, misty, gray; see **hazy** 1.

foible, *n.* —*Syn.* mannerism, oddity, singularity; see **characteristic.**

foil, *n.* **1.** [Leaf metal]—*Syn.* lead foil, aluminum foil, gold foil, tin foil, film, flake, leaf.
2. [A defense]—*Syn.* parry, guard, counterblow; see **defense** 1.

fold, *n.* **1.** [Folded material]—*Syn.* lap, pleat *or* plait, lapel, tuck, overlap, folded portion, part turned over, part turned back, shirring, smocking, gathers, gatherings, doubled material.
2. [The line at which material is folded]—*Syn.* crease, turn, folded edge, crimp, wrinkle, knife-edge, pleat *or* plait.
3. [Animal pen]—*Syn.* cage, corral, coop; see **pen** 1.

fold, *v.* **1.** [To enclose]—*Syn.* envelop, involve, do up; see **wrap** 2.
2. [To place together, or lay in folds]—*Syn.* double, plait, crease, curl, crimp, wrinkle, laminate, ruffle, corrugate, pucker, gather, double over, telescope, lap, overlap, overlay.—*Ant.* unfold*, straighten, expand.
3. [(D) To fail]—*Syn.* become insolvent, declare oneself bankrupt, close; see **fail** 4.

folder, *n.* **1.** [A folded sheet of printed matter]—*Syn.* circular, pamphlet, paper, circular letter, broadsheet, broadside, bulletin, advertisement, enclosure, stuffer, brochure, throwaway (D).
2. [A light, flexible case]—*Syn.* envelope, binder, portfolio, wrapper, wrapping, sheath, pocket, manila folder.

folk, *n.* **1.** [A people]—*Syn.* race, nation, community, tribe, society, body politic, nationality, population, state, group, settlement, culture group, ethnic group, clan, confederation.
2. [The common people]—*Syn.* the lower orders, the masses, proletariat; see **people** 3.

folklore, *n.* —*Syn.* traditions, (folk) tales, oral tradition, folk wisdom, oral literature, ballad lore, customs, superstitions, legends, fables, folkways, folk wisdom, traditional lore; see also **myth.**

folks, (D), *n.* —*Syn.* relatives, relations, kin; see **family** 1.

follow, *v.* **1.** [To be later in time]—*Syn.* come next, ensue, postdate; see **succeed** 2.
2. [To regulate one's action]—*Syn.* conform, observe, imitate, copy, take after, match, walk in the steps of, mirror, reflect, follow the example of, do as, mimic, hold fast, follow suit, do like, emulate, tag along, obey, abide by, adhere to, string along, comply, be in keeping, harmonize, be consistent with, attend, accord.—*Ant.* disregard, neglect*, depart from.
3. [To be a follower]—*Syn.* serve, support, be with; see **obey** 2.
4. [To hunt]—*Syn.* chase, seek, track; see **pursue** 1.
5. [To observe]—*Syn.* heed, regard, keep an eye on; see **watch** 1.
6. [To understand]—*Syn.* comprehend, catch, realize; see **understand** 1.
7. [To result]—*Syn.* proceed *or* spring *or* come from, happen, ensue; see **begin** 2.
as follows—*Syn.* the following, next, succeeding; see **following.**

follower, *n.* —*Syn.* henchman, attendant, hanger-on, companion, vassal, lackey, helper, partisan, recruit, disciple, pupil, protegé, imitator, worshiper, satellite, votary, apostle, proselyte, adherent, supporter, zealot, backer, participant, sponsor, evangelist, witness, devotee, believer, advocate, member, admirer, patron, promoter, true believer, auxiliary, coadjutor, sectary, seconder, upholder; *all* (D): stooge, copycat, yes man.—*Ant.* opponent*, deserter, apostate.

following, *mod.* —*Syn.* succeeding, next, ensuing, subsequent, later, after a while, by and by, when, later on, a while later, then, henceforth, afterwards, presently, afterward, coming after, directly after, in the wake of, pursuing, in pursuit (of), in search (of), on the scent, loaded for bear, in full cry, resulting, latter, posterior, rear, hinder, back.—*Ant.* preceding*, former, earlier.

following, *n.* —*Syn.* coterie, group, discipleship, clientele, public, audience, train, retinue, adherents, supporters, hangers-on, patrons, dependents, retainers.

folly, *n.* —*Syn.* absurdity, vice, silliness; see **stupidity** 2.

fond, *mod.* —*Syn.* enamored, attached, affectionate; see **loving.**

fondle, *v.* —*Syn.* pet, dandle, make love to; see **caress.**

fondness, *n.* —*Syn.* partiality, attachment, kindness; see **affection.**—*Ant.* hate, dislike, disgust.

food, *n.* —*Syn.* victuals, foodstuffs, meat and drink, meat, nutriment, pabulum, refreshment, food web, viands, edibles, table, comestibles, provisions, stores, sustenance, subsistence, rations, mess, board, aliment, cooking, food to go, cookery, cuisine, nourishment, larder, fleshpots, fare; *all* (D): grub, vittles, eats, chow; see also **feed, meal** 2.
For food in the menu; see also **bread, butter, cake** 2, **candy, cheese, delicatessen** 1, **dessert, drink** 2, 3, **egg, entree** 2, **fish, flavoring, fowl, fruit** 1, **hors d'oeuvres, jam** 1, **jelly, milk, meat, nut** 1, **oil, pastry, pudding, salad, sauce** 1, 2, **soup, spice, stew, vegetable.**
Food as diet includes the following—cellulose, carbohydrates, fats, fibers, iron, minerals, oils, protein, proteids, salts, starches, sugars, vitamins.

food for thought, *n.* —*Syn.* meditations, reflections, point to ponder, something to think about, stimulation, stimulus.

fool, *n.* **1.** [A simple-witted person]—*Syn.* nitwit, simpleton, dunce, oaf, ninny, cretin, nincompoop, bore, dolt, idiot, jackass, ass, buffoon, blockhead, numbskull, booby, boob, clodplate, dunderhead, goose, ignoramus, imbecile, moron, clown, tomfool, wiseacre, witling, donkey, looby, noddy, noodle, innocent, loon, dullard, jolthead, fathead, halfwit, mooncalf, lightweight, dotard, babbler, driveler, Simple Simon, silly; *all* (D): bonehead, simp, dope, nerd, turkey, dumbdumb, meathead, sap, birdbrain, lamebrain, noodlehead, dumb ox, lunkhead, numbskull, dimwit, dumbbell, jerk, chump, crackpot.—*Ant.* philosopher*, sage, scholar.
2. [One made to seem foolish]—*Syn.* butt, laughingstock, victim, clown, poor fish, schlemiel, dupe, gull, gudgeon, cully, stooge, fair game; *all* (D): goat, sucker, fall guy, pushover, mess, lug, screwball, crackpot, setup, (easy) mark.
no (*or* **nobody's**) **fool**—*Syn.* shrewd, calculating, capable; see **able** 1, 2, **intelligent** 1.
play the fool—*Syn.* be silly, show off, clown; see **joke.**

fool, *v.* —*Syn.* trick, dupe, mislead; see **deceive.**

fool around, *v.* —*Syn.* waste time, idle, dawdle; see **waste** 1, 2, **play** 1, 2.

fool away, *v.* —*Syn.* waste money, spend, squander; see **waste** 2.

fooled, *mod.* —*Syn.* tricked, duped, deluded; see **deceived** 1.

foolery, *n.* —*Syn.* absurdity, foolishness, folly; see **nonsense** 1, 2.

foolhardy, *mod.* —*Syn.* impetuous, precipitate, headlong; see **rash.**

fooling, *mod.* —*Syn.* joking, jesting, quippish, humorous, deceitful, waggish, gay, roguish, impish, bantering, trifling, jovial, witty, smart, frivolous, flippant, droll, laughable, insincere, misleading, prankish, light, frolicking, absurd, clever, facetious, jocular, playful, merry, sportive, pointed, trivial; *all* (D): kidding, joshing, spoofing, jollying.—*Ant.* serious*, grave, earnest.

foolish, *mod.* —*Syn.* silly, simple, irrational, halfwitted; see **stupid** 1.

foolishly, *mod.* —*Syn.* stupidly, irrationally, idiotically, witlessly, fatuously, insanely, injudiciously, imprudently, weakmindedly, unintelligently, uncomprehendingly, ineptly, mistakenly, illogically, unwisely, ill-advisedly, crazily, thoughtlessly, carelessly, irresponsibly, regrettably, absurdly, preposterously, ridiculously, with bad judgment, without good sense; *all* (D): boneheadedly, dumbly, like a jackass.—*Ant.* intelligently*, wisely, advisedly.

foolishness, *n.* **1.** [The quality of lacking good sense] —*Syn.* folly, weakness, silliness; see **stupidity** 1.
2. [Conduct or acts lacking good sense]—*Syn.* nonsense, mistake, indiscretion; see **stupidity** 2, 3.

foot, *n.* **1.** [A unit of measurement]—*Syn.* twelve inches, running foot, front foot, board foot, square foot, cubic foot.
2. [End of the leg]—*Syn.* pedal extremity, *pes* (Latin), hoof, paw, pad; *all* (D): barker, dog, tootsie, kicker, trotter, purp.
3. [A foundation]—*Syn.* footing, base, pier; see **foundation** 2.
4. [A metrical unit in verse]—*Syn.* measure, accent, interval, meter, duple meter, triple meter.
Metrical feet include the following—iamb, dactyl, spondee, trochee, anapest, dipod, amphibrach.
on foot—*Syn.* running, hiking, moving; see **walking.**
on one's feet—*Syn.* **1.** standing, erect, vertical; see **upright** 1. **2.** sound, settled, secure; see **established** 1.
on the wrong foot (D)—*Syn.* unfavorably, ineptly, incapably; see **wrongly** 2.
put one's best foot forward (D)—*Syn.* do one's best, appear at one's best, try hard; see **display** 1.
put one's foot down (D)—*Syn.* be firm, act decisively, determine; see **resolve** 1.
put one's foot in it *or* **in one's mouth**—*Syn.* embarrass oneself and others, blunder, be indiscreet; see **botch.**
under foot—*Syn.* on the ground *or* the floor, at one's feet, in one's way; see **under** 1.

football, *n.* **1.** [A sport]—*Syn.* American football, Association football, rugby, soccer; *all* (D): the pigskin sport, grid game, gridiron pastime, moleskin tussle.
2. [The ball used in football, sense 1]—*Syn.* regulation football; *all* (D): oval, inflated oval, apple, bacon, hide, porkhide, leather oval, pigskin, peanut, pineapple, porker, moleskin, sphere, swineskin, watermelon.
The National League football teams include the following—National Conference: Atlanta Falcons, Chicago Bears, Dallas Cowboys, Detroit Lions, Green Bay Packers, Los Angeles Rams, Minnesota Vikings, New Orleans Saints, New York Giants, Philadelphia Eagles, St. Louis Cardinals, San Francisco 49ers, Tampa Bay Buccaneers, Washington Redskins; American Conference: Buffalo Bills, Cincinnati Bengals, Cleveland Browns, Denver Broncos, Houston Oilers, Indianapolis Colts, Kansas City

Chiefs, Los Angeles Raiders, Miami Dolphins, New England Patriots, New York Jets, Pittsburgh Steelers, San Diego Chargers, Seattle Seahawks.

football player, *n.* —*Syn.* *all* (D): footballer, pigskin player, gridder, booter.
In the United States, football players include the following—right end, left end, right tackle, left tackle, right guard, left guard, center, quarterback, left halfback, right halfback, fullback; safety, linebacker, tight end, wide end, cornerback, flanker, nose guard.

footboy, *n.* —*Syn.* squire, page, lackey; see **servant.**

footfall, *n.* —*Syn.* tread, step, pace; see **gait** 1.

foothold, *n.* —*Syn.* ledge, crevice, footing, purchase, space, niche.

footing, *n.* —*Syn.* basis, resting place, foot; see **foothold.**

footman, *n.* —*Syn.* man in waiting, liveryman, lackey; see **servant.**

footpath, *n.* —*Syn.* bridle path, way, trail; see **path** 1.

footprint, *n.* —*Syn.* trace, trail, footstep; see **track** 2.

foot soldier, *n.* —*Syn.* infantryman, trooper, regular; see **soldier.**

footstep, *n.* —*Syn.* trace, trail, evidence; see **track** 2.
follow in (someone's) footsteps—*Syn.* emulate, succeed, resemble a predecessor; see **imitate** 2.

footstool, *n.* —*Syn.* footrest, ottoman, hassock; see **stool.**

fop, *n.* —*Syn.* dude, dandy, beau, exquisite, fashion plate, coxcomb, buck, dasher, silk stocking, macaroni, blade, man about town, fine gentleman, swell (D).

foppery, *n.* —*Syn.* coxcombry, showiness, ostentation; see **pretense** 1.

foppish, *mod.* —*Syn.* dapper, natty, vain; see **egotistic** 2.

for, *conj.* —*Syn.* as, since, in consequence of the fact that; see **because.**

for, *prep.* —*Syn.* toward, to, in favor of, intended to be given to, in order to get, under the authority of, in the interest of, during, in order to, in the direction of, to go to, to the amount of, to the extent of, in place of, in exchange for, as, in spite of, supposing, to counterbalance, concerning, with respect *or* regard to, conducive *or* beneficial to, notwithstanding, with a view to, for the sake of, in contemplation of, in consideration of, in furtherance of, in the name of, on the part of, in pursuance of.

forage, *v.* —*Syn.* search, pilfer, plunder; see **raid, ravage.**

forasmuch (as), *conj.* —*Syn.* since, inasmuch as, whereas; see **because.**

for a time, *mod.* —*Syn.* for a (long) while, for a long time, for some time, for hours, for days, for weeks, for *or* during the next few days, weeks, etc.

for a while, *mod.* —*Syn.* for a short time, for a few minutes, briefly; see **awhile.**

foray, *n.* —*Syn.* raid, invasion, inroad; see **attack** 1.

forbear, *v.* —*Syn.* cease, refrain, pause; see **abstain.**

forbearance, *n.* —*Syn.* avoidance, temperance, restraint; see **abstinence.**

for better or for worse, *mod.* —*Syn.* regardless, in any event, no matter what happens; see **anyhow** 1, 2.

forbid, *v.* —*Syn.* prohibit, debar, embargo, restrain, interdict, inhibit, preclude, oppose, cancel, hinder, obstruct, bar, prevent, enjoin, censor, outlaw, declare illegal, withhold, restrict, deny, block, check, disallow, deprive, exclude, ban, taboo, proscribe, say No to, put under the ban, put under an injunction; see also **halt** 2.—*Ant.* approve*, recommend, authorize.

forbidden, *mod.* —*Syn.* denied, taboo, kept back; see **refused.**

forbidding, *mod.* [Having an unfriendly appearance]—*Syn.* unpleasant, offensive, repulsive; see **grim** 1. **1.** [Having an ominous look]—*Syn.* sinister, threatening, frightening; see **ominous.**

force, *n.* **1.** [Force conceived as a physical property] —*Syn.* power, might, energy; see **strength** 1.
2. [Force conceived as a form of energy]—*Syn.* horsepower, potential, dynamism; see **energy** 3.
3. [Force conceived as part of one's personality] —*Syn.* forcefulness, dominance, competence, energy, persistence, willpower, drive, determination, effectiveness, efficiency, authority, impressiveness, ability, capability, potency, puissance, sapience; *all* (D): push, gumption, guts, intestinal fortitude. —*Ant.* indifference*, impotence, incompetence.
4. [A body of men capable of exerting force] —*Syn.* band, organization, troop, cell, division, unit; see **army** 2.
in force—*Syn.* **1.** in full strength, totally, all together; see **all** 2. **2.** operative, valid, in effect; see **working.**

force, *v.* **1.** [To use force]—*Syn.* compel, coerce, press, drive, make, impel, constrain, oblige, urge (forward), obligate, necessitate, require, enforce, demand, order, decree, command, force upon, inflict, burden, impose, fix, apply, insist, exact, draft, blackmail, force out of hiding, bind, put under obligation, contract, charge, restrict, limit, pin down, choke out, bring pressure to bear upon, bear hard upon, bear down (against *or* upon), obtrude on, break through; *all* (D): ram down one's throat, put the squeeze on, high-pressure, strong-arm, put the screws to, smoke out.
2. [To break open]—*Syn.* burst, pry *or* prize open, break in *or* into, extort, undo, use a bar on, assault; *both* (D): jimmy, crack *or* bust (wide open).
3. [To rape]—*Syn.* violate, attack, assault; see **rape.**
4. [To encourage growth]—*Syn.* quicken, cultivate, culture; see **farm** 1.
5. [To capture by assault]—*Syn.* take, win, overcome; see **seize** 2.

forced, *mod.* —*Syn.* compelled, coerced, constrained; see **bound** 2.

forceful, *mod.* —*Syn.* commanding, dominant, electric; see **powerful** 1.

forcefully, *mod.* —*Syn.* forcibly, stubbornly, willfully; see **vigorously.**

forcible, *mod.* —*Syn.* effective, vigorous, cogent; see **persuasive.**

forcibly, *mod.* —*Syn.* coercively, powerfully, effectively; see **vigorously.**

ford, *n.* —*Syn.* portage, passage, shallow; see **crossing** 1.

fore, *mod.* —*Syn.* forward, near, nearest; see **front.**

forebear, *n.* —*Syn.* ancestor, forerunner, progenitor; see **forefather.**

forebode, *v.* —*Syn.* forewarn, portend, prophesy; see **foretell.**

foreboding, *n.* **1.** [A feeling of impending evil] —*Syn.* premonition, dread, presentiment; see **anticipation** 2.

2. [An omen]—*Syn.* prediction, omen, prophecy; see **warning.**

forecast, *n.* —*Syn.* prediction, guess, estimate, budget, prognostication, prognosis, divination, forethought, foresight, prescience, foreknowledge, precognition, foretoken, conjecture, prophecy, foretelling, calculation, foreseeing, prevision, vaticination, augury.—*Ant.* reminiscence*, retrospect, retrospection.

forecast, *v.* **1.** [To foresee]—*Syn.* divine, augur, prophesy; see **anticipate** 1.

2. [To predict]—*Syn.* prognosticate, prophesy, gauge, calculate, determine, predetermine, presage, portend, infer, reason, demonstrate, guess; *both* (D): dope (out), figure out; see also **foretell.**

foreclose, *v.* **1.** [To exclude]—*Syn.* shut out, exclude, deprive; see **bar** 1, 2.

2. [To hinder]—*Syn.* impede, obstruct, preclude; see **hinder.**

foredoom, *v.* —*Syn.* doom, predestine, foreordain; see **condemn** 1.

forefather, *n.* —*Syn.* ancestor, progenitor, forebear, founder of the family, father, parent, sire, grandsire, forerunner, author, predecessor, originator, precursor, primogenitor, grandfather, procreator, patriarch, paterfamilias, relative, begetter, founder, kinsman; *all* (D): gaffer, grandpa, grandpop.

for effect, *mod.* —*Syn.* insincerely, artificially, hypocritically, ostentatiously, demonstratively, purposely, deliberately.

forefinger, *n.* —*Syn.* index finger, pointer, digit; see **finger.**

forego, *v.* —*Syn.* quit, relinquish, waive; see **abandon** 1.

foregoing, *mod.* —*Syn.* prior, former, previous; see **preceding.**

foregone, *mod.* —*Syn.* prior, previous, earlier; see **preceding.**

foreground, *n.* —*Syn.* face, forefront, frontage, façade, anteriority, nearer view, (immediate) prospect, neighborhood, proximity, propinquity, nearness, contiguity, adjacency, purview, immediate survey, range, reach, view.—*Ant.* background*, shadow, perspective.

forehanded, *mod.* **1.** [Wealthy]—*Syn.* wealthy, provident, well-to-do; see **rich** 1.

2. [Prudent]—*Syn.* sparing, thrifty, frugal; see **careful.**

forehead, *n.* —*Syn.* brow, front, aspect, visage, countenance, temples, foretop (D).

foreign, *mod.* **1.** [Concerning a country, idea, or way of life not one's own]—*Syn.* remote, exotic, strange, far, distant, inaccessible, unaccustomed, different, unknown, unfamiliar, outside, expatriate, exiled, from abroad, coming from another land, derived from another country, not native, not domestic, nonresident, alienated, estranged, extraneous, antipodal, faraway, far-off, hyperborean, beyond the rainbow, unexplored, transoceanic, transmarine, ultramontane, at the far corners of the earth, at the uttermost end of the earth, extralocal, nonnative, beyond the pale, outlandish.—*Ant.* local*, national, indigenous.

2. [Coming from a country not one's own]—*Syn.* alien, imported, borrowed, far-fetched, immigrant, barbarian, barbaric, adopted.—*Ant.* native*, homemade, aboriginal.

3. [Organically or essentially different]—*Syn.* heterogeneous, unassimilable, obstructive; see **unusual** 2.

foreigner, *n.* —*Syn.* stranger, immigrant, newcomer; see **alien.**

foreignism, *n.* —*Syn.* alienism, exoticism, idiom; see **language** 1.

foreknowledge, *n.* —*Syn.* foresight, prescience, premonition; see **feeling** 4, **forecast.**

foreland, *n.* —*Syn.* promontory, cliff, bluff; see **cape** 1.

foreman, *n.* —*Syn.* overseer, manager, supervisor, superintendent, taskmaster, head, head man, shop foreman, gang foreman; *all* (D): boss, straw boss, bossman, slavedriver.

foremost, *mod.* —*Syn.* fore, original, primary; see **first** 1.

forenoon, *n.* —*Syn.* morn, early part of the day, cool of the day; see **morning** 2.

forensic, *mod.* **1.** [Judicial]—*Syn.* juridical, legal, juristic; see **judicial.**

2. [Argumentative]—*Syn.* disputative, debatable, rhetorical; see **controversial.**

foreordain, *v.* —*Syn.* predestine, forshadow, destine; see **foretell.**

forerunner, *n.* —*Syn.* herald, harbinger, precursor; see **forefather, messenger.**

foresee, *v.* —*Syn.* prophesy, understand, predict; see **foretell.**

foreseen, *mod.* —*Syn.* anticipated, predictable, prepared for; see **expected** 2, **likely** 1.

foreshadow, *v.* —*Syn.* imply, presage, suggest; see **foretell.**

foresight, *n.* **1.** [Power to imagine the future] —*Syn.* forethought, forehandedness, premeditation; see **feeling** 4.

2. [Provision for the future]—*Syn.* economy, carefulness, husbandry; see **prudence.**

forest, *n.* —*Syn.* wood, woods, jungle, timber, timberland, growth, stand of trees, grove, woodland, virgin forest, the forest primeval, park, greenwood, cover, covert, clump, area below timberline, timbered *or* forested land *or* area, shelter, chase, brake, copse, coppice, holt, wold, weald, hurst, spinney, backwoods, tall timber; see also **tree.**

forestall, *v.* **1.** [To hinder]—*Syn.* thwart, prevent, preclude; see **hinder.**

2. [To anticipate]—*Syn.* await, provide against, look forward to; see **anticipate** 2.

forest fire, *n.* —*Syn.* holocaust, blaze, conflagration; see **fire** 1, 2.

forestry, *n.* —*Syn.* forest ranging, ranger service, management of growing timber, arboriculture, horticulture, dendrology, woodcraft, afforestation, silviculture, forestation, reclamation, tree-planting, woodmanship, conservation.

foretaste, *n.* —*Syn.* antepast, first experience, prelibation; see **anticipation** 1.

foretell, *v.—Syn.* predict, prophesy, foreshow, prognosticate, divine, foresee, announce in advance, tell before the occurrence, auspicate, cast a horoscope, foreknow, forebode, augur, betoken, portend, foreshadow, adumbrate, presage, call one's shot (D).—*Ant.* record*, confirm, recount.

forethought, *n.—Syn.* provision, planning, foresight; see **prudence.**

forever, *mod.* **1.** [For all time]—*Syn.* everlastingly, permanently, immortally, until the Day of Judgment *or* the end of time *or* Doomsday, on and on, ever, perpetually, always, evermore, aye, in perpetuity, world without end, *saecula saeculorum* (Latin), lastingly, eternally, interminably, enduringly, unchangingly, durably, ever and again, indestructibly, endlessly, infinitely, forevermore; *all* (D): for good (and all), till hell freezes over, for keeps, from the cradle to the grave, for life, for always, without cease, now and forever, in all ages, till death do us part.—*Ant.* temporarily*, for a time, at present.
2. [Continuously]—*Syn.* perpetually, unendingly, ceaselessly; see **regularly** 2.

forewarn, *v.—Syn.* premonish, admonish, alarm; see **warn** 1.

foreword, *n.—Syn.* preface, prologue, preamble; see **introduction** 4.

for example, *mod.—Syn.* for instance, as a model, *exempli gratia or* e.g. (Latin), as an example, to illustrate, to cite an instance, to give *or* offer *or* provide an illustration, a case in point, like (D).

forfeit, *v.—Syn.* sacrifice, give up, give over, relinquish; see **abandon** 1.

forfeiture, *n.—Syn.* abandonment, giving up, relinquishment; see **loss** 1.

forfend, *v.—Syn.* protect, fortify, secure; see **defend** 1, 2.

for fun, *mod.—Syn.* for no reason, for the fun of it, in fun; *all* (D): for kicks, for laughs, (just) for ducks.

forgather, *v.—Syn.* congregate, convene, assemble; see **gather** 1,

forge, *v.—Syn.* falsify, counterfeit, fabricate, imitate fraudulently, trump up, coin, invent, frame, feign, make, fashion, design, imitate, produce, copy, transcribe, duplicate, reproduce, trace.

forger, *n.—Syn.* falsifier, counterfeiter, coiner; see **criminal.**

forgery, *n.—Syn.* imitation, copy, imposture, cheat, counterfeit, fake, fabrication, sham, imposition; *all* (D): bogus, phony, funny, pseudo.—*Ant.* work*, real thing, original.

forget, *v.* **1.** [To lose memory]—*Syn.* lose consciousness of, put out of one's head, fail to remember, misremember, let bygones be bygones, be forgetful, have a short memory, consign to oblivion, think no more of; *all* (D): disremember, clean forget, go blotto, close one's eyes to, not give another thought, draw a blank, dismiss from the mind, kiss off, laugh off *or* away.—*Ant.* remember*, recall, recollect.
2. [To neglect accidentally]—*Syn.* overlook, ignore, omit, neglect, slight, disregard, pass over, lose sight of, skip, drop it (D); see also **neglect** 2. —*Ant.* perform*, attend to, discharge.
3. [To forget oneself]—*Syn.* transgress, act badly, trespass; see **misbehave.**

forget about, *v.—Syn.* omit, let slip one's memory, miss; see **forget** 2, **neglect** 2.

forgetful, *mod.* **1.** [Absent-minded]—*Syn.* preoccupied, dreamy, distracted; see **absent-minded.**
2. [Careless]—*Syn.* inattentive, neglectful, heedless; see **careless** 1.

forgetfulness, *n.—Syn.* negligence, heedlessness, inattention; see **carelessness.**

forget oneself, *v.—Syn.* offend, trespass, daydream; see **misbehave.**

forgivable, *mod.—Syn.* venial, trivial, pardonable; see **excusable.**

forgive, *v.* **1.** [To cease to resent]—*Syn.* pardon, dismiss from the mind, efface from the memory, pocket the affront, forgive and forget, let pass, palliate, excuse, condone, remit, forget, relent, bear no malice, exonerate, exculpate; *all* (D): let bygones be bygones, laugh it off, charge off, let up on, let it go, kiss and make up, bury the hatchet, turn the other cheek, charge to experience, make allowance, write off.—*Ant.* hate*, resent, retaliate.
2. [To absolve]—*Syn.* acquit, pardon, release; see **excuse** 1.

forgiven, *mod.—Syn.* reinstated, taken back, welcomed home; see **pardoned.**

forgiveness, *n.—Syn.* absolution, pardon, acquittal, exoneration, remission, dispensation, exculpation, extenuation, reprive, quittance, justification, amnesty, respite, memory.

forgiving, *mod.—Syn.* noble, open-hearted, free; see **kind** 1.

for good, *mod.—Syn.* permanently, for all time, henceforth; see **forever.**

forgotten, *mod.—Syn.* not remembered *or* recalled *or* recollected, unremembered, unrecalled, unrecollected, unretained, obliterated, lost, lapsed, (clear *or* clean) out of one's mind, gone out of *or* erased from one's mind *or* recollection *or* consciousness, beyond *or* past recollection *or* recall, consigned to *or* buried in *or* sunk in oblivion, not recoverable, blotted *or* blanked out, become a victim of amnesia; see also **abandoned.**

fork, *n.* **1.** [A furcated implement]—*Syn.* table fork, hay fork, pitchfork, manure fork, trident, prong, spear, scepter.
2. [A branch of a road or river]—*Syn.* bend, turn, crossroad, crotch, tributary, byway, junction, confluence, branch, stream, creek.

forked, *mod.—Syn.* angled, zigzag, pronged, branching, bifurcate(d), furcate(d), trident(ed), branched.

forlorn, *mod.—Syn.* forsaken, forgotten, miserable; see **abandoned** 1.

form, *n.* **1.** [Shape]—*Syn.* figure, appearance, plan, arrangement, design, outline, conformation, configuration, formation, structure, style, stance, construction, fashion, mode, scheme, framework, *Gestalt* (German), contour, profile, silhouette, skeleton, anatomy, articulation.
2. [The human form]—*Syn.* body, frame, torso; see **figure** 2.
3. [The approved procedure]—*Syn.* manner, mode, custom; see **method** 2.
4. [Anything intended to give form]—*Syn.* pattern, model, die; see **mold** 1.

5. [A standard letter or blank]—*Syn.* mimeographed letter, duplicate, routine letter, pattern, form letter, data sheet, information blank, chart, card, reference form, order form, questionnaire, application; see also **copy.**
6. [A rite]—*Syn.* ritual, formality, custom; see **ceremony** 2.
7. [Type]—*Syn.* make, sort, class; see **kind** 2.
8. [Arrangement]—*Syn.* organization, placement, scheme; see **order** 3.
9. [Convention]—*Syn.* habit, practice, usage; see **custom** 1, 2.

form, *v.* **1.** [To give shape to a thing]—*Syn.* mold, pattern, model, arrange, make, block out, block, fashion, construct, devise, plan, design, contrive, produce, invent, frame, scheme, plot, compose, erect, build, cast, cut, carve, chisel, hammer out, put together, plane, whittle, assemble, conceive, create, outline, trace, develop, cultivate, work, complete, finish, consummate, perfect, fix, regulate, put *or* knock together, establish, sculpture, pat, bend, twist, knead, set, determine, arrive at, reach, settle, articulate.—*Ant.* destroy*, demolish, shatter.
2. [To give character to a person]—*Syn.* instruct, rear, breed; see **teach** 1, 2.
3. [To comprise]—*Syn.* constitute, figure in, act as; see **compose** 1.
4. [To take form]—*Syn.* accumulate, condense, harden, set, settle, rise, appear, take shape, grow, develop, unfold, mature, materialize, eventuate, become a reality, take on character, assume definite characteristics, become visible; *all* (D): round into shape, shape up, fall into place, get into shape *or* shaped up, be finalized.—*Ant.* disappear*, dissolve, waste away.

formal, *mod.* **1.** [Notable for arrangement]—*Syn.* orderly, precise, set; see **regular** 3.
2. [Concerned with etiquette and behavior] —*Syn.* reserved, distant, stiff; see **conventional** 2, 3, **polite** 1.
3. [Official]—*Syn.* confirmed, directed, lawful; see **approved, legal** 1.
4. [In evening clothes]—*Syn.* full dress, black tie, white tie, in tails and top hat, dressed up, ceremonious, social; *all* (D): dressy, be in one's glad rags, in a soup and fish.

formality, *n.* **1.** [Propriety]—*Syn.* decorum, etiquette, correctness; see **behavior** 1.
2. [Custom]—*Syn.* rule, convention, conventionality; see **custom** 2.

format, *n.*—*Syn.* make-up, arrangement, construction; see **form** 1.

formation, *n.* **1.** [The process of forming]—*Syn.* arrangement, crystallization, deposit, accumulation, production, composition, development, fabrication, generation, creation, genesis, induction, embodiment, synthesis, compilation, constitution. —*Ant.* destruction*, dissolution, annihilation.
2. [An arrangement]—*Syn.* disposition, dispersal, phalanx; see **order** 3.

formative, *mod.*—*Syn.* impressionable, impressible, moldable; see **immature, sensitive** 3.

formed, *mod.*—*Syn.* shaped, molded, patterned, modeled, carved, outlined, developed, cultivated, completed, finished, built, created, invented, forged, concocted, designed, accomplished, manufactured, produced, born, authored, consummated, perfected, fixed, established, solidified, hardened, set, determined, arrived at, reached, settled, articulated.—*Ant.* shapeless*, formless, nebulous.

former, *mod.*—*Syn.* earlier, previous, foregoing; see **preceding.**

formerly, *mod.*—*Syn.* before now, some time ago, once, once upon a time, already, in former times, previously, aforetime, erewhile, earlier, radically, time out of mind, in the early days, eons *or* centuries ago, anciently, in the past, in the olden days, used to be, long ago, earlier, before this, in time past, heretofore; *both* (D): a while back, in Grandad's *or* Grandfather's *or* Grandmother's time. —*Ant.* recently*, subsequently, immediately.

formidable, *mod.*—*Syn.* fearful, dangerous, impregnable; see **terrible** 1.

form in *or* into line, *v.*—*Syn.* line up, dress right, form in a column of twos, fours, etc.; see **line up.**

formless, *mod.*—*Syn.* chaotic, vague, indeterminate; see **shapeless** 1.

formula, *n.* **1.** [A prescription]—*Syn.* direction, specifications, description, formulary, recipe; see also **method** 2.
2. [A set speech or form]—*Syn.* rote, creed, credo, ritual, established mode of speech, code, formal statement; see also **custom** 1, 2.
3. [A statement of a supposed truth]—*Syn.* ratio, logarithm, equation, recipe, prescription, theorem. For formulas of the elements; see **element** 2.

formulary, *n.*—*Syn.* formula, model, form; see **method** 2.

formulate, *v.*—*Syn.* express, give form to, set down; see **form** 1.

fornication, *n.*—*Syn.* adultery, whoredom, incontinence, lubricity, carnality, lechery, improper *or* illicit intercourse, unlicensed intercourse, unchastity, lewdness, libidinousness, licentiousness, venery, unfaithfulness, harlotry, prostitution, concubinage, concupiscence, promiscuousness, coitus, debauchery, libertinism; see also **copulation.**

for rent, *mod.*—*Syn.* on the market, renting, selling, for hire, saleable, available, offering, offered, advertised, to let.

forsake, *v.* **1.** [To relinquish]—*Syn.* renounce, disclaim, surrender; see **abandon** 1.
2. [To abandon]—*Syn.* desert, leave, quit; see **abandon** 2.

forsaken, *mod.*—*Syn.* destitute, deserted, lorn; see **abandoned** 1.

for sale, *mod.*—*Syn.* selling, saleable, on the market, on auction, under the hammer, on the (auction) block, advertised, listed, for clearance; *all* (D): up (for sale), to be cleared (out), *or* knocked down.

for some time, *mod.*—*Syn.* for a long while, a long time, for hours; see **for a time.**

forsooth, *mod.*—*Syn.* truly, really, certainly, definitely; see **surely.**

forswear, *v.*—*Syn.* abjure, renounce, deny; see **abandon** 1, 2.

forswear oneself, *v.*—*Syn.* recant, swear falsely, bear false witness; see **lie** 1.

fort, *n.*—*Syn.* fortress, citadel, acropolis; see **fortification** 2.

forte, *n.* —*Syn.* gift, strong point, talent; see **specialty.**

forth, *mod.* —*Syn.* first, out, into; see **ahead** 2.
and so forth—*Syn.* and so on, similarly, and other; see **et cetera.**

forthcoming, *mod.* —*Syn.* expected, inevitable, anticipated, future, resulting, impending, pending, awaited, destined, fated, predestined, approaching, in store, at hand, inescapable, imminent, in prospect, prospective, in the wind, in preparation, in the cards (D).

for the time being, *mod.* —*Syn.* at the moment, for now, for the present; see **temporarily.**

forthright, *mod.* **1.** [Candid]—*Syn.* forward, sincere, blunt; see **frank.**
2. [Directly]—*Syn.* at once, straight away, forthwith; see **immediately.**

forthwith, *mod.* —*Syn.* at once, instantly, directly; see **immediately.**

fortification, *n.* **1.** [The process of fortification] —*Syn.* trench digging, consolidating, defensive preparation, castle, entrenchment, arming, defending, trenching, fortifying, pouring concrete, redoubt, preparing bases *or* air strips *or* landing fields, digging in (D).
2. [Works prepared for defense]—*Syn.* fort, fortress, breastwork, defense, dugout, trench, entrenchment, gun emplacement, barricade, battlement, blockhouse, stockade, outpost, citadel, support, outwork, wall, barrier, groin, buffer, block, barbican, earthwork, barbette, parapet, castle, pillbox, riflepit, bastion, bulwark, defense in depth, hedgehog defense, Maginot line, bolt position, hill position, orillon.

fortified, *mod.* —*Syn.* defended, guarded, safeguarded, protected, manned, garrisoned, barricaded, armed, barbed, electrified, entrenched, secured, strong, covered, strengthened, supported, surrounded, fortressed, walled, enclosed, stockaded, bulwarked, bastioned, armored, dug in, deeply entrenched, hidden, camouflaged, revetted, bristling with guns, supplied with antiaircraft guns, defended from the air, equipped with air bases *or* an antimissile system *or* an early warning system.—*Ant.* open*, unprotected, unguarded.

fortify, *v.* **1.** [To strengthen against attack]—*Syn.* barricade, entrench, buttress; see **defend** 1.
2. [To strengthen physically or emotionally] —*Syn.* hearten, cheer, sustain, encourage, invigorate; see also **strengthen.**

fortify oneself (D), *v.* —*Syn.* take nourishment, dine, prepare; see **eat** 1.

fortitude, *n.* —*Syn.* firmness, valor, fearlessness; see **determination** 2.

fortress, *n.* —*Syn.* stronghold, fort, citadel; see **fortification** 2.

fortuitous, *mod.* —*Syn.* accidental, casual, chance; see **incidental** 2.

fortunate, *mod.* **1.** [*Said of persons*]—*Syn.* lucky, blessed, prosperous, successful, having a charmed life, in luck, as luck would have it, favored, well-to-do, happy, triumphant, victorious, overcoming, winning, gaining, affluent, thriving, flourishing, healthy, wealthy, in good estate; *all* (D): well-fixed, well-heeled, lousy with dough, in the gravy, born with a silver spoon in one's mouth, born on the sunny side, rolling in sugar.—*Ant.* unfortunate*, unlucky, cursed.
2. [*Said of things*]—*Syn.* auspicious, fortuitous, advantageous; see **helpful** 1, **hopeful** 2.

fortunately, *mod.* —*Syn.* luckily, happily, by a happy chance, providentially, opportunely, seasonably, in good time, in good season, auspiciously, favorably, prosperously; in the nick of time (D). —*Ant.* unfortunately*, by an evil chance, unhappily.

fortune, *n.* **1.** [Chance]—*Syn.* luck, fate, certainty; see **destiny** 1.
2. [Great riches]—*Syn.* possessions, inheritance, estate; see **wealth** 2.
a small fortune (D)—*Syn.* a high price *or* cost, a great expense, a large amount of money; see **price.**
tell one's fortune—*Syn.* predict, prognosticate, foretell; see **forecast** 2.

fortuneteller, *n.* —*Syn.* spiritualist, medium, seer, crystal gazer, soothsayer, augur, oracle, prophet, sibyl, fatiloquist, chiromancer, palmist, palmreader, tea-leaf reader, tarot reader, phrenologist, mantic, clairvoyant, Cassandra, mind-reader.

forum, *n.* —*Syn.* hearing, mass meeting, consideration; see **discussion** 1.

forward, *mod.* **1.** [Going forward]—*Syn.* advancing, progressing, leading on, ahead, progressive, onward, propulsive, in advance.—*Ant.* backward*, retreating, regressive.
2. [At a forward position]—*Syn.* front, first, foremost; see **ahead** 2.
3. [Bold]—*Syn.* presumptuous, impertinent, fresh (D); see **rude** 2.

forwarded, *mod.* —*Syn.* shipped, expressed, dispatched; see **delivered.**

forwardness, *n.* —*Syn.* boldness, presumptuousness, impertinence; see **rudeness.**

fossil, *n.* —*Syn.* (organic) remains, reconstruction, specimen, skeleton, relic, impression, trace, petrified deposit, petrifaction.

foster, *v.* **1.** [To support]—*Syn.* cherish, nurse, nourish; see **raise** 2.
2. [To harbor]—*Syn.* encourage, nurture, cultivate; see **promote** 1.

foul, *mod.* **1.** [Soiled]—*Syn.* unclean, filthy, impure; see **dirty** 1.
2. [Disgusting]—*Syn.* nasty, vulgar, coarse; see **offensive** 2.
3. [Unfair]—*Syn.* vicious, inequitable, unjust; see **dishonest** 2.

foul, *v.* **1.** [To make dirty]—*Syn.* defile, pollute, sully; see **dirty.**
2. [To become dirty]—*Syn.* soil, spot, discolor, stain, be clogged *or* coated *or* encrusted *or* covered *or* blocked *or* filled, become filthy, soot, clog.
run *or* **fall** *or* **go foul of** (D)—*Syn.* get into trouble (with), encounter, err; see **meet** 6, **misbehave.**

foul-mouthed, *mod.* —*Syn.* coarse, obscene, indecent; see **offensive** 2.

foul play, *n.* —*Syn.* unfairness, assault, violation; see **crime** 1, **injustice** 2.

found, *mod.* **1.** [Discovered]—*Syn.* unearthed, described, detected; see **discovered.**
2. [Occurring customarily]—*Syn.* common, native to *or* in, characteristic of; see **conventional** 1.

found, *v.* —*Syn.* establish, endow, set up; see **organize** 2.

foundation, *n.* **1.** [An intellectual basis]—*Syn.* reason, justification, authority; see **basis** 1.
2. [A physical basis]—*Syn.* footing, base, foot, basement, pier, groundwork, bed, ground, resting place, bottom, substructure, wall, understructure, underpinning, solid rock, rest, roadbed, support, substratum, prop, stand, bolster, stay, skid, shore, pediment, post, pillar, infrastructure, skeleton, column, shaft, pedestal, buttress, abutment, framework, scaffold, beam, chassis, skewback, pile.
3. [That which has been founded]—*Syn.* institution, organization, endowment, institute, society, plantation, establishment, company, guild, trusteeship, corporation, company, association, charity.

founded, *mod.* —*Syn.* organized, endowed, set up; see **established** 2.

founder, *n.* —*Syn.* originator, patron, prime mover; see **author** 1, **forefather.**

founding, *mod.* —*Syn.* establishing, endowing, instituting, originating, setting up, planting, colonizing, authorizing.

founding, *n.* —*Syn.* originating, setting up, starting; see **establishing** 1.

foundling, *n.* —*Syn.* castaway, derelict, waif; see **orphan.**

foundry, *n.* —*Syn.* plant, shop, forge; see **factory.**

fountain, *n.* **1.** [A source]—*Syn.* cause, spring, font; see **origin** 2.
2. [A jet of water]—*Syn.* spray, jet, stream, gush, bubbler, drinking fountain, spout, geyser, pump, spurt, play.
3. [A soda-water dispensary]—*Syn.* soda fountain, bar, soda bar, ice-cream parlor, drugstore fountain.

fountainhead, *n.* —*Syn.* source, rise, cause; see **origin** 2, 3.

fountain pen, *n.* —*Syn.* self-filling pen, reservoir pen, filler (British); see **pen** 3.

fourflusher (D), *n.* —*Syn.* fake, cheat, pretender; see **imposter.**

fourfold, *mod.* —*Syn.* fourscore, four-cycle, four times as many; see **quadruple.**

four-handed, *mod.* —*Syn.* quadrumanous, requiring two players, involving four hands, rendering a duet.

four hundred, *n.* [*Used with* the]—*Syn.* jet set, (high) society, elite; see **aristocracy.**

foursome (D), *n.* —*Syn.* quarter, team, party, ensemble, group, four-handed game.

foursquare, *mod.* **1.** [Geometrical]—*Syn.* quadrangular, rectangular, geometrical; see **square.**
2. [Firm]—*Syn.* stable, solid, hard; see **firm** 1.
3. [Frank]—*Syn.* direct, honest, forthright; see **frank.**

fowl, *n.* —*Syn.* barnyard fowl, wild fowl, game, poultry; see also **bird** 1, **chicken** 1, **pigeon.**
Fowl include the following—chicken, duck, goose, turkey, guinea, peafowl, capon, cock, hen, Cornish hen, pheasant, partridge, prairie chicken, woodcock, grouse, ptarmigan, moorfowl, swan.

fox, *n.* **1.** [A clever person]—*Syn.* reynard, Volpone, artful dodger, cheat, trickster; *both* (D); con man, flimflam man; see also **rascal.**
2. [An animal]—*Syn.* canine, red fox, gray fox, silver fox, arctic fox.

fox trot, *n.* —*Syn.* one-step, tango, slow dance; see **dance** 1.

foxy, *mod.* **1.** [Shrewd]—*Syn.* subtle, experienced, knowing; see **intelligent** 1.
2. [Cunning]—*Syn.* wily, crafty, artful; see **sly** 1.

foyer, *n.* —*Syn.* anteroom, hall, lobby; see **room** 2.

fracas, *n.* —*Syn.* dispute, tumult, brawl; see **fight** 1.

fraction, *n.* —*Syn.* section, portion, part; see **division** 2.

fractional, *mod.* —*Syn.* partial, constituent, sectional, fragmentary, incomplete, divided, segmented, compartmented, parceled, apportioned, dismembered, dispersed, by fractions, piecemeal, fractionary.—*Ant.* whole*, total, complete.

fractious, *mod.* —*Syn.* perverse, touchy, cross; see **irritable.**

fracture, *n.* **1.** [The act of breaking]—*Syn.* rupture, disjunction, cleaving, cleavage, disseverment, riving, displacement, dismemberment, dislocation, sharing, severing, separating, dismembering.
2. [The result of being broken]—*Syn.* wound, cleft, mutilation, crack, shattering, breach, fragmentation; see **sense** 1.
3. [A break in the skeletal system]—*Syn.* broken bone, broken limb, simple fracture, closed fracture, compound fracture, greenstick fracture, ruptured cartilage; see **sense** 1 and 2.

fragile, *mod.* —*Syn.* brittle, frail, delicate; see **dainty** 1, **weak** 1, 2.

fragility, *n.* —*Syn.* frangibleness, frailty, brittleness; see **delicacy** 1.

fragment, *n.* —*Syn.* piece, scrap, remnant; see **bit** 1.

fragmentary, *mod.* —*Syn.* broken, incomplete, fractional; see **broken** 1.

fragrance, *n.* —*Syn.* perfume, aroma, redolence; see **smell** 1.

fragrant, *mod.* —*Syn.* aromatic, redolent, perfumed; see **odorous** 2.

frail, *mod.* —*Syn.* feeble, breakable, tender; see **dainty.**

frailty, *n.* **1.** [Quality of being weak]—*Syn.* fragility, weakness, debility, delicacy, infirmity, feebleness, decrepitude, daintiness, puniness, frangibility, susceptibility, brittleness, softness, flaccidity, effeminacy, unsubstantiality, flimsiness, limpness; *both* (D): wobbliness, rustiness.—*Ant.* strength*, indestructibility, firmness.
2. [A moral or social weakness]—*Syn.* foible, solecism, error; see **fault** 2.

frame, *n.* **1.** [The structural portion]—*Syn.* skeleton, scaffold, truss, framework, scaffolding, casing, framing, support, stage, groundwork, organization, anatomy, carcass, gantry, fabric, warp, architecture.
2. [An open structure]—*Syn.* case, enclosure, support, shutter, girdle, span, clasp, jamb, mold, block, stay, window frame, doorjamb.
3. [A border intended as an ornament]—*Syn.* margin, verge, fringe, hem, valance, flounce, trim, trimming, wreath, outline, mounting, molding, frieze.

frame, *v.* **1.** [To make]—*Syn.* construct, erect, raise; see **build** 1.
2. [To prepare a written statement]—*Syn.* draft, draw up, devise; see **write** 1.

3. [To enclose in a frame]—*Syn.* mount, border, enclose, encase, back, mat.

4. [To act as a frame]—*Syn.* encircle, set off, fringe, envelop, outline, block out, limit, confine, enshrine, enclose, wreath, wrap, clasp, girdle, compass.

5. [(D) To cause a miscarriage of justice]—*Syn.* conspire against, make take the blame; *all* (D): double-cross, set up, shop (British), plant, put up a job on, kangaroo, fix.

framed, *mod.* **1.** [Surrounded by a frame]—*Syn.* mounted, enclosed, bordered, encircled, fringed, enveloped, outlined, confined, enclosed, wreathed, wrapped, clasped, girdled, compassed.

2. [(D) Arranged beforehand]—*Syn.* faked; *all* (D): fixed, planted, cooked up, set up, trumped up.

3. [Made of wood]—*Syn.* timbered, beamed, raftered, girdered, scaffolded, trussed, constructed, carpentered.

frame of mind, *n.*—*Syn.* temper, attitude, outlook; see **mood** 1.

framer, *n.*—*Syn.* organizer, creator, composer; see **author** 1.

frame-up (D), *n.*—*Syn.* hoax, dodge, frame; see **trick** 1.

framework, *n.*—*Syn.* skeleton, structure, core; see **frame** 1.

France, *n.*—*Syn.* French nation, French people, French Republic, Fourth Republic, French Union, French empire, lands of the Franks, Gaul, *Gallia, la Patrie, La France, La belle France, l'esprit gallois* (*all* French).

franchise, *n.*—*Syn.* right, freedom, suffrage; see **vote** 3.

frank, *mod.*—*Syn.* artless, candid, sincere, free, easy, familiar, open, free in speaking, unreserved *or* bold in speech, direct, undissembling, unreserved, uninhibited, downright, apparent, ingenuous, unsophisticated, unaffected, plain, aboveboard, forthright, outspoken, open-faced, straightforward, saying what one thinks, plainspoken, natural, guileless, blunt, openhearted, matter-of-fact; *all* (D): straight from the shoulder, flat-out, putting one's finger on, calling a spade a spade.—*Ant.* secretive*, dishonest, insincere.

frankfurter, *n.*—*Syn.* wiener, wiener sausage; *all* (D): weenie, hot dog, chili dog, frank, dog, link.

frankincense, *n.*—*Syn.* perfume, resin, olibanum; see **incense.**

frankly, *mod.*—*Syn.* freely, honestly, candidly; see **openly** 1.

frankness, *n.*—*Syn.* openness, sincerity, ingenuousness; see **honesty** 1.

frantic, *mod.*—*Syn.* distracted, mad, wild, frenetic, furious, raging, raving, frenzied, violent, agitated, deranged, crazy, delirious, insane, rabid, angry; see also **excited** 1.—*Ant.* calm, composed, subdued.

fraternal, *mod.*—*Syn.* friendly, intimate, congenial; see **brotherly.**

fraternity, *n.*—*Syn.* brotherhood, Greek letter society, fellowship; see **organization** 3.

fraternize, *v.*—*Syn.* consort, associate, league; see **join** 2.

fraud, *n.* **1.** [Deceit]—*Syn.* trickery, duplicity, guile; see **deception** 1.

2. [An imposter]—*Syn.* pretender, charlatan, quack; see **cheat** 1, **imposter.**

fraudulent, *mod.*—*Syn.* deceitful, tricky, swindling; see **dishonest** 1, 2.

fraught, *mod.*—*Syn.* abounding, filled, laden; see **full** 1.

fray, *n.*—*Syn.* conflict, quarrel, brawl; see **fight** 1.

fray, *v.*—*Syn.* shred, tatter, wear away; see **ravel.**

frazzle, *n.* **1.** [Exhaustion]—*Syn.* enervation, prostration, collapse; see **lassitude.**

2. [A frayed end]—*Syn.* shred, remnant, rag; see **tear.**

freak, *n.* **1.** [A caprice]—*Syn.* vagary, whim, crotchet; see **fancy** 3.

2. [An abnormality]—*Syn.* monstrosity, monster, abortion, rarity, abnormity, anomaly, malformation, mutation, *lusus naturae* (Latin), grotesquerie, freak of nature, oddity, aberration, curiosity, *rara avis* (Latin), queer fish, black swan, sport, hybrid, mooncalf, changeling, hermaphrodite, androgyne, missing link, anthropophagite.

freakish, *mod.*—*Syn.* abnormal, odd, strange; see **unusual** 2.

freckle, *n.*—*Syn.* pigmentation, macula, lentigo, mole, patch, blemish, blotch.

free, *mod.* **1.** [Not restricted politically]—*Syn.* sovereign, independent, released, unregimented, autonomous, autonomic, autarchic, freed, liberated, enjoying democracy *or* political independence, self-directing, not subject to regulation, exempt from external authority, saved *or* removed from bondage, self-governing, democratic, self-ruling, enfranchised, at liberty, unconstrained.—*Ant.* restricted*, enslaved, subject.

2. [Not restricted in space; *said of persons*]—*Syn.* unconfined, at large, cast loose, clear of, escaped, let out *or* off, unshackled, unfettered, scot-free, free as air, free to come and go, foot-loose and fancy-free; *both* (D): freewheeling, on the loose.—*Ant.* confined*, imprisoned, restrained.

3. [Not restricted in space; *said of things*]—*Syn.* unimpeded, unobstructed, unhampered, unattached, loose, not held fast, not attached, not in contact with something else, clear from, unentangled, clear, unengaged, disengaged, extricated, untrammeled, unfastened.—*Ant.* fixed*, fastened, rooted.

4. [Given without charge]—*Syn.* gratuitous, gratis, for nothing, for love, without charge, free of cost, complimentary; *all* (D): for free, for love, on the house, cuffo, as a comp, for a thank-you, free for nothing—*Ant.* paid*, charged, costly.

5. [Not restricted in speech or conduct]—*Syn.* liberal, lax, loose; see **easy** 1, **frank.**

for free (D)—*Syn.* without cost, gratis, unencumbered; see **free** 4.

give a free hand (D)—*Syn.* permit, give permission, encourage; see **allow** 1.

make free with (D)—*Syn.* exploit, utilize, appropriate; see **use** 1.

set free—*Syn.* release, liberate, discharge, emancipate; see **free** 1.

with a free hand—*Syn.* **1.** easily, voluntarily, purposely; see **freely** 1, 2. **2.** unrestrained, unlimited, unchecked; see **free** 1, 2.

free, *v.* **1.** [To liberate]—*Syn.* release, discharge, deliver, save, emancipate, rescue, extricate, loose, loosen, unfix, unbind, disengage, undo, set free, let out *or* loose, bail out, cut loose, relieve, reprieve, restore, absolve, acquit, dismiss, pardon, clear, enfranchise, affranchise, ransom, redeem, unfetter, unbind, unshackle, manumit, unchain, disentangle, disenthrall, disimprison, demobilize, untie, let go, unlock, unhand, unbar, let out of prison, open the cage, turn loose (D).—*Ant.* seize*, capture, incarcerate.

2. [To disburden]—*Syn.* decontaminate, desterilize, disencumber, relieve, discharge, unload, cast *or* put off, disengage, empty, unburden, disembarrass.

freebooter, *n.*—*Syn.* buccaneer, robber, highwayman; see **pirate.**

freed, *mod.*—*Syn.* liberated, released, discharged; see **free** 1, 2, 3.

freedom, *n.* **1.** [Political liberty]—*Syn.* independence, sovereignty, autonomy, democracy, self-government, enfranchisement, franchise, citizenship, prerogative, autarchy, self-determination, representative government; see also **liberty** 4. —*Ant.* slavery*, bondage, regimentation.

2. [Exemption from necessity]—*Syn.* privilege, immunity, license, carte blanche, licentiousness, indulgence, unrestraint, facility, range, latitude, scope, bent, play, own accord, free rein, full play, laissez faire, leeway; *both* (D): lazy fair, plenty of rope.—*Ant.* restraint*, constraint, hindrance.

3. [Natural ease and facility]—*Syn.* readiness, forthrightness, spontaneity; see **ease** 2.

4. [Liberty of action]—*Syn.* right to decide, freedom to choose *or* of choice, license; see **choice** 1, **choosing.**

free-for-all (D), *n.*—*Syn.* riot, battle, knock-down, drag-out fight; see **fight** 1.

freehand, *mod.*—*Syn.* drawn, sketched, unrestrained; see **easy** 1, **original** 2.

free hand, *n.*—*Syn.* scope, latitude, facility, opportunity, complete liberty, discretion, authority.

freehanded, *mod.*—*Syn.* charitable, liberal, openhanded; see **generous** 1.

freeing, *n.*—*Syn.* emancipation, liberation, releasing, deliverance, manumission, delivery, saving, salvation, restoration, ransoming, extrication, loosing, unfettering, unlocking, unchaining, unbinding, reprieve, discharging, loosening, pardoning, granting freedom, letting loose, setting free, removing fetters, setting at liberty, giving to the open air, freeing from prison *or* jail *or* concentration camp, demobilizing, untying.

free-lance, *mod.*—*Syn.* not under contract, unattached, independent, vagrant, amateur.

freely, *mod.* **1.** [Without physical restriction] —*Syn.* loosely, without encumbrance, unhindered, without restraint, as one pleases, without let *or* hindrance, unobstructedly, easily, without stint (D). —*Ant.* with difficulty*, under obstacles, in clogs.

2. [Without mental restriction]—*Syn.* voluntarily, willingly, fancy-free, of one's own accord, at will, at pleasure, at discretion, of one's own free will, purposely, deliberately, intentionally, advisedly, designedly, without urging, spontaneously, frankly, openly, unreservedly.—*Ant.* unwillingly*, under compulsion, hesitantly.

free on board, *mod.*—*Syn.* at the factory, plus shipping costs, net, F.O.B.

free-spoken, *mod.*—*Syn.* candid, outspoken, blunt; see **frank.**

freethinker, *n.*—*Syn.* atheist, schismatic, heretic; see **radical.**

free trade, *n.*—*Syn.* unrestricted commerce, tariff-free trade, duty-free trade.

freeway, *n.*—*Syn.* turnpike, superhighway, skyway, toll road; see **highway, road.**

free will, *n.*—*Syn.* willingness, volition, intention, purpose, choice, free choice, power of choice, voluntary decision, unrestrained will, will and pleasure, velleity, freedom, pleasure, discretion, inclination, desire, wish, intent, full intent and purpose, option, determination, mind, consent, assent. —*Ant.* constant*, compulsion, unwillingness.

freeze, *v.* **1.** [To change to a solid state]—*Syn.* congeal, harden, solidify, ice, quick-freeze, glaciate, ice up (D).—*Ant.* melt*, thaw, liquefy.

2. [To make cold]—*Syn.* chill, refrigerate, benumb, nip, bite, cool, pierce, chill to the marrow, make one's teeth chatter.—*Ant.* cook*, heat, bake.

3. [To discourage]—*Syn.* dishearten, depress, dampen; see **discourage** 1.

freezing, *mod.*—*Syn.* frosty, wintry, frigid; see **cold** 1.

freight, *mod.*—*Syn.* rail, railway, railroad, shipping, delivery, transportation, carrying, handling, moving, storage, express, trunk, baggage.

freight, *n.* **1.** [That which is carried]—*Syn.* burden, load, contents, weight, bulk, encumbrance, ballast, fardel, lading, cargo, shipping, consignment, goods, tonnage, bales, packages, ware.

2. [Charges for transportation]—*Syn.* shipping *or* transportation costs, carrying *or* handling charges, transfer charges, storage charges, rates, bill, rail charges.

freighter, *n.*—*Syn.* tanker, tramp, cargo ship; see **ship.**

French, *mod.* **1.** [Referring to the French culture or people]—*Syn.* Gallic, Latin, Frenchified, Parisian.

2. [Referring to the French language]—*Syn.* Romance, Romantic, Romanic, Provençal, Parisian, Gallic.

French, *n.* **1.** [The French people]—*Syn.* Gallic nation, Latins, Auvergnats, Basques, Bretons, Burgundians, Gascons, Gauls, Normans, Picards, Provençals, Savoyards, overseas French, French provincials.

2. [The French tongue]—*Syn.* Romance language, modern French, Middle French, Old French, Norman, Anglo-Norman, French of Paris, Parisian French, provincial French, *langue d'oc, langue d'oïl* (both French).

frenetic, *mod.*—*Syn.* fanatical, frenzied, frantic; see **excited.**

frenzy, *n.*—*Syn.* rage, craze, furor; see **excitement, insanity** 1.

frequency, *n.* **1.** [The state or quality of being frequent]—*Syn.* recurrence, number, reiteration; see **regularity.**

2. [The number of occurrences in a unit of time] —*Syn.* beat, pulse, cycle, wave length, radio wave, periodicity, pulsation, oscillation, rhythm, meter, round, rotation, rota, rate.

frequent, *mod.* **1.** [Happening often]—*Syn.* many, repeated, numerous, common, successive, habitual, thick, numberless, reiterated, reiterative, monotonous, redundant, profuse, pleonastic, incessant, continual, perpetual, customary, intermittent, familiar, commonplace, expected, ubiquitous, various, manifold, a good many (D).—*Ant.* rare*, infrequent, occasional.

2. [Happening regularly]—*Syn.* recurrent, usual, periodic; see **regular** 3.

frequent, *v.* —*Syn.* visit often, go to, resort to, visit repeatedly, be seen at daily, visit and revisit, attend regularly, be at home in, be often in, be habitually in, be accustomed to; *both* (D): hang around, hang out; see also **visit** 2.

frequenter, *n.* —*Syn.* haunter, habitué, customer, regular attendant, habitual resorter, frequent visitor, fan, daily customer.

frequently, *mod.* —*Syn.* often, regularly, usually, commonly, successively, many times, in many instances, repeatedly, intermittently, generally, every now and then, at times, not infrequently, often enough, not seldom, periodically, at regular intervals, spasmodically, oftentimes; *all* (D): heaps of times, more times than you can shake a stick at; see also **regularly** 1.—*Ant.* seldom*, infrequently, rarely.

fresh, *mod.* **1.** [Newly produced]—*Syn.* new, green, crisp, raw, recent, current, late, this season's, factory-fresh, garden-fresh, farm-fresh, new-crop, newly born, brand-new, newborn, immature, young, beginning; *all* (D): hot off the press, just out, newfangled.—*Ant.* old*, stale, musty.

2. [Novel]—*Syn.* unconventional, radical, different; see **unusual** 1, 2.

3. [Additional]—*Syn.* further, increased, supplementary; see **extra.**

4. [Not preserved]—*Syn.* unsalted, uncured, unpickled, undried, unsmoked; see **sense** 1.

5. [Unspoiled]—*Syn.* uncontaminated, green, not stale, good, unwilted, undecayed, well-preserved, odor-free, in good condition, unwithered, unblemished, unspotted, preserved, faultless, new, virgin, unimpaired.—*Ant.* decayed*, spoiled, contaminated.

6. [Not faded]—*Syn.* colorful, vivid, sharp; see **bright** 2, **definite** 2.

7. [Not salt; *said of water*]—*Syn.* potable, drinkable, cool, clear, pure, clean, sweet, fit to drink, safe.—*Ant.* dirty*, brackish, briny.

8. [*Said of a brisk wind*]—*Syn.* cool, refreshing, bracing, invigorating, quickening, quick, fair, spanking, refreshing, steady, stimulating, clear, stiff.

9. [Energetic]—*Syn.* spry, sprightly, alert; see **active** 2.

10. [Refreshed]—*Syn.* rested, restored, rehabilitated, like new, like a new man, unused, new, relaxed, stimulated, relieved, freshened, reinvigorated, revived.—*Ant.* tired*, exhausted, worn-out.

11. [Inexperienced]—*Syn.* untrained, untried, unskilled; see **inexperienced.**

12. [(D) Impudent]—*Syn.* saucy, disrespectful, impertinent; see **rude** 2.

freshen, *v.* **1.** [To sweeten]—*Syn.* desalinate, cleanse, purify; see **clean.**

2. [To activate]—*Syn.* invigorate, rouse, refresh; see **revive** 1, 2.

freshet, *n.* —*Syn.* overflow, deluge, surge; see **flood** 1.

freshman, *n.* —*Syn.* beginner, first-year student, novice, recruit, lowerclassman, tenderfoot, greenhorn, learner, apprentice, tyro, neophyte, probationer; *all* (D): frosh, freshie, plebe, rat, yearling, rookie, beanie.

fret, *v.* **1.** [To cause annoyance]—*Syn.* disturb, agitate, vex; see **bother** 2, 3.

2. [To suffer annoyance]—*Syn.* anguish, chafe, grieve; see **worry** 2.

3. [To rub painfully]—*Syn.* chafe, gall, corrode; see **rub** 1.

fretful, *mod.* —*Syn.* peevish, cross, captious; see **irritable.**

friable, *mod.* —*Syn.* brittle, fragile, breakable; see **dainty** 1.

friar, *n.* —*Syn.* brother, religious clerk, monk, mendicant, begging friar, abbot, brother, father, padre, abbé, curé, prior, pilgrim, penitent, holy man, palmer, Dominican, Franciscan, Carmelite, Augustinian; see also **monk.**

friction, *n.* **1.** [The rubbing of two bodies]—*Syn.* attrition, abrasion, wearing away, erosion, rasping, filing, grinding, massage, irritation.

2. [The results of rubbing]—*Syn.* agitation, soreness, resistance; see **irritation** 1.

3. [Trouble between individuals or groups]—*Syn.* animosity, quarrel, discontent; see **hatred** 1, 2.

4. [Resistance]—*Syn.* impedance, counteraction, interference; see **resistance** 3.

fried, *mod.* —*Syn.* grilled, cooked, rendered; see **done** 3.

friend, *n.* **1.** [A person with whom one has mutual attachment]—*Syn.* familiar, schoolmate, playmate, best friend, roommate, bedfellow, companion, intimate, confidant, comrade, fellow, fast friend, bosom friend, boon companion, mate; *all* (D): pal, birds of a feather, other self, chum, amigo, mate (British), crony, buddy, sidekick.—*Ant.* foe, enemy*, stranger.

2. [An ally]—*Syn.* compatriot, confrere, colleague; see **associate.**

3. [A patron]—*Syn.* supporter, accomplice, adherent; see **patron** 1.

make *or* **be friends** (with)(with)—*Syn.* befriend, stand by, become familiar (with); see **associate** 1.

friendless, *mod.* —*Syn.* unfriended, alone, forlorn; see **abandoned** 1.

friendliness, *n.* —*Syn.* kindness, amiability, geniality; see **friendship** 2.

friendly, *mod.* **1.** [Well-intentioned]—*Syn.* kind, kindly, helpful, sympathetic, amiable, amicable, well-disposed, neighborly, well-intentioned, sociable, civil, peaceful, loving, affectionate, fond, warm-hearted, attentive, brotherly, agreeable, genial, benevolent, accommodating, acquiescent, unoffensive, nonbelligerent, hearty, solicitous, fair-spoken, pleasant, affable, tender, complaisant, companionable, with open arms, cordial, familiar, intimate, confiding, on borrowing terms, close, devoted, dear, attached, loyal, faithful, steadfast, fair, true, staunch, responsive, in favor, trusted, fast, understanding, in with, fraternal, congenial, approachable, respectful, on visiting terms, cheerful, convivial, benign, good-humored, good-natured, generous, gracious, cooperative, wholehearted; *all* (D): big-hearted, folksy, chummy, solid, thick, palsy-walsy, arm in arm.—*Ant.* unfriendly*, antagonistic, spiteful.

2. [Helpful]—*Syn.* favorable, beneficial, amicable; see **helpful** 1.

friendship, *n.* **1.** [The state of being friends] —*Syn.* association, brotherhood, companionship, alliance, confraternity, amity, fellowship, fraternization, reciprocal feeling, fraternity, comity, mutual esteem, affinity, league, pact, sympathy, understanding, knowledge, agreement, fellow feeling, attachment, intercourse, intimacy, familiarity. —*Ant.* hatred*, hostility, enmity.

2. [Friendly feeling]—*Syn.* amity, concord, harmony, good will, friendliness, favor, devotion, regard, brotherly love, affection, consideration, esteem, good intentions, good disposition, kindness, kindliness, amiability, amicability, *rapprochement* (French), neighborliness, sociability, loving-kindness, respect, attention, attentiveness, appreciation, tenderness, geniality, congeniality, heartiness, affability, complaisance, companionability, cordiality, familiarity, intimacy, good faith, confidence, attachment, loyalty, steadfastness, staunchness, responsiveness, understanding, sympathy, good humor, good nature, graciousness, benevolence, wholeheartedness, sincerity, generosity; *both* (D): clubbability, chumminess.—*Ant.* hatred*, animosity, disfavor.

fright, *n.* **1.** [Alarm]—*Syn.* panic, terror, dread, horror; see **fear** 1.

2. [(D) Anything disapproved or disliked]—*Syn.* pitiable object, eyesore, nauseous article; see **ugliness.**

3. [(D) An unpleasant or unwelcome person] —*Syn.* frump, scarecrow, bother; see **nuisance** 3.

frighten, *v.* **1.** [To alarm]—*Syn.* scare, scare away *or* off, daunt, affright, appall, dismay, terrify, cow, shock, dishearten, abash, dispirit, throw into a fright, confound with dread, raise apprehension, intimidate, deter, strike with overwhelming fear, threaten, prey on the mind, badger, petrify, panic, demoralize, disrupt, give cause for alarm, put in fear, terrorize, horrify, astound, awe, perturb, disturb, startle, disquiet, discomfort, harrow, unman: *all* (D): bluff off, frighten one out of one's wits, take one's breath away, chill to the bone, make one's hair stand on end, make one's blood run cold, make one's flesh creep, put one's heart in his mouth, faze, give one a turn, scare one stiff, freeze the blood, curdle the blood.—*Ant.* encourage*, hearten, reassure.

2. [To drive off, because of alarm]—*Syn.* intimidate, discourage, repel, stave off, frighten away, stampede, put to flight, deter, browbeat, bulldoze (D).—*Ant.* fascinate*, inveigle, entice.

frightened, *mod.* —*Syn.* terrorized, affrighted, startled; see **afraid** 2.

frightful, *mod.* **1.** [Causing fright]—*Syn.* fearful, awful, awesome, direful, dreadful, horrifying, horrible, lurid, awe-inspiring, gruesome, traumatic, ghastly, grisly, macabre, petrifying, unnerving, atrocious, repellent, terrifying, harrowing, appalling, frightening, alarming, unspeakable, inconceivable, ominous, portentous, horrendous, dismaying, demoralizing, disturbing, disquieting.—*Ant.* charming*, reassuring, alluring.

2. [Very unpleasant]—*Syn.* calamitous, shocking, terrible; see **offensive** 2.

3. [(D) Bad]—*Syn.* vile, lewd, wrong; see **wicked** 1, 2.

frigid, *mod.* **1.** [Thermally cold]—*Syn.* freezing, frosty, refrigerated; see **cold** 1.

2. [Unresponsive]—*Syn.* unloving, undersexed, chilly; see **cold** 2, **indifferent** 1.

frigidity, *n.* —*Syn.* impassivity, inattention, coldness; see **indifference** 1.

frill, *n.* **1.** [Anything thought to be unnecessary] —*Syn.* affection, mannerism, frippery, gewgaw, gimcrack, furbelow, foppery; *all* (D): spinach, fandangle, doodad, tomfoolery.

2. [A lacy decoration]—*Syn.* lace, tuck, gore; see **decoration** 2.

fringe, *n.* **1.** [The extreme edge]—*Syn.* border, borderline, outside; see **edge** 1.

2. [A raveled or decorative edge]—*Syn.* flounce, hem, trimming, rickrack, edging, lace, knitting, tatting, crochet, needle point, border, binding, tape, bias, pinking.

fringed, *mod.* —*Syn.* edged, befringed, bordered; see **ornate** 1.

frippery, *n.* —*Syn.* nonsense, waste, gewgaws; see **frill** 1.

frisk, *v.* —*Syn.* romp, skip, leap; see **play** 2.

frisky, *mod.* —*Syn.* spirited, dashing, playful; see **active** 2.

fritter, *n.* —*Syn.* fried cake, batter cake, hotcake; see **pancake.**

frivolity, *n.* —*Syn.* flightiness, triviality, silliness, levity, lightness, puerility, trifling, folly, frippery, flummery, giddiness.

frivolous, *mod.* **1.** [Trivial]—*Syn.* superficial, petty, trifling; see **trivial.**

2. [Silly]—*Syn.* idiotic, senseless, foolish; see **stupid** 1.

frizzle, *v.* —*Syn.* sizzle, crisp, fry; see **cook.**

frock, *n.* —*Syn.* gown, habit, apron; see **clothes, dress** 2.

frog, *n.* **1.** [An amphibian]—*Syn.* bullfrog, flying frog, leopard frog, pickerel frog, *Rana* (Latin), polliwog.

2. [(D) Hoarseness]—*Syn.* catch, obstruction, infection; see **cold** 3.

3. [An ornamental braiding or buttonhole]—*Syn.* loop, eye, clasp, fastening, twist, curlicue.

frolic, *n.* **1.** [Gaiety]—*Syn.* joviality, fun, play; see **merriment** 2.

2. [A joke]—*Syn.* trick, antic, prank; see **joke** 1.

frolic, *v.* —*Syn.* caper, gambol, frisk; see **play** 1, 2.

frolicsome, *mod.* —*Syn.* gay, merry, jovial; see **happy** 1.

from, *prep.* —*Syn.* in distinction to, out of possession of, outside of; see **of.**

from hand to mouth (D), *mod.* —*Syn.* scrimpily, scantily, meagerly, precariously, poorly, by bare subsistence, as chance provides, without any margin, as want necessitates, scrimpingly, improvidently, scarcely, skimpily.

from pillar to post (D), *mod.*—*Syn.* transient, moving about, here today and gone tomorrow (D); see **driven.**

from side to side, *mod.*—*Syn.* back and forth, wobbly, unstable; see **irregular** 1.

front, *mod.*—*Syn.* fore, forward, frontal, foremost, head, headmost, leading, anterior, in the foreground.—*Ant.* rear*, back, hindmost.

front, *n.* **1.** [The forward part or surface]—*Syn.* frontage, exterior, fore part, anterior, obverse, façade, bow, foreground, face, head, breast, frontal area.—*Ant.* posterior, back, rear.

2. [The fighting line]—*Syn.* front line, van, no man's land, advance position, line of battle, vanguard, outpost, advance guard.

3. [The appearance one presents before others] —*Syn.* mien, carriage, port, demeanor, aspect, countenance, face, presence, expression, figure, exterior.

4. [Something attached for show]—*Syn.* façade, false front, mask, exterior, display, window dressing (D).

5. [Impudence]—*Syn.* effrontery, assurance, face (D); see **rudeness.**

in front of—*Syn.* before, preceding, leading; see **ahead** 2.

front, *v.*—*Syn.* border, look out on, front toward; see **face** 1.

frontier, *n.* **1.** [Boundary]—*Syn.* edge, verge, limit; see **boundary.**

2. [Backwoods]—*Syn.* hinterland, remote districts, outskirts; see **country** 1.

frontispiece, *n.*—*Syn.* façade, panel, ornament; see **decoration** 1, 2.

frost, *n.* **1.** [Temperature that causes freezing] —*Syn.* freeze, drop, killing frost; see **cold** 1.

2. [Frozen dew or vapor]—*Syn.* blight, hoar frost, black frost, white frost, rime.

frosting, *n.*—*Syn.* finish, covering, coating; see **icing.**

frosty, *mod.*—*Syn.* frigid, freezing, chilly; see **cold** 1.

froth, *n.*—*Syn.* bubbles, scum, fizz, effervescence, foam, ferment, head, fume, lather, suds, scud, spume, spray, spindrift, barm, ebullition, meerschaum.

frothy, *mod.* **1.** [Fizzing]—*Syn.* fizzing, bubbling, foaming, soapy, sudsy, bubbly, fizzy, foamy, with a head on (D).

2. [Trivial]—*Syn.* unsubstantial, trite, frivolous; see **trivial.**

froward, *mod.*—*Syn.* disobedient, intractable, naughty; see **obstinate** 1.

frown, *n.*—*Syn.* scowl, grimace, wry face, gloomy countenance, forbidding aspect, stern visage, dirty look (D).

frown, *v.*—*Syn.* scowl, grimace, lower, make a wry face, pout, glare, look black, knit the brow(s), sulk, glower, gloom, look stern.—*Ant.* smile*, laugh, grin.

frowning, *mod.*—*Syn.* scowling, grim, sulky; see **irritable.**

frowzy, *mod.* **1.** [Slovenly]—*Syn.* disorderly, unkempt, slatternly; see **dirty** 1.

2. [Stinking]—*Syn.* rancid, fetid, stale; see **rotten** 1.

frozen, *mod.*—*Syn.* chilled, frosted, iced; see **cold** 1, 2.

fructify, *v.*—*Syn.* impregnate, fecundate, pollinate; see **fertilize** 2.

frugal, *mod.*—*Syn.* thrifty, saving, prudent, parsimonious; see **careful.**

frugality, *n.*—*Syn.* economy, carefulness, conservation, husbandry, management, thrift, prudence, saving, parsimony, parsimoniousness, miserliness, scrimping, niggardliness, stinginess, avarice, avariciousness, penuriousness.—*Ant.* waste*, lavishness, prodigality.

fruit, *n.* **1.** [The edible growth of a plant]—*Syn.* fruitage, berry, drupe, grain, nut, root, tuber, pome; see also **apple** 1, **cherry, melon, orange, peach, pear, vegetable.**

Common fruits include the following—apple, pear, peach, plum, orange, grapefruit, banana, pineapple, watermelon, cantaloupe, honeydew melon, casaba, papaya, mango, kiwi, guava, grape, lime, lemon, persimmon, pomegranate, raspberry, blackberry, loganberry, blueberry, olive, date, fig, apricot, cherry, raisin, avocado, huckleberry, gooseberry, quince, kumquat, durian, strawberry.

2. [The ripened ovary of a seed plant]—*Syn.* seed pod, envelope, capsule, follicle, grain, nut, schizocarp, legume, silicle.

3. [The reward of labor; *often plural*]—*Syn.* profits, consequences, outcome; see **pay** 1, **result.**

fruitful, *mod.* **1.** [Fertile in a literal sense]—*Syn.* prolific, productive, fecund; see **fertile** 1, 2.

2. [Producing results, or likely to produce results] —*Syn.* productive, conducive, useful; see **profitable.**

fruition, *n.* **1.** [Achievement]—*Syn.* attainment, fulfillment, achievement; see **success** 1, 2.

2. [Gratification]—*Syn.* enjoyment, pleasure, content; see **satisfaction** 1, 2.

fruitless, *mod.*—*Syn.* vain, unprofitable, empty; see **futile** 1.

frump, *n.*—*Syn.* slob, slattern, drab woman, slovenly person, (old) bag (D); see also **prostitute.**

frustrate, *v.*—*Syn.* defeat, foil, balk; see **prevent.**

frustration, *n.*—*Syn.* disappointment, inpediment, failure; see **defeat** 3.

fry, *v.*—*Syn.* sauté, sear, singe, brown, grill, fricasse, pan-fry, deep-fry *or* French fry, frizzle, sizzle; see also **cook.**

small fry—*Syn.* children, infant(s), toddler(s); see **baby, child.**

frying pan, *n.*—*Syn.* skillet, spider, griddle; see **pan.**

out of the frying pan and into the fire—*Syn.* from bad to worse, worse off, having suffered defeat; see **in trouble.**

fuddle, *v.*—*Syn.* muddle, puzzle, intoxicate, inebriate, stupefy, make drunk, confound; see also **confuse.**

fuddled, *mod.*—*Syn.* intoxicated, muddled, confused; see **doubtful** 2, **drunk.**

fudge, *n.*—*Syn.* penuche, chocolate fudge, divinity fudge; see **candy.**

fuel, *n.*—*Syn.* liquid *or* solid propellant, combustibles, firing material.

Fuels include the following—coal, coke, charcoal, anthracite, bituminous coal, peat, slack, stoker coal, lignite, carbon, briquette, turf, cordwood, firewood, log, faggot, kindling, slabs, blocks, waste products, furze, timber, touchwood, crude oil, fuel oil, gas, natural gas, artificial gas, gasoline, kerosene, wax; see also **wood** 2.

fuel, *v.* —*Syn.* supply with *or* take on fuel, stoke, feed, service, fill up; *all* (D): gas, tank up, gas up, fuel up.

fugitive, *n.* —*Syn.* outlaw, Ishmael, refugee, truant, runaway, exile, vagabond, waif, stray, derelict, outcast, banished man, hunted person, recluse, hermit; *all* (D): bolter, corner-turner, fly-by-night, walkout.

fugitive, *mod.* —*Syn.* criminal, escaping, wandering, running away, evading, avoiding, on the lam (D); see also **moving** 1.

fulcrum, *n.* —*Syn.* block, prop, support of a lever; see **support** 2.

fulfill, *v.* —*Syn.* accomplish, effect, complete; see **achieve** 1.

fulfilled, *mod.* —*Syn.* accomplished, completed, achieved, realized, satisfied, effectuated, effected, finished, obtained, perfected, attained, reached, actualized, consummated, executed, dispatched, concluded, compassed, brought about, performed, carried out, put into effect, made good, brought to a close, crowned, matured.—*Ant.* disappointed*, unfulfilled, unrealized.

fulfillment, *n.* —*Syn.* attainment, accomplishment, realization; see **achievement** 2.

full, *mod.* **1.** [Filled]—*Syn.* sated, replete, brimful, overflowing, running over, plethoric, abundant, burdened, depressed, weighted, freighted, borne down, satisfied, saturated, crammed, packed, stuffed, jammed, jam full, glutted, cloyed, gorged, surfeited, abounding, loaded, chock-full, stocked, satiated, crowded; *all* (D): full as a tick, stuffed to the gills, jampacked, crawling (with), up to the brim, packed like sardines, fit *or* likely to burst *or* bust.—*Ant.* empty*, exhausted, void.

2. [Occupied]—*Syn.* assigned, reserved, in use; see **taken** 2.

3. [Well supplied]—*Syn.* abundant, complete, copious, ample, bounteous, plentiful, plenteous, sufficient, adequate, competent, lavish, extravagant, profuse.—*Ant.* inadequate*, scanty, insufficient.

4. [Not limited]—*Syn.* broad, unlimited, extensive; see **absolute** 1, 2.

5. [Loose]—*Syn.* flapping, baggy, flowing; see **loose** 1.

6. [Mature]—*Syn.* grown, entire, complete; see **mature** 1.

7. [Deep]—*Syn.* resonant, rounded, throaty; see **loud** 1.

in full—*Syn.* for the entire amount *or* value, fully, thoroughly; see **completely.**

to the full—*Syn.* entirely, thoroughly, fully; see **completely.**

fullback, *n.* —*Syn.* backfield man, safety man, blocking back; see **football player.**

full blast (D), *mod.* —*Syn.* wide open, full throttle, to the hilt; see **fast** 1.

full dress, *n.* —*Syn.* livery, formal, finery; see **clothes.**

full-grown, *mod.* —*Syn.* adult, prime, grown-up; see **mature** 1.

fullness, *n.* —*Syn.* abundance, saturation, completion; see **plenty.**

fully, *mod.* **1.** [Completely]—*Syn.* entirely, thoroughly, wholly; see **completely.**

2. [adequately]—*Syn.* sufficiently, amply, enough; see **adequately** 1.

fulminate, *v.* **1.** [To explode]—*Syn.* blow up, discharge, detonate; see **explode** 1.

2. [To intimidate]—*Syn.* menace, bluster, upbraid; see **threaten** 1.

3. [To denounce]—*Syn.* swear (at), condemn, declaim; see **curse** 1, 2, **denounce.**

fulmination, *n.* **1.** [Detonation]—*Syn.* discharge, blast, outburst; see **explosion** 1.

2. [Intimidation]—*Syn.* intimidation, denunciation, curse; see **warning.**

fulsome, *mod.* —*Syn.* coarse, gross, sickening; see **offensive** 2.

fumble, *n.* —*Syn.* mistake, blunder, dropped ball; see **error** 1.

fumble, *v.* —*Syn.* mishandle, bungle, mismanage; see **botch.**

fumigate, *v.* —*Syn.* cleanse thoroughly, treat, disinfect; see **purify.**

fun (D), *mod.* —*Syn.* merry, enjoyable, boisterous; see **happy** 1, **pleasant** 2.

fun, *n.* —*Syn.* play, game, sport, jest, amusement, relaxation, pastime, diversion, frolic, gambol, mirth, entertainment, solace, merriment, jollity, jollification, pleasure, drollery, buffoonery, foolery, romping, joke, absurdity, playfulness, laughter, frolicsomeness, festivity, carnival, tomfoolery, escapade, antic, romp, prank, comedy, banter, teasing, junketing, high jinks, celebration, holiday, rejoicing, good humor, joking, enjoyment, gladness, good cheer, delight, glee, high glee, freak of humor, treat, lark, recreation, hilarity, blitheness, joy, jocundity, joviality; *all* (D): time of one's life, blast, whoopee, big time, picnic, riot.—*Ant.* unhappiness*, tedium, sorrow.

for *or* **in fun**—*Syn.* for amusement, not seriously, playfully; see **happily** 2.

make fun of—*Syn.* mock, satirize, poke fun at; see **ridicule.**

function, *n.* **1.** [Use]—*Syn.* employment, capacity, faculty; see **use** 1.

2. [A social gathering]—*Syn.* celebration, reception, get-together; see **meeting** 1, **party** 1.

function, *v.* —*Syn.* perform, run, work; see **operate** 2.

functional, *mod.* —*Syn.* occupational, utilitarian, anatomic; see **practical.**

functionary, *n.* —*Syn.* deputy, representative, official; see **agent** 1.

fund, *n.* —*Syn.* endowment, matching *or* trust *or* endowment fund, capital; see **gift** 1.

fundamental, *n.* —*Syn.* buttocks, bottom, rear, seat; see **rump.**

fundamental, *mod.* **1.** [Providing the foundation] —*Syn.* basic, underlying, basal, radical, primary, first, underived, rudimentary, elementary, substrative, supporting, axiomatic, key, crucial, vital, major, principal, grass roots, requisite, elementary, cardinal, organic, axiological, theoretical, structural, sustaining, central, original—*Ant.* superficial*, incidental, consequent.

2. [Essential]—*Syn.* primary, requisite, significant; see **necessary** 1.

fundamentally, *mod.* —*Syn.* basically, radically, centrally; see **essentially.**

fundamentals, *n.* —*Syn.* essentials, basics, foundation; see **basis** 1.

funds, *n.* —*Syn.* capital, cash, collateral, money, assets, corporate assets, currency, savings, pecuniary resources, revenue, substance, *de quoi* (French), wherewithal, proceeds, hard cash, fluid assets, specie, stocks and bonds, money in *or* on hand *or* in the bank, letters of credit, accounts receivable *or* collectible, property, means, affluence, belongings, wealth, resources, securities, stakes, earnings, winnings, possessions, profits, treasure(s), stocks, stores; *all* (D): pelf, nest egg, jack, scratch, stuff, lucre, filthy lucre.

funeral, *n.* **1.** [Rites for the dead]—*Syn.* obsequies, interment, last rites, burial, burial ceremony, sepulture, entombment, mortuary rites, requiem, funeration, inhumation, cremation, funeral solemnities, crematory *or* funerary *or* funeral services; *both* (D): buryin', planting.

2. [Those attending a dead body]—*Syn.* cortege, mourners, pall bearers, funeral procession *or* train.

be one's funeral—*Syn.* harm oneself, hurt, damage; see **ruin** 2.

funereal, *mod.* —*Syn.* melancholy, gloomy, mournful; see **sad** 1, 2.

fungus, *n.* —*Syn.* sponge, mushroom, toadstool, parasite, puff ball, saprophyte, lichen, mold, rust, mildew, rot, truffle, morbid growth.

funk (D), *n.* **1.** [Fear]—*Syn.* fright, alarm, panic; see **fear** 1.

2. [Depression]—*Syn.* gloom, despondency, misery; see **depression** 2.

funnel, *n.* —*Syn.* duct, shaft, conduit; see **pipe** 1.

funny, *mod.* **1.** [Stirring to laughter]—*Syn.* laughable, comic, droll, comical, whimsical, amusing, entertaining, diverting, humorous, witty, laughable, capricious, jocose, jocular, jocund, waggish, droll, facetious, clever, mirthful, laugh-provoking, ludicrous, jolly, absurd, ridiculous, gay, jesting, sly, sportive, playful, merry, antic, joyful, joyous, good-humored, glad, gleeful, hilarious, blithe, jovial, farcical, joking; *all* (D): rich, side-splitting, a laugh, too funny for words, killing.—*Ant.* sad*, serious, melancholy.

2. [(D) Likely to arouse suspicion]—*Syn.* curious, unusual, odd; see **suspicious** 2.

funny (D), *n.* —*Syn.* jest, curious instance *or* incident, odd one; see **joke** 1, 2.

fur, *n.* —*Syn.* pelt, hide, hair, coat, brush, fluff.
Types of fur include the following—sable, mink, chinchilla, Persian lamb, astrakhan, karakul, Alaska seal, Hudson seal, muskrat, silver muskrat, ermine, American broadtail, monkey, beaver, skunk, otter, marten, stone marten, weasel, Chinese weasel (Chinese mink), American mink, kolinsky, fitch, squirrel, leopard, leopard cat, raccoon, wolverine, Russian pony, fox, white fox, blue fox, cross fox, red fox, silver fox, gray fox, Manchurian dog, sheepskin, bearskin, calfskin, kidskin, mouton, lamb, rabbit, cony.

make the fur fly (D) **1.** —*Syn.* fight, bicker, stir up trouble; see **excite** 2. **2.** hasten, act hastily, rush (through); see **hurry** 1.

furbish, *v.* **1.** [To restore]—*Syn.* refurbish, improve, renovate; see **renew** 1.

2. [To burnish]—*Syn.* polish, clean, brighten; see **shine** 3.

furious, *mod.* **1.** [Very angry]—*Syn.* enraged, raging, fierce; see **angry.**

2. [Intense]—*Syn.* extreme, excessive, intensified; see **intense.**

3. [Turbulent]—*Syn.* violent, agitated, tumultuous; see **turbulent.**

furl, *v.* —*Syn.* wrap up, curl, roll; see **fold** 2.

furlough, *n.* —*Syn.* permission, permit, leave; see **vacation.**

furnace, *n.* —*Syn.* heater, heating system, boiler, (forced draft) hot-air furnace, pipeless furnace, steam furnace, hot-water furnace, oil burner, gas furnace, electric furnace, annealing furnace, kiln, reduction furnace, blast furnace, open-hearth furnace, BOF (basic oxygen furnace), stove, forge, smithy.

furnish, *v.* **1.** [To supply necessities]—*Syn.* fit out, equip, stock; see **provide** 1.

2. [To equip with furniture]—*Syn.* appoint, decorate, fit, make habitable, do interior decorating.

furnished, *mod.* —*Syn.* supplied, provided, fitted out; see **equipped.**

furnishings, *n.* —*Syn.* household goods, decorations, things (D); see **furniture.**

furniture, *n.* —*Syn.* movables, household goods, home furnishings, appointments, chattels.
Furniture includes the following—*home:* table, chair, rug, carpet(ing), drapes, sofa, davenport, couch, cabinet, picture, chest, bureau, highboy, buffet, cupboard, stove, washing machine *or* washer, (clothes) dryer, dishwasher, refrigerator, bed, dresser, vanity, mirror, commode, chiffonier, tapestry, footstool, secretary, press, sideboard, clock, bookcase; *office:* desk, filing cabinet, stool, chair, table, counter, typewriter table.
Styles of furniture include the following—modern, tubular, Swedish modern, Danish modern, early American, Shaker, colonial, Italian Renaissance, French Renaissance, Tudor, Jacobean, Georgian, Queen Anne, Victorian, Louis XIV *or* Louis Quatorze, Louis XV *or* Louis Quinze, Chinese, Ming, Japanese, Oriental, Moorish, Adam, Hepplewhite, Sheraton, Chippendale, Duncan Phyfe, Empire, French colonial, French provincial, Spanish colonial, mission, Biedermeier, Mediterranean, Monterey.

furor, *n.* **1.** [Commotion]—*Syn.* tumult, excitement, stir; see **disturbance** 1.

2. [Frenzy]—*Syn.* rage, madness, lunacy; see **excitement.**

furrier, *n.* —*Syn.* fur dealer, tailor, fur seller, modiste.

furrow, *n.* —*Syn.* ditch, dike, gutter; see **trench** 1.

furrowed, *mod.* —*Syn.* grooved, ribbed, channeled; see **corrugated.**

further, *mod.* —*Syn.* more, to *or* at a greater distance, in addition; see **distant** 2.

furtherance, *n.* —*Syn.* advancement, promotion, progression; see **progress** 1.

furthermore, *mod.* —*Syn.* moreover, too, in addition; see **besides.**

furthest, *mod.* —*Syn.* most remote, most distant, remotest, farthest, uttermost, outermost, ultimate, extreme, outmost.

furtive, *mod.* **1.** [Clandestine]—*Syn.* hidden, surreptitious, stealthy; see **secret** 3.
2. [Evasive]—*Syn.* sneaky, shifty, elusive; see **sly** 1.

fury, *n.* —*Syn.* wrath, fire, rage; see **anger.**

fuse, *n.* —*Syn.* wick, tinder, touchwood, kindling, igniter, brand.
blow a fuse (D)—*Syn.* become angry, lose one's temper, rant; see **rage** 1.

fusillade, *n.* —*Syn.* volley, cross fire, firing; see **fire** 3.

fusion, *n.* **1.** [A melting]—*Syn.* liquefaction, liquification, melting, heating, smelting, separation.
2. [Unification]—*Syn.* amalgamation, blending, coalition; see **union** 1.

fuss, *n.* —*Syn.* trouble, complaint, bother; see **disturbance** 2.

fuss, *v.* —*Syn.* whine, whimper, object; see **complain** 1.

fussy, *mod.* —*Syn.* fastidious, particular, meticulous; see **careful** 1.

fustian, *n.* —*Syn.* bombast, ranting, pomposity; see **eloquence** 1.

futile, *mod.* **1.** [Useless]—*Syn.* vain, unavailing, useless, in vain, fruitless, hopeless, impractical, worthless, impracticable, unprofitable, to no effect, not successful, to no purpose, profitless, valueless, unneeded, resultless, unsatisfactory, unsatisfying, ineffective, ineffectual, bootless, unproductive, idle, empty, nugatory, hollow, exhausted, unreal, delusive, unsubstantial, visionary.—*Ant.* hopeful*, practical, effective.
2. [Frivolous]—*Syn.* trifling, petty, small; see **trivial.**

futility, *n.* —*Syn.* uselessness, triviality, falseness, hollowness, frivolity, idleness, vanity, emptiness, fruitlessness, hopelessness, worthlessness, labor in vain, lost trouble, unprofitableness, insubstantiality, vainness, bootlessness, falsity, illusion, folly, want of substance, unimportance, triflingness; *all* (D): carrying water in a sieve, sowing the sand, wild-goose chase, labor of Sisyphus, carrying owls to Athens, running around in circles, beating the air, spinning one's wheels, carrying coals to Newcastle.—*Ant.* importance*, fruitfulness, significance.

future, *mod.* —*Syn.* coming, impending, imminent, forthcoming, destined, fated, prospective, to come, in the course of time, expected, inevitable, approaching, unfolding, eventual, ultimate, planned, scheduled, on the schedule, budgeted, in the planning stage, booked, in the plans for the future, not ruled out, looked toward, in the natural course of events, likely, provided for in over-all planning; *all* (D): up, coming up, in the cards, a gleam in someone's eye.—*Ant.* past*, completed, recorded.

future, *n.* **1.** [All time that is to come]—*Syn.* futurity, aftertime, infinity, eternity, world to come, subsequent time, coming time, events to come, prospect, tomorrow, (the) hereafter, by and by, the sweet by and by (D).—*Ant.* past*, historic ages, recorded time.
2. [One's personal time to come]—*Syn.* destiny, fate, expectation; see **doom** 1.
3. [The future tense]—*Syn.* simple futurity, conditional, periphrastic future.

fuzz, *n.* **1.** [Down]—*Syn.* nap, fluff, fur; see **hair** 1.
2. [(D) Police]—*Syn.* patrolmen, cop, policemen; see **police.**

fuzzy, *mod.* **1.** [Like or covered with fuzz]—*Syn.* hairy, wooly, furry; see **downy.**
2. [Not clear]—*Syn.* blurred, indistinct, indefinite, out of focus, shadowy, dim, misty, hazy, foggy; see also **obscure** 1, **hazy** 1.

G

gab, *n.* —*Syn.* gossip, idle talk, prattle; see **nonsense** 1.
gift of (the) gab (D)—*Syn.* loquacity, volubility, verbal ability; see **eloquence** 1.
gab, *v.* —*Syn.* gossip, jabber, chatter; see **babble.**
gabble, *v.* —*Syn.* jabber, gossip, chatter; see **babble.**
gable, *n.* —*Syn.* peak, end wall, roof, housetop, ridge.
gad, *v.* —*Syn.* ramble, wander, stray; see **walk** 1.
gadabout, *n.* —*Syn.* idler, rover, itinerant; see **loafer, traveler.**
gadget, *n.* —*Syn.* mechanical contrivance, object, contraption; see **device** 1.
gaffer, *n.* —*Syn.* an old man, veteran, hick; see **boor, oldster.**
gag, *v.* **1.** [To stop the mouth]—*Syn.* choke, muzzle, muffle, obstruct, stifle, throttle, garrote, silence by violence, tape (up), deaden.
2. [To forbid expression to]—*Syn.* silence, constrain, repress; see **quiet** 2.
3. [To retch]—*Syn.* be nauseated, sicken, choke; see **vomit.**
gage, *n.* —*Syn.* measure, mark, check; see **gauge.**
gage, *v.* —*Syn.* check, assess, calibrate; see **measure** 1.
gaiety, *n.* —*Syn.* jollity, mirth, exhilaration; see **happiness** 1.
gaily, *mod.* **1.** [In a gay mood]—*Syn.* merrily, laughingly, vivaciously; see **happily** 2.
2. [In a gay manner]—*Syn.* showily, brightly, vivaciously, spiritedly, brilliantly, splendidly, gaudily, expensively, colorfully, extravagantly, garishly, sparklingly, scintillatingly, glowingly, in a bright *or* vivacious *or* sprightly manner, with spirit *or* élan, in holiday attire, with spirit and force, *con brio, con spirito (both* Italian).—*Ant.* quietly*, modestly, neatly.
gain, *n.* **1.** [The act of increasing]—*Syn.* increase, accrual, accumulation; see **addition** 1.
2. [Excess of returns over expenditures]—*Syn.* receipts, earnings, winnings; see **addition** 2, **profit** 2.
gain, *v.* **1.** [To increase]—*Syn.* augment, expand, enlarge; see **grow** 1, **increase** 1.
2. [To advance]—*Syn.* progress, overtake, move forward; see **advance** 1.
3. [To win]—*Syn.* get, cash in on, earn; see **win** 1.
4. [To achieve]—*Syn.* attain, realize, reach; see **succeed** 1.
gainful, *mod.* —*Syn.* lucrative, productive, useful; see **profitable.**
gainfully, *mod.* —*Syn.* productively, profitably, usefully; see **profitably.**
gain ground, *v.* —*Syn.* advance, proceed, progress; see **improve** 2.
gainsay, *v.* **1.** [To deny]—*Syn.* disclaim, refute, repudiate; see **deny** 1.
2. [To contradict]—*Syn.* disagree, dispute, controvert; see **oppose** 1.
gait, *n.* **1.** [Manner of moving on foot]—*Syn.* walk, run, motion, step, tread, stride, pace, tramp, march, carriage, movements.
2. [Style of foot movement; *said of horses*]—*Syn.* walk, single-foot, rack, amble, canter, pace, trot, run, gallop.
gala, *mod.* —*Syn.* gay, colorful, festive; see **bright** 1, 2, **happy** 1.
gala, *n.* —*Syn.* affair, function, fete; see **party** 1.
galaxy, *n.* **1.** [A large system of stars]—*Syn.* cosmic system, star cluster, nebula; see **constellation.**
2. [Any brilliant group, as of persons]—*Syn.* gathering *or* assemblage of celebrities *or* notables, brilliant company, elite; see **gathering.**
gale, *n.* —*Syn.* hurricane, blow, typhoon; see **storm** 1, **wind** 1.
gall, *n.* **1.** [Spite]—*Syn.* cynicism, rancor, bitterness; see **malice.**
2. [(D) Impudence]—*Syn.* effrontery, insolence, impertinence; see **rudeness.**
gall, *v.* —*Syn.* annoy, irk, irritate; see **bother** 2.
gallant, *mod.* —*Syn.* bold, courageous, intrepid; see **brave** 1.
gallantry, *n.* —*Syn.* heroism, valor, bravery; see **courage** 1.
galleon, *n.* —*Syn.* man-of-war, argosy, sailing vessel; see **ship**
gallery, *n.* **1.** [An elevated section of seats]—*Syn.* arcade, upstairs, loggia; see **balcony.**
2. [Onlookers, especially from the gallery]—*Syn.* spectators, audience, public; see **attendance** 2.
3. [A room for showing works of art]—*Syn.* salon, museum, exhibition room, studio, hall, exhibit, showroom, wing.
play to the gallery (D)—*Syn.* show off, strut, ham (it up) (D); see **display** 1.
galley, *n.* **1.** [A ship]—*Syn.* galleon, quarter galley, galleass, galiot, bireme, trireme, penteconter, dinghy, rowboat, tender; see also **boat, ship.**
2. [A kitchen]—*Syn.* caboose, scullery, cookroom; see **kitchen.**
galling, *mod.* —*Syn.* annoying, irritating, bothersome; see **disturbing.**
gallivant, *v.* —*Syn.* meander, gad, stray; see **walk** 1.
gallon, *n.* —*Syn.* 231 cubic inches, 3.7853 liters, tun, measure of capacity, liquid measure, four quarts, eight pints.
gallop, *v.* —*Syn.* run, spring, leap, jump, ride at full speed, go at a gallop, move by leaps, bound, hurdle,

swing, stride, lope, amble, canter, trot, pace, rack, single-foot.

gallows, *n.* —*Syn.* gibbet, scaffold, yardarm, hangman's tree, Tyburn Tree, tree, noose, halter; *all* (D): drop, picture frame, stretching yard.

galoshes, *n.* —*Syn.* arctics, overshoes, rubbers, boots, toe rubbers.

galvanize, *v.* **1.** [To startle]—*Syn.* stun, shock, astonish; see **frighten** 1.

2. [To coat]—*Syn.* plate, protect, electroplate; see **cover** 1.

3. [To animate]—*Syn.* excite, stimulate, arouse; see **animate** 1, **incite.**

gamble, *n.* —*Syn.* chance, lot, loser (D); see **uncertainty** 3.

gamble, *v.* **1.** [To play for money]—*Syn.* game, wager, bet, play at hazard, play, plunge, play at dice, cut the cards, bet against, cast lots, be caught short, speculate, back, lay money on; *all* (D): take a flyer, try one's luck, go for broke, flip the coin, leap into the dark, shoot craps, shoot the moon, buy a pig in a poke, buck the tiger, double the blind.

2. [To take chances]—*Syn.* hazard, venture, risk; see **chance** 2.

gambler, *n.* —*Syn.* gamester, plunger, backer, layer, sharper, card-sharp, player for stakes, dicer, speculator, hazarder, trickster, bunco steerer, confidence man, bettor, operator, bookmaker, croupier, banker, player; *all* (D): spec, sport, high-roller, stabber, tinhorn, blackleg, shark, shell-worker, knight of the elbow, shill, bookie, con man.

gambling, *n.* —*Syn.* betting, staking, playing at hazard, venturing, plunging, gaming, backing, laying money on, speculating; *all* (D): taking a flier, taking a shot, laying dough.

Types of gambling include the following—dicing, betting on horse races, lottery, matching, bridge, casino, baccarat, *chemin de fer* (French), roulette, bingo, lotto, keno, faro, poker, (gin) rummy, stud poker, draw poker, strip poker, fan-tan, newmarket, nap, blackjack, twenty-one, seven-up, Napoleon, Wellington, chuck-farthing, playing slot machines, betting on gambling wheels; *all* (D): crap-shooting, shooting crap, rolling bones, playing the ponies, spit in the ocean, backing the cards, working the machines, penny-ante.

gambol, *v.* —*Syn.* frolic, caper, romp; see **play** 2.

game, *mod.* **1.** [Plucky]—*Syn.* spirited, hardy, resolute; see **brave** 1.

2. [(D) Lame]—*Syn.* bad, ailing, weak; see **disabled.**

game, *n.* **1.** [Entertainment]—*Syn.* festivity, amusement, diversion; see **entertainment** 2.

Card games include the following—poker, whist, bridgewhist, bridge, contract bridge, duplicate bridge, honeymoon bridge, auction bridge, five hundred, casino, war, euchre, taroc *or* tarok, railroad euchre, seven-up, cribbage, patience, solitaire, pedro, cinch, hearts, nap, Napoleon, Wellington, bezique, twenty-one *or* blackjack, baccarat, *chemin de fer* (French), Pan (trademark).

Children's games include—hide-and-go-seek, tag, tap on the icebox, hopscotch, hen-and-chickens, andy over *or* ante over, pretty girl station, prisoner's base, dare base, jacks, mumble-the-peg or mumbletypeg, ball, one old cat, fox and geese, red Rover, king of the hill, marbles, crack the whip, statues, London Bridge, ring around the roses, drop the handkerchief; clap in, clap out; puss in the corner, blindman's bluff, shinny, tin-tin-come-in, follow the leader, Simon says, giant step, catch, pom-pom-pullaway, post office, favors, Jerusalem, musical chairs, streets and alleys, run the gauntlet, cops and robbers, soldier, Indian, duck-on-a-rock, mother-may-I; red light, green light.

Party games include—charades, ha-ha, spin-the-bottle, post office, stagecoach, concentration, buzz, pin-the-tail-on-the-donkey.

Word games include—Scrabble (trademark), anagrams, ghost.

Board games include—chess, (Chinese) checkers, backgammon, go; Monopoly, Sorry, Clue, Trivial Pursuit, Parcheesi, Mah-Jongg (*all* trademarks).

Guessing games include—twenty questions, Botticelli, geography, adverb.

2. [Sport]—*Syn.* play, recreation, merrymaking; see **sport** 1.

3. [(D) A trick]—*Syn.* prank, practical joke, hoax; see **joke** 1.

4. [Wild meat, fish, or fowl]—*Syn.* quarry, prey, ravin; see **fish, fowl, meat.**

ahead of the game (D)—*Syn.* winning, doing well, thriving; see **successful.**

make game of—*Syn.* tease, mock, make fun of; see **ridicule.**

off (one's) game (D)—*Syn.* performing poorly, doing badly, failing; see **losing** 1.

play the game (D)—*Syn.* behave (properly), act according to custom, do what is expected; see **behave** 2.

gamin, *n.* —*Syn.* waif, foundling, urchin; see **orphan.**

gamut, *n.* —*Syn.* compass, range, sweep; see **extent.**

gamy, *mod.* —*Syn.* strong, plucky, courageous; see **brave** 1.

gander, *n.* —*Syn.* adult male goose, drake, brant; see **bird** 1.

gang, *n.* —*Syn.* horde, band, troop; see **organization** 3.

gangling, *mod.* —*Syn.* spindly, lanky, tall; see **thin** 2.

gangplank, *n.* —*Syn.* plank, bridge, gangway, ladder, approach, ramp.

gangrene, *n.* —*Syn.* gangrenous tissue, decay, infection; see **disease** 3.

gangster, *n.* —*Syn.* gunman, underworld leader, racketeer; see **criminal.**

gang up on *or* **against** (D), *v.* —*Syn.* combat, overwhelm, fight with; see **attack** 2.

gangway, *n.* —*Syn.* passage, passageway, corridor; see **hall** 2.

gap, *n.* **1.** [A breach]—*Syn.* cleft, break, rift; see **hole** 1, 2.

2. [A break in continuity]—*Syn.* hiatus, recess, lull; see **pause** 1, 2.

3. [A mountain pass]—*Syn.* way, chasm, hollow, cleft, passage, ravine, gorge, arroyo, canyon, defile, passageway, notch, *couloir* (French), *barranca* (Spanish), gully, gulch.

gape, *v.* **1.** [To stare]—*Syn.* goggle, gaze, peer; see **stare.**

2. [To split]—*Syn.* part, crack, cleave; see **divide** 1, **yawn** 2.

garage, *n.* **1.** [Housing for cars]—*Syn.* car stall, parking space, parking garage, parking, pigeonhole parking, parking lot, self-parking (D), lockup, carport.
2. [Commercial establishment]—*Syn.* automobile repair shop, storage garage, service garage, dead storage; chop shop (D).

garb, *n.* **1.** [Clothes]—*Syn.* clothing, outfit, attire; see **clothes.**
2. [Dress]—*Syn.* guise, form, semblance; see **appearance** 1.

garbage, *n.* —*Syn.* refuse, waste, table scrapings; see **trash** 1, 3.

garble, *v.* —*Syn.* misquote, falsify, distort; see **confuse, mislead.**

garden, *n.* —*Syn.* vegetable patch; taro *or* melon *or* berry *or* potato, etc., patch *or* garden; cultivated area, truck garden, enclosure, field, plot, bed, herb garden, rock garden, rose garden, Victory garden, formal garden, kitchen garden, hotbed, cold frame, greenhouse, patio, terrace, back yard, conservatory, nursery, flower garden, water garden, hanging garden, floating garden, cactus garden, desert garden, English garden, garden spot, oasis.

gardener, *n.* —*Syn.* vegetable grower, truck farmer, seedsman, caretaker, landscaper, greenkeeper.

gardening, *n.* —*Syn.* truck farming, vegetable raising, tillage.

gargantuan, *mod.* —*Syn.* enormous, huge, immense; see **large** 1.

gargle, *v.* —*Syn.* swash, rinse, trill, rinse the mouth, irrigate the throat, use a mouthwash.

gargoyle, *n.* —*Syn.* spout, grotesque figure, drain, waterspout, rainspout, gutter; see also **sculpture.**

garish, *mod.* —*Syn.* showy, gaudy, ostentatious; see **ornate** 1.

garland, *n.* **1.** [Wreath]—*Syn.* crown, festoon, laurel; see **wreath.**
2. [Collection]—*Syn.* excerpts, miscellany, anthology; see **collection** 2.

garment, *n.* —*Syn.* dress, attire, apparel; see **clothes.**

garner, *n.* —*Syn.* granary, silo, grain elevator; see **storehouse.**

garner, *v.* —*Syn.* store, reap, collect; see **accumulate** 1, **assemble** 2, **harvest.**

garnish, *v.* —*Syn.* embellish, beautify, deck; see **decorate.**

garret, *n.* —*Syn.* upper story, attic, loft, cupola, penthouse, tower, lookout, dormer, clerestory, top story, belfry.

garrison, *n.* **1.** [Militia]—*Syn.* militia, defenders, occupation troops; see **army** 1, 2.
2. [A fortress]—*Syn.* post, stronghold, blockhouse; see **fortification** 2.

garrison, *v.* —*Syn.* fortify, protect, guard; see **defend** 1, 2.

garrote, *v.* —*Syn.* throttle, strangle, suffocate; see **choke** 1.

garrulity, *n.* —*Syn.* loquacity, wordiness, verbosity, glibness, multiloquence, grandiloquence, talkativeness, garrulousness, volubility, loquaciousness, largiloquence, fecundity, effusion, verboseness, prolixity.

garrulous, *mod.* —*Syn.* talkative, loquacious, chattering; see **verbose.**

garter, *n.* —*Syn.* band, strap, tie; see **fastener.**

gas, *n.* **1.** [A state of matter]—*Syn.* vapor, volatile substance, fumes, aeriform fluid, gaseous mixture.
2. [(D) Gasoline]—*Syn.* propellant, petrol (British), motor fuel; see **gasoline.**
3. [Poisonous gas]—*Syn.* Varieties include the following—systemic poison, vesicant, lacrimator, incendiary gas, Lewisite, mustard gas, chloral gas, chlorine, benzyl, bromide, bromoacetone, phosgene, chloropicrin, Agent Orange, hydrocyanic acid, arsine, chloracetophenone, brombenzylcyanide, Adamsite, sneeze gas, tear gas, asphyxiating gas, sternutatory gas, lachrymatory gas, vesicatory gas, moldy hay (D).
4. [An anesthetic]—*Syn.* ether, general anesthetic, chloroform, nitrous oxide, laughing gas (D).
step on the gas (D)—*Syn.* rush, hasten, move fast; see **hurry** 1.

gaseous, *mod.* —*Syn.* vaporous, effervescent, aeriform; see **volatile** 1.

gash, *n.* —*Syn.* slash, slice, wound; see **cut** 2.

gasoline, *n.* —*Syn.* petrol (British), motor fuel, propellant, combustible material; *both* (D): gas, juice. Types of gasoline include the following—low octane gasoline, high octane gasoline, ethyl gasoline, unleaded, super unleaded, regular (leaded), airplane gasoline; 80-octane, 100-octane, 150-octane gasoline, etc.; *all* (D): high test, low test, white gas, soup, gasso.

gasp, *v.* —*Syn.* labor for breath, breathe convulsively, gulp, have difficulty in breathing, pant, puff, wheeze, blow, sniffle, snort; inspire *or* respire *or* inhale violently *or* jerkily.
at the last gasp (D)—*Syn.* at the last moment, just in time, penultimately; see **finally** 2.

gassy (D), *mod.* —*Syn.* bombastic, boastful, pompous; see **egotistic** 2.

gate, *n.* —*Syn.* entrance, ingress, passage, way, port, issue, bar, weir, conduit, turnstile, revolving door, means of access, portcullis, lichgate, barrier; see also **door.**
get the gate (D)—*Syn.* be dismissed *or* rejected, be asked *or* forced to leave, be thrown out; see **get it** 2.
give (someone) the gate (D)—*Syn.* dismiss, reject, force out; see **oust.**

gate-crasher, *n.* —*Syn.* interloper, meddler, trespasser; see **intruder.**

gatekeeper, *n.* —*Syn.* sentry, guard, doorkeeper; see **watchman.**

gather, *v.* **1.** [To come together]—*Syn.* assemble, forgather, meet, gather around, congregate, hang around, flock together, flock *or* pour in, rally, crowd, throng, come together, convene, collect, unite, reunite, associate, hold a reunion, resort, swarm, huddle, swoop up, draw in, fish up, group, converge, concentrate, close with; *all* (D): fish in *or* up, swoop up, glom onto.—*Ant.* scatter*, disperse, part.
2. [To bring together]—*Syn.* collect, aggregate, amass; see **accumulate** 1, **assemble** 2.
3. [To conclude]—*Syn.* infer, deduce, find; see **assume.**

4. [To harvest]—*Syn.* garner, reap, take in; see **harvest.**
5. [To choose]—*Syn.* pick, cull, select; see **choose** 1.
gathered, *mod.* —*Syn.* assembled, met, forgathered, congregated, joined, rallied, crowded together, thronged, collected, united, associated, swarmed, huddled, grouped, inspissated, massed, amassed, accumulated, picked, garnered, harvested, stored, gleaned, hoarded, culled, mustered, combined, brought together, convened, convoked, summoned, compiled, mobilized, lumped together, amalgamated, incorporated, collocated, raked up, concentrated, heaped, stacked, piled, stowed away.—*Ant.* scattered*, dispersed, separated.
be gathered to one's fathers—*Syn.* pass away *or* be deceased, expire; see **die** 1.
gathering, *n.* —*Syn.* assembly, meeting, conclave, caucus, parley, council, conference, band, congregation, junction, company, rally, crowd, throng, bunch, collection, union, association, society, committee, legislature, house, senate, parliament, diet, swarm, huddle, group, body, mass, aggregation, herd, turnout, forgathering, flock, muster, levy, combination, caravan, convention, discussion, mobilization, collocation, assemblage, panel, concourse, interchange, reunion, meet, congress, conflux, gathering of the clans, coven, eisteddfod, synod, reception, conventicle, vestry, posse, gemote, folkmoot, moot, witenagemot, attendance, multitude, ingathering, audience, press, rout, horde, mob, queue, crush, party, entertainment, social gathering, crew, gang, school, array, bevy, troop, drove, concentration, convocation, council meeting, council of war; *all* (D): get-together, confab, huddle, bull session.
gauche, *mod.* —*Syn.* uncouth, clumsy, inept; see **awkward** 1.
gaucherie, *n.* —*Syn.* clumsiness, boorishness, blunder; see **awkwardness** 1.
gaudy, *mod.* —*Syn.* showy, flashy, tawdry; see **ornate** 1.
gauge, *n.* —*Syn.* measure, mark, check, scale, criterion, standard.
gauge, *v.* —*Syn.* check, weigh, calibrate, calculate; see **measure** 1.
gaunt, *mod.* —*Syn.* emaciated, scraggy, skinny; see **thin** 2.
gauze, *mod.* —*Syn.* gauzy, lacy, delicate; see **sheer** 2.
gauze, *n.* —*Syn.* film, veil, cheesecloth, mosquito netting, bandage, sterile cloth, sterile dressings, dressings.
gauzy, *mod.* —*Syn.* filmy, light, transparent; see **sheer** 2.
gravel, *n.* —*Syn.* mallet, maul, symbol of office; see **hammer.**
gawk, *v.* —*Syn.* stare, ogle, gaze; see **look** 2.
gawky, *mod.* —*Syn.* clumsy, rustic, uncouth; see **awkward** 1, **rude** 1.
gay, *mod.* **1.** [Happy]—*Syn.* cheerful, merry, vivacious; see **happy** 1.
2. [Bright]—*Syn.* brilliant, intense, rich; see **bright** 1, 2.
3. [Homosexual]—*Syn.* homophile, homoerotic, Lesbian; see **homosexual.**
gaze, *v.* —*Syn.* stare, watch, gape; see **look** 2.
gazette, *n.* —*Syn.* journal, publication, periodical; see **newspaper.**
gear, *n.* **1.** [Equipment]—*Syn.* material, tackle, things; see **equipment.**
2. [A geared wheel]—*Syn.* cog, cogwheel, pinion, toothed wheel, spurwheel, sprocket, ragwheel, lanternwheel.
Types of gears include the following—spur, bevel, crown, worm, internal, inside, drive *or* driving, transmission, differential, timing, conical, Hooke's, spiral, stepped, angular, beveled, elliptical, hooked, idling, overhead, hypoid, nylon, plastic, first *or* low, second *or* intermediate, third *or* high, fourth, reverse, overdrive, multiplying, quick-return.
high gear (D)—*Syn.* high speed, productivity, activity; see **action** 2.
in gear (D)—*Syn.* usable, efficient, productive; see **working.**
low gear (D)—*Syn.* low speed, slowness, inactivity; see **idleness** 1.
out of gear (D)—*Syn.* inefficient, not working, broken; see **useless** 1.
shift gears (D)—*Syn.* alter one's method *or* approach, proceed along a different course, accelerate; see **change** 1.
gear, *v.* **1.** [Prepare]—*Syn.* organize, harness, ready; see **prepare** 1.
2. [Regulate]—*Syn.* adjust, match, blend; see **regulate** 2.
gelatinous, *mod.* —*Syn.* jellied, coagulated, viscous; see **thick** 3.
gem, *n.* **1.** [A jewel]—*Syn.* precious stone, bauble, ornament; see **jewel** 1.
Types of gems include the following—diamond, emerald, ruby, pearl, brilliant, aquamarine, amethyst, topaz, turquoise, jade, opal, sapphire, garnet, carnelian, jacinth, beryl, cat's eye, chrysoprase, chalcedony, agate, bloodstone, moonstone, onyx, sard, lapis lazuli, chrysolite, carbuncle, coral.
2. [Anything excellent, especially if small and beautiful]—*Syn.* jewel, pearl of great price, paragon, acme of perfection, Koh-i-noor, trump, ace, nonpareil, beau ideal.
geminate, *mod.* —*Syn.* coupled, binate, paired; see **matched.**
gender, *n.* —*Syn.* sexuality, sort, variety; see **kind** 2, **sex** 3.
genealogy, *n.* —*Syn.* derivation, pedigree, parentage, generation, descent, history, family tree, lineage, extraction; see also **family** 1.
general, *mod.* **1.** [Having wide application]—*Syn.* comprehensive, comprehending, widespread, universal, limitless, unlimited, extensive, ecumenical, all-embracing, ubiquitous, unconfined, broad, taken as a whole, not partial, not particular, not specific, blanket, inclusive, wide, infinite, worldwide, endless, far-reaching, ample.—*Ant.* particular*, special, limited.
2. [Of common occurrence]—*Syn.* usual, customary, prevailing; see **common** 1.
3. [Not specific]—*Syn.* indefinite, uncertain, imprecise; see **vague** 2.
in general—*Syn.* generally, usually, ordinarily; see **regularly** 1.

generality, *n.* —*Syn.* abstraction, indefinite *or* general *or* vague statement, general phrase, loose statement, half-truth, simplistic statement, observation, universality, principle; see also **law** 4.

generalize, *v.* **1.** [To make generally applicable] —*Syn.* theorize, hypothesize, conclude, induce, derive a law, establish a criterion, observe similarities, discover order in apparent disorder, establish rules of probability, discern affinities.—*Ant.* separate*, particularize, deduce*.

2. [To speak in general terms]—*Syn.* enunciate *or* offer principles without applications, vapor, theorize, speculate, postulate, be metaphysical, discuss in the abstract, speak in terms of the ideal, philosophize; *both* (D): stay out on cloud nine, stay up in the clouds.—*Ant.* specify*, apply, particularize.

generally, *mod.* —*Syn.* usually, commonly, ordinarily; see **regularly** 1.

generalship, *n.* —*Syn.* strategics, logistics, leadership; see **administration** 1.

generate, *v.* —*Syn.* form, make, beget, create; see **produce** 1.

generation, *n.* **1.** [The act of producing]—*Syn.* engendering, formation, creation; see **production** 1.

2. [The act of producing offspring]—*Syn.* procreation, propagation, reproduction, breeding, bearing, spawning, bringing forth, multiplying, fructifying. —*Ant.* perishing, dying out, becoming extinct.

3. [One cycle in the succession of parents and children]—*Syn.* age, crop, rank, step in continuous generation, contemporaries, peers, age group.

4. [The time required for a generation, sense 3] —*Syn.* span, 20 to 30 years, period; see **age** 3.

generic, *mod.* —*Syn.* universal, general, nonexclusive; see **universal** 3, **general** 1.

generosity, *n.* **1.** [Unselfish giving]—*Syn.* bounty, readiness in giving, free giving, hospitality, charitableness, largesse, benevolence, charity, liberality, bounteousness, profusion, hospitality, beneficence, alms-giving, philanthropy, open-handedness, munificence, altruism, unselfishness, playing Lady Bountiful (D).—*Ant.* greed*, miserliness, stinginess.

2. [Humane largeness of sympathy]—*Syn.* magnanimity, charity, humanity; see **kindness** 1.

generous, *mod.* **1.** [Open-handed]—*Syn.* bountiful, liberal, munificent, charitable, altruistic, free-handed, beneficent, lavish, profuse, unselfish, hospitable, philanthropic, prodigal, unsparing, unstinting.—*Ant.* stingy*, close, tightfisted.

2. [Considerate or favorable; *said of conditions, terms, etc.*]—*Syn.* liberal, magnanimous, unselfish, easy, fair, moderate, reasonable, handsome, ungrudging, acceptable, just, equitable.—*Ant.* unfair*, unreasonable, restrictive.

3. [Noble]—*Syn.* honorable, chivalrous, excellent; see **noble** 1, 2.

4. [Abundant]—*Syn.* overflowing, large, bountiful; see **plentiful** 1, 2.

generously, *mod.* **1.** [With a free hand]—*Syn.* bountifully, liberally, lavishly, unsparingly, unstintingly, in full measure, handsomely, freely, as a noble gesture, profusely, with open hands, abundantly, munificently, charitably, prodigally, copiously.—*Ant.* selfishly*, grudgingly, sparingly.

2. [With an open heart]—*Syn.* charitably, liberally, magnanimously, wholeheartedly, unreservedly, nobly, majestically, royally, genially, honestly, animatedly, candidly, enthusiastically, unselfishly, disinterestedly, chivalrously, benevolently, warmly; see also **politely.**—*Ant.* selfishly*, coldly, heartlessly.

genetic, *mod.* —*Syn.* genital, sporogenous, xenogenetic, hereditary, matriclinous, patrimonial, oögenetic, phytogenetic, digenetic, abiogenetic, dysmerogenetic; see also **ancestral, historical.**

genetic code, *n.* —*Syn.* universal heredity alphabet, ribonucleic acid (RNA), AGTCAC, language of heredity, adenine, thymine, guanine, cytocine, base pairing; see also **DNA.**

genetics, *n.* —*Syn.* heredity, genesiology, eugenics; see **heredity.**

genial, *mod.* **1.** [Friendly]—*Syn.* cordial, kind, warmhearted; see **friendly** 1.

2. [Pleasant or favorable; *said of the weather, surroundings, etc.*]—*Syn.* warm, cheering, cheerful; see **fair** 3, **mild** 2, **pleasant** 2.

geniality, *n.* —*Syn.* kindliness, cheerfulness, friendliness; see **happiness** 1.

genitals, *n.* —*Syn.* organs, sexual organs, genitalia, organs of generation, private parts, reproductory organs, organs of excretion, pudenda, gonads, testicles, testes; *all* (D): stones, seeds, nuts, privates.

genius, *n.* **1.** [The highest degree of intellectual capacity]—*Syn.* ability, talent, intellect, brains, intelligence, endowment, precocity, inspiration, imagination, gift, aptitude, propensity, wisdom, astuteness, penetration, grasp, discernment, acumen, acuteness, percipience, power, capability, accomplishment, sagacity, subtlety, perspicacity, understanding, reach, sympathy, daemon, afflatus, enthusiasm, creative gift; *all* (D): knack, bent, turn.

2. [One having genius, sense 1]—*Syn.* gifted person, prodigy, adept; see **artist** 1, 2, **author** 1, **doctor, philosopher, poet, writer.**

3. [Character or characteristics]—*Syn.* nature, taste, disposition; see **character** 1, 2.

genre, *n.* —*Syn.* sort, style, kind; see **class** 1.

genteel, *mod.* **1.** [Polite]—*Syn.* courteous, mannerly, well-behaved; see **polite** 1.

2. [Elegant]—*Syn.* polished, cultured, well-bred; see **refined** 2.

3. [Refined, but mannered and pompous]—*Syn.* affected, pretentious, formal, ostentatious, showy, artificial, hollow, conventional, imitative.—*Ant.* honest*, genuine, cultured.

gentile, *n.* —*Syn.* heathen, non-Jew, non-Mormon; see **Christian.**

gentility, *n.* —*Syn.* decorum, propriety, refinement; see **behavior** 1.

gentle, *mod.* **1.** [Soft]—*Syn.* tender, smooth, sensitive; see **faint** 3, **soft** 2, 3.

2. [Kind]—*Syn.* tender, considerate, benign; see **kind** 1.

3. [Tamed]—*Syn.* domesticated, housebroken, broken, disciplined, educated, trained, cowed, civilized, tractable, pliable, taught, cultivated, tame, obedient to the rein.—*Ant.* wild*, savage, untamed.

4. [Well-born]—*Syn.* highbred, blue-blooded, aristocratic; see **noble** 1, 2, 3.

gentlefolk, *n.* —*Syn.* lords and ladies, upper class, nobility; see **aristocracy, aristocrat.**

gentleman, *n.* **1.** [A courteous and honorable man] —*Syn.* man of honor, refined man, man of his word, polished man, cavalier, sir, don; *all* (D): Sir Galahad, gentleman and a scholar, brick, trump, the glass of fashion and the mold of form, playboy. —*Ant.* boor*, sneak, puppy.

2. [A well-born person]—*Syn.* nobleman, patrician, man of breeding; see **aristocrat, lord** 2.

gentlemanly, *mod.* —*Syn.* polite, polished, gallant; see **refined** 2.

gentleness, *n.* **1.** [Intentional mildness]—*Syn.* tenderness, carefulness, caution; see **kindness** 1.

2. [Physical sensitivity]—*Syn.* tenderness, softness, pliability, delicacy, smoothness, fragility, pliancy, sweetness.—*Ant.* roughness*, hardness, imperviousness.

3. [Docility]—*Syn.* meekness, obedience, tameness; see **docility.**

gentlewoman, *n.* —*Syn.* dame, noblewoman, woman of quality *or* breeding *or* culture; see **lady** 2, 3.

gently, *mod.* **1.** [Quietly and softly]—*Syn.* mildly, blandly, smoothly; see **lightly** 1.

2. [Kindly]—*Syn.* considerately, tenderly, benevolently; see **kindly** 2.

gentry, *n.* —*Syn.* nobility, high society, upper class; see **aristocracy.**

genuflect, *v.* —*Syn.* kneel, curtsy, stoop; see **bow** 1.

genuine, *mod.* **1.** [Authentic; *said of things*] —*Syn.* real, true, actual, original, veritable, unadulterated, unmixed, undisguised, unerring, official, certified, whole, accurate, proved, tested, ascertained, good, natural, unimpeachable, pure, unquestionable, authenticated, existent, essential, substantial, unalloyed, factual, demonstrable, palpable, exact, precise, very, positive, valid, literal, sound, plain, unvarnished, certain, legitimate, sterling, pucka; *all* (D): legit, for real, 18-karat, the real stuff, honest-to-goodness, in the flesh.—*Ant.* vulgar*, spurious, sham.

2. [Sincere]—*Syn.* real, actual, unaffected, veritable, unquestionable, certain, absolute, unimpeachable, definite, uncontradictable, incontrovertible, well-established, known, manifest, reliable, bona fide, staunch, trustworthy, certain, free from pretense, without artificiality, valid, positive, frank, candid, heartfelt, not dissimulated, without a taint of hypocrisy.—*Ant.* hypocritical*, affected, simulated.

genus, *n.* —*Syn.* sort, kind, classification; see **class** 1.

geographical, *mod.* —*Syn.* terrestrial, geographic, mundane, earthly, geological, topographical, cartographic, geophysical, physiographic, of the earth, concerning the earth; see also **social science.**

geography, *n.* —*Syn.* earth science, geology, topography, economic geography, political geography, geopolitics, geopolitical study, physiography, physiographics, cartography.

geology, *n.* —Divisions of geology include the following—dynamic geology, structural geology, geotectonic geology, selenology, diastrophism, earthquakes, vulcanism, applied geology, mineral *or* mining geology, historical geology, paleontology, physiography, petrology, oil geology, prognostic geology.

geometrical, *mod.* —*Syn.* square, many-sided, multilateral, bilateral, triangular, polyhedral, polyhedrous, dihedral, trilateral, tetrahedral, quadrilateral.

geopolitics, *mod.* —*Syn.* world politics, political geography, economic geography; see **science** 1.

germ, *n.* **1.** [Origin]—*Syn.* inception, source, root; see **origin** 3.

2. [Embryo]—*Syn.* seed, bud, sprig; see **egg.**

3. [Bacillus]—*Syn.* microbe, antibody, bacteria, disease germ, micro-organism, virus, bacterium, microscopic life, parasite, bug (D).

German, *mod.* —*Syn.* Germanic, *Deutsch, hoch Deutsch* (*both* German), Teutonic, Prussian, Saxon, Bavarian, Rhenish, Thuringian, Hanoverian, Swabian, Franconian, thorough, systematic, *gemütlich* (German).

German, *n.* **1.** [The German language]—*Syn.* Teutonic language, Proto-Germanic, West Germanic, High German, Low German, Old High German, Middle High German, Modern German, New High German, *Plattdeutsch* (German), High Dutch, *Deutsch* (German), Dutch (D); see also **language** 2. Languages grouped with German as belonging to the Germanic family are as follows—*East Germanic:* Gothic, Vandalic; *North Germanic:* Old Norse, Icelandic, Faroese, Norwegian, Danish, Swedish; *West Germanic:* English, Yiddish, Dutch, Afrikaans, Flemish, Frisian, *Plattdeutsch,* German.

2. [A German person]—*Syn.* East German, West German, Teuton, Berliner, East Berliner, West Berliner, Bavarian, Hanoverian, Prussian, Franconian, Rhinelander, Saxon, Swabian, Hitlerite, Nazi, Aryan.

germane, *mod.* —*Syn.* apropos, pertinent, relating; see **relevant.**

Germany, *n.* —*Syn.* German nation, *Deutsches Reich* (German), German Reich, German people, West Germany, *Bundesrepublik Deutschland (BRD)* (German), East Germany, Communist Germany, *Deutsche Demokratische Republik (DDR)* (German), Axis power, Third Reich, German Empire, Nazi state, totalitarian state, Weimar Republic, Occupied Germany.

germicide, *n.* —*Syn.* disinfectant, antitoxin, insecticide; see **antiseptic.**

germinate, *v.* —*Syn.* generate, live, develop; see **grow** 1.

gestation, *n.* **1.** [Development]—*Syn.* incubation, maturation, growth; see **development** 2.

2. [Pregnancy]—*Syn.* reproduction, gravidity, fecundation; see **pregnancy.**

gesticulate, *v.* —*Syn.* pantomime, motion, signal; see **gesture.**

gesture, *n.* **1.** [A deliberately significant motion] —*Syn.* gesticulation, indication, intimation; see **sign** 1.

2. [A formality or pretense]—*Syn.* pose, posture, attitude; see **appearance** 2.

gesture, *v.* —*Syn.* make a sign, motion, signal, pantomime, act out, use sign language, use one's hands, indicate, signalize, saw the air (D); see also **move** 1.

get, *v.* **1.** [To obtain]—*Syn.* gain, procure, acquire; see **obtain** 1.

2. [To become]—*Syn.* grow, develop into, go; see **become** 1.
3. [To receive]—*Syn.* be given, take, accept; see **receive** 1.
4. [To induce]—*Syn.* persuade, talk into, compel; see **urge** 2.
5. [To catch]—*Syn.* capture, take, occupy; see **seize** 2.
6. [(D) To hit]—*Syn.* sock, strike, touch; see **hit** 1.
7. [(D) To overcome]—*Syn.* beat, vanquish, overpower; see **defeat** 1, 2, 3.
8. [To prepare]—*Syn.* make, arrange, dress; see **prepare** 1.
9. [To adjust]—*Syn.* order, straighten, dispose; see **adjust** 1, 3.
10. [To beget]—*Syn.* produce, generate, procreate; see **propagate** 1.
11. [To contract; *said of bodily disorders*]—*Syn.* fall victim to, succumb (to), get sick; see **catch** 4.
12. [To remove]—*Syn.* carry *or* take away, displace, cart off; see **remove** 1.
13. [To learn]—*Syn.* acquire, gain, receive; see **learn** 1.
14. [(D) To understand]—*Syn.* comprehend, perceive, know; see **understand** 1.
15. [(D) To puzzle]—*Syn.* upset, bewilder, confound; see **confuse.**
16. [(D) To please]—*Syn.* gratify, satisfy, amuse; see **entertain** 1.
17. [(D) To irritate]—*Syn.* annoy, provoke, vex; see **bother** 2.
18. [(D) To excite]—*Syn.* arouse, stir up, stimulate; see **excite** 2.
19. [(D) To observe]—*Syn.* look at, perceive, notice; see **see** 1.
20. [(D) To arrive]—*Syn.* come to, reach, land; see **arrive** 1.
21. [To come]—*Syn.* converge, advance, draw near; see **approach** 2, 3.

get across (D), *v.*—*Syn.* impart, convey, pass on; see **communicate** 1.

get ahead, *v.*—*Syn.* climb, prosper, thrive; see **succeed** 1.

get along, *v.* **1.** [To be successful]—*Syn.* thrive, prosper, flourish; see **succeed** 1.
2. [To proceed]—*Syn.* progress, move on, push ahead; see **advance** 1.
3. [To grow old]—*Syn.* wane, decline, advance in years; see **age** 1.

get angry, *v.*—*Syn.* become *or* grow enraged *or* infuriated *or* furious, etc.; lose one's temper *or* self-control *or* sense of balance; *all* (D): get mad *or* sore, blow up, blow *or* lose one's cool, get hot under the collar, get steamed up, fly off the handle, blow a fuse.

get at, *v.* **1.** [To arrive at]—*Syn.* achieve, reach, ascertain; see **arrive** 1.
2. [To intend]—*Syn.* mean, aim, purpose; see **intend** 1.

get away (from), *v.*—*Syn.* flee, run away, elude; see **escape.**

get away with, *v.*—*Syn.* escape notice; *both* (D): get off cheap, fall on deaf ears; see also **achieve** 1, **satisfy** 3.

get back, *v.* **1.** [To return]—*Syn.* reappear, turn back, revisit; see **return** 1.
2. [To regain]—*Syn.* retrieve, reclaim, salvage; see **recover** 1.

get back at, *v.*—*Syn.* get even with, pay back, retaliate; see **revenge.**

get behind, *v.*—*Syn.* loiter, fall behind, hesitate; see **lag** 1.

get by (D), *v.*—*Syn.* manage, get along, do well enough; see **contrive** 2.

get down, *v.*—*Syn.* dismount, come down, alight; see **descend** 1.

get even with, *v.*—*Syn.* settle a score, avenge, pay back; see **revenge.**

get going, *v.*—*Syn.* start, progress, move; see **begin** 1, 2.

get in, *v.* **1.** [To arrive]—*Syn.* come, land, reach the airport *or* dock *or* hotel, etc.; see **arrive** 1.
2. [To enter]—*Syn.* get inside, find a way in, gain ingress; see **enter** 1.

get *or* **be in touch (with),** *v.*—*Syn.* call, telephone, write (to), contact, wire, telegraph, radio, be in radio contact (with), correspond (with), communicate (with), reach, maintain connections (with), keep in touch *or* in contact (with), make overtures (to).

get it (D), *v.* **1.** [To understand]—*Syn.* comprehend, perceive, know; see **understand** 1.
2. [To be punished]—*Syn.* suffer, get what is coming to one, get one's just deserts, be scolded *or* reprimanded *or* admonished *or* rebuked *or* upbraided, suffer for, suffer the consequences *or* penalty; *all* (D): catch it, get in trouble, get *or* catch it in the neck, get one's comeuppance.

get mad (D), *v.*—*Syn.* lose one's self-control *or* temper *or* sense of balance, become angry *or* infuriated *or* irate, rant and rave; see **rage** 1.

get off, *v.* **1.** [To go away]—*Syn.* depart, escape, go; see **leave** 1.
2. [To dismount]—*Syn.* alight, light, disembark; see **descend** 1.

get on, *v.* **1.** [To put on]—*Syn.* dress, attire, don; see **wear** 1.
2. [To mount]—*Syn.* go up, ascend, scale; see **climb** 2.
3. [To succeed]—*Syn.* manage, do well enough, get along; see **succeed** 1.
4. [To age]—*Syn.* grow old(er), advance in years, approach retirement; see **age** 1.

get out, *interj.*—*Syn.* leave, begone, be off, go away, get away, avaunt; *all* (D): scram! clear out, split, skiddoo, take a powder, skedaddle, beat it, get the hell out.

get out, *v.* **1.** [To leave]—*Syn.* go, depart, take one's departure; see **leave** 1.
2. [To escape]—*Syn.* break out, run away, flee; see **escape.**

get out of, *v.* **1.** [To obtain]—*Syn.* get (from), secure, gain; see **obtain** 1.
2. [To escape]—*Syn.* flee, fly, run away; see **escape.**
3. [To evade]—*Syn.* dodge, shun, avoid; see **evade** 1.
4. [To leave]—*Syn.* depart, go away, withdraw; see **leave** 1.
5. [To consume]—*Syn.* use (up), be out (of), need; see **consume** 2.

get over, *v.*—*Syn.* overcome, recuperate, survive; see **recover** 3.

get past, *v.* —*Syn.* progress, proceed, get on; see **advance** 1.
get ready, *v.* —*Syn.* make preparations, arrange, plan; see **prepare** 1.
get rid of, *v.* —*Syn.* eject, expel, remove; see **eliminate** 1.
get set, *v.* —*Syn.* be on the alert, be ready, consolidate one's position; see **prepare** 1.
get sick, *v.* —*Syn.* become sick or ill, contract a disease, take sick; see **sicken.**
get the best of, *v.* —*Syn.* master, win victory over, conquer; see **defeat** 1, 2, 3.
get the hang of (D), *v.* —*Syn.* comprehend, become acquainted with, grasp; see **understand** 1.
get the worst of, *v.* —*Syn.* fail, miss, be defeated *or* beaten; see **lose** 3.
get to, *v.* **1.** [To arrive]—*Syn.* reach, approach, land at; see **arrive** 1.
2. [(D) To make listen or understand]—*Syn.* reach, talk to, approach; see **influence.**
get through, *v.* **1.** [To complete]—*Syn.* discharge, enact, finish; see **achieve** 1.
2. [To endure]—*Syn.* live *or* come through, survive, subsist; see **endure** 1, 2.
get through to (D), *v.* —*Syn.* make understand *or* listen, reach, come to an agreement (with); see **influence.**
getting, *n.* **1.** [The act of procuring]—*Syn.* taking, obtaining, gaining, grasping, catching, earning, winning, seizing, clutching, pursuing, securing, capturing, mastering, possessing oneself of, confiscating, appropriating, assimilating, seeking out, snatching.—*Ant.* losing*, giving up, abandoning.
2. [The act of changing]—*Syn.* succumbing, growing, becoming, altering, accepting, submitting to, being subjected to.—*Ant.* refusal*, rejecting, throwing off.
get together, *v.* **1.** [To gather]—*Syn.* collect, accumulate, congregate; see **assemble** 2.
2. [To reach an agreement]—*Syn.* come to terms, settle, make a bargain; see **agree on.**
get up, *v.* **1.** [To climb]—*Syn.* ascend, mount, go up; see **climb** 2.
2. [To arise]—*Syn.* get out of bed, rise, turn out; see **arise** 1.
get wind of, *v.* —*Syn.* hear about, find out, learn; see **discover** 1, **hear** 2.
get wise (to) (D), *v.* —*Syn.* find out, understand, learn; see **discover** 1.
get with, *v.* —*Syn.* act, start, proceed; see **begin** 1.
geyser, *n.* —*Syn.* hot springs, water spout, jet; see **fountain** 2.
ghastly, *mod.* **1.** [Like a ghost]—*Syn.* spectral, wan, wraithlike, pallid, ashen, grim, deathlike, corpselike, funereal, cadaverous, ghostly, unearthly, weird, unnatural, supernatural, uncanny, grisly, gruesome, macabre.—*Ant.* natural, real, substantial.
2. [Terrifying]—*Syn.* hideous, horrible, frightening; see **frightful** 1.
3. [(D) Unpleasant]—*Syn.* repulsive, disgusting, abhorrent; see **offensive** 2.
ghost, *n.* **1.** [An unsubstantial being]—*Syn.* vision, specter, wraith, apparition, spirit, daemon, demon, shade, phantom, appearance, incorporeal *or* ethereal *or* etheric being, spook, supernatural visitant, phantasm, kelpie, zombie; see also **devil** 1.
2. [A disembodied human soul]—*Syn.* spirit, manes, revenant, shade, soul.
give up the ghost—*Syn.* succumb, perish, expire; see **die** 1.
ghostly, *mod.* **1.** [Concerning a ghost]—*Syn.* ghostlike, pale, wan; see **frightful** 1.
2. [Concerning the soul]—*Syn.* spiritual, holy, religious; see **divine** 1, 2.
ghoul, *n.* —*Syn.* fiend, demon, vampire; see **devil** 1.
giant, *mod.* —*Syn.* monstrous, colossal, enormous; see **large** 1.
giant, *n.* **1.** [A gigantic manlike being]—*Syn.* ogre, Cyclops, Titan, Olympian, colossus, Gargantuan creature, Goliath, Antaeus, Brobdingnagian, man-mountain, Hercules, Atlas; see also **monster.** —*Ant.* dwarf*, pigmy, mannikin.
2. [Anything very large]—*Syn.* mammoth, behemoth, colossus, monster, whale, elephant, jumbo, leviathan, mountain, hulk, lump, bulk; *both* (D): whopper, super-duper.—*Ant.* dwarf*, mite, midget.
gibberish, *n.* —*Syn.* jargon, chatter, claptrap; see **nonsense** 1.
gibbet, *n.* —*Syn.* yardarm, lynching tree, scaffold; see **gallows.**
gibe, *v.* —*Syn.* scoff, sneer, flout; see **ridicule.**
giddy, *mod.* **1.** [Fickle]—*Syn.* unsettled, capricious, inconstant; see **changeable** 1.
2. [Dizzy]—*Syn.* vertiginous, reeling, unsteady; see **dizzy** 1.
3. [Promoting dizziness]—*Syn.* steep, towering, awful, precipitate, lofty, confusing, whirling, stupendous, flashing, unaccustomed, tremendous, overpowering.—*Ant.* regular, steadying, balancing.
gift, *n.* **1.** [A present]—*Syn.* presentation, donation, benefaction, largesse, grant, gratuity, boon, alms, endowment, bequest, bounty, charity, provision, favor, lagniappe, legacy, bestowal, award, reward, dispensation, fairing, philanthropy, oblation, libation, offering, souvenir, premium, token, pittance, remembrance, courtesy, bonus, subsidy, tribute, subvention, contribution, subscription, donative, dole, relief, ration, benefit, offertory, tip, Peter's pence, honorarium, vail, *Trinkgeld* (German), *pourboire* (French), allowance, handsel, remittance; *all* (D): for free, handout, hand-me-down.
2. [An aptitude]—*Syn.* faculty, capacity, capability; see **ability** 1, 2.
look a gift horse in the mouth (D)—*Syn.* carp, criticize, be ungrateful; see **censure.**
gifted, *mod.* —*Syn.* smart, skilled, talented; see **able** 1, 2.
gigantic, *mod.* —*Syn.* massive, huge, immense; see **large** 1.
giggle, *n.* —*Syn.* titter, chuckle, snicker; see **laugh.**
gigolo, *n.* —*Syn.* paid companion, playboy, paramour; see **lover** 1, **pimp.**
gild, *v.* **1.** [To give the appearance of gold]—*Syn.* wash, plate, overlay, tinsel, electroplate, overlay with gold, coat with gold leaf.
2. [To adorn]—*Syn.* varnish, overlay, lay on color, give glitter to, impart a specious appearance, whitewash, paint in rosy colors.

gilt, *mod.* —*Syn.* plated, gold-washed, tinseled, glittering, showy, gaudy, specious, meretricious, painted, varnished, shiny, sparkling, gleaming, lustrous, golden, gold-filled, alloyed, overlaid, gold-edged, gilded, tinsel, trumpery, tawdry, cheap, brummagem (D).—*Ant.* genuine*, solid gold, 18-carat.

gimcrack, *n.* —*Syn.* trifle, bauble, knick-knack; see **trinket.**

gimmick (D), *n.* **1.** [Gadget]—*Syn.* apparatus, fixture, contrivance; see **device** 1.
2. [Means]—*Syn.* catch, secret device, method; see **trick** 1.

gin, *n.* —Types of gin include the following—dry gin, sloe gin, cordial gin, unflavored gin, English gin, Dutch gin, Holland gin, Schiedam; see **drink** 2.

gingerly, *mod.* —*Syn.* cautiously, warily, suspiciously; see **carefully** 2.

gipsy, *n.* —*Syn.* hobo, rover, vagabond; see **gypsy** 1, **tramp** 1, **traveler.**

gird, *v.* **1.** [To encircle]—*Syn.* girdle, secure, bind; see **fasten** 1, **surround** 1, 2.
2. [To support]—*Syn.* brace, fortify, strengthen; see **support** 1.

girder, *n.* —*Syn.* truss, rafter, mainstay; see **beam** 1.

girdle, *n.* —*Syn.* belt, cinch(er), sash; see **corset.**

girdle, *v.* —*Syn.* encircle, enclose, clasp; see **surround** 1, 2.

girl, *n.* **1.** [A young female]—*Syn.* schoolgirl, miss, lass, coed, lassie, damsel, damosel, maid, maiden, tomboy, nymph, colleen, mademoiselle, minx, señorita, senhorita, young thing, flibbertigibbet; *all* (D): filly, subdeb, junior miss, nymph, nymphet, bobby soxer, teen-ager, chick, bird, pigeon, kitten, minx, broad, deb, skirt, dame, babe.
2. [A female domestic]—*Syn.* maid, help, waitress; see **servant.**
3. [(D) A female beloved]—*Syn.* sweetheart, inamorata, fiancée; see **lover** 1.

girlish, *mod.* —*Syn.* juvenile, naive, mincing, boy-crazy, unsophisticated, fresh, affected, unaffected, hoydenish, teenage; see also **young** 1.—*Ant.* mature*, matronly, sophisticated.

girth, *n.* **1.** [Measurement around the waist]—*Syn.* circumference, distance around, bigness, compass, waist measure, expansion, size.
2. [A band]—*Syn.* strap, cinch, surcingle; see **band** 1.

gist, *n.* —*Syn.* substance, essence, significance; see **basis** 1, **summary.**

give, *v.* **1.** [To transfer]—*Syn.* grant, bestow, confer, impart, present, endow, bequeath, award, dispense, subsidize, contribute, parcel *or* hand *or* dole *or* give out, pass *or* hand *or* throw in, hand down *or* over, deliver, let have, tip, remit, pass down, convey, deed, sell, will, give *or* make over (to), put into the hands of, contribute to, lavish upon, consign, negotiate, relinquish, cede, lease, accord, invest, dispose of, part with, fob off, lay upon, turn over, heap upon, transmit, settle, take delivery on; *all* (D): come through *or* across with, shell out, dish *or* deal out, fork over, untie the purse strings, kick in, palm off.—*Ant.* maintain*, withhold, take.
2. [To provide]—*Syn.* furnish, proffer, supply; see **provide** 1.
3. [To produce]—*Syn.* yield, furnish, return; see **produce** 1.
4. [To yield under pressure]—*Syn.* give way, retreat, collapse, fall, contract, offer no resistance, shrink, recede, open, relax, sag, bend, flex, crumble, yield, bow to.—*Ant.* resist*, remain rigid, stand firm.
5. [To allot]—*Syn.* assign, dispense, deal; see **distribute** 1.
6. [To inflict]—*Syn.* strike, deliver, mete out; see **inflict** 1.
7. [To pass on]—*Syn.* communicate, transmit, transfer; see **carry** 2.
8. [To give a speech]—*Syn.* deliver, present, read; see **address** 2.
9. [To give a play]—*Syn.* put on, present, produce; see **perform** 2.
10. [To administer]—*Syn.* minister, provide with, dispense; see **administer** 2.
what gives (D)—*Syn.* what happened? what is going on? tell me the facts; see **what** 2.

give attention to, *v.* —*Syn.* pay attention, hearken, be attentive; see **listen** 1.

give away, *v.* **1.** [(D) To reveal]—*Syn.* betray, divulge, disclose; see **reveal** 1.
2. [To give]—*Syn.* bestow, award, present; see **give** 1.

give back, *v.* —*Syn.* return, refund, reimburse; see **repay** 1.

give chase, *v.* —*Syn.* go after, follow, chase; see **pursue** 1.

give ear, *v.* —*Syn.* attend, heed, hearken; see **listen** 1.

give forth, *v.* —*Syn.* expel, discharge, send forth; see **emit** 1.

give in, *v.* —*Syn.* capitulate, submit, surrender; see **admit** 2, 3, **yield** 1.

given, *mod.* —*Syn.* granted, supplied, donated, conferred, bestowed, presented, imparted, awarded, bequeathed, dispensed, doled *or* handed out, contributed, subscribed, remitted, transferred, conveyed, consigned, disposed of, communicated, furnished, allowed, expended, lavished, released, yielded, offered, ceded.—*Ant.* kept*, taken, withheld.

give notice, *v.* —*Syn.* inform, advise, warn; see **notify** 1.

given to, *v.* —*Syn.* inured, habituated, obsessed (with); see **addicted to.**

give off, *v.* —*Syn.* smell of, effuse, emanate; see **emit** 1, **smell** 1.

give (one) a black eye (D), *v.* —*Syn.* discredit, blame, vilify; see **damage** 1, **slander.**

give out, *v.* **1.** [To emit]—*Syn.* emanate, expend, exude; see **emit** 1, **smell** 1.
2. [To deliver]—*Syn.* deal, dole, hand *or* pass out; see **distribute** 1.
3. [To publish]—*Syn.* proclaim, make known, announce; see **advertise** 1, **declare** 1.
4. [To weaken]—*Syn.* faint, fail, break down; see **tire** 1, **weaken** 1.

give over, *v.* **1.** [To hand over]—*Syn.* give up, deliver, relinquish; see **give** 1.
2. [To cease]—*Syn.* desist, finish, end; see **stop** 2.

give place, *v.* —*Syn.* retire, withdraw, be succeeded; see **retreat** 1, 2.

giver, *n.* —*Syn.* provider, supplier, donator; see **donor.**

give rise to, *v.* —*Syn.* originate, institute, cause; see **begin** 1.

give up, *v.* **1.** [To surrender]—*Syn.* stop fighting, cede, hand over; see **yield** 1.
2. [To stop]—*Syn.* quit, halt, cease; see **end** 1.
3. [To despair]—*Syn.* lose heart *or* courage, give in, abandon hope; see **despair of.**

give way, *v.* **1.** [To collapse]—*Syn.* sag, fall, crumble; see **give** 4.
2. [To draw back]—*Syn.* recede, withdraw, retire; see **retreat** 1.
3. [To concede]—*Syn.* yield, accede, grant; see **admit** 2, 3.

giving, *n.* —*Syn.* bestowing, donating, granting, conferring, imparting, supplying, awarding, presenting, bequeathing, dispensing, doling *or* passing *or* handing out, contributing, distributing, remitting, transferring, conveying, consigning, communicating, yielding, giving up, furnishing, allowing, expending, lavishing, offering, ceding, permitting, tipping, parting with, endowing, producing, disgorging, pouring forth, discharging, emitting.—*Ant.* getting*, taking, appropriating.

giving up, *n.* —*Syn.* quitting, losing, giving in; see **stopping.**

glacial, *mod.* **1.** [Cold]—*Syn.* icy, frozen, polar; see **cold** 1.
2. [Indifferent]—*Syn.* cool, unfriendly, antagonistic; see **cold** 2, **indifferent** 1.

glacier, *n.* —*Syn.* ice floe, floe, iceberg, berg, glacial mass, snow slide, icecap, ice field, ice stream, ice torrent, glacial table, *névé, sérac, mer de glace* (*all* French).

glad, *mod.* **1.** [Happy]—*Syn.* exhilarated, animated, jovial; see **happy** 1.
2. [Encouraging]—*Syn.* cheering, exhilarating, pleasing; see **hopeful** 2.

gladden, *v.* —*Syn.* delight, please, hearten, encourage, elate, amuse, transport, titillate, cheer, make happy, warm; see also **entertain** 1.

glade, *n.* —*Syn.* dell, dale, meadow; see **valley.**

gladiator, *n.* —*Syn.* prize fighter, combatant, swordsman; see **fighter** 1.

gladly, *mod.* —*Syn.* joyously, happily, gaily, blithely, cheerfully, ecstatically, blissfully, contentedly, readily, gratefully, enthusiastically, merrily, heartily, jocundly, willingly, zealously, pleasantly, pleasurably, pleasingly, zestfully, complacently, delightfully, gleefully, cheerily, felicitously, enchantedly, paradisiacally, beatifically, warmly, rapturously, passionately, transportedly, ardently, delightedly, gloatingly, lovingly, cordially, genially, sweetly, joyfully, acquiescently, seraphically, with pleasure, with relish, with (deep) satisfaction, with active support, with full agreement, with (full) approval, with delight.—*Ant.* unwillingly*, sadly, gloomily.

gladness, *n.* —*Syn.* cheer, mirth, delight; see **happiness** 1.

glamorous, *mod.* —*Syn.* fascinating, alluring, captivating, bewitching, exciting, charismatic, magnetic, dazzling; see also **charming.**

glamour, *n.* —*Syn.* allurement, charm, attraction; see **beauty** 1.

glance, *n.* —*Syn.* glimpse, sight, fleeting impression; see **look** 3.

glance, *v.* **1.** [To look]—*Syn.* see, peep, glimpse; see **look** 2.
2. [To ricochet]—*Syn.* skip, slide, carom, rebound, careen, brush, skim, touch, graze, dart, bounce; see also **hit** 3.

gland, *n.* —*Syn.* (endocrine) organ, glandule, pancreas, kidney, liver, testicle, spleen, epithelial cells. Kinds of glands include the following—simple, compound, tubular, saccular, racemose, ductless, adrenal, carotid, endocrine, lymphatic, parathyroid, parotid, pineal, pituitary, thyroid, thymus, sebaceous, sudoriparous, tear, sweat, lacrimal, serous, muciparous, salivary, piloric, mammary, seminal, prostrate, urethral, vaginal.

glandular, *mod.* —*Syn.* glandulous, epithelial, secretory, glanduliferous.

glare, *v.* **1.** [To shine fiercely]—*Syn.* beam, glow, radiate; see **shine** 1, 2.
2. [To stare fiercely]—*Syn.* fix with a look, pierce, gaze, glower, scowl, lower, goggle, menace, stare icily, fix, wither, look daggers (D); see also **frown, look** 2.

glaring, *mod.* **1.** [Shining]—*Syn.* blinding, dazzling, blazing; see **bright** 1.
2. [Staring]—*Syn.* gazing, piercing, fixing, searching, intent, penetrating, sharp, burning, withering.
3. [Obvious]—*Syn.* evident, conspicuous, obtrusive; see **obvious** 2.

glass, *n.* **1.** Types of glass include the following—silica, potash-lime, safety, sodium, crown, flint, plate, cut, pressed, stained, crystal.
2. Objects referred to as *glass* include the following—tumbler, goblet, breaker, chalice, cup, jigger, shot glass, looking glass, mirror, barometer, thermometer, altiscope, hourglass, windowpane, watch crystal, monocle, telescope, microscope, spyglass, binocular, burning glass, eyeglass, lens, optical glass.
3. [The contents of a tumbler]—*Syn.* glassful, half-pint, libation; see **drink** 1.

glasses, *n.* —*Syn.* spectacles, eyeglasses, bifocals, trifocals, goggles, field glasses, opera glasses, contact lenses, sunglasses, steel-rimmed glasses, rimless glasses, silver-rimmed glasses, horn-rimmed glasses, tortoise-shell glasses, psychedelic glasses, nose glasses, pince nez; *all* (D): cheaters, windows, specs, shades, blinkers.

glassware, *n.* —*Syn.* vitreous ware, crystal, glasswork, glass.
Types of common glassware include the following—tumbler, jug, decanter, bottle, fruit jar, tableware, glass ovenware, vase, lampshade, lamp base, flower bowl, goblet, sherbet glass, wine glass, liqueur glass, champagne glass, tulip glass, cocktail glass, highball glass, old-fashioned glass, brandy snifter, pony, shot glass, Pilsener glass, beer shell, stein, cake tray, parfait glass, beer mug, aleyard.

glassy, *mod.* —*Syn.* vitreous, lustrous, polished; see **smooth** 1.

glaze, *n.* —*Syn.* enamel, polish, varnish; see **finish** 2.

glaze, *v.* —*Syn.* glass, incrust, coat, make vitreous, overlay, cover, enamel, glass (over), make lustrous, polish, burnish, vitrify; see also **shine** 3.

glazed, *mod.*—*Syn.* glassy, translucent, transparent, enameled, varnished, vitreous, filmed over, shiny, incrusted, burnished, lustrous, smooth; see also **finished** 2.—*Ant.* fresh, rough*, unglazed.

gleam, *n.*—*Syn.* glow, beam, shimmer; see **light** 1, 3.

gleam, *v.*—*Syn.* shimmer, glimmer, sparkle; see **shine** 1, 2.

glean, *v.*—*Syn.* garner, gather, pick up; see **accumulate** 1.

glee, *n.*—*Syn.* joviality, merriment, mirth; see **happiness** 1.

gleeful, *mod.*—*Syn.* joyous, jolly, merry; see **happy** 1.

glen, *n.*—*Syn.* dale, dell, glade; see **valley.**

glib, *mod.*—*Syn.* articulate, loquacious, vocal; see **fluent** 2.

glide, *n.* **1.** [A gradual downward motion]—*Syn.* sinking, descent, loss of altitude, downward spiral, landing operation, volplaning, slide—*Ant.* plunge, debacle, crash.

2. [A smooth motion]—*Syn.* floating, continuous motion, smooth movement, flowing, slide, drift, swoop, wafting, skimming, flight, soaring, slither, zoom (D).—*Ant.* shuffle, trot, jerk.

glide, *v.* **1.** [To move downward gradually]—*Syn.* descend, slip, decline, slide, stream, spiral, lose altitude.

2. [To move gently]—*Syn.* float, slide, drift, waft, skim, skip, trip, fly, coast, flit, wing, soar, coast *or* slide *or* skim, etc., along.—*Ant.* hit, rattle, lurch.

glider, *n.*—*Syn.* lighter-than-air craft, sailplane, engineless airplane; see **plane** 3.

glimmer, *n.*—*Syn.* gleam, flash, flicker; see **light** 1.

glimmer, *v.*—*Syn.* gleam, fade, shimmer; see **shine** 1.

glimpse, *n.*—*Syn.* flash, impression, sight; see **look** 3.

glint, *n.*—*Syn.* glimmer, gleam, shimmer; see **light** 1.

glisten, *v.*—*Syn.* sparkle, shimmer, flicker; see **shine** 1.

glitter, *n.*—*Syn.* sparkle, shimmer, gleam; see **light** 1.

glitter, *v.*—*Syn.* glare, shimmer, sparkle; see **shine** 1.

gloaming, *n.*—*Syn.* dusk, evening, twilight; see **night** 1.

gloat, *v.*—*Syn.* rejoice, revel, exult; see **celebrate** 3.

globe, *n.* **1.** [A sphere]—*Syn.* balloon, orb, spheroid; see **ball** 1.

2. [The earth; *usually with* the]—*Syn.* terrestrial globe, celestial globe, Copernican sphere; see **earth** 1.

globe-trotter, *n.*—*Syn.* voyager, wanderer, tourist; see **traveler.**

gloom, *n.* **1.** [Heavy shade]—*Syn.* shadow, murk, dark; see **darkness** 1.

2. [Heavy spirits]—*Syn.* woe, sadness, depression, dejection, melancholy, melancholia, dullness, despondency, misery, sorrow, morbidity, pensiveness, hypochondriasis, catatonia, dolor, malaise, vexation, pessimism, foreboding, low spirits, cheerlessness, heaviness of mind, weariness, apprehension, misgiving, distress, affliction, despair, oppression, anguish, grief, horror, mourning, bitterness, mortification, chagrin, discouragement, disconsolateness; *all* (D): the blues, the dumps, (the) doldrums, blue funk.—*Ant.* happiness*, optimism, gaiety.

gloomy, *mod.* **1.** [Dark]—*Syn.* dim, clouded, unlit; see **dark** 1.

2. [Melancholy]—*Syn.* downhearted, depressed, morose; see **sad** 1.

3. [Encouraging melancholy]—*Syn.* dreary, depressing, discouraging; see **dismal** 1.

glorify, *v.* **1.** [To praise]—*Syn.* laud, commend, acclaim; see **praise** 1.

2. [To worship]—*Syn.* exalt, honor, venerate; see **worship** 2.

glorious, *mod.* **1.** [Characterized by glory]—*Syn.* famous, renowned, far-famed, famed, well-known, distinguished, splendid, excellent, noble, venerable, exalted, grand, illustrious, notable, celebrated, esteemed, honored, eminent, preeminent, remarkable, brilliant, great, heroic, memorable, immortal, deathless, never-to-be-forgotten, immortalized, time-honored, admirable, praiseworthy, remarkable; *all* (D): for all time, from time out of mind, on every tongue; see also **famous.**—*Ant.* unimportant*, inglorious, ignominious.

2. [Characterized by splendor]—*Syn.* splendid, marvelous, grand; see **beautiful** 1.

3. [(D) Delightful]—*Syn.* gratifying, festive, agreeable; see **pleasant** 1, 2.

glory, *n.* **1.** [Renown]—*Syn.* honor, distinction, reputation; see **fame** 1.

2. [Splendor]—*Syn.* gorgeousness, brightness, grandeur, radiance, effulgence, majesty, brilliance, sumptuousness, richness, preciousness, beauty, fineness.—*Ant.* tawdriness, meanness, baseness.

gone to glory (D)—*Syn.* late, passed on, deceased; see **dead** 1.

in one's glory (D)—*Syn.* at one's best, successful, in one's prime; see **happy** 1.

3. [Heaven]—*Syn.* beatitude, bliss, eternal life; see **heaven** 2.

gloss, *n.*—*Syn.* gleam, shimmer, polish; see **finish** 2.

glossary, *n.*—*Syn.* gloss(es), lexicon, compendium; see **dictionary.**

glossy, *mod.*—*Syn.* shining, reflecting, lustrous; see **bright** 1.

glove, *n.*—*Syn.* gauntlet, mitten, *Handschuh* (German), gage, *gant* (French), mitt, finger mitten.

glow, *n.*—*Syn.* warmth, effulgence, ray; see **heat** 1, **light** 1.

glow, *v.*—*Syn.* gleam, redden, radiate; see **burn** 1, **shine** 1.

glower, *v.*—*Syn.* glare, scowl, sulk; see **frown.**

glowing, *mod.* **1.** [Radiating heat and light]—*Syn.* gleaming, lustrous, phosphorescent; see **bright** 1.

2. [Radiating enthusiasm]—*Syn.* ardent, zealous, fervent; see **enthusiastic** 1, 2.

gloze, *v.*—*Syn.* gloss over, cover up, extenuate; see **palliate.**

glue, *n.*—*Syn.* paste, mucilage, cement; see **adhesive.**

glue, *v.*—*Syn.* paste, gum, cement, fix, stick, adhere; see also **repair** 1.

gluey, *mod.*—*Syn.* glutinous, viscid, sticky; see **adhesive.**

glum, *mod.* —*Syn.* moody, morose, sullen; see **sad** 1.
glut, *n.* —*Syn.* oversupply, overabundance, excess; see **excess** 1.
glut, *v.* **1.** [To oversupply]—*Syn.* flood, overwhelm, overstock, fill, load, congest, inundate, overload, surcharge, burden, deluge, saturate, clog, choke, cloy, gorge.—*Ant.* save*, scant, undersupply.
2. [To eat to satiety]—*Syn.* surfeit, stuff, cram, gorge, overeat, hog, eat one's fill, gobble up, eat out of house and home, fill, cloy, feast, raven, wolf, bolt, devour, eat like a horse (D).—*Ant.* starve*, diet*.
glutton, *n.* —*Syn.* gourmand, greedy person, epicure, *Fresser* (German), sensualist, hog, pig, garbage hound (D).
gluttonous, *mod.* —*Syn.* ravenous, voracious, omnivorous; see **greedy** 2.
gluttony, *n.* —*Syn.* voracity, edacity, intemperance; see **greed.**
gnarled, *mod.* —*Syn.* knotted, twisted, contorted; see **bent.**
gnash, *v.* —*Syn.* grind, snap, rotate the teeth; see **bite** 1, **chew.**
gnaw, *v.* —*Syn.* crunch, champ, masticate; see **bite** 1, **chew.**
gnome, *n.* —*Syn.* dwarf, troll, elf; see **fairy** 1.
go, *v.* **1.** [To depart]—*Syn.* quit, withdraw, run away; see **leave** 1.
2. [To proceed]—*Syn.* travel, progress, proceed; see **advance** 1, **move** 1.
3. [To function]—*Syn.* work, run, perform; see **operate** 2.
4. [To fit or suit]—*Syn.* conform, accord, harmonize; see **agree, agree with** 2, **fit** 1.
5. [To extend]—*Syn.* stretch, cover, spread; see **reach** 1.
6. [To belong]—*Syn.* mesh, fit in, be designed *or* adapted for; see **belong** 1, 2, **fit** 1.
7. [To elapse]—*Syn.* be spent, waste away, transpire; see **pass** 2.
8. [To fail]—*Syn.* decline, weaken, worsen; see **fail** 1.
9. [To continue]—*Syn.* maintain, carry on, persist; see **continue** 1.
10. [To appeal]—*Syn.* apply for a retrial, contest, reopen; see **appeal** 2.
11. [To die]—*Syn.* pass on, depart, succumb; see **die** 1.
12. [To end]—*Syn.* terminate, finish, conclude; see **stop** 2.
13. [To endure]—*Syn.* persevere, go on, persist; see **endure** 1.
14. [(D) To bet]—*Syn.* wager, gamble, hazard; see **bet.**
15. [(D) To tolerate]—*Syn.* let, permit, consent to; see **allow** 1.
as people (*or* **things**) **go**—*Syn.* in comparison with other people *or* things, by all standards, according to certain criteria; see **compared.**
from the word "go" (D)—*Syn.* from the outset, at the start, beginning with; see **at first.**
have a go at (D)—*Syn.* attempt, endeavor, try one's hand at; see **try** 1.
let go—*Syn.* let free, give up, abandon; see **release.**
let oneself go—*Syn.* be unrestrained *or* uninhibited, free oneself, have fun; see **relax.**
no go (D)—*Syn.* impossible, worthless, without value; see **useless** 1.
on the go (D)—*Syn.* in constant motion, moving, busy; see **active** 2.
what goes (D)—*Syn.* what is happening? give me the facts, what is going on?; see **what** 2.
go about, *v.* **1.** [To be occupied]—*Syn.* engage in, busy oneself with, be employed; see **work** 1, 2.
2. [To circulate]—*Syn.* move about, pass around, wander; see **circulate** 1, **travel** 2.
goad, *v.* —*Syn.* prod, urge, prick, prompt, spur, drive, rowel, whip, press, push, impel, force, stimulate, provoke, tease, excite, needle, instigate, inspirit, arouse, animate, encourage, bully, coerce, propel, thrust.—*Ant.* restrain*, curb, rein in.
go after, *v.* **1.** [To chase]—*Syn.* seek, run *or* go after, hunt; see **pursue** 1.
2. [To follow in time]—*Syn.* come after, supersede, supplant; see **succeed** 2.
go against, *v.* —*Syn.* be opposed to, contradict, counteract; see **oppose** 1, 2.
go ahead, *v.* —*Syn.* move on, proceed, progress; see **advance** 1.
goal, *n.* —*Syn.* object, aim, intent; see **end** 2, **purpose** 1.
go all out (D), *v.* —*Syn.* attempt, make a (great) effort, strive; see **try** 1.
go all the way, *v.* **1.** [To yield]—*Syn.* agree completely, give in, capitulate; see **agree, yield** 1.
2. [(D) To engage in sexual intercourse]—*Syn.* sleep with, fornicate, make love; see **copulate.**
go along, *v.* —*Syn.* carry on, keep up, go; see **continue** 1.
go along with, *v.* **1.** [To agree with]—*Syn.* concur, conspire, collaborate; see **agree to.**
2. [To cooperate]—*Syn.* work together, act jointly, share in; see **cooperate** 1.
3. [To accompany]—*Syn.* escort, squire, go with; see **accompany** 1.
goat, *n.* —*Syn.* *Capra* (Latin), nanny goat, buck, kid, he-goat, she-goat, billy (D).
Varieties of goatlike animals include the following—ibex, markhor, bezoar, dzeren, Rocky Mountain goat, Angora goat, Cashmere goat, dwarf goat, Guinean goat, Egyptian goat, Nubian goat, Maltese goat, Nepal goat, Syrian goat, Alpine goat, Toggenburg goat, Saanen goat; see also **animal** 2.
get one's goat (D)—*Syn.* annoy, irritate, bother; see **anger** 1.
go at, *v.* —*Syn.* blame, impugn, criticize; see **censure.**
go back on, *v.* **1.** [(D) To fail to keep]—*Syn.* renege, leave in the lurch, run out on; see **abandon** 2.
2. [To betray]—*Syn.* desert, be unfaithful, forsake; see **betray** 1.
go bad, *v.* —*Syn.* degenerate, deteriorate, rot; see **decay.**
go badly, *v.* —*Syn.* miscarry, fall short, dissatisfy; see **disappoint, fail** 1.
gobble, *v.* **1.** [To make a sound like a turkey]—*Syn.* gaggle, gurgle, cackle; see **sound** 1.
2. [(D) To eat rapidly]—*Syn.* bolt, cram, stuff; see **eat** 1.
go begging, *v.* —*Syn.* be unwanted *or* unpopular *or* in little demand, be rejected, be unneeded, find no takers (D).

go behind, *v.* —*Syn.* look *or* pry into, probe, investigate; see **examine** 1.

go better with, *v.* —*Syn.* progress, enhance, meliorate; see **improve** 2, **intensify.**

go-between, *n.* —*Syn.* middleman, referee, mediator; see **agent** 1, **messenger.**

go between, *v.* —*Syn.* intervene, mediate, arbitrate; see **meddle** 1, **reconcile** 2.

go beyond, *v.* —*Syn.* overdo, distance, surpass; see **exceed.**

goblet, *n.* —*Syn.* tumbler, beaker, grail; see **cup.**

goblin, *n.* —*Syn.* troll, hobgoblin, sprite; see **fairy** 1.

go by, *v.* **1.** [To pass]—*Syn.* move onward, make one's way, proceed; see **pass** 1.

2. [To conform to]—*Syn.* fall in with, comply, adjust to; see **agree, cooperate** 1.

go by the board, *v.* —*Syn.* be lost *or* ignored, miss, fall out; see **fail** 1.

go crazy, *v.* —*Syn.* become insane, lose one's wits, get angry; see **rage** 3.

god, *n.* **1.** [A supernatural being]—*Syn.* (male) deity, divinity, divine *or* superhuman being, spirit, numen, power, tutelary, Olympian, Valhallan, demigod, oversoul, prime mover, godhead, omnipotence, world spirit *or* soul, universal life force, infinite spirit, totem, idol, demon *or* daimon *or* daemon.

Greek gods and their Roman counterparts include —Zeus *or* Jupiter *or* Jove, Phoebus (Apollo) *or* Apollo, Ares *or* Mars, Hermes *or* Mercury, Poseidon *or* Neptune, Hephaestus *or* Vulcan, Dionysus *or* Bacchus, Hades *or* Pluto, Kronos *or* Saturn, Eros *or* Cupid.

Norse gods, known as the Aesir and Vanir, include —Balder, Frey *or* Freyr, Heimdall, Höder, Hoenir, Loki, Odin *or* Woden *or* Wotan, Thor *or* Donar, Tyr *or* Tiu, Ull *or* Ullr, Vali, Vidar, Ymir.

Hindu and Brahmanic gods include—Agni, Dyaus, Ganesa, Ganpati, Hanuman, Indra, Marut, Savitar, Soma, Surya, Varuna, Vayu, Yama.

For specific female deities; see also **goddess.**

The avatars of Vishnu include—Buddha, Kalki, Karma, Krishna, Matsya, Narsinh, Parshuram, Rama, Vaman, Varah, Jagannath.

Egyptian gods include—Anubis, Bast, Horus; Isis, Khem, Min, Neph, Nephthys, Nut, Osiris, Ptah, Ra *or* Amen-Ra, Set, Thoth.

Other gods include—Baal, Moloch, Shamash (*all* Semitic); Dagon (Philistine); Astarte *or* Ashtoreth (Phoenician); Anu, Bel, Ea (*all* Babylonian); Quetzalcoatl (Mexican).

2. [Capitalized, the Judeo-Christian deity]—*Syn.* Lord, Jehovah, Yahweh, YHWH, Jhvh, the Almighty, the King of Kings, the Omnipotent, the Godhead, the Creator, Demiurge, the Maker, the Supreme Being, the Ruler of Heaven, the All-holy, the Everlasting, the Divine Author, Our Father in Heaven, Almighty God, God Almighty, the Preserver, the Deity, the Divinity, the Omniscient, Providence, the All-knowing, the Infinite Spirit, the Absolute *or* Infinite *or* Eternal (Being), I Am, the All-father, the Author of All Things, the First Cause, the Lord of Lords, the Supreme Soul, the All-wise, the All-merciful, the All-powerful; the Trinity, the Holy Trinity, the Triune (God), Threefold Unity, Three in One and One in Three; Father, Son, and Holy Ghost; God the Son, Jesus Christ, Christ, Jesus, Jesus of Nazareth, the Nazarene, the Galilean, the Man of Sorrows, the Messiah, the Savior, the Redeemer, the Advocate, the Son of God, the Son of Man, the Son of Mary, the Only Begotten, the Lamb (of God), Immanuel *or* Emmanuel, the King of Glory, the King of the Jews, the Prince of Peace, the Good Shepherd, the Way, the Door, the Truth, the Life, the Light, the Christ Child, the Holy Spirit, the Spirit of God, Paraclete.

3. [Capitalized, the supreme deity of other religions]—*Syn.* Allah (Mohammedanism); Khuda (Hinduism); Brahma *or* the Supreme Soul, Atman *or* the Universal Ego, Vishnu *or* the Preserver, Shiva *or* the Destroyer (all Brahmanism); (the Lord) Buddha *or* the Blessed One (Buddhism); Mazda *or* Ormazd (Zoroastrianism).

goddess, *n.* —*Syn.* female deity, she-god; see also **god.**

Greek goddesses and their Roman counterparts include the following—Hera *or* Juno, Ceres *or* Demeter, Proserpina *or* Persephone, Artemis *or* Diana, Minerva *or* Athena, Aphrodite *or* Venus, Vesta *or* Hestia, Cybele *or* Rhea, Ge *or* Gaea, Nike.

Norse goddesses include—Freya *or* Freyja, Frigg *or* Frigga, Hel, Nanna, Ithunn *or* Idun, Sif, Sigyn.

Hindu and Brahmanic goddesses include—Chandi, Devi, Durga, Gauri, Kali, Lakshmi, Parvati, Sarasvati, Uma, Ushas.

godfather, *n.* —*Syn.* sponsor, elder, patron, gossip.

godhead, *n.* —*Syn.* divinity, deity, holiness; see **god** 1.

godless, *mod.* —*Syn.* agnostic, heathen, atheistic; see **impious** 1.

godlike, *mod.* —*Syn.* excellent, magnanimous, wise; see **holy** 1, 3.

godliness, *n.* —*Syn.* holiness, piety, sanctity; see **virtue** 1.

godly, *mod.* —*Syn.* righteous, devout, pious; see **holy** 1, 3.

godmother, *n.* —*Syn.* female sponsor, patroness, adoptive parent, gossip.

go down, *v.* **1.** [To sink]—*Syn.* descend, decline, submerge; see **sink** 1.

2. [To lose]—*Syn.* be defeated, submit, succumb; see **fail** 1, **lose** 3.

3. [To decrease]—*Syn.* reduce, make less, lessen; see **decrease** 1.

godsend, *n.* —*Syn.* benefit, gift, boon; see **blessing** 2.

go Dutch (D), *v.* —*Syn.* divide the bill, pay half, share expenses; see **share** 4.

go easy, *v.* —*Syn.* skimp, be sparing *or* careful, reprieve; see **pity** 2, **save** 3.

go far, *v.* **1.** [To contribute to]—*Syn.* assist, support, back up; see **contribute** 1, **help** 1.

2. [To extend]—*Syn.* reach, buy, reinforce; see **increase** 1.

3. [To succeed]—*Syn.* rise, achieve, go up in the world (D); see **succeed** 1.

go for, *v.* **1.** [To reach for]—*Syn.* stretch out for, outreach, clutch at; see **reach** 2.

2. [(D) To attack]—*Syn.* rush upon, run at, spring; see **attack** 1, 2, 4.

3. [(D) To like]—*Syn.* be fond of, fancy, care for; see **like** 2.

go for broke (D), *v.* —*Syn.* overextend, use all of one's resources, plunge; see **chance** 2, **gamble** 1.

go halves *or* **shares** (D), *v.* —*Syn.* divide *or* share expenses, pay one's way, go Dutch (D); see **share** 4.

go hard with, *v.* —*Syn.* be difficult, hinder, plague; see **oppress.**

go in for (D), *v.* **1.** [To advocate]—*Syn.* endorse, favor, back; see **promote** 1.

2. [To like]—*Syn.* care for, be fond of, fancy; see **like** 1.

going (D), *mod.* —*Syn.* flourishing, thriving, profitable; see **successful.**

be going to—*Syn.* shall, be intending to, be prepared to; see **will** 1, 3.

get one going (D)—*Syn.* annoy, excite, enrage; see **anger** 1.

have (something) going for one (D)—*Syn.* have an advantage, be successful *or* able *or* talented, have opportunity; see **succeed** 1.

go(ing) begging (D), *mod.* —*Syn.* unsought, unwanted, redundant, disdained, neglected, overlooked, refused, rejected, passed by *or* up; *both* (D): turned down, stood up; see also **superfluous, unnecessary.**

goings on (D), *n.* —*Syn.* events, deportment, conduct; see **behavior** 1.

going strong (D), *mod.* —*Syn.* flourishing, surviving, thriving; see **successful.**

going without saying, *mod.* —*Syn.* taken for granted, self-evident, apparent; see **obvious** 2.

go into, *v.* **1.** [To investigate]—*Syn.* analyze, probe, look into; see **examine** 1.

2. [To take up an occupation, hobby, etc.]—*Syn.* develop, undertake, enter into, participate in, take upon oneself, engage in, take up *or* on, get involved with, be absorbed in.

go in with, *v.* —*Syn.* form a partnership, join forces, consolidate; see **unite** 1.

gold, *mod.* **1.** [Made of gold, or plated with gold] —*Syn.* golden, aurous, gilded, beaten gold, carat metal, 24-carat, 18-carat.

2. [Of the color of gold]—*Syn.* yellow, aureate, gold-colored, red-gold, greenish gold, ochroid, flaxen, wheat-colored, deep tan, tawny.

gold, *n.* **1.** [A color]—*Syn.* dark *or* deep yellow, ochroid, tawny; see **color** 1, **gold,***mod.* 2.

2. [A precious metal]—*Syn.* aurum (AU), green gold, white gold, red gold, gold foil, gold leaf, gold plate, filled gold, commercial gold, gold alloy, cloth of gold *or* gold cloth, gold thread, gold wire, gold lace, gold tooling, rolled gold, mosaic gold, Mannheim gold, German gold, dead gold, Etruscan *or* Roman *or* colored gold; see also **metal.**

as good as gold (D)—*Syn.* very good, well behaved, obedient; see **excellent.**

goldsmith, *n.* —*Syn.* artisan, craftsman, lapidary; see **jeweler.**

golf, *n.* —*Syn.* match play, medal play, nine holes, eighteen holes, game; *all* (D): pasture pool, heather marbles, divot digging.

gone, *mod.* **1.** [Having left]—*Syn.* gone out *or* away, moved, removed, traveling, traveled, journeyed, transferred, displaced, shifted, withdrawn, retired, left, taken leave, departed, deserted, abandoned, quit, disappeared, not here, not a sign of, no more, flown, run off, decamped; *all* (D): AWOL, taken French leave, upped stakes, flown the coop, split, taken a powder.—*Ant.* come*, returned, remained.

2. [Being no longer in existence]—*Syn.* dead, vanished, passed, dissipated, disappeared, nonextant, dissolved, burned up, disintegrated, decayed, rotted away, turned to dust.

far gone (D)—*Syn.* **1.** advanced, deeply involved, absorbed; see **interested** 2. **2.** crazy, mad, eccentric; see **insane** 1.

gong, *n.* —*Syn.* tocsin, cymbal, bell, tambourine, alarum, drum, kettledrum, signal, carillon, tympanum, sounding board, fire alarm, dinner gong, doorbell, Chinese gong, tamtam.

gonorrhea, *n.* —*Syn.* venereal disease, social *or* sexual disease, clap (D); see **disease** 3.

good, *mod.* **1.** [Moral]—*Syn.* upright, honorable, charitable; see **righteous** 1.

2. [Kind]—*Syn.* considerate, tolerant, generous; see **kind** 1.

3. [Proper]—*Syn.* suitable, becoming, desirable; see **fit** 1, 2..

4. [Reliable]—*Syn.* trustworthy, dependable, loyal; see **reliable** 2.

5. [Sound]—*Syn.* safe, solid, stable; see **reliable** 1, 2.

6. [Pleasant]—*Syn.* agreeable, satisfying, enjoyable; see **pleasant** 1, 2.

7. [Honorable]—*Syn.* worthy, reputable, respectable; see **noble** 1, 2.

8. [Helpful]—*Syn.* beneficial, salutary, useful; see **helpful** 1.

9. [Qualified]—*Syn.* suited, competent, suitable; see **able** 1, 2.

10. [Skillful]—*Syn.* skilled, expert, qualified; see **able** 2.

11. [Of approved quality]—*Syn.* choice, select, high-grade; see **excellent.**

12. [Healthy]—*Syn.* sound, normal, vigorous; see **healthy** 1.

13. [Obedient]—*Syn.* dutiful, tractable, well-behaved; see **obedient** 1.

14. [Genuine]—*Syn.* valid, real, sound; see **genuine** 1.

15. [Thorough]—*Syn.* fussy, meticulous, painstaking; see **careful.**

16. [Orthodox]—*Syn.* conforming, regular, strict; see **conventional** 2, 3.

17. [Fresh]—*Syn.* unspoiled, uncontaminated, undecayed; see **fresh** 5.

18. [Considerable]—*Syn.* great, big, immeasurable; see **large** 1, **much** 2.

19. [Favorable]—*Syn.* approving, commendatory, commending; see **favorable** 3.

20. [Adequate]—*Syn.* sufficient, ample, satisfying; see **enough** 1.

21. [Sound, as an asset]—*Syn.* valid, cashable, backed, not void *or* counterfeit, worth it, safe, guaranteed, warranted, cleared, not debased, certified, not outlawed.

as good as—*Syn.* in effect, virtually, nearly; see **almost.**

come to no good—*Syn.* come to a bad end, get into trouble, have difficulty; see **fail** 1.

for good (and all) (D)—*Syn.* forever, always, permanently; see **finally** 1.

make good—*Syn.* fulfill, satisfy the requirement(s), accomplish; see **satisfy** 3.
no good—*Syn.* useless, valueless, unserviceable; see **worthless** 1.
to the good—*Syn.* favorable, advantageous, beneficial; see **profitable.**

good, *n.* **1.** [A benefit]—*Syn.* welfare, gain, asset; see **advantage** 3.
2. [That which is morally approved]—*Syn.* ethic, merit, ideal; see **virtue** 1.
3. [Good people]—*Syn.* the virtuous, the pious, children of light, elect, men of good will, philanthropists, God-fearing people, law-abiding citizens, enemies of darkness, just men.—*Ant.* rascal*, the wicked, the sinful.

good breeding, *n.*—*Syn.* civility, refinement, propriety; see **culture** 3.

good-by, *interj.*—*Syn.* farewell, Godspeed, fare you well, God bless you and keep you, God be with you, adieu, *adios* (Spanish), *au revoir* (French), *auf Wiedersehen* (German), *a rivederci* (Italian); *all* (D): so long, be good, bye-bye, ciao, see you later, toodle-oo, cheerio, don't take any wooden nickels, take it easy, don't work too hard; see you later, Alligator; have a nice day.

good fellowship, *n.*—*Syn.* companionship, brotherhood, fraternity; see **friendship** 1.

good for, *mod.* **1.** [Helpful]—*Syn.* useful, beneficial, salubrious; see **helpful** 1.
2. [Financially sound]—*Syn.* safe, competent, worth it; see **good** 21, **valid** 2.

good-for-nothing, *n.*—*Syn.* loafer, vagabond, bum; see **tramp** 1.

good fortune, *n.*—*Syn.* good luck, affluence, prosperity; see **success** 2.

Good Friday, *n.*—*Syn.* Crucifixion Day, Holy Friday, (solemn) fast (day), Friday before Easter *or* in Ember Week; see also **Easter, holiday.**

good graces, *n.*—*Syn.* affection, good will, favor; see **friendship** 2.

good-hearted, *mod.*—*Syn.* charitable, gracious, benevolent; see **kind** 1.

good humor, *n.*—*Syn.* amiability, levity, geniality; see **happiness** 1.

good-humored, *mod.*—*Syn.* cheerful, merry, amiable; see **happy** 1.

good-looking, *mod.*—*Syn.* clean-cut, attractive, impressive; see **beautiful** 1, 2, **handsome** 2.

good luck, *interj.*—*Syn.* cheers, *skaal* (Scandinavian), best wishes, Godspeed, *shalom* (Hebrew), *salaam* (Arabic), God bless you, peace be with you, *pax vobiscum* (Latin), *Gesundheit* (German), *bonne chance* (French), *salut* (French).

good luck, *n.*—*Syn.* prosperity, fortune, affluence; see **success** 2.

good morning, *interj.*—*Syn.* good day, good morrow, greetings, *bonjour* (French), *guten Morgen* (German), *buenos días* (Spanish), top o' the mornin' to you (D).

good nature, *n.*—*Syn.* tolerance, consideration, benevolence; see **kindness** 1.

good-natured, *mod.*—*Syn.* cordial, kindly, amiable; see **friendly** 1.

goodness, *n.*—*Syn.* decency, morality, honesty; see **virtue** 1, 2.

good night, *interj.*—*Syn.* *bon nuit, à demain* (both French), *gute Nacht* (German), *buenas noches* (Spanish), nighty-night (D).

good opinion, *n.*—*Syn.* esteem, approbation, honor; see **admiration** 1.

goods, *n.* pl. **1.** [Commodities]—*Syn.* merchandise, materials, wares; see **commodity.**
2. [Effects]—*Syn.* equipment, personal property, possessions; see **property** 1.
deliver the goods (D)—*Syn.* fulfill, accomplish, produce; see **satisfy** 3.
get (*or* **have**) **the goods on** (D)—*Syn.* uncover, obtain evidence on, prove the guilt of; see **expose** 1.

good will, *n.*—*Syn.* benevolence, charity, kindness, cordiality, sympathy, tolerance, helpfulness, favorable disposition, altruism.—*Ant.* hatred*, malevolence, animosity.

goody (D), *n.*—*Syn.* good thing, tidbit, reward; see **prize.**

goody-goody, *n.*—*Syn.* devout person, moralist, prig; see **prude.**

goof (D), *v.*—*Syn.* err, make a mistake, flub (D); see **fail** 1.

go off, *v.* **1.** [To leave]—*Syn.* quit, depart, part; see **leave** 1.
2. [To explode]—*Syn.* blow up, detonate, discharge; see **explode** 1.
3. [(D) To occur]—*Syn.* take place, pass, befall; see **happen** 2.

go on, *v.* **1.** [To act]—*Syn.* execute, behave, conduct; see **act** 1, 2.
2. [To happen]—*Syn.* occur, come about, take place; see **happen** 2.
3. [To persevere]—*Syn.* persist, continue, bear; see **endure** 1.
4. [To approach]—*Syn.* creep *or* loom up, near, advance; see **approach** 2.
5. [(D) To talk]—*Syn.* chatter, converse, speak; see **talk** 1.

goose, *n.* **1.** Types of geese include the following—gray goose, graylag, bean goose, pink-footed goose, white-fronted goose, snow goose, emperor goose, kelp goose, upland goose, black goose, barnacle goose, brant goose, Canada goose, Chinese goose, Egyptian goose, Orinoco goose.
2. [A stupid person]—*Syn.* loony, dope, silly; see **fool** 1.
cook one's goose (D)—*Syn.* ruin, spoil, defeat; see **destroy** 1.

go out, *v.* **1.** [To be extinguished]—*Syn.* cease, die, darken, flicker (out), flash out, become dark *or* black, burn out, stop shining; see also **shade** 3.
2. [To strike]—*Syn.* go on strike, walk out, picket; see **strike** 2.

go out of one's head, *v.*—*Syn.* go crazy *or* mad, become insane, flip (D); see **rage** 3.

go over, *v.* **1.** [To rehearse]—*Syn.* repeat, say something repeatedly, practice; see **rehearse** 3.
2. [To examine]—*Syn.* look at, investigate, analyze; see **examine** 1, **study** 1.
3. [(D) To succeed]—*Syn.* be successful, not fail, be impressive; see **succeed** 1.

gore, *n.*—*Syn.* blood, slaughter, massacre; see **carnage.**

gorge, *n.*—*Syn.* chasm, abyss, crevasse; see **ravine.**

gorge, *v.* —*Syn.* glut, surfeit, stuff oneself; see **eat** 1, **fill** 1.

gorgeous, *mod.* —*Syn.* superb, sumptuous, impressive; see **beautiful** 1, **grand** 2.

gory, *mod.* —*Syn.* blood-soaked, bloodstained, bloody; see **offensive** 2.

gosh (D), *interj.* —*Syn.* imagine, gee, golly, dear me, Lord, goodness gracious; see also **curse.**

go someone better, *v.* —*Syn.* surpass, excel, outshine; see **exceed.**

gospel, *n.* **1.** [A record of Christ]—*Syn.* New Testament, Christian Scripture, Evangelist; see **Bible.**
2. [A text]—*Syn.* authority, testament, scripture; see **Bible.**
3. [Belief or statement supposedly infallible] —*Syn.* creed, certainty, dogma; see **doctrine** 1, **faith** 2, **truth** 1.

gossamer, *n.* —*Syn.* cobweb, filament, tendril; see **fiber** 1, **thread.**

gossip, *n.* **1.** [Local, petty talk]—*Syn.* babble, chatter, meddling, small talk, malicious talk, whispering gallery, hearsay, rumor, scandal, news, slander, calumny, defamation, injury, blackening, grapevine telegraph (D).
2. [One who indulges in gossip, sense 1]—*Syn.* snoop, meddler, tattler, newsmonger, gossipmonger, scandalmonger, scandal-bearer, backbiter, magpie, chatterbox, talkative person, babbler, blatherskite, parrot; *all* (D): long-nose, sticky-beak, blabbermouth, telltale, old hen, fussbudget, Mrs. Grundy, gabbler.

gossip, *v.* —*Syn.* tattle, prattle, tell tales, talk idly, chat, chatter, rumor, report, tell secrets, blab, babble, repeat, prate, spread (a story) all over town, dish the dirt (D).

go straight, *v.* —*Syn.* lead a moral life, live within the law, improve; see **behave** 2, **reform** 2, 3.

go the rounds, *v.* —*Syn.* inspect, investigate, check; see **examine** 1, **guard** 2.

gothic, *mod.* —*Syn.* medieval, barbaric, grotesque; see **old** 3.

go through, *v.* **1.** [To inspect]—*Syn.* search, audit, investigate; see **examine** 1.
2. [To undergo]—*Syn.* withstand, survive, suffer; see **endure** 2.
3. [To spend]—*Syn.* consume, deplete, pay, expend; see **spend** 1.

go through with, *v.* —*Syn.* fulfill, finish, follow through (with); see **achieve** 1, **complete** 1.

go to bat for (D), *v.* —*Syn.* stand by, justify, protect; see **defend** 3.

go together, *v.* **1.** [To harmonize]—*Syn.* be suitable, match, fit; see **agree.**
2. [To keep company]—*Syn.* go steady, escort, go with; see **date** 2, **keep company with.**

go to law (D), *v.* —*Syn.* bring court action, file suit, take to court; see **accuse.**

go to the dogs, *v.* —*Syn.* deteriorate, backslide, decline; see **decay.**

gouge, *v.* **1.** [To hollow out]—*Syn.* scoop, chisel, channel; see **dig** 1.
2. [(D) To obtain illegally or immorally]—*Syn.* blackmail, take advantage, extort; see **steal.**

go under, *v.* **1.** [Drown]—*Syn.* sink, drown; suffocate; see **die** 1.
2. [To become bankrupt]—*Syn.* default, go broke, (go) bankrupt; see **fail** 4.

go up, *v.* —*Syn.* increase, rise, double; see **grow** 1.

gourd, *n.* **1.** [A melon]—*Syn.* squash, calabash, pumpkin; see **melon.**
2. [A cup]—*Syn.* bottle, dipper, flask; see **cup.**

gourmet, *n.* —*Syn.* gastronome, epicure, connoisseur; see **critic** 2.

govern, *v.* —*Syn.* command, administer, reign, legislate, oversee, hold dominion *or* sway, occupy the throne, assume (the) command, hold office, serve the people, administer the laws, exercise authority, be in power, supervise, superintend, direct, dictate, lay down the law, tyrannize; *all* (D): wield the sceptre, wear the crown, hold the reins of empire.

governable, *mod.* —*Syn.* manageable, submissive, controllable; see **docile.**

governed, *mod.* **1.** [Ruled]—*Syn.* commanded, administered, under authority, supervised, superintended, directed, overseen, tyrannized over, dictated to, conducted, guided, piloted, mastered, led, driven, subjugated, subordinate.—*Ant.* free*, autonomous, archic.
2. [Controlled]—*Syn.* determined, guided, influenced, swayed, inclined, regulated, directed, ordered, dependent, consequent, obedient, under one's jurisdiction.—*Ant.* unruly*, self-determined, capricious.

governess, *n.* —*Syn.* tutoress, mistress, duenna; see **guardian** 1, 2.

governing, *mod.* —*Syn.* commanding, administrative, executive, authoritative, supervisory, regulatory, controlling, directing, restraining, superintending, surveillant, overseeing, tyrannizing, dictatorial, arbitrary, conducting, guiding, mastering, potent, dominating, dominant, magisterial, determining, ascendant, ordering, compulsive, supreme, influential, gubernatorial, presidential, regal, absolute, ruling, checking, curbing, inhibiting, limiting, confining.—*Ant.* subordinate, powerless, tributary.

government, *n.* **1.** [The process of governing] —*Syn.* rule, control, command, regulation, bureaucracy, direction, equity, dominion, sway, authority, jurisdiction, hegemony, suzerainty, sovereignty, prerogative, polity, direction, power, management, authorization, patronage, mastery, predominance, superiority, supervision, superintendence, magistracy, supremacy, domination, preponderance, ascendancy, influence, presidency, politics, regimentation, state, statecraft, political practice, caretaker government, governmental procedure; see also **administration.**
2. [The instrument of governing]—*Syn.* administration, assembly, legislature, congress, cabinet, executive power, regime, supreme authority, ministry, party, chamber, council, parliament, senate, department of justice, soviet, synod, convocation, convention, court, directory, house (D). Types of government include the following—absolute monarchy, dictatorship, empire, tyranny, fascism, imperialism, colonialism, despotism, limited monarchy, constitutional monarchy, hereditary kingship, oligarchy, aristocracy, democracy, popular government, representative government, democratic so-

cialism, communism, socialism, party government. Divisions of government include—state, province, kingdom, territory, colony, dominion, commonwealth, soviet, republic, shire, city, county, canton, town, village, township, municipality, borough, commune, ward, district, suburb, department, *arrondissement, département* (*both* French), nome, nomarchy, parish.

governmental, *mod.* —*Syn.* political, administrative, executive, regulatory, bureaucratic, legal, magisterial, supervisory, sovereign, presidential, official, gubernatorial, national.

governor, *n.* **1.** [An administrator]—*Syn.* director, presiding officer, ruler; see **administrator.**

2. [Chief executive of a major political division] —*Syn.* (executive) head of a state, provincial magistrate, territorial executive, local executive, representative of the crown, gubernatorial leader, *gubernator* (Latin), governor of the state.

3. [A regulating mechanism]—*Syn.* automatic control, fuel control, heat control, thermocouple, thermostat, on-off thermostat, alarm, rheostat, butterfly valve; see also **valve.**

go well with, *v.* —*Syn.* match, correspond, harmonize; see **go with** 2.

go whole hog, *v.* —*Syn.* finish, do all of, bring to completion; see **complete** 1.

go with, *v.* **1.** [(D) To keep company with]—*Syn.* escort, attend, be with; see **accompany** 1, **date** 2, **keep company with.**

2. [To be appropriate to]—*Syn.* match, correspond, not clash, go well with, harmonize, complement, fit; see also **agree.**

go without, *v.* —*Syn.* lack, fall short, want; see **need.**

gown, *n.* —*Syn.* garb, garment, clothes; see **dress** 2.

go wrong, *v.* —*Syn.* slip, break down, go amiss; see **fail** 1.

grab (D), *n.* —*Syn.* prize, receipts, acquisition; see **booty, catch** 2.

up for grabs (D)—*Syn.* offered, obtainable, for the taking; see **available, free** 4.

grab, *v.* —*Syn.* clutch, grasp, take; see **seize** 1, 2.

grace, *n.* **1.** [The quality of being graceful]—*Syn.* suppleness, lithesomeness, lissomeness, ease (of movement), nimbleness, agility, pliancy, smoothness, form, address, poise, dexterity, adroitness, symmetry, balance, style, harmony.—*Ant.* awkwardness*, stiffness, maladroitness.

2. [Mercy]—*Syn.* forgiveness, love, charity; see **mercy** 1.

3. [Charm]—*Syn.* allure, attractiveness, comeliness; see **beauty** 1.

4. [A prayer at table]—*Syn.* invocation, thanks, thanksgiving, blessing, benediction, petition.

fall from grace—*Syn.* do wrong, misbehave, err; see **sin.**

have the grace—*Syn.* be proper or gracious, accept conditions, resign oneself; see **agree, obey** 1, 2.

in the bad graces of—*Syn.* in disfavor, rejected, disapproved; see **hated.**

in the good graces of—*Syn.* favored, accepted, admired; see **approved.**

with bad grace—*Syn.* sullenly, gracelessly, unwillingly; see **reluctantly.**

with good grace—*Syn.* graciously, willingly, generously; see **gracefully.**

graceful, *mod.* **1.** [*Said of movement*]—*Syn.* lissome, supple, limber, agile, lithe, pliant, nimble, elastic, springy, easy, dexterous, adroit, smooth, controlled, balletic, sylphlike, light-footed, willowy, poised, practiced, skilled, rhythmic, sprightly, elegant.—*Ant.* awkward*, fumbling, stiff.

2. [*Said of objects*]—*Syn.* elegant, neat, well-proportioned, trim, balanced, well-turned, symmetrical, dainty, pretty, harmonious, beautiful, comely, seemly, handsome, fair, delicate, tasteful, slender, decorative, artistic, exquisite, statuesque.—*Ant.* ugly*, shapeless, cumbersome.

3. [*Said of conduct*]—*Syn.* cultured, seemly, becoming; see **polite** 1.

gracefully, *mod.* —*Syn.* lithely, agilely, harmoniously, daintily, nimbly, elegantly, trimly, symmetrically, beautifully, felicitously, delicately, tastefully, artistically, pliantly, easily, dexterously, smoothly, skillfully, fairly, adroitly, handsomely, rhythmically, exquisitely, neatly, sprucely, delightfully, charmingly, imaginatively, becomingly, suitably, fitly, sweetly, pleasingly, congruously, appropriately, happily, decoratively, prettily.—*Ant.* awkwardly, insipidly, grotesquely.

graceless, *mod.* —*Syn.* corrupt, shameless, uncouth; see **rude** 1, 2.

gracious, *mod.* **1.** [Genial]—*Syn.* amiable, courteous, condescending; see **polite** 1.

2. [Merciful]—*Syn.* tender, loving, charitable; see **kind** 1.

gradation, *n.* —*Syn.* step, stage, scale; see **degree** 1.

grade, *n.* **1.** [An incline]—*Syn.* slope, inclined plane, gradient, slant, inclination, pitch, ascent, descent, obliquity, tangent, ramp, upgrade, acclivity, declivity, downgrade, climb, elevation, height; see also **hill.**

2. [An embankment]—*Syn.* fill, causeway, dike; see **dam** 1.

3. [Rank or degree]—*Syn.* class, category, classification; see **degree** 2.

4. [A division of a school]—*Syn.* standard, form, rank; see **class** 3.

5. [(D) A hybrid]—*Syn.* mixture, mongrel, ordinary specimen; see **hybrid.**

make the grade (D)—*Syn.* win, prosper, achieve; see **succeed** 1.

grade, *v.* —*Syn.* rate, give a grade *or* grades (to), assort; see **rank** 2.

graded, *mod.* —*Syn.* sorted, ranked, grouped; see **classified.**

gradient, *n.* —*Syn.* angle, slope, pitch; see **grade** 1, **inclination** 5.

gradual, *mod.* —*Syn.* creeping, regular, continuous; see **progressive** 1.

gradually, *mod.* —*Syn.* step by step, by degrees, steadily, increasingly, slowly, regularly, a little at a time, little by little, stone by stone, bit by bit, inch by inch, grade by grade, by installments, in small doses, continuously, in due succession, through all (the) gradations, by regular stages, progressively, successively, sequentially, serially, constantly, unceasingly, perceptibly, imperceptibly, insinuatingly, deliberately.—*Ant.* quickly*, haphazardly, by leaps and bounds.

graduate, *n.* —*Syn.* recipient of a degree *or* certificate, alumnus, alumna, former student, holder *or* bearer of a degree *or* certificate, baccalaureate, licentiate, gownsman, diplomate, product; *both* (D): old grad, alum.

graduate, *v.* **1.** [To give a degree]—*Syn.* grant a degree *or* diploma *or* certificate to, confer a degree *or* diploma *or* certificate on *or* upon, send out, certify, give a sheepskin to (D).
2. [To receive a degree]—*Syn.* receive *or* be awarded *or* win *or* earn *or* take a degree *or* certificate *or* diploma, become an alumna *or* alumnus, get out, finish (up), become qualified, be certificated, be commissioned; *all* (D): get a B.A., M.A., Ph.D., M.D., etc.; get a sheepskin.

graduated, *mod.* **1.** [Granted a degree]—*Syn.* certified, ordained, accredited, passed, invested, promoted.
2. [Arranged or marked according to a scale] —*Syn.* serialized, graded, tapered, sequential, measured, progressive, registered.

graduation, *n.* —*Syn.* commencement, convocation, conferring of new degrees, granting of diplomas, promotion, bestowal of honors, commissioning.

graffiti, *n.* pl.—*Syn.* scribbling, writing on walls, inscription, aphorism; see also **writing** 2.

graft, *n.* **1.** [A jointure for growth]—*Syn.* scion, shoot, union, slip, hybridization, graff, grafting.
2. [Dishonest gain]—*Syn.* fraud, peculation, thievery; see **corruption** 3.

graft, *v.* **1.** [To join for growth]—*Syn.* engraft, unite, propagate, splice.
2. [(D) To gain dishonestly]—*Syn.* thieve, cheat, swindle; see **steal.**

grail, *n.* —*Syn.* sacred vessel, hold dish, chalice; see **cup.**

grain, *n.* **1.** [Seeds of domesticated grasses]—*Syn.* cereal(s), corn (British), small grain, seed, maize.
Varieties of grain include the following—rice, wheat, oats, barley, corn, rye, millet.
2. [A particle]—*Syn.* speck, pellet, fragment; see **bit** 1.
3. [Character imparted by fiber]—*Syn.* texture, warp and woof, striation, tendency, fabric, staple, tissue, weft, current, direction, tooth, nap.
against the grain (D)—*Syn.* disturbing, irritating, bothersome; see **offensive** 2.

grammar, *n.* —*Syn.* syntax, accidence, morphology, structure, morphophonemics, syntactic structure, sentence structure, language *or* sentence pattern, linguistic science, rationalized language, stratification *or* stratificational grammar, transform *or* transformational grammar, universal grammar, tagmemics *or* tagmemic grammar, PS *or* phrase structure grammar, incorporating grammar, synthetic *or* inflectional grammar, analytic *or* distributive *or* isolating grammar, traditional grammar, the new grammar (D).
Terms in grammar include the following—tense, mood, aspect, case, sandhi, modification, incorporation, inflection, concord *or* agreement, sentence, nexus, coordination, subordination, structure, phrase structure, structural linguistics, phoneme, phonemics, string, stratification, particle, wave, field, knot, head word, transformation, morphophoneme, morpheme, morphemics, sememe, slot, tagmeme, tree, transform; see also **language** 2, **part** 2.

grammarian, *n.* —*Syn.* philologist, grammatist, rhetorician; see **linguist** 1.

grammatical, *mod.* **1.** [Having to do with grammar] —*Syn.* linquistic, syntactic, morphophonemic, sememic, morphological, logical, philological, analytic, analytical.
2. [Conforming to rules of grammar]—*Syn.* grammatically correct, conventional, accepted.—*Ant.* ungrammatical, solecistic, irregular.

grammatical construction, *n.* —*Syn.* structure, locution, sequence; see **clause** 2, **phrase, sentence** 2, **transformation** 2.

granary, *n.* —*Syn.* bin, crib, barn; see **storehouse.**

grand, *mod.* **1.** [Sumptuous]—*Syn.* rich, splendid, magnificent; see **sumptuous.**
2. [Exalted]—*Syn.* majestic, lofty, stately, dignified, elevated, high, regal, awful, noble, illustrious, sublime, great, ambitious, august, solemn, grave, pre-eminent, extraordinary, monumental, stupendous, huge, chief, soaring, vaulting, aspiring, transcendent, commanding, towering, overwhelming, impressive, imposing, foremost, awe-inspiring, mighty, empyrean; *all* (D): sensational, the cat's whiskers, terrif, great, swell.—*Ant.* poor, low, mediocre.
3. [Strongly approved of]—*Syn.* first-class, good, superb; see **excellent.**

grandeur, *n.* —*Syn.* splendor, superbity, magnificence, pomp, circumstance, impressiveness, eminence, distinction, fame, glory, brilliancy, opulence, richness, sumptuousness, luxuriousness, stateliness, beauty, handsomeness, ceremony, importance, exalted rank, celebrity, solemnity, fineness, majesty, sublimity, nobility, scope, dignity, loftiness, elevation, preeminence, height, greatness, transcendency, might, breadth, expansiveness, immensity, amplitude, vastness, sway, inclusiveness.—*Ant.* meanness, commonness, baseness.

grandfather, *n.* —*Syn.* grandsire, (paternal) forebear, elder, forefather, ancestor, patriarch; *all* (D): grandpa, granddaddy, grandpappy.

grandiloquent, *mod.* —*Syn.* pompous, histrionic, bombastic; see **oratorical.**

grandiose, *mod.* —*Syn.* pompous, flamboyant, theatrical; see **egotistic** 2.

grandly, *mod.* —*Syn.* royally, regally, sumptuously; see **wonderfully.**

grandmother, *n.* —*Syn.* grandam, matriarch, dowager, ancestor, (maternal) forebear, *Grossmutter* (German), *babushka* (Russian); *all* (D): grandma, gram, granny.

grandstand, *n.* —*Syn.* amphitheater, stadium, stall(s), stand(s), field house, coliseum, field, benches, boxes, bleachers, pit; see also **field** 2, **theater** 1.

grange, *n.* **1.** [Manor]—*Syn.* plantation, farm, hacienda; see **ranch.**
2. [Farmer's organization]—*Syn.* society, secret society, farmer's union, farmer's guild, *Turnverein* (German), agricultural party, farm vote, grass-roots movement.

granite, *mod.* —*Syn.* stone, igneous, durable; see **firm** 2.

grant, *n.* —*Syn.* gift, boon, reward, present, allowance, stipend, donation, matching grant, benefaction, gratuity, endowment, concession, bequest, privilege; federal grant, NDEA grant, HEW grant, NEH grant, Ford Foundation grant, etc.—*Ant.* deprivation, deduction, detriment.

grant, *v.* **1.** [To permit]—*Syn.* yield, cede, impart; see **allow** 1.
2. [To accept as true]—*Syn.* concede, accede, acquiesce; see **admit** 3.
3. [To bestow]—*Syn.* confer, award, invest; see **give** 1.

granted, *mod.* **1.** [Awarded]—*Syn.* conferred, bestowed, awarded; see **given.**
2. [Allowed]—*Syn.* accepted, admitted, acknowledged; see **assumed** 1.
take for granted—*Syn.* accept, presume, consider true *or* settled; see **assume** 1.

granulate, *v.* —*Syn.* grate, pulverize, powder; see **grind** 1.

grape, *n.* —Types of grapes *(Vitis vinifera)* include the following—wine grapes, raisin grapes, lambrusca, Concord, scuppernong, summer, plum, chicken, frost, winter, fox, muscadine, Catawba, Delaware, Hartford, Iona, Adirondack, Rogers, Old World, Mission, Vinifera, Euvitis, Niagara, bullace, viparia, rotundifolia, Malaga, Muscat, black Hamberg, Isabella.

grapevine, *n.* —*Syn.* climber, creeper, trailer; see **vine.**

graph, *n.* —*Syn.* diagram, chart, linear representation; see **design** 1, **plan** 1.

graphic, *mod.* **1.** [Pictorial]—*Syn.* visible, illustrated, descriptive, photographic, visual, depicted, seen, drawn, portrayed, traced, sketched, outlined, pictured, painted, limned, marked *or* blocked out, in full color, engraved, etched, graven, chiseled, hewn, in bold relief, stenciled, penciled, printed. —*Ant.* unreal*, imagined, chimerical.
2. [Vivid]—*Syn.* forcible, telling, picturesque, intelligible, comprehensible, clear, explicit, striking, definite, lucid, distinct, precise, expressive, eloquent, moving, stirring, unequivocal, concrete, energetic, colorful, strong, figurative, poetic.—*Ant.* obscure*, ambiguous, abstract.

grapple, *v.* **1.** [Fasten]—*Syn.* hook, catch, close; see **fasten** 1, **join** 1.
2. [Fight hand to hand]—*Syn.* engage, close, wrestle; see **fight** 2.

grasp, *v.* **1.** [To clutch]—*Syn.* grip, enclose, clasp; see **seize** 1, 2.
2. [To comprehend]—*Syn.* perceive, apprehend, follow; see **understand** 1.

grasp, *n.* —*Syn.* hold, clutch, cinch; see **grip** 2.

grasping, *mod.* —*Syn.* niggardly, rapacious, penurious; see **greedy** 1.

grasping, *n.* —*Syn.* hold, taking, grabbing; see **catch** 2.

grass, *n.* **1.** Wild grasses include the following—Johnson grass, salt grass, blue grass, beach grass, bent grass, foxtail, sedge, buffalo grass, bulrush, sand-bur, couch grass, carpet grass, crab grass, crowfoot, deer grass, bunch grass, meadow grass, fescue, heath grass, joint grass, orchard grass, pampas grass, June grass, redtop, river grass, slough grass, ribbon grass, stink grass, sweet grass, tickle grass, brome, canary grass, cat-tail, wild rice.
2. Domesticated grasses include the following—cane, millet, oats, wheat, barley, maize, rye, broomcorn, timothy, kaffir corn, Milo maize, Kentucky blue grass, rice, sesame, sorghum.
3. [Grassed area]—*Syn.* grassland, meadow, lawn, turf, green, fairway, sward, greensward, pasture, prairie(s), bottom(s), bottomland, hayfield; see also **field** 1, **yard** 1.
4. [(D) A drug]—*Syn.* marijuana, *Nicotanea glauca* (Latin), hemp, cannabis; *all* (D): pot, weed, maryjane, boo; see also **drug** 2.
let the grass grow under one's feet (D)—*Syn.* waste time, be lazy, fail; see **neglect** 1.

grasshopper, *n.* —Insects commonly called grasshoppers include the following—katydid, locust, cricket, green grasshopper, short-horned grasshopper, long-horned grasshopper, red-legged grasshopper, Rocky Mountain grasshopper, Mormon cricket, hateful grasshopper, *Acristida* (Latin), *Locusta* (Latin), *Gryllus* (Latin); *both* (D): hopper, hoppergrass.

grassland, *n.* —*Syn.* plains, meadow, prairie; see **field** 1.

grassy, *mod.* —*Syn.* grass-grown, verdant, green, sedgy, reedy, lush, matted, tangled, carpeted, lawnlike, turfy, sodded, sowed, luxurious, deep.

grate, *n.* —*Syn.* firebox, bed, furnace, stove, andiron, firepot.

grate, *v.* —*Syn.* rasp, grind, abrade; see **rub** 1.

grateful, *mod.* **1.** [Thankful]—*Syn.* appreciative, beholden, obliged; see **thankful.**
2. [Welcome]—*Syn.* agreeable, delectable, pleasing; see **pleasant** 2.

gratefully, *mod.* —*Syn.* appreciatively, thankfully, with a sense of obligation, delightedly, responsively, admiringly.—*Ant.* rudely*, ungratefully, thanklessly.

gratification, *n.* **1.** [Satisfaction]—*Syn.* enjoyment, pleasure, delight; see **satisfaction** 2.
2. [A source of satisfaction]—*Syn.* delight, regalement, luxury; see **satisfaction** 2, 3.

gratify, *v.* —*Syn.* indulge, humor, delight; see **satisfy** 1.

gratifying, *mod.* —*Syn.* satisfying, delightful, pleasing; see **pleasant** 2.

grating, *mod.* —*Syn.* offensive, strident, harsh; see **shrill.**

gratis, *mod.* —*Syn.* without charge, complimentary, as a gift; see **free** 4.

gratitude, *n.* —*Syn.* thankfulness, appreciation, gratefulness, acknowledgment, response, sense of obligation *or* indebtedness, feeling of obligedness *or* obligation, responsiveness, thanks, praise, guerdon, requital, recognition, honor, thanksgiving, grace.—*Ant.* ingratitude, indifference*, thanklessness.

gratuitous, *mod.* **1.** [Voluntary]—*Syn.* for nothing, gratis, complimentary; see **free** 4.
2. [Uncalled-for]—*Syn.* needless, unwarranted, unessential; see **unnecessary.**

gratuity, *n.* —*Syn.* present, donation, tip; see **gift** 1.

grave, *mod.* **1.** [Important]—*Syn.* momentous, weighty, consequential; see **important** 1.

2. [Dangerous]—*Syn.* critical, serious, ominous; see **dangerous** 1.
3. [Solemn]—*Syn.* serious, sober, earnest; see **solemn** 1.

grave, *n.* **1.** [A burial place]—*Syn.* vault, sepulcher, tomb, pit, crypt, mausoleum, catacomb, long home, six feet of earth, last resting place, narrow house, place of interment, mound, barrow, cromlech, clay, cairn, tumulus, dolmen; *all* (D): cold mud, pine, wooden shroud, pit for the dead, burial place, charnel house, last home, permanent address.
2. [Death]—*Syn.* dissolution, decay, last sleep; see **death** 2.
make one turn (over) in one's grave (D)—*Syn.* do something shocking *or* disrespectful, sin, err; see **misbehave.**
one foot in the grave (D)—*Syn.* old, infirm, near death; see **dying** 2.

gravel, *n.* —*Syn.* sand, pebbles, shale, pea gravel, marl, macadam, screenings, crushed rock, washings, alluvium, tailing.

graven, *mod.* —*Syn.* etched, sculptured, cut; see **engraved.**

graveyard, *n.*—*Syn.* burial ground, necropolis, God's acre; see **cemetery.**

gravitate, *v.*—*Syn.* drift, be attracted to, incline toward; see **approach** 2.

gravitation, *n.* —*Syn.* mutual attraction of bodies, agitation, settling together, planetary motion, earthward motion, gravity, resistless tendency.

gravity, *n.* **1.** [Weight]—*Syn.* heaviness, pressure, force; see **gravitation.**
2. [Importance]—*Syn.* seriousness, concern, significance; see **importance** 1.

gravy, *n.* —*Syn.* sauce, dressing, brown gravy, white gravy, milk gravy, pan gravy, meat gravy, white sauce, butter sauce.

gray, *mod.* **1.** [Between black and white]—*Syn.* neutral, dusky, silvery, livid, dingy, somber, sere, shaded, drab, leaden, grayish, ashen, grizzly, grizzled.
Shades of gray include the following—Oxford gray, blue-gray, silver-gray, smoke-gray, slate, bat, mouse-colored, iron-gray, lead, ash-gray, pepper and salt, grizzled, powder, dusty, smoky, heather, battleship gray.
2. [Aged]—*Syn.* grizzled, hoary, decrepit; see **old** 1, 2.

gray, *n.* —*Syn.* shade, drabness, dusk; see **color** 1.

graze, *v.* **1.** [To touch or score lightly]—*Syn.* brush, scrape, rub; see **touch** 1, 2.
2. [To pasture]—*Syn.* browse, feed, batten, crop, gnaw, nibble, bite, uproot, pull grass, forage, eat, champ, munch, crunch, masticate, ruminate.

grazing, *mod.* **1.** [Browsing]—*Syn.* battening, cropping, feeding, gnawing, nibbling, biting, uprooting, pasturing, pulling grass, foraging, eating, champing, munching, crunching, masticating, ruminating.
2. [Keeping livestock on the range]—*Syn.* herding, pasturing, feeding, ranging, running cattle *or* stock, stocking, fattening.

grease, *n.* —*Syn.* oil, wax, fat, lubricant, salve, Vaseline (trademark), unguent, goose grease, shmaltz, chicken fat, olive oil, cottonseed oil, peanut oil; see also **fat.**
Lubricating greases include the following—axle grease, hard oil, graphite, hypoid lubricant, differential grease, transmission grease.

grease, *v.* —*Syn.* oil, lubricate, smear, slave, coat *or* rub with oil, cream, daub, inunct, pomade, grease the wheels, anoint, swab, give a grease job (D).

grease job, *n.* —*Syn.* lubricating, lubrication service, lube (job) (D); see **lubrication.**

greasy, *mod.* —*Syn.* creamy, fat, oleaginous, fatty; see **oily** 1.

great, *mod.* **1.** [Eminent]—*Syn.* noble, grand, august, majestic, dignified, exalted, commanding, puissant, famous, renowned, widely acclaimed, Olympic, famed, celebrated, distinguished, noted, illustrious, highly regarded, conspicuous, elevated, prominent, high, stately, honorable, lordly, princely, magnificent, glorious, regal, royal, kingly, imposing, peerless, preeminent, unrivaled, fabulous, fabled, storied, a bit of all right (D).—*Ant.* obscure*, retired, anonymous.
2. [Large]—*Syn.* numerous, big, vast; see **large** 1.
3. [(D) Excellent]—*Syn.* exceptional, surpassing, transcendant; see **excellent.**
4. [Extensive]—*Syn.* inclusive, all-embracing, sweeping; see **comprehensive.**

Great Britain, *n.* —*Syn.* Britain, British Isles, United Kingdom; see **England.**

greatly, *mod.* —*Syn.* exceedingly, considerably, hugely; see **very.**

greatness, *n.* **1.** [Eminence]—*Syn.* prominence, renown, importance; see **fame** 1.
2. [Size]—*Syn.* bulk, extent, largeness; see **size** 2.
3. [Character]—*Syn.* magnanimity, merit, morality; see **virtue** 1.

Greece, *n.* —*Syn.* Hellas, Graecia, Achaia, Argos, Greek peninsula, Hellenic peoples, the Peloponnesus, the Peloponnese.

greed, *n.* —*Syn.* greediness, avidity, selfishness, eagerness, avarice, voracity, excess, rapacity, gluttony, piggishness, indulgence, hoggishness, gormandism *or* gourmandism, ravenousness, avariciousness, voraciousness, niggardliness, acquisitiveness, intemperance, cupidity, graspingness, covetousness, desire; *all* (D): grabbiness, an itching palm, taking ways.—*Ant.* generosity*, liberality, munificence.

greedy, *mod.* **1.** [Avaricious]—*Syn.* avid, grasping, rapacious, selfish, miserly, parsimonious, close, close-fisted, tight, tight-fisted, niggardly, exploitative, grudging, sordid, mercenary, illiberal, stingy, covetous, penurious, acquisitive, pennypinching (D).—*Ant.* generous*, munificent, bountiful.
2. [Gluttonous]—*Syn.* rapacious, swinish, voracious, devouring, hoggish, ravening, ravenous, omnivorous, carnivorous, insatiate, gorging, belly-worshiping, surfeiting, crapulous, intemperate, gormandizing, guzzling, gobbling, gulping, selfish, indulging one's appetites.—*Ant.* ascetic*, fasting, abstemious.

Greek, *mod.* —*Syn.* Hellenic, Hellenistic, Helladic, Minoan, Dorian, Attic, Boeotian, Athenian, Spartan, Peloponnesian, Ionian, Corinthian, Thessalian, ancient, classic; see also **classical** 2.

Greek, *n.* **1.** [A citizen of Greece]—*Syn.* Hellene, Athenian, Spartan, Achaean, Dorian, Ionian, Corinthian, Thessalian, Arcadian, Boeotian, Argolid, Laconian, Messenian, Attican, Peloponnesian.

2. [The Greek language]—*Syn.* Hellenic, Ionic, New Ionic, Attic, Æolic, Doric, Modern Greek, Romaic, Neo-Hellenic, language of Homer, koine.

Greeks, *n.* —*Syn.* Greek culture, Hellenes, the Ancients, Hellenism, classical times, Athens, the Golden Mean, the glory that was Greece, the Golden Age.

green, *mod.* **1.** [Of the color green]—*Syn.* greenish, virid, virescent.

Tints and shades of green include the following—emerald, sage, vert, verdigris, malachite, beryl, aquamarine, chartreuse, lime, kelly, glaucous, olive drab, Mittler's green, Prussian green, bronze-green, Lincoln green, yellow-green, bottle-green, pea-green, sea-green, apple-green, grass-green, forest-green, spinach-green, moss-green, pine-green, Nile green, olive-green, jade, Oriental emerald, Oriental aquamarine, viridian, Veronese green.

2. [Verdant]—*Syn.* foliate, growing, leafy, bosky, sprouting, visculent, pullulating, grassy, grass-grown, burgeoning, flourishing, lush.—*Ant.* withered*, sere, yellow.

3. [Immature]—*Syn.* young, growing, unripe, maturing, developing, half-formed, half-baked, fresh, sappy.—*Ant.* mature*, ripe, gone to seed.

4. [Inexperienced]—*Syn.* youthful, callow, raw; see **inexperienced.**

5. [Pale, usually from illness, envy, or jealousy] —*Syn.* pallid, peaked, wan; see **pale** 1.

green, *n.* **1.** [A color]—*Syn.* greenness, verdure, virescence, emerald, chlorophyl, verdantness, greenhood, viridity; see also **color** 1.

2. [A grass plot]—*Syn.* lawn, field, park; see **grass** 3.

long green (D), **folding green** (D)—*Syn.* bills, paper money, greenbacks; see **money** 1.

greenhorn, *n.* **1.** [Beginner]—*Syn.* apprentice, new hand, novice; see **amateur.**

2. [A boor]—*Syn.* yokel, crude fellow, rustic; see **boor.**

greenhouse, *n.* —*Syn.* hothouse, conservatory, glasshouse, arboretum, coolhouse, planthouse, potting shed, nursery, warmhouse (British).

greensward, *n.* —*Syn.* verdancy, verdure, greenery, viridity, virescence, viridescence.

greet, *v.* —*Syn.* welcome, accost, speak to, salute, address, hail, recognize, embrace, shake hands, nod, bow, curtsy, receive, call to, stop, acknowledge, bow to, approach, give one's love, hold out the hand, extend the right of friendship, herald, bid good day *or* hello *or* welcome, exchange greetings, move to, usher in, attend, pay one's respects. —*Ant.* ignore*, snub, slight.

greeting, *n.* **1.** [A salutation]—*Syn.* welcome, address, notice, reception, attention, accosting, speaking to, heralding, ushering in, acknowledgement, salutation, one's compliments, regards.

Common greetings include the following—hello, how do you do? how are you? *shalom* (Hebrew), *wie geht's?* (German), *comment allez-vous?* (French), good morning, good day, good afternoon, good evening, good morrow, *bonjour, bon soir, bonne nuit* (all French), *guten Morgen, guten Abend* (both German), *buenos días, buenas tardes, buenas noches* (all Spanish), *buona notte* (Italian); *all* (D): hi, hey, howdy, you, say, I say, what's new? how's it going? what's up? what do you know? how's tricks? how goes it? how's things?

2. [A message of courtesy]—*Syn.* testimonial, note, card; see **letter** 2.

gremlin, *n.* —*Syn.* demon, sprite, pixie; see **fairy** 1.

grenade, *n.* —*Syn.* shell, projectile, missile; see **weapon** 1.

grey, *mod.* —*Syn.* dun, drab, grayish; see **gray** 1.

grid, *n.* —*Syn.* plate, terminal, layer; see **electrode.**

griddle, *n.* —*Syn.* grill, gridiron, broiler, broiler pan, frying pan, spider, skillet.

gridiron, *n.* **1.** [(D) A football field]—*Syn.* turf, playing field, griddle (D); see **field** 2.

2. [A broiler]—*Syn.* griddle, roaster, barbecue rack; see **broiler.**

grief, *n.* **1.** [Mental distress]—*Syn.* sorrow, sadness, regret, melancholy, vexation, mourning, misery, trouble, anguish, bereavement, painful regret, distress over loss, depression, despondency, pain, worry, harassment, anxiety, woe, heartache, repining, lamentation, dole, dolor, malaise, disquiet, discomfort, smart, mortification, affliction, gloom, unhappiness, wretchedness, infelicity, desolation, despair, agony, torture, purgatory.—*Ant.* happiness*, exhilaration, pleasure.

2. [The cause of distress]—*Syn.* affliction, tribulation, vexation; see **difficulty** 2.

come to grief—*Syn.* be ruined *or* unsuccessful *or* harmed, etc.; have trouble, suffer; see **fail** 1.

grievance, *n.* —*Syn.* complaint, injury, case; see **objection** 1, 2.

grieve, *v.* —*Syn.* lament, bewail, regret, sorrow (for); see **mourn** 1.

grievous, *mod.* **1.** [Distressing]—*Syn.* disquieting, upsetting, troublesome; see **disturbing.**

2. [Mournful]—*Syn.* dismal, tragic, pathetic; see **sad** 1, 2.

3. [Painful]—*Syn.* severe, hurtful, sharp; see **painful** 1.

4. [Atrocious]—*Syn.* villainous, flagrant, heinous; see **outrageous.**

grill, *n.* **1.** [A broiler]—*Syn.* grid, griddle, rack; see **broiler.**

2. [A restaurant, especially one that grills food] —*Syn.* barbecue, lunchroom, cafeteria, diner, short order restaurant, café; see **restaurant.**

grill, *v.* **1.** [To broil]—*Syn.* roast, sauté, barbecue; see **cook.**

2. [To question closely]—*Syn.* cross-examine, interrogate, catechise; see **question** 1.

grim, *mod.* **1.** [Sullen]—*Syn.* crabbed, sour, repellent, crusty, gloomy, intractable, sulky, morose, somber, sullen, splenetic, churlish, forbidding, glum, grumpy, scowling, grouchy, glowering, dogged, stubborn, cantankerous.—*Ant.* happy*, cheerful, gay.

2. [Stern]—*Syn.* austere, strict, harsh; see **severe** 1.

3. [Relentless]—*Syn.* unrelenting, implacable, inexorable; see **severe** 2, **wicked** 2.

grimace, *n.* —*Syn.* smirk, smile, sneer; see **expression** 4.

grime, *n.* —*Syn.* soil, smudge, dirt; see **filth.**

grimy, *mod.* —*Syn.* begrimed, dingy, soiled; see **dirty** 1.

grin, *n.* —*Syn.* smirk, simper, wry face; see **smile.**

grin, *v.* —*Syn.* smirk, simper, beam; see **smile.**

grind, *n.* **1.** [A difficult or tedious job]—*Syn.* drudgery, toil, labor; see **work** 2.

2. [A drudge]—*Syn.* hard worker, toiler, crammer; see **drudge.**

grind, *v.* **1.** [To pulverize]—*Syn.* crush, powder, mill, grate, reduce to powder, attenuate, granulate, disintegrate, comminute, triturate, rasp, scrape, reduce to fine particles, levigate, file, abrade, pound, pestle, bray, beat into particles, crunch, crumple, roll *or* pound out, shiver, atomize, chop up, crumble.—*Ant.* organize*, mold, solidify.

2. [To sharpen]—*Syn.* whet, rub, give an edge to; see **sharpen** 1.

3. [Oppress]—*Syn.* persecute, harass, annoy; see **oppress.**

grinder, *n.* **1.** [A chopper or pulverizer]—*Syn.* food chopper, food processor, blender, mill, meat grinder, sausage stuffer, coffee grinder.

2. [An abrasive]—*Syn.* grindstone, whetstone, stone; see **abrasive.**

grinding, *mod.* —*Syn.* abrasive, crushing, pulverizing, grating, fricative, rasping, rubbing, milling, powdering, granulating, disintegrating, cracking, reducing to dust, comminutive, triturative, bonecrushing, crunching, splintering, shivering, smashing, crumbling, scraping, chopping, wearing away, eroding.

grind out (D), *v.* —*Syn.* create, manufacture, compose; see **produce** 2.

grindstone, *n.* —*Syn.* stone, emery wheel, wheel; see **abrasive.**

grip, *n.* **1.** [The power of gripping]—*Syn.* grasp, hold, manual *or* digital strength, ligature, musculature, purchase, goverment, governance.

2. [Application of the power to grip]—*Syn.* hold, grasp, clutch, gripe, purchase, clasp, catch, cinch, vise, clench, clinch, embrace, handclasp, handhold, fist, handgrip, handshake, snatch, grapple, anchor, squeeze, wrench, grab, cincture, enclosing, enclosure, fixing, fastening, crushing, clamp, clamping, iron grip, hoops of steel, vicelike grip, jaws; *all* (D): snag, glom, nip.

3. [Something suited to grasping]—*Syn.* knocker, knob, ear; see **handle** 1.

4. [(D) A traveling bag]—*Syn.* valise, suitcase, satchel; see **bag.**

grip, *v.* —*Syn.* clutch, grasp, clasp; see **seize** 1.

come to grips—*Syn.* engage, encounter, cope with; see **fight** 1, 2, **try** 1.

gripe (D), *n.* **1.** [An objection]—*Syn.* complaint, grievance, beef (D); see **objection** 2.

2. [Illness]—*Syn.* infirmity, indisposition, disorder; see **illness** 1.

gripe, *v.* **1.** [(D) To disturb]—*Syn.* annoy, vex, irritate; see **bother** 2, 3.

2. [(D) To complain]—*Syn.* grumble, mutter, fuss; see **complain** 1.

grippe, *n.* —*Syn.* influenza, epidemic catarrh, flu (D); see **disease** 3.

grisly, *mod.* —*Syn.* horrible, terrible, disgusting; see **offensive** 2.

grist, *n.* —*Syn.* seed, meal, milling; see **grain** 1.

gristle, *n.* —*Syn.* ossein, cartilage, osseous matter; see **bone.**

grit, *n.* **1.** [Fine particles]—*Syn.* gravel, sand, abrasive powder, dust, lumps, bits of foreign matter, crushed rock.

2. [Courage]—*Syn.* pluck, resolution, daring; see **courage** 1.

gritty, *mod.* **1.** [Containing grit]—*Syn.* rough, abrasive, sandy, rasping, lumpy, calculous, gravelly, muddy, dusty, powdery, pulverent, granular, friable, branny, floury, crumbly, permeable, porous, sabulous, arenose, loose, raspy, scratchy.

2. [Brave]—*Syn.* plucky, determined, resolute; see **brave** 1.

grizzled, *mod.* —*Syn.* silvery, grizzly, leaden; see **gray** 1, **old** 1, 2.

grizzly, *mod.* —*Syn.* grizzled, graying, hoary; see **gray** 1.

groan, *n.* —*Syn.* moan, sob, grunt; see **cry** 1.

groan, *v.* —*Syn.* moan, murmur, keen; see **cry** 1.

grocer, *n.* —*Syn.* greengrocer, food merchant, operator of a market, chain store manager, prune peddler (D).

groceries, *n.* —*Syn.* food, edibles, produce, comestibles, foodstuffs, perishables, vegetables, viands, staples, green groceries, produce, fruits, dairy products, processed foods, frozen foods, freeze-dried foods, dried *or* desiccated foods, packaged foods, canned foods.

grocery, *n.* —*Syn.* food store, vegetable market, corner store; see **market** 1.

groggy, *mod.* —*Syn.* drunken, dizzy, reeling; see **tired.**

groin, *n.* —*Syn.* crotch, *inguen, inguina* (both Latin), intersection of thighs and abdomen, joint (D).

groom, *n.* **1.** [A male servant]—*Syn.* hostler, stable boy, equerry; see **servant.**

2. [A man being married]—*Syn.* bridegroom, benedict, married man, successful suitor.

groom, *v.* —*Syn.* make presentable *or* attractive *or* acceptable, rub down, remove crudity, refine, get into being, comb, brush, ready, tidy, refresh, curry; *all* (D): spruce up, pretty up, slick up; see also **prepare** 1.

groove, *n.* —*Syn.* channel, trench, gouge, depression, score, scratch, canal, valley, notch, furrow, crimp, rut, incision, slit, scallop, chamfer, gutter, fluting, corrugation, corduroy, pucker, ditch, crease, crimp, vallecula.

in the groove (D)—*Syn.* efficient, skillful, operative; see **working.**

grope, *v.* —*Syn.* fumble, touch, feel blindly; see **feel** 1.

gross, *mod.* **1.** [Fat]—*Syn.* corpulent, obese, porcine; see **fat** 1.

2. [Obscene]—*Syn.* foul, swinish, indecent; see **lewd** 1, 2.

3. [Coarse]—*Syn.* corporeal, low, fleshly; see **rude** 1, 2.

4. [Without deduction]—*Syn.* in sum, total, entire; see **whole** 1.

gross, *n.* —*Syn.* total, aggregate, sum total, total amount; see **whole.**

gross, *v.* —*Syn.* earn, bring in, take in; see **earn** 2.

grotesque, *mod.* **1.** [Ludicrously incongruous] —*Syn.* odd, abnormal, queer; see **unusual** 2.
2. [Incongruous in form]—*Syn.* malformed, ugly, distorted; see **deformed.**
3. [Deliberately incongruous for artistic purposes] —*Syn.* fantastic, surrealistic, dadaist; see **artistic** 2.

grotto, *n.* —*Syn.* cavern, cave, hollow; see **hole** 3.

grouch (D), *n.* —*Syn.* complainer, grumbler, growler; *all* (D): bear, sourpuss, sorehead, crab, crank, griper, bellyacher, grouser, kicker.

grouch (D), *v.* —*Syn.* mutter, grumble, gripe (D); see **complain** 1.

grouchy, *mod.* —*Syn.* surly, ill-tempered, crusty; see **irritable.**

ground, *n.* **1.** [Soil]—*Syn.* sand, dirt, soil; see **earth** 2.
2. [An area]—*Syn.* spot, terrain, territory; see **area** 2.
break ground—*Syn.* start, initiate, commence; see **begin** 1.
cover ground—*Syn.* move, go on, progress; see **advance** 1.
cut the ground from under one (*or* **one's feet**) (D) —*Syn.* deprive, prove wrong, talk down; see **defeat** 1.
from the ground up—*Syn.* thoroughly, wholly, entirely; see **completely.**
gain ground—*Syn.* move, go on, progress; see **advance** 1.
get off the ground (D)—*Syn.* start, commence, come into being; see **begin** 2.
give ground—*Syn.* withdraw, yield, retire; see **retreat** 1.
hold (*or* **stand**) **one's ground**—*Syn.* maintain one's position, defend, sustain; see **endure** 2.
lose ground—*Syn.* withdraw, fall behind, drop back; see **lag** 1.
on delicate ground—*Syn.* in a sensitive position, unsteady, insecure; see **weak** 3, 6.
on firm ground—*Syn.* reliable, secure, supported; see **safe** 1.
on one's own ground (D)—*Syn.* comfortable in, capable, proficient; see **able** 1, 2.
run into the ground (D)—*Syn.* exaggerate, do too much, press; see **overdo** 1.
suit (right) down to the ground (D)—*Syn.* suit, be suitable *or* appropriate for, fulfill; see **fit** 1, 2.

ground, *v.* **1.** [To bring to the ground]—*Syn.* floor, bring down, prostrate; see **fell.**
2. [To restrict]—*Syn.* cause to remain on the ground, bar from flying, take wings away, prevent from driving (D); see also **restrict** 2.
3. [To instruct in essentials]—*Syn.* train, indoctrinate, educate; see **teach** 1.

ground hog, *n.* —*Syn.* woodchuck, chuck, rockchuck, marmot, rodent, aardvark, *wejak* (American Indian), woodshock (D).

groundless, *mod.* —*Syn.* causeless, baseless, unfounded.; see **illogical.**

grounds, *n.* **1.** [Real estate]—*Syn.* lot, environs, territory; see **property** 2.
2. [Basis]—*Syn.* reasons, arguments, proof; see **basis** 1.
3. [Sediment]—*Syn.* dregs, lees, leavings; see **residue.**

groundwork, *n.* —*Syn.* background, base, origin; see **basis** 1, **foundation** 2.

group, *mod.* —*Syn.* family, kindred, tribal, communal, racial; see also **common** 5.

group, *n.* **1.** [A gathering of persons]—*Syn.* assembly, assemblage, crowd; see **gathering.**
2. [Collected things]—*Syn.* accumulation, assortment, combination; see **collection** 2.
3. [An organized body of people]—*Syn.* association, club, society; see **organization** 3.

group, *v.* —*Syn.* file, assort, arrange; see **classify.**

grove, *n.* —*Syn.* woods, stand, spinney; see **forest.**

grovel, *v.* —*Syn.* crawl, cringe (to), fawn (upon), beg, sneak, stoop, kneel, crouch (before), truckle, kowtow (to), implore, today (to), sponge, cower, snivel, beseech, wheedle, blandish, flatter, cater to, humor, pamper, curry favor with, make much of, court, act up to, play up to, beg for mercy, prostrate, reverence; *all* (D): eat humble pie, soft-soap, butter up, make up to, kiss one's feet, lick the dust, dance attendance on, lick another's boots, knuckle under, polish the apple, eat dirt, brown-nose. —*Ant.* hate*, spurn, scorn.

groveling, *mod.* —*Syn.* servile, cringing, fawning; see **docile, humble** 1.

grow, *v.* **1.** [To become larger]—*Syn.* increase, expand (in size), swell, wax, pullulate, thrive, gain, enlarge, swell in substance, augment, advance, dilate, stretch, mount, build, burst forth, spread, burgeon, amplify, germinate, multiply, develop, abound, mature, jump up, flourish, luxuriate, grow up, rise, sprout, shoot *or* start *or* spring up; *all* (D): spread like wildfire, pop up, jump up, branch *or* fill *or* puff out.—*Ant.* lessen*, shrink, wither.
2. [To change slowly]—*Syn.* become, develop, alter, tend, pass, evolve, flower, shift, flow, progress, advance, get, wax, turn into, work up, turn, improve, mellow, age, better, ripen (into), blossom, assume the form of, open out, resolve itself into, mature.—*Ant.* continue*, regress, preserve.
3. [To cultivate]—*Syn.* raise, nurture, tend, nurse, foster, produce, plant, breed, market.—*Ant.* harm*, impede, neglect.
4. [To begin]—*Syn.* originate, start, arise; see **begin** 2.
5. [To become]—*Syn.* develop into, grow to be, change to; see **become** 1.

grower, *n.* —*Syn.* raiser, producer, breeder; see **farmer.**

growing, *mod.* —*Syn.* increasing, ever-widening, crescive, crescent, expanding, budding, germinating, maturing, burgeoning, fructifying, waxing, enlarging, amplifying, swelling, developing, mushrooming, spreading, thriving, flourishing, pullulating, dilating, augmenting, stretching, living, sprouting, cloning, viable, organic, animate, spreading like wildfire (D).—*Ant.* lessening, withering, shrinking.

growl, *n.* **1.** [A low, beastlike sound]—*Syn.* snarl, gnarl, gnarr, moan, bark, bellow, rumble, roar, howl, grumble, grunt.
2. [Speech resembling a growl, sense 1]—*Syn.* grumble, rumble, mumble; see **noise** 1.

growl, *v.* **1.** [To make a low, deep sound]—*Syn.* snarl, gnarr, gnarl; see **grumble** 2.

2. [To speak as if growling]—*Syn.* snarl, grumble, upbraid; see **complain** 1, **scold.**

grown, *mod.* —*Syn.* of age, adult, grown up; see **mature** 1.

grown-up, *n.* —*Syn.* adult, grown man, grown woman, grown person; see **adult.**

growth, *n.* **1.** [The process of growing]—*Syn.* extension, (organic) development, germination; see **increase** 1.

2. [The result of growing]—*Syn.* completion, adulthood, fullness; see **majority** 2, **maturity** 3.

3. [An organic excrescence]—*Syn.* tumor, cancer, swelling, mole, fungus, parasite, outgrowth, button, thickening, fibrousness, fribrous tissue, cancroid, X-ray shadow.

grub, *n.* **1.** [A larva]—*Syn.* entozoon, caterpillar, maggot; see **worm** 1.

2. [(D) Food]—*Syn.* victuals, comestibles, chow (D); see **food.**

grub, *v.* **1.** [To dig]—*Syn.* delve, burrow, excavate; see **dig** 1.

2. [To clear land]—*Syn.* uproot stumps, prepare for the plow, break; see **clean.**

3. [(D) To work laboriously]—*Syn.* moil, toil, drudge; see **work** 1.

grubby, *mod.* —*Syn.* dirty, sloppy, grimy; see **dirty** 1.

grudge, *n.* —*Syn.* spite, rancor, animosity; see **hatred** 1, 2, **malice.**

grudge, *v.* —*Syn.* begrudge, covet, be reluctant; see **envy.**

grueling, *mod.* —*Syn.* exhausting, tiring, fatiguing; see **difficult** 1, 2.

gruesome, *mod.* —*Syn.* grim, grisly, fearful; see **frightful** 1, **offensive** 2.

gruff, *mod.* **1.** [Brusque]—*Syn.* blunt, impolite, crude; see **abrupt** 2, **rude** 2.

2. [Hoarse]—*Syn.* harsh, grating, rough; see **hoarse.**

grumble, *v.* **1.** [To complain]—*Syn.* whine, protest, fuss; see **complain** 1.

2. [To growl]—*Syn.* snarl, gnarl, gnarr, snap, bark, grunt, mutter, rumble, croak, roar, splutter, snuffle, whine.

3. [To mutter]—*Syn.* murmur, mumble, whine; see **mutter** 2.

grumbling, *mod.* —*Syn.* discontented, sour, grouchy; see **irritable.**

grumpy, *mod.* —*Syn.* sullen, grouchy, cantankerous; see **irritable.**

grunt, *v.* —*Syn.* snort, squawk, squeak; see **cry** 3.

guarantee, *v.* **1.** [To certify]—*Syn.* attest, testify, aver, vouch for, declare, assure, answer for, be responsible for, stand behind, become surety for, evince, evidence, endorse, secure, make sure *or* certain, warrant, insure, witness, prove, reassure, support, affirm, confirm, cross one's heart (D).

2. [To give security]—*Syn.* pledge, give bond, go bail, wager, stake, give a guarantee, stand good for, mortgage, pawn, back, sign for.

3. [To promise]—*Syn.* swear, assure, insure; see **promise** 1.

guaranteed, *mod.* —*Syn.* warranted, certified, bonded, secured, endorsed, insured, pledged, plighted, confirmed, assured, ascertained, approved, attested, sealed, certificated, protected, on ice, affirmed, sure-fire (D).—*Ant.* unsupported, anonymous*, unendorsed.

guarantor, *n.* —*Syn.* bailsman, underwriter, patron; see **sponsor.**

guaranty, *n.* **1.** [Assurance]—*Syn.* pledge, attestation, certification; see **promise** 1.

2. [A document giving assurance]—*Syn.* warrant, warranty, bond, contract, recognizance, certificate, charter, testament, security.

guard, *n.* —*Syn.* sentry, sentinel, protector; see **watchman.**

off one's guard—*Syn.* unaware, unprotected, defenseless; see **unprepared.**

on one's guard—*Syn.* alert, mindful, vigilant; see **watchful.**

guard, *v.* **1.** [To protect]—*Syn.* secure, shield, safeguard; see **defend** 1, 2.

2. [To watch over]—*Syn.* watch, observe, superintend, stand sentinel, patrol, picket, police, look out *or* after, see after, supervise, tend, keep in view, keep an eye on, keep under surveillance, attend, overlook, keep a prisoner, hold in custody, stand over, babysit, care for, keep vigil, look *or* see to, chaperone, shepherd, oversee; *all* (D): keep a weather eye, ride herd on, keep tab(s) (on), be a father to.—*Ant.* disregard, neglect*, forsake.

guarded, *mod.* **1.** [Protected]—*Syn.* safeguarded, secured, defended; see **safe** 1.

2. [Cautious]—*Syn.* circumspect, attentive, overcautious; see **careful.**

guardian, *n.* **1.** [One who regulates or protects]—*Syn.* overseer, safeguard, curator, guard, vigilante, protector, conservator, preserver, trustee, custodian, keeper, patrol, warden, defender, paladin, member of a vigilance committee, supervisor, babysitter, sponsor, superintendent, sentinal, member of the Watch and Ward (D).

2. [A foster parent]—*Syn.* adoptive parent, foster mother, foster father, nurse, protector, custodian.

guardsman, *n.* —*Syn.* sentry, patrol, guard; see **watchman.**

guerrilla, *mod.* —*Syn.* auxiliary, independent, predatory; see **fighting.**

guerrilla, *n.* —*Syn.* irregular soldier, saboteur, independent; see **soldier.**

guess, *n.* —*Syn.* conjecture, surmise, supposition, theory, hypothesis, presupposition, presumption, opinion, postulate, estimate, divination, association of ideas, surmisal, suspicion, thesis, guesswork, view, belief, assumption, speculation, supposal, postulation, fancy, inference, conclusion, deduction, induction; *both* (D): guesstimate, shot in the dark.

guess, *v.* **1.** [To attempt an answer on inadequate evidence]—*Syn.* conjecture, presume, infer, suspect, speculate, imagine, surmise, theorize, opine, hypothesize, predicate, hazard a supposition *or* conjecture, suggest, figure, incline to a view, divine, reckon, calculate.

2. [To make a choice, almost at hazard]—*Syn.* chance, take a leap in the dark, light on, venture, suppose, presume, imagine, think likely, jump at a conclusion; *all* (D): guess maybe, make a stab at, lump it, have a shot at, hazard a guess.

3. [To choose rightly on little or no evidence]—*Syn.* pick, select, happen upon; see **choose** 1.

guess at, *v.* —*Syn.* reckon, calculate, survey; see **estimate** 1, 2, 3.

guessing, *n.* —*Syn.* guesswork, supposition, imagination, fancy, inference, deduction, presumption, predisposition, reckoning, surmise, theorizing, taking for granted, positing, postulating, assuming, presuming, opinion, going by dead reckoning; *both* (D): leaping to conclusions, going by guess and by God.

guest, *n.* **1.** [One to whom hospitality is extended] —*Syn.* visitor, caller, house guest, dinner guest, luncheon guest, etc.; visitant, company, partaker of hospitality, sharer, recipient of one's bounty, inmate, confidant *or* confidante, fellow, messmate, boon companion, bedfellow.

2. [One who is received for pay]—*Syn.* tenant, boarder, patron, customer, paying guest, roomer, habitué, sojourner, frequenter, lodger, renter.

guffaw, *n.* —*Syn.* roar, cachinnation, horselaugh; see **laugh, laughter.**

guidance, *n.* —*Syn.* direction, leadership, supervision; see **administration** 1.

guide, *n.* **1.** [One who guides others]—*Syn.* pilot, captain, pathfinder, scout, escort, cicerone, convoy, courier, director, exhibitor, vanguard, discoverer, explorer, lead, modernist, guru, conductor, usher, docent, pioneer, leader, superintendent, chaperone.

2. [A model]—*Syn.* pattern, design, example; see **model** 2.

guide, *v.* **1.** [Direct]—*Syn.* supervise, oversee, control; see **manage** 1.

2. [To lead]—*Syn.* conduct, escort, show the way; see **lead** 1.

guidebook, *n.* —*Syn.* guide, chart, manual; see **handbook.**

guild, *n.* —*Syn.* profession, society, trade; see **organization** 3.

guile, *n.* —*Syn.* craft, cunning, duplicity; see **dishonesty.**

guileless, *mod.* —*Syn.* honest, frank, sincere; see **naïve.**

guilt, *n.* —*Syn.* culpability, blame, error, fault, lapse, slip, crime, sin, offence, answerability, liability, misstep, solecism, criminality, blameworthiness, sinfulness, misconduct, dereliction, misbehavior, malpractice, peccability, frailty, delinquency, transgression, dereliction, indiscretion, weakness, failing, malefaction, malfeasance, felonious conduct.—*Ant.* innocence*, freedom from fault, blamelessness.

guiltless, *mod.* —*Syn.* harmless, above suspicion, free; see **innocent** 1.

guilty, *mod.* **1.** [Convicted]—*Syn.* found guilty, guilty as charged, condemned, sentenced, criminal, censured, impeached, incriminated, indicted, liable, condemned, proscribed, having violated law, weighed and found wanting, judged, damned, doomed, cast into outer darkness.—*Ant.* cleared, vindicated, absolved.

2. [Culpable]—*Syn.* in *or* at fault, sinful, on one's head, to blame, in the wrong, in error, accusable, censurable, wrong, blameworthy, blameable, reproachable, derelict, chargeable, indictable, convictable, looking like the cat that swallowed the canary (D).—*Ant.* blameless, innocent*, right.

3. [Wicked]—*Syn.* evil, depraved, licentious; see **wicked** 1.

guise, *n.* —*Syn.* form, mien, mode; see **appearance** 1.

gulch, *n.* —*Syn.* gully, ditch, gorge; see **ravine.**

gulf, *n.* **1.** [Chasm]—*Syn.* abyss, abysm, depth; see **ravine.**

2. [An arm of the sea]—*Syn.* inlet, sound, cove; see **bay.**

3. [A vast interval]—*Syn.* distance, hiatus, interregnum; see **expanse.**

gull, *n.* —*Syn.* sucker, dope, puppet; see **fool** 2.

gullet, *n.* —*Syn.* neck, gorge, maw; see **throat.**

gullible, *mod.* —*Syn.* innocent, trustful, simple; see **naïve.**

gully, *n.* —*Syn.* ditch, chasm, crevasse; see **ravine.**

gulp, *v.* —*Syn.* pour, swill, bolt, take in one draught, swig, choke down, toss off (D); see also **swallow.**

gum, *n.* —*Syn.* resin, glue, pitch, tar, pine tar, cohesive substance, rosin, amber, wax.

Commercial gums include the following—chewing gum, sealing wax, rosin, mucilage, caoutchouc, crude rubber, chicle, latex, gum arabic, wattle gum, Kordofan, British gum, cherry-gum, Sonora gum, gutta-percha, sweet gum, mesquite gum, gum maguey, gum ledon.

Varieties and flavors of chewing gum include the following—bubble gum, spearmint, peppermint, wintergreen, teaberry, licorice, charcoal, synthetic fruit, pepsin.

gummy, *mod.* —*Syn.* sticky, cohesive, viscid; see **adhesive.**

gumption (D), *n.* —*Syn.* shrewdness, sagacity, initiative; see **acument, industry** 1.

gun, *n.* **1.** [A cannon]—*Syn.* piece, ordnance, heavy ordnance, rifle.

Types of cannon include the following—long gun, siege gun, coast defense gun, howitzer, mortar, mobile tank gun, antitank gun, culvern, field piece, rifled cannon, 240 millimeter trench mortar, 155 millimeter howitzer, 170 millimeter field gun, 105 millimeter antiaircraft gun, ack ack (D); see **artillery** 1, **cannon, rocket.**

2. [A portable firearm]—Types include the following—rifle, automatic rifle, repeating rifle, repeater (D), recoilless rifle, air rifle, air gun, shotgun, double-barreled shotgun, magazine shotgun, pump gun (D), fowling piece, musket, flintlock, wheel lock, hand gun, muzzle-loader, breech-loader, squirrel gun, needle gun, blunderbuss, carbine, machine pistol, long rifle, space gun, laser gun, matchlock, revolver, pistol, horse pistol; *all* (D): gat, persuader, rod, burp gun, Saturday night special, zip gun; see also **machine gun, pistol.**

3. [A device suggestive of a gun]—*Syn.* spray gun, air brush, grease gun, atomizer, syringe.

give it the gun (D)—*Syn.* quicken, stimulate, accelerate; see **hasten** 2.

go great guns (D)—*Syn.* do well, succeed, triumph; see **prosper.**

jump the gun (D)—*Syn.* start too soon, act inappropriately, give oneself away; see **begin** 1, **hurry** 1.

stick to one's guns—*Syn.* maintain one's position, defend, sustain; see **endure** 2.

gunfire, *n.* —*Syn.* cannonading, bombardment, fire to pin down (someone), artillery support, air support, air strike, mortar fire, heavy arms attack, explosion, shooting, shot, report, artillery, shellburst, volley, discharge, enfilade, detonation, blast, firing, burst, thunder, crackle, barrage, creeping barrage, curtain, curtain of fire, cannonade, box of fire, salvo, fire power, superiority of fire.

gunman, *n.* —*Syn.* killer, thug, gangster; see **criminal.**

gunner, *n.* —*Syn.* machine gunner, mortar man *or* specialist, rocket man *or* rocketeer, missile man *or* launcher, bazooka carrier *or* launcher, sniper, sharpshooter, BAR man, rifleman, aerial gunner, artilleryman, cannoneer; *both* (D): body snatcher, Archie.

gunpowder, *n.* —*Syn.* black powder, high explosive, smokeless powder; see **explosive.**

gurgle, *v.* —*Syn.* ripple, murmur, purl; see **flow** 1.

gush, *n.* —*Syn.* jet, spray, spout; see **fountain** 2.

gush, *v.* **1.** [To spout]—*Syn.* pour, well, spew; see **flow** 2.

2. [To emit copiously]—*Syn.* pour fourth, flood, surge; see **flow** 1.

3. [(D) To act or speak effusively]—*Syn.* prate, prattle, gloze; see **babble.**

gushing, *mod.* **1.** [Flowing]—*Syn.* spouting, pouring out, emitting; see **flowing.**

2. [(D) Sentimental]—*Syn.* enthusiastic, blubbery, mushy (D); see **sentimental.**

gust, *n.* —*Syn.* blast, blow, breeze; see **wind** 1.

gusto, *n.* —*Syn.* zeal, fervor, ardor; see **enthusiasm** 1.

gusty, *mod.* —*Syn.* breezy, hearty, robust; see **windy** 1.

gut, *n.* —*Syn.* small intestine, large intestine, duodenum; see **abdomen.**

guts, *n.* **1.** [(D) Bowels]—*Syn.* viscera, insides, belly; see **abdomen.**

2. [(D) Fortitude]—*Syn.* pluck, hardihood, effrontery; see **courage** 1.

hate someone's guts (D)—*Syn.* detest, dislike, despise; see **hate** 1.

gutter, *n.* **1.** [A ditch]—*Syn.* canal, runnel, gully, sewer, watercourse, channel, dike, drain, moat, fosse, trough; see also **trench** 1.

2. [A drain for a roof]—*Syn.* eaves trough, rainspout, rain pipe, eavespout, gargoyle, eaves, conduit, cistern pipe, funnel.

guttural, *mod.* —*Syn.* throaty, hoarse, gruff, rough, grating, harsh, rasping, glottal, deep, sepulchral, growling, thick, inarticulate.—*Ant.* high-pitched, shrill, nasal.

guy, *n.* **1.** [Lateral tensile support]—*Syn.* cable, truss, sling, hawser, guy wire, guy rope, tent rope, tackle, cinch, bond, line, stay, painter, chain, tie, thong, bowline, strap, lanyard, brace, tendon, vinculum, copula.

2. [(D) Fellow]—*Syn.* chap, lad, person; see **fellow** 1.

guzzle, *v.* —*Syn.* swill, quaff, swig; see **drink** 1.

gymnasium, *n.* —*Syn.* health *or* recreation center, playing floor, exercise room, sports center, athletic department, *Turnverein* (German), field house, court, athletic club, arena, coliseum, theater, circus, stadium, ring, rink, pit, amphitheater, course, platform, floor, hippodrome, canvas, alley, garden, gallery, gym (D).

gymnast, *n.* —*Syn.* acrobat, tumbler, jumper; see **athlete.**

gymnastics, *n.* —*Syn.* trapeze performance, health exercises, acrobatics, aerobatics, therapeutics, body-building exercises, tumbling, vaulting, free exercise, floor exercise, dancercise, Jazzercise (trademark), work on the rings, bars, balance beam, horizontal bars, horse, etc.; slimnastics (D).

gyp, *n.* —*Syn.* cheat, fraud, trick; see **fake, trick** 1.

gyp, *v.* —*Syn.* cheat, defraud, swindle; see **deceive.**

gypsy, *n.* **1.** [A dark-skinned vagrant]—*Syn.* Egyptian, Caucasian, *Rom* (Gypsy), *Bohémien* (French), *Zingaro* (Italian), *Gitano* (Spanish).

2. [One who lives a roving life]—*Syn.* tramp, Bohemian, vagrant; see **traveler.**

gyrate, *v.* —*Syn.* spin, rotate, revolve; see **whirl.**

gyro, *n.* —*Syn.* gyrator, whirligig, spinner, gyroscope, gyroscopic control, gyrostat, gyroscopic governor.

H

habit, *n.* **1.** [Tendency to repeated action]—*Syn.* disposition, way, fashion, manner, propensity, bent, turn, gravitation, proclivity, inclination, addiction, impulsion, predisposition, susceptibility, weakness, bias, proneness, fixed attitude, persuasion, second nature, penchant; see also **attitude** 3, **inclination** 1.
2. [A customary action]—*Syn.* mode, practice, rule; see **custom** 1.
3. [An obsession]—*Syn.* addiction, fixation, hang-up (D); see **obsession.**
4. [Dress]—*Syn.* costume, riding costume, habiliment; see **clothes, dress** 1.
habitable, *mod.*—*Syn.* inhabitable, fit for habitation, livable; see **comfortable** 2.
habitat, *n.*—*Syn.* locality, territory, (natural) surroundings; see **environment, home** 1, **position** 1.
habitation, *n.*—*Syn.* abode, dwelling, occupancy; see **home** 1.
habitual, *mod.* **1.** [Of the nature of a habit]—*Syn.* ingrained, confirmed, frequent, periodic, continual, routine, mechanical, automatic, perfunctory, seasoned, iterated, permanent, perpetual, fixed, rooted, inveterate, systematic, recurrent, periodical, methodical, repeated, iterative, reiterative, disciplined, practiced, accustomed, established, set, repetitious, cyclic, reiterated, settled, trite, stereotyped, formal, addicted, acting by force of habit, being such by habit, in a groove *or* rut (D); see also **chronic, constant** 1, **regular** 3.—*Ant.* different*, exceptional, departing.
2. [Usual]—*Syn.* customary, accustomed, normal; see **common** 1, **conventional** 1.
habitué, *n.*—*Syn.* devotee, customer, patron; see **client, frequenter.**
hack, *n.* **1.** [A literary drudge]—*Syn.* scribbler, pulp-story writer, ghost writer, propaganda writer, inferior writer, writer of potboilers, free-lance writer, commercial writer, popular novelist; *all* (D): ghost, free lance, tenth rater, penny-a-liner; see also **writer.**—*Ant.* artist*, literary master, literary genius.
2. [A coach for hire]—*Syn.* hackney, hackney-coach, taxicab; see **carriage** 2, **vehicle** 1.
3. [A cut]—*Syn.* notch, nick, cleavage; see **cut** 2.
4. [A horse for hire]—*Syn.* nag, hackney, crowbait (D); see **horse** 1.
5. [(D) Commercial driver, especially of a taxicab]—*Syn.* taxi *or* cab driver, chauffeur, cabbie (D); see **driver.**
hack, *v.*—*Syn.* chop, whack, mangle; see **cut** 1.
hackle, *n.*—*Syn.* plumage, mantle, feathers; see **feather.**
hackles, *n.*—*Syn.* temper, dander, passion; see **anger.**
hackneyed, *mod.*—*Syn.* worn-out, old, trite; see **common** 1, **dull** 4.
hag, *n.*—*Syn.* old woman, crone, virago, vixen, withered old woman, shrew, ogress, hellhag, hellcat, grandmother, fishwife, gorgon, harridan, old witch, Xanthippe, Medusa; *both* (D): battle-ax, old cat; see also **witch, woman** 1.
haggard, *mod.*—*Syn.* gaunt, careworn, fretted; see **thin** 2, **weak** 1.
haggle, *v.* **1.** [To bargain]—*Syn.* deal, wrangle, argue; see **buy** 1, **sell** 1.
2. [To mangle]—*Syn.* whack, hack, chop; see **cut** 1.
hail, *n.*—*Syn.* hailstorm, sleet, icy particles, ice; see also **rain** 1.
hail, *v.* **1.** [To salute]—*Syn.* cheer, welcome, honor; see **greet.**
2. [To call to]—*Syn.* signal, address, speak to; see **summon** 1.
3. [To praise]—*Syn.* applaud, recognize, acclaim; see **praise** 1.
hail from (D), *v.*—*Syn.* come from, be born in, be a native of, claim origin in, claim as one's birthplace, originate; see also **begin** 2.
hair, *n.* **1.** [Threadlike growth]—*Syn.* locks, wig, moustache, whiskers, eyebrow, eyelash, thatch, sideburn, down, tress, wool, shock, mane, filament, fluff; see also **beard, fur.**
2. [One threadlike growth]—*Syn.* cilium, bristle, vibrissa, striga, villus; see also **fiber** 1, **thread.**
3. [Anything suggesting the thickness of a hair]—*Syn.* a hairbreadth, a narrow margin, hair trigger, hairspring, splinter, shaving, sliver; see also **bit** 3.
get in one's hair (D)—*Syn.* irritate, annoy, disturb; see **bother** 2.
have by the short hairs (D)—*Syn.* have at one's mercy, victimize, have over a barrel; (D); see **defeat** 1.
let one's hair down (D)—*Syn.* be informal, have fun, let oneself go; see **relax** 1.
make one's hair stand on end—*Syn.* terrify, scare, horrify; see **frighten** 1.
split hairs—*Syn.* quibble, cavil, nag; see **fight** 1.
to a hair—*Syn.* precisely, perfectly, right in every detail; see **exactly.**
hairbreadth, *mod.*—*Syn.* hazardous, narrow, close; see **dangerous** 1, **unsafe.**
hairbreadth, *n.*—*Syn.* (small) margin, fraction, job; see **bit** 3, **hair** 3.
haircut, *n.*—*Syn.* trim, trimming, shingling, bob, crew cut, page boy, pompadour, feather cut, bangs, convict cut, GI haircut, butch, D.A. *or* D.T. (D); see also **hairstyle.**

hair-do, *n.* —*Syn.* coiffure, hairdressing, do (D); see **haircut, hair style.**

hairdresser, *n.* —*Syn.* beauty culturist, beautician, beauty specialist; see **barber.**

hairiness, *n.* —*Syn.* shagginess, downiness, pubescence, pilosity, hispidity, crinosity, bristliness, hirsuteness, furriness, fluffiness.

hairless, *n.* —*Syn.* glabrescent, glabrous, shorn, tonsured, whiskerless, clean-shaven, beardless, shaven, smooth-faced; see also **bald** 1, **smooth** 3.—*Ant.* hairy*, shaggy, bearded.

hairpin, *n.* —*Syn.* hair fastener, pin, bobby pin, clasp, hair clip, barette; see also **fastener.**

hairsplitting, *mod.* —*Syn.* unimportant, minute, subtle; see **trivial, irrelevant, unimportant.**

hair style, *n.* —*Syn.* hair-do, coiffure, haircut, bob, headress; see also **haircut.**

Some of the common types of hair styles include the following—crew cut, butch, flat-top, Beatle, Prince Valiant, Yul Brynner, bubble, page boy, bouffant, flip, pigtails, French roll, bun, ponytail, braid, chignon, Afro, dreadlocks.

hairy, *mod.* **1.** [Bushy]—*Syn.* bristly, shaggy, wooly, unshorn, downy, fleecy, whiskered, pileous, pubescent, setaceous, tufted, unshaven, bearded, bewhiskered, furry, fuzzy, hirsute, pilose, flocculent, nappy, lanate, tufted, piliferous, ulotrichous, comose, strigose, fluffy, villous, crinite.—*Ant.* hairless*, bald, smooth.

2. [(D) Dangerous]—*Syn.* hazardous, difficult, perilous; see **dangerous** 1, **uncertain** 2.

hale, *mod.* —*Syn.* sound, robust, vigorous; see **healthy** 1, **strong** 1.

half, *mod.* —*Syn.* partly, partial, divided by two, equally distributed in halves, mixed, divided, halved, bisected; see also **halfway, two.**—*Ant.* all, full*, filled.

by half—*Syn.* considerably, many, very much; see **much** 1, 2.

in half—*Syn.* into halves, split, divided; see **half.**

not the half of it—*Syn.* not all of it, partial, incomplete; see **unfinished** 1.

halfback, *n.* —*Syn.* right halfback, left halfback, back; see **football player.**

half-baked, *mod.* —*Syn.* senseless, brainless, indiscreet; see **stupid** 1.

half-breed, *mod.* —*Syn.* half-blooded, crossed, half-caste, mestizo, crossbred; see also **hybrid, outcast.**

half-brother, *n.* —*Syn.* sibling, kin, brother by one parent; see **brother** 1, **relative.**

half dollar, *n.* —*Syn.* fifty cents, fifty-cent piece; *all* (D): silver half, four bits, turkey, fifty-center; see also **money** 1.

halfhearted, *mod.* —*Syn.* lukewarm, impassive, irresolute; see **indifferent** 1.

half measure, *n.* —*Syn.* partial action, halfhearted enthusiasm, apathy; see **indifference** 1.

half sister, *n.* —*Syn.* kin, stepsister, sister by one parent; see **sister, relative.**

halfway, *mod.* —*Syn.* midway, half the distance, in the middle, incomplete, unsatisfactory, compromising, conciliatory, partially, fairly, medially, in the midst, imperfectly, in part, partly, nearly, pretty, insufficiently, to a degree, to some extent, restrictedly, comparatively, rather with divided effort, moderately, by *or* in half measures, mediumly, to *or* at half the distance, in some measure, in *or* within the mean, middling (D); see also **half.** —*Ant.* wholly, completely*, entirely.

halfway house, *n.* —*Syn.* midpoint, country place, intermediate point; see **hotel, restaurant.**

half-wit, *n.* —*Syn.* imbecile, simpleton, idiot; see **fool** 1.

half-witted, *mod.* —*Syn.* moronic, imbecilic, mentally deficient; see **ignorant** 2, **stupid** 1.

half-yearly, *mod.* —*Syn.* semestral, semi-annual, twice a year; see **biannual.**

hall, *n.* **1.** [A large public or semi-public building or room]—*Syn.* legislative chamber, assembly (room), meeting place, banquet hall, town hall, concert hall, dance hall, music hall, arena, ballroom, clubroom, church, lyceum, exchange, drawing room, salon, refectory, lounge, bourse, chamber, mart, stateroom, gymnasium, dining hall, armory, amphitheater, *sala* (Spanish), rotunda, council chamber, reception room, waiting room, lecture room, gallery, casino; *both* (D): gym, mess hall; see also **auditorium, building** 1, **room** 2, **theater** 1.

2. [An entrance way]—*Syn.* vestibule, passage, lobby, foyer, gallery, anteroom, propylaeum, corridor, hallway, pass, entry; see also **entrance** 2, **room** 2.

3. [Rural seat of a titled person]—*Syn.* manor, manor house, country estate; see **castle, estate** 1.

hallelujah, *interj.* —*Syn.* praise God, praise the Lord, *Deo gratias* (Latin), praise ye the Lord, hosanna, alleluia, praise ye Jehovah, glory be, praise be, huzza, lift up your hearts, heaven be praised, thanks be to God, thank God, glory be to God in the highest, bless the Lord, thank heaven, hurray (D).

hallmark, *n.* —*Syn.* certification, mark *or* indication of excellence *or* genuineness *or* quality, device, endorsement, symbol, sign, sigil, authentication, signet, seal (of approval), stamp showing conformity to standards, mark of acceptance, ratification; see also **emblem, trademark.**

hallow, *v.* —*Syn.* consecrate, sanctify, beatify; see **bless** 3, **praise** 1.

hallowed, *mod.* —*Syn.* sacred, sacrosanct, consecrated; see **divine** 2.

Halloween, *n.* —*Syn.* All Hallows *or* Saints Evening *or* Even *or* E'en, (Feast of) All Saints, Hallowmas; see **autumn, holiday** 1.

hallucinate, *v.* —*Syn.* fantasize, have visions, visualize; see **dream** 1, **illusion** 1.

hallucination, *n.* —*Syn.* phantasm, mirage, delusion; see **dream** 1, **illusion** 1.

hallucinogen, *n.* —*Syn.* psychedelic *or* mind-expanding drug, stimulant; see **drug** 2.

hallway, *n.* —*Syn.* foyer, entrance way, corridor; see **entrance, hall** 2.

halo, *n.* —*Syn.* corona, aurora, crown of light, radiance, nimbus; see also **light** 1.

halt, *v.* **1.** [To cease]—*Syn.* stand still, pause, rest; see **stop** 1.

2. [To cause to cease]—*Syn.* pull up, check, terminate, suspend, put an end to, interrupt, intermit, break into, punctuate, block, cut short, bar someone's way, cut into, adjourn, hold off, cease fire, keep at arm's length, hold at bay, stop an advance, cause to halt, stem, balk, deter, stay, bring to a stand *or* standstill, stall, bring to an end, curb, stop, restrict, arrest, hold (in check), foil, defeat, thwart, hamper, frustrate, suppress, clog, abate, intercept, extinguish, blockade, obstruct, repress, inhibit, hinder, barricade, impede, undermine, constrain, preclude, overthrow, vanquish, disconcert, override, dam, forbid the banns, upset, stand in the way of, baffle, discountenance, confound, debar, contravene, overturn, reduce, counteract, worst, quell, outwit, prohibit, rout, outdo, put down, quash, subdue, discomfit, finish, forbid, oppose, crush, disallow; *all* (D): spike one's guns, scotch, choke off, nip in the bud, lay by the heels, shut down on, break (it) up, freeze, put on the brakes, hang fire, ring down on, hold on, steal one's thunder, throw a wet blanket on, throw a (monkey) wrench in the works, clip one's wings, tie one's hands, faze, dash the cup from one's lips, cut the ground from under one, hang like a millstone round one's neck, scotch the wheel, take the wind out of one's sails, squelch; see also **end** 1, **prevent, restrain** 1.—*Ant.* begin*, start, instigate.

halter, *n.* —*Syn.* noose, tie, strap, holder, leash, bridle, headstall, hackamore, rein; see also **bit** 4, **rope.**

halting, *mod.* —*Syn.* hesitant, uncertain, indecisive; see **doubtful** 2, **slow** 2.

halve, *v.* —*Syn.* split, bisect, cut in two; see **divide** 1.

ham, *n.* **1.** [Smoked pork thigh]—*Syn.* rump, gammon, sugar-cured ham, whole ham, half ham, butt, shank, York ham, Brandenburg ham, Virginia ham, Smithfield ham, Canadian bacon, peach-fed ham, picnic ham; see also **meat, pork.**

2. [The thigh of an animal]—*Syn.* buttocks, hind part, hind leg, rear, back part, hind quarter; see also **thigh.**

3. [(D) An incompetent actor]—*Syn.* failure, inferior player, nonprofessional; *all* (D): palooka, Johnny Sap, ham actor, hamateur; see also **amateur.**

hamburger, *n.* —*Syn.* chopped beefsteak, minute steak, Salisbury steak, ground round, ground chuck, ground beef; *both* (D): burger, wimpy; see also **beef** 1, **meat.**

hamlet, *n.* —*Syn.* villa, settlement, pueblo; see **village.**

hammer, *n.* —*Syn.* maul, mallet, mace, club, gavel, sledge, peen, rammer, ram, flatter; *all* (D): nailer, slug, knocker; see also **stick.**

Hammers include the following—claw, boilermaker's, bricklayer's, blacksmith's, machinist's, riveting, stone *or* spalling, prospecting, cross-peen, ball-peen, Exeter, joiner's, Canterbury claw, sealing, raising, welding, rawhide-laced, veneering, blocking, die, Nasmyth, set, double, dental, tilt hammer, steam hammer, triphammer, jackhammer.

hammer, *v.* —*Syn.* strike, whack, bang, bear down upon, pound (away at); see also **beat** 2, **hit** 1.

hammer and tongs, *mod.* —*Syn.* hard, as hard as possible, mightily; see **fiercely.**

hammer away, *v.* —*Syn.* try hard *or* repeatedly, continue, endeavour; see **hit** 1, **try** 1.

hammer out, *v.* —*Syn.* work out, fight through, get settled; see **decide.**

hammock, *n.* —*Syn.* (porch) swing, swinging couch, hanging bed, bunk, sailor's bed; see also **bed** 1.

hamper, *n.* —*Syn.* creel, pannier, laundry box; see **basket** 1.

hamper, *v.* —*Syn.* impede, thwart, embarrass; see **hinder.**

hamstring, *v.* —*Syn.* cripple, disable, injure; see **hurt** 1, **weaken** 2.

hand, *n.* **1.** [The termination of the arm]—*Syn.* fingers, palm, grip, grasp, hold, phalanges, metacarpus, knuckles; *all* (D): paw, duke, hook, shaker, grappler, forelift; see also **fist.**

2. [(D) A workman]—*Syn.* helper, worker, hired hand; see **laborer.**

3. [Handwriting]—*Syn.* chirography, script, penmanship; see **handwriting.**

4. [Aid]—*Syn.* help, guidance, instruction; see **aid** 1, **support** 3.

5. [Ability]—*Syn.* control, knack, skill; see **ability** 2.

6. [(D) Applause]—*Syn.* (standing) ovation, thunderous reception, handclapping; see **praise** 2.

7. [Round of cards]—*Syn.* good *or* poor *or* strong, etc., hand; deal, round; see **game** 1.

at first hand—*Syn.* from the original source, directly, originally; see **original** 1.

at hand—*Syn.* immediate, approximate, close by; see **near** 1.

at second hand—*Syn.* by the way, on hearsay, by rumor; see **indirectly.**

at the hand of—*Syn.* done by, responsible for, in charge of; see **by** 2.

by hand—*Syn.* handcrafted, home-made, manual; see **handmade.**

change hands—*Syn.* transfer, pass on, shift; see **give** 1.

eat out of one's hand—be devoted to one, be subordinated, obey; see **serve** 2.

force one's hand—*Syn.* drive, force, pressure; see **press** 1.

from hand to hand—*Syn.* shifted, given over, changed; see **transferred.**

from hand to mouth—*Syn.* from day to day *or* paycheck to paycheck, by necessity, in poverty; see **poor** 1.

hold hands—*Syn.* touch, press, squeeze; see **hold** 1.

in hand—*Syn.* under control, in order, all right; see **managed.**

join hands—*Syn.* unite, associate, agree; see **join** 1.

keep one's hand in—*Syn.* carry on, continue, make a practice of; see **practice** 1.

lay hands on—*Syn.* take, arrest, apprehend; see **seize** 1, 2.

not lift a hand—*Syn.* do nothing, be lazy, not try; see **neglect** 1, 2.

off one's hands—*Syn.* out of one's responsibility, no longer one's concern, not accountable for; see **irresponsible.**

on every hand—*Syn.* on all sides, at all times, all over; see **everywhere.**

on hand—*Syn.* ready, close by, usable; see **available.**

on one's hands—*Syn.* in one's care or responsibility, chargeable to one, accountable to; see **responsible** 1.

on the other hand—otherwise, conversely, from the opposite position; see **opposing** 2.

out of hand—*Syn.* out of control, wild, unmanageable; see **unruly.**

show (*or* **tip**) **one's hand**—disclose, divulge, confess; see **reveal** 1.

take in hand—*Syn.* take control of *or* responsibility for, take over, handle; see **try** 1.
throw up one's hands—*Syn.* give up, resign, quit; see **yield** 1.
to hand—*Syn.* close by, at hand, immediate; see **near** 1.
turn (*or* **put**) **one's hand to**—*Syn.* attempt, endeavor, try one's hand at; see **try** 2.
wash one's hands of—*Syn.* deny, reject, refuse; see **denounce.**
with a heavy hand—*Syn.* oppressive, harsh, coercive; see **cruel** 2, **severe** 2.
with a high hand—*Syn.* arbitrarily, tyrannically, oppressively; see **arrogantly.**
with clean hands—*Syn.* guiltless, blameless, inculpable; see **innocent** 1.

hand, *v.* —*Syn.* deliver, give to, return; see **give** 1.

hand and foot, *mod.* —*Syn.* entirely, fully, absolutely; see **completely.**

hand in glove, *mod.* —*Syn.* allied, working together, (closely) associated; see **together** 2, **united** 1.

hand around, *v.* —*Syn.* hand out, pass out *or* around, allot; see **distribute** 1, **give** 1.

handbag, *n.* —*Syn.* lady's pocketbook, bag, clutch purse; see **purse.**

handbill, *n.* —*Syn.* leaflet, flyer, throwaway; see **announcement** 2, **pamphlet.**

handbook, *n.* —*Syn.* textbook, directory, guidebook, basic text, instruction book, book of fundamentals, enchiridion; see also **book** 1, **manual, text** 1.

handcart, *n.* —*Syn.* wheelbarrow, pushcart, tumbrel; see **cart, vehicle** 1, **wagon.**

handcuffs, *n.* —*Syn.* manacles, fetters, shackles, iron rings; *all* (D): bracelets, wristlets, cuffs, clamps, braces, snaps; see also **chains.**

hand down, *v.* —*Syn.* pass on, bequeath, grant; see **give** 1.

handed, *mod.* —*Syn.* given to, conveyed, bestowed; see **given.**

handful, *n.* —*Syn.* a small quantity, some, a sprinkling; see **few.**

handicap, *n.* **1.** [A disadvantage]—*Syn.* hindrance, obstacle, block; see **impediment** 1.
2. [A physical injury]—*Syn.* impairment, affliction, chronic disorder; see **impediment** 2, **injury** 1.
3. [Advantage]—*Syn.* favor, upper hand, additional points; see **advantage** 1.

handicapped, *mod.* —*Syn.* thwarted, crippled, disabled, physically challenged, impeded, burdened, hampered, obstructed, encumbered, foiled, balked, put at a disadvantage, deterred, under handicap, disadvantaged, checked, blocked, limited, restrained, wounded, curbed, put behind; *all* (D): queered, stymied, behind the eight ball; see also **restricted.**—*Ant.* aided, helped*, supported.

handicraft, *n.* —*Syn.* creation, embroidery, craftsmanship; see **handiwork, workmanship.**

handily, *mod.* —*Syn.* skillfully, intelligently, smoothly; see **cleverly** 2, **easily** 1.

hand in, *v.* —*Syn.* deliver, submit, return; see **give** 1, **offer** 1.

hand in hand, *mod.* —*Syn.* (closely) associated, working together, related; see **together** 2, **united** 1.

handiwork, *n.* —*Syn.* personal work, handicraft, creation, doing, invention, design, manual effort, handwork, needlework, embroidery; see also **workmanship.**

handkerchief, *n.* —*Syn.* kerchief, napkin, neckerchief, headband, tissue, paper handkerchief; *both* (D): rag, hanky; see also **towel.**

handle, *n.* **1.** [A holder]—*Syn.* handhold, hilt, ear, grasp, tiller, crank, knocker, haft, bail, knob, stem, grip, arm; see also **holder** 1.
2. [(D) A title]—*Syn.* nickname, designation, moniker (D); see **name** 1, **title** 3.
fly off the handle (D)—*Syn.* become angry, lose one's temper, blow off steam (D); see **rage** 1.

handle, *v.* **1.** [To deal in]—*Syn.* retail, market, offer for sale; see **sell** 1.
2. [To touch]—*Syn.* finger, check, examine; see **feel** 2, **touch** 1.
3. [To direct]—*Syn.* supervise, control, manage; see **advise** 1, **command** 2.
4. [To do whatever is necessary]—*Syn.* manipulate, operate, work; see **manage** 1.

handled, *mod.* —*Syn.* controlled, organized, taken care of; see **directed, managed.**

handling, *n.* —*Syn.* treatment, approach, styling; see **administration** 1.

handmade, *mod.* —*Syn.* made by hand, handicraft, handsewn, hand-carved, hand-knit, improvised, hand-tailored, handcrafted; see also **homemade.** —*Ant.* factory-made, manufactured*, machine-made.

hand-me-down, *mod.* —*Syn.* used, inherited, handed down; see **old** 2, **secondhand, worn** 2.

hand-me-down, *n.* —*Syn.* secondhand article, discard(s), old clothes *or* articles *or* utensils, etc.; see **rummage** 2.

hand on, *v.* —*Syn.* pass on, bequeath, hand down; see **give** 1.

handout (D), *n.* —*Syn.* contribution, donation, free meal; see **gift** 1, **grant** 1.

hand out, *v.* —*Syn.* give to, deliver, disseminate; see **distribute** 1, **give** 1, **provide** 1.

hand over, *v.* —*Syn.* deliver, surrender, give up; see **give** 1, **yield** 1.

hands down (D), *mod.* —*Syn.* handily, with no trouble, completely; see **easily** 1, **surely** 1.

hands off, *interj.* —*Syn.* keep off, don't touch, leave (it) alone, don't, keep away, leave me alone, stay back, keep your distance; see also **avoid.**

handsome, *mod.* **1.** [Beautiful or elegant]—*Syn.* fine, aristocratic, comely; see **beautiful** 1, **dignified, refined** 2.
2. [Having good masculine appearance]—*Syn.* smart, spruce, dapper, impressive, clean-cut, virile, stately, well-proportioned, good-looking, attractive, athletic, personable, jaunty, strong, muscular, robust, well-dressed; *all* (D): slick, smooth, sharp; easy on the eyes; tall, dark and handsome; see also **manly.**—*Ant.* homely, ugly*, unsightly.
3. [Large or extensive]—*Syn.* full, ample, considerable; see **extensive** 1, **large** 1.
4. [Noble]—*Syn.* gracious, princely, magnanimous; see **noble** 2, **worthy.**

handsomely, *mod.* —*Syn.* nobly, liberally, magnanimously; see **abundantly, generously** 1.

hand-to-hand, *mod.* —*Syn.* face-to-face, facing, close; see **near** 1.

handwriting, *n.* —*Syn.* penmanship, hand, writing, script, longhand, chirography, scrawl, scribble, manuscript, style of penmanship, autography, writing done with the hand, holographic writing, a kind *or* style of writing, scription, calligraphy, scrivening, penscript, pencraft, scrivenery, griffonage; *all* (D): hieroglyphics, pothooks, scratching, chicken tracks, fist; see also **autograph, signature.**

handwritten, *mod.* —*Syn.* in manuscript *or* writing, transcribed, not typed; see **reproduced, written** 2.

handy, *mod.* **1.** [Near]—*Syn.* nearby, at hand, close by; see **convenient** 2, **near** 1.
2. [Useful]—*Syn.* beneficial, advantageous, gainful; see **helpful** 1, **profitable, usable.**
3. [Dexterous]—*Syn.* apt, skillful, ingenious; see **able** 1, 2, **fit** 1, 2.

handy man, *n.* —*Syn.* jack-of-all-trades, helper, hired man; see **laborer, man-of-all-work, servant.**

hang, *v.* **1.** [To suspend]—*Syn.* dangle, attach, drape, hook (up), put in a sling, hang up, nail on the wall, put on a clothesline, fix, pin *or* tack up, drape on the wall, fasten up; see also **fasten** 1.—*Ant.* drop*, throw down, let fall.
2. [To be suspended]—*Syn.* overhang, be held aloft, wave, flap, be loose *or* pendent, droop, flop, be in mid air, swing, dangle, jut, be fastened, impend, hover, stay up.—*Ant.* fall*, come down, drop.
3. [To kill by hanging]—*Syn.* execute, lynch, hang by the neck until dead; see **kill** 1.
4. [To depend]—*Syn.* cling, turn on, be determined by; see **depend** 1, 2.
get (*or* **have) the hang of**—*Syn.* have the knack of, comprehend, learn; see **understand** 1.
not care (*or* **give) a hang about**—*Syn.* be indifferent toward, not care about, ignore; see **neglect** 2.

hang about, *v.* —*Syn.* hang around, haunt, roam; see **frequent, loiter.**

hangar, *n.* —*Syn.* shed, aircraft shelter, stall, nest (D); see also **airport, garage** 1.

hang around, *v.* —*Syn.* associate (with), get along with, have relations with; see also **associate** 1.

hang back, *v.* —*Syn.* hesitate, pull away, recoil; see **avoid.**

hanged, *mod.* —*Syn.* lynched, strung up, brought to the gallows; see **executed** 2.

hanger, *n.* —*Syn.* (coat) hook, nail, peg, coat hanger, clothes hanger, holder, clothes rod, wire hanger, multiple hanger *or* rack, collapsible hanger; see also **rack** 1, **rod** 1.

hanger-on, *n.* —*Syn.* leech, nuisance, parasite; see **dependent, sycophant.**

hang fire, *v.* —*Syn.* drag on, remain unsettled *or* unfinished, recommence; see **continue** 2, **resume.**

hanging, *mod.* —*Syn.* dangling, swaying, swinging, jutting, overhanging, beetling, projecting, pendent, suspended, fastened to, pendulous, drooping.

hangman, *n.* —*Syn.* garroter, lyncher, public executioner; see **executioner, killer.**

hang on, *v.* —*Syn.* persist, remain, continue; see **endure** 1, 2.

hang one's head (in shame), *v.* —*Syn.* be ashamed, be embarrassed about, crawl; see **apologize, regret.**

hang-out (D), *n.* —*Syn. all* (D): bar, joint, hole; see **dive** 2.

hang out, *v.* —*Syn.* loiter, spend time, haunt; see **frequent.**

hangover, *n.* —*Syn.* result of intemperance, crapulence, headache; see **drunkenness, illness** 1.

hang together, *v.* —*Syn.* work together, comply with, assist one another; see **co-operate** 1.

hang-up (D), *n.* —*Syn.* problem, predicament, disturbance; see **difficulty** 1, 2.

hang up, *v.* —*Syn.* cease speaking, replace the receiver, finish a telephone call, ring off, hang up the phone, put off, buzz off (D).

hank, *n.* —*Syn.* knot, portion, length; see **part** 1, **piece** 1.

hanker, *v.* —*Syn.* crave, desire, wish for; see **want** 1.

hankering, *n.* —*Syn.* craving, longing, wish; see **desire** 1.

haphazard, *mod.* **1.** [Aimless]—*Syn.* offhand, casual, random, careless, slipshod, incidental, unthinking, unconscious, uncoordinated, slovenly, reckless, unconcerned, unpremeditated, loose, indiscriminate, unsystematic, unrestricted, unselected, irregular, adulterated, alloyed, motley, multifarious, blind, purposeless, unplanned; *all* (D): hit-or-miss, devil-may-care, willy-nilly, what-the-hell, slapbang; see also **aimless.**—*Ant.* careful, studied, planned.
2. [Accidental]—*Syn.* chance, sudden, unexpected; see **incidental** 2, **spontaneous.**

haphazardly, *mod.* —*Syn.* unexpectedly, casually, randomly, aimlessly, inconstantly, every now and then, every once in a while; see also **accidentally, carelessly.**

happen, *v.* **1.** [To be by chance]—*Syn.* come up *or* about, turn *or* crop up, chance, stumble *or* light upon, occur unexpectedly, come face to face with, befall; *all* (D): hit one like a ton of bricks, be one's luck, fall to one's lot, smack right up against.
2. [To occur]—*Syn.* take place, (come to) pass, arrive, ensue, befall, eventuate, come after, arise, take effect, come into existence, recur, come into being, spring, proceed, issue, follow, come about, fall, repeat, appear, go on, become a fact, turn out, become known, supervene, be found, come to mind, come and go, come around *or* round, come forth; *both* (D): transpire, come off; see also **result.**

happening, *n.* —*Syn.* incident, affair, accident; see **event** 1.

happenstance (D), *n.* —*Syn.* happening, fate, incident; see **event** 2, **luck** 1.

happily, *mod.* **1.** [Fortunately]—*Syn.* gracefully, successfully, felicitously; see **fortunately.**
2. [In a happy mood]—*Syn.* contentedly, joyously, exultantly, gladly, joyfully, cheerily, blithely, gaily, laughingly, smilingly, jovially, merrily, brightly, vivaciously, hilariously, sportively, chucklingly, mockingly, exhilaratingly, jauntily, with pleasure, delightedly, peacefully, blissfully, cheerfully, gleefully, playfully, heartily, lightheartedly, lightly, to one's delight, optimistically, with all one's heart, delightfully, with relish, with good will, buoyantly, in a happy manner, *de bonne volonté, de bonne grace* (both French), with zeal, with good grace, zestfully, of one's own accord, with open arms, sincerely, willingly, with willingness, heart and soul, in

happy circumstances, with right good will, freely, graciously, *con amore* (Italian), tactfully, lovingly, without demur *or* reluctance, devotedly, elatedly, agreeably *ex animo* (Latin).—*Ant.* morosely, sadly*, dejectedly.

happiness, *n.* **1.** [Good humor]—*Syn.* mirth, merrymaking, cheer, merriment, joyousness, vivacity, laughter, delight, gladness, good spirits, hilarity, playfulness, exuberance, gaiety, cheerfulness, buoyancy, good will, rejoicing, joviality, exhilaration, felicity, jollity, jocularity, glee, geniality, good cheer, lightheartedness, joy; see also **humor** 3. —*Ant.* sadness*, sorrow, unhappiness.

2. [Inner satisfaction]—*Syn.* exhilaration, contentment, bliss, blissfulness, joyfulness, beatitude, blessedness, enchantment, sanctity, ecstasy, rapture, transport, exultation, entrancement, peace, felicity, euphoria, peace of mind, tranquillity, inner joy, freedom from care, pleasure, elation, delirium, optimism, self-satisfaction, benignity, hopefulness, serenity, comfort, blitheness, complacency, gratification; *both* (D): paradise, seventh heaven; see also **comfort** 1, **ease** 1, **satisfaction** 2.—*Ant.* melancholy, depression*, dejection.

happy, *mod.* **1.** [In good humor]—*Syn.* joyous, joyful, merry, mirthful, glad, gleeful, delighted, cheerful, gay, captivated, blest, laughing, contented, genial, convivial, satisfied, rapturous, enraptured, relieved, congenial, cheery, blithe, jolly, hilarious, sparkling, enchanted, unalloyed, transported, rejoicing, blissful, jovial, jocund, delightful, delirious, exhilarated, cloudless, rhapsodic, rapt, enrapt, gladsome, pleased, gratified, peaceful, comfortable, beatific, intoxicated, debonair, light, bright, buoyant, ecstatic, charmed, bonny, pleasant, exultant, hearty, overjoyed, well, lighthearted, lightsome, radiant, vivacious, sunny, smiling, content, sprightful, zesty, animated, zestful, lively, spirited, exuberant, good-humored, elated, frisky, frolicsome, expressing happiness, jubilant, sportive, rollicking, playful, thrilled, dashing, fun-loving, gladdened, Elysian, jaunty, breezy, carefree, at peace, in good *or* high spirits, happy as a lark *or* a king *or* as the day is long, of good cheer, in ecstasies, flushed with excitement *or* pleasure; *all* (D): chipper, perky, peppy, fit, beside oneself, swinging, full of beans, bubbling over, having no kick coming, tickled, happy-go-lucky, in third *or* seventh heaven.—*Ant.* sorrowful, sad*, melancholy.

2. [Expressive of good humor]—*Syn.* laughing, smiling, shouting, cheering, cavorting, sparkling, giggling, chuckling, jesting, amusing, backslapping, joking, roaring, applauding, guffawing, celebrating, carousing, reveling, festive; *all* (D): making whoopee, kicking up one's heels, having a hot time, raising hell.—*Ant.* crying, weeping*, mourning.

3. [Fortunate or apt]—*Syn.* nice, felicitous, right; see **fortunate** 1.

happy-go-lucky, *mod.*—*Syn.* cheerful, easygoing, unconcerned; see **happy** 1.

harangue, *n.*—*Syn.* lecture, discourse, sermon; see **discussion** 1, **speech** 3.

harass, *v.* **1.** [To annoy an individual]—*Syn.* tease, vex, irritate; see **bother** 2.

2. [To make small, persistent attacks]—*Syn.* despoil, harry, raid; see **attack** 1.

harbinger, *n.*—*Syn.* indication, sign, signal; see **messenger, signal.**

harbor, *n.* **1.** [A place of refuge]—*Syn.* refuge, retreat, sanctuary; see **shelter.**

2. [A roadstead]—*Syn.* anchorage, port, haven, pier, breakwater, landing place, navigable bay, arm of the sea, harborage, inlet, jetty, embankment, wharf, mole; see also **dock** 1.

harbor, *v.* **1.** [To protect]—*Syn.* shelter, provide refuge, secure; see **defend** 2.

2. [To consider]—*Syn.* entertain, cherish, regard; see **consider** 1.

3. [To keep hidden]—*Syn.* suppress, withhold, hold back; see **hide** 1.

hard, *mod.* **1.** [Compact]—*Syn.* solid, unyielding, dense; see **firm** 2, **thick** 3.

2. [Difficult]—*Syn.* arduous, troublesome, laborious; see **difficult** 1, 2.

3. [Cruel]—*Syn.* perverse, unrelenting, vengeful; see **cruel** 1, 2.

4. [Persistent or energetic]—*Syn.* obdurate, stubborn, tough; see **active** 2, **obstinate** 1.

5. [Severe]—*Syn.* harsh, exacting, grim; see **severe** 1, 2.

6. [Alcoholic]—*Syn.* intoxicating, inebriating, stimulating; see **strong** 8.

7. [With difficulty]—*Syn.* strenuously, laboriously, with great effort; see **carefully** 1, **vigorously.**

be hard on—*Syn.* treat severely, be harsh toward, be painful to; see **abuse** 1.

hard and fast (D), *mod.*—*Syn.* rigid, unchangeable, unalterable; see **firm** 5, **resolute** 2.

hard-core, *mod.* **1.** [Devoted]—*Syn.* dedicated, steadfast, unwaivering; see **faithful.**

2. [Unyielding]—*Syn.* determined, intransigent, uncompromising; see **obstinate** 1, **resolute** 2.

harden, *v.* **1.** [To make less pervious]—*Syn.* steel, temper, anneal, solidify, mineralize, vitrify, precipitate, hornify, cornify, crystallize, freeze, amalgamate, coagulate, clot, granulate, make callous *or* firm *or* compact *or* tight *or* hard, convert to stone, congeal, ossify, petrify, starch, cure, bake, dry, flatten, cement, compact, consolidate, concentrate, sun, fire, fossilize, desiccate, braze, vulcanize, Harveyize, callous, incrassate, indurate, deposit, candy, toughen, fix, concrete, inspissate, encrust, lapidify; see also **compress, press** 1, **stiffen** 2, **thicken** 2.—*Ant.* soften*, unloose, melt.

2. [To become less penetrable]—*Syn.* solidify, congeal, jell, become dense, fix, settle, become fast, petrify, ossify, freeze over, fossilize, clot, cake, set, firm, curdle, coagulate, close, contract; see also **freeze** 1, **stiffen** 1, **thicken** 1.—*Ant.* liquefy, thaw*, soften.

3. [To toughen]—*Syn.* acclimate, acclimatize, indurate, habituate, inure, season, make callous *or* unfeeling *or* obdurate, discipline, accustom, train, coarsen, roughen, sear, embitter, develop, strengthen, brutalize, render insensitive *or* insensible *or* unimpressible, blunt, dull, envenom, numb, stupefy, benumb, stun, paralyze, steel; see also **deaden** 1, **stiffen** 2, **teach** 2.—*Ant.* weaken*, debilitate, soften.

hardened, *mod.* **1.** [Made hard]—*Syn.* compacted, stiffened, stiff; see **firm** 2.

2. [Inured to labor or hardship]—*Syn.* disciplined, trained, accustomed, habituated, indurated, inured, resistant, steeled, toughened, callous, seasoned, physically prepared, obdurate, inveterate, impenitent, unrepenting, impenetrable, unyielding, bad, shameless, irreclaimable, lost, incorrigible, irreligious, profane, abandoned, irredeemable, unhallowed, unfeeling, depraved, degenerate, tough, reprobate, insensible, chronic, hard, deadened, benumbed, habituated, unashamed, confirmed in error *or* vice, uncaring, hardhearted, inaccessible, untouched, uncontrite, sacrilegious, obtuse, unsubmissive, implacable, disdainful, habitual, seared, cold, blasphemous, irreverent, impious, unrelenting, contemptuous, indurate, unbending; *both* (D): hard as nails, hard-boiled; see also **cruel** 2, **ruthless** 1, 2, **stiff** 1.—*Ant.* unaccustomed, inexperienced*, raw.

hardening, *mod.*—*Syn.* stiffening, solidifying, strengthening, settling, freezing, fixing, fossilizing, coagulating.

hardening, *n.*—*Syn.* thickening, crystallization, setting; see **solidification** 1.

hard-favored, *mod.*—*Syn.* forbidding, hideous, grotesque; see **ugly.**

hard-featured, *mod.*—*Syn.* rough-featured, severe, austere; see **ugly.**

hard-fisted, *mod.*—*Syn.* selfish, miserly, niggardly; see **stingy.**

hard going, *mod.*—*Syn.* tough, laborious, tight; see **difficult** 1, 2.

hardheaded, *mod.* **1.** [Obstinate]—*Syn.* willful, stubborn, headstrong; see **obstinate** 1.

2. [Practical]—*Syn.* sensible, rational, shrewd; see **practical.**

hardhearted, *mod.*—*Syn.* brutish, unfeeling, heartless; see **cruel** 1.

hardihood, *n.* **1.** [Courage]—*Syn.* fearlessness, resolution; see **confidence** 2, **courage** 1.

2. [Presumption]—*Syn.* effrontery, impudence, impertinence; see **rudeness.**

hardly, *mod.*—*Syn.* scarcely, barely, just merely, detectably, infinitesimally, perceptibly, imperceptibly, noticeably, not noticeably, gradually, measurably, not measurably, not markedly *or* notably *or* mainly, etc.; no more than, not likely, not a bit, almost not, only just, with difficulty *or* trouble, by a narrow margin, not by a great deal, only in spite of difficulties, with much ado, seldom, sporadically, almost not at all, but just, in no manner, by no means, little, infrequently, somewhat, not quite, here and there, simply, not much, rarely, faintly, comparatively, scantly, almost inconceivably, miserably, uncommonly, slightly, sparsely, not often, rather, with little likelihood; *all* (D): once in a blue moon *or* a coon's age, within two whoops and a holler, by the skin of one's teeth, just enough to swear by; see also **moderately, only** 1.—*Ant.* easily*, without difficulty, readily.

hard-nosed, *mod.*—*Syn.* stubborn, unyielding, hard-headed; see **obstinate** 1, **resolute** 2.

hard of hearing, *mod.*—*Syn.* almost deaf, having a hearing problem, in need of a hearing device; see **deaf** 1.

hard on, *mod.*—*Syn.* unjust *or* unkind *or* cruel to, brutal, inclined to blame; see **cruel** 2, **harmful.**

hardship, *n.* **1.** [Injury]—*Syn.* misfortune, calamity, accident; see **catastrophe, disaster.**

2. [Burden]—*Syn.* trial, sorrow, worry; see **difficulty** 2, **grief** 1.

hard up, *mod.*—*Syn.* in trouble, poverty-stricken, in the lower income brackets; see **poor** 1.

hardware, *n.*—*Syn.* domestic appliances, fixtures, metal manufactures, hollowware, castings, plumbing, metalware, implements, tools, housewares, fittings, fasteners, nails, brads, screws, bolts, nuts, aluminum ware, cutlery, house furnishings, kitchenware, household utensils, appointments, accouterments; see also **appliance, device** 1, **tool** 1.

hardware store, *n.*—*Syn.* metalware store, household utensil store, kitchenware store, tool shop; see also **store** 1.

hardwood, *n.*—*Syn.* oak, beech, elm, ash, mahogany, chestnut, walnut, maple, teak, sycamore, greenheart, rosewood; see also **tree, wood** 2.

hardy, *mod.* **1.** [Strong]—*Syn.* vigorous, firm, tough; see **strong** 2.

2. [Suited to rigorous climates]—*Syn.* inured, tough, toughened, in good shape *or* condition, hardened, resistant, solid, staunch, seasoned, capable of endurance, able-bodied, physically fit, tenacious, well-equipped, acclimatized, Herculean, Atlantean, rugged, lusty, mighty, well, fit, robust, hearty, rigorous, wiry, stout, sound, sinewy, fresh, hale, brawny, able, vigorous, enduring, burly, powerful, firm, sturdy, leathery, staunch, virile, stalwart, solid, muscular, substantial, hefty (D); see also **healthy** 1, **strong** 1.—*Ant.* weak*, unaccustomed, unhabituated.

3. [Brave]—*Syn.* resolute, dauntless, bold; see **brave** 1.

hare, *n.*—*Syn.* cottontail, coney, bunny; see **animal** 1, **rabbit.**

harebrained, *mod.*—*Syn.* foolish, flighty, irresponsible; see **changeable** 1, 2, **stupid** 1.

harem, *n.*—*Syn.* seraglio, concubines, zenana, gynaeceum, oda, kept women.

hark, *v.*—*Syn.* harken, pay attention, give heed; see **listen** 1.

harlot, *n.*—*Syn.* whore, strumpet, call girl; see **prostitute.**

harm, *n.* **1.** [Injury]—*Syn.* hurt, infliction, impairment; see **injury** 1.

2. [Evil]—*Syn.* wickedness, outrage, foul play; see **abuse** 3, **evil** 2, **wrong** 2.

harm, *v.*—*Syn.* injure, wreck, cripple; see **hurt** 1.

harmed, *mod.*—*Syn.* damaged, injured, wounded; see **hurt.**

harmful, *mod.*—*Syn.* injurous, detrimental, hurtful, noxious, evil, mischievous, ruinous, malefic, demolitionary, internecine, adverse, inimical, harassing, sinister, subversive, incendiary, virulent, calamitous, cataclysmic, corroding, toxic, baleful, nocuous, consumptive, painful, wounding, crippling, bad, malicious, malignant, sinful, pernicious, baneful, unwholesome, pestilential, pestiferous, deleterious, annihilative, corrupting, menacing, ill-omened, dire, morbific, devouring, prejudicial, damaging, corrupt, vicious, insidious, treacherous, catastrophic, disastrous, wild, murderous, undetermining, sapping, destructive, unhealthy, stunting, habit-forming, killing, fatal, mortal, serious, fraught with *or* doing harm *or* evil, painful, sore, extirpative, afflicting, distressing, fell, diabolic, brutal, unhealthful, satanic, demoniac, ill, grevious, mortal, lethal, malevolent, mephitic, venomous, cruel, unfortunate, disadvantageous, felonious, aching, pricking, objectionable, fiendish, maleficent, unpropitious, unlucky, malign, sinistrous, noisome, devilish, corrosive; see also **dangerous** 1, 2. **deadly, ominous, poisonous, wicked.**—*Ant.* pure, healthful*, good.

harmless, *mod.* **1.** [*Unusually said of persons*] —*Syn.* inoffensive, naive, simple; see **kind** 1.
2. [*Usually said of things*]—*Syn.* pure, undefiled, spotless, unblemished, innocent, painless, unoffending, innoxious, navigable, powerless, controllable, manageable, safe, innocuous, not habit-forming, sure, nonirritating, reliable, noninjurious, trustworthy, sanitary, germproof, sound, not hurtful, out of operation, out of gear, inoffensive, sterile, without power *or* tendency to harm, inoperative, disarmed; see also **gentle** 3, **kind** 1, **weak** 5, 6. —*Ant.* injurious, harmful*, poisonous.

harmonic, *mod.*—*Syn.* consonant, tuneful, symphonious; see **harmonious.**

harmonica, *n.*—*Syn.* mouth organ, Panpipe, harmonicon; *all* (D): blue's-harp, French harp, corn-on-the-cob, mouth harp, mouth Steinway; see also **musical instrument.**

harmonious, *mod.* **1.** [Harmonic]—*Syn.* melodious, tuneful, musical, rhythmical, dulcet, sweet-sounding, melodic, symphonic, sonorous, in tune, in chorus, silvery, in unison; *both* (D): tuny, earful. —*Ant.* shrill*, jangling, dissonant.
2. [Congruous]—*Syn.* agreeable (to), accordant, concordant, consonant, corresponding, suitable, adapted, similar, like, peaceful, in accord, amicable, co-operative, congenial, on borrowing terms, in step, in accordance with, in concord *or* favor *or* harmony (with), on a footing with, friendly, of one accord, in concert, conforming, well-matched, evenly balanced, symmetrical, congruent; see also **fit** 1, 2.—*Ant.* incongruous, incompatible, opposed*.

harmonize, *v.* **1.** [To render harmonic]—*Syn.* blend, arrange, put to harmony, adapt, set, orchestrate, symphonize, tune, sing a duet, play *or* sing a many-part harmony, make contrapuntal, put on an even keel.
2. [To accord with one another]—*Syn.* correspond, be in harmony (with), fit in with; see **agree.**

harmony, *n.* **1.** [Musical concord]—*Syn.* chord, consonance, triad, diapason, accord, euphony, tunefulness, symphony, harmonics, counterpoint, concert, concordance, music, chorus, organum, sympathy, blending, unity, accordance, attunement, symphoniousness, chime, polyphony, unison, richness, overtone, musical pattern, musical concurrence, musical blend, concinnity.
2. [Social concord]—*Syn.* compatibility, equanimity, unanimity; see **agreement** 2, **peace** 2.
3. [Logical concord]—*Syn.* form, symmetry, accord, balance; see **agreement** 2, **consistency** 1, **regularity, symmetry.**
4. [Musical composition]—*Syn.* melody, piece, arrangement; see **composition** 2, **music** 1, **tune.**

harness, *n.*—*Syn.* tackle, gear, yoke, apparatus, bridle, accounterments, rigging, fittings.
Parts of a horse's harness include the following—bellyband, breeching, breeching strap, crupper, front, blind, crownpiece, overcheck *or* facepiece, cheekpiece, breast collar *or* breastband, throatlatch, bit, martingale, blinker, browband, noseband, neck strap, terret, checkhook, overcheck rein, hipstrap, trace *or* tug, collar, collar pad, hame, surcingle; see also **bit** 4, **halter, saddle.**
in harness—*Syn.* at work, occupied, working; see **busy** 1.
in harness with—*Syn.* in co-operation with, associated with, joined to; see **together** 2.

harness, *v.*—*Syn.* fetter, saddle, yoke, equip, outfit, bridle, hold in leash, hitch up, control, limit, govern, fit out for work, cinch, tame, strap, domesticate, accouter, tackle, gear, collar, put in harness, rig up *or* out, furnish, enchain, tie, secure, rein in, curb, check, constrain, fit for electric power; see also **bind** 1, **fasten** 1, **muzzle** 1, 2, **provide** 1.**restrain** 1.

harp, *n.*—*Syn.* lyre, multi-stringed instrument, claviharp; see also **musical instrument.**

harp on, *v.*—*Syn.* repeat, pester, nag; see **bother** 2, **disturb** 2.

harpoon, *n.*—*Syn.* missile, lance, javelin; see **spear, weapon** 1.

harpy, *n.*—*Syn.* vampire, temptress, demon; see **devil** 1, **monster** 1, **witch.**

harrow, *n.*—*Syn.* disk, cultivator, drag; see **plow, shovel, tractor.**
Types of harrows include the following—disk harrow, Scotch harrow, cultipacker, double-action harrow, cutaway harrow, spading harrow.

harrow, *v.* **1.** [To use a harrow on land]—*Syn.* drag, dig, cultivate; see **plow, shovel.**
2. [To torment]—*Syn.* tormenting, trying, nerve-racking; see also **disturbing.**

harrowing, *mod.*—*Syn.* tormenting, trying, nerve-racking; see also **disturbing.**

harry, *v.* **1.** [To raid]—*Syn.* pillage, sack, lay waste; see **attack** 1, **raid, ravage, steal.**
2. [To harass]—*Syn.* annoy, pester, torment; see **bother** 2, **disturb** 2.

harsh, *mod.* **1.** [Inharmonious]—*Syn.* discordant, jangling, cacophonous, grating, rusty, dissonant, absonant, inconsonant, strident, creaking, clashing, sharp, jarring, jangled, clamorous, cracked, hoarse, out of tune, unmelodious, rasping, screeching, earsplitting, caterwauling, stridulous, disturbing, off balance, noisy, flat, sour, out of key, tuneless, unmusical, off key, disagreeing, uncongenial, unsympathetic, uncomforting, incompatible; see also **loud** 1, 2, **raucous** 1, **shrill.**
2. [Discourteous]—*Syn.* gruff, ungracious, uncivil; see **rude** 1, 2, **ungrateful**
3. [Severe]—*Syn.* rigid, unrelenting, hard; see **firm** 1, **resolute** 1, **severe** 2.

harshly, *mod.*—*Syn.* sternly, powerfully, grimly; see **brutally, firmly** 2, **loudly, seriously** 1, 2.

harshness, *n.*—*Syn.* crudity, brutality, acerbity; see **anger, cruelty, tyranny.**

harum-scarum, *mod.*—*Syn.* reckless, harebrained, disconnected; see **careless** 1, **irresponsible, loose** 1, **thoughtless** 1, 2.

Harvard, *n.*—*Syn.* Harvard University, Harvard College, oldest college in the United States; *both* (D): the Yard, the Crimson; see also **college, university.**

harvest, *n.* **1.** [Crop]—*Syn.* reaping, yielding, fruitage; see **crop, fruit** 1, **grain** 1, **produce, vegetable.**

2. [Product]—*Syn.* intake, results, return; see **product** 2, **result.**

3. [A season]—*Syn.* harvest time, summer, fall; see **autumn, month, season.**

harvest, *v.*—*Syn.* gather (in), accumulate, pile up, collect, garner, crop, cut, pluck, pick, cull, take *or* draw in, glean, amass, gather the harvest, hoard, mow, take the yield *or* the (second) crop, strip the fields, put in barns, gather the first fruits; see also **reap** 1, **store** 2.—*Ant.* sow*, plant, seed.

harvester, *n.* **1.** [A harvesting machine]—*Syn.* binder, reaper, header, combine, harvesting machinery; see also **cat** 3, **equipment, tractor.**

2. [A man]—*Syn.* farm hand, worker, helper; see **farmer, laborer, workman.**

harvesting, *n.*—*Syn.* gathering, collecting, reaping; see **accumulation, collection** 1.

hash, *n.* **1.** [A dish of meat and vegetables]—*Syn.* ground meat and vegetables, baked ground meat, meat loaf, gallimaufry, leftovers, *fricandeau* (French), mash, chowchow, ragout, stew, hashed meat, olla-podrida, casserole, salmagundi, olio, minced meat, *réchauffé* (French); *both* (D): insult to a square meal, great unknown; see also **meat, stew.**

2. [A mixture]—*Syn.* mess, jumble, hodgepodge; see **confusion** 2, **mixture** 1.

hash out (D), *v.*—*Syn.* settle, conclude, get a decision on; see **decide.**

hash over (D), *v.*—*Syn.* debate, argue about, review; see **discuss.**

hasp, *n.*—*Syn.* hook, catch, clasp; see **fastener.**

hassle (D), *n.*—*Syn.* quarrel, squabble, row; see **dispute** 1.

hassle (D), *v.*—*Syn.* bother, annoy, harass; see **bother** 2.

hassock, *n.*—*Syn.* footrest, cushion, stool; see **furniture, seat** 1.

haste, *n.* **1.** [Rapidity]—*Syn.* rapidness, hurry, swiftness; see **speed.**

2. [Undue rapidity]—*Syn.* scramble, bustle, scurry, precipitation, flurry, hurly-burly, impetuousity, rashness, scuttle, impetuousness, foolhardiness, want of caution, untimeliness, hurriedness, scamper, hustling, undue celerity, press, recklessness, rush, hastiness, incautiousness, carelessness, irrationality, rashness, inexpedience, giddiness, precipitancy, impatience, heedlessness, plunge, unrestraint, vehemence, testiness, unwise *or* rash rapidity, excitation, fretfulness, outburst, abruptness, anticipation, intempestivity, prematureness; *all* (D): leap in the dark, speed-up, speedomania, smoke.—*Ant.* prudence*, caution, attention.

3. [Urgency]—*Syn.* promptness, promptitude, dispatch; see **importance** 2.

in haste—*Syn.* hastening, in a hurry, moving fast; see **hurrying.**

make haste—*Syn.* hurry, move *or* act quickly, speed up; see **hasten** 1.

hasten, *v.* **1.** [To make haste]—*Syn.* rush, sprint, spurt, scurry, move quickly, bestir oneself, dash (off), plunge, bustle, waste *or* lose no time, fly, be in a hurry, cover ground, not lose a moment, hurry (up), press (on), express, (move *or* act *or* proceed with) haste, flee, be on the run, skip, tear, post, scamper, pace, move speedily, push on, hie, hustle, bolt, scuttle, careen, make haste *or* time, dart, trip, be quick, ride hard, leap, clip, bound, zoom, skim, brush, spring, make forced marches, whip off *or* away, jump, speed up, work under pressure, make the best of one's time, make short work of, go at full blast *or* tilt, run like mad, march in double time, put on more speed, carry sail, take wing, make strides, go all out, trot, go *or* run wide open, pack off *or* away, gallop; *all* (D): make a dash for, step on it, shake a leg, beat the devil around a stump, go like sixty, work against time, put on steam, hie on, break one's neck, fall all over oneself, make up for lost time, hop to *or* on it, scoot, spin, whiz, beat a retreat, sweep, bundle, get cracking, skedaddle, outstrip the wind, fly on the wings of the wind, shoot, bowl *or* cut along, clap spurs to one's horse, swoop, wing one's way, crowd sail, rip, go on the double, stir one's stumps, go like (greased) lightning, go like a shot, whisk, go hell-bent, burn up the road, zip, go like a bat out of hell, flit, rip, step lively *or* along *or* on the gas, give her the gas; see also **race** 1, **run** 2, **speed.**—*Ant.* creep, crawl*, plod.

2. [To expedite]—*Syn.* accelerate, dispatch, speed up, fillip, advance, move up, quicken, stimulate, hurry (up), push, make short work of, urge, goad, press, whip on, agitate, push forward *or* ahead, put into action, get started, give a start, drive on, set in motion, take in hand, take over; *all* (D): put on wheels, blast off, railroad through, gear up, cut the red tape; see also **speed.**—*Ant.* defer, delay*, put off.

hastily, *mod.* **1.** [Rapidly]—*Syn.* hurriedly, speedily, nimbly; see **quickly** 1.

2. [Carelessly]—*Syn.* thoughtlessly, recklessly, rashly; see **carelessly.**

hasty, *mod.* **1.** [Hurried]—*Syn.* quick, speedy, swift; see **fast** 1.

2. [Careless]—*Syn.* ill-advised, precipitate, foolhardy; see **careless** 1, **rash.**

hat, *n.*—*Syn.* headgear, millinery, headpiece, helmet, chapeau, bonnet; *all* (D): lid, roof, bean pod; see also **helmet.**

Hatlike coverings include the following—for men: cap, service cap, forage cap, skullcap, yarmulke, kipa, overseas cap, derby, straw hat, felt hat, sombrero, cowboy's hat, Stetson, southwestern, ten-gallon hat, top hat, opera hat, crush hat, stovepipe, tall silk hat, collapsible, topper, miter, bowler, panama, leghorn, tam-o'-shanter, beret, cocked hat, tricornered hat, sailor hat, boater, digger, bycocket, fez, turban, shako, kepi, bearskin, tarboosh, toque, busby, sun helmet, trench helmet, steel helmet, mortarboard, soft-brimmed hat, fedora, homburg, deerstalker, domino; for women: hood, wimple, snood, cowl, kerchief, turban, cloche, calot, straw, skimmer, beret, bandanna, mobcap, Talbot, Louise Bourbon, Princesse Eugénie, Descat, pillbox, Gainsborough, scarf, chapel cap, whimsey, babushka.

pass the hat—*Syn.* take up a collection, gather funds, collect; see **accumulate** 1,
take one's hat off to—*Syn.* salute, cheer, congratulate; see **praise** 1.
talk through one's hat (D)—*Syn.* chatter, talk nonsense, make foolish statements; see **babble.**
throw one's hat into the ring—*Syn.* enter a contest, run for office, enter politics; see **campaign** 1.
under one's hat (D)—*Syn.* confidential, private, hidden; see **secret** 1.

hatch, *v.* **1.** [To bring forth]—*Syn.* bear, lay eggs, give birth; see **produce** 1.
2. [To plan]—*Syn.* prepare, scheme, plot; see **invent** 1, **plan** 1.

hatched, *mod.*—*Syn.* contrived, concluded, devised; see **planned.**

hatchery, *n.*—*Syn.* brooder, incubator, breeding place, fish hatchery; place for hatching eggs of poultry, fish, etc.

hatchet, *n.*—Types of hatches include the following—bench hatchet, lathing hatchet, roofer's hatchet, claw hatchet, broad hatchet, tomahawk, pipe-tomahawk, battleax; see also **ax.**

hatchway, *n.*—*Syn.* trap door, scuttle, hatch; see **door** 1, **entrance** 2, **gate.**

hate, *mod.*—*Syn.* intolerant, bigoted; anti-Semitic *or* anti-Negro, etc.; see **derogatory, opprobrious** 1, 2, **prejudiced.**

hate, *n.*—*Syn.* ill will, venom, disgust, antipathy, aversion, destination, rancor, malevolence, rankling, revenge, malignity, loathing, abomination, abhorrence, animosity, enmity; *all* (D): frost, scunner, dog-eye, nasty look, no love lost; see also **hatred** 1, 2, **malice, resentment** 1, 2.—*Ant.* love*, favor, desire.

hate, *v.* **1.** [To detest]—*Syn.* abhor, execrate, abominate, loathe, scorn, despise, have an aversion (toward), look at with loathing, spit upon, anathematize, curse, contemn, swear eternal enmity, dislike intensely, shudder at, not care for, sicken at, have enough of, be repelled by, feel repulsion for, have no use for, object to, bear malice, have ill feelings toward, bear a grudge against, spurn, shrink *or* recoil from, disparage, shun, nauseate, tread *or* trample underfoot, denounce, resent, esteem slightly, curse, be sick *or* tired of, reject, revolt against, hold cheap, deride, have no taste *or* stomach for, disfavor, look down upon, feel malice toward, hold aloof from, mislike, be malevolent, hold in contempt, have no use for, be disgusted with, view with horror, owe a grudge to; *all* (D): be down on, look daggers at, have it in for, hate like poison; see also **dislike.**—*Ant.* love*, adore, worship.
2. [(D) To dislike; *often used with infinitive or participle*]—*Syn.* object to, rebel, recoil *or* shrink from, shudder at, think nothing of, not like, have no liking for, find abhorrent, be set against, find obnoxious, not relish the idea, shun, avoid, mind, have no taste *or* stomach for, be disinclined, disapprove of, wish to avoid *or* evade, struggle against, shun, pull *or* draw back from, demur, feel sick at, put off, hesitate, eschew, not have the heart to, wish to abstain from, keep *or* steer clear of, quail *or* turn *or* wince *or* blench from, be reluctant, regard as distasteful *or* unpleasant *or* difficult; *all* (D): shy away, turn up one's nose at, look coldly upon, look down upon, speak ill of, look down one's nose, get on one's high horse, hold cheap, be cold about.—*Ant.* like*, favor, approve.

hated, *mod.*—*Syn.* despised, loathed, abhorred, abominated, detested, disliked, execrated, cursed, anathematized, unpopular, avoided, shunned, out of favor, condemned; see also **offensive** 2, **undesirable.**

hateful, *mod.*—*Syn.* odious, detestable, repugnant; see **offensive** 2, **undesirable.**

hater, *n.*—*Syn.* enemy of, execrator, ill-wisher, racist, abominator, calumniator, militant, antagonist, advocate of race hatred, jingoist; see also **bigot, enemy** 1, 2.

hatred, *n.* **1.** [Strong aversion]—*Syn.* abhorrence, loathing, rancor, detestation, revulsion, malignance, antipathy, repugnance, repulsion, disgust, contempt, (intense) dislike, scorn, abomination, distaste, disapproval, horror, hard feelings, displeasure; see also sense 2; see also **hate, malice, resentment** 2.—*Ant.* liking, affection*, attraction.
2. [Personal enmity]—*Syn.* ill will, antipathy, bitterness, antagonism, animosity, acrimony, pique, grudge, malice, malevolence, animus, revulsion, repugnance, militancy, disfavor, ignominy, prejudice, invidiousness, spite, revenge, hate, venom, envy, spleen, coldness, distaste, pitilessness, contempt, asperity, derision, race prejudice, malignity, hostility, odium, alienation, disaffection; *all* (D): bad blood, chip on one's shoulder, grudge; see also sense 1; see also **anger, opposition** 2, **resentment** 1.—*Ant.* friendship, devotion*, affection.

haughtiness, *n.*—*Syn.* insolence, aloofness, snobbishness; see **arrogance.**

haughty, *mod.*—*Syn.* arrogant, disdainful, proud; see **egotistical** 2.

haul, *n.* **1.** [A pull]—*Syn.* tug, lift, wrench; see **pull** 1.
2. [The distance something is hauled]—*Syn.* trip, voyage, yards; see **distance** 3.
3. [(D) Something obtained, especially loot]—*Syn.* find, spoils, take; see **booty, catch** 2.
in (*or* **over) the long haul**—*Syn.* over a long period of time, for a long time, in the end; see **for a time.**

haul, *v.*—*Syn.* pull, drag, bring; see **draw** 1.

haul off, *v.*—*Syn.* take, cart *or* truck *or* drag off, appropriate; see **remove** 1.

haunch, *n.*—*Syn.* backside, side, hindquarter; see **hip, rump.**

haunt, *n.* **1.** [A retreat]—*Syn.* den, resort, headquarters, lair, meeting place, rendezvous, trysting place; see also **bar** 2, **refuge** 1, **retreat** 2.
2. [A spirit]—*Syn.* poltergeist, spook, phantom; see **ghost** 1, 2.

haunt, *v.* **1.** [To frequent persistently]—*Syn.* habituate, visit often, resort to; see **frequent.**
2. [To frequent as a spirit]—*Syn.* come as a ghost, appear as a phantom, permeate, pervade, rise, float, before the eyes, dwell in, walk, be disclosed, inhabit, hover about, return from the dead, manifest itself, materialize, reappear frequently to after death, visit habitually after death; *both* (D): spook, ha'nt.
3. [To prey upon]—*Syn.* recur in one's mind, obsess, torment, beset, possess, trouble, weigh on one's mind, touch one's conscience, craze, madden,

hound, terrify, bedevil, plague, dwell heavily upon, intrude upon continually, vex, harass, weigh *or* prey on, infest, pester, be ever present, besiege, worry, tease, terrorize, disquiet, recur to persistently, frighten, annoy, possess one's mind, cause regret *or* sorrow, molest, harrow, appall, agitate, rack, overrun, sting, nettle, hang over one's head, agonize, unman, drive one nuts (D); see also **bother** 2, **disturb** 2.

haunted, *mod.* —*Syn.* frequented, visited by, preyed upon; see **obsessed.**

haunting, *mod.* —*Syn.* eerie, unforgettable, seductive; see **frightful** 1, **remembered.**

have, *v.* **1.** [To be in possession of]—*Syn.* possess, take unto oneself, hold; see **own** 1.
2. [To bear]—*Syn.* beget, give birth to, bring forth; see **produce** 1.
3. [To be obliged; *used with infinitive*]—*Syn.* be compelled *or* forced to, should, ought, be one's duty to, rest with, become, fall on, devolve upon; *both* (D): be up to, have got to; see also **must.**
4. [To have sexual intercourse with]—*Syn.* seduce, sleep with, deflower; see **copulate.**

have a ball (D), *v.* —*Syn.* revel, have fun, celebrate; see **enjoy oneself, play** 1.

have a heart (D), *v.* —*Syn.* take pity on, be merciful (to), be considerate (of); see **pity** 1, 2.

have at, *v.* —*Syn.* thrust, strike, attack; see **hit** 1.

have done, *v.* —*Syn.* leave, quit, outgrow; see **achieve** 1.

have had it (D), *v.* —*Syn.* be out, be defeated, come to the end of things *or* everything; see **lose** 3, **suffer** 1.

have in mind, *v.* —*Syn.* expect, foresee, hope; see **anticipate** 1, **think** 1.

have it good (D), *v.* —*Syn.* do well, thrive, have it easy (D); see **prosper.**

haven, *n.* —*Syn.* port, harbor, roadstead; see **refuge** 1, **shelter.**

have on, *v.* —*Syn.* be clothed in, be wearing, try on; see **wear** 1.

haversack, *n.* —*Syn.* saddlebag, knapsack, satchel; see **bag.**

have something on one, *v.* —*Syn.* be able to expose, have special knowledge of, be able to control; see **convict, know** 1.

have something on the ball (D), *v.* —*Syn.* be alert, be quick, be in tune, have a keen mind, be industrious, be with it (D).

have the law on one (D), *v.* —*Syn.* bring court action, file *or* bring suit, take it to court; *both* (D): tell it to the judge, tell it to the Marines; see also **accuse, sue.**

having, *mod.* —*Syn.* owning, possessing, enjoying, commanding, holding, controlling; see also **retaining.**

havoc, *n.* —*Syn.* devastation, plunder, ruin; see **destruction** 2.

hawk, *n.* **1.** [A member of the Accipitridae]—*Syn.* bird of prey, one of the Falconiformes, falcon; see **bird** 1.
Terms for hawks and hawklike birds include the following—red-tailed, zone-tailed, white tailed, short-tailed, broad-winged, short-winged, American sparrow, English sparrow, bush, duck, hen, fish, prairie, marsh, gray, blue, Cooper's, Harlan's, Swanson's, Harris', noble, ignoble, ferruginous, sharp-shinned, rough-legged, goshawk, windhover, night-hawk, (English) hobby, merlin, jack merlin, peregrine, tiercel, osprey, harrier, kite, kestrel, caracara, lugar, lanner, saker, eyas, haggard, gyrefalcon.
2. [A warlike person]—*Syn.* militarist, chauvinist, jingoist, belligerent, promoter *or* escalator *or* supporter, etc. of (all-out) war, warmonger, chauvin, jingo, hothead; see also **conservative, radical.**

hawker (D), *n.* —*Syn.* vendor, seller, peddler; see **businessman, merchant, salesman** 2.

hay, *n.* —*Syn.* provender, fodder, roughage, forage, feed; see also **grass** 1.
Hay includes the following—red clover, wild hay, timothy, sweetgrass, alsike, sweet clover, soybeans, swamp hay, alfalfa, oat hay, millet.
hit the hay (D)—*Syn.* go to bed, rest, recline; see **sleep.**
make hay out of—*Syn.* profit by, utilize, turn to one's advantage; see **use** 1.
make hay while the sun shines—*Syn.* opportunize, take advantage, make the most of an opportunity; see **use** 1.
not hay (D)—*Syn.* very much, a great deal, many; see **much.**

haycock, *n.* —*Syn.* sheaf, stack, loft; see **haystack.**

hayfield, *n.* —*Syn.* pasture, mead, grassland; see **field** 1, **meadow.**

hayloft, *n.* —*Syn.* barn, silo, storage space; see **storehouse.**

haymow, *n.* —*Syn.* hayloft, storage space, barn; see **storehouse.**

hayseed, *n.* —*Syn.* grass, chaff, hay; see **grain** 1, **seed** 2.

haystack, *n.* —*Syn.* sheaf, stack, hay, haycock, pile.

hazard, *n.* **1.** [Danger]—*Syn.* risk, peril, jeopardy; see **danger** 1.
2. [Luck]—*Syn.* chance, possibility, accident; see **risk** 2, **uncertainty** 3, **venture.**

hazard, *v.* —*Syn.* stake, try, guess; see **chance** 2, **gamble** 1, **risk, venture.**

hazardous, *mod.* —*Syn.* perilous, uncertain, precarious; see **dangerous** 1.

haze, *n.* —*Syn.* mist, smokiness, indistinctness, fume, smog, steam, cloudiness, miasma, film, haziness; see also **fog** 1.

hazel, *mod.* —*Syn.* brownish-gray, hazel-gray, bluish-green, greenish-brown, yellowish-green; see also **brown, colour** 1, **mellow.**

hazy, *mod.* **1.** [Obscured to the sight]—*Syn.* cloudy, foggy, smoggy, murky, misty, unclear, overcast, steaming, screened, fuliginous, fumy, rimy, filmy, gauzy, vaporous, smoky, dim, dull, indistinct, nebulous, spraylike, shadowy, dusky, obscure, wavering, thick, opaque, bleared, obfuscated, frosty, lowering, obfuscous, veiled, blurred, glimmering, semitransparent, blurry, crepuscular, faint, bleary, characterized by the presence of haze; see also **dark** 1.—*Ant.* bright, clear*, cloudless.
2. [Obscured to the understanding]—*Syn.* unclear, unsound, unintelligible; see **obscure** 1.

he, *pron.* —*Syn.* this one, the male, the abovenamed, the man, the boy, third person, masculine singular.

head, *n.* **1.** [The skull]—*Syn.* brainpan, scalp, brain box, pate, crown, headpiece, pow (Scotch), poll; *all* (D): bean, noggin, coconut, noodle, nut, nob; see also **cranium.**
2. [A leader or supervisor]—*Syn.* commander, commanding officer, ruler; see **administrator, leader** 2.
3. [The top]—*Syn.* summit, peak, crest; see **top** 1.
4. [The beginning]—*Syn.* front, start, source; see **origin** 2.
5. [A climax]—*Syn.* acme, turning point, end; see **climax, crisis.**
6. [Stored power]—*Syn.* latent force, static energy, potential energy; see **energy** 3.
7. [An attachment]—*Syn.* cap, bottle top, cork; see **cover** 1, **fixture** 1.
8. [(D) Intelligence]—*Syn.* brains, foresight, ingenuity; see **judgment** 1.
9. [A newspaper headline]. Types and parts of headlines include the following—deck, bank, line, streamer, banner, pyramid, inverted pyramid, read-out, two-line head, three-line head, subhead, ribbon, drop head.
10. [(D) A drug user]—*Syn.* hippie; *both* (D): acidhead, pothead; see **addict.**
come to a head—*Syn.* culminate, reach a crisis, come to a climax; see **climax** 1.
get it through one's head—*Syn.* learn, comprehend, see; see **understand** 1.
give one his head—*Syn.* permit, condone, approve; see **allow** 1.
go to one's head—*Syn.* stir mentally, stimulate, intoxicate; see **excite** 1.
hang (*or* **hide**) **one's head**—repent, be sorry, grieve; see **regret.**
keep one's head—*Syn.* remain calm, keep one's self-control, hold one's emotions in check; see **restrain** 1.
lose one's head—become excited *or* angry, go mad, rave; see **rage** 1.
make head—*Syn.* progress, go forward, proceed; see **advance** 1.
make head or tail of—*Syn.* comprehend, apprehend, see; see **understand** 1.
one's head off—*Syn.* greatly, extremely, considerably; see **much** 1.
on (*or* **upon**) **one's head**—*Syn.* burdensome, taxing, strenuous; see **difficult** 1.
out of (*or* **off**) **one's head**—*Syn.* crazy, delirious, raving; see **insane** 1.
over one's head—*Syn.* incomprehensible, not understandable, hard; see **difficult** 2.
put (*or* **lay**) **heads together**—*Syn.* consult, talk over, confer; see **discuss.**
take it into one's head—*Syn.* conceive, concoct, devise; see **invent** 2.

head, *v.* —*Syn.* direct, oversee, supervise; see **command** 2, **manage** 1.

headache, *n.* **1.** [A pain in the head]—*Syn.* migraine, sick headache, bilious headache, neuralgia, organic headache, megrim, cephalalgia, hemialgia, hemicrania, reflex headache; *both* (D): head-on, big head; see also **pain** 2.
2. [(D) A source of vexation and difficulty]—*Syn.* problem, jumble, mess; see **difficulty** 1, 2, **trouble** 2.

headdress, *n.* —*Syn.* bonnet, helmet, hood; see **crown** 2, **hat.**
headed, *mod.* —*Syn.* in transit, in motion, en route, going, directed, started, aimed, slated for, on the way to, pointed toward, in process of reaching, on the road to; see also **moving** 1.—*Ant.* stopping*, landed, disembarked.
headfirst, *mod.* —*Syn.* recklessly, hastily, rashly; see **carelessly.**
head for, *v.* —*Syn.* go *or* set out *or* make a dash *or* break for, start toward, hit for (D); see **travel** 2.
heading, *n.* —*Syn.* headline, subtitle, inscription, address, caption, legend, head, banner head, subject, overline, docket, section head, frontispiece, capital, superscription, ticket, headnote, display line, preface, imprint, prologue, streamer, banner (line), preamble, topic, title page, designation, specification, indication of contents; *both* (D): scarehead, screamer; see also **label, title** 1.
headland, *n.* —*Syn.* bluff, cliff, cape; see **hill, cape.**
headless, *mod.* **1.** [Unthinking]—*Syn.* witless, fatuous, brainless; see **dull** 3, **stupid** 1.
2. [Without a head]—*Syn.* decapitated, lifeless, truncated; see **dead** 1.
headlight, *n.* —*Syn.* searchlight, automobile light, front light, beacon, fog lamp, spotlight; see also **light** 3.
headline, *n.* —*Syn.* heading, caption, title; see **head** 9.
headlong, *mod.* —*Syn.* reckless, precipitate, impetuous; see **rash.**
headmaster, *n.* —*Syn.* dean, director, superintendent; see **administrator, principal.**
headmost, *mod.* —*Syn.* initial, outstanding, main; see **principal.**
head off (D), *v.* —*Syn.* block (off), interfere (with), intervene; see **stop** 1.
head on, *mod.* —*Syn.* headfirst, with full force, body to body; see **opposed.**
head over heels (D), *mod.* —*Syn.* entirely, precipitately, unreservedly; see **completely.**
headquarters, *n.* —*Syn.* main *or* home *or* chief office, (central) station *or* place, distributing center, police station, office of the commanding officer, meeting place *or* house, haunt, manager's office, quarters, base, military station *or* town, club, post, cantonment, center *or* base of operations *or* authority, offices from which orders are issued, H.Q. (D); see also **office** 3.
headship, *n.* —*Syn.* primacy, authority, control; see **administration** 1, **command** 2, **leadership** 1, **power** 2.
headsman, *n.* —*Syn.* hangman, beheader, public executioner; see **killer.**
headstone, *n.* —*Syn.* gravestone, marker, stone; see **grave** 1, **tombstone.**
headstrong, *mod.* —*Syn.* determined, strong-minded, stubborn; see **obstinate** 1.
headway, *n.* —*Syn.* advance, increase, promotion; see **progress** 1.
heady, *mod.* —*Syn.* overwhelming, intoxicating, powerful; see **strong** 8.
heal, *v.* **1.** [To cure]—*Syn.* restore, renew, treat, attend, make healthy, minister to, return to health, renovate, fix, repair, make whole, regenerate, bring round *or* around, remedy, meliorate, set, pu-

rify, cicatrize, rejuvenate, medicate, recall to life, reinvigorate, make clean, dress (a wound), rebuild, revive, rehabilitate, revivify, purge, reanimate, work a cure, cause to heal up, resuscitate, salve, help to get well, physic, free from ailment, make sound *or* whole, ameliorate; *all* (D): snatch from the jaws of death, doctor, set *or* fix up, put one on one's feet again, breathe new life into, skin over; see also **improve** 1, **nurse.**—*Ant.* make ill, expose*, infect.

2. [To recover]—*Syn.* get well, knit, mend; see **improve** 2, **recover** 3.

healing, *mod.*—*Syn.* restorative, invigorating, medicinal; see **remedial.**

health, *n.* **1.** [Physical or mental well-being]—*Syn.* vigor, haleness, wholeness, good condition, healthfulness, good health, fitness, robustness, bloom, soundness of body, freedom from disease *or* ailment, lustiness, tone, hardiness, hardihood, well-being, wellness, stamina, salubriousness, energy, euphoria, full bloom, eupepsia, salubrity; *all* (D): rosy cheeks, fine *or* high feather, fine fettle, good form, top shape, clean bill of health; see also **sanity** 1, **strength** 1, **vitality.**

2. [Condition of body or mind]—*Syn.* fitness, physical *or* mental state, form, shape, tone, constitution, well-being, circumstance, fettle, complexion, state of health, tendency.

healthful, *mod.*—*Syn.* nutritious, restorative, body-building, sanative, sanitary, hygienic, salutary, invigorating, tonic, stimulating, bracing, salubrious, wholesome, beneficial, health-giving, nutritive, nourishing, energy-giving, fresh, pure, clean, corrective, compensatory, cathartic, sedative, conducive to health, sustentative, regenerative, digestible, restoring, substantial, sustaining, promoting health, benign, good for one, aseptic, sanatory, desirable, clean, harmless, innocuous, healing, preventive, untainted, disease-free, unpolluted, unadulterated, uninjurious, favorable, advantageous, innoxious; see also **healthy, remedial.**—*Ant.* sickly, unwholesome*, noxious.

healthy, *mod.* **1.** [In good health]—*Syn.* sound, trim, all right, normal, robust, hale, vigorous, well, hearty, husky, athletic, stout, lusty, rosy-cheeked, potent, hardy, able-bodied, virile, muscular, blooming, sturdy, safe and sound, in good *or* sound condition, combat-ready, in full possession of one's faculties, in *or* enjoying *or* possessing good health, full of pep, never feeling better, as well as can be expected, bursting with health, fresh, of a sound constitution, whole, healthful, firm, stout, unimpaired, buxom, lively, undecayed, flourishing, good, ruddy, cured, fit, clear-eyed, plump, full of life and vigor, spirited, in fine fettle, burly, restored, tough, youthful, sound of wind and limb, free from disease *or* infirmity; *all* (D): in fine whack, fine, bobbish, at the peak of good health, fine and dandy, hunky-dory, chipper, in good shape, sound as a bell, in fine *or* high feather, in the pink (of condition), rugged, fit as a fiddle, sound as a dollar, looking like a million, fit and fine, full of beans, feeling one's oats, hard as nails; see also **sane** 1, **strong** 1.—*Ant.* unhealthy*, ill, diseased.

2. [Healthful]—*Syn.* salubrious, salutary, wholesome; see **healthful.**

heap, *n.*—*Syn.* pile, accumulation, mass, agglomeration, stack, load, collection, aggregation, stock, store, hoard, mountain, mound, abundance, profusion, bulk, fullness, volume, plenty, lump, total, sum, whole, huddle, mow, barrow, cartload, swell, harvest, hillock, deposit, carload, cargo, cock, wagonload, block, pyre, packet, jumble, pyramid, hill, cluster, confused mass, drift, bale, clump, shock, batch, bundle, bunch, gathering, amassment, acervation, concentration, assemblage of things lying one on another; *all* (D): haul, junk pile, full house, lots; see also **quantity.**—*Ant.* handful, bit*, a few specks.

heap, *v.* **1.** [To place in a heap]—*Syn.* pile, add, swell, (throw in a) bunch, lump, stack, rank, order, cord, bank, fill up, arrange, pile high, dike, hill, barricade, fill to overflowing, throw *or* rake *or* batch *or* bunch *or* draw together, fill *or* pile *or* heap up, mass, barrow, ruck, gather, dump, concentrate, mound, coacervate, deposit, dredge, group, throw *or* cast *or* gather in a heap, shock; see also **load** 1, **pack** 2.—*Ant.* scatter*, flatten, level.

2. [To amass]—*Syn.* gather, pile *or* lay up, store; see **accumulate** 1.

heaped, *mod.*—*Syn.* amassed, collected, stored; see **gathered.**

heaping, *mod.*—*Syn.* sated, running over, abundant; see **full** 1, **large** 1.

hear, *v.* **1.** [To perceive by ear]—*Syn.* listen to, hearken, hark, give attention, attend to, make out, auscultate, become aware of, catch, descry, apprehend *or* take in, eavesdrop, detect, perceive by the ear, overhear, take cognizance of, listen with both ears, keep one's ears open, have the sense of hearing, have perception of sound by the ear; *all* (D): give ear to, read (loud and clear), strain one's ears, listen in, devour someone's words, get (an earful); see also **listen** 1.

2. [To receive information aurally]—*Syn.* overhear, eavesdrop, be advised, find out, catch, learn, have it on good authority, learn by general report, have an account, ascertain, descry, pick up *or* glean *or* obtain *or* receive knowledge *or* appreciation of, receive information, discover, gather, apperceive, be told, understand, hear of, be led to believe, be made aware of, be informed, learn by the ear *or* by being told; *all* (D): hear say, hear tell of, get wise to, get an earful, get wind of, get the signal, sit in on, tune in; see also **listen** 2.

3. [To hold a hearing]—*Syn.* preside over, put on trial, summon to court; see **try** 3.

not hear of—*Syn.* not allow, refuse to consider, reject; see **forbid.**

heard, *mod.*—*Syn.* perceived, listened to, witnessed, caught, made out, understood, heeded, noted, made clear.

hearer, *n.*—*Syn.* listener, witness, bystander; see **auditor** 1.

hear from, *v.*—*Syn.* have *or* get *or* receive word *or* a communication (from), be informed, learn through; see **hear** 2, **receive** 1.

hearing, *mod.*—*Syn.* heeding, auditive, hearkening; see **auditory, listening, sensory** 1.

hearing, *n.* **1.** [An opportunity to be heard]—*Syn.* audition, interview, test, fair hearing, tryout, attendance, congress, conference, audit, notice, per-

formance, admittance, consultation, council, reception, presentation, audience, attention; see also **discussion** 1, **gathering, trial** 2.
2. [The act of hearing]—*Syn.* detecting, recording, distinguishing; see **listening.**
3. [The faculty for hearing]—*Syn.* ear, auditory faculty, aural apparatus, perception, listening ear, faculty *or* sense by which sound is perceived, sense of hearing, audition, act of perceiving sound, accoustic sensation.
4. [Range of hearing]—*Syn.* earshot, hearing distance, reach, sound, carrying distance, range, earreach, acoustical effect, auditory range; see also **extent.**

hearken, *v.* —*Syn.* notice, attend, observe; see **hear** 1, **listen** 1.

hear of, *v.* —*Syn.* hear *or* know about, be *or* become aware of, discover; see **know** 1, 3.

hear out, *v.* —*Syn.* listen to, yield (the floor) to, remain silent; see **listen** 2.

hearsay, *n.* —*Syn.* noise, scandal, report; see **gossip** 1, **rumor** 1, 2.

hearse, *n.* —*Syn.* funeral van *or* coach *or* vehicle, conveyance for a coffin, undertaker's limousine; *both* (D): meat wagon, dead wagon; see also **automobile, vehicle** 1.

heart, *n.* **1.** [The pump in the circulatory system] —*Syn.* vital organ, vascular organ, blood pump, cardiac organ; *both* (D): ticker, clock; see also **organ** 2.
2. [Feeling]—*Syn.* response, sympathy, sensitivity; see **emotion, feeling, pity** 1.
3. [The center]—*Syn.* core, middle, pith; see **center** 1.
4. [The most important portion]—*Syn.* gist, quintessence, root; see **essence** 1, **soul** 2.
5. [Courage]—*Syn.* fortitude, gallantry, spirit; see **courage** 1, **mind** 1, **soul** 4.
6. [The breast]—*Syn.* bosom, marrow, soul; see **breast** 3.
after one's own heart—*Syn.* suitable, pleasing, lovable; see **pleasant** 2.
at heart—*Syn.* basically, fundamentally, privately; see **originally** 1.
break one's heart—*Syn.* grieve, disappoint, pain; see **hurt** 1.
by heart—*Syn.* from memory, memorized, learned; see **remembered.**
change of heart—*Syn.* change of mind, reversal, alteration; see **change** 2.
do one's heart good—*Syn.* please, make content, delight; see **satisfy** 1.
eat one's heart out—*Syn.* worry, regret, nurse one's troubles; see **brood** 2.
from the bottom of one's heart—*Syn.* deeply, honestly, frankly; see **sincerely.**
have a heart—*Syn.* be kind, empathize, take pity; see **sympathize.**
have one's heart in one's mouth—*Syn.* be frightened, have anxiety, become nervous; see **fear** 1.
have one's heart in the right place—*Syn.* well-intentioned, well-meaning, kind; see **generous** 2.
in one's heart of hearts—*Syn.* fundamentally, basically, privately; see **secretly.**
lay to heart—*Syn.* take into account, take to heart, believe; see **consider** 1.
lose one's heart to—*Syn.* love, cherish, adore; see **fall in love.**
near one's heart—*Syn.* important, dear, cherished; see **beloved.**
set one's heart at rest—*Syn.* calm, placate, soothe; see **comfort** 1.
set one's heart on—*Syn.* long for, need, desire; see **want** 1.
take heart—*Syn.* cheer up, be comforted, take or give courage; see **encourage** 2.
take to heart—*Syn.* lay to heart, take into account, believe; see **consider** 1.
to one's heart's content—*Syn.* satisfactory, sufficient, plenty; see **enough** 1.
wear one's heart on one's sleeve—*Syn.* disclose, divulge, confess; see **reveal** 1.
with all one's heart—*Syn.* honestly, deeply, frankly; see **sincerely.**
with half a heart—*Syn.* half-heartedly, apathetically, listlessly; see **indifferent** 1.

heartache, *n.* —*Syn.* sorrow, despair, anguish; see **grief** 1, **regret.**

heart and soul, *mod.* —*Syn.* entirely, devotedly, absolutely; see **completely.**

heartbeat, *n.* —*Syn.* pulsation, throb of the heart, cardiovascular activity; see **beat** 2, **pulse.**

heartbreaking, *mod.* —*Syn.* cheerless, deplorable, joyless; see **pitiful** 1, **sad** 2, **tragic.**

heartbroken, *mod.* —*Syn.* melancholy, sorrowful, doleful; see **sad** 1.

heartburn, *n.* —*Syn.* pyrosis, indigestion, cardialgia, ulceritis, stomach upset, water qualm; see also **disease** 2.

heart disease, *n.* —*Syn.* heart failure, coronary illness, thrombosis; see **disease** 3.

hearten, *v.* —*Syn.* rouse, cheer, inspirit; see **encourage** 2.

heartfelt, *mod.* —*Syn.* sincere, deep, ardent; see **genuine** 2, **honest** 1.

hearth, *n.* **1.** [A fireplace]—*Syn.* grate, fireside, hearthstone; see **fireplace.**
2. [Home]—*Syn.* dwelling, abode, residence; see **home** 1.

heartily, *mod.* **1.** [Sincerely]—*Syn.* enthusiastically, earnestly, cordially; see **seriously** 2, **sincerely.**
2. [Vigorously]—*Syn.* zealously, enthusiastically, energetically; see **vigorously.**
3. [Completely]—*Syn.* totally, thoroughly, wholly; see **completely.**

heartless, *mod.* —*Syn.* unkind, unthinking, insensitive; see **cruel** 2, **ruthless** 1, 2, **savage** 2.

heart-rending, *mod.* —*Syn.* moving, piteous, mournful; see **pitiful** 1, **sad** 2.

hearty, *mod.* **1.** [Cordial]—*Syn.* warm, zealous, sincere, cheery, cheerful, jovial, wholehearted, neighborly, well-meant, vivacious, gay, animated, jolly, ardent, genial, fervid, zestful, glowing, enthusiastic, genuine, avid, deepest, passionate, frank, glad, deep, intense, exuberant, profuse, eager, unalloyed, effusive, gushing, devout, deep-felt, unfeigned, unrestrained, fervent, warmhearted, authentic, amicable, heartwarming, impassioned, heartfelt, brotherly, responsive; see also **friendly** 1, **happy** 1, 2.—*Ant.* false*, mock, sham.
2. [Healthy]—*Syn.* good, lively, full; see **healthful.**

heat, *n.* **1.** [Warmth]—*Syn.* calefaction, calidity, torridity, high temperature, hot wind, heat wave, fever, hot weather, temperature, incandescence, hotness, warmness, tepidity, incalescence, sultriness, red *or* white heat, torridness, tropical heat, dog days (D); see also **warmth, weather.**—*Ant.* cold*, frost, frigidity.
2. [Fervor]—*Syn.* ardor, passion, excitement; see **desire** 2, **enthusiasm** 1.
3. [Anger]—*Syn.* agitation, fury, ferocity; see **anger, rage** 2.
4. [A section of a race]—*Syn.* run, course, trial; see **race** 3.
5. [Sources of heat]—*Syn.* radioactivity, flame, radiation, atomic energy, solar energy; see also **energy** 3, **fire** 1, 2.

heat, *v.* **1.** [To make hot]—*Syn.* warm, fire, heat up, enflame, inflame, kindle, enkindle, calcine, calefy, tepefy, subject to heat, put on the fire, make hot *or* warm, calorify, smelt, scald, flush, carbonize, thaw, mull, boil, char, superheat, roast, chafe, seethe, oxidate, toast, oxidize, set fire to, melt, cauterize, sun, reheat, steam, incinerate, sear, singe, scorch, fuse, raise the temperature of, liquefy, gasify, fry, frizzle, use a blowtorch on, turn on the heat; see also **burn** 2, **cook, ignite.**—*Ant.* cool*, freeze, reduce the temperature.
2. [To become hot]—*Syn.* glow, warm (up), rise in temperature, become fevered *or* feverish, grow hot, incandesce, blaze, flame, flush, seethe, burst into flame, kindle, ignite, liquefy, gasify, thaw, swelter, perspire, reek, begin to pant, record a higher temperature, reach a higher thermal register; see also **boil** 2, **burn** 1, **sweat** 1.

heated, *mod.* **1.** [Warmed]—*Syn.* toasted, fired, cooked, broiled, fried, burnt, parched, scorched; see also **baked, boiled, burned** 1.—*Ant.* cool*, frozen, iced.
2. [Fervent]—*Syn.* fiery, ardent, avid; see **excited, passionate** 2.

heater, *n.*—*Syn.* radiator, auto heater, oil *or* gas *or* electric heater; see **furnace.**

heathen, *mod.*—*Syn.* idolatrous, pagan, unchristian, non-Jewish, non-Muslim, uncivilized, uncircumcised, unconverted, barbaric, amoral, ungodly, atheistic, agnostic, irreligious, paganish, gentile, sun-worshiping, ethnic, idolistic, henotheistic, polytheistic, demonolatrous, paynim, fetishistic, infidelic; see also **impious** 1, **primitive** 3.—*Ant.* Christian*, religious, moral.

heathen, *n.*—*Syn.* infidel, non-Christian, gentile; see **barbarian** 1, **pagan, skeptic.**

heating, *n.*—*Syn.* calefaction, steaming, boiling, scalding, roasting, broiling, melting, baking, warming, cooking, grilling; see also **heat** 1.—*Ant.* refrigeration*, freezing, cooling.

heave, *n.*—*Syn.* throw, hurl, fling, cast, wing, toss; see also **pitch** 2.

heave, *v.* **1.** [To raise laboriously]—*Syn.* lift, hoist, boost; see **raise** 1.
2. [To rise and fall]—*Syn.* rock, bob, pitch, go up and down, lurch, roll, reel, sway, swell, pant, palpitate, dilate, expand, billow, swirl, throb, waft, ebb and flow, wax and wane, undulate, puff, slosh, wash; see also **flow** 3, **toss** 2, **wave** 3, 4.—*Ant.* rest*, lie still, quiet.
3. [To throw]—*Syn.* hurl, fling, cast; see **throw** 1.

heaven, *n.* **1.** [The sky; *often plural*]—*Syn.* welkin, empyrean, firmament, stratosphere, heights, atmosphere, azure, beyond, heavenly spheres; *all* (D): the blue, the Great Unknown, upstairs; see also **air** 1, **sky.**
2. [The abode of the blessed]—*Syn.* Paradise, Elysian fields, Elysium, (Great) Beyond, Abode of the Dead, Olympus, Arcadia, Home of the Gods, Heavenly Home, God's Kingdom, Valhalla, Asgard, (abodes of) bliss, Zion, Holy City, Nirvana, welkin, inheritance of the saints, City Celestial, throne of God, (Land of) Beulah, (Garden of) Eden, Happy Isles, the New Jerusalem, afterworld, the divine abode, heavenly city, the city of God, abode of God and angels, our eternal home, the abode of saints, Kingdom of Heaven, next world, world to come, our Father's house, life *or* world beyond the grave, islands *or* isles of the blessed, abode of spirits of the righteous after death, Fortunate Isles *or* Islands, place of existence of the blessed after mortal life; *all* (D): happy hunting grounds, the eternal rest, Kingdom Come, Abraham's bosom, sweet by-and-by, the hereafter, the house not built with hands; see also **paradise** 3.—*Ant.* hell*, underworld, inferno.
3. [A state of great comfort]—*Syn.* bliss, felicity, harmony; see **happiness** 2.
4. [Supernatural power; *capital* H]—*Syn.* God Almighty, Providence, Divine Love; see **god.**
move heaven and earth—*Syn.* do all one can do, exert the most influence, do one's best; see **try** 1.

heavenly, *mod.* **1.** [Concerning heaven]—*Syn.* paradisiacal, celestial, supernal; see **angelic, divine** 1, **holy** 1.
2. [(D) Much approved of or liked]—*Syn.* blissful, sweet, enjoyable; see **excellent, pleasant** 1, 2.

heavily, *mod.*—*Syn.* laboriously, tediously, weightily, massively, ponderously, dully, gloomily, with difficulty, wearily, dejectedly, profoundly, with force *or* energy, densely; see also **gradually, slowly.**—*Ant.* lightly*, gently, easily.

heaviness, *n.*—*Syn.* burden, denseness, ballast; see **density** 1, **mass** 1, **weight** 1.

heavy, *mod.* **1.** [Weighty]—*Syn.* bulky, massive, cumbersome, unwieldy, ponderous, huge, overweight, top-heavy, of great weight, burdensome, portly, weighty, cumbrous, stout, big, heaved *or* lifted with labor, hard to lift *or* carry, having much weight in proportion to bulk, dense, elephantine, fat, substantial, ample, corpulent, abundant; *all* (D): beefy, hefty, chunky; see also **large** 1.—*Ant.* light*, buoyant, feather-light.
2. [Viscous]—*Syn.* dense, viscid, syrupy; see **thick** 3.
3. [Burdensome]—*Syn.* troublesome, oppressive, vexatious; see **difficult** 1, **disturbing, onerous** 1.
4. [Dull]—*Syn.* listless, slow, apathetic; see **dull** 6, **indifferent** 1.
5. [Gloomy]—*Syn.* dejected, cloudy, overcast; see **dark** 1, **dismal** 1, **sad** 2.
6. [Difficult]—*Syn.* complicated, troublesome, knotty; see **complex** 2, **confused** 2, **difficult** 2, **obscure** 1.

7. [Soggy]—*Syn.* inedible, damp, sodden; see **indigestible, wet** 1.

hang heavy—*Syn.* pass tediously, go slowly, be tedious; see **drag** 2.

heavy-handed, *mod.* **1.** [Strict]—*Syn.* oppressive, harsh, coercive; see **cruel** 2, **severe** 2.

2. [Awkward]—*Syn.* clumsy, inept, unskillful; see **awkward** 1.

heavy-hearted, *mod.* —*Syn.* forlorn, cheerless, melancholy; see **sad** 1, **sorrowful.**

heckle, *v.* —*Syn.* torment, disturb, pester; see **bother** 2, **ridicule.**

hectic, *mod.* —*Syn.* unsettled, boisterous, restless; see **confused** 2, **disordered.**

hedge, *n.* —*Syn.* fence, hedgerow, thornbush, shrubbery, enclosure, boundary, bushes, thicket, hurdle, obstacle, windbreak, quickset; see also **bush** 1, **plant.**

Shrubs and plants used for hedges include the following—boxwood *or* box, Russian privet, Japanese *or* California privet, mock privet *or* jasmine box, hawthorn *or* hedge thorn, Osage orange, honey locust, Russian olive, rose, honeysuckle, white willow, hedge laurel, dogrose, juniper, Glastonbury thorn, wait-a-bit thorn, Washington thorn, furze, broom, gorse, yucca, prickly pear cactus, ocatilla cactus, organ-pipe cactus, forsythia, barberry.

hedonism, *n.* —*Syn.* sensualism, gratification, debauchery; see **enjoyment** 2, **indulgence** 3.

hedonist, *n.* —*Syn.* sensualist, libertine, profligate, man of pleasure, pleasure-lover, thrill-seeker, Sybarite, voluptuary, eudaemonist, epicurean, gourmand, rake, debauchee, Sardanapalus, Lucullus; see also **glutton, lecher.**

heed, *v.* —*Syn.* pay attention (to), notice, be aware; see **regard** 1, **see** 3.

heedful, *mod.* —*Syn.* attentive, discreet, conscientious; see **careful, observant** 2.

heedless, *mod.* —*Syn.* thoughtless, negligent, inconsiderate; see **careless** 1, **rash.**

heel, *n.* **1.** [Hind part of the foot]—*Syn.* hock, spur, hind toe, Achilles' tendon; see also **foot** 2.

2. [The portion of the shoe under the heel, sense 1]. Varieties include the following—French, military, Cuban, low, spike, sensible, rubber, leather, plastic, wooden, spring, wedge sole; see also **bottom** 1, **foundation** 2.

3. [An object resembling a heel]—*Syn.* crust, spur, base, after-end, cyma reversa; see also **bottom** 1, **end** 4.

4. [(D) A worthless individual]—*Syn.* scamp, skunk, trickster; see **rascal.**

at heel—*Syn.* close behind, in back of, behind; see **following.**

cool one's heels (D)—*Syn.* be kept waiting, loiter, linger; see **wait** 1.

down at the heel(s)—*Syn.* shabby, seedy, rundown; see **worn** 2.

kick up one's heels—*Syn.* be lively, have fun, enjoy oneself; see **play** 1, 2.

on (*or* **upon) the heels of**—*Syn.* close behind, in back of, behind; see **following.**

out at the heel(s)—*Syn.* shabby, seedy, rundown; see **worn** 2.

show one's heels—*Syn.* run away, flee, take flight; see **escape.**

take to one's heels—*Ant.* run away, flee, take flight; see **escape.**

turn on one's heel—*Syn.* turn around, reverse, shift; see **turn** 1, 2.

heel, *v.* —*Syn.* follow, stay by one's heel, attend; see **obey** 1.

hefty, *mod.* —*Syn.* strong, husky, sturdy, stout, heavy, beefy, strapping, bulky, muscular, hearty, substantial, massive; see also **strong** 1.

hegemony, *n.* —*Syn.* dominion, authority, leadership; see **administration** 1, **command** 2, **power** 2.

hegira, *n.* —*Syn.* flight, fleeing, exodus; see **departure** 1, **escape** 1, **journey, retreat** 1.

heifer, *n.* —*Syn.* yearling, baby cow, springer; see **animal** 1, **calf, cow.**

height, *n.* **1.** [Altitude]—*Syn.* elevation, extent upward, pitch, prominence, loftiness, highness, perpendicular distance, angular measurement, upright distance, tallness, stature; see also **expanse, extent, length** 2.—*Ant.* depth, breadth*, width.

2. [Climax]—*Syn.* crowning point, end, crisis; see **climax, maximum, top** 1.

3. [An eminence]—*Syn.* rise, slope, alp; see **hill, mountain** 1.

heighten, *v.* **1.** [Increase]—*Syn.* sharpen, redouble, emphasize; see **increase** 1, **intensify, strengthen.**

2. [Raise]—*Syn.* uplift, elevate, lift; see **raise** 1.

heinous, *mod.* —*Syn.* atrocious, horrendous, flagrant; see **frightful** 1, **offensive** 2.

heir, *n.* —*Syn.* scion, male inheritor, heir presumptive, future possessor, legal heir, heir apparent, successor, descendent, one who inherits, heiress, beneficiary, heir expectant, heir general, heir at law, coheir, inheritor, grantee, devisee, crown prince, Prince of Wales.—*Ant.* predecessor, incumbent, parent.

heiress, *n.* —*Syn.* female inheritor, crown princess, inheritress, inheritrix, wealthy girl, debutante; see also **heir.**

heirloom, *n.* —*Syn.* inheritance, legacy, heritage, patrimony, antique, bequest, birthright, reversion; see also **gift** 1.

held, *mod.* —*Syn.* grasped, controlled, occupied, guarded, taken, gripped, clutched, defended, adhered, stuck, detained, sustained, believed; see also **retained** 1.—*Ant.* released, freed*, lost.

held over, *v.* —*Syn.* returned, presented again, retold; see **repeated** 1.

held up, *mod.* **1.** [Robbed]—*Syn.* assaulted, shot at, beaten; see **attacked.**

2. [Postponed]—*Syn.* withheld, put off, delayed; see **postponed.**

hell, *n.* **1.** [Place of the dead, especially of the wicked dead; *often capital H*]—*Syn.* underworld, inferno, place of departed spirits, the lower world, the grave, infernal regions, Sheol, Tartarus, Gehenna, abyss, realms of Pluto, Tophet, Styx, Acheron, Dis, Cocytus, Avernus, Abaddon, Satan's Kingdom, abode of the damned *or* the dead, realm of Pluto, everlasting fire, purgatory, Erebus, nether world, Pandemonium, Avichi, hell-fire, Malebolge, Hades, bottomless pit, perdition, lake of fire and brimstone, place of the lost, place of torment, limbo, habitation of fallen angels, place *or* state of punishment of the wicked after death; *all* (D): blue blazes, Halifax, Hoboken, hot place, you-know-

where, the hereafter.—*Ant.* heaven*, earth, paradise.
2. [A condition of torment]—*Syn.* trial, hell-fire, ordeal; see **crisis, difficulty** 1, 2, **emergency.**
be hell on (D)—*Syn.* be painful for, be difficult to, be harsh with; see **abuse** 1.
catch (*or* **get**) **hell** (D)—*Syn.* get into trouble, be scolded, receive punishment; see **get it** 2.
for the hell of it (D)—*Syn.* for no reason, for the fun of it, playfully; see **lightly** 1.

Hellenic, *mod.* —*Syn.* serene, refined, academic; see **ancient** 2, **classical** 2.

Hellenist, *n.* —*Syn.* stylist, classicist, philosopher; see **professor, scholar** 2.

hellish, *mod.* **1.** [Concerning hell]—*Syn.* Stygian, Tartarean, Hadean, chthonian, devilish, fiery; see also **infernal** 1.—*Ant.* divine*, heavenly, blessed.
2. [Extremely bad or unpleasant]—*Syn.* diabolical, fiendish, destructive; see **wicked** 2.

hello, *interj.* —*Syn.* how do you do, greetings, welcome, how are you, good morning, good day, *ciao* (Italian), *bonjour* (French), *buenos días, buenas tardes, buenas noches* (*all* Spanish), *shalom* (Hebrew); *all* (D): howdy, 'lo, hyah, h'arya, put it there, how goes it; see also **greeting** 1.—*Ant.* goodbye*, *au revoir* (French), *adiós* (Spanish).

hell of a (D), *mod.* —*Syn.* helluva (D), bad, awful; see **faulty, poor** 2.

hell on (D), *mod.* —*Syn.* hard *or* severe on, prejudiced (against), strict *or* exacting *or* firm with; see **cruel** 1, 2, **firm** 5, **harmful.**

helm, *n.* —*Syn.* tiller, steering wheel, rudder, steerage, steering apparatus; see also **wheel** 1.

helmet, *n.* Helmets include the following—crest, casque, sallet, burgonet, morion, armet, beaume, Roman helmet, stephane, Greek helmet, basinet, football helmet, sun helmet, diver's helmet, hard hat, trench helmet, motorcyclist's helmet, fencing helmet: *all* (D): tin hat, battle bowler, chamber pot, jerry, steel derby; see also **hat.**

help, *n.* **1.** [Assistance]—*Syn.* advice, co-operation, guidance; see **aid** 1.
2. [Employees]—*Syn.* aides, representatives, hired help; see **assistant, faculty** 2, **staff** 2.
3. [Physical relief]—*Syn.* maintenance, sustenance, nourishment; see **relief** 4, **remedy** 2.
cannot help but—*Syn.* be compelled *or* obliged to, cannot fail to, have to; see **must.**
cannot help oneself—*Syn.* be compelled to, have a need to, be the victim of circumstance *or* habit; see **must.**
so help me (God)—*Syn.* as God is my witness, by God, I swear; see **oath** 1.

help, *v.* **1.** [To aid]—*Syn.* assist, abet, uphold, advise, encourage, stand by, co-operate, intercede for, patronize, befriend, accommodate, work for, back up, maintain, sustain, prop, benefit, bolster, lend a hand, do a service, see through, do one's part, cheer, give a hand, be of use, come to the aid of, be of some help, help along, do a favor, promote, endorse, sanction, back, advocate, abet, stimulate, uphold, second, further, work for; *all* (D): stick up for, take under one's wing, go to bat for, side with, give a lift, boost, take in tow, pitch in, set to; see also **support** 2.—*Ant.* oppose*, rival, combat.
2. [To assist in recovery]—*Syn.* attend, nourish, doctor (D); see **heal** 1, **nurse, revive** 2, **treat** 3.
3. [To serve at table]—*Syn.* wait on, accommodate, tend to; see **serve** 4.
4. [To improve]—*Syn.* better, correct, ease; see **improve** 1.

helped, *mod.* —*Syn.* aided, maintained, supported, advised, abetted, befriended, relieved, sustained, nursed, patronized, encouraged, assisted, accompanied, taken care of, subsidized, bolstered, upheld; see also **backed** 2.—*Ant.* impeded, hindered, harmed*.

helper, *n.* —*Syn.* apprentice, aide, secretary; see **assistant, supporter.**

helpful, *mod.* **1.** [Useful]—*Syn.* valuable, important, significant, crucial, essential, co-operative, symbiotic, serviceable, invaluable, profitable, advantageous, favorable, convenient, suitable, practical, pragmatic, operative, effectual, efficacious, usable, accessible, applicable, conducive, utilitarian, improving, bettering, of service, serendipitous, all-purpose, desirable, instrumental, contributive, good for, to (one's) advantage, at one's command; see also **effective, necessary** 1.—*Ant.* useless*, ineffective, impractical.
2. [Curative]—*Syn.* healthy, salutary, restorative; see **healthful, remedial.**
3. [Obliging]—*Syn.* accommodating, considerate, neighborly; see **kind** 1.

helpfully, *mod.* —*Syn.* usefully, beneficially, constructively, kindly, profitably, to the good, advantageously; see also **effectively, excellently.**

helpfulness, *n.* —*Syn.* assistance, convenience, help; see **aid** 1, **use** 2, **usefulness.**

helping, *mod.* —*Syn.* aiding, assisting, co-operating, collaborating, synergistic, working *or* co-operating *or* collaborating (with), being assistant *or* consultant to, in co-operation *or* collaboration *or* combination (with), contributing (to), accessory (to), going along (with), acceding to; *all* (D): in cahoots (with), hand in glove (with), thick as thieves, in the same boat (with), up to one's ears in; see **helpful** 1, **practical.**

helping, *n.* —*Syn.* serving, plateful, order, course, portion, ration, piece, allowance; see also **food, meal** 2, **share.**

helpless, *mod.* **1.** [Dependent]—*Syn.* feeble, unable, invalid; see **dependent** 2, **disabled, weak** 1, 6.
2. [Incompetent]—*Syn.* incapable, unfit, inexpert; see **incompetent.**

helplessness, *n.* **1.** [Disability]—*Syn.* poor health, disorder, convalescence; see **illness** 1, **weakness** 1, 2.
2. [Incompetence]—*Syn.* incapacity, weakness, failure; see **inability** 1.

helpmate, *n.* —*Syn.* spouse, companion, aide; see **assistant, associate.**

help oneself, *v.* —*Syn.* aid *or* promote *or* further, etc., oneself, live by one's own efforts, get on *or* along; see **help** 1, **prosper.**

help oneself to, *v.* —*Syn.* take, grab, pick (up); see **appropriate, seize** 1, 2, **steal.**

helter-skelter, *mod.* **1.** [Carelessly]—*Syn.* incautiously, unmindfully, rashly; see **carelessly.**
2. [Confused]—*Syn.* tumultuous, jumbled, cluttered; see **disorderly** 1, **irregular** 1, 4.

hem, *n.* —*Syn.* border, skirting, edging, piping, selvage; see also **edge** 1, **fringe** 2, **rim, trimming.**
hem and haw, *v.* —*Syn.* stutter, hesitate in speech, falter; see **hesitate, pause, stammer.**
hemisphere, *n.* —*Syn.* half of the globe, Western Hemisphere, Eastern Hemisphere, Northern Hemisphere, Southern Hemisphere, realm, territory; see also **earth** 1.
hemorrhage, *n.* —*Syn.* discharge, bleeding, issue, emission of blood, hemorrhea, bloody flux, effusion; see also **illness** 1, **injury** 1.
hemp, *n.* —*Syn.* burlap, sacking, jute; see **cloth.**
hen, *n.* —*Syn.* female chicken, pullet, egger (D); see **bird** 1, **chicken** 1, **fowl.**
hence, *mod.* **1.** [Therefore]—*Syn.* consequently, for that reason, on that account; see **so** 2, **therefore.**
2. [From now]—*Syn.* henceforth, henceforward, from here; see **hereafter.**
3. [Away]—*Syn.* forward, onward, out; see **away** 1, **from.**
henceforth, *n.* —*Syn.* from now on, hence, in the future; see **hereafter.**
henchman, *n.* —*Syn.* partner, advocate, aid; see **associate, follower.**
henna, *mod.* —*Syn.* reddish-orange, reddish-brown, dyed with henna; see **brown, red.**
henpeck, *v.* —*Syn.* bully, suppress, intimidate; see **bother** 2, **threaten** 1.
henpecked, *mod.* —*Syn.* dominated by a wife, in fear of one's wife, subjected to nagging, browbeaten, intimidated, passive, constrained, compliant, in bondage, yielding, without freedom or independence, acquiescent, in subjection, subject, obedient, resigned, submissive, wife-ridden, docile, meek, cringing, unresisting, unassertive; *all* (D): led by the nose, under one's thumb, at one's beck and call, tied to one's apron strings, nagged, in harness; see also **dependent** 2, **subordinate, timid** 1, 2.
herald, *n.* —*Syn.* bearer, prophet, adviser; see **messenger, reporter, runner** 1.
herald, *v.* —*Syn.* proclaim, publicize, announce; see **advertise** 1, **declare** 1.
heraldry, *n.* —*Syn.* (study of) genealogies, heraldic device(s), coat(s) of arms, ceremony, pomp; see also **ceremony** 2, **ostentation** 1.
herb, *n.* Herbs include the following—those used mainly in medicine: foxglove *or* digitalis, belladonna, verbena, lemon verbena, vervain, coltsfoot, madder, baneberry, betony, herb-of-grace, herb-robert, leopard's-bane, thoroughwort, hyssop, hedge-hyssop, musk root, cinchona, camomile, castor-oil plant, boneset, horehound, wormwood, valerian; those used mainly in cookery; ginger, peppermint, thyme, summer savory, winter savory, mustard, chicory, chives, chervil, sweet chervil, needle chervil, cardamom, coriander, sweet basil, borage, peppergrass, parsley, anise, sweet cicely, cumin, fennel, caraway, rosemary, tarragon, oregano, wintergreen, Oswego tea, bergamot; see also **flavoring, pickle** 2, **plant, spice.**
herbal, *mod.* —*Syn.* herbaceous, verdant, grassy, vegetal, vegetative; see also **green** 2.
herbalist, *n.* —*Syn.* planter, greenskeeper, cultivator; see **gardener, scientist.**
herbarium, *n.* —*Syn.* garden, hothouse, nursery; see **greenhouse.**
herculean, *mod.* **1.** [Laborious]—*Syn.* strenuous, heavy, arduous; see **difficult** 1.
2. [Gigantic]—*Syn.* titanic, colossal, enormous; see **large** 1.
herd, *n.* **1.** [A number of animals]—*Syn.* flock, drove, pack, brood, swarm, lot, bevy, covey, gaggle, nest, brood, flight, school, clan; see also **gathering.**
2. [Disparaging term for common people]—*Syn.* rabble, mob, multitude; see **crowd** 1, **people** 3.
herdsman, *n.* —*Syn.* shepherd, herder, sheepherder, cowherd, goatherd, ranch hand, cattleman, range rider, buckaroo, vaquero, gaucho; *all* (D): cowhand, cowpuncher, saddle stiff, bull nurse, wrangler; see also **cowboy** 1, **rancher.**
here, *mod.* —*Syn.* in this place, hereabout(s), in this direction, hither, on this spot over here, up here, down here, right here, on hand *or* board *or* deck, in the face of, within reach or call.
hereafter, *mod.* —*Syn.* hence, henceforth, henceforward, from now on, after this, in the future, hereupon, in the course of time.
hereafter, *n.* —*Syn.* underworld, abode of the dead, the great beyond (D); see **heaven** 2, **hell** 1.
here and there, *mod.* —*Syn.* scatteringly, patchily, sometimes; see **everywhere, scattered.**
hereby, *mod.* —*Syn.* at this moment, with these means, with this, thus, herewith.
hereditable, *mod.* —*Syn.* congenital, genetic, intrinsic; see **ancestral, inherent.**
hereditary, *mod.* —*Syn.* inherited, genetic, paternal; see **ancestral.**
heredity, *n.* —*Syn.* inheritance, ancestry, hereditary transmission, hereditary succession, Mendelism, Mendelianism, genetics, eugenics.
herein, *mod.* —*Syn.* included, in this place, here; see **within.**
hereof, *mod.* —*Syn.* concerning this, in this regard, on this subject; see **about** 2.
heresy, *n.* —*Syn.* nonconformity, dissidence, revisionism, protestantism, dissent, heterodoxy, sectarianism, doctrinal divergence, apostasy, agnosticism, schism, unorthodoxy, secularism; see also **blasphemy, paganism, sin.**
heretic, *n.* —*Syn.* schismatic, apostate, sectarian; see **cynic, pagan, skeptic.**
heretical, *mod.* —*Syn.* skeptical, unorthodox, apostate; see **atheistic.**
heretofore, *mod.* —*Syn.* since, until now, up to this time; see **before** 1, **formerly.**
hereupon, *mod.* —*Syn.* subsequently, hence, next; see **hereafter.**
heritage, *n.* **1.** [Inheritance]—*Syn.* patrimony, legacy, birthright, heirship, ancestry, lot, right, dowry; see also **division** 2, **heredity, share.**
2. [Tradition]—*Syn.* convention, endowment, cultural inheritance; see **culture** 2, **custom** 2, **fashion** 2, **method** 2, **system** 2.
hermaphrodite, *n.* —*Syn.* bisexual, intersex, queer (D); see **homosexual, pervert** 2.
hermaphroditic, *mod.* —*Syn.* homosexual, inner-oriented, queer (D); see **bisexual, perverted** 2.
hermetic, *mod.* **1.** [Closed]—*Syn.* sealed, shut, airtight; see **tight** 2.

2. [Magical]—*Syn.* alchemical, mystical, occult; see **magic, mysterious** 2, **secret** 1.

hermit, *n.* —*Syn.* holy man, ascetic, anchorite, cenobite, solitary, recluse, eremite, santon, Hieronymite, stylite, hermitress, Marabout, solitarian, pillarist, anchoress, pillar saint; see also **ascetic, misanthrope, skeptic.**

hermitage, *n.* **1.** [Isolation]—*Syn.* seclusion, withdrawal, self-exile; see **isolation, privacy.**

2. [A retreat]—*Syn.* shelter, asylum, monastery; see **retreat** 2.

hero, *n.* **1.** [One distinguished for action]—*Syn.* brave man, model, conqueror, victorious general, god, martyr, champion, paladin, ace, exemplar, prize athlete, master, man of distinguished valor *or* performance, brave, warrior, demigod, saint, man of courage *or* mettle, lion, star, combatant, worthy, popular figure, great man, knight-errant, a man among men, man of the hour *or* day, intrepid warrior, fearless soldier, dauntless flier, tin god (D); see also **celebrity** 2, **idol** 2, **victor.**

2. [Principal male character in a literary composition]—*Syn.* protagonist, male lead, gallant, main actor, tragedian, leading man, chief character, principal male character, antihero, matinee idol; *all* (D): heavy, heavy (lead), Horatio Alger boy, Sir Galahad, Romeo; see also **actor, cast** 2, **star** 3.

heroic, *mod.* —*Syn.* valiant, valorous, fearless; see **brave** 1, **noble** 1, 2.

heroine, *n.* **1.** [A female hero]—*Syn.* courageous woman, champion, goddess, ideal, intrepid *or* resourceful *or* supremely courageous woman, demigoddess, woman of heroic character, woman of the hour *or* day; see also **celebrity** 2, **hero** 1, **idol** 2.

2. [Leading female character in a literary composition]—*Syn.* feminine lead, protagonist, leading lady, diva, prima donna, principal female character, female star *or* lead; *all* (D): romantic interest, heart interest, girl; see also **actress, cast** 2, **star** 3.

heroism, *n.* —*Syn.* rare fortitude, valor, bravery; see **courage** 1, **strength** 1, **valor.**

hesitancy, *n.* **1.** [Doubt]—*Syn.* indecision, skepticism, irresolution; see **doubt** 2, **uncertainty** 1.

2. [Delay]—*Syn.* wavering, delaying, procrastination; see **delay** 1, **hesitation** 2, **pause** 1, 2.

hesitant, *mod.* **1.** [Doubtful]—*Syn.* skeptical, unpredictable, irresolute; see **doubtful** 2, **uncertain** 2.

2. [Slow]—*Syn.* delaying, wavering, dawdling; see **lazy** 1, **slow** 2.

hesitantly, *mod.* —*Syn.* dubiously, falteringly, shyly; see **carefully** 2.

hesitate, *v.* —*Syn.* falter, stutter, fluctuate, vacillate, pause, stop, hold off *or* back, be dubious *or* uncertain, flounder, alternate, straddle, hover, scruple, balk, ponder, think about, defer, stay one's hand, delay, wait, think it over, change one's mind, trim, recoil, shy at, demur, dally, seesaw back and forth, not know what to do, be uncertain *or* irresolute, pull back, catch one's breath, weigh and consider, oscillate, hang back, swerve, tergiversate, debate, shift, shrink, wait, deliberate, linger, balance, equivocate; *all* (D): think twice, drag one's feet, hang off, shilly-shally, hem and haw, blow hot and cold, dillydally, straddle the fence, leave up in the air, make bones about, hang in the air, do figure eights; see also **stammer, waver.**—*Ant.* decide, resolve*, conclude.

hesitating, *mod.* **1.** [Doubtful]—*Syn.* skeptical, unsure, irresolute; see **doubtful** 2, **uncertain** 2.

2. [Slow]—*Syn.* delaying, wavering, dawdling; see **slow** 2.

hesitation, *n.* **1.** [Doubt]—*Syn.* equivocation, skepticism, irresolution; see **doubt** 2, **uncertainty** 2.

2. [Delay]—*Syn.* wavering, delaying, procrastination, dawdling, vacillation, fluctuation, oscillation, faltering; see also **delay** 1, **pause** 1, 2.

heterodox, *mod.* —*Syn.* heretical, skeptical, iconoclastic; see **atheistic, doubtful** 2.

heterogeneous, *mod.* —*Syn.* miscellaneous, variant, varied, nonhomogeneous, mingled, discordant, dissimilar, conglomerate, confused, inharmonious, unrelated, variegated, amalgamate, diversified, multiplex, unallied, motley, unmatched, independent, mosaic, mongrel, incompatible, composite, jumbled, assorted, odd; *both* (D): job-lot, mixy; see also **complex** 1, **different** 1, 2, **mixed** 1, **unlike, various.**

heterosexual, *mod.* —*Syn.* attracted to the opposite sex, sexually normal, straight (D); see **female** 2, **male.**

heterosexual, *n.* —*Syn.* sexually normal male *or* female, one who desires the opposite sex, hetero (D); see **man** 2, **woman** 1.

hew, *v.* —*Syn.* slit, slash, fell; see **cut** 1.

hey (D), *interj.* —*Syn.* you there, say, hey there, I say, hold on *or* up (D); see also **halt** 2, **hello, stop.**

heyday, *n.* —*Syn.* adolescence, bloom, prime (of life); see **youth** 1.

hiatus, *n.* —*Syn.* interval, gap, break; see **blank** 1, **pause** 1, 2.

hibernate, *v.* —*Syn.* sleep through the winter, winter, vegetate, enclose *or* immure oneself, keep out of society, lie dormant, lie torpid for the winter, hole up (D); see also **sleep.**

hidden, *mod.* **1.** [Secret]—*Syn.* esoteric, clandestine, surreptitious; see **secret** 3, **obscure** 3, **unknown** 1.

2. [Concealed from view]—*Syn.* secreted, secluded, out of sight, private, covert, concealed, undercover, occult, arcane, in the dark, in a haze *or* fog, in darkness, masked, screened, veiled, cloaked, obscured, disguised, socked in, invisible, clouded, sealed, unobserved, blotted, in eclipse, impenetrable, unseen, eclipsed, unexposed, camouflaged, enshrouded, undetected, shrouded, shadowy, unknown, indiscernible, latent, buried, opaque, undetected, deep, unsuspected, inscrutable, unapparent, inexplicable, illegible, unintelligible, imperceptible, puzzling, unobserved, out of view, dim, recondite, overlaid, clandestine, subterranean, cloistered, suppressed, secured, hermetic, dark, inward, underground, unrevealed, undisclosed, imperceivable, inert, withheld, surreptitious, sequestered, underhand, unsearchable; *all* (D): kept in the dark, under wraps, kept dark; see also **covered** 1, **isolated, obscure** 1, **withdrawn.** —*Ant.* obvious*, open, apparent.

3. [Mysterious]—*Syn.* symbolical, abstruse, cryptic; see **magic** 1, **mysterious** 2, **secret** 1.

hide, *n.* **1.** [Skin of an animal]—*Syn.* pelt, fell, rawhide, pigskin, chamois *or* shammy, bearskin, goatskin, jacket, integument, sheepskin, sealskin, snakeskin, alligator skin, calfskin; see also **coat** 2, **fur, leather, skin.**

2. [(D) Human skin]—*Syn.* integument, epidermis, pellicle; see **skin.**

neither hide nor hair—*Syn.* nothing whatsoever, no indication, not at all; see **nothing.**

hide, *v.* **1.** [To conceal]—*Syn.* shroud, curtain, veil, camouflage, cover, mask, cloak, keep in ignorance, not give away, ensconce, screen, adumbrate, blot out, reserve, bury, suppress, withhold, keep underground, stifle, tuck away, keep secret, hush up, shield, shade, eclipse, not tell, lock up, confuse, put out of sight, put out of the way, hold back, keep from, secrete, dissemble, smuggle, cache, harbor, overlay, shadow, conceal from sight, keep out of sight, entomb, stow away, protect, couch, obstruct the view of, hoard, store, seclude, closet, inter, conceal, put in concealment, hush, darken, obscure, render invisible, wrap, shelter, envelop, throw a veil over; *all* (D): keep in the shade *or* dark, keep under one's hat, seal one's lips, put the lid on, plant, put in lavender, sink, salt away, drop, dump; see also **censor, disguise.**—*Ant.* expose*, lay bare, uncover.

2. [To keep oneself concealed]—*Syn.* disguise oneself, change one's identity, cover one's traces, travel incognito, keep out of sight, go underground, lie in ambush, sneak, prowl, hermitize, burrow, skulk, avoid notice, lie in wait, hibernate, lie *or* be concealed, stand *or* hold oneself aloof, take refuge in a hiding place, lie low, conceal oneself, lie snug *or* close, rusticate, lie in ambush, lurk, shut oneself up, seclude oneself, lie hid *or* hidden, keep out of the way, go *or* stay in hiding, retire from sight; *all* (D); hide out, cover up, duck, keep shady, lie hid, keep in the background; see also **deceive, disappear, sneak.**

hide-and-seek, *n.*—*Syn.* evasion, mystification, elusiveness; see **game** 1.

hidebound, *mod.*—*Syn.* unchangeable, traditional, stubborn; see **conservative, dogmatic** 2, **obstinate** 1, **prejudiced.**

hide one's head, *mod.*—*Syn.* be ashamed, be embarrassed for *or* about, crawl; see **apologize, regret.**

hideous, *mod.* **1.** [Extremely ugly]—*Syn.* ghastly, grisly, frightful; see **ugly** 1.

2. [Shocking]—*Syn.* repulsive, hateful, revolting; see **frightful** 1, **offensive** 2.

hideout, *n.*—*Syn.* lair, den, hermitage; see **refuge** 1, **retreat** 2, **sanctuary** 2, **shelter.**

hiding, *mod.*—*Syn.* concealing, masking, screening, covering, going underground, veiling, suppressing, cloaking, in ambush, in concealment, out of sight.—*Ant.* obvious*, in plain view, in evidence.

hierarchy, *n.*—*Syn.* ministry, regime, theocracy; see **authority** 3, **bureaucracy** 1, **government** 1, 2.

hieroglyph, *n.*—*Syn.* pictograph, code, cryptograph; see **symbol.**

high, *mod.* **1.** [Tall]—*Syn.* towering, gigantic, big, colossal, tremendous, great, giant, huge, formidable, immense, lank, lanky, long, sky-scraping; *both* (D): steep, sky-high; see also **large** 1.—*Ant.* short*, diminutive, undersized.

2. [Elevated]—*Syn.* lofty, uplifted, upraised, soaring, aerial, high-reaching, flying, hovering, overtopping, beetling, jutting, cloud-swept (D); see also **above** 1, **raised** 1.—*Ant.* low*, depressed, underground.

3. [Exalted]—*Syn.* eminent, leading, powerful; see **distinguished** 2, **important** 2, **noble** 1, 2.

4. [Important]—*Syn.* essential, chief, crucial; see **important** 1, **necessary** 1.

5. [Expensive]—*Syn.* high-priced, costly, precious; see **expensive.**

6. [To an unusual degree]—*Syn.* great, extraordinary, special; see **unusual** 1, 2.

7. [Shrill]—*Syn.* piercing, sharp, penetrating; see **loud** 1, **shrill.**

8. [(D) Drunk]—*Syn.* intoxicated, tipsy, inebriated; see **drunk.**

9. [(D) Under the influence of drugs]—*Syn. all* (D): stoned, hopped-up, freaked-out, wasted, spaced out, tuned-in, turned-on, potted, on a trip, tripping, tripped-out, hyped-up, psyched.

on high—*Syn.* high in position, up in space, in heaven; see **above** 1.

high and dry (D), *mod.*—*Syn.* marooned, stranded, left helpless; see also **abandoned, dry** 1.

high and low, *mod.*—*Syn.* in every nook and corner, in all possible places, exhaustively; see **completely, everywhere.**

high and mighty, *mod.*—*Syn.* pompous, vain, conceited; see **egotistic** 2.

highball, *n.*—*Syn.* beverage, alcoholic drink, long drink; see **cocktail, drink** 2.

Highballs include the following—rye, Bourbon, Scotch, Irish, brandy, rum, applejack.

highborn, *mod.*—*Syn.* patrician, aristocratic, lordly; see **noble** 1, 2, 3.

higher, *mod.*—*Syn.* taller, more advanced, superior to, over, larger than, ahead, surpassing, more towering, bigger, greater; see also **above** 1, **beyond.**—*Ant.* smaller, shorter*, inferior.

highest, *mod.*—*Syn.* topmost, superlative, supreme, maximal, most, top-notch, top, overmost, apical, maximum, head, pre-eminent, capital, chief, paramount, acmic, tiptop, zenithal, crown; see also **best** 1, **principal.**

high-flown, *mod.*—*Syn.* extravagant, pretentious, haughty; see **egotistic** 2.

high-handed, *mod.*—*Syn.* oppressive, arbitrary, overbearing; see **autocratic** 1, **severe** 2.

highland, *n.*—*Syn.* uplands, plateau, high country; see **mountain** 1, **ridge** 2.

highly, *mod.*—*Syn.* extremely, profoundly, deeply; see **very.**

high-minded, *mod.*—*Syn.* honorable, conscientious, ethical; see **decent** 2, **honest** 1, **noble** 1, 2.

highness, *n.* **1.** [Quality of being high]—*Syn.* length, tallness, loftiness; see **height** 1.

2. [Term of respect, usually to royalty; *often capital*]—*Syn.* majesty, lordship, ladyship, excellency, honor, sire, grace, reverence, worship; see also **royalty.**

high on the hog (D), *mod.*—*Syn.* extravagantly, expensively, beyond one's means; see **wastefully.**

high-pressure, *mod.*—*Syn.* forceful, potent, compelling; see **powerful** 1.

high-pressure (D), *v.* —*Syn.* plead, adjure, ask; see **urge** 2.

high-priced, *mod.* —*Syn.* costly, precious, extravagant; see **expensive**

high school, *n.* —*Syn.* public school, secondary school, preparatory school, *lycée* (French), *Gymnasium, Realschule* (*both* German), Latin school, private academy, military school, upper grades, trade school, seminary, middle school, junior high school, intermediate school, vocational school; *all* (D): high, junior high, prep school; see also **academy** 1, **school** 1.

high-sounding, *mod.* —*Syn.* artificial, pompous, ostentatious; see **egotistic** 2.

high-speed, *mod.* —*Syn.* swift, rapid, quick; see **fast** 1.

high-spirited, *mod.* —*Syn.* daring, dauntless, reckless; see **brave** 1, **valiant** 1.

high-strung, *mod.* —*Syn.* nervous, tense, impatient; see **excitable, restless** 1.

high-toned, *mod.* **1.** [High-pitched]—*Syn.* raucous, sharp, piercing; see **loud** 1, **shrill.**
2. [(D) Dignified]—*Syn.* grand, noble, righteous; see **cultured, dignified, refined** 2.

highway, *n.* —*Syn.* roadway, parkway, superhighway, freeway, turnpike, toll road, skyway, post road *or* way, state *or* national highway, *Autobahn* (German); two-lane highway, four-lane highway, six-lane highway, etc.; see also **road** 1.

highwayman, *n.* —*Syn.* bandit, outlaw, thief; see **criminal, robber.**

high, wide, and handsome (D), *mod.* —*Syn.* extravagantly, expansively, without restraint; see **widely** 1.

hijack, *v.* —*Syn.* highjack, privateer, capture; see **seize** 2.

hike, *n.* —*Syn.* tramp, trip, backpack, tour, trek, excursion, ramble; see also **journey, walk** 3.

hike, *v.* **1.** [To tramp]—*Syn.* take a hike, tour, explore; see **travel** 2, **walk** 1.
2. [(D) To raise]—*Syn.* lift, advance, pull up; see **increase** 1.

hiking, *mod.* —*Syn.* tramping, hitchhiking, backpacking, rambling, wandering, exploring; see also **marching, walking.**

hilarious, *mod.* —*Syn.* amusing, lively, witty; see **entertaining, funny** 1.

hilarity, *n.* —*Syn.* play, amusement, excitement; see **entertainment** 1, **fun, laugh.**

hill, *n.* —*Syn.* mound, knoll, hillock, butte, mesa, bluff, promontory, precipice, cliff, range, rising ground, headland, monadnock, upland, hummock, mount, downgrade, inclination, descent, slope, ascent, slant, grade, incline, eminence, height, dune, highland, rise, helicline, *kopje* (South African), *tope* (Hindu), foothill, chine, spine, barrow, steep, down, fell, tumulus, climb, elevation, protuberance, ridge, heap, acclivity, hillside, talus, upgrade, hilltop, tor, vantage point *or* ground, pitch, swell, declivity, knap, gradient, Acropolis, hold, summit, esker, kop; see also **mountain** 1.

hillside, *n.* —*Syn.* grade, gradient, acclivity; see **hill**

hilltop, *n.* —*Syn.* peak, acme, elevation; see **height** 1, **hill, top** 1.

hilly, *mod.* —*Syn.* bumpy, uneven, undulating, rangy, steep, sloping, craggy, rocky, broken, rugged, precipitous; see also **abrupt** 1, **irregular** 4, **mountainous, rough** 1.—*Ant.* level*, even, regular.

hilt, *n.* —*Syn.* hold, handhold, grip; see **handle** 1.

hind, *mod.* —*Syn.* rear, hindmost, after; see **back.**

hinder, *v.* —*Syn.* impede, obstruct, interfere with, check, retard, fetter, block, thwart, bar, clog, encumber, burden, cripple, handicap, cramp, preclude, inhibit, debar, shackle, interrupt, arrest, contravene, curb, resist, oppose, baffle, muzzle, balk, deter, hamper, frustrate, nullify, checkmate, outwit, foil, entangle, stop, counteract, offset, neutralize, derange, tie *or* hold up, repress, obviate, embarrass, delay, defer, postpone, keep *or* set back, dam, close, box in, end, terminate, shut out, stay, choke, intercept, overreach, bottleneck, entrap, defeat, interpose, trammel, trap, antagonize, control, conflict with, deadlock, hold from *or* back, repulse, clash with, circumscribe, be an obstacle *or* impediment to, repel, cross, exclude, limit, keep in bounds, shorten, hamstring, filibuster, go against, prohibit, withhold, forestall, hedge, stem, slow down, stall, bring to a standstill, forbid, cause to delay, pinion, disallow, smother, stanch, disappoint, spoil, throttle, countervail, gag, bind *or* tie hand and foot, annul, silence, invalidate, vitiate, cancel out, hobble, constrict, cage, detain, deprive, stalemate, taboo, suspend, render difficult, set *or* pit against, put back; *all* (D): clip one's wings, fly in the face of, tie one's hands, set one's face against, get in the way of, hold up, jam, throw a monkey wrench into the works, snafu, scotch, spike (one's guns), hang fire, bog down, stymie, put the lid on, hang up, knock the bottom out of, knock the props from under; see also **prevent, restrain** 1.—*Ant.* help*, assist, aid.

hindmost, *mod.* —*Syn.* final, terminal, concluding; see **last** 1.

hindrance, *n.* —*Syn.* obstacle, intervention, trammel; see **barrier, impediment** 1, **interference** 1.

Hindu, *mod.* —*Syn.* Rajput, Sanskrit, Brahminic, East Indian; see also **Asiatic** 1, 2.

Hindu, *n.* —*Syn.* Asian, Buddhist, Brahmin; see **Indian** 2.

hinge, *n.* —*Syn.* hook, pivot, juncture, articulation, link, elbow, ball-and-socket, knee, butt, lifting butt, strap, cross garnet, articulated joint, flap; see also **joint** 1.
Hinges include the following—gate, blind, T, flap, strap, loose-pin, backflap, hook-and-eye, skew, H, turnover, spring, fast-joint, rising, sliding.

hinge, *v.* —*Syn.* connect, add, couple; see **join** 1.

hinged, *mod.* —*Syn.* linked, coupled, put together; see **joined.**

hint, *n.* **1.** [An intimation]—*Syn.* allusion, inkling, insinuation, implication, reference, advice, observation, adumbration, reminder, communication, notice, information, announcement, inside information, tip, clue, implied warning, token, idea, omen, scent, cue, trace, whiff, iota, suspicion, notion, whisper, taste, suspicion, evidence, reminder, memorandum, innuendo, prompter, signification, symptom, connotation, smattering, sign, wink, bare suggestion, glimmering, impression, denotation, supposition, tinge, vague knowledge, inference, prefigurement, premonition, broad *or* gentle hint, word to the wise, memorandum, mnemonic device, manifestation, foretoken, indirection, indication, slight knowledge; *all* (D): tip-off, pointer, dope; see also **suggestion** 1.

2. [A guarded remark]—*Syn.* innuendo, whisper, reflection, aside, insinuation, admonition, sign, suggestion, mention; see also sense 1, **allusion, warning.**

hint, *v.* —*Syn.* touch on, refer *or* allude to, intimate, apprise, inform, hint at, imply, infer, acquaint, remind, impart, bring up, recall, cue, prompt, insinuate, indicate, wink, broach, signify, foreshadow, advise, adumbrate, cause to remember, inform by indirection, make an allusion to, jog the memory, give a hint of, make indirect suggestion, suggest, give indirect information, make mention of, remark in passing, drop a hint, whisper; *all* (D): give an inkling of, tip off, put a bug *or* flea in one's ear, tip the wink, slip the dope; see also **mention, propose** 1, **refer** 2, **warn** 1.—*Ant.* hide*, conceal, cover.

hinted at, *mod.* —*Syn.* signified, intimated, referred to; see **implied, suggested.**

hip (D), *mod.* —*Syn.* aware, in the know, informed, unsquare, enlightened, *au courant* (French); *all* (D): groovy, with it, out of sight, with the beat, in the groove, boss, bad, hep, cool, in, too much; see also **modern** 1, **observant** 1.

hip, *n.* —*Syn.* haunch, side, hipbone, pelvis; *all* (D): beam, hench, ham; see also **bone.**

hipped (D), *mod.* —*Syn.* crazy, doting, foolish; see **insane** 1, **stupid** 1.

hippie (D), *mod.* —*Syn.* unorthodox, psychedelic, mod (D); see **beat** 2, **radical** 2, **unusual** 2.

hippie, *n.* —*Syn.* dissenter, Bohemian, nonconformist; see **beatnik, radical.**

hire, *v.* **1.** [To employ]—*Syn.* engage, sign up, draft, obtain, secure, take into one's employ, enlist, give a job to, take on, give work *or* employment to, put *or* set to work, bring in, occupy, use, fill a position, appoint, delegate, authorize, retain, commission, promise, empower, book, utilize, select, pick, pledge, bespeak, contract (for), procure, fill an opening, find help, find a place for, exploit, make use of, use another's services, add to the payroll; *both* (D): carry, give someone a break; see also **approve** 1, **choose** 1.—*Ant.* discharge, dismiss*, fire.

2. [To let]—*Syn.* lease, charter, contract for; see **borrow** 1, **let** 2, **rent** 1.

hired, *mod.* —*Syn.* contracted, signed up, given work; see **busy** 1, **employed, engaged** 3, **working.**

hireling, *n.* —*Syn.* hack, worker, aid; see **employee, laborer, workman.**

hiring, *n.* —*Syn.* chartering, leasing, letting, engaging, contracting, employing.

hiring hall, *n.* —*Syn.* union hall, union employment office, employment office, labor office, labor temple.

hirsute, *mod.* —*Syn.* woolly, bearded, furry; see **hairy** 1, **shaggy.**

hiss, *n.* —*Syn.* buzz, sibilance, escape of air; see **noise** 1.

hiss, *v.* **1.** [To make a hissing sound]—*Syn.* sibilate, fizz, seethe; see **buzz, sound** 1.

2. [To condemn]—*Syn.* boo, disapprove, shout down; see **censure, ridicule.**

historian, *n.* —*Syn.* history, professor, recorder, annalist, archivist, chronicler, historiographer, writer of history, biographer; see **antiquarian, archaeologist.**

historic, *mod.* —*Syn.* well-known, celebrated, memorable; see **famous, important** 2.

historical, *mod.* —*Syn.* actual, authentic, factual, important in history, constituting history, archival, traditional, commemorated, chronicled; see **ancient** 2, **classical** 2, **old** 3, **past** 1.

history, *n.* **1.** [A narrative]—*Syn.* account, memoir, tale; see **story.**

2. [The systematic, documented account of the past]—*Syn.* annals, records, archives, recorded history, chronicle, historical knowledge, historical writings, historical evidence, historical development, description of a movement.

Specific divisions of the study of history include the following—local, state, national, American, European, Asian, African, modern, medieval, classical, ancient, Roman, Greek, literary, cultural, intellectual; history of culture *or* mankind *or* philosophy *or* religion *or* science, etc.; archaeology, anthropology, prehistory; see also **record** 1, 2, **social science.**

3. [Past events]—*Syn.* antiquity, the past, the old days, ancient times; *both* (D): the good old days, ancient history; see also **antiquity** 3, **past** 1.

make history—*Syn.* accomplish, do something important, achieve; see **succeed** 1.

histrionic, *mod.* —*Syn.* dramatic, artificial, theatrical; see **affected** 2.

histrionics, *n.* **1.** [Acting]—*Syn.* dramatics, showmanship, performing; see **acting, drama** 1, 2, **performance** 2.

2. [Affection]—*Syn.* deceit, pretension, put-on (D); see **deception** 1, **pretense** 1.

hit, *mod.* —*Syn.* shot, struck, slugged, cuffed, slapped, smacked, pummeled, clouted, punched, boxed, slammed, knocked, beat, pounded, thrashed, spanked, banged, smashed, cudgeled, basted, slogged, smitten, tapped, rapped, whacked, thwacked, thumped, kicked; *all* (D): swatted, mugged, pasted, plastered, biffed, binged, poked, rocked, knocked out; see also **hurt.**—*Ant.* unhurt*, unscathed, untouched.

hit, *n.* **1.** [A blow]—*Syn.* slap, rap, punch; see **blow** 1.

2. [A popular success]—*Syn.* favorite, achievement, masterstroke; *all* (D): sellout, smash, knockout, wow, click; see also **success** 2.

3. [In baseball, a batted ball that cannot be fielded] —*Syn.* base hit *or* single (D), two-base hit *or* double (D), three-base hit *or* triple (D), home run; *all* (D): wallop, bagger, wham; see also **run** 3, **score** 1.

hit, *v.* **1.** [To strike]—*Syn.* knock, beat, sock, slap, punch, punish, smite, thump, bump, hammer, strike down, bang, whack, thwack, jab, clap, tap, dab, smack, kick at, pelt, flail, thrash, cuff, kick, rap, cudgel, clout, club, buffet, bat *or* kick around, lay low, lash out at, not hold one's punches, hit at, hit out (at), make a dent in, let have it, give a black eye, crack, squail; *all* (D): mug, pop, biff, hook, bash, nail one on, let fly at, box off, ride roughshod over, box the ears, whang, hang a mouse on; see also **knock out.**

2. [To bump against]—*Syn.* jostle, butt, knock against, scrape, bump, run against, thump, collide (with), bump into, meet head-on; see also **crash** 4.
3. [To fire in time; *said of an internal combustion motor*]—*Syn.* catch, respond, go, explode, run, connect, function, hit on all fours (D); see also **operate** 2.
4. [In baseball, to hit safely]—*Syn.* make a hit, make a two-base *or* three-base hit *or* a home run; *all* (D): hit safe, get on, rip a single *or* double *or* triple, blast one, make a homer; see also **score** 1.

hit-and-run, *mod.* —*Syn.* leaving illegally *or* without offering assistance, fugitive, illegally departed; see **illegal, wicked** 2.

hitch, *n.* **1.** [A knot]—*Syn.* loop, noose, yoke; see **knot** 1, **tie** 1.
2. [A difficulty]—*Syn.* block, obstacle, tangle; see **difficulty** 1, **impediment** 1.

hitch, *v.* **1.** [To harness]—*Syn.* yoke, tie up, strap, couple, lash, moor, chain, hook; see also **fasten** 1, **join** 1.
2. [To move with a jerk]—*Syn.* hobble, waggle, hop; see **limp, reel, totter** 2, **wobble.**

hitchhike, *v.*—*Syn.* take a lift, hitch *or* bum *or* catch *or* thumb a ride, thumb (D); see **ride** 1, **travel** 2.

hither, *mod.* —*Syn.* to, next, forward; see **near** 1, **toward.**

hitherto, *mod.* —*Syn.* until now, previously, heretofore; see **before** 1, **formerly.**

hit it off (D), *v.* —*Syn.* get on *or* along (well), become friends *or* acquaintances, become friendly; see **agree, like** 1, 2.

hit on *or* **upon,** *v.* —*Syn.* realize, come upon, stumble on; see **discover** 1, **find** 1, **recognize** 1.

hit or miss, *mod.* —*Syn.* at random, uncertainly, scatteringly; see **irregularly, scattered, unevenly.**

hit the jackpot (D), *v.* —*Syn.* be lucky, be well paid, strike it rich (D); see **win** 1.

hit the hay (D), *v.* —*Syn.* go to bed *or* to sleep, retire, get some sleep; see **sleep.**

hitting, *mod.* **1.** [Striking]—*Syn.* slapping, beating, punishing, whipping, slamming, thumping, whacking, smacking, cuffing, clubbing, clouting.
2. [Exploding smoothly; *said of an internal combustion engine*]—*Syn.* functioning, operating, going; see **running** 2, **working.**

hit town (D), *v.* —*Syn.* enter, approach, land; see **arrive** 1.

hive, *n.* —*Syn.* apiary, swarm, colony; see **beehive.**

hiway (D), *n.* —*Syn.* highway, freeway, parkway; see **road** 1.

hoard, *n.* —*Syn.* riches, treasure, cache; see **wealth** 1.

hoard, *v.* —*Syn.* store up, acquire, keep; see **accumulate** 1, **save** 3.

hoarse, *mod.* —*Syn.* grating, rough, uneven, harsh, raucous, discordant, gruff, strident, husky, throaty, thick, growling, croaking, cracked, ragged, guttural, gravelly, dry, piercing, whispering, blatant, breathy, scratching, absonant, indistinct, squawking, unmusical, jarring, rasping; see also **loud** 1, **shrill.**—*Ant.* sweet, pure*, mellifluous.

hoary, *mod.* —*Syn.* ancient, aged, antique; see **old** 1, 3.

hoax, *n.* —*Syn.* falsification, fabrication, deceit; see **deception** 1, **lie** 1.

hobble, *v.* **1.** [To restrict]—*Syn.* clog, fetter, shackle; see **hinder, restrain** 1.
2. [To move as though hobbled]—*Syn.* totter, dodder, halt; see **limp, stumble** 1.

hobby, *n.* —*Syn.* avocation, pastime, diversion, side interest, leisure-time activity, personal obsession, specialty, whim, fad, unremunerative occupation, favorite occupation *or* pursuit, pet topic, fancy, caprice, relaxation, whimsy, labor of love, play, craze, *divertissment* (French), sport, amusement, quest, craft, fun, art, game, sideline, vagary; see also **distraction** 2, **entertainment** 2.

hobgoblin, *n.* —*Syn.* imp, ghost, ogre; see **bugbear, fairy** 1.

hobnob, *v.* —*Syn.* fraternize, consort with, associate with; see **associate** 1, **join** 2.

hobo, *n.* —*Syn.* vagrant, vagabond, wanderer; see **beggar** 1, **tramp** 1.

hock (D), *v.* —*Syn.* sell temporarily, pledge, deposit; see **pawn, sell** 1.

hockey, *n.* —*Syn.* ice hockey, field hockey, hockey game; *both* (D): shinny, block-and-bunt; see also **game** 1, **sport** 3.

hocus-pocus, *n.* **1.** [Charm]—*Syn.* incantation, spell, chant; see **magic** 1.
2. [A trick]—*Syn.* fraud, hoax, flimflam (D); see **deception** 1, **trick** 1.

hod, *n.* —*Syn.* trough, tray, pail; see **bucket, container.**

hodgepodge, *n.* —*Syn.* jumble, combination, mess; see **mixture** 1.

hoe, *n.* —*Syn.* digger, scraper, scuffle hoe, warren hoe, garden hoe, grub hoe, weeding hoe, wheel hoe *or* cultivator; see also **tool** 1.

hog, *n.* **1.** [A pig]—*Syn.* swine, sow, boar, shoat, razorback, wild boar, wart hog, babirusa, truffle pig, peccary, collared peccary, white-lipped peccary; *all* (D): porker, piggy, pork, cob-roller, scrub, runt; see also **animal** 1.
Breeds of hogs include the following—Duroc, Duroc-Jersey, Hampshire, Berkshire, Chester White, Poland China, Tamworth, Lincolnshire, Cumberland, Essex, Wessex Saddleback, Large Yorkshire.
2. [A person whose habits resemble a pig's]—*Syn.* pig, selfish person, filthy person; see **glutton, slob.**
go the whole hog (D)—*Syn.* go all the way, do something fully, complete something; see **achieve** 1.
high on (*or* **off**) **the hog** (D)—*Syn.* luxurious, extravagant, rich; see **expensive.**

hoggish, *mod.* **1.** [Squalid]—*Syn.* smelly, foul, unclean; see **dirty** 1, **squalid.**
2. [Greedy]—*Syn.* grasping, rapacious, gluttonous; see **greedy** 2.

hogtie, *v.* —*Syn.* fetter, shackle, tie up; see **bind** 1.

hogwash, *n.* **1.** [Garbage]—*Syn.* scum, debris, refuse; see **trash** 1, 3.
2. [Nonsense]—*Syn.* foolishness, absurdity, ridiculousness; see **nonsense** 1.

hog-wild (D), *mod.* —*Syn.* extravagant, outlandish, unrestrained; see **extreme** 2, **unruly, wild** 1.

hoi polloi (Greek), *n.* —*Syn.* the masses, proletariat, crowd; see **people** 3.

hoist, *n.* —*Syn.* crane, lift, derrick; see **elevator** 1.

hold, *n.* —*Syn.* grasp, clutch, clasp; see **grip** 2.
catch hold of—*Syn.* take, grasp, catch; see **seize** 1.
get hold of—*Syn.* **1.** take, grasp, catch; see **seize** 1.
2. get, acquire, receive; see **obtain** 1.
lay (*or* **take**) **hold of**—*Syn.* take, grasp, get; see **seize** 1.
no holds barred (D)—*Syn.* without rules, unrestricted, unrestrained; see **unlimited.**

hold, *v.* **1.** [To have in one's grasp]—*Syn.* grasp, grip, clutch, carry, embrace, clench, cling to, detain, enclose, restrain, confine, check, take hold of, contain, hold down *or* onto, not let go, never let go, hang on, have a firm hold of, squeeze, press, secure, hug, handle, fondle, have *or* keep in hand, keep fast, cause to remain in a given place, retain, keep, keep *or* maintain a grasp on, clasp, hold fast *or* tight, keep a firm hold on, tie, keep close, unite, palm, take, catch, clinch, fasten upon, cradle; *both* (D): have an iron grip on, hang on to; see also **seize** 1.—*Ant.* let fall, release*, let go.
2. [To have in one's possession]—*Syn.* keep, retain, possess; see **maintain** 3, **own** 1.
3. [To remain firm]—*Syn.* resist, persevere, keep staunch; see **continue** 1, **endure** 2.
4. [To adhere]—*Syn.* attach, cling, take hold; see **adhere, fasten** 1, **stick** 1.
5. [To be valid]—*Syn.* exist, continue, remain true, have bearing, be the case, endure, be in effect, operate, be in force; see also **be** 1.—*Ant.* stop*, expire, be out-of-date.
6. [To believe]—*Syn.* regard, aver, judge; see **believe** 1, **think** 1.
7. [To contain]—*Syn.* have capacity for, carry, be equipped for; see **include** 1.
8. [To support; *often used with up*]—*Syn.* sustain, brace, buttress, prop, lock, stay, shoulder, underpin, uphold, underprop, shore *or* bear *or* bolster up; see also **support** 1.

hold back, *v.* **1.** [To restrain]—*Syn.* inhibit, control, curb; see **check** 2, **prevent, restrain** 1.
2. [To refrain]—*Syn.* desist, hesitate, forbear; see **abstain, avoid.**

hold down, *v.* —*Syn.* fix, pin down, control; see **prevent, restrain** 1.

holder, *n.* **1.** [An instrument used in holding] —*Syn.* sheathe, container, folder, holster, bag, sack, fastener, clip, handle, rack, arm, crank, knob, stem; see also **container, fastener.**
2. [An owner or occupant]—*Syn.* leaseholder, renter, dweller; see **owner, possessor, resident, tenant.**

hold fast, *v.* —*Syn.* clasp, lock, clamp; see **adhere, fasten** 1, **stick** 1.

hold firm, *v.* —*Syn.* retain, keep, preserve; see **maintain** 3.

hold forth, *v.* —*Syn.* speak, soliloquize, declaim; see **address** 2, **lecture.**

hold high, *v.* —*Syn.* exalt, observe, celebrate; see **admire** 1, **praise** 1.

holding, *mod.* —*Syn.* impeding, stopping, closing; see **blocking.**

holdings, *n.* —*Syn.* lands, possessions, security; see **estate** 2, **property** 1.

hold off, *v.* —*Syn.* be above, keep aloof, stave off; see **avoid, prevent.**

hold office, *v.* —*Syn.* be in (office), direct, rule; see **command** 2, **govern, manage** 1.

hold on, *v.* —*Syn.* hang on, attach oneself to, cling (to); see **seize** 1.

hold oneself, *v.* —*Syn.* stand up, carry oneself, walk; see **behave** 2, **stand** 1.

hold one's horses (D), *v.* —*Syn.* be calm, keep one's head (D), restrain oneself; see **stop** 2, **wait** 1.

hold one's own, *v.* —*Syn.* keep one's advantage, stand one's ground, do well, keep up; see also **succeed** 1.

hold one's tongue *or* **one's peace,** *v.* —*Syn.* be silent, conceal, keep secret, not say a word; see also **hide** 1.

holdout, *n.* —*Syn.* obstructionist, adversary, diehard, resister, objector, damper; *both* (D): wet blanket, spoilsport; see also **resister.**

hold out, *v.* **1.** [To offer]—*Syn.* proffer, tempt (with), grant; see **give** 1, **offer** 1.
2. [To endure]—*Syn.* suffer, hold on, withstand; see **continue** 1, **endure** 2.

hold out for, *v.* —*Syn.* persist, go on supporting, stand firmly for; see **continue** 1.

holdover, *n.* —*Syn.* remnant, relic, surplus; see **remainder.**

hold over, *v.* —*Syn.* do again *or* over, show again, play over; see **redo, repeat** 1.

hold the line, *v.* —*Syn.* wait, be patient, be quiet; see **quiet down.**

hold the road, *v.* —*Syn.* track, cling to *or* hug the road, ride well; see **ride** 5, **travel** 2.

hold together, *v.* —*Syn.* attach, clip, cling; see **adhere, fasten** 1, **stick** 1.

holdup (D), *n.* —*Syn.* robbery, burglary, stick-up (D); see **crime** 2, **theft.**

hold up, *v.* **1.** [To show]—*Syn.* exhibit, raise high, elevate; see **display** 1.
2. [To delay]—*Syn.* stop, pause, interfere with; see **delay** 1, **hinder, interrupt** 2.
3. [(D) To rob at gunpoint]—*Syn.* waylay, burglarize, steal from; see **rob.**
4. [To support]—*Syn.* brace, prop, shoulder; see **hold** 8. **support** 1.

hole, *n.* **1.** [A perforation]—*Syn.* notch, puncture, slot, eyelet, keyhole, porthole, buttonhole, peephole, loophole, air hole, stop, mousehole, window, crack, rent, split, tear, cleft, opening, fissure, gap, gash, rift, rupture, fracture, break, leak, nostril, *oeil-de-boeuf* (French), aperture, space, chasm, breach, slit, nick, cut, chink, scission, vent, incision, orifice, scissure, spiracle, leak, interstice, vent hole, scupper, foramen, eye, rime, acupuncture; see also **sense** 2.
2. [A cavity]—*Syn.* crater, mouth, gorge, throat, gullet, orifice, aperture, cranny, foramen, manhole, dent, opening, depression, indentation, impression, corner, shell hole, pockmark, swimming hole, pocket, dimple, dip, void, lacuna, vacuum, drop, gulf, depth, pit, abyss, hollow, chasm, vent, crevasse, trench, foxhole, mine, concavity, shaft, chamber, defile, scoop, valley, ravine, burrow, rift, fossa, cell, cistern, niche, alveolus, spider hole (D); see **sense** 1.
3. [A cave]—*Syn.* burrow, den, lair, grotto, cavern, cove, tunnel, excavation, mound, passage, refuge,

retreat, furrow, dugout, honeycomb, warren, covert, shelter; see also sense 2.
4. [(D) Serious difficulty]—*Syn.* impasse, tangle, mess; see **crisis, difficulty** 1, **emergency.**
5. [In golf, a depression made for the ball]—*Syn.* drop, cup, pocket, first to 18th hole; *both* (D): pot, mocking cup.
burn a hole in one's pocket—*Syn.* entice, lure, attract; see **tempt.**
in the hole (D)—*Syn.* broke, without money, in debt; see **poor** 1.
make a hole in—*Syn.* use up, consume, expend; see **spend** 1.
pick holes in—*Syn.* criticize, disprove, pick out errors in; see **analyze** 1.

hole up (D), *v.*—*Syn.* take cover, go into hiding, withdraw; see **hide** 2.

holiday, *n.* **1.** [A memorial day]—*Syn.* feast day, fiesta, saint's day, legal holiday, holy day, festival, fete, centennial, bicentennial, tercentenary, carnival, gala day, jubilee, red-letter day, fast day; see also **anniversary, celebration** 1, 2.
Common holidays include the following—United States: Sunday, Independence Day, Veterans Day, Memorial Day *or* Decoration Day, New Year's Day, Martin Luther King's Birthday, Christmas, Easter Sunday, Lincoln's Birthday, Thanksgiving Day, Washington's Birthday, Presidents' Day, Columbus Day, Labor Day, Election Day; Great Britain: (bank holidays) Good Friday, Easter Monday, Spring Holiday (formerly Whitsun), Late Summer, Christmas Day, Boxing Day, New Year's Day (in Scotland). Saints' days include the following—All Saints', Saint Alban's, Saint Augustine's, Saint Michael's, Saint Bartholomew's, Saint Swithin's, Thomas à Becket's, Saint Patrick's, Saint Denis', Saint Crispin's, Saint George's, Saint Andrew's, Saint David's, Saint Nicholas's.
2. [A vacation]—*Syn.* weekend, time off, leave; see **vacation.**

holiness, *n.* **1.** [Piety]—*Syn.* devoutness, humility, asceticism, saintliness, righteousness, godliness, beatitude, religiosity, blessedness, grace, reverence, faith, religiousness; see also **devotion, worship** 1. —*Ant.* evil*, impiety, wickedness.
2. [Sanctity]—*Syn.* sanctification, venerableness, sacredness, unction, inviolability, divine protection; see also **consecration.**—*Ant.* sin*, blasphemy, profaneness.

Holiness, *n.*—*Syn.* head of the Roman Catholic church, Vicar of Christ, bishop of Rome; see **Pope.**

hollow, *mod.* **1.** [Empty]—*Syn.* vacant, unfilled, void; see **empty** 1.
2. [Concave]—*Syn.* rounded *or* curving inward, bellshaped, curved, carved out, sunken, depressed, arched, vaulted, cup-shaped, excavated, infundibular, hollowed out, indented, calathiform, incurved, cupped, cyathiform, poculiform, incurving, incurvate, troughlike; see also **bent, round** 3.—*Ant.* convex, raised*, elevated.
3. [Sounding as though from a cave]—*Syn.* cavernous, echoing, deep, resonant, ghostly, deep-toned, blooming, roaring, rumbling, reverberating, muffled, nonresonant, plangent, dull, resounding, vibrant, muffled, sepulchral, vibrating, low, booming, ringing, clangorous, deep, mute, deep-mouthed, deep-toned, muted, thunderous; see also **loud** 1.—*Ant.* dead*, mute, silent.
4. [False]—*Syn.* flimsy, artificial, unsound; see **false** 2.
5. [(D) Hungry]—*Syn.* unsatisfied, ravenous, starved; see **hungry.**
beat all hollow (D)—*Syn.* outdo, beat, overcome; see **surpass.**

hollow, *n.* **1.** [A cavity]—*Syn.* depression, dip, pit; see **hole** 2.
2. [(D) A valley]—*Syn.* dale, bowl, basin; see **valley.**

hollow (out), *v.*—*Syn.* excavate, indent, remove earth; see **dig** 1, **shovel.**

Hollywood, *n.*—*Syn.* Movie Capital of America, Screenland, City of Glamour Girls; *all* (D): Filmdom, Flicker City, the great intellectual desert, Sin City.

holocaust, *n.*—*Syn.* ruin, fire, ravage; see **catastrophe, destruction** 1, **disaster.**

holy, *mod.* **1.** [Sinless]—*Syn.* devout, pious, blessed, righteous, moral, just, good, angelic, godly, venerable, immaculate, pure, spotless, clean, blameless, humble, saintly, guileless, innocent, godlike, saintlike, perfect, faultless, uncorrupt, undefiled, untainted, chaste, upright, virtuous, incorrupt, revered, dedicated *or* devoted to the service of God, sainted, heaven-sent, believing, heavenly minded, profoundly good, sanctified, inviolable, devotional, reverent, pietistic, spiritual, unstained, unworldly, pure in heart, zealous, seraphic, dedicated, right-minded, unspotted; see also **faithful, religious** 2. —*Ant.* evil, wicked*, sinful.
2. [Concerned with worship]—*Syn.* devotional, religious, ceremonial; see **divine** 2.
3. [Associated with a deity, especially with Christ; *often capitalized*]—*Syn.* Apostolic, Almighty, Omnipotent, True, Good, Eternal, Infinite, Blessed, Merciful.

Holy Ghost, *n.*—*Syn.* Holy Spirit, the Dove, third person of the Holy Trinity; see **god** 2, **trinity** 2.

Holy Writ, *n.*—*Syn.* Scriptures, the Gospel, the Canon; see **Bible** 2.

homage, *n.*—*Syn.* piety, earnestness, faithfulness; see **devotion, praise** 1, **reverence** 2, **worship** 1.

home, *mod.* **1.** [At home]—*Syn.* in one's home *or* house, at ease, in the family, at rest, about home, homely, domestic, familiar, being oneself, before one's own fireside, homey, in the bosom of one's family, down home, in one's element; see also **comfortable** 1.
2. [Toward home]—*Syn.* to one's home, back, homeward bound; see **homeward.**

home, *n.* **1.** [A dwelling place]—*Syn.* house, dwelling, residence, habitation, habitat, tenement, abode, lodging, quarters, homestead, hospice, hostel, domicile, dormitory, seat, berth, apartment, condominium, flat, living quarters, messuage (British), palace, shelter, asylum, *pied à terre* (French), hut, haunt, resort, cabin, bungalow, cottage, mansion, castle, summer home, rooming house, country home, place, address, diggings, shanty, wigwam, igloo, topek, hovel, cave, *isba* (Russian), lodge, villa, hotel, inn, manor, tepee, farmhouse, tavern, resthouse, barrack, tent; *all* (D): pad, hide-out, dump, hang-out, headquarters, parking place, digs, nest, condo, where one hangs his hat; see also **apartment, trailer.**

2. [The whole complex associated with domestic life]—*Syn.* homestead, hearth, fireside, birthplace, hometown, haven, rest, roof, the farm, the ancestral halls, the hills, the land; *all* (D): neck of the woods, camping ground, home-sweet-home; see also sense 1.

3. [An asylum]—*Syn.* orphanage, orphan asylum, rest home, home for the aged, soldiers' home, shelter, sanatorium, insane asylum, mental hospital, poorhouse, poor farm; *all* (D): almshouse, booby hatch, bathouse; see also **hospital, sanitarium.**

4. [In baseball, the base at which the batter stands] —*Syn.* home plate, batter's box, head of the diamond; *all* (D): the rubber, the plate, the platter; see also **base** 5.

at home—*Syn.* relaxed, at ease, familiar; see **comfortable** 1, **home** 1.

bring (something) home to—*Syn.* impress upon, make clear to, convince; see **persuade** 1.

come home—*Syn.* come or go back, return home, regress; see **return** 1.

homecoming, *n.* —*Syn.* homecoming celebration, entry, revisitation; see **arrival** 1, **return** 1.

homeland, *n.* —*Syn.* fatherland, motherland, home; see **country** 3.

homeless, *mod.* —*Syn.* desolate, outcast, destitute, vagrant, wandering, uncared-for, itinerant, friendless, banished, estranged, derelict, without a country, exiled, having no home, vagabond, forsaken, unplaced, unhoused, friendless, unsettled, houseless, unwelcome, dispossessed, disinherited, unestablished; *all* (D): left to shift for oneself, beyond the pale, outside the gates, without a roof over one's head; see also **abandoned** 1, **poor** 1.—*Ant.* at home, established*, settled.

homelike, *mod.* —*Syn.* cozy, cheerful, informal; see **comfortable** 2.

homely, *mod.* **1.** [Unpretentious]—*Syn.* snug, simple, cozy; see **modest** 2.

2. [Ill-favored]—*Syn.* plain, unattractive, uncomely; see **ugly** 1.

homemade, *mod.* —*Syn.* homespun, domestic, do-it-yourself, indigenous, home-loomed, self-made, home-wrought, home-worked, made at home, of domestic manufacture, home, not foreign; see **handmade, manufactured, native** 2.

home rule, *n.* —*Syn.* independence, sovereignty, autonomy; see **freedom** 1.

home run, *n.* —*Syn.* four-base hit, run; *all* (D): homer, circuit clout, four-bagger, grand tour, grand slam, round trip, looper.

homesick, *mod.* —*Syn.* nostalgic, pining, yearning for home, ill with longing, unhappy, unoriented, alienated, estranged, rootless; see also **lonely** 1.

homesickness, *n.* —*Syn.* nostalgia, rootlessness, longing, alienation, isolation, unhappiness, yearning for home; see also **loneliness.**

homespun, *mod.* **1.** [Made at home]—*Syn.* handicrafted, domestic, handspun; see **handmade, homemade.**

2. [Plain or coarse]—*Syn.* simple, unsophisticated; see **rustic** 3.

homestead, *n.* —*Syn.* house, residence, home place, farm, ranch, home grounds, place of settlement, home and grounds, grange, manor, farmstead, country house *or* seat, messuage, plantation, estate, demesne, hacienda; see also **home** 1, **property** 2.

homeward, *mod.* —*Syn.* toward home, back home, on the way home, homewards, homewardly, home, homeward bound, to one's family *or* native land.

homework, *n.* —*Syn.* outside assignment, library assignment, home study, preparation; *all* (D): fit, grind, noodling, skulldragging; see also **study** 2. —*Ant.* classwork, examination*, recitation.

homey, *mod.* **1.** [Having the qualities of a home] —*Syn.* enjoyable, livable, familiar; see **comfortable** 2, **pleasant** 2.

2. [Genial]—*Syn.* warm-hearted, homespun, unassuming; see **friendly** 1.

homicidal, *mod.* —*Syn.* maniacal, lethal, destructive; see **murderous, violent** 4.

homicide, *n.* —*Syn.* killing, manslaughter, death; see **crime** 2, **murder.**

homiletic, *mod.* —*Syn.* persuasive, moralizing, sermonizing, instructive, sermonic, preaching, edifying, expository, disciplinary, instructional, disquisitional, doctrinal, teaching, admonitory, didactic, relating to sermons, propagative, of the nature of a homily, of homilies *or* sermons; see **educational** 1.

homiletics, *n.* —*Syn.* moralizing, theology, rhetoric; see **preaching.**

homily, *n.* —*Syn.* lesson, doctrine, lecture; see **sermon.**

hominid, *n.* —*Syn.* cave dweller, cliff dweller, troglodyte, aborigine, savage, stone-age man, Paleolithic man, early man, ape man, dawn man, primitive man, *Homo sapiens fossilis* (Latin); see **man** 2. Terms for early men or manlike creatures include the following—Acheulean, Aurignacian, Australopithecus afarensis ("Lucy"), Azilian, Chellean, Combe-Capelle, Creopithecus, Cro-Magnon, Eolithic, Heidelberg, *Homo habilis, Homo soloensis* (*both* Latin), Kenyapithecus, Magdalenian, Mousterian, Neanderthal man, neolithic man, paleolithic, Peking man, Pithecanthropus *or* Java man, Prechellean, Proconsul africanus, Rhodesian, Solutrean, Steinheim man, Swanscombe man, Trinil, Zinjanthropus.

homogeneity, *n.* —*Syn.* congruity, analogy, correlation; see **agreement** 2.

homogeneous, *mod.* —*Syn.* comparable, similar, analogous; see **alike** 2, **like.**

homosexual, *mod.* —*Syn.* monoclinous, gynandrous, hermaphroditic, Lesbian, Sapphic, androgynous, epicene, gay.

homosexual, *n.* —*Syn.* Lesbian, gay, gynandroid, androgyne, hermaphrodite, transvestite; all (D): queen, butch, homo.

hone, *v.* —*Syn.* point, smooth, set; see **sharpen** 1.

honest, *mod.* **1.** [Truthful]—*Syn.* true, trustworthy, correct, exact, verifiable, undisguised, respectable, factual, sound, veritable, unimpeachable, legitimate, unquestionable, realistic, true-to-life, reasonable, aboveboard, unvarnished, naked, irrefutable, literal, plain, intrinsic, precise; *all* (D): straight, square, honest as the day is long, on the level *or* the legit, kosher, fair and square; see also **accurate** 1, 2. —*Ant.* deceptive, false*, misleading.

2. [Honorable]—*Syn.* upright, respectable, worthy; see **noble** 1, 2, **reliable** 1.
3. [Frank]—*Syn.* candid, straightforward, aboveboard; see **sense** 1; see **frank.**
4. [Fair]—*Syn.* just, equitable, impartial; see **fair** 1.

honestly, *mod.* **1.** [In an honest manner]—*Syn.* uprightly, fairly, genuinely; see **justly** 1, 2, **sincerely.**
2. [Really]—*Syn.* indeed, truly, naturally; see **really** 1.

honesty, *n.* **1.** [Integrity]—*Syn.* probity, honor, uprightness, veridicality, fidelity, scrupulousness, self-respect, straight-forwardness, trustworthiness, confidence, soundness, veracity, rectitude, right, principle, truthfulness, candor, frankness, openness, incorruptibility, morality, goodness, responsibility, loyalty, faithfulness, good faith, constancy, courage, quality *or* fact of being honest, moral strength, virtue, reliability, character, veraciousness, conscience, worth, impeccability, conscientiousness, trustiness, faith, freedom from fraud, justice, respectability, honorableness; see also **sincerity.**—*Ant.* dishonesty*, deception, deceit.
2. [Fair dealing]—*Syn.* probity, justice, rectitude; see **fairness.**

honey, *n.* Types of honey include the following—comb, extracted, strained, wild, mountain, desert, select, grated, linn *or* basswood, white clover, sweet clover, buckwheat, goldenrod, alfalfa, orange blossom, locust, sage, currant, cleome, cotton, eucalyptus, sycamore, teasel, thyme, barberry, heather, hawthorn; see also **food, syrup.**

honeycomb, *n.*—*Syn.* sieve, pattern, filter; see **screen.**

honeycombed, *mod.*—*Syn.* riddled, perforated, patterned; see **porous.**

honeyed, *mod.*—*Syn.* sugary, candied, enticing; see **persuasive, sweet** 1.

honeymoon, *n.*—*Syn.* post-nuptial vacation, married couple's first holiday, wedding trip, first month after marriage; see also **vacation.**

honk, *n.*—*Syn.* croak, quack, blare; see **noise** 1.

honk, *v.*—*Syn.* blow a horn, blare, quack, croak, signal, sound a klaxon, make a noise like a duck, trumpet, bellow; see also **sound** 1.

honor, *n.* **1.** [Respect]—*Syn.* reverence, esteem, worship, adoration, veneration, high reward, trust, faith, confidence, recognition, praise, attention, deference, notice, consideration, renown, reputation, repute, homage, account, laurel, elevation, approbation, wreath, credit, eulogium, adulation, laud, tribute, celebration, popularity, exaltation, good report, apotheosis, lionization, immortalization, fealty, mark of approval, deification, dignification, glorification, canonization, aggrandizement, righteousness; see also **admiration** 1.—*Ant.* opprobrium, disgrace*, disrepute.
2. [Glory]—*Syn.* exaltation, greatness, renown; see **fame** 1.
3. [Integrity]—*Syn.* courage, character, truthfulness; see **honesty** 1.
do honor to—*Syn.* show respect for, please, bring honor to; see **honor.**
do the honors—*Syn.* act as host or hostess, present, host; see **serve** 1.
on (*or* **upon**) **one's honor**—*Syn.* by one's faith, on one's word, staking one's good name; see **sincerely.**

honor, *v.* **1.** [To treat with respect]—*Syn.* worship, sanctify, venerate; see **praise** 1.
2. [To recognize worth]—*Syn.* esteem, value, look up to; see **admire** 1.
3. [To recognize as valid]—*Syn.* clear, pass, accept; see **acknowledge** 2.

Honor, *n.*—*Syn.* Excellency, Lordship, Majesty, Honorable Sir, Reverence, Justice, Governor; see also **judge** 1.

honorable, *mod.*—*Syn.* proud, reputable, creditable; see **distinguished, famous, important** 2, **noble** 2, 3.

honorably, *mod.*—*Syn.* nobly, fairly, virtuously; see **justly** 1.

honorarium, *n.*—*Syn.* complimentary fee, gratuity, reward; see **compensation, pay** 2, **payment** 1, **return** 3, **tip** 2.

honorary, *mod.*—*Syn.* titular, ex officio, gratuitous, nominal, favored, privileged; see also **complimentary.**

honored, *mod.*—*Syn.* respected, reversed, decorated, privileged, celebrated, reputable, well-known, esteemed, eminent, distinguished, dignified, noble, recognized, highly regarded, venerated; see also **famous, important** 2.—*Ant.* dishonored, disgraced*, shamed.

honors, *n.* **1.** [Courtesies]—*Syn.* ceremony, privilege, duties.
2. [Distinction]—*Syn.* high honors, award, prize, medal, laurels, wreath, garland, favor, feather in one's cap (D).

hood, *n.* **1.** [Covering worn over the head]—*Syn.* cowl, shawl, bonnet, protector, coif, capuche, veil, wimple, capuchin, kerchief, mantle, babushka, yashmak, purdah; see also **hat.**
2. [A covering for vehicles and the like]—*Syn.* canopy, awning, bonnet, shade, carriage top, auto top, calash, chimney top, convertible top; see also **cover** 1.
3. [(D) A criminal]—*Syn.* gangster, hoodlum, crook; see **criminal.**

hoodlum, *n.*—*Syn.* outlaw, gangster, crook; see **criminal.**

hoodwink, *v.*—*Syn.* blind, cheat, outwit; see **deceive.**

hoof, *n.*—*Syn.* unguis, ungula, cloven foot, animal foot, paw, coffin bone, trotter; see also **foot** 2.

hook, *n.* **1.** [An implement for snagging]—*Syn.* lock, catch, clasp; see **fastener.**
2. [A curved implement for cutting]—*Syn.* sickle, bill, billhook, machete, adze, scythe; see also **tool** 1.

hook, *v.* **1.** [To curve in the shape of a hook]—*Syn.* angle, crook, curve; see **arch** 1.
2. [To catch on a hook]—*Syn.* pin, catch, secure; see **fasten** 1.
3. [(D) To attain one's end by trickery]—*Syn.* cheat, defraud, dupe; see **deceive.**

hooked, *mod.*—*Syn.* curved, angled, arched; see **bent, crooked** 1.

hooked in, *mod.*—*Syn.* fastened, attached, connected; see **joined, wired.**

hooked up, *mod.*—*Syn.* connected, circuited, attached; see **joined, wired.**

hook, line, and sinker (D), *mod.* —*Syn.* whole, entire(ly), gullibly; see **completely.**

hookup, *n.* —*Syn.* attachment, connection, consolidation; see **junction** 2, **link, union** 1.

hook up, *v.* —*Syn.* combine, connect, attach; see **join** 1, **unite** 1.

hoop, *n.* —*Syn.* wooden wheel, band, circlet; see **circle** 1.

hoot, *n.* —*Syn.* howl, whoo, boo; see **cry** 2.

hoot, *v.* —*Syn.* cry out against, boo, howl down; see **cry** 3.

hop, *n.* **1.** [A quick jump]—*Syn.* spring, bounce, leap; see **jump** 1.
2. [(D) A short flight]—*Syn.* test flight, trip, jaunt; see **flight** 2, **journey.**

hop, *v.* —*Syn.* leap, jump on one leg; see **bounce** 1, **jump** 1.

hope, *n.* **1.** [Reliance upon the future]—*Syn.* faith, expectation, confidence; see **anticipation** 1, **optimism** 2.
2. [The object of hope]—*Syn.* wish, concern, aspiration, goal, promise, dream, utopia, promised land, fortune, reward, gain, achievement; see also **desire** 1, **end** 2, **purpose** 1.
3. [A reason for hope]—*Syn.* support, prop, mainstay, strength, bet, investment, faith, endurance; see also **belief** 1.

hope, *v.* —*Syn.* be hopeful, lean on *or* upon, wish, desire, live in hope, rely *or* depend *or* count on *or* upon, aspire to, doubt not, keep one's fingers crossed, hope for the best, be of good cheer, pray, cherish the hope, look forward to, await, contemplate, dream, presume, watch for, bank *or* reckon *or* calculate on, foresee, think to, promise oneself, suppose, deem likely, believe, suspect, surmise, hold, be assured, be *or* feel confident, anticipate, be prepared for, make plans for, rest on the hope, hold in prospect, aspire, assume, have faith, rest assured, entertain hope, feel confident, be sure of, take as a certainty, be reassured, take heart; *all* (D): hope to hell, knock on wood, catch at a straw, look on the bright *or* sunny side; see also **expect, trust** 1.

hopeful, *mod.* **1.** [Optimistic]—*Syn.* expectant, assured, sanguine, buoyant, enthusiastic, trustful, reassured, emboldened, full of hope, faithful, cheerful, anticipative, anticipating, trusting, inspirited, expecting, anticipatory, at ease, in hopes of, forward-looking, lighthearted, serene, calm, poised, comfortable, blithe, eager, elated; *all* (D): Pollyannaish, beamish, looking through rose-colored glasses; see also **confident** 3, **trusting** 2.
2. [Encouraging]—*Syn.* promising, reassuring, assuring, favorable, bright, cheering, flattering, gracious, opportune, timely, fortunate, propitious, auspicious, well-timed, fit, suitable, convenient, beneficial, reasonable, fair, uplifting, heartening, inspiring, exciting, pleasing, fine, inspiriting, fortifying, rousing, arousing, enlivening, lucky, stirring, making glad, gladdening, elating, providential, helpful, rose-colored, rosy, animating, attractive, satisfactory, refreshing, probable, good, conducive, advantageous, of good omen, pleasant, consoling, of promise, happy, cheerful, comforting, calming, proper, expeditious, enlivening.—*Ant.* discouraging, unfortunate*, unfavorable.

hopefully, *mod.* **1.** [Optimistically]—*Syn.* confidently, expectantly, sanguinely, with confidence *or* with (good) hope, trustingly, naively, with some reassurance, trustfully; see also **boldly** 1, **positively** 1, **surely.**—*Ant.* doubtfully, hopelessly*, gloomily.
2. [Probably]—*Syn.* expectedly, conceivably, feasibly; see **probably.**

hopeless, *mod.* **1.** [Despairing]—*Syn.* despondent, pessimistic, cynical; see **sad** 1.
2. [Discouraging]—*Syn.* unfortunate, threatening, bad, sinister, unyielding, irrevocable, irredeemable, incurable, beyond recall, past hope *or* cure, irretrievable, vain, unmitigable, irreversible, irreparable, irreclaimable, irrecoverable, cureless, without hope, with no hope, impracticable, ill-fated, disastrous, menacing, foreboding, unfavorable, dying, worsening, past recall, tragic, fatal, desperate, helpless, unavailing, lost, unreclaimable, to no avail, forlorn, remediless, relapsing, abandoned, gone, empty, idle, recidivous, valueless, incorrigible, useless, unserviceable, pointless, worthless, insurmountable; see **futile** 1, **impossible** 1.—*Ant.* favorable*, heartening, cheering.

hopelessly, *mod.* **1.** [Without hope]—*Syn.* cynically, pessimistically, despondently, despairingly, dejectedly, disconsolately, desperately, mechanically, automatically, emptily, spiritlessly, darkly, gloomily, dismally, desolately; *all* (D): down in the mouth, under the weather, fit to be tied; see also **sadly.**—*Ant.* confidently, hopefully*, expectantly.
2. [Giving small ground for hope]—*Syn.* impossibly, incurably, desperately, fatally, unavailingly, unfortunately, badly; *both* (D): without a chance in the world, with all odds against.

hoping, *mod.* —*Syn.* believing, expecting, wishing, assuming, anticipating, looking forward; see also **trusting** 2.

hopper, *n.* —*Syn.* receptacle, storage place, tank; see **storehouse.**

horde, *n.* —*Syn.* pack, throng, swarm; see **crowd** 1, **gathering.**

horizon, *n.* —*Syn.* range, border, limit; see **boundary, extent.**

horizontal, *mod.* **1.** [Level]—*Syn.* plane, aligned, parallel; see **flat** 1, **level** 3, **straight** 1.
2. [Even]—*Syn.* flush, uniform, regular; see **flat** 1, **smooth** 1.

horn, *n.* **1.** [A hornlike sounding instrument] —*Syn.* wood wind, brass wind, trumpet, air horn, electric horn.
Horns include the following—bugle, trombone, cornet, fluegelhorn, French horn, baritone, tuba, sax-tuba, brass tuba, bombardon, serpent, alpenhorn, hunting horn, conch, lure, ram's horn, shofar; see also **musical instrument.**
2. [Hard process protruding from the head of certain animals]—*Syn.* tusk, antler, outgrowth, pronghorn, hornbill, frontal bone, epiphysis, apophysis, quill, corniculum, spine, spike, corniplume, point, cornu, cornicle, cornule; see also **bone, tooth** 1.
3. [The material comprising horns, sense 2]—*Syn.* keratin, elastin, epidermal tissue, corneous *or* corneate matter.
blow one's own horn (D)—*Syn.* praise oneself, gloat, brag; see **boast** 1.

lock horns—*Syn.* disagree, conflict, defy; see **oppose** 1.
on the horns of a dilemma—*Syn.* torn between two alternatives, having to make a difficult decision, between the devil and the deep blue sea (D); see **in trouble** 1.
pull (*or* **draw** *or* **haul) in one's horns**—*Syn.* withdraw, recant, hold oneself back; see **restrain** 1.

horn in (on) (D), *v.* —*Syn.* intrude, impose (upon), get in on (D); see **enter** 1, **meddle** 1.

horny, *mod.* **1.** [Callous]—*Syn.* hard, firm, tough; see **bony** 1.
2. [(D) Sexually excited]—*Syn.* sensual, aroused, lecherous; see **excited, lewd** 2.

horrendous, *mod.* —*Syn.* horrible, frightful, terrible; see **poor** 2, **faulty.**

horrible, *mod.* **1.** [Offensive]—*Syn.* repulsive, dreadful, disgusting; see **offensive** 2.
2. [Frightful]—*Syn.* shameful, shocking, awful; see **frightful** 1, **terrible** 1.

horrid, *mod.* —*Syn.* hideous, disturbing, shameful; see **offensive** 2, **pitiful** 1.

horrified, *mod.* —*Syn.* frightened, repelled, aghast; see **afraid** 2, **shocked, troubled.**

horrify, *v.* —*Syn.* terrify, appall, petrify; see **frighten** 1.

horror, *n.* **1.** [Dread]—*Syn.* awe, terror, fright; see **fear** 2.
2. [Abhorrence]—*Syn.* aversion, dislike, loathing; see **hate, hatred** 1.

horror-stricken, *mod.* —*Syn.* petrified, paralyzed, shocked, overcome with fear *or* horror, aghast, scared to death, horrified, freaked (D); see also **afraid** 2.

hors d'oeuvre, *n.* —*Syn.* appetizers, canapés, relishes, caviar, *antipasto* (Italian), *zakuska* (Russian), smörgasbord, antepast; see also **appetizer.**

horse, *n.* [A domestic animal]—*Syn.* nag, draft animal, plow horse, racer, saddlehorse, steed, mount, charger, stallion, gelding, hack, mare, dobbin, roadster, palfrey, pad, thoroughbred, pacer, trotter, cob, hunter, courser, posthorse, piebald, calico pony, equine, quadruped, *Pferd* (German), *cheval* (French), *caballo* (Spanish); see also **animal, pony.** Kinds of horses include the following—Clydesdale, Shire, Belgian, Percheron, Appaloosa, French coach, Morgan, Suffolk, Flemish, Arabian, Barbary *or* barb, mustang, bronco, pinto, palomino, Hambletonian. **1.** [An upright structure]—*Syn.* trestle, support, bench, stage, scaffold, easel, tripod, bolster, clotheshorse, sawhorse, vaulting block.
back the wrong horse—*Syn.* choose *or* support the losing side, pick the loser, misjudge; see **lose** 3.
beat (*or* **flog) a dead horse** (D)—*Syn.* argue an issue that is already settled, nag, harp on; see **overdo** 1.
from the horse's mouth (D)—*Syn.* originally, from an authority, according to the source of the information; see **officially** 1.
hold one's horses (D)—*Syn.* curb one's impatience, slow down, relax; see **restrain** 1.
on one's high horse (D)—*Syn.* arrogant, haughty, disdainful; see **egotistic** 2.

horse around (D), *v.* —*Syn.* fool around (D), cavort, cause trouble; see **misbehave, play** 2.

horseback, *mod.* —*Syn.* by horse, on a horse, in the saddle, bareback, equestrian, mounted; see also **moving** 1.

horseman, *n.* —*Syn.* equestrian, equerry, roughrider, cavalry man, horse guard, dragoon, horse driver, horse trainer, keeper of horses, gaucho, pricker, buckaroo, postilion; *all* (D): broncobuster, saddle sitter, live weight, monkey, gypsy; see also **cowboy** 1, **jockey, rider** 1.

horsemanship, *n.* —*Syn.* riding skill, management of horses, equestrian skill, *manège* (French).

horseplay, *n.* —*Syn.* clowning, play, fooling around; see **fun, joke** 1.

horsepower, *n.* —*Syn.* strength, pull, power; see **energy** 3.

horticulture, *n.* —*Syn.* cultivation of gardens, agriculture, floriculture; see **farming, gardening.**

hose, *n.* **1.** [Stocking]—*Syn.* men's *or* women's hose, tights, panty hose; see **hosiery.**
2. [A flexible conduit]—*Syn.* garden hose, fire hose, line, tubing; see also **conduit, pipe** 1, **tube** 1.

hosiery, *n.* —*Syn.* silk *or* rayon *or* nylon *or* woolen stockings, full-fashioned hose, seamless hose, trunk hose, half hose, socks, anklets, tights, panty hose, leotards, knee stocks, ankle socks, bobby socks *or* sox, knitted *or* crotcheted *or* bulky stockings, body stocking.

hospitable, *mod.* —*Syn.* cordial, courteous, open; see **friendly** 1.

hospital, *n.* —*Syn.* clinic, infirmary, sanatorium, sanitarium, dispensary, Red Cross hospital, mental hospital, army hospital, city hospital, public hospital, ship's hospital, veteran's hospital, institution for the physically *or* mentally sick, medical center, valetudinarium, lying-in hospital, health service, outpatient ward, sick bay; *all* (D): sick house, repair shop, croaker joint.
Common hospital terms and their abbreviations include the following—abdomen (abd.), axillary (ax.), basic metabolic rate (B.M.R.), blood pressure (B.P.), centigrade (C.); eye, ear, nose, throat (E.E.N.T.); electrocardiogram (E.C.G.), electroencephalogram (E.E.G.), gastrointestinal (G.I.), genitourinary (G.U.), hemoglobin (Hb.), intramuscular (I.M.), infusion (inf.), intensive care unit (I.C.U.), intravenous (I.V.), left lower quadrant (L.L.Q.), nonprotein nitrogen (N.P.N.), obstetrics (O.B.), right eye (O.D.), outpatient department (O.P.D.), mouth (os.), left eye (O.S.), pulse (P), phenolsulfonphthalein (P.S.P.), rectal (R.), respiration (R.), red blood cell (R.B.C.), right lower quadrant (R.L.Q.), specimen (spec.), specific gravity (sp. gr.), tuberculosis (T.B.), tension (tn.); temperature, pulse, respiration (T.P.R.); white blood cell (W.B.C.), verbal order (V.O.), gurney-rolling cart for patients, Levin stomach tube, Foley type of catheter, incision and drainage (I and D), first pregnancy (para.), heavy with child *or* gravida, first fetal movement felt by mother *or* quickening.

hospitality, *n.* **1.** [Entertainment]—*Syn.* accommodation, good cheer, warm welcome *or* reception, conviviality, companionship, good fellowship, comradeship, one's best; see also **entertainment** 1, **welcome.**
2. [Generosity in offering entertainment]—*Syn.* bountifulness, liberality, graciousness, geniality, heartiness, obligingness, affability, consideration,

amiability, cordiality; see also **courtesy** 1, **generosity** 1.

host, *n.* **1.** [A man who entertains]—*Syn.* man of the house, entertainer, toastmaster, master, talk-show moderator, master of ceremonies; *both* (D): Goodtime Charlie, handshaker.
2. [A man who operates a place of public hospitality]—*Syn.* innkeeper, hotel keeper, tavern keeper, saloon keeper, barkeeper *or* barkeep, restaurant owner, restaurateur, manager, maitre d', night club owner, proprietor; see also **owner.**
3. [A large group]—*Syn.* throng, multitude, army; see **crowd** 1, **gathering.**
4. [Organism on which a parasite subsists]—*Syn.* host mother, host body, animal; see **organism.**
5. [Sacramental bread; *capitalized*]—*Syn.* Bread of the Last Supper, wafer, Communion loaf, altar bread, Eucharist; see also **communion** 2, **sacrament.**

host, *v.*—*Syn.* receive, treat, wine and dine; see **entertain** 2.

hostage, *n.*—*Syn.* security, guaranty, captive, pawn, scapegoat, victim of a kidnapping, sacrificial victim; see also **prisoner.**

hostel, *n.*—*Syn.* youth hotel, accommodations for bicyclists, inn; see **hotel.**

hostel, *v.*—*Syn.* travel by bicycle, hitchhike, make a (walking) tour; see **travel** 2.

hostess, *n.* **1.** [A woman who entertains extensively]—*Syn.* society lady, socialite, clubwoman, social leader, social climber, entertainer; *all* (D): lion hunter, queen bee, lorgnette juggler.
2. [A woman in charge of public hospitality]—*Syn.* proprietress, madame, owner, airline hostess, taxi dancer, receptionist, satin front (D); see also **administration** 2, **administrator.**
3. [A woman who hosts visitors]—*Syn.* lady of the house, mistress of the household, toastmistress, mistress of ceremonies.

hostile, *mod.*—*Syn.* antagonistic, hateful, opposed; see **unfriendly** 1.

hostility, *n.*—*Syn.* abhorrence, aversion, bitterness; see **hatred** 1, **malice, resentment** 2.

hot, *mod.* **1.** [Having a high temperature]—*Syn.* torrid, burning, fiery, flaming, blazing, very warm, feverish, baking, roasting, smoking, scorching, blistering, searing, sizzling, tropical, warm, calescent, broiling, igneous, red-hot, grilling, piping-hot, white-hot, scalding, parching, sultry, on fire, at high temperature, incandescent, ovenlike, smoldering, thermal, calid, toasting, simmering, thermogenic, recalescent, decalescent; *all* (D): blazing hot, boiling hot, like an oven, hotter than blazes; see also **boiling, cooking** 1, **heated** 1, **molten.**—*Ant.* cold*, frigid, chilly.
2. [Close]—*Syn.* sultry, humid, stuffy; see **close** 5.
3. [Eager]—*Syn.* ardent, passionate, distracted; see **enthusiastic** 2, 3, **excited.**
4. [Aroused]—*Syn.* furious, ill-tempered, indignant; see **angry.**
5. [(D) Erotic]—*Syn.* spicy, salacious, carnal; see **lascivious** 2, **lewd** 1, 2, **sensual.**
get hot (D)—*Syn.* become excited or enthusiastic, burn with fervor *or* anger, rave; see **rage** 1.
make it hot for (D)—*Syn.* create discomfort for, cause trouble for, vex; see **disturb** 1.

hot and bothered (D), *mod.*—*Syn.* upset, excited, disturbed; see **troubled.**

hotel, *n.*—*Syn.* stopping place, inn, lodging house, halfway house, boarding house, hostel, hospice, country *or* health *or* mountain resort, watering place, tavern, house, spa, rooming house, khan, caravansary; *all* (D); flophouse, bughouse, dump, boatel; see also **lodge, motel, resort** 2.

hotheaded, *mod.* **1.** [Impetuous]—*Syn.* unmanageable, wild, reckless; see **rash, unruly.**
2. [Irritable]—*Syn.* quick-tempered, crabby, touchy; see **irritable.**

hothouse, *n.*—*Syn.* glasshouse, conservatoire, nursery; see **greenhouse.**

hot plate, *n.*—*Syn.* electric burner, warmer, portable stove; see **stove.**

hot rod, *n.*—*Syn.* dragster, speedster, stock car; see **automobile, racer** 2, **vehicle** 1.

hot under the collar (D), *mod.*—*Syn.* furious, mad, resentful; see **angry.**

hound, *n.* Types of hounds include the following—greyhound, bloodhound, foxhound, staghound, deerhound, wolfhound, otterhound, harrier, basset, beagle, dachshund; see also **animal** 1, **dog** 1.

hound, *v.*—*Syn.* badger, provoke, annoy; see **bother** 2, 3.

hour, *n.* **1.** [A period of time]—*Syn.* time unit, sixty minutes, man-hour, ampere-hour, planetary hour, horsepower hour, recitation hour, lecture hour, class hour, supper hour, study hour, rush hour; see also **time** 1.
2. [An appointed time]—*Syn.* moment, minute, term; see **appointment** 2.
of the hour—*Syn.* most important, significant, relevant; see **important** 1.
one's hour—*Syn.* the time of one's death, one's dying, one's time (D); see **death** 1.
the small (*or* **wee**) **hours**—*Syn.* midnight, middle of the night, early morning; see **morning** 1, **night** 1.

hour after hour, *mod.*—*Syn.* continually, steadily, on and on; see **continuing, regularly** 2.

hourly, *mod.*—*Syn.* hour by hour, each hour, every hour, every sixty minutes, continually, at the striking of the hour; see also **frequently, regularly** 2.

house, *n.* **1.** [A habitation]—*Syn.* dwelling, apartment house, residence; see **apartment, home** 1.
2. [A large business establishment]—*Syn.* corporation, partnership, stock company; see **business** 4, **organization** 3.
3. [A family]—*Syn.* line, family tradition, ancestry; see **family** 1.
4. [A legislative body]—*Syn.* congress, council, parliament; see **legislature.**
bring down the house (D)—*Syn.* receive applause, create enthusiasm, please; see **excite** 2.
clean house—*Syn.* arrange, put in order, tidy up; see **clean.**
keep house—*Syn.* manage a home, run a house, be a housekeeper; see **manage** 1.
like a house on fire—*Syn.* actively, vigorously, energetically; see **quickly** 1.
on the house—*Syn.* without expense, gratis, for nothing; see **free** 4.
play house—*Syn.* make-believe, play games, play at keeping a home; see **pretend** 1.

set (*or* **put**) **one's house in order**—*Syn.* arrange, put in order, manage; see **order** 3.

housebreaker, *n.*—*Syn.* thief, lock-picker, burglar; see **criminal, robber.**

household, *n.*—*Syn.* family unit, house, domestic establishment; see **family** 1, **home.**

householder, *n.*—*Syn.* proprietor, landlord, mortgagee; see **owner.**

housekeeper, *n.*—*Syn.* wife and mother, caretaker, serving woman; see **housewife, servant.**

housekeeping, *n.*—*Syn.* household management, domestic science, home economy, housewifery, stewardship, husbandry, hotel administration; see also **housework.**

housetop, *n.*—*Syn.* shingles, gables, chimney; see **gable.**

housewife, *n.*—*Syn.* mistress *or* lady of the house, housekeeper, mother to one's children, *Hausfrau* (German), *mater familias* (Latin), home economist, home engineer, homemaker, mistress of a family, family manager, wife and mother, stay-at-home (D); see also **wife.**

housework, *n.*—*Syn.* housewifery, house cleaning, spring cleaning, window-washing, sweeping, cooking, baking, dusting, mopping, washing, laundering, bed-making, sewing, ironing, mending; see also **housekeeping, job** 2.

housing, *n.*—*Syn.* habitation, home construction, problem of providing houses, house-building program, sheltering, installation, covering, protection, abode, domicile, cantonment, house, accommodations, lodgment, quarters, roof, dwelling, lodging, residence, headquarters, stopping place, diggings (D); see also **home, shelter.**

hovel, *n.*—*Syn.* cottage, shed, cabin; see **hut, shack.**

hover, *v.*—*Syn.* float, flutter, waver; see **fly** 1, **hang** 2.

hovering, *mod.* **1.** [Floating]—*Syn.* gliding, swaying, airborne; see **flying** 1, **hanging.**

2. [Attending carefully]—*Syn.* considerate, attentive, shielding; see **protective, thoughtful** 2.

how, *conj.* and *mod.*—*Syn.* in what way, to what degree, by what method, in what manner, after what precedent, according to what specifications, from what source, by whose help, whence, wherewith, by virtue of what, whereby, through what agency *or* medium, by what means *or* aid.

however, *conj.* and *mod.* **1.** [But]—*Syn.* still, though, nevertheless; see **but** 1, **yet** 1.

2. [In spite of]—*Syn.* despite, without regard to, nonetheless; see **notwithstanding.**

howl, *n.*—*Syn.* moan, wail, lament; see **cry** 2, **yell** 1.

howl, *v.*—*Syn.* bawl, wail, lament; see **cry** 3, **yell.**

one's night to howl—*Syn.* time for fun, relaxation, recreation; see **leisure.**

howling, *mod.*—*Syn.* noisy, crying, moaning; see **loud** 2, **yelling.**

hub, *n.*—*Syn.* core, heart, middle; see **center** 1.

hubbub, *n.*—*Syn.* turmoil, fuss, disorder; see **confusion** 2, **noise, uproar.**

huckster, *n.*—*Syn.* hawker, vendor, hustler; see **businessman, salesman.**

huddle, *n.*—*Syn.* group, assemblage, cluster; see **bunch** 1, **crowd** 1, **gathering.**

huddle, *v.*—*Syn.* crouch, press close, crowd, bunch, draw together, mass, cluster, throng, nestle, cuddle, hug, curl up, snuggle, make oneself small; see also **gather** 1, **press** 1.

hue, *n.* **1.** [A shade of color]—*Syn.* hue, value, dye; see **shade** 2, **tint, tone** 4.

2. [A color]—*Syn.* tincture, tone, chroma; see **color** 1.

hue and cry (D), *n.*—*Syn.* clamor, shout, pursuit; see **cry** 1, **hunt** 2.

huff, *n.*—*Syn.* annoyance, offense, perturbation; see **anger, rage** 2.

huffy, *mod.*—*Syn.* offended, piqued, huffish; see **angry, insulted, irritable.**

hug, *n.*—*Syn.* embrace, squeeze, tight grip, fond pressure, caress, demonstration of affection; *all* (D): clinch, bunny hug, bear hug; see also **touch** 2.

hug, *v.*—*Syn.* embrace, squeeze, clasp, press close, hold to one's heart, love, keep close to, catch hold of, be near to, clasp tightly in the arms, cling, fold in the arms, clutch, seize, envelop, press, grasp, enfold, embosom, nestle, welcome, cuddle, lock, press to the bosom, snuggle, lie close, cling together, receive warmly, fold to the breast *or* heart; *all* (D): go into a clinch, clinch, do the bear; see also **caress, hold** 1, **touch** 1.

huge, *mod.*—*Syn.* tremendous, enormous, immense; see **large** 1.

hug the road, *v.*—*Syn.* track, cling to the road, drive well; see **ride** 5, **travel** 2.

hulk, *n.* **1.** [A large, unshapely object]—*Syn.* bulk, blob, hunk, chunk, lump, clump, clod, slather (D); see also **mass** 1, **part** 1.

2. [A wreck]—*Syn.* shell, remains, ruins, shambles, skeleton, frame, hull, dismasted ship, derelict, body; see also **wreck** 2.

hulking, *mod.*—*Syn.* bulky, cumbersome, clumsy; see **awkward** 1.

hull, *n.* **1.** [The body of a vessel]—*Syn.* framework, skeleton, main structure, wetted surface, underbody, water lines, decks, covering, cast, mold, sides; see also **frame** 1.

2. [A shell]—*Syn.* peeling, husk, shuck; see **peel, shell** 1.

hull, *v.*—*Syn.* husk, shuck, peel; see **skin.**

hullabaloo, *n.*—*Syn.* tumult, chaos, clamor; see **confusion** 2, **noise, uproar.**

hum, *v.*—*Syn.* buzz, drone, murmur, sing low, hum a tune, croon, sing in and undertone, whisper, sing without articulation, zoom, moan, make a buzzing sound, bombinate, thrum, bum, whir, vibrate, bombilate, purr; see also **sound** 1.

human, *mod.*—*Syn.* anthropoid, animal, biped, civilized, man-made, anthropomorphic, anthropocentric, anthropological, manlike, of man, belonging to man, humanistic, individual, man's, hominid, proper to man, personal, hominal; see also **mortal** 2, **rational** 1, **social** 1.—*Ant.* divine*, bestial, nonhuman.

human being, *n.*—*Syn.* being, mortal, individual; see **man** 1, 2, 3, **person** 1, **woman** 1.

humane, *mod.* **1.** [Kindly]—*Syn.* benevolent, sympathetic, understanding, pitying, compassionate, kindhearted, human, tenderhearted, forgiving, gracious, charitable, benignant, gentle, tender, clement, benign, obliging, friendly, indulgent, generous, lenient, tolerant, democratic, accommodating, good-natured, liberal, humanitarian, righteous, open-minded, broad-minded, altruistic, philanthropic, helpful, magnanimous, amiable, genial, cordial, unselfish, warmhearted, large-hearted, bighearted, beneficent, soft-hearted, sympathizing, freehearted, liberal, pitying, good; *both* (D): soft, easy; see also **kind** 1, **merciful** 1.—*Ant.* cruel*, barbaric, inhuman.

2. [Cultural]—*Syn.* civilized, advanced, cultured; see **educated** 1, **refined** 2.

humanist, *n.* —*Syn.* classicist, altruist, scholastic; see **philanthropist, philosopher, scholar** 2.

humanitarian, *mod.* —*Syn.* considerate, public-spirited, idealistic; see **generous** 1, **humane, kindly** 2, **philanthropic** 1, 2.

humanitarian, *n.* —*Syn.* altruist, helper, benefactor; see **patron** 1, **philanthropist.**

humanities, *n.* —*Syn.* liberal arts, letters, belles-lettres, arts, the fine arts, languages, the classics; see also **art** 2, **history** 2, **language** 2, **literature** 1, **philosophy** 1.

hunanity, *n.* **1.** [The human race]—*Syn.* man, mankind, men; see **man** 1.

2. [An ideal of human behavior]—*Syn.* tolerance, sympathy, understanding; see **kindness** 1, **virtue** 1, 2.

humanize, *v.* —*Syn.* acculturate, cultivate, refine; see **civilize, teach** 1, 2.

humanizing, *mod.* —*Syn.* civilizing, refining, uplifting; see **cultural.**

humble, *mod.* **1.** [Meek]—*Syn.* lowly, submissive, gentle, quiet, unassuming, diffident, simple, retiring, bashful, shy, timid, reserved, docile, deferential, backward, self-conscious, soft-spoken, coy, demure, blushing, sheepish, standoffish, mild, timorous, withdrawn, unpretentious, unobtrusive, hesitant, apprehensive, fearful, tentative, self-belittling, poor in spirit, tractable, sedate, unpretending, supplicatory, small, biddable, unpresuming, self-effacing, little, slavish, broken, ductile, obsequious, reverential, manageable, subservient, ordinary, unambitious, commonplace, free from pride, peaceful, placid, without arrogance, peaceable, obedient, passive, broken in spirit, tame, clement, restrained, enduring, stoic, yielding, stoical, acquiescent, unostentatious, unimportant, of little *or* small importance, gentle as a lamb, meek-spirited, meek-hearted, low, unresisting, resigned, subdued, tolerant, content, compliant; *all* (D): underdogmatic, mealy-mouthed, Micawberish, eating humble pie; see also **modest** 2.—*Ant.* proud*, haughty, conceited.

2. [Lowly]—*Syn.* unpretentious, unassuming, modest, seemly, becoming, homespun, natural, plebeian, low, cringing, out-of-the-way, proletarian, servile, undistinguished, pitiful, sordid, shabby, underprivileged, meager, beggarly, log-cabin, commonplace, menial, unimportant, insignificant, small, poor, untouched, unvarnished, unaffected, rough, hard, severe, unpretending, earthborn, base, meek, little, of low birth, obscure, inferior, baseborn, mean, inglorious, low-ranking, plain, common, homely, ignoble, low in rank, of low rank, simple, lowbred, uncouth, ignominious, of mean parentage, measly, contemptible, miserable, scrubby, ordinary, inferior, puny, humdrum, poorish, trivial, ill-bred, petty, underbred, paltry, unequal, vulgar, unrefined, wretched, unfit.—*Ant.* upper-class, noble*, privileged.

humble, *v.* —*Syn.* shame, mortify, chasten, demean (oneself), demote, lower, crush, abash, hide one's face, bring low, put to shame, silence, reduce, humiliate, degrade, overcome, strike dumb, take *or* put *or* pull *or* bring down, override, snub, confuse, discredit, deflate, upset, abase, make ashamed, put out of countenance, confound, meeken, deny, discomfit; *all* (D): take down a peg, pull (one) off his high horse, put down, squelch, squash, hide one's light under a bushel, kiss the rod; see also **disgrace, embarrass** 1.—*Ant.* exalt, praise*, glorify.

humbly, *mod.* —*Syn.* meekly, submissively, abjectly, simply, poorly, ingloriously, obscurely, on bended knee, apologetically.—*Ant.* haughtily, proudly*, boastfully.

humbug, *n.* —*Syn.* lie, fraud, faker; see **deception** 1, **fake, nonsense.**

humdrum, *mod.* —*Syn.* monotonous, common, uninteresting; see **dull** 4.

humid, *mod.* —*Syn.* stuffy, sticky, muggy; see **close** 5, **wet** 1.

humidity, *n.* —*Syn.* moisture, wetness, dampness, mugginess, dankness, heaviness, sogginess, thickness, fogginess, wet, sultriness, steaminess, steam, vaporization, dankness, evaporation, sweatiness, humectation, dewiness, humidification, liquidity, stickiness, moistness, swelter, oppressiveness; see also **rain** 1.—*Ant.* dryness*, aridity, drought.

humiliate, *v.* —*Syn.* debase, chasten, mortify, make a fool of, put to shame, humble, degrade, denigrate, crush, shame, discomfit, abash, make lowly, deny, confuse, snub, confound, lower, dishonor, depress, fill with shame, chagrin, break, demean, bring low, base, conquer, make ashamed, vanquish, pout out of countenance, cast *or* take *or* put *or* bring *or* pull down; *both* (D): take down a peg, put one's nose out of joint; see also **disgrace, embarrass** 1.

humiliated, *mod.* —*Syn.* humbled, abashed, disgraced; see **ashamed.**

humiliating, *mod.* —*Syn.* mortifying, humbling, disgracing; see **embarrassing, opprobrious** 1.

humiliation, *n.* —*Syn.* chagrin, mortification, mental pain; see **disgrace** 1, **embarrassment** 1, **shame** 2.

humility, *n.* —*Syn.* meekness, timidity, self-abasement, self-abnegation, submissiveness, servility, obsequiousness, mortification, reserve, lowliness, demureness, unobtrusiveness, subservience, subjection, humbleness, submission, abasement, diffidence, self-effacement, fawning, obedience, passiveness, nonresistance, resignation, bashfulness, shyness, timorousness, inferiority complex; see also **docility, modesty** 1.—*Ant.* pride*, vainglory, conceit.

hummock, *n.* —*Syn.* bump, knob, hump; see **bulge, hill, lump.**

humor, *n.* **1.** [Comedy]—*Syn.* amusement, jesting, raillery, joking, merriment, buffoonery, tomfoolery, badinage, clowning, jocularity, jocoseness, farce, drollery, facetiousness, black humor, salt, whimsicality; *both* (D): comedy stuff, laugh business; see also **entertainment** 1, **fun.**

2. [An example of humor]—*Syn.* witticism, pleasantry, banter; see **joke** 1, 2.

3. [The ability to appreciate comedy]—*Syn.* good humor, sense of humor, wittiness, high spirits, merry disposition, joviality, jolliness, jocularity, jocundity, gaiety, joyfulness, playfulness, happy frame of mind, jauntiness; see also **happiness** 1.
4. [Mood]—*Syn.* disposition, frame of mind, temper; see **mood** 1.
out of humor—*Syn.* cross, disagreeable, grouchy; see **irritable.**

humor, *v.* —*Syn.* indulge, pamper, baby, play up to, gratify, please, pet, coddle, tickle, gladden, mollycoddle, spoil, oblige, comply with, appease, placate, soften, be playful with; see also **comfort** 1, **entertain** 1, **satisfy** 1.—*Ant.* provoke, anger, enrage.

humorous, *mod.* —*Syn.* comical, comic, entertaining; see **funny** 1, **witty.**

humorously, *mod.* —*Syn.* comically, ridiculously, playfully, absurdly, ludicrously, amusingly, jokingly, mirthfully, ironically, satirically, facetiously, merrily, genially, jovially, jocosely, jocundly, not seriously *or* solemnly, screamingly, archly, in a comical *or* amusing *or* ridiculous, etc., manner; as ridiculously *or* absurdly *or* ludicrously, etc., as possible; *all* (D): just for fun *or* for ducks, crazily as crazy, like he was crazy *or* nuts *or* off his rocker, etc.

hump, *n.* —*Syn.* protuberance, mound, bump, swelling, camel hump, humpback, hunchback, hummock, protrusion, elevation, convexity, knob, knap, convexedness, excrescence, prominence, knurl, monticle, eminence, boss, projection, swell, hunch, barrow, gibbosity, lump, dune, tumescence, kopje; see also **bulge, hill.**

hump (D), *v.* —*Syn.* rush, work hard, speed up; see **hurry** 1.

humpback, *n.* —*Syn.* cripple, deformed person, Quasimodo; see **hunchback.**

humpbacked, *mod.* —*Syn.* stooped, malformed, distorted; see **deformed, disabled.**

hunch, *n.* **1.** [Hump]—*Syn.* protuberance, bump, swelling; see **bulge, hump, hill, lump.**
2. [(D) Intuition]—*Syn.* idea, notion, feeling, premonition, presage, forecast, presentiment, instinct, expectation, anticipation, foreknowledge, preconceived notion, forewisdom, omination, precognition, preapprehension, prescience, forewarning, clue, presagement, foreboding, boding, prenotice, prenotation, augury, auguration, hint, portent, apprehension, misgiving, qualm, suspicion, inkling, glimmer; see also **thought** 2.

hunch, *v.* —*Syn.* draw together, cower, bunch; see **bow** 1, **lean** 1.

hunchback, *n.* —*Syn.* humpback, cripple, crookbacked, humpbacked person, Quasimodo.

hundred, *n.* —*Syn.* ten tens, five score, century; see **number** 1.

hung, *mod.* —*Syn.* suspended, swaying, dangling; see **hanging.**

hunger, *n.* —*Syn.* craving, longing, yearning, mania, ravenousness, voracity, lust, desire for food, famine, starvation, appetite, gluttony, hungriness, panting, drought, appetition, glut, appetence, want, polydipsia, appetency, vacancy, void, greed, greediness; *all* (D): bottomless pit, peckishness, the munchies, a stomach for, sweet tooth, aching void; see also **appetite** 1, **desire** 1, **starvation.** —*Ant.* satisfaction*, satiety, glut.

hungry, *mod.* —*Syn.* starved, famished, craving, ravenous, desirous, hankering, unsatisfied, unfilled, starving, edacious, insatiate, voracious, of keen appetite, famishing, half-starved, hungered, ravening, omnivorous, carnivorous, supperless, greedy as a hog, dinnerless, piggish, hoggish, peckish, half-famished; *all* (D): on an empty stomach, hungry as a wolf, empty; see also **greedy** 2.—*Ant.* satisfied, full*, fed.

hung up (D), **1.** [Troubled]—*Syn.* disturbed, psychotic, psychopathic; see **neurotic, troubled** 2.
2. [Intent]—*Syn.* absorbed, engrossed, preoccupied; see **enthusiastic** 2, **rapt** 2, **thoughtful** 1.

hunk, *n.* —*Syn.* lump, large piece, good-sized bit, portion, a fair quantity, a good bit, chunk, bunch, mass, clod, a pile, thick slice, morsel, a lot, slice, gob, hank, loaf, nugget, block, loads, bulk, batch, wad (D); see also **part** 1, **piece** 1.

hunt, *n.* **1.** [The pursuit of game]—*Syn.* chase, sporting, shooting, coursing; lion hunt, tiger hunt, fox hunt, deer hunt, duck hunt, etc.; tracking, hawking, steeplechase, venery, *battue* (French), course, race, angling, fishing, game, gunning, pursuit, field sport, riding to hounds, piscation, beagling, piscatology; see also **hunting, sport** 3.
2. [A search]—*Syn.* investigation, probe, inquiry, raid, quest, pursuit, exploration, research, sifting, seeking, pursuance, hounding, prosecution, trailing, inquisition, scrutiny, inquest, study, interrogation, prying, meddling, tracing, snooping, research, rummage, following, pursuing, reconnaissance; *both* (D): look-see, frisking; see also **examination** 1.

hunt, *v.* **1.** [To pursue with intent to kill]—*Syn.* follow, give chase, stalk, hound, trail, dog, seek, capture, kill, shoot, press on, track, heel, shadow, chase (after), hunt out, ride to hounds, snare, look for, fish, run, ride, drive, fish for, hawk, poach, grouse, ferret, drag, course, start game; *all* (D): beagle, gun for, go gunning for; see also **pursue** 1.
2. [To try to find]—*Syn.* investigate, seek for, sift, winnow, drag, probe, fish out *or* for, look for, be on the lookout for, go after, trail, cast about, ransack, trace, ferret out, spoor, inquire, hunt for *or* out, search (for *or* out), grope in the dark, leave no stone unturned, delve for, scour, prowl after, examine, interrogate, question, catechise; *both* (D): nose around, rummage; see also **seek** 1.

hunted, *mod.* —*Syn.* pursued, followed, tracked, sought (for), trailed, chased, stalked, hounded, tracked, dogged, tailed, harried, outcast, outlawed, wanted, the object of hunt *or* search, *or* pursuit, driven out, searched for.

hunted down, *mod.* —*Syn.* found, brought to bay *or* to earth, taken; see **captured** 1.

hunter, *n.* **1.** [A person who hunts]—*Syn.* huntsman, stalker, chaser, sportsman, pursuer, ferreter, big-game hunter, hawker, falconer, beater, gunner, poacher, nimrod, pigsticker, horsewoman, huntress, horseman, archer, deerstalker, pursuant, equestrian, fisher, angler, equestrienne, piscator, fisherman, piscatorian, piscatorialist, toxophile, Waltonian, toxophilite, toxophilist, bowman, shooter; see also **trapper.**

2. [A dog or horse bred for hunting]—*Syn.* hunting dog, gun dog, hound, hound dog, courser, foxhound, rabbit hound, chaser, steed, equine, garran, stalking *or* hunting *or* riding horse, mount; see also **animal** 1, **dog** 1, **horse** 1.
Hunting dogs include the following—pointer, setter, boarhound, Great Dane, retriever, spaniel, bloodhound, whippet, borzoi, saluki, terrier, foxhound, wolfhound, Rhodesian ridgeback, beagle.

hunting, *mod.*—*Syn.* looking for *or* around, seeking, in search (of); see **searching** 2.

hunting, *n.*—*Syn.* the chase, the hunt, sporting, shooting, coursing, venery, stalking, falconry, trapping, big-game hunting, deer hunting, boar hunting, fox hunting, pheasant shooting, fowling, field, chevy, angling, pursuit, falconry, fishing, hawking, still hunt, venatics, fishery, steeplechase, fox hunting, riding to hounds, piscation, gunning, halieutics, beagling (D); see also **hunt, sport** 3.

hurdle, *n.* **1.** [A physical barrier]—*Syn.* barricade, earthwork, blockade; see **barrier.**
2. [Something in one's way]—*Syn.* complication, obstacle, obstruction; see **difficulty** 1, **impediment** 1, **interference** 1.

hurdle, *v.*—*Syn.* jump over *or* across, scale, vault, surmount, leap over, overcome, hop the sticks (D); see also **jump** 1.

hurl, *v.*—*Syn.* cast, fling, heave; see **throw** 1.

hurly-burly, *n.*—*Syn.* restlessness, turmoil, turbulence; see **confusion** 2, **uproar.**

hurrah, *interj.*—*Syn.* three cheers, hurray, rahrah, huzza; *all* (D): yippee, whoopee; hear, hear; hip-hip; see also **cheer** 3, **cry** 1, **encouragement** 2, **yell** 1.

hurricane, *n.*—*Syn.* whirlwind, line storm, typhoon, tempest, monsoon, blow (D); see also **storm.**

hurried, *mod.*—*Syn.* quick, speedy, in a hurry; see **fast** 1.

hurriedly, *mod.*—*Syn.* rapidly, speedily, fast; see **quickly** 1.

hurry, *interj.*—*Syn.* run, hasten, speed, move, get on it, hustle, gain time, look alive, get a move on, bear down on it, on the double, hump it (D).

hurry, *n.* **1.** [The press of time]—*Syn.* rush, drive, scurry, dash, push, precipitateness, hustle (D).
2. [Confusion]—*Syn.* bustle, flurry, fluster; see **confusion** 2.
3. [Haste]—*Syn.* dispatch, expedition, rush; see **speed.**

hurry, *v.* **1.** [To act hastily]—*Syn.* hasten, be quick, make haste, bestir oneself, bustle, rush, make short work of, scoot, work at high speed, dash on, hurry about, bundle on, run off, sally, work under pressure, hurry up, lose no time, make time, speed, act on a moment's notice; *all* (D): turn on the steam, step on the gas, get cracking, don't spare the horses, step on it, fly about, put on a burst of speed, dig out, dart to and fro, race one's motor, floor it, shake a leg.—*Ant.* delay*, lose time, procrastinate.
2. [To move rapidly]—*Syn.* fly, bustle, dash off; see **race** 1, **run** 2.
3. [To urge others]—*Syn.* push, spur, goad on; see **drive** 1, **goad, urge** 2.

hurrying, *mod.*—*Syn.* bustling, scurrying, darting, hastening, speeding, in a hurry, running, rushing, dashing, flying, expediting, propelling, racing, racing against time.—*Ant.* creeping*, crawling, inching along.

hurt, *mod.*—*Syn.* injured, damaged, harmed, marred, impaired, shot, warped, struck, contused, bruised, stricken, battered, buffeted, mauled, hit, stabbed, mutilated, lacerated, disfigured, blemished, pained, in pain, disturbed, suffering, distressed, tortured, agonized, in a serious state, unhappy, slightly wounded, grazed, scratched, severely wounded, sorely hurt; *both* (D): nicked, winged; see also **wounded.**—*Ant.* aided*, helped, assisted.

hurt, *n.* **1.** [A wound]—*Syn.* blow, gash, ache; see **injury** 1, **pain** 1.
2. [Damage]—*Syn.* ill-treatment, harm, persecution; see **damage** 1, **disaster, misfortune** 1.

hurt, *v.* **1.** [To cause pain]—*Syn.* cramp, squeeze, cut, bruise, tear, pain, torment, try, afflict, kick, puncture, do violence, slap, abuse, administer punishment, flog, whip, whack, torture, gnaw, stab, pierce, maul, cut up, harm, injure, wound, lacerate, harrow, convulse, prick, sting, do evil, chafe, bite, flail, give pain, grate, martyr, inflict pain, rasp, excruciate, burn, grind, rack, wring, nip, fret, crucify, martyrize, tweak, gripe, agonize, thrash, punch, prolong the agony, pinch, gall, spank, chastise, punish, pommel, lace, flail, buffet, drub, smite, trounce, scourge, flagellate, lambaste, baste, lash, cudgel, bastinado, belabor, birch, cane, switch, sandbag, cause *or* bring *or* occasion pain, anguish, distress, displease, discommode, discompose, incommode, put out; *all* (D): faze, give someone the works, give no quarter, barb the dart, work over, lay *or* wrack up, hang a shanty on, wallop, blackjack, belt, make someone yell murder, slug; see also **beat** 2.—*Ant.* comfort*, ease, soothe.
2. [To harm]—*Syn.* maltreat, injure, spoil; see **damage** 1, **destroy** 1.
3. [To distress]—*Syn.* worry, outrage, trouble; see **bother** 2, 3, **disturb** 2.
4. [To give a feeling of pain]—*Syn.* be sore, ache, throb, pain, be tender, be bruised, sting.

hurtful, *mod.*—*Syn.* aching, injurious, bad; see **dangerous** 1, 2, **deadly, harmful, ominous, poisonous.**

hurtle, *v.*—*Syn.* collide, bump, push; see **crash** 4.

husband, *n.*—*Syn.* spouse, married man, mate, bedmate, benedict, helpmate, consort, bridegroom, groom, breadwinner, provider, man, polygynist, polygamist, cuckold, goodman, monogamist, monogynist, bigamist, commonlaw husband *or* spouse; *all* (D): hubby, lord, head of the house, the man of the house, lord and master, meal ticket, old man; see also **man** 2.

husbandman, *n.*—*Syn.* planter, agriculturalist, forester; see **farmer.**

husbandry, *n.* **1.** [Farming]—*Syn.* agriculture, tillage, land management; see **farming.**
2. [Management of one's private affairs]—*Syn.* home management, personal transactions, budgeting, housekeeping, domestic arrangement, business dealings, management, managership, stewardship, retrenchment; see also **administration** 1.
3. [Thrift]—*Syn.* providence, wise administration, thriftiness; see **economy** 2, **frugality.**

hush, *interj.* —*Syn.* quiet, be quiet, stop talking, soft, less noise; *all* (D): pipe down, sign off, hush up; see also **shut up.**

hush, *n.* —*Syn.* peace, stillness, quiet; see **silence** 1.

hush, *v.* —*Syn.* silence, still, muffle, gag, stop, stifle, force into silence; see also **quiet** 2.

hush money, *n.* —*Syn.* graft, blackmail, extortion; see **bribe, theft.**

hush (up), *v.* —*Syn.* cover, conceal, suppress (mention of); see **hide** 1.

husk, *n.* —*Syn.* shuck, covering, outside; see **cover** 1, **shell** 1.

husky, *mod.* **1.** [Hoarse]—*Syn.* throaty, growling, gruff; see **hoarse, loud** 1.
2. [Strong]—*Syn.* muscular, sinewy, strapping; see **strong** 1.

hussar, *n.* —*Syn.* cavalryman, trooper, horse soldier; see **cavalry, soldier.**

hussy, *n.* —*Syn.* whore, slut, harlot; see **prostitute.**

hustle (D), *v.* **1.** [To hurry]—*Syn.* act quickly, rush, push; see **hasten** 1, **hurry** 1, **race** 1, **run** 2, **speed.**
2. [To work zealously]—*Syn.* do a thriving business, be conscientious, make many sales, apply oneself, do a good job, press one's business, give all one's energy to; *all* (D): at it all the time, keep humming, get on the ball; see also **work** 1.

hustler (D), *n.* **1.** [A professional gambler]—*Syn.* gamester, bookmaker, plunger; see **gambler.**
2. [A prostitute]—*Syn.* whore, harlot, call girl; see **prostitute.**
3. [A fast worker]—*Syn.* person with initiative, man of action, fanatic, cohort, busy bee, enthusiast, human dynamo, worker, pusher, workaholic, devotee; *all* (D): bug, nut, freak, live wire, go-getter, Johnny-on-the-spot, speed-up man; see also **zealot.**

hustling, *mod.* —*Syn.* fast-moving, bustling, occupied; see **active** 2, **busy** 1.

hut, *n.* —*Syn.* shanty, lean-to, crib, bungalow, bunkhouse, refuge, lodge, hutch, igloo, dugout, hovel, cottage, cabin, A-frame, hogan, tepee, tupek, cot, log house *or* cabin, cote, wigwam, wickiup, mean dwelling, poor cottage; *all* (D): pigeonhole, dump, rathole; see also **home** 1, **shack, shelter** 1, **shed.**

hutch, *n.* **1.** [A pen]—*Syn.* cage, coop, corral; see **pen** 1.
2. [A cupboard]—*Syn.* sideboard, buffet, cabinet; see **cupboard, furniture.**

hybrid, *mod.* —*Syn.* crossed, alloyed, crossbred, cross, variegated, mongrel, amphibious, half-blooded, half-breed, half-caste, heterogeneous, commingled, impure, mutated, intermingled, interbred, composite, half-and-half; see also **bred.**

hybrid, *n.* —*Syn.* crossbreed, cross, mixture, composite, half-breed, half-blood, half-caste, mongrel, combination, mestizo, quadroon, Eurasian, outcross, Ladino, mustee, octoroon; see also **mixture** 1.

hydrant, *n.* —*Syn.* tap, spigot, fire hydrant, water plug, water outlet, stop valve, discharge pipe, cock, fireplug; see also **faucet.**

hydraulic, *mod.* —*Syn.* water-pumping, using water, pressure-driven, water-powered.

hydraulics, *n.* —*Syn.* laws of the motion of water, science of the movement of liquids, science of liquids in motion, hydrodynamics, hydrostatics, hydrokinetics, hydromechanics, hydrography, hydrology, fluviology, hydrometry, pegology; see also **science** 1.

hydropathy, *n.* —*Syn.* physiotherapy, water treatment, cure; see **therapy, treatment** 2.

hygiene, *n.* —*Syn.* cleanliness, hygienics, hygiology, regimen, preventive medicine, hygienization, healthful living, public health, hygiantics, sanitary measures *or* provisions; see also **health** 1, **sanitation.**

hygienic, *mod.* —*Syn.* healthful, sanitary, clean; see **pure** 2, **sterile** 3.

hymn, *n.* —*Syn.* religious song, song of worship, ode, chant, psalm, paean, carol, evensong, litany, hosanna, motet, canticle, oratorio; see also **song.**

hyperbole, *n.* —*Syn.* overstatement, metaphor, distortion; see **exaggeration.**

hypercritical, *mod.* —*Syn.* fussy, strict, scrupulous; see **critical** 2, **sarcastic, severe** 1.

hypersensitive, *mod.* —*Syn.* high-strung, fastidious, jumpy; see **emotional** 2, **neurotic.**

hypertrophy, *n.* —*Syn.* profusion, excess, exaggeration, overgrowth, overexpansion, enlargement of an organ, excessive growth *or* accumulation, superfluity, amplitude, redundance, surfeit, oversupply, prolixity, overflow, profusion, exuberance, superabundance, affluence, prodigality, surplus, copiousness, overdevelopment; see also **growth** 3.

hypnosis, *n.* —*Syn.* trance, anesthesia, lethargy; see **stupor.**

hypnotic, *mod.* —*Syn.* soporose, sleep-inducing, mesmeric opiate, narcotic, anesthetic, anodyne, lenitive, pertaining to hypnosis, soporific, sleep-producing, soothing, somniferous, somnolent, calmative, somnific, somnifacient, soporiferous, trance-inducing.

hypnotism, *n.* —*Syn.* bewitchment, suggestion, mesmerism, hypnotherapy, deep sleep, spell-casting, self-hypnosis, hypnoanalysis, autohypnosis, hypnotic suggestion, induction of hypnosis, sleep production, fascination, psychokinesis.

hypnotize, *v.* **1.** [To put in a trance]—*Syn.* mesmerize, put *or* lull to sleep, dull the will, hold under a spell, entrance, bring under one's control, induce hypnosis, place in a trance, stupefy, drug, narcotize, soothe, psychologize, anesthetize, subject to suggestion, place under control, make drowsy or sleepy.
2. [To charm]—*Syn.* magnetize, captivate, entrance; see **charm** 1, **fascinate.**

hypnotized, *mod.* —*Syn.* entranced, mesmerized, enchanted; see **charmed.**

hypochondria, *n.* —*Syn.* depression, anxiety, melancholia, imagined ill-health, melancholy, despondency, doldrums, low spirits, dejection, anxiety neurosis; see also **neurosis, pretense** 1.

hypochondriac, *n.* —*Syn.* malingerer, melancholic, masochist, hypochondriast, mope, dispirited person, self-tormenter; see also **imposter, neurotic.**

hypocrisy, *n.* —*Syn.* quackery, casuistry, pharisaism, sanctimoniousness, affectation, pietism, false guise, bad faith, hollowness, display, charlatanry, lip service, bigotry, dissimulation, sham, fraud, pretense of virtue *or* piety, false goodness, lip homage, formalism, false *or* assumed piety, empty ceremony, tartuffism, solemn mockery, tartuffery, lip reverence, sanctimony, false profession, cant; see also **deception** 1, **dishonesty, lie** 1, **pretense** 1. —*Ant.* virtue*, devotion, piety.

hypocrite, *n.* —*Syn.* pretender, fraud, faker, dissembler, deceiver, casuist, charlatan, bigot, quack, tartuffe, backslider, whited sepulcher, sham, actor, cheat, informer, trickster, one given to hypocrisy, sophist, mountebank, adventurer, sharper, confidence man, malingerer, humbug, swindler, informer, knave, rascal, traitor, Judas, Uriah Heep, decoy, wolf in sheep's clothing, Pecksniff, actor, masquerader, dissimulator, attitudinizer, ass in lion's skin; *all* (D): bluenose, four-flusher, two-timer, two-face, God on wheels, Holy Joe, goody-goody, Holy Willie, bunko steerer, crook, spieler, stool pigeon, faker; see also **imposter.**

hypocritical, *mod.* —*Syn.* deceiving, deceptive, deluding, double-dealing, shamming, sanctimonious, dissembling, pious, unctuous, unreliable, mealy-mouthed, canting, insincere, double-faced, smooth-tongued, affected, false, caviling, dissimulating, lying, artificial, two-faced, smooth-spoken, spurious, captious, feigning, deceitful, assuming, unnatural, faithless, plausible, pretentious, mannered, Janus-faced, phoney; see also **dishonest** 1, 2.—*Ant.* upright, honest*, sincere.

hypodermic, *n.* —*Syn.* syringe, injector, shot; see **needle.**

hypothesis, *n.* —*Syn.* supposition, surmise, speculation, scheme, system, conjecture, assumption, presumption, condition, suggestion, thesis, proposal, working hypothesis, preliminary layout, tentative plans, basis for discussion, unproved theory, apriority, working hypothesis, law, inference, antecedent, reason, position, assignment, starting point, basis, derivation, philosopheme, ground, term, scheme, belief, foundation, postulate, axiom, presupposition, premise, data, attribution, interpretation, deduction, conclusion drawn from accepted truths *or* facts, demonstration, tentative law, principle, lemma, explanation, theorem, rationale, philosophy, *all* (D): shot in the dark, guess-so, clotheshorse; see also **guess, opinion** 1, **theory** 1.

hypothetical, *mod.* **1.** [Supposed]—*Syn.* presupposed, suppositious, suppositional, conditional, conjectural, imagined, indeterminate, speculative, indefinite, questionable, unconfirmed, equivocal, doubtful, conjecturable, concocted, suspect, stochastic, stochastical, assumed by hypothesis, possible, uncertain, debatable, imaginary, of the nature of hypothesis, vague, theoretical, pretending, open, provisory, casual, disputable, refutable, postulational, contestable, presumptive, hypothesized, assumptive, contingent, theoretic, postulated, based on incomplete knowledge, imaginary; see also **assumed** 1, **likely** 1.—*Ant.* proved*, demonstrated, confirmed.

2. [Characterized by hypothesis]—*Syn.* postulated, academic, philosophical; see **theoretical.**

hysteria, *n.* —*Syn.* delirium, agitation, feverishness; see **confusion** 2, **excitement, nervousness** 1.

hysterical, *mod.* —*Syn.* convulsed, uncontrolled, raving, delirious, wildly emotional, psychoneurotic, unnerved, neurotic, resembling *or* suggesting hysteria, spasmodic, emotional, rabid, emotionally disordered, distracted, morbidly excited, fuming, distraught, unrestrained, possessed, wrought-up, fanatical, irrepressible, harrowed, convulsive, carried away, frothing, seething, beside oneself, rampant, out of one's wits, turbulent, mad, affected with *or* suffering from hysteria, uncontrollable, agitated, raging, frenzied, uproarious, incensed, confused, tempestuous, maddened, blazing, crazy, impetuous, crazed, furious, violent, boiling, impassioned, panic-stricken, nervous, vehement, overwrought, fiery, passionate; *all* (D): cracked wide open, in a frazzle, in a fit, jittery, amuck, tempest-tossed, wild-eyed, on a laughing *or* crying jag; see also **angry, excited, frantic, troubled** 1.

I

I, *pron.* —*Syn.* myself, *ego* (Latin), self; see **character** 2, **id.**

iambic, *n.* **1.** [Verse]—*Syn.* iambic pentameter, rhyme, versification; see **poetry, verse** 1.
2. [A poetic meter]—*Syn.* metrical foot, iambus, iamb; see **foot** 4, **meter.**

ibidem, (Latin),*mod.* —*Syn. ibid.* (Latin), in the same place, in the work, in the same book, on the same page, in the same chapter.

ICBM, *n.* —*Syn.* Intercontinental Ballistic Missile, guided missile, strategic deterrent; see **rocket, weapon** 1, **missile.**

ice, *n.* —*Syn.* crystal, hail, floe, glacier, icicle, ice cube, cube ice, dry ice, black ice, white ice, chunk ice, iceberg, permafrost; see also **frost** 2.
break the ice—*Syn.* make a start, initiate, commence; see **begin** 1.
cut no ice (D)—*Syn.* have no influence *or* effect, not matter, be unimportant; see **fail** 1.
on ice (D)—*Syn.* in reserve, held, in abeyance; see **saved** 2.
on thin ice (D)—*Syn.* in a dangerous situation, imperiled, insecure; see **endangered.**

ice, *v.* **1.** [To become covered with ice]—*Syn.* frost, coat, mist; see **freeze** 1.
2. [To cover with icing]—*Syn.* frost, coat, trim; see **decorate.**

iceberg, *n.* —*Syn.* mass of land ice, ice mass, ice sheet, ice field, floe, berg, snowberg, icecap; see also **ice.**

icebox, *n.* —*Syn.* cooler, quick *or* fast freezer, fridge (D); see **refrigerator.**

ice cream, *n.* —*Syn.* mousse, spumoni, *glacé* (French), sherbet, tofutti, ice, parfait, frozen custard, frozen dessert; see also **dessert.**

icing, *n.* —*Syn.* frosting, coating, sugar coating, topping, fudge.

icon, *n.* —*Syn.* image, likeness, representation; see **picture** 2.

iconoclast, *n.* **1.** [A pagan]—*Syn.* fanatic, heathen, antichrist; see **pagan, skeptic.**
2. [A nonconformist]—*Syn.* individualist, agnostic, dissenter; see **radical, rebel** 1.

iconoclastic, *mod.* **1.** [Skeptical]—*Syn.* individualistic, nonconforming, dissident; see **radical** 2.
2. [Pagan]—*Syn.* heretical, fanatical, heathenish; see **heathen, impious** 1, **pagan.**

icy, *mod.* **1.** [Covered with ice]—*Syn.* frozen over, iced, glaring, freezing, glacial, frostbound, glassy, sleeted, frosted, frosty, smooth as glass; see also **slippery.**
2. [Cold]—*Syn.* freezing, glacial, polar; see **cold** 1.

id, *n.* —*Syn.* self, source of ego and libido, generative *or* instinctive force, inner nature, *Es* (German), reservoir of the ego, psyche; see also **character** 2.

idea, *n.* **1.** [A concept]—*Syn.* conception, mental impression, notion; see **opinion** 1, **thought** 2.
2. [A conviction]—*Syn.* opinion, doctrine, conception; see **belief** 1, **faith** 2.
3. [A plan]—*Syn.* intention, design, approach; see **plan** 2, **purpose** 1.
4. [Fancy]—*Syn.* whimsy, whim, fantasy; see **fancy** 2, 3, **imagination** 1.
5. [(D) Meaning]—*Syn.* sense, import, purport; see **meaning.**

ideal, *mod.* **1.** [Typical]—*Syn.* prototypical, model, archetypical; see **typical.**
2. [Perfect]—*Syn.* supreme, fitting, exemplary; see **excellent, perfect** 2.
3. [Characterizing the unattainable]—*Syn.* utopian, imaginary, fanciful, unreal, abstract, quixotic, Panglossian, high-flown, impracticable, chimerical, extravagant, theoretical, in the clouds, mercurial, out of reach, dreamlike, fictitious, unearthly; see **impractical, romantic** 1, **visionary** 1.—*Ant.* practical*, practicable, down-to-earth.

ideal, *n.* —*Syn.* paragon, goal, prototype; see **model** 1.

idealism, *n.* **1.** [Devotion to high principles]—*Syn.* perfectionism, aspiration, duty, humanitarianism, meliorism, religion, principle, virtue, conscience, philosophy.
2. [The conception of the universe as idea]—*Syn.* Platonism, metaphysical idealism, epistemological idealism, metaphysics, immateriality, subjective idealism, Hegelianism, Transcendentalism, Fichteism.

idealist, *n.* —*Syn.* visionary, romanticist, romantic, escapist, optimist, enthusiast, utopist, dreamer, theorizer, Platonist; see also **radical.**

idealistic, *mod.* —*Syn.* lofty, noble, exalted; see **impractical, visionary** 1.

idealization, *n.* —*Syn.* glorification, ennoblement, magnification; see **honor** 1.

idealize, *v.* —*Syn.* romanticize, glorify, rhapsodize, build castles in the air (D); see also **dream** 2, **invent** 1, 2.

ideals, *n.* —*Syn.* standards, principles, goals; see **ethics, morals.**

idea man, *n.* —*Syn.* thinker, consultant, originator; see **administration** 2, **specialist.**

idem (Latin), *mod.* —*Syn.* likewise, ditto, the same, as before, self-same, the same as given above; see also **alike** 3.

identical, *mod.* —*Syn.* like, twin, indistinguishable; see **alike** 1.

identification, *n.* **1.** [The act of identifying]—*Syn.* classifying, naming, cataloging; see **classification, description** 1.
2. [Means of identifying]—*Syn.* credentials, letter of introduction, testimony, letter of credit, badge, papers, ID (D); see also **passport.**

identify, *v.* —*Syn.* classify, catalog, analyze; see **describe, name** 1, 2.

identity, *n.* **1.** [Distinctive character]—*Syn.* individuality, uniqueness, integrity; see **character** 2, **personality** 1.
2. [The state of fulfilling a description]—*Syn.* identification, antecedents, true circumstances, parentage, status, citizenship, nationality, connections; see also **character** 2, **name** 1.

ideology, *n.* —*Syn.* belief(s), ideas, philosophy; see **culture** 2.

idiocy, *n.* **1.** [Folly]—*Syn.* foolishness, madness, insipidity; see **stupidity** 1.
2. [Mental derangement]—*Syn.* imbecility, cretinism, lunacy; see **insanity** 1.

idiom, *n.* —*Syn.* expression, idiosyncrasy of speech, argot; see **dialect, jargon** 1, 2, **language** 1, **phrase.**

idiomatic, *mod.* —*Syn.* vernacular, dialectal, peculiar; see **informal, local** 1.

idiosyncrasy, *n.* —*Syn.* eccentricity, characteristic, peculiarity; see **quirk.**

idiosyncratic, *mod.* —*Syn.* peculiar, distinctive, personal; see **characteristic, typical.**

idiot, *n.* —*Syn.* simpleton, nincompoop, booby; see **fool** 1.

idiotic, *mod.* **1.** [Having the mind of an idiot] —*Syn.* thick-witted, dull, moronic; see **stupid** 1.
2. [(D) Characterized by bad judgment or taste] —*Syn.* fatuous, asinine, dumb (D); see **silly, stupid** 1.

idle, *mod.* **1.** [Unused or inactive]—*Syn.* unoccupied, workless, unemployed, jobless, laid-off, uncultivated, untilled, fallow, vacant, deserted, not in use *or* operation, waste, barren, void, empty, abandoned, still, quiet, motionless, inert, dead, untouched; *all* (D): rusty, gathering dust, dusty, out of trim, out of action, out of a job, out of collar, on the bum, resting; see also **unemployed, unused** 1. —*Ant.* active*, busy, engaged.
2. [Useless]—*Syn.* pointless, rambling, vain; see **futile** 1, **irrelevant.**
3. [Lazy]—*Syn.* indolent, shiftless, slothful; see **lazy** 1.

idle, *v.* —*Syn.* slack, shirk, slow down; see **loaf** 1.

idleness, *n.* **1.** [State of being inactive]—*Syn.* loitering, time-killing, dawdling, inertia, inactivity, voluntary inertia, indolence, sluggishness, unemployment, joblessness, torpor, otiosity, torpidity, dormancy, lethargy, stupor, pottering, truancy, droning, loafing, vegetation, trifling, shilly-shallying.—*Ant.* industry, action*, occupation.
2. [Disinclination to activity]—*Syn.* slowness, indolence, slothfulness; see **laziness.**

idler, *n.* —*Syn.* drone, lounger, slacker; see **loafer.**

idling, *mod.* —*Syn.* lounging (around), drifting, lolling; see **loafing** 2, **resting** 1.

idol, *n.* **1.** [A deified image]—*Syn.* icon, graven image, effigy, god, Buddha, false god, figurine, fetish, totem, joss, golden calf, avatar, simulacrum, pagan deity, eidolon, mumbo-jumbo (D); see also **image** 2, **statue.**
2. [A venerated object or person]—*Syn.* god, goddess, desire, true-love, center of one's affections, inamorata.

idolater, *n.* —*Syn.* fetishist, zealot, heathen; see **pagan.**

idolatrous, *mod.* —*Syn.* fetishistic, ardent, idol-worshiping; see **pagan.**

idolatry, *n.* **1.** [The worship of idols]—*Syn.* idolism, adoration, burnt offering; see **worship** 1.
2. [Extreme devotion]—*Syn.* infatuation, fervor, transport; see **enthusiasm** 1.

idolize, *v.* —*Syn.* glorify, adore, canonize; see **worship** 2.

I don't know, *interj.* —*Syn.* (It) beats me! Who knows? The Lord knows! How should I know? You've got me! Ask me another! *Quien sabe?* (Spanish).

idyllic, *mod.* —*Syn.* pastoral, bucolic, pleasing; see **comfortable** 2, **pleasant** 2, **simple** 1.

if, *conj.* —*Syn.* provided that, with the condition that, supposing that, conceding that, on the assumption that, granted that, assuming (that), on the occasion that, whenever, wherever.
as if—*Syn.* as though, as the situation would be, in a way like; see **as if** 1.

iffy, *mod.* —*Syn.* unsettled, doubtful, uncertain; see **uncertain** 2.

igneous, *mod.* —*Syn.* formed by heat, volcanic, fiery; see **bright** 1, **molten.**

ignite, *v.* —*Syn.* enkindle, light, strike a light, start up, burst into flames, touch off, touch a match to, set off; see also **burn** 1, 2.

ignition, *n.* **1.** [Igniting]—*Syn.* combustion, bursting into flame, kindling; see **fire** 1.
2. [A system for igniting]—*Syn.* timing system, timer, distributor, sparking system, firing system, wiring system, spark (D).
Types of ignition include the following—impulse ignition, electronic ignition, make-and-break ignition, magneto ignition, spark ignition, sparkplug ignition; see also **engine, machine** 1, **motor.**

ignoble, *mod.* **1.** [Shameful]—*Syn.* disgraceful, degenerate, dishonorable; see **corrupt** 3, **lewd** 1, **shameful** 1, 2, **wicked** 1, **wrong** 1.
2. [Lowly]—*Syn.* mean, base, abject; see **humble** 2, **vulgar** 1.

ignominious, *mod.* **1.** [Offensive]—*Syn.* vicious, vile, nasty; see **mean** 3, **offensive** 2, **rotten** 3.
2. [Humiliating]—*Syn.* shocking, outrageous, mortifying; see **mean** 3, **opprobrious** 1, **shameful** 1, 2.

ignominy, *n.* **1.** [Offensive behavior]—*Syn.* lowness, baseness, sordidness; see **evil** 1, **meanness** 1, **vice** 2.
2. [Shame]—*Syn.* mortification, dishonor, humiliation; see **disgrace** 2.

ignoramus, *n.* —*Syn.* simpleton, imbecile, idiot; see **fool** 1, **moron.**

ignorance, *n.* **1.** [Lack of specific knowledge] —*Syn.* unawareness, unconsciousness, incomprehension, bewilderment, incapacity, inexperience, simplicity, disregard, insensitivity, sciolism, nescience, shallowness, fog, vagueness, half-knowledge, a little learning, no more than a tyro's *or* a

beginner's *or* an apprentice's background *or* preparation; see also **sense** 2, **confusion** 2, **deception** 1, **nonsense** 2.—*Ant.* ability*, learning, erudition.
2. [Lack of general knowledge]—*Syn.* illiteracy, unenlightenment, mental incapacity, denseness, dumbness, empty-headedness, crudeness, vulgarity, obtuseness, unfamiliarity, unintelligence, rawness, denseness, benightedness, superstition, blindness, simplicity, stolidity, unscholarliness; lack of learning *or* education *or* erudition *or* background, etc.; see also **sense** 1, **stupidity** 1.—*Ant.* knowledge*, acquaintance, understanding.

ignorant, *mod.* **1.** [Unaware]—*Syn.* unconscious (of), uninformed (about), unknowing, uninitiated, inexperienced, unwitting, unmindful, disregarding, misinformed, unsuspecting, unaware (of), insensible (to), unmindful *or* unconscious (of), mindless, witless, destitute of *or* without knowledge, unconversant (with), unintelligent, obtuse, thick, dense, moronic, imbecilic, shallow-brained, cretinous, unbookish, inept at *or* not adapted to *or* not gifted in learning, unscholarly, unscientific, half-learned; *all* (D): bird-brained, lowbrow, sappy, green; see also **sense** 2, **dull** 3, **oblivious, shallow** 2, **stupid** 1.—*Ant.* intelligent*, alert, aware.
2. [Untrained]—*Syn.* illiterate, uneducated, unlettered, untaught, uninstructed, uncultivated, unenlightened, untutored, unread, unschooled, nescient, benighted, superstitious, shallow, superficial, gross, coarse, vulgar, crude, callow, green, ingenuous, inerudite, knowing nothing, destitute of *or* without knowledge, misinformed, misguided, just beginning, undergoing apprenticeship, apprenticed, unbriefed; see also **inexperienced, naïve, unaware.**—*Ant.* learned*, cognizant, tutored.

ignore, *v.* —*Syn.* disregard, overlook, pass over; see **discard, neglect** 2, **omit** 1.

ill, *mod.* **1.** [Bad]—*Syn.* harmful, evil, noxious; see **wicked** 1.
2. [Sick]—*Syn.* unwell, unhealthy, ailing; see **sick.**
go ill with—*Syn.* be unfortunate for, be unfavorable to, hurt; see **disturb** 2.
take ill—*Syn.* **1.** become sick, become unwell, fall ill; see **sicken** 1, **weaken** 1. **2.** be annoyed at, be offended by, take offense; see **mistake.**

ill, *n.* —*Syn.* depravity, misfortune, mischief; see **evil** 2, **insult, wrong** 1, 2.

ill-advised, *mod.* —*Syn.* foolish, reckless, inappropriate; see **confused** 2, **rash, wrong** 3.

ill at ease, *mod.* —*Syn.* anxious, uneasy, uncomfortable; see **doubtful** 2, **restless** 1, **suspicious** 1, 2.

illative, *mod.* —*Syn.* deductive, consequential, inferential; see **implied, intended, suggested.**

ill-bred, *mod.* —*Syn.* uncouth, vulgar, uncivil; see **rude** 1, 2.

illegal, *mod.* —*Syn.* illicit, unlawful, contraband, unwarranted, unwarrantable, banned, unconstitutional, outside the law, extralegal, outlawed, not legal, unauthorized, unlicensed, lawless, actionable, *verboten* (German), *sub rosa* (Latin), illegitimate, prohibited, taboo, forbidden, interdicted, proscribed, misbegotten, irregular, criminal, against the law, after-hours, not approved, uncertified, unlicensed, smuggled; *both* (D): bootlegged, hot; see also **refused, stolen.**—*Ant.* lawful, legal*, authorized.

illegible, *mod.* —*Syn.* faint, unintelligible, difficult to read; see also **confused** 2, **obscure** 1.

illegibly, *mod.* —*Syn.* faintly, unintelligibly, indistinctly; see **obscurely.**

illegitimacy, *n.* —*Syn.* illegitimateness, bastardy, bastardism, illegitimation.

illegitimate, *mod.* **1.** [Unlawful]—*Syn.* contraband, wrong, illicit; see **illegal, wicked** 1, 2.
2. [Misbegotten]—*Syn.* born out of wedlock, natural, unlawfully begotten, hedgeborn, baseborn, by-blown, unfathered; see also **bastard** 1.
3. [Illogical]—*Syn.* twisted, unsound, incorrect; see **illogical, wrong** 2.

ill-fated, *mod.* —*Syn.* ill-starred, catastrophic, disastrous; see **destroyed, doomed, ruined** 1.

ill-favored, *mod.* —*Syn.* horrible, unattractive, unpleasant; see **disturbing, offensive** 2, **ugly** 1.

ill-humor, *n.* —*Syn.* moodiness, testiness, irritability; see **anger, annoyance** 1, **gloom** 2.

ill-humored, *mod.* —*Syn.* touchy, crabby, cross; see **bothered, irritable, sullen.**

illiberal, *mod.* **1.** [Miserly]—*Syn.* selfish, niggardly, miserly; see **greedy** 1, 2, **stingy.**
2. [Prejudiced]—*Syn.* partial, reactionary, bigoted; see **prejudiced, selfish** 1.

illicit, *mod.* —*Syn.* unlawful, prohibited, unauthorized; see **illegal, wicked** 1, **wrong** 1.

illiteracy, *n.* —*Syn.* lack of education, stupidity, idiocy; see **ignorance** 2.

illiterate, *mod.* —*Syn.* uneducated, unenlightened, dumb (D); see **ignorant** 2.

ill-mannered, *mod.* —*Syn.* impolite, uncouth, rough; see **rude** 2.

ill-natured, *mod.* —*Syn.* touchy, cross, crabby; see **irritable, sullen.**

illness, *n.* **1.** [The state of being sick]—*Syn.* sickness, failing health, seizure, ailing, poor health, infirmity, queasiness, vomiting, indisposition, disorder, relapse, attack, fit, convalescence, complaint, delicate health, collapse, breakdown, confinement, interesting condition, prostration, disability, disturbance, ill health; see also **weakness** 1.
2. [A particular disease]—*Syn.* sickness, ailment, malady; see **disease** 1, 3, **insanity** 1.

illogical, *mod.* —*Syn.* irrational, unreasonable, absurd, specious, fallacious, sophistic, sophistical, inconsequent, unsubstantial, incorrect, inconsistent, false, casuistic, Jesuitical, unscientific, paralogistic, paralogical, contradictory, untenable, unsound, preposterous, invalid, self-contradictory, Kafkaesque, unproved, groundless, implausible, hollow, irrelevant, inconclusive, fatuous, incongruous, prejudiced, biased, unconnected, without foundation, not following, out of bounds, without basis; *all* (D): without rhyme or reason, nutty, screwy, not ringing true, wacky, far out, dopey, having the cart before the horse; see also **fallible, wrong** 2.—*Ant.* sound, reasonable, logical*.

ill-proportioned, *mod.* —*Syn.* distorted, grotesque, disfigured; see **deformed.**

ill-smelling, *mod.* —*Syn.* rancid, putrefied, stale; see **decaying, rotten** 1, 3.

ill-sounding, *mod.* —*Syn.* cacophonous, jangling, dissonant; see **harsh** 1, **loud** 1, 2, **raucous** 1, **shrill.**

ill-starred, *mod.* —*Syn.* luckless, unhappy, futile; see **unfortunate** 2.

ill-suited, *mod.* —*Syn.* inappropriate, unsuitable, mismatched; see **unsuitable.**

ill temper, *n.* —*Syn.* petulance, animosity, indignation; see **anger, hatred** 2, **opposition** 2, **resentment** 1.

ill-tempered, *mod.* —*Syn.* cross, touchy, querulous; see **irritable, sullen.**

ill-timed, *mod.* —*Syn.* inopportune, awkward, inappropriate; see **unfavorable** 2, **untimely.**

ill-treat, *v.* —*Syn.* persecute, victimize, annoy; see **abuse** 1, **bother** 2.

illuminate, *v.* **1.** [To make light(er)]—*Syn.* lighten, irradiate, illume; see **brighten** 1, **light** 1.
2. [To explain]—*Syn.* interpret, elucidate, clarify; see **explain.**
3. [To decorate]—*Syn.* illustrate, ornament, trim; see **decorate.**

illuminated, *mod.* —*Syn.* lighted (up), having adequate illumination, light enough; see **bright** 1.

illumination, *n.* **1.** [A light]—*Syn.* gleam, flame, brilliance, lighting; see also **flash** 1, **light** 1, 3.
2. [Instruction]—*Syn.* teaching, education, information; see **knowledge** 1.
3. [Decoration]—*Syn.* flourish, ornament, embellishment; see **decoration** 2.

illumine, *v.* **1.** [To light up]—*Syn.* light up, irradiate, brighten; see **light** 1.
2. [To explain]—*Syn.* interpret, clarify, elucidate; see **explain.**

illusion, *n.* **1.** [Unreal appearance]—*Syn.* fancy, hallucination, mirage, apparition, ghost, chimera, delusion, deception, figment of the imagination, phantasm, image, trick of vision, myth, make-believe, *déjà vu* (French), paramnesia, castles in Spain (D); see also **dream** 1, **fantasy** 2, **vision** 3, 4.
2. [Misconception]—*Syn.* delusion, confusion, false impression; see **mistake** 2, **misunderstanding** 1.

illusory, *mod.* —*Syn.* deceptive, ideal, whimsical; see **fanciful** 1, **imaginary.**

illustrate, *v.* **1.** [To make clear by illustration] —*Syn.* picture, exemplify, represent, delineate, portray, depict, allegorize, imitate; see also **draw** 2, **paint** 1.
2. [To adorn with illustrations]—*Syn.* embellish, adorn, illuminate; see **decorate.**

illustrated, *mod.* —*Syn.* pictorial, pictured, adorned, engraved, embellished, decorated, delineated, portrayed, depicted, illuminated, wrought, garlanded, embossed, exemplified, in rotogravure; see also **graphic** 1.

illustration, *n.* **1.** [An example]—*Syn.* instance, model, sample; see **example** 1.
2. [An illustrative picture]—*Syn.* engraving, tailpiece, frontispiece, cartoon, vignette, etching, line drawing, halftone, inset picture, newsphoto; see also **picture** 3.

illustrative, *mod.* —*Syn.* exemplifying, corroborative, clarifying, specifying, explicatory, interpretive, explicative, illuminative, symbolic, emblematic, representative, imitative, indicative, pictorial, imagistic, comparative, metaphoric, figurative, allegorical, expository, revealing; see also **descriptive, explanatory, graphic** 1, 2.

illustrator, *n.* —*Syn.* commercial artist, worker of the art department, painter; see **artist** 1.

illustrious, *mod.* —*Syn.* celebrated, renowned, eminent; see **distinguished** 2, **famous, glorious** 1, **important** 2.

ill will, *n.* —*Syn.* malevolence, dislike, hostility; see **blame** 1, **hate, hatred** 1, 2, **objection** 1.

image, *n.* **1.** [Mental impression]—*Syn.* concept, conception, perception; see **thought** 2.
2. [Representation]—*Syn.* idol, carved figure, effigy, icon, form, drawing, model, illustration, portrait, photograph, reproduction, reflection, copy, likeness, facsimile, counterpart, replica; *all* (D): spittin' image, dead ringer, chip off the old block; see also **painting** 1, **picture** 3, **representation, statue.**

imagery, *n.* —*Syn.* illustration, metaphor, representation; see **comparison** 2.

imaginable, *mod.* —*Syn.* conceivable, comprehensible, apprehensible, credible, thinkable, sensible, possible, plausible, believable, conjecturable, reasonable, calculable; see also **convincing, likely** 1. —*Ant.* unimaginable, unbelievable*, inconceivable.

imaginary, *mod.* —*Syn.* fancied, illusory, visionary, shadowy, chimerical, dreamy, dreamlike, hypothetical, theoretical, delusive, deceptive, imagined, hallucinatory, ideal, notional, whimsical, fabulous, unsubstantial, nonexistent, apocryphal, fantastic, mythological, legendary, fictitious, imaginative; see also **fanciful** 1, **unreal.**—*Ant.* real*, factual, existing.

imagination, *n.* **1.** [Power to visualize]—*Syn.* intelligence, thoughtfulness, inventiveness, creativity, ingenuity, artistry, impressionableness, perceptibility, acuteness, mental agility, wittiness, wit, sensitivity, fancy, mental receptivity, suggestibility, visualization, realization, cognition, awareness, dramatization, pictorialization, insight, mental adaptability; see also **mind** 1.
2. [A product of the power to visualize]—*Syn.* creation, invention, fabrication; see **thought** 2.

imaginative, *mod.* —*Syn.* creative, inventive, originative; see **artistic** 3, **original** 2.

imagine, *v.* **1.** [To visualize mentally]—*Syn.* conceive, picture, conjure up, envisage, envision, see in one's mind, invent, fabricate, formulate, devise, think of, make up, conceptualize, dream, nurture, harbor, perceive, fancy, dramatize, pictorialize, receive the impression of, figure to oneself, create, build castles in the air (D); see also **visualize.**
2. [(D) To suppose]—*Syn.* think, guess, presume; see **assume** 1.

imagined, *mod.* —*Syn.* not real, insubstantial, thought up; see **false** 1, 2, 3, **imaginary.**

imbalance, *n.* —*Syn.* lack of balance, unevenness, inequality, shortcoming, disproportion; see also **irregularity** 1.

imbecile, *n.* —*Syn.* dolt, bungler, idiot; see **fool** 1.

imbecilic, *mod.* —*Syn.* imbecile, deranged, feeble-minded; see **insane** 1, **stupid** 1.

imbecility, *n.* **1.** [Stupid action]—*Syn.* folly, foolishness, tactlessness; see **stupidity** 2.

2. [Mental derangement]—*Syn.* moronity, feeble-mindedness, cretinism; see **insanity** 1.

imbibe, *v.* **1.** [To drink]—*Syn.* ingest, gorge, guzzle; see **drink** 1, **swallow.**

2. [To absorb]—*Syn.* take in, suck, soak up; see **absorb** 1.

imbue, *v.* —*Syn.* tutor, inculcate, indoctrinate; see **teach** 1.

imitate, *v.* **1.** [To follow the example of]—*Syn.* emulate, follow suit, do likewise; see **follow** 2.

2. [To mimic]—*Syn.* impersonate, mirror, copy, mime, ape, simulate, personate, duplicate, assume, act like, repeat, echo, do like, (re-)echo, reflect, pretend, play a part; *both* (D): take off, put on; see also **parody.**

3. [To copy]—*Syn.* duplicate, counterfeit, falsify; see **copy** 2, **reproduce** 1.

4. [To resemble]—*Syn.* look *or* be like, simulate, parallel; see **resemble.**

imitated, *mod.* —*Syn.* copied, duplicated, mimicked, mocked, aped, counterfeited, caricatured, parodied, burlesqued, made similar *or* to resemble, done *or* made in facsimile; see also **printed, reproduced.**

imitating, *mod.* —*Syn.* copying, following, reflecting, emulating, echoing, matching, paralleling, in imitation of.

imitation, *mod.* —*Syn.* copied, feigned, bogus; see **false** 3.

imitation, *n.* **1.** [The act of imitating]—*Syn.* simulation, counterfeiting, copying, duplication, patterning (after), picturing, representing, mimicry, aping, impersonation, impression, paraphrasing, parroting, echoing, matching, mirroring, paralleling; see also **reproduction** 1.

2. [An object made by imitating]—*Syn.* counterfeit, mime, simulacrum, sham, fake, picture, replica, echo, reflection, match, parallel, opposite number, animation, resemblance, transcription, image, mockery, take-off, substitution, forgery, artist's copy, ersatz; see also **copy, duplicate** 1, **reproduction** 2.—*Ant.* original, novelty*, pattern.

imitative, *mod.* **1.** [Copying]—*Syn.* mimicking, copying, reflecting; see **mimetic.**

2. [Counterfeit]—*Syn.* forged, sham, deceptive; see **false** 2, 3.

imitator, *n.* —*Syn.* copyist, follower, copier, impersonator, mime, mimic, pretender, counterfeiter, forger.

immaculate, *mod.* **1.** [Clean]—*Syn.* unsullied, spotless, stainless; see **bright** 1, **clean** 1.

2. [Morally pure]—*Syn.* undefiled, sinless, unsullied; see **innocent** 4, **religious** 2.

immanent, *mod.* —*Syn.* native, intrinsic, inborn; see **inherent.**

immaterial, *mod.* **1.** [Inconsequential]—*Syn.* insignificant meaningless, unimportant; see **irrelevant, trivial, unnecessary.**

2. [Insubstantial]—*Syn.* incorporeal, spiritual, bodiless, disembodied, without substance, intangible, ethereal, aerial, shadowy, ghostly, metaphysical, impalpable, incorporate.—*Ant.* real, physical*, substantial.

immature, *mod.* —*Syn.* youthful, sophomoric, half-grown; see **naive.**

immaturity, *n.* **1.** [Childhood]—*Syn.* ignorance, adolescence, infancy; see **childhood, youth** 1.

2. [Inexperience]—*Syn.* imperfection, incompleteness, childlike behavior; see also **instability.**

immeasurable, *mod.* —*Syn.* limitless, vast, extensive; see **endless** 1, **large** 1.

immediate, *mod.* **1.** [Without delay]—*Syn.* at once, instant, on the instant, live, now, on the moment, at this moment, at the present time, next, prompt; see also **following.**—*Ant.* someday*, later, any time.

2. [First]—*Syn.* pressing, critical, paramount; see **important** 1, **urgent** 1.

immediately, *mod.* —*Syn.* at once, without delay, instantly, directly, right away, instanter, at the first opportunity, forthwith, straightway, in a trice, in that instant, at short notice, now, this instant, speedily, quickly, promptly, on the spot *or* dot, rapidly, summarily, instantaneously, shortly; *all* (D): in a couple of humps, before you could say Jack Robinson, at a blow, on the double, now or never, in a jiffy, straight off; see also **urgently** 1.—*Ant.* in the future, later*, in a while.

immemorial, *mod.* —*Syn.* olden, primeval, ancient; see **old** 3, **traditional** 2.

immense, *mod.* **1.** [Huge]—*Syn.* gigantic, tremendous, enormous; see **extensive** 1, **large** 1.

2. [Boundless]—*Syn.* eternal, limitless, endless; see **infinite** 1.

immensity, *n.* —*Syn.* infinity, vastness, greatness, massiveness, hugeness, enormousness, immeasurableness, bulkiness, sizableness, immenseness, bigness, gigantism, tremendousness, stupendousness, monstrousness; see also **extent.**—*Ant.* bit*, tininess, minuteness.

immerse, *v.* **1.** [To put under water]—*Syn.* submerge, dip, douse, plunge, bury, duck, cover with water, drown, bathe, steep, soak, drench, dunk, souse; *both* (D): slop, put in the drink; see also **baptize** 1, **cover** 9, **sink** 1.—*Ant.* raise up, uncover*, draw out.

2. [Engross]—*Syn.* interest, engage, involve; see **fascinate.**

immersed, *mod.* —*Syn.* drowned, plunged, bathed; see **dipped, soaked, wet** 1.

immersible, *mod.* —*Syn.* sinkable, water soluble, aqueous; see **waterproof.**

immigrant, *n.* —*Syn.* newcomer, naturalized citizen, adoptive citizen; see **alien, emigrant.**

immigrate, *v.* —*Syn.* migrate, colonize, emigrate; see **leave** 1.

immigration, *n.* —*Syn.* colonization, settlement, migration, change of allegiance; see also **entrance** 1. —*Ant.* emigration*, leave-taking, exile.

imminent, *mod.* —*Syn.* approaching, impending, in store, at hand, brewing, about to happen, near, immediate, next, following, expectant, on its way, looming, to come, in view, in the offing, forthcoming, expected; *all* (D): in the wind, on the horizon, on the verge, in the cards; see also **coming** 1, **destined** 1.—*Ant.* remote, possible*, future.

immobile, *mod.* **1.** [Stable]—*Syn.* fixed, stationary, still; see **firm** 1.

2. [Inexpressive]—*Syn.* vacant, imperturbable, inscrutable; see **motionless** 1.

immobility, *n.* **1.** [Stability]—*Syn.* stabilization, constancy, quietus; see **stability** 1.
2. [Inflexibility]—*Syn.* rigidity, stolidity, stiffness; see **stability** 2.
immoderate, *mod.* —*Syn.* unbalanced, extravagant, excessive; see **extreme** 2.
immodest, *mod.* —*Syn.* brazen, shameless, bold; see **egotistic** 1, **rude** 2.
immodesty, *n.* —*Syn.* boldness, obscenity, indecency; see **rudeness.**
immoral, *mod.* —*Syn.* sinful, corrupt, shameless; see **noncompliant, wicked** 1.
immorality, *n.* —*Syn.* vice, depravity, dissoluteness; see **evil** 1, **nonconformity.**
immorally, *mod.* —*Syn.* sinfully, wickedly, unrighteously; see **wrongly** 1.
immortal, *mod.* **1.** [Deathless]—*Syn.* undying, permanent, phoenixlike, imperishable, endless, timeless, everlasting, sempiternal, interminable, death-defying, unfading, evergreen, amaranthine, never-ending, perennial, constant, ceaseless, never-ceasing, undecaying, indestructible, indissoluble, ever living, never-dying, enduring, godlike; see also **eternal** 2, **perpetual** 1.—*Ant.* mortal*, perishable, corrupt.
2. [Illustrious]—*Syn.* celebrated, eminent, glorious; see **famous.**
immortality, *n.* **1.** [Eternal life]—*Syn.* deathlessness, permanence, endlessness, timelessness, everlastingness, divinity, unceasingness, indestructibility, athanasy, unending life, continuity, perpetuation, sempiternity, imperishability, endless life, everness, unlimited existence, eternal continuance, perpetuity, everlasting life; see also **eternity** 1.—*Ant.* mortality, death*, decease.
2. [Life after death]—*Syn.* resurrection, eternal life, beatitude, afterlife, heaven, eternal bliss, redemption; see also **immortality** 2, **salvation** 2.
3. [Enduring fame]—*Syn.* glory, eminence, renown; see **fame** 1.
immortalize, *v.* —*Syn.* ennoble, canonize, deify; see **praise** 1.
immortalized, *mod.* —*Syn.* made famous, canonized deathless; see **famous.**
immovable, *mod.* —*Syn.* solid, stable, fixed; see **firm** 1.
immune, *mod.* —*Syn.* free, unaffected by, resistant, invulnerable, hardened to, unsusceptible, privileged, irresponsible, not liable, excused, unliable, unanswerable, licensed, favored, let off (D); see also **exempt, safe** 1.
immunity, *n.* **1.** [Exemption]—*Syn.* favor, privilege, license; see **freedom** 2.
2. [Freedom from disease]—*Syn.* resistance, immunization, protection, active immunity, passive immunity; see also **safety** 1.
immutable, *mod.* —*Syn.* stable, changeless, perpetual; see **permanent** 2.
imp, *n.* —*Syn.* demon, fiend, pixie; see **devil** 1.
impact, *n.* —*Syn.* shock, impression, contact; see **collision** 1.
impair, *v.* **1.** [To damage]—*Syn.* spoil, injure, hurt; see **break** 2, **damage** 1, **destroy** 1.
2. [Weaken]—*Syn.* diminish, lose strength, lessen; see **weaken** 1.
impaired, *mod.* —*Syn.* injured, spoiled, harmed; see **damaged** 2, **hurt.**
impalatable, *mod.* —*Syn.* unsavory, nauseous, sickening, unfit to be eaten, not pleasant tasting, inedible, uneatable, loathsome; see also **offensive** 2.
impale, *v.* —*Syn.* spear, spike, pierce; see **kill** 1, **stab.**
impalpable, *mod.* —*Syn.* imperceptible, intangible, indistinct; see **vague** 2.
impart, *v.* **1.** [To give]—*Syn.* bestow, grant, present; see **allow** 1, **give** 1.
2. [To inform]—*Syn.* tell, announce, divulge; see **admit** 2, **expose** 1, **reveal** 1.
impartial, *mod.* —*Syn.* unbiased, unprejudiced, disinterested; see **equal, fair** 1.
impartiality, *n.* —*Syn.* probity, candor, justice; see **equality, fairness.**
impassable, *mod.* —*Syn.* closed, blockaded, not fit for travel, obstructed, pathless, trackless, untrodden, impenetrable, forbidden, insurmountable; see also **difficult** 1.—*Ant.* open*, passable, traveled.
impasse, *n.* **1.** [Stalemate]—*Syn.* deadlock, standstill, cessation; see **pause** 2, **rest** 2.
2. [A cul-de-sac]—*Syn.* dead end, obstacle, blind alley; see **ambush, cul-de-sac, trap** 1.
impassible, *mod.* **1.** [Unfeeling]—*Syn.* unconcerned, passionless, insensible; see **indifferent** 1, **listless** 1, **nonchalant** 1.
2. [Invulnerable]—*Syn.* strong, invincible, secure; see **protected, safe** 1, **strong** 2.
impassioned, *mod.* —*Syn.* moving, fervid, ardent; see **intense, passionate** 2, **powerful** 1.
impassive, *mod.* —*Syn.* sedate, insensitive, emotionless; see **callous, indifferent** 1.
impatience, *n.* **1.** [Irritability]—*Syn.* fretfulness, hastiness, quick temper; see **anger, annoyance** 1.
2. [Restlessness]—*Syn.* agitation, disquietude, anxiety; see **care** 2, **excitement, nervousness** 2.
impatient, *mod.* **1.** [Irritable]—*Syn.* excitable, quick-tempered, fretful; see **bothered, irritable, troubled** 1.
2. [Restless]—*Syn.* anxious, eager, feverish; see **excitable, restless** 1.
impeach, *v.* —*Syn.* criticize, charge, arraign, impugn, denounce, indict, discredit, reprehend, reprimand, accuse of misconduct in office, reprobate, arraign for malfeasance, indict for maladministration, call to account, blame, incriminate, try, bring charges against, question, hold at fault; see also **accuse, censure.**—*Ant.* free*, acquit, absolve.
impeccable, *mod.* —*Syn.* faultless, pure, flawless; see **excellent, perfect** 2.
impecunious, *mod.* —*Syn.* insolvent, destitute, broke (D); see **poor** 1.
impede, *v.* —*Syn.* thwart, block, deter; see **bar** 1, 2, **hinder, oppose** 1.
impediment, *n.* **1.** [An obstruction]—*Syn.* hindrance, obstacle, block, bar, clog, encumbrance, difficulty, check, retardment, retardation, stoppage, restriction, stricture, restraint, blockage, prohibition, inhibition, hurdle, wall, barricade, trammel, shackle, handicap, disadvantage, deterrent, detriment, delay, traffic hazard, manacle, chain, tie, hitch, setback, drag, burden, load, dead weight, drawback, stumbling block, fault, flaw, rub; *all* (D): road block, holdup, catch-22, catch, cramp, bot-

tleneck, millstone around one's neck, red tape, monkey wrench in the machinery, crimp, catch, joker; see also **barrier.**—*Ant.* help*, aid, assistance.
2. [An obstruction in speech]—*Syn.* speech impediment *or* difficulty *or* block *or* trouble, stutter, stuttering, stammer, stammering, lisp, lisping, lallation, lambdacism, halting, hairlip, cleft palate.

impedimenta, *n.* —*Syn.* paraphernalia, gear, junk (D); see **equipment.**

impeding, *mod.* —*Syn.* encumbering, holding, hampering; see **blocking, stopping.**

impel, *v.* **1.** [To urge]—*Syn.* induce, instigate, animate; see **drive** 1, **excite** 1, **urge** 2.
2. [To press]—*Syn.* move, push, actuate, prod, start, set in motion, propel, activate, thrust forward, drive, jog, shove, poke, boost, boom, give someone a start; *both* (D): lend one's weight to, elbow one's way; see also **force** 1.

impend, *v.* **1.** [To threaten]—*Syn.* menace, approach, hover; see **threaten** 2.
2. [To project]—*Syn.* overhang, protrude, be suspended; see **hang** 2, **project** 1.

impending, *mod.* —*Syn.* in the offing, threatening, menacing; see **imminent, ominous.**

impenetrable, *mod.* **1.** [Dense]—*Syn.* impervious, hard, compact; see **firm** 2, **thick** 3.
2. [Incomprehensible]—*Syn.* unintelligible, inscrutable, unfathomable; see **obscure** 1.

impenitent, *mod.* —*Syn.* hard, insensitive, obdurate; see **obstinate** 1.

imperative, *mod.* **1.** [Necessary]—*Syn.* inescapable, immediate, crucial; see **important** 1, **necessary** 1, **urgent** 1.
2. [Authoritative]—*Syn.* masterful, commanding, dominant; see **aggressive** 2, **autocratic, powerful** 1.

imperceptible, *mod.* —*Syn.* vague, intangible, indistinct; see **obscure** 1.

imperceptibly, *mod.* —*Syn.* slowly, (just) barely, scarcely; see **gradually, hardly.**

imperfect, *mod.* —*Syn.* flawed, incomplete, deficient; see **damaged** 2, **faulty.**

imperfection, *n.* —*Syn.* fault, flaw, stain; see **blemish.**

imperial, *mod.* **1.** [Concerning an emperor or empress]—*Syn.* sovereign, supreme, hegemonic, imperatorial, august; see also **royal** 1.
2. [Suited to the dignity of an emperor]—*Syn.* regal, princely, magnificent; see **royal** 2.

imperialism, *n.* —*Syn.* empire, hegemony, sway, colonialism, international domination, rule of subject peoples, power politics, white man's burden (D); see also **administration** 1, **dominion** 1, **power** 2.

imperil, *v.* —*Syn.* jeopardize, expose, hazard; see **endanger, risk.**

imperious, *mod.* **1.** [Domineering]—*Syn.* tyrannical, oppressive, dictatorial; see **aggressive** 2, **autocratic, powerful** 1.
2. [Urgent]—*Syn.* pressing, critical, imperative; see **crucial** 1, **important** 1, **urgent** 1.

imperishable, *mod.* —*Syn.* enduring, immortal, perpetual; see **permanent** 2.

impersonal, *mod.* —*Syn.* detached, disinterested, cold; see **indifferent** 1.

impersonate, *v.* —*Syn.* mimic, portray, mime, act out, pose as, pass *or* double for, assume the character of, put on an act, pretend to be, act *or* take the part of, act a part, dress as, represent; see also **imitate** 2.

impersonation, *n.* **1.** [Performance]—*Syn.* imitation, role, enactment; see **performance** 2.
2. [Personification]—*Syn.* characterization, incarnation, manifestation; see **representation.**

impertinence, *n.* **1.** [Disrespectfulness]—*Syn.* impudence, insolence, disrespectfulness; see **rudeness.**
2. [Unsuitability]—*Syn.* unsuitability, inappropriateness, impropriety; see **incongruity.**

impertinent, *mod.* **1.** [Not to the point]—*Syn.* pointless, inapplicable, inappropriate; see **irrelevant.**
2. [Disrespectful]—*Syn.* saucy, insolent, impudent; see **rude** 2.
3. [Inappropriate]—*Syn.* incongruous, unfit, ill-suited; see **unsuitable.**

imperturbable, *mod.* —*Syn.* sedate, stoical, immovable; see **calm** 1.

impervious, *mod.* **1.** [Unreceptive]—*Syn.* inaccessible, unapproachable, impassive; see **indifferent** 1.
2. [Impermeable]—*Syn.* impenetrable, watertight, hermetic; see **tight** 2.

impetuosity, *n.* —*Syn.* rashness, recklessness, hastiness; see **carelessness, nonsense** 2.

impetuous, *mod.* —*Syn.* impulsive, hasty, precipitate; see **careless** 1, **changeable** 1, **rash.**

impetuously, *mod.* —*Syn.* hastily, thoughtlessly, heedlessly; see **carelessly, foolishly, rashly.**

impetus, *n.* —*Syn.* force, impulsion, stimulus; see **incentive, purpose** 1, **reason** 3.

impiety, *n.* **1.** [Ungodliness]—*Syn.* reprobation, profanity, godlessness; see **blasphemy, heresy, hypocrisy.**
2. [An impious act]—*Syn.* error, iniquity, sacrilege; see **injustice** 2, **sin, wrong** 1.

impinge, *v.* **1.** [To infringe upon]—*Syn.* encroach, intrude, invade; see **disturb** 2, **meddle** 1, **pry** 2.
2. [To hit]—*Syn.* strike, ricochet, crash against; see **beat** 2, **hit** 1.

impious, *mod.* **1.** [Irreligious]—*Syn.* godless, sinful, profane, blasphemous, sacrilegious, unholy, satanic, sanctimonious, hypocritical, canting, desecrating, defiling, disrespectful, diabolic, deceitful, disobedient, unethical, immoral, apostate, pietistical, unctuous, hardened, perverted, recusant, lacking reverence for God, unsanctified, unhallowed, desecrative, iniquitous, unrighteous, irreligious, agnostic, unregenerate, reprobate, irreverent, ungodly; see also **atheistic, wicked** 1.—*Ant.* pious*, virtuous, devout.
2. [Wicked]—*Syn.* sinful, iniquitous, nefarious; see **vicious** 1, **wicked** 1, 2.

impish, *mod.* —*Syn.* fiendish, elvish, mischievous; see **jaunty, naughty, rude** 2.

implacability, *n.* —*Syn.* cruelty, rancor, revengefulness; see **bitterness** 2, **hatred** 1, **malice.**

implacable, *mod.* —*Syn.* inexorable, unyielding, remorseless; see **cruel** 1, 2, **ruthless** 1, 2, **vindictive.**

implant, *v.* —*Syn.* stick in, insert, root; see **embed** 1, **plant.**

implausible, *mod.* —*Syn.* inconceivable, improbable, unreasonable; see **impossible, obscure** 1, **unbelievable.**

implement, *n.* —*Syn.* utensil, device, instrument; see **equipment, machine** 1, **tool** 1.

implement, *v.* —*Syn.* realize, make good, fulfill; see **achieve** 1, **complete** 1, **resolve** 1.

implicate, *v.* **1.** [To imply]—*Syn.* insinuate, suggest, give out; see **hint** 1, **mean** 1.
2. [To involve]—*Syn.* connect, cite, impute, associate, tie up with, charge, stigmatize, link, catch up in, relate, compromise; see also **accuse, entangle.**

implicated, *mod.* —*Syn.* under suspicion, suspected, known to have been associated (with); see **guilty** 2, **involved, suspicious** 1, 2.

implication, *n.* **1.** [Assumption]—*Syn.* reference, indication, inference; see **assumption** 1, **guess, hypothesis.**
2. [A link]—*Syn.* connection, involvement, entanglement; see **joint** 1, **link, union** 1.

implicit, *mod.* —*Syn.* unquestionable, certain, absolute; see **accurate** 2, **definite** 1, **inevitable.**

implicitly, *mod.* —*Syn.* inevitably, by nature, essentially; see **inherently, naturally** 2, **simply** 1.

implied, *mod.* —*Syn.* implicit, indicated, foreshadowed adumbrated, involved, parallel, tacit, signified, figured intended, meant, connoted, alluded to, latent, hidden insinuated, perceptible, hinted at, understood, symbolized, occult, lurking, indicative, potential, indirectly meant, inferred, significative, allusive, tacitly assumed, inferential, undeclared; see also **suggested.**

implore, *v.* —*Syn.* supplicate, beseech, entreat; see **beg** 1, **urge** 2.

imply, *v.* **1.** [To indicate]—*Syn.* intimate, hint at, suggest; see **hint, mention, refer** 2.
2. [To mean]—*Syn.* import, indicate, signify; see **designate** 1, **intend** 2, **mean** 1.
3. [To assume]—*Syn.* infer, presuppose, presume; see **assume** 1, **intend** 1, **propose** 1.

impolite, *mod.* —*Syn.* discourteous, moody, churlish; see **irritable, rude** 2, **sullen.**

impolitic, *mod.* —*Syn.* unwise, indiscreet, inconsiderate; see **careless** 1, **rash, stupid** 1.

imponderable, *mod.* —*Syn.* inestimable, incalculable, incomputable; see **endless** 1, **impossible** 1, **unbelievable.**

import, *v.* **1.** [To bring in]—*Syn.* introduce, ship *or* carry *or* transport *or* ferry *or* truck *or* freight in, buy abroad; see **carry** 1, **send** 1, **ship.**—*Ant.* export*, ship out, send away.
2. [To signify]—*Syn.* allude to, denote, imply; see **mean** 1.

importance, *n.* **1.** [Significance]—*Syn.* import, signification, drift, force, sense, tenor, consequence, purport, bearing, denotation, gist, effect, distinction, influence, usefulness, moment, weightiness, momentousness, materialness, emphasis, standing, caliber, stress, accent, weight, concern, attention, interest, seriousness, point, substance, relevance, notable feature, sum and substance, cardinal point; see also **essence** 1, **meaning, value** 1, 3. —*Ant.* insignificance*, triviality, emptiness.
2. [Prominence]—*Syn.* greatness, consequence, moment; see **fame** 1, **quality** 3, **rank** 2, 3.

important, *mod.* **1.** [Weighty; *said usually of things*] —*Syn.* significant, considerable, momentous, essential, great, decisive, critical, determining, chief, paramount, primary, foremost, principal, earnest, importunate, influential, marked, salient, imperative, exigent, of great consequence, mattering much, of moment, ponderous, of importance, never to be forgotten, of note, valuable, crucial, substantial, material, vital, serious, grave, relevant, pressing, far-reaching, extensive, conspicuous; *all* (D): heavy, front-page, big-league, standout, smash, big; see also **necessary** 1, **urgent** 1.—*Ant.* trivial*, inconsequential, unimportant.
2. [Eminent; *said usually of persons*]—*Syn.* illustrious, well-recognized, well-known, influential, imposing, distinguished, extraordinary, notable, prominent, remarkable, powerful, noteworthy, signal, grand, majestic, outstanding, noted, noble, upper-class, aristocratic, high-ranking, honored, esteemed, talented, distinctive, first-class, superior, foremost, incomparable, leading; *all* (D): top-notch, high-level, solid, four-star, high-up, high-muck-a-muck, double-distilled; see also **dignified, famous.**—*Ant.* obscure*, unknown, unrecognized.
3. [Relevant]—*Syn.* material, influential, significant; see **fit** 1, **related** 2, **relevant.**

importation, *n.* —*Syn.* borrowing, shipping *or* bringing in, admission, entrance, acceptance, reception, introduction, purchase abroad, adoption; see also **shipment, transportation.**

imported, *mod.* **1.** [Coming from abroad]—*Syn.* shipped in, produced abroad, exotic, alien; see also **foreign** 2.—*Ant.* native*, domestic, made in America.
2. [Rare]—*Syn.* expensive, choice, difficult to obtain; see **excellent, preferred, unusual** 1, 2.

importer, *n.* —*Syn.* international merchant, foreign buyer, importing wholesaler, import-export jobber; see also **merchant, salesman** 2.

importunate, *mod.* —*Syn.* overly solicitous, harassing, clamorous; see **disturbing, insistent.**

importune, *v.* —*Syn.* ask, plead, implore; see **beg** 1, **urge** 2.

importunity, *n.* —*Syn.* petition, address, insistence; see **appeal** 1, **claim, request.**

impose, *v.* —*Syn.* force upon, compel, fix; see **command** 2, **force** 1, **require** 2.

impose on *or* **upon,** *v.* **1.** [To disturb]—*Syn.* intrude, interrupt, presume; see **bother** 2, **disturb** 2.
2. [To deceive]—*Syn.* trick, cheat, delude; see **anger, deceive.**

imposing, *mod.* —*Syn.* stirring, exciting, overwhelming; see **impressive** 1, **striking.**

imposition, *n.* **1.** [A constraint]—*Syn.* demand, restraint, encumbrance; see **command** 1, **pressure** 2.
2. [A deception]—*Syn.* craftiness, trickery, fraud; see **deception** 1, **hypocrisy, trick** 1.

impossibility, *n.* —*Syn.* hopelessness, unattainability, unreasonableness, contrariety, impracticality, unfeasibility, impracticability, difficulty, unlikelihood, failure, unworkability; see also **futility.** —*Ant.* probability*, feasibility, practicality.

impossible, *mod.* **1.** [Incapable of being considered] —*Syn.* inconceivable, vain, infeasible, unachievable, unattainable, out of the question, too much (for), insurmountable, useless, impassable, inaccessible, unworkable, preposterous, unimaginable, unobtainable, not to be thought of, hardly possible, beyond the bounds of possibility; *all* (D): like finding a needle in a haystack, a hundred to one,

out of the question; see also **futile** 1, **hopeless** 2. —*Ant.* possible*, likely, reasonable.
2. [Having little likelihood of accomplishment] —*Syn.* improbable, unlikely, doubtful; see **difficult** 1, 2, **uncertain** 2.
3. [Undesirable; *said of things*]—*Syn.* improper, objectionable, incongruous; see **offensive** 2, **undesirable, unsuitable.**
4. [Undesirable; *said of persons*]—*Syn.* incapable, inefficient, inexpert; see **incompetent, undesirable.**

impostor, *n.* —*Syn.* pretender, empiric, charlatan, quack, fraud, impersonator, masquerader, scorner, mocker, mountebank, dissembler; *all* (D): ass in lion's skin, sharper, con man; see also **cheat** 1.

imposture, *n.* —*Syn.* deceit, deception, hoax; see **trick** 1.

impotence, *n.* **1.** [Sterility]—*Syn.* unproductiveness, frigidity, infecundity; see **barrenness.**
2. [Weakness]—*Syn.* inability, feebleness, infirmity; see **weakness** 1.

impotent, *mod.* **1.** [Weak]—*Syn.* powerless, inept, infirm; see **unable, weak** 1.
2. [Sterile]—*Syn.* barren, frigid, unproductive; see **sterile** 1.

impound, *v.* **1.** [To imprison]—*Syn.* encage, incarcerate, confine; see **enslave, imprison.**
2. [To seize]—*Syn.* appropriate, take, usurp; see **seize** 2.

impounded, *mod.* —*Syn.* kept, seized, confiscated; see **held, retained** 1.

impoverish, *v.* —*Syn.* make poor, bankrupt, exhaust; see **ruin** 2.

impoverished, *mod.* —*Syn.* poverty-stricken, bankrupt, broke (D); see **insolvent, poor** 1, **ruined** 4.

impracticability, *n.* —*Syn.* hopelessness, uselessness, emptiness; see **futility, impossibility.**

impracticable, *mod.* **1.** [Not feasible]—*Syn.* infeasible, inconceivable, unworkable; see **impossible** 1.
2. [Obstinate]—*Syn.* unreasonable, unyielding, headstrong; see **obstinate** 1.

impractical, *mod.* —*Syn.* unreal, unrealistic, unworkable, improbable, illogical, unreasonable, impracticable, inefficacious, speculative, absurd, wild, quixotic, chimerical, abstract, impossible, idealistic, infeasible, unfeasible, unwise, out of the question; see also **visionary** 1.—*Ant.* practical*, logical, reasonable.

impracticality, *n.* —*Syn.* inefficiency, lack of use *or* usefulness, inapplicability; see **worthlessness.**

imprecation, *n.* —*Syn.* blasphemy, malediction, swearing; see **curse.**

impregnable, *mod.* —*Syn.* immovable, powerful, invulnerable; see **safe** 1.

impregnate, *v.* **1.** [To infuse]—*Syn.* catechize, indoctrinate, implant; see **teach** 1.
2. [To permeate]—*Syn.* fill up, pervade, overflow; see **fill** 2, **saturate, soak** 1.
3. [To beget]—*Syn.* procreate, conceive, reproduce; see **produce** 1, **propagate** 1.

impregnated, *mod.* **1.** [Full]—*Syn.* saturated, shot through and through, full of; see **full** 1.
2. [Pregnant]—*Syn.* bred, *enceinte* (French), with child; see **pregnant** 1.

impresario, *n.* —*Syn.* producer, stage director, manager; see **director** 2, **leader** 3.

impress, *v.* **1.** [To make an impression]—*Syn.* indent, emboss, imprint; see **dent, mark** 1, **print** 2.
2. [To attract attention]—*Syn.* stand out, be conspicuous, cause a stir, create *or* make an impression, direct attention to, make an impact upon, engage the thoughts, engage attention, come forward, be listened to, find favor with, excite notice, arouse comment; *all* (D): make a hit, cut a figure, make a dent in, play to the gallery; see also **fascinate.**
3. [To command respect]—*Syn.* awe, dazzle, overawe; see **influence.**

impressed, *mod.* —*Syn.* aroused, awakened, snowed (D); see **affected** 1, **excited.**

impressibility, *n.* —*Syn.* susceptibility, sentimentality, flexibility, pliancy, plasticity, affectibility, tenderness, impressionability, perceptivity, emotionality, sensitiveness, susceptibleness, sensibility; see also **feeling** 4, **sensitivity.**

impressible, *mod.* —*Syn.* penetrable, sensuous, impressionable, easily affected, susceptible to impression, tender, emotional, sensible, facile, sentient, perceptive, sympathetic, amenable, empathetic, excitable; see also **affected** 1, **responsive, sensitive** 3.

impression, *n.* **1.** [An imprint]—*Syn.* print, footprint, fingerprint, dent, mold, indentation, depression, cast, form, track, spoor, pattern, matrix; see also **mark** 1.
2. [An effect]—*Syn.* response, consequence, reaction; see **result.**
3. [A notion based on scanty evidence]—*Syn.* theory, conjecture, supposition; see **guess, hypothesis, opinion** 1.

impressionable, *mod.* —*Syn.* perceptive, impressible, receptive; see **affected** 1, **responsive, sensitive** 3.

impressive, *mod.* **1.** [Striking]—*Syn.* stirring, moving, inspiring, effective, affecting, eloquent, impassioned, thrilling, excited, intense, rousing, well-done, well-organized, dramatic, absorbing, deep, profound, penetrating, remarkable, consequential, extraordinary, notable, awe-inspiring, soul-stirring, resounding, high-sounding, important, momentous, vital; *both* (D): big-time, darn good; see also **striking.**—*Ant.* dull*, uninteresting, common.
2. [Grand]—*Syn.* majestic, noble, stately; see **grand** 2.

imprimatur, *n.* —*Syn.* approval, charter, permit; see **permission.**

imprint, *n.* **1.** [A printed identification]—*Syn.* firm name, banner, trademark, sponsorship, direction, heading, colophon; see also **emblem, signature.**
2. [An impression]—*Syn.* dent, indentation, print; see **mark** 1.

imprint, *v.* —*Syn.* print, stamp, designate; see **mark** 1, 2, 3.

imprinted, *mod.* —*Syn.* branded, printed, impressed; see **marked** 1, **stamped.**

imprison, *v.* —*Syn.* jail, lock *or* box *or* bottle *or* coop up, confine, incarcerate, immure, impound, detain, keep (in), hold, intern, circumscribe, shut *or* bottle *or* lock *or* bolt *or* rail *or* box *or* fence in, cage, send to prison, keep as captive, hold as hostage, enclose, keep in custody, hold captive, put behind bars, commit to an institution; *all* (D): put away, slap in the can, dress in steel, lay in lavender, clap under hatches, send up; see also **enslave.**—*Ant.* free*, liberate, release.

imprisoned, *mod.* —*Syn.* arrested, jailed, incarcerated; see **confined** 3.

imprisonment, *n.* **1.** [Forcible detention]—*Syn.* captivity, isolation, incarceration, duress, durance, bondage, thralldom, quarantine, limbo, immuration; see also **arrest** 1, **confinement** 1, **restraint** 2. —*Ant.* freedom*, liberty, enlargement.

2. [Placing in forcible detention]—*Syn.* confining, jailing, capturing, incarcerating, mewing up, subjecting, enthralling, quarantining, immuring, imprisoning.—*Ant.* release*, liberating, discharge.

improbability, *n.* —*Syn.* implausibility, rarity, doubt; see **futility, impossibility.**

improbable, *mod.* —*Syn.* not likely, doubtful, not to be expected; see **unlikely.**

impromptu, *mod.* —*Syn.* extempore, unprepared, offhand; see **extemporaneous.**

improper, *mod.* **1.** [Unsuitable]—*Syn.* at odds, ill-advised, unsuited, indecorous, incongruous, out of place, ludicrous, incorrect, preposterous, unwarranted, undue, imprudent, unadapted, abnormal, irregular, inexpedient, unseasonable, inadvisable, untimely, inopportune, unfit, malapropos, unfitting, inappropriate, unapt, unbefitting, unmeet, ill-timed, awkward, inharmonious, discordant, discrepant, inapplicable, ill-assorted, odd; see also **unsuitable.**

2. [Immoral]—*Syn.* naughty, suggestive, smutty; see **lewd** 1, 2.

improperly, *mod.* —*Syn.* poorly, inappropriately, clumsily; see **awkwardly, badly** 1, **inadequately.**

impropriety, *n.* —*Syn.* incongruity, indecency, impudence; see **rudeness.**

improve, *v.* **1.** [To make better]—*Syn.* mend, amend, cultivate, revise, update, elevate, polish, refine, purify, edit, enlarge, touch up, emend, civilize, meliorate, ameliorate, landscape, develop, revamp, better, upgrade, give color to, set right, reorganize, promote, reform, raise, lift, rectify, rehabilitate, refashion, regenerate, retread, fix, straighten out, distill, change for the better; *all* (D): give a good going over, doctor up, be the making of; see also **adjust** 3, **change** 1, **correct** 1, **repair.** —*Ant.* destroy*, abolish, overthrow.

2. [To become better]—*Syn.* ameliorate, regenerate, advance, progress, renew, enrich, enhance, augment, gain strength, develop, get *or* grow better, grow, make progress, rally, profit, widen, increase, mellow, mature; *all* (D): come *or* get along *or* on, take a new lease on life, look up, shape *or* pick *or* perk up, come around, make headway, snap out of, blow one's mind, make strides; see also **recover** 2, 3.—*Ant.* weaken*, worsen, grow worse.

improved, *mod.* **1.** [Made better]—*Syn.* augmented, processed, corrected, ameliorated, bettered, amended, mended, reformed, elaborated, refined, modernized, brought up-to-date, enhanced, repaired, bolstered up, rectified, remodeled, reorganized, made over; *all* (D): better for, doctored up, polished up; see also **changed** 2, **revised.**—*Ant.* damaged*, injured, worsened.

2. [In better health]—*Syn.* recovering, convalescent, making a rapid recovery; see **well** 1.

improvement, *n.* **1.** [The process of becoming better]—*Syn.* melioration, amelioration, betterment, rectification, change, alteration, reformation, progression, advance, advancement, development, growth, rise, reclamation, civilization, gain, cultivation, progressiveness, increase, enrichment, promotion, elevation, preferment, ennoblement, recovery, regeneration, furtherance, renovation, reorganization, amendment, reform, emendation, revision, elaboration, refinement, modernization, enhancement, remodeling; *both* (D): shaking down, knocking the bugs out.—*Ant.* decay*, deterioration, retrogression.

2. [That which has been improved]—*Syn.* addition, supplement, repair, extra, attachment, correction, reform, remodeling, repairing, betterment, refinement, luxury, advance, advancement, step forward, enhancement, new model, deluxe model; *both* (D): latest thing, last word; see also **change** 2, **review** 1, **revision.**

improve on *or* **upon,** *v.* —*Syn.* make better, develop, refine; see **adjust** 3, **change** 1, **correct** 1, **improve** 1, **repair.**

improvidence, *n.* —*Syn.* slackness, wastefulness, extravagance; see **carelessness, indifference** 1, **neglect** 1, **waste** 1.

improvident, *mod.* —*Syn.* spendthrift, extravagant, lavish; see **wasteful.**

improvidently, *mod.* —*Syn.* impulsively, unwisely, thoughtlessly; see **foolishly, rashly.**

improving, *mod.* —*Syn.* reconstructing, repairing, elaborating, bettering, correcting, developing, fixing, remodeling, on the mend (D).

improvisation, *n.* —*Syn.* improvising, impulsive *or* impromptu creation, makeshift device; see **discovery** 2.

improvise, *v.* —*Syn.* ad-lib, coin, devise; see **invent** 1.

imprudence, *n.* —*Syn.* indiscretion, foolishness, indifference; see **carelessness, neglect** 1.

imprudent, *mod.* —*Syn.* incautious, brash, indiscreet; see **rash.**

imprudently, *mod.* —*Syn.* unwisely, inadvisedly, indiscreetly; see **foolishly, rashly.**

impudence, *n.* —*Syn.* insolence, impertinence, effrontery; see **rudeness.**

impudent, *mod.* —*Syn.* forward, insolent, shameless; see **rude** 2.

impudently, *mod.* —*Syn.* saucily, brashly, crudely; see **rudely.**

impugn, *v.* —*Syn.* question, attack, challenge, call in question, contradict, assail, knock (D); see **doubt** 1, 2.

impulse, *n.* **1.** [A throb]—*Syn.* surge, vibration, thrust, push, impetus, pulse, pulsation, pressure, augmentation, rush, motivation, impulsion, propulsion, stroke, momentum, shove, shock, bump, movement; see also **beat** 2.

2. [A sudden urge]—*Syn.* fancy, whim, caprice, motive, motivation, actuation, spontaneity, drive, appeal, notion, inclination, disposition, vagary, freak, wish, whimsy, inspiration, hunch, flash, thought, extemporization; see also **desire** 1.

impulsive, *mod.* **1.** [Spontaneous]—*Syn.* offhand, unpremeditated, extemporaneous; see **automatic** 2, **spontaneous.**

2. [Impetuous]—*Syn.* violent, sudden, hasty; see **careless** 1, **rash.**

impulsively, *mod.*—*Syn.* imprudently, hastily, abruptly; see **carelessly, rashly.**

impunity, *n.*—*Syn.* exemption, dispensation, privilege; see **exception** 1, **freedom** 2.

impure, *mod.* **1.** [Adulterated]—*Syn.* not pure, loaded, weighted, salted, diluted, debased, contaminated, mixed, watered (down), polluted, corrupted, raw, tainted, sugared, cut, adulterated, dilute; *both* (D): doctored, tampered with; see also **unclean.**

2. [Not chaste]—*Syn.* unclean, unchaste, corrupt; see **lewd** 2, **wicked** 1.

3. [Dirty]—*Syn.* nasty, tainted, filthy; see **dirty** 1, **polluted.**

impurity, *n.* **1.** [Lewdness]—*Syn.* indecency, profligacy, pornography; see **lewdness.**

2. [Filth]—*Syn.* dirt, defilement, excrement; see **contamination, filth, infection** 1, **pollution.**

imputation, *n.*—*Syn.* castigation, insinuation, incrimination; see **accusation** 2.

impute, *v.* **1.** [To attribute]—*Syn.* ascribe, assign, credit; see **attribute.**

2. [To charge]—*Syn.* brand, stigmatize, blame; see **accuse, censure.**

imputed, *mod.*—*Syn.* supposed, claimed, charged; see **likely** 1.

in, *prep.* **1.** [Within]—*Syn.* surrounded by, in the midst of, within the boundaries of, in the area of, within the time of, concerning the subject of, as a part of, inside of, enclosed in, protected by, not out of; see also **within.**

2. [Into]—*Syn.* to the center *or* midst of, in the direction of, within the extent of, under, near, against; see also **into, toward.**

3. [While engaged in]—*Syn.* in the act of, during the process of, while occupied with; see **during, meanwhile, while** 1.

have it in for (D)—*Syn.* wish to harm, be out to destroy, detest; see **hate** 1.

in a bad way, *mod.*—*Syn.* dangerously ill, in critical condition, destitute; see **dying** 1, 2, **miserable** 1, **poor** 1, 2, **sick, weak** 1, 2, 3.

inability, *n.* **1.** [Lack of competence]—*Syn.* incapacity, incompetence, inadequacy, shortcoming, insufficiency, impotence, powerlessness, ineptitude, ineptness, inefficacy, inutility, unfitness, inefficiency; see also **failure** 1, **weakness** 1, 2. —*Ant.* ability*, capability, capacity.

2. [A temporary lack]—*Syn.* disability, incapacitation, frailty; see **lack** 2, **necessity** 2.

inaccessible, *mod.*—*Syn.* unobtainable, far, unachievable, insurmountable, impracticable, aloof, unapproachable, unfeasible, unworkable, unavailable, unrealizable, insoluble, impassable, impervious, unavailable, not at hand, out of reach, elusive; see also **away** 1, **beyond, difficult** 2, **distant** 1, 2, **rare** 2, **remote** 1, **separated, tight** 2.

inaccuracy, *n.*—*Syn.* exaggeration, mistake, deception; see **error** 1.

inaccurate, *mod.*—*Syn.* fallacious, in error, incorrect; see **mistaken** 1, **wrong** 2.

inaccurately, *mod.*—*Syn.* inexactly, clumsily, crudely; see **badly** 1, **inadequately.**

inactive, *mod.* **1.** [Inert]—*Syn.* dormant, stable, still; see **idle** 1, **latent, motionless** 1.

2. [Indolent]—*Syn.* limp, slothful, lethargic; see **lazy** 1.

inadequacy, *n.* **1.** [Inferiority]—*Syn.* ineptitude, incompetence, insufficiency; see **inability** 1.

2. [A defect]—*Syn.* flaw, drawback, shortcoming; see **blemish, defect** 2, **lack** 2.

inadequate, *mod.* **1.** [Insufficient]—*Syn.* lacking, scanty, short, meager, failing, unequal, not enough, sparing, stinted, stunted, feeble, sparse, (too) little, small, thin, deficient, incomplete, inappreciable, inconsiderable, spare, bare, parsimonious, niggardly, miserly, scarce, unsubstantial, barren, depleted, low, weak, flaccid, impotent, unproductive, dry, sterile, jejune, imperfect, defective, lame; *all* (D): skimpy, shy, at low-water mark; see also **faulty, poor** 2, **unfinished** 1, **unsatisfactory, wanting.** —*Ant.* enough*, adequate, sufficient.

2. [Incompetent]—*Syn.* unequal, falling short, impotent; see **incompetent.**

inadequately, *mod.*—*Syn.* insufficiently, not enough, partly, partially, incompletely, scantily, deficiently, perfunctorily, ineffectively, inefficiently, ineptly, not up to standard(s) *or* specifications *or* requirements, meagerly, not in sufficient quantity *or* quality, in a limited manner, to a limited degree, not up to snuff (D); see also **badly** 1.

inadmissible, *mod.*—*Syn.* unsuited, inappropriate, unsatisfactory; see **unfit** 2.

in advance, *mod.*—*Syn.* ahead (of), earlier, in time; see **before.**

inadvertence, *n.*—*Syn.* neglect, indifference, oversight; see **omission** 1.

inadvertent, *mod.* **1.** [Careless]—*Syn.* unconcerned, reckless, negligent; see **careless** 1.

2. [Unintentional]—*Syn.* accidental, unpremeditated, unintentional; see **incidental** 1, 2.

inadvertently, *mod.* **1.** [Carelessly]—*Syn.* rashly, negligently, recklessly; see **carelessly.**

2. [Unintentionally]—*Syn.* unwittingly, involuntarily, not purposely; see **accidentally, incidentally.**

inadvisable, *mod.*—*Syn.* unsuitable, inappropriate, inconvenient; see **improper** 1, **wrong** 3.

inadvisedly, *mod.*—*Syn.* impulsively, regrettably, unwisely; see **foolishly, rashly.**

inalienable, *mod.*—*Syn.* inbred, basic, natural; see **absolute** 1, **inherent.**

in all respects, *mod.*—*Syn.* entirely, outright, wholly, thoroughly, altogether, totally, utterly, at all points, in every respect, quite, throughout, out-and-out (D); see also **completely.**

in a minute, *mod.*—*Syn.* before long, shortly, presently; see **soon** 1.

inamorata, *n.*—*Syn.* paramour, mistress, sweetheart; see **lover** 1.

in and about *or* **around,** *mod.*—*Syn.* close to, there, approximately; see **about** 2, **near** 1.

inane, *mod.*—*Syn.* pointless, foolish, ridiculous; see **illogical, silly, stupid** 1.

inanimate, *mod.* **1.** [Inorganic]—*Syn.* lifeless, mineral, non-animal, non-vegetable, azoic; see also **inorganic.**

2. [Inactive]—*Syn.* dull, inert, inoperative; see **idle** 1, **motionless** 1.

inanition, *n.* **1.** [Emptiness]—*Syn.* vacuum, gap, void; see **emptiness.**
2. [Starvation]—*Syn.* exhaustion, malnutrition, collapse; see **starvation.**

inanity, *n.* —*Syn.* silliness, asininity, foolishness; see **stupidity** 1, 2.

in any case, *mod.* —*Syn.* regardless, nonetheless, no matter what; see **anyhow** 1, 2.

in a pinch (D), *mod.* —*Syn.* in an emergency, if necessary, under pressure; see also **in case of.**

inapplicable, *mod.* —*Syn.* impertinent, inconsistent, remote; see **irrelevant.**

inappropriate, *mod.* —*Syn.* improper, irrelevant, inapplicable; see **unsuitable.**

inaptitude, *n.* —*Syn.* inexperience, unskillfulness, incompetence; see **inability** 1.

in arrears, *mod.* —*Syn.* behind, payable, overdue; see **due, late** 1, **unpaid** 1, 2.

inarticulate, *mod.* **1.** [Mute]—*Syn.* reticent, wordless, mute; see **dumb** 1.
2. [Indistinct]—*Syn.* unintelligible, inaudible, vague; see **obscure** 1.

inasmuch as, *conj.* —*Syn.* in view of (the fact that), making allowance for (the fact that), while; see **because, since** 1.

inattention, *n.* —*Syn.* heedlessness, negligence, obsession; see **carelessness, indifference, neglect** 1.

inattentive, *mod.* —*Syn.* preoccupied, indifferent, negligent; see **careless, diverted.**

inaudible, *mod.* —*Syn.* low, indistinct, silent; see **obscure** 1, **vague** 2.

inaudibly, *mod.* —*Syn.* unintelligibly, indistinctly, vaguely; see **obscurely.**

inaugurate, *v.* —*Syn.* introduce, initiate, originate; see **begin** 1.

inaugurated, *mod.* —*Syn.* originated, started, introduced; see **initiated** 1, 3.

inauguration, *n.* —*Syn.* initiation, commencement, installment; see **introduction** 1.

inauspicious, *mod.* —*Syn.* foreboding, unlucky, impending; see **ominous, sinister.**

inbred, *mod.* —*Syn.* innate, inborn, ingrained; see **inherent, native** 1.

inborn, *mod.* —*Syn.* essential, intrinsic, inbred; see **inherent, native** 1.

in brief, *mod.* —*Syn.* concisely, shortly and sweetly, to the point, cut short, abbreviated; see also **briefly.**

incalculable, *mod.* **1.** [Immense]—*Syn.* inestimable, limitless, boundless; see **infinite** 1, **vast** 2.
2. [Unpredictable]—*Syn.* unpredictable, unforeseen, unfixed; see **uncertain** 2.

incandescence, *n.* —*Syn.* radiance, luster, brilliance; see **light** 1.

incandescent, *mod.* —*Syn.* radiant, glowing, brilliant, intense.

incantation, *n.* **1.** [Invocation]—*Syn.* invocation, charm, chant; see **hymn, magic** 2.
2. [Witchcraft]—*Syn.* sorcery, black magic, enchantment; see **charm** 2, **magic** 1.

incapability, *n.* —*Syn.* incapacity, incompetence, impotence; see **inability** 1.

incapable, *mod.* —*Syn.* unsuited, poor, inadequate; see **incompetent, inexperienced, naive.**

incapable of, *mod.* **1.** [Incompetent]—*Syn.* ineffective, inadequate, unsuited; see **incompetent.**
2. [Innocent]—*Syn.* tame, irreproachable, innocuous; see **innocent** 1, **naive.**

incapacitate, *v.* —*Syn.* cripple, hinder, undermine; see **damage** 1, **hurt** 1, **weaken** 2.

incapacity, *n.* —*Syn.* inadequacy, insufficiency, uselessness; see **inability** 1.

incarcerate, *v.* —*Syn.* jail, detain, confine; see **imprison, restrict** 2.

incarceration, *n.* —*Syn.* bondage, captivity, restraint; see **confinement** 1, **imprisonment** 1.

incarnate, *mod.* —*Syn.* real, personified, tangible; see **human, physical** 1.

incarnation, *n.* **1.** [Personification]—*Syn.* manifestation, embodiment, incorporation; see **image** 2.
2. [Matter]—*Syn.* substance, body, flesh-and-blood; see **matter** 1.

in case, *mod.* —*Syn.* in the event that, provided, if it should happen (that); see **if.**

in case of, *mod.* —*Syn.* in the event of, in order to be prepared for, as a provision against; see also **if.**

incautious, *mod.* —*Syn.* hasty, reckless, indiscreet; see **rash.**

incautiously, *mod.* —*Syn.* brashly, thoughtlessly, heedlessly; see **carelessly, rashly.**

incendiary, *mod.* **1.** [Combustible]—*Syn.* ignitable, burnable, combustible; see **burning** 1, **inflammable.**
2. [Treacherous]—*Syn.* malevolent, provocative, subversive; see **dangerous** 1, **treacherous** 2, **wicked** 1, 2.

incendiary, *n.* **1.** [Arsonist]—*Syn.* pyromaniac, firebug, *petroleur* (French); see **arsonist, criminal.**
2. [An agitator]—*Syn.* insurgent, rioter, demonstrator; see **agitator, rebel** 1.

incense, *n.* —*Syn.* scent, fragrance, fuel, punk, joss stick, flame, odor, frankincense, essence, burnt offering, aroma, redolence, myrrh; see also **perfume.**

incense, *v.* —*Syn.* irritate, disgust, make angry; see **anger** 1, **bother** 2.

incensed, *mod.* —*Syn.* irate, indignant, furious; see **angry.**

incentive, *n.* —*Syn.* spur, inducement, motive, stimulus, stimulation, spring, impetus, ground, provocation, enticement, temptation, bait, consideration, determinant, excuse, rationale, goad, whip, urge, influence, lure, come-on (D), allurement, persuasion, inspiration, exhortation, encouragement, insistence, instigation, incitement, reason why; see also **impulse** 2, **motivation, purpose** 1, **reason** 3.

inception, *n.* —*Syn.* initiation, start, beginning; see **origin** 1.

incertitude, *n.* —*Syn.* hesitation, perplexity, misgiving; see **doubt** 2, **uncertainty** 1.

incessant, *mod.* —*Syn.* ceaseless, continuous, monotonous; see **constant** 1, **perpetual** 1, 2.

incessantly, *mod.* —*Syn.* steadily, monotonously, perpetually; see **regularly** 2.

incest, *n.* —*Syn.* inbreeding, interbreeding, Caunian love, Oedipal *or* Electral love, mother-son relationship, father-daughter relationship, brother-sister relationship; see also **lewdness, sex** 1.

incestuous, *mod.* —*Syn.* depraved, interbred, carnal; see **lewd** 2.

inch, *n.* **1.** [Twelfth of a foot]—*Syn.* fingerbreadth, 2.54 centimeters, measurement, 1/36 yard, length; see **measure** 1.

2. [Small degree]—*Syn.* jot, tittle, iota; see **bit** 3.
every inch—*Syn.* in all respects, thoroughly, entirely; see **completely.**
by inches—*Syn.* slowly, by degrees, step by step; see **gradually.**
within an inch of—*Syn.* very close to, near to, nearly; see **almost.**

inch, *v.* —*Syn.* creep, barely move, make some progress; see **crawl** 1.

inchoate, *mod.* —*Syn.* incipient, rudimentary, preliminary, beginning, just begun, not fully formed; see also **unfinished** 1.

incidence, *n.* —*Syn.* slope, tendency, degree, direction, trend, line, aim, occurrence; see also **drift** 1, 2, **grade** 1.

incident, *n.* —*Syn.* episode, happening, occurrence; see **event** 1.

incidental, *mod.* —*Syn.* subsidiary, as an incident of, contributing to; see **related** 2, **subordinate.**

incidentally, *mod.* —*Syn.* subordinately, by chance, by the way, in an incidental *or* subsidiary *or* related manner, as a side effect, as a by-product, unexpectedly, not by design, remotely; see also **accidentally.**

incidentals, *n.* —*Syn.* (minor) needs *or* requirements *or* necessities, incidental expenses, per diem; see **expenses, necessity** 2.

incinerate, *v.* —*Syn.* cremate, parch, burn up; see **burn** 2.

incipient, *mod.* —*Syn.* initial, elementary, basic; see **fundamental** 1.

incise, *v.* **1.** [To cut]—*Syn.* dissect, chop, split; see **cut** 1, **divide** 1, **sever.**
2. [To engrave]—*Syn.* chisel, etch, mold; see **carve** 1, **engrave** 2.

incised, *mod.* —*Syn.* etched, engraved, cut; see **carved.**

incision, *n.* —*Syn.* gash, slash, surgery; see **cut** 2, **hole** 1.

incisive, *mod.* **1.** [Sarcastic]—*Syn.* penetrating, sharp, severe; see **sarcastic.**
2. [Intelligent]—*Syn.* clever, bright, profound; see **intelligent** 1.

incisor, *n.* —*Syn.* tusk, eyetooth, canine tooth; see **tooth.**

incite, *v.* —*Syn.* arouse, rouse, impel, stimulate, instigate, provoke, excite, spur, sic, goad (on), exhort, persuade, influence, induce, prick, taunt, actuate, activate, animate, inspirit, coax, stir up, fire up, motivate, prompt, urge on, inspire, abet, force, foment; *all* (D): work up, lash into a fury, talk into, whip *or* egg on, hold sway over, blow the coals, fan the flame; see also **drive** 1, **encourage** 1, **push** 2, **urge** 2.—*Ant.* discourage*, dissuade, check.

incited, *mod.* —*Syn.* driven, pushed, motivated; see **urged** 2.

incitement, *n.* —*Syn.* vulgarity, boorishness, impudence; see **rudeness.**

inclemency, *n.* **1.** [Bitterness; *said of weather*] —*Syn.* wintriness, arctic conditions, low temperature, raininess, coldness, rawness, harshness, weather, severity; see also **rain** 1, **snow** 2, **storm** 1, **wind** 1.
2. [Strictness]—*Syn.* savagery, barbarity, unkindness; see **cruelty, severity.**

inclement, *mod.* **1.** [Bitter; *said of weather*]—*Syn.* wintry, severe, raw; see **cold** 1.
2. [Ruthless]—*Syn.* unkind, savage, harsh; see **cruel** 1, **ruthless** 1, **severe** 1, 2.

inclination, *n.* **1.** [A tendency]—*Syn.* bias, bent, propensity, predilection, partiality, penchant, predisposition, attachment, capability, capacity, proneness, aptness, leaning, fondness, disposition, liking, preference, movement, susceptibility, weakness, proclivity, drift, trend, turn, slant, impulse, attraction, affection, desire, temperament, whim, idiosyncrasy, urge, persuasion.
2. [A bow]—*Syn.* bend, bending, bowing; see **bow** 2.
3. [A slope]—*Syn.* grade, downgrade, incline; see **hill.**
4. [A trend]—*Syn.* slant, direction, bent; see **drift** 1.
5. [A slant]—*Syn.* pitch, slope, incline, angle, ramp, declivity, bevel, acclivity, bank, lean, list; see also **grade** 1.

incline, *n.* —*Syn.* slope, inclined plane, approach; see **grade** 1, **inclination** 5.

incline, *v.* **1.** [To cause to lean or bend]—*Syn.* tilt, twist, slant; see **bend** 1, **turn** 6, **veer.**
2. [To lean]—*Syn.* bow, nod, cock; see **lean** 1.
3. [To tend toward]—*Syn.* prefer, be disposed, be predisposed; see **favor** 1.

inclined, *mod.* **1.** [Disposed]—*Syn.* prone, slanted, willing; see **likely** 5.
2. [Diagonal]—*Syn.* tilted, slanted, tipped; see **oblique** 1.

inclose, *v.* —*Syn.* lock up, encircle, surround; see **enclose** 1.

include, *v.* **1.** [To contain]—*Syn.* hold, admit, cover, embrace, involve, consist of, take in, entail, incorporate, constitute, accommodate, be comprised *or* composed of, embody, implicate, be made up of, number among, carry, bear; see also **compose** 1, **comprise.**—*Ant.* omit*, be outside of, stand outside of.
2. [To place into or among]—*Syn.* enter, append, introduce, take in, incorporate, subsume, make room for, build, work in, inject, interject, add on, interpolate, insert, combine, make a part of, make allowance for, give consideration to, count in (D); see also **add** 1.—*Ant.* discard*, exclude, reject.

included, *mod.* —*Syn.* counted, numbered, admitted, covered, involved, constituted, embodied, given a place among, inserted, entered, incorporated, combined, placed, fused, merged; see also **within.**—*Ant.* excluded, left out, refused*.

including, *mod.* —*Syn.* together *or* along *or* coupled with, as well as, inclusive of, in conjunction with, not to mention, to say nothing of, among other things, with the addition of, in addition to, counting, made up of; see also **plus.**—*Ant.* besides*, not counting, aside from.

inclusion, *n.* —*Syn.* admittance, incorporation, embodiment, comprisal, formation, composition; see also **addition** 2, **insertion.**—*Ant.* exclusion*, elimination, exception.

inclusive, *mod.* —*Syn.* all together, from beginning to end, *in toto* (Latin); see **comprehensive, full** 3, **general** 1, **whole** 1.

incognito, *mod.* —*Syn.* camouflaged, masked, concealed; see **hidden** 2, **isolated, obscure** 1.

incoherence, *n.* —*Syn.* disagreement, dissimilarity, incongruity; see **inconsistency.**

incoherent, *mod.* **1.** [Not hanging together]—*Syn.* loose, uneven, uncoordinated; see **irregular** 4.
2. [Inarticulate]—*Syn.* mumbling, stammering, confused, speechless, uncommunicative, puzzling, indistinct, faltering, stuttering, unintelligible, voiceless, muttered, mumbled, jumbled, gasping, breathless, disconnected, rambling, disjointed, tongue-tied, muffled, indistinguishable, incomprehensible, muddled; see also **dull** 3, **dumb** 1, **mute** 1, **obscure** 1.—*Ant.* clear*, eloquent, distinct.

incoherently, *mod.* —*Syn.* frantically, frenziedly, drunkenly, confusedly, discontinuously, spasmodically, chaotically, randomly, ineptly, unsystematically, aimlessly, casually, sloppily, ambiguously, equivocally, illegibly, incomprehensibly, unrecognizably, uncertainly, inaudibly, mysteriously; *all* (D): by fits and starts, in snatches, light-headedly; see also **irregularly, obscurely, wildly** 1.

in cold blood, *mod.* **1.** [Deliberately]—*Syn.* intentionally, willfully, consciously; see **carefully** 2, **deliberately.**
2. [Cruelly]—*Syn.* heartlessly, ruthlessly, unmercifully; see **brutally.**

incombustible, *mod.* —*Syn.* non-flammable, noncombustible, unburnable; see **fireproof.**

income, *n.* —*Syn.* earnings, salary, wages, livelihood, returns, profit, dividends, assets, proceeds, benefits, receipts, gains, commission, drawings, avails, rent, royalty, honorarium, income after taxes, net income, gross income, taxable income; *all* (D): bottom line, cash, pickings, take; see also **pay** 2, **revenue** 1, 2.—*Ant.* expense*, expenditures, outgo.

incommensurate, *mod.* —*Syn.* not proportional, unequal, disproportionate; see **unfair** 1.

incommode, *v.* —*Syn.* discommode, inconvenience, annoy; see **bother** 2.

incommodious, *mod.* —*Syn.* awkward, troublesome, inconvenient; see **disturbing.**

incommunicable, *mod.* —*Syn.* not contagious, not catching, retained, kept in.

incommunicado, *mod.* —*Syn.* concealed, in retreat, secluded; see **hidden** 2, **isolated.**

incommunicative, *mod.* —*Syn.* quiet, secretive, silent; see **reserved** 3.

incomparable, *mod.* —*Syn.* unequaled, exceptional, superior; see **excellent, perfect** 2.

incomparably, *mod.* —*Syn.* exceptionally, eminently, superlatively; see **especially** 1.

incompatibility, *n.* —*Syn.* variance, conflict, animosity; see **disagreement** 1.

incompatible, *mod.* —*Syn.* inconsistent, contrary, clashing, inappropriate, contradictory, disagreeing, inconstant, factious, unadapted, opposite, jarring, discordant, incoherent, inadmissible; see also **opposed, unsuitable.**

incompetence, *n.* —*Syn.* inadequacy, inexperience, worthlessness; see **inability** 1.

incompetent, *mod.* —*Syn.* incapable, inefficient, inept, unskillful, inadequate, unfit, unskilled, disqualified, bungling, inexpert, floundering, ineffectual, unsuitable, untrained, maladroit, unhandy, clumsy, awkward, uninitiated, raw, inexperienced, unadapted, not equal to, amateurish; see also **unable.**—*Ant.* able*, fit, qualified.

incompetently, *mod.* —*Syn.* poorly, ignorantly, clumsily; see **awkwardly, badly** 1.

in competition with, *mod.* —*Syn.* opposed to, competing against; see **opposed.**

incomplete, *mod.* **1.** [Unfinished]—*Syn.* rough, half-done, under construction; see **unfinished** 1.
2. [Partial]—*Syn.* sketchy, meager, garbled; see **inadequate** 1.

incompletely, *mod.* —*Syn.* imperfectly, not entirely *or* completely, faultily; see **inadequately.**

incomprehensible, *mod.* —*Syn.* unintelligible, unclear, impenetrable; see **obscure** 1.

incompressible, *mod.* —*Syn.* dense, impenetrable, compact; see **thick** 1, 3.

inconceivable, *mod.* —*Syn.* fantastic, unimaginable, incredible; see **impossible** 1.

inconclusive, *mod.* —*Syn.* indecisive, deficient, lacking; see **faulty, inadequate** 1, **unsatisfactory.**

in condition, *mod.* —*Syn.* physically fit, prepared, trained, ready, conditioned; *all* (D): in the pink, ready to go, systems up and running, in fine fettle, primed; see also **healthy** 1, **strong** 1.

incongruity, *n.* —*Syn.* irrelevancy, inequality, anachronism; see **difference** 1, **inconsistency.**

incongruous, *mod.* **1.** [Inconsistent]—*Syn.* uncoordinated, unconnected, twisted, contradictory, incoherent, distorted, incompatible, irreconcilable, unintelligible, unrelated, divergent, irregular, unpredictable, shifting, uneven, loose, rambling, lopsided, disparate, discordant, conflicting, jumbled, fitful, unbalanced, incongruent, unanswerable, unavailing, screwy (D); see also **illogical.**—*Ant.* like, coordinated, related.
2. [Unsuitable]—*Syn.* inappropriate, incompatible, mismatched; see **unsuitable.**

in consequence of, *mod.* —*Syn.* because of, owing to, consequently; see **because.**

inconsequential, *mod.* —*Syn.* unimportant, immaterial, insignificant; see **irrelevant, trivial, unnecessary.**

inconsiderable, *mod.* —*Syn.* minute, unimportant, insignificant; see **trivial, worthless** 1.

inconsiderate, *mod.* —*Syn.* boorish, impolite, discourteous; see **rude** 2, **thoughtless** 2.

in consideration of, *mod.* —*Syn.* because of, in view of, taking into account; see **considering.**

inconsistency, *n.* —*Syn.* discrepancy, disagreement, dissimilarity, disparity, variance, contrariety, incongruity, inequality, unlikeness, divergence, deviation, inconsonance, disproportion, disproportionateness, paradox; see also **difference** 1.—*Ant.* consistency*, congruity, similarity.

inconsistent, *mod.* —*Syn.* contradictory, illogical, incoherent; see **incongruous** 1.

inconsistently, *mod.* —*Syn.* unpredictably, illogically, eccentrically; see **differently** 1.

inconsolable, *mod.* —*Syn.* heartbroken, forlorn, discouraged; see **sad** 1.

inconspicuous, *mod.* —*Syn.* concealed, indistinct, retiring; see **hidden** 2, **obscure** 1, 3, **secretive.**

inconspicuously, *mod.* —*Syn.* slyly, surreptitiously, not openly *or* noticeably; see **secretly.**

inconstant, *mod.* —*Syn.* fickle, variable, capricious; see **changeable** 1, 2.

in consultation with, *mod.* —*Syn.* advising, consulting, in co-operation with; see **helpful** 1, **practical.**

in contact with, *mod.* **1.** [Contiguous]—*Syn.* meeting, joining, connecting, coterminous, bordering, abutting, adjacent, close; see also **contiguous, near** 1.—*Ant.* distant*, out of contact, far.

2. [Communicating with]—*Syn.* in touch (with), writing (to), corresponding (with), in communication.

incontinence, *n.* —*Syn.* lust, obscenity, lechery; see **desire** 3, **lewdness.**

incontinent, *mod.* —*Syn.* lustful, carnal, shameless; see **lewd** 2, **wicked** 1.

in contrast to *or* **with,** *mod.* —*Syn.* as against, opposed to, contrasting; see **against** 3, **opposed.**

incontrovertible, *mod.* —*Syn.* established, undeniable, authentic; see **accurate** 1.

inconvenience, *n.* —*Syn.* bother difficulty, awkward detail; see **trouble** 2.

inconvenient, *mod.* —*Syn.* bothersome, awkward, badly arranged; see **disturbing.**

inconveniently, *mod.* —*Syn.* inappropriately, in an inconvenient manner, to an inconvenient degree; see **awkwardly.**

in cooperation (with), *mod.* —*Syn.* cooperating, collaborating, assisting; see **helping.**

incorporate, *v.* **1.** [To include]—*Syn.* add to, combine, fuse; see **consolidate** 2, **include** 2, **join** 1.

2. [To organize]—*Syn.* form a company, charter, start a business; see **organize** 2.

incorporated, *mod.* **1.** [Included]—*Syn.* entered, placed, fused; see **included, joined.**

2. [Organized]—*Syn.* united, consolidated, coordinated; see **organized.**

incorporation, *n.* **1.** [Inclusion]—*Syn.* embodiment, adding, fusion; see **addition** 2, **inclusion.**

2. [The act of becoming a corporate body]—*Syn.* chartering, consolidation, amalgamation, federation, establishment, confederation, affiliation, merger, unification, alliance, fraternization, unionization; see also **association** 1, **business** 4. —*Ant.* division*, dissolution, disbanding.

incorporeal, *mod.* **1.** [Insubstantial]—*Syn.* spiritual, bodiless, ethereal; see **immaterial** 2.

2. [Divine]—*Syn.* celestial, angelic, deistic; see **divine** 1, **eternal** 2.

incorrect, *mod.* —*Syn.* inaccurate, not trustworthy, false; see **mistaken** 1, **unreliable** 1, **wrong** 2.

incorrectly, *mod.* —*Syn.* mistakenly, inaccurately, clumsily; see **badly** 1, **wrongly** 1, 2.

incorrectness, *n.* —*Syn.* fault, blunder, inaccuracy; see **error** 1, **mistake** 2.

incorrigible, *mod.* —*Syn.* incurable, uncorrectable, useless; see **hopeless** 2, **irreparable.**

incorruptibility, *n.* **1.** [Persistence]—*Syn.* immortality, continuance, perpetuity; see **continuation** 1, **persistence.**

2. [Honesty]—*Syn.* integrity, honor, loyalty; see **honesty** 2, **reliability.**

incorruptible, *mod.* —*Syn.* honorable, scrupulous, just; see **accurate** 2, **honest** 1.

increase, *n.* **1.** [Growth]—*Syn.* development, spread, enlargement, expansion, escalation, elaboration, optimization, burgeoning, swelling, addition, accession, incorporation, merger, inflation, heightening, extension, dilation, multiplication, augmentation, rise, broadening, advance, intensification, deepening, swell, amplification, progression, uptick, improvement; *all* (D): boost, hike, jump, boom, appreciation; see also **progress** 1. —*Ant.* reduction*, decline, decrease.

2. [An addition]—*Syn.* increment, accession, accretion; see **addition** 2.

on the increase—*Syn.* growing, developing, spreading; see **increasing** 1.

increase, *v.* **1.** [To add to]—*Syn.* extend, enlarge, expand, dilate, broaden, widen, thicken, deepen, heighten, build, lengthen, magnify, add on, augment, escalate, let out, branch *or* open out, further, mark up, sharpen, build up, raise, enhance, amplify, reinforce, supplement, annex, distend, double, triple, stretch, multiply, intensify, exaggerate, aggravate, protract, prolong, aggrandize, redouble; *all* (D): boost, raise the ante, step up, rev up; see also **develop** 1, **improve** 1, **strengthen.**—*Ant.* decrease*, reduce, abridge.

2. [To grow]—*Syn.* rise, progress, develop; see **grow** 1.

increased, *mod.* —*Syn.* marked up, raised, heightened, elevated, added on, doubled.

increasing, *mod.* **1.** [Becoming larger]—*Syn.* developing, maturing, multiplying, broadening, widening, augmenting, waxing, sprouting, flourishing, rising, ever-widening, expanding, enlarging, accumulating, piling up, crescent, shooting up, getting big, swelling; *all* (D): on the rise, on the increase, on the upgrade, booming; see also **growing.**

2. [Becoming more intense]—*Syn.* intensifying, heightening, growing, dominant, advancing, growing louder, sharpening, accentuating, aggravating, emphasizing, accelerating, deepening.

increasingly, *mod.* —*Syn.* with (continual) acceleration, more and more, with (steady) increase *or* build-up; see **more** 1, 2.

incredible, *mod.* —*Syn.* unbelievable, improbable, ridiculous; see **impossible** 1.

incredibly, *mod.* —*Syn.* amazingly, astonishingly, uncommonly; see **especially** 1.

incredulity, *n.* —*Syn.* disbelief, skepticism, amazement; see **doubt** 1.

incredulous, *mod.* —*Syn.* skeptical, unbelieving, suspect; see **doubtful** 2, **suspicious** 1.

increment, *n.* —*Syn.* accretion, supplement, gain; see **addition** 2, **increase** 1, **profit** 2.

incriminate, *v.* —*Syn.* implicate, blame, charge; see **accuse, implicate** 2.

incriminating, *mod.* —*Syn.* inculpating, damning, damaging, convicting, condemnatory, final, accusatory.

incrust, *v.* —*Syn.* coat, enamel, plate; see **cover** 1, **paint** 2.

incubate, *v.* —*Syn.* hatch, brood, breed; see **produce** 1.

inculcate, *v.* —*Syn.* instill, implant, impress; see **instill, teach** 1.

incumbent, *mod.* —*Syn.* obligatory, binding, compelling; see **necessary** 1, **urgent** 1.

incur, *v.* —*Syn.* meet with, get, acquire; see **catch** 4, **obtain** 1.

incurable, *mod.* —*Syn.* fatal, serious, hopeless; see **deadly.**

incurious, *mod.* —*Syn.* apathetic, uninterested, tedious; see **dull** 3, **indifferent** 1.
incursion, *n.* —*Syn.* intrusion, aggression, invasion; see **attack** 1.
in danger, *mod.* —*Syn.* imperiled, threatened, in jeopardy; see **endangered.**
indebted, *mod.* —*Syn.* obligated, in debt, beholden, bounden, obliged, under obligation, owing, grateful, appreciative, liable, answerable for, chargeable, accountable, bound; see also **responsible** 1, **thankful.**
indebtedness, *n.* —*Syn.* deficit, responsibility, obligation; see **debit, debt** 1.
indecency, *n.* **1.** [The quality of being indecent] —*Syn.* coarseness, grossness, vulgarity; see **lewdness.**
2. [An instance of indecency]—*Syn.* impurity, immodesty, offense, incivility, impropriety, ribaldry, indelicacy, obscenity, raciness, four-letter word, lewdness, drunkenness, quadriliteral, foulness, gluttony, scandalmongering; see also **evil** 1.—*Ant.* chastity*, purity, delicacy.
indecent, *mod.* —*Syn.* immoral, shocking, shameless; see **lewd** 1, 2, **shameful** 1, **wicked** 1.
indecipherable, *mod.* —*Syn.* mysterious, unreadable, vague; see **illegible, obscure** 1.
indecision, *n.* —*Syn.* hesitation, question, irresolution; see **doubt** 2, **uncertainty** 2.
indecisive, *mod.* —*Syn.* irresolute, unstable, wishy-washy (D); see **changeable** 1, **doubtful** 2.
indecorous, *mod.* —*Syn.* coarse, vulgar, uncouth; see **rude** 1, 2.
indecorum, *n.* —*Syn.* vulgarity, indiscretion, impropriety; see **rudeness.**
indeed, *mod.* **1.** [Surely]—*Syn.* naturally, of course, certainly; see **really** 1, **surely.**
2. [Really]—*Syn.* For sure? Honestly? So?; see **really** 3.
indefatigable, *mod.* —*Syn.* inexhaustible, unwearied, tireless; see **active** 2, **tireless.**
indefensible, *mod.* **1.** [Submissive]—*Syn.* yielding, vincible, defenseless; see **weak** 1, 3, 6.
2. [Inexcusable]—*Syn.* bad, inexpiable, unpardonable; see **unforgivable.**
indefinite, *mod.* **1.** [Vague]—*Syn.* unsure, unsettled, loose; see **uncertain** 2, **vague** 2.
2. [Unlimited]—*Syn.* interminable, inexhaustible, innumerable; see **infinite** 1, **unlimited.**
indefinitely, *mod.* **1.** [Vaguely]—*Syn.* loosely, unclearly, ambiguously, indistinctly, incoherently, obscurely, indecisively, incompletely, lightly, briefly, momentarily, equivocally, inexactly, amorphously, generally, irresolutely, undecidedly; see also **vaguely.**—*Ant.* positively*, clearly, exactly.
2. [Without stated limit]—*Syn.* endlessly, continually, considerably; see **frequently, regularly** 2.
indelible, *mod.* —*Syn.* ingrained, enduring, strong; see **permanent** 2.
indelicacy, *n.* —*Syn.* impertinence, immodesty, impropriety; see **rudeness.**
indelicate, *mod.* —*Syn.* indecent, brash, improper; see **rude** 2.
in demand, *mod.* —*Syn.* desired, requisite, on the market; see **wanted.**
indemnify, *v.* **1.** [To repay]—*Syn.* return, remit, reimburse; see **pay** 1, **repay** 1.
2. [To answer for]—*Syn.* register, assure, insure; see **guarantee** 1, 2.
indemnity, *n.* —*Syn.* reimbursement, reward, restitution; see **compensation, pay** 2, **payment** 1, **return** 3.
indent, *v.* —*Syn.* make a margin, range, space inward; see **order** 3, **paragraph.**
indentation, *n.* **1.** [Gouge]—*Syn.* imprint, recession, depression; see **dent.**
2. [Division]—*Syn.* arrangement, topic, section; see **paragraph.**
indented, *mod.* —*Syn.* depressed, sectioned, paragraphed; see **organized.**
indenture, *n.* —*Syn.* agreement, compact, arrangement; see **contract** 1.
indentured, *mod.* —*Syn.* obligated, contracted, enslaved; see **bound** 1, 2.
independence, *n.* **1.** [Liberty]—*Syn.* sovereignty, autonomy, license; see **freedom** 1, 2.
2. [Competence]—*Syn.* qualification, aptitude, skill; see **ability** 1, 2.
independent, *mod.* **1.** [Free]—*Syn.* self-ruling, autonomous, unregimented; see **free** 1.
2. [Competent]—*Syn.* capable, fit, qualified; see **able** 1, 2.
independently, *mod.* —*Syn.* alone, unrestrictedly, autonomously, without support, separately, exclusive of, without regard to, of one's own volition, by oneself; *both* (D): on one's own, all by one's lonesome; see also **freely** 2, **individually.**
indescribable, *mod.* —*Syn.* indefinable, nondescript, incredible; see **impossible** 1.
indestructible, *mod.* —*Syn.* durable, unchangeable, immortal; see **permanent** 2.
in detail, *mod.* —*Syn.* minutely, item by item, part by part, step by step, inch by inch, systematically, circumstantially, intimately; see also **specifically** 2. —*Ant.* vaguely*, generally, indefinitely.
indeterminate, *mod.* —*Syn.* vague, general, indefinite; see **uncertain** 2.
index, *n.* **1.** [An indicator]—*Syn.* pointer, token, basis for judgment, formula, ratio, rule, average (rate *or* price), symbol, indicant, guide; see also **model** 2.
2. [An alphabetic arrangement]—*Syn.* tabular matter, book index, guide to publications, bibliography, bibliographical work, card file, book list, appendix, end list, directory, dictionary; see also **catalog** 1, **file** 2, **list, record** 1, **table** 2.
index, *v.* —*Syn.* alphabetize, arrange, tabulate; see **file** 1, **list** 1, **record** 1.
indexed, *mod.* —*Syn.* alphabetized, tabulated, filed; see **recorded.**
India, *n.* —*Syn.* The Indian Empire, Hither India, Farther India, Southern Asia, The Orient, The East, The Fabulous East, Country of the Indus, British India, Land of the Gold of Ophir, the brightest jewel in the British Crown, Crown Jewel, Mother India, Hindustan; see also **Asia.**
India ink, *n.* —*Syn.* drawing ink, black pigment, tusche; see **ink.**
Indian, *mod.* —*Syn.* native American, West Indian, Antillean, aboriginal American, primitive American, pre-Columbian, Amerindian, prehistoric American.

Indian, *n.* **1.** [American native]—*Syn.* Native American, Homo Americanus, American aborigine, American Indian, Amerindian, red man (D). Terms for Indian groups having had historical or social importance include the following—*United States and Canada: Arctic Indians:* Inuit, Eskimo, Aleut, Sitka; *eastern* or *Woods Indians:* Iroquois *or* Six Nations, Mohawk, Oneida, Seneca, Onandaga, Cayuga, Ottowa, Huron *or* Wyandot, Algonkin, Pequod, Micmac, Narragansett, Mohican, Delaware, Penobscot, Conestoga, Tuscarora, Ojibway *or* Chippewa, Menominee, Sauk, Fox, Pottawattamie, Seminole, Cherokee, Choctaw, Chicasaw, Creek *or* Muskogee, Natchez, Biloxi, Winnebago; *Plains Indians:* Sioux, Missouri, Oglala, Mandan, Iowa, Omaha, Comanche, Dakota, Crow, Kaw, Osage, Ponca, Apache, Kiowa, Arapahoe, Cheyenne, Pawnee, Caddo; *Great Basin Indians:* Blackfoot, Ute, Paiute, Shoshone, Bannock, Modoc, Digger, Pueblo, Hopi, Navaho, Pima, Moqui, Papago, Zuni, Folsom; *west coast Indians:* Athabascan, Salish, Costanoa, Chinook, Coos, Nez Percé, Maidu, Tlingit, Flathead, Pend d'Oreille, Coeur d'Alene, Kwakiutl, Bella Coola, Thompson, Miwok, Yuma, Klamath, Shasta, Luiseño, Pomo, Nutka, Haida; *Mexico and Central America:* Maya, Aztec, Toltec, Mixtec, Nahuat, Nahuatl, Pepil, Tabasco, Zacateca, Huasteco, Serrano, Seri, Macateco, Quiche; *South America:* Inca, Quechua, Carib, Aymara, Otuke, Chiquito, Fuega, Patagonia, Tupi, Arawak, Calchaquia, Tocomona, Charrua, Mataguaya, Chango; for terms arranged by language; see **language** 2.
2. [A native of India]—*Syn.* Asian, Hindu, Muslim, Brahmin, Kshatriya, Shudra.

India rubber, *n.* —*Syn.* fiber, latex, elastic; see **rubber.**

indicate, *v.* **1.** [To signify]—*Syn.* symbolize, betoken, intimate; see **mean** 1.
2. [To designate]—*Syn.* show, point out *or* to, register; see **designate** 1.

indicated, *mod.* —*Syn.* pointed out, delegated, determined; see **marked** 2.

indication, *n.* —*Syn.* evidence, sign, implication; see **hint** 1, **suggestion** 1.

indicative, *mod.* —*Syn.* characteristic, significatory, connotative; see **suggestive, symbolic.**

indicator, *n.* —*Syn.* notice, pointer, symbol; see **sign** 1.

indict, *v.* —*Syn.* charge, face with charges, arraign; see **accuse, censure.**

indictable, *mod.* **1.** [Guilty]—*Syn.* chargeable, blamable, accountable; see **guilty** 2.
2. [Indefensible]—*Syn.* criminal, illicit, felonious; see **illegal.**

indictment, *n.* **1.** [The act of indicting]—*Syn.* detention, censure, incrimination; see **blame** 1.
2. [A legal document]—*Syn.* bill, true bill, summons, statement, citation, replevin; see also **warrant, writ.**
3. [An accusation supported by evidence]—*Syn.* charge, presentment, findings; see **accusation** 2.

indifference, *n.* **1.** [Apathy]—*Syn.* unconcern, nonchalance, aloofness, impassiveness, impassivity, impassibility, coldness, insensitivity, callousness, alienation, disregard, disinterest, insouciance, noninterference, inertia, neutrality, isolationism, insusceptibility, immunity, phlegm, heedlessness, detachment, dullness, sluggishness, torpor, stupor, cold-bloodedness, disdain, stoicism, cool (D).
2. [Insignificance]—*Syn.* unimportance, worthlessness, triviality; see **insignificance.**

indifferent, *mod.* **1.** [Lacking interest]—*Syn.* unaroused, listless, cold, cool, lighthearted, unemotional, unsympathetic, passionless, heartless, unresponsive, lymphatic, unfeeling, uncommunicative, nonchalant, impassive, detached, callous, uninterested, supine, stony, reticent, remote, reserved, distant, unsocial, diffident, scornful, supercilious, blasé, phlegmatic, stoical, stolid, unimpressed, apathetic, heedless, unmoved, not inclined toward, neutral, uncaring, aloof, silent, disdainful, haughty, superior, condescending, snobbish, arrogant, not caring (about); *all* (D): offish, highbrow, lukewarm, snooty; see also **unconcerned.**—*Ant.* excited*, aroused, warm.
2. [Ordinary]—*Syn.* usual, temperate, average; see **common** 1, **conventional** 1, 3, **dull** 4, **fair** 2.

indifferently, *mod.* **1.** [Rather badly]—*Syn.* poorly, not (very) well (done), in a mediocre *or* ordinary *or* routine manner; see **badly** 1, **inadequately.**
2. [In an indifferent manner]—*Syn.* nonchalantly, coolly, detached; see **calmly, casually** 2.

indigence, *n.* —*Syn.* want, need, destitution; see **poverty** 1.

indigenous, *mod.* **1.** [Native]—*Syn.* domestic, primitive, original; see **native** 2.
2. [Inborn]—*Syn.* natural, congenital, innate; see **inherent.**

indigent, *mod.* —*Syn.* penniless, destitute, poverty-stricken; see **poor** 1.

indigestible, *mod.* —*Syn.* inedible, rough, hard, unripe, green, unpalatable, tasteless, unhealthy, undercooked, raw, poisonous, toxic, moldy, bad-smelling, malodorous, rotten, putrid, uneatable, unprepared; *both* (D): icky, hard on the stomach; see also **unwholesome.**—*Ant.* appetizing*, tasty, delicious.

indigestion, *n.* —*Syn.* dyspepsia, bad *or* upset *or* gaseous stomach, gas, heartburn, nausea, acid indigestion, acidosis; see also **illness** 1, **pain** 2.

indignant, *mod.* —*Syn.* upset, displeased, piqued; see **angry.**

indignation, *n.* —*Syn.* pique, wrath, ire; see **anger.**

indignity, *n.* —*Syn.* discourtesy, affront, outrage; see **insult.**

indirect, *mod.* —*Syn.* roundabout, out-of-the-way, tortuous, twisting, long, complicated, devious, aberrant, erratic, sidelong, zigzag, crooked, backhanded, obscure, circuitous, sinister, discursive, rambling, long-winded, secondary, subsidiary, auxiliary, implied, oblique.—*Ant.* direct*, straight, immediate.

indirectly, *mod.* —*Syn.* by implication *or* indirection, in a roundabout way, from a secondary source, secondhand, not immediately, diffusely, circumlocutorily, periphrastically, discursively, obliquely, lengthily.—*Ant.* immediately*, directly, primarily.

indiscernible, *mod.* —*Syn.* imperceptible, indistinct, vague; see **obscure** 1.

indiscreet, *mod.* —*Syn.* naïve, inopportune, misguided; see **rash, tactless.**

indiscreetly, *mod.* —*Syn.* incautiously, inadvisedly, naïvely; see **foolishly, rashly.**

indiscretion, *n.* **1.** [The quality of lacking prudence and judgment]—*Syn.* recklessness, imprudence, heedlessness, indiscreetness, bullheadedness, excitability, tactlessness, rashness, crudeness, misjudgment, thoughtlessness, unseemliness, hotheadedness, foolishness, stupidity, naïveté, ingenuousness, simple-mindedness; see also **carelessness.** —*Ant.* prudence*, caution, thoughtfulness.
2. [An example of indiscretion]—*Syn.* blunder, slip, fault; see **error** 1.

indiscriminate, *mod.* —*Syn.* random, confused, chaotic; see **aimless.**

indispensable, *mod.* —*Syn.* required, needed, essential; see **necessary** 1.

indispose, *v.* **1.** [To disqualify]—*Syn.* disallow, disable, incapacitate; see **bar** 2.
2. [To discourage]—*Syn.* dissuade, dishearten, convince; see **depress** 2, **discourage** 1.

indisposed, *mod.* **1.** [Sick]—*Syn.* ill, ailing, infirm; see **sick.**
2. [Unwilling]—*Syn.* hesitant, hostile, uncaring; see **reluctant, unwilling.**

indisposition, *n.* **1.** [Illness]—*Syn.* ailment, sickness, fever; see **illness** 1.
2. [Aversion]—*Syn.* hesitancy, dislike, unwillingness; see **hate, hatred** 1, **malice, resentment** 2.

indisputable, *mod.* —*Syn.* undeniable, undoubted, unquestionable; see **accurate** 1, **certain** 3.

indissoluble, *mod.* **1.** [Stable]—*Syn.* infusible, lasting, firm, insoluble, infragible, irrefragable; see also **constant** 1, **firm** 1, **whole** 1.
2. [Binding]—*Syn.* durable, unchangeable, enduring; see **permanent** 2, **perpetual** 1, **regular** 3.

indistinct, *mod.* —*Syn.* vague, confused, indefinite; see **obscure** 1.

indistinguishable, *mod.* **1.** [Identical]—*Syn.* like, same, equivalent; see **alike** 1, **equal.**
2. [Indistinct]—*Syn.* vague, invisible, dull; see **obscure** 1, **uncertain** 2.

individual, *mod.* **1.** [Separate]—*Syn.* specific, personal, proper, own, particular, singular, especial, definite, lone, alone, solitary, secluded, original, distinct, distinctive, personalized, individualized, exclusive, select, single, only, indivisible, reserved, separate, sole; see also **private, special** 1.—*Ant.* collective*, public, social.
2. [Unusual]—*Syn.* uncommon, singular, peculiar; see **different** 1, 2, **unique** 1, **unusual** 2.

individual, *n.* —*Syn.* human being, self, somebody; see **child, man** 3, **person** 1, **woman** 1.

individuality, *n.* **1.** [The quality of being individual] —*Syn.* peculiarity, distinctiveness, particularity, separateness, dissimilarity, singularity, idiosyncrasy, air, manner, habit, eccentricity, oddity, rarity, way of doing things; see also **difference** 1, **originality.**
2. [Character]—*Syn.* personality, uniqueness, selfhood; see **attitude** 3, **behavior** 1, **character** 2.

individually, *mod.* —*Syn.* separately, severally, one by one, one at a time, personally, restrictedly, exclusively, singly, by oneself, alone, independently, without help, distinctively, apart; see also **only** 1.—*Ant.* together*, collectively, co-operatively.

indivisible, *mod.* —*Syn.* indissoluble, unified, impenetrable; see **inseparable** 1, **permanent** 2, **unbreakable.**

indoctrinate, *v.* —*Syn.* inculcate, imbue, implant; see **convince, influence, teach** 1, 2, **train** 4.

indoctrinated, *mod.* —*Syn.* convinced, perverted, brainwashed; see **educated** 1, **persuaded, trained.**

indoctrination, *n.* —*Syn.* propagandism, instruction, brainwashing; see **education** 1, **persuasion** 1, **training.**

indolence, *n.* —*Syn.* sloth, disinclination, procrastination; see **idleness** 1, **laziness.**

indolent, *mod.* —*Syn.* slow, resting, sluggish; see **idle** 1, **lazy** 1, **listless** 1.

indomitable, *mod.* —*Syn.* unyielding, willful, stubborn; see **obstinate** 1, **ruthless** 1.

indoors, *mod.* —*Syn.* in the house, at home, under a roof; see **inside** 2, **within.**

indorse, *v.* —*Syn.* sign, support, underwrite; see **endorse** 1, 2.

in doubt, *mod.* —*Syn.* unsure, dubious, perplexed; see **doubtful** 2, **questionable** 1, **uncertain** 2.

induce, *v.* **1.** [To prevail on]—*Syn.* persuade, convince, wheedle; see **influence, urge** 2.
2. [To cause]—*Syn.* produce, effect, make; see **begin** 1.

induced, *mod.* **1.** [Persuaded]—*Syn.* convinced, cajoled, lured; see **persuaded.**
2. [Brought about]—*Syn.* effected, achieved, caused; see **finished** 1.
3. [Inferred]—*Syn.* thought, concluded, reasoned, rationalized, ratiocinated, explained, argued, debated, discussed, analyzed, posited, postulated, hypothesized; see also **assumed** 1, **considered** 1, **determined** 1.

inducement, *n.* —*Syn.* bait, lure, stimulus; see **desire** 1, **incentive, temptation.**

induct, *v.* —*Syn.* conscript, initiate, draft; see **enlist** 1, **recruit** 1.

inducted, *mod.* —*Syn.* conscripted, called up, drafted; see **initiated** 3.

induction, *n.* **1.** [Logical reasoning]—*Syn.* inference, rationalization, generalization, conclusion, ratiocination, judgment, conjecture; see also **reason** 2.
2. [The process of electrical attraction]—*Syn.* electric induction, magnetic induction, electromagnetic action, electrostatic induction; see also **electricity** 2.
3. [The process of being initiated]—*Syn.* initiation, introduction, ordination, consecration, instatement, investiture, conscription, entrance into service; see also **draft** 6, **installation** 1, **selection** 1.

in due time, *mod.* —*Syn.* eventually, at an appropriate time, in the natural course of events; see **finally** 2, **ultimately.**

indulge, *v.* **1.** [To humor]—*Syn.* tickle, nourish, coddle; see **entertain** 1, **humor.**
2. [To tolerate]—*Syn.* bear, allow to pass, oblige; see **endure** 2.
3. [To take part in]—*Syn.* go in for, revel, give way to; see **join** 2.

indulgence, *n.* **1.** [Humoring]—*Syn.* coddling, pampering, petting, overweening attention, fondling, babying, spoiling, placating, pleasing, toadying, favoring, kowtowing, gratifying.

2. [Forbearance]—*Syn.* allowance, lenience, toleration; see **endurance** 2, **patience** 1, **tolerance** 1.
3. [Revelry]—*Syn.* prodigality, dissipation, intemperance, drunkenness, overindulgence, luxury, waste, self-indulgence, hedonism; see also **greed, waste** 1.

indulgent, *mod.*—*Syn.* fond, considerate, tolerant; see **kind, lenient.**

industrial, *mod.*—*Syn.* manufacturing, manufactured, mechanized, automated, industrialized, factory-made, machine-made, modern, streamlined, in industry, technical, metropolitan; see also **mechanical** 1.—*Ant.* handmade*, domestic, handcrafted.

industrialist, *n.*—*Syn.* tycoon, owner, manager; see **businessman, financier.**

industrious, *mod.*—*Syn.* intent, involved, diligent; see **active** 2, **busy** 1.

industriously, *mod.*—*Syn.* diligently, steadily, laboriously, energetically, actively, busily; see also **carefully** 1, **vigorously.**

industry, *n.* **1.** [Attention to work]—*Syn.* activity, assiduity, persistence, application, applicability, patience, intentness, perseverance, enterprise, hard work, zeal, energy, dynamism, pains, inventiveness; see also **attention** 2, **care** 1, **diligence.**—*Ant.* laziness*, lethargy, idleness.
2. [An industrial organization]—*Syn.* trade, monopoly, manufactory; see **business** 4.
3. [Business as a division of society]—*Syn.* big business, management, corporation officers, monopolists, shareholders, high finance, entrepreneurs, capital, private enterprise, monied interests, stockholders.

inebriate, *v.*—*Syn.* exhilarate, stimulate, make drunk; see **intoxicate** 1.

inebriated, *mod.*—*Syn.* intoxicated; *both* (D): tipsy, plastered; see **drunk.**

inebriety, *n.*—*Syn.* alcoholism, intoxication, insobriety; see **drunkenness.**

ineffable, *mod.*—*Syn.* incredible, unspeakable, indescribable; see **impossible** 1.

ineffaceable, *mod.*—*Syn.* ingrained, ineradicable, indelible; see **permanent** 2.

in effect, *mod.*—*Syn.* in reality, in fact, absolutely; see **really** 1.

ineffective, *mod.*—*Syn.* not effective, worthless, neutralized; see **incompetent, weak** 1, 2.

ineffectively, *mod.*—*Syn.* inefficiently, poorly, crudely; see **badly** 1, **inadequately.**

ineffectual, *mod.*—*Syn.* impotent, unable (to), useless; see **incompetent, weak** 1, 2.

inefficiency, *n.*—*Syn.* incompetence, incapability, incapacity; see **failure** 1, **inability** 1, **weakness** 1, 2.

inefficient, *mod.* **1.** [Wasteful]—*Syn.* extravagant, prodigal, improvident; see **wasteful.**
2. [Lacking competence]—*Syn.* incapable, faulty, unfit; see **incompetent.**

inefficiently, *mod.*—*Syn.* poorly, ineffectively, crudely; see **badly** 1, **inadequately.**

inelastic, *mod.*—*Syn.* rigid, unyielding, stable; see **stiff** 1.

inelegant, *mod.*—*Syn.* coarse, crude, vulgar; see **rude** 2.

ineligible, *mod.*—*Syn.* inappropriate, unavailable, unsuitable; see **incompetent, unfit** 1.

ineluctable, *mod.*—*Syn.* certain, inevitable, unavoidable; see **inevitable.**

inept, *mod.* **1.** [Unsuitable]—*Syn.* not adapted, inappropriate, out of place; see **unfit** 2, **unsuitable.**
2. [Awkward]—*Syn.* clumsy, gauche, ungraceful; see **awkward** 1.

ineptitude, *n.*—*Syn.* incapacity, clumsiness, ungracefulness; see **awkwardness** 1, **inability** 1.

inequality, *n.*—*Syn.* disparity, dissimilarity, irregularity; see **contrast** 1, **difference** 1, **variation.**

inequitable, *mod.*—*Syn.* unjust, biased, foul; see **unfair** 1.

in error, *mod.*—*Syn.* mistaken(ly), inaccurate(ly), by mistake; see **badly** 1, **wrong** 2, **wrongly** 1.

inert, *mod.*—*Syn.* still, dormant, inactive; see **idle** 1.

inertia, *n.*—*Syn.* passivity, indolence, inactivity; see **laziness.**

in escrow, *mod.*—*Syn.* held, bonded, deposited; see **in trust, retained** 1.

in essence, *mod.*—*Syn.* ultimately, fundamentally, basically; see **essentially.**

inestimable, *mod.*—*Syn.* priceless, exquisite, precious; see **valuable** 1.

inevitable, *mod.*—*Syn.* fated, sure, unavoidable, impending, inescapable, necessary, ineluctable, unpreventable, irresistible, prescribed, destined, assured, ineludible, compulsory, obligatory, binding, irrevocable, inexorable, without fail, undeniable, fateful, doomed, determined, decreed, fixed, ordained, foreordained, decided, unalterable; *all* (D): sure as shooting, sure as blazes, as sure as your name is . . . , in the cards, come rain or shine; see also **certain** 3, **imminent.**—*Ant.* doubtful*, contingent, indeterminate.

inevitably, *mod.*—*Syn.* unavoidably, inescapably, surely; see **necessarily.**

inexact, *mod.*—*Syn.* inaccurate, ambiguous, unsubstantial; see **obscure** 1, **vague** 2, **wrong** 2.

inexcusable, *mod.*—*Syn.* unpardonable, reprehensible, indefensible; see **unforgivable, wrong** 1.

inexcusably, *mod.*—*Syn.* unforgivably, unpardonably, crudely; see **badly** 1, **wrongly** 1.

inexhaustible, *mod.* **1.** [Tireless]—*Syn.* never-ending, indefatigable, unwearied, unflagging, unsleeping; see **active** 2, **tireless.**
2. [Unlimited]—*Syn.* limitless, unbounded, boundless; see **endless** 1, **infinite** 1, **unlimited, vast** 2.

inexorable, *mod.* **1.** [Obstinate]—*Syn.* unyielding, stubborn, obdurate; see **obstinate** 1.
2. [Necessary]—*Syn.* relentless, compulsory, unalterable; see **necessary** 1.

inexorably, *mod.*—*Syn.* relentlessly, irresistibly, inevitably; see **necessarily.**

inexpedient, *mod.*—*Syn.* extravagant, unwise, inept; see **careless** 1, **rash, wasteful.**

inexpensive, *mod.*—*Syn.* thrifty, low-priced, modest; see **cheap** 1, **economical** 2.

inexpensively, *mod.*—*Syn.* economically, advantageously, luckily; see **cheaply.**

inexperience, *n.*—*Syn.* naïveté, ignorance, incompetence; see **inability** 1.

inexperienced, *mod.*—*Syn.* unused, unaccustomed, unhabituated, unadapted, unskilled, common, ordinary, unlicensed, untried, youthful, beardless, chaste, virgin, undeveloped, naïve, amateur, untrained, untutored, unschooled, inefficient, fresh, unversed, ignorant, innocent, uninformed, callow, unacquainted, undisciplined, new, immature, unripe, tender, unseasoned; *all* (D): not dry behind the ears, tenderfoot, soft, raw, green; see also **incompetent, young** 2.—*Ant.* experienced*, seasoned, hardened.

inexpert, *mod.*—*Syn.* incompetent, unskillful, inept; see **awkward** 1, **inexperienced.**

inexplicable, *mod.*—*Syn.* unexplainable, incomprehensible, puzzling; see **obscure** 1

inexpressible, *mod.*—*Syn.* unspeakable, indefinable, indescribable; see **impossible** 1.

inexpressive, *mod.*—*Syn.* vacant, impassive, expressionless; see **dull** 3.

inextinguishable, *mod.*—*Syn.* irrepressible, insatiable, unquenchable, eternal, ever-burning, indestructible, irreducible, imperishable, undying, fiery, rampant; see also **active** 2, **violent** 2.

in extremis (Latin), *mod.*—*Syn.* moribund, at one's end, on one's deathbed; see **dying** 1, **weak** 1.

inextricable, *mod.*—*Syn.* complicated, involved, intricate; see **complex** 1.

inextricably, *mod.*—*Syn.* totally, indistinguishably, inevitably; see **completely.**

in fact, *mod.*—*Syn.* certainly, in truth, truly; see **really** 1.

infallibility, *n.* **1.** [Reliability]—*Syn.* dependability, faithfulness, safety; see **reliability.**
2. [Perfection]—*Syn.* supremacy, impeccability, consummation; see **perfection** 3.

infallible, *mod.*—*Syn.* unerring, exact, perfect, unfailing, sure, reliable, dependable, trustworthy, unquestionable, true, authoritative, positive, irrefutable, apodictic, incontrovertible; *both* (D): sure-fire, double-sure; see also **accurate** 1, 2, **certain** 3. —*Ant.* false*, fallacious, erroneous.

infamous, *mod.* **1.** [Bad]—*Syn.* base, foul, vile; see **wicked** 1.
2. [Scandalous]—*Syn.* shocking, disgraceful, heinous; see **offensive** 2, **shameful** 2.

infamy, *n.* **1.** [Scandal]—*Syn.* notoriety, disapprobation, ignominy; see **disgrace** 1, **scandal, shame** 2.
2. [An infamous act]—*Syn.* impropriety, wickedness, immorality; see **evil** 2.

infancy, *n.* **1.** [The time of life's beginning]—*Syn.* cradle, babyhood, early childhood; see **childhood.**
2. [Any period of beginning]—*Syn.* outset, start, opening; see **origin** 1.

infant, *n.*—*Syn.* small child, tot, little one; see **baby** 1, **child.**

infanticide, *n.*—*Syn.* child-murder, puericide, abortion; see **murder.**

infantile, *mod.*—*Syn.* babyish, childlike, juvenile; see **childish** 1, **naïve.**

infantry, *n.*—*Syn.* foot soldiers, infantrymen, rifles, riflemen, dogfaces (D), combat troops, shock troops; see also **army, soldier.**
Infantrymen include the following—hoplite, arquebusier, crossbowman, pikeman, spearman, longbowman, archer, arbalester, *soldad* (Spanish), *fantassin* (French), swordsman, fusilier, skirmisher, scout, grenadier, *sepoy* (Hindu), Zouave, uhlan, sniper-scout, intelligence and reconnaissance (I&R), sharpshooter, air-borne infantry, paratrooper.

in fashion, *mod.*—*Syn.* stylish, modish, à la mode; see **fashionable, popular** 1.

infatuate, *v.*—*Syn.* beguile, captivate, charm; see **charm** 1, **fascinate.**

infatuated, *mod.*—*Syn.* spellbound, intoxicated, bewitched, inflamed, seduced, beguiled; see also **charmed, fascinated.**

infatuation, *n.*—*Syn.* absorption, fascination, crush (D); see **attraction** 1, **enthusiasm** 1.

in favor, *mod.*—*Syn.* favored, feted, honored; see **approved, popular** 1.

in favor of, *mod.*—*Syn.* approving, supporting, encouraging; see **enthusiastic.**

infect, *v.*—*Syn.* defile, taint, spoil; see **poison.**

infection, *n.* **1.** [The spread of a disease]—*Syn.* corruption, contagiousness, contagion, communicability, epidemic; see also **contamination, pollution.**
2. [Disease]—*Syn.* virus, impurity, germs; see **disease** 1, 2, **germ** 3.

infectious, *mod.*—*Syn.* transferable, diseased, communicable; see **catching, contagious, dangerous** 2.

infelicitous, *mod.*—*Syn.* inappropriate, unfavorable, awkward; see **uncomfortable** 1, **unfriendly** 2.

infer, *v.* **1.** [To conclude]—*Syn.* deduce, gather, come *or* reach the conclusion that, draw the inference that, induce, conjecture, arrive at, reason, construe, understand, reckon, read between the lines, mean to say; see also **assume** 1, **reason** 2, **understand** 1.
2. [To assume]—*Syn.* suppose, presume, presuppose; see **assume** 1, **understand** 2.
3. [To imply]—*Syn.* insinuate, suggest, indicate; see **hint** 1.

inference, *n.* **1.** [A judgment]—*Syn.* deduction, conclusion, answer; see **judgment** 3, **result.**
2. [A concluding]—*Syn.* reasoning, inferring, deducing; see **thought** 1.
3. [A supposition]—*Syn.* presumption, conjecture, surmise; see **assumption** 1, **opinion** 1.

inferential, *mod.*—*Syn.* probable, presumed, to be inferred *or* expected; see **likely** 1.

inferior, *mod.* **1.** [Low in rank]—*Syn.* secondary, minor, junior; see **subordinate, under** 2.
2. [Low in quality]—*Syn.* mediocre, common, second-rate; see **poor** 2.

inferiority, *n.*—*Syn.* deficiency, mediocrity, inadequacy; see **failure** 1, **inability** 1, **weakness** 1, 2.

infernal, *mod.* **1.** [Pertaining to hell]—*Syn.* underworld, nether, Stygian, subterranean, chthonian, Hadean, Tartarean, Plutonian.—*Ant.* ethereal*, divine, supernal.
2. [Hellish]—*Syn.* damned, devilish, diabolical; see **wicked** 1, 2.

infernally, *mod.*—*Syn.* hellishly, unbelievably, horribly; see **badly** 1.

infertility, *n.*—*Syn.* unproductiveness, impotence, sterility; see **barrenness.**

infest, *v.* **1.** [To contaminate]—*Syn.* pollute, infect, defile; see **corrupt** 1, **dirty.**
2. [To swarm]—*Syn.* overrun, swarm about, crowd, press, harass, beset, jam, pack, teem, abound, overwhelm, assail, fill, flood, throng, flock, be thick as flies (D); see also **swarm.**

infested, *mod.* **1.** [Overrun]—*Syn.* beset, crowded, overwhelmed; see **full** 1, **jammed** 2.

2. [Diseased]—*Syn.* ravaged, wormy, lousy, pediculous, pedicular, ratty, grubby; see also **sick.**

infidel, *n.* —*Syn.* nonbeliever, agnostic, atheist; see **cynic, skeptic.**

infidelity, *n.* **1.** [Lack of belief]—*Syn.* incredulity, impiety, skepticism; see **doubt** 1, **uncertainty** 1.
2. [Disloyalty]—*Syn.* treachery, adultery, betrayal; see **disloyalty, fornication, lewdness.**

infield, *n.* —*Syn.* diamond, right infield, center infield, left infield, short field; *both* (D): pasture, inner works; see also **field** 2.

infielder, *n.* —*Syn.* first baseman *or* first sacker (D) *or* first (D), second baseman *or* second (D) *or* keystone man (D), third baseman *or* third (D) *or* hot-corner man (D), shortstop *or* shortfielder (D).

infiltrate, *n.* —*Syn.* permeate, pervade, penetrate; see **filter** 1, **join** 2.

infinite, *mod.* **1.** [Unlimited]—*Syn.* unbounded, boundless, illimitable, unconfined, countless, incalculable, interminable, measureless, untold, inexhaustible, bottomless, unfathomable, without number *or* end *or* limit, limitless, tremendous, immense, having no limit *or* end, never-ending, immeasurable; see also **endless** 1, **unlimited.** —*Ant.* limited, bounded*, restricted.
2. [Endless]—*Syn.* without end, unending, incessant; see **constant** 1, **eternal** 2, **perpetual** 2.
3. [Absolute]—*Syn.* supreme, perpetual, enduring; see **absolute** 1, **immortal** 1.

infinite, *n.* —*Syn.* boundlessness, infinity, the unknown; see **eternity** 1, **space** 1.

infinitely, *mod.* —*Syn.* extremely, very much, unbelievably; see **very.**

infinitesimal, *mod.* —*Syn.* tiny, microscopic, miniature; see **little** 1, **minute** 1.

infinitesimally, *mod.* —*Syn.* imperceptibly, barely, minutely; see **hardly.**

infinitude, *n.* —*Syn.* endlessness, vastness, boundlessness; see **extent, immensity.**

infinity, *n.* —*Syn.* boundlessness, endlessness, the beyond, infinitude, limitlessness, expanse, extent, continuum, eternity, continuity, infinite space, ubiquity; see also **space** 1.

infirm, *mod.* **1.** [Sick]—*Syn.* decrepit, ill, anemic; see **sick.**
2. [Weak]—*Syn.* delicate, faint, decrepit; see **feeble** 1, **weak** 1.

infirmary, *n.* —*Syn.* clinic, sickroom, sick bay; see **hospital.**

infirmity, *n.* **1.** [Weakness]—*Syn.* frailty, deficiency, debility; see **weakness** 1.
2. [Illness]—*Syn.* sickness, ailing, confinement; see **illness** 1.

inflame, *v.* **1.** [To irritate]—*Syn.* vex, annoy, madden; see **anger, bother** 2.
2. [To arouse emotions]—*Syn.* incense, aggravate, disturb; see **excite** 1.
3. [To cause physical soreness]—*Syn.* congest, redden, chafe, erupt, break into a rash, infect, swell, raise the temperature; see also **hurt** 4, **irritate** 2.
4. [To burn]—*Syn.* kindle, set on fire, scorch; see **burn** 2, **ignite.**

inflamed, *mod.* **1.** [Stirred to anger]—*Syn.* aroused, incited, angered; see **angry.**
2. [Congested]—*Syn.* sore, fevered, chafed, irritated, festered, festering, infected, raw, blistered, burnt, scalded, swollen, bloodshot, red, septic; see also **hurt, painful** 1, **sore.**

inflammability, *n.* —*Syn.* flammability, ignitability, combustibility; see also **danger** 1.

inflammable, *mod.* —*Syn.* combustible, ignitable, burnable, liable to burn, risky, hazardous, dangerous, unsafe, flammable.—*Ant.* safe*, fireproof, nonflammable.

inflammation, *n.* —*Syn.* congestion, soreness, infection; see **pain** 2, **sore.**

inflammatory, *mod.* —*Syn.* incendiary, riotous, insurgent; see **rebellious** 2.

inflate, *v.* **1.** [To fill with air or gas]—*Syn.* blow *or* pump *or* puff out *or* up, expand, swell; see **fill** 1.
2. [To distend]—*Syn.* exaggerate, bloat, cram, expand, balloon, swell up, widen, augment, spread out, enlarge, magnify, aggrandize, exalt, build up, raise, maximize, overestimate, surcharge; see also **increase** 1, **stretch** 1, 2, **swell.**—*Ant.* underestimate*, deflate, minimize.

inflated, *mod.* —*Syn.* distended, swollen, extended, puffed, filled, grown, stretched, dilated, spread, enlarged, amplified, augmented, pumped up, exaggerated, bloated, crammed, aggrandized, magnified, overestimated, surcharged, turgid, tumid, bombastic, flatulent, pretentious, pompous, fustian, euphuistic, verbose; see also **full** 1, **increased.** —*Ant.* reduced*, deflated, minimized.

inflation, *n.* **1.** [Increase]—*Syn.* expansion, extension, build-up; see **increase** 1.
2. [General rise in price levels]—*Syn.* boom, financial crisis, inflationary pattern *or* trend *or* cycle, move toward higher price levels *or* structures; see also **rise** 2.

inflect, *v.* —*Syn.* turn, curve, crook; see **arch, bend** 1.

inflection, *n.* —*Syn.* pitch variation, pronunciation, enunciation, voice change, change of grammatical form, intonation, modulation, articulation, emphasis; see also **accent** 2, **pitch** 3, **sound** 2.

inflexibility, *n.* **1.** [Solidity]—*Syn.* stability, toughness, rigidity, stiffness, inflexibleness, temper, induration, ossification, petrifaction, fossilization, glaciation, crystallization, vitrification; see also **firmness** 2.
2. [Stubbornness]—*Syn.* obduracy, tenacity, obstinacy; see **determination** 2, **stubbornness.**

inflexible, *mod.* **1.** [Stiff]—*Syn.* rigid, hardened, taut; see **firm** 2, **stiff** 1.
2. [Firm of purpose]—*Syn.* determined, relentless, fixed; see **resolute** 2.

inflexibly, *mod.* —*Syn.* rigidly, unalterably, unchangeably; see **firmly** 1, 2, **obstinately.**

inflict, *v.* **1.** [To deal]—*Syn.* lay on, deliver, mete *or* deal out, strike, do to, dispense, give (out), wreck, bring (down) upon; see also **cause** 2.
2. [To impose]—*Syn.* force upon, apply, exact; see **command** 2, **force** 1, **require** 2.

infliction, *n.* —*Syn.* curse, indictment, castigation; see **pain** 1, **punishment.**

influence, *n.* **1.** [Attraction]—*Syn.* sway, spell, magnetism; see **attraction** 1.
2. [Power to influence others]—*Syn.* control, weight, authority, supremacy, command, domination, prerogative, esteem, (political) influence, monopoly, rule, fame, prominence, prestige, char-

acter, reputation, force, importance, significance, money, notoriety; *all* (D): power behind the throne, clout, juice, pull; see **leadership** 1, **power** 2.

influence, *v.* —*Syn.* sway, affect, impress, carry weight, count, be influential, determine, make oneself felt, have influence over, lead to believe, get into favor, bring (pressure) to bear, bribe, seduce, talk (one) into, alter, change, act upon *or* on, lead, brainwash, direct, modify, regulate, rule, compel, urge, incite, have a part in, bias, prejudice, turn, train, channel, mold, form, shape, instrumentalize, argue into, carry weight, exercise *or* exert influence, bear upon, get at, gain the confidence, gain a hold upon, be recognized, affect one's mind, bend to one's will, induce, cajole, convince, persuade, inveigle, motivate, actuate, prevail over; *all* (D): have an in, pull strings, fix, wear the pants, have pull *or* clout, twist around one's little finger, have a finger in the pie, lead by the nose, come to the front, have one's ear, lobby through, have the inside track.

influenced, *mod.* —*Syn.* changed, swayed, turned, altered, persuaded, inveigled, shaped, formed, instrumentalized, determined, moved; see also **affected** 1.

influential, *mod.* —*Syn.* prominent, substantial, powerful; see **famous, important** 2.

influenza, *n.* —*Syn.* grippe, flu, severe cold; see **disease** 3.

influx, *n.* —*Syn.* introduction, penetration, coming in; see **entrance** 1.

infold, *v.* —*Syn.* encompass, enfold, circle; see **surround** 2.

inform, *v.* —*Syn.* instruct, relate, teach; see **notify** 1, **tell** 1.

informal, *mod.* **1.** [Without formality]—*Syn.* intimate, relaxed, unceremonious, frank, open, straightforward, free, extempore, spontaneous, congenial, easygoing, unrestrained, unconventional, without ceremony; see also **friendly** 1. —*Ant.* restrained*, ceremonial, ritualistic.

2. [Not requiring formal dress]—*Syn.* ordinary, everyday, inconspicuous, habitual, motley, mixed, urbane, democratic, sociable, hail fellow well met; see also **common** 1.—*Ant.* special*, formal, exclusive.

informality, *n.* —*Syn.* casualness, familiarity, naturalness, affability, comfort, relaxation, warmness, friendliness, ease; see also **comfort** 1.

informant, *n.* **1.** [One who provides information] —*Syn.* newsman, journalist, interviewer; see **announcer, messenger, reporter.**

2. [A source of (scientific) information]—*Syn.* native, local *or* native person *or* speaker, qualified *or* cooperating person; see **citizen, savage** 2, **source** 2.

information, *n.* **1.** [Derived knowledge]—*Syn.* acquired facts, learning, erudition; see **data, knowledge** 1.

2. [News]—*Syn.* report, notice, message; see **news** 1, 2.

informative, *mod.* —*Syn.* instructive, enlightening, communicative, informing, free-spoken, advisory, informational; see also **educational** 1.

informed, *mod.* —*Syn.* versed, knowledgeable, well-read; see **educated** 1, **learned** 1.

informer, *n.* —*Syn.* squealer, tattletale; *all* (D): ratfink, stool pigeon, stoolie, fink.

infraction, *n.* —*Syn.* violation, infringement, breach; see **violation** 1.

infrastructure, *n.* —*Syn.* foundation, basic structure, base; see **foundation** 2.

infrequency, *n.* —*Syn.* rarity, unpredictability, scarcity; see **irregularity** 2.

infrequent, *mod.* —*Syn.* sparse, occasional, scarce; see **rare** 2.

infrequently, *mod.* —*Syn.* scarcely, not habitually *or* regularly, occasionally, uncommonly, sparingly, now and then, rarely, unusually, hardly ever; see also **seldom.**

infringe, *v.* —*Syn.* transgress, violate, trespass; see **meddle** 1.

infringement, *n.* —*Syn.* misbehavior, invasion, transgression; see **violation** 1.

in full, *mod.* —*Syn.* complete, entire, inclusive; see **whole** 1.

in full measure, *mod.* —*Syn.* completely, sufficiently, amply; see **adequately** 1.

infuriate, *v.* —*Syn.* aggravate, enrage, provoke; see **anger.**

infuriated, *mod.* —*Syn.* furious, enraged, incensed; see **angry.**

infuse, *v.* —*Syn.* inspire, introduce, implant; see **instill.**

infusion, *n.* —*Syn.* immersion, strain, admixture; see **liquid, mixture** 1.

in general, *mod.* —*Syn.* on the whole, usually, generally; see **regularly** 1.

ingenious, *mod.* **1.** [Clever]—*Syn.* original, skillful, gifted; see **able** 1, 2, **intelligent** 1.

2. [Inventive]—*Syn.* creative, imaginative, resourceful; see **artistic** 3, **original** 2.

ingenuity, *n.* —*Syn.* inventiveness, imagination, productiveness; see **originality.**

ingenuous, *mod.* **1.** [Frank]—*Syn.* outspoken, straightforward, undisguised; see **frank.**

2. [Simple]—*Syn.* unsophisticated, artless, plain; see **naïve.**

ingenuously, *mod.* —*Syn.* frankly, naïvely, freely; see **openly** 1.

ingenuousness, *n.* —*Syn.* frankness, openness, honesty; see **innocence** 2, **simplicity** 2, **sincerity.**

inglorious, *mod.* —*Syn.* ignoble, ignominious, undignified; see **offensive** 2, **shameful** 2.

in good part, *mod.* —*Syn.* graciously, magnanimously, understandingly; see **generously** 2, **kindly** 2.

ingot, *n.* —*Syn.* bullion, nugget, casting; see **bar, metal.**

ingrain, *v.* —*Syn.* imbue, fix, instill; see **teach** 1.

ingrained, *mod.* —*Syn.* congenital, inborn, indelible; see **inherent.**

ingrate, *n.* —*Syn.* self-seeker, bounder, thankless person; see **opportunist.**

ingratiate, *v.* —*Syn.* captivate, attract, charm; see **fascinate.**

ingratiating, *mod.* —*Syn.* fascinating, interesting, attractive; see **charming, pleasant** 1.

ingratitude, *n.* —*Syn.* thanklessness, ungratefulness, callousness, boorishness, disloyalty, lack of appreciation, inconsiderateness, thoughtlessness; see also **rudeness.**—*Ant.* gratitude*, appreciation, consideration.

ingredient, *n.* —*Syn.* constituent, component, element; see **fundamental** 1, **integral.**
ingredients, *n.* —*Syn.* parts, elements, additives, constituents, pieces, components; *all* (D): makings, fixings, innards.
ingress, *n.* **1.** [An intrusion]—*Syn.* incursion, admission, entrance; see **intrusion.**
2. [Opening]—*Syn.* doorway, entry, portal; see **door, entrance** 1, **gate.**
inhabit, *v.* —*Syn.* occupy, stay, live in; see **dwell, reside.**
inhabitant, *n.* —*Syn.* occupant, dweller, denizen, settler, lodger, permanent resident, incumbent, roomer, boarder, renter, lessee, occupier, indweller, householder, addressee, inmate, tenant, squatter, settler, colonist, native; see also **citizen, resident.**—*Ant.* alien*, transient, nonresident.
inhabited, *mod.* —*Syn.* settled, possessed, owned, lived *or* dwelt in, sustaining human life, peopled, occupied, colonized, developed, pioneered, supplied with people, filled with human beings.
inhalation, *n.* —*Syn.* puff, gasp, inhaling; see **breath** 1.
inhale, *v.* —*Syn.* gasp, smell, sniff; see **breathe** 1.
inharmonious, *mod.* —*Syn.* discordant, tuneless, dissonant; see **harsh** 1, **loud** 1, 2, **shrill.**
inharmoniously, *mod.* —*Syn.* inconsistently, inappropriately, brutally; see **badly** 1, **rudely.**
inherent, *mod.* —*Syn.* innate, inborn, latent, inbred, indigenous (to), intrinsic, internal, original, connate, native, deep-rooted, implicit, ingrained, immanent, congenital, fixed, indwelling, inseparable, unalienable, subjective, indispensable, essential, hereditary, constitutional, integral, integrated; *all* (D): bred in the bone, built in, running in the blood *or* family, in the grain, part and parcel of; see also **natural** 1, **native** 1.—*Ant.* incidental*, extrinsic, superficial.
inherently, *mod.* —*Syn.* inseparably, naturally, intrinsically, natively, immanently, by birth; see also **essentially.**
inherit, *v.* —*Syn.* succeed to, acquire, receive, get one's inheritance, fall heir to, be granted a legacy, come into, derive from, take into possession, take over, receive an endowment, come in for (D); see also **obtain** 1.—*Ant.* lose*, be disowned, miss.
inheritance, *n.* —*Syn.* patrimony, legacy, heritage; see **gift** 1.
inheritor, *n.* —*Syn.* recipient, successor, grantee; see **beneficiary, heir, heiress.**
inhibit, *v.* —*Syn.* repress, frustrate, hold back; see **hinder, restrain** 1.
inhibition, *n.* —*Syn.* prevention, restraint, hindrance; see **barrier, impediment** 1, **interference** 1.
inhospitable, *mod.* —*Syn.* short, brusque, cold; see **rude** 2.
inhospitality, *n.* **1.** [Unfriendliness]—*Syn.* narrowness, solitude, unfriendliness; see **rudeness.**
2. [Isolation]—*Syn.* seclusion, desertion, unsociability; see **isolation, retirement** 2.
inhuman, *mod.* —*Syn.* mean, heartless, cold-blooded; see **cruel** 1, **fierce** 1, **ruthless** 1, 2, **savage** 2.
inhumanity, *n.* —*Syn.* savagery, barbarity, brutality; see **cruelty, evil** 1, **tyranny.**
inhumanly, *mod.* —*Syn.* cruelly, viciously, immorally; see **brutally, rudely.**
inimical, *mod.* —*Syn.* antagonistic, hostile, contrary; see **unfriendly** 1.
inimitable, *mod.* —*Syn.* matchless, supreme, incomparable; see **perfect** 2.
inimitably, *mod.* —*Syn.* uniquely, distinctively, characteristically; see **excellently.**
iniquitous, *mod.* —*Syn.* unjust, vicious, evil; see **unfair** 1.
iniquity, *n.* —*Syn.* unfairness, immorality, evil; see **injustice** 2, **wrong** 1.
initial, *mod.* —*Syn.* basic, primary, elementary; see **first** 1, **fundamental** 1.
initially, *mod.* —*Syn.* at first, in *or* at the beginning, originally; see **first** 1.
initiate, *v.* —*Syn.* open, start, inaugurate; see **begin** 1.
initiated, *mod.* **1.** [Introduced into]—*Syn.* proposed, sponsored, originated, entered, brought into, admitted, inserted, put into, instituted; see also **proposed.**
2. [Begun]—*Syn.* inaugurated, established, started; see **begun.**
3. [Having undergone initiation]—*Syn.* installed, inducted, instated, instructed, grounded, passed, admitted, approved, made part of, made a member of, received, acknowledged, accepted, introduced, conscripted, drafted, called up, levied, confirmed, approved; *both* (D): volunteered, hazed.
initiation, *n.* **1.** [Initial experiences]—*Syn.* first trials, early adventures, grounding, process of learning, elementary steps, start, beginning, preliminaries.
2. [Formal introduction]—*Syn.* investment, induction, indoctrination; see **introduction** 1.
initiative, *n.* **1.** [Eagerness to start things]—*Syn.* vigor, energy, inventiveness; see **enthusiasm** 1.
2. [The starting of things]—*Syn.* action, enterprise, first step; see **force** 3, **responsibility** 1.
inject, *v.* **1.** [To vaccinate]—*Syn.* inoculate, shoot, mainline (D); see **vaccinate.**
2. [To include]—*Syn.* insert, interject, force into, introduce, place into, impregnate, implant, imbue, instill, interpolate, infuse, stick *or* throw in, add; see also **include** 2.
injection, *n.* —*Syn.* dose, enema, vaccination, inoculation; *all* (D): shot, jab, hypo, needle; see also **treatment** 2, **vaccination** 1.
injudicious, *mod.* —*Syn.* imprudent, foolish, impulsive; see **rash.**
injunction, *n.* —*Syn.* order, demand, embargo; see **command** 1, **writ.**
injure, *v.* —*Syn.* harm, damage, wound; see **hurt** 1.
injured, *mod.* —*Syn.* spoiled, damaged, harmed; see **hurt, wounded.**
injurious, *mod.* **1.** [Harmful]—*Syn.* detrimental, damaging, bad; see **dangerous** 1, 2, **deadly, harmful, poisonous.**
2. [Slanderous]—*Syn.* abusive, insulting, libeling; see **insulting, opprobrious** 1.
injuriously, *mod.* —*Syn.* harmfully, seriously, ruinously; see **badly** 1.
injury, *n.* **1.** [A physical hurt]—*Syn.* harm, sprain, damage, mutilation, impairment, blemish, cut, gash, scratch, stab, lesion, bite, fracture, hemorrhage, sting, bruise, sore, cramp, twinge, trauma,

abrasion, burn, swelling, wound, scar, distress, laceration, affliction, deformation; see also **pain** 1.
2. [A moral hurt]—*Syn.* abuse, slander, libel; see **insult, wrong** 2.

injustice, *n.* **1.** [Unfairness]—*Syn.* favoritism, inequality, partisanship; see **prejudice.**
2. [An unfair act]—*Syn.* miscarriage, unfairness, partiality, wrongdoing, malpractice, malfeasance, misfeasance, offense, crime, villainy, injury, iniquity, encroachment, infringement, violation, maltreatment, abuse, criminal negligence, transgression, tort, grievance, breach, damage, infraction; *both* (D): rotten deal, a crying shame; see also **evil** 1, **wrong** 2.—*Ant.* right*, just decision, honest verdict.

ink, *n.*—*Syn.* tusche, paint, watercolor.
Kinds of ink include the following—printing *or* printer's, drawing, indelible, India, sympathetic, copying, marking, logwood, Chinese, tannin, aniline, permanent, safety, lithographic, invisible, disappearing, erasable, rotogravure, engraver's, soluble, waterproof.

inkling, *n.*—*Syn.* indication, innuendo, suspicion; see **hint** 1, **suggestion** 1.

inky, *mod.*—*Syn.* sooty, murky, dull; see **black** 1, **dark** 1.

inlaid, *mod.*—*Syn.* checkered, parqueted, enameled; see **ornate** 1.

inland, *mod.*—*Syn.* toward the interior, back-country, backland, hinterland, interior, midland, provincial, boondock (D), domestic, inward, upland, intranational, intrastate; see also **central** 1.—*Ant.* foreign*, international, frontier.

inlay, *v.*—*Syn.* tool, emboss, parquet; see **decorate, trim** 2.

inlet, *n.*—*Syn.* delta, gulf, channel; see **bay.**

in light of, *mod.*—*Syn.* in view of, since, taking into account; see **considering.**

in line, *mod.*—*Syn.* even, regular, balanced; see **flat** 1.

in line with, *mod.*—*Syn.* similar to, in accord *or* agreeing with, consonant; see **harmonious** 2, **fit** 1, 2.

inmate, *n.*—*Syn.* patient, convict, internee; see **patient, prisoner.**

in memory, *mod.*—*Syn.* commemorating, honoring, recognizing, celebrating, for, in honor of, in memoriam.

inmost, *mod.* **1.** [Deep]—*Syn.* deepest, intestinal, innermost; see **deep** 1.
2. [Inherent]—*Syn.* intrinsic, ingrained, individual; see **inherent, private.**

in motion, *mod.*—*Syn.* traveling, going, under way; see **moving.**

inn, *n.*—*Syn.* tavern, hostel, saloon; see **bar** 2, **hotel, lodge, motel, resort** 2.

innate, *mod.*—*Syn.* intrinsic, inborn, inbred; see **inherent, natural** 1, **native** 1.

inner, *mod.*—*Syn.* innate, inherent, essential, inward, internal, interior, inside, focal, nuclear, central, spiritual, private, deep-seated, deep-rooted, subconscious, intrinsic, intuitive; see also **fundamental, private.**—*Ant.* outer*, surface, external.

innermost, *mod.*—*Syn.* ingrained, personal, deep; see **inherent, native** 1, **private.**

inning, *n.*—*Syn.* chance to bat, turn, period; *all* (D): stanza, session, heat; see **opportunity.**

innkeeper, *n.*—*Syn.* landlord, concierge, proprietor; see **host** 2, **owner, possessor.**

innocence, *n.* **1.** [Freedom from guilt]—*Syn.* guiltlessness, blamelessness, integrity, probity, impeccability, inculpability, clear conscience, faultlessness, clean hands (D); see **honesty** 1.—*Ant.* guilt*, culpability, dishonesty.
2. [Freedom from guile]—*Syn.* guilelessness, artlessness, naiveté, frankness, candidness, simple-mindedness, unaffectedness, plainness, forthrightness, ingenuousness, inoffensiveness; see **simplicity** 2, **sincerity.**—*Ant.* trickery*, shrewdness, wariness.
3. [Lack of experience]—*Syn.* purity, virginity, naiveté; see **chastity, ignorance** 1, **virtue** 1.

innocent, *mod.* **1.** [Guiltless]—*Syn.* not guilty, blameless, inculpable, impeccable, faultless, safe, unoffending, free of, uninvolved, above suspicion, clean (D); see also **honest** 1, **upright** 2.—*Ant.* guilty*, culpable, blameworthy.
2. [Without guile]—*Syn.* open, fresh, guileless; see **frank, childish, naïve, natural** 3, **simple** 1.
3. [Inexperienced]—*Syn.* youthful, raw, green (D); see **inexperienced, young** 2.
4. [Morally pure]—*Syn.* sinless, unblemished, pure, unsullied, undefiled, spotless, wholesome, upright, unimpeachable, clean, virtuous, virginal, immaculate, impeccable, righteous, uncorrupted, irreproachable, unstained, stainless, unspotted, incorrupt, moral, angelic; see also **chaste** 2, 3, **perfect** 2.—*Ant.* dishonest*, sinful, corrupt.
5. [Harmless]—*Syn.* innocuous, free, inoffensive; see **harmless** 2, **safe** 1.

innocently, *mod.*—*Syn.* without guilt, with good *or* the best of intentions, ignorantly; see **kindly** 2, **nicely** 1, **politely.**

innocuous, *mod.*—*Syn.* inoffensive, painless, weak; see **harmless** 2, **kind** 1.

innocuously, *mod.*—*Syn.* harmlessly, innocently, without harm *or* damage; see **kindly** 2, **nicely** 1.

innovation, *n.*—*Syn.* change, alteration, newness, newfangled idea, deviation, shift, modification, modernization, addition, novel contribution; see also **change** 2, **novelty** 2, **variation.**

innuendo, *n.*—*Syn.* aside, intimation, insinuation; see **allusion, hint** 1, **suggestion** 1.

innumerable, *mod.*—*Syn.* numberless, frequent, multitudinous; see **many, much.**

inoculate, *v.*—*Syn.* immunize, shoot, prick; see **inject, treat** 3, **vaccinate.**

inoculation, *n.*—*Syn.* hypodermic, injection, shot (D); see **treatment** 2, **vaccination** 2.

inoffensive, *mod.*—*Syn.* innocuous, pleasant, peaceable; see **calm** 1, **friendly** 1, **innocent** 4.

inoperative, *mod.*—*Syn.* ineffectual, unworkable, defective; see **broken** 2, **disabled, faulty, incompetent, weak** 2, 5.

inopportune, *mod.*—*Syn.* unfavorable, troublesome, unsuitable; see **disturbing, untimely.**

inordinate, *mod.*—*Syn.* immoderate, overmuch, undue; see **extreme** 2, **wasteful.**

inorganic, *mod.*—*Syn.* mineral, inanimate, azoic, lithoidal, unliving, without life.—*Ant.* organic*, vegetable, animal.

in part, *mod.*—*Syn.* partially, somewhat, to some extent *or* degree; see **partly, unfinished.**

in particular, *mod.* —*Syn.* especially, particularly, mainly; see **principally.**

in phase, *mod.* —*Syn.* corresponding, coordinated, at the same frequency; see **alike** 1, 2, 3, **equal, like.**

in pieces, *mod.* —*Syn.* shattered, damaged, busted (D); see **broken** 1, **destroyed, ruined** 1, 2.

input, *n.* —*Syn.* information, knowledge, facts; see **data.**

inquest, *n.* —*Syn.* investigation, hearing, inquiry; see **examination** 1, **trial** 2.

in question, *mod.* —*Syn.* up *or* open for discussion, on the floor, in debate, on the agenda, under revision, at issue; see also **controversial, questionable** 1, **uncertain** 2.

inquietude, *n.* —*Syn.* anxiety, disquiet, upset; see **disturbance** 1.

inquire, *v.* **1.** [To ask about]—*Syn.* make an inquiry, probe, interrogate; see **ask** 1, **question** 1.
2. [To seek into]—*Syn.* investigate, analyze, study; see **examine** 1.

inquiring, *mod.* —*Syn.* questioning, analytical, curious, examining, probing, Socratic, investigatory, fact-finding, maieutic, heuristic, speculative, searching; see also **inquisitive, interested.**

inquiry, *n.* **1.** [A question]—*Syn.* interrogation, request, questioning; see **question** 1.
2. [An investigation]—*Syn.* probe, analysis, hearing; see **examination** 1.

inquisition, *n.* —*Syn.* official inquiry, cross-examination, prosecution; see **examination** 1, **trial** 2.

inquisitive, *mod.* —*Syn.* curious, inquiring, speculative, questioning, intrusive, meddling, meddlesome, searching, challenging, analytical, poking, sifting, scrutinizing, prying, forward, presumptuous, impertinent; *all* (D): snoopy, nosy, long-nosed, rubber-necked, big-eyed; see also **interested.** —*Ant.* indifferent*, unconcerned, aloof.

in reality, *mod.* —*Syn.* in truth, truly, honestly; see **really** 1.

in regard *or* **respect to,** *mod.* —*Syn.* as to, concerning, with regard to; see **about, regarding.**

in reserve, *mod.* —*Syn.* withheld, withdrawn, out of circulation, stored away, in stock *or* storage, in preparation, saved, waiting, prepared, ready; see also **kept** 2, **retained** 1, **saved** 2.

inroad, *n.* —*Syn.* encroachment, invasion, incursion; see **intrusion.**

insane, *mod.* **1.** [Deranged]—*Syn.* crazy, crazed, deranged, wild, raging, frenzied, lunatic, balmy, schizophrenic, psychotic, psychopathic, psychoneurotic, paranoid, *non compos mentis* (Latin), maniacal, raving, demented, rabid, moonstruck, unhinged, unsettled, mentally unsound *or* diseased, suffering from hallucinations, bereft of reason, daft, deluded, possessed, stark mad, having a devil *or* demon, out of one's head *or* mind, obsessed, disordered, touched; *all* (D): mad as a March hare, pixilated, cracked, addlebrained, addlepated, addleheaded, schizo, schizzy, teched, balmy, loony, screwy, nutty, nuts, loco, daft, off the wall, wacko, bughouse, crazy as a coot, gone, derailed, half-cocked, haywire, bats batty, off the beam, having bats in the belfry, round the bend, bonkers, unglued, nutty as a fruitcake, nutty, off one's nut *or* base *or* chump *or* rocker, dotty, devoured by, having a button missing, one can short of a six-pack, frothing at the mouth, not playing with a full deck, out to lunch, not all there, psychoceramic; see also **sick, violent** 2, 4.—*Ant.* sane*, rational, sensible.
2. [Utterly foolish]—*Syn.* madcap, daft, idiotic; see **stupid** 1.

insanely, *mod.* **1.** [Crazily]—*Syn.* furiously, psychopathically, fiercely; see **crazily** 1, **violently** 1, 2, **wildly** 1.
2. [Stupidly]—*Syn.* idiotically, witlessly, irrationally; see **foolishly.**

insanity, *n.* **1.** [Mental illness]—*Syn.* mental derangement *or* abnormality *or* unbalance *or* aberration, psychopathy, madness, dementia, amentia, lunacy, psychosis, alienation, neurosis, psychoneurosis, phobia, mania; see also **complex** 1, **disease** 3.
Psychoses with organic pathology include the following—general paralysis *or* paresis, toxic psychosis, senile dementia, Korsakov's *or* polyneuritic psychosis, delirium tremens, traumatic psychosis.
Psychoses with no demonstrable organic pathology include or are characterized by the following—dementia praecox, paranoia, schizophrenia, manic-depressive insanity, circular insanity, melancholia, catatonia, catalepsy, mutism, negativism, euphoria, hebephrenia, morbid depression, delusions, hallucinations.
Neuroses or psychoneuroses include or are manifested by the following—hysteria; hysterical paralysis, hysterical anaesthesia, hysterical blindness, etc.; anxiety state, shock, shell shock, occupational neurosis, psychopathic personality, emotional instability, alcoholism, sexual perversion, homosexuality, psychasthenia, obsession, compulsion, amnesia, fugue; kleptomania, pyromania, etc.; sadism, masochism; claustrophobia, agoraphobia, etc.
Pathological states accompanied by impaired mentality include the following—Mongolism, cretinism, hydrocephaly, microcephaly, amaurotic family idiocy.
Feeblemindedness or subnormal mental states include the following—idiocy, imbecility, moronity *or* moronism.—*Ant.* sanity*, reason, normality.
2. [Utter folly]—*Syn.* oddity, idiosyncrasy, eccentricity; see **stupidity** 2.

insatiable, *mod.* —*Syn.* voracious, unsatisfied, unappeasable; see **greedy** 1, 2.

inscribe, *v.* —*Syn.* list, engrave, impress; see **write** 1.

inscription, *n.* —*Syn.* engraving, saying, legend; see **writing** 2.

inscrutable, *mod.* —*Syn.* incomprehensible, mysterious, ambiguous; see **difficult** 2, **secret** 1.

in season, *mod.* —*Syn.* legal *or* ready to hunt *or* pick, game, mature; see **legal** 1, **ready** 2, **ripe** 1, 3.

insect, *n.* —*Syn.* bug, beetle, arthropod, scarab, mite, vermin, cootie (D); see also **pest** 1.
Kinds of insects include the following—bristletail, spider, springtail, earwig, stone fly, May fly, dragonfly, darning needle, termite, thrips, plant bug, cicada, aphid, scale insect, leaf insect, alder fly, lacewing, mealy wing, mantis, ant lion, beetle, scorpion fly, caddis fly, butterfly, moth, true fly, sawfly, wasp, ichneumon fly, seventeen-year locust, bedbug, caterpillar, (short-horned) grasshopper, house cricket, walking stick, daddy-longlegs, wasp, bum-

blebee, honeybee, cockroach, potato bug, corn borer, boll weevil, stinkbug, firefly, Japanese beetle, yellow jacket; see also **ant, bee** 1, **flea, fly** 1, **mosquito.**

insecticide, *n.* —*Syn.* DDT, insect poison, pesticide; see **poison.**

insecure, *mod.* **1.** [Apprehensive]—*Syn.* anxious, vague, uncertain; see **troubled** 1.
2. [Defenseless]—*Syn.* immature, vulnerable, unstable; see **weak** 1, 3.

insecurity, *n.* **1.** [Anxiety]—*Syn.* vacillation, indecision, instability; see **doubt** 1, **uncertainty** 2.
2. [Danger]—*Syn.* risk, hazard, vulnerability; see **chance** 1, **danger** 1.

insensate, *mod.* **1.** [Indifferent]—*Syn.* impassive, apathetic, dispassionate; see **indifferent** 1, **unmoved** 2.
2. [Stupid]—*Syn.* senseless, irrational, dumb (D); see **stupid** 1.

insensibility, *n.* —*Syn.* inactivity, apathy, unconsciousness; see **indifference** 1.

insensible, *mod.* **1.** [Unconscious]—*Syn.* swooning, torpid, lethargic; see **unconscious** 1.
2. [Indifferent]—*Syn.* impassive, apathetic, cold; see **indifferent** 1, **unmoved** 2.

inseparable, *mod.* **1.** [Not separable]—*Syn.* indivisible, as one, tied up, molded together, intertwined, interwoven, entwined, integrated, integral, whole, connected, attached, conjoined, united; see also **joined, unified.**—*Ant.* separable, divisble*, apart.
2. [Very congenial]—*Syn.* loving, close, brotherly; see **friendly** 1, **intimate** 1.

insert, *n.* —*Syn.* inclusion, introduction, new material; see **addition** 2, **insertion.**

insert, *v.* **1.** [To put in]—*Syn.* imbed, root, stick *or* place in; see **embed** 1.
2. [To introduce]—*Syn.* enter, interpolate, inject; see **include** 2.

inserted, *mod.* —*Syn.* introduced, added, interpolated, placed with, infused, stuck in; see also **included.**

insertion, *n.* —*Syn.* insert, interpolation, injection, infusion, introduction, inclusion; see also **addition** 2.

in short, *mod.* —*Syn.* in summary, to put it briefly, (and) so; see **briefly.**

inside, *mod.* **1.** [Within]—*Syn.* within the boundaries *or* circumference of, bounded, surrounded by; see **under.**—*Ant.* after, beyond*, outside.
2. [Within doors]—*Syn.* indoors, under a roof, in a house, out of the open, behind closed doors, under a shelter, in (under), in the interior; see also **within.** —*Ant.* outside*, out-of-doors, in the open.
3. [(D) Based on intimate acquaintance]—*Syn.* esoteric, limited, exclusive; see **private, secret** 1.
4. [Toward the center]—*Syn.* inner, inward, internal, close up; see also **central** 1.

inside, *n.* —*Syn.* inner wall, sheathing, plaster, plastering, facing, bushing, wadding, *doublure* (French), inlayer; see also **lining.**

insides, *n.* —*Syn.* interior, inner portion, bowels, recesses, inland, hinterland, middle, belly, womb, heart, soul, breast; see also **abdomen, center** 1.

insidious, *mod.* —*Syn.* deceptive, ensnaring, treacherous; see **corrupt** 3, **dishonest** 1, **false** 1, **secret** 3, **sly** 1.

insight, *n.* —*Syn.* penetration, perspicacity, shrewdness; see **acumen.**

insignia, *n.* —*Syn.* ensign, coat of arms, symbol; see **decoration** 2, **emblem.**

insignificance, *n.* —*Syn.* unimportance, worthlessness, indifference, triviality, negligibility, nothingness, smallness, meanness, pettiness, paltriness, immateriality, matter of no consequence, trifling matter, nothing to speak of, nothing particular; *all* (D): drop in the bucket, molehill, drop in the ocean.

insignificant, *mod.* —*Syn.* irrelevant, petty, trifling; see **trivial, unimportant.**

insincere, *mod.* —*Syn.* deceitful, pretentious, shifty; see **dishonest** 2, **false** 1, **hypocritical, sly.**

insincerity, *n.* —*Syn.* distortion, falsity, lies; see **deception** 1, **dishonesty, hypocrisy** 2.

insinuate, *v.* **1.** [To make an indirect hint]—*Syn.* imply, suggest, purport; see **hint, mention, propose** 1, **refer** 2.
2. [To force a way into]—*Syn.* infuse, introduce slowly, ingratiate, slip into, wedge through, insert gradually, infiltrate, force through, inject; *both* (D): horn in, muscle in; see also **instill.**—*Ant.* push*, dash, crowd.

insinuation, *n.* —*Syn.* implication, veiled remark *or* observation, innuendo; see **hint** 1, 2, **suggestion** 1.

insipid, *mod.* **1.** [Tasteless]—*Syn.* flat, stale, vapid; see **tasteless** 1.
2. [Uninteresting]—*Syn.* weak, lifeless, characterless; see **dull** 4.

insistence, *n.* —*Syn.* demand, perseverance, determination; see **persistence.**

insistent, *mod.* —*Syn.* persistent, reiterative, continuous; see **obstinate** 1, **resolute** 2.

insist (that) *or* **upon,** *v.* —*Syn.* expect, request, order; see **ask** 1, **command** 1, **require** 2.

insobriety, *n.* —*Syn.* alcoholism, inebriety, intoxication; see **drunkenness.**

insolence, *n.* —*Syn.* effrontery, boldness, audacity; see **rudeness.**

insolent, *mod.* —*Syn.* offensive, overbearing, arrogant; see **rude** 2.

insolently, *mod.* —*Syn.* insultingly, crassly, crudely; see **rudely.**

insoluble, *mod.* —*Syn.* insolvable, unconcluded, unresolved, unsolved, mysterious; see also **difficult** 2.

insolvency, *n.* —*Syn.* distress, destitution, liquidation; see **bankruptcy, poverty** 1.

insolvent, *mod.* —*Syn.* bankrupt, indebted, foreclosed, failed, unbalanced, out of credit *or* funds *or* money, broken, in the hands of receivers, in receivership in chapter XI; *all* (D): broke, on the rocks, flat, busted, wiped out, done for, gone to the wall, in the red, in a hole, sent to the cleaners; see also **ruined** 4.—*Ant.* solvent*, running, in good condition.

insomnia, *n.* —*Syn.* wakefulness, sleeplessness, restlessness, insomnolence, indisposition *or* inability to sleep.

insomniac, *n.* —*Syn.* one afflicted with *or* victim of sleeplessness *or* insomnolence, light *or* broken sleeper, insomniac *or* insomnious patient; see **patient.**

insouciant, *mod.* —*Syn.* careless, heedless, thoughtless; see **unconcerned.**

inspect, *v.* —*Syn.* scrutinize, probe, investigate; see **examine** 1.
inspected, *mod.* —*Syn.* tried, checked, authorized; see **approved, investigated, tested.**
inspection, *n.* **1.** [An examination]—*Syn.* inventory, investigation, inquiry; see **examination** 1.
2. [A military review]—*Syn.* maneuvers, pageant, dress parade; see **drill** 3, **parade** 1, **review** 4.
inspector, *n.* —*Syn.* police inspector, chief detective, investigating officer, railroad inspector, customs officer, immigration inspector, government inspector, checker; see also **detective, investigator, policeman.**
inspiration, *n.* **1.** [An idea]—*Syn.* notion, hunch, whim; see **fancy** 2, 3, **impulse** 2, **thought** 2.
2. [A stimulant to creative activity]—*Syn.* stimulus, spur, influence; see **incentive, motivation.**
inspire, *v.* **1.** [To encourage]—*Syn.* inspirit, invigorate, spur; see **encourage** 2.
2. [To stimulate to creative activity]—*Syn.* fire, quicken, be the cause of, start off, put one in the mood, set aglow, give one the idea for, motivate, touch the imagination, give an impetus; see also **cause** 2, **urge** 2.
inspired, *mod.* **1.** [Stimulated]—*Syn.* roused, animated, inspirited, energized, motivated, stirred, excited, exhilarated, influenced, set going, started, activated, galvanized, moved; see also **encouraged.**
2. [Seemingly moved by supernatural powers] —*Syn.* possessed, in a frenzy, ecstatic, transported, carried away, fired, exalted, uplifted, caught on fire, held, guided, touched.
inspiring, *mod.* —*Syn.* rousing, encouraging, heartening, enlivening, animating, refreshing, exhilarating, revealing, illuminating; see also **exciting, stimulating.**
inspirit, *v.* —*Syn.* arouse, stimulate, animate; see **excite** 1, **urge** 2.
in spite of, *mod.* —*Syn.* nevertheless, in defiance of, despite; see **notwithstanding.**
instability, *n.* —*Syn.* inconstancy, changeability, immaturity, mutability, variability, non-uniformity, inconsistency, irregularity, imbalance, disequilibrium, unsteadiness, vulnerability, pliancy, fluidity, restlessness, inquietude, disquiet, anxiety, fluctuation, alternation, oscillation, fitfulness, impermanence, transience, vacillation, hesitation, flightiness, capriciousness, wavering, irresolution, fickleness; see also **change** 1, **mobility, uncertainty** 2, 3.
install, *v.* —*Syn.* set up, establish, induct, build *or* put in, place, invest, introduce, inaugurate, furnish with, put *or* fix up, line.
installation, *n.* **1.** [The act of installing]—*Syn.* placing, induction, investiture, ordination, inauguration, launching, accession, investment, coronation, establishment, furnishing.
2. [That which has been installed]—*Syn.* machinery, wiring, electrification, lighting, insulation, power, power plant, heating system, furnishings, foundation, base.
3. [Naval and military installations]—*Syn.* fort, bunker, ammo dump (D); see **fortification** 1, **harbor** 2, **munitions.**
installed, *mod.* —*Syn.* set *or* put up, started, put in; see **established** 2, **finished** 1.
installment, *n.* —*Syn.* partial payment, periodic payment, down payment, contract payment, section, chapter, episode, portion; see also **part** 1, **payment** 1.
instance, *n.* —*Syn.* case, situation, occurrence; see **example** 1.
instance, *v.* —*Syn.* exemplify, show, cite examples; see **cite** 2, **mention, refer** 2.
for instance—*Syn.* as an example, by way of illustration, in this fashion; see **for example.**
instant, *n.* —*Syn.* short while, second, flash, trice, split second, wink *or* bat of the eye; *all* (D): jiffy, two jerks of a lamb's tail, jiff; see **moment** 1.
on the instant—*Syn.* instantly, without delay, simultaneously; see **immediately.**
instantaneous, *mod.* —*Syn.* momentary, spontaneous, in a flash; see **immediate** 1.
instantaneously, *mod.* —*Syn.* promptly, directly, at once; see **immediately.**
instantly, *mod.* —*Syn.* directly, at once, without delay; see **immediately, spontaneously.**
instead, *mod.* —*Syn.* in place of, as a substitute, alternative, on second thought, in lieu of, on behalf of, alternatively; see also **rather** 2.
instead of, *prep.* —*Syn.* rather than, in place *or* lieu of, as a substitute *or* alternative *or* proxy for.
instigate, *v.* —*Syn.* prompt, stimulate, induce; see **urge** 2.
instigation, *n.* —*Syn.* prompting, influence, stimulation; see **incentive, motivation.**
instill, *v.* —*Syn.* infuse, suffuse, transfuse, intermix, imbue, inject, infiltrate, interject, inoculate, impregnate, implant, impress into the mind, impart (gradually), disseminate, inspire, diffuse, impress, propagandize, catechize, brainwash, introduce, inculcate, insinuate, indoctrinate, impart, insert, impenetrate, inseminate, force in, put into someone's head (D); see also **teach** 1.—*Ant.* remove*, draw out, extract.
instinct, *n.* —*Syn.* sentiment, sense, intuition; see **feeling** 4.
instinctive, *mod.* **1.** [Automatic]—*Syn.* mechanical, intuitive, reflex; see **automatic** 2, **habitual** 1.
2. [Natural]—*Syn.* spontaneous, accustomed, normal; see **natural** 2.
instinctively, *mod.* —*Syn.* inherently, intuitively, by *or* on instinct; see **naturally** 2.
institute, *v.* **1.** [To organize]—*Syn.* found, establish, launch; see **organize** 2.
2. [To begin]—*Syn.* initiate, start, open; see **begin** 1.
institution, *n.* **1.** [An organization]—*Syn.* system, company, association; see **business** 4, **office** 3, **university.**
2. [A welfare school]—*Syn.* academy, orphanage, reformatory; see **school** 1.
institutionalize, *v.* —*Syn.* standardize, incorporate into a system, make official; see **order** 3, **regulate** 2, **systematize.**
institutionalized, *mod.* —*Syn.* standardized, regularized, incorporated into a system; see **regulated.**
instruct, *v.* **1.** [To teach]—*Syn.* educate, give lessons, guide; see **teach** 1.
2. [To order]—*Syn.* tell, direct, bid; see **command** 1.

3. [To inform]—*Syn.* reveal, disclose, apprise; see **notify** 1, **tell** 1.
instructed, *mod.* —*Syn.* told, advised, informed; see **educated** 1, **learned** 1.
instruction, *n.* —*Syn.* guidance, preparation, direction; see **education** 1.
instructions, *n.* —*Syn.* orders, plans, directive; see **advice, directions.**
instructive, *mod.* —*Syn.* illuminating, enlightening, informative; see **education** 1.
instructor, *n.* —*Syn.* professor, tutor, lecturer; see **teacher** 1, 2.
instrument, *n.* —*Syn.* means, apparatus, implement; see **device** 1, **machine** 1, **tool** 1.
instrumental, *mod.* —*Syn.* partly responsible for, contributory, conducive; see **effective, helpful** 1, **necessary** 1.
instrumentality, *n.* —*Syn.* contribution, help, assistance; see **aid** 1.
in style, *mod.* —*Syn.* current, modish, stylish; see **fashionable, popular** 1.
insubordinate, *mod.* —*Syn.* disobedient, treacherous, defiant; see **rebellious** 2.
insubordination, *n.* —*Syn.* mutiny, treason, rebellion; see **revolution** 2.
insubstantial, *mod.* **1.** [Imaginary]—*Syn.* ephemeral, illusory, intangible; see **fanciful** 1, **imaginary, unreal.**
2. [Flimsy]—*Syn.* petty, slight, decrepit; see **flimsy** 1, **poor** 2.
insufferable, *mod.* —*Syn.* unbearable, intolerable, unendurable; see **painful** 1.
insufficient, *mod.* —*Syn.* skimpy, meager, thin; see **faulty, inadequate** 1, **poor** 2, **unfinished** 1, **unsatisfactory, wanting.**
insufficiently, *mod.* —*Syn.* barely, incompletely, partly; see **badly** 1, **inadequately.**
insular, *mod.* **1.** [Isolated]—*Syn.* detached, alone, separate; see **isolated, separated.**
2. [Biased]—*Syn.* narrow-minded, bigoted, provincial; see **prejudiced.**
insulate, *v.* —*Syn.* protect, cork, coat, inlay, separate, treat, isolate, apply insulation, tape up, glass in; see also **line** 1.
insulation, *n.* **1.** [The act of insulating]—*Syn.* taping, covering, caulking, furring, protecting, padding, packing, surrounding, isolating, defending, neutralizing, cording; see also **lining.**
2. [An insulator]—*Syn.* nonconductor, protector, resistant material.
Insulators include the following—knob, standoff, split-knob, double-cup, shackle, covering, pad, padding, sleeve, tape, air space, tube, tubing, rock wool, wool bat, asbestos, conduit, pack, packing, rubber, tarred felt, silk, furring, oiled silk, vacuum hair, lead, polarized layer.
insulator, *n.* —*Syn.* nonconductor, nonconveyor, nontransmitter; see **insulation** 2.
insult, *n.* —*Syn.* indignity, offense, affront, abuse, contumely, ill treatment, scurrility, opprobrium, outrage, vilification, incivility, impudence, insolence, blasphemy, mockery, derision, impertinence, discourtesy, invective, slight, ignominy, disrespect, slander, libel; *both* (D): slap in the face, black eye; see also **curse, rudeness.**—*Ant.* praise*, tribute, homage.
insult, *v.* —*Syn.* revile, vilify, libel, offend, outrage, abuse, humiliate, mock, vex, tease, irritate, annoy, aggravate, provoke, deride, taunt, laugh down, ridicule, jibe at, jeer, underestimate; *both* (D): take a slap at, step on one's toes; see also **curse** 2, **slander.**
Insulting remarks include the following—nuts, nerts, says you, go jump in the creek, in my eye, don't make me laugh, shut your face, shut up, so's your old man, you're crazy, don't give me any of your lip, baloney, bull, nuts to you, in a pig's eye, up yours, horse manure, tell it to the marines, oh yeah? my foot, my eye, does your mother know you're out? another country heard from.—*Ant.* praise*, extol, glorify.
insulted, *mod.* —*Syn.* slandered, libeled, vilified, reviled, cursed, defamed, dishonored, mocked, ridiculed, jeered at, humiliated, mistreated, aggrieved, offended, hurt, maltreated, outraged, affronted, slighted, shamed, underestimated, cut to the quick (D); see also **disgraced.**—*Ant.* praised*, admired, extolled.
insulting, *mod.* —*Syn.* affronting, outrageous, offensive, debasing, degrading, humiliating, humbling, scoffing, deriding, contemptuous, dyslogistic; see also **embarrassing, opprobrious** 1.—*Ant.* respectful*, complimentary, honoring.
insuperable, *mod.* —*Syn.* impassable, unattainable, inaccessible; see **impossible** 1.
insupportable, *mod.* —*Syn.* insufferable, dreadful, intolerable; see **painful** 1.
in support of, *mod.* —*Syn.* for, condoning, approving; see **supporting.**
insurance, *n.* —*Syn.* indemnity, assurance, warrant, backing, allowance, safeguard, support, something to fall back on (D); see also **protection** 2, **security** 2.
insure, *v.* —*Syn.* register, warrant, protect; see **guarantee** 1.
insured, *mod.* —*Syn.* safeguarded, defended, warranteed; see **guaranteed, protected, warranted.**
insurgent, *mod.* —*Syn.* riotous, insubordinate, anarchical; see **rebellious** 2.
insurgent, *n.* —*Syn.* rioter, anarchist, demonstrator; see **agitator, radical, rebel** 1.
insurmountable, *mod.* —*Syn.* insuperable, unconquerable, unbeatable; see **impossible** 1.
insurrection, *n.* —*Syn.* insurgence, revolt, rebellion; see **disorder** 2, **revolution** 2.
insurrectionary, *mod.* —*Syn.* mutinous, insurgent, riotous; see **rebellious** 2.
insusceptible, *mod.* —*Syn.* impassive, unfeeling, unemotional; see **callous, indifferent** 1.
intact, *mod.* —*Syn.* together, entire, uninjured; see **whole** 2.
intake, *n.* **1.** [Contraction]—*Syn.* alteration, shortening, constriction; see **abbreviation** 2, **contraction** 1, **reduction** 1, **shrinkage.**
2. [Profit]—*Syn.* harvest, gain, accumulation; see **profit** 2.
intangible, *mod.* **1.** [Uncertain]—*Syn.* indefinite, unsure, hypothetical; see **uncertain** 2, **vague** 2.
2. [Ethereal]—*Syn.* impalpable, airy, ephemeral; see **immaterial** 2.
intangibly, *mod.* —*Syn.* barely, slightly, undetectably; see **hardly, moderately, only** 1.

integer, *n.* —*Syn.* integral, whole number, individual; see **whole.**

integral, *mod.* —*Syn.* complete, indivisible, aggregate, undivided, unbroken, elemental; see also **whole** 1.

integrate, *v.* **1.** [To unify]—*Syn.* mix, blend, combine; see **mix** 1, **unite** 1.
2. [To abolish racial segregation]—*Syn.* desegregate, remove racial barriers, provide equal access, abolish segregation, make available to everyone.

integrated, *mod.* **1.** [Joined]—*Syn.* combined, interspersed, mingled; see **joined, unified.**
2. [Open to all races]—*Syn.* nonsegregated, not segregated, (for) both black and white, interracial, nonracial, for all races, nonsectarian, without restriction (as to race, creed, or color), making no racial distinctions, combined; see also **free** 1, 2, **open** 3.

integration, *n.* —*Syn.* unification, combination, co-operation; see **alliance** 1, **mixture** 1, **union** 1.

integrity, *n.* —*Syn.* uprightness, honor, probity; see **honesty** 1, **sincerity.**

intellect, *n.* **1.** [The power to reason]—*Syn.* understanding, comprehension, ability; see **acumen, judgment** 1.
2. [The mind]—*Syn.* intelligence, brain, mentality; see **mind** 1.

intellectual, *mod.* —*Syn.* mental, inventive, creative; see **intelligent** 1, **learned** 1.

intellectual, *n.* —*Syn.* pundit, genius, philosopher, academician, highbrow, member of the intelligentsia; *all* (D): egghead, brain, Einstein, longhair, bluestocking, braintruster; see also **scholar** 2.

intelligence, *n.* **1.** [Understanding]—*Syn.* perspicacity, discernment, comprehension; see **acumen, judgment** 1.
2. [Ability]—*Syn.* capacity, skill, aptitude; see **ability** 1, 2.
3. [Secret information]—*Syn.* report, statistics, facts, inside information, account; *both* (D): info, the dope; see also **data, knowledge** 1, **news** 1, **secret.**
4. [The mind]—*Syn.* intellect, brain, mentality; see **mind** 1.

intelligent, *mod.* **1.** [*Said of persons or beings*] —*Syn.* clever, bright, exceptional, astute, acute, smart, brilliant, perceptive, well-informed, resourceful, profound, penetrating, original, perspicacious, keen, racy, imaginative, inventive, reasonable, capable, able, ingenious, knowledgeable, creative, alive, responsible, understanding, alert, quick-witted, keen-witted, clear-headed, quick, sharp, witty, ready, vivid, calculating, amusing, comprehending, listening to reason, discerning, having one's wits about one, having it in one, discriminating, knowing, intellectual, on the qui vive, sagacious, studious, contemplative, having a head on one's shoulders, talented, apt, deep, sage, wise, shrewd; *all* (D): brainy, smart as a whip, all there, on the ball *or* beam, not born yesterday, crazy like a fox; see also **judicious.**—*Ant.* dull*, slow-minded, shallow.
2. [*Said of conduct*]—*Syn.* sensible, farsighted, rational; see sense 1, **judicious.**

intelligently, *mod.* —*Syn.* well, skillfully, admirably, reasonably, logically, judiciously, capably, diligently, sharply, sagaciously, astutely, discerningly, perspicaciously, comprehendingly, knowingly, knowledgeably, farsightedly, sensibly, prudently, alertly, keenly, resourcefully, aptly, discriminatingly; see also **completely, effectively.**—*Ant.* badly*, foolishly, stupidly.

intelligentsia, *n.* —*Syn.* the learned, intellectuals, eggheads (D); see **intellectual.**

intelligibility, *n.* —*Syn.* readability, understandability, lucidity; see **accuracy, clarity, simplicity** 1.

intelligible, *mod.* —*Syn.* plain, clear, obvious; see **understandable.**

intemperance, *n.* —*Syn.* insobriety, immoderation, alcoholism; see **drunkenness.**

intemperate, *mod.* **1.** [Drunken]—*Syn.* inebriated, dissipated, soused (D); see **drunk.**
2. [Excessive]—*Syn.* immoderate, inordinate, unrestrained; see **extreme** 2.

intend, *v.* **1.** [To propose]—*Syn.* plan, purpose, aim, expect, be resolved *or* determined (to), aspire to, have in mind *or* view, hope to, contemplate, think, aim at, take into one's head; see also **resolve.**
2. [To destine for]—*Syn.* design, mean, devote to, reserve, appoint, purpose, set apart, aim at *or* for, have in view; see also **assign** 1, **dedicate** 2, **designate** 1.
3. [To mean]—*Syn.* indicate, signify, denote; see **mean** 1.

intendant, *n.* —*Syn.* director, foreman, manager; see **superintendent.**

intended, *mod.* —*Syn.* designed, advised, contemplated, expected, predetermined, calculated, prearranged, predestined, meant; see also **planned, proposed.**

intense, *mod.* —*Syn.* intensified, deep, profound, extraordinary, exceptional, heightened, strained, marked, vivid, ardent, undue, powerful, passionate, impassioned, diligent, hard, full, great, supreme, exaggerated, violent, excessive, acute, keen, piercing, cutting, bitter, severe, concentrated, intensive, forceful, all-consuming, sharp, biting, stinging, shrill, high-pitched, fervid, strenuous, fervent, earnest, zealous, vehement, harsh, strong, pungent, brilliant; see also **extreme** 2.

intensely, *mod.* —*Syn.* deeply, profoundly, strongly; see **very.**

intensify, *v.* —*Syn.* raise, point, step up, set off, tone up, escalate, heighten, sharpen, emphasize, brighten, lighten, darken, concentrate, redouble, aggravate, augment, reinforce, magnify, add to; *both* (D): hop up, jazz up; see also **increase** 1, **strengthen.**—*Ant.* decrease*, loosen, relax.

intensity, *n.* **1.** [A high degree of application] —*Syn.* strain, force, concentration, power, vehemence, violence, passion, fervor, ferment, ardor, extreme, severity, acuteness, depth, deepness, weightiness, forcefulness, high pitch, sharpness, emphasis, magnitude; see also **energy** 3, **pressure** 1.
2. [Ferocity]—*Syn.* ferociousness, wildness, fury; see **anger.**
3. [Nervousness]—*Syn.* perturbation, anxiety, tenseness; see **excitement, nervousness** 2.

intensive, *mod.* —*Syn.* accelerated, speeded up, hard; see **fast** 1, **severe** 1, 2.

intensive care room, *n.* —*Syn.* hospital room, emergency unit, critical room; see **hospital.**

intent, *mod.* —*Syn.* engrossed, attentive, concentrating; see **enthusiastic** 1, 3.
to all intents and purposes—*Syn.* in almost every respect, practically, virtually; see **almost.**
intention, *n.* —*Syn.* aim, end, plan; see **purpose** 1.
intentional, *mod.* —*Syn.* intended, meditated, prearranged; see **deliberate** 1.
intentionally, *mod.* —*Syn.* specifically, with malice aforethought, in cold blood (D); see **carefully** 2, **deliberately.**
intently, *mod.* —*Syn.* hard, with concentration, keenly; see **closely.**
inter, *v.* —*Syn.* tomb, entomb, inhume; see **bury** 1.
intercede, *v.* —*Syn.* intervene, arbitrate, mediate; see **negotiate** 1, **reconcile** 2.
intercept, *v.* —*Syn.* cut off, stop, ambush, block, catch, take away, interpose, appropriate, interlope, make off with, seize midway; *both* (D): hijack, head off; see also **hinder, prevent.**
interception, *n.* —*Syn.* blocking, interfering (with), interposing; see **stopping.**
intercession, *n.* —*Syn.* prayer, negotiation, petition; see **appeal** 1, **request.**
intercessor, *n.* —*Syn.* mediator, negotiator, arbitrator; see **judge** 2.
interchange, *n.* **1.** [The act of giving and receiving reciprocally]—*Syn.* barter, trade, reciprocation; see **exchange** 2.
2. [Alternation]—*Syn.* varying, altering, exchange, transposition, shift, change of places; see also **variation.**
3. [A highway intersection]—*Syn.* cloverleaf, intersection, off-ramp; see **highway, road** 1.
interchangeably, *mod.* —*Syn.* correspondently, reciprocally, conversely; see **mutually, vice versa.**
intercommunication, *n.* —*Syn.* broadcast, news, communiqué; see **announcement** 2, **communication** 2, **report** 1.
intercom system, *n.* —*Syn.* telephone, two-way radio, public address system; see **communications, radio** 2.
intercourse, *n.* **1.** [Communication]—*Syn.* association, dealings, interchange; see **communication** 1.
2. [Sex act]—*Syn.* coitus, coition, sexual relations; see **copulation, fornication, sex** 1.
interdependence, *n.* —*Syn.* reliance, mutuality, confidence; see **dependence** 1, **necessity** 3.
interdict, *v.* —*Syn.* hinder, prohibit, stop; see **forbid, halt** 2, **prevent.**
interest, *n.* **1.** [Concern]—*Syn.* attention, curiosity, excitement; see **care** 2.
2. [Advantage]—*Syn.* profit, benefit, gain; see **advantage** 3.
3. [Premium]—*Syn.* credit, due, discount, percentage, gain, bonus, earnings, accrual; see also **addition** 2, **profit** 2.
4. [Share]—*Syn.* mortgage, piece, title; see **credit** 2, **share.**
5. [Affair]—*Syn.* concern, matter, case; see **business** 5.
6. [Persons with a common trade or purpose; *often plural*]—*Syn.* class, powers, business interests; see **industry** 3.
in the interest(s) of—*Syn.* for the sake of, on behalf of, in order to promote; see **for.**
interest, *v.* —*Syn.* intrigue, amuse, please; see **entertain** 1, **fascinate.**
interested, *mod.* **1.** [Having one's interest aroused] —*Syn.* stimulated, sympathetic, attentive, enticed, lured, curious, drawn, touched, moved, affected, inspired, inspirited, responsive, struck, impressed, roused, awakened, stirred, open to suggestion; *all* (D): keen on, all for, all wrapped up in; see also **charmed, excited.**—*Ant.* bored*, tired, annoyed.
2. [Concerned with or engaged in]—*Syn.* occupied, engrossed, partial, prejudiced, biased, taken, obsessed with, fired, absorbed in, personally interested in, having investments *or* owning stock in, likely to profit from; see also **busy** 1, **involved** —*Ant.* indifferent*, impartial, disinterested.
interesting, *mod.* —*Syn.* pleasing, pleasurable, fine, satisfying, fascinating, arresting, entrancing, riveting, engaging, readable, absorbing, stirring, enthralling, affecting, alluring, exotic, unusual, exceptional, lovely, gracious, impressive, striking, attractive, captivating, enchanting, beautiful, inviting, winning, magnetic, prepossessing, elegant, delightful, amusing, genial, refreshing; *both* (D): swell, dandy; see also **charming, exciting.**—*Ant.* dull*, shallow, boring.
interfere, *v.* **1.** [To meddle]—*Syn.* intervene, interpose, interlope; see **meddle** 1.
2. [To prevent]—*Syn.* stop, oppose, conflict; see **hinder, prevent.**
interference, *n.* **1.** [The act of obstructing]—*Syn.* intervention, resistance, retardation, impedance, checking, blocking, barring, hampering, clashing, collision, tackling, hindrance, shutting off, clogging, choking, arrest, barricading, thrusting between, interposition; see also **opposition** 1, **restraint** 2. —*Ant.* removal*, clearance, releasing.
2. [Taking forcible part in the affairs of others] —*Syn.* meddling, interposition, interruption, prying, trespassing, tampering, intermeddling, advising; *all* (D): kibitzing, butting in, horning in, barging in, back-seat driving; see also **intrusion.**
3. [That which obstructs]—*Syn.* obstruction, check, obstacle; see **barrier, impediment** 1, **restraint** 2.
interim, *n.* —*Syn.* interval, the meantime, interlude; see **pause** 1.
interior, *mod.* —*Syn.* inner, internal, inward; see **central** 1, **inside** 2.
interior, *n.* **1.** [Inside]—*Syn.* inner part, lining, heart; see **center** 1, **inside.**
2. [The inside of a building]—*Syn.* rooms, hall(s), stairway, hearth, vestibule, cloister, nave, lobby, transept, chapel, choir, gallery, basement.
interject, *v.* —*Syn.* introduce, interpose, insert, ingrain, interpolate, parenthesize, infiltrate, intersperse, infuse, splice, import, insinuate, implant, force in; see also **add** 1, **include** 2, **inject.**
interjection, *n.* **1.** [Insertion]—*Syn.* interpolation, insinuation, inclusion; see **insertion, parenthesis.**
2. [Exclamation]—*Syn.* utterance, ejaculation, exclamation; see **cry** 1.
interlace, *v.* **1.** [To weave]—*Syn.* intertwine, braid, entangle; see **knit** 1, **twist, weave** 1.
2. [To mingle]—*Syn.* blend, combine, connect; see **join** 1, **merge, mix** 1.

interline, *v.* **1.** [To write between the lines]—*Syn.* interpolate, interscribe, annotate; see **explain.**
2. [To put in an interlining]—*Syn.* pack, fill, back, stuff, pad, quilt, bush, insulate, upholster, cushion; see also **face** 3, **line** 1.

interlocutor, *n.*—*Syn.* spokesman, orator, conversationalist; see **speaker** 2, **talker.**

interloper, *n.*—*Syn.* meddler, trespasser, alien; see **intruder.**

interlude, *n.* **1.** [A recess]—*Syn.* hiatus, interruption, wait; see **delay** 1, **pause** 2, **recess** 1.
2. [A masquerade]—*Syn.* charade, play, farce; see **comedy, drama** 1, **masquerade.**

intermediary, *n.*—*Syn.* emissary, mediator, go-between; see **agent** 1, **delegate.**

intermediate, *mod.*—*Syn.* mean, between, medium, halfway, compromising, intermediary, neutral, standard, median, moderate, average, about the fiftieth percentile; see also **central** 1, **common** 1, **middle.**

interment, *n.*—*Syn.* entombment, burial, inhumation; see **funeral** 1.

intermezzo, *n.*—*Syn.* musical interlude, intermission, independent musical composition; see **music** 1.

interminable, *mod.*—*Syn.* long, boring, dragging (on and on); see **dull** 4, **eternal** 2.

interminably, *mod.*—*Syn.* continually, going on and on, persistently; see **frequently, forever** 1, **regularly** 2.

intermingle, *v.*—*Syn.* mingle, fuse, combine with; see **join** 1, **merge, mix** 1.

intermission, *n.*—*Syn.* interim, wait, respite; see **pause** 2, **recess** 1.

intermit, *v.*—*Syn.* suspend, cease, discontinue; see **interrupt** 2, **pause.**

intermittent, *mod.*—*Syn.* periodic, alternate, shifting, coming and going, recurrent, broken, seasonal, rhythmic, serial, epochal, cyclical, cyclic, discontinuous, every other, spasmodic, on and off, sporadic, fitful, occasional, now and then; *both* (D): by snatches, here and there; see also **changing, irregular** 1.—*Ant.* constant*, lasting, incessant.

intern, *n.*—*Syn.* apprentice doctor, assistant resident, medical graduate; see **doctor** 1.

internal, *mod.* **1.** [Within]—*Syn.* inside, inward, interior, private, intrinsic, innate, inherent, under the surface, intimate, subjective, enclosed, circumscribed; see also **inner.**—*Ant.* external, outer*, outward.
2. [Within the body]—*Syn.* intestinal, constitutional, physiological, physical, neurological, abdominal, ventral, visceral; see also **bodily** 1, **organic.** —*Ant.* foreign*, alien, external.
3. [Within a group or area]—*Syn.* indigenous, centralized, intrastate; see **domestic** 1, **native** 2.

internally, *mod.*—*Syn.* within the body, beneath *or* below the surface, inwardly, deep down, spiritually, mentally, invisibly, orally, by injection, within the limits *or* termini, out of sight; see also **inside** 1, **within.**

international, *mod.*—*Syn.* world-wide, worldly, world, intercontinental, between nations, all over the world, all-embracing, foreign, cosmopolitan, inter-Allied; see also **general** 1, **universal** 3.—*Ant.* domestic*, national, internal.

internationalize, *v.*—*Syn.* universalize, hold between nations, establish on an international basis, make worldwide *or* universal, include everybody, give international equality, exploit co-operatively, demilitarize; see also **unite** 1.—*Ant.* divide*, claim, exploit.

internationally, *mod.*—*Syn.* interculturally, interracially, co-operatively, like a man of the world, globally, in the spirit of the United Nations, interreliantly, concerning the intercourse of nations *or* peoples, not provincial *or* bigoted; see also **abroad, everywhere, universally.**

internecine, *mod.*—*Syn.* exterminatory, destructive, murderous; see **dangerous** 1, 2, **deadly.**

interpellate, *v.*—*Syn.* challenge, interrogate, summon; see **examine** 2, **question** 1.

interpellation, *n.*—*Syn.* interrogation, inquiry, investigation; see **examination** 1.

interplay, *n.*—*Syn.* interaction, transaction, reciprocation; see **exchange** 1, 2.

interpolate, *v.*—*Syn.* inject, insert, introduce; see **add** 1, **include** 2.

interpolation, *n.*—*Syn.* injection, interjection, incorporation; see **addition** 2, **insertion.**

interpose, *v.* **1.** [To break into]—*Syn.* intrude, intervene, interfere; see **interrupt** 2.
2. [To insert]—*Syn.* introduce, insert, inject; see **add** 1, **include** 2.

interposing, *mod.*—*Syn.* interceding, interfering, mediating; see **advisory** 1, **judicial, meddlesome.**

interposition, *n.*—*Syn.* insertion, intrusion, intercession; see **intervention** 1.

interpret, *v.* **1.** [To convey the meaning of; *said especially of a work of art*]—*Syn.* give one's impressions of, render, play, perform, depict, delineate, enact, portray, make sense of, read (into), improvise on, re-enact, mimic, gather from, view as, give one an idea about, make of (D); see also **define, describe, represent** 2.
2. [To explain]—*Syn.* translate, paraphrase, render; see **explain.**

interpretation, *n.* **1.** [An explanation]—*Syn.* account, rendition, exposition, paraphrase, statement, diagnosis, description, representation, definition, elucidation, presentation, argument, paraphrase, gloss, answer, solution; see also **explanation** 1, **translation.**
2. [A conception]—*Syn.* version, reading, deduction, point of view, commentary, annotation, idea, analysis, recreation, criticism, dissertation, essay, discussion, appreciation, theme, critique, examination, study; see also **exposition** 2, **review** 2, **thesis** 2.

interpreted, *mod.*—*Syn.* elucidated, explained, made clear; see **known** 2, **obvious** 2.

interpreter, *n.*—*Syn.* preacher, commentator, paraphraser, writer, artist, editor, reviewer, annotator, biographer, expositor, analyst, scholar, spokesman, delegate, speaker, exponent, demonstrator, philosopher, professor, glossographer, translator, simultaneous interpreter, linguist, language expert; see also **critic** 2.

interregnum, *n.*—*Syn.* interval, suspension, interruption; see **pause** 1, 2, **respite.**

interrogate, *v.*—*Syn.* cross-examine, ask, give the third degree; see **examine** 2, **question** 1.

interrogation, *n.* —*Syn.* inquiry, query, investigation; see **examination** 1.

interrogative, *mod.* —*Syn.* quizzical, curious, questioning; see **inquisitive, interested** 1.

interrupt, *v.* **1.** [To hinder]—*Syn.* impede, obstruct, get in the way of; see **hinder, prevent.**
2. [To break in on]—*Syn.* intrude, intervene, cut in on, break in *or* into, interfere, infringe, obtrude, chime in, cut off, break (someone's) train of thought, come between, work *or* crowd *or* edge *or* insinuate *or* inject *or* put in; *all* (D): break the thread, worm *or* muscle *or* butt *or* horn *or* barge *or* bust in, crash; see also **meddle** 1.

interrupted, *mod.* —*Syn.* stopped, checked, held up, obstructed, delayed, parenthetical, interfered *or* meddled with, deranged, disordered, hindered, suspended, cut short; see also **late** 1, **postponed.**

interruption, *n.* —*Syn.* check, break, hiatus, gap, lacuna, cessation, suspension, parenthesis, intrusion, obstruction, holding over; see also **arrest** 2, **delay** 2, **interference** 2.

intersect, *v.* **1.** [To divide]—*Syn.* cut across, break in two, intercross; see **divide** 1, **separate** 2.
2. [To come together]—*Syn.* meet, converge, touch; see **cross** 1, **join** 1.

intersection, *n.* —*Syn.* traffic circle, cloverleaf, four-way stop; see **crossing** 1, **crossroad, junction** 2.

intersperse, *v.* —*Syn.* sprinkle, distribute, interlard; see **scatter** 1, 2.

interstate, *mod.* —*Syn.* interterritorial, between states, internal, interior, domestic; see also **local** 1.

interstice, *n.* —*Syn.* interval, crack, space; see **hole** 1.

intertwine, *v.* —*Syn.* twist, braid, tangle; see **weave** 1.

interval, *n.* —*Syn.* period, interlude, interim; see **pause** 1, 2.

intervene, *v.* **1.** [To settle]—*Syn.* step in, intercede, mediate; see **negotiate** 1, **reconcile** 2.
2. [To happen]—*Syn.* take place, occur, be; see **happen** 2.
3. [To meddle]—*Syn.* come between, interpose, intrude; see **interrupt** 2, **meddle** 1.

intervening, *mod.* —*Syn.* intermediary, interceding, sandwiched; see **intermediate, middle.**

intervention, *n.* **1.** [The act of intervening]—*Syn.* interposition, mediation, intercession, interruption, breaking in, entrance in support of, entrance of a third party; see also **interference** 2, **intrusion.**
2. [Armed interference]—*Syn.* invasion, military occupation, armed intrusion; see **attack** 1.

interview, *n.* **1.** [A relatively formal conversation] —*Syn.* meeting, audience, conference; see **conversation, communication.**
2. [The record of a conversation]—*Syn.* statement, account, case history; see **record** 1.

interview, *v.* —*Syn.* converse with, hold a colloquy with, get one's opinion, consult with, interrogate, hold an inquiry, give (one) an oral examination, get something for the record (D); see also **question** 1, **talk** 1.

interweave, *v.* —*Syn.* entwine, twist, braid; see **weave** 1.

interwoven, *mod.* —*Syn.* knit, mingled, intermixed; see **knitted, woven.**

intestinal, *mod.* —*Syn.* inner, visceral, rectal, ventral, duodenal, celiac; see also **abdominal, internal** 2.

intestine, *n.* —*Syn.* alimentary canal, large intestine, small intestine, bowels, rectum, food passage; *all* (D): gut, pipe, spaghetti; see also **organ** 2.

intestines, *n.* —*Syn.* entrails, bowels, viscera, vitals, digestive organs, splanchnic *or* visceral parts, tubular portion of the alimentary canal, guts (D); see also **abdomen, insides.** Parts of the human intestine include the following—large intestine, small intestine, duodenum, jejunum, ileum, colon, rectum.

in the air, *mod.* —*Syn.* prevalent, abroad, current; see **fashionable, popular** 1.

in the background, *mod.* —*Syn.* retiring, unseen, out of sight; see **obscure** 3, **unnoticed, withdrawn.**

in the bag (D), *mod.* —*Syn.* assured, definite, clinched; see **certain** 3.

in the black, *mod.* —*Syn.* prosperous, thriving, successful; see **balanced** 1, **rich** 1.

in the cards, *mod.* —*Syn.* possible, predicted, imminent; see **likely** 1.

in the dark, *mod.* —*Syn.* uninformed, uninstructed, confused; see **deceived** 1, **ignorant** 1.

in the end, *mod.* —*Syn.* at length, in conclusion, as a result; see **finally** 2.

in the future, *mod.* —*Syn.* eventually, sometime, in due time; see **finally** 2, **someday.**

in the lead, *mod.* —*Syn.* ahead, winning, leading; see **triumphant.**

in the market, *mod.* —*Syn.* buying, negotiating, purchasing, prepared to buy, looking (for), open to, needing, desiring, wanting.

in the meantime, *mod.* —*Syn.* in anticipation, at the same time, for the nonce (D); see **during, meanwhile, while** 1.

in the offing, *mod.* —*Syn.* in the near future, before long, in a short time; see **immediately, soon** 1.

in the way, *mod.* —*Syn.* bothersome, nagging, obstructing; see **disturbing, meddlesome.**

intimacy, *n.* —*Syn.* closeness, familiarity, confidence; see **affection, friendship** 1.

intimate, *mod.* **1.** [Personal]—*Syn.* close, guarded, near, familiar, trusted, confidential, inmost, innermost, uptight with (D); see also **private, secret** 1, **special** 1.—*Ant.* public*, open, unguarded.
2. [Close]—*Syn.* devoted, fond, fast; see **faithful, friendly** 1.

intimate, *n.* —*Syn.* associate, (constant) companion, close friend; see **fiancé, friend** 1, **lover** 1.

intimate, *v.* —*Syn.* suggest, imply, infer; see **hint** 1.

intimately, *mod.* —*Syn.* closely, personally, informally, familiarly, confidentially, without reserve, privately, in detail, off the record; see also **lovingly, secretly.**—*Ant.* openly*, reservedly, publicly.

intimation, *n.* —*Syn.* implication, innuendo, tip (D); see **allusion, hint** 1, **suggestion.**

in time, *mod.* —*Syn.* eventually, in the end, at the last; see **finally** 2, **ultimately.**

intimidate, *v.* —*Syn.* scare, awe, overawe; see **frighten** 1, 2, **threaten** 1.

intimidated, *mod.* —*Syn.* frightened, terrified, cowed; see **afraid** 1, 2, **horror-stricken.**

intimidation, *n.* —*Syn.* fright, perturbation, dread; see **fear** 2, **terror.**

into, *prep.* —*Syn.* inside, in the direction of, through to, to the middle of; see also **in** 1, 2, **toward, within.**

intolerable, *mod.* —*Syn.* insufferable, insupportable, unendurable, unbearable, enough to drive one mad, extreme, past bearing *or* enduring; see also **impossible** 1, **offensive** 2, **painful** 1, **undesirable.**

intolerance, *n.* **1.** [Lack of willingness to tolerate] —*Syn.* bigotry, dogmatism, narrow-mindedness; see **fanaticism, jingoism.**

2. [An example of intolerance, sense 1]—*Syn.* racism, race hatred, chauvinism, super-patriotism, religious fanaticism, provincialism, class prejudice, sexism, ageism, Aryanism, rugged individualism, sectionalism, regionalism, nationalism, conservatism, fascism, communism, imperialism, ism (D); see also **fanaticism, prejudice.**

intolerant, *mod.* —*Syn.* dogmatic, narrow, bigoted; see **prejudiced, stupid** 1.

intonation, *n.* —*Syn.* tone, sonority, accent; see **pitch** 3, **sound** 2.

intone, *v.* —*Syn.* articulate, utter, chant; see **hum, sing** 1.

in toto (Latin), *mod.* —*Syn.* fully, totally, entirely; see **completely.**

in touch, *mod.* —*Syn.* knowing, acquainted with, in communication; see **familiar with.**

intoxicant, *n.* **1.** [Alcohol]—*Syn.* alcoholic drink, liquor, booze (D); see **alcohol, drink** 2.

2. [Drug]—*Syn.* narcotic, hallucinogen, dope (D); see **drug** 2, **marijuana.**

intoxicate, *v.* **1.** [To make drunk]—*Syn.* befuddle, dope up, muddle; see **confuse, drug.**

2. [To excite]—*Syn.* exhilarate, stimulate, turn on (D); see **excite** 1.

intoxicated, *mod.* **1.** [Unduly elated]—*Syn.* stimulated, captivated, absorbed; see **excited.**

2. [Drunk]—*Syn.* inebriated; *both* (D): wired, gassed; see **dizzy** 1, **drunk.**

intoxication, *n.* —*Syn.* infatuation, inebriation, intemperance; see **drunkenness.**

intractability, *n.* —*Syn.* mulishness, tenacity, obstinacy; see **determination, stubbornness.**

intractable, *mod.* —*Syn.* unmanageable, contrary, stubborn; see **obstinate** 1, **resolute** 2, **unruly.**

intransigent, *mod.* —*Syn.* uncompromising, tenacious, stubborn; see **obstinate** 1, **resolute** 2.

intransigently, *mod.* —*Syn.* stubbornly, obdurately, uncompromisingly; see **firmly** 1, 2, **obstinately.**

intrench, *v.* **1.** [To prepare trenches]—*Syn.* make a ditch, dig trenches, bulwark, fortify with trenches, trench, dig in; see also **dig** 1, **shovel.**

2. [To prepare for attack]—*Syn.* arm (oneself), get a firm foothold, stand ready; see **defend** 1.

intrenched, *mod.* —*Syn.* bulwarked, dug in, barricaded; see **fortified, safe** 1.

intrepid, *mod.* —*Syn.* courageous, bold, dauntless; see **brave** 1.

intrepidity, *n.* —*Syn.* bravery, assurance, boldness; see **courage** 1, **determination** 2, **endurance** 2.

intricacy, *n.* —*Syn.* complication, elaborateness, complexity; see **confusion** 2, **difficulty** 1, 2.

intricate, *mod.* —*Syn.* involved, tricky, abstruse; see **complex** 2, **difficult** 1, 2, **obscure** 1.

intrigue, *n.* **1.** [Plot]—*Syn.* scheme, conspiracy, cabal, machination, plan, secret arrangement, complication, ruse, artifice, design, dodge, contrivance, collusion, maneuver, fraud, secret plot, graft; *both* (D): wire-pulling, deal; see also **trick** 1.

2. [Love affair]—*Syn.* attachment, intimacy, liaison, amour, affair, interlude, infatuation, flirtation, romance; *both* (D): hush-hush show, case; see also **affair** 2.

intrigue, *v.* —*Syn.* delight, please, attract; see **charm** 1, **entertain** 1, **fascinate.**

intrigued, *mod.* —*Syn.* attracted, delighted, pleased; see **charmed, entertained** 2, **fascinated.**

intriguing, *mod.* **1.** [Fascinating]—*Syn.* engaging, attractive, delightful; see **beautiful** 1, 2, **charming, handsome** 2, **pleasant** 1.

2. [Sly]—*Syn.* crafty, clever, tricky; see **sly** 1.

intrinsic, *mod.* —*Syn.* essential, central, natural; see **fundamental** 1, **inherent.**

introduce, *v.* **1.** [To bring in]—*Syn.* freight, carry in, transport; see **carry, import** 1, **send** 1, **ship.**

2. [To present]—*Syn.* set forth, submit, advance; see **offer** 1, **propose** 1.

3. [To make strangers acquainted]—*Syn.* present, give an introduction, make known, hold a debut for, put on speaking terms with; *all* (D): do the honors, give a knockdown, break the ice.

4. [To institute]—*Syn.* launch, found, plan; see **organize** 2.

5. [To insert]—*Syn.* put in, add, enter; see **include** 2, **inject.**

6. [To begin]—*Syn.* start, open, inaugurate; see **begin** 1.

introduced, *mod.* **1.** [Brought in]—*Syn.* made current *or* known, imported, popularized; see **received.**

2. [Made acquainted]—*Syn.* acquainted with, on speaking terms, not unknown to each other *or* one another; see **familiar with.**

introduction, *n.* **1.** [The act of bringing in]—*Syn.* admittance, initiation, inception, installation, influx, ingress, institution, induction; see also **entrance** 1.

2. [The act of making strangers acquainted] —*Syn.* presentation, debut, meeting, formal acquaintance, preliminary encounter.

3. [Introductory knowledge]—*Syn.* first acquaintance, elementary statement, first contact, start, awakening, first taste, baptism, preliminary training, basic principles; see also **initiation** 1, **knowledge** 1.

4. [An introductory explanation]—*Syn.* preface, preamble, prefatory note, foreword, prologue, prelude, overture, intro (D), proem, prolegomena; see also **explanation** 2.

5. [A work supplying introductory knowledge] —*Syn.* primer, basic text, beginner's book, elements, foundation, manual, handbook, first book, grammar, survey, essentials; see also **book** 1, **text** 1.

introductory, *mod.* **1.** [Preliminary]—*Syn.* prefatory, initial, incipient, initiatory, opening, early, prior, starting, beginning, precursory, preparatory, primary, original, anterior, preparative, provisional; see also **first** 1.—*Ant.* principal*, substantial, secondary.

2. [Elementary]—*Syn.* rudimentary, basic, beginning; see **fundamental** 1.

introspection, *n.* —*Syn.* self-examination, rumination, brooding, introversion, egoism; see also **thought** 1.
introspective, *mod.* —*Syn.* contemplative, subjective, inner-directed; see **thoughtful** 1.
in trouble, *mod.* **1.** [In difficulty]—*Syn.* in a quandary, never free from, in chancery; *all* (D): in bad, in hot water, in for it, in the doghouse, in a jam, out on a limb; see also **troubled** 1.
2. [(D) Pregnant]—*Syn.* with child; *both* (D): expecting, knocked up; see **pregnant** 1.
introversion, *n.* —*Syn.* self-centeredness, inner-directedness, a preoccupation with *or* a centering upon (one's own) self; see **egotism.**
introvert, *n.* —*Syn.* brooder, self-observer, egoist, egotist, narcissist, autist, solitary; *both* (D): loner, lone wolf.
introverted, *mod.* —*Syn.* self-centered, indrawn, introvertive; see **egotistic** 1.
intrude, *v.* —*Syn.* interfere, interrupt, interpose; see **meddle** 1.
intruder, *n.* —*Syn.* prowler, thief, unwelcome guest, meddler, interloper, invader, snooper, unwanted person, crasher (D), interferer, interrupter, disrupting element, trespasser; see also **criminal, nuisance** 3, **robber.**
intrusion, *n.* —*Syn.* interruption, forced entrance, trespass, intervention, interposition, meddling, obtrusion, encroachment, invasion, infraction, overrunning, unwelcome suggestion, overstepping, transgression, seizure; *all* (D): nose-in, horn-in, muscle-in; see also **interference** 2.
intrusive, *mod.* —*Syn.* untimely, impertinent, nosey (D); see **meddlesome, rude** 2.
intrust, *v.* —*Syn.* entrust, give over, consign; see **assign** 1, **trust** 3.
in trust, *mod.* —*Syn.* in escrow, on deposit, in the custody of, deposited (with), under agreement with, in one's keeping, in account with, given as surety, bonded, held; see also **retained** 1.
intuition, *n.* —*Syn.* presentiment, foreknowledge, inspiration; see **feeling** 4.
intuitive, *mod.* —*Syn.* instantaneously apprehended, emotional, instinctive; see **automatic** 2, **habitual** 1, **inherent, natural** 1, **spontaneous, understood** 1.
inundate, *v.* —*Syn.* submerge, engulf, pour down on; see **flood, immerse** 1.
inundation, *n.* —*Syn.* deluge, torrent, tide; see **flood** 1.
inure, *v.* —*Syn.* accustom, habituate, toughen (up); see **familiarize, strengthen, teach** 1.
invade, *v.* **1.** [To enter with armed force]—*Syn.* force a landing, penetrate, fall on; see **attack** 1.
2. [To encroach upon]—*Syn.* infringe on, trespass, interfere with; see **meddle** 1.
invader, *n.* —*Syn.* trespasser, alien, attacking force; see **attacker, enemy** 1.
in vain, *mod.* —*Syn.* futilely, purposelessly, unprofitably; see **vainly.**
invalid, *mod.* —*Syn.* irrational, unreasonable, fallacious; see **illogical, wrong** 2.
invalid, *n.* —*Syn.* disabled person, incurable, paralytic, cripple, weakling, consumptive, tubercular, leper, inmate; *both* (D): bed case, chair case; see also **patient.**
invalidate, *v.* —*Syn.* annul, refute, nullify; see **cancel** 2, **revoke.**
invalidism, *n.* —*Syn.* feebleness, infirmity, sickness; see **weakness** 1.
invalidity, *n.* —*Syn.* falsity, inconsistency, unsoundness; see **fallacy** 1.
invaluable, *mod.* —*Syn.* priceless, expensive, dear; see **valuable** 1.
invariable, *mod.* —*Syn.* unchanging, uniform, static; see **constant** 1, **perpetual** 1, **regular** 3.
invariableness, *n.* —*Syn.* constancy, uniformity, lack of change; see **stability** 1.
invariably, *mod.* —*Syn.* perpetually, constantly, habitually; see **customarily, regularly** 2.
invasion, *n.* —*Syn.* forced entrance, intrusion, aggression; see **attack** 1.
invective, *n.* —*Syn.* denunciation, vituperation, condemnation; see **accusation** 2, **blame** 1.
inveigh, *v.* —*Syn.* scold, reproach, admonish; see **censure, denounce.**
inveigle, *v.* —*Syn.* coax, entice, persuade; see **influence, urge** 2.
invent, *v.* **1.** [To create or discover]—*Syn.* originate, devise, fashion, form, project, design, find, coin, improvise, contrive, execute, carry into execution, come upon, conceive, author, plan, think *or* make up, bring into being, bear, turn out, forge, make; *all* (D): ad-lib, hatch, wing it, dream *or* cook up; see also **compose** 3, **create** 2, **discover** 1, **produce** 2.
2. [To fabricate]—*Syn.* misrepresent, create out of thin air, simulate, fake, feign, make believe, trump up, equivocate, falsify, conjure *or* think up, misstate, concoct, cook up (D); see also **lie** 1.
invention, *n.* **1.** [Ingenuity]—*Syn.* inventiveness, imagination, creativeness; see **originality.**
2. [An original device]—*Syn.* contrivance, contraption, design; see **discovery** 2.
inventive, *mod.* —*Syn.* productive, imaginative, fertile; see **artistic** 3, **original** 2.
inventor, *n.* —*Syn.* author, originator, creator; see **architect** 1, **artist** 1, **designer.**
inventory, *n.* **1.** [A list]—*Syn.* stock book, itemization, register; see **catalogue** 1, **file** 2, **index** 2, **list, record** 1, **table** 2.
2. [The act of taking stock]—*Syn.* inspection, review, examination, tabulation, checking, counting, accounting, investigation; see also **summary.**
inventory, *v.* —*Syn.* take stock of, look *or* go over, account for, count, tabulate, check, investigate, review, examine, inspect, list, catalogue, audit; see also **file** 1, **list** 1, **record** 1.
inverse, *mod.* —*Syn.* inverted, converse, transposed; see **opposite** 3.
inversion, *n.* —*Syn.* transposition, reversion, contradiction; see **conversion** 1, **opposite.**
invert, *v.* **1.** [To upset]—*Syn.* overturn, turn upside-down, tip; see **upset** 1.
2. [To reverse]—*Syn.* change, rearrange, transpose; see **exchange** 1.
3. [To change]—*Syn.* alter, modify, convert; see **change** 1.
invertebrate, *mod.* —*Syn.* cowardly, hesitant, indecisive; see **irresolute.**
invertebrate, *n.* —*Syn.* nonskeletal *or* spineless creature, protozoan, member of the Vermes

group; see also **clam, crab, jellyfish, lobster, shellfish, worm.**

invest, *v.* —*Syn.* lay out, spend, put one's money into, lend on security, advance, intrust, give money over, buy stocks, make an investment, loan, lend; *all* (D): plant cabbages, buy into, salt away *or* down, sink money in, put up the dough; see also **buy** 1.

investigate, *v.* —*Syn.* look over *or* into, interrogate, review; see **examine** 1, **study** 1.

investigated, *mod.* —*Syn.* examined, tried, tested, inspected, searched, questioned, probed, considered, measured, checked, studied, researched, made the subject of an investigation *or* hearing *or* trial *or* probe, subjected to scrutiny *or* investigation, worked on, thought out *or* through, scrutinized, put to the test, gone over *or* into, cross-examined; see also **reviewed.**

investigating, *mod.* —*Syn.* fact-finding, investigative, inspecting; see **research.**

investigation, *n.* —*Syn.* inquiry, search, research; see **examination** 1, **study** 2.

investigator, *n.* —*Syn.* inquirer, tester, inspector, reviewer, analyst, auditor, reviewing board member, prosecutor; see also **examiner.**
Investigators include the following—sleuth, police inspector, district attorney, prosecuting attorney, government agent, census taker, insurance investigator, FBI agent, Gestapo agent, ombudsman, plain-clothes man, secret police, secret agent, informer; *all* (D): G-man, snooper, dick, undercover man, flatfoot; see also **detective, policeman, spy.**

investiture, *n.* —*Syn.* admission, investing, inauguration; see **installation** 1.

investment, *n.* —*Syn.* endowment, grant, loan, expenditure, expense, backing, speculation, disintermediation, financing, finance, purchase, advance, bail, interests, vested interests; *all* (D): grease, stake, nut; see also **money** 3, **property** 1.
Types of investment include the following—stocks, bonds, shares, securities, property, real estate, mortgage, capital goods, insurance liens, debentures, futures, mining stock, bonded liquor.

inveterate, *mod.* —*Syn.* ingrained, confirmed, deep-rooted; see **chronic, habitual** 1, **permanent** 2.

invidious, *mod.* —*Syn.* repugnant, odious, detestable; see **offensive** 2.

in view of, *mod.* —*Syn.* in consideration of, because, taking into consideration; see **considering.**

invigorate, *v.* —*Syn.* stimulate, freshen, exhilarate; see **animate** 1, **excite** 1.

invigorating, *mod.* —*Syn.* refreshing, exhilarating, bracing; see **stimulating.**

invincible, *mod.* —*Syn.* unconquerable, insuperable, impregnable; see **powerful** 1, **strong** 1, 2.

inviolability, *n.* —*Syn.* indestructibility, purity, sanctity; see **consecration, holiness** 2, **stability** 1, **strength** 1.

inviolable, *mod.* **1.** [Divine]—*Syn.* holy, sacred, sacrosanct; see **divine** 2.
2. [Indestructible]—*Syn.* durable, unbreakable, stable; see **permanent** 2.

inviolate, *mod.* —*Syn.* unbroken, intact, whole; see **perfect** 2.

invisibility, *n.* —*Syn.* obscurity, concealment, camouflage, indistinctness, imperceptibility, invisibleness, indefiniteness, seclusion, latency, cloudiness, haziness, fogginess, mistiness, duskiness, nebulousness, darkness, gloominess, gloom, insubstantiality, incorporeality, immateriality, intangibility, disappearance, vagueness, indefiniteness, indiscernibility, indistinguishability, unnoticeability.

invisible, *mod.* **1.** [Beyond unaided vision]—*Syn.* intangible, ungraspable, out of sight, unfinitesimal, microscopic, beyond the visual range, unseeable, unviewable, supernatural, ghostly, wraithlike, unseen, undisclosed, covert, occult, airy, impalpable, ethereal, ideal, unreal, vaporous, gaseous, supersensory; see also **dark** 1, **transparent** 1.—*Ant.* real*, substantial, material.
2. [Not apparent]—*Syn.* imperceptible, deceptive, inconspicuous; see **obscure** 1, **vague** 2.

invisibly, *mod.* —*Syn.* imperceptibly, undetectibly, out of sight, not visibly, uncertainly, obscurely, in a hidden *or* secret *or* unknown manner; see also **vaguely.**

invitation, *n.* **1.** [The act of inviting]—*Syn.* summons, solicitation, bidding, dating, compliments; *both* (D): bid, invite; see also **request.**
2. [That which invites]—*Syn.* note, card, message, encouragement, proposition, proposal, call, petition, overture, offer, enticement, temptation, attraction, allurement, lure, prompting, urge, pressure, reason, motive, ground; see also **appeal** 1, **letter** 2, **suggestion** 1.

invite, *v.* **1.** [To ask guests]—*Syn.* bid, ask, have over *or* out *or* in, formally invite, request (the pleasure of one's company), issue *or* send *or* give an invitation (to), include in the guest list, request an R.S.V.P., bid come; see also **ask** 1.
2. [To ask politely]—*Syn.* bid, request, induce, beg, suggest, encourage, entice, solicit, entreat, pray, supplicate, petition, persuade, prevail on, insist, ask insistently, press, ply, propose, lure, court, beseech, importune, crave, appeal to, implore, call upon, sue, beg leave, beg a boon; see also **urge** 2.—*Ant.* discourage*, repulse, rebuff.

inviting, *mod.* —*Syn.* appealing, alluring, cordial, tempting, attractive, winning, winsome, captivating, agreeable, engaging, open, encouraging, delightful, pleasing, enticing, persuasive, magnetic, fascinating, provocative, bewitching; see also **charming.**—*Ant.* painful*, unbearable, insufferable.

in vogue, *mod.* —*Syn.* stylish, current, à la mode; see **fashionable, popular** 1.

invoice, *n.* **1.** [An inventory]—*Syn.* manifest, itemized account, check list; see **inventory** 2.
2. [A bill of goods]—*Syn.* bill of lading, receipt, bill of shipment; see **statement** 3.

invoke, *v.* **1.** [To call upon]—*Syn.* request, entreat, appeal to; see **beg** 1.
2. [To summon]—*Syn.* send for, bid, conjure up; see **summon** 1.

involuntary, *mod.* —*Syn.* unintentional, uncontrolled, instinctive; see **automatic** 2, **habitual** 1.

involution, *n.* —*Syn.* intricacy, complication, complexity; see **difficulty** 1, 2.

involve, *v.* —*Syn.* draw into, compromise, implicate, entangle, link, connect, incriminate, associate, relate, catch up, wrap up in, denote, argue, suggest, prove, comprise, point to, commit, mix up, bring up; see also **include** 1, **mean** 1, **occupy** 3, **require** 2.

involved, *mod.* —*Syn.* brought into difficulties, entangled in a crime, incriminated, implicated, embarrassed, embroiled, caught *or* wrapped up *or* immersed in; see also **included.**

involvement, *n.* **1.** [Difficulty]—*Syn.* quandary, crisis, embarrassment; see **difficulty** 1, 2.

2. [Engrossment]—*Syn.* intentness, study, preoccupation; see **reflection** 1.

invulnerability, *n.* —*Syn.* assurance, impenetrability, strength; see **protection** 2, **safety** 1, **security** 1.

invulnerable, *mod.* —*Syn.* strong, invincible, secure; see **safe** 1.

inward, *mod.* **1.** [Moving into]—*Syn.* penetrating, ingoing, through, incoming, entering, inbound, inpouring, infiltrating, inflowing; see also **penetrating** 1.

2. [Placed within]—*Syn.* inside, internal, interior; see **in** 1, **within.**

3. [Private]—*Syn.* spiritual, intellectual, intimate; see **private, religious** 2.

inwardly, *mod.* —*Syn.* by nature, from within *or* the inside, from deep down, deeply rooted, fundamentally, basically, not outwardly *or* visibly, well-grounded, below the surface; see also **naturally** 2, **within.**

ion, *n.* —*Syn.* cation, anion, electrically charged particle; see **atom** 1, 2.

iota, *n.* —*Syn.* grain, particle, speck; see **bit** 1.

irascibility, *n.* —*Syn.* wrath, irritability, irritation; see **anger.**

irascible, *mod.* —*Syn.* peevish, cranky, irritable; see **angry.**

irate, *mod.* —*Syn.* enraged, furious, incensed; see **angry.**

ire, *n.* —*Syn.* wrath, fury, rage; see **anger.**

iridescence, *n.* —*Syn.* luminosity, phosphorescence, radiance; see **color** 1, **light** 1.

iridescent, *mod.* —*Syn.* pearly, nacreous, shimmering, prismatic, rainbow-colored, opalescent, lustrous; see also **bright** 1, 2.

iris, *n.* —*Syn.* flag, blue flag, yellow flag, fleur-de-lis, flower-de-luce, orris-root, gladdon, roast-beef plant, *Iris Germanica* (Latin); see also **flower** 2, **plant.**

Irish, *mod.* —*Syn.* Celtic, Hibernian, Ulster, Eire, Gael, Gaelic, Goidelic, Eirenic, Old Irish, Middle Irish, from the old sod (D).

irk, *v.* —*Syn.* annoy, harass, disturb; see **bother** 2, 3.

irksome, *mod.* —*Syn.* tiresome, tedious, troublesome; see **disturbing.**

iron, *mod.* **1.** [Made of iron]—*Syn.* ferrous, ironclad, ironcased, ironshod.

2. [Having the qualities of iron]—*Syn.* hard, robust, strong, unyielding, dense, insensible, inflexible, adamant, cruel, stubborn, implacable, heavy; see also **firm** 2, **thick** 3.

iron, *n.* **1.** [A metallic element]—*Syn.* pig iron, cast iron, wrought iron, sheet iron, coke, *Fe* (chemical symbol); see also **alloy, metal.** Instruments referred to as irons, and usually or originally made of iron, include the following—flatiron, branding iron, golf club, midiron, heavy iron, driving iron, light iron, manacle, iron pan, sadiron, electric iron, press, harpoon, gun, mangle, hardware, curling iron.

2. [Bitterness]—*Syn.* hurt, remorse, resentment; see **bitterness** 2, **distress** 1.

3. [An appliance]—*Syn.* pressing device, presser, steam iron, teflon iron, travel iron; see also **appliance.**

iron, *v.* —*Syn.* use a flatiron *or* electric *or* steam *or* gas iron (on), press, mangle, roll, finish, smooth (out), give a *coup de fer* (French); see also **flatten** 2, **smooth** 1.

have many irons in the fire—*Syn.* engaged, active, occupied; see **busy** 1.

in irons—*Syn.* shackled, fettered, tied; see **bound** 1.

ironed, *mod.* —*Syn.* pressed, flat, flattened; **see smooth** 1.

ironical, *mod.* **1.** [*Said of events, works, statements, and the like*]—*Syn.* contradictory, twisted, ridiculous, backbiting, mocking, satiric, paradoxical, unexpected, implausible, critical, chaffing, derisive, disparaging, uncomplimentary, exaggerated, caustic, biting, trenchant, incisive, scathing, pungent, satirical, spicy, bitter, acrid, jibing; see also **sense** 2, **sarcastic.**

2. [*Said especially of persons*]—*Syn.* sarcastic, sardonic, contemptuous, defiant, arrogant, quick-witted, clever, alert, quip-making, keen, sharp; see also **witty.**

ironing, *n.* —*Syn.* pressing, steam-pressing, mangling, smoothing, doing flatwork, flatting.

iron out, *v.* —*Syn.* compromise, settle differences, reach an agreement about; see **agree, arbitrate, negotiate** 1, **settle** 9.

irons, *n.* —*Syn.* shackles, manacles, fetters; see **chains, handcuffs.**

ironworks, *n.* —*Syn.* furnace, hearth, forge; see **factory.**

irony, *n.* —*Syn.* satire, wit, ridicule, raillery, mockery, burlesque, quip, banter, derision, criticism, paradox, jibe, twist, taunt, contempt, humor, reproach, repartee, backhanded compliment (D); see also **sarcasm.**

irradiate, *v.* —*Syn.* illuminate, lighten, brighten; see **light** 1.

irradiation, *n.* —*Syn.* reflection, radiation, radiance; see **light** 1.

irrational, *mod.* **1.** [Illogical]—*Syn.* unreasonable, specious, fallacious; see **illogical, wrong** 2.

2. [Stupid]—*Syn.* senseless, silly, ridiculous; see **stupid** 1.

irrationality, *n.* **1.** [Nonsense]—*Syn.* absurdity, fallibility, invalidity; see **nonsense** 1, 2.

2. [Incoherence]—*Syn.* unreasonability, insanity, idiocy; see **inconsistency.**

irrationally, *mod.* —*Syn.* illogically, unreasonably, stupidly; see **foolishly.**

irreclaimable, *mod.* —*Syn.* irreparable, incorrigible, beyond hope; see **hopeless** 2.

irreconcilable, *mod.* —*Syn.* hostile, reluctant, opposed; see **unfriendly** 1.

irrecoverable, *mod.* —*Syn.* irretrievable, unrectifiable, unremediable; see **lost** 1.

irredeemable, *mod.* —*Syn.* irreparable, incurable, beyond redemption; see **hopeless** 2.

irreducible, *mod.* —*Syn.* immutable, irrevocable, unchangeable, intransmutable, irresoluble, incapable of being diminished, indelible, indestructible, imperishable, indissoluble, inextinguishable; see also **firm** 1, **permanent.**

irrefragable, *mod.* —*Syn.* incontestable, undeniable, indisputable; see **certain** 3, **inevitable.**

irrefutable, *mod.* —*Syn.* evident, final, proven; see **accurate** 1, 2, **obvious** 1, 2.

irregular, *mod.* **1.** [Not even]—*Syn.* uneven, spasmodic, fitful, uncertain, aberrant, random, unsettled, inconstant, unsteady, fragmentary, unsystematic, occasional, infrequent, fluctuating, faltering, wavering, recurrent, intermittent, discontinuous, sporadic, changeable, capricious, casual, variable, shifting, unmethodical, jerky, up and down (D); see also **changing, shaky** 1, **unreliable** 2. —*Ant.* regular*, even, punctual.

2. [Not customary]—*Syn.* unique, extraordinary, abnormal; see **different** 1, **unusual** 2.

3. [Questionable]—*Syn.* strange, overt, debatable; see **questionable** 2, **suspicious** 2.

4. [Not regular in form or in outline]—*Syn.* not uniform, devious, unsymmetrical, asymmetrical, nonsymmetrical, uneven, unequal, craggy, hilly, broken, jagged, aberrant, notched, serrate, eccentric, elliptic, elliptical, bumpy, meandering, zigzagged, unaligned, amorphous, variable, wobbly, lumpy, off balance, off center, protuberant, lopsided, pockmarked, scarred, crinkled, bristling, bumpy, sprawling, out of proportion; *both* (D): cockeyed, gallywampus; see also **bent, crooked** 2.

irregularity, *n.* **1.** [Unevenness]—*Syn.* stop, break, uncertainty, aberration, shift, change, twist, bump, hump, flaw, imperfection, dent, hole, variability, spasm, deviation, inconsistency, distortion; see also **variation.**

2. [Something that is irregular]—*Syn.* peculiarity, singularity, anomaly, abnormality, strangeness, uniqueness, exception, excess, unorthodoxy, malfunction, malformation, deviation, dispensation, allowance, exemption, privilege, nonconformity, unconformity, innovation, oddity, eccentricity, rarity, looseness, laxity; see also **characteristic, quirk.** —*Ant.* custom*, regularity, rule.

3. [A suspicious or illegal occurrence]—*Syn.* breach, infringement, violation; see **crime** 1, **sin.**

irregularly, *mod.* —*Syn.* by snatches, periodically, at (irregular) intervals, intermittently, by fits and starts, fitfully, by jerks, by turns, off and on, hit or miss (D); see also **unevenly.**

irrelevant, *mod.* —*Syn.* inapplicable, impertinent, off the topic, inappropriate, inconsequent, unrelated, extraneous, unconnected, inapropros, inappropriate, not germane, off the point, foreign, outside *or* beside the question, out of order *or* place, pointless, beside the point, not connected with, not pertaining to, without reference to, out of the way, remote, neither here nor there (D); see also **trivial, unnecessary.**

irreligion, *n.* —*Syn.* atheism, disbelief, skepticism; see **doubt** 1.

irreligious, *mod.* —*Syn.* ungodly, profane, sacrilegious; see **atheistic, impious** 1, **wicked** 1.

irremediable, *mod.* —*Syn.* irreparable, malignant, dire; see **deadly, hopeless** 2, **inevitable.**

irremovable, *mod.* —*Syn.* stable, unchangeable, fixed; see **constant** 1, **permanent.**

irreparable, *mod.* —*Syn.* incorrigible, incurable, hopeless, irreversible, irretrievable, irredeemable; see also **broken** 1, **destroyed, ruined** 1.

irrepressible, *mod.* —*Syn.* insuppressible, unconstrained, tumultuous; see **rebellious** 2, **unruly.**

irreproachable, *mod.* —*Syn.* faultless, blameless, good; see **innocent** 4, **pure** 3.

irresistible, *mod.* **1.** [Overwhelming]—*Syn.* compelling, overpowering, invincible; see **overwhelming** 1, **powerful** 1.

2. [Fascinating]—*Syn.* lovable, alluring, enchanting; see **charming, tempting.**

irresolute, *mod.* —*Syn.* indecisive, wavering, faltering, vacillating, fickle, uncertain, fluctuating, unsettled, hesitant, hesitating, doubting, unstable, inconstant, fickle, fearful, timid, undetermined, wobbly, halfhearted; see **changing, shaky** 1, **undecided.** —*Ant.* resolute*, firm, determined.

irrespective, *mod.* —*Syn.* separate, distinct, independent; see **regardless** 2, **separated.**

irresponsible, *mod.* —*Syn.* untrustworthy, capricious, flighty, fickle, giddy, thoughtless, rash, undependable, unstable, loose, lax, immoral, shiftless, unpredictable, wild, devil-may-care; see **changeable** 1, **unreliable** 1.—*Ant.* responsible*, trustworthy, dependable.

irresponsive, *mod.* —*Syn.* taciturn, unmoved, secretive; see **indifferent** 1, **unconcerned.**

irretrievable, *mod.* —*Syn.* incorrigible, irrevocable, unrecoverable; see **absent, gone** 2, **lost** 1.

irreverence, *n.* **1.** [Blasphemy]—*Syn.* sinfulness, profanity, impiety; see **blasphemy, heresy, sin.**

2. [Indignity]—*Syn.* ridicule, discourtesy, disrespect; see **insult, rudeness.**

irreverent, *mod.* —*Syn.* profane, sacrilegious, disrespectful; see **rude** 2.

irreversible, *mod.* —*Syn.* unchangeable, invariable, immutable; see **constant** 1.

irrevocable, *mod.* —*Syn.* permanent, indelible, lost; see **certain** 3, **doomed, inevitable.**

irrigate, *v.* —*Syn.* water, pass water through, build an artificial watering system, obtain water rights, inundate; see **flood.**

irrigation, *n.* —*Syn.* watering, flooding, inundation, inundating, fertilization, fertilizing, making productive.

irritability, *n.* —*Syn.* anger, peevishness, impatience; see **anger, annoyance** 1, **sensitivity.**

irritable, *mod.* —*Syn.* sensitive, irascible, touchy, testy, ill-tempered, huffy, peevish, petulant, fractious, tense, contentious, disputatious, resentful, fretting, carping, crabbed, hypercritical, out of humor, bearish, quick-tempered, easily offended, choleric, glum, complaining, brooding, dissatisfied, plaintive, snarling, grumbling, surly, gloomy, ill-natured, morose, moody, fidgety, snappish, waspish, cantankerous, captious, fretful, querulous,

hypersensitive, ill-humored, annoyed, cross, churlish, grouchy, shrewish, sulky, sullen; *all* (D): high-strung, crusty, snappy, having a short fuse, thin-skinned, pickle-pussed, grumpy, sour-bellied; see **critical** 2, **excitable, troubled 1.**—*Ant.* pleasant*, agreeable, good-natured.

irritant, *n.* —*Syn.* bother, burden, nuisance; see **annoyance** 1, **trouble** 2.

irritate, *v.* **1.** [To bother]—*Syn.* provoke, exasperate, pester; see **bother** 2, **confuse, disturb** 2.
2. [To inflame]—*Syn.* redden, chafe, swell, erupt, pain, sting; see **burn** 6, **hurt** 4, **itch.**

irritated, *mod.* —*Syn.* disturbed, upset, bothered; see **troubled.**

irritating, *mod.* —*Syn.* vexatious, bothersome, trying; see **disturbing.**

irritation, *n.* **1.** [The result of irritating]—*Syn.* soreness, susceptibility, tenderness, excitability, rawness, tenseness, irritability, oversensitiveness, hypersensitivity, oversensitivity, (extreme) sensibility, susceptibleness; see **feeling** 4, **sensitivity.**
2. [A disturbed mental state]—*Syn.* excitement, upset, provocation; see **anger, annoyance, stress** 3.

irruption, *n.* —*Syn.* aggression, inflation, invasion; see **attack** 1.

is, *v.* —*Syn.* lives, breathes, subsists, transpires, happens, amounts to, equals, comprises, signifies, means.

Islam, *n.* —*Syn.* Moslemism, Mohammedanism, Islamism; see **church** 3, **religion** 2.

island, *n.* **1.** [Land surrounded by water]—*Syn.* isle, islet, bar, key, atoll, holm, *adal* (Malay), *jima* (Japanese), archipelago; see also **land** 1, **reef.**
2. [An isolated spot]—*Syn.* haven, retreat, refuge, sanctuary; see **refuge** 1, **shelter.**

ism, *n.* —*Syn.* dogma, belief, opinion; see **doctrine** 1.

isolate, *v.* —*Syn.* confine, detach, seclude; see **divide** 1, **separate** 2.

isolated, *mod.* —*Syn.* secluded, apart, backwoods, insular, segregated, confined, sequestered, screened, withdrawn, rustic, separate, lonely, forsaken, hidden, remote, out-of-the-way, unfrequented, lonesome, in a backwater, God-forsaken; see **alone** 1, **private, solitary.**

isolation, *n.* —*Syn.* detachment, solitude, loneliness, seclusion, segregation, confinement, separation, self-sufficiency, obscurity, retreat, privacy; see **retirement** 2, **withdrawal.**

isolation, *n.* —*Syn.* segregation, nonintervention, neutrality; see **noninterference.**

isolationist, *n.* —*Syn.* nationalist, high-tariff advocate, neutralist, conservative; *all* (D): America-firster, jingoist, super-patriot, ultra-nationalist, Bircher, 100% American; see **Conservative, patriot.**—*Ant.* liberal*, internationalist, free trader.

Israel, *n.* **1.** [The land of Israel]—*Syn.* Palestine, Judea, Canaan, the State of Israel, Jerusalem, Zion; *all* (D): the land of milk and honey, the Promised Land, the Homeland; see **Asia.**
2. [The Jewish people]—*Syn.* Hebrews, the children of God *or* Abraham, Israelites; see **Jew.**

Israelite, *n.* —*Syn.* Hebrew, sabra, Israeli; see **Jew.**

issue, *n.* **1.** [Question]—*Syn.* point, matter, problem, concern, point in question, matter of contention, argument, point of departure; see **puzzle** 2, **subject** 1.
2. [Result]—*Syn.* upshot, culmination, effect; see **result.**
3. [Edition]—*Syn.* number, copy, impression; see **edition.**
4. [Release]—*Syn.* issuance, circulation, delivery; see **distribution** 1.
5. [That which has been released on the market] —*Syn.* stocks, issue of stock, bond issue; see **investment**
at issue—*Syn.* in dispute, unsettled, controversial; see **undecided.**
take issue—*Syn.* differ, disagree, take a stand against; see **oppose** 1.

issue, *v.* **1.** [To emerge]—*Syn.* flow out, proceed, come forth; see **appear** 1.
2. [To be a result of]—*Syn.* rise from, spring, originate; see **begin** 2, **result.**
3. [To release]—*Syn.* circulate, send out, announce; see **advertise** 1, **declare** 1, **publish** 1.
4. [To distribute]—*Syn.* allot, dispense, assign; see **distribute** 1.
5. [To emit]—*Syn.* exude, give off, send forth; see **emit** 1.

issued, *mod.* —*Syn.* circulated, broadcast, televised, made public, announced, disseminated, published, sent out, promulgated, expressed, spread; see **delivered, distributed.**

isthmus, *n.* —*Syn.* land passage *or* bridge, neck of land, portage; see **land** 1.

it, *pron.* —*Syn.* such a thing, that which, the object, this thing, the subject; see **that, this.**
with it (D)—*Syn.* alert, aware, up-to-date; see **hip.**

Italian, *mod.* —*Syn.* Latin, Etruscan, Umbrian, Ligurian, Tuscan, Florentine, Milanese, Venetian, Neapolitan, Sicilian, Calabrian, Ibero-insular, Cevenole, Littoral, Adriatic, sub-Adriatic.

Italicism, *n.* —*Syn.* Italianism, Latinism, Italian idiom, Romanism.

italicize, *v.* —*Syn.* stress, underline, print in italic type, draw attention to; see **distinguish** 1, **emphasize.**

Italy, *n.* —*Syn.* Italia, Etruria, country of the Latins, Italian peninsula, Italian people, Italian Republic, Rome, *Latium* (Latin), Italian boot (D).

itch, *n.* **1.** [An uncomfortable sensation in the skin] —*Syn.* tingling, prickling, crawling, creeping sensation, rawness, scabbiness, pruritus, psoriasis, psora; see also **irritation** 1.
2. [A strong desire]—*Syn.* hankering, yearning, craving; see **desire** 1.

itch, *v.* **1.** [To have a tingling sensation]—*Syn.* creep, prickle, prick, be irritated, crawl, tickle; see also **tingle.**
2. [To have a strong desire]—*Syn.* yearn, crave, long for; see **want** 1.

itchy, *mod.* —*Syn.* itching, having an itch, tingling, pricking, crawly, crawling; see also **tender** 6.

item, *n.* —*Syn.* piece, article, matter; see **detail** 1, **part** 1.

itemize, *v.* —*Syn.* inventory, enumerate, number; see **count, detail** 1, **list** 1.

itemized, *mod.* —*Syn.* counted, particularized, enumerated; see **detailed.**

iterate, *v.* —*Syn.* say again, go over, emphasize; see **repeat** 3.

iteration, *n.* —*Syn.* redundancy, monotony, emphasis; see **repetition.**

itinerant, *mod.* —*Syn.* roving, nomadic, peripatetic; see **vagrant** 2, **wandering** 1.

itinerant, *n.* —*Syn.* nomad, wanderer, vagrant; see **tramp** 1.

itinerary, *n.* —*Syn.* course, travel plans, route; see **path** 1, **plan** 2, **program** 2, **way** 2.

ivory, *mod.* —*Syn.* creamy, cream-colored, tawny, fulvous; see also **tan, white** 1.

ivory, *n.* —*Syn.* animal tusk, whalebone, boar teeth, horn, hippo ivory, walrus ivory, hard ivory, soft ivory, live ivory, dead ivory; see also **bone.** Objects called ivory include the following—piano key, die, billiard ball, chessman, statuette, false tooth, ivory carving, cameo.

ivy, *n.* —*Syn.* climber, creeper, Hedera; see **vine.** Ivies include the following—American, German, English, true, wild, ground, Boston, European, African, Asiatic, Irish, Dutch, Indian, poison, black, five-leaf; woodbine, Virginia creeper.

Ivy League (D), *mod.* —*Syn.* mannerly, stylish, posh (D); see **fashionable.**

J

jab, *n.* —*Syn.* poke, punch, hit; see **blow** 1.
jabber, *v.* **1.** [To make a chattering sound]—*Syn.* gibber, babble, mutter; see **cry** 3, **murmur** 1, **sound** 1.
2. [To talk as though jabbering]—*Syn.* rattle, prate, jaw; see **babble, mutter** 2, **talk** 1, **utter.**
jack, *n.* **1.** [An instrument for elevating]—*Syn.* jackscrew, ratchet, jack, automobile jack, pneumatic jack, hydraulic jack; see also **device** 1, **tool** 1.
2. [(D) Money]—*Syn.* cash, coin, change; see **money** 1.
3. [The male of certain animals]—*Syn.* buck, stud, stag; see **animal** 2, **bull** 1.
every man jack—*Syn.* every man, everyone, all; see **everybody.**
jackanapes, *n.* —*Syn.* wiseacre, coxcomb, scamp; see **rascal, upstart.**
jackass, *n.* **1.** [The male ass]—*Syn.* he-ass, burro, Rocky Mountain canary (D); see **animal** 2, **donkey, horse.**
2. [(D) Term of opprobrium]—*Syn.* dolt, blockhead, nut; see **fool** 1, **rascal.**
jacket, *n.* —*Syn.* tunic, jerkin, parka; see **cape** 2, **clothes, coat** 1.
jackknife, *n.* —*Syn.* clasp knife, case knife, Barlow knife; see **knife.**
jackknife, *v.* —*Syn.* double up, fold (up), be wrecked, skid into a jackknife (D); see also **bend** 1, 2, **crash** 4, **twist.**
jack-of-all-trades, *n.* —*Syn.* handy man, factotum, versatile person; see **laborer, man-of-all-work, workman.**
jackpot, *n.* —*Syn.* bonanza, find, winnings; see **luck** 1, **profit** 2, **success** 2.
hit the jackpot (D)—*Syn.* succeed, achieve, attain; see **win** 1.
jack up (D), *v.* —*Syn.* lift, add to, accelerate; see **increase** 1, **raise** 1.
jade, *mod.* **1.** [Made from jade]—*Syn.* jadeite, true jade, nephrite, pyroxene, *yu* or *yu-shih, fei ts'ui* (both Chinese).
2. [Having the color of jade]—*Syn.* jade-green, yellow-green, pale green; see **green** 1.
jaded, *mod.* **1.** [Exhausted]—*Syn.* spent, fatigued, worn; see **tired, weak** 3.
2. [Insensitive]—*Syn.* cold, nonchalant, impassive; see **indifferent** 1, **unconcerned.**
jag, *n.* **1.** [(D) A moderate drunkenness or a narcotic state]—*Syn.* inebriety; *both* (D): buzz, pipe dream; see **drunkenness.**
2. [(D) A very small load]—*Syn.* pickup load, cargo, freight; see **load** 1.
3. [(D) A spree]—*Syn.* revelry, revel, trip (D); see **celebration** 2.
jagged, *mod.* —*Syn.* serrated, ragged, rugged; see **irregular** 4, **notched, rough** 1.
jail, *n.* —*Syn.* goal, carcel, penitentiary, cage, cell, dungeon, bastille, oubliette, bridewell, house of correction, guardroom, pound, reformatory, stockade, detention camp, concentration camp, penal institution, penal settlement *or* colony, house of detention, debtor's prison; *all* (D): black hole, hulks, lockup, limbo, death house, slammer, cooler, big house, sponging house, pen, stir, clink, jug, can, calaboose, coop, hoosegow; see also **prison.**
Some well-known jails and prison camps include the following—Sing Sing, Devils' Island, Attica, Alcatraz *or* the Rock (D), Dartmoor *or* the Moor (D), Newgate, Bridewell, Tower of London, Fleet, Marshalsea, Wormwood Scrubs, Holloway, Dannemora, Broadmoor, the Bastille, Belsen, Botany Bay, Andaman Islands.
jail, *v.* —*Syn.* confine, lock up, incarcerate, sentence, throw into the dungeon, impound, detain, put behind bars; *all* (D): jug, put in the clink, throw in stir, throw away the keys; see also **imprison.** —*Ant.* liberate*, discharge, let out.
jailbird (D), *n.* —*Syn.* convict, felon, culprit; see **criminal, prisoner.**
jailbreak, *n.* —*Syn.* break out, forcible *or* planned escape, breaking out of jail; see **escape** 1.
jailed, *mod.* —*Syn.* arrested, incarcerated, in jail; see **confined** 3, **held, under arrest.**
jailer, *n.* —*Syn.* gaoler, turnkey, keeper; see **warden, watchman.**
jam, *n.* **1.** [Preserves]—*Syn.* conserve, fruit butter, spread, marmalade, sweet, sugarplums, candied fruit; blackberry jam, plum, jam, strawberry jam, etc.; see also **jelly.**
2. [(D) A troublesome situation]—*Syn.* dilemma, problem, trouble; see **difficulty** 1.
jam, *v.* **1.** [To force one's way]—*Syn.* jostle, squeeze, crowd, throng, press, elbow, thrust, pack; see also **push** 1.
2. [To compress]—*Syn.* bind, squeeze, push; see **compress, pack** 2, **press** 1.
3. [To obscure by jamming]—*Syn.* drown out, garble, scramble; see **confuse, muddle** 1.
jamb, *n.* —*Syn.* pillar, support, lintel; see **column** 1, **post** 1.
jamboree, *n.* —*Syn.* festival, ceremony, gathering; see **celebration** 1, 2.
jammed, *mod.* **1.** [Stuck fast]—*Syn.* out of order, malfunctioning, obstructed, blocked, barred, trammeled, wedged, caught, close-coupled, warped, swollen, stiff, immovable, fast, fastened, fixed, frozen, unworkable; see also **tight** 2.—*Ant.* loose*, operating, in working order.

2. [Thronged]—*Syn.* crowded, populous, busy, humming, multitudinous, filled, overflowing, lively, deluged, teeming, flooded, swarming, congested, packed, crammed, burdened, loaded; see also **full** 1.—*Ant.* empty*, vacant, silent.

jam-packed, *mod.* —*Syn.* stuffed, overcrowded, loaded down; see **full** 1, **jammed** 2.

jangle, *v.* —*Syn.* jingle, clink, clatter; see **sound** 1.

janitor, *n.* —*Syn.* cleaning man, watchman, doorman; see **attendant, custodian** 2.

January, *n.* —*Syn.* New Year(s), the new year, first month of the year, post-holiday season, time of sales *or* inventories; see also **month, winter.**

Japan, *n.* —*Syn.* The Japanese Empire, the Island Kingdom, Zipangu, Yamato, (Dai) Nihon, Great Nihon, Nippon, the Land of the Rising Sun, the Flowery Kingdom, the Land of Cherry Blossoms.

Japanese, *mod.* —*Syn.* Ainu, Nipponese, East Asiatic; see **Asiatic** 1, 2.

Japanese, *n.* —*Syn.* Ainus, Orientals, Nipponese, Nisei, Issei, East Asiatics.

jar, *n.* **1.** [A glass or earthen container]—*Syn.* crock, pot, fruit jar, can, vessel, basin, beaker, jog, cruet, vat, decanter, pitcher, ewer, bottle, flagon, flask, cruse, burette, phial, toby, gallipot, vase, amphora, ampulla, chalice, urn, Canopic jar, *potiche* (French), *olla, cacharro, jarro* (all Spanish), *pithos* (Greek), *dolium* (Latin); see also **container.**

2. [The contents of a jar]—*Syn.* pot, quart, pint, jarful, jugful, tin; see also **contents** 1.

3. [A jolt]—*Syn.* jounce, thud, thump; see **bump** 1.

jar, *v.* **1.** [To cause to tremble]—*Syn.* shake (up), agitate, jolt, bounce, jounce, jiggle, jump, bump, thump, bang, wiggle, rock, jerk, slam, rattle, wobble; see also **crash** 4, **hit** 1, 3.

2. [To create discordant sounds]—*Syn.* clash, clang, bang; see **sound** 1.

jargon, *n.* **1.** [Trite speech]—*Syn.* cant, banality, insipidity, patter, hackneyed term, overused words, commonplace term *or* phrase, stale utterance, shopworn language, trite vocabulary, fustian, bombast, hocus-pocus (D); see **cliché, nonsense** 1.

2. [Hybrid language]—*Syn.* patois, lingo, broken English, calque, idiom, pidgin English, creole, vernacular, Chinook, koine, lingua franca; see **language** 1.

3. [Specialized vocabulary *or* pronunciation, etc.] —*Syn.* argot, shoptalk, slang, colloquialism, neologism, coined word(s), dog *or* pig Latin, localism, Romany, thieves' Latin, peddler's French, St. Giles Greek, rhyming slang, doubletalk, doublespeak, Double Dutch, op-talk; *all* (D): jargantua, novelese, officialese, legalese, bureaucratese, schoolese, newspeak, computerese, journalese, gobbledygook, slanguage; see also **dialect, slang.**

jarring, *mod.* **1.** [Discordant]—*Syn.* unharmonious, grating, rasping; see **harsh** 1, **loud** 1, 2, **shrill.**

2. [Jolting]—*Syn.* bumpy, rough, shaking, unsettling, agitating, uneven, bouncy, jouncy, jumpy, wobbly, crushing, smashing, jerky, rocky, staggering; *all* (D): jiggly, wiggly, slam-bang, walloping. —*Ant.* firm*, steadying, supporting.

jaundice, *n.* —*Syn.* icterus, biliousness, hepatitis, leptospirosis; see also **disease** 3.

jaundiced, *mod.* —*Syn.* envious, hostile, disapproving; see **jealous, opproprious** 1, **prejudiced, unfriendly** 1, 2.

jaunt, *n.* —*Syn.* excursion, sally, trip, saunter, stroll, safari, tour, round, run, gallop, canter, expedition, circuit, peregrination, trek, amble, tramp, hike, promenade, constitutional, turn, airing, outing, ride, drive, march, picnic, voyage, jog, ramble, prowl, course, patrol, beat, frolic, adventure; see also **journey, walk** 3.

jauntily, *mod.* —*Syn.* gaily, briskly, frivolously; see **cheerfully, happily** 2.

jaunty, *mod.* —*Syn.* swaggering, cocky, bold, rakish, devil-may-care, reckless, careless, swashbuckling, gay, dashing, venturesome, impudent, provocative, joking, jovial, jolly, frisky, hoydenish, frolicsome, jocose, rollicking, gamesome, hilarious, high-spirited, vivacious, animated, lively, prankish, debonair, airy, free (and easy), easy, light, sportive, sporty, dapper, natty (D), breezy, playful, cocksure, impish, devilish, brash, forward, exhilarated, impetuous, assured, presumptuous, riotous, sporting, facetious, scampish, merry, waggish, irreverent, roistering, arrogant, insolent, conceited, egotistic, affected, strutting, vainglorious, vaunting, ranting, flippant, flip, audacious, bumptious, impertinent, saucy, cheeky, brazen, cavalier, pert, malapert, fresh, rowdy; see also **happy** 1, **nonchalant** 1. —*Ant.* reserved*, staid, sedate.

javelin, *n.* —*Syn.* lance, shaft, harpoon; see **spear, weapon** 1.

jaw, *n.* **1.** [The bones of the mouth]—*Syn.* jawbone, muzzle, jowl, mandible, maxilla, chops; see also **bone.**

2. [A jawlike object]—*Syn.* clamp, grip, wrench, clasp, clutch; see also **vise.**

jaw (D), *v.* —*Syn.* criticize, vituperate, blame; see **censure, scold.**

jay, *n.* —*Syn.* bluejay, pie, European jay; see **bird** 1.

jaywalk, *v.* —*Syn.* cross (a street) obliquely, walk in a forbidden traffic zone, walk *or* cross against a light, cut across, cross illegally; see also **misbehave.**

jazz, *n.* —*Syn.* Dixieland, ragtime, modern jazz, progressive jazz, syncopated music, improvisation; *all* (D): hot music, jungle music, jungle style, cold jazz, straight jazz, le jazz hot, boogie-woogie, third-stream, bop, doo-wop, swing, jive; see also **music** 1.

jazz up (D), *v.* —*Syn.* enliven, speed up, make livelier *or* sexier *or* more salacious, etc.; see **excite** 1, **inspire** 2, **speed.**

jazzy (D), *mod.* —*Syn.* sexy, lively, salacious; see **exciting.**

jealous, *mod.* —*Syn.* possessive, demanding, monopolizing, envious, watchful, covetous, resentful, begrudging, mistrustful, skeptical, doubting, jaundiced, apprehensive; *all* (D): green-eyed, yellow-eyed, horn-mad; see also **suspicious** 1.—*Ant.* trusting*, confiding, believing.

jealousy, *n.* —*Syn.* resentment, possessiveness, suspicion; see **doubt** 1, **envy.**

jeep, *n.* —*Syn.* four-wheel drive vehicle, general purpose *or* G.P. vehicle, army car; see **automobile, vehicle** 1.

Jeeplike vehicles include the following—Jeep, Jeepster, Scout, Land Rover, Land Cruiser, Bronco (all trade marks).

jeeplike, *mod.* —*Syn.* four-wheel drive, reconnaissance, rough- *or* back-country, general purpose, multipurpose.
jeer, *v.* —*Syn.* scoff, poke fun, mock; see **ridicule.**
jeering, *mod.* —*Syn.* mocking, raucous, taunting; see **loud** 1, 2, **rude** 2, **yelling.**
jeering, *n.* —*Syn.* taunting, shouting, mocking; see **cry** 1, **rudeness.**
jell, *v.* —*Syn.* set, crystallize, condense; see also **freeze** 1, **harden** 2, **stiffen** 1, **thicken** 1.
jelly, *n.* **1.** [Jam]—*Syn.* jell, extract, preserve, gelatin, pulp, mass, pectin; apple jelly, currant jelly, raspberry jelly, etc.; see also **jam** 1.
2. [Cream]—*Syn.* ointment, unction, balm; see **salve.**
jellyfish, *n.* —*Syn.* medusa, coelenterate, ctenophore, hydrozoan, scyphozoan; see also **fish.**
jeopardize, *v.* —*Syn.* imperil, expose, venture; see **endanger, risk.**
jeopardy, *n.* —*Syn.* risk, peril, exposure; see **chance** 1, **danger** 1.
jerk, *n.* **1.** [A twitch]—*Syn.* tic, shrug, wiggle, shake, quiver, flick, jounce, jiggle; see also **bump** 1.
2. [(D) A rascal]—*Syn.* scamp, brute, rat (D); see **rascal.**
jerk, *v.* **1.** [To undergo a spasm]—*Syn.* shrug, have a convulsion, wriggle, quake, quiver, shiver, wiggle, dance; see also **shake** 1, **twitch** 2.
2. [To move an object with a quick tug]—*Syn.* snatch, grab, whisk, pluck, snag, hook, flip, flop, bounce, fling, hurtle, flick; see also **seize** 1, 2.
jerry-built, *mod.* —*Syn.* flimsy, inadequate, cheap; see **faulty, unfinished** 1, **unsatisfactory.**
jersey, *n.* —*Syn.* pullover, T-shirt, turtle neck; see **clothes, sweater.**
jest, *n.* —*Syn.* jape, prank, quip; see **joke** 1.
jester, *n.* —*Syn.* comedian, buffoon, joker; see **actor, clown, fool** 2.
jesting, *n.* —*Syn.* buffoonery, joking, clowning; see **humor** 1, **wit** 2.
Jesus, *n.* —*Syn.* Saviour, Redeemer, the Son of God; see **Christ, God** 1.
jet, *mod.* —*Syn.* ebony, raven, obsidian; see **black** 1, **dark** 1.
jet, *n.* —*Syn.* jet-propelled ship *or* aircraft *or* vehicle, jet plane, twin jet, strato-jet; jet bomber *or* fighter, etc.; supersonic *or* jet-age plane *or* airplane *or* aircraft, etc.; jet prop (D); see also **plane** 3.
jet, *n.* **1.** [A stream of liquid or gas]—*Syn.* spray, stream, spurt; see **fountain** 2.
2. [A jet-propelled airplane]—*Syn.* jet plane, twin jet, supersonic jet *or* airplane *or* plane, supersonic transport (SST); see **plane** 3.
jet, *v.* **1.** [To gush out in a stream]—*Syn.* spout, spurt, squirt; see **flow** 2.
2. [(D) To travel by jet airplane]—*Syn.* take a jet, go by jet, fly, travel; see **travel** 2.
jet set, *n.* —*Syn.* élite, younger set, international set; see **society** 3.
jettison, *v.* —*Syn.* eject, cast off, throw away; see **discard.**
jetty, *n.* —*Syn.* pier, wharf, quay; see **dock** 1, **harbor** 2.
Jew, *n.* —*Syn.* Hebrew, Israelite, Jewess, son of Israel, Judaist, Semite, Israeli, Ashkenazi, Sephardi, sabra, descendant of Abraham, wandering Jew.
jewel, *n.* **1.** [A precious stone]—*Syn.* bauble, brilliant, bijou, trinket; see also **gem** 1, **stone.**
Jewels include the following—emerald, amethyst, sapphire, jade, aquamarine, moonstone, agate, beryl, ruby, turquoise, topaz, garnet, carbuncle, cornelian, jasper, coral, peridot, chrysoprase, lapis lazuli, bloodstone, onyx, zircon; see also **diamond** 1, **opal, pearl** 1.
2. [An excellent person or thing]—*Syn.* phenomenon, specialty, genius; see **gem** 2, **prodigy.**
jeweler, *n.* —*Syn.* goldsmith, diamond setter, gem dealer, watchmaker, lapidary; see also **artist** 2, **craftsman, specialist.**
jewelry, *n.* —*Syn.* gems, precious stones, jewels, baubles, trinkets, adornments, frippery, bijoux, ornaments, costume jewelry; *all* (D): bangles, knickknacks, gewgaws, gimcrackery; see also **jewel** 1.
Jewelry includes the following—diadem, coronet, tiara, cross, locket, brooch, lavalliere, watch chain, pendant, armlet, anklet, earrings, cameo, chain, beads, charm; see also **bracelet, crown** 2, **necklace, pin** 2, **ring** 2.
Jewish, *mod.* —*Syn.* Hebrew, Hebraic, Mosaic, Semitic, Ashkenazic, Sephardic, Yiddish, Israelitish, Judaic, Zionist.
jibe (D), *v.* —*Syn.* agree, correspond, match; see **resemble, agree.**
jig, *n.* —*Syn.* song and dance, contredanse, hop; see **dance** 1, **music** 1.
jiggle, *v.* —*Syn.* shake, twitch, wiggle; see **jerk** 2.
jilt, *v.* —*Syn.* betray, forsake, desert; see **abandon** 2.
jilted, *mod.* —*Syn.* left, neglected, forsaken; see **abandoned** 1.
jingle, *n.* —*Syn.* tinkle, jangle, clank; see **noise** 1.
jingle, *v.* —*Syn.* tinkle, clink, rattle; see **ring** 3, **sound** 1.
jingoism, *n.* —*Syn.* chauvinism, overpatriotism, exaggerated patriotism, patriolatry; see also **patriotism.**
jinx, *n.* —*Syn.* evil eye, hex, spell; see **curse.**
jitterbug, *n.* —*Syn.* bop, fling, caper; see **dance** 1.
jitterbug, *v.* —*Syn.* hop, skip, cut a rug (D); see **dance** 1.
job, *n.* **1.** [Gainful employment]—*Syn.* situation, place, post, position, appointment, operation, task, line, calling, vocation, handicraft, career, craft, paying job, pursuit, office, function, faculty, means of livelihood, *métier* (French); see also **business** 1, **profession** 1, **trade** 2, **work** 2.
2. [Something to be done]—*Syn.* task, stint, business, burden, action, act, mission, assignment, affair, concern, obligation, enterprise, undertaking, project, chore, errand, care, matter (in hand), commission, function, responsibility, charge, province, deed, office, tour of duty, operation; *all* (D): lookout, scutwork, kick, (the whole) bit; see also **duty** 2.
3. [The amount of work done]—*Syn.* assignment, day's work, throughput, output, input, block of work, responsibility; see also **duty** 2.
odd jobs—*Syn.* miscellaneous duties, chores, occasional labor; see **work** 1.
on the job—*Syn.* busy, engaged, occupied; see **working.**
jobber, *n.* —*Syn.* middleman, wholesaler, business agent; see **businessman, merchant.**

job lot, *mod.* —*Syn.* by lot price, reduced, at a cut rate; see **cheap** 1.

jockey, *n.* —*Syn.* racer; *all* (D): saddle-sitter, monkey, jock, jocker, live weight; see also **horseman, rider** 1.

jockey, *v.* —*Syn.* maneuver, slip into, manage; see **insinuate** 2.

jocund, *mod.* —*Syn.* cheerful, lively, jolly; see **happy** 1.

jog, *n.* **1.** [A slow run]—*Syn.* trot, amble, pace; see **run** 1.

2. [A bump]—*Syn.* jiggle, whack, hit; see **blow** 1, **bump** 1.

jog, *v.* —*Syn.* jog along, take one's exercise, trot; see **run** 2.

joggle, *v.* —*Syn.* fuss, wiggle, jiggle; see **fidget.**

jog (someone's) memory, *v.* —*Syn.* bring up, recall, suggest; see **remind** 2.

John, *n.* —*Syn.* Jonathan, Jon, Jack, Jean, Johannes, Johann, Hans, Gino, Juan, Giovanni, Ivan, Jan, Ian, Yohahnan, Johnnie; see also **name** 1.

John Bull, *n.* —*Syn.* Englishman, Briton; see **England.**

John Doe (D), *n.* —*Syn.* the average citizen, John Q. Public, Mr. and Mrs. America, Joe Doakes, Mr. Taxpayer, man in the street, fictitious character, anyone, stock legal personage, unknown person; see also **mister.**

John Hancock (D), *n.* —*Syn.* autograph, mark, initials; see **signature.**

join, *v.* **1.** [To unite]—*Syn.* put *or* piece together, blend, combine, juxtapose, bring in contact with, touch, connect (up), couple, conjoin, affix, mix, unite in, assemble, stick *or* bind *or* lump together, fasten, append, attach, annex, agglutinate, bracket, span, intermix, cross *or* pair with, link, leash, yoke, marry, wed, melt into one, copulate, cement, weld, clasp, fuse, lock, grapple, clamp, interlace, entwine, subjoin, involve together, clip; see also **unite** 1. —*Ant.* separate*, sunder, sever.

2. [To enter the company of]—*Syn.* go to, mingle with, seek, associate *or* enlist with, join forces, enroll, go to the aid of, place by the side of, follow, rejoin, register, team *or* take *or* tie *or* line up with, be in, sign on *or* up, go *or* fall in with, align, consort, fraternize, throw in with, pair with, affiliate, act *or* side *or* align with, make one of, take part in, seek a place among, advance toward, seek reception, go to meet; see also **associate** 1, **unite** 1.—*Ant.* leave*, desert, abandon.

3. [To adjoin]—*Syn.* lie next to, be contiguous to, neighbor, border, fringe, butt, trench on, verge upon, be adjacent to, open into, be close to, bound, lie beside *or* near, be at hand, abut (on), touch, skirt, parallel, rim, hem, abound and abut upon.

join battle, *v.* —*Syn.* engage (with), fight against *or* with, open the fight *or* conflict *or* combat; see **attack** 2, **fight** 2.

joined, *mod.* —*Syn.* linked, yoked, coupled, conjoined, allied, akin, cognate, interallied, intertwined, blended, connected, united, federated, banded, wedded, married, interfused, mixed, put *or* tied together, interdependent, combined, touching, interclasped, clasped together, cemented, welded, fused, locked, grappled, interlaced, clipped together, conjugated, accompanying, associated, confederated, mingled, intermixed, clutched, hitched, spliced, engrafted, affixed, reciprocally attached, joint, conjoint, assimilated, mortised, interlaid, corporate, incorporated, involved, inseparable, bracketed, affiliated, related, pieced *or* fastened *or* stuck together, coupled with, bound up with *or* in; see also **unified.**—*Ant.* separated*, disparate, apart.

joint, *n.* **1.** [A juncture]—*Syn.* union, crux, nexus, articulation, coupling, hinge, tie, swivel, link, connection, interconnection, point of union, vinculum, bond, splice, bend, copula, hyphen, bracket, junction, tangency, bridge, conjuncture, impingement, confluence; joining *or* linking *or* combining structure *or* process *or* device, etc.; see also **association** 2, **piece** 1.

2. [A section]—*Syn.* piece, member, unit, digit, portion, division, block, step, chink, sector, fragment, segment, limb, bone, lobe, cell, offshoot, constituent, slab, chunk; see also **link, part** 3.

3. [(D) An establishment, particularly one providing entertainment]—*Syn. all* (D): hangout, hole in the wall; see **dive** 2.

4. [(D) A marijuana cigarette]—*Syn.* hemp, cannabis, grass (D); see **drug** 2.

out of joint—*Syn.* dislocated, disjointed, wrong; see **disordered.**

jointly, *mod.* —*Syn.* conjointly, mutually, together, combined, in federation *or* unison *or* conjunction *or* partnership *or* concert *or* assembly *or* alliance *or* association, connectedly, unitedly, federally, cooperatively, corporately, harmoniously, reciprocally, inseparably, with mutual reliance, concomitantly, companionably, hand in hand, hand in glove, collectively, in a body, similarly, alike, with one accord *or* assent, accordingly, in company with, arm in arm, side by side, en masse, in a group, in ensemble, with one another, agreeably, simultaneously, coincidentally, synchronically, concurrently, inextricably, contemporaneously; cheek by jowl (D).—*Ant.* singly*, separately, severally.

join up (D), *v.* —*Syn.* enter the armed forces, respond to the call of duty, come forward; see **volunteer** 2.

joist, *n.* —*Syn.* girder, scantling, strip; see **beam** 1, **post** 1, **support** 2.

joke, *n.* **1.** [An action intended to be funny]—*Syn.* prank, buffoonery, game, hoodwinking, sport, frolic, practical joke, trick, revel, mummery, clowning, caper, caprice, mischief, escapade, tomfoolery, pleasantry, play, gambol, antic, lark, drollery, spree, vagary, farce; *all* (D): monkeyshine, shenanigan, snow job, horseplay, stunt, gag, lark, skylark, put-on; see also sense 2, **trick** 1.

2. [Words intended to be funny]—*Syn.* jest, jape, pun, witticism, play on words, quip, bon mot, quibble, pleasantry, *jeu d'esprit* (French), banter, drollery, retort, conceit, repartee, rejoinder, sally, persiflage, mot, chestnut, epigram, saw, crank, badinage, smart answer; *all* (D): bull, crack, wisecrack, shaggy dog story, Joe Miller; see also sense 1.

3. [Ridiculous person]—*Syn.* laughingstock, jackass, butt; see **fool** 2.

joke, *v.* —*Syn.* jest, quip, banter, laugh, raise laughter, poke fun, play, sport, frolic, revel, play tricks, pun, twit, trick, fool, make merry (with), play the fool *or* the clown, be waggish; *both* (D): wisecrack, pull one's leg; see also **deceive, trifle** 1.

joker, *n.* **1.** [Comedian]—*Syn.* jester, comic, fool; see **actor, clown.**
2. [Supplement]—*Syn.* supplement, rider, addendum; see **addition** 2.

joking, *mod.*—*Syn.* humorous, facetious, not serious; see **funny** 1.

jokingly, *mod.*—*Syn.* facetiously, amusingly, not seriously; see **humorously.**

jollity, *n.*—*Syn.* vivacity, merriment, sport; see **fun, happiness.**

jolly, *mod.* **1.** [Cheerful]—*Syn.* gay, merry, joyful; see **happy** 1.
2. [Festive]—*Syn.* enjoyable, delightful, holidayish (D); see **entertaining, pleasant** 2.

jolt, *n.* **1.** [A bump]—*Syn.* jar, punch, bounce; see **blow** 1, **bump** 1.
2. [A surprise]—*Syn.* jar, start, shock; see **surprise** 2, **wonder** 1.

jostle, *v.*—*Syn.* nudge, elbow, shoulder; see **press** 1, **push** 1.

jot, *v.*—*Syn.* scribble (down), indicate, list; see **record** 1, **write** 1.

jotting, *n.*—*Syn.* item, entry, scrawl; see **note** 2, **record** 1.

jounce, *v.*—*Syn.* jerk, vibrate, bump; see **bounce** 1, **jump** 3.

journal, *n.* **1.** [A daily record]—*Syn.* diary, account, memoir, jotting, reminiscence, contemporary account, almanac, annual, chronology, daybook, commonplace book, chronicle, yearbook, annals, register, calendar, note, minutes, observation, statement, memento, reminder; see also **record** 1.
2. [A periodical]—*Syn.* publication, organ, weekly, monthly, annual, daily; see also **magazine** 2, **newspaper.**

journalese (D), *n.*—*Syn.* newspaper idiom, editorial style, newspeak (D); see **dialect, jargon** 3, **language** 1.

journalism, *n.*—*Syn.* newspaper writing, newspaper publishing, reporting, reportage, newsmaking, news coverage, the fourth estate; see also **social science, writing** 3.

journalist, *n.*—*Syn.* commentator, publicist, member of the fourth estate; see also **announcer, newspaperman, reporter, writer.**

journalistic, *mod.* **1.** [Concerning newspapers]—*Syn.* periodical, publishing, editorial, reportorial, commentative.
2. [Having the qualities of hasty writing]—*Syn.* ephemeral, sensational, current, timely, dated, prosy, slangy, stereotyped.

journey, *n.*—*Syn.* transit, passage, tour, excursion, wayfaring, jaunt, pilgrimage, saunter, voyage, junket, package tour, crossing, expedition, odyssey, range, patrol, beat, sally, venture, adventure, itinerary, course, route, circuit, Grand Tour, peregrination, ramble, wandering, *Wanderjahr* (German), traverse, visit, sojourn, traveling, lunar probe, travels, campaign, trek, migration, caravan, transmigration, roaming, quest, safari, exploration, vagabondage, vagrancy, trip, round, stroll, run, tramp, hike, promenade, constitutional, turn, airing, outing, drive, march, picnic, jog, prowl, look, survey, setting forth, crusade, perambulation, cruise, flight, sail, navigation, circumnavigation of the globe, nonstop flight, mission, ride; see also **travel** 1, **walk** 3.

journey, *v.*—*Syn.* tour, jaunt, take a trip; see **travel** 2.

journeyman, *n.*—*Syn.* apprentice, artisan, tradesman; see **artist, craftsman, laborer, specialist.**

Jove, *n.*—*Syn.* Jupiter, Zeus, Odin, Wotan, Dyaus, Ammon, Amen-Ra, Min, the Father of the Gods, All Father, the Lord of Olympus, the Ruler of all things, he who rules gods and men; see also **god** 1.

jovial, *mod.* **1.** [Convivial]—*Syn.* affable, amiable, merry; see **happy** 1.
2. [Pleasant]—*Syn.* enjoyable, festive, delightful; see **pleasant** 2.

joviality, *n.*—*Syn.* joy, geniality, good humor; see **merriment** 2.

jowl, *n.*—*Syn.* mandible, dewlap, cheek; see **jaw** 1.

joy, *n.* **1.** [Inner contentment]—*Syn.* ecstasy, rapture, cheer; see **happiness** 2, **satisfaction** 2.
2. [Delight]—*Syn.* amusement, gladness, gaiety; see **happiness** 1, **humor** 3.
3. [The exhibition of joy]—*Syn.* mirth, mirthfulness, cheerfulness, revelry, hilarity, hilariousness, blitheness, frolic, playfulness, gaiety, heartiness, geniality, good humor, sprightliness, merriment, merrymaking, joviality, sportiveness, jocularity, jollity, jocundity, levity, rejoicing, exulting, elation, friskiness, animation, liveliness, high *or* good spirits, transport, vivacity, sunniness, jocosity, jubilation, celebration, game; see also **laughter.**—*Ant.* weeping*, wailing, complaining.
4. [The cause of joy]—*Syn.* delight, solace, treasure, pride and joy, pleasure, gratification, alleviation, treat, regalement, diversion, sport, refreshment, delectation, dainty, indulgence; see also **comfort** 1, **ease** 1, **luxury** 1.—*Ant.* thorn in the flesh, care*, burden.

joyful, *mod.*—*Syn.* joyous, cheery, glad; see **happy** 1.

joyless, *mod.*—*Syn.* doleful, heavy, dreary; see **dismal** 1, **sad** 2.

joyous, *mod.*—*Syn.* blithe, glad, gay; see **happy** 1.

joy ride (D), *n.*—*Syn.* dangerous *or* reckless trip *or* travel, pleasure trip, drive for the fun of it; see **drive** 1, **race** 3.

joy rider (D), *n.*—*Syn.* fast *or* reckless driver, speeder, drag racer; see **driver.**

jubilant, *mod.*—*Syn.* gay, rejoicing, celebrating; see **happy** 1, 2.

jubilation, *n.*—*Syn.* delight, pleasure, enjoyment; see **celebration** 1, **happiness** 2.

Judaic, *mod.*—*Syn.* Semitic, Yiddish, Hebrew; see **Jewish.**

Judaism, *n.*—*Syn.* Jewish religion, Hebraism, orthodox Judaism, conservative Judaism, reform Judaism, reconstructionism, Zionism; see also **religion** 2.

Judaist, *n.*—*Syn.* Hebrew, Israelite, Son of Israel; see **Jew.**

Judas, *n.*—*Syn.* betrayer, fraud, informer; see **hypocrite, traitor.**

judge, *n.* **1.** [A legal official]—*Syn.* justice, chancellor, magistrate, justice of the peace, chief justice, associate justice, judiciary, magister, master of assize, circuit judge, marshal of assize, chancery judge, county judge, judge of the district court, appeal judge, hanging judge (D); see also **administrator.**

2. [An umpire]—*Syn.* moderator, referee, arbitrator, arbiter, adjudicator, mediator, interpreter, warden, inspector, negotiator, intercessor, final authority, go-between, assessor.

3. [A connoisseur]—*Syn.* expert, man of taste, professional; see **critic** 2, **specialist.**

judge, *v.* **1.** [To pass judgment]—*Syn.* adjudge, adjudicate, sit in judgment, doom, sentence, act on, give a hearing to, hold the scales (D); see also **condemn** 1, **convict.**

2. [To form an opinion]—*Syn.* conclude, infer, suppose; see **decide, resolve.**

judged, *mod.* —*Syn.* found guilty *or* innocent, convicted, settled; see **determined** 1, **guilty** 1, 2.

judging, *n.* —*Syn.* determining (policy), deciding, reaching *or* arriving at a decision; see **judgment** 2.

judgment, *n.* **1.** [Discernment]—*Syn.* discrimination, taste, penetration, shrewdness, sapience, sagacity, understanding, knowledge, wit, keenness, sharpness, critical faculty, reason, reasoning power, rationality, rational faculty, intuition, mentality, acuteness, perception, incisiveness, intelligence, awareness, sophistication, ingenuity, experience, profundity, depth, brilliance, mentality, subtlety, intellectual power, critical spirit, capacity, comprehension, sanity, mother wit, quickness, readiness, grasp, apprehension, perspicacity, perspicuousness, soundness, genius, reach, range, (good) sense, breadth, astuteness, prudence, wisdom, *sagesse* (French); *all* (D): savvy, gray matter, brains, a good head, horse sense; see also **acumen.**—*Ant.* stupidity*, simplicity, naïveté.

2. [The act of judging]—*Syn.* decision, consideration, appraisal, examination, weighing, sifting, assaying, determination, inspection, assessment, estimation, probing, appreciation, evaluation, review, contemplation, analysis, inquiry, inquisition, inquest, search, quest, pursuit, scrutiny, exploration, reconnaissance, close study, observation, exhaustive inquiry, regard; see also **research** 2, **study** 2.

3. [A pronouncement]—*Syn.* conclusion, appraisal, estimate, opinion, report, view, summary, belief, idea, conviction, inference, resolution, deduction, induction, moral, critique, determination, dictum, decree, best opinion, supposition, comment, commentary, finding, recommendation; see also **sentence** 1, **verdict.**

4. [An act of God]—*Syn.* retribution, visitation, manifestation, chastisement, correction, castigation, mortification, affliction, infliction, Nemesis; see also **punishment.**

Judgment Day, *n.* —*Syn.* doomsday, day of judgment, day of the Apocalypse, end of the world, last day, private *or* particular judgment, great *or* general judgment day; see also **judgment** 1, 2.

judicial, *mod.* —*Syn.* legal, legalistic, juristic, pontifical, authoritative, equitable, regular, principled, jurisdictional, administrative, constitutional, statutory; see also **lawful** 1.

judiciary, *n.* —*Syn.* judge, justices, bench, assize, tribunal, bar, judicature, courts of justice, legal profession, members of the bar, judicial branch, interpreters of the law, Star Chamber; see also **court** 2, **jury.**

judicious, *mod.* —*Syn.* well-advised, prudent, sensible, seasonable, timely, sagacious, proper, thoughtful, thorough, efficacious, perceptive, acute, shrewd, discriminating, judicial, keen, astute, sage, discerning, sharp, careful, wary, worldly-wise, far-sighted, clear-sighted, quick-witted, sophisticated, calculating, profound, perspicacious, accurate, penetrating, informed, sane, practical, wise, seemly, decorous, cautious, politic, diplomatic, circumspect, prudential, precautionary, precautious, expedient, capable, ready, tactful, cool, calm, considerate, deliberated, prescient, knowing, sapient, well-timed, moderate, temperate; see also **discreet, intelligent** 1, **rational** 1, **reasonable** 1.—*Ant.* rash*, ill-advised, hasty.

judo, *n.* —*Syn.* jujitsu, defense, wrestling; see **fight** 1, **sport** 3.

jug, *n.* —*Syn.* crock, pot, canteen, bottle, flagon, demijohn, cruet, flask, stone jar, pitcher, cruse; see also **container.**

juggle, *v.* **1.** [To keep in the air by tossing]—*Syn.* toss, poise, keep in motion, perform sleight of hand; see also **balance** 2.

2. [To alter, usually to deceive]—*Syn.* shuffle, trim, delude; see **deceive.**

juggler, *n.* **1.** [An acrobat]—*Syn.* balancer, trickster, entertainer; see **acrobat, athlete.**

2. [An imposter]—*Syn.* con man, charlatan, swindler; see **cheat** 1, **impostor.**

juice, *n.* —*Syn.* sap, extract, oil, water, fluid, sirup, sauce, milk, spirit; see also **liquid.**

juicy, *mod.* **1.** [Succulent]—*Syn.* moist, wet, watery, humid, dewy, sappy, viscid, dank, slushy, slippery, oozy, dripping, sodden, soaked, saturated, liquid, oily, sirupy, sauced; see also **delicious** 1. —*Ant.* dry*, dehydrated, bone-dry.

2. [(D) Full of interest]—*Syn.* spicy, piquant, intriguing, racy, risqué, tantalizing, fascinating, sensational, exciting, colorful, provocative.

3. [(D) Profitable]—*Syn.* lucrative, fruitful, favorable; see **profitable.**

July, *n.* —*Syn.* summer month, midsummer, baseball season, time of summer school *or* summer session, harvest (season); see also **month, summer, vacation.**

jumble, *n.* —*Syn.* clutter, mess, hodgepodge; see **confusion** 1, **mixture** 1.

jumbo, *mod.* —*Syn.* immense, mammoth, gigantic; see **large** 1.

jump, *n.* **1.** [A leap up or across]—*Syn.* skip, hop, hopping, rise, upsurge, rising, pounce, lunge, leaping, jumping, skip, skipping, running jump, broad jump, high jump, vault, bounce, hurdle, spring, bound, saltation, buckjump, leapfrogging, caper, dance, gambol.

2. [A leap down]—*Syn.* precipitation, plunge, diving, nosedive, plummet, headlong fall, airborne assault *or* attack, casting *or* hurling oneself down *or* off, fall; see also **dive** 1, **drop** 2.

3. [An obstacle]—*Syn.* hurdle, bar, fence; see **barrier, impediment.**

4. [Distance jumped]—*Syn.* leap, stretch, vault; see **height** 1, **length** 1.

5. [(D) An advantage]—*Syn.* upper hand, handicap, head start; see **advantage** 1.
6. [A sudden rise]—*Syn.* ascent, spurt, inflation; see **increase** 1, **rise** 2.
get (*or* **have**) **the jump on** (D)—*Syn.* get an advantage over, exceed, beat; see **surpass.**

jump, *v.* **1.** [To leap across or up]—*Syn.* vault, leap (over), spring, surge, lurch, lunge, pop up *or* out, bound, hop, skip, high-jump, broad-jump, take, hurdle, top; see also **bounce** 2.
2. [To leap down]—*Syn.* drop, plummet, plunge; see **dive, fall** 1.
3. [To pass over]—*Syn.* cover, take, skip, traverse, remove, nullify; see also **cancel** 2, **cross** 2.
4. [To vibrate]—*Syn.* jiggle, wobble, jounce, waver, rattle, quiver, shake, rebound, dance, jerk, skip, ricochet, slither, hurtle; see also **bounce** 1.
5. [(D) To leave]—*Syn.* skip, abandon, clear out; see **leave** 1.
6. [(D) To board]—*Syn.* mount, climb on, spring upon; see sense 1, **board** 2, **catch** 6.
7. [(D) To accost belligerently]—*Syn.* halt, hold up, approach; see **attack.**

jump a claim, *v.*—*Syn.* pre-empt, stake out, attach; see **seize** 2, **steal.**

jump at (D), *v.*—*Syn.* accept, agree to, embrace; see **seize** 1.

jump bail, *v.*—*Syn.* abscond, run off, leave town; see **escape, leave** 1.

jumping, *mod.*—*Syn.* vaulting, hopping, skipping, bounding, leaping, hurdling, buoyant, active, beating, vibrant, irregular, dynamic, pulsating, quivering, quaking, trembling, unsteady, throbbing, hammering, thudding, agitated, tripping.—*Ant.* calm*, steady, straightforward.

jump in with both feet (D), *v.*—*Syn.* act blindly, rush in, be impetuous; see **hurry** 1.

jump on *or* **all over** (D), *v.*—*Syn.* blame, charge, berate; see **accuse, attack** 2.

jump ship (D), *v.*—*Syn.* run off, depart, take (French) leave; see **escape, leave** 1.

jump the track, *v.*—*Syn.* leave the rails, be wrecked, go into a ditch; see **crash** 4.

jumpy, *mod.*—*Syn.* sensitive, restless, nervous; see **excitable, excited.**

junction, *n.* **1.** [A meeting]—*Syn.* joining, coupling, reunion; see **joint** 1, **union** 1.
2. [A place of meeting, especially of roads]—*Syn.* crossroads, confluence, terminal, collocation, crossing, four corners, intersection; see also **crossroad.**

juncture, *n.*—*Syn.* choice, turning point, meeting point; see **circumstance** 1, **crisis, meeting** 1, **position** 1, **time** 2.

June, *n.*—*Syn.* spring *or* summer (month), month of brides *or* graduation *or* roses, baseball season, beginning of summer; see also **month, summer, vacation.**

jungle, *n.*—*Syn.* bush, wilderness, undergrowth, primeval forest, wood, boscage, trackless waste; see also **forest.**—*Ant.* clearing*, cultivation, settlement.

junior, *mod.*—*Syn.* subordinate, lesser, lower; see **subordinate.**

junk, *n.* **1.** [Rubbish]—*Syn.* waste, garbage, filth; see **trash** 1.
2. [Salvage]—*Syn.* scraps, odds and ends, miscellany; see **rummage** 2, **trash** 3.

junk (D), *v.*—*Syn.* dump, (sell for) scrap, wreck; see **discard.**

junket, *n.* **1.** [Pudding]—*Syn.* custard, milk dessert, rennet; see **delicatessen** 1, **pudding.**
2. [A festivity]—*Syn.* excursion, picnic, outing; see **celebration** 2, **ceremony** 2, **feast.**
3. [A journey]—*Syn.* trip, voyage, political tour *or* inspection; see **journey.**

junkie (D), *n.*—*Syn.* dope addict, dope peddler, dealer (D); see **addict, criminal.**

junkman, *n.*—*Syn.* salvage man, ragpicker, garbage man, junk dealer, beachcomber, trashman, scavenger.

junta, *n.* **1.** [Administrative body]—*Syn.* council, assembly, meeting; see **committee, gathering.**
2. [Political faction]—*Syn.* cabal, party, insurrectionary force; see **faction** 1.

jurisdiction, *n.*—*Syn.* authority, purview, range, supervision, control, legal direction, discretion, judicature, bailiwick, province, magistracy, commission, inquisition, scope, arbitration, prerogative, right, reign, domain, extent, empire, hegemony, sovereignty; see also **administration** 1, **command** 2, **power** 2.

jurisprudence, *n.*—*Syn.* statute, constitution, legal science; see **law** 5.

jurist, *n.*—*Syn.* attorney, judge, legal adviser; see **lawyer.**

juror, *n.*—*Syn.* juryman, peer, hearer, good man and true (D); see also **witness.**

jury, *n.*—*Syn.* tribunal, judges, peers, panel, board, grand jury, petit jury, coroner's jury.

just, *mod.* **1.** [Precisely]—*Syn.* exactly, correctly, perfectly; see **accurately.**
2. [Hardly]—*Syn.* barely, scarcely, by very little; see **hardly.**
3. [Only]—*Syn.* merely, simply, plainly; see **only** 2.
4. [At the present]—*Syn.* right *or* just now, at this moment, presently; see **now** 1.
5. [Recently]—*Syn.* just a while ago, lately, a moment ago; see **recently.**
6. [(D) Very]—*Syn.* really, simply, quite; see **very.**
7. [Fair]—*Syn.* impartial, equal, righteous; see **fair** 1.

justice, *n.* **1.** [Fairness]—*Syn.* right, truth, equity; see **fairness.**
2. [Lawfulness]—*Syn.* legality, equity, prescriptive *or* statutory *or* established right, legitimacy, sanction, legalization, constitutionality, authority, code, charter, creed, credo, decree, legitimization, rule, regularity, legal process, ritual character, authorization; see also **custom** 1, **law** 2, **power** 2.—*Ant.* illegality*, illegitimacy*, inequity.
3. [The administration of law]—*Syn.* judicature, adjudication, equity, settlement, arbitration, hearing, legal process, the forms of the law, due process, judicial procedure, jury trial, trial by law *or* jury, regulation, decision, pronouncement, review, appeal, sentence, consideration, rehearsing, pleading, taking evidence, litigation, prosecution, presentment; see also **judgment** 1, **law** 3, **trial** 2.—*Ant.* lawlessness, disorder*, despotism.
4. [A judge]—*Syn.* magistrate, umpire, chancellor; see **judge** 1.

bring to justice—*Syn.* capture, try, exact punishment from; see **arrest** 1.
do justice to—*Syn.* treat fairly, do right by, help; see **treat** 1.
do oneself justice—*Syn.* be fair to oneself, give oneself credit, be fair; see **justify.**

justifiable, *mod.* —*Syn.* proper, suitable, probable; see **fit** 1, 2, **logical** 1.

justification, *n.* —*Syn.* excuse, defense, pretext, reason, argument, palliation, extenuation, vindication, redemption, approval, validation, warrant, response, exoneration, exculpation, mitigation, explanation, rationalization, reply, palliative, apology, apologia, acquittal, salvation, answer, *raison d'être* (French), advocacy, plea, support, confirmation, sanctification, rebuttal, whitewashing (D); see also **appeal** 1, **explanation** 2.—*Ant.* blame*, conviction, incrimination.

justify, *v.* **1.** [To vindicate]—*Syn.* absolve, acquit, clear; see **excuse.**
2. [To give reasons for]—*Syn.* plead, argue for, support, apologize (for), palliate, excuse, sustain, maintain, advocate, brief, answer for, be answerable for, put in a plea (for), stand up for, make allowances, rationalize, exculpate, speak in favor (of), favor, make a plea, acquit oneself (of), show sufficient grounds (for), countenance, do justice to, condone, pardon, make good, confirm, rebut, show cause; see also **defend** 3, **explain.**—*Ant.* convict*, condemn, implicate.
3. [To prove by the event]—*Syn.* warrant, verify, bear out; see **prove.**

justly, *mod.* **1.** [Honorably]—*Syn.* impartially, honestly, frankly, unreservedly, candidly, fairly, straightforwardly, uprightly, reasonably, moderately, temperately, evenhandedly, rightly, righteously, piously, equitably, equably, tolerantly, charitably, virtuously, beneficently, respectably, benevolently, dutifully, duteously, lawfully, legally, legitimately, helpfully, rightfully, properly, duly, benignly, in justice, as it ought to be; see also **morally, openly** 1.
2. [Exactly]—*Syn.* judiciously, fittingly, properly, well, closely, particularly, discriminatingly, distinctly, clearly, precisely, lucidly, realistically, rationally, credibly, nicely, delicately, correctly, scrupulously, meticulously, sedulously, strictly, faithfully, punctiliously, unerringly, unimpeachably, rigorously, severely, religiously, sharply, critically, shrewdly, painstakingly, painfully, factually, objectively, detachedly, pictorially, unimaginatively, in detail, verbatim, with mathematical exactitude; see also **accurately.**

just now, *mod.* —*Syn.* very or quite recently, a moment *or* a minute *or* a little while *or* a short time *or* not long ago, a little back *or* earlier; see **recently.**

just the same, *mod.* and *prep.* —*Syn.* nevertheless, all the same, nonetheless, not withstanding, in spite of that; see **but** 1.

jut, *v.* —*Syn.* extend, bulge, stick out; see **project** 1.

juvenile, *mod.* **1.** [Immature]—*Syn.* youthful, adolescent, pubescent, tender, infantile, growing, undeveloped, babyish, beardless, boyish, formative, budding, unfledged, teen-age, junior, younger, developing, fresh, milk-fed, blooming, unweaned; *all* (D): green, plastic, sappy, kiddish; see **young** 1. —*Ant.* old*, elder, elderly.
2. [Suited to youth]—*Syn.* callow, puerile, childish; see **naïve, young** 2.

juxtapose, *v.* —*Syn.* place next to, put close together, put side by side; see **place.**

K

kaleidoscopic, *mod.* **1.** [Brightly colored]—*Syn.* colorful, multicolored, vivid; see **bright** 1, 2.
2. [Ever changing]—*Syn.* protean, plastic, fluid; see **changeable** 2, **changing.**

keel, *n.*—*Syn.* coal barge, board, bottom timber; see **boat, ship.**
on an even keel—*Syn.* steady, level, stable; see **balanced.**

keel over, *v.*—*Syn.* overturn, capsize, pitch; see **upset** 1.

keen, *mod.* **1.** [Sharp]—*Syn.* pointed, edged, acute; see **sharp** 1, 2.
2. [Astute]—*Syn.* bright, clever, shrewd; see **intelligent** 1, **judicious.**
3. [Intense]—*Syn.* cutting, piercing, strong; see **extreme** 2, **intense.**
4. [Eager]—*Syn.* ardent, interested, intent; see **enthusiastic** 1, 2.
5. [Sensitive]—*Syn.* perceptive, penetrating, sharp; see **observant** 1.

keenly, *mod.*—*Syn.* acutely, sharply, perceptively, astutely, cleverly, penetratingly, precisely, alertly, distinctly, eagerly, with acumen *or* perception *or* precision, etc.; *all* (D): on the ball, in the running, keeping an eye out; see also **clearly** 1, 2, **very, vigorously.**

keenness, *n.*—*Syn.* insight, sharpness, shrewdness; see **acumen, judgment.**

keen-sighted, *mod.*—*Syn.* clear-sighted, sharp-eyed, sharp-sighted, farsighted, telescopic; *all* (D); hawk-eyed, Argus-eyed, cat-eyed.

keep, *v.* **1.** [To hold]—*Syn.* retain, grip, grasp; see **hold** 1.
2. [To maintain]—*Syn.* preserve, conserve, care for; see **maintain** 3.
3. [To continue]—*Syn.* keep going, carry on, sustain; see **continue** 1, **endure** 1.
4. [To operate]—*Syn.* administer, run, direct; see **command** 2, **manage** 1.
5. [To tend]—*Syn.* care for, minister to, attend; see **tend** 1.
6. [To remain]—*Syn.* stay, continue, abide; see **remain** 1.
7. [To store]—*Syn.* deposit, cache, put; see **save** 3, **store** 2.
8. [To prevent; *used with from*]—*Syn.* stop, block, avert; see **hinder, prevent.**
9. [Retain]—*Syn.* not spoil, season, put up; see **preserve** 3.
for keeps (D)—*Syn.* permanently, changelessly, perpetually; see **forever** 1.

keep after, *v.* **1.** [To pursue]—*Syn.* track, trail, follow; see **pursue** 1.
2. [To nag]—*Syn.* push, remind, pester; see **bother** 2, **disturb** 2.

keep an appointment, *v.*—*Syn.* show up, be on time, be there; see **arrive** 1.

keep an eye on, *v.*—*Syn.* observe, investigate, look after; see **guard** 2, **watch** 1.

keep at, *v.*—*Syn.* persist, persevere, endure; see **continue** 1.

keep away, *v.* **1.** [To remain]—*Syn.* stay away, hold back, not come *or* appear; see **remain** 1.
2. [To restrain]—*Syn.* keep off, hold back, defend oneself (from); see **hinder, prevent, restrict** 2.

keep back, *v.* **1.** [To delay]—*Syn.* check, hold, postpone; see **delay** 1, **hinder, suspend** 2.
2. [To restrict]—*Syn.* inclose, inhibit, oppose; see **forbid, restrict** 2.

keep calm, *v.*—*Syn.* take (one's) time, keep cool, be patient; see **calm down, relax.**

keep company with, *v.*—*Syn.* fraternize, accompany, associate, go steady with, go together, consort with, date, go with, usher, guard; *all* (D): take up with, hang around with, pal around with.

keep dark, *v.*—*Syn.* suppress, keep quiet, conceal; see **hide** 1.

keep down, *v.*—*Syn.* reduce, deaden, muffle; see **decrease** 2, **soften** 2.

keeper, *n.* **1.** [Operator]—*Syn.* manager, owner, entrepreneur; see **administrator.**
2. [Watchman]—*Syn.* guard, official, attendant; see **warden, watchman.**

keep from, *v.* **1.** [To abstain]—*Syn.* desist, refrain, avoid; see **abstain.**
2. [To prevent]—*Syn.* prohibit, forestall, impede; see **hinder, prevent, restrain** 1.

keep going, *v.*—*Syn.* progress, promote, proceed; see **advance** 1, **improve** 2.

keeping, *n.* **1.** [A safeguard]—*Syn.* resistance, maintenance, security; see **defense** 1, **protection** 2.
2. [A consistency]—*Syn.* uniformity, balance, harmony; see **agreement** 2, **consistency** 1, **symmetry.**
in keeping with—*Syn.* similar to, much the same, in conformity with; see **alike** 2.

keep in line, *v.* **1.** [To behave]—*Syn.* obey, be good, restrain oneself; see **behave** 2.
2. [To manage]—*Syn.* check, watch over, be responsible for; see **manage** 1, **restrain** 1.

keep off *or* **out,** *interj.*—*Syn.* Hands off! Stay away! Stop! Keep off the grass! No trespassing! No hunting *or* fishing! Private property!

keep off *or* **out,** *v.* **1.** [To avoid]—*Syn.* stay away, evade, resist; see **avoid.**

2. [To restrain]—*Syn.* hold back, keep away, defend (oneself) from; see **hinder, restrain** 1, **restrict** 2.
keep on, *v.* —*Syn.* finish, repeat, pursue; see **continue** 1, **endure** 1.
keep pace with, *v.* —*Syn.* keep abreast of, keep up with, pace; see **compete, rival.**
keep safe, *v.* —*Syn.* care for, chaperone, protect; see **guard** 2, **watch** 1.
keepsake, *n.* —*Syn.* memento, token, remembrance; see **souvenir.**
keep to, *v.* —*Syn.* adhere to, be devoted to, restrict oneself *or* one's activities to; see **follow** 2, **regulate** 2.
keep to oneself, *v.* —*Syn.* be a recluse *or* a hermit *or* a lone wolf, cultivate solitude, avoid human companionship, stay away, keep one's own counsel; see also **hibernate.**
keep under, *v.* —*Syn.* suppress, prevent, subdue; see **check** 2, **restrain** 1.
keep up, *v.* —*Syn.* support, care for, safeguard; see **maintain** 3, **sustain** 2.
keep up with, *v.* —*Syn.* keep pace *or* step, pace, run with; see **compete, rival.**
keep up with the Joneses (D), *v.* —*Syn.* climb (socially), be socially self-conscious, scramble for position; see **compete, imitate.**
keg, *n.* —*Syn.* cask, drum, vat; see **barrel, container.**
kennel, *n.* —*Syn.* doghouse, den, pound; see **enclosure** 1, **pen** 1.
kept, *mod.* **1.** [Preserved]—*Syn.* put up, pickled, stored; see **preserved** 2.
2. [Retained]—*Syn.* maintained, withheld, held, clutched, guarded, watched over, reserved, on file, at hand, prolonged, engrossed; see also **retained** 1, **saved** 2.
3. [Observed]—*Syn.* obeyed, honored, solemnized, commemorated, continued, regarded, discharged, maintained, carried on, held inviolate; see also **fulfilled.**—*Ant.* abandoned*, dishonored, forgotten.
kept woman, *n.* —*Syn.* concubine, harlot, white slave; see **mistress** 2, **prostitute.**
kerchief, *n.* —*Syn.* shawl, veil, muffler; see **handkerchief.**
kernel, *n.* **1.** [Grain]—*Syn.* nut, core, heart, germ, fruit; see also **grain** 1, **seed** 1.
2. [Essential portion]—*Syn.* heart, center, root; see **essence** 1.
3. [A small piece]—*Syn.* piece, atom, morsel; see **bit** 1, **division** 2, **part** 1.
kerosene, *v.* —*Syn.* fuel, petroleum, distillate, coal oil, lighting oil, lamp oil; see also **fuel, oil.**
ketchup, *n.* —*Syn.* tomato sauce, mushroom sauce, condiment; see **relish, sauce.**
kettle, *n.* —*Syn.* cauldron, saucepan, stewpot; see **pot** 1.
kettledrum, *n.* —*Syn.* timpano, tabla, tambour; see **drum, musical instrument.**
key, *n.* **1.** [Instrument to open a lock]—*Syn.* latchkey, opener, master key, passkey, skeleton key, *passe-partout* (French).
2. [A means of solution]—*Syn.* clue, index, pointer, pivot, hinge, crux, fulcrum, lever, nexus, core, root, taproot, nucleus, earmark, marker, symptom, sign, brand, cipher, code, indicator, blueprint, signboard, tip-off (D); see also **answer** 2.
keyboard, *n.* —*Syn.* row of keys, clavier, console, piano keys, claviature; *both* (D): blacks and whites, the eighty-eight, ivories; see also **piano.**
keyed up (D), *mod.* —*Syn.* stimulated, spurred on, nervous; see **excited.**
keynote, *mod.* —*Syn.* main, leading, official; see **important** 1, **principal.**
keynote, *n.* —*Syn.* basic idea, ruling principle, standard; see **criterion, measure** 2.
keystone, *n.* —*Syn.* buttress, prop, mainstay; see **brace, foundation** 2, **support** 2.
kick, *n.* **1.** [A blow with the foot]—*Syn.* boot, swift kick, jolt, jar, fillip; see also **blow** 1.
2. [In sports, a kicked ball]—*Syn.* punt, drop kick, place kick, free kick, boot (D).
3. [(D) An objection]—*Syn.* complaint, reproof, animadversion; see **objection** 2.
4. [(D) Pleasant reaction]—*Syn.* joy, pleasant, sensation, refreshment; see **enjoyment** 2, **thrill.**
kick, *v.* **1.** [To give a blow with the foot]—*Syn.* boot, jolt, punt, dropkick, place kick, kick off; see also **beat** 2, **hit** 1.
2. [(D) To object]—*Syn.* make a complaint, criticize, carp; see **complain** 1, **oppose** 1.
kick about *or* **around,** *v.* —*Syn.* mistreat, treat badly, misuse; see **abuse** 1.
kickback (D), *n.* —*Syn.* payment, percentage, payola (D); see **bribe, refund.**
kick back (D), *v.* —*Syn.* pay in, repay, return; see **pay** 1, **refund** 1.
kick in (D), *v.* —*Syn.* donate, add to, give (to); see **contribute** 1, **give** 1.
kickoff (D), *mod.* —*Syn.* opening, starting, initial; see **first** 1.
kickoff, *n.* —*Syn.* opening, beginning, launching; see **origin** 1.
kick off (D), *v.* —*Syn.* start, open, get under way; see **begin** 1.
kick out (D), *v.* —*Syn.* reject, throw out, eject; see **dismiss** 1, **oust, remove** 1.
kick over the traces (D), *v.* —*Syn.* mutiny, revolt, break away; see **rebel** 1.
kick the bucket (D), *v.* —*Syn.* perish, succumb, pass away; see **die** 1.
kid, *n.* **1.** [The young of certain animals]—*Syn.* billikin, nannikin, lamb, lambkin, fawn, calf, weanling; see also **animal** 1.
2. [(D) A child]—*Syn.* son, daughter, tot; see **boy, child, girl** 1.
kid (D), *v.* —*Syn.* tease, pretend, fool; see **bother** 2, **joke.**
kiddish, *mod.* —*Syn.* juvenile, immature, babyish; see **childish** 1, **naive, young** 2.
kidnap, *v.* —*Syn.* abduct, ravish, capture, steal, rape, carry away, hold for ransom, waylay, shanghai, carry off, make off *or* away with, grab, remove, lay hands on, put under duress, impress, spirit away, violate the Lindbergh law; *all* (D): pirate, bodysnatch, snatch, bundle off; see also **seize** 2. —*Ant.* ransom, rescue*, release.
kidnapped, *mod.* —*Syn.* made off with, transported, abducted, ravished, snatched, stolen, raped, carried away, held for ransom, shanghaied, waylaid, manhandled, kept under duress, held in durance vile, impressed, spirited away, seized, held

under illegal restraint; see also **captured** 1.—*Ant.* free*, rescued, freed.

kidnapper, *n.*—*Syn.* felon, abductor, shanghaier; see **criminal.**

kidnapping, *n.*—*Syn.* abduction, felony, child stealing; see **crime** 2.

kidney, *n.*—*Syn.* excretory organ, urinary organ, abdominal gland; see **organ** 2.

kill, *v.* **1.** [To deprive of life]—*Syn.* slay, slaughter, murder, assassinate, massacre, butcher, garrote, hang, lynch, electrocute, dispatch, execute, knife, immolate, sacrifice, shoot, strangle, stifle, poison, choke, smother, suffocate, asphyxiate, drown, behead, hack, guillotine, crucify, dismember, decapitate, disembowel, quarter, tear limb from libm, destroy, give the death blow, give the *coup de grâce,* put to death, deprive of life, put an end to, victimize, exterminate, stab, cut the throat, shoot down, put to the sword, mangle, cut *or* bring *or* mow down, machine gun, decimate, carry *or* pick off, liquidate, eliminate, remove, put one out of his misery, starve, bludgeon, make *or* do away with, commit murder; *all* (D): bump off, rub *or* wipe out, hit, erase, waste, grease, take for a ride, do in, knock off, heave overboard, put away, finish off, spill blood, blow one's brains out, send to glory, tick off, put to sleep, brain, zap.—*Ant.* rescue*, resuscitate, animate.

2. [To deprive of existence]—*Syn.* exterminate, ruin, annihilate; see **abolish, destroy** 1.

3. [To cancel]—*Syn.* annul, nullify, counteract; see **cancel** 2, **recant, revoke.**

4. [To turn off]—*Syn.* turn out, shut off, stop; see **halt** 2, **turn off** 1.

5. [To veto]—*Syn.* cancel, prohibit, refuse; see **forbid.**

killer, *n.*—*Syn.* murderer, manslayer, gunman, gangster, shooter, butcher, Nazi, SS man, hangman, assassin, assassinator, hit man (D) slayer, sniper, electrocutioner, headsman, axman, cutthroat, ruffian, garroter; see **criminal, executioner.**

killing, *mod.* **1.** [Destructive]—*Syn.* mortal, lethal, fatal; see **deadly, destructive** 2.

2. [(D) Funny]—*Syn.* ludicrous, overpowering, irresistible; see **funny** 1.

killing, *n.*—*Syn.* slaying, assassination, slaughter; see **crime** 2, **murder.**

kill time, *v.*—*Syn.* dawdle, procrastinate, dally; see **loaf** 1.

kiln, *n.*—*Syn.* hearth, pottery oven, reduction furnace; see **furnace, oven.**

kilowatt-hour, *n.*—*Syn.* one thousand watts acting for an hour, unit of work *or* energy *or* electricity, kwh; see **electricity** 1, 2.

kin, *n.*—*Syn.* (blood) relation *or* relative, member of the family, sibling; see **family** 1, **relative.**

kind, *mod.*—*Syn.* careful, tender, well-meaning, considerate, charitable, loving, pleasant, amiable, soft, softhearted, compassionate, sympathetic, understanding, solicitous, sweet, compliant, serviceable, generous, helpful, obliging, neighborly, accommodating, indulgent, noble-minded, womanly, delicate, tactful, gentle, tenderhearted, kindhearted, good-natured, benign, good-hearted, inoffensive, benevolent, altruistic, other-directed, complaisant, lenient, acquiescent, easy-going, patient, tolerant, mellow, genial, sensitive, courteous, agreeable, thoughtful, assisting, well-disposed, willing, mollifying, Christian doing unto others, etc.; see also **humane** 1, **merciful** 1.—*Ant.* rough*, brutal, harsh.

kind, *n.* **1.** [Class]—*Syn.* classification, species, genus; see **class** 1.

2. [Type]—*Syn.* sort, variety, description, fiber, stamp, ilk, character, complexion, tendency, gender, habit, breed, feather, set, tribe, denomination, persuasion, manner, connection, designation.

kindergarten, *n.*—*Syn.* class for small children, pre-elementary grade, preschool training; see **nursery** 1, **school** 1.

in kind—*Syn.* in the same way, with something like that received, in a similar fashion; see **similarly.**

of a kind—*Syn.* similar, same, like; see **alike** 1.

kindhearted, *mod.*—*Syn.* amiable, generous, good; see **humane** 1, **kind** 1, **merciful** 1.

kindheartedness, *n.*—*Syn.* generosity, benevolence, goodness; see **kindness** 1.

kindle, *v.* **1.** [To start a fire]—*Syn.* light, set fire; see **burn** 1, 2, **ignite.**

2. [To excite]—*Syn.* arouse, inspire, animate; see **excite** 1, 2.

kindliness, *n.*—*Syn.* generosity, charity, benevolence; see **kindness** 1.

kindling, *n.* **1.** [Firewood]—*Syn.* firewood, tinder, coals; see **fuel, wood** 2.

2. [Combustion]—*Syn.* ignition, combustion, burning; see **fire** 1.

kindly, *mod.* **1.** [Kind]—*Syn.* generous, helpful, good; see **humane** 1, **kind, merciful** 1.

2. [In a kind manner]—*Syn.* cordially, considerately, benevolently, genially, affectionately, tenderly, solicitously, good-naturedly, humanely, carefully, helpfully, sympathetically, courteously, thoughtfully, compassionately, benignly, understandingly, charitably, tolerantly, delicately; see also **generously** 2.

kindness, *n.* **1.** [The quality of being kind]—*Syn.* tenderness, good intention, consideration, sympathy, sweetness, serviceability, helpfulness, indulgence, delicacy, tact, benignity, mildness, courtesy, thoughtfulness, humanity, courteousness, understanding, solicitude, solicitousness, compassion, unselfishness, altruism, agreeableness, amicableness, commiseration, warmheartedness, softheartedness, politeness, kindliness, clemency, benevolence, goodness, beneficence, philanthropy, charity, friendliness, good disposition, mercy, affection, loving-kindness, cordiality, amiability, forbearance, graciousness, kindheartedness, Christianity, virtue; see also **generosity** 1, **tolerance** 1.—*Ant.* brutality, cruelty, selfishness.

2. [A kindly act]—*Syn.* (good) service, relief, succor, charity, benevolence, philanthropy, boon, favor, good deed, good turn, kind office, alms, bounty, benefaction, self-sacrifice, mercy; *all* (D): lift, boost, good lick; see also **aid** 1.—*Ant.* transgression, injury*, wrong.

kind of (D), *mod.*—*Syn.* somewhat, having the nature of, sort of (D); see **moderately.**

kindred, *mod.*—*Syn.* similar, like, germane; see **alike** 2, **related** 2, 3.

kindred, *n.* **1.** [Relationship]—*Syn.* kinship, connection, blood relationship; see **relationship.**
2. [Those with whom one is in relationship]—*Syn.* kin, relations, relatives; see **family** 1, **relative.**

kinetic, *mod.* —*Syn.* motor, transitional, motive; see **active** 1, **moving** 1.

king, *n.* **1.** [A male sovereign]—*Syn.* monarch, despot, tyrant, potentate, prince, lord temporal, autocrat, czar, tsar, caesar, kaiser, emperor, *rex* (Latin), suzerain, overlord, crowned head, imperator, majesty, regal personage, sultan, caliph, shah, pasha, Dalai Lama, mogul, rajah, maharajah, khan, mikado, gerent; see also **ruler** 1.—*Ant.* servant, slave, subordinate.
2. [A very superior being]—*Syn.* lord, chief, head, dictator, ruler, commander, boss, mogul, tycoon, sahib, master, authority, power, senior, *duce* (Italian), *Fuehrer* (German), *caudillo* (Spanish), governor, tyrant; *all* (D): high muckamuck, big shot, bigwig, noise; see also **administrator, leader** 2.—*Ant.* servant*, menial, flunky.

kingdom, *n.* —*Syn.* realm, domain, suzerainty, country, empire, lands, possessions, principality, state, dominions, sway, rule, scepter, crown, throne, subject territory; see also **area** 2, **nation** 1, **territory** 2.

kingdom come (D), *n.* —*Syn.* afterlife, the hereafter, abode of the blessed; see **heaven** 2.

kingly, *mod.* —*Syn.* majestic, regal, aristocratic; see **grand** 2, **noble** 1, 3, **royal** 1.

kingship, *n.* —*Syn.* supremacy, divinity, majesty; see **power** 2, **royalty.**

king-size, *mod.* —*Syn.* big, large-size, giant; see **broad** 1, **large** 1.

kink, *n.* **1.** [A twist]—*Syn.* tangle, crimp, crinkle; see **curl, curve** 1.
2. [A muscle spasm]—*Syn.* cramp, knot, twinge; see **pain** 2.
3. [An eccentricity]—*Syn.* notion, whim, peculiarity; see **quirk.**
4. [A difficulty]—*Syn.* hitch, defect, complication; see **difficulty** 1, **impediment** 1.

kinky, *mod.* **1.** [Full of kinks]—*Syn.* curled, knotted, frizzled; see **knotted, curly** 1, **rolled** 1.
2. [(D) Bizarre]—*Syn.* weird, odd, sick (D); see **unusual** 2.

kinsfolk, *n.* —*Syn.* lineage, descent, kin; see **family** 1, **relative.**

kinship, *n.* —*Syn.* affiliation, connection, alliance; see **family** 1, **relationship.**

kinsman, *n.* —*Syn.* sibling, parent, kin; see **family** 1, **relative.**

kiosk, *n.* —*Syn.* pavilion, newsstand, stall; see **booth.**

kipper, *v.* —*Syn.* pickle, marinate, put up; see **preserve** 3.

kirk, *n.* —*Syn.* tabernacle, shrine, chapel; see **church** 1, **temple.**

kismet, *n.* —*Syn.* karma, fortune, fate; see **chance** 1, **destiny** 1, **doom** 1.

kiss, *n.* —*Syn.* salutation, embrace, salute, endearment, osculation, touch of the lips, butterfly kiss, caress; *all* (D): buss, smack, smooch, peck; see also **touch** 2.

kiss, *v.* —*Syn.* salute, osculate, *baiser* (French); *all* (D): play post office, smack, smooch, pet, buss, neck, make out, blow a kiss; see also **caress, love** 2, **touch** 1.

kiss goodby (D), *v.* —*Syn.* give up, suffer the loss of, sign away; see **give** 1, **lose** 2.

kissing, *n.* —*Syn.* osculation, exchange of kisses, fondling, love-making; *all* (D): spooning, necking, bussing, parking, petting; see also **love** 1.

kit, *n.* **1.** [A set]—*Syn.* assortment, selection, stock; see **collection** 2.
2. [Equipment]—*Syn.* material, tools, outfit; see **equipment.**
3. [A pack]—*Syn.* poke, knapsack, satchel; see **bag, container.**
the whole kit and caboodle (D)—*Syn.* lot, collection, all; see **everything.**

kitchen, *n.* —*Syn.* scullery, gallery, galley, cuisine, canteen, cook's room, cookhouse, kitchenette, mess (D).

kite, *n.* —*Syn.* box kite, Hargrave kite, Chinese kite, cellular kite, Eddy kite, tailless kite, tetrahedral kite; see also **toy** 1.

kith and kin, *n.* —*Syn.* relatives, relations, siblings; see **family** 1, **relative.**

kitten, *n.* —*Syn.* pussy, kitty, catkin, pussycat, kittycat, kit, tabbykin, baby cat; see **animal** 1, **cat.**

kittenish, *mod.* —*Syn.* playful, mischievous, childish; see **flirtatious, jaunty.**

kleptomania, *n.* —*Syn.* compulsion to steal, thievishness, light-fingeredness (D); see **neurosis.**

kleptomaniac, *n.* —*Syn.* thief, pilferer, compulsive stealer; see **criminal, neurotic, robber.**

knack, *n.* —*Syn.* trick, skill, faculty; see **ability** 1, 2.

knapsack, *n.* —*Syn.* (back)pack, kit, rucksack; see **bag, container.**

knave, *n.* —*Syn.* scamp, fraud, villain; see **rascal.**

knavery, *n.* —*Syn.* thievery, rascality, fraud; see **deception** 1, **dishonesty** 1, **hypocrisy** 2, **lie** 1.

knavish, *mod.* —*Syn.* felonious, hypocritical, fraudulent; see **dishonest** 2.

knead, *v.* —*Syn.* work, mix, ply, shape, alter, twist, aerate, blend; see also **press** 1.

knee, *n.* —*Syn.* (knee) joint, crook, bend, hinge, kneecap, patella, ginglymus joint, processes of the knee, articulation of the femur and the tibia; see also **bone, joint** 1.
bring to one's knees—*Syn.* beat, force to submit, coerce; see **defeat** 1, 2.

knee breeches, *n.* —*Syn.* knickers, britches, shorts; see **clothes, pants** 1.

kneel, *v.* —*Syn.* bend the knee, rest on the knees, do obeisance, genuflect, bend, stoop, bow down, curtsey; see also **bow** 1.

knell, *n.* —*Syn.* ring, signal, death bell; see **bell** 2, **noise** 1.

knell, *v.* —*Syn.* peal, toll, chime; see **ring** 3, **sound** 1.

knickerbocker, *n.* —*Syn.* knickers, breeches, trousers; see **clothes, pants** 1.

knickknack, *n.* —*Syn.* gadget, *objet d'art* (French), conversation piece, bric-a-brac, curio, curiosity, ornament, trifle, bauble, trinket, toy, plaything, frill, furbelow, showpiece, embellishment, trapping; *all* (D): gimcrack, gingerbread, gewgaw, whimsy, flummery; see also **decoration** 2, **device** 1, **thing** 1.

knife, *n.* —*Syn.* blade, cutter, sword, bayonet, cutting edge, dagger, stiletto, lance, lancet, bit, cutlass, machete, creese, whittle, poniard, scalpel, edge,

dudgeon, dirk, sickle, scythe, sabre, scimitar, claymore, broadsword, bodkin, snickersnee, point, skiver, skewer, spit, guillotine, skean, misericord; *all* (D): pigsticker, toad-stabber, tickler, left-hander, shiv; see **razor.**
Knives include the following—carving, chopping, table, dinner, breakfast, dessert, grapefruit, fish, pocket, clasp, hunting, Bowie, corn, cane, butcher, skinning, surgical, castrating, paper, pruning, oyster, putty, palette, ferrule, bread, butter, cake, serving, wood carver's, molding, paper hanger's, miter, excelsior, switchblade, Boy Scout, Swiss Army.

knife, *v.* **1.** [To stab]—*Syn.* spit, lance, thrust through; see **hurt** 1, **kill** 1, **stab.**
2. [To injure in an underhanded way]—*Syn.* trick, give a coward's blow, strike below the belt; see **deceive.**

knife through, *v.* —*Syn.* dash, shoot *or* plunge *or* drive *or* slip *or* slide through, pierce; see **dart** 1, **slide** 1.

knight, *n.* —*Syn.* cavalier, *caballero* (Spanish), gentleman, champion, knight-errant, thane, bachelor, man-at-arms, Templar, Hospitaler; see **aristocrat, sir** 1.

knight-errantry, *n.* **1.** [Bravery]—*Syn.* boldness, gallantry, chivalry; see **courage** 1, **strength** 1.
2. [Recklessness]—*Syn.* craziness, quixotism, irresponsibility; see **carelessness, indiscretion** 1.

knighthood, *n.* —*Syn.* chivalry, gentility, courtliness; see **courtesy** 1, **kindness** 2.

knightly, *mod.* —*Syn.* gallant, courteous, *gentil* (French); see **brave** 1, **chivalrous, noble** 1.

knit, *v.* **1.** [To form by knitting]—*Syn.* spin, crochet, purl, web, cable, net; see also **sew, weave** 1.
2. [To combine or join closely]—*Syn.* intermingle, connect, affiliate; see **join** 1.
3. [To grow together]—*Syn.* heal, mend, repair; see **improve** 2, **join** 3.

knitted, *mod.* —*Syn.* knit, purled, crocheted, stitched, spun, meshed, webbed, wefted; see also **sewn, woven.**

knob, *n.* **1.** [A projection]—*Syn.* hump, bump, protuberance; see **bulge, lump.**
2. [A door handle]—*Syn.* doorknob, latch, door latch; see **handle** 1.

knobby, *mod.* —*Syn.* knobbed, lumpy, bumpy; see **bent, crooked** 1, **irregular** 4.

knock, *n.* —*Syn.* rap, thump, whack; see **beat** 1, **blow** 1, **injury** 1.

knock, *v.* —*Syn.* tap, rap, thump; see **beat** 2, **hit** 1, **hurt** 1.

knock about (D), *v.* —*Syn.* rove, drift, wander; see **roam** 1, **walk** 1.

knock down, *v.* **1.** [To ruin]—*Syn.* devastate, damage, trample; see **destroy** 1, **ravage.**
2. [To hit]—*Syn.* thrash, drub, kayo (D); see **beat** 2, **hit** 1, **knock out** 2.

knock off (D), *v.* **1.** [To kill]—*Syn.* murder, stab, shoot; see **kill** 1.
2. [To accomplish]—*Syn.* complete, finish, eliminate; see **achieve** 1, **succeed** 1.

knock oneself out (D), *v.* —*Syn.* slave, labor, do one's utmost; see **work** 1.

knockout, *n.* **1.** [A blow that knocks unconscious] —*Syn.* knockout blow, finishing or final blow, technical knockout (TKO), *coup de grâce* (French); *all* (D): blackout, cold pack, hearts and flowers, the count, kayo; see also **blow** 1.
2. [(D) A success]—*Syn.* excellent thing, sensation, perfection; see **success** 1, **triumph** 1.

knock out, *v.* **1.** [(D) To anesthetize]—*Syn.* etherize, put to sleep, stupefy; see **deaden** 1, **drug.**
2. [To strike down]—*Syn.* strike senseless, render unconscious, knock a person out of his senses; *all* (D): knock down for the count, knock cold, kayo, knock for a loop, put a silencer on, put out like a light *or* an empty milk bottle; see also **beat** 2, **defeat** 3, **hit** 1, **hurt** 1.

knock together (D), *v.* —*Syn.* make, toss together, construct; see **build** 1, **create** 2.

knock up (D), *v.* —*Syn.* impregnate, make pregnant, inseminate; see **propagate** 1.

knoll, *n.* —*Syn.* rise, mound, hillock; see **hill, mountain** 1.

knot, *n.* **1.** [An arrangement of strands]—*Syn.* tie, hitch, splice, ligature, bond.
Knots include the following—anchor knot, sheet bend, timber hitch, bowknot, clove hitch, carrick bend, half crown knot, diamond hitch, figure-of-eight, fisherman's bend, flat knot, square knot, granny knot, half hitch, inside clinch, thief knot, outside clinch, lanyard knot, loop knot, mesh knot, midshipman's hitch, open hand knot, overhand knot, rolling hitch, round seizing, bowline on a bight, running bowline, sheepshank, shroud knot, running knot, slide knot, single knot, slip knot, stopper knot, surgeon's knot, trefoil knot, weaver's hitch, stevedore's knot, harness hitch, reef knot, cat's-paw, Blackwall hitch, magnus hitch, halyard bend.
2. [A hard or twisted portion]—*Syn.* snarl, gnarl, snag, bunch, contortion, coil, spiral, warp, screw, helix, perplexity, entanglement, tangle, twist, twirl, whirl, whorl.
3. [A group]—*Syn.* cluster, assortment, gathering; see **bunch** 1, **collection** 2.
tie the knot (D)—*Syn.* wed, join in marriage, get hitched (D); see **marry** 2.

knot, *v.* —*Syn.* bind, tie, cord; see **fasten** 1.

knotted, *mod.* —*Syn.* tied, twisted, tangled, snarled, entangled, bunched, clustered, clumped, snagged, whirled, engaged, perplexed, looped, hitched, spliced, fastened, bent, warped, lashed, clinched, meshed, seized, banded, lassoed, braided, snarled together, linked, involved; see also **tight** 2. —*Ant.* free*, loose, separate.

knotty, *mod.* —*Syn.* hard troublesome, tricky; see **difficult** 2.

know, *v.* **1.** [To possess information]—*Syn.* be cognizant *or* acquainted *or* informed, be in possession of the facts, have knowledge of, be schooled *or* read *or* learned *or* versed in, be conversant with, appreciate, prize, ken, recognize, wot, be *or* become aware *or* sensible of, know full well, ween, trow, have at one's fingertips, be master of, know by heart, know inside and out, know by rote, be instructed, awaken to, keep up on, have information about, know what's what, know all the answers; *all* (D): have one's number, have the jump on, have down cold, have the goods on, get *or* be hep to, know one's stuff, know the score *or* ropes.—*Ant.* be oblivious of, neglect*, overlook.

2. [To understand]—*Syn.* comprehend, apprehend, see into; see **understand** 1.

3. [To recognize]—*Syn.* perceive, discern, be familiar with, have the friendship of, acknowledge, be accustomed to, associate with, be *or* get acquainted; see also **associate** 1.

in the know—*Syn.* informed, knowing, aware; see **educated** 1, **learned** 1.

knowable, *mod.* —*Syn.* distinct, visible, plain; see **obvious** 1, **understandable.**

know-how, *n.* —*Syn.* skill, background, wisdom; see **ability** 1, **experience** 3, **knowledge** 1.

know how, *v.* —*Syn.* be able, have the (necessary) background *or* training, be trained in *or* for; see **understand** 1.

knowing, *mod.* —*Syn.* sharp, clever, acute; see **intelligent** 1, **judicious, reasonable** 1.

knowingly, *mod.* —*Syn.* intentionally, purposely, consciously; see **carefully** 2, **deliberately** 2.

knowledge, *n.* **1.** [Information]—*Syn.* learning, lore, erudition, scholarship, facts, wisdom, instruction, book-learning, cognizance, enlightenment, expertise, intelligence, light, doctrine, dogma, theory, science, principles, data base, philosophy, awareness, insight, proficiency, attainments, accomplishments, education, substance, observation, store of learning; *all* (D): know-how, the scoop, the goods, the know; see **data, experience** 3.—*Ant.* emptiness, ignorance*, pretension.

2. [Culture]—*Syn.* dexterity, cultivation, learning; see **culture** 3, **experience** 3, **refinement** 2.

known, *mod.* **1.** [Open]—*Syn.* discovered, disclosed, revealed; see **observed** 1, **obvious** 1, **public.**

2. [Established]—*Syn.* well-known, published, recognized, notorious, received, accepted, noted, proverbial, hackneyed, certified, down pat (D); see also **established** 2, **familiar** 1.

know-nothing, *n.* —*Syn.* imbecile, clod, illiterate; see **fool** 1, **moron.**

knuckle down (D), *v.* —*Syn.* try hard, labor, work (at); see **improve** 1, **try** 1

knuckle under, *v.* —*Syn.* give in, give up, acquiesce; see **abandon** 1, **retreat** 1, **yield** 1.

kook (D), *n.* —*Syn.* eccentric; *all* (D): crackpot, harebrain, lamebrain, loony, cuckoo, ding-a-ling, nut, screwball, crazy, weirdo, wacko, flake, fruitcake, dingbat.

kosher, *mod.* —*Syn.* proper, genuine, on the up and up (D); see **conventional** 2, **fit** 1, 2, **official** 3.

kowtow to (D), *v.* —*Syn.* stoop, fawn, prostrate; see **grovel.**

kudos (D), *n.* —*Syn.* praise, credit, glory, fame, honor; see **praise** 2, **honor** 1.

Ku Klux Klan, *n.* —*Syn.* secret racist society, white supremacy group, hate group; *all* (D): KKK, (the) klan, cloaked avengers, bedsheet nightriders.

L

label, *n.* —*Syn.* tag, marker, ticket, mark, stamp, hallmark, insignia, design, number, identification, description, classification, copyright label, characterization, epithet, sticker, bumper sticker, price mark; see also **emblem, name** 1.

label, *v.* —*Syn.* specify, mark, identify; see **designate** 1, **name** 1, 2.

labeled, *mod.* —*Syn.* identified, provided with identification, stamped; see **marked** 1, 2.

labor, *n.* **1.** [The act of doing work]—*Syn.* activity, toil, operation; see **work** 2.

2. [Work to be done]—*Syn.* task, employment, undertaking; see **job** 2.

3. [Exertion required in work]—*Syn.* exertion, energy, industry, diligence, strain, stress, pull, push, drudgery, travail; see also **effort** 1, **exercise** 1.

4. [The body of workers]—*Syn.* laborers, workers, workingmen, operatives, proletariat, blue-collar workers, work *or* labor force, working people, employee(s); see also **workman.**—*Ant.* employer*, capitalist, businessman.

5. [Childbirth]—*Syn.* parturition, giving birth, labor pains; see **birth** 1.

labor, *v.* —*Syn.* toil, strive, get cracking (D); see **work** 1.

laboratory, *n.* —*Syn.* workroom, experiment room, research room, testing room, experiment laboratory; *both* (D): lab, kitchen.

Labor Day, *n.* —*Syn.* first Monday in September, Knights of Labor day, end of summer; see **autumn, holiday.**

labored, *mod.* —*Syn.* forced, strained, heavy; see **difficult** 2.

laborer, *n.* —*Syn.* day laborer, unskilled worker, toiler, blue-collar worker, manual laborer; carpenter's helper, bricklayer's helper, etc.; ranch hand, farm hand, construction hand, etc.; apprentice, learner, hired man, hand, transient worker, seasonal laborer, ditch-digger, pick-and-shovel man, roust-about, stevedore, miner, street cleaner, thrall, helot, serf, villein, galley slave, wage slave, chattel, instrument, stooge, robot, automaton, peon, mercenary, flunky, lackey, hireling, hack; *all* (D): beast of burden, doormat, chaingauger; see also **workman.**

laborious, *mod.* **1.** [Difficult]—*Syn.* arduous, hard, stiff; see **difficult** 1.

2. [Industrious]—*Syn.* assiduous, indefatigable, diligent; see **active** 2.

laboriously, *mod.* **1.** [Strenuously]—*Syn.* with difficulty, resolutely, tiresomely; see **painfully** 1, **vigorously.**

2. [Diligently]—*Syn.* earnestly, eagerly, steadily; see **carefully** 1, **industriously.**

labor union, *n.* —*Syn.* organized labor, American Federation of Labor and Congress of Industrial Organizations (AFL-CIO), (independent) union, craft union, guild, industrial union, local, labor party; see also **labor** 4, **organization** 3.

American labor unions include the following—International Ladies' Garment Workers' Union (ILGWU), International Union of Electrical, Radio, and Machine Workers (IUE), United Steelworkers of America (USW), American Federation of Teachers (AFT), American Federation of Television and Radio Artists (AFTRA), International Longshoremen's and Warehousemen's Union (ILWU), United Mine Workers of America (UMWA), United Farm Workers of America (UFWA), International Brotherhood of Teamsters, Chauffeurs, Warehousemen, and Helpers of America (Teamsters' Union).

labyrinth, *n.* —*Syn.* problem, complication, complexity; see **maze, puzzle** 2.

labyrinthian, *mod.* —*Syn.* twisted, complicated, gnarled; see **confused** 2, **difficult** 2.

lace, *n.* **1.** [Ornamental threadwork]—*Syn.* edging, trimming, banding, border, tatting, insertion, ornament, mesh, tissue, net; see also **decoration** 2.

Laces include the following—needle-point, Valenciennes, bobbin, pillow, Venetian, flat, Venetian point, Alençon, bone, cutwork, *merletti a piombini* (Italian), reticella, point d'esprit, torchon, macramé, blond, d'Angleterre, Mechlin, Brussels, point de Gaze, Duchesse, point appliqué, Bruges, Binche, filet, plat appliqué, Irish crochet, Limerick, Carrickmacross, passementerie, guipure.

2. [Material for binding through openings]—*Syn.* thong, cord, band; see **rope, thread.**

lace, *v.* —*Syn.* strap, bind, close; see **fasten** 1, **tie** 2.

lacerate, *v.* **1.** [To tear]—*Syn.* slash, rip (open), stab; see **break** 1, **cut** 2.

2. [To injure]—*Syn.* wound, harm, maim; see **hurt** 1.

laceration, *n.* —*Syn.* tear, gash, incision; see **cut** 2, **injury** 1.

lachrymose, *mod.* —*Syn.* weeping, tearful, crying; see **sad** 1, 2.

lacing, *n.* —*Syn.* bond, hitch, tie; see **fastener, knot** 1.

lack, *n.* **1.** [The state of being lacking]—*Syn.* destitution, absence, need, dearth, shortage, paucity, deprivation, deficiency, scarcity, exiguity, exigency, insufficiency, inadequacy, privation, poverty, distress, scantiness.—*Ant.* plenty*, sufficiency, abundance.

2. [That which is lacking]—*Syn.* need, decrease, want, loss, depletion, shrinkage, shortage, shortness, short fall, abridgment, defect, meagerness, scantiness, slightness, inferiority, paucity, stint, curtailment, retrenchment, reduction; see also **necessity** 2.—*Ant.* wealth*, overflow, satisfaction.

lack, *v.* —*Syn.* want, require, have need (of); see **need.**

lackadaisical, *mod.* —*Syn.* idle, inattentive, lazy; see **dull** 6, **listless** 1.

lackey, *n.* —*Syn.* attendant, manservant, footman; see **servant.**

lacking, *mod.* —*Syn.* needed, deprived of, missing; see **wanting.**

lackluster, *mod.* —*Syn.* dim, colorless, obscure; see **dark** 1, **dull** 2.

laconic, *mod.* —*Syn.* pithy, curt, brief; see **short** 2.

lacquer, *n.* —*Syn.* stain, veneer, finish; see **coat** 3, **cover** 2, **varnish.**

lacuna, *n.* —*Syn.* gap, hiatus, space; see **blank** 1, **emptiness.**

lacy, *mod.* **1.** [Transparent]—*Syn.* sheer, thin, gauzy; see **transparent** 1.

2. [Fancy]—*Syn.* frilly, patterned, elegant; see **fancy** 2, **ornate** 1.

lad, *n.* —*Syn.* fellow, youth, stripling; see **boy, child.**

ladder, *n.* —*Syn.* stairway, step-stool, scale; see **stairs.**

Ladders include the following—stepladder, rope ladder, ship's ladder, accommodation ladder, fireman's scaling (extension) ladder, companionway, collapsing ladder, Jacob's ladder, gangway, fire escape, standing ladder.

lade, *v.* **1.** [To fill]—*Syn.* replenish, stuff, pack; see **fill** 1.

2. [To dip]—*Syn.* scoop, bail, spoon; see **dip** 2.

laden, *mod.* —*Syn.* weighted, loaded, burdened; see **full** 1.

lading, *n.* —*Syn.* cargo, shipment, shipping; see **freight** 1.

ladle, *n.* —*Syn.* skimmer, scoop, vessel; see **dipper, silverware, spoon.**

lady, *n.* **1.** [A woman]—*Syn.* female, adult, matron; see **woman** 1.

2. [A ladylike woman]—*Syn.* well-bred woman, dame, woman of good taste *or* breeding *or* quality, woman of education, cultured woman.

3. [A woman of gentle breeding]—*Syn.* gentlewoman, high-born lady, mistress of a manor *or* estate, noblewoman, titled lady.

Titles for ladies include the following—queen, princess, empress, duchess, archduchess, marchioness, viscountess, countess, contessa, baroness, maharani, sultana.

ladylike, *mod.* —*Syn.* womanly, cultured, well-bred; see **polite** 1, **refined** 2.

ladylove, *n.* —*Syn.* sweetheart, girl friend, darling; see **lover** 1.

lag, *n.* —*Syn.* slack, retardation, slowness, belatedness, tardiness, falling behind, interval, pulling back, delay, slowdown, drag, sluggishness, backwardness.—*Ant.* progress*, progression, advance.

lag, *v.* **1.** [To move slowly]—*Syn.* dawdle, linger, fall *or* hold back, loiter, tarry, straggle, saunter, be retarded, inch along, inch, get behind, slacken, slow up, fall *or* lag behind, procrastinate; *both* (D): have lead in one's rear, get no place fast; see also **delay** 1.—*Ant.* hasten, hurry*, keep pace with.

2. [To move without spirit]—*Syn.* plod, trudge, toddle, slouch, lounge, shuffle, falter, stagger, hobble, limp, shamble.—*Ant.* dance*, scamper, bound.

laggard, *n.* —*Syn.* loiterer, straggler, slowpoke, dawdler.

lagoon, *n.* —*Syn.* inlet, sound, pool; see **bay, lake.**

lair, *n.* —*Syn.* cave, pen, den; see **hole** 3.

laissez faire, *n.* —*Syn.* isolationism, neutrality, indifference; see **noninterference.**

laity, *n.* —*Syn.* believers, congregation, parish; see **laymen.**

lake, *n.* —*Syn.* pond, creek, mouth, tarn, loch, mere, pool, inland sea; see also **sea.**

Famous lakes include the following—Titicaca, Yellowstone, Geneva *or* Leman, Lucerne, Constance, Ladoga, Great Salt, Superior, Huron, Michigan, Erie, Ontario, Finger Lakes, Champlain, Tahoe, Millac, Victoria, Nyanza, Tanganyika, Nyasa, Como, Maggiore, Windermere, Coniston Water, Derwentwater, Crummock Water, Wastwater, Haweswater, Ennerdale Water, Lake of the Woods, Buttermere, Bassenthwaite Water, Baikal, Lyn Cawlyd, Loch Tay, Loch Lomond, Lough Neagh, Lough Erne.

lamb, *n.* —*Syn.* young sheep, young one, yeanling; see **animal** 1, **sheep.**

lambaste (D), *v.* —*Syn.* punish, thrash, whip; see **beat** 2, **hit** 1.

Lamb of God, *n.* —*Syn.* the Christ Child, Jesus, the Saviour; see **Christ, God** 1.

lame, *mod.* **1.** [Forced to limp]—*Syn.* crippled, defective, limping; see **deformed, disabled.**

2. [Sore]—*Syn.* bruised, stiff, raw; see **painful** 1.

3. [Weak; *usually used figuratively*]—*Syn.* inefficient, ineffective, faltering; see **faulty, inadequate** 1, **poor** 2, **unfinished** 1, **unsatisfactory, wanting.**

lame duck, *n.* —*Syn.* defeated candidate, pensioner, superannuated man; see **failure** 2, **victim** 1.

lament, *v.* **1.** [To express sorrow]—*Syn.* regret, grieve, sorrow; see **mourn** 1.

2. [To weep]—*Syn.* sob, bawl, wail; see **cry** 1, **weep.**

3. [To regret]—*Syn.* deplore, rue, repine; see **regret.**

lamentable, *mod.* —*Syn.* unfortunate, deplorable, regrettable; see **sad** 1, **unfavorable** 2.

lamentation, *n.* **1.** [Mourning]—*Syn.* weeping, complaining, sobbing; see **mourning** 1.

2. [A cry]—*Syn.* lament, wail, sob; see **cry** 3, **tears.**

lamenting, *mod.* —*Syn.* sobbing, regretting, mournful; see **sad** 1.

laminate, *v.* —*Syn.* stratify, overlay, layer; see **cover** 1, **plate.**

laminated, *mod.* —*Syn.* flaky, scaly, layered; see **covered** 1, **stratified.**

lamp, *n.* —*Syn.* light, light bulb, lighting device; see **light** 3.

Types and forms of lamps include the following—wick, oil, gas, electric, sun, hanging, bracket, portable, table, standing, floor, torchier, bridge, safety, miner's, street, arc, incandescent, vapor, gasoline, temple, domestic, terra cotta, clay, pottery, vase, bronze, brass, iron, glass, night, gooseneck, chandelier, gaselier, lantern, torch.

lampoon, *n.* —*Syn.* satire, invective, pasquinade; see **parody** 2.

lampoon, *v.* —*Syn.* satirize, caricature, parody; see **ridicule.**

lance, *n.*—*Syn.* lancet, foil, point; see **spear, weapon** 1.

lance-shaped, *mod.* —*Syn.* spearklike, hastate, lanceolate, spear-shaped, pointed, lanciform, lancelike; see also **sharp** 2.

land, *n.* **1.** [The solid surface of the earth]—*Syn.* ground, soil, dirt, earth, clay, loam, leaf mold, glebe, marl, gravel, subsoil, clod, sand, rock, mineral, metal, pebble, stone, dry land, terra firma, valley, desert, tableland, hill, bank, seaboard, seaside, shore, beach, strand, crag, cliff, boulder, ledge, peninsula, delta, promontory, neck, tongue; see also **earth** 2, **mountain** 1, **plain.**—*Ant.* sea*, stream, ocean.

2. [Land as property]—*Syn.* estate, tract, real estate; see **area** 2, **property** 2.

3. [Land as an agent of production]—*Syn.* ranch, quarry, field; see **farm, mine** 1.

4. [A country]—*Syn.* continent, province, region; see **country** 3, **home** 2, **nation** 1.

land, *v.* **1.** [To bring a boat to shore]—*Syn.* dock, set on shore, set down, bring in, come to land, pilot, steer, bring into her slip, drop *or* cast anchor, put in, make land.—*Ant.* leave*, weigh anchor, cast off.

2. [To come into port]—*Syn.* dock, berth, come to berth; see **arrive** 1.

3. [To go ashore]—*Syn.* disembark, debark, come ashore, invade, arrive, alight, leave the boat, light on, leave the ship, go down the gangplank; *both* (D): hit the beach, lift anchor and pack gear; see also **descend** 1.—*Ant.* leave*, go on shipboard, go up the gangplank.

4. [To bring an airplane to earth]—*Syn.* touch *or* get down, ground, take down, arrive, alight, get into the field, come in, bring in the ship; maneuver a nosecone, spaceship, etc.; settle, land into the wind, level off, flatten out, come down, descend upon, make a forced landing; *all* (D): set it on the deck, balloon in, bounce in, crash-land, up-wind, fishtail down, build a wooden horse, nose over, overshoot, splash down, check in, undershoot, pancake, settle her down hot, fishtail down; see also **arrive** 1.

landed, *mod.*—*Syn.* property-holding, secure, wealthy; see **rich** 1.

landing, *n.* **1.** [The act of reaching shore]—*Syn.* arriving, docking, berthing, wharfing, piloting, making port, steering, casting anchor, anchoring, dropping anchor; see also **arrival** 1.

2. [The place where landing, sense 1, is possible] —*Syn.* marina, pier, wharf; see **dock** 1, **harbor** 2.

3. [The act of reaching the earth]—*Syn.* setting down, grounding, getting in, arriving, deplaning, reaching an airport, splashing down, completing a mission, vertical landing, settling, alighting, making a crash landing; *all* (D): ballooning in, setting it on the deck, bouncing in, upwinding, nosing over, pancaking, splashdown.

landing field, *n.*—*Syn.* airfield, flying field, airstrip; see **airport.**

landlady, *n.*—*Syn.* lodginghouse mistress, lessor, innkeeper; see **owner.**

landlord, *n.*—*Syn.* landowner, lessor, property *or* house owner, innkeeper; see **owner.**

landmark, *n.* **1.** [A notable relic]—*Syn.* survival, remnant, historic structure, vestige, fragment, souvenir, ruins, specimen, trace, memorial, museum, battleground; see **monument** 1, **relic** 1, **ruin** 2.

2. [A crisis]—*Syn.* milestone, turning point, stage; see **crisis, event** 1.

3. [A point from which a course may be taken] —*Syn.* vantage point, mark, benchmark, blaze, guide, marker, stone, tree, hill, mountain, bend, promontory, duck on a rock (D); see also **position** 1.

landscape, *n.* **1.** [Natural scenery]—*Syn.* scene, scenery, panorama; see **view** 1, 2.

2. [Scenic art]—*Syn.* mural, photograph, scene; see **painting** 1, **sketch** 1.

landscape, *v.* —*Syn.* provide *or* do the landscaping, finish off *or* up, put in the lawn and shrubbery; see **decorate, trim** 2.

landscaping, *n.*—*Syn.* lawn, shrubbery, garden, (the) grounds, beautification program, urban development, setting, background; see **decoration** 2.

landslide (D), *mod.*—*Syn.* conclusive, lopsided, decisive; see **large** 1, **many, overwhelming** 2.

landslide, *n.* —*Syn.* (earth *or* rock) mass, slide, slip, avalanche, *Lawine* (German); snow slide, rock slide, mud slide, etc.; see also **descent** 2.

lane, *n.*—*Syn.* way, alley, passage; see **path** 1, **road** 1.

language, *n.* **1.** [A means of communication] —*Syn.* voice, utterance, expression, vocalization, sound, phonation, (native *or* mother) tongue, articulation, meta-language, object language, sense-datum language, thing-language, physical language; language of diplomacy, language of chemistry, language of flowers, etc.; accent, word, sign, signal, pantomime, (facial) gesture, vocabulary, diction, dialect, idiom, local speech, broken *or* pidgin English, lingo, brogue, polyglot, patois *or* vernacular, lingua franca *or* trade language, gibberish, pig Latin, debased speech, inscription, picture writing, hieroglyphics, cuneiform, printing, writing, poetry, prose, song, style, phraseology; see **communication** 1, **conversation, speech** 2.

2. [The study of language, sense 1]—*Syn.* morphology, phonology, phonemics, morphemics, morphophonemics, phonics, phonetics, semantics, semasiology, criticism, letters, linguistic studies, history of language, etymology, dialectology, linguistic geography, anthropological linguistics, sociolinguistics, lexicostatistics, glottochronology, structural linguistics, descriptive *or* taxonomic linguistics, historical *or* diachronic linguistics, comparative *or* synchronic linguistics, contrastive grammar, descriptive grammar, prescriptive grammar, phrase-structure *or* PS grammar, generative grammar, immediate-constituent *or* IC grammar, transform(ational) grammar, tagmemics, stratificational grammar, glossematics, Prague school of linguistics, London *or* Firthian school of linguistics; see also **anthropology, etymology, grammar, linguistics, literature** 1.

Types of languages include the following—synthetic *or* inflectional, analytic *or* isolating *or* distributive, incorporating, agglutinative, computer, artificial, polysynthetic.

Languages mainly by phyla or family include the following—Indo-European, Finno-Ugric, Altaic,

Basque, Caucasian, Afro-Asiatic, Nilo-Saharan, Niger-Congo, Khoisan, Malayo-Polynesian, Dravidian, Austro-Asiatic, Sino-Tibetan, Kadai, Eskimo-Aleut, Athabaskan, Algonquian, Mosan, Iroquoian, Natchez-Muskogean, Siouan, Penutian, Hokan, Uto-Aztecan, Mayan.

Indo-European languages include the following—Germanic: Gothic, Old Saxon, Old English *or* Anglo-Saxon, English, Frisian, Old High German, German, Yiddish, Dutch, Afrikaans, Flemish, Old Norse, Danish, Swedish, Norwegian, Icelandic; Celtic: Breton, Welsh *or* Cymric, Cornish, Irish *or* Erse, Scots Gaelic, Manx; Italic: Oscan, Umbrian, Venetic, Latin; Romance: Portuguese, Galician, Spanish, Catalan, Provençal, French, Haitian Creole, Walloon, Italian, Sardinian, Romanian, Rhaeto-Romanic *or* Romansh *or* Ladin; Greek: Attic, Ionic, Doric, Koine; Slavic: Old Church Slavonic, Russian, Byelorussian, Ukrainian, Polish, Czech, Slovak, Slovene, Serbo-Croatian, Bulgarian; Baltic: Old Prussian, Lithuanian, Latvian *or* Lettish; Albanian; Armenian; Iranian: Old Persian, Avestan, Pahlavi, Kurdish, Persian, Pushtu *or* Afghan; Indie: Sanskrit, Pali, Prakrit, Hindi, Urdu; Tocharian; Hittite.

Other Eurasian languages include the following—Uralic: Finnish, Estonian, Hungarian, Samoyed; Altaic: Turkish, Mongolian; Georgian; Abkhasian, Kabardian, Chechen; Basque; Etruscan.

African and Asian languages include the following—Afro-Asiatic *or* Hamito-Semitic: Akkadian *or* Assyro-Babylonian, Aramaic, Syriac, Phoenician, Talmudic, Hebrew, Arabic, Amharic, Egyptian *or* Coptic, Tuareg, Somali, Hausa; Sumerian; Niger-Congo: Wolof, Mande, Ewe, Yoruba, Ibo, Efik, Tiv, Swahili, Kikuyu, Rwanda, Zulu, Xhosa, Swazi, Venda; Nilo-Saharan: Songhai, Kanuri, Nilotic, Dinka, Nuer, Masai; Khoisan: Sandawe, Hatsa, Bushman-Hottentot.

Asian and Malayo-Polynesian languages include the following—Japanese, Ryukyu; Korean; Sino-Tibetan: Burmese, Tibetan, Mandarin, Cantonese; Kadai: Thai *or* Siamese, Laotian *or* Lao; Miao-Yao; Malayo-Polynesian: Malay, Indonesian, Javanese, Balinese, Tagalog *or* Filipino, Malagasy, Micronesian, Hawaiian, Tahitian, Samoan, Maori, Fijian; Papuan, Australian; Tasmanian; Dravidian: Telegu, Tamil, Kanerese *or* Kannada, Malayalam; Austro-Asiatic: Santali, Palaung, Mon-Khmer, Vietnamese.

North, Central, and South American languages include the following—Algonquian: Massachusetts, Delaware, Mohegan, Penobscot, Pasamaquoddy, Fox-Sauk-Kickapoo, Cree, Menomini, Shawnee, Blackfoot, Arapaho, Cheyenne; Wiyot, Yurok; Kutenai; Salishan: Tillamook, Lillooet; Wakashan: Nootka, Kwakiutl; Muskogean: Creek, Choctaw-Chickasaw, Seminole; Natchez, Chitimacha; Iroquoian: Cherokee, Huron *or* Wayondot, Erie, Oneida, Mohawk, Seneca, Cayuga, Susquehanna *or* Conestoga; Siouan: Biloxi, Dakota, Mandan, Winnebago, Hidatsa, Crow; Caddoan: Caddo, Wichita, Pawnee; Yuchi; Aleut, Eskimo; Penutian: Tsimshian, Maidu, Miwok, Klamath-Modoc; Zuni; Hokan: Karok, Shasta, Washo, Pomo; Subtiaba-Tlapanec, Tequistlatec, Jicaque; Comecrudo, Tonkawa; Mayan: Kekchi, Quiche, Tseltal-Tsotzil, Tojolabal, Yucatec; Totonac; Mixe, Zoque, Vera Cruz; Huave; Zapotec, Chatino; Mixtec; Pueblo *or* Popoluca; Otomi, Pame; Tarascan; Uto-Aztecan: Tubatulabal, Luiseño, Tepehuan, Pima-Papago, Hopi, Huichol, Nahuatl *or* Aztec, Northern Paiute *or* Paviotso, Mono, Shoshoni-Comanche, Southern Paiute-Ute, Chemehuevi; Kiowa-Tanoan; Keresan; Na-Dené: Haida, Tlingit, Athabaskan (Chipewyan, Apachean, Navaho, Hupa); Yukian; Quechua; Aymara; Araucanian.

speak the same language—*Syn.* understand one another, communicate, get along; see **agree.**

languid, *mod.* **1.** [Weak]—*Syn.* feeble, weary, infirm; see **weak** 1.

2. [Dull]—*Syn.* sluggish, heavy, lethargic; see **dull** 6.

3. [Listless]—*Syn.* dull, inattentive, spiritless; see **indifferent** 1, **listless** 1, **unconcerned.**

languidly, *mod.*—*Syn.* nonchalantly, indifferently, gently; see **calmly, easily** 1, **slowly.**

languidness, *n.* **1.** [Dullness]—*Syn.* listlessness, sluggishness, apathy; see **indifference** 1, **slowness** 1.

2. [Weakness]—*Syn.* feebleness, impotence, prostration,; see **weakness** 1.

languish, *v.* **1.** [To weaken]—*Syn.* fade, fail, droop; see **weaken** 1.

2. [To want]—*Syn.* hunger, pine, desire; see **need, want** 1.

languishing, *mod.* **1.** [Weak]—*Syn.* droopy, dull, sluggish; see **slow** 1, 2, **weak** 1.

2. [Pensive]—*Syn.* pining, melancholy, longing; see **sad** 1.

languor, *n.*—*Syn.* lethargy, listlessness, lassitude; see **indifference** 1, **laziness.**

lank, *mod.*—*Syn.* lean, slender, meager; see **thin** 2.

lanky, *mod.*—*Syn.* lean, bony, rangy; see **thin** 2.

lantern, *n.*—*Syn.* torch, lamp, lighting device; see **light** 3.

Lanterns include the following—lighthouse, magic, cupola, tower, barn, searchlight, police, dark, bull's eye, railroad, flashlight, oil, gas, electric, horn, glass, paper, architectural, hand, hanging, Chinese, Japanese, ship's, poop, optical, lantern of the dead.

lanyard, *n.*—*Syn.* cord, line, string; see **rope.**

lap, *n.* **1.** [That portion of the body that is formed when one sits down]—*Syn.* knees, legs, thighs, front, seat.

2. [The portion that overlaps]—*Syn.* extension, projection, fold; see **flap, overlap.**

3. [Part of a race]—*Syn.* circuit, round, course; see **distance** 3, **race** 3.

drop into someone's lap—*Syn.* transfer responsibility, shift blame, pass the buck (D); see **give** 1.

in the lap of luxury—*Syn.* surrounded by luxury, living elegantly, prospering; see **rich** 1.

in the lap of the gods—*Syn.* superhuman, extraordinary, beyond human control *or* understanding; see **supernatural.**

lapse, *n.*—*Syn.* slip, mistake, failure; see **error** 1.

lapse, *v.* **1.** [To fail slowly]—*Syn.* slip, deteriorate, decline; see **weaken** 1.

2. [To become void]—*Syn.* end, cease, terminate; see **stop** 2.

lapsed, *mod.*—*Syn.* past, extinct, dead; see **finished** 1.

larceny, *n.* —*Syn.* burglary, thievery, robbery; see **crime** 2, **theft.**

lard, *n.* —*Syn.* bacon, pork, fat, leaf lard; see **fat, grease.**

larder, *n.* —*Syn.* pantry, storeroom, scullery; see **pantry, room** 2, **storehouse.**

lardy, *mod.* —*Syn.* fat, buttery, greasy; see **oily** 1.

large, *mod.* **1.** [Of great size]—*Syn.* huge, big, wide, grand, great, considerable, substantial, vast, massive, immense, spacious, bulky, capacious, colossal, gigantic, mountainous, immeasurable, extensive, extended, plentiful, copious, populous, ample, abundant, liberal, comprehensive, lavish, swollen, bloated, puffy, blowsy, corpulent, obese, tumid, turgid, herculean, titanic, monstrous, towering, mighty, magnificent, commodious, enormous, cyclopean, giant, jumbo, Brobdingnagian, tremendous, prodigious, monumental, stupendous, enlarged, voluminous, overgrown, cumbrous, cumbersome, ponderous, Gargantuan, Antaean, distended, dilated, gross, immoderate, extravagant, prodigal; *all* (D): super, kingsized, booming, blooming, bumper, whopping; see also **broad** 1, **deep** 2, **extensive** 1, **high** 1, **long** 1.—*Ant.* little*, small, tiny.

2. [Involving great plans]—*Syn.* extensive, extended, considerable; see **comprehensive, general** 1.

3. [Magnanimous]—*Syn.* open, noble, bighearted; see **generous** 1, **kind.**

largely, *mod.* **1.** [In large measure]—*Syn.* mostly, mainly, chiefly; see **principally.**

2. [In a large way]—*Syn.* extensively, abundantly, comprehensively, on a large scale, broadly, magnificently, grandly, lavishly, liberally, prodigiously, voluminously, generously, expansively, imposingly, considerably, copiously, commodiously, extravagantly, immoderately, prodigally, in a big way, in the grand manner, open-handedly; see also **widely.**

largeness, *n.* —*Syn.* magnitude, proportion, breath; see **measure** 1, **measurement** 2, **quantity, size** 2.

largess, *n.* —*Syn.* present, donation, contribution; see **gift** 1.

lariat, *n.* —*Syn.* lasso, tether, *reata* (Spanish); see **rope.**

lark, *n.* —*Syn.* songbird, warbler, philomel; see **bird** 1.

Larks include the following—skylark, horned lark, shore lark, Sprague's lark, pipit, wagtail, titlark, meadowlark.

larva, *n.* —*Syn.* maggot, grub, caterpillar; see **invertebrate, worm** 1.

lascivious, *mod.* **1.** [Filled with lust]—*Syn.* ruttish, lustful, immoral; see **lewd** 1, 2, **sensual.**

2. [Suggestive of intercourse]—*Syn.* fleshly, carnal, orgiastic, bodily, earthly, animal, natural, voluptuous; see also **sensual.**—*Ant.* ascetic, spiritual*, abstemious.

lasciviousness, *n.* —*Syn.* lechery, wantonness, lustfulness; see **desire** 3, **lewdness.**

lash, *n.* —*Syn.* cane, thong, rod; see **whip.**

lash, *v.* **1.** [To whip]—*Syn.* cane, scourge, strap; see **whip.**

2. [To tie up]—*Syn.* bind, fasten, truss; see **bind** 1.

lash (out), *v.* —*Syn.* strike, thrash, scourge; see **beat** 2, **hit** 1.

lashing, *mod.* —*Syn.* thrashing, beating, floundering; see **hitting** 1, **punishment.**

lass, *n.* —*Syn.* young woman *or* lady, damsel, maiden; see **girl** 1, **woman** 1.

lassitude, *n.* —*Syn.* languor, faintness, weariness, tiredness, fatigue, heaviness, stupor, dullness, drowsiness, yawning, exhaustion, burnout, prostration, drooping, torpor, torpidity, lethargy, apathy, ennui, stupefaction, inappetence, phlegm, hebetude, supineness, inertia; *all* (D): (brain) fag, the dumps, spring fever; see also **indifference** 1. —*Ant.* action*, vivaciousness, sprightliness.

lasso, *n.* —*Syn.* tether, lariat, noose; see **rope.**

last, *mod.* **1.** [Final]—*Syn.* ultimate, utmost, lowest, meanest, least, latest, end, extreme, remotest, furthest, outermost, farthest, uttermost, conclusive, concluding, hindmost, far, far-off, aftermost, hindermost, determinative, determinate, ulterior, once and for all, definitive, after all others, ending, at the end, terminal, eventual, antipodal, terminative, terminating, directing, settling, resolving, decisive, crowning, climactic, closing, ending, finishing, unanswerable, irrefutable.—*Ant.* first*, foremost, beginning.

2. [Most recent]—*Syn.* latest, newest, current, freshest, immediate, most fashionable, in the fashion, modish, the last word (D); see also **fashionable, modern** 1.—*Ant.* old*, stale, outmoded.

last, *n.* **1.** [The end]—*Syn.* tail end, last *or* terminal *or* final one, ending; see **end** 4.

2. [A shoemaker's mold]—*Syn.* form, cast, shape; see **mold** 1, 2.

at (long) last—*Syn.* after a long time, in the end, ultimately; see **finally** 2.

see the last of—*Syn.* see for the last time *or* never again, dispose of, get rid of; see **end** 1.

last, *v.* **1.** [To endure]—*Syn.* remain, persist, go on; see **continue** 1, **endure** 1, 2.

2. [To be sufficient]—*Syn.* hold out, be adequate *or* enough *or* ample *or* satisfactory, serve, do, accomplish the purpose, answer; see also **satisfy** 3.

lasting, *mod.* —*Syn.* enduring, abiding, constant; see **permanent** 2, **perpetual** 1.

lastly, *mod.* —*Syn.* in conclusion, at last, ultimately; see **finally** 2.

latch, *n.* —*Syn.* catch, hook, bar; see **fastener, lock** 1.

latch, *v.* —*Syn.* lock, cinch, close up; see **close** 4, **fasten** 1.

latch onto (D), *v.* —*Syn.* grab, take, steal; see **seize** 1, 2.

late, *mod.* **1.** [Tardy]—*Syn.* too late, held up, overdue, stayed, postponed, put off, not on time, belated, behind time, lagging, delayed, remiss, behindhand, backward, not in time; *all* (D): in the lurch, later than you think, at the eleventh hour; see also **slow** 2, 3.—*Ant.* early*, punctual, on time.

2. [Recently dead]—*Syn.* defunct, deceased, departed; see **dead** 1.

3. [Recent]—*Syn.* new, just out, recently published; see **fresh** 1.

4. [Far into the night]—*Syn.* nocturnal, night-loving, after hours, advanced, tardy, toward morning, after midnight.

5. [At an advanced cultural stage]—*Syn.* developed, cultured, advanced; see **modern** 1, 3.

of late—*Syn.* lately, in recent times, a short time ago; see **recently.**

lately, *mod.* —*Syn.* a short time ago, in recent times, of late; see **recently.**

lateness, *n.* —*Syn.* belatedness, tardiness, retardation, protraction, prolongation, slowness, backwardness, advanced hour, late date; see also **delay** 1.—*Ant.* anticipation*, earliness, promptness.

latent, *mod.* —*Syn.* implied, inherent, underdeveloped, torpid, potential, dormant, quiescent, suspended, in abeyance, abeyant, involved, inactive, in the making, possible, intrinsic, sleeping, inert, lurking, unexposed, covert, inoperative, suppressed, passive, underlying, contained, unexpressed, tacit, inferred, escaping notice, inferential, between the lines (D); see also **hidden** 2, **idle** 1. —*Ant.* active*, developed, operative.

later, *mod.* —*Syn.* succeeding, next, more recent; see **following.**

lateral, *mod.* —*Syn.* oblique, sidelong, side by side; see **side.**

laterally, *mod.* —*Syn.* alongside, next to, sideways; see **parallel** 1.

latest, *mod.* —*Syn.* most recent, immediately prior (to), just done *or* finished *or* completed; see **last** 1, 2.

lath, *n.* —*Syn.* strip, slat, mesh, groundwork.

Kinds of laths include the following—wooden, metal, sheet metal, perforated metal, wire mesh, chicken wire, single, double, thinnest, ¼-inch, ½-inch.

lathe, *n.* —*Syn.* turret lathe, turning lathe, cutter; see **machine** 1, **tool** 1.

lather, *n.* —*Syn.* suds, foam, bubbles; see **froth.**

lather, *v.* —*Syn.* foam, scrub, soap; see **wash** 2.

lathery, *mod.* —*Syn.* sudsy, foamy, bubbly; see **frothy** 1.

Latin, *mod.* **1.** [Pertaining to ancient Rome or to its language]—*Syn.* Roman, Romanic, Latinic; see **classical** 2.

2. [Pertaining to southwestern Europe]—*Syn.* Latinate, Roman, Gallic, Mediterranean, Italian, Spanish, French, Portuguese.

Latin, *n.* —*Syn.* Roman language, Romance language, language of Latium; see **language** 2.

Divisions of Latin include the following—classical Latin, Latin of the Golden Age, Latin of the Silver Age, provincial Latin, Late Latin, low Latin, medieval Latin, Middle Latin, Vulgar Latin, monks' Latin, made Latin, New Latin, Modern Latin.

Languages descended from Latin include the following—Portuguese, Spanish, Catalan, Provençal, Rhaeto-Romanic *or* Ladin, Italian, Romanian, French.

latitude, *n.* **1.** [Freedom within limits]—*Syn.* range, scope, independence; see **extent, freedom** 2.

2. [A point in its relationship to the equator] —*Syn.* (meridional) distance, degree, measure, degrees of latitude; see also **measure** 1.

latitudinarian, *mod.* —*Syn.* tolerant, libertine, accepting; see **lenient, liberal** 2.

latrine, *n.* —*Syn.* privy, lavatory, restroom; see **bath** 3, **toilet** 2.

latter, *mod.* —*Syn.* late, last, recent; see **following, last** 1.

latter, *n.* —*Syn.* the nearest *or* most recent *or* subsequent *or* second, third, etc., person referred to; the last named; see **end** 4, **last** 1.

latterly, *mod.* —*Syn.* lately, hitherto, of late; see **recently.**

lattice, *n.* —*Syn.* screen, web, mesh, structure, framework, trellis, grating; see also **frame** 1, **net.**

laud, *v.* —*Syn.* eulogize, flatter, commend; see **admire** 1, **praise** 1, **compliment** 1, 2.

laudable, *mod.* —*Syn.* praiseworthy, commendable, of note; see **excellent, worthy.**

laudatory, *mod.* —*Syn.* flattering, approving, eulogistic; see **complimentary.**

laugh, *n.* —*Syn.* mirth, sound, merriment, amusement, rejoicing, facial contortion, facial gesture, emotional expression, crow, shout, chuckle, chortle, cackle, fit *or* peal of laughter, horselaugh, guffaw, titter, snicker, snigger, giggle, roar, belly laugh, snort; see also **laughter.**—*Ant.* sob, cry*, whimper.

have the last laugh—*Syn.* defeat (finally), beat in the end, overcome all obstacles; see **win** 1.

no laughing matter—*Syn.* serious, grave, significant; see **important** 1.

laugh, *v.* —*Syn.* chuckle, chortle, guffaw, laugh off, smile away, snicker, snigger, titter, giggle, burst out (laughing), be convulsed, shriek, roar, cachinnate, beam, grin, smile, smirk, roar, shout, crow; *all* (D): have a hemorrhage, die laughing, break up, howl, haw-haw, split one's sides, bust up, roll in the aisles, tee-hee, snort, be in stitches; see also **smile.**—*Ant.* cry*, sob, weep.

laugh out of court—*Syn.* mock, deride, laugh at; see **ridicule.**

laugh out the other side of one's mouth—*Syn.* be disappointed, be sorry, have qualms about; see **regret.**

laughable, *mod.* **1.** [Exciting humor]—*Syn.* ludicrous, comic, comical; see **funny** 1.

2. [Exciting humor and some contempt]—*Syn.* eccentric, bizarre, fantastic; see **unusual** 2.

laugh at, *v.* —*Syn.* deride, taunt, make fun of; see **ridicule.**

laughing, *mod.* —*Syn.* chortling, giggling, chuckling; see **happy** 2.

laughingstock, *n.* —*Syn.* target, butt, victim; see **fool** 2.

laugh off, *v.* —*Syn.* deride, avoid by ridicule, dismiss *or* forget by laughing; see **scorn** 2.

laughter, *n.* —*Syn.* chortling, chuckling, guffawing, tittering, giggling, shouting, roaring, crowing, merriment, hilarity; *all* (D): howling, haw-hawing, snorting; see also **laugh.**—*Ant.* cry*, weeping, wailing.

launch, *n.* —*Syn.* motorboat, cabin cruiser, ship's launch; see **boat, ship.**

launch, *v.* **1.** [To initiate]—*Syn.* originate, start, set going; see **begin** 1.

2. [To send off]—*Syn.* set in motion, propel, drive, lance, thrust, fire off, send forth, eject; see **drive** 1, 3, **propel.**

launched, *mod.* —*Syn.* started, sent, set in motion, floated, begun, aloft, afloat, lofted, put *or* placed *or* sent *or* lofted into orbit, made airborne, put in motion *or* on the water *or* sea *or* in the air, having completed take-off; see **begun, driven, sent.**

launder, *v.* —*Syn.* cleanse, do the wash, wash and iron; see **clean, wash** 2.

laundress, *n.* —*Syn.* washerwoman, cleaning lady, domestic; see **servant.**

laundry, *n.* —*Syn.* ironing, washing, clothes; see **wash** 1.

laurel, *n.* **1.** [An evergreen tree]—*Syn.* bay, evergreen tree, shrub; see **tree.**

2. [A crown]—*Syn.* crown, honor, garland; see **wreath.**

rest on one's laurels—*Syn.* be satisfied, stop *or* quit (trying to achieve), give up *or* in; see **stop** 2.

lava, *n.* —*Syn.* basalt, pumice, volcanic rock; see **rock** 1.

lavatory, *n.* —*Syn.* privy, bathroom, washroom; see **bath** 3, **toilet** 2.

lavender, *mod.* or *n.* —*Syn.* lilac, lilac-purple, bluish-red; see **color** 1, **purple.**

lavish, *mod.* **1.** [Profuse]—*Syn.* generous, unstinted, unsparing; see **plentiful** 1, 2.

2. [Prodigal]—*Syn.* extravagant, inordinate, excessive; see **wasteful.**

lavish, *v.* —*Syn.* scatter freely, give generously, squander; see **spend** 1, **waste** 2.

lavishly, *mod.* —*Syn.* profusely, richly, expensively; see **carelessly, foolishly, wastefully.**

lavishness, *n.* **1.** [Extravagance]—*Syn.* wastefulness, dissipation, squandering; see **waste** 1.

2. [Plenty]—*Syn.* profuseness, plentitude, abundance; see **excess** 1, **plenty.**

law, *n.* **1.** [The judicial system]—*Syn.* judicial procedure, judicature, legal process, the (legal) authorities, the police, writ (of habeas corpus), (due) process, precept, summons, notice, (bench) warrant, search warrant, warrant of arrest, subpoena, garnishment, They (D); see also **authority** 3, **government** 1, 2, **legality.**

2. [Bodies of the law]—*Syn.* code, constitution, organic act, criminal law, statute law, civil law, law of the press, maritime law, martial law, military law, private law, public law, commercial law, probate law, substantive law, statutory law, chancery, statutes, civil code, ordinances, precepts, equity, cases, archives, common law, canon law, decisions, unwritten law, natural law; see also **system** 2.

3. [An enactment]—*Syn.* statute, edict, decree, order, ordinance, judicial decision, ruling, injunction, summons, act, charge, prescription, caveat, enactment, requirement, demand, divestiture, rescript, canon, regulation, commandment, mandate, dictate, precept, instruction, behest, bidding, legislation; see also **command** 2, **indictment** 2, **warrant, writ.**

4. [A principle]—*Syn.* foundation, fundamental, origin, source, (ultimate) cause, truth, axiom, maxim, ground, base, reason, rule (of action), theorem, guide, precept, usage, postulate, proposition, generalization, proposal, assumption, hard and fast rule; see also **basis** 1.

5. [The study of law, sense 1]—*Syn.* jurisprudence, legal precedent, legal science, equity, legal practice.

6. [Officers appointed to enforce the law]—*Syn.* district attorney, prosecuting attorney, sheriff, constable, state police, city police, the Man (D); see also **judge** 1, **lawyer, police.**

7. [The Bible]—*Syn.* Word, Old and New Testaments, the Book, Gospel, Scripture, Revelation; see also **Bible.**

go to law (D)—*Syn.* take legal action, take to court, prosecute; see **sue.**

lay down the law—*Syn.* establish rules, order, prohibit; see **command** 1.

read law—*Syn.* prepare for a career as lawyer, study law, practice law; see **study** 1.

lawbreaker, *n.* —*Syn.* felon, offender, violator; see **criminal.**

lawbreaking, *n.* —*Syn.* felony, violation, offense; see **crime** 1, 2.

lawful, *mod.* —*Syn.* legalized, legitimate, statutory, passed, decreed, judged, judicial, juridical, commanded, ruled, enjoined, ordained, ordered, mandated, authorized, according to edict, constitutional, adjudged, legislated, enacted, official, according to fiat, enforced, protected, licit, vested, juris-prudent, jurisprudential, within the law, statutory, in conformity to *or* conformable with the law, jural, nomothetic, legitimatized, canonical, established; see also **legal** 1, **permitted.**—*Ant.* illegal*, unlawful, illegitimate.

lawfully, *mod.* —*Syn.* licitly, in accordance with the law, by law; see **legally** 1.

lawfulness, *n.* —*Syn.* authenticity, validity, legitimacy; see **legality.**

lawless, *mod.* **1.** [Without law]—*Syn.* wild, untamed, uncivilized, savage, native, uncultivated, barbarous, fierce, violent, turbulent, unpeaceful, tempestuous, disordered, agitated, disturbed, warlike; see also **uncontrolled.**—*Ant.* cultured*, cultivated, controlled.

2. [Not restrained by law]—*Syn.* uncomfortable, insurgent, mutinous, riotous, ungovernable, nihilistic, nonconformist, unorthodox, seditious, in defiance of the law, traitorous, recusant, contumacious, seditious, revolutionary, insubordinate, disobedient, piratical, terrorizing, tyrannous, anarchic, anarchistic, anarchical, heterodox, despotic, bad, criminal, evil, infringing, noncompliant, defiant, rude, recalcitrant, refractory, transgressive; see also **mobbish, rebellious** 2, **unruly.**

lawlessness, *n.* —*Syn.* irresponsibility, terrorism, chaos; see **disorder** 2, **disturbance** 2.

lawmaker, *n.* —*Syn.* lawgiver, congressman, councilman; see **administrator, legislator.**

lawn, *n.* —*Syn.* garden, park, green, grassplot, grassland; see also **grass** 3, **yard** 1.

lawsuit, *n.* —*Syn.* action, prosecution, suit; see **claim, trial** 2.

lawyer, *n.* —*Syn.* professional man, legal adviser, practitioner, jurist, defender, prosecuting attorney, prosecutor, attorney, counsel, counselor, counselor-at-law, attorney-at-law, solicitor, barrister, legist, sergeant, advocate, professor of law, attorney at law, deputy, agent, public attorney, private attorney, counselor of embassy, counselor of legation, prosecutor of the pleas, attorney general, solicitor general, proctor, procurator, district attorney (D.A), friend of the court, federal attorney; *both* (D) Philadelphia lawyer, shyster, ambulance chaser, mouthpiece, legal eagle.

lax, *mod.* —*Syn.* slack, remiss, soft; see **careless** 1, **indifferent** 1.

laxative, *mod.* —*Syn.* relaxing, loosening, opening, freeing, unbinding, purgative, purging, diarrheic, diarrheal, diuretic, unconstipative, physicking, cathartic.—*Ant.* binding, confining*, restricting.

laxative, *n.* —*Syn.* physic, aperient, purgative, diuretic, cathartic, purge, medicament, remedy, cure, specific, dose, drench; see also **medicine** 2. Common laxatives include the following—castor oil, mineral oil, agar-agar, cascara sagrada, flaxseed, milk of magnesia, croton oil, epsom salts, cascarin compound, psyllium seeds.

laxity, *n.* —*Syn.* indulgence, indecision, leniency; see **carelessness, indifference** 1.

lay, *n.* —*Syn.* order, arrangement, situation; see **position** 1.

lay, *v.* **1.** [To knock down]—*Syn.* trounce, defeat, club; see **beat** 2, **hit** 1.
2. [To place]—*Syn.* put, deposit, set; see **place** 1.
3. [To put in order]—*Syn.* arrange, organize, systematize; see **order** 3.
4. [To bring forth]—*Syn.* generate, deposit, yield; see **produce** 1.
5. [To smooth out]—*Syn.* steam, lay flat, iron out; see **iron, press** 2, **smooth** 1.
6. [To bet]—*Syn.* game, wager, lay odds; see **bet, gamble** 1.
7. [To work out]—*Syn.* devise, concoct, design; see **plan** 1, 2.

lay about one, *v.* **1.** [To act]—*Syn.* move, do, operate; see **act** 1, **perform** 1.
2. [To attack]—*Syn.* hurt, punch, thrash; see **attack** 2, **beat** 2, **hit** 1.

lay a course, *v.* —*Syn.* chart, outline, project; see **plan** 1, 2.

lay aside, *v.* **1.** [To place]—*Syn.* deposit, put, set; see **place** 1.
2. [To save]—*Syn.* lay away, collect, keep; see **save** 3, **store** 2.
3. [To bury]—*Syn.* entomb, inter, inhume; see **bury** 1.

lay away, *v.* **1.** [To save]—*Syn.* lay aside, keep, collect; see **save** 3, **store** 2.
2. [To bury]—*Syn.* entomb, inter, inhume; see **bury** 1.

lay bare, *v.* —*Syn.* reveal, show, disclose; see **expose** 1, **undress.**

lay by, *v.* —*Syn.* hoard, put aside, build up savings; see **save** 3, **store** 2.

lay by the heels, *v.* —*Syn.* thrash, overcome, overpower; see **beat** 2, **defeat** 1, 2, 3, **win** 1.

lay claim to, *v.* —*Syn.* appropriate, demand, take; see **require** 2, **seize** 2.

lay down, *v.* **1.** [To declare]—*Syn.* assert, state, affirm; see **declare** 1, **report** 1, **say.**
2. [To bet]—*Syn.* game, put up, wager; see **bet, gamble** 1.

lay down one's life (for), *v.* —*Syn.* die for, sacrifice, perish; see **die** 1.

lay down the law, *v.* —*Syn.* demand, stress, emphasize; see **require** 2.

layer, *n.* —*Syn.* stratum, bed, thickness, fold, band, overlay, lap, overlap, ply, seam, coping, course, substratum, floor, story, tier, zone, stripe, girdle, lamination, lamella, lamina, delamination, film, slab, coating, flap, panel.

lay eyes on, *v.* —*Syn.* stare, view, notice; see **see** 1.

lay figure, *n.* —*Syn.* zero, non-person, unimportant person; see **nobody** 2.

lay for, *v.* —*Syn.* await, waylay, wait; see **ambush, attack** 1.

lay hands on, *v.* —*Syn.* get, acquire, grasp; see **obtain** 1.

lay hold of, *v.* —*Syn.* get, grasp, grab; see **seize** 1, 2.

lay in, *v.* —*Syn.* collect, gather, amass; see **accumulate** 1, **store** 2.

laying, *n.* —*Syn.* arranging, setting, putting; see **placing.**

lay into, *v.* —*Syn.* battle, invade, fire at; see **attack** 1, **fight** 2.

lay it on (D), *v.* —*Syn.* flatter, commend, glorify; see **compliment** 1, 2, **encourage** 2, **praise** 1.

lay low (D), *v.* —*Syn.* go underground, disappear, hide out; see **hide** 2, **sneak.**

layman, *n.* **1.** [One who does not make religion a profession]—*Syn.* secular, one of the laity, laic, catechumen, neophyte, proselyte, convert, parishioner, communicant, believer, one of the people *or* flock, congregation; see also **follower, member** 1. —*Ant.* priest*, ecclesiastic, cleric.
2. [One who is not versed in a subject]—*Syn.* nonprofessional, novice, dilettante; see **amateur, recruit.**

laymen, *n.* —*Syn.* laity, converts, congregation, neophytes, parish, parishioners, the faithful, communicants, members, believers, the uninitiated; see also **following.**

lay off, *v.* **1.** [To discharge employees, usually temporarily]—*Syn.* fire, discharge, let go; see **dismiss** 2, **oust.**
2. [(D) To stop]—*Syn.* cease, halt, desist; see **end** 1, **stop** 2.

lay on, *v.* —*Syn.* invade, besiege, beat; see **attack** 1, **fight** 2.

lay open, *v.* —*Syn.* incise, knife, slice; see **cut** 2.

layout, *n.* —*Syn.* arrangement, design, draft; see **organization** 2, **plan** 1, **purpose** 1.

lay out, *v.* —*Syn.* lend, put out (at interest), put up; see **invest, spend** 1.

layover, *n.* —*Syn.* break, hiatus, rest; see **delay** 1, **pause** 1, 2, **respite.**

lay over, *v.* —*Syn.* delay, stay over, break a journey; see **rest** 2, **stop** 1.

lay plans (for), *v.* —*Syn.* draft, design, think out; see **form** 1, **intend** 1, **plan** 2.

lay the foundation for, *v.* —*Syn.* construct, put up, fabricate; see **build** 1, **create** 2, **form** 1.

lay to, *v.* —*Syn.* (give) credit, ascribe, pin on (D); see **assign** 1, **attribute.**

lay to rest, *v.* —*Syn.* inter, give burial (to), take to a last resting place; see **bury** 1.

lay up, *v.* **1.** [To save]—*Syn.* conserve, preserve, hoard; see **save** 3, **store** 2.
2. [To disable]—*Syn.* injure, harm, beat up; see **hurt** 1.

lay waste, *v.* —*Syn.* ravage, devastate, ruin; see **destroy** 1.

lazily, *mod.* —*Syn.* indolently, nonchalantly, slackly; see **gradually, slowly.**

laziness, *n.* —*Syn.* indolence, slothfulness, sloth, lethargy, inactivity, slackness, sluggishness, dullness, lackadaisicalness, torpidness, heaviness, inertia, inertness, drowsiness, supineness, passivity, languidness, langurousness, laggardliness, listlessness, otiosity, otioseness, laxness, negligence, sleepiness, neglectfulness, remissness, dullness, stupidity, dormancy, torpescence, leadenness, dreaminess, weariness, apathy, stolidity, somnolence, somnolency, somnolescence, indifference, unconcern, laggardness, dilatoriness, tardiness, shiftlessness, deliberateness, leisureliness, procrastination; see **idleness** 1.—*Ant.* action*, promptitude, agility.

lazy, *mod.* **1.** [Indolent]—*Syn.* indolent, slothful, idle, slack, remiss, laggard, sluggish, heavy-footed, lagging, apathetic, loafing, dallying, languid, passive, asleep on the job, procrastinating, neglectful, unconcerned, indifferent, dilatory, tardy, inattentive, careless, unready, unpersevering, lethargic, lifeless, flagging, logy (D), weary, tired, supine, lackadaisical; see **listless** 1.—*Ant.* active*, businesslike, indefatigable.

2. [Slow]—*Syn.* slothful, inactive, lethargic; see **dull** 6, **slow** 1, 2.

leach, *v.* —*Syn.* remove, purge, percolate; see **filter** 1, 2.

lead, *mod.* —*Syn.* leading, head, foremost; see **best** 1, 2, **first** 1, **principal.**

lead, *n.* **1.** [The position at the front]—*Syn.* head, advance, first place, contact, point, edge, fore part, van, advanced guard, façade, front rank, first line, line of battle, scout, outpost, scouting party, patrol, sniper scouts, advance position, cutting edge, forerunner; see **front** 2, **vanguard.**—*Ant.* end*, rear, last place.

2. [Leadership]—*Syn.* direction, guidance, headship; see **administration** 1, **leadership** 1.

3. [A clue]—*Syn.* evidence, trace, hint; see **proof** 1, **sign** 1.

4. [A leading performer]—*Syn.* diva, prima donna, star; see **actor, actress.**

5. [A leading role]—*Syn.* principal part, important role, chief character; *all* (D): heavy, fat lines, lead spot, standout role, top bracket, top spot; see **role.**

lead, *n.* —*Syn.* metallic lead, galena, blue lead; see **element** 2, **metal.**

lead, *v.* **1.** [To conduct]—*Syn.* guide, precede, steer, pilot, attend, show *or* point (the way), show in *or* to *or* up *or* about *or* around, convoy, point out, squire, escort, chaperone, accompany, protect, guard, safeguard, watch over, convey, go along with, drive, shepherd, feel out the path, discover the way, find a way through, be responsible for; see also **manage** 1.—*Ant.* follow*, be conveyed, be piloted.

2. [To exercise leadership]—*Syn.* direct, manage, supervise; see **command** 2, **manage** 1.

3. [To influence]—*Syn.* prevail on, affect, spur (on); see **influence, motivate.**

4. [To play a first card]—*Syn.* start, commence, play first, take the initiative, make the start; see **begin** 1.

5. [To extend]—*Syn.* traverse, pass along, span; see **reach** 1.

leaden, *mod.* **1.** [Made of lead]—*Syn.* plumbic, plumbean, plumbiferous, pewter, galena; see **metallic** 1.

2. [Heavy]—*Syn.* burdensome, oppressive, weighty; see **heavy** 1, **onerous** 1.

3. [Lead-colored]—*Syn.* dull, pewter, blue-gray; see **gray.**

leader, *n.* **1.** [A guide]—*Syn.* conductor, lead, pilot; see **guide** 1.

2. [One who provides leadership]—*Syn.* general, commander, pacesetter, director, floor leader, manager, head, officer, captain, master, chieftain, headman, governor, ruler, *Füher* (German), *duce* (Italian), *caudillo* (Spanish), *vozhd* (Russian), executor; *both* (D): boss (man), brains; see **administration** 2, **administrator, chief** 1.

3. [One who directs a musical group]—*Syn.* conductor, director, choir leader, bandleader, impresario, maestro, manager: *both* (D): baton, stick waver; see **musician.**

4. [An article sold to attract trade]—*Syn.* bargain, introduction, novelty; see **commodity.**

leadership, *n.* **1.** [The quality notable in leaders] —*Syn.* authority, control, executiveness, administration, effectiveness, activity, primacy, superiority, supremacy, supremeness, skillfulness, skill, initiative, foresight, energy, capacity; see **influence** 2, **power** 2.

2. [The action of leading]—*Syn.* direction, guidance, management; see **administration** 1.

leading, *mod.* **1.** [Principal]—*Syn.* foremost, chief, dominating; see **best** 1, 2, **principal.**

2. [First]—*Syn.* front, head, escorting; see **first** 1.

lead off, *v.* —*Syn.* start, open, initiate; see **begin** 2.

lead on, *v.* —*Syn.* lure, entice, intrigue; see **deceive.**

lead one's life, *v.* —*Syn.* persist, endure, live (on); see **be** 1.

lead up to, *v.* —*Syn.* prepare (for), introduce, make preparations for; see **begin** 2, **propose** 1.

lead with one's chin (D), *v.* —*Syn.* blunder into, be indiscreet *or* rash, act foolishly; see **dare** 1, 2, **risk.**

leaf, *n.* **1.** [The leafy organ of a plant]—*Syn.* leaflet, needle, bract, petiole, blade, stalk, stipule, scale, protective leaf, floral leaf, leaf stalk, seed leaf, calyx leaf, bracteole, sepal, lithophyl, caulis, perianth, petal.

2. [Matter in thin, smooth form]—*Syn.* skin, coat, sheath; see **sheet** 2.

in leaf—*Syn.* foliate(d), in foliage, fully leaved (out); see **green** 2.

take a leaf from someone's book—*Syn.* follow someone's example, take after, copy; see **imitate** 2.

turn over a new leaf—*Syn.* make a new start, redo, begin again; see **change** 4.

leaflet, *n.* —*Syn.* handbill, circular, broadside; see **pamphlet.**

leafy, *mod.* —*Syn.* leaf-covered, leafed (out), in foliage *or* leaf, verdant, abounding, abundant, springlike, summery, covered, hidden, secluded, shady, shaded, umbrageous; see **green** 2.—*Ant.* bare*, leafless, austere.

league, *n.* —*Syn.* band, group, unit; see **organization** 3.

leagued, *mod.* —*Syn.* related, allied, joined; see **united** 2.

leak, *n.* **1.** [Loss through leakage]—*Syn.* leakage, loss, flow, seepage, drop, escape, outgoing, incom-

ing, detriment, short circuit, falling off, destruction, expenditure, decrease; see **waste** 1.
2. [An aperture through which a leak may take place]—*Syn.* puncture, chink, crevice; see **hole** 1.
3. [(D) Surreptitious news]—*Syn.* news leak, exposure, slip; see **advertisement** 1, **news** 1.

leak, *v.* **1.** [To escape by leaking]—*Syn.* drip, ooze, drool; see **flow** 2.
2. [To permit leakage]—*Syn.* be cracked *or* broken *or* split, have a fissure *or* hole, be out of order *or* in disrepair, permit wastage, have a slow leak.

leakproof, *mod.*—*Syn.* watertight, impervious, waterproof; see **tight** 2.

leaky, *mod.*—*Syn.* punctured, cracked, split; see **broken** 1, **open** 4.

lean, *mod.* **1.** [Thin]—*Syn.* lank, meager, slim; see **thin** 2.
2. [Containing little fat]—*Syn.* fibrous, muscular, sinewy, meaty, free from fat, all-meat, protein-rich; see **strong** 1.

lean, *v.* **1.** [To incline]—*Syn.* slope, slant, sag, sink, decline, list, tip, bow, nod, twist, cock, place, careen, roll, veer, droop, drift, dip, pitch, cant, bend, heel, be not perpendicular, be slanting *or* slanted, be off; see **bend** 2, **tilt** 1.
2. [To tend]—*Syn.* favor, be disposed, incline; see **tend** 2.

leaning, *mod.*—*Syn.* inclining, tilting, out of perpendicular; see **oblique** 1.

lean on *or* **upon,** *v.* **1.** [To be supported by]—*Syn.* rest on, be upheld by, bear on, put one's weight on, hang on *or* upon, fasten on; see **lean** 1.
2. [To rely upon]—*Syn.* believe in, count on, put faith in; see **depend on, trust** 1.

lean-to, *n.*—*Syn.* shelter, shanty, cabin; see **hut, shack, shed.**

leap, *v.*—*Syn.* spring, vault, bound; see **bounce** 2, **jump** 1.

learn, *v.* **1.** [To acquire mentally]—*Syn.* acquire, receive, imbibe, get, take *or* drink in, pick up, read, master, ground oneself in, peruse, con, pore over, study, gain (information), ascertain, determine, unearth, hear, find out, learn by heart, memorize, be taught a lesson, become well-versed in, soak in, collect one's knowledge, improve one's mind, build one's background; *both* (D): get up on, get the signal; see **study** 1.
2. [To find out]—*Syn.* uncover, ascertain, discern; see **discover** 1.

learned, *mod.* **1.** [Having great learning; *said of people*]—*Syn.* scholarly, erudite, scholastic, academic, accomplished, conversant with, lettered, instructed, collegiate, well-informed, bookish, pansophic, omniscient, polymathic, pedantic, professorial; see **cultured, educated** 1.—*Ant.* ignorant*, incapable, illiterate.
2. [Showing evidence of learning; *said of productions*]—*Syn.* scholarly, scientific, deep, solid, sound, sage, philosophic, philosophical, literary, erudite, grave, solemn, sober, judicious, studied, studious, sapient, abstract, recondite, esoteric, arcane, far out (D); see **profound** 2.—*Ant.* superficial*, unscholarly, shallow.

learned, *mod.*—*Syn.* memorized, word for word, by heart, by rote.

learner, *n.*—*Syn.* pupil, apprentice, scholar; see **student.**

learning, *n.*—*Syn.* lore, scholarship, training; see **education** 1, **knowledge** 1.

lease, *n.*—*Syn.* document of use, permission to rent, charter; see **contract** 1, **record** 1.
new lease on life—*Syn.* another chance, new perspective *or* outlook, opportunity; see **change** 2.

lease, *v.*—*Syn.* let, charter, rent out; see **rent** 1.

leash, *n.*—*Syn.* cord, chain, strap; see **rope.**
hold in leash—*Syn.* check, curb, control; see **restrain** 1.
strain at the leash—*Syn.* be impatient, act hastily, get excited; see **hurry** 1.

least, *mod.* **1.** [Smallest]—*Syn.* tiniest, minutest, infinitesimal, molecular, microcosmic, microscopic, atomic; see **minute** 1.
2. [Least important]—*Syn.* slightest, most trivial, niggling, piddling, finical, next to nothing; see **trivial, unimportant.**
3. [In the lowest degree]—*Syn.* minimal, at the nadir, most inferior, bottom; see **lowest, minimum.**—*Ant.* maximum*, highest, at the zenith.
at (the) least—*Syn.* in any event, with no less than, at any rate; see **anyhow** 1.
not in the least—*Syn.* not at all, in no way, not in the slightest degree; see **never.**

leather, *n.*—*Syn.* tanned hide, parchment, vellum, kangaroo hide, calfskin, horsehide, buckskin, deerskin, elk hide, goatskin, sheepskin, scarfskin, capeskin, rawhide, cowhide, buffalo hide *or* robe, snakeskin, sharkskin, lizard, shoe leather, glove leather, chamois skin, sole leather, alligator hide; see **hide** 1, **skin.**
Leathers include the following—pebble grain, cordovan, kid, natural, split, Scotch grain, suede, patent, Morocco, shagreen, tooled, embossed.

leathery, *mod.*—*Syn.* rugged, coriaceous, durable; see **strong** 2, **tough** 2.

leave, *n.* **1.** [Permission]—*Syn.* consent, dispensation, allowance; see **permission.**
2. [Authorized absence]—*Syn.* leave of absence, holiday, furlough; see **vacation.**
beg leave—*Syn.* ask permission, request, inquire; see **ask** 1.
by your leave—*Syn.* with your permission, if your permission is granted, if you please; see **please.**
on leave—*Syn.* away, gone, on a vacation; see **absent** 1.
take leave of—*Syn.* say good-by (to), bid farewell, leave alone; see **leave** 1.
take one's leave—*Syn.* go away, depart, remove oneself; see **leave** 1.

leave, *v.* **1.** [To go away]—*Syn.* go, depart, take leave, withdraw, move, set out, come away, go forth, take off, start, remove oneself, step down, quit (a place), part (company), defect, vanish, elope, retire, walk *or* get *or* slip *or* break *or* ride *or* go *or* move out *or* off *or* away, vacate, issue, decamp, abscond, flee, get out, flit, migrate, fly, run along, embark, emplane, sally (forth), say good-by, entrain, emigrate, astronavigate, escape (from) the earth's atmosphere *or* gravitational pull; *all* (D): clear *or* pull *or* cut out, push *or* cast off, scram, split, blow, head out for, ditch, give the slip, trip off, vamoose, sign *or* check out, beat it, take a powder,

take to the tall timber(s), be rolling, fade away, pull up stakes, get along, make oneself scarce, break squares with, bid a long farewell; see also **disappear, resign** 2, **retreat** 1, 2.—*Ant.* arrive*, get to, reach.
2. [To abandon]—*Syn.* back out, forsake, desert; see **abandon** 2.
3. [To allow to remain]—*Syn.* let be *or* stay, leave behind, let continue, let go, drop, lay down, omit, forget; see also **neglect** 1, 2.—*Ant.* seize*, take away, keep.
4. [To allow to fall to another]—*Syn.* bequeath, will, devise, leave behind, bequest, hand down, transmit; see also **give** 1.

leave home, *v.*—*Syn.* run away *or* off, play *or* become truant, depart; see **leave** 1.

leave incomplete, *v.*—*Syn.* leave unfinished *or* undone *or* deficient, forbear; see **abandon** 1.

leave in the lurch, *v.*—*Syn.* leave, forsake, desert; see **abandon** 2.

leaven, *v.* **1.** [To ferment]—*Syn.* raise, pepsinate, lighten; see **ferment.**
2. [To influence]—*Syn.* change, cause, affect; see **influence.**

leave no stone unturned, *v.*—*Syn.* persist, move ahead, persevere; see **continue** 1, **endure** 1.

leave off, *v.*—*Syn.* cease, end, halt; see **stop** 2.

leave out, *v.*—*Syn.* cast aside, reject, dispose of; see **discard, eliminate** 1.

leave out in the cold, *v.*—*Syn.* ignore, slight, neglect; see **abandon** 2.

leave-taking, *n.*—*Syn.* farewell, parting, departing; see **departure** 1.

leave to, *v.*—*Syn.* bequeath, hand down, pass on; see **give** 1.

leave tracks, *v.*—*Syn.* clue, give information, leave traces; see **neglect** 2.

leave up in the air (D), *v.*—*Syn.* leave unfinished, neglect, give up; see **abandon** 1, **stop** 2.

leave word, *v.*—*Syn.* inform, let know, report; see **notify** 1, **tell** 1.

leavings, *n.*—*Syn.* remains, residue, garbage; see **trash** 1, 3.

lecher, *n.*—*Syn.* debaucher, reprobate, libertine, adulterer, philanderer, rake, Don Juan, Casanova, (grossly) sensual man, corrupter, sensualist, sex deviate, one who commits *or* is guilty of adultery, roué.

lecherous, *mod.*—*Syn.* carnal, lustful, corrupt; see **lewd** 2, **sensual.**

lechery, *n.*—*Syn.* lust, debauchery, sensuality; see **desire** 3, **passion.**

lectern, *n.*—*Syn.* platform, podium, rostrum, pulpit, stand, desk; see also **furniture.**

lecture, *n.* **1.** [A speech]—*Syn.* discourse, address, talk; see **speech** 3.
2. [A reprimand]—*Syn.* rebuke, talking-to, dressing-down; see **rebuke.**

lecture, *v.* **1.** [To give a speech]—*Syn.* talk, speak, expound; see **address** 2, **teach** 1.
2. [To rebuke]—*Syn.* scold, reprimand, admonish; *both* (D): give a going-over, give a piece of one's mind; see also **censure, scold.**

lecturer, *n.*—*Syn.* preacher, orator, instructor; see **speaker** 2, **teacher** 1, 2.

led, *mod.*—*Syn.* taken, escorted, guided; see **accompanied.**

ledge, *n.*—*Syn.* shelf, mantle, jut, strip, bar, setback, offset, step, ridge, reef, rim, bench, berm, edge, path, route, way, walk, track, trail; see also **projection.**

ledger, *n.*—*Syn.* entries, books, account book; see **record** 1.

lee, *n.*—*Syn.* protection, harbor, shield; see **refuge** 1, **shelter.**

leech, *n.* **1.** [A parasite]—*Syn.* tapeworm, hookworm, bloodsucker; see **parasite** 1.
2. [(D) Dependent]—*Syn.* parasite, hanger-on, sponger (D); see **sycophant.**

leer, *n.*—*Syn.* smirk, squint, evil grin; see **sneer.**

leery, *mod.*—*Syn.* cautious, doubting, uncertain; see **suspicious** 1, 2.

lees, *n.*—*Syn.* remains, deposit, dregs; see **residue, sediment.**

leeward, *mod.*—*Syn.* lee, sheltered, leeside, quiet, peaceful, still, secure, undisturbed, serene, smooth, shielded, protected, screened, safe; see also **calm** 2. —*Ant.* windward, stormy*, windy.

leeway, *n.*—*Syn.* space, margin, latitude; see **extent.**

left, *mod.* **1.** [Opposite to right]—*Syn.* leftward, left-hand, near, sinister, sinistral, sinistrous, larboard, port, portside, nigh side (D).—*Ant.* right*, right-hand, starboard.
2. [Remaining]—*Syn.* staying, continuing, over; see **extra, remaining.**
3. [Radical]—*Syn.* left-wing, liberal, progressive; see **radical** 2, **revolutionary** 1.
4. [Departed]—*Syn.* gone out; *both* (D): taken a powder, split; see **gone** 1.

left, *n.*—*Syn.* left hand *or* side *or* direction *or* part, port, not the right *or* center; see **position** 1.

left-handed, *mod.*—*Syn.* clumsy, careless, gauche; see **awkward** 1.

leftist, *n.*—*Syn.* socialist, anarchist, communist; see **agitator, liberal, radical.**

left out, *mod.*—*Syn.* lost, neglected, removed; see **omitted.**

leftover, *mod.*—*Syn.* remaining, unwanted, unused, residual, uneaten, unconsumed, untouched, (perfectly) good; see also **extra.**

leftovers, *n.*—*Syn.* leavings, scraps, debris; see **food, trash** 1, 3.

left-wing, *mod.*—*Syn.* leftist, not conservative, reform; see **liberal** 2, **radical** 2.

leg, *n.* **1.** [The limb of a creature]—*Syn.* part, member, lower appendage, hind leg, foreleg, back leg, front leg, left leg, right leg, shank; *all* (D): shank's mare, underpinning, gam, stem, pin, bender, landing gear; see also **limb** 2.
2. [A relatively long, narrow support]—*Syn.* post, column, stake; see **brace, support** 2.
get up on one's hind legs (D)—*Syn.* assert oneself, be aggressive, take a stand; see **declare** 1.
give a leg up (D)—*Syn.* aid, support, assist; see **help** 1.
not have a leg to stand on (D)—*Syn.* be illogical *or* unreasonable, make rash statements, have no defense *or* excuse *or* justification; see **mistake.**
on one's (*or* **it's**) **last legs** (D)—*Syn.* decaying, not far from exhaustion *or* death *or* breakdown, old; see **dying** 2, **worn** 2.

pull someone's leg (D)—*Syn.* make fun of, fool, play a trick on; see **deceive.**
shake a leg (D)—*Syn.* hasten, act hastily, get moving; see **hurry** 1.
stretch one's legs (D)—*Syn.* exercise, go for a walk, move about; see **walk** 1.
take to one's legs (D)—*Syn.* walk *or* run away, depart, take flight; see **leave** 1.

legal, *mod.* **1.** [In accordance with the law]—*Syn.* lawful, constitutional, statutory, permissible, allowable, allowed, proper, legalized, sanctioned, legitimate, licit, right, just, justifiable, justified, fair, prescribed, authorized, hereditary, accustomed, due, rightful, precedented, warranted, admitted, sound, conceded, granted, acknowledged, ordained, condign, equitable, according to equity, within the law, protected, enforced, enforcible, judged, enjoined, decreed, statutory, contracted, contractual, passed, from time out of mind, customary, chartered, *de jure* (Latin); *all* (D): clean, legit, straight, on the up and up; see also **permitted.**—*Ant.* illegal*, unlawful, prohibited.
2. [Concerning the law]—*Syn.* statutory, juridical, constitutional; see **judicial, lawful** 1.

legality, *n.* —*Syn.* legitimacy, lawfulness, authority, permissibility, validity, justice, defendability, *status de jure* (Latin), status before the law *or* in court; see also **right** 1, 2.

legalize, *v.* —*Syn.* authorize, formulate, sanction; see **approve** 1.

legally, *mod.* **1.** [In accordance with the law] —*Syn.* lawfully, legitimately, permissibly, authorized, conceded, warranted, licitly, allowably, admittedly, enforcibly, juridically, constitutionally, with due process of law, by statute *or* law, as developed by the courts, in the eyes of the law, in accordance with law *or* the statute *or* the constitution *or* the ordinance, in view of the legal requirements *or* limitations; see also **rightfully.**—*Ant.* illegal*, unauthorized, illicitly.
2. [In a manner suggestive of the law]—*Syn.* legislatively, judicially, constitutionally, juridically, in legal terminology, with legal phrasing, professionally.

legatee, *n.* —*Syn.* heiress, inheritor, receiver; see **beneficiary, heir.**

legation, *n.* —*Syn.* committee, deputation, assignment; see **appointment** 1, **commission** 1, **delegation** 1, **installation** 1.

legend, *n.* **1.** [An improbable, traditional story] —*Syn.* folk tale, saga, fable; see **myth, story.**
2. [A brief piece of written matter]—*Syn.* caption, motto, inscription; see **writing** 2.

legendary, *mod.* **1.** [Traditional]—*Syn.* handed-down, customary, related; see **told, traditional** 1.
2. [Probably fictitious]—*Syn.* fabulous, mythical, mythological, fabricated, fanciful, imaginative, created, invented, allegorical, apocryphal, improbable, imaginary, dubious, doubtful, romantic, unhistoric, unhistorical, figmental, storied, unverifiable; see also **false** 2.—*Ant.* historical*, historic, actual.

legerdemain, *n.* —*Syn.* deceit, trickery, deception; see **deception** 1, **trick** 1.

leggings, *n.* —*Syn.* gaiters, stockings, chaps, puttees, half-boots, buskins, cothurnus; *all* (D): putts, chaps, leggins; see also **clothes.**

legibility, *n.* —*Syn.* lucidity, intelligibility, coherence; see **clarity.**

legible, *mod.* —*Syn.* distinct, plain, sharp; see **clear** 2.

legion, *n.* **1.** [An army]—*Syn.* division, phalanx, brigade; see **army** 2, **troops.**
2. [A crowd]—*Syn.* multitude, body, group; see **crowd** 1, **gathering.**

legislate, *v.* —*Syn.* make *or* enforce laws, pass, constitute; see **enact** 1.

legislation, *n.* —*Syn.* bill, enactment, act; see **law** 3.

legislative, *mod.* —*Syn.* lawmaking, enacting, decreeing, ordaining, lawgiving, legislational, legislatorial, congressional, juridical, jurisdictive, parliamentarian, nomothetic, senatorial, synodical, parliamentary, aldermanic, statute-making, from *or* by the legislature; see also **authoritative** 2.

legislator, *n.* —*Syn.* lawmaker, lawgiver, assemblyman, congressman, congresswoman, representative, senator, member of parliament (M.P.), floor leader, deputy, councilman, alderman; see also **administrator.**

legislature, *n.* —*Syn.* lawmakers, congress, parliament, chamber, assembly, senate, house, congress, house of representatives, council, soviet, plenum, law-making body, diet, voice of the people, duly constituted legislative body, bicameral legislature; see also **authority** 3, **bureaucracy** 1, **government** 1, 2.
Important legislatures include the following—Congress of the United States, Parliament of Great Britain, National Assembly of France, Supreme Soviet of the Soviet Union, United Nations Assembly, Riksdag of Sweden, Congresso Nacional of Brazil, State Council of China, Parliament of Canada, Federal Parliament of Australia, Parliament of the Union of South Africa, Oireachtas of the Irish Free State, Knesset of Israel, Congresso Nacional of Argentina, Eduskunta of Finland, Congresso of Mexico, Nationalrat of Switzerland, General Assembly of New Zealand, Congresso Nacional of Chile, Congresso of Cuba.

legitimate, *mod.* **1.** [In accordance with legal provisions]—*Syn.* licit, statutory, authorized; see **lawful** 1, **legal** 1.
2. [Logical]—*Syn.* reasonable, probable, consistent; see **logical** 1, **understandable.**
3. [Authentic]—*Syn.* verifiable, valid, reliable; see **genuine** 1, 2.
4. [Born of wedded parents]—*Syn.* accredited, received, accepted, authentic, genuine, certain, sure, true, recognized, sired in wedlock.—*Ant.* illegitimate*, bastard, unrecognized.

legume, *n.* —*Syn.* pea, fruit, pod; see also **bean** 2, **plant, vegetable.**
Legumes include the following—pea, clover, alfalfa *or* lucerne, soybean *or* soya bean, vetch, pulse.

leisure, *n.* —*Syn.* freedom, (free) time, spare time *or* moments, vacant hour, relaxation, recreation, repose, ease, intermission, recess, holiday, leave of absence, scope, range, convenience, idle hours, opportunity; see also **rest** 1, **vacation.**—*Ant.* work*, toil, travail.

at leisure—*Syn.* idle, resting, not busy; see **unoccupied** 2.
at one's leisure—*Syn.* when one has time, at one's convenience, at an early opportunity; see **whenever.**

leisurely, *mod.* **1.** [Enjoying leisure]—*Syn.* lax, slow, free; see **comfortable** 1, **lazy** 1.
2. [In a manner suggestive of leisure]—*Syn.* slowly, unhurriedly, lazily, deliberately, laggardly, dilatorily, with delay, calmly, composedly, lingeringly, tardily, inactively, taking one's time, gradually, languidly, langorously, sluggishly, lethargically, indolently, listlessly.—*Ant.* quickly*, rapidly, hastily.

leitmotiv, *n.* —*Syn.* recurrent musical phrase *or* situation *or* idea, suggestive melody, motif; see also **theme** 2.

lemon, *n.* **1.** [Citrus fruit]—*Syn.* juicy fruit, citron, food; see **fruit** 1.
2. [(D) An inadequate object or person]—*Syn.* bad one, blunder, worthless person *or* thing; see **failure** 1, 2.

lend, *v.* **1.** [To make a loan]—*Syn.* advance, provide with, let out, furnish, permit to borrow, allow, trust with, lend on security, extend credit, entrust, place *or* put at interest, loan (D), accommodate.—*Ant.* borrow*, repay, pay back.
2. [To impart]—*Syn.* confer, grant, present; see **give** 1.
3. [To adapt oneself]—*Syn.* suit oneself, adjust, comply; see **accommodate** 2, **conform.**

lend a hand, *v.* —*Syn.* assist, aid, succor; see **help** 1.

lender, *n.* —*Syn.* bestower, granter, usurer, moneylender, bank, pawnshop, loan company; *all* (D): golden balls, uncle, loan shark, moneymonger, angel, stakeman, Shylock; see also **banker** 1, **donor.**

lend itself to, *v.* —*Syn.* be adaptable to, fit in, suit; see **fit** 1, 2.

lend oneself to, *v.* —*Syn.* agree to, consent, give support to; see **agree.**

length, *n.* **1.** [Linear distance]—*Syn.* space, measure, span, reach, range, longitude, remoteness, stride, magnitude, compass, portion, dimension, unit, radius, diameter, linearity, longness, mileage, stretch; see also **extent.**
2. [Extent in space]—*Syn.* extensiveness, spaciousness, farreachingness, ranginess, endlessness, continuance, tallness, height, loftiness, lengthiness, expansion; see also **breadth** 2, **expanse, width.** —*Ant.* shortness, nearness*, closeness.
3. [Duration]—*Syn.* period, interval, season, year, month, week, day, minute, continuance, limit, lastingness; see also **term** 2, **time** 1.
at full length—*Syn.* extended, stretched out, lengthwise; see **long** 1.
at length—*Syn.* **1.** after a long time, eventually, in the end; see **finally** 2. **2.** extensively, in full, wholly; see **completely.**
go to any (*or* **great**) **length(s)**—*Syn.* do anything, stop at nothing, achieve by any means; see **try** 1.

lengthen, *v.* **1.** [To make longer]—*Syn.* extend, stretch, reach, elongate, protract, prolongate, prolong, distend, dilate, amplify, draw out, expand, augment, proceed, continue; *both* (D): string out, let out; see also **increase** 1.—*Ant.* decrease*, contract, draw in.
2. [To grow longer]—*Syn.* produce, increase, expand; see **grow** 1.

lengthwise, *mod.* —*Syn.* longitudinally, the long way, along, endlong, from end to end, from stem to stern, overall, fore and aft, from head to foot, from top to toe *or* bottom; see also **alongside.**—*Ant.* crosswise, across, from side to side.

lengthy, *mod.* —*Syn.* prolix, not brief, long; see **dull** 4.

leniency, *n.* —*Syn.* forbearance, tolerance, charity; see **kindness** 1, **mercy** 1.

lenient, *mod.* —*Syn.* loving, soft, soft-hearted, favoring, mild, tender, yielding, complaint, pampering, clement, indulgent, humoring, tolerant, forbearing, pardoning, letting, permitting, allowing, gratifying, sympathetic, assuaging, assuasive, emollient; see also **kind.**—*Ant.* severe*, firm, austere.

lens, *n.* —*Syn.* optical instrument, microscope, camera, eyeglass, spectacles.
Types of lenses include the following—spherical, planoconcave, double concave, biconcave, planoconvex, double convex, biconvex, diverging concavo-convex, converging concavo-convex, diverging, converging, diverging meniscus, converging meniscus, achromatic, anastigmatic, photographic, simple.

Lent, *n.* —*Syn.* Easter preparation, Great Lent, Great Fast, forty weekdays preceding Easter; see also **celebration** 1, **fast.**

lent, *mod.* —*Syn.* loaned, out at interest, borrowed; see **given.**

leonine, *mod.* —*Syn.* like a lion, powerful, kingly; see **brave** 1, **strong** 1.

leopard, *n.* —*Syn.* panther, hunting leopard, jaguar; see **animal** 2, **cat** 2.

leper, *n.* —*Syn.* infected person, outcast, leprosy case; see **invalid, patient.**

leprechaun, *n.* —*Syn.* goblin, brownie, gnome; see **fairy** 1.

leprosy, *n.* —*Syn.* leprous infection *or* inflammation, nerve paralysis, lepra; see **disease** 3.
Terms for leprous diseases include the following —elephantiasis, joint-evil, black leprosy, dry leprosy, nontuberculated lepra, *lepra cutanea, lepra nervosum* (*both* Latin).

leprous, *mod.* —*Syn.* unclean, infected, diseased; see **sick.**

Lesbian, *n.* —*Syn.* gay, sapphist, homosexual; see **homosexual.**

lèse-majesté, *n.* —*Syn.* mutiny, betrayal, revolt; see **dishonesty, treason.**

lesion, *n.* —*Syn.* wound, tumor, sore; see **injury.**

less, *mod.* —*Syn.* smaller, lower, not so much as, not as much, lesser, minor, fewer, reduced, declined, not as great, not so significant, in decline, depressed, inferior, secondary, subordinate, beneath, minus, deficient, diminished, shortened, circumcised, limited; see also **shorter.**—*Ant.* more*, more than, longer.

less and less, *mod.* —*Syn.* declining, decreasing, shrinking; see **lessening.**

lessee, *n.* —*Syn.* boarder, resident, rentee; see **renter.**

lessen, *v.* **1.** [To grow less]—*Syn.* diminish, dwindle, decline; see **decrease** 1.

2. [To make less]—*Syn.* reduce, diminish, slack up; see **decrease** 2.

lessening, *mod.* —*Syn.* decreasing, declining, waning, ebbing, dropping, diminishing, abating, slowing (down), dwindling, sinking, sagging, subsiding, moderating, slackening, ebbing, lowering, shrinking *or* drying *or* shriveling (up), depreciating, softening, quieting, lightening, weakening, decaying, narrowing (down), drooping, wasting, running low *or* down, dying away *or* down, withering *or* fading (away), wearing off *or* out *or* away *or* down, falling *or* slacking (away *or* off *or* down), growing less (and less); losing momentum *or* impetus *or* spirit, etc.; slumping, in a slump, plunging, plummeting, going down *or* back *or* backward, in reverse; getting worse *or* lower *or* slower, etc.

lessening, *n.* —*Syn.* decrease, decline, shrinkage; see **discount, reducing, reduction** 1.

lesser, *mod.* —*Syn.* inferior, minor, secondary; see **subordinate.**

lesson, *n.* **1.** [An instructive assignment]—*Syn.* recitation, drill, reading; see **exercise** 2.

2. [Instruction]—*Syn.* teaching, tutoring, schooling; see **education** 1.

3. [Anything instructive]—*Syn.* helpful word, good example, noble action; see **model** 2.

lessor, *n.* —*Syn.* landlady, property owner, landlord; see **owner.**

lest, *conj.* —*Syn.* for fear that, so that, in order to avoid *or* prevent; see **or.**

let, *v.* **1.** [To permit]—*Syn.* suffer, tolerate, leave; see **allow** 1.

2. [To award; *said especially of contracts*]—*Syn.* make, sign, grant, assign, engage, let *or* hire out; see also **give** 1.—*Ant.* cancel*, repudiate, break.

3. [To rent]—*Syn.* lease, hire, sublet; see **rent** 1.

let alone, *v.* —*Syn.* ignore, leave (to oneself *or* itself), abandon; see **leave** 3, **neglect** 2.

letdown, *n.* —*Syn.* frustration, setback, disillusionment; see **disappointment** 1.

let down, *v.* —*Syn.* disappoint, disillusion, not support; see **abandon** 2, **fail** 1.

let go, *v.* —*Syn.* relinquish, dismiss, release, part with; see **abandon** 1.

lethal, *mod.* —*Syn.* fatal, mortal, malignant; see **deadly** 1, **harmful, poisonous.**

lethargic, *mod.* —*Syn.* inert, sluggish, indifferent; see **lazy** 1, **listless** 1.

lethargy, *n.* —*Syn.* inactivity, apathy, sloth; see **laziness.**

let in, *v.* —*Syn.* admit, allow to enter, give admission to; see **allow** 1.

let off, *v.* —*Syn.* leave, excuse, let go, remove; see **abandon** 1, **drop** 1.

let on (D), *v.* —*Syn.* imply, indicate, suggest; see **hint.**

let out, *v.* —*Syn.* liberate, let go, eject; see **free** 1.

letter, *n.* **1.** [A unit of the alphabet]—*Syn.* capital (also (D): cap), upper case, lower case (also (D): LC, l.c.), small letter, majuscule, minuscule, rune, uncial, alphabet, stop *or* plosive, fricative, affricate, surd, diphthong, mute, sonant, liquid, nasal, labial, bilabial, velar, uvular, interdental, palatal, dental, glottal, guttural, logotype, ligature; see also **consonant, vowel.**

The Greek letters are as follows—alpha, beta, gamma, delta, epsilon, zeta, eta, theta, iota, kappa, lambda, mu, nu, xi, omicron, pi, rho, sigma, tau, epsilon, phi, chi, psi, omega.

2. [A written communication]—*Syn.* note, epistle, missive, message, billet, memorandum, report, line (D); see also **word** 3.

Types of letters include the following—business, form, circular, drop, open, chain, personal; billet-doux, postcard, postal, direct mail advertising, junk mail (D).

to the letter—*Syn.* just as written *or* directed, perfectly, precisely; see **exactly.**

letter carrier, *n.* —*Syn.* courier, mail carrier, postman; see **mailman, messenger.**

lettered, *mod.* —*Syn.* literate, erudite, scholarly; see **educated** 1, **learned** 1.

let the cat out of the bag, *v.* —*Syn.* divulge, let out; see **reveal** 1, **tell** 1.

letup, *n.* —*Syn.* interval, recess, respite; see **pause** 1, 2.

let up, *v.* —*Syn.* cease, release, slow down; see **slow** 1, **stop** 2.

levee, *n.* —*Syn.* embankment, dike, ridge, obstruction, block; see also **dam** 1.

level, *mod.* **1.** [Smooth]—*Syn.* polished, rolled, planed; see **flat** 1, **smooth** 1.

2. [Of an even height]—*Syn.* regular, equal, uniform, flush, of the same height, common, same, constant, straight, equable, balanced, steady, unfluctuating, stable, trim, trimmed, precise, exact, matching, matched, unbroken, on a line, lined up, aligned, uninterrupted, continuous; see also **parallel** 1, **smooth** 1.—*Ant.* irregular*, uneven, crooked.

3. [Horizontal]—*Syn.* plane, leveled, planetary, recumbent, supine, lying prone, in the same plane, on one plane; see also **flat** 1.—*Ant.* upright*, vertical, perpendicular.

find one's (*or* **its**) **level**—*Syn.* develop, find the proper place *or* station *or* occupation, suit; see **fit** 1, 2.

one's level best (D)one's best, the best one can do, all one's effort; see **best.**

on the level (D)—*Syn.* fair, sincere, truthful; see **honest** 1.

level, *v.* **1.** [To straighten]—*Syn.* surface, bulldoze, equalize; see **smooth** 1, **straighten.**

2. [To demolish]—*Syn.* ruin, waste, wreck; see **destroy** 1.

3. [(D) To be honest with]—*Syn.* be frank *or* straight (with), come to terms, be open and aboveboard.

level-headed, *mod.* —*Syn.* wise, practical, prudent; see **discreet, judicious, rational** 1, **reasonable** 1.

level off, *v.* —*Syn.* level out, find a level, reach an equilibrium; see **decrease** 1, **straighten.**

lever, *n.* —*Syn.* lifter, pry, leverage, prise, (prying *or* pinch) bar, crowbar, crow, handspike, arm, advantage; see also **machine** 1, **tool** 1.

leverage, *n.* —*Syn.* purchase, lift, hold; see **support** 2.

levied, *mod.* —*Syn.* exacted, taken, collected, raised, assessed, imposed, conscripted, mustered, drafted, required, demanded, called out, tasked, made liable (to *or* for); see also **taxed** 1.

levity, *n.* —*Syn.* flippancy, high spirits, giddiness; see **frivolity, happiness** 1.

levy, *n.* —*Syn.* toll, duty, custom; see **tax** 1.

lewd, *mod.* **1.** [Suggestive of lewdness]—*Syn.* ribald, smutty, risqué, dirty, indecent, loose, foulmouthed, obscene, vulgar, bawdy, naughty, off-color, questionable, taboo, unconventional, immoral, racy, impure, immodest, unclean, suggestive, indelicate, scandalous, scurrilous, coarse, rakish, vile, ungentlemanly, unladylike, unvirtuous, salacious, pornographic, gross, shameless, erotic, in bad taste, unfit for the young; see also **sense** 2, **sensual.**—*Ant.* decent*, refined, clean.

2. [Inclined to lewdness]—*Syn.* lustful, wanton, lascivious, libidinous, licentious, lecherous, libertine, lubricious, profligate, dissolute, voluptuous, reprobate, carnal, orgiastic, sensual, debauched, corrupt, unchaste, depraved, unbridled, Rabelaisian, unregenerate, polluted, ruttish, nymphomaniacal, satyric, prurient, concupiscent, incontinent, masochistic, sadistic, incestuous, fornicative, unbridled, beastly, goatish, hircine, caprine; *all* (D): horny, horsing, in heat, hot-pants, storkmade; see also **vulgar** 1.—*Ant.* chaste, pure*, modest.

lewdly, *mod.* —*Syn.* wantonly, shockingly, indecently, lasciviously, lecherously, libidinously, unchastely, carnally, dissolutely, immodestly, voluptuously, sensually, profligately, depravedly, orgiastically, incontinently, indelicately, like a wanton *or* roué *or* loose woman, in a lewd manner, with lewd gestures, in a suggestive manner, with phallic implications, suggesting the libido, unbecoming polite society.

lewdness, *n.* —*Syn.* indecency, unchastity, incontinence, fleshliness, vulgarity, lechery, wantonness, lubricity, lasciviousness, aphrodisia, bodily appetite, libidinousness, sensuality, licentiousness, voluptuousness, lecherousness, profligacy, dissoluteness, obscenity, salacity, scurrility, coarseness, carnal passion, grossness, boorishness, sensuous desire, vileness, salaciousness, pornography, fleshly lust, depravity, brutishness, lustfulness, carnality, ruttishness, pederasty, nymphomania, pruriency, prurience, incontinency, corruptness, satyriasis, corruption, raunchiness, unnatural desires, dirtiness, ribaldry, incest, indelicacy, incestuousness, concupiscence, eroticism, sadism, erotism, smut, smuttiness, evil, evilness, evil-mindedness, impurity, debauchery; see also **evil** 1.—*Ant.* modesty*, decency, continency.

lexicographer, *n.* —*Syn.* etymologist, philologist, polyglot, dictionary maker, dictionarist, lexicologist, lexicographist, glossarian, glossarist, glossologist, glossographer, glottologist, philologer, vocabulist, phonologist, philologian, phonetician, phoneticist; see also **linguist** 1.

lexicography, *n.* —*Syn.* dictionary making, philology, derivation, etymology, origin, genesis, glossography, terminology, orismology, glottogony, glossology, lexicology, phonology; see also **grammar, language** 2.

lexicon, *n.* —*Syn.* glossary, thesaurus, vocabulary; see **dictionary.**

liability, *n.* **1.** [The state of being liable]—*Syn.* obligation, indebtedness, owing, susceptibility, subjection to, amenability, answerability, accountability, accountableness, exposedness, compulsion, amenableness, being made accountable; see also **responsibility** 2.—*Ant.* freedom*, exemption, immunity.

2. [A source of liability, sense 1]—*Syn.* balance, burden, arrearage, arrears, account, debit, remainder, pledge, accident, chance, involvement, responsibility, encumbrance, exposed position, contingency, indebtment, possibility, misfortune, onus, contract, lease, mortgage; see also **debt** 1.

liable, *mod.* **1.** [Responsible]—*Syn.* answerable, subject, accountable; see **responsible** 1.

2. [Likely]—*Syn.* verisimilar, apt, inclined; see **likely** 5.

liaison, *n.* —*Syn.* love affair, romance, amour; see **affair** 2.

liar, *n.* —*Syn.* prevaricator, false witness, deceiver, dissimulator, romancer, maligner, deluder, untruther, trickster, cheat, misleader, falsifier, storyteller, equivocator, fibber, one who lies, fabricator, pseudologue, perjurer, fabulist, pseudologist; see also **cheat** 1.

libation, *n.* —*Syn.* oblation, gift, offering; see **drink** 1, **sacrifice** 1.

libel, *n.* —*Syn.* calumny, slander, lying; see **lie** 1.

libelous, *mod.* —*Syn.* derogatory, slanderous, sarcastic; see **opprobrious** 1.

liberal, *mod.* **1.** [Openhanded]—*Syn.* unselfish, bountiful, benevolent; see **generous** 1, **kind.**

2. [Open-minded]—*Syn.* tolerant, receptive, receiving, intelligent, progressive, libertarian, advanced, left, radical, interested, wide-awake, broadminded, understanding, permissive, indulgent, unprejudiced, impartial, disinterested, reasonable, rational, unbiased, detached, dispassionate, unorthodox, unconventional, avant-garde, broad-gauge, left-wing, uncolored, objective, magnanimous; see also **fair** 1, **lenient.**—*Ant.* prejudiced*, intolerant, biased.

3. [Plentiful]—*Syn.* abundant, profuse, bountiful; see **plentiful** 1.

liberal, *n.* —*Syn.* reformer, progressive, libertarian, insurgent, rebel, revolutionary, anarchist, socialist, communist, individualist, extremist, eccentric, freethinker, leftist, left-winger; see also **agitator.**

liberalism, *n.* —*Syn.* broad-mindedness, liberality, free-thinking, freedom, radicalism, humanitarianism, free thought, progressivism, universality, forward view, breadth of mind, latitudinarianism.

liberality, *n.* **1.** [Generosity]—*Syn.* benevolence, charity, giving; see **generosity** 1.

2. [Broad-mindedness]—*Syn.* free thought, progressivism, universality; see **liberalism.**

liberalize, *v.* —*Syn.* expand, increase, grow; see **change** 1, **improve** 1.

liberate, *v.* **1.** [To free from bondage]—*Syn.* set free, loose, release; see **free** 1.

2. [To free from chemical or physical restraint] —*Syn.* disengage, render gaseous, extract, separate, aerify, etherify, set free from combination, drive off, purify, gasify, make volatile, sublimate, analyze, catalyze, subject to catalysis, induce catalysis; see also **release.**

liberation, *n.* **1.** [Emancipation]—*Syn.* rescue, freedom, deliverance; see **freeing.**

2. [Release; *said of chemicals*]—*Syn.* freeing, separation, displacement, hydrolysis, diffusion, breaking ionic *or* covalent bonding, evaporation, osmosis, end products of respiration *or* photosynthesis, breakdown of organic *or* inorganic compounds, splitting *or* dividing of molecular structure.

liberator, *n.* —*Syn.* preserver, emancipator, deliverer, rescuer, freer, manumitter, redeemer, emancipator of a nation, freer of a people, martyr; see also **savior** 1.

liberty, *n.* **1.** [Freedom from bondage]—*Syn.* deliverance, emancipation, enfranchisement; see **freedom** 1.

2. [Freedom from occupation]—*Syn.* rest, leave, relaxation; see **freedom** 2, **leisure, recreation.**

3. [Freedom to choose]—*Syn.* permission, alternative, decision; see **choice** 1, **selection** 1.

4. [The rights supposedly natural to man]—*Syn.* freedom, free speech, suffrage, autonomy, sovereignty, franchise, independence, enfranchisement, freedom from arbitrary *or* despotic government, power of choice, right of habeas corpus, affranchisement, opportunity, right, immunity, privilege, exemption, birthright, self-government, education, enlightenment, bail, life, self-development, self-determination, autarchy; see also **democracy** 2.

at liberty—*Syn.* unrestricted, unlimited, not confined; see **free** 1, 2.

take liberties—*Syn.* be too familiar *or* impertinent, act too freely, use carelessly; see **abuse** 1.

libidinous, *mod.* —*Syn.* lustful, licentious, salacious; see **lewd** 2, **sensual.**

libido, *n.* —*Syn.* urge, impulse, psychic energy; see **desire** 3.

librarian, *n.* —*Syn.* custodian, keeper, caretaker, curator, bibliosoph, bibliothecary, cataloger, officer in charge of the library, bibliognost; see also **administrator.**

Librarians include the following—reference, children's, county, state, college, university, museum, departmental.

library, *n.* —*Syn.* books, book collection, manuscripts, manuscript collection, institution, public library, ambry, bookery, athenaeum, private library, book room, lending library, collection of manuscripts, circulating library, reference library *or* collection, archives, museum, treasury, thesaurus, muniments, memorabilia, rare books, incunabula, incunables, reading room; see also **building** 1.

Great libraries of the world include the following—Bibliothéque Nationale, Paris; British Museum, London; Bodleian Library, Oxford; Cambridge University Library; Biblioteca Vaticana, Biblioteca Nazionale Centrale Vittorio Emanuele, Rome; Biblioteca Laurentiana, Biblioteca Nazionale Centrale, Florence; Biblioteca Ambrosiana, Milan; Biblioteca Marciana, Venice; Bibliothèque Royale, Brussels; Biblioteca Nacional, Madrid; Biblioteca Nacional, Lisbon; Koninklijke Bibliotheek, The Hague; Kongelige Bibliothek, Copenhagen; Gosudarstvennaya Publichnaya Biblioteka, Leningrad; Staatsbibliothek, Berlin; National Library, Athens; Metropolitan Library, Beijing, Library of the Imperial Cabinet, Tokyo; Biblioteca Nacional, Mexico City; Biblioteca Nacional, Rio de Janeiro; Library of Congress, Folger Shakespeare Library, Washington, D.C.; Widener Library, Harvard University; Columbia University Library, New York Public Library, Morgan Library, New York; Boston Public Library; Cleveland Public Library; Harper Library, University of Chicago; Huntington Library, Pasadena, Calif.; Sterling Library, Yale University; University of California Libraries; Hoover War Library, Stanford University; Robert Frost Memorial Library, Amherst College.

librettist, *n.* —*Syn.* writer, poet, lyricist; see **author** 2.

libretto, *n.* —*Syn.* song book, lyrics, lines, words, book, opera; see also **writing** 2.

license, *n.* **1.** [Unbridled use of freedom]—*Syn.* looseness, excess, laxity, slackness, relaxedness, effrontery, arrogance, sauciness, immoderation, debauchery, sensuality, gluttony, audacity, forwardness, temerity, boldness, complacency, wantonness, prodigality, epicureanism, wild living, lawlessness, indulgence, presumptuousness, unrestraint, licentiousness, self-indulgence, profligacy, unruliness, refractoriness; *all* (D): gall, brass, crust.

2. [A formal permission]—*Syn.* permit, consent, grant; see **permission.**

license, *v.* —*Syn.* permit, authorize, privilege; see **allow** 1.

licensed, *mod.* —*Syn.* authorized, permitted, allowed; see **approved.**

licentious, *mod.* —*Syn.* lascivious, sensuous, desirous; see **lewd** 2, **sensual.**

lichen, *n.* —*Syn.* fungus growth, fungus-alga, thallophyte, epiphyte, symbiont; see also **plant.**

Types of lichen include the following—foliaceous lichens, crustaceous lichens, fruticose lichens, gelatinous lichens, Iceland moss, reindeer moss (reindeer lichen), *Rocella tinctoria, Rocella fuciformis* (both Latin).

lick, *v.* **1.** [To pass the tongue over]—*Syn.* stroke, rub, touch, pass over *or* across, move *or* gloss over, caress, wash, play, graze, brush, glance, sweep, tongue, ripple, fondle, soothe, tranquilize, calm, quiet.

2. [To play over; *said of flames*]—*Syn.* run over, shoot, rise and fall, advance, fluctuate, flutter, vibrate, fly to and fro, leap, waver, vacillate, quiver, tremble, palpitate, blaze; see also **burn** 1, **dart** 1, **wave** 3.—*Ant.* burn*, smoke, smolder.

3. [(D) To beat]—*Syn.* whip, trim, thrash; see **beat** 2.

4. [(D) To defeat]—*Syn.* overcome, vanquish, frustrate; see **defeat** 1.

licking (D), *n.* —*Syn.* whipping, beating, thrashing; see **defeat** 3, **mauling.**

lid, *n.* —*Syn.* cap, top, roof; see **cover** 1, **hood** 2.

lie, *n.* **1.** [An intentional misstatement]—*Syn.* falsehood, untruth, fiction, hyperbole, fraudulence, inaccuracy, misstatement, myth, fable, deceptiveness, disinformation, barefaced lie, dirty lie, misrepresentation, inoperative statement, lying, untruthfulness, prevarication, mendacity, falsification, falseness, falsifying, subterfuge, defamation, detraction, tall story, calumny, fabrication, deception, slander, backbiting, calumniation, aspersion, revilement, untruism, vilification, reviling, tale, false swearing, perjury, libel, forgery, distortion, obloquy, garbled version, guile, fib, white lie; *all* (D): corker, fish story, lollapalooza, whopper; see also **dishonesty.**—*Ant.* truth*, veracity, truthfulness.

2. [Anything calculated to mislead another] —*Syn.* falsification, evasion, deceit; see **deception** 1, **trick** 1.

give the lie to—*Syn.* dispute, belie, prove false; see **disprove.**

lie, *v.* **1.** [To utter an untruth]—*Syn.* falsify, prevaricate, tell a lie, lie out of, deceive, mislead, misguide, misinstruct, misteach, misinform, exaggerate, distort, misstate, misspeak, concoct, equivocate, tell a falsehood, be untruthful, forswear, be a liar, dupe, victimize, pervert, overdraw, break one's word, bear false witness, go back on, say one thing and mean another, misrepresent, dissimulate, dissemble, perjure oneself, delude, malign, invent, palter, beguile; *both* (D): spin a long yarn, bull.—*Ant.* declare*, tell the truth, be honest.

2. [To be situated]—*Syn.* extend, be (on), be beside, be located *or* fixed *or* established *or* placed *or* seated *or* set, be level *or* smooth *or* even *or* plane, exist in space, prevail, endure, stretch *or* reach *or* spread along; see also **occupy** 2.

3. [To be prostrate]—*Syn.* be recumbent *or* helpless *or* supine *or* exhausted *or* flat *or* prone, sprawl, loll, laze, be stretched out, be powerless, be thrown down; see also **sense** 4, **rest** 2.—*Ant.* stand*, be upright, sit.

4. [To assume a prostrate position]—*Syn.* lie down, recline, repose, stretch out, couch, go to bed, turn in, retire, take a nap *or* siesta, hit the hay (D); see also **rest** 1, **sleep.**—*Ant.* rise*, get up, arise.

take lying down—*Syn.* submit, surrender, be passive; see **yield** 1.

lie down on the job (D), *v.* —*Syn.* dawdle, slack off, fool around; see **loiter.**

liege, *n.* —*Syn.* master, lord, sovereign; see **owner.**

lie low, *v.* —*Syn.* keep out of sight, conceal oneself, go underground; see **hide** 2, **sneak.**

lien, *n.* —*Syn.* right to dispose of property, hold on property, charge, security on property, real security; see also **claim.**

lie over, *v.* —*Syn.* stay over, break a journey, stop off; see **halt** 2, **pause, stop** 1.

lieutenant, *n.* —*Syn.* army *or* navy man *or* officer, military man, soldier, platoon leader, fighter, commissioned officer, commander, leader; *all* (D): second looie, 90-day wonder, shavetail; see **officer** 3. Lieutenants include the following—first lieutenant, second lieutenant, lieutenant junior grade, sublieutenant.

life, *n.* **1.** [The fact or act of living]—*Syn.* being, entity, growth, animation, (animate) existence, endurance, survival, presence, living, consciousness, subsistence, symbiosis, breath, continuance, flesh and blood, animateness, viability, substantiality, mortal being, reproduction, metabolism, vitality, vital spark; see also **experience** 1.—*Ant.* death*, discontinuance, nonexistence.

2. [The sum of one's experiences]—*Syn.* life experience, conduct, behavior, way *or* manner of life, reaction, response, participation, enjoyment, joy, suffering, happiness, dread, nausea, tide of events, circumstances, unhappiness, realization, knowledge, enlightenment, attainment, development, growth, retardation, frustration, personality; see also **world** 1.

3. [A biography]—*Syn.* life story, memoir, memorial; see **biography, journal** 1, **story.**

4. [Duration]—*Syn.* lifetime, one's natural life, longevity, actuarial expectancy, period of existence, duration of life, endurance, continuance, span, history, career, course, era, epoch, century, decade, days, generation, time, period, life span, season, cycle, record, one's born days (D); see also **extent, length** 3.

5. [One who promotes gaiety]—*Syn.* life-giver, spirit, animator, entertainer, invigorator; *both* (D): life of the party, master of ceremonies; see also **host** 1, **hostess** 1, 3.

6. [Vital spirit]—*Syn.* vital force, vital principle, *élan vital* (French); see **enthusiasm** 1, **excitement.**

as large (*or* **big**) **as life**—*Syn.* actually, truly, in (actual) fact; see **accurately.**

bring to life—*Syn.* inspirit, activate, liven; see **animate** 1.

come to life—*Syn.* revive, awaken, show signs of life; see **recover** 2, 3.

for dear life (D)—*Syn.* intensely, desperately, for all one is worth; see **strongly.**

for life—*Syn.* for the duration of one's life, for a long time, as long as one lives; see **forever** 1.

for the life of me (D)—*Syn.* by any means, as if one's life were at stake, whatever happens; see **anyhow** 1.

from life—*Syn.* from a living model, descriptive, representational; see **genuine** 1.

matter of life and death—*Syn.* crisis, grave concern, something vitally important; see **importance** 1.

not on your life (D)—*Syn.* by no means, certainly not, never; see **no.**

see life—*Syn.* experience, do, act; see **live** 2.

take life—*Syn.* deprive of life, murder, destroy; see **kill** 1.

take one's own life—*Syn.* kill oneself, die by one's own hand, murder; see **commit suicide.**

true to life—*Syn.* true to reality, realistic, representational; see **genuine** 1.

lifeboat, *n.* —*Syn.* quarter boat, rowboat, scull; see **boat, raft.**

life expectancy, *n.* —*Syn.* probable future, statistical probability, chances; see **future** 1.

life-giving, *mod.* **1.** [Fertile]—*Syn.* prolific, generative, productive; see **fertile** 1, 2.

2. [Inspiring]—*Syn.* invigorating, animating, revealing; see **inspiring, stimulating.**

lifeless, *mod.* **1.** [Without life]—*Syn.* inert, inanimate, departed; see **dead** 1.

2. [Lacking spirit]—*Syn.* lackluster, listless, heavy; see **dull** 3, 4, **slow** 2.

lifelike, *mod.* —*Syn.* simulated, exact, imitative; see **graphic** 1, 2.

lifeline, *n.* —*Syn.* help, salvation, line; see **aid** 1, **rope.**

lifelong, *mod.* —*Syn.* lifetime, enduring, livelong; see **permanent** 2.

life of Riley (D), *n.* —*Syn.* contentment, prosperity, luxury; see **comfort** 1, **ease** 1, **satisfaction** 2.

life or death, *mod.* —*Syn.* decisive, necessary, critical; see **important** 1.

life story, *n.* —*Syn.* autobiography, memoir, profile; see **biography, journal** 1, **record** 1.

lifetime, *mod.* —*Syn.* lifelong, continuing, enduring; see **permanent** 2.

lifetime, *n.* —*Syn.* existence, endurance, continuance; see **life** 3, 4, **record** 2.

lifework, *n.* —*Syn.* occupation, career, vocation; see **business** 1, **profession** 1, **purpose** 1.

lift, *n.* **1.** [The work of lifting]—*Syn.* pull, lifting, upthrow, ascension, raising, weight, foot-pounds, elevation, sub-elevation, escalation, ascent, mounting.
2. [(D) A ride]—*Syn.* transportation, drive, passage; see **journey.**
3. [(D) Aid]—*Syn.* help, assistance, support; see **aid** 1.

lift, *v.* —*Syn.* hoist, elevate, upheave; see **raise** 1.

lifter, *n.* —*Syn.* jackscrew, pry, lift; see **jack** 1, **lever.**

ligature, *n.* —*Syn.* link, bond, connection; see **band** 2, **rope.**

light, *mod.* **1.** [Having illumination]—*Syn.* illuminated, radiant, luminous; see **bright** 1.
2. [Having color]—*Syn.* vivid, rich, clear; see **bright** 2.
3. [Having little content]—*Syn.* superficial, slight, frivolous; see **trivial, unimportant.**
4. [Having gaiety and spirit]—*Syn.* lively, merry, animated; see **jaunty.**
5. [Having little weight]—*Syn.* airy, fluffy, feathery, imponderable, slender, downy, floating, lighter than air, light as air, floatable, gossamery, light as a feather, frothy, buoyant, easy, dainty, filmy, veil-like, tissuelike, thin, sheer, gaseous, effervescent, unsubstantial, insubstantial, ethereal, graceful, charming, weightless, atmospheric; see also **volatile** 1.—*Ant.* heavy*, ponderous, weighty.
6. [Digestible]—*Syn.* slight, edible, moderate; see **eatable.**
7. [Small in quantity or number]—*Syn.* wee, small, tiny, minute, thin, inadequate, minuscule, insufficient, hardly enough, not much, hardly *or* scarcely any, not many, slender, scanty, slight, moderate, puny, sparse, fragmentary, fractional, shredlike; see also **dainty** 1, **few.**—*Ant.* large*, great, immense.
8. [Wanton]—*Syn.* carnal, immodest, indecent; see **lewd** 2, **sensual.**

light, *n.* **1.** [The condition opposed to darkness] —*Syn.* radiance, luminous energy, luminosity, brilliance, splendor, irradiation, glare, brightness, clearness, lightness, brilliancy, coruscation, incandescence, scintillation, shine, fulgor, refulgence, emanation, lucency, luster, sheen, sparkle, glitter, glimmer, glister, effulgence, resplendence, flood of light, blare, radiation, gleam.—*Ant.* darkness*, blackness, blankness.
2. [Emanations from a source of light]—*Syn.* radiation, stream, blaze; see **beam** 2, **flash** 1, **ray.**
3. [A source of light]—*Syn.* match, wick, sun, planet, star, moon, lightning, torch, flashlight, chandelier, spotlight, halo, nimbus, northern light *or* aurora borealis, aureole, corona; see also **bulb, candle, lamp.**
4. [Day]—*Syn.* daylight, sun, sunrise; see **day** 2.
5. [Aspect]—*Syn.* point of view, condition, standing; see **circumstances** 2.
6. [Basis for understanding]—*Syn.* enlightenment, information, education; see **data, knowledge** 1.
in (the) light of—*Syn.* with knowledge of, because of, in view *or* consideration of; see **considering.**
see the light (of day)—**1.** *Syn.* come into being, exist, begin; see **be. 2.** comprehend, realize, be aware; see **understand** 1.
stand in one's own light—*Syn.* harm oneself, act carelessly *or* thoughtlessly, err; see **fail** 1.
strike a light—*Syn.* inflame, cause to burn, kindle; see **burn** 2, **ignite.**

light, *v.* **1.** [To provide light]—*Syn.* illuminate, illumine, illume, lighten, give light to, shine upon, furnish with light, light up, turn on the electricity, make a light, make visible, provide adequate illumination *or* candlepower, turn *or* switch on a light, floodlight, cast *or* throw light upon, make bright, flood with light, animate, fill with light, irradiate; see also **brighten** 1.—*Ant.* shade*, put out, darken.
2. [To cause to ignite]—*Syn.* inflame, spark, kindle; see **burn** 2, **ignite.**
3. [To become ignited]—*Syn.* take fire, become inflamed, flame; see **burn** 1, **ignite.**
4. [To come to rest from flight *or* travel]—*Syn.* perch, roost, rest, alight, fly *or* come down, settle on, stop, drop, sit down, debus, come to rest, get down, detrain, unhorse, settle (down); see also **arrive** 1.—*Ant.* fly*, soar off, take off.
make light of—*Syn.* make fun of, mock, belittle; see **neglect** 1, **ridicule.**

lighted, *mod.* **1.** [Illuminated]—*Syn.* brilliant, alight, glowing; see **bright** 1.
2. [Burning]—*Syn.* blazing, flaming, aflame; see **afire, burning** 1.

lighten, *v.* **1.** [To make lighter]—*Syn.* unburden, disburden, make lighter, reduce the load of, lessen (the weight of), uplift, buoy up, mitigate, levitate, alleviate, make less burdensome, disencumber, take off a load, remove, take from, pour out, throw overboard, jettison, reduce, cut down, put off, facilitate, upraise, make buoyant, take off weight, eradicate, shift, change; see also **decrease** 1, **empty** 2, **unload.**—*Ant.* load*, burden, overload.
2. [To ease]—*Syn.* assuage, comfort, free; see **ease** 1, **relieve** 2.

lighter, *n.* **1.** [Boat]—*Syn.* craft, barge, keel; see **boat.**
2. [Mechanical igniter]—*Syn.* cigar *or* cigarette *or* pipe lighter, igniter, flame; see **light** 3, **match** 1.

light-fingered, *mod.* —*Syn.* thievish, stealthy, pilfering, filching, stealing.

light-footed, *mod.* —*Syn.* swift, buoyant, adroit; see **agile, graceful** 1.

lightheaded, *mod.* **1.** [Giddy]—*Syn.* inane, fickle, frivolous; see **changeable** 1, **silly** 1.
2. [Faint]—*Syn.* tired, delirious, dizzy; see **weak** 1.

lighthearted, *mod.* —*Syn.* gay, joyous, cheerful; see **happy** 1.

lighthouse, *n.* —*Syn.* guide, lightship, beam; see **beacon, tower.**

lighting, *n.* **1.** [Illumination]—*Syn.* brilliance, flame, brightness; see **flash** 1, **illumination** 1, **light** 1, 3.

2. [Ignition]—*Syn.* kindling, setting aflame, burning; see **fire** 1.

light in the head, *mod.* —*Syn.* foolish, senseless, incompetent; see **silly, stupid** 1.

light into, *v.* —*Syn.* rebuke, blame, assault; see **censure, scold.**

lightless, *mod.* —*Syn.* unilluminated, dusky, without light; see **black** 1, **dark** 1.

lightly, *mod.* **1.** [With lightness]—*Syn.* delicately, airily, buoyantly, daintily, readily, gently, subtly, exquisitely, ethereally, mildly, softly, tenderly, carefully, leniently, tenuously, unsubstantially, effortlessly, nimbly, agilely, smoothly, blandly, sweetly, comfortably, restfully, peacefully, quietly, ripplingly, soaringly; see also **easily** 1, **gracefully.** —*Ant.* heavily*, ponderously, roughly.

2. [With indifference]—*Syn.* slightingly, carelessly, indifferently; see **casually** 2.

light-minded, *mod.* —*Syn.* capricious, flighty, frivolous; see **changeable** 1.

lightness, *n.* **1.** [Illumination]—*Syn.* sparkle, blaze, shine; see **flash, light** 1, 3.

2. [The state of being light]—*Syn.* airiness, volatileness, etherealness, downiness, thinness, sheerness, fluffiness, featheriness; see also **buoyancy** 1, **delicacy** 1.

3. [Agility]—*Syn.* balance, deftness, nimbleness; see **agility, grace** 1.

lightning, *n.* —*Syn.* electrical discharge, fulmination, streak of lightning, thunderball, thunderstroke, firebolt, thunderlight, thunderbolt, bolt (from the blue); see also **electricity** 2.

Types of lightning include the following—ball, globular, chain, forked, heat, summer, sheet.

light out, *v.* —*Syn.* run, abscond, depart; see **leave** 1.

lightweight (D), *n.* —*Syn.* incompetent, bungler, stupid person; see **failure** 2, **fool** 1.

likable, *mod.* —*Syn.* agreeable, amiable, attractive; see **friendly** 1.

like, *mod.* —*Syn.* similar, same, near, resembling, close, not far from, according to, conforming with, matching, equaling, jibing, allying, not unlike, akin, related, analogous, twin, corresponding, allied to, much the same, or the same form, comparable, identical, congeneric, congenerous, approximative, in the manner of, parallel, homologous, to the effect that, consistent, of a piece, approximating; see also **alike** 1, 2.—*Ant.* different*, far, unrelated.

like, *prep.* —*Syn.* similar (to), same, near to; see **alike** 2, **like.**

like, *n.* —*Syn.* counterpart, resemblance, parallelism; see **similarity.**

and the like—*Syn.* and so forth, etc., similar kinds; see **others, same.**

more like it (D)—*Syn.* acceptable, good, improved; see **better** 2.

nothing like—*Syn.* dissimilar, contrasting, opposed; see **different** 1, 2.

something like—*Syn.* similar, resembling, akin; see **like.**

like, *v.* **1.** [To enjoy]—*Syn.* take delight in, relish, take *or* derive pleasure in *or* from, be pleased by, revel *or* indulge *or* rejoice in, find agreeable *or* congenial *or* appealing, be gratified by, take satisfaction in, be keen on, exclaim over, savor, fancy, dote on, take an interest in, develop interest for, delight *or* bask *or* luxuriate in, regard with favor, have a liking for, love, have a taste for, care to, feast on; *all* (D): get a kick out of, feast one's eyes on, swim in, be tickled by, eat up, go in for, lick one's lips over.—*Ant.* endure*, detest, dislike.

2. [To be fond of]—*Syn.* have a fondness for, admire, hold in regard, take a fancy to, feel warmly *or* affectionately toward, prize, esteem, hold dear, dote on, care about *or* for, approve, be pleased with; *all* (D): take to, have a soft spot in one's heart for, go for in a big way, hunger and thirst after, hanker for, have a yen for, become attached to, be sweet on, cotton to, have eyes for; see also **cherish** 1, **love** 1.—*Ant.* hate*, disapprove, dislike.

3. [To be inclined]—*Syn.* choose, feel disposed, wish, desire, have a preference for, prefer, fancy, feel like, incline toward; see also **want** 1.

like anything *or* **blazes** *or* **crazy** etc. (D), *mod.* —*Syn.* very much, exceedingly, greatly; see **much** 1, 2, **very.**

liked, *mod.* —*Syn.* popular, loved, admired; see **beloved, honored.**

like father, like son, *mod.* —*Syn.* similar, resembling each other, showing a family resemblance; see **alike** 1, 2, 3.

likelihood, *n.* —*Syn.* plausibility, reasonableness, possibility; see **probability.**

likely, *mod.* **1.** [Probable]—*Syn.* apparent, probable, seeming, credible, possible, feasible, presumable, conceivable, reasonable, conjecturable, practicable, workable, attainable, achievable, ostensible, surmisable, inferable, believable, rational, thinkable, imaginable, plausible, to be supposed, supposable, to be guessed, anticipated, expected, imminent, destined, assumable, grantable, persuasive, warrantable, as like as not (D).—*Ant.* impossible*, doubtful, questionable.

2. [Promising]—*Syn.* suitable, apt, assuring; see **fit** 1, 2, **hopeful** 2.

3. [Believable]—*Syn.* plausible, true, acceptable; see **convincing** 2.

4. [Apt]—*Syn.* inclined, tending, disposed, predisposed, prone, liable, subject to, on the verge *or* point of, in the habit of, given to, in favor of, having a weakness for.

like-minded, *mod.* —*Syn.* compatible, unanimous, agreeable; see **fit** 1, **harmonious** 2.

liken, *v.* —*Syn.* parallel, set beside, contrast; see **compare** 1, **distinguish** 1.

likeness, *n.* **1.** [Similarity]—*Syn.* resemblance, correspondence, affinity; see **similarity.**

2. [A representation]—*Syn.* image, effigy, portrait; see **copy, picture** 3, **representation.**

likewise, *mod.* —*Syn.* in like manner, furthermore, moreover; see also **besides.**

liking, *n.* —*Syn.* desire, fondness, devotion; see **affection, love** 1.

Lilliputian, *mod.* —*Syn.* diminutive, dwarfed, small; see **little** 1.

lily, *n.* —*Syn.* bulb, *Lilium* (Latin), fleur-de-lis; see **flower** 1, **plant.**

Lilies include the following—wood, meadow, Easter, Bermuda, Canada, canadense, superbum, golden-banded, tiger, Madonna, Annunciation, coral, Turk's-cap, showy, Washingtonianum, Phila-

delphicum, auratum, common white, Jacob's, wild orange-red, southern red.
The following are popularly called lilies—sego, lily of the valley, fleur-de-lis, iris, amaryllis, belladonna lily, daffodil, narcissus, spider lily, Guernsey lily, star grass, agapanthus, day lily, mariposa lily, water lily, calla lily, yellow calla.
gild the lily—*Syn.* overdo, exaggerate, try to improve something already perfect; see **improve** 1.

limb, *n.* **1.** [A branch]—*Syn.* arm, bough, offshoot; see **branch** 2.
2. [A bodily appendage]—*Syn.* arm, leg, appendage, part, wing, pinion, fin, flipper, lobe; see also **member** 3.

limber, *mod.* **1.** [Agile]—*Syn.* nimble, spry, deft; see **agile, graceful** 1.
2. [Pliant]—*Syn.* supple, lithe, plastic; see **flexible** 1.

limbo, *n.*—*Syn.* nothingness, purgatory, nether regions; see **hell** 1, **oblivion** 2.

limelight, *n.*—*Syn.* publicity, spotlight, recognition; see **attention** 1, 2, **fame** 1.

limit, *n.* **1.** [The boundary]—*Syn.* end, frontier, border; see **boundary.**
2. [The ultimate]—*Syn.* utmost, bourne, ultimate, farthest point, farthest reach, destination, goal, conclusion, extremity, eventuality, termination, absolute, ultima Thule; *all* (D): the bitter end, deadline, cut-off point, the nines; see also **end** 4, **finality, purpose** 1.—*Ant.* origin*, incipience, start.

limit, *v.*—*Syn.* bound, confine, curb; see **define** 1, **restrict** 2.

limitation, *n.* **1.** [The act of limiting]—*Syn.* restriction, obstruction, deprivation, hindrance, restraint, deterrence, control, determent, prohibition, repression, suppression, discouragement, interdiction, cutoff, interception, stoppage; see also **arrest** 2, **interference** 1, **interruption, prevention.**—*Ant.* increase*, permission, toleration.
2. [That which limits]—*Syn.* condition, definition, qualification, reservation, control, curb, check, injunction, bar, obstruction, stricture, taboo, circumspection, inhibition, modification; see also **arrest** 1, **barrier, boundary, impediment** 1, **refusal, restraint** 2.—*Ant.* freedom*, latitude, liberty*.
3. [A shortcoming]—*Syn.* inadequacy, insufficiency, deficiency, shortcoming, weakness, want, imperfection, weak spot, failing, fault, frailty, flaw, incompleteness; see also **blemish, defect** 2, **lack** 2. —*Ant.* strength*, perfection*, ability*.

limited, *mod.* **1.** [Restricted]—*Syn.* confined, checked, curbed; see **bound** 1, 2, **bounded, restrained, restricted.**
2. [Having only moderate capacity]—*Syn.* cramped, insufficient, short; see **faulty, inadequate** 1, **poor** 2, **unsatisfactory.**

limitless, *mod.*—*Syn.* unending, boundless, immeasurable; see **endless** 1, **infinite** 1, **unlimited.**

limp, *mod.* **1.** [Without stiffness]—*Syn.* pliant, soft, flaccid, flabby, formative, supple, pliable, limber, relaxed, bending readily, ductile, plastic, impressible, yielding, lax, slack, droopy, loose, flimsy, unsubstantial; see also **flexible** 1.—*Ant.* stiff*, rigid, wooden.
2. [Weak]—*Syn.* feeble, infirm, debilitated; see **weak** 2.

limp, *n.*—*Syn.* halt, lameness, hobble, falter, hitch, flat wheel (D).

limp, *v.*—*Syn.* halt, walk lamely, proceed slowly, flag, shuffle, teeter, proceed in a lame manner, lag, stagger, claudicate, totter, dodder, hobble, hitch, falter; *both* (D): dot along, dot and go one; see also **stumble** 1.

limpid, *mod.* **1.** [Transparent]—*Syn.* pellucid, filmy, thin; see **clear** 2, **pure** 1, **transparent** 1.
2. [Intelligible]—*Syn.* clear, distinct, lucid; see **definite** 2, **obvious** 1.

Lincoln's Birthday, *n.*—*Syn.* February 12, birthday of the Great Emancipator, Old *or* Honest Abe's day; see also **holiday** 1, **winter.**

line, *n.* **1.** [A row]—*Syn.* length, list, rank, file, catalogue, array, order, group, arrangement, furrow, ridge, range, seam, band, border, block, series, sequence, succession, chain, train, string, column, procession, formation, division, queue, magazine, concatenation, trench, channel, groove, drain, mark, scar, thread, fissure, crack, straight line; see also **seam, series.**
2. [A mark]—*Syn.* outline, tracing, stroke; see **mark** 1.
3. [A rope]—*Syn.* cord, filament, steel tape; see **rope, wire** 1.
4. [Lineal descent]—*Syn.* descent, pedigree, lineage; see **family** 1, **heredity.**
5. [A border line]—*Syn.* border, mark, limit; see **boundary, edge** 1.
6. [A course]—*Syn.* street, lane, path; see **road** 1, **route** 1.
7. [Policy]—*Syn.* belief, principle, course; see **plan** 2, **policy, route** 2.
8. [Matter printed in a row of type]—*Syn.* row, words, letters; see **copy.**
9. [A military front]—*Syn.* disposition, formation, position; see **front** 2.
10. [A railroad]—*Syn.* trunk line, sideline, mainline; see **railroad, track** 1.
11. [An organization supplying transportation] —*Syn.* steamship line, airline, stage company; see **transportation.**
12. [(D) The kind or materials of trade]—*Syn.* materials, trade, involvement; see **business** 1, **industry** 3.
13. [(D) Goods handled by a given house]—*Syn.* wares, merchandise, produce; see **commodity, material** 2.
14. [(D) Talk intended to influence another] —*Syn.* prepared speech, patter, persuasion; see **conversation, speech** 3.
all along the line—*Syn.* at every turn, completely, constantly; see **everywhere.**
bring (*or* **come** *or* **get**) **into line**—*Syn.* align, make uniform, regulate; see **order** 3.
down the line—*Syn.* entirely, thoroughly, wholly; see **completely.**
draw the (*or* **a**) **line**—*Syn.* set a limit, prohibit, restrain; see **restrict** 2.
get a line on (D)—*Syn.* find out about, investigate, expose; see **discover** 1.
in line—*Syn.* agreeing, conforming, uniform; see **regular** 3.

in line for—*Syn.* being considered for, ready, thought about; see **considered** 1.
in line of duty—*Syn.* authorized, prescribed, required; see **approved, legal** 1.
lay (*or* **put**) **it on the line** (D)—*Syn.* elucidate, define, clarify; see **explain.**
on a line—*Syn.* linear, lined, level; see **direct** 1, **straight** 1.
out of line—*Syn.* misdirected, not uniform, not even; see **irregular** 1, 2.
read between the lines—*Syn.* read meaning into, discover a hidden meaning, expose; see **understand** 1.

line, *v.* **1.** [To provide a lining]—*Syn.* interline, encrust, stuff, wad, panel, incrust, reinforce the back of, pad, quilt, fill, overlay, bush, sheath, wainscot, double (British); see also **face** 3.
2. [To provide lines]—*Syn.* trace, delineate, outline; see **draw** 2, **mark** 1.
3. [To be in a line]—*Syn.* border, edge, outline, rank, rim, bound, skirt, fall in, fall into line, fringe, follow; see also **succeed** 2.
4. [To arrange in a line]—*Syn.* align, queue, marshal, dress (up), face in, arrange, range, array, group, set out, bring into a line with others, fix, place, list space, line right *or* left, rank, draw up; see **file** 1, **line up, order** 3.—*Ant.* disarrange, disperse, scatter.

lineage, *n.*—*Syn.* forefathers, ancestors, progenitors; see **family** 1, **heredity.**

lineal, *mod.* **1.** [Having to do with a line]—*Syn.* longitudinal, on a line, marking; see **linear.**
2. [Hereditary]—*Syn.* inherited, transmitted, descended; see **ancestral, inherent.**

lineament, *n.*—*Syn.* detail, form, quality; see **characteristic, feature** 1.

linear, *mod.*—*Syn.* lineal, lined, long, extended in a line, elongated, resembling a thread, continuing, unintermitting, looking like a line, rectilinear, successive, in the direction of a line, undeviating, narrow, threadlike, outstretched, extended; see also **direct** 1, **straight** 1.

lined, *mod.*—*Syn.* interlined, stuffed, encrusted, coated, wadded, faced, brushed, sheathed, wainscoted, ceiled.

linen, *n.*—*Syn.* cloth, material, flaxen fabric, sheeting, linen cloth.
Linens include the following—damask, single damask, five-leaf damask, eight-leaf damask, linen duck, linen huckaback, linen crash, dowlas, osnaburg, low sheeting, low brown linen, plain bleached linen, twilled linen, linen drilling, diaper linen, cambric linen, lawn, handkerchief linen, printed linen, hand-blocked linen, dyed linen; see also **bedding, cloth, sheet** 1, **towel.**
Articles called linens include the following—handkerchiefs, towels, bedding, sheets, pillowcases, underwear, shirts, dishtowels, tablecloths, napkins, doilies.

liner, *n.*—*Syn.* ocean liner, airship, cruiser; see **plane** 3, **ship.**

linesman, *n.*—*Syn.* umpire, referee, arbiter; see **judge** 2, **official** 2.

lineup (D), *n.*—*Syn.* starters, entrants, first string (D); see **list, register** 1.

line up, *v.*—*Syn.* fall in, form in *or* into (a) line, take one's proper place in line, queue up, form ranks; form a column by two's, four's, etc.; get in line *or* formation; see also **march.**

linger, *v.* **1.** [To go reluctantly]—*Syn.* tarry, saunter, lag, trail, hesitate, delay, plod, trudge, traipse, falter, totter, stagger, dawdle, lumber, procrastinate, slouch, shuffle, trifle, potter, fritter away time, shilly-shally, dillydally, idle, crawl, loll, vacillate, take one's time, wait, putter, hobble, be dilatory, be tardy, be long; *all* (D): sit around, hang around, hang back, let the grass grow under one's feet; see also **loiter.**—*Ant.* hasten, hurry*, speed.
2. [To go slowly]—*Syn.* hang on, remain, be moribund; see **delay** 1, **hinder.**

lingerie, *n.*—*Syn.* women's underwear; *both* (D): dainties, unmentionables; see **clothes, underwear.**

lingo, *n.*—*Syn.* dialect, idiom, jargon; see **language** 1.

linguist, *n.* **1.** [Student of language]—*Syn.* etymologist, philologist, philologer, structuralist, structural linguist, usagist, transformationalist, transformational grammarian, phonologist, dialectician, vocabulist, glossographer, glossologist, phoneticist, phonetician, phonemist, grammatist, grammarian, lexiconist, lexicographer, philologue, linguistician, stratificationalist, stratificational grammarian, tagmemist, glottochronologist, comparativist, comparative (Indo-European) grammarian, reconstructionist, linguistic geographer, semanticist.
2. [Speaker of many languages]—*Syn.* polyglot, translator, polyglottist, savant, conversant, Pangloss; see also **scholar** 2.

linguistic, *mod.*—*Syn.* semantic, dialectal, philological, etymological, phonological, morphological, lingual, phonetic, phonemic, grammatical, syntactical, usagistic, glottal, scientific, exact, oral, lexical, lexemic.

linguistics, *n.* pl.—*Syn.* grammar, semantics, phonology, morphology, syntax, philology; see also **etymology, grammar, language** 2.
Branches of the study of linguistics include the following—historical *or* diachronic, descriptive, comparative *or* synchronic, geographical, anthropological; psycholinguistics, sociolinguistics, symbolic logic, glottochronology.

liniment, *n.*—*Syn.* ointment, cream, lotion; see **balm** 2, **medicine** 2, **salve.**

lining, *mod.*—*Syn.* edging, skirting, fringing, outlining. rimming, insulating; see also **bordering.**

lining, *n.*—*Syn.* interlining, inner coating *or* layer *or* surface, filling, quilting, stuffing, wadding, padding, brushing, sheathing, wainscoting, covering, wall, reinforcement, in layer, brattice, partition, doublure, paneling; see also **facing** 2, **insulation** 2.

link, *n.*—*Syn.* ring, loop, coupling, coupler, section, seam, weld, ligation, connective, hitch, intersection, nexus, copula, connection, fastening, splice, interconnection, junction, joining, ligature, vinculum, articulation; see also **bond** 2, **fastener, joint** 1, **knot** 1, **tie** 1.

link, *v.*—*Syn.* connect, associate, combine; see **join** 1.

linked, *mod.*—*Syn.* connected, combined, associated; see **joined.**

linking, *mod.* —*Syn.* combining, joining, associating; see **connecting.**

links, *n.* —*Syn.* golf course, greens, fairways, club course, public course, golf links, country club; *all* (D): cow pasture, spinach plot, divot garden.

linoleum, *n.* —*Syn.* linoxyn, floor covering, cork composition, Congoleum, Linowall (both trademarks); see also **floor** 1, **flooring, tile.**

lint, *n.* —*Syn.* raveling, fluff, fibre; see **dust.**

lion, *n.* **1.** [Celebrity]—*Syn.* favorite, wonder, prodigy; see **celebrity**2.

2. [A leonine carnivore]—*Syn.* leo, *Felis leo* (Latin), king of beasts *or* the jungle, African *or* Asian cat, lioness; see also **animal** 2, **cat** 2.

Kinds of lions include the following—Arabian *or* Persian, Barbary, Bengal, Cape, Gambian, Senegal; lion of Gujerat.

lionhearted, *mod.* —*Syn.* strong, noble, courageous; see **brave** 1.

lionize, *v.* —*Syn.* dignify, celebrate, honor; see **praise** 1.

lip, *n.* **1.** [A fleshy portion of the mouth]—*Syn.* speech organ, fold of flesh, edge *or* border of the mouth, liplike part, labium, labrum; see also **mouth**1.

2. [An edge]—*Syn.* spout, margin, brim, flange, portal, nozzle, overlap, projection, flare; see also **edge** 1, **rim.**

bite one's lips—*Syn.* show restraint, keep back one's anger, hold one's temper in check; see **restrain oneself.**

hang on the lips of—*Syn.* attend to, heed, hand on one's every word; see **listen** 2.

keep a stiff upper lip (D)—*Syn.* take heart, be encouraged, remain strong; see **suffer** 3.

smack one's lips—*Syn.* express satisfaction, enjoy, be delighted; see **appreciate** 1.

liquefy, *v.* —*Syn.* deliquesce, condense, flux; see **dissolve** 1, **melt** 1.

liqueur, *n.* —*Syn.* cordial, brandy, after-dinner drink; see **cocktail, drink** 2.

liquid, *mod.* **1.** [In a state neither solid nor gaseous] —*Syn.* watery, liquescent, fluidic, liquiform, molten, damp, moist, aqueous, liquefied, dissolved, deliquescent, melted, thawed; see also **fluid, wet** 1. —*Ant.* solid*, solidified, frozen.

2. [Having qualities suggestive of fluids]—*Syn.* flowing, running, splashing, sappy, thin, ichorous, solvent, moving, viscous, diluting; see also **fluid, juicy.**—*Ant.* dense, imporous, impenetrable.

3. [Readily available in cash]—*Syn.* ready, free, realizable, marketable, quick, fluid; see also **usable.** —*Ant.* tied up, permanent, fixed.

liquid, *n.* —*Syn.* liquor, fluid, flux, inelastic fluid, aqueous *or* liquid *or* liquefied *or* melted material, juice, sap, extract, secretion, flow, matter in a liquid *or* fluid state; see also **water** 1.

liquidate, *v.* **1.** [To pay]—*Syn.* settle, repay, reimburse; see **pay** 1.

2. [To change into money]—*Syn.* sell, convert, change; see **cash, exchange** 2.

3. [To abolish]—*Syn.* annul, cancel, destroy; see **abolish, eliminate** 1.

4. [(D) To kill]—*Syn.* annihilate, murder, do in (D); see **kill** 1.

liquor, *n.* **1.** [Matter in liquid form]—*Syn.* water, drink, extract, potable, fluid, decoction, infusion, dissolvent, solvent; see also **liquid.**

2. [Strong alcoholic drink]—*Syn.* whiskey; *both* (D): booze, alcohol; see **cocktail, drink** 2.

liquor store, *n.* —*Syn.* liquor dealer *or* counter *or* dispensary *or* wholesaler *or* supplier, state liquor control *or* commission store *or* branch, package store, carryout (D); see also **bar** 2, **store** 1.

lisp, *v.* —*Syn.* falter, mispronounce, sputter, stutter, clip one's words, drawl; see also **utter.**

lissome, *mod.* —*Syn.* lithe, supple, flexible; see **agile, flexible** 1.

list, *n.* —*Syn.* roll, record, schedule, agenda, arrangement, enrollment, gazette, slate, archive, enumeration, draft, panel, brief, invoice, register, memorandum, inventory, account, outline, syllabus, tally, manifest, prospectus, bulletin, directory, roster, list of names, subscribers, subscription list, panel, muster, poll, ballot, table of contents, menu, bill of fare, dictionary, glossary, lexicon, vocabulary, thesaurus, bill of lading, docket; see also **catalogue** 1, **file** 2, **index** 2, **table** 2.

list, *v.* **1.** [To enter in a list]—*Syn.* set down, arrange, bill, catalogue, schedule, enter, note, place, chronicle, post, insert, classify, file, enroll, register, manifest, inscribe, tally, inventory, enumerate, record, index, calendar, tabulate, book, invoice, census, draft, poll, impanel, slate, post, docket, keep count of, run down, call the roll; see also **file** 1, **record** 1. —*Ant.* remove*, wipe out, obliterate.

2. [To cultivate with a lister]—*Syn.* cultivate, seed, prepare; see **plow** 1.

3. [To lean]—*Syn.* pitch, slant, incline; see **lean** 1.

listed, *mod.* —*Syn.* filed, catalogued, indexed; see **recorded.**

listen, *v.* **1.** [To endeavor to hear]—*Syn.* attend, keep one's ears open, be attentive, listen in, pick up, overhear, give attention *or* a hearing to, give ear, hearken, hark, listen to, pay *or* give attention, hear, monitor; *all* (D): tune in, give ear to, incline an ear to, not miss a trick, lend an ear, strain one's ears, prick up *or* cock one's ears.—*Ant.* be deaf to, turn a deaf ear to, ignore.

2. [To receive advice cordially]—*Syn.* (give) heed, receive, take advice, take under advisement, welcome, accept, entertain, admit, take into consideration, adopt, hear out (D).—*Ant.* discard*, scorn, refuse.

listener, *n.* —*Syn.* hearer, heeder, witness; see **auditor** 1.

listening, *mod.* —*Syn.* hearing, paying attention, heeding, attending, overhearing, hearkening, giving ear, straining to hear, receiving, accepting; *both* (D): lending an ear, pricking up one's ears; see also **interested** 1, **involved.**—*Ant.* indifferent*, giving no attention, inattentive.

listless, *mod.* **1.** [Lacking spirit or desire]—*Syn.* dull, stupid, spiritless, inattentive, drowsy, sleepy, languid, dreamy, thoughtless, indolent, heedless, lifeless, abstracted, absent, laggard, faint, lacking zest, slack, mopish, supine, inanimate, phlegmatic, dormant, insouciant, lukewarm, nonchalant, careless, torpid, sluggish, leaden, heavy, lethargic, bored, uninterested, languorous, neutral, lackadaisical, enervated, apathetic, easy-going; see also **in-**

different 1, **unconcerned.**—*Ant.* active*, vivacious, vigorous.

2. [Lacking action]—*Syn.* passive, sluggish, indolent; see **slow** 2.

listlessness, *n.*—*Syn.* idleness, lethargy, inactivity; see **indifference** 1, **laziness.**

lit, *mod.*—*Syn.* illuminated, lighted, resplendent; see **afire, bright** 1, **burning** 1.

litany, *n.*—*Syn.* petition, invocation, act of devotion; see **prayer** 2.

literacy, *n.*—*Syn.* refinement, scholarship, ability; see **education** 1, **knowledge** 1.

literal, *mod.* **1.** [Word for word]—*Syn.* verbatim, *literatim* (Latin), verbal, written, natural, usual, ordinary, apparent, real, not figurative *or* metaphorical *or* allegorical, strict, following the exact words, unerring, veracious, scrupulous, veritable, accurate, critical, authentic, undeviating; of, at *or* to the letter;—*Ant.* free*, interpretive, figurative.

2. [Exact]—*Syn.* true, veritable, methodical; see **accurate** 1.

literally, *mod.*—*Syn.* really, actually, precisely, exactly, completely, undeviatingly, unerringly, indisputably, undisputably, correctly, strictly, to the letter, faithfully, rigorously, straight, unmistakably, veritably, truly, not metaphorically *or* figuratively, rightly, word for word, verbatim, unimaginatively, letter by letter; see also **accurately** 1.—*Ant.* freely*, figuratively, fancifully.

literary, *mod.*—*Syn.* arcane, bookish, belletristic; see **learned** 2.

literate, *mod.*—*Syn.* informed, scholarly, erudite; see **educated** 1, **intelligent** 1, **learned** 1.

literature, *n.* **1.** [Artistic production in language]—*Syn.* letters, lore, belles-lettres, literary works, literary productions, the humanities, classics, books, polite literature *or* letters, republic of letters, writings; see also **biography, drama** 1, **exposition** 2, **history** 2, **novel, poetry, record** 1, 2, **story, writing** 2.

Great bodies of literature include the following—Greek, Latin, Egyptian, Sanskrit, Icelandic, Hebraic, Arabic, Coptic, Chinese, Japanese, Persian, Hindu, French, Italian, Spanish, German, Russian, English, Danish, Swedish, Norwegian, Provençal, Slavic.

Periods in western literature include the following—classical, heroic, medieval, neoclassical, renaissance, Georgian, pseudoclassical, Augustan, Romantic, Victorian, modern *or* recent *or* twentieth-century.

2. [Written matter treating a given subject]—*Syn.* discourse, composition, treatise, dissertation, thesis, tract, paper, theme, treatment, disquisition, essay, discussion, research, observation, comment, findings, abstract, précis, report, critique, summary; see also **article** 3, **exposition** 2.

lithe, *mod.*—*Syn.* supple, pliant, pliable; see **flexible** 1.

litigant, *n.*—*Syn.* claimant, disputant, contestant; see **defendant, prosecution** 2.

litigate, *v.*—*Syn.* dispute, contest, prosecute; see **sue.**

litigation, *n.*—*Syn.* case, prosecution, lawsuit, action; see **trial** 2.

litigious, *mod.*—*Syn.* belligerent, hostile, argumentative; see **quarrelsome** 1.

litter, *n.* **1.** [A mess]—*Syn.* scattering, jumble, hodgepodge; see **rash** 1, 3.

2. [The young of certain animals]—*Syn.* cubs, pigs, piglets, puppies, kittens; see also **offspring.**

litter, *v.*—*Syn.* scatter, confuse, jumble; see **dirty.**

litterbug (D), *n.*—*Syn.* delinquent, offender, slob (D); see **malefactor.**

little, *mod.* **1.** [Small in size]—*Syn.* diminutive, dwarfish, small, tiny, shrunk, atomic, wee, undersized, not big *or* large, stunted, limited, cramped, wizened, scraggy, imperceptible, light, slight, microscopic, short, Lilliputian, runty, embryonic, elfin, invisible, shriveled, amoebic, microzoic, animalcular, pugged, vestigial, stubby, truncated, snub, molecular, microbic, toy, miniature, scrubby, cramped, puny, pygmy, dwarfed, inappreciable, bantam; *all* (D): half-pint, pocket-sized, pint-sized; see also **minute** 1.—*Ant.* large*, big, huge.

2. [Small in quantity]—*Syn.* inappreciable, inconsiderable, insufficient; see **inadequate** 1.

3. [Few in number]—*Syn.* scarce, not many, hardly any; see **few.**

4. [Brief]—*Syn.* concise, succinct, abrupt; see **short** 2.

5. [Small in importance]—*Syn.* trifling, insignificant, inconsiderable; see **trivial, unimportant.**

6. [Small in character]—*Syn.* base, mean, petty; see [**vulgar** 1, **wicked** 1.

7. [Weak]—*Syn.* stunted, runty, undersized; see **weak** 1.

make little of—*Syn.* make fun of, mock, abuse; see **ridicule.**

little, *n.*—*Syn.* trifle, modicum, whit; see **bit** 1.

littleness, *n.*—*Syn.* small size, petiteness, insignificance; see **smallness.**

liturgical, *mod.*—*Syn.* ceremonial, solemn, ritual; see **conventional** 2, **divine** 2.

liturgy, *n.*—*Syn.* rite, formula, ritual; see **ceremony** 2.**sacrament.**

livable, *mod.*—*Syn.* habitable, tenantable, inhabitable; see **bearable, comfortable** 2.

live, *mod.* **1.** [Active]—*Syn.* energetic, vital, vivid; see **active** 2.

2. [Not dead]—*Syn.* aware, conscious, existing; see **alive** 1.

3. [Not taped or filmed]—*Syn.* broadcast direct, unrehearsed, in the flesh (D); see **real** 2.

live, *v.* **1.** [To have life]—*Syn.* exist, breathe, be alive; see **be** 1.

2. [To enjoy life]—*Syn.* relish, savor, experience, love, delight in, live richly, make every moment count, have rich experiences, experience life to the full, live abundantly, make the most of life, take the earth's bounty, have a meaningful existence, take pleasure in, get a great deal from life.—*Ant.* suffer*, endure pain, be discouraged.

3. [To dwell]—*Syn.* live in, inhabit, abide; see **dwell, reside.**

4. [To gain subsistence]—*Syn.* remain, continue, earn a living, support oneself, acquire a livelihood, earn money, get ahead, provide for one's needs, make ends meet, maintain oneself; see also **earn** 2, **profit** 2, **subsist.**

5. [To persist in human memory]—*Syn.* prevail, remain, survive, last, be remembered, be unforgotten, live on in men's minds; see also **endure** 1.
where one lives (D)—*Syn.* personally, in a sensitive *or* vulnerable area, at one's heart; see **painfully** 2.
live and let live, *v.* —*Syn.* be tolerant *or* broad-minded, accept, ignore; see **allow** 1, **tolerate** 1.
live at, *v.* —*Syn.* inhabit, tenant, occupy; see **dwell, reside.**
live by, *v.* —*Syn.* survive, maintain life, acquire a livelihood; see **live** 4, **subsist.**
live down, *v.* —*Syn.* overcome, survive, outgrow; see **endure** 2.
live it up (D), *v.* —*Syn.* have fun, enjoy, paint the town red (D); see **celebrate** 3.
livelihood, *n.* **1.** [The supporting of life]—*Syn.* living, sustenance, maintenance; see **subsistence** 1.
2. [The means of supporting life]—*Syn.* means, circumstances, resources; see **subsistence** 2.
liveliness, *n.* —*Syn.* animation, spiritedness, briskness; see **action** 1.
livelong, *mod.* —*Syn.* everlasting, entire, complete; see **whole**1.
lively, *mod.* **1.** [Energetic]—*Syn.* vigorous, brisk, industrious; see **active** 1, 2.
2. [Gay]—*Syn.* cheerful, merry, joyful; see **happy** 1.
3. [Festive]—*Syn.* hospitable, entertaining, enjoyable; see **pleasant** 2.
4. [Exciting]—*Syn.* rousing, provocative, stimulating; see **exciting.**
5. [Eventful]—*Syn.* involved, complex, industrious; see **active** 2, **busy** 1.
6. [Stimulating]—*Syn.* invigorating, refreshing, exhilarating; see **stimulating.**
live on, *v.* —*Syn.* be supported, earn, augment; see **live** 4, **subsist.**
liver, *n.* —*Syn.* innard, glandular organ, vital part; see **organ** 2.
livery, *n.* —*Syn.* attire, costume, clothing; see **clothes.**
livestock, *n.* —*Syn.* cows, sheep, domestic animals; see **cattle, herd** 1.
live up to, *v.* —*Syn.* meet (expectations), do well, give satisfaction; see **satisfy** 3.
live with, *v.* —*Syn.* dwell *or* reside with, commit adultery, live in sin, cohabit, dwell as man and wife, play house (D); see also **misbehave.**
livid, *mod.* **1.** [Purplish]—*Syn.* discolored, lead-colored, black and blue; see **colored** 1, **purple.**
2. [Angry]—*Syn.* outraged, offended, black (D); see **angry.**
living, *mod.* **1.** [Alive]—*Syn.* existing, breathing, (having) being; see **alive** 1.
2. [Vigorous]—*Syn.* awake, brisk, alert; see **active** 2.
living, *n.* **1.** [A means of survival]—*Syn.* existence, sustenance, maintenance; see **subsistence** 2.
2. [Those not dead; *usually used with* the]—*Syn.* the quick, real people, flesh and blood (D).
living room, *n.* —*Syn.* lounge, front room, den; see **parlor, room** 2.
lizard, *n.* —*Syn.* reptile, saurian.
Lizards include the following—alligator, crocodile, dinosaur, horned toad, (horned) iguana, gecko, gila monster, European green lizard, bearded lizard, chameleon, basilisk, dragon lizard, Komodo dragon *or* monitor lizard.
Lizardlike creatures include the following—(giant) salamander, water dog, mud puppy, hellbender, newt, triton; see also **reptile.**
load, *n.* **1.** [A physical burden]—*Syn.* weight, encumbrance, carload, wagonload, hindrance, shipload, parcel, pressure, cargo, haul, incubus, lading, charge, pack, mass, payload, shipment, bale, contents, capacity, bundle, fardel, base load, peak load, heft (D); see also **freight** 1, **shipment.**—*Ant.* lightness*, buoyancy, weightlessness.
2. [Responsibility]—*Syn.* charge, obligation, trust; see **duty** 1.
3. [A charge: *said especially of firearms*]—*Syn.* powder, shot, clip, round, shell, projectile, powder and shot; see also **ammunition.**
4. [A measure]—*Syn.* shot, amount, part; see **measurement** 2, **quantity.**
get a load of (D)—*Syn.* be aware of, listen, attend; see **hear** 2, **see** 1.
have a load on (D)—*Syn.* intoxicated, tipsy, inebriated; see **drunk.**
load, *v.* **1.** [To place a load]—*Syn.* place, arrange, stow (away), store, lumber, burden, stuff, put good in *or* on, containerize, freight, weight, pile, heap, fill(up), cram, mass, ballast, lade, heap on, put aboard, stack, pour in, take on cargo, take on ballast; see also **pack** 1.—*Ant.* unload, unpack*, take off cargo.
2. [To overload]—*Syn.* encumber, saddle, weigh down; see **burden, oppress.**
3. [to charge; *said especially of firearms*]—*Syn.* prime, ready, make ready to fire, prepare for shooting, insert a clip.
loaded, *mod.* **1.** [Supplied with a load]—*Syn.* laden, burdened, weighted; see **full** 1.
2. [Ready to discharge; *said of firearms*]—*Syn.* charged, primed, ready to shoot, readied, ready to fire.—*Ant.* uncharged, unloaded*, unprimed.
3. [(D) Intoxicated]—*Syn. all* (D): wired, tanked, gassed; see **drunk.**
4. [(D) Tricky]—*Syn.* deceitful, leading, touchy; see **mean** 3, **tricky** 3.
loading, *n.* —*Syn.* stowing, storing, arranging cargo, putting on cargo *or* freight, taking on freight *or* passengers, filling, lading, weighing down, ballasting, cramming, burdening, encumbering, charging, priming, readying, cumbering, containerization, putting on a load, filling the hold, receiving a consignment; see **packing** 1.
loaf, *n.* —*Syn.* dough, roll, twist, bun, pastry, mass, lump, cube; see **bread** 1, **cake** 2.
loaf, *v.* **1.** [To do nothing useful]—*Syn.* idle, trifle, lounge, kill time, be inactive *or* unoccupied *or* slothful *or* indolent, vegetate, dally, take it easy, laze, twiddle the thumbs, not lift a finger, be lazy, loll, malinger, potter, drift, relax, slack, shirk, waste time, slow down, evade, dillydally, sit *or* stand around, slack off, fritter time away, dream, let down; *all* (D): goof off, bum, goldbrick, stall, lollygag, hand out, hold up a corner, piddle; see also **relax, rest** 1.
2. [To travel at an easy pace]—*Syn.* loiter, stroll, saunter; see **walk** 1.
loafer, *n.* —*Syn.* idler, lounger, lazy person, ne'er-do-well, good-for-nothing, lazybones, sluggard, malingerer, waster, wastrel, slacker, shirker, beach-

comber, wanderer, sundowner, ski bum; *all* (D): bum, lizard, goldbrick, lollygagger, deadbeat.

loafing, *mod.* **1.** [Doing nothing useful]—*Syn.* rambling, worthless, futile; see **lazy** 1.
2. [Ostensibly employed, but wasting time]—*Syn.* slacking, shirking, evading, letting *or* slowing down *or* up, putting in time, apathetic, indifferent, uninterested, careless, pretending; *both* (D): sojering, whipping the cat; see also **resting** 1.—*Ant.* active*, toiling, energetic.

loam, *n.*—*Syn.* topsoil, dirt, wood's earth; see **earth2.**

loan, *n.*—*Syn.* (act of) lending, accommodation, trust, advance, permission to borrow, investment, giving credit, mortgage, advancing, time payment; *all* (D): touch, bite, coins; see also **allowance** 2, **credit** 4.—*Ant.* promise*, borrowing, pledge.

loan, *v.*—*Syn.* provide with, advance, let out; see **lend** 1.

loaned, *mod.*—*Syn.* lent, advanced, on trust *or* security *or* credit, invested, granted, furnished, bestowed, afforded, ventured, intrusted, put out at interest, let, risked, leased; see also **given.**—*Ant.* borrowed*, pledged, pawned.

loath, *mod.*—*Syn.* averse, indisposed, remiss; see **opposed, reluctant, unwilling.**

loathe, *v.*—*Syn.* abhor, detest, abominate; see **dislike, hate** 1.

loathing, *n.*—*Syn.* dislike, aversion, disgust; see **hate, hatred** 1, **malice, resentment** 2.

loathsome, *mod.*—*Syn.* obnoxious, deplorable, disgusting; see **offensive** 2, **repulsive.**

lob, *v.*—*Syn.* toss, heave, launch; see **throw** 2.

lobate, *mod.*—*Syn.* divided, lobular, globular; see **round** 1.

lobby, *n.*—*Syn.* vestibule, entryway, antechamber; see **hall** 2, **room** 2.

lobby, *v.*—*Syn.* procure, sway, change, alter, advance, solicit (votes), exercise influence, further, induce, bring pressure to bear, put pressure on, jawbone, press, pressure, affect, modify, promote, request, urge, carry by solicitation; *all* (D): pull strings *or* wires, wirepull, politick (D); see also **influence.**

lobe, *n.*—*Syn.* flap, fold, section, projection, portion, part, lap, convexity, ear section, wattle, excurvation; see also **bulge, ear** 1.

lobster, *n.*—*Syn.* crustacean, invertebrate, crawfish; see also **shellfish.**
Lobsters include the following—American, Maine, European, Norway, spiny, black, grasshopper, rock, sea-crawfish.

local, *mod.* **1.** [Associated with a locality]—*Syn.* sectional, insular, divisional, territorial, situal, district, provincial, neighborhood, town, civic, topographical, geographical, descriptive, historical, legendary, geologic, geodetic, botanical, small-town, parochial, zoological, social, economic; see also **political, regional, traditional** 2.
2. [Restricted to a locality]—*Syn.* limited, confined, bounded; see **restricted.**

locale, *n.*—*Syn.* vicinity, territory, district; see **area** 2, **region** 1.

localism, *n.*—*Syn.* idiom, idiosyncrasy, provincialism; see **custom** 2, **dialect.**

locality, *n.* **1.** [Area]—*Syn.* district, section, sector; see **area** 2, **region** 1.
2. [Position]—*Syn.* spot, location, site; see **position** 1.
3. [Neighborhood]—*Syn.* block, vicinity, district; see **neighborhood.**

localize, *v.*—*Syn.* surround, confine, limit; see **restrict** 2.

locally, *mod.*—*Syn.* regionally, sectionally, provincially, in the neighborhood, in the town, nearby, restrictedly, in a limited manner, narrowly.—*Ant.* distantly, nationally, widespread.

locate, *v.* **1.** [To determine a location]—*Syn.* discover, search out, find, come on *or* across, meet with, position, ferret out, stumble on, discover the location *or* place of, get at, hit *or* light *or* come *or* happen *or* fix upon, lay one's fingers *or* hands on, track down, establish, determine, station, place, unearth; see also **designate** 1.
2. [To take up residence]—*Syn.* settle down, establish oneself, inhabit; see **dwell, reside, settle** 7.

located, *mod.* **1.** [Determined in space]—*Syn.* traced, found, happened on; see **discovered.**
2. [Situated]—*Syn.* positioned, seated, fixed; see **placed, resting** 2.

locating, *n.*—*Syn.* finding, discovering, unearthing, searching *or* tracing out, digging up, coming *or* stumbling on, happening *or* lighting upon, unclosing, placing, spotting, settling (upon), establishing.

location, *n.* **1.** [The act of locating]—*Syn.* finding, discovering, searching out; see **locating.**
2. [A position]—*Syn.* place, spot, section; see **position** 1.
3. [A site]—*Syn.* situation, place, scene; see **area** 2, **neighborhood** 1.

lock, *n.* **1.** [A device for locking]—*Syn.* hook, catch, latch, bolt, bar, staple, hasp, clinch, bond, fastening, padlock, safety catch, clamp, holdfast, clasp, link, junction, connection, barrier, canal gate, device, fixture, grip, grapple; see also **fastener.**
Types of locks include the following—single acting tumbler, double acting tumbler, pin-tumbler cylinder, sash ward, fine ward, solid ward, lever, safety lever, cylinder, keyless, combination, cabinet, duplex key, action, rim, mortise, padlock, timelock.
2. [A tuft or ringlet of hair]—*Syn.* tuft, tress, ringlet, bunch, twist, portion of hair, snip, braid, plait; see also **curl, hair** 1.
under lock and key—*Syn.* locked up, imprisoned, in jail; see **confined** 3.

lock, *v.*—*Syn.* bolt, bar, turn the key; see **fasten** 1.

locked, *mod.*—*Syn.* secured, padlocked, cinched; see **tight** 2.

locker, *n.*—*Syn.* cabinet, wardrobe, cupboard; see **closet, furniture.**

locket, *n.*—*Syn.* miniature case, memento case, pendant; see **bracelet, jewelry, necklace.**

lockup, *n.*—*Syn.* prison, jail, penitentiary; see **jail.**

lock up, *v.*—*Syn.* confine, put behind bars, shut up; see **imprison.**

locomotion, *n.*—*Syn.* velocity, headway, travel; see **movement** 1.

locomotive, *n.*—*Syn.* steam engine, electric locomotive, diesel locomotive, wood-burner, coal-burner, passenger *or* freight locomotive; *all* (D):

boiler, smokolotive, teakettle, cowcatcher; see also **engine** 1, **train** 2.

locust, *n.* —*Syn.* (dog-day) cicada, short-horned grasshopper, migratory grasshopper, beetle; see also **grasshopper, insect.**
Locusts include the following—Rocky Mountain (western cricket, stone-cricket, Mormon cricket), seventeen-year, migratory, clumsy, bald, green-striped.

lode, *n.* —*Syn.* ore deposit, vein, strike (D); see **mine** 1.

lodestone, *n.* —*Syn.* magnetic ore *or* stone, loadstone, magnetite; see **magnet.**

lodge, *n.* —*Syn.* abode, dwelling place, home, stopover, inn, ski lodge, dormitory, (youth) hostel, chalet; see also **hotel, motel, resort** 2.

lodge, *v.* **1.** [To become fixed]—*Syn.* catch, stick, abide; see **remain** 1, **stay** 1.
2. [To take (temporary) residence]—*Syn.* room, stay *or* stop over, abide, hostel, board, dorm (D); see also **dwell, reside.**

lodger, *n.* —*Syn.* guest, roomer, resident; see **boarder, tenant.**

lodging, *n.* **1.** [Personal accommodation]—*Syn.* harbor, asylum, *pied-á-terre* (French), port, protection, cover, roof over one's head; see also **refuge** 1, **shelter.**
2. [A (temporary) living place; *usually plural*] —*Syn.* inn, tourist camp, lodging place, lodgment, address, chambers, domicile, residence, habitation, apartment, home, room, tourist court; see also **hotel, lodge, motel, resort** 2.

loft, *n.* —*Syn.* upper room, hayloft, storage area; see **attic.**

lofty, *mod.* **1.** [High]—*Syn.* tall, elevated, towering; see **high** 2, **raised** 1.
2. [Idealistic]—*Syn.* exalted, enhanced, heightened; see **grand** 2.

log, *n.* **1.** [The main stem of a fallen or cut tree] —*Syn.* bole, timber, stick, length; see also **trunk** 3, **wood** 2.
2. [The record of a voyage]—*Syn.* account, chart, diary; see **journal** 1, **record** 1.

loge, *n.* —*Syn.* stall, gallery, box; see **balcony.**

logger, *n.* —*Syn.* rafter, bucker, cutter; see **lumberjack.**

logging, *n.* —*Syn.* felling trees, woodcutting, woodchopping, lumberjacking, cutting off *or* over; see also **lumbering.**

logic, *n.* —*Syn.* reasoning, dialectic, doctrine of terms *or* judgment *or* inference, deduction, syllogism, induction, inference, course of argument or thought; thesis, antithesis and synthesis; see also **philosophy** 1, **thought** 1.
Branches of logic include the following—traditional *or* Aristotelian, modern *or* epistemological, pragmatic, instrumental *or* experimental, psychological, symbolic *or* mathematical, deductive, inductive *or* Baconian.

logical, *mod.* **1.** [Being in logical agreement] —*Syn.* deducible, coherent, consistent, inferential, probable, sound, extensional, cogent, pertinent, germane, legitimate, relevant, congruent *or* consistent with, as it ought to be; see also **valid** 1.
2. [Rational]—*Syn.* perceptive, sensible, discerning; see **judicious, rational** 1, **reasonable** 1.

logically, *mod.* —*Syn.* rationally, by logic *or* reason, inevitably; see **reasonably** 1, 2.

logician, *n.* —*Syn.* rationalist, syllogist, sophist; see **philosopher, scholar** 2.

logrolling (D), *n.* —*Syn.* promotion, help, chicanery; see **aid** 1, **improvement** 1, **influence** 2.

logy (D), *mod.* —*Syn.* dull, sluggish, drowsy; see **lazy** 1.

loiter, *v.* —*Syn.* saunter, stroll, dawdle, linger (idly), dally, delay, lag, shuffle, waste time, potter, procrastinate, traipse, shamble, pass time in idleness, halt, tarry, fritter away time, loll, dabble, wait, hover, pause, dillydally, hang back, shilly-shally, amble, slacken, trail, drag, slough, flag, ramble, laze along, idle, let the grass grow under one's feet (D); see also **loaf** 1.—*Ant.* hurry*, hasten, stride along.

loll, *v.* —*Syn.* lounge, lean, recline; see **rest** 1.

lollipop, *n.* —*Syn.* sucker, sweet, confection; see **candy.**

lone, *mod.* —*Syn.* solitary, lonesome, deserted; see **alone** 1.

loneliness, *n.* —*Syn.* detachment, separation, solitude, desolation, aloneness, solitariness, lonesomeness, desertedness, forlornness; see also **homesickness, isolation.**

lonely, *mod.* **1.** [Without company]—*Syn.* abandoned, forlorn, comfortless, forsaken, friendless, deserted, desolate, homeless, left, lone, lonesome, solitary, uncompanioned, troglodytic, withdrawn, anchoritic, secluded, unattended, by oneself, empty, apart, companionless, unsocial, reclusive, single, renounced, lorn, rejected, unaccompanied, unbefriended, disconsolate, uncherished; see also **homesick.**—*Ant.* accompanied, joined*, associated.
2. [Inaccessible or unfrequented]—*Syn.* alone, desolate, unfrequented; see **isolated.**

loner, *n.* —*Syn.* independent, self-reliant person, lone wolf; see **hermit, misanthrope.**

lonesome, *mod.* —*Syn.* solitary, forlorn, alone; see **homesick, lonely** 1.

long, *mod.* **1.** [Extended in space]—*Syn.* lengthy, extended, outstretched, elongated, interminable, boundless, unending, limitless, stretching, great, high, deep, drawn out, enlarged, expanded, spread, tall, lofty, towering, continued, lengthened, stringy, long-limbed, rangy, lanky, gangling, far-reaching, far-seeing, distant, running, faraway, far-off, remote; see also **endless** 1, **large** 1.—*Ant.* short*, small, stubby.
2. [Extended in time]—*Syn.* protracted, prolonged, enduring, unending, meandering, long-winded, spun out, lengthy, for ages, without end, forever and a day, day after day, hour after hour, etc.; lasting, prospective, continued, long-lived, sustained, tardy, dilatory, delayed, lingering; see also **eternal** 1, **perpetual** 1.—*Ant.* short*, brief, uncontinued.
3. [Tedious]—*Syn.* hard, longspun, long-drawn; see **dull** 4.
4. [Having (a certain commodity) in excess]—*Syn.* rich, profuse, abundant; see **plentiful** 1.

long, *v.* —*Syn.* desire, yearn for, wish; see **want** 1.

long and short of it (D), *n.* —*Syn.* conclusion, totality, upshot; see **result, whole.**

longevity, *n.* —*Syn.* survival, perpetuity, durability, persistence, long life, endurance, continuance; see also **continuation** 1.
longing, *mod.* —*Syn.* wanting, desirous, ravenous; see **enthusiastic** 2.
longing, *n.* —*Syn.* yearning, pining, hunger; see **desire** 1, **wish** 1.
longitude, *n.* —*Syn.* longitude in arc, longitude in time, celestial longitude; see **distance** 3, **measure** 1.
as (*or* **so) long as**—*Syn.* seeing that, provided, since; see **because.**
before long—*Syn.* in the near future, immediately, shortly; see **soon** 1.
long-lived, *mod.* —*Syn.* long-lasting, macrobiotic, enduring; see **permanent** 2, **perpetual** 1.
long-suffering, *mod.* —*Syn.* tolerant, uncomplaining, forgiving, easygoing, clement, forbearing, resigned, lax, lenient, indulgent; see also **patient** 1.
long-winded, *mod.* —*Syn.* redundant, wordy, prolix; see **verbose.**
look, *n.* **1.** [Appearance]—*Syn.* aspect, presence, mien; see **appearance** 1, **expression** 4.
2. [An effort to see]—*Syn.* gaze, stare, scrutiny, inspection, contemplation, visual search, reconnaissance, introspection, speculation, attending, noticing, regarding, marking, observation, keeping watch; *both* (D): once-over, eye-tape; see also **attention** 1, **examination** 1.
3. [A quick use of the eyes]—*Syn.* glance, quick cast of the eyes, survey, squint, glimpse, peek, peep, twinkle of an eye, *coup d'oeil* (French), leer, flash; *both* (D): peekaboo, the eye.
look, *v.* **1.** [To appear]—*Syn.* seem to be, look like, resemble; see **seem.**
2. [To endeavor to see]—*Syn.* view, gaze, glance (at), scan, stare, behold, contemplate, watch, survey, scrutinize, regard, inspect, discern, spy, observe, attend, examine, mark, gape, turn the eyes upon, give attention, peer, ogle, have an eye on, study, peep, look on *or* at *or* upon *or* through; *all* (D): cock the eye, take a gander at, get a load of; see also **see** 1.
it looks like—*Syn.* probably, it seems that there will be, it seems as if; see **seem.**
look after, *v.* —*Syn.* look out for, support, watch; see **guard** 2.
look for, *v.* —*Syn.* research, pry, follow; see **hunt** 2, **search, seek** 1.
looking glass, *n.* —*Syn.* hand glass, pier, full-length mirror; see **mirror.**
look into, *v.* —*Syn.* investigate, study, probe; see **examine** 1, 2.
lookout, *n.* **1.** [A place of vantage]—*Syn.* outlook, view, prospect, panorama, post, scene, beacon, cupola, crow's nest, watchtower, observation tower, observatory, belvedere, observation post, signal station, patrol station, sentry box; *all* (D): captain's lookout, widow's walk, sea-widow's roost; see also **tower.**
2. [One stationed at a lookout, sense 1]—*Syn.* watcher, sentinel, scout; see **watchman.**
look out, *interj.* —*Syn.* be careful, pay attention, hearken, listen, notice, have a care, heads up (D); see also **watch out.**
look up, *v.* **1.** [(D) To improve]—*Syn.* get better, advance, progress; see **improve** 2.
2. [To find by search]—*Syn.* come upon, research, find; see **discover** 1, **search, seek** 1.
look up to, *v.* —*Syn.* respect, adulate, honor; see **admire** 1.
loom, *n.* —*Syn.* weaver, knitting machine, table loom; see **machine** 1.
Types of looms include the following—hand, draw, Jacquard, bar, power, dobby, small ware, double pile, single pile, terry, lappet, horizontal, vertical.
loom, *v.* **1.** [To appear]—*Syn.* come into view, come on the scene, rise; see **appear** 1.
2. [To appear large or imposing]—*Syn.* menace, emerge (in mist), overshadow, shadow, bulk, figure, show, tower, hulk, be seen in shadow, issue, emanate, top, overtop, impress, hang over, rise gradually, seem large *or* huge, be coming *or* near *or* imminent, hover, approach, impend, come forth, break through the clouds; see also **threaten** 2.
looming, *mod.* —*Syn.* rising, appearing, emerging; see **imminent.**
loop, *n.* —*Syn.* ring, eye, circuit; see **circle** 1.
knock (*or* **throw) for a loop** (D)—*Syn.* confuse, disturb, startle; see **shock** 2.
loop, *v.* **1.** [To form a loop]—*Syn.* curve, connect, tie together; see **bend** 1.
2. [To be in the form of a loop]—*Syn.* fold, coil, ring; see **circle.**
loophole, *n.* **1.** [An evasion]—*Syn.* avoidance, means of escape, deception; see **lie** 1, **trick** 1.
2. [An opening]—*Syn.* slot, knothole, aperture; see **hole** 1.
loose, *mod.* **1.** [Unbound]—*Syn.* unfastened, undone, unsewed, untied, unpinned, insecure, unsecure, unsecured, unshackled, relaxed, unhasped, unattached, unconnected, disconnected, untethered, unfettered, uncaged, liberated, unbuttoned, unclasped, unhooked, slack, loosened, baggy, unconfined, unlatched, unlocked, unbolted, unscrewed, unhinged, worked free; see also **free** 3. —*Ant.* tight*, confined, bound.
2. [Movable]—*Syn.* unattached, free, wobbly; see **movable.**
3. [Vague]—*Syn.* disconnected, detached, random; see **obscure** 1, **vague** 2.
4. [Wanton]—*Syn.* unrestrained, dissolute, disreputable; see **lewd** 2.
break loose—*Syn.* free oneself, shake off restraint, flee; see **escape.**
cast loose—*Syn.* set free, untie, release; see **free** 1.
let loose (with) (D)—*Syn.* give out, come out with, issue; see **release.**
on the loose (D)—*Syn.* unconfined, unrestrained, wild; see **free** 2, 3.
set (*or* **turn) loose**—*Syn.* set free, release, untie; see **free** 1.
loosen, *v.* **1.** [To make loose]—*Syn.* extricate, release, unfix; see **free** 1.
2. [To become loose]—*Syn.* relax, slacken, work loose *or* free, go slack, break up, let go, become unfastened *or* unbound *or* undone, become unstuck (D).—*Ant.* tighten*, tighten up, become rigid.
loot, *n.* —*Syn.* spoils, plunder, take (D); see **booty.**
loot, *v.* —*Syn.* plunder, thieve, rifle; see **rob, steal.**

lop, *v.* **1.** [To hang]—*Syn.* slump, flop, droop; see **hang** 2.
2. [To cut off; *said especially of branches*]—*Syn.* crop, prune, chop; see **cut** 1, **trim** 1.
lopsided, *mod.*—*Syn.* uneven, unbalanced, crooked; see **irregular** 4.
loquacious, *mod.*—*Syn.* voluble, chattering, fluent; see **talkative, verbose.**
loquacity, *n.*—*Syn.* talkativeness, verboseness, wordiness; see **conversation, discussion** 1.
Lord, *n.*—*Syn.* Divinity, the Supreme Being, Jehovah; see **God** 1.
lord, *n.* **1.** [A master]—*Syn.* ruler, governor, prince; see **master** 1.
2. [A member of the nobility]—*Syn.* peer, nobleman, count, don, patrician, hidalgo, grandee, seigneur, magnate, titled person; see also **aristocrat, royalty.**
Noblemen sometimes called lords include the following—duke, marquis, earl, viscount, baron, baronet, bishop, Scottish Lord of Session, younger sons of dukes and marquises.
lord it over (D), *v.*—*Syn.* boss, order (about *or* around), dictate (to); see **abuse** 1, **command** 2.
lordly, *mod.* **1.** [Noble]—*Syn.* grand, dignified, honorable; see **noble** 1, 2, 3.
2. [Pompous]—*Syn.* overbearing, imperious, haughty; see **egotistic** 1, 2.
lore, *n.*—*Syn.* enlightenment, wisdom, learning; see **knowledge** 1.
lose, *v.* **1.** [To bring about a loss]—*Syn.* mislay, forget, be careless with; see **misplace.**
2. [To incur loss]—*Syn.* suffer, miss, be deprived of, fail to keep, suffer loss, be reduced by, be impoverished from, become poorer by, be at a disadvantage because of; *both* (D): let slip through the fingers, come out of the small end of the horn; see also **waste** 1.—*Ant.* profit*, gain, improve.
3. [To fail to win]—*Syn.* be defeated, suffer defeat, be worsted, be left behind, be outdistanced, go down in defeat, succumb, fall, be the loser, miss, have the worst of it, be humbled, take defeat at the hands of; *all* (D): drop, go down for the count, get it in the neck, come out on the short end of the score, be sunk; see also **fail** 1.—*Ant.* win*, triumph, be victorious.
4. [To suffer financially]—*Syn.* squander, expend, dissipate; see **spend** 1, **waste** 2.
loser, *n.*—*Syn.* sufferer, defeated, deprived, worsted, bereaved, forfeiter, incurrer, dispossessed, destroyed, ruined, wrecked, undone, overthrown, underdog, disadvantaged, underprivileged, fallen, bereft, denuded, unredeemed; see also **failure** 2.—*Ant.* winner*, gainer, conqueror.
losing, *mod.* **1.** [*Said of one who loses*]—*Syn.* failing, falling, being undone *or* defeated *or* worsted *or* ruined, doomed, being wrecked *or* destroyed *or* shorn of *or* denuded *or* deprived (of), being bereft of, having the worst of it, coming to grief; *both* (D): quit of, on the way out; see also **sad** 2.
2. [*Said of an activity in which one must lose*]—*Syn.* futile, desperate, lost; see **hopeless** 2.
loss, *n.* **1.** [The act or fact of losing]—*Syn.* ruin, destruction, perdition, mishap, misfortune, forfeiture, giving up, bereavement, ill fortune, misadventure, ill luck, accident, calamity, trouble, disaster, death, sacrifice, catastrophe, cataclysm, trial, failure, misplacing, mislaying.
2. [Damage suffered by loss, sense 1]—*Syn.* hurt, injury, wound; see **damage** 1, 2.
3. [The result of unprofitable activity]—*Syn.* privation, want, bereavement, deprivation, need, destitution, being without, lack, waste, deterioration, impairment, degeneration, retrogression, retardation, decline, disadvantage, wreck, wreckage, extermination, eradication, extinction, undoing, dissolution, annihilation, extirpation, perdition, bane, end, undoing, disorganization, breaking up, immolation, suppression, relapse; see also **bankruptcy.**—*Ant.* advantage*, advancement, supply.
at a loss—*Syn.* confused, puzzled, unsure; see **undecided.**
losses, *n.*—*Syn.* casualties, accretion, deaths; see **casualty** 2.
lost, *mod.* **1.** [Not to be found]—*Syn.* misplaced, mislaid, invisible, cast away, missing, hidden, obscured, (gone) astray, nowhere to be found, strayed, lacking, wandered off, forfeited, vanished, wandering, minus, without, gone out of one's possession; see also **absent, gone** 2.—*Ant.* found*, come back, returned.
2. [Ignorant of the way]—*Syn.* perplexed, bewildered, ignorant; see **doubtful** 2.
3. [Destroyed]—*Syn.* demolished, devastated, wasted; see **destroyed, ruined** 1.
4. [No longer to be gained]—*Syn.* gone, passed, costly; see **destroyed, ruined** 1.
5. [No longer to be gained]—*Syn.* gone, passed, costly; see **unprofitable** 1.
6. [Helpless]—*Syn.* feeble, sickly, disabled; see **weak** 1, 3.
get lost (D)—*Syn.* go away, leave, begone; see **get out.**
lot, *n.* **1.** [A small parcel of land]—*Syn.* parcel, part, division, patch, clearing, piece of ground, plat, plot, field, tract, block, portion, allotment, apportionment, parking lot, piece, plottage, acreage; see also **area** 2, **property** 2.
2. [A number of individual items, usually alike]—*Syn.* number, quantity, group, batch, set, order, consignment, requisition; see also **shipment.**
3. [Destiny]—*Syn.* doom, portion, fate; see **chance** 1, **destiny** 1.
4. [(D) A great quantity]—*Syn.* large amount, abundance, amplitude, considerable amount, plenitude, great numbers, bundle, bunch, cluster, group, pack, batch, large numbers, (very) much *or* many, ever so much, quantities, enough and to spare, quite a lot *or* bit, quite a sum, a good deal; *all* (D): oodles and gobs, a whole bunch, loads, heaps, zillion, gobs, oodles; see also **plenty.**
cast (*or* **throw**) **in one's lost with**—*Syn.* associate with, share, unite; see **join** 1, 2.
draw (*or* **cast**) **lots**—*Syn.* choose, pick, elect; see **decide.**
lotion, *n.*—*Syn.* liniment, hand lotion, cream, solution, embrocation, liquid preparation, wash, lenitive, abirritant, unguent, palliative, demulcent; see also **balm** 2, **cosmetic, medicine** 2, **salve.**
loud, *mod.* **1.** [Having volume of sound]—*Syn.* deafening, ringing, ear-rending, ear-piercing, ear-

splitting, booming, fulminating, intense, resounding, piercing, high-sounding, trumpet-toned, blaring, sonorous, resonant, crashing, deep, full, powerful, emphatic, vehement, thundering, heavy, big, deep-toned, full-tongued, roaring, strident, enough to wake the dead (D); see also **shrill.**—*Ant.* soft*, faint, feeble.

2. [Producing loud sounds]—*Syn.* clamorous, noisy, uproarious, blatant, vociferous, stentorian, turbulent, tumultuous, blustering, clarion-voiced, lusty, loud-voiced, boisterous, obstreperous, rambunctious, cacophonous, raucous, loud-tongued; see also **harsh** 1.—*Ant.* quiet*, soft-voiced, calm.

3. [(D) Lacking manners and refinement]—*Syn.* loud-mouthed, brash, offensive; see **rude** 2, **vulgar** 1.

4. [(D) Lacking good taste, especially in colors] —*Syn.* garish, flashy, tawdry; see **ornate** 1.

loudly, *mod.*—*Syn.* audibly, vociferously, ringingly, fully, powerfully, crashingly, shrilly, deafeningly, piercingly, resonantly, emphatically, vehemently, thunderingly, ear-splittingly, in a full-toned voice, full-sounding, articulately, with full tongue, in full cry, clamorously, noisily, uproariously, plainly, blatantly, lustily, in a loud-mouthed manner, vulgarly, rudely, obstreperously, ostentatiously, boorishly, garishly, flashily, tawdrily, gaudily, conspicuously, cheaply, tastelessly, obtrusively, showily, theatrically, in full cry, aloud, resoundingly, at the top of one's lungs (D).

loud-speaker, *n.*—*Syn.* speaker, amplifier, public address system, speaker cone, diaphragm, electrodynamic speaker, high-fidelity speaker, full- *or* high-frequency speaker, low-frequency speaker, woofer, tweeter, sound truck; *both* (D): bullhorn, hog caller.

lounge, *n.* **1.** [A bedlike seat]—*Syn.* couch, settee, divan; see **davenport, furniture.**

2. [A social room]—*Syn.* reception room, parlor, mezzanine, club room, cocktail lounge, public room, (hotel) lobby; see also **bar** 2, **room** 2.

lounge, *v.*—*Syn.* idle, repose, kill time (D); see **loaf** 1, **rest** 1.

louse, *n.*—*Syn.* *Hemiptera* (Latin), pediculus, mite; see **insect.**

Lice include the following—sucking, biting, bird, chicken, turkey, plant, fish, carp, bee, body, crab; *both* (D): cootie, livestock.

lousy, *mod.* **1.** [Infested with lice]—*Syn.* pediculous, pediculate, pedicular, hemipteroid, with lice; see also **infested** 2.

2. [(D) Bad]—*Syn.* horrible, disliked, unwelcome; see **faulty, harmful, poor** 2, **unpopular.**

lout, *n.*—*Syn.* hick, peasant, rustic; see **boor.**

loutish, *mod.*—*Syn.* bungling, rustic, clumsy; see **awkward** 1, **rude** 2, **vulgar** 1.

lovable, *mod.*—*Syn.* winning, winsome, lovely; see **friendly** 1.

love, *n.* **1.** [Passionate and tender devotion]—*Syn.* attachment, devotedness, passion, passionate affection, amativeness, infatuation, yearning, flame, rapture, enchantment, ardor, emotion, sentiment, amorousness, free love, fondness, enjoyment, cherishing, tenderness, adoration, crush (D); see also **affection.**—*Ant.* hate*, aversion, antipathy.

2. [Affection based on esteem]—*Syn.* respect, regard, appreciation; see **admiration** 1.

3. [A lively and enduring interest]—*Syn.* involvement, concern, enjoyment; see **devotion.**

4. [A beloved]—*Syn.* dear one, loved one, cherished one; see **lover** 1.

fall in love (with)—*Syn.* begin to feel love (for), adore, be infatuated; see **fall in love.**

for love—*Syn.* as a favor, pleasurably, without payment; see **freely** 2.

for the love of—*Syn.* for the sake of, with fond concern for, because of; see **for.**

in love—*Syn.* enamored, infatuated, charmed, besotted; see **loving.**

make love—*Syn.* fondle, embrace, caress; see **love** 2.

not for love or money—*Syn.* under no conditions, by no means, no; see **never.**

with no love lost between—*Syn.* unkindly, vengefully, full of dislike; see **angrily.**

love, *v.* **1.** [To be passionately devoted]—*Syn.* adore, be in love with, care for, delight in, hold dear, choose, fancy, venerate, be enchanted by, be passionately attached to, have affection for, be enamored of, dote on, glorify, exalt, idolize, prize, put on a pedestal, hold in affection, deify, be fascinated by, hold high, canonize, think the world of, treasure, prefer, yearn for, esteem, be captivated *or* enraptured by, lose one's heart to, be fond of, admire, long for, be oneself with, thrive with; *all* (D): flip over, fall for, be nuts *or* crazy about, go for, have it bad, cotton to; see also **cherish** 1, **like** 2. —*Ant.* hate*, detest, loathe.

2. [To express love by caresses]—*Syn.* cherish, fondle, make much of, feast one's eyes on, embrace, cling to, clasp, hug, take into one's arms, hold, pet, soothe, stroke, encircle with one's arms, press to the heart, draw close, remain near to, bring to one's side, look tenderly at, look deeply into one's eyes; *all* (D): chase after, make a play for, shine up to, neck, pet, love up, make (love), make it; see also **caress, kiss, make love.**—*Ant.* exclude, spurn, refuse.

3. [To possess a deep and abiding interest]—*Syn.* enjoy, delight in, relish; see **admire** 1, **like** 1.

loved, *mod.*—*Syn.* desired, cherished, well beloved; see **beloved.**

loveless, *mod.* **1.** [Rejected]—*Syn.* disliked, forsaken, unloved; see **refused.**

2. [Heartless]—*Syn.* cold, hard, insensitive; see **cruel** 2, **ruthless** 1.

loveliness, *n.*—*Syn.* appeal, charm, fairness; see **beauty** 1.

lovely, *mod.* **1.** [Beautiful]—*Syn.* attractive, comely, fair; see sense 2, **beautiful** 1, 2, **handsome** 2.

2. [Charming]—*Syn.* engaging, enchanting, captivating; see **charming.**

3. [(D) Very pleasing]—*Syn.* nice, splendid, delightful; see **pleasant** 1, 2.

lover, *n.* **1.** [A suitor]—*Syn.* wooer, sweetheart, darling, dear, dearest, beloved, admirer, courter, escort, infatuate, paramour, fiancé, swain, inamorato, petitioner, suppliant, applicant, solicitor, entreater; *all* (D): gentleman friend, boyfriend, beau, flame, steady.

2. [A willing student or practitioner; *used only in phrases*]—*Syn.* dilettante, amateur, practitioner,

fan, hobbyist, fanatic, neophyte; see also **enthusiast** 1, **zealot.**
3. [An epithet for a beloved]—*Syn.* beloved, sweetheart, dear; see **darling** 2.

loving, *mod.* —*Syn.* admiring, respecting, valuing, liking, fond, tender, kind, enamored, attached, devoted, appreciative, having a good will toward, attentive, thoughtful, ardent, solicitous, amiable, warm, amorous, enamored, warm-hearted, affectionate, zealous for, anxious, concerned, sentimental, amatory, benign, earnest, benevolent, cordial, caring, considerate, loyal, generous; see also **friendly** 1, **passionate** 2.

lovingly, *mod.* —*Syn.* tenderly, devotedly, adoringly, warmly, ardently, fervently, zealously, earnestly, loyally, generously, kindly, considerately, thoughtfully, dotingly, fondly, affectionately, passionately, impassionedly, yearningly, longingly, endearingly, enrapturedly, rapturously, admiringly, respectfully, appreciatively, reverently, with friendship toward, with love, attentively.

low, *mod.* **1.** [Close to the earth]—*Syn.* squat, flat, level, low-lying, profound, decumbent, prostrate, crouched, below, ankle-high, not far above the horizon, low-hanging, lowering, knee-high, beneath, under, depressed, sunken, nether, inferior, unelevated, lying under; see also **deep** 1.—*Ant.* high*, lofty, elevated.
2. [Far down on a scale]—*Syn.* muffled, hushed, quiet; see **faint** 3.
3. [Low in spirits]—*Syn.* dejected, moody, blue (D); see **sad** 1.
4. [Vulgar]—*Syn.* base, mean, coarse; see **vulgar** 1.
5. [Faint]—*Syn.* ill, dizzy, feeble; see **sick, weak** 1.
6. [Simple]—*Syn.* economical, moderate, inexpensive; see **cheap** 1.
lay low—*Syn.* bring to ruin, overcome, kill; see **destroy** 1.
lie low—*Syn.* wait, conceal oneself, take cover; see **hide** 2.

lower, *v.* —*Syn.* scale down, demote, de-escalate, push down, bring low, set *or* let *or* cast down, ground, depress; see also **decrease** 1, 2, **drop** 2.

lowering, *mod.* —*Syn.* threatening, overhanging, menacing; see **ominous.**

lowest, *mod.* —*Syn.* shortest, littlest, smallest, slightest, bottom, rock-bottom, ground, base, undermost, nethermost; see also **least** 1, **minimum.**

low-grade, *mod.* —*Syn.* inferior, bad, second-rate (D); see **poor** 2.

low-key, *mod.* —*Syn.* subdued, restrained, understated, subtle, toned-down, relaxed, easygoing; *all* (D): laid-back, loose, soft-sell.

lowland, *n.* —*Syn.* bog, bottom land, marsh; see **swamp, valley.**

lowly, *mod.* —*Syn.* unpretentious, cast down, meek; see **humble** 2.

loyal, *mod.* —*Syn.* true, dependable, firm; see **faithful.**

loyalist, *n.* —*Syn.* supporter, follower, chauvinist; see **patriot.**

loyally, *mod.* —*Syn.* faithfully, conscientiously, trustworthily, devotedly, constantly, sincerely, obediently, resolutely, stanchly, earnestly, submissively, steadfastly, with fidelity *or* fealty *or* allegiance *or* constancy, in good faith; see also **truly** 2.

loyalty, *n.* —*Syn.* allegiance, submission, homage, fealty, faithfulness, subjection, fidelity, trustworthiness, constancy, integrity, attachment, trueness, sincerity, steadfastness, adherence, stanchness, adherence to duty, singleness of heart, bond, tie, group feeling, probity, uprightness, honor, reliability, (good) faith, incorruptibility, scrupulousness, conscientiousness, singlemindedness, inviolability, dependability, devotedness, support, zeal, ardor, earnestness, resolution, obedience, duty, *esprit de corps* (French), honesty, truthfulness; see also **devotion.**—*Ant.* disloyalty*, perfidy, faithlessness.

lozenge, *n.* —*Syn.* troche, capsule, pill; see **medicine** 2, **tablet** 3.

lubber, *n.* —*Syn.* rustic, clod, slob; see **boor, peasant.**

lubberly, *mod.* —*Syn.* clumsy, rough, crude; see **awkward** 1, **rude** 1, 2.

lubricant, *n.* —*Syn.* cream, ointment, oil; see **grease.**

lubricate, *v.* —*Syn.* oil, anoint, cream; see **grease.**

lubrication, *n.* —*Syn.* lubricating *or* greasing *or* oiling (service), oiling and greasing (up); *all* (D): lubing, lube (job), grease monkey job *or* service, grease job.

lucid, *mod.* **1.** [Clear to the sight]—*Syn.* pellucid, transparent, diaphanous; see **clear** 2, **obvious** 1.
2. [Clear to the understanding]—*Syn.* plain, evident, explicit; see **obvious** 2.
3. [Bright]—*Syn.* shining, resplendent, luminous; see **bright** 1.

lucidity, *n.* —*Syn.* clearness, purity, transparency; see **clarity.**

luck, *n.* **1.** [Good fortune]—*Syn.* good luck, prosperity, weal, wealth, favorable issue, fluke, master stroke, run *or* piece *or* streak of luck, windfall, advantage, profit, triumph, victory, kismet, karma, win, health, friends, happiness, blessings, godsend, opportunity, low probability, lucky break, occasion, turn of the wheel (of fortune); *all* (D): break, walkover, the breaks, smiles of fortune; see also **success** 2.—*Ant.* failure*, ill-fortune, bad luck.
2. [Chance]—*Syn.* unforeseen occurrence, hap, fate; see **accident** 2, **chance** 1.
crowd (*or* push) one's luck (D)—*Syn.* gamble, take risks, chance; see **risk.**
down on one's luck (D)—*Syn.* in misfortune, unlucky, discouraged; see **unfortunate** 2.
in luck—*Syn.* lucky, successful, prosperous; see **fortunate** 1.
out of luck—*Syn.* unlucky, in misfortune, in trouble; see **unfortunate** 2.
try one's luck—*Syn.* attempt, risk, endeavor; see **try** 1.
worse luck—*Syn.* unhappily, unluckily, unfavorably; see **unfortunately** 1.

luckily, *mod.* —*Syn.* opportunely, happily, favorably; see **fortunately**

luckless, *mod.* —*Syn.* cursed, hopeless, stricken; see **unfortunate** 2.

lucky, *mod.* **1.** [Enjoying good luck]—*Syn.* blessed, successful, prosperous; see **fortunate** 1.
2. [Characterized by good luck]—*Syn.* favorable, advantageous, serendipitous; see **hopeful** 2.

3. [Supposed to bring good luck]—*Syn.* providential, propitious, auspicious; see **magic** 1.
lucrative, *mod.* —*Syn.* fruitful, productive, gainful; see **profitable.**
lucre, *n.* —*Syn.* gain, spoils, profit; see **wealth** 2.
ludicrous, *mod.* —*Syn.* comical, odd, farcical; see **funny** 1.
lug, *v.* —*Syn.* carry, tug, lift; see **draw** 1.
luggage, *n.* —*Syn.* trunks, bags, valises; see **baggage.**
lugubrious, *mod.* —*Syn.* dismal, mournful, pensive; see **sad** 2.
lukewarm, *mod.* —*Syn.* cool, tepid, chilly; see **warm** 1.
lull, *n.* **1.** [A cessation of sound]—*Syn.* quiet, stillness, hush; see **silence** 1.
2. [A cessation of activity]—*Syn.* hiatus, calm, quiet; see **pause** 2.
lull, *v.* —*Syn.* calm, quiet down, bring *or* encourage repose; see **quiet** 1, 2.
lullaby, *n.* —*Syn.* good-night song, bedtime song, sleepsong; see **song.**
lumber, *n.* —*Syn.* cut timber, logs, sawed timber, forest products, boards, hardwood, softwood, lumbering products; see also **timber** 1, **tree, wood** 2.
Lumber includes the following—matched flooring, tongue and groove, matched siding, sheeting, shingle, trim, finish, lath, clapboard, walk board, timbers, tie, molding, plywood, welded wood, pressed wood, shake, scantling, two-by-four, two-by-six, two-by-eight, two-by-twelve, four-by-four, six-by-eight, one-by-four, one-by-six, one-by-twelve; see also **beam** 1.
Uses of lumber include the following—joist, rafter, plate, stringer, frame(s), ridge, planking, clapboarding, roofing, flooring, siding, studding, door, door jamb, tread.
Grades of lumber include the following—select, choice, clear, FAS *or* first and second clear, common, FAS common, cull.
lumbering, *mod.* —*Syn.* clumsy, blundering, overgrown; see **awkward** 1, **crude** 1, **heavy** 1.
lumbering, *n.* —*Syn.* timbering, felling trees, cutting logs, getting out lumber, cutting off *or* over, lumberjacking, milling, tree farming, sawing, logging; *all* (D): ground-hogging, donkey-setting, river-driving.
lumberjack, *n.* —*Syn.* lumberer, logger, lumber cutter, feller, trimmer, cruiser, scaler, skid man, rafter, topper, birler, choker, rigger, bucker, bellman; *all* (D): whistle punk, brush rat, bushwhacker, sawdust-eater; see also **laborer, woodsman, workman.**
lumberman, *n.* —*Syn.* logger, woodman, forester; see **laborer, lumberjack, woodsman, workman.**
luminary, *n.* **1.** [A light]—*Syn.* star, lamp, radiance; see **light** 3.
2. [A philosopher]—*Syn.* teacher, prophet, notable; see **intellectual, personage** 2.
luminescence, *n.* —*Syn.* fluorescence, fire, radiance; see **light** 1.
luminescent, *mod.* —*Syn.* glowing, luminous, radiant; see **bright** 1.
luminosity, *n.* —*Syn.* radiance, fluorescence, glow; see **light** 1.
luminous, *mod.* —*Syn.* lighted, glowing, radiant; see **bright** 1.
lump, *n.* —*Syn.* handful, protuberance, bunch, bump, agglomeration, block, bulk, chunk, piece, portion, section; see also **mass** 1, **part** 1.
get (*or* **take**) **one's lumps** (D)—*Syn.* be punished, undergo, receive punishment; see **suffer** 1.
in the lump—*Syn.* amassed, aggregated, collected; see **gathered.**
lumpish, *mod.* —*Syn.* heavy, clumsy, bungling; see **awkward** 1, **stupid** 1.
lumpy, *mod.* —*Syn.* knotty, clotty, uneven; see **irregular** 4, **thick** 1, 3.
lunacy, *n.* —*Syn.* madness, dementia, mania; see **insanity** 1.
lunate, *mod.* —*Syn.* semicircular, crescent-shaped, horned, crescent; see also **round** 1.
lunatic, *mod.* **1.** [Insane]—*Syn.* demented, deranged, psychotic; see **insane** 1.
2. [Foolish]—*Syn.* irrational, idiotic, daft; see **stupid** 1.
lunatic, *n.* —*Syn.* crazy person, demoniac, insane person; see **madman, neurotic.**
lunch, *n.* —*Syn.* meal, light repast, luncheon, refreshment, sandwich, snack, (high) tea.
lunch, *v.* —*Syn.* dine, have lunch, take a (lunch) break; see **eat** 1.
lunge, *n.* —*Syn.* plunge, jab, thrust; see **jump** 1, 2.
lunge, *v.* —*Syn.* surge, lurch, bound; see **jump** 1.
lurch, *v.* —*Syn.* stagger, weave, sway; see **reel.**
lure, *n.* —*Syn.* bait, decoy, fake; see **camouflage** 1, **trick** 1.
lure, *v.* **1.** [To draw]—*Syn.* attract, pull, haul; see **draw** 1.
2. [To entice]—*Syn.* enchant, bewitch, allure; see **charm** 1, **fascinate.**
lurid, *mod.* **1.** [Shocking]—*Syn.* startling, offensive, sensational; see **unusual** 2, **violent** 4.
2. [Vivid]—*Syn.* distinct, extreme, deep; see **bright** 2, **intense.**
lurk, *v.* —*Syn.* wait, crouch, conceal oneself; see **hide** 2, **sneak.**
lurking, *mod.* —*Syn.* hiding out, sneaking, hidden; see **hiding.**
luscious, *mod.* —*Syn.* sweet, toothsome, palatable; see **delicious** 1.
lush, *mod.* **1.** [Green]—*Syn.* verdant, dense, grassy; see **green** 2.
2. [Delicious]—*Syn.* rich, juicy, succulent; see **delicious** 1.
3. [Elaborate]—*Syn.* extensive, luxurious, ornamental; see **elaborate** 1, **ornate** 1.
lust, *n.* —*Syn.* appetite, passion, concupiscence; see **desire** 3.
lust (after), *v.* —*Syn.* long (for), desire, hunger *or* wish for; see **want** 1.
luster, *n.* **1.** [Brightness]—*Syn.* glow, brilliance, radiance; see **light** 1.
2. [Fame]—*Syn.* glory, respect, renown; see **fame** 1, **honor** 1.
lusterless, *mod.* —*Syn.* pale, colorless, drab; see **dull** 2.
lustful, *mod.* —*Syn.* lecherous, wanton, lascivious; see **lewd** 2, **sensual.**
lustrous, *mod.* —*Syn.* shiny, radiant, glowing; see **bright** 1.

lusty, *mod.*—*Syn.* hearty, robust, vigorous; see **healthy** 1.

luxuriant, *mod.*—*Syn.* lush, dense, rank; see **green** 2.

luxuriate, *v.* **1.** [To indulge]—*Syn.* overdo, indulge in, live extravagantly; see **prosper.**

2. [To flourish]—*Syn.* abound, increase, thrive; see **grow** 1.

luxurious, *mod.*—*Syn.* self-indulgent, voluptuous, comfortable, pleasurable, costly, gratifying, sybaritic, hedonistic, epicurean, sensuous, deluxe, sumptuous, self-pampering, languorous, languishing, easy, affluent, inordinate, immoderate, opulent, fit for a king, deeply comfortable, in the lap of luxury (D); see also **expensive, rich** 2, **sensual.** —*Ant.* poor*, ascetic, self-denying.

luxury, *n.* **1.** [Indulgence of the senses, regardless of the cost]—*Syn.* gratification, softness, costliness, expensiveness, richness, idleness, leisure, luxuriousness, high-living, prodigality, epicureanism, sybaritism, hedonism, lavishness; see also **enjoyment** 2, **indulgence** 3.—*Ant.* poverty*, poorness, lack.

2. [An indulgence beyond one's means]—*Syn.* expensive rarity, extravagance, intemperance, immoderation, unrestraint, exorbitance, wastefulness; *all* (D): high-flying, spree, splurging; see also **excess** 1, **waste** 1.

lyceum, *n.* **1.** [School]—*Syn.* secondary school, institute, private school; see **academy** 1, **school** 1.

2. [Hall]—*Syn.* gallery, lecture room, saloon; see **auditorium, hall** 1.

lying, *mod.* **1.** [In the act of lying]—*Syn.* falsifying, prevaricating, swearing falsely, committing perjury, fibbing, misstating, misrepresenting, inventing, dissimulating, equivocating, malingering. —*Ant.* frank*, truthful, veracious.

2. [Given to lying]—*Syn.* deceitful, unreliable, double-dealing; see **dishonest** 1, 2.

3. [Not reliable]—*Syn.* unsound, tricky, treacherous; see **false** 2, **unreliable** 2.

4. [Prostrate]—*Syn.* supine, reclining, jacent, resting, horizontal, procumbent, resupine, reposing, recumbent, flat, fallen, prone, crashed, dropped, tumbled, powerless.

lying down, *mod.*—*Syn.* reclining, reposing, sleeping; see **asleep, resting** 1.

lymphatic, *mod.*—*Syn.* indecisive, listless, dull; see **indifferent** 1, **unconcerned.**

lynch, *v.*—*Syn.* hang, mob, murder; see **kill** 1.

lynx-eyed, *mod.*—*Syn.* observant, attentive, aware; see **sharp-sighted.**

lyric, *n.* **1.** [A libretto]—*Syn.* opera text, words *or* story of the opera, words of a choral; see **libretto.**

2. [Verses set to music]—*Syn.* the words, the poem, the verse; see **poem.**

3. [A short, songlike poem]—*Syn.* lyrical poem, ode, sonnet, hymn, roundel; see also **poetry, song, verse** 1.

lyrical, *mod.*—*Syn.* emotional, expressive, songful, melodious, sweet, rhythmical; see also **musical** 1, **poetic.**

M

ma (D), *n.* —*Syn.* mama, *mater* (Latin), mom; see **mother.**

macabre, *mod.* —*Syn.* horrible, ghastly, grim; see **offensive** 2.

mace, *n.* **1.** [A weapon or symbol of authority] —*Syn.* staff, weapon, battle hammer; see **club** 3, **stick.**
2. [A compound]—*Syn.* Chemical Mace (trademark), fear gas, nerve gas; see **gas** 3, **weapon** 1.

machete, *n.* —*Syn.* sickle, steel, blade; see **knife, sword.**

Machiavellian, *mod.* —*Syn.* cunning, crafty, ambitious; see **sly** 1.

machination, *n.* —*Syn.* scheme, plot, ruse; see **plan** 2.

machine, *n.* **1.** [A mechanical contrivance]—*Syn.* instrument, implement, gadget; see **computer, device** 1, **engine** 1, **motor, press** 3, **tool** 1.
Types of machines include the following—hydraulic welder, steam welder, electric-motor welder, drill press, belt-driven press, hydraulic press, pillar press, pendulum press, steam hammer, drop hammer, radial drill, gang drill, die sinker, rough grinder, precision grinder, lathe-tool grinder, planer-tool grinder, jig borer, rip saw, crosscut saw, jigsaw, band saw, speed lathe, lathe-planer, engine lathe, turret lathe, automatic lathe, vertical lathe, crank planer, plate planer, shaper, slotter, broacher, milling machine, gear-cutting machine, die-threading machine, pipe-threading machine.
2. [(D) A political organization]—*Syn.* movement; *both* (D): ring, line-up; see **organization** 3.
3. [A person who resembles a machine]—*Syn.* automaton, grind, robot; see **drudge, laborer.**

machine, *v.* —*Syn.* tool, shape, plane, turn, drill, weld, die, grind, thread, bore, lathe; see also **manufacture** 1.

machine gun, *n.* —*Syn.* automatic rifle, semiautomatic rifle, automatic arms, light arms, light ordnance; *all* (D): Tommy gun, burp gun, Chicago mowing machine, put-put, stutterer, squirt gun; see also **gun** 1, 2, **weapon** 1.
Types of machine guns include the following—pom-pom, mitrailleuse, Garrand, M-14, M-16, M-60, Gatling gun, submachine gun, light 30-caliber machine gun, heavy 30-caliber machine gun, 50-caliber machine gun.
Makes of machine guns include the following—Bofors, Lewis, Chauchat, Thompson, Browning *or* BAR *or* Browning Automatic Rifle, Maxim, Vickers, Spaundau, Johnson, Nambu.

machinery, *n.* **1.** [Mechanical equipment]—*Syn.* appliances, implements, tools; see **appliance, device** 1, **engine, machine** 1, **motor.**
2. [Devices]—*Syn.* contrivances, shifts, plans, artifices; see also **device** 2, **means, method** 2.

machinist, *n.* —*Syn.* machine operator, engineer, skilled workman; see **mechanic, workman.**

macrocosm, *n.* —*Syn.* cosmos, nature, totality; see **universe, whole.**

macroscopic, *mod.* —*Syn.* visible, apparent to the naked eye, perceptible; see **obvious** 1.

mad, *mod.* **1.** [Insane]—*Syn.* demented, deranged, psychotic; see **insane** 1.
2. [Angry]—*Syn.* provoked, enraged, exasperated; see **angry.**
3. [Distraught]—*Syn.* distracted, frenetic, badly upset; see **excited** 1, **frantic.**
4. [Afflicted with rabies]—*Syn.* frenzied, raging, foaming at the mouth; see **rabid** 3.

madam, *n.* **1.** [A title of address]—*Syn.* Mrs., madame, dame, *Frau* (German), madonna, *signora* (Italian), *señora* (Spanish); *both* (D): ma'am, marm.
2. [A woman in charge of an establishment] —*Syn.* matron, housekeeper, housemother, (faculty) adviser, manageress; see also **administrator, hostess** 2.
3. [The mistress of a house of ill fame]—*Syn.* procuress, bawd, whore; see **prostitute.**

madcap, *mod.* —*Syn.* frivolous, foolish, wild; see **rash, stupid** 1.

madcap, *n.* —*Syn.* daredevil, desperado, adventuress; see **adventurer** 1.

madden, *v.* —*Syn.* craze, infuriate, enrage; see **anger** 1.

maddening, *mod.* —*Syn.* annoying, infuriating, offensive; see **disturbing.**

made, *mod.* —*Syn.* fashioned, shaped, finished; see **built** 1, **formed, manufactured.**
have (got) it made (D)—*Syn.* confident, secure, prosperous; see **successful.**

made easy, *mod.* —*Syn.* reduced, made plain, uncomplicated; see **easy** 2, **simplified.**

made over, *mod.* —*Syn.* remade, rebuilt, redecorated; see **improved** 1, **remodeled, repaired.**

made-up, *mod.* **1.** [False]—*Syn.* invented, prepared, fictitious; see **false** 2, 3, **unreal.**
2. [Marked by the use of make-up]—*Syn.* rouged, powdered, colored, freshened, reddened, cosmeticized.

made work, *n.* —*Syn.* work, employment, welfare; see **job** 1.

madhouse, *n.* —*Syn.* mental hospital, asylum, bedlam; see **hospital, sanitarium.**

madly, *mod.* **1.** [Insanely]—*Syn.* psychopathically, psychotically, irrationally; see **crazily** 1, **violently** 2.
2. [Wildly]—*Syn.* rashly, crazily, hastily; see **violently** 1, **wildly** 1.

madman, *n.* —*Syn.* lunatic, one who is mentally ill, maniac, raver, bedlamite, insane man, deranged person, psychiatric patient; *all* (D): Tom o'Bedlam, nut, cuckoo, psychotic, crazyman, screwball, oddball, psycho, stir-nut; see also **fool** 1, **psychopath.**

madness, *n.* —*Syn.* derangement, aberration, delusion; see **insanity** 1.

maelstrom, *n.* **1.** [Whirlpool]—*Syn.* vortex, undertow, eddy; see **storm** 1, **whirlpool.**

2. [Disturbance]—*Syn.* commotion, turmoil, fury; see **confusion** 2, **storm** 2.

magazine, *n.* **1.** [A storage chamber]—*Syn.* armory, ammunition storehouse, cache; see **arsenal, storehouse.**

2. [A periodical]—*Syn.* publication, broadside, pamphlet, booklet, manual, circular, brochure; see also **journal** 2, **review** 2.

Types of magazines include the following—critical review, literary review, weekly, monthly, bimonthly, quarterly, annual, supplement, digest, art magazine, picture *or* pictorial magazine, theatrical magazine, moving picture magazine, poetry magazine, news magazine, science fiction magazine, home magazine, scholarly *or* scientific *or* professional journal, outing magazine, women's magazine, men's magazine, fashion magazine, house organ, trade journal, mystery story magazine, western story magazine, horror story magazine, adventure story magazine, magazine of reprints, love story magazine, college magazine, humorous magazine, little magazine, fanzine, radio magazine; *all* (D): mag, rag, sheet, pulp, slick.

Famous magazines include the following—United States: Reader's Digest, Ebony, Time, Newsweek, U.S. News & World Report, Playboy, Saturday Review, Vogue, Glamor, McCall's, Fortune, Harper's Bazaar, Harper's, Atlantic Monthly, Holiday, New Republic, Nation, National Review, People, New York Times Magazine, New Yorker, Sports Illustrated, National Geographic, Field and Stream; Britain: New Statesman, Spectator, Economist, New Society, Nature, Encounter, London Illustrated News, Punch; France: Paris Match, La Revue, Réalités; Germany: Der Stern, Der Spiegel, Bunte, Illustrierte, Quick; U.S.S.R.: Kulturali Zhizn, Mezhnunarodnaia Zhizn, Novoe Vremia, Sovetskii Soyuz, Krokodil.

magenta, *n.* —*Syn.* maroon, fuchsia, vermilion; see **color** 1.

maggot, *n.* —*Syn.* grub, slug, larva; see **parasite** 1, **worm** 1.

maggoty, *mod.* —*Syn.* wormy, gone bad, tainted; see **infested, rancid** 1, **rotten** 1, 2.

magic, *mod.* **1.** [Occult]—*Syn.* sorcerous, wizardly, witchlike, Circean, Chaldean, thaumaturgic, theurgic, mystic, diabolic, Satanic, theurgical, necromantic, fiendish, demoniac, malevolent, shamanist, voodooistic, runic, conjuring, witching, spellbinding, enchanting, fascinating, cabalistic, cryptic, transcendental, supernatural, alchemistic, necromantic, spooky, ghostly, haunted, weird, uncanny, eldritch, eerie, numinous, spectral, apparitional, wraithlike, disembodied, discarnate, immaterial, ectoplasmic, astral, spiritualistic, mediumistic, psychic, phenomenological, magical, otherworldly, fairylike, mythical, mythic, amuletic, talismanic, phylacteric, tutelary, charmed, enchanted, bewitched, ensorcelled, tranced, entranced, charmed, fay, spellbound, under a spell *or* charm, under the evil eye, under a curse, cursed, mantological, prophetic, telepathic, clairvoyant, clairaudient, thought-reading, telekinetic, spirit-rapping, paranormal, parapsychological, metapsychological, hyperpsychological, hyperphysical; see also **mysterious** 2.

2. [Mysterious]—*Syn.* wonderful, miraculous, fantastical; see **imaginary, unusual** 2.

magic, *n.* **1.** [The controlling of supernatural powers]—*Syn.* occultism, legerdemain, thaumaturgy, necromancy, incantation, spell, wizardry, alchemy, bewitchery, superstition, enchantment, conjury, sorcery, sortilege, shamanism, prestidigitation, legerdemain, slight of hand, prophecy, divination, diabolism, vaticination, augury, astrology, horoscopy, taboo, witchcraft, astromancy, black magic, black art, voodooism, fire worship, *pishogue* (Irish), *myalism* (West Indian); see also **witchcraft.**

2. [An example of magic]—*Syn.* incantation, prediction, soothsaying, fortunetelling, presage, evil eye, presaging, foreboding, exorcism, ghost dance; see also **charm** 2, **divination, forecast.**

magical, *mod.* —*Syn.* occult, enchanting, mystic; see **magic** 1, **mysterious** 2.

magician, *n.* —*Syn.* enchanter, necromancer, conjurer, seer, soothsayer, diviner, evocator, sorceror, wizard, warlock, medicine man, talismanic, powwow, voodoo, Magian, Shaman, exorcist; see also **prophet, witch.**

magic lantern, *n.* —*Syn.* slide projector, tachistoscope, optical projector; see **projector.**

magisterial, *mod.* —*Syn.* domineering, judicial, authoritative; see **egotistic** 2, **impressive** 1.

magistrate, *n.* —*Syn.* justice, officer, police judge; see **judge** 1.

magnanimity, *n.* —*Syn.* benevolence, unselfishness, altruism; see **generosity** 1, **kindness** 1, 2.

magnanimous, *mod.* —*Syn.* high-minded, unselfish, great-hearted; see **generous** 2, **kind** 1, **noble** 1, 2.

magnate, *n.* **1.** [One powerful in a specific area] —*Syn.* industrialist, capitalist, tycoon; see **businessman, financier.**

2. [A person of rank or importance]—*Syn.* nobleman, notable, peer; see **aristocrat.**

magnet, *n.* —*Syn.* lodestone, magnetite, magnetic iron ore, natural magnet, artificial magnet, bar magnet, electromagnet, horseshoe magnet; see also **attraction** 2.

magnetic, *mod.* —*Syn.* irrestible, captivating, fascinating; see **inviting.**

magnetism, *n.* —*Syn.* lure, influence, charm; see **attraction** 1.

magnetize, *v.* —*Syn.* lure, charm, attract; see **draw** 1, **fascinate.**

magnificence, *n.* —*Syn.* grandeur, sublimity, exaltedness, majesty, stateliness, nobleness, impressiveness, glory, radiance, show, ostentation, grace, beauty, pulchritude, style, flourish, luxuriousness, glitter, nobility, greatness, loftiness, lavishness, brilliance, sumptuousness, splendor, ostentatiousness, richness, pomp, resplendency, spectacularity; *both*

(D): swank, posh; see also **elegance** 1, **plenty.** —*Ant.* dullness*, simplicity, unostentatiousness.

magnificent, *mod.* **1.** [Grand]—*Syn.* exalted, great, majestic; see **grand** 2.
2. [Gorgeous]—*Syn.* brilliant, radiant, glittering; see **luxurious, sumptuous.**
3. [Noble]—*Syn.* chivalric, magnanimous, high-minded; see **noble.**

magnificently, *mod.* —*Syn.* (very) well, superbly, gorgeously; see **splendidly.**

magnify, *v.* **1.** [To enlarge]—*Syn.* amplify, blow up, expand; see **increase** 1.
2. [To exaggerate]—*Syn.* overstate, intensify, embroider; see **exaggerate.**

magniloquence, *n.* —*Syn.* pomposity, bombast, grandiloquence; see **eloquence** 1, **speech** 2.

magnitude, *n.* **1.** [Size]—*Syn.* extent, breadth, dimension; see **measure** 1, **measurement** 2, **quantity, size** 2.
2. [Importance]—*Syn.* greatness, consequence, significance; see **degree** 2, **importance** 1.

magpie, *n.* **1.** [Gossip]—*Syn.* chatterer, windbag, idle talker; see **gossip** 2.
2. [Black bird]—*Syn.* crow, raven, jackdaw; see **bird** 1.

maid, *n.* **1.** [A female servant]—*Syn.* maidservant, *bonne* (French), *matranee* (Hindi), nursemaid, housemaid, domestic, cleaning woman, chambermaid, barmaid, charwoman; see also **servant.**
2. [A girl]—*Syn.* child, virgin, maiden, kid (D); see **girl** 1, **woman** 1.

maiden, *mod.* —*Syn.* earliest, beginning, virgin; see **first, virgin** 2.

maidenhood, *n.* —*Syn.* modesty, purity, virginity; see **chastity, innocence** 3.

maidenly, *mod.* —*Syn.* girlish, gentle, reserved; see **chaste** 2, **feminine** 2.

maiden name, *n.* —*Syn.* family *or* inherited name, surname, cognomen; see **name** 1.

maid of all work, *n.* —*Syn.* domestic, servant, housekeeper; see **maid** 1, **servant.**

maidservant, *n.* —*Syn.* waitress, domestic, housemaid; see **maid** 1, **servant.**

mail, *n.* —*Syn.* letter, post, communication, air-mail letter(s), postal, junk mail, post card, printed matter; see also **letter** 2, **post** 2.

mail, *v.* —*Syn.* post, send by post *or* mail, drop into a letter box; see **send** 1.

mailed, *mod.* —*Syn.* posted, sent by post, transmitted by post, in the mail, shipped, consigned, dispatched, sent by mail, dropped in the post office; see also **delivered, sent.**

mailing, *n.* —*Syn.* posting, airmailing, expressing, making up *or* getting out *or* handling *or* processing the mail *or* the post, getting the mail out, addressing, stamping, stuffing; see also **transportation.**

mailing list, *n.* —*Syn.* recipients, prospects, subscribers; see **list.**

mailman, *n.* —*Syn.* postman, carrier, mail carrier, letter carrier, mail clerk, R.F.D. carrier.

maim, *v.* —*Syn.* mutilate, mangle, cripple, incapacitate, disable, disfigure, injure, hack, truncate, impair, disqualify, damage, hurt, castrate, spoil, mar, blemish, deface, warp, dismember, hamstring; see also **damage** 1, **hurt** 1.

maimed, *mod.* —*Syn.* injured, damaged, wounded; see **hurt.**

main, *mod.* **1.** [Principal]—*Syn.* chief, foremost, leading; see **principal.**
2. [Only]—*Syn.* utter, pure, simple; see **absolute.**

main, *n.* —*Syn.* trunk, channel, trough; see **pipe** 1.

mainland, *n.* —*Syn.* shore, beach, dry land; see **continent, land** 1, **region** 1.
in the main—*Syn.* mainly, chiefly, mostly; see **principally.**

mainly, *mod.* —*Syn.* chiefly, largely, essentially; see **principally.**

mainspring, *n.* —*Syn.* heart, root, power; see **origin** 3.

mainstay, *n.* —*Syn.* pillar, backbone, strength; see **aid** 1.

maintain, *v.* **1.** [To uphold]—*Syn.* hold up, advance, keep; see **support** 2, **sustain** 1.
2. [To assert]—*Syn.* state, affirm, attest; see **declare** 1, **report** 1, **say.**
3. [To keep ready for use]—*Syn.* preserve, keep, conserve, repair, withhold, renew, cache, reserve, defer, hold back, have in store, keep on, care for, save, put away, set aside, store up, husband, keep for, keep prepared, lay aside *or* away, set by, keep on hand, keep in reserve, set apart, keep in condition *or* readiness, keep up, keep aside, control, hold over, manage, direct, have, own, sustain, secure, stick to, stand by; see also **prepare** 1.—*Ant.* waste*, neglect, consume.
4. [To continue]—*Syn.* carry on, persevere, keep up *or* on; see **continue** 1.
5. [To support]—*Syn.* provide *or* care for, take care of, keep; see **support** 5, **sustain** 2.

maintenance, *n.* **1.** [The act of maintaining] —*Syn.* keeping, sustaining, continuance, upholding, carrying; see also **preservation, support** 3, **subsistence** 1.
2. [The means of maintaining]—*Syn.* sustenance, livelihood, resources; see **pay** 1, 2, **subsistence** 2.

majestic, *mod.* —*Syn.* dignified, sumptuous, exalted; see **grand** 2, **noble** 1, 3.

majestically, *mod.* —*Syn.* grandly, royally, regally; see **wonderfully.**

majesty, *n.* **1.** [Grandeur]—*Syn.* nobility, illustriousness, greatness; see **grandeur.**
2. [The power of a ruler]—*Syn.* sovereignty, divine right, supremacy; see **power** 2.
3. [A form of address; *usually capital*]—*Syn.* Lord, King, Emperor, Prince, Royal Highness, Highness, Sire, Eminence, Queen; see also **title** 3.

major, *mod.* **1.** [Greater]—*Syn.* higher, larger, dominant, primary, upper, exceeding, extreme, ultra, over, above; see also **better** 2, **older, senior, superior.**
2. [Important]—*Syn.* significant, main, influential; see **important** 1, 2, **principal.**

major-domo, *n.* —*Syn.* butler, steward, retainer; see **servant.**

majority, *n.* **1.** [The larger part]—*Syn.* more than half, preponderance, greater number; see **bulk** 2.
2. [Legal maturity]—*Syn.* manhood, full age, adulthood, man's estate, prime of life, middle age, voting age.

make, *v.* **1.** [To manufacture]—*Syn.* construct, fabricate, produce; see **build** 1, **manufacture** 1.

2. [To total]—*Syn.* add up to, come to, equal; see **amount to.**
3. [To create]—*Syn.* originate, cause, conceive; see **compose** 3, **create** 2, **invent** 1, **produce** 2.
4. [To acquire]—*Syn.* gain, get, secure; see **obtain** 1.
5. [To force]—*Syn.* constrain, compel, coerce; see **force** 1.
6. [To reach]—*Syn.* progress, reach, arrive at; see **arrive** 1.
7. [To cause]—*Syn.* start, effect, initiate; see **begin** 1, **cause** 2.
8. [To appoint]—*Syn.* name, select, constitute; see **assign** 1, **delegate** 1, 2.
9. [To offer]—*Syn.* proffer, tender, advance; see **offer** 1.
10. [To wage]—*Syn.* carry on, conduct, engage in; see **wage.**
11. [To enact]—*Syn.* decree, legislate, establish; see **declare** 1, **enact** 1.
12. [To prepare]—*Syn.* get ready, arrange, adjust; see **cook, prepare** 1.
13. [To perform]—*Syn.* do, carry through, execute; see **perform** 1.
14. [To move]—*Syn.* proceed, advance, go; see **move** 1.
on the make (D)—*Syn.* belligerent, desirous, lustful; see **aggressive** 2.

make a clean sweep, *v.*—*Syn.* triumph, succeed, win everything; see **win** 1.

make after, *v.*—*Syn.* trail, follow, chase; see **pursue** 1.

make a joke of, *v.*—*Syn.* jest, make light of, josh; see **joke.**

make amends, *v.*—*Syn.* atone, make up for, compensate; see **reconcile** 2, **repay** 1, **settle** 9.

make as if *or* **as though,** *v.*—*Syn.* make believe, simulate, affect; see **pretend** 1.

make a speech, *v.*—*Syn.* give, present, deliver; see **address** 2.

make a trip, *v.*—*Syn.* tour, journey, trek; see **travel** 2.

make away with, *v.*—*Syn.* rape, carry off, abduct; see **steal.**

make-believe, *mod.*—*Syn.* pretended, fraudulent, acted; see **false** 3, **fantastic, unreal.**

make-believe, *n.*—*Syn.* sham, unreality, fairy tale; see **fancy** 2, **fantasy** 2, **pretense** 2.

make believe, *v.*—*Syn.* feign, simulate, counterfeit; see **dream** 2, **pretend** 1.

make certain (of), *v.*—*Syn.* make sure of, check into, find out, investigate; see also **examine** 1, **guarantee** 1.

make do, *v.*—*Syn.* employ, suffice, accept; see **endure** 2, **survive** 1, **use** 1.

make ends meet, *v.*—*Syn.* survive, subsist, get along; see **budget** 1, **estimate** 3, **manage** 1.

make eyes at, *v.*—*Syn.* wink at, flirt with, tease; see **flirt** 1.

make for, *v.*—*Syn.* aim for, travel to, go *or* head toward; see **advance** 1, **approach** 2.

make fun of, *v.*—*Syn.* tease, embarrass, mimic; see **bother** 2, **imitate** 2, **parody.**

make good, *v.* **1.** [To repay]—*Syn.* compensate, adjust, reimburse; see **pay** 1, **repay** 1.
2. [To justify]—*Syn.* maintain, support, uphold; see **justify** 2.
3. [To complete]—*Syn.* succeed, finish, accomplish; see **achieve** 1, **end** 1.
4. [To succeed]—*Syn.* arrive, pay off, prove oneself; see **pay** 2, **succeed** 1.

make headway, *v.*—*Syn.* progress, achieve, become better; see **advance** 1, **improve** 2.

make into, *v.*—*Syn.* transform, reform, alter; see **change** 1, **convert** 2, **revise.**

make it (D), *v.*—*Syn.* achieve, triumph, accomplish; see **succeed** 1.

make known, *v.*—*Syn.* tell, advise, announce; see **advertise** 1, **declare** 1, 2.

make like (D), *v.*—*Syn.* fake, feign, simulate; see **pretend** 1.

make love, *v.*—*Syn.* sleep with, unite sexually, have intercourse *or* sexual relations; see **copulate, join** 1, **love** 2.

make merry, *v.*—*Syn.* frolic, revel, enjoy; see **enjoy oneself, play** 1.

make much of, *v.* **1.** [To enlarge]—*Syn.* magnify, overstate, blow up (D); see **exaggerate.**
2. [To favor]—*Syn.* advance, tout, praise; see **encourage** 2, **favor** 1, 2, **promote** 1.

make of, *v.*—*Syn.* interpret, translate, understand; see **think** 1.

make off, *v.*—*Syn.* depart, run, go; see **leave** 1.

make off with, *v.*—*Syn.* abduct, rob, kidnap; see **steal.**

make out, *v.* **1.** [To understand]—*Syn.* perceive, recognize, see; see **understand** 1.
2. [To succeed]—*Syn.* accomplish, achieve, prosper; see **succeed** 1.
3. [(D) To kiss]—*Syn.* neck, fondle, pet; see **kiss.**
4. [To see]—*Syn.* discern, perceive, detect; see **discover** 1, **see** 1.
5. [To do moderately well]—*Syn.* manage, do well enough, get along; see **contrive** 2, **endure** 2.

make over, *v.* **1.** [To improve]—*Syn.* amend, correct, restore; see **improve** 1, **redecorate, remodel.**
2. [To transfer]—*Syn.* deliver, convey, pass; see **give** 1.
3. [To rebuild]—*Syn.* renovate, refashion, refurbish; see **repair** 1, **restore** 3.

make overtures, *v.*—*Syn.* woo, attend, pursue; see **court** 1.

make peace, *v.*—*Syn.* propitiate, negotiate, make up; see **reconcile** 2.

make progress, *v.*—*Syn.* go forward, progress, proceed; see **advance, improve** 2.

Maker, *n.*—*Syn.* The Creator, Omniscience, Providence; see **god.**

maker, *n.*—*Syn.* creator, producer, inventor; see **author** 1.

make ready, *v.*—*Syn.* arrange, get ready, prearrange; see **cook, prepare** 1.

make sense, *v.*—*Syn.* be reasonable *or* plausible *or* probable *or* intelligible *or* clear *or* lucid *or* understandable *or* logical *or* coherent, articulate, scan, add up, follow, infer, deduce, induct; *all* (D): hang together, hold water, put two and two together, pull oneself together, straighten up *or* out, stand to reason; see also **reason** 2, **think** 1.

makeshift, *mod.*—*Syn.* substitute, alternative, stopgap; see **temporary.**

makeshift, *n.* —*Syn.* stopgap, substitute, replacement; see **device** 1, 2.
make sport of, *v.* —*Syn.* tease, deride, mock; see **ridicule.**
make sure of, *v.* —*Syn.* ensure, determine, review; see **check** 3, **discover** 1.
make the most of, *v.* —*Syn.* take advantage (of), employ, promote; see **improve** 1, **use** 1.
make the rounds, *v.* —*Syn.* inspect, scrutinize, check up (on); see **examine** 1, **visit** 4.
make time, *v.* —*Syn.* gain, speed up, make good *or* fast *or* quick *or* rapid time; see **speed** 1, **travel.**
make uneasy, *v.* —*Syn.* disturb, upset, trouble; see **frighten** 1.
make-up, *n.* **1.** [Cosmetics]—*Syn.* grease paint, mascara, (eye) liner, clown white, burnt cork, Vaseline (trademark), powder, pomade, pomatum; see also **cosmetic.**
Types of make-up include the following—theatrical, straight, character, juvenile, middle age, old age, fantastic, grotesque, impressionist, expressionist, concert, mime.
2. [(D) Anything offered to make good a shortage] —*Syn.* atonement, compensation, conciliation; see **payment** 2, **reparation** 2.
3. [Composition]—*Syn.* scheme, scructure, arrangement; see **composition** 2, **design** 1, **formation** 1.
4. [The arrangement of printed matter]—*Syn.* layout, dummy, spread; see **order** 3, **plan** 1.
make up, *v.* **1.** [To compose]—*Syn.* compound, combine, mingle; see **join** 1, **mix** 1.
2. [To constitute]—*Syn.* comprise, include, consist of; see **compose** 1.
3. [To invent]—*Syn.* fabricate, devise, fashion; see **compose** 3, **create** 2, **invent** 1, 2.
4. [To provide]—*Syn.* furnish, fill, supply; see **provide** 1.
5. [To reconcile]—*Syn.* conciliate, pacify, accommodate; see **reconcile** 2.
6. [To apply cosmetics]—*Syn.* powder, rouge; apply face powder *or* lipstick *or* eyeshadow *or* eye make-up, etc.; beautify, do up (D).
make up for, *v.* —*Syn.* compensate, balance, counter-balance; see **offset.**
make up (one's) mind, *v.* —*Syn.* choose, pick, elect; see **decide, resolve.**
make up to (D), *v.* —*Syn.* flatter, cater to, humor; see **grovel, praise** 1.
make use of, *v.* —*Syn.* need, employ, utilize; see **use** 1.
make war, *v.* —*Syn.* battle, combat, encounter; see **fight** 2.
make way, *v.* —*Syn.* progress, proceed, break ground *or* trail (D); see **advance** 1.
make with (D), *v.* **1.** [To give]—*Syn.* hand over, deliver, part with; see **give** 1.
2. [To do]—*Syn.* put on, act, carry out; see **perform** 1.
3. [To display]—*Syn.* present, exhibit, show; see **display** 1.
making, *mod.* **1.** [Preparing]—*Syn.* forming, fashioning, manufacturing, producing, fabricating, constructing, forging, turning out, executing, effecting, shaping, building, creating, accomplishing, generating, originating, composing.
2. [Totaling]—*Syn.* computing, constituting, reckoning, concluding, consisting (of), aggregating, summing, adding up to, producing, arriving at, completing.
making, *n.* —*Syn.* imagination, conception, formulation, devising, fancying, producing, constituting, occasioning, causation, performing, fashioning, building, origination, shaping, forging, designing, planning, fabrication, composition, authoring, contriving; see also **construction** 1, **production** 1.
maladministration, *n.* —*Syn.* mismanagement, misrule, incompetency; see **disorder** 2.
maladroit, *mod.* —*Syn.* clumsy, gauche, inept; see **awkward** 1.
malady, *n.* —*Syn.* ailment, sickness, illness; see **disease** 1, 2.
malaise, *n.* —*Syn.* uneasiness, discomfort, despair; see **depression** 2, **pain** 1.
malapert, *mod.* —*Syn.* bold, impudent, presumptuous; see **rude** 2.
malapropos, *mod.* —*Syn.* out of place, inexpedient, irrelevant; see **unfit** 2, **untimely.**
malaria, *n.* —*Syn.* malarial fever, sickness, jungle fever (D); see **disease** 3.
malarious, *mod.* —*Syn.* fetid, unwholesome, noxious; see **harmful, poisonous.**
malcontent, *mod.* —*Syn.* disobedient, restless, discontented; see **rebellious** 2, 3, **unruly.**
malcontent, *n.* —*Syn.* anarchist, extremist, dissenter; see **agitator, radical.**
male, *mod.* —*Syn.* masculine, manlike, manful, virile, macho, vigorous, powerful, stouthearted, potent, forceful, courageous, sturdy, tenacious; see also **manly.**—*Ant.* feminine*, unmanly, effeminate.
male, *n.* —*Syn.* male sex, man-child, he; see **boy, father.**
malediction, *n.* —*Syn.* imprecation, denunciation, damnation; see **curse.**
malefactor, *n.* —*Syn.* evildoer, wrongdoer, transgressor, convict, villain, rascal, scoundrel, hellhound, wretch, jailbird, culprit, delinquent, outlaw, felon, murderer, scamp, scapegrace, outcast, vagabond, varlet, rapscallion, rogue, ruffian, black sheep, hoodlum, sinner, *larrikin* (Australian); *all* (D): tough, rough, rowdy, rounder, bad egg, holy terror, thug, bum, bad actor, tough bunny, gorilla, rubber-outer; see also **criminal.**
malevolence, *n.* —*Syn.* ill will, enmity, indignity; see **evil** 1, **hate, hatred** 1, 2, **malice, resentment** 1, 2.
malevolent, *mod.* —*Syn.* spiteful, malicious, evil; see **wicked** 1, 2.
malfeasance, *n.* —*Syn.* wrongdoing, misbehavior, impropriety; see **mischief** 3.
malformation, *n.* —*Syn.* distortion, abnormality, deformity; see **contortion** 1.
malformed, *mod.* —*Syn.* distorted, grotesque, abnormal; see **deformed, twisted** 1.
malfunction, *n.* —*Syn.* slip, bad *or* faulty performance, failure to work *or* function *or* perform, etc.; see **failure** 1.
malice, *n.* —*Syn.* spite, rancor, animosity, ill-feeling, hostility, grudge, implacability, bitterness, antipathy, umbrage, repugnance, dislike, resentment, venom, acerbity, mordacity, malignance,

malignity, bad blood, viciousness; *all* (D): pure cussedness, dirt, cat bite; see also **evil** 1, **hatred** 1, 2. —*Ant.* kindness*, benevolence, goodness.

malicious, *mod.* —*Syn.* ill-disposed, spiteful, hateful; see **wicked** 1, 2.

malign, *v.* —*Syn.* accuse, misrepresent, scandalize; see **censure, curse** 2, **insult, slander.**

malignancy, *n.* —*Syn.* fatality, virulence, hatred; see **malice.**

malignant, *mod.* **1.** [Diseased]—*Syn.* cancerous, fatal, lethal, deadly, poisonous, destructive, internecine, mortal, pestilential; see also **deadly, poisonous.**

2. [Harmful]—*Syn.* deleterious, corrupt, sapping; see **dangerous** 1, 2, **harmful.**

maligned, *mod.* —*Syn.* reviled, scorned, rejected; see **abused.**

malignity, *n.* **1.** [Fatality]—*Syn.* deadliness, virulence, noxiousness; see **fatality.**

2. [Hostility]—*Syn.* hostility, envy, spite; see **hate, hatred** 1, 2, **malice, resentment** 1, 2.

mall, *n.* —*Syn.* court, walk, lane; see **lawn, park** 1, **road** 1.

malleable, *mod.* —*Syn.* pliant, tractable, manageable; see **flexible** 1.

mallet, *n.* —*Syn.* maul, mall, club; see **hammer.**

malnutrition, *n.* —*Syn.* scurvy, consumption, rickets; see **hunger, illness** 1, **starvation.**

malodorous, *mod.* —*Syn.* infested, stinking, rancid; see **rank** 2, **rotten** 1.

malpractice, *n.* —*Syn.* negligence, misbehavior, neglect; see **carelessness, violation** 1.

malt, *n.* —*Syn.* slops, malt liquor, ale; see **beer.**

maltreat, *v.* —*Syn.* injure, damage, ill-treat; see **abuse** 1, **hurt** 1.

maltreatment, *n.* —*Syn.* punishment, injury, injustice; see **abuse** 3, **violation** 2.

mama, *n.* —*Syn.* female progenitor, mamma, parent; see **mother** 1.

mammal, *n.* —*Syn.* vertebrate, creature, beast; see **animal** 1.

mammoth, *mod.* —*Syn.* gigantic, immense, enormous; see **high** 1, **large** 1, **long** 1, 2.

mammy, *n.* **1.** [A negro nurse]—*Syn.* negress; *both* (D): black mammy, aunty; see **nurse** 3.

2. [(D) Mother]—*Syn.* female parent, mom, mama; see **mother** 1.

man, *n.* **1.** [The human race]—*Syn.* men and women, mankind, humankind, human beings, race, humanity, human species, human nature, persons, mortals, populace, individuals, earthlings, civilized society, *Homo faber* (Latin), creatures, fellow creatures, people, folk, society, *Homo sapiens* (Latin); see also **hominid.**

2. [An adult male]—*Syn.* he, gentleman, Sir, Mr., esquire, swain, fellow, blade, yeoman, mister, master, beau; *all* (D): chap, guy, buck; see also **boy.**

3. [Anyone]—*Syn.* human being, an individual, fellow creature; see **person** 1.

4. [Male quality]—*Syn.* manliness, manhood, bravery, resolution, forcefulness, machismo, aggression, tenacity; see also **courage** 1.

5. [(D) Husband]—*Syn.* married man, spouse, partner; see **husband.**

as a man—*Syn.* in unison, united, all together; see **unanimously.**

be one's own man—*Syn.* be independent, stand alone, be free; see **endure** 1.

man and boy (D)—*Syn.* all of a man's life, a lifetime, a long time; see **boy, man** 2.

to a man—*Syn.* all, everyone, with no exception; see **everybody.**

man, *v.* —*Syn.* garrison, protect, fortify; see **defend** 1, **guard** 2.

manacle, *n.* —*Syn.* handcuffs, irons, fetters; see **band** 2, **chains.**

manage, *v.* **1.** [To direct]—*Syn.* lead, oversee, indicate, designate, instruct, mastermind, engineer, show, carry on, disburse, distribute, execute, handle, watch, guide, supervise, conduct, engage in, officiate, pilot, steer, minister, regulate, administer, manipulate, officiate, superintend, preside, recommend, suggest, advocate, counsel, request, call upon, admonish, maintain, care for, take over, take care of, carry on, watch over, have in one's charge, look after, see to, urge, inspect, animate, propose; *all* (D): occupy the chair, run the show, hold down, call the shots, take the helm, run a tight ship; see **advise** 1, **command** 2.—*Ant.* obey*, follow, take orders.

2. [To contrive]—*Syn.* accomplish, bring about, effect; see **achieve** 1, **contrive** 2, **succeed** 1.

3. [To get along]—*Syn.* bear up, survive, scrape *or* get by (D); see **endure** 2.

manageable, *mod.* —*Syn.* controllable, docile, compliant, pliant, governable, teachable, tractable, willing, obedient, submissive, yielding, adaptable, flexible, dutiful, humble, meek, easy, soft, malleable; see **gentle** 3, **obedient** 1, **willing** 2.—*Ant.* rebellious*, ungovernable, unruly.

managed, *mod.* **1.** [Trained]—*Syn.* handled, guided, persuaded, influenced, driven, counseled, urged, taught, instructed, coached; *all* (D): groomed, primed, shined *or* tuned up, trained fine, given a workout; see **educated** 1, **trained.**—*Ant.* wild*, undisciplined, uneducated.

2. [Governed]—*Syn.* ruled, controlled, dominated, commanded, directed, swayed, mastered, run, regulated, ordered, compelled, supervised, piloted, cared for, taken care of; see **governed** 1, 2.—*Ant.* ungoverned, free*, unsupervised.

management, *mod.* —*Syn.* business, governmental, supervisory; see **administrative, official.**

management, *n.* **1.** [Direction]—*Syn.* supervision, superintendence, control; see **administration** 1, **command** 2.

2. [Those who undertake management; *usually preceded by* the]—*Syn.* directors, administrators, executives; see **administration** 2, **authority** 3.

manager, *n.* —*Syn.* director, handler, superintendent, supervisor; see **administrator.**

managing, *mod.* —*Syn.* directing, supervising, superintending, advising, admonishing, overseeing, controlling, guiding, operating, taking charge of, caring for, husbanding, administering, executing, organizing, regulating, inspecting, leading, piloting, steering, handling, charging, manipulating; see also **governing.**

mandate, *n.* —*Syn.* command, decree, behest, order, commission, fiat, charge; see **command** 1.

mandated, *mod.* —*Syn.* administered, assigned, ordered, commanded, decreed, charged, dictated, proclaimed, summoned, requisitioned, bid.

mandatory, *mod.* —*Syn.* compulsory, forced, obligatory; see **necessary** 1.

mandible, *n.* —*Syn.* mouth, lower jaw, jawbone; see **bone, jaw** 1.

mane, *n.* —*Syn.* brush, ruff, fringe; see **fur, hair** 1.

man-eater, *n.* —*Syn.* vampire, anthropophage, carnivore; see **cannibal, savage.**

man-eating, *mod.* —*Syn.* cannibal, carnivorous, creophagous; see **dangerous** 1, 2, **deadly, ferocious, murderous.**

maneuver, *n.* **1.** [A movement, usually military] —*Syn.* stratagem, movement, procedure; see **plan** 2, **tactics.**
2. [A trick]—*Syn.* subterfuge, finesse, ruse; see **trick** 1.
3. [Extensive practice in arms; *plural*]—*Syn.* sham battle, imitation war, exercises, war games, summer maneuvers; see **drill** 3, **exercise** 1, **parade** 1.

maneuver, *v.* —*Syn.* plot, scheme, machinate, intrigue, move, finesse, manage, contrive, design, devise, trick, cheat, conspire, shift, sham, proceed; *both* (D): angle for, wangle into; see **plan** 1.

maneuverer, *n.* —*Syn.* operator, manager, wheeler-dealer (D); see **agent** 1, **diplomat** 2, **politician** 1, 3.

mange, *n.* —*Syn.* rash, scales, eruption, psoriasis, eczema, skin disease, scabies, scab, scurvy, sores; see also **disease** 3.

manger, *n.* **1.** [A feed rack]—*Syn.* rack, trough, receptacle, feed box, crib; see **bin, storehouse.**
2. [The birthplace of Christ]—*Syn.* Bethlehem, crèche, stable, cradle, Holy Cradle, the lowly cattle shed, the oxen's stall; see **bed** 1.

mangle, *n.* —*Syn.* press, machine, household appliance, electric ironer; see **iron** 3.

mangle, *v.* **1.** [To mutilate]—*Syn.* tear, lacerate, wound, injure, cripple, maim, rend, hamstring, disfigure, cut, slay, flay, slit, hash, butcher, slash, slice, carve, bruise, separate, mutilate; see **break** 2, **damage** 1, **destroy** 1.
2. [To iron with a power roller]—*Syn.* steam press, smooth, iron; see **press** 2.

mangy, *mod.* **1.** [Scabby]—*Syn.* psoriatic, rashy, scabby; see **dirty** 1, **sick.**
2. [Poverty-stricken]—*Syn.* impoverished, shabby, indigent; see **poor** 2, **squalid.**

manhandle, *v.* —*Syn.* damage, maul, mistreat; see **abuse** 1, **beat** 2.

man-hater, *n.* —*Syn.* misanthropist, solitary, eremite; see **hermit, misanthrope.**

manhole, *n.* —*Syn.* vent, scuttle, hatch; see **hole** 2, **sewer.**

manhood, *n.* **1.** [Male maturity]—*Syn.* post-pubescence, coming of age, adulthood; see **majority** 2.
2. [Manly qualities]—*Syn.* virility, valor, resoluteness, honor, gallantry, nobility, forcefulness, machismo, daring, chivalry, boldness, tenacity, potency, sturdiness, self-reliance, tenderness, gentleness; see **courage** 1, **strength** 1.

mania, *n.* —*Syn.* craze, lunacy, madness; see **desire** 1, **insanity** 1, **obsession.**

maniac, *n.* —*Syn.* lunatic, insane person, crazy man; see **madman, psychopath.**

maniacal, *mod.* —*Syn.* raving, mad, deranged; see **insane** 1.

manicure, *v.* —*Syn.* trim, beautify, cut, polish, color, shape; see **trim** 1.

manifest, *mod.* —*Syn.* clear, visible, unmistakable; see **obvious** 1, 2.

manifest, *v.* **1.** [To display]—*Syn.* show, exhibit, disclose; see **display** 1, **expose** 1, **reveal** 1.
2. [To evidence]—*Syn.* confirm, declare, demonstrate; see **prove.**

manifestation, *n.* —*Syn.* phenomenon, explanation, indication; see **meaning, sign** 1.

manifesto, *n.* —*Syn.* publication, decree, proclamation; see **announcement** 1.

manifold, *mod.* —*Syn.* various, numerous, diverse; see **complex** 1, **different** 2.

manikin, *n.* —*Syn.* puppet, marionette, figure; see **doll, model** 3, 4.

manipulate, *v.* —*Syn.* handle, shape, mold; see **form** 1, **manage** 1, **plan** 1.

manipulation, *n.* —*Syn.* guidance, use, direction; see **administration** 1.

manipulator, *n.* —*Syn.* director, mastermind, liaison *or* personnel man; see **administrator.**

mankind, *n.* —*Syn.* humanity, human race, society; see **man** 1.

manlike, *mod.* —*Syn.* anthropoid, simian, anthropomorphic; see **human.**

manliness, *n.* —*Syn.* masculinity, manlikeness, virility; see **courage** 1, **manhood** 2, **strength** 1.

manly, *mod.* —*Syn.* masculine, courageous, undaunted, fearless, firm, staunch, dignified, stately, noble, valiant, valorous, high-spirited, plucky, lion-hearted, intrepid, gallant, resolute, bold, macho, audacious, stout-hearted, confident, self-reliant; see also **brave** 1.—*Ant.* cowardly*, timid, effeminate.

man-made, *mod.* —*Syn.* manufactured, artificial, unnatural, counterfeit, not genuine; see also **false** 3, **synthetic** 2.

manna, *n.* —*Syn.* nourishment, sustenance, maintenance; see **bread, food, subsistence** 1.

manner, *n.* **1.** [Personal conduct]—*Syn.* mien, deportment, demeanor; see **behavior** 1.
2. [Customary action]—*Syn.* use, way, practice; see **custom** 1, 2, **habit** 1.
3. [Method]—*Syn.* mode, fashion, style; see **method** 2.
by all manner of means—*Syn.* certainly, of course, without doubt; see **surely.**
by any manner of means—*Syn.* in any way, at all, however; see **anyhow** 2.
by no manner of means—*Syn.* in no way, not at all, definitely not; see **never.**
in a manner of speaking—*Syn.* in a way, so to speak, so to say; see **rather.**
to the manner born—*Syn.* naturally fit, suited, accustomed from birth; see **able** 1.

mannered, *mod.* —*Syn.* artificial, self-conscious, posed; see **affected** 2.

mannerism, *n.* —*Syn.* idiosyncrasy, pretension, peculiarity; see **characteristic, quirk.**

mannerly, *mod.* —*Syn.* polished, considerate, charming; see **polite** 1.

manners, *n.* **1.** [Personal behavior]—*Syn.* conduct, deportment, bearing; see **behavior** 1.

2. [Culture]—*Syn.* urbanity, taste, refinement; see **courtesy** 1, **culture** 3, **dignity** 1, **elegance** 1, **sophistication.**

mannish, *mod.* —*Syn.* manlike, manful, masculine; see **manly.**

man-of-all-work, *n.* —*Syn.* jack-of-all-trades, handyman, servant, factotum, caretaker, servant, seneschal; *both* (D): major-domo, do-all; see also **laborer, workman.**

man of means, *n.* —*Syn.* capitalist, tycoon, rich man; see **financier, millionaire.**

man-of-war, *n.* —*Syn.* battleship, destroyer, naval vessel; see **ship, warship.**

manor, *n.* —*Syn.* manor house, mansion, hotel; see **estate** 1, **hotel.**

manor house, *n.* —*Syn.* lodge, villa, mansion; see **home** 1, **hotel.**

manpower, *n.* —*Syn.* youth, men of military age, males; see **labor** 4.

manse, *n.* —*Syn.* rectory, vicarage, minister's residence; see **parsonage.**

manservant, *n.* —*Syn.* valet, steward, attendant; see **servant.**

mansion, *n.* —*Syn.* villa, house, hall; see **estate** 1, **home** 1.

manslaughter, *n.* —*Syn.* killing, homicide, assassination; see **crime** 2, **murder.**

manslayer, *n.* —*Syn.* assassin, murderer, gangster; see **criminal, killer.**

mantel, *n.* —*Syn.* fireplace, mantelpiece, chimney piece; see **shelf.**

mantilla, *n.* —*Syn.* kerchief, scarf, lace covering; see **veil.**

manual, *mod.* —*Syn.* by hand, hand-operated, not automatic, standard; see also **old-fashioned.**

manual, *n.* —*Syn.* guidebook, reference book, textbook, exercise book, manual of arms; see also **handbook, text** 1.

manufacture, *n.* —*Syn.* fashioning, forming, assembling; see **production** 1.

manufacture, *v.* **1.** [To make a product]—*Syn.* make, construct, fabricate, produce, form, fashion, carve, mold, cast, frame, put together, forge, turn out, stamp out, print out, cut out, have in production *or* on the assembly line, print, erect, shape, execute, accomplish, complete, tool, machine, mill, make up, reduce; see **assemble** 3, **build** 1.—*Ant.* destroy*, demolish, tear down.

2. [To devise from almost nothing]—*Syn.* make up, fabricate, contrive; see **create** 2, **invent** 1, **produce** 2.

manufactured, *mod.* —*Syn.* made, produced, constructed, fabricated, erected, fashioned, shaped, forged, turned out, tooled, machined, executed, done, assembled, ready for the market, in shape, complete, completed, fresh off the assembly line (D); see **built** 1, **formed.**

manufacturer, *n.* —*Syn.* maker, producer, fabricator, constructor, builder, operator, smith, forger, artificer, craftsman, corporation, entrepreneur, company; see **business** 4.

manufacturing, *mod.* —*Syn.* producing, industrial, fabricative; see **making** 1.

manufacturing, *n.* —*Syn.* fabrication, building, construction, assembling, casting, tooling, preparing for market, putting in production, continuing *or* keeping in production *or* on the assembly line, mass production, forging, formation, erection, composition, composing, accomplishment, completion, finishing, doing, turning out; see **making, production** 1.—*Ant.* destruction, wreck*, demolition*.

manumit, *v.* —*Syn.* liberate, emancipate, release; see **free** 1.

manure, *n.* —*Syn.* guano, plant-food, compost; see **dung, fertilizer.**

manuscript, *n.* —*Syn.* composition, papyrus, parchment, vellum, tablet, stone, paper, document, original, copy, typescript, scroll, letterpress, autograph, translation, facsimile, palimpsest, book, piece of music, typewritten copy, script; see **writing** 2.

Famous manuscripts include the following—*Syn.* Bankes Homer, Harris Homer, Codex Argentus of Ulfilas, the Vatican Virgils, Codex Vaticanus (Bible), Codex Sinaiticus (Bible), Codex Alexandrinus (Bible), Dead Sea Scrolls, Laurentian Herodotus, Gospels of Vercelli, Charter of King Edgar, Iliad of the Ambrosian, Lindesfarne Gospels, the Book of Deir, the Book of Kells, the Book of the Dun Cow, Gospel Book of Charlemagne, Paris Psalter, Oxford Euclid, Oxford Plato, Cotton Vitellius A-15 (Beowulf), Ellesmere Manuscript (Canterbury Tales), Finnsburg Fragment, the Book of the Dead, Rosetta Stone, Widner Eve of St. Agnes.

many, *mod.* —*Syn.* numerous, multiplied, manifold, multifold, multitudinous, multifarious, multiplex, diverse, divers, sundry, profuse, innumerable, not a few, numberless, a world of, countless, uncounted, untold, alive with, teeming, in heaps, several, of every description, prevalent, no end of *or* to, everywhere, thick (with), crowded, common, usual, plentiful, abundant; *all* (D): galore, lousy with, bursting out all over; see **multiple** 1, **various.**—*Ant.* few*, meager, scanty.

many, *n.* —*Syn.* a great number, abundance, thousands (D); see **plenty.**

a good *or* **(great) many**—*Syn.* a great number, abundance, thousands; see **plenty.**

as many (as)—*Syn.* as much (as), an equal number, a similar amount; see **same.**

be one too many for—*Syn.* overwhelm, overcome, beat down; see **defeat** 1, 2.

many-colored, *mod.* —*Syn.* varicolored, kaleidoscopic, prismatic; see **bright** 2, **multicolored.**

many-sided, *mod.* **1.** [Multilateral]—*Syn.* polyhedral, geometric, bilateral, polyhedrous, dihedral, trilateral, quadrilateral, tetrahedral; see **geometrical.**

2. [Gifted]—*Syn.* endowed, talented, adaptable; see **able** 1, 2, **versatile.**

map, *n.* —*Syn.* chart, graph, plat, sketch, diagram, projection, delineation, drawing, picture, portrayal, draft, tracing, outline, ground plan; see **plan** 1.

Types of maps include the following—topographical, relief, model, political, isothermic *or* isothermal, isobaric, contour, gravity, industrial, military, geodetic, marine, weather, road, railroad, cartographic, cartogramic, ichnogramic, air, aerial; globe.

put on the map (D)—*Syn.* make famous, bring fame to, glorify; see **establish** 2.

wipe off the map (D)—*Syn.* eliminate, put out of existence, ruin; see **destroy** 1.
map, *v.* —*Syn.* outline, draft, chart; see **plan** 2.
mar, *v.* **1.** [To damage slightly]—*Syn.* harm, bruise, scratch; see **break** 2, **damage** 1.
2. [To impair]—*Syn.* deform, deface, warp; see **destroy** 1.
maraud, *v.* —*Syn.* plunder, rape, pillage; see **attack** 1, **raid, ravage.**
marauder, *n.* —*Syn.* raider, privateer, thief; see **pirate, robber.**
marauding, *mod.* —*Syn.* thieving, ravaging, extortionate; see **rapacious** 2.
marble, *mod.* **1.** [Composed of marble]—*Syn.* marmoreal, adamant, flinty, vitreous, horny, corneus, bony, osseous, petrified, granitelike, unyielding, indurated; see **rock** 1, **stone.**
2. [Giving the effect of marble]—*Syn.* marbled, mottled, marmoreal, veined, flecked, striated, barred, striped, watered, pied, variegated, mosaic, diapered.
marble, *n.* **1.** [Metamorphic limestone]
Marbles include the following—Parian, Pentelic, Carrara, Carrian, Serpentine, Algerian, Tecali (onyx marbles), Siena *or* Tuscan, Gibraltar, Vermont, Georgia, fire, black, rance, cipolin, giallo antico, brocatello, verdantique, ophicalcite; see **stone.**
2. [A piece of carved marble]—*Syn.* carving, figurine, figure; see **art** 2, **sculpture, statute.**
3. [A ball used in marbles]—*Syn. all* (D): marb, nib, ivory, mig, shooter, ante, bait; see **toy** 1.
marbles, *n.* —*Syn. all* (D): marbs, nibs, funs, keeps, taw, date up, ante up; see **game** 1.
March, *n.* —*Syn.* spring month, beginning of spring, Lent, windy month, month that comes in like a lion and goes out like a lamb; see **month, spring** 2.
march, *n.* **1.** [The act of marching]—*Syn.* progression, movement, advancing, advancement, double march, countermarch, goose step, military parade, quick step, double time, quick march, route march; see **step** 1, **walk** 3.
2. [The distance or route marched]—*Syn.* walk, trek, hike; see **journey, route** 2.
3. [Music for marching]—*Syn.* martial music, wedding march, processional; see **music.**
march, *v.* —*Syn.* move, advance, step out, go on, proceed, space, step, tread, tramp, journey, stroll, saunter, patrol, prowl, walk, promenade, parade, goose-step, file, mount a patrol, range, strut, maintain contact, proceed, progress, go ahead, file off, do the lock step, forge ahead; see **travel** 2, **walk** 1. —*Ant.* pause*, halt, retreat.
on the march—*Syn.* proceeding, advancing, tramping; see **marching.**
steal a march on (D)—*Syn.* outdo, gain an advantage over, overcome; see **surpass.**
marching, *mod.* —*Syn.* advancing, parading, filing, proceeding, tramping, hiking, pacing, stepping, double-marching, patrolling, policing, checking, in motion, being brought up, en route, retreating, being flown in *or* out, quick-marching, route-marching; see **moving** 1, **traveling** 2, **walking.**
Mardi Gras, *n.* —*Syn.* fat *or* Shrove Tuesday, last day of carnival *or* of Folly *or* before Lent, carnival, festival in New Orleans; see **Easter, holiday, spring** 2.
mare, *n.* —*Syn.* female horse, brood mare, breeding stock; see **animal** 2, **horse.**
mare's-nest, *n.* —*Syn.* deception, hoax, lie; see **trick** 1.
margin, *n.* —*Syn.* border, lip, shore; see **boundary, edge** 1.
marginal, *mod.* —*Syn.* rimming, edging, verging; see **bordering.**
marijuana, *n.* —*Syn. cannabis sativa, cannabis indica* (*both* Latin), hemp, bhang, ganja, hashish, charas, majoon, cannabin, cannabidiol, synthetic marijuana *or* THC; *all* (D): cannabis, dope, grass, pot, weed, boo, maryjane, maui wowi, shit, sensimilla, queen mary, hash, (acapulco) gold, (California) brown; see also **drug** 2.
marine, *mod.* —*Syn.* maritime, of the sea, oceanic; see **maritime** 2, **nautical.**
mariner, *n.* —*Syn.* seaman, tar, navigator; see **sailor.**
marines, *n.* —*Syn.* United States Marines, Royal Marines, landing party, amphibious forces, sea soldiers; *all* (D): devil dogs, grunts, Seabees, leathernecks; see also **troops.**
marionette, *n.* —*Syn.* mannikin, model, puppet; see **doll, toy** 1.
marital, *mod.* —*Syn.* conjugal, connubial, nuptial; see **matrimonial.**
maritime, *mod.* **1.** [Bordering on the sea]—*Syn.* seaside, seashore, shore, oceanic.—*Ant.* inland*, hinterland, continental.
2. [Concerned with the sea]—*Syn.* naval, marine, oceanic, seagoing, hydrographic, seafaring, aquatic, natatorial, pelagic, Neptunian; see also **nautical.**
Mark, *n.* —*Syn.* "John whose name was Mark," John Mark, the second Gospel; see **disciple, saint** 2.
mark, *n.* **1.** [The physical result of marking]—*Syn.* brand, stamp, blaze, imprint, impression, line, trace, check, stroke, streak, dot, point, nick, underlining.
2. [A target]—*Syn.* butt, prey, bull's eye; see **target.**
3. [A record]—*Syn.* register, record, trade-mark, impression, price tag, price mark, ticket, label, score, representation.
4. [Effect]—*Syn.* manifestation, consequence, value; see **result.**
5. [A symbol]—*Syn.* sign, image, badge; see **emblem.**
6. [An evidence of character]—*Syn.* idiosyncrasy, particularity, indication; see **characteristic, trait.**
7. [The point at which a race begins]—*Syn.* starting line, start, holes, gun.
8. [A limit]—*Syn.* end, rim, trim-line; see **boundary, edge** 1.
beside the mark—*Syn.* beside the point, extraneous, immaterial; see **irrelevant.**
hit the mark (D)—*Syn.* achieve, accomplish, do right *or* well; see **succeed** 1.
make one's mark—*Syn.* accomplish, prosper, become famous; see **succeed** 1.
miss the mark—*Syn.* be unsuccessful, err, mistake; see **fail** 1.
wide of the mark—*Syn.* erring, mistaken, inaccurate; see **wrong** 2.

mark, *v.* **1.** [To make a mark]—*Syn.* brand, stamp, imprint, blaze, print, check, chalk, label, sign, impress, identify, check off, trace, stroke, streak, dot, point, nick, underline, score, inscribe, seal.
2. [To designate]—*Syn.* earmark, point out, stake out, indicate, signalize, check *or* mark off, signify, remark, denote; see also **designate** 1.
3. [To distinguish]—*Syn.* characterize, signalize, qualify; see **distinguish** 1.
4. [To note carefully]—*Syn.* chronicle, register, write down; see **list** 1, **record** 1.
5. [To put prices upon]—*Syn.* ticket, label, tag; see **price.**

mark down, *v.* —*Syn.* reduce, put on sale, cut the price (of); see **lower, price.**

marked, *mod.* **1.** [Carrying a mark]—*Syn.* branded, signed, sealed, stamped, blazed, imprinted, impressed, inscribed, characterized by, distinguished by, recognized *or* identified by.
2. [Priced]—*Syn.* labeled, trade-marked, price-marked, marked down, marked up, ticketed, priced, tagged; see also **costing.**

marked down, *mod.* —*Syn.* lowered, priced lower, discounted; see **reduced** 2.

markedly, *mod.* —*Syn.* notably, particularly, considerably; see **especially** 1.

marked up, *mod.* —*Syn.* added on, more expensive, raised; see **increased.**

marker, *n.* —*Syn.* ticket, price mark, trademark, seal, brand, stamp, pencil, pen, boundary mark, tombstone, inscription; see also **label, tag** 2.

market, *n.* **1.** [A place devoted to sale]—*Syn.* trading post, mart, shopping mall, shopper's square, emporium, exchange, city market, public market, farmer's market, supermarket, green-grocer's, grocery store, meat market, fish market, curb market, flea market, stock market, stock exchange, Bourse, fair, dime store, drug store, department store, variety store, general store, bazaar, stall, booth, warehouse, business, delicatessen; see also **shop, store** 1.
2. [The state of trade]—*Syn.* supply and demand, sale, run; see **business** 1, 5, **demand** 2.
be in the market (for)—*Syn.* want (to buy), be willing to purchase, need; see **want** 1.
on the market—*Syn.* saleable, ready for purchase, available; see **for sale.**

market, *v.* —*Syn.* vend, exchange, barter; see **sell** 1.

marketable, *mod.* —*Syn.* for the consumer, wholesale, for sale; see **commercial** 1, **retail.**

marketing, *n.* —*Syn.* shopping, retailing, purchasing; see **buying, selling** 1.

market place, *n.* —*Syn.* selling place, department store, curb market; see **market** 1, **shop, store** 1.

marking, *mod.* and *n.* **1.** [Designating]—*Syn.* pointing out, characterizing, noticing, recognizing, distinguishing, showing, specifying, indicating, naming, terming, calling, denominating; see also **sense** 2.
2. [Making a mark upon]—*Syn.* imprinting, scoring, blazing, stamping, tagging, branding, ticketing, labeling, notching, lettering, initialing, inscribing, impressing, earmarking, signing; see also **sense** 1.

mark off, *v.* —*Syn.* segregate, separate, indicate; see **designate** 1, **mark** 2.

marksman, *n.* —*Syn.* sharpshooter, sniper, shooter; see **rifleman.**

mark time, *v.* —*Syn.* put off, postpone, kill time (D); see **delay** 1, **wait** 1.

markup, *n.* —*Syn.* raise, margin, gross profit; see **increase** 1, **profit** 2.

mark up, *v.* —*Syn.* raise the price, adjust, add to; see **increase** 1.

marmalade, *n.* —*Syn.* preserves, conserve, apple butter, swish (D); see also **jam** 1.

maroon, *v.* —*Syn.* desert, isolate, forsake; see **abandon** 2.

marriage, *n.* **1.** [The act of marrying]—*Syn.* wedding, espousal, spousal, nuptials, pledging, mating; see **ceremony** 2, **sacrament.**—*Ant.* divorce*, separation, annulment.
2. [The state following marriage]—*Syn.* matrimony, conjugality, nuptial tie *or* knot, union, match, connubiality, wedlock, wedded state, wedded bliss, holy matrimony; *all* (D): holy bedlock, double harness, tie that binds, fatal step, life sentence.—*Ant.* chastity*, bachelorhood, spinsterhood.
3. [A close union]—*Syn.* intimacy, compatibility, comradeship; see **friendship** 1.

marriageable, *mod.* —*Syn.* nubile, grown-up, adult; see **mature** 1.

married, *mod.* —*Syn.* wedded, mated, espoused, united, given *or* pledged in marriage, living in the married state, in the state of matrimony; *all* (D): doubled, anchored, grabbed off, knotted, handcuffed; see also **joined.**—*Ant.* single*, unwedded, unmarried.

marrow, *n.* —*Syn.* nucleus, kernel, heart; see **essence** 1.

marry, *v.* **1.** [To take a spouse]—*Syn.* wed, espouse, enter the matrimonial state, contract matrimony, promise *or* pledge in marriage, mate, take a helpmate, lead to the altar; *all* (D): bestow one's hand upon, take the vows, plight one's troth, become one, tie the knot, double up, drop anchor, get hooked *or* yoked.—*Ant.* divorce*, put away, reject.
2. [To join in wedlock]—*Syn.* unite, give, join in matrimony, pronounce man and wife; *all* (D): church, couple, hook, pronounce sentence; see **join** 1.—*Ant.* divorce*, annul, separate.

marry off (D), *v.* —*Syn.* give in marriage, bestow, make a match (for), find a mate (for); see **give** 1.

marsh, *n.* —*Syn.* morass, bog, quagmire; see **swamp.**

marshal, *n.* **1.** [A high military officer]—*Syn.* provost marshal, field marshal, air marshal; see **officer** 3.
2. [A local policeman]—*Syn.* constable, patrolman, deputy; see **policeman, sheriff.**

marshal, *v.* —*Syn.* order, dispose, direct; see **lead** 1.

marshy, *mod.* —*Syn.* swampy, boggy, low, wet, spongy, sopping, swamplike, fenny, mucky, low-lying, moory, plashy, soft, squashy, damp, sloppy, poachy; see **muddy** 1, 2.

mart, *n.* —*Syn.* emporium, mall, bazaar; see **market, shop, store** 1.

martial, *mod.* —*Syn.* warlike, soldierly, combative; see **military.**

martinet, *n.* —*Syn.* taskmaster, disciplinarian, overseer; see **dictator, master** 1.

martyr, *n.* —*Syn.* sufferer, offering, scapegoat; see **saint** 2, **victim** 1.

martyrdom, *n.* —*Syn.* torment, agony, pain, distress, ordeal, affliction, suffering, devotion, eternal glory, life everlasting; see **sacrifice** 1, **torture.** —*Ant.* self-gratification, indulgence*, worldliness.

marvel, *n.* —*Syn.* miracle, phenomenon, curiosity; see **wonder** 2.

marvel, *v.* —*Syn.* stare, stand in awe, stare with open mouth; see **wonder** 1.

marvelous, *mod.* **1.** [Wonderful]—*Syn.* fabulous, astonishing, spectacular; see **unusual** 1.
2. [So unusual as to suggest the supernatural] —*Syn.* miraculous, phenomenal, supernatural; see **unusual** 2.

marvelously, *mod.* **1.** [Strangely]—*Syn.* wondrously, magically, unusually; see **strangely.**
2. [Excellently]—*Syn.* (very) well, superbly, admirably; see **excellently.**

mascot, *n.* —*Syn.* luck piece, talisman, amulet; see **charm** 2.

masculine, *mod.* **1.** [Male]—*Syn.* virile, generative, potent; see **male.**
2. [Manly]—*Syn.* courageous, adult, honorable; see **brave** 1, **manly.**

masculinity, *n.* —*Syn.* virility, power, manliness; see **manhood** 2, **strength** 1.

mash, *n.* —*Syn.* mix, brew, bran mash, chicken feed, pulp, paste, dough, batter, pap, emulsion, poultice, sponge, jam, infusion, decoction, *masa* (Mexican); see **feed, mixture** 1.

mash, *v.* —*Syn.* crush, hash, bruise, squash, chew, masticate, macerate, smash, pound, reduce, squeeze, batter in, brew, infuse, decoct, steep, pulverize; see **grind** 1, **press** 1.

mashed, *mod.* —*Syn.* crushed, pressed, brewed, mixed, pulped, pulpy, battered, pounded, smashed, squashed, softened, reduced, spongy, pasty, doughy, hashed, steeped, infused, decocted, pulverized, masticated, chewed, macerated, bruised; see **limp** 1, **soft** 2.—*Ant.* whole*, hard, uncrushed.

mask, *n.* **1.** [A disguise]—*Syn.* cover, false face, veil, domino, hood, costume, theater device; see **camouflage** 1, **disguise.**
2. [A protection]—*Syn.* gas mask, catcher's mask, fencing mask, fireman's mask, welder's mask, respirator; see also **protection** 2.
3. [A masquerade]—*Syn.* revel, party, carnival; see **masquerade.**

mask, *v.* —*Syn.* cloak, conceal, veil; see **disguise, hide** 1.

Mason, *n.* —*Syn.* a member of the Masonic order.
Degrees of Masons include the following—Blue Lodge: First *or* Entered Apprentice, Second *or* Fellowcraft, Third *or* Master Mason, Fifth *or* Past Master, Twelfth *or* Knight Templar; Scottish Rite: Fourth *or* Secret Master, Fifth *or* Perfect Master, Twelfth *or* Master Architect; Thirty-third Degree.

mason, *n.* —*Syn.* bricklayer, builder, craftsman; see **workman.**

masonry, *n.* —*Syn.* stone wall, brick wall, mason work, handiwork, artifact; see **workmanship.**

masquerade, *n.* —*Syn.* revel, circus, mask, festivity, mummery, Mardi Gras, Shrove Tuesday, masked ball, mask-ball, masking, pretense, imposture; see **carnival** 1, **dance** 1, **entertainment** 2, **party** 1.

masquerade, *v.* —*Syn.* mask, revel, frolic; see **disguise, pretend** 2.

masquerader, *n.* —*Syn.* mimic, masked *or* costumed *or* disguised person, guest at a masked ball; see **actor, dancer.**

mass, *n.* **1.** [A body of matter]—*Syn.* lump, bulk, piece, portion, section, batch, block, body, core, clot, coagulation; *both* (D): wad, gob; see **hunk.**
2. [A considerable quantity]—*Syn.* heap, volume, crowd; see **quantity, size** 2.
3. [The greater portion]—*Syn.* majority, plurality; see **bulk** 2.
4. [Size]—*Syn.* magnitude, volume, span; see **extent, size** 2.
in the mass—*Syn.* en masse, as a whole, collectively; see **gathered.**

mass, *n.* —*Syn.* eucharistic rite, Catholic service, Eucharist, Lord's Supper, Holy Communion, ceremony, observance, form; see **celebration** 3, **worship** 1.
Masses include the following—High Mass, Low Mass, Solemn High Mass, Requiem Mass, Votive Mass.
Parts of the Mass include the following—Prayers at the Foot of the Altar, Introit, Kyrie Eleison, Gloria, Collect, Epistle, Gradual and Hallelujah, Gospel, Credo, Offertory, Sanctus, Consecration, Elevation of the Host, Pater Noster, Last Gospel.
The following are sometimes called masses—Mission, Missal, Kermis, Lamas.

massacre, *n.* —*Syn.* butchering, killing, slaughter; see **carnage, murder.**

massacre, *v.* —*Syn.* exterminate, mass murder, annihilate; see **depopulate, kill** 1.

massage, *v.* —*Syn.* stimulate, caress, press; see **knead, rub** 1.

massed, *mod.* —*Syn.* collected, assembled, brought (together); see **jammed** 2, **joined.**

masses, *n.* —*Syn.* proletariat, the rank and file, multitude; see **people** 3.

massive, *mod.* —*Syn.* huge, heavy, cumbersome; see **extensive, large** 1.

mass media, *n.* —*Syn.* news media, audio-visual media, press and radio; see **advertisement** 1, 2, **broadcasting, magazine** 2, **newspaper, radio** 1, 2, **television.**

mass meeting, *n.* —*Syn.* public *or* open meeting, assemblage, group; see **gathering.**

mass production, *n.* —*Syn.* mass producing, assembly-line methods, automation, automated production; see **manufacturing, production** 1.

mast, *n.* —*Syn.* spar, pole, post, timber, trunk, Maypole, flagstaff (D); see **column** 1.
Masts include the following—mainmast, foremast, mizzen, mizzenmast, topmast, topgallant mast, lower mast, jurymast, jigger.

master, *mod.* —*Syn.* leading, supreme, main; see **excellent, major** 1, **principal.**

master, *n.* **1.** [One who directs others]—*Syn.* chief, leader, governor, ruler, director, lord, overseer, supervisor, superintendent, boss, judge, patriarch, chieftan, commander, commandant; see also **administrator.**—*Ant.* servant*, underling, subject.

2. [A teacher]—*Syn.* instructor, preceptor, mentor; see **teacher** 1.
3. [One who possesses great skill]—*Syn.* genius, maestro, savant, sage, scientist, past master, champion, prima donna, protagonist, connoisseur, academician, pundit, fellow, doctor; *both* (D): top sawyer, boss; see **artist** 1, 2, **scholar** 2.—*Ant.* disciple*, beginner, undergraduate.
4. [A supreme being, especially Christ]—*Syn.* supreme being, Christ, Messiah; see **god** 1, 2, 3.
5. [The source of copies]—*Syn.* original, control, file copy; see **copy.**

master, *v.* **1.** [To conquer]—*Syn.* subdue, rule, humble; see **defeat** 1.
2. [To become proficient in]—*Syn.* gain mastery in, understand, comprehend; see **learn** 1, **study** 1.

masterful, *mod.* —*Syn.* commanding, bossy, dictatorial; see **autocratic** 1, **tyrannical.**

masterly, *mod.* —*Syn.* superior, skillful, superb; see **excellent.**

mastermind, *n.* —*Syn.* leader, expert, genius; see **administrator, artist** 1, 2, **author** 1, **doctor, philosopher.**

mastermind, *v.* —*Syn.* direct, supervise, engineer; see **manage** 1.

master of ceremonies, *n.* —*Syn.* chairman, presiding officer, emcee (D); see **speaker** 3.

masterpiece, *n.* —*Syn.* perfection, model, standard, cream of the crop, cream, flower, masterwork, *magnum opus* (Latin), *chef d'oeuvre, coup de maître, pièce de résistance* (all French), prize, gem, jewel, classic, showpiece, treasure.

mastership, *n.* —*Syn.* control, command, authority; see **leadership** 1, **power** 2.

master stroke, *n.* —*Syn.* conquest, advantage, achievement; see **triumph** 1, **victory** 1, 2.

mastery, *n.* **1.** [Control]—*Syn.* dominance, sovereignty, government; see **command** 2, **power** 2.
2. [Ability to use to the full]—*Syn.* power, influence, force, backing, skill, cunning, adroitness, capacity, knowledge, expertness, proficiency, genius, adeptness; see **ability** 2, **education** 1.

masticate, *v.* —*Syn.* gnaw, nibble, chew up; see **bite** 1, **chew, eat** 1.

mastication, *n.* —*Syn.* rumination, chewing, deglutition; *both* (D): Fletcherizing, Fletcherism; see **bite** 1, **digestion.**

mat, *n.* —*Syn.* covering, floor covering, doormat, table runner, (table) doily, place mat, landing mat, boat fender, network, table mat, place setting, intertexture, web, mesh, wattle, woven fabric, cloth, straw mat; see **cover** 1, **rug, tablecloth.**

mat, *v.* —*Syn.* plait, twine, felt, entwine, braid, tangle, snarl, entangle, dishevel; see **twist, weave** 1.

matador, *n.* —*Syn.* bullfighter, toreador, tauromachist, killer of bulls; see **contestant, fighter** 1.

match, *n.* **1.** [An instrument to produce fire] —*Syn.* safety match, sulphur match, matchstick, fuse, lucifer, locofoco (D); see **light** 3.
2. [An article that is like another]—*Syn.* peer, equivalent, mate, analogue, counterpart, approximation; see **equal.**
3. [A formal contest]—*Syn.* race, event, rivalry; see **competition** 2, **sport** 3.
4. [A marriage or engagement]—*Syn.* mating, union, espousal; see **marriage** 2.

match, *v.* **1.** [To find or make equals]—*Syn.* equalize, liken, equate, make equal, pair, coordinate, level, even, match up, balance, mate, marry, unite; see **equal.**
2. [To be alike]—*Syn.* harmonize, suit, be twins, be counterparts, be doubles, match *or* check with, go together, go with, rhyme with, take after; see **agree, resemble.**—*Ant.* differ*, be unlike, bear no resemblance.
3. [To meet in contest]—*Syn.* equal, keep pace with, run side by side, come up with, be on a level with, cope with, meet, compete with; see **rival.**

matched, *mod.* —*Syn.* doubled, similar, equated, evened, coordinated, harmonized, paired, mated; see **alike** 1, **balanced** 1.—*Ant.* unlike*, unequal, different*.

matching, *mod.* —*Syn.* comparable, analogous, parallel; see **equal.**

matchless, *mod.* —*Syn.* incomparable, unparalleled, unequaled; see **excellent, perfect** 2, **superior.**

matchmaker, *n.* —*Syn.* arranger, marriage counselor, agent; see **cupid.**

mate, *n.* **1.** [One of a pair]—*Syn.* complement, analog, counterpart; see **match** 2.
2. [A companion]—*Syn.* partner, comrade, schoolfellow, stable companion, helpmate, playmate, classmate; *all* (D): buddy, pal, chum, roomie; see **friend** 1.
3. [A marriage partner]—*Syn.* spouse, bride, groom, bedmate; *both* (D): (the) old man, (the) old lady; see **husband, wife.**
4. [A naval officer]—*Syn.* warrant officer, skipper, petty officer, next in command to a captain *or* chief specialist, first mate, second mate, third mate, boatswain's mate; see **officer** 3.

material, *mod.* **1.** [Composed of matter]—*Syn.* palpable, sensible, corporeal; see **physical** 1, **real** 2, **tangible.**
2. [Large in quantity]—*Syn.* considerable, substantial, notable; see **appreciable, much** 2.

material, *n.* **1.** [Matter]—*Syn.* body, corporeality, substance; see **element** 2, **matter** 1.
2. [Unfinished matter; *often plural*]—*Syn.* raw material, stuff, stock, staple, ore, stockpile, crop, supply, accumulation; see **alloy, cloth, cotton, element, linen, metal, mineral, plastic, rock** 1, **rubber, wool** 1, 2.

materialist, *n.* —*Syn.* realist, self-seeker, capitalist; see **opportunist.**

materialistic, *mod.* —*Syn.* mundane, carnal, earthly-minded, object-oriented, possessive, acquisitive, unspiritual, secular, earthy, material; see **greedy** 1, **worldly** 1.—*Ant.* impractical*, spiritual, ascetic.

materialize, *v.* **1.** [To become matter]—*Syn.* be realized, take (on) form, become real, actualize, reify, become embodied, be incarnate, coalesce, become concrete, metamorphose, reintegrate; see **form** 4.—*Ant.* dissolve*, disintegrate*, disperse.
2. [To develop]—*Syn.* unfold, emerge, evolve; see **develop** 3, **grow** 2.

materially, *mod.* **1.** [Concerning matter]—*Syn.* physically, corporeally, bodily, really, objectively, sensibly, actually, tangibly, palpably, ponderably, mundanely; see also **physically.**—*Ant.* unsubstantially, slightly, immaterially.

2. [To a considerable degree]—*Syn.* markedly, notably, substantially; see **very.**

materiel, *n.* —*Syn.* machinery, implements, war equipment; see **equipment.**

maternal, *mod.* —*Syn.* parental, sympathetic, protective; see **motherly.**

maternity, *n.* —*Syn.* parenthood, mothership, motherliness; see **motherhood.**

mathematical, *mod.* **1.** [Concerning mathematics] —*Syn.* scientific, geometrical, arithmetical, numerical, computative, measurable; see **analytical** 2.

2. [Exact]—*Syn.* precise, verified, substantiated; see **accurate** 2.

mathematics, *n.* —*Syn.* science of (real) (positive) numbers, language of numbers, computation, reckoning, calculation, correlation and deduction of numbers; *both* (D): new math, math; see **arithmetic, science** 1.

Types of mathematics include the following—arithmetic, algebra ((*also* (D): algy), plane *and* solid geometry, plane *and* spherical trigonometry *or* trig (D), analytic(al) geometry, differential *and* integral calculus *or* calc (D), programming, applied mathematics, probability, statistics, complex function, topology, transforms, logarithms *or* log (D).

Terms in mathematics include the following—number, symbol, equation, function, variable, constant, locus, graph, formula, square, volume, cube, curve, circle, sector, segment, derivative, tangent, progression, parabola, hyperbola, ellipse, calculus, theorem, hypothesis, logarithm.

matinee, *n.* —*Syn.* afternoon performance, play, show; see **entertainment** 2, **movie.**

matriarch, *n.* —*Syn.* female ruler, dowager, matron; see **queen.**

matriculate, *v.* —*Syn.* sign up for, enroll, enter; see **join** 2, **register** 4.

matriculation, *n.* **1.** [Registration]—*Syn.* entry, registering, enlisting; see **enrollment** 1, **registration** 1.

2. [Instruction]—*Syn.* practice, drill, preparation; see **education** 3, **training.**

matrimonial, *mod.* —*Syn.* conjugal, connubial, hymeneal, wedded, spousal, engaged, espoused, bridal, betrothed, nuptial, marital.

matrimony, *n.* —*Syn.* conjugality, wedlock, union; see **marriage** 2.

matrix, *n.* —*Syn.* form, cast, pattern; see **model** 2, **mold** 1.

matron, *n.* **1.** [A woman in a supervisory position] —*Syn.* housekeeper, superintendent, housemother; see **administrator.**

2. [An older married woman]—*Syn.* dame, lady, dowager, wife, mother; see also **woman** 1.

matronly, *mod.* —*Syn.* middle-aged, wifely, grave, sedate, womanly, ladylike; see also **mature** 1, **motherly.**—*Ant.* inexperienced*, immature, girlish.

matted, *mod.* —*Syn.* snarled, rumpled, disordered; see **tangled, twisted** 1.

matter, *n.* **1.** [Substance]—*Syn.* body, material, substantiality, corporeality, corporeity, protoplasm, constituents, stuff, materialness, object, thing, physical world; see also **element** 2.—*Ant.* nothing*, nihility, immateriality.

2. [Difficulty]—*Syn.* trouble, distress, perplexity; see **difficulty** 2.

3. [Subject]—*Syn.* interest, focus, resolution; see **subject** 1, **theme** 1, **topic.**

4. [An affair]—*Syn.* undertaking, circumstance, concern; see **affair** 1.

5. [Pus]—*Syn.* suppuration, maturation, purulence, ulceration, infection; see also **sore.**

as a matter of fact—*Syn.* in fact, in actuality, truly; see **really** 1.

for that matter—*Syn.* in regard to that, as far as that is concerned, concerning that; see **and.**

no matter—*Syn.* it doesn't matter, it is of no concern, regardless of; see **regardless** 2.

matter, *v.* **1.** [To be of importance]—*Syn.* value, carry weight, weigh, signify, be substantive *or* important, have influence, import, imply, denote, express, be of consequence, involve, be worthy of notice, cut ice (D); see also **mean** 1.

2. [To form or discharge pus]—*Syn.* suppurate, come to a head, fester; see **decay.**

matter-of-course, *mod.* —*Syn.* routine, usual, ordinary; see **natural** 1, 2, **regular** 3.

matter of course, *n.* —*Syn.* expected *or* anticipated result, routine event *or* happening, the usual thing; see **event** 1, **result.**

matter-of-fact, *mod.* —*Syn.* objective, prosaic, feasible; see **practical.**

matter of life or death (D), *n.* —*Syn.* significance, seriousness, concern; see **importance** 1.

matter of no consequence, *n.* —*Syn.* unimportance, immateriality, trifling matter; see **insignificance.**

Matthew, *n.* —*Syn.* Levi the tax-gatherer, apostle, first Gospel; see **disciple, saint** 2.

matting, *n.* —*Syn.* floor covering, door mat, drugget, table covering, straw matting, tatami, fiber mat; see also **cover** 1, **mat, rug.**

mattock, *n.* —*Syn.* pick, hoe, hatchet; see **ax, tool** 1.

mattress, *n.* —*Syn.* pallet, innerspring, springs, box spring, bedding, cushion, crib mattress; see **bed** 1.

mature, *mod.* **1.** [Adult]—*Syn.* full-grown, middle-aged, prime, grown, grown-up, of age, in full bloom, in one's prime, womanly, manly, matronly, manlike, developed, prepared, settled, cultivated, cultured, sophisticated; see also **experienced.** —*Ant.* adolescent, young*, immature.

2. [Ripe]—*Syn.* ready, seasoned, perfected; see **mellow** 1, **ripe** 1, 2.

3. [Considered]—*Syn.* thought about, reasoned, seasoned; see **considered** 1, **thoughtful** 1.

mature, *v.* **1.** [To come to maturity]—*Syn.* grow up, become a man *or* woman, come of age, become experienced, settle down, become full-blown, ripen (into), reach perfection, become prime, attain majority, culminate, become wise, become perfected, grow skilled, fill out, cut one's eyeteeth (D); see also **age** 1, **develop** 1.

2. [To grow]—*Syn.* ripen, mellow, evolve; see **grow** 2.

matured, *mod.* —*Syn.* ripened, grown, full-grown, mellowed, aged, middle-aged, developed, prime, advanced, full-blown, perfected, prepared, consummated, evolved, reasoned, considered, complete, cured, culminated, cultivated, cultured, at a high peak, brought to perfection, reached its goal, manly, womanly, sophisticated, experienced; see also **finished.**—*Ant.* young*, childish*, adolescent.

maturing, *mod.* —*Syn.* ripening, growing, sweetening, mellowing, developing, near prime, approaching middle age, nearing the meridian, moving, stirring, advancing, preparing, evolving, perfecting, consummating; see also **increasing** 1.—*Ant.* dying*, fading, declining.

maturity, *n.* **1.** [Mental competence]—*Syn.* development, sophistication, cultivation, culture, civilization, advancement, mental power, mentality, capability; see also **ability** 1, 2.—*Ant.* immaturity, undevelopment, adolescence.
2. [Physical development]—*Syn.* prime of life, post-pubescence, adulthood; see **majority** 2.
3. [Ripeness]—*Syn.* readiness, mellowness, fitness, full growth, sweetness; see also **development** 2.

maudlin, *mod.* —*Syn.* weak, insipid, gushing; see **emotional** 2, **sentimental.**

maul, *n.* —*Syn.* mallet, club, sledge; see **hammer, tool** 1.

maul, *v.* —*Syn.* pound, whip, trample; see **beat** 2, **hit** 1.

mauling, *n.* —*Syn.* clubbing, whipping, beating, man-handling, drubbing, thrashing, threshing, pommeling, thumping, pounding, strapping, ill-treatment, flogging, licking, trouncing, chastisement, caning, rawhiding, rain of blows (D); see also **defeat** 3.

maunder, *v.* **1.** [To digress]—*Syn.* drift, stray (from a subject), wander; see **deviate, ramble** 2.
2. [To mumble]—*Syn.* mutter, mouth, drivel; see **mumble.**

mausoleum, *n.* —*Syn.* crypt, catacomb, monolith; see **grave** 1, **memorial, monument** 1.

mauve, *mod.* —*Syn.* violet, lavender, lilac; see **purple.**

maverick, *mod.* —*Syn.* in opposition *or* revolt, contentious, aberrant; see **quarrelsome** 1, **radical** 2, **unusual** 2.

maverick, *n.* **1.** [Calf]—*Syn.* baby cow, yearling, renegade calf; see **animal** 2, **calf.**
2. [Nonconformist]—*Syn.* dissenter, malcontent, extremist; see **nonconformist, radical.**

maw, *n.* —*Syn.* gorge, craw, gullet, jaws, mouth; see also **throat.**

mawkish, *mod.* —*Syn.* tasteless, nauseating, garish; see **emotional** 2, **sentimental**

maxim, *n.* —*Syn.* aphorism, adage, epithet; see **proverb, saying.**

maximum, *mod.* —*Syn.* supreme, highest, greatest; see **best** 1.

maximum, *n.* —*Syn.* supremacy, height, pinnacle, preeminence, culmination, matchlessness, preponderance, apex, peak, greatest number, highest degree, summit, nonpareil; see also **climax.**—*Ant.* minimum*, foot, bottom.

May, *n.* —*Syn.* spring month, (opening of the) fishing season, baseball season, garden month, fifth month, Mother's Day season; see also **month, spring** 2.

may, *v.* **1.** [Grant permission]—*Syn.* be permitted, be allowed, can, be privileged to, be authorized, be at liberty to.
2. [Concede possibility]—*Syn.* will, shall, be going to, should, be conceivable, be possible, be credible, be practicable, be within reach, be obtainable; see also **will** 3.

Mayan, *mod.* —*Syn.* Maya, pre-Columbian, Yucatan; see **Indian** 1.

maybe, *mod.* —*Syn.* mayhap, perhaps, possibly, can be, might be, could be, maybe so, as it may be, conceivable, credible, feasible, obtainable, wind and weather permitting; *both* (D): on the cards, God willing.—*Ant.* hardly*, scarcely, probably not.

Mayflower, *n.* —*Syn.* hawthorn, marsh marigold, hepatica, anemone, spring beauty, trailing arbutus, May apple, greater stitchwort, cuckooflower; see also **flower** 1, **plant.**

mayhem, *n.* —*Syn.* maiming, mutilating, dismembering, dismemberment, great bodily injury, disfiguring, crippling, *immedicable vulnus* (Latin), deforming, deformation; see also **crime** 2.

mayor, *n.* —*Syn.* magistrate, Lord Mayor, borough president, perfect, burgomaster, chairman *or* president of a city council, civil administrator, civil judge, *maire* (French), *Burgermeister* (German), city father (D); see also **administrator.**

maze, *n.* —*Syn.* tangle, entanglement, twist, labyrinth, winding, convolution, intricacy, confusion, meandering, torsion, puzzle; see also **network** 1. —*Ant.* order*, disentanglement, simplicity.

meadow, *n.* —*Syn.* grass, pasture, mead, lea, mountain meadow, upland pasture, alp, meadow land, bottom land, bottoms, grassland, pasturage; hay meadow, clover meadow, bluegrass meadow, etc.; salt marsh, polder, veldt, high veldt, sweet veldt, sour veldt, bush-veldt, steppe, *Heide* (German), heath, *champ* (French), pampa, llano, savanna; see also **field** 1, **plain.**

meager, *mod.* **1.** [Thin]—*Syn.* lank, lanky, gaunt, starved, emaciated, lean, bony, slender, slim, spare, little, sparing, bare, scant, stinted, lacking, wanting, niggard, scraggy, scrawny, withered, wandlike, willowlike, willowy, lithe, narrow, tenuous, slightly-made, skinny; *all* (D): weedy, peaked, slab-sided; see also **thin** 2, 4.—*Ant.* fat*, plump, stout.
2. [Scanty]—*Syn.* short, deficient, insufficient; see **inadequate** 1, **unfinished** 1, **wanting.**

meagerly, *mod.* —*Syn.* scantily, skimpily, not much; see **inadequately.**

meagerness, *n.* **1.** [Lack]—*Syn.* scarcity, aridity, need; see **lack** 1, **poverty** 2.
2. [Dullness]—*Syn.* flatness, tedium, sameness; see **boredom, dullness** 1, **monotony** 1, **slowness** 1.

meal, *n.* **1.** [Ground feed]—*Syn.* bran, farina, grits, groats, fodder, provender, forage; see also **feed, flour, grain** 1.
Types of meal include the following—corn meal, corn grits, hominy (grits), corn starch, corn gluten, barley meal, oatmeal, linseed meal, soybean meal, soybean flour, cottonseed meal, bonemeal, tankage, alum meal.
2. [The quantity of food taken at one time]—*Syn.* repast, feast, refection, collation, refreshment; *all* (D): mess, feed (bag), eats, grub, bag, chow, spread, stand-up, square meal, munchies, carry-out, snack, from soup to nuts, blowout, grubfest.
Meals include the following—banquet, brunch, snack, tea, high tea, picnic, luncheon, dessert, supper; see also **breakfast, dinner, lunch.**

mealy, *mod.* —*Syn.* powdery, friable, crumbly; see **gritty.**

mealy-mouthed, *mod.* —*Syn.* pretentious, insincere, theatrical; see **affected** 2, **euphemistic.**

mean, *mod.* **1.** [Small-minded]—*Syn.* base, low, debased; see **vulgar** 1.
2. [Of low estate]—*Syn.* servile, pitiful, shabby; see **humble** 2.
3. [Vicious]—*Syn.* shameless, dishonorable, degraded, malign, contemptible, evil, infamous, treacherous, crooked, fraudulent, perjured, blackguard, faithless, ill-tempered, dangerous, despicable, degenerate, rotten (D), scurrilous, arrant, perfidious, knavish, unscrupulous, hard as nails (D); see also **vicious** 1.
4. [Stingy]—*Syn.* miserly, niggardly, rapacious; see **greedy** 1, **stingy.**
5. [Average]—*Syn.* mediocre, middling, halfway; see **common** 1, 2, **conventional** 1, 3, **popular** 1, 3, **traditional** 2.

mean, *n.* —*Syn.* middle, median, midpoint; see **average** 1, **center** 1.

mean, *v.* **1.** [To have as meaning]—*Syn.* indicate, spell, denote, signify, betoken, import, add up, determine, symbolize, imply, involve, allude, speak of, touch on, stand for, drive at, point to, connote, suggest, express, designate, intimate, tell the meaning of, purport.
2. [To have in mind]—*Syn.* anticipate, propose, expect; see **intend** 1.
3. [To design for]—*Syn.* destine for, aim at, set apart; see **intend** 2.

meander, *v.* **1.** [To turn]—*Syn.* recoil, change, twine; see **turn** 2, **wind** 3.
2. [To wander]—*Syn.* twist and turn, roam, drift; see **ramble** 3, **walk** 1.

meandering, *mod.* —*Syn.* rambling, nomadic, circular; see **travelling** 2, **wandering** 1.

meanie (D), *n.* —*Syn.* brute, tyrant, cruel *or* nasty *or* brutal, etc., person; see **beast** 2, **rascal.**

meaning, *n.* —*Syn.* sense, denotation, import, purport, purpose, definition, object, implication, application, intent, suggestion, connotation, symbolization, aim, drift, context, significance, essence, worth, intrinsic value, interest.—*Ant.* nonsense*, aimlessness, absurdity.

meaningful, *mod.* —*Syn.* significant, exact, essential; see **important** 1.

meaningless, *mod.* —*Syn.* vague, absurd, insignificant; see **trivial, unimportant.**

meanly, *mod.* —*Syn.* niggardly, meagerly, miserly; see **selfishly.**

meanness, *n.* **1.** [The quality of being mean] —*Syn.* smallmindedness, debasement, degradation, abjection, shamelessness, infamy, degeneracy, blackguardism, knavishness, unscrupulousness, stinginess, closeness, niggardliness, frugality, churlishness, corruptness, cupidity, sordidness, contemptibleness, disrepute, rapacity, malice, malignity, unworthiness, ill-temper, unkindness, covetousness, avarice, miserliness, parsimony; see also **greed.**—*Ant.* generosity*, nobility, worthiness.
2. [A mean action]—*Syn.* belittling, defaming, groveling, cheating, sneaking, quarreling, scolding, taking advantage of, deceiving, coveting, grudging, grasping, dishonoring, defrauding, perjuring, shaming, degrading, beggaring, stealing.

means, *n.* **1.** [An instrumentality or instrumentalities]—*Syn.* machinery, mechanism, agency, organ, channel, medium, factor, agent, auspices, power, organization; see also **method** 2, **system** 2.
2. [Wealth]—*Syn.* resources, substance, property; see **wealth** 2.
by all means—*Syn.* of course, certainly, yes indeed; see **surely, yes.**
by any means—*Syn.* in any way, at all, somehow; see **anyhow** 2.
by means of—*Syn.* with the aid of, somehow, through; see **by** 2.
by no (manner of) means—*Syn.* in no way, not possible, (definitely) not; see **never, no.**

mean-spirited, *mod.* —*Syn.* base, timid, servile; see **afraid** 1, **cowardly, weak** 3.

meanwhile, *mod.* —*Syn.* meantime, during the interval, in the interim, ad interim, for the time being, until, till, up to, in the meantime, when; see also **during, while** 1.

measurable, *mod.* **1.** [Estimable]—*Syn.* weighable, fathomable, assessable; see **calculable.**
2. [Limited]—*Syn.* moderate, proscribed, measured; see **restricted.**

measure, *n.* **1.** [A unit of measurement]—*Syn.* dimension, capacity, weight, volume, distance, degree, quantity, area, mass, frequency, density, viscosity, intensity, rapidity, speed, caliber, bulk, sum, duration, magnitude, amplitude, size, pitch, ratio, depth, scope, height, strength, breadth, amplification.
Common units of measure include the following —*linear:* inch, foot, yard, rod, mile (U.S. and Britain); millimeter, centimeter, decimeter, meter, kilometer (continental Europe); *surface:* square inch, square foot, square yard, acre, square rod, square mile (U.S. and Britain); centaire, are, hectare (Europe); *volume:* dram, gill, pint, quart, gallon (U.S. and Britain); centiliter, liter, hectoliter (Europe); *weight:* gram, ounce, pound (U.S. and Britain); milligram, gram, kilogram (Europe); *relationship:* F-number, revolutions per minute (r.p.m.), miles per hour (m.p.h.), feet per second (f.p.s.), per second per second, erg, foot-pound, kilowatt-hour, acre-foot, decibel, man-hour, frequency modulation (FM), ohm, watt, volt, octane number *or* rating, percentage.
Common units of measure and their abbreviations used in medicine include the following—amount (amt.), centigrade (C.), cubic centimeter (cc.), dram (dr.), Fahrenheit (F.), gram (gm.), grain (gr.), drop (gtt.), hour (hr.), pound (lb.), minim (m.), milligram (mg.), minute (min.), number (no.), pint (O), ounce (oz.), by (per.), one half (ss.), tablespoon (tbsp.), teaspoon (tsp.), unit (U).
2. [Anything used as a standard]—*Syn.* rule, test, trial, example, standard, yardstick, norm, canon, pattern, type, model; see also **criterion.**
3. [A beat]—*Syn.* rhythm, tempo, time, step, throb, stroke, accent, meter, cadence, tune, melody, stress, vibration, division; see also **beat** 3.
4. [A bill]—*Syn.* project, proposition, proposal; see **bill** 3.

5. [A preventive or counteractive action]—*Syn.* agency, device, stratagem; see **action** 2, **means** 1.
beyond (*or* **above**) **measure**—*Syn.* immeasurably, exceedingly, extremely; see **much** 1, 2.
for good measure—*Syn.* added, as a bonus, additionally; see **extra.**
in a measure—*Syn.* to some extent, somewhat, in a way; see **rather.**
made to measure—*Syn.* suited, custom-made, made to order; see **tailored.**
take measures—*Syn.* take action, do things to accomplish a purpose, employ; see **act** 1.
take someone's measure (D)—*Syn.* measure, judge, weigh; see **estimate** 1, 2.

measure, *v.* **1.** [To apply a standard of measurement]—*Syn.* rule, weigh, mark, lay off *or* out, grade, graduate, gauge, sound, pitch, beat, stroke, time, mete, mark off, pace off, plumb, scale, rank, even, level, gradate, shade, blend, rhyme, line, align, line out, regulate, portion, set a criterion *or* standard, average, equate, encircle, square, calibrate, block in, survey, telemeter, chromatograph, map; see also **estimate** 1, 2.
2. [To contain by measurement]—*Syn.* hold, cover, contain; see **include** 1.

measured, *mod.* **1.** [Steady]—*Syn.* steady, systematic, deliberate; see **regular** 3.
2. [Moderate]—*Syn.* limited, restrained, confined; see **restricted.**
3. [Determined]—*Syn.* checked, evaluated, calculated; see **determined** 1.

measure for measure, *n.*—*Syn.* retaliation, vengeance, repayment; see **revenge** 1.

measureless, *mod.*—*Syn.* bottomless, immense, indefinite; see **endless** 1, **infinite** 1, **unlimited.**

measurement, *n.* **1.** [The act of measuring]—*Syn.* estimation, determination, analysis, computation; see also **judgment** 2.
2. [The result of measuring]—*Syn.* distance, dimension, weight, degree, pitch, time, height, width, depth, density, volume, area, length, measure, thickness, quantity, magnitude, extent, range, altitude, scope, reach, amount, capacity, frequency, viscosity, intensity, pressure, speed, acceleration, rapidity, caliber, hardness, grade, span, step, calibration, strength, mass; see also **size** 2.
3. [A set of measures]—*Syn.* inch, foot, yard; see **measure** 1.

measure off, *v.*—*Syn.* mark out, limit, determine *or* set up boundaries; see **divide** 1, **mark** 1.

measure out, *v.*—*Syn.* allot, deal, apportion; see **distribute** 1.

measuring, *n.*—*Syn.* weighing, grading, gauging, graduating, scaling, calibrating, rhyming, aligning, blending, leveling, mapping, squaring, surveying, shading, averaging, spanning, stepping (off), cruising, checking, calculating.

meat, *n.* veal, mutton, lamb, chicken, turkey, goose, duck, rabbit, venison, goat's meat, horsemeat; see also **beef** 1, **pork.**
Cuts and forms of meat include the following—roast, cutlet, steak, filet, leg, shoulder, loin, tenderloin, rib, round, rump, chuck, brisket, plate, flank, chop, liver, brains, kidneys, heart, bacon, ham, tripe, oxtail, sausage, frankfurter, ground meat, chipped meat, dried *or* jerked meat, salt *or* pickled meat.
Grades of meats include the following—prime, grade A, first, second, utility, canners and cutters, choice, good, commercial, top.

meaty, *mod.* **1.** [Full of substance]—*Syn.* fat, tough, sinewy; see **lean** 2.
2. [Full of content]—*Syn.* significant, factual, weighty; see **important** 1.

mechanic, *n.*—*Syn.* machinist, skilled workman, fender bender (D); see **workman.**
Mechanics include the following—automobile mechanic, fender and body man, tuneup man, metalworker, automobile parts assembler, automobile motor repairman, radio tester, radio chassis aligner, airplane electrician, electric appliance service man, electric-acetylene-welder operator, acetylene cutter, acetylene welder, bolt-cutter, bolt-threader operator, boring-mill operator, circular-saw operator, drill-press operator, engine-lathe operator, layout man, steel erector, steel-forging upsetter, steel pourer, steel cutter, bridge crane operator, derrick boat operator, armature bander, armature-shaft repairman.

mechanical, *mod.* **1.** [Concerning machinery]—*Syn.* engineering, production, manufacturing, tooling, tuning, implementing, fabricating, fabrication, forging, machining, building, construction, constructing.
2. [Like a machine]—*Syn.* made to a pattern, machinelike, stereotyped, standardized, without variation, fixed, unchanging, monotonous.—*Ant.* original*, varied, changing*.
3. [Operated by the use of machinery]—*Syn.* power-driven, involuntary, programmed; see **automated, automatic.**

mechanically, *mod.*—*Syn.* automatically, unreasoningly, unchangeably; see **regularly** 1.

mechanics, *n.*—*Syn.* kinetics, aeromechanics, pure mechanics, rational mechanics, machine technology, technical details; see also **physics, science** 1.

mechanism, *n.*—*Syn.* working parts, mechanical action, system of parts; see **device** 1, **tool** 1.

mechanistic, *mod.*—*Syn.* monotonous, Godless, inhuman; see **arbitrary** 2, **automatic** 2, **mechanical** 2, **ruthless** 1, 2.

mechanization, *n.*—*Syn.* automation, industrialization, trade; see **business** 4.

mechanize, *v.*—*Syn.* equip, computerize, industrialize, motorize, automate, put on the assembly line, make mechanical, introduce machinery into.

medal, *n.*—*Syn.* reward, commemoration, badge; see **decoration** 3.

medallion, *n.*—*Syn.* ornament, emblem, necklace; see **jewelry.**

meddle, *v.* **1.** [To interfere in others' affairs]—*Syn.* intermeddle, interpose, interfere, obtrude, interlope, intervene, pry, snoop, impose oneself, infringe, break in upon, advance upon, make it one's business, abuse one's rights, push in, chime in, force an entrance, encroach, intrude, be officious, obstruct, impede, hinder, encumber, busy oneself with, come uninvited, tamper with, inquire, be curious: *all* (D): stick one's nose in, crash the gates, monkey with, bust in, muscle in, barge in, worm in,

have a finger in, fool with, butt in, horn in; see also **interrupt** 2.—*Ant.* neglect*, ignore, let alone.
2. [To handle others' things]—*Syn.* tamper, molest, pry, fool with, trespass, snoop, nose, dabble in, use improperly, monkey with (D).

meddlesome, *mod.* —*Syn.* obtrusive, interfering, officious, meddling, intrusive, impertinent, interposing, interrupting, obstructive, impeding, hindering, encumbering, curious, tampering, prying, snooping, troublesome; *all* (D): snoopy, nosy, kibitzing, chiseling in, making snoopee; see also **inquisitive, interested** 1, **rude** 2.

meddling, *n.* —*Syn.* interfering, interrupting, snooping; see **interference** 2, **rudeness.**

medial, *mod.* —*Syn.* average, mean, between, intermediate, innermost; see also **center, central** 1, **middle.**

median, *mod.* —*Syn.* medial, middle, halfway; see **center** 1, **central** 1.

median, *n.* —*Syn.* mean, mid-point, norm; see **average** 1, **center** 1.

mediate, *v.* —*Syn.* propitiate, interfere, intercede; see **negotiate** 1, **reconcile** 2.

mediation, *n.* —*Syn.* interposition, arbitration, negotiation; see **agreement** 1, **intervention** 1.

mediator, *n.* —*Syn.* intercessor, medium, negotiator; see **judge** 2.

medic, *n.* —*Syn.* physician, practitioner, surgeon; see **doctor** 1.

medical, *mod.* —*Syn.* healing, medicinal, curative, therapeutic, restorative, prophylactic, preventive, alleviating, medicating, pharmaceutical, salutary, sedative, narcotic, tonic, disinfectant, corrective, pathological, cathartic, health-bringing, peptic, corroborant, lenitive, demulcent, balsamic, depuritory, emollient; see also **remedial.**—*Ant.* destructive*, disease-giving, harmful*.
Common medical terms and their abbreviations include the following—of each (aa), before meals (a.c.), as desired (ad lib), water (aq), twice a day (b.i.d.), dilute (dil), dram (dr.), elixir (elix.), extract (ext.), fluid (fld.), divided doses (fract. dos.), gram (gm.), grain (gr.), drop (gtt.), hour (hr.), at bedtime (H.S.), kilogram (kg.), pound (lb.), liquid (liq.), milligram (mg.), minute (min.), pint (O), oil (Ol), ounce (oz.), after meals (p.c.), by (per), afternoon (P.M.), whenever necessary (p.r.n.), every day (q.d.), every hour (q.h.), every two hours (q.2.h.), every three hours (q.3.h.), four times a day (q.i.d.), sufficient quantity (q.s.), solution (sol.), dissolve (solv.), if necessary (s.o.s.), spirit (sp.), one half (ss.), soap solution (S.S.), temperature (T.), tablet (tab.), tablespoon (tbsp.), three times a day (t.i.d.), tincture (tinct.), teaspoon (tsp.), unit (U.), ointment (ung.), volume (V.), weight (wt.), medications (meds.), immediately (stat.).

medicament, *n.* —*Syn.* antidote, remedy, drug; see **medicine** 2.

Medicare, *n.* —*Syn.* socialized medicine, social security, old-age *or* hospitalization insurance, public health; see also **insurance, security** 2.

medication, *n.* —*Syn.* remedy, pill, vaccination; see **medicine** 2, **prescription.**

medicinal, *mod.* —*Syn.* curative, healing, therapeutic; see **remedial.**

medicine, *n.* **1.** [The healing profession]—*Syn.* medical men, healers, practitioners, doctors, physicians, surgeons, osteopaths, chiropractors, the profession, American Medical Association (A.M.A.).
2. [A medical preparation]—*Syn.* drug, dose, potion, prescription, pill(s), tablet, capsule, draft, curative preparation, patent medicine, remedy, cure, antivenin, anti-poison, antibiotic, medicament, medication, vaccination, inoculation, injection, draught, simple, herb, specific, nostrum, elixir, tonic, balm, alterant, salve, lotion, ointment, emetic, pharmacopoeia, shot (D).
Common medicines include the following—physic, steroid, cathartic, counteractive, stimulant, counterirritant, anodyne, depurgatory, antiseptic, antidote, alterative, febrifuge, liniment, tincture, antitoxin, serum, vaccine, immuno-suppressive drugs, purgative, enema, anesthetic, sedative.
3. [The study and practice of medicine]—*Syn.* medical science, physic, healing art, medical profession; *both* (D): doctoring, bed-panology.
Branches of medicine include the following—surgery, therapy, therapeutics, anesthesiology, internal medicine, oral surgery, general practice, experimental medicine, psychiatry, psychotherapy, psychoanalysis, ophthalmology, obstetrics, gynecology, pediatrics, orthopedics, bariatrics, neurology, cardiology, dermatology, pathology, endocrinology, immunology, laryngology, urology, diathermy, hematology, diagnostics, radiotherapy, psychopathology, psychosomatics, geriatrics, chiropody, veterinary medicine, otology; eye, ear, nose and throat; inhalation therapy.
The following are not always recognized as branches of medicine—osteopathy, homeopathy, chiropractic.

medieval, *mod.* —*Syn.* pertaining to the Middle Ages, feudal, antiquated; see **old** 3.

mediocre, *mod.* —*Syn.* average, ordinary, standard; see **common** 1, **conventional** 1, 3, **dull** 4, **fair** 2.

mediocrity, *n.* **1.** [Ordinariness]—*Syn.* commonplaceness, commonness; see **normality** 1.
2. [A mediocre person]—*Syn.* upstart, cipher, nonentity; see **citizen, commoner, nobody** 2.

meditate, *v.* **1.** [To muse]—*Syn.* ponder, study, contemplate, ruminate, muse (on *or* over *or* upon), revolve, say to oneself, reflect, view, brood over, cogitate, be in an abstraction, cherish *or* entertain the idea, dream; *all* (D): mull, be in a brown study, chew the cud; see also **consider** 3.
2. [To think over]—*Syn.* weigh, consider, speculate; see **think** 1.

meditation, *n.* —*Syn.* examination, contemplation, speculation; see **reflection** 1, **study** 2, **thought** 1.

meditative, *mod.* —*Syn.* reflective, pensive, absorbed; see **studious, thoughtful** 1.

Mediterranean, *mod.* —*Syn.* south European, Latinate, Italianate; see **classical** 2, **European, Latin** 2.

medium, *mod.* —*Syn.* commonplace, mediocre, ordinary; see **common** 1.

medium, *n.* **1.** [A means]—*Syn.* mechanism, tool, factor; see **means** 1, **part** 3.
2. [A means of expression]—*Syn.* symbol, sign, token, interpretation, exponent, manifestation, revelation, evidence, mark, statement, delinea-

tion; see also **communication** 1, **communications, speech** 2.
Common modes of expression include the following—speech, facial expresison, gesture, signs, pantomime, music, drama, writing, painting, sculpture, radio, television.
3. [A supposed channel of supernatural knowledge] —*Syn.* oracle, seer, spiritualist; see **fortuneteller, prophet.**

medley, *n.* **1.** [A mixture]—*Syn.* mingling, melee, conglomeration; see **mixture** 1, **variety** 1.
2. [A composition made from musical snatches] —*Syn.* potpourri, miscellany, *pasticcio* (Italian), pastiche; see also **composition** 4, **music** 1.

meed, *n.* —*Syn.* pay, award, reward; see **honors** 2, **prize.**

meek, *mod.* **1.** [Humble]—*Syn.* unassuming, plain, mild; see **humble** 1, **modest** 2.
2. [Long-suffering]—*Syn.* passive, resigned, serene; see **patient** 1.
3. [Lacking spirit]—*Syn.* submissive, compliant, subdued; see **docile, resigned.**

meekness, *n.* —*Syn.* submission, mildness, timidity; see **docility, humility.**

meet, *mod.* —*Syn.* fitting, apt, expedient; see **fair** 1, **fit** 1, 2, **timely.**

meet, *n.* —*Syn.* match, athletic event, tournament; see **competition** 2, **event** 3.

meet, *v.* **1.** [To come together]—*Syn.* converge, get together, enter in; see **gather** 1.
2. [To go to a place of meeting]—*Syn.* resort, be present at, gather together, foregather, convene, congregate, muster, appear, go to the meeting (D); see also **assemble** 2, **attend** 2.—*Ant.* leave*, disperse, scatter.
3. [To touch]—*Syn.* reach, coincide, adhere; see **join** 1.
4. [To become acquainted]—*Syn.* make the acquaintance of, be presented to, be introduced, present oneself, make oneself known; *both* (D): get next to, get to know; see also **familiarize (oneself with).**
5. [To fulfill]—*Syn.* answer, fit, suffice; see **satisfy** 3.
6. [To encounter]—*Syn.* fall in with, come on *or* upon, meet by accident, come across, meet face to face, face up to, bump into, touch shoulders with, meet at every turn, engage, join issue with, battle, grapple with, match, jostle, push, brush against, shove; see also **face** 1, **fight** 2.—*Ant.* abandon*, turn one's back on, leave.

meeting, *n.* **1.** [The act of coming together]—*Syn.* encounter, juxtaposition, juxtaposing, joining, confluence, juncture, apposition, unifying, unification, adherence, rencounter, convergence, confrontation, abutment, contacting, connection, recontact possibility, conflict, contention, accord, agreement, compromising, reception, harmonizing; *all* (D): teach-in, love-in, sit-in.—*Ant.* departure*, separation, dispersal.
2. [A gathering, usually of people]—*Syn.* conference, assemblage, rally; see **gathering.**

meetinghouse, *n.* —*Syn.* church, hall, auditorium; see **headquarters, room** 2.

meeting of minds, *n.* —*Syn.* approval, assent, negotiation; see **agreement** 3.

meet one's responsibilities, *v.* —*Syn.* transact, complete, carry out; see **achieve** 1, **perform** 1.

meet up with (D), *v.* —*Syn.* encounter, become acquainted (with), be introduced; see **meet** 4.

meet with, *v.* —*Syn.* observe, experience, encounter; see **find** 1.

megalith, *n.* —*Syn.* boulder, monolith, concretion; see **rock** 1, **stone.**

megalomania, *n.* —*Syn.* compulsion, instability, mental disorder; see **insanity** 1, **neurosis, obsession.**

megalopolis, *n.* —*Syn.* municipality, group of cities, metropolis; see **city** 1.

megaphone, *n.* —*Syn.* bull horn, sound device, microphone; see **amplifier.**

melancholia, *n.* —*Syn.* despondency, melancholy, despair; see **depression** 2, **sadness.**

melancholy, *mod.* **1.** [Sad; *said of persons*]—*Syn.* depressed, unhappy, dispirited; see **sad** 1.
2. [Depressing; *said of information or events*] —*Syn.* dreary, unfortunate, saddening; see **sad** 2.

melancholy, *n.* —*Syn.* wistfulness, despair, unhappiness; see **depression** 2, **grief** 1, **sadness.**

mélange (French), *n.* —*Syn.* medley, combination, jumble; see **mixture** 1.

meld, *v.* —*Syn.* blend, merge, unite; see **mix** 1, **unite** 1.

melee, *n.* —*Syn.* scuffle, rumpus, skirmish; see **fight** 1.

meliorate, *v.* —*Syn.* amend, advance, correct; see **improve** 1.

mellifluous, *mod.* —*Syn.* resonant, smooth, liquid; see **harmonious** 1, **melodious, musical** 1.

mellow, *mod.* **1.** [Ripe]—*Syn.* sweet, soft, perfected, full-flavored, seasoned, aged, cured, tender, well-matured; see also **matured, ripe** 1.—*Ant.* green*, hard, unripe.
2. [Culturally mature]—*Syn.* cultured, fully developed, broad-minded; see **matured.**

mellowed, *mod.* —*Syn.* mature, ripened, softened; see **matured, ripe** 1, 2, **soft** 2, 3.

melodeon, *n.* —*Syn.* harmonium, wind instrument, accordion; see **musical instrument, organ** 3.

melodious, *mod.* —*Syn.* agreeable, pleasing, euphonic, sweet, tuneful, dulcet, accordant, assonant, mellifluous, resonant, mellow, in tune, well tuned, harmonic, symphonic, symphonious, unisonant, soft, clear, silvery, silver-toned, euphonious; see also **harmonious** 1, **musical** 1.—*Ant.* harsh*, grating, discordant.

melodrama, *n.* —*Syn.* play, opera, theater; see **drama** 1.

melodramatic, *mod.* —*Syn.* artificial, spectacular, sensational; see **exaggerated.**

melody, *n.* **1.** [The quality of being melodious] —*Syn.* consonance, assonance, concord, unison, euphony, resonance, inflection, chime; see also **harmony** 1.—*Ant.* noise*, discord, disharmony.
2. [A melodious arrangement]—*Syn.* air, lyric, strain; see **composition** 2, **music** 1, **song, tune.**

melon, *n.* —*Syn.* pepo, *Cucurbitaceae* (Latin), gourd; see also **food, fruit** 1.
Types of melons include the following—watermelon, muskmelon, *Cucumis melo, Citrullus vulgaris* (both Latin), nutmeg melon, cantaloupe, Rocky Ford, gourd melon, apple-cucumber, winter melon, casaba, Cranshaw, honeydew.

melt, *v.* **1.** [To liquefy]—*Syn.* thaw, deliquesce, render, fuse, blend, merge, soften, flow, run, disintegrate, waste away; see also **dissolve** 1.—*Ant.* freeze*, harden, coagulate.
2. [To relent]—*Syn.* forgive, show mercy, become lenient; see **yield** 1.
3. [To decrease]—*Syn.* vanish, pass away, go; see **decrease** 1.

melted, *mod.* —*Syn.* softened, thawed, molten, liquefied, dwindled, deliquesced, run away, rendered, fused, blended, merged, wasted away, disintegrated, vanished, decreased, diminished, tempered, abated, mitigated, mollified, relaxed.

melting, *mod.* —*Syn.* softening, liquefying, reducing; see **soft** 2.

melting pot, *n.* —*Syn.* mingling, common ground, international meeting place; see **mixture** 1.

member, *n.* **1.** [A person or group]—*Syn.* constituent, charter member, active member, member in good standing, honorary member, affiliate, affiliate member, brother, sister, comrade, *tovarich* (Russian), chapter, post, branch, lodge, canton, district, county, town, township, state, country, countries, company, battalion, regiment, division.
2. [A part]—*Syn.* portion, segment, fragment; see **division** 2, **part** 1.
3. [A part of the body]—*Syn.* organ, feature, segment, arm, leg; see also **limb** 2.

membership, *n.* —*Syn.* club, society, association, body of members, fellowship, company, group, brotherhood.

membrane, *n.* —*Syn.* layer, sheath, lamina; see **film** 1.

memento, *n.* —*Syn.* token, relic, keepsake; see **souvenir.**

memoir, *n.* —*Syn.* life story, diary, autobiography; see **biography, journal** 1.

memorable, *mod.* **1.** [Historic]—*Syn.* momentous, critical, unforgettable, surpassing, crucial, famous, illustrious, distinguished, great, notable, significant, decisive, enduring, lasting, monumental, eventful, interesting; see also **important** 1.
2. [Unusual]—*Syn.* remarkable, exceptional, singular; see sense 1, **unusual** 1.

memorandum, *n.* —*Syn.* notice, record, jotting; see **note** 2, **reminder.**

memorial, *mod.* —*Syn.* dedicatory, commemorative, remembering, consecrating, canonizing, enshrining, memorializing, deifying, in tribute.

memorial, *n.* —*Syn.* remembrance, testimonial, tablet, slab, pillar, tombstone, headstone, column, shaft, obelisk, monolith, mausoleum, record, inscription, memento, statue, *hic jacet, requiescat in pace* (both Latin), R.I.P., slat (D); see also **celebration** 1, **ceremony** 2, **monument** 1, **souvenir.**

Memorial Day, *n.* —*Syn.* Decoration Day, Confederate Memorial Day, May 10 *or* 30 *or* April 26 *or* June 3; see also **holiday** 1, **spring** 2.

memorize, *v.* —*Syn.* fix in the memory, make memorable, record, commemorate, memorialize, retain, commit to memory, imprint in one's mind, bear in mind, treasure up, enshrine, learn by rote, use mnemonics, give word for word; *all* (D): get down pat, have in one's head, have at one's fingertips, bottle up, learn by heart; see also **learn** 1, **remember** 2.—*Ant.* neglect*, forget, fail to remember.

memory, *n.* **1.** [The power to call up the past] —*Syn.* recollection, retrospection, reminiscence, thought, mindfulness, consciousness, subconsciousness, unconscious memory, retentive memory, *déjà vu* (French), ready memory, exact *or* photographic memory, visual memory, auditory memory; *both* (D): camera-eye, dead-eye; see also **mind** 1, **remembrance** 1.
2. [That which can be recalled]—*Syn.* (mental) image, picture, vision, sound image, representation, fantasy, concept; see also **thought** 2.

menace, *n.* **1.** [A threat]—*Syn.* caution, intimidation, foretelling; see **warning.**
2. [An imminent danger]—*Syn.* hazard, peril, threat; see **danger** 1.

menace, *v.* —*Syn.* intimidate, portend, loom; see **threaten** 2.

menacing, *mod.* —*Syn.* approaching, impending, threatening; see **imminent, ominous.**

menagerie, *n.* —*Syn.* zoological garden, terrarium, vivarium; see **zoo.**

mend, *v.* **1.** [To repair]—*Syn.* heal, patch, fix; see **reconstruct, repair** 1, **restore** 3.
2. [To improve]—*Syn.* aid, remedy, cure; see **correct** 1, **improve** 1.
3. [Reform]—*Syn.* regenerate, behave, mend one's manners; see **improve** 2, **reform** 3.
4. [To get well]—*Syn.* recover, respond to medication, knit; see **heal** 1, **recover** 3.
on the mend—*Syn.* getting better, recuperating, recovering; see **improving.**

mendacious, *mod.* —*Syn.* lying, untrue, spurious; see **false** 2.

mendacity, *n.* —*Syn.* lying, prevarication, falsification; see **deception** 1, **lie** 1.

mended, *mod.* —*Syn.* restored, put in shape, patched up, renovated, refreshed, renewed, corrected, helped, bettered, abated, lessened, ameliorated, remedied, cured, relieved, rectified, rejuvenated, refurbished, emended, enhanced, remodeled, altered, changed, fixed, regulated, rebuilt, regenerated, reorganized, revived, touched up, cobbled, tinkered; *both* (D): gone over, doctored; see also **improved** 1, **repaired.**

mendicant, *n.* —*Syn.* hobo, vagabond, pauper; see **beggar** 1, 2, **tramp** 1.

mending, *n.* —*Syn.* restoring, renovating, repairing, renewing, putting into shape, patching up, refreshing, freshening, helping, bettering, ameliorating, relieving, remedying, curing, rectifying, correcting, enhancing, emending, changing, altering, rebuilding, remodeling, renovation, repair, restoration, reviving, tinkering, going over (D); see also **correction** 1, **fixing** 1.

menial, *mod.* —*Syn.* common, servile, abject; see **humble** 1, 2.

menial, *n.* —*Syn.* domestic, maid, lackey; see **servant.**

mensurable, *mod.* —*Syn.* assayable, estimable, measurable; see **calculable, determinable.**

mensuration, *n.* —*Syn.* survey, measure, evaluation; see **estimate** 1, **judgment** 2.

mental, *mod.* **1.** [Concerning the mind]—*Syn.* reasoning, cerebral, thinking; see **rational** 1, **thoughtful** 1.
2. [Existing only in the mind]—*Syn.* subjective, subliminal, subconscious, telepathic, psychic, clairvoyant, unreal, imaginative; see also **mysterious** 2. —*Ant.* objective*, bodily*, sensual*.

mental health, *n.*—*Syn.* normality, mental balance *or* stability, freedom from mental illness *or* disease; see **sanity** 1.

mentality, *n.*—*Syn.* intellect, comprehension, reasoning; see **brain** 1, **mind** 1.

mentally, *mod.*—*Syn.* rationally, thoughtfully, psychically, intellectually, inwardly, pensively, psychologically, introspectively, subjectively.

mention, *n.*—*Syn.* notice, naming, specifying; see **allusion, remark.**
make mention of—*Syn.* notice, consider, cite; see **mention.**
not to mention—*Syn.* in addition, too, without even mentioning; see **also.**

mention, *v.*—*Syn.* notice, specify, cite, adduce, introduce, state, declare, quote, refer to, discuss, touch on, instance, acquaint with, infer, intimate, notify, communicate, suggest, make known, point out, point to *or* at, speak of, throw out (D); see also **consider** 2, **designate** 1, **name** 2.—*Ant.* overlook*, take no notice of, disregard.

mentioned, *mod.*—*Syn.* noticed, cited, specified, named, quoted, introduced, referred to, discussed, declared, intimated, revealed, brought to one's attention, brought up, considered, communicated, made known, spoken of; see also **suggested, told.**

mentioning, *mod.*—*Syn.* remarking, noting, observing; see **saying.**

mentioning, *n.*—*Syn.* speaking of, taking note of, referring to, introduction, inferring, intimating, making known, specifying, citing; see also **naming, suggesting.**

mentor, *n.*—*Syn.* instructor, guide, coach; see **teacher** 1, **trainer.**

menu, *n.*—*Syn.* bill of fare, carte, cuisine, table, cover, spread, card, food (D); see also **list.**

mercantile, *mod.*—*Syn.* trading, business, marketing; see **commercial** 1, **industrial.**

mercenary, *mod.*—*Syn.* acquisitive, selfish, miserly; see **greedy** 1, **stingy.**

mercenary, *n.*—*Syn.* legionnaire, professional soldier, warrior; see **soldier.**

merchandise, *n.*—*Syn.* wares, commodities, stock; see **commodity.**

merchandise, *v.*—*Syn.* market, distribute, promote; see **sell** 1.

merchant, *n.*—*Syn.* trader, storekeeper, retailer, shopkeeper, wholesaler, handler, sender, consigner, exporter, shipper, dealer, local representative, jobber, tradesman; see also **businessman.**

merchantable, *mod.*—*Syn.* in demand, marketable, salable; see **commercial** 1, **in the market.**

merchantman, *n.*—*Syn.* galleon, steamship, commercial vessel; see **boat, ship.**

merciful, *mod.* **1.** [Giving evidence of mercy] —*Syn.* lenient, clement, feeling, compassionate, pitiful, soft-hearted, mild, sparing, tolerant, kindly, indulgent, benign, benignant; see also **humane** 1, **kind.**—*Ant.* cruel*, pitiless, unsparing.
2. [Having mercy as a character trait]—*Syn.* gentle, tender, gracious; see **kind, thoughtful** 2.

merciless, *mod.*—*Syn.* pitiless, unsparing, relentless; see **cruel** 2, **fierce** 1, **ruthless** 1.

mercurial, *mod.*—*Syn.* variable, fluctuating, inconstant; see **changeable** 1, 2, **irregular** 1.

mercy, *n.* **1.** [Willingness to spare others]—*Syn.* leniency, lenience, soft-heartedness, mildness, clemency, tenderness, lenity, gentleness, compassion, benignancy; see also **generosity** 1, **tolerance** 1. —*Ant.* intolerance, indifference*, selfishness.
2. [The act of sparing or forgiving]—*Syn.* forbearance, toleration, forgiveness; see **kindness** 1.
3. [Compassionate assistance to those in distress] —*Syn.* compassion, commiseration, sympathy; see **aid** 1, **pity** 1.
at the mercy of—*Syn.* in the power of, vulnerable to, controlled by; see **subject** 1.

mere, *mod.*—*Syn.* small, minor, insignificant; see **little** 1, **poor** 2.

merely, *mod.*—*Syn.* slightly, solely, simply; see **hardly, only** 3.

meretricious, *mod.*—*Syn.* gaudy, flashy, loud; see **ornate** 1.

merge, *v.*—*Syn.* fuse, join, synthesize, amalgamate, blend, marry, absorb, consolidate, coalesce, conglomerate, centralize, impregnate, assimilate, melt into one, immerge, submerge; see also **mix** 1, **unite** 1.

merger, *n.*—*Syn.* pool, consolidation, alliance; see **incorporation** 2, **organization** 1.

meridian, *n.* **1.** [Noon]—*Syn.* noontime, midday, noonday; see **noon, time** 1, 2.
2. [Summit]—*Syn.* apex, extremity, peak; see **climax.**

meridional, *mod.* **1.** [Noon]—*Syn.* midday, noontime, sunny, resplendent, blazing, radiant; see also **bright** 1.
2. [Southern]—*Syn.* austral, southerly, to the south; see **southeast, southern, southwest.**

merit, *n.* **1.** [Worth]—*Syn.* credit, benefit, advantage; see **quality** 3, **value** 3.
2. [A creditable quality]—*Syn.* worthiness, excellence, honor; see **character** 2, **virtue** 1.

merit, *v.*—*Syn.* be worth, warrant, justify; see **deserve.**

merited, *mod.*—*Syn.* earned, proper, fitting; see **deserved, fit** 1, **warranted.**

meritorious, *mod.*—*Syn.* praiseworthy, commendable, honorable; see **noble** 1, 2, **worthy.**

merrily, *mod.*—*Syn.* joyfully, gleefully, genially; see **cheerfully, happily** 2.

merriment, *n.* **1.** [A merry feeling]—*Syn.* joy, cheerfulness, gaiety; see **happiness** 1, **humor** 3.
2. [A merry occasion]—*Syn.* carousal, sport, frolic, festivity, good time, recreation, tomfoolery, buffoonery, mummery, merry-making; see also **fun, party** 1.—*Ant.* funeral*, wake, work.

merry, *mod.* **1.** [Happy]—*Syn.* gay, joyous, mirthful; see **happy** 1.
2. [Festive]—*Syn.* enjoyable, amusing, lively; see **entertaining, pleasant** 2.

merry-go-round, *n.*—*Syn.* carousel, revolving platform, amusement device, whirligig, the dizzy rounds (D).

merrymaking, *n.* —*Syn.* frolic, amusement, revelry; see **entertainment** 1, **fun.**
mesa, *n.* —*Syn.* plateau, table, tableland, butte, table mountain; see also **hill, mountain** 1.
mesh, *n.* —*Syn.* snare, trap, screen; see **net, web** 1, 2.
mesh, *v.* —*Syn.* coincide, suit, be in gear; see **agree, fit** 1.
mesmerism, *n.* —*Syn.* hypnosis, entrancing, hypnotism; see **numbness, stupor.**
mesmerize, *v.* —*Syn.* render unconscious, control, stupefy; see **deaden** 1, **drug, hypnotize**
mess, *n.* **1.** [A mixture]—*Syn.* combination, compound, blend; see **mash, mixture** 1.
2. [A confusion]—*Syn.* jumble, mayhem, hodgepodge (D); see **confusion** 2, **disorder** 2.
3. [Military term for meals]—*Syn.* rations; *both* (D): chow, grub; see **meal** 2.
message, *n.* **1.** [Communicated information]—*Syn.* tidings, information, intelligence; see **advice, broadcast, communication** 2, **directions.**
2. [A communication]—*Syn.* note, word, paper; see **communications, letter** 2, **news** 1, 2, **report** 1.
get the message (D)—*Syn.* get the hint, comprehend, perceive; see **understand** 1.
mess around *or* **about (with)** (D), *v.* —*Syn.* dawdle, fool around, play the fool (with); see **loiter, play** 1, 2.
messenger, *n.* —*Syn.* bearer, minister, angel, prophet, dispatcher, herald, carrier, courier, runner, crier, errand boy, intermediary, envoy, emissary, internuncio, go-between, ambassador, commissionaire, flag-bearer; *all* (D): gofer, boy, hotboot, speed; see also **agent** 1.
Messiah, *n.* —*Syn.* Saviour, Redeemer, Jesus Christ; see **Christ, god** 2.
messmate, *n.* —*Syn.* comrade, buddy, shipmate; see **friend** 1, **mate** 2.
mess up, *v.* —*Syn.* spoil, ruin, foul up, damage; see **botch, destroy** 1.
messy, *mod.* —*Syn.* rumpled, untidy, slovely; see **dirty** 1, **disordered.**
metal, *n.* —*Syn.* element, native rock, metalliferous ore, ore deposit, free metal, refined ore, smelted ore; see also **alloy, mineral.**
Types of metal include the following—gold, silver, copper, iron, steel, aluminum, manganese, nickel, lead, cobalt, platinum, zinc, tin, barium, cadmium, chromium, tungsten, mercury, iridium, molybdenum, antimony, vanadium, alunite, corundum, lithium, sodium, potassium, ribidium, caesium, casium, strontium, radium, beryllium, magnesium, gallium, indium, thallium, cerium, calcium, celtium, anthanium, terbium, holmium, titanium, germanium, arsenic, bismuth, uranium, dysprosium, erbium, rhodium, ruthenium, palladium, osmium, indium, lanthanum, entecium, neodymium, niobium, praseodymion, samarium, tantalum, thorium, thulium, ytterbium, zirconium.
metallic, *mod.* **1.** [Made of metal]—*Syn.* hard, rocklike, fusible, ory, iron, leaden, silvery, golden, tinny, stannic, metallurgic, mineral, geologic.
2. [Suggestive of metal; *said especially of sound*] —*Syn.* ringing, resounding, resonant, trumpet-tongued, bell-like, clanging, clangorous; see also **loud** 1, 2.
metamorphic, *mod.* —*Syn.* variable, mobile, versatile; see **changeable** 2, **growing.**
metamorphose, *v.* —*Syn.* alter, diverge, transform; see **change** 1, **vary** 1.
metamorphosis, *n.* —*Syn.* transformation, evolution, modification; see **change** 1, 2, **variety** 1.
metaphor, *n.* —*Syn.* trope, simile, implied comparison; see **comparison** 2.
mix metaphors—*Syn.* be inconsistent, garble, talk illogically; see **confuse.**
metamorphic, *mod.* —*Syn.* allegorical, symbolic, descriptive; see **illustrative.**
metaphorical, *mod.* —*Syn.* symbolical, allegorical, figurative, referential, allusive, comparative, mystical, anagogic, metonymic, poetic, anagogical, contrastive, exegetical, symbolistic, involved, imaginative, mythic, antonomastic, catachrestic; see also **descriptive, graphic** 1, 2, **illustrative, symbolic.**
metaphysical, *mod.* —*Syn.* mystical, abstract, spiritual; see **difficult** 2, **transcendental.**
metaphysics, *n.* —*Syn.* epistemology, ontology, cosmology, mysticism, transcendentalism; see also **philosophy, religion** 1.
mete, *v.* —*Syn.* allot, measure out, administer; see **distribute** 1, **give** 1.
metempsychosis, *n.* —*Syn.* rebirth, transmigration, reincarnation, incarnation, reanimation; see also **renewal, spiritualism** 1.
meteor, *n.* —*Syn.* falling star, shooting star, meteorite, fireball, bolide, meteroid; see also **satellite** 1, **star** 1.
meteoric, *mod.* —*Syn.* brilliant, swift, transient; see **bright** 1, **fleeting.**
meteoroid, *n.* —*Syn.* meteorite, shooting star, falling stone; see **meteor, star** 1.
meteorology, *n.* —*Syn.* climate science, atmospheric conditions, climatology, aerology, climatography, aerography; see also **science** 1, **weather.**
meter, *n.* —*Syn.* measure, rhythm, metrical feet, quantitative feet, syllabic groups, metrical structure *or* pattern, common meter, long meter, ballad meter, tetrameter, pentameter, hendecasyllable, heptameter, sprung rhythm, dipodic rhythm; see also **beat** 3, **music** 1, **poetry.**
method, *n.* **1.** [Order]—*Syn.* classification, organization, arrangement; see **order** 3, **system** 1.
2. [A procedure]—*Syn.* mode, style, standard procedure, fashion, way, means, tenor, process, proceeding, adjustment, disposition, disposal, practice, routine, technic, technique, method of attack, mode of operation, manner of working, ways and means, habit, custom, *modus operandi* (Latin), manner, formula, process, course, rule; see also **system** 2.
3. [Plan]—*Syn.* design, outline, scheme; see **opinion** 1, **plan** 2, **purpose** 1.
methodical, *mod.* —*Syn.* well-regulated, systematic, exact; see **regular** 3, **orderly** 2.
Methodist, *n.* —*Syn.* Trinitarian, Protestant, Southern Methodist, Methodist-Episcopal; see **Christian, Christianity** 2, **church** 3.
meticulous, *mod.* —*Syn.* scrupulous, fastidious, precise; see **accurate** 1, 2, **careful.**
métier, *n.* —*Syn.* trade, profession, occupation; see **job** 1, **profession** 1, **trade** 2.

metropolis, *n.* —*Syn.* capital, megalopolis, municipality; see **center** 2, **city.**

metropolitan, *mod.* —*Syn.* city, municipal, cosmopolitan; see **modern** 2, **urban** 2.

mettle, *n.* **1.** [Spirit]—*Syn.* animation, energy, spunk; see **force** 3, **life** 1, **vitality.**
2. [Hardihood]—*Syn.* stamina, bravery, pluck; see **courage** 1, **strength** 1.

mettlesome, *mod.* **1.** [High-spirited]—*Syn.* spirited, vigorous, spunky; sèe **active** 2.
2. [Gallant]—*Syn.* plucky, valiant, dauntless; see **brave** 1.

Mexican, *mod.* —*Syn.* Latin American, (from) south of the border, Hispanic; see **American** 1.

Mexico, *n.* —*Syn. Mejico, El Pais* (*both* Spanish), the other side of the Rio Grande, land south of the border, a sister republic, the republic to the south; see also **America** 1.

mezzanine, *n.* —*Syn.* second floor, balcony, intermediate floor; see **attic, floor** 2.

mezzo, *mod.* —*Syn.* medium, medial, mean; see **central** 1.

mezzotint, *n.* —*Syn.* half tone, line engraving, black and white; see **engraving** 2, **plate** 3.

miasma, *n.* —*Syn.* vapor, steam, fume; see **gas** 1, **haze.**

miasmatic, *mod.* —*Syn.* dangerous, contagious, lethal; see **deadly, poisonous.**

mickey mouse (D), *mod.* —*Syn.* trite, platitudinous, simplistic; see **dull** 4, **easy** 2, **naïve, simple** 2.

microbe, *n.* —*Syn.* microorganism, bacterium, bacillus; see **germ** 3.

microphone, *n.* —*Syn.* sound transmitter, receiver, pickup instrument; *all* (D): mike, miker, duck, talkback mike, bug, mike boom, walkie-talkie; see also **amplifier.**

microscope, *n.* —*Syn.* lens, magnifying glass, optical instrument; *both* (D): scope, mike; see also **lens.** Microscopes include the following—high-powered, compound, photographic, electron, electronic.

microscopic, *mod.* —*Syn.* diminutive, tiny, infinitesimal; see **little** 1, **minute** 1.

mid, *mod.* —*Syn.* intervening, medial, median; see **halfway, intermediate, middle.**

middle, *mod.* —*Syn.* between, mean, midway, medial, average, mezzo, equidistant; see also **central** 1, **halfway, intermediate.**

middle, *n.* —*Syn.* mean, media, midpoint; see **center** 1.

middle age, *n.* —*Syn.* adulthood, prime, maturity; see **majority** 2.

middle-aged, *mod.* —*Syn.* adult, in one's prime, matronly; see **mature** 1, **matured.**

middle-class, *mod.* —*Syn.* white-collar, bourgeois, substantial; see **common** 1, **popular** 1, 3.

middle classes, *n.* —*Syn.* white-collar class, the rank and file, (the) bourgeoisie; see **people** 3.

middleman, *n.* —*Syn.* representative, broker, salesman; see **agent** 1.

middle-sized, *mod.* —*Syn.* fair-sized, moderate-sized, average, normal, ordinary, so-so, indifferent, in-between, fair to middling (D); see also **common** 1.

Middle Western, *mod.* —*Syn.* Midwestern, midland, prairie, prairie-state, Middle American; see also **western** 1, 3.

middling, *mod.* —*Syn.* mediocre, ordinary, average; see **common** 1, **conventional** 1, 3, **traditional** 2.
fair to middling (D)—*Syn.* moderately good, ordinary, average; see **fair** 2.

midget, *n.* —*Syn.* homunculus, pygmy, dwarf, small person, mannikin; see also **runt.**

midnight, *n.* —*Syn.* dead of night, stroke of midnight, 12:00 P.M., noon of night, witching hour; see also **night** 1.
burn the midnight oil (D)—*Syn.* stay up late, work *or* study (late), keep late hours; see **study** 1, **work** 1.

midshipman, *n.* —*Syn.* seaman, mariner, navigator; see **sailor.**

midst, *n.* —*Syn.* midpoint, nucleus, middle; see **center** 1.
in our (*or* **your** *or* **their**) **midst**—*Syn.* between us, with, accompanying; see **among.**
in the midst of—*Syn.* in the course of, engaged in, in the middle of; see **central** 1.

midsummer, *n.* —*Syn.* solstice, June 22, longest day of the year; see **summer.**

midway, *mod.* —*Syn.* in the thick of, between, in the middle; see **central** 1, **halfway, intermediate, middle.**

midwife, *n.* —*Syn.* accoucheuse, attendant, practitioner, assistant, one who delivers, *sage-femme* (French).

mien, *n.* —*Syn.* aspect, mannerism, look; see **appearance** 1.

miff, *n.* —*Syn.* huff, tantrum, fit; see **anger, rage** 2.

miff, *v.* **1.** [To annoy]—*Syn.* provoke, pester, offend; see **bother** 2.
2. [To frown]—*Syn.* scowl, frown, seethe; see **rage** 1.

might, *n.* —*Syn.* strength, force, sway; see **strength** 1.

mightily, *mod.* —*Syn.* energetically, strongly, forcibly; see **powerfully, vigorously.**

mighty, *mod.* **1.** [Strong]—*Syn.* powerful, stalwart, muscular; see **strong** 1.
2. [Powerful through influence]—*Syn.* great, all-powerful, omnipotent; see **powerful** 1.
3. [Imposing]—*Syn.* great, remarkably large, extensive, impressive, gigantic, magnificent, majestic, towering, dynamic, irresistible, notable, extraordinary, grand, considerable, monumental, titanic, tremendous, high and mighty; see also **large** 1.—*Ant.* plain*, unimpressive, ordinary.

mighty (D), *mod.* —*Syn.* great, exceedingly, extremely; see **very.**

migrate, *v.* —*Syn.* move, emigrate, immigrate; see **leave** 1.

migration, *n.* —*Syn.* emigration, immigration, voyage; see **departure** 1, **journey, movement** 2.

migratory, *mod.* **1.** [Having fixed habits of migration; *said especially of birds*]—*Syn.* seasonal, transient, impermanent, emigrating, immigrating, passing over, like birds of passage, here for the winter, arrived for the summer, in a flyway.—*Ant.* local*, hibernating, nonmigratory.
2. [Given to moving; *said especially of transient labor*]—*Syn.* shifting, changing, unsettled, casual, roving, wandering, nomadic, tramp, vagrant, on

the move, wetback (D); see also **temporary.**—*Ant.* permanent*, steady, settled.

mild, *mod.* **1.** [Gentle; *said especially of persons*] —*Syn.* meek, easygoing, patient; see **kind.**
2. [Temperate; *said especially of weather*]—*Syn.* bland, untroubled, tropical, peaceful, pacific, summery, tepid, medium, cool, balmy, breezy, gentle, soft, lukewarm, clement, clear, moderate, genial, mellow, fine, uncloudy, sunny, warm; see also **calm** 2, **fair** 3.—*Ant.* rough*, cold*, stormy*.
3. [Easy; *said especially of burdens or punishment*] —*Syn.* soft, light, tempered; see **moderate** 4.
4. [Not irritating]—*Syn.* bland, soothing, soft, smooth, gentle, moderate, easy, mollifying, mellow, delicate, temperate.

mildew, *n.* —*Syn.* smut, fungus, rust; see **decay** 2, **mold** 3.

mildew, *v.* —*Syn.* mold, spoil, must; see **decay.**

mildly, *mod.*—*Syn.* gently, meekly, blandly, calmly, genially, tranquilly, tepidly, softly, lightly, moderately, tenderly, compassionately, tolerantly, patiently, imperturbably, temperately, indifferently, quietly, soothingly, indulgently, mollifyingly; see also **kindly** 2.—*Ant.* violently*, harshly, roughly.

mildness, *n.* —*Syn.* tolerance, tenderness, gentleness; see **kindness** 1.

mile, *n.* —*Syn.* 5,280 feet, statute mile, geographical mile, nautical mile, Admiralty mile; see also **distance** 3, **measure** 1.

mileage, *n.* —*Syn.* rate, space, measure; see **distance** 3, **length** 1.

milestone, *n.* **1.** [Sign]—*Syn.* post, pillar, stone; see **sign** 1.
2. [Event]—*Syn.* discovery, breakthrough, anniversary; see **event** 1, 2.

militant, *mod.*—*Syn.* combative, belligerent, offensive; see **aggressive** 2, **militaristic.**

militant, *n.* —*Syn.* rioter, violent objector, demonstrator; see **protester.**

militarism, *n.* —*Syn.* martial policy, regimentation, militancy; see **power** 2, **war.**

militarist, *n.* —*Syn.* warlord, warmonger, combatant; see **soldier.**

militaristic, *mod.* —*Syn.* warmongering, jingoistic, chauvinistic, warlike, antagonistic, belligerent; see also **aggressive** 2.

military, *mod.*—*Syn.* armed, martial, militant, fighting, combatant, soldierly, combative, concerning the armed forces, noncivil, warlike, for war; see also **aggressive** 2, **army, militaristic.**

militia, *n.* —*Syn.* military force, civilian army. National Guard; see **army** 1.

milk, *n.* —*Syn.* fluid, juice, whey, sap; see also **liquid.** Types of milk include the following—whole, skim, raw, pasteurized, homogenized, certified; grade-A, grade-B, etc.; loose, acidophilous, condensed, dried, evaporated, powdered, two-percent, four-percent, etc.; reducing, dietary, goat's, ewe's, mare's, mother's; cream, half-and-half, baby formula, buttermilk, koumiss, kefir.
cry over spilt milk—*Syn.* mourn, lament, sulk; see **regret.**

milking, *n.* —*Syn.* drawing from, pumping, draining, suction, sapping, emptying, suckling, sucking; see also **extraction** 2.

milkman, *n.* —*Syn.* dairyman, dairy farmer, cowherd, one who delivers milk, iceman, dairymaid, milkmaid.

milksop, *n.* —*Syn.* pantywaist, milquetoast, sissy; see **coward.**

milky, *mod.* —*Syn.* opaque, pearly, cloudy; see **white** 1.

Milky Way, *n.* —*Syn.* galactic circle, stars and planets, galaxy; see **constellation.**

mill, *n.* **1.** [A factory]—*Syn.* manufactory, plant, millhouse; see **factory.**
2. [A machine for grinding, crushing, pressing, etc.] Types of mills include the following—flour, coffee, bone, cotton, weaving, spinning, powder, rolling, cider, cane, lapidary; sawmill, *arrastra* (Spanish), coin press, diesinking machine.
in the mill—*Syn.* in production, developing, in the works (D); see **growing.**
through the mill (D)—*Syn.* tested, completed, produced; see **finished** 1.

millennium, *n.* —*Syn.* happiness, golden age, golden dream, kingdom come, heaven on earth, thousand years of peace; see also **utopia.**

miller, *n.* —*Syn.* mill operator, meal grinder, mill owner; see also **workman.**

milliner, *n.* —*Syn.* modiste, hat salesman, hatter, hat maker.

millinery, *n.* —*Syn.* bonnet, cap, headgear; see **hat.**

millionaire, *n.* —*Syn.* man of wealth *or* means, capitalist, tycoon, rich man, moneyed man, man of substance, plutocrat, Croesus, nabob, Midas, Dives, man of millions; *all* (D): tippybob, doughbag, butter-and-egg man, big-money man, money baron, robber baron, bankroll; see also **financier.**—*Ant.* beggar*, poor man, pauper.

millions (D), *n.* **1.** [*Said of people*]—*Syn.* the masses, population, populace; see **people** 3.
2. [*Said of money*]—*Syn.* a fortune, great wealth, profits; see **wealth** 1, 2.

millstone, *n.* **1.** [A grinder]—*Syn.* stone, chopper, mill; see **grinder** 1, **tool** 1.
2. [A burden]—*Syn.* impediment, load, responsibility; see **difficulty** 2.

mime, *n.* **1.** [An imitator]—*Syn.* mimic, impersonator, comedian; see **actor, imitator.**
2. [An imitation]—*Syn.* mockery, caricature, mimicry; see **imitation** 2, **parody** 1.

mime, *v.* —*Syn.* impersonate, mimic, pretend; see **act** 1, **imitate** 2, **parody.**

mimetic, *mod.* —*Syn.* imitative, reflective, mocking, mimicking, copying, make-believe, echoic.

mimic, *n.* —*Syn.* mime, impersonator, comedian; see **actor, imitator.**

mimic, *v.* **1.** [To imitate]—*Syn.* copy, simulate, impersonate; see **imitate** 2.
2. [To mock]—*Syn.* make fun of, burlesque, caricature; see **parody, ridicule.**

mimicry, *n.* —*Syn.* mime, pretense, mockery; see **imitation** 2, **parody** 1.

minaret, *n.* —*Syn.* steeple, spire, belfry; see **tower.**

mince, *v.* **1.** [To chop]—*Syn.* dice, hash, divide; see **chip.**
2. [To minimize]—*Syn.* mitigate, alleviate, lessen; see **decrease** 2.

mincing, *mod.* —*Syn.* insincere, unnatural, artificial; see **affected** 2.

mind, *n.* **1.** [Intellectual potentiality]—*Syn.* soul, spirit, intellect, brain, consciousness, thought, mentality, intuition, perception, conception, intelligence, intellectuality, apperception, percipience, capacity, judgment, understanding, wisdom, genius, talent, reasoning, instinct, ratiocination, thinking principle, wit, mental *or* intellectual faculties, creativity, ingenuity, intellectual powers *or* processes; *all* (D): gray matter, brainstuff, brainpower, milk in the coconut, what it takes.
2. [Purpose]—*Syn.* intention, inclination, determination; see **purpose** 1.
3. [Memory]—*Syn.* subconscious, remembrance, cognizance; see **memory** 1
bear (*or* **keep) in mind**—*Syn.* heed, recollect, recall; see **remember** 1.
be in one's right mind—*Syn.* be mentally well, be rational, be sane; see **reason** 2.
be of one mind—*Syn.* have the same opinion *or* desire, concur, be in accord; see **agree.**
be of two minds—*Syn.* be undecided *or* irresolute, vacillate, ride the fence (D); see **waver.**
call to mind—*Syn.* recall, recollect, bring to mind; see **remember** 1.
change one's mind—*Syn.* alter one's opinion, change one's views, disagree with oneself; see **change one's mind.**
give someone a piece of one's mind—*Syn.* rebuke, confute, criticize; see **censure.**
have a good (*or* **great) mind to**—*Syn.* be inclined to, propose, tend to; see **intend** 1.
have half a mind to—*Syn.* be inclined to, propose, tend to; see **intend** 1.
have in mind—*Syn.* **1.** recall, recollect, think of; see **remember** 1. **2.** purpose, propose, be inclined to; see **intend** 1.
know one's own mind—*Syn.* know oneself, be deliberate, have a plan; see **know** 1.
make up one's mind—*Syn.* form a definite opinion, choose, finalize; see **decide** 1.
meeting of the minds—*Syn.* concurrence, unity, harmony; see **agreement** 2.
never mind—*Syn.* don't be concerned, it doesn't matter, it is of no importance; see **never mind.**
on one's mind—*Syn.* occupying one's thoughts, causing concern, worrying one; see **important** 1.
out of one's mind—*Syn.* mentally ill, raving, mad; see **insane** 1.
put in mind—*Syn.* recall, inform, call attention to; see **remind** 2.
set one's mind on—*Syn.* determine, intend, plan; see **decide** 1.
take one's mind off—*Syn.* turn one's attention from, divert, change; see **distract** 1.
to one's mind—*Syn.* in one's opinion, as one sees it, according to one; see **personally** 2.

mind, *v.* **1.** [To obey]—*Syn.* be under the authority of, heed, do as told; see **behave** 2, **obey** 1.
2. [To give one's attention]—*Syn.* heed, attend, be attentive to; see **regard** 1.
3. [To be careful]—*Syn.* tend, watch out for, have oversight of, take care, trouble, be wary, be concerned for, be solicitous, dislike, object; *all* (D): mind one's *p*'s and *q*'s, have a care, sleep with one eye open, keep one's chin in; see also **care** 2. —*Ant.* neglect*, ignore, be careless.
4. [To remember]—*Syn.* recollect, recall, bring to mind; see **remember** 1.
5. [To object to]—*Syn.* complain, deplore, be opposed to; see **dislike, object** 1.

minded, *mod.* —*Syn.* disposed, inclined, liking, turned *or* leaning toward, desirous, intending, purposing, planning, contemplating, convinced, determined, resolved, decided, settled on, fixed on, harboring a design, proposing to oneself, aspiring to, aiming at, driving for, thinking of, having a good mind to; see also **willing** 2.—*Ant.* unwilling*, disinclined, undetermined.

mindful, *mod.* —*Syn.* attentive, heedful, watchful; see **careful.**

mindless, *mod.* **1.** [Careless]—*Syn.* inattentive, oblivious, neglectful; see **careless** 1, **indifferent** 1, **rash.**
2. [Stupid]—*Syn.* foolish, senseless, unintelligent; see **stupid** 1.

mind one's *p*'s and *q*'s (D), *v.* —*Syn.* act properly, conform, mind; see **behave** 2.

mind's eye (D), *n.* —*Syn.* imagination, fantasy, vision; see **thought** 2.

mine, *mod.* —*Syn.* my own, belonging to me, possessed by me, mine by right, owned by me, left to me, from me, by me; see also **our.**

mine, *n.* **1.** [A source of natural wealth]—*Syn.* pit, well, shaft, diggings, excavation, adit, workings, quarry, deposit, vein, lode, dike, ore bed, placer (deposit), matrix; *all* (D): pay dirt, pay streak, bonanza; see also **tunnel.**
Types of mines, sense 1, include the following—placer, surface, open pit, strip; quartz, coal, iron, copper, silver, gold, diamond, etc.; underhand *or* bottom stope, overhand *or* top stope, rill stope, opencast stope, shrinkage stope.
2. [An explosive charge]—*Syn.* landmine, ambush, trap; see **bomb, explosive, weapon** 1.
Types of mines, sense 2, include the following—floating, anchor, ratchet, magnetic, aerial, antipersonnel *or* castrator (D) *or* Bouncing Betty (D) *or* Leaping Lena (D); S-mine, *Teller* (German), claymore, delayed action mine, time bomb, booby trap.

mine, *v.* **1.** [To dig for minerals]—*Syn.* excavate, burrow, pan, stope, drill, work, quarry, wash for gold; see also **dig** 1.
2. [To lay mines]—*Syn.* sow with mines, prepare mine fields, set booby traps; see **defend** 1.

miner, *n.* —*Syn.* excavator, digger, driller, dredger, mineworker, prospector; *all* (D): desert rat, sourdough, forty-niner; see also **laborer, workman.**
Types of miners include the following—*Syn.* gold, coal, diamond, amber, quarry, placer; collier, tarrier, driller, blaster, prospector, hard-rock geologist, caisson worker, gold panner, geologist, geological *or* mining engineer, mine superintendent; *all* (D): mucker, donkey engineer, muckman, highgrader, rusher, pocket hunter, hardrocker.

mineral, *mod.* —*Syn.* geologic, rock, metallurgic; see **metallic** 1.

mineral, *n.* —*Syn.* earth's crust, geologic formation, geologic rock, rock deposit, country rock, ore deposit, gangue, igneous rock, metamorphic rock, morphologic rock, magma, petroleums, crystal; see also **metal, ore.**
Common minerals include the following—quartz, feldspar, mica, hornblende, pyroxene, olivine, cal-

cite, dolomite, pyrite, chalcopyrite, barite, garnet, diopside, gypsum, staurolite, tourmaline, obsidian, malachite, azurite, limonite, galena, aragonite, magnetite, ilmenite, serpentine, epidote, fluorite, cinnabar, talc, bauxite, corundum, cryolite, spinel, sheelite, wolframite.

mingle, *v.* —*Syn.* combine, blend, admix; see **mix** 1.

mingling, *n.* —*Syn.* compound, composite, blend; see **mixture** 1.

miniature, *mod.* —*Syn.* diminutive, small, tiny; see **little** 1, **minute** 1.

minimal, *mod.* —*Syn.* insignificant, smallest, minimum; see **least** 1.

minimize, *v.* —*Syn.* lessen, depreciate, reduce; see **decrease** 2.

minimum, *mod.* —*Syn.* smallest, tiniest, merest; see **least** 1.

minimum, *n.* —*Syn.* smallest, least, lowest, narrowest, modicum, atom, molecule, particle, dot, jot, iota, point, spark, shadow, whit, tittle, soupçon, scintilla, trifle, gleam, grain, scruple.

mining, *n.* —*Syn.* excavating, hollowing, opening, digging, scooping, tapping, boring, drilling, pitting, undermining, delving, burrowing, tunneling, staving in, honeycombing, placer mining, stoping, hard-rock mining, prospecting.

minion, *n.* —*Syn.* creature, slave, dependent; see **follower.**

minister, *n.* **1.** [One authorized to conduct Christian worship]—*Syn.* pastor, parson, preacher, clergyman, rector, monk, abbot, prelate, curate, vicar, deacon, chaplain, pulpiteer, servant of God, shepherd, churchman, cleric, padre, ecclesiastic, bishop, archbishop, suffragan, confessor, reverend, dean, archdeacon, abbé, curé, prebendary, canon, diocesan, primate, metropolitan, reverence, reader, lecturer, divine, shepherd, Bible-reader, missionary; *all* (D): sky pilot, black coat, psalm singer; see also **priest.**—*Ant.* layman*, church member, parishioner.

2. [A high servant of the state]—*Syn.* ambassador, consul, liaison officer; see **diplomat** 1, **representative** 2, **statesman.**

minister, *v.* —*Syn.* administer to, tend, wait on; see **help** 1.

ministerial, *mod.* **1.** [Priestly]—*Syn.* pastoral, ecclesiastical, canonical; see **clerical** 2, **religious** 1.

2. [Official]—*Syn.* valid, consular, diplomatic; see **official** 3.

ministration, *n.* —*Syn.* assistance, help, support; see **aid** 1.

ministry, *n.* **1.** [The functions of the clergy]—*Syn.* pastoral care, preaching, exhortation, administration of the sacraments, prayer, spiritual leadership, service.

2. [The clergy]—*Syn.* the cloth, clergymen, ecclesiastics, clerics, the clerical order, priesthood, the pulpit, clericals, prelacy, vicarage, the desk, clergy.

3. [A department of state]—*Syn.* bureau, administrative agency, executive branch; see **department** 2.

minor, *mod.* —*Syn.* secondary, lesser, insignificant; see **trivial, unimportant.**

minor, *n.* —*Syn.* person under eighteen *or* twenty-one, underage person, boy, girl, child, infant, little one, lad, slip, spring, schoolboy, schoolgirl, lassie, miss, maid; see also **youth** 3.

minority, *n.* **1.** [An outnumbered group]—*Syn.* opposition, less than half, the outvoted, the few, the outnumbered, the losing side; *both* (D): splinter group, the outs.

2. [The time before one is of legal age]—*Syn.* childhood, immaturity, adolescence; see **youth** 1.

minor-league, *mod.* —*Syn.* second-rate, minor, small-time; see **unimportant, trivial.**

minstrel, *n.* —*Syn.* ballad singer, balladeer, bard, minnesinger, troubadour, jongleur, street singer, songsmith, *trovatore* (Italian), *trouvère* (French), *Meistersinger* (German); see also **musician, poet.**

minstrelsy, *n.* —*Syn.* balladry, folk music, *Lieder* (German); see **song.**

mint, *v.* **1.** [To print or press money]—*Syn.* strike, mold, punch, coin, cast, forge, stamp, issue, provide legal tender; see also **print** 2.

2. [To invent a word, etc.]—*Syn.* coin, devise, create; see **invent** 1.

minus, *mod.* —*Syn.* diminished, short of, deficient; see **less.**

minute, *mod.* **1.** [Extremely small]—*Syn.* microscopic, diminutive, wee, tiny, atomic, miniature, puny, infinitesimal, inframicroscopic, microbic, molecular, exact, precise, pulverized, fine, exiguous, inconsiderable; *all* (D): teeny, weeny, teensy, peewee, itsy(-bitsy), invisible; see also **little** 1. —*Ant.* large*, huge, immense.

2. [Trivial]—*Syn.* immaterial, nonessential, paltry; see **trivial, unimportant.**

3. [Exact]—*Syn.* particular, circumstantial, specialized; see **detailed, elaborate** 2.

minute, *n.* **1.** [The sixtieth part of an hour]—*Syn.* sixty seconds, unit *or* measure of time, space of time; see also **time** 1.

2. [A brief time]—*Syn.* short time, second, trice, flash, twinkling, breath; *all* (D): jiffy, bat of an eye, shake of a lamb's tail, couple of humps, tick, twink; see also **instant, moment** 1, **time** 2.—*Ant.* eternity*, long time, forever*.

up to the minute (D)—*Syn.* **1.** modern, contemporary, in the latest style; see **fashionable. 2.** current, prompt, recent; see **modern** 1.

(the) minute that, *conj.* —*Syn.* as soon as, the second that, at the time that; see **when** 1, 2, **whenever.**

minutiae, *n.* —*Syn.* trivia, particulars, items; see **details.**

minx, *n.* —*Syn.* wench, malapert, saucy young woman; see **girl** 1.

miracle, *n.* —*Syn.* marvel, revelation, supernatural occurrence; see **wonder** 2.

miraculous, *mod.* **1.** [Caused by divine intervention]—*Syn.* supernatural, marvelous, superhuman, beyond understanding, phenomenal, anomalous, unimaginable, stupendous, stupefying, awesome, monstrous; see also **mysterious** 2, **unknown** 1. —*Ant.* natural*, familiar*, imaginable.

2. [So unusual as to suggest a miracle]—*Syn.* extraordinary, freakish, wondrous; see **unusual** 1, 2.

mirage, *n.* —*Syn.* phantasm, delusion, hallucination; see **fantasy** 2, **illusion** 1.

mire, *n.* —*Syn.* marsh, bog, ooze; see **mud, swamp.**

mirror, *n.* —*Syn.* looking glass, speculum, reflector, polished metal, imager, hand glass, cheval glass, pier glass, mirroring surface, camera finder, hand mirror, full-length mirror; see also **glass** 2.

mirth, *n.* —*Syn.* frolic, jollity, entertainment; see **fun, merriment** 2.

miry, *mod.* —*Syn.* slimy, swampy, grimy; see **dirty** 1, **marshy, muddy** 1.

misadventure, *n.* —*Syn.* adversity, ill luck, catastrophe; see **misfortune** 1.

misanthrope, *n.* —*Syn.* misanthropist, misogynist, doubter, hater of mankind *or* men, hater of women, recluse, isolate, loner (D); see also **cynic, skeptic.**

misanthropic, *mod.* —*Syn.* cynical, egotistical, selfish; see **sarcastic.**

misanthropy, *n.* —*Syn.* cynicism, selfishness, egoism; see **egotism, pride** 1.

misapply, *v.* —*Syn.* misdirect, waste, distort; see **misunderstand.**

misapprehend, *v.* —*Syn.* err, blunder, confuse; see **mistake, misunderstand.**

misapprehension, *n.* —*Syn.* misconception, fallacy, delusion; see **mistake** 2, **misunderstanding** 1.

misappropriate, *v.* —*Syn.* plunder, appropriate, abuse; see **rob, steal.**

misbegotten, *mod.* —*Syn.* natural, baseborn, unlawful; see **illegal, illegitimate** 2, **poor** 2.

misbehave, *v.* —*Syn.* do wrong *or* evil, sin, fail, trip, blunder, work iniquity, offend, trespass, behave badly, misdo, err, lapse, be delinquent, be at fault, be culpable *or* blameworthy *or* guilty *or* censurable, be reprehensible, be bad, misdemean oneself, forget oneself, misconduct oneself, be immoral *or* dissolute *or* disreputable *or* indecorous, carry on, be naughty, go astray, take a wrong course, deviate from the path of virtue; *all* (D): sow one's wild oats, cut up, screw up; see also **transgress.**—*Ant.* behave*, be good, do well.

misbehaved, *mod.* —*Syn.* uncivil, discourteous, ill-mannered; see **naughty, rude** 2.

misbehavior, *n.* —*Syn.* transgression, misconduct, fault; see **mischief** 3.

misbelief, *n.* —*Syn.* skepticism, suspicion, scruple; see **doubt** 2, **uncertainty** 2.

misbelieve, *v.* —*Syn.* distrust, suspect, mistrust; see **doubt** 2.

misbeliever, *n.* —*Syn.* doubter, pessimist, questioner; see **cynic, skeptic.**

miscalculate, *v.* —*Syn.* blunder, miscount, err; see **mistake.**

miscall, *v.* —*Syn.* call by a wrong name, misterm, mistitle, misname, use a pseudonym; see also **mistake.**

miscarriage, *n.* **1.** [Failure]—*Syn.* malfunction, defeat, mistake; see **failure** 1.

2. [A too premature delivery]—*Syn.* unnatural birth, untimely delivery, birth interruption; see **abortion** 1.

miscarry, *v.* —*Syn.* abort, lose, go wrong; see **fail** 1.

miscellaneous, *mod.* **1.** [Lacking unity]—*Syn.* diverse, disparate, unmatched; see **different** 2.

2. [Lacking order]—*Syn.* mixed, muddled, scattered; see **confused** 2, **disordered.**

miscellany, *n.* **1.** [Medley]—*Syn.* jumble, collection, hodgepodge; see **mixture** 1.

2. [Anthology]—*Syn.* collectanea, extracts, symposium, compilation, excerpta, miscellanea; see also **collection** 2.

mischance, *n.* —*Syn.* casualty, accident, emergency; see **catastrophe, disaster, misfortune** 1.

mischief, *n.* **1.** [Damage]—*Syn.* hurt, injury, harm; see **damage** 1.

2. [Evil]—*Syn.* atrocity, ill, catastrophe; see **evil** 2, **wrong** 2.

3. [Prankishness]—*Syn.* troublesomeness, harmfulness, impishness, waggishness, sportiveness, roguishness, rascality, misbehavior, misconduct, fault, transgression, wrongdoing, misdoing, playfulness, frolicsomeness, naughtiness, mischief-making, devilment, friskiness; *both* (D): katzenjammers, shenanigans, funny business.—*Ant.* dignity*, demureness, sedateness.

mischief-maker, *n.* —*Syn.* scoundrel, troublemaker, rogue; see **rascal.**

mischievous, *mod.* —*Syn.* playful, roguish, prankish; see **naughty, rude** 2.

misconceive, *v.* —*Syn.* deceive, misinterpret, err; see **mistake, misunderstand.**

misconception, *n.* —*Syn.* delusion, blunder, fault; see **error** 1, **mistake** 2, **misunderstanding** 1.

misconduct, *n.* —*Syn.* misbehavior, offense, wrongdoing; see **evil** 2, **mischief** 3.

misconduct, *v.* **1.** [Mismanage]—*Syn.* misapply, mishandle, misdirect; see **confuse, mismanage.**

2. [Misbehave oneself]—*Syn.* err, transgress, do wrong; see **misbehave.**

misconstruction, *n.* —*Syn.* distortion, misunderstanding, fallacy; see **error** 1, **mistake** 2.

misconstrue, *v.* —*Syn.* exaggerate, distort, pervert; see **mistake, misunderstand.**

miscount, *n.* —*Syn.* miscalculation, wrong total, incorrect sum; see **error** 1, **mistake** 2.

miscount, *v.* —*Syn.* misestimate, err, miscalculate; see **mistake.**

miscreant, *n.* —*Syn.* wretch, villain, knave, rogue, ruffian, rapscallion, scamp, caitiff, sneak, scoundrel, culprit, reprobate, delinquent, bully, malefactor, felon, criminal, convict, outlaw, jailbird, drunkard, bootlegger, blackguard, outcast, scapegrace, scallawag, racketeer, hoodlum, pickpocket, loafer, rounder, rowdy, rough; see also **rascal.**—*Ant.* gentleman*, lady*, good man.

misdate, *v.* —*Syn.* date wrongly *or* in error, predate, postdate; see **mistake.**

misdeed, *n.* —*Syn.* fault, transgression, offense; see **crime** 1.

misdemeanor, *n.* —*Syn.* misconduct, misbehavior, misdeed; see **crime** 2.

misdirect, *v.* —*Syn.* lead astray, misinform, instruct badly; see **deceive, mislead.**

misdoer, *n.* —*Syn.* malefactor, offender, evildoer; see **criminal, miscreant.**

misdoing, *n.* —*Syn.* fault, betrayal, transgression; see **error** 1, **mistake** 2.

misemploy, *v.* —*Syn.* misuse, waste, mistreat; see **abuse** 1.

miser, *n.* **1.** [A hoarder of gold]—*Syn.* extortioner, usurer; *all* (D): skinflint, hoarder, harpy, lickpenny, screw, hunks, scrimp, rake-renter, Scrooge, money-grubber.—*Ant.* beggar*, spendthrift, waster.

2. [A niggardly person]—*Syn.* churl, misanthropist; *all* (D): skinflint, piker, cheapskate, pinchpenny, cheeseparer, penny pincher, tightwad, muckworm; see also **misanthrope.**—*Ant.* patron*, philanthropist, benefactor.

miserable, *mod.* **1.** [In misery]—*Syn.* distressed, afflicted, sickly, ill, wretched, sick, ailing, unfortunate, pitiable, uncomfortable, suffering, hurt, wounded, tormented, tortured, in pain, strained, racked, injured, anguished, agonized, fevered, burning, convulsed; see also **troubled** 1, 2.—*Ant.* helped*, aided, comfortable*.

2. [Unhappy]—*Syn.* pained, discontented, sorrowful; see **sad** 1.

3. [Of very low standard]—*Syn.* sorry, worthless, inferior; see **poor** 2.

miserably, *mod.*—*Syn.* poorly, unsatisfactorily, imperfectly; see **badly** 1, **inadequately.**

miserly, *mod.*—*Syn.* covetous, parsimonious, close-fisted; see **stingy.**

misery, *n.* **1.** [Pain]—*Syn.* distress, suffering, agony; see **pain** 2.

2. [Dejection]—*Syn.* worry, despair, desolation; see **depression** 2, **grief** 1, **sadness.**

3. [Trouble]—*Syn.* grief, anxiety, problem; see **difficulty** 2.

misfire, *v.*—*Syn.* fail to fire, miss, fizzle out (D); see **explode** 1, **fail** 1.

misfit, *n.*—*Syn.* paranoid, psychotic, maladjusted *or* disoriented person; see **neurotic.**

misfortune, *n.* **1.** [Bad luck]—*Syn.* misadventure, ill luck, ill *or* bad *or* adverse chance *or* fortune, disadvantage, mischance, disappointment, adversity, vexatiousness, discomfort, burden, annoyance, nuisance, unpleasantness, unsatisfactoriness, inconvenience, untowardness, worry, anxiety; see **difficulty** 1.—*Ant.* advantage*, good fortune, stroke of fortune.

2. [Disaster]—*Syn.* mishap, calamity, accident; see **sense** 1.

misgiving, *n.*—*Syn.* distrust, mistrust, unbelief; see **doubt** 2, **uncertainty** 2.

misguided, *mod.*—*Syn.* misled, deceived, confused; see **mistaken** 1.

mishandle, *v.*—*Syn.* mistreat, harm, misemploy; see **abuse** 1.

mishap, *n.*—*Syn.* accident, mischance, misadventure; see **catastrophe, disaster, misfortune** 1.

mishmash (D), *n.*—*Syn.* hodgepodge, combination, jumble; see **mixture** 1.

misinform, *v.*—*Syn.* mislead, report inaccurately (to), misstate; see **deceive, lie** 1.

misinterpret, *v.*—*Syn.* falsify, distort, miscalculate; see **mistake, misunderstand.**

misinterpretation, *n.*—*Syn.* distortion, misreckoning, delusion; see **error** 1, **mistake** 2, **misunderstanding** 1.

misjudge, *v.* **1.** [To make a wrong judgment, usually of a person]—*Syn.* presume, prejudge, suppose, presuppose, misapprehend, be partial, be overcritical, be unfair, be one-sided, be misled, come to a hasty conclusion; see also **misunderstand.**—*Ant.* understand*, discern, detect.

2. [To make an inaccurate estimate]—*Syn.* miss, miscalculate, misconceive, misthink, misconstrue, overestimate, underestimate, dogmatize, bark up the wrong tree (D); see also **mistake.**—*Ant.* estimate*, predict, calculate.

misjudgment, *n.* **1.** [Mistake]—*Syn.* distortion, misinterpretation, misconception; see **error** 1, **mistake** 2.

2. [Prejudice]—*Syn.* unfairness, bias, partiality; see **prejudice.**

mislaid, *mod.*—*Syn.* gone, misplaced, disarranged; see **lost** 1.

mislay, *v.*—*Syn.* disorder, displace, disarrange; see **misplace.**

mislead, *v.*—*Syn.* delude, cheat, defraud, cozen, bilk, take in, overreach, outwit, ensnare, trick, enmesh, entangle, victimize, lure, beguile, inveigle, hoax, dupe, gull, bait, misrepresent, bluff; *all* (D): give a bum steer, throw off the scent, lead one on a merry chase, bamboozle, gull, dupe, scam, humbug, hoodwink, put (someone) on; see also **deceive, lie** 1.

misled, *mod.*—*Syn.* misguided, deluded, wronged; see **deceived** 1, **mistaken** 1.

mislike, *v.*—*Syn.* condemn, disdain, not care for; see **dislike.**

mismanage, *v.*—*Syn.* bungle, blunder, overlook, confound, misconduct, fumble; *all* (D): mess *or* foul up, kill the goose that lays the golden eggs, bark up the wrong tree; see also **fail** 1.

mismatched, *mod.*—*Syn.* incompatible, discordant, inconsistent; see **incongrous** 1, **unsuitable.**

misname, *v.*—*Syn.* nickname, label incorrectly, miscall, mistitle, misterm, mislabel, misidentify, misdenominate, title *or* label *or* identify wrongly, misstyle, misconstrue; see also **mistake.**

misogynist, *n.*—*Syn.* celibate, misanthrope, woman-hater, bachelor, agamist, misogamist, encratite; see also **cynic, skeptic.**

misplace, *v.*—*Syn.* mislay, displace, shuffle, disarrange, remove, disturb, take out of its place, disorder, tumble, dishevel, confuse, mix, scatter, unsettle, muss, disorganize; see also **lose** 2.—*Ant.* find*, locate*, place*.

misplaced, *mod.*—*Syn.* displaced, mislaid, out of place; see **lost** 1.

misprint, *n.*—*Syn.* typing error, fault, typo (D); see **error** 1, **mistake** 2.

misprision, *n.*—*Syn.* indiscretion, offense, misdemeanor; see **crime** 2.

misprize, *v.*—*Syn.* ridicule, miscalculate, disregard; see **underestimate.**

mispronounce, *v.*—*Syn.* falter, misspeak, murder the Queen's English (D); see **hesitate, stammer.**

mispronunciation, *n.*—*Syn.* misaccentuation, cacology, cacoepy; see **error** 1, **mistake** 2.

misquote, *v.*—*Syn.* distort, overstate, misrepresent; see **exaggerate.**

misreport, *v.*—*Syn.* distort, falsify, misquote; see **exaggerate.**

misrepresent, *v.*—*Syn.* distort, falsify, understate; see **deceive, lie** 1, **mislead.**

misrepresentation, *n.*—*Syn.* counterfeit, untruth, mask, cloak, mendacity, deceit, dissembling, disguise, simulation, feigning, misstatement, distortion, falsification, understatement, overdrawing, exaggeration, caricature, travesty, burlesque, parody, extravaganza, imitation, bad likeness, misapprehension, misconception, misunderstanding, misapplication, misinterpretation, misconstruction, misguidance, misdirection, perversion, sophistry; *all* (D): phoney, lollapalooza, barnumism; see also **deception** 1, **lie** 1.—*Ant.* truth*, honesty*, candor.

misrule, *n.*—*Syn.* mismanagement. chaos, anarchy; see **disorder** 2.

miss, *n.* **1.** [A failure]—*Syn.* slip, blunder, mishap; see **error** 1, **mistake** 2.
2. [A young woman]—*Syn.* lass, lassie, female; see **girl** 1.
a miss is as good as a mile—*Syn.* err, miscalculate, misjudge; see **mistake.**

miss, *v.* **1.** [To feel a want]—*Syn.* desire, crave, yearn; see **need, want** 1.
2. [To fail to catch]—*Syn.* snatch at, drop; *all* (D): butter a catch, foozle, fumble the ball, blow, have butterfingers, juggle, louse, muff, boot.—*Ant.* catch*, grab, hold*.
3. [To fail to hit]—*Syn.* miss one's aim, miss the mark, be wide of the mark, overshoot, undershoot, go above *or* below *or* to the side; *both* (D): carve the breeze, fan the air.—*Ant.* hit*, shoot, get.
4. [To fail to use]—*Syn.* avoid, refrain, give up; see **abstain.**

missal, *n.*—*Syn.* hymnal, Mass book, psalter; see **prayer book.**

missed, *mod.* **1.** [Not found or noticed]—*Syn.* gone, misplaced, mislaid, forgotten, unrecalled, unnoticed, not in sight, put away, in hiding, hidden, strayed, wandered off, moved, removed, borrowed, unseen; see also **lost** 1.—*Ant.* remembered*, found, located.
2. [Longed for]—*Syn.* needed, desired, wished for, pined for, wanted, yearned for, clung to, craved, hungered *or* thirsted for.—*Ant.* hated*, disliked, unwanted.

misshapen, *mod.*—*Syn.* distorted, disfigured, twisted; see **deformed.**

missile, *n.*—*Syn.* cartridge, projectile, ammunition; see **bullet, shot** 2, **weapon** 1.
Terms for types of missiles include the following—*Syn.* Polaris, Poseidon, SLBM *or* Submarine-Launched Ballistic Missile, Titan II, Pershing, Cruise, MX, Minuteman, ICBM *or* Intercontinental Ballistic Missile, ABM *or* Anti-Ballistic Missile, FOBS *or* Fractional Orbital Bombardment System, MIRV *or* Multiple Independently Targetable Reentry Vehicle.

missing, *mod.*—*Syn.* disappeared, lacking, removed; see **absent, lost** 1.

missing link, *n.*—*Syn.* connection, needed *or* necessary part, pertinent evidence; see **link, man** 2, **savage** 1.

mission, *n.*—*Syn.* charge, sortie, commission; see **purpose** 1.

missionary, *n.*—*Syn.* apostle, evangelist, revivalist, preacher, teacher, pastor, herald, padre; see also **messenger, minister** 1.

missish, *mod.*—*Syn.* prudish, formal, priggish; see **prim.**

Mississippi River, *n.*—*Syn.* Great Water, Father of Waters, *Missi sepe* (Algonquin); *both* (D): Old Man River, the Big Drink; see also **river** 1.

missive, *n.*—*Syn.* word, note, message; see **letter** 2.

misspend, *v.*—*Syn.* squander, exhaust, lavish; see **waste** 2.

misspent, *mod.*—*Syn.* wasted, squandered, thrown away; see **wasted.**

misstate, *v.*—*Syn.* deceive, misrepresent, misquote; see **exaggerate.**

misstatement, *n.*—*Syn.* exaggeration, distortion, falsity; see **error** 1, **mistake** 2.

misstep, *n.*—*Syn.* slip, miss, trip, bungle, stumble; see also **failure** 1.

mist, *n.*—*Syn.* cloud, rain, haze; see **fog** 1.

mist, *v.*—*Syn.* shower, drizzle, fog; see **mizzle, rain.**

mistake, *n.* **1.** [A blunder]—*Syn.* false step, blunder, slip; see **error** 1.
2. [A misunderstanding]—*Syn.* misapprehension, confusion, misconception, misconstruction, delusion, illusion, overestimation, underestimation, impression, aberration, muddle, bemuddling, confounding, disregarding, misinterpretation, misapplication, misdoubt, misstatement, perversion, perplexity, bewilderment, misjudgment; see also **exaggeration** 1, **misunderstanding** 1.—*Ant.* knowledge*, certainty, interpretation.

mistake, *v.*—*Syn.* err, blunder, slip, lapse, miss, overlook, omit, underestimate, overestimate, fail to know *or* recognize, substitute, misjudge, misapprehend, misconceive, misunderstand, confound, misinterpret, misconstrue, confuse, botch, bungle, be at cross purposes, have the wrong impression, tangle, snarl, slip up, mix; *all* (D): make a mess of (it), come a cropper, miss the boat, slip a cog, open one's mouth and put one's foot in it.—*Ant.* succeed*, be accurate, explain.

mistaken, *mod.* **1.** [In error]—*Syn.* misinformed, deceived, confounded, confused, misinterpreting the facts, misconceiving the meaning, misunderstanding *or* misapprehending the situation, misjudging the facts, having the wrong impression, deluded, misinformed, misguided, at fault, off the track, having been too credulous; see also **wrong** 2.
2. [Ill-advised]—*Syn.* unadvised, duped, fooled, misled, tricked, unwarranted; see also **deceived** 1.
3. [Taken for another]—*Syn.* improperly *or* wrongly identified, unrecognized, confused with, taken for, in a case of mistaken identity, misnamed, miscataloged, misconstrued.

mistakenly, *mod.*—*Syn.* badly, falsely, inadvisedly; see **wrongly** 1, 2.

mister, *n.*—*Syn.* title, Mr., man, *monsieur* (French), *Herr* (German), *signor* (Italian), *señor* (Spanish), *gospodin, grazhdanin, tovarishch* (*all* Russian).

misterm, *v.*—*Syn.* mislabel, miscall, mistitle; see **misname.**

mistimed, *mod.*—*Syn.* untimely, unfavorable, inappropriate; see **unsuitable.**

mistiness, *n.*—*Syn.* cloudiness, dimness, fogginess; see **fog** 1.

mistranslate, *v.*—*Syn.* misinterpret, distort, falsify; see **mistake, misunderstand.**

mistreat, *v.*—*Syn.* harm, injure, wrong; see **abuse** 1.

mistreatment, *n.*—*Syn.* injury, harm, violation; see **abuse** 3.

mistress, *n.* **1.** [A woman in authority]—*Syn.* housekeeper, schoolmistress, caretaker, chaperone, housemother, manager, wife, mother, consort; see also **lady** 2, **matron** 2.

2. [An illegitimate consort]—*Syn.* courtesan, paramour, sweetheart, ladylove, voluptuary, woman of easy virtue, concubine, kept woman, the other woman (D); see also **prostitute.**

mistrial, *n.* —*Syn.* malfeasance *or* miscarriage (of justice), (legal) slip, blunder; see **error** 1, **failure** 1, **mistake** 2.

mistrust, *n.* —*Syn.* scruple, skepticism, suspicion; see **doubt** 2, **uncertainty** 2.

mistrust, *v.* —*Syn.* suspect, distrust, scruple; see **doubt** 2.

mistrustful, *mod.* —*Syn.* skeptical, dubious, unsure; see **doubtful** 2, **suspicious** 1.

misty, *mod.* —*Syn.* dim, foggy, hazy, murky, shrouded, obscure, enveloped *or* hidden in spume *or* spray; see also **dark** 1.

misunderstand, *v.* —*Syn.* err, misconceive, misinterpret, miscomprehend, misjudge, miscalculate, misreckon, misapply, misconstrue, be at cross-purposes, be perplexed, be bewildered, confuse, confound, have the wrong impression, fail to understand, misapprehend, overestimate, underestimate, be misled, be unfamiliar with, be unconversant with; *all* (D): have the wrong slant on, not understand all one knows, not register; see also **mistake.**—*Ant.* understand*, grasp, apprehend.

misunderstanding, *n.* **1.** [Misapprehension]—*Syn.* delusion, misreckoning, miscalculation, confusion, misinterpretation, confounding; see also **error** 1, **mistake** 2.—*Ant.* conception*, understanding, apprehension.

2. [Mutual difficulty]—*Syn.* debate, dissension, quarrel; see **disagreement** 1, **dispute** 1.

misunderstood, *mod.* —*Syn.* misinterpreted, badly *or* falsely interpreted, misconceived; see **mistaken** 1, **wrong** 2.

misusage, *n.* —*Syn.* cacology, antiphrasis, solecism, catachresis, malapropism, mispronunciation, spoonerism, ungrammaticalness, barbarism, improper use of words; see also **error** 1, **mistake** 2.

misuse, *n.* —*Syn.* ill-usage, misapplication, perversion; see **abuse** 1.

misuse, *v.* —*Syn.* maltreat, mistreat, ill-treat; see **abuse** 1.

mite, *n.* —*Syn.* parasite, bug, tick; see **insect, vermin.**

Mites include the following—clover, house, itch, cheese, blister, chicken.

mitigate, *v.* —*Syn.* alleviate, lessen, moderate; see **decrease** 1.

mitigation, *n.* —*Syn.* alleviation, reduction, remission; see **moderation** 2, **relief** 1.

mitt, *n.* —*Syn.* baseball glove; *both* (D): catcher's mitt, first baseman's mitt; see **glove.**

mitten, *n.* —*Syn.* mitt, gauntlet, boxing glove; see **glove.**

mix, *v.* **1.** [To blend]—*Syn.* fuse, merge, coalesce, embody, brew, unite, combine, cross, hybridize, interbreed, immix, admix, commix, intermix, amalgamate, incorporate, alloy, mingle, compound, agitate, commingle, intermingle, weave, throw together, interweave, adulterate, infiltrate, intertwine, knead, stir, suffuse, instill, transfuse, synthesize, stir around, infuse, saturate, tincture, dye, season; see also **join** 1.

2. [To confuse]—*Syn.* mix up, jumble, tangle; see **confuse.**

3. [To associate]—*Syn.* fraternize, get along, consort with; see **associate** 1.

mixed, *mod.* **1.** [Commingled]—*Syn.* admixed, blended, fused, mingled, commixed, compounded, combined, amalgamated, united, brewed, tied, merged, embodied, infused, transfused, crossed, hybridized, assimilated, married, woven, kneaded, incorporated; see also **joined.**—*Ant.* separated*, severed, raveled.

2. [Various]—*Syn.* miscellaneous, unselected, diverse; see **different** 2, **various.**

3. [Confused]—*Syn.* mixed up, jumbled, disordered; see **confused** 2.

mixed-up kid (D), *n.* —*Syn.* dupe, well-intentioned person, young punk (D); see **fool** 1, 2.

mixer, *n.* **1.** [An instrument used to mix materials] —*Syn.* blender, Osterizer (trademark), food processor, juicer, egg beater, cake mixer, food mixer, cocktail shaker, converter, carburetor, concrete *or* cement mixer, paint mixer, turbine beater; see also **appliance, machine** 1.

2. [A substance used in a mixture]—*Syn.* ingredient, component, combining element; see **part** 1.

3. [Liquids used in prepared drinks]—*Syn.* carbonated water, soda water, tonic, quinine (water), tap water, distilled water, seltzer, mineral water, ginger ale; see also **drink** 3, **soda, water** 1.

4. [(D) A party]—*Syn.* tea, social gathering, cocktail party; see **party** 1.

mixture, *n.* **1.** [A combination]—*Syn.* blend, compound, composite, amalgam, miscellany, intermixture, admixture, mingling, medley, mix, potpourri, salmagundi, alloy, fusion, jumble, mishmash, mash, brew, merger, adulteration, hybridization, hybrid, crossing, infiltration, magma, transfusion, infusion, mélange, interweavement, saturation, assimilation, incorporation, stew, dough, batter, hodgepodge (D).

2. [A mess]—*Syn.* mix-up, muddle, disorder; see **confusion.** 2.

mix-up, *n.* —*Syn.* turmoil, chaos, commotion; see **confusion** 2, **disorder** 2.

mizzle, *v.* —*Syn.* mist, drizzle, sprinkle, shower, trickle, ooze, dribble, rain in small drops; see also **rain.**

mnemonic, *mod.* —*Syn.* of the memory, reminiscential, intended to assist the memory, mnemotechnic; see also **helpful** 1.

moan, *n.* —*Syn.* plaint, groan, wail; see **cry** 1.

moan, *v.* —*Syn.* groan, wail, whine; see **cry** 1.

moaning, *n.* —*Syn.* groan, whine, murmur; see **cry** 1.

moat, *n.* —*Syn.* ditch, canal, furrow; see **channel** 1, **trench** 1.

mob, *n.* **1.** [A disorderly crowd of people]—*Syn.* swarm, rabble, throng, press, multitude, populace, horde, rout, riot, host, lawless element; see also **crowd** 1, **gathering.**

2. [The lower classes]—*Syn.* burgeoisie, plebeians, proletariat; see **people** 3.

mob, *v.* —*Syn.* hustle, crowd, swarm; see **attack** 1, **rebel** 1, **riot.**

mobbish, *mod.* —*Syn.* vulgar, disorderly, ignoble, mean, vile, base, beggarly, proletarian, sorry, lowbred, unpolished, plebeian, uncivilized, boorish, churlish, boisterous, rude, barbarous, savage, frenzied, hysteric, wild, impetuous, explosive, fierce; see also **unruly.**

mobile, *mod.* **1.** [Movable]—*Syn.* unstationary, loose, free; see **movable.**

2. [Capable of rapid motion]—*Syn.* motile, motor-activated; see also **motorized.**

Types of mobile units of the armed forces include the following—motorized,. tank, paratroop, air, naval, torpedoboat, patrol-boat, task-force, search-and-destroy, patrol.

mobility, *n.* —*Syn.* changeability, versatility, flow, flux, plasticity, fluidity, changefulness, mutability; see also **movement** 1.

mobilize, *v.* —*Syn.* assemble, prepare, gather; see **enlist** 1.

mob law, *n.* —*Syn.* mob rule, anarchy, lawlessness; see **disorder** 2.

mobocracy, *n.* —*Syn.* anarchy, lawlessness, mob rule; see **disorder** 2.

moccasin, *n.* —*Syn.* heelless shoe, slipper, sandal, wedgie, play-shoe, *huarache* (Spanish), deerskin moccasin, elkhide moccasin, beaded moccasin, fringed moccasin; see also **shoe.**

mock, *mod.* —*Syn.* counterfeit, sham, pretended; see **false** 3, **unreal.**

mock, *v.* **1.** [To ridicule]—*Syn.* deride, scorn, taunt; see **ridicule.**

2. [To mimic]—*Syn.* mime, burlesque, caricature; see **parody.**

3. [To dare]—*Syn.* brave, defy, challenge; see **dare** 2.

mocker, *n.* —*Syn.* charlatan, scorner, pretender; see **cheat** 1, **imposter.**

mockery, *n.* —*Syn.* disparagement, imitation, sham; see **ridicule.**

mocking, *mod.* —*Syn.* uncivil, insulting, unkind; see **rude** 2.

mode, *n.* **1.** [Manner]—*Syn.* tone, form, style; see **method** 2.

2. [The prevailing fashion]—*Syn.* style, convention, vogue; see **fashion** 2.

model, *n.* **1.** [A person worthy of imitation]—*Syn.* archetype, prototype, exemplar, paradigm, ideal, role model, beau ideal, man of probity, good man, good woman, good example, hero, demigod, saint; see also **paragon.**—*Ant.* rascal*, scoundrel, reprobate.

2. [Anything that serves as a copy]—*Syn.* original, text, type, guide, copy, tracing, facsimile, duplicate, pattern, design, touchstone, gauge, ideal, shape, form, specimen, mold, principle, basis, standard, sketch, cartoon, painting, precedent, archetype, antitype, prototype, exemplar; see also **criterion.**

3. [A duplicate on a small scale]—*Syn.* miniature, image, illustration, representation, reduction, statue, statuette, figure, figurine, effigy, idol, mock-up, skeleton, portrait, photograph, relief, print, engraving; see also **copy, duplicate** 1.

4. [One who poses professionally]—*Syn.* poser, sitter, mannequin; see **nude.**

Kinds of models include the following—portrait, artist's, fashion, sculptor's, photographic.

model, *v.* **1.** [To form]—*Syn.* shape, mold, fashion; see **create** 2, **form** 1.

2. [To imitate a model]—*Syn.* trace, duplicate, sketch, reduce, represent, print, die, counterfeit, caricature, parody, burlesque; *both* (D): steal one's stuff, register; see also **illustrate** 1, **paint** 1.

3. [To serve as a model]—*Syn.* sit, act as model, set an example; see also **pose** 2.

4. [To demonstrate]—*Syn.* show (off), wear, parade *or* pose in; see **display** 1.

modeled, *mod.* —*Syn.* designed, shaped, cast; see **formed.**

moderate, *mod.* **1.** [Not expensive]—*Syn.* inexpensive, low-priced, medium-priced, reasonable, modest, inexorbitant, not excessive, not dear, average, nominal, at par, usual, inconsiderable, marked down, at a bargain, half-price, reduced, worth the money, relatively low, of small yield; see also **cheap** 1, **economical** 2.—*Ant.* expensive*, dear, exorbitant.

2. [Not violent]—*Syn.* modest, cool, tranquil; see **calm** 1, **reserved** 3.

3. [Not radical]—*Syn.* tolerant, judicious, nonpartisan, middle-of-the-road, unopinionated, undogmatic, not given to extremes, measured, low-key, evenly balanced, neutral, impartial, straight, midway, in the mean, average, restrained, dispassionate, sound, cautious, considered, considerate, respectable, middle-class, preserving the middle course, striking the golden mean, compromising; see also **conservative.**—*Ant.* radical*, unbalanced, partial.

4. [Not intemperate]—*Syn.* pleasant, gentle, soft, balmy, inexcessive, equable, tepid, clement, easy, not rigorous *or* severe, temperate, favorable, tolerable, bearable, tame, pacific, untroubled, unruffled, monotonous, even; see also **fair** 3, **mild** 2.—*Ant.* severe*, rigorous, bitter.

5. [Not indulgent]—*Syn.* sparing, abstemious, frugal, regulated, self-denying, abstinent, non-indulgent, self-controlled, within compass, disciplined, careful; *all* (D): on the wagon, sworn off, teetotaling; see also **restrained, sober** 3.—*Ant.* wasteful*, excessive, self-indulgent.

moderate, *v.* **1.** [To become less]—*Syn.* abate, modify, decline; see **decrease** 1.

2. [To make less]—*Syn.* check, curb, reduce; see **decrease** 2.

moderately, *mod.* —*Syn.* tolerantly, tolerably, temperately, somewhat, to a degree, enough, to some *or* a certain extent, a little, to some degree, fairly, more than not, not exactly, quite a bit, in moderation, within reason *or* bounds *or* restrictions, within reasonable limits, as far as could be expected, within the bounds of reason, in reason, in a tempered manner; *both* (D): pretty, tolerable; see also **reasonably** 2, **slightly.**—*Ant.* much*, extremely, remarkably.

moderation, *n.* **1.** [Restraint]—*Syn.* toleration, steadiness, sobriety, coolness, the golden mean, temperateness, quiet, temperance, lenity, patience, sedation, fairness, justice, constraint, forbearance, reasonableness, dispassionateness, poise, balance; see also **restraint** 1.

2. [The act of moderating]—*Syn.* mediation, settlement, governance, regulation, restriction, limitation, reduction, controlling, assuagement, alleviation, composing, soothing, quieting, placating, sobering, tempering; see also **restraint** 2.—*Ant.* increase*, license, misgovernance.

moderator, *n.* —*Syn.* chairman, arbitrator, mediator; see **judge** 2.

modern, *mod.* **1.** [Up to date]—*Syn.* stylish, modish, chic, smart, conforming, swank, in the trend, up-to-the-minute, late, current, recent, of the mode, of the present, prevailing, prevalent, in the fad, avant-garde, classy (D), present-day, latest, advanced, streamlined, breaking with tradition, untraditional, new-fashioned, having the new look, contemporary, in vogue, in use, common; *all* (D): with it, in the swim, newfangled, sharp, smooth, just out, mod, cool, in the air, jet-age; see also **fashionable, fresh** 1.—*Ant.* old-fashioned*, out-of-date, out-of-style.

2. [Having the comforts of modern life]—*Syn.* modernistic, modernized, renovated, functional, with modern conveniences, done over, having modern improvements, strictly modern; see also **convenient** 1, **improved** 1.—*Ant.* Victorian*, dilapidated, run down.

3. [Concerning recent times]—*Syn.* contemporary, contemporaneous, recent, concurrent, present-day, coincident, synchronous, twentieth-century, latter-day, mechanical, of the Machine Age, automated, of modern times, modernist; see also **now** 1, **present** 1.—*Ant.* old*, medieval, primordial.

modernism, *n.* —*Syn.* innovation, fashion, newness; see **fad, novelty** 1.

modernist, *n.* —*Syn.* innovator, futurist, pioneer; see **guide** 1, **leader** 2.

modernistic, *mod.* —*Syn.* surrealistic, futuristic, highstyle; see **fashionable, modern** 1.

modernize, *v.* —*Syn.* regenerate, refurbish, bring up to date; see **improve** 1, **renew** 1, **revive** 1.

modest, *mod.* **1.** [Humble]—*Syn.* unassuming, meek, diffident; see **humble** 1, **resigned.**

2. [Not showy]—*Syn.* unpretentious, unostentatious, unobtrusive, demure, quiet, seemly, proper, decorous, unstudied, plain, simple, natural, unassuming, humble, unornamented, tasteful, unadorned, unembellished, unvarnished, unaffected, homely; *both* (D): taking a back seat, hiding one's face; see also **dignified, reserved** 3.—*Ant.* immodest*, ostentatious, pretentious.

3. [Moderate]—*Syn.* reasonable, inexpensive, average; see **cheap** 1, **economical** 2, **moderate** 1.

4. [Proper]—*Syn.* pure, chaste, seemly; see **decent** 2, **honest** 1, **prudish.**

5. [Lowly]—*Syn.* plain, simple, unaffected; see **humble** 2.

modestly, *mod.* **1.** [In a modest manner]—*Syn.* unobtrusively, retiringly, quietly, simply, unpretentiously, unpresumptuously, diffidently, bashfully, unassumingly, chastely, virtuously, purely, shyly, demurely, shrinkingly.—*Ant.* boldly*, boastfully, pretentiously.

2. [Within reasonable limits]—*Syn.* reasonably, coolly, sensibly; see **cheaply, moderately.**

modesty, *n.* **1.** [The attitude that leads one to make a modest self-estimate]—*Syn.* intelligent humility, unpretentiousness, unassumingness, delicacy, unostentatiousness, reticence, constraint, unobtrusiveness, self-effacement, meekness; see also **courtesy** 1, **dignity** 1, **restraint** 1.—*Ant.* vanity*, conceit, egotism*.

2. [Shyness]—*Syn.* inhibition, timidity, diffidence; see **shyness.**

3. [Chastity]—*Syn.* decency, innocence, celibacy; see **chastity, purity** 1, **virtue** 1.

modicum, *n.* —*Syn.* trifle, fraction, particle; see **bit** 1.

modification, *n.* —*Syn.* qualification, alteration, correction; see **adjustment** 1, **change** 2.

modified, *mod.* **1.** [Changed]—*Syn.* varied, mutated, adjusted; see **changed** 2.

2. [Reduced]—*Syn.* qualified, limited, diminished; see **reduced** 1.

modifier, *n.* —*Syn.* limiter, conditioner, alterant, alterer, transformer.

Types of grammatical modifiers include the following—adjective, adjectival, adverb, adverbial, pronominal adjective, pronominal, phrasal modifier, verbal adjective, adjectival clause, adverbial clause; see also **word** 1.

modify, *v.* **1.** [To alter]—*Syn.* repair, transform, remodel; see **change** 1, **turn** 2.

2. [To change]—*Syn.* alter, modify, vary; see **become** 1, **change** 4.

3. [To moderate]—*Syn.* mitigate, restrain, curb; see **decrease** 2, **restrict** 2.

modish, *mod.* —*Syn.* stylish, smart, mod (D); see **fashionable, modern** 1.

modiste, *n.* —*Syn.* clothier, seamstress, designer; see **dressmaker, tailor.**

modulate, *v.* —*Syn.* inflect, accentuate, vibrate; see **change** 1, **sound** 1.

modulation, *n.* —*Syn.* timbre, intonation, inflection; see **pitch** 3, **sound** 2.

modus operandi (Latin), *n.* —*Syn.* operation, organization, procedure; see **method** 2, **system** 2.

mogul, *n.* —*Syn.* personage, czar, notable; see **lord** 2, **royalty.**

Mohammedan, *mod.* —*Syn.* Muslim, Sulmanic, Islamic; see **Moslem.**

moiety, *n.* **1.** [Part]—*Syn.* half, section, fraction; see **division** 2, **part** 1.

2. [Clan]—*Syn.* affiliation, kinship, group; see **family** 1.

moist, *mod.* **1.** [Damp]—*Syn.* humid, dank, moistened; see **wet** 1.

2. [Rainy]—*Syn.* drizzly, muggy, clammy; see **wet** 2.

moisten, *v.* —*Syn.* sprinkle, dampen, saturate, drench, moisturize, waterlog, steep, sog, sop, dip, rinse, wash (over), wet (down), humidify, water (down), squirt, shower, rain on, splash, splatter, bathe, steam, bedew, spray, mist, sponge; see also **soak** 1.

moisture, *n.* —*Syn.* precipitation, mist, drizzle; see **fog** 1, **rain** 1.

mold, *n.* **1.** [A form]—*Syn.* matrix, womb, cavity, shape, frame, pattern, design, die, cast, dish, fossil cavity, depression, cup, image, mold-board, core; see also **form** 1, **model** 2.

2. [The body shaped in a mold, sense 1]—*Syn.* cast, kind, molding, casting, image, reproduction, form, pottery, shell, core; see also **impression** 1.

3. [A parasitic growth]—*Syn.* rust, smut, blue mold, mould, black mold, parasite, pennicillium, fungus, lichen; see also **decay** 2.

mold, *v.* **1.** [To give physical shape to]—*Syn.* make, round into, fashion; see **form** 1.
2. [To determine a course of action or an opinion] —*Syn.* devise, plot, scheme; see **plant** 1.
3. [To decay through the action of mold]—*Syn.* molder, mildew, rust; see **decay.**

molding, *n.* **1.** [A molded or carved strip]—*Syn.* architectural ornament, embellishment, decoration, frieze, picture holder *or* frame, cornice; see also **frame** 2.
Types of molding include the following—fillet and fascia, sunk fillet, quarter round, torus, bead, reed, ovolo, ogee, cavetto, scotia, conge, cyma recta, cyma reversa, beak, splay.
2. [Forming as in a mold]—*Syn.* shaping, creating, casting; see **making.**

moldy, *mod.*—*Syn.* musty, mildewed, dank; see **rotten** 1.

mole, *n.* **1.** [Dike]—*Syn.* hill, mound, breakwater; see **dam** 1.
2. [Blemish]—*Syn.* flaw, birthmark, blotch; see **blemish.**

molecular, *mod.*—*Syn.* miniature, microscopic, atomic; see **little** 1, **minute** 1.

molecule, *n.* **1.** [Unit]—*Syn.* particle, fragment, unit; see **bit** 1.
2. [Atom]—*Syn.* electron, ion, particle; see **atom** 2.

molest, *v.* **1.** [To disturb objects]—*Syn.* displace, meddle, disorganize; see **disturb** 2.
2. [To disturb people]—*Syn.* interrupt, break in upon, intrude, obtrude oneself, encroach upon, annoy, worry, disquiet, irritate, discommode, discompose, plague, badger, abuse sexually, bait, pester, hinder, tease, irk, vex, trouble, confuse, perturb, frighten, terrify, scare, misuse, maltreat; see also **bother** 2.

mollify, *v.* **1.** [To quiet one who is angry]—*Syn.* soothe, appease, calm; see **quiet** 1.
2. [To lessen]—*Syn.* ameliorate, alleviate, diminish; see **decrease** 2.

mollycoddle, *n.*—*Syn.* recreant, craven, weakling; see **coward.**

mollycoddle, *v.*—*Syn.* pamper, spoil, baby; see **pamper, baby,** *v.*

molt, *v.*—*Syn.* lose, cast off, remove skin; see **shed.**

molten, *mod.*—*Syn.* heated, melted, fused, liquefied, running, fluid, seething; see also **hot** 1. —*Ant.* cold*, cool*, solid.

moment, *n.* **1.** [A brief time]—*Syn.* minute, instant, millisecond, trice, second, bit, while, flash, twinkling; *all* (D): jiff, jiffy, three winks; see also **time** 2.
2. [Importance]—*Syn.* significance, note, consequence; see **importance** 2.

momentarily, *mod.*—*Syn.* immediately, right now, instantly; see **now** 1.

momentary, *mod.*—*Syn.* fleeting, flying, quick, summary, passing, flitting, flashing, transient, evanescent, fugitive, impermanent, shifting, spasmodic, ephemeral, vanishing, cursory, temporary, fugacious, like lightning, like a summer shower, bubblelike, dreamlike, gone in a flash; *both* (D): in the bat *or* wink of an eye, quicker than one can say Jack Robinson.—*Ant.* eternal*, continual, ceaseless.

momentous, *mod.*—*Syn.* far-reaching, serious, consequential; see **important** 1.

momentum, *n.*—*Syn.* impulse, force, drive; see **energy** 3.

mommy (D), *n.*—*Syn.* mom, female parent, mama; see **mother** 1, **parent.**

monarch, *n.*—*Syn.* despot, sovereign, autocrat; see **king** 1.

monarchal, *mod.*—*Syn.* regal, autocratic, eminent; see **noble** 3, **royal** 2.

monarchy, *n.*—*Syn.* kingship, sovereignty, command; see **power** 2.

monastery, *n.*—*Syn.* abbey, priory, religious community; see **cloister.**

monastic, *mod.*—*Syn.* humble, pious, devout; see **religious** 2.

monasticism, *n.*—*Syn.* priesthood, cloistered life, celibacy; see **ministry** 2.

monetary, *mod.*—*Syn.* pecuniary, financial, fiscal; see **commercial** 1.

money, *n.* **1.** [A medium of exchange]—*Syn.* gold, silver, cash, currency, check, bills, coin (of the realm), notes, coinage, specie, legal tender; *all* (D): Almighty Dollar, beans, gravy, wampum, shekels, dough, roll, long green, coins, lucre, folding money, jack, wad, bucks, ducats, pesos, dineros, cabbage, hard cash, mazuma, bread.
Money includes the following—cent, dollar (United States; penny, pound (England); *centime, franc* (France); *centesimo,lira* (Italy); *centavo, peso* (Mexico); *kopek, ruble* (Russia); *øre, krone* (Denmark); *fen, yuan* (China); *sen, yen* (Japan); *Pfennig, Mark* (Germany).
2. [Wealth]—*Syn.* funds, capital, property; see **wealth** 1, 2.
3. [Merged interests]—*Syn.* financiers, corporate interests, capitalists, capital, financial structure(s), vested interests, moneyed group; see also **banking, business** 4.
4. [Pay]—*Syn.* payment, salary, wages; see **pay** 2.
for one's money (D)—*Syn.* for one's choice, in one's opinion, to one's mind; see **personally** 2.
in the money (D)—*Syn.* wealthy, flush (D), loaded (D); see **rich** 1.
make money—*Syn.* gain profits, become wealthy, earn; see **profit** 2.
one's money's worth—*Syn.* full value, gain, benefit; see **value** 1, 3.
place (*or* **put) money on**—*Syn.* risk, bet, wager; see **gamble** 1.
put money into—*Syn.* invest (money) in, support, underwrite; see **invest.**

moneybags (D), *n.*—*Syn.* tycoon, capitalist, banker; see **financier, millionaire.**

moneyed, *mod.*—*Syn.* wealthy, well-to-do, affluent; see **rich** 1.

moneyless, *mod.*—*Syn.* bankrupt, destitute, indigent; see **poor** 1, **ruined** 4.

(one's) money's worth, *n.*—*Syn.* return, payment, reimbursement; see **pay** 1, **value** 1.

mongrel, *mod.*—*Syn.* crossbred, halfbred, hybrid; see **confused** 2, **mixed** 1.

monitor, *n.*—*Syn.* counselor, informant, director; see **adviser.**

monitor, *v.* —*Syn.* watch, observe, control; see **advise** 1.
monitory, *mod.* —*Syn.* sinister, warning, portentous; see **ominous.**
monk, *n.* —*Syn.* hermit, eremite, cenobite, religious, anchorite, ascetic, solitary, recluse, abbot, prior; see also **friar, priest.**
Monks include the following—Benedictine, Cistercian, Carthusian, Trappist, Franciscan, Capuchin, Dominican, Carmelite, Augustinian, Jesuit, Templar, Bernardine.
monkey (D), *n.* —*Syn.* primate, lemur, anthropoid ape; see also **animal** 2.
Monkeys include the following—chimpanzee, orangutan, ouakari, baboon, marmoset, gibbon, gorilla, guenon, guereza, douroucouli, colobus, langur, mandrill; common green, woolly (saki), spider, squirrel, capuchin, proboscis, diana monkey.
a monkey on one's back—*Syn.* addiction, compulsion, need; see **obsession.**
monkey, *v.* —*Syn.* pry, fool around, tamper with; see **meddle** 2.
monkey business (D), *n.* —*Syn.* deceit, conniving, misconduct; see **deception** 1, **lie** 1.
monkeyshines (D), *n.* —*Syn.* jokes, amusement, antics; see **joke** 1.
monody, *n.* —*Syn.* dirge, chant, lament; see **cry** 3, **song.**
monolithic, *mod.* —*Syn.* solid (stone *or* rock *or* concrete, etc.), unified, of one sort, inflexible, unyielding, consistent; see also **firm** 2, **uniform, united.**
monologue, *n.* —*Syn.* talk, speech, discourse; see **address** 2.
monomania, *n.* —*Syn.* fanaticism, furor, compulsion; see **neurosis, obsession.**
monoplane, *n.* —*Syn.* airplane, single-seater, aircraft; see **plane** 3.
monopolize, *v.* —*Syn.* engross, acquire, exclude, own exclusively, absorb, consume, manage, have, hold, corner, cartelize, syndicate, restrain, patent, copyright, corner the market (D)—*Ant.* include*, give, invite.
monopoly, *n.* —*Syn.* trust, corner, pool, syndicate, cartel, copyright, patent.—*Ant.* business*, open market, trade*.
monotonous, *mod.* **1.** [Tiresome]—*Syn.* tedious, wearisome, wearying; see **dull** 4.
2. [Having but one tone]—*Syn.* monotonic, monotonical, unvarying, lacking variety, in one key, unchanged, reiterated, recurrent, single, uniform.—*Ant.* varying*, various*, multiple.
monotony, *n.* —*Syn.* invariability, likeness, sameness, tediousness, similarity, continuity, continuance, oneness, identicalness, evenness, levelness, flatness, dreariness, unchangeableness, equability; *all* (D): jog trot, even tenor, the same old thing; see also **boredom, dullness** 1.—*Ant.* difference*, variability, variety*.
monsoon, *n.* —*Syn.* typhoon, hurricane, tempest; see **storm** 1.
monster, *n.* **1.** [A great beast]—*Syn.* beastlike creature, basilisk, imaginary monster, centaur, monstrosity, Gorgon, sphinx, Minotaur, Hydra, kraken, Python, salamander, chimera, lamia, unicorn, echidna, dragon, griffin, cyclops, cockatrice, hippocampus, phoenix, mermaid, hippogriff, gyascutus, androsphinx, dipsas, sagittary, sea serpent, hippocentaur, manticore, hippocert, whangdoodle, roe, bucentaur, rhinoceros, elephant, lycanthrope, werewolf, uturuncu.
2. [An unnatural creation]—*Syn.* abnormality, abnormity, monstrosity; see **freak** 2.
monstrous, *mod.* **1.** [Huge]—*Syn.* stupendous, prodigous, enormous; see **large** 1.
2. [Unnatural]—*Syn.* abnormal, preposterous, uncanny; see **unnatural** 1, **unusual** 2.
3. [Shocking]—*Syn.* horrible, terrible, atrocious; see **frightful** 1, **terrible** 1.
monstrously, *mod.* —*Syn.* horribly, cruelly, outrageously; see **badly** 1, **brutally.**
month, *n.* —*Syn.* measure of time, thirty days, one-twelfth of a year, four weeks, moon, period.
Types of months include the following—calendar, lunar, synodical, anomalistic, nodical, tropical, sidereal, solar.
Months of the year are the following—January, February, March, April, May, June, July, August, September, October, November, December.
monthly, *mod.* —*Syn.* once a month, every month, menstrual, mensal, phaseal, phasic, punctually, steadily, recurrent, cyclic, cyclical, repeated, rhythmic, methodically, periodically, from month to month, in its turn; see also **regularly** 2.
monument, *n.* **1.** [Anything erected to preserve a memory]—*Syn.* tomb, shaft, column, pillar, headstone, tombstone, gravestone, cenotaph, mausoleum, obelisk, shrine, statue, building, erection, pile, tower, monolith, tablet, slab, stone; see also **memorial.**
2. [A landmark in the history of creative work] —*Syn.* work of art, magnum opus, permanent contribution; see **achievement** 2, **masterpiece.**
monumental, *mod.* —*Syn.* lofty, impressive, majestic; see **grand** 2, **great** 1.
mood, *n.* **1.** [A state of mind]—*Syn.* state, condition, frame of mind, temper, cue, humor, disposition, inclination, caprice, whim, fancy, vein, pleasure, vagary, crotchet, freak, wish, desire.
2. [A quality of mind]—*Syn.* bent, propensity, tendency; see **attitude** 3.
3. [Grammatical mode]—*Syn.* aspect, inflection, mode.
Moods in English grammar include the following —indicative, subjunctive, imperative, interrogative, conditional, potential.
moody, *mod.* —*Syn.* pensive, unhappy, low-spirited; see **sad** 1.
moon, *n.* —*Syn.* celestial body, heavenly body, planet, secondary planet, planetoid, crescent, new moon, halfmoon, full moon, old moon; *all* (D): orb of night, Diana, Luna, Phoebe, Cynthia, moon goddess, dry moon, wet moon, green cheese, sailor's friend; see also **satellite** 1.
moonbeam, *n.* —*Syn.* light, stream, gleam, streak, glint, spark, glitter, sparkle, scintillation, lambency, play of moonlight, pearl blue (D); see also **beam** 2, **flash** 1, **ray.**
mooncalf, *n.* —*Syn.* idiot, simpleton, incompetent; see **fool.**
moonlight, *n.* —*Syn.* effulgence, radiance, luminescence; see **light** 3.

moon-shaped, *mod.* —*Syn.* lunar, sickle-shaped, crescent; see **bent.**

moonshine, *n.* **1.** [Moonlight]—*Syn.* effulgence, radiance, luminosity; see **light** 3.

2. [Whisky distilled illicitly]—*Syn. all* (D): mountain dew, swamp root, donk, jackass, mule, white lightning, white mule; see **whisky.**

moonshiner (D), *n.* —*Syn.* illicit *or* illegal distiller *or* dealer, racketeer; *all* (D): legger, shiner, (mountain) moonlighter, hootcher, boozelegger; see also **criminal.**

moonstruck, *mod.* —*Syn.* infatuated, lovesick, foolish; see **insane** 1.

moor, *n.* —*Syn.* wasteland, rough country, upland; see **field** 1.

Moorish, *mod.* —*Syn.* Arab, Mohammedan, Moresque; see **Arab.**

moory, *mod.* —*Syn.* muddy, spongy, swampy; see **marshy.**

moot, *mod.* —*Syn.* unsettled, debatable, disputable; see **controversial, questionable** 1, **uncertain** 2.

mop, *n.* —*Syn.* swab, duster, sweeper; see also **broom.**

Mops include the following—oil, floor, dust, dish, rag, wet, dry, soldering, metalworker's polishing, surgical; gun swab, miner's swab stick.

mop, *v.* —*Syn.* swab, wipe, rub, dab, pat, polish, wash, dust, wipe up; see also **clean.**

mope, *v.* —*Syn.* be low-spirited, fret, pine away, grieve, despond, droop, sink, lose heart, brood, pine, yearn, repine, despair, grumble, chafe, lament, regret, look glum, sulk; *all* (D): be in a funk, give way, look blue, croak, be sunk in the doldrums, pull a long face; see also **mourn** 1.—*Ant.* revive*, celebrate*, cheer up.

mopped, *mod.* —*Syn.* swabbed, washed, polished; see **clean** 1.

mop the floor *or* **the earth (with)** (D), *v.* —*Syn.* beat, thrash, trounce; see **defeat** 1, 2.

mop up (D), *v.* —*Syn.* finish off, dispatch, clean (up); see **achieve** 1, **defeat** 1, 2, **eliminate** 1.

moral, *mod.* **1.** [Characterized by conventional virtues]—*Syn.* trustworthy, kindly, courteous, respectable, proper, scrupulous, conscientious, good, truthful, decent, just, honorable, honest, high-minded, saintly, pure, exemplary, laudable, worthy, correct, decorous, meet, praiseworthy, seemly, aboveboard, dutiful, principled, godly, conscientious, chaste, ethical; see also **noble** 1, 2, **reliable** 1, **upright** 2.—*Ant.* unscrupulous*, lying*, dishonest*.

2. [Having to do with approved relationships between the sexes]—*Syn.* virtuous, immaculate, decent; see **chaste** 2, **innocent** 4.

3. [Virtual]—*Syn.* substantial, virtual, implicit; see **practical.**

morale, *n.* —*Syn.* assurance, resolve, spirit; see **confidence** 2.

morality, *n.* **1.** [Virtue]—*Syn.* righteousness, uprightness, honesty; see **virtue** 1.

2. [Probity in sexual relationships]—*Syn.* purity, gentleness, decency; see **chastity.**

moralize, *v.* —*Syn.* sermonize, admonish, pontificate; see **lecture, scold.**

morally, *mod.* **1.** [In accordance with accepted standards of conduct]—*Syn.* conscientiously, truthfully, honestly, honorably, appropriately, laudably, respectably, courteously, scrupulously, uprightly, righteously, trustworthily, decently, properly, in a manner approved by society; see also **justly** 1, 2, **sincerely.**—*Ant.* wrongly*, worthlessly, dishonorably.

2. [In a chaste manner]—*Syn.* chastely, virtuously, purely; see **modestly** 1.

3. [Practically]—*Syn.* potentially, implicitly, substantially; see **probably.**

morals, *n.* —*Syn.* ideals, customs, standards, mores, policies, beliefs, dogmas, social standards, principles; see also **ethics.**

morass, *n.* —*Syn.* marsh, bog, quagmire; see **swamp.**

moratorium, *n.* —*Syn.* halt, cessation, interim; see **end** 2.

morbid, *mod.* **1.** [Diseased]—*Syn.* sickly, unhealthy, ailing; see **sick.**

2. [Pathological]—*Syn.* abnormal, unsound, gruesome, gloomy, melancholic, irascible, suspecting, depressed, morose, sullen, hypochondriac, despondent, ill-natured, ill-balanced, aberrant, eccentric, unnatural, unusual, unsound, psychotic, paranoid, deranged, demented; see also **insane** 1, **sad** 1. —*Ant.* sane*, normal, usual.

morbidly, *mod.* —*Syn.* unnaturally, insanely, weirdly; see **crazily, sick.**

mordacity, *n.* —*Syn.* sharpness, acerbity, acridity; see **bitterness** 1, 2.

mordant, *mod.* —*Syn.* stringent, bitter, sharp; see **severe** 2.

more, *mod.* **1.** [Additional]—*Syn.* also, likewise, and, over and above, more than that, further, in addition, beside(s), added; see also **extra.**—*Ant.* less than, less, subtracted from.

2. [Greater in quantity, amount, degree, or quality] —*Syn.* expanded, increased, major, augmented, extended, expanded, enhanced, aggrandized, added to, larger, higher, wider, deeper, heavier, solider, stronger, amassed, massed, over *or* above the mark.—*Ant.* lessened, weaker, decreased.

3. [Greater in numbers]—*Syn.* exceeding, too many for, numerous, innumerable, bounteous, extra; see also **infinite** 1, **plentiful** 2.—*Ant.* too few (for), scanty, scarce.

more and more, *mod.* —*Syn.* increasingly, more frequently; increasing in weight *or* size *or* number, etc.; see **frequently, increasing** 2.

more or less, *mod.* —*Syn.* about, somewhat, in general; see **approximate** 3, **approximately, moderately.**

moreover, *mod.* —*Syn.* further, by the same token, furthermore; see **besides.**

Moresque, *mod.* —*Syn.* Arabic, Mohammedan, Moorish; see **Arabian, Moslem.**

morgue, *n.* **1.** [A place where the dead are received] —*Syn.* deadhouse, the undertaker's mortuary, charnel house; *all* (D): cold-meat tray, packing house, stiffville; see also **building** 1.

2. [The library of a newspaper]—*Syn.* reference room, photographic collection, file; see **library, museum.**

moribund, *mod.* —*Syn.* incurable, on one's deathbed, sinking; see **dying** 1.

Mormon, *mod.* —*Syn.* concerning the Church of Jesus Christ of Latter-day Saints, concerning the State of Desert, saintly, churchly; see also **religious** 1, **Protestant.**

morning, *n.* **1.** [Dawn]—*Syn.* aurora, Eos, the East, morn, daybreak, dayspring, break of day, first blush *or* flush of morning, daylight, cockcrow, sun-up, the small hours; *all* (D): the wee small hours, crack of dawn, milk-wagon time; see also **day** 2, **time** 1.
2. [The time before noon]—*Syn.* forenoon, morningtide, prime, after midnight, before noon, breakfast time, before lunch; see also **A.M., day** 2.

mornings, *mod.* —*Syn.* in the morning(s), every morning, before noon, in the A.M., early, in good season; see also **daily, regularly** 1, 2.

morning star, *n.* —*Syn.* Venus, evening star, eastern star; see **planet, star** 1.

moron, *n.* —*Syn.* feeble-minded person, retardate, imbecile, idiot, simpleton, natural, goose, addlepate, dullard, dunce, gawk, blockhead, mental defective, cretin, tomfool, dunce; *all* (D): dunderhead, lunkhead, muttonhead, numskull, dimwit, halfwit, boob, dingbat, saphead, mutt, loony; see also **fool** 1.—*Ant.* philosopher*, sage, scientist.

moronic, *mod.* —*Syn.* foolish, mentally retarded, dumb (D); see **stupid** 1.

morose, *mod.* **1.** [Gloomy]—*Syn.* depressed, dolorous, melancholy; see **sad** 1, **troubled** 1.
2. [Ill-humored]—*Syn.* sour, splenetic, acrimonious, ill-natured, gruff, perversive, ill-tempered, sulky, gloomy, crusty, grouchy, surly, saturnine, churlish, mumpish, cantankerous, crabbed, cross, snappish, frowning, cross-grained, harsh; see also **irritable, sullen.**

morsel, *n.*—*Syn.* bite, chunk, piece; see **bit** 1, **part** 1.

mortal, *mod.* **1.** [Causing death]—*Syn.* malignant, fatal, lethal; see **deadly, poisonous.**
2. [Subject to death]—*Syn.* human, transient, temporal, passing, frail, impermanent, evanescent, fugacious, perishable, precarious, fading, passing away, ephemeral, momentary; see also **temporary.** —*Ant.* eternal*, perpetual*, everlasting.
3. [(D) Very great]—*Syn.* extreme, deadly, last, ending; see also **grand** 2.

mortal, *n.* —*Syn.* creature, being, human; see **animal** 1, **man** 1.

mortality, *n.* **1.** [Destruction]—*Syn.* dying, extinction, fatality; see **death** 1, **destruction** 1.
2. [Humanity]—*Syn.* being, mankind, human race; see **man** 1.

mortar, *n.* **1.** [A receptacle to be used with a pestle] —*Syn.* basin, pot, caldron; see **bowl.**
2. [The heaviest ordnance commonly used by infantrymen]—*Syn.* trench mortar, knee mortar, training mortar; *all* (D): spigot mortar, stovepipe, tock Emma, bubbly-wubbly; see also **cannon, weapon** 1.

mortgage, *n.* —*Syn.* lease, title, debt; see also **contract.**
Types of mortgages include the following—construction, installment, leasehold, anticipating, trust, chattel, first, second.

mortgaged, *mod.* —*Syn.* tied, bound, pledged, obligated, held under mortgage, liable, under lien; see also **guaranteed, promised.**

mortification, *n.* **1.** [Humiliation]—*Syn.* regret, remorse, chagrin; see **disgrace** 1, **embarrassment** 1, **shame** 2.
2. [Penance]—*Syn.* purgation, flagellation, discipline; see **penance** 1.

mortify, *v.* —*Syn.* shame, discipline, belittle; see **disgrace, humiliate, ridicule.**

mortuary, *n.* —*Syn.* charnel house, funeral parlor, funeral home; see **morgue** 1.

mosaic, *mod.* —*Syn.* diapered, varied, inlaid; see **ornate** 1.

Moslem, *mod.* —*Syn.* Muslim, Mohammedan, Islamic, Musselmanic, worshiping Allah, believing in Mohammed, looking toward Mecca, following the Koran; see also **Arabian.**

mosquito, *n.* Mosquitoes include the following—anopheles, culex, aedes, stegomyia, trichopronsoon, corethra, psorophora, mansonia; see also **insect, pest** 1.

moss, *n.* Mosses include the following—musci, bryophyta, sphagnum, peat moss, mosslike lichen, Iceland moss, rock moss, club moss; see also **plant.**

mossback (D), *n.* —*Syn.* right-winger, reactionary, die-hard; see **conservative.**

mossy, *mod.* —*Syn.* tufted, velvety, plushy, downy, mosslike, smooth, fresh, damp, moist, cushiony, resilient, soft, covered, overgrown; see also **green** 2. —*Ant.* dry*, bare, prickly.

most, *mod.* —*Syn.* nearly all, all but, well-nigh all, not quite all, close upon all, in the majority.
at the most—*Syn.* in toto, not more than, at the outside (D); see **most.**
make the most of—*Syn.* exploit, utilize, take advantage of; see **use** 1.

mostly, *mod.* **1.** [Frequently]—*Syn.* often, many times, in many instances; see **frequently, regularly** 1.
2. [Largely]—*Syn.* chiefly, essentially, for the most part; see **principally.**

mot, *n.* —*Syn.* remark, adage, maxim; see **proverb, saying.**

mote, *n.* —*Syn.* speck, scrap, crumb; see **bit** 1.

motel, *n.* —*Syn.* motor hotel, motor inn, cabins, stopping place, road house, court, motor court; see also **hotel, lodge, resort** 2.

moth, *n.* —*Syn.* (moth) miller, tineid, *Heterocera* (Latin); see **insect.**
Mothlike creatures include the following—carpet beetle, dermestid beetle, silk(worm); gypsy, clothes, honeycomb, death's head, buffalo, lappet, luna, emperor, harlequin, deltoid, cabbage, tiger, lackey, ermine, plume moth.

mother, *n.* **1.** [A female parent]—*Syn.* parent, ancestress, matriarch, mamma, dam, materfamilias, mater; *all* (D): mama, mammy, motherkin, mum, mummy, ma, mom, mommy, muddy, mudder, mumma, muzzer, maw; see also **parent, relative.**
2. [A matron]—*Syn.* superintendent, mother superior, housemother; see **administrator.**
3. [The source]—*Syn.* fountainhead, font, beginning; see **origin** 2.

mother country, *n.* —*Syn.* motherland, native land *or* country, homeland; see **country** 3, **nation** 1.

motherhood, *n.* —*Syn.* maternity, mothership, parenthood.

mother-in-law, *n.* —*Syn.* husband's *or* wife's mother, mother by marriage; *both* (D): mater-in-law, back-seat driver; see also **relative.**

motherly, *mod.* —*Syn.* maternal, devoted, careful, watchful, kind, warm, gentle, tender, comprehending, sympathetic, caretaking, supporting, protective, protecting; see also **loving.**

mother tongue, *n.* —*Syn.* native speech *or* language *or* tongue, dialect, ideolect, local idiom; see also **language** 1.

mother wit, *n.* —*Syn.* common sense, perception, reason; see **wisdom** 2.

motif, *n.* —*Syn.* subject, main feature, topic; see **theme** 1.

motion, *n.* **1.** [A movement]—*Syn.* change, act, action; see **movement** 2.
2. [The state of moving]—*Syn.* passage, translating, changing; see **movement** 1.
3. [An act formally proposed]—*Syn.* suggestion, consideration, proposition; see **plan** 2.

motionless, *mod.* **1.** [Not moving]—*Syn.* still, unmoving, dead, deathly still, inert, stock-still, stagnant, becalmed, quiet, quiescent, at a dead calm, at a full stop, in a deadlock, lying at anchor.—*Ant.* moving*, shifting, changing*.
2. [Firm]—*Syn.* unmovable, fixed, stationary; see **firm** 1.

motion picture, *n.* —*Syn.* moving picture, cinema, (the silver) screen; see **movie.**

motivate, *v.* —*Syn.* impel, inspire hope, stimulate, incite, propel, spur, goad, move, induce, prompt, arouse, whet, instigate, fire, provoke, actuate, cause; *all* (D): touch off, egg on, trigger; see also **drive** 1, **excite** 1, **urge** 2.

motive, *n.* —*Syn.* cause, purpose, idea; see **reason** 3.

motley, *mod.* **1.** [Varied]—*Syn.* multiform, mixed, heterogeneous; see **various.**
2. [Varicolored]—*Syn.* prismatic, mottled, kaleidoscopic; see **bright** 2, **multicolored.**

motor, *n.* —*Syn.* machine, device, instrument; see also **engine** 1.
Types of motors include the following—internal combustion, Wankel, diesel, spark diesel, compound, steam, turbine, gas turbine, jet, rotary, radial, in line, airplane, automobile, truck, A.C. *or* D.C. electric, V-type, T-head, L-head, high compression, low compression.

motor, *v.* —*Syn.* tour, drive, ride; see **travel** 2.

motorboat, *n.* —*Syn.* speedboat; *all* (D): putt-putt, hop-up, bronco, skip-jack; see also **boat.**
Types of motorboats include the following—open, out-board, electric-powered, gasoline-powered; cruiser, run-about, whaleboat, yawl, auxiliary yacht, sea sled.

motorcycle, *n.* —*Syn.* motorized two-wheeled vehicle, cycle; *all* (D): pig, hog, bike, chopper, sickle; see also **racer** 2, **vehicle** 1.
Makes of motorcycles include the following—BSA, Triumph, Bultaco, Greeves, Yamaha, Cimatti, Vespa, Ducati, Garelli, Lambretta, Matchless, Norton, Suzuki, Indian, Volocette, BMW, Jawa, Royal Enfield, Bridgestone, Maico, Harley Davidson, Kawasaki, Hodaka.

motorist, *n.* —*Syn.* automobile operator; *both* (D): autoist, gear grinder; see **driver.**

motorized, *mod.* —*Syn.* motor-driven, motor-powered, electric-driven, gasoline-driven, oil-driven, motor-equipped, motor-operated; see also **mobile** 2.

motorman, *n.* —*Syn.* operator, engineer, man at the controls; see **driver.**

motto, *n.* —*Syn.* maxim, adage, saw, epigram, aphorism, apothegm, pretty sentiment, slogan, catchword, watchword, byword, catch phrase, axiom, sententious phrase; see also **proverb, saying.**
Familiar mottoes include the following—in God we trust, one from many *or e pluribus unum* (Latin), time flies *or tempus fugit* (Latin), art for art's sake *or ars pro arte* (Latin), art is long and time is fleeting *or ars longa, vita brevis* (Latin), hail and farewell *or ave atque vale* (Latin), rest in peace *or requiescat in pace* (Latin) *or* R.I.P., peace be with you *or pax vobiscum* (Latin), peace on earth, good will toward men, one for all and all for one *or gung ho* (Chinese); I came, I saw, I conquered *or veni, vidi, vici* (Latin); home sweet home, God bless our home, don't tread on me, thus be it always with tyrants *or sic semper tyrannis* (Latin); we must all hang together, or assuredly we shall all hang separately; give me liberty or give me death, all or nothing, you can't take it with you; it is sweet to die for one's country *or dulce et decorum est pro patria mori* (Latin), all men are created free and equal; liberty, equality, fraternity *or liberté, égalité fraternité* (French); God and my right *or Dieu et mon droit* (French), for God and country, a man's a man for a' that, what's worth doing is worth doing well, *tout bien ou rien* (French), all is lost save honor *or tout est perdu fors l'honneur* (French); *tout passe, tout casses, tout lasse* (French); don't give up the ship; don't fire until you see the whites of their eyes; remember the Alamo *or* the Maine *or* Pearl Harbor, etc.; Our Country! In her intercourse with foreign nations may she always be in the right, but our Country, right or wrong; he will hew to the line of the right, let the chips fall where they may; *espérance* (French); pray and paddle, praise the Lord and pass the ammunition; put your trust in God, my boys, and keep your powder dry; take the cash and let the credit go; abandon hope, all ye who enter here; to err is human, to forgive divine; make hay while the sun shines, infinite riches in a little room, through these portals pass the most beautiful girls in the world; *all* (D): get there fustest with the mostest; in God we trust, all others pay cash; Pike's Peak or bust, Berlin or bust, etc.; rest in pieces.

mound, *n.* —*Syn.* pile, heap, knoll; see **hill.**

mount, *v.* **1.** [To rise]—*Syn.* ascend, arise, uprise; see **rise** 1.
2. [To climb (until one can stand or sit on the top)] —*Syn.* ascend, scale, clamber; see **climb** 2.

mountain, *mod.* —*Syn.* towering, weighty, steep, isolated, lofty, elevated, plateau, broken, ski-country, snow-capped, above the timber line, above the snow line; see also **mountainous.**—*Ant.* level*, flat*, hollow.

mountain, *n.* **1.** [A lofty land mass]—*Syn.* mount, elevation, peak, sierra, butte, hill, alp, range, ridge, pike, bluff, headland, knap, steeps, palisade, volcano, crater, lava cap, lava plug, tableland, mesa, plateau, height, crag, tor, precipice, cliff, massif, earth mass.—*Ant.* valley*, ravine, flatland.

Famous chains of mountains include the following—Alps, Himalayas, Caucasus, Urals, Pyrenees, Ruwenzori, Andes, Rockies, Canadian Rockies, Appalachians, Cascades, Adirondacks, White Mountains, Sierra Nevada, Sierra Madre, Cordillera, Apennine chain, Sentinel Range, Grampian Mountains.
Famous peaks include the following—Mont Blanc, Mt. Aetna, Vesuvius, the Matterhorn, Pike's Peak, Mt. Whitney, Mt. Shasta, Mt. Washington, the Jungfrau, Wetterhorn, Dent du Midi, the Grand Teton, Mt. McKinley, Mt. St. Elias, Mt. Logan, Mt. Robson, Krakatoa, Pelee, Citlaltepetl, Cotopaxi, Chimborazo, Popocatepetl, Iztaccihuatl, Mt. Cook, Mt. Everest, Annapurna, Mt. Dhaulagiri, Nanga Parbat, Lhotse, Nupseg, K2 *or* Godwin Austen, Mt. Ushba, Mount of Olives, Mt. Sinai, Fujiyama, Mt. Kenya, Mt. Kilimanjaro.
2. [A pile]—*Syn.* mass, mound, glob (D); see **heap.**

mountaineer, *n.*—*Syn.* mountain man, mountain dweller, hillman, highlander, uplander, native of mountains, mountain climber, rock climber, mountain guide, mountain scaler, hillbilly (D).

mountainous, *mod.*—*Syn.* mountainlike, mountain, with mountains, difficult, barbarous, wild, untamed, strange, remote, uncivilized, rude, crude, unpopulated, solitary, unfamiliar, hard to penetrate, isolated, steep, lofty, hilly, alpine, upland, aerial, elevated, volcanic, towering, ridged, craggy, cliffy, rugged; see also **high** 2, **rocky.**—*Ant.* low*, small, flat*.

mountebank, *n.*—*Syn.* pretender, charlatan, mocker; see **cheat** 1, **imposter.**

mounted, *mod.* **1.** [On horseback]—*Syn.* seated, riding, in the saddle, cavalry, provided with a horse; *both* (D): horsed, up.—*Ant.* afoot*, unhorsed, dismounted.
2. [Firmly fixed]—*Syn.* supported, set, attached; see **firm** 1.
3. [Backed]—*Syn.* pasted on, set off, strengthened; see **reinforced.**

mourn, *v.* **1.** [To lament]—*Syn.* deplore, grieve, fret, sorrow, rue, regret, bemoan, sigh, long for, miss, droop, languish, yearn, ache, pine, anguish, complain, agonize, repine, weep (over), bewail, suffer, wring one's hands, be brokenhearted, be in distress, be sad, beat one's breast, take on (D).—*Ant.* celebrate*, rejoice, be happy.
2. [To cry]—*Syn.* sob, wail, moan; see **cry.**

mourner, *n.*—*Syn.* lamenter, bereaved person, griever, keener, weeper, wailer, repiner, sorrower, willow-wearer, pallbearer, commiserator, bemoaner, condoler, friend of the deceased, member of the family.

mournful, *mod.* **1.** [Afflicted with sorrow]—*Syn.* sorrowful, mourning, unhappy; see **sad** 1.
2. [Suggestive of sorrow]—*Syn.* distressing, pitiable, pathetic; see **sad** 2.

mournfully, *mod.*—*Syn.* sorrowfully, regretfully; with sorrow *or* weeping *or* tears, etc.; see **sadly.**

mourning, *n.* **1.** [The act of expressing grief]—*Syn.* sorrowing, grieving, yearning, aching, sorrow, lamentation, lamenting, pining, repining, sighing, regretting, deploring, weeping over, drooping, languishing, wailing, crying, moaning, murmuring, complaining, bemoaning, sobbing, keening; see also **depression** 1, **grief** 1, **sadness.**—*Ant.* celebration*, rejoicing, being glad.
2. [Symbols of mourning]—*Syn.* black, mourning coach, mourning ring, mourning cloak, arm band, mourning veil, mourning garb, widow's weeds, black suit, black tie, sackcloth and ashes, rent garment.

mouse, *n.*—*Syn.* rodent, vermin, rat.
Mice include the following—white-footed, meadow, field, house, church, pocket *or* kangaroo, jumping; see also **animal** 2, **pest** 1.

mouth, *n.* **1.** [The principal facial opening] Parts of the mouth include the following—lips, orifice, roof, floor, tongue, jaws, gums, teeth, pharynx, soft palate, alveolar ridge, hard palate, alveoli, uvula.
2. [Any opening resembling a mouth]—*Syn.* orifice, entrance, aperture; see **opening** 1.
3. [The end of a river]—*Syn.* estuary, firth, delta, portal, harbor, roads, sound, tidewater.
down in (*or* **at**) **the mouth** (D)—*Syn.* depressed, discouraged, unhappy; see **sad** 1.
give mouth to—*Syn.* express, tell, reveal; see **say.**
have a big mouth (D)—*Syn.* talk loudly, exaggerate, brag; see **talk** 1.

mouthful, *n.*—*Syn.* portion, piece, morsel; see **bite** 1.

mouthpiece (D), *n.*—*Syn.* spokesman, adviser, counselor; see **adviser.**

mouthy (D), *mod.*—*Syn.* bombastic, loudmouthed, pompous; see **oratorical.**

movable, *mod.*—*Syn.* not fastened, portable, adjustable, adaptable, not fixed, unstationary, mobile, transportable, motile, liftable, conveyable, demountable, detachable, turnable, removable, separable, drawable, deployable, pullable, derangeable, transferable, shiftable, ambulatory, unfixate, loose, unfastened, free, unattached, in parts, in sections, knocked down, on wheels.—*Ant.* fixed*, fastened, stationary.

movables, *n.*—*Syn.* household equipment, wares, goods; see **furniture.**

move, *n.*—*Syn.* motility, transit, progress; see **movement** 1, 2.
get a move on (D)—*Syn.* go faster, start moving, get cracking (D); see **hurry** 1.
on the move—*Syn.* moving, busy, acting; see **active** 2.

move, *v.* **1.** [To be in motion]—*Syn.* go, walk, run, glide, travel, drift, budge, stir, shift, pass, cross, roll, metastasize, flow, march, travel, progress, proceed, traverse, drive, off-load, ride, fly, hurry, head for, bustle, climb, crawl, jump, leap; *all* (D): shove along, jump to it, get a move *or* wiggle on, take off, get going; see also **advance** 1.—*Ant.* stop*, remain stationary, stay quiet.
2. [To set in motion]—*Syn.* impel, actuate, propel; see **push** 2.
3. [To arouse the emotions of]—*Syn.* influence, affect, stir, instigate, stimulate, touch, play on, sway, quicken, excite, induce, rouse, inspirit, prevail upon, work upon, touch a (sympathetic) chord (D); see also **drive** 1, **encourage** 1, **excite** 1.—*Ant.* quiet*, lull, pacify.
4. [To propose an action formally]—*Syn.* suggest, introduce, submit; see **propose** 1.

moved, *mod.* **1.** [Transported]—*Syn.* conveyed, carried, sent, taken, shifted, transferred, reassigned, reallocated, changed, flown, driven, drawn, pushed, lifted, elevated, lowered, let down, displaced, withdrawn, replaced, sent abroad, put abroad, trucked, hauled, dragged, lugged; *all* (D): kicked upstairs, snaked, toted; see also **transported.**
2. [Gone to a different residence]—*Syn.* transferred, relocated, emigrated, migrated, vacated, removed, at a new *or* different address, departed, gone away, changed residences, left, gone for good (D); see also **gone** 1.—*Ant.* resident*, remaining, still there *or* here.
3. [Proposed]—*Syn.* recommended, submitted, introduced; see **proposed.**

movement, *n.* **1.** [The state of moving]—*Syn.* move, transit, passage, progress, journey, advance, velocity, motility, mobility, change, movableness, shift, translating, alteration, ascension, descension, propulsion, flow, flux, action, flight, declination, wandering, journeying, voyaging, migration, emigration, transplanting, evolving, shifting, changing, locomotion, drive, evolution, undertaking, regression.—*Ant.* stationariness, quiet, fixity.
2. [An example of movement]—*Syn.* immigration, migration, march, demonstration, crusade, patrol, sweep, emigration, evolution, unrest, transition, change, transfer, displacement, withdrawal, ascension, descension, progression, regression, transportation, removal, departure, trip, day's trip, shift, flight, slip, slide, step, footfall, stride, gesture, act, action, vacating, campaign, mobilization, pilgrimage, expedition, procession, locomotion, cavalcade; see also **journey.**
3. [A trend]—*Syn.* drift, tendency, bent; see **inclination** 1.

movie, *mod.*—*Syn.* screen, cinematic, motion, sound, picture, photographic.

movie, *n.*—*Syn.* moving *or* motion picture, photoplay, cinema, film, show, screenplay, talking picture, silent picture, photodrama, cinematograph, cartoon, animated cartoon, serial, comedy, foreign film, travelogue, short, documentary, videotape; *all* (D): talkie, stick flick, flicker; see also **drama, entertainment** 2.

movies, *n.* **1.** [(D) A showing of a moving picture]—*Syn.* motion picture, film, photoplay; see **movie.**
2. [The motion picture industry]—*Syn.* moving pictures, screen pictures, cinema, the cinematic industry, cinematography, Hollywood, the screen world; *all* (D): the silver screen, the industry, pictures, the flicks, celluloids; see also **theatre** 2.

move in, *v.*—*Syn.* take up residence, take occupancy (of), get a home; see **arrive** 1, **establish** 2.

move off, *v.*—*Syn.* depart, be in motion, go; see **leave** 1.

move on, *v.*—*Syn.* keep moving *or* going, continue, go; see **travel** 2, **walk** 1.

move up, *v.*—*Syn.* go forward, do well, go *or* get ahead; see **advance** 1, **prosper, rise** 1.

moving, *mod.* **1.** [In motion]—*Syn.* going, changing, progressing, advancing, shifting, evolving, withdrawing, rising, going down, descending, ascending, getting up, traveling, on the track, journeying, on the march, moving up, starting, proceeding, traversing, flying, climbing; *all* (D): up-tempo, on the jump, on the wing, under sail, going great guns.—*Ant.* unchanging, unmoving, let be.
2. [Going to another residence]—*Syn.* migrating, emigrating, vacating, removing, departing, leaving, going away, changing residences; *both* (D): going for good, flitting.—*Ant.* remaining, staying, stopping.

mow, *n.*—*Syn.* loft, hayloft, haymow, hay barn; see also **attic.**

mow, *v.*—*Syn.* scythe, reap, lay in swaths; see **harvest.**

much, *mod.* **1.** [To a great degree or extent]—*Syn.* important, weighty, notable, signal, considerable, prominent, memorable, salient, momentous, stirring, eventful, serious, urgent, pressing, critical, paramount, principal, leading, significant, telling, trenchant; *all* (D): first-rate, high-flying, in the front rank.—*Ant.* little*, inconsiderable, trivial.
2. [In great quantity]—*Syn.* full, many, very many, abundant, satisfying, enough, sufficient, adequate, considerable, substantial, ample, everywhere, copious, voluminous, plentiful, profuse, complete, lavish, generous, immeasurable, endless, countless, fabulous, extravagant, preposterous, overwrought, overcharged; *all* (D): hell of a lot, all over the place, no end.—*Ant.* inadequate*, insufficient, limited.
3. [Very]—*Syn.* greatly, enormously, extremely; see **very.**

much, *pron.*—*Syn.* a great quantity, abundance, quantities, a great deal, (a) sufficiency, riches, wealth, amplitude, plethora, volume, very much, breadth, copiousness, plentifulness, fullness, profuseness, exuberance, completeness, fruitfulness, lavishness, generousness; *all* (D): lot, great lot, quite a bit, gobs, thousands, tons, oodles; see also **plenty.**—*Ant.* penury*, scarcity, little.
as much as—*Syn.* practically, virtually, in effect; see **almost, equal.**
make much of—*Syn.* treat with importance, expand, exaggerate; see **overdo** 1.
not much of a—*Syn.* inferior, mediocre, unsatisfactory; see **poor** 2.

mucilage, *n.*—*Syn.* paste, cement, glue; see **adhesive.**

mucilaginous, *mod.*—*Syn.* viscid, gummy, sticky; see **adhesive.**

muck, *n.*—*Syn.* refuse, dung, waste; see **trash** 1, 3.

muckraker, *n.*—*Syn.* exposer, scandalbearer, meddler; see **gossip** 2.

mucky, *mod.*—*Syn.* foul, filthy, unclean; see **dirty.**

mucus, *n.*—*Syn.* snot, phlegm, excretion, slime.

mud, *n.*—*Syn.* dirt, muck, clay, alluvia, mire, slush, silt, muddiness, turbidity, stickiness, ooze, clayeyness, bog, marsh, swamp, hardpan, percolation, viscidity; *both* (D): soup, axle grease; see also **filth.**

muddle, *n.* **1.** [Confusion]—*Syn.* trouble, disarrangement, disarray; see **confusion** 2, **disorder** 2.
2. [Difficulty]—*Syn.* perplexity, quandary, predicament, pother, dilemma, complication, intricacy, complexity, awkwardness, involvement, emergency, struggle, unmanageableness, encumbrance; *both* (D), jam, pickle; see also **difficulty** 2, **puzzle.**

muddle, *v.* **1.** [To confuse; *said of affairs*]—*Syn.* stir up, misarrange, disarrange, entangle, foul, mix,

jumble, bungle, derange, shake up, mess, botch, potter, clutter, snarl, pi, complicate, disorder; see also **confuse.**
2. [To confuse; *said usually of people*]—*Syn.* disturb, perturb, ruffle; see **confuse.**
muddled, *mod.* **1.** [Drunk]—*Syn.* tipsy, inebriated, intoxicated; see **drunk.**
2. [Confused]—*Syn.* uncertain, addled, stupid; see **confused** 2.
muddle through, *v.* —*Syn.* manage, get by, make it; see **succeed** 1, **survive** 1.
muddy, *mod.* **1.** [Containing sediment]—*Syn.* stirred, turbid, roiled, roily, dull, dark, cloudy, murky, indistinct, confused, obscure, opaque, reddened; see also **dirty** 1.—*Ant.* clear*, translucent, pellucid.
2. [Deep with mud]—*Syn.* sloppy, swampy, soggy, sodden, slushy, watery, miry, fenny, boggy, soaked; see also **marshy.**—*Ant.* dry*, barren, parched.
muff, *v.* —*Syn.* miscarry, fumble, blunder; see **fail** 1.
muffin, *n.* —*Syn.* quick bread, biscuit, bun; see **bread.**
muffle, *v.* —*Syn.* deaden, mute, stifle; see **decrease** 2, **soften** 2.
muffled, *mod.* —*Syn.* suppressed, stifled, indistinct; see **obscure** 1.
muffler, *n.* —*Syn.* fascinator, chest protector, tippet, neckpiece, babushka, neckerchief, kerchief, neckband, neck cloth, wimple, Ascot, fur piece, choker, mantle, stole, boa, fichu, veil; see also **scarf.**
mug, *n.* —*Syn.* vessel, stein, flagon; see **cup.**
muggy, *mod.* —*Syn.* damp, humid, moist; see **wet** 1.
mulct, *v.* **1.** [To cheat someone]—*Syn.* defraud, trick, swindle; see **deceive, lie** 1.
2. [Punish]—*Syn.* penalize, fine, reprove; see **punish.**
mule, *n.* —*Syn.* hinney, army mule, Missouri mule; see **animal** 2.
mulish, *mod.* —*Syn.* opinionated, headstrong, stubborn; see **obstinate** 1.
mull, *v.* —*Syn.* reflect, meditate, ponder; see **think** 1.
multicolored, *mod.* —*Syn.* prismatic, mottled, varicolored, kaleidoscopic, dappled, motley, spotted, polychrome, marbled, speckled, checkered, piebald, flecked, veined, streaked, pied; see also **bright** 2.
multifarious, *mod.* —*Syn.* heterogeneous, mixed, diverse; see **different** 2, **various.**
multiform, *mod.* —*Syn.* various, many-shaped, manifold; see **multiple** 1.
multiple, *mod.* **1.** [Various]—*Syn.* complicated, more than one, many, manifold, compound, having many uses, multifold, multiplex, multitudinous, aggregated, many-sided, multifarious, versatile, increased, varied, compound, added; see also **various.** —*Ant.* simple*, united*, centralized.
2. [Repeated]—*Syn.* reoccurring, repetitious, duplicated; see **multiplied.**
multiplication, *n.* —*Syn.* duplication, reproduction, addition, increase, repetition, compounding, recurrence, amplification, augmentation, manifolding, reduplication, making more, reduplication, reproducing, repeating, augmenting; see also **arithmetic.**—*Ant.* reduction*, subtraction, decrease.
multiplied, *mod.* —*Syn.* manifolded, compounded, aggregated, added, reproduced, amplified, repeated, augmented, duplicated, reduplicated, made many; see also **increased.**—*Ant.* reduced*, divided, decreased.
multiply, *v.* **1.** [To increase]—*Syn.* add, augment, double; see **increase** 1.
2. [To bring forth young]—*Syn.* generate, produce, populate; see **propagate** 1, **reproduce** 3.
3. [To employ multiplication as an arithmetical process]—*Syn.* repeat, compound, aggregate, manifold, raise, square, cube, raise to a higher power, employ a function, calculate; see also **increase** 1. —*Ant.* divide, decrease*, subtract.
multitude, *n.* **1.** [The state of being numerous] —*Syn.* aggregation, plenitude, abundance; see **number** 1.
2. [A great crowd]—*Syn.* throng, drove, mob; see **crowd** 1, **gathering, people** 3.
mum, *mod.* —*Syn.* hushed, soundless, without a word; see **quiet** 2.
mumble, *v.* —*Syn.* mutter, utter, whine, whimper, rumble, grumble, murmur, maunder, ramble on, whisper, speak indistinctly, articulate poorly; *all* (D); say to oneself, swallow one's words, speak with mush in the mouth; see also **hesitate, stammer.** —*Ant.* say*, articulate, enunciate.
mumjo jumbo, *n.* **1.** [Nonsense]—*Syn.* jabber, gibberish, hocus-pocus, double talk, drivel, gobbledegook, psychobabble, doublespeak, wish-wash; *both* (D): jazz, guff; see also **nonsense** 1.
2. [Red tape]—*Syn.* smoke screen, run-around, officialism; see **details.**
mummer, *n.* —*Syn.* quizzer, masker, harlequin; see **actor, clown.**
mummery, *n.* —*Syn.* revel, amusement, performance; see **masquerade.**
mummify, *v.* —*Syn.* embalm, dry up, mortify; see **preserve** 3.
mummy, *n.* —*Syn.* remains, cadaver, corpse; see **body** 2.
mumpish, *mod.* —*Syn.* sulky, morose, dull; see **irritable.**
munch, *v.* —*Syn.* crunch, bite, grind, masticate, ruminate, crush, mash, smash, reduce, soften, press, break up; see also **chew, eat** 1.
mundane, *mod.* —*Syn.* normal, ordinary, everyday; see **worldly** 1.
municipal, *mod.* —*Syn.* self-governing, metropolitan, city, town, community, local, civil, borough, incorporated, corporate; see also **public.**—*Ant.* national, state, world-wide.
municipality, *n.* —*Syn.* district, village, borough; see **city, town** 1.
munificence, *n.* —*Syn.* generosity, consideration, benevolence; see **kindness** 1.
munificent, *mod.* —*Syn.* open-handed, charitable, benevolent; see **generous** 1, **kind.**
muniment, *n.* —*Syn.* deed, warrant, document; see **certificate, record** 1.
munitions, *n.* —*Syn.* materiel, weapons, war material, preparations for defense, offensive material, equipment, military provisions, military stores, arms, armament, ordnance; see also **ammunition,**

bomb, bullet, cannon, explosive, gun 1, 2, **machine gun, mine** 2, **mortar** 2, **plane** 3, **rocket, shell** 2, **shot** 2, **tank** 2, **tank-destroyer.**

Common types of munitions include the following—artillery, cannon, rocket, automatic rifle, machine gun, antiaircraft gun, rifle, cartridge, shell, bayonet, hand grenade, mortar, grenade launcher, bomb, guided missile, aerial bomb, depth charge, torpedo, mine, detection equipment, radio, radar, flame thrower, atom bomb, hydrogen bomb, communication equipment.

mural, *n.* —*Syn.* wall painting, decoration, representation; see **painting** 1.

murder, *n.* —*Syn.* killing, homicide, unlawful homicide, death, destruction, annihilation, carnage, putting an end to, slaying, shooting, knifing, assassination, terrorism, dispatching, lynching, crime, felony, killing with malice aforethought, murder in the first degree, first degree murder, contract killing, murder in the second degree, murder in the third degree, manslaughter, massacre, genocide, butchery, mayhem, patricide, matricide, infanticide, fratricide, genocide, the Holocaust, suicide, foul play; *all* (D): ride, dust-off, bump-off, the works, the business, one-way ticket, dowser; see also **crime** 2.

get away with murder (D)—escape (punishment), take flight, avoid prosecution *or* punishment; see **evade** 1.

murder, *v.* **1.** [To kill unlawfully]—*Syn.* slay, assassinate, butcher; see **kill** 1.

2. [(D) To ruin, especially by incompetence] —*Syn.* spoil, mar, misuse; see **botch, destroy** 1, **fail** 1.

murdered, *mod.* —*Syn.* killed, assassinated, massacred; see **dead** 1.

murderer, *n.* —*Syn.* slayer, assassin, butcher; see **criminal, killer.**

murderous, *mod.* —*Syn.* destroying, killing, felonious, lethal, law-breaking, fell, sanguinary, cruel, bloodthirsty, savage, criminal; see also **deadly, destructive** 2.

murderously, *mod.* —*Syn.* cruelly, viciously, wickedly; see **brutally.**

murky, *mod.* **1.** [Dark]—*Syn.* dim, dusky, dingy; see **dark** 1, **dirty** 1.

2. [Gloomy]—*Syn.* cheerless, dismal, somber; see **sad** 1.

3. [Having the natural light obscured]—*Syn.* overcast, darkened, misty; see **stormy** 1.

murmur, *v.* **1.** [To make a low, continuous sound] —*Syn.* purl, ripple, moan, trickle, burble, babble, tinkle, gurgle, ooze, drip, meander, flow gently; see also **hum, whisper.**—*Ant.* noise*, peal, clang.

2. [To mutter]—*Syn.* mumble, rumble, growl; see **grumble** 2.

mumurer, *n.* —*Syn.* grumbler, complainer, malcontent; see **agitator, radical.**

murmurous, *mod.* —*Syn.* indistinct, muffled, low; see **faint** 3.

murrain, *n.* —*Syn.* anthrax, hoof-and-mouth disease, cattle disease, epizootic disease, murr, Texas fever, pox, pestilence, cattle plague; see also **disease** 3.

muscle, *n.* —*Syn.* fiber, flesh, protoplasm, meat, brawn; *both* (D): beef, horseflesh; see also **tissue** 3.

Muscles include the following—striated, nonstriated, voluntary, involuntary, reflex, heart, cardiac, frontal, temporal, trapesial, splenial, *splenius cervicis, pectoralis major* (*both* Latin), pectoral, external oblique, dorsal, subclavial, scapular, intercostal, biceps, triceps, rotator cuff, branchial, extensor, flexor, palmar, dorsal, interosseal, aponeurotic, sartorial, gluteal, adductor, adductorial, biceps femoris, lateral, medial, anterior tibial, digital.

muscular, *mod.* —*Syn.* brawny, powerful, husky; see **strong** 1.

muse, *v.* —*Syn.* ponder, meditate, reflect; see **think** 1.

Muses, *n.* —*Syn.* goddesses, sacred Nine, the tuneful Nine, Nine goddesses, the Graces, the arts, classical deities.

Names of the classical Muses include the following—Calliope, Clio, Erato, Euterpe, Melpomene, Polyhymnia, Terpsichore, Thalia, Urania.

museum, *n.* —*Syn.* institution, building, hall, place of exhibition, foundation, art gallery, library, picture gallery, archives, treasury, storehouse, depository, vault, repository, aquarium, menagerie, zoological garden *or* park, zoo, botanical garden, herbarium, arboretum.

Famous museums include the following—Museum of the Archaeological Society, National Museum of Antiquities, Athens; Archaeological Museum, Cairo; Louvre, Musée de l'Homme, Paris; British Museum, National Gallery, Victoria and Albert Museum, London; Museo Nazionale, Naples; Vatican Gallery, Museo Nazionale, Rome; Museo del Prado, Madrid; Kaiser Friedrich Museum, Berlin; Rumiantsov Museum, Moscow; Hermitage, Imperial Academy of Science, Leningrad; Museo Nacional, Mexico City; Museum of Fine Arts, Boston; Peabody Museum of American Archaeology and Ethnology, Cambridge; National Museum, Library of Congress, Smithsonian Institution, Washington; Field Museum, Art Institute, Chicago; Cleveland Museum of Art, Metropolitan Art Gallery, American Museum of Natural History, Heye Foundation, Museum of the American Indian, New York; Huntington Library, Pasadena, California.

mush, *n.* **1.** [Boiled meal]—*Syn.* Indian meal, hasty pudding, supawn, samp, hominy, cereal, grain; *both* (D): spoon, victual; see also **food.**

2. [Any soft mass]—*Syn.* pulp, slush, dough; see **mash.**

3. [(D) Sentimentality]—*Syn.* sentimentalism, excessive sentiment, mawkishness, affectation, superficiality, superficial sentiment, exaggerated sentiment, romanticism, maudlinism, a sentiment about sentiment; *all* (D): puppy love, gush, flapdoodle, hearts and flowers, sob stuff; see also **love.**

mushroom, *n.* —*Syn.* toadstool, fungus, *champignon* (French).

Edible mushrooms include the following—morel, chanterelle, puffball, earth star, honey, agaric, button, cèpe, meadow mushroom, Caesar's mushroom, fairy ring, shaggy mane, inky cap, oyster mushroom, parasol, golden clavaria, bear's head, hedgehog, jew's ear, trembling mushroom, liver fungus, soft-skinned crepidotus, green russula, tan-colored

russula, Mary russula, sheathed amanitopsis, large-sheathed amanitopsis, smooth lepiota, American lepiota, *Lactarius deliciosus, Lactarius camphoratus, Hypholoma incertum, Cantharellus crispus, Hydrophorus pratensis, Amanita caesarea* (*all* Latin).
Poisonous mushrooms or toadstools include the following—jack-my-lantern, fetid russula, fly agaric, *Amanita muscaria* (Latin), death angel, death cup, *Amanita phallordes* (Latin).

mushroom, *v.* —*Syn.* augment, spread, sprout; see **grow** 1, **increase** 1.

mushy, *mod.* **1.** [Soft]—*Syn.* pulpy, mashy, muddy; see **soft** 2.
2. [(D) Sentimental]—*Syn.* romantic, maudlin, effusive; see **emotional** 2, **sentimental.**

music, *n.* **1.** [A combination of tone and rhythm] —*Syn.* harmony, melody, tune, air, strain, harmonics, song, minstrelsy, measure, refrain, phrasing, modulation cadence, the Nine (D).
Terms used in music include the following—scale, chromatic scale, tempered scale, clef, note, tone, pitch, sharp, flat, accidental, major, minor, key, mode, orchestral coloring, orchestration, instrumentation, transposition, variation, improvisation, rhythm, accent, beat, down-beat, up-beat, off-beat, syncopation, chord, dominant chord, subdominant chord, tonic chord, counterpoint, interval, timbre, volume, resonance. Musical forms for the voice include the following—art song, folk song, aria; see **song.**
Musical forms for instruments include the following—symphony (the conventional four movements of a symphony are sonata, andante, scherzó, finale), concerto, concerto grosso, suite, partita; trio *or* quartet *or* quintet, etc., for strings *or* woodwinds, etc.; overture, prelude, sonata, sonatina, mass, scherzo, rondo, nocturne, caprice, invention, concertino, toccata, chaconne, passacaglia, fugue, étude, exercise, tone poem, symphonic poem, symphonic fantasy, fantasia, variations, rhapsody, ballet music, serenade, ballade, march, canzonetta, rhythm and blues, rondino, pastorale, dance.
Musical dance forms include the following—waltz, tango, polka; see **dance** 1.
General styles of music include the following—classical *or* long-hair (D), serious, medieval, modern, folk, primitive, popular, national, sacred, secular, impressionistic, neoteric, baroque, neoclassical, neo-Bachian, modernistic, formal, romantic, *a cappella* (Italian), program, pure, jazz; *all* (D): blues, jive, ragtime, boogiewoogie, hot music, folk rock, acid rock, heavy metal, rock-and-roll, bebop *or* bop, third stream, soul rock, soul, le jazz hot, ragtime, swing, barrelhouse, rap.
Styles of music according to its technical form include the following—melodic, polyphonic, contrapuntal, homophonic, Gregorian, strict, free, harmonic, lyric, epic, dramatic, pastoral, mensurable, figured, atonal, whole toned, diatonic, pentatonic, twelve-tone, aleatoric, modal, syncopated.
Styles of music according to its method of performance include the following—vocal, instrumental, solo, choral, orchestral.
Styles of music according to its use include the following—operatic, symphonic, chamber, dance, concert, motion picture, theatrical, ecclesiastical, church, military, concert, ballet.
2. [The study or writing of music]—*Syn.* musicology, musicography, hymnology, hymnography.
3. [Responsiveness to music]—*Syn.* musical appreciation, sensitivity, aesthetic sense; see **appreciation** 3, **feeling** 4.
face the music (D)—*Syn.* accept the consequences (of one's actions), suffer, undergo; see **endure** 2.
set to music—*Syn.* compose music for, write a song around, provide a musical setting (for); see **compose** 3.

musical, *mod.* **1.** [Having the qualities of music] —*Syn.* tuneful, dulcet, sweet, pleasing, agreeable, euphonious, melic, symphonious, symphonic, lyric, mellow, vocal, choral, silvery, canorous, assonant, unisonant, unisonous, homophonous, consonant, rhythmical; see also **harmonious** 1, **melodious.** —*Ant.* tuneless, discordant, harsh.
2. [Having aptitude for music]—*Syn.* gifted, talented, musically inclined; see **artistic** 3.

musical, *n.* —*Syn.* musicale, choral service, songfest, musical comedy, song-and-dance, minstrel show, oratorio, burlesque; see also **opera, performance** 2, **show** 1.

musical instrument, *n.* Types of musical instruments include the following—lyre, bell, pipes of Pan, flute, piccolo, flageolet, oboe, clarinet *or* licorice stick (D), alto clarinet, bass clarinet, A clarinet, E-flat clarinet, B-flat clarinet, bassoon, contrabassoon, fife, bagpipe, ocarina (sweet potato) (D): trombone, bazooka, French horn, English horn, basset horn, tuba, baritone, sousaphone, helicon, cornet, A-flat cornet, B-flat cornet, trumpet, fluegelhorn, alpenhorn, saxophone, virginal, dulcimer, spinet, harpsichord, harmonica, *Hammer Klavier* (German), piano, clavichord, organ, pipe organ, reed organ, mouth organ, jew's harp, harp, vina, calabash, tambourine, ukelele, Hawaiian guitar, guitar, electric guitar, flamenco guitar, banjo, mandolin, lute, theorbo, viola, violin *or* fiddle (D), violoncello *or* cello, bass viol, xylophone, marimba, *Glockenspiel* (German), vibraharp, vibraphone *or* vibes (D), cymbal, drum, accordian, concertina, zamar, tom-tom, magoudhi, balalaika, kokiri, samisen, cheng, siao, kin, che, koto, sitar, crowd, recorder, grand piano, concert piano, baby grand piano, upright piano, spinet, player piano, tuning fork, calliope; see also **drum, flute, horn** 1, **organ, piano,**

musician, *n.* —*Syn.* player, performer, composer; see **artist** 1, **genius** 2.
Musicians include the following—singer, director, teacher, instrumentalist, soloist, soprano, first soprano, second soprano, alto, contralto, tenor, baritone, bass, basso, basso profundo, coloratura soprano, mezzosoprano, folk singer, drummer, pianist, flautist *or* flutist, violinist, cellist; performer on a woodwind instrument, performer on a brass instrument, percussion performer, etc.; cello, flute, first violin, second violin, viola, etc; *both* (D): jazzmen, blues men.

musing, *mod.* —*Syn.* pensive, introspective, absorbed; see **thoughtful** 1.

musing, *n.* —*Syn.* absorption, meditation, deliberation; see **reflection** 1, **thought** 1.

musket, *n.* —*Syn.* flintlock, carbine, matchlock; see **gun** 2, **rifle, weapon** 1.

musketeer, *n.* —*Syn.* enlisted man, rifleman, hussar; see **fighter** 1, **soldier.**

muskrat, *n.* —*Syn.* musk shrew, Pyrenean desman, Muscovitic desman, civet cat, musquash; *both* (D): musk cat, muskbox; see also **animal** 2.

muss (D), *n.* —*Syn.* chaos, disarrangement, turmoil; see **confusion** 2, **disorder** 2.

muss, *v.* —*Syn.* rumble, tousle, dishevel, ruffle, crumple, jumble, disarrange, disturb, mess up; see also **tangle.**

mussy, *mod.* —*Syn.* messy, chaotic, rumpled; see **tangled.**

must (D), *n.* —*Syn.* requirement, need, obligation; see **necessity** 2.

must, *v.* —*Syn.* ought, should, have, have (got) (to), be compelled (to), be necessitated, be obliged *or* required, be doomed *or* destined, be ordered *or* directed, be made *or* driven; *all* (D): must needs, have no choice, be pushed to the wall, be one's fate; see also **need.**

mustache, *n.* —*Syn.* moustachio; *both* (D): handlebars, soup-strainer; see **beard, whiskers.**

mustang, *n.* —*Syn.* bronc, colt, wild stallion; see **horse** 1.

muster, *v.* —*Syn.* call together, marshal, summon; see **assemble** 2, **gather** 1.

musty, *mod.* **1.** [Spoiled]—*Syn.* moldy, putrid, rank; see **rotten** 1, **spoiled.**
2. [Stale with age]—*Syn.* fusty, dusty, moth-eaten, crumbling, dry, dried-out, antediluvian, mummyish, decrepit; see also **wasted, withered.**—*Ant.* new*, well-cared-for, in good condition.
3. [Trite]—*Syn.* worn, commonplace, hackneyed; see **common** 1, **dull** 4.

mutability, *n.* —*Syn.* instability, indecision, inconstancy, variableness, changeableness, volatility, versatility, fickleness, vacillation, indecision, irresolution, changefulness; see also **uncertainty** 2, 3.

mutable, *mod.* —*Syn.* fickle, uncertain, doubtful; see **changeable** 2, **unreliable** 2.

mutation, *n.* —*Syn.* modification, deviation, variation; see **change** 1, 2, **variety** 1, 2.

mute, *mod.* **1.** [Without power of speech]—*Syn.* tongueless, aphonic, deaf and dumb, inarticulate, voiceless, tonguetied; see also **dumb** 1, **quiet** 2. —*Ant.* vocal*, noisy, unimpaired.
2. [Suddenly deprived of speech]—*Syn.* speechless, wordless, silent; see **bewildered, surprised.**

mute, *v.* —*Syn.* silence, reduce, benumb; see **soften** 2.

mutilate, *v.* **1.** [To maim]—*Syn.* cut, batter, scratch; see **maim, weaken** 2.
2. [To damage]—*Syn.* injure, deface, ravage; see **damage** 1, **hurt** 1.

mutilated, *mod.* —*Syn.* garbled, disfigured, distorted, castrated, maimed, mangled, dismembered, truncated, amputated, butchered, excised, defaced, dislimbed; see also **deformed, twisted** 1, **weakened.**

mutineer, *n.* —*Syn.* insurgent, revolutionary, subversive; see **radical, rebel** 1.

mutinous, *mod.* —*Syn.* insubordinate, riotous, anarchistic; see **lawless** 1, 2, **radical** 2, **rebellious** 1, 2, 3.

mutiny, *n.* —*Syn.* insurrection, revolt, resistance; see **revolution** 2.

mutter, *v.* **1.** [To make a low, mumbling sound] —*Syn.* rumble, growl, snarl; see **grumble** 2, **sound** 1.
2. [To speak as if to oneself]—*Syn.* murmur, grunt, grumble, sputter, whisper, speak *sotto voce* (Italian), speak inarticulately *or* indistinctly, articulate poorly, speak in an undertone; *both* (D): speak with mush in one's mouth, swallow one's words; see also **mumble, utter.**
3. [To complain]—*Syn.* grumble, moan, groan; see **complain** 1.

mutton, *n.* —*Syn.* lamb, sheep flesh, *mouton* (French); see also **meat, sheep.**
Cuts of mutton include the following—shoulder, leg, spigot (Scotch), rib chop, loin chop, lamb chop, leg of lamb, brisket, breast, stew meat, neck.

mutual, *mod.* **1.** [Reciprocal]—*Syn.* interchangeable, correlative, done reciprocally, convertible, acting reciprocally, alternate, interchanged, responded to, respective, two-sided, bilateral, given and taken, received and offered; see also **exchangeable.**—*Ant.* unreciprocated, inconvertible, noninterchangeable.
2. [Common]—*Syn.* joint, shared, belonging equally to; see **common** 1, **sharing.**

mutual fund, *n.* —*Syn.* trust fund, investment corporation, cushioned stock list; see **bank** 3, **funds.**

mutuality, *n.* —*Syn.* reciprocity, correlation, alternation; see **exchange** 2, **sale** 1, 2, **transaction.**

mutually, *mod.* —*Syn.* commonly, co-operatively, respectively, reciprocally, in cooperation *or* collaboration *or* combination, by common consent *or* agreement *or* contract, in conjunction (with), to (the) common profit *or* advantage, each to each, to one another, all at once, en masse; as a group *or* company *or* organization, etc.; see also **jointly, together** 2.—*Ant.* individually*, independently, separately.

muzzle, *v.* **1.** [To fasten a muzzle upon]—*Syn.* cage, sheathe, cover, wrap, muffle, envelop, deaden; see also **bind** 1, **gag** 1.—*Ant.* release*, unfasten, unbind.
2. [To silence]—*Syn.* gag, restrain, trammel, restrict, repress, suppress, check, stop, stop one's mouth, hush, still, shush (D); see also **prevent, quiet** 2.

muzzled, *mod.* —*Syn.* silenced, gagged, quieted; see **abused, trapped.**

myopia, *n.* —*Syn.* nearsightedness, astigmatism, strabismus, blindness; see also **sight** 1, **vision** 1.

myopic, *mod.* —*Syn.* nearsighted, astigmatic, bleary-eyed, shortsighted, halfsighted, dimsighted, presbyopic; *all* (D): moon-eyed, mole-eyed, goggle-eyed, blind.

myriad, *mod.* —*Syn.* variable, infinite, innumerable; see **endless** 1, **multiple** 1.

myself, *pron.* —*Syn.* me, personally, in my proper person, I *or* me personally; the speaker *or* author *or* writer, etc.; on my own authority *or* responsibility; *all* (D): yours truly, your humble servant, me myself, my own sweet self; see also **ID.**

mysterious, *mod.* **1.** [Puzzling]—*Syn.* enigmatic, enigmatical, strange; see **difficult** 2, **unnatural** 1.

2. [Concerning powers beyond those supposedly natural]—*Syn.* mystic, occult, dark, mystifying, arcane, transcendental, cabalistic, spiritual, symbolic, subjective, mystical, magical, abstruse, dark, veiled, strange, alchemistic, supernormal, necromantic, astrological, unknowable, unfathomable, ineffable, esoteric, numinous, cryptic, oracular, unrevealed, incredible; see also **magic** 1, **secret** 1.
3. [Not generally known]—*Syn.* obscure, hidden, ambiguous; see **secret** 1.

mystery, *n.* **1.** [The quality of being mysterious] —*Syn.* inscrutability, inscrutableness, unfathomableness, unfathomability, undiscoverability, unanswerableness, unexplainableness, inexplicableness, abstruseness, equivocality, esoterism, occultism, cabalism; see also **irregularity** 2, **magic** 1, 2, **strangeness.**—*Ant.* clarity*, discoverability, scrutability.
2. [Something difficult to know]—*Syn.* riddle, conundrum, enigma; see **difficulty** 2, **puzzle** 2.
3. [A trick]—*Syn.* sleight-of-hand, trick of magic, juggle; see **trick** 1.
4. [(D) A mystery story]—*Syn.* detective story, mystery play, mystery movie; see **story.**

mystic, *mod.*—*Syn.* occult, transcendental, spiritual; see **mysterious** 2, **secret** 1.

mysticism, *n.*—*Syn.* occultism, pietism, ontologism, cabala, cabalism, quietism, orphism, divine afflatus, enthusiasm; see also **spiritualism** 1.

mystification, *n.*—*Syn.* bewilderment, uncertainty, complexity; see **confusion** 2, **wonder** 1.

mystify, *v.*—*Syn.* perplex, trick, hoodwink; see **deceive, lie** 1.

mystique, *n.*—*Syn.* attitude, complex, nature; see **character** 1, **temperament.**

myth, *n.*—*Syn.* fable, folk tale, legend, lore, saga, folk ballad, *mythos* (Greek), allegory, parable, tale; see also **story.**

mythical, *mod.*—*Syn.* mythological, fabricated, fictitious; see **false** 3, **unreal.**

mythological, *mod.*—*Syn.* whimsical, fictitious, chimerical; see **fanciful** 1, **fantastic, imaginary.**

mythology, *n.*—*Syn.* belief, conviction, mythicism; see **faith** 2, **religion** 1.
Mythologies include the following—Latin, Chaldean, Semitic, Bantu, Sumerian, Greek, Egyptian, Norse *or* Germanic, Celtic, Hindu, American Indian.

N

nab, *v.* **1.** [(D) To arrest]—*Syn.* apprehend, capture, catch; see **arrest** 1.
2. [To seize]—*Syn.* grab, take, snatch; see **seize** 2.

nadir, *n.* —*Syn.* depth(s), lowest point, foot; see **bottom** 1, **opposite** 3.

nag, *n.* —*Syn.* plug, mount, hack; see **animal** 2, **horse** 1.

nag, *v.* —*Syn.* vex, annoy, pester; see **bother** 2, 3.

naiad, *n.* —*Syn.* nymph, sprite, undine; see **fairy** 1.

nail, *n.* —*Syn.* brad, pin, peg, hob, stud; see also **spike** 1.
Types and sizes include the following—common wire, copper, coated, cement-coated, galvanized, finishing, flooring, shingle, roofing, staging, boat, hinge, chair, horseshoe, brad, cut, upholsterer's, clout, box, shoe, headless, hobnail; twopenny, fourpenny, sixpenny, eightpenny, tenpenny, twelvepenny.

nail, *v.* **1.** [To hammer]—*Syn.* drive, pound, spike; see **beat** 2, **hammer, hit** 1.
2. [To fasten with nails]—*Syn.* secure, hold, bind; see **fasten** 1.
3. [(D) To arrest]—*Syn.* capture, detain, apprehend; see **arrest** 1, **seize** 2.
hard as nails—*Syn.* callous, unfeeling, remorseless; see **cruel** 2.
hit the nail on the head (D)—*Syn.* do *or* say what is exactly right, be accurate, come to the point; see **define** 2.

naive, *mod.* —*Syn.* unaffected, ingenuous, plain, artless, innocent, untrained, countrified, callow, jejune, *naïf* (French), natural, unschooled, ignorant, untaught, provincial, unsophisticated, unworldly, guileless, spontaneous, instinctive, impulsive, simple-minded, innocuous, unsuspecting, harmless, confiding, gullible, credulous, trusting, fresh, unjaded, original, rustic, boorish, unpolished, rude, primitive, sincere, unfeigned, open, candid, forthright, aboveboard, romantic, fanciful, unpretentious, transparent, unsuspicious, straightforward, uncomplicated, easily imposed upon; see also **childish** 1, **frank, inexperienced, simple** 1.—*Ant.* experienced*, sophisticated, complicated.

naively, *mod.* —*Syn.* childishly, ingenuously, stupidly; see **foolishly, openly** 1.

naiveté, *n.* —*Syn.* ingenuousness, childishness, inexperience; see **innocence** 2, **simplicity** 2.

naked, *mod.* **1.** [Nude]—*Syn.* unclothed, undressed, stripped, unclad, unrobed, disrobed, divested, threadbare, leafless, hairless, bare, undraped, exposed, ungarmented, having nothing on, in dishabille, unappareled, denuded, unveiled, uncovered, uncloaked, stark naked, bald, bareheaded, barren, dismantled; *all* (D): in the altogether, in one's birthday suit, in the buff, peeled, without a stitch, in the raw, topless, bottomless, in native buff, in a state of nature.—*Ant.* clothed*, clad, dressed.
2. [Without covering]—*Syn.* bared, unconcealed, unprotected; see **exposed** 2, **open** 4.
3. [Unadorned]—*Syn.* plain, simple, artless; see **modest** 2, **natural** 3.

nakedness, *n.* —*Syn.* nudity, bareness, nature in the raw, undress, baldness, exposure, *both* (D): state of nature, the raw.

namby-pamby, *mod.* —*Syn.* insipid, wishy-washy, simpering; see **cowardly** 1, 2, **irresolute, sentimental.**

name, *n.* **1.** [A title]—*Syn.* proper name, Christian name, given name, cognomen, appellation, designation, first name, family name, compellation, title, prenomen, denomination, surname, agnomen, agname, style, sign, patronymic, matronymic, eponym; *both* (D): moniker, handle; see also **signature.**
2. [Reputation]—*Syn.* renown, honor, repute; see **fame** 1.
3. [An epithet]—*Syn.* nickname, pen name, pseudonym, sobriquet, stage name, *nom de plume, nom de guerre* (both French), pet name, fictitious name; see also **alias.**
Insulting names include the following—devil, imbecile, idiot, blackguard, rat, skunk, dog, pig, fool, moron, brute, *cochon, canaille* (both French), *ladrón, galopin* (both Spanish), *Schweinhund, Schweinigel, Lausejunge, Lausehund* (all German); *all* (D): bum, boob, oaf, goon, sourpuss, dumb Dora, specks, four-eyes, skinny, fatty, windbag, buttinski, meshugana; see also **curse, insult.**
4. [A famous person]—*Syn.* star, hero, lion, a person of renown; *all* (D): celeb, headline attraction, blue-booker, headliner; see also **celebrity** 2, **personage** 2.
call names—*Syn.* swear at, castigate, slander; see **censure** 1.
in the name of—*Syn.* by authority of, in reference to, as representative of; see **for.**
know only by name—*Syn.* be familiar with, not know personally, have heard of; see **know** 3.
to one's name—*Syn.* belonging to one, in one's possession, possessed by; see **owned.**

name, *v.* **1.** [To give a name]—*Syn.* call, christen, baptize, style, term, label, identify, provide with nomenclature, classify, denominate, designate, title, entitle, nickname, characterize, label, ticket; *all* (D): dub, pin a moniker on, put the tag on, give a handle; see also **describe, define.**
2. [To indicate by name]—*Syn.* refer to, specify, signify, denote, single out, mark, suggest, connote,

point to, note, remark, index, list, cite; see also **mention, refer** 2.
3. [To appoint]—*Syn.* elect, nominate, select; see **delegate** 1.

name calling, *n.* —*Syn.* insulting, abusing, derogating; see **insult.**

named, *mod.* **1.** [Having as a name]—*Syn.* called, designated, entitled, titled, termed, specified, styled, appellated, denominated, christened, baptized, nicknamed, labeled; *both* (D): tagged, dubbed.
2. [Chosen]—*Syn.* appointed, commissioned, delegated, deputed, authorized, nominated, returned, elected, invested, vested, assigned, ordained, entrusted, picked, selected, chosen, decided *or* fixed upon, determined *or* settled on, picked out, preferred, favored, supported, approved, certified, called, anointed, consecrated, sanctioned, drafted, opted, declared, announced, singled out.

name-dropper, *n.* —*Syn.* snob, poseur, showoff; see **braggart.**

name-dropping, *n.* —*Syn.* posing, showing off, assuming a pose; see **boast.**

nameless, *mod.* **1.** [Without an acknowledged name]—*Syn.* unacknowledged, unknown, unnamed; see **anonymous.**
2. [Without a well-known name]—*Syn.* inconspicuous, undistinguished, obscure; see **unknown** 2.
3. [Better left without being named]—*Syn.* unmentionable, disreputable, despicable; see **offensive** 2.

namely, *mod.* —*Syn.* to wit, that is to say, particularly, by way of explanation, strictly speaking, as much as to say, in other words, in plain English, *id est (i.e.), videlicet (viz.), scilicet* (all Latin); see also **specifically** 1.

naming, *n.* —*Syn.* identifying, pinning down, giving a name (to), finding a name (for), providing an identification (for); see also **classification** 1, **description** 1.

nap, *n.* **1.** [A short sleep]—*Syn.* siesta, cat nap, doze; see **rest** 1, **sleep.**
2. [The finish of certain goods, especially fabric] —*Syn.* pile, shag, surface, feel, grit, ingrain, tooth, fiber, woof, wale, warp and weft, roughness, smoothness; see also **grain** 3, **outside** 1, **texture** 1.

nape, *n.* —*Syn.* the back of the neck, cervix, cervical area, scruff (of the neck), poll, occiput; see also **neck** 1.

napkin, *n.* —*Syn.* serviette, paper napkin, (table) linen; see **towel.**

narcotic, *mod.* —*Syn.* deadening, numbing, dulling, analgesic, anesthetic, stupefying.

narcotic, *n.* —*Syn.* stupefacient, anodyne, opiate; see **drug** 2.

narrate, *v.* —*Syn.* recite, make known, rehearse, detail, enumerate, describe, recount, set *or* hold forth, depict, characterize, delineate, portray, picture, proclaim, unfold, paint, disclose, reveal, chronicle, repeat, relate (the particulars), give an account (of), tell a story; *all* (D): spin a yarn, unfold a tale, hand a lingo, spin a windy; see also **report** 1, **tell** 1.

narration, *n.* —*Syn.* description, narrative, account; see **report** 1, **story.**

narrative, *mod.* —*Syn.* storylike, fictional, retold, recounted, narrated, sequential, reported; see also **chronological, historical.**

narrator, *n.* —*Syn.* teller of tales, reciter, raconteur; see **storyteller.**

narrow, *mod.* **1.** [Lacking breadth]—*Syn.* close, cramped, tight, confined, shrunken, compressed, slender, thin, fine, linear, threadlike, tapering, tapered, slim, spare, scant, scanty, incapacious, attenuated, strait, coarctate, lanky, spindling, small, meager; see also **restricted.**—*Ant.* broad, wide, extensive.
2. [Lacking tolerance]—*Syn.* dogmatic, narrow-minded, parochial; see **conservative, conventional** 3, **prejudiced.**
3. [Lacking understanding]—*Syn.* ill-advised, imprudent, irrational; see **stupid** 1.
4. [Lacking a comfortable margin]—*Syn.* close, near, precarious; see **dangerous** 1, **endangered, unsafe.**

narrowing, *n.* —*Syn.* shortening, restricting, lessening; see **abbreviation** 2, **contraction** 1, **reduction** 1.

narrowly, *mod.* —*Syn.* nearly, close(ly), by a (narrow) margin; see **almost.**

narrow-minded, *mod.* —*Syn.* bigoted, biased, provincial; see **conservative, conventional** 3, **prejudiced.**

narrow-mindedness, *n.* —*Syn.* intolerance, bigotry, provincialism; see **prejudice.**

narrowness, *n.* **1.** [A physical restriction]—*Syn.* confinement, slimness, restriction; see **barrier, impediment** 1, **interference** 1.
2. [A mental restriction]—*Syn.* intolerance, bigotry, bias; see **prejudice, stubborness.**

narrows, *n.* —*Syn.* strait, neck, canal; see **channel** 1.

nasty, *mod.* **1.** [Offensive to the senses]—*Syn.* foul, gross, revolting; see **offensive** 2, **vulgar** 1.
2. [Indecent]—*Syn.* immoral, immodest, smutty; see **lewd** 1, 2, **shameful** 1, **wicked** 1.
3. [Likely to be harmful]—*Syn.* injurious, damaging, noxious; see **dangerous** 1, **harmful, poisonous.**
4. [Unkind]—*Syn.* sarcastic, critical, mean; see **cruel** 1, **fierce** 1, **ruthless** 1.

nation, *n.* **1.** [An organized state]—*Syn.* realm, country, commonwealth, republic, democracy, state, monarchy, dominion, body politic, land, domain, empire, kingdom, principality, sovereignty, colony; see also **government** 1.
2. [A people having some unity]—*Syn.* populace, community, public; see **population, race** 2, **society** 2.

national, *mod.* **1.** [Concerning a nation]—*Syn.* ethnic, political, sovereign, state, social, societal, politic, civic, civil, communal, royal, imperial, federal; see also **governmental, public** 2.
2. [Operative throughout a nation]—*Syn.* nationwide, inland, internal, country-wide, interstate, social, widespread, sweeping; see also **general** 1.

nationalism, *n.* —*Syn.* provincialism, chauvinism, jingoism; see **loyalty, patriotism.**

nationality, *n.* **1.** [Citizenship]—*Syn.* native land, allegiance, adopted country, political home; see also **country** 3, **origin** 2.
2. [A national group]—*Syn.* body politic, society, community; see **citizen, population, race** 2.

nationally, *mod.* **1.** [Concerning a nation]—*Syn.* politically, governmentally, as a state, as a country, publicly, of the people, throughout the country, transcending state boundaries, for the general welfare.

2. [Everywhere]—*Syn.* generally, commonly, entirely; see **everywhere, universally** 2, 3.

nationwide, *mod.* —*Syn.* general, federal, universal; see **national** 2, **regional, public** 1, 2.

native, *mod.* **1.** [Natural]—*Syn.* innate, inherent, inborn, implanted, inbred, ingrained, inwrought, congenital, fundamental, hereditary, inherited, essential, constitutional; see also **natural** 1.—*Ant.* unnatural*, foreign, alien.

2. [Characteristic of a region]—*Syn.* aboriginal, indigenous, original, primitive, autochthonous, autochthonal, primary, primeval, vernacular, domestic, local, found locally; see also **regional.**—*Ant.* imported*, brought in, transplanted.

3. [Born in a region]—*Syn.* belonging, native-born, (coming) from; see **related** 2.

go native—*Syn.* adopt a different way of life, live simply, vegetate; see **change** 4.

native, *n.* **1.** [Aborigine]—*Syn.* primitive, ancient, man of old; see **savage** 1.

2. [Citizen]—*Syn.* national, inhabitant, indigene; see **citizen, resident.**

native son, *n.* —*Syn.* local candidate, favorite son, home *or* local boy (D); see **candidate, favorite, resident.**

Nativity, *n.* —*Syn.* the birth of Christ, Holy Night, coming of the Christ-child; see **Christmas.**

natty, *mod.* —*Syn.* smart, chic, well-dressed; see **clean** 1, **fashionable, neat** 1.

natural, *mod.* **1.** [Rooted in nature]—*Syn.* intrinsic, original, essential, true, fundamental, inborn, ingrained, inherent, instinctive, implanted, innate, inbred, subjective, inherited, congenital, genetic, incarnate, bred in the bone; see also **native** 1. —*Ant.* foreign*, alien, acquired.

2. [To be expected]—*Syn.* normal, typical, characteristic, usual, customary, habitual, accustomed, involuntary, spontaneous, uncontrolled, uncontrollable, wonted, familiar, common, universal, prevailing, prevalent, general, uniform, constant, consistent, probable, ordinary, logical, reasonable, anticipated, looked for, hoped for, counted on, relied on, generally occurring, in the natural course of events; see also **regular** 3.—*Ant.* unknown*, unexpected, unheard of.

3. [Not affected]—*Syn.* ingenuous, simple, artless, innocent, spontaneous, impulsive, childlike, unfeigned, unaffected, open, frank, candid, unsophisticated, homey, unpretentious, forthright, sincere, unstudied, straightforward, undesigning, being oneself, unsuspecting, credulous, trusting, plain, unassumed, direct, unpolished, rustic; see also **naive.**—*Ant.* ornate* pretentious, affected.

4. [Concerning the physical universe]—*Syn.* actual, tangible, according to nature; see **physical** 1, **real.**

natural child, *n.* —*Syn.* love child, illegitimate offspring, *nullius filius* (Latin); see **baby** 1, **bastard** 1, **child.**

naturalist, *n.* —*Syn.* botanist, zoologist, biologist; see **scientist.**

naturalization, *n.* —*Syn.* adoption, acclimatization, acculturation, adapting, conditioning, habituation, accustoming, inurement, making new allegiances, rooting, grounding; see also **adjustment** 2.

naturalize, *v.* —*Syn.* adapt, acclimate, accustom; see **adopt** 2, **change** 1, **conform.**

naturally, *interj.* —*Syn.* certainly, absolutely, of course; see **surely, yes.**

naturally, *mod.* **1.** [In an unaffected manner] —*Syn.* artlessly, spontaneously, innocently, candidly, openly, impulsively, freely, readily, easily, without restraint, unceremoniously, unconstrainedly, directly; see also **simply** 1, **sincerely.** —*Ant.* awkwardly*, restrainedly, clumsily.

2. [As a matter of course]—*Syn.* casually, according to expectation, as anticipated, characteristically, typically, normally, commonly, usually, ordinarily, habitually, instinctively, intuitively, by nature, by birth, uniformly, generally, consistently; see also **customarily.**—*Ant.* strangely*, astonishingly, amazingly.

natural science, *n.* —*Syn.* popular science, organic and inorganic science, physical science, science of nature; see also **science** 1.

nature, *n.* **1.** [The external universe]—*Syn.* cosmos, creation, macrocosm; see **universe, world** 1.

2. [The complex of essential qualities]—*Syn.* characteristics, quality, constitution; see **character** 1, **essence** 1.

3. [Natural surroundings]—*Syn.* outside world, out-of-doors, scenery, rural *or* natural setting, view, seascape, landscape, (the) outdoors, external nature, natural scenery, God's hand, recreational facilities, forest primeval; *both* (D): the great outdoors, the birds and the bees; see also **environment, reality** 1.

4. [Natural forces]—*Syn.* natural law, natural order, underlying cause, cosmic process, physical energy, kinetic energy, potential energy, water power, fission, fusion, hydrogen atom, heavy water, atomic power, the sun, radiation, rays; beta rays, gamma rays, etc; see also **energy** 3, **physics.**

5. [Vital forces in an organism]—*Syn.* creation, generation, regeneration, restoration, vivification, animation, energy, quickening, reproductiveness, life force, the nature of the beast (D); see also **life** 1, 2, **strength** 1.

6. [Kind]—*Syn.* species, sort, type; see **kind** 2, **variety** 1, 2.

by nature—*Syn.* inherently, by birth, as a matter of course; see **naturally** 2.

in a state of nature—*Syn.* uncultivated, not tamed, primitive; see **wild** 3.

of (*or* **in**) **the nature of**—*Syn.* similar to, having the essential character of, as compared to; see **like.**

naught, *n.* —*Syn.* nought, zero, not anything; see **nothing.**

naughty, *mod.* —*Syn.* wayward, disobedient, mischievous, impish, fiendish, badly behaved, roguish, bad, unmanageable, ungovernable, refractory, recalcitrant, wanton, froward, insubordinate; see also **unruly.**

nausea, *n.* **1.** [Sickness]—*Syn.* motion sickness, queasiness, vomiting; see **illness** 1.

2. [Disgust]—*Syn.* offense, revulsion, aversion; see **hatred** 1.

nauseate, *v.* —*Syn.* sicken, offend, repulse; see **bother** 3, **disgust, disturb** 2.

nauseated, *mod.* **1.** [Sick]—*Syn.* squeamish, ill, queasy; see **sick.**

2. [Disgusted]—*Syn.* revolted, sickened, offended; see **disgusted, insulted, shocked.**

nauseating, *mod.* —*Syn.* sickening, repulsive, disgusting; see **offensive** 2.

nauseous, *mod.* **1.** [Sick]—*Syn.* queasy, ill, squeamish; see **sick.**

2. [Disgusting]—*Syn.* revolting, loathsome, sickening; see **offensive** 2.

nautical, *mod.* —*Syn.* ocean-going, marine, naval, oceanic, deep-sea, aquatic, sailing, seafaring, seaworthy, sea-going, boating, rowing, oceanographic, sea-loving, navy-trained, yachting, whaling, cruising, navigating, salty, pelagic, thalassic, abyssal; see also **maritime** 2.

naval, *mod.* —*Syn.* seagoing, marine, aquatic; see **maritime** 2, **nautical.**

nave, *n.* —*Syn.* hub, core, middle; see **center** 1.

navel, *n.* —*Syn.* omphalos, depression, umbilicus; see **abdomen, center** 1.

navicert, *n.* —*Syn.* assurance, safe conduct, papers; see **passport, promise** 1.

navigable, *mod.* —*Syn.* off-soundings, passable, open; see **safe** 1.

navigate, *v.* —*Syn.* pilot, steer, lie to, head out for, ride out, lay the course, operate; see also **drive** 3.

navigation, *n.* —*Syn.* navigating, seamanship, piloting, pilotage, aeronautics, flying, sailing, seafaring, ocean travel, exploration, voyaging, shipping, cruising, steerage, plotting a course, aquatics, boating, yachting, transoceanic *or* transatlantic *or* transpacific travel, arctic travel, coasting, island-hopping, plane sailing, traverse sailing, sailing against the wind, middle sailing, parallel sailing, latitude sailing, mercator sailing, great-circle sailing, spherical navigation; see also **travel** 1.

navigator, *n.* —*Syn.* seaman, explorer, mariner; see **airman, pilot** 1, **sailor.**

navy, *n.* —*Syn.* fleet, first line of defense, squadron, flotilla, armada, task force, scouting force, submarine force, amphibious force, marine air arm, coast guard.

nazi, *mod.* —*Syn.* fascist, totalitarian, right-wing; **absolute** 3, **autocratic** 1, **tyrannical.**

Nazi, *n.* —*Syn.* National Socialist; see **agitator, radical.**

near, *mod.* **1.** [Not distant in space]—*Syn.* nigh, adjacent, adjoining, proximal, neighboring, not remote, close at hand, proximate, contiguous, handy, near *or* hard by, next door to, at close quarters, beside, side by side, in close proximity; see also **bordering.**—*Ant.* distant*, removed, far off.

2. [Not distant in relationship]—*Syn.* touching, affecting, akin; see **friendly** 1, **related** 3.

3. [Not distant in time]—*Syn.* at hand, approaching, next; see **coming** 1, **expected** 2, **imminent.**

nearing, *mod.* —*Syn.* coming, impending, threatening; see **approaching, imminent.**

nearly, *mod.* —*Syn.* within a little, all but, approximately; see **almost.**

nearness, *n.* **1.** [Nearness in time or space]—*Syn.* closeness, contiguity, adjacency, proximity, propinquity, vicinity, vicinage, approximation, approach, intimacy, resemblance, likeness, handiness, close quarters, imminence, immediacy, loom, threat, menace, prospectiveness; see also **neighborhood, similarity.**—*Ant.* distance*, remoteness, difference.

2. [Nearness in feeling]—*Syn.* familiarity, dearness, intimacy; see **admiration** 1, **affection, friendship** 2.

nearsighted, *mod.* —*Syn.* shortsighted, astigmatic, mope-eyed; see **myopic.**

nearsightedness, *n.* —*Syn.* shortsightedness, blindness, astigmatism; see **myopia.**

neat, *mod.* **1.** [Clean and orderly]—*Syn.* tidy, trim, prim, spruce, natty, dapper, smart, correct, shipshape, methodical, regular, orderly, systematic, spotless, finical, nice, dainty, elegant, spick-and-span, immaculate, meticulous, trig, chic, well-groomed, exact, precise, proper, neat as a pin, in good order, spruced up, put to right; see also **clean** 1.—*Ant.* unkempt, disordered*, slovenly.

2. [Clever; *said of something done*]—*Syn.* dexterous, deft, skillful, expert, proficient, handy, apt, ready, quick, artful, nimble, agile, adept, speedy, finished, practiced, easy, effortless; see also **able** 2. —*Ant.* awkward*, clumsy, fumbling.

3. [Pure]—*Syn.* unadulterated, unmixed, unalloyed; see **clear** 2, **pure** 1.

neatly, *mod.* **1.** [Arranged so as to present a neat appearance]—*Syn.* tidily, orderly, systematically, methodically, immaculately, correctly, exactly, trimly, primly, uniformly, levelly, flatly, smoothly, regularly, precisely; see also **evenly** 1, **organized.** —*Ant.* unevenly*, untidily, unsystematically.

2. [In an adroit manner]—*Syn.* skillfully, deftly, agilely; see **cleverly** 2, **easily** 1.

neatness, *n.* **1.** [Neatness in persons]—*Syn.* cleanness, tidiness, orderliness; see **cleanliness.**

2. [Neatness in things]—*Syn.* cleanness, clearness, correctness; see **order** 3, **system** 1.

nebula, *n.* —*Syn.* galaxy, galactic vapor, cloud cluster, nimbus, rarified gas, interstellar dust, luminous vapor.

Kinds of nebulae include the following—spiral, planetary, diffuse, galactic, anagalactic, dark; see also **constellation.**

nebulous, *mod.* —*Syn.* indistinct, dim, vague; see **dark** 1, **hazy** 1, **obscure** 1, 3.

necessarily, *mod.* —*Syn.* vitally, cardinally, fundamentally, importantly, indispensably, momentously, unavoidably, undeniably, certainly, as a matter of course, inexorably, inescapably, ineluctably, inevasively, unpreventably, irresistibly, inevitably, assuredly, exigently, pressingly, significantly, undoubtedly, indubitably, positively, unquestionably, no doubt, without fail, of necessity, of course, by force, come what may, willy-nilly, without recourse, beyond one's control, by its own nature, from within, by definition; see also **surely.**

necessary, *mod.* **1.** [Essential]—*Syn.* requisite, expedient, needful, indispensable, needed, required, urgent, wanted, imperative, prerequisite, exigent, pressing, vital, cardinal, fundamental, significant, momentous, compulsory, mandatory, basic, paramount, obligatory, essential, compelling, incumbent on *or* upon, all-important, nuts-and-bolts, binding, specified, unavoidable, decisive, crucial,

elementary, quintessential, chief, principal, prime, intrinsic, fixed, constant, permanent, determinate, inherent, ingrained, innate, without choice *or* appeal; see also **important** 1.—*Ant.* unimportant*, unessential, insignificant.
2. [Inevitable]—*Syn.* unavoidable, undeniable, assured; see **certain** 2, **imminent, inevitable.**

necessitate, *v.* —*Syn.* compel, constrain, oblige; see **command** 1, **force** 1, **require** 2.

necessity, *n.* **1.** [The state of being required] —*Syn.* needfulness, essentiality, indispensability, undeniability, requisiteness, prerequisiteness; see also **requirement** 2.—*Ant.* chance*, fortuity, possibility.
2. [That which is needed]—*Syn.* need, want, requisite, vital part, essential, demand, imperative, fundamental, claim, exaction, desideratum; see also **lack** 2.
3. [The state of being forced by circumstances] —*Syn.* exigency, pinch, stress, urgency, extremity, destitution, privation, obligation, inexorableness, inescapableness, case of life or death; see also **emergency, poverty** 1, 2.
of necessity—*Syn.* inevitably, importantly, surely; see **necessarily.**

neck, *n.* **1.** [The juncture of the head and the trunk] —*Syn.* cervix, cervical vertebrae, nape, scruff; see also **throat.**
2. [The part of a dress at the neck, sense 1]—*Syn.* neckband, neckline, collar line; see **collar.**
get it in the neck (D)—*Syn.* be punished, be discharged, undergo; see **suffer** 1.
risk one's neck—*Syn.* endanger oneself, gamble, take a chance; see **risk.**
stick one's neck out (D)—*Syn.* endanger oneself, take a chance, gamble; see **risk.**
win or lose by a neck—*Syn.* win or lose by a close margin, come too close, barely win *or* lose; see **lose** 3, **win** 1.

necklace, *n.* —*Syn.* ornament, accessory, (string of) beads, jewels, chain, neckband, necklet, lavaliere, pearls, diamonds, choker; see also **jewelry.**

neck of the woods (D), *n.* —*Syn.* locality, area, section; see **place** 3.

necktie, *n.* —*Syn.* neckwear, knot, ascot; see **tie** 2. Neckties include the following—cravat, flowing tie, bow tie, stock, four-in-hand (tie), string tie, bolo tie, white *or* black tie, Windsor tie.

necromancer, *n.* —*Syn.* sorcerer, warlock, conjuror; see **magician, wizard** 1.

necromancy, *n.* —*Syn.* wizardry, thaumaturgy, sorcery; see **magic** 1, **witchcraft.**

necrosis, *n.* —*Syn.* corruption, rot, putrefaction; see **decay** 2, **disease** 3.

need, *n.* **1.** [Poverty]—*Syn.* indigence, penury, pennilessness; see **poverty** 1.
2. [Lack]—*Syn.* insufficiency, shortage, inadequacy; see **lack** 1, 2.
3. [A requirement]—*Syn.* obligation, compulsion, urgency; see **necessity** 1, **requirement** 2.
have need to—*Syn.* be compelled to, require, want; see **must.**
if need be—*Syn.* if it is required, if the occasion demands, if necessary; see **if.**

need, *v.* —*Syn.* lack, require, feel the necessity for, be in need (of), suffer privation, be in want, be destitute, be short, be inadequate, have occasion for, feel a dearth, have use *or* need for, miss, be *or* do without, be needy *or* poor, be bereft *or* deprived (of), be deficient (in), go hungry, not approach, live from hand to mouth; *all* (D): feel the pinch, be down and out, be hard up, be up against it, do with; see also **want** 1.—*Ant.* own*, have, hold.

needed, *mod.* —*Syn.* wanted, required, desired; see **necessary** 1.

needle, *n.* **1.** [Sewing instrument]—*Syn.* awl, spike, skewer, pin, darner.
Varieties and sizes of needles include the following —sewing, sewing-machine, tacking, darning, upholsterer's, shoemaker's sail-maker's, surgeon's, knitting, crochet, straw, (long-eyed) sharp, ground-down, between, blunt, embroidery, crewel.
2. [Sharp, pointed wirelike instrument]—*Syn.* hypodermic (needle), syringe, phonograph needle, stylus, electric needle, electrolytic needle, probe.
3. [A pointing instrument]—*Syn.* gauge, indicator, director; see **pointer** 1.

needle, *v.* —*Syn.* quiz, question, nag; see **bother** 2, 3, **examine** 1, 2.

needless, *mod.* —*Syn.* unwanted, excessive, groundless; see **unnecessary, useless** 1.

needlework, *n.* —*Syn.* fancywork, tailoring, stitchery; see **embroidery** 1, **sewing.**

need to, *v.* —*Syn.* have to, be obligated to, have reason to; see **must.**

needy, *mod.* —*Syn.* destitute, indigent, penniless; see **poor** 1.

ne'er-do-well, *n.* —*Syn.* idler, bum, vagrant; see **loafer.**

nefarious, *mod.* —*Syn.* bad, treacherous, evil; see **wicked** 1.

negate, *v.* **1.** [To nullify]—*Syn.* repeal, retract, neutralize; see **cancel** 2.
2. [To contradict]—*Syn.* belie, oppose, refute; see **deny.**

negation, *n.* **1.** [Opposite]—*Syn.* contradiction, converse, contrary; see **opposite.**
2. [Denial]—*Syn.* opposition, contradiction, repudiation; see **denial** 1, **refusal.**

negative, *mod.* **1.** [Involving a refusal]—*Syn.* denying, negatory, dissentient, disavowing, contradictory, contrary, repugnant, recusant, gainsaying, impugning, contravening, rejecting, naysaying, disallowing.—*Ant.* admissible*, assenting, accepting.
2. [Lacking positive qualities]—*Syn.* unaffirmative, absent, removed, privative, neutralizing, counteractive, annulling, abrogating, invalidating. —*Ant.* emphatic*, validating, affirmative.

negative, *n.* **1.** [A refusal]—*Syn.* contradiction, disavowal, refutation; see **denial** 1, **refusal.**
2. [A negative image]—*Syn.* film, plate, developed film; see **image** 2, **picture** 2.

neglect, *n.* **1.** [The act of showing indifference to a person]—*Syn.* slight, disregard, thoughtlessness, disrespect, carelessness, scorn, oversight, inadvertence, heedlessness, inattention, unconcern, inconsideration, disdain, coolness; see also **indifference** 1.
2. [The act of neglecting duties or charges]—*Syn.* negligence, slovenliness, neglectfulness; see **carelessness.**

3. [The result of neglecting]—*Syn.* chaos, default, lapse; see **delay** 1, **failure** 1.

neglect, *v.* **1.** [To treat with indifference]—*Syn.* slight, scorn, overlook, disregard, contemn, disdain, detest, rebuff, affront, despise, ignore, depreciate, spurn, underestimate, undervalue, shake off, make light of, laugh off, keep one's distance, forget oneself, pass over *or* up *or* by, have nothing to do with, let slip, let alone, let tomorrow take care of itself, keep aloof (from), let go, not care for, pay no attention to, leave alone, not give a hoot *or* darn *or* damn, pay no heed *or* mind, turn one's shoulder upon, set at nought; *all* (D): let the grass grow under one's feet, leave well enough alone, let (it) ride, play possum, keep at arms length.—*Ant.* consider*, appreciate, value.

2. [To fail to attend to responsibilities]—*Syn.* pass over, defer, procrastinate, suspend, dismiss, discard, let pass *or* slip, miss, skip, gloss over, let go, ignore, be remiss *or* derelict, trifle, slur, skimp, postpone, lose sight of, look the other way, let (it) go, dismiss from the mind, not trouble oneself with, be slack, evade, be careless *or* irresponsible; see also **omit** 1.—*Ant.* watch*, care for, attend.

neglected, *mod.*—*Syn.* slighted, disregarded, scorned, disdained, despised, affronted, overlooked, ignored, spurned, contemned, undervalued, deferred, dismissed, passed over, postponed, evaded, deteriorated, underestimated, declined, decayed, unheeded, lapsed, uncared for, unwatched, depreciated, unconsidered, unthought of, shaken off, unused, unwanted, tossed aside, abandoned, forgotten; *all* (D): (out) in the cold, hid under a bushel basket, dropped, put on the shelf; see also **omitted.**—*Ant.* considered*, cared for, heeded.

neglectful, —*Syn.* heedless, negligent (of), inattentive; see **careless** 1, **indifferent** 1, **lazy** 1.

neglecting, *mod.*—*Syn.* disregarding, ignoring, slighting; see **omitting, overlooking** 2.

negligee, *n.*—*Syn.* kimono, nightdress, pajamas; see **clothes, nightgown, robe.**

negligence, *n.*—*Syn.* remissness, oversight, heedlessness; see **carelessness, indifference** 1, **neglect** 1.

negligent, *mod.*—*Syn.* indifferent, inattentive, neglectful; see **careless** 1.

negligently, *mod.*—*Syn.* heedlessly, indifferently, sloppily; see **carelessly.**

negotiable, *mod.*—*Syn.* variable, transactional, debatable; see **transferable.**

negotiate, *v.* **1.** [To make arrangements for]—*Syn.* arrange, bargain, confer, consult, parley, transact, mediate, make peace, contract, settle, adjust, conciliate, concert, accommodate, bring to terms, make terms, make the best of, treat with, moderate, umpire, referee, work out; *all* (D): dicker, haggle, bury the hatchet; see also **arbitrate.**

2. [To transfer]—*Syn.* barter, allocate, transmit; see **assign** 1, **sell** 1.

negotiating, *n.*—*Syn.* transacting, trading, bargaining, conferring.

negotiation, *n.* **1.** [Arbitration]—*Syn.* compromise, intervention, mediation; see **agreement** 1.

2. [A conference]—*Syn.* meeting, consultation, colloquy; see **discussion** 1.

negotiator, *n.*—*Syn.* mediator, moderator, arbitrator; see **judge** 2.

Negro, *n.*—*Syn.* black, Ethiopian, African, Afro-American, Afro-Asian, Sudanese, Hamite, Krooman, colored *or* Negroid person, black man, Black Panther, Black Muslim, Bantu.

neigh, *v.*—*Syn.* nicker, whinny, call; see **sound** 1.

neighbor, *n.*—*Syn.* acquaintance, bystander, next-door-neighbor, nearby resident; see also **friend** 1.

neighborhood, *n.*—*Syn.* environs, block, vicinity, vicinage, locality, proximity, purlieus, district, adjacency, quarter, parish, closeness, nearness, precinct, ward, propinquity, community, contiguity, region, area, zone, section, suburb, part, tract; see also **area** 2.

in the neighborhood of (D)—*Syn.* about, approximately, close to; see **near** 1.

neighboring, *mod.*—*Syn.* adjacent, adjoining, contiguous; see **bordering, near** 1.

neighborly, *mod.*—*Syn.* sociable, hospitable, helpful; see **friendly** 1.

neither, *conj.* and *mod.*—*Syn.* nor yet, also not, not either, not, not at all.

neither, *pron.*—*Syn.* not one or the other, neither one, not this one, none of two, nor this nor that, no one of two, not the one, not any one; see also **none** 1, **nothing.**

neologism, *n.*—*Syn.* coinage of words, neology, new word, new phrase, nonce word, synthetic word, vogue word; see also **phrase, word** 1.

neophyte, *n.*—*Syn.* novice, student, beginner; see **amateur.**

nephew, *n.*—*Syn.* brother's *or* sister's son, grandnephew, son of a brother-in-law *or* sister-in-law, nephew by marriage; see also **niece, relative.**

Neptune, *n.*—*Syn.* god of the sea, Poseidon, Oceanus; see **god** 1.

nerve, *n.* **1.** [The path of nervous impulses]—*Syn.* nerve fiber, nerve tissue, nerve filament, nerve cord, nervure, venation; see also **tissue** 3.

Types of nerves include the following—motor, sensory, efferent, afferent, effectors, receptors.

Important nerves include the following—optic, auditory, acoustic, vagus, cardiac, digastic, inferior cardiac, axillary, cervicofacial, ciliary, fourth, fifth, lacrymal, lingual, middle cardiac, ophthalmic.

2. [Courage]—*Syn.* resolution, spirit, mettle; see **courage** 1.

3. [Impudence]—*Syn.* temerity, audacity, effrontery; see **rudeness.**

nerveless, *mod.* **1.** [Weak]—*Syn.* spineless, nervous, feeble; see **afraid** 1, **cowardly** 1, **weak** 3.

2. [Calm]—*Syn.* controlled, intrepid, impassive; see **calm** 1, **patient** 2, **tranquil** 2.

nerve oneself, *v.*—*Syn.* take *or* pluck (up) one's courage, prepare (for), get ready (for); see **fight** 2, **oppose** 2, **prepare** 1, **resist** 1.

nerve-racking, *mod.*—*Syn.* exhausting, horrible, wearisome; see **difficult** 1, **painful** 1.

nerves, *n.* **1.** [*Stamina*]—*Syn.* fortitude, firmness, pluck; see **endurance** 2.

2. [(D) A nervous excitement]—*Syn.* strain, tension, hysteria, emotional stress, sleeplessness, neurasthenia; see also **nervousness** 1.

get on one's nerves (D)—*Syn.* exasperate, irritate, annoy; see **bother** 2, 3.

nervous, *mod.* **1.** [Excitable]—*Syn.* sensitive, high-strung, neurotic; see **excitable.**
2. [Excited]—*Syn.* agitated, bothered, annoyed; see **excited.**
3. [Timid]—*Syn.* apprehensive, shy, shrinking; see **afraid** 1, **timid** 2.

nervously, *mod.*—*Syn.* tensely, apprehensively, restlessly; see **excitedly.**

nervousness, *n.* **1.** [The state of being temporarily nervous]—*Syn.* stimulation, agitation, perturbation, inspiration, animation, intoxication, disquietude, delirium, discomfiture, elation, feverishness, anger; *all* (D): the jerks, mike *or* stage fright, butterflies in the stomach, the jitters, the shakes; see also **embarrassment** 1, **excitement.**—*Ant.* rest*, calm, relaxation.
2. [The quality of being nervous in temperament] —*Syn.* sensitiveness, mettlesomeness, demonstrativeness, excitability, irascibility, impulsiveness, impetuosity, uncontrollability, turbulence, moodiness, hastiness, vehemence, hypersensitivity, neuroticism, impatience, neurasthenia; see also **sensitivity.**—*Ant.* composure*, poise, steadiness.

nervy (D), *mod.*—*Syn.* crass, pushy, inconsiderate; see **crude** 1, **rude** 1, 2.

nescience, *n.*—*Syn.* naïveté, inexperience, rawness; see **ignorance** 2.

nest, *n.*—*Syn.* den, haunt, cradle, aerie, womb, incubator; see also **retreat** 2.

nest egg (D), *n.*—*Syn.* personal *or* accumulated savings, personal property, something for a rainy day (D); see **money** 1, **property** 1, **savings** 1.

nestle, *v.*—*Syn.* cuddle, snuggle, settle down, take shelter, lie close, make oneself snug, huddle, move close to, lie against, curl up (to).

nestling, *n.*—*Syn.* fledgling, suckling, infant; see **baby** 1, **bird** 1.

net, *mod.*—*Syn.* clear, pure, remaining, exclusive, excluding, after deductions, irreducible, undeductible.

net, *n.*—*Syn.* screen, mesh, fabric; see also **cloth, web** 1.
Varieties of nets include the following—hair, mosquito, tennis, ping-pong, volleyball, goal, bird, butterfly, fish, gill, dip, beating, draw, drag, drift, drop, hand, landing, set, stake, scoop, bag, purse, bull, casting, clues.

net, *v.*—*Syn.* make, clear, gain above expenses; see **profit** 2.

nether, *mod.*—*Syn.* beneath, below, lower; see **under** 1.

netlike, *mod.*—*Syn.* spun, meshlike, webbed; see **woven.**

netted, *mod.* **1.** [Webbed]—*Syn.* spun, interwoven, mesh; see **woven.**
2. [(D) Caught]—*Syn.* enmeshed, apprehended, seized; see **captured** 1, **under arrest.**

netting, *n.*—*Syn.* mesh, trellis, screen; see **cloth, material** 2, **web** 2.

nettle, *v.*—*Syn.* annoy, pester, irritate; see **bother** 3, **disgust, disturb** 2, **insult.**

nettled, *mod.*—*Syn.* vexed, irritated, disturbed; see **angry.**

network, *n.* **1.** [System of channels]—*Syn.* tracks, circuitry, channels, system, labyrinth, reticule, artery, arrangement, jungle (D); see also **chain** 1, **wiring** 2, 3.
2. [Netting]—*Syn.* fabric, fiber, weave, knitting, mesh, plexus, grillwork, wattle, screening; see also **cloth, material** 2, **web** 2.

neurosis, *n.*—*Syn.* compulsion, deviation, instability, mental disorder, emotional disturbance, neurotic condition, aberration; see also **insanity** 1, **obsession.**

neurotic, *mod.*—*Syn.* disoriented, disturbed, unstable, erratic, psychoneurotic, aberrant, upset, sick; see also **insane** 1, **troubled** 1.

neurotic, *n.*—*Syn.* paranoid, psychoneurotic, sick person, psychotic, hypochondriac, neuropath, kleptomaniac.

neuter, *mod.*—*Syn.* barren, infertile, sexless, asexual, unfertile, impotent, frigid, fallow; see also **sterile** 1.

neutral, *mod.* **1.** [Not fighting]—*Syn.* noncombatant, nonpartisan, on the side lines, nonparticipating, inactive, disengaged, uninvolved, bystanding, standing by, inert, on the fence (D).—*Ant.* engaged*, involved, active*.
2. [Without opinion]—*Syn.* nonchalant, disinterested, impartial; see **indifferent** 1, **unconcerned.**
3. [Without distinctive color]—*Syn.* drab, indeterminate, vague; see **dull** 2.

neutrality, *n.*—*Syn.* aloofness, nonpartisanship, disinterest; see **noninterference.**

neutralize, *v.*—*Syn.* counterbalance, counterpoise, compensate; see **offset.**

neutrally, *mod.*—*Syn.* impartially, without taking sides, equally; see **objectively.**

never, *mod.*—*Syn.* not ever, at no time, not at any time, not in the least, not in any way, in no way, not at all, not under any condition, nevermore, never again, no way (D).

never-ceasing, *mod.*—*Syn.* persistent, steady, neverending; see **constant** 1, **perpetual** 1, **regular** 3.

never-dying, *mod.*—*Syn.* sempiternal, endless, undying; see **eternal** 2, **immortal** 1, **perpetual** 1.

never-ending, *mod.*—*Syn.* timeless, endless, persistent; see **constant** 1, **eternal** 2, **perpetual** 1, **regular** 3.

never mind, *interj.*—*Syn.* forget it, it doesn't matter, ignore it, don't bother, let it go, *macht nichts* (German), drop it (D); see also **stop** 2.

nevertheless, *mod.*—*Syn.* not the less, nonetheless, notwithstanding; see **although, but** 1.

never-tiring, *mod.*—*Syn.* diligent, tenacious, persevering; see **busy** 1, **resolute** 2.

new, *mod.* **1.** [Recent]—*Syn.* current, late, just out; see **fresh** 1.
2. [Modern]—*Syn.* modish, latest, *au courant* (French); see **fashionable, modern** 1.
3. [Novel]—*Syn.* unique, original, bizarre; see **unusual** 1, 2.
4. [Different]—*Syn.* unlike, dissimilar, distinct; see **different** 1, 2.
5. [Additional]—*Syn.* further, increased, supplementary; see **extra.**
6. [Inexperienced]—*Syn.* unseasoned, unskilled, untrained; see **incompetent, inexperienced.**
7. [Fresh]—*Syn.* unspoiled, uncontaminated, undecayed; see **fresh** 5.

8. [Recently]—*Syn.* newly, freshly, lately; see **recently.**

new blood (D), *n.* —*Syn.* replacements, younger personnel, another generation; see **recruit, youth** 2.

newborn, *mod.* —*Syn.* infant, recent, new; see **fresh** 1, **young** 1.

newcomer, *n.* —*Syn.* immigrant, outsider, foreigner, neophyte, *all* (D): tenderfoot, rookie, maverick, Johnny-come-lately, youngtimer, blow-in; see also **alien, stranger.**

newfangled, *mod.* —*Syn.* novel, unique, new; see **fashionable, modern** 1.

new-fashioned, *mod.* —*Syn.* current, avant-garde, stylish; see **fashionable, modern** 1.

newly, *mod.* —*Syn.* lately, anew, afresh; see **recently.**

newlywed, *n.* —*Syn.* blushing bride, bridegroom, honeymooner; see **bride, groom** 2, **husband, wife.**

newness, *n.* —*Syn.* originality, uniqueness, modernity, recentness; see also **novelty** 1.

news, *n.* **1.** [Information]—*Syn.* intelligence, tidings, advice, discovery, enlightenment, recognition, cognizance; *all* (D): the scoop, the goods, headlines, front-page news; see also **data, knowledge** 1, **revelation** 1.

2. [A specific report]—*Syn.* telling, narration, recital, account, description, specification, particularization, itemization, message, copy, communication, release, communiqué, telegram, cable, radiogram, broadcast, telecast, bulletin, dispatch; *all* (D): (news) story, scoop, big news, eye-opener; see also **announcement** 2, **report** 1.

make news—*Syn.* become famous *or* notorious, accomplish, create events; see **expose** 1, **reveal** 1.

newsboy, *n.* —*Syn.* (town) crier, paperboy, paper carrier; *all* (D): newsy, news distrib, rag man, sheet hustler.

newscast, *n.* —*Syn.* news broadcasting, telecast, newscasting; see **announcement** 2, **broadcast, news** 2, **report** 1.

newscaster, *n.* —*Syn.* news analyst, commentator, broadcaster; see **reporter, writer.**

newsmonger, *n.* —*Syn.* gossipmonger, scandalmonger, busybody; see **gossip** 2.

newspaper, *n.* —*Syn.* publication, (daily) paper, press, fourth estate, public press, sheet, tabloid, gazette; see also **journal** 1, **record** 1.

Varieties of newspapers include the following—daily, weekly, bi-weekly, metropolitan, rural, county, country, trade, provincial, community.

Parts of newspapers include the following—front page section, news section, foreign news section, editorial page, local news section, domestic news section, magazine, business section, society section, women's section, sports section, entertainment *or* amusement section, rotogravure section, comics *or* comic page, school section, advertising section, syndicated section *or* boiler plate (D).

Editions of newspapers include the following—morning, afternoon, evening, home, final home, extra, suburban, city, final, sports final, green sports final, pink sports final, mail, second mail, state, stocks, final stocks, Sunday.

Famous newspapers include the following—England: *The Times, Financial Times, Daily Mail, Daily Express, Daily Mirror, Guardian,* France: *Le Temps, Le Figaro, Le Monde,* Russia: *Pravda, Izvestia,* Germany: *Die Welt, Frankfurter Allgemeine,* U.S.: *Washington Post, New York Times, The News, Chicago Sun-Times, Christian Science Monitor, Wall Street Journal,* Baltimore *Sun, Chicago Tribune, Milwaukee Journal,* San Francisco *Examiner-Chronicle, Los Angeles Times.*

newspaperman, *n.* —*Syn.* newsman, journalist, member, of the editorial department; see **author** 2, **editor, reporter, writer.**

newsy, *mod.* —*Syn.* significant, informative, instructive; see **detailed, elaborate** 2.

New York, *n.* —*Syn.* Manhattan, Greater New York, Metropolitan New York *all* (D): the Big Apple, Gotham, Father Knickerbocker, little old New York, Babylon-on-Hudson, the Town, the (Big) City, City of Towers, the Garment Capital, Metropolis of America, Modern Gomorrah, Wall Street, Financial Capital of the World; see also **city.**

The boroughs of New York City include the following—Manhattan, the Bronx, Queens, Brooklyn, Richmond.

Sections of New York City include the following—Staten Island, Harlem, Greenwich Village, the East Village, the Bowery, Chinatown, the Battery, Washington Heights, Morningside Heights, Tenderloin, Wall Street, Times Square, Long Island City, Jamaica, Flushing, Far Rockaway, Van Cortland Park.

Greater New York includes the following—Hoboken, Bayonne, Jersey City, Newark, Westchester, Yonkers, White Plains, New Rochelle, Garden City, Great Neck.

next, *mod.* **1.** [Following in order]—*Syn.* succeeding, subsequent, ensuing; see **following.**

2. [Adjacent]—*Syn.* beside, close, alongside, on one *or* the side, adjoining, neighboring, meeting, hard by, touching, cheek by jowl, side by side, coterminous, attached, abutting, back to back, to the left *or* right; see also **bordering, contiguous, near** 1.

get next to (D)—*Syn.* become friendly with, befriend, join the company of; see **associate** 1.

next-door (to), *mod.* —*Syn.* adjacent (to), neighboring, adjoining; see **beside, near** 1, **next** 2.

nib, *n.* —*Syn.* neb, tip, pen; see **point** 2.

nibble, *n.* —*Syn.* morsel, peck, cautious bite; see **bit** 1, **bite** 1.

nibble, *v.* —*Syn.* nip, gnaw, snack; see **bite** 1, **eat** 1.

nice, *mod.* **1.** [Approved]—*Syn.* likable, superior, admirable; see **excellent.**

2. [Behaving in a becoming manner]—*Syn.* pleasing, agreeable, winning, winsome, prepossessing, refined, cultured, amiable, delightful, charming, inviting, pleasant, cordial, courteous, ingratiating, considerate, kind, kindly, helpful, gracious, obliging, genial, gentle, *simpático* (Spanish), seemly, decorous, becoming, unassuming, unpresumptuous, modest, demure; see also **friendly** 1.—*Ant.* rude*, indecorous, crude.

3. [Involving a careful distinction]—*Syn.* delicate, minute, exacting, fastidious, finical, finicking, discerning, discriminating, fine, critical, distinguishing, trivial, finicky (D); see also **careful.**—*Ant.* careless*, broad, sweeping.

4. [Accurate]—*Syn.* correct, exact, right; see **accurate** 1.

nice and (D), —*Syn.* exceptionally, unusually, agreeably; see **very.**

nicely, *mod.* **1.** [In a welcome manner]—*Syn.* pleasantly, pleasingly, amiably, winningly, creditably, acceptably, excellently, distinctively, happily, felicitously, triumphantly, admirably, desirably, pleasurably, attractively, likably, enjoyably, beautifully, graciously, finely; see also **agreeably, perfectly** 1.—*Ant.* badly*, unfortunately, unsuccessfully.

2. [In a becoming manner]—*Syn.* winsomely, invitingly, charmingly; see **modestly** 1, **politely.**

3. [Carefully]—*Syn.* rightly, correctly, conscientiously; see **accurately, carefully** 1.

niceness, *n.* **1.** [Accuracy]—*Syn.* exactitude, surety, precision; see **accuracy** 2.

2. [Kindness]—*Syn.* discernment, taste, refinement; see **care** 1, **discretion** 1, **kindness, prudence, tact.**

nice to, *mod.*—*Syn.* helpful *or* kindly to *or* with, thoughtful of, generous; see **kind.**

nicety, *n.*—*Syn.* taste, delicacy, finesse; see **culture** 3, **refinement** 2.

niche, *n.*—*Syn.* cranny, corner, cubbyhole; see **hole** 2.

nick, *n.*—*Syn.* jag, indent, indentation, notch, slit, knock, dint, impression; see also **cut** 2, **dent.**

nick, *v.*—*Syn.* indent, notch, slit; see **cut** 2, **dent.**

nickel, *n.* **1.** [A mineral]—*Syn. Ni,* metallic *or* chemical element, plating material; see **element** 2, **metal, mineral.**

2. [A coin made of nickel, sense 1]—*Syn.* five-cent piece, coin, five cents; *all* (D): chit, chitney, fish scale, five-center, jip, jitney, picayune; see also **money** 1.

niece, *n.*—*Syn.* sister's *or* brother's daughter, niece by marriage, grandniece, daughter of a brother-in-law *or* sister-in-law; see also **nephew, relative.**

niggard, *n.*—*Syn.* tightwad, Scrooge, skinflint; see **miser** 2.

niggardliness, *n.*—*Syn.* thrift, frugality, stinginess; see **greed.**

niggardly, *mod.*—*Syn.* miserly, parsimonious, stingy; see **greedy** 1.

niggling, *mod.*—*Syn.* trifling, petty, piddling; see **trivial, unimportant.**

nigh, *mod.*—*Syn.* near, close, close at hand; see **near, close.**

night, *n.* **1.** [The diurnal dark period]—*Syn.* after dark, evening, from dusk to dawn, nightfall, after nightfall, twilight, eventide, nighttime, bedtime, midnight, before dawn, the dark hours, obscurity, witching hour, dead of night; *both* (D): nite, whoopee time.

2. [The dark]—*Syn.* blackness, duskiness, gloom; see **darkness** 1.

make a night of it (D)—*Syn.* enjoy, have fun, party; see **celebrate** 3.

night clothes, *n.*—*Syn.* negligee, nightshirt, nightwear; see **clothes, nightgown, pajamas, robe.**

night club, *n.*—*Syn.* casino, discotheque, cabaret, tavern, café, roadhouse, floor show, night spot, nitery (D); see also **restaurant, saloon** 3, **theatre** 1.

nightfall, *n.*—*Syn.* dusk, twilight, evening; see **night** 1.

nightgown, *n.*—*Syn.* nightdress, nightrobe, negligee, bedgown, lingerie, night gear, nightshirt, shift, muu-muu, sleeping clothes, lounging pajamas, nightwear; *all* (D): sleeper, nightie, PJ's, 'jamas; see also **clothes, pajamas, robe.**

nightingale, *n.*—*Syn.* songbird, warbler, philomel; see **bird** 1.

nightly, *mod.*—*Syn.* nocturnal, night inhabiting, in the hours of night, every twenty-four hours, during the hours of darkness, at night, each night, every night, by night; see also **regularly** 1.—*Ant.* daily*, by day, diurnal.

nightmare, *n.*—*Syn.* bad dream, horror, incubus; see **dream** 1, **fantasy** 2, **illusion** 1, **vision** 3, 4.

night school, *n.*—*Syn.* (night) classes, (university *or* college) extension, community college; see **school** 1, **university.**

nighttime, *n.*—*Syn.* darkness, bedtime, midnight; see **night** 1.

nihilism, *n.* **1.** [Rejection]—*Syn.* repudiation, atheism, renunciation; see **denial** 1, **refusal.**

2. [Anarchy]—*Syn.* apolitical situation, lawlessness, mob rule; see **disorder** 2.

nihilist, *n.*—*Syn.* revolutionary, insurgent, anarchist; see **agitator, rebel** 1.

nihilistic, *mod.*—*Syn.* insurgent, unruly, anarchic; see **lawless** 2, **rebellious** 2.

nil, *n.*—*Syn.* zero, naught, nihil; see **nothing.**

nimble, *mod.* **1.** [Agile]—*Syn.* quick, spry, active; see **agile, graceful** 1.

2. [Alert]—*Syn.* quick-witted, bright, clever; see **intelligent** 1, **judicious.**

nimble-fingered, *mod.*—*Syn.* proficient, skillful, capable; see **agile, graceful** 1.

nimble-footed, *mod.*—*Syn.* swift, active, adept; see **agile, graceful** 1.

nimbleness, *n.*—*Syn.* grace, vivacity, skill; see **agility.**

nimble-witted, *mod.*—*Syn.* shrewd, clever, alert; see **intelligent** 1, **judicious.**

nimbly, *mod.*—*Syn.* swiftly, rapidly, agilely; see **gracefully.**

nimbus, *n.*—*Syn.* aura, radiance, glow, circle of light, aureole, nebula, aurora, cloud, nebulous light, effulgence, emanation; see also **halo, light** 1.

nincompoop, *n.*—*Syn.* imbecile, simpleton, dope (D); see **fool** 1.

ninefold, *mod.*—*Syn.* novenary, nonary, three times three, ninth, nonahedral, nonuple, enneahedral.

ninth, *mod.*—*Syn.* three times three, nonary, novenary; see **ninefold.**

nip, *n.*—*Syn.* nibble, morsel, catch; see **bite** 1, **pinch.**

nip, *v.*—*Syn.* nibble, snap, munch; see **bite** 1, **pinch.**

nipple, *n.*—*Syn.* mammilla, papilla, areola, mammary gland, dug, teat, tit, teatlike object, breast, udder.

nitty-gritty (D), *n.*—*Syn.* essentials, reality, lowdown (D); see **facts.**

nitwit, *n.*—*Syn.* blockhead, dummy, dimwit; see **fool** 1.

no, *mod.* and *interj.*—*Syn.* (absolutely) not, not at all, by no means, the answer is in the negative, not by any means, *nyet* (Russian), *nein* (German), negative (D), nix (D); see also **negative** 2, **neither, never, none.**

nobility, *n.* **1.** [Magnificence]—*Syn.* grandeur, majesty, greatness; see **dignity** 1, **magnificence.**

2. [Aristocracy; *usually used with* the]—*Syn.* ruling class, gentry, peerage; see **aristocracy, royalty, society** 3.

noble, *mod.* **1.** [Possessing an exalted mind and character]—*Syn.* generous, princely, magnanimous, magnificent, courtly, lofty, elevated, splendid, excellent, august, reputable, supreme, eminent, pre-eminent, lordly, dignified, sublime, great, good, superior, chivalric, chivalrous, great-hearted, high-minded, honorable, distinguished, liberal, tolerant, gracious, benign, beneficient, humane, benevolent, charitable, sympathetic, bounteous, brilliant, extraordinary, remarkable, self-denying, devoted, self-forgetful, heroic, resolute, lion-hearted, mettlesome, valorous; see also **worthy.** —*Ant.* corrupt*, low, ignoble.

2. [Possessing excellent qualities or properties] —*Syn.* meritorious, virtuous, worthy, valuable, useful, incorrupt, first-rate, refined, cultivated, chivalrous, trustworthy, candid, liberal, gracious, princely, munificent, magnanimous, generous, distinctive, sincere, truthful, constant, faithful, upright, honest, warmhearted, true, veracious, distinctive, reputable, respectable, admirable, good, above-board, fair, manly, just, estimable; see also **excellent, perfect** 2.—*Ant.* poor*, inferior, second-rate.

3. [Belonging to the nobility]—*Syn.* titled, aristocratic, patrician, highborn, wellborn, blue-blooded, gentle, of gentle birth *or* blood, imperial, lordly, highbred, princely, of good breed, kingly, born to the purple (D); see also **royal** 2.—*Ant.* common*, plebeian, lowborn.

4. [Grand]—*Syn.* stately, impressive, imposing; see **grand** 2.

nobleman, *n.*—*Syn.* peer, noble, member of the nobility; see **lord** 2, **royalty.**

noble-minded, *mod.*—*Syn.* just, principled, generous; see **fair** 1, **kind.**

noblesse, *n.*—*Syn.* nobility, gentility, gentry; see **aristocracy, royalty, society** 3.

noblewoman, *n.*—*Syn.* gentlewoman, countess, empress; see **lady** 2, 3, **royalty.**

nobly, *mod.* **1.** [Majestically]—*Syn.* aristocratically, illustriously, royally; see **generously** 2, **politely.**

2. [Honorably]—*Syn.* fairly, respectably, honestly; see **justly** 1.

nobody, *mod.* **1.** [No one at all]—*Syn.* no person, no one, not anybody; see **none** 1.

2. [A person of little importance]—*Syn.* upstart, cipher, nonentity, nullity, jackstraw, parvenu, whippersnapper; *all* (D): no great shakes, man of straw, punk, a nothing, nix, nixie, zero; see also **sycophant.**

nocturnal, *mod.*—*Syn.* at night, night-loving, nighttime; see **late** 4, **nightly.**

nocturne, *n.*—*Syn.* lullaby, evening song, serenade; see **song.**

nocuous, *mod.*—*Syn.* noxious, malignant, injurious; see **dangerous** 1, 2, **deadly, harmful, poisonous.**

nod, *n.* **1.** [A slight bow]—*Syn.* dip, inclination, greeting; see **bow** 2.

2. [(D) Approval; *usually used with* the]—*Syn.* acceptance, affirmative answer, yes; see **permission.**

nod, *v.* **1.** [To make a nodding movement]—*Syn.* assent, sign, signal, greet, salaam, bend, curtsy, incline the head, nod yes, acquiesce, consent, respond, fall in with, concur, acknowledge, recognize; see also **agree, approve** 1, **bow** 1.—*Ant.* deny*, dissent, disagree.

2. [To become sleepy or inattentive]—*Syn.* drowse, nap, drift (off); see **sleep.**

node, *n.*—*Syn.* bump, swelling, clot; see **bulge, lump.**

nodule, *n.*—*Syn.* bud, protuberance, knob; see **bulge.**

noise, *n.* **1.** [A sound]—*Syn.* sound, sonance, something heard *or* audible, impact of sound waves. Kinds of noises include the following—brief, loud noises: bang, boom, crash, thud, blast, blast off, roar, bellow, blat, shout, peal, cry, yelp, squawk, yawp, hee-haw, blare, clang, ring, shot, sonic boom, jangle, eruption, explosion, detonation; *all* (D): blowup, zowie, whang, cachunk, kerboom, biff-bang; brief faint noises: peep, squeak, squawk, cackle, cluck, tweet, clink, tinkle, pop, whisper, stage whisper, sigh, splash, swish, note, sough, sob, whine, whimper, plink, plunk, plop, plump, pad, pat, ping, rustle, murmur, beat, stir, purr, twitter; soft *or* stifled *or* dulled *or* suppressed, etc. sound, still small voice (D); continuing noises: reverberation, ringing, tone, tune, clangor, clanging, tinkling, sonorousness, resonance, cacophany, rock, rattle, rattling, whistle, whistling, piping, twittering, dissonance, discord, shouting, roaring, bellowing, rumble, rumbling, grunting, murmuring, drone, droning, thunder(ing), bombarding, bombardment, shelling, fire, firing, tramp(ing), whine, whining, screech(ing), scream(ing), banging, clanging, hum, humming, laugh(ing), chuckle, chuckling, whir, whirring, purr, purring, swishing, rustling, ripple, rippling, strumming, thrumming, beating, patter(ing), clatter(ing), tintinnabulation, ululation, trill(ing), whinney(ing), neigh(ing), caw(ing), clucking, cackling, (semi)quaver; soft *or* low *or* muffled, etc. voice; surge *or* swell *or* sweep, etc. of sound.

2. [Clamor]—*Syn.* tumult, racket, hullabaloo, fanfare, cry, outcry, shouting, yelling, fracas, din, pandemonium, turbulence, uproariousness, drumming, caterwauling, hubbub, lamentation, bewailing, boisterousness, clamorousness, babel, stridency, blatancy; see also **uproar.**—*Ant.* silence*, lull, quietness.

noised about (D), *mod.*—*Syn.* (generally *or* commonly *or* well) known, recognized, revealed; see **advertised, discovered.**

noiseless, *mod.* **1.** [Containing no noise]—*Syn.* silent, still, soundless; see **quiet** 2.

2. [Making no noise]—*Syn.* voiceless, speechless, wordless; see **dumb** 1, **mute** 1.

noiselessly, *mod.*—*Syn.* inaudibly, quietly, without a sound; see **silently.**

noisome, *mod.* **1.** [Harmful]—*Syn.* baneful, pernicious, unwholesome; see **dangerous** 1, 2, **deadly.**

2. [Evil-smelling]—*Syn.* putrid, malodorous, mephitic; see **rank** 2, **rotten** 1.

noisy, *mod.*—*Syn.* clamorous, vociferous, boisterous; see **loud** 1, 2.

nomad, *n.* —*Syn.* wanderer, migrant, vagabond; see **traveler.**
nomadic, *mod.* —*Syn.* roaming, drifting, roving; see **traveling** 2, **wandering.**
nom de plume, *n.* —*Syn.* alias, pen name, stage name; see **pseudonym.**
nomenclature, *n.* —*Syn.* terminology, locution, vocabulary; see **classification** 1.
nominal, *mod.* **1.** [In name only]—*Syn.* titular, stated, mentioned, suggested, formal, simple, ostensible, professed, purported, theoretical, pretended, so-called, in effect only; see also **given, named** 1.—*Ant.* real*, obvious, genuine*.
2. [Insignificant]—*Syn.* meaningless, trifling, low; see **trivial, unnecessary.**
nominate, *v.* —*Syn.* propose as a candidate, designate for election, call, specify, put up, draft (D); see also **choose** 1, **decide.**
nominated, *mod.* —*Syn.* designated, called, suggested; see **approved, named** 2.
nomination, *n.* —*Syn.* naming, designation, proposal; see **appointment** 1.
nominee, *n.* —*Syn.* aspirant, solicitor, political contestant; see **candidate, contestant.**
nonacceptance, *n.* —*Syn.* renunciation, disapproval, rejection; see **refusal.**
nonage, *n.* —*Syn.* immaturity, childhood, adolescence; see **youth** 1.
nonaligned, *mod.* —*Syn.* uncommitted, undecided, not committed; see **neutral** 1.
nonappearance, *n.* —*Syn.* avoidance, truancy, failure to appear; see **absence** 1.
nonchalance, *n.* —*Syn.* apathy, disregard, insouciance; see **indifference** 1.
nonchalant, *mod.* **1.** [Cool and casual]—*Syn.* uncaring, insouciant, untroubled, apathetic, cold, frigid, cool, unfeeling, impassive, imperturbable, easygoing, listless, lackadaisical, apathetic, lukewarm, unruffled, unexcited, composed, collected, aloof, detached, unflappable, calm, serene, placid, incurious, disinterested, easy, effortless, light, smooth, neutral, unimpressible; see also **indifferent** 1, **unconcerned.**—*Ant.* warm*, ardent, enthusiastic.
2. [Careless]—*Syn.* negligent, neglectful, trifling; see **careless** 1.
nonchalantly, *mod.* —*Syn.* coolly, indifferently, casually; see **calmly.**
noncommittal, *mod.* —*Syn.* reserved, wary, cautious; see **careful, judicious, tactful.**
non-completion, *n.* —*Syn.* inadequacy, fault, deficiency; see **blemish, defect** 2, **lack** 2.
noncompliance, *n.* —*Syn.* nonconformity, refusal, dissent; see **disagreement** 1, **objection** 2, **protest.**
noncompliant, *mod.* —*Syn.* negative, divergent, irregular, refusing, declinatory, refractory, impatient, contumacious; see also **rebellious** 2.
non compos mentis (Latin), *mod.* —*Syn.* crazy, deranged, lunatic; see **insane** 1, **sick, violent** 2, 4.
nonconformist, *n.* —*Syn.* rebel, eccentric, maverick, iconoclast, malcontent, dissenter, dissentient, demonstrator, hippie, protester, dissident, Bohemian, a different breed of cat (D); see also **beatnik, liberal, radical.**
nonconformity, *n.* —*Syn.* dissent, opposition, contumaciousness, lawlessness, transgressiveness, heresy, heterodoxy, recusance, violation, breach of custom, denial, unorthodoxy, iconoclasm, uniqueness, strangeness, disobedience, unruliness, mutinousness, insubordination, recalcitrance, noncompliance, unconventionality, originality, Bohemianism, disagreement, recusancy, contumacy, obstinacy, refusal, refusing, nonagreement, disaffection, discordance, disapproval, nonconsent, rejection, nonacceptance, negation, disapprobation, opposition, objection, exception, veto, nonobservance; see also **individuality** 1.
nondescript, *mod.* —*Syn.* uninteresting, empty, indescribable; see **common** 1, **dull** 4.
none, *pron.* **1.** [No person]—*Syn.* no one, not one, not anyone, no one at all, not a person, not a soul, neither one (nor the other); see also **neither.** —*Ant.* many*, some, a few.
2. [No thing]—*Syn.* not a thing, not anything, not any; see **nothing.**
nonentity, *n.* —*Syn.* nullity, upstart, no-account (D); see **nobody** 2, **sycophant.**
nonessential, *mod.* —*Syn.* superfluous, insignificant, petty; see **trivial, unimportant.**
nonesuch, *n.* —*Syn.* quintessence, select, nonpareil; see **paragon.**
nonetheless, *mod.* —*Syn.* nevertheless, in spite of that, anyway; see **although, but** 1.
nonexistence, *n.* —*Syn.* nonbeing, negation, nothingness; see **oblivion** 2.
nonexistent, *mod.* —*Syn.* missing, unsubstantial, fictitious; see **imaginary, unreal.**
nonfulfillment, *n.* —*Syn.* incompletion, miscarriage, disappointment; see **failure** 1.
nonhero, *n.* —*Syn.* antihero, protagonist, untraditional *or* nontraditional hero; see **hero** 2.
noninterference, *n.* —*Syn.* nonintervention, neutrality, laissez faire, isolationism, nonresistance, refraining, refusal to become involved, failure to intervene, nonpartisanship, adherence to the Monroe Doctrine.
nonintervention, *n.* —*Syn.* apathy, dormancy, neutrality; see **noninterference.**
nonjuror, *n.* —*Syn.* dissenter, heretic, eccentric; see **nonconformist, radical.**
nonlegal, *mod.* —*Syn.* unlawful, prohibited, forbidden; see **illegal.**
nonobjective, *mod.* —*Syn.* subjective, free-form, modern (istic), not traditional, unconventional, revolutionary; see also **free** 2, **irregular** 2, **unusual** 2.
nonobservance, *n.* —*Syn.* infidelity, inattention, failure; see **carelessness, indifference** 1, **neglect** 1.
no-nonsense, *mod.* —*Syn.* matter-of-fact, practical, serious, earnest, purposeful, serious-minded, solemn, dedicated, resolute; see **practical, resolute** 2.
nonpareil, *n.* —*Syn.* quintessence, the best, nonesuch; see **paragon.**
nonpartisan, *mod.* —*Syn.* unprejudiced, just, nonaligned, unbiased, independent, uninfluenced, unaffected, uninvolved, unimplicated, unbigoted, objective; see also **neutral** 1.
nonpayment, *n.* —*Syn.* failure, delinquency, bankruptcy; see **default.**
nonplus, *v.* —*Syn.* baffle, bewilder, confound; see **confuse.**
nonplussed, *mod.* —*Syn.* baffled, confused, at a loss (for words); see **bewildered, doubtful** 2.

nonproductive, *mod.* **1.** [Profitless]—*Syn.* unproductive, unprofitable, not producing; see **idle** 1, **useless** 1.
2. [Unconcerned; *said of students*]—*Syn.* disinterested, lazy, under-achieving; see **indifferent** 1, **unconcerned.**
nonprofit, *mod.*—*Syn.* charitable, altruistic, humane; see **generous** 1, **philanthropic** 2.
nonproliferation, *n.*—*Syn.* restriction, limiting, holding down *or* back *or* in; see **restraint** 2.
nonresident, *mod.*—*Syn.* absentee, out-of-state, living abroad; see **foreign** 1.
nonresistance, *n.*—*Syn.* tolerance, submission, conformity; see **docility.**
nonresistant, *mod.*—*Syn.* yielding, tolerant, submissive; see **docile, obedient** 1.
nonsense, *n.* **1.** [Matter that has no meaning]—*Syn.* balderdash, rubbish, twaddle, trash, gobbledygook, drivel, scribble, scrawl, inanity, senselessness, babble, palaver, buncombe, idle chatter, pretense, prattle, blather, nonsensicalness, rant, bombast, claptrap; *all* (D): bull, baloney, trash, gas, tripe, hooey, soft soap, bunk, rant, poppycock, mumbo jumbo, gab, twaddle, garbage, rubbish, hogwash, rot, hot air.
2. [Frivolous behavior]—*Syn.* unsteadiness, flightiness, thoughtlessness, fickleness, foolishness, fatuousness, giddiness, rashness, infatuation, extravagance, imprudence, irrationality, madness, senselessness, inconsistency, shallowness; see also **stupidity** 2.—*Ant.* consideration*, steadiness, thoughtfulness.
3. [Pure fun]—*Syn.* absurdity, jest, joke; see **fun.**
nonsensical, *mod.*—*Syn.* absurd, silly, senseless; see **stupid** 1.
nonsentient, *mod.*—*Syn.* apathetic, impervious, senseless; see **indifferent** 1, **paralyzed.**
non sequitur, *n.*—*Syn.* illogical conclusion, conclusion that does not follow, non seq. (D); see **nonsense** 1, **stupidity** 2.
nonspiritual, *mod.*—*Syn.* substantial, tangible, material; see **real** 2.
nonstop, *mod.*—*Syn.* uninterrupted, unbroken, continuous, round-the-clock; see **constant** 1.
nonsubjective, *mod.*—*Syn.* impersonal, scientific, detached; see **objective** 1.
nonviolent, *mod.*—*Syn.* passive, passively resistant, without violence; see **peaceful** 2, **quiet** 4.
nook, *n.*—*Syn.* niche, cubbyhole, cranny; see **hole** 2, **recess** 2.
noon, *n.*—*Syn.* noontime, noontide, noonday, noonlight, midday, twelve noon, high noon, meridian, noon hour; see also **time** 1, 2.
noonday, *n.*—*Syn.* twelve o'clock, noontide, meridian; see **noon, time** 1.
no one, *pron.*—*Syn.* no man, not one, nobody; see **neither, none** 1.
noose, *n.*—*Syn.* hitch, running knot, lasso; see **knot** 1, **rope.**
nor, *conj.*—*Syn.* and not, not any, not either, not one, nor yet; see also **neither.**
norm, *n.*—*Syn.* pattern, scale, standard; see **average** 1, **criterion, measure** 2, **model** 1, 2.
normal, *mod.* **1.** [Usual]—*Syn.* ordinary, run-of-the-mill, typical; see **common** 1, **conventional** 1, 3, **traditional** 2.
2. [Regular]—*Syn.* routine, orderly, methodical; see **regular** 3.
3. [Sane]—*Syn.* lucid, wholesome, right-minded; see **rational, reasonable, sane** 1.
4. [Showing no abnormal bodily condition]—*Syn.* in good health, whole, sound; see **healthy** 1.
normality, *n.* **1.** [Mediocrity]—*Syn.* ordinariness, commonplaceness, uniformity, standardness, averageness, commonness, commonality, unremarkableness; see also **regularity.**
2. [Sanity]—*Syn.* normalcy, mental balance, reason; see **sanity** 1.
normally, *mod.*—*Syn.* usually, commonly, in accordance with the *or* a norm; see **frequently, regularly** 1, 2.
normative, *mod.*—*Syn.* normalizing, regulating, regularizing; see **standardizing.**
north, *mod.* **1.** [Situated to the north]—*Syn.* northward, northern, in the north, on the north side of, northerly, northmost, northernmost.
2. [Moving toward the north]—*Syn.* northerly, northbound, northward, to the north, headed north, toward the North Pole, in a northerly direction; see also **south** 4.
3. [Coming from the north]—*Syn.* northerly, southbound, headed south, out of the north, moving toward the equator, moving toward the South Pole; see also **south** 3.
4. [Associated with the north]—*Syn.* polar, hyperborean, boreal; see **arctic, cold** 1.
North, *n.*—*Syn.* Federals, Northerners, Yankees, Yanks, the men in blue, carpetbaggers, damyankees (D); see also **confederacy, south, union** 2.
north, *n.*—*Syn.* the Barrens, tundra, northern section, northland, Northern Hemisphere, the north country, the north woods, Arctic regions, polar regions, the frozen north, land of ice and snow; see also **direction** 1.
northeast, *mod.*—*Syn.* NE, nor'east, northeastern, northeasterly, northeastward(s), north-north-east (NNE), northeast by east (NEbE), northeast by north (NEbN); see also **direction** 1.
northerly, *mod.*—*Syn.* boreal, northern, polar; see **arctic, north** 2.
northern, *mod.*—*Syn.* northerly, boreal, polar; see **arctic, north** 1.
North Pole, *n.*—*Syn.* arctic, Arctic Circle *or* Zone, home of Santa Claus; see **north.**
Northstar, *n.*—*Syn.* polestar, lodestar, Polaris; see **star** 1.
northward(s), *mod.*—*Syn.* to *or* toward the north, northerly, up; see **north** 2.
northwest, *mod.*—*Syn.* NW, nor'west, northwestern, northwesterly, northwestward(s), north-northwest (NNW), northwest by west (NWbW), northwest by north (NWbN); see also **direction** 1.
nose, *n.* **1.** [The organ of smell]—*Syn.* nasal organ, nasal cavity, nares, nasal passages, nostrils, olfactory nerves; *all* (D): snoot, proboscis, beak, bill; see also **organ** 2.
2. [A projection]—*Syn.* snout, nozzle, muzzle; see **projection.**
by a nose (D)—*Syn.* by a very small margin, too close for comfort, barely; see **almost.**
count noses (D)—*Syn.* add, total, sum up; see **count.**

cut off one's nose to spite one's face—*Syn.* injure one's own interests, hurt oneself, be self-destructive; see **hurt** 1.
follow one's nose—*Syn.* go (straight) forward, continue blindly, keep going; see **advance** 1, **continue** 1.
look down one's nose at (D)—*Syn.* disdain, snub, be disgusted by; see **scorn** 1.
on the nose (D)—*Syn.* precisely, to the point, correctly; see **exactly.**
pay through the nose—*Syn.* pay an unreasonable price, pay heavily, get taken (D); see **pay** 1.
put one's nose out of joint (D)—*Syn.* harm, substitute for, hurt; see **anger** 1, **replace** 1.
turn up one's nose at—*Syn.* sneer at, refuse, disdain; see **scorn** 1.
under one's very nose—*Syn.* in plain sight, visible, at one's fingertips; see **obvious** 1.

nose, *v.* —*Syn.* search, inspect, pry; see **examine** 1.

nose for news (D), *n.* —*Syn.* news sense, an eye for the unusual, interest; see **curiosity** 1.

nose out (D), *v.* —*Syn.* beat, win from, better; see **defeat** 1.

nostalgia, *n.* —*Syn.* remorse, wistfulness, sentimentality; see **homesickness, loneliness.**

nostalgic, *mod.* —*Syn.* lonesome, regretful, sentimental; see **homesick, lonely** 1.

nostril, *n.* —*Syn.* nasal passage, nasal opening, snout; see **nose** 1.

nostrum, *n.* —*Syn.* formula, patent medicine, panacea; see **medicine** 2, **remedy** 2.

nosy, *mod.* —*Syn.* snoop, snooping, curious; see **inquisitive, interested** 2.

not, *mod.* —*Syn.* no, non-, un-, in-; see also **negative** 2.

notability, *n.* —*Syn.* precedence, notoriety, esteem; see **fame** 1.

notable, *mod.* **1.** [Remarkable]—*Syn.* distinguished, important, striking; see **unusual** 1.
2. [Famous]—*Syn.* well-known, celebrated, renowned; see **famous.**

notable, *n.* —*Syn.* leading *or* important person *or* figure, person in the news, V.I.P. (D); see **leader** 2, **personality** 3.

notably, *mod.* —*Syn.* reputably, prominently, distinctly; see **very.**

not a little, *mod.* —*Syn.* great, large, copious; see **many, much** 1, 2.

not a little, *n.* —*Syn.* not a few, profusion, abundance; see **lot** 4, **much, plenty.**

not always, *mod.* —*Syn.* not usually, sometimes, occasionally; see **seldom.**

notarize, *v.* —*Syn.* sign (legally), attach *or* affix a legal signature, make legal; see **approve** 1.

notary, *n.* —*Syn.* public accountant, attorney, official; see **accountant, clerk** 2, **lawyer.**

not at all, *mod.* —*Syn.* by no (manner of) means, not by any means *or* in any way, no way (D); see also **no.**

notation, *n.* **1.** [Arithmetic]—*Syn.* mathematical system, algebra, math (D); see **arithmetic, mathematics.**
2. [Symbols]—*Syn.* signs, figures, characters; see **notes, representation, symbol, system** 1.

notch, *n.* —*Syn.* nock, nick, indent; see **cut** 2, **dent, groove.**

notch, *v.* —*Syn.* indent, nick, chisel; see **cut** 1, **dent.**

notched, *mod.* —*Syn.* nicked, jagged, saw-toothed; see **irregular** 4, **rough** 1.

not completely, *mod.* —*Syn.* incompletely, not fully, not thoroughly; see **halfway, unfinished** 1.

note, *n.* **1.** [A representation]—*Syn.* sign, figure, mark; see **representation, symbol.**
2. [A brief record]—*Syn.* notation, jotting, scribble, reminder, scrawl, annotation, agenda, datum, minute, entry, memorandum, journal, inscription, calendar, diary; see also **mark** 3, **notes, record** 1, **summary.**
3. [A brief communication]—*Syn.* dispatch, epistle, announcement; see **letter** 2, **word** 3.
4. [A musical tone, or its symbol]—*Syn.* tone, key, scale, shape note, interval, degree, step, sharp, flat, natural; see also **pitch** 3.
Musical notes, include the following—whole note *or* semibreve, double whole note *or* breve, half note *or* minim, quarter note *or* crotchet, eighth note *or* quaver, sixteenth note *or* semiquaver, thirty-second note *or* demisemiquaver, sixty-fourth note *or* hemidemisemiquaver, triplet, grace note *or* appoggiatura.

note, *v.* **1.** [To notice]—*Syn.* remark, heed, perceive; see **regard** 1, **see** 1.
2. [To record]—*Syn.* write down, enter, transcribe; see **record** 1, **write.**

notebook, *n.* —*Syn.* memorandum book, record book, diary; see **journal** 1, **record** 1.

noted, *mod.* —*Syn.* well-known, celebrated, notorious; see **famous.**

not entirely, *mod.* —*Syn.* incompletely, not perfectly, not thoroughly; see **halfway, unfinished** 1.

notes, *n.* —*Syn.* commentary, interpretation, explanation, findings, recordings, field notes, observations; see also **data, records.**
compare notes—*Syn.* exchange views, confer, go over; see **discuss.**
strike the right note—*Syn.* be correct, do what is expected *or* pleasing, respond correctly; see **succeed** 1.
take notes—*Syn.* write down, keep a record, enter; see **record** 1.

not especially, *mod.* —*Syn.* somewhat, to a degree, within limits; see **moderately.**

noteworthy, *mod.* —*Syn.* outstanding, remarkable, exceptional; see **unique** 1, **unusual** 1.

nothing, *n.* —*Syn.* not anything, no thing, trifle, bagatelle, nothingness, nonexistence, inexistence, nonbeing, nullity, zero, nihility, extinction, oblivion, obliteration, annihilation, nonentity, neither hide nor hair; *all* (D), goose egg, zip, zilch; see also **blank** 1, **emptiness.**
for nothing—*Syn.* **1.** gratis, without cost, unencumbered; see **free** 4. **2.** in vain, for naught, emptily; see **unnecessary.**
have nothing on—*Syn.* have no evidence, be without proof, be only guessing; see **guess** 1.
in nothing flat (D)—*Syn.* in almost no time at all, speedily, rapidly; see **quickly** 1.
make nothing of—*Syn.* minimize, underplay, play down; see **neglect** 1.
think nothing of—*Syn.* minimize, underplay, disregard; see **neglect** 1.

nothing but, *mod.* and *prep.* —*Syn.* only that, nothing else, without exception; see **only** 1, 2, 3.
nothing doing (D), *interj.* —*Syn.* certainly not, by no means, the reply is in the negative; see **no.**
nothing for it (D), *mod.* —*Syn.* without recourse *or* exception *or* escape *or* change, certainly, of necessity; see **necessarily, surely.**
nothing less than, *n.* —*Syn.* the absolute *or* outside limit, boundary, restriction; see **limit** 2.
nothingness, *n.* **1.** [Void]—*Syn.* vacuum, blank, hollowness; see **emptiness, nothing, oblivion** 2.
2. [Worthlessness]—*Syn.* pettiness, unimportance, smallness; see **insignificance.**
nothing to it (D), *mod.* —*Syn.* facile, slight, like taking candy from a baby (D); see **easy** 2, **simple** 3.
notice, *n.* **1.** [A warning]—*Syn.* note, notification, intimation; see **sign** 1, **warning.**
2. [An announcement]—*Syn.* comments, remark, enlightenment; see **announcement** 2, **declaration** 2, **report** 1.
serve notice—*Syn.* give warning, declare, announce; see **notify** 1.
take notice—*Syn.* become aware, pay attention, observe; see **regard** 1, **see** 1.
notice, *v.* **1.** [To observe]—*Syn.* mark, remark, look at; see **regard** 1, **see** 1.
2. [To publish a notice]—*Syn.* mention, comment on, notify; see **publish** 1.
noticeable, *mod.* —*Syn.* observable, appreciable, conspicuous; see **obvious** 1.
noticed, *mod.* —*Syn.* seen, remarked, recorded; see **observed** 1.
noticing, *mod.* —*Syn.* perceiving, regarding, heeding; see **observant** 2, **saying, seeing.**
notification, *n.* —*Syn.* information, advice, intelligence; see **announcement** 2, **publicity** 3, **warning.**
notify, *v.* **1.** [To provide with information]—*Syn.* declare, announce, inform, enlighten, make known, publish, express, acquaint, apprise, mention, advise, state, proclaim, convey, herald, blazon, circulate, disseminate, report, pass out, reveal, divulge, disclose, teach, air, vent, assert, send word, let know, promulgate, telephone, write, speak to, radio, cable, wire, broadcast, circularize, spread abroad; *all* (D): tip off, spill, brief, debrief, cue in, squeal, sing, talk, give a straight steer, wise up, give a gilt-edged tip, let in on the know; see also **advertise** 1, **communicate** 1, **tell** 1.
2. [To warn]—*Syn.* caution, apprise, suggest; see **hint.**
noting, *mod.* —*Syn.* noticing, seeing, perceiving; see **observant** 2, **saying, seeing.**
notion, *n.* **1.** [Opinion]—*Syn.* idea, assumption, sentiment; see **opinion** 1, **thought** 2.
2. [Conception]—*Syn.* concept, understanding, inkling, intimation, conceit, whim, fancy, imagination, perception, impression, insight, consciousness, mental apprehension, inclination, indication, intuition, comprehension, penetration, discernment; see also **awareness, knowledge** 1.
not less than, *mod.* —*Syn.* more (than), at least, at a minimum; see **more** 1, 2, 3.
not noticeably, *mod.* —*Syn.* obscurely, indeterminately, invisibly; see **vaguely.**
not now, *mod.* —*Syn.* sometime, later, at another time; see **someday.**
notoriety, *n.* —*Syn.* repute, renown, name; see **fame** 1, **reputation** 1, 2.
notorious, *mod.* —*Syn.* ill-famed, infamous, disreputable; see **famous, wicked** 1, 2.
notoriously, *mod.* —*Syn.* particularly, notably, spectacularly; see **especially** 1.
not particularly, *mod.* —*Syn.* not expressly *or* exclusively, barely, scarcely; see **hardly.**
not really, *mod.* —*Syn.* not entirely, doubtful, uncertain; see **questionable** 1.
not usually, *mod.* —*Syn.* sometimes, occasionally, now and then; see **seldom.**
not with it (D), *mod.* —*Syn.* uninformed, lacking understanding, uncomprehending; see **ignorant** 1, **stupid** 1, **unaware.**
notwithstanding, *mod.* and *prep.* —*Syn.* despite, in spite of, in any case *or* event, regardless of, for all that, on the other hand, after all, however, at any rate, at all events, to the contrary, nevertheless, nonetheless, though, howbeit, yet; see also **although, but** 1.
not worth it, *mod.* —*Syn.* not good enough, too poor, inadequate; see **poor** 2, **worthless** 1.
nought, *n.* —*Syn.* naught, not anything, cipher; see **nothing.**
noun, *n.* —*Syn.* substantive, term, part of speech, nominal, common noun, proper noun; see also **label, language** 2, **name** 1.
nourish, *v.* —*Syn.* feed, supply, sustain; see **provide** 1, **support** 5.
nourishing, *mod.* —*Syn.* macrobiotic, healthy, nutritious; see **healthful.**
nourishment, *n.* —*Syn.* nurture, nutriment, provender; see **food.**
nouveau riche, *n.* —*Syn.* parvenu, newly-rich, status-seeker; see **upstart.**
novel, *mod.* —*Syn.* new, odd, strange; see **unique** 1, **unusual** 1, 2.
novel, *n.* —*Syn.* paperback, best-seller, fiction; see also **book** 1, **story.**
Types of novels include the following—romance, detective story, love story, *Bildungsroman* (German), *roman fleuve, roman à clef* (both French), novella, adventure story, ghost story, mystery, western, science fiction *or* fantasy, novel of the soil; historical, sectional, regional, naturalistic, Gothic, problem, biographical, psychological, pornographic, satirical, picaresque, social, adventure, supernatural, etc., novel; *all* (D): thriller, chiller, shocker, sci-fi *or* SF, pulp, porn.
novelist, *n.* —*Syn.* fiction writer, fictionist, storyteller, narrative writer, writer of novels, writer of prose fiction; see also **author** 2, **writer.**
novelty (D), *mod.* —*Syn.* curious, odd, fashionable; see **unusual** 2.
novelty, *n.* **1.** [The quality of being novel]—*Syn.* originality, recentness, modernity, freshness; see also **newness.**
2. [Something popular because it is new]—*Syn.* innovation, origination, creation; see **fad.**
3. [A striking article, usually one that is cheap and garish]—*Syn.* oddity, curiosity, gimcrack; see **knick-knack.**
November, *n.* —*Syn.* fall *or* autumn (month), Thanksgiving (season), football season, hunting season; see also **month, autumn.**

novice, *n.* —*Syn.* beginner, learner, neophyte; see **amateur.**

novitiate, *n.* **1.** [Apprenticeship]—*Syn.* internship, tutelage, trial period; see **origin** 1.
2. [Novice]—*Syn.* intern, beginner, apprentice; see **amateur.**

now, *mod.* **1.** [At the present]—*Syn.* at this time, right now, at this *or* the moment, just now, momentarily, this day, these days, here and now, for the nonce.
2. [In the immediate future]—*Syn.* promptly, in a moment, presently, in a minute; see **soon** 1.
3. [Immediately]—*Syn.* at once, forthwith, instantly; see **immediately.**

nowadays, *mod.* —*Syn.* in these days, in this age, in the present age; see **now** 1.

now and then, *mod.* —*Syn.* sometimes, infrequently, occasionally; see **seldom.**

noway, *mod.* —*Syn.* not at all, on no account, by no means, not a jot, not a bit of it, nowhere(s) near, in no case *or* respect.

nowhere, *mod.* —*Syn.* not anywhere, not in any place, not at any place, nowhere at all, in no place, to no place.

noxious, *mod.* **1.** [Harmful]—*Syn.* baneful, pernicious, deleterious; see **dangerous** 1, 2.
2. [Foul]—*Syn.* noisome, spoiled, putrid; see **offensive** 2, **rotten** 1.
3. [Poisonous]—*Syn.* toxic, virulent, venomous; see **deadly, harmful, poisonous.**

nozzle, *n.* —*Syn.* spout, nose, mouthpiece, beak, outlet, vent, hose end; see also **end** 4.

nuance, *n.* —*Syn.* subtlety, refinement, distinction; see **difference** 1.

nub (D), *n.* —*Syn.* essence, crux, core, nitty-gritty (D); see **essence** 1.

nuclear, *mod.* —*Syn.* endoplastic, endoplasmic, concerning a nucleus; see **atomic** 2.

nuclear bomb, *n.* —*Syn.* nuclear armament *or* warhead; hydrogen bomb *or* H-bomb, atomic bomb *or* A-bomb, neutron bomb, cobalt bomb *or* C-bomb, etc.; atomic *or* nuclear weapon; see also **arms** 1.

nuclear fission, *n.* —*Syn.* fusion, atomic power, splitting the atom; see **energy** 3, **power** 2.

nucleus, *n.* **1.** [Essence]—*Syn.* core, gist, kernel; see **essence** 1, **matter.**
2. [Basis]—*Syn.* foundation, premise, crux; see **basis** 1.
3. [Center]—*Syn.* hub, focus, pivot; see **center** 1.

nude, *mod.* —*Syn.* stripped, unclothed, bare; see **naked** 1.

nude, *n.* —*Syn.* naked body *or* man *or* woman, nudist, gymnosophist, pin-up, ecdysiast, model; *both* (D): stripper, peeler.

nudge, *n.* —*Syn.* tap, poke, shove; see **bump** 1, **push, touch** 2.

nudge, *v.* —*Syn.* poke, bump, tap; see **push** 1, **touch** 1.

nudity, *n.* —*Syn.* bareness, nudeness, undress; see **nakedness.**

nugatory, *mod.* —*Syn.* ineffectual, inadequate, impotent; see **faulty, useless** 1.

nugget, *n.* —*Syn.* ingot, bullion, chunk; see **gold** 2, **lump, mass** 1, **rock** 1.

nuisance, *n.* **1.** [A bother]—*Syn.* annoyance, vexation, bore; see **trouble** 2.
2. [An offense, against the public]—*Syn.* breach, infraction, affront; see **crime** 1.
3. [(D) An unpleasant *or* unwelcome person] —*Syn.* pest, bore, annoyance, problem (child), frump, bother; *all* (D): holy terror, prune, bad egg, foul ball, insect, human mistake, louse, pain in the neck, nudnik, poor excuse, bum; see also **trouble** 2.

null, *mod.* **1.** [Void]—*Syn.* invalid, vain, unsanctioned; see **void** 1.
2. [Nonexistent]—*Syn.* absent, nothing, negative; see **imaginary, unreal.**
3. [Useless]—*Syn.* ineffective, valueless, barren; see **useless** 1, **worthless** 1.

nullification, *n.* —*Syn.* neutralization, repeal, revocation; see **cancellation, withdrawal.**

nullify, *v.* —*Syn.* repeal, invalidate, quash; see **cancel** 2, **revoke.**

numb, *mod.* **1.** [Insensible]—*Syn.* deadened, dead, unfeeling, insensate, (be)numbed, asleep, senseless, anesthetized, stupefied, comatose; see also **paralyzed.**
2. [Insensitive]—*Syn.* apathetic, lethargic, phlegmatic; see **callous, indifferent** 1, **listless** 1.

numb, *v.* —*Syn.* paralyze, stun, dull; see **deaden** 1.

number, *n.* **1.** [A quantity]—*Syn.* amount, sum total, totality, aggregate, whole, whole number, product, measurable quantity, recorded total, estimate, the lot, conglomeration, plenty, manifoldness, plentitude, abundance; see also **quantity.**
2. [A representation of quantity]—*Syn.* character, sign, emblem; see **representation, symbol.**
beyond number—*Syn.* too many *or* much to count, innumerable, countless; see **many.**
get (*or* **have**) **one's number** (D)—*Syn.* discover one's true character, find out about, know; see **understand** 1.
one's number is up (D)—*Syn.* one's time to die has arrived, one's time has come, one's destiny is fulfilled; see **doomed.**
without number—*Syn.* too numerous to be counted, innumerable, countless; see **many.**

number, *v.* —*Syn.* calculate, enumerate, estimate; see **add** 1, **count, total** 1.

numbered, *mod.* **1.** [Given numbers]—*Syn.* designated, told, enumerated, checked, specified, indicated; see also **marked** 1.
2. [Approaching an end]—*Syn.* fixed, limited, fated; see **doomed.**

numbering, *mod.* —*Syn.* totaling, adding up to, reaching; see **making** 2.

numbering, *n.* —*Syn.* count, tally, valuation; see **estimate** 1.

numberless, *mod.* —*Syn.* countless, limitless, numerous; see **infinite** 1, **many.**

number one (D), *n.* —*Syn.* numero uno, I, me, your self, my self, his *or* her self, himself, herself; see also **myself.**

numbness, *n.* —*Syn.* deadness, anesthesia, stupefaction, dullness, insensitivity, insensibility, paralysis, loss of motion *or* sensation.

numeral, *n.* —*Syn.* character, cipher, digit; see **number** 1.

numerate, *v.* —*Syn.* number, measure, enumerate; see **add** 1, **count, total** 1.

numerical, *mod.* —*Syn.* arithmetical, fractional, exponential, logarithmic, differential, integral, digital, mathematical, binary; see also **statistical.**

numerous, *mod.* —*Syn.* copious, various, diverse; see **infinite** 1, **many.**

numskull, *n.* —*Syn.* simpleton, jackass, nitwit; see **fool** 1.

numskulled, *mod.* —*Syn.* brainless, inane, dumb; see **dull** 3, **stupid** 1.

nun, *n.* —*Syn.* abbess, postulant, sister, religious woman, anchorite, prioress, mother superior, canoness.

nunnery, *n.* —*Syn.* priory, abbey, convent; see **cloister, retreat** 2.

nuptial, *mod.* —*Syn.* conjugal, connubial, marital; see **matrimonial.**

nuptials, *n.* —*Syn.* wedding, matrimony, marriage ceremony; see **marriage** 2.

nurse, *n.* **1.** [One who cares for the sick]—*Syn.* attendant, male nurse, practical nurse, licensed practical nurse (LPN), private nurse, registered nurse (R.N.), floor nurse, night nurse, day nurse, doctor's assistant, student nurse, nurse's aide, therapist, Red Cross nurse; *both* (D): Lady in Gray, Florence Nightingale.
Specialists in nursing include the following—psychiatric, pediatric, geriatric, surgical, public health, etc., nurse; hospital *or* nurses' supervisor, floor nurse, nurse in charge of in-service training.
2. [One who cares for the young]—*Syn.* servant, nursemaid, caretaker, attendant, babysitter; *all* (D): nanny, minder, nurserymam.
3. [One who suckles the young]—*Syn.* wet nurse, *amah* (India), foster mother, mammy.

nurse, *v.* —*Syn.* attend *or* minister (to), aid, medicate, irradiate, X-ray, immunize, inoculate, vaccinate, care for, take care *or* charge of, look after, look *or* see to, cherish, nurture, foster, mother, father, be a mother *or* father to, suckle, cradle, dry-nurse, wet-nurse, feed; see also **heal** 1, **sustain** 2, **tend** 1, **treat** 3.

nursery, *n.* **1.** [A place for children]—*Syn.* child's room, playroom, nursery school, preschool, day nursery, crèche, kindergarten; *all* (D): brattery, His Royal Highness' Palace, tottery; see also **school** 1.
2. [A place for plants]—*Syn.* hothouse, hotbed, plantation; see **greenhouse.**

nursing, *mod.* **1.** [Acting as a nurse]—*Syn.* fostering, cherishing, watching over, caring for, attending, devoting oneself to, bringing up; see also **tending** 2.
2. [Gaining nourishment by suckling]—*Syn.* taking nourishment, sucking, milking, feeding, suckling.

nursing, *n.* —*Syn.* nurse's training, profession *or* duties of a nurse, healing, treating.

nurture, *n.* **1.** [Nourishment]—*Syn.* pabulum, nutriment, sustenance; see **food, subsistence** 1.
2. [Training]—*Syn.* upbringing, breeding, care; see **education** 1, **training.**

nurture, *v.* —*Syn.* nourish, care for, provide (for); see **feed, sustain** 2.

nurturing, *n.* —*Syn.* maintenance, development, sustenance; see **subsistence** 2.

nut, *n.* **1.** [A dry fruit]—*Syn.* seed, kernel, stone, achene, caryopsis, utricle; see also **fruit** 1.
Common nuts include the following—acorn, beechnut, hazelnut, black walnut, English walnut, almond, nutmeg, pecan, filbert, coconut, pistachio, cashew, hognut, water chestnut, butternut, kola; (swamp) hickory, pine, Brazil, groundnut, ginkgo, quandong, betel nut.
2. [A threaded metal block]—*Syn.* bur, lock nut, cap, ratchet nut, bolt nut, screw nut, jam nut; see also **bolt** 1.
3. [(D) An eccentric or insane person]—*Syn.* eccentric, fanatic, maniac; see **zealot.**
4. [(D) The head]—*Syn.* crown, skull, brain; see **cranium, head** 1.
hard (*or* **tough**) **nut to crack**—*Syn.* problem, responsibility, burden; see **difficulty** 1, 2.
off one's nut (D)—*Syn.* silly, crazy, eccentric; see **insane** 1.

nutbrown, *mod.* —*Syn.* roan, chestnut, brownish; see **brown.**

nutriment, *n.* —*Syn.* nourishment, provisions, sustenance; see **food, subsistence** 1.

nutrition, *n.* —*Syn.* diet, nourishment, victuals; see **food, menu, subsistence** 1.

nutritive, *mod.* —*Syn.* edible, wholesome, nutritious; see **healthful.**

nuts (D), *mod.* —*Syn.* crazy, deranged, ridiculous; see **insane** 1, **unusual.**

nutty, *mod.* —*Syn.* deranged, eccentric, irrational; see **insane** 1.

nuzzle, *v.* —*Syn.* caress, cuddle, snuggle; see **nestle.**

nylon, *n.* —*Syn.* synthetic(s), polyamide product; synthetic fiber *or* cloth *or* plastic, etc.; see **cloth, fiber** 1, **plastic.**

nymph, *n.* —*Syn.* nature goddess, sprite, mermaid; see **fairy** 1.

O

oaf, *n.* —*Syn.* blockhead, goon, lout; see **fool** 1, **moron.**

oak, *n.* **1.** [An oak tree]—*Syn. Quercus, Lithocarpus* (*both* Latin), casuarina; see also **tree.**
Varieties of oaks include the following—white, red, scarlet, Spanish, black, live, bur, British, pin, jack, scrub, valley, swamp white, willow, laurel, California blue.
2. [Oak woods]—*Syn.* hardwood, oaken wood, oak paneling; see also **wood** 2.
Kinds of finishes of oak include the following—plain-sawed, quarter-sawed, light oak, dark oak, golden oak, weathered oak, distressed oak.

oar, *n.* —*Syn.* pole, sweep, scull; see **paddle.**

oarsman, *n.* —*Syn.* gondolier, oar, ferryman, boatman, rower, boatswain *or* bo's'n (D); see also **sailor.**

oasis, *n.* —*Syn.* green *or* fertile area, irrigated land(s), watered tract, garden spot, desert garden, water hole, watering place, desert resting place; see also **refuge** 1, **retreat** 2, **sanctuary** 2.

oath, *n.* **1.** [An attestation of the truth]—*Syn.* affirmation, affidavit, vow, sworn statement, testimony, word, deposition, sworn declaration, contract, adjuration, avowal, pledge, ironclad oath (D); see also **declaration** 1, **promise** 1.—*Ant.* denial*, disavowal, lie.
2. [The name of the Lord taken in vain]—*Syn.* malediction, swearword, blasphemy; see **curse.**

oatmeal, *n.* —*Syn.* rolled oats, steel-cut oats, porridge; see **breakfast food, grain** 1.

obdurate, *mod.* —*Syn.* stubborn, inflexible, unyielding; see **callous, obstinate** 1.

obedience, *n.* —*Syn.* willingness, submission, compliance; see **docility.**

obedient, *mod.* **1.** [Dutiful]—*Syn.* amenable, loyal, lawabiding, governable, tractable, resigned, devoted, respectful, complaisant, controllable, attentive, obliging, willing, deferential, under the control of, at one's command *or* nod, obeisant, faithful, honoring, reverential, venerating; *all* (D): at one's beck and call, on a string, wrapped around one's (little) finger; see also **faithful.**—*Ant.* unruly*, disobedient, undutiful.
2. [Docile]—*Syn.* pliant, acquiescent, compliant; see **docile.**

obediently, *mod.* —*Syn.* dutifully, submissively, devotedly, loyally, faithfully, compliantly, at one's orders; see also **willingly.**

obeisance, *n.* —*Syn.* courtesy, homage, deference; see **praise** 1, **reverence** 2.

obelisk, *n.* —*Syn.* pillar, pyramid, monolith; see **column** 1, **tower.**

obese, *mod.* —*Syn.* corpulent, plump, stout; see **fat** 1.

obey, *v.* **1.** [To act in accordance with orders]—*Syn.* submit, answer (to), respond, act (upon *or* on), bow to, surrender, yield, perform, do, carry out, attend to orders, do what one is told, accept, accord, consent, do what is expected of one, do one's duty, redeem one's pledge, do as one says, come at call, serve, concur, accede, assent, conform, acquiesce, mind, take orders, do the will of, do one's bidding, comply, fulfill, play second fiddle (D); see also **agree.**—*Ant.* rebel*, disobey, mutiny.
2. [To act in accordance with a recognized principle]—*Syn.* live by, set one's course by, accept, agree, give allegiance to, be loyal to, reconcile, adjust, accommodate to, adopt, own, make one's own, abide by, hold fast, embrace, practice, adhere *or* conform to, be devoted *or* attached to, serve, exercise; see also **behave** 2, **conform, follow** 2.—*Ant.* oppose*, refuse, cast off.

obfuscate, *v.* —*Syn.* obscure, muddle, confuse; see **muddle** 1, **confuse.**

obituary, *n.* —*Syn.* death notice, mortuary tribute, eulogy, necrology, obit (D); see also **announcement** 2.

object, *n.* **1.** [A corporeal body]—*Syn.* article, something, gadget; see **thing** 1.
2. [A purpose]—*Syn.* objective, aim, wish; see **purpose** 1.
3. [One who receives]—*Syn.* recipient, target, victim; see **receiver.**

object, *v.* —*Syn.* protest, take exception (to), dispute; see **complain** 1.

objectify, *v.* —*Syn.* actualize, substantiate, make objective; see **materialize** 1.

objection, *n.* **1.** [The reason for disapproval]—*Syn.* disapproval, scruple, hesitation, question, demurring, reluctance, disinclination, declination, unwillingness, rejection, dislike, dissatisfaction, discontent, displeasure, repugnancy, disesteem, disapprobation, shrinking, boggling, shunning, revulsion, repudiation, low opinion, abhorrence, hesitancy, unacceptance, discarding, dubiousness; see also **doubt** 1, 2.—*Ant.* permission*, acceptance, desire.
2. [The statement or instance of an objection, sense 1]—*Syn.* protestation, criticism, complaint, charge, accusation, remonstrance, expostulation, gainsaying, reprimand, exception, execration, admonition, disapproval, reproach, dispute, opposition, adverse comment, rejection, ban, countercharge, grievance, contradiction, contravention, invective, censure, abuse, scolding, denunciation, lecture, disagreement, vituperation, difference, disdain, reprehension, plaint, upbraiding, chiding, insistence, condemnation, depreciation, animad-

version, grumbling, caviling, clamor, faultfinding, tongue-lashing, vilification, carping, reproof, depreciation, revilement, dissent, indictment, imputation, demurrer, insinuation, complaining, frown, blame, sarcasm, odium, whining, croaking, gravamen, moaning, wail, groan, murmur, lament, regret, lamentation, aspersion; *all* (D): beef, problem, gripe, kick, crack, dressing-down, knock; see also **rebuke.**—*Ant.* praise*, commendation, recommendation.

objectionable, *mod.* **1.** [Revolting]—*Syn.* gross, repugnant, abhorrent; see **offensive** 2.
2. [Undesirable]—*Syn.* unacceptable, unsatisfactory, inexpedient; see **undesirable.**

objective, *mod.* **1.** [Existing independently of the mind]—*Syn.* actual, external, material, scientific, sure, extrinsic, nonsubjective, measurable, extraneous, unintrospective, reified, tactile, corporeal, bodily, palpable, physical, phenomenal, sensible, outward, outside, determinable, eliminating the human equation, unchangeable, invariable; see also **real** 2.—*Ant.* mental*, subjective, introspective.
2. [Free from personal bias]—*Syn.* detached, impersonal, unbiased; see **accurate** 2, **fair** 1.

objective, *n.* —*Syn.* goal, aim, aspiration; see **purpose** 1.

objectively, *mod.* —*Syn.* impartially, indifferently, neutrally, open-mindedly, dispassionately, justly, equitably, detachedly, soberly, accurately, candidly, considerately, not subjectively; with objectivity *or* impartiality *or* (due) consideration *or* (good) judgment, etc.; without prejudice *or* bias *or* partiality *or* passion, etc.; *all* (D): squarely, on the square, like a square shooter, on the up and up.

object to, *v.* —*Syn.* disapprove, doubt, question; see **oppose** 1.

obligate, *v.* —*Syn.* bind, restrict, constrain; see **force** 1, **restrain** 1.

obligation, *n.* —*Syn.* conscience, burden, debt; see **duty** 1, **responsibility** 2.

obligatory, *mod.* —*Syn.* required, essential, binding; see **necessary** 1.

oblige, *v.* **1.** [To accommodate]—*Syn.* assist, aid, contribute; see **accommodate** 1, **help** 1, **serve** 1.
2. [To require]—*Syn.* compel, coerce, bind; see **command** 1, **force** 1, **require** 2.

obliged, *mod.* —*Syn.* compelled, obligated, required; see **bound** 2.

obliging, *mod.* —*Syn.* amiable, accommodating, helpful; see **kind.**

obligingly, *mod.* —*Syn.* helpfully, agreeably, thoughtfully; see **kindly** 2.

oblique, *mod.* **1.** [Slanting]—*Syn.* inclined, inclining, diverging, leaning, sloping, angled, diagonal, cater-cornered, unperpendicular, unvertical, skew, askew, asymmetrical, turned, twisted, awry, strained, askance, distorted, unhorizontal, off level, sideways, slanted, tipping, tipped, aslant, athwart, at an angle, skewwise, on the bias; *all* (D): skewy, slaunchwise, kitty-cornered, geewhacky, northeast by southwest; see also **bent, crooked** 1.—*Ant.* vertical*, perpendicular, straight.
2. [Indirect]—*Syn.* obscure, circuitous, roundabout; see **indirect, vague** 2.

obliquely, *mod.* —*Syn.* cornerways, diagonally, catercorner; see **cornerwise.**

obliterate, *v.* **1.** [To destroy]—*Syn.* liquidate, annihilate, level; see **defeat** 2, **destroy** 1, **ravage.**
2. [To erase]—*Syn.* delete, wipe *or* mark out, rub off; see **cancel** 1, **eliminate** 1.

obliterated, *mod.* —*Syn.* eliminated, wiped out, removed; see **destroyed.**

oblivion, *n.* **1.** [Blankness]—*Syn.* forgetfulness, unmindfulness, obliviousness, Lethe, insensibleness, waters of oblivion, amnesia; see also **carelessness, indifference** 1.—*Ant.* memory*, remembrance, recollection.
2. [Nothingness]—*Syn.* nonexistence, Nirvana, obscurity, nullity, nihility, void, limbo; see also **emptiness, nothing.**—*Ant.* existence*, fullness, being.

oblivious, *mod.* —*Syn.* abstracted, preoccupied, inattentive, absorbed, absent, heedless, distracted, forgetful, unmindful, forgetting, unrecognizing, unnoticing, blundering, unobservant, unconscious, unaware, overlooking, gauming (D); see also **absent-minded, dreamy** 1.—*Ant.* observant*, attentive, mindful.

obliviously, *mod.* —*Syn.* thoughtlessly, heedlessly, ignorantly; see **carelessly.**

oblong, *mod.* —*Syn.* elongated, rectangular, ovate, ovaliform, ovated, oval, elliptical, ellipsoidal, ovaloid, egg-shaped, elongate, ovopyriform.—*Ant.* square*, circle, circular.

obloquy, *n.* **1.** [Disgrace]—*Syn.* infamy, ill repute, dishonor; see **disgrace** 1, **shame** 2.
2. [Slanderous matter]—*Syn.* slander, backbiting, defamation; see **accusation** 2, **blame** 1, **insult, objection** 2.

obnoxious, *mod.* —*Syn.* annoying, disagreeable, displeasing; see **offensive** 2.

obnoxiously, *mod.* —*Syn.* cruelly, indecently, unwelcomely; see **badly** 1, **brutally.**

obscene, *mod.* **1.** [Foul]—*Syn.* unwholesome, filthy, unclean; see **offensive** 2.
2. [Lewd]—*Syn.* wanton, lustful, lascivious; see **lewd** 1, 2, **ribald, sensual.**

obscenely, *mod.* —*Syn.* indecently, viciously, suggestively; see **lewdly.**

obscenity, *n.* **1.** [The state or quality of being obscene]—*Syn.* salacity, vulgarity, scurrility; see **lewdness.**
2. [That which is obscene]—*Syn.* vulgarity, impropriety, smut; see **indecency** 2, **pornography.**

obscure, *mod.* **1.** [Vague]—*Syn.* indistinct, ambiguous, indeterminate, indefinite, indecisive, unintelligible, impenetrable, inscrutable, unfathomable, unclear, insoluble, involved, undecisive, undefined, intricate, illegible, incomprehensible, hazy, dark, dim, abstruse, unaccountable, inexplicable, inconceivable, unbelievable, incredible, complicated, enigmatical, illogical, imprecise, unreasoned, mixed up, doubtful, questionable, dubious, inexact, unexact, unreasoned, loose, ill-defined, unidentified, invisible, undisclosed, perplexing, cryptic, escaping notice, mystical, secret, equivocal, enigmatic, concealed, mysterious, recondite, esoteric, puzzling, lacking clarity, unreadable, contradictory, wanting precision, in need of clarifying, lacking organization, out of focus, in need of translations, unrelated; *all* (D): clear as mud, too much for, over one's head, deep, cockeyed, far out; see also

complex 2, confused 2, confusing, difficult 2, uncertain 2, vague 2.—*Ant.* clear*, definite, distinct.
2. [Dark]—*Syn.* cloudy, dense, hazy; see **dark** 1.
3. [Little known]—*Syn.* unknown, rare, hidden, covered, remote, removed, retired, reticent, secretive, seldom seen, unseen, inconspicuous, humble, invisible, abstruse, mysterious, deep, cryptic, oracular, enigmatic, esoteric, arcane, undisclosed, cabalistic, inexpressible, unapprehended, dark; see also **distant** 1, **irrelevant, profound** 2, **secret** 1.

obscure, *v.* **1.** [To dim]—*Syn.* shadow, cloud, screen; see **shade** 2.
2. [To conceal]—*Syn.* cover, veil, wrap (up); see **disguise, hide** 1.

obscurely, *mod.* —*Syn.* dimly, darkly, thickly, duskily, nebulously, dingily, tenebrously, generally, dully, indistinctly, gloomily, hazily, unintelligibly, indefinitely, indefinably, indecisively, unobtrusively; see also **vaguely.**

obscurity, *n.* —*Syn.* vagueness, dimness, fuzziness; see **uncertainty** 1, 2, 3.

obsequious, *mod.* —*Syn.* cringing, slavish, sycophantic, deferential, servile, subject, enslaved, subordinate, parasitical, stipendiary, toadyish, toadying, fawning, truckling, groveling, spineless, crouching, cringing, mealy-mouthed, subservient, abject, beggarly, sniveling, prostrate, sneaking, oily; *all* (D): bootlicking, brown-nosing, kowtowing, apple-polishing, flunkyish, toad-eating; see also **docile, obedient** 1.—*Ant.* insulting*, proud, haughty.

obsequiously, *mod.* —*Syn.* servilely, slavishly, subserviently, sycophantically, ingratiatingly, fawningly, abjectly, grovelingly, on one's knees.

observable, *mod.* —*Syn.* perceptible, noticeable, discernible; see **obvious** 1.

observably, *mod.* —*Syn.* noticeably, obviously, notably; see **clearly** 1, 2.

observance, *n.* **1.** [A custom]—*Syn.* ritual, practice, rite; see **custom** 2.
2. [Attention]—*Syn.* awareness, observation, notice; see **attention** 1.

observant, *mod.* **1.** [Given to observing]—*Syn.* keen, alert, penetrating, wide-awake, discerning, perceptive, sharp, eager, interested, discovering, detecting, discriminating, searching, understanding, questioning, deducing, surveying, alive, contemplating, regardful, considering, sensitive, clear-sighted, comprehending, bright, intelligent; *both* (D): on the ball *or* beam, on one's toes; see also **intelligent** 1, **judicious.**—*Ant.* thoughtless*, unobservant, insensitive.
2. [Engaged in observing]—*Syn.* watchful, gazing, attentive, alert, awake, wide-awake, sleepless, wakeful, noticing, viewing, vigilant, reconnoitering, guarding, mindful, on guard, regardful, listening, heedful, on the watch *or* lookout, on the qui vive, looking out, intent on, alive to, careful, undistracted, intent, open-eyed, sharp-eyed, circumspect, cautious, wary, prudent, marking, inspecting, scrutinizing, examining, surveying, all ears *or* eyes (D); see also **watching.**—*Ant.* careless*, heedless, inattentive.

observation, *n.* **1.** [The power of observing]—*Syn.* noticing, recognizing, view, regard, overlook, mark, heedfulness, note, perception, measurement, estimation, conclusion, inspection, scrutiny, investigation, research, search, probe, check, detection, ascertainment, once-over (D); see also **acumen, sight** 1.—*Ant.* indifference*, obstruction, blindness.
2. [A remark]—*Syn.* comment, note, commentary; see **remark, speech** 3.

observatory, *n.* —*Syn.* watchtower, observation post, beacon; see **lookout** 1, **tower.**

observe, *v.* **1.** [To notice]—*Syn.* look at, perceive, recognize; see **see** 1, **witness.**
2. [To watch]—*Syn.* scrutinize, inspect, examine; see **watch** 1.
3. [To comment]—*Syn.* note, remark, mention; see **comment** 1.
4. [To commemorate]—*Syn.* dedicate, solemnize, keep; see **celebrate** 1.
5. [To abide by]—*Syn.* conform to, comply, adopt; see **follow** 2, **obey** 2.

observed, *mod.* **1.** [Noticed]—*Syn.* seen, noted, marked, attended, detected, perceived, viewed, espied, regarded, looked at *or* over, found, overlooked, heeded, ascertained, pointed out, minded, watched, noticed, inspected, discerned, discovered, surveyed, descried, beheld, contemplated, scrutinized, revealed, realized, examined, listened to, heard, checked (off); see also **recognized.** —*Ant.* unnoticed*, unseen, unperceived.
2. [Commemorated]—*Syn.* recalled, memorialized, preserved, respected, freshened, kept, celebrated, solemnized, esteemed, reverenced, honored, venerated, sanctified, regarded, worshiped, kept in mind, minded, consecrated; see also **remembered.**—*Ant.* abandoned*, forgotten, desecrated.

observer, *n.* **1.** [One who watches]—*Syn.* watcher, watchman, sentinel, lookout, sentry, guard, detective, policeman, reconnoiterer, spectator, eyewitness, beholder, onlooker, bystander, passer-by, meddler, peeper, voyeur, prying person, peeping Tom (D); see also **spy, witness.**
2. [One who offers original comment]—*Syn.* commentator, novelist, columnist; see **author** 2, **historian, writer.**

observing, *mod.* **1.** [Observant]—*Syn.* alert, keen, penetrating; see **intelligent** 1, **observant** 1.
2. [Engaged in observing]—*Syn.* attentive, watchful, looking on; see **observant** 2, **watching.**

obsess, *v.* —*Syn.* dominate, possess, hound; see **haunt** 3.

obsessed, *mod.* —*Syn.* haunted, beset, controlled, preoccupied, overpowered, captivated, perplexed, seized, bedeviled, plagued, fixated, hung up (D); see also **troubled** 1, 2.

obsession, *n.* —*Syn.* fixation, fascination, passion, fancy, phantom, craze, delusion, mania, infatuation, fixed idea, *idée fixe* (French), compulsion; *both* (D): bee in one's bonnet, hang-up; see also **attraction** 1, **neurosis.**

obsolescent, *mod.* —*Syn.* becoming obsolete, growing old *or* out of fashion, senescent; see **aging.**

obsolete, *mod.* —*Syn.* antiquated, archaic, out-of-date; see **old** 2, 3, **old-fashioned.**

obstacle, *n.* —*Syn.* restriction, obstruction, hindrance; see **barrier, impediment** 1.

obstetrics, *n.* —*Syn.* tocology, midwifery, O.B. (D); see **medicine** 3.

obstinacy, *n.* —*Syn.* stubbornness, tenacity, reluctance; see **determination** 2, **purpose** 1.

obstinate, *mod.* —*Syn.* stubborn, firm, headstrong, dogged, pertinacious, opinionated, strong-minded, contumacious, opinionative, contradictory, inflexible, positive, perverse, contrary, cantankerous, unimpressible, determined, convinced, resolved, indomitable, adamant, intractable, crotchety, obdurate, self-willed, refractory, unamenable, unalterable, unconquerable, restive, unflinching, unyielding, unbending, immovable, tenacious, decided, heady, unmanageable, bull-headed, mulish, pigheaded, plucky, sulky, case-hardened, fixed, stiff-necked, callous, hard, hardened, relentless, recalcitrant, unrelenting, resistant, repulsive, willful, unwavering, prejudiced, biased, bigoted, dogmatic, unreasonable, unreasoning; *all* (D): hellbent, diehard, set in one's ways; see also **resolute** 2.—*Ant.* docile*, submissive, amenable.

obstinately, *mod.* —*Syn.* doggedly, stubbornly, tenaciously, pertinaciously, mulishly, stiffneckedly, pigheadedly, bullheadedly, like a bull, persistently, unwaveringly, determinedly, unyieldingly, fixedly, resolutely, unreasonably, unreasoningly, perversely, stolidly, resistantly, intractably, inflexibly, headstrongly, willfully, recalcitrantly, obdurately, steadfastly, stanchly, unflinchingly, resolvedly, opinionatedly, immovably, unimpressibly, unconquerably, contumaciously, indomitably, unrelentingly, unamenably, stubbornly as a mule, like a jackass; see also **firmly** 2.—*Ant.* obediently*, docilely, graciously.

obstreperous, *mod.* —*Syn.* boisterous, noisy, raucous; see **loud** 2.

obstruct, *v.* **1.** [To impede with an obstruction] —*Syn.* stop, interfere, terminate; see **hinder, prevent, restrain** 1.

2. [To place an obstruction]—*Syn.* block, clog, barricade; see **bar** 1.

obstruction, *n.* **1.** [The act of obstructing]—*Syn.* circumvention, blocking, checkmate; see **interference** 1, **restraint** 2.

2. [That which obstructs]—*Syn.* difficulty, trouble, roadblock; see **barrier, impediment** 1.

obtain, *v.* **1.** [To gain possession]—*Syn.* occupy, reach, invade, capture, recover, take, grab, accomplish, acquire, procure, get, force from, make use of, fetch and carry, bring out *or* back *or* forth, attain, gain, win, secure, achieve, glean, reap, retrieve, recover, collect, gather, earn, pick (up), purchase, effect, receive, inherit, salvage, pocket, compass, realize, save, hoard, lay up; *all* (D): corral, drum up, scrape up *or* together, come by, score, nab, gobble up, get at, get hold of; beg, borrow, or steal; see also **seize** 2.—*Ant.* give*, donate, present.

2. [Pertain]—*Syn.* be pertinent to, appertain to, bear upon; see **concern** 1.

obtainable, *mod.* —*Syn.* ready, attainable, achievable; see **available.**

obtrusive, *mod.* **1.** [Protruding]—*Syn.* jutting, bulging, projecting; see **prominent** 1.

2. [Presumptuous]—*Syn.* forward, intrusive, impertinent; see **rude** 2.

obtrusively, *mod.* —*Syn.* obviously, crassly, bluntly; see **clearly** 1, 2.

obtuse, *mod.* **1.** [Stupid]—*Syn.* dense, stolid, insensible; see **dull** 3.

2. [Not sharp]—*Syn.* round, blunt, greater than 90°; see **dull** 1.

obtusely, *mod.* —*Syn.* stupidly, dully, unintelligently; see **foolishly.**

obverse, *n.* —*Syn.* face, opposite side, main surface; see **front** 1.

obviate, *v.* —*Syn.* preclude, forestall, block; see **hinder, prevent, restrain** 1.

obvious, *mod.* **1.** [Clearly apparent to the eye] —*Syn.* clear, visible, apparent, public, transparent, observable, perceptible, exposed, undisguised, noticeable, plain, conspicuous, overt, glaring, prominent, standing out, light, bright, open, unmistakable, evident, recognizable, discernible, in evidence, exoteric, in view *or* sight, perceivable, discoverable, distinguishable, accessible, precise, patent, manifest, palpable, distinct; *all* (D): clear as a bell *or* day, sticking out a mile, plain as the nose on one's face, hitting one in the face, leaping to the eye; see also **definite** 2.—*Ant.* obscure*, hidden, indistinct.

2. [Clearly apparent to the mind]—*Syn.* lucid, apparent, conclusive, explicit, understood, intelligible, comprehensible, self-evident, patent, indisputable, unquestionable, undeniable, axiomatic, proverbial, aphoristic, reasonable, broad, unequivocal, unambiguous, on the surface, unmysterious; *all* (D): as plain as the nose on one's face, going without saying, staring one in the face, open and shut; see also **definite** 1, **understandable.** —*Ant.* profound*, ambiguous, equivocal.

3. [Naive]—*Syn.* simple, innocent, unsophisticated; see **inexperienced, naive, young** 2.

obviously, *interj.* —*Syn.* of course, yes, evidently; see **surely.**

obviously, *mod.* —*Syn.* without doubt, unmistakably, certainly; see **clearly** 1, 2.

occasion, *n.* **1.** [An event]—*Syn.* occurrence, incident, happening; see **event** 1, 2.

2. [An opportunity]—*Syn.* chance, excuse, opening; see **opportunity** 1, **possibility** 2.

3. [A time]—*Syn.* moment, instant, season; see **time** 2.

4. [An (immediate) cause]—*Syn.* prompting, incident, antecedent; see **cause** 1, 3, **circumstance** 1.

on occasion—*Syn.* once in a while, sometimes, occasionally; see **hardly, seldom.**

rise to the occasion—*Syn.* do what is necessary, meet an emergency, carry on; see **succeed** 1.

take the occasion—*Syn.* seize *or* use the opportunity, do something, bring about; see **act** 1, **use** 1.

occasion, *v.* —*Syn.* bring about, introduce, do; see **cause.**

occasional, *mod.* **1.** [Occurring at odd times] —*Syn.* sporadic, random, infrequent; see **irregular** 1, **rare** 2.

2. [Associated with a special occasion]—*Syn.* uncommon, not habitual, exceptional; see **unusual** 1, 2.

3. [Intended for special use]—*Syn.* especial, particular, specific; see **exclusive, special** 1.

occasionally, *mod.* —*Syn.* infrequently, at random, irregularly; see **hardly, seldom.**

occlude, *v.* —*Syn.* block, curb, impede; see **close** 2, **prevent.**

occult, *mod.* **1.** [Hidden]—*Syn.* unrevealed, esoteric, obscure; see **hidden** 2, **secret** 1, 3.
2. [Concerning powers beyond those supposedly natural]—*Syn.* mystical, magical, supernatural; see **mysterious** 2, **secret** 1.

occupancy, *n.* —*Syn.* possession, occupation, inhabitance; see **deed** 2, **ownership, title** 2.

occupant, *n.* —*Syn.* lessee, inhabitant, renter; see **resident, tenant.**

occupation, *n.* **1.** [The act of occupying]—*Syn.* seizure, entering, invasion; see **attack** 1, **capture.**
2. [A vocation]—*Syn.* calling, affair, chosen work; see **job** 1, **profession** 1, **trade** 2.
3. [The state of being in possession]—*Syn.* control, use, holding; see **ownership, title** 2.

occupational, *mod.* —*Syn.* professional, career, technical, functional, workaday, official, industrial; see also **vocational.**

occupied, *mod.* **1.** [Busy]—*Syn.* engaged, working, engrossed; see **busy** 1.
2. [Full]—*Syn.* in use, leased, utilized; see **busy** 3, **rented, taken** 2.

occupy, *v.* **1.** [To take possession]—*Syn.* conquer, take over, invade; see **obtain** 1, **seize** 2.
2. [To fill space]—*Syn.* remain, tenant, reside, live in, hold, take up, pervade, keep, own, (be in) command, extend, control, fill an office, maintain, involve, permeate; see also **fill** 2, **sit** 2.—*Ant.* empty*, remove, move.
3. [To absorb attention]—*Syn.* engage, employ, engross, attend, monopolize, fill, interest, immerse, arrest, absorb, take up, utilize, involve, employ one's time in, keep busy, busy, be active with, be concerned with; see also **fascinate.**

occupying, *mod.* **1.** [Filling a place]—*Syn.* holding, obtaining, remaining, situated, posted, assigned to, tenanting, residing, living in, taking up, possessing, permeating, pervading, covering, settled on, controlling, maintaining, commanding, sitting, staying, established in *or* at, owning; *both* (D): set up, running; see also **placed, resting** 2.—*Ant.* gone*, leaving, removing.
2. [Engaging attention]—*Syn.* absorbing, concentrated upon, utilizing, engrossing, attending upon, concerned with, embarking upon, monopolizing, engaging, arresting, working at, attracting, focusing, drawing, exacting, requiring; see also **exciting, interesting.**

occur, *v.* —*Syn.* take place, transpire, befall; see **happen** 1, 2.

occurrence, *n.* **1.** [A usual happening]—*Syn.* happening, incident, episode; see **event** 1.
2. [A strange and unexpected event]—*Syn.* occasion, accident, adventure; see **event** 2.

occur to, *v.* —*Syn.* come to mind, present *or* offer *or* suggest itself, spring, issue, rise, appear, catch one's attention, arrest the thoughts, pass through one's mind, impress one; *all* (D): enter *or* cross one's mind, crop up, strike one.

occur with, *v.* —*Syn.* happen with, coexist, appear with; see **accompany** 3.

ocean, *n.* —*Syn.* great sea, high seas, salt water, seashore, seaside, shores, Oceanus, Neptune, the mighty deep, the main, the great waters, the Seven Seas, mare; *all* (D): big pond, puddle, briny deep, Davy Jones' locker, the cradle of the deep; see also **sea.**
Oceans include the following—Atlantic, Pacific, Arctic, Antarctic, Indian, North Atlantic, South Atlantic, North Pacific, South Pacific.—*Ant.* continent*, lake, river.

ocean floor, *n.* —*Syn.* sea bed, bottom of the sea, offshore lands; see **sea bottom.**

ocean-going, *mod.* —*Syn.* seagoing, seafaring, marine; see **maritime** 2, **nautical.**

oceanic, *mod.* —*Syn.* marine, aquatic, pelagic; see **maritime** 2, **nautical.**

October, *n.* —*Syn.* fall *or* autumn *or* harvest month, football season, "October's bright blue weather," Indian summer, hunting season; see also **autumn, month.**

ocular, *mod.* —*Syn.* viewed, perceived visually, beheld; see **visual.**

oculist, *n.* —*Syn.* ophthalmologist, eye specialist, optometrist; see **doctor** 1.

odd, *mod.* **1.** [Unusual]—*Syn.* queer, unique, strange; see **unusual** 2.
2. [Indefinite]—*Syn.* doubtful, insecure, inexplicit; see **obscure** 1, **uncertain** 2, **vague** 2.
3. [Miscellaneous]—*Syn.* fragmentary, odd-lot, varied; see **different** 2, **various.**
4. [Single]—*Syn.* sole, unpaired, unmatched; see **alone** 1, **single** 1.
5. [Not even]—*Syn.* uneven, remaining, over and above, additional, exceeding, spare, leftover; see also **irregular** 1, 4.—*Ant.* regular*, even, even-numbered.

oddity, *n.* —*Syn.* eccentricity, abnormality, peculiarity; see **characteristic, irregularity** 2, **quirk.**

oddly, *mod.* —*Syn.* curiously, ridiculously, inexplicably; see **foolishly, strangely.**

oddment, *n.* —*Syn.* scrap, shred, fragment; see **bit** 1.

odds, *n.* **1.** [An advantage]—*Syn.* allowance, edge, benefit, difference, superiority; *all* (D): overlay, square odds, place money, show money; see also **advantage** 1.
2. [A probability]—*Syn.* favor, superiority, chances; see **probability.**

odds and ends, *n.* —*Syn.* miscellany, scraps, particles; see **remnants, rummage** 2.

ode, *n.* —*Syn.* formal *or* Pindaric ode, lyric, *canzone* (Italian); see **poetry.**

odious, *mod.* —*Syn.* repellent, repulsive, disgusting; see **offensive** 2.

odium, *n.* **1.** [Hostility]—*Syn.* enmity, malice, aversion; see **hatred** 2, **resentment** 1, 2.
2. [Disgrace]—*Syn.* dishonor, opprobrium, disfavor; see **disgrace** 1, **shame** 2.

odor, *n.* —*Syn.* perfume, fragrance, bouquet; see **smell** 1, 2.

odorless, *mod.* —*Syn.* flat, scentless, unaromatic, unperfumed, unsmelling, unscented, without odor, odor-free, unfragrant, lacking fragrance.—*Ant.* odorous*, fragrant, perfumed.

odorous, *mod.* **1.** [Having an offensive odor] —*Syn.* smelly, stinking, fetid, musty, putrid, foul, redolent, odoriferous, odoriferant, emitting an odor, strong, malodorous, mephitic, tumaceous, stenchladen, nauseous, cloying, cloacal, unsavory,

effluvious, moldy, stale, dank, miasmic; *all* (D): stinky, skunky, pewy; see also **offensive 2, rotten** 1.
2. [Having a pleasant odor]—*Syn.* sweet, spicy, pungent, sweet-scented, sweet-smelling, savory, fragrant, aromatic, perfumed, scented, scent-laden, redolent, odoriferous, odoriferant, olent, spice-laden, "full of the warm south," honeyed, perfumy, perfumatory, balmy, savorous, flower-scented, nectar-scented, rose-scented.—*Ant.* odorless*, stinking, smelly.

of, *prep.*—*Syn.* from, out of *or* from, away from, proceeding *or* coming *or* going from, about, concerning, as concerns, pertaining *or* appertaining *or* peculiar *or* attributed to, characterized by, regarding, as regards, in regard to, referring to, with *or* in reference to, appropriate to, like, belonging *or* related to, having relation to, native to, consequent to, based on, akin to, consanguineous to, connected with; see also **about** 2.

off, *mod.* and *prep.* **1.** [Situated at a distance] —*Syn.* ahead, behind, up front, to one side, divergent, beside, aside, below, beneath, above, far, afar, absent, not here, removed, apart, in the distance, at a distance, gone, away; see also **distant** 1.—*Ant.* here*, at hand, present.
2. [Moving away]—*Syn.* into the distance, away from, farther away, disappearing, vanishing, removing, sheering off, turning aside; see also **away** 1.—*Ant.* returning*, coming, approaching.
3. [Started]—*Syn.* initiated, commenced, originated; see **begun.**
4. [Mistaken]—*Syn.* erring, in error, confused; see **mistaken** 1, **wrong** 2.
5. [(D) Crazy]—*Syn.* odd, peculiar, queer; see **insane** 1.
6. [(D) Not employed]—*Syn.* not on duty, on vacation, gone; see **unemployed.**

offal, *n.*—*Syn.* garbage, refuse, waste; see **trash** 1, 3.

off and on, *mod.*—*Syn.* now and again *or* then, sometimes, occasionally; see **seldom.**

off balance, *mod.*—*Syn.* unbalanced, tipsy, eccentric; see **irregular** 1, 2, **unsteady.**

off base (D), *mod.*—*Syn.* incorrect, faulty, erroneous; see **mistaken** 1, **wrong** 2.

offbeat (D), *mod.*—*Syn.* strange, unique, idiosyncratic; see **unusual** 2.

off-Broadway, *mod.*—*Syn.* noncommercial, not commercialized, *avant-garde* (French), experimental, off-off-Broadway, unconventional, low-cost; see also **artistic** 2, 3.

off center, *mod.*—*Syn.* off-centered, not centered, eccentric; see **irregular** 1, 2, **unsteady.**

off-color, *mod.*—*Syn.* racy, spicy, indelicate; see **risqué.**

off course, *mod.*—*Syn.* strayed, drifting, misguided; see **lost** 1.

offend, *v.*—*Syn.* annoy, affront, outrage; see **anger** 1.

offended, *mod.*—*Syn.* vexed, provoked, exasperated; see **angry, insulted.**

offense, *n.* **1.** [A misdeed]—*Syn.* misdemeanor, malfeasance, transgression; see **crime** 1, 2, **sin.**
2. [An attack]—*Syn.* assault, aggression, battery; see **attack** 1.
Styles of offense in football include the following —*all* (D): running attack, shotgun offense, T-formation, wishbone, passing attack, straight football, power plays, cross-bucks and spinners, flying wedge, razzle-dazzle, the aerial route, the bust-em philosophy.
Styles of offense in basketball include the following —*all* (D): five-man attack, four-man offense, center fan, cartwheel, slow-breaking attack, fast-breaking attack.
3. [Resentment]—*Syn.* umbrage, pique, indignation; see **anger.**

offensive, *mod.* **1.** [Concerned with an attack] —*Syn.* assaulting, attacking, invading; see **aggressive** 2.
2. [Revolting]—*Syn.* obnoxious, odious, opprobrious, disagreeable, displeasing, abhorrent, reprehensible, detestable, repulsive, repugnant, shocking, horrible, horrid, hideous, repellent, nauseating, invidious, nauseous, revolting, distasteful, impious, blasphemous, unspeakable, accursed, unutterable, dreadful, terrible, grisly, ghastly, bloody, gory, infamous, hateful, low, foul, corrupt, bad, indecent, nasty, dirty, unclean, filthy, sickening, malignant, rancid, disgusting, feculent, lousy, verminous, macabre, putrid, vile, impure, beastly, monstrous, coarse, ribald, noxious, loathsome, abominable, stinking, reeking, execrable, purulent, obscene, saprogenous, pernicious, smutty, damnable, distressing, irritating, uncongenial, putrid, unpleasant, uninviting, contaminated, unsympathetic, frightful, malodorous, unattractive, forbidding, disagreeing, adverse, inimical, repelling, incompatible, unsavory, intolerable, unpalatable, dissatisfactory, unpleasing, inharmonious, unsuited, objectionable, annoying, antipathetic, in disfavor, to one's disgust, beneath contempt; *all* (D): bad vibes, cussed, blankety, helluva, gosh-awful, hell-fired, icky, jerkwater, lousy, mangy, rummy, snide, two-bit, pewy; see also **rotten** 1, 3, **shameful** 1, 2, **ugly** 1, 2, **vulgar** 1, **wicked** 1, 2. —*Ant.* pleasant*, agreeable, likable.
3. [Insolent]—*Syn.* impertinent, impudent, insulting; see **rude** 2.

offensive, *n.*—*Syn.* position of attack, invasion, assault; see **attack** 1.

offer, *n.*—*Syn.* proposal, presentation, proposition; see **suggestion** 1.

offer, *v.* **1.** [To present]—*Syn.* proffer, tender, administer, donate, put forth, advance, extend, submit, hold out, grant, allow, award, volunteer, accord, place at one's disposal; *both* (D): lay at one's feet, put up; see also **contribute** 1, **give** 1.—*Ant.* refuse*, withhold, keep.
2. [To propose]—*Syn.* suggest, submit, advise; see **propose** 1.
3. [To try]—*Syn.* attempt, endeavor, strive; see **try** 1.
4. [To occur]—*Syn.* happen, present itself, appear; see **occur to.**

offering, *n.* **1.** [Something contributed]—*Syn.* contribution, donation, present; see **gift** 1.
2. [Something offered to a deity]—*Syn.* oblation, expiation, atonement; see **sacrifice** 1.

offer up, *v.*—*Syn.* present, proffer, immolate; see **sacrifice** 1.

off for *or* **to,** *mod.*—*Syn.* going, departing, leaving; see **traveling** 2.

offhand, *mod.* —*Syn.* at the moment, unprepared, impromptu, informal, extemporary, unpremeditated, ad-lib, off-the-cuff, off-the-record, spontaneous, off the top of one's head (D), unstudied, unrehearsed, improvised, by ear; see also **extemporaneous.**

offhandedly, *mod.* —*Syn.* nonchalantly, heedlessly, thoughtlessly; see **carelessly, indifferently.**

office, *n.* **1.** [A position involving responsibility] —*Syn.* employment, business, occupation; see **job** 1, **profession** 1, **trade** 2.
2. [A function]—*Syn.* performance, province, service; see **duty** 2.
3. [A place in which office work is done]—*Syn.* room, office building, factory, bureau, agency, warehouse, facility, school building, suite; see also **building** 1, **department** 2.
Types of offices include the following—consular, customs, foreign, ambassadorial, ministerial, governmental, business, school principal's, counseling, secretarial, stenographic, filing, typing, insurance, accountant, data processing, real estate, brokerage, bookkeeping, journalistic, recording, law, bank, doctor's, dentist's, psychiatrist's, advertising agency, theater; booking office, box office.

officer, *n.* **1.** [An executive]—*Syn.* manager, director, president; see **administrator, leader** 2.
2. [One who enforces civil law]—*Syn.* magistrate, military police, deputy; see **policeman, sheriff.**
3. [One holding a responsible post in the armed forces]—American officers include the following —*Army commissioned and special officers:* Commander in Chief, Five-star General, Four-star General, Three-star General, Two-star General, One-star general, General of the Army, General *or* Brass Hat (D), Lieutenant General, Major General, Brigadier General, Colonel, Lieutenant Colonel, Major, Captain, First Lieutenant *or* the Brass (D) *or* Brass Looie (D), Second Lieutenant *or* Shave tail (D) *or* Sears-Roebuck Lieutenant (D), Adjutant General, Aide-de-Camp, Chief of Staff, Assistant Chief of Staff, Chaplain *or* Padre (D), Inspector General, Judge Advocate General, Provost Marshal General, Quartermaster General, Surgeon General; *Navy commissioned officers:* Admiral of the Fleet *or* Fleet Admiral, Admiral *or* Five-starrer (D) *or* Four-starrer (D) *or* the Man (D), Rear Admiral *or* Rear (D) *or* Two-starrer (D), Vice Admiral *or* Vice (D), Captain *or* Mister (D) *or* the Old Man (D), Commander *or* Big Gun (D) *or* Three-striper, Lieutenant Commander, Lieutenant *or* Loot (D), Lieutenant, junior grade; Ensign *or* One-striper (D); *Army noncommissioned officers:* Chief Warrant Officer; Warrant Officer, junior grade; Master Sergeant, First Sergeant *or* Top Kick (D) *or* Sarge (D), Technical Sergeant, Staff Sergeant, Sergeant, Mate, Corporal *or* Corp (D) *or* Corpuscle (D), *temporary officers:* Officer Commanding, Commanding Officer *or* CO (D), officer in command of a given area or theater.

official, *mod.* **1.** [Having to do with one's office] —*Syn.* formal, fitting, suitable, befitting, precise, established, ceremonious, according to precedent *or* protocol, proper, correct, accepted, recognized, customary; see also **conventional** 1, 2, 3, **fit** 1, 2. —*Ant.* informal*, unceremonious, ill-fitting.
2. [Authorized]—*Syn.* ordered, endorsed, sanctioned; see **approved.**
3. [Reliable]—*Syn.* authoritative, authentic, trustworthy, true, unquestionable, indubitable, veritable, real, sure, absolute, canonical, positive, clear, unequivocal, unmistakable, decisive, conclusive, unimpeachable, valid, authenticated, credible, bona fide, accurate, faithful, standard, irrefutable, incontestable, verified, proven, indisputable, not to be questioned, definite, assured, decided, to be depended on, to be trusted, worthy of confidence, undeniable, guaranteed, insured; see also **certain** 3, **genuine** 1, **reliable** 2.—*Ant.* unreliable*, unauthentic, unverified.

official, *n.* **1.** [Administrator]—*Syn.* comptroller, director, executive; see **administrator, leader** 2.
2. [A sports official]—*Syn.* referee, umpire, linesman, adjudicator; *all* (D): ref, ump, chain gang; see also **judge** 2.

officially, *mod.* **1.** [In an official manner]—*Syn.* regularly, formally, orderly, befittingly, fittingly, suitably, according to form, ceremoniously, in set form, precisely, according to precedent, conventionally, in an established manner, as prescribed, according to protocol, all in order, according to etiquette, correctly, properly, customarily.—*Ant.* casually*, informally, unceremoniously.
2. [With official approval]—*Syn.* authoritatively, authorized, sanctioned; see **approved, authoritative** 2.

officiate, *v.* —*Syn.* govern, umpire, direct; see **command** 2, **manage** 1.

officious, *mod.* —*Syn.* interfering, self-important, impertinent; see **meddlesome, rude** 2.

off one's hands, *mod.* —*Syn.* free from *or* of, released from, out of one's charge; see **free** 1, 2, 3.

offprint, *n.* —*Syn.* reprint, impression, photostat; see **copy.**

offscouring, *n.* —*Syn.* refuse, rubbish, waste; see **trash** 1, 3.

offset, *v.* —*Syn.* balance, counterbalance, compensate, equalize, set off, requite, recompense, be equivalent, make amends, allow for, charge *or* place against, equipoise, counterpoise, neutralize, counteract, countervail, equal, counterpose, negate, account, rob Peter to pay Paul (D).—*Ant.* burden*, overbalance, overload.

offshoot, *n.* —*Syn.* offspring, by-product, limb; see **branch** 1, 2.

offshore, *mod.* —*Syn.* oceanic, in the sea, marine; see **maritime** 2, **nautical.**

offside (D), *mod.* —*Syn.* foul, faulty, not in *or* on the line; see **illegal, wrong** 1, 2, 3.

offspring, *n.* —*Syn.* progeny, issue, descendant(s), children, sibling(s), lineage, 'scion, generation, posterity, brood, seed, family, heirs, offshoot(s), heredity, succession, successor(s), next generation, chip(s) off the old block (D); see also **baby** 1, **child.**

off-street parking (D), *n.* —*Syn.* private *or* reserved *or* restricted parking, parking lot, designated area; see **parking area.**

off the beam (D), *mod.* —*Syn.* in error, misdirected, confused; see **mistaken** 1, **wrong** 1, 2.

off the cuff (D), *mod.* —*Syn.* impromptu, spontaneous, on the spur of the moment; see **oral, original** 3, **spoken.**

off the record, *mod.* —*Syn.* not for publication, restricted, confidential; see **secret** 1, 3.

off the top of one's head (D), *mod.* —*Syn.* without previous thought, impromptu, spontaneous; see **carelessly, quickly** 1, 2.

off the track (D), *mod.* —*Syn.* ill-advised, bad, crazy; see **mistaken** 1, 2, **wrong** 2, 3.

off work, *mod.* —*Syn.* not on duty *or* working, gone (home), not employed; see **unemployed.**

off year, *n.* —*Syn.* bad *or* poor *or* slack year *or* time *or* period, off season; time of reduced activity *or* voting *or* production, etc.; see **time** 2, **year.**

often, *mod.* —*Syn.* usually, many times, oftentimes; see **frequently, regularly** 1.

ogle, *v.* —*Syn.* gaze, gape, stare; see **look** 2.

ogre, *n.* —*Syn.* fiend, demon, monstrosity; see **freak** 2, **monster** 1.

oh, *interj.* —*Syn.* indeed! oh-oh! oh, no! oh, yes! oops (D); see also **no, yes.**

oil, *n.* **1.** [Liquid, greasy substance]—*Syn.* melted fat, unction, lubricant; see **fat, grease.**
Common oils include the following—vegetable, animal, mineral, fixed, fatty, volatile, essential, machine, crude, lubricating, cottonseed, olive, castor, palm, corn, whale, sperm, cocoa, linseed, drying, semidrying, nondrying, wormwood, pimento, candlenut, poppy-seed, soybean, sesame, cinnamon-bark, tung, cassia, tarragon, vetiver, bergamot, wintergreen, cameline, palmarosa, chenopodium, ilang-ilang, cod-liver, halibut-liver, hake, fish; petroleum, kerosene, lard, tallow, oil of bitter almonds, oleo, Vaseline (trademark), oil of amber, oil of spike lavender, kokum butter, turpentine.
2. [Liquid substance used for power or illumination]—*Syn.* petroleum, kerosene, coal oil, crude oil, liquid coal, rock *or* fossil oil, cerate, liquid gold (D); see also **fuel, petroleum.**

oil, *v.* —*Syn.* lubricate, smear, coat with oil; see **grease.**

oilcloth, *n.* —*Syn.* tablecloth, oilskin, waterproof, shower cloth, oil silk, linoleum, rubberized cloth, tarpaulin; see also **cloth.**

oily, *mod.* **1.** [Rich with oil]—*Syn.* oleaginous, fatty, greasy, buttery, oil-soaked, rich, adipose, pinguid, lardy, bland, soapy, soothing, creamy, oil-bearing, oil-rich, saponaceous, petroliferous.—*Ant.* dry*, dried, gritty.
2. [Having a surface suggestive of oil]—*Syn.* oiled, waxy, sleek, slippery, smooth, polished, lustrous, bright, brilliant, gleaming, glistening, shining, smeary; see also **smooth.**—*Ant.* rough*, dull, unpolished.
3. [Unctuous]—*Syn.* fulsome, supple, suave, compliant, insinuating, flattering, cajoling, coaxing, ingratiating, glib, smooth-tongued, smooth, gushing, smarmy (D); see also **affected** 2.—*Ant.* frank*, candid, brusque.

ointment, *n.* —*Syn.* unguent, lotion, cream; see **balm** 2, **medicine** 2, **salve.**

O.K., *interj.* —*Syn.* all right, correct, surely; see **yes.**

O.K., *n.* —*Syn.* approval, endorsement, affirmation; see **permission.**

O.K., *v.* —*Syn.* confirm, condone, notarize; see **approve** 1, **endorse** 2.

old, *mod.* **1.** [No longer vigorous]—*Syn.* aged, elderly, partriarchal, superannuated, gray, grizzled, venerable, hoary, not young, of long life, past one's prime, far advanced in years, matured, having lived long, full of years, seasoned, debilitated, infirm, inactive, deficient, enfeebled, decrepit, exhausted, tired, impaired, anemic, broken down, wasted, doddering, senile; *all* (D): on the shelf, ancient, gone to seed, with one foot in the grave and the other on a banana peel.—*Ant.* young*, fresh, youthful.
2. [Worn]—*Syn.* time-worn, worn-out, thin, patched, ragged, faded, used, in holes, rubbed off, mended, broken-down, fallen to pieces, tumbled down, fallen in, given way, long used, out of use, rusted, crumbled, past usefulness, dilapidated, weather-beaten, ramshackle, battered, shattered, shabby, castoff, decayed, antiquated, decaying, stale, useless, tattered, in rags, torn, moth-eaten; see also sense 1, **worn** 2.—*Ant.* fresh*, new, unused.
3. [Ancient]—*Syn.* archaic, time-honored, prehistoric, bygone, early, antique, forgotten, pristine, immemorial, antediluvian, olden, remote, past, distant, former, of old, gone by, classic, medieval, in the Middle Ages, unmodern, out of the dim past, primordial, primeval, before history, moss-grown, mossy, belonging to antiquity, uncontemporary, dateless, unrecorded, handed down, of earliest time, of the old order, ancestral, traditional, time out of mind, trogloditic, before the Flood, in the dawn of history, old as the hills (D); see also senses 1, 2.—*Ant.* modern*, recent, late.
4. [Cherished]—*Syn.* good, dear, adored; see **beloved.**
5. [(D) Wonderful]—*Syn.* great, magnificent, superb; see **excellent.**
6. [Grown up]—*Syn.* adult, of (legal) age, grown; see **experienced, mature** 1.
7. [Old-fashioned]—*Syn.* antiquated, obsolete, outmoded; see **old-fashioned.**

old age, *n.* —*Syn.* seniority, dotage, infirmity; see **age** 2, **senility.**

Old English, *mod.* —*Syn.* early English, Anglian, Alfredian; see **Anglo-Saxon.**

older, *mod.* —*Syn.* elder, senior, sooner, former, preceding, of the greater age, prior, more aged, less young, not so new, earlier, first, first-born, having come before, more antique, more antiquated, more ancient, lower, of an earlier time, of an earlier vintage, of a former period; see also **old** 3.—*Ant.* young*, newer, of a later vintage.

oldest, *mod.* —*Syn.* most aged, initial, primeval; see **first** 1, **original** 1.

old-fashioned, *mod.* —*Syn.* antiquated, out-of-date, obsolete, obsolescent, outmoded, demoded, unfashionable, traditional, unstylish, passé, *démodé* (French), before the War, Victorian, not modern, old-time, unaccepted, disapproved, time-honored, not current, antique, ancient, no longer prevailing, bygone, disused, archaic, grown old, superannuated, antediluvian, Neanderthal, primitive, quaint, amusing, odd, neglected, outworn, of long standing, dowdy, musty, unused, in the old ways, of great age, of the old times, past, oldfangled, behind the times, exploded, gone by, of the old school, extinct, out, gone out, out of it; *all* (D): Model-T, out of the swim, back number, old hat, moss-backed, olden; see also **old** 3.—*Ant.* modern*, fashionable, stylish.

old hand, *n.*—*Syn.* old-timer, master, one of the old guard (D); see **veteran** 1.

old lady (D), *n.*—*Syn.* female parent *or* spouse, woman, lover, female member of the family; see **mother** 1, **parent, wife.**

old man (D), *n.* **1.** [Father or husband]—*Syn.* head of the house, male parent *or* spouse, lover, man; see **father** 1, **husband, parent.**

2. [An affectionate address]—*Syn.* my friend, old boy, old chap, old fellow, old bean, buddy; see also **friend** 1.

Old Nick, *n.*—*Syn.* Satan, Prince of Darkness, Evil One; see **devil** 1.

oldster (D), *n.*—*Syn.* old man, veteran, patriarch, dowager, golden-ager, senior citizen, senior adult, retired man *or* woman; *all* (D): old duffer, old codger, geezer, old coot, old goat, old bag, no spring chicken; see also **grandfather, grandmother.**

Old Testament, *n.*—*Syn.* the Covenant, Hebrew Scripture, Jewish *or* Mosaic Law, Pentateuch, Hexateuch, Heptateuch, the Law *or* Torah, the Prophets *or* Neviim, Hagiographa *or* Ketubim, Apocrypha; see also **Bible** 2.

The Hebrew Testament includes the following—Torah: Genesis, Exodus, Leviticus, Numbers, Deuteronomy; Neviim: Joshua, Judges, I Samuel, II Samuel, I Kings, II Kings, Isaiah, Jeremiah, Ezekiel, Hosea, Joel, Amos, Obadiah, Jonah, Micah, Nahum, Habakkuk, Zephaniah, Haggai, Zechariah, Malachi; Ketubim: Psalms, Proverbs, Job, Song of Songs, Ruth, Lamentations, Ecclesiastes, Esther, Daniel, Ezra, Nehemiah, I Chronicles, II Chronicles.

The Christian version (the Old Testament) contains the same books but changes the order somewhat and titles the Song of Songs the Song of Solomon.

old-time, *mod.*—*Syn.* outmoded, ancient, obsolete; see **old-fashioned.**

old-world, *mod.*—*Syn.* Hellenic, archaic, European; see **ancient** 2, **classical** 2.

Old World, *n.*—*Syn.* Eastern Hemisphere; Europe, Asia, and Africa; Eurasia, the cradle of civilization, the Hither-East, the Fertile Crescent; see also **East** 2, **Europe.**

oleaginous, *mod.*—*Syn.* suety, greasy, adipose; see **fatty, oily** 1.

oligarchy, *n.*—*Syn.* theocracy, thearchy, diarchy, triarchy, duarchy, duumvirate, triumvirate, regency, gerontocracy, aristocracy; see also **government** 2.

olive, *mod.*—*Syn.* greenish yellow, blackish green, yellowish green, olive-drab, khaki; see also **drab** 2, **green,** n.

olive, *n.*—*Syn.* stuffed olive, pitted olive, ripe olive, black olive, green olive; see also **fruit** 1.

Olympics, *n.*—*Syn.* Olympian *or* Olympic Games, world championships, international amateur athletic competition; see **competition** 2, **sport** 3.

Modern winter Olympic competitions include the following—two- and four-man bobsledding, ice hockey; 500-meter, 1,500-meter, 3,000-meter (women), 5,000-meter, 10,000-meter speed skating; men's and women's figure skating, figure skating pairs, downhill skiing, cross-country skiing (from women's 5-kilometer through men's 50-kilometer), ski jumping, Nordic combined ski race and jump, ski relay, combined downhill and slalom skiing, giant slalom, slalom biathlon (cross-country and shooting), tobogganing singles and doubles, luge.

Modern summer Olympic competitions include the following—swimming: 100-meter, 200-meter, 400-meter, 1,500-meter freestyle, 100-meter and 200-meter backstroke, 100-meter and 200-meter breaststroke, 100-meter and 200-meter butterfly, 400-meter and 800-meter freestyle relay; track and field: 100-meter, 200-meter, 400-meter, 800-meter, 1,500-meter, 3,000-meter, 5,000-meter and 10,000-meter runs, marathon, 20,000-meter and 50,000-meter walk, 110-meter and 400-meter hurdles, running high and long jumps, 400-meter and 1,600-meter relays, pole vault, hammer throw, discus throw, javelin, triple jump, shot put, modern pentathlon, decathlon, archery, boxing, fencing, shooting, team games, and the like.

Olympus, *n.*—*Syn.* Mount Olympus, abode of the gods, home of the Olympians; see **heaven** 2.

omelet, *n.*—*Syn.* omelette, fried egg, soufflé; see **egg, food.**

Kinds of omelet include the following—plain, jelly, ham, cheese, spinach, parsley, mushroom, Spanish, Denver, chicken-liver, western.

omen, *n.*—*Syn.* portent, augury, indication; see **sign** 1.

ominous, *mod.*—*Syn.* threatening, forbidding, baleful, foreboding, menacing, dark, suggestive, portentous, fateful, ever-threatening, premonitory, dire, direful, ill-omened, grim, gloomy, haunting, perilous, ill-starred, ill-fated, impending, fearful, clouded, unpropitious, inauspicious, presaging, augural, precursive, prescient, prophetic, vatic, vaticinal; see also **dangerous** 2, **dismal** 1, **doomed, frightful** 1, **imminent, sinister.**—*Ant.* favorable*, encouraging, auspicious.

omission, *n.* **1.** [The act of omitting]—*Syn.* overlooking, missing, leaving out, withholding, disregard, oversight, ignoring, failing to mention, not inserting, not naming, preclusion, prohibition, elision, breach, cancellation, repudiation, elimination, cutting out, excluding, passing over, slighting; see also **carelessness, exclusion, neglect** 1.—*Ant.* inclusion*, mentioning, inserting.

2. [Something omitted]—*Syn.* need, want, imperfection; see **lack** 2.

omit, *v.* **1.** [To fail to include]—*Syn.* leave out, except, reject, preclude, repudiate, prohibit, exclude, pass over *or* by, count out, cast aside, delete, drop, cut out, cancel, void, withhold; see also **bar** 2, **discard, dismiss** 1, **eliminate** 1.—*Ant.* include*, accept, put in.

2. [To neglect]—*Syn.* ignore, slight, overlook; see **disregard, neglect** 2.

omitted, *mod.*—*Syn.* left out, overlooked, missing, wanting, slighted, unmentioned, unnamed, not included, uninserted, absent, not present, unnoted, unnoticed, voided, lacking, ignored, withheld, excluded, disregarded, passed over *or* by, counted out, excepted, repudiated, barred, rejected, canceled, cut out, excised, deleted, dropped, precluded, prohibited, kept out; see also **missed** 1, **neglected.**—*Ant.* included*, present, mentioned.

omitting, *mod.* —*Syn.* leaving out, missing, failing to mention, not naming, not including *or* inserting, discarding, withholding, ignoring, neglecting, repudiating, passing over *or* by, excluding, slighting, disregarding, excepting, canceling, casting aside, prohibiting, precluding; see also **overlooking** 2.—*Ant.* including*, mentioning, inserting.

omitting, *n.* —*Syn.* neglecting, ignoring, excluding; see **omission** 1.

omnibus, *n.* **1.** [Anthology]—*Syn.* readings, compilation, selection; see **collection** 2.

2. [Vehicle]—*Syn.* autobus, tram, streetcar; see **bus.**

omnipotence, *n.* —*Syn.* mastery, authority, control; see **dominion** 1, **power** 2.

omnipotent, *mod.* —*Syn.* all-powerful, unlimited in power, godlike; see **almighty** 2.

omnipresent, *mod.* —*Syn.* infinite, everywhere, unbiquitous; see **almighty** 2.

omniscient, *mod.* —*Syn.* infinite, pre-eminent, all-knowing; see **almighty** 2.

omnivorous, *mod.* —*Syn.* rapacious, voracious, gluttonous; see **greedy** 1, 2.

on, *mod.* and *prep.* **1.** [Upon]—*Syn.* above, in contact with, touching, supported by, situated upon, resting upon, on top of, about, held by, moving across *or* over, covering; see also **upon** 1.—*Ant.* under*, underneath, below.

2. [Against]—*Syn.* in contact with, close to, leaning on; see **against** 2, **next** 2.

3. [Toward]—*Syn.* proceeding, at, moving; see **approaching, toward.**

4. [Forward]—*Syn.* onward, ahead, advancing; see **forward** 1.

5. [Near]—*Syn.* beside, close to, adjacent to; see **bordering, near** 1.

and so on—*Syn.* and so forth, also, in addition; see **et cetera.**

have something on someone (D)—*Syn.* know something, have proof, be able to discredit; see **expose** 1.

on account, *mod.* —*Syn.* on credit, payable, credited; see **bought, charged** 1, **due.**

on account of, *mod.* —*Syn.* since, for the sake of, for the reason that; see **because.**

on again, off again (D), *mod.* —*Syn.* intermittently, sometimes, occasionally; see **varying.**

on and off, *mod.* —*Syn.* now and then, sometimes, infrequently; see **seldom.**

on approval, *mod.* —*Syn.* on trial, on probation, subject to refusal, on examination, guaranteed, on a money-back guarantee; see also **temporarily.**

on arrival, *mod.* —*Syn.* having arrived *or* entered *or* landed *or* reached, etc.; upon *or* after landing *or* arriving *or* reaching, etc.; when due, upon arrival.

on board, *mod.* —*Syn.* loaded, shipped, in transit; see **aboard.**

on call, *mod.* —*Syn.* alerted, ready, handy; see **available.**

once, *mod.* **1.** [One time]—*Syn.* this time, but once, once only, before, one time before, already, one, just this once, for the nonce, not more than once, never again, a single time, one time previously, on one occasion, only one time.—*Ant.* twice*, many times, frequently.

2. [Formerly]—*Syn.* long ago, previously, earlier; see **formerly.**

all at once—*Syn.* simultaneously, all at the same time, unanimously; see **together** 2.

at once—*Syn.* now, quickly, this moment; see **immediately.**

for once—*Syn.* for at least one time, once only, uniquely; see **once** 1.

once and for all (D), *mod.* —*Syn.* with finality, permanently, unalterably; see **finally** 1.

once in a blue moon (D), *mod.* —*Syn.* rarely, infrequently, unusually; see **seldom.**

once in a while, *mod.* —*Syn.* sometimes, occasionally, on occasion; see **seldom.**

once more, *mod.* —*Syn.* once again, another time, (done) over; see **again.**

once or twice, *mod.* —*Syn.* a few times, infrequently, not much; see **seldom.**

once-over (D), *n.* —*Syn.* look, inspection, checkup; see **examination** 1.

once over lightly (D), *mod.* —*Syn.* hastily, sketchily, with a lick and a promise (D); see **lightly** 1, **quickly** 1.

once upon a time, *mod.* —*Syn.* in the olden days, long ago, in ancient times; see **formerly.**

oncoming, *mod.* —*Syn.* impending, expected, imminent; see **approaching.**

on demand, *mod.* —*Syn.* payable, collect, C.O.D., when due, on call; see also **bought, due.**

one, *mod.* —*Syn.* individual, peculiar, especial, specific, separate, single, lone, singular, odd, one and only, solitary, singular, precise, definite, sole, uncommon; see also **different** 1, 2, **special** 1, **unique** 1, **unusual** 2.—*Ant.* common*, several, imprecise.

one, *n.* **1.** [A single item]—*Syn.* unit, 1, whole, person, thing, identity, ace, integer, item, example, digit, singleness, individual, individuality, individuation.—*Ant.* plural, many*, several.

2. [The quality of being united]—*Syn.* unitedness, totality, entirety; see **unity** 1.

all one—*Syn.* making no difference, (be) insignificant, of no importance; see **unimportant.**

at one—*Syn.* in accord, agreeing, of the same opinion; see **united.**

tie one on (D)—*Syn.* go on a drinking spree, get drunk, imbibe; see **drink** 2.

one another, *pron.* —*Syn.* each other, reciprocally, each to the other; see **each.**

one-horse (D), *mod.* —*Syn.* small, inadequate, junky (D); see **little** 1, **poor** 2.

one-man, *mod.* —*Syn.* small, limited, restricted; see **little** 1, **single** 5.

one man, one vote, *mod.* —*Syn.* by direct representation, constitutional, representative; see **democratic.**

oneness, *n.* —*Syn.* integrity, harmony, indivisibility; see **unity** 1.

onerous, *mod.* —*Syn.* oppressive, heavy, serious, exacting, demanding, burdensome, galling, troublesome, formidable, grinding, laborious, strenuous, tedious, tiresome, hard, embittering, arduous, plodding, backbreaking, grueling, toilsome, cumbersome, weighty, ponderous, responsible, rigorous, severe, vexatious, harsh, painful, overpowering, crushing, excessive, merciless, overtaxing, taxing, fatiguing, pressing, tiring, exhausting, intolerable, austere, causing care, irksome, distressing, grievous, heartbreaking, afflictive; see also **difficult** 1, 2.—*Ant.* easy*, light, trifling.

one-shot (D), *mod.* —*Syn.* singular, unique, not repeatable; see **once** 1, **single** 5.

one-sided, *mod.* **1.** [Unilateral]—*Syn.* single, uneven, partial; see **irregular** 4, **unilateral.**
2. [Prejudiced]—*Syn.* biased, partial, narrow-minded; see **prejudiced, unfair** 1.

one-time, *mod.* —*Syn.* prior, former, previous; see **past** 1.

one-to-one, *mod.* —*Syn.* made even, in accord, coordinated; see **balanced** 1.

one-way, *mod.* —*Syn.* directional, with no return, restricted; see **directed, narrow** 1.

one-way street (D), *n.* —*Syn.* unreciprocated effort; project *or* affair *or* action, etc., without help *or* cooperation; lone venture; unassisted *or* unsupported operation *or* action *or* attempt, etc.; see also **barrier, impediment** 1.

one with, *mod.* —*Syn.* like, similar (to), following (after); see **alike** 1, 2.

on file, *mod.* —*Syn.* preserved, at hand, filed; see **recorded.**

on fire, *mod.* —*Syn.* aflame, blazing, glowing; see **afire, burning** 1.

ongoing, *mod.* —*Syn.* open-ended, continuous, in process; see **continuing.**

on hand, *mod.* —*Syn.* in stock, stocked, present; see **available.**

on loan, *mod.* —*Syn.* leased, lent, on lease; see **loaned.**

onlooker, *n.* —*Syn.* eyewitness, sightseer, spectator; see **observer** 1.

only, *mod.* **1.** [Solely]—*Syn.* exclusively, uniquely, wholly, entirely, severally, particularly, and no other, and no more, and nothing else, undividedly, nothing but, totally, utterly, first and last, one and only; see also **individually, singly.**
2. [Merely]—*Syn.* just, simply, plainly, barely, solely; see also **hardly.**
3. [Sole]—*Syn.* single, without another companionless, by oneself, isolated, apart, unaccompanied, exclusive, unique, unclassified; see also **alone** 1, **solitary.**

on occasion, *mod.* —*Syn.* occasionally, at certain *or* appropriate times, sometimes; see **seldom.**

onomatopoeia, *n.* —*Syn.* imitation of sounds, echo, mimesis; see **figure of speech.**

on one hand, *mod.* —*Syn.* on one side of the question, from one viewpoint, from one direction.

on one's hands, *mod.* —*Syn.* in one's care, charged with, responsible for; see **responsible** 1.

on or about, *prep.* —*Syn.* at about, approximately, in the vicinity (of); see **at** 1.

on or before, *prep.* —*Syn.* at about the time (of), prior to, in anticipation of; see **before.**

on purpose, *mod.* —*Syn.* knowingly, meaningfully, consciously; see **deliberately.**

onrush, *n.* —*Syn.* rush, assault, surge; see **attack** 1.

on sale, *mod.* —*Syn.* marked down, at a bargain, at a cut rate, on the bargain counter, in the bargain basement, among the remnants; see also **reduced** 2.

on second thought, *mod.* —*Syn.* on mature consideration, as afterthought, in reality; see **incidentally.**

onset, *n.* **1.** [An attack]—*Syn.* rush, assault, encounter; see **attack** 1.
2. [A beginning]—*Syn.* incipience, opening, start; see **origin** 1.

onshore, *mod.* —*Syn.* aground, inland, toward shore; see **ashore**

onslaught, *n.* —*Syn.* assault, invasion, onrush; see **attack** 1.

on tap, *mod.* —*Syn.* fresh from the barrel, ready to be drawn, on draft, free-flowing, on hand; see also **available.**

on the air, *mod.* —*Syn.* broadcasting, going on, televising, in progress, speaking, performing, telecasting, being telecast, live.

on the ball (D), *mod.* —*Syn.* competent, qualified, alert; see **able** 1, 2.

on the beam (D), *mod.* —*Syn.* on course, straight, correct; see **direct** 1.

on the button (D), *mod.* —*Syn.* precisely, squarely, explicitly; see **accurately.**

on the contrary, *mod.* —*Syn.* conversely, antithetically, contrariwise, inversely, contrasting, on the other hand, at the opposite pole, on the other side; see also **oppositely.**

on the market, *mod.* —*Syn.* on *or* for sale, available, purchasable; see **procurable.**

on the mend (D), *mod.* —*Syn.* improving, recovering, getting better; see **convalescent.**

on the occasion of, *prep.* —*Syn.* at the time when, because of, since; see **at** 1, **because, on** 1.

on the part of, *prep.* —*Syn.* in support of, to help, in the interest of; see **for.**

on the side of, *mod.* —*Syn.* in favor of, supporting, working with; see **for, helping.**

on the spur of the moment (D), *mod.* —*Syn.* suddenly, spontaneously, without a second thought; see **quickly** 2.

on the verge (of), *mod.* —*Syn.* not quite, at the point of, almost; see **about to.**

on time, *mod.* —*Syn.* prompt, on schedule, dependable; see **punctual.**

onto, *mod.* and *prep.* **1.** [To]—*Syn.* toward, in contact with, adjacent; see **against** 1.
2. [Upon]—*Syn.* over, out upon, above; see **upon** 1.

ontology, *n.* —*Syn.* science of existence, the nature of being, cosmology; see **metaphysics, philosophy.**

on tour, *mod.* —*Syn.* away, missing, removed; see **absent, traveling** 2.

on trial, *mod.* **1.** [In court]—*Syn.* in litigation, at law, up for investigation *or* hearing, at the bar, before the bar, before a judge *or* jury, being tried *or* judged, indicated; see also **accused.**
2. [Experimentally]—*Syn.* on a trial basis, for a trial period, on approval; see **experimentally.**

on vacation, *mod.* —*Syn.* vacationing, on leave, touring; see **resting** 1, **traveling** 2.

onward, *mod.* —*Syn.* on ahead, beyond, in front of; see **forward** 1, **moving** 1.

onward and upward (D), *mod.* —*Syn.* getting better, profiting, going ahead; see **improving** 1, **rising.**

oodles (D), *n.* —*Syn.* mass, heap, abundance; see **much.**

oops (D), *interj.* —*Syn.* sorry, I beg your pardon, excuse me; see **exclamation.**

ooze, *n.* —*Syn.* slime, fluid, mire; see **mud.**

ooze, *v.* —*Syn.* seep, exude, leak; see **flow** 2.

oozy, *mod.* —*Syn.* muddy, sloppy, slimy; see **wet** 1.

opacity, *n.* —*Syn.* cloudiness, obscurity, murkiness; see **darkness** 1.

opal, *n.* —*Syn.* silica, semiprecious stone, opaline; see **gem** 1, **jewel** 1.
Types of opals include the following—precious, noble, harlequin, black, common, resin, pitch, wood, cacholong, girasol, hyalite, geyserite, menilite.

opalescent, *mod.* —*Syn.* prismatic, rainbow-colored, nacreous; see **bright** 1, 2, **iridescent.**

opaque, *mod.* **1.** [Relatively impervious to light] —*Syn.* nontransparent, dim, dusky, darkened, darkling, murky, gloomy, lusterless, smoky, thick, misty, cloudy, clouded, shady, turbid, muddy, dull, blurred, frosty, filmy, foggy, sooty, dirty, dusty, fuliginous, nubilous, nontranslucent, absorbing light, coated over, covered; see also **dark** 1, **hazy** 1. —*Ant.* clear*, transparent, translucent.
2. [Relatively impervious to understanding]—*Syn.* concealed, enigmatic, perplexing; see **obscure** 1, **vague** 2.

op art, *n.* —*Syn.* optical illusion, abstraction, distortion; see **art** 2, **painting** 1, **sculpture.**

open, *mod.* **1.** [Not closed]—*Syn.* unclosed, accessible, clear, open to view, uncovered, disclosed, divulged, introduced, initiated, inaugurated, begun, full-blown, unfurled, susceptible, ajar, agape, gaping, yawning, wide, rent, torn, spacious, broad gauge, unshut, expansive, extensive, spread out, vistaed, revealed, unenclosed; see also senses 2, 4. —*Ant.* tight*, closed, shut.
2. [Not obstructed]—*Syn.* unlocked, unbarred, unbolted, unblocked, unfastened, cleared (away), removed, made passable, unsealed, unobstructed, unoccupied, vacated, unburdened, emptied; see also sense 1.—*Ant.* taken*, barred, blocked.
3. [Not forbidden]—*Syn.* free (of entrance), unrestricted, permitted, allowable, free of access, public, welcoming, not posted; see also **admissible, permitted.**—*Ant.* refused*, restricted, forbidden.
4. [Not protected]—*Syn.* unguarded, unsecluded, liable, exposed, out in the weather, uncovered, apart, fallen open, unshut, unroofed, insecure, unsafe, conspicuous, unhidden, unconcealed, subject, sensitive; see also **sense** 1, **unsafe.**—*Ant.* safe*, secluded, secure.
5. [Not decided]—*Syn.* in question, up for discussion, debatable; see **controversial, questionable** 1, **uncertain** 2.
6. [Not solid]—*Syn.* airy, fretted, fretworked, openworked, intersticed, filigree; see also **penetrable.**—*Ant.* firm*, solid, impenetrable.
7. [Frank]—*Syn.* plain, candid, straightforward; see **frank.**
8. [Obvious]—*Syn.* apparent, well-known, clear; see **obvious** 1.

open, *v.* **1.** [To begin]—*Syn.* start, inaugurate, initiate; see **begin** 1, 2.
2. [To move aside a prepared obstruction]—*Syn.* unbar, unlock, unclose, clear, admit, turn back, reopen, open the lock, lift the latch, free, loosen, disengage, throw *or* lay open, swing wide, unfasten, undo, unbolt, throw back the bolt, turn the key *or* knob.—*Ant.* close*, shut, lock.
3. [To make an opening]—*Syn.* force an entrance, breach, make an aperture, cut in, tear down, push in, shatter, destroy, burst in, break open, cave in, burst out from, penetrate, cleave, pierce, force one's way into, smash, prick, punch a hole into, slit, puncture, crack; *both* (D): muscle in, jimmy; see also **force** 2, **remove** 1.—*Ant.* repair*, seal, mend.
4. [To make available]—*Syn.* make accessible, put on sale *or* view, open to the public, make public, put forward, free, make obtainable, make usable, prepare, present, make convenient, make ready. —*Ant.* remove*, put away, lock up.
5. [To expose to fuller view]—*Syn.* unroll, unfold, uncover; see **expose** 1, **reveal** 1.

open-air, *mod.* —*Syn.* spacious, outside, outdoors; see **airy** 1.

open-door, *mod.* —*Syn.* unrestricted, unlimited, hospitable; see **free** 1, 2, 3.

opened, *mod.* —*Syn.* unlocked, made *or* thrown open, not closed; see **free** 3, **open** 2.

open-ended, *mod.* —*Syn.* going on, without specified limits, optional; see **continuing.**

open-eyed, *mod.* **1.** [Amazed]—*Syn.* intrigued, astounded, startled; see **surprised.**
2. [Watchful]—*Syn.* gazing, aware, perceptive; see **observant** 2, **watching.**

open fire, *v.* —*Syn.* start, blast, explode; see **begin, shoot** 1.

openhanded, *mod.* —*Syn.* benevolent, charitable, altruistic; see **generous** 1, **kind.**

openhandedly, *mod.* —*Syn.* freely, unstintingly, lavishly; see **generously** 1.

openhearted, *mod.* —*Syn.* true, good, candid; see **frank, honest** 1.

open house, *n.* —*Syn.* hospitality, big party, celebration; see **party** 1.

open housing, *n.* —*Syn.* renting *or* selling without regard to race, creed, or color; unrestricted rentals, fair housing, integrated neighborhood, integration, housing available to anyone, civil rights; see also **choice** 1, **freedom** 1, **liberty** 4, **union** 1.

opening, *mod.* —*Syn.* initial, beginning, primary; see **first** 1.

opening, *n.* **1.** [A hole]—*Syn.* break, crack, tear; see **hole** 1, 2.
2. [An opportunity]—*Syn.* chance, availability, occasion; see **opportunity** 1, **possibility** 2.

openly, *mod.* **1.** [Frankly]—*Syn.* naturally, simply, artlessly, naively, ingenuously, unsophisticatedly, (out) in the open, candidly, aboveboard, forthrightly, straightforwardly, honestly, unreservedly, fully, readily, willingly, without restraint, plainly, undisguisedly, unabashedly, unhesitatingly, without reserve, to one's face, in public; *all* (D): straight from the shoulder, face to face, in the marketplace; see also **sincerely.**—*Ant.* secretly*, furtively, surreptitiously.
2. [Shamelessly]—*Syn.* immodestly, unblushingly, brazenly, not caring, regardlessly, insensibly, unconcernedly, crassly, arrantly, brassily, insolvently,

flagrantly, wantonly, notoriously, affronting decency, without pretense, in defiance of the law; see also **carelessly, lewdly.**—*Ant.* carefully*, prudently, discreetly.

open-minded, *mod.*—*Syn.* tolerant, fair-minded, just; see **fair** 1, **liberal** 2.

open-mouthed, *mod.*—*Syn.* astonished, amazed, aghast; see **surprised.**

open out, *v.*—*Syn.* fan (out), diverge, enlarge; see **grow** 1, **spread** 2.

open sea, *n.*—*Syn.* high seas, the (briny) deep, (the) waves; see **ocean.**

open season (D), *n.*—*Syn.* license to kill, unrestricted hostility, freedom to criticize *or* denounce; see **objection** 1.

open sesame (D), *n.*—*Syn.* means of admission, code, sign; see **key** 2, **password.**

open shop, *n.*—*Syn.* non-union labor *or* employment, anti-union business, free business; see **labor** 4, **labor union.**

open up, *v.*—*Syn.* enlarge, become fluid, start; see **begin** 2, **grow** 1, **spread** 2.

opera, *n.*—*Syn.* musical drama, opera score, libretto, opera performance; see also **performance** 2, **show** 1.
Kinds of operas include the following—grand, light, comic; *opéra bouffe, opéra comique* (*both* French), *opera buffa* (Italian), opera ballet, operetta, chorale.

operate, *v.* **1.** [To keep in operation]—*Syn.* manipulate, conduct, administer; see **command** 2, **manage** 1.
2. [To be in operation]—*Syn.* function, work, serve, carry on, run, revolve, act, behave, fulfill, turn, roll, spin, pump, lift, spark, explode, burn, move, progress, advance, proceed, go, contact, hit, engage, transport, convey, contain, exert; *all* (D): click, tick, percolate; see also **perform** 1.—*Ant.* stop*, stall, break down.
3. [To produce an effect]—*Syn.* react, act on, influence, bring about, determine, turn, bend, contrive, work, accomplish, fulfill, finish, complete, benefit, compel, promote, concern, enforce, take *or* have effect, work on, succeed; *all* (D): get results, get across, turn the trick; see also **achieve** 1, **produce** 1.
4. [To carry out a surgical procedure]—*Syn.* excise, cut, remove diseased tissue, amputate, transplant (an organ), set (a bone), explore, carve up (D); see also **treat** 3.

operated, *mod.*—*Syn.* conducted, handled, run, carried on, regulated, ordered, maintained, supervised, superintended, governed, administered, wielded, transacted, performed, conveyed, transported, moved, determined, achieved, contrived, accomplished, fulfilled, promoted, enforced, worked, served, guided, executed, sustained, used, practiced, put into effect, revolved, turned, spun, finished, driven, brought about, bent, manipulated, negotiated; see also **directed, managed** 2.

operating, *mod.* **1.** [Causing to function]—*Syn.* managing, conducting, directing, executing, manipulating, administering, ordering, regulating, supervising, running, wielding, transacting, guiding, putting into effect, sustaining, maintaining, performing, practicing, revolving, promoting, determining, moving, turning, spinning, driving, contriving, fulfilling, accomplishing, finishing, effecting, bringing about, serving, enforcing, in operation, at work; see also **using.**
2. [Functioning]—*Syn.* acting, producing, going; see **running** 2, **working.**

operating, *n.*—*Syn.* management, direction, control; see **managing, operation** 1.

operation, *n.* **1.** [The act of causing to function]—*Syn.* execution, guidance, superintendence, carrying out, ordering, order, maintenance, handling, manipulating, manipulation, supervision, control, conduct, agency, compelling, promoting, enforcing, enforcement, advancement, controlling, administering, regulating, running, supervising, directing, transacting, transaction, conducting; see also **administration** 1, **regulation** 1.
2. [An action]—*Syn.* performance, act, employment, labor, service, carrying on, transaction, deed, doing, proceeding, handiwork, workmanship, exploitation, enterprise, movement, progression, progress, development, engagement, transference, conveyance, undertaking; see also **action** 1, **work** 2.
3. [A method]—*Syn.* process, formula, procedure; see **method** 2, **plan** 2.
4. [Surgical treatment]—*Syn.* dismemberment, surgery, vivisection, dissection, biopsy, emergency operation, acupuncture, exploratory operation, clinical trial, section, excision, removal, the knife (D); see also **medicine** 3, **surgery, transplant.**
Common operations include the following—appendectomy, cystectomy, hysterectomy, mastectomy, tonsillectomy, gastrectomy, hemorrhoidectomy, colostomy, castration, abortion, lobotomy, psychosurgery, caesarian section, plastic surgery *or* facelifting (D), dermoplasty, rhinoplasty, amputation, autopsy *or* post-mortem.

operative, *mod.*—*Syn.* influential, adequate, efficient; see **effective.**

operator, *n.* **1.** [One who operates a machine]—*Syn.* engineer, operative, operant, skilled *or* trained employe(e); see also **laborer, workman.**
Kinds of operators include the following—telephone, computer, switchboard, PBX, long-distance, information, emergency; typist, copyist, mimeographer, Xerographer (trademark).
2. [One who operates workable property]—*Syn.* executive, supervisor, director; see **administrator.**
3. [(D) Manipulator]—*Syn.* speculator, scoundrel, fraud; see **rascal.**

ophthalmologist, *n.*—*Syn.* eye doctor, eye specialist, optic surgeon; see **doctor** 1.

opiate, *n.* **1.** [Anything that pacifies]—*Syn.* pacifier, sedative, anodyne; see **tranquilizer** 2.
2. [A pacifying drug]—*Syn.* morphine, codeine, opium derivative; see also **drug** 2, **medicine** 2, **opium.**

opinion, *n.* **1.** [A belief]—*Syn.* notion, view, sentiment, conception, idea, surmise, impression, inference, conjecture, inclination, fancy, imagining, supposition, suspicion, notion, assumption, guess, theory, thesis, theorem, postulate, hypothesis, point of view, presumption, presupposition, persuasion, mind; see also **belief** 1, **viewpoint.**
2. [A considered judgment]—*Syn.* estimation, conviction, conclusion; see **judgment** 3, **verdict.**

opinionated, *mod.*—*Syn.* bigoted, stubborn, unyielding; see **obstinate, prejudiced.**

opium, *n.*—*Syn.* opiate, soporific, dope (D); see **drug** 2.
Derivatives of opium include the following—morphine, laudanum, codeine, narcotine, narceine, papaverine, thebaine, paramorphine, diamorphine, heroin, laudanidine, diacetylmorphine, cryptopine, oxydimorphine, rheadine, oxynarcotine, laudanum, gnoscopine, lanthopine, laudanine, meconin, deuteropine, laudanosine, protopine, hydrocotarnine, chandu.

opponent, *n.* **1.** [A rival]—*Syn.* competitor, claimant, emulator, striver, contender, challenger, candidate, equal, entrant, the opposition oppositionist, aspirant, bidder; see also **contestant.**—*Ant.* supporter*, defender, abettor.
2. [An opposing contestant]—*Syn.* antagonist, disputant, contestant, filibusterer, litigant; *all* (D): clasher, scrapper, tangler; see also **player** 1.—*Ant.* associate*, partner, colleague.
3. [An enemy]—*Syn.* foe, adversary, assailant; see **enemy** 1, 2.

opportune, *mod.*—*Syn.* fitting, suitable, fortuitous; see **convenient** 1, **helpful** 1, **timely.**

opportunism, *n.*—*Syn.* expediency, timeliness; *both* (D): making hay while the sun shines, striking while the iron is hot; see also **advantage** 3.

opportunist, *n.*—*Syn.* vacillator, carpetbagger, timeserver, trimmer, ingrate, bounder, self-seeker, go-getter; see also **businessman, politician** 3, **rascal.**

opportunity, *n.* **1.** [Favorable circumstances]—*Syn.* chance, occasion, suitable circumstance, juncture, excuse, happening, contingency, event, befalling, probability, fitness, fortuity, good fortune, luck, hap; *both* (D): fair go, (even) break; see also **possibility** 2.
2. [A suitable time]—*Syn.* occasion, moment, time and tide; see **timeliness.**

oppose, *v.* **1.** [To hold a contrary opinion]—*Syn.* object, expose, disapprove, debate, dispute, contradict, argue, search out, deny, run counter to, protest, defy, cross, taunt, controvert, cope, speak against, gainsay, confront, thwart, neutralize, reverse, turn the tables, not countenance, be opposed to, oppose change, not have any part of, face down, militate against, interfere with, disapprove of, cry out against, disagree (with), not conform, run against *or* counter to, come in conflict with, not abide, go contrary to, part company with, frown at, not be good for, not accept, call in question, be at cross purposes, contrast *or* conflict *or* grapple with, doubt, be reluctant *or* against *or* unwilling, reject, dislike, demur, deprecate, take exception, repudiate, repugn, question, probe, resist, confound, confute, refute, stand up for the other side; *all* (D): cry out against, buck, turn thumbs down, cry down, swim against the stream, have a brush with; see also sense 2, **dare** 2, **face** 1.—*Ant.* agree*, approve, accept.
2. [To fight]—*Syn.* resist, battle, encounter, bombard, assault, attack, assail, storm, protest, clash, meet, skirmish, engage, contest, face, restrain, go *or* match *or* turn *or* count *or* mark against, uphold, defend, rebel, revolt, secede, mutiny, strike back, combat, run counter to, defy, snub, infringe, strive (against), run against, grapple with, fight off, withstand, repel, guard, safeguard, act, shield, counterattack, struggle, outflank, antagonize, retaliate, impede, overpower; *all* (D): take on all comers, scrap, lock horns (with), go to the mat, fly in the face of; see also **fight** 2.

opposed, *mod.*—*Syn.* antagonistic (to), averse, opposite, against, contrary, restrictive, hostile (to), at odds, disputed, counter (to), at cross-purposes; *all* (D): up against, against the grain, at the other end of the spectrum; see also **reluctant, unwilling.**

opposing, *mod.* **1.** [In the act of opposition]—*Syn.* conflicting, clashing, combating, objecting, disagreeing, exposing, disputing, denying, protesting, controverting, crossing, gainsaying, battling, confronting, reversing, neutralizing, facing, stemming, meeting, breasting, withstanding, repelling, defending, resisting, counteracting, outflanking, in defiance of, at variance, at cross-purposes, in disagreement with, in opposition to; *all* (D): at loggerheads *or* odds *or* feud, on the outs, at daggers drawn.—*Ant.* helping*, agreeing, defending.
2. [Belonging to the opposition or constituting the opposition]—*Syn.* inimical, antonymous, hostile, adverse, antithetic, obstructive, recalcitrant, antagonistic, conflicting, calumniating, competitive, rival, aspiring, contesting, defensive, resistive, resistant, challenging, disputative, litigative, defying, unfavorable, sinister, contradictory; see also **unfriendly.**—*Ant.* friendly*, favorable, allied.
3. [Situated opposite]—*Syn.* contrary, facing, fronting; see **opposite** 3.

opposing, *n.*—*Syn.* opposition to, denial, contest; see **fight** 1, **opposition** 1.

opposite, *mod.* **1.** [Contrary]—*Syn.* antithetical, diametric, reversed; see **different** 1.
2. [In conflict]—*Syn.* adverse, inimical, hostile; see **opposing** 2.
3. [So situated as to seem to oppose]—*Syn.* facing, fronting, in front of, abreast, on different sides of, on opposite sides, in opposition to, contrasting, on the other side of, contrary, (over) against, front to front, back to back, nose to nose, on the farther side, retrograde, opposing, diametrical, vis-à-vis, eyeball to eyeball (D).—*Ant.* matched*, on the same side, side by side.

opposite, *n.*—*Syn.* contradiction, contrary, converse, direct opposite, opposition, foil, vice versa, antithesis, antipodes, antistrophe, antonym, counter term, counterpart, inverse, reverse, adverse, the opposite pole, the other extreme, the other side, the opposite term *or* force *or* idea, etc.; see also **contrast** 2.—*Ant.* alike*, same, a related *or* similar thing.

oppositely, *mod.*—*Syn.* contrarily, reversely, counter, opposed, in the negative, any rather; see also **otherwise** 1.

opposition, *n.* **1.** [The act of opposing]—*Syn.* hostilities, conflict, clash, strife, combat, contention, facing, confronting, coping with, breasting, meeting, stemming, belieing, struggle, encounter, buffeting, resisting, resistance, defense, counterattack, outflanking, neutralizing, grapple, war, warfare, skirmish, brush, fray, engagement, action, withstanding, repelling, duel, trial by battle, collision, contest, overpowering, running counter to, race, handicap, check, counteraction, contradiction, debate, countervail, vying with, obstruction, thwart; *all* (D): competish, bucking, opposish, cross (up), slough; see also **battle** 2, **fight** 1.—*Ant.* peace*, cessation, surrender.

2. [The attitude suggestive of opposition]—*Syn.* dislike, repugnance, hostility, antagonism, defiance, objectionableness, antipathy, abhorrence, detestation, aversion, constraint, restriction, restraint, hindrance, tyranny, misrule, discord, want of harmony, incompatibility, distaste, disfavor, dissatisfaction, discontent, displeasure, irritation, offense, chagrin, humiliation, mortification, disagreement, anger, loathing, disapproval, complaint, discontentment, inconvenience; see also **hate, hatred** 1, 2, **malice, resentment.**—*Ant.* support*, enthusiasm, accord.

3. [The individual or group that opposes]—*Syn.* antagonist, disputant, adversary; see **enemy** 1, 2, **opponent** 1, 2.

oppress, *v.* —*Syn.* trouble, plague, suppress, trample, harass, worry, crush, annoy, maltreat, hinder, vex, handicap, overload, hamper, strain, encumber, press *or* beat down, saddle, smother, hound, ride roughshod over, burden with, depress, dispirit, dishearten, bear hard upon, go ill with, lie on, keep under *or* down, take liberties (with), put upon; see also **abuse** 1, **bother** 2.

oppressed, *mod.* —*Syn.* misused, downtrodden, browbeaten, enslaved, henpecked, mistreated, maltreated, burdened, taxed, hampered, like dirt (under one's feet); see also **abused.**

oppression, *n.* **1.** [Organized cruelty]—*Syn.* tyranny, hardness, domination, coercion, dictatorship, fascism, persecution, severity, harshness, subjugation, abusiveness, abuse, subduing, conquering, overthrowing, compulsion, force, forcibleness, torment, military control, martial law; see also **cruelty.** —*Ant.* freedom*, liberalism, voluntary control.

2. [Low spirits]—*Syn.* melancholy, weariness, worry; see **depression** 2, **grief** 1.

oppressive, *mod.* —*Syn.* troublesome, confining, burdensome; see **difficult** 1, 2.

oppressively, *mod.* —*Syn.* severely, hard, restrictively; see **brutally.**

opprobrious, *mod.* **1.** [Expressing slander]—*Syn.* scurrilous, slanderous, abusive, insulting, libeling, defaming, shaming, reproaching, offending, dishonoring, disgracing, pejorative, abasing, humiliating, calumniating, damaging, injuring, injurious, hurting, causing disrepute, maligning, detractive, derogative, disparaging, depreciative, debasing, denigrating, vituperative, spiteful, contumelious, reviling, malevolent, malignant, malign, despiteful; see also **embarrassing, insulting.**—*Ant.* appreciative*, praising, eulogizing.

2. [Involving slander]—*Syn.* hateful, infamous, disgraceful, scandalous, vulgar, vile, abusive, ignoble, contemptuous, ignominious, dishonorable, base, libelous, defamatory, odious, atrocious, detestable, malicious, abominable, nefarious, ill-willed, heinous, outrageous, shocking, flagrant, execrable; see also **offensive** 2, **shameful** 1, 2.—*Ant.* friendly*, honorable, commendable.

opprobrium, *n.* —*Syn.* disrepute, ignominy, stigma; see **disgrace** 2, **insult** 1.

opt (for), *v.* —*Syn.* choose, decide, pick; see **choose** 1, **decide.**

optic, *mod.* —*Syn.* ocular, of the vision, optical; see **visual.**

optical, *mod.* —*Syn.* ocular, seeing, visible; see **visual.**

optimism, *n.* **1.** [Belief in the essential goodness of the universe]—*Syn.* mysticism, logical realism, philosophy of goodness, belief in progress, Leibnitz's doctrine; see also **faith, idealism** 2.—*Ant.* sadness*, pessimism, cynicism.

2. [An inclination to expect or to hope for the best] —*Syn.* cheerfulness, hopefulness, confidence, assurance, sanguineness, encouragement, happiness, brightness, enthusiasm, good cheer, exhilaration, buoyancy, trust, looking on the bright side, seeing through rose-colored glasses, calmness, elation, expectancy, expectation, anticipation, easiness, sureness, Pollyannaism, certainty.—*Ant.* gloom*, despair, melancholy.

optimist, *n.* —*Syn.* Pollyanna, dreamer, positivist; see **idealist.**

optimistic, *mod.* **1.** [Inclined to hope for the best, or to expect it]—*Syn.* cheerful, sanguine, assured; see **confident** 3, **hopeful** 1, **trusting** 2.

2. [Predicting improvement]—*Syn.* promising, cheering, encouraging; see **hopeful** 2.

optimistically, *mod.* —*Syn.* expectantly, encouragingly, with good hope(s) *or* expectation(s); see **favorably** 1, **hopefully** 1.

optimum, *mod.* —*Syn.* select, choice, maximum; see **best** 1, **excellent.**

option, *n.* **1.** [A choice]—*Syn.* selection, alternative, dilemma; see **choice** 3, **preference.**

2. [A privilege to purchase]—*Syn.* right, prerogative, grant, claim, license, lease, franchise, advantage, security, immunity, benefit, title, prior claim, dibs (D).

3. [The power to choose]—*Syn.* free will, discretion, opportunity; see **choice** 1, **choosing.**

4. [The act of choosing]—*Syn.* decision, consideration, appraisal; see **judgment** 2.

optional, *mod.* —*Syn.* discretionary, elective, nonobligatory, noncompulsory, free, unrestricted, arbitrary, unforced, volitional, not required, according to one's will; *both* (D): with no strings attached, take it or leave it; see also **voluntary.**—*Ant.* necessary*, compulsory, enforced.

opulent, *mod.* **1.** [Rich]—*Syn.* affluent, prosperous, wealthy; see **rich** 1.

2. [Plentiful]—*Syn.* profuse, abundant, luxuriant; see **plentiful** 1, 2.

opulently, *mod.* —*Syn.* richly, wealthily, luxuriously; see **largely** 2, **well** 2, 3.

opus, *n.* —*Syn.* piece, creation, product; see **literature** 2, **music** 1, **work** 3.

or, *conj.* **1.** [A suggestion of choice]—*Syn.* or only, or but, as an alternative *or* choice *or* substitute, on the other hand, in turn, conversely, in other words, or else, in preference to, preferentially; see also **either.**—*Ant.* neither*, nor, without choice.

2. [A suggestion of correction]—*Syn.* or not, or not exactly, in reverse, reversing it, on the contrary, contrary to, oppositely, or rather, instead of, correctly speaking; see also **instead, rather** 2.

3. [A suggestion of approximation]—*Syn.* roughly, about, practically; see **approximately.**

oracle, *n.* **1.** [A revelation]—*Syn.* commandment, edict, canon; see **law** 3.

2. [A prophet]—*Syn.* soothsayer, Cassandra, fortuneteller; see **prophet.**

oracular, *mod.* **1.** [Vague or obscure]—*Syn.* ambiguous, mysterious, cryptic; see **obscure** 1, 3, **vague** 2.

2. [Prophetic]—*Syn.* soothsaying, foretelling, prophesying, forecasting, predicting, presaging, foreboding, auguring, portending, prognosticating, discovering, divining, foreknowing, foreseeing, clairvoyant, divulging, anticipating, apprehending, declaring, proclaiming, fatidic, occult, sibylline, vaticinal, vatic, interpretive; see also **mysterious** 2. —*Ant.* objective*, scientific, realistic.

3. [Authoritative]—*Syn.* dogmatic, peremptory, imperious; see **authoritative** 2.

oral, *mod.* —*Syn.* vocal, verbal, uttered, voiced, lingual, unwritten, phonetic, phonic, articulate, ejaculatory, phonated, sounded, from the lips *or* mouth, in the mouth, not written, nuncupative, acroamatic, by word of mouth; see also **spoken.** —*Ant.* written*, unspoken, printed.

orally, *mod.* —*Syn.* verbally, not written, by word of mouth; see **literally, personally** 2, **spoken.**

orange, *mod.* —*Syn.* reddish, ocherous, glowing; see **orange,** *n.* 1.

orange, *n.* **1.** [Color]—*Syn.* red-yellow, apricot, tangerine, burnt orange, peach, coral, salmon; see also **color** 1.

2. [Fruit]—*Syn.* citrus fruit, tropical fruit, sour orange; see also **food, fruit** 1.

Classes and varieties of oranges include the following—wild, China, sweet, common, bitter, Seville, bergamot, mandarin, tangerine, ugli (fruit), navel, Bahia, Washington navel, St. Michael's, egg, Bittencourt, Dom Louise, Maltese, Excelsior, Brown's white, silver, Plata, Jaffa, blood, Valencia, king, Satsuma, Florida.

oration, *n.* —*Syn.* discourse, sermon, address; see **speech** 3.

orator, *n.* —*Syn.* lecturer, declaimer, pleader; see **speaker** 2.

oratorical, *mod.* —*Syn.* rhetorical, eloquent, declamatory, bombastic, loud, noisy, pompous, theatrical, stylistic, expressive, forceful, persuasive, fervid, vivid, elocutionary, intoning, senatorial, gesturing, gesticulative, elaborate, impassioned, lofty, noble, high-sounding, inflated, orotund, tumid, grandiloquent, dramatic, histrionic, artificial, important, stagy, imposing, ostentatious, in the grand style, Periclean; see also **fluent** 2, **verbose.** —*Ant.* natural*, undramatic, simple.

oratorically, *mod.* —*Syn.* wordily, bombastically, rhetorically; see **loudly, spoken, verbosely.**

oratory, *n.* —*Syn.* rhetoric, eloquence, elocution; see **speech** 3.

orb, *n.* —*Syn.* sphere, globe, ball; see **circle** 1.

orbit, *n.* **1.** [Path described by one body revolving around another]—*Syn.* ellipse, circle, ring, circuit, apogee, course, perigee, lap, round, cycle, curve, parabolic orbit, synchronous orbit, hold pattern, transfer orbit, flight path; see also **revolution** 1.

2. [Range of activity or influence]—*Syn.* arena, range, field, boundary, limit, circumference, compass, circle, bounds, department, domain, dominion, jurisdiction, precinct, province, realm; see also **area** 2.

orbit, *v.* **1.** [To revolve around another body] —*Syn.* encircle, (en)compass, ring, move in a circuit, go around, revolve; see also **circle.**

2. [To put into orbit]—*Syn.* fire, blast *or* lift off, project; see **launch** 2.

orbited, *mod.* —*Syn.* put *or* placed *or* lofted *or* sent into orbit, put *or* sent up, rocketed; see **driven, launched, sent.**

orbiting, *mod.* —*Syn.* circling, encircling, going around; see **moving** 1, **revolving** 1.

orchard, *n.* —*Syn.* fruit trees, nut trees, fruit plantation *or* farm; apple orchard, peach orchard, etc.; see also **farm.**

orchestra, *n.* —*Syn.* musical ensemble, symphony, *Kapelle* (German); see **band** 4.

Types of orchestras include the following—concert, symphony, philharmonic, chamber, string, dance, jazz, radio, television, studio, theater, swing, sinfonietta, jazz band; *all* (D): battery, menagerie, hot orchestra.

orchestral, *mod.* —*Syn.* symphonic, operatic, instrumental, concert, philharmonic, scored for orchestra; see also **musical** 1.

orchestrate, *v.* —*Syn.* harmonize, score, arrange; see **compose** 3.

ordain, *v.* **1.** [To establish]—*Syn.* install, institute, appoint; see **enact** 1.

2. [To destine]—*Syn.* determine, foreordain, intend; see **predetermine.**

3. [To invest with priestly functions]—*Syn.* install, confer holy orders upon, consecrate, frock, delegate, invest; see also **bless** 3.

ordained, *mod.* **1.** [Ordered]—*Syn.* commanded, determined, established by law *or* ordinance *or* edict *or* declaration, etc.; see **established** 2, **ordered** 2.

2. [Invested into the ministry]—*Syn.* consecrated, anointed, received into the ministry; see **graduated** 1, **named** 2.

ordeal, *n.* —*Syn.* tribulation, distress, calamity; see **difficulty** 1, 2, **trial** 3.

order, *n.* **1.** [A command]—*Syn.* direction, mandate, injunction; see **command** 1, **law** 3.

2. [Sequence]—*Syn.* progression, succession, procession; see **line** 1, **sequence** 1, **series.**

3. [Orderly arrangement]—*Syn.* regulation, plan, disposition, management, establishment, method, distribution, placement, scale, rule, computation, adjustment, adaptation, ordering, ranging, standardizing, marshaling, aligning, lining up, trimming, grouping, composition, cast, assortment, disposal, scheme, form, routine, array, procedure, method, index, cosmos, regularity, uniformity, symmetry, harmony, placement; *all* (D): layout, line-up, setup; see also **classification** 1, **system** 1.—*Ant.* confusion*, disarray, displacement.

4. [Organization]—*Syn.* society, sect, company; see **organization** 3.

5. [A formal agreement to purchase]—*Syn.* engagement, reserve, application, requisition, request, stipulation, booking, arrangement; see also **buying, reservation** 1.

6. [The amount purchased in an order, sense 5] —*Syn.* amount, purchase, bulk; see **quantity, shipment.**
7. [Peace]—*Syn.* calm, quiet, peacefulness; see **peace** 1, 2.
8. [Kind]—*Syn.* hierarchy, rank, degree; see **class** 1, **classification** 1.
9. [Customary method]—*Syn.* ritual, rite, plan; see **custom** 2, **tradition** 1.
10. [Social rank]—*Syn.* station, status, position; see **rank** 3.
by order of—*Syn.* according to, by the authority of, under the command of; see **for.**
call to order—*Syn.* ask to be quiet, start a meeting, congregate; see **assemble** 1.
in order—*Syn.* working, efficient, operative; see **effective.**
in order that—*Syn.* so that, to the end that, for; see **because.**
in order to—*Syn.* for the purpose of, as a means to, so that; see **to** 6.
in short order—*Syn.* rapidly, without delay, soon; see **quickly** 1.
on order—*Syn.* requested, on the way, sent for; see **ordered** 1.
on the order of—*Syn.* approximately, roughly, similar to; see **like.**
tall order (D)—*Syn.* a difficult task, problem, responsibility; see **difficulty** 2.

order, *v.* **1.** [To give a command]—*Syn.* direct, dictate, decree; see **command** 1, **require** 2.
2. [To authorize a purchase]—*Syn.* secure, reserve, request; see **buy** 1, **obtain** 1.
3. [To put in order]—*Syn.* arrange, furnish, regulate, establish, dispose, manage, systematize, space, methodize, file, put away, classify, distribute, alphabetize, regularize, normalize, get information, pattern, formalize, settle, fix, locate, dress up, get things into proportion, sort out, index, put to rights, set *or* establish *or* lay down guide lines *or* parameters (for), adjust, adapt, set in order, assign, place, regiment, trim, range, align, standardize, marshal, plan, group; see also **line** 3, **organize** 1,—*Ant.* confuse*, disarrange, disarray.

ordered, *mod.* **1.** [On order]—*Syn.* requested, requisitioned, applied *or* sent for, bespoken, spoken for, engaged, booked, arranged for, stipulated, retained, written for, telephoned for; see also **reserved** 1.
2. [Commanded]—*Syn.* directed, ordained, commanded, charged, dictated, regulated, decreed, ruled, enjoined, bidden, imposed, authorized, proclaimed, exacted, forbidden, interdicted, required, proscribed, prescribed, announced, by order *or* command, as ordered, under one's jurisdiction; see also **approved, requested.**—*Ant.* omitted*, revoked, optional.
3. [Put in order]—*Syn.* arranged, regulated, placed; see **classified, organized.**

ordering, *n.*—*Syn.* regulation, organization, systemization; see **order** 3, **system** 1.

orderly, *mod.* **1.** [Ordered; *said of objects and places*]—*Syn.* neat, tidy, arranged; see **clean** 1, **neat** 1.
2. [Methodical; *said of persons*]—*Syn.* systematic, correct, formal, businesslike, systematical, exact, tidy, neat, uncluttered, shipshape, thorough, precise; see also **careful, regular** 3.—*Ant.* irregular*, inaccurate, unmethodical.
3. [Peaceful]—*Syn.* quiet, at peace, submissive; see **calm** 1, 2, **tranquil** 1.

orderly, *n.*—*Syn.* aide, steward, valet; see **attendant.**

ordinance, *n.*—*Syn.* direction, mandate, authorization; see **command** 1, **law** 3.

ordinarily, *mod.*—*Syn.* usually, generally, habitually; see **customarily, frequently, regularly** 1.

ordinary, *mod.* **1.** [In accordance with a regular order or sequence]—*Syn.* customary, normal, everyday; see **common** 1, 2, **popular** 1, 3, **regular** 3, **traditional** 2.
2. [Lacking distinction]—*Syn.* average, mediocre, normal; see **common** 1, **conventional** 3, **dull** 4, **fair** 2.
out of the ordinary—*Syn.* extraordinary, uncommon, special; see **unusual** 2.

ordination, *n.* **1.** [An installation]—*Syn.* consecration, coronation, investiture; see **installation** 1.
2. [A system]—*Syn.* plan, classification, organization; see **order** 3, **system** 1.

ordnance, *n.*—*Syn.* arms, military weapons, artillery; see **ammunition.**

ore, *n.*—*Syn.* metalliferous earth, unrefined earth *or* rock, ore bed, parent rock, native mineral, matrix; see also **mineral.**

organ, *n.* **1.** [An instrument]—*Syn.* medium, means, way; see **device** 1, **tool** 1.
2. [A part of an organism having a specialized use] —*Syn.* vital part *or* structure, functional division, process; see **gland.**
Human organs include the following—brain, heart, eye, ear, nose, tongue, lung, kidney, stomach, intestine, pancreas, gall bladder, liver, penis, womb.
3. [A musical instrument]—*Syn.* wind instrument, keyboard instrument, harmonium, melodeon, calliope, hurdy-gurdy, accordion; *all* (D): groan box, toot tub, wheezer; see also **musical instrument.**
Types of organs include the following—great, swell, choir, orchestral, solo, pipe, echo, pedal, altar, chancel, antiphonal, gallery, floating, barrel, reed, electric, electronic, hand, grind, street.

organic, *mod.*—*Syn.* structural, constitutional, systemic, organized, systematic, co-ordinated, fundamental, vital, radical, necessary, inherent, elemental, basic, primary, basal, important, original, initial, principal, prime, primitive, essential, biotic, plasmic, cellular, nuclear, amoebic, protoplasmic, vacuolated, vacuolar, amoeboid, protozoan; see also **alive, natural** 1, **whole** 1.—*Ant.* unimportant*, unessential, inorganic.

organically, *mod.*—*Syn.* by nature, inevitably, wholly; see **essentially, naturally** 2.

organism, *n.*—*Syn.* person, organic structure, bion, morphon, physiological individual, morphological individual; see also **animal** 1, **body** 1, **plant.**

organist, *n.*—*Syn.* instrumentalist, hurdy-gurdy man, organ-player; *both* (D): wheezer, monkey hurdler; see also **musician.**

organization, *n.* **1.** [The process of organizing] —*Syn.* establishment, formulation, schematization, plan, planning, disposition, ordering, creation, molding, grouping, projection, design, provision, working out, assembling, construction, deliberation, institution, foundation, preparation, rehearsal, direction, structure, situation, formation, association; see also **classification** 1.—*Ant.* confusion*, confounding, disintegration.

2. [The manner of organizing]—*Syn.* regulation, systematization, system, method, methodizing, co-ordination, adjustment, harmony, unity, correlation, standard, standardization, settlement, arrangement, disposition, classification, alignment, group, symmetry, uniformity; see also **order** 3. —*Ant.* confusion*, bedlam, chance.

3. [An organized body]—*Syn.* aggregation, association, federation, combine, corporation, union, institute, trust, cartel, confederation, monopoly, combination, machine, business, industry, company, society, league, club, fraternity, house, order, alliance, party, co-operative, guild, profession, trade, coalition, syndicate, fellowship, lodge, brotherhood, concord, confederacy, affiliation, body, band, sodality, sorority, team, squad, crew, clique, circle, set, coterie, troupe, group; see also **system** 1.

organize, *v.* **1.** [To put in order]—*Syn.* arrange, compose, combine, systematize, methodize, co-ordinate, adjust, synthesize, dispose, put in order, line up, regulate, harmonize, range, adapt, settle, fit, straighten, reorganize, correlate, standardize; *all* (D): whip into shape, fall into, keep in line; see also **classify, order** 3.—*Ant.* upset*, disarrange, disturb.

2. [To form an organization]—*Syn.* establish, constitute, prepare, scheme, formulate, lay out, form, create, mold, fashion, project, design, build, found, authorize, raise, appoint, fix, secure, instate, erect, assemble, make, direct, construct, institute; see also **plan** 2.—*Ant.* destroy*, eradicate, break down.

organized, *mod.* —*Syn.* established, methodized, co-ordinated, systematized, systematic, constituted, directed, adjusted, assigned, distributed, grouped, fixed up, standardized, in place *or* order, in turn *or* succession, in good form, placed, put away, orderly, in series *or* sequence, arranged, prepared, made ready, regimented, constructed, synthesized, settled, composed, marshaled, framed, planned, schematized, ranked, put in order, ordered, regulated, ranged, disposed, formulated, formed, fashioned, shaped, made, projected, designed, harmonized, related, interrelated, correlated, oriented, founded, associated; see also **classified.**—*Ant.* shapeless*, unplanned, formless.

organizing, *n.* —*Syn.* co-ordination, systemization, formation; see **organization** 1.

orgy, *n.* —*Syn.* revelry, debauch, revel, spree, feast, bout, debauchery, bacchanal(ia), saturnalia, carousal, dissipation; *all* (D): fling, nude-in, be-in, bash, bust, jag, binge, (hell)bender; see also **celebration** 2, **indulgence** 3.

orient, *v.* **1.** [To direct]—*Syn.* determine, turn, locate; see **lead** 1.

2. [To adjust]—*Syn.* get (one's) bearings, familiarize, adapt; see **conform.**

Orient, *n.* **1.** [Eastern Asia]—*Syn.* Far East, Asia, China, Hong Kong, Macao, India, Japan, Vietnam, Siam *or* Thailand, Laos, Indo-China, Cambodia, Korea, Burma, the mysterious East, Celestial Kingdom, land of the rising sun, land of Confucianism; see also **east** 2.—*Ant.* Europe*, Occident, Western World.

2. [Southwestern Asia]—*Syn.* Near East, Middle East, Levant, Egypt, Mohammedan world, Turkey, Syria, Lebanon, Israel, Jordan, Iraq, Iran, Persia, Moslem world, Hither-East, Arabia, the Golden *or* Fertile Crescent, the cradle of mankind; see also **east** 2.

Oriental, *mod.* —*Syn.* (Far) Eastern, Near Eastern, Asian; see **Asiatic** 1, 2.

orientation, *n.* —*Syn.* familiarization, bearings, introduction; see **adjustment** 1, **introduction** 3, 4.

orifice, *n.* —*Syn.* opening, cleft, crack; see **hole** 1, 2.

origin, *n.* **1.** [The act of beginning]—*Syn.* rise, start, starting, genesis, alpha, commencement, outset, incipience, inception, initiation, nativity, dawn, introduction, embarkation, forging, entrance, ingress, entry, outbreak, onset, first move *or* act *or* step, foundation, origination, authoring, ascent, first appearance, creation, induction, launching, inauguration, forming, fashioning, molding, devising, invention; see also **birth** 1.—*Ant.* end*, close, termination.

2. [The place or time of beginning]—*Syn.* source, spring, issue, fountain, inlet, derivation, provenance, provenience, root, stem, shoot, twig, sapling, portal, door, gate, gateway, fountainhead, wellspring, spring head, font, fount, *source* (French), natural well, *fons et origo* (Latin), birthplace, square one (D), omphalos, cradle, nest, womb, hotbed, reservoir, forge, infancy, babyhood, childhood, youth.—*Ant.* result*, outcome, issue.

3. [Cause]—*Syn.* seed, germ, stock, parentage, ancestry, parent, ancestor, *raison d'être* (French), egg, sperm, embryo, principle, element, nucleus, first cause, First Great Cause, author, creator, heart, prime mover, *primum mobile* (Latin), begetter, progenitor, producer, determinant, agent, leaven, mainspring, causality, causation, impulse, source, influence, prime motive, generator, ultimate cause, remote cause, occasion, root, first act, spring, antecedent, motive, inducement, activation, inspiration; see also **cause** 3.—*Ant.* result*, consequence, conclusion.

original, *mod.* **1.** [Pertaining to the source]—*Syn.* primary, primeval, primordial, rudimentary, rudimental, aboriginal, elementary, inceptive, in embryo, fundamental, protogenic, primitive, initial, beginning, commencing, starting, opening, dawning, incipient; see also **first** 1.—*Ant.* late*, recent, developed.

2. [Creative]—*Syn.* originative, productive, causal, causative, generative, imaginative, inventive, innovative, ingenious, unconventional, constitutive, formative, demiurgic, resourceful, ready, quick, seminal, envisioning, sensitive, archetypal, inspiring, devising, conceiving, fertile, fictive, fashioning, molding.—*Ant.* stupid*, imitative, unproductive.

3. [Not copied]—*Syn.* primary, principal, first, genuine, new, firsthand, uncopied, fresh, novel, underived, independent, one, sole, lone, single, solitary, neoteric, authentic, pure, new-fashioned, untranslated, nonimitative, unexampled, elemental, real, absolute, sheer; see also **unique** 1, **unusual** 1.—*Ant.* imitated*, copied, repeated.

originality, *n.* —*Syn.* creativeness, inventiveness, innovation, invention, ingenuity, ingeniousness, conception, realization, authenticity, novelty, freshness, nonconformity, newness, modernity, individuality, brilliance, intellectual independence, a creative spirit *or* mind; see also **imagination** 1. —*Ant.* imitation*, dependency, imitativeness.

originally, *mod.* **1.** [In an original manner]—*Syn.* imaginatively, creatively, ingeniously, inventively, novelly, freshly, startlingly, modernly, in a new fashion, in the first instance *or* place, in a new manner, independently, originatively, artistically, with genius.

2. [In the beginning]—*Syn.* first, incipiently, basically; see **formerly.**

originate, *v.* **1.** [To have a beginning]—*Syn.* start, rise, dawn; see **begin** 2.

2. [To bring about a beginning]—*Syn.* start, introduce, found; see **begin** 1.

originated, *mod.* —*Syn.* introduced, started, commenced; see **begun.**

originating, *mod.* —*Syn.* rising, starting, beginning, commencing, issuing, springing from, emanating, arising, deriving, flowing from, dawning, given birth, generated, induced, produced, determined, caused, activated, motivated, begot, given source, leavened, inspired, descending, formed, fashioned, made, incepted, created, authored, cradled, forged.

ornament, *n.* —*Syn.* embellishment, adornment, beautification; see **decoration** 2, **embroidery** 1, **trimming** 1.

ornamental, *mod.* **1.** [Providing ornament]—*Syn.* embellishing, adorning, decorative, decorating, making pleasing, rendering attractive, decking, setting off, gracing, garnishing, enhancing, heightening, furbishing, ornamentive, dressy, accessory, florid.—*Ant.* ugly*, detractive, plain.

2. [Intended for ornament]—*Syn.* fancy, luxurious, showy; see **elaborate** 1, **ornate** 1.

3. [Beautiful]—*Syn.* delicate, exquisite, spiritual; see **beautiful** 1.

ornamentation, *n.* —*Syn.* adornment, embellishment, elaboration; see **decoration** 1.

ornate, *mod.* **1.** [Overly decorated]—*Syn.* showy, flamboyant, bedight, superficial, curved, flowery, resplendent, sumptuous, lavish, bespangled, many-colored, brilliant, parti-colored, bright, colored, tinseled, jeweled, embroidered, begilt, glossy, tesselated, burnished, polished, gorgeous, pompous, stylish, magnificent, adorned, festooned, trimmed, gilded, embellished, furbished, encrusted, striped, waved, scrolled, inlaid, illuminated, garnished, decked, bedecked, flowered, glowing, vivid, variegated, radiant, fine, gay, alluring, dazzling, sparkling, scintillating, shining, flashing, glistening, glamorous, glittering, grotesque, ornamented, artificial, ostentatious, pretentious, flaunting, baroque, rococo, gaudy, glitzy, tawdry, flashy, meretricious; see also **elaborate** 1.

2. [Referring to writing or speech]—*Syn.* adorned, ornamented, embellished; see **elegant** 4.

orphan, *n.* —*Syn.* foundling, ragamuffin, parentless child, orphaned child, waif, stray; see also **child.**

orphanage, *n.* —*Syn.* orphans' home, asylum for orphaned children, institution, foundling home, orphanotrophy; see also **school** 1.

orthodox, *mod.* —*Syn.* standard, customary, doctrinal; see **conservative, conventional** 3.

orthodoxy, *n.* —*Syn.* dogma, tradition, doctrine; see **faith** 2, **religion** 2.

oscillate, *v.* **1.** [To swing]—*Syn.* palpitate, vibrate, sway; see **swing** 1, **wave** 3, **waver.**

2. [To fluctuate]—*Syn.* be unsteady, waver, vacillate; see **change** 4.

oscillation, *n.* **1.** [Swinging]—*Syn.* waving, swaying, quivering; see **vibration.**

2. [Fluctuation]—*Syn.* hesitancy, misgiving, faltering; see **doubt** 2, **uncertainty** 2.

osculate, *v.* —*Syn.* touch lips; *both* (D): buss, smack; see **kiss.**

osculation, *n.* —*Syn.* endearment, embrace, caress; see **kiss, touch** 2.

osseous, *mod.* —*Syn.* bony, rigid, stiff, calcified, ossified, skeletal, callous, inflexible, unyielding; see also **firm** 2, **thick** 3.

ossification, *n.* —*Syn.* fossilization, induration, hardening, bone formation, ostosis, calcification.

ossify, *v.* —*Syn.* congeal, fossilize, turn to bone; see **harden** 2, **stiffen** 1, **thicken** 1.

ostensible, *mod.* —*Syn.* manifest, demonstrative, notable; see **likely** 1.

ostensibly, *mod.* —*Syn.* superficially, to all intents and purposes, for show; see **apparently.**

ostentation, *n.* **1.** [The quality of being ostentatious] —*Syn.* exhibitionism, showiness, pomp, pompousness, pomposity, parading, bravado, vaunting, magnificence, pageant, pageantry, splendor, spectacle, flourish, flamboyance, garishness, array, demonstration, pretending, boasting, bragging, swaggering, vainglory, braggartism; see also **pretense** 1. —*Ant.* reserve*, diffidence, timidity.

2. [Ostentatious conduct]—*Syn.* show, brag, boast, vaunt, swagger, flourish, parade, fuss, exhibition, braggadocio, pretension; see also **display** 2, **vanity** 1.—*Ant.* reserve*, modest behavior, quiet.

ostentatious, *mod.* —*Syn.* pretentious, showy, pompous; see **egotistic** 2.

ostentatiously, *mod.* —*Syn.* blatantly, showily, proudly; see **pompously.**

ostracism, *n.* —*Syn.* segregation, elimination, eviction; see **exclusion, exile** 1, **removal** 1.

ostracize, *v.* —*Syn.* exile, expel, deport; see **banish** 1.

ostracized, *mod.* —*Syn.* banished, treated like a pariah, ignored; see **punished.**

other, *mod.* —*Syn.* one of two, the remaining one, another, one beside, some beside, additional, different, separate, distinct, opposite, across from, lately, recently, not long ago, other than; see also **extra.**

other, *pron.* —*Syn.* the one remaining, the part remaining, the alternate, the alternative; see also **another.**—*Ant.* this*, that, the first choice.

of all others—*Syn.* superior (to), highest, supreme; see **best** 1, 2.

the other day (*or* **night**)—*Syn.* not long ago, a while back *or* ago, yesterday *or* the day before; see **recently.**

others, *n.* —*Syn.* unnamed persons, the remainder, some, a few, any others, a number, a handful, a small number, not many, hardly any, two or three, more than one, many, a great number, a great many; *all* (D): they, folks, the rest; see also **everybody.**—*Ant.* no one*, none, not any.

otherwise, *mod.* **1.** [In another way]—*Syn.* in a different way, contrarily, in an opposed way, under other conditions, in different circumstances, on the other hand, in other respects, in other ways; see also **oppositely.**—*Ant.* like*, so, in like manner.

2. [Introducing an alternative threat]—*Syn.* unless you do, with this exception, except on these conditions, barring this, in any other circumstances, except that, without this, unless . . . then, other than; see also **unless.**—*Ant.* therefore*, hence, as a result.

otherworldly, *mod.*—*Syn.* spectral, abstract, metaphysical; see **mysterious** 2, **supernatural.**

otiose, *mod.* **1.** [Lazy]—*Syn.* indolent, slothful, idle; see **lazy** 1, **listless** 1.

2. [Futile]—*Syn.* vain, useless, hopeless; see **futile** 1.

ottoman, *n.*—*Syn.* footstool, footrest, hassock; see **furniture, stool.**

ouch, *interj.*—*Syn.* oh; *all* (D): oh dear, ooh, gosh, ach, darn, dannation, damn, gee, geez, great Scot, dash it all, shoot, oops, oy, hooee, goldarn, good land, gracious, great Caesar, great guns, oh Lawdy, blazes, the deuce, hell.

ought (to), *v.*—*Syn.* should, have to, is necessary *or* fitting *or* becoming *or* expedient, behooves, is reasonable *or* logical *or* natural, requires, is in need of, is responsible for; see also **must.**

ounce, *n.*—*Syn.* uncia, measure, troy ounce, avoirdupois ounce, fluid ounce, one sixteenth of a pound (avoirdupois), one sixteenth of a pint, one twelfth of a pound (troy); see also **measure** 1.

our, *mod.*—*Syn.* ours, our own, belonging to us, owned *or* used by us, due to us, inherent in us, a part of us, of interest to us, done *or* accomplished by us, in our employ, with *or* near *or* of us.

ourselves, *pron.*—*Syn.* us, our own selves, the speakers, individually, personally, privately, without help, our very own selves (D); see also **we.**

oust, *v.*—*Syn.* eject, discharge, dispossess, evict, dislodge, remove, deprive, expel, drive *or* force out, show the door, chase out, cast out, depose, dethrone, distrain, disinherit, banish; *all* (D): boot out, bundle off, send packing, bounce, buck off, wash out, give the gate, sack, pack off, send to Coventry; see also **dismiss** 1, 2.—*Ant.* restore*, reinstate, commission.

ousted, *mod.*—*Syn.* removed, fired, defeated; see **beaten** 1.

out, *mod.* and *prep.* **1.** [In motion from within]—*Syn.* out of, away from, from, from within, out from, out toward, outward, on the way.—*Ant.* in from*, in, into.

2. [Not situated within]—*Syn.* on the outer side, on the surface, external, extrinsic, extraneous, outer, outdoors, out-of-doors, unconcealed, open, exposed, in the open; see also **outside** 1, **without.**—*Ant.* within*, inside, on the inner side.

3. [Beyond]—*Syn.* distant, removed, removed from; see **away** 1, **beyond.**

4. [Continued to the limit or near it]—*Syn.* ended, accomplished, fulfilled, over, passed; see also **done** 1, **finished** 1.—*Ant.* unfinished*, unaccomplished, unfulfilled.

5. [Not at home or at one's office]—*Syn.* not in, away, busy, on vacation, at lunch, gone, left; see also **absent.**—*Ant.* in*, receiving, not busy.

6. [No longer at bat; *in sport*]—*Syn.* retired, put out, in the field, struck out; *all* (D): away, down, fanned.

7. [(D) Unconscious]—*Syn.* insensible; *both* (D): out cold, blotto; see **unconscious** 1.

8. [Wanting]—*Syn.* lacking, missing, without; see **wanting.**

9. [Completely]—*Syn.* out and out, utterly, totally; see **completely.**

10. [(D) Not acceptable]—*Syn.* out-of-date, outmoded, unfashionable; see **old-fashioned, unpopular.**

all out (D)—*Syn.* wholeheartedly, with great effort, entirely; see **completely.**

on the outs (D)—*Syn.* on unfriendly terms, disagreeing, fighting; see **opposing** 1.

out (D), *n.*—*Syn.* means of escape, way out, excuse; see **escape** 1, 2, **explanation** 2.

outage, *n.*—*Syn.* interruption of service, blackout, dim-out, brownout; failure of electrical service *or* electricity *or* gas *or* utilities, etc.; see also **interruption.**

out-and-out, *mod.*—*Syn.* complete, entire, total; see **completely.**

out back, *mod.*—*Syn.* behind, in back of, to the rear; see **back.**

outbalance, *v.*—*Syn.* outweigh, transcend, outdo; see **exceed.**

outbid, *v.*—*Syn.* bid *or* offer higher *or* more (than), raise the price, bid something up; see **bid** 1, **pay** 1.

outboard motor, *n.*—*Syn.* marine *or* two-cycle *or* portable *or* detachable motor, boat motor, boating equipment; see **motor.**

outbreak, *n.* **1.** [A sudden violent appearance]—*Syn.* eruption, irruption, ebullition, explosion, outburst, disruption, burst, bursting (forth), detonation, thunder, commotion, rending, break, breaking out, breaking forth, gush, gushing forth, outpouring, pouring forth, breaking bonds, tumult, spurt, sundering, snapping apart, discharge, volley, blast, blowup, crash, roar, earthquake, temblor, squall, paroxysm, spasm, convulsion, fit, ictus, effervescence, boiling, flash, flare, crack.—*Ant.* peace*, tranquility, quiet.

2. [Sudden violence]—*Syn.* fury, mutiny, brawl; see **disorder** 2, **revolution** 2.

outbuilding, *n.*—*Syn.* outhouse, stable, barn, backhouse, outside building, storehouse; see also **building** 1, **hut, shed.**

outburst, *n.*—*Syn.* discharge, upheaval, eruption; see **disturbance** 2, **outbreak** 1.

outcast, *mod.*—*Syn.* vagabond, proscribed, driven out, hounded, untouchable, rejected, thrown aside, pushed out, hunted, Ishmaellike, not accepted by society, cast out, degraded, expelled, outlawed, cast away, exiled, expatriated, made a vagabond, serving a life sentence, having a price on one's head; see also **disgraced.**

outcast, *n.* **1.** [One who has been cast out]—*Syn.* fugitive, pariah, untouchable; see **refugee.**

2. [A vagabond]—*Syn.* gypsy, bum, tramper; see **rascal, tramp** 1.
outclass, *v.* —*Syn.* outdo, excel, surpass; see **exceed.**
outcome, *n.* —*Syn.* issue, upshot, consequence; see **end** 2, **result.**
outcrop, *n.* —*Syn.* bared rock *or* soil, exposed surface, projecting land mass; see **earth** 2, **land** 1.
outcry, *n.* —*Syn.* complaint, clamor, scream; see **objection** 2.
outdated, *mod.* —*Syn.* outmoded, out of fashion, antiquated; see **old** 3.
outdistance, *v.* —*Syn.* exceed, better, beat; see **defeat** 3.
outdo, *v.* —*Syn.* surpass, overdo, beat; see **defeat** 1, **exceed.**
outdone, *mod.* —*Syn.* defeated, bettered, improved upon; see **beaten** 1.
outdoor, *mod.* —*Syn.* outside, out-of-doors, open-air, alfresco, picnic, out of the house, out in the open, free, unrestricted, rustic, informal, free and easy, healthful, invigorating, nature-loving, given to outdoor sports; see also **airy** 1.—*Ant.* interior*, indoor, in the house.
outdoors, *mod.* —*Syn.* out-of-doors, outdoor, without, out of the house, outside, on the outside, in the yard, in the open, in the garden *or* patio, into the street.
outdoors, *n.* —*Syn.* the out-of-doors, natural scenery, fresh air, garden, patio, woods, hills, mountains, streams, Mother Nature, the great outdoors, God's great outdoors, countryside, the country; see also **environment, nature** 2.—*Ant.* inside*, domestic matters, household concerns.
outer, *mod.* —*Syn.* outward, without, external, exterior, extrinsic *or* extraneous to, foreign *or* alien to, beyond, exposed; see also **outside.**—*Ant.* inner*, inward, inside.
outermost, *mod.* —*Syn.* surface, peripheral, external; see **outside.**
outer space, *n.* —*Syn.* infinity, (the) heavens, (the) universe; see **space** 1.
outface, *v.* —*Syn.* confront, oppose, defy; see **dare** 2, **face** 1.
outfield, *n.* —*Syn.* *all* (D): pasture, garden, outer works, playpen; see also **baseball, field** 2.
In baseball, the outfield consists of the following —left field, over third base, over shortstop; *all* (D): left, deep left, short left, over short, left patrol; center field, just over second base; *all* (D): center, deep center, short center, center garden; right field, over first base; *all* (D): deep right, short right, over first, sunfield, sun, dexter pasture.
outfielder, *n.* —*Syn.* *all* (D): pasture police, gardener, fly hawk, flypaper, fly chaser; see also **fielder, player** 1.
In baseball, outfielders are as follows—left fielder, center fielder, right fielder.
outfight, *v.* —*Syn.* excel, beat, whip; see **defeat** 1, **exceed.**
outfit, *n.* —*Syn.* trappings, outlay, gear; see **equipment.**
outfit, *v.* —*Syn.* equip, fit out, supply; see **provide** 1.
outfitted, *mod.* —*Syn.* ready, provided with *or* for, suited (up); see **equipped.**
outfitter, *n.* —*Syn.* clothier, seamstress, costumer; see **tailor.**
outflank, *v.* —*Syn.* bypass, surround, outmaneuver; see **defeat** 1, 2, **pass** 1.
outflow, *n.* —*Syn.* current, drainage, movement of tide; see **ebb, flow.**
outfly, *v.* —*Syn.* fly past, exceed in speed, outdistance; see **defeat** 3, **leave** 1, **pass** 1.
out front, *mod.* —*Syn.* ahead, winning, victorious; see **triumphant.**
outgo, *n.* —*Syn.* costs, losses, outflow; see **expenses, loss, reduction** 1.
outgoing, *mod.* —*Syn.* sociable, civil, kind; see **friendly** 1.
outgrow, *v.* —*Syn.* relinquish, discontinue, give up; see **abandon** 1, **discard.**
outgrowth, *n.* **1.** [A product]—*Syn.* end result, outcome, effect; see **end** 2, **result.**
2. [A projection]—*Syn.* prominence, jut, protuberance; see **bulge, projection.**
outguess, *v.* —*Syn.* predict (successfully), outmaneuver, think faster (than); see **defeat** 1, **think** 1.
outhouse, *n.* —*Syn.* latrine; *both* (D): pot, quacken; see **bath** 3, **toilet** 2.
outing, *n.* —*Syn.* excursion, airing, drive; see **vacation.**
out in left field (D), *mod.* —*Syn.* unlikely, crazy, wild; see **impractical, insane** 1.
outlander, *n.* —*Syn.* foreigner, *Ausländer* (German), immigrant; see **alien, stranger.**
outlandish, *mod.* **1.** [Uncouth]—*Syn.* gauche, boorish, clumsy; see **awkward** 1, **rude** 1, 2.
2. [Ridiculous]—*Syn.* odd, queer, strange; see **unusual** 2.
outlandishly, *mod.* —*Syn.* ridiculously, insanely, crazily; see **foolishly.**
outlast, *v.* —*Syn.* outlive, outwear, remain; see **endure** 1, **survive** 1.
outlaw, *n.* —*Syn.* fugitive, bandit, badman; see **criminal.**
outlaw, *v.* —*Syn.* make illegal, stop, ban; see **banish, condemn** 1, **prevent.**
outlawed, *mod.* —*Syn.* stopped, banned, made illegal; see **illegal.**
outlay, *n.* —*Syn.* expenditure, cost, charge; see **expense** 1.
outlet, *n.* **1.** [An opening]—*Syn.* break, crack, tear; see **hole** 1, 2.
2. [An electric terminal]—*Syn.* plug-in, terminal, electrical device; see **socket.**
outline, *n.* **1.** [A skeletonized plan]—*Syn.* frame, skeleton, framework; see **plan** 1, **sketch** 1.
2. [A preliminary plan]—*Syn.* sketch, drawing, draft; see **plan** 2.
3. [The line surrounding an object; *often plural*] —*Syn.* contour, side, boundary; see **edge** 1, **frame** 3.
4. [A shape seen in outline]—*Syn.* silhouette, profile, configuration, shape, figure, formation, lineament, aspect, appearance, representation; see also **form** 1.
outline, *v.* **1.** [To draw]—*Syn.* sketch, paint, describe; see **draw** 2.
2. [To plan]—*Syn.* rough *or* block out, draft, sketch; see **plan** 2.
outlined, *mod.* **1.** [Marked in outline]—*Syn.* bounded, delineated, edged, bordered, circum-

scribed, marked, zoned, girdled, banded, configurated, delimited.
2. [Given in summary]—*Syn.* epitomized, generalized, charted, diagramed, mapped, graphed; see also **summarized.**

outlining, *mod.* —*Syn.* edging, bounding, marking, zoning, circumscribing, girdling, banding, configurating, delimiting; see also **bordering.**

outlining, *n.* —*Syn.* sketching, planning, delineating, tracing, diagraming, drafting, plotting, circumscribing, delineating, blocking out, charting, mapping, bounding, girdling, banding, delimiting, depicting, aligning, drawing up, designing, projecting; see also **drawing** 1.

outlive, *v.* —*Syn.* live longer (than), outlast, last; see **endure** 1, **survive.**

outlook, *n.* **1.** [Point of view]—*Syn.* scope, vision, standpoint; see **viewpoint.**
2. [Apparent future]—*Syn.* probability, prospect(s), likelihood, possibility, expectation, chance(s), opportunity, appearances, probable future, openings, normal course of events, probabilities, risk, mathematical chances, law of averages; see also **forecast.**

out loud, *mod.* —*Syn.* aloud, above a whisper, audible; see **heard, loud** 1, **loudly.**

outlying, *mod.* —*Syn.* afar, far-off, external; see **distant** 1, **remote** 1.

outmaneuver, *v.* —*Syn.* outwit, outdo, excel; see **defeat** 1, **exceed.**

outmoded, *mod.* —*Syn.* out of date, old-fashioned, superannuated; see **old** 1, 2, 3.

outnumbered, *mod.* —*Syn.* exceeded, bested, overcome; see **beaten** 1.

out of, *mod.* **1.** [Having none in stock]—*Syn.* all out of stock, not in stock, gone; see **depleted, sold out.**
2. [From]—*Syn.* out from, away from, from within; see **from.**
3. [Beyond]—*Syn.* outside of, on the border of, in the outskirts; see **beyond.**

out of bounds, *mod.* —*Syn.* outlawed, forbidden, controlled; see **illegal.**

out of breath, *mod.* —*Syn.* exhausted, gasping, winded; see **breathless.**

out of control, *mod.* —*Syn.* gone, doomed, uncontrolled; see **lost, ruined** 1, 2, **unruly.**

out of curiosity, *mod.* —*Syn.* being curious (about) *or* interested (in), out of interest, stimulated (by); see **accordingly.**

out-of-date, *mod.* —*Syn.* obsolete, passé, antiquated; see **old-fashioned.**

out-of-doors, *mod.* —*Syn.* in the open, outside, not in(side); see **out** 2, 5, **outdoor, outdoors.**

out of hand, *mod.* —*Syn.* beyond control, out of control, unchecked; see **uncontrolled, unruly.**

out of it (D), *mod.* —*Syn.* uninformed, behind the times, square (D); see **ignorant** 1, **old-fashioned.**

out of line, *mod.* **1.** [Crooked]—*Syn.* not lined up, uneven, devious; see **crooked, irregular** 4.
2. [Disrespectful]—*Syn.* outspoken, dissident, insolent; see **radical** 2, **rebellious** 2, **unruly.**

out of one's mind *or* **head,** *mod.* —*Syn.* crazy, deranged, irresponsible; see **insane** 1.

out of order, *mod.* —*Syn.* broken down, defective, ineffective; see **broken** 2, **faulty.**

out of place, *mod.* —*Syn.* mislaid, displaced, gone; see **lost** 1.

out of pocket, *mod.* —*Syn.* lost, gone, spent; see **wasted.**

out of print, *mod.* —*Syn.* sold out, not available, (all) gone; see **sold.**

out of range, *mod.* —*Syn.* out of earshot, *sotto voce,* indistinct; see **distant** 1.

out of the blue, *mod.* —*Syn.* unforeseen, sudden, unanticipated; see **unexpected.**

out-of-the-way, *mod.* **1.** [Remote]—*Syn.* far-off, secluded, isolated; see **distant** 1, **remote** 1.
2. [Strange]—*Syn.* bizarre, odd, weird; see **unusual** 2.

out of time, *mod.* —*Syn.* misfiring, out of adjustment, fast, late, early, ahead, behind; see also **slow** 2.

out of touch, *mod.* —*Syn.* stranger to, estranged, uninstructed; see **ignorant** 1, **inexperienced, naive, unaware.**

out of work, *mod.* —*Syn.* out of a job *or* employment, dismissed, without work *or* job; see **unemployed.**

out on bail, *mod.* —*Syn.* released, out, bailed out; see **discharged** 1, **free** 2.

out on bond, *mod.* —*Syn.* released, freed, let go; see **discharged** 1, **free** 2.

outperform, *v.* —*Syn.* beat, better, exceed; see **defeat** 1, 3.

outplay, *v.* —*Syn.* overcome, surpass, beat; see **defeat** 1, **exceed.**

outpost, *n.* —*Syn.* advance(d) *or* forward post *or* position *or* station, listening post, point of attack; see **boundary, position** 1.

outpouring, *n.* —*Syn.* overflow, emission, drainage; see **ebb, flow.**

output, *n.* **1.** [Production]—*Syn.* producing, making, manufacturing; see **production** 1.
2. [Product]—*Syn.* yield, amount, crop; see **product** 2.

outrage, *n.* —*Syn.* indignity, abuse, affront; see **insult.**

outrage, *v.* —*Syn.* offend, wrong, affront; see **abuse** 1, **insult.**

outrageous, *mod.* —*Syn.* wanton, shaming, opprobrious, notorious, shameless, disgracing, disgraceful, brazen, barefaced, gross, scandalous, contemptible, turbulent, disorderly, insulting, affronting, abusive, oppressive, dishonorable, reprehensible, malignant, injurious, glaring, rank, immoderate, extreme, inordinate, flagrant, despicable, glaring, contemptible, ignoble, contumelious, malevolent, scurrilous, odious, monstrous, heinous, atrocious, flagitious, nefarious, vicious, iniquitous, wicked, shocking, violent, unbearable, villainous, horrendous, infamous, corrupt, degenerate, criminal, sinful, depraving, debasing, debauching, abandoned, vile, horrifying, abominable, execrable; see also **offensive** 2, **shameful** 1, 2.—*Ant.* excellent*, laudable, honorable.

outrageously, *mod.* —*Syn.* horribly, shamefully, awfully; see **badly** 1, **brutally, foolishly.**

outrank, *v.* —*Syn.* rank above, excel, rival; see **exceed.**

outreach, *v.* —*Syn.* excel, predominate, surpass; see **exceed.**

outrider, *n.* —*Syn.* guardian, attendant, guide; see **escort.**

outright, *mod.* —*Syn.* out-and-out, unmitigated, arrant; see **completely, obvious** 1, **unconditional.**

outrun, *v.* —*Syn.* beat, win, forge ahead; see **defeat** 1, **exceed.**

outsell, *v.* —*Syn.* excel, surpass, sell more than; see **exceed.**

outset, *n.* —*Syn.* starting, source, rise; see **origin** 1.

outshine, *v.* **1.** [To obscure]—*Syn.* cloud, dim, eclipse; see **shade** 2.
2. [To outdo]—*Syn.* transcend, surpass, excel; see **defeat** 1, **exceed.**

outside, *mod.* —*Syn.* extreme, outermost, farthest, apart from, external, away from, farther; see also **outer.**—*Ant.* inner*, inside, interior.

outside, *n.* **1.** [An outer surface]—*Syn.* exterior, outer side, surface, integument, covering, sheath, façade, topside, upper side, front side, face, appearance, outer aspect, seeming; see also **body** 4, **cover** 1, 2, **skin.**—*Ant.* interior, inside*, inner side.
2. [The limit]—*Syn.* outline, border, bounds; see **boundary, edge** 1, **end** 4.
at the outside—*Syn.* at the most, at the absolute limit, no *or* not more than; see **most.**

outsider, *n.* —*Syn.* foreigner, stranger, refugee; see **alien.**

outskirts, *n.* —*Syn.* border, suburbs, limits; see **boundary, edge** 1.

outsmart, *v.* —*Syn.* outguess, outdo, get the better of; see **deceive, defeat** 1, **trick.**

outspoken, *mod.* —*Syn.* blunt, candid, artless; see **abrupt** 2, **frank.**

outspread, *mod.* —*Syn.* spread (out *or* wide), spread far, expanded, expensive, extended, unlimited, beyond limits, unbounded, beyond boundaries, unheld, unrestrained, unrestricted, unconfined, unenclosed, uncircumscribed, free; see also **extensive** 1, **widespread.**—*Ant.* narrow*, contracted, bounded.

outstanding, *mod.* —*Syn.* conspicuous, leading, notable; see **distinguished** 2, **important** 1, 2.

outstandingly, *mod.* —*Syn.* superbly, notably, supremely; see **excellently, well** 2, 3.

outstay, *v.* —*Syn.* outwait, stay longer (than), hang on; see **endure** 1, **wait** 1.

outstrip, *v.* —*Syn.* surpass, outdo, excel; see **exceed.**

outthink, *v.* —*Syn.* outguess, outplan, see *or* think better than; see **defeat** 1.

outvote, *v.* —*Syn.* overwhelm, out-ballot, snow under (D); see **defeat** 1.

outward, *mod.* **1.** [In an outwardly direction] —*Syn.* out, toward the edge, from within; see **outer, outside** 1.
2. [To outward appearance]—*Syn.* on the surface, visible, to the eye; see **obvious** 1, **open** 1.

outward bound, *mod.* —*Syn.* going, leaving, departed; see **afloat, gone** 1, **traveling** 1, 2.

outwardly, *mod.* —*Syn.* superficially, in appearance, on the surface; see **apparently.**

outwear, *v.* **1.** [To survive]—*Syn.* sustain, last longer than, outlast; see **continue** 1, **endure** 1, **survive** 1.
2. [To exhaust]—*Syn.* spend, wear out, deplete; see **tire** 1, 2, **weary** 1, 2.

outweigh, *v.* **1.** [To exceed in weight]—*Syn.* overbalance, overweigh, weigh more (than), go beyond; see also **burden.**
2. [To exceed in importance]—*Syn.* excel, surpass, outrun; see **exceed.**

outwit, *v.* —*Syn.* baffle, trick, bewilder; see **confuse, deceive.**

outwitted, *mod.* —*Syn.* tricked, outsmarted, taken (D); see **deceived** 1.

outwork, *v.* —*Syn.* work better *or* faster *or* harder *or* more efficiently, etc. (than); improve upon, out-perform; see **defeat** 1, **work** 1.

outworn, *mod.* **1.** [Obsolete]—*Syn.* out of use, archaic, extinct; see **old** 2, **old-fashioned.**
2. [Exhausted]—*Syn.* consumed, run-down, weary; see **spent** 2, **tired.**

oval, *mod.* —*Syn.* egg-shaped, elliptical, ellipsoidal; see **oblong.**

ovation, *n.* —*Syn.* laudation, acclaim, applause; see **praise** 2.

oven, *n.* —*Syn.* hot-air chamber, oil burner, broiler; see **furnace, stove.**
Types of ovens include the following—baking, coke, annealing, pottery, metallurgical, Aladdin's, charcoal, electric, gas, Egyptian, firing, bush, Dutch, beehive, drying; kiln, leer, hot-air sterilizer.

over, *mod.* and *prep.* **1.** [Situated above]—*Syn.* aloft, overhead, overtop, up beyond, covering, roofing, protecting, higher than, farther up, upstairs, in the sky, at the zenith, straight *or* high up, up there, in the clouds, among the stars, in heaven, just over, up from, outer, on top of; see also **above** 1, **up** 1, **upper.**—*Ant.* under*, below, beneath.
2. [Passing above]—*Syn.* overhead, aloft, up high; see **across.**
3. [Again]—*Syn.* once more, afresh, another time; see **again.**
4. [Beyond]—*Syn.* past, farther on, out of sight; see **beyond.**
5. [Done]—*Syn.* accomplished, ended, completed; see **done** 2, **finished** 1.
6. [(D) In addition]—*Syn.* over and above, extra, additionally; see **besides.**
7. [Having authority]—*Syn.* superior to, in authority, above; see **higher, superior.**

over a barrel (D), *mod.* —*Syn.* in trouble, worsted, defeated; see **beaten** 1.

overabundance, *n.* —*Syn.* surplus, profusion, superfluity; see **excess** 1.

overact, *v.* —*Syn.* assume, overdo, act; see **exceed, exaggerate.**

over-all, *mod.* —*Syn.* complete, thorough, comprehensive; see **general** 1.

overalls, *n.* —*Syn.* an over-all garment, jump suit, coveralls; see **clothes, pants** 1.

overbalance, *v.* **1.** [To exceed]—*Syn.* pass over, surpass, transcend; see **exceed.**
2. [To upset]—*Syn.* subvert, capsize, overturn; see **upset** 1.

overbearing, *mod.* **1.** [Haughty]—*Syn.* arrogant, proud, insolent; see **egotistic** 2.
2. [Autocratic]—*Syn.* despotic, oppressive, dictatorial; see **absolute** 3, **autocratic** 1, **tyrannical.**

overblown, *mod.* —*Syn.* superfluous, excessive, profuse; see **oratorical, verbose.**

overboard, *mod.* —*Syn.* over the side, from on board, off the ship, out of the boat, into the water.
overbuilt, *mod.* —*Syn.* overly promoted, overgrown, built up too much *or* excessively; see **exaggerated.**
overcast, *mod.* —*Syn.* cloudy, clouded, not clear *or* fair; see **dark** 1.
overcharge, *v.* —*Syn.* overtax, cheat, charge to excess, overburden, strain, lay it on (D); see also **deceive.**
overcoat, *n.* —*Syn.* greatcoat, topcoat, raincoat; see **clothes, coat** 1.
overcome, *mod.* **1.** [Beaten]—*Syn.* conquered, overwhelmed, overthrown; see **beaten** 1.
2. [Seized]—*Syn.* apprehended, appropriated, pre-empted; see **captured** 1, **held.**
overcome, *v.* —*Syn.* overwhelm, subdue, master; see **defeat** 1, **win** 1.
overcompensate, *v.* —*Syn.* correct *or* revise *or* improve unduly *or* excessively *or* too much, overdo a good thing, blunder; see **correct** 1, **destroy** 1, **overdo** 1.
overconfident, *mod.* —*Syn.* reckless, impudent, heedless; see **careless** 1, **rash.**
overcritical, *mod.* —*Syn.* domineering, harsh, hypercritical; see **severe** 1, 2.
overcrowd, *v.* —*Syn.* crowd, stuff, fill; see **pack** 2, **press** 1.
overcrowded, *mod.* —*Syn.* congested, overbuilt, overpopulated; see **full** 1.
overcrowding, *n.* —*Syn.* overpopulation, overbuilding, population explosion; see **congestion.**
overdeveloped, *mod.* —*Syn.* congested, pushed *or* promoted too much, overbuilt; see **growing.**
overdevelopment, *n.* —*Syn.* overbuilding, overexpansion, overoptimistic handling *or* treatment; see **congestion.**
overdo, *v.* **1.** [To do too much]—*Syn.* magnify, pile up *or* on, amplify, overestimate, overreach, stretch, overvalue, go *or* carry too far, overplay, overrate, exaggerate, hyperbolize, go to extremes, overstate, enlarge, enhance, exalt; *all* (D): bite off more than one can chew, run into the ground, do to death, go overboard, butter one's bread on both sides, carry coals to Newcastle, burn the candle at both ends, lay it on, have too many irons in the fire, have one's cake and eat it too; see also **exceed.**—*Ant.* neglect*, underdo, slack.
2. [To overtax oneself physically]—*Syn.* overlabor, overwork, overload, overlade, overdrive, strain, overstrain, fatigue, exhaust, overtire, wear down, collapse; see also **tire** 1, **weary** 2.—*Ant.* loaf*, take it easy, dawdle.
overdone, *mod.* —*Syn.* excessive, too much, pushed too far; see **exaggerated.**
overdose, *n.* —*Syn.* excessive *or* heavy dose *or* dosage, too much, overtreatment; see **excess** 1, 3, **treatment** 2.
overdrawn, *mod.* —*Syn.* exhausted, depleted, (all) paid out; see **gone** 2.
overdue, *mod.* —*Syn.* delayed, belated, tardy; see **late** 1.
overeager, *mod.* —*Syn.* overzealous, vigorous, overenthusiastic; see **enthusiastic** 1, 2, 3.
overeat, *v.* —*Syn.* overindulge, stuff, gorge; see **eat** 1.
overemphasize, *v.* —*Syn.* stress; *both* (D): make a big thing of, make something out of (nothing); see **emphasize, exceed.**
overestimate, *v.* —*Syn.* overvalue, overprice, overrate; see **exaggerate, exceed.**
overexcite, *v.* —*Syn.* quicken, provoke, arouse; see **excite** 1.
overexcited, *mod.* —*Syn.* aroused, overstimulated, incited; see **excited.**
overexert, *v.* —*Syn.* fatigue, strain, exhaust; see **tire** 2.
overexpand, *v.* —*Syn.* grow *or* develop too much *or* too fast, overdevelop, overextend; see **grow** 1.
overextended, *mod.* —*Syn.* overexpanded, spread too thin, spread out; see **enlarged.**
overfeed, *v.* —*Syn.* overfill, satiate, stuff; see **eat** 1.
overfill, *v.* —*Syn.* cram, overload, stuff; see **compress, pack** 2, **press** 1.
overflight, *v.* —*Syn.* survey, reconnaissance flight, spy mission; see **flight** 2, **spying.**
overflow, *n.* **1.** [The act of overflowing]—*Syn.* redundancy, inundation, exuberance, overproduction, congestion, deluge, spillover, overabundance, engorgement, flooding, spilling (over), submergence, submersion, overspreading, superabounding, overcrowding, enforcement, push, propulsion, encroachment, advance, infringement, overtopping, overwhelming, overbrimming; see also **flood** 1.—*Ant.* lack*, deficiency, scarcity.
2. [That which overflows]—*Syn.* superfluity, surplus, surplusage; see **excess** 1.
3. [The vent through which overflow occurs] —*Syn.* outlet, passage, exit; see **hole** 1, 2.
overflow, *v.* **1.** [To flow over the top, or out at a vent]—*Syn.* spill over, fall, run *or* pour (out *or* over), waste, shed, cascade, spout (forth), jet, spurt, drain, leak, squirt, spray, shower, gush, shoot, issue, rush, irrupt, wave, surge, overtop, overbrim, brim *or* lap *or* bubble *or* flow over; see also **flow** 2, **spill.**
2. [To flow out upon]—*Syn.* inundate, water, wet; see **flood.**
overflowing, *mod.* —*Syn.* abundant, in (God's) plenty, bountiful; see **plentiful** 2.
overfly, *v.* —*Syn.* survey, fly across *or* over, inspect; see **fly** 1, 4.
overgrown, *mod.* **1.** [Grown to an unnatural size] —*Syn.* disproportionate, excessive, huge; see **large** 1.
2. [Grown without being tended]—*Syn.* thick, crowded, disordered; see **green** 2, **wild** 3.
overgrowth, *n.* —*Syn.* growth, abundance, luxuriance; see **excess** 1.
overhang, *n.* —*Syn.* protrusion, obtrusion, overlap, overlie, droop, suspension, imbrication, beetling, jutting, extension; see also **projection.**
overhang, *v.* **1.** [To hang over]—*Syn.* jut, be suspended, beetle, impend, command, overtop, swing *or* dangle *or* droop *or* flap over; see also **project** 1, **protrude.**
2. [To threaten]—*Syn.* be imminent, endanger, menace; see **threaten** 2.
overhaul, *v.* —*Syn.* modernize, fix, renew; see **improve** 1, **reconstruct, repair** 1, **restore** 3.
overhead, *mod.* —*Syn.* above, aloft, hanging; see **over** 1.

overhead, *n.* —*Syn.* rent, insurance, depreciation, current expense, factory cost, burden; see also **expenses.**

overhear, *v.* —*Syn.* hear intentionally, listen in on, catch; see **eavesdrop, hear** 1, 2, **listen** 1.

overheard, *mod.* —*Syn.* listened to, recorded, bugged (D); see **heard.**

overheat, *v.* —*Syn.* heat (up) too much, bake, blister; see **heat** 2.

overindulgence, *n.* —*Syn.* overeating, overdrinking, eating *or* drinking too much; see **drunkenness, eating, greed.**

overjoyed, *mod.* —*Syn.* enraptured, transported, charmed; see **happy** 1, **thrilled.**

overkill, *n.* —*Syn.* (needless) slaughter, extermination, genocide; see **carnage, destruction** 1, 2.

overland, *mod.* —*Syn.* transcontinental, coast-to-coast, fast, west-coast, east-coast, plane, train, stage, bus, air, Pullman, through (D); see also **cross-country.**

overlap, *n.* —*Syn.* extension, overlay, addition; see **flap, overhang, projection.**

overlap, *v.* —*Syn.* overlie, overhang, imbricate, lap *or* fold over, extend (alongside), flap, extend *or* project *or* fold upon, overlay; see also **project** 1, **protrude.**

overlapping, *mod.* —*Syn.* coincidental, overlying, super-imposed, extending, protruding, projecting.

overlay, *v.* **1.** [To burden]—*Syn.* overload, cram, encumber; see **burden** 1, **load** 1.
2. [To overlap]—*Syn.* extend, superimpose, cover; see **overlap.**

overleap, *v.* **1.** [To jump over]—*Syn.* spring, leap over, pass; see **jump** 1.
2. [To omit]—*Syn.* reject, overlook, miss; see **omit** 1.

overload, *v.* —*Syn.* oppress, weigh down, encumber; see **burden, load** 1.

overlook, *v.* **1.** [To occupy a commanding height] —*Syn.* look over, top, survey, inspect, watch over, look out, view, give upon *or* on, front on, command, tower over, have a prospect of, surmount, mount over; see also **face** 4.
2. [To ignore deliberately]—*Syn.* slight, make light of, disdain; see **neglect** 1.
3. [To fail to see]—*Syn.* miss, leave out, neglect; see **omit** 1.

overlooked, *mod.* —*Syn.* missed, left out, forgotten; see **neglected, omitted.**

overlooking, *mod.* **1.** [Providing a view]—*Syn.* viewing, topping, surmounting, looking over, giving on, looking out on, giving a survey of, giving a vantage point, lofty, commanding.
2. [Disregarding]—*Syn.* missing, neglecting, forgetting, passing over, disdaining, scorning, snubbing, cutting, slighting, being inattentive to, being unobservant, making light of, passing; see also **omitting.**

overnight, *mod.* —*Syn.* one night, lasting one night, during one *or* the night; see **late** 4.

over (one's) dead body (D), *mod.* —*Syn.* not if one can help it, (only) with (great) difficulty, by no means; see **never.**

overpass, *n.* —*Syn.* span, footbridge, gangplank; see **bridge** 1.

overpay, *v.* —*Syn.* pay (too much), pay excessively, overcompensate, overrecompense, over-reward, over-remunerate, overreimburse, overyield, overexceed, oversettle, pay the Devil (D).—*Ant.* deceive*, deprive, cheat.

overpayment, *n.* —*Syn.* overcharge, too much, payment warranting *or* requiring a refund; see **money** 1, **payment** 1.

overplay, *v.* —*Syn.* overdo, labor (at), show off; see **promote** 1, **work** 1.

overpower, *v.* —*Syn.* overwhelm, master, subjugate; see **defeat** 2.

overpowering, *mod.* —*Syn.* irresistible, uncontrollable, overwhelming; see **intense.**

overproduction, *n.* —*Syn.* excess, excessive production, overstock; see **production** 1, 2.

overrate, *v.* —*Syn.* build up, magnify, overestimate; see **exaggerate, exceed.**

overrated, *mod.* —*Syn.* not (very) good, overblown, not satisfactory; see **poor** 2, **unsatisfactory.**

overreach, *v.* **1.** [To exceed]—*Syn.* overact, outreach, overdo; see **exceed.**
2. [To outwit]—*Syn.* outsmart, cheat, fool; see **deceive.**
3. [To spread over]—*Syn.* overlay, encroach (on *or* upon), overlap; see **cover** 1, **spread** 4.

overridden, *mod.* —*Syn.* defeated, rejected, voted down; see **refused.**

override, *v.* **1.** [To dismiss]—*Syn.* pass over, not heed, take no account of; see **disregard, neglect** 1.
2. [To thwart]—*Syn.* make void, reverse, annul; see **cancel** 2, **revoke.**

overriding, *mod.* —*Syn.* dominant, main, determining; see **major** 1.

overripe, *mod.* —*Syn.* decayed, decaying, overmature; see **rotten** 1.

overrule, *v.* **1.** [To nullify]—*Syn.* invalidate, rule against, override; see **cancel** 2, **revoke.**
2. [To rule]—*Syn.* direct, control, manage; see **govern** 1.

overrun, *v.* **1.** [To defeat]—*Syn.* overwhelm, invade, occupy; see **defeat** 2.
2. [To infest]—*Syn.* ravage, invade, overwhelm; see **infest, swarm.**

overseas, *mod.* —*Syn.* away, across, in foreign countries; see **abroad.**

oversee, *v.* —*Syn.* superintend, supervise, look after; see **command** 2, **manage** 1.

overseer, *n.* —*Syn.* supervisor, manager, superintendent; see **foreman.**

oversell, *v.* —*Syn.* glut (the market), overpromote, push *or* promote too hard *or* much; see **sell** 1.

overshadow, *v.* **1.** [To dominate]—*Syn.* manage, tower above, rule; see **command** 2, **dominate, govern.**
2. [To shade]—*Syn.* shadow, dim, cloud; see **shade** 2.

overshoes, *n.* —*Syn.* rubber shoes, galoshes, rubbers, arctics, gums (D); see also **shoe.**

overshoot, *v.* —*Syn.* overreach, overdo, overact; see **exceed.**

oversight, *n.* —*Syn.* failure, overlooking, mistake; see **error** 1, **omission** 1.

oversimplification, *n.* —*Syn.* (too great a) reduction, excessive simplification, simplism; see **simplicity.**

oversimplified, *mod.* —*Syn.* simplistic, simple, made easy; see **simplified.**
oversimplify, *v.* —*Syn.* (over)reduce, make too simple *or* easy *or* simplistic, restrict; see **simplify.**
oversleep, *v.* —*Syn.* sleep late *or* in, miss the alarm (clock), stay in bed; see **sleep.**
overspecialize, *v.* —*Syn.* limit (oneself), specialize too much, be a specialist; see **restrain** 1, **restrict** 2.
overspread, *v.* —*Syn.* envelop, sheathe, coat; see **cover** 1.
overstaffed, *mod.* —*Syn.* having *or* with too many men *or* employees, having excess *or* unneeded labor *or* help, having *or* with no openings; see **full** 1, 3.
overstate, *v.* —*Syn.* expand upon, amplify, emphasize; see **exaggerate, exceed.**
overstay, *v.* —*Syn.* stay (too long), stop, outstay one's welcome; see **remain** 1.
overstep, *v.* —*Syn.* violate, encroach, trespass; see **exceed, meddle** 1.
overstock, *v.* —*Syn.* overfill, cram, overload; see **burden, load** 1.
overstress, *v.* —*Syn.* overemphasize, stress too much, promote *or* push out of proportion; see **emphasize.**
overstrung, *mod.* —*Syn.* distraught, hypersensitive, nervous; see **excited, frantic, hysterical, troubled** 1.
oversubscribed, *mod.* —*Syn.* contributed to, overpurchased, put over the top (D); see **bought, given.**
oversubscription, *n.* —*Syn.* oversubscribing, lively market, generous contributions; see **gift** 1, **sale** 1, 2.
overt, *mod.* —*Syn.* clear, open, plain; see **definite** 2, **obvious** 1.
overtake, *v.* —*Syn.* overhaul, catch up with, get to; see **catch** 3, **reach** 1.
overtaken, *mod.* —*Syn.* caught (up with *or* to), reached, apprehended; see **beaten** 1, **captured** 1.
overtax, *v.* —*Syn.* exhaust, strain, trouble; see **oppress, tire** 2, **weary** 1.
over the hill (D), *mod.* —*Syn.* past, removed, departed; see **dead** 1, **gone** 1, 2, **old** 1, 2.
overthrow, *v.* **1.** [To defeat]—*Syn.* overcome, overrun, overpower; see **defeat** 2.
2. [To abolish]—*Syn.* eradicate, exterminate, terminate; see **abolish, destroy** 1.
overthrown, *mod.* —*Syn.* overcome, overwhelmed, vanquished; see **beaten** 1.
overtime, *mod.* —*Syn.* additional, added, supplementary; see **extra, late** 4.
overtime, *n.* —*Syn.* extra *or* additional pay *or* wages, late hours, larger *or* bigger check; see **pay** 2.
overtone, *n.* —*Syn.* tone, inference, hint; see **meaning, suggestion** 1.
overtop, *v.* —*Syn.* dominate, command, surpass; see **exceed.**
overture, *n.* **1.** [Preliminary negotiations; *sometimes plural*]—*Syn.* approach, advance, tender; see **suggestion** 1.
2. [A musical introduction]—*Syn.* prelude, prologue, *Vorspiel* (German), voluntary, proem, preface; see also **introduction** 1.
overturn, *v.* —*Syn.* reverse, upturn, overthrow; see **upset** 1.
overuse, *v.* —*Syn.* use too much *or* too frequently, wear out, misuse; see **abuse** 1, **use** 1.
overvalue, *v.* —*Syn.* magnify, overestimate, overemphasize; see **exaggerate, exceed, overdo** 1.
overview, *n.* —*Syn.* survey, sketch, (general) outlook; see **summary.**
overweening, *mod.* —*Syn.* haughty, insolent, arrogant; see **egotistic** 2.
overweigh, *v.* —*Syn.* weigh down, overload, strain; see **burden, outweigh.**
overwhelm, *v.* **1.** [To defeat]—*Syn.* overcome, overthrow, conquer; see **confute, defeat** 1, **win** 1.
2. [To drown]—*Syn.* submerge, inundate, waste; see **sink** 1.
3. [To astonish]—*Syn.* puzzle, bewilder, confound; see **confuse, surprise** 1.
overwhelmed, *mod.* —*Syn.* beaten, worsted, overpowered, vanquished, devastated, repulsed, engulfed, submerged; see also **beaten** 2, **drowned.**
overwhelming, *mod.* **1.** [In the act of destroying] —*Syn.* conquering, subjugating, defeating, subduing, overpowering, overthrowing, crushing, routing, ruining, smashing, wiping out, extinguishing, invading, occupying, ravaging, devastating, breaking, reducing, overturning, overriding, overrunning, upsetting; see also **triumphant.**—*Ant.* protective*, saving, defending.
2. [In the act of submerging]—*Syn.* wasting, inundating, drowning, deluging, surging, overspreading, desolating, obliterating, dissolving, blotting out, wrecking, erasing, effacing, expunging, burying, immersing, engulfing, engrossing, covering. —*Ant.* floating*, reclaiming, raising.
3. [Astonishing]—*Syn.* amazing, terrifying, awful; see **frightful** 1, **might** 3, **powerful** 1, **strong** 1, 2, 8.
4. [Unbelievable]—*Syn.* remarkable, strange, baffling; see **unbelievable, unusual** 1, 2.
overwhelming, *n.* —*Syn.* ruining, destroying, overrunning; see **destruction** 1, **wreck** 1.
overwork, *n.* —*Syn.* extra work, overtime, exploitation, overburdening, overloading, exhaustion, going too far, overdoing it; see also **abuse** 3.
overwork, *v.* —*Syn.* overdo, exhaust, wear out; see **burden, tire** 1, 2, **weary** 1.
overworked, *mod.* —*Syn.* too busy, overburdened, worked too hard; see **tired.**
overwrought, *mod.* **1.** [Weary from exhaustion] —*Syn.* affected, worn, weary; see **spent** 2, **tired.**
2. [Excitable from exhaustion]—*Syn.* emotional, nervous, neurotic; see **excitable.**
overzealous, *mod.* —*Syn.* overeager, carrying a good thing too far, bossy; see **enthusiastic** 1, 2, 3.
owe, *v.* —*Syn.* be under obligation, be indebted *or* obligated to *or* for, have an obligation, ought to, be bound, become beholden, get on credit, feel bound, be bound to pay, be contracted to, be subject to draft for, be in debt for, have signed a note for, have borrowed, have lost, bind out (D).
owed, *mod.* —*Syn.* owing, becoming due, indebted; see **due, unpaid** 1.
owing, *mod.* —*Syn.* owed, attributable, in debt; see **due.**
owl, *n.* —*Syn.* owlet, bird of prey, night bird, nocturnal bird, owl pigeon, satinette, turbit, Bubo, Strix; see also **bird** 1.
Kinds of owls include the following—hoot, barn, burrowing, great horned, screech, spotted, eagle,

snow, snowy, tawny, long-eared, short-eared, pigmy, boobook, saw-whet, hissing, African, Chinese; hawk owl.

own, *mod.* —*Syn.* mine, yours, his, hers, its, theirs, personal, individual, owned, very own (D); see also **private.**

own, *v.* **1.** [To possess]—*Syn.* hold, have, enjoy, have inherited, fallen heir to, have title to, have rights to, be master of, occupy, control, dominate, have claim upon, boast, reserve, retain, keep, have in hand, have a deed for; see also **maintain** 3. —*Ant.* lack*, want, need.

2. [To acknowledge]—*Syn.* assent to, grant, recognize; see **admit** 2, 3, **declare** 2.

owned, *mod.* —*Syn.* possessed, had, bought, purchased, kept, inherited, enjoyed, fallen into the possession of, seized by, in the seizin of, in *or* on hand, bound over, descended upon, dowered upon, in the possession of, among the possessions of, the property of; see also **held, retained** 1.

come into one's own—*Syn.* receive what one deserves, gain proper credit *or* recognition, thrive; see **prosper.**

of one's own—*Syn.* personal, private, belonging to one; see **owned.**

on one's own—*Syn.* by oneself, acted independently, singly; see **independently.**

owner, *n.* —*Syn.* one who has *or* retains, possessor, keeper, buyer, purchaser, heir, heiress, coinheritor, joint heir, heritor, legatee, proprietor, proprietress, landlord, landlady, sharer, partner, titleholder, master, heir-apparent; see also **possessor.**

ownership, *n.* —*Syn.* possession, having, holding, claim, deed, title, control, buying, purchasing, purchase, falling heir to, heirship, possessorship, proprietorship, occupancy, tenure, use, residence, tenancy, dominion, seizin.

own up (D), *v.* —*Syn.* be honest, admit error, confess; see **admit** 2.

ox, *n.* —*Syn.* castrated bull, bullock, steer, *Bos taurus* (Latin); see also **animal** 1, **bull** 1, **cow.**

Kinds of oxen include the following—wild, musk, Indian, Galla, gayal, gaur.

oxford, *n.* —*Syn.* low shoe, walking shoe, tie shoe, blucher, brogue, comfort shoe, nurse's shoe; see also **shoe.**

oyster, *n.* —*Syn.* bivalve, mollusk, sea food; see also **clam, fish, shellfish.**

Types of oysters include the following—blue point, rock, American-Canadian, Portuguese, Japanese (Gigantic), Chinese, European, British Columbian, Australian mud, flat, saddlerock, cove, box, wild, tonged, dredged.

P

pa (D), *n.* —*Syn.* sire, papa, dad; see **father** 1, **parent.**

pabulum, *n.* —*Syn.* sustenance, nutrition, diet; see **food.**

pace, *n.* —*Syn.* step, velocity, movement; see **speed.**
change of pace—*Syn.* variation, alteration, diversity; see **change** 2.
go through one's paces—*Syn.* show one's abilities, perform, exhibit; see **display** 1.
keep pace (with)—*Syn.* go at the same speed, maintain the same rate of progress, keep up with; see **equal.**
off the pace—*Syn.* out of first place, behind the leader, trailing after; see **behind** 3.
put through one's paces— challenge, put to the test, run through a routine; see **test** 1.
set the pace—*Syn.* begin, initiate, establish criteria; see **lead** 1.

pace, *v.* **1.** [To stride]—*Syn.* trot, canter, gallop; see **walk** 1.
2. [To measure by pacing]—*Syn.* determine, pace off, step off; see **measure** 1.

pacer, *n.* **1.** [A horse]—*Syn.* pony, mount, steed; see **animal** 2, **horse** 1.
2. [A criterion]—*Syn.* standard, example, pacemaker; see **criterion, measure** 2.

pacifiable, *mod.* —*Syn.* forgiving, peaceable, appeasable, placable, conciliable, propitiable, pacificatory, propitiatory.

Pacific, *n.* —*Syn.* North Pacific, South Pacific, Central Pacific, South Seas; see also **ocean.**

pacific, *mod.* —*Syn.* peaceable, peaceful, tranquil, untroubled, smooth, gentle, quiet, still, composed, restful, unruffled, halcyon, appeasing, conciliatory, mild, kindly, placid, serene, easygoing; see also **calm** 1, 2.—*Ant.* quarrelsome*, turbulent, rough.

pacification, *n.* —*Syn.* accommodation, settlement, adjustment; see **agreement** 3.

pacifist, *n.* —*Syn.* man of peace, peace-lover, peace monger, passive resister, Satyagrahist, noncooperator, civil disobedience campaigner; *all* (D): conchie, sit-downer, flower child, dove; see also **radical, conscientious objector, resister.**

pacify, *v.* **1.** [To mollify]—*Syn.* conciliate, appease, placate; see **quiet** 1.
2. [To quiet]—*Syn.* soothe, silence, lull; see **quiet** 2.

pack, *n.* **1.** [A package]—*Syn.* bundle, parcel, load; see **package** 1.
2. [Kit]—*Syn.* outfit, baggage, luggage; see **equipment.**
3. [A group]—*Syn.* number, gang, mob; see **crowd** 1.
4. [A medical dressing]—*Syn.* application, hot pack, ice pack, pledget, pad, sponge, tampon, compress, bandage, wet dressing; see also **dressing** 3.
5. [A set of cards]—*Syn.* canasta *or* poker *or* rummy *or* bridge *or* pinochle deck, set, assortment; see **deck** 2.

pack, *v.* **1.** [To prepare for transportation]—*Syn.* prepare, gather, collect, (make) ready, get ready, put in (order), stow away, dispose, cinch, sock up, tie with a diamond hitch, tie, bind, brace, fasten. —*Ant.* undo*, untie, take out.
2. [To stow compactly]—*Syn.* stuff, squeeze, bind, compress, condense, arrange, ram, cram, jam, insert, press, contract, put away, pack *or* thrust *or* drive *or* run in.—*Ant.* scatter*, loosen, fluff up.
3. [To fill by entering; *often used with* in]—*Syn.* crowd, throng, mob; see **press** 1, **push** 1.
4. [To transport by using pack animals; *often used with* in *or* out]—*Syn.* freight, journey, trek, haul around, go by muleback, take a pack train; see also **carry** 1.

package, *n.* **1.** [A bundle]—*Syn.* parcel, packet, bundle, burden, load, kit, bunch, sheaf, pack, batch, baggage, luggage, grip, suitcase, bag, handbag, valise, trunk, box, carton, crate, can, tin, sack, bottle; see also **container.**
2. [The contents of a package, sense 1]—*Syn.* parcel, bale, bundle, crate, tin, load, bunch, assortment, stack, pile, roll, lot, dunnage, faggot.

packed, *mod.* **1.** [Ready for storage or shipment] —*Syn.* arranged, prepared, bundled, wrapped, consigned; see also **ready** 2.
2. [Pressed together]—*Syn.* compact, compressed, pressed down; see **full** 1, **jammed** 2.

packet, *n.* **1.** [A small bundle or container]—*Syn.* pack, receptacle, parcel; see **container, package** 1.
2. [A ship with a regular schedule]—*Syn.* mail ship, mail steamer, steamboat; see **ship.**

packhorse, *n.* —*Syn.* nag, pack animal, transportation; see **animal** 2, **horse** 1.

packing, *n.* **1.** [The preparation of goods for shipment or storage]—*Syn.* preparation, arrangement, compression, consignment, disposal, disposition, sorting, grading, laying away.
2. [Material used to fill space]—*Syn.* stuffing, wadding, waste; see **filling.**

packing house, *n.* —*Syn.* packing *or* processing plant, meat packers, butchery; see **butcher, factory.**

packsaddle, *n.* —*Syn.* mule chair, seat, cushion; see **saddle.**

pack train, *n.* —*Syn.* caravan, safari, supply train; see **equipment.**

pact, *n.* —*Syn.* settlement, compact, bargain; see **agreement** 3, **treaty.**

pad, *n.* **1.** [Material for writing]—*Syn.* note paper, note pad, memorandum, block, foolscap, parchment, *tabula rasa* (Latin); see also **paper** 5, **tablet** 2.
2. [Material for padding]—*Syn.* stuffing, wadding, waste; see **filling.**
3. [(D) a residence]—*Syn.* room, apartment, living quarters; see **home** 1, 2.

pad, *v.* **1.** [To thicken]—*Syn.* stuff, fill out, pad out; see **fill** 1.
2. [To increase]—*Syn.* lengthen, expand, augment, amplify, inflate, spread, stretch, enlarge; see also **increase** 1.

padded, *mod.* —*Syn.* stuffed, filled, quilted; see **full** 1, **jammed** 2.

padding, *n.* **1.** [Filling]—*Syn.* stuffing, wadding, waste; see **filling.**
2. [Verbosity]—*Syn.* diffuseness, redundancy, triteness; see **wordiness.**

paddle, *n.* —*Syn.* oar, pole, scull, sweep, paddle wheel; see also **propeller.**

paddle, *v.* **1.** [To propel by paddling]—*Syn.* scull, boat, cruise, drift, navigate, cut water, run rapids; see also **drive** 3, **propel.**
2. [To beat, usually rather lightly]—*Syn.* spank, thrash, rap; see **beat** 2, **punish.**

paddled, *mod.* —*Syn.* beaten, spanked, pounded; see **hit, punished.**

paddle one's own canoe (D), *v.* —*Syn.* do without assistance, go alone, ask no favors, manage, rely upon oneself.

paddock, *n.* —*Syn.* corral, pen, stockyard; see **barnyard.**

padlock, *n.* —*Syn.* latch, fastener, catch; see **lock** 1.

padre, *n.* —*Syn.* clergyman, pastor, monk; see **minister** 1, **priest.**

padrone, *n.* —*Syn.* operator, supervisor, chief; see **master** 1.

paean, *n.* —*Syn.* ovation, oratorio, anthem; see **hymn, song.**

pagan, *mod.* —*Syn.* unchristian, idolatrous, heathenish; see **atheistic, heathen, impious** 1.

pagan, *n.* —*Syn.* idolater, idolist, gentile, pantheist, heathen, Pyrrhonist, doubter, scoffer, heretic, unbeliever, infidel, paynim, Gheber, Philistine, Zoroastrian, animist, fireworshipper, freethinker, atheist, agnostic; see also **skeptic.**—*Ant.* Christian*, Jew, Mohammedan*.

paganism, *n.* —*Syn.* heathenism, agnosticism, idolatry, pagandom, mythology, mysticism, henotheism, ditheism, dualism, pantheism, cosmotheism, nonbelief, infidelity, doubt, heresy, demonism, demon worship, devil worship, sun worship, heliolatry, pyrolatry, fetishism, heathenry; see also **atheism.**

page, *n.* **1.** [One side of a sheet]—*Syn.* leaf, sheet, folio, side, surface, recto, verso.
2. [A youth]—*Syn.* attendant, footboy, boy; see **servant.**

page, *v.* **1.** [To call]—*Syn.* hunt for, seek for, call the name of; see **summon** 1.
2. [To mark the pages]—*Syn.* number, check, paginate, foliate; see also **count.**

pageant, *n.* —*Syn.* exhibition, celebration, pomp; see **parade** 1.

pageantry, *n.* —*Syn.* pomp, show, spectacle; see **display** 2, **parade** 1.

paged, *mod.* —*Syn.* summoned, called *or* asked for, sought; see **requested** 1.

paid, *mod.* —*Syn.* rewarded, paid off, reimbursed, compensated, indemnified, remunerated, solvent, unindebted, unowed, recompensed, salaried, hired, out of debt, refunded; see also **repaid.**

paid for, *mod.* —*Syn.* purchased, bought and paid for, owned; see **bought.**

paid off, *mod.* —*Syn.* out of debt, solvent, (in the) clear; see **bought.**

pail, *n.* —*Syn.* pot, receptacle, jug; see **bucket, container.**

pain, *n.* **1.** [Suffering, physical or mental]—*Syn.* hurt, anguish, distress, discomfort, disorder, agony, misery, crucifixion, martyrdom, wretchedness, shock, torture, torment, passion; see also **injury** 1. —*Ant.* health*, well-being, ease.
2. [Suffering, usually physical]—*Syn.* ache, twinge, catch, throb, throe, spasm, cramp, gripe, stitch, torture, malady, sickness, rack, laceration, paroxysm, soreness, fever, burning, prick, torment, distress, agony, affliction, discomfort, hurt, pang, wound, strain, sting, burn, crick; see also **illness** 1, **injury** 1. Specific kinds of pains (including aches) include the following—housemaid's knee, tennis elbow, shin splint, arthritis, arthritic pain, rheumatism, inflammatory rheumatism, gout, peritonitis, bursitis, earache, headache, stomachache *or* bellyache, toothache, backache.
3. [Suffering, usually mental]—*Syn.* despondency, worry, anxiety; see **depression** 2, **grief** 1, **sadness.**
feeling no pain (D)—*Syn.* intoxicated, inebriated, stoned (D); see **drunk.**
upon (*or* **under) pain of**—*Syn.* at the risk of, in danger of, risking; see **gambling.**

pain, *v.* —*Syn.* distress, grieve, trouble; see **hurt** 1.

pained, *mod.* —*Syn.* upset, worried, distressed; see **hurt, troubled** 1.

painful, *mod.* **1.** [Referring to physical anguish] —*Syn.* raw, aching, throbbing, burning, torturing, hurtful, biting, piercing, sharp, severe, caustic, tormenting, smarting, extreme, grievous, griping, stinging, lacerating, bruised, sensitive, tender, irritated, irritable, vexatious, distressing, grievous, inflamed, burned, unpleasant, ulcerated, abcessed, uncomfortable; see also **sore.**—*Ant.* healthy*, comfortable, well.
2. [Referring to mental anguish]—*Syn.* worrying, depressing, saddening; see **disturbing.**

painful, *mod.* **1.** [With pain]—*Syn.* in pain, achingly, in suffering, racked by pain, sorely, with difficulty.
2. [With extreme care]—*Syn.* painstakingly, slowly, tortuously; see **carefully** 1, 2.

painstaking, *mod.* —*Syn.* scrupulous, exacting, meticulous; see **careful.**

paint, *n.* **1.** [Pigment]—*Syn.* coloring material, chroma, chlorophyll; see **color** 1.
Paints and colorings include the following—*artist's materials:* oil, acrylic, pastel, gouache, crayon, charcoal, water color, showcard color, tempera; *architectural finishes:* house paint, enamel, varnish, calcimine, casein paint, stain, oil, wax, whitewash, tempera, fresco, encaustic, anticorrosion paint, antifouling paint, metallic paint, fireproof paint, cellulose paint, luminous paint, barn paint, inside

paint, outside paint, flat paint, white lead, linseed oil paint.
2. [(D) Make-up]—*Syn.* cosmetics, tint, rouge; see **cosmetic, make-up** 1.
3. [Covering]—*Syn.* overlay, varnish, veneer; see **cover** 2.
paint, *v.* **1.** [To represent by painting]—*Syn.* portray, paint in oils, sketch, outline, picture, depict, delineate, draft, catch a likeness, limn, design, shade, tint, compose, apply pigment, fresco, wash; see also **draw** 2.
2. [To protect, or decorate by painting]—*Syn.* coat, decorate, apply, brush, tint, touch up, stipple, ornament, gloss over, swab, daub, slap on, (use an) airbrush; see also **cover** 1, **spread** 4.
3. [(D) To apply cosmetics]—*Syn.* cosmeticize, rouge, powder; see **make up** 6.
paintable, *mod.* —*Syn.* scenic, pictorial, graphic; see **picturesque** 1.
painted, *mod.* **1.** [Portrayed]—*Syn.* outlined, pictured, drawn, sketched, composed, designed, depicted, delineated, frescoed, limned, washed on; see also **colored** 1.
2. [Finished]—*Syn.* coated, covered, enameled, decorated, ornamented, brushed over, tinted, washed, daubed, touched up, smeared; see also **ornate** 1.
3. [(D) Made-up]—*Syn.* rouged, reddened, colored, powdered, freshened, daubed; see also **made-up** 2.
painter, *n.* **1.** [A house painter]—*Syn.* interior decorator, calciminer; *both* (D): dauber, paint-slinger; see also **workman.**
2. [An artist]—*Syn.* craftsman, artisan, illustrator, landscapist, portrait painter, miniaturist, draftsman, etcher, sketcher, cartoonist, artificer, animator, dauber; see also **artist** 1.
Major painters include the following—Cimabue, Giotto, Sandro Botticelli, Andrea del Sarto, Veronese, Jan van Eyck, Albrecht Dürer, Lucas Cranach, Hieronymus Bosch, Pieter Breughel (the elder and the younger), Hans Holbein (the elder and the younger), Frans Hals, Leonardo da Vinci, Michelangelo Buonarroti, Raphael, Titian, Tintoretto, El Greco, Correggio, Caravaggio, Canaletto, Tiepolo, Peter Paul Rubens, Anthony Van Dyck, Rembrandt van Rijn, Jan Vermeer, Nicolas Poussin, Antoine Watteau, Sir Joshua Reynolds, Thomas Gainsborough, John Constable, J. M. W. Turner, J. S. Copley, William Hogarth, Diego Velázquez, Francisco Goya, Eugène Delacroix, Auguste Renoir, Edgar Degas, James Whistler, Winslow Homer, Édouard Manet, Claude Monet, Walter Sickert, Paul Cézanne, Vincent van Gogh, Paul Gauguin, Henri de Toulouse-Lautrec, Pablo Picasso, Henri ("le Douanier") Rousseau, Amedeo Modigliani, Marc Chagall, Georges Braque, Henri Matisse, Piet Mondrian, Paul Klee, Salvador Dali, Jackson Pollock.
painting, *n.* **1.** [A work of art]—*Syn.* oil painting, water color, abstract design, landscape, cityscape, seascape, composition, sketch, portrait, picture, likeness, art work, canvas, mural, depiction, delineation; see also **art** 3.
Schools of painting include the following—primitive, Romanesque, Medieval, Florentine, Sienese, Flemish, Venetian, Mannerist, Dutch, Spanish, French, *tableau de genre* (French), pre-Raphaelite, impressionist, postimpressionist, *plein air* (French), Fauvism, primitivism, Naturalism, Expressionist, Cubism, Futurism, Symbolism, Dadaism, Surrealism, Mexican mural, pop, op.
2. [The act of applying paint]—*Syn.* enameling, covering, coating, varnishing, decorating, calcimining, daubing, splashing, brushing, airbrushing, the brush (D); see also **art** 2.
pair, *n.* —*Syn.* couple, mates, two, two of a kind, duo, twosome, combination, combo (D), twins, brace, deuce, fellows, yoke, duality, biformation; see also **both.**
pair, *v.* —*Syn.* combine (with), match, balance (off); see **join** 1, 2.
pajamas, *n.* —*Syn.* nightwear, lounging pajamas, lounging robe, slacks; *all* (D): PJ's, 'jamas, nightie.
pal (D), *n.* —*Syn.* companion, bosom friend, buddy; see **friend** 1.
palace, *n.* —*Syn.* royal residence, official residence, hall, manor, mansion, dwelling; see also **castle.**
palatable, *mod.* —*Syn.* tasty, appetizing, savory; see **delicious** 1.
palate, *n.* —*Syn.* roof of the mouth, velum, hard palate, soft palate; see also **mouth** 1.
palatial, *mod.* —*Syn.* regal, illustrious, magnificent; see **grand** 2, **stately** 2.
palatinate, *n.* —*Syn.* country, province, mandate; see **area** 2, **territory** 2.
palatine, *n.* —*Syn.* minister, chamberlain, official; see **lord** 2, **royalty.**
palaver, *n.* —*Syn.* speech, babble, conversation; see **nonsense** 1.
pale, *mod.* **1.** [Wan]—*Syn.* pallid, sickly, anemic, bloodless, ghastly, cadaverous, haggard, deathlike, ghostly, spectral, lurid; see also **dull** 2.
2. [Lacking light]—*Syn.* dim, wan, faint; see **dark** 1.
3. [Lacking color]—*Syn.* white, colorless, bleached; see **dull** 2.
pale, *v.* —*Syn.* grow pale, lose color, blanch; see **faint, whiten** 1.
paleness, *n.* **1.** [Pallor]—*Syn.* sickness, whiteness, anemia, pallidness, colorlessness.
2. [Dimness]—*Syn.* translucency, dullness, obscurity; see **darkness** 1.
paleology, *n.* —*Syn.* paleontology, archaism, prehistory; see **archaeology, science** 1.
palimpsest, *n.* —*Syn.* inscription, document, writing; see **manuscript.**
palindrome, *n.* —*Syn.* wordplay, play on words, witticism; see **pun.**
paling, *n.* —*Syn.* enclosure, hedge, picket; see **fence** 1.
palisade, *n.* —*Syn.* stockade, defense, bank; see **barrier, fortification** 2, **wall** 1.
palisades, *n.* —*Syn.* cliff, face, slope; see **mountain** 1, **wall** 1.
pall, *n.* —*Syn.* cloak, cloth, covering; see **cover** 1.
pall, *v.* —*Syn.* satiate, surfeit, glut; see **disgust, weary** 1.
pallet, *n.* —*Syn.* cot, stretcher, couch; see **bed** 1.
palliate, *v.* —*Syn.* apologize for, make light of, screen, hide, conceal, cover, veil, gloss over, cloak, mitigate, assuage, varnish, veneer, whitewash, soften, subdue, moderate, gloze, bolster up, excul-

pate, vindicate, justify, alleviate; see also **excuse, extenuate.**

pallid, *mod.* —*Syn.* gray, colorless, wan; see **pale** 1.

pallor, *n.* —*Syn.* wanness, whiteness, lack of color; see **paleness.**

palm, *n.* Types of palms include the following—feather, fan, date, Washington, doom, wax, cabbage, curly, fern, coconut, sea-coconut, rattan, oil, para, walkstick, wine, betel, palmyra, Bourbon, raphia, royal, umbrella, palmetto, piasava; see also **tree.**

palmate, *mod.* —*Syn.* jagged, scalloped, toothed, dentate, lobed, nicked, serrated, escalloped; see also **irregular** 4, **notched.**

palmist, *n.* —*Syn.* spiritualist, clairvoyant, prophet; see **fortuneteller.**

palmistry, *n.* —*Syn.* fortunetelling, prediction, prophecy; see **divination, forecast.**

palmy, *mod.* —*Syn.* prosperous, glorious, delightful; see **rich** 1, **successful, triumphant.**

palpable, *mod.* —*Syn.* plain, manifest, unmistakable; see **obvious** 1, **tangible.**

palpitate, *v.* —*Syn.* pulse, throb, vibrate; see **beat** 3.

palpitation, *n.* —*Syn.* throbbing, tremble, pulsation; see **beat** 2.

palsied, *mod.* —*Syn.* disabled, paralyzed, paralytic, neurasthenic, weak, debilitated, atonic, helpless, tremorous, shaking, diseased; see also **sick.**

palsy, *n.* —*Syn.* disability, paralysis, cerebral palsy; see **disease** 3.

paltriness, *n.* —*Syn.* unimportance, irrelevance, triviality; see **insignificance.**

paltry, *mod.* —*Syn.* small, insignificant, trifling; see **trivial, unimportant.**

pampas, *n.* —*Syn.* prairie, tundra, plains; see **plain.**

pamper, *v.* —*Syn.* spoil, indulge, baby, pet, cater to, humor, gratify, yield to, coddle, overindulge, please, cosset, spare the rod and spoil the child (D); see also **satisfy** 1.

pamphlet, *n.* —*Syn.* booklet, brochure, pocketbook, chapbook, leaflet, bulletin, compilation, circular, broadside, throwaway, handbill; see also **announcement** 3.

pamphleteer, *n.* —*Syn.* carper, commentator, essayist; see **critic** 1.

pan, *n.* —*Syn.* vessel, kettle, container, pail, bucket, baking pan, gold pan; see also **container, utensils** 1. Kitchen pans include the following—kettle, stew pan, sauce pan, double boiler, roaster, casserole, cake pan, bread pan, pie pan, cookie sheet, frying pan *or* skillet *or* spider, dishpan.

pan, *v.* **1.** [To obtain gold]—*Syn.* wash, shake, agitate, separate, placer, mine, secure, obtain.
2. [(D) To disparage]—*Syn.* criticize, review unfavorably, jeer at; see **censure.**
3. [To swing; *said of a camera*]—*Syn.* sweep, pan to *or* toward, follow; see **move** 1.

panacea, *n.* —*Syn.* relief, elixir, cure; see **remedy** 2.

pancake, *n.* —*Syn.* flapjack, hot cake, batter cake, griddlecake, cake, fried bread, fried mush, sourdough, *latke* (Yiddish), **tortilla** (Spanish), *crêpe* (French), *crêpes suzette* (French); see also **food.**

pandemonium, *n.* **1.** [Confusion]—*Syn.* uproar, anarchy, riot; see **confusion** 2.
2. [Hell]—*Syn.* underworld, inferno, abyss; see **hell** 1.

pander, *n.* —*Syn.* procurer, white slaver, whoremonger; see **pimp.**

pane, *n.* —*Syn.* window glass, stained glass, mirror; see **glass** 2.

panegyric, *mod.* —*Syn.* laudatory, acclamatory, flattering; see **complimentary.**

panegyric, *n.* —*Syn.* compliment, honor, eulogy; see **praise** 2.

panel, *n.* —*Syn.* ornament, tablet, inset, wainscoting, plyboard, hanging, tapestry, arras; see also **decoration** 2.

pang, *n.* —*Syn.* throb, sting, bite; see **pain** 1.

panhandle (D), *v.* —*Syn.* solicit, ask alms, bum (D); see **beg** 2.

panhandler, *n.* —*Syn.* vagrant, bum, mendicant; see **beggar** 1, **tramp** 1.

panic, *n.* **1.** [Overpowering fright]—*Syn.* dread, alarm, fright; see **fear** 1.
2. [Mob action, impelled by panic, sense 1]—*Syn.* mob hysteria, group hysteria, frenzy, crush, rush, jam; see also **confusion** 2.
3. [A wave of financial hysteria]—*Syn.* run on the bank, crash, economic decline; see **depression** 3.
push the panic button (D)—*Syn.* panic, become afraid, dread; see **fear** 1.

panic-stricken, *mod.* —*Syn.* terrified, hysterical, fearful; see **afraid** 2.

panoply, *n.* —*Syn.* covering, shield, protection; see **armor** 1.

panorama, *n.* —*Syn.* spectacle, scenery, prospect; see **view** 2.

panoramic, *mod.* —*Syn.* pictorial, general, scenic; see **picturesque** 1.

pan out (D), *v.* —*Syn.* yield, net, come *or* work out; see **result.**

pansy, *n.* —*Syn.* *Viola tricolor hortensis* (Latin), *pensée* (French), heartsease; see **flower** 2, **plant.**

pant, *v.* —*Syn.* wheeze, throb, palpitate; see **breathe** 1, **gasp.**

pantaloons, *n.* —*Syn.* trousers, breeches, knickers; see **clothes, pants** 1.

pantheism, *n.* —*Syn.* heathenism, polytheism, agnosticism; see **paganism.**

panther, *n.* **1.** [A wild beast]—*Syn.* jaguar, puma, wild cat; see **animal** 2, **cat** 2.
2. [A member of the Black Panthers]—*Syn.* (black *or* Negro) militant, dissident, ghetto reformer; see **protester.**

panties (D), *n.* —*Syn.* pants, underpants, briefs; see **underwear.**

panting, *n.* **1.** [Breathing]—*Syn.* respiring, gasping, heaving; see **breathing.**
2. [A desire]—*Syn.* passion, lust, hunger; see **desire** 3.

pantomime, *v.* —*Syn.* sign, sign language, dumb show, mimicry, play without words, acting without speech, charade, mime; see also **parody** 1.

pantry, *n.* —*Syn.* storeroom, scullery, larder, cupboard, cooler; see also **closet, room** 2.

pants, *n.* **1.** [Trousers]—*Syn.* breeches, slacks, jeans, denims, dungarees, overalls, cords, shorts, corduroys, pantaloons, jodhpurs, bell bottoms, toreador pants, riding breeches, chaps, short pants, knee pants, knickerbockers, knickers, bloomers, rompers, sun suit; see also **clothes.**

2. [(D) Underclothing, especially women's]—*Syn.* shorts, drawers, briefs, panties, bikinis, scanties, *cache-sexe* (French), knickers (British); see also **clothes, underwear.**

papa, *n.* —*Syn.* dad, daddy, male parent; see **father** 1, **parent.**

papacy, *n.* —*Syn.* the Vatican, the Holy See, Pontificate, popedom, bishopric.

papal, *mod.* —*Syn.* pontifical, emanating from the Pope *or* the Vatican, papist, papistic, papistical, popish, Romanistic, Romish.

paper, *mod.* —*Syn.* unsubstantial, flimsy, cardboard; see **thin** 1.

paper, *n.* **1.** [A piece of legal or official writing] —*Syn.* document, official document, legal paper; see **record** 1.

Papers, sense 1, include the following—abstract, affidavit, bill, certificate, citation, contract, instrument, credentials, data, deed, diploma, indictment, grant, order(s), passport, visa, plea, records, safe-conduct, subpoena, summons, testimony, true bill, voucher, warrant, will.

2. [A newspaper]—*Syn.* journal, daily, daily journal; see **newspaper.**

3. [A piece of writing]—*Syn.* essay, article, theme; see **exposition** 2, **writing** 2.

4. [Means of commercial exchange]—*Syn.* paper money, bills, bank notes; see **money** 1.

5. [A manufactured product] Paper, sense 5, includes the following—*writing material:* typing *or* typewriter, writing stationery, bond paper, letterhead, personal stationery, ruled, rag, handmade, handtorn, deckle-edge, laid, crown, post paper, correspondence card, foolscap, second sheet, onion skin, manifold, carbon paper, note pad, note card, filing card; *printing paper:* enameled *or* glazed, enameled book, coated stock, free sheet, machine-finished book, publication book, poster, linen finish, ripple finish, vellum, eggshell, parchment, India, wove, four-ply blank, six-ply blank, writing; 50-pound, 60-pound, 80-pound, etc.; newsprint, strawboard; *miscellaneous:* art, rice, Chinese *or* Japanese rice, Japanese tea oatmeal, crêpe, butcher's, wrapping, tissue, brown, tar, roofing, building, tracing, graph, Whatman, transfer, filter, toilet, wax, photographic *or* sensitive *or* sensitized paper; wallpaper, Cellophane, Pliofilm (trademarks), paper towel, cleansing tissue.

on paper—*Syn.* **1.** recorded, signed, official; see **written** 2; **2.** in theory, assumed to be feasible, not yet in practice; see **theoretical.**

paper, *v.* —*Syn.* hang, paste up, plaster; see **cover** 1.

paperback, *n.* —*Syn.* paperbacked *or* paperbound book, paperback original, reprint; see **book** 1.

papered, *mod.* —*Syn.* hung, decorated, ornamented, papercovered, plastered over, placarded; see also **covered** 1.

paper money, *n.* —*Syn.* currency, folding money (D); bill, silver certificate, Federal Reserve note, greenback, legal tender; see also **money** 1.

papers, *n.* **1.** [Evidence of identity or authorization] —*Syn.* naturalization papers, identification card, ID (D); see **identification** 2, **passport.**

2. [Documentary materials]—*Syn.* writings, documents, private; see **record** 1.

paper work, *n.* —*Syn.* office *or* desk *or* inside work, keeping up with *or* handling the correspondence, keeping one's desk clear, doing the office chores, keeping records, filing, preparing *or* getting up reports, taking dictation, typing, keeping books; see also **administration** 1, **letter** 2.

papery, *mod.* —*Syn.* flimsy, insubstantial, slight; see **poor** 2, **thin** 1.

papism, *n.* —*Syn.* Romanism, Catholicity, Catholicism, Roman Catholicism, popery, popism.

papist, *n.* —*Syn.* Roman Catholic, Romanist, Christian; see **Catholic** 3.

papistry, *n.* —*Syn.* the Roman Catholic Church, Roman Catholicism, Catholicism; see **papism.**

papoose, *n.* —*Syn.* infant, child, nursling; see **baby** 1, **Indian** 1.

pappy (D), *n.* —*Syn.* papa, daddy, pa; see **father** 1, **parent.**

par, *n.* —*Syn.* standard, level, norm; see **criterion, model** 2.

parable, *n.* —*Syn.* fable, moral story, tale; see **story.**

parabolic, *mod.* **1.** [Figurative]—*Syn.* figurative, metaphorical, allegorical; see **descriptive, explanatory, illustrative.**

2. [Curved]—*Syn.* warped, hyperbolic, intersected; see **bent.**

parachute, *n.* —*Syn.* chute, seat pack parachute, lap pack parachute, harness and pack; *all* (D): umbrella, brolly, bailer, silk; see also **equipment.**

parachute, *v.* —*Syn.* make a lift-off jump, make a free fall, side-slip, glide down, fall, plummet, hurtle, bail out; *all* (D): come downstairs, brolly hop, hit the silk; see also **jump** 1.

parade, *n.* **1.** [A procession]—*Syn.* spectacle, ceremony, cavalcade, motorcade, demonstration, review, line of floats, line of march, pageant, ritual; see also **march** 1.

2. [An ostentatious show]—*Syn.* show, ostentation, ceremony; see **display** 2.

parade, *v.* **1.** [To participate in a parade]—*Syn.* roll *or* march past, march in review, demonstrate, display, exhibit; see also **march.**

2. [To make an ostentatious show]—*Syn.* show off, exhibit, flaunt; see **display** 1.

paradigm, *n.* —*Syn.* chart, sample, standard; see **criterion, model** 2.

paradise, *n.* **1.** [The other world]—*Syn.* Kingdom Come, Celestial Home, By-and-By; see **heaven** 2.

2. [The home of Adam and Eve]—*Syn.* Garden of Eden, Eden, the Garden.

3. [An idyllic land]—*Syn.* Arcadia, Cockaigne, Carcassonne, El Dorado, Elysium *or* the Elysian Fields, Erewhon, Eden, Valhalla; see also **utopia.**

paradox, *n.* **1.** [A seeming contradiction]—*Syn.* mystery, enigma, ambiguity; see **puzzle** 2.

2. [An actual contradiction]—*Syn.* absurdity, inconsistency, nonsense; see **error** 1, **mistake** 2.

paradoxical, *mod.* —*Syn.* contradictory, incomprehensible, ambiguous; see **obscure** 1.

paragon, *n.* —*Syn.* ideal, perfection, sublimation, original, paradigm, best, nonpareil, nonesuch; see also **model** 1.

paragraph, *n.* —*Syn.* passage, section, division of thought, topic, statement, verse, article, item, notice.

paragraph, *v.* —*Syn.* group, section, divide, arrange, break.

parallel, *mod.* **1.** [Equidistant at all points]—*Syn.* side by side, never meeting, running parallel, coordinate, coextending, lateral, laterally, in the same direction, extending equally.
2. [Similar in kind, position, or the like]—*Syn.* identical, equal, conforming; see **alike** 1, 2.

parallel, *n.* —*Syn.* resemblance, likeness, correspondence; see **similarity.**

parallel, *v.* —*Syn.* match, correspond, correlate; see **equal.**

parallelism, *n.* —*Syn.* affinity, correspondence, likeness; see **similarity.**

paralysis, *n.* —*Syn.* insensibility, loss of motion, loss of sensation; see **disease** 3.

paralytic, *mod.* —*Syn.* powerless, immobile, inactive, paralyzed, crippled, insensible, physically disabled, palsied, siderated, paraplegic, diplegic, palsified; see also **disabled, sick.**

paralytic, *n.* —*Syn.* paralysis victim, paretic, cripple, paralyzed person, palsy victim; see also **patient.**

paralyze, *v.* —*Syn.* strike with paralysis, make inert, render nerveless; see **deaden** 1.

paralyzed, *mod.* —*Syn.* insensible, nerveless, benumbed, stupefied, inert, inactive, unmoving, helpless, torpid; see also **disabled, paralytic.**

paramount, *mod.* —*Syn.* supreme, eminent, preeminent; see **predominant** 1.

paramour, *n.* —*Syn.* concubine, courtesan, lover; see **mistress** 2.

paranoia, *n.* —*Syn.* mental disorder, fright, fear; see **complex** 1, **insanity** 1.

paranoiac, *n.* —*Syn.* psychopath, maniac, neuropath; see **neurotic.**

paranoid, *mod.* —*Syn.* affected by paranoia, unreasonably distrustful, overly suspicious, having a persecution complex; see **neurotic.**

parapet, *n.* —*Syn.* rampart, obstruction, hindrance; see **barrier, wall** 1.

paraphernalia, *n.* —*Syn.* gear, material, apparatus; see **equipment.**

paraphrase, *n.* —*Syn.* digest, restatement, explanation; see **interpretation** 1, **summary.**

paraphrastic, *mod.* —*Syn.* expository, translatory, interpretive; see **explanatory.**

parasite, *n.* **1.** [A plant or animal living on another] —*Syn.* bacteria, parasitoid, saprophyte, epiphyte; see also **fungus.**
2. [A hanger-on]—*Syn.* dependent, slave, sponger; see **sycophant.**

parasitical, *mod.* —*Syn.* ravenous, parasitic, ravening, wolfish, predacious; see also **predatory.**

parasitism, *n.* —*Syn.* bloodsucking, sponging, dependency, predatoriness, predaciousness, ravenousness; see also **dependence** 1.

parasol, *n.* —*Syn.* sunshade, shade, canopy; see **umbrella.**

paratrooper, *n.* —*Syn.* commando, parachute jumper, shock trooper; see **soldier.**

paravane, *n.* —*Syn.* antisubmarine device, antimine device, explosive paravane; see **weapon** 1.

parboil, *v.* —*Syn.* simmer, steam, partially cook; see **boil** 2, **cook.**

parcel, *n.* —*Syn.* bundle, packet, carton; see **package** 1.

parceling, *n.* —*Syn.* division, allotment, distribution; see **share.**

parcel out, *v.* —*Syn.* allot, allocate, measure (out); see **distribute** 1, **give** 1.

parcel post, *n.* —*Syn.* post, postal service, express, C.O.D.; see also **mail.**

parch, *v.* —*Syn.* dessicate, dehydrate, brown; see **dry** 1.

parched, *mod.* —*Syn.* burned, withered, dried; see **dry** 1.

parching, *mod.* —*Syn.* burning, drying, withering; see **dry** 1.

parchment, *b.* —*Syn.* vellum, Parthian leather, goatskin, sheepskin; see also **paper** 5.

pardon, *n.* **1.** [The reduction or removal of punishment]—*Syn.* absolution, grace, remission, amnesty, exoneration, discharge, exculpation; see also **acquittal, mercy** 1.—*Ant.* punishment*, condemnation, conviction.
2. [Forgiveness]—*Syn.* excuse, forbearance, conciliation; see **forgiveness, kindness** 1.
3. [A statement granting pardon, sense 1]—*Syn.* reprieve, acquital, exoneration, indulgence, amnesty, release, discharge; see also **acquittal, freeing.**

pardon, *v.* **1.** [To reduce punishment]—*Syn.* exonerate, exculpate, clear, absolve, remit, reprieve, acquit, set free, liberate, discharge, spring (D), rescue, justify, suspend charges, put on probation, grant amnesty to; see also **free** 1, **release.**—*Ant.* punish*, chastise, sentence.
2. [To forgive]—*Syn.* condone, overlook, exculpate; see **excuse, forgive** 1.

pardonable, *mod.* —*Syn.* passable, forgivable, venial; see **excusable.**

pardoned, *mod.* —*Syn.* forgiven, freed, excused, released, granted amnesty, given a pardon, reprieved, exonerated, granted a reprieve, acquitted, manumitted; *all* (D): let off, whitewashed, outside the wall, sprung, back in circulation; see also **discharged** 1, **free** 1.—*Ant.* accused*, convicted, condemned.

pare, *v.* **1.** [To peel]—*Syn.* scalp, strip, flay; see **cut** 1, **shave** 1, **skin.**
2. [To trim]—*Syn.* clip, crop, trim off; see **carve** 1, **cut** 1, **trim** 1.

parent, *n.* —*Syn.* immediate forebear, procreator, progenitor, sire, he *or* she from whom one has one's being; see also **father** 1, **mother** 1, **origin** 3.

parentage, *n.* —*Syn.* ancestry, origin, paternity; see **family** 1, **heredity.**

parental, *mod.* —*Syn.* paternal, maternal, familial, patrimonial, phylogenetic, phyletic, hereditary; see also **ancestral.**

parenthesis, *n.* —*Syn.* brackets, braces, enclosure, punctuation marks, crotchets; see also **punctuation.**

parenthetical, *mod.* —*Syn.* episodic, intermediate, incidental; see **related** 2, **subordinate.**

par excellence, *mod.* —*Syn.* superior, pre-eminent, the very finest; see **excellent, supreme.**

pariah, *n.* —*Syn.* scapegoat, one in disgrace, untouchable; see **outcast.**

Paris, *n.* —*Syn.* capital of France, city on the Seine, city of love, fashion capital, gay Paree (D); see also **France.**

parish, *n.* —*Syn.* ecclesiastical unit, charge, archdiocese, congregation, demesne, cure, parochial unit, territory, county (in Louisiana), diocese; see also **area** 2, **church** 3.

parity, *n.* —*Syn.* affinity, equivalence, similarity; see **equality.**

park, *n.* **1.** [A place designated for outdoor recreation]—*Syn.* square, plaza, place, lawn, green, village green, esplanade, promenade, boulevard, tract, recreational area, pleasure ground, national park *or* forest, national monument, enclosure, market place, woodland, parkland, parkway, meadow; see also **grass** 3, **lot** 1, **playground.**

2. [A place designed for outdoor storage]—*Syn.* parking lot, parking space, lot; see **garage** 1, **parking area.**

park, *v.* —*Syn.* mass, collect, order, place in order, station, place in rows, leave, store, impound, deposit; see also **line up, place** 1.

parked, *mod.* —*Syn.* stationed, standing, left, put, ranked, lined up, in rows, by the curb, in the parking lot, stored, halted, unmoving; see also **placed.**

parking area, *n.* —*Syn.* space, car space, off-street parking, parking lot, parking garage, parking building, pigeonhole (D); see also **garage** 1, **lot** 1.

parking lot, *n.* —*Syn.* lot, parking building, parking space; see **parking area.**

parking orbit, *n.* —*Syn.* temporary orbit *or* maneuver, interim stage *or* phase, orbital holding pattern; see **orbit** 1.

parking space, *n.* —*Syn.* space, car space, pigeonhole (D); see **parking area.**

parkway, *n.* —*Syn.* thoroughfare, toll road, turnpike; see **highway, road** 1.

parlance, *n.* —*Syn.* speech, manner of speech, tongue; see **language** 1.

parley, *n.* —*Syn.* meeting, council, conference; see **conversation, discussion** 1.

parley, *v.* —*Syn.* speak, negotiate, confer; see **discuss, talk** 1.

Parliament, *n.* —*Syn.* national legislative body of Great Britain, House of Commons, House of Lords; see **authority** 3. **committee, government** 2, **legislature.**

parliamentary, *mod.* —*Syn.* congressional, administrative, lawmaking; see **authoritative** 2, **governmental, legislative, political.**

parlor, *n.* —*Syn.* living room, sitting room, drawing room, front room, reception room, salon, waiting room, guest room; see also **room** 2.

parlous, *mod.* —*Syn.* risky, perilous, hazardous; see **dangerous** 1, **deadly, unsafe.**

parochial, *mod.* **1.** [Regional]—*Syn.* provincial, insular, sectional; see **local** 1, **regional.**

2. [Narrow-minded]—*Syn.* biased, provincial, shallow; see **conservative, conventional** 3, **prejudiced.**

parodist, *n.* —*Syn.* cartoonist, humorist, satirist, author, caricaturist, poetaster, ridiculer; see also **critic** 2.

parody, *n.* **1.** [Presentation through exaggerated imitation]—*Syn.* travesty, burlesque, mimicry, copy, cartoon, misrepresentation, satire, lampoon, pasquinade, roast, caricature, mockery, derision, mime, irony, satire, raillery; see also **imitation** 1, 2, **joke** 1, **ridicule.**—*Ant.* truth*, accuracy, exactness.

2. [A work using parody]—*Syn.* travesty, burlesque, cartoon, farce, extravaganza, copy, caricature, mock-heroic, jest, lampoon, take-off, satirical imitation, satiric drama, satiric poetry; see also **imitation** 2, **joke** 2.

parody, *v.* —*Syn.* mimic, copy, burlesque, travesty, exaggerate, deride, mime, caricature, jest, distort, mock, laugh at, jeer, lampoon, roast, disparage; see also **imitate** 2, **impersonate, joke, ridicule.**

parole, *v.* —*Syn.* discharge, pardon, liberate; see **free** 1, **release.**

paronomasia, *n.* —*Syn.* wordplay, ambiguity, phrase; see **pun, word** 1.

paroxysm, *n.* **1.** [Violent emotion]—*Syn.* passion, hysterics, outbreak, outburst, frenzy, furor, fury, violence, agitation, explosion, frothing, fuming, (berserk) fit; see also **anger, excitement, rage** 2. —*Ant.* peace*, tranquillity, equanimity.

2. [A fit]—*Syn.* attack, spasm, convulsion; see **outbreak** 1.

parquet, *n.* —*Syn.* tiling, inlay, mosaic; see **flooring, tile.**

parricide, *n.* —*Syn.* patricide, matricide, killing; see **crime** 2, **murder.**

parrot, *n.* **1.** [A bird]—*Syn.* psittaciformes, parakeet, lovebird, cockatoo, macaw, quetzal, trogon, lory, lorikeet; see also **bird** 1.

2. [One who copies others]—*Syn.* plagiarist, mimic, mimicker, ape, disciple, impersonator, imposter, mocker, copycat (D); see also **imitator.**

parry, *v.* **1.** [To ward off]—*Syn.* rebuke, rebuff, hold one's own; see **repel** 1, **resist** 1.

2. [To avoid]—*Syn.* shun, elude, dodge; see **avoid, evade** 1.

parsimonious, *mod.* —*Syn.* selfish, tight, frugal; see **greedy** 1, **stingy.**

parsimony, *n.* —*Syn.* stinginess, selfishness, providence; see **frugality, greed.**

parson, *n.* —*Syn.* clergyman, cleric, preacher; see **minister** 1.

parsonage, *n.* —*Syn.* rectory, pastor's dwelling, minister's residence, manse, parsonage house, vicarage, mansion.

part, *n.* **1.** [A portion]—*Syn.* piece, fragment, fraction, section, sector, member, segment, division, allotment, apportionment, ingredient, element, rasher, subsystem, slab, subdivision, partition, particle, installment, component, constituent, bit, slice, scrap, chip, chunk, lump, sliver, splinter, shaving, molecule, atom, electron, proton, neutron; see also **share.**—*Ant.* whole*, total, aggregate.

2. [A part of speech]—*Syn.* pronoun, modifier, adjective, adverb, preposition, conjunction, interjection; see also **noun, verb.**

3. [A machine part]—*Syn.* molding, casting, fitting, lever, shaft, cam, spring, band, belt, chain, pulley, clutch, spare part, replacement; see also **bolt** 1, **brace, frame** 1, 2, **gear** 2, **machine** 1, **nut** 2, **rod** 1, **wheel** 1.

4. [A character in a drama]—*Syn.* hero, heroine, character; see **role.**

for one's (own) part—*Syn.* privately, so far as one is concerned, in one's opinion; see **personally** 2.

for the most part—*Syn.* mainly, mostly, to the greatest part *or* extent; see **largely.**

in good part—*Syn.* good-naturedly, without offense, cordially; see **agreeably.**

in part—*Syn.* to a certain extent, somewhat, slightly; see **partly.**

on one's part—*Syn.* privately, as far as one is concerned, coming from one; see **personally** 2.

play a part—*Syn.* **1.** behave unnaturally, put on, disguise; see **deceive. 2.** share, join, take part; see **participate** 1.

take someone's part—*Syn.* act in behalf of someone, aid, help; see **support** 2.

part, *v.* **1.** [To put apart]—*Syn.* separate, break, sever; see **divide** 1.

2. [To depart]—*Syn.* withdraw, take leave, part company; see **leave** 1.

partake, *v.*—*Syn.* participate, divide, take; see **share** 2.

partaking, *n.*—*Syn.* communion, collectivism, partition; see **sharing.**

parted, *mod.*—*Syn.* divided, severed, sundered; see **separated.**

parterre, *n.*—*Syn.* seats, orchestra circle, balcony seats, boxes, parquet circle; see also **balcony.**

part from, *v.*—*Syn.* separate, part, break up with; see **leave** 1.

parthenogenesis, *n.*—*Syn.* parthenogeny, birth, virgin birth; see **reproduction** 1.

partial, *mod.* **1.** [Not complete]—*Syn.* unperformed, incomplete, half done; see **unfinished** 1.

2. [Showing favoritism]—*Syn.* unfair, influenced, biased; see **prejudiced.**

partiality, *n.* **1.** [Bias]—*Syn.* favoritism, unfairness, intolerance; see **prejudice.**

2. [Liking]—*Syn.* fondness, inclination, preference; see **affection.**

partially, *mod.*—*Syn.* partly, somewhat, in part; see **partly.**

participant, *n.*—*Syn.* partaker, co-operator, partner, sharer, co-partner, shareholder, a party to; see also **associate.**

participate, *v.* **1.** [To take part in]—*Syn.* share, partake, aid, co-operate, join in, come in, associate with, be a party to, bear a hand, have a finger *or* hand in, concur, take an interest in, take part in, answer the call of duty, enter into, have to do with, get in the act, go into, chip in (D); see also **associate** 1, **join** 2.—*Ant.* retire*, withdraw, refuse.

2. [To engage in a contest]—*Syn.* play, strive, engage; see **compete.**

participation, *n.*—*Syn.* partnership, joining in, sharing, support, aid, assistance, help, encouragement, concurrence, seconding, standing by, taking part; see also **co-operation** 1.

participator, *n.*—*Syn.* sharer, cooperator, partaker; see **associate, participant.**

particle, *n.*—*Syn.* jot, scrap, shred; see **bit** 1.

particle accelerator, *n.*—*Syn.* atom smasher, linear accelerator, cyclotron; see **accelerator.**

parti-colored, *mod.*—*Syn.* kaleidoscopic, colorful, prismatic; see **bright** 2, **multicolored.**

particular, *mod.* **1.** [Specific]—*Syn.* distinct, singular, appropriate; see **special** 1.

2. [Exact]—*Syn.* precise, minute, circumstantial; see **accurate** 1, 2.

3. [Fastidious]—*Syn.* discriminating, finicky, hard to please; see **careful.**

4. [Notable]—*Syn.* remarkable, singular, odd; see **unusual** 1.

in particular—*Syn.* expressly, particularly, individually; see **especially** 1.

particular, *n.*—*Syn.* fact, specification, item; see **detail** 1.

particularize, *v.*—*Syn.* itemize, enumerate, specify; see **file** 1, **list** 1, **record** 1.

particularly, *mod.*—*Syn.* unusually, expressly, individually; see **especially.**

parting, *n.* **1.** [The act of separating]—*Syn.* leave-taking, good-bye, farewell; see **departure.**

2. [The time or place of separating]—*Syn.* split, crossroads, Y break, divergence, hour of parting, parting of the ways, where the path divides, where the brook and river meet (D).

3. [The act of dividing]—*Syn.* bisection, severance, separation; see **division** 1.

partisan, *mod.*—*Syn.* factional, biased, sympathetic, blind, devoted, fanatic, warped, zealous, overzealous, unreasoning, cliquish, cliquey, conspiratorial, exclusive, accessory, adhering, leagued together, unjust, unconsidered, ganged-up (D).

partisan, *n.*—*Syn.* adherent, supporter, sympathizer, disciple, satellite, sycophant, devotee, zealot, accessory, backer; see also **follower.**

partition, *n.* **1.** [Division]—*Syn.* apportionment, separation, severance; see **distribution** 1.

2. [That which divides or separates]—*Syn.* bar, obstruction, hindrance; see **barrier, wall** 1.

partly, *mod.*—*Syn.* in part, partially, to a degree, in some degree *or* measure, measurably, somewhat, noticeably, notably, in some part, incompletely, insufficiently, inadequately, up to a certain point, so far as possible, insofar as was then possible, not wholly *or* entirely, as much as could be expected, to some *or* a certain extent, within limits, slightly, to a slight degree, in a portion only, in some ways, in certain particulars, only in details, in a general way, not strictly speaking, not in accordance with the letter of the law, in bits and pieces, by fits and starts, carelessly, with large omissions, short of the end, at best *or* worst *or* most *or* least, at the outside.—*Ant.* completely*, wholly, entirely.

partner, *n.*—*Syn.* co-worker, ally, comrade; see **associate.**

partnership, *n.*—*Syn.* alliance, union, co-operation, company, combination, corporation, cartel, connection, brotherhood, society, lodge, club, fellowship, fraternity, confederation, band, body, crew, coterie, clique, gang, ring, faction, party, community, conjunction, joining, companionship, friendship, help, assistance, chumminess (D); see also **business** 4, **organization** 3.

part of, *pron.*—*Syn.* portion, section, division; see **some.**

part of speech, *n.*—*Syn.* grammatical form *or* shape *or* unit *or* construct *or* construction, word *or* phrase *or* locution having a certain privilege of occurrence, lexeme; see **adjective, adverb, conjunction, grammar, noun, preposition, pronoun, verb, word.**

partway, *mod.*—*Syn.* started, toward the middle, somewhat; see **begun, some.**

part with, *v.*—*Syn.* let go (of), suffer loss, give up; see **lose** 2.

party, *n.* **1.** [A social affair]—*Syn.* at-home, tea, luncheon, dinner party, dinner, cocktail hour, sur-

prise party, house party, social, bee, reception, banquet, feast, affair, gathering, soirée, function, gala, fete, ball, recreation, fun, jollification, cheer, beguilement, accommodation, amusement, entertainment, festive occasion, carousal, diversion, performance, high tea, kaffee-klatsch; *all* (D): binge, spree, toot, riot, splurge, tear, shindig, blowout, bash.
2. [A group of people]—*Syn.* multitude, mob, company; see **crowd** 1, **gathering.**
3. [A political organization]—*Syn.* organized group, body, electorate, combine, combination, bloc, ring, junta, partisans, cabal; see also **faction** 1. Well-known political parties include the following —*historical:* Guelph, Ghibelline, Jacobin, Girondist, Yorkist, Lancastrian, Puritan, Roundhead, Politique, Tory, Whig, Know-Nothing, Grangers, Greenback, People's, Mugwump, Prohibition, Bull Moose, Farmer-Labor, Progressive, Populist; *twentieth-century:* Republican, Democratic, Liberal, Conservative, Labour (Britain), Popular Front, National Socialist *or* Nazi, Fascist, Falangist, Congress Party (India), Kuomintang, Comintern *or* Third International, Socialist, Communist, Cooperative Commonwealth Federation, Independent, Peace and Freedom, Black Panther, American Independent, Townsendite, Epic.
4. [An individual or group involved in legal proceedings]—*Syn.* litigant, participant, contractor, agent, plotter, confederate, cojuror, compurgator; see also **defendant.**
Types of parties, sense 4, include the following—plaintiff, defendant, purchaser, seller, lessor, lessee, employer, employee, licenser, licensee.
5. [(D) A specified but unnamed individual]—*Syn.* party of the first, second, third, etc., part; someone, individual; see **person** 1, **somebody.**

party line, *n.*—*Syn.* principles, official stand, orders; see **policy, propaganda.**

parvenu, *mod.*—*Syn.* arrogant, forward, snobbish; see **egotistic** 2.

parvenu, *n.*—*Syn.* status-seeker, snob, nouveau riche; see **upstart.**

pass, *n.* **1.** [An opening through mountains]—*Syn.* defile, gorge, ravine, crossing, track, way, path, passageway, water gap, *col* (French); see also **route** 1.
2. [A document assuring permission to pass] —*Syn.* ticket, passport, visa, order, admission, furlough, permission, right, license; see also **permit.**
3. [In sports, the passing of the ball from one player to another]—*Syn.* toss, throw, hurl, fling, flip; see also **pitch** 2.
Types of passes, sense 3, include the following—forward pass, lateral pass, line pass, bounce pass; *all* (D): touchdown pass, bullet pass, shovel pass, lateral, spot pass, flat pass, passback, snapback.
4. [(D) An advance]—*Syn.* approach, sexual overture, proposition; see **suggestion** 1.

pass, *v.* **1.** [To move past]—*Syn.* go *or* run by *or* past, flit by, come by, shoot ahead of, catch, come to the front, go beyond, roll on, fly past, reach, roll by, cross, flow past, glide by, go in opposite directions, blow over (D); see also **move** 1.
2. [To elapse]—*Syn.* transpire, slip *or* pass away *or* by, fly, fly by, linger, glide by, run out; *both* (D): drag, crawl.
3. [To complete a course successfully]—*Syn.* matriculate, be graduated, pass with honors; see **succeed** 1.
4. [To hand to others]—*Syn.* transfer, relinquish, hand over; see **give** 1.
5. [To enact]—*Syn.* legislate, establish, vote in; see **enact** 1.
6. [To become enacted]—*Syn.* carry, become law, become valid, be ratified, be established, be ordained, be sanctioned.
7. [To refuse to act]—*Syn.* decline, ignore, omit; see **disregard, neglect** 1, **refuse.**
8. [To exceed]—*Syn.* excel, transcend, go beyond; see **exceed, surpass.**
9. [To spend time]—*Syn.* fill, occupy oneself, while away (D); see **spend** 2.
10. [To pronounce formally]—*Syn.* announce, claim, state; see **declare** 1.
11. [To proceed]—*Syn.* progress, get ahead, move *or* go on; see **advance** 1.
12. [To emit]—*Syn.* give off, send forth, exude; see **emit** 1.
bring to pass—*Syn.* bring about, initiate, start; see **cause** 1.
come to pass—*Syn.* occur, develop, come about; see **happen** 2.

passable, *mod.* **1.** [Capable of being crossed or traveled]—*Syn.* open, fair, penetrable, navigable, traversable, beaten, accessible, traveled, easy, broad, graded, travelable; see also **available.**—*Ant.* impassable*, impossible, inaccessible.
2. [Admissible]—*Syn.* all right, mediocre, tolerable; see **common** 1, **fair** 2.

passage, *n.* **1.** [A journey]—*Syn.* voyage, crossing, trek; see **journey.**
2. [A passageway]—*Syn.* way, exit, entrance; see **hall** 2.
3. [A reading]—*Syn.* section, portion, paragraph; see **reading** 3.

passageway, *n.*—*Syn.* gate, door, way; see **hall** 2.

pass away, *v.*—*Syn.* depart, expire, pass on; see **die** 1.

pass by, *v.* **1.** [To go past]—*Syn.* travel, move past, depart from; see **leave** 1, **pass** 1.
2. [To neglect]—*Syn.* pass over, not choose, omit; see **abandon** 1, **neglect** 1.

passé, *mod.*—*Syn.* old-fashioned, out-of-date, outmoded; see **old-fashioned.**

passenger, *n.*—*Syn.* wayfarer, voyager, fellow traveler, fellow passenger, rider, customer, patron, commuter, tourist, excursionist, pilgrim, wanderer, straphanger (D); see also **traveler.**

passer-by, *n.*—*Syn.* witness, traveler, bystander; see **observer** 1.

passing, *mod.* **1.** [In the act of going past]—*Syn.* departing, crossing, going by, gliding by, flashing by, speeding by, going in opposite directions, passing in the night; see also **moving** 1.
2. [Of brief duration]—*Syn.* fleeting, transitory, transient; see **temporary.**

passion, *n.* **1.** [Sexual desire]—*Syn.* lust, craving, sexual excitement; see **desire** 3.

2. [Strong emotion]—*Syn.* outburst, feeling, intensity; see **emotion.**

passionate, *mod.* **1.** [Excitable]—*Syn.* vehement, hotheaded, tempestuous; see **excitable.**
2. [Ardent]—*Syn.* intense, impassioned, loving, fervent, fervid, moving, inspiring, dramatic, melodramatic, romantic, amorous, lustful, concupiscent, poignant, swelling, enthusiastic, tragic, stimulating, wistful, stirring, thrilling, warm, burning, glowing, vehement, deep, affecting, eloquent, spirited, fiery, expressive, forceful, heated, hot, flaming; *all* (D): high-powered, steamed-up, high-pressure, hot, horny, in hot blood; see also **exciting, stimulating.**
3. [Intense]—*Syn.* strong, vehement, violent; see **intense.**

passionately, *mod.* —*Syn.* deeply, dearly, devotedly; see **angrily, excitedly, lovingly.**

passionless, *mod.* —*Syn.* uncaring, apathetic, cold; see **indifferent** 1, **unconcerned.**

passive, *mod.* **1.** [Being acted upon]—*Syn.* receptive, stirred, influenced; see **affected** 1.
2. [Not active]—*Syn.* inactive, inert, lifeless; see **idle** 1, **latent, motionless** 1.
3. [Patient]—*Syn.* enduring, forbearing, quiet; see **patient** 1, **resigned.**

passively, *mod.* —*Syn.* indifferently, without resistance, quietly; see **calmly.**

passiveness, *n.* —*Syn.* apathy, resignation, unconcern; see **indifference** 1.

pass judgment, *v.* —*Syn.* sentence, decide, consider; see **condemn** 1, **judge** 1.

pass off, *v.* **1.** [To pretend]—*Syn.* pass for, make a pretense of, palm off (D); see **pretend** 1.
2. [To emit]—*Syn.* give off, send forth, eject; see **emit** 1.
3. [To disappear]—*Syn.* vanish, fade out, fall away; see **disappear.**

pass on, *v.* **1.** [To decide]—*Syn.* determine, conclude, make a judgment; see **decide, judge** 1.
2. [To die]—*Syn.* expire, depart, succumb; see **die** 1.

pass out, *v.* **1.** [To faint]—*Syn.* swoon, lose consciousness, black out (D); see **faint.**
2. [To distribute]—*Syn.* hand out, circulate, deal out; see **distribute** 1, **give** 1.

pass over, *v.* **1.** [To traverse]—*Syn.* travel through, go *or* move over, go across; see **cross** 1.
2. [To ignore]—*Syn.* dismiss, overlook, neglect; see **disregard.**

passport, *n.* —*Syn.* pass, license, permit, safe-conduct, visa, travel permit, authorization, warrant, credentials; see also **identification** 2.

pass the buck (D), *v.* —*Syn.* transfer responsibility, assign, refer; see **avoid, delegate** 2.

pass up, *v.* **1.** [To refuse]—*Syn.* dismiss, send away, reject; see **deny** 1, **refuse.**
2. [To disagree]—*Syn.* ignore, overlook, neglect; see **disregard.**

password, *n.* —*Syn.* countersign, signal, phrase, secret word, watchword, parole, identification, open sesame (D); see also **key** 2.

past, *mod.* **1.** [Having occurred previously]—*Syn.* former, preceding, gone by, foregoing, elapsed, anterior, antecedent, prior.
2. [No longer serving]—*Syn.* ex-, retired, earlier; see **preceding.**

not put it past someone—*Syn.* suspect, accuse, expect; see **anticipate** 1, **fear** 1, **guess** 2.

past, *n.* **1.** [Past time]—*Syn.* antiquity, long ago, past times, old times, years ago, good old days, *or* times, ancient times, former times, days gone by, (auld) lang-syne, yore, days of old *or* yore, yesterday.—*Ant.* future*, the present, tomorrow.
2. [Past events]—*Syn.* knowledge, happenings, events; see **history.**
3. [Concealed experiences]—*Syn.* secret affair, love affair, amour, hidden past, bronzed *or* scarlet past, scarlet letter, scarlet A.

past, *prep.* —*Syn.* through, farther than, behind; see **beyond.**

paste, *n.* —*Syn.* cement, glue, mucilage; see **adhesive.**

paste, *v.* —*Syn.* glue, fix, affix, repair, patch; see also **stick** 1.

pasteboard, *n.* —*Syn.* paper board, bristol board, cardboard, tagboard, oak tag, corrugated paper, carton material, backing; see also **paper** 5.

pastel, *n.* **1.** [A sketch]—*Syn.* portrait, depiction, design; see **drawing** 1, **picture** 3, **representation, sketch** 1.
2. [A pale color]—*Syn.* hue, tone, delicate color; see **color** 1.

pasteurize, *v.* —*Syn.* render *or* make germ-free, sterilize, make safe (for human consumption); see **clean, heat** 2.

pastime, *n.* —*Syn.* recreation, amusement, sport; see **distraction** 2, **entertainment** 1, 2, **game** 1, **hobby.**

pastor, *n.* —*Syn.* priest, rector, clergyman; see **minister** 1.

pastoral, *mod.* —*Syn.* rustic, agrarian, simple; see **rural.**

pastoral, *n.* —*Syn.* verse, play, idyll; see **poem.**

pastorate, *n.* —*Syn.* pastorship, clergy, priesthood; see **ministry** 2.

pastry, *n.* —*Syn.* baked goods, dainty, delicacy, patisserie, bread; *all* (D): goodies, yum-yums, fixings, trimmings, indigestion, ambrosia, bellyache; see also **cake** 2, **doughnut.**
Pastries include the following—French, Danish; tart, pie, turnover, phyllo, oatcake, shortbread, rusk, pudding, brioche, *frangipane* (Italian), *croissant* (French), eclair, panettone, *Strudel* (German), cakes, sweet roll.

pasturage, *n.* —*Syn.* grassland, grazing land, pasture; see **field** 1, **meadow, plain.**

pasture, *n.* —*Syn.* grazing land, pasturage, hayfield; see **field** 1, **meadow, plain.**

pasty, *mod.* **1.** [Like paste]—*Syn.* gluey, gelatinous, gooey (D), doughy; see **sticky, adhesive.**
2. [Pale]—*Syn.* wan, pallid, sickly, ashen, sallow, anemic, bloodless; see also **pale** 1, **dull** 2.

pat, *v.* **1.** [To strike lightly]—*Syn.* tap, beat, punch; see **hit** 1.
2. [To strike lightly and affectionately]—*Syn.* stroke, pet, rub; see **caress.**

patch, *n.* —*Syn.* piece, mend, bit, scrap, spot, application, appliqué.

patch, *v.* —*Syn.* darn, mend, cover; see **repair.**

patch up, *v.* —*Syn.* appease, adjust, compensate; see **settle** 9.

patchwork, *n.* —*Syn.* jumble, hodgepodge, muddle; see **confusion** 2, **disorder** 2.

patchy, *mod.* —*Syn.* sketchy, uneven, varying; see **irregular.**

patent, *mod.* **1.** [Concerning a product for which a patent has been obtained]—*Syn.* controlled, monopolized, patented, licensed, limited, copyrighted, protected, exclusive.—*Ant.* free*, unpatented, uncontrolled.

2. [Obvious]—*Syn.* evident, open, clear; see **obvious** 1.

patent, *n.* —*Syn.* patent right, protection, concession, control, limitation, license, copyright, privilege; see also **monopoly.**

patent, *v.* —*Syn.* license, secure, control, limit, monopolize, safeguard, exclude, copyright.

patented, *mod.* —*Syn.* copyright(ed), patent applied for, trademarked, under patent *or* copyright, patent pending; see also **restricted.**

patent medicine, *n.* —*Syn.* manufactured *or* prepared *or* packaged medicine, drugs, nostrum, panacea, cure-all, patented medicine; see also **medicine** 2.

paternal, *mod.* —*Syn.* patrimonial, fatherly, protective; see **parental.**

paternalism, *n.* —*Syn.* collectivism, totalitarianism, socialism, jurisdiction, Fourierism.

paternity, *n.* **1.** [Fatherhood]—*Syn.* progenitorship, paternal parentage, fathership; see **fatherhood.**

2. [Authorship]—*Syn.* creation, derivation, origin; see **authorship.**

path, *n.* **1.** [A trodden way]—*Syn.* trail, way, track, short cut, footpath, crosscut, footway, roadway, walkway, cinder track, trod (British), byway; see also **route** 1.

2. [A course]—*Syn.* route, beat, beaten path; see **way** 2.

pathetic, *mod.* —*Syn.* touching, affecting, moving; see **pitiful** 1.

pathfinder, *n.* —*Syn.* explorer, searcher, discoverer; see **scout** 1.

pathless, *mod.* —*Syn.* unpenetrated, impassable, untrodden, impervious; see also **unused** 1.

pathological, *mod.* —*Syn.* unhealthy, disordered, diseased; see **neurotic, sick.**

pathology, *n.* —*Syn.* diagnostics, bacteriology, pathogeny; see **medicine** 3.

pathos, *n.* —*Syn.* passion, desolation, sentiment; see **emotion, feeling** 4.

patience, *n.* **1.** [Willingness to endure]—*Syn.* forbearance, fortitude, composure, submission, endurance, impeturbability, nonresistance, longanimity, self-control, passiveness, bearing, serenity, humility, yielding, poise, sufferance, long-suffering, moderation, leniency; see also **resignation** 1.—*Ant.* nervousness*, fretfulness, restlessness.

2. [Ability to continue]—*Syn.* submission, perseverance, persistence; see **endurance** 2.

patient, *mod.* **1.** [Enduring without complaint]—*Syn.* submissive, meek, forbearing, mild-tempered, composed, tranquil, serene, long-suffering, unruffled, imperturbable, passive, cold-blooded, easy-going, philosophic, tolerant, gentle, unresentful; see also **resigned.**—*Ant.* irritable*, violent, resentful.

2. [Quietly persistent in an activity]—*Syn.* steady, dependable, calm, reliable, placid, stable, composed, unwavering, imperturbable, quiet, serene, unimpassioned, dispassionate, enduring; see also **regular** 3.—*Ant.* restless*, irrepressible, feverish.

patient, *n.* —*Syn.* case, inmate, victim, sufferer, sick *or* ill individual; medical *or* surgical *or* psychiatric *or* dental, etc., case *or* patient, one seeking help *or* cure *or* relief, outpatient, bed patient, emergency (ward) patient, convalescent, convalescent *or* walking *or* ambulatory case *or* patient, one recovering from an illness *or* sickness *or* injury, hospital case, hospitalized person, subject.

patiently, *mod.* **1.** [Suffering without complaint]—*Syn.* enduringly, bravely, impassively, resignedly, numbly, forbearingly, imperturbably, dispassionately, tolerantly, submissively, meekly; see also **calmly.**

2. [Continuing without impatience]—*Syn.* steadily, firmly, unabatingly; see **regularly** 2.

patio, *n.* —*Syn.* porch, piazza, courtyard, court, square, open porch; see also **yard** 1.

patriarch, *n.* —*Syn.* master, head of family, ancestor; see **chief** 2, **ruler** 1.

patrician, *mod.* —*Syn.* highborn, grand, aristocratic; see **noble** 3, **royal** 1.

patrician, *n.* —*Syn.* nobleman, gentleman, noble; see **aristocrat, lord** 2.

patriciate, *n.* —*Syn.* nobility, gentry, peerage; see **aristocracy, royalty.**

patricide, *n.* —*Syn.* father killing, homicide, killing; see **crime** 2, **murder.**

patrimony, *n.* —*Syn.* inheritance, birthright, dowry; see **gift** 1.

patriot, *n.* —*Syn.* lover of his country, good citizen, statesman, nationalist, volunteer, loyalist, jingoist, chauvinist.

patriotic, *mod.* —*Syn.* devoted, zealous, public-spirited, consecrated, dedicated, fervid, statesman-like, nationalistic, jingoistic, chauvinistic.—*Ant.* traitorous*, antisocial, misanthropic.

patriotism, *n.* —*Syn.* love of country, public spirit, *amor patriae* (Latin), good citizenship, civism, nationality, nationalism; see also **loyalty.**

patrol, *n.* **1.** [A unit engated in patrolling]—*Syn.* guard, watch, protection; see **army** 2.

2. [The action of patrolling]—*Syn.* guarding, watching, safeguarding, protecting, defending, escorting, convoying, scouting.

patrol, *v.* —*Syn.* watch, walk, inspect; see **guard** 2.

patrolman, *n.* —*Syn.* police, police officer, constable; see **policeman.**

patron, *n.* **1.** [One who provides support]—*Syn.* philanthropist, benefactor, benefactress, helper, protector, encourager, supporter, champion, backer, financer, advocate, defender, guide, leader, friend, ally, sympathizer, well-wisher, partisan, employer, buyer; *all* (D): angel, sugar daddy, booster, philanthropoid; see also **supporter.**—*Ant.* enemy*, obstructionist, adversary.

2. [One who uses facilities]—*Syn.* client, habitué, purchaser; see **buyer.**

patronage, *n.* **1.** [The support provided by a patron]—*Syn.* assistance, grant, financing, special privileges, protection, aegis, support, benefaction, aid, sponsorship, commercial backing, recommenda-

tion, guardianship, encouragement, help; see also **subsidy.**
2. [Trade]—*Syn.* commerce, trading, shopping; see **business** 1.
3. [Condescension]—*Syn.* deference, civility, condescendence, patronization, toleration, insolence, sufferance, brazenness, condescending favor.

patronize, *v.* **1.** [To trade with]—*Syn.* habituate, buy *or* purchase from, shop with; see **buy** 1, **sell** 1.
2. [To assume a condescending attitude]—*Syn.* talk down to, be overbearing, stoop, be gracious to, indulge, favor, pat on the back, play the snob, snub, lord it over; see also **condescend.**

patronizing, *mod.* —*Syn.* condescending, gracious, stooping; see **polite** 1.

patronymic, *n.* —*Syn.* surname, family name, cognomen; see **name** 1.

patter, *n.* —*Syn.* tapping, patting, sound; see **noise** 2.

patter, *v.* —*Syn.* tap, chatter, rattle; see **sound** 1.

pattern, *n.* **1.** [Example]—*Syn.* original, guide, copy; see **model** 2.
2. [Markings]—*Syn.* decoration, trim, ornament; see **design** 1.

paucity, *n.* —*Syn.* insufficiency, scarcity, absence; see **lack** 1.

Paul, *n.* —*Syn.* Saul, Saul of Tarsus, the Apostle Paul, Jew of Tarsus, writer of the Pauline epistles; see also **disciple.**

paunch, *n.* —*Syn.* stomach, epigastrium, belly; see **abdomen.**

pauper, *n.* —*Syn.* dependent, indigent, destitute person, have-not, poverty-stricken person, suppliant; see also **beggar** 1, 2.

pause, *n.* **1.** [A break]—*Syn.* intermission, suspension, discontinuance, breathing space, hitch, hesitancy, interlude, hiatus, abeyance, interim, lapse, cessation, stopover, interval, rest period, gap, stoppage; see also **recess** 1.—*Ant.* continuation*, prolongation, progression.
2. [Temporary inaction]—*Syn.* lull, rest, stop, halt, truce, suspension of active hostilities, stay, respite, interregnum, standstill, stand, deadlock, stillness. —*Ant.* persistence*, steadiness, ceaselessness.
give one pause—*Syn.* frighten, cause doubt, create suspicion *or* uncertainty; see **confuse.**

pause, *v.* —*Syn.* delay, halt, rest, catch (one's) breath, cease, hold back, reflect, deliberate, suspend, think twice, discontinue, interrupt, rest one's oars (D); see also **hesitate.**

pave, *v.* —*Syn.* flag, lay concrete, lay asphalt, asphalt, gravel, macadamize, floor, hard-surface (D); see also **cover** 1.

paved, *mod.* —*Syn.* hard-surfaced, flagged, cobblestone, corduroy, asphalt, concrete, brick, bricked, surfaced with wood blocks; see also **covered** 1.

pavement, *n.* **1.** [A hard surface for traffic]—*Syn.* hard surface, paving, paving stone, paving tile, flagging, pave; see also **asphalt.**
Road surfaces include the following—concrete, asphalt, Bitulithic (trademark), stone, brick, tile, macadam, gravel, cobblestone, wood blocks, flagstone.
2. [A paved road or area]—*Syn.* highway, thoroughfare, street; see **road** 1, **sidewalk.**

pavilion, *n.* **1.** [Tent]—*Syn.* canopy, covering, awning; see **cover** 1, **tent.**
2. [Light building]—*Syn.* structure, dome, circus house; see **building** 1.

paving, *n.* —*Syn.* hard surface, concrete, paved highway; **asphalt, pavement** 1.

paw, *n.* —*Syn.* forefoot, talon, hand; see **claw.**

paw, *v.* **1.** [To strike wildly]—*Syn.* clutch, grasp, smite; see **hit** 1.
2. [To scrape with the front foot]—*Syn.* scratch, rake, rub, claw, search, rasp, grate; see also **dig** 1.
3. [To handle clumsily]—*Syn.* fondle, handle, stroke, pat, clap, slap, maul, make passes at (D); see also **botch.**

pawn, *n.* —*Syn.* cat's-paw, dupe, fool; see **victim** 2.

pawn, *v.* —*Syn.* deposit, pledge, give in earnest; *all* (D): hock, hang up, leave with uncle, lay in lavender, soak, pop; see also **sell** 1.

pawnbroker, *n.* —*Syn.* moneylender, broker, usurer, moneymonger, lumberer (D); see also **lender.**

pawned, *mod.* —*Syn.* deposited, pledged, hocked, borrowed on, given security, on deposit, in hock (D); see also **sold.**

pawnshop, *n.* —*Syn.* pawnbrokery; **both** (D): hock shop, pop shop; see **shop, store.**

pay, *n.* **1.** [Monetary return]—*Syn.* profit, proceeds, interest, return, recompense, indemnity, reparation, rake-off, reward, perquisite, consideration, defrayment.—*Ant.* expense*, disbursement, outlay.
2. [Wages]—*Syn.* compensation, salary, payment, hire, remuneration, commission, redress, fee, stipend, indemnity, earnings, settlement, consideration, reimbursement, recompensation, reckoning, satisfaction, honorarium, meed, reward, requital, emolument; *all* (D): time, time and a half, double time, overtime.
in the pay of—*Syn.* working for, engaged by, in the service *or* employ of; see **employed.**

pay, *v.* **1.** [To give payment]—*Syn.* pay up, compensate, recompense, make payment, reward, remunerate, discharge, recoup, refund, requite, settle, get even with, reckon with, lay *or* put down, make restitution *or* reparation, hand over, repay, liquidate, handle, take care of, give, confer, bequeath, defray, meet, prepay, disburse, clear, adjust, satisfy, reimburse; *all* (D): kick in, dig up, plank down, put up, stake, foot the bill, get square with the world, sweeten the kitty, bear the cost *or* expense, put one's money on the line, pay as you go, cashout, fork out *or* over, come down *or* through with, even the score, chip in, square off, clear off old scores, square oneself, ante.—*Ant.* deceive*, swindle, victimize.
2. [To produce a profit]—*Syn.* return, pay off, pay out, show *or* yield profit, yield excess, show gain, pay dividends; *all* (D): sweeten, kick back, weigh out.—*Ant.* fail*, lose, become bankrupt.
3. [To retaliate]—*Syn.* repay, punish, requite; see **revenge.**

payable, *mod.* —*Syn.* owed, owing, obligatory; see **due.**

pay back, *v.* —*Syn.* discharge a responsibility, even up, compound (for); see **return** 2.

pay down on, *v.* —*Syn.* make a payment on, pay in on, start (the) purchase (of); see **pay** 1.

payee, *n.* —*Syn.* recipient, receiver, wage-earner, laborer, worker, seller.

pay for, *v.* —*Syn.* atone for, make amends for, do penance for, compensate for, make up for, make satisfaction for, expiate, make reparation for, give satisfaction for, pay the penalty for, make compensation for.

paying, *mod.* —*Syn.* productive, good, sound; see **profitable.**

paymaster, *n.* —*Syn.* purser, bursar, cashier; see **accountant, clerk** 2, **treasurer.**

payment, *n.* **1.** [The act of paying or being paid] —*Syn.* recompense, reimbursement, restitution, subsidy, return, redress, refund, remittance, reparation, disbursement, down, amends, cash, salary, wage, fee, sum, pay-off, repayment, indemnification, requital, defrayment, retaliation; see also **pay** 1.
2. [An installment]—*Syn.* portion part, amount; see **adjustment** 2, **debt** 1, **installment, mortgage.**

pay-off, *n.* —*Syn.* settlement, conclusion, reward; see **adjustment** 2, **pay** 1, **payment** 1.

pay off, *v.* —*Syn.* discharge, let go, drop (from the payroll); see **dismiss** 2.

payroll, *n.* **1.** [Those receiving pay]—*Syn.* employees, workers, pay list; see **faculty** 2, **staff.**
2. [Wages for a period]—*Syn.* salary, receipts, payment; see **pay** 2.

pea, *n.* —*Syn.* Plants commonly called peas include the following—garden, early June, dwarf, brush, everbearing, field, sweet, chick-pea, cowpea; *Pisum sativum, Pisum Arvense, Lathyrus odoratus, Vigna sinensis, Cicer arietinum* (all Latin), *ceci* (Italian), *garbanzo* (Spanish); see also **flower** 1, **plant, vegetable.**
as like as two peas in a pod (D)—*Syn.* identical, the same, similar; see **alike** 1.

peace, *n.* **1.** [The state of being without war] —*Syn.* armistice, pacification, conciliation, order, concord, amity, union, unity, reconciliation, fraternalism, fraternization, brotherhood, love, unanimity, stand-down (D); see also **agreement** 2, **friendship** 1, 2.—*Ant.* war*, warfare, battle.
2. [State of being without disturbance]—*Syn.* calm, repose, quiet, tranquillity, harmony, lull, hush, congeniality, equanimity, silence, stillness; see also **rest** 1.—*Ant.* fight*, noisiness, quarrel.
3. [Mental or emotional calm]—*Syn.* calmness, repose, harmony, concord, contentment, sympathy; see also **composure, reserve** 2, **tranquillity.** —*Ant.* distress*, disturbance, agitation.
at peace—*Syn.* peaceful, quiet, tranquil; see **calm** 1, 2.
hold (*or* **keep**) **one's peace**—*Syn.* be silent, keep quiet, not speak; see **shut up.**
keep the peace—*Syn.* avoid violating the law, keep order, obey the law; see **obey** 1, 2.
make one's peace with—*Syn.* conciliate, submit to, appease; see **quiet** 1.
make peace—*Syn.* end hostilities, settle, reconcile; see **quiet** 1.

peaceable, *mod.* **1.** [At peace]—*Syn.* serene, quiet, balmy; see **calm** 1, 2, **tranquil** 1, 2.
2. [Inclined to peace]—*Syn.* conciliatory, pacific, peaceful; see **friendly** 1.

peaceful, *mod.* **1.** [At peace]—*Syn.* quiet, tranquil, serene; see **calm** 1, 2.
2. [Inclined to peace]—*Syn.* well-disposed, sociable, amiable; see **friendly** 1, **pacific.**

peacefully, *mod.* **1.** [Calmly]—*Syn.* tranquilly, quietly, composedly; see **calmly, resting** 1.
2. [Without making trouble]—*Syn.* pacifically, conciliatingly, harmoniously, fraternally, placatingly, inoffensively, temperately, civilly; see also **modestly** 1.—*Ant.* angrily*, belligerently, hostile.

peacemaker, *n.* —*Syn.* arbitrator, negotiator, mediator; see **diplomat** 1, **statesman.**

peace offering, *n.* —*Syn.* placation, sacrifice, overture; see **appeasement, gift** 1.

peace officer, *n.* —*Syn.* policeman, (police) (officer), member of the police force; see **police.**

peach, *n.* Varieties of peaches include the following —North China, South China, Peen-to, Indian, Persian, cling(stone), freestone, white-fleshed, yellow-fleshed, Elberta, Hale, Golden Jubilee, Halehaven, South Haven, Red Bird Cling, Heath Cling, Orange Cling, May Flower, Champion, Alexander, Rochester, Belle of Georgia, Early Crawford, Crawford's Late Red-Elberta; see also **fruit** 1.

peak, *n.* **1.** [A mountain]—*Syn.* summit, top, crown; see **hill, mountain** 1.
2. [The maximum]—*Syn.* zenith, highest point, greatest quantity; see **height** 1, **tip** 1, **top** 1.

peak, *v.* —*Syn.* top (out), reach a peak *or* a climax *or* the top *or* apex *or* ultimate, crest; see **climax** 1.

peaked, *mod.* **1.** [Sharp]—*Syn.* pointed, topped, triangle-topped; see **sharp** 1.
2. [(D) Appearing ill]—*Syn.* sickly, ailing, poorly; see **pale** 1, **sick.**

peal, *n.* —*Syn.* ring, ringing, clang; see **noise** 1, **sound** 2.

peal, *v.* —*Syn.* chime, ring out, resound; see **ring** 3, **sound** 1.

peanut, *n.* —*Syn.* goober, groundpea, groundnut, Bambara, goober pea.

pear, *n.* Varieties of pears include the following— Bartlett, Gorham, Royal Riviera, Clapp's Favorite, Keiffer's Hybrid, Parrish Favorite, Seckel, Winter Nellis, Beurre d'Anjou; see also **fruit** 1, **tree.**

pearl, *mod.* —*Syn.* blue-gray, silver-white, nacreous, mother-of-pearly, pearly, lustrous, gray-white; see also **iridescent, silver** 1.

pearl, *n.* **1.** [A concretion in a mollusk shell] —*Syn.* nacre, margarite, cultured pearl; see **gem** 1, **jewel** 1.
2. [A droplet]—*Syn.* dewdrop, raindrop, globule; see **drop** 1.
cast pearls before swine—*Syn.* throw *or* give something away, be unappreciated, be misunderstood; see **confuse, waste.**

pearly, *mod.* —*Syn.* opaline, opalescent, nacreous; see **iridescent, pearl, silver** 1.

peasant, *n.* —*Syn.* small farmer, rustic, provincial, tenant farmer, farm-laborer, farm worker, kulak, sharecropper; see also **farmer, laborer, rancher, workman.**

peasantry, *n.* **1.** [The masses]—*Syn.* rank and file, commonality, proletariat; see **people** 3.
2. [Vulgarity]—*Syn.* crudity, impropriety, indelicacy; see **meanness** 1, **rudeness.**

pea soup (D), *n.* —*Syn.* smog, traffic *or* driving hazard, pea-souper (D); see **fog.**

pebble, *n.* —*Syn.* pebblestone, gravel, cobblestone, cobble; see also **rock** 1, **stone.**

peccadillo, *n.* —*Syn.* mistake, violation, error; see **fault** 2, **sin.**

peck, *n.* **1.** [A slight, sharp blow]—*Syn.* pinch, tap, rap; see **blow** 1.
2. [The impression made by a peck, sense 1] —*Syn.* depression, blemish, mark; see **hole** 1, **scar.**
3. [One fourth of a bushel]—*Syn.* eight quarts, quater-bushel, large amount; see **measure** 1, **quantity.**

peck, *v.* —*Syn.* nip, pick, hit, tap, rap; see also **bite** 1, **pinch.**

pectoral, *mod.* —*Syn.* intimate, inner, subjective; see **emotional** 2.

peculiar, *mod.* **1.** [Unusual]—*Syn.* wonderful, singular, outlandish; see **strange** 1, 2, **unusual** 2.
2. [Characteristic of only one]—*Syn.* strange, uncommon, eccentric; see **characteristic, unique** 1.

peculiarly, *mod.* —*Syn.* oddly, queerly, unusually; see **especially** 1, **strangely.**

peculiarity, *n.* —*Syn.* distinctiveness, unusualness, singularity; see **characteristic.**

pecuniary, *mod.* —*Syn.* financial, fiscal, monetary; see **commercial** 1.

pedagogic, *mod.* —*Syn.* professorial, academic, scholastic; see **educational** 1, **learned** 1, **profound** 2.

pedagogue, *n.* **1.** [Instructor]—*Syn.* schoolmaster, educator, lecturer; see **teacher** 1, 2.
2. [Bigot]—*Syn.* conventionalist, sophist, dogmatist; see **bigot.**

pedagogy, *n.* —*Syn.* instruction, guidance, teaching; see **education** 1, 3.

pedal, *n.* —*Syn.* treadle, foot lever, pedal keyboard, clutch, brake, foot feed, gas feed, accelerator; see also **lever.**

pedal, *v.* —*Syn.* treadle, operate, control, accelerate, clutch, brake, work; see also **drive** 3, **propel.**

pedant, *n.* —*Syn.* formalist, doctrinaire, dogmatist, methodologist, precisian, bluestocking, bookworm, pedagogue.

pedantic, *mod.* —*Syn.* formal, precise, pompous, ostentatious of learning, pedagogic, bookish, didactic, doctrinaire, academic, scholastic; see also **egotistic** 2.

pedantry, *n.* —*Syn.* sophistry, meticulousness, precision, display of knowledge, bookishness, exactness, pretension, dogmatism, finicalness; see also **egotism.**

peddle, *v.* —*Syn.* hawk, vend, trade; see **sell** 1.

peddler, *n.* —*Syn.* hawker, vender, seller; see **businessman, salesman** 2.

pedestal, *n.* —*Syn.* stand, foundation, footstall, plinth; see also **column** 1, **support** 2.

pedestrian, *n.* —*Syn.* foot-traveler, one who walks, hiker; see **walker.**

pedigree, *n.* —*Syn.* lineage, clan, ancestry; see **family** 1, **heredity.**

peek, *n.* —*Syn.* sight, glimpse, glance; see **look** 3.

peek, *v.* —*Syn.* glance, peep, glimpse; see **see** 1.

peel, *n.* —*Syn.* peeling, husk, bark, shuck, shell; see also **cover** 2, **skin.**

peel, *v.* —*Syn.* pare, strip, tear *or* pull off, flay, uncover, decorticate; see also **skin.**

peeling, *n.* —*Syn.* paring, strip, sliver; see **skin.**

peep, *n.* **1.** [A peek]—*Syn.* glimpse, glance, sight; see **look** 3.
2. [A peeping sound]—*Syn.* cheep, chirp, hoot; see **cry** 2.

peep, *v.* **1.** [To look cautiously]—*Syn.* peek, glimpse, glance; see **see** 1.
2. [To make a peeping sound]—*Syn.* cheep, chirp, squeak; see **cry** 3.

peephole, *n.* —*Syn.* slit, crevice, slot; see **hole** 1.

peer, *n.* **1.** [An equal]—*Syn.* match, rival, companion; see **equal.**
2. [A lord]—*Syn.* nobleman, titled person, count; see **lord** 2.

peer, *v.* —*Syn.* gaze, inspect, scrutinize; see **see** 1.

peerage, *n.* —*Syn.* gentry, nobility, ruling class; see **aristocracy, royalty.**

peer group, *n.* —*Syn.* equals, age *or* social group *or* class, one's peers; see **associate, fellowship** 2, **equal.**

peerless, *mod.* **1.** [Not equaled]—*Syn.* unequaled, supreme, best; see **excellent.**
2. [Faultless]—*Syn.* unique, superior, unexampled; see **perfect** 2.

peeve, *v.* —*Syn.* irritate, annoy, anger; see **bother** 2.

peeved (D), *mod.* —*Syn.* sullen, irritated, upset; see **angry.**

peevish, *mod.* **1.** [Having a sour disposition]—*Syn.* perverse, pertinacious, morose; see **obstinate.**
2. [Inclined to complain]—*Syn.* querulous, complaining, growling; see **irritable.**
3. [In bad humor]—*Syn.* cross, fretful, fretting; see **angry.**

peg, *n.* —*Syn.* pin, holder, marker, tack, screw, fastener, plug, bolt, dowel, treenail, linchpin; see also **nail.**
round peg in a square hole *or* **square peg in a round hole**—*Syn.* misfit, sorry figure, odd ball (D); see **misanthrope.**
take down a peg (D)—*Syn.* humiliate, criticize, diminish; see **humble.**

peg, *v.* —*Syn.* clinch, tighten, secure; see **fasten** 1.

peignoir, *n.* —*Syn.* gown, dressing gown, negligee; see **clothes, nightgown, robe.**

pejorative, *mod.* —*Syn.* irreverent, deprecatory, derisive; see **rude** 2.

pelf, *n.* —*Syn.* profit, gain, spoils; see **money** 1, **wealth** 2.

pellet, *n.* —*Syn.* pill, globule, bullet, bead, pebble, grain, orblet, spherule; see also **rock** 2, **stone.**

pell-mell, *mod.* —*Syn.* impetuously, hurriedly, indiscreetly; see **foolishly, rashly.**

pellucid, *mod.* **1.** [Transparent]—*Syn.* lucid, gauzy, translucent; see **clear** 2, **transparent** 1.
2. [Explicit]—*Syn.* simple, clear, plain; see **understandable.**

pelt, *n.* —*Syn.* fell, hair, wool; see **hide** 1.

pelt, *v.* —*Syn.* swat, wham, knock; see **beat** 2, **hit** 1.

pen, *n.* **1.** [An enclosed place]—*Syn.* coop, cage, corral, sty, close, concentration camp, penitentiary; see also **enclosure** 1.
2. [The means of enclosure]—*Syn.* wire fence, hedge, wall; see **fence** 1.
3. [A writing instrument] Pens and pen points include the following—fountain, common, desk, drawing, ruling, marker, artist's, reed, quill, steel, ball point pen, biro (British); nib, stub, fine, coarse,

Spencerian; Speedball, Osmiroid (both trademarks).

pen, *v.* **1.** [To enclose]—*Syn.* close *or* fence in, confine, coop up (D); see **enclose** 1.

2. [To write]—*Syn.* compose, indict, commit to writing; see **write** 1, 2.

penal, *mod.* —*Syn.* punitive, causing suffering, retributive, chastening, reformatory, corrective, punishing, punitory.

penalize, *v.* —*Syn.* scold, chasten, castigate; see **punish.**

penalty, *n.* —*Syn.* fine, mortification, discipline; see **punishment.**

penance, *n.* **1.** [Voluntary punishment]—*Syn.* mortification, purgation, repentance, retribution, compensation, self-imposed atonement, self-flagellation, fasting, suffering, expiation, *paenitentia* (Latin), *Beichte* (German), sackcloth and ashes, hair shirt, inward penance, outward penance, reparation; see also **punishment.**

2. [A sacrament]—*Syn.* repentance, penitence, confession, absolution, sorrow for sin, contrition, remorse, forgiveness for sin; see also **repentance, sacrament.**

penchant, *n.* —*Syn.* inclination, attachment, affinity; see **affection.**

pencil, *n.* **1.** [A graphic instrument] Types of pencils include the following—lead, mechanical, colored, drawing, slate, indelible, charcoal, eyebrow, cosmetic, drafting; chalk, crayon, stylus.

2. [Anything suggestive of a pencil]—*Syn.* shaft, gleam, streak, line, pointer, indicator.

pendant, *n.* **1.** [Ornament]—*Syn.* earring, locket, lavalière; see **decoration** 2, **jewelry.**

2. [Correlative]—*Syn.* parallel, one of a pair, equal; see **match** 2, **mate** 1.

pendent, *mod.* —*Syn.* pendant, dependent, suspended; see **hanging.**

pending, *mod.* —*Syn.* continuing, indeterminate, awaiting; see **imminent, ominous.**

pendulous, *mod.* —*Syn.* swaying, dangling, swinging; see **hanging.**

pendulum, *n.* —*Syn.* swing, pendant, oscillator, suspended body; see also **device** 1, **machine** 1.

penetrable, *mod.* —*Syn.* permeable, susceptible, receptive, pervious, open, passable, accessible; see also **porous.**

penetrate, *v.* **1.** [To pierce]—*Syn.* bore, perforate, enter, insert, go through, make an entrance, stick into, jab, thrust, stab, force (a way), make a hole, run into, seep *or* filter in, run through, punch, puncture, drive into, stick, drill, ream, eat through, spear, impale, wound, gore, sting, prick, transfix, sink into, knife, bayonet, go *or* pass through. —*Ant.* leave*, withdraw, turn aside.

2. [To permeate]—*Syn.* enter, infiltrate, seep; see **filter.** 1.

3. [To understand]—*Syn.* discern, perceive, grasp; see **understand** 1.

penetrating, *mod.* **1.** [Entering]—*Syn.* piercing, boring, going through, puncturing, sticking into, permeating, infiltrating, forcing, passing through, punching into, edged, pointed; see also **sharp** 2. —*Ant.* dull*, blunt, rounded.

2. [Mentally keen]—*Syn.* astute, shrewd, sharp; see **intelligent** 1.

penetration, *n.* **1.** [Act of entering]—*Syn.* insertion, invasion, boring into, perforation, thrusting, stabbing, punching, forcing, infiltration, seepage, ingress, diffusion, sticking *or* driving into, osmosis, piercing; see also **entrance** 1.—*Ant.* departure*, evacuation, egress.

2. [Mental acuteness]—*Syn.* discernment, perception, keen-sightedness; see **acumen.**

peninsula, *n.* —*Syn.* point, foreland, promontory, cape, headland, neck, spit, chersonese; see also **land** 1.

penitence, *n.* —*Syn.* remorse, sorrow, contrition; see **penance** 1, 2, **regret** 1, **repentance.**

penitent, *mod.* —*Syn.* repentant, sorrowful, contrite; see **sorry** 1.

penitentiary, *mod.* —*Syn.* punitive, disciplinary, refractory; see **penal.**

penitentiary, *n.* —*Syn.* reformatory, penal institution, pen (D); see **jail, prison.**

penknife, *n.* —*Syn.* pocketknife, jackknife, Boy Scout knife; see **knife.**

penman, *n.* **1.** [Scribe]—*Syn.* clerk, recorder, copyist; see **scribe** 1, **secretary** 2.

2. [Writer]—*Syn.* journalist, essayist, novelist; see **author** 2, **writer.**

penmanship, *n.* —*Syn.* script, longhand, chirography; see **handwriting.**

pen name, *n.* —*Syn.* *nom de plume* (French), anonym, pseudonym; see **alias, name** 3.

pennant, *n.* —*Syn.* streamer, decoration, emblem; see **flag** 1.

penniless, *mod.* —*Syn.* poverty-stricken, lacking means, indigent; see **poor** 1.

pennon, *n.* —*Syn.* banner, pennant, streamer; see **flag** 1.

penny, *n.* —*Syn.* cent, copper, red cent (D); see **money** 1.

a pretty penny (D)—*Syn.* a large sum of money, fortune, riches; see **wealth.**

turn an honest penny—*Syn.* profit, earn money honestly, gain; see **earn** 2.

penny ante (D), *mod.* —*Syn.* trifling, insignificant, petty; see **trivial, unimportant.**

pension, *n.* —*Syn.* annuity, premium, payment, grant, social security, gift, reward, subvention, rocking-chair money (D); see also **allowance** 2, **subsidy.**

pensioner, *n.* —*Syn.* retired person, dependent, grantee, accipient; see also **beneficiary.**

pensive, *mod.* —*Syn.* ruminating, serious, musing; see **thoughtful** 1.

pent-up, *mod.* —*Syn.* held in check, repressed, restrained; see **restrained, restricted.**

Pentecost, *n.* —*Syn.* seventh Sunday after Easter, Whitsunday, festival, the descent of the Holy Spirit on the Apostles.

penurious, *mod.* —*Syn.* mean, frugal, niggardly; see **stingy.**

penury, *n.* —*Syn.* need, bankruptcy, destitution; see **poverty** 1.

people, *n.* **1.** [Humankind]—*Syn.* humanity, mankind, the human race; see **man** 1.

2. [A body of persons having racial or social ties] —*Syn.* nationality, tribe, community; see **race** 2.

3. [The humbler portions of society]—*Syn.* mass, folk, proletariat, rabble, masses, plebeians, the multitude, the majority, democracy, crowd, submerged tenth, common people, common herd, rank and file, the underprivileged, underdogs, the public, the man in the street, commons, commonalty, *hoi polloi* (Greek), *bourgeoisie* (French), *los de abajo* (Spanish); *all* (D): riffraff; rag, tag and bobtail; the common peepul, the mob, the herd, the horde, the many, the great unwashed, John *or* Jane Q. Public.

4. [Family]—*Syn.* close relatives, kinsmen, siblings; see **family** 1.

5. [Society in general]—*Syn.* they, anybody, the public; see **everybody.**

peopled, *mod.* —*Syn.* lived in, dwelt in, sustaining human life; see **inhabited.**

pep (D), *n.* —*Syn.* energy, vigor, liveliness; see **vigor** 1, 3, **action** 1.

pepper, *n.* Common peppers include the following—red, sweet, black, cayenne, green *or* stuffing, pimiento, jalapeño, paprika *or* bonnet pepper; see also **spice.**

Varieties of pepper include the following—California Wonder, Chinese Giant, Ruby King, Perfection, King of the North, Yellow Giant, Sweet Mango, Hungarian Wax *or* Banana.

peppery, *mod.* **1.** [Seasoned]—*Syn.* hot, piquant, pungent; see **spicy** 1.

2. [Incisive; *said of speech*]—*Syn.* acute, keen, sharp; see **sarcastic.**

peppy (D), *mod.* —*Syn.* lively, vigorous, sprightly; see **active** 1, 2.

per, *prep.* —*Syn.* to each, for each, contained in each, according to, through, by, by means of.

perambulate, *v.* **1.** [To ramble]—*Syn.* wander, stroll, hike; see **walk** 1.

2. [To inspect]—*Syn.* study, scan, patrol; see **examine** 1.

perceivable, *mod.* —*Syn.* open, observable, visible; see **obvious** 1.

perceive, *v.* **1.** [See]—*Syn.* observe, note, notice; see **look** 2, **regard** 1, **see** 1.

2. [Understand]—*Syn.* comprehend, sense, grasp; see **distinguish** 1, **learn** 1, **recognize** 1, **understand** 1.

perceived, *mod.* —*Syn.* seen, felt, touched, reacted to, witnessed, made out, heeded, observed, noted, sensed, grasped, noticed, anticipated, overheard, picked up; see also **heard, recognized, understood** 1.

perceiving, *mod.* —*Syn.* alert, aware, cognizant; see **discreet, judicious, rational** 1, **sensitive** 3.

per cent, *mod.* —*Syn.* by the hundred, reckoned on the basis of a hundred, percentaged, in a hundred, percentile; see also **fractional.**

percentage, *n.* —*Syn.* per cent, rate, rate per cent, portion, section, allotment, duty, discount, commission, winnings; *all* (D): washout rate, cut, rake-off, holdout, corner, pay-off, slice, split, shake, squeeze; see also **division** 2, **interest** 3.

perceptible, *mod.* —*Syn.* perceivable, discernible, cognizable; see **audible, obvious** 1.

perception, *n.* **1.** [The act of perceiving]—*Syn.* realizing, understanding, apprehending; see **attention** 2, **judgment** 2, **study** 2, **thought** 1.

2. [The result of perceiving]—*Syn.* insight, knowledge, observation; see **attitude** 3, **opinion** 1, **plan** 2, **thought** 2, **viewpoint.**

3. [The power to perceive]—*Syn.* discernment, perspicacity, sagacity; see **acumen, judgment** 1.

perceptive, *mod.* **1.** [Aware]—*Syn.* alert, incisive, keen; see **conscious** 1, **observant** 1.

2. [Discerning]—*Syn.* perspicacious, sharp, sagacious; see **discreet, judicious, rational** 1.

perch, *n.* —*Syn.* seat, pole, landing place; see **roost.**

perch, *v.* —*Syn.* roost, settle down, land; see **rest** 1, **sit** 1, 2.

percolate, *v.* —*Syn.* pass through, pervade, permeate, penetrate, bubble; see also **filter** 1.

percussion, *n.* —*Syn.* shock, blow, impact; see **collision** 1, **crash** 4.

per diem, *n.* —*Syn.* costs, daily *or* routine expense(s), outlay; see **expense** 1.

perdition, *n.* —*Syn.* condemnation, destruction, doom; see **blame** 1, **damnation.**

perdurable, *mod.* —*Syn.* lasting, stable, enduring; see **permanent** 2, **perpetual** 1.

peregrinate, *v.* —*Syn.* wander, ramble, rove; see **roam** 1, **travel** 2.

peremptory, *mod.* **1.** [Not subject to revision]—*Syn.* fixed, authoritative, uncompromising; see **absolute** 1, **comprehensive, finished** 1, **firm** 1.

2. [Harsh]—*Syn.* rigorous, firm, stringent; see **cruel** 2, **sarcastic, severe** 2.

3. [Dictatorial]—*Syn.* overbearing, decisive, assertive; see **absolute** 3, **autocratic** 1, **tyrannical.**

perennial, *mod.* —*Syn.* enduring, sustained, continuing; see **permanent** 2, **perpetual** 1.

perfect, *mod.* **1.** [Having all necessary qualities]—*Syn.* complete, sound, entire; see **absolute** 1, **comprehensive, whole** 1, 2.

2. [Without defect]—*Syn.* excelling, faultless, flawless, impeccable, immaculate, unblemished, defectless, foolproof, untainted, unspotted, consummate, absolute, matchless, unequaled, impeccable, peerless, taintless, classical, stainless, spotless, crowning, culminating, supreme, pure, ideal, sublime, beyond all praise, beyond compare; see also **excellent, pure** 2, **whole** 2.—*Ant.* ruined*, damaged, faulty.

3. [Exact]—*Syn.* precise, sharp, distinct; see **accurate** 1, 2, **certain** 3, **definite** 1, 2.

4. [(D) Excessive]—*Syn.* very great, flagrant, gross; see **extreme** 2, **superfluous.**

perfect, *v.* —*Syn.* fulfill, realize, develop; see **achieve** 1, **complete** 1.

perfected, *mod.* —*Syn.* completed, consummate, developed, mature, conclusive, full, elaborate, thorough; see also **finished** 1, **fulfilled, ripe** 3.

perfection, *n.* **1.** [The act of perfecting]—*Syn.* completion, fulfillment, finishing, consummation, ending, realization, touching up; see also **achievement** 2.—*Ant.* ruin*, destruction*, neglect*.

2. [The state of being complete]—*Syn.* ripeness, completeness, completion; see **end** 2, **maturity** 3, **result.**

3. [A high degree of excellence]—*Syn.* consummation, supremacy, impeccability, crown, ideal, paragon, phoenix, faultlessness.

perfectly, *mod.* **1.** [In a perfect manner]—*Syn.* excellently, fitly, correctly, flawlessly, faultlessly, supremely, ideally.—*Ant.* badly*, poorly, incorrectly.

2. [To a sufficient degree]—*Syn.* quite, utterly, absolutely; see **well** 2, 3.

perfervid, *mod.* —*Syn.* ardent, zealous, intense; see **enthusiastic** 2, 3.

perfidious, *mod.* —*Syn.* treacherous, mean, corrupt; see **dishonest** 2.

perfidy, *n.* —*Syn.* deceit, falseness, disloyalty; see **dishonesty.**

perforate, *v.* —*Syn.* drill, slit, stab; see **penetrate** 1.

perforation, *n.* —*Syn.* break, aperture, slit; see **hole** 1.

perform, *v.* **1.** [To accomplish an action]—*Syn.* do, make, achieve, rehearse, accomplish, fulfill, execute, transact, carry out *or* off *or* through, discharge, effect, enforce, administer, complete, consummate, operate, finish, realize, go about *or* through (with), discharge the duties of, put through, work out, devote oneself to, come through (with), be engrossed *or* engaged in, see to (it), bring off *or* about *or* through, engage in, concern oneself with, have effect, fall to, do justice to, do one's part, give oneself up to, make a move, put in motion *or* force, follow through, apply oneself to, put across, deal with, carry into execution, do something, look to, take measures, acquit oneself, act on, lose oneself in, make it one's own business, dispose of, bring to pass, do what is expected of one, put into effect, occupy oneself with, take action, address oneself to, put in action; *all* (D): do one's stuff, lift a finger, keep one's hand in, muddle through, have a free play, go in for, make short work of, pull off, do up brown; see also **act** 1.—*Ant.* fail*, neglect, ignore.

2. [To present a performance]—*Syn.* give, present, enact, play, offer, impersonate, show, exhibit, display, act out, dramatize, execute, put on the stage, produce, act the part of, tread the boards, put on an act, act one's part, go through one's repertoire, go through tricks; see also **act** 3.

3. [(D) To behave in a ludicrous manner]—*Syn.* clown, play the fool, show off; see **joke, misbehave.**

4. [(D) To complete an action]—*Syn.* finish, complete, knock off (D); see **achieve** 1.

performance, *n.* **1.** [The fulfilling of a function] —*Syn.* completion, fulfillment, attainment, doing, achievement, accomplishment, execution, carrying out, administration, enforcement, consummation, realization, fruition.—*Ant.* failure*, unfulfillment, frustration.

2. [A public presentation]—*Syn.* production, appearance, rehearsal, exhibition, offering, representation, pageant, burlesque, spectacle, review, revue, opera, masque, play, drama, dance recital, concert, exhibit, display, special (D); see also **act** 2, **drama** 1, **show** 1.

performing, *mod.* **1.** [Fulfilling a function]—*Syn.* doing, acting, operating, carrying out, in the act (of), fulfilling, achieving, effecting.

2. [Taking part in a presentation]—*Syn.* playing, displaying, exhibiting, going through paces *or* routine *or* repertoire *or* tricks.

performing, *n.* —*Syn.* making, acting, accomplishing; see **doing.**

perfume, *n.* —*Syn.* scent, fragrance, aroma, odor, sweetness, redolence, bouquet, sachet, incense; see also **smell** 1.

Perfumes include the following—attar of roses, sandalwood, balm, bergamot, bay, rosemary, bay rum, palm oil, frankincense, myrrh, civet, Eau de Cologne (trademark), musk, orange-flowers, potpourri, muscadine, spice, sachet, lavender, rose geranium.

perfumed, *mod.* —*Syn.* aromatic, scented, fragrant; see **odorous** 2.

perfunctory, *mod.* —*Syn.* apathetic, mechanical, routine; see **careless** 1, **indifferent** 1.

pergola, *n.* —*Syn.* trellis, kiosk, arbor; see **lattice.**

perhaps, *mod.* —*Syn.* conceivably, possibly, reasonably; see **maybe.**

perilous, *mod.* —*Syn.* precarious, unsafe, uncertain; see **dangerous** 1.

perimeter, *n.* —*Syn.* margin, outline, border; see **boundary, edge** 1.

period, *n.* **1.** [A measure of time]—*Syn.* epoch, time, era; see **age** 3.

2. [An end]—*Syn.* limit, conclusion, close; see **end** 2.

3. [A mark of punctuation]—*Syn.* point, full stop, full pause, dot, ending-pitch; see also **punctuation.**

periodical, *mod.* —*Syn.* periodic, rhythmic, regular, cyclic, cyclical, fluctuating, orbital, pendulum-like, recurrent, recurring, intermittent, alternate, serial, hourly, daily, weekly, monthly, yearly, at various times, at regular *or* fixed intervals, on certain occasions, at predetermined *or* regular times, annual, perennial, centennial; see also **regular** 3.

periodical, *n.* —*Syn.* review, number, publication; see **magazine** 2, **newspaper.**

periodically, *mod.* —*Syn.* rhythmically, systematically, annually; see **regularly** 2.

peripatetic, *mod.* —*Syn.* roaming, itinerant, roving; see **wandering** 1.

peripheral, *mod.* —*Syn.* external, outer, surface; see **outside.**

periphery, *n.* —*Syn.* covering, perimeter, border; see **outside** 1.

periphrase, *n.* —*Syn.* circumlocution, ambiguity, evasion; see **wordiness.**

periphrastic, *mod.* —*Syn.* equivocal, roundabout, circumlocutory; see **obscure** 1.

perish, *v.* —*Syn.* pass away, be lost, depart; see **die** 1.

perjure, *v.* —*Syn.* prevaricate, swear falsely, falsify; see **lie** 1.

perjurer, *n.* —*Syn.* prevaricator, falsifier, deceiver; see **liar.**

perjury, *n.* —*Syn.* false statement, violation of an oath, willful falsehood; see **lie** 1.

perk (up), *v.* **1.** [Be refreshed]—*Syn.* revive, recuperate, liven up; see **recover** 3.

2. [Cheer or refresh]—*Syn.* invigorate, shake, enliven; see **renew** 1, **revive** 1.

perky, *mod.* **1.** [Proud]—*Syn.* dignified, haughty, jaunty; see **proud** 1.

2. [Alert]—*Syn.* aware, brisk, lively; see **active** 2.

permanence, *n.* —*Syn.* continuity, dependability, durability; see **stability** 1.

permanent, *mod.* **1.** [Perpetual]—*Syn.* unchanging, continual, changeless; see **perpetual** 1.

2. [Intended to last for a considerable time] —*Syn.* durable, enduring, abiding, uninterrupted, stable, continuing, unremitting, unremittent, lasting, perdurable, firm, hard, tough, strong, rocklike, hardy, robust, sound, sturdy, steadfast, imperishable, surviving, living, long-lived, long-standing, invariable, persisting, tenacious, persevering, unyielding, resisting, resistant, impenetrable, recurring, wearing, constant, changeless, holding, persistent, perennial.

permanently, *mod.* —*Syn.* for all time, enduringly, lastingly; see **forever** 1.

permeable, *mod.* —*Syn.* pory, pervious, penetrable; see **porous.**

permeate, *v.* —*Syn.* pervade, saturate, fill; see **filter** 1.

permeation, *n.* —*Syn.* diffusion, saturation, seepage; see **penetration** 1.

permissible, *mod.* —*Syn.* allowable, sanctioned, to be permitted; see **admissible.**

permissibly, *mod.* —*Syn.* fittingly, allowably, lawfully, legitimately, properly, by one's leave; see also **legally** 1.

permission, *n.* —*Syn.* leave, liberty, consent, assent, acquiescence, acceptance, letting, approbation, agreement, license, permit, allowance, authority, tolerance, toleration, authorization, imprimatur, approval, acknowledgment, admission, verification, recognition, concurrence, promise, avowal, support, corroboration, guarantee, guaranty, warrant, visa, advocacy, carte blanche, commendation, encouragement, ratification, grace, authority, sanction, dispensation, confirmation, endorsement, affirmation, concordance, assurance, empowering, legalization, grant, indulgence, trust, connivance, concession, adjustment, settlement, accord, subscription; *all* (D): nod, O.K., rubber stamp, the go-ahead, high-sign, green light.—*Ant.* denial*, injunction, interdiction.

permissive, *mod.* **1.** [Permitting]—*Syn.* authorizing, allowing, agreeable; see **lenient, permitting.**

2. [Authorized]—*Syn.* allowed, licensed, permitted; see **approved.**

permit, *n.* —*Syn.* license, grant, consent, favor, toleration, authorization, empowering, charter, sanction, legalization, concession, indulgence, privilege; see also **permission.**—*Ant.* denial*, veto, prohibition.

permit, *v.* —*Syn.* sanction, tolerate, let; see **allow** 1.

permitted, *mod.* —*Syn.* granted, allowed, licensed, authorized, legalized, tolerated, empowered, sanctioned, conceded, consented, favored, suffered, chartered, accorded, vouchsafed, let, indulged, privileged; see also **approved.**—*Ant.* refused*, denied, prohibited.

permitting, *mod.* —*Syn.* consenting, allowing, tolerating, authorizing, empowering, chartering, sanctioning, granting, suffering, licensing, letting, vouchsafing; see also **lenient.**

permutation, *n.* —*Syn.* alteration, transformation, shift; see **change** 2.

pernicious, *mod.* **1.** [Extremely harmful]—*Syn.* detrimental, prejudicial, malignant; see **harmful.**

2. [Noxious]—*Syn.* virulent, venomous, baneful; see **deadly, poisonous.**

perorate, *v.* **1.** [To harangue]—*Syn.* speak, lecture, recite; see **address** 2.

2. [To summarize]—*Syn.* epitomize, conclude, sum up; see **decrease** 2, **summarize.**

peroration, *n.* **1.** [A speech]—*Syn.* discourse, talk, lecture; see **speech** 3.

2. [A conclusion]—*Syn.* restatement, outline, end; see **summary.**

peroxide (D), *mod.* —*Syn.* fair, light, flaxen; see **blond.**

perpendicular, *mod.* —*Syn.* vertical, plumb, straight; see **upright** 1.

perpetrate, *v.* —*Syn.* commit, act, do; see **perform** 1.

perpetual, *mod.* **1.** [Never stopping]—*Syn.* continuous, unceasing, constant, never-ceasing, incessant, permanent, lasting, uninterrupted, eternal, everlasting, enduring, continued, without end, ceaseless, imperishable, undying, immortal, sempiternal; see also **endless** 1.—*Ant.* short*, transitory, fleeting.

2. [Continually repeating]—*Syn.* incessant, repetitious, continual, reoccurring, repeating, recurrent, intermittent, going on and on, returning, annual; see also **constant** 1, **regular** 3.

perpetually, *mod.* —*Syn.* enduringly, unceasingly, permanently; see **forever** 1, 2.

perpetuate, *v.* —*Syn.* keep alive, preserve, keep in existence; see **continue** 1.

perpetuation, *n.* —*Syn.* maintenance, permanence, propagation; see **continuation** 1.

perpetuity, *n.* —*Syn.* constancy, endurance, continuance; see **continuity** 1.

perplex, *v.* —*Syn.* puzzle, confound, bewilder; see **confuse.**

perplexed, *mod.* **1.** [Confused]—*Syn.* troubled, uncertain, bewildered; see **doubtful** 2.

2. [Involved]—*Syn.* intricate, bewildering, confusing; see **complex** 2, **difficult** 2.

perplexing, *mod.* —*Syn.* bewildering, confusing, mystifying; see **difficult** 2.

perplexity, *n.* **1.** [Uncertainty based on doubt] —*Syn.* bewilderment, confusion, quandary; see **doubt** 2, **uncertainty** 2.

2. [Difficulty causing uncertainty]—*Syn.* complication, crisis, emergency; see **difficulty** 2.

perquisite, *n.* —*Syn.* income, proceeds, gain; see **profit** 2, **tip** 2.

per se, *mod.* —*Syn.* as such, intrinsically, alone, singularly, fundamentally, in essence, in *or* by itself, virtually; see also **essentially.**

persecute, *v.* **1.** [To oppress, especially for religious reasons]—*Syn.* afflict, harass, hector, bait, victimize, tyrannize, outrage, ill-treat, oppress, imprison, torment, torture, rack, flog, strike, beat, scourge, kill, crucify, maltreat, banish, expel, exile; see also **abuse** 1.—*Ant.* encourage*, endorse, patronize.

2. [To torment persistently]—*Syn.* annoy, worry, tease; see **bother** 2.

persecution, *n.* —*Syn.* affliction, infliction, torture, ill-treatment, maltreatment, torment, killing, murder, massacre, banishment, expulsion, exile, imprisonment, mistreatment, annoyance, teasing, galling, provoking, pestering; see also **abuse** 3, **oppression** 1, **torture.**—*Ant.* help*, succor, stimulation.

perseverance, *n.* **1.** [The act of perseverance] —*Syn.* continuance, prolonging, pursuance; see **continuation** 1.
2. [The attitude of mind]—*Syn.* grit, resolution, pluck; see **determination** 2.

persevere, *v.* —*Syn.* persist, remain, pursue; see **endure** 1.

persist, *v.* —*Syn.* persevere, pursue, strive; see **continue** 1, **endure** 1.

persistence, *n.* —*Syn.* steadfastness, tenacity, constancy, indefatigability, resolution, grit, stamina, pluck; see also **endurance** 2.—*Ant.* indifference*, indolence, idleness.

persistent, *mod.* —*Syn.* tenacious, steadfast, determined; see **resolute** 2.

persnickety (D), *mod.* —*Syn.* fussy, fastidious, particular; see **careful.**

person, *n.* **1.** [An individual]—*Syn.* (human) being, child, somebody, self, oneself, I, me, soul, spirit, character, individuality, personage, personality, (personal) identity; see also **man** 2, **woman** 1.
2. [An individual enjoying distinction]—*Syn.* distinguished person, personality, success; see **character** 4, **personage** 2.
3. [Bodily form]—*Syn.* physique, frame, form; see **body** 1.
in person—*Syn.* personally, in the flesh, present; see **near, there.**

personable, *mod.* —*Syn.* agreeable, pleasant, attractive; see **charming.**

personage, *n.* **1.** [An individual]—*Syn.* human being, someone, individual; see **man** 3, **person** 1, **woman** 1.
2. [A notable]—*Syn.* personality, individual, distinguished person, dignitary, well-known person, person in the limelight, celebrity, cynosure, star; *all* (D): somebody, big man, big boss, bigwig, brass, chief, prince, nabob, very important person *or* VIP, big man on campus *or* BMOC; see also **success** 3.

personal, *mod.* **1.** [Private]—*Syn.* secluded, secret, retired; see **private.**
2. [Individual]—*Syn.* claimed, peculiar, particular; see **individual** 1, **special** 1.
3. [Pertaining to one's person]—*Syn.* fleshly, corporeal, corporal; see **bodily** 1.

personality, *n.* **1.** [The total of one's nature] —*Syn.* self, onself, being; see **character** 2.
2. [Individual characteristics]—*Syn.* disposition, nature, temper; see **character** 1.
3. [A notable person]—*Syn.* celebrity, star, cynosure; see **character** 4, **personage** 2.

personally, *mod.* **1.** [Viewed in a personal manner] —*Syn.* directly, narrowly, pettily, small-mindedly, ungenerously, blindly, with concern for self, keenly, hard; see also **egotistically, selfishly.** —*Ant.* publicly*, generally, broadly.
2. [From the point of view of the speaker]—*Syn.* for me, myself, by *or* for myself, for my part, as I see it, according to my opinion; see also **individually, mentally, subjectively.**—*Ant.* certainly*, objectively, scientifically.

persona non grata (Latin), *n.* —*Syn.* trespasser, antagonist, undesirable; see **enemy.**

personification, *n.* —*Syn.* metaphor, anthropomorphism, imagery; see **representation.**

personify, *v.* **1.** [To impersonate]—*Syn.* represent, live as, act out; see **imitate** 2, **impersonate.**
2. [To embody]—*Syn.* substantiate, contain, materialize; see **complete** 1.
3. [To represent]—*Syn.* copy, symbolize, exemplify; see **represent** 3.

personnel, *n.* —*Syn.* workers, employees, faculty, corps, cadre, organization, group, troop; see also **staff** 2.

perspective, *n.* —*Syn.* aspect, attitude, outlook; see **viewpoint.**

perspicacious, *mod.* —*Syn.* observant, perceptive, alert; see **judicious.**

perspicacity, *n.* —*Syn.* insight, discrimination, penetration; see **acumen.**

perspicuity, *n.* —*Syn.* lucidity, plainness, clearness; see **clarity.**

perspicuous, *mod.* —*Syn.* lucid, distinct, apparent; see **clear** 2, **obvious** 1.

perspiration, *n.* —*Syn.* water, exudation, beads of moisture; see **sweat.**

perspire, *v.* —*Syn.* secrete, exude, lather; see **sweat** 1.

persuade, *v.* **1.** [To influence]—*Syn.* convince, move, induce, satisfy, inveigle, assure, cajole, incline, talk (someone) into something, win over, bring around *or* over, lead to believe *or* to act *or* to do something, gain the confidence of, prevail on *or* upon, overcome another's resistence, wear down, bring a person to his senses, win an argument, make *or* carry one's point, gain the confidence of; *all* (D): make (someone) see the light, cram down one's throat, sell (a bill of goods), sell on, turn (someone) on (to); see also **influence.**—*Ant.* dissuade*, neglect, dampen.
2. [To urge]—*Syn.* exhort, coax, prompt; see **urge** 1, 2.

persuaded, *mod.* —*Syn.* convinced, won over, moved (to), led, influenced, motivated, lured, allured, attracted (to), prevailed upon, decoyed, seduced, wheedled, inveigled, impelled, having given in *or* succumbed to pressure; *both* (D): brought to see the light, turned on (to).

persuasion, *n.* **1.** [The act of persuading]—*Syn.* inducing, suasiòn, influencing, enticing, enticement, exhorting, exhortation, seducing, seduction, inveigling, inveiglement, alluring, wheedling, cajoling, cajolery, winning over, talking over *or* around; *all* (D): making (someone) see the light *or* the facts of life, bringing to heel, talking someone into something, turning (someone) on (to something).—*Ant.* prevention*, dissuasion, confusion.
2. [A belief]—*Syn.* creed, tenet, religion; see **faith.**

persuasive, *mod.* —*Syn.* convincing, alluring, plausible, luring, seductive, wheedling, influential, winning, enticing, impelling, moving, actuating, inspiriting, efficient, efficacious, effectual, compelling, touching, forceful, potent, powerful, swaying, cogent, pointed, strong, energetic, forcible, inveigling; see also **effective, stimulating.**

persuasiveness, *n.* —*Syn.* control, forcefulness, strength; see **influence** 2, **power** 2.

pert, *mod.* —*Syn.* bold, daring, saucy; see **rude** 2.

pertain, *v.* —*Syn.* relate to, belong to, refer to; see **concern** 1.

pertaining, *mod.* —*Syn.* belonging to, appropriate to, connected with; see **referring.**

pertinacious, *mod.* **1.** [Resolute]—*Syn.* determined, attentive, tenacious; see **resolute** 2.
2. [Obstinate]—*Syn.* insistent, perverse, persistent; see **obstinate.**

pertinence, *n.* —*Syn.* consistency, congruity, relevance; see **importance** 1.

pertinent, *mod.* —*Syn.* appropriate, suitable, related; see **relevant.**

pertness, *n.* —*Syn.* insolence, arrogance, audacity; see **rudeness.**

perturb, *v.* **1.** [To annoy]—*Syn.* pester, worry, irritate; see **bother** 2.
2. [To confuse]—*Syn.* perplex, confound, bewilder; see **confuse.**

perturbation, *n.* —*Syn.* distress, disturbance, anxiety; see **confusion** 1, 2, **disorder** 2.

perturbed, *mod.* —*Syn.* uneasy, anxious, restless; see **troubled** 1.

perusal, *n.* —*Syn.* scrutiny, inspection, research; see **examination** 1.

peruse, *v.* **1.** [To inspect]—*Syn.* study, scrutinize, analyze; see **examine** 1.
2. [To read]—*Syn.* glance over, scan, skim; see **read** 1.

pervade, *v.* —*Syn.* suffuse, permeate, spread through; see **penetrate** 1.

perverse, *mod.* **1.** [Obstinate]—*Syn.* headstrong, obdurate, self-willed; see **obstinate** 1.
2. [Inclined to opposition and bad temper]—*Syn.* cranky, contrary, unreasonable; see **irritable.**
3. [Erring]—*Syn.* wayward, delinquent, capricious; see **wicked** 1.

perversion, *n.* **1.** [A distortion]—*Syn.* involution, regression, abuse; see **contortion** 1.
2. [Deviation]—*Syn.* corruption, debasement, depravity, wickedness, depredation, degeneration, vitiation, degradation, impairment, self-defilement, vice, bestiality.

pervert, *v.* —*Syn.* ruin, vitiate, divert; see **corrupt** 1.

perverted, *mod.* —*Syn.* distorted, deviating, corrupt; see **wicked** 1.

pervious, *mod.* —*Syn.* pory, permeable, penetrable; see **porous.**

pesky, *mod.* —*Syn.* troublesome, provoking, annoying; see **disturbing.**

peso (D), *n.* —*Syn.* cash, legal tender, coin; see **money** 1.

pessimism, *n.* —*Syn.* unhappiness, gloom, low spirits, despondency, melancholy, blighted hope, lack of expectation; see also **depression** 2, **grief** 1, **sadness.**

pessimist, *n.* —*Syn.* misanthrope, worrier, melancholic, depreciator, complainer; *all* (D): croaker, Cassandra, crepehanger, worrywart, gloomy Gus.

pessimistic, *mod.* **1.** [Discouraging]—*Syn.* worrisome, troublesome, troubling; see **dismal** 1.
2. [Inclined to a discouraging view]—*Syn.* hopeless, gloomy, cynical, misanthropic, melancholy, depressed, sullen, morose, morbid, despairing, distrustful, sullen, sneering; see also **sad** 1.—*Ant.* confident*, optimistic, sanguine.
3. [Believing in philosophic pessimism]—*Syn.* fatalistic, deterministic, mechanistic, rationalistic, realistic.

pest, *n.* **1.** [Anything destructive]—*Syn.* virus, germ, insect pest, bug, harmful bird, bird of prey, destructive animal; see also **disease** 2, **insect.** Common pests include the following—house fly, mosquito, flea, louse, mite, bedbug, ant, cockroach, termite, carpenter ant, tick, botfly, screw-worm fly, leaf hopper, aphid, codling moth, peachtree borer, Japanese beetle, Colorado beetle, corn borer, boll weevil, San Jose scale, oyster shell scale, squash bug, peach moth, gypsy moth, hawk moth, wireworm, cutworm, tent caterpillar, plum curculio, pear slug, tomato slug, mouse, rat, gopher, prairie dog, woodchuck, groundhog, rabbit, mole, weasel, coyote, hawk.
2. [A nuisance]—*Syn.* bore, tease, annoyance; see **trouble** 2.

pester, *v.* —*Syn.* annoy, harass, provoke; see **bother** 2.

pestiferous, *mod.* —*Syn.* virulent, toxic, unhealthy; see **harmful, deadly, poisonous.**

pestilence, *n.* —*Syn.* epidemic, endemic, sickness; see **disease** 1.

pestilential, *mod.* **1.** [Deadly]—*Syn.* infectious, pestiferous, malignant; see **dangerous** 1, 2, **deadly.**
2. [Harmful]—*Syn.* destructive, troublesome, contaminating; see **harmful.**

pestle, *n.* —*Syn.* grinder, pulverizer, pounder, brayer, muller, masher; see also **device** 1, **tool** 1.

pet, *mod.* —*Syn.* beloved, dear, preferred; see **favorite.**

pet, *n.* **1.** [A term of endearment]—*Syn.* lover, dear, love; see **darling** 2.
2. [Favorite]—*Syn.* darling, idol, adored one; see **favorite.**
3. [A creature kept as an object of affection] Common pets include the following—pony, horse, goldfish, rabbit, guinea pig, lamb, mouse, white rat, chicken, pigeon, canary, parrot; see also **animal** 1, **bird** 1, **cat** 1, **dog.**

pet, *v.* **1.** [To caress]—*Syn.* fondle, cuddle, kiss; see **touch** 2.
2. [To make love]—*Syn.* neck (D), embrace, hug; see **caress, kiss, love** 2.

petal, *n.* —*Syn.* floral leaf, corolla, floral envelope, perianth, leaf, bract, scale.

petard, *n.* —*Syn.* firecracker, explosive, squib; see **fireworks.**

peter out (D), *v.* —*Syn.* stop, dwindle, miscarry; see **fail** 1.

petition, *n.* —*Syn.* prayer, request, supplication; see **appeal** 1.

petition, *v.* —*Syn.* request, seek to obtain by petition, appeal; see **ask** 1.

petitioner, *n.* —*Syn.* applicant, solicitor, claimant; see **candidate.**

petrifaction, *n.* —*Syn.* fossilization, solidification, hardening, toughening, firmness, compactness, ossification, calcification.

petrified, *mod.* **1.** [Hardened]—*Syn.* stone, hardened, calcified, silicified, ossified, infiltrated, mineralized; see also **firm** 2.
2. [Frightened]—*Syn.* terrorized, startled, scared; see **afraid** 2.

petrify, *v.* **1.** [To harden]—*Syn.* mineralize, clarify, solidify; see **harden** 2.

2. [To frighten]—*Syn.* startle, alarm, astonish; see **frighten** 1.

petroleum, *n.* —*Syn.* crude oil, paraffin-base oil, asphalt-base oil, naphthene-base oil, coal oil; see also **oil.**

petticoat, *n.* —*Syn.* skirt, underskirt, slip; see **clothes, underwear.**

pettifogger, *n.* —*Syn.* inferior lawyer, trickster, fraud; see **cheat** 1, **lawyer, rascal.**

pettifoggery, *n.* —*Syn.* treachery, fraud, deceit; see **deception** 1, **dishonesty, lie** 1.

pettifogging, *mod.* —*Syn.* shifty, evasive, deceitful; see **dishonest** 1, 2, **sly** 1.

petty, *mod.* **1.** [Trivial]—*Syn.* small, insignificant, frivolous; see **trivial, unimportant.**

2. [Mean]—*Syn.* shallow, scurvy, contemptible; see **vulgar** 1.

3. [Inferior]—*Syn.* puny, weak, undersized; see **poor** 2.

petulance, *n.* —*Syn.* malevolence, ill-humor, cynicism; see **bitterness** 2.

petulant, *mod.* —*Syn.* grouchy, testy, cross; see **irritable.**

pew, *n.* —*Syn.* slip, place, stall; see **bench** 1, **seat** 1.

phantasm, *n.* —*Syn.* apparition, vision, illusion; see **ghost** 1.

phantasmal, *mod.* —*Syn.* fancied, fanciful, unreal; see **imaginary.**

phantom, *n.* —*Syn.* apparition, specter, shade; see **ghost** 1.

pharisaic, *mod.* —*Syn.* sanctimonious, insincere, deceiving; see **hypocritical.**

Pharisee, *n.* —*Syn.* fraud, faker, dissembler; see **bigot, hypocrite.**

pharmacist, *n.* —*Syn.* chemist, apothecary, pharmaceutist; see **druggist.**

pharmacy, *n.* **1.** [Pharmacology]—*Syn.* medicine, drug manufacturing, chemistry; see **science.**

2. [A drugstore]—*Syn.* drugstore, medical distributor, variety store; see **store** 1.

phase, *n.* —*Syn.* condition, stage, appearance, point, aspect; see also **state** 2.

phase out, *v.* —*Syn.* slowly get rid of, gradually dispose of, weed out (D); see **eliminate** 1.

pheasant, *n.* Pheasants include the following—Reeves, silver, golden, Lady Amherst, peacock, Chinese ring-necked, argus, kallege, Mongolian, tragopan *or* Indian horned, monal *or* Impeyan; see also **bird** 1, **fowl.**

phenomenal, *mod.* —*Syn.* extraordinary, unique, remarkable; see **unusual** 1.

phenomenon, *n.* —*Syn.* aspect, appearance, happening; see **event** 1.

phial, *n.* —*Syn.* cruet, test tube, vial; see **bottle, container, flask.**

philander, *v.* —*Syn.* sue for, coquet, flirt; see **court** 1, **love** 1.

philanderer, *n.* —*Syn.* flirt, adulterer, debaucher; see **lecher, pimp.**

philanthropic, *mod.* **1.** [Kindly]—*Syn.* kindhearted, benevolent, humanitarian; see **humane** 1, **kind.**

2. [Generous for the public good]—*Syn.* public-spirited, liberal, bountiful, magnanimous, helpful, civic-minded, openhanded, charitable, altruistic, patriotic; see also **generous** 1.—*Ant.* pessimistic*, misanthropic, cynical.

philanthropist, *n.* —*Syn.* sympathizer, donor, humanitarian, altruist, giver, contributor, donor, benefactor, friend to man; see also **patron** 1.

philanthropy, *n.* —*Syn.* benevolence, humanitarianism, beneficence; see **generosity** 1, **patronage** 1.

philippic, *n.* —*Syn.* tirade, reproach, exchange; see **discussion** 1, **speech** 3.

Philistine, *n.* —*Syn.* conformist, conventionalist, pedant; see **follower, sycophant.**

Philistinism, *n.* —*Syn.* pedantry, conventionalism, conformity; see **docility.**

philologist, *n.* —*Syn.* historical linguist, etymologist, grammarian; see **linguist** 1, **scholar** 2.

philology, *n.* —*Syn.* etymology, lexicography, linguistics; see **grammar, language** 2.

philosopher, *n.* —*Syn.* logical, wise man, sage, savant, Sophist, Solon; see also **scholar** 2.

Major philosophers include the following—Epicurus, Plato, Aristotle, Marcus Aurelius, St. Augustine, St. Thomas Aquinas, Boethius, Baruch Spinoza, René Descartes, Edmund Burke, Thomas Hobbes, John Locke, Immanuel Kant, John Stuart Mill, George Berkeley, Friedrich Schiller, Jean Jacques Rousseau, Arthur Schopenhauer, G. W. F. Hegel, Soren Kierkegaard, Friedrich Nietzsche, William James, Martin Heidegger, Karl Marx, Ernst Cassirer, Jean-Paul Sartre, Martin Buber.

philosophic, *mod.* —*Syn.* pensive, profound, sapient; see **learned** 2, **thoughtful** 1.

philosophical, *mod.* **1.** [Given to thought]—*Syn.* reflective, cogitative, rational; see **judicious, thoughtful** 1.

2. [Embodying deep thought]—*Syn.* erudite, thoughtful, deep; see **learned** 2, **profound** 2.

3. [Calm]—*Syn.* composed, cool, unmoved; see **calm** 1, **patient** 2.

philosophize, *v.* —*Syn.* ponder, weigh, deliberate (upon); see **think** 1.

philosophy, *n.* **1.** [The study of knowledge]—*Syn.* theory, reasoned doctrine, explanation of phenomena, logical concept, systematic view, theory of knowledge, early science, natural philosophy; see also **knowledge** 1.

Fields of philosophy include the following—aesthetics, logic, ethics, metaphysics, epistemology, psychology, axiology.

Schools of philosophy include the following—Egyptian, Ionian *or* Milesian, Pythagorean, Eleatic, Sophist, Cyrenaic, Cynic, Megarian, Platonic, Aristotelian, Epicurean, Stoic, Sceptic, Gnostic, Neo-Platonic, Eclectic, Patristic, Arabian, Jewish, Cabalist, Scholastic, Modern.

Philosophic attitudes include the following—idealism, realism, existentialism, nihilism, mechanism, naturalism, determinism, natural realism, intuitionism, utilitarianism, teleology, nominalism, conceptualism, pragmatism, ontology, pejorism, Kantianism, Hegelianism, logical empiricism, absolutism, transcendentalism, logical positivism.

2. [A fundamental principle]—*Syn.* truth, axiom, conception; see **basis** 1, **law** 4, **theory** 1.

3. [A personal attitude or belief]—*Syn.* outlook, view, *Weltanschauung* (German); see **belief** 1, **opinion** 1, **viewpoint.**

phlebotomy, *n.* —*Syn.* drainage, bloodletting, bleeding, lancing, leeching, sanguisage, draining; see also **blood** 1, **transfusion.**

phlegm, *n.* **1.** [Apathy]—*Syn.* nonchalance, unconcern, stoicism; see **indifference** 1.
2. [Sputum]—*Syn.* spittle, discharge, slime, viscous matter, morbid matter, spit (D); see also **mucus, saliva.**

phlegmatic, *mod.* —*Syn.* apathetic, tiresome, cold; see **dull** 4, **indifferent** 1.

phobia, *n.* **1.** [Neurosis]—*Syn.* dread, unreasoned fear, *Angst* (German); see **fear** 2, **neurosis.**
2. [Dislike]—*Syn.* disgust, avoidance, aversion; see **hatred** 1, 2, **resentment** 2.

Phoebus, *n.* —*Syn.* deity, Apollo, god of the sun; see **god** 3.

phoenix, *n.* —*Syn.* bird, symbol of immortality, mythical monster; see **idol** 1, **statue.**

phone, *n.* —*Syn.* wireless, radiophone, private phone; see **telephone.**

phoneme, *n.* —*Syn.* meaningful unit of sound, ceneme, minimal distinctive unit of sound; see **grammar.**

phonemics, *n.* —*Syn.* linguistic analysis, study of phonemes, linguistics; see **language** 2.

phonetics, *n.* —*Syn.* study of sounds, phonetic system, science of language speaking; see **language** 2.

phonics, *n.* —*Syn.* sounds, sound system, learning pronunciation; see **pronunciation.**

phonograph, *n.* —*Syn.* graphophone, gramophone, juke box; see **record player.**

phonology, *n.* —*Syn.* phonics, acoustics, linguistics; see **language** 2.

phony, *mod.* —*Syn.* affected, imitation, artificial; see **false** 3.

phosphorescence, *n.* —*Syn.* brightness, luminescence, glowing; see **light** 1.

phosphorescent, *mod.* —*Syn.* radiant, glowing, luminous; see **bright** 1.

photo finish (D), *n.* —*Syn.* close race *or* finish, almost a tie, a close one (D); see **end** 2, **race** 3.

photograph, *n.* —*Syn.* photo, print, portrait, image, likeness, Kodachrome (trademark), snapshot, Kodak (trademark), photogram, microcopy, microfilm, bibliofilm, tactical photograph, photomicrogram, photomicrograph, radiograph, photomontage, photomural; *all* (D): snap, shot, pic, close-up, candid (photo); see also **picture** 2, 3.

photograph, *v.* —*Syn.* take a picture, get a likeness, film, snapshot, copy, reproduce, illustrate, make an exposure, make a picture, catch a likeness, get a film, make a moving picture of, microfilm, photogram; *all* (D): snap, shoot, get a close-up; see also **record** 3.

photographer, *n.* —*Syn.* picture-taker, camera man, photographist, cameraman, cinematographer, daguerreotypist; see also **artist** 1, 2.
Kinds of photographers include the following—aerial, portrait, news, professional, amateur; X-ray operator, radiographer, photogrammetrist.

photographic, *mod.* —*Syn.* accurate, detailed, exact; see **graphic** 1.

photography, *n.* —*Syn.* picture-taking, portrait photography, view photography, aerial photography, tactical photography, photogrammetry, candid camera photography, snapshooting (D); see also **reproduction** 1.

phrase, *n.* —*Syn.* group of words, expression, slogan, catchword, maxim, wordgroup.
Grammatical phrases include the following—prepositional, gerund, gerundive, participial, infinitive, noun, adjective *or* adjectival, adverbial, conjunctive, absolute, attributive, headed, nonheaded, exocentric, endocentric.

phraseology, *n.* —*Syn.* style, manner, idiom; see **diction.**

phrenetic, *mod.* —*Syn.* delirious, maniacal, deranged; see **insane** 1.

phrenology, *n.* —*Syn.* craniology, metoposcopy, physiognomy, cranioscopy, physiognomics, craniometry, craniognomy.

phylum, *n.* —*Syn.* variety, species, kind; see **class** 1.

physic, *n.* —*Syn.* cathartic, purge, purgative; see **laxative.**

physical, *mod.* **1.** [Concerning matter]—*Syn.* material, corporeal, visible, tangible, environmental, palpable, substantial, natural, sensible, somatic, concrete, ponderable, materialistic; see also **real** 2.
2. [Concerning the body]—*Syn.* corporal, corporeal, fleshly; see **bodily** 1.
3. [Concerning physics]—*Syn.* mechanical, motive, electrical, sonic, vibratory, vibrational, thermal, radioactive, radiational, atomic, relating to matter, relating to motive forces, dynamic.

physical (D), *n.* —*Syn.* medical checkup, health examination, exam (D); see **examination** 3.

physically, *mod.* —*Syn.* corporally, really, actually; see **bodily** 1, **materially** 1.

physician, *n.* —*Syn.* practitioner, doctor of medicine, surgeon; see **doctor** 1.

physicist, *n.* —*Syn.* natural philosopher, aerophysicist, astrophysicist, biophysicist, geophysicist, nuclear physicist, plasma physicist, physiochemist, radiation physicist; see also **scientist.**

physics, *n.* —*Syn.* natural philosophy, science of the material world, science of matter and motion; see **science** 1.
Divisions of physics include the following—heat, light, electricity, electronics, sound, mechanics, dynamics, kinetics, atomic structure, radiant energy, spectroscopy, supersonics, hydraulics, pneumatics, aerodynamics, engineering.

physiognomy, *n.* —*Syn.* countenance, features, look; see **appearance** 1.

physiology, *n.* —*Syn.* study of living organisms, study of organic functions, biology; see **anatomy** 1, **biology, science** 1.
Divisions of physiology include the following—metabolism, catabolism, angriology, kinesiology, endocrinology, cerebrology, lymphology, ophthalmology, genetics, eugenics, anthropometry, neurology.

physique, *n.* —*Syn.* build, structure, constitution, configuration, frame, strength, power, physical nature, bodily character; see also **anatomy** 2.

pi, *v.* —*Syn.* jumble, disarrange, mix (up); see **disorganize.**

pianist, *n.* —*Syn.* *pianiste* (French), performer, piano player, artist, virtuoso; *all* (D): keyboard artist, ivory tickler, ivory pounder, piano tinkler, piano thumper; see also **musician.**

piano, *n.* —*Syn.* grand, baby grand, upright, square, concert grand, apartment grand, boudoir, cabinet, cottage piano; spinet, clavichord, pianoforte, pianette, *bibi* (French), pianino, oblique pianoforte, sostinente pianoforte, electric piano, player piano, digitorium, dumb piano; see also **musical instrument.**

piazza, *n.* —*Syn.* veranda, yard, patio; see **court** 1.

picaresque, *mod.* —*Syn.* roguish, bold, adventurous; see **brave** 1.

picayune, *mod.* —*Syn.* trivial, petty, small; see **trivial, unimportant.**

piccolo, *n.* —*Syn.* woodwind (instrument), pipe, flute; see **musical instrument.**

pick, *n.* **1.** [An implement for picking]—*Syn.* pickax, mattock, rock hammer; see **tool** 1.
2. [A blow with a pointed instrument]—*Syn.* peck, nip, dent; see **blow** 1.
3. [(D) A choice selection]—*Syn.* best, elect, select, cream, upper per cent, top; *both* (D): topnotchers, aces; see also **best.**

pick, *v.* **1.** [To choose]—*Syn.* select, pick out, separate; see **choose** 1.
2. [To gather]—*Syn.* pluck, pull, choose; see **accumulate** 1.
3. [To deprive, especially by pecking or plucking] —*Syn.* pluck, strip, defeather, pinfeather, pull off.
4. [To use a pointed instrument]—*Syn.* dent, indent, strike; see **hit** 2.

pick a fight, *v.* —*Syn.* provoke, start, foment; see **incite.**

pick apart, *v.* —*Syn.* dissect, break up *or* down, pick to pieces; see **break** 2, **cut** 1.

pickax, *n.* —*Syn.* implement, pick, ax; see **tool** 1.

picked, *mod.* —*Syn.* elite, special, exclusive; see **excellent.**

picket, *n.* **1.** [A stake]—*Syn.* stake, pole, pillar; see **post** 1.
2. [A watchman]—*Syn.* patrolman, guard, union member, vedette, sentry, inlying picket.

picket, *v.* **1.** [To strike]—*Syn.* walk out, blockade, boycott; see **strike** 2.
2. [To enclose]—*Syn.* imprison, fence, corral; see **enclose** 1.

picking, *n.* —*Syn.* gathering, culling, separating; see **choice** 3, **preference.**

pickings (D), *n.* —*Syn.* profits, earnings, proceeds; see **booty.**

pickle, *n.* **1.** [A preservative solution]—*Syn.* solution, alcohol, formaldehyde solution; see **brine, vinegar.**
2. [A relish] Varieties of pickles include the following—cucumber, gherkin, beet, green tomato, dill, bread-and-butter, sweet, mustard, garlic, half-sour, kosher, pickled peppers, pickled beans, pickled apricots, pickled cherries, pickled peaches, pickled pears, pickled quince, pickled pineapple, pickled watermelon rind, ginger tomatoes, piccalilli, chow-chow, chutney, corn relish, cranberry-orange relish, spiced currants, spiced gooseberries, beet relish, mango relish, chili sauce, catsup; see also **flavoring, herb, relish** 1, **spice.**
3. [(D) A troublesome situation]—*Syn.* disorder, dilemma, evil plight; see **difficulty** 2.

pickle, *v.* —*Syn.* keep, cure, can; see **preserve** 3.

pick-me-up, *n.* —*Syn.* highball, whiskey, eye-opener (D); see **cocktail, drink** 1.

pick off (D), *v.* —*Syn.* snipe, get, shoot; see **kill** 1, **remove** 1.

pick one's way, *v.* —*Syn.* move cautiously, find one's way, work through; see **find** 1, **sneak, walk** 1.

pick out, *v.* —*Syn.* select, make a choice of, notice; see **choose.**

pickpocket, *n.* —*Syn.* cutpurse, thief, purse snatcher; see **criminal, robber.**

pickup (D), *n.* —*Syn.* loose woman, streetwalker; *all* (D): trick, number, (easy) mark; see also **date** 3.

pick up, *v.* **1.** [To acquire incidentally]—*Syn.* happen upon, find, secure; see **obtain** 1.
2. [To take up in the hand or arms]—*Syn.* lift, uplift, cuddle; see **raise** 1.
3. [To receive]—*Syn.* get, take, acquire; see **receive** 1.
4. [(D) To increase]—*Syn.* pay better, swell, swell out; see **increase** 1.
5. [(D) To improve]—*Syn.* get better, get well, recover health; see **recover** 3.
6. [(D) To call for]—*Syn.* call *or* go *or* stop *or* drop in for, bring (along), go to get, accompany, get, apprehend, invite; see also **arrest** 1, **invite** 1.
7. [(D) To make an indecent proposal]—*Syn.* give the glad eye, offer oneself, proposition (D); see **solicit** 3.

pickup truck, *n.* —*Syn.* van, autotruck, pickup (D); see **truck** 1, **vehicle** 1.

picnic, *n.* **1.** [A meal]—*Syn.* barbecue, cookout, weiner roast, clambake, fish fry; see also **meal** 2.
2. [(D) An easy time]—*Syn.* party, good time, lark, child's play, short *or* light work, smooth sailing, joy ride, sure thing, no trouble; *all* (D): piece of cake, cakewalk, cinch.

pictorial, *mod.* **1.** [Having the quality of a picture] —*Syn.* graphic, scenic, striking; see **picturesque** 1.
2. [Making use of pictures]—*Syn.* decorated, embellished, adorned; see **illustrated.**

picture, *n.* **1.** [A scene before the eye or the imagination]—*Syn.* spectacle, panorama, pageant; see **view** 1.
2. [A human likeness]—*Syn.* portrait, representation, photo, photograph, snapshot, cartoon, image, effigy, icon, statue, statuette, figure, figurine, close-up (D).
3. [A pictorial representation]—*Syn.* illustration, engraving, etching, woodcut, cut, outline, cartoon, hologram, draft, crayon sketch, pastel, water color, aquarelle, poster, graph, oil, mezzotint, chart, map, plot, trademark, mosaic, blueprint, tapestry, show-card, advertisement, aquatint, aquatone, facsimile, animation, tracing, photograph, lithograph, zinc etching, photoengraving, collotype, halftone, rotogravure, print; *all* (D): ad, pix, still, commercial; see also **design** 1, **drawing** 2, **painting** 1.
Types of pictures, as works of art, include the following—landscape, seascape, cityscape, genre painting, chiaroscuro, historical work, religious work, madonna, ascension, annunciation, Last Judgment, crucifixion; St. Anthony, St. Anne, etc.; birth of Christ, battle scene, triumphal entry, detail, veronica, vernicle, icon, illumination, miniature, portrait, self-portrait, illustration, *danse macabre* (French), nude, fresco, mural, collage,

pin-up, figure, still life, center spread, animal picture, hunting print, fashion plate, photomural, photomontage, *papier collé* (French).
4. [A motion picture]—*Syn.* cinema, cinerama, cartoon; see **movie.**
5. [A description]—*Syn.* depiction, delineation, portrayal; see **description** 1.
6. [(D) Adequate comprehension; *usually with* the] —*Syn.* (the) idea, understanding, survey; see **knowledge** 1.
in the picture (D)—*Syn.* involved, concerned, part of; see **considered** 1.
out of the picture (D)—*Syn.* immaterial, not considered, unimportant; see **irrelevant.**

picture, *v.* **1.** [To depict]—*Syn.* sketch, delineate, portray; see **draw** 2.
2. [To imagine]—*Syn.* portray, create, conceive; see **imagine** 1.

picturesque, *mod.* **1.** [Having the qualities of a picture]—*Syn.* pictorial, scenic, graphic, striking, arresting.
2. [Romantic and striking, but lacking depth and power]—*Syn.* pretty, charming, unusual; see **pleasant** 2.

piddle, *v.*—*Syn.* loaf, delay, idle; see **loiter.**

piddling, *mod.*—*Syn.* insignificant, petty, trifling; see **trivial, unimportant.**

pie, *n.* Varieties of pies include the following—*meat pies:* fish, chicken, lamb, pork, beef, steak-and-kidney, shepherd's, cottage; *dessert pies:* apple, banana, banana cream, chocolate cream, Boston cream, chiffon, apricot, peach, pear, raisin, custard, coconut cream, rice custard, fig and pecan, caramel, caramel nut, chocolate, lemon, key lime, cranberry and raisin, orange, mince, prune, cherry, gooseberry, huckleberry, blueberry, strawberry, strawberry cream, raspberry, blackberry, Washington; see also **dessert, pastry.**
as easy as pie (D)—*Syn.* not difficult, simple, uncomplicated; see **easy** 2.

piebald, *mod.*—*Syn.* mottled, dappled, varicolored; see **multicolored.**

piece, *n.* **1.** [Part]—*Syn.* portion, share, section, bit, item, lump, hunk, scrap, interest, lot, cut, allotment, end, half, quota, percentage, dole; see also **part** 1.
2. [Work of art]—*Syn.* study, composition, creation; see **art** 2.
3. [Musical, literary, or theatrical composition] —*Syn.* suite, orchestration, production, opus, song, aria, harmonization, study, arrangement, treatise, exposition, sketch, play, novel, thesis, dissertation, discourse, discussion, treatment, essay, causerie, article, paper, memoir, descant, homily, poem, theme, monograph, commentary, review, paragraph, criticism, play, drama, melodrama, pageant, monologue, opera, ballet; see also **composition** 2, 4.
4. [Theatrical role]—*Syn.* part, lines, bit (D); see **part** 2.
go to pieces—*Syn.* **1.** come *or* fall apart, break (up), fail; see **break down** 3. **2.** (D) quit, collapse, lose control; see **cry** 1, **stop** 2, **worry** 2.
speak one's piece—*Syn.* air one's opinions, talk, reveal; see **tell** 1.

piecemeal, *mod.*—*Syn.* partially, bit by bit, step by step; see **gradually.**

piece together, *v.*—*Syn.* combine, make, create; see **assemble** 3.

pied, *mod.*—*Syn.* dappled, varicolored, spotted; see **multicolored.**

pier, *n.*—*Syn.* wharf, landing, quay; see **dock** 1.

pierce, *v.*—*Syn.* go *or* pass *or* break through *or* into, stab, intrude; see **penetrate** 1.

piercing, *mod.* **1.** [Shrill]—*Syn.* deafening, earsplitting, sharp; see **loud** 1, **shrill.**
2. [Penetrating]—*Syn.* entering, boring, puncturing; see **penetrating** 1.

piety, *n.* **1.** [Devotion to duty]—*Syn.* fealty, filial allegiance, application; see **loyalty.**
2. [Devotion to the service of God]—*Syn.* reverence, duty, zeal; see **devotion, holiness** 1.
3. [Pious remarks]—*Syn.* lecture, preachment, preaching; see **sermon.**

pig, *n.*—*Syn.* piglet, swine, shoat; see **animal** 2, **hog** 1.
buy a pig in a poke (D)—*Syn.* take a chance, buy (something) sight unseen, gamble; see **risk.**

pigeon, *n.*—*Syn.* dove, culver, *columba* (Latin), squab; see also **bird** 1.
Pigeons include the following—mourning dove, ground dove, turtledove, ringdove, stock dove; carrier, pouter, homing, fantail, rock, wood, passenger, Cape, bronze-wing, crowned, fruit, tooth-billed pigeon.

pigeonhole, *n.*—*Syn.* niche, slot, compartment; see **hole** 2, **place** 2.

pigeon-house, *n.*—*Syn.* aviary, coop, roost; see **birdhouse.**

piggery, *n.*—*Syn.* pigsty, stockyard, pigpen; see **enclosure** 1, **pen** 1.

piggish, *mod.*—*Syn.* selfish, dirty, ravenous; see **greedy** 1.

pigheaded, *mod.*—*Syn.* recalcitrant, insistent, stubborn; see **obstinate** 1.

pigment, *n.*—*Syn.* paint, oil paint, dye, coloring matter, orpiment, artist's material; see also **color** 1.

pigskin (D), *n.*—*Syn.* regulation football, (the) ball, (the) oval (D); see **football** 2.

pigtail, *n.*—*Syn.* plait, hairdo, twine; see **braid.**

pike, *n.*—*Syn.* roadway, drive, turnpike; see **highway, road** 1.

piker (D), *n.*—*Syn. all* (D): tightwad, skinflint, cheapskate; see **miser** 2.

pilaster, *n.*—*Syn.* prop, pillar, minaret; see **column** 1, **post** 1.

pile, *n.* **1.** [A heap]—*Syn.* collection, mass, quantity; see **heap.**
2. [(D) Money]—*Syn.* affluence, riches, dough (D); see **wealth** 2.

pile, *v.* **1.** [To amass]—*Syn.* hoard, store, gather; see **accumulate** 1.
2. [To place one upon another]—*Syn.* rank, stack, bunch; see **heap** 1.

piled, *mod.* **1.** [Heaped]—*Syn.* joined, accumulated, collected; see **gathered.**
2. [Ranked]—*Syn.* stacked, heaped, arranged; see **organized, ranked.**

pilfer, *v.*—*Syn.* rob, embezzle, appropriate; see **steal.**

pilgrim, *n.*—*Syn.* wayfarer, wanderer, sojourner; see **traveler.**

pilgrimage, *n.—Syn.* travel, wayfaring, trip; see **journey.**

pill, *n.* **1.** [A tablet]—*Syn.* capsule, pilule, pellet; see **medicine** 2, **tablet** 3.
2. [(D) A contraceptive tablet; *usually with* the] —*Syn.* contraceptive drug, oral contraceptive, prophylactic; see **contraceptive.**

pillage, *n.* **1.** [The act of pillaging]—*Syn.* robbery, stealing, rapine; see **destruction** 1, **theft.**
2. [That which is pillaged]—*Syn.* plunder, loot, spoils; see **booty.**

pillage, *v.—Syn.* plunder, loot, rob; see **destroy** 1, **steal.**

pillar, *n.* **1.** [A column]—*Syn.* pedestal, mast, shaft; see **column** 1, **post** 1.
2. [A support]—*Syn.* mainstay, dependence, guider; see **support** 2.
from pillar to post (D)—*Syn.* back and forth, fluctuating, vacillating; see **undecided.**

pillow, *n.—Syn.* feather pillow, down pillow, pneumatic cushion, foam rubber cushion, bolster, pad, padding, rest, bag, support, headrest; see also **cushion.**

pillowcase, *n.—Syn.* pillow slip, pillow casing, pillow cover, pillow sham, pillow tie; see also **cover** 1.

pilot, *n.* **1.** [Flier]—*Syn.* airman, fighter pilot, commercial pilot, bomber pilot, automatic pilot, mechanical pilot, aeronaut, aerial navigator, navigator, aerialist; *all* (D): auto pilot, jet jockey, birdman; see also **aviator.**
2. [One who conducts ships]—*Syn.* helmsman, steersman, man at the wheel, man at the controls, wheelman, coxswain.
3. [Guide]—*Syn.* scout, leader, director; see **guide** 1.

pilot, *v.—Syn.* guide, conduct, manage; see **lead** 1.

pilot program, *n.—Syn.* experimental *or* initial *or* model program, test (case), trial run; see **model** 2, **experiment** 2.

pimp, *n.—Syn.* procurer, whoremonger, pander, white-slaver, runner, flesh-peddler (D); see also **criminal.**

pimple, *n.—Syn.* pustule, papule, papula, swelling, acne, whitehead, blackhead, inflammation, bump, lump, boil, furuncle, carbuncle, blister, excrescence, caruncle, zit (D); see also **blemish.**

pin, *n.* **1.** [A device to fasten goods by piercing or clasping]—*Syn.* clip, catch, needle, bodkin, quill, clasp, nail; see also **fastener.**
Pins include the following—common, safety, straight, hat, knitting, hair, clothes, bobby, toggle, cotter, push.
2. [A piece of jewelry]—*Syn.* tiepin, stickpin, brooch, fibula, ouch, badge, stud, sorority *or* fraternity pin, school pin; see also **jewelry.**
3. [A rod inserted through a prepared hole] —*Syn.* bolt, bar, dowel; see **brace.**

pin, *v.—Syn.* close, clasp, bind; see **fasten** 1.

pinafore, *n.—Syn.* smock, frock, overskirt; see **apron.**

pince-nez, *n.—Syn.* bifocals, eyepieces, spectacles; see **glasses.**

pincers, *n.—Syn.* pinchers, pair of pincers, wrench, pliers, nippers, tongs, instrument, tweezers, grippers, wire cutters; see also **tool** 1.

pinch, *n.—Syn.* squeeze, compression, nip, nipping, grasp, grasping, pressure, cramp, contraction, confinement, limitation, hurt, torment.

pinch, *v.* **1.** [To squeeze]—*Syn.* nip, crimp, cramp, tweak, compress, press, grasp.
2. [(D) To steal]—*Syn.* take, filch, rob; see **steal.**
3. [(D) To arrest]—*Syn.* apprehend, detain, hold; see **arrest** 1.

pinchbeck, *mod.—Syn.* imitation, fake, deceptive; see **false** 3.

pinchers, *n.—Syn.* pliers, pair of pincers, wrench; see **pincers, tool** 1.

pinch-hit (D), *v.—Syn.* replace, act for, succeed; see **substitute** 2.

pinch hitter (D), *n.—Syn.* replacement, substitute, successor; see **agent** 1, **delegate, representative** 2.

pine, *n.* Pines include the following—white, stone, whitebark, foxtail, bristle-cone, nut, singleleaf, piñon, Weymouth, sugar, longleaf, loblolly, western yellow, pond, Arizona, Monterey, digger, Chihuahua, jack, gray, lodge-pole, Georgia pitch *or* yellow, Torrey, bull, imou, red, Corsican; Scotch fir *or Pinus sylvestris* (Latin); see also **tree, wood** 2.

ping, *n.—Syn.* ting, clink, sonar echo; see **sound** 2.

pink, *mod.—Syn.* rosy, reddish, pinkish, flushed, dawn-tinted.

pink, *n.—Syn.* rose, red, roseate, blush-rose, salmon, shocking pink, blushing pink; see also **color** 1.
in the pink (D)—*Syn.* in good health, well, fit; see **healthy** 1.

pinnacle, *n.* **1.** [A tower]—*Syn.* belfry, spire, steeple; see **tower.**
2. [An apex]—*Syn.* zenith, crest, summit; see **climax.**

pinup, *n.—Syn.* calendar girl, playmate, centerfold girl, gatefold girl; see also **nude.**

pioneer, *mod.—Syn.* pioneering, initial, untried; see **brave** 1, **early** 1, **experimental.**

pioneer, *n.* **1.** [One who prepares the way]—*Syn.* pathfinder, scout, explorer; see **guide** 1.
2. [One in the vanguard of civilization]—*Syn.* early settler, colonist, pilgrim, immigrant, colonizer, halutz, homesteader, squatter.
3. [A military engineer]—*Syn.* fortification engineer, member of demolition squad, bridge builder, road builder, miner, sapper; *both* (D); bridge monkey, road monkey; see also **engineer** 1.

pioneer, *v.—Syn.* discover, explore, found; see **colonize, establish** 2, **settle** 1.

pious, *mod.* **1.** [Religious]—*Syn.* divine, holy, devout; see **religious** 2.
2. [Divine]—*Syn.* hallowed, sacred, holy; see **divine** 2.
3. [Related to those who profess piety]—*Syn.* clerical, priestly, ecclesiastical; see **religious** 1.

pipe, *n.* **1.** [A tube]—*Syn.* pipeline, drain pipe, sewer, waterpipe, aqueduct, trough, passage, duct, cloaca, tubular runway, canal, vessel; see also **channel** 1, **conduit, tube** 1.
2. [A device for smoking]—*Syn. all* (D): nosewarmer, hayburner, hod, boiler, smokestack.
Varieties of smoking pipes include the following —meerschaum, corncob (*also* (D): Missouri meerschaum); bulldog pipe, brierwood pipe, clay pipe, churchwarden, narghile, hookah, Turkish pipe,

opium pipe, calabash, calumet, Indian peace, water pipe, hashish pipe *or* hash pipe (D).
3. [A musical instrument]—*Syn.* wind instrument, flageolet, piccolo; see **flute, musical instrument.**

pipe down (D), *v.*—*Syn.* become quiet, hush, speak lower; see **stop** 2.

piper, *n.*—*Syn.* flute player, flautist, fifer, tooter (D); see also **musician.**
pay the piper—*Syn.* take *or* suffer the consequences, be responsible, settle (for); see **pay** 1.

pipe up (D), *v.*—*Syn.* speak (up), volunteer, shout; see **say, talk** 1.

piquancy, *n.*—*Syn.* seasoning, relish, zest; see **flavoring.**

piquant, *mod.* **1.** [Stimulating the interest]—*Syn.* charming, sparkling, enticing; see **exciting, interesting.**
2. [Stimulating the taste]—*Syn.* high-flavored, well-flavored, spicy; see **delicious** 1, **savory.**

pique, *n.*—*Syn.* umbrage, resentment, offense; see **anger, annoyance** 1.

pique, *v.* **1.** [To anger]—*Syn.* irritate, fret, nettle; see **anger** 1, **bother** 2.
2. [To excite]—*Syn.* arouse, rouse, stimulate; see **excite** 1.

piqued, *mod.*—*Syn.* bothered, irritated, annoyed; see **angry, troubled** 1.

piracy, *n.* **1.** [Larceny]—*Syn.* pillage, holdup, robbery; see **crime** 2, **theft.**
2. [Plagiarism]—*Syn.* copying, lifting, cheating; see **forgery.**

piranha, *n.*—*Syn.* serrosalmo, caribe, man-eating fish; see **fish.**

pirate, *n.*—*Syn.* thief, freebooter, plunderer, pillager, marauder, privateer, soldier of fortune, corsair, buccaneer, ranger, sea rover, sea-robber, Barbary pirate, plagiarist; see also **criminal, robber.**

piratical, *mod.*—*Syn.* plundering, stealing, marauding; see **lawless** 2, **rebellious** 2, 3.

piscatorial, *mod.*—*Syn.* piscine, angling, fishing, piscatory, piscatorian, piscatorious.

piss (D), *v.*—*Syn.* pass *or* make water, go to the bathroom, pee (D); see **urinate.**

pistol, *n.*—*Syn.* revolver, automatic pistol, automatic, six-shooter; *all* (D): gat, rod, Saturday night special, cannon, six-gun, pepper pot, barker, pill shooter, iron, forty-five, thirty-eight; see also **gun** 2, **weapon** 1.
Pistols include the following—automatic, repeating, six-shooter, seven-shooter, Derringer, pocket, .22-caliber, .32-caliber, .38-caliber, .45-caliber, Colt, Webley, Smith and Wesson, Mauser, Nagant, Steyr, Browning, *modèle d'ordonnance* (French), *Luger, Parabellum* (both German).

piston, *n.*—*Syn.* plunger, ram, disk, cylinder, sucker; see also **device** 1.

pit, *n.*—*Syn.* abyss, cavity, depression; see **hole** 2.

pitch, *n.* **1.** [Slope]—*Syn.* slant, incline, angle; see **grade** 1, **inclination** 5.
2. [A throw]—*Syn.* toss, fling, hurl, heave, cast, pitched ball, ball, strike; *all* (D): delivery, offering, the old apple.
3. [Musical frequency]—*Syn.* frequency of vibration, rate of vibration, tone; see also **sound** 2.
Standards of pitch include the following—concert, classic, high, low, international, French, Stuttgart, philharmonic, philosophical.
4. [A viscous liquid]—*Syn.* resin, gum resin, rosin; see **gum, tar** 1.
make a pitch for (D)—*Syn.* urge, promote, aid; see **support** 2.

pitch, *v.* **1.** [To throw]—*Syn.* hurl, fling, toss; see **throw** 1.
2. [To fall forward]—*Syn.* plunge, flop, vault; see **dive, fall** 1.
3. [To slope abruptly]—*Syn.* rise, fall, ascend; see **bend** 2, **lean** 1, **tilt** 1.

pitcher, *n.* **1.** [A utensil for pouring liquid]—*Syn.* cream pitcher, milk pitcher, water pitcher, jug, vessel, amphora; see also **container.**
2. [In baseball, one who pitches to the batter]—*Syn. all* (D): right-hander, left-hander, southpaw, hurler, ace hurler, fireball hurler, twirler, pill feeder, tosser, heaver, chucker; see also **player** 1.

pitchfork, *n.*—*Syn.* fork, hayfork, three-tined fork, header fork; see also **tool** 1.

pitch in, *v.*—*Syn.* volunteer, work, aid; see **help** 1.

pitch into, *v.*—*Syn.* assault, blame, scold; see **attack** 1, **fight** 2.

pitchy, *mod.*—*Syn.* shadowy, gloomy, black; see **dark** 1.

piteous, *mod.*—*Syn.* ruined, wretched, miserable; see **poor** 1.

pitfall, *n.*—*Syn.* snare, meshes, deadfall; see **trap** 1.

pith, *n.*—*Syn.* center, stem, medulla; see **fiber** 1.

pithy, *mod.*—*Syn.* forceful, useful, terse; see **effective.**

pitiful, *mod.* **1.** [Affecting]—*Syn.* miserable, mournful, sorrowful, woeful, distressed, distressing, cheerless, comfortless, lamentable, deplorable, joyless, dismal, touching, pathetic, affecting, stirring, arousing, poignant, heart-breaking, human, dramatic, impressive, pitiable, tearful, heart-rending, depressing, piteous, afflicted, suffering, pathetic, moving, base, low, vile; see also **sad** 2.—*Ant.* happy*, cheerful, joyful.
2. [Tragically inadequate]—*Syn.* wretched, pathetic, paltry; see **inadequate** 1.

pitiless, *mod.* **1.** [Lacking pity]—*Syn.* unfeeling, obdurate, unpitying, callous, soulless, heartless, cold, frigid, stony, insensible, uncaring, iron-hearted, unsympathetic, unmerciful, hardhearted, austere, cold-blooded, relentless; see also **indifferent** 1, **remorseless** 1, **unconcerned.**—*Ant.* kind*, kindly, compassionate.
2. [Cruel]—*Syn.* satanic, merciless, brutal; see **cruel** 2, **ruthless** 1, 2.

pitman, *n.*—*Syn.* excavator, tunneler, laborer; see **miner, workman.**

pittance, *n.*—*Syn.* wage, pension, pay; see **allowance** 2.

pitter-patter, *n.*—*Syn.* thump, patter, tap; see **noise** 1.

pity, *n.* **1.** [Compassionate feeling]—*Syn.* sympathy, compassion, charity, soft-heartedness, tenderness, goodness, compunction, understanding, mercy, forbearance, ruth, warmheartedness, kindliness, brotherly love, unselfishness, benevolence, favor, condolence, fellow feeling, philanthropy, commiseration, largeheartedness, clemency, humanity; see also **kindness** 1.—*Ant.* hatred*, severity, ferocity.

2. [Anything that might move one to pity, sense 1] —*Syn.* mishap, mischance, ill luck; see **catastrophe, disaster, misfortune** 1.

have (*or* **take**) **pity on**—*Syn.* show pity to, spare, pardon; see **forgive** 1, **pity** 2.

pity, *v.* **1.** [To feel pity for]—*Syn.* feel for, sympathize with, commiserate, be sorry for, condole, be sympathetic to, show sympathy, express sympathy for, feel with *or* for, bleed for, grieve with, weep for; see also **comfort** 1, **sympathize.**—*Ant.* censure*, rebuke, become angry.

2. [To be merciful to]—*Syn.* spare, take pity on, show pity to, show forgiveness to, be merciful to, pardon, give quarter, put out of one's misery, reprieve, grant amnesty to; see also **forgive** 1. —*Ant.* destroy*, condemn, accuse.

pitying, *mod.* —*Syn.* tender, compassionate, sympathetic; see **kind.**

pivot, *n.* —*Syn.* axle, shaft, swivel; see **axis.**

pivot, *v.* —*Syn.* whirl, swivel, rotate; see **turn** 1.

pivotal, *mod.* —*Syn.* focal, crucial, middle; see **central** 1.

pixilated, *mod.* —*Syn.* frivolous, whimsical, eccentric; see **insane** 1.

pixy, *n.* —*Syn.* dryad, sprite, leprechaun; see **fairy** 1.

placard, *n.* —*Syn.* circular, bulletin, notice; see **poster.**

placard, *v.* —*Syn.* publicize, declare, announce; see **advertise** 1.

placate, *v.* —*Syn.* pacify, cheer, appease; see **comfort** 2, **satisfy** 1, 3.

place, *n.* **1.** [Position]—*Syn.* station, point, spot; see **position** 1.

2. [Space]—*Syn.* room, compass, stead, void, distance, area, seat, volume, berth, reservation, accommodation; see also **extent.**

3. [Locality]—*Syn.* spot, locus, site, community, district, suburb, country, section, habitat, home, residence, abode, house, quarters; see also **area** 2, **neighborhood, region** 1.

4. [Rank]—*Syn.* status, position, station; see **rank** 3.

5. [An office]—*Syn.* position, situation, occupation; see **job** 1, **profession** 1, **trade** 2.

6. [A courtlike space]—*Syn.* square, park, plaza; see **court** 1, **yard** 1.

give place (to)—*Syn.* make room for, move over for, surrender to; see **yield** 3.

go places (D)—*Syn.* attain success, achieve, advance; see **succeed** 1.

in place—*Syn.* fitting, timely, appropriate; see **fit** 1, 2.

in place of—*Syn.* as a substitute for, instead, taking the place of; see **instead of.**

know one's place—*Syn.* adapt, accept one's station *or* restrictions, remain in one's position; see **conform.**

out of place—*Syn.* inappropriate, unsuitable, not fitting; see **improper** 1.

put someone in his place—*Syn.* humiliate, reprimand, derogate; see **humble.**

take place—*Syn.* occur, come into being, be; see **happen** 2.

take the place of—*Syn.* replace, act in one's stead, serve as proxy for; see **substitute** 2.

place, *v.* **1.** [To put in a place]—*Syn.* locate, dispose, allot, allocate, settle, assign, deposit, distribute, put, plant, lodge, quarter, store, stow, set, situate, fix in, put in place, consign to a place, lay; see also **install.** —*Ant.* remove*, displace, dislodge.

2. [To put in order]—*Syn.* fix, arrange, group; see **order** 3.

3. [(D) To be among the winners]—*Syn.* conquer, overwhelm, gain victory; see **defeat** 1, **win** 1.

placed, *mod.* —*Syn.* established, settled, fixed, located, alloted, rated, allocated, deposited, lodged, quartered, planted, set, arranged, stowed, stored, installed, situated, implanted, set up, ordered; see also **resting** 2.

place mat, *n.* —*Syn.* cloth, cover, doily; see **mat.**

placement, *n.* **1.** [Installation]—*Syn.* induction, employment, placing; see **installation** 1.

2. [An arrangement]—*Syn.* situation, position, arrangement; see **organization** 1.

placement service, *n.* —*Syn.* employment service, job placement, appointing occupations; see **employment** 1.

placid, *mod.* —*Syn.* quiet, unruffled, still; see **calm** 2, **tranquil** 2.

placing, *n.* —*Syn.* putting, setting, laying, arranging, depositing, fixing, allocating, allotting, lodging, quartering, locating, installing, establishing, settling.

plagiarism, *n.* **1.** [Forgery]—*Syn.* appropriation, literary theft, falsification, counterfeiting, piracy, fraud.

2. [Something forged]—*Syn.* copy, fraud, counterfeit; see **forgery, imitation** 1.

plagiarist, *n.* —*Syn.* counterfeiter, imitator, forger, literary vandal, plagiarizer, pirate, copier, lifter (D); see also **cheat** 1, **impostor.**

plagiarize, *v.* —*Syn.* forge, paraphrase, appropriate; see **copy** 2.

plague, *n.* —*Syn.* epidemic, Black Death, influenza; see **disease** 3.

plague, *v.* —*Syn.* disturb, trouble, irk; see **bother** 2.

plaid, *n.* —*Syn.* tartan, crossbarred cloth, checkered cloth, Highland plaid, Scotch Highland plaid, kilt, filibeg; see also **check** 5, **cloth.**

plain, *mod.* **1.** [Obvious]—*Syn.* open, manifest, clear; see **definite** 1, 2, **obvious** 1, 2, **understandable.**

2. [Simple]—*Syn.* unadorned, unostentatious, unpretentious; see **modest** 2.

3. [Ordinary]—*Syn.* everyday, average, commonplace; see **common** 1, **conventional** 1, 3, **dull** 4, **traditional** 2.

4. [Homely]—*Syn.* plain-featured, coarse-featured, unattractive; see **ugly** 1.

5. [In blunt language]—*Syn.* outspoken, candid, impolite; see **abrupt** 2, **rude** 2.

plain, *n.* —*Syn.* prairie, steppe, pampas, champaign, reach, expanse, open country, lowland, flat, level land, mesa, savanna, llano, moorland, moor, heath, wold, tundra, playa, veldt, downs, peneplain, the High Plains; see also **field** 1, **meadow.**

plainly, *mod.* —*Syn.* manifestly, evidently, visibly; see **clearly** 1, 2.

plain song, *n.* —*Syn.* canto, chant, melody; see **song.**

plain-spoken, *mod.* —*Syn.* candid, direct, artless; see **frank.**

plaint, *n.* —*Syn.* lament, moan, sorrow; see **cry** 3.

plaintive, *mod.* —*Syn.* melancholy, pitiful, mournful; see **sad** 2.

plait, *n.* —*Syn.* pleat, pleating *or* plaiting, crease, tuck, braid, weaving; see also **fold** 1, 2.
Plaits include the following—box, knife, accordion, inverted, unpressed, machine, umbrella, trouser.

plan, *n.* **1.** [A preliminary sketch]—*Syn.* draft, diagram, map, chart, delineation, time line, design, outline, representation, form, drawing, view, projection, rough draft, road map (D); see also **sketch** 1.
2. [A proposed sequence of action]—*Syn.* scheme, project, scope, outline, idea, flow chart, handling, manipulating, projection, undertaking, method, design, tactics, procedure, treatment, intention, policy, course of action, plot, conspiracy, expedient, strategy, stratagem, arrangement, way of doing things; *both* (D): angle, the picture; see also **program** 2, **purpose** 1.
3. [Arrangement]—*Syn.* layout, method, disposition; see **order** 3.

plan, *v.* **1.** [To plot an action in advance]—*Syn.* prepare, scheme, devise, invent, outline, project, contrive, shape, design, map, plot (a course), form (a plan), think out, engineer, figure on *or* for, intrigue, conspire, frame, concoct, steer one's course, establish *or* set guidelines *or* parameters (for), work up *or* out, line up, plan an attack, come through, calculate on, be at, make arrangements, put up a job, reckon on, ready up, take measures, lay in provisions, bargain for; *all* (D): cook up, fix to *or* for, pack the deal, bore from within, dope out, put on ice.
2. [To arrange in a preliminary way]—*Syn.* outline, draft, sketch, lay out, map out, organize, prepare a sketch, chart, map, draw, trace, design, illustrate, depict, delineate, represent, shape, preprint, chalk out, rough in, block out, block in.
3. [To have in mind]—*Syn.* propose, think, purpose; see **intend** 1.
4. [To program]—*Syn.* feed through, feed in, activate a computer; see **program** 2.

plane, *mod.* —*Syn.* even, flush, level; see **flat** 1, **smooth** 1.

plane, *n.* **1.** [A plane surface]—*Syn.* level, extension, horizontal, flat, sphere, face, stratum, dead level (D).
2. [A tool for smoothing wood] Types include the following—jack, smoothing, jointing, block, circular, reed, rabbet, grooving, routing, toothing, thumb, match, dovetail, sash, beading, scraper, dado, bullnose, trying, chamfer; electric planer, jointer, foreplane; see also **tool** 1.
3. [An airplane]—*Syn.* aircraft, airliner, aeroplane, airship, heavier-than-air craft, *avion* (French); *all* (D): jet, bird, ship, boat, crate, heap, hack, taxi, bus.
Kinds of planes include the following—propeller, jet, rocket, scout, observation, reconnaissance, transport, supersonic transport (SST), pursuit, passenger; biplane, triplane, monoplane, dirigible *or* blimp, racer, glider, bomber, clipper, seaplane, hydroplane, fighter, fighter-bomber, interceptor, turbojet, stratojet, helicopter (*also* (D): whirlybird *or* puddle-jumper *or* egg-beater), gyroplane, amphibian, zeppelin, sailplane.
Makes of airplanes include the following—*United States: commercial:* Boeing 707, 720, 727, 707-32C, 747, 767, McDonnell Douglas DC-8, DC-8F, DC-9, DC-10; *military:* Beechcraft T-34, Boeing KC-135, 3-135A, C-135B, B-52H, McDonnell Douglas H-4, A-3, F-15, F-18, Grumman HU-16B, OV-1, A-6A, General Dynamics F-111, F-16 Convair F-106A, U-2, Lockheed YF-12A, F-104 Starfighter, McDonnell Phantom F-4, Puff (C-47); *helicopters:* Doman D-10B, Bell UH-LB, UH-LD, UH-LE, UH-LF, 47G-4, 47G-3B-1, 47J-2A Ranger, Hiller 12E, Sikorsky S-65A, Boeing Vertol 107, CH-47A Chinook; *USSR: commercial:* Antonov An-24, Ilyshin IL-62, Tupolev TU-114 "Cleat," LI-2; *military:* Ilyushin IL-18 Moscow, IL-18, IL-28, "Fishbed-D" (E-66A), Myasishchev "Bounder," MYA-4 "Bison," Sukhoi "Fitter," "Fishpot," Tupolev TU-16 "Kipper," TU-20 "Bear," Yakovlev YAK-25, "Brewer," "Flashlight-D," Mig-17, Mig-21, Mig-23, Supersonic; *helicopters:* Kamov KA-22 Vintokryl, Kamov KA-26, KA-20 "Harp," Mil V-2 "Hoplite," Mil V-8 "Hip"; *England: commercial:* BAC V10 model 1103, Viscount 843, Vickers Vanguard 953, BAC 1-11 model 203; *military:* BAC Lightning F.MK3, T.MK, TSR2, Handley Page Victor B.MK, BK.MK1, Hawker Siddeley Sea Vixen, Trident 1, Short Sc.1; *helicopters:* Westland Wessex HC.MK2, HC.MK1, Westland Scout AH.MK1, Wasp HAS.MK1; *France: commercial:* Dassault Mystère 20, Potez 840, Sud-Aviation Caravelle Super 8, series VI-R; *military:* Dassault Etendard IV-P, Mirage 111-T, Mirage IV-A, Potez CM170; *helicopters:* Sud-Aviation SE3130 Alouette 11, Super Frelon SA3210, Sud-Aviation SA3180.

plane, *v.* —*Syn.* finish, smooth, level; see **flatten** 2.

planet, *n.* —*Syn.* celestial body, heavenly body, luminous body, wandering star, planetoid, asteroid, star.
The known planets are as follows—Mercury, Venus, Earth, Mars, Jupiter, Saturn, Uranus, Neptune, Pluto, the planetoids *or* asteroids.

planetarium, *n.* —*Syn.* observatory, building, watchtower; see **lookout** 1.

planetary, *mod.* **1.** [Nomadic]—*Syn.* vagrant, gypsy, restless; see **traveling** 2, **wandering** 1.
2. [Earthly]—*Syn.* tellurian, terrestrial, mundane; see **worldly** 1, 2.

plangent, *mod.* —*Syn.* roaring, pounding, thundering, beating, dashing, butting, smashing, striking, throbbing, buffeting; see also **hitting** 1.

plank, *n.* —*Syn.* board, planking, 2-inch piece; see **lumber.**

planned, *mod.* —*Syn.* projected, on the drawing board, programmed, in the making, under consideration, on the docket *or* anvil *or* carpet, prospective, cut out, cut and dried, under advisement, prelogisticated, prepared; see also **outlined** 2.

planner, *n.* —*Syn.* executive, member of the executive committee *or* board, member of the planning commission *or* board, director, detailer, long-range *or* master planner, one who lays down guidelines *or* draws up a long-range *or* long-term *or* master plan; see also **administrator.**

planning, *mod.* —*Syn.* devising, arranging, preparing, preparatory, plotting, shaping, scheming, contriving, considering, designing, laying down guide lines, developing a (master) plan, thinking of, looking into, masterminding (D).

planning, *n.* —*Syn.* preparation, devising, outlining; see **plan** 2.

plans, *n.* —*Syn.* outline, expectations, planned procedure(s); see **program** 4, **sketch** 1.

plant, *n.* —*Syn.* shrub, weed, corn, bush, slip, shoot, cutting, sprout, seedling, plantlet; see also **bulb, cactus, flower** 1.

plant, *v.* —*Syn.* put in the ground, sow, set (out), pot, start, transplant, seed, stock, colonize, settle, establish, locate, be in; see also **farm** 1.

plantation, *n.* —*Syn.* acreage, estate, ranch; see **farm.**

planted, *mod.* —*Syn.* cultivated, sown, seeded, stocked, implanted, strewn, drilled.

planter, *n.* —*Syn.* rancher, agriculturist, cultivator; see **farmer.**

planting, *n.* —*Syn.* sowing, seeding, drilling; see **farming.**

plaque, *n.* —*Syn.* plate, slab, tablet; see **decoration** 2.

plash, *n.* —*Syn.* plop, drop, drip; see **splash.**

plash, *v.* —*Syn.* trickle, burble, splatter; see **splash.**

plaster, *mod.* —*Syn.* plaster of Paris, imitation, sham, cardboard, lath and plaster, plastered.

plaster, *n.* —*Syn.* mortar, binding, coat, Portland cement, gypsum, lime, plaster of Paris; see also **cement.**

plaster, *v.* —*Syn.* coat, bind, cement; see **cover** 1, **face** 3.

plastic, *mod.* **1.** [Pliant]—*Syn.* pliable, supple, impressionable; see **flexible** 1.

2. [Made from plastics]—*Syn.* substitute, synthetic, *ersatz* (German), molded, cast, cellulose; see also **chemical.**

plastic, *n.* —*Syn.* synthetic, synthetic *or* artificial product, substitute, plastic material, processed material, polymerized substance.

Common plastics include the following—thermoplastic, thermoplastic product, thermosetting material, resin *or* cellulose *or* soybean *or* protein derivative, latex, synthetic rubber, butadiene, diolefin, chloroprene, polysulfide, polyethylene, nylon, cellophane, synthetic wool, vinylidene chloride, phenolic (phenolformaldehyde *and* phenolfurfura), ethyl cellulose, urea, cellulose nitrate, acrylic *or* methyl methacrylate, styrene, vinyl chloride *or* polyvinyl chloride, melamine, copolymer vinyl, polyvinal butyral, lignocellulose, artificial shellac.

The following are trademarked plastics—Perbunan, Buna N, Chemigum, Buna S, Butyl, Methyl Rubber *or* SKA *and* SKB, Sovprene, Neoprene, Thiokil, Aralac, Velon, Saran, Orlon, Bakelite, Durez, Phenolite, Textolite, Lumarith, Ethocel, Celluloid, Nitron, Lucite, Plexiglass, Polystyrene, Styron, Lustron, Vinylite, Zinlac, Fortisan.

plasticity, *n.* —*Syn.* mobility, pliancy, resilience; see **flexibility** 1.

plate, *n.* **1.** [Domestic utensils]—*Syn.* service, silver service, tea service; see **silverware.**

2. [A flat surface]—*Syn.* lamina, slice, stratum; see **plane** 1.

3. [A full-page illustration]—*Syn.* photography, lithograph, etching, woodcut, electrotype, cut, engraving, mezzotint, photoengraving; see also **illustration** 2, **picture** 3.

4. [A flattish dish]—*Syn.* dinner plate, soup plate, salad plate, casserole, *patera* (Latin), dessert plate, platter, trencher; see also **china, dish** 1.

5. [Food served on a plate, sense 4]—*Syn.* helping, serving, course; see **meal** 2.

6. [(D) In baseball, the base immediately before the catcher]—*Syn.* home base, home plate, home; see **base** 5.

plate, *v.* —*Syn.* laminate, stratify, layer, scale, flake, overlay, gild, nickel, bronze, chrome, silver, enamel, encrust, platinize; see also **cover** 1.

plateau, *n.* —*Syn.* tableland, mesa, elevation; see **hill, plain.**

platform, *n.* **1.** [A stage]—*Syn.* dais, pulpit, speaker's platform, rostrum, stand, floor, staging, terrace, belvedere; see also **stage.**

2. [A program]—*Syn.* principles, policies, the party planks (D); see **program** 4.

platitude, *n.* **1.** [A trite expression]—*Syn.* truism, proverb, triviality; see **cliché, motto.**

2. [Triteness]—*Syn.* flatness, boredom, evenness; see **dullness** 1, **monotony** 1.

platitudinous, *mod.* —*Syn.* commonplace, common, trite; see **dull** 4, **trivial, unimportant.**

platonic, *mod.* —*Syn.* idealistic, utopian, quixotic; see **visionary** 1.

platoon, *n.* —*Syn.* detachment, military unit, company; see **army** 2.

platter, *n.* —*Syn.* tray, serving platter, well-and-tree platter, meat platter, silver platter, trencher; see also **dish** 1, **plate** 4.

plaudit, *n.* —*Syn.* applause, approval, acclamation; see **praise** 2.

plausible, *mod.* —*Syn.* probable, credible, supposable; see **likely** 1.

plausibly, *mod.* —*Syn.* understandably, believably, with good reason; see **reasonably** 1, 2.

play, *n.* **1.** [Amusement]—*Syn.* enjoyment, diversion, pleasure; see **entertainment** 1.

2. [Recreation]—*Syn.* relaxation, game, sport; see **entertainment** 2.

3. [Fun]—*Syn.* frolic, happiness, sportiveness; see **fun.**

4. [A drama]—*Syn.* piece, musical, theatrical; see **drama** 1, **performance** 2, **show** 2.

5. [Sport]—*Syn.* exhibition, match, tryout; see **sport** 1, 3.

6. [Action]—*Syn.* activity, movement, working; see **action** 1.

make a play for (D)—*Syn.* make advances to, court, try for; see **try** 1.

play, *v.* **1.** [To amuse oneself]—*Syn.* entertain oneself, revel, make merry, carouse, play games, rejoice, have a good time, idle away, horse around (D).—*Ant.* mourn*, grieve, sulk.

2. [To gambol]—*Syn.* frisk, sport, cavort, joke, dance, romp, frolic, play games, make jokes, be a practical joker, jump (about), skip, frolic, caper; *all* (D): cut capers, cut up, show off, be the life of the

party, play the fool, carry on.—*Ant.* drag*, mope, droop.
3. [To produce music]—*Syn.* perform, execute, operate, work, cause to sound, finger, pedal, bow, plunk, tinkle, pipe, toot, mouth, pump, fiddle, sound, strike, saw, scrape, twang, pound, thump, tickle.
4. [To display light, erratic movement]—*Syn.* waltz, spout, flicker; see **dance** 1, 2.
5. [To act in a play]—*Syn.* impersonate, present, represent; see **act** 3, **perform** 2.
6. [To engage in sport]—*Syn.* participate, engage, rival; see **compete, contest** 2.
7. [To pretend]—*Syn.* imagine, suppose, think; see **pretend** 1.
8. [To gamble]—*Syn.* chance, risk, hazard; see **gamble** 1.

play around (D), *v.*—*Syn.* fool around, take lightly, philander; see **flirt** 1, **trifle with.**

play ball (D), *v.*—*Syn.* collaborate, work together, stand together; see **cooperate** 1, 2.

playbill, *n.*—*Syn.* program, notice, placard; see **advertisement** 2, **poster.**

play down (D), *v.*—*Syn.* belittle, hold down *or* back, minimize; see **restrain** 1.

played, *mod.*—*Syn.* presented, produced, interpreted; see **given.**

player, *n.* **1.** [One who takes part in a game] —*Syn.* member, athlete, sportsman, sportswoman, amateur, professional, gymnast, acrobat, swimmer, diver, trackman; *all* (D): flash, champ, pro, semipro, nonpro, jock, sweat; see also **contestant, opponent** 1.
2. [An actor]—*Syn.* performer, vaudeville performer, ham (D); see **actor, actress.**
3. [A reproducing device]—*Syn.* record player, tape player *or* set *or* deck, video cassette recorder (VCR), home music center; see **record player, tape recorder.**

play fair, *v.*—*Syn.* be good *or* civil, mind, obey; see **behave** 2.

playful, *mod.* **1.** [Humorous]—*Syn.* joking, whimsical, comical; see **funny** 1.
2. [Frolicsome]—*Syn.* gay, merry, spirited; see **happy** 1, **jaunty.**

playgoer, *n.*—*Syn.* one who frequents the theatre, play attender, habitué; see **frequenter.**

playground, *n.*—*Syn.* playing field, park, school ground, municipal playground, yard, school yard, diamond, gridiron; see also **lot** 1.

playing, *mod.*—*Syn.* sportive, sporting, gamboling; see **active** 1, 2.

playmate, *n.*—*Syn.* comrade, neighbor, companion; see **friend** 1.

plaything, *n.*—*Syn.* gadget, amusement, trinket; see **doll, game** 1, **toy** 1.

playtime, *n.*—*Syn.* vacation, holiday, freedom; see **leisure.**

playwright, *n.*—*Syn.* scripter, scenarist, tragedian; see **author** 2, **dramatist, writer.**

plaza, *n.*—*Syn.* square, village square, public square; see **court** 1.

plea, *n.* **1.** [An appeal]—*Syn.* overture, request, supplication; see **appeal** 1.
2. [A form of legal defence]—*Syn.* pleading, argument, case; see **defense** 3.

plead, *v.* **1.** [To beg]—*Syn.* implore, beseech, solicit; see **ask** 1, **beg** 1.
2. [To enter a plea]—*Syn.* present, allege, cite; see **declare** 1.
3. [To discuss in court]—*Syn.* defend, advocate, allege, give evidence, prosecute, argue, debate, answer charges, respond, vouch, avouch, examine, cross-examine, cross-question, question.

plead guilty, *v.*—*Syn.* confess, repent, concede; see **admit** 3.

pleading, *mod.*—*Syn.* imploring, supplicating, desirous; see **begging.**

pleasant, *mod.* **1.** [Affable]—*Syn.* agreeable, attractive, obliging, charming, mild, amusing, kindly, mild-mannered, gracious, genial, amiable, polite, urbane, cheerful, sympathetic, civil, cordial, genteel, engaging, social, bland, diplomatic, civilized, convivial, good-humored, good-natured, soft, fun, delightful, jovial, jolly; see also **kind.**—*Ant.* sullen*, unsympathetic, unkind.
2. [Giving pleasure; *said of occasions, experiences, and the like*]—*Syn.* gratifying, pleasurable, agreeable, cheering, amusing, welcome, refreshing, satisfying, all right, satisfactory, adequate, acceptable, comfortable, diverting, fascinating, adorable, droll, enjoyable, delightful, sociable, lively, exciting, convivial, glad, jocose, festive, cheerful, entertaining, relaxing, joyous, joyful, merry, happy, pleasing, favorable, bright, sunny, brisk, catchy, sparkling, enlivening, colorful, light, humorous, sporting, laughable, comforting; *all* (D): not so bad, not half bad, not bad.—*Ant.* sad*, unhappy, disagreeable.
3. [Encouraging pleasure; *said of climate*]—*Syn.* temperate, agreeable, balmy; see **fair** 3, **mild** 2.

pleasantly, *mod.* **1.** [Agreeably]—*Syn.* pleasingly, charmingly, welcomely; see **agreeably.**
2. [Courteously]—*Syn.* gallantly, civilly, thoughtfully; see **politely.**

pleasantry, *n.* **1.** [Humor]—*Syn.* comedy, joking, merriment; see **humor** 1.
2. [A joke]—*Syn.* game, quip, jest; see **joke** 2.

please, *interj.*—*Syn.* if you please, if it please you, may it please you, by your leave, *bitte* (German), *s'il vous plait* (French), *por favor* (Spanish), *se v'è grato* (Italian).

please, *v.* **1.** [To give pleasure]—*Syn.* gratify, satisfy, make up to; see **entertain** 1.
2. [To desire]—*Syn.* wish, demand, command; see **want** 1.
if you please—*Syn.* if you will, if I may, by your leave; see **please.**

pleased, *mod.*—*Syn.* gratified, satisfied, charmed; see **happy** 1.

pleasing, *mod.*—*Syn.* charming, agreeable, delightful; see **pleasant** 1.

pleasure, *n.* **1.** [Enjoyment]—*Syn.* bliss, delight, ease; see **happiness** 2.
2. [Will]—*Syn.* want, preference, wish; see **desire** 1.
3. [Amusement]—*Syn.* hobby, game, diversion; see **entertainment** 1, 2, **fun.**
4. [Gratification]—*Syn.* revelry, self-indulgence, gluttony; see **indulgence** 3.

pleat, *n.*—*Syn.* pleating, tuck, crease; see **fold** 1, **plait.**

pleat, *v.*—*Syn.* ruffle, crease, gather; see **fold** 2.

pleated, *mod.* —*Syn.* plaited, box-pleated, knife-pleated, accordion-pleated, tucked, folded.
plebeian, *mod.* —*Syn.* vulgar, ordinary, coarse; see **common** 1, **conventional** 1, 3, **traditional** 2.
plebiscite, *n.* —*Syn.* poll, referendum, ticket; see **vote** 1.
pledge, *n.* —*Syn.* guarantee, token, agreement; see **promise.**
take the pledge—*Syn.* vow, swear (off), vouch; see **promise** 1.
pledge, *v.* **1.** [To give security]—*Syn.* sign for, pawn, give bond; see **guarantee** 2.
2. [To promise]—*Syn.* swear, vow, vouch; see **promise** 1.
pledged, *mod.* —*Syn.* plighted, bound, enforced; see **guaranteed, promised.**
plenary, *mod.* —*Syn.* entire, complete, inclusive; see **whole** 1.
plenipotentiary, *n.* —*Syn.* diplomat, spokesman, emissary; see **agent** 1.
plenitude, *n.* —*Syn.* wealth, excess, abundance; see **plenty.**
plentiful, *mod.* **1.** [Bountiful]—*Syn.* prolific, fruitful, profuse, lavish, bounteous, unstinted, liberal, prodigal, unsparing, inexhaustible, replete, generous, abundant, liberal, extravagant, improvident, excessive, plenteous, copious, full-handed, superabundant, over-liberal, superfluous, overflowing, flowing, fulsome, affluent, flowing with milk and honey (D).—*Ant.* stingy*, niggardly, skimpy.
2. [Existing in plenty]—*Syn.* sufficient, abundant, copious, ample, luxuriant, exuberant, plenteous, overflowing, large, chock-full, teeming, unlimited, well-provided, flowing, full, flush, lush with, pouring, fruitful, swarming, swimming, abounding. —*Ant.* poor*, scant, scanty.
plenty, *n.* —*Syn.* abundance, fruitfulness, profuseness, fullness, lavishness, deluge, torrent, sufficiency, bounty, profusion, adequacy, plethora, plentifulness, plentitude, copiousness, great plenty, God's own plenty, flood, avalanche, good store, limit, capacity, adequate stock, enough and to spare, everything, *Hülle und Fülle* (German), all kinds of, all one wants, all one can eat *or* drink, more than one knows what to do with, too much of a good thing, a good bit, all one needs, all one can use, a great deal, bonanza; *all* (D): a bunch, a lot, loads (of), oodles and gobs, full house, egg in one's beer; see also **excess** 1.
pleonasm, *n.* —*Syn.* redundancy, verbiage, circumlocution; see **repetition, wordiness.**
pleonastic, *mod.* —*Syn.* repetitious, wordy, redundant; see **oratorical, verbose.**
plethora, *n.* —*Syn.* surplus, overabundance, plenty; see **excess** 1.
plethoric, *mod.* —*Syn.* swollen, grown, filled; see **full** 1, **inflated.**
plexus, *n.* —*Syn.* net, mesh, web; see **network** 1.
pliability, *n.* **1.** [Flexibility]—*Syn.* facility, elasticity, mobility; see **flexibility** 1.
2. [Adaptability]—*Syn.* susceptibility, passivity, obedience; see **docility.**
pliable, *mod.* **1.** [Flexible]—*Syn.* limber, supple, plastic; see **flexible** 1.
2. [Tractable]—*Syn.* pliant, manipulable, irresolute; see **docile, obedient** 1.
pliant, *mod.* **1.** [Yielding under influence]—*Syn.* tractable, yielding, pliable; see **docile, obedient** 1.
2. [Yielding under physical pressure]—*Syn.* limber, supple, plastic; see **flexible** 1.
pliers, *n.* —*Syn.* pinchers, forceps, tweezers; see **pincers.**
plight, *n.* —*Syn.* impasse, dilemma, tight situation; see **difficulty** 1, **predicament.**
plod, *v.* —*Syn.* trudge, hike, plug; see **walk** 1.
plop, *v.* —*Syn.* thump, thud, bump; see **sound** 1.
plot, *n.* **1.** [An intrigue]—*Syn.* conspiracy, scheme, artifice; see **trick** 1.
2. [The action of a story]—*Syn.* plan, scheme, outline, design, development, progress, unfolding, movement, story line, climax, denouement, events, incidents, enactment, suspense, structure, build-up, scenario.
3. [A piece of ground]—*Syn.* parcel, land, division; see **area** 2, **lot** 1.
plot, *v.* **1.** [To devise an intrigue]—*Syn.* frame, contrive, scheme; see **plan** 1.
2. [To plan]—*Syn.* sketch, outline, draft; see **plan** 2.
3. [To determine a course]—*Syn.* map out, put forward, propose, outline, consider, plan.
plow, *n.* Plows include the following—moldboard, gang, steam, tractor, double, straddle, sulky, wheel, mole, skim, hillside, shovel, sod *or* paring, bullnose, hand; lister, hoe plow *or* horse-hoe, garden plow *or* wheel hoe, harrow, cultivator, corn-hoe (D); see also **tool** 1
plow, *v.* **1.** [To use a plow]—*Syn.* break, furrow, cultivate, harrow, turn, plow up, turn over, till, list, ridge, break ground, do the plowing, start the spring work; *both* (D): turn it over, give it the gang; see also **farm** 1.
2. [To act like a plow]—*Syn.* smash into, rush through, shove apart; see **dig** 1, **push** 1.
3. [(D) To fail; *British usually spelled 'plough'*] —*Syn.* suspend, send home, dismiss; see **fail** 5.
plowed, *mod.* —*Syn.* cultivated, turned, tilled, furrowed, broken.
plowing, *n.* —*Syn.* tilling, furrowing, cultivating, breaking, turning, listing; see also **farming.**
plowman, *n.* —*Syn.* cultivator, farm laborer, planter; see **farmer.**
pluck, *n.* —*Syn.* bravery, boldness, determination; see **courage** 1.
plucky, *mod.* —*Syn.* dauntless, courageous, undaunted; see **brave** 1.
plug, *n.* **1.** [An implement to stop an opening] —*Syn.* cork, stopper, stopple, filling, stoppage, bung, spigot, river, wedge.
2. [An electrical fitting]—*Syn.* attachment plug, fitting, connection, wall plug, floor plug, plug fuse.
3. [A large pipe with a discharge valve]—*Syn.* water plug, fire hydrant, fire plug; see **hydrant.**
4. [Tobacco prepared for chewing]—*Syn.* cake of tobacco, chewing tobacco, twist, cut; *all* (D): baccy, chawin', chewin', pack of scrap; see also **tobacco.**
5. [(D) An inferior horse]—*Syn.* hack, plowhorse, scrub; see **horse** 1.
plug, *v.* —*Syn.* stop, fill, obstruct, secure, ram, make tight, drive in; see also **close** 2.
plug in, *v.* —*Syn.* connect, make a connection, bring in electricity; see **join** 1, 3.

plugging, *mod.*—*Syn.* deterring, holding (back), closing; see **blocking, stopping.**

plum, *n.* Plums and plumlike fruits include the following—freestone, Damson, Satsuma, Duarte, Elephant Heart, Green Gage, Reine Claude, Sugar plum; French prune, improved French prune, Italian-Fellemberg prune, Stanley prune; see also **fruit** 1.

plumage, *n.*—*Syn.* down, mantle, feathers; see **feather.**

plumb, *mod.*—*Syn.* erect, straight, perpendicular; see **upright** 1, **vertical.**

plumb, *v.*—*Syn.* fathom, explore, search; see **measure** 1.

plumber, *n.*—*Syn.* steam fitter, tradesman, metal worker, handy man; see also **workman.**

plumbing, *n.*—*Syn.* pipes, water pipes, sewage pipes, heating pipes, bathroom fixtures, sanitary provisions; see also **pipe** 1.

plume, *n.*—*Syn.* quill, crest, tuft; see **feather.**

plummet, *v.*—*Syn.* plunge, fall, nosedive; see **dive, fall** 1.

plump, *mod.* **1.** [Somewhat fleshy; *said of persons*] —*Syn.* obese, stout, fleshy; see **fat** 1.

2. [Filled so as to be rounded; *said of things*] —*Syn.* plethoric, round, filled; see **full** 1.

plunder, *n.*—*Syn.* loot, winnings, spoil; see **booty.**

plunder, *v.*—*Syn.* burn, steal, lay waste; see **raid, ravage.**

plunge (D), *n.*—*Syn.* rash *or* heavy investment, purchase, buying spree; see **venture.**

take the plunge (D)—*Syn.* start, commence, attempt; see **begin** 1.

plunge, *v.*—*Syn.* fall, throw oneself, rush; see **dive, jump** 1.

plural, *mod.* **1.** [Concerning plural number]—*Syn.* few, a number of, abundant; see **many.**

2. [Concerning plural marriage]—*Syn.* bigamous, digamous, polygamous, polyandrous, morganatic.

plurality, *n.*—*Syn.* majority, advantage *or* lead in votes cast, favorable returns; see **majority** 2, **lead** 1.

plus, *mod.* and *prep.*—*Syn.* added to, additional, additionally, increased by, with the addition of, surplus, positive; see also **extra.**—*Ant.* less*, minus, subtracted from.

plush (D), *mod.*—*Syn.* elegant, luxurious, sumptuous; see **rich** 2.

plush, *n.*—*Syn.* rayon plush, silk plush, wool plush, cotton plush, mohair plush, velvet, velveteen, plushette; see also **cloth.**

plutocrat, *n.*—*Syn.* magnate, tycoon, capitalist; see **aristocrat.**

ply, *n.* **1.** [A sheet]—*Syn.* thickness, fold, overlay; see **layer.**

2. [An inclination]—*Syn.* tendency, bent, bias; see **inclination** 1.

ply, *v.* **1.** [To use]—*Syn.* utilize, employ, wield; see **use** 1.

2. [To practice]—*Syn.* work at, exercise, pursue; see **practice** 2.

3. [To supply]—*Syn.* replenish, equip, furnish; see **provide** 1.

4. [To beat]—*Syn.* hurt, whip, strike; see **beat** 2.

pneumatic, *mod.*—*Syn.* breezy, atmospheric, ethereal; see **airy** 1.

pneumonia, *n.*—*Syn.* lung fever, pneumonitis, lobar pneumonia, croupous pneumonia; see also **disease** 3.

poach, *v.* **1.** [To steal]—*Syn.* filch, pilfer, smuggle; see **steal.**

2. [To blend]—*Syn.* mash, mingle, stir; see **cook, mix** 1.

pock, *n.*—*Syn.* flaw, hole, mark; see **blemish, scar.**

pocket, *mod.*—*Syn.* small, tiny, miniature; see **little** 1, **minute** 1.

pocket, *n.* **1.** [A cavity]—*Syn.* hollow, opening, airpocket; see **hole** 2.

2. [A pouch sewed into a garment]—*Syn.* pouch, poke, sac, pod.

Kinds of pockets include the following—patch, slash, inset, watch, coin, invisible, pants, jacket, coat, vest, side, back, rear, inner, outer, inside, outside.

3. [Small area]—*Syn.* isolated group, secluded section of persons, separated group.

in one's pocket (D)—*Syn.* controlled, under control, regulated; see **managed.**

in pocket (D)—*Syn.* gained, usable, ready; see **available.**

pocket, *v.*—*Syn.* conceal, hide, enclose; see **steal.**

pocketbook, *n.*—*Syn.* wallet, pouch, coin purse; see **bag, purse.**

pocketknife, *n.*—*Syn.* jackknife, blade, penknife; see **knife.**

pockmark, *n.*—*Syn.* pit, smallpox scar, mark; see **blemish, scar.**

pod, *n.*—*Syn.* seed vessel, bean pod, pea pod; see **seed** 1.

poem, *n.*—*Syn.* poetry, lyric, sonnet, edda, ballad, quatrain, blank verse, free verse, song, composition, creation; see also **writing** 2.

poet, *n.*—*Syn.* writer, poemwriter, bard, versifier, dilettante, minstrel, troubadour, jongleur, verse maker, maker of verses, scribbler of verses, metrist, lyrist, parodist, author of the lyric *or* the book, lyricist, librettist, dramatic poet, dramatist, lyric poet, writer of lyrics, rhymester, poetaster; see also **artist** 1, **writer.**

Major poets include the following—*British:* Geoffrey Chaucer, Edmund Spenser, William Shakespeare, John Donne, John Milton, John Dryden, Alexander Pope, Samuel Johnson, Robert (Bobbie) Burns, William Blake, William Wordsworth, Samuel Taylor Coleridge, Lord Byron, John Keats, Percy Bysshe Shelley, Alfred Lord Tennyson, Robert Browning, Gerard Manley Hopkins, William Butler Yeats, Thomas Stearns Eliot, Dylan Thomas; *American:* Edward Taylor, Edgar Allan Poe, Walt Whitman, Emily Dickinson, Edwin Arlington Robinson, Robert Frost, Carl Sandburg, Edna St. Vincent Millay, Ezra Pound, Wallace Stevens, E. E. Cummings, Marianne Moore, Robert Lowell; *Classical Greek:* Homer, Pindar, Aeschylus, Sophocles, Euripides; *Latin:* Virgil, Lucretius, Ovid, Horace, Catullus, Juvenal; *Italian:* Dante Alighieri, Petrarch, Ludovico Ariosto, Gabriele d'Annunzio; *French:* François Villon, Jean de La Fontaine, Charles Baudelaire, Stéphane Mallarmé, Paul Verlaine, Arthur Rimbaud, Victor Hugo, Guillaume Apollinaire; *Spanish:* St. John of the Cross, Pedro Calderón de la Barca, Federico Garcia Lorca, Pablo

Neruda; *Portuguese:* Luis Vaz de Camões; *German:* Wolfgang von Goethe, Friedrich Schiller, Heinrich Heine, Rainer Maria Rilke, Bertolt Brecht; ***Russian:*** Mikhail Yurievich Lermontov, Alexander Pushkin, Vladimir Mayakovski, Boris Pasternak, Yevgeni Yevtushenko.

poetic, *mod.* —*Syn.* poetical, lyric, lyrical, metrical, idyllic, rhythmical, tuneful, melodious, epodic, elegiac, odic, epical, romantic, dramatic, iambic, dactylic, spondaic, trochaic, anapestic, Heliconian, Parnassian, Pierian, Ionic, Sapphic, Alcaic, Pindaric, Dircaean, imaginative, dipodic.—*Ant.* unpoetical, unimaginative, prosaic.

poetize, *v.* —*Syn.* score, sing, versify; see **compose** 3.

poetry, *n.* —*Syn.* poem, paean, song, versification, metrical composition, rime, rhyme, poesy, stanza, rhythmical composition, poetical writings; see also **verse** 1.

Types of poetry include the following—idyllic, lyric, pastoral, epic, heroic, dramatic, elegiac, ballad, narrative, symbolic, light, humorous, satiric, didactic.

Forms of verse include the following—sonnet, Shakespearean sonnet, Italian sonnet, Miltonic sonnet, Wordsworthian sonnet; Chaucerian stanza, Spenserian stanza; heroic couplet (*also* (D): rocking-horse couplet), Alexandrine, iambic pentameter, rhyme royal, ottava rima, couplet, distich, ode, epode, triolet, rondeau, rondel, rondelet, tanka, haiku, kyrielle, quinzain, ballade, sestine, sloka, triad, gazel, shaped whimsey, villanelle, limerick, parody; blank verse, free verse, stop-short, stichic verse, strophic verse, stanzaic verse, assonance, accentual verse, alliterative verse.

pogrom, *n.* —*Syn.* slaughter, mass murder, massacre; see **carnage, murder.**

poignancy, *n.* **1.** [Intensity]—*Syn.* concentration, sharpness, piquancy; see **intensity** 1.

2. [Emotion]—*Syn.* feeling, sadness, sentimentality; see **emotion.**

poignant, *mod.* **1.** [Sharp]—*Syn.* piquant, bitter, acute; see **sarcastic.**

2. [Touching]—*Syn.* emotional, sorrowful, pitiful; see **passionate** 2, **sentimental.**

point, *n.* **1.** [A position having no extent]—*Syn.* location, spot, locality; see **position** 1.

2. [A sharp, tapered end]—*Syn.* end, pointed end, apex, needle point, pin point, barb, prick, spur, spike, tine, snag, spine, claw, tooth, calk, rowel, stabber, sticker, prickler; see also **thorn, tip** 1.

3. [Anything having a point, sense 2]—*Syn.* sword, dagger, stiletto; see **knife, needle** 1.

4. [Purpose]—*Syn.* aim, object, intent; see **purpose** 1.

5. [Meaning]—*Syn.* force, drift, import; see **meaning.**

6. [A time]—*Syn.* period, limit, duration; see **time** 1.

7. [A detail]—*Syn.* case, feature, point at issue; see **circumstance, detail** 1.

8. [A tally]—*Syn.* count, notch, mark; see **score** 1.

at the point of—*Syn.* on the verge of, close to, almost; see **near** 1.

beside the point—*Syn.* immaterial, not pertinent, not germane; see **irrelevant.**

in point—*Syn.* apt, pertinent, germane; see **relevant.**

in point of—*Syn.* in the matter of, as concerns, as relevant to; see **about** 2.

make a point of—*Syn.* stress, emphasize, do as a rule *or* on principle, insist upon; see **emphasize.**

stretch (*or* **strain**) **a point**—*Syn.* allow, make an exception, concede; see **yield** 1.

to the point—*Syn.* pertinent, apt, exact; see **relevant.**

point, *v.* **1.** [To indicate]—*Syn.* show, name, denote; see **designate** 1.

2. [To direct]—*Syn.* guide, steer, influence; see **lead** 1.

3. [To face]—*Syn.* look, aim, tend; see **face** 4.

4. [To sharpen]—*Syn.* taper, whet, barb; see **sharpen** 1.

point-blank, *mod.* —*Syn.* straight, plainly, directly; see **frank.**

pointed, *mod.* **1.** [Sharp]—*Syn.* fine, keen, spiked; see **sharp** 2.

2. [Biting or insinuating]—*Syn.* caustic, tart, trenchant; see **sarcastic.**

pointer, *n.* **1.** [A pointing instrument]—*Syn.* hand, rod, indicator, dial, gauge, director, index, mark, arrow, signal, needle, register.

2. [A variety of dog]—*Syn.* hunting dog, gun dog, game dog; see **dog** 1.

3. [(D) A hint]—*Syn.* clue, tip, warning; see **hint** 1.

pointing, *mod.* **1.** [Indicating]—*Syn.* showing, signifying, denoting, evidencing, designating, evincing, manifesting, declaring, specifying, revealing, disclosing, displaying, placing, spotting, directing to, guiding, steering, marking.

2. [Directed]—*Syn.* looking, fronting, turned, stretched toward, headed (toward), facing.

pointing out, *mod.* —*Syn.* mentioning, noting, declaring; see **saying.**

pointless, *mod.* **1.** [Dull]—*Syn.* uninteresting, prosaic, not pertinent; see **irrelevant, trivial, unnecessary.**

2. [Blunt]—*Syn.* worn, obtuse, rounded; see **dull** 1.

3. [Ineffective]—*Syn.* useless, powerless, impotent; see **incompetent, weak** 1, 2.

point off, *v.* —*Syn.* separate, group, detach; see **divide** 1.

point of no return, *n.* —*Syn.* last chance, extremity, turning point; see **end** 4.

point of view, *n.* —*Syn.* outlook, position, approach; see **attitude** 1.

point out, *v.* —*Syn.* indicate, show, denote; see **designate** 1.

point up, *v.* —*Syn.* accent, stress, make clear; see **emphasize.**

poise, *n.* —*Syn.* balance, gravity, equilibrium; see **composure, dignity** 1.

poison, *n.* —*Syn.* virus, bane, toxin, infection, germ, bacteria, oil, vapor, gas; see also **venom** 1.

Poisons include the following—rattlesnake, copperhead, black-widow-spider, tarantula venom; smallpox, yellow-fever, common-cold, flu virus; poison oak, poison ivy, carbon monoxide gas, cooking gas, arsenic, lead, strychnine, corrosive sublimate; oxalic, sulphuric, hydrochloric, nitric, carbolic, prussic, hydrocyanic acid; cyanide, cantharides, caustic soda, lye, belladonna, aconite, Paris green, lead arsenate, blue vitriol *or* copper sulfate, nicotine, DDT, Agent Orange.

poison, *v.* —*Syn.* infect, injure, kill, murder, destroy, vitiate, corrupt, pervert, undermine, defile, harm, taint, envenom, make ill, cause violent illness.—*Ant.* benefit, help*, purify.

poisoned, *mod.* **1.** [Suffering from poisoning] —*Syn.* infected, indisposed, diseased; see **sick.**
2. [Dying of poison]—*Syn.* fatally poisoned, beyond recovery, succumbing; see **dying** 1.
3. [Polluted with poison]—*Syn.* contaminated, tainted, defiled, corrupted, venomous, virulent, impure, malignant, noxious, deadly, toxic, pernicious; see also **poisonous.**—*Ant.* pure*, fresh, untainted.

poisoning, *n.* Varieties of poisoning include the following—blood poisoning *or* septicemia, food poisoning, ptomaine, toxemia, lead poisoning, systemic poisoning, corrosive poisoning, irritant poisoning.

poisonous, *mod.* —*Syn.* bad, noxious, hurtful, dangerous, pestiferous, baneful, malignant, infective, venomous, virulent, peccant, vicious, corrupt, deleterious, noisome, morbid, morbific, morbiferous, fatal, pestilential, miasmatic, toxic, toxiferous, deadly, destructive; see also **harmful.**—*Ant.* healthy*, wholesome, nourishing.

poke, *n.* —*Syn.* jab, thrust, punch; see **blow** 1.

poke, *v.* —*Syn.* jab, punch, crowd; see **push** 1.

poker, *n.* **1.** [A fire iron]—*Syn.* metal bar, iron rod, fireplace implement, fire-stirrer; see also **iron** 1.
2. [A gambling game] Varieties of poker include the following—draw, straight, bluff, stud, whisky, jack pot, table stake; see also **gambling, game** 1.

polar, *mod.* **1.** [Concerning polar regions]—*Syn.* extreme, terminal, farthest; see **arctic.**
2. [Cold]—*Syn.* glacial, frozen, frigid; see **cold** 1.

polarity, *n.* —*Syn.* duality, contradiction, contrariety; see **opposition** 1, 2.

Polaroid (trademark), *mod.* —*Syn.* Land (trademark), polarizing, polarized; see also **camera.**

pole, *n.* —*Syn.* shaft, flagpole, flagstaff; see **post** 1.

polemic, *mod.* —*Syn.* discursive, argumentative, contestable; see **controversial, questionable** 1, **uncertain** 2.

polemics, *n.* —*Syn.* debate, contention, argument; see **discussion** 1.

polestar, *n.* —*Syn.* Polaris, guide, north star; see **star** 1.

police, *n.* —*Syn.* arm of the law, law enforcement body, FBI, police officers, policemen, police force, custodians of the law, detective force, military police (*also* (D): M.P.'S), Royal Canadian Mounted Police (*both* (D): RCMP, Mounties), canine corps, New York's Finest (D).

police, *v.* —*Syn.* watch, control, patrol; see **guard** 2.

policeman, *n.* —*Syn.* patrolman, officer of the law, magistrate, process server, constable; *all* (D): bluecoat, beat pounder, cop, copper, flatfoot, fuzz, the Man, John Law, the heat, bull, speed cop, bobby, redneck.
Policemen include the following—man on a beat, mounted police, motorcycle police, traffic police, squad-car police, municipal police, state police, highway patrol, detective, SWAT (Special Weapons and Tactics) team, federal agent *or* investigator, *all* (D): fed, narc, F.B.I. man.

police state, *n.* —*Syn.* dictatorship, authoritarian *or* fascist *or* rightest government, result of a *Putsch*; see **autocracy.**

policy, *n.* —*Syn.* course, procedure, method, system, strategy, tactics, administration, management, theory, tenet, doctrine, behavior, scheme, design, arrangement, organization, plan, order.

polish, *n.* —*Syn.* shine, burnish, glaze; see **finish** 2.

polish, *v.* —*Syn.* burnish, furbish, finish; see **shine** 3.

polished, *mod.* **1.** [Bright]—*Syn.* glossy, shining, gleaming; see **bright** 1.
2. [Refined]—*Syn.* polite, well-bred, cultured; see **refined** 2.
3. [Referring to writing or speech]—*Syn.* perfected, elaborate, ornate; see **elegant** 4.

polite, *mod.* **1.** [Courteous]—*Syn.* obliging, thoughtful, mannerly, attentive, pleasant, gentle, mild, nice, concerned, considerate, solicitous, conciliatory, conciliative, bland, obsequious, condescending, honey-tongued, amiable, gracious, cordial, considerate, good-natured, sympathetic, interested, smooth, chivalric, diplomatic, politic, benign, propitiatory, kindly, kind, kindly-disposed, courtly, benignant, affable, agreeable, civil, complacent, complaisant, respectful, amenable, gallant, genteel, gentlemanly, mannered, punctilious, sociable, ingratiating, neighborly, friendly, respectful.—*Ant.* egotistic*, insolent, pompous.
2. [Refined]—*Syn.* polished, well-bred, cultured; see **refined** 2.

politely, *mod.* —*Syn.* thoughtfully, considerately, attentively, solicitously, concernedly, cordially, graciously, amiably, kindheartedly, compassionately, gently, benignantly, urbanely, affably, agreeably, civilly, gallantly, complacently, sociably, elegantly, gracefully, charmingly, ingratiatingly, winningly, blandly, tactfully, in good humor, with good grace, with old-fashioned courtesy, with easy graciousness; see also **respectfully.**

politeness, *n.* —*Syn.* refinement, culture, civility; see **courtesy** 1.

politic, *mod.* **1.** [Prudent]—*Syn.* diplomatic, sensible, sagacious; see **discreet, judicious.**
2. [Adroit]—*Syn.* bland, smooth, urbane; see **intelligent** 1.

political, *mod.* —*Syn.* legislative, partisan, executive, administrative, concerning public affairs, having to do with politics, pertaining to government affairs, civic, state, federal; see also **governmental.**

political science, *n.* —*Syn.* political economy, science of government, politics, political theory, study of government, government science; see also **social science.**

political scientist, *n.* —*Syn.* political researcher, Kremlinologist, sovietologist; see **professor, teacher** 2.

politician, *n.* **1.** [One who follows politics professionally]—*Syn.* officeholder, office seeker, party man, partisan, legislator, congressman, member of parliament, politico.
2. [A statesman]—*Syn.* student of statecraft, lawmaker, governmental leader; see **statesman.**
3. [One who plays politics]—*Syn.* agitator, demagogue, timeserver, political panderer, poser, rabble

rouser; *all* (D): baby-kisser, arm-waver, spoilsmonger, Man on Horseback.

politics, *n.* **1.** [Political science]—*Syn.* practical government, functional government, systematic government, domestic affairs, internal affairs, foreign affairs, matters of state.
2. [The business of obtaining public office]—*Syn.* campaigning, getting votes, seeking nomination, electioneering; *all* (D): being up for election, running for office, standing to run, throwing one's hat in the ring, stumping the country, taking the stump.

polity, *n.*—*Syn.* republic, commonwealth, country; see **nation** 1.

poll, *n.* **1.** [A census]—*Syn.* vote, consensus, ballot; see **census.**
2. [A voting place; *usually plural*]—*Syn.* ballot box(es), voting machines, polling place *or* area; see **voting.**

poll, *v.*—*Syn.* question, register, enroll; see **examine** 1, **list** 1.

pollen, *n.*—*Syn.* microspores, powder, fine particles; see **dust.**

pollinate, *v.*—*Syn.* pollen, cross-fertilize, breed; see **fertilize** 2.

pollute, *v.*—*Syn.* deprave, soil, stain; see **dirty, poison.**

polluted, *mod.*—*Syn.* soiled, corrupted, defiled, poisoned, filthy, smelly; see also **dirty** 1.

pollution, *n.*—*Syn.* corruption, defilement, demoralization, adulteration, blight, soiling, fouling, foulness, taint, tainting, polluting, decomposition, desecration, profanation, abuse, deterioration, rottenness, spoliation, impairment, misuse, infection, besmearing, besmirching, smirching; see also **contamination.**
Some common pollutants of the air and water include the following—sewage, soapsuds, garbage, factory waste, radiation, detergent, carbon monoxide, automobile *or* bus *or* truck exhaust, pesticides, Agent Orange, factory smoke.

poltergeist, *n.*—*Syn.* spirit, spook, supernatural visitant; see **ghost** 1, 2.

poltroon, *n.*—*Syn.* deserter, dastard, recreant; see **coward, weakling.**

polygamy, *n.*—*Syn.* (fraternal) polyandry, (sororal) polygyny, plural marriage, bigamy; see also **marriage** 1.

polyglot, *mod.*—*Syn.* bilingual, polyglottic, polylingual, learned in languages, diglottic, diglot, hexaglot, Panglossian.

polyphonic, *mod.*—*Syn.* orchestral, choral, harmonic; see **harmonious** 1.

polytechnic, *n.*—*Syn.* technological institute, occupational school, trade school; see **school** 1.

polytheism, *n.*—*Syn.* tritheism, ditheism, paganism, henotheism; see also **religion** 2.

pomade, *n.*—*Syn.* hair oil, hair cream, hair dressing, hair lotion, ointment, balm, salve; see also **cosmetic.**

pomade, *v.*—*Syn.* make up, anoint, oil; see **grease.**

pommel, *n.*—*Syn.* saddle horn, handle, hilt, knob, ball, horn.

pommel, *v.*—*Syn.* strike, pound, hurt; see **beat** 2, **hit** 1.

pomp, *n.*—*Syn.* magnificence, affectation, splendor; see **ostentation** 2.

pompon, *n.*—*Syn.* tuft, plume, tassel, topknot, knob, crest, cockade; see also **decoration** 2.

pomposity, *n.* **1.** [Pretension]—*Syn.* presumption, conceit, overconfidence; see **arrogance.**
2. [Grandiloquence]—*Syn.* balderdash, pretension, bombast; see **nonsense** 1.

pompous, *mod.*—*Syn.* arrogant, haughty, proud; see **egotistic** 2.

pompously, *mod.*—*Syn.* pretentiously, conceitedly, boastfully, snobbishly, imperiously, insolently, autocratically, disdainfully, magisterially, overbearingly, proudly, ostentatiously, bombastically, theatrically, spectacularly, flamboyantly, gaudily; see also **arrogantly, egotistically.**—*Ant.* quietly*, humbly, modestly.

pond, *n.*—*Syn.* fishpond, millpond, lily pond; see **lake, pool** 1.

ponder, *v.*—*Syn.* meditate, deliberate, consider; see **think** 1.

ponderable, *mod.*—*Syn.* substantial, weighty, massive; see **heavy** 1.

ponderous, *mod.*—*Syn.* dull, weighty, lifeless; see **heavy** 1.

poniard, *n.*—*Syn.* dagger, blade, sword; see **knife.**

pontiff, *n.*—*Syn.* prelate, cardinal, His Holiness; see **Pope.**

pontifical, *mod.*—*Syn.* papist, apostolic, ecclesiastical; see **papal.**

pontificate, *n.*—*Syn.* popedom, bishopric, the Vatican; see **papacy.**

pontoon, *n.*—*Syn.* barge, float, craft; see **boat, raft.**

pony, *n.*—*Syn.* Shetland pony, Welsh pony, Galloway horse, bronco, cayuse, mustang, Indian pony, Russian pony; see also **horse** 1.

poodle, *n.*—*Syn.* French poodle, French barbet, fancy dog; see **dog** 1, **pet** 3.

pool, *n.* **1.** [Small body of liquid, usually water] —*Syn.* puddle, mudpuddle, pond, lake, fishpond, millpond, swim tank, natatorium, tarn; see also **lake.**
2. [Supply]—*Syn.* funds, provisions, amount available; see **equipment, supply** 2.
3. [Game]—*Syn.* snooker, 8-ball, billards; see **game** 1.

pool, *v.*—*Syn.* combine, merge, blend; see **join** 1.

poop, *n.*—*Syn.* deck of a ship, stern, back end; see **deck** 1.

poor, *mod.* **1.** [Lacking worldly goods]—*Syn.* indigent, penniless, moneyless, impecunious, destitute, needy, poverty-stricken, underprivileged, fortuneless, starved, straitened, penurious, pinched, distressed, reduced, beggared, famine-stricken, underdeveloped, stinted, empty-handed, meager, scanty, insolvent, beggarly, ill-provided, ill-furnished, in want, in penury, suffering privation, in need; *all* (D): behind the eight ball, poor as a church mouse, broke, hard up, on the dole, strapped (for money), down and out; see also **wanting** 1.—*Ant.* wealthy*, well-to-do, affluent.
2. [Lacking excellences]—*Syn.* pitiful, paltry, contemptible, miserable, pitiable, dwarfed, insignificant, diminutive, ordinary, common, mediocre, trashy, shoddy, worthless, sorry, base, mean, coarse, vulgar, inferior, imperfect, smaller, lesser, below

par, subnormal, under average, second-rate, reduced, defective, deficient, lower, subordinate, minor, secondary, humble, second-hand, pedestrian, beggarly, homely, homespun, fourth-rate, tawdry, petty, unimportant, bad, cheap, flimsy, threadbare, badly made, less than good, unwholesome, lacking in quality, dowdy, undergrade, second-class, shabby, shoddy, valueless, easy, gaudy, mass-produced, gimcrack, squalid, catchpenny, trivial, sleazy, trifling, unsuccessful, second-best, tasteless, insipid, barbarous, vile, disgusting, despicable, rustic, crude, outlandish, odd, rock-bottom, garish, flashy, showy, inelegant, loud, unsightly, inartistic, affected, ramshackle, pretentious, tumble-down, glaring, artificial, flaunting, newfangled, out-of-date, old-fashioned; *all* (D): crummy, junky, two-bit, schlock, third-rate, kitschy, raunchy, corny, cheesy; see also **faulty, inadequate** 1, **unsatisfactory.**

3. [Lacking strength]—*Syn.* puny, feeble, infirm; see **weak** 1.

4. [Lacking vigor or health]—*Syn.* indisposed, impaired, imperfect; see **sick.**

5. [Lacking fertility]—*Syn.* infertile, unproductive, barren; see **sterile** 1, 2, **worthless** 1.

poor, *n.*—*Syn.* needy, forgotten man, the unemployed, underdogs, the underprivileged, beggars, the impoverished masses, second-class citizen, have-nots (D); see also **pauper, people** 3.

poorhouse, *n.*—*Syn.* retreat, debtor's prison, asylum, harbor, house for paupers, almshouse; see also **shelter.**

poorly, *mod.* **1.** [In an inferior manner]—*Syn.* defectively, crudely, unsuccessfully; see **badly** 1, **inadequately.**

2. [Ill]—*Syn.* indisposed, ailing, unwell; see **sick.**

poorness, *n.*—*Syn.* want, need, destitution; see **poverty** 1, **starvation.**

poor-spirited, *mod.*—*Syn.* wretched, miserable, mean; see **afraid** 1, **cowardly** 1.

pop, *n.* **1.** [A slight explosive sound]—*Syn.* report, burst, shot; see **noise** 1.

2. [A carbonated drink]—*Syn.* soda pop, ginger pop, soda water, beverage, soft drink; see also **drink** 3.

pop, *v.*—*Syn.* dart, leap, protrude; see **jump** 1, **rise** 1.

pop art, *n.*—*Syn.* abstraction from the everyday, avant-garde, corn (D); see **art** 2, **painting** 1, **sculpture.**

Pope, *n.*—*Syn.* head of the Roman Catholic Church, bishop of Rome, Primate of Italy, Roman Pontiff, vicar of Jesus Christ on earth, Metropolitan of the Roman Province, successor to Peter in the See of Rome, Patriarch of the West, His Holiness, the Holy Father, *Servus servorum Dei* (Latin); see also **father** 5, **master** 1, **priest.**

poppy, *n.*—*Syn.* bloom, blossom, herb; see also **drug** 2, **flower** 1, 2.

Varieties of poppies, include the following—opium, corn, Iceland, black, California, field, garden, horn, horned, long-headed, Mexican, Oriental, prickly, red, Shirley, seaside, dwarf,

poppycock (D), *n.*—*Syn.* humbug, gibberish, foolishness; see **nonsense** 1, **stupidity** 2.

populace, *n.*—*Syn.* masses, commonality, multitude; see **man** 1, **people** 3.

popular, *mod.* **1.** [Generally liked]—*Syn.* favorite, well-liked, approved, pleasing, suitable, well-received, sought, fashionable, stylish, beloved, likable, lovable, attractive, praised, promoted, recommended, in the public eye, celebrated, noted, admired, famous, in (high) favor, celebrated, run after (D); see also **common** 1, **conventional** 1, 2, **traditional** 2.—*Ant.* unknown*, in disrepute, out of favor.

2. [Cheap]—*Syn.* low-priced, popular-priced, marked down; see **cheap** 1, **economical** 2.

3. [Commonly accepted]—*Syn.* general, familiar, demanded, in demand, prevalent, prevailing, current, rife, in use, widespread, ordinary, adopted, embraced, having caught on, in the majority, having caught the popular fancy; see also **fashionable, modern** 1.

4. [Pertaining to the common people]—*Syn.* proletarian, accessible, neighborly; see **democratic** 1, **republican.**

popularity, *n.*—*Syn.* approval, general esteem, widespread acceptance, following, prevalence, universality, demand, fashionableness, the rage (D).

popularize, *v.*—*Syn.* familiarize, catch on, cheapen, give currency to, spread, universalize, produce in quantity, gear down (D); see also **generalize** 1, **simplify.**

popularly, *mod.*—*Syn.* commonly, usually, ordinarily; see **regularly** 1.

population, *n.*—*Syn.* inhabitants, dwellers, number *or* group of people, citizenry, natives, group, residents, culture, community, state, populace; see also **society** 2.

populous, *mod.*—*Syn.* peopled, crowded, populated, serried, dense, thronged, thick, swarming, teeming, crawling (with people) (D).

porcelain, *n.*—*Syn.* earthenware, ceramic(s), enamel(ware); see also **china.**

Porcelains include the following—Alcora, Amstel, Arita, Berlin, Brandenburg, bone, Bow, Bristol, Burslem, Chelsea, Cookworthy, Crown Derby, Meissen, Dresden, Belleek, Mayflower, Royal Worcester, Swansea, Lowestoft, Budweis, Caen, Chantilly, Limoges, Luneville, Sèvres, Copenhagen, Dresden, Iamri, Hizen, Imperial yellow, Kouan-Ki, Mandarin, rose, Capodimonte, Medici, cast, fusible, ironstone, chemical, majolica, eggshell, embossed, hybrid.

porch, *n.*—*Syn.* piazza, portico, breezeway, entrance, doorstep, stoop, gallery, entrance platform, carriage porch, galilee, stoa; see also **balcony, veranda.**

porcine, *mod.*—*Syn.* hoggish, rapacious, piggish; see **greedy** 2.

pore, *n.*—*Syn.* opening, foramen, orifice, vesicle; see also **hole** 1, 2.

pork, *n.* Common cuts of pork include the following—ham, loin, bacon, back, spare ribs, side meat, shoulder, loin roast, loin chops, shoulder chops, hock, Boston butt, plate, jowl, pig's feet; see also **meat.**

pork barrel (D), *n.*—*Syn.* (local) appropriations, graft, government funds *or* projects; see **corruption** 3.

porker (D), *n.* —*Syn.* swine, pig, boar; see **animal** 2, **hog** 1.

pornographic, *mod.* —*Syn.* immoral, dirty, obscene; see **lewd** 1.

pornography, *n.* —*Syn.* obscene literature, prurience, salaciousness, vulgarity, quadriliteral, obscenity, grossness, four-letter word, smut; see also **indecency** 2.

porous, *mod.* —*Syn.* pervious, permeable, acceptable, pory; see also **penetrable.**

port, *mod.* —*Syn.* lefthand(ed), to *or* toward the left, larboard; see **left** 1.

port, *n.* —*Syn.* haven, anchorage, gate; see **harbor** 2.

portable, *mod.* —*Syn.* transportable, conveyable, transferable, easily transported, manageable; see also **movable.**

portage, *n.* —*Syn.* hauling, carriage, conveyance; see **transportation.**

portal, *n.* —*Syn.* gateway, opening, ingress; see **door** 1, **entrance** 2, **gate.**

portend, *v.* —*Syn.* forecast, predict, herald; see **hint, warn** 1.

portent, *n.* —*Syn.* omen, clue, caution; see **sign** 1, **warning.**

portentous, *mod.* **1.** [Ominous]—*Syn.* looming, prophetic, forewarning; see **imminent, ominous, sinister.**

2. [Unusual]—*Syn.* rare, extraordinary, significant; see **unusual** 2.

porter, *n.* **1.** [A gatekeeper]—*Syn.* doorkeeper, doorman, lodgekeeper, gamekeeper, caretaker, ostiary, janitor; see also **watchman.**

2. [A person, who carries another's things]—*Syn.* carrier, transporter, bellboy, pullman porter; *all* (D): redcap, George, boy, buttons, bellhop, hop.

portfolio, *n.* **1.** [A flat container]—*Syn.* briefcase, attaché case, folder; see **bag, case** 7, **container.**

2. [A collection, especially of stocks and bonds] —*Syn.* holdings, selection, documents; see **collection** 2.

3. [An assignment]—*Syn.* office, responsibility, duties; see **duty** 2, **job** 1, 2.

porthole, *n.* —*Syn.* peephole, hole, opening; see **window** 1.

portico, *n.* —*Syn.* covered wall, colonnade, arcade; see **patio, porch.**

portion, *n.* —*Syn.* section, piece, part; see **division** 2, **share.**

portly, *mod.* **1.** [Fat]—*Syn.* corpulent, heavy, stout; see **fat** 1.

2. [Dignified]—*Syn.* majestic, grand, remarkable; see **impressive** 1, **striking.**

portrait, *n.* —*Syn.* likeness, portraiture, representation; see **painting** 1, **picture** 2.

portraiture, *n.* —*Syn.* representation, portrait, painting; see **art** 3, **picture** 2.

portray, *v.* **1.** [To represent]—*Syn.* depict, characterize, reproduce; see **define** 2, **describe, represent** 2.

2. [To imitate]—*Syn.* copy, simulate, mimic; see **imitate** 2, **impersonate, parody.**

portrayal, *n.* —*Syn.* depiction, replica, likeness; see **copy, description** 1, **imitation** 2.

pose, *n.* —*Syn.* artificial position, affectation, attitudinizing; see **fake, pretense** 1.

pose, *v.* **1.** [To pretend]—*Syn.* profess, feign, make believe; see **act** 1, **pretend** 1.

2. [To assume a pose for a picture]—*Syn.* sit, attitudinize, strike an attitude, adopt a position, posture; see also **model** 3.

posed, *mod.* —*Syn.* formal, stiff, unnatural; see **awkward** 1, **conventional** 2, 3.

poser, *n.* **1.** [A pretender]—*Syn.* mimic, hypocrite, pretender; see **cheat** 1, **impostor.**

2. [A mystery]—*Syn.* problem, enigma, perplexity; see **puzzle** 2, **riddle** 1.

posh (D), *mod.* —*Syn.* elegant, deluxe, opulent; see **rich** 2.

posit, *v.* **1.** [To place]—*Syn.* set, fix, secure; see **fasten** 1, **place** 1.

2. [To state]—*Syn.* announce, assert, pronounce; see **declare** 1, **say.**

position, *n.* **1.** [A physical position]—*Syn.* location, locality, spot, seat, ground, environment, post, whereabouts, bearings, station, point, place, stand, space, surroundings, situation, site, topography, chorography, geography, region, tract, district, scene, setting; see also **area** 2, **place** 3.

2. [An intellectual position]—*Syn.* view, belief, attitude; see **judgment** 3, **opinion** 1.

3. [An occupational position]—*Syn.* office, employment, occupation; see **job** 1, **profession** 1, **trade** 2.

4. [A social position]—*Syn.* station, state, status; see **rank** 3.

5. [Posture]—*Syn.* pose, carriage, bearing, deportment, stance, stand, condition, situation, status, state, mien, form, manner, habit; see also **attitude** 3, **posture** 1.

position, *v.* —*Syn.* put, locate, settle in; see **place.**

positive, *mod.* **1.** [Definite]—*Syn.* decisive, actual, concrete; see **definite** 1, **real** 2.

2. [Emphatic]—*Syn.* peremptory, assertive, obstinate; see **emphatic** 1, **resolute** 2.

3. [Certain]—*Syn.* sure, convinced, confident; see **accurate** 1, **certain** 1, 3.

positively, *mod.* **1.** [In a positive manner]—*Syn.* peremptorily, assertively, uncompromisingly, dogmatically, arbitrarily, stubbornly, obstinately, emphatically, dictatorially, imperatively, oracularly, decidedly, absolutely, insistently, authoritatively, assuredly, confidently, unhesitatingly, with conviction *or* emphasis; see also **boldly** 1.

2. [Without doubt]—*Syn.* undoubtedly, unmistakably, undeniably; see **surely.**

posse, *n.* —*Syn.* vigilante, party, civilian police, detachment, lynch mob, force armed with legal authority, armed band, group of deputies, police force; see also **law** 6, **police.**

possess, *v.* —*Syn.* hold, occupy, control; see **maintain** 3, **own** 1.

possessed, *mod.* **1.** [Insane]—*Syn.* mad, crazed, violent; see **insane** 1.

2. [Owned]—*Syn.* kept, enjoyed, in one's possession; see **held, owned, retained** 1.

possessing, *mod.* —*Syn.* holding, occupying, owning; see **retaining.**

possession, *n.* **1.** [Ownership]—*Syn.* proprietary rights, hold, mastery; see **ownership.**

2. [Property]—*Syn.* personal property, real estate, something possessed; see **property** 1, 2.

3. [A colony]—*Syn.* settlement, territory, (part of) an overseas empire; see **colony** 1.

possessions, *n.*—*Syn.* belongings, goods, effects; see **estate** 1, 2, **property** 1.

possessor, *n.*—*Syn.* holder, proprietor, proprietress, inheritor, occupant, occupier, retainer, master, buyer, purchaser, sharer, partner, landlord, landowner, lessee, legatee, landlady, mistress, lord of the manor, laird, trustee, beneficiary, inheritor, heir, heiress; see also **owner.**

possibility, *n.* **1.** [The condition of being possible] —*Syn.* plausibility, feasibility, workableness; see **chance** 1, **probability.**

2. [A possible happening]—*Syn.* hazard, chance, contingency, occasion, circumstance, hope, occurrence, fortuity, hap, happening, outside chance, incident, instance; see also **accident** 2, **event** 1, **opportunity** 1.

possible, *mod.* **1.** [Within the realm of possibility] —*Syn.* conceivable, imaginable, thinkable; see **likely** 1.

2. [Acceptable]—*Syn.* expedient, desirable, welcome; see **pleasant** 2.

3. [Contingent upon the future]—*Syn.* indeterminate, fortuitous, adventitious; see **dependent** 3, **likely** 1, **uncertain** 2.

possibly, *mod.*—*Syn.* perhaps, by chance, mayhap; see **likely** 1, **maybe, probably.**

post, *n.* **1.** [An upright in the ground]—*Syn.* prop, support, pillar, pedestal, stake, stud, upright, doorpost; see also **column** 1, **mast.**

2. [The mails]—*Syn.* mail *or* postal service, post office, P.O.; see **mail.**

postal, *mod.*—*Syn.* post office, mail, messenger, carrier, epistolary, airmail, express, special delivery, registered, insured.

post-bellum, *mod.*—*Syn.* postwar, after the war, cease-fire; see **calm** 2.

postcard, *n.*—*Syn.* postal card, note, letter card; see **letter** 2.

postdate, *v.* **1.** [To anticipate]—*Syn.* assume, overdate, date after; see **anticipate** 1.

2. [To succeed]—*Syn.* replace, ensue, follow; see **succeed** 2.

poster, *n.*—*Syn.* placard, bill, sign, banner, *affiche* (French), sheet, billboard, signboard, handbill, broadside; see also **advertisement** 1, 2.

posterior, *mod.* **1.** [Subsequent]—*Syn.* coming after, succeeding, next; see **following.**

2. [Behind]—*Syn.* in back of, last, after; see **back.**

posterity, *n.*—*Syn.* progeny, descendants, seed, breed, children, issue, heirs, rising generation, new generation, younger generation, successors, lineage, future time; see also **family** 1, **offspring.**

posthaste, *mod.*—*Syn.* swiftly, speedily, hastily; see **quickly** 1.

posthumous, *mod.*—*Syn.* after death, continuing, future; see **post-mortem.**

postlude, *n.*—*Syn.* epilogue, finale, close; see **end** 2.

postman, *n.*—*Syn.* mail carrier, letter carrier, carrier; see **mailman.**

post-mortem, *mod.*—*Syn.* after death, posthumous, subsequent, post-obit, future, more recent, later, following, post-mortal, postmundane.

post mortem, *n.*—*Syn.* dissection, examination after death, coroner's examination; see **autopsy, examination** 3.

post office, *n.*—*Syn.* mail office, postal service, P.O.; see **mail, post** 2.

postpone, *v.*—*Syn.* defer, put off, hold over; see **delay** 1, **suspend** 2.

postponed, *mod.*—*Syn.* deferred, delayed, retarded, put off, set for a later time, to be done later, withheld, staved off, shelved, tabled, prorogued, adjourned, intermitted, suspended; see also **late** 1, **witheld.**

postponement, *n.*—*Syn.* respite, suspension, adjournment; see **delay** 1, **pause** 1, 2.

postscript, *n.*—*Syn.* P.S., note, supplement, appendix, appendage; see also **addition** 2.

postulate, *v.* **1.** [To theorize]—*Syn.* hypothesize, suppose, speculate; see **estimate** 1, **guess** 1.

2. [To implore]—*Syn.* beg, request, demand; see **ask** 1, **question** 1.

posture, *n.* **1.** [Stance]—*Syn.* pose, carriage, demeanor, bearing, aspect, presence, condition.

2. [Attitude]—*Syn.* way of thinking, feeling, sentiment; see **attitude** 3.

posture, *v.*—*Syn.* sit, display, attitudinize; see **pose** 2.

postwar, *mod.*—*Syn.* post-bellum, after the war, peaceful; see **peacetime.**

posy, *n.*—*Syn.* corsage, garland, bouquet; see **flower** 1, **wreath.**

pot, *n.* **1.** [Container]—*Syn.* vessel, kettle, pan, jug, jar, mug, tankard, cup, can, crock, canister, receptacle, bucket, urn, pitcher, bowl, cauldron, mortar, melting pot, crucible; see also **container.**

2. [(D) Marijuana]—*Syn.* *cannabis sativa* (Latin); *all* (D): grass, weed, maryjane, boo; see also **drug** 2, **marijuana.**

go to pot—*Syn.* deteriorate, go to ruin, fall apart; see **decay.**

potable, *mod.*—*Syn.* fit for drinking, uncontaminated, drinkable, potulent, clean, unpolluted, fresh; see also **pure** 2, **sanitary.**

potato, *n.*—*Syn.* tuber, white potato, sweet potato, yam, rhizome; *both* (D): spud, tater; see also **root** 1, **vegetable.**

Potatoes include the following—Irish Cobbler, Early Ohio, Green Mountain, Rural, Burbank, Epicure, Great Scot, Kerr's Pink, King Edward VII, Arran Chief, Bliss Triumph, Idaho Russet, new.

potbellied, *mod.*—*Syn.* obese, paunchy, bloated; see **fat** 1.

potency, *n.* **1.** [Strength]—*Syn.* power, energy, vigor; see **manhood** 2, **strength** 1.

2. [Authority]—*Syn.* influence, control, dominion; see **command** 2, **power** 2.

potent, *mod.* **1.** [Strong]—*Syn.* vigorous, robust, sturdy; see **strong** 1, 2.

2. [Powerful]—*Syn.* mighty, great, influential; see **dominant** 2, **powerful** 1.

3. [Convincing]—*Syn.* effective, swaying, cogent; see **impressive** 1, **persuasive.**

4. [Effective]—*Syn.* useful, stiff, efficient; see **effective.**

potentate, *n.*—*Syn.* monarch, sovereign, overlord; see **king** 1, **master** 1, **ruler** 1.

potential, *mod.*—*Syn.* implied, inherent, dormant; see **likely** 1.

potentiality, *n.*—*Syn.* capacity, possibility, energy; see **ability** 1, 2, **probability.**

potentially, *mod.*—*Syn.* conceivably, imaginably, possibly; see **likely** 1, **maybe, probably.**

pothouse (D), *n.*—*Syn.* tavern, inn, saloon; see **bar** 2.

potion, *n.*—*Syn.* dose, tonic, elixir, draft, liquor, dram, nip, cordial, stimulant, libation, restorative, philter, spirits, aromatics, remedy; see also **drink** 2, 3, **liquid, medicine** 2.

potpourri, *n.*—*Syn.* medley, hodgepodge, blend; see **mixture.**

pottery, *n.*—*Syn.* ceramics, porcelain, crockery, earthenware, clay ware; see also **utensils.**
Varieties of pottery include the following—Abruzzi, Etruscan, Apulian, Cypriote, Cambrian, Assyrian, Anatolian, Awata, Damascus, Persian, Bizen, Bendigo, Amstel, Faenza, Castelli, Sicilian, Broussa, Celtic, Chartreuse, Cognac, Sèvres, Varges, Rouen, Dresden, Burslem, Quimper, Upchurch, Mexican, Indian, peasant, inlaid, hard, soft, unglazed, glazed, roughcast.

pouch, *n.*—*Syn.* sack, receptacle, poke; see **bag, container.**

poultice, *n.*—*Syn.* plaster, application, dressing; see **medicine** 2, **treatment** 2.

poultry, *n.*—*Syn.* domesticated birds, pullets, barnyard fowls; see **chicken** 1, **fowl, turkey.**

pounce, *v.*—*Syn.* bound, surge, dart; see **dive** 1, **jump** 1.

pound, *n.* **1.** [Measure of weight]—*Syn.* sixteen ounces, Troy pound, avoirdupois pound, commercial pound, pint; see also **measure** 1, **weight** 1.
2. [Kennel]—*Syn.* coop, doghouse, cage; see **pen** 1.

pound, *v.*—*Syn.* strike, crush, pulverize; see **beat** 2, 3, **hit** 1.

pour, *v.* **1.** [To flow]—*Syn.* discharge, emit, issue; see **drain** 3, **flow** 2.
2. [To allow to flow]—*Syn.* replenish with, spill, splash; see **empty** 2.
3. [To rain heavily]—*Syn.* stream, flood, drench; see **rain.**

pourboire (French), *n.*—*Syn.* present, gratuity, tip; see **gift** 1.

pouring, *mod.*—*Syn.* streaming, gushing, spouting, rushing, raining, flooding, showering, discharging, emitting, issuing, escaping, emanating, welling out, spurting, spilling, shedding, draining, running (down *or* away *or* out); see also **flowing.**

pour it on (D), *v.*—*Syn.* overwork, overburden, add to; see **burden, increase** 1.

pout, *v.*—*Syn.* make a long face, protrude the lips, be sullen; see **frown, sulk.**

poverty, *n.* **1.** [Want of earthly goods]—*Syn.* beggary, destitution, pennilessness, penury, indigence, mendicancy, pauperism, want, need, insufficiency, starvation, famine, underdevelopment, dearth, abjection, privation, reduced circumstances, insolvency, impoverishment, broken fortune, straits, scantiness, deficiency, meagerness, aridity, sparingness, exiguity, stint, depletion, reduction, emptiness, vacancy, deficit, debt, poorness; *all* (D): wolf at the door, deep water, hard spot, pinch, bite, tough going; see also **lack** 1.—*Ant.* wealth*, prosperity, comfort.
2. [Want of any desirable thing]—*Syn.* shortage, shortness, insufficiency, inadequacy, exigency, scarcity, incompleteness, failing, defect; see also **lack** 2.

poverty-stricken, *mod.*—*Syn.* penniless, broke, bankrupt; see **poor** 1, **wanting** 1.

powder, *n.*—*Syn.* particles, film, pulverulence, powderiness, explosive powder, medicinal powder, cosmetic powder; see also **cosmetic, explosive, medicine** 2.
keep one's powder dry (D)—*Syn.* be ready, be prepared, alert oneself; see **prepare** 1.
take a powder (D)—*Syn.* run away, abandon, desert; see **leave** 1.

powdery, *mod.*—*Syn.* sandy, gravelly, dusty; see **gritty.**

power, *n.* **1.** [Strength]—*Syn.* vigor, energy, stamina; see **strength** 1.
2. [Controlling sway]—*Syn.* authority, command, jurisdiction, dominion, ascendency, superiority, domination, dominance, mastery, preponderance, control, sway, sovereignty, prerogative, hegemony, suzerainty, prestige, regency, omnipotence, puissance, supreme authority, the last word, rule, law, first strike capability, warrant, supreme authority, the last word, rule of law, law of the jungle, brute force, authorization, supremacy, student power, youth power, Black power, legal sanction, government, absolutism, carte blanche, say-so (D); see also **influence** 2, **leadership** 1—*Ant.* incompetence*, ineptitude, collapse.
3. [Ability; *often plural*]—*Syn.* skill, endowment, capability; see **ability** 1, 2.
4. [Force]—*Syn.* compulsion, coercion, duress; see **pressure** 2, **restraint** 2.
5. [Energy]—*Syn.* horsepower, potential, dynamism; see **energy** 3.
in power—*Syn.* ruling, authoritative, commanding; see **powerful** 1.

powerful, *mod.* **1.** [Wielding power]—*Syn.* mighty, all-powerful, almighty, superhuman, omnipotent, overpowering, great, invincible, dominant, influential, authoritative, overruling, potent, puissant, forceful, forcible, compelling, ruling, prevailing, pre-eminent, commanding, supreme, highest, important, authoritarian, charismatic, paramount, ruthless, in the saddle, having the upper hand, in control; see also **predominant** 1.—*Ant.* weak*, incompetent, impotent.
2. [Strong]—*Syn.* robust, stalwart, sturdy; see **strong** 1, 2.
3. [Effective]—*Syn.* efficacious, effectual, convincing; see **persuasive.**

powerfully, *mod.*—*Syn.* forcibly, forcefully, effectively, severely, intensely, with authority; see also **vigorously.**

powerhouse, *n.*—*Syn.* central station, generating plant, electric-power station, substation, dynamo station.

powerless, *mod.*—*Syn.* impotent, feeble, infirm; see **weak** 1, 2.

(the) powers that be (D), *n.*—*Syn.* boss(es), higher authorities, (the) higher-ups (D); see **administration** 2.

powwow (D), *n.* —*Syn.* council, meeting, conference; see **discussion** 1.
pox, *n.* —*Syn.* smallpox, measles, chicken pox; see **disease** 3.
practicability, *n.* —*Syn.* potentiality, possibility, feasibility; see **probability.**
practicable, *mod.* —*Syn.* usable, workable, functional; see **practical.**
practical, *mod.* —*Syn.* matter-of-fact, pragmatic, unimaginative, solid, practicable, feasible, workable, functional, useful, sound, sound-thinking, down-to-earth, unromantic, unsentimental, unidealistic, realistic, sensible, sane, reasonable, rational, to (one's) advantage, operative, utilitarian, possible, usable, serviceable, efficient, effective, working, in action, in operation, with both feet on the ground (D).—*Ant.* unreal*, imaginative, unserviceable.
practically, *mod.* **1.** [In a practical manner]—*Syn.* unimaginatively, pragmatically, efficiently, functionally, sensibly, rationally, reasonably, realistically, with regard to use, considered as to service, from a workable standpoint; see also **effectively.**
2. [Virtually]—*Syn.* for ordinary purposes, nearly, just about; see **almost.**
practical nurse, *n.* —*Syn.* attendant, nurse's helper, nursemaid; see **nurse** 1, 2, **servant.**
practice, *n.* **1.** [A customary action]—*Syn.* usage, use, wont; see **custom** 2, **tradition** 1.
2. [A method]—*Syn.* mode, manner, fashion; see **method** 2, **system** 2.
3. [Educational repetition]—*Syn.* exercise, drill, repetition, iteration, rehearsal, recitation, recounting, relating; *both* (D): tune-up, prepping.
4. [A practitioner's custom]—*Syn.* work, patients, clients, clientele, professional business.
practice, *v.* **1.** [To seek improvement through repetition]—*Syn.* drill, train, exercise, study, rehearse, repeat, recite, iterate, put in practice, make it one's business, work at, accustom oneself, act up to, habituate oneself; *all* (D): polish up, sharpen up, woodshed, build up.
2. [To employ one's professional skill]—*Syn.* function, work at, follow, put into effect, hang out one's shingle, employ oneself in, practice medicine *or* law.
practiced, *mod.* —*Syn.* trained, expert, exercised; see **able** 1, 2.
praenomen, *n.* —*Syn.* first name, Christian name, cognomen; see **name** 1.
pragmatic, *mod.* —*Syn.* realistic, utilitarian, philistine, extensional, logical; see also **practical.**
prairie, *n.* —*Syn.* steppe, savanna, grassland; see **field** 1, **meadow, plain.**
praise, *n.* **1.** [The act of praising]—*Syn.* applause, applauding, adulation, blandishment, esteem, commendation, approval, approbation, appreciation, cheering, advocacy, acclamation, adoration, acclaim, recognition, obeisance, sycophancy, homage, extolling, magnifying, glorifying, celebrating, exalting, giving thanks, saying grace, crying up, singing the praises of; see also **admiration** 1. —*Ant.* hatred*, contempt, dislike.
2. [An expression of praise]—*Syn.* laudation, eulogy, encomium, regard, applause, panegyric, recommendation, hand-clapping, hurrahs, huzzah(s), bravos, ovation, cheers, cries, whistling, tribute, compliment, elogium, acclaim, flattery, plaudit, paean, blessing, benediction; *all* (D): boost, kudos, rave, a big hand, chit, puff.—*Ant.* censure, blame*, condemnation.
sing someone's praise(s)—*Syn.* commend, acclaim, congratulate; see **praise** 1.
praise, *v.* **1.** [To commend]—*Syn.* recommend, applaud, cheer, acclaim, endorse, sanction, admire, eulogize, adulate, elevate, aggrandize, smile on, cajole, give an ovation to, clap, pay tribute to, do credit to, have a good word for, make much of, extend credit, bestow humor *or* honor upon, bow down and worship, pay homage to, sound the praises of, advocate, compliment, appreciate, admire, celebrate, honor, congratulate, flatter; *all* (D): root for, rave over, boost, give a big hand, buildup, tout, talk *or* cry up, raise the roof; see also **approve** 1.
2. [To speak or sing in worship]—*Syn.* glorify, adore, reverence; see **worship** 2.
praised, *mod.* —*Syn.* admired, aided, helped, flattered, worshiped, lauded, belauded, extolled, glorified, exalted, blessed, celebrated, paid tribute to, magnified.
praiseworthy, *mod.* —*Syn.* select, worthy, admirable; see **excellent.**
prance, *v.* —*Syn.* cavort, frisk, gambol; see **dance** 2.
prank, *n.* —*Syn.* game, escapade, caper; see **joke** 1.
prankish, *mod.* —*Syn.* playful, capricious, mischievous; see **naughty.**
pranks, *n.* —*Syn.* antics, capers, frolics; see **trick** 1.
prattle, *n.* —*Syn.* twaddle, drivel, chatter; see **nonsense** 1.
prattle, *v.* —*Syn.* gush, jabber, chatter; see **babble.**
pray, *v.* **1.** [To ask or beg]—*Syn.* importune, petition, plead; see **ask** 1, **beg** 1.
2. [To call upon God]—*Syn.* hold communion (with God), supplicate, implore, petition, entreat, invocate, commend someone to God; *all* (D): pull on the skies, take hold of the horns of the altar, hang onto God, get down on one's prayerbones.
prayer, *n.* **1.** [An earnest request]—*Syn.* entreaty, request, petition; see **appeal** 1.
2. [An address to the deity]—*Syn.* orison, invocation, act of devotion, supplication, (private) devotions, benediction, litany, rogation, *brocho or berakah* (Hebrew).
Prayers, sense 2, include the following—Lord's Prayer, Pater Noster, Ave Maria, grace (at meals), *Kiddush, Kaddish, shma (Yisroel), amidah* (all Hebrew), matins, vespers, Angelus, general confession, Miserère, collects, hours, stations of the cross, evensong.
prayer book, *n.* —*Syn.* liturgy, mass book, missal, hymnal, holy text, guide; see also **bible** 2.
prayerful, *mod.* —*Syn.* devout, orthodox, pious; see **religious** 2.
pray for, *v.* —*Syn.* ask earnestly, invocate, recite the rosary; see **pray** 2.
preach, *v.* —*Syn.* exhort, discourse, moralize, teach, lecture, talk, harangue, inform, address.
preacher, *n.* —*Syn.* missionary, parson, evangelist; see **minister** 1.
preaching, *n.* —*Syn.* moralizing, teaching, exhortation, doctrine, instruction, homily.

preachy, *mod.* —*Syn.* sanctimonious, holier-than-thou, monitory; see **moral** 1, **talking.**
preamble, *n.* —*Syn.* prelude, preface, introductory part; see **introduction** 1.
precarious, *mod.* —*Syn.* doubtful, uncertain, dubious; see **dangerous** 1.
precaution, *n.* —*Syn.* anticipation, forethought, regard; see **care** 1.
precautionary, *mod.* —*Syn.* prudent, discreet, alert; see **careful.**
precede, *v.* —*Syn.* go before, come first, be *or* move ahead of, take precedence over, preface, introduce, usher *or* ring in, herald, forerun, antecede, head, lead, run *or* go ahead, scout, light the way, go in advance, come before, antedate, come to the front, forge ahead, head up (D).—*Ant.* succeed*, come after, come last.
precedence, *n.* —*Syn.* preference, precession, the lead (D); see **priority.**
precedent, *n.* —*Syn.* authoritative example, exemplar, pattern; see **criterion, example** 1, **model** 2.
preceding, *mod.* —*Syn.* antecedent, precedent, previous, other, prior, aforesaid, ahead of, earlier, former, forerunning, past, foregoing, above-mentioned, above-named, above-cited, *supra* (Latin), afore-mentioned, before-mentioned, above, before, precursory, prefatory, front, forward, anterior, preliminary, preparatory, introductory, preexistent, aforeknown, already indicated, previously mentioned.
precept, *n.* —*Syn.* doctrine, statute, rule; see **law** 3.
preceptor, *n.* —*Syn.* instructor, mentor, lecturer; see **teacher** 1.
pre-Christian, *mod.* —*Syn.* before Christianity, before Christ, pagan; see **heathen.**
precinct, *n.* —*Syn.* limit, confine, boundary; see **area** 2.
precious, *mod.* **1.** [Valuable]—*Syn.* high-priced, costly, dear; see **expensive, valuable** 1.
2. [Beloved]—*Syn.* cherished, inestimable, prized; see **beloved, favorite.**
3. [Refined and delicate]—*Syn.* overrefined, overnice, fragile; see **dainty** 1, **refined** 2.
precious metal, *n.* —*Syn.* silver, platinum, pewter; see **gold** 2, **metal.**
precious stone, *n.* —*Syn.* emerald, diamond, ruby; see **gem** 1.
precipice, *n.* —*Syn.* crag, cliff, bluff; see **hill, mountain** 1.
precipitate, *v.* —*Syn.* accelerate, press, hurry; see **hasten** 2, **speed.**
precipitately, *mod.* —*Syn.* hastily, speedily, swiftly; see **immediately, quickly** 1.
precipitation, *n.* **1.** [Carelessness]—*Syn.* rashness, presumption, impetuosity; see **carelessness, rudeness.**
2. [Condensation]—*Syn.* rainfall, hail, rain, snow, sleet, hailstorm; see also **storm** 1.
precipitous, *mod.* —*Syn.* craggy, dizzying, steep; see **abrupt** 1, **sharp** 2.
précis, *n.* —*Syn.* condensation, abridgement, abstract; see **summary.**
precise, *mod.* **1.** [Exact]—*Syn.* decisive, well-defined, strict; see **accurate** 1, 2, **definite** 1, 2.
2. [Fussily or prudishly careful]—*Syn.* rigid, inflexible, uncompromising; see **careful, severe** 1.
precisely, *mod.* —*Syn.* correctly, exactly, definitely; see **accurately, specifically** 2.
precision, *n.* —*Syn.* exactness, correctness, sureness; see **accuracy** 2.
preclude, *v.* —*Syn.* prevent, interrupt, impede; see **hinder, restrain** 1.
precocious, *mod.* —*Syn.* developed, forward, presumptuous; see **intelligent** 1, **mature** 1.
precolonial, *mod.* —*Syn.* preprovincial, prerevolutionary, preimperial; see **historical.**
pre-Columbian, *mod.* —*Syn.* before the discovery of America, old-world, pre-American, Mayan, Aztecan, Indian, Eskimo; see also **ancient** 2.
preconception, *n.* —*Syn.* prejudice, bias, assumption; see **inclination** 1.
precursor, *n.* **1.** [A messenger]—*Syn.* forerunner, herald, vanguard; see **messenger.**
2. [A predecessor]—*Syn.* ancestor, antecedent, parent; see **forefather.**
precursory, *mod.* —*Syn.* previous, prior, preliminary; see **before** 1, **preceding.**
predatory, *mod.* —*Syn.* preying, voracious, carnivorous, rapacious, predacious, raptorial, ravening, wolfish, bloodthirsty; see also **greedy** 2, **hungry.**
predecessor, *n.* —*Syn.* antecedent, forerunner, ancestor; see **forefather.**
predestination, *n.* **1.** [A forecast]—*Syn.* prediction, intention, predetermination; see **forecast.**
2. [Fate]—*Syn.* doom, fortune, decree; see **destiny** 1.
predetermine, *v.* —*Syn.* destine, predestine, fate, doom, decide.
predetermined, *mod.* —*Syn.* calculated, deliberate, fated; see **planned, proposed.**
predicament, *n.* —*Syn.* strait, quandary, plight, puzzle, perplexity, dilemma, scrape, corner, hole, impasse, tight situation, state, condition, position, lot, circumstance, mess, muddle, imbroglio, exigency, deadlock, pinch, crisis; *all* (D): bind, fix, pickle, hot water, pretty kettle of fish, jam; see also **difficulty** 1, 2.
predicate, *n.* —*Syn.* verbal phrase, part of speech, word; see **verb.**
predicate, *v.* —*Syn.* assert, declare, state; see **mean** 1.
predict, *v.* —*Syn.* prophesy, prognosticate, divine; see **foretell.**
predictable, *mod.* —*Syn.* anticipated, foreseen, prepared for; see **expected** 2, **likely** 1.
prediction, *n.* —*Syn.* prophecy, foresight, prognostication; see **forecast.**
predictive, *mod.* —*Syn.* portentous, forbidding, auspicious; see **imminent, ominous, sinister.**
predilection, *n.* —*Syn.* partiality, bias, prejudice; see **inclination** 1.
predispose, *v.* **1.** [To stimulate]—*Syn.* urge, inspire, activate; see **animate** 1.
2. [To prepare]—*Syn.* make expectant, cultivate, indoctrinate; see **teach** 1.
predisposed, *mod.* —*Syn.* willing, inclined, eager; see **enthusiastic** 1.
predisposition, *n.* **1.** [A tendency]—*Syn.* leaning, bent, predilection; see **inclination** 1.
2. [A preference]—*Syn.* option, partiality, liking; see **choice** 3, **preference.**

predominance, *n.* —*Syn.* reign, supremacy, control; see **administration** 1, **command** 2, **power** 2.

predominant, *mod.* **1.** [Supreme in power]—*Syn.* mighty, almighty, supreme, omnipotent, all-powerful, ascendant, reigning, ruling, overruling, prevailing, prevalent, controlling, supervisory, directing, influential, dominant, dominating, authoritative, arbitrary, paramount, preponderant, imperious, absolute, executive, official, potent, weighty, effective, efficacious, overpowering, governing, holding the reins; see also **powerful** 1.—*Ant.* incompetent*, submissive, inferior.

2. [Of first importance]—*Syn.* transcendent, surpassing, superlative; see **principal.**

predominate, *v.* —*Syn.* dominate, prevail, rule; see **command** 2, **govern, manage** 1.

preeminent, *mod.* —*Syn.* dominant, incomparable, superior; see **predominant** 1.

preeminently, *mod.* —*Syn.* conspicuously, notably, incomparably; see **very.**

preempt, *v.* —*Syn.* acquire, seize, appropriate; see **obtain** 1.

preen, *v.* —*Syn.* spruce, trim, primp; see **dress** 1, **dress up.**

prefab (D), *n.* —*Syn.* prefabricated *or* mass-produced building, (temporary) structure, standardized housing; see **building** 1.

prefabricate, *v.* —*Syn.* fabricate, perform, set up, coordinate, pre-assemble; see also **assemble** 3.

preface, *n.* —*Syn.* prelude, prolegomenon, preliminary; see **explanation** 2, **introduction** 4.

preface, *v.* —*Syn.* introduce, commence, precede; see **begin** 1.

prefatory, *mod.* —*Syn.* opening, initiative, preliminary; see **introductory** 1.

prefect, *n.* —*Syn.* official, consul, regent; see **administrator.**

prefecture, *n.* **1.** [Presidency]—*Syn.* officials, directorship, directors; see **administration** 2.

2. [Jurisdiction]—*Syn.* area, consulate, embassy; see **office** 3.

prefer, *v.* —*Syn.* single out, fix upon, fancy; see **favor** 1.

preferable, *mod.* —*Syn.* more eligible, more desirable, good; see **excellent.**

preferably, *mod.* —*Syn.* by preference, by *or* at choice, by selection, in preference, first, sooner, before, optionally, at pleasure, willingly, at will; see also **rather** 2.

preference, *n.* —*Syn.* favorite, election, option, decision, selection, pick; see also **choice** 3.

preferential, *mod.* —*Syn.* favored, special, advantageous; see **favorite, preferred, unusual** 1.

preferment, *n.* **1.** [Promotion]—*Syn.* elevation, raise, advancement; see **promotion** 1.

2. [Priority]—*Syn.* attention, precedence, station; see **rank** 3.

preferred, *mod.* —*Syn.* chosen, selected, fancied, adopted, picked out, taken, elected, liked, favored, set apart, culled, handpicked, singled out, endorsed, settled upon, sanctioned, decided upon; see also **approved, named** 2.—*Ant.* neglected*, unpreferred, overlooked.

prefigure, *v.* —*Syn.* symbolize, signify, indicate; see **mean** 1.

prefix, *n.* **1.** [An addition]—*Syn.* affix, adjunct, preflex, prefixture.

2. [A designation]—*Syn.* title, cognomen, designation; see **name** 1.

pregnancy, *n.* —*Syn.* reproduction, fertilization, gestation, gravidity, propagation, parturiency, germination, fecundation, productivity, fertility.

pregnant, *mod.* **1.** [With child]—*Syn.* gestating, gravid, fruitful, *enceinte* (French), with child, big with child, parturient, hopeful, anticipating; *both* (D): in a family way, expecting.

2. [Meaningful]—*Syn.* significant, consequential, weighty; see **important** 1.

prehistoric, *mod.* —*Syn.* preceding history, very early, unknown; see **old** 3.

prejudge, *v.* —*Syn.* presuppose, forejudge, presume; see **decide.**

prejudice, *n.* —*Syn.* partiality, unfairness, spleen, bias, detriment, prepossession, enmity, prejudgment, dislike, disgust, aversion, antipathy, racism, sexism, ageism, apartheid, misjudgment, xenophobia, disrelish, umbrage, pique, coolness, animosity, contemptuousness, bad opinion, one-sidedness, narrow-mindedness, displeasure, repugnance, revulsion, preconception, foregone conclusion, quirk, slant, warp, twist; see also **hatred** 1, 2, **inclination** 1, **objection** 2, **spite.**—*Ant.* admiration*, appreciation, good opinion.

without prejudice—*Syn.* **1.** unbiased, objective, unprejudiced; see **fair** 1. **2.** not damaged *or* discredited, unaltered, without implied comment; see **unchanged.**

prejudiced, *mod.* —*Syn.* preconceived, prepossessed, biased, directed against, influenced, inclined, leaning, conditioned, presupposing, predisposed, dogmatic, doctrinaire, pedantic, opinionated, partisan, extreme, intransigent, hidebound, narrow, intolerant, canting, illiberal, racist, sexist, xenophobic, blind, partial, narrow-minded, wedded to an opinion, insular, parochial, provincial, one-sided, not seeing an inch beyond one's nose, squint-eyed, intolerant of, disliking, having a predilection, closed against, judging on slight knowledge, smug.—*Ant.* generous*, open-minded, receptive.

prejudicial, *mod.* —*Syn.* unjust, unfavorable, biased; see **prejudiced.**

prelacy, *n.* **1.** [Hierarchy]—*Syn.* rank, episcopacy, prelatism; see **ministry** 2.

2. [Episcopate]—*Syn.* diocese, pontificate; see **bishopric.**

prelate, *n.* —*Syn.* bishop, cardinal, pope; see **minister** 1, **priest.**

preliminary, *mod.* —*Syn.* preparatory, preceding, prefatory; see **introductory** 1.

prelude, *n.* **1.** [Introduction]—*Syn.* preface, preliminary preparation, prelusion; see **introduction** 1.

2. [Musical piece]—*Syn.* fugue, toccata, overture; see **music** 1.

premarital, *mod.* —*Syn.* before the vows, before marriage, during courtship; see **before** 1.

premature, *mod.* —*Syn.* unanticipated, precipitate, rash; see **early** 2, **untimely.**

prematurely, *mod.* —*Syn.* too early, rash, precipitately; see **early** 2, **untimely.**

premeditate, *v.*—*Syn.* propose, aim, plot; see **intend** 1.

premeditated, *mod.*—*Syn.* intentional, conscious, contrived; see **deliberate** 1, **planned.**

premeditation, *n.*—*Syn.* intention, plot, design; see **plan** 2, **purpose** 1.

premiere, *n.*—*Syn.* first night, beginning, opening; see **performance** 1.

premise, *n.*—*Syn.* proposition, evidence, assumption; see **basis** 1, **proof** 1.

premise, *v.* **1.** [To introduce]—*Syn.* commence, start, announce; see **begin** 1.
2. [To assume]—*Syn.* presuppose, suppose, postulate; see **assume** 1.

premises, *n.* **1.** [Evidence]—*Syn.* testimony, reason, support; see **basis** 1, **proof** 1.
2. [Real estate]—*Syn.* bounds, limits, land; see **property** 2.

premium, *mod.*—*Syn.* prime, superior, select(ed); see **excellent.**

premium, *n.*—*Syn.* remuneration, bonus, annual installment; see **prize.**
at a premium—*Syn.* costly, expensive, rare; see **valuable** 1.

premonition, *n.*—*Syn.* omen, portent, forewarning; see **sign** 1, **warning.**

premonitory, *mod.*—*Syn.* threatening, dismal, indicative; see **imminent, ominous, sinister.**

prenatal, *mod.*—*Syn.* before birth, during pregnancy, fetal; see **before** 1.

preoccupation, *n.*—*Syn.* absorption, daydreaming, amusement; see **distraction** 2.

preoccupied, *mod.*—*Syn.* removed, absorbed, distracted; see **rapt** 2.

preordain, *v.*—*Syn.* appoint, doom, set; see **bless** 3, **predetermine.**

prepaid, *mod.*—*Syn.* shipped paid, with charges paid, settled for (D); see **paid.**

preparation, *n.* **1.** [The act of preparing]—*Syn.* preparing, fitting, making ready, manufacture, readying, putting in order, establishment, compounding, adapting, rehearsal, incubation, gestation, building, construction, formation, maturing, anticipation, founding, foreseeing, development, evolution, furnishing, build-up (D).
2. [The state of being prepared]—*Syn.* preparedness, readiness, fitness, adaptation, suitability, capacity, qualification, background, ripeness, mellowness, maturity, training, education, equipment.
3. [Something that is prepared]—*Syn.* arrangement, product, compound; see **mixture** 1.

preparatory, *mod.*—*Syn.* preliminary, prefatory, previous; see **introductory** 1.

prepare, *v.* **1.** [To make oneself ready]—*Syn.* get ready, foresee, arrange, make preparations *or* arrangements, fit, adapt, qualify, put in order, adjust, set one's house in order, prime, fix, settle, fabricate, appoint, furnish, elaborate, perfect, develop, prepare the ground, lay the foundations, block out, roughhew, smooth the way, man, arm, set for, cut out, warm up, lay the groundwork, contrive, devise, lay by, lay in, make provision, put in readiness, build up (for), provide (for *or* against), make snug, clear the decks, hold oneself in readiness, be prepared, be ready; see also **anticipate** 2, **plan** 1.
2. [To make other persons or things ready]—*Syn.* outfit, equip, fit out; see **provide** 1.
3. [To cook and serve]—*Syn.* concoct, dress, brew; see **cook, serve** 4.

prepared, *mod.* **1.** [Fitted]—*Syn.* adapted, qualified, adjusted; see **able** 2, **fit** 1, 2.
2. [Subjected to a special process or treatment]—*Syn.* treated, frozen, pre-cooked, ready-to-eat, processed; see also **preserved** 2.
3. [Ready]—*Syn.* combat-ready, on the drawing board, instant, programmed, systems "go" (D); see also **ready** 2.

preparedness, *n.*—*Syn.* readiness, mobility, zeal; see **preparation** 2, **willingness.**

preparing, *n.*—*Syn.* fitting, adapting, qualifying; see **preparation** 1.

preponderance, *n.*—*Syn.* supremacy, superiority, dominance; see **advantage** 2, **command** 2, **power** 2.

preponderant, *mod.*—*Syn.* overpowering, significant, dominant; see **predominant** 1, **powerful** 1.

preponderate, *v.*—*Syn.* excel, outdo, predominate; see **exceed, surpass.**

preposition, *n.*—*Syn.* part of speech, word of relationship, conjunctive *or* copulative *or* prefixed element, function word, form word; see also **grammar, word** 1.

prepossessed, *mod.*—*Syn.* biased, opinionated, inclined; see **prejudiced.**

prepossessing, *mod.*—*Syn.* handsome, captivating, attractive; see **charming, pleasant** 1.

prepossession, *n.* **1.** [Preoccupation]—*Syn.* dreaming, pastime, problem; see **distraction** 2.
2. [Bias]—*Syn.* tendency, aversion, partiality; see **inclination** 1, **prejudice.**

preposterous, *mod.*—*Syn.* impossible, fantastic, extreme; see **stupid** 1, **unusual** 2.

preposterousness, *n.*—*Syn.* extravagance, ridiculousness, absurdity; see **impossibility, nonsense** 1, 2, **stupidity** 2.

prepotent, *mod.*—*Syn.* potent, effective, dynamic; see **powerful** 1, **strong** 8.

prerequisite, *mod.*—*Syn.* essential, required, expedient; see **important** 1, **necessary** 1.

prerequisite, *n.*—*Syn.* essential, necessity, need; see **requirement** 1.

prerevolutionary, *mod.*—*Syn.* before a revolution, pre-American Revolution, before the war; see **before** 1.

prerogative, *n.*—*Syn.* privilege, advantage, exemption; see **right** 1.

presage, *v.*—*Syn.* augur, forecast, predict; see **foretell.**

presbyter, *n.*—*Syn.* pastor, priest, clergyman; see **minister** 1.

Presbyterian, *n.*—*Syn.* Christian, non-Catholic, churchgoer; see **Protestant.**

presbytery, *n.* **1.** [Parsonage]—*Syn.* manse, rectory, vicarage; see **parsonage.**
2. [Clergy]—*Syn.* the pulpit, clerics, priesthood; see **ministry** 2.

prescience, *n.*—*Syn.* foresight, prediction, anticipation; see **acumen.**

prescient, *mod.*—*Syn.* perceptive, cautious, foresighted; see **discreet, judicious.**

prescribe, *v.* **1.** [To give directions]—*Syn.* guide, order, appoint; see **command** 2.

2. [To give medical directions]—*Syn.* designate, direct, write a prescription, write directions to a pharmacist.

prescription, *n.* —*Syn.* direction, prescript, medical recipe, formula, prescribed remedy; see also **medicine** 2.

prescriptive, *mod.* —*Syn.* authoritarian, rigid, cut and dried; see **arbitrary** 1, 2, **authoritative, determined** 1.

presence, *n.* **1.** [The fact of being present]—*Syn.* occupancy, occupation, residence, inhabitance, habitancy, ubiquity, ubiety; see also **attendance** 1.
2. [The vicinity of a person]—*Syn.* propinquity, nearness, closeness; see **neighborhood.**
3. [One's appearance and behavior]—*Syn.* carriage, port, demeanor; see **appearance** 1, **behavior** 1.

presence of mind, *n.* —*Syn.* sensibility, alertness, sobriety; see **acumen, watchfulness.**

present, *mod.* **1.** [Near in time]—*Syn.* existing, being, in process, in duration, begun, started, commenced, going on, under consideration, at this time, contemporary, contemporaneous, coeval, ad hoc, immediate, instant, prompt, at this moment, at present, today, nowadays, already, even now, but now, just now, for the time being, for the nonce, for the occasion; see also **modern** 1, **now** 1.—*Ant.* past*, over, completed.
2. [Near in space]—*Syn.* in view, at hand, within reach; see **near** 1.

present, *n.* **1.** [The present time]—*Syn.* instant, this time, present moment; see **today.**
2. [A gift]—*Syn.* grant, donation, offering; see **gift** 1.

present, *v.* **1.** [To introduce]—*Syn.* make known, acquaint with, give an introduction; see **introduce** 3.
2. [To display]—*Syn.* exhibit, show, manifest; see **display** 1.
3. [To suggest]—*Syn.* imply, infer, intimate; see **hint.**
4. [To submit]—*Syn.* donate, proffer, put forth; see **offer** 1.
5. [To give]—*Syn.* grant, bestow, confer; see **give** 1.
6. [To give a play, etc.]—*Syn.* put on, do, impersonate; see **act** 3, **perform** 2.

presentable, *mod.* —*Syn.* attractive, prepared, satisfactory; see **fit** 1, 2.

presentation, *n.* **1.** [The act of presenting]—*Syn.* bestowal, donation, delivering; see **giving.**
2. [Something presented]—*Syn.* present, offering, remembrance; see **gift** 1.

presented, *mod.* —*Syn.* bestowed, granted, conferred; see **given.**

presentiment, *n.* —*Syn.* expectation, apprehension, intuition; see **anticipation** 2.

presently, *mod.* —*Syn.* directly, without delay, shortly; see **immediately, soon** 1.

preservation, *n.* —*Syn.* security, safety, protection, conservation, maintenance, saving, keeping, storage, curing, tanning, freezing, sugaring, pickling, evaporation, canning, refrigeration.

preservative, *mod.* —*Syn.* saving, conservative, protective, preservatory, conservatory, precautionary.

preservative, *n.* —*Syn.* hygenic preserver, chemical, preserving agent, prophylaxis.

preserve, *v.* **1.** [To guard]—*Syn.* protect, shield, save; see **defend** 2.
2. [To maintain]—*Syn.* keep up, care for, conserve; see **maintain** 3.
3. [To keep]—*Syn.* can, conserve, process, save, put up, put down, souse, store, cure, bottle, do up, season, salt, pickle, put in brine, put in vinegar, pot, tin, dry, sun-dry, smoke, corn, dry-cure, smoke-cure, freeze, quick freeze, keep up, cold-pack, refrigerate, dehydrate, seal up, kipper, marinate, evaporate, embalm, mummify, mothball, fill. —*Ant.* waste*, allow to spoil, let spoil.

preserved, *mod.* **1.** [Saved]—*Syn.* rescued, guarded, secured; see **saved** 1.
2. [Prepared for preservation]—*Syn.* conserved, dried, freeze-dried, sun-dried, dehydrated, evaporated, smoked, seasoned, pickled, canned, salted, brined, jerked, put down, put up, kippered, cured, corned, marinated, tinned, potted, bottled, cyanized, embalmed, mummified.

preserves, *n.* —*Syn.* spread, sweet, conserve, marmalade, jell, pickles, extract, gelatin, pectin; see also **jam** 1, **jelly** 1.

preside, *v.* —*Syn.* direct, lead, control; see **advise** 1, **manage** 1.

presidency, *n.* —*Syn.* office of the president, chairmanship, position; see **administration** 2.

president, *n.* —*Syn.* presiding officer, chief director, Great White Father (D); see **administrator.**

presidential, *mod.* —*Syn.* official, regulatory, of the chief executive; see **administrative.**

presiding, *n.* —*Syn.* supervising, controlling, directing; see **managing, organization** 1, 2.

press, *n.* **1.** [The pressure of circumstances]—*Syn.* rush, confusion, strain; see **haste** 2.
2. [Publishing as a social institution]—*Syn.* the Fourth Estate, publishers, publicists, newsmen, newspapermen, journalists, journalistic writers, editors, correspondents, political writers, columnists, periodicals, print media, periodical press, papers, newspapers; see also **newspaperman, reporter.**
3. [A printing press] Types of presses include the following—rotary, web, automatic, hand, unit-type, multicolor, twelve cylinder, twenty-four cylinder, universal-unit multi-color, flatbed, high-speed, rotogravure; see also **machine** 1.

press, *v.* **1.** [To subject to pressure]—*Syn.* thrust, crowd, bear upon, bear down on *or* upon, squeeze, hold *or* pin *or* screw *or* force down, throng, crush, drive, weight, urge; see also **compress, push** 1. —*Ant.* raise*, release, relieve.
2. [To smooth, usually by heat and pressure] —*Syn.* finish, mangle, roll; see also **iron, smooth** 1.
3. [To embrace]—*Syn.* clasp, encircle, enfold; see **caress, hold** 1, **hug, touch** 1.

press agent, *n.* —*Syn.* publicizer, advertiser, publicist; see **reporter.**

press conference, *n.* —*Syn.* interview, public report *or* statement, briefing; see **announcement** 1, **hearing.**

pressed, *mod.* —*Syn.* rushed, in a hurry, pushed, rushing, closely timed, fast, urged (on), short, limited, pressured.

pressing, *mod.* —*Syn.* importunate, constraining, distressing; see **important, urgent** 1.

pressman, *n.* **1.** [A printer]—*Syn.* compositor, linotypist, typesetter; see **printer.**
2. [A reporter]—*Syn.* journalist, newspaperman, correspondent; see **reporter.**

pressure, *n.* **1.** [Physical pressure]—*Syn.* force, burden, mass, load, encumbrance, stress, thrust, tension, shear, squeeze (D); see also **strength** 1, **weight** 1.—*Ant.* release*, relief, deliverance.
2. [Some form of social pressure]—*Syn.* compulsion, constraint, urgency, demand, persuasion, stress, affliction, coercion, trouble, hardship, humiliation, misfortune, necessity, requirement, repression, confinement, unnaturalness, obligation, discipline; see also **influence** 2, **oppression** 1, **restraint** 2, **urging.**—*Ant.* aid*, assistance, encouragement.

pressure, *v.* —*Syn.* press, compel, constrain; see **urge** 2, 3.

pressure group, *n.* —*Syn.* clique, special interest(s), lobbyist; see **organization** 3.

presswork, *n.* —*Syn.* typography, publishing, copying; see **printing.**

prestige, *n.* —*Syn.* renown, éclat, influence; see **fame** 1.

presumable, *mod.* —*Syn.* seeming, probable, apparent; see **likely** 1.

presumably, *mod.* —*Syn.* reasonable, credible, likely; see **probably.**

presume, *v.* —*Syn.* consider, suppose, take for granted; see **assume** 1.

presuming, *mod.* —*Syn.* arrogant, proud, presumptuous; see **egotistic** 2.

presumption, *n.* **1.** [An assumption]—*Syn.* conjecture, guess, hypothesis; see **assumption** 1.
2. [Impudence]—*Syn.* arrogance, audacity, effrontery; see **rudeness.**

presumptive, *mod.* —*Syn.* assumptive, circumstantial, possible; see **hypothetical** 1, **likely** 1.

presumptuous, *mod.* —*Syn.* arrogant, insolent, bold; see **egotistic** 2, **rude** 2.

presuppose, *v.* —*Syn.* presume, suppose, consider; see **assume** 1.

pretend, *v.* **1.** [To feign]—*Syn.* affect, simulate, claim falsely, imitate, counterfeit, sham, make as if *or* though, dissimulate, mislead, beguile, delude, pass (off) for, cheat, cozen, dupe, hoodwink, be deceitful, bluff, falsify, be hypocritical; *all* (D): pull a phoney, fake, put on, let on, go through the motions, sail under false colors, keep up appearances; see also **deceive.**
2. [To make believe]—*Syn.* mimic, fill a role, take a part, represent, portray, put on a front, dash off, make out like, play, make as if, make believe, act the part of; *all* (D): put on big looks, put on (an act), act a part, put on lugs, put on airs, playact; see also **act** 3, **imitate** 2, **impersonate, reproduce** 2.

pretended, *mod.* —*Syn.* feigned, counterfeit, assumed, affected, shammed, bluffing, simulated, dissimulated, lying, falsified, put on, concealed, covered, masked, cheating; see also **false** 3.

pretender, *n.* —*Syn.* fraud, hypocrite, rogue; see **cheat** 1.

pretending, *n.* —*Syn.* feigning, assumption, shamming, bluffing, dissembling, counterfeiting, simulation, dissimulation, concealment, covering, masking, cheating, screening.

pretense, *n.* **1.** [The act of pretending]—*Syn.* affectation, misrepresentation, falsification, act, deceit, fabrication, trickery, double-dealing, misstatement, shuffling, falsifying, simulation, excuse, insincerity, profession, ostentation, assumption, dissembling, dissimulation, evasion, equivocation, prevarication, egotism, brazenness, arrogance, dandyism, foppery, servility, toadyism, obsequiousness, sycophancy, cringing, truckling, timeserving, complacency, smugness, priggishness, prudishness, coyness, formality, stiffness; *both* (D): blind, smoke screen; see also **dishonesty, imitation** 1.—*Ant.* honesty*, candor, sincerity.
2. [Something pretended]—*Syn.* gloss, falsehood, lie, falseness, affectedness, affectation, mask, cloak, show, excuse, subterfuge, pretext, fraud, appearance, seeming, semblance, wile, ruse, sham, airs, claim, mannerism; see also **deception** 1, **imitation** 2, **trick** 1.

pretension, *n.* **1.** [A claim]—*Syn.* assertion, demand, declaration; see **claim.**
2. [A pretense]—*Syn.* allegation, pretext, maintenance; see **ostentation** 2.

pretentious, *mod.* —*Syn.* gaudy, ostentatious, conspicuous; see **ornate** 1.

preterit, *mod.* —*Syn.* past time, past action, preceding; see **past** 1.

preternatural, *mod.* —*Syn.* ghostly, irregular, unnatural; see **mysterious** 2, **supernatural.**

pretext, *n.* —*Syn.* appearance, affection, guise; see **pretense** 1.

prettily, *mod.* —*Syn.* pleasingly, gently, quietly; see **politely.**

pretty, *mod.* **1.** [Attractive]—*Syn.* comely, lovely, good-looking; see **beautiful** 1.
2. [Pleasant]—*Syn.* delightful, cheerful, pleasing; see **pleasant** 2.
3. [(D) Considerable]—*Syn.* ample, sizeable, notable; see **large** 1, **much** 1, 2.
4. [Somewhat]—*Syn.* rather, tolerably, a little; see **moderately.**
sitting pretty (D)—*Syn.* in a favorable position, prospering, thriving; see **successful.**

prevail, *v.* —*Syn.* predominate, preponderate, control; see **command** 2.

prevailing, *mod.* —*Syn.* prevalent, general, popular, current, regular, steady, predominant, universal, catholic, worldwide, sweeping, all-embracing, comprehensive, widespread, ecumenical; see also **common** 1.

prevail upon, *v.* —*Syn.* convince, sway, persuade; see **influence.**

prevalence, *n.* —*Syn.* dissemination, occurrence, currency; see **regularity.**

prevalent, *mod.* —*Syn.* widespread, accepted, frequently met; see **common** 1, **prevailing.**

prevaricate, —*Syn.* exaggerate, distort, falsify; see **lie** 1.

prevarication, *n.* —*Syn.* deception, dishonesty, falsehood; see **lie** 1.

prevaricator, *n.* —*Syn.* perjurer, hypocrite, deceiver; see **liar.**

prevent, *v.* —*Syn.* preclude, obviate, forestall, anticipate, block, arrest, stop, thwart, debar, repress, interrupt, halt, impede, check, avert, frustrate, balk, foil, retard, obstruct, counter, countercheck, counteract, inhibit, restrict, block off, limit, hold back *or* off, stop from, deter, intercept, override, circumvent, bar, ward off, keep from happening, nip in the bud, put a stop *or* an end to, stave *or* keep *or* draw off, turn aside; see also **hinder, restrain** 1. —*Ant.* help*, aid, encourage.

preventative, *n.* —*Syn.* safeguard, remedy, protection; see **medicine** 2.

prevented, *mod.* —*Syn.* obviated, stopped, interfered with; see **interrupted.**

prevention, *n.* —*Syn.* anticipation, forestalling, arresting, preclusion, obviating, bar, debarring, halt, impeding, foil, retardation, repression, restraint, restriction, inhibition, interception, overriding, circumvention, hindering, counteraction, obstruction, opposition, warding *or* staving *or* drawing *or* keeping off, stopping, thwarting, blocking; see also **refusal.**—*Ant.* aid*, encouragement, help.

preventive, *mod.* —*Syn.* deterrent, precautionary, tending to prevent; see **defensive.**

preview, *n.* —*Syn.* preliminary showing *or* viewing, presurvey, preliminary view, research, prior examination, preliminary study; see also **show** 1.

previous, *mod.* **1.** [Earlier]—*Syn.* antecedent, prior, former; see **preceding.**

2. [(D) Too early]—*Syn.* premature, unfounded, unwarranted; see **early** 2.

previously, *mod.* —*Syn.* long ago, earlier, beforehand; see **before** 1.

prewar, *mod.* —*Syn.* before a war, prerevolutionary, time of peace; see **peacetime.**

prey, *n.* —*Syn.* spoil, pillage, loot; see **victim** 1.

prey on, *v.* **1.** [To destroy]—*Syn.* seize, raid, pillage; see **destroy** 1.

2. [To eat]—*Syn.* feed on, devour, consume; see **eat** 1.

price, *n.* —*Syn.* expenditure, outlay, expense, cost, value, worth, figure, impost, dues, tariff, valuation, appraisement, quotation, fare, hire, wages, exactment, return, disbursement, rate, appraisal, reckoning, equivalent, payment, demand, barter, consideration, amount, marked price, asking price, wholesale price, list price, retail price, discount price, sticker price, estimate, output, exaction, ransom, reward, carry charge, pay, prize, return, guerdon, par value, requital, money's worth, price ceiling, ceiling; see also **charge** 1.

at any price—*Syn.* whatever the cost, expense no object, anyhow; see **regardless.**

beyond price—*Syn.* invaluable, inestimable, priceless; see valuable 1.

price, *v.* —*Syn.* put a price on, fix the price of, appraise, assess, estimate a price, mark up, mark down, reduce, sticker (D); see also **rate, value** 2.

priced, *mod.* —*Syn.* valued, estimated, worth; see **costing.**

priced out of the market, *mod.* —*Syn.* (too) high-priced, unreasonable, not competitive; see **expensive.**

priceless, *mod.* —*Syn.* invaluable, inestimable, without price; see **valuable** 1.

prick, *n.* —*Syn.* tap, stab, probing; see **cut** 1.

prick, *v.* —*Syn.* pierce, puncture, spur; see **cut** 1, **hurt** 1.

prickle, *n.* **1.** [A needle]—*Syn.* pin, spine, spike; see **needle** 1, 2.

2. [A sensation]—*Syn.* chill, tingling, tickle; see **feeling** 1.

prickle, *v.* —*Syn.* provoke laughter, sting, tingle; see **tickle** 1.

prickly, *mod.* —*Syn.* thorny, pointed, spiny; see **sharp** 2, **stimulating.**

prick up one's ears, *v.* —*Syn.* pay attention (to), notice, listen to; see **listen** 1.

pride, *n.* **1.** [The quality of being vain]—*Syn.* vainglory, egoism, egotism, self-esteem, self-love, self-exaltation, self-glorification, self-admiration, smugness, pretension; *all* (D): big-headedness, proud flesh, chest expansion.—*Ant.* humility*, self-effacement, unpretentiousness.

2. [Conduct growing from pride, sense 1]—*Syn.* haughtiness, vanity, disdain; see **arrogance.**

3. [Sense of personal satisfaction]—*Syn.* self-respect, self-satisfaction, self-sufficiency; see **happiness** 2.

4. [A source of satisfaction]—*Syn.* enjoyment, repletion, sufficiency; see **satisfaction** 2.

5. [A group of animals, especially lions]—*Syn.* pack, drove, bunch; see **herd** 1.

pride oneself on, *v.* —*Syn.* take pride in, flatter oneself, be proud of; see **boast** 1.

priest, *n.* —Names for priests in various sects include the following—father confessor, spiritual father, priest-vicar, high priest, minor canon, pontiff, vicar, care of souls, clergyman, rector, preacher, presbyter, elder, *kohen* (Hebrew), rabbi, lama, monk, friar; see also **minister** 1.

priestcraft, *n.* —*Syn.* priesthood, clergy, monasticism; see **ministry** 2.

priestess, *n.* —*Syn.* clergywoman, ministress, lady preacher; see **minister** 1.

priesthood, *n.* —*Syn.* clergy, Holy Orders, monasticism; see **ministry** 2.

priestly, *mod.* —*Syn.* ecclesiastic, episcopal, ministerial; see **clerical** 2.

prig, *n.* —*Syn.* prude, puritan, formalist; see **bigot.**

priggish, *mod.* —*Syn.* vain, proud, pompous; see **egotistic** 2.

priggishness, *n.* —*Syn.* simulation, puritanism, affectation; see **hypocrisy, pretense** 1.

prim, *mod.* —*Syn.* stiff, formal, precise, demure, decorous, nice, orderly, tidy, cleanly, trim, spruce, pat; see also **polite** 1.

primacy, *n.* —*Syn.* supremacy, prelacy, authority; see **power** 2.

prima donna, *n.* —*Syn.* star, actress, vocalist; see **singer.**

prima-facie (Latin), *mod.* —*Syn.* superficial, seemingly, by all appearances; see **apparently.**

primarily, *mod.* —*Syn.* originally, fundamentally, in the first place; see **essentially, principally.**

primary, *mod.* **1.** [Earliest]—*Syn.* primitive, initial, first; see **original** 1.

2. [Fundamental]—*Syn.* elemental, basic, central; see **fundamental** 1.

3. [Principal]—*Syn.* chief, prime, main; see **principal.**

primary school, *n.* —*Syn.* elementary school, first *or* lower grades, kindergarten; see **school** 1.
primate, *n.* —*Syn.* gorilla, chimpanzee, orangutan, gibbon, great ape, cercopithecoid, animal capable of fully erect *or* semi-erect posture, hominoid, brachiator; see also **hominid, man** 1.
prime, *mod.* **1.** [Principal]—*Syn.* earliest, beginning, original; see **principal.**
2. [Excellent]—*Syn.* top, choice, superior; see **best** 1, **excellent.**
primed, *mod.* —*Syn.* qualified, prepared, educated; see **able** 2, **fit** 1, 2.
prime minister, *n.* —*Syn.* executive, leader, PM (D); see **administrator.**
prime mover, *n.* —*Syn.* supreme being, creator, author; see **god** 2, 3.
primer, *n.* —*Syn.* beginner's book, preparatory book, hornbook; see **introduction** 3, 5.
primeval, *mod.* —*Syn.* ancient, primitive, primal; see **old** 3.
primitive, *mod.* **1.** [Simple]—*Syn.* rudimentary, first; see **fundamental** 1.
2. [Ancient]—*Syn.* primeval, archaic, primordial; see **old** 3.
3. [Uncivilized]—*Syn.* crude, rough, simple, rude, atavistic, uncivilized, savage, uncultured, natural, barbaric, barbarous, barbarian, fierce, untamed, uncouth, Gothic, ignorant, undomesticated, wild, animal, brutish, raw, untaught, aboriginal, green, unlearned, untutored, underdeveloped; see also **fierce** 1, **savage** 1, 3.
primp (D), *v.* —*Syn.* make one's toilet, paint and powder, get (all) dressed up (D); see **dress** 1, **groom, prepare** 1.
prince, *n.* —*Syn.* sovereign, ruler, monarch, potentate; see also **royalty.**
princely, *mod.* —*Syn.* sovereign, regal, august; see **royal** 1.
princess, *n.* —*Syn.* female ruler, sovereign, monarch, dauphiness, czarina, infanta; see also **royalty.**
Princeton, *n.* —*Syn.* Princeton University, Princeton College, College of New Jersey, Nassau Hall; *all* (D): Orange and Black, one of the Big Three, Old Nassau, Tiger; see also **university.**
principal, *mod.* —*Syn.* leading, chief, first, head, prime, main, foremost, cardinal, essential, capital, important, preeminent, highest, supreme, prominent, dominant, predominant, predominating, supereminent, controlling, superior, prevailing, paramount, greatest, front rank, incomparable, unapproachable, unapproached, peerless, matchless, transcendant, unequaled, unrivaled, maximum, crowning, unparalleled, sovereign, second to none; *both* (D): mainline, high mucky-muck. —*Ant.* unimportant*, secondary, accessory.
principal, *n.* —*Syn.* chief, head, chief party, master; see also **administrator.**
principality, *n.* —*Syn.* realm, country, state; see **territory** 2.
principally, *mod.* —*Syn.* chiefly, mainly, essentially, substantially, materially, eminently, pre-eminently, superlatively, supremely, vitally, especially, particularly, peculiarly, notably, importantly, fundamentally, dominantly, predominantly, basically, largely, first and foremost, in large measure, first of all, to a great degree, prevailingly, prevalently, generally, universally, mostly, above all, cardinally, in the first place, to crown all, for the most part, for the greatest part, before anything else, in the main. —*Ant.* slightly*, somewhat, tolerably.
principle, *n.* **1.** [A fundamental law]—*Syn.* origin, source, postulate; see **law** 4.
2. [A belief or set of beliefs; *often plural*]—*Syn.* system, opinion, teaching; see **belief** 1, **faith** 2, **policy.**
in principle—*Syn.* in theory, ideally, in essence; see **theoretically.**
principles, *n.* —*Syn.* ideals, standard of conduct, beliefs; see **attitude** 3, **character** 1, 2.
print, *n.* **1.** [Printed matter]—*Syn.* impression, reprint, issue; see **copy, edition.**
Forms of print include the following—line, galley proof, page proof, slip, pull, trial impression, foundry proof, page, sheet, spread, throwaway, first printing, second printing, letterpress, offset, inkjet.
2. [A printed picture]—*Syn.* engraving, lithograph, photograph; see **picture** 3, **sketch** 1.
in print—*Syn.* printed, available, obtainable; see **published.**
out of print—*Syn.* O.P., unavailable, remaindered; see **sold** 1.
print, *v.* **1.** [To make an impression]—*Syn.* impress, imprint, indent; see **mark** 1.
2. [To reproduce by printing]—*Syn.* run off, print up, issue, reissue, reprint, disseminate, bring out, go to press, set type, compose, see through the press, pull proof, start the presses, take an impression; *all* (D): put to bed, machine off, let them roll; see also **publish** 1.—*Ant.* talk*, write, inscribe.
3. [To simulate printing]—*Syn.* letter, do lettering, calligraph; see **write** 2.
printed, *mod.* —*Syn.* impressed, imprinted, engraved, stamped, lithographed, multilithed, Xeroxed (trademark), printed by (photo-)offset, printed by cold *or* hot type, silkscreened; see also **reproduced.**
printer, *n.* —Workers in print shops include the following—typesetter, compositor, linotype operator, pressman, proofreader, stereotyper, mat man, printer's devil; see also **workman.**
printing, *n.* **1.** [A process of reproduction]—*Syn.* typography, composition, type-setting, presswork.
2. [Printed matter]—*Syn.* line, page, sheet; see **print** 1.
3. [Publication]—*Syn.* issuing, issuance, distribution; see **publication** 1.
printing press, *n.* —*Syn.* rotary press, cylinder press, machine; see **press** 3.
prior, *mod.* —*Syn.* antecedent, above-mentioned, foregoing; see **preceding.**
priority, *n.* —*Syn.* superiority, preference, precedence, antecedence, precedency, previousness, pre-existence, preterition, earliness, preclude, pre-eminence, right of way; see also **advantage** 1, 2.
priory, *n.* —*Syn.* convent, monastery, hermitage; see **cloister.**
prism, *n.* **1.** [A stone]—*Syn.* crystal, pebble, gem; see **rock** 2, **stone.**
2. [A refractor]—*Syn.* optical instrument, kaleidoscope, spectroscope, spectrometer; see also **crystal.**
prismatic, *mod.* —*Syn.* chromatic, kaleidoscopic, colorful; see **bright** 1, 2, **multicolored.**

prison, *n.* —*Syn.* penitentiary, reformatory, prison house, panopticon, guardhouse, stockade; see also **jail.**

prisoner, *n.* —*Syn.* captive, convict, culprit, jailbird, detainee, the legally retarded, escapee, hostage, con (D); see also **defendant.**

prisoner of war, *n.* —*Syn.* captive *or* captured *or* interned person *or* personnel, person in captivity, one not liberated, person covered by international law or agreements, POW (D); see also **prisoner.**

prison ward, *n.* —*Syn.* maximum security, pen, confinement area; see **cell** 3, **room** 2.

pristine, *mod.* —*Syn.* primitive, initial, primary; see **fundamental** 1.

privacy, *n.* —*Syn.* seclusion, solitude, retreat, isolation, sequestration, separateness, aloofness, separation, concealment; see also **retirement** 2, **secrecy.**

private, *mod.* —*Syn.* special, separate, sequestered, retired, secluded, withdrawn, removed, not open, behind the scenes, off the record, privy, *in camera* (Latin), clandestine, single; see also **hidden** 2, **individual** 1, **isolated, own, secret** 1, **solitary.**—*Ant.* public*, open, exposed.

in private—*Syn.* privately, personally, not public; see **secretly.**

private, *n.* —*Syn.* enlisted man, infantryman; private first class, second class, etc.; see **sailor, soldier.**

privateer, *n.* **1.** [Pirate ship]—*Syn.* private vessel, armed vessel, freebooter; see **ship.**

2. [Pirate]—*Syn.* buccaneer, corsair, freebooter; see **pirate.**

privately, *mod.* —*Syn.* confidentially, clandestinely, alone; see **personally** 1, **secretly.**

private parts, *n.* —*Syn.* (genital) organs, organs of reproduction, privates; see **genitals.**

privation, *n.* —*Syn.* want, destitution, penury; see **poverty** 1.

privilege, *n.* **1.** [A customary concession]—*Syn.* due, perquisite, prerogative; see **right** 1.

2. [An opportunity]—*Syn.* chance, fortunate happening, event; see **opportunity** 1.

privileged, *mod.* —*Syn.* free, vested, furnished; see **exempt.**

privy, *mod.* —*Syn.* confidential, personal, separate; see **private.**

privy, *n.* —*Syn.* outhouse, backhouse, outdoor toilet, latrine, outside privy; see also **toilet** 2.

privy to, *mod.* —*Syn.* conscious of, acquainted with, aware (of); see **conscious** 1.

prize, *n.* —*Syn.* reward, advantage, privilege, possession, honor, inducement, premium, meed, guerdon, bounty, bonus, spoil, booty, plunder, pillage, loot, award, accolade, recompense, requital, acquisitions, acquirements, laurel, decoration, medal, trophy, palm, crown, citation, scholarship, fellowship, feather in one's cap, blue ribbon, title, championship, first place, mark of honor; *all* (D): pay-off, bacon, cake, gravy, plum, hand-painted doormat, swag.

prize, *v.* —*Syn.* guess, count, esteem; see **estimate** 1, **rate, value** 2.

prize fight, *n.* —*Syn.* boxing match, fight, ring (D); see **boxing, sport** 3.

prize fighter, *n.* —*Syn.* boxer, pugilist, contender; see **fighter** 2.

prize ring, *n.* —*Syn.* the ring, gymnasium, arena; see **ring** 5.

probability, *n.* —*Syn.* contingency, hazard, plausibility, reasonableness, conceivability, prospect, likeliness, promise, likelihood, possibility, chance, credibility, expectation, presumption, anticipation, practicability, feasibility, odds; see also **chance** 1, **possibility** 2.—*Ant.* doubt*, improbability, doubtfulness.

probable, *mod.* —*Syn.* seeming, presumable, feasible; see **likely** 1.

probably, *mod.* —*Syn.* presumably, seemingly, apparently, believably, reasonably, imaginably, feasibly, practicably, expediently, plausibly, most likely, everything being equal, as like as not, as the case may be, one can assume, like enough, no doubt, to all appearance, in all probability.—*Ant.* unlikely*, doubtfully, questionably.

probation, *n.* —*Syn.* period of trial, ordeal, moral trial; see **punishment.**

probe, *n.* —*Syn.* exploration, scrutiny, inquiry; see **examination** 1.

probe, *v.* —*Syn.* investigate, pierce deeply, penetrate; see **examine** 1.

probity, *n.* —*Syn.* fidelity, honor, integrity; see **honesty** 1.

problem, *n.* **1.** [A difficulty]—*Syn.* dilemma, quandary, obstacle; see **difficulty** 1, 2, **predicament.**

2. [A question to be solved]—*Syn.* query, intricacy, enigma; see **puzzle** 2.

problematic, *mod.* —*Syn.* problematical, unsettled, doubtful; see **questionable** 1, **uncertain** 2.

procedure, *n.* **1.** [Method]—*Syn.* fashion, style, mode; see **method** 2, **system** 2.

2. [Plan]—*Syn.* course of action, idea, scheme; see **plan** 2.

proceed, *v.* —*Syn.* move, progress, continue; see **advance** 1.

proceeding, *n.* [*Often plural*]—*Syn.* process, transaction, deed, experiment, performance, measure, step, course, undertaking, venture, adventure, occurrence, incident, casualty, circumstance, happening, movement, operation, procedure, exercise, maneuver; see also **action** 2.

proceedings, *n.* —*Syn.* documents, minutes, account; see **records.**

proceeds, *n.* **1.** [Product]—*Syn.* result(s), reward, income; see **profit** 2.

2. [A return]—*Syn.* gain, interest, yield; see **return** 3.

process, *n.* —*Syn.* means, rule, manner; see **method** 2.

in (the) process of—*Syn.* while, when, in the course of; see **during.**

process, *v.* —*Syn.* treat, make ready, concoct; see **prepare** 1.

processed, *mod.* —*Syn.* treated, handled, fixed; see **prepared** 2.

procession, *n.* —*Syn.* train, advance, cavalcade; see **parade** 1.

proclaim, *v.* —*Syn.* advertise, give out, blazon; see **declare** 1.

proclamation, *n.* —*Syn.* promulgation, official publication, advertisement; see **announcement** 1.

procrastinate, *v.* —*Syn.* defer, pause, gain time; see **delay** 1, **hesitate.**

procreation, *n.* —*Syn.* conception, impregnation, generation, breeding, propagation; see also **reproduction** 1.
proctor, *n.* —*Syn.* appointee, minister, representative; see **agent** 1, **delegate.**
procurable, *mod.* —*Syn.* attainable, obtainable, on the market, for sale, purchasable, on sale; see also **available.**
procure, *v.* —*Syn.* get, secure, gain; see **obtain** 1.
procurement, *n.* —*Syn.* obtainment, acquirement, appropriation; see **acquisition** 1.
procurer, *n.* —*Syn.* pander, whoremonger, runner; see **pimp.**
procuress, *n.* —*Syn.* whoremonger, whore, madam; see **prostitute.**
procuring, *n.* —*Syn.* obtaining, acquiring, gaining; see **acquisition** 1.
prod, *v.* —*Syn.* provoke, crowd, shove; see **push** 1.
prodigal, *mod.* —*Syn.* lavish, luxuriant, squandering; see **wasteful.**
prodigality, *n.* **1.** [Affluence]—*Syn.* money, profusion, abundance; see **wealth** 2.
2. [Wastefulness]—*Syn.* dissipation, lavishness, extravagance; see **waste** 1.
prodigious, *mod.* —*Syn.* huge, immense, monstrous; see **large** 1.
prodigy, *n.* —*Syn.* marvel, portent, miracle, monster, enormity, spectacle, freak, curiosity; see also **wonder** 2.
produce, *n.* —*Syn.* product, fruitage, harvest, result, resultant, crop, return, effect, consequence, amount, profit, ingathering, outcome, outgrowth, aftermath, gain, emolument, realization; see also **butter, cheese, cream** 1, **food, fruit** 1, **grain** 1, **milk, vegetable.**
produce, *v.* **1.** [To bear]—*Syn.* yield, bring *or* give forth, give birth (to), propagate, bring out, come through, blossom, flower, deliver, generate, engender, breed, contribute, give, afford, furnish, return, render, show fruit, fructify, fetch, bring in, present, offer, provide, contribute, sell for, bear (fruit), accrue, allow, admit, proliferate, be delivered of, bring to birth, reproduce, foal, lamb, drop, be brought to bed, calve, fawn, whelp, cub, kitten, hatch, farrow, throw, usher into the world, spawn; see also **yield** 2.
2. [To create by mental effort]—*Syn.* originate, author, procreate, bring forth, conceive, engender, effectuate, write, design, fabricate, imagine, turn out, devise; see also **compose** 3, **create** 2, **invent** 1, 2.
3. [To cause]—*Syn.* effect, occasion, bring about; see **begin** 1.
4. [To show]—*Syn.* exhibit, present, unfold; see **display** 1.
5. [To make]—*Syn.* assemble, build, construct; see **manufacture** 1.
6. [To present a performance]—*Syn.* present, play, put on the stage; see **act** 3, **perform** 2.
produced, *mod.* **1.** [Created]—*Syn.* originated, composed, made; see **formed.**
2. [Presented]—*Syn.* performed, acted, put on, shown, staged, brought out, offered, presented, imparted, rendered.
3. [Caused]—*Syn.* occasioned, propagated, begot, bred, engendered, generated, hatched, induced.
producer, *n.* —*Syn.* raiser, yielder, generator; see **farmer.**
producing, *mod.* —*Syn.* bearing, bringing forth, generating; see **fertile** 1, 2.
product, *n.* **1.** [A result]—*Syn.* output, outcome, produce; see **result.**
2. [*Often plural;* goods produced]—*Syn.* stock, goods, merchandise, manufactured product; see also **commodity.**
production, *n.* **1.** [The act of producing]—*Syn.* origination, creation, authoring, reproduction, yielding, giving, bearing, rendering, giving forth, increasing, augmentation, accrual, return, procreation, occasioning, generation, engendering, fructification, fruiting, blooming, blossoming; see also **making.**
2. [The amount produced]—*Syn.* crop, result, stock; see **product** 2.
make a production out of (D)—*Syn.* fuss over, elaborate, exaggerate; see **overdo** 1.
productive, *mod.* —*Syn.* rich, fruitful, prolific; see **fertile** 1, 2.
productivity, *n.* —*Syn.* richness, potency, fecundity; see **fertility** 1.
profanation, *n.* —*Syn.* profanity, impiety, abuse; see **blasphemy, heresy, sin.**
profane, *mod.* **1.** [Worldly]—*Syn.* temporal, transitory, transient; see **worldly** 2.
2. [Irreverent]—*Syn.* godless, irreligious, sacrilegious; see **atheistic, impious** 1.
profane, *v.* —*Syn.* despoil, commit sacrilege, befoul, revile, commit sin, be irreligious, scorn, mock, indulge in vice, be evil, do wrong, blaspheme, swear, curse, cuss (D).
profanity, *n.* —*Syn.* abuse, cursing, swearing; see **blasphemy.**
profess, *v.* —*Syn.* avow, confess, pretend; see **declare** 1.
professed, *mod.* —*Syn.* avowed, declared, pledged; see **announced, told.**
professedly, *mod.* —*Syn.* slyly, deceptively, basely; see **falsely.**
profession, *n.* **1.** [A skilled or learned occupation] —*Syn.* calling, business, avocation, vocation, employment, occupation, engagement, office, situation, position, lifework, chosen work, billet, role, service, pursuit, undertaking, concern, post, berth, craft, sphere, field, specialty, walk of life; see also **church** 3, **education** 3, **journalism, law** 5, **medicine** 3, **trade** 2.
2. [A declaration]—*Syn.* pretense, avowal, vow; see **declaration** 1, **oath** 1.
professional, *mod.* **1.** [Skillful]—*Syn.* expert, learned, adept; see **able** 1, **trained.**
2. [Well-qualified]—*Syn.* acknowledged, known, licensed; see **able** 2.
professional, *n.* —*Syn.* expert, trained *or* experienced personnel, specially trained person; see **specialist.**
professor, *n.* —*Syn.* schoolmaster, pedagogue, educator, faculty member, dominie, pundit, don (British), savant, sage; see also **teacher** 2.
Teachers popularly called professors include the following—full professor, associate professor, assistant professor, professor emeritus, instructor, lecturer, graduate assistant, teaching assistant *or*

T.A. (D), tutor, school principal, fellow, teaching fellow, master docent.

professorial, *mod.* —*Syn.* academic, scholastic, scholarly; see **learned** 1, 2.

proficiency, *n.* —*Syn.* learning, skill, knowledge; see **ability** 1, 2.

proficient, *mod.* —*Syn.* skilled, expert, skillful; see **able** 2.

profile, *n.* —*Syn.* silhouette, shape, figure; see **form** 1, **outline** 4.

profit, *n.* **1.** [Advantage]—*Syn.* avail, good, value; see **advantage** 3.
2. [Excess of receipts over expenditures]—*Syn.* gain, return(s), proceeds, receipts, take, gate, emolument, acquisition, rake-off, accumulation, saving, aggrandizement, augmentation, interest, remuneration, earnings.—*Ant.* loss*, debits, costs.

profit, *v.* **1.** [To be of benefit]—*Syn.* benefit, assist, avail; see **help** 1.
2. [To derive gain]—*Syn.* benefit, capitalize on, cash in on, realize, clear, gain, reap profits, make a profit, recover, thrive, prosper, harvest, make money.—*Ant.* lose*, lose out on, miss out on.

profitable, *mod.* —*Syn.* lucrative, useful, sustaining, self-sustaining, aiding, remunerative, beneficial, gainful, advantageous, paying, successful, favorable, assisting, productive, serviceable, valuable, contributive, conducive, instrumental, practical, pragmatic, effective, to advantage, effectual, sufficient, paying its way, bringing in returns, making money, paying well; *both* (D): paying out, in the black; see also **helpful** 1.—*Ant.* unprofitable*, unsuccessful, unproductive.

profitably, *mod.* —*Syn.* lucratively, remuneratively, gainfully, usefully, advantageously, successfully, favorably, for money, productively, practically, effectively, effectually, sufficiently, sustainingly.

profiteer, *n.* —*Syn.* exploiter, chiseler, cheater; see **cheat** 1.

profitless, *mod.* —*Syn.* vain, futile, ineffectual; see **useless** 1, **worthless** 1.

profligate, *mod.* —*Syn.* dissolute, abandoned, depraved; see **lewd** 2, **wicked** 1.

profound, *mod.* **1.** [Physically deep]—*Syn.* fathomless, bottomless, subterranean; see **deep** 1.
2. [Intellectually deep]—*Syn.* recondite, heavy, erudite, scholarly, abstruse, mysterious, sage, serious, sagacious, penetrating, discerning, knowing, wise, reflective, knowledgeable, intellectual, enlightened, thorough, informed, of great learning, immensely learned; see also **intelligent** 1, **learned** 2, **solemn** 1.—*Ant.* superficial*, shallow, flighty.
3. [Emotionally deep]—*Syn.* heartfelt, deep-felt, great; see **intense.**

profoundly, *mod.* —*Syn.* deeply, extremely, thoroughly; see **very.**

profundity, *n.* **1.** [Depth]—*Syn.* pitch, deepness, lowness; see **depth** 1.
2. [Perception]—*Syn.* acuity, sagacity, authority; see **acumen.**

profuse, *mod.* **1.** [Extravagant]—*Syn.* liberal, extreme, prodigal; see **wasteful.**
2. [Abundant]—*Syn.* bountiful, overflowing, superfluous; see **plentiful** 1.

profusely, *mod.* —*Syn.* extensively, lavishly, richly; see **much** 1, 2.

profuseness, *n.* **1.** [Plenty]—*Syn.* abundance, surplus, affluence; see **plenty.**
2. [Verbosity]—*Syn.* prolixity, verbiage, grandiloquence; see **wordiness.**

profusion, *n.* —*Syn.* abundance, lavishness, prodigality; see **plenty.**

progenitor, *n.* —*Syn.* forebear, begetter, ancestor; see **forefather, parent.**

progeny, *n.* —*Syn.* issue, descendants, children; see **offspring.**

prognosis, *n.* —*Syn.* forecast, prophecy, prediction, diagnosis; see also **guess.**

program, *n.* **1.** [A list of subjects]—*Syn.* schedule, memoranda, printed program; see **list, record** 2.
2. [A sequence of events]—*Syn.* happenings, schedule, agenda, order of business, calendar, plans, business, affairs, details, arrangements, catalog, curriculum, order of the day, series of events, appointments, things to do, chores, preparations, necessary acts, meetings, getting and spending, all the thousand and one things; see also **plan** 2.
3. [An entertainment]—*Syn.* performance, show, presentation; see **performance** 2.
4. [A sequence of coded instructions for a computer]—*Syn.* computer language; see **computer.**

program, *v.* **1.** [To schedule]—*Syn.* slate, book, bill, budget, poll, register, list, draft, empanel, line up (D).
2. [To work out a sequence to be performed] —*Syn.* feed through *or* in, activate a computer, compute, reckon, figure, calculate, estimate, enter, compile, feed, edit, process, prioritize, concatenate, extend, delete, add.

programmed, *mod.* —*Syn.* scheduled, slated, lined up (D); see **planned.**

programmed learning, *n.* —*Syn.* instruction, audio-visual learning, learning with the use of a teaching machine.

progress, *n.* **1.** [Movement forward]—*Syn.* progression, advance, headway, impetus, velocity, pace, momentum, motion, rate, step, stride, current, flow, tour, circuit, transit, journey, voyage, march, expedition, locomotion, ongoing, passage, course, procession, process, lapse of time, march of events, course of life, movement of the stars, motion through space.—*Ant.* stop*, stay, stand.
2. [Improvement]—*Syn.* advancement, development, growth; see **improvement** 1.
in progress—*Syn.* advancing, going on, continuing; see **moving** 1.

progress, *v.* **1.** [To move forward]—*Syn.* proceed, move onward, move on; see **advance** 1.
2. [To improve]—*Syn.* advance, become better, grow; see **improve** 2.

progression, *n.* —*Syn.* progress, rise, change; see **improvement** 1.

progressive, *mod.* **1.** [In mounting sequence] —*Syn.* advancing, mounting, rising, increasing, growing, continuous, successive, following, adding, multiplying, consecutive, gradual, serial, unbroken, uninterrupted, endless, regular, methodical, uniform; see also **moving** 1.—*Ant.* firm*, stationary, immovable.

2. [Receptive to new ideas]—*Syn.* tolerant, lenient, openminded; see **liberal** 2.

prohibit, *v.* **1.** [To forbid]—*Syn.* interdict, put under the ban, obstruct; see **forbid, halt** 2, **prevent.**
2. [To hinder]—*Syn.* obstruct, impede, inhibit; see **hinder, prevent, restrain** 1.

prohibited, *mod.* —*Syn.* forbidden, restricted, not approved; see **illegal, refused.**

prohibition, *n.* **1.** [The act of prohibiting]—*Syn.* forbiddance, interdiction, repudiation; see **refusal.**
2. [Restrictions placed upon the handling or consumption of liquor; *often capital*]—*Syn.* Volstead Act, temperance, Eighteenth Amendment, Prohibition Amendment; *all* (D): the Noble Experiment, the Lost Cause, the Eighteenth Amusement; see also **amendment** 2.

prohibitionist, *n.* —*Syn.* temperance advocate, abstinent, teetotaler; see **abstainer.**

prohibitive, *mod.* —*Syn.* limiting, preventing, restrictive; see **conditional.**

project, *n.* —*Syn.* outline, design, scheme; see **plan** 2.

project, *v.* **1.** [To thrust out]—*Syn.* protrude, hang over, extend, jut, bulge, beetle, stretch *or* push *or* stand *or* stick *or* hang *or* jut out, be prominent, be conspicuous, be convex.—*Ant.* withdraw*, regress, revert.
2. [To throw]—*Syn.* pitch, heave, propel; see **throw** 1.

projectile, *n.* —*Syn.* bullet, shell, missile; see **weapon** 1.

projecting, *mod.* —*Syn.* jutting, protruding, protuberant; see **prominent** 1.

projection, *n.* **1.** [Bulge]—*Syn.* prominence, jut, protuberance, step, ridge, rim; see also **bulge.**
2. [Forecast]—*Syn.* prognostication, prediction, guess; see **forecast.**

proletarian, *mod.* —*Syn.* low, humble, destitute; see **poor** 1.

proletariat, *n.* —*Syn.* the masses, commonality, the rank and file; see **people** 3.

proliferate, *v.* —*Syn.* engender, procreate, generate; see **propagate** 1, **reproduce** 3.

proliferation, *n.* —*Syn.* conception, propagation, generation; see **procreation, reproduction** 1.

prolific, *mod.* —*Syn.* yielding, rich, fecund; see **fertile** 1, 2.

prolix, *mod.* —*Syn.* diffuse, wordy, tedious; see **verbose.**

prologue, *n.* —*Syn.* preface, preamble, proem; see **introduction** 1.

prolong, *v.* —*Syn.* continue, hold, draw out; see **increase** 1, **lengthen** 1.

prolonged, *mod.* —*Syn.* extended, lengthened, continued; see **dull** 4.

promenade, *n.* **1.** [A walk]—*Syn.* ramble, hike, stroll; see **walk** 3.
2. [A dance]—*Syn.* reception, ball, prom (D); see **dance** 2.

promenade, *v.* —*Syn.* stroll, hike, pace; see **walk** 1.

prominence, *n.* **1.** [A projection]—*Syn.* jut, protrusion, bump; see **bulge, projection.**
2. [Notability]—*Syn.* reknown, influence, distinction; see **fame** 1.

prominent, *mod.* **1.** [Physically prominent]—*Syn.* protuberant, extended, jutting, beetling, conspicuous, protruding, projecting, noticeable, rugged, rough, hummocky, obtrusive, extrusive, shooting out, salient, hilly, raised, embossed, relieved, bossy, convex, rounded.—*Ant.* hollow*, depressed, sunken.
2. [Socially prominent]—*Syn.* notable, pre-eminent, leading; see **famous.**
3. [Conspicuous]—*Syn.* remarkable, striking, noticeable; see **conspicuous** 1.

promiscuity, *n.* —*Syn.* lechery, looseness, indiscrimination; see **evil** 1, **lewdness.**

promiscuous, *mod.* **1.** [Mixed]—*Syn.* confused, jumbled, diverse; see **mixed** 1.
2. [Morally lax]—*Syn.* indiscriminate, indiscriminative, unrestricted; see **lewd** 2.

promise, *n.* **1.** [A pledge]—*Syn.* assurance, agreement, pact, oath, engagement, covenant, consent, avowal, warrant, asseveration, affirmation, swearing, plight, word, troth, vow, profession, guarantee, insurance, obligation, stipulation, commitment, betrothal, affiance, espousal, plighted faith, marriage contract, giving one's word, gentleman's agreement, attestation, word of honor, parole, warranty, foretaste.
2. [Hope]—*Syn.* outlook, good omen, good appearance; see **encouragement** 2, **hope** 2.

promise, *v.* **1.** [To give one's word]—*Syn.* plight, engage, declare, agree, vow, swear, espouse, consent, asseverate, affirm, profess, undertake, pledge, covenant, contract, bargain, affiance, betroth, assure, guarantee, warrant, give assurance *or* warranty, insure, cross one's heart, keep a promise, live up to, plight faith *or* troth, bind *or* commit *or* obligate oneself, make oneself answerable, secure, give security, underwrite, subscribe, lead one to expect, answer for, pledge one's honor.—*Ant.* deceive*, deny, break faith.
2. [To appear promising]—*Syn.* ensure, insure, assure; see **encourage** 2.

promised, *mod.* —*Syn.* pledged, sworn, plighted, vowed, agreed, covenanted, as agreed upon, undertaken, professed, consented, affirmed, asseverated, insured, warranted, vouched for, underwritten, subscribed, stipulated, assured, ensured; see also **guaranteed.**

promising, *mod.* —*Syn.* likely, assuring, encouraging; see **hopeful** 2.

promontory, *n.* —*Syn.* projection, foreland, point; see **land** 1, **peninsula.**

promote, *v.* **1.** [To further]—*Syn.* forward, urge, encourage, succor, profit, patronize, help, aid, assist, develop, support, back, uphold, champion, propagandize, advertise, advocate, cultivate, improve, push, bolster, develop, speed, foster, nourish, nurture, subsidize, second, befriend, benefit, subscribe to, favor, expand, subserve, improve, better, cooperate, avail, boom, bestead; *all* (D): lobby for, get behind, plug, hype, boost.—*Ant.* discourage*, weaken, enfeeble.
2. [To advance in rank[—*Syn.* raise, advance, elevate, graduate, move up, exalt, aggrandize, magnify, prefer, favor, increase, ascend, better, ennoble, dignify; *both* (D): kick upstairs, up.—*Ant.* humble*, demote, reduce.

promotion, *n.* **1.** [Advancement in rank]—*Syn.* preferment, elevation, raise, improvement, ad-

vance, lift, betterment, ennobling, favoring. —*Ant.* removal*, demotion, lowering.
2. [Improvement]—*Syn.* advancement, progression, development; see **improvement** 1, **increase** 1.
3. [Publicity]—*Syn.* public relations *or* PR job, advertising, notice; see **advertisement** 1, **publicity** 3.

prompt, *mod.* —*Syn.* early, timely, precise; see **punctual.**

prompt, *v.* **1.** [To instigate]—*Syn.* arouse, provoke, inspire; see **incite, urge** 2.
2. [To suggest]—*Syn.* bring up, indicate, imply; see **hint** 1, **mention, propose** 1.
3. [To help]—*Syn.* aid, assist, advise; see **help** 1.

prompted, *mod.* —*Syn.* moved, incited, suggested; see **inspired** 1, **urged** 2.

prompter, *n.* —*Syn.* memo, notice, memorandum; see **note** 2, **reminder.**

promptly, *mod.* —*Syn.* on time, punctually, hastily; see **immediately, quickly** 1, 2.

promptness, *n.* —*Syn.* preparedness, agility, readiness; see **preparation** 2.

promulgate, *v.* —*Syn.* publish, declare, proclaim; see **advertise** 1.

prone, *mod.* —*Syn.* inclined, predisposed, devoted; see **likely** 4.

prong, *n.* —*Syn.* spine, spur, spike; see **fastener.**

pronoun, *n.* —Pronouns include the following—personal, possessive, demonstrative, relative, definite, indefinite, interrogative, intensive, reflexive, reciprocal.

pronounce, *v.* **1.** [To speak formally]—*Syn.* proclaim, say, assert; see **declare** 1.
2. [To articulate]—*Syn.* enunciate, phonate, vocalize; see **utter.**

pronounced, *mod.* —*Syn.* notable, noticeable, clear; see **definite** 2, **famous, obvious** 1, 2, **strong** 2, 8, **unusual** 1.

pronouncement, *n.* —*Syn.* report, declaration, statement; see **announcement** 1.

pronunciation, *n.* —*Syn.* articulation, utterance, voicing; see **diction.**

proof, *n.* **1.** [Evidence]—*Syn.* demonstration, verification, averment, case, reasons, exhibits, credentials, data, warrant, confirmation, substantiation, attestation, corroboration, affidavit, facts, witness, testimony, deposition, trace, record, criterion.
2. [Process of proving]—*Syn.* test, attempt, assay; see **trial** 2.
3. [A printed proof sheet]—*Syn.* trial proof, pull, slip, revise, (trial) impression, galley (proof), page proof, stereo (proof), foundry proof.

proofread, *v.* —*Syn.* improve, scan, proof; see **correct** 1.

prop, *n.* —*Syn.* aid, assistance, strengthener; see **post** 1.

propaganda, *n.* —*Syn.* promotion, publicity, advertisement, publication, announcement, evangelism, proselytism, promulgation; *both* (D): ballyhoo, handout.

propagandist, *n.* —*Syn.* disseminator, advocate, devotee, pamphleteer, advocator, indoctrinator, proselytizer, evangelist, missionary, catechizer, teacher, salesman, zealot, hawker (D).

propagandize, *v.* —*Syn.* instill, indoctrinate, instruct; see **teach** 1.

propagate, *v.* **1.** [To beget]—*Syn.* breed, engender, create, originate, father, sire, fertilize, inseminate, make pregnant, spermatize, generate, produce, reproduce, impregnate, fecundate.
2. [To spread]—*Syn.* disseminate, diffuse, develop; see **scatter** 1, 2.

propagation, *n.* **1.** [Procreation]—*Syn.* conception, generation, impregnation; see **procreation, reproduction** 1.
2. [Diffusion]—*Syn.* spread, circulation, dispersion; see **distribution** 1.

propel, *v.* —*Syn.* impel forward, move, press onward; see **drive** 3.

propellant, *n.* —*Syn.* charge, gunpowder, combustible; see **explosive, fuel.**

propeller, *n.* —Propellers include the following—screw, Archimedean, fishtail, variable-pitch, feathering, marine, airplane, two-bladed, three-bladed, four-bladed, weedless, pusher, pulling; propeller-wheel.

propensity, *n.* —*Syn.* talent, capacity, competence; see **ability** 1, 2.

proper, *mod.* **1.** [Suitable]—*Syn.* just, decent, fitting; see **fit** 1, 2.
2. [Conventional]—*Syn.* customary, usual, decorous; see **conventional** 1, 2.
3. [Prudish]—*Syn.* prim, precise, strait-laced; see **prudish.**
4. [Personal]—*Syn.* private, own, peculiar; see **individual** 1.

properly, *mod.* —*Syn.* correctly, fitly, suitably; see **accurately, well** 3.

property, *n.* **1.** [Possession]—*Syn.* belongings, lands, assets, holdings, inheritance, capital, equity, investment(s), goods (and chattel), earthly possessions, real property, personal property, taxable property, resources, private property, public property, wealth; see also **business** 5, **estate** 1, **farm, home** 1.
2. [A piece of land]—*Syn.* section, quarter section, estate, tract, part, realty, real estate, farm, park, ranch, homestead, yard, grounds, frontage, acres, acreage, premises, campus, grant, landed property, field, claim, holding, plot, leasehold, freehold; see also **lot** 1.
3. [Characteristic]—*Syn.* peculiarity, feature, trait; see **characteristic.**

prophecy, *n.* —*Syn.* prediction, prognostication, augury; see **divination.**

prophesy, *v.* —*Syn.* predict, prognosticate, divine; see **foretell.**

prophet, *n.* —*Syn.* seer, seeress, oracle, soothsayer, clairvoyant, wizard, augur, sibyl, sorcerer, predictor, forecaster, prognosticator, diviner, haruspex, evocator, medium, witch, palmist, fortuneteller, palmist, tea-leaf reader, reader of the future, weather forecaster, meteorologist, ovate, bard, druid, *vates sacer* (Latin), magus, astrologer, horoscopist.

prophetess, *n.* —*Syn.* seeress, sorceress, Cassandra; see **prophet.**

prophetic, *mod.* —*Syn.* predictive, occult, veiled; see **oracular** 2.

prophylactic, *mod.* —*Syn.* protective, preventive, preventative; see **contraceptive.**

prophylactic, *n.* —*Syn.* diaphragm, condom, birth-control device; see **contraceptive.**
prophylaxis, *n.* —*Syn.* precaution, sanitation, prevention; see **treatment** 2.
propinquity, *n.* **1.** [Proximity]—*Syn.* nearness, contiguity, concurrence; see **proximity.**
2. [Kinship]—*Syn.* affiliation, connection, consanguinity; see **relationship.**
propitiate, *v.* —*Syn.* conciliate, appease, atone; see **satisfy** 1, 3.
propitious, *mod.* **1.** [Favorable]—*Syn.* auspicious, encouraging, promising; see **hopeful** 2.
2. [Kindly]—*Syn.* benignant, helpful, generous; see **kind.**
proponent, *n.* —*Syn.* defender, advocate, champion; see **protector.**
proportion, *n.* —*Syn.* relationship, dimension, share; see **balance** 2, **part** 1.
proportional, *mod.* —*Syn.* proportionate, equivalent, comparable; see **comparative, equal.**
proposal, *n.* **1.** [Offer]—*Syn.* overture, recommendation, proposition; see **suggestion** 1.
2. [Plan]—*Syn.* scheme, program, prospectus; see **plan** 2.
3. [An offer of marriage]—*Syn.* offer, overture, proposition, asking of one's hand, betrothment, engagement.
propose, *v.* **1.** [To make a suggestion]—*Syn.* suggest, offer, put forward, move, set forth, come up with, state, proffer, advance, propound, introduce, put to, contend, assert, tender, recommend, advise, counsel, lay before, submit, adduce, affirm, volunteer, press, urge (upon), hold out, make a motion, lay (something) on the line.—*Ant.* oppose*, dissent, protest.
2. [To mean]—*Syn.* purpose, intend, aim; see **mean** 1.
3. [To propose marriage]—*Syn.* offer marriage, ask in marriage, make a proposal, ask for the hand of, press one's suit; *both* (D): pop the question, fire the question.
proposed, *mod.* —*Syn.* projected, prospective, advised, scheduled, expected, arranged, advanced, suggested, moved, proffered, put forward, submitted, recommended, urged, volunteered, pressed, intended, determined, anticipated, designed, schemed, purposed, considered, referred to, contingent; see also **planned.**
proposition, *n.* —*Syn.* proposal, scheme, project; see **plan** 1.
proposition, *v.* —*Syn.* ask, accost, approach; see **solicit** 3.
proprietary, *mod.* —*Syn.* fashionable, restrictive, established; see **exclusive.**
proprietor, *n.* —*Syn.* heritor, master, proprietary; see **owner, possessor.**
propriety, *n.* **1.** [Suitability]—*Syn.* aptness, suitability, advisability, accordance, agreeableness, recommendability, compatibility, correspondence, consonance, seemliness, appropriateness, congruity, modesty, good breeding, dignity, concord, harmony, expedience, convenience, pleasantness, welcomeness; see also **fitness.**—*Ant.* inconsistency*, incongruity, inappropriateness.
2. [Conventional conduct]—*Syn.* good manners, good behavior, correctness; see **behavior** 1.

propulsion, *n.* —*Syn.* push, impulsion, impetus, momentum, drive; see also **thrust** 3.
prorate, *n.* —*Syn.* allocate, divide, allot; see **distribute** 1.
prosaic, *mod.* —*Syn.* common, mundane, trite; see **dull** 4.
proscribe, *v.* —*Syn.* banish, outlaw, exile; see **forbid.**
prose, *n.* fiction, non-fiction, composition; see **exposition** 2, **literature** 2, **story, writing** 2.
prosecute, *v.* **1.** [To pursue]—*Syn.* follow up, put through, execute; see **continue** 1.
2. [Involve in a legal action]—*Syn.* contest, indict, involve in litigation; see **sue.**
prosecution, *n.* **1.** [The act of furthering a project] —*Syn.* pursuit, pursuance, undertaking; see **achievement** 2.
2. [The prosecuting party in a criminal action] —*Syn.* state, government, prosecuting agent, prosecuting attorney, state's attorney; see also **accuser, lawyer.**
proselyte, *n.* —*Syn.* neophyte, disciple, convert; see **follower.**
prosody, *n.* —*Syn.* versification, metrics, poem; see **poetry.**
prospect, *n.* **1.** [A view]—*Syn.* sight, landscape, vista; see **view** 1.
2. [A probable future]—*Syn.* expectancy, promise, hope; see **forecast, outlook** 2.
3. [A possible candidate]—*Syn.* possibility, likely person, interested party; see **candidate, recruit.**
in prospect—*Syn.* hoped for, planned, anticipated; see **expected** 2.
prospective, *mod.* —*Syn.* considered, hoped for, promised; see **planned, proposed.**
prospectus, *n.* —*Syn.* outline, design, scheme; see **plan** 1.
prosper, *v.* —*Syn.* become rich *or* wealthy, be enriched, thrive, turn out well, fare *or* do well, be fortunate, have good fortune, flourish, get on, rise (in the world), fatten, batten, increase, bear fruit, bloom, blossom, flower, make money, make a fortune, benefit, advance, gain; *all* (D): make good, do right by oneself, make one's mark, roll in the lap of luxury, feather one's nest, come along, catch on, come on, do wonders; see also **succeed** 1.
prosperity, *n.* **1.** [Good fortune]—*Syn.* accomplishment, victory, successfulness; see **success** 2.
2. [Inflation]—*Syn.* expansion, exorbitance, affluence; see **increase** 1.
prosperous, *mod.* —*Syn.* flourishing, well-off, well-to-do; see **rich** 1.
prostitute, *n.* —*Syn.* harlot, strumpet, lewd woman, whore, bawd, streetwalker, loose woman, fallen woman, courtesan, abandoned woman, concubine, vice girl, hustler, call girl, *fille de joie* (French), tramp, slut, lady of assignation; *all* (D): tart, hooker, lady of the evening, bimbo, pro, white slave, *poule* (French); see also **criminal.**
prostitution, *n.* —*Syn.* fornication, whoredom, hustling, harlotry, adultery, wantonness, hooking (D); see also **lewdness.**
prostrate, *mod.* **1.** [Defenseless]—*Syn.* open, overcome, beaten; see **weak** 1, 3, 6.
2. [Submissive]—*Syn.* given in, obedient, subservient; see **docile.**

prostrate, *v.* **1.** [To submit]—*Syn.* give in, obey, surrender; see **yield** 1.
2. [To overthrow]—*Syn.* wreck, destroy, ruin; see **defeat** 2.

prostration, *n.* **1.** [Submission]—*Syn.* surrender, downfall, destruction; see **docility.**
2. [Exhaustion]—*Syn.* tiredness, weariness, collapse; see **lassitude.**

prosy, *mod.* —*Syn.* stale, trite, common; see **dull** 4.

protagonist, *n.* —*Syn.* leading character, lead, exemplar, warrior, combatant; see also **hero** 1, **idol** 2.

protean, *mod.* —*Syn.* mutable, variable, unsettled; see **changeable** 2.

protect, *v.* —*Syn.* shield, guard, preserve; see **defend** 1, 2.

protected, *mod.* —*Syn.* shielded, safeguarded, cared for, watched over, preserved, defended, guarded, secured, kept safe, sheltered, harbored, screened, under the aegis of, fostered, cherished, ensconced, curtained, shaded, disguised, camouflaged; see also **covered** 1, **safe** 1.—*Ant.* weak*, insecure, unsheltered.

protection, *n.* **1.** [A covering]—*Syn.* shield, screen, camouflage; see **shelter.**
2. [A surety]—*Syn.* certainty, safeguard, safekeeping, assurance, invulnerability, impregnability, reassurance, security, stability, strength; see also **guaranty** 2.—*Ant.* insecurity, weakness, frailty.

protective, *mod.* —*Syn.* protecting, emergency, as a last resort, having built-in protection, guarding, shielding.

protector, *n.* —*Syn.* champion, defender, patron, sponsor, safeguard, benefactor, supporter, advocate, partisan, guardian angel, guard, shield, bulwark; guide, philosopher, and friend; Maecenas, abettor, savior, stand-by, promoter, mediator, friend at court, counsel, second, backer, upholder, sympathizer, tower of strength in time of need, tutelary, genius; *all* (D): big brother, big sister, angel, cover, front; see also **guardian.**

protectorate, *n.* **1.** [Protection]—*Syn.* surety, guidance, jurisdiction; see **protection** 2.
2. [Province]—*Syn.* mandate, colony, dominion; see **territory** 2.

protein, *n.* —*Syn.* proteid, amino acid, nitrogenous matter.

protest, *n.* —*Syn.* mass meeting, rally, demonstration, peace demonstration, draft demonstration, peace rally, race riot, clamor, tumult, turmoil, student *or* campus revolt, moratorium; *all* (D): sit-in, teach-in, study-in, mill-in, love-in; see also **objection** 2.

protest, *v.* —*Syn.* demur, disagree, object; see **oppose** 1.

Protestant, *n.* —Some Protestant sects include the following—Evangelist, Adventist, Baptist, Congregational, Episcopal, Lutheran, Methodist, Presbyterian.

protestant, *mod.* —*Syn.* evangelical, reform(ed), non-Catholic, new; Adventist, Baptist, Congregational *or* Congregationalist, etc.; see also **Protestant.**

protester, *n.* —*Syn.* demonstrator, heckler, opposer of those in power *or* administration, dissident, rebel; see also **agitator, liberal** 2, **radical.**

protocol, *n.* **1.** [Contract]—*Syn.* obligation, compact, treaty; see **contract** 1.
2. [Standards]—*Syn.* order, rules, etiquette; see **custom** 1, 2.

prototype, *n.* —*Syn.* criterion, ideal, archetype; see **model** 1.

protract, *v.* —*Syn.* postpone, defer, procrastinate; see **delay** 1.

protrude, *v.* —*Syn.* come through, stick out, jut out, swell, point, obtrude, project, extrude, stick up, distend, pop out (D).

protuberance, *n.* —*Syn.* bump, knob, jutting; see **bulge.**

proud, *mod.* **1.** [Having a creditable self-respect]—*Syn.* self-respecting, self-sufficient, self-satisfied, ambitious, mettlesome, spirited, vigorous, valiant, high-spirited, honorable, great-hearted, pleased with oneself, fiery, dignified, stately, lordly, lofty-minded, high-souled, high-minded, high-mettled, impressive, imposing, fine, splendid, looking one in the face *or* eye, on one's high horse, high and mighty, having no false modesty, holding up one's head.—*Ant.* humble, unpretentious, unassuming.
2. [Egotistic]—*Syn.* egotistical, vain, vainglorious; see **egotistic** 2.
do oneself proud (D)—*Syn.* achieve, prosper, advance; see **succeed** 1.

proudly, *mod.* —*Syn.* boastfully, haughtily, insolently, contemptuously, like a lord; see also **arrogantly.**

provable, *mod.* —*Syn.* inferable, deductible, testable, demonstrable, in evidence; see also **certain** 3, **conclusive.**

prove, *v.* —*Syn.* justify, substantiate, authenticate, corroborate, testify, explain, attest, show, warrant, uphold, determine, settle, fix, certify, back, sustain, validate, bear out, affirm, confirm, make evident, convince, evidence, be evidence of, witness, declare, testify, betoken, have a case, manifest, demonstrate, document, establish, settle once and for all, (just) go to show (D); see also **verify.**—*Ant.* disprove*, break down, disqualify.

proved, *mod.* —*Syn.* confirmed, established, demonstrated; see **establish** 3.

provenance, *n.* —*Syn.* birthplace, derivation, home; see **origin** 2.

proverb, *n.* —*Syn.* maxim, adage, aphorism, precept, saw, saying, motto, dictum, text, witticism, repartee, axiom, truism, apothegm, byword, catch phrase, mot, epigram, moral, folk wisdom, platitude.

proverbial, *mod.* —*Syn.* current, general, unquestioned; see **common** 1, **dull** 4, **familiar** 1.

proverbially, *mod.* —*Syn.* as the saying is, as the fellow says, as they say, as the story goes, aphoristically, axiomatically, epigrammatically, platitudinously, traditionally; see also **customarily.**

provide, *v.* **1.** [To supply]—*Syn.* furnish, equip, grant, replenish, provide with, accommodate, care for, indulge *or* favor with, contribute, give, proffer, outfit, fit, stock, store, minister, administer, render, procure, afford, present, bestow, purvey, cater, rig (up), fit out *or* up, provision, ration, implement.—*Ant.* refuse*, take away, deny.
2. [To yield]—*Syn.* render, afford, give; see **produce** 1.

provided, *conj.* —*Syn.* on the assumption (that), in the event, in the case that; see **if, supposing.**

provided that, *conj.* —*Syn.* on condition, in the event, with that understood; see **if, supposing.**

provide for *or* **against,** *v.* —*Syn.* make provision, make ready, prepare for, arrange, care for, support, plan ahead; see also **prepare** 1.

providence, *n.* —*Syn.* divine government, divine superintendence, Deity; see **god.**

provident, *mod.* —*Syn.* cautious, prepared, prudent; see **judicious.**

providential, *mod.* —*Syn.* fortunate, timely, opportune; see **hopeful** 2.

providing, *conj.* —*Syn.* provided, in the event *or* the case that, on the assumption (that); see **if, supposing.**

providing, *n.* —*Syn.* provision, supplying, furnishing, equipping, replenishing, replenishment, contributing, outfitting, stocking, filling, procurement, affording, presenting, preparing, preparation, arrangement, planning, putting by, laying by *or* in, putting in readiness, granting, bestowing, giving, offering, tendering, accumulating, storing, saving.

province, *n.* —*Syn.* area, region, dependency; see **territory** 2.

provincial, *mod.* —*Syn.* rude, unpolished, countrified; see **rural.**

provincialism, *n.* **1.** [Dialect]—*Syn.* vernacular, localism, idiosyncrasy; see **dialect.**
2. [Narrow-mindedness]—*Syn.* bias, intolerance, xenophobia; see **inclination** 1, **prejudice.**

proving, *n.* —*Syn.* trying, examining, justifying, verifying; see also **testing.**

provision, *n.* **1.** [Arrangement]—*Syn.* preparation, outline, procurement; see **plan** 2.
2. [Supplies; *usually plural*]—*Syn.* stock, store, emergency; see **equipment, reserve** 1.
3. [A proviso]—*Syn.* stipulation, prerequisite, terms; see **requirement** 1.

provisional, *mod.* —*Syn.* transient, passing, ephemeral; see **temporary.**

provisionally, *mod.* —*Syn.* conditionally, on these *or* certain conditions, for the time being; see **temporarily.**

proviso, *n.* —*Syn.* provision, clause, conditional stipulation; see **limitation** 2, **requirement** 1.

provocation, *n.* —*Syn.* incitement, stimulus, inducement; see **incentive.**

provocative, *mod.* —*Syn.* alluring, arousing, intriguing; see **interesting, stimulating.**

provoke, *v.* **1.** [To vex]—*Syn.* irritate, put out, aggravate; see **bother** 2.
2. [To incite]—*Syn.* stir, rouse, arouse; see **incite.**
3. [To cause]—*Syn.* make, produce, bring about; see **begin** 1.

provoked, *mod.* —*Syn.* exasperated, incensed, enraged; see **angry.**

provoking, *mod.* —*Syn.* vexing, annoying, tormenting; see **disturbing.**

provost, *n.* —*Syn.* executive, supervisor, officer; see **administrator.**

prow, *n.* —*Syn.* head, bowsprit, fore; see **bow** 1.

prowess, *n.* —*Syn.* bravery, valor, intrepidity; see **courage** 1.

prowl, *v.* —*Syn.* slink, lurk, rove; see **sneak.**

proximity, *n.* —*Syn.* contiguity, concurrence, closeness; see **nearness** 1.

proxy, *n.* —*Syn.* substitute, broker, representative; see **agent** 1, **delegate** 1.

prude, *n.* —*Syn.* prig, puritan, old maid, prudish person; *all* (D): prune, priss, sourpuss, Mrs. Grundy, stick-in-the-mud, spoilsport, wet blanket, bluenose, goody-goody, tattletale.

prudence, *n.* —*Syn.* caution, circumspection, judgment, providence, considerateness, judiciousness, sagacity, deliberation, wisdom, foresight, forethought, care, carefulness, frugality, watchfulness, precaution, heedfulness, heed, economy, husbandry, concern, conservatism, conservation, discrimination, cunning, vigilance, coolness, calculation, presence of mind; see also **discretion** 1, **tact.** —*Ant.* carelessness*, imprudence, rashness.

prudent, *mod.* **1.** [Cautious and careful]—*Syn.* cautious, circumspect, wary; see **careful, discreet.**
2. [Sensible and wise]—*Syn.* discerning, sound, reasonable; see **judicious.**

prudery, *n.* —*Syn.* stuffiness, primness, strictness; see **behavior** 1, **courtesy** 1.

prudish, *mod.* —*Syn.* overnice, stilted, mincing, precise, narrow-minded, illiberal, bigoted, prissy, priggish, over-refined, fastidious, stuffy, conventional, offish, stiff, smug, strait-laced, demure, narrow, puritanical, blue-nosed (D), affected, artificial, scrupulous, overexact, pedantic, pretentious, strict, rigid, rigorous, simpering, finical, finicking, finicky, squeamish, schoolgirlish, oldmaidish, like a maiden aunt, prudish as an old maid; see also **prim.**—*Ant.* sociable*, broad-minded, genial.

prune, *n.* Varieties of prunes include the following —French, Stanley, Italian-Fellemberg, St. Julien, myrobalan, Bosnian; see also **fruit** 1.

prune, *v.* —*Syn.* lop, clip, dock; see **cut** 1.

pry, *v.* **1.** [To move with a lever]—*Syn.* push, lift, raise, pull, prize, move, tilt, hoist, heave, uplift, upraise, elevate, turn out, jimmy (D); see also **force** 2, **open** 2.
2. [To endeavor to discover; *often used with* into] —*Syn.* search, ferret out, seek, ransack, reconnoiter, peep, peer, peek, snoop, gaze, look closely, spy, stare, gape, nose, be curious, inquire; *both* (D): rubber, rubberneck; see also **hunt** 2, **meddle** 1.

prying, *mod.* —*Syn.* quizzical, curious, inquiring; see **inquisitive, interested** 1.

psalm, *n.* —*Syn.* sacred song, praise, verse; see **song.**

psalter, *n.* —*Syn.* the Psalms, hymnbook, songbook; see **book** 1.

pseudo, *mod.* —*Syn.* imitation, quasi, sham; see **false** 3.

pseudonym, *n.* —*Syn.* pen name, anonym, assumed name; see **alias, name** 3.

psyche, *n.* —*Syn.* subconscious, mind, ego, (subliminal) self, individuality, personality; see also **character** 2.

psychedelic, *mod.* —*Syn.* hallucinatory, mind-expanding, mind-changing, experimental, consciousness-expanding, psychotomimetic, hallucinogenic; *all* (D): mind-bending, mind-blowing, trippy, freaky.

psychedelic, *n.* —*Syn.* stimulant, mind-expanding drug, hallucinogen; see **drug** 2.

psychiatrist, *n.*—*Syn.* analyst, therapist, shrink (D); see **doctor** 1, **psychoanalyst.**

psychiatry, *n.*—*Syn.* psychopathology, psychotherapeutics, psychotherapy, psychoanalysis, alienism, mental hygiene, mental health, psychiatrics, neuropsychiatry; see also **medicine** 1, **science** 1.

psychic, *mod.* **1.** [Mental]—*Syn.* analytic, intellectual, psychological; see **mental** 2.

2. [Spiritual]—*Syn.* telepathic, mystic, immaterial; see **supernatural.**

psycho (D), *mod.*—*Syn.* mad, crazy, psychopathic, loony, crazed, screwy (D); see also **insane** 1.

psychoanalysis, *n.*—*Syn.* analysis, psychotherapy, depth psychiatry, depth psychology, dream analysis, interpretation of dreams, depth interview, psychoanalytic therapy, group therapy, games (D); see also **therapy.**

psychoanalyst, *n.*—*Syn.* psychiatrist, analyst, neuropsychiatrist, psychoanalyzer, alienist, psychopathist, psychopathologist, psychometrician; *all* (D): deficiency expert, head-shrinker, shrink; see also **doctor** 1.

psychological, *mod.* **1.** [Concerning psychology] —*Syn.* directly experimental, subjective, experimental; see **mental** 2.

2. [(D) Suitable]—*Syn.* fitting, timely, opportune; see **fit** 1.

psychologist, *n.*—*Syn.* psychiatrist, analyst, clinician; see **doctor** 1, **psychoanalyst.**

psychology, *n.*—*Syn.* science of mind, study of personality, medicine, therapy; see also **science** 1, **social science.**

Divisions and varieties of psychology include the following—rational, existential, functional, structural, self, dynamic, organismic, motor, physiological, abnormal, differential, Gestalt, Freudian, Adlerian, Jungian, genetic, applied, psychotechnological, academic, popular, introspective, analytical, comparative, child, animal, mass, individual, social, racial; behaviorism, parapsychology.

psychopath, *n.*—*Syn.* lunatic, mental case, bedlamite, psychopathic *or* unstable *or* aggressive *or* antisocial personality, sociopath, maniac; see also **fool** 1, **madman.**

Specific kinds of psychopaths include the following —hysteric, neurotic, neuropath, psychotic, paranoic, manic-depressive, hypomanic, schizophrenic, monomaniac, dipsomaniac, drug addict, hypochondriac, melancholic.

psychopathic, *mod.*—*Syn.* psychotic, deranged, (mentally) unbalanced; see **insane** 1.

psychotic, *mod.*—*Syn.* insane, mad, psychopathic; see **insane** 1.

pub (D), *n.*—*Syn.* public house, bar, drinking establishment; see **saloon** 3.

puberty, *n.*—*Syn.* boyhood, pubescence, adolescence; see **youth** 1.

public, *mod.* **1.** [Available to the public]—*Syn.* free to all, without charge, open (to the public), unrestricted, not private, known; see also **free** 4.

2. [Owned by the public]—*Syn.* governmental, government, civil, civic, common, communal; owned *or* deeded to the federal government *or* state *or* county *or* city, etc.; publicly owned, municipal, metropolitan, state, federal, country, city, township, not taken up *or* homesteaded, given *or* deeded in perpetuity.—*Ant.* private*, personal, restricted.

public, *n.*—*Syn.* men, society, the community; see **people** 3.

in public—*Syn.* candidly, plainly, above board; see **openly** 1.

publication, *n.* **1.** [The act of making public] —*Syn.* writing, printing, broadcasting, announcement, notification, promulgation, issuing, statement, divulgation, ventilation, acquaintance, advisement, advertisement, communication, revelation, disclosure, discovery, dissemination, making current, making available.

2. [Something published]—*Syn.* news, tidings, information; see **book** 1, **magazine** 2, **newspaper.**

publicist, *n.*—*Syn.* announcer, columnist, correspondent; see **journalist, newspaperman, reporter, writer.**

publicity, *n.* **1.** [Public distribution]—*Syn.* notoriety, currency, publicness; see **distribution** 1.

2. [Free advertising]—*Syn.* public relations copy, release, report; see **advertising** 1, **reporting.**

3. [Activity intended to advertise]—*Syn.* promotion, promoting, publicizing, advertising, announcing, broadcasting, pushing, billing, making use of (available mass) media; getting out *or* distributing publicity, advertising, etc.; *all* (D): clout, puff, boost, plug, going on the air (with); see also **advertisement** 1, 2.

publicize, *v.*—*Syn.* announce, broadcast, promulgate; see **advertise** 1.

publicly, *mod.*—*Syn.* candidly, plainly, aboveboard; see **openly** 1.

public opinion, *n.*—*Syn.* public pressure, power of the press, popular pressure; see **force** 3, **influence, opinion** 1.

public relations, *n.*—*Syn.* promotion, public image, favorable climate (of opinion); see **advertising** 1, **propaganda.**

public-spirited, *mod.*—*Syn.* altruistic, humanitarian, openhanded; see **generous** 1.

public utility, *n.*—*Syn.* (public) service(s), natural monopoly, light and power; see **utilities.**

publish, *v.* **1.** [To print and distribute]—*Syn.* reprint, issue, reissue, distribute, bring out, write, do publishing, bring into the open, become a publisher, get off *or* out, put to press, put forth *or* about, enter the publishing field, be in the newspaper *or* magazine *or* book business, own a publishing house, send forth, give out *or* forth; see also **print** 2.

2. [To make known]—*Syn.* announce, promulgate, proclaim; see **advertise** 1, **declare** 1.

published, *mod.*—*Syn.* written, printed, made public, circulated, broached, proclaimed, promulgated, propagated, pronounced, ventilated, divulged, made current, made known, broadcast, circulated, spread abroad, disseminated, got out, appeared, released, coming forth, seeing the light, presented, offered, voiced, blazoned, noised abroad, given to the world, given publicity, brought before the public; see also **advertised, an-**

nounced, issued, reported.—*Ant.* unknown*, unpublished, unwritten.
publisher, *n.*—*Syn.* publicist, businessman, administrator; see **journalist.**
puck, *n.*—*Syn.* fay, sprite, elf; see **fairy** 1.
pucker, *n.*—*Syn.* plait, crease, furrow; see **fold** 1, **wrinkle.**
pucker, *v.*—*Syn.* condense, squeeze, purse; see **contract** 1, **wrinkle** 1.
puckish, *mod.*—*Syn.* impish, mischievous, playful; see **naughty.**
pudding, *n.*—*Syn.* mousse, custard, junket, tapioca; see also **dessert.**
Puddings include the following—blanc mange, charlotte russe, Russian cream, Spanish cream, apple snow, fruit cobbler, rice, bread, batter, cornstarch, fig, plum, Christmas, chocolate, Indian Delmonico, fruit sago, graham pudding.
puddle, *n.*—*Syn.* plash, mud puddle, rut; see **pool** 1.
pudgy, *mod.*—*Syn.* chubby, chunky, stout; see **fat** 1.
puerile, *mod.*—*Syn.* boyish, inexperienced, immature; see **childish** 1, **naive, young** 2.
puerility, *n.*—*Syn.* absurdity, frivolity, rubbish; see **nonsense** 2, **stupidity** 2.
puff, *n.*—*Syn.* whiff, sudden gust, quick blast; see **wind.**
puff, *v.* **1.** [To flatter]—*Syn.* commend, admire, congratulate; see **praise** 1.
2. [To inflate]—*Syn.* distend, enlarge, swell; see **fill** 1.
3. [To blow]—*Syn.* exhale, pant, whiff; see **blow** 1.
puffed, *mod.*—*Syn.* expanded, swollen, bloated; see **full** 1, **increased, inflated.**
puffy, *mod.* **1.** [Windy]—*Syn.* airy, gusty, breezy; see **windy** 1.
2. [Conceited]—*Syn.* egocentric, pompous, mettlesome; see **egotistic** 2.
3. [Swollen]—*Syn.* distended, expanded, blown; see **full** 1, **increased, inflated.**
pugilism, *n.*—*Syn.* fighting, sparring, fisticuffs; see **boxing, sport** 3.
pugilist, *n.*—*Syn.* boxer, prize fighter, contender; see **fighter** 2.
pugnacious, *mod.*—*Syn.* belligerent, defiant, antagonistic; see **rebellious** 2.
puke, *v.*—*Syn.* throw up, retch, barf (D); see **vomit.**
pull, *n.* **1.** [The act of pulling]—*Syn.* tow, drag, haul, jerk, twitch, wrench, extraction, drawing, rending, tearing, uprooting, weeding, row, paddle; *both* (D): snake, yank.
2. [Exerted force]—*Syn.* work, strain, tug; see **strength** 1.
3. [(D) Influence]—*Syn.* inclination, inducement, weight; see **influence** 2.
pull, *v.* **1.** [To exert force]—*Syn.* tug, pull at, draw in; see **work.**
2. [To move by pulling]—*Syn.* pick, rend, gather; see **draw** 1.
3. [To incline]—*Syn.* slope, tend, move toward; see **lean** 1.
pull apart, *v.*—*Syn.* separate, split, force apart; see **divide** 1.
pull away, *v.*—*Syn.* depart, pull off, go; see **leave** 1.
pull down, *v.*—*Syn.* raze, wreck, remove; see **destroy** 1.
pullet, *n.*—*Syn.* young hen, fowl, rooster; see **bird** 1, **chicken** 1.
pulley, *n.*—*Syn.* sheave, block, lift, lifter, crowbar, crow, pry; see also **tool** 1.
pulling, *n.*—*Syn.* plucking, shaking, contesting, twitching, struggling, towing, stretching.
pull into, *v.*—*Syn.* come in, land, make a landing; see **arrive** 1.
Pullman, *n.*—*Syn.* sleeping car, chair car, sleeper (D); see **car** 2, **train** 2.
pull off, *v.* **1.** [To remove]—*Syn.* detach, separate, yank *or* wrench off; see **remove** 1.
2. [(D) To achieve]—*Syn.* accomplish, manage, succeed; see **achieve** 1.
pull oneself together, *v.*—*Syn.* recover, revive, get on one's feet (D); see **improve** 2.
pull out, *v.*—*Syn.* go, depart, stop participating; see **leave** 1, **stop** 2.
pull over, *v.*—*Syn.* drive or turn to the side, pull up, park; see **stop** 1, **turn** 6.
pull rank (D), *v.*—*Syn.* order, demand, bid; see **command** 1.
pull through (D), *v.*—*Syn.* get better, get over something, triumph; see **recover** 2, 3, **survive** 1.
pull up, *v.* **1.** [To remove]—*Syn.* dislodge, elevate, pull *or* dig out; see **remove** 1.
2. [To stop]—*Syn.* arrive, come to a halt *or* a stop, get there; see **stop** 1.
pulmonary, *mod.*—*Syn.* of the lungs, pneumonic, lunglike, affecting the lungs, consumptive, lobar.
pulp, *n.*—*Syn.* sarcocarp, pap, mash, sponge, paste, pomace, dough, batter, curd, grume, jam, poultice; see also **flesh** 2.
pulpit, *n.* **1.** [The ministry]—*Syn.* priesthood, clergy, ecclesiastics; see **ministry** 2.
2. [A platform in a church]—*Syn.* desk, rostrum, stage; see **platform.**
pulpy, *mod.*—*Syn.* smooth, thick, fleshy; see **soft** 2.
pulsate, *v.*—*Syn.* throb, quiver, vibrate; see **beat** 3.
pulsation, *n.*—*Syn.* quiver, shiver, throb; see **beat** 2.
pulse, *n.*—*Syn.* pulsation, vibration, oscillation, throb; see also **beat** 2.
pulverize, *v.*—*Syn.* comminute, triturate, levigate; see **grind** 1.
pump, *n.* Pumps include the following—air, chain, force, Geissler, lift, mercury, sand, shell, Sprengel, suction, vacuum, oscillating, rotary displacement, piston, centrifugal, volute centrifugal, turbine centrifugal, jet, bucket; pulsometer, hydraulic ram; see also **machine** 1, **tool** 1.
pump, *v.*—*Syn.* elevate, draw out *or* up, tap; see **draw** 1.
pun, *n.*—*Syn.* conceit, witticism, quip, quibble, play upon words; see also **joke** 2.
punch, *n.* **1.** [A blow]—*Syn.* thrust, knock, stroke; see **blow** 1.
2. [An instrument for denting or perforating] Varieties include the following—blacksmith's, cooper's, nail, leather, ticket, duplex, center, drift, belt, blanking, culling, forming, drawing, redrawing, bending, coining, embossing, extruding, curling,

seeming, trimming, doming, tracer, grounder, planisher, perloir, beading; see also **tool** 1.

punch, *v.* **1.** [To hit]—*Syn.* strike, knock, thrust against; see **hit** 1.

2. [To perforate]—*Syn.* pierce, puncture, bore; see **penetrate** 1.

punched, *mod.*—*Syn.* perforated, dented, pierced, pricked, punctured, needled, stamped, embossed, imprinted, bored, dinted, wounded, bitten, tapped, transpierced, impaled, pinked, spiked, gored, speared, stabbed, spitted, stuck.

punctilious, *mod.*—*Syn.* formal, particular, exact; see **careful.**

punctual, *mod.*—*Syn.* prompt, precise, particular, on time, on schedule, exact, timely, seasonable, expeditious, periodic, regular, cyclic, dependable, recurrent, constant, steady, scrupulous, punctilious, meticulous; *both* (D): under the wire, on the nose; see also **accurate** 2, **reliable** 2.—*Ant.* unreliable*, careless, desultory.

punctuality, *n.*—*Syn.* readiness, promptness, steadiness; see **preparation** 2, **regularity.**

punctuation, *n.*—Marks of punctuation include the following—period, colon, semicolon, comma, interrogation, exclamation, parentheses, dash, brackets, apostrophe, hyphen, quotation marks, brace, ellipsis.

puncture (D), *n.*—*Syn.* punctured tire, flat tire, flat (D); see **hole** 1.

puncture, *v.*—*Syn.* prick, perforate, pierce; see **penetrate** 1.

punctured, *mod.*—*Syn.* deflated, let down, no longer inflated; see **damaged, reduced** 1, 2, **ruined** 2.

pundit, *n.*—*Syn.* intellectual, savant, thinker; see **scholar** 2.

pungent, *mod.*—*Syn.* sharp, acid, tart; see **sour** 1.

punish, *v.*—*Syn.* correct, discipline, chasten, castigate, chastise, sentence, train, reprove, lecture, penalize, fine, incarcerate, immure, expel, execute, exile, behead, hang, electrocute, dismiss, debar, disbench, defrock, whip, masthead, keelhaul, smite, spank, paddle, trounce, flog, birch, switch, cuff, inflict penalty, visit punishment; *all* (D): come down (upon), do in, beat up, attend to, crack down on, make it hot for, pitch into, give a dressing-down, dust one's jacket, lick, bring to book, give a lesson to, polish to within an inch of one's life, lower the boom, ground, throw the book at, blacklist, blackball, give one his comeuppance, visit upon; see also **banish** 1, **beat** 2, **censure, imprison, kill** 1, **scold.**

punishable, *mod.*—*Syn.* culpable, criminal, condemned; see **guilty** 1.

punished, *mod.*—*Syn.* corrected, disciplined, chastened, penalized, sentenced, trained, reproved, chastised, castigated, lectured, scolded, imprisoned, incarcerated, immured, expelled, exiled, transported, dismissed, debarred, disbenched, defrocked, whipped, spanked, trounced, flogged, birched, switched, cuffed; *all* (D): cracked down on, given the deuce, pitched into, grounded, licked, given one's deserts; see also **beaten** 1, **confined** 3, **executed** 2.—*Ant.* cleared*, exonerated, released.

punishment, *n.*—*Syn.* correction, discipline, reproof, penalty, infliction, suffering, deprivation, unhappiness, trial, penance, retribution, (just) deserts, mortification, sequestration, disciplinary action, amercement, fine, mulct, reparation, forfeiture, forfeit, confiscation; *all* (D): dose of strap oil, carrot-and-stick treatment, bit of one's mind, rap on the knuckles; see also **execution** 2, **sentence** 1.—*Ant.* freedom*, exoneration, release.

punitive, *mod.*—*Syn.* punitory, vindictive, disciplinary; see **penal.**

punk (D), *mod.*—*Syn.* bad, inadequate, not good; see **poor** 2.

puny, *mod.*—*Syn.* feeble, inferior, diminutive; see **weak** 1.

pup, *n.*—*Syn.* puppy, whelp, young dog; see **animal** 2, **dog** 1.

pupa, *n.*—*Syn.* nymph, chrysalis, cocoon; see **cover** 2, **insect.**

pupil, *n.* **1.** [A follower]—*Syn.* adherent, attendant, satellite; see **follower.**

2. [A student]—*Syn.* undergraduate, co-ed, learner; see **student.**

puppet, *n.* **1.** [A marionette]—*Syn.* manikin, figurine, moppet; see **doll.**

2. [An instrument]—*Syn.* follower, mercenary, servant; see **victim.**

puppetry, *n.*—*Syn.* exhibition, mummery, play; see **act** 2, **performance** 2, **show** 1.

puppy, *n.*—*Syn.* pup, whelp, young dog; see **animal** 2, **dog** 1.

purchasable, *mod.* **1.** [Marketable]—*Syn.* salable, wholesale, for sale; see **commercial** 1, **retail.**

2. [Treacherous]—*Syn.* fraudulent, deceiving, unscrupulous; see **corrupt** 3, **dishonest** 1, **mean** 3.

purchase, *n.* **1.** [The act of buying]—*Syn.* acquirement, procurement, getting, obtaining, shopping, installment plan *or* buying, bargaining, marketing, investing; see also **acquisition** 1, **buying.**

2. [Something bought]—*Syn.* property, possession, gain, booty, acquirement, investment; see also **acquisition** 2, **bargain** 2.

purchase, *v.*—*Syn.* obtain, acquire, buy up; see **buy** 1.

purchaser, *n.*—*Syn.* shopper, obtainer, procurer; see **buyer.**

purchasing, *n.*—*Syn.* obtaining, procuring, acquiring; see **buying.**

pure, *mod.* **1.** [Not mixed]—*Syn.* unmixed, unadulterated, unalloyed, unmingled, simple, clear, genuine, undiluted, classic, real, true, fair, bright, unclouded, transparent, limpid, lucid, straight, pellucid, neat; see also **clear** 2, **genuine** 1, **simple** 1, **transparent** 1.—*Ant.* mixed*, mingled, blended.

2. [Clean]—*Syn.* immaculate, spotless, stainless, unspotted, germ-free, unstained, unadulterated, unblemished, untarnished, unsoiled, disinfected, sterilized, pasteurized, uncontaminated, sanitary, unpolluted, unsullied, purified, refined.—*Ant.* dirty*, sullied, contaminated.

3. [Chaste]—*Syn.* virgin, continent, celibate; see **chaste** 3.

4. [Innocent]—*Syn.* sinless, spotless, unsullied; see **innocent** 4.

5. [Theoretical]—*Syn.* unproved, tentative, philosophical; see **theoretical.**
6. [Absolute]—*Syn.* sheer, utter, complete; see **absolute** 1.

purebred, *mod.* —*Syn.* papered, full-blooded, pedigreed; see **thoroughbred.**

purely, *mod.* —*Syn.* entirely, totally, essentially; see **completely.**

purgative, *n.* —*Syn.* physic, emetic, purge; see **laxative.**

purgatory, *n.* —*Syn.* limbo, hell, torture, penance, hell on earth, place of the dead, hereafter.

purge, *n.* **1.** [Cleansing]—*Syn.* abstersion, clarification, expurgation; see **cleaning, purification.**
2. [Excretion]—*Syn.* defecation, evacuation, catharsis; see **excretion** 1.
3. [Elimination]—*Syn.* eradication, disposal, murder, removal, liquidation, extermination, annihilation, extirpation, assassination, abolition, extinction, disposition, expulsion, ejection; see also **destruction** 1.

purge, *v.* **1.** [To cleanse]—*Syn.* clear, purify, clarify; see **clean, excrete.**
2. [To eliminate]—*Syn.* liquidate, exterminate, dispose of; see **abolish, forbid, kill** 1, **prevent.**

purification, *n.* —*Syn.* purifying, cleansing, ablution, lustration, purgation, catharsis, refinement, laving, washing, bathing, lavation, disinfection; see also **cleaning.**—*Ant.* pollution*, defilement, contamination.

purify, *v.* —*Syn.* cleanse, chasten, clear, refine, wash, disinfect, fumigate, deodorize, depurate, clarify, deterge, rarify, sublimate, edulcorate, purge, filter; see also **clean.**

puritan, *mod.* —*Syn.* puritanical, strict, proper; see **prejudiced.**

puritanical, *mod.* —*Syn.* strict, rigid, prudish; see **severe** 2.

puritanism, *n.* —*Syn.* austerity, prudishness, strictness; see **severity.**

purity, *n.* **1.** [The state of being pure]—*Syn.* pureness, cleanness, cleanliness, immaculateness, stainlessness, whiteness, clearness, untaintedness, immaculacy, unsulliedness.
2. [Innocence]—*Syn.* artlessness, guilelessness, blamelessness; see **innocence** 2, **simplicity** 2, **sincerity.**
3. [Chastity]—*Syn.* abstemiousness, continence, self-command; see **chastity, virtue** 1.

purlieu, *n.* **1.** [Border]—*Syn.* fringe, outskirts, periphery; see **boundary, edge** 1.
2. [Environment]—*Syn.* vicinity, locale, district; see **area** 2, **neighborhood.**

purple, *mod.* —*Syn.* purplish, purply, purpled, reddish blue, bluish red; see also **color** 1.
Tints and shades of purple include the following —lilac, violet, mauve, heliotrope, magenta, plum, lavender, pomegranate, royal purple, Tyrian purple, Indian purple, dahlia purple, wine purple, solferino.

purport, *n.* —*Syn.* import, significance, intent; see **meaning.**

purport, *v.* —*Syn.* indicate, imply, claim (to be); see **mean** 1.

purpose, *n.* **1.** [Aim]—*Syn.* intention, end, goal, mission, objective, object, idea, design, hope, resolve, meaning, view, scope, desire, dream, expectation, ambition, intent, destination, direction, scheme, prospect, proposal, target, aspiration; see also **plan** 2.
2. [Resolution]—*Syn.* tenacity, constancy, persistence; see **confidence** 2, **determination** 2, **faith** 1.
on purpose—*Syn.* purposefully, intentionally, designedly; see **deliberately.**
to good purpose—*Syn.* profitably, usefully, advantageously; see **helpfully.**
to little (*or* **no**) **purpose**—*Syn.* profitlessly, uselessly, worthlessly; see **unnecessarily.**
to the purpose—*Syn.* to the point, pertinent, apt; see **relevant.**

purpose, *v.* —*Syn.* aim, plan, propose; see **intend** 1.

purposeful, *mod.* **1.** [Determined]—*Syn.* obstinate, stubborn, persistent; see **resolute** 2.
2. [Worthwhile]—*Syn.* deliberate, profitable, useful; see **helpful** 1.

purposely, *mod.* —*Syn.* intentionally, designedly, advisedly; see **deliberately.**

purr, *v.* —*Syn.* hum, drone, sigh, sing, mutter; see also **sound** 1.

purse, *n.* —*Syn.* pouch, pocketbook, receptacle, *portemonnaie* (French), moneybag, wallet, pocket, coin purse, billfold, reticule, money belt, sack, vanity case, vanity bag, halfpenny-purse, belt-purse *or* sporran, bursa, saccule, *poche, pochette* (*both* French).
hold the purse strings (D)—*Syn.* be in control of money, finance, manage a household *or* business; see **manage** 1.
tighten the purse strings (D)—*Syn.* scrimp, be sparing, hoard; see **save** 3.

purser, *n.* —*Syn.* banker, cashier, teller; see **accountant.**

pursuant, *mod.* —*Syn.* compatible, following, agreeable; see **harmonious** 2.

pursue, *v.* **1.** [To chase]—*Syn.* seek, hound, track (down), dog, shadow, search for *or* out, give chase (to), drive out *or* away, stalk, run *or* search *or* get *or* go *or* make *or* send *or* prowl *or* look after, gun *or* hunt down, trail, tag with, direct *or* bend one's steps, camp on the trail of, follow close upon, move behind, hunt *or* fish *or* scout out, nose *or* poke around, fasten oneself upon, keep on foot, follow up, attach oneself to ask *or* dig *or* go running *or* gun *or* delve *or* look about for.
2. [To seek]—*Syn.* strive *or* try for, aspire to, attempt; see **try** 1.
3. [To continue]—*Syn.* persevere, proceed, carry on; see **continue** 1.

pursuing, *mod.* —*Syn.* out for, out to, in pursuance of, in the market for, on the lookout for.

pursuit, *n.* —*Syn.* chase, race, pursuance; see **hunt** 2.

purvey, *v.* —*Syn.* furnish, serve, supply; see **provide** 1.

pus, *n.* —*Syn.* infection, discharge, mucus; see **matter** 5.

push, *n.* —*Syn.* shove, force, bearing, propulsion, drive, exertion, weight, straining, putting forth one's strength, shoving, thrusting, forcing, driving, exerting of pressure, lean, inducement, kinetic energy, mass, potential, reserve, impact, blow; see also **pressure** 1, **thrust** 3.

push, *v.* **1.** [To press against]—*Syn.* thrust, shove, butt, crowd, gore, ram, shove *or* crush *or* bear against, jostle, push out of one's way, bear *or* lie on, shoulder, elbow, struggle, strain, exert, contend, set one's shoulder to, rest one's weight on, put forth one's strength; see also **force** 1.
2. [To move by pushing]—*Syn.* impel, accelerate, drive onward, launch, start, set *or* put in motion, actuate, push forward, shift, start going *or* rolling, budge, stir, inch *or* shove along; see also **drive** 3, **propel.**
3. [To promote]—*Syn.* advance, expedite, urge; see **promote** 1.
4. [(D) To sell illegally]—*Syn.* sell under the counter, blackmarket, bootleg, moonshine; see also **sell** 1.

pushcart, *n.*—*Syn.* handcar, trolley, wheelbarrow; see **cart.**

pushed (D), *mod.*—*Syn.* crowded, in trouble, in difficulty; see **embarrassed.**

pusher (D), *n.* **1.** [Intruder]—*Syn.* pest, meddler, interrupter; see **intruder.**
2. [A seller of drugs]—*Syn.* black-market salesman, dope peddler, connection (D); see **criminal.**

push off, *v.*—*Syn.* depart, start, take off; see **leave** 1.

push on, *v.*—*Syn.* keep going, go, make progress; see **continue** 1, 2.

pushover, *n.*—*Syn.* sucker, easy pickings, fool; see **victim** 2.

pussyfoot (D), *v.*—*Syn.* evade, avoid, dodge, sidestep, hedge; see **avoid, evade** 1.

put, *v.* **1.** [To place]—*Syn.* set, seat, settle; see **place** 1.
2. [To establish]—*Syn.* install, quarter, fix; see **establish** 2.
3. [To deposit]—*Syn.* invest in, insert, embed; see **plant.**

put about, *v.*—*Syn.* vary, veer, turn; see **change** 1.

put across *or* **over** (D), *v.*—*Syn.* succeed, fulfill, complete; see **achieve** 1.

put aside, *v.*—*Syn.* deposit, save, put out of the way; see **store** 2.

putative, *mod.*—*Syn.* presumed, supposed, accepted; see **assumed** 1.

put away, *v.*—*Syn.* deposit, save, put out of the way; see **store** 2.

put back, *v.*—*Syn.* bring back, make restitution (for), put in (its) place; see **replace** 1, **return** 2.

put by, *v.*—*Syn.* secure, keep, save; see **preserve** 3.

put-down (D), *n.*—*Syn.* suppression, indignity, cut (D); see **insult.**

put down, *v.*—*Syn.* silence, repress, crush; see **defeat** 1, 2.

put emphasis on, *v.*—*Syn.* stress, dramatize, make clear; see **emphasize.**

put forth, *v.*—*Syn.* produce, form, constitute; see **compose** 3, **create** 2, **invent** 1.

put forward, *v.*—*Syn.* further, urge, present; see **propose** 1.

put in, *v.*—*Syn.* sail for, move toward, land; see **approach** 2.

put (someone) in his place, *v.*—*Syn.* tell off, reprimand, correct; see **censure.**

put off, *v.*—*Syn.* postpone, defer, retard; see **delay.**

put-on, *mod.*—*Syn.* feigned, simulated, calculated; see **pretended.**

put-on (D), *n.* **1.** [A trick]—*Syn.* deception, device, job (D); see **trick** 1.
2. [A joke]—*Syn.* hoax, satire, pretense; see **fake, joke** 1, 2.

put on, *v.* **1.** [To pretend]—*Syn.* feign, sham, make believe; see **pretend** 1.
2. [(D) To deceive]—*Syn.* trick, confuse, confound; see **deceive.**

put on airs, *v.*—*Syn.* brag, show off, make pretensions; see **strut.**

put one's cards on the table, *v.*—*Syn.* say, display, show; see **reveal** 1, **tell** 1.

put one through his paces, *v.*—*Syn.* test, try, try out; see **examine** 1.

put out, *v.*—*Syn.* discard, throw away, turn adrift; see **eject** 1.

put over (D), *v.*—*Syn.* manage, do, get done; see **achieve** 1.

putrefy, *v.*—*Syn.* rot, putresce, decompose; see **decay.**

putrid, *mod.*—*Syn.* corrupt, putrified, decayed; see **rotten** 1.

putter, *v.*—*Syn.* dawdle, fritter, poke; see **loiter.**

put through, *v.*—*Syn.* do, manage, finish; see **achieve** 1.

put to sleep (D), *v.*—*Syn.* knock out, subject to euthanasia, murder; see **kill** 1.

put up, *mod.*—*Syn.* canned, pickled, tinned; see **preserved** 1.

put up, *v.* **1.** [To preserve]—*Syn.* can, smoke, pickle; see **preserve** 3.
2. [To build]—*Syn.* erect, fabricate, construct; see **build** 1.
3. [To bet]—*Syn.* speculate, wager, put one's money on; see **gamble** 1.
4. [To entertain]—*Syn.* house, provide *or* give bed and board, make welcome; see **entertain** 2.

put up with, *v.*—*Syn.* undergo, tolerate, stand; see **endure** 2.

puzzle, *n.* **1.** [The state of being puzzled]—*Syn.* uncertainty, hardship, vexation; see **confusion** 2.
2. [A problem]—*Syn.* tangle, bafflement, question, frustration, intricacy, maze, coil, issue, enigma, proposition, mystification, bewilderment, befuddlement, labyrinth, query, conundrum, mystery, dilemma, oracle, cabala, muddle, esoterica, secret, riddle, ambiguity, difficulty, perplexity, confusion, entanglement, stickler, paradox.—*Ant.* answer*, solution, development.
3. [A problem to be worked for amusement] Varieties include the following—riddle, conundrum, cryptogram, logogram, crossword puzzle, jigsaw puzzle, anagram, acrostic, charade, rebus, puzzle-ring, Chinese puzzle.

puzzle, *v.* **1.** [To perplex]—*Syn.* obscure, bewilder, complicate; see **confuse.**

2. [To wonder]—*Syn.* marvel, be surprised, be astonished; see **wonder** 1.

puzzled, *mod.* —*Syn.* perplexed, bewildered, mystified; see **doubtful** 2.

puzzle out, *v.* —*Syn.* figure out, work out, decipher; see **solve.**

puzzle over, *v.* —*Syn.* think about, consider, debate; see **think** 1.

puzzling, *mod.* **1.** [Obscure]—*Syn.* uncertain, ambiguous, mystifying; see **obscure** 1.
2. [Difficult]—*Syn.* perplexing, abstruse, hard; see **difficult** 2.

pygmy, *n.* —*Syn.* bantam, pixy, dwarf; see **midget, runt.**

pylon, *n.* **1.** [Arch]—*Syn.* span, entrance, door; see **arch.**
2. [Pillar]—*Syn.* shaft, tower, post; see **column** 1.

pyramid, *n.* —*Syn.* tomb, shrine, remains; see **monument.**

pyre, *n.* —*Syn.* pile to be burned, combustible material, fuel; see **fire** 1.

pyromaniac, *n.* —*Syn.* demented person, incendiary, firebug (D); see **arsonist.**

pyrotechnics, *n.* —*Syn.* combustible devices, rockets, sparklers; see **fireworks.**

Q

quack, *mod.* —*Syn.* unprincipled, pretentious, dissembling; see **dishonest** 2.
quack, *n.* —*Syn.* rogue, charlatan, humbug; see **cheat** 1, **impostor.**
quackery, *n.* —*Syn.* duplicity, pretense, misrepresentation; see **dishonesty.**
quadrangle, *n.* **1.** [Quadrilateral]—*Syn.* geometrical foursided figure, parallelogram, rhombus; see **rectangle.**
2. [A court]—*Syn.* courtyard, forum, square; see **court** 1, **yard** 1.
quadrangular, *mod.* —*Syn.* rectangular, quadrilateral, plane; see **angular** 1, **square.**
quadroon, *n.* —*Syn.* mulatto, one-fourth Negro, cross-breed; see **hybrid, Negro.**
quadruped, *n.* —*Syn.* four-legged animal, domestic beast, mammal; see **animal** 1.
quadruple, *mod.* —*Syn.* fourfold, four-way, four times as great, consisting of four parts, quadruplex, four-cycle, quadruplicate, quadripartite, biquadratic, quadrigeminal.
quaff, *v.* —*Syn.* gulp, swallow, guzzle; see **drink** 1, **swallow.**
quagmire, *n.* **1.** [Swamp]—*Syn.* marsh, bog, mire; see **swamp.**
2. [Dilemma]—*Syn.* perplexity, involvement, trouble; see **difficulty** 1, 2, **predicament.**
quail, *v.* —*Syn.* shrink, cower, tremble; see **wince.**
quaint, *mod.* **1.** [Queer]—*Syn.* odd, old, freakish; see **unusual** 2.
2. [Old-fashioned but charming]—*Syn.* fanciful, cute, pleasing, captivating, curious, ancient, antique, picturesque, whimsical, affected, enchanting, baroque, Victorian, French Provincial, Early American, Colonial; see also **charming.**—*Ant.* modern*, up-to-date, fashionable.
quake, *n.* —*Syn.* temblor, tremor, shock; see **earthquake.**
quake, *v.* —*Syn.* tremble, shrink, cower; see **shake** 1.
qualification, *n.* —*Syn.* need, requisite, essential; see **requirement** 1.
qualifications, *n.* —*Syn.* endowments, acquirements, attainments; see **experience** 3.
qualified, *mod.* **1.** [Limited]—*Syn.* conditional, modified, confined; see **restricted.**
2. [Competent]—*Syn.* adequate, equipped, fitted; see **able** 1, 2.
qualify, *v.* **1.** [To limit]—*Syn.* reduce, restrain, temper; see **change** 1.
2. [To fulfill requirements]—*Syn.* fit, suit, pass, be capacitated for, have the requisites, meet the demands, be endowed by nature for, measure up, meet the specifications.—*Ant.* fail*, become unfit, be unsuited.
quality, *n.* **1.** [A characteristic]—*Syn.* attribute, trait, endowment; see **characteristic.**
2. [Essential character]—*Syn.* nature, essence, genius; see **character** 2.
3. [Grade]—*Syn.* class, kind, state, condition, merit, worth, excellence, stage, step, variety, standing, rank, group, place, position, repute; see also **degree** 2.
qualm, *n.* **1.** [Doubt]—*Syn.* indecision, scruple, suspicion; see **doubt** 2, **uncertainty** 2.
2. [Nausea]—*Syn.* faintness, dizziness, queasiness; see **illness** 1.
quandary, *n.* —*Syn.* dilemma, plight, puzzle; see **predicament.**
quantity, *n.* —*Syn.* amount, number, bulk, mass, measure, extent, abundance, volume, capacity, lot, deal, pile, magnitude, multitude, amplitude, portion, carload, sum, profusion, mountain, load, barrel, shipment, consignment, bushel, supply, ton, ocean, flood, sea, flock, the amount of, score, swarm, quite a few, army, legion, host, pack, crowd; *all* (D): bunch, heap, mess, gob, batch, all kinds of, all sorts of; see also **size** 2.
quarantine, *v.* —*Syn.* isolate, hospitalize, interdict, restrain, dock for contagious disease, put under *or* place in quarantine, hold at a distance; see also **separate** 2.
quarantined, *mod.* —*Syn.* shut up *or* away, in *or* under quarantine, hospitalized, restrained, separated; see also **isolated.**
quarrel, *n.* **1.** [An angry dispute]—*Syn.* wrangle, squabble, dissension; see **disagreement** 1, **dispute** 1.
2. [A personal encounter]—*Syn.* fisticuffs, combat, struggle; see **fight** 1.
3. [Objection]—*Syn.* complaint, disapproval, disagreement; see **objection** 1.
quarrel, *v.* —*Syn.* wrangle, dispute, contend, fight, squabble, embroil, clash, altercate, dissent, bicker, struggle, strive, contest, object, complain, disagree, be at loggerheads, argue, charge, allegate, feud, strike, engage in blows, come to an encounter; *all* (D): mix it up with, pick a bone with, tread on one's toes, get tough with, lock horns, have words with, fall foul of, have a brush with, have it out, fall out (with), break with, make the fur fly, kick up a row; see also **oppose** 1.—*Ant.* agree*, accord, harmonize.
quarreling, *mod.* —*Syn.* disagreeing, at odds, at loggerheads, at swords' points, not on speaking terms, at variance, out of line with, in contempt of, in disagreement, out of accord, discordant, inharmonious.
quarrelsome, *mod.* **1.** [Inclined to fight]—*Syn.* factious, combative, pugnacious, litigious, turbulent,

unruly, passionate, violent, contentious, disputatious, dissentious, fiery, impassioned, hotheaded, excitable, hasty, tempestuous, with a chip on one's shoulder (D).—*Ant.* calm*, peaceful, unresisting.
2. [Bad-tempered]—*Syn.* fractious, cross, cross-grained, irascible, snappish, waspish, peevish, petulant, churlish, cantankerous, thin-skinned, touchy, huffy, pettish, peppery; see also **irritable.**—*Ant.* agreeable*, good-natured, unruffled.

quarry, *n.* **1.** [A mine]—*Syn.* shaft, vein, lode; see **mine** 1.
2. [The hunted]—*Syn.* game, chase, prey; see **victim** 1.

quart, *n.*—*Syn.* two pints, thirty-two ounces, one-fourth gallon; see **measure** 1.

quarter, *n.* **1.** [One of four equal parts]—*Syn.* fourth, one-fourth part, portion, farthing, division, span, three months, semester, school term, quarter of an hour, quarter section; see also **part** 1.
2. [One quarter of a dollar; *United States*]—*Syn.* twenty-five cents, one-fourth of a dollar, coin; *both* (D): two bits, white money; see also **money** 1.
3. [Direction]—*Syn.* bearing, region, point; see **direction** 1.
4. [A section of a community]—*Syn.* neighborhood, district, section; see **area** 2.
at close quarters—*Syn.* at close range, cramped, restricted; see **near** 1.
cry quarter—*Syn.* beg for mercy, surrender, quit; see **beg** 1, **stop** 2.

quarter, *v.* **1.** [To divide into quarters]—*Syn.* cleave, dismember, cut up; see **cut** 1, **divide** 1.
2. [To provide living quarters]—*Syn.* lodge, shelter, assign to lodgings, settle, establish, quarter upon, house.

quarterback, *n.*—*Syn.* back, Q.B., quarter; *all* (D): gridironer, signal caller, field general, barker; see also **football player.**

quarterly, *mod.*—*Syn.* by quarters, once every three months, once a quarter, periodically; see also **regularly** 1.

quartermaster, *n.*—*Syn.* commissioned officer, petty officer, supply officer; see **officer** 3.

quarters, *n.*—*Syn.* house, apartment, room, barracks, tent, lodge, cabins, cottage, car trailer.

quartet, *n.*—*Syn.* four persons, four voices, four musicians, string quartet, principals, four-voice parts.

quartz, *n.* Types of quartz include the following—amethyst, false topaz, rock crystal, rose quartz, smoky quartz, bloodstone, agate, onyx, sardonyx, carnelian, chrysoprase, prase, flint, jasper; see also **rock** 1.

quash, *v.* **1.** [To crush]—*Syn.* squash, subdue, repress; see **defeat** 2.
2. [To revoke]—*Syn.* nullify, repeal, revoke; see **cancel** 2.

quasi, *mod.*—*Syn.* supposedly, to a certain extent, apparently; see **almost.**

quaver, *v.*—*Syn.* tremble, vibrate, quiver; see **shake** 1.

quay, *n.*—*Syn.* key, wharf, pier; see **dock** 1.

queasy, *mod.*—*Syn.* squeamish, sick, uneasy; see **uncomfortable** 1.

queen, *n.*—*Syn.* ruler, female ruler, female sovereign, woman monarch, queen mother, regent, wife of a king, czarina, consort, queen consort, queen dowager, queen regent, fairy queen, May Queen, matriarch.

queenly, *mod.*—*Syn.* imperial, grand, noble; see **royal** 1.

queen-size (D), *mod.*—*Syn.* medium large, outsize, not king-size; see **broad** 1, **large** 1.

queer, *mod.* **1.** [Odd]—*Syn.* odd, peculiar, uncommon; see **unusual** 2.
2. [Slightly ill]—*Syn.* qualmy, qualmish, faint; see **sick.**
3. [(D) Unsatisfactory]—*Syn.* incomplete, incompetent, inefficient; see **inadequate** 1.
4. [(D) Suspicious]—*Syn.* strange, questionable, curious; see **suspicious** 2.

quell, *v.* **1.** [To subdue]—*Syn.* put down, stop, silence; see **defeat** 2.
2. [To allay]—*Syn.* reduce, calm, check; see **quiet** 1.

quench, *v.* **1.** [To satisfy]—*Syn.* slake, glut, gorge; see **drink** 1.
2. [To smother]—*Syn.* stifle, dampen, douse (D); see **moisten.**

querulous, *mod.*—*Syn.* fretful, irascible, peevish; see **irritable.**

quest, *n.*—*Syn.* journey, search, crusade; see **examination** 1, **hunt** 2.

question, *n.* **1.** [A query]—*Syn.* inquiry, inquiring, interrogatory, interrogation, inquisition, feeler, catechism, inquest, rhetorical question, burning question, crucial question, leading question, catch question, academic question, vexed question, sixty-four dollar question (D).—*Ant.* answer*, solution, reply.
2. [A puzzle]—*Syn.* enigma, mystery, problem; see **puzzle** 2.
3. [A subject]—*Syn.* proposal, topic, discussion; see **subject** 1.
beside the question—*Syn.* not germane, beside the point, unnecessary; see **irrelevant.**
beyond question—*Syn.* beyond dispute, without any doubt, sure; see **certain** 3.
in question—*Syn.* being considered, under discussion, controversial; see **considered** 1.
out of the question—*Syn.* not to be considered, by no means, no; see **impossible** 1.

question, *v.* **1.** [To ask]—*Syn.* inquire, interrogate, query, quest, seek, search, sound out, petition, solicit, ask about, catechize, show curiosity, pry into, ask a leading question, challenge, raise a question, pick one's brains, make inquiry, quiz, cross-examine, probe, investigate, put to the question, bring into question; *all* (D): grill, pump, give the third degree to; see also **ask** 1.
2. [To doubt]—*Syn.* distrust, suspect, dispute; see **doubt** 1, 2.

questionable, *mod.* **1.** [Justifying doubt]—*Syn.* doubtful, undefined, equivocal, disputable, arguable, obscure, occult, indecisive, controversial, vague, unsettled, open to doubt, indeterminate, debatable, moot, unconfirmed, problematical, cryptic, apocryphal, hypothetical, mysterious, oracular, enigmatic, ambiguous, indefinite, contingent, provisional, paradoxical, under advisement *or* examination, open to question, up for discussion, in question, to be voted on, to be decided, hard to believe,

incredible; see also **uncertain** 2.—*Ant.* definite*, undoubted, credible.
2. [Having a poor appearance or reputation] —*Syn.* dubious, disreputable, notorious, opprobrious, obnoxious, of ill repute, unsatisfactory, of little account, thought ill of, under a cloud, unesteemed, ill-favored, unpopular, unpleasing, ugly, unattractive, offensive, disagreeable, evil-looking, illegitimate, discreditable, unhonored, unliked, unloved; see also **suspicious** 2.—*Ant.* honored*, esteemed, liked.

questioner, *n.* **1.** [An inspector]—*Syn.* quizzer, analyst, examiner; see **investigator.**
2. [A skeptic]—*Syn.* doubter, scoffer, agnostic; see **cynic.**

questioning, *n.* —*Syn.* interrogation, catechism, inquest; see **examination** 2.

questionless, *mod.* —*Syn.* without doubt, indisputable, unquestionable; see **certain** 3.

questionnaire, *n.* —*Syn.* set of questions, inquiry, outline, opinionnaire, classification, survey, poll, canvass; see also **census.**

queue, *n.* **1.** [A braid]—*Syn.* pony tail, plait, pigtail; see **braid.**
2. [A series]—*Syn.* tail, chain, file; see **line** 1.

quibble, *n.* —*Syn.* equivocation, quiddity, dodge; see **lie** 1.

quibble, *v.* —*Syn.* dodge, avoid, beat about the bush; see **evade** 1.

quibbling, *mod.* —*Syn.* ambiguous, evasive, elusive; see **sly** 1.

quick, *mod.* **1.** [Rapid]—*Syn.* swift, expeditious, fleet; see **fast** 1.
2. [Almost immediate]—*Syn.* posthaste, prompt, instantaneous; see **immediate** 1.
3. [Hasty]—*Syn.* impetuous, mercurial, quick-tempered; see **rash.**
4. [Alert]—*Syn.* ready, sharp, vigorous; see **active** 2.

quicken, *v.* **1.** [To hasten]—*Syn.* speed, hurry, make haste; see **hasten** 1.
2. [To cause to hasten]—*Syn.* expedite, urge, promote; see **hasten** 2.
3. [To increase]—*Syn.* grow, strengthen, energize; see **increase** 1.
4. [To come or bring to life]—*Syn.* spring, grow, rise, spring up, be revived, be resuscitated, be animated, activate, arouse, revitalize; see also **animate** 1, **revive** 1.

quickie (D), *n.* **1.** [A hasty action]—*Syn.* brief attempt; limited *or* short *or* small, etc., deed *or* performance *or* operation, etc.; quick one; see **action** 2.
2. [A quick drink]—*Syn. all* (D): short shot, one for the road, wee drappy; see **drink** 2.

quickly, *mod.* **1.** [Rapidly]—*Syn.* speedily, swiftly, fleetly, flying, wingedly, with dispatch, scurrying, hurrying, rushing, shooting, bolting, darting, flashing, dashing, suddenly, in (great) haste, in a hurry, just now, this minute, in a moment, on the instant, in an instant, right away, by forced marches, at a greater rate, without delay, under press of sail, in full sail, against the clock, racing, galloping, loping, sweeping, light-footedly, briskly, at once; *all* (D): like a bat out of hell, on the double, like all forty, in a flash *or* jiffy, to beat the band, on the nail, at full blast, in full sail, hellbent for leather, hand over fist, like mad, at one jump, by leaps and bounds, like a house afire, double-time, like crazy, like fury, full steam ahead, in high gear.—*Ant.* slowly*, sluggishly, creepingly
2. [Soon]—*Syn.* at once, instantly, promptly; see **immediately, soon.**

quickness, *n.* —*Syn.* swiftness, haste, agility; see **speed.**

quicksand, *n.* —*Syn.* snare, trap, quagmire; see **swamp.**

quicksilver, *n.* —*Syn.* mercury, ore, liquid mercury; see **mineral.**

quick-tempered, *mod.* —*Syn.* temperamental, quarrelsome, sensitive; see **irritable.**

quick-witted, *mod.* —*Syn.* sharp, humorous, clever; see **intelligent** 1.

quid, *n.* —*Syn.* chewing tobacco, cud, chew; see **tobacco.**

quid pro quo (Latin), *n.* —*Syn.* retribution, remuneration, return; see **compensation.**

quiescence, *n.* —*Syn.* repose, quiet, calm; see **rest** 1.

quiescent, *mod.* —*Syn.* quiet, cool, serene; see **calm** 1.

quiet, *mod.* **1.** [Calm]—*Syn.* peaceful, unexcited, unanxious; see **calm** 1, 2.
2. [Silent]—*Syn.* hushed, muffled, noiseless, still, stilled, mute, muted, soundless, dumb, quieted, speechless, unspeaking, quiescent, taciturn, reserved, reticent, unuttered, unexpressed, close-mouthed, close, tight-lipped, uncommunicative, secretive.
3. [Motionless]—*Syn.* unruffled, placid, level; see **smooth** 1.
4. [In peaceful circumstances]—*Syn.* secure, settled, retired; see **calm** 2.

quiet, *n.* **1.** [Rest]—*Syn.* calm, tranquillity, relaxation; see **peace** 2.
2. [Silence]—*Syn.* hush, stillness, speechlessness; see **silence** 1.

quiet, *v.* **1.** [To make calm]—*Syn.* calm, cool, relax, compose, tranquilize, satisfy, please, pacify, mollify, assuage, console, subdue, reconcile, gratify, calm down, soften, moderate, smooth, ameliorate, allay, becalm, lull, appease, restrain, palliate, sober, slacken, soothe; see also **comfort** 2, **ease** 1, 2. —*Ant.* excite*, increase, agitate.
2. [To make silent]—*Syn.* still, deaden, silence, reduce *or* lower the sound level, muffle, smother, mute, stop, check, restrain, suppress, break in, preclude, confute, eliminate, repress, refute, confound, answer, quell, insulate; *all* (D): to stop the mouth, floor, put the lid on, button up, choke off, kibosh, put the stopper on; see also **hush, soften** 2. —*Ant.* sound*, ring, cause to sound.

quiet down (D), *v.* —*Syn.* grow silent, be hushed, hush, be subdued, be suppressed, become speechless, fall quiet, break off, be answered.

quietly, *mod.* **1.** [Calmly]—*Syn.* peacefully, unconcernedly, confidently; see **calmly.**
2. [Almost silently]—*Syn.* noiselessly, speechlessly, as quietly as possible; see **silently.**
3. [Without attracting attention]—*Syn.* humbly, unostentatiously, simply; see **modestly.**

quietus, *n.* **1.** [Death]—*Syn.* decease, end, dissolution; see **death** 1.

2. [Defeat]—*Syn.* overcoming, beating, overthrow; see **defeat** 2.

quill, *n.* **1.** [A feather]—*Syn.* down, plume, pinion; see **feather.**

2. [A pen]—*Syn.* fountain pen, goose quill, reed; see **pen** 3.

quilt, *n.* —*Syn.* bed covering, coverlet, comforter, feather bed, puff, down puff, batt, bed quilt, patchwork quilt, pieced quilt, bedspread, pad; see also **cover** 2.

quintessence, *n.* —*Syn.* core, pith, spirit; see **essence** 1.

quip, *n.* **1.** [A jeer]—*Syn.* mockery, satire, offense; see **insult.**

2. [A witticism]—*Syn.* jest, repartee, banter; see **pun.**

quirk, *n.* —*Syn.* vagary, whim, caprice, fancy, whimsy, conceit, humor, turn, twist, knack, peculiarity, foible, idiosyncrasy, crotchet, quibble, equivocation, subterfuge, bee in the bonnet (D); see also **characteristic, irregularity** 2.

quisling, *n.* —*Syn.* fifth columnist, turncoat, secret agent; see **traitor.**

quit, *v.* **1.** [Abandon]—*Syn.* surrender, renounce, relinquish; see **abandon** 1.

2. [To cease]—*Syn.* discontinue, end, desist; see **stop** 2.

3. [To leave]—*Syn.* go away from, depart, vacate; see **leave** 1.

4. [To resign]—*Syn.* leave, cease work, give notice; see **resign** 2.

quite, *mod.* **1.** [Completely]—*Syn.* entirely, wholly, totally; see **completely.**

2. [Really]—*Syn.* truly, positively, actually; see **really** 1.

3. [(D) To a considerable degree]—*Syn.* pretty, more or less, considerably; see **very.**

quitter, *n.* —*Syn.* shirker, dropout, deserter; *all* (D): gold-bricker, piker, ratter, striker, slacker.

quiver, *n.* —*Syn.* shudder, shiver, tremble; see **vibration.**

quiver, *v.* —*Syn.* vibrate, shudder, shiver; see **wave** 3.

quivering, *mod.* —*Syn.* shuddering, shivering, shaking, tremulous, fluttering, trembling, vibrating.

quixotic, *mod.* —*Syn.* daring, fanciful, whimsical; see **romantic** 1.

quiz, *n.* —*Syn.* test, questioning, query; see **examination** 2.

quiz, *v.* —*Syn.* question, test, cross-examine; see **examine** 1.

quiz program *or* **show,** *n.* —*Syn.* question-and-answer game *or* program *or* show, panel, battle of brains, College Bowl (trademark), quiz kids (D); see also **show** 2.

quizzical, *mod.* —*Syn.* eccentric, odd, amusing; see **unusual** 2.

quondam, *mod.* —*Syn.* former, past, extinct; see **preceding.**

quorum, *n.* —*Syn.* enough to transact business, majority of the membership, legal minimum; see **attendance** 2, **member** 1.

quota, *n.* —*Syn.* portion, part, division; see **share.**

quotation, *n.* **1.** [Quoted matter]—*Syn.* excerpt, passage, citation, citing, extract, recitation, repetition, sentence, quote, plagiarism.

2. [A quoted price]—*Syn.* market price, current price, published price, stated price, price named; see also **price.**

quote, *v.* **1.** [To repeat verbatim]—*Syn.* recite, excerpt, extract; see **cite** 2.

2. [To state a price]—*Syn.* give *or* name a price, request, demand; see **price, rate, value** 2.

quoted, *mod.* **1.** [Repeated from another]—*Syn.* recited, excerpted, extracted, cited, instanced, copied.—*Ant.* original*, created, made.

2. [Offered or mentioned at a stated price]—*Syn.* asked, stated, announced, published, named, marked, given, priced, price-marked, ticketed, tagged.

quotient, *n.* —*Syn.* outcome, remainder, computation; see **result.**

quoting, *mod.* —*Syn.* repeating, reciting, citing, excerpting, copying, instancing, announcing, stating, naming, publishing.

R

rabbi, *n.* —*Syn.* Jewish teacher *or* minister, graduate of a rabbinical school, Hebrew doctor of laws, rabbin, rav, master, teacher, preacher, expounder of the law, Talmudist, religious functionary, Hebrew theologian; see also **priest.**

rabbit, *n.* —*Syn.* cony, hare, pika, leveret, lagomorph, *lapin* (French), *Sylvilagus, Lepus* (*both* Latin), bunny, Easter bunny; see also **animal** 2, **rodent.**
Kinds of rabbits include the following—jack, cottontail, snowshoe, Angora, Ostend, Polish, Flemish, Siberian, Silver, Normandy, Patagonian; Belgian hare, Chinchilla hare, tapeti.

rabble, *n.* —*Syn.* mob, masses, riffraff; see **crowd** 1, **people** 3.

rabid, *mod.* **1.** [Fanatical]—*Syn.* obsessed, zealous, keen; see **enthusiastic** 2, **radical** 2.
2. [Insane]—*Syn.* mad, raging, deranged; see **violent** 2.
3. [Affected with rabies]—*Syn.* poisoned, bitten, attacked by a mad dog, hydrophobic, extremely violent, frothing *or* foaming at the mouth, frenzied, raging, virulent; see also **sick.**

rabies, *n.* —*Syn.* canine madness, hydrophobia, lyssa; see **disease** 3.

race, *n.* **1.** [A major division of mankind]—*Syn.* species, culture, variety, type, kind, strain, breed, family, cultural group, color; see also **man** 1.
The supposed races, sense 1, include the following —Caucasian *or* white, Mongolian *or* yellow, Negroid *or* black, American *or* red, Malay *or* brown.
2. [Roughly, people united by blood or custom] —*Syn.* nationality, caste, variety, type, (a) people, mankind, tribe, sept, group, ethnic stock, human race, class, population connected by common descent, kind, nation, folk, group of persons connected by blood *or* heredity, main varieties of the human species, coterie, clique, gene pool, pedigree, lineage, community, inhabitants, population, populace, public, clan, body politic, breeding population; see also **culture** 2, **heredity, society** 2.
3. [A contest, usually in speed]—*Syn.* competition, run, dash, sprint, relay, clash, meet, event, engagement, competitive trial of speed, competitive action, scurry, spurt, clip, pursuit, rush, steeplechase, handicap, round pace, chase, match, *concours* (French), derby, regatta, sweepstakes, turf, lampadephoria, lampadedromy, marathon; *all* (D): heat, grind, speedfest; see also **sport** 3.
Famous races, sense 3, include the following—*automobile:* New Zealand Grand Prix, Australian Grand Prix, Sebring 12-Hour Endurance Race, Pan Formula Two Grand Prix, Targa Florio Road Race, Grand Prix of Monaco, Nürburgring Sports Car Race, Grand Prix of Belgium, Le Mans 24-Hour Race, Grand Prix of France, European Grand Prix, Dutch Grand Prix, Grand Prix of Italy, Indianapolis 500 Speedway, British Grand Prix, German Grand Prix, United States Road Racing Championship; *horse:* Kentucky Derby, Grand National, Derby, Belmont Stakes, Aqueduct Stakes, Preakness, Man O'War Stakes, San Juan Capistrano Handicap, American Derby, Arlington Classic; *yacht:* Bacardi Cup Sailing Championship, St Petersburg-Fort Lauderdale Race, Lipton Cup Race, Newport-Bermuda Yacht Race, One Ton Cup; *bicycle:* Tour de France, Tour d'Italie, New York Six-Day, Tour of Marin, Montreal Six-Day, Kugler-Anderson Memorial Tour of Somerville, U.S. National Championships, Eastern Collegiate International, Tour de St Laurent, Tour de Mexico, Grand Prix of Long Island, Eastern Seaboard Championship, Connecticut Valley Championship; *track:* 50-yard dash, 100-yard dash, 100-meter dash, 200-yard dash, quarter-mile run, half-mile run, mile run, two-mile run, cross-country run, 1500-meter run, 5000-meter run, 120-yard high hurdles, 220-yard low hurdles, marathon; *swimming:* Men's National A.A.U. Championships, Women's A.A.U. Indoor Championships, Men's National A.A.U. Outdoor Championships, Women's National A.A.U. Outdoor Championships, NAIA National Championships, Pan-American Games, Summer Olympic Games.
Famous race tracks include the following—*horse:* Epsom Downs, Churchill Downs, Pimlico Track, Hialeah Park, Aintree, Leopardstown, Longchamp Racecourse, Gavea, Ascot, Siena; *automobile:* Sebring, Monza, Le Mans, Indianapolis, Bonneville, Brands Hatch, Silverstone.

race, *v.* **1.** [To move at great speed]—*Syn.* speed, hurry, run, pursue, chase, tear (around), bustle, spurt, post, skim, press *or* dash on, run swiftly, hasten, trip, fly, hustle, hie, scud, scorch, dash, rush, sprint, swoop, scuttle, move at an accelerated rate of speed, dart, scamper, haste, plunge ahead, whiz, bolt, scramble, whisk, shoot; *all* (D): ride hard, hotfoot it, run like mad, crowd sail, wing one's way, outstrip the wind, burn up the road, gun the motor, skedaddle.
2. [To compete]—*Syn.* run a race, compete in a race, contend in running, follow a course, engage in a contest of speed, try to beat in a contest of speed, contend, enter a competition.

racecourse, *n.* —*Syn.* course, path, turf; see **race track.**

race prejudice, *n.* —*Syn.* racism, race hatred, antisemitism, bigotry, Aryanism, apartheid, intolerance, bias, partiality, unfairness; see also **prejudice.**

racer, *n.* **1.** [A runner]—*Syn.* track man, competitor, sprinter; see **athlete.**
2. [A vehicle designed for racing]—*Syn.* racing auto *or* bicycle *or* motorcycle, etc.; racing model, model stripped for racing, speedboat, yacht; *all* (D): flying coffin, motor bullet, bronco, sea flea, race bike, scow.

race riot, *n.* —*Syn.* civil disturbance, color riot, demonstration; see **fight** 1, **protest.**

race track, *n.* —*Syn.* speedway, track circuit, course, path, drive, runway, cinder path; *all* (D): the cinders, oval, speed oval, ring, platter.

racial, *mod.* —*Syn.* lineal, hereditary, ancestral, genetic, ethnic, genealogical, phyletic, phylogenic, phylogenetic, phylogenetical, ethnological, patriarchal, paternal, parental.

raciness, *n.* **1.** [Sharpness]—*Syn.* tang, pungency, piquancy; see **bitterness** 1.
2. [Vigor]—*Syn.* vitality, liveliness, spirit; see **excitement.**
3. [Indecency]—*Syn.* suggestiveness, indelicacy, pornography; see **lewdness.**

racing, *mod.* —*Syn.* speeding, running, galloping, rushing, hurrying, sailing, whizzing, darting, flying, tearing, shooting, whisking, hastening, at full speed; *all* (D): burning up the road, making time, with the throttle wide open.—*Ant.* crawling*, creeping, going at a snail's pace.

racing, *n.* —*Syn.* sporting, the turf, running, galloping, rushing, hurrying, sailing, whizzing, darting, flying, tearing, shooting, whisking; see also **competition** 1.

racism, *n.* —*Syn.* racial prejudice, racial bias, bigotry, racial discrimination, apartheid, segregation; see also **prejudice.**

racist, *mod.* —*Syn.* white supremacist, favoring racism, bigoted; see **prejudiced.**

racist, *n.* —*Syn.* white supremacist, believer in racism, supporter of the color line; see **bigot.**

rack, *n.* **1.** [A frame]—*Syn.* holder, receptacle, framework, stand, shelf, ledge, perch, frame, bracket, whatnot, arbor, trivet, box, counter, trestle, hat *or* clothes *or* cake *or* bottle *or* pen *or* gun *or* tie *or* folder *or* feed rack; see also **frame** 1.
2. [An engine of torture]—*Syn.* instrument of torture that stretches the body, wheel, iron heel, wooden horse, thumbscrew, iron maiden, boot, water rack, bed of Procrustes, *peine forte et dure* (French), Oregon boot (D); see also **torture.**

racket, *n.* **1.** [Disturbing noise]—*Syn.* uproar, clatter, din; see **disturbance** 2, **noise** 2.
2. [Confusion accompanied by noise]—*Syn.* squabble, scuffle, fracas, clash, row, wrangle, agitation, babel, pandemonium, turbulence, vociferation, clamor, outcry, hullabaloo, tumult, hubbub, commotion, blare, turmoil, stir, noisy fuss, uproar, clatter, charivari, babble, roar, shouting, rumpus, riot, squall, clangor, brawl, fight, pitched battle; *all* (D): free-for-all, (great) to-do, fuss; see also **confusion** 2.
3. [(D) A means of extortion]—*Syn.* illegitimate business, confidence game (*also* (D): con game), conspiracy, plot, intrigue, underworld activity, systematic cheating, numbers pool, policy racket, protection, swindling, illegitimate undertaking, extortion, organized illegal activity, illicit scheme, graft, trick, dishonest game, lawlessness; *all* (D): shakedown, game, push, lay, dodge, the squeeze; see **corruption** 3, **crime** 2, **theft.**
4. [A web and frame used as a bat] Types of rackets include the following—tennis racket, squash racket, fivesbat, lacrosse net, badminton racket; see also **frame** 2.

racketeer, *n.* —*Syn.* gang leader, trickster, dealer in illicit goods; see **criminal.**

racy, *mod.* **1.** [Full of zest]—*Syn.* rich, pungent, piquant, spicy, sharp, spirited, saucy, forcible, appetizing, smart, clever, witty, exhilarating, vigorous, forcible, lively, vivacious, animated, exciting, sprightly, buoyant, playful, sportive, forceful, energetic, keen, bright, stimulating, fiery, gingery, peppery, snappy.—*Ant.* dull*, doughy, flat.
2. [(D) Not quite respectable]—*Syn.* indecent, erotic, indelicate; see **lewd** 1, **risqué.**

radar, *n.* —*Syn.* radio *d*etecting *a*nd *r*anging, radio locator (British), radar principle, AWACS, Missile Site Radar (MSR), Multi-Function Array Radar (MAR); see also **detector, electronics.**

radial, *mod.* —*Syn.* branched, outspread, radiated; see **spiral, spreading.**

radiance, *n.* —*Syn.* brightness, brilliance, effulgence; see **light** 1.

radiant, *mod.* —*Syn.* shining, luminous, radiating; see **bright** 1.

radiate, *v.* **1.** [To send forth from a center]—*Syn.* shed, diffuse, spread, disperse, shoot in all directions, irradiate, emit (in straight lines), transmit, disseminate (from a center), broadcast, dispel, strew, sprinkle, circulate, send out in rays from a point, throw out; see also **scatter** 2.
2. [To shed light or heat]—*Syn.* beam, light up, illumine, heat, warm, circulate, expand, widen, brighten, illuminate, irradiate, glitter, glisten, glow, glare, gleam, glimmer, flare, blaze, flicker, sparkle, flash, scintillate, shimmer, fulgurate, coruscate, reflect; see also **light** 1, **shine** 1, **spread** 3.

radiation, *n.* **1.** [Dissemination]—*Syn.* propagation, dissipation, divarication, polarization, scattering, spread, diffraction, transmission, broadcast, emission, ramification, diffusion, dispersion, circulation, divergence, dispersal; see also **distribution** 1, **extent.**
2. [Fallout]—*Syn.* nuclear *or* radioactive particles, radioactivity, radiant energy; see **fallout, pollution.**

radical, *mod.* **1.** [Fundamental]—*Syn.* original, primitive, native; see **fundamental** 1, **organic.**
2. [Advocating extreme change]—*Syn.* extreme, thorough, complete, rabid, insurgent, revolutionary, iconoclastic, advanced, forward, insurrectionary, progressive, abolitionist, militant, uncompromising, intransigent, recalcitrant, mutinous, recusant, seditious, restive, riotous, refractory, lawless, racist, white supremacist, insubordinate, anarchistic, unruly, nihilistic, communistic, Bolshevistic, liberal, leftist, immoderate, freethinking; *both* (D): ultra, red; see also **fanatical, rebellious** 2. —*Ant.* conservative*, reformist, gradualist.
3. [Believing in violent political and social change] —*Syn.* leftist, communistic, heretical; see **revolutionary** 1.

radical, *n.* —*Syn.* insurgent, objector, revolutionist, revolutionary, insurrectionist, leftist, Bolshevist, anarchist, socialist, communist, pacifist, syndicalist, nihilist, avant-garde, traitor, rebel, revolter, mutineer, firebrand, anarcho-syndicalist, renegade, extremist, crusader, individualist, fascist, Nazi, racist, white supremacist, fetishist, misfit, iconoclast, eccentric, freethinker, rightist, yippie, hippie, fanatic, Black nationalist, demonstrator, peace marcher, rioter, fifth columnist, nonconformist, left-winger, right-winger; *all* (D): (John) Bircher, pinko, red; see also **agitator, rebel.**

radically, *mod.* **1.** [Completely]—*Syn.* wholly, thoroughly, entirely; see **completely.**
2. [Originally]—*Syn.* basically, primitively, firstly; see **essentially, formerly.**

radio, *n.* **1.** [The study and practice of wireless communication]—*Syn.* radio transmission, radio reception, signaling, radio engineering, radiotelephony, radiotelegraphy, television, radio work, radio operation, radionics, radio-telephonics; see also **broadcasting, communication** 2, **communications.**
2. [A receiving device]—*Syn.* wireless, ship's radio, radio set, home radio, transistor radio (*or* (D): transistor), portable radio, pocket radio, car radio, Walkman (trademark), walkie-talkie; *all* (D): ghetto blaster, boom box, squawk box; see also **communications.**

radioactive, *mod.* —*Syn.* active, energetic, radiating poison, dangerous, hot (D); see also **poisonous.**

radioactivity, *n.* —*Syn.* radiant energy *or* heat, radioactive particles, Roentgen rays; see **energy** 3, **fallout.**

radiogram, *n.* —*Syn.* telegram, cablegram, message; see **communication** 2.

radiograph, *n.* —*Syn.* negative, roentgenogram, gamma-ray picture; see **photograph, X-rays.**

radio wave, *n.* —*Syn.* FM (frequency modulation), AM (amplitude modulation), sound wave; see **frequency** 2.

radius, *n.* —*Syn.* space, sweep, range, semidiameter, spoke, compass, reach, span, interval, limit; see also **boundary, expanse.**

raffle, *n.* —*Syn.* sweepstakes, pool, lottery, disposition of a prize among shareholders by lot, drawing, lots, stake, wager, flier, wagering, game of chance, bet, betting, tossup, speculation, gaming, long odds, random shot; see also **gambling.**

raft, *n.* —*Syn.* flatboat, barge, float, pontoon, lighter, catamaran, life raft, swimming raft, rubber raft, balsa, jangada; see also **boat.**

rafter, *n.* —*Syn.* crossbeam, roof beam, rib, common rafter, hip rafter, jack rafter, valley rafter; see also **beam** 1, **timber** 2.

rag, *n.* —*Syn.* remnant, wiper, dishrag, discarded material, hand rag, tatter, shred; see also **cloth.**
chew the fat *or* the rag (D)—*Syn.* chat, converse, have a talk; see **talk** 1.

rag (D), *v.* —*Syn.* nag, annoy, scold; see **abuse** 1, **bother** 2.

ragamuffin, *n.* —*Syn.* beggar, waif, hobo; see **orphan, tramp** 1.

rage, *n.* **1.** [Violent anger]—*Syn.* fury, wrath, ferocity; see **anger.**
2. [A fit of anger]—*Syn.* frenzy, tantrum, uproar, paroxysm, hysterics, explosion, storm, outburst, spasm, convulsion, eruption, furor, excitement, extreme agitation, madness, vehemence, fury, rampage, huff, wrath, raving, violent anger, choler, spleen, ire, resentment, bitterness, acerbity, gall, ferment, acrimony, irritation, animosity, exasperation, passion, indignation, tantrum, heat, temper, umbrage, squall; *all* (D): blowup, apoplexy, fireworks, conniption (fit), hemorrhage; see also **fit** 2, **violence** 2.
3. [The object of enthusiasm and imitation]—*Syn.* style, mode, fashion, vogue, craze, mania, the last word, the latest; *all* (D): quite the cheese, the latest scream, the in thing, the newest wrinkle, all the go; see also **fad.**
all the rage (D)—*Syn.* modish, in style *or* vogue, (much) in demand; see **fashionable, popular** 1.

rage, *v.* **1.** [To give vent to anger]—*Syn.* rant, fume, rave, foam, splutter, flame, yell, scream, roar, rail at, boil (over), shake, quiver, fulminate, seethe, shout, scold, go into a tantrum, have a fit, run amok, run riot, rampage, fly apart, flare *or* blaze *or* flame *or* fire *or* bristle up, carry *or* go on, show violent anger, act with fury, act with unrestrained violence, be violently agitated with passion, bluster, storm, be furious, fret, chafe, lose one's temper; *all* (D): work oneself into a sweat, go berserk, go into a tailspin, go up in the air, have a (conniption) fit, blow one's top, breathe fire and fury, go on the warpath *or* rampage, put one's fur up, gnash one's teeth, raise Cain *or* the devil, take on, throw a fit, go into orbit, fly off *or* out, fly off the handle, fly into a passion, explode, vent one's spleen, stamp with rage, look black, snap at, run mad, raise a storm, bridle *or* blow up, blow a fuse, champ at the bit, fly off at a tangent, cut loose, have a hemorrhage, get one's hair up, get one's quills up, foam *or* froth at the mouth, make a fuss over, kick up a row, have a nervous breakdown, let off steam, look daggers, get oneself into a lather, lose one's head.—*Ant.* cry*, be calm, pout.
2. [To be out of control]—*Syn.* storm, overflow, break out, erupt, explode, flare, roar; see also **burn** 1, **run** 1.
3. [To become insane]—*Syn.* go crazy *or* insane, become mentally ill; *all* (D): go nuts *or* haywire *or* balmy *or* loony, break down, go off the deep end, crack (up), take leave of one's senses, run amok.

ragged, *mod.* —*Syn.* tattered, in shreds, patched, rough-edged, badly worn, rough, worn out, broken, worn to rags, frayed, frazzled, threadbare, shoddy, out at the seams, shredded, battered, the worse for wear, worn to a thread, having loose-hanging shreds, down at the heels, motheaten, full of holes, torn, rent, unpressed, poorly made, badly dressed; see also **shabby** 1, **worn** 2.—*Ant.* whole*, new, unworn.
run ragged (D)—*Syn.* exhaust, harass, beat; see **defeat** 1, **tire** 2.

raging, *mod.* —*Syn.* furious, irate, enraged; see **angry.**

ragout, *n.* —*Syn.* hash, *pot-au-feu* (French), goulash; see **soup, stew.**

ragpicker, *n.* —*Syn.* garbage man, junk dealer, dumpman; see **beggar** 1, **junkman, tramp** 1.

rags, *n.* —*Syn.* old clothes, patched clothing, tatters, torn garments, shreds and patches, scraps, castoff clothes, shreds, frazzles, patches, remnants; see also **clothes.**

ragtime, *n.* —*Syn.* jazz, swing, blues; see **music** 1.

raid, *n.* **1.** [A predatory attack]—*Syn.* invasion, assault, forced entrance, sortie, sweep, reconnaissance in force, incursion, foray; see also **attack** 1.
2. [An armed investigation]—*Syn.* seizure, surprise entrance, police raid, roundup; *all* (D): bustup, tipover, pull, bust, shootup; see also **arrest** 1, **capture.**

raid, *v.* —*Syn.* assail, storm, fire on, march on, bomb, shell, bombard, rake, torpedo, strafe, strike at, charge, loot, assault, forage, pirate, maraud, sack, ransack, despoil, invade, force an entrance, make away with, besiege, plunder, pillage, blockade; see also **attack** 1.—*Ant.* surrender, defend*, protect.

raider, *n.* **1.** [A person who makes raids]—*Syn.* bandit, thief, plunderer, rifler, assaulter, highwayman, pillager, privateer, hijacker, cattle lifter, predator, wrecker, depredator, free-booter, holdup man, sharper, pilferer, looter, poacher, viking, bushranger, spoiler, corsair, filibuster, picaroon, filcher, rustler, cavalryman, guerrilla, marauder, brigand, buccaneer, invader, despoiler, abductor; see also **criminal, pirate, robber.**
2. [A vessel engaged in raiding]—*Syn.* privateer, pirate ship, brigantine, corsair, submarine, U-boat, mosquito boat, torpedo boat; see also **ship.**

rail, *n.* **1.** [A polelike structure]—*Syn.* post, railing, barrier, picket, rail fence, siding, balustrade, banister, paling, rest, hand rail, guard rail, brass rail; see also **bar** 1, **fence** 1.
2. [A track; *often plural*]—*Syn.* railway, monorail, railroad track; see **railroad, track** 1.
go off the rails (D)—*Syn.* go crazy, run amok, become insane; see **rage** 3.
ride on a rail (D)—*Syn.* drive away, exile, run out of town; see **banish** 1.

rail at, *v.* —*Syn.* thunder against, rant, fume; see **rage** 1.

railing, *n.* —*Syn.* balustrade, fence, banister; see **rail** 1.

raillery, *n.* —*Syn.* derision, caricature, satire; see **parody** 1, **ridicule.**

railroad, *n.* —*Syn.* track, line, railway, trains, rails, elevated, underground, subway, *métro* (French), commuter line, sidetrack, siding, passing track, loading track, feeder line, main line, double track, single track, trunk line, transcontinental railroad, system; *all* (D): el, iron horse, dinky; see also **train** 2.

railway, *n.* —*Syn.* track, line, route; see **railroad.**

raiment, *n.* —*Syn.* attire, garments, clothing; see **clothes.**

rain, *n.* **1.** [Water falling in drops]—*Syn.* drizzle, mist, sprinkle, sprinkling, damp day, spring rain, rainfall, shower, precipitation, wet weather; *all* (D): cat-and-dog weather, liquid sunshine, sizzle-sozzle, drizzle-drazzle, sky-juice, Scotch mist.
2. [A rainstorm]—*Syn.* thunderstorm, tempest, cloudburst; see **storm** 1.

rain, *v.* —*Syn.* pour, drizzle, drop, fall, shower, sprinkle, mist, mizzle, spit, set in, lay the dust, patter; *all* (D): rain cats and dogs, come down in bucketfuls, rain pitchforks and hammer-handles; see also **storm.**

rainbow, *n.* —*Syn.* iris, prism, colors; see **spectrum.**

raincoat, *n.* —*Syn.* oilskin, canvas coat, rubber coat, mackintosh *or* mac (D), London Fog (trademark), treated canvas coat, waterproof, protector, sou' wester, windbreaker, parka, reversible, overcoat; see also **coat** 1, **clothes.**

raindrop, *n.* —*Syn.* drop, sprinkle, dewdrop; see **rain** 1.

rainfall, *n.* —*Syn.* precipitation, downpour, moisture; see **rain** 1.

rain gauge, *n.* —*Syn.* hyetometer, hyetograph, ombrometer, instrument for measuring rainfall, udomograph, ombrograph, pluviograph, udometer, pluviometer, hyetometrograph; see also **gauge.**

rain or shine (D), *mod.* —*Syn.* fated, unavoidable, sure; see **certain** 3, **inevitable.**

rainproof, *mod.* —*Syn.* watertight, impermeable, waterproof; see **dry** 1, **protected.**

rainy, *mod.* —*Syn.* moist, coastal, drizzly; see **stormy** 1, **wet** 2.

raise, *n.* —*Syn.* raising, salary increment, advance; see **addition** 2, **promotion** 1.

raise, *v.* **1.** [To lift]—*Syn.* uplift, upraise, upheave, elevate, hoist, run *or* pull *or* set *or* lift *or* tilt *or* throw *or* take *or* bring *or* place *or* move *or* put *or* hold *or* block *or* stand *or* cock up, heave, set upright, put on its end, shove, boost, upcast, lever, exalt, rear, mount, pry, prise.—*Ant.* lower*, bring down, take down.
2. [To nurture]—*Syn.* bring up, rear, nurse, suckle, nourish, wean, breed, cultivate, train, foster; see also **provide** 1, **support** 5.
3. [To collect or make available]—*Syn.* gather, allocate, procure, bring together, borrow, have ready; see also **accumulate** 1, **appropriate** 2.
4. [To erect]—*Syn.* construct, establish, put up; see **build** 1.
5. [To ask]—*Syn.* bring up, suggest, put; see **ask** 1, **propose** 1.
6. [To advance in rank]—*Syn.* exalt, dignify, honor; see **promote** 2.

raise Cain (D), *v.* —*Syn.* break up, shatter, storm; see **damage** 1, **destroy** 1.

raised, *mod.* **1.** [Elevated]—*Syn.* lifted, hoisted, built high, heightened, set high, in relief, erected, constructed, set up, jerry-built; see also **built** 1. —*Ant.* reduced*, lowered, taken down.
2. [(D) Nurtured]—*Syn.* reared, brought up, trained, prepared, educated, fostered, bred, nourished, nursed.
3. [Produced]—*Syn.* grown, harvested, cultivated, made, mass-produced, assembly-lined (D).

raise hell (D), *v.* —*Syn.* carry on, celebrate, carouse; see **drink** 2, **riot.**

raise money, *v.* —*Syn.* make money (by), collect, procure; see **earn** 2.

rajah, *n.* —*Syn.* Indian monarch, ruler, maharajah; see **chief** 2, **leader** 2.

rake, *n.* **1.** [A debauched person]—*Syn.* lecher, roué, libertine, profligate, sensualist, seducer, philanderer, gigolo, Don Juan, Casanova, Lothario; see also **drunkard, rascal.**
2. [A pronged implement] Rakes include the following—refuse, clam, lawn, garden, gleaning, moss, hay, buck, stubble, weeding, oyster, horse,

revolving, sweep, dump, side-delivery; leaf sweeper; see also **tool.**

rake, *v.* **1.** [To use a rake]—*Syn.* clear up, collect, scratch, gather, scrape, clean up, furrow, weed, clear, grade, level; see also **clean, smooth** 1, **sweep.**
2. [To sweep with gunfire]—*Syn.* strafe, machine-gun, blister; see **shoot** 1.

rake-off (D), *n.* —*Syn.* illegal fee, illegitimate commission, cream (D); see **booty, commission** 5, **pay** 1, **profit** 2.

rakish, *mod.* —*Syn.* smart, dashing, chic; see **fashionable.**

rally, *n.* —*Syn.* celebration, mass meeting, session; see **gathering.**

rally, *v.* **1.** [To return to the attack]—*Syn.* unite against, reassemble, renew, redouble, counterattack, come together, charge, come round *or* about, surge forward; see also **attack** 1, **return** 1, **revenge.**—*Ant.* disperse, scatter*, disintegrate.
2. [To urge others to rally, sense 1]—*Syn.* call to arms, cry havoc, inspirit; see **encourage** 2, **urge** 2.
3. [To regain strength]—*Syn.* surge, recuperate, grow stronger; see **recover** 3, **revive** 2.

ram, *n.* **1.** [An object used to deliver a thrust]—*Syn.* plunger, pump, beam, prow, hammerhead, arm piece, weight, pole, shaft, lever, spike, battering-ram, pile driver, tamping iron, punch, sledge hammer, rammer, tamper, monkey, bat, maul, hydraulic ram, spar, piston, drop weight, bow; see also **bar** 1, **hammer.**
2. [A male sheep]—*Syn.* tup, wild ram, buck, bucksheep; see also **animal** 2, **sheep.**
Breeds of rams include the following—Leicester, Rambouillet, Merino, Lincoln, Oxforddown, Hampshire, Cotswold, Southdown, Suffolk, Shropshire, Cheviot.

ram, *v.* **1.** [To strike head-on]—*Syn.* bump, collide, hook; see **butt** 1, **hit** 1, 2.
2. [To pack forcibly]—*Syn.* cram, jam, stuff; see **pack** 2.

ramble, *v.* **1.** [To saunter]—*Syn.* stroll, promenade, roam; see **walk** 1.
2. [To speak or write aimlessly]—*Syn.* drift, stray, diverge, meander, gossip, talk nonsense, chatter, babble, digress, maunder, get off the point *or* subject, go on and on, talk discursively, write without sequence of ideas, expiate, protract, enlarge, descant, be diffuse, prose, dwell on, amplify, go astray, drivel, rant and rave, talk at random; *all* (D): talk off the top of one's head, dote, blather, harp on, go off on a tangent, beat around the bush.
3. [To go in various directions; *said especially of vines*]—*Syn.* twist, wander, roam, branch off, climb, spread, fork, straggle, stray, extend, grow, clamber, trail; see also **turn** 6, **wind** 3.
4. [(D) To move at a lively pace]—*Syn.* go fast, step lively, trot; see **run** 2.

rambler, *n.* **1.** [One who rambles]—*Syn.* globe-trotter, nomad, pilgrim; see **traveler.**
2. [A rambling flower or vine]—*Syn.* rambling rose, climber, climbing shrub; see **rose, vine.**

rambling, *mod.* **1.** [Strolling]—*Syn.* hiking, promenading, roaming, sauntering, roving, taking a walk, moving about, wandering about aimlessly, perambulatory, straggling, wayfaring, nomadic, meandering, taking an irregular course, vagrant, zigzagging, itinerant, migratory, ambulatory, peripatetic; see also **walking, wandering** 1.
2. [Incoherent]—*Syn.* discursive, disconnected, confused; see **incoherent** 2, **incongruous** 1.
3. [Covering considerable territory without much plan]—*Syn.* spread out, strewn, straggling, trailing, random, here and there, at length, widely thrown, unplanned, sprawling, gangling; see also **scattered.**—*Ant.* closely formed, planned*, compact.

rambunctious, *mod.* —*Syn.* boisterous, noisy, rough; see **loud** 2, **rude** 2.

ramification, *n.* **1.** [The process of branching]—*Syn.* forking, divarication, bifurcation, radiation, breaking, branching, dividing, subdividing, shooting off, partition; see also **division** 1.—*Ant.* concentration*, centralization, uniting.
2. [A result of ramification, sense 1]—*Syn.* offshoot, bough, river; see **branch** 1, **division** 2.

ramp, *n.* —*Syn.* incline, slope, grade; see **hill, inclination** 5.

rampage, *n.* —*Syn.* turmoil, uproar, ferment; see **disturbance** 2, **violence** 1.

rampageous, *mod.* —*Syn.* boisterous, uncontrollable, wild; see **violent** 4.

rampant, *mod.* —*Syn.* raging, uncontrolled, growing (without check), violent, vehement, impetuous, rank, turbulent, luxuriant, blustering, tumultuous, exuberant, profuse, boisterous, furious, unruly, wanton, rife, prevalent, dominant, predominant, excessive, clamorous, fanatical, impulsive, exceeding all bounds, impassioned, intolerant, unrestrained, epidemic, pandemic, extravagant, overabundant, sweeping the country, like wildfire (D); see also **plentiful** 2, **wild** 3.—*Ant.* modest*, mild, meek.

rampart, *n.* **1.** [A barrier]—*Syn.* barricade, protection, earthwork; see **barrier, support** 2.
2. [An embankment]—*Syn.* bulwark, elevation, mound of earth; see also **hill, ridge** 2, **wall** 1.

ramshackle, *mod.* —*Syn.* crumbling, rickety, decrepit; see **shabby** 1, **shaky** 1, **unsteady** 1.

ranch, *n.* —*Syn.* plantation, grange, farmstead, ranchland(s), ranch house, ranch buildings, hacienda; poultry, fruit, cattle, etc., ranch; Western cattle farm; *all* (D): horse *or* sheep *or* cattle spread, holdout, rancho; see also **farm, property** 2.

rancher, *n.* —*Syn.* ranch-owner, ranchman, stockman, breeder, cattle farmer, cowkeeper, cowherder, shepherd, drover, grazier, stock breeder, horse trainer, herdsman, herder, ranchero, broncobuster, granger, cattleman, cowboy, cattle baron *or* king; see also **farmer.**

rancid, *mod.* **1.** [Decaying]—*Syn.* contaminated, rotten, tainted, stale, bad, polluted, unhealthy, noxious, moldy, carious, putrescent, impure, decomposing, putrefied, musty, rank, fetid, foul, offensive.—*Ant.* fresh*, fragrant, sweet.
2. [Having a rank taste and odor]—*Syn.* foul, fetid, stinking, putrid, offensive, smelly, sour, disagreeable, malodorous, strong-smelling, saprogenous, cloacal, feculent, mephitic, sharp, nasty, disgusting, evil-smelling, gamy, high, strong, putrefactive, turned, musty, reeky, noisome; see also **rank** 2.

rancor, *n.* —*Syn.* malignity, spite, hatred, malice, enmity, ill will, malevolence, ill feeling, animosity, animus, hostility, bitterness, unfriendliness, antagonism, variance, antipathy, aversion, uncharitableness, vindictiveness, hardness of heart, acrimony, harshness, venom, mordacity, acerbity, ruthlessness, umbrage, pique, bile, spleen, virulence, spitefulness, vengeance, grudge, dudgeon, vengefulness, revengefulness, retaliation; see also **hate.** —*Ant.* friendship*, love, respect.

random, *mod.* —*Syn.* haphazard, chance, accidental; see **aimless, irregular** 1.

at random—*Syn.* haphazardly, by chance, aimlessly; see **accidentally.**

range, *n.* **1.** [Distance]—*Syn.* reach, span, horizontal projection; see **expanse.**
2. [Extent]—*Syn.* length, area, expanse; see **extent.**
3. [A series of mountains]—*Syn.* highlands, alps, sierras; see **mountain** 1.
4. [Land open to grazing]—*Syn.* pasture, grazing land, field, meadow, lea, plain, grassland, prairie land; see also **country** 1.
5. [A kitchen stove]—*Syn.* gas range, electric range, portable range; see **appliance, stove.**

range, *v.* **1.** [To vary]—*Syn.* differ, fluctuate, diverge from; see **change** 1, **vary** 1.
2. [To traverse wide areas]—*Syn.* encompass, reach, spread *or* sweep *or* pass over, cover, stray, cruise, stroll, wander, ramble, explore, scour, search, reconnoiter, traverse, roam, rove; see also **cross** 1, **travel** 2.
3. [To place in order]—*Syn.* line up, classify, arrange; see **order** 3, **rank** 1.

range fire, *n.* —*Syn.* brush fire, holocaust, blaze; see **fire** 1.

ranger, *n.* **1.** [Forester]—*Syn.* game warden, woodsman, range rider; see **watchman.**
2. [Trooper]—*Syn.* mounted policeman, patrolman, guard; see **policeman, soldier.**

ranging, *mod.* **1.** [Grazing]—*Syn.* feeding, nibbling grass, browsing, chewing cud, pasturing; see also **grazing** 1.
2. [Varying]—*Syn.* fluctuating, differing, shifting, extending; see also **changing, different** 1.
3. [Moving over wide areas]—*Syn.* roaming, flying over, roving, sweeping, spanning, overrunning, speeding through, stretching; see also **traveling** 2.

rangy, *mod.* —*Syn.* skinny, lanky, gangling; see **thin** 2.

rank, *mod.* **1.** [Having luxurious growth]—*Syn.* wild, dense, lush, vigorous, tall of growth, tropical, semitropical, overabundant, jungly, fertile, rich, productive, high-growing, fructiferous, coarse, overgrown, luxuriant, exuberant, profuse, prolific, lavish, excessive, extreme; see also **green** 2, **thick** 1. —*Ant.* sparse, thin*, scanty.
2. [Having a foul odor]—*Syn.* smelly, fetid, putrid, stinking, rancid, disagreeable, smelling, offensive, sour, foul, fusty, noisome, noxious, graveolent, stale, tainted, gamy, musty, strong, putrescent, rotten, moldy, high, ill-smelling, turned, nauseating, obnoxious, disgusting, reeking, mephitic, malodorous, ordurous, nasty, feculent, strong-smelling.—*Ant.* fragrant, sweet*, fresh.
3. [Corrupt]—*Syn.* gross, coarse, indecent; see **wicked** 1.

rank, *n.* **1.** [A row]—*Syn.* column, file, string; see **line** 1.
2. [Degree]—*Syn.* seniority, standing, station, authority, status, grade, class, order, sphere; see also **degree** 2.
3. [Social eminence]—*Syn.* station, position, distinction, note, nobility, caste, privilege, standing, reputation, quality, situation, esteem, condition, state, place (in society), status, circumstance, footing, grade, blood, family, pedigree, ancestry, stock, parentage, birth.

pull rank on (D)—*Syn.* take advantage, exploit, abuse subordinates; see **command** 1, 2, **insult.**

rank, *v.* **1.** [To arrange in a row, or rows]—*Syn.* put in line, line up, place in formation; see **order** 3.
2. [To evaluate comparatively]—*Syn.* place, put, regard, judge, assign, give precedence to, fix, establish, settle, estimate, value, valuate, include, list, rate; see also **classify.**
3. [To possess relative evaluation]—*Syn.* be worth, stand, have a place head, go ahead of *or* before, be anterior to, come first, forerun, antecede, have supremacy (over) *or* the advantage (of), precede, outrank, take the lead, take precedence (over), belong, count among, be classed, stand in relationship.

rank and file, *n.* **1.** [Soldiers]—*Syn.* infantry, militia, privates; see **soldier, troops.**
2. [The common people]—*Syn.* masses, the common people, proletariat; see **people** 3.

ranked, *mod.* —*Syn.* ordered, piled, (neatly) stacked, corded, arranged, heaped; see also **organized.**—*Ant.* disordered*, disarranged, strewn.

rankle, *v.* —*Syn.* annoy, bother, pester, pain, rile, nettle, mortify, chafe, fret, hurt, gall, irritate, inflame, lie embedded; see also **anger.**

rankling, *n.* **1.** [Decay]—*Syn.* festering, putrefaction, soreness, decay, putrescence, suppuration, matter, pus.
2. [Hatred]—*Syn.* malevolence, hostility, resentment; see **anger, hate, malice.**

ranks, *n.* —*Syn.* rank and file, lower strata, common soldiery, men, enlisted men; see also **army** 1, **soldier.**

ransack, *v.* **1.** [To search thoroughly]—*Syn.* rummage, explore, turn upside down, look all over for, look high and low for, leave no stone unturned, scour, seek everywhere, ferret *or* nose *or* hunt out, overhaul, sound, spy, peer, look around, pry, scan, probe, look into, investigate, scrutinize; see also **hunt** 2, **search.**
2. [To loot]—*Syn.* pillage, plunder, ravish, rape, strip, despoil, rifle, forage, maraud, make off with, take away, seize, appropriate, spoil, poach, gut, rustle, lift, thieve, ravage, lay waste, pilfer, bag, rob, steal, filch, purloin; *both* (D): crib, pinch; see also **raid.**

ransom, *n.* —*Syn.* redemption (money), compensation, expiation; see **bribe.**

ransom, *v.* —*Syn.* release, rescue, deliver, recover, regain, emancipate, manumit, unchain, unfetter, buy off, extricate, reprieve, liberate, save; see also **free** 1, **redeem** 1.—*Ant.* imprison*, confine, lock up.

rant, *n.* —*Syn.* bombast, racket, patter; see **nonsense** 1.

rant, *v.* —*Syn.* rave, fume, rail; see **rage** 1, **yell.**

ranting, *mod.* —*Syn.* raging, crazy, mad; see **angry.**
rap, *n.* —*Syn.* knock, thump, slap; see **blow** 1.
beat the rap (D)—*Syn.* avoid punishment, evade, be acquitted; see **escape.**
bum rap (D)—*Syn.* unfair sentence, blame, frame (D); see **punishment.**
take your rap (D)—*Syn.* be punished, suffer, take the blame; see **pay for.**
rap, *v.* **1.** [To tap sharply]—*Syn.* knock, strike, whack; see **beat** 2, **hit** 1.
2. [(D) To talk, often compulsively]—*Syn.* chatter, jabber, run off at the mouth (D); see **babble, talk** 1.
rapacious, *mod.* **1.** [Greedy]—*Syn.* grasping, avaricious, miserly; see **greedy** 1, 2.
2. [Living on prey]—*Syn.* ravening, ravenous, predatory, predacious, carnivorous, devouring, voracious, omnivorous, depredatory, extortionate, murderous, raptorial, vulturous; see also **greedy** 2, **savage** 2.
rapacity, *n.* **1.** [Greed]—*Syn.* grossness, avarice, covetousness; see **greed.**
2. [Plunder]—*Syn.* thieving, thievery, marauding; see **theft.**
rape, *n.* —*Syn.* seduction, violation, deflowering, criminal attack, assault, abduction, statutory offense, defilement, abuse, molestation, devirgination, defloration, ill-usage, maltreatment, criminal ravishment, forcible violation of a woman, (gang) bang (D); see also **crime** 2.
rape, *v.* —*Syn.* violate, seize, outrage, compromise, force a woman, molest, ravish, attack, assault, defile, deflower, wrong, despoil, devirginate, debauch, ruin, corrupt, seduce, maltreat, abuse, bang (D).
raped, *mod.* —*Syn.* attacked, assaulted, ravished; see **ruined** 3.
rapid, *mod.* **1.** [Swift]—*Syn.* speedy, accelerated, hurried; see **fast** 1.
2. [Quick]—*Syn.* nimble, light-footed, fleet, mercurial, brisk, expeditious, winged, lively, ready, prompt, spry; see also **active** 1, **agile.**—*Ant.* listless*, sluggish, languid.
rapidity, *n.* —*Syn.* swiftness, celerity, dispatch; see **speed.**
rapidly, *mod.* —*Syn.* fast, swiftly, posthaste; see **immediately, quickly** 1.
rapier, *n.* —*Syn.* cutlass, skean, blade; see **sword.**
rapist, *n.* —*Syn.* raper, ravager, ravisher, defiler, seducer, despoiler, attacker, betrayer, debaucher, deceiver; see also **rascal.**
rapport, *n.* —*Syn.* harmony, compatibility, affinity; see **agreement** 2.
rapprochement (French), *n.* —*Syn.* harmony, cordiality, friendliness; see **agreement** 2, **friendship** 2.
rapscallion, *n.* —*Syn.* scoundrel, scamp, rogue; see **rascal.**
rapt, *mod.* **1.** [Enraptured]—*Syn.* transported, entranced, enchanted, bewitched, charmed, hypnotized, captivated, fascinated, ecstatic, enthralled, overwhelmed, beguiled, delighted, enamored, ravished, taken, held; see also **happy** 1.—*Ant.* unaffected, impassive*, unconcerned.
2. [Engrossed]—*Syn.* absorbed, occupied, intent, engaged, preoccupied, lost, unconscious, employed, involved, inattentive, dreaming, oblivious, abstracted, absent, absentminded; *both* (D): caught up in, hung up; see also **busy** 1.—*Ant.* unconcerned*, uninterested, disinterested.
rapture, *n.* **1.** [Delight]—*Syn.* pleasure, cheer, satisfaction, enjoyment, felicity, exhilaration, contentment, gladness, gratification, elation, jubilation, well-being, gaiety, buoyancy, good spirits; *all* (D): plush, cushions, altitudes, seventh heaven; see also **happiness** 2.—*Ant.* pain*, grief, affliction.
2. [An ecstatic state]—*Syn.* ecstasy, bliss, transport, beatitude, enchantment, passion, glory, elysium, paradise, inspiration, enthusiasm, divine communion, mystical trance, at-oneness; see also **sense** 1.
rapturous, *mod.* —*Syn.* enchanted, charmed, delighted; see **happy** 1.
rare, *mod.* **1.** [Uncommon]—*Syn.* exceptional, singular, extraordinary; see **unusual** 1, 2.
2. [Scarce]—*Syn.* sparse, few, scanty, meager, limited, short, expensive, precious, out of circulation, off the market, in great demand, occasional, uncommon, isolated, scattered, infrequent, deficient, almost unobtainable, few and far between (D); see also **unique** 1.—*Ant.* profuse, cheap*, tawdry.
3. [Choice]—*Syn.* select, matchless, superlative; see **excellent.**
4. [Thin]—*Syn.* tenuous, light, flimsy; see **thin** 1, 5.
5. [Not cooked]—*Syn.* not cooked *or* done, imperfectly cooked, nearly raw, underdone, red, rarely *or* moderately done, *saignant* (French), not thoroughly cooked; see also **raw** 1.
rare bird, *n.* —*Syn.* rarity, phenomenon, curiosity; see **irregularity** 2, **wonder** 2.
rarefy, *v.* **1.** [To refine]—*Syn.* cleanse, refine, wash; see **clean, purify.**
2. [To thin]—*Syn.* expand, make rare *or* less solid *or* less dense, disperse; see **thin.**
rarely, *mod.* —*Syn.* unusually, occasionally, once in a great while; see **infrequently, seldom.**
rarity, *n.* **1.** [Infrequency]—*Syn.* rareness, scarcity, uncommonness; see **irregularity** 2.
2. [A phenomenon]—*Syn.* curiosity, spectacle, exhibition; see **wonder** 2.
rascal, *n.* —*Syn.* scoundrel, rogue, rake, knave, villain, robber, fraud, scamp, hypocrite, sneak, shyster, cad, trickster, charlatan, swindler, grafter, cardsharp, cheat, black sheep, ruffian, tough, rowdy, bully, scalawag, mountebank, liar, blackguard, wretch, quack, fellow, tramp, beggar, bum, idler, wastrel, prodigal, hooligan, ne'er-do-well, varlet, miscreant, reprobate, misdoer, felon, sinner, delinquent, rakehell, recreant, malfeasor, malefactor, profligate, loafer, rapscallion, renegade, beachcomber, mendicant, *gamine* (French), impostor, opportunist, vagrant, pretender, gambler, mischief-maker, sharper, faker; *all* (D): skunk, bastard, fink, rat, rotten *or* bad egg, con man, con artist, flimflammer, dirty dog, good-for-nothing, worm, two-timer, stool pigeon, case, double-dealer, phony, four-flusher, slicker; see also **criminal.** —*Ant.* hero*, nice guy, philanthropist.
rascality, *n.* —*Syn.* roguery, villainy, baseness, meanness, knavery, wickedness, culpability, guile, profligacy, chicanery, treachery, trickery, worthlessness, blackguardism, double-dealing, ruffianism, improbity, disreputability; see also **crime** 1, **dishonesty.**

rascally, *mod.* —*Syn.* bad, vicious, vile; see **wicked** 1.

rash, *mod.* —*Syn.* precipitate, impetuous, impulsive, foolish, hotheaded, thoughtless, reckless, headstrong, bold, careless, determined, audacious, heedless, madcap, unthinking, headlong, incautious, wild, precipitant, overhasty, unwary, injudicious, venturous, foolhardy, imprudent, venturesome, adventurous, daring, jumping to conclusions, insuppressible, breakneck, irrational, fiery, furious, frenzied, passionate, immature, hurried, aimless, excited, feverish, indomitable, tenacious, frantic, indiscreet, quixotic, uncalculating, ill-advised, unconsidered, without thinking, imprudent, unadvised, irresponsible, brash, precipitous, premature, sudden; *all* (D): burning one's fingers, harebrained, hot-brained, harum-scarum, game to the last, devil-may-care, daredevil, rushing in where angels fear to tread; see also **rude** 1.—*Ant.* calm*, cool, level-headed.

rasher, *n.* —*Syn.* chip, cut, slice; see **part** 1, **piece** 1.

rashly, *mod.* —*Syn.* brashly, impulsively, unwisely, abruptly, foolishly, impetuously, incautiously, carelessly, precipitately, precipitantly, precipitously, imprudently, recklessly, boldly, indiscreetly, inadvisedly, ill-advisedly, thoughtlessly, unthinkingly, furiously, hurriedly, heedlessly, boldly, headstrongly, unpreparedly, excitedly, overhastily, wildly, frantically, irrepressibly, without (due) consideration *or* thinking (about it) *or* forethought *or* planning *or* investigation *or* research; in a hasty *or* rash *or* thoughtless, etc., manner; with (great) indiscretion *or* thoughtlessness *or* bad judgment, etc.; passionately, fiercely, feverishly, indomitably, headily; see also **rudely.**

rashness, *n.* —*Syn.* frenzy, recklessness, foolhardiness; see **carelessness.**

rasp, *v.* —*Syn.* grate, irritate, scratch; see **rub** 1.

rasping, *mod.* —*Syn.* hoarse, grating, grinding; see **harsh** 1, **raucous** 1.

rat, *n.* **1.** [A rodent]—*Syn.* mouse, muskrat, vermin; see **pest** 1, **rodent.**
Rats include the following—white, black, brown, house, longtailed, water, swamp, tree, giant, field, bamboo, cotton, kangaroo, jerboa, river, pack.
2. [A deserter]—*Syn.* informer, turncoat, fink (D); see **deserter, traitor.**

ratchet, *n.* —*Syn.* catch, sprocket (wheel), cogwheel; see **cog, wheel** 1.

rate, *n.* **1.** [Ratio]—*Syn.* proportion, degree, standard, scale, fixed amount, quota, relation, relationship, comparison, relative, weight, percentage, numerical progression, diagrammatic estimate; see also **measure** 1, 2.
2. [Price]—*Syn.* valuation, allowance, estimate; see **price.**
3. [Speed]—*Syn.* velocity, flow, motion, movement, pace, clip, gallop, tread, hop, spurt, dash, time; see also **speed.**

rate, *v.* **1.** [To rank]—*Syn.* judge, estimate, evaluate, grade, relate to a standard, fix, tag, calculate, assess, deem, class, determine, apprise, assay, guess at; see also **measure** 1, **price, rank** 2.
2. [(D) To be well-thought-of]—*Syn.* be a favorite *or* accepted *or* welcome, etc.; triumph, succeed; see **prosper.**

rated, *mod.* —*Syn.* ranked, classified, graded, classed, put, thought of, given a rating, weighted, measured; see also **placed.**

rather, *interj.* —*Syn.* I should say, certainly, of course, by all means, most assuredly, no doubt about it; *both* (D): and how! you're telling me.

rather, *mod.* **1.** [To some degree]—*Syn.* fairly, somewhat, a little; see **moderately, reasonably** 2.
2. [By preference]—*Syn.* first, by choice, in preference, sooner, more readily, willingly, much sooner, just as soon, as a matter of choice; see also **preferably.**

ratification, *n.* —*Syn.* acceptance, confirmation, sanction; see **permission.**

ratify, *v.* —*Syn.* sanction, establish, substantiate; see **approve** 1, **endorse** 2.

rating, *n.* —*Syn.* grade, commission, number; see **class** 1, **degree** 2, **rank** 2.

ratio, *n.* —*Syn.* proportion, quota, quotient; see **degree** 1, **rate** 1.

ration, *n.* —*Syn.* allotment, portion, quota; see **division** 2, **share.**

ration, *v.* —*Syn.* proportion, allot, apportion; see **distribute** 1.

rational, *mod.* **1.** [Acting in accordance with reason] —*Syn.* stable, calm, cool, deliberate, discerning, discriminating, level-headed, collected, ratiocinative, logical, thoughtful, knowing, sensible, of sound judgment *or* good sense, impartial, exercising reason, intelligent, wise, reasoning, prudent, circumspect, intellectual, reflective, philosophic, objective, far-sighted, enlightened, well-advised, judicious, analytical, deductive, synthetic, perspicacious, conscious, balanced, sober, systematic; *both* (D): all there, together; see also **reasonable** 1. —*Ant.* rash*, reckless, wild.
2. [Of a nature that appeals to reason]—*Syn.* intelligent, sensible, wise; see **judicious, reasonable** 1.
3. [Sane]—*Syn.* normal, lucid, responsible; see **sane** 1.

rationale, *n.* —*Syn.* hypothesis, motive, exposition; see **reason** 3.

rationalism, *n.* —*Syn.* humanism, realism, reasoning; see **logic, reason** 2.

rationalize, *v.* **1.** [Reason]—*Syn.* think, deliberate, intellectualize; see **reason** 2.
2. [To justify]—*Syn.* explain away, vindicate, reconcile; see **excise, justify** 2.

rationally, *mod.* —*Syn.* sensibly, normally, intelligently; see **reasonably** 1.

rattle, *n.* —*Syn.* clatter, shaking, patter, noise, racket, rattling, din, knock, clack, roll, rumble, drumming, pitapat, ratatat; see also **noise** 1.

rattle, *v.* **1.** [To make a rattling sound]—*Syn.* drum, clack, knock; see **sound** 1.
2. [(D) To talk with little meaning]—*Syn.* chatter, gush, prattle; see **babble.**
3. [(D) To disconcert]—*Syn.* bother, put out, unnerve; see **confuse, disturb** 2, **embarrass** 1.

rattlebrained (D), *mod.* —*Syn.* giddy, irrational, scatterbrained; see **stupid** 1.

rattlesnake, *n.* —*Syn.* rattler, diamondback, sidewinder, prairie rattler, timber rattler, copperhead, water moccasin, belltail, pit viper; see also **snake.**

rattletrap, *mod.* —*Syn.* tottery, rickety, makeshift; see **unstable** 1, **weak** 2.

rattletrap, *n.* —*Syn.* heap, old car, jalopy; see **automobile, wreck** 2.

raucous, *mod.* **1.** [Harsh]—*Syn.* hoarse, loud, gruff, strident, rough, grating, dissonant, jarring, rasping, stertorous, thick, cacophonous, absonant, squawking, ear-piercing, blatant, sharp, acute, blaring, dry, braying, atonal, grinding, unharmonious, unmusical, piercing, husky, discordant; see also **harsh** 1.
2. [Disorderly]—*Syn.* intemperate, rowdy, drunk; see **unruly.**

ravage, *v.* —*Syn.* pillage, overrun, devastate, destroy, crush, desolate, despoil, overspread, wreck, waste, disrupt, disorganize, demolish, annihilate, overthrow, overwhelm, break up, pull down, smash, shatter, scatter, batter down, exterminate, extinguish, prostrate, trample (down), dismantle, stamp out, lay waste, lay in ruins, sweep away, raze, ruin, plunder, strip, impair, sack, consume, spoil, harry, ransack, maraud, wrest, prey, forage, crush, foray, rape, rob, raid, pirate, seize, spoliate, capture, gut, loot; see also **damage** 1.—*Ant.* build, improve*, rehabilitate.

rave, *v.* **1.** [To babble]—*Syn.* gabble, jabber, rattle on; see **babble.**
2. [To rage]—*Syn.* storm, splutter, rail; see **rage** 1.

ravel, *v.* —*Syn.* untwist, come apart, wind *or* weave *or* smooth out, untangle, disentangle, unsnarl, unbraid, untwine, unweave, unravel, make plain; see also **free** 1, **loosen** 2.

ravenous, *mod.* —*Syn.* voracious, omnivorous, starved; see **hungry, rapacious** 2.

ravine, *n.* —*Syn.* gully, gorge, canyon, gulch, arroyo, valley, gap, chasm, abyss, break, crevice, crevasse, coulee.

raving, *mod.* —*Syn.* violent, shouting, fuming; see **insane** 1.

ravish, *v.* **1.** [To charm]—*Syn.* delight, please, enchant, bewitch, captivate, attract, allure, enthrall, hold, draw, mesmerize, magnetize, hypnotize; see also **charm** 1, **fascinate.**
2. [To rape]—*Syn.* seduce, abduct, deflower; see **rape.**

raw, *mod.* **1.** [Uncooked]—*Syn.* fresh, rare, hard, unprepared, undercooked, underdone, fibrous, coarse-grained, unpasteurized, unbaked, unfried; see also **rare** 5.—*Ant.* cooked*, baked*, fried.
2. [Unfinished]—*Syn.* natural, untreated, rough, newly cut, unprocessed, crude, unrefined, unstained, untanned, coarse, newly mined, uncut, virgin; see also **unfinished** 2.—*Ant.* manufactured, refined*, processed.
3. [Untrained]—*Syn.* immature, new, fresh; see **inexperienced.**
4. [Cold]—*Syn.* biting, windy, bleak; see **cold** 1.
5. [Without skin]—*Syn.* peeled, skinned, dressed, galled, scraped, blistered, cut, wounded, pared, uncovered, chafed, bruised.—*Ant.* coated, covered*, healed.
6. [(D) Nasty]—*Syn.* low, dirty, unscrupulous; see **mean** 3, **vulgar** 1.
in the raw (D)—*Syn.* nude, bare, unclothed; see **naked** 1.

rawboned, *mod.* —*Syn.* gaunt, lean, lanky; see **thin** 2.

ray, *n.* —*Syn.* beam, flash, light, stream, gleam, blaze, sunbeam, wave, moonbeam, radiation, flicker, spark, irradiation, emanation, radiance, streak, shaft, pencil, patch, blink, glimmer, glitter, glint, sparkle.
Rays include—Roentgen, cosmic, ultraviolet, infrared, gamma, beta, alpha; X-ray.

rayon, *n.* —*Syn.* cellulose fiber, artificial fabric, synthetic; see **cloth, fiber** 1.

raze, *v.* —*Syn.* wreck, demolish, dismantle, ruin, scatter, overthrow, tumble, pull *or* knock *or* break *or* mow *or* blow *or* tear *or* batter *or* cast down, reduce, fell, break *or* tear up, annihilate, capsize, spill, exterminate, level, overturn, flatten, topple, dynamite, bomb, subvert, smash, crash; see also **destroy** 1, **turn** 2, **upset** 1.—*Ant.* build*, raise, erect.

razor, *n.* —*Syn.* shaving instrument, cutting edge, blade; *all* (D): scraper, mower, cutter, hook, shivy *or* shiv; see also **knife.**
Razors include the following—double-edged, single-edged, straight-back, safety, hollow-ground, electric; *all* (D): electric shaver, dry-shave, blade.

reach, *n.* —*Syn.* compass, range, scope, grasp, ken, stretch, extension, orbit, horizon, gamut; see also **ability** 1.

reach, *v.* **1.** [To extend to]—*Syn.* touch, span, encompass, pass along, continue *or* get *or* go to, roll *or* go on, stretch, go as far as, attain, equal, approach, lead, stand, terminate, end, overtake, join, come up (to), sweep; see also **spread** 3.
2. [To extend a part of the body to]—*Syn.* lunge, strain, move, reach out, feel for, come at, make contact with, shake hands, throw out a limb, make for, put out, touch, strike, seize, grasp; see also **stretch** 1.
3. [To arrive]—*Syn.* get to, come to, enter; see **arrive** 1.
4. [To give an object to another]—*Syn.* hand over, relinquish, give over, give away, carry to, turn over, transfer; see also **give** 1.

reaching, *mod.* **1.** [Extending to a point]—*Syn.* going up to, ending at, stretching, encompassing, taking in, spanning, spreading to, embracing, joining, sweeping on to.
2. [Arriving]—*Syn.* coming to, landing, touching down, entering, disembarking, making port, getting off at, alighting, putting in, getting to, stopping at; see also **landing** 1.
3. [Extending a part of the body]—*Syn.* stretching, straining, making for, lunging, feeling for, putting out, outstretching, touching, grasping, seizing, striking; see also **extending.**

react, *v.* **1.** [To act in response]—*Syn.* reciprocate, respond, counter, reply, behave, give back, act; see also **answer** 1.
2. [To feel in response]—*Syn.* be affected, take, be struck, be impressed, be involved, find; *both* (D): catch the infection, catch the flame; see also **feel** 2.

reaction, *n.* **1.** [An answer]—*Syn.* reply, rejoinder, reception, receptivity, response, return, feeling, opinion, reflection, backlash, attitude, retort, reciprocation, repercussion, reflex; see also **answer** 1, **opinion** 1.
Reactions to stimuli include the following—contraction, expansion, jerk, knee jerk, tropism, heliotropism, phototropism, cognition, shock, relapse, exhaustion, stupor, anger, disgust, revulsion, fear, illness, joy, laughter, wonder.

2. [A backward tendency, especially in politics] —*Syn.* conservatism, backlash, status quo, right wing, toryism, retrenchment, regression, relapse, retrogression, retreat, withdrawal, backsliding; *both* (D): return to normalcy, return to the good old days; see also **stability** 1.

reactionary, *mod.* —*Syn.* rigid, retrogressive, regressive; see **conservative.**

reactionary, *n.* —*Syn.* die-hard, reactionist, conservative; see **radical** 2.

read, *mod.* —*Syn.* examined, gone *or* checked over, scanned; see **understood** 1.

read, *v.* **1.** [To understand by reading]—*Syn.* comprehend, go through, peruse, scan, glance *or* go over, gather, see, know, skim, perceive, apprehend, grasp, learn; *all* (D): flip through the pages, dip into, scratch the surface, bury oneself in; see also **understand** 1.

2. [To interpret]—*Syn.* view, render, translate, decipher, make out, unravel, express, explain, expound, construe, perceive, paraphrase, restate, put; see also **interpret** 1.

3. [To contain when read]—*Syn.* state, hold, indicate, express, assert, affirm.

readable, *mod.* **1.** [Capable of being read]—*Syn.* clear, legible, coherent, distinct, intelligible, lucid, comprehensible, plain, unmistakable, decipherable, regular, orderly, fluent, tidy, flowing, precise, graphic, understandable, unequivocal, explicit, straightforward, simple.—*Ant.* illegible*, unintelligible, undecipherable.

2. [Likely to be read with pleasure]—*Syn.* interesting, absorbing, fascinating, pleasurable, engrossing, satisfying, amusing, entertaining, enjoyable, rewarding, gratifying, pleasing, worth reading, pleasant, inviting, engaging, eloquent, well-written, smooth, exciting, attractive, pungent, clever, brilliant, ingenious, relaxing, stimulating, appealing; see also **trenchant** 2.—*Ant.* dreary, depressing, dull*.

read between the lines (D), *v.* —*Syn.* surmise, conclude, suspect; see **guess** 1.

reader, *n.* **1.** [One who reads habitually]—*Syn.* bibliophile, editor, book reviewer, literary critic, proofreader, editorial assistant, scholar, bookworm, bibliomaniac, man of learning, savant, walking encyclopedia (D); see also **writer.**

2. [One who makes a profession of reading]—*Syn.* lecturer, elocutionist, reciter, rhetorician, soliloquist, monologist, mime, *diseur, diseuse* (*both* French); see also **teacher** 1, 2.

3. [Anyone admitted to a library]—*Syn.* library patron, user, browser, research worker, scholar, grind (D); see also **student.**

4. [A book intended for the study of reading] —*Syn.* primer, storybook, graded text, companion volume, selected readings, anthology, omnibus, models; see also **book** 1, **text** 1.

5. [A grader of papers]—*Syn.* teaching assistant *or* T.A., lab assistant, professor; see **teacher** 1, 2.

read for, *v.* —*Syn.* try out, go out for, audition; see **perform** 2, **try out for.**

readily, *mod.* —*Syn.* quickly, promptly, immediately; see **eagerly, easily** 1, **willingly.**

readiness, *n.* —*Syn.* aptness, predisposition, eagerness; see **willingness, zeal** 2.

reading, *n.* **1.** [The act of interpreting written matter]—*Syn.* expression, utterance, delivery, recitation, recital, rendition, enactment.

2. [Interpretation]—*Syn.* version, treatment, commentary; see **interpretation** 2, **translation.**

3. [A selection from written matter]—*Syn.* brief, excerpt, digest, extract, passage, quotation, section, installment; see also **recitation** 3.

4. [A version]—*Syn.* account, paraphrase, rendering; see **interpretation** 1, **version** 1.

readjust, *v.* —*Syn.* reconcile, compromise, methodize; see **regulate** 2.

readjustment, *n.* —*Syn.* rearrangement, rehabilitation, reconstruction; see **adjustment** 1.

read the riot act to (D), *v.* —*Syn.* rebuke, tell, put someone in his place; see **scold.**

read up on, *v.* —*Syn.* prepare, investigate, research; see **study** 1.

ready, *mod.* **1.** [Prompt]—*Syn.* quick, spontaneous, alert, wide-awake, swift, fleet, fast, sharp, immediate, instant, animated; see also **active** 2, **observant** 2, **punctual.**—*Ant.* slow*, dull, dilatory.

2. [Prepared]—*Syn.* fit, apt, skillful, ripe, handy, in readiness, waiting, on call, in line for, in position, on the brink of, equipped to do the job *or* perform the services, open to, fixed for, on the mark, in harness, in the saddle, equal to, at one's beck and call, expectant, available, at hand, anticipating, in order; *all* (D): all systems go, (all) squared away, in a go condition; see also **able** 1, **intelligent** 1.—*Ant.* unprepared*, unready, unavailable.

3. [Enthusiastic]—*Syn.* eager, zealous, ardent; see **enthusiastic** 3.

at the ready—*Syn.* prepared, equipped, on the brink; see **ready** 2.

make ready—*Syn.* order, prepare for something, equip; see **prepare** 1.

ready-made, *mod.* **1.** [Prepared]—*Syn.* instant, prefabricated, ready-to-wear, off-the-rack, store-bought (D), built; see **prepared** 2, **preserved** 2.

2. [Trite]—*Syn.* mundane, banal, ordinary; see **common** 1, **dull** 4.

real, *mod.* **1.** [Genuine]—*Syn.* true, authentic, original; see **genuine** 1.

2. [Having physical existence]—*Syn.* actual, solid, firm, substantive, material, live, substantial, existent, tangible, existing, present, palpable, factual, sound, concrete, corporal, corporeal, bodily, incarnate, embodied, physical, sensible, stable, in existence, *de facto* (Latin), perceptible, evident, undeniable, irrefutable, practical, true, true to life. —*Ant.* unreal*, unsubstantial, hypothetical.

3. [(D) Very much]—*Syn.* exceedingly, exceptionally, uncommonly; see **very.**

for real (D)—*Syn.* actually, in fact, certainly; see **really** 1.

real estate, *n.* —*Syn.* land, property, lots, realty, houses, landed interests, freehold, ground, acres, messuage, holdings; see also **building** 1, **estate** 1, **farm, home** 1.

realism, *n.* —*Syn.* authenticity, naturalness, actuality; see **reality** 1.

realist, *n.* —*Syn.* pragmatist, naturalist, scientist, rationalist, pessimist, cynic, defeatist; see also **philosopher.**

realistic, *mod.*—*Syn.* authentic, original, representative; see **genuine** 1.

reality, *n.* **1.** [The state of being real]—*Syn.* authenticity, factual basis, truth, actuality, realness, substantiality, existence, substance, materiality, being, presence, actual existence, sensibility, corporeality, solidity, perceptibility, true being, absoluteness, tangibility, palpability.
2. [Anything that has become real]—*Syn.* realness, certainty, deed; see **fact** 2.

realization, *n.*—*Syn.* understanding, comprehension, consciousness; see **awareness.**

realize, *v.* **1.** [To bring to fulfillment]—*Syn.* perfect, make good, actualize; see **complete** 1.
2. [To understand]—*Syn.* recognize, apprehend, discern; see **understand** 1.
3. [To receive]—*Syn.* get clear, make a profit from, obtain; see **earn** 2, **profit** 2, **receive** 1.

realized, *mod.* **1.** [Fulfilled]—*Syn.* completed, accomplished, done, finished, concluded, actualized, come true, materialized, executed, achieved, performed, effected, consummated, substantiated, made real.—*Ant.* unfinished*, unfulfilled, unsubstantiated.
2. [Earned]—*Syn.* gained, gotten, acquired, received, accrued, made, reaped, harvested, gathered, inherited, profited, taken, cleared, obtained, gleaned, netted.

realizing, *mod.* **1.** [Achieving]—*Syn.* accomplishing, performing, completing, consummating, effecting, fulfilling, doing, coming through, attaining, reaching, perfecting, discharging, rounding out.
2. [Earning]—*Syn.* making, netting, getting, acquiring, obtaining, receiving, inheriting, clearing, being paid, accruing, taking in, being allowed.
3. [Understanding]—*Syn.* recognizing, discerning, comprehending, appreciating, knowing, being aware, finding, suspecting, grasping, seeing through.

really, *mod.* **1.** [In fact]—*Syn.* actually, indeed, genuinely, certainly, surely, absolutely, in effect, positively, veritably, in fact *or* reality, authentically, upon my honor, legitimately, precisely, literally, indubitably, unmistakably, undoubtedly, categorically, in point of fact, for fair, I assure you, I'll answer for it, be assured, believe me, as a matter of fact, of course, honestly, truly, admittedly, nothing else but, beyond (any) doubt, in actuality, unquestionably; *all* (D): as sure as you're alive, no buts about it, without the shadow of a doubt, it is written, you said it.
2. [To a remarkable degree]—*Syn.* surprisingly, remarkably, extraordinarily; see **very.**

really, *interj.*—*Syn.* indeed? honestly? for a fact? yes? is that so? are you sure? no fooling? *all* (D): cross your heart and hope to die? on your honor? you don't say? the deuce you say! blow me down! ain't it the truth? I doubt not; you said it! do tell? no kidding?

realm, *n.*—*Syn.* domain, area, sphere; see **department** 1, **expanse, region** 1.

real McCoy (D), *n.*—*Syn.* the real thing, something genuine, the original; see **the genuine article.**

realtor, *n.*—*Syn.* real estate agent, broker, dealer; see **salesman.**

reanimate, *v.*—*Syn.* restore, invigorate, resuscitate; see **renew** 1, **revive** 1.

reap, *v.* **1.** [To harvest]—*Syn.* cut, mow, glean, gather, produce, crop, pick, take the yield, gather the fruit, strip the fields, pluck, cull; see also **harvest.**—*Ant.* plant*, sow, seed.
2. [To gain]—*Syn.* get, acquire, procure, collect, glean, realize, draw, derive, secure, recover, retrieve, take in, profit, obtain, gain, make capital of, pick up, receive, come to have.—*Ant.* lose*, relinquish, give up.

reaper, *n.*—*Syn.* binder, farm equipment, grain harvester; see **harvester** 1.

reappear, *v.*—*Syn.* come again, re-enter, crop up again; see **appear** 1, **repeat** 2.

reapportion, *v.*—*Syn.* redistribute, redistrict, resection, distribute, divide, allot.

rear, *n.*—*Syn.* hind part, back seat, rear end, rumble seat, tail end, posterior, rump, butt (D); see also **back** 1.

rear, *v.*—*Syn.* lift, elevate, turn *or* bring up; see **raise** 1, **support** 5.

rearrange, *v.*—*Syn.* do over, reset, replace, reconstruct, shift, rework, revamp; see also **order** 3, **prepare** 1.

reason, *n.* **1.** [The power of reasoning]—*Syn.* intelligence, mind, sanity; see **acumen, judgment** 1.
2. [A process of reasoning]—*Syn.* logic, intellection, dialectics, speculation, generalization, rationalism, argumentation, inference, induction, deduction, discernment, analysis, ratiocination, rationalization.
3. [A basis for rational action]—*Syn.* end, object, rationale, intention, (ulterior) motive, basis, wherefore, aim, intent, cause, design, ground, impetus, idea, motivation, root, incentive, goal, purpose, the why and wherefore (D); see also **purpose** 1.
4. [The mind]—*Syn.* brain, mentality, intellect; see **mind** 1.
by reason of—*Syn.* because of, for, by way of; see **because.**
in *or* **within reason**—*Syn.* in accord with what is reasonable, rationally, understandably; see **reasonably** 1.
out of all reason—*Syn.* unreasonable, irrational, irresponsible; see **illogical.**
stand to reason—*Syn.* be plausible *or* logical *or* feasible *or* practical, etc.; seem all right, appeal; see **convince.**
with reason—*Syn.* understandably, soundly, plausibly; see **reasonably** 1.

reason, *v.* **1.** [To think logically]—*Syn.* reflect, deliberate, contemplate; see **think** 1.
2. [To seek a reasonable explanation]—*Syn.* suppose, infer, deduce, gather, draw from, conclude, generalize, adduce, rationalize, think through, study, analyze, examine, figure out, thresh out (D); see also **assume** 1.
3. [To discuss persuasively]—*Syn.* argue, trace, contend, dispute, debate, demonstrate, point out, prove, establish, discourse, justify; see also **discuss.**

reasonable, *mod.* **1.** [Amenable to reason]—*Syn.* rational, sane, level-headed, intelligent, clear-cut, tolerant, endowed with reason, conscious, cerebral, capable of reason, thoughtful, reflective, percipient, reasoning, ratiocinative, cognitive, perceiving,

consistent, broad-minded, liberal, generous, sensible, unprejudiced, unbiased, persuasible, malleable, flexible, agreeable; see **rational** 1.—*Ant.* prejudiced*, intolerant, biased.
2. [Characterized by justice]—*Syn.* fair, right, just, prudent, equitable, rational, impartial, reflective, sensible, humane, politic, knowing, sapient, discreet, analytical, objective, circumspect, judicious, making sense, standing to reason, moderate; see also **honest** 1.—*Ant.* excessive, immoderate*, extreme.
3. [Likely to appeal to the reason]—*Syn.* feasible, sound, plausible; see **understandable.**
4. [Moderate in price]—*Syn.* inexpensive, reduced, fair; see **cheap** 1.

reasonably, *mod.* **1.** [In a reasonable manner] —*Syn.* rationally, sanely, logically, understandably, plausibly, sensibly, soundly, persuasively, fairly, justly, honestly, wisely, judiciously, plainly, intelligently, soberly, unaffectedly, agreeably, in *or* within (all) reason, within the limits *or* bounds of reason, as far as possible, as far as could be expected, as much as good sense dictates, within reasonable limitations *or* the bounds of possibility, with due restraint.
2. [To a moderate degree]—*Syn.* mildly, prudently, fairly, moderately, inexpensively, temperately, evenly, calmly, gently, leniently, sparingly, frugally, indulgently, tolerantly, within bounds.

reasoning, *mod.* —*Syn.* logical, inductive, analytical; see **judicious, rational** 1.

reasoning, *n.* —*Syn.* thinking, rationalizing, drawing conclusions; see **acumen, thought** 1.

reassure, *v.* —*Syn.* convince, console, give confidence; see **comfort** 1, **encourage** 1, 2, **guarantee** 1.

rebate, *n.* —*Syn.* allowance, deduction, remission; see **discount.**

rebel, *n.* **1.** [A person engaged in a political revolution]—*Syn.* insurrectionist, revolutionist, revolutionary, agitator, insurgent, insurrectionary, traitor, seditionist, mutineer, subverter, anarchist, overthrower, nihilist, guerrilla, member of the uprising, rioter, demagogue, revolter, separatist, malcontent, schismatic, deserter, recreant, dissenter, seceder, apostate, sectarian, turncoat, counterrevolutionary, renegade, secessionist, Sinn Feiner, Trotskyite, underground worker; *both* (D): Third Worlder, refusenik; see also **radical.**
2. [A person of independent opinions]—*Syn.* independent, individualist, iconoclast, innovator, experimenter, experientialist.

rebel, *v.* **1.** [To endeavor to overthrow a government]—*Syn.* rise (up), resist, revolt, turn against, defy, resist lawful authority, fight in the streets, strike, boycott, break with, overturn, mutiny, riot (against), take up arms (against), start a confrontation, secede, renounce, combat, oppose, be insubordinate, be treasonable, upset, overthrow, dethrone, disobey; *all* (D): raise hell, kick up a row, run amok.—*Ant.* submit, obey*, be contented.
2. [To object]—*Syn.* remonstrate, denounce, criticize; see **censure, oppose** 1.

rebellion, *n.* —*Syn.* insurrection, revolt, defiance; see **disobedience, revolution** 2.

rebellious, *mod.* **1.** [Engaged in armed rebellion] —*Syn.* revolutionary, insurgent, counterrevolutionary, warring, insurrectionary, attacking, rioting, mutinous; see also sense 2, 3.—*Ant.* beaten*, overwhelmed, conquered.
2. [Inclined toward rebellion]—*Syn.* dissident, factious, seditious, fractious, disobedient, treasonable, refractory, defiant, resistant, restless, riotous, insubordinate, quarrelsome, bellicose, sabotaging, disloyal, disaffected, alienated, ungovernable, threatening.—*Ant.* docile*, peaceful, gentle.
3. [Apt to oppose authority]—*Syn.* anarchistic, iconoclastic, individualistic, radical, pugnacious, quarrelsome, independent-minded, stubborn, contemptuous, insolent, contumacious, alienated, scornful, uncontrollable, intractable, unyielding, recalcitrant; see also **lawless** 2.—*Ant.* dutiful, tractable, yielding*.

rebirth, *n.* —*Syn.* resurrection, rejuvenation, rehabilitation; see **renewal, restoration** 1, **revival.**

rebound, *v.* —*Syn.* reflect, ricochet, repercuss; see **bounce** 1.

rebuff, *n.* —*Syn.* repulse, snub, reprimand; see **insult, rebuke.**

rebuff, *v.* **1.** [To reject]—*Syn.* refuse, repel, check, snub, dismiss, repudiate, spurn, send *or* turn away, ignore, slight, disregard, put in one's place, reprove, rebuke, oppose, chide, repulse, cross, reject, decline, resist, keep at a distance, keep at arm's length, disallow; *all* (D): give the cold shoulder, give the go-by, cut, turn down, slam the door in one's face, rake over the coals, not hear of, put off, lash out at, tell (where to get) off, give the deuce, put down, give the works; see also **deny, neglect** 1.
2. [To beat back]—*Syn.* drive *or* push back, ward *or* fend *or* stave *or* hold *or* keep *or* beat off, keep at bay; see also **repel** 1, **resist** 1.

rebuild, *v.* **1.** [To repair]—*Syn.* touch up, patch, build up; see **repair** 1.
2. [To restore]—*Syn.* refurbish, make restoration, reconstruct historically; see **reconstruct, restore** 3.

rebuilt, *mod.* —*Syn.* remodeled, restored, reorganized; see **built** 1, **repaired.**

rebuke, *n.* —*Syn.* condemnation, reproof, reprimand, rebuff, snub, refusal, repulse, disapproval, scolding, censure, criticism, chiding, admonition, ostracism, blame, upbraiding, reprehension, berating, reproach, reproval, expostulation, blame, punishment, rating, objurgation, correction, affliction, castigation, admonishment, remonstrance; *all* (D): tongue-lashing, dressing-down, chewing-out, lecture, put-down, slap in the face; see also **insult.** —*Ant.* compliment*, congratulations, applause.

rebuke, *v.* —*Syn.* reprove, reprimand, admonish; see **censure, oppose** 1.

rebut, *v.* —*Syn.* confute, prove false, invalidate; see **deny, disprove, refute.**

rebuttal, *n.* —*Syn.* reply, return, confutation; see **answer** 1, **refusal.**

recalcitrant, *mod.* —*Syn.* radical, resistant, stubborn; see **obstinate** 1, **rebellious** 3.

recall, *v.* **1.** [To call to mind]—*Syn.* recollect, think of, revive; see **remember** 1.
2. [To remove from office]—*Syn.* discharge, disqualify, suspend; see **dismiss** 2.
3. [To summon again]—*Syn.* call back, reconvene, reassemble; see **summon** 1.

recalled, *mod.* **1.** [Remembered]—*Syn.* recollected, brought to mind, summoned up; see **remembered.**
2. [Relieved of responsibility]—*Syn.* brought back, stripped of office, dismissed, cast out, displaced, fired, laid off, made redundant (British), replaced, ousted, suspended, pensioned, made emeritus, let out, let go, removed (from office), retired, replaced, superannuated; *all* (D): kicked upstairs, canned, busted, cashiered, washed out; see also **discharged** 1.

recant, *v.*—*Syn.* retract, abjure, deny, take back, revoke, cancel, renounce, disavow, disclaim, back down *or* out, withdraw, rescind, abrogate, forswear, contradict, repudiate, abnegate, annul, void, countermand, take *or* call back, disown, unsay, nullify, repeal; *all* (D): draw in one's horns, eat crow, be of another mind, eat humble pie, back down, eat one's words *or* hat; see also **abandon** 1.—*Ant.* acknowledge*, admit, proclaim.

recapitulate, *v.*—*Syn.* restate, sum up, reiterate; see **repeat** 3, **summarize.**

recapture, *v.*—*Syn.* regain, reobtain, reacquire; see **recover** 1.

recede, *v.* **1.** [To go backward]—*Syn.* fall *or* draw back, shrink (from), withdraw; see **retreat** 1.
2. [To sink]—*Syn.* ebb, drift away, lower, turn down, abate, decline, die *or* move *or* go away, drop *or* wash back, drop, fall off, lessen; see also **decrease** 1, **fall** 2.—*Ant.* rise*, flow, increase.

receipt, *n.* **1.** [The act of receiving]—*Syn.* receiving, acquisition, accession, acceptance, taking, arrival, recipience, getting, admitting, intaking (D), acquiring, reception; see also **admission** 2.—*Ant.* shipment, delivery*, giving.
2. [An acknowledgment of receipt, sense 1]—*Syn.* letter, voucher, release, cancellation, slip, signed notice, stub, discharge, quittance, declaration, paid bill, chit (D); see also **certificate.**

receipted, *mod.*—*Syn.* certified, marked paid, stamped, signed, approved, acknowledged, attached with a receipt.

receive, *v.* **1.** [To take into one's charge]—*Syn.* accept, be given, admit, get, gain, inherit, acquire, gather up, collect, reap, procure, derive, appropriate, seize, take possession, redeem, pocket, pick up, hold, come by, earn, take (in), assume, draw, arrogate, win, secure; *all* (D): spike, come into, come in for, catch, get from, corral; see also **obtain** 1.—*Ant.* discard*, abandon, refuse.
2. [To endure]—*Syn.* undergo, experience, suffer; see **endure** 2.
3. [To support]—*Syn.* bear, sustain, prop; see **support** 1.
4. [To make welcome]—*Syn.* accommodate, initiate, induct, install, make welcome, shake hands with, admit, permit, welcome (home), accept, entertain, host, invite *or* let *or* show *or* bring *or* usher in, let through, make comfortable, be at home to, bring as a guest into, introduce, give a party, give access to, allow entrance to; *all* (D): roll out the red carpet (for), give the red-carpet treatment (to), get out the welcome mat (for); see also **greet.**—*Ant.* visit*, be a guest, call.

received, *mod.*—*Syn.* taken, gotten, acquired, obtained, honored, brought in, signed for, admitted, collected, gathered; see also **accepted, acknowledged.**—*Ant.* given*, disbursed, delivered.

receiver, *n.* **1.** [One who receives]—*Syn.* consignee, customer, recipient, heir, beneficiary, grantee, acceptor, teller, collector, object, target, victim, subject, trustee, assignee, creditor, guinea pig (D).
2. [A device for receiving]—*Syn.* telephone, handset, headphone, television, radio, receiving set, mission control, control center, detection *or* detecting *or* listening device, transceiver, lunar receiving laboratory (LRL), hydrophone.

receiving, *mod.*—*Syn.* taking, getting, acquiring, accepting, being given, inheriting, collecting, making, drawing, earning, gaining.—*Ant.* giving*, disbursing, awarding.
be on the receiving end (D)—*Syn.* be the recipient, get, (have to) take; see **receive** 1.

recension, *n.*—*Syn.* reprint, new version, reexamination; see **edition, review** 2, **revision.**

recent, *mod.* **1.** [Lately brought into being]—*Syn.* fresh, novel, newly born; see **modern** 1, **unusual** 1, 2.
2. [Associated with modern times]—*Syn.* contemporary, up-to-date, streamlined; see **modern** 1, 3.

recently, *mod.*—*Syn.* lately, in recent times, just now, just a while ago, not long ago, a short while ago, of late, latterly, newly, freshly, new, the other day, within the recent past.—*Ant.* once*, long ago, formerly.

receptacle, *n.*—*Syn.* box, wastebasket, holder; see **container.**

reception, *n.* **1.** [The act of receiving]—*Syn.* acquisition, acceptance, accession; see **receipt** 2.
2. [The manner of receiving]—*Syn.* meeting, encounter, introduction, gathering, welcome, salutation, induction, admission, disposition; see also **greeting** 1.
3. [A social function]—*Syn.* tea, gathering, party, soiree, matinee, cocktail party, dinner, buffet (luncheon *or* supper).

receptive, *mod.*—*Syn.* alert, sensitive, perceptive; see **observant** 2, **sympathetic.**

recess, *n.* **1.** [An intermission]—*Syn.* respite, rest, pause, hiatus, interlude, break, cessation, stop, suspension, interregnum, interval, intervening period, halt, coffee break (D).
2. [An indentation]—*Syn.* break, dent, corner, niche, pigeonhole, mouth, opening, embrasure, hollow, crutch, fork, angle; see also **hole** 2.
3. [A recessed space]—*Syn.* cell, cubicle, carrel, alcove, nook, cranny, oriel, hiding place, ambush, apse, closet, crypt, cove, bay; see also **hole** 3.

recession, *n.* **1.** [A relapse]—*Syn.* collapse, return, reversal; see **retreat** 1.
2. [An economic decline]—*Syn.* unemployment, inflation, decline; see **bankruptcy, depression** 3.

recessive, *mod.*—*Syn.* passive, latent, inactive, not dominant, receding, regressive, suspended, refluent, relapsing, dormant; see also **idle** 1.—*Ant.* dominant*, prevailing, overbalancing.

recharge, *v.*—*Syn.* charge again, restore, put new life into; see **renew** 1, **revive** 1.

recipe, *n.*—*Syn.* formula, compound, receipt, instructions, prescription, cookery formula, directions, method.

recipient, *mod.* —*Syn.* on the receiving end, getting, taking; see **receiving.**

recipient, *n.* —*Syn.* heir, object, legatee; see **beneficiary, receiver.**

reciprocal, *mod.* —*Syn.* interchangeable, correlative, convertible; see **exchangeable, mutual** 1.

reciprocate, *v.* **1.** [To exchange]—*Syn.* alternate, retaliate, return; see **exchange** 2.

2. [To vacillate]—*Syn.* share, swing, interchange; see **alternate** 1, **wave** 3.

reciprocation, *n.* —*Syn.* return, trade, buying and selling; see **exchange** 2.

reciprocity, *n.* —*Syn.* interchange, transfer, exchange; see **buying, selling** 1.

recital, *n.* **1.** [A concert]—*Syn.* presentation, portrayal, musical; see **performance** 2, **show** 2.

2. [A narration]—*Syn.* account, fable, tale; see **report** 1, **story.**

recitation, *n.* **1.** [The act of reciting]—*Syn.* delivery, speaking, playing, narrating, reading, recounting, declaiming, discoursing, soliloquizing, discussion, holding forth, performance, recital, rehearsal, monologue, discourse.

2. [A meeting for recitation, sense 1]—*Syn.* quiz period, recitation period, examination, oral questioning, schoolroom exercise, discussion hour, class discussion; see **gathering.**

3. [A composition used for recitation, sense 1] —*Syn.* soliloquy, address, oration, talk, proclamation, poetry, reading selection, sermon, appeal, report; see also **speech** 3, **writing** 2.

recite, *v.* **1.** [To repeat formally]—*Syn.* declaim, address, read, render, discourse, hold forth, enact, dramatize, deliver from memory, interpret, soliloquize.

2. [To report on a lesson]—*Syn.* answer, give a report, explain, reel off, reply to questions, give a verbal account; see also **discuss, report** 2.

3. [To relate in detail]—*Syn.* expatiate, enumerate, enlarge, report, account for, give an account of, impart, chant, convey, quote, communicate, utter, describe, relate, state, tell, mention, narrate, recount, retell, picture, delineate, portray; see also **explain, tell** 1.

reckless, *mod.* —*Syn.* thoughtless, breakneck, wild; see **rash.**

recklessly, *mod.* —*Syn.* dangerously, heedlessly, with abandon; see **bravely, carelessly.**

reckon, *v.* —*Syn.* compute, consider, calculate, enumerate, count, evaluate, judge; see also **estimate** 1.

reckoning, *n.* **1.** [An estimate]—*Syn.* computation, adding, count; see **calculation** 1, **estimate** 1.

2. [Charge]—*Syn.* cost, fee, debt; see **charge** 1.

reclaim, *v.* **1.** [To bring into usable condition] —*Syn.* rescue, work over, regenerate, redeem, recondition, recover from refuse, convert, reform, enhance, remodel, develop; see also **restore** 3.

2. [To reform]—*Syn.* resolve, mend, improve; see **reform** 3.

reclamation, *n.* —*Syn.* redemption, repair, repossession; see **recovery** 3, **restoration** 1.

recline, *v.* —*Syn.* sprawl, lean, lounge; see **rest** 1.

recluse, *n.* —*Syn.* troglodyte, anchorite, eremite; see **ascetic, hermit.**

recognition, *n.* **1.** [The act of recognizing]—*Syn.* recalling, remembering, identifying, perceiving, verifying, apprehending, acknowledging, noticing, recollection, memory, identification, recall, re-identification, recognizance, remembrance, mental reproduction *or* recurrence, cognizance.

2. [Tangible evidence of recognition, sense 1] —*Syn.* greeting, acknowledgment, identification, perception, admission, verification, comprehension, appreciation, renown, esteem, notice, attention, acceptance, regard, honor.

recognize, *v.* **1.** [To know again]—*Syn.* be familiar, make out, distinguish, verify, recollect, sight, diagnose, place, espy, descry, recall, remember, see, perceive, admit knowledge of, notice; see also **know** 1.

2. [To acknowledge]—*Syn.* assent, appreciate, realize; see **admit** 3.

3. [To acknowledge the legality of a government] —*Syn.* exchange diplomatic representatives, have diplomatic relations with, sanction, approve, extend formal *or* de jure *or* de facto recognition to; see also **acknowledge** 2.

recognized, *mod.* —*Syn.* sighted, caught, perceived, realized, acknowledged, known, appreciated, admitted, recalled, remembered.

recoil, *v.* —*Syn.* withdraw, turn away, shrink (from), draw *or* step *or* pull back, flinch, demur, blink, shirk, falter, dodge, swerve, wince, cringe, duck, quail; see also **retreat** 1.

recollect, *v.* —*Syn.* recall, bring to mind, look back on; see **remember** 1.

recollection, *n.* —*Syn.* remembrance, reminiscence, retrospection; see **memory** 1.

recommend, *v.* **1.** [To lend support or approval] —*Syn.* agree to, sanction, hold up, commend, extol, compliment, applaud, celebrate, praise, speak well *or* highly of, acclaim, eulogize, confirm, laud, second, favor, back, advocate, stand by, magnify, glorify, exalt, think highly of, be satisfied with, esteem, value, prize, uphold, justify, endorse, vouch for; *all* (D): go on record for, be all for, front for, go to bat for; see also **approve** 1, **support** 2. —*Ant.* censure*, disesteem, denounce.

2. [To make a suggestion or prescription]—*Syn.* prescribe, suggest, counsel; see **advise** 1, **urge** 1.

recommendation, *n.* **1.** [The act of recommending] —*Syn.* advocacy, guidance, order, counsel, direction, tip, proposal, instruction, judgment, sanction, commendation, endorsement, support, approbation, charge, injunction, esteem, eulogy, praise; see also **advice, suggestion** 1.—*Ant.* disapproval, opposition*, antagonism.

2. [A document that vouches for character or ability]—*Syn.* certificate, testimonial, reference, character, character reference, letter of recommendation, letter in support; see also **letter** 2.

recommended, *mod.* —*Syn.* urged, sanctioned, mentioned, praised, commended, endorsed, supported, suggested, advocated, persuaded; see also **approved.**—*Ant.* refused*, declined, disapproved.

recompense, *n.* —*Syn.* return, repayment, reward; see **payment** 1.

reconcile, *v.* **1.** [To adjust]—*Syn.* adapt, arrange, regulate; see **adjust** 1, 3.

2. [To bring into harmony]—*Syn.* conciliate, assuage, pacify, propitiate, mitigate, make up, mediate, arbitrate, intercede, bring together, accustom oneself to, harmonize, accord, dictate peace, accommodate, appease, reunite, make peace between, bring to terms, bring into one's camp, win over; *all* (D): bury the hatchet, patch up, kiss and make up; see also **settle** 9.—*Ant.* bother*, irritate, alienate.

reconciled, *mod.*—*Syn.* settled, regulated, arranged, adjusted, agreed to, adapted, conciliated, propitiated, harmonized, reunited, brought to conclusion; see also **determined.**—*Ant.* opposed*, alienated, antagonized.

reconciliation, *n.*—*Syn.* conciliation, settlement, payment; see **adjustment** 2, **agreement** 3.

reconnaissance, *n.*—*Syn.* observation, survey, preview; see **examination** 1.

reconnoiter, *v.*—*Syn.* inspect, inquire, survey; see **examine** 1.

reconsider, *v.*—*Syn.* re-evaluate, think *or* go *or* work over, rearrange, consider again, recheck, reinquire, re-examine, correct, amend, revise, retrace, emend, rework, replan, review, withdraw for consideration, reweigh, amend one's judgment; see also **consider** 1.

reconstruct, *v.*—*Syn.* rebuild, remodel, construct again, make over, revamp, recondition, reconstitute, reproduce, re-establish, restore, refashion, reorganize, replace, overhaul, renovate, modernize, rework, construct from the original, copy, remake; see also **build** 1, **repair.**

reconstruction, *n.*—*Syn.* rebuilding, resetting, remodeling, modernization, reorganization, reformation, regeneration, rehabilitation, restoration, replotting, replanning, reestablishment, remaking; see also **repair.**

record, *n.* **1.** [Documentary evidence]—*Syn.* manuscript, inscription, transcription, account, history, legend, story, writing, written material, document. Types of records include the following—register, catalog, list, inventory, memo, memorandum, registry, schedule, chronicle, docket, scroll, archive, note, contract, statement, will, testament, petition, calendar, log(book), letter, memoir, reminiscence, dictation, confession, deposition, inscription, official record, sworn document, evidence, license, bulletin, gazette, newspaper, magazine, annual report, journal, Congressional Record, transactions, debates, bill, annals, presidential order, state paper, white paper, blue book, budget, report, entry, book, publication, autograph, signature, vital statistics, deed, paper, diary, stenographic notes, ledger, daybook, almanac, proceedings, minutes, description, affidavit, certificate, muniment, memorabilium, transcript, dossier, roll.

2. [One's past]—*Syn.* career, experience, work, accomplishment, background, case history, studies, way of life, past behavior, reign, administration, official conduct; see also **life** 2.

3. [A device for the reproduction of sound]—*Syn.* recording, disk, compact disk, wax cylinder, phonograph record, laser disk, wax plate, steel plate, recording wire, transcription; *all* (D): canned music, cut, take, platter.

go on record—*Syn.* assert, attest, state; see **declare** 2.

off the record—*Syn.* confidential, unofficial, secret; see **private.**

on the record—*Syn.* recorded, stated, official; see **public** 1.

record, *v.* **1.** [To write down]—*Syn.* register, write (in), put *or* mark *or* jot *or* set *or* note *or* write *or* take down, put on record, transcribe, list, note, file, mark, inscribe, log, catalog, tabulate, matriculate, put in writing, put in black and white, chronicle, keep accounts, keep an account of, spill ink, make a written account of, put on paper, preserve, make an entry in, chalk up, write (up), enter, enroll, report, book, post, journalize, copy, document, insert, enumerate; see also **write** 1.

2. [To indicate]—*Syn.* point out *or* to, explain, show; see **designate** 1.

3. [To record electronically]—*Syn.* tape, cut, photograph, make a record of, make a tape, tape-record, videotape, film, cut a record (D).

recorded, *mod.*—*Syn.* listed, filed, on file, in black and white, in writing, inscribed, put down, registered, documented, entered, written, published, noted down, described, reported, catalogued, mentioned, certified, kept, chronicled, booked.

recorder, *n.*—*Syn.* dictaphone, recording instrument, stereophonic recorder; see **tape recorder.**

recording, *n.*—*Syn.* documentation, recounting, self-debriefing; see **reporting.**

record player, *n.*—*Syn.* phonograph, stereo, high fidelity set, hi-fi, component set, sound system, victrola, talking machine, music box, juke box, graphophone, gramophone; see also **tape recorder**
Record player parts include the following—changer, turntable, tone arm, amplifier, preamplifier (*or* (D): preamp), speakers, stylus, cartridge, woofer, tweeter, spindle, needle.

records, *n.*—*Syn.* documents, chronicles, archives, public papers, registers, annals, memorabilia, memoranda, lists, return, diaries, accounts.

recount, *v.*—*Syn.* state, portray, convey; see **narrate.**

recoup, *v.*—*Syn.* regain, make up for, get back; see **recover** 2.

recourse, *n.*—*Syn.* help, appeal, support; see **aid** 1.

recover, *v.* **1.** [To obtain again]—*Syn.* redeem, salvage, retrieve, rescue, reclaim, recoup, find again, recapture, repossess, bring *or* get *or* win back, reacquire, regain, rediscover, resume, catch up, replevin, replevy, become seized of; see also **obtain** 1.—*Ant.* lose*, let slip, fall behind.

2. [To improve one's condition]—*Syn.* gain, increase, better, realize, reach, (out) grow, collect, forge ahead, pick up, produce, succeed to, inherit, purchase, make money; *both* (D): become something, make a name; see also **improve** 2, **profit** 2.—*Ant.* fail*, go bankrupt, give up.

3. [To regain health]—*Syn.* rally, come around *or* back *or* up *or* to *or* out of it, get out of danger, improve, convalesce, heal, get the better of, overcome, start anew, be restored, mend, revive, be oneself again, perk up, gain (strength), recuperate, be reanimated, get well *or* back *or* over *or* better; *all* (D): pull through, make a comeback, get back in shape, snap out of, sober up, get through, return to form.—*Ant.* die*, fail, become worse.

recovered, *mod.* —*Syn.* renewed, found, replaced, reborn, rediscovered, reawakened, retrieved, redeemed, reclaimed, regained, revived, returned, resumed; see also **discovered.**—*Ant.* lost*, missed, dropped.

recovering, *mod.* —*Syn.* getting better, improving, mending; see **convalescent.**

recovery, *n.* **1.** [The act of returning to normal] —*Syn.* re-establishment, resumption, restoration, reinstatement, rehabilitation, reconstruction, return, reformation, recreation, replacement, readjustment, improving, getting back to normal *or* normalcy; see also sense 2, **improvement** 1.
2. [The process of regaining health]—*Syn.* convalescence, recuperation, revival, rebirth, renaissance, renascence, reanimation, resurgence, resurrection, regeneration, cure, improvement, reawakening, renewal, reinvigoration, resuscitation, rejuvenation, revivification, post-operative care, rehabilitation, return of health, bodily *or* physical improvement, healing, betterment.
3. [The act of regaining possession]—*Syn.* repossession, retrieval, reclamation, redemption, indemnification, reparation, compensation, recapture, replevin, return, recouping, restoration, remuneration, reimbursement, retaking, recall, replevy.

recreant, *mod.* —*Syn.* cowardly, craven, false, base, low, mean-spirited, faithless, cowering, yielding, afraid, hesitant, timorous, unfaithful, apostate, renegade, erring, timid, fearful, dastard(ly), skulking, sneaking, weak-minded, pigeonhearted, unmanly, spiritless, falsehearted, arrant, perfidious, defecting, treacherous, vile; see also **vulgar** 1.—*Ant.* brave*, courageous, gallant.

recreation, *n.* —*Syn.* amusement, relaxation, diversion, play, fun, entertainment, enjoyment, festivity, hobby, holiday, vacation, pastime, pleasure, game, avocation, refreshment; see also **sport** 1.

recruit, *n.* —*Syn.* new man, novice, tyro, beginner, selectee, draftee, trainee, volunteer, enlisted man, serviceman, soldier, sailor, marine; *all* (D): rookie, Johnny Raw, jeep, greenie, G.I. Joe; see also **soldier.**

recruit, *v.* **1.** [To raise troops]—*Syn.* draft, call up, select, supply, muster, deliver, sign up, induct, take in, find manpower, call to arms *or* colors, augment the army, bring into service; see also **enlist** 1.
2. [To gather needed resources]—*Syn.* restore, store up, replenish, strengthen, revive, recuperate, recover, fill up, recoup, repair, improve, better, gain, regain, reanimate; see also **obtain** 1, **raise** 3.

recruited, *mod.* —*Syn.* inducted, called up, accepted into the armed forces; see **initiated** 3.

rectangle, *n.* —*Syn.* geometrical figure, square, box, oblong, four-sided figure, right-angled parallelogram; see also **form** 1.

rectangular, *mod.* —*Syn.* square, four-sided, right-angled, orthogonal, foursquare, boxy (D); see also **angular** 1.

rectify, *v.* —*Syn.* redress, reform, amend; see **correct** 1, **improve** 1, **revise.**

rectitude, *n.* —*Syn.* integrity, honesty, uprightness; see **honesty** 1.

rector, *n.* —*Syn.* pastor, vicar, pontiff; see **minister** 1.

rectory, *n.* —*Syn.* vicarage, presbytery, manse; see **parsonage.**

recumbent, *mod.* —*Syn.* reclining, prostrate, lying down; see **lying** 4.

recuperate, *v.* —*Syn.* heal, pull through, get back on one's feet; see **recover** 3.

recur, *v.* —*Syn.* return, reappear, crop up again; see **happen** 2, **repeat** 1.

recurrent, *mod.* —*Syn.* reoccurring, repetitive, habitual; see **repeated** 1.

recycle, *v.* —*Syn.* start *or* do over, start again, restart; see **begin** 1, **resume.**

red, *n.* Tints and shades of red include the following —scarlet, carmine, vermilion, crimson, cerise, cherry-red, ruby, garnet, maroon, brick-red, infrared, far infrared, near infrared, claret, rust, red-gold, magenta, pink, damask, coral-red, blood-red, solferino, fuchsia, russet, terra cotta, bittersweet, geranium lake, nacarat *or* nacarine, hyacinth red, Chinese red, Morocco red *or* caldron, Turkey red, Alizarin red, aniline red, aurora red, Bengal red, Congo red, Venetian red, Indian red *or* Indian ocher, chrome-red, carthamus red, rose, rose de Pompadour, rose blush, rose du Barry, old rose, Tyrian purple; see also **color** 1, **pink.**
in the red (D)—*Syn.* in debt, losing money, going broke (D); see **indebted.**
see red (D)—*Syn.* become angry, lose one's temper, get mad (D); see **rage** 1.

red-blooded, *mod.* —*Syn.* vigorous, high-spirited, robust; see **strong** 1, **healthy** 1.

redden, *v.* **1.** [To grow red]—*Syn.* blush, color, flush, crimson, turn red, bloody, rust.
2. [To make red]—*Syn.* color, rouge, apply lipstick, tint, dye, put paint on, ruddle *or* reddle, rubricate, flush, tint, encarmine, encarnadine.

reddish, *mod.* —*Syn.* flushed, somewhat red, rose; see **red,** *n.*

redecorate, *v.* —*Syn.* refurbish, refresh, renew, paint, restore, recondition, remodel, renovate, revamp, rearrange, touch *or* patch up, plaster, refurnish, readorn, wallpaper, clean (up), carpet; *both* (D): do over, fix (up); see also **decorate.**

redeem, *v.* **1.** [To recover through a payment] —*Syn.* buy back, repay, ransom, purchase, repurchase, reclaim, retrieve, regain, settle, replevy, discharge, cash in, buy off, get back, take *or* call in, cover, defray, make good, restore, reinstate, recapture, replevin, recoup, repossess, buy *or* pay off; see also **obtain** 1.
2. [To save]—*Syn.* liberate, set free, deliver; see **ransom, rescue** 1.

redeemed, *mod.* —*Syn.* acquired, gotten back, taken; see **recovered.**

redeemer, *n.* —*Syn.* rescuer, deliverer, liberator; see **savior** 1.

redeem oneself, *v.* —*Syn.* atone, expiate, remedy, redress, propitiate, reform, keep faith, apologize, do penance, appease, give satisfaction, vindicate *or* clear *or* absolve oneself, prove oneself innocent, beg pardon, express regrets, make amends; see also **pay for.**

redemption, *n.* **1.** [Recovery]—*Syn.* retrieval, reclamation, reparation; see **recovery** 3, **return** 2.
2. [Salvation]—*Syn.* regeneration, sanctification, rebirth; see **salvation** 3.

red-handed (D), *mod.* —*Syn.* blatantly, caught in the act, while one is at it; see **openly** 2.

redheaded, *mod.* —*Syn.* auburn-haired, red-haired, sandy-haired, titian-haired, strawberry blonde; *both* (D): carrot-topped, brick-topped.

red-hot (D), *mod.* **1.** [Burning]—*Syn.* heated, sizzling, scorching; see **burning** 1, **hot** 1.
2. [Zealous]—*Syn.* heated, fanatical, eager; see **excited.**
3. [Raging]—*Syn.* excessive, rabid, very; see **extreme** 2.
4. [Newest]—*Syn.* latest, recent, hippest (D); see **modern** 1.

redo, *v.* —*Syn.* start over, redesign, rethink, go back to the drawing board, revamp, do over again; see also **repeat** 1.

redolent, *mod.* —*Syn.* sweet, perfumed, fragrant; see **odorous** 2.

redone, *mod.* —*Syn.* done over, refinished, fixed up; see **improved** 1, **revised.**

redouble, *v.* —*Syn.* reinforce, raise, magnify; see **increase** 1, **strengthen.**

redoubt, *n.* —*Syn.* bulwark, stronghold, fortress; see **fortification** 2.

redoubtable, *mod.* —*Syn.* fearful, dreadful, frightening; see **frightful** 1.

redress, *n.* **1.** [Correction]—*Syn.* revision, amendment, remedy, change, reformation, renewal, remodeling, reworking, re-establishment, rectification, relief, rehabilitation, repair.
2. [Amends]—*Syn.* compensation, satisfaction, payment, reward, indemnity, retribution, requital, return, reparation, recompense, allowance, atonement, propitiation, adjustment, correction, conciliation, remission, indemnification, restitution, restoration; see also **pay** 2, **prize.**

redress, *v.* —*Syn.* change, revise, rectify; see **correct** 1.

red tape (D), *n.* **1.** [Delay]—*Syn.* wait; *both* (D): roadblock, holdup; see **impediment** 1.
2. [Bureaucracy]—*Syn.* officialism, inflexible routine, officialdom; see **bureaucracy** 1, 2.

reduce, *v.* **1.** [To make less]—*Syn.* lessen, diminish, cut down; see **decrease** 2.
2. [To defeat]—*Syn.* conquer, overcome, subdue; see **defeat** 1, 2, 3.
3. [To humble]—*Syn.* degrade, demote, abase; see **humble, humiliate.**

reduced, *mod.* **1.** [Made smaller]—*Syn.* lessened, decreased, diminished, shortened, abridged, abbreviated, condensed, miniaturized, transistorized, compressed, foreshortened, economized, cut down, down-sized, shrunk, subtracted, contracted, melted, boiled down.—*Ant.* enlarged, stretched, spread*.
2. [Made lower]—*Syn.* lowered, abated, sunk, deflated, leveled, cheapened, marked *or* taken down, discounted, weakened, debilitated, humbled, demoted, degraded.—*Ant.* heightened, raised*, elevated.
3. [Made orderly]—*Syn.* standardized, classified, regulated, controlled, ordered, formulated, systematized, unified; see also **organized.**

reducing, *n.* —*Syn.* lowering, (fore)shortening, condensing, compressing, cutting down, lessening, diminishing, paring down, contracting, shriveling; see also **contraction** 1, **reduction** 1.

reduction, *n.* **1.** [The process of making smaller] —*Syn.* conversion, contraction, abatement, reducing, deoxidation, refinement, diminution, lowering, lessening, shortening, retrenchment, attenuation, atrophy, condensation, decrease, loss, compression, depression, subtraction, discount, shrinkage, concision, constriction, subduction, modification, minimization, curtailment, abbreviation, decrescence, syncope, miniaturization, down-sizing, ellipsis, elision, abridgment, assuagement, modulation, moderation, mitigation, decline, remission, decrement, decline.—*Ant.* increase*, increasing, enlargement.
2. [An amount that constitutes reduction, sense 1] —*Syn.* decrease, rebate, cut; see **discount.**

redundancy, *n.* —*Syn.* verbosity, tautology, excess; see **repetition, wordiness.**

redundant, *mod.* **1.** [Needless]—*Syn.* superfluous, irrelevant, excessive; see **extreme** 2, **unnecessary.**
2. [Repetitious]—*Syn.* wordy, bombastic, loquacious; see **oratorical, verbose.**

reduplicate, *v.* —*Syn.* double, duplicate, ditto (D); see **copy** 2, **repeat.**

re-echo, *v.* —*Syn.* reverberate, reiterate, rebound; see **repeat** 3.

reed, *n.* —*Syn.* cane, stalk, grass; see **plant, weed** 1.

re-educate, *v.* —*Syn.* reinstruct, readjust, rehabilitate; see **improve** 1, **teach** 1.

reedy, *mod.* —*Syn.* piercing, sharp, loud; see **shrill.**

reef, *n.* —*Syn.* ridge, shoal, (sand) bar, rock, bank, beach, coral reef, atoll, ledge, rock barrier.

reefer (D), *n.* —*Syn.* marijuana cigarette; *all* (D): joint, roach, toke, stick; see also **drug** 2, **marijuana, tobacco.**

reek, *n.* —*Syn.* stench, stink, smell; see **smell** 2.

reek, *v.* —*Syn.* smell of, give off (an odor), emit stench; see **smell** 1, **stink.**

reel, *n.* —*Syn.* spool, bobbin, windlass, spindle, wound strip, roll (of film).

reel, *v.* —*Syn.* roll, whirl, sway, stagger, weave, feel giddy, bob, waver, walk drunkenly, totter, careen.

re-enter, *v.* —*Syn.* reappear, come back, re-emerge; see **enter** 1, **return** 1.

re-establish, *v.* —*Syn.* rehabilitate, put in place again, go back to; see **organize** 2.

re-examine, *v.* —*Syn.* go back over, review, check thoroughly; see **examine** 1.

refer, *v.* **1.** [To concern]—*Syn.* regard, relate, have relation, have to do with, apply, be about, answer (to), involve, connect, be a matter of, have a bearing on, correspond with, bear upon, comprise, include, belong, pertain, have reference, take in, cover, appertain, point, hold, encompass, incorporate, touch, deal with; see also **concern** 1.
2. [To mention]—*Syn.* allude to, bring up, direct a remark *or* mention, make reference *or* allusion, advert, ascribe, direct attention, attribute, cite, quote, hint at, point to, notice, indicate, speak about, suggest, touch on, give as example, associate, adduce, exemplify, instance, excerpt, extract; see also **mention.**
3. [To direct]—*Syn.* send to, put in touch with, relegate, commit, submit to, assign, give a recommendation to, introduce; see also **designate** 1, **lead** 1.

referee, *n.* —*Syn.* arbitrator, conciliator, ref (D); see **judge** 2, **umpire.**

reference, *n.* **1.** [The act of referring]—*Syn.* indicating, pointing out, mentioning, bringing up, stating, attributing, connecting, associating, relating.
2. [An allusion]—*Syn.* mention, hint, implication; see **allusion.**
3. [A source]—*Syn.* original (text), book, article, writing, standard work, dictionary, thesaurus, encyclopedia, reference book, guidebook, footnote, eyewitness, informant, evidence; see also **source** 2.
4. [A person vouching for another]—*Syn.* friend, employer, patron, associate, backer, booster (D).

referendum, *n.*—*Syn.* election, poll, choice; see **vote** 2.

referred (to), *mod.* **1.** [Mentioned]—*Syn.* brought up, alluded to, spoken about; see **mentioned, suggested.**
2. [Directed]—*Syn.* recommended, sent on, introduced; see **proposed.**

referring, *mod.*—*Syn.* alluding, suggesting, hinting, indicating, attributing, mentioning, citing, quoting, bringing up, touching on, remarking, implying, imputing, ascribing.

refine, *v.* **1.** [To purify]—*Syn.* rarefy, strain, filter; see **clean, purify.**
2. [To improve]—*Syn.* make clear, better, clarify; see **explain, improve** 1.

refined, *mod.* **1.** [Purified]—*Syn.* cleaned, cleansed, aerated, strained, washed, clean, expurgated, rarefied, boiled down, distilled, clarified, tried, drained, elutriated; see also **pure** 2.—*Ant.* raw*, crude, unrefined.
2. [Genteel]—*Syn.* cultivated, civilized, polished, elegant, urbane, well-bred, gracious, enlightened, free from coarseness, courtly, mannerly, suave, gentlemanly, ladylike, restrained, gentle, mannerly, high-minded, subtle, courteous; see also **polite** 1.

refinement, *n.* **1.** [The act of refining]—*Syn.* cleaning, cleansing, purification, distillation, clarifying, draining, elutriation, depuration, detersion, cracking.
2. [Culture]—*Syn.* civilization, cultivation, erudition, sophistication, breeding, enlightenment, wide knowledge, lore, subtlety, science, artistic attainments, scholarship, learning; see also **culture** 3.
3. [Genteel feelings and behavior]—*Syn.* elegance, politeness, polish, good manners, suavity, courtesy, grace, gentleness, tact, cultivation, graciousness, civility, affability, taste, discrimination, fineness, delicacy, dignity, urbanity, *savoir faire* (French); see also **culture** 2.

refinery, *n.*—*Syn.* smelting works, oil refinery, sugar refinery; see **factory.**

refining, *mod.*—*Syn.* cleansing, purifying, modernizing, making *or* rendering pure(r) *or* clean(er) *or* more useful, etc.; cleaning up, sharpening; see also **cleaning, helpful.**

refinished, *mod.*—*Syn.* redone, remodeled, fixed up; see **clean** 1, **changed** 3, **repaired.**

reflect, *v.* **1.** [To contemplate]—*Syn.* speculate, concentrate, weigh; see **consider** 2, **think** 1.
2. [To throw back]—*Syn.* echo, re-echo, repeat, match, take after, return, resonate, reverberate, copy, resound, reproduce, reply, repercuss, be resonant, emulate, imitate, follow, catch, rebound; see also **bounce** 1, **sound** 1.
3. [To throw back an image]—*Syn.* mirror, shine, reproduce, show up on, flash, cast *or* give back, return, give forth.
4. [To discredit]—*Syn.* (cast) blame, reproach, disesteem; see **censure.**

reflected, *mod.*—*Syn.* mirrored, repeated, reproduced, echoed, followed, derived from, returned, sent *or* cast back, emulated, imitated, brought to mind.

reflection, *n.* **1.** [Thought]—*Syn.* consideration, absorption, imagination, observation, pensiveness, thinking, contemplation, rumination, speculation, musing, deliberation, study, pondering, meditation, concentration, cogitation; see also **thought** 1.
2. [An image]—*Syn.* impression, rays, light, shine, glitter, appearance, idea, reflected image, likeness, shadow, duplicate, picture, echo, representation, reproduction; see also **copy, image** 2.
3. [Discredit]—*Syn.* censure, reproach, disesteem; see **blame** 1.

reflective, *mod.*—*Syn.* contemplative, studious, pensive; see **thoughtful** 1.

reflector, *n.*—*Syn.* shiny metal, glass, reverberator; see **mirror.**

reflex, *mod.*—*Syn.* mechanical, unthinking, habitual; see **automatic** 2, **spontaneous.**

reform, *n.*—*Syn.* reformation, betterment, new law; see **change** 2, **improvement** 2.

reform, *v.* **1.** [To change into a new form]—*Syn.* reorganize, remodel, revise, repair, reconstruct, rearrange, transform, ameliorate, redeem, rectify, better, rehabilitate, improve, correct, cure, remedy, convert, mend, emend, amend, restore, rebuild, reclaim, revolutionize, regenerate, refashion, renovate, renew, rework, reconstitute, make over, remake; see also **change** 1.—*Ant.* degrade, corrupt*, botch.
2. [To correct evils]—*Syn.* amend, clean out, give a new basis, abolish, repeal, uplift, ameliorate, rectify, regenerate, give new life to, remedy, stamp out, make better, standardize, bring up to code, denazify; see also **improve** 1.
3. [To change one's conduct for the better]—*Syn.* resolve, mend, regenerate, uplift, make amends, have a new conscience, make a new start, make (New Year) resolutions; *all* (D): turn over a new leaf, put on the new man, go straight, change one's ways, clean up one's act, throw it all over, get religion, wipe one's nose, swear off; see also sense 2.

Reformation, *n.*—*Syn.* Renaissance, Lutheranism, Protestantism, Puritanism, Calvinism, Anglicanism, Unitarianism, Counter Reformation, Protestant Movement; see also **revolution** 2.

reformation, *n.* **1.** [The act of reforming]—*Syn.* reorganization, reconstruction, renewal, repair, rearrangement, renovation, transformation, reworking, shifting, realignment.
2. [The state of being reformed]—*Syn.* reawakening, repeal, abolition, rebirth, remaking, re-establishment; see also **recovery** 1, **restoration** 1.

reformatory, *n.*—*Syn.* house of correction, penal institution, penitentiary, asylum for young delinquents, boys' reformatory, girls' reformatory; *all*

(D): kids' pen, young-stir, little house, Junior College; see also **jail, school** 1.

Reformed, *mod.* —*Syn.* denominational, unorthodox, nonconforming, sectarian, dissenting, heterodox, enlightened, Protestant.—*Ant.* Catholic*, Roman Catholic, Papist.

reformed, *mod.* **1.** [Changed]—*Syn.* altered, transformed, shifted, reconstituted, reorganized, shuffled, re-established, revolutionized, rectified, amended, reset, reworked, renewed, regenerated; see also **changed** 2, **improved** 1.—*Ant.* degenerated, vicious, corrupt*.

2. [Changed for the better in behavior]—*Syn.* converted, improved, redeemed, gone straight (D), made a new man of, turned over a new leaf (D); see also **polite** 1, **righteous** 1.

refractory, *mod.* **1.** [Stubborn]—*Syn.* opinionated, headstrong, willful; see **obstinate** 1.

2. [Inflexible]—*Syn.* hard, impliable, rigid; see **firm** 2, **stiff** 1.

refrain, *n.* —*Syn.* undersong, theme, strain; see **chorus** 2, **music** 1, **song.**

refrain, *v.* —*Syn.* cease, avoid, forbear; see **abstain.**

refresh, *v.* **1.** [To renew]—*Syn.* invigorate, animate, exhilarate; see **renew** 1.

2. [To revive]—*Syn.* resuscitate, restore, bring around; see **revive** 1.

refreshing, *mod.* **1.** [Bracing]—*Syn.* invigorating, rousing, exhilarating; see **stimulating.**

2. [Novel]—*Syn.* delightful, extraordinary, unique; see **unusual** 1, 2.

refreshment, *n.* —*Syn.* tidbit, ice cream, cakes; see **drink** 1, **food.**

refrigerate, *v.* —*Syn.* chill, make cold, freeze; see **cool** 2.

refrigeration, *n.* —*Syn.* cooling, chilling, freezing, preservation by cold, glacification, infrigidation, glaciation, regelation; see also **preservation.**

refrigerator, *n.* —*Syn.* icebox, Frigidaire (trademark) (*or* (D): fridge), automatic cooler, cold-storage box, refrigerator car, electric refrigerator, cooling apparatus, refrigeration equipment, quick freezer.

refuge, *n.* **1.** [A place of protection]—*Syn.* shelter, asylum, ambush, sanctuary, protectory, covert, home, retreat, anchorage, nunnery, convent, monastery, poorhouse, safe place, hiding place, game farm *or* refuge *or* preserve, harbor (of refuge), haven, fortress, stronghold.

2. [A means of resort]—*Syn.* alternative, escape, resource, last resort, outlet, way out, retreat, exit, opening.

refugee, *n.* —*Syn.* exile, expatriate, fugitive, emigrant, *émigré* (French), renegade, foreigner, political refugee, expellee, defector, castaway, derelict, foundling, homeless person, leper, pariah, outlaw, Ishmael, prodigal, displaced person (*or* (D): DP), alien, outcast, fugitive, evacuee.

refund, *n.* —*Syn.* return, reimbursement, repayment, remuneration, compensation, allowance, payment for expenses, rebate, discount, settlement, discharge, acquittance, retribution, satisfaction, consolation, money back (D); see also **payment** 1.

refund, *v.* **1.** [To return]—*Syn.* pay back, reimburse, remit, repay, relinquish, indemnify, make good, balance, recoup, adjust, reward, restore, redeem, make repayment (to), compensate, recompense, make amends, redress, remunerate, give back, settle, honor a claim; *all* (D): kick back, make good, make up for; see **pay** 1, **return** 2.

2. [To put financial obligations on a new basis] —*Syn.* borrow, redeem, discharge, transmit, transfer, make over, resubscribe, commit, undertake, tax, renegotiate, renew, compensate, sell bonds, raise revenue, increase the public debt, issue securities.

refunded, *mod.* **1.** [Returned]—*Syn.* acquitted, reimbursed, discharged; see **paid, repaid, returned.**

2. [Placed on a new financial basis]—*Syn.* renewed, reestablished, redeemed, resubscribed, borrowed, renegotiated, reissued, revised, reconstituted.

refurbish, *v.* —*Syn.* fix up, renovate, restore; see **renew** 1, **repair** 1.

refusal, *n.* —*Syn.* repudiation, renunciation, rebuff, snub, rejection, turndown, nonacceptance, denial, disavowal, noncompliance, forbidding, veto, interdiction, proscription, ban, writ, enjoinment, exclusion, discountenancing, disallowance, negation, refutation, renouncement, repulse, withholding, disclaimer, nonconsent, unwillingness, regrets, abnegation, declination, repulsion, reversal, dissent, prohibition, disfavor, disapproval, curb, restraint; see also **opposition** 2.—*Ant.* consent*, approval, acceptance.

refuse, *n.* —*Syn.* leavings, remains, residue; see **trash** 1, 3.

refuse, *v.* —*Syn.* dissent, desist, repel, rebuff, scorn, pass up, reject, disallow, have no plans to *or* for, not anticipate, demur, protest, withdraw, hold back, withhold, shun, evade, dodge, ignore, spurn, regret, turn down, turn from, beg to be excused, send regrets, send off, not budge, cut out of the budget, not budget, not care to, refuse to receive, dispense with, not be at home to, disaccord with, say no, make excuses, disapprove, set aside, turn away; *all* (D): beg off, brush off, not buy, thumbs down, hold out *or* off, turn one's back on turn a deaf ear to; see also **confute, deny.**—*Ant.* allow*, admit, consent.

refused, *mod.* —*Syn.* declined, rejected, rebuffed, vetoed, repudiated, forbidden, denied (to), disowned, disavowed, forsaken, blocked, repelled, closed to, dismissed, turned down, unbudgeted, not budgeted, not in *or* cut from *or* removed from the budget.—*Ant.* permitted*, allowed, consented to.

refutation, *n.* —*Syn.* rebuttal, confutation, contradiction; see **denial, refusal.**

refute, *v.* —*Syn.* disprove, confute, show up, rebut, explode, expose, prove false, overthrow, show the weakness in, provide refutation for, argue against, oppose, tear down, demolish, squelch, take a stand against, invalidate, cancel (out), repudiate, contradict, negate, dispute, discredit, contravene, parry, contend, debate, disclaim, convict, reply to, quash, crush, gainsay, dispose of, abnegate; *all* (D): knock holes into, knock into a cocked hat, give the lie to, not leave a leg to stand on; see also **answer** 3, **deny** 1.—*Ant.* support*, uphold, stand by.

regain, *v.* —*Syn.* recapture, retrieve, reacquire; see **recover** 1.

regal, *mod.* —*Syn.* sovereign, noble, majestic; see **royal** 1.

regale, *v.* **1.** [To satisfy]—*Syn.* delight, please, nurture; see **entertain** 1.
2. [To feast]—*Syn.* entertain, amuse, gratify; see **celebrate** 3.

regalia, *n.* **1.** [Finery]—*Syn.* best clothes; *both* (D): best bib and tucker, Sunday-go-to-meetings; see **clothes.**
2. [A symbol of royalty]—*Syn.* insignia, decoration(s), crown; see **emblem, symbol.**

regard, *n.* **1.** [A look]—*Syn.* gaze, glance, notice, view, scrutiny, attention, once-over (D); see also **look** 3.
2. [A favorable opinion]—*Syn.* esteem, respect, honor, favor, liking, interest, fondness, attachment, deference, opinion, sympathy, estimation, appreciation, reverence, homage, consideration, love, affection, value, devotion; see also **admiration** 1.
as regards—*Syn.* concerning, with respect *or* reference to, about; see **regarding.**
without regard to—*Syn.* despite, without considering, regardless of; see **notwithstanding.**

regard, *v.* **1.** [To look at]—*Syn.* observe, notice, mark, view, watch, heed, look on, mind, give attention to, advert to, attend, gaze, note, stare at, see, witness, contemplate.—*Ant.* neglect*, overlook, turn away.
2. [To have an attitude]—*Syn.* surmise, look upon, view; see **consider** 2, **think** 1.
3. [To hold in esteem]—*Syn.* respect, esteem, value; see **admire** 1.

regarding, *mod.* and *prep.* —*Syn.* concerning, with respect *or* reference *or* regard to, in relation to, as regards; see also **about** 2.

regardless, *mod.* **1.** [Heedless]—*Syn.* negligent, careless, unobservant, unheeding, inattentive, reckless, nonobservant, inconsiderate, inadvertent, blind, unfeeling, deaf, coarse, crude, neglectful, mindless, insensitive, lax, indifferent, listless, uninterested, unconcerned.—*Ant.* alert*, watchful, vigilant.
2. [In spite of; *usually used with of*]—*Syn.* despite, aside from, distinct from, without regard to, without considering, at any cost, leaving aside; see also **although, but** 1, **notwithstanding.**

regards, *n.* —*Syn.* best wishes, compliments, greetings, salutations, remembrances, respects, love, deference, commendations, love and kisses (D); see also **greeting.**

regatta, *n.* —*Syn.* boat race, rowing competition, yacht race; see **race** 3.

regency, *n.* —*Syn.* regiment, rule, authority; see **dominion** 1, **power** 2.

regenerate, *v.* —*Syn.* raise from the dead, recreate, exhilarate; see **produce** 2, **revive** 1.

regeneration, *n.* **1.** [Reconstruction]—*Syn.* rebuilding, rehabilitation, renovation; see **reconstruction.**
2. [Conversion]—*Syn.* revival, redemption, rebirth; see **salvation** 3.

regent, *n.* —*Syn.* governor, minister, director; see **agent** 1, **ruler** 1.

regime, *n.* —*Syn.* administration, management, political system; see **government** 2.

regiment, *n.* —*Syn.* corps, soldiers, military organization; see **army** 2, **troops.**

regiment, *v.* —*Syn.* order, control, rank; see **classify.**

regimentation, *n.* —*Syn.* massing, collectivization, organization, planned economy, standardization, methodization, regulation, uniformity, arrangement, mechanization, institutionalization, classification, division, lining up, adjustment, harmonization, grouping, ordering, overorganization; see also **control, regulation** 1, **restraint** 2.

regimented, *mod.* —*Syn.* disciplined, controlled, rigid; see **governed** 1, 2.

region, *n.* **1.** [An indefinite area]—*Syn.* country, district, territory, section, sector, province, zone, realm, vicinity, quarter, locale, locality, environs, precinct, county, neighborhood, terrain, domain, range.
2. [A limited area]—*Syn.* precinct, ward, block; see **area** 2.
3. [Scope]—*Syn.* sphere, province, realm; see **field** 4.

regional, *mod.* —*Syn.* provincial, territorial, local, zonal, environmental, regionary, positional, regionalistic, geographical, parochial, sectional, topical, locational, locationary, insular, topographic.

register, *n.* **1.** [A list]—*Syn.* file, registry, roll, annals, entry, guest book, roster, membership, personnel; see also **list, record** 1.
2. [A heating regulator]—*Syn.* grate, hot-air opening, radiator, heating unit.

register, *v.* **1.** [To record]—*Syn.* check in, enroll, file; see **list** 1, **record** 1.
2. [To indicate]—*Syn.* point out, point to, record; see **designate** 1.
3. [To show]—*Syn.* express, disclose, manifest; see **display** 1.
4. [To enlist or enroll]—*Syn.* go through registration, check into, make an entry, sign up for, check in, sign in, join.

registered, *mod.* **1.** [Recorded]—*Syn.* cataloged, described, noted down; see **recorded.**
2. [Pedigreed]—*Syn.* purebred, thoroughbred, blooded, pure-blooded, full-blooded.

registrar, *n.* —*Syn.* recorder, head of the registering office, register, receiving clerk, registering clerk, university administrator, director of admissions, admissions officer; see also **clerk** 2.

registration, *n.* **1.** [The act of registering]—*Syn.* enrolling, signing up, certification, matriculation, recording, listing, filing, cataloging, booking, noting down, stamping, authorizing, notarization; see also **enrollment** 1.
2. [Those who have registered]—*Syn.* enrollment, turnout, registrants, voters, hotel guests, students, matriculants, student body, delegation.

regress, *v.* —*Syn.* backslide, relapse, revert; see **retreat** 1, **sink** 1.

regressive, *mod.* —*Syn.* conservative, reverse, reactionary; see **backward** 1.

regret, *n.* **1.** [Remorse]—*Syn.* concern, compunction, worry, repentance, self-reproach, self-condemnation, self-disgust, misgiving, regretfulness, nostalgia, self-accusation, contrition, qualm, scruple, penitence, bitterness, disappointment, dissatisfaction, uneasiness, conscience, discomfort, annoyance, spiritual disturbance; see also **care** 2.—*Ant.* comfort*, satisfaction, ease.

2. [Grief]—*Syn.* sorrow, pain, anxiety; see **grief** 1.

regret, *v.* **1.** [To be sorry for]—*Syn.* mourn, bewail, lament, cry over, rue, grieve, repent, repine, have compunctions about, look back upon, feel conscience-stricken, bemoan, moan, have a bad conscience, have qualms about, weep over, be disturbed over, feel uneasy about; *all* (D): laugh out of the other side of one's mouth, kick oneself, bite one's tongue, cry over spilled milk.—*Ant.* celebrate*, be satisfied with, be happy.

2. [To disapprove of]—*Syn.* deplore, be averse *or* opposed to, deprecate; see **censure, denounce, dislike.**

regretful, *mod.*—*Syn.* penitent, frustrated, remorseful; see **sorry** 1.

regrettable, *mod.*—*Syn.* dreadful, pitiful, unfortunate; see **unfavorable** 2.

regular, *mod.* **1.** [In accordance with custom]—*Syn.* customary, usual, routine; see **conventional** 1, 2.

2. [In accordance with law]—*Syn.* normal, legitimate, lawful; see **legal** 1.

3. [In accordance with an observable pattern]—*Syn.* orderly, methodical, routine, symmetrical, precise, exact, systematic, arranged, organized, patterned, constant, congruous, consonant, accordant, consistent, invariable, formal, regulated, rational, steady, rhythmic, periodic, measured, classified, in order, unconfused, harmonious, systematic, normal, natural, cyclic, successive, momentary, alternating, probable, recurrent, general, usual, expected, serial, automatic, mechanical, alternate, hourly, daily, monthly, weekly, annual, seasonal, yearly, pulsating, rotational, diurnal, quotidian, tertian, quartan, hebdomadal, menstrual, anticipated, looked *or* hoped for, counted *or* relied on *or* upon, generally occurring, in the natural course of events, punctual, steady, uniform, regular as clockwork (D).—*Ant.* irregular*, sporadic, erratic.

regularity, *n.*—*Syn.* evenness, steadiness, uniformity, routine, constancy, consistency, invariability, rhythm, recurrence, system, congruity, homogeneity, punctuality, periodicity, swing, rotation, conformity, proportion, symmetry, balance, cadence, harmony.

regularly, *mod.* **1.** [As a matter of usual practice]—*Syn.* customarily, habitually, punctually, systematically, unchangingly, right along, as a rule, usually, commonly, as a matter of course, tirelessly, conventionally, ordinarily, repeatedly, frequently, orthodoxly, faithfully, religiously, mechanically, automatically, without once missing.

2. [With little or no deviation]—*Syn.* normally, periodically, evenly, methodically, exactly, monotonously, rhythmically, steadily, unbrokenly, typically, continually, like clockwork, cyclically, day in and day out, constantly, always, ceaselessly, time and time again, invariably, redundantly, hourly, incessantly, daily, perpetually, over and over again, weekly, monthly, annually, diurnally, exactly.—*Ant.* irregularly*, unevenly, brokenly.

regulate, *v.* **1.** [To control]—*Syn.* rule, legislate, direct; see **command** 2, **manage** 1.

2. [To adjust]—*Syn.* arrange, methodize, dispose, classify, systematize, put in order, fix, settle, adapt, standardize, co-ordinate, allocate, readjust, reconcile, rectify, correct, improve, temper, set; see also **adjust** 1, **order** 3, **organize** 1.

regulated, *mod.*—*Syn.* fixed, adjusted, arranged, directed, controlled, supervised, methodized, systematized, settled, adapted, coordinated, reconciled, improved, standardized, tempered, ruled; see also **classified, managed** 2, **organized.**—*Ant.* confused*, disarranged, upset.

regulation, *n.* **1.** [The act of regulating]—*Syn.* handling, direction, control, supervision, superintendence, governing, regimentation, classification, coordination, settlement, systematization, arrangement, reorganization, management, guidance, moderation, reconciliation, standardization, codification; see also **administration** 1.

2. [A rule]—*Syn.* law, statute, ordinance; see **command** 1, **law** 3.

regulative, *mod.*—*Syn.* supervisory, authoritative, managerial; see **administrative.**

regulator, *n.*—*Syn.* damper, adjuster, transformer, thermostat, clock, lever, governor, index, valve, knob, button, controlling instrument, pressure valve, safety device, switch; see also **machine** 1.

rehabilitate, *v.*—*Syn.* restore, change, re-establish; see **improve** 1, **renew** 1.

rehabilitation, *n.*—*Syn.* rebuilding, re-establishment, remaking; see **improvement** 1, **restoration** 1, **reconstruction, repair.**

rehash, *v.*—*Syn.* say again, discuss, reiterate; see **repeat** 1, 3.

rehearsal, *n.*—*Syn.* recitation, recital, trial *or* practice performance, experiment, test flight, reading, run-through, dress rehearsal; *all* (D): prep, trial balloon, readying, call; see also **performance** 2, **practice** 3.

rehearse, *v.* **1.** [To tell]—*Syn.* describe, recount, relate; see **narrate.**

2. [To repeat]—*Syn.* tell again, retell, do over, recapitulate, re-enact; see also **perform** 1, **repeat** 3, **talk** 1.

3. [To practice for a performance]—*Syn.* drill, test, experiment, hold rehearsals, speak from a script, go *or* run through, hold a reading, learn one's part; see also **practice** 1, **try out for.**

reheat, *v.*—*Syn.* rewarm, recook, warm; see **heat** 1.

reign, *v.*—*Syn.* hold power *or* sovereignty, sit on the throne, wear the crown, dominate, be supreme, hold sway over, prevail, administer; see also **command** 2, **govern, manage** 1.

reigning, *mod.*—*Syn.* powerful, authoritative, ruling, in power, governing, dominating, supreme, prevailing.

reimburse, *v.*—*Syn.* repay, compensate, make reparations; see **pay** 1, **refund** 1.

reimbursed, *mod.*—*Syn.* repaid, satisfied, paid off; see **paid.**

reimbursement, *n.*—*Syn.* compensation, restitution, recompense; see **payment** 1.

rein, *n.*—*Syn.* bridle strap, line, control; see **halter.**

draw rein *or* **draw in the reins**—*Syn.* slow down, cease, end; see **halt** 2.

give (free) rein to—*Syn.* authorize, permit, condone; see **allow** 1.

keep a rein on—*Syn.* control, check, have authority over; see **manage** 1.

reincarnation, *n.* —*Syn.* incarnation, reanimation, rebirth; see **metempsychosis, renewal.**

reindeer, *n.* —*Syn.* caribou, European reindeer, *Rangifer tarandus* (Latin); see **animal** 2, **deer.**

reinforce, *v.* —*Syn.* buttress, pillar, add to; see **strengthen.**

reinforced, *mod.* —*Syn.* supported, assisted, strengthened, augmented, buttressed, fortified, pillowed, banded, backed, braced, built-up, stiffened, thickened, cushioned, lined; see also **strong** 2.

reinforcement, *n.* **1.** [Support]—*Syn.* coating, concrete block, pillar; see **support** 2.
2. [Military aid; *usually plural*]—*Syn.* fresh troops, additional matériel, new ordnance; see **aid** 1.

reinstate, *v.* —*Syn.* reinstall, put back, reelect, return, reinvest, put in power again, reclassify, restore, replace, rehire, redeem.

reinstated, *mod.* —*Syn.* rehired, reinstalled, (back) on the payroll *or* in office, returned, restored, reelected, reused, reinaugurated, replaced, reinvested, reclassified.

reiterate, *v.* —*Syn.* restate, retell, rewarn; see **decrease** 2, **repeat** 3.

reiteration, *n.* —*Syn.* recapitulation, restatement, redundancy; see **repetition.**

reject, *v.* **1.** [To refuse]—*Syn.* repudiate, decline, renounce; see **deny** 1, **refuse** 1.
2. [To discard]—*Syn.* cast off *or* out, throw out, expel; see **discard.**

rejected, *mod.* —*Syn.* returned, given back, denied; see **refused.**

rejection, *n.* —*Syn.* repudiation, denial, dismissal; see **refusal.**

rejoice, *v.* —*Syn.* exult, enjoy, revel; see **celebrate** 3.

rejoicing, *n.* —*Syn.* exhilaration, triumph, festivity; see **celebration** 1, 2.

rejoin, *v.* —*Syn.* assemble, congregate, crowd; see **join** 2.

rejoinder, *n.* —*Syn.* response, retort, reply; see **answer** 1.

rejuvenate, *v.* —*Syn.* reinvigorate, exhilarate, refresh; see **strengthen.**

rejuvenation, *n.* —*Syn.* reinvigoration, stimulation, revivification; see **renewal, revival** 1.

relapse, *n.* —*Syn.* reversion, recidivism, return; see **loss** 3.

relapse, *v.* —*Syn.* lapse, retrogress, fall, backslide, become a backslider *or* a recreant, revert, regress, suffer a relapse, deteriorate, degenerate, retrovert, fall from grace, fall back *or* off, weaken, sink back, fall into again, slide *or* slip back, be overcome *or* overtaken, give in to again.

relate, *v.* **1.** [Tell]—*Syn.* recount, recite, retell; see **describe, narrate, report** 1.
2. [Connect]—*Syn.* bring into relation, associate, correlate; see **compare** 1.

related, *mod.* **1.** [Told]—*Syn.* narrated, described, recounted, explained, recorded, mentioned, stated, recited, detailed, said; see also **told.**
2. [Connected]—*Syn.* associated, in touch with, linked, tied up, knit together, allied, affiliated, complementary, analogous, correspondent, akin, alike, like, enmeshed, parallel, correlated, intertwined, interrelated, similar, mutual, dependent, interdependent, interwoven, of that ilk, in the same category, reciprocal, interchangeable.
3. [Akin]—*Syn.* kindred, of the same family, germane, fraternal, cognate, consanguine, of one blood, agnate; see also sense 2.

relate to, *v.* —*Syn.* be associated to, be connected with, have a relation to, have reference to, affect, be joined with, concern, identify with, bring to bear upon, correspond to, tie in with (D); see also **concern** 1, **refer** 1.

relation, *n.* **1.** [Relationship]—*Syn.* connection, association, similarity; see **relationship.**
2. [A relative]—*Syn.* family connection, sibling, kinsman; see **relative.**
in relation to—*Syn.* concerning, with reference to, about; see **regarding.**

relationship, *n.* —*Syn.* relation, connection, tie, association, consanguinity, affinity, likeness, link, kinship, bond, dependence, relativity, proportion, rapport, appositeness, analogy, homogeneity, interrelation, correlation, nearness, alliance, relevance, accord; *both* (D): hookup, contact; see also **similarity.**—*Ant.* difference*, dissimilarity, oppositeness.

relative, *mod.* **1.** [Pertinent]—*Syn.* dependent, contingent, applicable; see **related** 2, **relevant.**
2. [In regard to]—*Syn.* with respect to, concerning, relating to; see **about** 2, **referring.**

relative, *n.* —*Syn.* kin, family connection, relation, member of the family, blood relation, next of kin, sibling *or* sib, kinsman.
Relatives include the following—mother, father, parent, grandmother, grandfather, great-grandmother, great-grandfather, ancestor, aunt, uncle, great-aunt, great-uncle, (first) cousin, second cousin, third cousin, fourth cousin, cousin once removed, distant cousin, wife, husband, spouse, daughter, son, child, nephew, niece, brother, sister, sibling, kinsman, kinswoman, mother-in-law, father-in-law, brother-in-law, sister-in-law, aunt by marriage, cousin by marriage, in-law (D).

relatively, *mod.* —*Syn.* comparatively, proportionately, comparably, approximately, nearly; see also **almost.**

relativity, *n.* **1.** [The physical theory of the relativity and interdependence of matter, time, and space] —*Syn.* restricted relativity, special relativity, theory of general relativity, the curvilinear universe, the denial of the absolute, time as space, fourth dimension; see also **physics.**
2. [The state of being dependent]—*Syn.* dependence, pertinency, relevancy, interdependence, comparability, proportionality, interconnection, contingency, conditionality; see also **relationship.**

relax, *v.* —*Syn.* repose, recline, settle back, make oneself at home, breathe easy, take one's time, take a break, sit around *or* back, stop work, lie down, unbend, be at ease; *all* (D): cool one's heels, take a breather, ease off, take five; see also **rest** 1.

relaxation, *n.* —*Syn.* repose, reclining, loosening; see **rest** 1.

relaxed, *mod.* —*Syn.* untroubled, carefree, at ease; see **comfortable** 1.

relay, *v.* —*Syn.* communicate, transfer, send forth, transmit, hand over *or* on *or* down, turn over, deliver, communicate, pass on; see also **carry** 1, **send** 1.

release, *n.* **1.** [Freedom]—*Syn.* liberation, discharge, freeing; see **ease** 2, **freedom** 1, 2.

2. [That which has been released; *usually, printed matter*]—*Syn.* news story, publicity, news flash, public notice, new song, latest publication, recent stock, propaganda.

release, *v.* —*Syn.* liberate, deliver, discharge, let go, acquit, loose, exempt, open up, give out for circulation, set free, let *or* pay *or* get *or* bail out, hand over, let off, rescue, let loose, clear, untie, loosen, emancipate; see also **free** 1.

released, *mod.* **1.** [Freed]—*Syn.* discharged, dismissed, liberated; see **free** 1, 2.

2. [Announced]—*Syn.* broadcast, stated, made public; see **published.**

relegate, *v.* **1.** [To assign]—*Syn.* commit, entrust, confide; see **assign** 1.

2. [To remove]—*Syn.* banish, eliminate, expel; see **dismiss** 1, 2.

relent, *v.* —*Syn.* soften, comply, relax; see **yield** 1.

relentless, *mod.* —*Syn.* unmerciful, vindictive, hard; see **pitiless** 1, **ruthless** 1.

relevance, *n.* —*Syn.* connection, significance, pertinence; see **importance** 1.

relevant, *mod.* —*Syn.* suitable, appropriate, fit, proper, pertinent (to), becoming, pertaining to, apt, applicable, important, fitting, congruous, apposite, germane, cognate, related, conforming, concerning, suitable, conformant, compatible, accordant, referring, harmonious, correspondent, consonant, congruent, consistent, correlated, associated, allied, relative, affinitive, connected, to the point, bearing on the question, having direct bearing, having to do with, related to; *all* (D): pat, on the nose, on the beezer.—*Ant.* opposed*, discrepant, antagonistic.

reliability, *n.* —*Syn.* dependability, trustworthiness, constancy, loyalty, faithfulness, sincerity, devotion, honesty, authenticity, steadfastness, fidelity, safety, security.

reliable, *mod.* **1.** [Having a sound character] —*Syn.* firm, unimpeachable, sterling, strong, positive, stable, dependable, solid, staunch, decisive, unequivocal, steadfast, definite, conscientious, constant, steady, trustworthy, faithful, loyal, good, true, sure, devoted, tried, trusty, honest, honorable, veracious, candid, true-hearted, high-principled, responsible, sincere, altruistic, determined, reputable, careful, proved, respectable, righteous, decent, incorrupt, truthful, upright; *all* (D): regular, all right, kosher, sure, O.K., on the up and up, square-shooting, true blue, tried and true, straight-shooting.—*Ant.* false*, insincere, unfaithful.

2. [Worthy of trust]—*Syn.* safe, honest, sound, stable, solid, steady, guaranteed, sure, certain, substantial, secure, unquestionable, conclusive, irrefutable, incontestable, dependable, good, firm, strong, solvent, unfailing, infallible, authentic, competent, assured, workable; *both* (D): foolproof, sure-fire.—*Ant.* dangerous*, insecure, undependable.

reliably, *mod.* —*Syn.* assuredly, presumably, certainly; see **probably, surely.**

reliance, *n.* —*Syn.* confidence, trust, hope; see **faith** 1.

relic, *n.* **1.** [Something left from an earlier time] —*Syn.* vestige, trace, survival, heirloom, antique, keepsake, memento, curio, curiosity, token, souvenir, testimonial, evidence, monument, trophy, remain(s), artifact, remembrance, bric-a-brac; see also **souvenir.**

2. [A ruin]—*Syn.* remnant, residue, remains, shard, potsherd, broken stone; see also **ruin** 2.

relief, *n.* **1.** [The act of bringing succor]—*Syn.* mitigation, easement, alleviation, assuagement, softening, comforting, remission, deliverance, extrication, amelioration.

2. [Aid]—*Syn.* assistance, support, maintenance; see **aid** 1.

3. [A relieved state of mind]—*Syn.* satisfaction, relaxation, ease, comfort, release, happiness, contentment, cheer, restfulness, a load off one's mind (D); see also **comfort** 1.

4. [The person or thing that brings relief]—*Syn.* diversion, relaxation, consolation, solace, reinforcement, supplies, food, shelter, clothing, release, respite, remedy, nursing, medicine, medical care, redress, reparations, indemnities, variety, change, palliative, hypodermic, cure; see also **aid** 1.

5. [The raised portions of a sculptural decoration or map]—*Syn.* embossment, projection, *rilievo* (Italian), high relief, half relief, bas-relief, low relief, hollow relief, intaglio, frieze, contour, configuration; see also **decoration** 1.

relieve, *v.* **1.** [To replace]—*Syn.* discharge, throw out, force to resign; see **dismiss** 1, 2.

2. [To lessen; *said especially of pain*]—*Syn.* assuage, alleviate, soothe, comfort, allay, divert, free, ease, lighten, soften, diminish, mitigate, console, cure, aid, assist; see also **decrease** 2, **help** 1.

relieved, *mod.* **1.** [Eased in mind]—*Syn.* comforted, solaced, consoled, reassured, satisfied, allayed, soothed, relaxed, put at ease, restored, reconciled, appeased, placated, alleviated, mollified, disarmed, pacified, adjusted, propitiated, breathing easy (D); see also **comfortable** 1.—*Ant.* sad*, worried, distraught.

2. [Deprived of something, or freed from it] —*Syn.* replaced, dismissed, separated (from), disengaged, released, made free of, rescued, delivered, supplanted, superseded, succeeded, substituted, interchanged, exchanged; see also **discharged** 1.

3. [Lessened; *said especially of pain*]—*Syn.* mitigated, palliated, softened, assuaged, eased, abated, diminished, allayed, salved, soothed, lightened, alleviated, drugged, anesthetized.

relight, *v.* —*Syn.* light again, reillumine, refire; see **burn** 2.

religion, *n.* **1.** [All the centers about man's belief in or relationship to a superior being or beings] —*Syn.* belief, devotion, piety, spirituality, persuasion, godliness, sense of righteousness, morality, religiosity, theology, faithfulness, devoutness, creed, myth, superstition, doctrine, cult, denomination, mythology, communion, religious conscience, fidelity, conscientiousness, spiritual-mindedness, religious bent, ethical standard; see also **faith** 2.

2. [Organized worship or service of a deity] —*Syn.* veneration, adoration, consecration, sanctification, prayer, ritual, rites, ceremonials, holy sacrifice, incantation, holiday, observance, pietism, orthodoxy, reformism; see also **ceremony** 2.
Religions include the following—Christianity, (Zen) Buddhism, Hinduism, Islam, Jainism, Judaism, Theosophy, Zoroastrianism, Shintoism, Taoism, Bahai, deism, theism, polytheism, dualism; see also **church** 3.
get religion (D)—*Syn.* become converted, believe, change; see **reform** 2, 3.

religious, *mod.* **1.** [Pertaining to religion]—*Syn.* ethical, spiritual, moral, ecclesiastical, clerical, theological, canonical, divine, supernatural, holy, sacred, sacrosanct, churchly, theistic, deistic, sacerdotal, priestly, pontifical, ministerial.—*Ant.* secular, worldly*, earthly.
2. [Devout]—*Syn.* pious, puritanical, sanctimonious, pietistic, godly, god-fearing, orthodox, reverend, reverential, believing, faithful, Christian, fanatic, evangelistic, revivalistic, church-going; see also **holy** 1.—*Ant.* atheistic*, agnostic, nonbelieving.
3. [Scrupulous]—*Syn.* methodical, minute, thorough; see **careful.**

relinquish, *v.* —*Syn.* quit, surrender, give up; see **abandon** 1.

relish, *n.* **1.** [A condiment]—*Syn.* seasoning, herb, savor; see **flavoring, pickle** 2, **spice.**
Relishes include the following—catsup *or* ketchup, piccalilli, Indian *or* corn *or* beet *or* horseradish *or* cucumber *or* pepper *or* pickle *or* tomato *or* green bean *or* orange *or* mango *or* pear relish, chow-chow, spiced currants *or* gooseberries *or* grapes, ginger tomatoes, (pear) mincemeat, pepper hash, pickled pears *or* peaches *or* apricots *or* pineapple *or* watermelon rind, chili *or* chutney *or* bardo *or* hot *or* cranberry sauce.
2. [Obvious delight]—*Syn.* gusto, joy, great satisfaction; see **zest** 1.

relish, *v.* —*Syn.* enjoy, fancy, be fond of; see **like** 1.

reluctance, *n.* —*Syn.* disinclination, qualm, hesitation; see **doubt** 2.

reluctant, *mod.* —*Syn.* disinclined, loath, unwilling, averse, opposed, tardy, backward, adverse, laggard, remiss, slack, squeamish, demurring, grudging, involuntary, uncertain, hanging back, hesitant, hesitating, diffident, with bad grace, indisposed, disheartened, discouraged, queasy.—*Ant.* willing*, eager, disposed.

reluctantly, *mod.* —*Syn.* under protest, unwillingly, squeamishly, involuntarily, slowly, with a heavy heart (D).

rely on *or* **upon,** *v.* —*Syn.* hope, have faith in, count on; see **depend on, trust** 1, 3.

remade, *mod.* —*Syn.* rebuilt, redone, made over; see **improved** 1, **revised.**

remain, *v.* **1.** [To stay]—*Syn.* abide, dwell, reside, inhabit, sojourn, make camp, stop, live, tarry, pause, stay over, rest (with), linger, sit through, stick around, sit out, stay in, hold over, spend one's days; see also **settle** 7.—*Ant.* leave*, be off, depart.
2. [To endure]—*Syn.* keep on, go on, prevail; see **continue** 1, **endure** 1.
3. [To be left]—*Syn.* remain standing, outlive, outlast; see **survive** 1.

remainder, *n.* —*Syn.* remaining portion, leftover, residue, remains, relic, remnant, dregs, surplus, leavings, balance, residuum, excess, overplus, scrap, fragment, small piece, carry-over, obverse, rest, residual portion, whatever is left, salvage, remaindered portion, cross remainder, contingent remainder, vested remainder.

remaindered, *mod.* —*Syn.* sold out, discontinued, dropped; see **sold** 1.

remaining, *mod.* —*Syn.* tarrying, waiting, stopping, halting, resting, sojourning, pausing, passing the night.

remains, *n.* —*Syn.* corpse, cadaver, relics; see **body** 2.

remake, *v.* —*Syn.* transform, revise, alter; see **change** 1.

remark, *n.* —*Syn.* statement, saying, utterance, annotation, note, mention, reflection, illustration, point, *bon mot* (French), conclusion, consideration, talk, observation, expression, comment, assertion, witticism.

remark, *v.* —*Syn.* speak, mention, observe; see **say, talk** 1.

remarkable, *mod.* —*Syn.* exceptional, extraordinary, uncommon; see **unusual** 1.

remarkably, *mod.* —*Syn.* exceptionally, singularly, notably; see **especially, very.**

remedial, *mod.* —*Syn.* healing, therapeutic, corrective, invigorating, medicinal, recuperative, tonic, health-giving, antidotal, restorative, purifying, reformative, restitutive, soothing, alleviative, antiseptic; see also **healthful.**

remedy, *n.* **1.** [A medicine]—*Syn.* antidote, pill, drug; see **medicine** 2, **treatment** 2.
2. [Effective help]—*Syn.* relief, cure, corrective, redress, support, improvement, solution, plan, panacea, cure-all, assistance, counteraction; see also **relief** 4.

remedy, *v.* —*Syn.* cure, solve, help, aid, assist, correct, right, renew, rectify, set right, relieve, treat, attend, change, revise, amend, palliate, mitigate; see also **heal** 1.

remember, *v.* **1.** [To recall]—*Syn.* recollect, recognize, summon up, relive, dig into the past, refresh one's memory, be reminded of, think of, revive, bring *or* call to mind, cast *or* think *or* look *or* go back, brood over, conjure up, call in *or* back *or* up, carry one's thoughts back, look back upon, have memories of, commemorate, memorialize, reminisce, carry in one's thoughts, keep a memory alive, enshrine in the memory; *both* (D): spot, date back. —*Ant.* lose*, forget, neglect.
2. [To bear in mind]—*Syn.* keep in mind, memorize, know by heart, learn, master, get, be impressed on one's mind, fix in the mind, retain, treasure, hold dear, dwell upon, brood over, keep forever.—*Ant.* neglect*, ignore, disregard.

remembered, *mod.* —*Syn.* thought of, recalled, recollected, rewarded, summoned up, brought to *or* borne in mind, memorialized, haunting one's thoughts, commemorated, dug up (D).—*Ant.* forgotten, lost*, overlooked.

remembering, *mod.* —*Syn.* recalling, recollecting, bringing back, summoning up, thinking of, recognizing, memorializing, commemorating, celebrating.

remembrance, *n.* **1.** [Memory]—*Syn.* recall, recollection, afterthought, hindsight, retrospection, recognition, reconstruction, mental image; see also **memory** 1.
2. [A gift]—*Syn.* reward, token, keepsake; see **gift** 1.

remind, *v.* **1.** [To bring into the memory]—*Syn.* bring back, make one think of, intimate; see **hint** 1.
2. [To call the attention of another]—*Syn.* caution, point out, jog *or* refresh the memory, remind one of, mention to, call attention to, bring up, prompt, prod, stress, emphasize, note, stir up; *both* (D): put a flea in one's ear, give a cue; see also **warn** 1.

reminded, *mod.* —*Syn.* warned, cautioned, prompted, put in mind (of), made aware, advised, forewarned, notified, awakened, prodded.

reminder, *n.* —*Syn.* warning, notice, admonition, note, memorandum, memo, hint, suggestion, memento, token, keepsake, trinket, remembrance, souvenir.

reminisce, *v.* —*Syn.* recall, recollect, call up; see **remember** 1.

reminiscence, *n.* —*Syn.* account, version, memory, memoirs, chronicle, recollection, firsthand account, primary source, eyewitness account, old-timer's version, anecdotage, personal history, local history; see also **story.**

reminiscent, *mod.* —*Syn.* implicative, recollective, nostalgic; see **suggestive.**

remiss, *mod.* —*Syn.* uninterested, negligent, neglectful; see **careless** 1, **indifferent** 1.

remission, *n.* **1.** [An alleviation]—*Syn.* abatement, lessening, release; see **relief** 1.
2. [An interruption]—*Syn.* pause, lull, break; see **delay** 1.
3. [An acquittal]—*Syn.* mercy, discharge, forgiveness; see **acquittal, pardon** 1.

remit, *v.* **1.** [To send]—*Syn.* make payment, forward, dispatch; see **pay** 1.
2. [To pardon]—*Syn.* absolve, exonerate, release; see **forgive** 1, **pardon** 1.

remittance, *n.* —*Syn.* transmittal, money sent, enclosure; see **payment** 1.

remitted, *mod.* —*Syn.* made less, commuted, not (strictly) enforced; see **reduced** 1, 2.

remnant, *n.* **1.** [A remaining part]—*Syn.* residue, leavings, dregs; see **excess** 1, **remainder.**
2. [The last of a bolt of goods]—*Syn.* strip, piece, part, portion, surplus, shred, endpiece, scrap, odds and ends.

remnants, *n.* —*Syn.* scraps, odds and ends, leftovers, particles, surplus, endpieces, remains, leavings; see also **excess** 1, **remainder.**

remodel, *v.* —*Syn.* renovate, refurnish, refurbish, readjust, reconstruct, readapt, rearrange, redecorate, refashion, improve, reshape, recast, rebuild, repair, modernize, repaint; see also **change** 1.

remodeled, *mod.* —*Syn.* refurnished, redecorated, rebuilt, repaired, modernized, altered, improved, reconstructed, readjusted, renovated, rearranged, made over; see also **changed** 3.

remodeling, *n.* —*Syn.* rearrangement, readjustment, reconstruction, reshaping, recasting, refurnishing, refurbishing, restoration, modernization, renovation, regeneration, redecoration; see also **improvement** 2.

remonstrance, *n.* —*Syn.* rebuke, reproach, complaint; see **objection** 2.

remonstrate, *v.* —*Syn.* protest, expostulate, demur, criticize, find fault, pick flaws, animadvert, censure, scold, nag, deprecate, recriminate, decry, frown upon, disparage, blame, disapprove; see also **complain** 1.—*Ant.* approve*, favor, support.

remorse, *n.* —*Syn.* compunction, contrition, self-reproach; see **grief** 1, **regret** 1.
without remorse—*Syn.* cruel, pitiless, relentless; see **remorseless** 1, 2.

remorseful, *mod.* —*Syn.* contrite, penitent, repentant; see **sorry** 1.

remorseless, *mod.* **1.** [Lacking remorse as a quality of character]—*Syn.* shameless, hardened, obdurate, barbarous, inhuman, pitiless, indurate, tyrannical, merciless, hard-hearted, cruel, impenitent, unregenerate, uncontrite, unrepenting, ruthless, fierce, savage, unchristian, hard, intolerant, insensitive, greedy, avaricious, bloody, murderous.—*Ant.* sorry*, remorseful, apologetic.
2. [Relentless]—*Syn.* implacable, inexorable, sanguinary, unyielding, unforgiving, vindictive, avenging, stern, harsh, exacting, bitter, hard-bitten, sour, grim, adamant, inflexible, perverse, intractable, strict, rigorous, tough, unrelenting, crazed, forbidding, maddening; see also **severe** 1, 2. —*Ant.* kind*, forgiving, indulgent.

remote, *mod.* **1.** [Distant]—*Syn.* far-off, faraway, out-of-the-way, removed, beyond, secluded, inaccessible, isolated, unknown, alien, foreign, undiscovered; *all* (D): off the beaten track, over the hills and far away, in a backwater, godforsaken; see also **distant** 1.—*Ant.* near*, close, accessible.
2. [Ancient]—*Syn.* forgotten, past, hoary, aged, antiquated, timeworn, archaic, prehistoric, primitive, antediluvian, immemorial, antique, olden, unrecorded, primeval; see also **ancient, old** 3.
3. [Separated]—*Syn.* unrelated, irrelevant, unconnected, obscure, abstracted, indirect, inappropriate, farfetched, exclusive, alone, extraneous, apart, detached; see also **separated.**—*Ant.* relevant*, pointed, related.

remote control, *n.* —*Syn.* electrical control, radio-circuit control, control from a distance, mechanization, electric eye.

removable, *mod.* —*Syn.* demountable, detachable, loose; see **movable.**

removal, *n.* **1.** [The state of being removed]—*Syn.* dismissal, discharge, expulsion, exile, deportation, banishment, elimination, extraction, dislodgment, evacuation, ejection, transference, eradication, extermination, extirpation, replacement, translocation, the can *or* chuck *or* gate *or* bounce (D). —*Ant.* entrance*, induction, introduction.
2. [The act of moving]—*Syn.* change of residence, reallocation, change of address; see **departure** 1.

remove, *v.* **1.** [To move physically]—*Syn.* take away from, cart *or* clear *or* carry *or* take *or* tear *or* brush away, transfer, skim, transport, dislodge, uproot, excavate, displace, unload, discharge, lift up, doff, raise, evacuate, shift, switch, lift, push, draw away *or* in, withdraw, separate, extract, cut *or* dig *or* dip *or* tear *or* pull *or* take *or* burn *or* smoke *or* rip out, take down, tear *or* draw *or* take *or* skip *or* carry *or* cart *or* clear *or* strike *or* cut *or* rub *or* scrape off, take *or* pull in.

2. [To eliminate]—*Syn.* get rid of, do away with, exclude; see **eliminate** 1.

3. [To kill]—*Syn.* assassinate, murder, liquidate; see **kill** 1.

4. [To dismiss]—*Syn.* discharge, displace, discard; see **dismiss** 1, 2.

removed, *mod.* **1.** [Taken out]—*Syn.* extracted, eliminated, withdrawn, evacuated, dislodged, ejected, pulled out, amputated, excised, expunged, extirpated.—*Ant.* left, ignored*, established.

2. [Distant]—*Syn.* faraway, out-of-the-way, far-off; see **away** 1, **beyond, distant** 1.

3. [Dismissed]—*Syn.* banished, relieved of office, retired; see **discharged** 1, **recalled** 2.

remove from, *v.*—*Syn.* extract, separate, withdraw; see **remove** 1.

remunerate, *v.*—*Syn.* compensate, recompense, reward; see **pay** 1.

remuneration, *n.*—*Syn.* reward, commission, compensation; see **pay** 2, **profit** 2.

remunerative, *mod.*—*Syn.* useful, lucrative, gainful; see **profitable.**

renaissance, *n.*—*Syn.* rebirth, reconstruction, renascence; see **resurrection.**

rend, *v.*—*Syn.* rip, sever, sunder; see **break** 1.

render, *v.* **1.** [To give]—*Syn.* present, hand over, distribute; see **give** 1.

2. [To perform, especially a service]—*Syn.* do, act, execute; see **perform** 1.

3. [To interpret; *said especially of music*]—*Syn.* play, perform, depict; see **interpret** 1.

4. [To provide]—*Syn.* furnish, contribute, minister; see **provide** 1.

5. [To state formally]—*Syn.* pass, state, deliver; see **declare** 1.

6. [To translate]—*Syn.* transliterate, paraphrase, transpose; see **translate** 1.

rendered, *mod.* **1.** [Performed]—*Syn.* carried out, concluded, effected; see **done** 2.

2. [Interpreted]—*Syn.* played, executed, performed, enacted, delivered, translated, depicted, demonstrated, delineated, represented, presented.

rendezvous, *n.*—*Syn.* assignation, tryst, gathering place; see **meeting** 1.

rendezvous, *v.*—*Syn.* meet secretly *or* privately, be closeted with (someone), meet behind closed doors; see **meet** 2.

rendition, *n.*—*Syn.* interpretation, version, reading; see **translation.**

renegade, *mod.*—*Syn.* unfaithful, revolutionary, reactionary; see **radical** 2.

renegade, *n.* **1.** [A rebel]—*Syn.* recreant, apostate, heretic; see **rebel** 1, **traitor.**

2. [A fugitive]—*Syn.* escapee, exile, runaway; see **refugee.**

renew, *v.* **1.** [To refresh]—*Syn.* revive, reawaken, regenerate, re-establish, rehabilitate, gentrify, reinvigorate, replace, revive, rebuild, reconstitute, remake, refinish, refurbish, redo, repeat, invigorate, exhilarate, restore, resuscitate, reconceive, recondition, overhaul, recodify, replenish, go over, cool, brace, freshen, stimulate, recreate, remodel, revamp, redesign, modernize, rejuvenate, give new life to, recover, renovate, reintegrate, make a new beginning, bring up *or* down to date; *all* (D): do over, make like new, rehab, give a recondition job, bring up to code; see also **revive** 1.

2. [To repeat]—*Syn.* resume, reiterate, recommence; see **repeat** 1.

3. [To replace]—*Syn.* resume, supplant, substitute; see **replace** 1.

renewal, *n.*—*Syn.* recurrence, resurrection, recommencement, new start, redoubling, renovation, rehabilitation, gentrification, resumption, reissue, revival, comeback, reopening, reconditioning, recharging, regeneration, restoration, re-establishment, reversion, rejuvenation, reformation, rearrangement, replacing, rebirth, revision; see also **revival** 1.—*Ant.* destruction*, exhaustion, impoverishment.

renewed, *mod.*—*Syn.* revived, readapted, refitted; see **repaired.**

renounce, *v.* **1.** [To abandon]—*Syn.* relinquish, forsake, quit; see **abandon** 1.

2. [To repudiate]—*Syn.* disown, disavow, give up; see **deny, discard.**

renovate, *v.*—*Syn.* make over, remake, rehabilitate; see **renew** 1, **restore** 3.

renovated, *mod.*—*Syn.* renewed, remodeled, redone; see **clean** 1, **changed** 3, **repaired.**

renovation, *n.*—*Syn.* reform, revision, change; see **improvement** 1, **renewal, restoration** 1.

renown, *n.*—*Syn.* distinction, prestige, eminence; see **fame** 1.

renowned, *mod.*—*Syn.* notable, celebrated, distinguished; see **famous.**

rent, *v.* **1.** [To sell the use of property]—*Syn.* lease, lend, let, make available, allow the use of, take in roomers, sublet, put on loan.

2. [To obtain use by payment]—*Syn.* hire, pay rent for, charter, contract, sign a contract for, engage, borrow, pay for services; see also **pay** 1.

rental, *n.*—*Syn.* rent, renting price, rentage, amount paid for rent.

rented, *mod.*—*Syn.* leased, lent, hired, contracted, engaged, let, chartered, taken, on lease, allocated to a lessee, out of the market, with a tenant; *both* (D): sewed up, out.

renter, *n.*—*Syn.* lease holder, roomer, tenant, lessee, rentee, occupant.

renunciation, *n.* **1.** [Denial]—*Syn.* rejection, remission, disclaimer; see **denial** 1.

2. [Refusal]—*Syn.* repeal, veto, rebuff; see **cancellation, refusal.**

reopen, *v.*—*Syn.* revive, re-establish, begin again; see **open** 2, **renew** 1.

reorganization, *n.*—*Syn.* re-establishment, reconstitution, reorientation; see **change** 2, **improvement** 1.

reorganize, *v.*—*Syn.* rebuild, renovate, regenerate; see **organize** 2, **reconstruct.**

repaid, *mod.*—*Syn.* remunerated, reimbursed, compensated, recompensed, requited, refunded, indemnified, paid back, restored, returned; see also **paid.**

repair, *n.*—*Syn.* reconstruction, substitution, reformation, rehabilitation, new part, patch, restoration, restored portion, replacement, brazure, soldering; see also **improvement** 2, **repairing.**—*Ant.* break*, tear, fracture.

repair, *v.*—*Syn.* fix, adjust, emend, improve, correct, settle, put into shape, reform, patch, rejuvenate, refurbish, retread, touch up, put in order, revive, refresh, renew, mend, darn, sew, revamp, rectify, right, ameliorate, calk, cobble, renovate, reshape, rebuild; *all* (D): work over, fix up, dirty one's hands with; see also **reconstruct, restore** 3.—*Ant.* wreck*, damage, smash.

repaired, *mod.*—*Syn.* fixed, adjusted, rearranged, adapted, settled, remodeled, rectified, mended, corrected, righted, restored, renewed, remedied, improved, renovated, retouched, in (working) order, cobbled, patched up, calked, put together, put back into shape, sewn, reset, stitched up. —*Ant.* damaged*, worn, torn.

repairing, *n.*—*Syn.* mending, fixing, sewing, patching, adjusting, calking, remodeling, cobbling, retouching, renovating, remedying, restoring; see also **improvement** 2.

reparable, *mod.*—*Syn.* redeemable, corrigible, improvable, restorable, curable, rectifiable, remediable, recoverable, emendable.

reparation, *n.* **1.** [The act of atoning]—*Syn.* atonement, expiation, apology, penance, propitiation, satisfaction, self-condemnation, self-commitment.

2. [Whatever is given in reparation, sense 1] —*Syn.* indemnity, retribution, amends, requital, atonement, satisfaction, repayment, restitution, payment, compensation, redress, indemnification, emolument, remuneration, recompense, reward, settlement, adjustment.

repartee, *n.*—*Syn.* reply, retort, quip; see **answer** 1.

repay, *v.* **1.** [To pay back]—*Syn.* reimburse, recompense, refund, return, indemnify, give back, make amends, requite, compensate; *both* (D): square oneself, settle up; see also **pay** 1.

2. [To retaliate]—*Syn.* get even with, square accounts, reciprocate; see **revenge.**

repayment, *n.*—*Syn.* compensation, indemnity, restitution; see **payment** 1, **preparation** 2.

repeal, *n.*—*Syn.* abrogation, annulment, cancellation, revocation, abolition; see also **withdrawal.**

repeal, *v.*—*Syn.* annul, abolish, abrogate; see **cancel** 2.

repeat, *v.* **1.** [To do again]—*Syn.* redo, remake, do *or* play over, recur, rehash, reciprocate, return, rework, reform, refashion, recast, (re)duplicate, renew, reconstruct, reerect, revert, hold over, go over again and again.

2. [To happen again]—*Syn.* reoccur, recur, revolve, reappear, occur again, come again, return; see also **happen** 2.

3. [To say again]—*Syn.* (re)iterate, restate, reissue, republish, reutter, echo, recite, re-echo, rehearse, retell, go over, play *or* read back, recapitulate, name over; *all* (D): drum into, rehash, come again, sing the same old song; see also **say.**

repeated, *mod.* **1.** [Done again]—*Syn.* redone, remade, copied, imitated, reworked, refashioned, recast, done over, reciprocated, returned, reverted, (re)duplicated.

2. [Said again]—*Syn.* reiterated, restated, reannounced, reuttered, recited, reproduced, seconded, paraphrased, reworded, retold.

repeatedly, *mod.*—*Syn.* again and again, many times, time and again; see **frequently, regularly.**

repeating, *mod.*—*Syn.* recurrent, repetitious, reiterative, imitating, copying, echoing, re-echoing, (re)duplicating, reproducing; see also **perpetual** 2, **verbose.**

repel, *v.* **1.** [To throw back]—*Syn.* rebuff, resist, stand up against, oppose, check, repulse, put to flight, keep at bay, knock down, drive *or* chase away, drive *or* beat *or* hold *or* force *or* push back, beat *or* ward *or* chase *or* stave *or* fight off.—*Ant.* fall*, fail, retreat.

2. [To cause aversion]—*Syn.* nauseate, offend, revolt; see **disgust.**

3. [To reject]—*Syn.* disown, dismiss, cast aside; see **refuse.**

repellent, *mod.*—*Syn.* repulsive, foul, smelly; see **offensive** 2.

repelling, *n.*—*Syn.* repulsing, scattering, dispersing; see **refusal.**

repent, *v.*—*Syn.* be sorry, have qualms, be penitent; see **apologize, regret.**

repercussion, *n.*—*Syn.* consequence, result, effect; see **result.**

repentance, *n.*—*Syn.* sorrow, remorse, regret, penitence, contriteness, attrition, contrition, compunction, self-denunciation, self-abasement, self-reproach, self-condemnation, self-humiliation, prick *or* sting of conscience.—*Ant.* happiness*, content, impenitence.

repentant, *mod.*—*Syn.* penitent, regretful, contrite; see **sorry** 1.

repertory, *n.*—*Syn.* stockroom, depot, cache; see **storehouse.**

repetition, *n.*—*Syn.* recurrence, reoccurrence, reappearance, reproduction, copy, rote, duplication, renewal, recapitulation, reiteration, return; see also **wordiness.**

repetitious, *mod.*—*Syn.* boring, wordy, repeating; see **dull** 4, **verbose.**

repetitive, *mod.*—*Syn.* repetitious, repeated, redundant; see **dull** 4, **verbose.**

replace, *v.* **1.** [To supply an equivalent]—*Syn.* reestablish, reconstitute, refund, reimburse, repay, redress, compensate, mend, patch, redeem; see also **rearrange, reconstruct, renew** 1, **repair** 1. —*Ant.* lose*, damage, injure.

2. [To take the place of]—*Syn.* take over, supplant, displace; see **substitute** 2.

3. [To put back in the same place]—*Syn.* restore, reinstate, put back; see **return** 2.

replaced, *mod.* **1.** [Returned to the same place] —*Syn.* restored, reinstated, reintegrated, recovered, recouped, reacquired, regained, repossessed, resumed, rewon, retrieved.

2. [Having another in one's place; *said of persons*] —*Syn.* dismissed, cashiered, dislodged; see **recalled** 2.

3. [Having another in its place; *said of things*] —*Syn.* renewed, interchanged, replenished; see **changed** 1.

replacing, *n.*—*Syn.* substitution, restoration, rearrangement, rehabilitation, reconstitution, renewal, reinstatement.

replenish, *v.*—*Syn.* supply, refresh, provision; see **renew** 1.

replete (with), *mod.* **1.** [Full]—*Syn.* filled, stuffed, packed; see **full** 1.
2. [Abundant]—*Syn.* complete, lavish, plenteous; see **full** 3, **luxurious.**

replica, *n.* —*Syn.* copy, likeness, model; see **duplicate** 1, **imitation** 2.

reply, *n.* —*Syn.* response, return, retort; see **answer** 1.

reply, *v.* —*Syn.* retort, rejoin, return; see **answer** 1.

replying, *mod.* —*Syn.* answering, acknowledging, in response to, responding, in rejoinder *or* answer *or* return, reacting.

report, *n.* **1.** [A transmitted account]—*Syn.* tale, narration, narrative, description, announcement, wire, cable, telegram, recital, acquisition of signal, broadcast; see also **news** 1, 2, **story.**
2. [An official summary]—*Syn.* pronouncement, proclamation, address, résumé, précis, outline, brief, digest, opinion, release, write-up (D); see also **record** 1, **summary.**
Reports include the following—bank statement, dispatch, communiqué, court decision, inventory, treasurer's report.
3. [A loud, explosive sound]—*Syn.* detonation, bang, blast; see **noise** 1.

report, *v.* **1.** [To deliver information]—*Syn.* describe, recount, narrate, provide (the) details (of *or* for), give an account (of), set forth, inform, advise, communicate, retail, wire, cable, telephone, radio, broadcast, notify, relate, state; see also **tell** 1.
2. [To make a summary statement]—*Syn.* summarize, publish, proclaim, announce, enunciate, promulgate, make known, list, itemize, account for, give the facts, write up, present a paper, read an address.
3. [To present oneself]—*Syn.* be at hand, arrive, come, get to, reach; *both* (D): show up, turn up.
4. [To record]—*Syn.* take minutes, inscribe, note down; see **record** 1.

reported, *mod.* —*Syn.* stated, recited, recounted, narrated, described, set forth, announced, broadcast, rumored, noted, expressed, proclaimed, made known, according to rumor, revealed, communicated, disclosed, imparted, divulged, recorded; *both* (D): in the air, all over town.—*Ant.* unknown*, verified, certain.

reporter, *n.* —*Syn.* newspaperman, news writer, columnist, journalist, newsman, newsperson, newscaster, anchorperson, anchorman, anchorwoman, correspondent, interviewer, cub reporter, star reporter, newsgatherer; *all* (D): legman, newshound, goat, newshawk; see also **writer.**

reporting, *mod.* —*Syn.* filing a report, sending *or* mailing *or* broadcasting *or* wiring a story, broadcasting; see **saying.**

reporting, *n.* —*Syn.* newsgathering, recounting, describing, writing up, recording, noting down, narrating, publicizing, making public, summarizing; *both* (D): newscasting, covering a beat; see also **broadcasting, writing** 1.

repose, *n.* —*Syn.* relaxation, inaction, relaxing; see **rest** 1.

repose, *v.* **1.** [To recline]—*Syn.* slant, lie, tilt; see **lean** 1.
2. [To rest]—*Syn.* loll, loaf, lounge; see **relax, rest** 1, **sleep.**

repository, *n.* —*Syn.* argosy, locker, treasury; see **closet, storehouse.**

reprehend, *v.* —*Syn.* rebuke, reprove, reprimand; see **censure, scold.**

reprehensible, *mod.* —*Syn.* objectionable, culpable, blamable; see **guilty** 2, **wicked** 1, 2.

represent, *v.* **1.** [To act as a delegate]—*Syn.* be an agent for, serve, speak *or* act for, hold office, be deputy for, be attorney for, act *or* stand in place of, factor, steward, act as broker, be sent to a convention, sell for, buy for, be proxy for, do business for, be spokesman for, be ambassador for, exercise power of attorney for.
2. [To present as a true interpretation]—*Syn.* render, depict, enact, realize, delineate, describe, draw, outline, portray, design, mirror, picture, body forth, interpret.—*Ant.* misinterpret, distort*, falsify.
3. [To serve as an equivalent]—*Syn.* copy, imitate, reproduce, symbolize, exemplify, typify, signify, substitute, stand for, impersonate, personify.

representation, *n.* —*Syn.* description, narration, delineation, reproduction, copy, design, imitation, exhibition, enactment, personification, impersonation, setting forth, delegation, adumbration, depiction, portrayal, illustration, pictorialization.

representative, *n.* **1.** [An emissary]—*Syn.* deputy, salesman, messenger; see **agent** 1, **delegate.**
2. [One who is elected to the lower legislative body]—*Syn.* congressman, congresswoman, assemblyman, councilman, councilwoman, councilperson, member of congress *or* parliament, deputy, legislator, senator, councilor; see also **diplomat** 1.
Diplomatic and consular representatives include the following—envoy, ambassador, consul, plenipotentiary, nuncio, attaché, diplomatic agent, resident commissioner.

represented, *mod.* **1.** [Depicted]—*Syn.* portrayed, interpreted, delineated, drawn, pictured, illustrated, defined, revealed, sketched, personified, symbolized, mirrored, characterized, brought out, described.
2. [Presented]—*Syn.* rendered, exhibited, enacted; see **displayed, shown** 1.

representing, *mod.* **1.** [Purporting to depict]—*Syn.* depicting, portraying, delineating, picturing, presenting, illustrating, showing, exhibiting, bringing out, characterizing, reproducing, describing, defining, mirroring, interpreting, symbolizing, reporting, revealing, personifying, limning.—*Ant.* misrepresentation*, distorting, misrepresenting.
2. [Acting as an agent]—*Syn.* serving, substituting for, being deputy for, acting by authority of, attorney for, factoring for, stewarding for, selling for, buying for, acting as broker for.

repress, *v.* —*Syn.* control, curb, check; see **hinder, restrain** 1.

repression, *n.* —*Syn.* constraint, control, suppression; see **restraint** 1.

repressive, *mod.* —*Syn.* oppressive, restrictive, unprecedented; see **difficult** 1, **extreme** 2.

reprieve, *n.* —*Syn.* release, absolution, clearance; see **acquittal, freeing, pardon** 3.

reprieve, *v.* **1.** [To pardon]—*Syn.* postpone, absolve, forgive; see **excuse** 1.

2. [To alleviate]—*Syn.* comfort, lessen, soothe; see **relieve** 2.

reprimand, *v.* —*Syn.* reproach, denounce, criticize; see **censure.**

reprint, *n.* —*Syn.* republication, facsimile, second edition; see **copy, edition.**

reprint, *v.* —*Syn.* republish, reproduce, bring out a new edition; see **print** 2.

reprisal, *n.* —*Syn.* retribution, retaliation, paying back; see **revenge** 1.

reproach, *n.* —*Syn.* discredit, censure, rebuke; see **blame** 1.

reproach, *v.* —*Syn.* condemn, blame, cavil; see **censure.**

reproachful, *mod.* —*Syn.* caustic, censorious, scolding; see **critical** 2.

reprobate, *mod.* **1.** [Wicked]—*Syn.* immoral, lewd, lascivious, vicious, dissolute, profligate, corrupt, vile, demoralized, vitiated, degraded, disreputable, worthless, base, disgusting, repulsive, repellent, forbidding; see also **wicked** 1.—*Ant.* good, honest*, fine.

2. [Rejected by the Lord]—*Syn.* sinful, blasphemous, diabolical, unregenerate, iniquitous, malevolent, godforsaken, damned, cursed, accursed; see also **doomed.**—*Ant.* virtuous, moral*, God-fearing.

reprobate, *n.* —*Syn.* wretch, sinner, transgressor, rake, scoundrel, viper, debauchee, scamp, degenerate, seducer, sot, drunkard, toper, guzzler, sneak, libertine, scapegrace, ne'er-do-well, good-for-nothing, waster, spendthrift, hellhound, devil, rogue; *all* (D): cuss, varmint, bastard; see also **rascal.**

reproduce, *v.* **1.** [To make an exact copy]—*Syn.* photograph, photostat, xerograph, Xerox (trademark), print, mimeograph, multigraph, type, reprint, portray, transcribe, electrotype, stereotype, reimpress, restamp; see **copy** 2.

2. [To make a second time]—*Syn.* repeat, duplicate, recreate, recount, revive, re-enact, redo, reawaken, relive, remake, reflect, follow, mirror, echo, re-echo, represent.

3. [To multiply]—*Syn.* procreate, engender, breed, generate, propagate, fecundate, hatch, father, beget, impregnate, progenerate, sire, repopulate, multiply, give birth.

reproduced, *mod.* —*Syn.* copied, printed, traced, duplicated, transcribed, dittoed, recorded, multiplied, Xeroxed (trademark), repeated, made identical, typed, set up, set in type, in facsimile, transferred, photographed, blueprinted, photostated, mimeographed, multigraphed, electrotyped, electroplated, engraved, photoengraved; reproduced in facsimile, in duplicate, in triplicate, etc.; see also **manufactured.**

reproduction, *n.* **1.** [The process of reproducing] —*Syn.* reprinting, duplication, reduplication, transcription, photographing, photography, xerography, mirroring, re-enactment, recreation, revival, renewal, portrayal, propagation, imitating.

2. [A copy]—*Syn.* imitation, print, offprint; see **copy.**

3. [A photographic reproduction]—*Syn.* photostat, photoengraving, rotograph, photogram, rotogravure, xerograph, telephoto, wirephoto, X-ray, radiograph, radiogram, skiagraph, skiagram, shadowgraph, shadowgram; *all* (D): candid photo, closeup, roto, pic, pix, blowup, sneak photo, flash-photo.

reproductive, *mod.* —*Syn.* generative, creative, conceptive; see **sexual** 1.

reproof, *n.* **1.** [Censure]—*Syn.* disapproval, disapprobation, blame; see **objection** 1.

2. [An oral or written statement intended to censure]—*Syn.* rebuke, reprimand, admonition; see **objection** 2.

reprove, *v.* —*Syn.* criticize, blame, condemn; see **censure.**

reptile, *n.* —*Syn.* serpent, saurian, amphibian, naked reptile, one of the reptilia, sauropod, one of the sauria; see **lizard, snake, turtle.**

republic, *n.* —*Syn.* democracy, democratic state, constitutional government, commonwealth, self-government, representative government, government by popular sovereignty; see also **government** 2.

Republican, *n.* —*Syn.* registered Republican, Young Republican, Old Line Republican; see **Conservative.**

republican, *n.* —*Syn.* democrat, Jacobin, liberal, progressive, socialist, constitutionalist, Rousseauist.

republican, *mod.* —*Syn.* democratic, constitutional, popular, electoral, autonomous, sovereign, representative; see also **Conservative, democratic** 1.—*Ant.* authoritarian, autocratic*, fascist.

Republicans, *n.* —*Syn.* party in *or* out of office, G.O.P., Grand Old Party; *all* (D): Elephant, lily-whites, Old Guard.

repudiate, *v.* **1.** [To disown]—*Syn.* disinherit, banish, renounce; see **discard, oust.**

2. [To refuse]—*Syn.* demur, decline, spurn; see **refuse.**

3. [To disavow]—*Syn.* retract, repeal, revoke; see **recant.**

repudiated, *mod.* —*Syn.* rejected, thrown out, discredited; see **disgraced, refused.**

repudiation, *n.* —*Syn.* disagreement, cancellation, abrogation; see **refusal.**

repugnant, *mod.* **1.** [Basically opposed]—*Syn.* antagonistic, antipathetic, inimical, hostile, opposite, contrary, adverse, counter, conflicting, unconformable, contradictory, against, unfitted, incompatible, in opposition, alien; see also **different** 1, **opposed, opposing** 2, **unfriendly** 1.—*Ant.* harmonious*, agreeable, conformable.

2. [Disgusting]—*Syn.* repulsive, distasteful, disagreeable; see **offensive** 2.

repulse, *n.* —*Syn.* rebuff, setback, snub; see **defeat** 2.

repulse, *v.* **1.** [To throw back]—*Syn.* set back, overthrow, resist; see **repel** 1.

2. [To rebuff]—*Syn.* spurn, repel, snub; see **rebuff** 1.

repulsion, *n.* **1.** [Rejection]—*Syn.* rebuff, denial, snub; see **refusal.**

2. [Aversion]—*Syn.* hate, disgust, resentment; see **hatred** 1, 2, **malice.**

repulsive, *mod.* **1.** [Capable of repelling]—*Syn.* offensive, resistant, unyielding, stubborn, opposing, retaliating, insurgent, counteracting, attacking, counterattacking, defensive, combative, aggressive, pugnacious; see also **obstinate.**—*Ant.* yielding*, surrendering, capitulating.

2. [Disgusting]—*Syn.* odious, forbidding, horrid; see **offensive** 2.

reputable, *mod.* **1.** [Enjoying a good reputation] —*Syn.* distinguished, celebrated, honored, notable, renowned, prominent, esteemed, well-known, illustrious, favored, famous, popular, acclaimed, in high favor, conspicuous, eminent, high-ranking, famed; see also **important** 2.—*Ant.* disgraced*, ignominious, infamous.

2. [Honorable]—*Syn.* trustworthy, dignified, noble, estimable, worthy, creditable, respectable, constant, faithful, conscientious, truthful, honest, sincere, fair, reliable, dependable, just, high-principled, righteous, upright, straightforward.—*Ant.* dishonest*, dishonorable, disloyal.

reputation, *n.* **1.** [Supposed character]—*Syn.* reliability, trustworthiness, respectability, dependability, credit, esteem, estimation; see also **character** 2.

2. [Good name]—*Syn.* standing, prestige, stature, regard, favor, account, respect, privilege, acceptability, social approval; see also **admiration** 1, **honor** 1.

3. [Fame]—*Syn.* prominence, eminence, notoriety; see **fame** 1.

repute, *n.* —*Syn.* (good) standing, reputation, (high) station; see **fame** 1.

repute, *v.* —*Syn.* esteem, regard, affirm; see **admire** 1, **believe** 1.

request, *n.* —*Syn.* call, inquiry, application, petition, question, invitation, offer, solicitation, supplication, prayer, requisition, recourse, suit, entreaty, demand; see also **appeal** 1.

by request—*Syn.* asked for, sought for, wanted; see **requested** 1, 2.

request, *v.* **1.** [To ask]—*Syn.* demand, inquire, call for; see **ask** 1.

2. [To solicit]—*Syn.* beseech, entreat, sue; see **beg** 1.

requested, *mod.* **1.** [Wanted]—*Syn.* asked, demanded, wished, desired, sought, hunted, needed, solicited, petitioned, appealed, requisitioned, in demand; see also **popular** 1, **wanted.**

2. [Called for]—*Syn.* summoned, paged, asked for, called up *or* in *or* back, phoned, telephoned, had a request *or* a call (for), sought (out), drafted; see also sense 1.

requesting, *mod.*—*Syn.* asking, calling for; demanding, wanting, wishing, soliciting, petitioning, requisitioning, appealing for.

requiem, *n.*—*Syn.* dirge, Mass for the dead, threnody; see **funeral** 1, **Mass.**

require, *v.* **1.** [To need]—*Syn.* want, feel the necessity for, have need for; see **need.**

2. [To demand]—*Syn.* oblige, necessitate, obligate, requisition, command, exact, challenge, insist upon, expect, entail, look *or* push for, assert oneself, call for, take no denial; see also **ask** 1.

required, *mod.*—*Syn.* requisite, imperative, essential; see **necessary** 1.

requirement, *n.* **1.** [A prerequisite]—*Syn.* (preliminary) condition, essential, imperative, element, requisite, (indispensable) provision, terms, necessity, stipulation, fundamental, first principle, precondition, reservation, specification, proviso, fulfillment, qualification, vital part, *sine qua non* (Latin); see also **basis** 1.

2. [A need]—*Syn.* necessity, necessary, lack, want, demand, claim, obsession, preoccupation, prepossession, engrossment, stress, extremity, exigency, pinch, obligation, pressing concern, urgency, compulsion, exaction, the decencies (D).

requiring, *mod.*—*Syn.* needing, demanding, calling for, necessitating, involving, compelling, forcing, exacting, enjoining; see also **urgent** 1.

requisite, *mod.*—*Syn.* imperative, demanded, needed; see **important** 1, **inevitable, necessary** 1.

requisition, *v.*—*Syn.* call for, order, request; see **buy** 1, **require** 2.

requite, *v.*—*Syn.* remunerate, repay, recompense, compensate, reward, satisfy, pay off, settle with, retaliate, revenge, quit; see also **pay** 1, **redeem** 1. —*Ant.* pardon*, slight, overlook.

reread, *v.*—*Syn.* re-examine, study again, go over; see **read** 1.

rescind, *v.*—*Syn.* remove, abrogate, annul; see **abolish, cancel** 1, 2, **revoke.**

rescue, *n.* **1.** [The act of rescuing]—*Syn.* deliverance, saving, release, extrication, liberation, ransom, redemption, salvation, reclamation, reclaiming, emancipation, disentanglement, disembarrassment, affranchisement, recovering, heroism; see also **freeing.**

2. [An instance of rescue]—*Syn.* action, deed, feat, performance, exploit, accomplishment, heroics; see also **achievement** 2.

rescue, *v.* **1.** [To save]—*Syn.* preserve, recover, redeem, recapture, salvage, retain, hold over, keep (back), safeguard, protect, retrieve, withdraw, take to safety; see also **ransom, save** 1.—*Ant.* lose*, slip from one's hands, relinquish.

2. [To free]—*Syn.* deliver, liberate, extricate, release, emancipate, ransom, set free, unloose, put at liberty, unleash, manumit; see also **free** 1.—*Ant.* imprison*, capture, jail.

research, *mod.*—*Syn.* investigating, investigative, fact-finding, scientific, scientifically based exploratory, planning, analytic, specialized, involved in research; see also **explanatory.**

research, *n.*—*Syn.* investigation, analysis, experimentation; see **examination** 1, **study** 2.

research, *v.*—*Syn.* get *or* read up on, do research, look into *or* up; see **examine** 1, **study** 1.

resemblance, *n.*—*Syn.* likeness, correspondence, coincidence; see **similarity.**

resemble, *v.*—*Syn.* be *or* look *or* seem *or* sound like, follow, take after, parallel, match, correspond to, coincide, relate, mirror, bear analogy, approximate, give indication *or* remind one of, bring to mind, catch a likeness, have all the signs of, be the very image of, be similar to, come close to, appear like, bear a resemblance to, come near, pass for, have all the earmarks of, echo, compare with, be comparable to; *all* (D): smack of, be the spit and image of, be a dead-ringer for, have the same pieprint as; see also **agree.**—*Ant.* differ*, contradict, oppose.

resent, *v.*—*Syn.* frown at, be vexed, be insulted; see **dislike.**

resentment, *n.* **1.** [Anger]—*Syn.* ire, wrath, fury, vehemence, passion, displeasure, ill will, malice, vexation, exasperation, choler, annoyance, irritation; see also **anger.**—*Ant.* friendship*, friendliness, affection.

2. [A rankling sense of wrong]—*Syn.* bitterness, cynicism, indignation, pique, displeasure, animus, antagonism, hurt, perturbation, acrimony, acerbity, exacerbation, umbrage, grudge, outrage; see also **hate, hatred** 1, 2.

reservation, *n.* **1.** [The act of reserving]—*Syn.* restriction, limitation, isolation, withholding, setting aside, exclusive possession, booking, bespeaking, retainment, retaining; see also **restraint** 2.

2. [An instrument for reserving]—*Syn.* ticket, pass, license, badge, stipulation, card, two-fer (D).

3. [The space reserved]—*Syn.* seat, car, room, bus, train, box, stall, place, parking spot, table, berth, compartment.

reserve, *n.* **1.** [A portion kept against emergencies]—*Syn.* savings, insurance, resources, reserved funds, store, provisions, assets, supply, hoard, backlog, nest egg; *both* (D): something in the sock, something for a rainy day; see also **security** 2.

2. [Calmness]—*Syn.* backwardness, restraint, reticence, modesty, unresponsiveness, uncommunicativeness, caution, inhibition, coyness, demureness, aloofness.

3. [A reserve player]—*Syn.* substitute, second-string man, alternate; *all* (D): bench polisher, spare tire, sub, scrub.

4. [Unexpected fund]—*Syn.* sinking fund, funded reserve, government securities, negotiable bonds, floating assets; see also **resources, wealth** 1.

in reserve—*Syn.* withheld, kept back *or* aside, saved; see **reserved** 2.

reserve, *v.* **1.** [To save]—*Syn.* store up, set aside, put away; see **maintain** 3, **save** 3.

2. [To retain]—*Syn.* keep, possess, have; see **hold** 1, **own** 1.

reserved, *mod.* **1.** [Held on reservation]—*Syn.* appropriated, pre-empted, claimed, private, booked, engaged, spoken for, set apart, roped off, taken, arrogated, held; see also **saved** 2.—*Ant.* public*, open, unreserved.

2. [Held in reserve]—*Syn.* saved, withheld, kept aside, preserved, conserved, stored away, funded, put in a safe, on ice (D).—*Ant.* used*, spent, exhausted.

3. [Restrained]—*Syn.* shy, modest, backward, reticent, secretive, private, quiet, composed, retiring, controlling oneself, self-contained, mild, gentle, peaceful, soft-spoken, sedate, collected, serene, placid.—*Ant.* loud*, ostentatious, boisterous.

reserves, *n.*—*Syn.* reinforcements, enlisted reserves, volunteers; see **army** 2, **troops.**

reservoir, *n.*—*Syn.* storage (place), tank, reserve, store, pool, cistern, water supply.

reside, *v.*—*Syn.* dwell, occupy, tenant, lodge, populate, remain, continue, stay, sojourn, take up residence in.

residence, *n.* **1.** [A dwelling]—*Syn.* house, habitation, living quarters; see **apartment, home** 1.

2. [An official seat]—*Syn.* headquarters, residency, cantonment.

Residences include the following—capital, royal palace, presidential home, vicarage, bishop's palace, deanery, governor's mansion, White House, Vatican, Buckingham Palace, Kremlin, Elysée, Castel Gandolfo, Escorial.

resident, *n.*—*Syn.* house-dweller, citizen, suburbanite, tenant, inhabitant, native, denizen, occupant, inmate, householder, boxholder, dweller.

residential, *mod.*—*Syn.* home-owning, living, suburban, domestic, private.

residual, *mod.*—*Syn.* left over, remaining, surplus, continuing, extra, enduring, lingering.

residue, *n.*—*Syn.* residual, residuum, remainder, leavings, scraps, scourings, scobs, parings, raspings, shavings, dregs, debris, remainder, sewage, silt, slag, soot, scum; see also **trash** 1.

resign, *v.* **1.** [To relinquish]—*Syn.* surrender, capitulate, give up; see **abandon** 1, **yield** 1.

2. [To leave one's employment]—*Syn.* quit, separate oneself from, retire, step down, drop out, stand down *or* aside, sign off, end one's services, leave, hand in one's resignation, cease work, give notice; *all* (D): ask for one's time, chuck one's job, walk out of, toss up one's job.

resignation, *n.* **1.** [Mental preparation for something unwelcome]—*Syn.* submission, humility, passivity, patience, deference, docility, submissiveness, abandonment, renunciation, self-abnegation, resignedness, acquiescence, endurance, compliance, yieldingness, unresistingness.—*Ant.* resistance*, unsubmissiveness, unwillingness.

2. [The act of resigning]—*Syn.* retirement, departure, leaving, quitting, giving up, abdication, surrender, withdrawal, relinquishment, vacating, tendering one's resignation, giving up office, termination of one's connection.

resigned, *mod.*—*Syn.* quiet, peaceable, docile, tractable, submissive, yielding, relinquishing, gentle, obedient, manageable, willing, agreeable, ready, amenable, pliant, compliant, easily managed, genial, cordial, well-disposed, satisfied, acquiescent, quiescent, patient, unresisting, tolerant, calm, reconciled, adjusted, adapted, accommodated, tame, biddable, nonresisting, passive, philosophical, renouncing, unassertive, subservient, deferential.—*Ant.* rebellious*, recalcitrant, resistant.

resilience, *n.*—*Syn.* elasticity, snap, recoil; see **flexibility** 1.

resilient, *mod.*—*Syn.* rebounding, elastic, springy; see **flexible** 1.

resin, *n.*—*Syn.* copal, pitch, gum; see **tar** 1.

resinous, *mod.*—*Syn.* pitchy, lacquered, gummy; see **adhesive, sticky.**

resist, *v.* **1.** [To withstand]—*Syn.* hold, remain, maintain, endure, bear, continue, persist, obtain, occur, repeat, stay, retain, brook, suffer, abide, tolerate, be unalterable *or* immune *or* unsusceptible *or* fixed *or* permanent *or* hard *or* strong, persevere, last, oppose change, bear up against, stand up to, put up a struggle, hold off, repel, remain firm; *all* (D): fight to the last ditch, die hard, arch one's back.—*Ant.* stop*, desist, cease.

2. [To oppose]—*Syn.* combat, antagonize, assault; see **oppose** 1, 2.

resistance, *n.* **1.** [A defense]—*Syn.* parrying, stand, holding, withstanding, warding off, rebuff, obstruction, defiance, striking back, copying, check, halting, protecting, protection, safeguard, shield, screen, cover, watch, support, fight, impeding, blocking, opposition; see also **defense** 1.—*Ant.* retirement*, withdrawal*, withdrawing.

2. [The power of remaining impervious to an influence]—*Syn.* unsusceptibility, immunity, immovability, unalterableness, hardness, imperviousness, endurance, unyieldingness, fixedness, fastness, stability, stableness, permanence.—*Ant.* vacillation*, variability, susceptibility.

3. [The power of holding back another substance] —*Syn.* retardation, nonconduction, friction, nonpromotion, attrition, reserve, surface resistance, detention, volume resistance, impedance.

4. [An opposition]—*Syn.* underground movement, *maquis* (French); anti-Fascist, anti-Communist, anti-American, etc., movement; boycott, strike, walkout, slowdown, front, stand, guerrilla movement; see also **revolution** 2.

resistant, *mod.*—*Syn.* contrary, defiant, unyielding; see **opposing** 2, **rebellious** 2.

resister, *n.*—*Syn.* wet blanket, damper, spoilsport, killjoy, obstructor, staller, obstructionist, saboteur, opponent, adversary, activist, antagonist, opposition, die-hard, bitter-ender, last-ditcher, objector, conscientious objector *or* CO, passive resister, noncooperator, dissenter, disputer, contender, militant, guerrilla, combatant.

resolute, *mod.* **1.** [Brave]—*Syn.* courageous, intrepid, valiant; see **brave** 1.

2. [Strong-minded]—*Syn.* steady, steadfast, firm, true, set, determined, serious, decided, unshaken, persevering, unflagging, unfaltering, persistent, persisting, constant, set *or* intent upon, unchanging, bent on, immutable, fixed, settled, loyal, unwavering, staunch, strong, stubborn, obstinate, faithful, knowing one's own mind, resolved, uncompromising, unyielding, strong-willed, tenacious, dogged, self-reliant, enduring, indefatigable, purposeful, established, adamant, adamantine, inflexible, independent, radical, irreconcilable, unremovable, intransigent, inveterate, obdurate, pertinacious; *all* (D): gritting one's teeth, out for blood, putting one's foot down, putting one's heart into, having one's heart set on, hellbent.—*Ant.* unsteady*, vacillating, wavering.

resolutely, *mod.*—*Syn.* with all one's heart, bravely, with a will; see **firmly** 2, **obstinately.**

resolution, *n.* **1.** [Fixedness of mind]—*Syn.* fortitude, perseverance, resolve; see **determination** 2.

2. [A formal statement of opinion]—*Syn.* verdict, formal expression, decision, recommendation, analysis, elucidation, interpretation, exposition, presentation, declaration, recitation, assertion; see also **judgment** 3.

resolve, *v.*—*Syn.* determine, settle (on), conclude, fix, purpose, propose, choose, fix upon, make up one's mind, take a firm stand, take one's stand, take a decisive step, make a point of, pass upon, decree, elect, remain firm; *all* (D): buckle to, burn one's bridges, take the bull by the horns; see also **decide.**

resonance, *n.*—*Syn.* thunder, vibration, boom; see **noise** 1.

resonant, *mod.*—*Syn.* resounding, reverberating, booming; see **loud** 1.

resort, *n.* **1.** [A relief in the face of difficulty] —*Syn.* expedient, shift, makeshift, stopgap, substitute, surrogate, resource, device, refuge, recourse, hope, relief, possibility, opportunity.

2. [A place for rest or amusement] Resorts include the following—seaside, mountain, curative-bath, spa, health camp, rest, camping, skiing, sports, winter, lake, summer, gambling, amusement **park,** night club, restaurant, dance hall, club, watering place (D); see also **hotel, lodge, motel.**

as a last resort—*Syn.* in desperation, lastly, in the end; see **finally** 1, 2.

resort to, *v.*—*Syn.* turn to, refer to, apply, go to, use, try, employ, utilize, have recourse to, benefit by, put to use, make use of, recur to, take up.

resound, *v.*—*Syn.* vibrate, rumble, reverberate; see **sound** 1.

resounding, *mod.*—*Syn.* reverberating, thunderous, booming; see **loud** 1.

resource, *n.*—*Syn.* reserve, supply, support, source, stock, store, means, expedient, stratagem, relief, resort, recourse, artifice, device, refuge.

resourceful, *mod.*—*Syn.* original, ingenious, capable; see **active** 2, **intelligent** 1.

resources, *n.*—*Syn.* means, money, stocks, bonds, products, revenue, riches, assets, belongings, effects, collateral, capital, income, savings; see also **property** 1, **reserve** 1, 4, **wealth** 1.

respect, *n.*—*Syn.* esteem, honor, regard; see **admiration** 1, **praise** 1.

pay one's respects—*Syn.* wait upon, show regard, be polite; see **visit** 1.

in respect of—*Syn.* about, concerning, in reference to; see **regarding.**

respect, *v.* **1.** [To esteem]—*Syn.* regard, value, look up to; see **admire** 1.

2. [To treat with consideration]—*Syn.* appreciate, heed, notice, consider, note, recognize, defer *or* do honor *or* be kind *or* show courtesy to, spare, take into account, attend, uphold; see also **regard** 1. —*Ant.* ridicule*, mock, scorn.

respectability, *n.*—*Syn.* integrity, decency, propriety; see **honesty** 1, **virtue** 1.

respectable, *mod.*—*Syn.* presentable, upright, fair, moderate, mediocre, tolerable, passable, ordinary, virtuous, modest, honorable, admirable, worthy, estimable, decorous, decent, correct, seemly, proper, *comme il faut* (French); see also **decent** 2, **honest** 1, **reputable** 2.—*Ant.* dishonest*, indecorous, dissolute.

respected, *mod.*—*Syn.* regarded, appreciated, valued; see **honored, important** 2.

respectful, *mod.*—*Syn.* deferential, considerate, appreciative, courteous, admiring, reverent, revering, reverencing, attending, upholding, regarding, valuing, venerating, taking thought for, recognizing, deferring to, showing respect for; see also **polite** 1.—*Ant.* rude*, impudent, contemptuous.

respectfully, *mod.*—*Syn.* deferentially, regardfully, reverentially, decorously, ceremoniously, attentively, courteously, considerately, with all respect, with due respect, with the highest respect, in deference to; see also **politely.**—*Ant.* rudely*, disrespectfully, impudently.

respecting, *mod.*—*Syn.* regarding, concerning, in relation to, relating to, pertaining to, relevant to, pertinent to, in respect to, with reference to, referring to, in connection with, anent, about, as for, as to, with regard to, in the matter of.

respective, *mod.* —*Syn.* particular, several, individual, each separately, each to each.

respectively, *mod.* —*Syn.* severally, each, by lot, each to each, in particular; individually, distributively, apiece.

respects, *n.* —*Syn.* deference, courtesies, kind wishes, best wishes, greetings, cordial regards, salaam, kowtow; see also **greeting** 1, **regards.**

respiration, *n.* —*Syn.* inhalation, exhalation, expiration; see **breath** 1.

respite, *n.* —*Syn.* reprieve, suspension, commutation, postponement, pause, interval, stop, intermission, deferment, acquittal, exculpation, pardon, forgiveness, discharge, immunity, halt, stay, deliverance, truce, cessation, interregnum, deadlock, interruption, protraction, adjournment, release; see also **delay** 1.—*Ant.* punishment*, condemnation, penalty.

resplendent, *mod.* —*Syn.* shiny, glossy, radiant; see **bright** 1.

respond, *v.* —*Syn.* reply, rejoin, acknowledge; see **answer** 1.

response, *n.* —*Syn.* rejoinder, reply, acknowledgment; see **answer** 1.

responsibility, *n.* **1.** [State of being reliable]—*Syn.* trustworthiness, reliability, trustiness, dependability, dependableness, loyalty, faithfulness, capableness, capacity, efficiency, competency, uprightness, firmness, steadfastness, stability, ability; see also **honesty** 1.

2. [State of being accountable]—*Syn.* answerability, accountability, liability, amenability, subjection, boundness, obligatoriness, incumbency, engagement, pledge, contract, constraint, restraint; see also **duty** 1.—*Ant.* freedom*, exemption, immunity.

3. [Anything for which one is accountable]—*Syn.* obligation, trust, contract; see **duty** 1.

responsible, *mod.* **1.** [Charged with responsibility] —*Syn.* accountable, answerable (for), amenable, liable, subject, susceptive, bound, incumbent *or* devolving on, under obligation, beholden to, constrained, tied, fettered, bonded, censurable, chargeable, obligated, obliged, compelled, contracted, hampered, held, pledged, sworn *or* bound to, under contract, engaged; see also **bound** 2. —*Ant.* free*, unconstrained, unbound.

2. [Capable of assuming responsibility]—*Syn.* trustworthy, trusty, reliable, capable, efficient, loyal, faithful, dutiful, dependable, tried, self-reliant, able, competent, qualified, effective, upright, firm, steadfast, steady, stable; see also **able** 2. —*Ant.* irresponsible*, capricious, unstable.

responsive, *mod.* —*Syn.* answering, replying, acknowledging, respondent, impressionable, sympathetic, sensitive, warm, warmhearted, compassionate, tender; see also **active** 2, **conscious** 1.—*Ant.* indifferent*, cold*, cool.

rest, *n.* **1.** [Repose]—*Syn.* quiet, quietude, quiescence, quietness, ease, tranquillity, slumber, calm, calmness, peace, peaceableness, peacefulness, pacification, relaxation, rest, recreation, coffee break, rest period, siesta, doze, nap, somnolence, dreaminess, comfort, breathing spell, lounge, lounging period, loafing period, vacation, lull, leisure, respite, composure; see **sense** 2.—*Ant.* strain*, restlessness, sleeplessness.

2. [State of inactivity]—*Syn.* intermission, cessation, stillness, stop, stay, stand, standstill, lull, discontinuance, interval, hush, silence, dead calm, stagnation, stagnancy, fixity, immobility, inactivity, motionlessness, catalepsy, caesura, pause, full stop, deadlock, recess, noon hour (D); see **sense** 1; **peace** 1.—*Ant.* continuance*, activity, endurance.

3. [Anything upon which an object rests]—*Syn.* support, prop, stay, seat, trestle, pillar, pedestal, base, bottom, pediment; see also **foundation** 2.

4. [(D) The remainder]—*Syn.* residue, surplus, remnant; see **excess** 4, **remainder.**

5. [Death]—*Syn.* release, demise, mortality; see **death** 1.

at rest—*Syn.* in a state of rest, immobile, inactive; see **resting** 1.

lay to rest—*Syn.* inter, assign to the grave, entomb; see **bury** 1.

rest, *v.* **1.** [To take one's rest]—*Syn.* sleep, slumber, doze, repose, compose oneself for sleep, lie (down), lounge, let down, ease off, recuperate, rest up, take a rest *or* a break, break the monotony, lean, recline, couch, pillow, relax, unbend, settle (down), dream, drowse, take one's ease, be comfortable, stretch out, nap, nod, snooze (D).

2. [To be still]—*Syn.* be quiet, lie *or* stand still, pause, halt, stop (short), hold, cease, pull up, lie to, rest on one's oars.

3. [To depend upon]—*Syn.* be supported *or* upheld, hang *or* lie upon, be seated on, be propped by, be founded *or* based on; see also **depend** 2.

restaurant, *n.* —*Syn.* eating house, eating place, dining room, café; *all* (D): beanery, lobster palace, chow dump, eatery, greasy spoon, hashhouse,

Types of restaurants include the following—café, hotel, dining room, inn, coffee shop, coffee house, fast food place, coffee room, chophouse, tearoom, luncheon, luncheonette, lunch-wagon, hamburger stand, fast-food outlet, sea-food grotto, coffee deck, *trattoria* (Italian), *estaminet, bistro* (*both* French), creamery, dining car, dining coach, dining saloon, diner, lunch bar, soda fountain, milk bar, hot-dog stand, snack bar, automat, rathskeller, rotisserie, cabaret, night club, cafeteria, grill *or* grillroom, oyster house, barbecue, spaghetti house, pizzeria, canteen.

rested, *mod.* —*Syn.* restored, refreshed, relaxed, strengthened, renewed, unwearied, unfatigued, untired, awake, revived, recovered, brought back, revivified, reanimated, revitalized, reintegrated, unworn; see also **fresh** 10.—*Ant.* tired*, wearied, fatigued.

restful, *mod.* —*Syn.* untroubling, untroubled, tranquil, tranquilizing, calm, peaceful, quiet, reposeful, serene, pacific, comfortable, easy, placid, mild, still, soothing, relaxing, refreshing, restoring, revitalizing, reviving, renewing.—*Ant.* loud*, irritating, agitating.

resting, *mod.* **1.** [Taking rest]—*Syn.* relaxing, unbending, reposing, composing oneself, reclining, lying down, sleeping, stretched out, at ease, quiet, quiescent, dormant, comfortable, lounging, loafing, taking a breathing spell *or* a breather, enjoying a lull, sleeping, dozing, drowsing, napping, taking a siesta, recessing, taking a vacation, having a holiday.

2. [Situated]—*Syn.* located, based on, established, set *or* settled on, seated, standing *or* propped on, supported *or* held by, reposing, lying; see also **occupying 1, placed.**

rest in peace, *n.* —*Syn.* prayer, *Requiescat in Pace* (Latin), may the earth rest light on thee, here lies; see also **epitaph.**

restitution, *n.* —*Syn.* compensation, return, restoration; see **payment** 1, **reparation** 2.

restive, *mod.* —*Syn.* unyielding, unruly, stubborn; see **obstinate.**

restless, *mod.* **1.** [Not content when still]—*Syn.* fidgety, skittish, feverish, sleepless, jumpy, nervous, unquiet, flurried, restive, peeved, annoyed, impatient, flustered, twitching, trembling, tremulous; *both* (D): rattled, jittery; see also **active** 2, **excited.** —*Ant.* quiet*, sedate, lethargic.

2. [Not content with conditions]—*Syn.* disturbed, uneasy, disquieted, anxious, up in arms, discontented, vexed, excited, agitated, angry, disaffected, estranged, alienated, resentful, refractory, recalcitrant, fractious, insubordinate, contumacious, perverse; see also **rebellious** 2, 3.—*Ant.* calm*, content, satisfied.

3. [Not content with a settled life]—*Syn.* roving, transient, wandering, discontented, unsettled, roaming, nomadic, footloose, peripatetic, itinerant, moving, straying, ranging, gadding, gallivanting, meandering, traipsing; see also **rambling** 3.—*Ant.* firm*, immovable, settled.

restlessness, *n.* —*Syn.* uneasiness, discomfort, excitability; see **excitement, nervousness** 1, 2.

restoration, *n.* **1.** [The act of restoring]—*Syn.* revival, healing, return, cure, remaking, renovation, renewal, reclamation, reformation, rehabilitation, recreation, alteration, replacing, remodeling, rejuvenation, rebuilding; see also **recovery** 1.

2. [The act of reconstructing]—*Syn.* rehabilitation, reconstruction, reparation; see **repair.**

restorative, *mod.* —*Syn.* medicinal, corrective, therapeutic; see **healthful, remedial.**

restore, *v.* **1.** [To give back]—*Syn.* make restitution, replace, put back; see **return** 2.

2. [To recreate]—*Syn.* re-establish, revive, recover; see **renew** 1.

3. [To rebuild in a form supposed to be original] —*Syn.* rebuild, put back, alter, make restoration, rehabilitate; see also **reconstruct, repair.**

4. [To reinstate]—*Syn.* reinstall, put back, reerect; see **reinstate.**

5. [To bring back to health]—*Syn.* refresh, cure, make healthy; see **heal** 1.

restored, *mod.* —*Syn.* rebuilt, re-established, revived; see **built** 1, **repaired.**

restrain, *v.* **1.** [To hold in check]—*Syn.* check, control, curb, bridle, rein *or* hem *or* keep in, handle, regulate, keep in line, guide, direct, keep down *or* from, repress, harness, muzzle, hold in leash, govern, inhibit, hold, bind, prescribe, deter, hold in *or* back, hamper, constrain, restrict, stay, gag, limit, impound, box *or* bottle up, tie *or* crack *or* pin down, hold *or* choke *or* pull back, contain, sit on, come down on.

2. [To restrict]—*Syn.* limit, circumscribe, delimit; see **restrict** 2.

restrained, *mod.* —*Syn.* under control, in check, in leading strings, under restraint, on leash, under wraps (D).

restraining, *mod.* —*Syn.* controlling, restrictive, coercive; see **governing.**

restrain oneself, *v.* —*Syn.* hold aloof *or* back, forgo, get organized, desist from, show restraint, curb *or* discipline *or* limit *or* efface *or* get hold of *or* mortify oneself; see also **abstain.**

restraint, *n.* **1.** [Control over oneself]—*Syn.* control, self-control, reserve, reticence, constraint, artistic economy, withholding, caution, coolness, forbearance, silence, secretiveness, stress repression, self-government, self-restraint, stiffness, abstinence, self-denial, self-repression, unnaturalness, constrained manner, abstemiousness, abstention, self-discipline, self-censorship; see also **attention** 2, **limitation** 1.—*Ant.* laziness*, slackness, laxity.

2. [An influence that checks or hinders]—*Syn.* repression, deprivation, limitation, hindrance, abridgment, reduction, decrease, prohibition, confinement, check, barrier, obstacle, obstruction, restriction, bar, curb, blockade, order, command, instruction, coercion, impediment, compulsion, duress, force, violence, deterrence, determent, discipline, assignment, definition, prescription, moderation, tempering, qualifying.—*Ant.* liberty*, license, incitement.

restrict, *v.* **1.** [To restrain]—*Syn.* curb, check, bind; see **restrain** 1.

2. [To hold within limits]—*Syn.* delimit, limit, circumscribe, assign, contract, shorten, narrow, decrease, inclose, keep in *or* within bounds, demark, define, encircle, surround, shut in, tether, chain, diminish, reduce, moderate, modify, temper, qualify; *both* (D): come down on, pin down.—*Ant.* increase*, extend, expand.

restricted, *mod.* —*Syn.* limited, confined, restrained, circumscribed, curbed, bound, prescribed, checked, bounded, inhibited, hampered, marked, defined, delimited, encircled, surrounded, shut in, hitched, tethered, chained, snaffled, fastened, secured, bridled, held in *or* back *or* down, reined in, controlled, governed, deterred, impeded, stayed, stopped, suppressed, repressed, prevented, trammeled, fettered, deprived, blocked, barred, obstructed, dammed, clogged, manacled, frustrated, embarrassed, baffled, foiled, shrunken, narrowed, shortened, decreased, diminished, reduced, moderated, tempered, modified, qualified, out of bounds; see also **bound** 1, 2.

restriction, *n.* —*Syn.* custody, limitation, contraction; see **confinement** 1, **restraint** 2.

restrictive, *mod.* **1.** [Contrary]—*Syn.* prohibitory, prohibitive, confining; see **opposed.**

2. [Provisional]—*Syn.* definitive, limiting, qualificatory; see **conditional.**

result, *n.* —*Syn.* consequence, issue, event, execution, effect, outcome, end, finish, termination, consummation, completion, aftereffect, aftermath, upshot, sequel, sequence, fruit, fruition, eventuality, proceeds, emanation, outgrowth, outcropping, ensual, returns, backwash, backlash, repercussion, settlement, determination, decision, arrangement, denouement, payoff (D); see also **end** 2, 4.—*Ant.* origin*, source, root.

result, *v.* —*Syn.* issue, grow *or* spring *or* rise *or* proceed *or* emanate *or* germinate *or* flow *or* accrue *or* arise *or* derive *or* come from, originate in, (be)-come of, spring, emerge, rise, ensue, emanate, effect, produce, fruit, follow, happen, occur, come about *or* out *or* forth *or* of, pan *or* fall *or* crop *or* work out, appear, end, finish, terminate, conclude.

result from, *v.* —*Syn.* proceed *or* spring *or* come from, emerge, start; see **begin** 2.

result in, *v.* —*Syn.* end *or* terminate in, conclude, finish; see **achieve** 1, **end** 1.

resulting in, *mod.* —*Syn.* leading to, having the result *or* effect that, eventuating as, becoming.

resume, *v.* —*Syn.* take up again, reassume, begin again, recommence, reoccupy, go on (with), renew, recapitulate, return, keep *or* carry on, keep up; see also **continue** 2.—*Ant.* stop*, cease, discontinue.

résumé, *n.* **1.** [A summary]—*Syn.* abstract, synopsis, précis; see **summary.**

2. [A summary of personal and professional history] —*Syn.* curriculum vitae, work history, biography; *all* (D): CV, vita, bio.

Resurrection, *n.* **1.** [Christ's rising from the tomb] —*Syn.* Easter, Return from the Dead, the Ascension *or* Assumption, Rolling Away the Stone, Reappearance on Earth, Overcoming Death.

2. [The rising of souls]—*Syn.* the Last Judgment, the Harrowing of Hell, the Second Coming of Christ, Judgment Day; see also **salvation** 3.

resurrection, *n.* —*Syn.* return to life, reanimation, transformation, restoration, resuscitation, revival, revivifying, rebirth, renewal, renaissance *or* renascence, reincarnation, transmigration, transmogrification.

resuscitate, *v.* —*Syn.* cure, bring around, restore; see **revive** 1.

retail, *mod.* —*Syn.* direct, in small lots, by the piece, by the pound, singly, local, to the consumer, in small quantities, by the package.—*Ant.* wholesale*, in large amounts, in quantity.

retail, *v.* —*Syn.* distribute, dispense, dispose of; see **sell** 1.

retain, *v.* **1.** [To hold]—*Syn.* cling to, grasp, clutch; see **hold** 1.

2. [To keep]—*Syn.* preserve, put away, husband; see **maintain** 3.

3. [To reserve services]—*Syn.* employ, maintain, engage; see **hire** 1.

4. [To remember]—*Syn.* recall, recollect, recognize; see **remember** 1.

retained, *mod.* **1.** [Kept]—*Syn.* had, held, possessed, owned, enjoyed, secured, preserved, husbanded, saved, maintained, restrained, confined, curbed, detained, contained, received, admitted, included, withheld, put away, treasured, sustained, celebrated, remembered, commemorated; see also **kept** 2.—*Ant.* lost*, wasted, refused.

2. [Employed]—*Syn.* hired, engaged, contracted, promised, chosen, selected, given a position, secured, bespoken; see also **employed.**—*Ant.* unemployed*, disengaged, let go.

retainer, *n.* —*Syn.* valet, attendant, lackey; see **servant.**

retaining, *mod.* —*Syn.* maintaining, sustaining, securing, saving, preserving, holding, keeping, owning, possessing, having, withholding, taking, seizing, confining, suppressing, curbing, arresting, restraining, holding *or* keeping back, receiving, admitting, comprehending, accommodating, embracing, treasuring, cherishing, commemorating, employing, engaging, hiring, bespeaking.

retaliate, *v.* —*Syn.* requite, return, repay; see **revenge.**

retaliating, *mod.* —*Syn.* taking revenge, getting back, turning the tables, getting even, paying off, exchanging.

retaliation, *n.* —*Syn.* vengeance, reprisal, punishment; see **revenge** 1.

retard, *v.* **1.** [To dawdle]—*Syn.* falter, hesitate, poke (D); see **loaf** 1, **loiter.**

2. [To hinder]—*Syn.* postpone, delay, impede; see **hinder.**

retardation, *n.* —*Syn.* obstacle, delay, hindrance; see **impediment** 1.

retarded, *mod.* **1.** [*Said of persons*]—*Syn.* backward, underachieving, stupid; see **dull** 3.

2. [*Said of activities*]—*Syn.* delayed, slowed down *or* up, held back; see **slow** 1, 2, 3.

retch, *v.* —*Syn.* spew, eject, throw up; see **vomit.**

retention, *n.* **1.** [Custody]—*Syn.* charge, reservation, hold; see **custody** 1.

2. [Memory]—*Syn.* recall, recognition, recollection; see **memory** 1, **remembrance.**

reticence, *n.* —*Syn.* silence, closeness, hesitation; see **reserve** 2, **shyness.**

reticent, *mod.* —*Syn.* taciturn, hesitant, quiet; see **reserved** 3.

retinue, *n.* —*Syn.* procession, convoy, cortege; see **escort.**

retire, *v.* **1.** [To draw away]—*Syn.* separate, withdraw, part, recede, retreat, regress, draw back, seclude oneself, secede, keep aloof *or* apart, shut oneself up, deny oneself, rusticate; see also **leave** 1. —*Ant.* join*, accompany, take part in.

2. [To go to bed]—*Syn.* lie down, turn in, rest; see **lie** 4, **sleep.**

3. [To cease active life]—*Syn.* resign, give up work, leave active service, sever one's connections, relinquish, make vacant, hand over, lead a quiet life, reach retirement age, sequester oneself.

4. [To remove]—*Syn.* revoke, rescind, repeal; see **withdraw** 2.

retired, *mod.* **1.** [Having withdrawn from active life] —*Syn.* resigned, relinquished, laid down, handed over, reached retirement age, emeritus, leading a quiet life, secluding oneself, separating oneself, rusticating, aloof.—*Ant.* active*, working*, busy*.

2. [Having been withdrawn]—*Syn.* removed, withdrawn, drawn back, gone (away), drawn away from, vacated, abandoned, evacuated, retreated, separated, apart, departed; see also **discharged** 1, **recalled** 2.—*Ant.* present*, advanced, brought forward.

retirement, *n.* **1.** [The act of retiring]—*Syn.* relinquishment, resignation, abandonment, vacating, evacuation, separation, removal, handing over, laying down, egressing, exiting, retreating, withdrawal, going away, leaving, secession, departure,

recession, retreat, regression, abdication, severance.—*Ant.* arrival*, entrance, taking up.
2. [The state of being retired]—*Syn.* seclusion, sequestration, aloofness, apartness, separateness, privacy, concealment, solitude, solitariness, isolation, remoteness, loneliness, quiet, retreat, tranquillity, refuge, serenity, inactivity; see also **silence** 1. —*Ant.* exposure*, activity, association.

retiring, *mod.* —*Syn.* quiet, withdrawing, not forward; see **modest** 2, **reserved** 3.

retort, *n.* —*Syn.* counter, repartee, response; see **answer** 1.

retort, *v.* —*Syn.* reply, rejoin, snap back; see **answer** 1.

retouch, *v.* —*Syn.* amend, modify, revise; see **correct** 1.

retrace, *v.* —*Syn.* reinspect, recall, reverse one's steps; see **copy** 2, **follow** 2.

retract, *v.* **1.** [To draw in]—*Syn.* withdraw, draw away, take in; see **remove** 1.
2. [To disavow]—*Syn.* countermand, take back, withdraw; see **recant.**

retraction, *n.* —*Syn.* abjuration, denial, revocation, recantation, disowning, disavowal, recall, withdrawal, annulment, forswearing, unsaying, repudiation, nullification, quashing, abrogation, reversal, rescindment, renouncing, disclaimer, negative, contradiction, abnegation, setting aside, contraversion, gainsaying; *all* (D): backdown, backwater, renege, stand-down; see also **cancellation, denial** 1. —*Ant.* confirmation*, reaffirmation, corroboration.

retreading (D), *n.* —*Syn.* renewing, updating, improving; see **improvement** 1.

retreat, *n.* **1.** [The act of retreating]—*Syn.* retirement, removal, evacuation, departure, escape, withdrawal, drawing back, reversal, retrogression, backing out, flight, recession, retraction, going, running away, eluding, evasion, avoidance, recoil. —*Ant.* advance*, progress, progression.
2. [A place to which one retreats]—*Syn.* seclusion, solitude, privacy, shelter, refuge, asylum, safe place, defense, sanctuary, security, cover, ark, harbor, port, haven, place of concealment, hiding place, hideaway (D), resort, haunt, habitat, hermitage, cell, convent, cloister.—*Ant.* front*, exposed position, van.
beat a retreat—*Syn.* evacuate, abandon, withdraw; see **leave** 1, **retreat** 2.

retreat, *v.* **1.** [To retire]—*Syn.* recede, retrograde, back (out), retract, go, depart, recoil, shrink, quail, run, draw back, reel, start back, reverse, seclude oneself, keep aloof *or* apart, hide, separate from, regress, resign, relinquish, lay down, hand over, sequester oneself, retrocede, withdraw, backtrack, leave, back off *or* down, chicken out (D).—*Ant.* stay*, remain continue.
2. [In battle, to execute a forced retirement] —*Syn.* evacuate, abandon, leave, withdraw, draw *or* back out, vacate the position, retire, remove, pull *or* march out, disengage, turn *or* fall *or* draw *or* break *or* move back, give ground, move behind, beat a retreat, back down *or* out, escape, decamp, fly, be routed, give way, flee (in disorder), execute a strategic withdrawal, shorten one's lines, avoid, evade, elude.—*Ant.* attack*, progress, drive forward.

retrench, *v.* —*Syn.* save, conserve, scrimp; see **economize.**

retrenchment, *n.* **1.** [A reduction]—*Syn.* abatement, decrease, deduction; see **reduction** 1.
2. [Thrift]—*Syn.* curtailing, thriftiness, frugality; see **economy** 2.

retribution, *n.* —*Syn.* requital, reprisal, retaliation; see **revenge** 1.

retrieve, *v.* —*Syn.* regain, bring back, reclaim; see **recover** 1.

retrograde, *mod.* **1.** [Backward]—*Syn.* retrogressive, regressive, recessive; see **backward** 1, **opposite** 3.
2. [Degenerate]—*Syn.* crumbling, decrepit, rotting; see **decaying.**

retrogression, *n.* **1.** [Regression]—*Syn.* retroaction, recession, regression, throwback, backward movement, retirement; see also **retreat** 1.
2. [Deterioration]—*Syn.* decline, degeneration, decadence; see **decay** 1, 2.

retrospect, *n.* —*Syn.* remembering, recollection, review; see **memory** 1.

retrospective, *mod.* —*Syn.* deliberative, absorbed, pensive; see **resolute** 2, **thoughtful** 1.

return, *mod.* —*Syn.* coming back, repeat, repeating, repetitive, recurring, intermittent, reappearing, sent back, answering, replying, retorting, rotating, turning, rebounding, recurrent; see also **repeated** 1.

return, *n.* **1.** [The act of coming again]—*Syn.* restoring, recompensing, entrance, homecoming, revisitation, recovery, arrival, repossession, coming, appearance, occurrence, bounding back, entry, recoiling, rotating; see also **sense** 2.—*Ant.* departure*, exit, going out.
2. [The act of being returned]—*Syn.* restoration, restitution, rejoinder, recompense, acknowledgment, answer, reaction, reversion, repetition, reverberation, reappearance, reoccurrence, rebound, recoil, reconsideration; see also **sense** 1. —*Ant.* departure*, disappearance, taking.
3. [Proceeds]—*Syn.* profit, income, results, gain, avail, revenue, advantage, yield, accrual, accruement, interest.—*Ant.* failure*, loss, disadvantage.
4. [Reports]—*Syn.* account, statements, tabulation; see **records, report.**
in return—*Syn.* in exchange, as payment *or* repayment, for *or* as a reward; see **pay** 1, 2.

return, *v.* **1.** [To go back]—*Syn.* go *or* come again, come back, recur, reappear, reoccur, repeat, revert, reconsider, re-enter, re-examine, reinspect, bounce back up, turn back, retrieve *or* retrace one's steps, turn, rotate, revolve, renew, revive, recover, regain, rebound, circle *or* double *or* move *or* track *or* reel *or* turn *or* come back, reverberate, repercuss, recoil, retrace, hark back to, revisit, retire, retreat.—*Ant.* move*, advance, go forward.
2. [To put *or* send something back]—*Syn.* send *or* bring *or* toss *or* put *or* thrust *or* roll *or* hand *or* give back, restore, replace, restitute, render, reseat, reestablish, reinstate, react, recompense, refund, repay, make restitution.—*Ant.* hold*, keep, hold back.
3. [To answer]—*Syn.* reply, respond, retort; see **answer** 1.

4. [To repay]—*Syn.* reimburse, recompense, refund; see **repay** 1.
5. [To yield a profit]—*Syn.* pay off, show profit, pay dividends; see **pay** 2.
6. [To speak formally]—*Syn.* deliver, pass, state; see **declare** 1.
7. [To reflect]—*Syn.* echo, sound, mirror; see **reflect** 2, 3.

returned, *mod.* —*Syn.* restored, restituted, given *or* gone *or* sent *or* brought *or* turned *or* come back, reappeared, recurred, reoccurred, repeated, reverted, re-entered, rotated, revolved, rebounded, reverberated, refunded, acknowledged, answered, rejoindered, repaid, yielded; see also **refused.** —*Ant.* kept*, held, retained.

returning, *n.* **1.** [The act of coming back]—*Syn.* return, reappearance, repetition, reoccurrence, reoccurring, recurrence, reverberation, reentrance, retracing, revolving, revolution, rotation, rotating, rebound, reversion, retreat, turning back, homecoming.
2. [The act of sending back]—*Syn.* restoring, bringing back, repayment, recompensing, giving back, answering, responding, replying.

reunion, *n.* —*Syn.* reuniting, meeting (again), homecoming, rejoining, reconciliation, reconcilement, restoration, harmonizing, bringing together, healing the breach, get-together (D).

reunite, *v.* —*Syn.* meet (again), reassemble, reconvene, join, rejoin, become reconciled, have a reconciliation, be restored to one another, remarry, heal the breach, get together; *all* (D): patch it up, make up, reheat the ashes, be rewelded.—*Ant.* separate*, go separate ways, be disrupted.

revamp, *v.* —*Syn.* rejuvenate, replenish, recondition; see **reconstruct, renew** 1, **repair.**

reveal, *v.* **1.** [To divulge]—*Syn.* disclose, betray a confidence, make known, confess, impart, publish, lay bare, betray, avow, admit, acknowledge, give utterance to, bring *or* let *or* give *or* open out, make public, unfold, bring to light, communicate, announce, declare, inform, notify, utter, make plain, break the news, unbosom, broadcast, concede, come out with, explain, bring into the open, affirm, report; *all* (D): let the cat out of the bag, blab, talk, rat, stool, make a clean breast of, put one's cards on the table, bring to light, let fall, show one's colors, get (something) out of one's system, give the low-down, squeal, blow the whistle, let on; see also **tell** 1.
2. [To expose]—*Syn.* show, exhibit, unveil; see **expose** 1.

reveille, *n.* —*Syn.* signal, bell, bugle; see **alarm** 1.

revel, *n.* —*Syn.* carousal, frolic, festivity; see **entertainment** 1, 2.

revel, *v.* **1.** [To play]—*Syn.* frolic, carouse, rejoice; see **play** 1.
2. [To indulge oneself]—*Syn.* indulge, delight, enjoy; see **celebrate** 3.

revelation, *n.* **1.** [A disclosure]—*Syn.* discovery, announcement, divulgement, disclosure, betrayal, telling, showing.—*Ant.* secrecy*, hiding, refusal to tell.
2. [The act of revealing divine truth]—*Syn.* prophecy, vision, apocalypse, inspiration, sign, foreshadowing, shadowing forth, adumbration, oracle, divine manifestation; see also **divination.**
3. [Divine truth revealed]—*Syn.* divine word, God's word, apocalypse, cabala; see also **doctrine** 1, **faith** 2.

revelry, *n.* —*Syn.* spree, festivity, festival; see **entertainment** 1, **party** 1.

revenge, *n.* **1.** [The act of returning an injury] —*Syn.* vengeance, requital, reprisal, measure for measure, repayment, counterplay, sortie, counterinsurgency, retaliation, retribution, avenging, avengment, getting even (D); see also **attack** 1, **fight** 1.—*Ant.* pardon*, forgiveness, excusing.
2. [The desire to obtain revenge]—*Syn.* vindictiveness, rancor, implacability, ruthlessness, malevolence, vengefulness, an eye for an eye, return of evil for evil, spitefulness, ill-will, animus; see also **hate, malice.**

revenge, *v.* —*Syn.* retaliate, vindicate, requite, take revenge, have accounts to settle, have one's revenge, breathe vengeance, wreak one's vengeance, pay back *or* off, make reprisal, get even with, punish for, repay (in kind), return (like for like *or* blow for blow), retort, match, reciprocate, square accounts, settle up, pay back in his own coin, take an eye for an eye, turn the tables on, get *or* hit back at, fight back, be out for blood, give an exchange, give and take, give one his deserts, even (up) the score; *all* (D): get, fix, give one his comeuppance, pay off old scores, get square with, score off, give tit for tat, return the compliment, pay back in spades. —*Ant.* forgive*, condone, pardon.

revengeful, *mod.* —*Syn.* spiteful, malevolent, hateful; see **cruel** 1, **vindictive.**

revenue, *n.* **1.** [Income]—*Syn.* return, earnings, result, yield, wealth, receipts, proceeds, resources, funds, stocks, credits, dividends, interest, perquisites, salary, profits, means, fruits, emoluments, annuity, acquirements, rents; see also **income, pay** 1, 2.—*Ant.* expenses*, outgoes, obligations.
2. [Governmental income]—*Syn.* wealth, revenue, taxation; see also **income** 1, **tax** 1.
Types of revenue include the following—direct tax, indirect tax, bonds, loans, customs, duties, tariff, tax surcharge, excise, property tax, income tax, inheritance and death tax, land tax, poll tax, gasoline tax, school tax, franchise, license, grants, rates, bridge and road tolls, harbor dues, countervailing duties, differential duties, special taxation, patent stamps, stamp duties, registration duties, internal revenue, tax on spirits, tobacco tax, revenue on fermented liquors, lease of land, sale of land, subsidy.

reverberate, *v.* —*Syn.* resound, echo, reflect; see **sound** 1.

reverberation, *n.* —*Syn.* vibration, echo, repercussion; see **noise** 1.

revere, *v.* —*Syn.* venerate, regard, respect; see **admire** 1.

reverence, *n.* **1.** [A reverential attitude]—*Syn.* respect, admiration, love, regard, approval, approbation, esteem, obsequiousness, deference, awe, fear, veneration, honor, devotion, adoration; see also **praise** 1.—*Ant.* hatred*, contempt, disdain.
2. [The expression of reverence]—*Syn.* honor, veneration, prostration, genuflection, devotion, obei-

sance, homage, bow, piety, devoutness, religiousness; see also **praise** 2, **worship** 1.—*Ant.* ridicule*, scoffing, mockery.

reverend, *mod.* —*Syn.* revered, respected, venerated; see **divine** 2, **religious** 2.

reverend, *n.* —*Syn.* divine, (ordained) clergy (man), priest; see **minister** 1.

reverent, *mod.* —*Syn.* venerating, esteeming, honoring; see also **respectful.**

reverential, *mod.* —*Syn.* pious, holy, devout; see **religious** 2.

reverie, *n.* —*Syn.* meditation, contemplation, preoccupation; see **thought** 2.

reversal, *n.* —*Syn.* renunciation, repudiation, repeal; see **cancellation, refusal, withdrawal.**

reverse, *n.* **1.** [The opposite]—*Syn.* converse, other side, contrary; see **opposite.**
2. [A defeat]—*Syn.* vanquishment, catastrophe, conquering; see **defeat** 2.

reverse, *v.* **1.** [To turn]—*Syn.* go back, shift, invert; see **turn** 2.
2. [To alter]—*Syn.* turn around, modify, convert; see **change** 1.
3. [To annul]—*Syn.* nullify, invalidate, repeal; see **cancel** 2.
4. [To exchange]—*Syn.* transpose, rearrange, shift; see **exchange** 1.

reversed, *mod.* —*Syn.* turned (around *or* back), backward, end for end, inverted, contrariwise, out of order, everted, inside out, regressive, retrogressive, undone, unmade.—*Ant.* ordered*, established*, in (proper) order.

reversion, *n.* **1.** [Return]—*Syn.* rotation, reaction, reversal; see **return** 2.
2. [A rebirth]—*Syn.* resurrection, restoration, renascence; see **renewal, revival** 1.

revert, *v.* —*Syn.* go back, reverse, recur to; see **return** 1.

reverted, *mod.* —*Syn.* unclaimed, confiscated, seized; see **returned.**

review, *n.* **1.** [A re-examination]—*Syn.* reconsideration, second thought, revision, retrospection, second view, reflection, study, survey, retrospect.
2. [A critical study]—*Syn.* survey, critique, criticism, analysis, commentary, dissertation, study, investigation, discourse, theme, thesis, essay, monograph, critical review, article, treatise, book review, exposition, discussion, inspection, canvass, evaluation, appraisal; see also **examination** 1.
3. [A summary]—*Syn.* synopsis, abstract, outline; see **summary.**
4. [A formal inspection]—*Syn.* parade, inspection, dress parade, drill, march, procession, cavalcade, column, file, military display, march past, the once-over (D); see also **display** 2.

review, *v.* **1.** [To correct]—*Syn.* criticize, revise, re-edit; see **correct** 1.
2. [To inspect]—*Syn.* analyze, re-examine, check thoroughly; see **examine** 1.

reviewed, *mod.* —*Syn.* inspected, examined, reconsidered, studied, surveyed, analyzed, judged, epitomized, abridged, abstracted, outlined, summarized, commented on, criticized; see **considered** 1.

reviewer, *n.* —*Syn.* commentator, analyst, inspector; see **critic** 2.

reviewing, *mod.* —*Syn.* criticizing, inspecting, examining, surveying, studying, analyzing, judging, epitomizing, abridging, abstracting, outlining, summarizing, commenting on.

revile, *v.* —*Syn.* belittle, malign, reproach; see **censure.**

revise, *v.* —*Syn.* reconsider, rewrite, redraft, correct, re-examine, look over, change, rework, improve, amend, develop, compare, scan, scrutinize, overhaul; see also **edit** 1.—*Ant.* discard*, set aside, disregard.

revised, *mod.* —*Syn.* corrected, edited, redacted, revisioned, amended, overhauled, improved, altered, changed, rectified, polished, redone, rewritten, reorganized, restyled, emended.

revision, *n.* —*Syn.* re-examination, revisal, correction, editing, redaction, re-editing, overhauling, amendment, emendation, improvement, alteration, change, reconsideration, review, rectifying, rectification, polish, restyling, rewriting.

revisit, *v.* —*Syn.* visit again, stay, call on; see **visit** 2, 4.

revival, *n.* **1.** [The act of reviving]—*Syn.* renewal, renascence *or* renaissance, refreshment, arousal, awakening, rebirth, reversion, resurrection, enkindling, restoration, invigoration, vivification, resuscitation, reawakening, improvement, freshening, recovery, cheering, consolation.
2. [That which is revived]—*Syn.* life of a past era, customs, manners, crafts, former success, forgotten masterpiece, dated work.
3. [An evangelical service]—*Syn.* meeting, (revival) service, evangelistic meeting; *all* (D): preaching, tent meeting, camp meeting; see also **ceremony.**

revivalist, *n.* —*Syn.* preacher, missionary, evangelist; see **minister** 1.

revive, *v.* **1.** [To give new life]—*Syn.* enliven, enkindle, refresh, renew, vivify, revivify, animate, reanimate, resuscitate, recondition, rejuvenate, bring to *or* around, wake up, resurrect, make whole, exhilarate, energize, invigorate, put *or* breathe new life into, bring to, reproduce, regenerate, restore, touch up, repair.—*Ant.* decrease*, wither, lessen.
2. [To take on new life]—*Syn.* come around, freshen, improve, recover, flourish, awake, reawake, rouse, arouse, strengthen, overcome, come to life, grow well, be cured.—*Ant.* die*, faint, weaken.
3. [To hearten]—*Syn.* cheer, comfort, brighten, encourage, inspirit, solace, console, relieve, divert, gladden, raise the spirits, applaud, soothe, appreciate, please, make joyful, delight, rejoice.

revived, *mod.* —*Syn.* restored, reinstituted, reestablished; see **built** 1, **repaired.**

revocation, *n.* —*Syn.* annulment, repeal, repudiation; see **cancellation.**

revoke, *v.* —*Syn.* forswear, recant, recall, retract, disclaim, abjure, renounce, repudiate, abrogate, disown, dismiss, deny, annul, quash, abolish, rescind, remove, erase, expunge, nullify, void, repeal, obliterate, vacate, wipe out, rub off, countermand, counterorder, eat one's words (D); see also **cancel** 2. —*Ant.* approve*, endorse, ratify.

revolt, *n.* —*Syn.* uprising, mutiny, sedition; see **revolution** 2.

revolt, *v.* **1.** [To rebel]—*Syn.* mutiny, rise up, resist; see **rebel** 1.

2. [To repel]—*Syn.* sicken, offend, nauseate; see **disgust.**

revolting, *mod.* —*Syn.* awful, loathsome, repulsive; see **offensive** 2, **shameful** 1, 2.

revolution, *n.* **1.** [A complete motion about an axis] —*Syn.* rotation, spin, turn, revolving, circuit, round, whirl, gyration, circumvolution, cycle, roll, reel, twirl, swirl, pirouette.

2. [An armed uprising]—*Syn.* revolt, rebellion, mutiny, insurrection, riot, anarchy, outbreak, *coup (d'état)* (French), destruction, overturn, upset, overthrow, reversal, rising, crime, violence, bloodshed, turbulence, insubordination, disturbance, reformation, plot, cabal, underground activity, guerrilla activity, public unrest, upheaval, tumult, disorder, foment, turmoil, uproar, uprising, row, strife, strike, *junta* (Spanish), *Putsch* (German), subversion, breakup, secession, convulsion, throe; see also **change** 2.—*Ant.* law*, order, control.

Important revolutions include the following—Protectorate, 1653, "Glorious Revolution," 1688, England; French Revolution, 1789; Revolutionary War, 1775, United States; Overthrow of the Manchus, 1911, Maoist Communist State, 1949, China; Rise of the German Republic, 1918; Nazi Seizure of Government, 1933, Germany; War of Independence, 1821, Greece; March on Rome of Fascisti, 1920, Italy; Russian Revolution, 1917; Mexican Revolution, 1911; Polish Revolt Against Russia, 1830, Poland; Overthrow of Alphonso XIII, 1931, Spain; Rise of the Young Turks, 1908; Revolt against the Netherlands, 1949, Indonesia; Revolt of the French Indo-Chinese states, 1954.

3. [A reversal]—*Syn.* change, substitution, end of an era, epoch, reconstruction, overturn, upset, overthrow, debacle, revolution in ideas, political upheaval, disintegration, falling apart; see also **sense** 2.

revolutionary, *mod.* **1.** [Concerned with a revolution]—*Syn.* rebellious, revolting, mutinous, insurrectionary, destructive, anarchistic, radical, reformist, subverting, insurgent, overturning, upsetting, destroying, breaking up, convulsive, subversive, seceding, riotous, agitating, disturbing, working underground, working beneath the surface, seditious, seditionary, factious, treasonable. —*Ant.* patriotic*, loyal, constructive.

2. [New and unusual]—*Syn.* novel, advanced, forward; see **different** 1, 2, **unusual** 2.

revolutionary, *n.* —*Syn.* revolutionist, traitor, insurrectionist; see **rebel** 1, **resister.**

revolutionize, *v.* —*Syn.* recast, remodel, refashion; see **change** 1, **reform** 1.

revolve, *v.* —*Syn.* spin, rotate, twirl; see **turn** 1.

revolver, *n.* Types of revolvers include the following—forty-five caliber, forty-four caliber, thirty-eight caliber, thirty-two caliber; *all* (D): Colt, .45, .44, .38, .32, .22, Dewey, pepper pot, blue lightning, six-shooter; see also **gun** 2, **pistol.**

revolving, *mod.* **1.** [Rotating]—*Syn.* turning, spinning, whirling, gyrating, rolling, reeling, twirling, swirling, pirouetting, circulating, encircling.

2. [Capable of rotating]—*Syn.* rotatory, rotary, rotational, rotative, trochilic, whirling, gyral, gyratory, gyrational, vertiginous, vortical, vorticose, circumvolutory, circumgyratory, circumrotary, circumrotatory.

revulsion, *n.* **1.** [A withdrawal]—*Syn.* removal, recoil, repercussion; see **withdrawal.**

2. [Disgust]—*Syn.* dislike, distaste, repugnance; see **objection** 1.

reward, *n.* **1.** [Payment]—*Syn.* compensation, remuneration, recompense; see **pay** 1, 2.

2. [A prize]—*Syn.* premium, bonus, award; see **prize.**

reward, *v.* —*Syn.* compensate, repay, remunerate; see **pay** 1.

rewarded, *mod.* —*Syn.* paid, recompensed, compensated, satisfied, remunerated, requited, given an award, awarded a prize.

rework, *v.* —*Syn.* do over; *both* (D): go back to the drawing board, touch up; see **edit** 1, **redo.**

rewrite, *v.* —*Syn.* recast, write, edit, write a story, fill out, pad, cut; *both* (D): doctor, rehash; see also **revise.**

rhapsody, *n.* —*Syn.* fantasia, improvisation, instrumental; see **composition** 4.

rhetoric, *n.* **1.** [Address]—*Syn.* composition, discourse, oratory; see **speech** 3.

2. [Grandiloquence]—*Syn.* oration, verbosity, elocution; see **wordiness.**

rhetorical, *mod.* —*Syn.* oratorical, bombastic, eloquent; see **verbose.**

rhetorician, *n.* —*Syn.* orator, soliloquist, lecturer; see **speaker** 2.

rheumatism, *n.* —*Syn.* stiff joints, rheumatic fever, inflammation of the joints, painful joints, rheumatoid arthritis; *all* (D): crimps, rheumatiz, screwmatics; see also **disease** 3.

rhyme, *n.* —*Syn.* verse, rhyming verse, vowelchime; see **poetry.**

rhythm, *n.* —*Syn.* swing, accent, rise and fall; see **beat** 2, 3.

rhythmic, *mod.* —*Syn.* melodious, measured, balanced; see **musical** 1, **regular** 3.

rib, *n.* **1.** [One part of the bony frame of the thorax] —*Syn.* true rib, false rib, floating rib; *all* (D): slat, slab, rod, floater, phoney; see also **bone.**

2. [A rod]—*Syn.* girder, bar, strip; see **rod** 1, **support** 2.

3. [A ridge]—*Syn.* fin, nervure, vaulting; see also **sense** 2, **ridge** 1.

ribald, *mod.* —*Syn.* earthy, obscene, lewd, bawdy; lascivious, vulgar, salacious, indecorous, unbecoming, coarse, vile, ungentlemanly, unladylike, foulmouthed, base, spicy, racy, risqué, indecent; *all* (D): dirty, hot, fast, blue, juicy.—*Ant.* refined*, decent, decorous.

ribaldry, *n.* —*Syn.* pornography, smuttiness, obscenity; see **humor** 1, **indecency** 2.

ribbon, *n.* —*Syn.* band, fillet, trimming, decoration, fabric, strip.

rich, *mod.* **1.** [Possessed of wealth]—*Syn.* wealthy, moneyed, affluent, opulent, well-to-do, well provided for; *all* (D): worth a million, well off, well fixed, bloated, gilded, plastered with dough, in clover, swimming in gravy, in the money *or* in funds *or* good case.—*Ant.* poor*, poverty-stricken, destitute.

2. [Sumptuous]—*Syn.* luxurious, magnificent, resplendent, lavish, sumptuous, chic, embellished, ornate, costly, expensive, opulent, deluxe, lavish, fancy, splendid, superb, elegant, gorgeous, valuable, precious, extravagant, grand; *all* (D): posh, plush, classy, ritzy, swank, swanky, snazzy, lush, swell, smart, stylish, high-class, spiffy, sharp, tony, high-toned; see also **beautiful** 1.—*Ant.* cheap*, plain, simple.

3. [Fertile]—*Syn.* exuberant, lush, copious, plentiful, generous, fruitful, profuse, luxuriant, teeming, abundant, prolific, productive, fecund, fruit-bearing, bearing, propagating, yielding, breeding, superabounding, prodigal; see also **fertile** 1.—*Ant.* sterile*, unfruitful, barren.

4. [Having great food value]—*Syn.* nourishing, luscious, sweet, fatty, oily, nutritious, sustaining, strengthening, satisfying; see also **healthful.**—*Ant.* inadequate*, not nourishing, deficient.

5. [Laughable]—*Syn.* absurd, preposterous, ridiculous, funny, amusing, entertaining, queer, odd, strange, diverting, droll, comical, ludicrous, farcical, humorous, incongruous, foolish; *both* (D): slaying, splitting.—*Ant.* reasonable*, intelligent, normal.

rich, *n.* —*Syn.* the wealthy, the well-to-do, capitalists, the haves (D).

riches, *n.* —*Syn.* fortune, possessions, money; see **wealth** 2.

richly, *mod.* —*Syn.* sumptuously, wealthily, opulently; see **largely** 2, **well** 2, 3.

rich man, *n.* —*Syn.* plutocrat, tycoon, capitalist; see **financier, millionaire.**

richness, *n.* **1.** [Abundance]—*Syn.* copiousness, bounty, abundance; see **plenty.**

2. [Harmony]—*Syn.* melodiousness, resonance, sonority; see **harmony** 1.

rickets, *n.* —*Syn.* rachitis, inflammation of the spine, sickness; see **disease** 3.

rickety, *mod.* **1.** [Rachitic]—*Syn.* diseased, affected with rickets, inflamed; see **sick.**

2. [Feeble]—*Syn.* infirm, shakey, fragile; see **weak** 2.

ricochet, *v.* —*Syn.* reflect, rebound, glance off; see **bounce** 1.

rid, *mod.* —*Syn.* relieved, quit, delivered; see **free** 2.

be rid of—*Syn.* be freed, evade, have done with; see **escape.**

get rid of—*Syn.* clear, relieve, shed; see **free** 2.

rid, *v.* —*Syn.* clear, relieve, shed; see **free** 2.

riddance, *n.* —*Syn.* release, liberation, discharge; see **freedom** 2.

riddle, *n.* **1.** [A difficult problem]—*Syn.* problem, question, knotty question, doubt, quandary, entanglement, dilemma, embarrassment, perplexity, enigma, confusion, complication, complexity, intricacy, strait, labyrinth, predicament, plight, distraction, bewilderment; see also **puzzle** 2.—*Ant.* simplicity*, clarity, disentanglement.

2. [An obscure question to be solved for amusement]—*Syn.* mystery, conundrum, puzzle, charade, rebus, maze, enigma, brain twister (D). —*Ant.* answer*, solution, explanation.

ride, *n.* —*Syn.* drive, trip, transportation; see **journey.**

take for a ride (D)—*Syn.* murder, abduct, trick; see **deceive, kill** 1.

ride, *v.* **1.** [To be transported]—*Syn.* be carried, tour, journey, motor, drive, go for an airing, go by automobile *or* train *or* plane, sail, go by boat *or* water; see also **fly** 1, **travel** 1.

2. [To control a beast of burden by riding]—*Syn.* manage, guide, sit well, have a good seat, post, direct, curb, restrain, urge on, handle, handle well, ride hard.

3. [To allow oneself to be dominated by circumstances]—*Syn.* drift, float, go with the current, move aimlessly, be without ambition, take the line of least resistance, go with the tide (D).

4. [(D) To treat with unusual severeity]—*Syn.* domineer over, override, be autocratic, persecute, harass, hound, hector, harry, badger, bait, treat overbearingly, disparage, revile, reproach, berate, upbraid, rate, scold, afflict, annoy, be arbitrary, tyrannize; see also **bother** 2.

5. [To move as a carrier]—*Syn.* perform (well), ride well *or* evenly, remain stable, corner well, hold on the curves, give evidence of good design *or* engineering, hold *or* cling to *or* hug the road, keep an even keel, maintain balance *or* equilibrium.

rider, *n.* **1.** [One who rides]—*Syn.* driver, passenger, motorist, horseman; *all* (D): critter-hopper, broncster, hitchhiker.

2. [An additional clause or provision, usually not connected with the main body of the work] —*Syn.* addition, amendment, addendum, appendix, supplement, adjunct, appendage, codicil.

ridge, *n.* **1.** [A long, straight, raised portion]—*Syn.* rib, seam, rim, backbone, spinal column, ridge pole, parapet.

2. [Land forming a ridge, sense 1]—*Syn.* mountain ridge, range, elevation, hill, moraine, terminal moraine, medial moraine, esker, kame, hogback.

ridged, *mod.* —*Syn.* crinkled, furrowed, ribbed; see **corrugated.**

ridicule, *n.* —*Syn.* scorn, contempt, mockery, disdain, derision, jeer, leer, disparagement, sneer, rally, flout, fleer, twit, taunt, burlesque, caricature, satire, parody, travesty, irony, sarcasm, persiflage, chaff, raillery, badinage, farce, buffoonery, buffoonism, horseplay, foolery; *all* (D): needle, razoo, razz, rib, roast, raspberry, horse laugh.—*Ant.* praise*, commendation, approval.

ridicule, *v.* —*Syn.* gibe *or* scoff *or* sneer *or* laugh *or* rail *or* point *or* grin at, mock, taunt, banter, mimic, jeer, deride, twit, quiz, chaff, disparage, flout, deride, scorn, make sport of, make fun of, fleer, rally, burlesque, caricature, show up, unmask, expose, satirize, parody, cartoon, travesty, run down, make fun of; *all* (D): put down, deflate, send up, takeoff, brush off, guy, rag, raz, rib, cast in one's teeth, give the Bronx cheer, pull one's leg, point the finger of scorn, have a fling at, roast, pan.—*Ant.* encourage, approve*, applaud.

ridiculous, *mod.* —*Syn.* ludicrous, absurd, preposterous; see **funny** 1, **unusual** 2.

ridiculously, *mod.* —*Syn.* foolishly, insanely, stubbornly, absurdly, stupidly, inanely; see also **humorously.**

riding, *mod.* —*Syn.* traveling, astride, mounted, driving, touring, in transit; see also **moving** 1.

riding, *n.* —*Syn.* traveling, journeying, horseback riding; see **journey, travel** 1.

rife, *mod.* **1.** [Widespread]—*Syn.* prevalent, extensive, common; see **widespread.**

2. [Abundant]—*Syn.* plentiful, abounding, profuse; see **plentiful** 1.

riffraff, *n.* —*Syn.* mob, masses, rabble; see **people** 3.

rifle, *n.* Rifles include the following—Albini-Braendlin, Berdan, Berthier, Chassepot, Francini-Martini, Lebel, Martini-Henry, Mannlicher, Schulhof, Sober, Peabody-Martini, Lee-Metford, Remington, Krag-Jorgensen, Sharps, Johnson, Springfield, Winchester, Garrand, Enfield, breech-loading, double-barrelled, repeating, Mauser, high-powered, low-powered, Lee straight-pull, match, Minie, muzzle-loading, rook and rabbit, saloon, Schneider repeating, United States magazine, carbine, M-1, M-14, M-16, automatic, semi-automatic; *both* (D): stick, iron; see also **gun** 2, **machine gun.**

rifleman, *n.* —*Syn.* shooter, sharpshooter, marksman, crack shot, dead shot, huntsman, musketeer, trooper, carabineer, dragoon, shot, sniper; see also **gunner, hunter** 1.

rift, *n.* —*Syn.* opening, split, crack; see **break** 1, **parting** 2.

rig, *n.* —*Syn.* tackle, apparatus, gear; see **equipment.**

rigging, *n.* —*Syn.* gear, apparatus, implements; see **equipment.**

right, *mod.* **1.** [Correct]—*Syn.* true, precise, correct; see **accurate** 1, **valid** 1.

2. [Just]—*Syn.* lawful, legitimate, honest; see **fair** 1.

3. [Suitable]—*Syn.* apt, proper, appropriate; see **fit** 1, 2.

4. [Sane]—*Syn.* reasonable, rational, sound, wise, normal, discerning, discreet, enlightened, circumspect, penetrating, judicious, far-sighted; see also **sane.**—*Ant.* insane*, unreasonable, unsound.

5. [Justly]—*Syn.* fairly, evenly, equitably, honestly, decently, sincerely, legitimately, lawfully, conscientiously, squarely, impartially, objectively, reliably, dispassionately, without bias, without prejudice; see also **justly** 1.

6. [Straight]—*Syn.* directly, undeviatingly, immediately; see **direct** 1.

7. [Opposite to left]—*Syn.* dextral, dexter, right-handed, clockwise, on the right.—*Ant.* left*, sinistral, counterclockwise.

8. [The side intended for show]—*Syn.* outward, outer, top, finished, decorated, ornamented, trimmed, best, in good condition, unworn, best-looking, clean.—*Ant.* inner*, bottom, unfinished.

right, *n.* **1.** [A privilege]—*Syn.* prerogative, immunity, exemption, license, benefit, advantage, favor, franchise, preference, priority, perquisite; see also **freedom** 2.

2. [Justice]—*Syn.* equity, freedom, liberty, independence, emancipation, enfranchisement, self-determination, natural expectation; see also **fairness.**

3. [The conservative element]—*Syn.* reactionaries, conservatives, traditionalists, right wing, Tories, Old Guard, Ku Klux Klan, Republicans, Republican Party; *all* (D): Dixiecrats, John Birchers, the Klan. —*Ant.* radical*, left, liberals.

4. [The part opposite the left]—*Syn.* right hand, dexter, right side, strong side, active side.

by rights—*Syn.* properly, justly, suitably; see **rightly.**

in one's own right—*Syn.* individually, acting as one's own agent, by one's own authority; see **independently.**

in the right—*Syn.* correct, true, accurate; see **valid** 1.

right, *v.* **1.** [To make upright]—*Syn.* set *or* bring *or* put up, make straight, bring around, turn up, put in place, balance; see also **straighten, turn** 2.—*Ant.* upset*, turn upside down, spill.

2. [To repair an injustice]—*Syn.* adjust, correct, repair, restore, vindicate, do justice, recompense, reward; see **fair play, remedy, rectify, mend, amend, set right**; see also **repair.**—*Ant.* wrong*, hurt, harm.

right away, *mod.* —*Syn.* presently, directly, without delay; see **immediately, now, urgently** 1.

righteous, *mod.* **1.** [Virtuous]—*Syn.* just, upright, good, honorable, honest, worthy, exemplary, noble, right-minded, goodhearted, dutiful, trustworthy, equitable, scrupulous, conscientious, ethical, moral, fair, impartial, fairminded, commendable, praiseworthy, guiltless, blameless, sinless, peerless, sterling, matchless, whole-souled, meritorious, deserving, laudable, punctilious, creditable, charitable, philanthropic, philanthropical, having a clear conscience; see also **reliable** 2.—*Ant.* corrupt*, sinful, profligate.

2. [Religiously inclined]—*Syn.* devout, pious, saintly, godly, godlike, angelic, devoted, reverent, reverential, faithful, fervent, strict, rigid, devotional, zealous, spiritual; see also **holy** 1, **religious** 2. —*Ant.* impious*, irreligious, profane.

3. [Conscious of one's own virtue]—*Syn.* self-righteous, hypocritical, self-esteeming; see **egotistic** 2.

righteousness, *n.* **1.** [Justice]—*Syn.* uprightness, nobility, fairness; see **honor** 1.

2. [Devotion to a sinless life]—*Syn.* piety, saintliness, devoutness, devotion, reverence, religiousness, godliness, spirituality, zeal, worship; see also **holiness** 1.—*Ant.* blasphemy*, irreverence, impiety.

rightful, *mod.* —*Syn.* proper, just, honest; see **fair** 1, **legal** 1, **permitted.**

rightfully, *mod.* —*Syn.* lawfully, justly, fairly, properly, truly, equitably, honestly, impartially, fittingly, legitimately, in all conscience, as is fitting, in equity, by right, in reason, dispassionately, objectively, according to his due; *all* (D): fair and square, on the level, by rights; see also **legally** 1.

rightly, *mod.* —*Syn.* uprightly, justly, in reason, in justice, properly, fitly, correctly, appropriately, suitably, exactly, truly; see **accurately, well** 2. —*Ant.* wrongly*, without reason, erroneously.

right track (D), *n.* —*Syn.* right way, good *or* sound method *or* procedure, standard *or* professional approach; see **means** 1, **method** 2, **system** 2, **track** 1.

right-wing, *mod.* —*Syn.* conservative, reactionary, hidebound; see **prejudiced.**

rigid, *mod.* **1.** [Stiff]—*Syn.* unyielding, inflexible, solid; see **firm** 1, **stiff** 1, **unbreakable.**

2. [Strict]—*Syn.* exact, rigorous, fight (D); see **resolute** 2, **severe** 1, 2.
3. [Fixed]—*Syn.* set, unmoving, solid; see **definite** 1, **determined** 1.

rigmarole, *n.* —*Syn.* drivel, red tape, inanity; see **nonsense** 1.

rigor, *n.* —*Syn.* rigidity, stiffness, inflexibility, hardness, sternness, harshness, austerity, severity, strictness, stringency, inexorability, obduracy, exactitude, preciseness, intolerance, obstinacy, freedom from deviation, uncompromisingness, inclemency, tenacity, traditionalism, conventionalism, relentlessness, rigorousness; see also **stubborness.**—*Ant.* peace*, lenity, mildness.

rigorous, *mod.* **1.** [Severe]—*Syn.* harsh, austere, uncompromising; see **severe** 1.
2. [Exact]—*Syn.* precise, meticulous, dogmatic; see **accurate** 1, 2, **definite** 1.

rile, *v.* —*Syn.* irritate, provoke, annoy; see **bother** 2, **disturb** 2.

rim, *n.* —*Syn.* edge, border, verge, brim, lip, brink, top, margin, line, outline, band, ring, strip, brow, curb, ledge, skirt, fringe, hem, limit, confine, end, terminus; see also **side** 2.—*Ant.* center*, middle, interior.

rime, *n.* —*Syn.* snow, sleet, icicle; see **frost** 2, **ice.**

rind, *n.* —*Syn.* peel, hull, shell, surface, coating, crust, bark, cortex, integument; see also **skin.** —*Ant.* inside*, center, interior.

ring, *n.* **1.** [A circle]—*Syn.* circlet, girdle, brim; see **circle** 1, **rim.**
2. [A circlet of metal]—*Syn.* hoop, band, circle; see **bracelet, jewelry.**
Rings include the following—finger, wedding, engagement, graduation, class, guard, signet, organization, umbrella, ankle, nose, key, harness, napkin, bracelet, earring, ear drop.
3. [A close association, often corrupt]—*Syn.* cabal, junta, junto, combine, party, bloc, faction, group, gang, monopoly, cartel, corner, pool, trust, syndicate; *all* (D): racket, gang, push, string; see **organization** 3.
4. [Pugilism]—*Syn.* prize ring, prize fighting, boxing, professional fighting, fist fighting; *all* (D): boxing game, cauliflower industry, fistic frivolity, fight racket; see also **sport** 3.
5. [The area roped for a fight]—*Syn.* arena; *all* (D): ropes, battle box, P. R., square, resin.
6. [A ringing sound]—*Syn.* clank, clangor, jangle; see **noise** 1.
give someone a ring (D)—*Syn.* call (up), phone, speak to *or* with; see **telephone.**
run rings around (D)—*Syn.* excel, overtake, beat; see **surpass.**

ring, *v.* **1.** [To encircle]—*Syn.* circle, rim, surround, encompass, girdle, enclose *or* inclose, move around, loop, gird, belt, confine, hem in.
2. [To cause to sound]—*Syn.* clap, clang, bang, beat, toll, strike, pull, punch, buzz, play, sound the brass (D); see also **sound** 1.
3. [To give forth sound by ringing]—*Syn.* resound, reverberate, peal, chime, tinkle, jingle, jangle, vibrate, chime, clang, tintinnabulate; see also **sound** 1.
4. [To call by ringing]—*Syn.* summon, call out, ring up, buzz for, press the buzzer, give a ring.

ring in, *v.* —*Syn.* start, initiate, open; see **begin** 1.

ringleader (D), *n.* —*Syn.* rabble rouser, demagogue, *agent provocateur* (French); see **leader** 2.

ringlet, *n.* —*Syn.* (lock of) hair, twist, spiral; see **curl, lock** 2.

ring out, *v.* **1.** [To resound]—*Syn.* thunder, boom, reverberate; see **sound** 1.
2. [To stop]—*Syn.* halt, close, shut down; see **stop** 1.

ring the changes (on), *v.* —*Syn.* go over, elaborate (upon), reiterate; see **repeat** 1, 3.

rink, *n.* —*Syn.* ice rink, skating rink, course; see **arena.**

rinse, *v.* —*Syn.* clean, flush, dip (in water); see **soak** 1, **wash** 2.

riot, *n.* —*Syn.* confusion, uproar, tumult; see **disorder** 2, **disturbance** 2, **protest, trouble** 2.
run riot—*Syn.* revolt, riot, fight; see **rebel** 1.

riot, *v.* —*Syn.* revolt, stir up trouble, fight in the streets; see **rebel** 1.

rioter, *n.* **1.** [Rebel]—*Syn.* mutineer, revolutionary, resister; see **agitator, liberal** 2, **radical, rebel** 1.
2. [Sensualist]—*Syn.* pimp, reveler, lech (D); see **lecher.**

riotous, *mod.* **1.** [Wanton]—*Syn.* reveling, roistering, excessive; see **lewd** 1, 2, **vulgar** 1.
2. [Rebellious]—*Syn.* tumultuous, brawling, disorderly; see **rebellious** 2, **unruly.**

rip, *n.* —*Syn.* rent, cleavage, split; see **cut** 2, **tear.**

rip, *v.* —*Syn.* rend, split, cleave, rive, tear, shred; see also **cut** 1.

ripe, *mod.* **1.** [Ready to be harvested]—*Syn.* fully grown, fully developed, ruddy, red, yellow, plump, filled out, matured, ready.—*Ant.* green*, undeveloped, half-grown.
2. [Improved by time and experience]—*Syn.* mellow, wise, sweetened, increased, perfected, matured, aged, experienced, discerning, sagacious, discreet, judicious, informed, learned, versed, skilled, skillful, subtle, enlightened, sound, tolerant, forbearing, understanding, sympathetic, enriched, full; see also **mature** 1.
3. [Ready]—*Syn.* prepared, seasoned, consummate, perfected, finished, usable, fit, conditioned, prime, available, on the mark, completed; see also **ready** 2.—*Ant.* unfit*, unready, unprepared.

ripen, *v.* **1.** [To mature]—*Syn.* grow up, come of age, reach perfection; see **age** 1, **mature** 1.
2. [To grow]—*Syn.* develop, evolve, advance; see **grow** 2.

ripple, *v.* —*Syn.* fret, curl, break; see **wave** 4.

rise, *n.* **1.** [The act of rising]—*Syn.* ascent, mount, climb, soaring, towering, surge, upsurge, lift, upward sweep, ascent stage, reach, going *or* coming *or* pushing up.—*Ant.* fall*, sinking, drop.
2. [An increase]—*Syn.* augmentation, growth, enlargement, multiplication, heightening, intensifying, distention, stacking up, piling up, addition, accession, inflation, acceleration, doubling, advance; see also **increase** 1.—*Ant.* reduction*, decrease, lessening.
3. [Source]—*Syn.* beginning, commencement, start; see **origin** 1.
get a rise out of (D)—*Syn.* tease, provoke, annoy; see **anger** 1.
give rise to—*Syn.* initiate, begin, start; see **cause** 2.

rise, *v.* **1.** [To move upward]—*Syn.* ascend, mount, climb, scale, surmount, soar, tower, rocket, levitate, surge, sweep upward, lift, get *or* bob *or* move *or* push *or* reach *or* come *or* go up, surge, sprout, grow, rear, uprise, blast off, curl upward; see also **fly** 1.—*Ant.* fall*, drop, come down.
2. [To get out of bed]—*Syn.* get up, rise up, wake; see **arise** 1.
3. [To increase]—*Syn.* grow, swell, intensify, mount, enlarge, spread, expand, extend, augment, heighten, enhance, distend, inflate, pile *or* stack up, multiply, accelerate, speed up, add to, wax, advance, raise, double; see also **increase** 1.—*Ant.* decrease*, lessen, contract.
4. [To begin]—*Syn.* spring, emanate, issue; see **begin** 2.
5. [To improve one's station]—*Syn.* prosper, flourish, thrive, succeed, advance, progress, be promoted, be elevated, be lifted up, better oneself, rise in the world; see also **improve** 1.—*Ant.* fail*, go down in the world, deteriorate.
6. [To stand]—*Syn.* be erected, be built, be placed, be located, be put up, go up, uprise, be founded, have foundation, be situated; see also **stand** 1.
7. [To swell; *said usually of dough or batter*] —*Syn.* inflate, billow, bulge; see **swell.**

rising, *mod.* —*Syn.* climbing, ascending, going *or* moving *or* surging *or* spiraling *or* swinging *or* slanting *or* inclining up *or* aloft, mounting, accelerating, attaining *or* gaining height *or* altitude, on the rise, in ascension, upgoing, upcoming, upsurging, upswinging, scandent, levitating; *all* (D): going upstairs, topping out, heading for the stars; see also **growing, increasing** 1, 2.

rising, *n.* —*Syn.* climbing, ascension, gaining altitude; see **increase** 1.

risk, *n.* **1.** [Danger]—*Syn.* hazard, peril, jeopardy; see **danger** 1.
2. [The basis of a chance]—*Syn.* good risk, gamble, fortuity, contingency, opportunity, prospect; see also **chance** 1, **uncertainty** 3.
run a risk—*Syn.* take a chance, gamble, venture; see **risk.**

risk, *v.* —*Syn.* gamble (on), hazard, venture, run the risk *or* chance *or* hazard, do at one's own peril; *all* (D): hang by a thread, play with fire, carry too much sail, go out of one's depth, be caught short, beard the lion (in his den), bell the cat, double the blind, fall to one's lot, make an investment, take the liberty, lay oneself open to, reckon without one's host, sit on a barrel of gun powder, pour money into, go through fire and water, leave to luck, expose oneself, leap before one looks, fish in troubled waters, skate on thin ice, defy danger, live in a glass house, go to sea in a sieve, sail too near the wind, buck the tiger.

risky, *mod.* —*Syn.* perilous, precarious, hazardous; see **dangerous** 1, **endangered, unsafe.**

risqué, *mod.* —*Syn.* indecent, erotic, ribald, indelicate, salty, earthy, blue, spicy, suggestive, lewd, sophisticated, smart, naughty, with a *double-entendre* (French) *or* double meaning, not a parlor story, not for mixed company, not for the ladies, not for Sunday school, like the *Decameron,* provocative, improper, offensive, indiscreet, salacious, immoral, amoral, bawdy; *all* (D): sexy, racy, dirty, naughty, smutty, off-color, shady, juicy, hot, breezy, blue, sizzling, choice, raw, strong, warm; see also **wanton** 1.—*Ant.* respectable*, decorous, modest.

rite, *n.* —*Syn.* observance, service, ritual; see **ceremony** 2, **custom** 2, **sacrament.**

ritual, *n.* —*Syn.* observance, rite, act; see **ceremony** 2, **custom** 2.

ritualistic, *mod.* —*Syn.* formal, reverent, ceremonial; see **conventional** 3.

ritzy (D), *mod.* —*Syn.* elegant, luxurious, stylish; see **rich** 2.

rival, *mod.* —*Syn.* competing, striving, combatant, combating, emulating, vying, opposing, disputing, contesting, contending, conflicting, battling, equal. —*Ant.* helpful*, aiding, assisting.

rival, *n.* —*Syn.* emulator, competitor, antagonist; see **contestant, opponent** 1.

rival, *v.* —*Syn.* equal, emulate, match, compare with, even off, approximate, near, come near to, approach, resemble, contend with, compete. —*Ant.* co-operate*, aid, be unequal.

rivalry, *n.* —*Syn.* competition, emulation, striving, contest, vying, struggle, battle, contention, opposition, dispute; see also **fight** 1.—*Ant.* co-operation*, combination, conspiracy.

river, *n.* **1.** [Flowing water]—*Syn.* stream, flow, course, current, tributary, rivulet, river system, creek, brook, watercourse.
Famous rivers include the following—Seine, Rhône, Loire, Thames, Severn, Avon, Clyde, Danube, Rhine, Elbe, Don, Volga, Yenisei, Dnieper, Vistula, Nile, Euphrates, Tigris, Ganges, Indus, Irrawaddy, Yellow, Yangste-Kiang, Congo, Zambesi, St. Lawrence, Saskatchewan, Mississippi, Missouri, Ohio, Platte, Delaware, Columbia, Gila, Colorado, Snake, Hudson, Rio Grande, Amazon, Orinoco, La Plata, Murray.
2. [Anything likened to a river, sense 1]—*Syn.* wave, swell, outpouring; see **flood.**
sell down the river (D)—*Syn.* betray, abuse, cheat; see **deceive.**
up the river (D)—*Syn.* imprisoned, jailed, in jail; see **confined** 3.

rivet, *v.* —*Syn.* nail, affix, fix; see **fasten** 1.

rivulet, *n.* —*Syn.* brook, stream, creek; see **river** 1.

roach, *n.* **1.** [An insect]—*Syn.* cockroach, bug, beetle; see **insect.**
2. [(D) The butt end of a marijuana cigarette] —*Syn. all* (D): joint, butt, last hit; see **marijuana.**

road, *n.* **1.** [A strip prepared for travel]—*Syn.* path, way, highway, roadway, street, avenue, thoroughfare, boulevard, highroad, drive, terrace, parkway, byway, lane, alley, alleyway, crossroad, viaduct, subway, overhead way, paving, slab, towpath, throughway, thruway, freeway, expressway, turnpike, trace, trackway, trail, post road, post way, secondary road, market road, national highway, state highway, county road, military road, Roman road, *Autobahn* (German), freeway; *all* (D): drag, big road, main drag.
Types of roads include the following—macadam, Tarvia (trademark), asphalt, concrete, brick, (oiled) gravel, graded earth, wood block, cobblestone, clay and sand, graded and drained, corduroy.
2. [A course]—*Syn.* scheme, way, plans; see **plan** 2.

3. [(D) A railroad]—*Syn.* railway, route, line; see **railroad.**
on the road—*Syn.* on tour, traveling, on the way; see **en route.**
one for the road (D)—*Syn.* cocktail, nightcap, toast; see **drink** 2.
take to the road—*Syn.* go, get underway, set out; see **leave, travel** 2.

roadbed, *n.* —*Syn.* crushed rock, gravel, ballast; see **foundation** 2.

roam, *v.* **1.** [To wander]—*Syn.* ramble, range, stroll, rove, walk, traverse, stray, straggle, meander, prowl, tramp, saunter, peregrinate, knock *or* bat around, scour, straggle, gallivant, struggle along; *both* (D): traipse, hike; see also **travel** 2.
2. [To frequent]—*Syn.* resort to, go to, visit often, be often in, be at home in, be habitually in; see also **frequent, visit** 4.

roar, *n.* —*Syn.* bellow, shout, boom, thunder, howl, bay, bawl, yell, bluster, uproar, din, clamor, clash, detonation, explosion, barrage, reverberation, rumble; see also **cry** 1, 2, **noise** 1.—*Ant.* silence*, whisper, sigh.

roar, *v.* —*Syn.* bellow, shout, boom, thunder, howl, bay, bawl, yell, clamor, rumble, drum, detonate, explode, reverberate, resound, re-echo; see also **cry** 3, **sound** 1.

roast, *n.* Roasts include the following—shoulder, breast, rib, cross rib, rump, chuck, brisket, crown, leg of lamb, beef, pork, lamb, veal; see also **meat.**

roast, *v.* —*Syn.* toast, broil, barbecue; see **cook.**

rob, *v.* —*Syn.* thieve, take, burglarize, strip, plunder, deprive of, withhold from, defraud, cheat, swindle, pilfer, break into, hold up, stick up, purloin, filch, lift, abscond with, embezzle, defalcate, peculate, despoil, pillage, sack, loot; *all* (D): snitch, pinch, push *or* knock over, swipe, cop; see also **steal.**

robber, *n.* —*Syn.* thief, cheat, despoiler, plunderer, pillager, brigand, bandit, freebooter, pirate, marauder, shanghaier, raider, forager, thug, desperado, forger, hold-up man, second-story man, corsair, privateer, buccaneer, swindler, highwayman, bank robber, mosstrooper, pilferer, shoplifter, cattle-thief, housebreaker, burglar, pickpocket, cutpurse, pickpurse, thimblerigger, cardsharper, sharper, safe-cracker; *all* (D): fence, grafter, rustler, crook, cat bandit, con man, cracksman, blaster, clip artist, come-on, chiseler, paper hanger, swagman, stick-up man; see also **criminal, rascal.**

robbery, *n.* —*Syn.* burglary, larceny, thievery; see **crime** 2.

robe, *n.* —*Syn.* gown, dress, garment, costume, mantle, draperies, covering, cape, dressing gown, bathrobe, negligee, tea gown, *robe-de-chambre* (French), kimono, house gown; see also **clothes.**

robot, *n.* **1.** [A mechanical man]—*Syn.* automaton, android, Frankenstein, mechanical monster, humanoid, thinking machine.
2. [A person who resembles a machine]—*Syn.* slave, menial, scullion; see **drudge, laborer.**

robust, *mod.* **1.** [Healthy]—*Syn.* hale, hearty, sound; see **healthy** 1.
2. [Strong]—*Syn.* sturdy, muscular, hardy; see **strong** 1.

rock, *n.* **1.** [A solidified form of earth]—*Syn.* stone, mineral mass, dike, mineral body, earth crust; see also **metal, mineral, ore.**
Rocks include the following—igneous, sedimentary *or* stratified, metamorphic; concretion, gypsum, alabaster, limestone, freestone, sandstone, conglomerate, marble, dolomite; chalk, soapstone, slate, shale, granite, lava, pumice, basalt, quartz, obsidian, porphyry, rhyolite, ironstone, gneiss, tufa, schist.
2. [A piece of rock, sense 1]—*Syn.* stone, boulder, cobblestone, pebble, fieldstone, cliff, crag, promontory, scarp, escarpment, reef, chip, flake, sliver, building stone, paving block, slab.
3. [Anything firm or solid]—*Syn.* defense, support, Rock of Gibralter; see **foundation** 2.
4. [(D) Lively dance music]—*Syn.* rock and roll, popular *or* modern *or* teenage dance, rhythm and blues (D); see **dance** 1, **music** 1.
on the rocks (D) **1.** —*Syn.* bankrupt, poverty-stricken, impoverished; see **poor** 1, **ruined** 4. **2.** over ice cubes, undiluted, straight; see **strong** 8.

rock, *v.* —*Syn.* sway, vibrate, reel, totter, swing, move, push and pull, agitate, roll, shake, shove, jolt, jiggle, quake, convulse, tremble, undulate, oscillate, quiver, quaver, wobble; see also **wave** 3.

rock-bottom, *mod.* —*Syn.* scant, inferior, insufficient; see **poor** 2.

rocket, *n.* —*Syn.* projectile, missile, retrorocket, flying missile; see also **spacecraft.**
Kinds of rockets include the following—intercosmic, air-to-air, air-to-ground (ATG), ground-to-air (GTA), barrage rocket, high velocity aircraft rocket (HVAR), ship-to-shore (STS), ship-to-ship, air-to-air, surface-to-air, lunar excursion module (LEM).

rocket, *v.* —*Syn.* fly, climb, shoot upward, upshoot, skyrocket, ascend, soar, spring up.

rocking chair, *n.* —*Syn.* easy chair, arm chair, rocker, Boston rocker, swing rocket, platform rocker; see also **chair** 1, **furniture, seat** 1.

rocky, *mod.* —*Syn.* stony, flinty, hard, inflexible, solid, petrified, pitiless, obdurate, ragged, jagged, rugged; see also **stone.**—*Ant.* soft*, plastic, flexible.

rococo, *mod.* —*Syn.* extravagant, gaudy, garish; see **ornate** 1.

rod, *n.* **1.** [A rodlike body]—*Syn.* staff, bar, pole, wand, stave, baton, spike, pin, rodule, cylinder, bacillus, bacillary *or* bacilliform *or* bacillar *or* bacillian body, cylindrical object, rodlet, scepter, twig, switch, whip, stock, stalk, trunk; see also **stick.**
2. [A fishing rod]—*Syn.* pole, bamboo, rod and reel, tackle.
Fishing rods include the following—steel, jointed, bamboo, willow, bait, trolling, casting *or* fly, trout, salmon, bass, deep-sea, tarpon, swordfish.

rodent, *n.* Common varieties of rodents include the following—rat, mouse, squirrel, chipmunk, beaver, porcupine, rabbit, muskrat, prairie dog, gopher, marmot, ground hog, woodchuck, spermophile, ground squirrel, chinchilla, capybara, vole, mole, hare, pika, little chief hare, paca, agouti, guinea pig.

rodeo, *n.* —*Syn.* riding unbroken horses, rounding up cattle, roundup, features of a roundup.
Some rodeo events include the following—broncobusting, bulldogging, closed event, re-riding, calf-roping, cutting (out steers).

rodomontade, *n.*—*Syn.* pretension, grandiloquence, exaggeration; see **pretense** 1, 2.

rogue, *n.*—*Syn.* outlaw, problem, miscreant; see **criminal, rascal.**

roguery, *n.*—*Syn.* betrayal, villainy, fraud; see **deception** 1, **dishonesty.**

roguish, *mod.* **1.** [Dishonest]—*Syn.* unscrupulous, sly, corrupt; see **dishonest** 1, **false** 1.
2. [Mischievous]—*Syn.* gay, playful, witty; see **jaunty.**

roil, *v.*—*Syn.* irritate, aggravate, annoy; see **bother** 2, 3.

roily, *mod.*—*Syn.* murky, filthy, mucky; see **dirty** 1, **muddy** 1.

role, *n.*—*Syn.* function, task, part, character, title role, impersonation, leading man, leading woman, hero, heroine, ingenue, performance, presentation, acting, characterization, execution.

roll, *n.* **1.** [The act of rolling]—*Syn.* turn, turning over, revolution, rotation, wheeling, trundling, whirl, gyration.
2. [A relatively flat object rolled upon itself]—*Syn.* scroll, volute, spiral, coil, whorl, convolution, cartouche, fold, shell, cone, cornucopia.
3. [A long, heavy sound]—*Syn.* thunder, roar, drumbeat; see **noise** 1.
4. [A small, fine bread] Types of rolls include the following—Parker House, potato, butter, finger, cinnamon, sweet, crescent, croissant, French, clover-leaf, poppy-seed, dinner, bagel, hot cross bun; see also **bread** 1, **pastry.**
5. [A list]—*Syn.* register, table, schedule; see **catalogue** 1, **index** 2, **list, record** 2.
strike from the rolls—*Syn.* expel, reject, cast-out; see **oust.**

roll, *v.* **1.** [To move by rotation, or in rotating numbers]—*Syn.* rotate, come around, swing around, wheel, come in turn, circle, alternate, follow, succeed, be in sequence, follow in due course; see also **sense** 3, **move** 1, **turn** 1.
2. [To cause to roll, sense 1]—*Syn.* drive, push, impel, propel, twirl, trundle.—*Ant.* stop*, let be, put down.
3. [To revolve]—*Syn.* turn (over), pivot, wind, spin, spiral, reel, gyre, whirl, twirl, swirl, swivel, eddy, pirouette; see also **sense** 1.
4. [To make into a roll]—*Syn.* twist, fold, curve, bend, arch, bow, coil, spiral.—*Ant.* spread*, stretch, flatten.
5. [To smooth with a roller]—*Syn.* press, level, flatten, spread, pulverize, grind.—*Ant.* cut*, roughen, toss up.
6. [To flow]—*Syn.* undulate, run, wave, surge, glide, billow; see also **flow** 1.
7. [To produce a relatively deep, continuous sound]—*Syn.* ruffle, drum, reverberate, cannonade, resound, echo, thunder; see also **roar, sound** 1.
8. [To travel]—*Syn.* journey, drive, make time; see **travel** 2.
9. [To function]—*Syn.* work, go, start production; see **operate** 2.

rolled, *mod.* **1.** [Made into a roll]—*Syn.* twisted, folded, curved, bent, bowed, coiled, spiraled, arched, voluted, convoluted.—*Ant.* spread*, unrolled, opened out.
2. [Flattened]—*Syn.* pressed, leveled, evened; see **flat** 1.

roller, *n.*—*Syn.* billow, breaker, surge; see **wave** 1.

rollick, *v.*—*Syn.* sport, revel, celebrate; see **play** 2.

rollicking, *mod.*—*Syn.* jovial, sportive, playful; see **jaunty.**

roll in (D), *v.* **1.** [To arrive]—*Syn.* enter, land, disembark; see **arrive** 1.
2. [To accumulate]—*Syn.* mass, collect, assemble; see **accumulate** 1.

roll off, *v.*—*Syn.* depart, start, go; see **leave** 1.

roll out, *v.*—*Syn.* start, initiate, provide; see **begin** 1.

Roman, *mod.* **1.** [Referring to the culture centered at Rome]—*Syn.* Latin, classic, classical, late classic, Augustan, ancient, Italic.
2. [Referring to the city of Rome]—*Syn.* imperial, papal, eternal; see **ancient** 2, **classical** 2.

romance, *n.* **1.** [Experiences that excite the imagination]—*Syn.* fancy, fantasy, the picturesque, idealization, poetic event, adventure, risk, hazard, daring enterprise, bold venture.
2. [A courtship]—*Syn.* enchantment, passion, fascination; see **love** 1.
3. [A tale of love and adventure]—*Syn.* ballad, lyric tale, metrical romance, Arthurian romance, *chanson de geste* (French), picaresque tale, adventure story, tale of heroes, romantic novel, novel, fiction, romaunt, *romanza* (Italian); see also **story.**

romantic, *mod.* **1.** [Referring to love and adventure]—*Syn.* adventurous, novel, daring, charming, enchanting, idyllic, lyric, poetic, fanciful, chivalrous, courtly, knightly.
2. [Referring to languages descending from Latin; *often capital*]—*Syn.* romantic, romance, Mediterranean, Italic, Latinic, Provençal, Catalan, Ladin *or* Rhaeto-Romanic *or* Romansh, Ladino *or* Judezmo, Andalusian, Aragonese, Castilian.
3. [Referring to the Romantic Movement; *often capital*]—*Syn.* Rousseauistic, Byronic, Wordsworthian, *Sturm und Drang* (German).

romanticist, *n.*—*Syn.* romantic, utopist, sentimentalist; see **author** 2, **idealist.**

Rome, *n.* **1.** [Leading city in the Italian peninsula]—*Syn.* city of the Caesars, the Eternal City, city on seven hills, imperial city.
2. [The Catholic Church]—*Syn.* the Vatican, Catholicism, the Pope, Holy See, Mother Church; see also **church** 3.

Romeo, *n.*—*Syn.* Sir Galahad, lecher, wolf (D); see **lover** 1.

romp, *n.*—*Syn.* gambol, caper, frisk, leap, dance, skip, hop, frolic, rollick, disport, sport, cavort; see also **play** 2.

romp, *v.*—*Syn.* gambol, celebrate, frolic; see **play** 1, 2.

rompers, *n.*—*Syn.* jumpers, play suit, overalls; see **pants** 1.

roof, *n.*—*Syn.* cover, shelter, tent, house, habitation, home.
Roofs include the following—gable, gambrel, jerkinhead, hip, break, mansard, French, pyramidal, flat, dormer-windowed, penthouse; see also **roofing.**

roofing, *n.* Varieties of roofing include the following—felt, composition, roll roofing, shingles, wood shingles, composition shingles, asbestos, slate shingles, tile, asphalt, shake, copper, galvanized iron, thatch, sod.

rook, *v.* —*Syn.* trick, swindle, cheat; see **deceive.**

rookery, *n.* —*Syn.* mating ground, sea bird breeding place, seal breeding place, colony; see also **home** 1, 3.

room, *n.* **1.** [Space]—*Syn.* vastness, reach, sweep; see **extent.**

2. [An enclosure]—*Syn.* chamber, apartment, cabin, cubicle, cubiculum, niche, vault; see also **dining room** 2, **porch.**

Rooms include the following—living, sitting, drawing, reception, bed, music, play, game, bath, guest, family, furnace, waiting, boudoir, cupboard, foyer, vestibule, study, library, den, kitchen, hall, master bedroom, parlor, wardrobe, closet, press, scullery, pantry, basement, utility, laundry, cellar, attic, garret, anteroom, dormitory, alcove, ward, nacelle, barrack, office, breakfast nook, nursery, studio, schoolroom, loft.

3. [The possibility of admission]—*Syn.* opening, place, resignation; see **vacancy** 2.

4. [A rented sleeping room]—*Syn.* lodging room, chambers, quarters, lodgings, one-room apartment, bed-sitting room (British), efficiency apartment, studio; *all* (D): bachelor apartment, flat, diggings, digs, pad; see also **apartment, bedroom.**

roomer, *n.* —*Syn.* lodger, occupant, dweller, paying guest; see also **renter, tenant.**

rooming house, *n.* —*Syn.* lodging house, boardinghouse, family hotel, hotel, quarters, chambers; *all* (D): diggings, digs, bunkhouse; see also **apartment house, home** 1.

roommate, *n.* —*Syn.* chum, comrade, bed-fellow, tentmate; *all* (D): roomie *or* roomy, bachy, bunky; see also **friend** 1.

roomy, *mod.* —*Syn.* spacious, extensive, ample; see **large** 1.

roost, *n.* —*Syn.* perch, resting place, lighting place, landing place.

rooster, *n.* —*Syn.* cock, chanticleer, cockalorum; see **chicken** 1.

root, *n.* **1.** [An underground portion of a plant] Types of roots include the following—conical, napiform, fusiform, fibrous, moniliform, nodulose, tuberous, adventitious, prop, aerial, tap.

2. [The cause or basis]—*Syn.* source, reason, motive; see **origin** 2, 3.

take root—*Syn.* begin growing, start, commence; see **grow** 3.

rooted, *mod.* —*Syn.* grounded, based (on), fixed (in); see **firm** 1.

rope, *n.* —*Syn.* cord, cordage, braiding, string, thread, strand, tape, cord, lace.

Kinds of rope include the following—ratline, shroud, halyard, lanyard, stay, brace, rope ladder, painter, cable, hawser, halter, lariat, lasso.

at the end of one's rope—*Syn.* desperate, despairing, in despair; see **extreme** 2, **hopeless** 2.

give someone enough rope (D)—*Syn.* permit, give freedom, concede; see **allow** 1.

know the ropes (D)—*Syn.* be experienced, comprehend, understand; see **know** 1.

on the ropes (D)—*Syn.* near collapse, close to ruin, in danger; see **endangered.**

roped, *mod.* —*Syn.* tied, fast, fastened; see **firm** 1.

ropedancer, *n.* —*Syn.* entertainer, circus entertainer, tightrope walker; see **athlete.**

roped off, *mod.* —*Syn.* segregated, private, restricted; see **marked** 1, **reserved** 2.

ropy, *mod.* —*Syn.* gelatinous, mucous, stringy; see **adhesive, fibrous.**

rosary, *n.* —*Syn.* prayers, beads, series of prayers, string of beads.

rose, *mod.* —*Syn.* rose-colored, rosy, dawn-tinted, flushed; see also **pink, red.**

rose, *n.* Classes of roses include the following—wild, tea, climbing tea, hybrid tea, hybrid perpetual, rugosa, hybrid rugosa, polyantha, sweet briar, shrub, multiflora, floribunda, chinensis, noisette, musk, cabbage, cinnamon, eglantine, rambler; see also **flower** 2.

Varieties of roses include the following—Jacqueminot *or* jack (D), American Beauty, Rubrifolia, Crimson Glory, Etoile de Hollande, Duquesa de Penaranda, President Hoover, Talisman, Condesa de Sastago, Santa Anita, Mlle. Cecile Brunner, Grand Duchess Charlotte, Heart's Desire, Kaiserin Auguste Viktoria, Christopher Stone, McGredy's Yellow, McGredy's Ivory, Rouge Mallerin, Mrs. Pierre Dupont, Frau Karl Druschki, Soeur Therese, Golden Dawn, King Midas, Betty Prior, Pink Aachen, White Aachen.

roseate, *mod.* —*Syn.* cherry, blushing, rosy; see **pink, red.**

roster, *n.* —*Syn.* names, subscribers, program; see **catalogue** 1, **list, index** 2, **record** 2, **register** 1.

rostrum, *n.* —*Syn.* desk, platform, pulpit; see **furniture, lectern.**

rosy, *mod.* **1.** [Rose-colored]—*Syn.* colored, deep pink, pale cardinal; see **pink, red.**

2. [Promising]—*Syn.* pleasing, alluring, optimistic, bright, favorable, cheerful, glowing; see also **hopeful** 2.

rot, *interj.* —*Syn.* humbug, nonsense, tush, twaddle, bosh (D).

rot, *n.* **1.** [The process of rotting]—*Syn.* decomposition, corruption, disintegration; see **decay** 1, 2.

2. [Nonsense]—*Syn.* trash, silliness, foolishness; see **nonsense** 1.

rot, *v.* —*Syn.* spoil, disintegrate, decompose; see **decay.**

rotary, *mod.* —*Syn.* rotating, whirling, encircling; see **revolving** 2, **turning.**

rotate, *v.* —*Syn.* twist, wheel, revolve; see **move** 1, **turn** 1.

rotation, *n.* —*Syn.* turn, circumrotation, circle; see **revolution** 1.

rote, *n.* —*Syn.* learning, routine, memorization; see **memory** 1, **repetition.**

rotten, *mod.* **1.** [Having rotted]—*Syn.* bad, rotting, putrifying, decaying, putrescent, putrified, spoiled, decomposed, decayed, offensive, disgusting, rancid, fecal, feculent, purulent, pustular, rank, foul, corrupt, polluted, infected, loathsome, over-ripe, bad-smelling, putrid, crumbled, disintegrated, stale, noisome, smelling, fetid, mephitic, noxious. —*Ant.* fresh*, unspoiled, good.

2. [Not sound]—*Syn.* unsound, defective, diseased, marred, impaired, bruised, injured, shaky, tottering, deteriorated, wasted, withering; see also **weak** 2.—*Ant.* strong*, sound, healthy.

3. [Corrupt]—*Syn.* vitiated, contaminated, polluted, filthy, tainted, defiled, impure, sullied, unclean, soiled, debauched, blemished, morbid, infected, dirtied, befouled, depraved, tarnished; see also **dirty** 1.—*Ant.* pure*, clean, healthy.

rotting, *mod.* —*Syn.* crumbling, breaking up, wasting away; see **decaying, rotten** 1, 3.

rotund, *mod.* **1.** [Round]—*Syn.* circular, spherical, globular; see **round** 1.

2. [Fluent]—*Syn.* resounding, vibrant, resonant; see **loud** 1.

rotunda, *n.* —*Syn.* arcade, cupola, dome; see **building** 1.

roué, *n.* —*Syn.* sensualist, playboy, reprobate; see **lecher.**

rouge, *n.* —*Syn.* red, reddener, dye, paint, cathamus red, carmine, eosin; *all* (D): war paint, blusher, drugstore complexion; see also **cosmetic, make-up** 1.

rough, *mod.* **1.** [Not smooth]—*Syn.* unequal, broken, coarse, choppy, ruffled, uneven, ridged, rugged, scabrous, irregular; needing sanding *or* finishing *or* smoothing, etc.; not sanded *or* smoothed *or* finished, etc.; unfinished, not completed, lacking *or* needing the finishing touches, bumpy, rocky, stony, jagged, grinding, knobby, sharpening, cutting, sharp, crinkled, crumpled, rumpled, scraggly, scraggy, hairy, shaggy, hirsute, bushy, tufted, bearded, woolly, nappy, unshaven, unshorn, gnarled, knotty, nodose, bristly.—*Ant.* level*, flat, even.

2. [Not gentle]—*Syn.* harsh, strict, stern; see **severe** 2.

3. [Crude]—*Syn.* boorish, uncivil, uncultivated; see **rude** 1.

4. [Not quiet]—*Syn.* buffeting, stormy, tumultuous; see **turbulent.**

5. [Unfinished]—*Syn.* incomplete, imperfect, uncompleted; see **unfinished** 1.

6. [Approximate]—*Syn.* inexact, unprecise, uncertain; see **approximate** 3.

rough, *n.* **1.** [A rowdy person]—*Syn.* roisterer, brawler, hooligan, yegg (D), tough, thug; see also **rascal.**—*Ant.* gentleman*, respectable citizen, good guy (D).

2. [Any roughness]—*Syn.* unevenness, irregularity, bumpiness; see **roughness** 1.

3. [In golf, any unkempt part of the course] —*Syn.* grass, weeds, brush, stoniness, off the fairway; *both* (D): fog, jungle.

in the rough—*Syn.* unfinished, unrefined, rough; see **crude** 1.

rough draft, *n.* —*Syn.* outline, blueprint, first draft; see **plan** 1.

roughhouse, *n.* —*Syn.* roughness, rowdiness, barbarity; see **violence** 1.

roughly, *mod.* **1.** [Approximately]—*Syn.* about, in round numbers, by guess; see **approximately.**

2. [In a brutal manner]—*Syn.* coarsely, cruelly, inhumanly; see **brutally.**

3. [In an uneven manner]—*Syn.* irregularly, bumpily, stumblingly; see **unevenly.**

roughness, *n.* **1.** [The quality of being rough on the surface]—*Syn.* unevenness, coarseness, brokenness, bumpiness, break, crack, (ragged) edge, scarification, irregularity, scratch, nick, raggedness, jaggedness, crinkledness, wrinkledness, shagginess, bushiness, beardedness, hairiness, bristling, wooliness; see also **hole** 2.—*Ant.* regularity*, smoothness, evenness.

2. [The quality of being rough in conduct]—*Syn.* harshness, severity, hardness, rudeness, brusqueness, incivility, crudity.—*Ant.* kindness*, gentility, courtesy.

round, *mod.* **1.** [Having the shape of a globe] —*Syn.* spherical, spheroid, globular, orbed, orbicular, orbiculate, globe-shaped, globose, ball-shaped, domical.

2. [Having the shape of a disk]—*Syn.* circular, cylindrical, ringed, annular, oval, disk-shaped.

3. [Curved]—*Syn.* arched, arced, rounded, bowed, looped, whorled, recurved, incurved, coiled, curled.

4. [Approximate]—*Syn.* rough, in tens, in hundreds; see **approximate** 3.

5. [Large]—*Syn.* liberal, generous, expansive, extensive; see also **large** 1.

6. [Complete]—*Syn.* rounded, done, accomplished; see **finished** 1.

7. [Around]—*Syn.* about, near, in the neighborhood of, close to; see also **almost, approximately.**

round, *n.* **1.** [A round object]—*Syn.* ring, orb, globe; see **circle** 1, **rim.**

2. [A period of action]—*Syn.* bout, course, whirl, cycle, circuit, routine, performance; see also **sequence** 1, **series.**

3. [A unit of ammunition]—*Syn.* cartridge, charge, load; see **bullet, ammunition, shell** 2, **shot** 2.

4. [A rung]—*Syn.* rundle, crosspiece, step, stair, tread; see also **ladder, rung.**

go the round—*Syn.* go about, go full course, complete; see **achieve** 1, **circulate** 1.

round, *v.* **1.** [To turn]—*Syn.* whirl, wheel, spin; see **turn** 1.

2. [To make round]—*Syn.* curve, convolute, bow, arch, bend, loop, whorl, shape, form, recurve, coil, fill out, curl, mold.—*Ant.* straighten*, flatten, level.

roundabout, *mod.* **1.** [Indirect]—*Syn.* circuitous, devious, deviating; see **indirect.**

2. [Surrounding]—*Syn.* encompassing, encircling, peripheral; see **outer, outside.**

rounder (D), *n.* —*Syn.* carouser, felon, vagrant; see **drunkard.**

roundly, *mod.* —*Syn.* thoroughly, soundly, wholly; see **completely.**

roundness, *n.* —*Syn.* fullness, completeness, circularity, oneness, inclusiveness, wholeness.

round off, *v.* —*Syn.* approximate, round off by tens, hundreds, etc.; accept rough figure for; see **estimate** 1, 2.

round out, *v.* —*Syn.* expand, fill in *or* up *or* out, enlarge; see **grow** 1.

roundup, *n.* —*Syn.* gathering of cattle, branding, ranching; see **rodeo.**

round up (D), *v.* —*Syn.* collect, gather (in), bring in; see **assemble** 2.

rouse, *v.* **1.** [To waken]—*Syn.* arouse, raise, awake; see **awaken** 1, **wake** 1.

2. [To stimulate]—*Syn.* stimulate, urge, provoke; see **animate** 1, **excite** 1.

roustabout, *n.* —*Syn.* worker, stevedore, longshoreman; see **laborer, workman.**

rout, *n.* —*Syn.* flight, retreat, confusion; see **defeat** 2, **loss** 1.

rout, *v.* —*Syn.* overcome, overthrow, scatter, hunt, beat, defeat, conquer, discomfit, overpower, overmaster, overmatch, outmaneuver, vanquish, drive off, put to flight, repulse, subjugate, subdue. —*Ant.* fail*, lose, suffer.

route, *n.* **1.** [A course being followed]—*Syn.* way, course, path, track, beat, tack, divergence, detour, digression, meandering, rambling, wandering, circuit, round, rounds, range; see also **road** 1.

2. [A projected course]—*Syn.* map, plans, order of march, line of march, sealed orders, layout, plot, diagram, chart, journey, itinerary; see **plan** 2, **program** 2.

routed, *mod.* **1.** [Provided with a route]—*Syn.* directed, laid out, ordered; see **prospered, sent.**

2. [Moved along a route]—*Syn.* forwarded, conveyed, carried; see **moved** 1, **transported.**

routine, *mod.* —*Syn.* usual, customary, methodical; see **conventional** 1, 2, **habitual** 1.

routine, *n.* —*Syn.* round, cycle, habit; see **method** 2, **system** 2.

rove, *v.* —*Syn.* walk, meander, wander; see **roam** 1.

roving, *n.* —*Syn.* wayfaring, traveling, moving; see **rambling** 1, **wandering** 1.

row, *n.* —*Syn.* series, order, file; see **line** 1.

hard row to hoe (D)—*Syn.* dilemma, problem, something difficult to do; see **difficulty** 1, 2.

in a row—*Syn.* in succession, successively, in a line; see **consecutively.**

row, *n.* —*Syn.* squabble, riot, trouble; see **disturbance** 1, **fight** 1.

rowboat, *n.* —*Syn.* vessel, skiff, dinghy; see **boat.**

rowdy, *mod.* —*Syn.* rebellious, rude, mischievous; see **lawless** 2, **unruly.**

royal, *mod.* **1.** [Pertaining to a king or his family] —*Syn.* high, elevated, highborn, monarchic, reigning, regnant, regal, ruling, authoritative, dominant, absolute, imperial, sovereign, paramount, supreme; see also **sense** 2, **noble** 3.—*Ant.* humble*, debased, lowborn.

2. [Having qualities befitting royalty]—*Syn.* great, grand, stately, lofty, illustrious, renowned, eminent, superior, worthy, honorable, dignified, chivalrous, courteous, kingly, great-hearted, large-hearted, princely, princelike, majestic, magnificent, splendid, courtly, impressive, commanding, aristocratic, lordly, august, imposing, superb, glorious, resplendent, gorgeous, sublime; see **sense** 1; **noble** 1, 2, **worthy.**—*Ant.* mean*, ignoble, base.

royally, *mod.* —*Syn.* magnanimously, liberally, munificently, bounteously, lavishly; see also **generously** 1.

royalty, *n.* —*Syn.* kingship, sovereignty, nobility, authority, eminence, distinction, blood, birth, high descent, rank, greatness, power, supremacy, primacy, the crown, mogul, suzerainty; see also **aristocracy.**

Degrees of royalty include the following—czar, czarina, czarevitch, czarevna, grand duke, grand duchess, shah, emperor, empress, king, queen, prince of Wales, princess of Wales, archduke, archduchess, princess royal, queen mother, prince consort, prince, princess, duke, duchess.

rub, *n.* **1.** [A rubbing action]—*Syn.* brushing, stroke, smoothing, scraping, scouring, grinding, rasping, friction, attrition; see also **touch** 2.

2. [A difficulty]—*Syn.* impediment, hindrance, dilemma; see **difficulty** 1, 2, **predicament.**—*Ant.* answer*, solution, resolving.

rub, *v.* **1.** [To subject to friction]—*Syn.* scrape, smooth, abrade, scour, grate, grind, wear away, graze, rasp, knead, fret, massage, polish, shine, burnish, curry, scrub, swab, erase, rub out *or* down, file, chafe, clean.

2. [To apply by rubbing]—*Syn.* brush, daub, bedaub, touch, stroke, paint, smear, spread, cover, coat, plaster, anoint, slather (D).

rubber, *mod.* —*Syn.* elastic, rubbery, soft, stretchable, stretching, rebounding, flexible, ductile, lively, buoyant, resilient.

rubber, *n.* Types of rubber include the following —India, native, wild, raw, crude, crepe, vulcanized, hard, reclaimed, synthetic, methyl.

rubbish, *n.* —*Syn.* litter, debris, waste; see **trash** 1.

rubicund, *mod.* —*Syn.* colored, rosy, reddish; see **red.**

rub out, *v.* **1.** [To cancel]—*Syn.* eradicate, erase, delete; see **cancel** 1, **eliminate** 1.

2. [(D) To kill]—*Syn.* destroy, butcher, shoot; see **kill** 1.

ruddy, *mod.* —*Syn.* rosy, reddish, bronzed; see **red.**

rude, *mod.* **1.** [Boorish]—*Syn.* rustic, ungainly, awkward, lubberly, crude, coarse, gross, rough, harsh, blunt, rugged, common, barbarous, lumpish, ungraceful, hulking, loutish, antic, rowdy, disorderly, rowdyish, brutish, boorish, clownish, stupid, ill-proportioned, unpolished, uncultured, uncultivated, unrefined, untrained, indecorous, unknowing, untaught, uncouth, slovenly, ill-bred, inelegant, ignorant, inexpert, illiterate, clumsy, awkward, gawky, slouching, graceless, ungraceful, lumbering, green, unacquainted, unenlightened, uneducated, vulgar, indecent, ribald, homely, outlandish, disgraceful, inappropriate; *all* (D): hayseed, bohunk, hick. —*Ant.* cultured*, urbane, suave.

2. [Not polite]—*Syn.* churlish, sullen, surly, sharp, harsh, gruff, snarling, ungracious, unkind, ungentle, obstreperous, overbearing, crabbed, sour, disdainful, unmannerly, ill-mannered, improper, shabby, ill-chosen, discourteous, ungentlemanly, fresh, abusive, forward, loud, loud-mouthed, bold, brazen, audacious, brash, arrogant, supercilious, blustering, impudent, crass, raw, saucy, imprudent, pert, unabashed, contumelious, sharp-tongued, loose, mocking, barefaced, insolent, impertinent, offensive, vituperative, naughty, impolite, hostile, insulting, disrespectful, scornful, flippant, presumptuous, sarcastic, defiant, outrageous, imperious, swaggering, disparaging, contemptuous, rebellious, disdainful, unfeeling, insensitive, scoffing, scurrilous, disagreeable, domineering, overbearing, high-handed, hypercritical, self-assertive, brutal, severe, hard, cocky, bullying, cheeky, nervy, assuming, dictatorial, magisterial, misbehaved, officious, meddling, intrusive, meddlesome, acrimonious, bitter, uncivilized, slandering, ill-tempered, bad-tempered; *all* (D): sassy, snotty, snooty, brassy,

uppity, crusty, bold as brass.—*Ant.* polite*, courteous, mannerly.
3. [Harsh]—*Syn.* rough, violent, stormy; see **turbulent.**
4. [Approximate]—*Syn.* guessed, surmised, unprecise; see **approximate** 3.
5. [Coarse]—*Syn.* rough, unrefined, unpolished; see **crude** 1.
6. [Primitive]—*Syn.* ignorant, uncivilized, barbarous; see **primitive** 3.

rudely, *mod.*—*Syn.* crudely, impudently, coarsely, impolitely, indecently, barbarously, roughly, harshly, bluntly, boorishly, ungraciously, uncouthly, vulgarly, illiterately, indecorously, insolently, contemptuously, brutally, dictatorially, churlishly, sullenly, gruffly, discourteously, impishly, loudly, brazenly, blusteringly, crassly, unabashedly, ribaldly, spunkily, mockingly; *all* (D): sassily, bitchily, snootily, snootingly.—*Ant.* kindly*, politely*, suavely.

rudeness, *n.*—*Syn.* discourtesy, bad manners, vulgarity, incivility, impoliteness, impudence, disrespect, misbehavior, barbarity, ungentlemanliness, unmannerliness, ill-breeding, crudity, brutality, barbarism, tactlessness, boorishness, unbecoming conduct, conduct not becoming a gentleman, lack *or* want of courtesy, crudeness, *gaucherie, brusquerie* (*both* French), grossness, coarseness, bluntness, effrontery, impertinence, insolence, audacity, boldness, shamelessness, presumption, officiousness, intrusiveness, brazenness, sauciness, defiance, bumptiousness, contempt, back talk, ill temper, irritability, disdain, asperity, bitterness, sharpness, acrimony, unkindness, ungraciousness, social breach, harshness; *all* (D): gall, sass, lip, nerve, brass, crust, cheek.

rudiment, *n.*—*Syn.* nucleus, beginning, source; see **origin** 2.

rudimentary, *mod.* **1.** [Primary]—*Syn.* basic, elemental, initial; see **fundamental** 1, **original** 1.
2. [Immature]—*Syn.* half-done, simple, uncompleted; see **unfinished** 1.

rue, *v.*—*Syn.* deplore, lament, be sorry; see **mourn** 1, **regret.**

rueful, *mod.* **1.** [Penitent]—*Syn.* contrite, remorseful, regretful; see **sorry** 1.
2. [Pitiful]—*Syn.* pathetic, sorrowful, despondent; see **pitiful** 1, **sad** 2.

ruffian, *n.*—*Syn.* miscreant, hoodlum, bully; see **rascal.**

ruffle, *v.* **1.** [To disarrange]—*Syn.* rumple, tousle, rifle; see **confuse, tangle.**
2. [To anger]—*Syn.* irritate, fret, nettle; see **anger** 1.

rug, *n.*—*Syn.* carpet, carpeting, floor covering, linoleum, straw mat, floor mat, woven mat, drugget. Types of rugs include the following—Axminster, velvet, Wilton velvet, fiber, rya, mohair, wool-and-fiber, skin, bearskin, sheepskin, goatskin, numdah, Navajo, Persian, paper fiber, rag, chenille, twist, shag, hand-hooked, Cambodia, camel's hair, tapestry, Chinese, Oriental, Symrna, Finnish, India drugget.

rugged, *mod.* **1.** [Rough; *said especially of terrain*]—*Syn.* hilly, broken, mountainous; see **rough** 1.
2. [Strong; *said especially of persons*]—*Syn.* hale, sturdy, hardy; see **healthy** 1, **strong** 1.

ruin, *n.* **1.** [The act of destruction]—*Syn.* extinction, demolition, overthrow; see **destruction** 1, **wreck** 1.
2. [A building fallen into decay; *often plural*]—*Syn.* remains, traces, residue, foundations, vestiges, remnants, relics, wreck, walls, detritus, rubble; see also **destruction** 2.
3. [The state of destruction]—*Syn.* dilapidation, waste, wreck; see **destruction** 2.

ruin, *v.* **1.** [To destroy]—*Syn.* injure, overthrow, demolish; see **destroy** 1, **ravage.**
2. [To cause to become bankrupt]—*Syn.* impoverish, bankrupt, beggar, reduce, pauperize, fleece, make penniless, bring to destitution, bring to want, drain, exhaust, deplore; *all* (D): bust, clean out, cook one's goose, do in, do for.—*Ant.* help*, pay, fund.
3. [To destroy chastity]—*Syn.* rape, despoil, ravish.

ruined, *mod.* **1.** [Destroyed]—*Syn.* demolished, overthrown, torn down, extinct, abolished, exterminated, annihilated, subverted, wrecked, desolated, ravaged, smashed, crushed, crashed, extinguished, extirpated, dissolved; *both* (D): totaled out, screwed up; see also **destroyed.**—*Ant.* protected*, saved, preserved.
2. [Spoiled]—*Syn.* pillaged, harried, robbed, plundered, injured, hurt, impaired, defaced, harmed, marred, past hope, mutilated, ghettoized, broken; *all* (D): gone to the dogs *or* devil *or* deuce, on the rocks, done for; see also **spoiled.**—*Ant.* repaired, restored*, mended.
3. [Rendered unchaste]—*Syn.* violated, defiled, ravished, raped, forced, despoiled, deflowered.
4. [Bankrupt]—*Syn.* pauperized, poverty-stricken, beggared, reduced, left in penury, penniless, fleeced, brought to want; *all* (D): gone under, sold up, busted, through the mill; see also **insolvent.**—*Ant.* rich*, prosperous, well off.

ruinous, *mod.* **1.** [Destructive]—*Syn.* baneful, pernicious, wasteful; see **destructive** 2.
2. [Leading to bankruptcy]—*Syn.* unfortunate, rash, speculative, suicidal, fatal, impoverishing, pauperizing, exhausting, draining, depleting, bringing to want, reducing to penury.

ruins, *n.*—*Syn.* remains, foundation, debris, walls, wreckage; see also **destruction** 2, **wreck** 2.

rule, *n.* **1.** [Government]—*Syn.* control, dominion, jurisdiction; see **government** 1.
2. [A regulation]—*Syn.* edict, command, commandment; see **law** 3.
3. [The custom]—*Syn.* habit, course, practice; see **custom** 1, 2.
as a rule—*Syn.* ordinarily, generally, habitually; see **customarily.**

rule, *v.* **1.** [To govern]—*Syn.* conduct, control, dictate; see **govern** 1.
2. [To regulate]—*Syn.* order, decree, direct; see **command** 2, **manage** 1.

ruled, *mod.* **1.** [Governed]—*Syn.* administered, controlled, managed; see **governed** 1.
2. [Having lines]—*Syn.* lined, marked, marked off, squared, graphed, prepared for graphs; see also **linear.**

rule of thumb, *n.*—*Syn.* approximation, estimate, conjecture; see **guess.**

rule out, *v.* —*Syn.* eliminate, not consider, recant; see **abolish, cancel** 2, **revoke.**

ruler, *n.* **1.** [One who governs]—*Syn.* governor, commander, chief, manager, adjudicator, monarch, regent, director; for types of rulers, sense 1, see **dictator, king** 1, **leader** 2.

2. [A straightedge] Types of rules, sense 2, include the following—foot rule, yardstick, carpenter's rule, slide rule, parallel rule, stationer's rule, T-square, try square, steel square, compositor's rule *or* ruler.

ruling, *n.* —*Syn.* order, decision, precept; see **law** 3, **rule.**

rum, *n.* Types of rum include the following—light, dark, spiced, West Indies, Jamaica, New England, Puerto Rican, Bacardi, arrack, Cape Horn rainwater (D); see also **drink** 2.

rumble, *n.* —*Syn.* reverberation, resounding, thunder, roll, drumbeat; see also **noise.**

rumble, *v.* —*Syn.* resound, growl, thunder; see **sound** 1.

ruminate, *v.* **1.** [Regurgitate]—*Syn.* rechew, spew, regurgitate; see **vomit.**

2. [To ponder]—*Syn.* ponder, contemplate, cogitate; see **meditate** 1, **think** 1.

rummage, *n.* **1.** [Trash]—*Syn.* odds and ends, refuse, scraps; see **trash** 1.

2. [Used or second hand goods]—*Syn.* antiques, stuff, frippery, old clothes, odds and ends, hand-me-downs.

rummage, *v.* —*Syn.* search, toss about, put in confusion; see **hunt** 2, **seek** 1.

rummage through, *v.* —*Syn.* look for *or* around, search high and low, look all over, scour, ransack, turn inside out; see also **hunt** 2, **search.**

rumor, *n.* **1.** [Common talk]—*Syn.* report, news, tidings, intelligence, dispatch, hearsay, gossip, bruit, scandal, tittle-tattle, notoriety, noise, cry, popular report, fame, repute; *all* (D): grapevine, scuttlebutt, buzz, breeze.

2. [An unsubstantial story]—*Syn.* canard, hoax, fabrication, suggestion, supposition, innuendo, story, tale, invention, fiction, falsehood; see also **lie** 1.

rumored, *mod.* —*Syn.* reported, told, said, noised, reputed, spread abroad, gossiped, bruited, given out, noised abroad, broadcast, it is said, as they say, all over town, current, circulating, in circulation, rife, prevailing, prevalent, persisting, general, in everyone's mouth; *all* (D): going around *or* the rounds, buzzed, in the breeze.

rump, *n.* —*Syn.* posterior, buttocks, sacrum, hind end, tail end, posterior, butt end, bottom, croup, crupper, rear, back, seat, breech, hunkers, hurdies (Scotch), fundament, *derrière* (French); *all* (D): ass, buns, can.

rumple, *v.* —*Syn.* crumple, crush, fold; see **wrinkle** 1, 2.

rumpus, *n.* —*Syn.* uproar, disturbance, tumult; see **confusion** 2, **fun.**

run, *n.* **1.** [The act of running]—*Syn.* sprint, pace, bound, flow, amble, gallop, canter, lope, spring, trot, dart, rush, dash, flight, escape, break, charge, swoop, race, scamper, tear, whisk, scuttle, scud, flow, fall, drop.

2. [A series]—*Syn.* continuity, succession, sequence; see **series.**

3. [In baseball, a score]—*Syn.* record, tally, count, point; see also **score** 1.

4. [The average]—*Syn.* par, norm, run of the mill; see **average** 1.

5. [A course]—*Syn.* way, route, field; see **track** 1.

in the long run (D)—*Syn.* in the final outcome, finally, eventually; see **ultimately.**

on the run (D) **1.** —*Syn.* busy, in a hurry, running; see **hurrying. 2.** retreating, defeated, routed; see **beaten** 1.

run, *v.* **1.** [To move, usually rapidly]—*Syn.* flow in *or* over, cut *or* chase along, fall, pour, tumble, drop, leap, spin, whirl, whiz, scud, sail.

2. [To go swiftly by physical effort]—*Syn.* rush, hurry, spring, bound, scurry, skitter, scramble, scoot, travel, run off *or* away, dash ahead *or* at *or* on, put on a burst of speed, go on the double, have effect, go on the double-quick, hasten (off), light out, have a free play, make tracks, dart (ahead), gallop, canter, lope, spring, trot, single-foot, amble, pace, flee, speed, spurt, swoop, bolt, race, shoot, tear, whisk, scamper, scuttle.

3. [To function]—*Syn.* move, work, go; see **operate** 2.

4. [To cause to function]—*Syn.* control, drive, govern; see **command** 2, **manage** 1.

5. [To extend]—*Syn.* encompass, cover, spread; see **reach** 1, **surround** 2.

6. [To continue]—*Syn.* last, persevere, go on; see **continue** 1.

7. [To read]—*Syn.* is worded, is written, appears; see **mean** 1.

8. [To complete]—*Syn.* oppose, contest, contend with; see **compete, race** 2.

run after, *v.* —*Syn.* follow, chase, hunt; see **pursue** 1.

run amok, *v.* —*Syn.* go crazy *or* insane, break down, lose one's head; *all* (D): go off the deep end, go haywire *or* nuts *or* balmy *or* looney, crack up; see also **rage** 3.

run-around, *n.* —*Syn.* postponement, diversion, bureaucratic inertia; see **delay** 1, **difficulty** 1.

runaway, *mod.* —*Syn.* fleeing, running, out of hand, out of control, beyond restraint, delinquent, wild; see also **disorderly** 1.

runaway, *n.* —*Syn.* juvenile offender, lawbreaker, truant; see **delinquent.**

run away, *v.* **1.** [To empty]—*Syn.* flow, wash, pour out; see **drain** 2, 3.

2. [Escape]—*Syn.* flee, depart, steal away; see **escape, leave** 1.

run-down, *mod.* —*Syn.* **1.** [Exhausted]—*Syn.* weak, debilitated, weary; see **weak** 1, 2, **tired.**

2. [Dilapidated]—*Syn.* broken-down, shabby, rickety, beat-up (D); see **old** 2, **crumbly.**

run-down, *n.* —*Syn.* report, outline, review; see **summary.**

run down, *v.* **1.** [To chase]—*Syn.* hunt, seize, apprehend; see **pursue** 1.

2. [To ridicule]—*Syn.* make fun of, belittle, depreciate; see **ridicule.**

run dry, *v.* —*Syn.* dry up, stop running, cease to flow; see **dry** 1.

(a) run for one's money, *n.* —*Syn.* one's money's worth, (adequate) payment, enough; see **pay** 1.

rung, *n.*—*Syn.* tread, rundle, round, crosspiece, bar, rod, crossbar, level, board.

run into, *v.* **1.** [To collide with]—*Syn.* bump (into), crash, have a collision; see **hit** 1, 2.
2. [To encounter]—*Syn.* come across, see, contact; see **meet** 6.
3. [To blend with]—*Syn.* mingle, combine with, osmose; see **enter** 1, **join** 1.

runner, *n.* **1.** [One who runs]—*Syn.* racer, entrant, contestant, sprinter, dash man, (long) distance runner, marathoner, middle distance runner, 220-man (D), cross-country runner *or* man, jogger, track man, hurdler, messenger, courier, post(rider), express, dispatch bearer; *all* (D): cinder man, cinder artist, century man; see **athlete.**
2. [A vine]—*Syn.* tendril, branch, offshoot; see **vine.**

running, *mod.* **1.** [In the act of running]—*Syn.* pacing, racing, speeding, galloping, cantering, trotting, scuttling, scudding, scampering, fleeing, bounding, whisking, sprinting, flowing, tumbling, falling, pouring.
2. [In the process of running]—*Syn.* producing, operating, working, functioning, proceeding, moving, revolving, guiding, conducting, administering, going, in operation, in action, executing, promoting, achieving, transacting, wielding, determining, bringing about.
3. [Extending]—*Syn.* spreading, reaching, encompassing; see **extending.**
4. [Flowing]—*Syn.* dashing, coursing, streaming, swamping, washing over, flowing along, laving, watering; see also **flowing.**

run-off, *n.*—*Syn.* spring run-off, drainage, surplus water; see **flow, river, water** 1.

run off, *v.* **1.** [To pour out]—*Syn.* empty, exude, draw off; see **drain** 2, 3.
2. [To abandon]—*Syn.* depart, flee, go; see **leave** 1.
3. [To produce]—*Syn.* turn out, make, publish; see **manufacture** 1, **print** 2.

run-of-the-mill, *mod.*—*Syn.* popular, mediocre, ordinary; see **common** 1.

run on, *v.*—*Syn.* chatter, maunder, gabble; see **gossip, ramble** 2.

run onto, *v.*—*Syn.* encounter, see, contact; see **meet** 6.

run out, *v.* **1.** [To squander]—*Syn.* lose, dissipate, exhaust; see **waste** 2.
2. [To stop]—*Syn.* expire, finish, end; see **stop** 2.
3. [To become exhausted]—*Syn.* weaken, wear out, waste away; see **tire** 1.
4. [To go away]—*Syn.* go, depart, run away; see **abandon** 2, **escape, leave** 1.
5. [To pour out]—*Syn.* flow, empty, leak; see **drain** 2, 3.
6. [To pass]—*Syn.* elapse, slip by, glide; see **pass** 2.
7. [To remove physically]—*Syn.* dislodge, throw out, put out; see **eject** 1.

run over, *v.*—*Syn.* trample on, drive over, kill, hurt, injure, hit and run (D).

runt, *n.* **1.** [A dwarf]—*Syn.* pygmy, mannikin, midget, homunculus; *both* (D): punk, scrub.
2. [A mediocrity]—*Syn.* little fellow, degenerate whippersnapper; see **nobody** 2.

run the gauntlet, *v.*—*Syn.* fire, open fire, kill; see **shoot** 1.

run through, *v.* **1.** [To examine]—*Syn.* check, inspect, look at; see **examine** 1, 2.
2. [To spend]—*Syn.* waste, squander, lose; see **spend** 1.

run together, *v.*—*Syn.* blend (with), mingle, combine (with); see **enter** 1, **join** 1.

run up bills, *v.*—*Syn.* squander money, throw money away, waste money *or* one's substance; see **spend** 1.

rupture, *n.*—*Syn.* hole, separation, crack; see **break** 1, **tear.**

rupture, *v.*—*Syn.* crack, tear, burst; see **break.**

rural, *mod.*—*Syn.* rustic, farm, agricultural, ranch, pastoral, bucolic, backwoods, country, Arcadian, country, sylvan, agrarian, georgic, agronomic, suburban.—*Ant.* urban*, industrial, commercial.

ruse, *n.*—*Syn.* artifice, gimmick, deceit; see **device** 2, **trick** 1.

rush, *n.*—*Syn.* haste, dash, charge; see **hurry** 1.
with a rush—*Syn.* suddenly, forcefully, rushing; see **fast** 1, **unexpectedly.**

rush, *v.*—*Syn.* hasten, speed, hurry up; see **hurry** 1.

rushed, *mod.*—*Syn.* hurried, driven, pressured; see **pressed.**

rush in, *v.*—*Syn.* take chances, hurry things, act precipitately *or* without caution; see **risk.**

rushing, *mod.* **1.** [Hurrying]—*Syn.* being quick, bestirring oneself, losing no time; see **hurrying.**
2. [Moving with great speed]—*Syn.* driving, darting, flying, running, dashing, scurrying, pushing, racing, galloping, plunging.

russet, *mod.*—*Syn.* reddish-brown, reddish-gray, yellowish-brown; see **brown, red.**

Russia, *n.*—*Syn.* Union of Soviet Socialist Republics, Soviet Union, U.S.S.R., Great Russia, Little Russia, White Russia, Muscovy, Russia in Europe, Siberia, the Soviets; *both* (D): Reds, Russian Bear; for divisions of Russia, see **Europe.**

Russian, *mod.*—*Syn.* Slavic, Slav, Muscovite, Siberian.

rust, *mod.*—*Syn.* reddish, red-yellow, reddish-brown; see **brown, red.**

rust, *n.*—*Syn.* decomposition, corruption, corrosion, oxidation, decay, rot, dilapidation, breakup, wear.

rust, *v.*—*Syn.* oxidize, become rusty, degenerate, decay, rot, corrode.

rustic, *mod.* **1.** [Rural]—*Syn.* agricultural, pastoral, agrarian; see **rural.**
2. [Boorish]—*Syn.* countrified, rude, clownish, outlandish, uncouth, unpolished, inelegant, awkward, coarse, rough, dull, stupid, foolish, loutish, lubberly, ungainly, lumpish, ignorant, unsophisticated, uneducated.—*Ant.* cultured*, refined, educated.
3. [Suggesting the idyllic qualities of rural places or people]—*Syn.* sylvan, verdant, unadorned, idyllic, bucolic, artless, simple, plain, honest, unsophisticated, pleasing, charming, picturesque, pastoral, natural, unaffected, sturdy; see also **pleasant** 2.—*Ant.* complex*, urbane, sophisticated.

rustle, *n.*—*Syn.* stir, whisper, ripple, swish, friction, crackle, purl, patter, secret sound; see also **noise** 1.

rustle, *v.*—*Syn.* stir, whisper, swish, crackle, purl, patter, ripple, crepitate, tap, sough, sigh, murmur; see also **sound** 1.

rustler, *n.* **1.** [A robber]—*Syn.* cattle thief, horse thief, outlaw; see **robber.**
2. [(D) An industrious person]—*Syn.* worker, driver, pusher; *both* (D): hustler, humper.

rustle up (D), *v.*—*Syn.* round up, collect, rob; see **assemble** 2, **steal.**

rustling, *mod.*—*Syn.* murmuring, swishing, stirring; see **whispering.**

rusty, *mod.* **1.** [Decayed]—*Syn.* unused, neglected, worn; see **old** 2, **weak** 2.
2. [Unpracticed]—*Syn.* out of practice, soft, ill-qualified; see **weak** 6.

rut, *n.* **1.** [A deeply cut track]—*Syn.* hollow, trench, furrow; see **groove.**
2. [Habitual behavior]—*Syn.* custom, habit, course, routine, practice, performance, round, circuit, circle, pattern, wont, usage, procedure.—*Ant.* change*, veer, mutation.

ruthless, *mod.* **1.** [Without pity; *said of persons*]—*Syn.* pitiless, unpitying, unmerciful, tigerish, ferine, feral, ferocious, stony-hearted, obdurate, cold-blooded, remorseless, vindictive, vengeful, revengeful, rancorous, implacable, unforgiving, malevolent, surly, hardhearted, hard, cold, unsympathetic, unforbearing, vicious, sadistic; see also **sense** 2, **cruel** 1, **powerful** 1.—*Ant.* merciful*, forgiving, compassionate.
2. [Showing little evidence of pity; *said of actions, policies, etc.*]—*Syn.* savage, brutal, cruel, tyrannical, merciless, relentless, barbarous, inhuman, grim, atrocious, flagrant, terrible, abominable, outrageous, inexorable, fiendish, oppressive, bloodthirsty, venomous, galling.—*Ant.* kind*, helpful, civilized.

rye, *n.*—*Syn.* cereal, grass, feed; see **grain** 1.
Varieties of rye include the following—fall, spring, spurred, Wallachian, Michel.

S

Sabbath, *n.* —*Syn.* seventh day, Lord's day, day of rest, *dies non* (Latin), Saturday, Sunday; see also **weekend.**

sabbatical, *n.* —*Syn.* leave, time off, holiday; see **vacation.**

sable, *mod.* —*Syn.* ebony, raven, dark; see **black** 1, **brown.**

sabotage, *n.* —*Syn.* demolition, overthrow, treason; see **destruction** 1, **revolution** 2.

sabotage, *v.* —*Syn.* subvert, wreck, undermine; see **attack** 1, **destroy** 1.

sac, *n.* —*Syn.* welt, pouch, cellblister; see **cyst, sore.**

saccharine, *mod.* —*Syn.* sugary, honeyed, candied; see **sweet** 1, 2.

sacerdotal, *mod.* —*Syn.* priestly, ministerial, apostolic; see **clerical** 2, **divine** 2.

sachet, *n.* —*Syn.* fragrance, scent-bag, potpourri; see **perfume, smell** 1.

sack, *n.* —*Syn.* sac, pouch, pocket; see **bag, container.**
hit the sack (D)—*Syn.* go to bed *or* to rest, go to sleep, retire; see **sleep.**

sack, *v.* —*Syn.* bag, package, pocket; see **pack** 1.

sackcloth, *n.* —*Syn.* canvas, burlap, hopsacking, denim, cloth, homespun.

sackcloth and ashes, *n.* —*Syn.* hair shirt, remorse, repentance, mortification; see also **mourning** 2, **regret** 1.

sacrament, *n.* **1.** [Christian rites]—*Syn.* holy observance, ceremonial, ritual, liturgy, act of divine worship, mystery *or* the mysteries; see also **ceremony** 2.
In the Roman Catholic and Eastern Orthodox churches, the seven sacraments are as follows—baptism, confirmation *or* the laying on of hands, penance, Communion *or* the Eucharist, extreme unction, holy orders, matrimony.
2. [The Eucharist and the bread and wine used in it]—*Syn.* intinction, consubstantiation, impanation, transsubstantiation, the body and the blood of Christ, (holy) wafer; see also **communion** 2.
3. [A sacred symbol or token]—*Syn.* pledge, bond, vow; see **oath** 1, **promise** 1.

sacramental, *mod.* —*Syn.* sacred, pure, solemn; see **holy** 1, **religious** 1.

sacred, *mod.* **1.** [Holy]—*Syn.* pure, pious, saintly; see **holy** 1.
2. [Dedicated]—*Syn.* consecrated, ordained, sanctioned; see **divine** 2.

sacred cow (D), *n.* —*Syn.* immune *or* favored *or* privileged person *or* individual, one above criticism, elite; see **favorite, pet** 3.

sacrifice, *n.* **1.** [An offering to a deity]—*Syn.* offering, tribute, oblation, expiation, atonement, reparation, penance, propitiation, immolation, execution victim.
2. [A loss]—*Syn.* discount, deduction, reduction; see **loss** 1.
3. [In baseball, a play that advances a runner at the expense of the batter]—*Syn.* fielder's choice, sacrifice fly, bunt, noble deed (D).

sacrifice, *v.* **1.** [To offer to a deity]—*Syn.* consecrate, immolate, dedicate, give up, devote, offer up, hallow, worship, dedicate to the service of the Lord, make an offering of; see also **bless** 3.
2. [To give up as a means to an end]—*Syn.* forfeit, forgo, relinquish, yield, suffer the loss of, permit injury to, renounce, spare, give up, let go, resign oneself to, endure the loss of, sacrifice oneself, abandon oneself to, surrender, part with, waive, go astray from.
3. [To sell at a loss]—*Syn.* cut, reduce, sell out, sell at a bargain, have a fire sale, mark down, take shrinkage, take a beating, incur a loss, sell for a song (D); see also **decrease** 2, **lose** 2.

sacrificed, *mod.* —*Syn.* gone, given up, thrown to the wolves (D); see **abandoned, lost** 1.

sacrificial, *mod.* —*Syn.* atoning, conciliatory, sacrificing, expiatory, propitiatory; see also **divine** 2.

sacrilege, *n.* —*Syn.* impiety, curse, violation; see **blasphemy, heresy.**

sacrilegious, *mod.* —*Syn.* sinful, blasphemous, profane; see **impious** 1, **wicked** 1.

sacristy, *n.* —*Syn.* vestry, vestibule, church room, vestry room.

sacrosanct, *mod.* —*Syn.* sacred, reverent, blessed; see **divine** 2, **religious** 1.

sad, *mod.* **1.** [Afflicted with sorrow]—*Syn.* unhappy, sorry, sorrowful, downcast, dismal, gloomy, glum, pensive, heavy-hearted, dispirited, dejected, depressed, desolate, troubled, melancholy, morose, grieved, pessimistic, melancholic, crushed, broken-hearted, heartbroken, heartsick, despondent, careworn, rueful, anguished, disheartened, lamenting, mourning, grieving, weeping, bitter, woebegone, doleful, spiritless, joyless, heavy, crestfallen, discouraged, moody, low-spirited, *mesto* (Italian), despairing, languishing, hopeless, worried, downhearted, cast down, in heavy spirits, morbid, oppressed, blighted, grief-stricken, foreboding, apprehensive, horrified, anxious, dolorous, *triste* (French), wretched, miserable, mournful, disconsolate, forlorn, saturnine, atrabilious, jaundiced, out of sorts, distressed, afflicted, bereaved, repining, harassed, dreary, bilious, lugubrious, woeful; *all* (D): in the doldrums, down (in the dumps), gone into mourning, in bad humor, out of humor, cut up, in the depths, (looking) blue, in grief, making a long

face, bathed in tears, feeling like hell, down in the mouth.—*Ant.* happy*, gay, cheerful.
2. [Suggestive of sorrow]—*Syn.* pitiable, unhappy, dejecting, saddening, disheartening, discouraging, dispiriting, joyless, dreary, dark, dismal, gloomy, poignant, moving, touching, mournful, lachrymose, disquieting, disturbing, dimming, somber, doleful, oppressive, funereal, discomposing, lugubrious, pathetic, tragic, pitiful, piteous, woeful, rueful, sorry, unfortunate, hapless, heart-rending, dire, distressing, depressing, grievous.
3. [(D) Inferior]—*Syn.* cheap, bad, second-class; see **common** 1, **poor** 2.

sadden, *v.* —*Syn.* oppress, dishearten, discourage, cast down, deject, depress; *all* (D): make one's heart bleed, cast a gloom upon, break one's heart.

saddle, *n.* —*Syn.* seat, montura; *all* (D): hack, hull, leather.
Saddles include the following—English, English cavalry, U.S. cavalry, Western, cowboy, stock, camel, Cossack, sidesaddle, packsaddle, cacolet *or* mule-chair.

sadism, *n.* —*Syn.* perversion, cruelty, malice, sexual abnormality *or* aberration, *psychopathia sexualis* (Latin), masochism.

sadistic, *mod.* —*Syn.* cruel, brutal, vicious; see **cruel** 1.

sadly, *mod.* —*Syn.* unhappily, morosely, dejectedly, wistfully, sorrowfully, dolefully, grievously, gloomily, joylessly, dismally, cheerlessly, in sorrow.

sadness, *n.* —*Syn.* sorrow, dejection, melancholy, depression, grief, despondency, sorrowfulness, oppression; *all* (D): downs, gloom, blues, dumps.

safe, *mod.* **1.** [Not in danger]—*Syn.* out of danger, secure, in safety *or* security, free from harm *or* danger, unharmed, unscathed, safe and sound, protected, guarded, housed, screened (from danger), unmolested, unthreatened, entrenched, impregnable, invulnerable, under the protection of, saved, safeguarded, secured, defended, supported, sustained, maintained, upheld, preserved, vindicated, shielded, nourished, sheltered, fostered, cared for, cherished, watched, impervious to, patrolled, looked after, ministered to, supervised, tended, attended, kept in view *or* order, surveyed, regulated; *all* (D): (with one's head) above water, undercover, out of harm's way *or* reach, on the safe side, on ice, in free, at anchor, in harbor, snug (as a bug in a rug), out of the meshes, under one's wing *or* the wing of *or* the shadow of, bearing a charmed life, under lock and key.—*Ant.* dangerous*, unsafe*, risky.
2. [Not dangerous]—*Syn.* innocent, innocuous, innoxious; see **harmless** 2.
3. [Reliable]—*Syn.* trustworthy, dependable, competent; see **reliable** 1, 2.
4. [Free from radioactivity]—*Syn.* clear, checked, pure, decontaminated, neutralized, cold (D).

safe, *n.* —*Syn.* strongbox, coffer, chest, repository, vault, case, reliquary, safe-deposit box.

safe-conduct, *n.* **1.** [Permit]—*Syn.* license, safeguard, permit, ticket; see **guaranty** 2, **passport.**
2. [Protection]—*Syn.* guard, convoy, consort; see **escort, guide** 1.

safeguard, *n.* **1.** [Protection]—*Syn.* guard, shield, surety; see **defense** 1, **protection** 2.
2. [License]—*Syn.* pass, safe-conduct, passport; see **escort, permission.**

safekeeping, *n.* —*Syn.* supervision, care, guardianship; see **custody** 1, **protection** 2.

safely, *mod.* —*Syn.* securely, with safety *or* impunity, without harm *or* risk *or* mishap *or* danger, harmlessly, carefully, cautiously, reliably.

safety, *n.* **1.** [Freedom from danger]—*Syn.* security, protection, impregnability, surety, sanctuary, refuge, shelter, invulnerability.
2. [(D) A lock]—*Syn.* lock mechanism, safetycatch, safety lock; see **fastener, lock** 1.

safety pin, *n.* —*Syn.* shield pin, lingerie pin, clasp pin; see **fastener, pin** 1.

sag, *n.* —*Syn.* depression, settling, sinking, droop, tilt, list, cant, dip, slant, fall, distortion, slump (D); see also **hole** 2.

sag, *v.* **1.** [To sink]—*Syn.* stoop, hang down, become warped; see **bend** 2, **lean** 1.
2. [To lose vigor]—*Syn.* droop, decline, fail; see **hesitate, weaken** 1.

saga, *n.* —*Syn.* epic, legend, adventure; see **story.**

sagacious, *mod.* **1.** [Intellectually keen]—*Syn.* perceptive, acute, astute; see **intelligent** 1, **witty.**
2. [Understanding and judicious]—*Syn.* discriminating, wise, sensible; see **judicious, rational** 1.

sagacity, *n.* —*Syn.* perspicacity, discernment, shrewdness; see **acumen, judgment** 1.

sage, *mod.* —*Syn.* prudent, philosophic, discerning; see **judicious, learned** 1, 2.

sage, *n.* —*Syn.* philosopher, savant, man of learning; see **master** 3, **scientist.**

sagely, *mod.* —*Syn.* learnedly, in an informed manner, shrewdly; see **wisely.**

said, *mod.* —*Syn.* pronounced, aforesaid, forenamed; see **preceding, spoken.**

sail, *n.* **1.** [Means of sailing a vessel]—*Syn.* sheet(s), canvas, muslin, cloth, rag (D).
Sails include the following—mainsail, foresail, topsail, jib, spanker, ringsail, skysail, spritsail, staysail, fisherman staysail, topgallant, mizzen, fore topsail, fore staysail, fore trysail, fore royal, studdingsail, storm trysail, flying jib, working sails, light sails *or* kites, mizzen topsail, main topsail, upper main topsail, main staysail, fore skysail, fore topgallant, trysail, mizzenroyal, balloon sail, spinnaker, spanker, balloon jib.
2. [A journey by sailing vessel]—*Syn.* voyage, cruise, trip; see **journey.**
set sail—*Syn.* go, depart, set out; see **leave** 1, **sail** 1, 2.

sail, *v.* **1.** [To embark]—*Syn.* take ship, put to sea, make sail, get under way, set sail, weigh anchor, leave, begin a voyage.
2. [To travel by sailing]—*Syn.* cruise, voyage, bear in with the land, go alongside, bear down on, bear for, direct one's course for, crowd *or* set sail, put on sail, put to sea, sail away from, navigate, travel, make headway, mis-stay, lie in, make at *or* for, heave to, lay in *or* for, fetch up, bring to, bear off, double a point, close with, back and fill, bear up for *or* to, run down *or* in, put off *or* in, gather way, hug the shore; *all* (D): plow the waves, hang out the washing, plow the deep.
3. [To fly]—*Syn.* float, soar, ride the storm, skim, glide.

sailing, *mod.* **1.** [In the act of sailing]—*Syn.* under (full) sail, on the high seas, under way, on the sea, at sea, under canvas (D); see also **boating, traveling** 2.

2. [Having to do with sailing, or intended for sailing]—*Syn.* rigged for sail, full-rigged, masted, square-rigged, fore-and-aft rigged, cutter-rigged, sloop-rigged, cat-rigged, three-masted, four-masted, sailed, provided with sails.

sailor, *n.* **1.** [A seafaring man]—*Syn.* seaman, mariner, seafarer, pirate, navigator, pilot, boatman, *matelot* (French), yachtsman, able-bodied seaman; *all* (D): A.B, Jack Tar, tar, hearty, sea-dog, limey, shellback, lascar, salt, bluejacket.

Kinds and ranks of sailors include the following—*crew:* (deck) hand, stoker *or* bakehead (D), cabin boy, yeoman, purser; ship's carpenter, cooper, tailor; steward, navigator, signalman, gunner, afterguard; *officers:* captain *or* commander *or* skipper (D), navigating officer, deck officer; first, second, third, boatswain's mate; boatswain (*or* (D): bos'n).

2. [A member of the marine forces]—*Syn.* navy man, marine, midshipman, (naval) cadet, coastguard, frogman; *all* (D): seabee, bluejacket, gob, leatherneck, middy.

sail under false colors, *v.*—*Syn.* misrepresent, feign, sham; see **deceive.**

saint, *n.* **1.** [A saintly person]—*Syn.* a true Christian, child of God, son of God, paragon, salt of the earth, godly person, man of God, unworldly person, altruist, the pure in heart, a believer; see also **philanthropist.**

2. [A holy person, especially one canonized by a church]—*Syn.* martyr, Christian martyr, religious exemplar.

Familiar saints include the following—St. Mary, St. Peter, St. Paul, St. Luke, St. John, St. Nicholas, St. Francis, St. Anne, St. Christopher, St. James, St. George, St. Thomas, St. Andrew, St. Patrick, St. Stephen, St. Anthony, St. Denis, St. Thomas à Becket.

saintly, *mod.*—*Syn.* virtuous, full of good deeds, angelic, righteous, worthy, pious, holy, divine.

sake, *n.* **1.** [End]—*Syn.* objective, consequence, final cause; see **result.**

2. [Purpose]—*Syn.* score, motive, principle; see **purpose** 1, **reason** 3.

3. [Welfare]—*Syn.* benefit, interest, well-being; see **advantage** 3, **welfare** 1.

salable, *mod.*—*Syn.* marketable, popular, suppliable; see **commercial** 2, **profitable.**

salacious, *mod.*—*Syn.* lascivious, wanton, lecherous; see **lwed** 2, **wicked** 1.

salad, *n.*—*Syn.* (salad) greens, slaw, mixture, combination, *mélange* (French).

Common salads include the following—green, tossed, vegetable, fruit, tomato, potato, macaroni, fruit, bean, combination, chef's, seafood, tuna, shrimp, lobster, crab, chicken, ham, Waldorf, Caesar, pineapple, banana, molded, frozen; cole slaw.

salamander, *n.*—*Syn.* eft, newt, triton; see **lizard, reptile.**

salary, *n.*—*Syn.* wage(s), recompense, payroll; see **pay** 2.

sale, *n.* **1.** [The act of selling]—*Syn.* commerce, business, traffic, exchange, barter, commercial enterprise, marketing, vending, trade; see also **economics.**

2. [An individual instance of selling]—*Syn.* deal, transaction, negotiation, turnover, trade, purchase, auction, disposal; see also **buying, selling** 1.

3. [An organized effort to promote unusual selling]—*Syn.* bargain sale, clearance, stock reduction, fire sale, unloading, dumping, remnant sale, going out of business sale, bankruptcy sale; *both* (D): closeout, sellout.

for *or* **on** *or* **up for sale**—*Syn.* (put) on the market, to be sold, marketable, available, (offered) for purchase, not withheld.

on sale—*Syn.* reduced, at a bargain, cut; see **cheap** 1.

sales, *n.*—*Syn.* (sales) receipts, day's *or* month's *or* week's *or* year's sales, business; see **income.**

salesman, *n.* **1.** [A sales clerk]—*Syn.* salesperson, seller, counterman; see **clerk** 1.

2. [A commercial traveler]—*Syn.* (out-of-town) representative, agent, canvasser, solicitor, seller, businessman, itinerant, field worker, traveler, traveling man, traveling salesman, Fuller Brush man, sales manager; *all* (D): runner, drummer, rep, sales rep, contact-man, gentleman of the road.

salesperson, *n.*—*Syn.* salesman, saleswoman, saleslady; see **clerk.**

sales resistance, *n.*—*Syn.* price consciousness, slow market, competition; see **opposition** 2, **trouble** 2.

sales talk, *n.*—*Syn.* promotion, (sales) patter, presentation; see **advertising** 1, **publicity** 3.

saleswoman, *n.*—*Syn.* saleslady, salesgirl, shopgirl, counter-girl, *vendeuse* (French); see also **clerk** 1.

salient, *mod.* **1.** [Prominent]—*Syn.* remarkable, notable, striking; see **conspicuous** 1, **famous.**

2. [Projecting]—*Syn.* jutting, swelling, bowed; see **hilly, prominent** 1.

saline, *mod.*—*Syn.* briny, brackish, alkaline; see **salty.**

saliva, *n.*—*Syn.* water, spittle, salivation, excretion, phlegm, enzyme, spit.

sallow, *mod.*—*Syn.* wan, pallid, ashy, ashen, colorless, waxy, yellow, olive, jaundiced, muddy (complexioned); see also **dull** 2, **pale** 1.

sally, *v.*—*Syn.* rush out, march out, go forth; see **hurry** 1.

salmon, *n.* **1.** [A fish] Varieties of salmon include the following—Atlantic, Pacific, quinnat, chinook, redback, blueback, humpback, silver, coho, dog; salmon trout, steelhead trout, red fish.

2. [The flesh of salmon, sense 1, used as food]—*Syn.* salmon steak, salmon filet, smoked salmon, kippered salmon, canned salmon, salmon salad, lox; *both* (D): goldfish, deep-sea turkey; see also **food.**

salon, *n.*—*Syn.* showroom, hall, reception room; see **gallery** 3, **room** 2.

saloon, *n.* **1.** [A large social room]—*Syn.* salon, apartment, ballroom; see **hall** 1, **lounge** 2.

2. [A dining hall, especially on a ship]—*Syn.* dining cabin, *salle à manger* (French), dining car; see **dining room.**

3. [A public drinking house]—*Syn.* bar, alehouse, tavern, publichouse, night club, cocktail lounge: *all* (D): grog shop, pub, beer parlor, poor man's club, joint, hangout, watering hole, place.

salt, *mod.* **1.** [Tasting of salt]—*Syn.* alkaline, saline, briny; see **salty.**
2. [Preserved with salt]—*Syn.* salted, brined, cured, pickled, corned, marinated, dilled, salt-pickled, preserved, soused (D).

salt, *n.* **1.** [A common seasoning and preservative] —*Syn.* sodium chloride, common salt, table salt, savor, condiment, flavoring, spice, seasoning. Common types of flavoring salts include the following—garlic, sea, celery, onion, barbecue, salad, seasoning, (hickory) smoked; poultry seasoning, kitchen bouquet, monosodium glutamate *or* MSG, salt substitute.
2. [A chemical compound] Common chemical salts include the following—Epsom, Glauber's, Rochelle, mineral, smelling; saltpeter, sal ammoniac, salts of tartar, baking soda.
3. [Anything that provides savor]—*Syn.* relish, pungency, smartness; see **humor** 1, **wit** 1.
below the salt—*Syn.* disfavored, not in favor, not socially acceptable; see **unpopular.**
not worth one's salt—*Syn.* good-for-nothing, bad, worthless; see **poor** 2.
salt of the earth—*Syn.* fine *or* good *or* excellent, *etc.* man *or* woman *or* people; solid citizen, one of nature's noblemen (D); see **gentleman** 1, **lady** 2.
with a grain *or* **pinch of salt**—*Syn.* doubtingly, skeptically, *cum grano salis* (Latin); see **suspiciously.**

salt, *v.* **1.** [To flavor with salt]—*Syn.* season, make tasty, make piquant; see **flavor.**
2. [To scatter thickly]—*Syn.* pepper, strew, spread; see **scatter** 1, 2.

salt a mine, *v.* —*Syn.* misrepresent, fix up to sell, deceive, mislead; *both* (D): plant, doctor.

salt away (D), *v.* —*Syn.* invest, put away, put in the bank, accumulate, save, set aside, hoard.

salt down, *v.* —*Syn.* pack in salt, cure, keep, preserve, put down, pickle.

salty, *mod.* —*Syn.* briny, brackish, pungent, alkaline, well-seasoned, flavored, well-flavored, highly flavored, sour, acrid.

salubrious, *mod.* —*Syn.* sanitary, healthy, wholesome; see **healthful.**

salutary, *mod.* **1.** [Healthful]—*Syn.* salubrious, healthy, wholesome, good, nutritious, health-giving.
2. [Beneficial]—*Syn.* tonic, helpful, remedial, bracing, advantageous, curative, restorative, invigorating.

salutation, *n.* —*Syn.* salute, address, welcome; see **greeting** 1, **regards.**

salutatory, *n.* —*Syn.* address, recitation, lecture; see **speech** 3.

salute, *v.* **1.** [To address]—*Syn.* speak, recognize, hail, accost, greet; see also **address** 2.
2. [To recognize with respect]—*Syn.* welcome, pay one's respects to, receive, bow, greet with a bow, greet with a kiss, congratulate.
3. [To perform a military salute]—*Syn.* present arms, snap to attention, dip the colors, fire a salute, touch one's cap, do honor to, break out a flag; see also **praise** 1.

salvage, *v.* —*Syn.* retrieve, recover, regain, rescue, restore, redeem, get back, glean.

salvation, *n.* **1.** [The act of preservation]—*Syn.* deliverance, extrication, liberation, emancipation, rescue, release, conservation, exemption, reprieve, pardon.
2. [A means of preservation]—*Syn.* buckler, safeguard, assurance; see **aid** 1, **protection** 2.
3. [In the Christian religion, saving a soul from damnation]—*Syn.* regeneration, rebirth, new birth, second birth, work of grace, forgiveness, mercy, justification, redemption, sanctification, entire sanctification.

salve, *n.* —*Syn.* ointment, cerate, unguent, lubricant, balm, medicine, emollient, unction, counterirritant, remedy, help, cure, cream. Common salves include the following—camphor ice, zinc oxide, menthol ice, lanolin; Vaseline, Mentholatum, Ben-Gay, Vaporub (all trademarks).

same, *mod.* **1.** [Like another in state]—*Syn.* equivalent, identical, corresponding; see **alike** 1, 2, **equal.**
2. [Like another in action]—*Syn.* similarly, in the same manner, likewise; see **alike** 3, **related** 2.

same, *pron.* —*Syn.* the very same, identical object, no other *or* different, substitute, equivalent, similar product, synthetic product, just-as-good (D).

sameness, *n.* —*Syn.* uniformity, unity, resemblance, analogy, similarity, alikeness, identity, standardization, equality, unison, no difference.

sample, *n.* —*Syn.* specimen, unit, individual; see **example** 1, **representation.**

sample, *v.* —*Syn.* taste, test, inspect; see **examine** 1, **experiment** 2.

sanatorium, *n.* —*Syn.* resort, health resort, hospital, sanitarium, spa, watering place, retreat, pump room.

sanctified, *mod.* —*Syn.* pure, anointed, hallowed; see **blessed** 2, **divine** 2.

sanctify, *v.* —*Syn.* deify, glorify, dedicate; see **bless** 3, **worship** 2.

sanctimonious, *mod.* —*Syn.* bigoted, deceiving, insincere; see **false** 1, **hypocritical.**

sanction, *n.* **1.** [Approval]—*Syn.* consent, acquiescence, assent; see **permission.**
2. [An instrumentality]—*Syn.* decree, command, writ, sentence, ban, embargo, injunction, loss of reward, penalty, punishment, punitive sanctions, civil sanctions, remuneratory sanctions.

sanction, *v.* —*Syn.* confirm, authorize, countenance; see **approve** 1, **endorse** 2.

sanctity, *n.* —*Syn.* sanctification, sacredness, piety; see **holiness** 2, **virtue** 1.

sanctuary, *n.* **1.** [A sacred place]—*Syn.* chancel, Holy of Holies, shrine, sanctum, church, temple; see also **church** 1, **temple.**
2. [A place to which one may retire]—*Syn.* asylum, resort, haven, convent, screen, defense, shield, protection, refuge, retreat, shelter.
3. [A refuge for wild life]—*Syn.* shelter, game refuge, park, national park.

sand, *mod.* —*Syn.* beach, chip, beige, sand beige, desert sand, ecru, natural, tan.

sand, *n.* **1.** [Rock particles]—*Syn.* sandy soil, sandy loam, silt, dust, grit, powder, gravel, rock powder, silica, rock flour, debris, detritus, dirt; see also **earth** 2.
2. [The beach]—*Syn.* strand, *plage* (French), seaside, seashore, coast, seaboard, sea bank.

sandal, *n.* —*Syn.* slipper, low shoe, evening slipper, thong, *huarache* (Spanish), wedgie, loafer, strapped pump, Jesus boot (D);

sand lot (D), *n.* —*Syn.* amateur baseball; *both* (D): Little League, Twilight League; see **baseball.**

sandstone, *n.* Varieties of sandstone include the following—arkrose, freestone, brownstone, flagstone, bluestone, grit, novaculite, Triassic brownstone, Berea sandstone, Medina sandstone, Potsdam quartzite, Old Red Sandstone, New Red Sandstone; see also **mineral** 1, **rock** 1.

sandstorm, *n.* —*Syn.* dust storm, high wind, Mormon rain (D); see **storm** 1, **wind** 1.

sandwich, *n.* —*Syn.* lunch, light lunch, quick lunch, wich (D).
Sandwiches include the following—hamburger *or* hamburg, burger (D), cheeseburger, wiener (*all* (D): dog, hot dog, red hot, pup), chili dog, Denver, Western, sloppy Joe, club, tuna fish, ham, chicken, roast beef, ham and egg, cheese, deviled meat, steak, hot roast meat, submarine, hero, poorboy, hoagie, bacon and cheese; bacon, lettuce and tomato (BLT); toasted cheese, tomato, egg salad, lettuce, open face, peanut butter and jelly, jelly, fruit and nut, pinwheel, ribbon, checkerboard, rolled.

sandy, *mod.* **1.** [Containing sand; *said especially of soil*]—*Syn.* light, loose, permeable, porous, easy to work, easily worked, friable, granular, powdery, gritty, sabulous, arenose.
2. [Suggestive of sand; *said especially of the hair*] —*Syn.* fair-haired, fair, blond, light, light-haired, towheaded, reddish, carrot-red, carroty, sandy-red, sandy-flaxen, sun-bleached, faded.

sane, *mod.* **1.** [Sound in mind]—*Syn.* rational, normal, lucid, right-minded, sober, sound-minded, sound, in one's right mind, self-possessed, with a healthy mind, mentally sound, balanced, healthy-minded, reasonable; *all* (D): having a head on one's shoulders, having all one's marbles, all there, in possession of one's faculties.—*Ant.* insane*, irrational, delirious.
2. [Sensible]—*Syn.* reasonable, fair-minded, open to reason, endowed with reason, sagacious, judicious, wise, logical, intelligent, steady, with good judgment, discerning, well-advised.—*Ant.* illogical*, unreasonable, senseless.

San Francisco, *n.* —*Syn.* City by the Golden Gate, City of St. Francis; *all* (D): Frisco, Queen City, Golden City, the City Cosmopolitan, Port o' Missing Men.

sanguinary, *mod.*—*Syn.* gory, cruel, bloodthirsty; see **ferocious, savage** 2.

sanguine, *mod.* —*Syn.* enthusiastic, expectant, optimistic; see **hopeful** 1, 2.

sanitarium, *n.* —*Syn.* health resort, sanatorium, spa, watering place, pump room, asylum, convalescent home, hospital, nursing home.

sanitary, *mod.*—*Syn.* hygienic, sanative, uncontaminated, wholesome, unpolluted, purified, sterile, healthful.

sanitation, *n.*—*Syn.* sanitary science, science of public cleanliness, hygiene, asepsis, disinfection.

sanity, *n.* **1.** [Freedom from mental disease]—*Syn.* sound mind, rationality, healthy mind, *mens sana* (Latin), saneness, heredity, a clear mind, clear-mindedness, wholesome outlook.
2. [Good sense]—*Syn.* common sense, intelligence, reason, reasonableness, prudence, good judgment, sagacity, acumen, understanding, comprehension.

sap, *n.* **1.** [The life fluid of a plant]—*Syn.* fluid, secretion, essence; see **juice.**
2. [A vital fluid]—*Syn.* lifeblood, precious fluid, substance; see **blood** 1.
3. [(D) A dupe]—*Syn.* dolt, gull, simpleton; see **fool** 1.

sap, *v.* —*Syn.* undermine, exhaust, subvert; see **drain** 1, 2, 3, **weaken** 2.

sapience, *n.* —*Syn.* intelligence, erudition, insight; see **knowledge** 1, **wisdom** 2.

sapient, *mod.*—*Syn.* sagacious, discriminating, wise; see **judicious.**

sapless, *mod.* **1.** [Dry]—*Syn.* shriveled, dehydrated, decayed; see **dry** 1, **withered.**
2. [Insipid]—*Syn.* spineless, ineffectual, lazy; see **dull** 4, **weak** 3.

sapling, *n.* —*Syn.* scion, seedling, slip, sprig, young tree; see also **tree.**

sapphire, *mod.*—*Syn.* sapphirine, greenish-blue; see **blue** 1.

sappy, *mod.* **1.** [Juicy]—*Syn.* lush, succulent, watery; see **juicy.**
2. [Forceful]—*Syn.* potent, effectual, dynamic; see **active** 2, **powerful** 1.
3. [(D) Idiotic]—*Syn.* foolish, silly, illogical; see **stupid** 1.

sarcasm, *n.*—*Syn.* satire, irony, banter, derision, contempt, scoffing, flouting, superciliousness, ridicule, burlesque, disparagement, criticism, cynicism, invective, censure, lampooning, aspersion, sneering, mockery.—*Ant.* flattery, fawning, cajolery.

sarcastic, *mod.*—*Syn.* scornful, mocking, ironical, satirical, taunting, severe, derisive, sardonic, bitter, saucy, hostile, sneering, snickering, quizzical, arrogant, Rabelaisian, Hudibrastic, disrespectful, scurrile, scurrilous, chaffing, twitting, offensive, irascible, carping, cynical, disillusioned, snarling, unbelieving, corrosive, acid, cutting, contemptuous, scorching, captious, sharp, acrimonious, pert, brusque, caustic, biting, harsh, austere, contumelious, grim.

sarcastically, *mod.*—*Syn.* cruelly, viciously, unkindly; see **brutally.**

sardines, *n.*—*Syn.* young herring, menhaden, sprats, *brisling* (Norwegian), pilchard, anchovy, *Sardinia pilchardus* (Latin).

sardonic, *mod.*—*Syn.* sarcastic, cynical, scornful; see **sarcastic.**

sash, *n.* —*Syn.* scarf, cincture, girdle; see **band** 1, 2.

Satan, *n.*—*Syn.* Mephistopheles, Lucifer, Beelzebub; see **devil** 1.

satanic, *mod.* —*Syn.* malicious, vicious, devilish; see **sinister, wicked** 2.

satchel, *n.*—*Syn.* handbag, traveling bag, reticule; see **bag, purse.**

satellite, *n.* **1.** [A small planet that revolves around a larger one]—*Syn.* moon, planetoid, minor planet, secondary planet, inferior planet, asteroid.
2. [A man-made object put into orbit around a celestial body]—*Syn.* space satellite, robot satellite, unmanned satellite, body satellite, orbital rocket, artificial moon, spacecraft, moonlet, man-made

moon, mouse, mouse-moon, sputnik, satellite station, spy-in-the-sky.
Satellites include the following—Tiros, Discoverer, Sputnik, Syncom, Early Bird, Echo, Telstar, Relay, Nimbus, Secor, Skylab, Soyuz, Challenger.
3. [A smaller country dependent upon a larger one] —*Syn.* iron-curtain country, captive nation, buffer state, mandate.

satiate, *v.* —*Syn.* surfeit, fill, gratify; see **satisfy** 1.

satin, *n.* —*Syn.* silk, glossy silk, cloth, fabric of royalty.
Types of satin include the following—satin de chine, royal weave, satin de laine, satin de Lyon, crèpe satin.

satiny, *mod.* —*Syn.* sericeous, glossy, smooth; see **silken.**

satire, *n.* **1.** [The exposing of vice or folly, especially by wit]—*Syn.* mockery, ridicule, caricature; see **irony, parody** 1.
2. [A work conspicuous for its satire, sense 1] —*Syn.* burlesque, lampoon, caricature; see **parody** 2.

satirical, *mod.* —*Syn.* mocking, abusive, paradoxical; see **ironical** 1, **sarcastic.**

satirist, *n.* —*Syn.* comedian, caricaturist, critic; see **author** 2, **writer.**

satirize, *v.* —*Syn.* mimic, mock, deride; see **ridicule.**

satisfaction, *n.* **1.** [The act of satisfying]—*Syn.* gratification, fulfillment, achievement, reparation, atonement, settlement, recompense, compensation, amends, indemnification, redemption, conciliation, propitiation, indulgence, liquidation, amusement.
2. [The state or feeling of being satisfied]—*Syn.* comfort, pleasure, well-being, content, contentment, gladness, delight, bliss, joy, happiness, relief, complacency, peace of mind, ease, heart's ease, serenity, contentedness, cheerfulness.—*Ant.* dissatisfaction*, unhappiness, discontent.
3. [Something that contributes to satisfaction, sense 2]—*Syn.* treat, entertainment, refreshment, remuneration, meed, prize, reward, prosperity, good fortune; see **aid** 1, **blessing** 2.
4. [Reparation]—*Syn.* reimbursement, repayment, compensation; see **reparation** 2.

satisfactorily, *mod.* **1.** [In a satisfactory manner] —*Syn.* convincingly, suitably, competently; see **adequately** 1, 2.
2. [Productive of satisfactory results]—*Syn.* amply, abundantly, thoroughly; see **agreeably.**

satisfactory, *mod.* —*Syn.* adequate, satisfying, pleasing; see **enough** 1.

satisfied, *mod.* —*Syn.* content, happy, contented, filled, supplied, fulfilled, paid, requited, compensated, appeased, convinced, gratified, *sans souci* (French), sated, at ease, with enough of, without care, satiated.

satisfy, *v.* **1.** [To make content]—*Syn.* comfort, cheer, elate, befriend, please, rejoice, delight, exhilarate, amuse, entertain, flatter, make merry, make cheerful, gladden, content, gratify, indulge, humor, conciliate, propitiate, capture, enthrall, enliven, animate, captivate, fascinate, fill, sate, be of advantage, surfeit, gorge, glut, cloy, satiate; *both* (D): tickle, brighten up.
2. [To pay]—*Syn.* repay, clear (up), disburse; see **pay** 1, **settle** 9.
3. [To fulfill]—*Syn.* do, fill, serve the purpose, be enough, assuage, observe, perform, comply with, conform to, meet requirements, keep a promise, accomplish, complete, be adequate, be sufficient, provide, furnish, qualify, answer, serve, equip, meet, avail, suffice, fill the want, come up to, content one, appease one; *all* (D): fill the bill, pass muster, get by, go in a pinch.—*Ant.* neglect*, leave open, fail to do.
4. [To convince]—*Syn.* induce, inveigle, win over; see **convince, persuade** 1.

satisfying, *mod.* —*Syn.* pleasing, comforting, gratifying; see **enough** 1, **pleasant** 2.

saturate, *v.* —*Syn.* overfill, drench, steep; see **immerse** 1, **soak** 1.

saturated, *mod.* —*Syn.* drenched, full, soggy; see **soaked, wet** 1.

saturation, *n.* —*Syn.* fullness, soaking, superabundance, overload, plethora, engorgement, congestion.

saturnalia, *n.* —*Syn.* spree, revelry, gang bang (D); see **orgy.**

saturnine, *mod.* —*Syn.* morose, passive, grave; see **dull** 4, **solemn** 1.

satyr, *n.* **1.** [Demigod]—*Syn.* (sylvan) deity, faun, Pan; see **god** 1.
2. [Lecher]—*Syn.* old goat, whoremonger, rake, reprobate, debaucher, wretch, dirty old man.

sauce, *n.* **1.** [A condiment]—*Syn.* appetizer, gravy, seasoning; see **flavoring, food.**
Varieties of sauce, sense 1, include the following —barbecue, Bernaise, caper, Colbert, hollandaise, tartar, horseradish, Worcestershire, Spanish, mushroom, mustard, *velouté* (French), gooseberry, raisin, madeira, chef's special.
2. [*United States,* stewed fruit]—*Syn.* cooked fruit, fruit butter, conserve, preserve.
Varieties of sauce, sense 2, include the following —apple, gooseberry, blueberry, blackberry, boysenberry, loganberry, raspberry, strawberry, pear, peach, plum, cherry, grape, apricot, nectarine, prune.

saucepan, *n.* —*Syn.* stewpan, vessel, utensil; see **pan.**

saucer, *n.* —*Syn.* small bowl, sauce dish, cereal dish; see **china, dish.**

saucily, *mod.* —*Syn.* pertly, impudently, impolitely; see **rudely.**

saucy, *mod.* —*Syn.* impudent, impertinent, insolent; see **rude** 2.

saunter, *v.* —*Syn.* roam, ramble, wander; see **walk** 1.

sausage, *n.* Sausages include the following—pork sausage, country sausage, link sausage, Vienna sausage *or* Wienerwurst, Bologna sausage, salami, liverwurst, knockwurst, capocola, cervelat, Braunschweiger, Thuringer, Holstein sausage, Göteborg, landjaeger, chorizos, coppa, frankfurter, knoblauch, goose-liver sausage, head cheese, lachsschinken, Lyons sausage, mettwurst, mortadella, pepperoni, kolbassy, kielbasa, bratwurst, summer sausage; see also **meat.**

savage, *mod.* **1.** [Primitive]—*Syn.* crude, simple, original, primary, first, earliest, primordial, fundamental, aboriginal, pristine, ancient, archaic, rustic, primeval, native, natural, in a state of nature, unchanged, unmodified.—*Ant.* forward*, advanced, sophisticated.

2. [Cruel]—*Syn.* barbarous, inhuman, brutal, brutish, ferine, feral, heartless, cold-blooded, destructive, blood-thirsty, bloody-minded, sanguinary, murderous, atrocious, fierce, ferocious, furious, frantic, violent, raging, malicious, malignant, malevolent, ravening, infuriate, ravenous, rapacious, merciless, remorseless, ruthless, relentless, hellish, devilish, demoniac, diabolical, infernal; see also **cruel** 1, 2.—*Ant.* kind*, generous, gentle.

3. [Wild]—*Syn.* untamed, uncivilized, uncultured, uncultivated, untaught, primitive, unspoiled, rude, heathenish, pagan, ungoverned, unrestrained, turbulent, wild.—*Ant.* tame*, broken, civilized.

savage, *n.* **1.** [Native]—*Syn.* aborigine, cannibal, troglodyte, barbarian, tribesman.

2. [Brute]—*Syn.* bully, ruffian, animal; see **beast** 2.

savagely, *mod.*—*Syn.* cruelly, viciously, indecently; see **brutally.**

savant, *n.*—*Syn.* philosopher, authority, intellectual; see **master** 3, **scholar** 2.

save, *v.* **1.** [To remove from danger]—*Syn.* deliver, extricate, rescue, free, set free, liberate, release, emancipate, ransom, redeem, come to the rescue of, snatch from the jaws of death, wrest from danger, defend.—*Ant.* leave*, desert, condemn.

2. [To assure an afterlife]—*Syn.* rescue from sin, reclaim, regenerate, bring into spiritual life, deliver from the power of Satan.—*Ant.* condemn*, damn, send to Hell.

3. [To hoard]—*Syn.* collect, store, lay up, lay apart, lay in, amass, accumulate, gather, treasure up, store up, pile up, hide away, cache, stow away, draw the purse strings (D).—*Ant.* waste*, spend, invest.

4. [To preserve]—*Syn.* conserve, keep, put up; see **preserve** 3.

5. [To reserve]—*Syn.* lay aside, lay away, set aside; see **maintain** 3.

6. [To avoid]—*Syn.* spare, curtail, lessen; see **avoid.**

saved, *mod.* **1.** [Kept from danger]—*Syn.* rescued, released, delivered, protected, defended, guarded, safeguarded, preserved, salvaged, reclaimed, regenerated, cured, healed, conserved, maintained, safe, secure, freed, free from harm, free from danger, unthreatened.—*Ant.* ruined*, lost, destroyed.

2. [Not spent]—*Syn.* kept, unspent, unused, untouched, accumulated, deposited, retained, laid away, hoarded, invested, husbanded, amassed, stored, spared.—*Ant.* wasted*, squandered, spent.

saving, *mod.* **1.** [Redeeming]—*Syn.* rescuing, reparatory, preserving; see **retaining.**

2. [Thrifty]—*Syn.* sparing, frugal, careful; see **economical** 1.

3. [Conditional]—*Syn.* provisional, qualificative, contingent; see **conditional.**

saving, *n.* **1.** [Conservation]—*Syn.* preservation, maintenance, thrift; see **conservation, economy** 2.

2. [Profit]—*Syn.* gain, proceeds, increase; see **addition** 2, **profit** 2.

savings, *n.*—*Syn.* means, property, resources, funds, reserve, competence, investment, provision, provisions, accumulation, store, riches, harvest, gleanings, hoard, cache; *all* (D): nest egg, money in the bank, anchor to windward, sheet anchor, provision for a rainy day.

savior, *n.* **1.** [One who saves another]—*Syn.* deliverer, rescuer, preserver, hero, knight, protector, guardian (angel), good genius, good Samaritan, benefactor; *both* (D): friend at court, friend in need.—*Ant.* enemy*, seducer, murderer.

2. [Christ; *often capital; usually Saviour*]—*Syn.* Redeemer, Messiah, Intercessor, Mediator, Advocate, Preserver and Finisher of our Faith, Surety, The Perfect Sacrifice, The Final Sacrifice, Our Exponent, Our Very Present Help in Time of Trouble, Friend and Helper; see also **Christ.**—*Ant.* devil*, demon, Power of Evil.

savoir-faire, *n.*—*Syn.* poise, courtesy, manners; see **tact.**

savor, *n.*—*Syn.* odor, flavor, relish, tang, taste, scent, tinge, zest, smack.

savor, *v.*—*Syn.* enjoy, relish, appreciate; see **like** 1.

savory, *mod.*—*Syn.* palatable, pleasing, appetizing, piquant, pungent, spicy, tangy, rich, flavorous, tasty, tempting, delectable, delicious, gustful, luscious, dainty, toothsome, nectareous, exquisite, ambrosial, good.

saw, *n.* Types of saws include the following—annular, circular, concave, mill, ice, crosscut, band, rip, hand, panel, pruning, whip, wood, buck, keyhole, back, butcher's, hack, double, jig; see also **tool** 1.

sawmill, *n.*—*Syn.* mill, lumber mill, portable mill; see **factory.**

saw-toothed, *mod.*—*Syn.* nicked, toothed, notched; see **irregular** 4.

saxophone, *n.*—*Syn.* horn, brass wind, sax (D); see **musical instrument.**

say, *v.*—*Syn.* tell, speak, relate, state, announce, remark, pronounce, declare, state positively, open one's mouth, have one's say, fling off, have one's ear, break silence, find words to express, rise to the occasion, put forth, let out, assert, maintain, express oneself, opine, answer, respond, reply, suppose, assume.

to say the least—*Syn.* at a minimum *or* the (very) least, to put it mildly, minimally.

saying, *mod.*—*Syn.* mentioning, making clear, revealing, pointing *or* giving out, remarking, noting, announcing, noticing, claiming, stating (emphatically), affirming, maintaining, asserting, attesting *or* certifying *or* testifying (to), alleging, informing, phrasing, stressing, demonstrating, averring, (a)-vouching, insisting (on), publicizing, advertising, making public, swearing, implying, propounding, observing, drafting a proposition, saying formally *or* officially *or* finally, *etc.;* making an announcement *or* a statement *or* declaration, *etc.*

saying, *n.*—*Syn.* aphorism, (wise) saw, adage, maxim, apothegm, epigram, gnome, byword, motto, proverb, precept, dictum.

scab, *n.* **1.** [A crust over a wound]—*Syn.* eschar, slough, crust.

2. [(D) One who replaces a union worker on strike]—*Syn.* turncoat, strikebreaker, traitor, apostate, deserter, knobstick (D).

scabbard, *n.*—*Syn.* casing, holder, covering; see **case** 7, **sheath.**

scabby, *mod.* —*Syn.* flaky, scurfy, scaly; see **rough** 1.

scabrous, *mod.* **1.** [Rough]—*Syn.* scaly, coarse, notched; see **rough** 1.
2. [Difficult]—*Syn.* treacherous, ominous, perilous; see **dangerous, difficult** 1.
3. [Improper]—*Syn.* immodest, unconventional, indiscreet; see **improper** 1, **risqué.**

scaffold, *n.* —*Syn.* framework, stage, structure; see **building** 1, **platform** 1.

scalawag, *n.* —*Syn.* rogue, scoundrel, trickster; see **rascal.**

scald, *v.* —*Syn.* char, blanch, parboil; see **burn** 2.

scale, *n.* **1.** [A series for measurement]—*Syn.* rule, computation, system; see **measure** 2, **order** 3.
2. [A flake or film]—*Syn.* thin coating, covering, incrustation; see **flake, layer.**
3. [A device for weighing; *often plural*]—*Syn.* steelyard, stilliard, balance, scale beam, spring scale, trebuchet, Roman balance, stapel scale, Danish balance.
Varieties of scales, sense 3, include the following—beam, automatic indicating, counter, cylinder, drum, barrel, flexure plate, plate fulcrum, platform, spring, electronic, digital, computing, household, miner's, assayer's.
4. [Musical tones]—*Syn.* range, diatonic *or* chromatic scale, major *or* minor scale, whole tone scale, harmonic *or* melodic scale; see also **music.**
on a large scale—*Syn.* extensively, grandly, expansively; see **generously.**
on a small scale—*Syn.* economically, in a small limited way, with restrictions; see **inadequate** 1, **unimportant.**

scale, *v.* **1.** [To climb]—*Syn.* ascend, surmount, mount; see **climb** 2.
2. [To peel]—*Syn.* exfoliate, strip off, flake; see **peel, skin.**
3. [To measure]—*Syn.* compare, balance, compute, size, allow due weight, estimate, calibrate, graduate, have a weight of, make of an exact weight.

scale down, *v.* —*Syn.* cut back, limit, restrict; see **decrease** 2.

scale up, *v.* —*Syn.* advance, augment, step up (D); see **increase** 1.

scallop, *n.* —*Syn.* serration, border, indentation; see **cut** 2, **edge** 1.

scalpel, *n.* —*Syn.* dissecting instrument, surgical tool, blade; see **knife.**

scalper (D), *n.* —*Syn.* ticket salesman, dealer, sharper, resale man, speculator.

scaly, *mod.* —*Syn.* rough, flaky, scabby, broken, skinned.

scamp, *n.* —*Syn.* rogue, knave, scoundrel; see **rascal**; see also **rough** 1.

scamper, *v.* —*Syn.* hasten, speed, haste; see **hurry** 1, **run** 2.

scan, *v.* **1.** [To analyze]—*Syn.* investigate, study, inquire into; see **examine** 1.
2. [To glance at]—*Syn.* browse, thumb over, consider; see **look** 2.

scandal, *n.* —*Syn.* shame, disgrace, embarrassment, infamy, turpitude, discredit, blot (on one's escutcheon), slander, disrepute, detraction, obloquy, calumny, defamation, opprobrium, reproach, aspersion, backbiting, gossip, eavesdropping, rumor, hearsay.—*Ant.* praise*, adulation, flattery.

scandalize, *v.* —*Syn.* calumniate, detract, defame, traduce, backbite, vilify, revile, malign, slander, offend, shock, disgust, asperse, libel, disparage, run down, lampoon, hold up to scorn, severely criticize, disgrace, decry, dishonor, embarrass, belittle, sneer at, blackball, blacken, blackguard, depreciate, condemn, deprecate, speak ill of.—*Ant.* praise*, laud, honor.

scandalous, *mod.* —*Syn.* infamous, disreputable, ignominious; see **lewd** 1, **shameful** 2.

scandalously, *mod.* —*Syn.* shamefully, indecently, cruelly; see **wrongly** 1, 2.

Scandinavian, *mod.* —*Syn.* Norse, Viking, Nordic, Germanic, Norwegian, Swedish, Danish, Icelandic, Gutnish, Faroese, Norwego-Danish, Northern, Scandahoovian (D).

scant, *mod.* —*Syn.* scarce, insufficient, meager; see **inadequate** 1.

scanty, *mod.* —*Syn.* scarce, few, pinched, meager, little, small, bare, ragged, insufficient, inadequate, slender, narrow, thin, scrimp, scrimpy, tiny, wee, sparse, diminutive, short, stingy.—*Ant.* much*, large, many.

scapegoat, *n.* —*Syn.* substitute, sacrifice, dupe; see **victim** 1.

scapegrace, *n.* —*Syn.* scamp, rogue, scoundrel; see **rascal.**

scar, *n.* —*Syn.* cicatrix *or* cicatrice, cat-face, mark, blemish, discoloration, disfigurement, defect, flaw, hurt, wound, injury.

scar, *v.* —*Syn.* mark up, cramp, cut, pinch, slash, belt, hurt, maim, pierce, stab, whip, beat, injure.

scarce, *mod.* —*Syn.* limited, infrequent, not plentiful; see **rare** 2, **uncommon.**
make oneself scarce (D)—*Syn.* go, depart, run (off); see **leave** 1.

scarcely, *mod.* —*Syn.* barely, only just, scantily; see **hardly.**

scarcity, *n.* —*Syn.* deficiency, inadequacy, insufficiency; see **lack** 2, **poverty** 2.

scare, *n.* —*Syn.* fright, terror, alarm; see **fear** 1.

scare, *v.* —*Syn.* panic, terrify, alarm; see **frighten** 1.

scared, *mod.* —*Syn.* startled, frightened, fearful; see **afraid** 1, 2.

scare off *or* **away,** *v.* —*Syn.* drive off *or* out *or* away, get rid of, dispose of; see **frighten** 2.

scare up (D), *v.* —*Syn.* produce, provide, get; see **find** 1.

scarf, *n.* —*Syn.* throw, sash, tippet, muffler, shawl, comforter, ascot, stole, wrapper, prayer shawl *or* tallit, chasuble, orarion, pallium; see also **clothes.**

scarfskin, *n.* —*Syn.* cuticle, rind, epidermis; see **skin.**

scarlet, *mod.* —*Syn.* cardinal, royal red, Chinese red, Mandarin red, Turkey red, Persian red, Indian red, Naples red, Majolica earth, Persian earth, Prussian red, scarlet ochre, vermilion, chrome scarlet, French vermilion, paprika, Dutch vermilion, Chinese vermilion, pimento, scarlet vermilion, orient red, oriental red, chrome red, Austrian vermilion, Austrian cinnabar, para vermilion, radium vermilion, antimony vermilion, English vermilion, orange vermilion; see also **red.**

scat, *interj.* —*Syn.* be off, begone, out of the way, get out of my way, get out from under my feet, away with you, out with you, be off with you, get out of my sight; *all* (D): scoot, scram, git, bug off, get out, shoo, shoo-fly, gangway, draw your sled, pull your freight, march, beat it, get going.

scathing, *mod.* —*Syn.* brutal, cruel, harsh; see **severe** 1, 2.

scathingly, *mod.* —*Syn.* viciously, cruelly, shrilly; see **angrily, brutally.**

scatological, *mod.* —*Syn.* scatologic, filthy, obscene; see **dirty 1, lewd** 1, 2.

scatter, *v.* **1.** [To become separated]—*Syn.* run apart, run away, go one's own way, diverge, disperse, disband, migrate, spread widely, go in different directions, blow off, go in many directions, be blown to the four points of the compass, be strewn to the four winds of heaven.—*Ant.* assemble*, convene, congregate.

2. [To cause to separate]—*Syn.* dispel, derange, dissipate, diffuse, strew, divide, disband, shed, distribute, intersperse, disseminate, separate, disunite, sunder, scatter to the wind, sever, set asunder.—*Ant.* unite*, join, mix.

3. [To seed]—*Syn.* disseminate, set, strew.

4. [To waste]—*Syn.* spend, expend, dissipate, fritter away, squander, lavish, be prodigal with one's substance, spend prodigally, sow, broadcast, pour out like water, exhaust; *all* (D): throw away (with both hands), throw around, scatter to the birds; see also **spend** 1, **waste** 2.

scatterbrained, *mod.* —*Syn.* silly, giddy, irrational; see **illogical, stupid** 1.

scattered, *mod.* —*Syn.* spread, strewed, rambling, sowed, sown, sprinkled, spread abroad, separated, disseminated, dispersed, strung out, distributed, widespread, diffuse, all over the place, separate, shaken out.—*Ant.* gathered*, condensed, concentrated.

scattering, *mod.* —*Syn.* uneven, some, not many; see **few, irregular** 1.

scatteringly, *mod.* —*Syn.* unevenly, not regularly *or* evenly, sometimes; see **irregularly.**

scavenger, *n.* —*Syn.* trash collector, cleaner, garbageman; see **junkman.**

scenario, *n.* —*Syn.* plot, outline, synopsis; see **summary.**

scene, *n.* —*Syn.* spectacle, exhibition, display; see **view** 1.

behind the scenes—*Syn.* surreptitiously, quietly, deviously; see **secret** 1, 3.

make the scene (D)—*Syn.* come, get there, make it (D); see **arrive** 1.

scenery, *n.* —*Syn.* landscape, prospect, spectacle; see **view** 1, 2.

scenic, *mod.* —*Syn.* beautiful, spectacular, dramatic; see **picturesque** 1.

scent, *n.* —*Syn.* odor, fragrance, redolence; see **perfume, smell** 1, 2.

scepter, *n.* **1.** [Rod]—*Syn.* baton, stick, staff; see **wand.**

2. [Authority]—*Syn.* supremacy, jurisdiction, authority; see **command** 2, **power** 2.

schedule, *n.* **1.** [List]—*Syn.* catalogue, inventory, registry; see **list, record** 1.

2. [Program]—*Syn.* agenda, order of business, calendar; see **plan** 2, **program** 2.

on *or* **up to schedule**—*Syn.* on time, not lagging *or* behind, being pushed along; see **accepted, early** 2, **enough** 1.

schedule, *v.* —*Syn.* record, register, catalogue; see **list** 1, **program** 1.

scheduled, *mod.* —*Syn.* listed, stated, arranged; see **planned, proposed.**

scheme, *n.* —*Syn.* project, course of action, purpose; see **plan** 2, **system** 2.

scheme, *v.* —*Syn.* intrigue, contrive, devise; see **plan** 1.

schemer, *n.* —*Syn.* conniver, rogue, deceiver; see **rascal.**

scheming, *mod.* —*Syn.* tricky, cunning, crafty; see **sly** 1.

schism, *n.* —*Syn.* split, section, cabal; see **division** 2, **faction** 1.

schismatic, *mod.* —*Syn.* discordant, heretical, dissident; see **atheistic, rebellious** 2.

schismatic, *n.* —*Syn.* heretic, rebel, dissenter; see **protestor, skeptic.**

scholar, *n.* **1.** [A pupil]—*Syn.* schoolboy, schoolgirl, learner; see **student.**

2. [An expert in humanistic studies]—*Syn.* philosopher, savant, sage, professor, academic, teacher, doctor, litterateur; see also **critic** 2, **scientist.** Scholars include the following—editor, textual critic, lexicographer, historian, biographer, bibliographer, comparativist, linguist, philologist, semanticist, paleographer, historiographer, archaeologist, Egyptologist, Americanist, geographer, geopolitician, political scientist, sociologist, philosopher, folklorist, anthropologist, economist, ethnologist, cartographer, classicist, dialectologist, rhetorician, grammarian, etymologist, musicologist, literary historian, theologian, orientalist.

scholarly, *mod.* —*Syn.* erudite, cultured, studious; see **educated** 1, **learned** 1.

scholarship, *n.* —*Syn.* ability to publish, scientific approach, learning, pedantry, accomplishments, intellectualism, erudition, bibliography, bibliomania, studentship, Ph.D-itis (D); see also **knowledge** 1.

scholastic, *mod.* —*Syn.* academic, literary, lettered; see **learned** 1, 2.

school, *n.* **1.** [An institution of learning]—Varieties of schools include the following—nursery school, elementary school, middle school, junior high school, high school, secondary school, parochial school, boarding school, military school, seminary, normal school, conservatory, trade school, technical school, graduate school, professional school, divinity school, art school, law school *or* college *or* college of law; college of engineering, etc.; of medicine *or* dentistry *or* liberal arts *or* pure science *or* applied science, etc.; preparatory school, junior college, community college, the grades (D); see also **academy** 1, **college, university.**

2. [Persons or products associated by common intellectual or artistic theories]—*Syn.* class, party, adherents, following, circle; see also **academy** 2.

3. [A building housing a school, sense 1]—*Syn.* schoolhouse, hall, establishment, institution; see also **building** 1.

go to school—*Syn.* attend school *or* kindergarten *or* college, etc.; of medicine *or* dentistry *or* liberal arts *or* pure science matriculate; see also **learn** 1, **register.**

school-age, *mod.* —*Syn.* youthful, old enough to go to school, of school age; see **childish** 1, **young** 1.

schoolbook, *n.* —*Syn.* primer, textbook, assigned reading; see **book** 1, **text** 1.

schoolboy, *n.* —*Syn.* lad, learner, pupil; see **student.**

schoolhouse, *n.* —*Syn.* structure, institution, house; see **building** 1, **school** 3.

schooling, *n.* —*Syn.* teaching, nurture, discipline; see **education** 1.

schoolmate, *n.* —*Syn.* roommate, comrade, classmate; see **friend** 1.

schoolteacher, *n.* —*Syn.* educator, lecturer, instructor; see **teacher** 1, 2, **professor.**

school year, *n.* —*Syn.* nine months, from September to June, period (that the) school or college or kindergarten, *etc.,* is in session; see **year.**

schooner, *n.* —*Syn.* clipper, yacht, vessel; see **boat, ship.**

science, *n.* **1.** [An organized body of knowledge] —*Syn.* classified information, department of learning, branch of knowledge, system of knowledge, body of fact.

For commonly recognized sciences see **anthropology, archaeology, biology, botany, chemistry, cybernetics, geography, geology, mathematics, medicine** 3, **physics, physiology, psychology, social science, sociology, zoology.**

2. [A highly developed skill]—*Syn.* craftsmanship, art, deftness; see **ability** 1, 2.

scientific, *mod.* **1.** [Objectively accurate]—*Syn.* precise, exact, clear; see **accurate** 2, **objective** 1.

2. [Concerning science]—*Syn.* experimental, deductive, methodically sound; see **logical** 1.

scientifically, *mod.* —*Syn.* reliably, accurately, dependably; see **carefully** 1, 2, **exactly.**

scientist, *n.* —*Syn.* expert, specialist, investigator, laboratory technologist *or* technician, savant, natural philosopher, student of natural history, student of natural phenomena, explorer, research worker, research assistant, laboratory man *or* worker, learned man, serious student, seeker after knowledge, Doctor of Science, Doctor of Philosophy in Chemistry *or* Physics, etc.; Ph.D., scientific thinker, pure scientist, applied scientist, a Steinmetz, a Pasteur, an Einstein, a Gottlieb.

Scientists include the following—anatomist, astronomer, botanist, zoologist, biologist, chemist, biochemist, geologist, geographer, mathematician, physicist, psychiatrist, psychologist, astrophysicist, spectroscopist, spectral analyst, ecologist, biophysicist, bacteriologist, marine botanist, oceanographer, geopolitician, systematic botanist, industrial chemist, manufacturing chemist, chemurgist, pharmacist, chemical engineer, sanitary engineer, agronomist, entomologist, ornithologist, endocrinologist, radiologist, graphologist, geophysicist, cartographer, neurologist, neurophysicist, paleontologist, paleobotanist, structural geologist, oil geologist, mineralogist, metallurgist, anthropologist, ethnologist, comparative anatomist, Egyptologist, archaeologist, ethnobiologist, sociologist, linguist, dialectologist, folklorist; student of *or* specialist in aerodynamics, supersonics, astrophysical spectral analysis, roentgenology, etc.; see also **dentist, doctor, professor.**

scintillate, *v.* —*Syn.* twinkle, glimmer, sparkle; see **shine** 1, 2.

scion, *n.* —*Syn.* descendant, heir, progeny; see **child, offspring.**

scissors, *n.* —*Syn.* shears, pair of scissors *or* shears, cutting instrument.

scoff, *v.* —*Syn.* mock, deride, jeer; see **ridicule.**

scold, *v.* —*Syn.* admonish, chide, berate, chasten, asperse, expostulate with, rebuke, censure, reprove, upbraid, reprimand, taunt, cavil, criticize, denounce, disparage, recriminate, rate, revile, rail, abuse, objurate, vituperate, reprobate, villify, find fault with, nag, lecture; *all* (D): have on the carpet, rake over the coals, give one a talking to, preach, tell off, chew *or* bawl out, get after, chew *or* dress *or* call down, lay down the law, blow up at, jump down one's throat, jump on, call, keep after, burn up, light into, take the wind out of one's sails, put down; see also **punish.**—*Ant.* praise*, commend, extoll.

scoop, *v.* —*Syn.* ladle, shovel, bail; see **dip** 1.

scoot, *v.* —*Syn.* dart, speed, rush; see **hasten** 1, **hurry** 1.

scooter (D), *n.* —*Syn.* motor bicycle *or* scooter, cheap transportation, motor bike (D); see **motorcycle.**

scope, *n.* —*Syn.* reach, range, field; see **extent.**

scorch, *v.* —*Syn.* roast, parch, shrivel; see **burn** 1.

scorching, *mod.* **1.** [Hot]—*Syn.* fiery, searing, sweltering; see **burning** 1, **hot** 1.

2. [Harsh]—*Syn.* caustic, derisive, curt; see **sarcastic, scornful** 1, 2.

score, *n.* **1.** [A tally]—*Syn.* stock, counterstock, countertally, reckoning, record, average, rate, account, count, number.

2. [The total of the scores, sense 1]—*Syn.* summation, aggregate, sum, addition, summary, amount, final tally, final account; see also **number** 1, **whole.**

3. [Written music]—*Syn.* transcript, arrangement, orchestration; see **music** 1, **composition.**

know the score (D)—*Syn.* grasp *or* know *or* understand a little *or* the elements, *etc.;* be aware (of), comprehend; see **know** 1, **understand** 1.

score, *v.* **1.** [To make a single score]—*Syn.* make a goal, gain a point, win a point, rack *or* chalk up (D).

2. [To compute the score]—*Syn.* total, calculate, reckon, tally, enumerate, count, add.

3. [To damage]—*Syn.* deface, mar, mark; see **damage** 1, **maim.**

4. [To compose a musical accompaniment]—*Syn.* orchestrate, arrange, adapt; see **compose** 3.

5. [(D) To purchase legally or illegally]—*Syn.* get, procure, secure; see **buy** 1, **obtain** 1.

6. [(D) To copulate]—*Syn.* have (sexual) intercourse (with), sleep *or* lie with, fornicate; see **copulate.**

scorn, *v.* **1.** [To treat with scorn]—*Syn.* hold in contempt, despise, disdain; see **hate** 1.

2. [To refuse as a matter of principle]—*Syn.* ignore, flout, defy, spurn, repudiate, reject, turn the back upon, avoid, shun, renounce; see also **confute, re-**

fuse, **refute.**—*Ant.* acknowledge*, accept, welcome.

scornful, *mod.* **1.** [Given to scorning]—*Syn.* contemptuous, disdainful, haughty, supercilious, overbearing, arrogant, insolent, cynical, sneering, hypercritical; *all* (D): with the nose in the air, toplofty, snooty; see also **egotistic** 2.—*Ant.* respectful*, admiring, gracious.
2. [Characterized by scorn]—*Syn.* derisive, opprobrious, contumelious, scurrilous, abusive, insulting, offensive, rude, sarcastic, malicious, jeering, mocking, sneering, ironical.—*Ant.* polite*, respectful, flattering.

scornfully, *mod.*—*Syn.* contemptuously, rudely, sneeringly; see **brutally, proudly.**

Scots, *mod.*—*Syn.* Scotch, Scottish, Caledonian, highland, from north of the border, Gaelic; see also **Anglo-Saxon.**

scotch, *v.*—*Syn.* thwart, stop, block; see **hinder.**

scot-free, *mod.*—*Syn.* uncontrolled, footloose, liberated; see **free** 2.

Scotland, *n.*—*Syn.* Scotia, the Highlands, Caledonia; see **Britain, England.**

Scotsman, *n.*—*Syn.* Gael, Highlander, clansman, Scotchman, Scot.

scoundrel, *n.*—*Syn.* rogue, scamp, villain; see **rascal.**

scour, *v.* **1.** [To cleanse]—*Syn.* scrub, cleanse, rub; see **clean, wash** 1, 2.
2. [To search]—*Syn.* seek, look for, inquire; see **hunt** 2, **search.**

scourge, *n.* **1.** [A whip]—*Syn.* strap, cord, stick; see **whip.**
2. [Punishment]—*Syn.* correction, penalty, infliction; see **punishment.**

scourge, *v.* **1.** [To whip]—*Syn.* flog, hit, thrash; see **beat** 2.
2. [To punish]—*Syn.* chastise, castigate, penalize; see **punish.**

scouring powder, *n.*—*Syn.* cleaner, scrubbing powder, detergent; see **cleanser, soap.**

scout, *n.* **1.** [One who gathers information]—*Syn.* explorer, pioneer, outpost, runner, advance guard, precursor, patrol, reconnoiterer.
2. [(D) A Boy Scout] Degrees of scouts, sense 2, include the following—Cub, Tenderfoot, Second Class, First Class, Star, Life, Eagle, Queen's (British), bronze palm, gold palm, silver palm.
3. [(D) A Girl Scout]—*Syn.* explorer, young adventurer, Bluebird, Campfire Girl, pioneer.
Girl Scout ranks include the following—Brownie, Junior, Cadette, Senior.

scow, *n.*—*Syn.* barge, cargo ship, freighter; see **boat, ship.**

scowl, *v.*—*Syn.* glower, disapprove, grimace; see **frown, glare** 2.

scramble, *v.* **1.** [To mix]—*Syn.* combine, blend, interfuse; see **mix** 1.
2. [To climb hastily]—*Syn.* clamber, push, struggle; see **climb** 2.

scrap, *n.* **1.** [Junk metal]—*Syn.* waste material, chips, cuttings; see **trash** 3.
2. [A bit]—*Syn.* fragment, particle, portion; see **bit** 1, **piece** 1.
3. [(D) A fight]—*Syn.* quarrel, brawl, squabble; see **fight** 1.

scrap, *v.* **1.** [To discard]—*Syn.* reject, forsake, dismiss; see **abandon** 2, **discard.**
2. [(D) To fight]—*Syn.* wrangle, battle, squabble; see **fight** 1, **quarrel.**

scrapbook, *n.*—*Syn.* portfolio, memorabilia, notebook; see **album, collection** 2.

scrape, *v.*—*Syn.* abrade, scour, rasp; see **irritate** 2, **rub** 1.

scraper, *n.*—*Syn.* grater, grader, rasp, eraser, abrasive; see also **hoe, tool** 1.

scratch, *n.*—*Syn.* hurt, cut, mark; see **injury** 1, **scar.**
from scratch (D)—*Syn.* from the start or the beginning, without preparation *or* a predecessor, solely; see **alone, original** 1.

scratch, *v.*—*Syn.* scrape, scarify, prick; see **damage** 1, **hurt** 1.

scratching, *mod.*—*Syn.* grating, abrading, abrasive, attritive, rasping, erosive, scratchy, scarifying; see also **rough** 1.

scratch the surface (D), *v.*—*Syn.* be superficial, analyze *or* inspect superficially, touch on *or* upon, mention, skim, scan, brush; see also **begin** 1, 2.

scrawl, *n.*—*Syn.* scribbing, scratch, *barbouillage* (French); see **handwriting.**

scrawl, *v.*—*Syn.* scribble, scratch, doodle; see **write** 2.

scrawled, *mod.*—*Syn.* scribbled, scratched, inscribed; see **written** 2.

scrawny, *mod.*—*Syn.* lanky, gaunt, lean; see **thin** 2.

scream, *n.*—*Syn.* screech, outcry, shriek; see **cry** 1, **yell** 1.

scream, *v.*—*Syn.* shriek, screech, squeal; see **cry** 3, **yell.**

screaming, *mod.*—*Syn.* shrieking, screeching, squealing; see **yelling.**

screech, *n.*—*Syn.* shriek, yell, outcry; see **cry** 1.

screech, *v.*—*Syn.* scream, shout, shriek; see **yell.**

screen, *n.* **1.** [A concealment]—*Syn.* cloak, cover, covering, curtain, shield, envelope, veil, mask, shade.
Smoke screens include the following—sulphur trioxide solution, white phosphorus, HC mixture.
2. [A protection]—*Syn.* shelter, guard, security; see **cover** 1, **protection** 2.

screen, *v.* **1.** [To hide]—*Syn.* veil, conceal, mask; see **hide** 1.
2. [To choose]—*Syn.* select, eliminate, sift; see **choose** 1.

screened, *mod.*—*Syn.* hidden, sheltered, concealed; see **secret** 3.

screw, *n.*—*Syn.* spiral, worm, bolt, pin; see also **fastener.**
Screws include the following—jack, lead, leveling, dowel, double, drive, Hindley's, lag, worm, male *or* outside, female *or* inside, Phillips (trademark), right-handed, left-handed, metric, milled, endless, reciprocal, regulating, set, winged, thumb, rigger's, right-and-left, setting up, society, spiral, triple, feed, wood, machine.
have a screw loose (D)—*Syn.* be insane *or* crazy *or* demented, *etc.;* be touched in the head, be off one's rocker *or* nut (D); see **insane** 1.
put the screw(s) on *or* **to** (D)—*Syn.* compel, coerce, give the treatment (D); see **force** 1.

screw, *v.*—*Syn.* twine, wind, contort; see **turn** 1, **twist.**

screw-up (D), *n.* —*Syn.* mistake, confusion, mess; see **error** 1, **confusion.**
screw up (D), *v.* —*Syn.* bungle, foul up, mishandle; see **botch.**
screwy (D), *mod.* —*Syn.* odd, crazy, inappropriate; see **insane** 1, **wrong** 2, 3.
scribble, *n.* —*Syn.* scrawl, scrabble, scratch; see **handwriting.**
scribble, *v.* —*Syn.* scrawl, scratch, scrabble; see **write** 2.
scribe, *n.* **1.** [One who transcribes professionally] —*Syn.* copyist, clerk, secretary, keeper of accounts, copier, transcriber.
2. [A writer]—*Syn.* reporter, correspondent, penman; see **author** 1, **editor, writer.**
scrimmage, *n.* —*Syn.* confusion, scramble, scrap; see **fight** 1.
scrimp, *v.* —*Syn.* limit, pinch, skimp; see **economize, save** 3.
script, *n.* **1.** [Handwriting]—*Syn.* writing, characters, chirography; see **handwriting.**
2. [Playbook]—*Syn.* lines, text, dialogue, book, scenario.
scriptural, *mod.* **1.** [Authoritative]—*Syn.* recorded, accepted, standard; see **authoritative** 2, **written** 2.
2. [Biblical]—*Syn.* ecclesiastical, canonical, divine; see **religious** 1.
scripture, *n.* **1.** [Writing]—*Syn.* document, manuscript, inscription; see **writing** 2.
2. [Truth]—*Syn.* reality, verity, final word; see **truth** 1.
3. [*Capital;* the Bible]—*Syn.* the Word, Holy Writ, the Book; see **Bible** 2.
scroll, *n.* **1.** [A rolled sheet, especially a manuscript] —*Syn.* parchment, scripture, document; see **manuscript, writing** 2.
2. [A curved ornament]—*Syn.* volute, spiral, convolution; see **decoration** 2.
scrub, *mod.* **1.** [Inferior]—*Syn.* second-rate, unimportant, mediocre; see **poor** 2.
2. [Dwarf]—*Syn.* stunted, puny, diminutive; see **little** 1.
scrub (D), *n.* —*Syn.* mongrel, cur, cull, dwarf, stunted individual, an undesirable, inferior example; see also **runt** 1.
scrub, *v.* —*Syn.* rub, cleanse, scour; see **clean, wash** 1, 2.
scrubbed, *mod.* —*Syn.* cleaned, polished, immaculate; see **clean** 1.
scrubbing, *n.* —*Syn.* rubbing, washing, cleansing; see **cleaning.**
scrubby, *mod.* —*Syn.* inferior, stunted, scrawny; see **inadequate** 1, **poor** 2.
scrumptious, *mod.* —*Syn.* appetizing, tasty, delectable; see **delicious** 1, **rich** 4.
scruple, *n.* —*Syn.* compunction, qualm, uneasiness; see **doubt** 2.
scruples, *n.* —*Syn.* overconscientiousness, point of honor, scrupulousness; see **attention** 2, **care** 1.
scrupulous, *mod.* —*Syn.* exact, punctilious, strict; see **careful.**
scrupulously, *mod.* —*Syn.* exactly, precisely, devotedly; see **carefully** 1.
scrutinize, *v.* —*Syn.* view, study, stare; see **examine** 1, **watch** 1.
scrutiny, *n.* —*Syn.* analysis, investigation, inspection; see **examination** 1.
scuff, *n.* —*Syn.* clamor, sound, scrape; see **noise** 2.
scuffle, *n.* —*Syn.* struggle, shuffle, strife; see **fight** 1.
sculptor, *n.* —*Syn.* artist, modeler, carver, stone carver, wood carver, worker in bronze (*or* metal). Major sculptors include the following—Phidias, Ghiberti, Donatello, Luca della Robbia, Michelangelo, Giovanni da Bologna, Benvenuto Cellini, Gian Lorenzo Bernini, Auguste Rodin, Constantin Brancusi, Henry Moore, Jacques Lipchitz, Aristide Maillol, Pisano, Saint-Gaudens.
sculpture, *n.* —*Syn.* carving, modeling, carving in stone, modeling in clay, kinetic sculpture, op art, casting in bronze, woodcutting, stone carving, plastic art; see also **art** 2, **image** 2, **statue.**
sculptured, *mod.* —*Syn.* formed, cast, molded, engraved, carved, in relief, chiseled.
scum, *n.* —*Syn.* froth, film, impurities; see **residue, trash** 1, 3.
scurrility, *n.* —*Syn.* slander, sarcasm, defilement; see **abuse** 1.
scurrilous, *mod.* —*Syn.* indecent, shameless, ribald; see **lewd** 1, 2.
scurry, *v.* —*Syn.* race, scamper, rush; see **hasten** 1, **run** 2.
scutcheon, *n.* —*Syn.* shield, insignia, crest; see **decoration** 3.
scuttle, *v.* **1.** [To destroy]—*Syn.* submerge, abandon, dismantle; see **destroy** 1, **sink** 2.
2. [To hurry]—*Syn.* scurry, scramble, sprint; see **hasten** 1, **run** 2.
scuttlebutt (D), *n.* —*Syn.* (common) talk, inside information, straight dope (D); see **facts, gossip** 1, **rumor** 1.
scythe, *n.* —*Syn.* cutter, sickle, machete; see **hoe, knife.**
sea, *n.* Important seas include the following—Bering, Caribbean, Baltic, North, Irish, Mediterranean, Adriatic, Ionian, Aegean, Tyrrhenian, Black, Caspian, Azov, Red, Dead, White, Barents, Tasman, Okhotsk, Japan, Yellow, South China, Arabian, East China, Java, Timor, Sulu, Celebes, Coral; see also **ocean.**
at sea (D)—*Syn.* confused, puzzled, upset; see **bewildered, uncertain** 2.
put (out) to sea—*Syn.* embark, go, start (out); see **leave** 1, **sail** 1.
sea bottom, *n.* —*Syn.* ocean *or* deep-sea floor, depths *or* bottom of the sea, offshore land(s), ocean bottom, abyssal *or* ocean depths, continental shelf, undersea topography, undersea park, marine farm, tidewater, the briny deep (D); see also **ocean.** Terms for undersea topography include the following—bank, sands, seamount *or* submarine mountain, ridge, guyot, hill, tablemount, escarpment, plateau, reef, basin, canal, province, shoal, sill, channel, deep, depth, plain, trench, trough, fracture zone, rift.
seacoast, *n.* —*Syn.* seashore, seaboard, seaside; see **shore.**
seafaring, *mod.* —*Syn.* naval, oceanic, marine; see **maritime** 2, **nautical.**
sea food, *n.* —*Syn.* halibut, mollusk, marine life; see **fish, lobster, shellfish.**

seal, *n.* **1.** [Approval]—*Syn.* authorization, permit, allowance; see **permission.**
2. [Fastener]—*Syn.* adhesive tape, sticker, tie; see **fastener, tape.**
sealed, *mod.*—*Syn.* secured, fixed, held together; see **firm** 1, **tight** 2.
seal off, *v.*—*Syn.* quarantine, close, segregate; see **forbid, restrict** 2.
seam, *n.*—*Syn.* joint, line of joining, union, stitching, line of stitching, closure, suture.
seaman, *n.*—*Syn.* A. B., navigator, tar; see **marines, sailor** 1, 2.
seamstress, *n.*—*Syn.* sewer, needleworker, designer; see **dressmaker, tailor.**
seamy, *mod.*—*Syn.* unpleasant, bad, disagreeable; see **disappointing, disturbing.**
séance, *n.*—*Syn.* divination, ritual, session; see **gathering.**
seaplane, *n.*—*Syn.* hydroplane, airplane, amphibian; see **plane** 3.
seaport, *n.*—*Syn.* port, haven, town; see **dock** 1, **harbor** 2.
sea power, *n.*—*Syn.* naval forces, task *or* mobile striking force, navy (in being); see **navy.**
sear, *v.* **1.** [To cook by searing]—*Syn.* scorch, brown, toast; see **cook.**
2. [To dry by searing]—*Syn.* tan, harden, cauterize; see **burn** 2, **dry** 2.
search, *n.*—*Syn.* exploration, quest, reserach; see **hunt** 2.
in search of—*Syn.* looking for, seeking, on the lookout (for); see **searching** 2.
search, *v.*—*Syn.* explore, examine, rummage, comb, ransack, look up and down, smell around, track down, look for, go through, cast *or* beat about, poke into, grope in the dark (D), scrutinize; see also **hunt** 2, **seek** 1.
searching, *mod.* **1.** [Careful]—*Syn.* exploring, scrutinizing, examining; see **careful.**
2. [Seeking]—*Syn.* hunting, (actively or seriously) looking (for), seeking out *or* for, pursuing, in search of, receptive (to), susceptible (to), ready for, in the market (for), in need of, needing, wanting; *all* (D): on the lookout (for), looking out (for), crazy about *or* for, all hot for.
searchlight, *n.*—*Syn.* arc light, beam, Half-mile Ray (trademark); see **light** 3.
search me (D), *interj.*—*Syn.* I do not *or* don't know, who knows? how should *or* would I know? that is not *or* that's not my affair *or* in my department; see also **uncertainty** 1.
sea shell, *n.* Common sea shells include the following—conch, periwinkle, abalone, ammonite, ram's horn, clam, oyster, starfish, sea urchin, sand dollar, sea snail, nautilus, scallop; see also **shell** 3.
seashore, *n.*—*Syn.* seaboard, seaside, seacoast; see **shore.**
seasick, *mod.*—*Syn.* nauseated, miserable, suffering from *mal de mer*; see **sick.**
seaside, *n.*—*Syn.* seaboard, seashore, seacost; see **resort** 2, **shore.**
season, *n.*—*Syn.* period, term, a while, division, certain months of the year; see also **fall** 5, **spring** 2, **summer, winter.**
in good season—*Syn.* not late, on time, fairly soon; see **early** 2.
in season—*Syn.* seasonable, on the market, (readily) available; see **available.**
seasonable, *mod.*—*Syn.* appropriate, opportune, convenient; see **timely.**
seasonal, *mod.*—*Syn.* once a season, out of season, periodically, biennial, occurring *or* available only at certain times of the year, with the times, once in a while; see also **annual, yearly.**
seasoned, *mod.* **1.** [Spicy]—*Syn.* tangy, sharp, aromatic; see **spicy** 1.
2. [Experienced]—*Syn.* established, settled, mature; see **able** 2, **experienced.**
seasoning, *n.*—*Syn.* sauce, relish, spice, pungency; see also **flavoring, pickle** 2.
seat, *n.* **1.** [A structure on which one may sit]—*Syn.* bench, settee, pew, chair, stool, thwart; see also **furniture.**
2. [Space in which one may sit]—*Syn.* situation, chair, accommodation; see **place** 2.
3. [(D) The part of the body with which one sits]—*Syn.* buttocks, rear, breech; see **rump.**
4. [An official situation]—*Syn.* post, position, office, chair, place; see also **job** 1, **profession** 1, **trade** 2.
5. [A place of support, usually a surface]—*Syn.* bed, fitting, bottom; see **foundation** 2, **support** 2.
have *or* **take a seat**—*Syn.* be seated, sit (down), occupy a place; see **sit** 1.
seated, *mod.*—*Syn.* situated, located, settled, installed, established, rooted, set, fitted in place, placed, arranged, accommodated with seats.
seating, *n.*—*Syn.* places, reservations, chairs, seats, room, accommodation, arrangement, seating space.
seaward, *mod.*—*Syn.* offshore, fresh, fresh from the sea, out to sea, over the sea, over the ocean; see also **coastal, maritime** 1, 2.
seaweed, *n.*—*Syn.* kelp, tangle, sea tangle, sea meadow, algae, marine meadow; see also **plant.** Seaweed includes the following—sea moss, Irish moss, Sargasso weed, dulse, rockweed, sea lettuce, kelp, giant kelp, agar-agar, gulf-weed, sea cabbage.
seaworthy, *mod.*—*Syn.* fit for sea, navigable, secure; see **safe** 1.
secede, *v.*—*Syn.* withdraw, retract, leave; see **retire** 1, **retreat** 1.
secession, *n.*—*Syn.* withdrawal, seceding, retraction; see **retirement** 1.
seclude, *v.* **1.** [To isolate]—*Syn.* quarantine, ostracize, evict; see **separate** 2.
2. [To hide]—*Syn.* screen out, conceal, cover; see **hide** 1.
secluded, *mod.*—*Syn.* screened, removed, sequestered; see **isolated, withdrawn.**
seclusion, *n.*—*Syn.* solitude, aloofness, privacy; see **retirement** 2.
second, *mod.*—*Syn.* secondary, subordinate, inferior, next, next in order, following, next to the first, next in rank, another, other; see also **unimportant.**
play second fiddle (to)—*Syn.* defer (to), be inferior (to), be less successful (than); see **fail** 1.
second, *n.*—*Syn.* flash, trice, flash of an eyelid; see **moment, instant.**
secondary, *mod.* **1.** [Derived]—*Syn.* dependent, developed, consequent, subsequent, proximate,

subordinate, subsidiary, auxiliary.—*Ant.* original*, primary, basic.
2. [Minor]—*Syn.* inconsiderable, petty, small; see **trivial, unimportant.**
seconded, *mod.* —*Syn.* backed, favored, supported; see **approved.**
secondhand, *mod.* —*Syn.* used, not new, reclaimed, renewed, re-used, old, worn, borrowed, derived, not original.
secondly, *mod.* —*Syn.* in the second place, furthermore, also, besides, next, on the other hand, in the next place, for the next step, next in order, further, to continue; see also **including.**
second-rate, *mod.* —*Syn.* mediocre, inferior, common; see **poor** 2.
secrecy, *n.* —*Syn.* concealment, confidence, hiding, seclusion, privacy, retirement, solitude, mystery, dark, darkness, isolation, reticence, stealth.
secret, *mod.* **1.** [Not generally known]—*Syn.* mysterious, ambiguous, hidden, unknown, arcane, cryptic, esoteric, abstruse, occult, mystic, mystical, classified, dark, veiled, enigmatical, enigmatic, strange, deep, buried in mystery, obscure, clouded, recondite, shrouded, unenlightened, unintelligible, cabalistic.—*Ant.* known*, revealed, exposed.
2. [Hidden]—*Syn.* latent, secluded, concealed; see **hidden** 2.
3. [Operating secretly]—*Syn.* clandestine, underhand, underhanded, stealthy, sly, surreptitious, close, in ambuscade *or* ambush, furtive, disguised, undercover, hush-hush (D), backdoor, confidential, backstairs, incognito, camouflaged, cryptographic, enigmatic, under false pretense, unrevealed, undisclosed, dissembled, dissimulated, *in camera* (Latin), under wraps (D); see also **secretive, sly** 1, **taciturn.** —*Ant.* open*, aboveboard, overt.
secret, *n.* —*Syn.* mystery, deep mystery, something veiled, something hidden, confidence, private matter, code, telegram, scrambled telephone conversation, personal matter, privileged information, top secret, enigma, puzzle, something forbidden, classified *or* confidential *or* inside information, an unknown, magic number, the unknown.
in secret—*Syn.* slyly, surreptitiously, quietly; see **secret** 3.
secretariat, *n.* —*Syn.* bureau, department, council; see **administration** 2, **committee.**
secretary, *n.* **1.** [A secondary executive officer] —*Syn.* director, manager, superintendent, cabinet member, cabinet officer, bureau chief, head of a department, department manager, administrator.
2. [An assistant]—*Syn.* clerk, typist, stenographer, copyist, amanuensis, recorder, confidential clerk, correspondent.
secrete, *v.* **1.** [To hide]—*Syn.* conceal, cover, seclude; see **disguise, hide** 1.
2. [To perspire]—*Syn.* discharge, swelter, emit; see **sweat** 1.
secretion, *n.* —*Syn.* discharge, issue, movement; see **excretion** 1, **flow.**
secretive, *mod.* —*Syn.* reticent, taciturn, tight-lipped, undercover, with bated breath, in private, in the dark, in chambers, by a side door, under the breath, in the background, between ourselves, in privacy, in a corner, under the cloak of, reserved.
secretly, *mod.* —*Syn.* privately, covertly, obscurely, darkly, surreptitiously, furtively, stealthily, clandestinely, underhandedly, slyly, behind one's back, intimately, personally, confidentially, between you and me, in (strict) confidence, in secret, behind the scenes, on the sly, behind closed doors, quietly, hush-hush (D); see also **secretive.**—*Ant.* openly*, obviously, publicly.
sect, *n.* —*Syn.* denomination, following, order; see **church** 3, **faction** 1.
sectarian, *n.* —*Syn.* dissenter, nonconformist, rebel; see **protestant, skeptic.**
section, *n.* **1.** [A portion]—*Syn.* subdivision, slice, segment; see **part** 1, **share.**
2. [An area]—*Syn.* district, sector, locality; see **region** 1.
sectional, *mod.* —*Syn.* partial, exclusive, narrow, selfish, local, regional, separate, divided, left-wing. —*Ant.* whole*, in one piece, united.
sector, *n.* —*Syn.* division, area, quarter; see **area** 2, **division** 2.
secular, *mod.* —*Syn.* temporal, profane, earthly; see **materialistic, worldly** 1.
secure, *mod.* **1.** [Firm]—*Syn.* fastened, adjusted, bound; see **firm** 1, **tight** 1.
2. [Safe]—*Syn.* guarded, unharmed, defended; see **protected, safe** 1.
3. [Self-confident]—*Syn.* assured, solid, determined, confident, strong, stable, sound, steady, steadfast, reliable, able, resolute.
secure, *v.* **1.** [To fasten]—*Syn.* settle, adjust, bind; see **fasten** 1, **tighten** 1.
2. [To obtain]—*Syn.* achieve, acquire, grasp; see **obtain** 1.
3. [To protect]—*Syn.* guard, make safe, ensure; see **defend** 1, 2.
securing, *n.* —*Syn.* acquiring, procuring, attaining; see **acquisition** 1.
security, *n.* **1.** [Safety]—*Syn.* protection, shelter, safety, refuge, retreat, defense, safeguard, preservation, sanctuary, ward, guard, immunity, freedom from harm, freedom from danger, redemption, salvation.—*Ant.* danger*, risk, hazard.
2. [A guarantee]—*Syn.* earnest, forfeit, token, pawn, pledge, surety, bond, collateral, assurance, gage, bail, certainty, promise, warranty, pact, compact, contract, covenant, agreement, sponsor, bondsman, hostage; see also **protection** 2.—*Ant.* doubt*, broken faith, unreliability.
3. [Stability]—*Syn.* soundness, assurance, surety; see **confidence** 2.
sedan, *n.* **1.** [Chair]—*Syn.* saddle, place, carriage; see **chair** 1.
2. [Vehicle]—*Syn.* car, sedan limousine, motor vehicle; see **automobile, vehicle** 2.
sedate, *mod.* —*Syn.* composed, unruffled, sober; see **calm** 1, **dignified.**
sedately, *mod.* —*Syn.* quietly, slowly, formally; see **deliberately, proudly.**
(under) sedation, *mod.* —*Syn.* quiet(ed), soothed, calmed down; see **calm** 1.
sedative, *mod.* —*Syn.* tranquilizing, calming, soothing; see **remedial.**
sedative, *n.* —*Syn.* tranquilizer, medication, narcotic; see **drug** 2, **medicine** 2.

sedentary, *mod.* —*Syn.* inactive, stationary, settled; see **idle** 1.

sediment, *n.* —*Syn.* settlings, residue, lees, dregs, dross, grounds, solids, silt, powder, sand, alluvium, loess, grit, gritty matter, soot, deposit, debris, precipitate, trash.

sedition, *n.* —*Syn.* revolt, mutiny, insurrection; see **revolution** 2, **treason.**

seditious, *mod.* —*Syn.* violent, dissident, insurgent; see **lawless** 2, **rebellious** 2.

seduce, *v.* —*Syn.* decoy, allure, inveigle, entice, abduct, attract, tempt, bait, bribe, lure, induce, captivate, stimulate, defile, deprave, lead astray, violate, prostitute, debauch, rape, deflower; see also **fascinate.**—*Ant.* preserve*, protect, guide.

seducer, *n.* —*Syn.* debaucher, corrupter, rake; see **lecher.**

seduction, *n.* —*Syn.* bewitchment, subjugation, corruption; see **rape, violation** 2.

seductive, *mod.* —*Syn.* alluring, beguiling, tempting; see **charming.**

seductress, *n.* —*Syn.* siren, enchantress, vamp; see **shrew, witch.**

sedulous, *mod.* —*Syn.* attentive, assiduous, unremitting, active, desirous, unwearied, industrious, diligent, busy, hustling, keen, eager, brisk, vivacious, stirring, painstaking, sleepless, avid, anxious, persevering, persistent, alert, spry, ardent; see also **busy** 1, **careful, observant** 1, 2.—*Ant.* careless*, indifferent, unconcerned.

see, *v.* **1.** [To perceive with the eye]—*Syn.* observe, look at, behold, descry, examine, inspect, regard, espy, view, look out on, gaze, stare, eye, lay eyes on, mark, perceive, pay attention to, heed, mind, detect, (take) notice, discern, scrutinize, scan, spy, survey, contemplate, remark, clap eyes on, be apprized of, make out, cast the eyes on, direct the eyes, catch sight of, cast the eyes over, get a load of (D).
2. [To understand]—*Syn.* perceive, comprehend, discern; see **recognize** 1, **understand** 1.
3. [To witness]—*Syn.* look on, be present, pay attention, notice, observe, regard, heed; see also **witness.**
4. [(D) To accompany]—*Syn.* escort, attend, bear company; see **accompany** 1.
5. [(D) To equal, especially to equal a bet in poker] —*Syn.* meet a bet, cover a bet, match a wager; see **equal.**
6. [To have an appointment (with)]—*Syn.* speak to *or* with, have a conference (with), get advice from; see **consult, discuss.**

see about, *v.* —*Syn.* attend (to), look after *or* to, provide for; see **perform** 1.

seed, *n.* **1.** [A botanical ovule]—Seeds and fruits commonly called seeds include the following—grain, kernel, berry, ear, corn, nut.
2. [Something to be planted]—*Syn.* grain, bulbs, cuttings, ears, tubers, roots; seed corn, seed potatoes, etc.
go *or* **run to seed**—*Syn.* decline, worsen, run out; see **decay, waste** 3.

seed, *v.* —*Syn.* scatter, strew, broadcast; see **plant, sow.**

seeding, *n.* **1.** [The act of planting seed]—*Syn.* sowing, broadcasting, implanting, strewing, scattering, spreading, propagating; see also **farming.**
2. [Ground on which seed has been sown]—*Syn.* planting, garden, cultivated ground, cultivated field, seeded ground, garden spot, lawn, grass plot, garden plot, sod, small grain, hay.

see fit to, *v.* —*Syn.* decide (to), be willing *or* determined (to), determine (to); see **want, wish** 2.

seeing, *mod.* —*Syn.* observing, looking, regarding, viewing, noticing, surveying, looking at, observant, wide awake, alert, awake, perceiving, inspecting, beholding, witnessing.

seek, *v.* **1.** [To look for]—*Syn.* investigate, explore, search *or* delve *or* gun *or* bob *or* dig *or* ransack *or* fish *or* go gunning for, look around *or* about for, look *or* hunt up, sniff *or* dig *or* hunt *or* root out, smell around, go *or* run *or* see *or* prowl after, go in pursuit *or* search of.
2. [To try]—*Syn.* endeavor, strive for, attempt; see **try** 1.
3. [To find out]—*Syn.* query, inquire, solicit; see **ask** 1.

seeking, *mod.* —*Syn.* hunting, searching, looking (for); see **pursuing.**

seem, *v.* —*Syn.* appear (to be), have the appearance, create *or* leave *or* give *or* convey the impression, impress one, appear to one, produce *or* induce the reaction, look, look like, resemble, make a show of, show, have the qualities *or* features *or* aspects of, resemble superficially, lead one to suppose something to be, have all the evidence of being, be calculated *or* likely to deceive one into believing, be suggestive of, have the expression *or* the mien *or* the deport *or* the demeanor, give the effect *or* feeling (of), sound like, take on the aspect *or* manner; *all* (D); make out to be, give the idea, have all the earmarks of, make a noise like.

seemingly, *mod.* —*Syn.* ostensibly, obviously, professedly; see **apparently.**

seemly, *mod.* **1.** [Suitable]—*Syn.* timely, appropriate, suitable; see **fit** 1, 2.
2. [Attractive]—*Syn.* pleasing, good-looking, comely; see **beautiful** 1, 2, **charming.**

seen, *mod.* —*Syn.* manifest, evident, viewed; see **observed** 1, **obvious** 1.

see off, *v.* —*Syn.* go with, bid farewell *or bon voyage* (French), go to the depot or the wharf or the airport, *etc.* (with); see **accompany** 1.

seep, *v.* —*Syn.* leak, flow gently, trickle; see **drain** 3, **flow** 2.

seepage, *n.* —*Syn.* infiltration, leakage, percolation; see **drainage, flow.**

seer, *n.* —*Syn.* predictor, soothsayer, vaticinator; see **prophet.**

seesaw, *n.* —*Syn.* alternation, teeterboard, hickey horse; see **teeter-totter.**

seethe, *v.* —*Syn.* simmer, stew, ebullate; see **boil** 2, 3, **cook.**

see through, *v.* **1.** [To complete]—*Syn.* finish (up), bring to a (successful) conclusion, wind up (D); see **complete** 1, **end** 1.
2. [To understand]—*Syn.* comprehend, penetrate, detect; see **understand** 1.

see to, *v.* —*Syn.* do, attend (to), look to *or* after; see **understand** 1.

segment, *n.* —*Syn.* section, portion, fragment; see **division** 2, **part** 1.
segregate, *v.* —*Syn.* isolate, sever, split up; see **divide** 1, **separate** 2.
segregated, *mod.* —*Syn.* divided into racial groups *or* by race(s) *or* color *or* along racial lines, *etc.*, isolated, in line with *or* according to Jim Crow restrictions, ghettoized; see **racial, separated.**
segregation, *n.* —*Syn.* dissociation, disconnection, separation; see **division** 1.
seignior, *n.* —*Syn.* Mr., master, *Herr* (German); see **mister, sir** 2.
seize, *v.* **1.** [To grasp]—*Syn.* take, take hold of, lay hold of *or* hands on, catch up, catch hold of, hang on *or* onto, catch, grip, clinch, clench, clasp, embrace, compass, grab, clutch, grapple, snag, pluck, appropriate, snatch, swoop up, enfold, enclose, pinch, squeeze, make *or* hold fast, possess oneself of, envelope.—*Ant.* leave*, pass by, let alone.
2. [To take by force]—*Syn.* capture, rape, occupy, win, take captive, pounce, conquer, take by storm *or* assault, subdue, overwhelm, overrun, overpower, ambush, snatch, incorporate, exact, extend protection to, retake, carry (off), apprehend, arrogate, arrest, secure, commandeer, force, gain, take, recapture, appropriate, take possession of, confiscate, take over, pounce on, usurp, overcome, impound, intercept, steal, purloin, expropriate, abduct; *all* (D): seize upon, snap up, nab, trap, throttle, lay hold of, lift, snap (up), hook, collar, fasten upon, wrench, claw, snare, bag, catch up, jerk, freeze onto, batten on, wring, cull, get one's clutches *or* fingers *or* hands on, kidnap, rustle, stick *or* hold up, swipe, clap hands on, scramble for, help oneself to, jump a claim.
3. [To comprehend]—*Syn.* perceive, see, know; see **understand** 1.
seized, *mod.* —*Syn.* confiscated, annexed, clutched; see **beaten** 1, **captured** 1.
seizure, *n.* **1.** [Capture]—*Syn.* seizing, taking, apprehending; see **capture.**
2. [A spasm]—*Syn.* spell, convulsion, breakdown; see **fit** 1, **illness** 1.
seldom, *mod.* —*Syn.* rarely, unusually, in a few cases, a few times, at times, seldom seen, on divers occasions, usually, sporadically, irregularly, inhabitually, whimsically, sometimes, when occasion permits, from time to time, infrequently, not often, not very often, occasionally, uncommonly, scarcely, hardly, hardly ever, scarcely ever, when the spirit moves, on and off, once in a while, once in a blue moon, once in a lifetime, every now and then; both (D): in a coon's age, not in a month of Sundays. —*Ant.* frequently*, often.
select, *mod.* —*Syn.* elite, picked, preferred; see **excellent.**
select, *v.* —*Syn.* decide, pick, elect; see **choose** 1.
selected, *mod.* —*Syn.* picked, chosen, elected; see **named** 2.
selecting, *mod.* —*Syn.* appointing, choosing, electing, recruiting, nominating.
selecting, *n.* —*Syn.* choosing, selection, choice, picking, culling, electing, sifting, gleaning, segregating, indicating, appointing, denominating, denomination, segregation, election, appointment, determining, determination, winnowing, separation, separating, isolation, isolating, marking off, marking out; *both* (D): winnowing the wheat from the chaff, separating the sheep from the goats.
selection, *n.* **1.** [The act of selecting]—*Syn.* choice, election, determination, choosing, preference, cooptation, appropriation, adoption, reservation, separation.
2. [Anything selected]—*Syn.* pick, collection, excerpt; see **choice** 3.
3. [An evolutionary process]—*Syn.* survival of the fittest, natural selection, sexual selection, unconscious selection, methodical selection, modification, change by sport, adaptation, Darwinian process, biogenesis, Mendelian fitness.
selective, *mod.* —*Syn.* discriminating, scrupulous, particular; see **careful, judicious.**
self, *mod.* —*Syn.* of one's self, by one's self, by one's own effort; see **alone** 1, **individual** 1.
self, *n.* —*Syn.* oneself, one's being, inner nature; see **character** 2.
self-abuse, *n.* —*Syn.* self-destruction, masochism, self-murder; see **abuse** 3, **suicide.**
self-acting, *mod.* —*Syn.* mechanical, self-propellent, automatic.
self-admiration, *n.* —*Syn.* pomposity, vanity, egotism, conceit; see also **arrogance, pride** 1.
self-amortizing, *mod.* —*Syn.* self-liquidating, paying for itself, funded.
self-assurance, *n.* —*Syn.* security, self-reliance, morale; see **confidence** 2.
self-assured, *mod.* —*Syn.* self-confident, assured, certain; see **confident** 2.
self-centered, *mod.* —*Syn.* self-indulgent, self-conscious, egotistical; see **egotistic** 1, 2, **selfish** 1.
self-confidence, *n.* —*Syn.* assurance, courage, self-reliance; see **confidence** 2.
self-confident, *mod.* —*Syn.* fearless, secure, self-assured; see **confident** 2.
self-conscious, *mod.* —*Syn.* unsure, uncertain, shy; see **doubtful** 2, **humble** 1.
self-consciously, *mod.* —*Syn.* bashfully, affectedly, upset; see **ashamed, modestly** 1.
self-contained, *mod.* **1.** [Austere]—*Syn.* reticent, constrained, uncommunicative; see **reserved** 3.
2. [Independent]—*Syn.* self-sustaining, complete, independent; see **free** 1, **whole** 1.
self-control, *n.* —*Syn.* poise, restraint, aplomb, self-government, reserve, reticence, self-restraint, discretion, balance, stability, sobriety, abstemiousness, dignity, repression, constraint, self-constraint, self-regulation.—*Ant.* nervousness*, timidity, talkativeness.
self-defense, *n.* —*Syn.* self-protection, the manly art (of self-defense), putting up a fight; see **fight** 1, **protection** 2.
self-denial, *n.* **1.** [Generosity]—*Syn.* asceticism, selflessness self-sacrifice; see **generosity** 1, **temperance.**
2. [Torture]—*Syn.* suffering, self-neglect, torment; see **martyrdom, sacrifice** 1.
self-destruction, *n.* —*Syn.* self-extinction, harakiri, masochism; see **death** 1, **suicide.**
self-determination, *n.* —*Syn.* privilege, spontaneity, initiative; see **will** 3.
self-esteem, *n.* —*Syn.* vanity, haughtiness, egotism; see **pride** 1.

self-evident, *mod.* —*Syn.* plain, visible, apparent; see **obvious** 2.
self-explanatory, *mod.* —*Syn.* plain, clear, distinct, certain, easy to understand, comprehensible, understandable, obvious, open, visible, easy to see, easily seen, manifest, self-evident, unmistakable, unequivocal; *all* (D): plain as the nose on one's face, clear as crystal, plain as day.—*Ant.* obscure*, vague, uncertain.
self-government, *n.* **1.** [Autonomy]—*Syn.* home rule, republic, independence; see **freedom** 1.
2. [Self-control]—*Syn.* conduct, character, stability; see **discipline** 2, **restraint** 1.
self-important, *mod.* —*Syn.* proud, egotistical, conceited; see **egotistic** 2.
self-imposed, *mod.* —*Syn.* accepted, self-determined, willingly adopted *or* enforced *or* established, *etc.*; see **deliberate** 1, **voluntarily.**
self-indulgence, *n.* —*Syn.* incontinence, excess, intemperance; see **greed, indulgence** 3.
selfish, *mod.* **1.** [Centered in self]—*Syn.* self-seeking, self-centered, self-indulgent, indulging oneself, wrapped up in oneself, narrow, narrow-minded, prejudiced, egotistical, egoistical, egoistic, egotistic, looking out for number one (D).
2. [Niggardly]—*Syn.* miserly, stingy, parsimonious; see **greedy** 1.
selfishly, *mod.* —*Syn.* egotistically, miserly, stingily, greedily, in one's own interest, meanly, cannily, ungenerously, illiberally, unchivalrously, to gain private ends, from *or* because of selfish *or* interested motives, lacking in generosity *or* magnanimity *or* consideration, *etc.*; see also **wrongly** 1, 2.
selfishness, *n.* —*Syn.* self-regard, self-indulgence, self-worship; see **greed.**
self-liquidating, *mod.* —*Syn.* self-amortizing, paying for itself, to be written off, funded, provided for; see also **paid.**
self-love, *n.* —*Syn.* vanity, conceit, self-esteem; see **arrogance, egotism.**
self-made, *mod.* —*Syn.* competent, self-reliant, audacious; see **able** 1, 2, **confident** 2.
self-possessed, *mod.* —*Syn.* placid, reserved, aloof; see **calm** 1, **reserved** 3.
self-possession, *n.* —*Syn.* self-assurance, poise, presence (of mind); see **confidence** 2, **restraint** 1.
self-regulating, *mod.* —*Syn.* mechanical, self-adjusting, motorized; see **automatic** 1, 2.
self-reliance, *n.* —*Syn.* self-trust, self-confidence, independence; see **confidence** 2.
self-reliant, *mod.* —*Syn.* determined, resolute, independent; see **able** 1, 2, **confident** 2.
self-renunciation, *n.* —*Syn.* altruism, heroism, magnanimity; see **generosity** 1, **temperance.**
self-reproach, *n.* —*Syn.* remorse, contrition, repentance; see **regret** 1.
self-respect, *n.* —*Syn.* morale, worth, pride; see **confidence** 2, **dignity** 1.
self-restraint, *n.* —*Syn.* patience, endurance, control; see **restraint** 1.
self-righteous, *mod.* —*Syn.* affected, sanctimonious, pharisaic; see **egotistical** 2, **hypocritical.**
self-righteously, *mod.* —*Syn.* smugly, pompously, boastfully; see **proudly.**
self-sacrifice, *n.* —*Syn.* altruism, free-giving, benevolence; see **generosity** 1, **kindness** 1, 2.
self-sacrificing, *mod.* —*Syn.* big-hearted, helpful, self-effacing; see **generous** 1, **noble** 1, 2.
selfsame, *mod.* —*Syn.* same, equivalent, similar; see **alike** 1, 2, **equal.**
self-satisfaction, *n.* —*Syn.* complacency, smugness, conceit; see **egotism.**
self-satisfied, *mod.* —*Syn.* smug, vain, conceited; see **egotistic** 2.
self-seeking, *mod.* —*Syn.* self-indulgent, rapacious, avaricious; see **greedy** 1.
self-styled, *mod.* —*Syn.* *soi-disant* (French), immodestly *or* boastfully called, said to be, by one's own admission; see also **egotistical** 1, 2, **egotistically.**
self-sufficient, *mod.* **1.** [Independent]—*Syn.* competent, self-confident, efficient; see **confident** 2.
2. [Arrogant]—*Syn.* haughty, smug, conceited; see **egotistic** 2.
self-taught, *mod.* —*Syn.* self-made, self-educated, amateur, nonprofessional; see also **educated** 1, **learned** 1, **local** 1.
self-willed, *mod.* —*Syn.* willful, opinionated, stubborn; see **obstinate** 1.
sell, *v.* **1.** [To convey for a consideration]—*Syn.* market, vend, auction, dispose of, put up for sale, barter, exchange, trade, bargain, peddle, retail, merchandise, sell at the market, sell on the curb, sell over the counter, sell futures on, contract, wholesale, transfer for a consideration *or* for value received *or* for one dollar and other valuable considerations, give title to *or* a deed for, put in escrow; see also **exchange** 2.—*Ant.* buy*, obtain*, get.
2. [To betray]—*Syn.* sell out (D), fail, violate; see **betray** 1, **deceive, disappoint.**
seller, *n.* —*Syn.* dealer, peddler, tradesman, salesman, retailer, agent, vender, merchant, auctioneer, shopkeeper, trader, marketer, storekeeper; see **businessman.**
selling, *n.* **1.** [The act of selling]—*Syn.* sale, auction, bartering, trading, vending, auctioning, transfer, transferring, commercial transaction, transacting, disposal, scoring, disposing, merchandising.—*Ant.* buying*, acquiring, purchasing.
2. [The occupation of selling]—*Syn.* commercial enterprise, traffic, merchandising; see **business** 1.
sell off, *v.* —*Syn.* trade, bargain, get rid of; see **sell** 1.
sell-out (D), *n.* —*Syn.* betrayal, deception, deal; see **trick** 1.
sell out (D), *v.* —*Syn.* thwart, trick, turn in, cop out (D); see also **betray** 1, **deceive, disappoint.**
sell short (D), *v.* —*Syn.* denigrate, derogate, belittle; see **depreciate** 2, **insult, ridicule.**
selvage, *n.* —*Syn.* edge, skirting, border; see **hem, rim.**
semantic, *mod.* —*Syn.* semiotic, connotative, denotative; see **grammatical** 1.
semantics, *n.* —*Syn.* meaning, semiotics, science *or* philosophy of meaning, general semantics, symbolic logic, semiology, connotation, denotation, exposition, explanation, explication, glossology, exegetics, symbolism, symbiology; see also **definition** 1, **interpretation** 1.
semblance, *n.* —*Syn.* likeness, analogy, resemblance; see **appearance** 2, **similarity.**

semester, *n.* —*Syn.* six-month period, eighteen weeks, four and one-half months; see **term** 2.
semiannual, *mod.* —*Syn.* twice a year, half-yearly, biannual, every six months, semiyearly; see also **annual, seasonal, yearly.**
semicircle, *n.* —*Syn.* arc, semicircumference, half a circle, 180 degrees, half-moon; see also **arch, curve** 1.
semicircular, *mod.* —*Syn.* crescentlike, bowed, curved; see **bent, round** 1.
semiconscious, *mod.* —*Syn.* half-conscious, half-awake, comatose; see **asleep, dying** 1.
semifinal, *n.* —*Syn.* next to the last, next to the final, just before the final, preliminary to the final, elimination test, elimination round; see also **round** 2.
semiliquid, *mod.* —*Syn.* pasty, gelatinous, gummy; see **liquid** 2, **thick** 3.
seminal, *mod.* —*Syn.* generative, primary, original; see **fundamental** 1.
seminar, *n.* —*Syn.* research, study, lesson; see **class** 3, **course** 4.
seminary, *n.* —*Syn.* secondary school, institute, theological school; see **academy** 1, **school** 1.
semiprofessional, *mod.* —*Syn.* amateur, not professional, (highly) skilled; see **able** 1, **trained.**
sempiternal, *mod.* —*Syn.* unchanging, incessant, everlasting; see **constant** 1, **eternal** 2.
Senate, *n.* —*Syn.* legislative body, United States Senate, State legislature, the lawgivers, upper branch of Congress, the Upper House; *all* (D): the Solons, the Elders, the bulwark of democracy, senatorium; see also **legislature.**
senate, *n.* —*Syn.* legislative body, lawgiving body, assembly, council, deliberative body; see also **legislature.**
senator, *n.* —*Syn.* Solon, elder statesman, statesman, legislator, politician, member of the senate; see also **representative** 2.
send, *v.* **1.** [To dispatch]—*Syn.* transmit, forward, convey, advance, express, ship, mail, send forth *or* out *or* in, delegate, expedite, hasten, accelerate, entrain, post, address, rush (off), hurry off, get under way, put under sail, give papers, provide with credentials, send out for, address to, commission, consign, drop (a letter); see also **export.**
2. [To deliver]—*Syn.* convey, transfer, pack' off, give, bestow, grant, confer, entrust, assign, impart, utter, give out; see also **sense** 1.
3. [To project]—*Syn.* propel, fling, hurl; see **throw** 1.
4. [To broadcast, usually electronically]—*Syn.* transmit, relay, wire, cable, broadcast, emit, televise, conduct, communicate; see also **carry** 2.
send about one's business *or* **away,** *v.* —*Syn.* discharge, get rid of, dispatch; see **dismiss** 1.
send around, *v.* —*Syn.* circulate, send to everybody *or* everyone, make available; see **distribute** 1.
send back, *v.* —*Syn.* reject, mail *or* ship back, decide against; see **return** 2.
send (away) for, *v.* —*Syn.* order, request, write away (for); see **ask** 1, **obtain** 1.
send in, *v.* —*Syn.* submit, mail, deliver; see **offer** 1, **ship.**
sending, *n.* —*Syn.* shipping, posting, dispatching; see **mailing, transportation.**
send-off, *n.* —*Syn.* going-away party, (auspicious) beginning, (good) start; see **celebration** 2, **encouragement.**
send packing (D), *v.* —*Syn.* reject, throw out (D), eject; see **dismiss** 1.
send word, *v.* —*Syn.* get in touch, communicate, report; see **telegraph, telephone, writer** 1, 2.
senile, *mod.* —*Syn.* aged, infirm, feeble; see **old** 1, **sick.**
senility, *n.* —*Syn.* old age, dotage, anecdotage, feebleness, anility, infirmity, decline, senile dementia, Alzheimer's disease, senescence, second childhood, sere and yellow leaf (D); see also **age** 2, **weakness** 1. —*Ant.* youth*, infancy, childhood.
senior, *mod.* —*Syn.* elder, older, higher in rank, more advanced, of greater dignity, of advanced standing, next older, next higher in rank; see also **superior.**
senior, *n.* —*Syn.* superior, elder, upper classman, dean, master, oldest, first born.
seniority, *n.* —*Syn.* (preferred) standing, rank(ing), station; see **advantage** 1, 2, **antiquity** 1, **preference.**
señor (Spanish), *n.* —*Syn.* gentleman, Mr., monsieur; see **mister, sir** 2.
señorita (Spanish), *n.* —*Syn.* young lady, maid, lass; see **girl** 1, **woman** 1.
sensation, *n.* **1.** [The sense of feeling]—*Syn.* sensibility, susceptibility, sensitiveness, consciousness, awareness, perception, impression; see also **emotion, thought** 1.—*Ant.* stupor*, apathy, torpor.
2. [A feeling]—*Syn.* response, sentiment, passion; see **feeling** 1.
sensational, *mod.* **1.** [Fascinating]—*Syn.* exciting, agitating, marvelous, moving, incredible, astonishing, superb, breathtaking, eloquent, surprising, thrilling, spectacular, dramatic, stirring; see also **impressive** 1, **interesting.**
2. [Melodramatic]—*Syn.* exaggerated, excessive, lurid, emotional, startling, stimulating.
sensationalism, *n.* —*Syn.* emotionalism, melodrama, photism, McCarthyism, sentimentality; see also **drama** 2, **emotion.**
sense, *n.* **1.** [One of the powers of physical perception]—*Syn.* kinesthesia, function, sensation; see **hearing** 3, **sight** 1, **smell** 3, **taste** 1, **touch** 1, 4.
2. [Mental ability]—*Syn.* intellect, understanding, reason, mind, spirit, soul, brains, judgment, wit, imagination, common sense, cleverness, reasoning, intellectual ability, mental capacity, knowledge; see also **thought** 1.—*Ant.* dullness*, idiocy, feeble wit.
3. [Reasonable and agreeable conduct]—*Syn.* reasonableness, fairmindedness, discretion; see **fairness.**
4. [Tact and understanding]—*Syn.* insight, discernment, social sense; see **feeling** 4, **judgment** 1.
in a sense—*Syn.* in a way, to a degree, somewhat; see **some, somehow.**
make sense—*Syn.* be *or* appear to be reasonable *or* logical, look all right, add up (D); see **appear** 1, **seem.**
senseless, *mod.* —*Syn.* ridiculous, silly, foolish; see **illogical, stupid** 1.
senses, *n.* —*Syn.* consciousness, mental faculties, feeling; see **awareness, life** 1, 2.

sensibility, *n.* —*Syn.* responsiveness, perceptivity, keenness; see **awareness, judgment** 1, **sensitivity.**

sensible, *mod.* **1.** [Showing good sense]—*Syn.* reasonable, discerning, thoughtful; see **judicious, rational** 1, **sane** 2.

2. [Perceptive]—*Syn.* aware, informed, attentive; see **conscious** 1.

sensitive, *mod.* **1.** [Tender]—*Syn.* delicate, sore, painful; see **tender** 6.

2. [Touchy]—*Syn.* high-strung, tense, nervous; see **irritable, unstable** 2.

3. [Sensory]—*Syn.* sentient, impressionable, sensible, perceptive, susceptible, receptive, psychic, alive to, sensorial, sensatory; *all* (D): psyched in, tuned in, soulful, turned on (to); see also **sympathetic.**

sensitivity, *n.* **1.** [Susceptibility]—*Syn.* allergy, irritability, ticklishness; see **irritation** 1.

2. [Emotional response or condition]—*Syn.* delicacy, sensibility, sensitiveness, nervousness, (acute) awareness, consciousness, acuteness, subtlety, feeling(s), sympathetic response, responsiveness, sympathy, impressionability, affectibility; see also **sensation** 1.

sensitize, *v.* —*Syn.* stimulate, refine, sharpen; see **animate** 1, **excite** 2.

sensory, *mod.* **1.** [Neurological]—*Syn.* sensible, relating to sensation *or* the senses, neural, conscious, afferent, receptive, sensatory, acoustic, auditory, aural, auricular, sonic, phonic, audio-visual, visual, ocular, optic, ophthalmic, olfactory, olfactive, gustatory, gustative, lingual, glossal, tactile, tactual; see also **sensitive** 3.

2. [Conveyed by the senses]—*Syn.* audible, perceptible, discernible, auricular, distinct, clear, plain, hearable; see also **obvious** 1, 2, **tangible.**

sensual, *mod.* **1.** [Sensory]—*Syn.* tactile, sensuous, stimulating, sharpened, pleasing, dazzling, feeling, being, heightened, enhanced, appealing, delightful, luxurious, fine, arousing, stirring, moving; see also **beautiful** 1, **emotional** 2, **exciting.**

2. [Carnal]—*Syn.* voluptuous, pleasure-loving, fleshly, lewd, unspiritual, hedonic, apolaustic, self-loving, self-indulgent, epicurean, intemperate, gluttonous, Sybaritical, rakish, debauched, orgiastic, Corybantic, sensuous, piggish, hoggish, bestial. —*Ant.* chaste*, ascetic, self-denying.

sensuality, *n.* —*Syn.* sensationalism, appetite, ardor; see **desire** 3, **emotion, love** 1.

sensuous, *mod.* —*Syn.* passionate, physical, exciting; see **sensual** 1.

sent, *mod.* —*Syn.* commissioned, appointed, ordained, delegated, dispatched, directed, issued, transmitted, discharged, gone, on the road, in transit, emitted, uttered, sent forth, driven, impelled, forced to go, consigned, ordered, committed; see also **shipped.**—*Ant.* kept*, restrained, held back.

sent around, *mod.* —*Syn.* handed out, spread around, circulated; see **distributed.**

sentence, *n.* **1.** [A pronounced judgment]—*Syn.* edict, dictum, decree, order, doom, determination, decision, pronouncement, considered opinion, censure, penalty, condemnation; see also **judgment** 3, **punishment, verdict.**

2. [An expressed thought] Types of sentences, sense 2, include the following—simple, complex, compound, compound-complex, kernel, transformed, declarative, interrogative, imperative, exclamatory, statement, question, command, exclamation.

sentence, *v.* —*Syn.* pronounce judgment, adjudge, adjudicate, send up, confine, impound, incarcerate, jail, judge, doom, send to prison; see also **condemn** 1, **convict, imprison, punish.**

sententious, *mod.* **1.** [Compact]—*Syn.* concise, aphoristic, pointed; see **obvious** 2.

2. [Theatrical]—*Syn.* bombastic, pretentious, showy; see **oratorical, ornate** 1.

sent for, *mod.* —*Syn.* applied for, written for, requested; see **ordered** 1.

sentient, *mod.* —*Syn.* aware, alert, perceptive; see **observant** 1, **sensitive** 3.

sentiment, *n.* —*Syn.* sensibility, predilection, tender feeling; see **emotion, feeling** 4, **thought** 2.

sentimental, *mod.* —*Syn.* emotional, romantic, romantical, dreamy, idealistic, visionary, mawkish, maudlin, bathetic, artificial, sickish, unrealistic, susceptible, silly, overemotional, affected, simpering, languishing, artificial, insincere, overacted, schoolgirlish; *both* (D): sappy, gushy, mushy, tear-jerking.

sentimentality, *n.* —*Syn.* sentimentalism, sentiment, melodramatics, bathos, melodrama, maudlinness, triteness, mawkishness, emotionalness; *both* (D): mushiness, gushiness; see also **emotion, romance** 1.

sentin, *mod.* —*Syn.* submitted, offered, presented, proffered, proposed.

sentinel, *n.* —*Syn.* lookout, sentry, guard; see **watchman.**

sent off, *mod.* —*Syn.* dispatched, consigned, in transit; see **shipped.**

sentry, *n.* —*Syn.* sentinel, watch, protector; see **watchman.**

separable, *mod.* —*Syn.* breakable, severable, detachable; see **divisible.**

separate, *v.* **1.** [To cause to part]—*Syn.* undo, distribute, part; see **divide** 1.

2. [To keep apart]—*Syn.* isolate, insulate, single out, sequester, seclude, rope off, segregate, intervene, stand between, draw apart, split *or* break up.

3. [To part company]—*Syn.* take leave, go away, depart; see **leave** 1.

4. [To classify]—*Syn.* assign, distribute, group; see **classify, order** 3.

separated, *mod.* —*Syn.* divided, parted, apart, disconnected, abstracted, apportioned, partitioned, distinct, disunited, disjointed, sundered, disembodied, cut in two, cut apart, set apart, distant, disassociated, removed, distributed, scattered, set asunder, put asunder, divorced, divergent, marked, severed, far between, in halves.—*Ant.* united*, together, whole.

separately, *mod.* —*Syn.* singly, definitely, distinctly; see **clearly** 1, 2, **individually.**

separation, *n.* **1.** [The act of dividing]—*Syn.* disconnection, severance, division, cut, disjoining, detachment.

2. [The act of parting]—*Syn.* leave-taking, farewell, embarkation; see **departure** 1.

September, *n.* —*Syn.* fall or autumn or summer (month), Indian summer, harvest (month), back-to-school season, opening of (the) school(s), opening of the football season.

septic, *mod.*—*Syn.* insanitary, toxic, putrefactive; see **rotten** 2, **unwholesome.**

septic tank, *n.*—*Syn.* (sewage) disposal system, tank for anaerobic bacteria *or* bacterial action, sanitary provisions; see also **sewer.**

sepulcher, *n.*—*Syn.* tomb, vault, crypt; see **grave** 1.

sepulchral, *mod.*—*Syn.* funereal, burial, somber; see **dismal** 1.

sequel, *n.*—*Syn.* consequence, continuation, progression; see **sequence** 1, **series.**

sequence, *n.* **1.** [Succession]—*Syn.* order, continuity, continuousness, concatenation, continuance, successiveness, progression, graduation, consecutiveness, flow, consecution, perpetuity, unbrokenness, catenation, subsequence, course.
2. [Arrangement]—*Syn.* placement, distribution, classification; see **order** 3.
3. [A series]—*Syn.* chain, string, array; see **series.**

sequential, *mod.* **1.** [Next]—*Syn.* subsequent, succeeding, later; see **consecutive, following.**
2. [Continuous]—*Syn.* incessant, steady, persistent; see **constant** 1, **regular** 3.

sequester, *v.* **1.** [To set apart]—*Syn.* separate, set off, segregate; see **separate** 2.
2. [To take over]—*Syn.* confiscate, seize, appropriate; see **seize** 2.
3. [To seclude]—*Syn.* withdraw, draw back, take leave; see **retire** 1, 3, **retreat** 1.

sere, *mod.*—*Syn.* dried up, scorched, burned; see **dry** 1, **withered.**

serenade, *n.*—*Syn.* melody, compliment, nocturne; see **music** 1, **song.**

serene, *mod.*—*Syn.* calm, clear, pellucid, limpid, unruffled, translucent, undisturbed, undimmed, tranquil, halcyon, smooth, quiet, still, composed, imperturbable, dispassionate, cool, cool-headed, sedate, level-headed, content, satisfied, patient, reconciled, easygoing, placid, comfortable, cheerful.—*Ant.* confused*, disturbed, ruffled.

serenity, *n.*—*Syn.* quietness, calmness, tranquility; see **composure, patience** 1, **peace** 2.

serf, *n.*—*Syn.* land-slave, thrall, villein; see **servant, slave** 1.

serge, *n.*—*Syn.* twill, wool serge, silk serge; see **cloth.**

sergeant, *n.* Types include the following—master sergeant, staff sergeant, technical sergeant, first sergeant, top sergeant, platoon sergeant, sergeant major, sergeant-at-arms, police sergeant; *both* (D): top kick, sarge; see also **officer** 3, **soldier.**

serial, *mod.*—*Syn.* consecutive, successive, ensuing, following, continued, continual, continuing; *both* (D): going on, continued in our next.

serial, *n.*—*Syn.* installment, serial picture, continued story; see **movie.**

series, *n.*—*Syn.* rank, file, line, row, set, train, range, list, string, chain, order, sequence, succession, group, procession, continuity, column, cordon, progression, suite, category, classification, tier, suit, scale, array, gradation.

serious, *mod.* **1.** [Involving danger]—*Syn.* grave, severe, pressing; see **dangerous** 1, 2.
2. [Involving earnestness]—*Syn.* grave, earnest, sober; see **solemn** 1.

seriously, *mod.* **1.** [In a manner fraught with danger]—*Syn.* dangerously, precariously, perilously, in a risky way, threateningly, menacingly, grievously, severely, harmfully, in a dangerous *or* menacing *or* perilous manner.—*Ant.* safely*, harmlessly, in no danger.
2. [In a manner that recognizes importance]—*Syn.* gravely, soberly, earnestly, solemnly, thoughtfully, sternly, sedately, with forethought, with sobriety, with great earnestness, all joking aside; see also **sincerely.**—*Ant.* lightly*, thoughtlessly, airily.

seriousness, *n.* **1.** [The quality of being dangerous]—*Syn.* gravity, weight, enormity; see **importance** 1.
2. [The characteristic of being sober]—*Syn.* earnestness, sobriety, solemnity, gravity, calmness, thoughtfulness, coolness, sedateness, sober-mindedness, staidness; see also **sincerity.**—*Ant.* fun*, gaiety, jollity.

sermon, *n.*—*Syn.* discourse, address, exhortation, lesson, doctrine, lecture; see also **speech** 3.

serpent, *n.*—*Syn.* reptile, viper, ophidian; see **snake.**

serpentine, *mod.*—*Syn.* snakelike, bowed, spiral; see **bent, twisted** 1.

serum, *n.*—*Syn.* antitoxin(s), antiserum, agglutinin(s), immunotoxin, blood serum, plasma, agglutinogen(s), agglutinoid.

servant, *n.*—*Syn.* servitor, attendant, retainer, helper, hireling, dependent, menial, domestic, drudge, slave, slavey (D); see also **assistant.**
Servants include the following—butler, housekeeper, chef, cook, second maid, scullery maid, kitchenmaid, maid of all work, 'tween maid, general maid, laundress, chambermaid, parlormaid, lady's maid, seamstress, nursemaid, nurse, valet, gentleman's gentleman, doorman, footman, lackey, wine steward, major-domo, squire, chauffeur, groom, stableboy, stableman, gardener, yardman, kennelman, handyman,

serve, *v.* **1.** [To fulfill an obligation]—*Syn.* hear duty's call, hearken to the call of duty, obey the call of one's country, acquit oneself of an obligation, subserve, discharge one's duty, live up to one's duty.—*Ant.* betray*, dishonor, disgrace.
2. [To work for]—*Syn.* be employed by, labor, toil, carry on a trade, be in the employ of; see also **work** 2.
3. [To help]—*Syn.* give aid, assist, be of assistance; see **help** 1.
4. [To serve at table]—*Syn.* wait (on), attend, help one to food, help.
5. [To obey]—*Syn.* follow, accept, agree; see **obey** 2.

served, *mod.*—*Syn.* dressed, prepared, offered, apportioned, dealt, furnished, supplied, provided, dished up (D).

serve notice, *v.*—*Syn.* inform, report, give word; see **notify** 1.

serve someone right, *v.*—*Syn.* deserve (it), have it coming, be fair, get one's dues, be rightly served, do justice to, do the right thing by, give the devil his due (D).

serve time, *v.*—*Syn.* stand committed, serve (out) a jail sentence, be incarcerated *or* in jail, pay one's debt to society, go to jail; *all* (D): do a term, be in stir, be in the joint, do time, be sent up.

service, *n.* **1.** [Aid]—*Syn.* co-operation, assistance, help; see **aid** 1.
2. [Tableware]—*Syn.* set, silver, setting; see **china, dish** 1, **pottery.**
3. [A religious service]—*Syn.* rite, worship, sermon; see **ceremony.**
4. [Military service]—*Syn.* army, duty, active service, stint.
at one's service—*Syn.* zealous, anxious to help *or* be of service, obedient; see **helpful** 1, **ready** 1, **willing** 1.
in service—*Syn.* functioning, repaired, in (good) condition; see **working.**
of service—*Syn.* useful, handy, usable; see **helpful** 1.

service, *v.* —*Syn.* maintain, sustain, keep up, preserve, keep safe; see also **repair.**

serviceable, *mod.* —*Syn.* practical, advantageous, beneficial; see **helpful** 1, **usable.**

service club, *n.* —*Syn.* luncheon club, community welfare group, business and professional group *or* society, *etc.*; see **organization** 3.
Service clubs include the following: Rotary International, Lions, Kiwanis, Toastmaster's, Soroptimist, Elks, I.O.O.F. (International Order of Odd Fellows), Shriners, Masons and Eastern Star, Knights of Pythias, Knights of Columbus.

service station, *n.* —*Syn.* filling station, gas station, shop (D); see **garage** 2.

servile, *mod.* —*Syn.* menial, beggarly, cringing; see **humble** 1, 2, **obsequious.**

serving, *mod.* —*Syn.* aiding, co-operating, helping; see **helpful.**

serving, *n.* —*Syn.* plateful, course, portion; see **helping, meal** 2.

servitude, *n.* —*Syn.* confinement, bondage, subjugation; see **slavery** 1, **subjection.**

session, *n.* —*Syn.* assembly, concourse, sitting; see **gathering.**

set, *mod.* **1.** [Firm]—*Syn.* stable, solid, settled; see **firm** 2.
2. [Determined]—*Syn.* concluded, steadfast, decided; see **determined** 1, **resolute** 2.
3. [Obstinate]—*Syn.* immovable, stubborn, relentless; see **obstinate** 1.

set, *n.* **1.** [Inclination]—*Syn.* attitude, position, bearing; see **inclination** 1.
2. [A social group]—*Syn.* clique, coterie, circle; see **faction** 1, **organization** 3.
3. [A collection of (like) items]—*Syn.* kit, assemblage, assortment; see **collection** 2.

set, *v.* **1.** [To place]—*Syn.* insert, deposit, arrange; see **place** 1.
2. [To establish]—*Syn.* anchor, fix, introduce; see **establish** 2, **install.**
3. [To become firm]—*Syn.* jell, solidify, congeal; see **harden** 2, **stiffen** 1, **thicken** 1.
4. [To value]—*Syn.* rate, fix a price, estimate; see **price, value** 2.
5. [To fasten]—*Syn.* lock, make fast, fix; see **fasten** 1.
6. [To start]—*Syn.* commence, initiate, put in motion; see **begin** 1.
7. [To brood]—*Syn.* incubate, hatch, hover; see **produce** 1.

set about, *v.* —*Syn.* start, begin a task, start doing; see **begin** 1.

set apart, *v.* —*Syn.* isolate, segregate, make separate *or* distinct *or* individual, *etc.*; see **distinguish** 1, **separate** 2.

set aside, *v.* **1.** [To save]—*Syn.* put away, reserve, lay up; see **maintain** 3, **save** 3.
2. [To discard]—*Syn.* abrogate, repeal, reject; see **cancel** 2, **discard.**

setback, *n.* —*Syn.* hindrance, check, reversal; see **delay** 1, **difficulty** 1, **impediment** 1.

set back, *v.* —*Syn.* retard, reverse, slow (down); see **defeat** 1, 3, **hinder.**

set down, *v.* —*Syn.* put on paper, register, write out; see **record** 1, **write** 1, 2.

set forth, *v.* —*Syn.* begin a journey, start out, take the first steps; see **begin** 2.

set free, *v.* —*Syn.* liberate, discharge, give freedom to; see **free** 1, **release.**

set in, *v.* —*Syn.* commence, begin to grow, turn; see **begin** 2.

set off, *v.* **1.** [To contrast]—*Syn.* be different, appear different, be the opposite; see **contrast** 1, **offset.**
2. [To explode]—*Syn.* touch off, set the spark to, detonate; see **explode** 1.

set out, *v.* —*Syn.* initiate, start, commence; see **begin** 2.

set sail, *v.* —*Syn.* launch, shove off, weigh anchor; see **leave** 1, **sail** 1, 2.

set straight, *v.* —*Syn.* revise, inform (properly), provide the facts *or* the evidence *or* a new insight, *etc.*; see **correct** 1, **improve** 1, 2.

settee, *n.* —*Syn.* couch, divan, sofa; see **davenport, furniture.**

set the pace, *v.* —*Syn.* take the lead, pace, provide a standard; see **lead** 1.

setting, *n.* —*Syn.* environment, surroundings, ambiance *or* ambience, mounting, backdrop, frame, framework, background, context, perspective, horizon, shadow, shade, distance, *mise en scene* (French).—*Ant.* front*, foreground, focus.

settle, *v.* **1.** [To decide]—*Syn.* make a decision, form judgment, come to a conclusion; see **decide.**
2. [To prove]—*Syn.* establish, verify, make certain; see **prove.**
3. [To finish]—*Syn.* end, make an end of, complete; see **achieve** 1.
4. [To sink]—*Syn.* descend, decline, fall; see **sink** 1.
5. [To cause to sink]—*Syn.* submerge, submerse, plunge; see **immerse** 1, **sink** 2.
6. [To quiet]—*Syn.* calm, compose, pacify; see **quiet** 1.
7. [To establish residence]—*Syn.* locate, lodge, become a citizen, reside, fix one's residence, abide, set up housekeeping, make one's home, establish a home, keep house; see also **dwell.**
8. [To take up sedentary life; *often used with* down] —*Syn.* follow regular habits, live an orderly life, become conventional, follow convention, buy a house, marry, marry and settle down, raise a family, forsake one's wild ways, regulate one's life; *all* (D): get in a groove, get in a rut, lead a humdrum existence, hang up one's hat, clear the land, mend one's fences; see also **improve** 1, 2, **live** 4.
9. [To satisfy a claim]—*Syn.* pay, compensate, make an adjustment, reach a compromise, make

payment, arrange a settlement, get squared away, reconcile, resolve, rectify, pay damages, pay out, settle out of court, settle *or* patch up, work out, settle *or* even the score, clear off old scores, dispose of, get quits with, account with.

settled, *mod.* —*Syn.* decided, resolved, ended; see **determined** 1.

settlement, *n.* **1.** [An agreement]—*Syn.* covenant, arrangement, compact; see **agreement** 3, **contract** 1.
2. [A payment]—*Syn.* compensation, remuneration, reimbursement; see **adjustment** 2, **pay** 2.
3. [A colony]—*Syn.* principality, plantation, establishment, foundation.

settler, *n.* —*Syn.* planter, immigrant, homesteader; see **pioneer** 2.

settle up, *v.* —*Syn.* meet one's obligations, make a settlement, pay up *or* one's bills; see **pay** 1.

setup, *n.* **1.** [Arrangement]—*Syn.* structure, composition, plan; see **order** 3, **organization** 2.
2. [(D) A gullible person]—*Syn.* dupe, gull, easy mark, sitting duck, trusting soul, sucker, fool; *all* (D): goat, butt, dummy, patsy, mark, Simple Simon, victim, pushover, cat's paw.
3. [Accompaniments for alcoholic beverages] —*Syn.* service (for drinks), tray from room service, settings.
Parts of a setup include the following—water, mixers, glasses, ice cubes; see also **drink** 3, **glassware.**

set up, *v.* **1.** [To make arrangements]—*Syn.* prearrange, inaugurate, work on; see **arrange** 2.
2. [To finance]—*Syn.* patronize, promote, support, pay for, subsidize.
3. [To establish]—*Syn.* found, originate, make provisions (for); see **begin** 1, **establish** 2.

set upon, *v.* —*Syn.* assail, fall upon, spring at from; see **attack** 1.

sever, *v.* —*Syn.* part, split, dissociate, rend, cleave; see also **cut** 1, **divide** 1.

several, *mod.* **1.** [Few]—*Syn.* some, any, a few, quite a few, not many, sundry, two or three, a small number of, scarce, sparse, hardly any, scarcely any, half a dozen, only a few, scant, scanty, rare, infrequent, in a minority, a handful, more or less, not too many.—*Ant.* many*, large numbers of, none.
2. [Various]—*Syn.* manifold, multiform, plural, a plurality, a number, not a few, numerous, diverse, a lot of, quite a lot of, a good deal; see also **many, various.**
3. [Distinct or separate]—*Syn.* certain, different, divers, definite, single, particular; see **individual** 1.

several, *n.* —*Syn.* not too many, various ones, different ones, a minority, a small number, quite a number, quite a few, quite a variety; see also **few.**

severally, *mod.* —*Syn.* exclusively, alone, singly; see **individually, only** 1.

severance, *n.* —*Syn.* section, split, separation; see **division** 1, 2.

severance pay, *n.* —*Syn.* pittance, stipend, allotment; see **pay** 2.

severe, *mod.* **1.** [Stern]—*Syn.* exacting, uncompromising, unbending, inflexible, unchanging, unalterable, inexorable, harsh, cruel, oppressive, close, grinding, peremptory, obdurate, resolute, austere, rigid, grim, earnest, stiff, forbidding, resolved, relentless, strait-laced, determined, unfeeling, insensate, with an iron will, strict, inconsiderate, firm, immovable, as firm as the Rock of Gibraltar, adamant, unyielding.—*Ant.* flexible*, yielding, genial.
2. [Difficult or rigorous]—*Syn.* overbearing, tyrannical, mordant, sharp, exacting, stringent, drastic, domineering, rigid, oppressive, despotic, unmerciful, bullying, uncompromising, obdurate, relentless, unrelenting, hard, rigorous, austere, grinding, ascetic, grim, implacable, cruel, pitiless, critical, unjust, barbarous, censorious, crusty, gruff, crabbed, unmitigated, intractable, stubborn, autocratic, Draconian, with a heart of granite, stony-hearted; *all* (D): hard-shell, rock-ribbed, hidebound; see also **difficult** 1.—*Ant.* easy*, easygoing, indulgent.

severely, *mod.* —*Syn.* critically, harshly, rigorously; see **firmly** 2, **seriously** 1.

severity, *n.* —*Syn.* asperity, sharpness, acerbity, grimness, hardness, unkindness, hardheartedness, strictness, austerity, rigor; see also **cruelty.**—*Ant.* pity*, kindness, softness.

sew, *v.* —*Syn.* stitch, seam, fasten, work with needle and thread, tailor, tack, embroider, bind, piece, baste, build (D).—*Ant.* ravel*, rip, undo.

sewage, *n.* —*Syn.* sewerage, excrement, offscum, offal, waste matter; see also **residue.**

sewer, *n.* —*Syn.* drain, drainpipe, drainage tube, conduit, gutter, disposal *or* sewage system, septic tank, dry well, leech field *or* ditches, city sewer(s), sewage disposal, sanitary provisions *or* facility *or* facilities, *etc.*; see also **trench** 1.

sewing, *n.* —*Syn.* stitching, seaming, backstitching, tailoring, embroidering, darning, mending, piecing, patching, dressmaking.

sewing machine, *n.* Varieties and types of sewing machines include the following—domestic, treadle, electric, cabinet, lock-stitch, portable, chain-stitch, heavy duty, commercial, factory, shoemaker's, bookbinder's, luggage maker's.

sewn, *mod.* —*Syn.* stitched, saddle-stitched, sewed, mended, embroidered, tailored.

sex, *n.* **1.** [Ideas associated with sexual relationships] —*Syn.* sex attraction, sex appeal, magnetism, sensuality, affinity, love, courtship, marriage, generation, reproduction.
2. [A group, either male or female]—*Syn.* men, women, males, females, the feminine world, the masculine world, androgynes.
3. [Gender]—*Syn.* sexuality, masculinity, femininity, womanliness, manhood, manliness.
4. [Sexual intercourse]—*Syn.* making love, (the) sexual act, going to bed (with someone); see **copulation, fornication.**
5. [Continuation of the species]—*Syn.* natural selection, breeding, eugenics, sexual selection, Mendelian fitness, improvement of the species, improvement of the race, contributing to the gene pool.

sexton, *n.* —*Syn.* warden, servant, janitor; see **custodian** 2.

sexual, *mod.* **1.** [Reproductive]—*Syn.* genitive, genital, generative, reproductive, procreative, coital; see also **original** 1.
2. [Intimate]—*Syn.* carnal, wanton, passionate, loving, sharing, between the sexes; see also **intimate** 1, **sensual** 2.

sexuality, *n.* —*Syn.* lust, sensuality, passion; see **desire** 3.

sexy (D), *mod.*—*Syn.* sensuous, libidinous, off-color; see **lewd** 1, 2, **sensual** 1, 2.

shabby, *mod.* **1.** [In bad repair]—*Syn.* ragged, threadbare, faded, ill-dressed, dilapidated, decayed, deteriorated, the worse for wear, run-down, broken-down, poor, pitiful, worn, meager, miserable, degenerated, wretched, poverty-stricken; *all* (D): scrubby, seedy, gone to seed, down at the heel, on one's uppers.—*Ant.* neat*, new, well-kept.

2. [Inconsiderate]—*Syn.* contemptible, low, mean, paltry, sordid, unkind, mercenary, miserly, selfish, thoughtless; *all* (D): stingy, piffling, tight-fisted; see also **rude** 2.—*Ant.* generous*, kindly, noble.

shack, *n.*—*Syn.* hut, shed, hovel, cabin, shanty, shotgun shack.

shackle, *v.*—*Syn.* hobble, fetter, chain; see **bind** 1.

shade, *n.* **1.** [Lack of light]—*Syn.* blackness, shadow, dimness; see **darkness** 1.

2. [A darkened color]—*Syn.* dark hue, dark tone, deep tone, grain, tinge, cast.—*Ant.* lightness*, pastel color, light saturation.

3. [A degree of color]—*Syn.* brilliance, saturation, hue; see **color** 1, **tint.**

4. [A slight difference]—*Syn.* variation, proposal, hint; see **suggestion** 1.

5. [An obstruction to light]—*Syn.* covering, blind, screen; see **curtain.**

6. [A ghost]—*Syn.* spirit, manes, revenant; see **ghost** 1, 2.

put in *or* **into the shade**—*Syn.* overcome, best, get the better of; see **defeat** 1, 2.

shade, *v.* **1.** [To intercept direct rays]—*Syn.* screen, shelter, shadow, cast a shadow over, overshadow, eclipse.

2. [To make darker]—*Syn.* darken, blacken, obscure, cloud, shadow, (make) dim, adumbrate, tone down, nigrify, black out, make dusky, deepen the shade, overshadow, make gloomy, screen, shut out the light, befog, keep out the light.

3. [To become darker]—*Syn.* grow dark, grow black, become dark, grow dim, blacken, turn to twilight, deepen into night, become gloomy, be overcast, grow dusky, cloud up *or* over, overcloud, grow shadowy.

4. [(D) To win by a narrow margin]—*Syn.* barely win, win by a hairbreadth, nose out (D); see **defeat.**

shadow, *n.*—*Syn.* umbra, obscuration, adumbration; see **darkness** 1.

be in *or* **under the shadow (of)**—*Syn.* threatened, in danger (of), in a dangerous situation; see **endangered.**

shadow, *v.* **1.** [To shade]—*Syn.* dim, veil, screen; see **shade** 1, 2, **shelter.**

2. [To follow secretly]—*Syn.* trail, watch, keep in sight; see **pursue** 1.

shadowy, *mod.*—*Syn.* dim, cloudy, in a fog; see **dark** 1, **hazy** 1.

shady, *mod.* **1.** [Shaded]—*Syn.* dusky, shadowy, adumbral, in the shade, sheltered, out of the sun, dim, cloudy, under a cloud, cool, indistinct, vague; see also **dark** 1.

2. [(D) Questionable]—*Syn.* suspicious, disreputable, dubious, dishonest, fishy (D), crooked, underhanded.

shaft, *n.* **1.** [Rod]—*Syn.* stem, handle, bar, cylinder, pole; see also **rod** 1.

2. [A weapon]—*Syn.* arrow, spear, lance, missile; see also **weapon** 1.

3. [Light ray]—*Syn.* wave, streak, beam of light; see **beam** 2, **ray.**

shaggy, *mod.*—*Syn.* rough, uncombed, unkempt, furry, hirsute, hairy, long-haired.

shake, *n.*—*Syn.* tremble, shiver, pulsation; see **movement** 1, 2.

no great shakes (D)—*Syn.* failure, mediocrity, poor *or* inferior person *or* thing *or* example, *etc.*; see **failure** 1, 2.

shake, *v.* **1.** [To vibrate]—*Syn.* tremble, quiver, quake, shiver, shudder, palpitate, waver, fluctuate, reel, flap, flutter, totter, thrill, wobble, stagger, waggle; see also **wave** 1, 3.

2. [To cause to vibrate]—*Syn.* agitate, rock, sway, swing, joggle, jolt, jounce, bounce, brandish, jar, move, flourish, set in motion, convulse.

shakedown (D), *n.*—*Syn.* exhortation, blackmail, badger game; see **theft.**

shake hands, *v.*—*Syn.* meet, welcome, receive; see **greet.**

shake hands on it, *v.*—*Syn.* come to terms, conclude a transaction *or* agreement, strike a bargain; see **agree.**

shaken, *mod.*—*Syn.* unnerved, upset, overcome; see **excited.**

shake off, *v.*—*Syn.* lose, get rid of, drop; see **remove** 1.

shake up, *v.*—*Syn.* disturb, unsettle, overturn; see **upset** 1.

shaky, *mod.* **1.** [Not firm]—*Syn.* quivery, trembling, jellylike, all-a-quiver, unsettled, not set, yielding, unsteady, tottering, unsound, insecure, tremulous, unstable, infirm, jittery, nervous.—*Ant.* firm*, settled, rigid.

2. [Not reliable]—*Syn.* uncertain, not dependable, not to be depended on, doubtful, questionable; see also **unreliable** 2, **unsteady** 2.

shale, *n.*—*Syn.* schistous clay, silt rock, sedimentary rock; see **rock** 1.

shall, *v.*—*Syn.* be going to, be about to, intend, want to, be obliged, must; see also **will** 3.

shallow, *mod.* **1.** [Lacking physical depth]—*Syn.* shoal, depthless, slight, inconsiderable, superficial, with the bottom in plain sight, with no depth, with little depth, not deep; *all* (D): as deep as a mud puddle, not deep enough to float a match, no deeper than a heavy dew.—*Ant.* deep*, bottomless, unfathomable.

2. [Lacking intellectual depth]—*Syn.* superficial, simple, silly, trifling, frothy, insane, frivolous, superficial, petty, foolish, farcical, idle, unintelligent; *all* (D): piffling, piddling, namby-pamby, lightweight, wishy-washy; see also **dull** 3, **stupid** 1. —*Ant.* profound*, philosophic, wise.

sham, *mod.*—*Syn.* misleading, lying, untrue; see **false** 3.

sham, *n.*—*Syn.* fakery, pretense, pretext; see **fake.**

shaman, *n.*—*Syn.* medicine man, witch doctor, angakok, obeah doctor, mundunugu; see also **priest.**

shamble, *v.*—*Syn.* hobble, dodder, shuffle; see **limp, walk** 1.

shambles, *n.*—*Syn.* mess, hodge-podge, confusion; see **disorder** 2.

shame, *n.* **1.** [A disgrace]—*Syn.* embarrassment, stigma, blot; see **disgrace** 2.
2. [A sense of wrongdoing]—*Syn.* bad conscience, mortification, confusion, humiliation, compunction, regret, chagrin, discomposure, irritation, remorse, stupefaction, embarrassment, abashment, self-reproach, self-reproof, self-disgust, stings of conscience, pangs of remorse; see also **guilt.**
3. [A condition of disgrace]—*Syn.* humiliation, dishonor, degradation; see **disgrace** 1, **scandal.**
put to shame—*Syn.* see **shame** *v.*

shame, *v.*—*Syn.* humiliate, mortify, dishonor; see **disgrace, humble.**

shamed, *mod.*—*Syn.* disgraced, embarrassed, humiliated, mortified, ashamed, chagrined, unable to show one's face.

shamefaced, *mod.* **1.** [Shy]—*Syn.* modest, restrained, retiring; see **humble** 1, **reserved** 3, **resigned.**
2. [Embarrassed]—*Syn.* crestfallen, humiliated, perplexed; see **ashamed.**

shameful, *mod.* **1.** [*Said of persons*]—*Syn.* immodest, corrupt, immoral, intemperate, debauched, drunken, profligate, villainous, knavish, degraded, reprobate, diabolical, indecent, indelicate, lewd, vulgar, impure, unclean, fleshly, carnal, sinful, wicked.—*Ant.* upright*, chaste, honorable.
2. [*Said of actions or conduct*]—*Syn.* dishonorable, disgraceful, contemptible, scandalous, flagrant, obscene, ribald, heinous, infamous, opprobrious, outrageous, shocking, ignominious, gross, infernal, disgusting, too bad, unworthy, evil, foul, hellish, disreputable, despicable; see also **corrupt** 3, **dishonest** 1, 2, **wrong.**—*Ant.* worthy*, admirable, creditable.

shamefully, *mod.*—*Syn.* cruelly, badly, outrageously; see **brutally, wrongly** 1, 2.

shameless, *mod.*—*Syn.* brazen, bold, forward; see **rude** 2, **lewd** 1, 2.

shamelessly, *mod.*—*Syn.* brazenly, audaciously, unblushingly; see **boldly** 1, **openly** 2.

shank, *n.*—*Syn.* long shank, foreleg, stem; see **leg** 1, **limb** 2.
shank of the evening (D)—*Syn.* early evening, not late *or* time to go, quite early; see **early, night** 1.

shanty, *n.*—*Syn.* cabin, hovel, cottage; see **hut, shack.**

shape, *n.* **1.** [Form]—*Syn.* contour, aspect, configuration; see **appearance** 1, **form** 1.
2. [An actual form]—*Syn.* pattern, stamp, frame; see **mold** 1, 2.
3. [A phantom]—*Syn.* apparition, shade, wraith; see **ghost** 1.
4. [(D) Condition]—*Syn.* state, physical state, health, fitness, lack of fitness.
out of shape—*Syn.* distorted, misshapen, battered; see **bent, broken** 1, **flat** 1, **ruined** 1, 2, **twisted.**
take shape—*Syn.* take (on) form, grow (up), fill out; see **develop** 1, **improve** 2.

shape, *v.* **1.** [To give shape]—*Syn.* mold, cast, fashion; see **form** 1.
2. [To take shape]—*Syn.* become, develop, take form; see **form** 4, **grow** 2.

shaped, *mod.*—*Syn.* made, fashioned, created; see **formed.**

shapeless, *mod.* **1.** [Formless]—*Syn.* indistinct, indefinite, invisible, amorphous, amorphic, vague, anomalous, without character *or* form *or* shape *or* definite form, lacking form, inchoate, unformed, unmade, not formed *or* made *or* created, with no definite outline; see also **uncertain** 2.—*Ant.* formed*, distinct, molded.
2. [Deformed]—*Syn.* misshapen, irregular, unshapely, unsymmetrical, mutilated, disfigured, malformed, ill-formed, abnormal; see also **deformed.**—*Ant.* regular*, symmetrical, shapely.

shapely, *mod.*—*Syn.* symmetrical, comely, proportioned; see **trim** 2.

shape up (D), *v.* **1.** [To obey]—*Syn.* mind, conform, observe; see **behave** 2, **improve** 2, **obey** 1.
2. [To develop]—*Syn.* enlarge, expand, refine; see **develop** 1.

share, *n.*—*Syn.* division, apportionment, part, portion, quota, helping, serving, piece, ration, slice, allotment, parcel, dose, fraction, fragment, allowance, pittance, dividend, percentage, heritage, commission; *all* (D): cut, whack, rake-off.
on shares—*Syn.* proportionally, in proportion, on the basis of investments; see **equally.**

share, *v.* **1.** [To divide]—*Syn.* allot, distribute, apportion, part, partition, deal, dispense, assign, administer.—*Ant.* unite*, combine, withhold.
2. [To partake]—*Syn.* participate, share in, experience, receive, have a portion of, have a share in, take part in, go in with, take a part of, take a share of; see also **like** 1.—*Ant.* avoid*, have no share in, take no part in.
3. [To give]—*Syn.* yield, bestow, accord; see **give** 1.
4. [To pay half of the expenses]—*Syn.* share expenses, pay half, go Dutch, go shares *or* halves, go fifty-fifty, give and take, divide with.

share and share alike (D), *mod.*—*Syn.* equally, fifty-fifty (D), shared.

shareholder, *n.*—*Syn.* stockholder, bondholder, part-owner, sharer.

sharing, *n.*—*Syn.* giving, dividing, communal living, partition, splitting, distribution, share and share alike, co-operative, partaking, participating, companionate.

shark, *n.* Sharks include the following—whale, basking, blue, man-eating, hammerhead, thresher, mackerel, gray, dog, bonnethead, shovelhead, dusky, Port Jackson, sharp-nose, spinous, white, sand, sleeper, tiger; see also **fish.**

sharp, *mod.* **1.** [Having a keen edge]—*Syn.* acute, edged, keen-edged, razor-edged, sharpened, ground fine, honed, honed to razor sharpness, razor-sharp, sharp-edged, fine, cutting, knifelike, knife-edged.—*Ant.* dull*, unsharpened, blunt.
2. [Having a keen point]—*Syn.* pointed, sharp-pointed, spiked, spiky, peaked, needle-pointed, keen, fine, salient, spiny, thorny, prickly, barbed, needlelike, briery, stinging, sharp as a needle, pronged, tapered, tapering, horned, unguiculate, acuate, acuminate, aculeate, muricate, aciculate, aciculated, aciculiform.
3. [Having a keen mind]—*Syn.* clever, astute, bright; see **intelligent** 1.

4. [Having the ability to wound with words] —*Syn.* caustic, biting, acrimonious; see **sarcastic.**
5. [Not quite honest or honorable]—*Syn.* crafty, designing, underhand; see **sly** 1.
6. [Distinct]—*Syn.* audible, visible, explicit; see **clear** 2, **definite** 2, **obvious** 1.
7. [Vigilant]—*Syn.* attentive, watchful, close; see **observant** 1, 2.
8. [Intense]—*Syn.* cutting, biting, piercing; see **intense.**
9. [Vigorous]—*Syn.* brisk, energetic, lively; see **active** 2.
10. [(D) Excellent]—*Syn.* fine, distinctive, first-class; see **excellent.**
11. [(D) Stylish]—*Syn.* dressy, chic, in style; see **fashionable.**

sharpen, *v.* **1.** [To make keen]—*Syn.* grind, file, hone, put an edge on, grind to a fine edge, hone to a razor edge, make sharp, make acute, whet, strop, give an edge *or* a fine edge to, put a point on, give a fine point to.—*Ant.* flatten*, thicken, turn.
2. [To make more exact]—*Syn.* focus, bring into focus, intensify, make clear, make clearer, clarify, outline distinctly, make more distinct.—*Ant.* confuse*, cloud, obscure.

sharper (D), *n.*—*Syn.* pretender, swindler, fraud; see **cheat** 1, **imposter.**

sharply, *mod.*—*Syn.* piercingly, pointedly, distinctly; see **clearly** 1, 2.

sharpshooter, *n.*—*Syn.* shooter, gunman, marksman; see **gunner, rifleman.**

sharp-sighted, *mod.*—*Syn.* alert, attentive, aware, observant, lynx-eyed.

sharp-witted, *mod.*—*Syn.* bright, smart, discriminating; see **intelligent** 1.

shatter, *v.*—*Syn.* shiver, split, burst; see **break** 3.

shattered, *mod.*—*Syn.* splintered, crushed, in smithereens (D); see **broken** 1.

shave, *v.* **1.** [To remove a shaving]—*Syn.* shear, graze, slice thin, cut into thin slices, skim, pare; see also **peel, skin.**
2. [To remove hair]—*Syn.* barber, cut, use a razor, clip closely, strip, strip the hair from tonsure, make bare.

shawl, *n.*—*Syn.* stole, tucker, shoulder shawl; see **muffler, wrap.**

she, *pron.*—*Syn.* this one, this girl, this woman, that girl, that woman, a female animal; see also **woman** 1.

sheaf, *n.*—*Syn.* package, cluster, collection; see **bunch** 1.

shear, *v.*—*Syn.* sever, cleave, shave; see **cut** 1.

shears, *n.*—*Syn.* cutters, clippers, scissors, snips, nippers, snippers.
Shears include the following—lever *or* alligator *or* crocodile, barber's, dressmaker's, metal-cutting, grass, sheepshearing, revolving, rotary, pruning, pinking, button-hole, guillotine, power; shearing machine.

sheath, *n.*—*Syn.* case, scabbard, cover, spathe, sheating, cere.
Specialized sheaths include the following—leaf sheath, dental sheath, Cirrus sheath, dentinal sheath, Neumann's sheath, Sheath of Schwann *or* primitive sheath *or neurilemma* (Latin), Sheath of Henle, preputial sheath *or* prepuce.

sheathe, *v.*—*Syn.* envelop, surround, cover; see **wrap** 2.

shed, *n.*—*Syn.* shelter, outbuilding, hut, lean-to, woodshed.

shed, *v.*—*Syn.* drop, let fall, send *or* give forth, shower down, cast, molt, exuviate, slough, discard, exude, emit, scatter, sprinkle.

shed blood, *v.* **1.** [To bleed]—*Syn.* lose blood, spill blood, be wounded; see **bleed** 1.
2. [To kill]—*Syn.* be violent, slaughter, murder; see **kill** 1.

shedding, *n.*—*Syn.* peeling, molting, casting off, losing hair, dropping, exuviating, exfoliating.

sheen, *n.*—*Syn.* shine, polish, gloss; see **finish** 2, **wax.**

sheep, *n.* Sheep include the following—Leicester, Cotswold, Southdown, Cheviot, blackfaced, Welsh, broadtailed, Iceland, Tartary, Astrakhan, Wallachian, Cretan, merino, Rambouillet, Shropshire, Dorset, Corriedale, Hampshire Down, Lincoln, Oxford, Romney, Suffolk, Mouflon, mountain, big horn, Rocky Mountain, Argali, Marco Polo's, Herny, Galway, Madras; see also **animal** 2, **goat.**

sheepish, *mod.*—*Syn.* timid, shy, retiring; see **docile, tame** 4.

sheer, *mod.* **1.** [Abrupt]—*Syn.* steep, very steep, precipitous; see **abrupt** 1.
2. [Thin]—*Syn.* transparent, diaphanous, delicate, fine, smooth, pure, lucid, translucent, gauzy, pellucid, limpid, soft, fragile, flimsy, slight, clear, lacy.
3. [Absolute]—*Syn.* utter, altogether, quite; see **absolute** 1.

sheet, *n.* **1.** [A bed cover]—*Syn.* covering, bed sheet, bedding, bed linen; see also **cloth, cover** 1.
2. [A thin, flat object]—*Syn.* lamina, leaf, foil, veneer, layer, stratum, coat, film, ply, covering, expanse.

shelf, *n.* **1.** [A ledge]—*Syn.* shoal, shallow, rock, reef, mantle, sandbank; see also **ledge, ridge** 2.
2. [A cupboard rack]—*Syn.* counter, cupboard, mantelpiece, rack.

shell, *n.* **1.** [A shell-like cover or structure]—*Syn.* husk, crust, nut, pod, case, pericarp, scale, shard, integument, eggshell, carapace, plastron.
2. [An explosive projectile]—Varieties include the following—armor-piercing, blind-loaded, high-explosive, anti-personnel, artillery shell, cannon shell, common, deck-piercing, torpedo, shrapnel, antiaircraft; see also **weapon** 1.
3. [A crustaceous covering]—Varieties include the following—tortoise, crustacean, conch, snail; see also **sea shell.**

shell, *v.*—*Syn.* strip, break off, remove the kernel, shuck, shell off, peel off, exfoliate, husk.

shellfish, *n.*—*Syn.* crustacean, mollusk, molluscoid, crustaceous animal, invertebrate, invertebrate *or* marine animal *or* creature, arthropod, gastropod, Arthropoda, molluskan type, bivalve, shell-meat.
Creatures often called shellfish include the following—crab, lobster, clam, shrimp, prawn, crawfish, crayfish, mussel, whelk, piddock, cockle, abalone, snail, boxfish, isopod, laemadipod, trilobite, branchiopod, corepod, malacostran.

shell out (D), *v.*—*Syn.* pay for *or* out, expend, fork over (D); see **pay** 1.

shellshocked (D), *mod.* —*Syn.* suffering from concussion, suffering from war nerves, psychoneurotic, neurotic, psychotic, hysterical, not oneself, upset, bomb-batty (D); see also **insane** 1.

shelter, *n.* —*Syn.* refuge, harbor, haven, sanctuary, asylum, retreat, covert, shield, screen, defense, security, safety, guardian, protector, house, roof, tent, shack, shed, hut, shade, shadow.

shelter, *v.* —*Syn.* screen, cover, hide, conceal, guard, take in, ward, harbor, defend, protect, shield, watch over, take care of, secure, preserve, safeguard, surround, enclose, house, lodge.—*Ant.* expose*, turn out, evict.

sheltered, *mod.* **1.** [Shaded]—*Syn.* screened, protected, shady, veiled, covered, protective, curtained.
2. [Protected]—*Syn.* guarded, ensured, shielded; see **safe** 1, **watched.**

shelve, *v.* **1.** [To arrange]—*Syn.* space, range, line up; see **file** 1, **line** 4, **order** 3, **organize** 1.
2. [To postpone]—*Syn.* hold, defer, prolong; see **delay** 1, **suspend** 2.

shepherd, *n.* —*Syn.* sheepherder, caretaker, protector; see **herdsman.**

sherbet, *n.* —*Syn.* ice, water ice, fruit ice; see **dessert, ice cream.**

sheriff, *n.* —*Syn.* county officer, county administrator, peace officer, reeve; see also **policeman.**

shield, *n.* —*Syn.* buckler, defense, absorber, buffer, bumper, protection, shelter, pavis, guard.

shield (from), *v.* —*Syn.* protect, conceal, fend (for *or* from); see **cover** 1, **defend** 2.

shift, *n.* **1.** [A change]—*Syn.* transfer, transformation, substitution, displacement, fault, alteration, variation; see also **change** 2.
2. [A working period]—*Syn.* turn, spell, working time; see **time** 1.
3. [Those who work a shift, sense 2]—*Syn.* gang, squad, relay, group, workmen; see also **team** 1.
make shift (to)—*Syn.* contrive (to), find a way (to), devise a means (of); see **manage, succeed** 1.

shift, *v.* **1.** [To change position]—*Syn.* slip, budge, fault, move, move over, turn, stir; see also **change** 4.
2. [To cause to shift, sense 1]—*Syn.* displace, remove, substitute; see **change** 1, **exchange** 1.
3. [To put in gear]—*Syn.* change gears, double-clutch, downshift, split-shift, put in drive; see also **drive** 3.

shiftless, *mod.* —*Syn.* idle, inactive, indolent; see **lazy** 1.

shifty, *mod.* —*Syn.* tricky, cunning, sneaky; see **sly** 1.

shilling, *n.* —*Syn.* ten (new) pence, one tenth of a pound; *both* (D): bob, bobstick; see also **money** 1.

shilly-shally, *v.* —*Syn.* falter, waver, fluctuate; see **hesitate, pause.**

shimmer, *v.* —*Syn.* glisten, glow, gleam; see **shine** 1.

shimmering, *mod.* —*Syn.* glimmering, sparkling, bright, scintillating, glimmery, twinkling, glistening, twinkly.

shin, *n.* —*Syn.* tibia, shankbone, limb; see **bone, leg** 1.

shin, *v.* —*Syn.* scramble, scale, ascend; see **climb** 2.

shindig (D), *n.* —*Syn.* party, dance, blow out (D); see **party** 1.

shine, *v.* **1.** [To give forth light]—*Syn.* radiate, beam, scintillate, glitter, sparkle, twinkle, glimmer, glare, glow, flash, blaze, shimmer, illumine, illuminate, blink, shoot out beams, irradiate, dazzle, bedazzle, flash, luminesce, flicker; see also sense 2, **light** 1.
2. [To reflect light]—*Syn.* glisten, gleam, glow, look good, be *or* grow bright, be effulgent, scintillate, have a gloss, give back, give light, deflect, mirror; see sense 1, **reflect** 3.
3. [To cause to shine, usually by polishing]—*Syn.* scour, brush, polish, put a gloss *or* finish on, finish, burnish, furnish, wax, buff, polish up, polish to a high luster, give a sheen to, make brilliant, make glitter; see also **clean, face** 2, **paint** 2.

shingle, *v.* —*Syn.* shear, decrease, trim; see **cut** 1.

shingles, *n.* —*Syn.* asbestos shingles, felt base shingles, shakes; see **roofing.**

shining, *mod.* **1.** [Bright]—*Syn.* radiant, gleaming, luminous; see **bright** 1, **shimmering.**
2. [Illustrious]—*Syn.* eminent, remarkable, brilliant; see **glorious** 1.

shiny, *mod.* —*Syn.* polished, sparkling, glistening; see **bright** 1.

ship, *n.* Types of ships include the following—dahabeah, junk, galleon, sampan, xebec, lugger, steamer, steamship, ocean greyhound, liner, freighter, landing barge, packet, ferry, clipper, square-rigged vessel, dhow, sailing ship, transport, tanker, fishing smack, lightship, pilot boat, cutter-yacht, pindjajap, lorcha, galiot, casco, patamar, caique, bilander, baghla, state barge, battleship, cruiser, destroyer, corvette, aircraft carrier, whaling vessel, bark, barkentine, brigantine, schooner, windjammer, yacht, dragger, cutter, ketch, yawl, bugeye, sloop, brig, tug, trawler, three-master, four-master, billyboy, hoy, felucca, caravel; see also **boat.**

ship, *v.* —*Syn.* send, consign, direct, dispatch, transmit, ship out, put into the hands of a shipper, export, put on board; see also **send** 1.

shipmate, *n.* —*Syn.* fellow, fellow sailor, comrade; see **sailor** 1.

shipment, *n.* —*Syn.* consignment, lot, load, goods shipped, cargo, carload, truckload, purchase; see also **commodity, freight** 2.

shipped, *mod.* —*Syn.* consigned, exported, delivered, transported, F.O.B., c.i.f., carried, expressed; see also **sent.**

shipper, *n.* —*Syn.* sender, consigner, exporter; see **merchant.**

shipping, *n.* **1.** [Ships]—*Syn.* steam, sailing, freight, passenger, war transport; see also **load** 1.
2. [Transportation]—*Syn.* freighting, trucking, airborne traffic; see **transportation.**

shipwreck, *n.* —*Syn.* destruction, loss, sinking; see **wreck** 3.

shipwrecked, *mod.* —*Syn.* sunk, cast away; see **destroyed, ruined** 1, **wrecked.**

shirk, *v.* —*Syn.* elude, cheat, malinger; see **avoid, evade** 1.

shirt, *n.* Shirts include the following—dress, undershirt, sport, work, cowboy, Western, lumberman's, long-sleeved, short-sleeved, cotton, silk, flannel, T-shirt, jersey, pullover, tank top, turtleneck, Mackinaw; see also **blouse, clothes.**

keep one's shirt on (D)—be calm *or* quiet *or* restrained, *etc.;* show restraint, remain calm; see **calm down.**
lose one's shirt (D)—*Syn.* lose everything, become bankrupt, go to the wall (D); see **fail** 4, **lose** 2.
shiver, *v.* —*Syn.* be cold, vibrate, quiver; see **shake** 1, **wave** 3.
shivery, *mod.* **1.** [Shaking]—*Syn.* tremulous, trembling, fluttering; see **quivering.**
2. [Brittle]—*Syn.* breakable, fragile, frail; see **weak** 1, 2.
shoal, *n.* —*Syn.* sandbank, sand bar, shallow, shallow water, underwater knoll, bank, bar, mudflat; see also **reef, shore.**
shock, *n.* **1.** [The effect of physical impact]—*Syn.* crash, clash, wreck; see **collision** 1.
2. [The effect of a mental blow]—*Syn.* excitement, hysteria, emotional upset; see **confusion** 2.
3. [The after-effect of physical harm]—*Syn.* concussion, stupor, collapse; see **illness** 1, **injury** 1.
shock, *v.* **1.** [To disturb one's self-control]—*Syn.* startle, agitate, astound; see **disturb** 2.
2. [To disturb one's sense of propriety]—*Syn.* insult, outrage, horrify, revolt, offend, appall, abash, astound, anger, floor, shake up, disquiet, dismay. —*Ant.* comfort*, humor, please.
3. [To jar]—*Syn.* shake, agitate, jolt; see **jar** 1.
shocked, *mod.* —*Syn.* startled, aghast, upset, astounded, offended, appalled, dismayed; see also **troubled.**
shocking, *mod.* —*Syn.* repulsive, hateful, revolting; see **frightful** 1, **offensive** 2.
shoddy, *mod.* —*Syn.* pretentious, gaudy, tacky (D); see **poor** 2.
shoe, *n.* —*Syn.* footwear, foot covering.
Footwear includes the following—Oxford, slipper, Turkish slipper, moccasin, low shoe, high shoe, boot, sandal, Roman sandal, chopine, balmoral, Crakow, blucher, patten, pump, sabot, clog, arctic, galosh, rubber shoe, leather shoe, fabric shoe, running *or* jogging *or* track shoes, tennis shoe; *all* (D): sneaker, loafer, heels, fruit boots, tennies, wedgie.
in another's shoes—*Syn.* in the position or place of another, in changed *or* different *or* other circumstances, reversal of roles; see **sympathetic, understood** 1.
where the shoe pinches—*Syn.* source of the trouble *or* difficulty, problem, complication; see **difficulty** 1, 2, **trouble** 2.
shoemaker, *n.* —*Syn.* cobbler, Crispin, shoe mender, shoe repairer, mender of shoes, bootmaker; see also **craftsman.**
shoestring, *n.* —*Syn.* lace, tie, shoelace, latchet; see also **fastener.**
on a shoestring—*Syn.* with too little backing *or* capital, impoverished, inadequately financed; see **dangerously, poor** 1.
shoo, *interj.* —*Syn.* get away, begone, leave; see **get out.**
shoot, *v.* **1.** [To discharge]—*Syn.* fire, shoot off, expel, pull the trigger, set off, torpedo, explode, ignite, blast, sharpshoot, open fire, rake, gauntlet, pump full of lead (D).
2. [To move rapidly]—*Syn.* dart, spurt, rush; see **hasten** 1, **hurry** 1.
3. [To kill by shooting]—*Syn.* dispatch, murder, execute; see **kill** 1.
4. [To hunt]—*Syn.* follow the chase, go afield, go gunning; see **hunt** 1.
5. [(D) To inquire]—*Syn.* request, solicit, ask; see **question** 1.
shoot at, *v.* **1.** [To fire a weapon at]—*Syn.* shoot, fire at, let off *or* fly, fire a shot at, fire upon, take a shot at (D); see also **attack** 1.
2. [(D) To strive for]—*Syn.* aim, endeavor, strive; see **try** 1.
shooting, *n.* **1.** [Firing a weapon]—*Syn.* gunning, firing, pulling the trigger, blasting, discharging, letting go, taking aim and firing, sighting a target; see also **gunfire, shot** 1.
2. [A sport]—*Syn.* pursuit of game animals, target shooting, field sport; see **hunting.**
shooting star, *n.* —*Syn.* meteor, falling star, fireball, bolide, meteorite.
shoot off one's mouth (D), *v.* —*Syn.* brag, bluster, blabber; see **boast** 1, **say, yell.**
shoot the bull (D), *v.* —*Syn.* exaggerate grossly, carry on a lengthy conversation, converse; see **boast** 1, **gossip.**
shoot up, **1.** [To grow rapidly]—*Syn.* spring up, thrive, prosper; see **grow** 1, **rise** 1, 3, **sprout.**
2. [To attack]—*Syn.* bombard, fire at, spray with slugs *or* bullets; see **attack** 1, 2.
shop, *n.* —*Syn.* store, department store, retail store, dry goods store, novelty shop.
set up shop—*Syn.* go into business, start, open (up) a shop *or* business *or* an office, *etc.*; see **begin** 1, 2.
shut up shop (D)—*Syn.* close (down *or* up), go out of business, cease functioning; see **close** 4, **stop** 2.
talk shop—*Syn.* talk business, exchange views, discuss one's speciality; see **gossip, talk** 1.
shop, *v.* —*Syn.* shop for *or* around, look *or* hunt for, try to buy; see **buy** 1.
shopkeeper, *n.* —*Syn.* manager, tradesman, storekeeper; see **businessman, merchant.**
shopper, *n.* —*Syn.* bargain hunter, professional shopper, purchaser; see also **buyer.**
shopping, *n.* —*Syn.* looking for bargains, inspecting goods, purchasing, comparing, looking, hunting for, matching, window-shopping; see also **buying.**
shopping center, *n.* —*Syn.* shops, trading center, parking lot; see **business** 4, **parking area.**
shore, *n.* —*Syn.* shingle, beach, strand, seaside, seashore, sand, coast, seacoast, brim, brink, bank, border, seaboard, margin, margent, sea beach, lakeside, lakeshore, river bank, riverside, raised beach, foreshore, lee shore, windward shore.
short, *mod.* **1.** [Not long in space]—*Syn.* low, skimpy, slight, not tall, not long, undersized, little, abbreviated, dwarfish, stubby, squat, stunted, stocky, diminutive, tiny, small, dwarf, dwarfed, close to the ground, dumpy, chunky, thickset, compact; *all* (D): stumpy, sawed-off, runty, pint-sized, pocket-sized, compact.
2. [Not long in time]—*Syn.* brief, curtailed, cut short, not protracted, concise, unprolonged, unsustained, laconic, condensed, terse, succinct, pithy, summary, pointed, precise, bare, abridged, summarized, aphoristic, epigrammatic, compressed, short-term, short-lived; see also **fleeting.**

3. [Inadequate]—*Syn.* deficient, insufficient, niggardly; see **inadequate** 1.
be *or* **run short (of)**—*Syn.* lack, want, run out of; see **need.**
fall short—*Syn.* not reach, be unsuccessful *or* inadequate, fall down (D); see **fail** 1, **miss** 3.
for short—*Syn.* as a nickname, familiarly, commonly; see **abbreviation** 1, **named** 1, **so-called.**
in short—*Syn.* that is, in summary, to make a long story short (D); see **briefly, finally** 1.

shortage, *n.*—*Syn.* short fall, scant supply, curtailment; see **lack** 1.

shortcake, *n.*—*Syn.* biscuit, cookie, teacake, Scottish shortbread; see also **cake** 2, **pastry.**

shortcoming, *n.*—*Syn.* fault, deficiency, lapse; see **weakness** 2.

short cut, *n.*—*Syn.* bypass, alternative, alternate route, timesaver, timesaving method *or* approach; see also **means** 1, **why** 2, 3.

shorten, *v.*—*Syn.* curtail, abridge, abbreviate; see **decrease** 2.

shorter, *mod.*—*Syn.* smaller, lower, not so long, briefer, more limited, more concise, more abrupt, lessened, diminished, reduced, curtailed.—*Ant.* higher*, longer, taller.

short for, *mod.* abbreviation, nickname, shortening (of); see **abbreviation** 1, **named** 1, **so-called.**

shorthand, *n.* Varieties of shorthand include the following—Pitman, Gregg, Fayet, Gabelsberger, Speedwriting; see also **handwriting.**

short-handed, *mod.*—*Syn.* understaffed, needing *or* in need of help, in the market (for laborers *or* hands *or* employees, *etc.*); see **wanting.**

short-lived, *mod.*—*Syn.* brief, momentary, temporary; see **fleeting, short** 2.

shortly, *mod.*—*Syn.* presently, quickly, right away; see **soon** 1.

shortness, *n.*—*Syn.* brevity, briefness, conciseness; see **length** 1.

short of, *mod.*—*Syn.* in need of, lacking, missing; see **wanting.**

shorts, *n.*—*Syn.* underpants, briefs, athletic underwear; see **clothes, underwear.**

shortsighted, *mod.* **1.** [Myopic]—*Syn.* nearsighted, astigmatic, blind; see **myopic.**
2. [Foolish]—*Syn.* unthinking, headlong, unwary; see **rash, stupid** 1.

short-tempered, *mod.*—*Syn.* touchy, gruff, harsh; see **irritable.**

shot, *mod.*—*Syn.* killed, injured, struck; see **attacked.**

shot, *n.* **1.** [The act of shooting]—*Syn.* firing, igniting, blasting, setting off, taking aim, sighting a target, pulling the trigger, discharge, loosing, letting fly; see also **gunfire, shooting** 1.
2. [A flying missile]—*Syn.* bullet, ball, pellet, lead, projectile, buckshot, grapeshot.
3. [An opportunity to shoot]—*Syn.* range, line of fire, reach, distance, chance, turn.
4. [One who shoots]—*Syn.* gunner, huntsman, marksman, hunter, rifleman.
call the shots (D)—*Syn.* direct, control, supervise; see **command** 2, **restrain** 1.
have *or* **take a shot at** (D)—*Syn.* endeavor, attempt, do one's best (at *or* in); see **try** 1.
like a shot (D)—*Syn.* rapidly, speedily, like a bat out of hell (D); see **fast** 1, **quickly.**
shot in the arm (D)—*Syn.* help, boost(er), assistance; see **aid** 1, **encouragement** 2.

shotgun, *n.* Sizes and types of shotguns include the following—10-gauge, 12-gauge, 16-gauge, 20-gauge, 26-gauge, single-barreled, double-barreled, hammerless, full-choke, modified choke, smooth bore, single shot, repeater, hand-loading, automatic, self-loading, pump, one-trigger, two-trigger; see also **gun** 2, **rifle.**

shoulder, *n.* **1.** [Juncture of the fore leg or arm and body]—*Syn.* upper arm *or* leg, shoulder cut, (shoulder) joint; see **arm** 1, 2, **joint** 1.
2. [A projection]—*Syn.* collar, protrusion, road *or* soft shoulder; see **ledge, ridge** 1, 2.
cry on someone's shoulder—*Syn.* weep, object, shed tears; see **cry** 1, **complain** 1.
put one's shoulder to the wheel—*Syn.* labor, attempt, strive; see **try** 1, **work** 1.
rub shoulders with—*Syn.* be acquainted *or* familiar with, know, see (frequently); see **associate** 1.
shoulder to shoulder—*Syn.* side by side, beside one another, together; see **loyally, near** 1.
straight from the shoulder (D)—*Syn.* honestly, frankly, openly; see **direct, sincerely, truly** 2.
turn *or* **give a cold shoulder to**—*Syn.* ignore, neglect, pass over; see **insult.**

shoulder, *v.*—*Syn.* shove, jostle, push aside.

shoulder blade, *n.*—*Syn.* shoulder bone, omoplate, scapula; see **bone.**

shout, *n.*—*Syn.* roar, bellow, scream; see **cry** 1, **yell** 1.

shout, *v.*—*Syn.* screech, roar, scream; see **yell.**

shout down, *v.*—*Syn.* silence, shut up, overcome; see **defeat** 1, 3, **quiet** 2.

shouting, *mod.*—*Syn.* jeering, screaming, raucous; see **loud** 2, **yelling.**

shouting, *n.*—*Syn.* cries, yelling, jeering; see **cry** 1.

shove, *v.*—*Syn.* jostle, push out of one's way, shoulder.

shovel, *n.* Shovels include the following—*Syn.* coal, snow, fire, miner's, irrigating, split, twisted, pronged, scoop, round-pointed; see also **tool** 1.

shovel, *v.*—*Syn.* take up, pick up, take up with a shovel, clean out, throw, move, pass, shift, delve; *both* (D): muck, handle a muck stick; see also **dig** 1, **load** 1.

shove off (D), *v.*—*Syn.* depart, go, start out; see **leave** 1.

show, *n.* **1.** [An exhibition]—*Syn.* presentation, exhibit, showing, exposition, occurrence, sight, appearance, program, flower show, boat show, home show, dog *or* cat show, bringing before the public, bringing to public view; see also **display** 2.
2. [A public performance]—*Syn.* carnival, representation, burlesque, production, appearance, concert, act, pageant, spectacle, light show, entertainment; see also **comedy, drama** 1, **movie.**
3. [Pretense]—*Syn.* sham, make believe, semblance; see **pretense** 1, 2.
for show—*Syn.* for (sake of) appearances, ostensibly, ostentatiously; see **apparently, pompously.**
get *or* **put the show on the road** (D)—*Syn.* start, open, get started; see **begin** 1.

stand *or* **have a show** (D)—*Syn.* stand *or* have a chance, be possible, admit of; see **allow** 1, 2.
steal the show (D)—*Syn.* triumph, get the best of it, win (out); see **defeat** 1, 3, **win** 1.

show, *v.* **1.** [To display]—*Syn.* exhibit, manifest, present; see **display** 1.
2. [To explain]—*Syn.* reveal, tell, explicate; see **explain.**
3. [To demonstrate]—*Syn.* attest, determine, confirm; see **prove.**
4. [To convince]—*Syn.* teach, prove to, persuade; see **convince.**
5. [To grant]—*Syn.* confer, bestow, dispense; see **give** 1.
6. [To indicate]—*Syn.* register, note, point; see **designate** 1, **record** 1.

showcase, *n.* —*Syn.* cabinet, display counter, museum case, exhibition, display case.

showdown, *n.* —*Syn.* crisis, exposé, unfolding; see **climax.**

shower, *n.* **1.** [Water falling in drops]—*Syn.* drizzle, mist, rainfall; see **rain** 1.
2. [Act of cleansing the body]—*Syn.* bathing, washing, sponging; see **bath** 1.
3. [An enclosure for showering]—*Syn.* showerstall, bath, shower room; see **bath** 3.

show in, *v.* —*Syn.* conduct, direct, guide; see **lead** 1.

showing, *n.* **1.** [A show]—*Syn.* exhibit, display, exhibition, production; see also **show** 1.
2. [An appearance]—*Syn.* occurrence, sight, manifestation; see **appearance** 3, **view** 1.

shown, *mod.* **1.** [Put on display]—*Syn.* displayed, demonstrated, advertised, exposed, set out, presented, exhibited, delineated, laid out, put up for sale; *both* (D): put up, put on the block.—*Ant.* withdrawn*, concealed, held back.
2. [Proved]—*Syn.* demonstrated, determined, made clear; see **established** 3, **obvious** 2.

show-off, *n.* —*Syn.* boaster, exhibitionist, egotist; see **braggart.**

show off, *v.* —*Syn.* brag, swagger, make a spectacle of oneself; see **boast** 1.

showpiece, *n.* —*Syn.* masterpiece, prime example, prize; see **masterpiece.**

show up, 1. [To arrive]—*Syn.* appear, come, turn up; see **arrive** 1.
2. [To expose]—*Syn.* discredit, worst, belittle; see **defeat** 1, 3, **convict, expose** 1.

show window, *n.* —*Syn.* display window, store window, picture window; see **display** 2.

showy, *mod.* —*Syn.* flashy, glaring, gaudy; see **ornate** 1.

shred, *n.* —*Syn.* fragment, piece, tatter; see **bit** 1, **rag.**

shred, *v.* —*Syn.* tear, strip, cut into small pieces, reduce to tatters, tear into rags, cut into slivers.

shrew, *n.* —*Syn.* vixen, virago, termagant, spitfire, she-devil, scold, porcupine, dragon, fury, fire-eater, Kate the Shrew, tigress, beldame, harridan, madcap, carper, defamer, detractor, calumniator, siren, reviler, backbiter, vituperator, muckraker, Biddy Moriarty, Xanthippe, barracker (Australian); *both* (D): hell cat, nag.

shrewd, *mod.* **1.** [Clever]—*Syn.* astute, ingenious, sharp; see **intelligent** 1.
2. [Cunning]—*Syn.* underhand, crafty, tricky; see **sly** 1.

shrewdly, *mod.* —*Syn.* knowingly, cleverly, slyly, foxily, trickily, sagaciously, astutely, skillfully, ably, smartly, guilefully, deceptively, cunningly, perspicaciously, intelligently, judiciously, neatly, cooly, handily, facilely, adroitly, deftly, with skill *or* cunning *or* shrewdness *or* sagacity, in a crafty manner, in a cunning manner, with consummate skill; *both* (D) with the know-how, knowing one's way around; see also **carefully** 2, **deliberately.**

shrewdness, *n.* —*Syn.* astuteness, perspicacity, sharpness; see **acumen, judgment** 1.

shrewish, *mod.* —*Syn.* pugnacious, petulant, peevish; see **irritable, quarrelsome** 2.

shriek, *n.* —*Syn.* scream, screech, howl; see **cry** 1, 3, **yell** 1.

shriek, *v.* —*Syn.* scream, screech, squawk; see **cry** 1, 3, **yell.**

shrieking, *mod.* —*Syn.* screaming, piercing, sharp; see **shrill.**

shrill, *mod.* —*Syn.* high-pitched, piercing, penetrating, sharp, strident, screeching, thin, piping, deafening, earsplitting, blatant, noisy, clanging, clangorous, harsh, blaring, raucous, metallic, discordant, cacophonous, acute; see also **loud** 1. —*Ant.* soft*, low, faint.

shrimp, *n.* Varieties include the following—British, common, deep-water, California, river; see also **fish, shellfish.**

shrine, *n.* —*Syn.* sacred place, sacred object, hallowed place, reliquary; see also **altar, church** 1.

shrink, *v.* —*Syn.* withdraw, blench, flinch; see **contract** 1, **recoil.**

shrinkage, *n.* —*Syn.* decrease, diminution, lessening, reduction, depreciation.

shrive, *v.* **1.** [To absolve]—*Syn.* redeem, purge, pardon; see **excuse, forgive** 1.
2. [To confess]—*Syn.* repent, atone, pray; see **confess** 3.

shrivel, *v.* —*Syn.* parch, dry up, shrink; see **contract** 1, **dry** 1, **wither.**

shroud, *n.* —*Syn.* garment, winding sheet, covering, graveclothes, cerements; see also **cloth, cover** 1.

shrub, *n.* —*Syn.* scrub, fern, dwarf tree; see **bush** 1, **hedge, plant.**

shrubbery, *n.* —*Syn.* shrubs, bushes, thick growth, ornamental planting *or* bushes, group of shrubs, hedge, arboretum; see also **brush** 4.

shrug (off), *v.* —*Syn.* forget, ignore, disapprove; see **doubt** 1, 2, **gesture.**

shrunken, *mod.* —*Syn.* withdrawn, withered, dwindled, contracted; see also **dry** 1, **wrinkled.**

shuck, *n.* —*Syn.* husk, pod, leaf; see **shell** 1.

shudder, *n.* —*Syn.* tremor, shuddering, shaking, trembling.

shudder, *v.* —*Syn.* quiver, quake, shiver; see **shake** 1, **wave** 1.

shuffle, *v.* **1.** [To move with a shuffling gait]—*Syn.* scuffle, scuff, scuff the feet; see **walk** 1.
2. [To mix cards]—*Syn.* change, change the order, rearrange, mix-up.

shun, *v.* —*Syn.* dodge, evade, keep away from, ignore, neglect; see also **avoid.**—*Ant.* accept, adopt*, take advantage of.

shut, *mod.* —*Syn.* stopped, locked, fastened; see **tight** 2.
shut, *v.* —*Syn.* close up, lock, seal; see **close** 4.
shutdown, *n.* —*Syn.* closing, closedown, cessation, abandonment.
shut down, *v.* —*Syn.* close up *or* down, shut up, abandon.
shut-in, *n.* —*Syn.* convalescent, sufferer, cripple; see **invalid, patient.**
shut off, *v.* —*Syn.* turn off, discontinue, put a stop to; see **close** 4, **stop** 1.
shut out, *v.* —*Syn.* keep out, evict, fence out *or* off; see **refuse.**
shutter, *n.* —*Syn.* blind, cover, shade; see **curtain, screen** 1.
shuttle, *v.* —*Syn.* seesaw, vacillate, come and go; see **alternate** 2.
shut up, *v.* **1.** [To cease speaking]—*Syn.* be quiet, stop talking, quiet, hush, quit (your) chattering, silence, dry up (D).
2. [To close]—*Syn.* padlock, close up *or* down *or* out, stop; see **close** 4.
shy, *mod.* —*Syn.* retiring, timorous, bashful; see **humble** 1, 2.
shyness, *n.* —*Syn.* bashfulness, reserve, timidity, modesty, timorousness, timidness, coyness, demureness, sheepishness, diffidence, apprehension, backwardness, nervousness, insecurity, reticence, mike fright (D); see also **restraint** 1.
sick, *mod.* —*Syn.* ill, ailing, unwell, disordered, diseased, feeble, weak, impaired, suffering, feverish, imperfect, sickly, declining, unhealthy, morbid, rabid, indisposed, distempered, infected, invalid, delicate, infirm, frail, rickety, broken down, physically run down, confined, laid up, coming down with, under medication, bedridden, in poor health, hospitalized, quarantined, incurable; *all* (D): on the blink, out of kilter, peaked, feeling poorly, sick as a dog, seedy, in a bad way, not so hot, at a low ebb, under the weather, down in the mouth, looking green about the gills.—*Ant.* healthy*, hearty, well.
sicken, *v.* **1.** [To contract a disease]—*Syn.* become ill *or* sick, take sick, fall ill, become diseased, fall victim to a disease, be stricken, run a temperature *or* a fever, be taken with, come down with, get *or* catch *or* pick up a disease *or* illness, acquire, incur, suffer a relapse, languish, waste away, break out (with *or* in); *all* (D): take *or* catch one's death, be laid by the heels, pick up a bug.
2. [To offend]—*Syn.* repel, nauseate, revolt; see **disgust.**
sickening, *mod.* **1.** [Contaminated]—*Syn.* sickly, tainted, diseased; see **sick.**
2. [Disgusting]—*Syn.* revolting, nauseous, putrid; see **offensive** 2.
sickly, *mod.* —*Syn.* ailing, weakly, feeble; see **sick.**
sickness, *n.* —*Syn.* ill health, ailment, infirmity; see **illness** 1.
sick of, *mod.* —*Syn.* tired (of), disgusted, fed up; see **disgusted with.**
side, *mod.* —*Syn.* at *or* to *or* from *or* by *or* into the side, indirect, not the main, off the main, roundabout, by a devious way, off to the side, lateral, sidewise, sideways, sidelong, off center, oblique, superficial.—*Ant.* middle*, direct, central.
side, *n.* **1.** [One of two opponents]—*Syn.* party, contestant, rival, foe, combatant, belligerent; see also **faction** 1.
2. [A face]—*Syn.* facet, front, front side, rear, surface, outer surface, inner surface, top, bottom, elevation, view; see also **plane** 1.
on the side—*Syn.* in addition (to), as a bonus, additionally; see **extra.**
side by side—*Syn.* adjacent, nearby, faithfully; see **loyally, near** 1,
take sides—*Syn.* join, fight for, declare oneself; see **help** 1, **support** 2.
sideboard, *n.* —*Syn.* closet, buffet, shelf; see **cupboard, table** 1.
sideburns, *n.* —*Syn.* burnsides, side-whiskers, face hair.
side dish, *n.* —*Syn.* dish, entree, meal; see **food.**
side effect, *n.* —*Syn.* influence, symptom, reaction; see **disease** 1, 2, **result.**
sidehill, *n.* —*Syn.* descent, declivity, decline; see **hill.**
side light, *n.* —*Syn.* opening, skylight, casement; see **window** 1.
side line, *n.* —*Syn.* avocation, interest, trade; see **hobby.**
sidelong, *mod.* —*Syn.* edgeways, laterally, indirectly; see **sideways.**
side show, *n.* —*Syn.* lesser *or* minor attraction, adjunct, related activity; see **addition** 2.
sidesplitting, *mod.* —*Syn.* laughable, comical, absurd; see **funny** 1.
side-step, *v.* —*Syn.* evade, elude, shun; see **avoid.**
sidetrack, *n.* —*Syn.* siding, turnout, shut; see **path** 1, **track** 1.
sidewalk, *n.* —*Syn.* footway, footpath, paved area, foot pavement; see also **path** 1, **track** 1.
sideways, *mod.* —*Syn.* indirectly, sloping, sidelong, in the lateral (direction), broadside on; see also **oblique** 1.
side with, *v.* —*Syn.* join, aid, incline to; see **favor** 1, 2, **help** 1, **support** 2.
siding, *n.* —*Syn.* (outside) finish, (outer) wall, covering; see **cover** 2, **finish** 2.
Sidings include the following—clapboards, shingles, stucco, pebbledash, brick veneer, matched siding, tongue and groove (siding), aluminum *or* steel *or* corrugated *or* enameled, *etc.,* sheets.
sidle, *v.* —*Syn.* veer, walk sideways, tilt; see **walk** 1.
siege, *n.* —*Syn.* offense, onslaught, assault; see **attack** 1.
siesta, *n.* —*Syn.* nap, doze, rest; see **sleep.**
sieve, *n.* —*Syn.* strainer, sifter, colander, screen, bolt, bolting cloth, mesh, searce, hair sieve, drum sieve, flat sieve, quarter-inch sieve, half-inch sieve, gravel sieve, flour sieve.
sift, *v.* **1.** [To evaluate]—*Syn.* investigate, scrutinize, probe; see **examine** 1.
2. [To put through a sieve]—*Syn.* bolt, screen, winnow, grade, sort, colander, size, searce, strain; see also **clean, filter** 2, **purify.**
sigh, *n.* —*Syn.* deep breath, sigh of relief, expression of sorrow; see **cry** 1.
sigh, *v.* —*Syn.* suspire, groan, lament; see **breathe** 1, **cry** 1, **gasp.**
sight, *n.* **1.** [The power of seeing]—*Syn.* perception, apperception, eyesight, eyes (for), range of vision,

apprehension, ken, keen *or* clear *or* good sight; see **vision** 1.
2. [Something worth seeing; *often plural*]—*Syn.* show, view, spectacle, display, scene, point of interest, local scene.
3. [(D) An unsightly person]—*Syn.* eyesore, hag, ogre, ogress, bum, scarecrow, fright; see also **slob, tramp** 1.
a sight for sore eyes (D)—*Syn.* beauty, welcome sight, delight; see **blessing** 2, **friend** 1, **view** 1.
at first sight—*Syn.* hastily, without much *or* due consideration, provisionally; see **quickly** 1, 2, **rashly.**
by sight—*Syn.* somewhat acquainted, not intimate(ly), superficially; see **unfamiliar** 1.
catch sight of—*Syn.* glimpse, notice, see momentarily *or* fleetingly *or* for a moment, etc.; see **see** 1.
lose sight of—*Syn.* miss, fail to follow, slip up on (D); see **forget** 2, **neglect** 1, **omit** 1.
on sight—*Syn.* at once, without hesitation, precipitately; see **immediately, quickly** 1, 2.
out of sight (of)—*Syn.* disappeared, vanished, indiscernible; see **gone** 1, **invisible** 1.

sighted, *mod.* —*Syn.* seen, in sight, located; see **observed** 1, **obvious** 1.

sightless, *mod.* —*Syn.* eyeless, visionless, unseeing; see **blind** 1.

sight-seeing, *n.* —*Syn.* vacationing, excursion, tour; see **touring** 2, **travel** 1.

sight-seer, *n.* —*Syn.* observer, wanderer, voyager; see **tourist, traveller.**

sign, *n.* **1.** [A signal]—*Syn.* indication, portent, clue, omen, prognostic, augury, presentiment, divination, presage, premonition, handwriting on the wall, foreshadowing, foreboding, foreknowledge, token, manifestation, foretoken, harbinger, herald, hint, symptom, assurance, precursor, prediction, mark, badge, auspice, symbol, caution, warning, beacon, flag, hand signal, wave of the arm, flash, whistle, warning bell, signal bell, signal light, high sign (D).
2. [An emblem]—*Syn.* insignia, badge, crest; see **emblem.**
3. [A symbol]—*Syn.* type, visible sign, token; see **symbol.**

sign, *v.* **1.** [Authorize]—*Syn.* endorse, confirm, acknowledge; see **approve** 1.
2. [Indicate]—*Syn.* express, signify, signal; see **mean** 1.
3. [Consecrate]—*Syn.* dignify, hallow, ordain; see **bless** 3.
4. [Hire]—*Syn.* engage, contract, employ; see **hire** 1.

signal, *n.* —*Syn.* beacon, flag, omen; see **sign** 1.

signal, *v.* —*Syn.* give a sign to, flag, wave, gesture, motion, semaphore, nod, beckon, warn, indicate.

signalize, *v.* —*Syn.* honor, acclaim, applaud; see **praise** 1.

signature, *n.* —*Syn.* sign, stamp, mark, name, written name, subscription, autograph, impression, indication, designation, trademark, one's John Hancock (D).

sign away, *v.* —*Syn.* transfer, dispose of, auction; see **sell** 1.

signed, *mod.* —*Syn.* marked, autographed, written, undersigned, countersigned, sealed, witnessed, subscribed, registered, receipted, enlisted, signed on the dotted line (D); see also **endorsed.**

signer, *n.* —*Syn.* cosigner, underwriter, endorser; see **sponsor, witness.**

signet, *n.* —*Syn.* stamp, badge, seal; see **emblem.**

significance, *n.* —*Syn.* weight, consequence, point; see **importance** 1.

significant, *mod.* —*Syn.* meaningful, notable, vital; see **important** 1.

signification, *n.* —*Syn.* connotation, significance, implication; see **meaning.**

signify, *v.* —*Syn.* imply, import, purport; see **mean** 1.

sign off, *v.* —*Syn.* cease, become silent, go off the air; see **stop** 1, 2.

sign on the dotted line, *v.* —*Syn.* notarize, countersign, underwrite; see **endorse** 1.

sign up (for), *v.* —*Syn.* subscribe (to *or* for), take, accept; see **join** 2, **volunteer** 2.

silence, *n.* **1.** [Absence of sound]—*Syn.* quietness, stillness, hush, utter stillness, the stillness of death, absolute quiet, calm, noiselessness, soundlessness, quiet, deep stillness, stillness of eternal night, loss of signal, cessation of all sound, quietude, hush of early dawn, radio silence, security silence, security blackout, censorship, iron curtain.—*Ant.* noise*, din, uproar.
2. [Absence of speech]—*Syn.* muteness, secrecy, taciturnity, reserve, reticence, inarticulateness, golden silence, respectful silence, sullen silence.—*Ant.* talkativeness*, glibness, loquacity.

silence, *v.* —*Syn.* overawe, quell, still; see **hush** 1, **quiet** 2.

silenced, *mod.* —*Syn.* quieted, calmed, stilled, restrained, repressed, held down *or* back, restricted, subdued, inhibited, gagged, coerced, suppressed, under duress *or* compulsion *or* restraint, etc., made subservient *or* obedient *or* inhibited, etc.; see also **beaten.**

silent, *mod.* **1.** [Without noise]—*Syn.* still, hushed, soundless; see **calm** 2, **quiet** 2.
2. [Without speech]—*Syn.* reserved, mute, speechless; see **dumb** 1.

silently, *mod.* —*Syn.* without noise, without a sound, as still as a mouse, like a shadow, in utter stillness, noiselessly, stilly, calmly, quietly, soundlessly, mutely, dumbly, in deathlike silence, like one struck dumb, morosely, speechlessly, wordlessly, as silently as falling snow.

silhouette, *n.* —*Syn.* contour, shape, profile; see **form** 1, **outline** 4.

silk, *n.* Silks include the following—taffeta, moiré, watered silk, jacquard, damask, crepe, satin crepe, satin de Lyon, satin, rajah, pongee, China silk, tissue, voile, mousseline de soie, shantung, tussah, matelassé, surah, twilled lining, crepe de Chine, georgette, chiffon, tapestry, upholstery, velvet, chiffon velvet, plush, ribbons, tie silk, silk shirting; see also **cloth.**

silken, *mod.* —*Syn.* soft, tender, delicate, luxurious, like silk, made of silk, resembling silk, smooth, satiny, glossy.

sill, *n.* —*Syn.* threshold, beam, bottom of the frame; see **ledge.**

silly, *mod.* —*Syn.* senseless, ridiculous, nonsensical, unreasonable, foolish, fatuous, irrational, inconsistent, stupid, absurd, simpleminded, harebrained, brainless, featherbrained, empty-headed, muddle-headed, illogical, ludicrous, preposterous.

silo, *n.* —*Syn.* rocket launcher *or* storage, pit, super-hardened silo; see **building** 1, **defense** 2.

silt, *n.* —*Syn.* deposit, sand, varbe; see **residue, sediment.**

silver, *mod.* **1.** [Suggestive of silver]—*Syn.* silvery, pale, white, lustrous, bright, resplendent, silvern, silvery white, silverlike, white as silver; see also **shimmering.**

2. [Concerning the use of silver]—*Syn.* of silver, made of silver, sterling, plated with silver, silver-gilt, silver-plated.

silver-tongued, *mod.* —*Syn.* oratorical, mellifluous, eloquent; see **fluent** 2.

silverware, *n.* —*Syn.* silver, service, cutlery, flatware, hollow ware, silver plate.

Common pieces of silverware include the following —knife, dinner knife, fish knife, butter spreader, butter knife, fork, salad fork, cold meat fork, tablespoon, soup spoon, dessert spoon, ice-cream spoon, bouillon spoon, iced-tea spoon, coffee spoon, teaspoon, soup ladle, gravy ladle, berry server, jelly server, sugar spoon, sugar tongs, pastry server, pickle fork, oyster fork, grapefruit spoon, demitasse spoon, salt spoon, nutpick, spatula.

silvery, *mod.* **1.** [Shining]—*Syn.* shiny, glittering, brilliant; see **bright** 1, **shimmering.**

2. [Musical]—*Syn.* melodious, resonant, sonorous; see **harmonious** 1, **musical** 1.

simian, *mod.* —*Syn.* anthropoid, apelike, primate; see also **animal** 1.

simian, *n.* —*Syn.* ape, gorilla, chimpanzee, orangutan; see **monkey.**

similar, *mod.* —*Syn.* much the same, comparable, related; see **alike** 2.

similarity, *n.* —*Syn.* correspondence, likeness, resemblance, similitude, parallelism, semblance, agreement, affinity, kinship, analogy, closeness, approximation, conformity, congruity, concordance, concurrence, coincidence, harmony, comparability, identity, community, relation, correlation, relationship, proportion, parity, comparison, simile, interrelation, homogeneity, association, connection, similar form, similar appearance, like quality, point of likeness.—*Ant.* difference*, variance, dissimilarity.

similarly, *mod.* —*Syn.* likewise, thus, furthermore, in a like manner, correspondingly, by the same token, in like fashion, in addition, then, as well, too; see also **so.**

simile, *n.* —*Syn.* metaphor, analogy, likeness, epic simile, explicit comparison of dissimilars; see also **comparison** 2, **figure of speech.**

similitude, *n.* —*Syn.* semblance, simulation, replica; see **copy, representation.**

simmer, *v.* **1.** [To boil]—*Syn.* seethe, stew, warm; see **boil** 2, **cook.**

2. [To be angry]—*Syn.* seethe, fret, fume; see **rage** 1.

simmer down (D), *v.* —*Syn.* cool (off), be reasonable, become calm *or* quiet *or* sensible, etc.; see **calm down.**

simmering, *mod.* —*Syn.* broiling, heated, boiling; see **hot** 1.

simmering, *n.* —*Syn.* boiling, stewing, ebullition, boil.

simon-pure, *mod.* —*Syn.* true, authentic, real; see **genuine** 1, **pure** 1, 2.

simper, *v.* —*Syn.* giggle, grin, snicker; see **smile, sneer.**

simple, *mod.* **1.** [Not complicated]—*Syn.* single, unmixed, unblended, mere, uncompounded, unalloyed, unadulterated, not complex, uncomplicated, without confusion, simplistic, not confusing, pure.

2. [Plain]—*Syn.* unadorned, unaffected, homely; see **modest** 2.

3. [Easy]—*Syn.* not difficult, mild, of little difficulty, not arduous, done with ease, with great facility, manageable, presenting no difficulty, not puzzling; see also **easy** 2.—*Ant.* obscure*, puzzling, difficult*.

4. [Stupid]—*Syn.* inane, dull, ignorant; see **shallow** 2, **stupid** 1.

5. [Unsophisticated]—*Syn.* ingenuous, plain, artless; see **innocent** 1, **naive.**

simple-minded, *mod.* —*Syn.* unintelligent, childish, moronic; see **dull** 3, **naive, stupid** 1.

simpleton, *n.* —*Syn.* clod, idiot, bungler; see **fool** 1.

simplicity, *n.* **1.** [The state of being without complication]—*Syn.* singleness, homogeneity, purity, uniformity, clearness, unity, integrity, monotony. —*Ant.* confusion*, intricacy, complexity.

2. [The quality of being plain]—*Syn.* plainness, stark reality, lack of ornament, unadornment, lack of sophistication, bareness, rusticity, homeliness, freedom from artificiality, severity.—*Ant.* sophistication*, ornamentation, elaboration.

3. [Artlessness]—*Syn.* naïveté, ingenuousness, primitiveness; see **innocence** 2.

simplified, *mod.* —*Syn.* made easy, abridged, made plain, uncomplicated, clear, interpreted, broken down, cleared up, reduced; see also **obvious** 1, 2.

simplify, *v.* —*Syn.* clear up, clarify, elucidate, interpret, reduce to essentials, make clear, make plain, break down, analyze; see **explain, order** 3.—*Ant.* mix*, complicate, confuse.

simplistic, *mod.* —*Syn.* simplest, (unduly *or* overly) simplified, characterized by simplism *or* oversimplification, condensed, oversimplified; see also **childish** 1, **naive, simple** 1.

simply, *mod.* **1.** [With simplicity]—*Syn.* clearly, plainly, intelligibly, directly, candidly, sincerely, modestly, easily, quietly, naturally, honestly, frankly,* unaffectedly, artlessly, ingenuously, without self-consciousness, commonly, ordinarily, matter-of-factly, unpretentiously, openly, guilelessly. —*Ant.* awkwardly*, affectedly, unnaturally.

2. [Merely]—*Syn.* utterly, just, solely; see **only** 2.

3. [Absolutely]—*Syn.* really, in fact, totally; see **completely.**

simulate, *v.* —*Syn.* pretend, dissemble, imitate, cheat, deceive, misrepresent, prevaricate, equivocate, feign, sham, fake (D), assume, fence, gloss over, fabricate, disguise, concoct, exaggerate, play the hypocrite, counterfeit, playact, invent, lie. —*Ant.* reveal*, speak out, speak the truth.

simultaneous, *mod.* —*Syn.* coincident, at the same time, concurrent, contemporaneous, in concert, in the same breath, in chorus, at the same instant; see also **equally.**

simultaneously, *mod.* —*Syn.* at the same time, as one, concurrently; see **together** 2.

sin, *n.* —*Syn.* error, wrongdoing, trespass, wickedness, evil-doing, iniquity, immorality, crime, ungodliness, unrighteousness, veniality, disobedience to the divine will, transgression of the divine law, violation of God's law.
Sins recognized as deadly include the following —pride, covetousness, lust, anger, gluttony, envy, sloth.—*Ant.* righteousness*, godliness, virtue.

sin, *v.* —*Syn.* err, do wrong, commit a crime, offend, break the moral law, break one of the Commandments, smash the Ten commandments, shatter the Decalogue, trespass, transgress, misbehave, misconduct oneself, go astray, stray from the path of duty, wander from the paths of righteousness, fall, lapse, fall from grace *or* virtue; *all* (D): sow one's wild oats, kick over the traces, let one's foot slip, take the primrose path, wallow in the mire, wander from the straight and narrow, follow the broad way, backslide, live in sin, sleep around; see also **curse** 1, **deceive, kill** 1, **steal.**

since, *mod.* and *prep.* **1.** [Because]—*Syn.* for, as, inasmuch as, considering, forasmuch as, in consideration of, after all, insomuch as, seeing that, in view of (the fact), for the reason that, by reason of, on account of, in view of; see also **because.**
2. [Between the present and a previous time] —*Syn.* ago, from the time of, subsequent to, after, following, more recently than, until now.

sincere, *mod.* **1.** [Genuine]—*Syn.* real, actual, bona fide; see **genuine** 2, **serious** 2.
2. [Honest]—*Syn.* truthful, faithful, trustworthy; see **honest** 1, **reliable** 1, 2.

sincerely, *mod.* —*Syn.* truthfully, truly, really, honestly, genuinely, earnestly, aboveboard, seriously, ingenuously, naturally, without equivocation, in all conscience, candidly, frankly, profoundly, deeply, to the bottom of one's heart.

sincerity, *n.* —*Syn.* honor, earnestness, innocence, trustworthiness, guilelessness, veracity, justice, impartiality, openness, frankness, truthfulness, genuineness; see also **honesty** 1, **reliability.**—*Ant.* cunning*, guile, deceit.

sinecure, *n.* —*Syn.* easy job, child's play, cinch, snap (D).

sinews of war, *n.* —*Syn.* finances, cash, financial resources; see **money** 1, **power** 2, **wealth** 2.

sinewy, *mod.* **1.** [Strong]—*Syn.* powerful, forceful, acute; see **strong** 2.
2. [Stringy]—*Syn.* elastic, threadlike, ropy; see **flexible** 1.

sinful, *mod.* —*Syn.* erring, immoral, corrupt; see **wicked** 1, 2, **wrong** 1.

sinfully, *mod.* —*Syn.* unrighteously, immorally, unjustly; see **wrongly** 1.

sing, *v.* **1.** [To produce vocal music]—*Syn.* chant, carol, warble, vocalize, trill, croon, choir, twitter, chirp, lilt, sing soprano *or* tenor *or* bass, etc.; raise a song, lift (up) the voice in song, pipe up, burst into song.—*Ant.* mumble*, squawk, screech.
2. [To produce a sound suggestive of singing] —*Syn.* buzz, resound, purr; see **hum, sound** 1.
3. [To write poetry]—*Syn.* celebrate in song, versify, tell in verse, compose, grow lyrical; see also **write** 1.

singe, *v.* —*Syn.* burn, sear, scorch; see **burn** 2.

singer, *n.* —*Syn.* vocalist, songster, chorister, soloist, minstrel, chanter; *all* (D): crooner, groaner, voice; see also **musician.**

singing, *mod.* —*Syn.* musical, humming, chanting, warbling, purring, whistling, twittering.

singing, *n.* —*Syn.* warbling, crooning, chanting; see **music** 1.

single, *mod.* **1.** [Unique]—*Syn.* sole, original, exceptional, singular, only, uncommon, without equal, unequaled, peerless, without a peer, without a rival, unrivaled; see also **rare** 2, **unique** 1, **unusual** 1.—*Ant.* many*, numerous, widespread.
2. [Individual]—*Syn.* particular, separate, indivisible; see **individual** 1, **private.**
3. [Unmarried]—*Syn.* unwed, divorced, celibate, eligible, living alone, companionless, spouseless, bachelor, maiden, unattached, free; *all* (D): footloose, unfettered, on the loose, free-lancing, in the market.—*Ant.* married*, united*, wed.
4. [Alone]—*Syn.* isolated, separated, deserted; see **alone** 1.
5. [For the use of one person]—*Syn.* private, individual, restricted, secluded, personal, one's own, not public, not general, exclusive.—*Ant.* public*, common, general.

single-handed, *mod.* —*Syn.* without help *or* assistance, courageously, self-reliantly; see **alone** 1, **bravely, individually.**

single-minded, *mod.* —*Syn.* stubborn, self-reliant, bigoted; see **determined** 1, **selfish** 1.

singly, *mod.* —*Syn.* alone, by itself, by oneself, separately, only, solely, one by one, privately, individually, singularly, once.—*Ant.* together*, in groups, in a crowd.

sing out, *v.* —*Syn.* call (out), cry, bellow; see **say, yell.**

singsong, *mod.* —*Syn.* tiresome, repetitious, monotonous; see **dull** 4.

singular, *mod.* **1.** [Referring to one]—*Syn.* sole, one only, single; see **unique** 1.
2. [Odd or strange]—*Syn.* peculiar, uncommon, extraordinary; see **rare** 2, **unusual** 2.

singularity, *n.* **1.** [Irregularity]—*Syn.* deviation, curiosity, abnormality; see **irregularity** 2.
2. [Idiosyncrasy]—*Syn.* peculiarity, propensity, manner; see **characteristic, quirk.**

singularly, *mod.* —*Syn.* notably, uniquely, remarkably; see **especially** 1.

sinister, *mod.* —*Syn.* evil, bad, corrupt, perverse, dishonest, inauspicious, menacing, foreboding, threatening, ominous, disastrous, malign, malignant, hurtful, harmful, injurious, baneful, baleful, obnoxious, dire, woeful, disastrous, pernicious, mischievous, deleterious, poisonous, adverse, unlucky, unfortunate, unfavorable, unpropitious; see also **wicked** 1, 2.—*Ant.* fortunate*, lucky, opportune.

sink, *n.* —*Syn.* sewer, basin, cesspool, washbasin, tub, pan, ewer, bowl.

sink, *v.* **1.** [To go downward]—*Syn.* descend, decline, fall, subside, drop, droop, regress, slump, go under, immerse, go to the bottom, be submerged, settle, go to Davy Jones's locker (D), hit a slump, touch bottom, go down with (the ship).—*Ant.* rise*, float, come up.

2. [To cause to sink, sense 1]—*Syn.* submerge, scuttle, depress, submerse, immerse, engulf, overwhelm, swamp, lower, bring down, force down, cast down, let down, send to Davy Jones's locker (D); see also **soak** 1.—*Ant.* raise*, float, bring up.
3. [To incline]—*Syn.* slant, tilt, list; see **lean** 1.
4. [To weaken]—*Syn.* decline, fail, fade; see **weaken** 1.
5. [To deteriorate]—*Syn.* spoil, degenerate, rot; see **decay, waste** 3.
6. [To decrease]—*Syn.* lessen, diminish, wane; see **decrease** 1.

sinker, *n.*—*Syn.* plummet, bob, plumb; see **weight** 2.

sink in (D), *v.*—*Syn.* impress, penetrate (the mind), take hold, make an impression; see also **influence.**

sinking, *mod.*—*Syn.* settling in, submerging, drowning, immersing, engulfing, dropping, falling, going under.

sinless, *mod.*—*Syn.* pure, perfect, upright; see **innocent** 4, **righteous** 1.

sinner, *n.*—*Syn.* wrongdoer, delinquent, miscreant, adulterer, adultress; see also **criminal, rascal.**

sinning, *mod.*—*Syn.* sinful, immoral, erring; see **wicked** 1, 2, **wrong** 1.

sinuous, *mod.* **1.** [Twisted]—*Syn.* crooked, circuitous, curved; see **indirect, twisted** 1.
2. [Indirect]—*Syn.* devious, vagrant, deviative; see **erring, wrong** 3.

sip, *v.*—*Syn.* taste, drink in, extract; see **drink** 1.

Sir, *n.* **1.** [A formal title]—*Syn.* lord, knight, baron, priest, governor, master.
2. [A form of address; not always capital]—*Syn.* sire, Your Honor, Your Excellency, Your Majesty, Your Reverence, Your Grace, My Lord, my dear sir; *all* (D): Mister, Bud, Chief, Big Boy, You.

sire, *n.*—*Syn.* procreator, parent, begetter, generator, creator; see **father** 1.

siren, *n.* **1.** [An alarm]—*Syn.* horn, whistle, signal; see **alarm** 1.
2. [Seductress]—*Syn.* temptress, vamp, charmer; see **shrew.**

sirup, *n.* Common sirups include the following—cane, corn, maple, simple, glucose, rock candy; molasses, sorghum, honey, treacle; see also **sugar, sweets.**

sissy (D), *mod.*—*Syn.* weak, afraid, nellie (D); see **cowardly** 1.

sister, *n.* **1.** [A sister by blood]—*Syn.* blood relative, female sibling, member of the family, stepsister, half sister; *all* (D): big sister, kid sister, own sister, sis; see also **relative.**
2. [A sister by religious profession]—*Syn.* nun, member of a sisterhood, inmate of a convent, devotee, deaconess, one who professes Christ, bride of Jesus.

sit, *v.* **1.** [To assume a sitting posture]—*Syn.* be seated, seat oneself, take a seat, sit down, sit up, squat, perch; *all* (D): hunker, park oneself, take a load off one's feet, take a load off one's mind.—*Ant.* rise*, stand up, get up.
2. [To occupy a seat]—*Syn.* have a place, have a chair, sit in, take a chair, take a seat, take a place; see also **occupy** 2.—*Ant.* stand*, give up one's seat, be without a seat.
3. [To lie]—*Syn.* remain, rest, bear on; see **lie** 2, **relax.**
4. [To hold an assemblage]—*Syn.* convene, come together, hold an assembly; see **assemble** 2, **meet** 2.

sit back, *v.*—*Syn.* ignore, relax, keep one's hands off (D); see **neglect** 1.

site, *n.*—*Syn.* locality, section, situation; see **place** 3, **position** 1.

sit-in, *n.*—*Syn.* demonstration, march, display; see **protest, strike** 1.

sit on *or* **upon,** *v.*—*Syn.* sit in (on), take part (in), be a part of; see **co-operate** 1, **join** 2, **work** 2.

sit out, *v.*—*Syn.* ignore, abstain (from), hold back; see **neglect** 1, 2.

sitter, *n.*—*Syn.* baby sitter, one who is baby-sitting, attendant, companion, someone to watch *or* mind *or* tend *or* attend to the children; see also **nurse** 2, **servant.**

sitting, *n.*—*Syn.* session, seance, appointment; see **gathering, meeting** 1.

sitting room, *n.*—*Syn.* front room, living room, reception room; see **drawing room, parlor, room** 2.

situate, *v.*—*Syn.* locate, take up residence, establish; see **dwell, reside, settle** 7.

situated, *mod.*—*Syn.* established, fixed, located; see **placed.**

situation, *n.* **1.** [Circumstance]—*Syn.* condition, state, state of one's affairs; see **circumstance** 1, **circumstances** 2.
2. [A physical position]—*Syn.* location, site, spot; see **place** 3, **position** 1.
3. [A social position]—*Syn.* station, status, sphere; see **rank** 2, 3.
4. [An economic position]—*Syn.* place, employment, post; see **job** 1, **profession** 1, **trade** 2.

sit up (for), —*Syn.* wait *or* stay (up), not (go to) sleep, wait for; see **wait** 1.

sit well with (D), *v.*—*Syn.* please, be acceptable *or* welcome *or* agreeable *or* pleasing, etc. to, gratify; see **satisfy** 1.

sixpence, *n.*—*Syn.* half a shilling, half-real, picayune; see **money** 1.

sixth sense, *n.*—*Syn.* foresight, clairvoyance, second sight, intuition, telepathy.

size, *n.* **1.** [Measurement]—*Syn.* extent, area, dimension; see **measurement** 2.
2. [Magnitude]—*Syn.* bulk, largeness, greatness, extent, vastness, amplitude, scope, immensity, enormity, stature, capaciousness, hugeness, humongousness (D), breadth, substance, volume, bigness, highness, mass, extension, intensity, capacity, proportion; see also **extent, quantity.**
of a size—*Syn.* similar, matched, paired; see **alike** 1.

sized, *mod.*—*Syn.* stiffened, varnished, filled; see **finished** 2, **glazed.**

size up (D), *v.*—*Syn.* judge, survey, scrutinize; see **examine** 1.

sizzle, *n.*—*Syn.* hiss, hissing, sputtering; see **noise** 1.

sizzle, *v.*—*Syn.* brown, grill, broil; see **cook, fry.**

skate, *v.*—*Syn.* slide, glide, skim, slip, skid, go quickly, race, ice skate, roller skate.

skeleton, *n.* **1.** [Bony structure]—*Syn.* skeletal frame, axial *and* appendicular skeleton, osseous processes, exoskeleton, endoskeleton, support; see also **bone.**

2. [Framework]—*Syn.* draft, design, sketch; see **frame** 1, 2.

skeptic, *n.* —*Syn.* doubter, unbeliever, cynic, questioner, infidel, heathen, freethinker, atheist, deist, agnostic, heretic, disbeliever, Pyrrhonist, pagan, anti-Christian, dissenter, latitudinarian, misbeliever, rationalist, profaner, materialist, positivist, nihilist, somatist, scoffer, apostate, blasphemer; see also **cynic.**

skeptical, *mod.* —*Syn.* cynical, dubious, unbelieving; see **doubtful** 2, **suspicious** 1.

skeptically, *mod.* —*Syn.* dubiously, doubtingly, not gullibly; see **suspiciously.**

skepticism, *n.* —*Syn.* suspicion, uncertainty, dubiousness; see **doubt** 2, **sarcasm.**

sketch, *n.* **1.** [A drawing or plan]—*Syn.* portrayal, picture, draft, design, outline, adumbration, form, shape, delineation, drawing, representation, painting, skeleton, figure, figuration, configuration, depiction, illustration, copy, likeness, *croquis* (French), fashion plate, rough *or* preliminary *or* tentative sketch; see also **picture** 3, **plan** 1.

2. [A description or plan]—*Syn.* summary, survey, draft; see **description** 1, **plan** 1, 2.

sketch, *v.* **1.** [To draw]—*Syn.* paint, describe, depict; see **draw** 2.

2. [To plan]—*Syn.* outline, chart, draft; see **plan** 2.

sketchily, *mod.* —*Syn.* hastily, patchily, incompletely; see **badly, inadequately.**

sketchy, *mod.* **1.** [Rough]—*Syn.* coarse, crude, preliminary; see **introductory** 1, **unfinished** 1.

2. [Imperfect]—*Syn.* defective, superficial, insufficient; see **faulty, inadequate** 1.

skid, *v.* —*Syn.* slip, glide, move; see **slide** 1.

skid road, *n.* —*Syn.* skid row, poor *or* red-light district, desolation row (D); see **ghetto, slum.**

skiff, *n.* —*Syn.* rowboat, dinghy, tender; see **boat.**

skill, *n.* **1.** [Ability]—*Syn.* dexterity, facility, craft; see **ability** 1, 2, **experience** 3, **talent.**

2. [Trade]—*Syn.* occupation, work, craft; see **job** 1, **profession** 1, **trade** 2.

skilled, *mod.* —*Syn.* skillful, a hand at, proficient; see **able** 2, **experienced.**

skillful, *mod.* —*Syn.* skilled, practiced, accomplished; see **able** 1, 2, **experienced.**

skim, *v.* **1.** [To pass lightly and swiftly]—*Syn.* soar, float, sail, dart; see also **fly** 1.

2. [To remove the top; especially, to remove cream] —*Syn.* brush, scoop, ladle, separate; see also **dip** 2, **remove** 1.

3. [To read swiftly]—*Syn.* look through, brush over, scan; see **examine** 1, **read** 1.

skimp, *v.* —*Syn.* scamp, slight, scrimp; see **sacrifice** 2, **save** 3.

skimpy, *mod.* **1.** [Deficient]—*Syn.* short, scanty, insufficient; see **inadequate** 1.

2. [Stingy]—*Syn.* tight, niggardly, miserly; see **stingy.**

skin, *n.* —*Syn.* tegument, integument, epithelium, epidermis, dermis, derma, cuticle, scarfskin, trueskin, bark, peel, husk, rind, hide, fell, coat, carapace, pelage, covering, surface, parchment, vellum.

be no skin off one's back *or* **nose** (D)—*Syn.* not hurt (one), do no harm, not affect one; see **prosper, survive** 1.

by the skin of one's teeth (D)—*Syn.* (just) barely, scarcely, narrowly; see **hardly.**

get under one's skin (D)—*Syn.* irritate, disturb, upset; see **anger** 1.

have a thick skin (D)—*Syn.* be indifferent, not care, shrug off; see **endure** 1, 2.

have a thin skin (D)—*Syn.* be sensitive *or* timid *or* readily hurt, etc., wince, cringe; see **suffer** 1.

save one's skin (D)—*Syn.* get away *or* out, evade, leave (just) in time; see **escape, leave** 1, **survive** 1.

with a whole skin (D)—*Syn.* safe, unharmed, undamaged; see **saved** 1, **unhurt.**

skin, *v.* —*Syn.* excoriate, decorticate, peel, pare, flay, scalp, slough, cast, shed, exuviate, strip, strip off, pull off, remove the surface from, skin alive, husk, shuck, bark, lay bare, bare.

skin-deep, *mod.* —*Syn.* shallow, desultory, ignorant; see **superficial, trivial.**

skin diver, *n.* —*Syn.* scuba diver, submarine diver, deep-sea diver, pearl diver, aquanaut, frogman (D); see also **diver.**

skin diving, *n.* —*Syn.* underwater swimming, swim at great sea depths, scuba diving.

Skin diving equipment includes the following—wet *or* dry suit, snorkle, air tanks, mask, fins, air regulator, buoyancy compensator (BC) vest, weight belt, depth gauge, spear gun.

skinflint, *n.* —*Syn.* scrimp, tightwad, hoarder; see **miser** 1.

skinny, *mod.* —*Syn.* lean, gaunt, slender; see **thin** 2.

skip, *v.* —*Syn.* caper, gambol, leap; see **jump** 1.

skipper, *n.* —*Syn.* commander, leader, operator; see **captain** 3, **officer** 3, **pilot** 2.

skirmish, *n.* —*Syn.* engagement, encounter, conflict; see **battle** 2, **fight** 1.

skirt, *n.* —*Syn.* kilt, fustanella, kirtle, petticoat, dirndl, tutu, hoopskirt, harem skirt, suit skirt, broomstick skirt, culottes, miniskirt, pleated skirt, divided skirt, hobble skirt, pannier, sarong, muumuu; see also **clothes, dress** 2.

skit, *n.* —*Syn.* sketch, burlesque, parody; see **drama** 1.

skittish, *mod.* **1.** [Frivolous]—*Syn.* lively, capricious, whimsical; see **changeable** 1, 2.

2. [Shy]—*Syn.* timid, restive, nervous; see **afraid** 2.

skulk, *v.* —*Syn.* prowl, slink, lurk; see **hide** 2, **sneak.**

skull, *n.* —*Syn.* scalp, pericranium, brain case; see **head** 1, **cranium.**

skunk (D), *n.* —*Syn.* knave, rogue, scoundrel; see **rascal.**

sky, *n.* —*Syn.* firmament, azure, the heavens, welkin, empyrean; see also **air** 1, **heaven** 1.

out of a clear (blue) sky (D)—*Syn.* without warning, suddenly, abruptly; see **quickly** 1, **soon** 1.

to the skies (D)—*Syn.* without restraint *or* limit, excessively, inordinately; see **unlimited.**

sky-blue, *mod.* —*Syn.* azure, cerulean, *bleu céleste* (French); see **blue** 1.

skylight, *n.* —*Syn.* fanlight, light, bay window; see **window** 1.

skyline, *n.* —*Syn.* horizon, shape, profile; see **outline** 4.

skyscraper, *n.* —*Syn.* tall building, tower, modern building, high-rise (building), eyesore (D); see also **building** 1.

slab, *n.* —*Syn.* plate, slice, bit, chunk, lump, chip, piece, cutting; see also **part** 1.

slack, *mod.* **1.** [Not taut]—*Syn.* relaxed, lax, limp; see **loose** 1.
2. [Not busy]—*Syn.* remiss, sluggish, inattentive; see **lazy** 1.

slack down *or* **off** *or* **up,** *v.* —*Syn.* decline, lessen, become slower *or* quieter, *etc.*; see **decrease** 1, **slow** 1.

slacken, *v.* —*Syn.* loosen, retard, reduce; see **decrease** 1, 2.

slacker, *n.* —*Syn.* recluse, milksop, recreant; see **cheat** 1, **coward.**

slag, *n.* —*Syn.* cinders, recrement, refuse; see **residue.**

slain, *mod.* —*Syn.* slaughtered, destroyed, assassinated; see **dead** 1.

slam, *v.* **1.** [To throw with a slam]—*Syn.* thump, fling, hurl; see **throw** 1.
2. [To shut with a slam]—*Syn.* bang, crash, push; see **close** 4.

slander, *n.* —*Syn.* defamation, calumny, scandal; see **lie** 1.

slander, *v.* —*Syn.* villify, defame, calumniate, asperse, decry, traduce, libel, defile, detract, depreciate, disparage, revile, dishonor, blaspheme, curse, attack, sully, tarnish, besmirch, denigrate, smirch, blot, cast a slur on, scandalize, belittle, backbite, derogate, blacken, sneer at, malign, falsify, speak evil of; *all* (D): give a bad name, blacken the fair name, dish the dirt, sling the mud, plaster, blackwash; see also **lower.**—*Ant.* praise*, applaud, eulogize.

slanderous, *mod.* —*Syn.* libelous, defamatory, disparaging; see **opprobrious** 1.

slang, *n.* —*Syn.* cant, argot, colloquialism, neologism, pidgin English, vulgarism, vulgarity, pseudology, lingo, thieves' Latin, peddlers' French, jargon, shoptalk, Billingsgate, Biddy Moriarty's vocabulary, bog Latin (Irish), dog Latin, St. Giles' Greek; *all* (D): slanguage, English as she is spoke, Franglais, Americanese; see also **jargon** 1, 3, **language** 1.

slant, *v.* —*Syn.* veer, lie obliquely, incline; see **bend** 2, **lean** 1, **tilt** 1.

slanting, *mod.* —*Syn.* inclining, sloping, tilting; see **bent, oblique** 1.

slap, *v.* —*Syn.* strike, pat, spank; see **hit** 1.

slapdash, *mod.* —*Syn.* hasty, sluggish, impetuous; see **careless** 1.

slap down (D), *v.* —*Syn.* rebuke, reprimand, worst; see **defeat** 1, **hush** 1, **quiet** 2.

slap-happy (D), *mod.* —*Syn.* out of one's wit(s) *or* head, badly beaten, dizzy; see **beaten** 1, **punished, silly.**

slapstick, *mod.* —*Syn.* absurd, droll, comical; see **funny** 1.

slash, *v.* —*Syn.* slit, gash, sever; see **cut** 1.

slashing, *mod.* —*Syn.* harsh, brutal, vicious; see **cruel** 1.

slat, *n.* —*Syn.* buttress, brace, lath; see **support** 2.

slate, *mod.* —*Syn.* dark, dark gray, slate gray; see **gray** 1.

slattern, *n.* —*Syn.* trollop, whore, pickup (D); see **prostitute.**

slatternly, *mod.* —*Syn.* messy, sloppy, untidy; see **dirty.**

slaughter, *n.* —*Syn.* butchery, killing, massacre; see **carnage.**

slaughter, *v.* —*Syn.* slay, murder, massacre; see **butcher** 1, **kill** 1.

slaughterhouse, *n.* —*Syn.* abattoir, butchery, butcher house, shambles, stockyhard, aceldama.

Slav, *n.* Slavs include the following—Russian, Bulgarian, Pole, Slovene, Slovak, Ukranian, Bohemian, Moravian, Czech, Serb, Croat, Sorb, Deniker.

slave, *mod.* —*Syn.* vassal, captive, enslaved; see **bound** 1, 2, **restricted.**

slave, *n.* **1.** [A person in bondage]—*Syn.* bondsman, bondservant, bondslave, thrall, chattel, serf, vassal, captive, bondsmaid, bondwoman, victim of tyranny, one of a subject people.
2. [A drudge]—*Syn.* toiler, menial, worker; see **drudge, laborer.**

slavery, *n.* **1.** [Bondage]—*Syn.* servitude, thralldom, enthrallment, subjection, subjugation, serfdom, constraint, captivity, restraint, bond service, vassalage, involuntary servitude; see also **captivity.**
2. [The use of slaves as an institution]—*Syn.* owning slaves, slaveholding, slave-owning, practicing slavery, holding slaves; see also sense 1.
3. [Drudgery]—*Syn.* toil, menial labor, grind; see **work** 2.

Slavic, *mod.* —*Syn.* Slav, Slavophile, Slavonic, Old Slavonic, Church Slavonic.
Words referring to Slavic peoples include the following—Cyrillic, Glagolitic, Russian, Polish, Bulgarian, Czech, Ukrainian, Bohemian, Serbian, Slovenian, Slovak, Croatian *or* Croat, Bosnian, Montenegrin, Yugoslavian.

slavish, *mod.* **1.** [Having the qualities of a slave] —*Syn.* servile, cringing, fawning; see **docile, obsequious.**
2. [Lacking originality]—*Syn.* uninspired, faithful, imitative; see **dull** 4.

slavishly, *mod.* —*Syn.* thoughtlessly, insensitively, scrupulously; see **accurately, blindly** 2, **carelessly.**

slay, *v.* —*Syn.* murder, slaughter, butcher, assassinate; see also **kill** 1.

sleazy, *mod.* —*Syn.* shoddy, cheap, shabby; see **shabby, poor** 2.

sled, *n.* **1.** [A sled intended for sport]—*Syn.* hand sled, coasting sled, coaster, child's sled, toboggan; *all* (D): belly-bumper, belly-slammer, pig-sticker.
2. [A sled intended as a vehicle]—*Syn.* sledge, bob, bobsled, bobsledge, bobsleigh, sleigh, cutter, chair, drag, stone drag, boat, stone boat; see also **vehicle** 1.

sleek, *mod.* —*Syn.* silken, silky, satin; see **smooth** 1.

sleep, *n.* —*Syn.* slumber, doze, nap, rest, repose, sound *or* deep sleep, nod, siesta, catnap, dream, hibernation, dormancy, Morpheus, the Sandman; *all* (D): snooze, shut-eye, the down.

sleep, *v.* —*Syn.* slumber, doze, drowse, rest, nap, snooze, hibernate, dream, snore, nod, yawn, languish, flag, relax, go to bed, rest in the arms of Morpheus, drop *or* fall asleep, lose oneself in slumber; *all* (D): take forty winks, catnap, turn in, go rockaby, hit the hay *or* sack, saw logs, sack up *or* out, catch a wink, roll in.

sleep around (D), *v.* —*Syn.* fornicate, be promiscuous, practice adultery; see **copulate.**
sleepily, *mod.* —*Syn.* dully, drowsily, as though asleep; see **slowly.**
sleepiness, *n.* —*Syn.* torpor, lethargy, drowsiness, tiredness, sand in the eyes (D); see also **laziness.**
sleeping, *mod.* —*Syn.* dormant, inert, inactive; see **asleep.**
sleepless, *mod.* —*Syn.* wakeful, insomnious, insomnolent; see **restless** 1.
sleeplessness, *n.* —*Syn.* restlessness, wakefulness, alertness; see **insomnia.**
sleep (something) off, *v.* —*Syn.* get over it, improve, sober up; see **recover** 2.
sleep on it, *v.* —*Syn.* think about it, consider, ponder; see **think** 1.
sleepy, *mod.* —*Syn.* dozy, somnolent, sluggish; see **tired.**
sleet, *n.* —*Syn.* sleet storm, hail, hail storm; see **rain** 1, **storm** 1.
sleeve, *n.* Types of sleeves include the following —coat, tight-fitting, flowing, short, elbow, three-quarter, bishop, raglan, leg-of-mutton, shirt, tailored, two-piece, one-piece, long, cape, puff, domino, kimona.
sleigh, *n.* —*Syn.* cutter, sledge, bobsled; see **sled** 1, 2.
sleight, *n.* **1.** [A trick]—*Syn.* craft, deception, hoax; see **cunning, trick** 1.
2. [Ability]—*Syn.* skill, dexterity, expertise; see **ability** 1, 2.
slender, *mod.* —*Syn.* slim, slight, spare; see **thin** 1.
slenderize, *v.* —*Syn.* starve oneself, lose weight, reduce; see **diet.**
slice, *n.* —*Syn.* thin piece, chop, collop; see **part** 1.
slick, *mod.* —*Syn.* sleek, sleeky, glossy; see **oily** 2, **smooth** 1.
slicker (D), *n.* —*Syn.* cheat, trickster, sharper; see **rascal.**
slide, *v.* **1.** [To move with a sliding motion]—*Syn.* glide, skate, skim, slip, coast, skid, toboggan, move along, move over, move past, pass along.
2. [To cause to slide, sense 1]—*Syn.* shove, thrust, ram, impel, urge, propel, drive, press against, butt, launch, start, accelerate; see also **push** 2.
let slide—*Syn.* ignore, pass over, allow to decline *or* get worse *or* decay, etc.; see **neglect** 1, 2.
sliding scale, *n.* —*Syn.* adjusted *or* variable scale, ratio, related scales *or* rates; see **rate** 1, **relationship.**
slight, *mod.* **1.** [Trifling]—*Syn.* insignificant, petty, piddling; see **trivial, unimportant.**
2. [Inconsiderable]—*Syn.* small, sparse, scanty; see **inadequate** 1.
3. [Delicate]—*Syn.* frail, slender, flimsy; see **dainty** 1.
slight, *v.* —*Syn.* disdain, snub, overlook; see **neglect** 1, **scorn** 2.
slighting, *mod.* —*Syn.* abusive, derisive, maligning; see **derogatory, opprobrious** 1, 2.
slightly, *mod.* —*Syn.* a little, to some *or* a small extent, more or less, ever so little, hardly at all, scarcely any, hardly noticeable, unimportantly, inconsiderably, insignificantly, lightly, inappreciably, imperceptibly, somewhat, rather on a small scale.
slim, *mod.* —*Syn.* slender, narrow, lank; see **thin** 2.
slime, *n.* —*Syn.* fungus, mire, ooze; see **mud.**
slimy, *mod.* —*Syn.* oozy, miry, mucky; see **muddy** 1, 2.
sling, *n.* **1.** [A hanging bandage]—*Syn.* cast, bandage, compress; see **dressing** 3.
2. [A weapon]—*Syn.* beany, mortar, slingshot; see **catapult, weapon** 1.
sling, *v.* **1.** [To throw]—*Syn.* hurl, send, shoot; see **throw** 1.
2. [To suspend]—*Syn.* hoist, raise, weight; see **hang** 1.
slink, *v.* —*Syn.* prowl, cower, lurk; see **sneak.**
slinky (D), *mod.* —*Syn.* sleek, sinuous, serpentine; see **graceful** 1, **smooth** 1, 2.
slip, *n.* **1.** [Error]—*Syn.* lapse, misdeed, indiscretion; see **error** 1.
2. [Misstep]—*Syn.* slide, skid, stumble; see **fall** 1.
3. [Undergarment]—*Syn.* underclothing, pantislip, bra-slip; see **clothes, underwear.**
4. [Piece of paper]—*Syn.* piece, sheet, leaf; see **paper** 1.
give someone the slip (D)—*Syn.* get away, slip away, escape (from); see **leave** 1.
slip, *v.* —*Syn.* glide, shift, move; see **slide** 1.
let slip—*Syn.* miss, fail (with), slip up (D); see **drop** 2, **neglect** 1, 2.
slip on, *v.* —*Syn.* put on, don, change (clothes), get on.
slip one over on (D), *v.* —*Syn.* get the better of, outguess, outmaneuver; see **deceive, defeat** 1, 3, **trick.**
slipper, *n.* —*Syn.* house shoe, sandal, pump, dancing shoe.
slippery, *mod.* —*Syn.* glassy, smooth, glazed, polished, oily, slick, waxy, lubricious, unctuous, soapy, greasy, slimy, icy, lustrous, satiny, silky, satin-smooth, glabrous, sleek, glistening, wet, *glacé* (French), unsafe, insecure, uncertain, untrustworthy, unreliable, tricky, shifty, slithery, slippy, skiddy, slippery as an eel (D)—*Ant.* rough*, sticky, tenacious.
slipping (D), *mod.* —*Syn.* failing, growing worse, in error; see **unsatisfactory.**
slip-up, *n.* —*Syn.* oversight, mishap, omission; see **error** 1.
slip up on (D), *v.* —*Syn.* overlook, miss, bungle; see **fail** 1.
slit, *n.* —*Syn.* split, cleavage, crevice; see **hole** 1, 2, **tear.**
slit, *v.* —*Syn.* tear, slice, split; see **cut** 1, 2.
slither, *v.* —*Syn.* slink, coast, glide; see **slide** 1.
sliver, *n.* —*Syn.* splinter, thorn, fragment; see **bit** 1, **flake.**
sliver, *v.* —*Syn.* rive, splinter, crush; see **break** 1, 2, **cut** 2.
slob (D), *n.* —*Syn.* pig, hog, slattern, tramp, sloven, slop (D), draggletail, yokel, ragamuffin, tatterdemalion, mudlark, street arab, dustman, chimney-sweep, wallower, leper; see also **sight** 3.
slobber, *v.* —*Syn.* drip, salivate, dribble; see **drool** 1.
slog, *v.* —*Syn.* toil, labor, perform; see **work** 1.
slogan, *n.* —*Syn.* catchword, rallying cry, trademark; see **motto, proverb.**
slop, *n.* **1.** [Waste]—*Syn.* slush, swill, refuse; see **trash** 1.

2. [A small quantity]—*Syn.* leavings, few drops, pile; see **bit** 1.

slop, *v.* —*Syn.* slosh, wallow, flounder, splash, drip, spill, dash, spatter, let run out, let run over.

slope, *n.* **1.** [A hillside]—*Syn.* rising ground, incline, grade; see **hill.**

2. [Inclination]—*Syn.* slant, tilt, declivity; see **inclination** 5.

sloping, *mod.* —*Syn.* askew, tilted, slanted; see **oblique** 1.

slop over (D), *v.* —*Syn.* blunder, flounder, good (D); see **fail** 1, **overdo** 1.

sloppy, *mod.* **1.** [Poor]—*Syn.* clumsy, amateurish, mediocre; see **awkward** 1, **careless** 1, **poor** 2.

2. [Wet]—*Syn.* slushy, splashy, muddy; see **wet** 1.

slot, *n.* —*Syn.* aperture, opening, cut; see **groove, hole** 1, 2.

sloth, *n.* —*Syn.* lethargy, torpidity, indolence; see **laziness.**

slothful, *mod.* —*Syn.* sluggish, lethargic, indolent; see **lazy.**

slouch, *n.* —*Syn.* bungler, incompetent, beginner; see **failure** 2.

no slouch—*Syn.* expert, professional, successful person; see **success** 3.

slouch, *v.* —*Syn.* droop, stoop, lounge; see **bow** 1, **loaf** 1.

slouchy, *mod.* —*Syn.* drooping, clumsy, stooping; see **awkward** 1.

slough, *n.* —*Syn.* quagmire, bog, marsh; see **swamp.**

slovenly, *mod.* —*Syn.* untidy, slipshod, frowzy; see **careless** 1.

slow, *mod.* **1.** [Slow in motion]—*Syn.* sluggish, laggard, deliberate, gradual, moderate, loitering, leaden, creeping, inactive, torpid, slow moving, ultra-slow, crawling, imperceptible, snaillike, slow-paced, leisurely; *both* (D): glue-footed, as slow as molasses in January.—*Ant.* fast*, swift, rapid.

2. [Slow in starting]—*Syn.* dilatory, procrastinating, delaying, postponing, idle, indolent, tardy, torpid, lazy, apathetic, phlegmatic, inactive, fabian, sluggish, heavy, quiet, drowsy, inert, dreamy, sleepy, lethargic, stagnant, slothful, supine, passive, slack, negligent, remiss, listless, languorous, lackadaisical, disinclined, reluctant, hesitant, enervated, dormant, abeyant, potential, latent; see also **late** 1. —*Ant.* immediate*, alert, instant.

3. [Slow in producing an effect]—*Syn.* belated, behindhand, backward, unpunctual, overdue, delayed, long-delayed, behindtime, regarded, impeded, detained, hindered, moss-backed.—*Ant.* busy*, diligent, industrious.

4. [Dull or stupid]—*Syn.* stolid, tame, uninteresting; see **dull** 3.

slow, *v.* **1.** [To become slower]—*Syn.* slacken, slow up *or* down, lag, loiter, quiet, relax, procrastinate, back water, back and fill; *all* (D): stall, let up, wind down, ease up *or* off; see also sense 2, **decrease** 1, **hesitate.**—*Ant.* rise*, accelerate, mount.

2. [To cause to become slower]—*Syn.* delay, postpone, decelerate, moderate, reduce, regulate, retard, detain, temper, qualify, decrease, diminish, hinder, impede, hold back, keep waiting, brake, curtail, check, curb, reef, shorten sail; *all* (D): cut down, rein in, cut back; see **sense** 1.

slowdown, *n.* —*Syn.* retardation, partial stoppage, slacking off; see **production** 1, **strike** 1.

slowly, *mod.* —*Syn.* moderately, gradually, languidly, nonchalantly, gently, haltingly, deliberately, leisurely, casually, at one's leisure, with deliberation *or* procrastination, taking one's (own sweet) time (D).

slowness, *n.* **1.** [Dullness]—*Syn.* sluggishness, languidness, listlessness, apathy, lethargy, drowsiness; see **indifference** 1, **stupidity** 1.

2. [Weakness]—*Syn.* inactivity, feebleness, impotence; see **weakness** 1.

sludge, *n.* **1.** [Mud]—*Syn.* muck, ooze, slop; see **mud.**

2. [Waste]—*Syn.* refuse, slime, filth; see **residue.**

slug, *n.* —*Syn.* goldbrick, laggard, idler; see **loafer** 1.

sluggish, *mod.* —*Syn.* inactive, torpid, indolent; see **lazy** 1, **slow** 1, 2.

sluggishness, *n.* —*Syn.* apathy, drowsiness, lethargy; see **fatigue, lassitude, laziness.**

sluice, *n.* **1.** [A gate]—*Syn.* floodgate, conduit, lock; see **gate.**

2. [A trough]—*Syn.* sluiceway, moat, ditch; see **channel** 1, **trench** 1.

slum, *mod.* —*Syn.* ghetto, tenemental, poverty-stricken, crowded; see **poor** 1.

slum, *n.* —*Syn.* low neighbourhood, cheap housing, poor district, tenement neighbourhood; *all* (D): tenderloin, cabbage patch, radio city, ratnest, the wrong side of the tracks, desolation row, Harlem, Watts, Hunter's Point, skid row, Tobacco Road; see **ghetto, tenement.**

slum (around), *v.* —*Syn.* go slumming, sight-see, look around; see **visit** 4.

slumber, *n.* —*Syn.* repose, nap, doze; see **rest** 1, **sleep.**

slump, *n.* **1.** [Decline]—*Syn.* depreciation, slip, descent; see **drop** 2, **fall** 1.

2. [Depression]—*Syn.* rut, routine, bad period; see **depression** 2.

slump, *v.* **1.** [Fall]—*Syn.* cave in, go to ruin, collapse; see **fall** 1.

2. [Decline]—*Syn.* blight, depreciate, sink; see **decay.**

slur, *n.* **1.** [Stain]—*Syn.* blot, smear, blemish; see **stain.**

2. [Aspersion]—*Syn.* stigma, reproach, exposé; see **accusation** 2.

slur, *v.* **1.** [To discredit]—*Syn.* cast aspersions on, disparage, slander; see **accuse.**

2. [To pronounce indistinctly]—*Syn.* blue, garble, mumble, mispronounce, drop words *or* sounds, hurry over; see **say.**

slush, *n.* —*Syn.* (melting) snow, mire, refuse; see **mud.**

slut, *n.* —*Syn.* wench, whore, hooker (D); see **prostitute.**

sly, *mod.* **1.** [Crafty]—*Syn.* wily, tricky, foxy, shifty, insidious, crafty, shrewd, designing, deceitful, guileful, scheming, deceiving, captious, intriguing, cunning, unscrupulous, deceptive, conniving, calculating, plotting, elusive, delusive, illusory, bluffing, dissembling, dishonest, mealy-mouthed, treacherous, underhanded, sneaking, double-deal-

ing, faithless, traitorous, sharp, smart, ingenious, cagey, canny, dishonorable; *all* (D): crooked, mean, dirty, ratty, double-crossing, slick, smooth, slippery, shady.—*Ant.* honest*, fair, just.
2. [Shrewd]—*Syn.* clever, sharp, astute; see **intelligent** 1.
3. [Secretive]—*Syn.* furtive, evasive, stealthy; see **secret** 3, **secretive.**

slyly, *mod.* —*Syn.* cleverly, stealthily, shrewdly, foxily, meanly, secretly, cunningly, intelligently, with downcast eyes, on the quiet, furtively.

smack (D), *mod.* —*Syn.* precisely, just, clearly; see **exactly.**

smack, *n.* **1.** [A sharp noise]—*Syn.* bang, crack, snap; see **noise** 1.
2. [A slap]—*Syn.* pat, hit, spank; see **below** 1.
3. [A small amount]—*Syn.* trace, suggestion, touch; see **bit** 1, 2.

smack, *v.* **1.** [To hit smartly]—*Syn.* slap, spank, cuff; see **hit** 1.
2. [To kiss]—*Syn.* greet, press the lips to, smooch; see **kiss.**

smack down (D), *v.* —*Syn.* rebuke, take aback, humiliate; see **defeat** 1, 3, **rebuff.**

smack of, *v.* —*Syn.* bear resemblance (to), bring to mind, suggest; see **resemble.**

small, *mod.* **1.** [Little in size]—*Syn.* tiny, diminutive, miniature; see **little** 1.
2. [Little in quantity]—*Syn.* scanty, short, meager; see **inadequate** 1.
3. [Unimportant]—*Syn.* trivial, insignificant, unessential; see **shallow** 2, **unimportant.**
4. [Ignoble]—*Syn.* mean, petty, base; see **vulgar** 1.
5. [Humble]—*Syn.* modest, poor, pitiful; see **humble** 2.

smaller, *mod.* —*Syn.* tinier, lesser, (more) petite; see **less, shorter.**

small talk, *n.* —*Syn.* chitchat, light conversation, banter, casual conversation, idle conversation, table talk; see also **babble.**

smallness, *n.* —*Syn.* littleness, smallishness, narrowness, minuteness, diminutiveness, infinitesimalness, small *or* little *or* minute *or* diminutive size *or* bulk *or* mass, shortness, brevity, atomity, slightness, microdimensions, scantiness, exiguity, tininess, petiteness, dapperness, dinkiness (D).

smallpox, *n.* —*Syn.* variola, cowpox, white man's disease (D); see **disease** 3.

smart, *mod.* **1.** [Intelligent]—*Syn.* clever, bright, quick; see **intelligent** 1.
2. [Impudent]—*Syn.* bold, brazen, forward; see **rude** 2.
3. [Vigorous]—*Syn.* brisk, lively, energetic; see **active** 2.
4. [Shrewd]—*Syn.* sharp, crafty, ingenious; see **sly** 1.
5. [Fashionable]—*Syn.* stylish, chic, in fashion; see **fashionable.**

smart, *v.* —*Syn.* sting, be painful, burn; see **hurt** 1.

smart aleck (D), *n.* —*Syn.* show-off, boaster, life of the party (D); see **braggart, clown.**

smarten, *v.* **1.** [To beautify]—*Syn.* adjust, tidy, polish; see **improve** 1.
2. [To stimulate]—*Syn.* educate, tutor, animate; see **teach** 1, 2.

smartly, *mod.* —*Syn.* in a lively or spirited or vivacious, *etc.,* manner, gaily, spirited; see **active** 1, 2.

smash, *n.* —*Syn.* crash, breakup, breaking; see **blow** 1.

smash, *v.* —*Syn.* crack, shatter, crush, burst, shiver, fracture, splinter, break, demolish, destroy, batter, crash, wreck, disrupt, break up, overturn, overthrow, lay in ruins, raze, topple, tumble.

smashed, *mod.* —*Syn.* wrecked, crushed, mashed; see **broken** 1.

smattering, *n.* —*Syn.* superficial knowledge, some half-truths, smatter; see **introduction** 3.

smear (D), *n.* —*Syn.* distortion, slander, put-up job (D); see **deception** 1, **lie** 1, **trick** 1.

smear, *v.* **1.** [To spread]—*Syn.* cover, coat, apply; see **paint** 2, **spread** 4.
2. [To slander]—*Syn.* defame, vilify, libel; see **insult, slander.**
3. [(D) To defeat]—*Syn.* beat, conquer, trounce; see **defeat** 2, 3.
4. [To dirty]—*Syn.* soil, spot, sully; see **dirty.**

smeary, *mod.* —*Syn.* sticky, messy, smudgy; see **dirty** 1, **oily** 1.

smell, *n.* **1.** [A pleasant smell]—*Syn.* fragrance, odor, scent, perfume, exhalation, redolence, essence, aroma, bouquet, trail, trace, emanation.
2. [An unpleasant smell]—*Syn.* malodor, stench, fetidness, stink, mephitis, mustiness, rancidity, effluvium, foulness, reek, uncleanness, fume.
3. [The sense of smell]—*Syn.* smelling, detection, olfactory perception, nasal sensory power, olfactory sensitivity, olfaction, response to olfactory stimuli.

smell, *v.* **1.** [To give off odor]—*Syn.* perfume, scent, exhale, emanate, stink, stench.
2. [To use the sense of smell]—*Syn.* scent, sniff, inhale, snuff, perceive, detect, nose out, get a whiff of (D); see also **breathe** 1.

smell out, *v.* —*Syn.* find, detect, identify; see **discover.**

smelly, *mod.* —*Syn.* stinking, foul, fetid; see **odorous** 1, **rancid** 2, **rank** 2.

smelt, *v.* —*Syn.* refine, extract, melt; see **clean, purify.**

smidgen (D), *n.* —*Syn.* drop, pinch, mite; see **bit** 1.

smile, *n.* —*Syn.* grin, smirk, simper, pleased look, amused countenance, tender look, friendly expression, delighted look, joyous look; see also **laugh.**

smile, *v.* —*Syn.* beam, be gracious, look happy *or* delighted *or* pleased, express friendliness, express tenderness, break into a smile, look amused, smirk, simper, greet, grin; see also **laugh** 1.

smile at, *v.* —*Syn.* grin *or* snicker at, deride, poke fun at; see **ridicule.**

smiling, *mod.* —*Syn.* bright, with a smile, sunny, beaming; see also **happy.**

smirch, *n.* **1.** [A smudge]—*Syn.* spot, blotch, smear; see **blemish, stain.**
2. [Dishonor]—*Syn.* stigma, slur, blemish; see **disgrace** 1, 2, **scandal.**

smirch, *v.* **1.** [To soil]—*Syn.* smudge, discolor, smear; see **dirty.**
2. [To degrade]—*Syn.* sully, discredit, malign; see **humble, slander.**

smirk, *n.* —*Syn.* leer, grin, smile; see **sneer.**

smirk at, *v.* —*Syn.* simper, grin at, make a face at; see **smile.**
smite, *v.* —*Syn.* strike, beat, belabor; see **hit** 1.
smith, *n.* —*Syn.* metalworker, forger.
Smiths include the following—blacksmith, farrier, gunsmith, goldsmith, silversmith, locksmith, tinsmith, whitesmith, bronzesmith, brass-smith, coppersmith, clocksmith, coachsmith, hammersmith, scissors-smith, swordsmith, firesmith, wiresmith, cooper, wheelwright; see also **craftsman, workman.**
smithereens, *n.* —*Syn.* particles, bits, fragments; see **bit** 1.
smock, *n.* —*Syn.* frock, work dress, coverall; see **clothes, dress** 2.
smog, *n.* —*Syn.* high fog, smoke haze, haze, mist, frost smoke, air pollution.
smoke, *n.* —*Syn.* vapor, fume, gas, soot, reck, smother, haze, smolder, smudge, smog, Pittsburgh perfume (D).
smoke, *v.* **1.** [To give off smoke]—*Syn.* burn, fume, vaporize, reek, smother, smoke up, smolder, smudge, reek.
2. [To use smoke, especially from tobacco]—*Syn.* puff, inhale, smoke a pipe, smoke cigarettes, use cigars, dip snuff, drag (D).
smoked, *mod.* —*Syn.* cured, treated with smoke, dried, exposed to smoke, kippered; see also **prepared** 2, **preserved** 2.
smoke out (D), *v.* —*Syn.* uncover, reveal, find; see **discover.**
smokestack, *n.* —*Syn.* funnel, pipe, stack, flue; see also **chimney.**
smoking, *n.* —*Syn.* using tobacco, pulling on a pipe; *both* (D): burning the weed, having a drag.
smoky, *mod.* **1.** [Smoldering]—*Syn.* fumy, vaporous, reeking; see **burning** 1.
2. [Sooty]—*Syn.* grimy, messy, dingy; see **dirty** 1.
3. [Gray]—*Syn.* smoke-colored, silvery, neutral; see **gray** 1.
smolder, *v.* —*Syn.* fume, consume, steam; see **burn** 1, **smoke** 1.
smooth, *mod.* **1.** [Without bumps]—*Syn.* flat, plane, flush, horizontal, unwrinkled, unvarying, level, monotonous, unrelieved, unruffled, mirrorlike, quiet, still, tranquil, sleek, glossy, glassy, lustrous, smooth as glass.—*Ant.* rough*, steep, broken.
2. [Without jerks]—*Syn.* uniform, regular, even, invariable, undeviating, steady, stable, fluid, flowing, rhythmic, constant, equable, singsong, continuous.—*Ant.* changeable*, spasmodic, erratic.
3. [Without hair]—*Syn.* shaven, beardless, whiskerless, clean-shaven, smooth-faced, smooth-chinned, glabrescent, glabrous; see also **bald.** —*Ant.* hairy*, bearded, unshaven.
4. [Without qualities that are socially disturbing] —*Syn.* suave, mild, genial; see **polite** 1.
5. [Without irritants to the taste]—*Syn.* bland, soft, creamlike; see **creamy, delicious** 1.
smooth, *v.* **1.** [To remove unevenness]—*Syn.* even, level, flatten, grade, macadamize, iron, burnish, polish, glaze, varnish, gloss, remove obstruction, remove roughness, sand, clear the way, smooth the path.—*Ant.* wrinkle*, roughen, corrugate.
2. [To mollify]—*Syn.* palliate, mellow, mitigate; see **decrease** 2, **ease** 2, **soften** 2.
smoothly, *mod.* —*Syn.* flatly, sleekly, placidly; see **easily** 1, **evenly** 1.
smoothness, *n.* —*Syn.* evenness, levelness, sleekness; see **regularity.**
smooth over (D), *v.* —*Syn.* conceal, cover (up), hush (up); see **hide** 1.
smorgasbord, *n.* —*Syn.* buffet, self-service (meal), salad course; see **food, lunch, meal** 2.
smother, *v.* —*Syn.* stifle, suffocate, suppress; see **choke** 1, 2, **extinguish** 1.
smothered, *mod.* **1.** [Extinguished]—*Syn.* drenched, consumed, drowned, put out, not burning, quenched, snuffed.
2. [Strangled]—*Syn.* choked, asphyxiated, breathless; see **dead** 1.
smudge, *n.* —*Syn.* smirch, spot, soiled spot; see **blemish.**
smug, *mod.* —*Syn.* self-satisfied, complacent, conceited, vainglorious, pleased with oneself, priggish, snobbish, superior, egotistical, egoistic, complacent, self-righteous; *both* (D): stuck up, stuck on oneself.—*Ant.* modest*, retiring, reserved.
smuggle (in), *v.* —*Syn.* bring in contraband, slip by the customs, get around the customs, run contraband (D); see also **hide** 1.
smuggler, *n.* —*Syn.* bootlegger, pirate, crook; see **criminal.**
smuggling, *n.* —*Syn.* bootlegging, stealing, hiding, running goods, clandestine importation; see also **importation, theft.**
smut, *n.* **1.** [Filth]—*Syn.* dirt, muck, grime; see **filth.**
2. [Pornography]—*Syn.* filth, indecency, ribaldry; see **pornography.**
smutty, *mod.* —*Syn.* indecent, pornographic, suggestive; see **lewd** 1, 2.
snack, *n.* —*Syn.* luncheon, slight meal, hasty repast; see **lunch, meal** 2.
snack bar, *n.* —*Syn.* cafeteria, lunchroom, lunch counter, hot-dog stand, luncheteria, automat, café; see also **restaurant.**
snafu (D), *n.* —*Syn.* hassle, muddle, chaos; see **confusion** 2.
snag, *n.* —*Syn.* obstacle, hindrance, knot; see **barrier, difficulty** 1, **impediment** 1.
snail-paced, *mod.* —*Syn.* snaillike, sluggish, crawling; see **slow** 1, 2.
snake, *n.* —*Syn.* reptile, serpent, vermin (D); see also **rattlesnake.**
Common snakes include the following—viper, pit, viper, moccasin, water moccasin, copperhead, rattlesnake, rattler, cottonmouth, black snake, bull snake, chicken snake, coachwhip snake, coral snake, fox snake, garter snake, gopher snake, king snake, milk snake, arrow snake, water snake, boa *or* boa constrictor, anaconda, cobra, aboma, adder, milk adder, puffing adder, blowing adder, puff adder, anaconda, death adder, krait, black mamba, green mamba, tiger snake, *fer-de-lance* (French).
snaky, *mod.* **1.** [Twisting]—*Syn.* twisting, serpentine, entwined; see **indirect, twisted** 1, **winding.**
2. [Sneaky]—*Syn.* subtle, crafty, treacherous; see **sly** 1.
snap, *n.* **1.** [Fastener]—*Syn.* clasp, fastening, catch; see **fastener.**
2. [(D) Cinch]—*Syn.* easy job, ease, no problem, breeze, easy as pie (D).

snap, *v.* —*Syn.* catch, clasp, lock; see **close** 4, **fasten** 1.

snap at, *v.* —*Syn.* vent one's anger (at), jump down one's throat, take it out on; see **get angry.**

snap back (D), *v.* —*Syn.* get better, revive, become stronger; see **improve** 2, **recover** 2, 3.

snap decision, *n.* —*Syn.* snap judgment, unpremeditation, rash act; see **impulse** 2.

snap one's finger(s) at (D), *v.* —*Syn.* defy, pay no attention (to), have contempt (for); see **dare** 2, **oppose** 1, 2.

snap out of it, *v.* **1.** [To recover]—*Syn.* pull through, get over, revive; see **recover** 2, 3.
2. [To cheer up]—*Syn.* perk up, take heart, keep one's spirits up (D); see **improve** 2, **smile.**

snappish, *mod.* —*Syn.* cross, angry, touchy; see **irritable.**

snappy (D), *mod.* —*Syn.* with style, in good style, chick, having that certain something (D); see also **active** 2, **fashionable.**

snapshot, *n.* —*Syn.* snap, candid camera shot, action shot; see **photograph, picture** 2, 3.

snare, *n.* —*Syn.* trap, lure, decoy; see **trick** 1.

snarl, *n.* **1.** [Confusion]—*Syn.* tangle, entanglement, complication; see **confusion** 2.
2. [A snarling sound]—*Syn.* growl, grumble, gnarl, surly speech, cross words, angry words, sullen growl; see also **noise** 1.

snarl, *v.* —*Syn.* growl, gnarl, gnar, grumble, mutter, threaten, bark, yelp, snap, gnash the teeth, fulminate, bully, bluster, quarrel, abuse; *both* (D): champ the bit, bite one's thumb; see **cry** 3.

snatch, *v.* —*Syn.* jerk, grasp, steal; see **seize** 1, 2.

snazzy (D), *mod.* —*Syn.* desirable, modern, attractive; see **excellent, fashionable.**

sneak, *n.* —*Syn.* cheater, confidence man, underhanded *or* unreliable person; see **cheat** 1, **rascal.**

sneak, *v.* —*Syn.* skulk, slink, creep, slip away, move secretly, steal, hide, move under cover, ambush oneself, prowl, lurk, secrete oneself, cheat, delude, deceive; *all* (D): soft heel away, gumshoe, ooze off; see also **evade** 1.

sneaking, *mod.* —*Syn.* unscrupulous, sinister, crafty; see **sly** 1.

sneak out of (D), *v.* —*Syn.* evade, get *or* worm *or* squirm, *etc.*, out (of), escape (from); see **avoid, escape.**

sneaky, *mod.* —*Syn.* tricky, deceitful, unreliable; see **dishonest** 1, 2.

sneer, *v.* —*Syn.* mock, scoff, jeer, gibe, taunt, disparage, slight, scorn, despise, underrate, decry, belittle, detract, lampoon, ridicule, deride, twit, flout, burlesque, caricature, travesty, laugh at, look down, insult, affront, disdain, curl one's lip, fleer, rally, satirize, condemn; *both* (D): give the raspberry, give the Bronx cheer; see also **doubt** 1.

sneeze, *n.* —*Syn.* wheezing, suspiration, sniffle; see **cold** 3, **fit** 1.

snicker, *v.* —*Syn.* giggle, titter, snigger; see **laugh** 1.

snide, *mod.* —*Syn.* base, malicious, mean; see **sarcastic, scornful** 1, 2.

sniff, *v.* —*Syn.* snuff, scent, inhale; see **smell** 2.

snip, *v.* —*Syn.* clip, slice, nip (off); see **cut** 1.

snipe, *v.* —*Syn.* ambush, shoot, murder; see **kill** 1.

sniper, *n.* —*Syn.* sharpshooter, gunman, hired assassin; see **killer, rifleman.**

snippet, *n.* —*Syn.* particle, fragment, scrap; see **bit** 1, **part** 1, **piece** 1.

snippy, *mod.* —*Syn.* curt, sharp, insolent; see **abrupt** 2, **rude** 2.

snivel, *v.* **1.** [To cry]—*Syn.* blubber, sniffle, weep; see **cry** 1.
2. [To complain]—*Syn.* whine, whimper, gripe (D); see **complain** 1.

snob, *n.* —*Syn.* parvenu, pretender, upstart; see **braggart.**

snobbery, *n.* —*Syn.* presumption, pretension, pomposity; see **arrogance.**

snobbish, *mod.* —*Syn.* ostentatious, pretentious, overbearing; see **egotistic** 2.

snooty (D), *mod.* —*Syn.* conceited, nasty, egotistical; see **egotistic** 2.

snooze, *n.* —*Syn.* slumber, drowse, nap; see **rest** 1, **sleep.**

snore, *v.* —*Syn.* snort, wheeze, sleep; see **breathe** 1.

snort, *v.* —*Syn.* grunt, snore, puff, blow; see also **breathe** 1.

snotty (D), *mod.* —*Syn.* impudent, like a (spoiled) brat, nasty; see **rude** 2.

snout, *n.* —*Syn.* muzzle, proboscis, nozzle; see **nose** 1.

snow, *n.* **1.** [A snowstorm]—*Syn.* blizzard, snowfall, snow flurry; see **storm** 1.
2. [Frozen vapor]—*Syn.* snow crystal, snowflake, slush, sleet, snowdrift, snowbank, snow blanket, powder snow, snow pack, snowfall, fall of snow, snow field.
3. [(D) A drug]—*Syn.* opium, cocaine, coke (D); see **drug** 2.

snow, *v.* —*Syn.* storm, whiten, blanket, spit snow, blizzard, cover, pelt, shower, sleet.

snow-bound, *mod.* —*Syn.* snowed in, frozen in *or* out, blocked off; see **isolated, trapped.**

snow job (D), *n.* —*Syn.* persuading, flattery, deceit; see **deception** 1.

snowy, *mod.* —*Syn.* niveous, snowlike, fluffy, fleecy, feathery, soft, icy, cold, wintry, blizzardlike, stormy, blanketing, drifting, drifted, glaring, white, gleaming, dazzling, powdery.

snub, *v.* **1.** [To slight]—*Syn.* ignore, disregard, disdain; see **neglect** 1, **scorn** 2, **shun.**
2. [To rebuke]—*Syn.* reprimand, reproach, admonish; see **censure, insult, scold.**

snug, *mod.* **1.** [Cozy]—*Syn.* homelike, compact, convenient; see **comfortable** 1, **warm** 1.
2. [Close in fit]—*Syn.* tight, trim, well-built, close.

snuggle, *v.* —*Syn.* curl up, cuddle, grasp; see **hug, nestle.**

so, *mod.* **1.** [To a degree]—*Syn.* very, this much, indeterminately, so large, vaguely, indefinitely, extremely, infinitely, remarkably, unusually, so much, uncertainly, extremely, in great measure, in some measure; see also **such.**
2. [Thus]—*Syn.* in such wise, on this wise, and so on *or* forth, in such manner, in this way, even so, in this degree, to this extent; see also **thus.**
3. [Accordingly]—*Syn.* then, therefore, and so, hence, consequently; see also **accordingly.**
4. [Exactly right]—*Syn.* exact, correct, just so; see **accurate** 1, **fit** 1.

(and) so much for that—*Syn.* enough of that, that is all, having finished; see **accordingly, enough** 1.

soak, *v.* **1.** [To drench]—*Syn.* wet, immerse, immerge, merge, dip, water, imbrue, infiltrate, percolate, permeate, drown, saturate, pour into, pour on, wash over, flood; see also **cover** 9, **moisten.**

2. [To remain in liquid]—*Syn.* steep, imbue, macerate, soften, be saturated, be infiltrated, be permeated, be pervaded, infuse, sink into, waterlog.

3. [To absorb]—*Syn.* dry, sop, mop; see **absorb** 1.

soaked, *mod.*—*Syn.* sodden, saturated, wet, wet through, seeping, drenched, soggy, reeking, dripping, permeated, softened, macerated, immersed, immerged, steeped, infiltrated, dipped, pervaded, infused, flooded, drowned, sunk into, waterlogged.

soak in (D), *v.*—*Syn.* be understood, penetrate; *both* (D): register, sink in.

soap, *n.*—*Syn.* saponin, solvent, softener, soapsuds; see also **cleanser.**

Varieties and forms of soap include the following—solid soap, hard soap, bar soap, a cake of soap, soap tablet, soap chips, soap powder, soft soap, liquid soap, settled soap, fitted soap, soap flakes, soap papers, glycerine soap, saddle soap, wash ball, tar soap, lead *or* metallic soap, amole, green soap, brown soap, guest soap, perfumed soap, gum soap, middle soap, neat soap, soap root, Castile soap, bath soap, laundry soap, naphtha soap.

soapy, *mod.*—*Syn.* sudsy, lathery, foamy; see **frothy** 1.

soar, *v.*—*Syn.* tower, sail, rise; see **fly** 1, **glide** 2.

sob, *n.*—*Syn.* weeping, bewailing, convulsive sighs; see **cry** 1, 3.

sob, *v.*—*Syn.* lament, sigh convulsively, snivel; see **cry** 1, **weep.**

sober, *mod.* **1.** [Solemn]—*Syn.* restrained, earnest, grave; see **solemn** 1, **serious** 2.

2. [Temperate]—*Syn.* abstemious, calm, pacific; see **moderate** 4.

3. [Not drunk]—*Syn.* abstinent, serious, sedate, clear-headed, abstaining, self-possessed, calm, ascetic, non-indulgent, steady; see also **moderate** 5.

soberly, *mod.*—*Syn.* moderately, temperately, solemnly, gravely, sedately, in a subdued manner, unpretentiously, quietly, abstemiously, regularly, steadily, calmly, coolly, collectedly, unimpassionedly, somberly, staidly, seriously, earnestly, dispassionately, fairly, justly.—*Ant.* hilariously*, excitedly, drunkenly.

sobersides (D), *n.*—*Syn.* prig, puritan, old maid (of either sex); see **prude.**

sobriety, *n.* **1.** [Temperance]—*Syn.* renunciation, self-denial, teetotalism; see **abstinence, temperance.**

2. [Gravity]—*Syn.* earnestness, serenity, placidity; see **seriousness** 2.

so-called, *mod.*—*Syn.* commonly named, doubtfully called, nominal, professed, thus termed, wrongly named, popularly supposed, erroneously accepted as, usually supposed; see also **allegedly.**

sociability, *n.*—*Syn.* social intercourse, geniality, hospitality; see **ability** 1, **cooperation** 1, **friendship** 2.

sociable, *mod.*—*Syn.* affable, genial, companionable; see **friendly** 1.

social, *mod.* **1.** [Concerning human affairs]—*Syn.* mundane, secular, worldly, human, philanthropic, cultural, eugenical, material, political, racial, humane, benevolent, charitable, altruistic; see also **common** 5, **group, universal** 2.

2. [Concerning polite intercourse]—*Syn.* diverting, genial, amusing, entertaining, companionable, pleasurable, informative, civil, polite, polished, mannerly, pleasure-seeking, hospitable, pleasant.

3. [Sociable]—*Syn.* communicative, convivial, familiar; see **friendly** 1, **pleasant** 2.

social climber, *n.*—*Syn.* one with an appetite for fame *or* position, upstart, parvenu, *nouveau riche* (French), manipulator, lickspittle, ambitious person; *all* (D): Johnny-come-lately, brown-noser, yes man, puppy dog, babbit, fixer, hanger-on; see also **opportunist, status seeker.**

socialism, *n.*—*Syn.* Communism, Fourierism, Saint Simonianism, Marxianism, Fabianism, Marxism, Leninism, Maoism, state socialism; see also **government** 2.

socialist, *n.*—*Syn.* Fourierite, Marxist, communist, Fabian; see also **democrat, radical.**

socialized medicine, *n.*—*Syn.* Medicare, Medicaid, free clinics; see **charity, medicine** 1, 3, **welfare** 2.

socially, *mod.* **1.** [With regard to the welfare of mankind]—*Syn.* humanly, culturally, eugenically, ethically, religiously, philosophically, psychologically, politically, anthropologically, racially.

2. [With regard to polite society]—*Syn.* politely, civilly, courteously, hospitably, companionably, convivially, entertainingly, amusingly, divertingly, cordially, genially, sociably.

social science, *n.*—*Syn.* study of man and social phenomena, study of human society, a science dealing with a certain phase or aspect of human society, science, social studies; see also **anthropology, economics, geography, history** 2, **journalism, political science, psychology, science** 1, **sociology.**

social security, *n.*—*Syn.* social insurance, old age *or* disability *or* unemployment, *etc.,* insurance, (the) dole, social security payments *or* system, retirement; see also **welfare** 2.

social service, *n.*—*Syn.* welfare work, aid for the needy, philanthropy; see also **charity** 2, **welfare** 2.

society, *n.* **1.** [Friendly association]—*Syn.* friendship, social intercourse, fellowship; see **organization** 3.

2. [Organized humanity]—*Syn.* the public, civilization, culture, nation, community, human groupings, the people, the world at large, social life.

3. [Those who indulge in wealth and leisure]—*Syn.* high life, élite, aristocracy, gentlefolk, polite society, wealthy class, *haut monde* (French); *both* (D): smart set, the Four Hundred.

sociology, *n.*—*Syn.* synecology, autecology, social anthropology, social psychology, study of human groups, (systematic) analysis of human institutions; see also **social science.**

Branches of sociology include the following—eugenics, collective behavior, population problems, gerontology, social service, labor problems, cultural anthropology, social theory, social security, racial relationships, social organization.

sock, *n.*—*Syn.* stocking, hose, ankle-length stocking; see also **clothes, hosiery.**

Stockings and socks include the following—silk hose, rayon hose, seamless hose, support hose, cotton hose, mercerized hose, nylon stockings, full-fashioned stockings, golf hose, mesh stockings, bed socks, baby socks, half hose.

sock (D), *v.* —*Syn.* strike, beat, soak (somebody) (one) (D); see **hit.**

socket, *n.* —*Syn.* holder, opening, standard, support, device, cavity, joint.

sod, *n.* —*Syn.* clod, turf, sward, peat, pasture, meadow, lawn, grassland, mead, prairie, pasturage, green, grassplot; see also **earth** 2, **grass** 1.

soda, *n.* —*Syn.* soda water, carbonated water, Seltzer (water), mineral water; *all* (D): fizz, fizz water, pop, mixer; see also **drink** 3.

sodden, *mod.* —*Syn.* saturated, drenched, steeped; see **soaked, wet** 1.

sodomy, *n.* —*Syn.* pederasty, homosexuality, bestiality; see **perversion** 2.

sofa, *n.* —*Syn.* couch, divan, love seat; see **davenport, furniture.**

so far, *mod.* —*Syn.* thus far, up to now, to here; see **here, now** 1.

soft, *mod.* **1.** [Pliable]—*Syn.* malleable, plaint, elastic; see **flexible** 1.
2. [Soft to the touch]—*Syn.* smooth, satiny, velvety, silky, delicate, fine, thin, flimsy, limp, fluffy, feathery, flocculent, downy, woolly, pulpy, mellow, pasty, doughy, spongy, pithy, punky, mushy, mashy, soppy.—*Ant.* harsh*, rough*, flinty.
3. [Soft to the eye]—*Syn.* dull, dim, quiet, shaded, pale, pallid, light, pastel, ashen, wan, faint, blond, misty, hazy, dusky, delicate, tinted; see also **gray** 1, **shady.**—*Ant.* bright*, glaring, brilliant.
4. [Soft to the ear]—*Syn.* low, melodious, faraway; see **faint** 3.
5. [Soft in conduct]—*Syn.* affectionate, considerate, courteous; see **kind.**
6. [Lacking training]—*Syn.* untrained, flabby, out of condition; see **fat** 1, **weak** 1.
7. [(D) Easy]—*Syn.* simple, effortless, manageable; see **easy** 2.
be soft on—*Syn.* treat lightly, not condemn *or* oppose, fail to attack; see **favor** 2, **neglect** 1.
soft in the head—*Syn.* foolish, dumb, not bright *or* intelligent; see **dull** 3, **stupid** 1.

soft drink, *n.* —*Syn.* nonalcoholic drink, soda (water), pop; see **soda.**

soften, *v.* **1.** [To become soft]—*Syn.* dissolve, lessen, diminish, disintegrate, become tender, become mellow, thaw, melt, moderate, bend, give, yield, relax, relent.—*Ant.* stiffen*, solidify, freeze.
2. [To make soft]—*Syn.* mollify, mellow, assurage, moisten, modify, palliate, appease, temper, tone down, qualify, lower, tenderize, enfeeble, weaken, deliberate, mash, knead; see also **decrease** 2. —*Ant.* strengthen*, increase, tone up.

softhearted, *mod.* —*Syn.* tender, kindhearted, humane; see **humane** 1, **kind** 1, **merciful** 1.

softness, *n.* —*Syn.* mellowness, impressibility, plasticity; see **flexibility** 1.

soft spot, *n.* —*Syn.* weak point, vulnerability, heel of Achilles; see **weakness** 2.

soggy, *mod.* —*Syn.* mushy, spongy, saturated; see **soaked, wet** 1.

soil, *n.* —*Syn.* dirt, loam, clay; see **earth** 2.

soil, *v.* **1.** [To dirty]—*Syn.* stain, sully, spoil; see **dirty.**
2. [To disgrace]—*Syn.* shame, debase, degrade; see **disgrace, slander.**

soiled, *mod.* —*Syn.* stained, tainted, ruined; see **dirty** 1.

sojourn, *n.* —*Syn.* stay, residence, temporary abode; see **vacation, visit.**

solace, *v.* —*Syn.* cheer, soothe, console; see **comfort** 1.

solar, *mod.* —*Syn.* planetary, lunar, astral, stellar, celestial, heavenly, sidereal, cosmic, empyreal, zodiacal.

solar system, *n.* —*Syn.* (the) heaven(s), heavenly bodies; the sun, moon, and stars; see **universe.**

sold, *mod.* **1.** [Sold out]—*Syn.* disposed of, bargained for; *both* (D): gone, taken; see also **sold out.**
2. [Convinced]—*Syn.* pleased (with), impressed, taken with; see **satisfied.**

solder, *v.* —*Syn.* mend, patch, cement; see **fasten** 1, **join** 1.

soldier, *n.* —*Syn.* warrior, fighter, private, officer, enlisted man, volunteer, conscript, commando, mercenary, musketeer, cadet, rank and file, ranks, selectee, commissioned officer, noncommissioned officer, warrant officer, recruit, veteran, Green Beret, Tommy (British), warmonger, militant; *all* (D): G.I., Joe, doughfoot, dogface, grunt.
Varieties of soldiers include the following—*Syn.* marine, infantryman, foot soldier, rifleman, sniper, guerrilla, scout, skirmisher, sniper-scout, guardsman, sharpshooter, artilleryman, gunner, cannoneer, engineer, cavalryman, knight, dragon, airman, bomber pilot, fighter pilot, torpedo operator, air gunner, radio operator, signalman, paratrooper, commando, air-borne trooper, tanker, Ranger, draftee, selectee, ski trooper, antiaircraft gunner, pioneer, machine-gunner, *sepoy* (Hindu), Zouave, grenadier.

soldierly, *mod.* **1.** [Militant]—*Syn.* antagonistic, combative, warlike; see **aggressive** 2, **fighting, militaristic.**
2. [Brave]—*Syn.* intrepid, heroic, bold; see **brave** 1.

sold out, *mod.* —*Syn.* out of, all sold, out of stock, not in stock, gone, depleted.

sole, *mod.* —*Syn.* only one, no more than one, remaining; see **individual** 1, **single** 1.

sole, *n.* —*Syn.* planta, tread, ball; see **bottom** 1, **foot** 2.

solecism, *n.* —*Syn.* misuse, blunder, cacology; see **abuse** 1, **misusage.**

solely, *mod.* **1.** [Exclusively]—*Syn.* singly, undividedly, singularly; see **individually, only** 1.
2. [Completely]—*Syn.* entirely, totally, wholly; see **completely.**

solemn, *mod.* **1.** [Appearing serious or thoughtful] —*Syn.* grave, serious, sober, portentous, earnest, intense, deliberate, heavy, austere, somber, dignified, staid, sedate, no-nonsense, awe-inspiring, pensive, brooding, moody, grim, stern, thoughtful, reflective.—*Ant.* happy*, gay, lighthearted.
2. [Impressive]—*Syn.* imposing, ceremonious, overwhelming; see **grand** 2.
3. [Sacred]—*Syn.* religious, holy, hallowed; see **divine** 2.

solemnity, *n.* —*Syn.* sobriety, gravity, impressiveness; see **seriousness** 2.

solemnize, *v.* —*Syn.* consecrate, sanctify, honor; see **bless** 3.

solemnly, *mod.* —*Syn.* sedately, gravely, impressively; see **seriously** 2.

solicit, *v.* **1.** [To ask]—*Syn.* request, query, inquire; see **ask** 1, **question** 1.

2. [To beg]—*Syn.* entreat, beseech, supplicate; see **beg** 1.

3. [To tempt for sexual purposes]—*Syn.* proposition, accost, give the come-on, approach, entice, hustle, angle on (D); see also **fascinate, seduce.**

solicited, *mod.* —*Syn.* sought, asked for, requested, petitioned, approached, invited.

soliciting, *n.* —*Syn.* solicitation, asking, requesting, inviting, approaching, seeking, petitioning, canvassing, inducing.

solicitor, *n.* —*Syn.* attorney-at-law, counselor, counsel, barrister, advocate, proctor, procurator; see **lawyer.**

solicitous, *mod.* —*Syn.* devoted, tender, loving; see **kind, thoughtful** 2.

solicitude, *n.* —*Syn.* anxiety, watchfulness, heed; see **care** 2.

solid, *mod.* **1.** [Firm in position]—*Syn.* stable, fixed, rooted; see **firm** 1.

2. [Firm or close in texture]—*Syn.* compact, hard, substantial; see **firm** 2, **thick** 1.

3. [Reliable]—*Syn.* dependable, trustworthy, steadfast; see **reliable** 1, 2.

4. [Continuous]—*Syn.* uninterrupted, continued, unbroken; see **consecutive** 1, **regular** 3.

solid, *n.* —*Syn.* a magnitude containing length, breadth, thickness, body, substance, and dimensional form.

Solids include the following—cube, cone, pyramid, cylinder, prism, sphere, tetrahedron, hexahedron, octahedron, pentahedron.

solidification, *n.* **1.** [Hardening]—*Syn.* petrification, stiffening, setting, concretion, casehardening, solidifying, crystallization, fossilization, ossification, glaciation, freezing, calcification, compression, coagulation, concentration.

2. [Combination]—*Syn.* coalition, affiliation, embodiment; see **union** 1.

solidify, *v.* **1.** [To harden]—*Syn.* set, fix, crystallize; see **compress, harden** 2, **thicken** 1.

2. [To make secure]—*Syn.* become solid, cause to acquire strength, make firm; see **join** 1, **thicken** 2.

soliloquize, *v.* —*Syn.* monologize, apostrophize, speak; see **address** 2, **lecture.**

soliloquy, *n.* —*Syn.* address, apostrophe, lecture; see **speech** 3.

solitary, *mod.* —*Syn.* sole, lone, only, alone, single, lonely, separate, retired, individual, secluded, isolated, singular, companionless.—*Ant.* accompanied*, thick, attended.

solitude, *n.* —*Syn.* isolation, seclusion, retirement; see **silence** 1.

solo, *n.* —*Syn.* aria, *pas seul* (French), song, single part; see also **music** 1, **song.**

soluble, *mod.* —*Syn.* capable of disintegration *or* decomposition, dissolvable, solvable, solvent, dissoluble, emulsifiable, dispersible, resolvable, water-soluble, fat-soluble.

solution, *n.* **1.** [Explanation]—*Syn.* explication, resolution, clarification; see **answer** 2.

2. [Fluid]—*Syn.* suspension, aqueous material, water, solvent, chemical dissolvent, extract, sap, enzyme, juice; see also **liquid.**

solvable, *mod.* **1.** [Soluble]—*Syn.* dissolvable, dissoluble, solvent; see **soluble.**

2. [Explainable]—*Syn.* reasonable, discernible, decipherable; see **understandable.**

solve, *v.* —*Syn.* figure *or* work *or* reason *or* think *or* find *or* make *or* puzzle out, decipher, unravel, elucidate, interpret, explain, resolve, answer, decode, get to the bottom of, fathom, get (right), hit upon a solution, work, do, settle *or* clear up, untangle, unlock, determine, divine; *all* (D): dope (out), hit the nail on the head, hit it, make a dent in a problem, put two and two together, have it.

solvency, *n.* —*Syn.* financial competence, freedom from financial worries, richness; see **safety** 1, **stability** 1, **wealth** 2.

solvent, *n.* **1.** [Dissolvent]—*Syn.* resolvent, moderator, water, alkahest, dissolvent, chemical solution, catalyst, enzyme; see also **solution** 2.

2. [Solution]—*Syn.* resolution, discovery, exposition; see **answer** 2, **explanation** 1.

somber, *mod.* **1.** [Dark]—*Syn.* shady, cloudy, drab; see **dark** 1, **dull** 2.

2. [Gloomy]—*Syn.* melancholy, dreary, dire; see **dismal** 1.

some, *mod.* **1.** [Few]—*Syn.* few, a few, a little, a bit, part of, more than a few, more than a little, any.

2. [(D) Extraordinary]—*Syn.* fascinating, amazing, remarkable; see **unusual** 1.

some, *pron.* —*Syn.* any, a few, a number, an amount, a part, a portion, more or less.

somebody, *pron.* —*Syn.* someone, some person, a person, one, anybody, he, a certain person, this person, so-and-so, whoever, whatcha-m' call-'im (D).

someday, *mod.* —*Syn.* sometime, one time, one time or another, at a future time, in a time to come, anytime, one day, on a day, one of these days, after a while, one fine day *or* morning, subsequently, finally, eventually.

somehow, *mod.* —*Syn.* in some way, in one way or another, in a way not yet known, by one means or another, by some means, somehow or other, by hook or by crook, anyhow, the best one can, by fair means or foul, after a fashion, with any means at one's disposal; *all* (D): any old how, every man for himself and the devil take the hindmost, by guess and by God.

someone, *pron.* —*Syn.* some person, one, individual; see **somebody.**

something, *pron.* —*Syn.* event, object, portion, anything, being; see **thing** 1.

sometime, *mod.* —*Syn.* one day, in a time to come, in the future; see **someday.**

sometimes, *mod.* —*Syn.* at times, at intervals, now and then; see **seldom.**

somewhat, *mod.* —*Syn.* a little, to a degree, to some extent; see **moderately, slightly.**

somewhere, *mod.* —*Syn.* in some place, here and there, around, in one place or another, somewhence, somewhither, in *or* to parts unknown, someplace, about; *all* (D): around somewhere, kicking around, any old place; see also **scattered.**

somnambulism, *n.*—*Syn.* noctambulation, sleepwalking, wandering; see also **insomnia.**
somnolence, *n.*—*Syn.* sluggishness, drowsiness, lethargy; see **fatigue, sleepiness.**
somnolent, *mod.*—*Syn.* drowsy, fatigued, sleepy; see **tired.**
son, *n.*—*Syn.* male child, offspring, descendant, foster son, dependent, scion, heir, boy; *all* (D): junior, chip off the old block, his father's son, sliver.
Son, *n.*—*Syn.* God's *or* His only begotten Son, Jesus, the Saviour; see **Christ.**
song, *n.*—*Syn.* melody, lyric, strain, verse, tune, ballad, ditty (D), number, poem, musical expression; see also **hymn.**
Songs include the following—lay, aria, air, carol, ballad, canticle, canzonet, canzone, roundelay, madrigal, ditty, cantata, opera, operetta, oratorio, refrain, chanson, chorale, minstrelsy, virelay, elegy, pastorale, nursery tune, canon, spiritual, berceuse, barcarolle, round, hymn, chant, folksong, art song, evensong, drinking song, love song, plainsong, descant, motet, chorus, lyric, chanty, dirge, psalm, marching song, battle song, *aubade* (French), *Lied* (German), lullaby, cradlesong, serenade, rock *or* country rock *or* acid-head rock, etc.
(big) song and dance (D)—*Syn.* drivel, boasting, pretense; see **lie** 1, **nonsense** 1, **talk** 5.
for a song—*Syn.* cheaply, at a bargain, for (almost) nothing; see **cheap** 1.
songster, *n.*—*Syn.* vocalist, sweet singer, warbler; see **musician.**
sonic boom, *n.*—*Syn.* report, crash, evidence of a pressure wave; see **explosion** 1, **sound** 2.
sonnet, *n.*
Types of sonnets include the following—Italian, Petrarchan, Shakespearian, Elizabethan, Miltonic, Spenserian, Meredithian, Cummings; see also **poem.**
sonority, *n.*—*Syn.* vibration, timbre, resonance; see **noise** 1.
sonorous, *mod.*—*Syn.* resonant, resounding, vibrant; see **loud** 1.
soon, *mod.* **1.** [In the near future]—*Syn.* before long, in a short time, shortly, forthwith, presently, quickly, in a minute *or* second, in short order, in due time; see also **someday.**
2. [Early]—*Syn.* in time, promptly, on time; see **early** 2.
sooner or later, *mod.*—*Syn.* eventually, inevitably, certainly; see **someday, surely.**
soot, *n.*—*Syn.* carbon, smoke, grit; see **residue, sediment.**
soothe, *v.*—*Syn.* quiet, mollify, tranquilize, calm, relax, assuage, alleviate, help, pacify, lighten, unburden, mitigrate, console, cheer; see also **comfort** 1, 2, **ease** 1, 2, **relieve** 2.
soothsayer, *n.*—*Syn.* seer, oracle, diviner; see **fortune-teller, prophet.**
sooty, *mod.* **1.** [Dirty]—*Syn.* dingy, grimy, smeared; see **dirty** 1.
2. [Dark]—*Syn.* dull, greyish, murky; see **black** 1, **dark** 1.
sophism, *n.*—*Syn.* paradox, irrationality, absurdity; see **deception** 1, **ostentation** 1.
sophist, *n.*—*Syn.* thinker, caviler, rhetorician; see **critic** 1, **pedant, philosopher.**
sophisticated, *mod.* **1.** [Cultured]—*Syn.* refined, adult, well-bred; see **cultured, mature** 1.
2. [Modern]—*Syn.* advanced, involved, complicated; see **complex** 1, **modern** 1.
sophistication, *n.*—*Syn. savoir faire, savoir vivre (both* French); tact, poise, refinement, finesse, social grace; see also **composure, elegance** 1.
sophistry, *n.*—*Syn.* delusion, irrationality, inconsistency; see **fallacy** 1, **pendantry.**
sophomore, *n.*—*Syn.* second-year man, lowerclassman, underclassman; see **student.**
sophomoric, *mod.*—*Syn.* reckless, brash, foolish; see **inexperienced, naive, young** 2.
soporific, *mod.* **1.** [Soothing]—*Syn.* balmy, mesmeric, sedative; see **hypnotic, tranquil** 2.
2. [Sleepy]—*Syn.* drowsy, dull, somnolent; see **tired.**
soporific, *n.*—*Syn.* narcotic, anesthetic, sedative; see **drug** 2.
soppy, *mod.*—*Syn.* wet, drenched, soaked, drippy, drizzling, saturated, damp, muggy, watery.
soprano, *n.*—*Syn.* falsetto, descant, treble; see **singer.**
sorcerer, *n.*—*Syn.* witch, wizard, alchemist; see **magician.**
sorcery, *n.*—*Syn.* enchantment, divination, alchemy; see **magic** 1, **witchcraft.**
sordid, *mod.*—*Syn.* low, degraded, abject; see **dirty** 1, **shameful** 1, 2.
sore, *mod.* **1.** [Tender]—*Syn.* painful, hurting, hurtful, severe, raw, aching, smarting, sensitive, tender, irritated, irritable, vexatious, distressing, grievous, bruised, angry, inflamed, burned, unpleasant, ulcerated, abscessed, uncomfortable.
2. [(D) Angry]—*Syn.* irked, resentful, irritated; see **angry.**
sore, *n.*—*Syn.* cut, bruise, wound, boil, ulcer, hurt, abscess, gash, stab, gall, soreness, discomfort, injury; see also **pain** 2.
sorely, *mod.*—*Syn.* extremely, grievously, painfully, woefully, distressfully, badly, severely, sadly, heartbrokenly; see also **so** 1, **very.**
sorority, *n.*—*Syn.* sisterhood, club, association; see **organization** 3.
sorrel, *mod.*—*Syn.* tawny, roan, sandy, red; see **brown, red.**
sorrow, *n.* **1.** [Grief]—*Syn.* sadness, anguish, pain; see **grief** 1.
2. [The cause of sorrow]—*Syn.* catastrophe, misfortune, affliction; see **difficulty** 2, **trouble** 2.
3. [Mourning]—*Syn.* weeping, grieving, lamenting; see **mourning** 1.
sorrow, *v.*—*Syn.* bemoan, bewail, regret; see **mourn** 1, **weep.**
sorrowful, *mod.*—*Syn.* grieved, afflicted, in sorrow, in mourning, depressed, dejected; see also **sad** 1.
sorrowfully, *mod.*—*Syn.* regretfully, weeping, in sorrow *or* sadness *or* dejection, *etc.*; see **sadly.**
sorry, *mod.* **1.** [Penitent]—*Syn.* contrite, repentant, conscience-stricken, remorseful, conscience-smitten, regretful, compunctious, touched, self-accusing, melted, sorrowful, apologetic, self-condemnatory, softened.
2. [Inadequate in quantity or quality]—*Syn.* poor, paltry, trifling, cheap, mean, shabby, scrubby, stunted, small, trivial, unimportant, beggarly, insig-

nificant, dismal, pitiful, worthless, despicable; see also **inadequate** 1.—*Ant.* plentiful*, adequate, enough.
3. [Sad]—*Syn.* grieved, mournful, melancholy; see **sad** 1.

sort, *n.* —*Syn.* species, description, class; see **kind** 2, **variety** 1.
of sorts *or* **a sort**—*Syn.* some, such as they are, ordinary; see **common** 1, **poor** 2.
out of sorts—*Syn.* irritated, upset, in a bad mood; see **angry, troubled.**

sort, *v.* —*Syn.* file, assort, class; see **classify, distribute** 1, **order** 3.

sortie, *n.* —*Syn.* foray, encounter, charge; see **attack** 1, **fight** 1.

sort of (D), *mod.* —*Syn.* somewhat, to a degree, kind of (D); see **moderately, slightly.**

so-so, *mod.* —*Syn.* ordinary, mediocre, average; see **common** 1, **dull** 4, **fair** 2.

sot, *n.* —*Syn.* alcoholic, inebriate, drunk; see **drunkard.**

sottish, *mod.* —*Syn.* inebriated, intoxicated, soused; see **drunk.**

sough, *v.* —*Syn.* moan, sigh, wail; see **cry** 1, **whisper.**

sought, *mod.* —*Syn.* wanted, needed, desired; see **hunted.**

soul (D), *mod.* —*Syn.* dear, congenial, intimate; see **beloved.**

soul, *n.* **1.** [A disembodied spirit]—*Syn.* phantom, ghost, shade, shadow, umbra, spirit, apparition, vision, specter, phantasm, wraith; *all* (D): haunt, spook, hant.
2. [Essential nature]—*Syn.* spiritual being, heart, substance, individuality, disposition, cause, personality, force, essence, genius, principle, ego, psyche, life, cause.
3. [Mind]—*Syn.* intellect, intelligence, thought; see **mind** 1.
4. [The more lofty human qualities]—*Syn.* courage, love, affection, honor, duty, idealism, philosophy, culture, heroism, art, poetry, reverence, sense of beauty.
5. [A person]—*Syn.* human being, man, being, man; see **person** 1.

soulful, *mod.* —*Syn.* sensitive, eloquent, deep; see **profound** 2.

soulfully, *mod.* —*Syn.* sorrowfully, religiously, spiritually; see **intelligently, sadly.**

soulless, *mod.* —*Syn.* hard, callous, insensitive; see **cruel** 2.

sound, *mod.* **1.** [Healthy]—*Syn.* hale, hearty, well; see **healthy** 1.
2. [Firm]—*Syn.* solid, stable, safe; see **reliable** 2.
3. [Sensible]—*Syn.* reasonable, rational, prudent; see **judicious.**
4. [Free from defect]—*Syn.* flawless, unimpaired, undecayed; see **whole** 2.
5. [Proper]—*Syn.* allowed, fair, sanctioned; see **legal** 1, **valid** 1, 2.
6. [Deep]—*Syn.* deep, intellectual, thoughtful; see **profound** 2.
7. [Complete]—*Syn.* thorough, effectual, total; see **absolute** 1.
8. [Trustworthy]—*Syn.* dependable, loyal, true; see **faithful, reliable** 1.

sound, *n.* **1.** [Something audible]—*Syn.* vibration, din, racket; see **noise** 1.
2. [The quality of something audible]—*Syn.* noise, resonance, note, timbre, tone, music, pitch, intonation, accent, tonality, tenor, sonorousness, character, quality, softness, loudness, reverberating, reverberation, sonority, ringing, mournfulness, joyousness, lightness, assonance, amplification, vibration, modulation, sweetness, harshness, discord, consonance, harmony.
3. [Water between an island and the mainland]—*Syn.* strait, bay, bight; see **channel** 2.

sound, *v.* **1.** [To make a noise]—*Syn.* vibrate, echo, resound, reverberate, give out sound, shout, sing, whisper, murmur, clatter, clank, rattle, blow, blare, bark, ring (out), detonate, explode, thunder, emit sound, spread sound, buzz, gabble, rumble, hum, jabber, jangle, jar, whine, crash, bang, reflect, burst, boom, shrill, clitter, ruckle, chatter, creak, clang, roar, babble, clap, patter, prattle, clink, toot, cackle, clack, thud, slam, smash, thump, snort, shriek, moan, play, quaver, trumpet, croak, caw, quack, squawk.
2. [To measure]—*Syn.* rule, mark, gauge; see **examine** 2, **measure** 1.
3. [To seem]—*Syn.* appear, give the impression, appear to be; see **seem.**
4. [To pronounce]—*Syn.* articulate, enunciate, verbalize; see **say, utter.**

sound effects, *n.* —*Syn.* background, accompaniment; offstage sound; see **music** 1, **noise** 1, 2.

sounding, *mod.* —*Syn.* ringing, thudding, bumping, roaring, calling, thundering, booming, crashing, clattering, clinking, clanging, tinkling, whispering, pinging, rattling, rumbling, ticking, crying, clicking, reverberating, echoing, pattering, clucking, chirping, peeping, growling, grunting, bellowing, murmuring, soughing, whirring, splattering, screeching, screaming, squealing, making a noise *or* a sound *or* a racket *or* a clatter, etc.; see also **noise** *n.* 1.

soundless, *mod.* —*Syn.* inaudible, silent, still; see **quiet** 2.

sound off (D), *v.* —*Syn.* brag, shout, shoot off one's mouth (D); see **boast** 1, **say, yell.**

sound out, *v.* —*Syn.* probe, feel out, sound, feel; *all* (D): put out a feeler, send up a trial balloon, run it up the flag pole, see how the land lies, get the lay of the land, see which way the wind blows; see also **examine** 1, **experiment** 2.

soundproof, *mod.* —*Syn.* soundproofed, silent, soundless; see **quiet** 2.

soup, *n.* Soups include the following—*soupe du jour* (French), beef broth, mutton broth, bouillon, consommé, oxtail soup, chicken soup, tomato soup, mushroom soup, celery soup, cream of tomato bisque, potato soup, purée of peas, soup à la Italienne, minestrone, borsch, vichyssoise, onion soup, clam broth, (clam *or* fish) chowder, vegetable soup, okra soup, Scotch broth, mulligatawny, turtle soup, mock turtle soup, wiener and lentil soup, mongole, navy bean soup, black bean soup, Philadelphia pepperpot, split-pea soup; see also **broth, food, stew.**

soupçon, *n.* —*Syn.* dash, drop, hint; see **dash** 4.

sour, *mod.* **1.** [Sour in taste]—*Syn.* acid, acidulated, tart, acetous, vinegary, fermented, rancid, musty, turned, acrid, acidulous, acetose, acidic, salty, bitter, acrid, caustic, cutting, stinging, peppery, harsh, irritating, unsavory, vitriolic, tangy, vinegarish, briny, brackish, astringent, dry, sharp, keen, biting, pungent, piquant, acerb, acetic, curdled, foxy, sourish, subacid, green, unripe, acescent, with a kick (D).—*Ant.* sweet*, mild, bland.

2. [Sour in temper]—*Syn.* on edge, ill-natured, grouchy; see **irritable.**

sour, *v.* —*Syn.* turn, ferment, spoil, acidulate, acidify, acetify, envenom, make sour, acerbate, curdle, tartarize.

source, *n.* **1.** [The origin]—*Syn.* beginning, cause, root; see **origin** 2, 3.

2. [A person or work supplying information] —*Syn.* expert, specialist, authorization, source material; see also **reference** 3.

3. [A fountain]—*Syn.* spring, reservoir, fount; see **origin** 2.

sourly, *mod.* —*Syn.* acidulously, uncivilly, impolitely; see **angrily.**

sourpuss (D), *n.* —*Syn.* killjoy, shrew, curmudgeon; see **grouch.**

souse, *v.* **1.** [To soak]—*Syn.* drown, wet, dunk; see **dip** 1, **immerse** 1.

2. [To preserve]—*Syn.* pickle, marinate, brine; see **preserve** 3.

South, *n.* —*Syn.* the Sunny South, South Atlantic States, the Old South, Pre-Civil War South, Southern United States, the New South, the Deep South, territory south of the Mason-Dixon line, cotton *or* tobacco states *or* belt, Sunbelt; *all* (D): (way) down south, Dixie (land), Southland; see also **Confederacy, United States.**

south, *mod.* **1.** [Situated to the south]—*Syn.* southern, southward, on the south side of, in the south, toward the equator, southmost, southernmost, toward the south pole, southerly, tropical, equatorial, in the torrid zone.

2. [Moving south]—*Syn.* southward, to the south, southbound, headed south, southerly, in a southerly direction, toward the equator.

3. [Coming from the south]—*Syn.* headed north, northbound, out of the south, from the south, toward the north pole; see also **north** 2.

south, *n.* —*Syn.* southland, southern section, southern region, tropics, tropical region, equatorial region, south pole, southern hemisphere, south arctic region.

southeast, *mod.*

Points of the compass between south and east include the following—east by south, east-southeast, southeast by east, southeast, southeast by south, south-southeast, south by east; see also **direction** 1.

Southern, *mod.* —*Syn.* South Atlantic, Confederate, south of the Mason-Dixon line, Gulf, Old South, New South, cotton-raising, tobacco-raising.

southern, *mod.* —*Syn.* in the south, of the south, from the south, toward the south, austral, meridional, southerly; see also **south** 1.

Southwest, *n.* —*Syn.* the Wild West, the Old West; *all* (D): the Great Open Spaces, the Cow Country, Cactus Country; see also **west** 3, **United States.**

southwest, *mod.*

Points of the compass between south and west include the following—south by west, south-southwest, southwest by south, southwest, southwest by west, west-southwest, west by south; see also **direction** 1.

souvenir, *n.* —*Syn.* memento, keepsake, reminder, token, relic, remembrance; see also **memorial.**

sovereign, *n.* —*Syn.* monarch, autocrat, supreme ruler; see **king.**

sovereignty, *n.* —*Syn.* supremacy, supreme power, sway; see also **government** 1.

soviet, *mod.* —*Syn.* socialist, communist, sovietized, collective, collectivized, in accordance with soviet *or* socialist *or* communistic *or* collective ideology; see also **Russian.**

soviet, *n.* —*Syn.* assembly, congress, council; *volost, uyezd, guberniya, oblast (all* Russian); see also **legislature.**

Soviet Union, *n.* —*Syn.* USSR *or* CCCP (Russian) *or* Union of Soviet Socialist Republics, New Russia, Soviet Russia, Iron Curtain country (D); see also **Europe, Russia.**

sow, *v.* —*Syn.* seed, disseminate, propagate, scatter, plant, broadcast, drill in, drill seed, use a drill seeder *or* broadcast seeder, strew, seed down, plant to wheat, barley, etc.; put in small grain, do the seeding.

sowed, *mod.* —*Syn.* scattered, cast, broadcast, spread, distributed, dispersed, disseminated, bestrewn, strewn, strewn abroad, planted.

sox, *n.* —*Syn.* hose, hosiery, stockings; see **socks.**

spa, *n.* —*Syn.* baths, spring, curative bath; see **bath** 3, **resort** 2.

space, *mod.* —*Syn.* outer-space, space-age, transearth, lunar, Martian, interplanetary, interstellar, selenologic(al); see also **infinite.**

space, *n.* **1.** [The infinite regions]—*Syn.* outer space, the heavens, infinite distance, infinity, interstellar *or* interplanetary space, the beyond, distance beyond the farthest stars, illimitable distance, measureless miles, the void, space-age distances, area of weightlessness, place where time and space are one; see also **expanse.**—*Ant.* limit, measure, definite area.

2. [Room]—*Syn.* expanse, scope, range; see **extent.**

3. [A place]—*Syn.* area, location, reservation; see **place** 3.

4. [An interval in time]—*Syn.* season, period, term; see **time** 1.

space, *v.* **1.** [Group]—*Syn.* align, range, apportion; see **order** 3.

2. [Interspace]—*Syn.* set at intervals, interval, keep apart; see **separate** 2.

space-age, *mod.* —*Syn.* twentieth-century, contemporary, recent; see **infinite, modern** 1, **space.**

spacecraft, *n.* —*Syn.* flying saucer, capsule, unidentified flying object (UFO), manned orbiting laboratory (MOL), orbiting vehicle (O.V.), re-entry vehicle (R.V.), lunar module (L.M.), command module (C.M.), service module (S.M.), spaceship, rocket, repulsor, flying missile, projectile rocket, warhead, space station, deep-space ship, reconnaissance rocket, moon messenger, remote-controlled spaceship, (solar) probe, lunar orbiter, weather satellite; see also **satellite** 2.

spaced, *mod.* —*Syn.* divided, distributed, dispersed; see **separated.**

space out, *v.* —*Syn.* distribute, disperse, divide; see **separate** 2.

space platform, *n.* —*Syn.* space station, orbiting vehicle (O.V.), manned orbiting laboratory (MOL); see **spacecraft.**

spacious, *mod.* —*Syn.* capacious, roomy, vast; see **large** 1.

spade, *n.* —*Syn.* implement, garden tool, digging tool; see **shovel.**

Spain, *n.* —*Syn.* Hispania, *España* (Spanish), Iberian Peninsula, country of Spain, Spanish people, Spanish monarchy, Spain under Franco, Falangist state, Hispanic peoples, Iberia, Castile, Hispanic totalitarianism.

span, *n.* —*Syn.* spread, compass, measure; see **extent.**

span, *v.* —*Syn.* traverse, pass over, ford; see **cross** 1.

spangled, *mod.* —*Syn.* burning, radiant, shiny; see **bright** 1, 2.

Spaniard, *n.*
Spaniards include the following groups—Iberian, Basque, Catalan, Castilian, Segovian, Cordoban, Galician, Andalusian, Aragonese, Asturian, Estremaduran.

Spanish, *mod.* —*Syn.* Spanish-speaking, Iberian, Romance, Hispanic, Catalan, Castilian, Galician, Andalusian, Basque, Hispano-Gallican, Spanish-American, Mexican, South American, Latin American.

Spanish, *n.* —*Syn.* Castilian, Hispanic, Old Spanish, Modern Spanish, *el Español* (Spanish), Spanish of Latin America, Mexican, Iberian dialects; see also **language** 2.

spank, *n.* —*Syn.* spat, whack, spanking; see **blow** 1.

spank, *v.* —*Syn.* whip, chastise, thrash; see **beat** 2, **punish.**

spar, *n.* —*Syn.* pugilism, fight, contest; see **boxing, sport** 1.

spar, *v.* —*Syn.* scrap, wrestle, exchange blows; see **box** 2, **fight** 2.

spare, *mod.* —*Syn.* superfluous, supernumerary, additional; see **extra.**

spare, *v.* —*Syn.* forbear, forgive, be merciful; see **pity** 2, **save** 1.
something to spare—*Syn.* surplus, what is left over *or* extra, bonus; see **excess** 1, **remainder.**

sparing, *mod.* **1.** [Niggardly]—*Syn.* close, tight, avaricious; see **economical** 1, **stingy.**
2. [Merciful]—*Syn.* compassionate, mild, tolerant; see **humane** 1, **merciful** 1.

spark, *n.* —*Syn.* glitter, glow, sparkle; see **fire** 1, **flash** 1.

sparkle, *v.* —*Syn.* glitter, glisten, twinkle; see **shine** 1.

sparkling, *mod.* —*Syn.* glinting, scintillating, gleaming; see **bright** 1, 2, **shimmering.**

sparrow, *n.*
Sparrows include the following—Belding, Bell, black-chinned, chipping, Brewer, desert, English, fived, Fox, Gambel, golden-crowned, Lincoln, rufus-crowned, swamp, song, silver-tongue, tree, vesper, western lark, white-crowned, white-throated; see also **bird** 1.

sparse, *mod.* —*Syn.* scattered, scanty, meager; see **inadequate** 1, **rare** 2.

Spartan, *mod.* —*Syn.* bold, fearless, virile; see **brave** 1.

spasm, *n.* —*Syn.* convulsion, seizure, contraction; see **fit** 1.

spasmodic, *mod.* **1.** [Twitchy]—*Syn.* jerky, convulsive, spastic; see **shaky** 1.
2. [Irregular]—*Syn.* uncertain, sporadic, periodic; see **irregular** 1.

spat, *n.* **1.** [A quarrel]—*Syn.* tiff, dispute, scrap; see **disagreement** 1.
2. [A blow]—*Syn.* slap, whack, spank; see **blow** 1.

spat, *v.* —*Syn.* punch, thump, slap; see **hit** 1.

spatter, *v.* —*Syn.* splash, spot, wet, soil, swash, sprinkle, scatter, strain, bespatter, dash, dot, speck, speckle, polka-dot, stipple, pebble-dash, bedew, shower, spangle, bespeckle, seed, dribble, spray, dapple, mottle, bestrew, star, star-scatter.

spawn, *v.* —*Syn.* generate, bring forth, issue; see **produce** 1, **reproduce** 3.

speak, *v.* **1.** [To utter]—*Syn.* vocalize, pronounce, express; see **utter.**
2. [To communicate]—*Syn.* converse, articulate, chat; see **talk** 1.
3. [To deliver a speech]—*Syn.* lecture, declaim, deliver; see **address** 2.
so to speak—*Syn.* that is to say, in a manner of speaking, as the saying goes (D); see **accordingly.**
to speak of—*Syn.* somewhat, a little, not much; see **some.**

speak-easy (D), *n.* —*Syn.* pub, (illicit) liquor establishment, blind pig (D); see **bar** 2, **saloon** 1.

speaker, *n.* **1.** [One who delivers an address] —*Syn.* speechmaker, orator, lecturer, public speaker, preacher, spellbinder, declaimer, rhetorician, platform orator, stump speaker, discourser, discussant, addresser, haranguer, demagogue, elocutionist, talker.
2. [A presiding officer; *frequently capital*]—*Syn.* chairman, spokesman, mouthpiece, presiding officer.

speak for itself, *v.* —*Syn.* account for, be self-explanatory, vindicate; see **explain** 1, **justify** 2.

speaking, *mod.* **1.** [Talking]—*Syn.* oral, verbal, vocal; see **talking.**
2. [Expressive]—*Syn.* meaningful, eloquent, forceful; see **fluent** 2.

speak out, *v.* —*Syn.* insist, assert, make oneself heard; see **declare** 1.

speak well of, *v.* —*Syn.* commend, recommend, support; see **praise** 1.

spear, *n.* —*Syn.* lance, pike, javelin, gar, halberd, half-pike, partisan, bill, lancet, bayonet, fish spear, hunting spear, weapon.

spearhead, *v.* —*Syn.* originate, create, induce; see **begin** 1.

special, *mod.* **1.** [Intended for a particular purpose] —*Syn.* specific, particular, appropriate, especial, peculiar, proper, individual, first, unique, personal, restricted, exclusive, defined, limited, reserved, specialized, determinate, distinct, select, choice, definite, marked, designated, earmarked.—*Ant.* general*, unrestricted, indefinite.
2. [Unusual]—*Syn.* distinctive, exceptional, extraordinary; see **unusual** 1.

special (D), *n.* —*Syn.* dish, course, *pièce de résistance* (French); see **breakfast, dinner, lunch, meal** 2.
specialist, *n.* —*Syn.* expert, adept, devotee, master, veteran, ace, scholar, professional, sage, savant, authority, connoisseur, maven (D), skilled practitioner, technician, virtuoso.—*Ant.* novice, amateur*, beginner.
specialize, *v.* **1.** [To study intensively]—*Syn.* concentrate on, develop oneself in, train; see **concentrate** 2.
2. [To practice exclusively]—*Syn.* work in exclusively, pursue specifically, go in for, limit oneself to; see also **practice** 1.
specialized, *mod.* —*Syn.* specific, for a particular purpose, functional, for a special purpose, specially designed, technoscientific, technoscientifically.
specially, *mod.* —*Syn.* particularly, uniquely, specifically; see **especially.**
specialty, *n.* **1.** [An object of attention]—*Syn.* pursuit, practice, object of study, object of attention, field of concentration, work, special project *or* product, hobby; see also **job** 1, **vocation** 2.
2. [A superior result]—*Syn.* *magnum opus* (Latin), *pièce de résistance* (French); see **masterpiece.**
specie, *n.* —*Syn.* cash, currency, coin; see **money** 1.
species, *n.* —*Syn.* class, variety, sort; see **division** 2, **kind** 2.
specific, *mod.* —*Syn.* particular, distinct, precise; see **definite** 1, 2, **special** 1.
specifically, *mod.* **1.** [As an example]—*Syn.* peculiarly, especially, indicatively, pointedly, particularly, specially, respectively, concretely, individually, characteristically.—*Ant.* universally*, generally, commonly.
2. [In a specific manner]—*Syn.* circumstantially, correctly, definitely, explicitly, expressly, categorically, in detail, precisely, minutely, exactly, clearly; see also **accurately.**—*Ant.* indirectly*, uncertainty, vaguely.
specification, *n.* —*Syn.* designation, term, written requirement, particularization, stipulation, blueprint, detailed statement, spec (D).
specified, *mod.* —*Syn.* particularized, detailed, precise; see **necessary** 1.
specify, *v.* —*Syn.* name, point out, designate, define, stipulate, show clearly, go into detail, particularize, blueprint, come to the *or* a point, pin down.
specimen, *n.* —*Syn.* individual, part, unit; see also **example** 1.
specious, *mod.* —*Syn.* plausible, colorable, beguiling, deceptive, misleading, ostensible, probable, presumable, presumptive, credible, likely, apparent, sophisticated, flattering, apparently right, seemingly just, showy, garish, pretentious, ostentatious, pompous.—*Ant.* unbelievable*, unlikely, incredible.
speck, *n.* —*Syn.* spot, iota, mite; see **bit** 1.
speckled, *mod.* —*Syn.* mottled, specked, variegated, dotted, spotted, dappled, particolored, motley, mosaic, tesselated.
spectacle, *n.* —*Syn.* scene, representation, exhibition; see **display** 2, **view** 1.
make a spectacle of oneself—*Syn.* show off, act ridiculously *or* like a fool, play the fool; see **misbehave.**
spectacular, *mod.* —*Syn.* striking, magnificent, dramatic; see **sensational** 1, **thrilling.**
spectacular, *n.* —*Syn.* play, movie, production; see **comedy, drama** 1, **show** 2.
spectator, *n.* —*Syn.* beholder, viewer, onlooker; see **observer** 1.
specter, *n.* —*Syn.* apparition, phantom, spirit; see **ghost** 1, **soul** 1.
spectral, *mod.* —*Syn.* phantom, unearthly, ghostlike; see **frightful** 1, **ghastly.**
spectrum, *n.* —*Syn.* color spectrum, chromatic spectrum, hue cycle, fundamental colors; see also **color** 1.
speculate, *v.* **1.** [To think]—*Syn.* contemplate, meditate, muse, reflect, conjecture, theorize, hypothesize, hazard an opinion, consider, cogitate; *both* (D): beat the brains, wear out the gray matter; see also **think.**—*Ant.* neglect*, take for granted, ignore.
2. [To gamble in business]—*Syn.* risk, hazard, venture; *all* (D): margin up, be long of the market, pour money into, play *or* overstay *or* scoop the market, take a chance; see also **gamble** 1.
speculation, *n.* **1.** [Thought]—*Syn.* meditation, consideration, thinking; see **thought** 1.
2. [Speculative business]—*Syn.* trading in futures, speculative enterprise, financial risk; *both* (D): a flier in stocks, risky deal; see **gambling.**—*Ant.* risk*, safe investment, legitimate business.
speculative, *mod.* **1.** [Thoughtful]—*Syn.* contemplative, meditative, pensive; see **thoughtful** 1.
2. [Involving risk]—*Syn.* unsafe, insecure, risky; see **dangerous** 1, **uncertain** 2.—*Ant.* safe*, certain, sure.
speculator, *n.* **1.** [A stockbroker]—*Syn.* stockholder, venturer, gambler; see **businessman.**
2. [An analyst]—*Syn.* theorist, philosopher, experimenter; see **critic** 2, **examiner.**
speech, *n.* **1.** [Language]—*Syn.* tongue, mother tongue, native tongue; see **language** 1.
2. [The power of audible expression]—*Syn.* talk, utterance, discourse, conversation, articulation, oral expression, diction, pronunciation, expression, locution, vocalization, enunciation, palaver, communication, prattle, parlance, intercourse, conversation, chatter.
3. [An address]—*Syn.* lecture, discourse, oration, disquisition, harangue, oratory, sermon, dissertation, homily, recitation, prelection, allocation, talk, rhetoric, tirade, panegyric, bombast, diatribe, exhortation, eulogy, commentary, declamation, appeal, invocation, salutation, travelogue, valedictory, paper, stump, speech, keynote address, political speech; *all* (D): speechification, elocuting, opus, pep talk, spiel; see also **communication** 2.
speechless, *mod.* —*Syn.* aphonic, inarticulate, mum; see **dumb** 1, **mute** 1.
speed, *n.* —*Syn.* swiftness, celebrity, briskness, activity, eagerness, haste, hurry, promptitude, acceleration, dispatch, velocity, readiness, agility, liveliness, quickness, momentum, promptness, expedition, fleetness, rapidity, alacrity, pace, precipitation, rush, precipitancy, urgency, legerity, rate, headway, fleetness; *all* (D): breeze, bat, clip, snap, steam.—*Ant.* slowness*, tardiness, dilatoriness.

speed, *v.* —*Syn.* ride hard, put on sail, go like the wind, cut along, crowd sail, go fast, bowl along, cover ground, gun the motor, give her the gas, go all out, gear up, go it, break the sound barrier; see also **race** 1.

speeded up, *mod.* —*Syn.* accelerated, intensified, bettered; see **fast** 1, **improved** 1.

speedily, *mod.* —*Syn.* rapidly, fast, abruptly; see **quickly** 1.

speeding, *n.* —*Syn.* exceeding the speed limit, breaking the (speed) law, reckless driving, driving recklessly *or* carelessly; see also **racing.**

speedster, *n.* —*Syn.* speeder, reckless driver, lawbreaker; see **criminal, driver.**

speed up, *v.* **1.** [To accelerate]—*Syn.* go faster, increase speed, move into a higher speed *or* bracket *or* level; see **improve** 2, **race** 1.

2. [To cause to accelerate]—*Syn.* promote, further, get things going *or* moving; see **improve** 1, **urge** 3.

speedway, *n.* —*Syn.* turnpike, highway, circuit; see **race track.**

speedy, *mod.* —*Syn.* quick, nimble, expeditious; see **fast** 1, **rapid** 2.

spell, *n.* **1.** [A charm]—*Syn.* abracadabra, talisman, amulet; see **charm** 2.

2. [A period of time]—*Syn.* term, interval, season; see **time** 1.

3. [(D) An illness or a seizure]—*Syn.* stroke, spasm, turn; see **fit** 1, **illness** 1.

cast a spell on *or* **over**—*Syn.* enchant, bewitch, beguile; see **charm** 1.

under a spell—*Syn.* enchanted, bewitched, unable to resist; see **charmed.**

spellbinder, *n.* —*Syn.* charismatic person, political orator, lecturer; see **actor, speaker** 2, **talker.**

spellbound, *mod.* —*Syn.* entranced, amazed, fascinated; see **bewildered, charmed** 1.

speller, *n.* —*Syn.* word book, spelling book, school text; see **book** 1, **text** 1.

spelling, *n.* —*Syn.* orthography, orthographic study, logography, visual aspect of language; see also **grammar.**

spell out, *v.* —*Syn.* make clear, go into (great *or* minute) detail, simplify; see **explain.**

spend, *v.* **1.** [To expend]—*Syn.* consume, deplete, waste, dispense, contribute, donate, give, liquidate, exhaust, squander, disburse, allocate, pay, discharge, lay out, pay up, settle, defray, drain one's resources, empty one's purse, bestow, use up, put in, confer, misspend, absorb, prodigalize, throw away, cast away; *all* (D): foot the bill, ante up, open the purse, fork out, shell out, pony up, shell out, blow.—*Ant.* save*, keep, conserve.

2. [To pass time]—*Syn.* while away, let pass, idle, fritter away, misuse, occupy oneself, employ, fill, put in, squander, kill, fool away, drift, laze; see also **consume** 2, **use** 1, **waste** 2.

spendthrift, *n.* —*Syn.* wastrel, squanderer, (high) spender, waster, improvident *or* imprudent *or* indiscreet person, prodigal, prodigal son, profligate, high-roller (D); see also **beggar** 1.

spent, *mod.* **1.** [Expended]—*Syn.* used, consumed, disbursed; see **finished** 1, **gone** 2.

2. [Exhausted]—*Syn.* done, finished, consumed, used up, depleted, dissipated, wasted, lost.

spew, *v.* —*Syn.* spread, spit, blow (out); see **blow** 1, **scatter** 2.

sphere, *n.* —*Syn.* ball, globule, orb; see **circle** 1.

spherical, *mod.* **1.** [Round]—*Syn.* circular, globular, rotund; see **round** 1, 2.

2. [Stellar]—*Syn.* celestial, astronomical, heavenly; see **stellar.**

spice, *n.* —*Syn.* seasoning, savor, relish; see **flavoring.**

Spices include the following—white pepper, black pepper, red pepper, cinnamon, allspice, nutmeg, mace, ginger, cloves, tumeric, coriander, cardamom, oregano, salt, chili pepper, cumin, anise, paprika, capsicum.

spicy, *mod.* **1.** [Suggestive of spice]—*Syn.* pungent, piquant, keen, fresh, aromatic, fragrant, seasoned, perfumed, distinctive, balsamic, tangy, highly seasoned, balmy, of *or* like cinnamon *or* cloves *or* cardamom, etc., juniperlike, sagelike, etc.; herbaceous, savory, flavory, flavorful, tasty, redolent of the South Seas, odoriferous, perfume-laden; see also **salty, sour** 1.

2. [Risqué]—*Syn.* racy, erotic, sophisticated; see **risqué.**

spider, *n.*

Common spiders include the following—tarantula, black widow, garden, diadem, grass, trapdoor, bird, brown, hermit, wolf, jumping, burrowing, hunting, water, violin back.

spigot, *n.* —*Syn.* plug, valve, tap; see **faucet.**

spike, *n.* **1.** [A large nail]—*Syn.* brad, peg, pin, hob, stud; see also **nail.**

Styles of spikes include the following—cut, wire, iron, railway, dock, forked, barbed.

Sizes of spikes include the following—twenty-penny, forty-penny, sixty-penny.

2. [A spikelike cluster]—*Syn.* raceme, inflorescence, head; see **bunch** 1, **stalk.**

spike, *v.* —*Syn.* nail, pin, make fast; see **fasten** 1.

spike a rumor (D), *v.* —*Syn.* refute, stop gossip, reveal the facts; see **deny** 1, **expose** 2.

spill, *v.* —*Syn.* lose, scatter, drop, spill over, run out; see also **empty** 2.

spilled, *mod.* —*Syn.* shed, poured out, lost, run out, squandered; see also **gone** 2.

spin, *n.* —*Syn.* circuit, rotation, gyration; see **revolution** 1, **turn** 1.

spin, *v.* **1.** [To make by spinning]—*Syn.* mold, produce, shape, twist into shape; see also **form** 1, **twist.**

2. [To whirl]—*Syn.* revolve, twirl, rotate; see **turn** 1, **whirl.**

spindle, *n.* —*Syn.* shaft, pivot, stem; see **axis, rod** 1.

spindling, *mod.* —*Syn.* skinny, lean, flat; see **thin** 1, 2.

spine, *n.* **1.** [A spikelike protrusion]—*Syn.* thorn, prick, spike, barb, thornlet, spinula, quill, ray, thistle, needle; see also **point** 2.

2. [A column of vertabrae]—*Syn.* spinal column, ridge, backbone, chine, rachis, vertebral process; see also **bone, vertebrae.**

spineless, *mod.* **1.** [Flexible]—*Syn.* pliable, limber, soft; see **flexible** 1.

2. [Weak]—*Syn.* timid, fearful, frightened; see **cowardly** 1, **weak** 3.

spin off, *v.* —*Syn.* set up, provide for, establish; see **develop** 4, **produce** 2.

spinster, *n.* —*Syn.* unmarried woman, virgin, single woman; *all* (D): old maid, bachelor girl, spin; see also **woman** 1.

spiny, *mod.* —*Syn.* pointed, barbed, spiked; see **sharp** 2.

spiral, *mod.* —*Syn.* winding, circling, cochlear, coiled, helical, whorled, radial, screw-shaped, circumvoluted, curled, rolled, scrolled, tendrillar, wound.

spire, *n.* —*Syn.* steeple, cone, pinnacle; see **tower.**

spirit, *n.* **1.** [Life]—*Syn.* breath, vitality, animation; see **life** 1.

2. [Soul]—*Syn.* psyche, essence, substance; see **soul** 2.

3. [A supernatural being]—*Syn.* vision, apparition, specter; see **ghost** 1, 2, **god** 1, **goddess.**

4. [Courage]—*Syn.* boldness, ardor, enthusiasm; see **courage** 1.

5. [A form of alcohol; *often plural*]—*Syn.* distillation, spiritous liquor, hard liquor; see **drink** 2.

6. [Feeling; *often plural*]—*Syn.* humor, tenor; see **feeling, mood** 1.

7. [Intent or meaning]—*Syn.* genius, quality, sense; see **character** 1, **meaning.**

spirited, *mod.* —*Syn.* lively, vivacious, effervescent; see **active** 2.

spiritless, *mod.* —*Syn.* dull, apathetic, unconcerned; see **indifferent** 1.

spiritual, *mod.* —*Syn.* refined, pure, holy; see **religious** 1.

spiritually, *mod.* —*Syn.* devoutly, religiously, mystically, in a spiritual *or* religious *or* devout, *etc.,* manner *or* mood *or* attitude; see also **happily** 2, **mentally, sadly.**

spiritualism, *n.* **1.** [Occultism]—*Syn.* occultism, necromancy, mysticism, cabalism, supernaturalism, theosophy.

2. [Idealism]—*Syn.* insubstantiality, metaphysics, immateriality; see **idealism** 2.

spit, *v.* —*Syn.* expectorate, splutter, eject, drivel, slobber, drool.

spit and image (D), *n.* —*Syn.* image, spitting image (D), replica; see **copy.**

spite, *n.* —*Syn.* umbrage, malice, malignity, resentment, ill will, hatred, contempt, harsh feeling, grudge, antipathy, enmity, animosity, rancor, venom, bad blood (D); see also **hate.**—*Ant.* love*, sympathy, affection.

spiteful, *mod.* —*Syn.* hateful, malicious, resentful; see **angry, cruel** 1, 2.

spitfire, *n.* —*Syn.* tigress, beldame, hag; see **shrew.**

spittle, *n.* —*Syn.* drool, rheum, mucous; see **phlegm, saliva, spit.**

splash, *n.* —*Syn.* plash, plop, dash, spatter, sprinkle, spray, slosh, slop.

make a splash (D)—*Syn.* show off (D), do something (big), get results (D); see **succeed** 1.

splash, *v.* —*Syn.* dash, splatter, bespatter, dabble, plash, get wet, throw; see also **moisten.**

splayed, *mod.* —*Syn.* wide, spread out, large; see **broad** 1.

spleen, *n.* —*Syn.* resentment, venom, wrath; see **anger, hatred** 2.

splendid, *mod.* **1.** [Magnificent]—*Syn.* grand, imposing, marvelous; see **beautiful** 1.

2. [Glorious]—*Syn.* illustrious, celebrated, distinguished; see **glorious** 1.

3. [(D) Very good]—*Syn.* premium, great, fine; see **excellent.**

splendidly, *mod.* —*Syn.* brilliantly, gorgeously, grandly, beautifully, excellently, magnificently, majestically, well, radiantly, elegantly, handsomely, illustriously.

splendor, *n.* —*Syn.* luster, brilliance, brightness; see **glory** 2.

splenetic, *mod.* —*Syn.* peevish, cross, fretful; see **irritable.**

splice, *v.* —*Syn.* knit, graft, mesh; see **join** 1, **weave** 1.

spliced, *mod.* **1.** [Joined]—*Syn.* tied (together), fitted, united; see **joined.**

2. [(D) Married]—*Syn.* united *or* joined in holy matrimony *or* wedlock, espoused, wedded; see **married.**

splint, *n.* **1.** [A support]—*Syn.* prop, rib, reinforcement; see **brace, support** 2.

2. [A sliver]—*Syn.* chip, slat, reed; see **splinter.**

splinter, *n.* —*Syn.* sliver, fragment, piece, flake, chip, wood; see also **bit** 1.

splinter, *v.* —*Syn.* shiver, shatter, rive; see **break** 2, **smash.**

split, *n.* **1.** [A dividing]—*Syn.* separating, breaking up, severing; see **division** 1.

2. [An opening]—*Syn.* crack, fissure, rent; see **hole** 1.

split, *v.* —*Syn.* burst, rend, cleave; see **break** 1, **cut** 1, **divide** 1.

split off, *v.* —*Syn.* separate, go (one's own way), divide; see **leave** 1.

splitting, *mod.* **1.** [Loud]—*Syn.* deafening, shrill, acute; see **loud** 1.

2. [Violent]—*Syn.* severe, harsh, acute; see **intense.**

split up (D), *v.* **1.** [To separate]—*Syn.* part, sunder, isolate; see **divide** 1.

2. [To be divorced]—*Syn.* separate, have a marriage annulled, have separate maintenance; see **divorce.**

splotch, *n.* —*Syn.* smudge, spot, blot; see **blemish, stain.**

splurge (D), *v.* —*Syn.* spend (lavishly), have *or* give a party, be extravagant; see **celebrate** 1, 3.

splutter, *v.* **1.** [Stammer]—*Syn.* stutter, stumble, gabble; see **stammer.**

2. [To spit]—*Syn.* spew, spray, hiss; see **spit.**

spoil, *v.* **1.** [To decay]—*Syn.* rot, decompose, become tainted; see **decay.**

2. [To ruin]—*Syn.* destroy, defile, plunder; see **disgrace.**

spoilage, *n.* —*Syn.* waste, decomposition, deterioration; see **decay** 1, 2.

spoiled, *mod.* —*Syn.* damaged, harmed, marred, injured, corrupted; see also **ruined** 2, **wasted.**

spoiling, *mod.* —*Syn.* rotting, breaking up, wasting away; see **decaying.**

spoils, *n.* —*Syn.* plunder, pillage, prize; see **booty.**

spoils system, *n.* —*Syn.* party politics, to the victor belong the spoils, corrupt practices; see **corruption** 3.

spoke, *n.* —*Syn.* rundle, handle, crosspiece; see also **part** 3, **rod** 1, **rung.**

spoken, *mod.* —*Syn.* uttered, expressed, told, announced, mentioned, communicated, oral, verbal, phonetic, voiced, lingual, unwritten.
spokesman, *n.* —*Syn.* deputy, mediator, substitute; see **agent** 1, **representative** 2, **speaker** 1.
spoliation, *n.* —*Syn.* plundering, raid, destruction; see **attack** 1.
sponge, *v.* **1.** [Clean]—*Syn.* wipe, wet, wash; see **clean, mop.**
2. [(D) To use another's money]—*Syn.* leach; *both* (D): mooch, bum; see **borrow** 1.
sponger, *n.* —*Syn.* dependent, bloodsucker, parasite; see **sycophant.**
spongy, *mod.* —*Syn.* springy, like a sponge, porous; see **wet** 1.
sponsor, *n.* —*Syn.* guarantor, advocate, patron, underwriter, supporter, adherent, sustainer, champion.
sponsorship, *n.* —*Syn.* sponsoring, favor, lending *or* giving one's name to; see **aid** 1, **support** 2, 3.
spontaneity, *n.* —*Syn.* inspiration, will, tendency; see **impulse** 2, **inclination** 1.
spontaneous, *mod.* —*Syn.* involuntary, instinctive, unbidden, unplanned, impromptu, ad-lib (D), casual, unintentional, impulsive, offhand, automatic, unforced, natural, inevitable, irrestible, unavoidable, resistless, unwilling, unconscious, uncontrollable.—*Ant.* deliberate*, willful, intended.
spontaneously, *mod.* —*Syn.* instinctively, impulsively, automatically, directly, at once; see also **immediately, unconsciously.**
spoof (D), *n.* —*Syn.* trickery, put on, satire; see **deception** 1.
spoof (D), *v.* —*Syn.* fool, play a trick on, kid (D); see **trick.**
spook, *n.* —*Syn.* visitant, spirit, disembodied spirit; see **ghost** 1.
spook (D), *v.* —*Syn.* alarm, startle, terrorize; see **frighten** 1.
spooky, *mod.* —*Syn.* weird, eerie, ominous; see **mysterious** 2, **uncanny.**
spool, *n.* —*Syn.* bobbin, spindle, quill, cop, bottom; see also **reel.**
spoon, *n.*
Spoons include the following—teaspoon, dessert, soup, tablespoon, salt, sugar, gravy, demitasse, grapefruit, runcible, spork; see also **silverware.**
spoon (D), *v.* —*Syn.* make love, fondle, pet (D); see **love** 2.
spoor, *n.* —*Syn.* trace, trail; see **path** 1, **track** 1.
sporadic, *mod.* —*Syn.* infrequent, occasional, uncommon; see **irregular** 1.
sport, *n.* **1.** [Entertainment]—*Syn.* diversion, recreation, play, amusement, merrymaking, jollification, festivity, revelry, revel, Saturnalia, carnival, pastime, pleasure, enjoyment; see also **entertainment** 2, **fun, game** 1.
2. [A joke]—*Syn.* raillery, pleasantry, mockery, jest, jesting, mirth, joke, joking, mummery, antics, trifling, tomfoolery, nonsense, jollity, laughter, drollery, escapade, practical joke.
3. [Athletic or competitive amusement]
Sports, sense 3, include the following—chase, hunt, hunting, shooting, horse racing, automobile racing, running, dog racing, cockfighting, fishing, angling, basketball, golf, bowling, billiards, pool, tennis, squash, handball, racquetball, table tennis, volleyball, soccer, gymnastics, acrobatics, football, baseball, track and field sports, cricket, lacrosse, hockey, skating, skiing, fencing, jumping, boxing, wrestling.
4. [(D) A person with sporting instincts] gambler, irresponsible fellow, horsey person, rake, one of the fast set; see **clown, rascal.**
for *or* **in sport**—*Syn.* jokingly, in fun, jestingly; see **humorously.**
sport (D), *v.* —*Syn.* don, have on, be dressed in; see **wear** 1.
sporting, *mod.* **1.** [Interested in sport]—*Syn.* gaming, showy, flashy; see **jaunty.**
2. [Fair or more than fair]—*Syn.* considerate, sportsmanlike, gentlemanly; see **generous** 1, **reasonable** 2.
sportive, *mod.* —*Syn.* gay, playful, sprightly; see **jaunty.**
sportsman, *n.* —*Syn.* huntsman, big game hunter, woodsman; see **fisherman, hunter** 1.
sportsmanship, *n.* **1.** [Skill]—*Syn.* facility, dexterity, cunning; see **ability** 2.
2. [Honor]—*Syn.* justice, integrity, truthfulness; see **honesty** 2.
spot, *mod.* —*Syn.* prompt, ready, instantaneous; see **immediate** 1.
spot, *n.* **1.** [A dot]—*Syn.* speck, flaw, pimple; see **bit** 1, **blemish.**
2. [A place]—*Syn.* point, locality, scene; see **place** 3.
3. [Small amount]—*Syn.* minute quantity, little bit, pinch; see **bit** 1.
hit the high spots (D)—*Syn.* **1.** hurry, travel rapidly, make (good) time (D); see **speed. 2.** treat hastily, go over lightly, touch up; see **neglect** 1, 2.
hit the spot (D)—*Syn.* please, delight, be (just) right; see **satisfy** 1.
in a bad spot (D)—*Syn.* in danger *or* trouble *or* difficulty, *etc.;* threatened, on the spot (D); see **dangerous** 1, 2.
spot, *v.* **1.** [Stain]—*Syn.* blemish, blotch, spatter; see **dirty, spatter.**
2. [Point out]—*Syn.* find, detect, recognize; see **locate** 1.
spotless, *mod.* —*Syn.* stainless, immaculate, without spot *or* blemish; see **clean** 1, **pure** 2.
spotlight, *n.* **1.** [Light]—*Syn.* limelight, floodlight, flashlight; see **lamp, light** 3.
2. [Publicity]—*Syn.* attention, notoriety, publicity; see **fame** 1.
spotted, *mod.* **1.** [Dotted]—*Syn.* marked, dappled, blotchy; see **speckled.**
2. [Blemished]—*Syn.* soiled, smudged, smeared; see **dirty** 1.
spotty, *mod.* —*Syn.* uneven, dotted, unequal; see **irregular** 4.
spouse, *n.* —*Syn.* marriage, partner, groom, bride; see **husband, mate** 3, **wife.**
spout, *v.* —*Syn.* squirt, discharge, pour; see **emit** 1.
spout off (D), *v.* —*Syn.* brag, chatter, shoot off one's mouth (D); see **boast, talk** 1, **yell.**
sprain, *n.* —*Syn.* twist, overstrain, strain; see **injury** 1.
sprained, *mod.* —*Syn.* wrenched, strained, pulled out of place; see **hurt, twisted** 1.

sprawl, *v.* —*Syn.* slouch, relax, lounge; see **lie** 3, **sit** 1.
spray, *n.* —*Syn.* splash, spindrift, fine mist; see **fog** 1, **froth.**
spray, *v.* —*Syn.* scatter, diffuse, sprinkle; see **spatter.**
spread, *mod.* —*Syn.* expanded, dispersed, extended, opened, unfurled, sown, scattered, diffused, strewn, spread thin, disseminated, overflowed, broadcast; see **distributed.**—*Ant.* restricted*, narrowed, restrained.
spread, *n.* **1.** [Extent]—*Syn.* scope, range, expanse; see **extent, measure** 1.
2. [A spread cloth]—*Syn.* blanket, coverlet, counterpane; see **bedspread, cover** 1, **tablecloth.**
3. [A spread food]—*Syn.* preserve, conserve, jelly; see **butter, cheese, preserves.**
4. [(D) A meal]—*Syn.* feast, banquet, informal repast; see **dinner, lunch, meal** 2.
spread, *v.* **1.** [To distribute]—*Syn.* cast, diffuse, disseminate; see **radiate** 1, **scatter** 2, **sow.**
2. [To become spread]—*Syn.* lie, flatten, level, flow, even out, be distributed, settle.
3. [To extend]—*Syn.* open, unfurl, roll out, unroll, unfold, reach, circulate, lengthen, widen, expand, untwist, unwind, uncoil, enlarge, increase, develop, radiate, branch off, diverge, expand; see also **flow** 2, **reach** 1.—*Ant.* close*, shorten, shrink.
4. [To apply over a surface]—*Syn.* cover, coat, smear, daub, overlay, overspread, plate, gloss, enamel, paint, spatter, spray, veneer, plaster, gild, pave, diffuse, wax, varnish.
5. [To separate]—*Syn.* part, sever, disperse; see **divide** 1, **separate** 2.
6. [To make known]—*Syn.* publish, broadcast, proclaim; see **advertise** 1, **declare** 1.
spreading, *mod.* —*Syn.* extended, extensive, spread out, growing, widening, ever-widening, fungous, parasitic, radial.
spread on, *v.* —*Syn.* coat, cover, smear (on); see **spread** 4.
spread oneself (D), *v.* —*Syn.* live *or* entertain lavishly, try to make an impression, go the whole hog (D); see **celebrate** 3, **spend** 1.
spread oneself (too) thin (D), *v.* —*Syn.* expand, proliferate, attempt (too much); see **increase** 1, **spread** 3, **try** 1.
spree, *n.* —*Syn.* revel, frolic, binge; see **celebration** 1, 2, **orgy.**
sprig, *mod.* —*Syn.* twig, slip, shoot; see **branch** 2, **stalk.**
sprightly, *mod.* —*Syn.* animated, brisk, lively, airy, frolicsome, light, joyous, gay, fairylike, nimble, agile, quick, jaunty, dapper, bright, spirited, jolly, alert, blithe, saucy, cheery.—*Ant.* dull*, dejected, morose.
spring, *n.* **1.** [A fountain]—*Syn.* flowing well, artesian well, sweet water; see **fountain** 2, **origin** 2.
2. [The season between winter and summer] —*Syn.* springtime, seedtime, vernal season, flowering, budding, sowing-time, vernal equinox, blackberry winter (D); see also **April, June, May, season.**
3. [Origin]—*Syn.* source, cause, beginning; see **origin** 3.
spring a leak, *v.* —*Syn.* start leaking, develop a leak, be perforated *or* punctured *or* leaky, etc.; see **leak** 2.
springy, *mod.* —*Syn.* pliable, wiry, light; see **flexible** 1.
sprinkle, *v.* —*Syn.* dampen, bedew, spray; see **moisten.**
sprinkling, *n.* —*Syn.* handful, few, mixture; see **several** 1.
sprint, *n.* —*Syn.* burst of speed, dash, supreme effort; see **race** 3.
sprint, *v.* —*Syn.* rush, dash, work at top speed; see **race** 1, **run** 2.
sprinter, *n.* —*Syn.* dash *or* short-distance man, one in the dashes *or* sprints, track man; see **runner.**
sprite, *n.* —*Syn.* nymph, elf, goblin; see **fairy** 1.
sprout, *v.* —*Syn.* germinate, take root, shoot (up), bud, burgeon; see also **grow** 1.
spruce, *mod.* —*Syn.* trim, tidy, well-groomed; see **neat** 1.
spry, *mod.* —*Syn.* nimble, fleet, vigorous; see **active** 2, **agile.**
spume, *n.* —*Syn.* spray, foam, scum; see **froth.**
spume, *v.* —*Syn.* boil, ferment, foam; see **bubble** 1.
spunk (D), *n.* —*Syn.* spirit, courage, nerve; see **courage** 1.
spur, *v.* —*Syn.* goad, prick, impel; see **drive** 1, 2, **push** 2.
spurious, *mod.* —*Syn.* counterfeit, apocryphal, deceptive; see **false** 2, 3.
spurn, *v.* —*Syn.* despise, disdain, look down on, hold in contempt; see also **evade** 1, **scorn** 2, **shun.**
spurt, *n.* **1.** [A stream]—*Syn.* squirt, jet, stream; see **fountain** 2.
2. [An eruption]—*Syn.* explosion, commotion, discharge; see **outbreak** 1.
spurt, *v.* —*Syn.* spout, jet, burst; see **flow** 2.
sputnik, *n.* —*Syn.* orbital rocket, artificial moon, lunik; see **satellite** 2, **spacecraft.**
sputter, *v.* —*Syn.* stumble, stutter, falter; see **stammer.**
spy, *n.* —*Syn.* secret agent, operative, espionage agent, double agent, emissary, scout, detective, observer, watcher, wiretapper, intelligencer, undercover man, secret-service agent; *all* (D): mole, spook, Mata Hari.
spy, *v.* **1.** [To see]—*Syn.* view, behold, descry; see **see** 1.
2. [To act as a spy]—*Syn.* scout, observe, watch, examine, scrutinize, take note, search, discover, look for, hunt, turn over, peer, pry, spy upon, set a watch on, hound, trail, follow; *all* (D): gumshoe, heel, sleuth, spot, fish out; see also **meddle** 1, 2.
spying, *n.* —*Syn.* overflight, watching, observing, prying, following, wiretapping, voyeurism; see also **interference** 2, **intrusion.**
squabble, *n.* —*Syn.* spat, quarrel, feud; see **dispute** 1.
squabble, *v.* —*Syn.* argue, disagree, fight; see **quarrel.**
squad, *n.* —*Syn.* company, small company, crew; see **team** 1, 2.
squadron, *n.* —*Syn.* unit, group, wing; see **fleet.**
squalid, *mod.* —*Syn.* dirty, filthy, unclean, poor, poverty-stricken, mean, grimy, soiled, foul, reeking, ordurous, nasty, abominable, slimy, slummocky, sloshy, ill-smelling, feculent, odious, repellent, gruesome, horrid, horrible, sordid, ramshackle, besmeared, sloppy, smutty, muddy, miry,

lutose, dingy, reeky, fetid, moldy, musty, fusty, offensive.—*Ant.* clean*, pure, spotless.

squall, *n.* —*Syn.* blast, gust, gale, brief gale, little hurricane, restricted storm; see also **storm** 1.

squall, *v.* —*Syn.* yell, whine, whimper; see **cry** 3.

squally, *mod.* —*Syn.* windy, raging, turbulent; see **stormy** 1.

squalor, *n.* —*Syn.* ugliness, disorder, uncleanness; see **filth, poverty** 1.

squander, *v.* —*Syn.* spend, spend lavishly, throw away; see **waste** 2.

square, *mod.* **1.** [Having right angles]—*Syn.* right-angled, four-sided, equal-sided, foursquare, squared, equilateral, rectangular, rectilinear.

2. [(D) Old-fashioned]—*Syn.* dated, stuffy, out-of-date; see **conservative, old-fashioned.**

square, *n.* **1.** [A rectangle]—*Syn.* equal-sided rectangle, plane figure, rectilinear plane; see **rectangle.**

2. [A park]—*Syn.* city *or* civic center, intersection, plaza, traffic circle, open space, recreational area; see also **park** 1.

on the square—*Syn.* just, fair, decent; see **honest** 1, **reasonable** 2.

square away *or* **off,** *v.* —*Syn.* box, threaten, put up one's fists; see **fight** 2.

square deal, *n.* —*Syn.* fair *or* honest *or* just, etc., transaction *or* agreement *or* treatment, etc., justice, consideration; see **business** 1, **honesty** 1.

squarely, *mod.* —*Syn.* honestly, considerately, fairly; see **justly** 1.

squash, *n.*

Varieties of squash include the following—winter, Hubbard, turban, winter crookneck, Canada crookneck, cushaw, summer, scallop, Italian, zucchini, straightneck, summer crookneck, acorn, white bush, white bush scalloped, warted Hubbard, green, banana, yellow crookneck, Danish; see also **vegetable.**

squashy, *mod.* —*Syn.* soft, marshy, pulpy; see **wet** 1.

squat, *mod.* —*Syn.* stocky, broad, heavy, thickset, stubby; see **fat** 1, **short** 1.

squat, *v.* —*Syn.* stoop, hunch, cower; see **bow** 1, **sit** 1.

squatter, *n.* —*Syn.* colonist, homesteader, settler; see **pioneer** 2.

squaw, *n.* —*Syn.* female Indian, Indian woman, wife (D); see **Indian** 1, **woman** 1.

squawk, *v.* —*Syn.* cackle, crow, yap; see **cry** 3.

squeak, *n.* —*Syn.* peep, squeal, shrill sound; see **cry** 2, **noise** 1.

squeak, *v.* —*Syn.* creak, screech, scritch, peep, squeal, scream, pipe; see also **cry** 3, **sound** 1.

squeak through (D), *v.* —*Syn.* manage, survive, get by (D); see **endure** 2, **succeed** 1.

squeal, *v.* —*Syn.* shout, yell, screech; see **cry** 1, 3.

squeamish, *mod.* —*Syn.* finicky, fussy, mincing, delicate, qualmish, hard to please, fastidious, hypercritical, particular, exacting, prim, prudish, strait-laced, puritanical, captious, easily nauseated, annoyed by trifles, readily disgusted, queasy, persnickety (D).

squeeze, *n.* —*Syn.* influence, restraint, force; see **pressure** 1, 2.

put the squeeze on (D)—*Syn.* compel, urge, use force *or* pressure *or* compulsion, *etc.* (with); see **force** 1, **influence.**

squeeze, *v.* —*Syn.* clasp, pinch, clutch; see **hug, press** 1.

squeeze through (D), *v.* —*Syn.* survive, accomplish, get by (D); see **endure** 1, **succeed** 1.

squelch, *v.* —*Syn.* crush, oppress, thwart; see **censure, suppress.**

squib, *n.* —*Syn.* satire, burlesque, spoof; see **parody** 2.

squint, *v.* —*Syn.* look askance, give a sidelong look, look asquint, cock the eye, screw up the eyes, peek, peep; see also **glare** 2, **look** 2.

squint-eyed, *mod.* **1.** [Cockeyed]—*Syn.* cross-eyed, wall-eyed, cockeyed; see **blind** 1.

2. [Skeptical]—*Syn.* suspicious, sinister, questioning; see **prejudiced.**

squire, *n.* **1.** [An attendant]—*Syn.* attendant, valet, assistant; see **servant.**

2. [An escort]—*Syn.* chaperon, gallant, cavalier; see **companion** 3, **date** 3, **escort.**

squire, *v.* —*Syn.* assist, conduct, escort; see **accompany** 1.

squirm, *v.* —*Syn.* wriggle, twist, fidget; see **wiggle.**

squirt, *v.* —*Syn.* spurt, spit, eject; see **emit** 1.

stab, *n.* —*Syn.* thrust, prick, cut, hurt, knife thrust, bayonet thrust, wound, puncture, blow, piercing, stick, transfixion.

make a stab at—*Syn.* endeavor, try to, do one's best (to); see **try** 1.

stab, *v.* —*Syn.* transfix, pierce, wound, stick, cut, hurt, thrust, prick, drive, puncture, hit, bayonet, saber, knife; see also **kill** 1.

stability, *n.* **1.** [Firmness of position]—*Syn.* steadiness, durability, solidity, endurance, substantiality, immobility, suspense, immovability, inaction, establishment, solidness, balance, permanence.

2. [Steadfastness of character]—*Syn.* stableness, aplomb, security, endurance, maturity, constancy, resoluteness, determination, perseverance, adherence, backbone, assurance, resistance; see also **confidence** 2.

stabilize, *v.* **1.** [To fix]—*Syn.* bolt, secure, steady; see **fasten** 1.

2. [To support]—*Syn.* maintain, uphold, preserve; see **support** 2, **sustain** 1.

stab in the back (D), *v.* —*Syn.* deceive, undercut, turn traitor; see **betray** 1, **trick.**

stable, *mod.* **1.** [Fixed]—*Syn.* steady, stationary, solid; see **firm** 1.

2. [Steadfast]—*Syn.* calm, firm, constant; see **resolute** 2.

3. [Permanent]—*Syn.* enduring, well-built, durable; see **permanent** 1.

stable, *n.* —*Syn.* shelter, barn, coop, corral, hutch, kennel; see also **pen** 1.

stable, *v.* —*Syn.* pen, corral, put up; see **tend** 1.

stableboy, *n.* —*Syn.* stableman, groom, hand (D); see **servant.**

stack, *n.* **1.** [A heap]—*Syn.* pile, mass mound; see **heap.**

2. [A tall chimney]—*Syn.* flue, smokestack, pipe; see **chimney.**

stack, *v.* —*Syn.* rick, pile, accumulate; see **heap** 1.

stacked, *mod.* **1.** [Put away]—*Syn.* stored, stashed, put aside; see **kept** 2, **saved** 1, 2.
2. [(D) Amply proportioned; *said of women*] —*Syn.* shapely, well-proportioned, built (D); see **buxom** 2.
stack the deck *or* **the cards** (D), *v.* —*Syn.* prearrange, deceive, set up; see **arrange** 2, **trick.**
stack up (D), *v.* —*Syn.* become, work out (to *or* as), resolve (into); see **result.**
stadium, *n.* —*Syn.* gymnasium, strand, amphitheater; see **arena.**
staff, *n.* **1.** [A stick]—*Syn.* wand, pole, stave; see **club** 3, **stick.**
2. [A corps of employees]—*Syn.* personnel, assistants, force, help, workers, crew, team, organization, agents, faculty, cadre, cast, operatives, deputies, servants, factotums, officers.
3. [An officer's assistants]—*Syn.* junior officers, corps, aides-de-camp, escort, guard of honor.
stage, *n.* **1.** [The theater]—*Syn.* theater, boards, scene, parascene; *both* (D): limelight, spotlight; see also **drama** 1.
2. [A platform]—*Syn.* frame, scaffold, staging; see **platform** 1.
3. [A level, period, or degree]—*Syn.* grade, plane, step; see **degree** 1.
by easy stages—*Syn.* easily, gently, taking one's time (D); see **slowly.**
stagecraft, *n.* —*Syn.* histrionics, theater, dramatics; see **acting.**
stagehand, *n.* —*Syn.* prompter, carpenter, costumer; see **workman.**
stagger, *v.* —*Syn.* totter, waver, vacillate; see **reel.**
staggering, *mod.* —*Syn.* monstrous, huge, tremendous; see **large** 1, **tremendously, unbelievable.**
staging, *n.* **1.** [A production]—*Syn.* presentation, preparation, adaptation; see **acting.**
2. [A stage]—*Syn.* enclosure, scaffold, stage; see **frame** 1, **platform** 1.
stagnant, *mod.* **1.** [Still]—*Syn.* inert, dead, inactive; see **idle** 1.
2. [Filthy]—*Syn.* putrid, foul, filthy; see **dirty** 1.
3. [Dull]—*Syn.* dormant, lifeless, passive; see **listless** 1.
stagnate, *v.* —*Syn.* deteriorate, rot, putrefy; see **decay.**
stagy, *mod.* —*Syn.* show, thespian, dramatic; see **theatrical** 1.
staid, *mod.* —*Syn.* sober, grave, steady; see **dignified.**
stain, *n.* —*Syn.* blot, smirch, blemish, spot, mottle, splotch, blotch, stained spot, smudge, discoloration, stigma, brand, blotch, blot on the escutcheon, something the matter, ink spot, spatter, drip, speck.
stain, *v.* **1.** [To soil]—*Syn.* spot, discolor, taint; see **dirty.**
2. [To color]—*Syn.* dye, tint, lacquer; see **color** 1, **paint** 2, **varnish.**
stairs, *n.* —*Syn.* stairway, staircase, flight, companionway, steps, stair, escalator, moving stair, spiral staircase, open *or* closed stairway, ascent.
stake, *n.* —*Syn.* rod, paling, pale; see **post** 1, **stick.**
at stake—*Syn.* at issue, in danger, risked; see **endangered.**
pull up stakes (D)—*Syn.* depart, move, decamp; see **leave** 1.
stale, *mod.* **1.** [Old or musty]—*Syn.* spoiled, dried, smelly; see **musty** 2, **old** 2.
2. [Dull and trite]—*Syn.* mawkish, hackneyed, fusty; see **dull** 4.
stalemate, *n.* —*Syn.* deadlock, standstill, check; see **delay** 1, **pause** 2.
stalk, *n.* —*Syn.* stem, support, axis, pedicle, petiole, peduncle, stipe, stipes, seta, upright, quill, stack, caulis, caulicle, spire, shaft, helm, bent, scape, funicle, spike, stipel, tigella, straw, boon, bennet, stock; see also **trunk** 3.
stalk, *v.* —*Syn.* approach stealthily, track, chase; see **hunt** 1, **pursue** 1.
stall, *v.* **1.** [To break down]—*Syn.* not start, not turn over, stop working; *both* (D): conk out, go dead; see also **break down** 3.
2. [To delay]—*Syn.* postpone, hamper, hinder; see **delay** 1.
stallion, *n.* —*Syn.* animal, quadruped, steed; see **horse** 1.
stalwart, *mod.* **1.** [Strong]—*Syn.* sturdy, robust, vigorous; see **strong** 1.
2. [Brave]—*Syn.* valiant, valorous, bold; see **brave** 1.
stamina, *n.* —*Syn.* strength, vigor, vitality; see **endurance.**
stammer, *v.* —*Syn.* falter, stop, stumble, hesitate, pause, block one's utterance, stutter, repeat oneself, sputter, halt, hem and haw.
stamp, *n.* —*Syn.* emblem, brand, cast; see **impression** 1, **imprint** 1, **mark** 1.
stamp, *v.* —*Syn.* impress, imprint, brand; see **mark** 1.
stamped, *mod.* —*Syn.* marked, branded, imprinted; *both* (D): okayed, O.K.'d; see also **approved.**
stampede, *n.* —*Syn.* rush, dash, flight; see **run** 1.
stampede, *v.* —*Syn.* bolt, rush, panic; see **run** 2.
stamp out, *v.* —*Syn.* eliminate, kill out *or* off, dispatch; see **destroy** 1, **kill** 1, **remove** 1.
stanchion, *n.* —*Syn.* stay, prop, bolster; see **beam** 1, **brace, support** 2.
stand, *n.* **1.** [Position]—*Syn.* notion, view, belief; see **attitude** 3, **opinion** 1.
2. [A platform]—*Syn.* stage, gantry, station; see **platform** 1.
make *or* **take a stand** (D)—*Syn.* insist, assert, take a position; see **declare** 1, **fight** 1, 2, **say.**
take the stand—*Syn.* bear witness, give evidence *or* testimony, be sworn in; see **testify.**
stand, *v.* **1.** [To be in an upright position]—*Syn.* be erect, be on one's feet, stand up, come to one's feet, rise, jump up (D).
2. [To endure]—*Syn.* last, hold, abide; see **endure** 1.
3. [To be of a certain height]—*Syn.* be, attain, come to; see **reach** 1.
4. [To be situated]—*Syn.* fill, hold, take up; see **occupy** 2.
5. [To oppose]—*Syn.* withstand, stand against, confront; see **compete, oppose** 1.
6. [(D) To pay for]—*Syn.* bear the cost, stand the expense, make payment; see **pay** 1.
stand a chance, *v.* —*Syn.* have a chance, be a likelihood, be a possibility, be a probability, have some-

thing in one's favor, have something on one's side, be preferred.

standard, *mod.* —*Syn.* regular, regulation, made to a standard; see **approved, official** 3.

standard, *n.* **1.** [Flag]—*Syn.* pennant, banner, colors; see **flag** 1.
2. [Emblem]—*Syn.* symbol, figure, insignia; see **emblem.**
3. [Measure]—*Syn.* example, rule, test; see **criterion, measure** 2.
4. [Model]—*Syn.* pattern, type, example; see **model** 2.

standard-bearer, *n.* —*Syn.* commander, demagogue, boss; see **leader** 2.

standardization, *n.* —*Syn.* uniformity, sameness, likeness, evenness, levelness, monotony; see also **regularity.**

standardize, *v.* —*Syn.* regulate, institue, normalize; see **order** 3, **systematize.**

standardized, *mod.* —*Syn.* patterned, graded, made alike; see **regulated.**

standardizing, *mod.* —*Syn.* normative, normalizing, regulating, regularizing, regulative, balancing, determining, controlling, shifting, directive, directing, influencing, making *or* bringing to *or* toward a norm *or* median *or* an average.

stand-by, *n.* —*Syn.* upholder, supporter, advocate; see **patron** 1, **protector.**

stand by, *v.* **1.** [To defend or help]—*Syn.* befriend, second, abet; see **defend** 2, 3, **help** 1, **sustain** 3.
2. [To wait]—*Syn.* be prepared, be ready, be near; see **wait** 1.

stand for, *v.* **1.** [To mean]—*Syn.* represent, suggest, imply; see **mean** 1.
2. [(D) To allow]—*Syn.* permit, suffer, endure; see **allow** 1.

stand-in, *n.* —*Syn.* double, second, understudy; see **assistant, substitute.**

standing, *n.* —*Syn.* position, status, reputation; see **rank** 3.

standoff, *n.* —*Syn.* stalemate, deadlock, dead end; see **delay** 1, **pause** 2.

standoffish, *mod.* —*Syn.* cool, aloof, distant; see **indifferent** 1.

stand one's ground, *v.* —*Syn.* oppose, fight (back *or* against), resist; see **fight** 1, 2.

stand out, *v.* —*Syn.* be prominent, be conspicuous, emerge; see **loom** 2.

stand pat (D), *v.* —*Syn.* stay, persist, insist (on no change); see **remain** 1.

standpoint, *n.* —*Syn.* attitude, point of view, station; see **judgment** 3, **opinion** 1.

standstill, *n.* —*Syn.* stop, halt, cessation; see **delay** 1, **pause** 2.

stand up for, *v.* —*Syn.* back, protect, champion; see **approve** 1, **defend** 3.

stand up to, *v.* —*Syn.* resist, oppose, challenge; see **fight** 1, 2.

Stanford, *n.* —*Syn.* Leland, Stanford Junior University; *all* (D): The Farm, Leland's Racehorse Farm, Indians, Red and White, Hoover's Hayfield; see also **university.**

stanza, *n.* —*Syn.* stave, refrain, strophe; see **verse** 2.

staple, *mod.* —*Syn.* standard, chief, essential; see **necessary** 1, **principal.**

star, *n.* **1.** [A luminous heavenly body]—*Syn.* sun, astral body, pulsar, quasar, seyfert galaxy, quasi-stellar object, sidereal body, fixed star, variable star; *both* (D): lamp, twinkler.
Classes of stars include the following—fixed star, binary star, multiple star, supergiant *or* red giant, medium yellow, white dwarf, planet, meteor, comet, meteorite, star of the first, second, third, etc., magnitude; member of a galaxy, star cluster, star cloud or globular cluster.
Familiar stars include the following—individual stars: Betelgeuse, Sirius, Vega, Spica, Arcturus, Aldebaran, Antares, Atlas, Castor, Pollux, Cappella, Algol, North Star *or* Polaris; constellations: Great Bear *or* Ursa Major, Little Bear *or* Ursa Minor, Great Dipper, Little Dipper, Orion, Coma Berenices *or* Berenice's Hair, The Gemini *or* Castor and Pollux, Cassiopeia, Pleiades, Hyades, Taurus, Canis Major *or* the Great Dog, Canis Minor *or* the Little Dog, Scorpion, Sagittarius, Corona Borealis *or* the Northern Crown, Pegasus, Leo, Hercules, Boötes, Cetus, Aquila *or* the Eagle, Cygnus *or* the Swan, Corona Australis *or* the Southern Crown, the Southern Cross.
2. [A conventional figure]
Forms of stars include the following—asterisk, pentacle, pentagram, estoile, mullet, six-pointed star, five-pointed star, Star of David; see also **form** 1.
3. [A superior performer]—*Syn.* headliner, leading lady, leading man, movie actor, movie actress, actor, actress, favorite, player, matinee idol, chief attraction; *all* (D): lead, starlet, topliner, luminary, the flash.

starch, *n.* **1.** [A laundering agent]—*Syn.* stiffening, sizing, *amidon* (French), laundry starch, cornstarch, arrowroot starch, spray starch.
2. [A complex carbohydrate]—*Syn.* glycogen, polysaccharide, $C_6 H_{10} O_5$; see **carbohydrate, sugar.**

starch, *v.* —*Syn.* dip in starch, add starch, make stiff; see **stiffen** 2, **thicken** 2.

stare, *v.* —*Syn.* gaze, gawk, look fixedly; see **look** 2, **watch** 1.

staring, *mod.* —*Syn.* bald, stary, fixed; see **dull** 3.

stark, *mod.* —*Syn.* stiff, firm, severe; see **abrupt** 2.

stark-naked, *mod.* —*Syn.* nude, without a stitch (of clothing), in the altogether (D); see **naked** 1.

starlight, *mod.* —*Syn.* luminous, lustrous, shining; see **bright** 1, **shimmering.**

starlight, *n.* —*Syn.* gleam, glimmer, twinkle; see **light** 3.

starlike, *mod.* —*Syn.* shining, radiant, shiny; see **bright** 1, **shimmering.**

starred, *mod.* —*Syn.* selected, choice, designated; see **excellent, special** 1.

starry, *mod.* **1.** [Shiny]—*Syn.* luminous, lustrous, shining; see **bright** 1, **shimmering.**
2. [Stellar]—*Syn.* celestial, heavenly, astronomical; see **stellar.**

start, *n.* **1.** [The beginning]—*Syn.* inception, commencement, inauguration; see **origin** 1.
2. [The point at which a start is made]—*Syn.* source, derivation, spring; see **origin** 2.

start, *v.* **1.** [To begin]—*Syn.* commence, rise, spring; see **begin** 2.
2. [To cause to start, sense 1]—*Syn.* inaugurate, start off, originate; see **begin** 1, **cause** 2.

3. [To arouse]—*Syn.* rouse, incite, light; see **excite** 2.
4. [To cause to ignite]—*Syn.* light, set on fire, fire; see **ignite.**

started, *mod.*—*Syn.* evoked, initiated, instituted; see **begun.**

starter, *n.*—*Syn.* innovator, initiator, beginner, opener, master, originator, pioneer, father (of), inventor, moving *or* leading spirit, one who sets guide lines *or* trends *or* patterns, spark plug (D); see also **author** 1.—*Ant.* follower*, adherent, successor.

start in, *v.*—*Syn.* commence, open, make a start *or* a beginning *or* a first move, *etc.*; see **begin** 2.

starting, *n.*—*Syn.* offset, outset, opening; see **origin** 2.

startle, *v.*—*Syn.* alarm, shock, astonish; see **frighten** 1, **surprise** 2.

startled, *mod.*—*Syn.* frightened, alarmed, shocked; see **surprised.**

startling, *mod.*—*Syn.* shocking, alarming, unexpected; see **frightful** 1.

start off *or* **out,** *v.*—*Syn.* depart, begin (a journey *or* trip), go; see **leave** 1.

start up, *v.* **1.** [To begin to rise]—*Syn.* recover, go up, shoot (up); see **rise** 1, 3.
2. [To activate]—*Syn.* make go *or* run, crank (up), get (something) started; see **begin** 1.

starvation, *n.*—*Syn.* deprivation, belt tightening, need, want, inanition; see also **hunger.**

starve, *v.* **1.** [To become weak or die from hunger] —*Syn.* famish, crave, perish; see **die** 1, **weaken** 1.
2. [To cause to starve, sense 1]—*Syn.* underfeed, undernourish, deprive (of food), kill, withhold nourishment; see also **weaken** 2.

starving, *mod.*—*Syn.* famished, weakening, dying; see **hungry.**

state, *n.* **1.** [A sovereign unit]—*Syn.* republic, land, kingdom; see **country** 3, **nation** 1.
2. [A condition]—*Syn.* circumstance, situation, welfare, phase, case, station, nature, estate, time, footing, status, standing, stipulation, proviso, contingency, juncture, occurrence, occasion, eventuality, element, prerequisite, imperative, essential, requirement, limitation, category, standing, reputation, environment, chances, outlook, position, event, accompaniment.
3. [A difficulty]—*Syn.* plight, pinch, quandary; see **difficulty** 1, **predicament.**
4. [Mood]—*Syn.* frame of mind, humor, disposition; see **mood**1.
in a state—*Syn.* disturbed, upset, badly off; see **confused, troubled** 1, 2.

state, *v.*—*Syn.* pronounce, assert, affirm; see **declare** 1.

statecraft, *n.*—*Syn.* statesmanship, diplomacy, senatorship; see **tact.**

stated, *mod.*—*Syn.* established, fixed, regular; see **told.**

stately, *mod.* **1.** [*Said of persons*]—*Syn.* lordly, dignified, proud, imperious, haughty, stiff, formal, noble, solemn, august, ceremonious, pompous, imperious, regal, royal, kingly, imperial, masterful. —*Ant.* simple*, unassuming, modest.
2. [*Said of objects*]—*Syn.* large, grand, spacious, lofty, imposing, elevated, high, majestic, magnificent, sumptuous, palatial, opulent, superb, luxurious, monumental, impressive.—*Ant.* poor*, cheap, lowly.

statement, *n.* **1.** [The act of stating]—*Syn.* utterance, comment, allegation, declaration, observation, remark, assertion, averment, profession, acknowledgment, avowal, protestation, assurance, asseveration, affirmation; see also **announcement** 1.
2. [A prepared announcement]—*Syn.* description, narrative, recital; see **announcement** 2, **declaration** 2.
3. [A statement of account]—*Syn.* bill, charge, reckoning, account, record, report, annual, report, budget, audit, affidavit, balance sheet.

statesman, *n.*—*Syn.* legislator, lawgiver, Solon, administrator, executive, minister, official, politician, strategist, diplomat, representative, elder statesman, veteran lawmaker.

statesmanship, *n.*—*Syn.* statecraft, diplomacy, legislation; see **tact.**

static, *mod.*—*Syn.* immobile, formant, inactive; see **latent.**

station, *n.* **1.** [Place]—*Syn.* situation, site, location; see **position** 1.
2. [Duty]—*Syn.* occupation, service, calling; see **duty** 2.
3. [Depot]—*Syn.* terminal, stop, stopping place; see **depot** 2.
4. [Headquarters]—*Syn.* main office, home office, base of operations; see **headquarters.**
5. [Social position]—*Syn.* order, standing, state; see **rank** 3.
6. [An establishment to vend petroleum products] —*Syn.* gas *or* gasoline *or* service *or* filling *or* petrol station, pumps, petroleum outlet *or* retailer; see **garage** 2.
7. [A broadcasting establishment]—*Syn.* (local) television *or* radio *or* transmission *or* transmitter *or* radar *or* microwave *or* broadcasting station, plant, studio(s), transmitter, Channel 1 *or* 2 *or* 3, etc.; see also **communications, radio** 2, **television.**
Specialized broadcasting stations include the following—AM station, FM *or* frequency modulation station, tracking station, monitor *or* monitoring station, amateur *or* ham (D) station, space station *or* control, spaceport, space platform *or* space island port station, moon *or* lunar *or* Martian, etc. station *or* base, transit station, direction finder (station), clear-channel station, shortwave station, educational radio *or* television station *or* center.

station, *v.*—*Syn.* place, commission, allot; see **assign** 1.

stationary, *mod.*—*Syn.* fixed, stable, permanent; see **motionless** 1.

stationery, *n.*—*Syn.* writing materials, office supplies, school supplies; see **paper** 5.

statistical, *mod.*—*Syn.* mathematical, demographic, arithmetical, analytical.

statistics, *n.*—*Syn.* enumeration, figures, demography; see **data.**

statuary, *n.*—*Syn.* statues, carving, art; see **image** 2, **sculpture.**

statue, *n.*—*Syn.* statuette, cast, figure, bust, representation, likeness, image, torso, piece, sculpture, statuary, marble, bronze, ivory, simulacrum, stabile, effigy, icon; see also **art** 2.

statuesque, *mod.* —*Syn.* stately, beautiful, grand; see **graceful** 2.
stature, *n.* —*Syn.* development, growth, tallness; see **height** 1, **size** 2.
status, *n.* —*Syn.* situation, standing, station; see **rank** 3.
status seeker, *n.* —*Syn.* manipulator, social climber, self-server, *nouveau riche* (French), junior executive, ambitious person; see also **opportunist.**
statute, *n.* —*Syn.* enactment, ordinance, canon; see **law** 3.
statutory, *mod.* —*Syn.* sanctioned, lawful, rightful; see **legal** 1.
staunch, *mod.* —*Syn.* steadfast, strong, constant; see **faithful, firm** 1.
stave, *n.* —*Syn.* stick, rod, staff; see **beam** 1, **support** 2.
stay, *n.* **1.** [A support]—*Syn.* prop, hold, truss; see **support** 2.
2. [A visit]—*Syn.* stop, sojourn, halt; see **visit.**
stay, *v.* —*Syn.* tarry, linger, sojourn; see **visit** 2, **wait** 1.
stay put (D), *v.* —*Syn.* remain, stand (still *or* fast *or* rigid *or* immovable, *etc.),* persist; see **endure** 1, **resist** 1.
stead, *n.* —*Syn.* advantage, service, avail; see **use** 2.
steadfast, *mod.* —*Syn.* staunch, stable, constant; see **faithful.**
steadily, *mod.* —*Syn.* firmly, unwaveringly, undeviatingly; see **regularly** 2.
steady, *mod.* **1.** [Showing little variation]—*Syn.* uniform, unvarying, patterned; see **consecutive** 1, **constant** 1, **regular** 3.
2. [Calm and self-possessed]—*Syn.* cool, poised, steadfast; see **calm** 1, **reserved** 3.
go steady (with) (D)—*Syn.* keep company (with), court *or* be courted, go with *or* together; see **court** 1, **love** 1.
steak, *n.*
Cuts of steak include the following—filet mignon, tenderloin, porterhouse, sirloin, strip, rib, T-bone, New York, Kansas City, London broil, minute, chip, club, cube, flank, chuck, Salisbury, string, round, ground round, hamburger, Swiss; see **food, meat.**
steal, *v.* —*Syn.* take, filch, bag, thieve, loot, rob, purloin, embezzle, defraud, keep, carry away *or* off, appropriate, take possession of, withdraw, divert, lift, remove, impress, abduct, shanghai, kidnap, spirit away, run off with, hold for ransom, rifle, sack, cheat, cozen, hold up, strip, poach, peculate, counterfeit, circulate bad money, swindle, plagiarize, misappropriate, housebreak, burglarize, blackmail, fleece, plunder, pillage, despoil, ransack; *all* (D): crib, burgle, stick up, hijack, skyjack, pinch, rustle, rip off, liberate, snatch, lift, freeze on to, annex, cop, swipe, pinch, mooch, gyp, dip one's hands into, make off with; see also **seize** 2.
stealing, *n.* —*Syn.* piracy, embezzlement, shoplifting; see **crime** 2, **theft.**
stealth, *n.* —*Syn.* slyness, furtiveness, underhandedness; see **secrecy.**
stealthy, *mod.* —*Syn.* enigmatic, clandestine, private; see **secret** 3.
steam, *n.* —*Syn.* vaporized water, fume(s), fog; see **cloud** 1, **vapor.**
steam, *v.* **1.** [To cook]—*Syn.* heat, brew, pressure cook; see **cook.**
2. [To speed]—*Syn.* rush, sail, hurry; see **drive** 1, **speed.**
steamboat, *n.* —*Syn.* steamer, steamship, liner; see **boat, ship.**
steamer, *n.* —*Syn.* steamship, steamboat, liner; see **boat, ship.**
steaming, *mod.* —*Syn.* piping (hot), boiling, just out of the oven *or* off the stove; see **cooking** 1, **hot** 1.
steamroller (D), *v.* —*Syn.* steamroll (D), overpower, railroad (through) (D); see **defeat** 1, **force** 1, **trick.**
steamy, *mod.* —*Syn.* vaporous, gaseous, evaporating; see **volatile** 1.
steed, *n.* —*Syn.* charger, warhorse, palfrey; see **horse** 1.
steel, *n.*
Forms and varieties of steel include the following—ingot, bar, slab, billet, rod, scrap, hot rolled sheet *or* strip, cold rolled sheet *or* strip, plate, skelp, angle, channel, round, flat, square, joist bar, Z-bar, reinforcing, wire rod; see also **alloy, metal.**
steep, *mod.* —*Syn.* precipitous, sheer, perpendicular; see **abrupt** 1.
steeple, *n.* —*Syn.* turret, pointed belfry, *tourelle* (French); see **tower.**
steeplechase, *n.* —*Syn.* sweepstakes, derby, handicap; see **race** 3.
steer, *n.* —*Syn.* beef, feeder, cattle; see **cow, ox.**
steer, *v.* —*Syn.* point, head for, direct; see **drive** 3.
steer clear of (D), *v.* —*Syn.* keep away (from), miss, escape; see **avoid.**
steersman, *n.* —*Syn.* helmsman, coxwain, wheelman; see **pilot** 2.
stellar, *mod.* —*Syn.* celestial, heavenly, astronomical, spherical, galactic, cosmic, astrological.
stem, *n.* —*Syn.* peduncle, petiole, pedice; see **stalk.**
from stem to stern—*Syn.* the full length, completely, entirely; see **everywhere, throughout.**
stench, *n.* —*Syn.* odor, stink, redolence; see **smell** 2.
stenographer, *n.* —*Syn.* stenographist, office girl, typist, shorthand, stenographer; see also **clerk** 2, **secretary** 2.
stenography, *n.* —*Syn.* phonography, stenotype, tachygraphy; see **shorthand.**
stentorian, *mod.* —*Syn.* blaring, sonorous, resounding; see **loud** 1, **raucous** 1.
step, *n.* **1.** [A movement of the foot]—*Syn.* pace, stride, gait, footfall, tread, stepping.
2. [One degree in a graded rise]—*Syn.* rest, run, tread, round, rung, level.
3. [The print of a foot]—*Syn.* footprint, footmark, print, imprint, impression, footstep, trail, trace, mark; see also **track** 2.
4. [An action, especially a first action]—*Syn.* start, move, measure; see **action** 2.
in step (with)—*Syn.* in agreement (with), coinciding (with), similar (to); see **alike** 1, 2, 3, **similarly.**
keep step—*Syn.* agree to *or* with, conform (to), keep in line (D); see **conform.**
out of step—*Syn.* inappropriate(ly), incorrect(ly), inaccurate(ly); see **wrong** 2, 3, **wrongly** 2.
take steps—*Syn.* do (something), start, intervene; see **act** 1.

watch one's step (D)—*Syn.* be careful, take precautions, look out; see **watch out** 2.

step, *v.* —*Syn.* pace, stride, advance, recede, go forward, go backward, go up, go down, ascend, descend, pass, walk, tread, march, move, hurry, move quickly, move forward, move backward, mince, hop; see also **climb** 2, **rise** 1.

step by step, *mod.* —*Syn.* by degrees, cautiously, tentatively; see **carefully** 2, **slowly.**

step down, *v.* —*Syn.* leave, go, get out (D); see **resign** 2, **retire** 3.

step in, *v.* —*Syn.* come (in), arrive, be invited (in); see **enter** 1.

step on it (D), *v.* —*Syn.* go *or* travel (fast), make (good) time, speed (up); see **speed.**

steppe, *n.* —*Syn.* prairie, pampas, savanna; see **plain.**

steppingstone, *n.* —*Syn.* help, agent, factor; see **aid** 1, **means** 1, **link.**

steps, *n.* —*Syn.* march, advance, rise; see **improvement** 1.

step up, *v.* —*Syn.* augment, improve, intensify; see **increase** 1.

stereo (D), *n.* —*Syn.* stereo (tape) recorder, stereo (record) player, stereo receiver; see **radio** 2, **record player, tape recorder.**

stereotype, *n.* —*Syn.* convention, fashion, institution; see **average** 1, **custom** 1, 2.

stereotype, *v.* —*Syn.* conventionalize, methodize, pigeon-hole, define, standardize, normalize, catalogue, institutionalize; see also **regulate** 2, **systematize.**

stereotyped, *mod.* —*Syn.* hackneyed, trite, ordinary; see **conventional** 1, 2, **dull** 4.

sterile, *mod.* **1.** [Incapable of producing young] —*Syn.* infertile, impotent, childless, infecund, barren, issueless, without issue.—*Ant.* fertile*, productive, potent.

2. [Incapable of producing vegetation]—*Syn.* desolate, fallow, waste, desert, arid, dry, barren, unproductive, fruitless, unfruitful, bleak, gaunt; see also **empty** 1.—*Ant.* rich*, productive, fertile.

3. [Scrupulously clean]—*Syn.* antiseptic, septic, sterilized, disinfected, decontaminated, germ-free, sterilized, uninfected, sanitary, hygienic, pasteurized; see also **pure** 2.—*Ant.* dirty*, infected, contaminated.

4. [Without intellectual interest]—*Syn.* uninspiring, stupid, stale; see **dull** 4, **shallow** 2.

5. [Unprofitable]—*Syn.* fruitless, profitless, unproductive; see **worthless** 1, **useless** 1.

sterility, *n.* —*Syn.* infertility, incapacity, fruitlessness; see **barrenness, worthlessness.**

sterilize, *v.* —*Syn.* ascepticize, aseptify, antisepticize, disinfect, decontaminate, incapacitate, make sterile, Tyndalize, pasteurize; see also **clean, purify.**

sterling, *mod.* —*Syn.* authentic, real, true; see **genuine** 1, **pure** 1.

sterling, *n.* —*Syn.* flatware, silver, cutlery; see **silverware.**

stern, *mod.* —*Syn.* rigid, austere, strict; see **severe** 1.

stevedore, *n.* —*Syn.* docker, lumper, loader; see **laborer, workman.**

stew, *n.* —*Syn.* ragout, goulash, Hungarian goulash, meat pie, cottage pie, steak-and-kidney pie, gallimaufry, *ollapodrida* (Spanish), *bouillabaisse* (French), beef stew, Irish stew, slumgullion (D), casserole, mutton stew, lamb stew, veal stew, *pot-au-feu* (French), matelote; see also **food, soup.**

stew, *v.* **1.** [To boil]—*Syn.* simmer, steam, seethe; see **boil** 2, **cook.**

2. [(D) To fret]—*Syn.* fume, fuss, chafe; see **worry** 2.

steward, *n.* —*Syn.* agent, chamberlain, purser; see **administrator, waiter.**

stew in one's own juice (D), *v.* —*Syn.* endure, be punished, (have to) take one's own medicine (D); see **suffer** 1.

stick, *n.* —*Syn.* shoot, twig, branch, stem, stalk, rod, wand, staff, stave, walking stick, cane, matchstick, club, baton, drumstick, timber, cudgel, ferrule, pole, bludgeon, bat, birch, rule, ruler, stock, joist, shillelagh, truncheon, cue, billet, spar, mast; see also **rod** 1.

the sticks (D)—*Syn.* rural area(s), (the) back country, outlying district(s); see **country** 1.

stick, *v.* **1.** [To remain fastened]—*Syn.* adhere, cling, fasten, attach, cleave, unite, cohere, hold, stick together, hug, clasp, hold fast, stick like wax, cling like a bur, cling like ivy, stick like a leech. —*Ant.* loosen*, let go, fall, come away.

2. [To penetrate with a point]—*Syn.* prick, impale, pierce; see **penetrate** 1, **stab.**

stick around (D), *v.* —*Syn.* stay, continue, be present; see **remain** 1.

stick by (someone) (D), *v.* —*Syn.* be loyal (to), stand by, believe in; see **support** 2.

sticker, *n.* —*Syn.* lackey, plugger, adherent; see **follower.**

stickiness, *n.* **1.** [Humidity]—*Syn.* mugginess, dampness, wetness; see **humidity.**

2. [Cohesion]—*Syn.* adhesiveness, gumminess, fusion; see **coherence** 1.

stick it out (D), *v.* —*Syn.* persist, endure, stay; see **remain** 1.

stickler, *n.* **1.** [A zealot]—*Syn.* devotee, fanatic, contender; see **follower, zealot.**

2. [A puzzle]—*Syn.* enigma, riddle, paradox; see **irony, puzzle** 2.

stick out, *v.* —*Syn.* jut, show, come through; see **protrude.**

stick-up (D), *n.* —*Syn.* burglary, robbery, stealing; see **crime** 2, **theft.**

stick up, *v.* —*Syn.* show, poke *or* bristle *or* fly up, come through; see **protrude.**

stick up for (D), *v.* —*Syn.* support, aid, fight for; see **defend** 1, 2, 3, **help** 1.

sticky, *mod.* —*Syn.* glutinous, ropy, viscous, gluey; see also **adhesive.**

stiff, *mod.* **1.** [Not easily bent]—*Syn.* solid, rigid, congealed, petrified, ossified, firm, tense, unyielding, inflexible, inelastic, hard, hardened, starched, annealed, cemented, stony, starchy, taut, contracted, thick, indurate, stubborn, obstinate, pertinacious, numb, unbending, thickened, wooden, steely, frozen, solidified, chilled, benumbed, refractory.—*Ant.* flexible*, softened, soft.

2. [Formal]—*Syn.* ungainly, ungraceful, unnatural; see **awkward.**

3. [Severe]—*Syn.* rigorous, exact, strict; see **severe** 1, 2.

4. [Obstinate]—*Syn.* stubborn, inflexible, headstrong; see **obstinate** 1.
5. [Potent]—*Syn.* hard, potent, powerful; see **strong** 8.
6. [(D) Difficult]—*Syn.* arduous, hard, laborious; see **difficult** 1.

stiffen, *v.* **1.** [To grow stiff]—*Syn.* jelly, thicken, clot, coagulate, solidify, congeal, condense, set, curdle, freeze, inspissate, cake, chill, candy, crystallize; see also **harden** 2.—*Ant.* soften*, melt, liquefy.
2. [To cause to become stiff]—*Syn.* harden, benumb, anneal, starch, petrify, ossify, brace, prop, cement, fix, precipitate, evaporate, strengthen, invigorate, revive, bring to, inflate.—*Ant.* relax*, moisten, limber.

stiff-necked, *mod.*—*Syn.* stubborn, unyielding, priggish; see **obstinate, prudish.**

stifle, *v.*—*Syn.* smother, suffocate, extinguish; see **choke** 1.

stigma, *n.*—*Syn.* reproach, brand, shame; see **blame** 1, **disgrace** 2.

stigmata, *n.*—*Syn.* mark, blot, defect; see **blemish.**

stigmatize, *v.*—*Syn.* brand, defame, discredit; see **disgrace.**

stiletto, *n.*—*Syn.* dagger, cutter, blade; see **knife.**

still, *mod.* **1.** [Silent]—*Syn.* calm, tranquil, noiseless; see **quiet** 2.
2. [Yet]—*Syn.* nevertheless, furthermore, however; see **besides, but** 1, **yet** 1.

stillness, *n.*—*Syn.* quietness, tranquillity, soundlessness; see **silence** 1.

stilt, *n.*—*Syn.* shore, prop, post; see **brace, support** 2.

stilted, *mod.*—*Syn.* pompous, affected, decorous; see **egotistic** 2, **prim.**

stimulant, *n.*—*Syn.* tonic, bracer, energizer; see **drug** 2.

stimulate, *v.*—*Syn.* support, foster, incite; see **excite** 1, **urge** 2.

stimulated, *mod.*—*Syn.* keyed up, speeded up, accelerated; see **excited.**

stimulating, *mod.*—*Syn.* intriguing, enlivening, arousing, high-spirited, bracing, rousing, inspiriting, energetic, refreshing, exhilarating, warming, strengthening, enjoyable, health-building, tonic, vivifying, sharp, keen, evocative, exciting, inspiring, intoxicating, provoking, animating.—*Ant.* dull*, dreary, humdrum.

stimulus, *n.*—*Syn.* inducement, provocation, motive; see **incentive.**

stimulus and response, *n.*—*Syn.* feeling, consequence, receptivity; see **reaction** 2.

sting, *n.* **1.** [An injury]—*Syn.* wound, cut, sore; see **injury** 1.
2. [Pain]—*Syn.* prick, bite, burn; see **pain** 2.

sting, *v.*—*Syn.* prick, prickle, tingle; see **hurt** 4.

stingy, *mod.*—*Syn.* parsimonious, niggardly, miserly, penurious, close, closefisted, sordid, greedy, covetous, tightfisted, avaricious, acquisitive, grasping, curmudgeonly, penny-pinching, grudging, cheeseparing, sparing, ignoble, cheap, scurvy, rapacious, near, narrow, shabby, scrimping, skimping, churlish, ungenerous, selfish, meagerly, meanly, skimpy, illiberal, extortionate.—*Ant.* generous*, bountiful, liberal.

stink, *n.*—*Syn.* stench, fetor, offensive odor; see **smell** 2.

stink, *v.*—*Syn.* smell bad, emit a stench, be offensive, make an offensive odor, smell up.

stint, *n.* **1.** [A limit]—*Syn.* restriction, limit, limitation; see **restraint** 2.
2. [A task]—*Syn.* assignment, work, consignment; see **job** 1, 2.

stint, *v.*—*Syn.* restrain, confine, limit; see **define** 1, **restrict** 2.

stipend, *n.*—*Syn.* wage, gratuity, pension; see **allowance** 2, **pay** 2.

stipple, *v.*—*Syn.* dapple, dot, dab; see **draw** 2, **paint** 1.

stipulate, *v.*—*Syn.* condition, bargain, arrange; see **designate** 1, **specify.**

stipulation, *n.*—*Syn.* designation, obligation, arrangement; see **requirement** 1, **specification.**

stir, *n.*—*Syn.* agitation, tumult, bustle; see **excitement.**

stir, *v.* **1.** [To excite]—*Syn.* provoke, inflame, awaken; see **excite** 1.
2. [To mix by stirring]—*Syn.* move, beat, agitate; see **mix** 1.

stirring, *mod.*—*Syn.* stimulating, lively, animating; see **interesting.**

stir up trouble (D), *v.*—*Syn.* cause difficulty, foment, agitate; see **bother** 2, **disturb** 2.

stitch, *v.*—*Syn.* join, make a seam, baste; see **sew.**

stock, *mod.*—*Syn.* trite, hackneyed, common; see **common** 1, **dull** 4.

stock, *n.* **1.** [Goods]—*Syn.* merchandise, produce, accumulation; see **commodity.**
2. [Livestock]—*Syn.* domestic animals, barnyard animals, farm animals; see **cow, fowl, hog** 1, **horse** 1, **sheep.**
3. [A stalk]—*Syn.* stem, plant, trunk; see **stalk.**
4. [A business share]—*Syn.* funds, assets, stocks and bonds, property, capital.
in stock—*Syn.* not sold out, stocked, not difficult to get; see **available.**
out of stock—*Syn.* sold (out *or* off), gone, not available; see **sold** 1.
take stock (of)—*Syn.* count up, inventory, figure; see **count, estimate** 1.
take stock in—*Syn.* invest (in), purchase, take a chance on; see **buy** 1.

stockade, *n.*—*Syn.* barrier, protection, enclosure; see **fence** 1.

stocking, *n.*—*Syn.* hose, hosiery, nylons; see **sock.**

stock market, *n.*—*Syn.* the market, the exchange, syndicate; see **business** 1.

stock-still, *mod.*—*Syn.* motionless, stagnant, inactive; see **idle** 1.

stock (up), *v.*—*Syn.* replenish, supply, furnish; see **buy** 1, **provide** 1.

stodgy, *mod.*—*Syn.* boring, uninteresting, tedious; see **dull** 4.

stoical, *mod.*—*Syn.* impassive, enduring, unmoved; see **indifferent** 1.

stoicism, *n.*—*Syn.* impassivity, patience, sobriety; see **indifference** 1.

stolen, *mod.*—*Syn.* taken, kept, bagged, robbed, filched, purloined, appropriated, impressed, lifted, diverted, abducted, kidnapped, shanghaied, spirited away, run off with, poached, sacked, cheated, rifled, plagiarized, embezzled, misappropriated; *all* (D): pinched, swiped, ripped off; see also **captured** 1.

stolid, *mod.* —*Syn.* unexcitable, impassive, apathetic; see **indifferent** 1.

stomach, *n.* —*Syn.* paunch, belly, breadbasket (D); see **abdomen.**

stomachache, *n.* —*Syn.* indigestion, acute indigestion, gastric upset; see **illness** 1, **pain** 1.

stone, *mod.* —*Syn.* rock, stony, rocky, flinty, adamantine, hard, rough, cragged, craggy, petrified, petrous, calciferous, calcific, lithic, calcified, become stone, petrographic, petrographical, crystallographic, lithographic, lithological, marble, granite.

stone, *n.* —*Syn.* concretion, mass, crag, cobblestone, cobble, boulder, gravel, pebble, rock, sand, grain, granite, marble, flint, gem, jewel.

cast the first stone—*Syn.* criticize, blame, reprimand; see **attack** 2, **scold.**

leave no stone unturned—*Syn.* take (great) pains *or* care, be scrupulous, try hard; see **pursue** 1, **work** 1.

stoned (D), *mod.* —*Syn.* under the influence (of drugs *or* LSD *or* heroin, etc.), drugged; *all* (D): ripped out, high, spaced out, tripping, turned on; see also **drunk, unconscious.**

stony, *mod.* —*Syn.* inflexible, cruel, unrelenting; see **firm** 2, **rough** 1.

stool, *n.* —*Syn.* seat, footstool, standrest, footrest, ottoman, hassock; see also **furniture.**

stoop, *v.* **1.** [To bow or bend]—*Syn.* incline, crouch, slant; see **bow** 1, **lean** 1.

2. [To condescend]—*Syn.* deign, patronize, look down (on); see **condescend.**

stop, *interj.* —*Syn.* cease, knock it off, cut it out, quit it, say, hey there; see also **halt** 2.

stop, *n.* **1.** [A pause]—*Syn.* halt, stay, standstill; see **end** 2, **pause** 1, 2.

2. [A stopping place]—*Syn.* station, passenger station, wayside stop; see **depot.**

pull out all the stops (D)—*Syn.* go the limit, do everything (possible), give it all one has (D); see **try** 1, **work** 1.

put a stop to—*Syn.* halt, interrupt, intervene; see **stop** 1.

stop, *v.* **1.** [To halt]—*Syn.* pause, stay, stand, lay *or* stay over, break the journey, tarry, stand still, shut down, rest, discontinue, come to a halt *or* a stand, pull up, reach a standstill, check, bivouac, cease marching, hold; *all* (D): stop dead in one's tracks, stop short, freeze (up), call it a day, stymie, box (in), knock on the head, cut short; see also **end** 1. —*Ant.* continue*, proceed, advance.

2. [To cease]—*Syn.* terminate, finish, conclude, withdraw, leave off, let *or* pull *or* fold *or* fetch *or* wind *or* bring up, relinquish, have done (with), desist, refrain, ring down, settle, discontinue, end, close, draw *or* tie *or* give up, call off, bring up, close down, break up, hold up, pull up, lapse, be at an end, cut out, die away, come off, go out, stay one's hand, run out, defect, surrender, close; *all* (D): peter out, call it a day, knock (it) off, lay off, throw in the towel, belay that, blow over, melt away, drop it, run out, write off, pipe down, save one's breath, give over, run its course; see also **halt** 2, **suspend** 2. —*Ant.* begin*, start, commence.

3. [To prevent]—*Syn.* hinder, obstruct, arrest; see **prevent.**

4. [To cause to cease]—*Syn.* arrest, check, suspend; see **halt** 2.

stop for, *v.* —*Syn.* get, accompany, go to get; see **obtain** 1, **pick up** 6.

stopgap, *mod.* —*Syn.* expedient, substitute, makeshift; see **practical, temporary.**

stopgap, *n.* —*Syn.* makeshift, expedient, resource; see **substitute.**

stopover, *n.* —*Syn.* layover, halt, pause; see **delay** 1.

stop over (*or* **by** *or* **in** *or* **off**), *v.* —*Syn.* stop to see, break a journey, stay; see **visit** 1, 2, 4.

stopped, *mod.* —*Syn.* at a halt, off the air, cut short; see **interrupted.**

stopping, *n.* —*Syn.* staying, remaining, halt, halting, holding, hesitation, pause, encumbering, wait, check, delay, block, stand-down, ending, closing, breaking off, deterring, desisting, terminating, ceasing, shutting up (D).

storage, *n.* —*Syn.* room, area, accommodation; see **storehouse, warehouse.**

store, *n.* **1.** [An establishment, especially for retail sales]—*Syn.* shop, department store, specialty shop, men's furnishing store, draper's, drygoods store, storehouse, repository, emporium, chain store, market, confectionary, business house, grocery store, *étape* (French), *godown* (Oriental), *golah* (Anglo-Indian); see also **building** 1.

2. [Stored goods]—*Syn.* wares, reserve, stocks; see **commodity, property** 1.

store, *v.* —*Syn.* put, deposit, cache, stock, store *or* stow away, lay by *or* in *or* up *or* down, put away *or* aside, lock away, bank, warehouse, stockpile, collect, squirrel away, pack away, set aside *or* apart, amass, file; *all* (D): stash, salt away *or* down, file and forget, put in moth balls, moth-ball; see also **save** 3. —*Ant.* spend*, draw out, withdraw.

stored, *mod.* —*Syn.* stocked, reserved, hoarded; see **saved** 1.

storehouse, *n.* —*Syn.* depository, warehouse, granary, magazine, silo, store, storage place, cornhouse, corncrib, barn, depot, cache, grain elevator, safe-deposit vault, armory, arsenal, argosy, repertory, repository.

storekeeper, *n.* —*Syn.* small businessman, purveyor, grocer; see **merchant.**

storied, *mod.* —*Syn.* famed, recognized, renowned; see **famous.**

storm, *n.* **1.** [A violent disturbance of the elements] —*Syn.* tempest, downpour, cloudburst, disturbance, waterspout, blizzard, snowstorm, purga, squall, hurricane, cyclone, tornado, twister, gust, blast, gale, blow, monsoon; see also **rain** 1, **wind** 1.

2. [An outbreak suggestive of a storm, sense 1] —*Syn.* anger, agitation, annoyance, commotion, turmoil, violence, perturbation, racket, temper, hubbub, rage, fury, passion, hysteria.—*Ant.* peace*, harmony, quiet.

storm, *v.* —*Syn.* blow violently, howl, blow a gale, roar, set in, squall, pour, drizzle, drop, rain, mizzle, spit, lay the dust, patter; *all* (D): rain cats and dogs, come down in bucketfuls, breathe fire and fury, rain pitchforks and hammer-handles; see also **snow.**

stormy, *mod.* **1.** [Characterized by storms]—*Syn.* rainy, wet, damp, cold, bitter, raging, roaring, frigid, windy, blustery, pouring, blustering, murky, tempestuous, turbulent, tumultuous, storming, wild, boisterous, rough, torrid, squally, dark, violent, threatening, menacing, riproaring (D).—*Ant.* mild*, clement, equable.

2. [Characterized by violent emotions]—*Syn.* savage, riotous, agitated; see **turbulent, violent** 2.

story, *n.* —*Syn.* imaginative writing, write-up, fable, narrative, tale, myth, fairy tale, anecdote, legend, account, recital, memoir, parable, apologue, fiction, novel, romance, allegory, epic, saga, fantasy, edda; see also **literature** 1.

Varieties of stories include the following—Long: novel, romance, realistic novel, comedy of manners, historical novel, biographical fiction, novelette, satire, saga, heroic poem, epic, mythological account, narrative, chronicle, *chanson de geste* (French); Short: jest, *Märchen* (German), folktale, fairy tale, apologue, fantasy, anecdote, short story, novella, ghost story, example, *exemplum* (Latin), fable, *conte devot* (French), detective story, saint's life, legend, beast tale, primitive tale, horror story, adventure story, idyll, pastoral, parable, allegory; *all* (D): short short, western, pulp.

storyteller, *n.* —*Syn.* author, relator, fabler, narrator, minstrel, teller, bard, poet, biographer, chronicler, raconteur, anecdotist, teller of tales, spinner of yarns, fabulist, fabricator, prose writer.

stout, *mod.* **1.** [Brave]—*Syn.* fearless, bold, undaunted; see **brave** 1.

2. [Heavy or fat]—*Syn.* corpulent, fleshy, portly; see **fat** 1.

3. [Strong]—*Syn.* sturdy, hardy, husky; see **strong** 1.

stove, *n.*

Varieties of stoves include the following—cooking, heating, circulating, Franklin, Norwegian, airtight, galvanized-iron, cast-iron, tile, wood, coal, oil, electric, infrared, microwave, high frequency, low frequency, atomic, portable, camp, car, tinmen's, Nuremberg; range, baseburner; see also **appliance, oven.**

stovepipe, *n.* —*Syn.* flue, funnel, smokestack; see **chimney.**

straddle, *v.* —*Syn.* bestride, ride, mount, bestraddle; see also **balance** 2, **sit** 1.

strafe, *v.* —*Syn.* bombard, storm, barrage; see **attack** 1.

straggle, *v.* —*Syn.* ramble, stray, wander; see **lag** 1, **loiter, roam** 1.

straggly, *mod.* **1.** [Rambling]—*Syn.* irregular, roving, hiking; see **rambling** 1.

2. [Untidy]—*Syn.* messy, tangled, dispersed; see **loose** 1.

straight, *mod.* **1.** [Not curved or twisted]—*Syn.* rectilinear, vertical, perpendicular, rectilineal, plumb, upright, erect, in line with, unbent, in *or* on a line *or* row, inflexible, undeviating, even, level.—*Ant.* bent*, curved, curving.

2. [Direct]—*Syn.* uninterrupted, continuous, through; see **direct** 1.

3. [Correct]—*Syn.* right, orderly, exact; see **accurate** 1.

4. [Honest]—*Syn.* good, reliable, honorable; see **decent** 2, **honest** 1, **moral** 1, **upright** 2.

5. [Unmixed]—*Syn.* out-and-out, undiluted, plain; see **concentrated** 1, **pure** 1.

go straight (D)—*Syn.* obey the law, avoid crime, live a decent life; see **behave** 2.

the straight and narrow path—*Syn.* good *or* proper conduct *or* behavior, righteousness, morality; see **honesty** 1, **virtue** 1, 2.

straighten, *v.* —*Syn.* order, compose, make straight, rectify, untwist, unsnarl, unbend, uncoil, unravel, uncurl, unfold, put straight, level, make plumb, arrange, arrange on a line, align, make upright, make perpendicular, make vertical.—*Ant.* bend*, twist, curl.

straighten out, *v.* —*Syn.* **1.** [To settle]—*Syn.* conclude, set at rest, figure out; see **decide, govern** 1.

2. [To put in order]—*Syn.* tidy, clean up, arrange; see **straighten.**

straighten up, *v.* **1.** [To make neat]—*Syn.* tidy, arrange, fix; see **clean, straighten.**

2. [To stand up]—*Syn.* rise up, arise, be upright; see **rise** 6, **stand** 1.

straightforward, *mod.* —*Syn.* sincere, candid, outspoken; see **frank, honest** 1.

straightway, *mod.* —*Syn.* at once, directly, promptly; see **immediately.**

strain, *n.* **1.** [Effort]—*Syn.* exertion, struggle, endeavor; see **effort** 1.

2. [Mental tension]—*Syn.* anxiety, tension, pressure; see **stress** 3.

3. [A bodily injury less than a sprain]—*Syn.* wrench, twist, stretch, ache, jerk, bruise.

4. [Pressure]—*Syn.* tension, force, pull; see **stress** 2.

strain, *v.* **1.** [To exert]—*Syn.* strive, endeavor, labor; see **try** 1.

2. [To wrench]—*Syn.* twist, sprain, distort; see **hurt** 1, **wrench.**

3. [To stretch]—*Syn.* rack, extend, draw (tight); see **stretch** 2, **tighten** 1.

4. [To filter]—*Syn.* refine, purify, screen; see **filter** 2, **sift** 2.

strained, *mod.* —*Syn.* forced, constrained, tense; see **difficult** 1.

strainer, *n.* —*Syn.* mesh, filter, colander; see **sieve.**

strait, *n.* **1.** [A channel]—*Syn.* inlet, canal, sound; see **channel** 1.

2. [Difficulty]—*Syn.* distress, crisis, plight; see **difficulty** 1, 2.

straiten, *v.* **1.** [Distress]—*Syn.* perplex, corner, fluster; see **confuse, embarrass** 1.

2. [To limit]—*Syn.* contract, confine, constrain; see **hinder, restrict** 2.

strait jacket, *n.* —*Syn.* jacket, confining jacket, jacket for violently insane people; see **chains.**

strait-laced, *mod.* —*Syn.* strict, severe, stiff; see **prudish.**

strand, *n.* —*Syn.* beach, coast, seacoast; see **shore.**

stranded, *mod.* —*Syn.* aground, beached, ashore; see **abandoned** 1.

strange, *mod.* **1.** [Little known]—*Syn.* foreign, external, exotic, outside, without, detached, apart, faraway, remote, alien, unexplored, isolated, unrelated, irrelevant; see also **unfamiliar** 2, **unknown** 1, 2, 3, **unnatural** 1.—*Ant.* familiar*, present, close.

2. [Not acquainted]—*Syn.* ignorant of, without knowledge of, uninformed about, unfamiliar, unheard of, newfangled, new, not versed in, unaccustomed to, novel.—*Ant.* old*, prevailing, current.

3. [Unusual]—*Syn.* exceptional, rare, uncommon; see **unusual** 1, 2.

strangely, *mod.* —*Syn.* oddly, queerly, newly, unfamiliarly, unnaturally, uncommonly, exceptionally, remarkably, rarely, fantastically, amazingly, surprisingly, startlingly, strikingly, singularly, unutterably, indescribably, peculiarly, ineffably, uniquely, unusually, uncustomarily, astonishingly, exotically, marvelously.—*Ant.* regularly*, commonly, usually.

strangeness, *n.* —*Syn.* newness, unfamiliarity, exoticism, novelty, abnormality, singularity, eccentricity, fantasticality, remoteness, indescribability, esotericism, esoterism, sense of being alien, unaccustomed quality, strange nature, unfamiliar surroundings, feeling of newness.—*Ant.* familiarity*, acquaintanceship, homelike quality.

stranger, *n.* —*Syn.* foreigner, outsider, outlander, newcomer, unknown *or* unexpected *or* uninvited *or* migrant *or* itinerant person, visitor, guest, immigrant, intruder, interloper, new boy *or* girl in town *or* in school, stranger within the gates, floater, drifter, squatter, migratory worker; *all* (D): perfect *or* complete stranger, foreign body, wetback, member of a different mob, gate *or* party crasher; see also **alien.**—*Ant.* inhabitant*, citizen, native.

strangle, *v.* **1.** [To smother]—*Syn.* asphyxiate, suffocate, kill; see **choke** 1.

2. [To suppress]—*Syn.* subdue, stifle, repress; see **restrain** 1, **suppress.**

strap, *n.*—*Syn.* thong, strop, leash; see **band** 1.

strapped (D), *mod.* —*Syn.* impoverished, out of money, broke (D); see **poor** 1.

strapping (D), *mod.* —*Syn.* big, tall, powerful; see **heavy** 1, **high** 1, **strong** 2.

stratagem, *n.* —*Syn.* trick, deception, plot, scheme; see **method** 2.

strategic, *mod.* **1.** [Clever]—*Syn.* cunning, diplomatic, tricky; see **dishonest** 1.

2. [Crucial]—*Syn.* vital, decisive, imperative; see **important** 1, **necessary** 1.

strategist, *n.* —*Syn.* tactician, schemer, contriver; see **administrator.**

strategy, *n.* **1.** [Tactics]—*Syn.* approach, maneuvering, procedure; see **tactics.**

2. [Cunning]—*Syn.* plan, artifice, craft; see **policy, tact.**

stratification, *n.* —*Syn.* tabular structure, lamination, scaliness, delamination; see also **layer.**

stratified, *mod.* —*Syn.* layered, flaky, laminated, stratiform, scaly, squamous.

stratify, *v.* —*Syn.* laminate, flake, scale; see **plate.**

stratum, *n.* —*Syn.* seam, tier, level; see **layer.**

straw, *n.* Straws and strawlike fibers include the following—oat, wheat, barley, rye, rice, buckwheat, bean, pea, buri, *jipijapa* (Spanish), palm, palmetto; see also **hay.**

grasp at straws *or* **a straw** (D)—*Syn.* panic attempt, be desperate *or* excited *or* frightened; see **fear** 1, **try** 1.

a straw in the wind (D)—*Syn.* evidence, indication, signal; see **sign** 1.

strawberry, *mod.* —*Syn.* carmine, strawberry-red, rose, rose-red, deep rose; see also **red, rose.**

strawberry, *n.* —*Syn.* bragaria; *all* (D): everbearing, queen of berries, the perfect berry; see also **berry** 1, **fruit** 1.

straw man, *n.* —*Syn.* weak *or* feeble argument *or* position, blind, statement to be refuted, Aunt Sally (British); see **fake, nonsense** 2.

straw vote, *n.* —*Syn.* opinion poll, unofficial ballot, dry run (D); see **opinion** 1, **vote** 1, 2.

stray, *v.* —*Syn.* rove, roam, swerve, go amiss *or* astray, deviate; see also **turn** 3, **walk** 1.

strayed, *mod.* —*Syn.* wandered, vagrant, roaming; see **lost** 1.

streak, *n.* —*Syn.* stripe, strip, ridge; see **band** 1.

like a streak—*Syn.* like lightning, swift, speedy; see **fast** 1, **rapid** 2.

streaky, *mod.* —*Syn.* streaked, smudgy, veined; see **striped.**

stream, *n.* —*Syn.* current, rivulet, brook; see **river** 1, **water** 2.

stream, *v.* —*Syn.* gush, run, flow; see **flow** 1, 2.

streamer, *n.* **1.** [Banner]—*Syn.* standard, pennant, banner; see **flag** 1.

2. [Headline]—*Syn.* title, screamer, caption; see **head** 9.

streamlined, *mod.* —*Syn.* modernized, sleek, offering low wind resistance; see **modern** 1, **smooth** 1.

street, *n.* —*Syn.* highway, way, lane, path, avenue, thoroughfare, boulevard, terrace, place, road, mews, route, artery, parkway, court, cross street, esplanade, boardwalk, row, embankment, square, piazza, close, alley, circle, dead end, passage, mall, circus, arcade, *via* (Italian), *rue* (French), *Strasse* (German).

streetcar, *n.* —*Syn.* tram, tramcar, trolley car, trolley, passenger car, bus, trackless trolley; see also **vehicle** 1.

streetwalker, *n.* —*Syn.* whore, hustler, harlot; see **prostitute.**

strength, *n.* **1.** [Power]—*Syn.* vigor, brawn, energy, nerve, vitality, sinews, muscle, backbone, physique, thews, stoutness, health, toughness, fortitude, sturdiness, hardiness, stalwartness, tenacity, mana, robustness, soundness, durability.—*Ant.* weakness*, feebleness, loss of energy.

2. [Intensity]—*Syn.* depth, concentration, fervor; see **force** 3, **intensity** 1.

on the strength of—*Syn.* reassured by, in view of, as a result (of); see **because, since** 1.

strengthen, *v.* —*Syn.* intensify, add, invigorate, fortify, encourage, confirm, increase, multiply, empower, arm, energize, harden, reactivate, steel, brace, buttress, stimulate, sustain, nerve, animate, reanimate, restore, reman, refresh, recover, hearten, establish, toughen, temper, bear out, rejuvenate, tone up, build up, make firm, stiffen, brace up, rally, sharpen, enliven, give weight, carry weight, substantiate, uphold, back, augment, enlarge, extend, mount, rise, ascend, wax, grow, back up, beef up (D).—*Ant.* weaken*, cripple, tear down.

strenuous, *mod.* —*Syn.* vigorous, ardent, zealous; see **difficult** 1.

strenuously, *mod.* —*Syn.* hard, laboriously, energetically; see **industriously, vigorously.**

stress, *n.* **1.** [Importance]—*Syn.* significance, weight, import; see **importance** 1.
2. [Pressure]—*Syn.* strain, tension, force, stretch, tautness, traction, pull, tensity, distention, eulogation, draw, extension, protraction, intensity, tightness, spring; see also **pressure** 1.
3. [Mental tension]—*Syn.* tension, strain, pressure, burden, hardship, overexertion, agony, trial, affliction, anxiety, nervousness, fearfulness, apprehensiveness, apprehension, impatience, fear, ferment, disquiet, disquietude, tenseness, passion, intensity, fluster, expectancy, restlessness, trepidation, misgiving, mistrust, alarm, dread, flutter, trembling, pinch, urgency; *both* (D): jitters, heeby-jeebies. —*Ant.* peace*, calm, quiet.

stress, *v.* —*Syn.* accent, make emphatic, accentuate; see **emphasize.**

stretch, *n.* —*Syn.* extent, compass, range, reach; see **time** 1.

stretch, *v.* **1.** [To become longer]—*Syn.* grow, expand, be extended, extend oneself, spread, unfold, increase, swell, spring up, shoot up, open, burst forth.—*Ant.* contract*, shrink, wane.
2. [To cause to stretch, sense 1]—*Syn.* tighten, strain, make tense, draw, draw out, elongate, extend, develop, distend, inflate, lengthen, magnify, amplify, spread out, widen, pull out of shape *or* into shape, draw tight, make taut, tauten.—*Ant.* relax*, let go, slacken.
3. [To occupy space]—*Syn.* extend across, range, extend to, spread over, cover a given distance; see also **occupy** 2, **reach** 1.

stretcher, *n.* —*Syn.* litter, cot, portable bed; see **bed** 1.

strew, *v.* —*Syn.* spread, toss, cover; see **scatter** 2.

stricken, *mod.* —*Syn.* wounded, injured, harmed; see **hurt.**

strict, *mod.* —*Syn.* stringent, stern, austere; see **severe** 2.

strictly, *mod.* —*Syn.* rigidly, rigorously, stringently; see **surely.**

stricture, *n.* **1.** [Censure]—*Syn.* criticism, obloquy, rebuke; see **blame** 1.
2. [Constriction]—*Syn.* tightness, choking, strangulation, check, squeezing, astringency, binding, control, contraction, compression, shrinking; see also **restraint** 2.

stride, *n.* —*Syn.* walk, pace, measured step; see **gait** 1.
hit one's stride (D)—*Syn.* become *or* get up to normal, get better, arrive; see **develop** 1, **improve.**
take in one's stride (D)—*Syn.* handle, do easily *or* naturally, deal with; see **manage** 1.

stride, *v.* —*Syn.* stamp, march, walk pompously; see **walk** 1.

strident, *mod.* —*Syn.* shrill, grating, vociferous; see **loud** 1.

strife, *n.* **1.** [Verbal contention]—*Syn.* quarrel, animosity, conflict; see **disagreement.**
2. [Physical struggle]—*Syn.* fighting, struggle, combat; see **fight** 1.

strike, *n.* **1.** [An organized refusal]—*Syn.* walkout, deadlock, work stoppage, quitting, sit-down (strike), job action, sickout, tie-up, *heuga* (Spanish) *brazos caidos* (Spanish), slowdown, called strike, sympathetic strike, general strike, wildcat strike, token strike, confrontation; *all* (D): sit-in, teach-in, study-in, blue flu, love-in, mill-in; see also **revolution** 2.
2. [A discovery]—*Syn.* gold strike, success, find, unfolding, exposure, disclosure, opening up, laying bare, bringing to light, uncovering; see also **discovery** 1.
3. [A blow]—*Syn.* hit, stroke, punch; see **blow** 1.
4. [A pitched ball]—*Syn.* ball one *or* two *or* three, pitch *or* one over the plate, called strike; see **pitch** 2.
have two strikes against one (D)—*Syn.* be in danger *or* trouble, be uncertain *or* troubled, be handicapped; see **doubt** 2, **fear** 1.
(out) on strike—*Syn.* striking, protesting, on the picket line; see **unemployed.**

strike, *v.* **1.** [To hit]—*Syn.* box, punch, thump; see **beat** 2, **hit** 1.
2. [To refuse to work]—*Syn.* walk out, tie up, sit down, slow down, go out, be on strike, sit in, arbitrate, negotiate a contract, picket, boycott, stop, quit, enforce idleness, resist, hold out for, hit the bricks (D); see also **oppose** 1, 2, **rebel** 1.
3. [To light]—*Syn.* kindle, inflame, scratch; see **burn** 1, **ignite.**
4. [To seem]—*Syn.* look, have the semblance, be plausible; see **seem.**
5. [To find]—*Syn.* uncover, open up, lay bare; see **discover** 1.

strike a balance, *v.* —*Syn.* compromise, make mutual concessions, make an adjustment, give and take, meet halfway; see also **adjust** 1, **arbitrate, negotiate** 1.

strike a light, *v.* —*Syn.* illuminate, strike a match, light up; see **burn** 1, **ignite, light** 1.

strike it rich (D), *v.* —*Syn.* strike *or* find oil *or* gold *or* iron, *etc.*, become wealthy, make money; see **prosper.**

strike out, *v.* **1.** [To begin something new]—*Syn.* start (out), initiate, find a new approach; see **begin** 1.
2. [To cancel]—*Syn.* obliterate, invalidate, expunge; see **cancel** 1, **remove** 1.
3. [In baseball, to be out on strikes]—*Syn.* be struck out, be called out, make an out; *all* (D): fan, whiff, bat the breeze, go down swinging, be unable to see 'em.

striker (D), *n.* —*Syn.* holdout, turnout; *both* (D): walk-outer, sit-downer; see also **protestor.**

striking, *mod.* —*Syn.* attractive, conspicuous, noticeable, impressive, surprising, astonishing, electrifying, stunning, staggering, confounding, unusual, unwonted, singular, remarkable, extraordinary, dazzling, startling, fascinating, noteworthy, distinguished, memorable, outlandish, bizarre; see also **beautiful** 1, 2, **charming, handsome** 2.—*Ant.* ugly*, common, dull.

string, *n.* **1.** [A sequence]—*Syn.* chain, succession, procession; see **line** 1, **order** 3, **sequence** 1, **series.**
2. [Twine]—*Syn.* cord, twist, strand; see **rope, twine.**

string along (with) (D), *v.* —*Syn.* bow *or* accede to, accept, tolerate; see **agree, follow** 2.

string bean, *n.* —*Syn.* green bean, snap bean. Varieties include the following—green, wax, pole, bush, Italian, Kentucky wonder, French-cut, stringless; see also **bean** 2, **food, vegetable.**

stringent, *mod.* **1.** [Strict]—*Syn.* acrimonious, rigorous, harsh; see **severe** 2.
2. [Compelling]—*Syn.* forceful, powerful, poignant; see **convincing** 2, **valid** 1, 2.

string of beads, *n.* —*Syn.* chain, beads, neckband; see **necklace.**

string up (D), *v.* —*Syn.* hang, kill *or* execute (by hanging), hang by the neck until dead; see **kill** 1.

stringy, *mod.* **1.** [Fibrous]—*Syn.* wiry, ropy, threadlike; see **fibrous.**
2. [Viscous]—*Syn.* pasty, gluey, gummy; see **sticky.**

strip, *n.* —*Syn.* tape, slip, shred; see **band** 1, **layer, piece** 1.

strip, *v.* **1.** [Undress]—*Syn.* divest, disrobe, become naked; see **undress.**
2. [Remove]—*Syn.* displace, tear, lift off; see **peel, remove** 1, **shred.**

stripe, *n.* —*Syn.* line, division, strip, discoloration, varicolor, contrasting color, band, border, decoration, demarcation, ribbon; see also **layer.**

striped, *mod.* —*Syn.* lined, barred, banded; see **ruled** 2.

stripling, *n.* —*Syn.* fledgling, youngster, minor; see **youth** 3.

strive, *v.* —*Syn.* endeavor, aim, attempt; see **try** 1.

stroke, *n.* —*Syn.* box, cuff, rap; see **blow** 1.

stroll, *v.* —*Syn.* ramble, saunter, gallivant; see **roam** 1, **walk** 1.

strong, *mod.* **1.** [Physically strong; *said especially of persons*]—*Syn.* robust, sturdy, firm, muscular, sinewy, thewy, vigorous, stout, hardy, big, heavy, husky, lusty, active, potent, energetic, tough, virile, doughty, mighty, athletic, able-bodied, powerful, manly, heavy-set, stalwart, brawny, burly, wiry, strapping; *all* (D): having what it takes, hard as nails, made of iron, in fine feather, having the makings.—*Ant.* weak*, emaciated, feeble.
2. [Physically strong; *said especially of things*] —*Syn.* solid, sturdy, firm, staunch, unimpaired, well-established, well-founded, well-built, secure, tough, durable, able, unyielding, steady, stable, fixed, sound, powerful, mighty, tough, well-made, rugged, substantial, reinforced.—*Ant.* unstable*, insecure, tottering.
3. [Healthy]—*Syn.* sound, hale, hearty; see **sense** 1, **healthy** 1.
4. [Firm]—*Syn.* steadfast, determined, staunch; see **resolute** 2.
5. [Intelligent]—*Syn.* sagacious, clear-headed, perceptive; see **intelligent** 1.
6. [Powerful]—*Syn.* great, mighty, influential; see **powerful** 1.
7. [Extreme]—*Syn.* drastic, forceful, strict; see **extreme** 2.
8. [Potent in effect]—*Syn.* powerful, potent, high-powered, stiff, power-packed, effective, hard, high-potency, stimulating, inebriating, intoxicating; *both* (D): hot, spiked.
9. [Undiluted]—*Syn.* straight, rich, unmixed; see **concentrated** 1.
10. [Intense]—*Syn.* sharp, acute, keen; see **intense.**
11. [Distinct]—*Syn.* clear, marked, sharp; see **definite** 2, **obvious** 1, 2.
12. [Competent]—*Syn.* adept, proficient, skilled; see **able.**
13. [Financially sound]—*Syn.* stable, solid, safe; see **reliable** 2.
14. [Convincing]—*Syn.* cogent, potent, forceful; see **persuasive.**
come on strong (D)—*Syn.* increase, develop, get better; see **improve.**

strongbox, *n.* —*Syn.* box, coffer, depository; see **safe, vault** 2.

stronger, *n.* —*Syn.* the better, the mightier, the more successful, the more capable, the stronger-willed, the more promising one, the more vigorous, the likelier (D).

strongest, *mod.* —*Syn.* mightiest, stoutest, firmest, hardiest, healthiest, most vigorous, most active, most intense, most capable, most masterful, sturdiest, most courageous, strongest-willed, most efficient, most efficacious.—*Ant.* weak*, feeblest, most timid.

strong for (D), *mod.* —*Syn.* approving, favorable (to), supporting; see **favorable** 3.

stronghold, *n.* —*Syn.* fortress, citadel, castle; see **fortification** 2.

strongly, *mod.* —*Syn.* stoutly, vigorously, actively, heavily, fully, completely, sturidly, robustly, energetically, firmly, stanchly, solidly, securely, immovably, steadily, heartily, forcibly, resolutely, capably, powerfully, invincibly, indomitably, influentially, greatly, richly, well.

strop, *v.* —*Syn.* strap, grind, hone; see **sharpen** 1.

struck, *mod.* **1.** [Hit]—*Syn.* smacked, pounded, hurt; see **hit** 1.
2. [Closed by a strike]—*Syn.* shut down, having labor trouble, idle; see **closed** 2.

structural, *mod.* —*Syn.* constructural, fundamental, basic, organic, formative, skeletal, anatomic, anatomical, formational, formalistic, architectural, tectonic, geotectonic.—*Ant.* tangled*, chaotic, unorganized.

structural linguistics, *n.* —*Syn.* structural analysis, structure, new grammar; see **grammar, language** 2.

structure, *n.* **1.** [Construction]—*Syn.* arrangement, composition, fabrication; see **formation** 1.
2. [A building]—*Syn.* house, pile, erection; see **building** 1.

struggle, *n.* —*Syn.* conflict, contest, strife; see **fight** 1.

struggle, *v.* —*Syn.* strive, grapple, cope; see **fight** 1.

strum, *v.* —*Syn.* tweak, pluck, pick; see **play** 3.

strumpet, *n.* —*Syn.* streetwalker, whore, harlot; see **prostitute.**

strut, *v.* —*Syn.* swagger, walk pompously, stride proudly, walk with a strut; see also **walk** 1.

stub, *n.* —*Syn.* stump, short end, snag, root, remainder, remnant, dock, counterfoil.

stubborn, *mod.* —*Syn.* unreasonable, unyielding, headstrong; see **obstinate** 1, **resolute** 2.

stubbornly, *mod.* —*Syn.* persistently, doggedly, tenaciously; see **firmly** 2, **obstinately.**

stubbornness, *n.* —*Syn.* obstinacy, doggedness, inflexibility, pertinacity, indomitability, perverseness, perversity, contumacy, obduracy, adamancy, refractoriness, mulishness, sullenness, pigheadedness, stupidity, intractableness, bullheadedness, moroseness; see also **determination** 2.—*Ant.* flexibility*, amenability, good nature.

stubby, *mod.* —*Syn.* chubby, stout, stocky; see **fat** 1, **short** 1.

stucco, *n.* —*Syn.* cement stucco, plaster, concrete, pebbledash; see also **cement.**

stuck, *mod.* **1.** [Tight]—*Syn.* fast, fastened, cemented; see **tight** 2.

2. [Stranded]—*Syn.* grounded, lost, high and dry (D); see **abandoned** 1.

3. [Perplexed]—*Syn.* at a loss, puzzled, baffled; see **doubtful** 2.

stud, *n.* —*Syn.* studding, framing, upright; see **post** 1, **stick.**

student, *n.* —*Syn.* learner, disciple, undergraduate, coed (D), novice, high school *or* junior college *or* college student, graduate (student), pupil, docent, apprentice, registrant.

studied, *mod.* **1.** [Deliberate]—*Syn.* plotted, prepared, premeditated; see **deliberate** 1, **planned.**

2. [Investigated]—*Syn.* thought about *or* through, examined, gone into; see **investigated, reviewed.**

studio, *n.* —*Syn.* workshop, atelier, workroom, salon, broadcasting room, radio station.

studious, *mod.* —*Syn.* industrious, thoughtful, contemplative, busy, well-read, well-informed, scholarly, lettered, academic, learned, bookish, earnest, diligent, assiduous, attentive, sedulous, loving study, given to study.—*Ant.* lazy*, unproductive, capricious.

study, *n.* **1.** [A place in which to study]—*Syn.* schoolroom, library, studio; see **office** 3, **room** 2.

2. [The act of studying]—*Syn.* research, investigation, memorizing, learning, reading, inquiry, examination, consideration, questioning, analyzing, comparison, thought, reflection, reasoning; see also **education** 1.

3. [That which one studies]—*Syn.* subject, branch of learning, field of knowledge, art; see also **knowledge** 1.

study, *v.* **1.** [To endeavor to learn]—*Syn.* read, go into, refresh the memory, read up on, burn the midnight oil, bone up, go over, cram, think, go in for, inquire, bury oneself in, dive into, plunge into.

2. [To endeavor to understand]—*Syn.* do research, compare, analyze; see **examine** 1, **learn** 1.

study up on (D), *v.* —*Syn.* prepare (oneself) (on), become conversant (with), go over *or* into, do one's homework (D); see also **prepare** 1, **study** 1.

stuff, *n.* **1.** [Material]—*Syn.* elemental part, principle, essence; see **material** 2.

2. [Cloth]—*Syn.* tissue, web, textile; see **cloth.**

stuff, *v.* —*Syn.* ram, pad, wad; see **fill** 1, **pack** 2.

stuffed, *mod.* —*Syn.* crowded, packed, crammed; see **full** 1.

stuffed shirt (D), *n.* —*Syn.* phony (D), pompous person *or* individual, incompetent; see **braggart, fake, imposter.**

stuffing, *n.* **1.** [Material used to pad]—*Syn.* packing, wadding, padding, quilting, calking, filler, packing material.

Stuffings include the following—wool, cotton, kapok, sisal, feathers, fur, waste, cotton waste, rags, batting, excelsior, horsehair, shredded paper, sawdust, moss.

2. [Material used to stuff fowl, fish, etc.]—*Syn.* dressing, forcemeat, filling; see **dressing.**

stuffy, *mod.* **1.** [Close]—*Syn.* confined, stagnant, muggy; see **close** 5.

2. [(D) Conservative]—*Syn.* conventional, stody, uninteresting; see **conservative, dull** 3, 4, **old-fashioned.**

stultify, *v.* **1.** [To ridicule]—*Syn.* scoff at, deride, mock; see **bother** 3, **ridicule.**

2. [To prevent]—*Syn.* check, stop, repress; see **prevent.**

stumble, *v.* **1.** [To move in a stumbling manner] —*Syn.* blunder, flounder, lurch, falter; see also **waver.**

2. [To trip]—*Syn.* pitch, tilt, topple; see **fall** 1, **trip** 1.

stumbling block, *n.* —*Syn.* obstacle, hindrance, barricade; see **barrier, difficulty** 1, 2.

stump, *n.* —*Syn.* butt, piece, projection; see **end** 4.

stumped (D), *mod.* —*Syn.* puzzled, baffled, up a stump (D); see **bewildered** 2, **uncertain** 2.

stumpy, *mod.* —*Syn.* stubby, short and thick, chunky; see **fat** 1, **heavy.**

stun, *v.* **1.** [To render unconscious]—*Syn.* hit, put to sleep, knock out; see **deaden** 1, **drug.**

2. [To astound]—*Syn.* astonish, bewilder, amaze; see **surprise** 1.

stunned, *mod.* —*Syn.* dazed, astonished, amazed; see **shocked.**

stunning, *mod.* —*Syn.* striking, astounding, marvelous, astonishing, remarkable; see also **beautiful** 1, 2, **charming, handsome** 2.

stunt (D), *n.* —*Syn.* act, skit, comic sketch; see **performance** 2.

stupefaction, *n.* —*Syn.* astonishment, amazement, surprise; see **stupor, wonder** 1.

stupefied, *mod.* —*Syn.* astonished, astounded, amazed; see **bewildered, surprised.**

stupefy, *v.* **1.** [To stun]—*Syn.* dull, numb, benumb; see **deaden** 1.

2. [To amaze]—*Syn.* astound, astonish, startle; see **surprise** 1.

stupendous, *mod.* —*Syn.* breathtaking, marvelous, miraculous; see **grand** 2.

stupid, *mod.* **1.** [Foolish]—*Syn.* senseless, brainless, idiotic, simple, shallow, ill-advised, imprudent, witless, irrational, inane, ridiculous, mindless, ludicrous, blind (to), muddled, absurd, half-witted, funny, comical, silly, laughable, nonsensical, daft, illogical, indiscreet, unintelligent, irresponsible, coquettish, shallow-brained, scatterbrained, crackbrained, addled, inconsistent, flirting, unwary, incautious, misguided, wild, injudicious, imbecile, addleheaded, lunatic, insane, mad, crazy, moronic, touched, freakish, comic, puerile, inexpedient, narrow-minded, incoherent, childish, anile, senile, monstrous, outrageous, far-fetched, extravagant, preposterous, unreasonable, chimerical, asinine, useless, unwise, thoughtless, careless, vain, fatuous, light, light-headed, flighty, madcap, giddy; *all* (D): cuckoo, dippy, not seeking for looking, boneheaded, goofy, cracked, dumb, half-baked, in the dark, having a block for a head, not knowing what's what, in darkness, dead to the world, in a daze, knowing nothing, groping in the dark, green, wacky, harebrained, tetched, damn-fool, block-

headed, not seeing an inch beyond one's nose, screwy, bats, cock-eyed, loony, batty, nutty.—*Ant.* sane*, wise, judicious.
2. [Dull]—*Syn.* dense, obtuse, dull-witted; see **dull** 3, **shallow** 2.

stupidity, *n.* **1.** [Dullness of mind]—*Syn.* stupor, stupefaction, apathy, slowness, inertia, heaviness, obtuseness, sluggishness, stolidity, feeble-mindedness, folly, weakness, silliness, nonsense, absurdity, imbecility, imprudence, lunacy, simplicity, idiocy, brainlessness, shallowness, weak-mindedness, fatuousness, fatuity, incapacity, short-sightedness, poverty of intellect, impracticality, addle-headedness, dullness of comprehension, puerility, senility, ineptitude, giddiness, thick-headedness, asininity, muddleheadedness, slowness, lack of judgment, injudiciousness, unfeelingness, stupidness, slowwittedness, bluntness, emptiness of mind, insensibility, doltishness, lack of intelligence, mental deficiency, fatuity; *all* (D): boobishness, nitwittedness, dippiness, battiness, balminess, goofiness, baloney, nertz, bull, hooey, piffle, phooey, blatherskite. —*Ant.* wisdom*, intelligence, judgment.
2. [Extreme folly]—*Syn.* witlessness, senselessness, idiocy, imbecility, lunacy, nonsensicality, nonsense, indiscretion, ludicrousness, absurdity, asininity, silliness, simplicity, ineptitude, madness, infatuation, giddiness, rashness, frivolity, irrationality; *both* (D): dadaism, damn-foolishness; see also **carelessness.** —*Ant.* acumen*, shrewdness, canniness.
3. [A stupid act]—*Syn.* foolishness, folly, madness, imbecility, misguidedness, the bright thing to do (D); see also sense 2.

stupidly, *mod.* —*Syn.* imprudently, stubbornly, obtusely; see **foolishly, rashly.**

stupor, *n.*—*Syn.* insensibility, lethargy, apathy, stupefaction, asphyxia, swoon, coma, fainting, swooning, unconsciousness, numbness, torpor, syncope, narcosis, somnolence, anaesthesia, trance, hypnosis, inertness, analgesia, suspended animation, amazement, bewilderment.

sturdy, *mod.* —*Syn.* firm, resolute, unyielding; see **strong** 1, 2.

stutter, *v.* —*Syn.* stumble, falter, sputter; see **stammer.**

sty, *n.*—*Syn.* den, hovel, tumble-down shack; see **dump, pen** 1.

stygian, *mod.* —*Syn.* infernal, dreary, gloomy; see **dark** 1, **dismal** 1.

style, *n.* **1.** [Distinctive manner]—*Syn.* way, form, technique; see **method** 2.
2. [Fashion]—*Syn.* vogue, habit, custom; see **fashion** 2.
3. [Behavior]—*Syn.* carriage, bearing, manner; see **behavior** 1, **characteristic, habit** 1.

stylish, *mod.* —*Syn.* chic, smart, in fashion; see **fashionable.**

stylist, *n.*—*Syn.* romanticist, impressionist, classicist; see **author** 1, 2, **composer, writer.**

stylize, *v.*—*Syn.* conventionalize, formalize, accord; see **conform.**

stylus, *n.*—*Syn.* graver, stylograph, burin; see **knife, pen** 3.

stymie (D), *v.* —*Syn.* block, impede, obstruct; see **hinder.**

suave, *mod.* —*Syn.* sophisticated, agreeable, urbane; see **cultured, pleasant** 1.

subaltern, *mod.* —*Syn.* servile, inferior, secondary; see **subject** 1, **subordinate.**

subaqueous, *mod.* —*Syn.* underwater, submarine, submersed; see **undersea.**

subconscious, *mod.* —*Syn.* subliminal, innermost, inmost; see **mental** 2.

subconscious, *n.* —*Syn.* subliminal, essence, mind; see **psyche, soul** 2.

subdivide, *v.* —*Syn.* part, redivide, partition; see **divide** 1.

subdivision, *n.* **1.** [A class]—*Syn.* group, subclass, smaller *or* lower *or* subsidiary *or* minor, etc., group *or* class; see **class** 1, **division** 2.
2. [A tract]—*Syn.* (new) development, (building) lots, community; see **tract.**

subject, *mod.* **1.** [Under rule]—*Syn.* governed, ruled, controlled, directed, obedient, submissive, subaltern, servile, slavish, subservient, subjected, at one's feet, at the mercy of.
2. [Dependent]—*Syn.* liable (to), contingent on, subject to, dependent on, open to, accountable to, answerable to; see also **subordinate.**

subject, *n.* **1.** [Matter for discussion]—*Syn.* substance, matter, theme, material, topic, thesis, text, question, problem, theorem, motion, resolution, point, case, gist, matter in hand, subject for inquiry, item on the agenda, topic under consideration, field of inquiry, head, chapter, proposition, argument, thought, discussion.
2. [A title]—*Syn.* head, caption, legend; see **name** 1, **title** 1.

subject, *v.* —*Syn.* control, tame, master, subdue, reduce, subjugate, enslave, vanquish, defeat, rule, enthrall, dominate, subordinate, make subservient, suppress, constrain, Finlandize, restrain, lead captive; see also **govern** 1, **hinder.**—*Ant.* liberate*, release, rescue.

subjection, *n.* —*Syn.* bondage, subservience, servitude, colonialism, servility, dependence, subordination; see also **slavery** 1.

subjective, *mod.* **1.** [Not objective]—*Syn.* nonobjective, biased, personal; see **individual** 1, **prejudiced.**
2. [Related to the mind]—*Syn.* illusory, fanciful, resulting from a mental construct; see **mental** 2.

subjectively, *mod.* —*Syn.* internally, intrinsically, individually, immanently, self-centeredly, egocentrically, mentally, nonobjectively, emotionally, inner, interior, inherently, introspectively; see also **personally** 2.

subject matter, *n.* —*Syn.* essentials, contents, essence; see **subject** 1, **topic.**

subject of (*or* **under**) **discussion,** *n.* —*Syn.* question, point, matter in hand; see **subject** 1, **topic.**

subjoin, *v.* —*Syn.* append, postfix, suffix; see **join** 1.

subjugate, *v.* **1.** [Subdue]—*Syn.* suppress, enslave, master; see **defeat** 1, **hinder, restrain** 1, **subject.**
2. [To conquer]—*Syn.* overcome, crush, triumph over; see **defeat** 2.

subjugated, *mod.* —*Syn.* ruled, controlled, directed; see **governed** 1, **subject** 1.

sublet, *v.* —*Syn.* sublease, underlet, lease; see **rent** 1, 2.

sublimate, *v.* **1.** [To purify]—*Syn.* cleanse, refine, uphold; see **clean, purify.**
2. [To repress]—*Syn.* hide, conceal, obscure; see **suppress.**
sublime, *mod.*—*Syn.* exalted, lofty, stately; see **grand** 2, **noble** 1, 2.
sublimity, *n.*—*Syn.* importance, eminence, esteem; see **grandeur.**
submarine, *n.*—*Syn.* underseas boat, submersible, sub (D); see **ship, warship.**
submerge, *v.* **1.** [To cause to sink]—*Syn.* submerse, engulf, swamp; see **immerse** 1, **sink** 2.
2. [To go downward]—*Syn.* descend, immerse, subside; see **sink** 1.
submersed, *mod.*—*Syn.* submerged, underwater, marine; see **wet** 1.
submission, *n.* **1.** [Resignation]—*Syn.* obedience, meekness, assent; see **docility, resignation** 1.
2. [Subjection]—*Syn.* prostration, servility, cringing; see **slavery** 1.
submissive, *mod.*—*Syn.* passive, tractable, yielding; see **docile.**
submit, *v.* **1.** [To offer]—*Syn.* tender, proffer, present; see **offer** 1.
2. [To surrender]—*Syn.* capitulate, resign, relinquish; see **obey** 1, **yield** 1.
3. [To suggest]—*Syn.* advise, suggest, offer; see **propose** 1.
subnormal, *mod.*—*Syn.* witless, inane, foolish; see **dull** 3, **stupid** 1.
subordinate, *n.*—*Syn.* assistant, helper, aide; see **assistant.**
subordinate, *mod.*—*Syn.* inferior, junior, smaller, sub, low, baser, underaverage, insignificant, subnormal, paltry, playing second fiddle, not hold a candle to, not up to snuff, below par, below the mark, unequal to, not comparable to, in the shade, nothing to brag about, at a low ebb, lower, minor, depending on, lower in rank, subject, subservient, being a satellite, submissive, subsidiary, accessory, auxiliary, ancillary; see also **secondary** 1, **under** 2, 3.—*Ant.* superior*, higher, excellent.
subordination, *n.*—*Syn.* subjection, submission, servitude; see **slavery.**
subpoena, *n.*—*Syn.* summons, warrant, citation; see **command** 1.
subpoena, *v.*—*Syn.* cite, arraign, call; see **summon** 1.
sub rosa (Latin), *mod.*—*Syn.* obscurely, privately, confidentially; see **secretly.**
subscribe, *v.* **1.** [To give personal support]—*Syn.* advocate, consent, second; see **support** 2.
2. [To give financial support]—*Syn.* support, give, promise; see **contribute** 1, **pay** 1.
3. [Suggest]—*Syn.* submit, propose, advise; see **recommend** 1.
4. [To obey]—*Syn.* consent, accept, acquiesce; see **obey** 1.
subscriber, *n.*—*Syn.* contributer, attester, signer, backer, sponsor, endorser, paying member, regular taker; see also **patron** 1, **supporter.**
subscript, *n.*—*Syn.* sequel, index, addendum; see **appendix.**
subscription, *n.*—*Syn.* consent, approval, agreement, support, acceptance, annual payment; see also **dues, recommendation** 1, **signature.**
subsequent, *mod.*—*Syn.* succeeding, consequent, after; see **following.**
subsequently, *mod.*—*Syn.* after, consequently, in the end; see **finally** 2.
subserve, *v.*—*Syn.* advance support, aid; see **promote** 1, **serve** 1.
subservient, *mod.*—*Syn.* submissive, obsequious, servile; see **docile.**
subside, *v.*—*Syn.* recede, sink, dwindle; see **ebb, fall** 1.
subsidiary, *mod.*—*Syn.* assistant, auxiliary, subject; see **helpful** 1, **secondary** 1, **subordinate.**
subsidize, *v.*—*Syn.* support, finance, back; see **contribute** 1, **promote** 1.
subsidy, *n.*—*Syn.* premium, indemnity, honorarium, bonus, tribute, gratuity, allowance, aid, bounty, support, pension, reward, subvention, endowment, grant, bequest, scholarship; see also **fellowship** 4, **gift** 1, **grant, payment** 1.
subsist, *v.*—*Syn.* stay alive, remain alive, scrape by *or* along, feed on, be, go it alone, eke out an existence, live on, barely exist; see also **live** 4.
subsistence, *n.* **1.** [The supporting of life]—*Syn.* living, sustenance, maintenance, support, keep, bread, bread and butter, necessities of life.—*Ant.* lack*, want, hunger.
2. [The means of supporting life]—*Syn.* means, circumstances, resources, property, money, riches, wealth, competence, capital, substance, affluence, independence, gratuity, fortune, dowry, legacy, earnings, wages, salary, income, pension; see also **funds.**—*Ant.* poverty*, penury, penniless.
subsoil, *n.*—*Syn.* loam, dirt, gravel; see **clay, earth** 2.
substance, *n.* **1.** [Essence]—*Syn.* body, core, pith; see **basis** 1, **essence** 1, **matter** 1.
2. [Object]—*Syn.* matter, material, being, object, item, person, animal, something, element; see also **thing** 1.
in substance—*Syn.* in essence, substantially, actually; see **essentially.**
substandard, *mod.*—*Syn.* inferior, second-rate, lower; see **cheap** 1, **poor** 2.
substantial, *mod.* **1.** [Strong]—*Syn.* solid, firm, stout; see **strong** 1, 2.
2. [Important]—*Syn.* valuable, extraordinary, principal; see **important** 1, 2.
3. [Real]—*Syn.* material, actual, visible; see **real** 2, **tangible.**
4. [Considerable]—*Syn.* ample, abundant, plentiful; see **large** 1, **much** 2.
5. [Wealthy]—*Syn.* affluent, well-to-do, opulent; see **rich** 1.
substantiality, *n.*—*Syn.* materiality, realness, actuality; see **reality** 1.
substantially, *mod.* **1.** [Essentially]—*Syn.* really, mainly, in essence *or* fact *or* reality, *etc.*; see **essentially.**
2. [Heavily]—*Syn.* extensively, considerably, largely; see **heavily, much** 1, 2.
substantiate, *v.* **1.** [To prove]—*Syn.* confirm, ratify, attest; see **approve** 1, **prove.**
2. [To actualize]—*Syn.* reify, realize, incarnate; see **complete** 1.
substantiation, *n.*—*Syn.* embodiment, approval, vindication; see **proof** 1.

substantive, *n.*—*Syn.* part of speech, common noun, proper noun; see **noun.**
substitute, *n.*—*Syn.* deputy, double, ghost writer, dummy, relief, fill-in, stand-in, understudy, proxy, alternate, surrogate, backup, replacement; *all* (D): ringer, ghost, sub, pinch-hitter; see also **agent** 1, **assistant, delegate.**
substitute, *v.* **1.** [To exchange]—*Syn.* interchange, change, replace; see **exchange** 1.
2. [To take the place of]—*Syn.* act for, do the work of, replace, supplant, displace, supercede, take another's place, double *or* answer *or* make way *or* count for, serve in one's stead, pass for, go for *or* as, step up, fill another's position, take over another's duties, fill in for; *all* (D): pinch-hit for, take the rap for, sub for, spell, go to bat for, ring in, front for, be in *or* fill someone's shoes.
substitution, *n.*—*Syn.* replacement, change, swap; see **exchange** 3.
substratum, *n.*—*Syn.* foundation, matter, frame; see **layer.**
substructure, *n.*—*Syn.* base, ground, infrastructure; see **foundation** 2.
subterfuge, *n.*—*Syn.* device, artifice, ploy; see **deception** 1, **trick** 1.
subterranean, *mod.* **1.** [Hidden]—*Syn.* secret, furtive, concealed; see **hidden** 2.
2. [Buried]—*Syn.* subsurface, sunk, subterraneous; see **underground.**
subtilize, *v.*—*Syn.* quibble, mislead, cavil; see **deceive, evade** 1.
subtle, *mod.* **1.** [Suggestive]—*Syn.* indirect, implied, insinuated, inferred, illusive; see also **mental, suggestive.**
2. [Precise]—*Syn.* definite, complex, exact; see **detailed.**
subtlety, *n.*—*Syn.* fine distinction, nuance, innuendo; see **distinction** 1.
subtract, *v.*—*Syn.* deduct, take away, withhold; see **decrease** 2.
subtraction, *n.*—*Syn.* deducting, subduction, diminution; see **discount, reduction** 1.
suburb, *n.*—*Syn.* outlying district, residential district, suburbia, outskirts, *banlieue* (French), neighbourhood; see also **area** 2.
suburban, *mod.*—*Syn.* provincial, in the country, rural, beyond the city limits, away from the city; see also **district, local** 1, **rural.**—*Ant.* urban*, metropolitan, cosmopolitan.
suburbanite, *n.*—*Syn.* resident, commuter, traveler; see **citizen.**
subvention, *n.*—*Syn.* subsidy, grant, help; see **aid** 1.
subversion, *n.*—*Syn.* ruin, overthrow, subversive activities, un-American activities, destruction; see also **defeat** 2, **revolution** 2.
subversive, *mod.*—*Syn.* ruinous, riotous, insurgent; see **rebellious** 2.
subvert, *v.*—*Syn.* overturn, overthrow, suppress, supplant, supersede, ruin, destroy, extinguish, invert, depress, upset, undermine, corrupt, pervert, demolish, tumble, topple, capsize, reverse, level, throw down, pull down; see also **defeat** 2.
subway, *n.*—*Syn.* Underground (British), tube, rapid transit, *Métro* (French); *both* (D): sub, chute; see also **railroad, train** 2.
succeed, *v.* **1.** [To attain success]—*Syn.* achieve, accomplish, get, propser, attain, reach, be successful, fulfill, earn, secure, succeed in, score, obtain, thrive, profit, realize, acquire, flourish, be victorious, capture, wrest, reap, benefit, recover, retrieve, gain, receive, master, triumph, possess, overcome, win (out), surmount, prevail, conquer, vanquish, distance, outdistance, avail, reduce, suppress, worst, outwit, outmaneuver, score a point, be accepted, be well-known, grow famous, carry *or* pull *or* go *or* come off, put *or* come through, make *or* work one's way, make one's fortune, carry all before one, satisfy one's ambition, make one's mark; *all* (D): come into money, hit it, hit the mark, live high, gain the day, arrive, come out with flying colors, beat the game, weather a storm, work well, overcome all obstacles, play one's cards well, crown, top, arrive at, do oneself proud, make it, die game, make good, do all right by oneself, be on top of the heap, make short work of, break good for, cover ground, get places, click, set the world on fire, carry out *or* off, gain one's end, bear oneself with credit, work, cut the mustard, make a killing, cut a swath, put across.—*Ant.* fail*, give up, go amiss.
2. [To follow in time]—*Syn.* follow after, come after, take the place of, ensue, supervene, supplant, supersede, replace, postdate, displace, come next, become heir to, result, be subsequent to, follow in order, bring up the rear (D).
succeeding, *mod.*—*Syn.* ensuing, following after, next in order; see **following.**
success, *n.* **1.** [The fact of succeeding]—*Syn.* achieving, gaining, prospering, attaining, accomplishing, progressing, advancing, triumphing, making a fortune, finishing, completion, consummation, doing, culmination, conclusion, termination, resolution, completion, end, attainment, realization, maturation, breakthrough, victory, triumph, accomplishment, benefiting, profiting, having good luck; *all* (D): being out in front, making a noise in the world, making a ten strike.—*Ant.* failure*, disappointment, failing.
2. [The fact of having succeeded to a high degree]—*Syn.* fortune, good luck, achievement, gain, benefit, prosperity, victory, advance, attainment, progress, profit, prosperous issue, the life of Riley, bed of roses, favorable outcome.—*Ant.* defeat*, loss, disaster.
3. [A successful person or thing]—*Syn.* celebrity, famous person, leader, authority, master, expert, man of fortune; *all* (D): somebody, star, gallery hit, bell-ringer, VIP, tops.—*Ant.* failure*, loser, nonentity.
successful, *mod.*—*Syn.* prosperous, fortunate, lucky, victorious, triumphant, auspicious, happy, unbeaten, favorable, fortuitous, strong, propitious, advantageous, encouraging, contended, satisfied, thriving, flourishing, wealthy; *all* (D): up in the world, ahead of the game, at the top of the ladder, in luxury, out in front, on the track, over the hump, in front of the parade.—*Ant.* unsuccessful*, poor, failing.
successfully, *mod.*—*Syn.* fortunately, triumphantly, luckily, victoriously, happily, favorably, fortuitously, strongly, thrivingly, flourishingly, fa-

mously, propitiously, auspiciously, prosperously, contentedly, with colors flying, beyond all expectation, swimmingly (D).

succession, *n.* —*Syn.* continuation, suite, set; see **sequence** 1, **series.**

in succession—*Syn.* consecutively, successively, in sequence, one after *or* behind the other; see also **consecutive, repeatedly.**

successive, *mod.* —*Syn.* serial, succeeding, in line; see **consecutive** 1.

successor, *n.* —*Syn.* heir, follower, replacement; see **candidate.**

succinct, *mod.* —*Syn.* terse, concise, curt; see **short** 2.

succor, *n.* —*Syn.* sustenance, help, assistance; see **aid** 1.

succor, *v.* —*Syn.* aid, assist, befriend; see **help** 1.

succulent, *mod.* —*Syn.* pulpy, tasty, lush; see **delicious** 1, **juicy.**

succulent, *n.* —*Syn.* one of the *Cactaceae or* the *Crassulacae* (both Latin), ground cover, desert vegetation *or* foliage *or* flora, houseleek, homewort, fouet, cactus, ice plant, live-forever, semperviva, house plant, hens and chickens; see also **cactus, plant.**

succumb, *v.* **1.** [To yield]—*Syn.* submit, surrender, accede; see **yield** 1.

2. [To die]—*Syn.* expire, drop, cease; see **die** 1.

such, *mod.* —*Syn.* so, so very, of this kind, of that kind, of the sort, of the degree, so much, beforementioned.

such, *pron.* —*Syn.* this, that, such a one, such an one, such a person, such a thing.

as such—*Syn.* in *or* of *or* in and of itself, by its (own) nature, more than in name only; see **accordingly, essentially.**

such as, *conj.* and *prep.* —*Syn.* for example, for instance, to give an example *or* instance; see **including, similarly, thus.**

such as it is, *mod.* —*Syn.* as is, however poor it may be, for whatever it is worth, a poor thing but mine own; see also **inadequate** 1, **poor** 2.

suck, *v.* —*Syn.* absorb, take up, swallow up, engulf.

sucker, *n.* **1.** [A fish]—Common suckers include the following—black horse, red horse, buffalo fish, lumpfish, sand sucker, remora, shark sucker, clingfish, chub sucker, hog sucker, hog molly, quillback, gourd-seed sucker, sweet sucker, jump rock, spotted sucker, brook sucker; see also **fish.**

2. [(D) A victim]—*Syn.* dupe, fool, cat's-paw; see **victim** 2.

3. [Candy]—*Syn.* sweet, confectionary, lollipop; see **candy.**

suckle, *v.* —*Syn.* nurse, nurture, nourish; see **sustain** 2.

suckling, *n.* —*Syn.* infant, babe, chick; see **baby** 1.

suction, *n.* —*Syn.* sucking, the force of air *or* the wind *or* a vacuum, effect of atmospheric pressures; see **attraction, power** 2, **pull** 1.

sudden, *mod.* —*Syn.* precipitate, swift, impromptu; see **immediate** 1, **unexpected.**

all of a sudden—*Syn.* unexpectedly, suddenly, precipitously; see **quickly** 1.

suddenly, *mod.* —*Syn.* without any warning, abruptly, swiftly; see **quickly** 1.

suds, *n.* —*Syn.* foam, bubbles, lather; see **froth, soap.**

sue, *v.* —*Syn.* prosecute, follow up, claim, demand, indict, solicit, beg, litigate, contest, pray, entreat, plead, petition, appeal, accuse, file a plea, enter a plea, claim damages, go to law, file suit, prefer a claim, enter a lawsuit, take one to court, file a claim; *all* (D): have the law on one, law, haul into court.

suet, *n.* —*Syn.* fat, lard, blubber; see **grease, oil** 1.

suffer, *v.* **1.** [To feel pain]—*Syn.* undergo, experience, ache, smart, be in pain, be wounded, agonize, grieve, be racked, be convulsed, languish, droop, flag, sicken, endure torture, get it in the neck, look green about the gills, complain of, get it, be affected with, go hard with, match it, flinch at, not feel like anything, labor under; see also **hurt** 4.—*Ant.* recover*, be relieved, be restored.

2. [To endure]—*Syn.* bear, sustain, put up with; see **endure** 2.

3. [To permit]—*Syn.* allow, acquiesce, admit, let, concede, indulge, connive at, stretch a point, authorize, license, sanction, yield, bow, submit.

sufferance, *n.* —*Syn.* toleration, fortitude, composure; see **endurance** 2, **patience** 1.

on sufferance—*Syn.* allowed, tolerated, endured; see **legal** 1, **permitted.**

sufferer, *n.* —*Syn.* the sick, injured person, patient; see **victim** 1.

suffering, *n.* —*Syn.* distress, misery, affliction; see **difficulty** 1, 2, **pain** 2.

suffice, *v.* —*Syn.* answer, avail, serve; see **satisfy** 3.

sufficiency, *n.* —*Syn.* adequacy, enough, supply; see **plenty.**

sufficient, *mod.* —*Syn.* adequate, ample, satisfactory; see **enough** 1.

sufficiently, *mod.* —*Syn.* to one's satisfaction, enough, amply; see **adequately** 1.

suffix, *n.* —*Syn.* affix, postfix, addition; see **appendix.**

suffocate, *v.* —*Syn.* stifle, smother, strangle; see **choke** 1.

suffrage, *n.* —*Syn.* voice, ballot, testimonial; see **vote** 3.

sugar, *n.* Common varieties and forms of sugar include the following—sucrose, cane sugar, corn sugar, brown sugar, beet sugar, grape sugar, dextrose, fruit sugar, levulose, maltrose, malt sugar, lactose, maple sugar, saccharose; see also **carbohydrate, food.**

sugary, *mod.* —*Syn.* sticky, granular, candied; see **sweet** 1.

suggest, *v.* **1.** [To make a suggestion]—*Syn.* submit, advise, recommend; see **propose** 1.

2. [To bring to mind]—*Syn.* imply, infer, intimate; see **hint.**

suggested, *mod.* —*Syn.* submitted, advanced, proposed, advocated, propounded, advised, recommended, counseled, tendered, reminded, prompted, summoned up, called up, offered, laid before, put forward.

suggesting, *mod.* —*Syn.* indicating, suggestive (of), implying; see **saying.**

suggesting, *n.* —*Syn.* propounding, advancing, proposing, submitting, moving, offering, proffering, tendering, recalling, prompting, summoning up; recommending, jogging the memory, laying before, putting forward, advising, with reference to, counseling.

suggestion, *n.* **1.** [A suggested detail]—*Syn.* hint, allusion, suspicion, intimation, implication, innuendo, insinuation, opinion, proposal, advice, opinion, recommendation, injunction, charge, instruction, submission, tender, reminder, approach, advance, bid, idea, tentative statement, presentation, proposition.
2. [A suggested plan]—*Syn.* scheme, idea, outline; see **plan** 2.
3. [A very small quantity]—*Syn.* trace, touch, taste; see **bit** 1.

suggestive, *mod.* —*Syn.* carrying a suggestion of, intriguing, giving an inkling of, symptomatic, indicative; see also **symbolic.**

suicidal, *mod.* —*Syn.* mortal, lethal, ruinous; see **deadly, harmful.**

suicide, *n.* —*Syn.* self-murder, self-slaughter, self-destruction, hara-kiri, self-homicide; see also **death** 1.

suit, *n.* **1.** [A series]—*Syn.* suite, set, group; see **series.**
2. [A case at law]—*Syn.* lawsuit, action, litigation; see **trial** 2.
3. [Clothes to be worn together]—*Syn.* costume, ensemble, outfit, livery, uniform; see also **clothes.** Kinds of suits include the following—women: sport suit, tailored suit, man-tailored suit, soft suit, dressmaker suit, cocktail suit, three-piece suit, jump suit, minisuit, slack suit, cardigan suit, evening suit, bathing suit, sun suit, play suit; men: sport suit, slack suit, business suit, leisure suit, full dress (also (D): tails, monkey suit, soup and fish), dinner jacket, tuxedo (also (D): tux, tuck), Palm Beach (trademark) suit, morning dress, bathing suit; children: snow suit, sun suit, play suit, bathing suit, Eton suit.
bring suit—*Syn.* prosecute, start (legal) proceedings, initiate a case; see **sue.**
follow suit (D)—*Syn.* accord with, regulate one's actions by, take a cue from (D); see **follow 2, imitate** 2.

suit, *v.* **1.** [To be in accord with]—*Syn.* befit, be agreeable, be appropriate to; see **agree, agree with** 2.
2. [To please]—*Syn.* amuse, fill, gratify; see **entertain** 1, **satisfy** 1.
3. [To adapt]—*Syn.* accommodate, revise, readjust; see **change** 1.

suitability, *n.* —*Syn.* rightness, appropriateness, agreement; see **fitness, propriety** 1.

suitable, *mod.* —*Syn.* fitting, becoming, proper; see **fit** 1, 2.

suitably, *mod.* —*Syn.* well, all to the good, pleasantly; see **fit** 1, 2.

suitcase, *n.* —*Syn.* case, grip, satchel; see **bag.**

suite, *n.* **1.** [Attendants]—*Syn.* retinue, faculty, followers; see **servant, staff** 2.
2. [A series]—*Syn.* sequence, scale, line; see **order** 3, **series.**
3. [Matched furniture]—*Syn.* set, bedroom suite, overstuffed set; see **furniture.**

suited, *mod.* —*Syn.* adapted, satisfactory, fitted; see **fit** 1, 2.

suit oneself, *v.* —*Syn.* do as one pleases, be self-indulgent, pamper oneself; see **satisfy** 1.

suitor, *n.* —*Syn.* gallant, supplicant, beau; see **lover** 1.

suit up, *v.* —*Syn.* prepare, make ready, get ready; see **dress** 1.

sulfa drug, *n.* Varieties include the following—sulfathiazole, sulfanilamide, sulfapyridine, sulfadiazole, sulmefrin; see also **drug** 2.

sulk, *v.* —*Syn.* scowl, pout, frown, be sullen, be morose, be silent, glower, lower; *both* (D): gripe, grouse.

sulkiness, *n.* —*Syn.* sourness, glumness, grouchiness; see **anger.**

sulky, *mod.* —*Syn.* cross, morose, surly; see **irritable, sullen.**

sullen, *mod.* —*Syn.* unsociable, silent, morose, glum, sulky, sour, cross, ill-humored, petulant, moody, grouchy, crabby, surly, fretful, ill-natured, ill-tempered, peevish, gloomy, gruff, querulous, churlish, saturnine; *all* (D): chumpish, sourpussed, fiddle-faced; see also **irritable.**—*Ant.* friendly*, sociable, jolly.

sullenly, *mod.* —*Syn.* morosely, glumly, sourly; see **angrily, silently.**

sullenness, *n.* —*Syn.* sulkiness, moodiness, acrimony; see **anger.**

sully, *v.* **1.** [To soil]—*Syn.* blot, stain, spot; see **dirty.**
2. [To defame]—*Syn.* shame, debase, denounce; see **disgrace.**

sultan, *n.* —*Syn.* soldian, grand-seignoir, emperor; see **king** 1, **ruler** 1.

sultriness, *n.* —*Syn.* mugginess, dampness, closeness; see **humidity.**

sultry, *mod.* —*Syn.* close, stifling, oppressive; see **hot** 1, **wet** 1.

sum, *n.* —*Syn.* amount, value, worth; see **whole.**

summarily, *mod.* —*Syn.* promptly, readily, speedily; see **immediately.**

summarize, *v.* —*Syn.* prune down, cut back, sum *or* cipher *or* abstract, skim over, review, count up, compile, shorten; *both* (D): memory up, put in a nutshell; see also **decrease** 2.

summarized, *mod.* —*Syn.* capsulated, decreased, diminished, outlined, shortened, summed up, reviewed.

summary, *n.* —*Syn.* outline, epitome, digest, synopsis, analysis, abstract, recapitulation, abbreviation, capitulation, compendium, résumé, essence, précis, extract, skeleton, brief, conspectus, prospectus, reduction, version, core, report, sense, essential, case, survey, sketch, syllabus, condensation, summing-up, pandect, aperçu; *all* (D): recap, sum and substance, the long and short of a thing, wrap-up. —*Ant.* increase*, extension, elaboration.

summer, *mod.* —*Syn.* summery, summertime, in summer, vacation; see also **hot** 1, **warm** 1.

summer, *n.* —*Syn.* summertime, summer season, full summer, dog days, sunny season, harvest, haying time, vacation, picnic days, fly time (D); see also **season.**—*Ant.* winter*, cold months, snowy season.

summer, *v.* —*Syn.* vacation, stay *or* spend the summer, take a holiday (at), holiday; see also **live** 2, **remain** 1.

summerhouse, *n.* —*Syn.* garden house, alcove, vinery; see **resort** 2, **retreat** 2.

summit, *n.* —*Syn.* apex, zenith, crown; see **mountain** 1, **top** 1.

summon, *v.* **1.** [To call]—*Syn.* request, beckon, send for, invoke, bid, ask, draft, petition, signal, motion, sign, order, command, direct, enjoin, conjure up, ring, charge, recall, call in *or* for *or* out *or* forth *or* up *or* away *or* down *or* together, volunteer (D).
2. [To convene]—*Syn.* call together, convoke, gather; see **assemble** 2.

summoned, *mod.*—*Syn.* called for *or* up, paged, drafted; see **requested** 2, **wanted.**

summons, *n.* **1.** [Legal call]—*Syn.* subpoena, writ, warrant; see **indictment.**
2. [Invocation]—*Syn.* cry, bell, calling; see **call** 4.

summon up, *v.*—*Syn.* recall, recollect, be reminded; see **remember** 1.

summum bonum (Latin), *n.*—*Syn.* height, highest good, contentment; see **best.**

sumptuous, *mod.*—*Syn.* costly, lavish, magnificent, gorgeous, imposing, opulent, impressive, beautiful, elegant, pompous, splendid, deluxe, luxurious; see also **rich** 2.

sum up, *v.*—*Syn.* summarize, review, conclude; see **examine** 1, **total** 1.

sun, *n.*—*Syn.* day-star, solar disk, solar orb, eye of heaven, great luminary, light of the day, lamp of the day, source of light, giver of light, Sol, Apollo; see also **star** 1.
a place in the sun—*Syn.* favorable position *or* situation, reward, prominence; see **advantage** 1, 2, **prize.**
under the sun—*Syn.* on earth, terrestrial, mundane; see **earthly** 1.

sunburned, *mod.*—*Syn.* tanned, burned, adust, sunburnt, brown, browned by the sun, suntanned, bronzed, ruddy, brown as a berry, nut-brown, baked brown, sunbaked.—*Ant.* pale*, white-skinned, pallid.

sundae, *n.*—*Syn.* ice cream, ice cream with topping, dish of ice cream, parfait, banana split; see also **dessert, treat.**

Sunday, *n.*—*Syn.* first day, day off, Lord's day; see **Sabbath.**

sunder, *v.*—*Syn.* separate, part, split; see **divide** 1.

sundry, *mod.*—*Syn.* divers, several, manifold; see **various.**

sunken, *mod.*—*Syn.* lowered, depressed, down; see **under** 1.

sunless, *mod.*—*Syn.* pitchy, overcast, gloomy; see **dark** 1.

sunlight, *n.*—*Syn.* daylight, sunshine, light of day; see **day** 2, **light** 1.

sunny, *mod.*—*Syn.* shining, brilliant, sunshiny; see **bright** 1.

sunrise, *n.*—*Syn.* peep of day, daybreak, aurora; see **morning** 1.

sunset, *n.*—*Syn.* sundown, evening, end of the day, eve, eventide, close of the day, sunsetting, nightfall, twilight, dusk; see also **night** 1.—*Ant.* dawn*, sunrise, morning.

sunshade, *n.*—*Syn.* parasol, canopy, awning; see **umbrella.**

sunshine, *n.*—*Syn.* sunlight, the sun, sunbeams, the sun's beams *or* rays; see also **light** 1.

sup, *v.*—*Syn.* feed, munch, dine; see **eat** 1.

superabundance, *n.*—*Syn.* surplus, exorbitance, overflow; see **excess** 1, **remainder.**

superabundant, *mod.*—*Syn.* surplus, excess, excessive; see **extreme** 2.

superannuated, *mod.*—*Syn.* obsolete, passé, outdated; see **old-fashioned.**

superb, *mod.*—*Syn.* magnificent, august, splendid, elegant, exquisite; see also **excellent, grand** 2.

supercilious, *mod.*—*Syn.* disdainful, haughty, contemptuous; see **egotistic** 2.

superficial, *mod.*—*Syn.* flimsy, cursory, perfunctory, hasty, desultory, shallow, summary, shortsighted, purblind, ignorant, narrow-minded, prejudiced, warped, partial, skin-deep, untrustworthy, outward, external, exterior, unenlightened.—*Ant.* learned*, deep, profound.

superficiality, *n.*—*Syn.* triviality, shallowness, lack of depth; see **indifference, nonsense** 1, 2, **nothing.**

superficially, *mod.*—*Syn.* lightly, at first glance, externally, on the surface, outwardly, extraneously, flimsily, partially, hastily, ignorantly, frivolously, not thoroughly *or* profoundly; see also **carelessly, casually** 2.—*Ant.* carefully*, thoroughly, thoughtfully.

superfluity, *n.*—*Syn.* surplus, abundance, plethora; see **excess** 1, **plenty.**

superfluous, *mod.*—*Syn.* unnecessary, excessive, superabundant, overflowing, redundant, overmuch, very great, abounding, inordinate, needless, exorbitant, on one's hands, in excess, extravagant, profuse, turgescent, supererogatory, pleonastic, lavish, overcharged; see also **extreme** 2.—*Ant.* wanting*, scanty, lacking.

superintend, *v.*—*Syn.* supervise, oversee, conduct; see **manage** 1, **watch** 2.

superintendence, *n.*—*Syn.* direction, management, supervision; see **administration** 1, **command** 2.

superintendent, *n.*—*Syn.* overseer, supervisor, inspector, director; see also **administrator.**

superior, *mod.*—*Syn.* higher, better, preferred, above, exceeding, finer, of higher rank, a cut above (D), in ascendency, more exalted; see also **excellent.**

superiority, *n.*—*Syn.* supremacy, preponderance, advantage; see **perfection.**

superlative, *mod.* **1.** [Supreme]—*Syn.* prime, highest, greatest; see **best** 1, **excellent.**
2. [Excessive]—*Syn.* exaggerated, effusive, inflated; see **extreme** 2.

supernatural, *mod.*—*Syn.* preternatural, superhuman, spectral, ghostly, occult, paranormal, hidden, mysterious, secret, unknown, unrevealed, dark, mystic, mythical, mythological, fabulous, legendary, misty, unintelligible, unfathomable, unearthly, inscrutable, incomprehensible, undiscernible, transcendental, metempiric, psychic, obscure, unknowable, impenetrable, invisible, concealed.—*Ant.* natural*, plain, common.

supernumerary, *mod.*—*Syn.* excessive, exaggerated, effusive; see **extreme** 2, **superfluous.**

superscription, *n.*—*Syn.* inscription, epigraph, title; see **identification** 2, **label.**

supersede, *v.*—*Syn.* outmode, succeed, take the place of; see **replace** 1.

superseded, *mod.*—*Syn.* out of date, outmoded, discarded; see **old** 2, 3, **old-fashioned, poor** 2.

supersensory, *mod.* —*Syn.* extrasensory, telepathic, psychic; see **mental** 2, **supernatural.**

superstition, *n.* —*Syn.* false belief, notion, irrationality, fear, superstitious fear.

superstitious, *mod.* —*Syn.* fearful, apprehensive, credulous; see **careful, stupid** 1.

supervene, *v.* —*Syn.* ensue, issue, occur; see **happen** 2.

supervise, *v.* —*Syn.* oversee, conduct, control; see **manage** 1.

supervised, *mod.* —*Syn.* directed, administered, superintended; see **managed** 2.

supervision, *n.* —*Syn.* guidance, surveillance, direction; see **administration** 1.

supervisor, *n.* —*Syn.* director, superintendent, executive; see **administrator.**

supine, *mod.* **1.** [Prone]—*Syn.* recumbent, prostrate, flat, lying, reclining.
2. [Indolent]—*Syn.* listless, languid, passive; see **indifferent.**

supper, *n.* —*Syn.* evening meal, tea, late refreshments; see **dinner, meal** 2.

supplant, *v.* —*Syn.* displace, transfer, supersede; see **remove** 1.

supple, *mod.* —*Syn.* yielding, pliant, agile; see **flexible** 1, **rubber.**

supplement, *n.* —*Syn.* sequel, continuation, complement; see **addition** 2, **appendix.**

supplement, *v.* —*Syn.* add to, supply, fill up, complete, extend, augment, supply a need, reinforce, strengthen, fortify, increase, buttress, subsidize, enhance, enrich, go hand in hand with; see also **improve** 1, **increase** 1.

supplementary, *mod.* —*Syn.* additional, completing, supplemental; see **extra.**

supplicate, *v.* —*Syn.* petition, appeal, beseech; see **beg** 1.

supplication, *n.* —*Syn.* entreaty, prayer, petition; see **appeal** 1, **request.**

supplied, *mod.* —*Syn.* provided, furnished, endowed; see **given.**

supply, *n.* **1.** [A quantity]—*Syn.* stock, hoard, accumulation, amount, number; see also **quantity.**
2. [Provisions; *plural*]—*Syn.* raw materials, materials on hand, stores, stocks, replenishments; see also **equipment.**

supply, *v.* —*Syn.* furnish, fulfill, outfit; see **provide** 1, **satisfy** 3.

supplying, *n.* —*Syn.* furnishing, stocking, replenishing; see **providing.**

support, *n.* **1.** [Aid]—*Syn.* help, assistance, comfort; see **aid** 1.
2. [A reinforcement]—*Syn.* lining, coating, concrete block, rib, stilt, stay, shore, supporter, buttress, pole, post, underpinning, dependence, prop, guide, backing, stiffener, flotation, collar, rampart, abutment, stave, stake, rod, pillar, column, timber; see also **brace.**
3. [Financial aid]—*Syn.* maintenance, living, provision, livelihood, subsidy, subsistence, upkeep, care, relief, allowance, sustenance, alimentation, alimony, responsibility for; see also **payment** 1.
4. [One who provides support]—*Syn.* backer, provider, second, preserver; see also **patron** 1, **supporter.**

support, *v.* **1.** [To hold up from beneath]—*Syn.* prop, hold *or* keep *or* bolster *or* shore *or* bear up, bolster, buttress, brace, sustain, shore, stay, mainstay, underpin, undergird, keep from falling, shoulder, carry, bear, be a foundation for.—*Ant.* drop*, let fall, break down.
2. [To uphold]—*Syn.* maintain, sustain, back up, abet, aid, assist, help, bolster, stay, comfort, carry, bear out, hold, foster, shoulder corroborate, cheer, establish, buoy, put forward, promote, advance, champion, advocate, countenance, approve, throw in with, stick by, stand behind, cast in on, substantiate, lot with, verify, get back of, stick up for, go to bat for, confirm, further, encourage, hearten, strengthen, second, preserve, recommend, take care of, stand in with, pull for, agree with, stand up for, keep up, stand back of, take the part of, rally round; *both* (D): give a lift to, boost.—*Ant.* hinder*, discourage, deter.
3. [To defend]—*Syn.* second, stand by, plead for; see **defend** 3.
4. [To continue]—*Syn.* carry on, keep up, maintain; see **continue** 1.
5. [To provide for]—*Syn.* take care of, keep an eye on, care for, attend to, look after, back, bring up, sponsor, underwrite, put up the money (for), set up in business, finance, pay for, subsidize, guard, chaperon, nurse, pay the expenses of; *all* (D): grubstake, stake, bank-roll, raise, bring home the bacon, earn one's keep; see also **sustain** 2.—*Ant.* abandon*, ignore, fail.

supportable, *mod.* —*Syn.* sustainable, endurable, tolerable; see **bearable.**

supported, *mod.* **1.** [Backed personally]—*Syn.* financed, promoted, sustained; see **backed** 2.
2. [Supported physically]—*Syn.* held up, propped (up), braced, bolstered, borne (up), floating (on *or* upon), floated, borne *or* buoyed *or* lifted (up), based *or* founded (upon *or* on), raised (up), having (an adequate *or* a sufficient) base *or* basis *or* foundation(s) *or* underpinning(s), etc.; see also **firm** 1.

supporter, *n.* —*Syn.* advocate, adherent, sustainer, sponsor, benefactor, upholder, confederate, champion, helper; see also **patron** 1, **subscriber.**

supporting, *mod.* —*Syn.* upholding, aiding, shielding, promoting, approving, back of; see also **helping.**

suppose, *v.* —*Syn.* conjecture, surmise, deem; see **assume** 1, **guess** 1.

supposed, *mod.* —*Syn.* assumed, presumed, presupposed; see **likely** 1.

supposedly, *mod.* —*Syn.* seemingly, supposably, believably; see **apparently, probably.**

supposing, *conj.* and *mod.* —*Syn.* if, in case that, in these circumstances, under these conditions, let us suppose, allowing that, granting that, presuming, assuming, presupposing, with the supposition that, taking for granted that.

supposition, *n.* **1.** [A guess]—*Syn.* surmise, notion, speculation; see **guess, guessing.**
2. [A theory]—*Syn.* idea, thesis, likelihood; see **hypothesis, opinion** 1.

suppositional, *mod.* —*Syn.* conjectural, hypothetical, presumptive; see **theoretical.**

suppositious, *mod.* —*Syn.* counterfeit, deceptive, fictitious; see **false** 2, 3.

suppress, *v.*—*Syn.* crush, overpower, overcome, contain, cut off, beat *or* slap *or* hold *or* put down, burke, subdue, keep in, quash, repress, quell, stifle; *all* (D): sit on, trample out, bottle up, keep in ignorance, choke off, come *or* clamp *or* crack down on; see also **defeat** 1, 2.

suppression, *n.*—*Syn.* abolition, burking, overriding, suppressing, overthrow, elimination; see also **defeat** 2, **destruction** 1.

suppurate, *v.*—*Syn.* fester, gather, putrefy; see **decay.**

supremacy, *n.*—*Syn.* domination, mastery, supreme authority; see **command** 2, **power** 2.

supreme, *mod.*—*Syn.* highest, greatest, paramount, chief; see also **best** 1, **excellent, principal.**

surcease, *n.*—*Syn.* deferment, interruption, cessation; see **delay** 1, **end** 2, **pause** 1, 2.

surcharged, *mod.*—*Syn.* overfull, superflous, replete; see **full** 1.

sure (D), *interj.*—*Syn.* certainly, of course, by all means, positively, absolutely, but definitely; see also **surely.**

sure, *mod.* **1.** [Confident]—*Syn.* positive, assured, convinced; see **certain** 1.

2. [Inevitable]—*Syn.* unfailing, unavoidable, indisputable; see **certain** 3, **inevitable.**

for sure—*Syn.* certainly, for certain, without doubt; see **surely.**

make sure—*Syn.* make certain, determine, establish; see **fix** 4, **guarantee** 2, **manage** 1.

to be sure—*Syn.* of course, certainly, obviously; see **surely.**

sure-fire (D), *mod.*—*Syn.* dependable, good, infallible; see **excellent, reliable** 2.

surely, *mod.*—*Syn.* doubtlessly, certainly, undoubtedly, fixedly, definitely, absolutely, evidently, explicitly, without doubt, beyond doubt *or* question, plainly, infallibly, to be sure, most assuredly, unshakably, decidedly, inevitably, indisputably, positively, unquestionably, irrefutably, unfailingly, without any doubt, admittedly, clearly, with assurance, beyond the shadow of a doubt, nothing else but, precisely, conclusively, unequivocally, distinctly, by all means, in all conscience, at any rate, with certainty, unerringly, unmistakably, at all events, undeniably, manifestly, indubitably, with confidence, as a matter of course, rain or shine (D).—*Ant.* doubtful*, with no assurance, in doubt.

sure thing (D), *n.*—*Syn.* no gamble, certainty, safe venture *or* investment *or* project, etc.; see **winner.**

surety, *n.*—*Syn.* pledge, bail, forfeit; see **guaranty** 2.

surf, *n.*—*Syn.* breakers, breaking waves, foam, froth, spindrift, rollers, combers; see also **ocean, tide, wave** 1.

surface, *n.*—*Syn.* exterior, covering, superficies; see **cover** 2, **outside** 1.

surfeit, *n.*—*Syn.* surplus, superfluity, profusion; see **excess** 1, **remainder.**

surfeit, *v.*—*Syn.* satiate, overindulge, gorge; see **eat** 1, **fill** 1, **satisfy** 3.

surge, *n.* **1.** [A wave]—*Syn.* swell, billow, breaker; see **surf, wave** 1, 2.

2. [A deluge]—*Syn.* rush, swell, roll; see **flood** 1.

surge, *v.* **1.** [To rise]—*Syn.* mount, tower, arise; see **climb** 2, **rise** 1, 3.

2. [To swell]—*Syn.* billow, heave, deluge; see **grow** 1, **swell.**

surgeon, *n.*—*Syn.* specialist, specialist in surgery, surgical expert, operator, interventionist, consultant; see also **doctor** 1.

surgery, *n.*—*Syn.* operative surgery, cyosurgery, surgical operation; see **medicine** 3, **operation** 4.

surgical, *mod.*—*Syn.* healing, curative, operational, with the surgeon's knife; see also **medical, remedial.**

surly, *mod.*—*Syn.* morose, testy, crabby; see **irritable, sullen.**

surmise, *n.*—*Syn.* conjecture, attempt, theory; see **guess, hypothesis, opinion** 1.

surmise, *v.*—*Syn.* conjecture, guess, suppose; see **assume** 1.

surmount, *v.*—*Syn.* conquer, overcome, subdue; see **defeat** 2.

surmountable, *mod.*—*Syn.* conquerable, bearable, attainable; see **inadequate** 1, **poor** 2, **weak** 2, 3.

surname, *n.*—*Syn.* cognomen, last name, patronymic; see **name** 1.

surpass, *v.*—*Syn.* excel, outdo, transcend, improve upon, go beyond, better; see also **exceed.**

surpassing, *mod.*—*Syn.* exceeding, excelling, dominant; see **excellent.**

surplus, *n.*—*Syn.* surplusage, residue, something extra; see **excess** 1, **remainder.**

surprise, *n.* **1.** [A feeling]—*Syn.* astonishment, wonderment, shock; see **wonder** 1.

2. [The cause of a feeling]—*Syn.* something unexpected, blow, sudden attack, unexpected good fortune, sudden misfortune, unawaited event, unsuspected plot.

take by surprise—*Syn.* startle, assault, sneak up on; see **attack** 1, 2, **surprise** 1, 2.

surprise, *v.* **1.** [To amaze]—*Syn.* astonish, astound, bewilder, confound, shock, overwhelm, dumbfound, unsettle, stun, electrify, petrify, startle, stupefy, stagger, nonplus, take aback, cause wonder, strike with wonder *or* awe, dazzle, daze, perplex, stagger one's belief, leave open-mouthed, leave aghast, make all agog; *all* (D): flabbergast, floor, bowl over, jar, flash upon one, carry one off his feet, jolt, take one's breath away, strike dumb, make one's hair stand on end, make one's head swim, come *or* creep up on, catch unaware; see also **confuse, frighten** 1.

2. [To take unaware]—*Syn.* take by surprise, catch one in the act of, burst in upon, startle; *all* (D): catch off-balance, catch flat-footed, catch one napping, catch asleep, nab, pop in on; see also **sense** 1.

surprised, *mod.*—*Syn.* upset, taken unaware, astounded, caught short *or* napping, astonished, bewildered, taken by surprise, shocked, struck with amazement, confounded, nonplussed, startled, staggered, not anticipating.—*Ant.* calm*, aware, poised.

surprising, *mod.*—*Syn.* extraordinary, remarkable, shocking; see **unexpected, unusual** 1, 2.

surrealistic, *mod.*—*Syn.* incoherent, unconnected, absurd; see **fantastic, illogical, incongruous** 1, **unreal.**

surrender, *n.*—*Syn.* capitulation, yielding, giving up, submission, giving way, unconditional surrender, white flag, cessation, abandonment, relinquishment, acquiescence, abdication, resignation, delivery.

surrender, *v.* **1.** [To accept defeat]—*Syn.* capitulate, quit, give in; see **yield** 1.
2. [To relinquish possession]—*Syn.* give up, let go, resign; see **abandon** 1.

surreptitious, *mod.*—*Syn.* clandestine, private, covert; see **hidden** 2, **secret** 3.

surreptitiously, *mod.*—*Syn.* confidentially, stealthily, privately; see **secretly.**

surrogate, *n.*—*Syn.* deputy, representative, proxy; see **agent** 1, **delegate, substitute.**

surround, *v.* **1.** [To be on all sides]—*Syn.* girdle, circle, environ, gird, enclose, shut *or* close in, fence in, close around, circle about, envelope, hem in, wall in.
2. [To take a position on all sides]—*Syn.* encompass, encircle, inundate, flow around, besiege, beset, invest, close in *or* around, house *or* hem in, compass about, go around, beleaguer, blockade; see also **circle.**—*Ant.* abandon*, flee from, desert.

surrounded, *mod.*—*Syn.* girdled, encompassed, encircled, hemmed in, fenced in, hedged in, circled about, girded, enclosed, fenced about, enveloped.—*Ant.* free*, unfenced, agape.

surrounding, *mod.*—*Syn.* enclosing, encircling, encompassing; see also **around** 1.

surroundings, *n.*—*Syn.* setting, environs, vicinity; see **environment.**

surveillance, *n.*—*Syn.* supervision, inspection, direction; see **examination** 1.

survey, *n.*—*Syn.* study, critique, outline; see **examination** 1, **review** 1, 2.

survey, *v.* **1.** [To look upon]—*Syn.* look over, take a view of, view; see **see** 1.
2. [To examine or summarize]—*Syn.* study, scan, inspect; see **examine** 1.

surveyor, *n.*—*Syn.* civil engineer, measurer, instrument man; see **engineer** 1.

survival, *n.*—*Syn.* endurance, durability, continuance; see **continuation** 1.

survive, *v.* **1.** [To live on]—*Syn.* outlive, outlast, outwear, live down *or* out, weather the storm, make out, persist, persevere, last, remain, keep the wolf from the door, pull *or* live *or* get *or* come through, keep afloat, get on; see also **endure** 1.
2. [To endure]—*Syn.* bear *or* suffer through, withstand, sustain; see **endure** 2.

survivor, *n.*—*Syn.* one who has escaped, one still living, one spared, one left behind, relict, posterity, descendant, heir, widow, widower, orphan, derelict.

susceptibility, *n.*—*Syn.* susceptivity, awareness, perceptivity; see **sensitivity** 2.

susceptible, *mod.*—*Syn.* responsive, receptive, susceptive; see **sensitive** 3.

suspect, *mod.*—*Syn.* dubious, questionable, suspected; see **suspicious** 2, **unlikely.**

suspect, *v.* **1.** [To doubt someone]—*Syn.* distrust, disbelieve, mistrust; see **doubt** 2.
2. [To suppose]—*Syn.* presume, surmise, speculate; see **assume** 1.

suspected, *mod.*—*Syn.* doubtful, imagined, fancied; see **questionable** 1, 2, **suspicious** 2.

suspend, *v.* **1.** [To debar]—*Syn.* reject, exclude, omit; see **bar** 2, **eject** 1, **refuse.**
2. [To cease temporarily]—*Syn.* postpone, defer, put off, discontinue, adjourn, interrupt, delay, procrastinate, prorogue, pigeonhole, shelve, waive, lay over, stave off, retard, protract, lay on the table, file, lay aside, break up, restrain, keep one waiting, desist, break off, halt, put a stop to, check, arrest, put an end to.—*Ant.* continue*, carry on, proceed.
3. [To hang]—*Syn.* dangle, swing, wave; see **hang** 2.
4. [To cause to hang]—*Syn.* hang up, swing, hook up; see **hang** 1.

suspended, *mod.*—*Syn.* pensile, postponed, pendulous; see **hanging.**

suspenders, *n.*—*Syn.* braces, straps, shoulder straps; see **brace.**

suspense, *n.* **1.** [Uncertainty]—*Syn.* apprehension, indecisiveness, dilemma; see **doubt** 2.
2. [Perplexity]—*Syn.* hesitancy, hesitation, anxiety; see **confusion** 2, **uncertainty** 3.

suspension, *n.* **1.** [A delay]—*Syn.* postponement, deferment, stay; see **delay** 1, **pause** 1, 2, **respite.**
2. [An end]—*Syn.* halt, discontinuing, stoppage; see **end** 2, **stopping.**

suspension bridge, *n.*—*Syn.* overhead bridge, cable bridge, walkway; see **bridge** 1.

suspicion, *n.*—*Syn.* misgiving, mistrust, surmise; see **doubt** 1.
above suspicion—*Syn.* honorable, cleared, gentlemanly; see **honest** 1, **innocent** 1, 4, **noble** 1, 2.
under suspicion—*Syn.* suspected, held *or* apprehended *or* arrested, etc., (for questioning), dubious; see **questionable** 1, 2, **suspicious** 2.

suspicious, *mod.* **1.** [Entertaining suspicion]—*Syn.* jealous, distrustful, suspecting, doubting, questioning, wary, leery, doubtful, dubious, suspect, in doubt, without faith, skeptical, unbelieving, without belief, wondering.—*Ant.* trusting*, trustful, without any doubt of.
2. [Arousing suspicion]—*Syn.* not quite trustworthy, questionable, queer, suspect, irregular, unusual, uncommon, different, peculiar, open to question, out of line, shady, equivocal, overt, debatable, disputable.—*Ant.* regular*, usual, common.

suspiciously, *mod.*—*Syn.* doubtingly, doubtfully, skeptically, dubiously, uncertainly, distrustfully, distrustingly, unbelievingly, questioningly, problematically, in doubt, in a doubtful manner, having *or* entertaining doubt *or* uncertainty *or* skepticism, etc.; causing *or* inducing *or* encouraging, etc., suspicion; with caution, with (some) reservation(s) *or* allowance(s), not gullibly *or* wholeheartedly *or* without reservations *or* doubts, etc., with a grain *or* a pinch of salt, *cum grano salis* (Latin), like a doubting Thomas (D).

sustain, *v.* **1.** [To carry]—*Syn.* bear, bear on the shoulder, carry on the back, hold up, support the weight of, keep from falling, keep from sinking, convey, transport, transfer, put a shoulder under; *all* (D): pack, tote, lug.—*Ant.* abandon*, drop, desert.
2. [To nourish]—*Syn.* keep up, maintain, provide food for, give food to, maintain the health of, keep in health, nurture, supply food for, nurse; see also **provide** 1, **support** 2.—*Ant.* neglect*, injure, starve.

3. [To defend]—*Syn.* befriend, favor, stand by, support, comfort; *all* (D): side with, back up, stand up for; see also **defend** 3,—*Ant.* oppose*, hinder*, forsake.

sustained, *mod.* —*Syn.* maintained, continued, supported; see **backed** 2.

sustenance, *n.* —*Syn.* nourishment, food, nutrition; see **aid** 1, **subsistence** 1, 2.

suture, *n.* —*Syn.* stitching, stitch, joint; see **seam.**

svelte, *mod.* —*Syn.* lithe, lissome, lean; see **smooth** 1, **thin** 2.

swab, *v.* —*Syn.* wash, sweep, scrub; see **clean, mop.**

swabbed, *mod.* —*Syn.* mopped (down *or* up), cleaned, scrubbed; see **clean** 1.

swacked (D), *mod.* —*Syn.* inebriated, drunken, high (D); see **drunk.**

swaddle, *v.* —*Syn.* swathe, enwrap, sheathe; see **clothe, wrap** 1, 2.

swag (D), *n.* —*Syn.* loot, plunder, graft; see **booty.**

swagger, *v.* **1.** [To strut]—*Syn.* sway, saunter, prance; see **strut.**

2. [To boast]—*Syn.* gloat, brag, show off; see **boast** 1.

swain, *n.* —*Syn.* wooer, beau, suitor; see **lover** 2.

swallow, *n.* Swallows include the following—bank, cliff, barn, tree, eave, rough-winged; purple martin; see also **bird** 1.

swallow, *v.* —*Syn.* consume, engulf, gulp, take, wash down, pour, swill, bolt, take in one draught, swig, choke down, ingurgitate, imbibe, swallow up, toss off (D); see also **drink** 1, **eat** 1.

swami, *n.* —*Syn.* lord, master, guru; see **priest, professor, teacher** 1.

swamp, *n.* —*Syn.* bog, fen, quagmire, morass, marsh, slough, soft ground, wet ground, mire, peat bog, holm, swale, bottoms, river bottoms, moor, spongy ground, lowland, bayou, bottomland, cattail swamp, tule swamp, fen land, boggy ground, swampy ground, polder, trembling prairie, Everglades, muskag; see also **mud.**—*Ant.* desert*, high ground, rocky ground.

swampy, *mod.* —*Syn.* boggy, wet, miry; see **marshy, muddy** 2.

swan, *n.* —*Syn.* aquatic bird, trumpeter, whooper; see **bird** 1.

swank, *n.* —*Syn.* spectacle, array, swagger; see **display** 2.

swanky (D), *mod.* —*Syn.* showy, ostentatious, swank (D); see **rich** 2, **expensive.**

swan song, *n.* —*Syn.* dirge, elegy, *chant du cygne* (French); see **song.**

swap, *v.* —*Syn.* interchange, trade, barter; see **exchange** 2.

sward, *n.* —*Syn.* turf, sod, lawn; see **grass** 1.

swarm, *n.* —*Syn.* throng, crowd, multitude, dense crowd, horde, pack, troop, drove, shoal, school. —*Ant.* one*, not any, none.

swarm, *v.* —*Syn.* gather like bees, rush together, crowd, cluster, move in a crowd, throng, flock together, gather in multitudes; see also **teem.**

swarthy, *mod.* —*Syn.* dark skinned, brown, tawny, dark hued, dark complexioned.

swastika, *n.* —*Syn.* cross, insignia, triskele; see **emblem.**

swat, *v.* —*Syn.* beat, knock, slap; see **hit** 1.

swatch, *n.* —*Syn.* sample, pattern, fragment; see **example** 1.

swath, *v.* —*Syn.* strip, row, ribbon; see **stripe, track** 2.

swathe, *v.* —*Syn.* drape, bandage, bind; see **clothe, wrap** 1.

sway, *n.* **1.** [Fluctuation]—*Syn.* swaying, swinging, swing, leaning, oscillation, vibration, undulation, wave, wavering, pulsation.

2. [Authority]—*Syn.* power, jurisdiction, rule; see **dominion** 1, **government** 1.

hold sway—*Syn.* rule, control, dominate; see **govern** 1, **reign.**

sway, *v.* **1.** [To fluctuate]—*Syn.* bend, oscillate, swagger; see **swing** 1, **wave** 3.

2. [To influence]—*Syn.* persuade, affect, direct; see **impress** 2, **influence.**

swear, *v.* **1.** [To curse]—*Syn.* blaspheme, utter profanity, cuss (D); see **curse** 1, 2.

2. [To take an oath]—*Syn.* avow, affirm, depose, testify, state, vow, attest, warrant, vouch, assert, swear by, make an affidavit, give witness, cross one's heart.

3. [To declare]—*Syn.* assert, affirm, maintain; see **declare** 1, **justify** 2.

swear by, *v.* —*Syn.* believe, commit, have faith in; see **trust** 1.

swear for, *v.* —*Syn.* guarantee, uphold, give assurance (for); see **back** 2, **help** 1, **support** 2.

swear in, *v.* —*Syn.* bring forward, call to testify, put on the (witness) stand, administer an oath, put upon oath.

swearing, *n.* —*Syn.* cursing, profanity, blaspheming; see **blasphemy, curse.**

swear off, *v.* —*Syn.* quit, reform, resolve; see **halt** 2, **suspend** 2, **stop** 1.

swear out, *v.* —*Syn.* charge (with), enter a charge (against), obtain a warrant; see **accuse.**

sweat, *n.* —*Syn.* perspiration, insensible perspiration, beads of sweat, sweating, excretion of the sweat glands, transudation, steam.

sweat, *v.* **1.** [To perspire]—*Syn.* perspire, secrete, transude, swelter, wilt, exude, break out in a sweat.

2. [To work hard]—*Syn.* toil, slave, exert; see **work** 1.

sweat blood (D), *v.* —*Syn.* slave, endure, labor; see **suffer** 1, **work** 1.

sweater, *n.* Types of sweaters include the following —coat, Norwegian, Fair Isle, twin, evening, sport, long-sleeved, short-sleeved, barrel, sleeveless, crew neck, turtle neck; pull-over, cardigan; see **clothes.**

sweat (it) out (D), *v.* —*Syn.* worry, agonize, be troubled *or* uncertain *or* doubtful *or* worried, etc.; see **endure** 2, **suffer** 1.

sweaty, *mod.* —*Syn.* perspiring, moist, wet with perspiration, wet with sweat, glowing, drenched in perspiration, bathed in *or* covered with sweat; see **hot** 1.

Swedish, *mod.* —*Syn.* from Sweden, from the far north, from the northland, North Germanic, Norse, Scandinavian, from the land of Svea, from Svealand.

sweep, *n.* **1.** [Movement]—*Syn.* course, progress, stroke; see **movement** 2, **swing.**

2. [Extent]—*Syn.* range, compass, scope; see **breadth** 2, **extent, length** 1, 2, 3.

sweep, *v.* —*Syn.* brush up, clear, clear up; *both* (D); tidy, ready up; see **clean, mop.**

sweeping, *mod.* —*Syn.* extensive, complete, all-embracing; see **comprehensive, full** 3.

sweepings, *n.* —*Syn.* dirt, litter, refuse; see **filth, trash** 1, 2.

sweeptstakes, *n.* —*Syn.* contest, competition, event; see **race** 3, **sport** 3.

sweep under the rug (D), *v.* —*Syn.* conceal, ignore, get *or* put something out of sight; see **hide** 1, **neglect** 1.

sweet, *mod.* **1.** [Sweet in taste]—*Syn.* toothsome, sugary, luscious, candied, sweet as honey, sweet as sugar, sugared, honeyed, syrupy, like honey, like sugar, honeyed, saccharine, cloying, like nectar, delicious; see **rich** 4.—*Ant.* sour*, bitter, sharp.

2. [Sweet in disposition]—*Syn.* agreeable, pleasing, engaging, winning, delightful, patient, reasonable, gentle, kind, generous, unselfish, sweet-tempered, even-tempered, good-humored, considerate, thoughtful, companionable; *all* (D): saccharine, mushy, gooey, soppy; see **friendly** 1.—*Ant.* selfish*, repulsive, inconsiderate.

3. [Not salt]—*Syn.* fresh, unsalted, uncured, unseasoned, freshened.—*Ant.* salty*, pickled, briny.

4. [Dear]—*Syn.* sympathetic, loving, winsome; see **beloved.**

sweet, *n.* **1.** [A term of affection]—*Syn.* dear, sweetheart, dearest; see **darling** 2.

2. [A dessert; *British*]—*Syn.* the sweet course, final course, end of the meal, top-off (D); see also **dessert.**

sweeten, *v.* **1.** [To make sweet]—*Syn.* sugar, add sugar, make sweet, add sweetening, make toothsome, give a sweet flavor to, mull; see also **flavor.** —*Ant.* sour*, make sour, make bitter.

2. [To make fresh]—*Syn.* purify, freshen, remove salt from, fumigate, disinfect, cleanse, revive, renew, ventilate.

sweetheart, *n.* —*Syn.* beloved, dear, loved one; see **darling** 2, **lover** 1.

sweetly, *mod.* **1.** [In a sweet manner]—*Syn.* agreeably, pleasantly, comfortably, gently, gratefully, softly, smoothly, kindly, with winsome ways, in a winning manner, charmingly, ingenuously, with naïveté.

2. [With a sweet sound]—*Syn.* like music, with the sound of silver bells, like a bell, musically, tunefully, melodiously, mellifluously, with the voice of an angel, like a bird, with a golden voice; see also **harmonious** 1, **lyrical, musical** 1.

sweetness, *n.* **1.** [Sweetness of taste]—*Syn.* freshness, sugar content, palatableness, sweet taste, a taste like honey, flavor of honey.

2. [Figurative sweetness]—*Syn.* mildness, gentleness, docility, unselfishness, generosity, consideration.

sweet potato, *n.*—*Syn.* *batata* (Haitian), *patata* (Spanish), *Ipomoea batatas* (Latin), potato, potato vine, yam; see also **food, vegetable.**

sweets, *n.* —*Syn.* bonbons, candy, confectionery, confection, sweetmeats, comfit, preserves, candied fruit, *glacé* fruit, *glacé* nuts; see also **dessert, ice cream.**

sweet-scented, *mod.* —*Syn.* fragrant, aromatic, perfumed; see **odorous** 2.

sweet-sounding, *mod.* —*Syn.* musical, resonant, melodic; see **harmonious** 1, **lyrical, melodious.**

sweet-tempered, *mod.* —*Syn.* good-natured, amiable, tranquil; see **calm** 1, **friendly** 1.

swell (D), *mod.* —*Syn.* just what one wants, desirable, fine; see **excellent.**

swell, *v.* —*Syn.* dilate, expand, distend, increase, enlarge, grow, grow larger, puff up, be inflated, become larger, bulge, balloon, puff, inflate, bulge out, blister, plump, round out, fill out, tumefy, become tumid *or* swollen.

swelling, *n.* —*Syn.* welt, wale, weal, wart, pimple, wen, carbuncle, boil, pock, pustule, inflammation, growth, corn, lump, bunion, tumor, suppuration, blister, abscess, contusion, abrasion, ridge; see also **injury** 1, **sore.**

swelter, *v.* —*Syn.* suffocate, simmer, perspire; see **sweat** 1.

sweltering, *mod.* —*Syn.* scorching, sultry, humid; see **close** 5, **hot** 1.

swiftly, *mod.* —*Syn.* quickly, speedily, space, without warning, with breath-taking speed.

swiftness, *n.* —*Syn.* acceleration, velocity, rapidity; see **speed.**

swerve, *v.* —*Syn.* move, bend, turn aside; see **turn** 6.

swift, *mod.* —*Syn.* flying, sudden, speedy; see **fast** 1.

swift-footed, *mod.* —*Syn.* nimble, fleet, speedy; see **active** 1, **agile, fast** 1.

swill, *n.* —*Syn.* slops, garbage, waste; see **trash** 1, 2.

swill (D), *v.* —*Syn.* gulp (down), drink (up), pour down one's gullet; see **drink** 1, **swallow.**

swim, *n.* —*Syn.* bath, dip, plunge, swimming race, aquatic contest, dive, jump, splash.

swim, *v.* —*Syn.* slip, bathe, float, glide, slip through the water, move, stroke, paddle, go swimming *or* for a swim, take a dip, do aquatic stunts, train or practice for the swimming team, swim free style *or* the breast stroke *or* the Australian crawl, etc.; see also **swimming, race** 2.

swimming, *n.* —*Syn.* water sport, diving, aquatics, floating, natation, bathing, summer sport; see also **sport** 3.

Strokes in swimming include the following—breast, back, elementary back, side, butterfly, crawl, modified crawl, Australian crawl, American crawl, dog paddle, trudgen.

swimmingly, *mod.* —*Syn.* successfully, smoothly, effectively; see **easily** 1, **quickly** 1.

swimming pool, *n.*—*Syn.* plunge, pool, natatorium, bathing pool, public pool, tank, swimming hole (D).

swindle, *n.* —*Syn.* imposition, deception, knavery; see **trick** 1.

swindle, *v.* —*Syn.* dupe, victimize, defraud; see **deceive.**

swindler, *n.* —*Syn.* cheat, cheater, thief, imposter, charlatan, mountebank, trickster, deceiver, falsifier, counterfeiter, double-dealer, forger, rogue, absconder, fraud; *all* (D): confidence man, con man, fourflusher, sharper, gypo, gyp artist, clip, grifter, scammer, bunco-steerer, black-leg; see also **criminal.**

swine, *n.* —*Syn.* pigs, porkers, peccaries; see **hog** 1.

swing, *n.* —*Syn.* sway, motion, undulation, fluctuation, stroke, vibration, oscillation, lilt, beat, rhythm; see also **wave** 3.

in full swing—*Syn.* lively, vigorous, animated; see **active** 2, **exciting.**

swing, *v.* **1.** [To describe an arc]—*Syn.* away, pivot, rotate, turn, turn about, revolve, fluctuate, waver, palpitate, oscillate, vibrate, turn on an axis; see also **rock, wave** 3.
2. [To cause to swing, sense 1]—*Syn.* wield, flourish, brandish, whirl, twirl, wave, hurl to and fro, throw around in a circle.

swinger (D), *n.*—*Syn.* celebrant, sophisticated *or* gay or lively *or* ultra-modern person, life of the party (D); see **clown, guest** 1, **sport** 4.

swinging, *mod.* **1.** [Moving backward and forward] —*Syn.* swaying, fluctuating, waving; see **moving** 1.
2. [(D) Lively]—*Syn.* vivacious, spirited, sophisticated; see **active** 2, **happy** 1, **modern** 1.

swing round the circle (D), *v.*—*Syn.* campaign; *all* (D): mend fences, work at the grass-roots level, beat the bushes *or* the back country; see **travel** 2.

swinish, *mod.*—*Syn.* boorish, piggish, coarse; see **beastly** 1, **rude** 1.

swirl, *n.* **1.** [Eddy]—*Syn.* whirl, twist, surge; see **eddy.**

swirl, *v.*—*Syn.* eddy, whirl, surge; see **roll** 3, 6, **wave** 4. **1.** [Twist]—*Syn.* coil, whirl, whorl; see **curl.**

swirling, *mod.*—*Syn.* swirly, twisting, in turmoil; see **writing.**

swish, *v.*—*Syn.* wheeze, whiz, whisper; see **sound** 1.

switch, *v.*—*Syn.* turnabout, shift, rearrange; see **change** 1, **turn** 2.

switch off, *v.*—*Syn.* turn off, cut (off) the current, break the connection, disconnect; see also **stop** 1.

switch on, *v.*—*Syn.* turn on, start, hook up, complete the connection; see also **begin** 1.

swivel, *n.*—*Syn.* caster, pivot, pin; see **axis.**

swollen, *mod.*—*Syn.* distended, puffed, swelled; see **enlarged, inflated.**

swoon, *v.*—*Syn.* pass out, lose consciousness, languish; see **faint.**

swoop, *n.*—*Syn.* plunge, fall, drop; see **descent** 2, **dive** 1.

swoop, *v.*—*Syn.* slide, plummet, plunge; see **descend** 1, **dive, fall** 1.

sword, *n.*—*Syn.* saber, epee, foil, rapier, scimitar, brand, cutlass, weapon, smallsword, broadsword, bilbo, bill, cavalry sword, Toledo blade, samurai sword; see also **knife.**
at swords' points—*Syn.* fighting, quarreling, at war; see **angry.**
cross swords—*Syn.* fight (with), battle, differ; see **attack** 1, 2, **fight** 2.

swordsman, *n.*—*Syn.* gladiator, fencer, dueler; see **contestant.**

sybarite, *n.*—*Syn.* voluptary, epicure, sensualist; see **glutton.**

sybaritic, *mod.*—*Syn.* voluptuous, luxurious, carnal; see **sensual** 2.

sycophant, *n.*—*Syn.* parasite, toady, flatterer, fawner, hanger-on, toadeater, tufthunter, lickspittle, flunkey, adulator, timeserver, cringer, crawler, truckler, slave, puppet, cat's-paw, groveler, spaniel, lap-dog, sniveler; *all* (D): apple-polisher, gofer, yes-man, bootlicker, stooge, back-scratcher, flunky, smoothie, soft-soap artist, baloneyer, apple-saucer, doormat.—*Ant.* ruler*, master, dictator.

sycophantic, *mod.*—*Syn.* slavish, servile, subservient; see **docile, obsequious.**

syllabus, *n.*—*Syn.* digest, outline, synopsis; see **plan** 1, **program** 2.

syllogism, *n.*—*Syn.* argument, dialectic, prologism; see **logic.**

sylph, *n.*—*Syn.* hobgoblin, nymph, dryad; see **fairy** 1.

sylphlike, *mod.*—*Syn.* willowy, diaphanous, charming; see **graceful** 1, 2, **gracefully.**

sylvan, *mod.*—*Syn.* wooded, shady, forestlike; see **rural.**

symbol, *n.*—*Syn.* type, representative, regalia, token, figure; see also **representation.**

symbolic, *mod.*—*Syn.* representative, typical, indicatory, indicative, suggestive, symptomatic, characteristic.

symbolism, *n.*—*Syn.* typology, metaphor, analogy; see **comparison** 2, **relationship.**

symbolize, *v.*—*Syn.* typify, signify, express; see **mean** 1.

symmetrical, *mod.*—*Syn.* balanced, well-formed, shapely, proportional, well-set; see also **regular** 3.

symmetry, *n.*—*Syn.* proportion, arrangement, order, equality, regularity, conformity, agreement, finish, shapeliness, centrality, evenness, balance, equivalence, equilibrium, equipoise, similarity.

sympathetic, *mod.*—*Syn.* compassionate, pitying, loving, considerate, sympathizing; see also **sensitive** 3, **thoughtful** 2.

sympathetically, *mod.*—*Syn.* sensitively, perceptively, responsively, harmoniously, in accord *or* harmony *or* concert, *en rapport* (French), understandingly, appreciatively, compatibly, feelingly, emotionally, with feeling, warmly, heartily, cordially, kindheartedly, warmheartedly, softheartedly, humanely, in tune (with).

sympathize, *v.*—*Syn.* condole, commiserate, pity, show mercy, show tenderness, comfort, understand, be understanding, love, be kind to, show kindliness, share another's sorrow, express sympathy.

sympathizer, *n.* **1.** [A comforter]—*Syn.* condoler, solacer, consoler; see **friend** 1.
2. [An advocate]—*Syn.* benefactor, partisan, backer; see **patron** 1, **supporter.**

sympathy, *n.* **1.** [Fellow feeling]—*Syn.* understanding, commiseration, compassion; see **pity** 1.
2. [An expression of sympathy, sense 1]—*Syn.* condolence, consolation, solace, comfort, cheer, encouragement, reassurance; see also **aid.**
3. [Connection]—*Syn.* unity, harmony, concord, alliance, close relation, accord, agreement.

symphonic, *mod.*—*Syn.* melodic, musical, consonant; see **harmonious** 1, **lyrical.**

symphony, *n.* **1.** [Harmony]—*Syn.* concord, chord, consonance; see **harmony** 1.
2. [A musical form]—*Syn.* ritornelle, symphonic composition, orchestral sonata, major work; see also **music** 1.

symposium, *n.*—*Syn.* parley, debate, convocation; see **discussion** 1.

symptom, *n.*—*Syn.* mark, sign, token, indication.

symptomatic, *mod.*—*Syn.* indicative, characteristic, significant; see **suggestive.**

synagogue, *n.* —*Syn.* place of worship, Jewish synagogue, house of God; see **church** 1.

syncopate, *v.* —*Syn.* shorten, slide, contract; see **decrease** 2.

syndicate, *n.* **1.** [An association]—*Syn.* company, union, partnership; see **business** 4, **organization** 3. **2.** [A council]—*Syn.* board, cabinet, chamber; see **committee.**

syndicate, *v.* —*Syn.* regulate, direct, merger; see **manage** 1.

syndrome, *n.* —*Syn.* prognostics, diagnostics, symptoms; see **complex** 2, **sign** 1.

synod, *n.* —*Syn.* congress, conclave, assembly; see **committee.**

synonym, *n.* —*Syn.* analogue, polyonym, equivalent; see also **word** 1.

synonymous, *mod.* —*Syn.* same, like, similar, equivalent, identical, correspondent, corresponding, alike, interchangeable, synonymic, convertible, apposite, compatible, coincident; see also **equal.**—*Ant.* conflicting*, divergent, contrary.

synopsis, *n.* —*Syn.* outline, digest, brief; see **summary.**

syntax, *n.* —*Syn.* order (of words), arrangement, grammatical rules; see **grammar, language** 2.

synthesis, *n.* **1.** [The process of putting together] —*Syn.* combination, organization, integration, constructing, construction, integrating, bringing into one, building a whole, forming into unity, making one of many; see also **union** 1.—*Ant.* separation*, disseminating, dissecting.

2. [The result of putting together]—*Syn.* organization, organism, structure, unit, whole, complete whole, entirety, rounded conception, assembly, the one out of many.

synthesize, *v.* —*Syn.* integrate, incorporate, amalgamate; see **manufacture** 1.

synthetic, *mod.* **1.** [False]—*Syn.* artificial, counterfeit, plastic; see **false** 3.

2. [Man-made]—*Syn.* chemically made, ersatz, makeshift, unnatural, polymerized; see also **manufactured.**

syrup, *n.* —*Syn.* sugar solution, treacle, sorghum; see **sirup, sugar, sweets.**

system, *n.* **1.** Order]—*Syn.* orderliness, regularity, conformity, logical order, definite plan, arrangement, rule, reduction to order, systematic procedure, systematic arrangement, logical process, orderly process; see also **order** 3.

2. [A method]—*Syn.* mode, way, scheme, arrangement, policy, artifice, usage, custom, practice, operation, course of action, modus operandi, definite procedure; see also **method** 2.

systematic, *mod.* —*Syn.* orderly, methodical, precise; see **regular** 3.

systematically, *mod.* —*Syn.* orderly, in order, in regular order; see **regularly** 2.

systematize, *v.* —*Syn.* plan, arrange, organize, order, contrive, project, devise, design, frame, establish, institute, arrange, put in order.—*Ant.* confuse*, jumble, disorder.

T

tab, *n.* —*Syn.* loop, stop, clip, handhold, filing tab, strip, flap, bookmark, slip, holder; see also **label, marker, tag** 2.

tabernacle, *n.* —*Syn.* recess, shrine, reliquary; see **church** 1, **temple.**

table, *n.* **1.** [A piece of furniture]—*Syn.* desk, pulpit, stand, board, counter, slab, dresser, bureau, lectern, sideboard, washstand, sink, horse, tea wagon, trivet; see also **furniture.**
Tables include the following—writing table, secretary, dining table, kitchen table, card table, drafting table, vanity table, operating table, altar table, retable, end table, drop-leaf table, laboratory table, library table, refectory table.
2. [A statement in tabulated form]—*Syn.* schedule, digest, synopsis, report, record, chart, register, compendium, index, appendix, table of contents, tabular illustration, statistics; see **summary.**
3. [Food]—*Syn.* meat and drink, things to eat, spread; see **food, meal** 2.
turn the tables (D)—*Syn.* reverse, alter, switch; see **change** 1.
under the table (D)—*Syn.* covertly, surreptitiously, not obviously; see **secretly.**

table, *v.* —*Syn.* postpone (action), defer, put off; see **delay** 1.

tableau, *n.* —*Syn.* scene, picture, illustration; see **view** 1.

tablecloth, *n.* —*Syn.* napkin, table-cover, covering, oilcloth, lace cloth, spread, luncheon cloth, bridge-table cloth, tea-cloth, breakfast set, place mats, luncheon set, doilies; see also **cover** 1.

tablet, *n.* **1.** [A thin piece of material bearing a legend]—*Syn.* slab, stone, slate, monument, plate, record, headstone, tombstone, gravestone, marker, inscription, codex; see also **epitaph.**
2. [Writing paper]—*Syn.* folder, pad, sheaf, sheets, memorandum pad, memo book, correspondence paper, ream; see also **paper** 5.
3. [A pharmaceutical preparation]—*Syn.* pill, dose, cake, square, capsule; see also **medicine** 2.

taboo, *mod.* —*Syn.* forbidden, out of bounds, reserved; see **holy** 3, **illegal, restricted.**

taboo, *n.* —*Syn.* restriction, reservation, stricture, limitation, law, regulation, superstition, prohibition, proscription, ban, no-no (D), interdiction, social convention, moral obligation, religious convention; see also **sanction** 2.

taboo, *v.* —*Syn.* inhibit, inderdict, prohibit, proscribe, forbid, prevent, debar, disallow, exclude, circumscribe, hinder, ban, frown upon, restrict, veto; see also **hinder, restrain** 1.—*Ant.* **allow*, permit, sanction.**

taboo, *mod.* —*Syn.* forbidden; see **holy** 3, **illegal.**

taboret, *n.* —*Syn.* stool, seat, table; see **bench** 1, **chair** 1, **furniture.**

tabulate, *v.* —*Syn.* formulate, enumerate, arrange, index, alphabetize, grade, codify, digest, classify, register, catalogue, systematize, methodize, put in tabular form, categorize; see also **file** 1, **list** 1, **record** 1.

tacit, *mod.* —*Syn.* implicit, assumed, unspoken; see **implied, understood** 2.

taciturn, *mod.* —*Syn.* reticent, uncommunicative, silent, mute, speechless, close, mum, curt, close-mouthed, sententious, sparing; see also **quiet** 2, **reserved** 3.—*Ant.* talkative*, loquacious, chatty.

tack, *n.* **1.** [A short, broad-headed nail]—*Syn.* thumbtack, glazier point, push pin, carpet tack, copper tack; see also **nail, pin** 1.
2. [An oblique course]—*Syn.* tangent, deviation, digression, variation, alteration, sweep, swerve, zigzag, yaw, echelon, sidling, siding, switch, turn-about-face (D); see also **turn** 6.

tack, *v.* **1.** [To fasten lightly]—*Syn.* pin, paste, baste, tie, nail, mount, sew, stitch, hem piece together; see also **fasten** 1.
2. [To steer an oblique course]—*Syn.* go in zigzags, zigzag, change course, turn in the wind, deviate, turn about-face, alter one's course, jibe, yaw, sheer, wear, shift, switch, shunt, bear (D); see also **turn** 6, **veer.**—*Ant.* straighten*, hold a course, take a straight course.

tackle, *n.* **1.** [Equipment]—*Syn.* rigging, ropes and pulleys, apparatus; see **equipment.**
2. [A contrivance having mechanical advantage]—*Syn.* pulleys, block-and-tackle, mechanical purchase, differential tackle (*also* (D): differential), movable pulley; see also **pulley.**
3. [In football, an attempt to down a ball-carrier]—*Syn.* flying tackle, low tackle, shoulder tackle, running tackle, sack, plunge, lunge, shoestring tackle (D); see also **block** 5.
4. [In football, one who plays between end and guard]—*Syn.* linesman, right tackle, left tackle, big block-and-tackle man (D); see also **football player.**
5. [In fishing, equipment]—*Syn.* gear, sporting goods, fishing apparatus *or* paraphernalia *or* outfit *or* machinery; see **equipment, net, rod** 2.
Fishing tackle includes the following—hook, line, fly, (casting) rod, (casting) reel, (cut) bait, (live) bait, minnow, grasshopper, fish *or* salmon eggs, worm, lure, spinner, seine, (fish) net, landing net, pole, gaff, float, bobber, cork, sinker, creel, tackle box, fly-typing materials, swivels, shot, deep-sea tackle, leader, number four *or* six *or* eight *or* ten hook, etc;

cod hook, bass hook, pike hook, etc; stringer, fish sack, basket.

tackle, *v.* **1.** [(D) To undertake]—*Syn.* launch, embark on, work on, set about, take up in earnest, turn one's hand to, begin, turn to, plunge into, devote oneself to, make an attempt; *all* (D): put one's shoulder to the wheel, dig in, start the ball rolling, square off, get going; see also **try** 1, **undertake.** —*Ant.* avoid*, hesitate, delay.

2. [In football, to endeavour to down an opponent] —*Syn.* grapple, seize, throw down, catch, grab, down, throw, throw for a loss, sack, upset, bring to the ground, stop; *all* (D): nail, smear, haul to earth, take, put the freeze on.

tact, *n.* —*Syn.* perception, discrimination, judgment, acuteness, penetration, intelligence, acumen, common sense, perspicacity, subtlety, discernment, *savoir-faire,* prudence, aptness, good taste, refinement, delicacy, the ability to get along with others, finesse; *both* (D): horse sense, good politics.—*Ant.* rudeness*, coarseness, misconduct.

tactful, *mod.* —*Syn.* urbane, suave, politic, diplomatic, civil, considerate, courteous, polished, perceptive, sympathetic, understanding, adroit, poised, observant, aware, gentle, wise, cautious, careful, prudent; see also **judicious, thoughtful** 2. —*Ant.* rude*, hasty, uncivil.

tactician, *n.* —*Syn.* engineer, strategist, planner; see **administrator, diplomat** 2.

tactics, *n.* —*Syn.* strategy, maneuvering, military art, generalship, plan of attack, plan of defense, procedure, stratagem, approach, disposition, map work, chalk work.

tactile, *mod.* —*Syn.* palpable, physical, tactual; see **real** 2, **tangible.**

tactless, *mod.* —*Syn.* stupid, unperceptive, unthoughtful, insensitive, inconsiderate, discourteous, unsympathetic, misunderstanding, impolitic, rash, hasty, awkward, clumsy, imprudent, rude, rough, crude, boorish, unpolished, gruff, uncivil, vulgar.—*Ant.* tactful*, urbane, politic.

tag, *n.* **1.** [A remnant or scrap]—*Syn.* rag, piece, shred, patch, snip, chip, fragment, snatch, trifle, scrap, waste, discard, junk, remainder, remains, leavings, refuse, stubble; see **cloth, remnant** 2.

2. [A mark of identification]—*Syn.* ticket, badge, card tab, trademark, stamp, stub, voucher, slip, label, check, chip, emblem, insignia, tally, motto, sticker, inscription, laundry mark, price tag, identification number, button, pin.

3. [A children's game]—*Syn.* cross tag, Chinese tag, squat tag; see **game** 1.

tag, *v.* **1.** [To fit with a tag]—*Syn.* check, hold, earmark; see **designate** 1, **mark** 2.

2. [(D) To follow closely]—*Syn.* pursue, track, chase, track down, trace, dog, follow the heels of, trail; *both* (D): shadow, trail; see also **hunt** 2.

tail, *n.* **1.** [The prolongation of the spinal column] —*Syn.* rear end, rear appendage, extremity, stub, hind part, caudal appendage, *cauda* (Latin), coccyx, brush, scut, flag, dock; *all* (D): rudder, cue, fly swatter, pole, tassel, wagger; see also **rear.**

2. [The end of anything, especially if elongated] —*Syn.* last part, hindmost part, tailpiece; see **end** 4.—*Ant.* origin*, head, beginning.

3. [Parts in the tail of an airplane include the following—empennage, tail group, rudder, tail assembly, tail skid, stabilizer, diving rudder, horizontal tail fin, elevator, airfoil.

on one's tail (D)—*Syn.* behind, shadowing, trailing; see **following.**

turn tail (D)—*Syn.* run away, evade, avoid; see **escape.**

with one's tail between one's legs (D)—*Syn.* in defeat *or* fear, humbly, dejectedly; see **fearfully.**

tail end, *n.* —*Syn.* extremity, tip, limit; see **end** 4.

tailor, *n.* —*Syn.* garment maker, clothier, tailoress, dress-maker, seamstress, habit-maker, modiste, pants-presser; *all* (D): needle-pusher, nip-and-tucker, whipstitch, sartor.

tailored, *mod.* —*Syn.* tailor-made, made-to-measure, simple, mannish; see also **sewn.**

taint, *v.* **1.** [To pollute]—*Syn.* spoil, infect, rot; see **decay.**

2. [To corrupt]—*Syn.* deprave, debase, defile; see **corrupt** 1.

tainted, *mod.* —*Syn.* infected, diseased, decayed, vitiated, contaminated, fetid, smelling, stinking, rank, putrid, rancid, graveolent, rotten, polluted, impaired; see also **spoiled.**—*Ant.* clean*, pure, fresh.

take, *n.* **1.** [Something that is taken]—*Syn.* part, cut, proceeds; see **profit** 2, **share.**

2. [Scene filmed or televised]—*Syn.* film, shot, motion picture; see **photograph.**

3. [(D) Something that is seized]—*Syn.* holding, catching, haul (D); see **booty, catch** 2.

on the take (D)—*Syn.* corruptible, avaricious, money-hungry; see **greedy** 1.

take, *v.* **1.** [To seize]—*Syn.* appropriate, pocket, carry off; see **seize** 1, 2.

2. [To collect]—*Syn.* gather up, accept, reap; see **receive** 1.

3. [To catch]—*Syn.* capture, grab, get hold of; see **catch** 1.

4. [To choose]—*Syn.* select, decide on, prefer; see **choose** 1, **decide.**

5. [To acquire]—*Syn.* win, attain, secure; see **earn** 2, **obtain** 1.

6. [To require]—*Syn.* necessitate, demand, call for; see **need.**

7. [To purchase]—*Syn.* pay for, procure, gain; see **buy** 1.

8. [To contract; *said of a disease*]—*Syn.* get, come down with, be seized with; see **catch** 4.

9. [To record]—*Syn.* note, register, take notes; see **record** 1.

10. [To transport]—*Syn.* move, drive, bear; see **carry** 1.

11. [To captivate]—*Syn.* charm, delight, overwhelm; see **entertain** 1, **fascinate.**

12. [To win]—*Syn.* prevail, triumph, beat; see **defeat** 1.

13. [To rent]—*Syn.* lease, hire, charter; see **rent** 2.

14. [To steal]—*Syn.* misappropriate, purloin, filch; see **steal.**

15. [To undergo]—*Syn.* tolerate, suffer, bear; see **endure** 2, **undergo.**

16. [To consider]—*Syn.* regard, look upon, hold; see **consider** 2.

17. [To comprehend]—*Syn.* apprehend, grasp, perceive; see **know** 1, **understand** 1.
18. [To lead]—*Syn.* guide, steer, pilot; see **lead** 1.
19. [To escort]—*Syn.* conduct, attend, go with; see **accompany** 1.
20. [To admit]—*Syn.* let in, welcome, give access to; see **receive** 4.
21. [To enjoy]—*Syn.* relish, delight in, luxuriate in; see **like** 1.
22. [To adopt]—*Syn.* utilize, assume, appropriate; see **adopt** 2.
23. [To apply]—*Syn.* put in practice, exert, exercise; see **practice** 1, **use** 1.
24. [To travel]—*Syn.* tour, journey, trek; see **travel** 2.
25. [To seek]—*Syn.* look for, search for, go after; see **hunt** 2, **seek** 1.
26. [To experience]—*Syn.* sense, observe, be aware of; see **feel** 2.
27. [(D) To cheat]—*Syn.* defraud, trick, swindle; see **deceive.**
28. [To grow]—*Syn.* germinate, develop into, grow to be; see **become** 1.

take aback, *v.* —*Syn.* astonish, astound, startle; see **frighten** 1, **surprise** 2.

take a chance (D), *v.* —*Syn.* venture, hazard, gamble; see **risk, try** 1.

take advantage of, *v.* —*Syn.* dupe, fool, outwit; see **deceive.**

take after, *v.* **1.** [To resemble]—*Syn.* look like, be like, seem like; see **resemble.**
2. [To follow]—*Syn.* follow suit, do like, emulate; see **follow** 2.
3. [To chase]—*Syn.* follow, trail, track; see **hunt** 1, 2, **pursue** 1.

take a (long) look at, *v.* —*Syn.* inspect, check (out), test; see **examine** 1.

take amiss, *v.* —*Syn.* bristle, bridle, grumble; see **complain** 1, **mistake.**

take a picture, *v.* —*Syn.* shoot, snap, film; see **photograph.**

take a shot at (D), *v.* **1.** [To try]—*Syn.* endeavour, risk, hazard; see **try** 1.
2. [To fire at]—*Syn.* shoot, fire at, fire a shot at; see **shoot at** 1.

take at one's word, *v.* —*Syn.* regard, accept, take one's word for; see **believe** 1.

take away, *v.* **1.** [To subtract]—*Syn.* deduct, take from, minus (D); see **decrease** 2.
2. [To carry off]—*Syn.* transport, cart off, carry away; see **remove** 1.

take back, *v.* **1.** [To regain]—*Syn.* retrieve, get back, reclaim; see **recover** 1.
2. [To restrict]—*Syn.* draw in, retire, pull in; see **remove** 1, **withdraw** 2.
3. [To disavow]—*Syn.* retract, back down, recall; see **deny, recant, withdraw** 2.

take care, *v.* —*Syn.* beware, heed, mind, take heed; see also **prepare** 1, **watch out.**

take care of, *v.* —*Syn.* superintend, oversee, protect; see **guard** 2.

take cognizance of, *v.* —*Syn.* observe, notice, record; see **regard** 1, **see** 1.

take down, *v.* **1.** [To dismantle]—*Syn.* disassemble, take apart, undo; see **dismantle.**
2. [To write down]—*Syn.* inscribe, jot down, note down; see **record** 1, **write** 2.

take down a peg (D), *v.* —*Syn.* meeken, demean, chasten; see **humble.**

take exception, *v.* —*Syn.* condemn, lament, disfavor; see **oppose** 1, **refuse.**

take five, *v.* —*Syn.* break, unwind, slow down; see **relax.**

take flight, *v.* —*Syn.* flee, desert, defect; see **escape, leave** 1.

take for, *v.* **1.** [To mistake]—*Syn.* misapprehend, misunderstand, err; see **mistake.**
2. [To assume]—*Syn.* presuppose, infer, accept; see **assume** 1.

take for a ride (D), *v.* **1.** [To murder]—*Syn.* shoot, machinegun, slay; see **kill** 1.
2. [To deceive]—*Syn.* defraud, swindle, trick; see **deceive.**

take from, *v.* —*Syn.* take, grab, appropriate; see **seize** 2.

take heed, *v.* —*Syn.* heed, beward, mind; see **take care, watch out.**

take in, *v.* **1.** [To include]—*Syn.* embrace, comprise, incorporate; see **include** 1.
2. [To understand]—*Syn.* comprehend, apprehend, perceive; see **understand** 1.
3. [(D) To cheat]—*Syn.* swindle, lie, defraud; see **deceive.**
4. [To give hospitality]—*Syn.* welcome, shelter, accept; see **receive** 1, 4.
5. [To shorten]—*Syn.* reduce, lessen, cut down; see **decrease** 2.

take in good part, *v.* —*Syn.* stand, tolerate, bear; see **endure** 2.

take in hand, *v.* —*Syn.* educate, instruct, exercise; see **teach** 1.

take in (one's) stride, *v.* —*Syn.* handle, do, manage; see **achieve** 1, **command** 2, **perform** 1, **succeed** 1.

take into account, *v.* —*Syn.* ponder, study, take under *or* into consideration; see **consider** 1, **think** 1.

take into consideration, *v.* —*Syn.* study, examine, ponder; see **consider** 1, **think** 1.

take into custody, *v.* —*Syn.* jail, apprehend, imprison; see **arrest** 1.

take inventory, *v.* —*Syn.* examine the books, take stock of, look over; see **examine** 1, **inventory.**

take it, *v.* **1.** [To assume]—*Syn.* suppose, presume, gather; see **assume** 1.
2. [To endure]—*Syn.* persevere, keep on, carry on; see **endure** 2.

take it out on (D), *v.* —*Syn.* get even with, get back at, settle with; see **revenge.**

take leave, *v.* —*Syn.* retire, depart, withdraw; see **leave** 1.

take liberties with, *v.* —*Syn.* take advantage of, capitalize on, exploit; see **use** 1.

take life, *v.* —*Syn.* murder, deprive of life, slaughter; see **kill** 1.

take measures, *v.* —*Syn.* arrange, provide, adjust; see **prepare** 1.

taken, *mod.* **1.** [Captured]—*Syn.* arrested, seized, appropriated; see **captured** 1.
2. [Employed or rented]—*Syn.* occupied, reserved, held, hired, contracted for; see also **rented.**

take notice, *v.* —*Syn.* heed, perceive, observe; see **regard** 1, **see** 1.

take-off, *n.* **1.** [(D) A burlesque]—*Syn.* cartoon, comedy, caricature; see **imitation** 1, **parody** 2, **ridicule.**

2. [The act of leaving the ground]—*Syn.* ascent, upward flight, forlanding, fly-off, climb, rise, hop, jump, vertical takeoff; see also **departure** 1, **rise** 1. —*Ant.* dive*, descent, tailspin landing.

take off, *v.* **1.** [To undress]—*Syn.* strip, divest, expose; see **undress.**

2. [To deduct]—*Syn.* lessen, subtract, take away; see **decrease** 2.

3. [(D) To mock]—*Syn.* satirize, mimic, burlesque; see **parody, ridicule.**

4. [To leave the earth]—*Syn.* blast off, ascend, soar; see **fly** 1, 4, **rise** 1.

5. [(D) To depart]—*Syn.* go away; *both* (D): split, shove off; see **leave** 1.

take on, *v.* **1.** [To hire]—*Syn.* employ, engage, give work to; see **hire** 1.

2. [To acquire an appearance]—*Syn.* emerge, develop, turn; see **become** 1, **seem.**

3. [To undertake]—*Syn.* attempt, handle, endeavor; see **try** 1, **undertake.**

4. [(D) To meet in fight or sport]—*Syn.* engage, battle, contest; see **attack** 1, 4, **complete.**

take one's chance(s), *v.* —*Syn.* hazard, jeopardize, try; see **chance** 2, **risk.**

take one's choice, *v.* —*Syn.* pick out, discriminate between, make a decision; see **choose** 1, **decide.**

take one's fancy, *v.* —*Syn.* attract, allure, catch the eye of; see **fascinate.**

take one's own life, *v.* —*Syn.* self-murder, die by one's own hand, kill oneself; see **commit suicide.**

take one's (own *or* own sweet) time, *v.* —*Syn.* dawdle, fool around, be lazy; see **loiter.**

take out, *v.* **1.** [To extract]—*Syn.* cut out, pull out, draw out; see **remove** 1.

2. [To escort]—*Syn.* lead, chaperon, attend; see **accompany** 1.

take out after (D), *v.* —*Syn.* chase, trail, follow; see **hunt** 1, 2, **pursue** 1.

take over, *v.* **1.** [To take control]—*Syn.* take charge, take command, assume charge *or* control, assume the leadership of; see also **lead** 1.

2. [To seize control]—*Syn.* take the reins of, take the helm of, overthrow; see **seize** 2.

3. [To convey]—*Syn.* transport, bear, move; see **carry** 1, **send** 1, 2.

take pains, *v.* —*Syn.* make an effort, care, endeavor; see **try** 1.

take part, *v.* —*Syn.* associate, co-operate, follow; see **join** 2, **participate** 1, **share** 2.

take (someone's) part, *v.* —*Syn.* aid, support, second; see **defend** 2, **help** 1.

take place, *v.* —*Syn.* befall, (come to) pass, ensue; see **happen** 2.

take precautions, *v.* —*Syn.* foresee, mind, adjust; see **prepare** 1, **watch out.**

take seriously, *v.* —*Syn.* consider, calculate on, work on; see **believe** 1, **trust** 1.

take stock (of), *v.* **1.** [To inventory]—*Syn.* enumerate, audit, take account of; see **examine** 1, **inventory.**

2. [To consider]—*Syn.* examine, study, review; see **consider** 1, **think** 1.

take the field, *v.* —*Syn.* initiate, start, go forth; see **begin** 1, **campaign** 1.

take the lead, *v.* **1.** [To lead]—*Syn.* direct, guide, head; see **lead** 1.

2. [To win]—*Syn.* run ahead of the pack, move out in front, take over; see **succeed** 1.

take the opportunity, *v.* —*Syn.* take advantage of, act, utilize; see **begin** 1, **use** 1.

take the place of, *v.* —*Syn.* replace, take over, supercede; see **substitute** 2.

take to, *v.* —*Syn.* enjoy, be fond of, admire; see **favor** 2, **like** 1, 2.

take to heart, *v.* —*Syn.* be affected by, feel deeply, trouble oneself, empathize, sympathize; see also **feel** 2, **understand** 1.

take to task, *v.* —*Syn.* reprove, criticize, judge; see **censure, scold.**

take up, *v.* **1.** [To begin]—*Syn.* start, initiate, commence; see **begin** 1.

2. [To raise]—*Syn.* lift, elevate, hoist; see **raise** 1.

3. [To shorten]—*Syn.* tighten, reduce, lessen; see **decrease** 2.

4. [To occupy]—*Syn.* consume, engage, fill; see **occupy** 2, **use** 1.

5. [To adopt as a cause]—*Syn.* appropriate, become involved in *or* with, assume, embrace; see **adopt** 2.

take up with (D), *v.* —*Syn.* associate with, befriend, become intimate with; see **associate** 1.

taking, *mod.* —*Syn.* engaging, refreshing, gracious; see **charming, pleasant** 1.

taking, *n.* —*Syn.* catching, grabbling, stealing; see **booty, catch** 2, **theft.**

talcum, *n.* —*Syn.* talc, talcum powder, powdered talc, baby powder, perfumed talc, toilet powder, after-shave powder, counterirritant; see also **powder.**

tale, *n.* **1.** [A story]—*Syn.* anecdote, fairy tale, folk tale; see **story.**

2. [A lie]—*Syn.* tall tale, fiction, exaggeration; see **lie** 1.

talent, *n.* **1.** [A gift]—*Syn.* aptitude, faculty, gift, genius, facility, skill, capability, expertise, inventiveness, turn, forte, knack (D); see also **ability** 1, 2.

2. [(D) A famous person]—*Syn.* celebrity, notable, find (D); see **star** 3.

talented, *mod.* —*Syn.* gifted, capable, skilled; see **able** 1.

talisman, *n.* —*Syn.* good luck piece, fetish, amulet; see **charm** 2.

talk, *n.* **1.** [Human speech]—*Syn.* utterance, locution, parlance; see **communication** 1, **speech** 2.

2. [A conference]—*Syn.* symposium, parley, consultation; see **conversation, discussion** 1.

3. [An address]—*Syn.* lecture, oration, sermon; see **speech** 3.

4. [Gossip]—*Syn.* report, hearsay, tittle-tattle; see **gossip** 1, **rumor** 1.

5. [Nonsense]—*Syn.* bombast, twaddle, cant, banter, persiflage, noise, palaver, badinage, racket, rubbish, rot; *all* (D): jive, trash, flapdoodle, raillery, bunk, fudge; see also **jargon** 1, **nonsense** 1.

big talk (D)—*Syn.* bragging, boasting, lying; see **exaggeration** 1.

make talk (D)—*Syn.* chat, converse, gossip; see **talk** 1.

talk, *v.* **1.** [To converse]—*Syn.* discuss, confer, chat, interview, speak, communicate, talk together, dialogue, engage *or* have *or* participate *or* indulge in a (meaningful) dialogue *or* a conversation *or* a meeting of the minds *or* a seance *or* a seminar *or* a coffee klatsch *or* a confrontation, chatter, gossip, yammer, remark, be on the phone with, be in contact with, talk over, reason with, visit with, parley, commune with, read, hold a discussion, confide in, argue, observe, notice, inform, rehearse, debate, have an exchange, exchange opinions, have a conference on *or* over *or* with; *all* (D): pop off, talk away, go on, gab, chew the rag *or* fat, match, *or* compare notes with, talk an arm *or* a leg off of, go over, pipe up, shoot off one's mouth, spit out, bat *or* shoot the breeze *or* bull, pass the time of day, be closeted with, engage in conversation.—*Ant.* hush*, be silent, be still.

2. [To lecture]—*Syn.* speak, give a talk, deliver a speech; see **address** 2, **lecture.**

3. [(D) To inform]—*Syn.* reveal, divulge, sing (D); see **notify** 1, **tell** 1.

4. [(D) To persuade]—*Syn.* induce, sway, count; see **influence, persuade** 1.

5. [To utter]—*Syn.* pronounce, express, speak; see **utter.**

talk about, *v.* —*Syn.* treat, take under *or* into consideration, deal with; see **consider** 1, **discuss.**

talkative, *mod.* —*Syn.* voluble, loquacious, wordy, verbose, garrulous, verbal, chattering, glib, chatty, long-winded, effusive, long-tongued, gossipy; *all* (D): gabbling, windy, crackling, full of hot air, yappy, all yaw, gassy, big-mouthed; see also **fluent** 2.—*Ant.* reserved*, laconic, speechless.

talk back (D), *v.* —*Syn.* sass, retort, defy; see **answer** 1.

talk big (D), *v.* —*Syn.* brag, gloat, bluster; see **boast** 1.

talk business (D), *v.* —*Syn.* be serious, talk shop, confer; see **consult, discuss.**

talk down to, *v.* —*Syn.* stoop, snub, be overbearing; see **condescend, humiliate, patronize** 2.

talker, *n.* —*Syn.* speaker, orator, speechmaker, mouthpiece, spokesman, lecturer, actor, performer, debater, story-teller, conversationalist, raconteur, barker, announcer, preacher, lawyer, reader, rhetorician, after-dinner speaker, stump speaker, gossip; *both* (D): windbag, empty barrel.

talking, *mod.* —*Syn.* eloquent, chattering, mouthing, repeating, echoing, pronouncing, expressing, articulating, enunciating, ranting, spouting, haranguing, waffling, speaking, vocalizing, verbalizing, declaiming, orating, conversing, discussing, holding forth; see also **fluent** 2, **verbose.**—*Ant.* listening*, hearing, witnessing.

talk (one) into, *v.* —*Syn.* win over, sway, affect; see **convince, influence, persuade** 1.

talk over, *v.* —*Syn.* consider, consult, deliberate; see **discuss.**

talk up, *v.* —*Syn.* acclaim, extol, commend; see **exaggerate, praise** 1.

tall, *mod.* **1.** [Lofty]—*Syn.* big, great, towering; see **high** 1.

2. [Exaggerated]—*Syn.* far-fetched, outlandish, unbelievable; see **exaggerated.**

tallow, *n.* —*Syn.* beef fat, mutton fat, wax; see **fat, grease.**

tally, *n.* **1.** [Account]—*Syn.* reckoning, summation, poll; see **score** 1, 2.

2. [Counterpart]—*Syn.* match, complement, partner, coordinate, companion, reciprocal.

3. [Label]—*Syn.* identification, emblem, insignia; see **tag** 2.

tally, *v.* **1.** [To record]—*Syn.* write down, register, mark down; see **record** 1.

2. [To count]—*Syn.* add up, sum, total; see **count.**

talon(s), *n.* —*Syn.* spur, clutches, nail, hook; see **claw.**

tame, *mod.* **1.** [Domesticated]—*Syn.* subdued, submissive, housebroken, harmless, trained, overcome, mastered, civilized, broken in, harnessed, yoked, acclimatized, muzzled, bridled; *all* (D): busted, gentled down, dehorned, halter-wise; see also **docile.**—*Ant.* wild*, undomesticated, untamed.

2. [Gentle]—*Syn.* tractable, obedient, kindly; see **gentle** 3.

3. [Uninteresting]—*Syn.* insipid, monotonous, routine; see **conventional** 3, **dull** 4, **uninteresting.**

4. [Without spirit]—*Syn.* limp, flat, weak, mild, denatured, diluted, feeble, halfhearted, spiritless, bloodless; *all* (D): boiled down, half-cooked, half-baked, without punch.—*Ant.* alive*, spirited, animated.

tamper (with), *v.* —*Syn.* alter, diversity, vary, mess (around) with; see also **change** 1, **destroy** 1.

tan, *mod.* —*Syn.* brownish, sun-tanned, leather-colored, unbleached, weathered; see also **brown, tan, tawny.**

tan, *n.* —*Syn.* light-brown, red-yellow, beige, cream, ecru, natural, saddle-tan, tanbark, buff, bronze, golden, citrine, khaki, drab, olive-brown, dun, umber, sand, tawny; see also **brown, gold** 2, **yellow** 1.

tandem, *mod.* —*Syn.* one behind the other, back to back, single, file, behind, in back of, in sequence, sequential, ordered, in order.

tang, *n.* —*Syn.* zest, flavor, taste, savor, pungency, piquancy, taste, thrill (D).

tangent, *mod.* —*Syn.* touching, tangential, in-contact; see **contiguous.**

go off on a tangent—*Syn.* swerve, get off the course *or* subject, lose track; see **deviate.**

tangible, *mod.* —*Syn.* perceptible, palpable, material, real, substantial, sensible, touchable, verifiable, physical, corporeal, solid, visible, stable, graspable, well-grounded, incarnated, embodied, manifest, factual, objective, tactile; *all* (D): big as life and twice as natural, sticking out like a sore thumb. —*Ant.* spiritual*, ethereal, intangible.

tangle, *n.* —*Syn.* snarl, snag, muddle; see **confusion** 2, **knot** 2.

tangle, *v.* —*Syn.* involve, complicate, confuse, obstruct, hamper, derange, mix up, discompose, disorganize, upset, unbalance, unhinge, embarrass, perplex, tie up, trap, mess up.—*Ant.* order*, fix, unravel.

tangled, *mod.* —*Syn.* tied up, confused, knit together, disordered, chaotic, out of place, mixed up, snarled, knotted, trapped, entangled, twisted, raveled, muddled; *all* (D): messed up, balled up, screwy, wires crossed.—*Ant.* organized*, ordered, unraveled.

tank, *n.* **1.** [A large container for liquids]—*Syn.* tub, basin, cistern, receptacle, vat, cauldron, keg, vessel, cask, tun; see also **container.**

2. [An armored caterpillar vehicle] Varieties include the following—light, medium, heavy, radio-controlled, baby, miniature, Goliath, Mark IV, Mark VI, etc.; M-3, M-4, etc.; Armstrong-Vickers, Royal Tiger, *Königstiger* (German), Hunting Panther, Panzer; *all* (D): General Grant, General Sherman, General Pershing, land cruiser, doodle-bug; see also **tank-destroyer, weapon** 1.

tankard, *n.*—*Syn.* mug, stein, flask; see **bottle, jug.**

tanker, *n.*—*Syn.* steel cargo boat, oiler, tank trailer, tank wagon, tank truck; see also **boat, truck** 1.

tank farming, *n.*—*Syn.* hydroponics, agriculture, horticulture; see **farming.**

tanned, *mod.*—*Syn.* brown, bronzed, tan-faced; see **sunburned, tan.**

tantalize, *v.*—*Syn.* tease, torment, frustrate; see **charm** 1, **fascinate.**

tantamount, *mod.*—*Syn.* equivalent, parallel, identical; see **equal.**

tantrum, *n.*—*Syn.* conniption, outburst, animosity; see **anger, fit** 2.

tap, *n.* **1.** [A light blow]—*Syn.* pat, rap, dab; see **blow** 1.

2. [A spigot]—*Syn.* faucet, petcock, bibcock; see **faucet.**

3. [A partial sole used for repair]—*Syn.* patch, guard, cover, reinforcement.

tap, *v.* **1.** [To strike lightly]—*Syn.* pat, touch, rap; see **hit** 1.

2. [To puncture in order to draw liquid]—*Syn.* perforate, pierce, bore, drill, broach, stab, spear, riddle, spike, lance; see also **penetrate** 1.—*Ant.* close*, seal, solder.

3. [To obtain by means of tapping]—*Syn.* draw, draw out, draw forth, pour out, drain, empty.

tape, *n.*—*Syn.* ribbon, line, rope.

Tapes include the following—braid, edging, bending, tapeline, tape measure, steel tape, surveyor's chain, adhesive tape, gummed tape, draftsman's tape, Scotch Tape (trademark), masking tape, reinforced tape, adhesive cellulose, videotape, mending tape.

tape, *v.* **1.** [To fasten]—*Syn.* tie up, bond, bind, rope, wire, hold together, support with tape; see also **fasten** 1.

2. [To record]—*Syn.* register, make a recording, put on tape; see **record** 2.

3. [To bandage]—*Syn.* tie, swathe, truss; see **bind** 1, **fasten** 1.

taper, *v.*—*Syn.* narrow, lessen, thin out, thin down, reduce, whittle down, grow less, taper off; see also **decrease** 1, 2.—*Ant.* increase*, thicken, expand.

tape recorder, *n.*—*Syn.* recording equipment, (monaural) recorder, stereo *or* stereophonic recorder, cassette *or* two-sided reel-to-reel cartridge recorder, videocassette recorder (VCR), dictaphone; see **record player.**

Tape recorder terms include the following—tape deck, tape head, monaural recorder, stereo *or* stereophonic recorder, take-up wheel, reel-to-reel, tape transport, input jack, output jack, two-track, four-track, eight-track, tape cartridge, cassette, digital counter, sound-on-sound, sound-with-sound, reverse-o-matic, automatic shutoff, hysteresis-synchronous motor, voice-activated tape machine, tape eraser, demagnetizer.

tapering, *mod.*—*Syn.* conical, pyramidal, pointed; see **sharp** 2.

taper off, *v.*—*Syn.* recede, rescind, diminish; see **decrease** 2, **taper.**

tapestry, *n.*—*Syn.* hanging, fabric, drapery; see **cloth, curtain, decoration** 2.

taproom, *n.*—*Syn.* barroom, tavern, pub; see **bar** 2, **saloon** 3.

taps, *n.*—*Syn.* drum taps, trumpet sound, bugle taps, bugle call, tribute for the dead, dirge, light-out signal; see also **call** 4.

tar, *n.* **1.** [A viscous liquid]—*Syn.* pitch, mineral pitch, coal tar, wood tar, lignite tar, distillate, asphalt, roofing cement, resin; see also **gum.**

2. [(D) A sailor]—*Syn.* seaman, navy man, blue jacket, mariner, seafarer; *all* (D): old salt, barnacle, Jack, Jack Tar, middy, limey (British); see also **sailor** 1, 2.

tardiness, *n.*—*Syn.* detention, slowness, delay; see **lateness.**

tardy, *mod.*—*Syn.* overdue, too late, behindhand; see **late** 1, **slow** 2, 3.

target, *n.* **1.** [A goal]—*Syn.* objective, aim, purpose, end, destination, mark.

2. [Bull's-eye]—*Syn.* point, spot, butt, mark, dummy.

3. [A prey]—*Syn.* quarry, game, scapegoat, papoose (D); see also **victim** 1, 2.

target date, *n.*—*Syn.* goal, finish, scheduled close; see **end** 2.

tariff, *n.*—*Syn.* duty, rate, charge; see **tax** 1.

tarnish, *v.* **1.** [To stain]—*Syn.* soil, smudge, smear; see **dirty.**

2. [To disgrace]—*Syn.* embarrass, defame, blacken; see **disgrace, slander.**

tarpaulin, *n.*—*Syn.* duck, oilcloth, sailcloth; see **canvas** 1, **cloth.**

tarry, *v.*—*Syn.* delay, dawdle, dally; see **linger** 1, **loiter.**

tart, *mod.*—*Syn.* bitter, acidulous, sharp; see **sour** 1.

tartar, *n.*—*Syn.* hun, hothead, beast; see **barbarian** 1, **savage** 1.

tartly, *mod.*—*Syn.* acidulously, sharply, curtly; see **angrily.**

tartness, *n.*—*Syn.* sourness, acidity, acridity; see **bitterness** 1.

task, *n.*—*Syn.* chore, responsibility, business; see **duty** 2.

taskmaster, *n.*—*Syn.* overseer, monitor, inspector; see **administrator, superintendent.**

taste, *n.* **1.** [The sense that detects flavor]—*Syn.* tongue, taste buds, palate, gustation, *goût* (French).

2. [The quality detected by taste, sense 1]—*Syn.* flavor, savor, savoriness, sapidity, aftertaste, palatableness, tang, piquancy, suggestion; *all* (D): zip, wallop, ginger, kick, smack, bang, jolt, umph, drive, nuttiness, zing, punch.

The basic tastes are distinguished as sweet, sour, bitter, and salt.

3. [Judgment, especially esthetic judgment]—*Syn.* discrimination, susceptibility, appreciation, good taste, discernment, acumen, penetration, acuteness, feeling, refinement, appreciation; see also **judgment** 1.
4. [Preference]—*Syn.* tendency, leaning, affection, attachment; see also **inclination** 1.
in bad taste—*Syn.* pretentious, rude, crass; see **tasteless** 2.
in good taste—*Syn.* delicate, pleasing, refined; see **tasteful** 2.
to one's taste—*Syn.* pleasing, satisfying, appealing; see **pleasant**

taste, *v.* **1.** [To experience flavor]—*Syn.* relish, smack one's lips, chew, eat, bite, enjoy.
2. [To test by the tongue]—*Syn.* sip, try, touch, sample, lick, suck, roll over in the mouth, partake of; see also **examine** 2.
3. [To recognize by flavor]—*Syn.* sense, savor, distinguish; see **know** 3.
4. [To experience]—*Syn.* feel, perceive, know; see **undergo.**

tasteful, *mod.* **1.** [Delicious]—*Syn.* delectable, pleasing, tasty, savory, rich; see also **delicious** 1.
2. [Esthetically pleasing]—*Syn.* gratifying, delicate, elegant, nice, fine, exquisite, esthetical, chaste, fastidious, classical, cultivated, refined, precise, pure, unaffected; see also **artistic** 3, **dainty** 1. —*Ant.* rude*, coarse, vulgar.

tasteless, *mod.* **1.** [Lacking flavor]—*Syn.* unsavory, dull, bland, unseasoned, vapid, savorless, flat, watery, flavorless, unpleasurable, without spice; see also **uninteresting.**—*Ant.* delicious*, seasoned, spicy.
2. [Plain]—*Syn.* homely, insipid, trite, commonplace, innocent, unaffected, simple, natural, innocuous, stereotyped, plain, homely, wholesome; see also **common** 1.—*Ant.* unusual*, extraordinary, sophisticated.
3. [Lacking good taste]—*Syn.* pretentious, ornate, showy, trivial, artificial, florid, ostentatious, garish, clumsy, makeshift, coarse, uncouth, useless, rude, ugly, unsightly, unlovely, hideous, foolish, stupid, crass.—*Ant.* simple*, effective, handsome.

tasty, *mod.* —*Syn.* savory, palatable, appetizing; see **delicious** 1.

tatters, *n.* —*Syn.* scraps, patches, shreds; see **rags, remnants.**

tattle, *v.* —*Syn.* prattle, tell on, chatter; see **gossip.** 2.

tattler, *n.* —*Syn.* muckraker, busybody, snoop; see **gossip** 2.

tattletale, *mod.* —*Syn.* gossipy, garrulous, revealing; see **talkative.**

tattletale, *n.* —*Syn.* informer, talebearer, tattler, busybody, troublemaker, blabbermouth; *all* (D): snitch, fink, squealer, stool pigeon, stoolie, rat, ratfink.

tattoo, *n.* —*Syn.* design, brand, symbol; see **emblem, mark** 1.

taught, *mod.* —*Syn.* instructed, informed, directed; see **educated** 1, **learned** 1.

taunt, *n.* —*Syn.* insult, mockery, gibe; see **ridicule.**

taunt, *v.* —*Syn.* jeer, mock, tantalize; see **bother** 2, 3, **ridicule.**

taut, *mod.* —*Syn.* stretched, firm, tightly drawn, tense, rigid, unyielding, set; see also **stiff** 1, **tight** 1. —*Ant.* loose*, slack, loosened.

tautological, *mod.* —*Syn.* repetitious, redundant, reiterative; see **illogical.**

tautology, *n.* —*Syn.* redundancy, pleonasm, reiteration; see **repetition.**

tavern, *n.* —*Syn.* taproom, alehouse, roadhouse; see **bar** 2, **saloon** 3.

tawdry, *mod.* —*Syn.* sleazy, showy, gaudy; see **common** 1, **poor** 2.

tawny, *mod.* —*Syn.* tanned, brownish-tan, leathery, dusky, reddish-tan, browned, brownish, dusky, dark, mulatto, russet, yellowish, golden, dark-gold, brownish-yellow, *tannè* (French); see also **brown, gold** 2, **red, tan, yellow.**

tax, *n.* **1.** [A pecuniary levy]—*Syn.* fine, charge, rate, obligation, price, cost, contribution, expense; see also **dues.**—*Ant.* discount*, interest, allowance.
Taxes include the following—processing tax, assessment tax, toll, excise, custom, levy, impost, duty, revenue tax, tariff, tribute, dues, capitation, tithe, towage, salvage, wharfage, brokerage, freightage, poll tax, income tax, sales tax, property tax, excise tax, inheritance tax, cigarette tax, luxury tax, county tax, city tax, state tax, federal tax, excess-profit tax, surtax, corporation tax, single tax.
2. [A burden]—*Syn.* strain, task, difficulty, imposition, demand; see **burden** 2.

tax, *v.* **1.** [To cause to pay a tax]—*Syn.* assess, exact from, demand, lay an impost, exact tribute, charge duty, demand toll, require a contribution, enact a tax; see also **require** 2.
2. [To accuse]—*Syn.* censure, charge, tax with, reprove, reproach; see **accuse.**
3. [To burden]—*Syn.* encumber, weigh down, overload; see **burden.**

taxable, *mod.* —*Syn.* assessable, ratable, dutiable, payable, chargeable; see also **due.**—*Ant.* free*, tax-exempt, deductible.

taxation, *n.* —*Syn.* laying taxes, imposing taxes, levying, assessment, money-gathering; see also **dues, tax** 1.

taxed, *mod.* **1.** [Paying taxes]—*Syn.* levied upon, demanded from, required from, assessed, drawn upon, imposed upon, subjected to tax; see also **levied.**
2. [Burdened]—*Syn.* overtaxed, strained, harassed, fatigued; see also **tired.**
3. [Accused]—*Syn.* ascribed, imputed, charged, arraigned, complained against; see also **accused.**

taxicab, *n.* —*Syn.* taxi, cab, tourist car, sightseeing car; *all* (D): tax, hack, crawler, nighthawk, curb cruiser; see **automobile.**

taxing, *mod.* —*Syn.* troublesome, exacting, tedious; see **difficult** 1, **disturbing.**

tea, *n.* **1.** [An infusion made from tea leaves] —*Syn.* beverage, brew, infusion, decoction; *all* (D): boiled leaves, English, Rosie Lee, scandal broth; see also **drink** 3.
Tea and tealike drinks include the following—black, Congou, Keemun Congou, Souchong, Lapsang Souchong, Oolong, Formosa, Oolong, Pouchong, Bohea, Darjeeling, Assam, orange pekoe, pekoe, green, Hyson, Young Hyson, Imperial

Hyson, Gunpowder *or* Pearl, Earl Grey, Moyune Gunpowder, Twankay, panfired, basket-fired, Paraguay, mixed, jasmine, blended, spider-leaf, butterfly's eyebrow, orange flower, sassafras, sage, mint, camomile, tansy, herb, ginger, Abyssinian, Labrador, horehound, cambric; tea of heaven, maté, chai.

2. [A light afternoon or evening meal]—*Syn.* snack, buffet, refreshment, refection, collation, tea party, five o'clock tea, tiffin, high tea, supper; see also **lunch, meal** 2.

teach, *v.* **1.** [To act as teacher]—*Syn.* instruct, tutor, coach, educate, profess, explain, expound, lecture, direct, give a briefing, edify, enlighten, guide, show, give lessons in ground, rear, prepare, fit, interpret, bring up *or* out, instill, inculcate, indoctrinate, brainwash, develop, form, address to, initiate, inform, nurture, illustrate, imbue, implant; *all* (D): break in, give the facts, point a moral, put up to, give an idea of, improve one's mind, open one's eyes, knock into one's head, bring home to, cram, stuff; see also **influence, motivate.**—*Ant.* learn*, gain, acquire.

2. [To drill]—*Syn.* exercise, train, discipline, rear, ground, prepare, familiarize with, school, qualify, mold, practice, prime, perfect a routine, rehearse, repeat, memorize, accustom, habituate, make familiar with, give drill *or* training, give directions, din into; *all* (D): pound into, sharpen up, lick into shape, polish up.—*Ant.* follow*, master, cultivate.

teachable, *mod.* —*Syn.* qualified, amenable, open to instructions, sympathetic, eager, willing to learn, docile, intelligent, bright, apt; see also **able** 1, **intelligent** 1, **willing** 1, 2.—*Ant.* stupid*, unteachable, dense.

teacher, *n.* **1.** [One who teaches, especially in the primary or secondary grades]—*Syn.* schoolmaster, schoolmistress, schoolman, educator, public school teacher, high school teacher, tutor, mentor, pedagogue, coach, master, guru, swami, mistress, kindergarten teacher, pupil teacher, teacher-in-training, substitute teacher, supervisor; *all* (D): teach, schoolmarm, wet-nurse.

2. [One who teaches advanced students]—*Syn.* professor, lecturer, instructor, docent, faculty member, graduate assistant.

teaching, *n.* —*Syn.* pedagogy, instruction, normal training; see **education** 1, 3.

teacup, *n.* —*Syn.* china cup, drinking cup, porcelain cup; see **china, cup, dish.**

teakettle, *n.* —*Syn.* teapot, tea urn, samovar; see **pot** 1, **urn.**

team, *n.* **1.** [People working together, especially on the stage]—*Syn.* partners, combination troupe, company; *all* (D): duo, trio, foursome, sextette, scream-mates, love team, heart team; see also **organization** 3.

2. [An organization, especially in sport]—*Syn.* contingent, aggregation, outfit, unit, crew, side, club; see also **organization** 3.

3. [Draft animals]—*Syn.* rig, four-in-hand, pair, span, tandem, cart horses, string, matched team.

team, *v.* —*Syn.* pull, couple, haul; see **draw.**

team up with, *v.* —*Syn.* attach oneself to, collaborate, corroborate; see **accompany** 1, **co-operate** 1, 2, **help** 1.

teamwork, *n.* —*Syn.* partisanship, collaboration, union; see **alliance** 1, **co-operation** 1, **partnership.**

tear, *n.* —*Syn.* teardrop, droplet, moisture, discharge, eyewash (D); see **drop** 1.

tear, *n.* —*Syn.* rent, rip, hole, slit, laceration, split, break, gash, rupture, fissure, crack, cut, breach, damage, imperfection.—*Ant.* repair*, patch, renovation.

tear, *v.* —*Syn.* rend, split, lacerate; see **cut,** 1, 2, **rend.**

tearful, *mod.* —*Syn.* weeping, mournful, lamenting, bathed in tears, teary, weepy, on the edge of tears.

tearing, *n.* —*Syn.* ripping, slicing, rending, cutting up, slashing, slitting, breaking, lacerating, severing, bursting, cleaving, parting in two, splitting, tearing down, destroying, knocking apart, sundering.

tears, *n.* —*Syn.* sobbing, sob, crying, cry, weeping, lamenting, whimpering, grieving, mourning, lamentation; *all* (D): waterworks, weeps, sob act; see also **grief** 1.

tease, *v.* —*Syn.* taunt, tantalize, torment; see **bother** 2, **ridicule.**

teasing, *mod.* —*Syn.* plaguing, pestering, exciting, tickling, badgering, harassing, bothering, taunting, gibing, twitting, irritating, tormenting, tantalizing, exasperating, vexing, provoking; *both* (D): ribbing, kidding; see also **disturbing.**—*Ant.* comforting*, regaling, praising.

teaspoon, *n.* —*Syn.* kitchen utensil, measuring spoon, 1/3 of a tablespoon, stirrer, sugar spoon, silver spoon; see also **spoon, utensils.**

teat, *n.* —*Syn.* nipple, mammilla, tit, pap, dug, mammary nipple; *all* (D): titty, boob, jug, knocker; see also **breast** 2.

technical, *mod.* —*Syn.* specialized, special, scientific, professional, scholarly, mechanical, methodological, restricted, abstruse, highly versed, technological, industrial.—*Ant.* artistic*, nontechnical, simplified.

technician, *n.* —*Syn.* practitioner, professional, engineer; see **craftsman, specialist.**

technique, *n.* —*Syn.* procedure, system, routine; see **method** 2.

tedious, *mod.* —*Syn.* slow, wearisome, tiresome; see **dull** 4.

tediousness, *n.* —*Syn.* tedium, dearth, dryness; see **dullness** 1.

tedium, *n.* —*Syn.* boredom, tediousness, dullness; see **monotony.**

teem, *v.* —*Syn.* abound, overflow, swell, pour, be plentiful, pour out, swarm, superabound, bristle with, swim *or* roll *or* wallow in, teem with, crawl *or* bristle *or* overflow *or* creep *or* abound with; see also **grow** 1, **prosper.**—*Ant.* need*, lack, become scarce.

teeming, *mod.* —*Syn.* replete, crammed, swarming; see **full** 3, **plentiful** 2.

teen-age, *mod.* —*Syn.* immature, youthful, adolescent; see **juvenile** 1.

teens, *n.* —*Syn.* boyhood, girlhood, adolescence, early adolescence, puberty, late adolescence, young adulthood; *all* (D): teen age, awkward age, kidhood, age of indiscretion; see also **youth** 1.

teeter, *v.* —*Syn.* tremble precariously, seesaw, totter, wobble, sway, waver, dangle, reel, quiver, flutter, teeter-totter, weave, wiggle-waggle (D).—*Ant.* fall*, rest, topple over.

teeter-totter, *n.*—*Syn.* teeter, teeterboard, teeteringboard, seesaw, hickey horse, tipitty bounce, teetery-bender; see also **game** 1, **toy** 1.

teeth, *n.*—*Syn.* dentition, fangs, tusks; see **tooth** 1.

teetotaler, *n.*—*Syn.* prohibitionist, prude, abstinent; see **abstainer.**

telegram, *n.*—*Syn.* wire, cable, cablegram, message, telegraphic message, teletype copy, radiogram, call, report, summons, night message, night letter, day letter, news message, code message; *all* (D): signal, flash, buzzer; see also **communication** 2.

telegraph, *n.*—*Syn.* Morse telegraph, electric telegraph, wireless, radio telegraph, wireless telegraph, transmitter; *all* (D): rig, she, Old Betsy; see also **communications, radio** 2.

telegraph, *v.*—*Syn.* wire, send a wire, send a cable, send a radiogram, communicate by telegram; *all* (D): flash, wire, buzz, send a flash, file; see also **communicate** 2.

telegraphed, *mod.*—*Syn.* sent by wire, wired, radioed, cabled, communicated, sent; *both* (D): flashed, buzzed; see also **sent.**

telegraphic, *mod.*—*Syn.* by code, by Morse code, by International code, abbreviated, short, worded like a telegram; see also **wireless.**

telepathy, *n.*—*Syn.* insight, premonition, extrasensory perception, mind reading, presentiment; see also **communication** 1, **sixth sense.**

telephone, *n.*—*Syn.* phone *or* 'phone, private phone extension phone, radiophone, radio telephone, car phone, speakerphone, conference phone, wireless telephone, cordless telephone, French phone, Princess Phone (trademark), mouthpiece; *all* (D): line, party line, local line, long distance, the horn, the blower (British), extension, pay phone, booth phone, nickel phone; see also **communications, radio** 2.

telephone, *v.*—*Syn.* call, call up, phone, ring, ring up, make a call to, dial, call on the phone, put in a call to; *all* (D): phone up, give a ring, give a buzz, buzz.

telephoned, *mod.*—*Syn.* phoned, radiophoned, called, communicated by telephone, reached by phone.

telescope, *n.*—*Syn.* field glasses, binoculars, opera glass, glass, optical instrument, reflecting telescope, refracting telescope, Galilean telescope, Gregorian telescope, mercurial telescope, helioscope, equatorial telescope, polemoscope, telelectroscope, telespectroscope, telestereoscope, telengiscope, teinoscope *or* prism telescope; *both* (D): lookstick, peeker; see also **glasses.**

television, *n.*—*Syn.* T.V., teevee, video, color television, home entertainment center; *all* (D): (boob) tube, the eye, box; see also **communications, station** 7.

tell, *v.* **1.** [To inform]—*Syn.* communicate, explain, instruct, direct, order, divulge, reveal, make known, utter, speak, report, recite, cue in, reel off, spit it out, paint in its true colors, put before, name over, let in on, let into, open up, give the facts, blow upon, lay open, fill one in, let on, let slip, level with, leave word, hand it to, lay before, break it to, break the news, break strike, add up, keep one posted, let know, give out, leak out, give notice, declare, acquaint, advise, confess, impart, notify, represent, assert, mention, give inside information; *all* (D): tell all, break down with, give away, cough up, come across with, shoot, come clean, make a clean breast of; see also **discuss, say.**—*Ant.* hide*, keep secret, be silent.

2. [To narrate]—*Syn.* describe, recount, set forth; see **narrate, report** 1.

3. [To deduce]—*Syn.* know, understand, make out, perceive, ascertain, find out, recognize, be sure, differentiate, discriminate, determine, know for certain, clinch (D).

teller, *n.*—*Syn.* cashier, clerk, bank clerk, bank employee, counting clerk, bank assistant, pay-off man (D); see also **workman.**

telling, *mod.*—*Syn.* crucial, conscpicuous, devastating, significant; see also **effective, important** 1.

tell off, *v.*—*Syn.* rebuke, reprimand, chide; see **censure.**

telltale, *mod.*—*Syn.* tattletale, significant, revealing; see **important** 1.

temblor, *n.*—*Syn.* shock, quake, tremor; see **earthquake.**

temerity, *n.*—*Syn.* audacity, boldness, hardihood, rashness, presumption, overconfidence, recklessness, venturesomeness, precipitancy, precipitation, hastiness, heedlessness, foolhardiness, thoughtlessness, carelessness, indiscretion, imprudence, impetuosity; see also **rudeness.**—*Ant.* prudence*, caution, deliberation.

temper, *n.* **1.** [State of mind]—*Syn.* disposition, frame of mind, humor; see **mood** 1.

2. [An angry state of mind]—*Syn.* furor, ire, passion; see **anger, rage** 2.

3. [The quality of being easily angered]—*Syn.* impatience, excitability, touchiness, sourness, sensitivity, fretfulness, peevishness, irritability, ill-humor, acerbity, petulence, irascibility, crossness, churlishness, pugnacity, sullenness, tartness; *all* (D): grouchiness, huffiness, cantankerousness.—*Ant.* patience*, calmness, equanimity.

4. [The quality of induced hardness or toughness in materials]—*Syn.* tensile strength, sturdiness, hardness; see **firmness** 2, **strength** 1.

5. [Composure]—*Syn.* equanimity, poise, tranquility; see **composure.**

keep one's temper—*Syn.* remain calm, control *or* compose oneself, not become angry; see **restrain** 1.

lose one's temper—*Syn.* become angry, get mad, fly off the handle (D); see **rage** 1.

temper, *v.* **1.** [To soften or qualify]—*Syn.* mitigate, pacify, moderate, abate, mollify, curb, restrain; see also **ease** 1, 2, **soften** 2.—*Ant.* attack*, violate injure.

2. [To toughen or harden]—*Syn.* steel, anneal, braze, bake, chill, stiffen, caseharden, cement, vulcanize, solidify, congeal, indurate, starch, petrify, mold, set, dry, toughen up (D); see also **strengthen.**—*Ant.* melt, dissolve, soften.

temperament, *n.*—*Syn.* character, disposition, constitution, nature, inner nature, quality, temper, spirit, mood, attitude, type, structure, make-up, humor, mood, outlook, peculiarity, individuality, idiosyncrasy, distinctiveness, psychological habits, mentality, intellect, intellectual capacity, susceptibility, ego, inclination, tendency, turn of mind (D).

temperamental, *mod.* —*Syn.* moody, sensitive, touchy; see **irritable.**

temperamentally, *mod.* —*Syn.* emotionally, typically, by nature; see **mentally.**

temperance, *n.* —*Syn.* moderation, restraint, abstinence, self-control, forbearance, self-denial, self-restraint, abnegation, frugality, sobriety, soberness, abstemiousness, tee-totalism, vegetarianism, water wagon (D).—*Ant.* drunkenness*, prodigality, inebriation.

temperate, *mod.* **1.** [Moderate]—*Syn.* regulated, reasonable, fair; see **moderate** 4.
2. [Neither hor nor cold]—*Syn.* medium, warm, balmy; see **fair** 3, **mild** 2.
3. [Not given to drink]—*Syn.* abstemious, abstinent, restrained; see **moderate** 5.

temperature, *n.* —*Syn.* heat, warmth, cold, body heat, weather condition, climatic characteristic, thermal reading, degrees of temperature, degrees above *or* below zero.

tempest, *n.* **1.** [A storm]—*Syn.* gale, typhoon, blizzard; see **storm** 1.
2. [A commotion]—*Syn.* tumult, chaos, turmoil; see **disturbance** 2.

tempestuous, *mod.* —*Syn.* raging, tumultuous, furious; see **stormy** 1, **turbulent.**

tempestuously, *mod.* —*Syn.* furiously, frantically, without restraint; see **violently** 1, 2.

temple, *n.* —*Syn.* house of prayer, synagogue, *aedes* (Latin), stupa, dagoba, pantheon, pagoda, tope; see also **church** 1.
Famous temples include the following—Solomon's Temple, Zerabbabel's Temple, Parthenon (Athens), Greek Doric Temple (Sicily), Pantheon (Rome), Temple of Fortuna Virilis (Rome), Dilwara Temple (India), Lama Temple (Peking), Shawe Dagon (Rangoon), Honganji Temple (Kyoto), Angkor Wat (Cambodia).

tempo, *n.* —*Syn.* pace, speed, meter; see **speed.**

temporal, *mod.* **1.** [Transitory]—*Syn.* temporary, transient, ephemeral; see **temporary.**
2. [Worldly]—*Syn.* secular, earthly, mundane; see **worldly** 1, 2, **materialistic.**

temporarily, *mod.* —*Syn.* momentarily, briefly, tentatively, for a while, for the moment, for a time, provisionally, transitorily, for the time being, pro tempore *or* pro tem.—*Ant.* forever*, perpetually, perennially.

temporary, *mod.* —*Syn.* transitory, transient, fleeting, short, brief, ephemeral, evanescent, fugitive, volatile, shifting, passing, summary, momentary, fugacious, stopgap, makeshift, substitute, for the time being, overnight, *ad hoc* (Latin), impermanent, irregular, changeable, unenduring, unfixed, unstable, perishable, provisional, short-lived, mortal, pro tem; *all* (D): on the go, on the fly, on the wing, here today and gone tomorrow; see also **momentary.**—*Ant.* permanent*, fixed, eternal.

temporize, *v.* —*Syn.* hedge, stall, balk; see **delay** 1, **hesitate.**

temporizer, *n.* —*Syn.* conniver, hedger, schemer; see **opportunist, social climber, status seeker.**

tempt, *v.* —*Syn.* lure, fascinate, seduce, appeal to, induce, intrigue, incite, provoke, allure, charm, captivate, tantalize, entice, draw out, bait, stimulate, move, motivate, rouse, instigate, wheedle, coax, inveigle; *all* (D): vamp, make a play for, make one's mouth water; see also **influence, persuade** 1.
—*Ant.* discourage*, repel, dissuade.

temptation, *n.* —*Syn.* lure, attraction, fascination, appeal, inducement, bait, fancy, hankering, provocation, yen (D).

tempted, *mod.* —*Syn.* desirous, desiring, inclined, bent on, allured, seduced, enticed, in the mood for, on the verge of, drawn by, on the point of, dying to (D); see also **charmed.**—*Ant.* indifferent*, averse to, disinclined.

tempter, *n.* —*Syn.* seducer, charmer, prompter; see **lecher.**

tempting, *mod.* —*Syn.* appetizing, attractive, fascinating, intriguing, rousing, tantalizing, provoking, provocation, alluring; *both* (D): mouth-watering, temptatious; see also **charming, tasteful** 1, 2.
—*Ant.* ugly*, repulsive, unwholesome.

ten, *mod.* —*Syn.* tenth, tenfold, decuple, denary, decimal.

tenable, *mod.* —*Syn.* defensible, impregnable, trustworthy; see **reliable** 2, **strong** 2.

tenacious, *mod.* **1.** [Adhesive]—*Syn.* retentive, sticky, inseparable, waxy, resisting, gummy, coriaceous, viscous, viscid, glutinous; see **adhesive, tough** 2.—*Ant.* loose*, lax, slack.
2. [Persistent]—*Syn.* pertinacious, purposeful, resolute; see **obstinate.**

tenacity, *n.* —*Syn.* perseverance, obstinacy, resolution; see **determination** 2, **stubbornness.**

tenancy, *n.* —*Syn.* tenure, occupancy, hold; see **ownership.**

tenant, *n.* —*Syn.* renter, lessee, householder, rent payer, dweller, inhabitant, occupant, resident, roomer, lodger, boarder, freeholder, holder, possessor, leaseholder, tenant farmer; see also **resident.**—*Ant.* owner*, proprietor, landlord.

tend, *v.* **1.** [To watch over]—*Syn.* care for, manage, direct, superintend, do, perform, accomplish, guard, administer, minister to, oversee, corral, wait upon, attend, serve, nurse, mind (D); see also **manage** 1.
2. [To have a tendency (toward)]—*Syn.* conduce, lead, point, direct, make for, result in, serve to, be in the habit of, favor, be disposed *or* predisposed (to) *or* biased *or* prejudiced (in favor of), be apt to, gravitate toward, incline (to), verge on.

tendency, *n.* **1.** [Direction]—*Syn.* aim, bent, trend; see **drift** 1.
2. [Inclination]—*Syn.* leaning, bias, bent; see **inclination** 1.

tender, *mod.* **1.** [Soft]—*Syn.* delicate, fragile, supple; see **soft** 2.
2. [Youthful]—*Syn.* immature, childish, childlike; see **young** 1.
3. [Kind]—*Syn.* loving, solicitous, compassionate; see **kind.**
4. [Weak]—*Syn.* fragile, frail, delicate; see **weak** 1.
5. [Touching]—*Syn.* moving, pathetic, affecting; see **pitiful** 1.

6. [Sensitive]—*Syn.* delicate, dainty, touchy, ticklish, oversensitive, hypersensitive, painful; see also **raw** 5, **sore.**

tender, *v.* —*Syn.* proffer, present, give; see **offer** 1.

tenderfoot (D), *n.* —*Syn.* apprentice, novice, greenhorn (D); see **amateur.**

tenderhearted, *mod.* —*Syn.* softhearted, tender, humane; see **humane** 1, **kind** 1, **merciful** 1.

tenderly, *mod.* **1.** [Softly]—*Syn.* gently, carefully, delicately; see **lightly** 1.

2. [Lovingly]—*Syn.* fondly, affectionately, accordingly; see **lovingly.**

tenderness, *n.* —*Syn.* fondness, lovingness, love, watchfulness, consideration, sympathy, courtesy, care; see also **friendship** 2, **kindness** 1.—*Ant.* hatred*, ruthlessness, brusqueness.

tending, *mod.* **1.** [Inclined (toward)]—*Syn.* apt to, leaning, disposed (to), predisposed (to), bent on, likely to, prone to, liable to, verging on, working toward; see also **likely** 5.

2. [Giving attention to]—*Syn.* caring for, managing, directing, supervising, administering, ministering to, serving, nursing, aiding, attending; *all* (D): playing wet-nurse to, babying.—*Ant.* omitting*, neglecting, avoiding.

tendon, *n.* —*Syn.* band, ligament, tie; see **cord** 2, **muscle.**

tenement, *n.* —*Syn.* apartment house, tenement house, slum dwelling; *both* (D); eyesore, firetrap; see also **ghetto, home** 1, **hotel.**

tenet, *n.* —*Syn.* view, conviction, belief, position, faith, trust, opinion, impression, doctrine, system, dogma, creed, principle, profession, credo, conception, self-conviction, presumption, assumption.

tennis, *n.* —*Syn.* lawn tennis, court tennis, platform tennis, table tennis, tennis tournament, match play, professional tennis, amateur tennis; *both* (D): net game, the tennis racket; see also **sport** 3.

tennis shoes, *n.* —*Syn.* canvas shoes, rubber-soled shoes, soft-heeled shoes; *all* (D): gums, sneakers, tennies, creepers, pussyfooters; see also **shoe.**

tenor, *n.* **1.** [One with a high masculine voice] —*Syn.* vocalist, singer, lyric tenor, bel canto tenor, countertenor, crooner; *all* (D): adenoid tenor, bathroom tenor, gelatine tenor, whiskey tenor; see also **musician.**

2. [Tendency]—*Syn.* tone, course, trend, drift; see also **inclination** 1.

tense, *mod.* **1.** [Nervous]—*Syn.* agitated, anxious, high-strung, on edge, fluttery, jumpy, jittery; see also **excited.**—*Ant.* calm*, unconcerned, indifferent.

2. [Stretched tight]—*Syn.* rigid, stiff, firm; see **tight** 1.

tension, *n.* **1.** [Stress]—*Syn.* tautness, force, tightness; see **balance** 2, **stress** 2.

2. [Mental stress]—*Syn.* pressure, strain, anxiety; see **stress** 3.

tent, *n.* —*Syn.* shelter, canvas, canopy, tarpaulin, covering; see also **cover** 1.

Tentlike coverings include the following—umbrella tent, awning, marquee, wigwam, tepee, booth, pavilion, kibitka *or* khirghiz tent, tambu, pup tent, fly tent, fly, canoe tent, lean-to tent, circus tent; *all* (D): rag, top, big top, round top.

tentacle, *n.* —*Syn.* tentaculum, arm, leg; see also **appendage** 2, **feeler** 1, **limb** 2.

tentative, *mod.* —*Syn.* provisional, probationary, unconfirmed, not final, not settled, conditional, indefinite, undecided, iffy (D), open to consideration, subject to change, trial, on trial, makeshift; see also **experimental.**—*Ant.* conclusive*, final, decisive.

tentatively, *mod.* —*Syn.* experimentally, conditionally, provisionally; see **temporarily.**

tenuous, *mod.* **1.** [Slender]—*Syn.* slim, fine, narrow; see **thin** 2, 5.

2. [Flimsy]—*Syn.* insubstantial, slight, flimsy; see **light** 5, **thin** 1.

tenure, *n.* —*Syn.* occupancy, occupation, ownership; see **security** 2.

tepee, *n.* —*Syn.* Indian tent, skin tent, comical tent, wigwam, wickiup, lodge; see also **tent.**

tepid, *mod.* —*Syn.* lukewarm, moderate, heated; see **warm** 1.

term, *n.* **1.** [A name]—*Syn.* expression, terminology, phrase, word, locution, indication, denomination, article, appellation, designation, title, head, caption, nomenclature; *both* (D): moniker, whatsis; see also **name** 1.

2. [A period of time]—*Syn.* span, interval, course, cycle, season, duration, phase, official period of tenure, quarter, course of time, semester, school period, session, period of confinement; see also **time** 2.

bring to terms—*Syn.* coerce, pressure, reduce to submission; see **force** 1.

come to terms—*Syn.* compromise, arrive at an agreement, arbitrate; see **agree.**

in terms of—*Syn.* in reference to, about, concerning; see **regarding.**

terminal, *mod.* —*Syn.* final, concluding, last; see **last** 1.

terminal, *n.* **1.** [An end]—*Syn.* limit, extremity, terminus; see **end** 4.

2. [Part of a computer]—*Syn.* data terminal, keyboard, CRT (cathode ray tube), monitor, printer, output device, input device, screen (D); see also **computer.**

terminate, *v.* **1.** [To abolish]—*Syn.* eliminate, annul, stop; see **cancel** 2, **end** 1.

2. [To finish]—*Syn.* complete, end, perfect; see **achieve** 1.

3. [To limit]—*Syn.* bound, tether, confine; see **define** 1, **restrict** 2.

4. [To come to an end]—*Syn.* finish, cease, desist; see **stop** 2.

termination, *n.* —*Syn.* finish, close, terminus; see **end** 2.

terminology, *n.* —*Syn.* nomenclature, technology, specification; see **jargon** 3, **language** 1.

terminus, *n.* —*Syn.* end, conclusion, limit; see **end** 4.

terms, *n.* **1.** [Conditions]—*Syn.* details, items, points, particulars; see also **circumstances** 2.

2. [An agreement]—*Syn.* understanding, treaty, conclusion; see **agreement** 3.

terrace, *n.* —*Syn.* patio, garden, step terrace, landscape, platform, solarium, raised bank, park strip, hanging garden, green, plot, lawn; see also **garden, yard** 1.

terra firma, *n.* —*Syn.* soil, ground, dry land; see **earth** 2.

terrain, *n.* —*Syn.* ground, region, territory; see **area** 2.

terra incognita, *n.* —*Syn.* unacquaintance, estrangement, unfamiliarity; see **alienation.**

terrestrial, *mod.* —*Syn.* physical, temporal, mundane; see **earthly** 1, **worldly** 1, 2.

terrible, *mod.* **1.** [Inspiring terror]—*Syn.* terrifying, appalling, fearful, awesome, horrifying, ghastly, awe-inspiring, petrifying, revolting, gruesome, shocking, unnerving; see also **frightful** 1.—*Ant.* happy*, joyful, pleasant.

2. [Unwelcome]—*Syn.* unfortunate, disastrous, inconvenient, disturbing; *both* (D): atrocious, lousy; see also **offensive** 2.—*Ant.* welcome*, good, attractive.

terribly (D), *mod.* —*Syn.* horribly, frightfully, badly, notoriously, unbelievably, seriously, fatally, fearfully, drastically, staggeringly, discouragingly, disturbingly, inconveniently, unhappily, unfortunately, intensely, markedly; see also **badly** 1, **very.** —*Ant.* fairly*, decently, encouragingly.

terrier, *n.* Terriers include the following—English terrier, black-and-tan terrier, Boston terrier, fox terrier, Scotch terrier, Skye terrier, toy terrier, rat terrier, bull terrier, Welsh terrier, Bedlington terrier, West Highland white terrier, Airedale, Sealyham, schnauzer; see also **dog.**

terrific, *mod.* —*Syn.* shocking, thunderous, deafening, world-shaking, immense, tremendous; see also **great** 1, **large** 1.—*Ant.* common*, ordinary, conventional.

terrifically, *mod.* —*Syn.* frightfully, mightily, horribly; see **badly** 1, **terribly, very.**

terrify, *v.* —*Syn.* shock, horrify, terrorize; see **frighten** 1.

territorial, *mod.* —*Syn.* regional, sectional*, provincial; see **national** 1.

territory, *n.* **1.** [A specified area]—*Syn.* region, township, empire; see **area** 2.

2. [An area organized politically under the central government]—*Syn.* commonwealth, colony, protectorate, dominion, province, mandate; see also **nation** 1.

3. [An indefinite area]—*Syn.* section, area, boundary; see **region** 1.

terror, *n.* —*Syn.* fright, horror, panic; see **fear** 1, 2.

terrorist, *n.* —*Syn.* subversive, revolutionary, incendiary; see **rebel** 1.

terrorize, *v.* —*Syn.* coerce, intimidate, browbeat; see **threaten** 1.

terse, *mod.* —*Syn.* short, pithy, laconic, taut, compact, brief, concise, pointed, neat, exact, trenchant, epigrammatic, cryptic, to the point, carefully edited, precise; see also **abrupt** 2.—*Ant.* verbose*, wordy, prolix.

test, *n.* **1.** [A check for adequacy]—*Syn.* inspection, analysis, countdown, probing, inquiry, inquest, elimination, proving ground(s), training stable, search, dry run (D); see also **examination** 1, **experiment** 1.

Tests include the following—engineering, technical, structural, mechanical, chemical, countdown, psychological, Rorschach, mental, intelligence, IQ *or* intelligence quotient, aptitude, vocational, qualifying, comprehensive, written, true-false, multiple choice, objective, diagnostic, semester, term, Scholastic Aptitude Test (SAT), association, psychiatric, toxicological, vascular, electro-cardiac, urinary, metabolic, neurological, reflex, eye, exhaustion, breaking point, burst, heat, strength, pressure, density, longitudinal, transverse, tensility, metallurgic, electronic, supersonic, ultrasonic, spectrographic, x-ray, pneumatic, hydrostatic, expansion, contraction, flattening, compression, corrosion, eddy-current, Rockwell hardness, metallographic, complex mixture.

2. [A formal examination]—*Syn.* quiz, questionnaire, essay; see **examination** 2.

test, *v.* —*Syn.* inquire, question, try out; see **examine** 2, **experiment** 2.

testament, *n.* —*Syn.* colloquy, covenant, evidence; see **proof** 1.

tested, *mod.* —*Syn.* examined, tried, essayed, assayed, processed, proved, experimented with, approved, certified, on approval, given a trial, exposed to test, measured; see also **established** 3. —*Ant.* unused*, untested, untried.

tester, *n.* —*Syn.* validator, examiner, lab assistant; see **checker, inspector.**

testify, *v.* **1.** [To demonstrate]—*Syn.* indicate, show, make evident; see **prove.**

2. [To bear witness]—*Syn.* affirm, give evidence, swear, swear to, attest, witness, give witness, give one's word, certify, warrant, depose, vouch, give the facts, stand up for, say a good word for.

3. [To declare]—*Syn.* assert, attest, claim; see **declare** 1.

testimonial, *n.* —*Syn.* voucher, credential, affidavit; see **certificate, degree** 3, **recommendation** 2.

testimony, *n.* **1.** [The act of stating]—*Syn.* attestation, statement, assertion; see **declaration** 1.

2. [Evidence]—*Syn.* grounds, facts, data; see **proof** 1.

3. [Statement]—*Syn.* deposition, affidavit, affirmation; see **declaration** 2.

testiness, *n.* —*Syn.* touchiness, irritability, asperity; see **annoyance** 1.

testing, *n.* —*Syn.* examination, examining, trying out, trial, proving, experimenting, experimentation, questioning, measuring, measurement; see also **experiment** 1.

testy, *mod.* —*Syn.* grouchy, touchy, peevish; see **irritable.**

tête-à-tête, *mod.* —*Syn.* confidential, private, familiar; see **intimate** 1, **secretive.**

tête-à-tête, *n.* —*Syn.* talk, parley, colloquy; see **conversation, discussion** 1.

tether, *n.* —*Syn.* picket, chain, harness; see **fastener, rope.**

tether, *v.* —*Syn.* secure, picket, baten; see **fasten** 1, **tie** 2.

Texas, *n.* —*Syn.* Lone Star State, Jumbo State, Longhorn State; see **South, Southwest, United States.**

text, *n.* **1.** [A textbook]—*Syn.* course book, class book, prescribed reading, required reading, manual, handbook, study book, assigned reference, syllabus; see also **book** 1.

2. [A subject, especially a verse from the Bible] —*Syn.* quotation, line, paragraph, stanza, passage, extract, topic, thesis, theme; see also **subject** 1.

3. [Writing, considered for its authenticity]—*Syn.* lines, textual evidence, document; see also **manuscript, writing** 2.

texture, *n.* **1.** [Quality]—*Syn.* character, disposition, surface, fineness, roughness, coarseness, feeling, feel, touch, sense, flexibility, stiffness, smoothness, weave, taste; see also **fiber** 2.
2. [Structure]—*Syn.* composition, weave, organization, arrangement, balance, strategy, intermixture; see also **construction** 2, **form** 2.

thank, *v.* —*Syn.* be obliged, show gratitude, give thanks, acknowledge, show appreciation, be obligated to, be indebted to, bless, praise, bow down to, kiss, smile on, show courtesy, express one's obligation to; see also **appreciate** 1.—*Ant.* neglect*, ignore, show indifference.

thanked, *mod.* —*Syn.* blessed, shown appreciation, lauded, applauded, appreciated; see also **praised.**

thankful, *mod.* —*Syn.* obliged, grateful, gratified, contented, satisfied, indebted to, beholden, pleased, kindly disposed, appreciative, giving thanks, overwhelmed.—*Ant.* ungrateful*, insensible, thankless.

thankfulness, *n.* —*Syn.* warmth of feeling, appreciation, gratefulness; see **gratitude, thanks.**

thanking, *mod.* —*Syn.* appreciating, being grateful, giving thanks, acknowledging appreciation, being satisfied, showing contentment, admitting indebtedness.—*Ant.* critical*, disparaging, finding fault.

thankless, *mod.* **1.** [Not returning thanks]—*Syn.* unappreciative, ungrateful, self-centered; see **cruel** 2, **rude** 2.
2. [Not eliciting thanks]—*Syn.* poorly paid, unappreciated, unrewarded, profitless, disagreeable, unrecognized, vain, barren, not worth it; see also **useless** 1.

thanks, *n.*—*Syn.* appreciation, thankfulness, acknowledgment, recognition, gratitude, gratefulness.—*Ant.* blame*, censure, criticism.

Thanksgiving, *n.*—*Syn.* ceremony of giving thanks, day of blessing, day of worship, Thanksgiving Day, festival of plenty, last Thursday in November, turkey day (D); see also **celebration** 1, 2, **feast, holiday** 1.

that, *conj.* —*Syn.* in that, so, so that, in order that, to the end that, for the reason that; see also **because.**

that, *mod.* —*Syn.* the, this, one, a certain, a (well) known, a particular, such.

that, *pron.* —*Syn.* the one, this one, the one in question, that fact, that other, who; see also **which.**
all that (D)—*Syn.* so very, so, rather less; see **not.**
at that (D)—*Syn.* even so, all things considered, anyway; see **anyhow** 1.

thatch, *n.*—*Syn.* roof covering, straw roofing, thatch palm, thatching, reed thatch, rush thatch; see also **roof, roofing.**

thaumaturgy, *n.*—*Syn.* alchemy, sorcery, black magic; see **magic** 1, **witchcraft.**

thaw, *v.* **1.** [To melt]—*Syn.* dissolve, liquefy, flow, run, deliquesce, liquate, fuse, become liquid; see also **dissolve** 1, **melt** 1.—*Ant.* freeze*, congeal, refrigerate.
2. [To unbend]—*Syn.* open up, loosen, become soft, relent, relax, mollify, grow genial; see also **soften** 1.—*Ant.* stiffen*, harden, grow cool.

the, *mod.* **1.** [The definite article]—*Syn.* some, a few, a particular one, a special one, a specific one, a certain one, an individual one, this, that, each, every, these, those, the whole, the entire.
2. [Special or unique; *often italics*]—*Syn.* preeminent, outstanding, particular, unparalleled, unequaled, supreme, unsurpassed, unusual, uncommon, rare, singular, unprecedented, exceptional, one, sole, single, significant, distinguished, especial, specific, choice, individual, peculiar, exceptional, occasional, unfamiliar, strange, spectacular, phenomenal, unheard of, unknown, unattainable, invincible, impregnable, almighty, all-powerful; see also **special** 1, **unique** 1.—*Ant.* common*, usual, ordinary.

theater, *n.* **1.** [A building intended for theatrical productions]—*Syn.* playhouse, concert hall, coliseum, hippodrome, circle theater, round theater, Greek theater, odeum, theater in the round, house, opera house, amphitheater, assembly hall; see also **auditorium.**
2. [The legitimate stage]—*Syn.* stage, drama, Broadway, the boards, theatrics, footlights; *all* (D): legit, the oak, the deck; see also **comedy, movies** 2, **show** 2.
3. [Any place of military action]—*Syn.* arena, combat area, battleground, sphere of operations, field, sector, terrain, bridgehead, front, salient, objective, target area, no-man's-land; see also **battlefield.**

theatrical, *mod.* **1.** [Concerning the theater] —*Syn.* dramatic, amateur, professional, vaudeville, touring, histrionic, comic, tragic, farcical, tragicomic, melodramatic, operatic, theater, show.
2. [Showy]—*Syn.* ceremonious, meretricious, superficial; see **affected** 2.

theft, *n.* —*Syn.* robbery, racket, thievery, larceny, stealing, swindling, swindle, cheating, defrauding, rapacity, fraud, piracy, burglary, pillage, pilfering, plunder, vandalism, pocket-picking, safecracking, extortion, embezzlement, credit-card misuse, deprivation, looting, appropriation, shoplifting; *all* (D): fleece, grab, holdup, reef, mugging, stickup; see also **crime** 2.

the genuine article, *n.*—*Syn. all* (D): the real cheese, the goods, not an illusion, the article, the Real McCoy; see also **reality** 1.

the hereafter, *n.*—*Syn.* (the) beyond, afterlife, post-existence; see **heaven** 2.

their, *mod.* —*Syn.* belonging to them, belonging to others, theirs, of them.

the limit (D), *n.*—*Syn.* the unbearable, the last straw, more than enough, *coup de grâce* (French); *both* (D): the pay-off, breaking point, boiling point.

theme, *n.* **1.** [A subject]—*Syn.* topic, proposition, argument, thesis, text, subject matter, matter in hand, problem, question, point at issue, affair, business, point, case, thought, idea; *all* (D): line, rag, stuff; see also **issue** 1, **subject** 1.
2. [A recurrent melody]—*Syn.* melody, motive, motif, leitmotif, thematic, statement, strain, air, tune, melodic subject, developed melody; see also **song.**
3. [A short composition]—*Syn.* essay, report, paper, dissertation, description, statement; see also **exposition** 2.

then, *mod.* —*Syn.* at that time, formerly, before, years ago, at that point, suddenly, all at once, soon after, before long, next, later, thereupon; see also **when** 1, 2.
but then—*Syn.* but at the same time, on the other hand, however; see **but** 1, 2.
what then?—*Syn.* in that case? and then? as a result?; see **what** 1.

thence, *mod.* —*Syn.* therefore, from there *or* then on, from that time, thenceforth.

theologian, *n.* —*Syn.* divine, theologist, ecclesiastic; see **philosopher, scholar** 2.

theological, *mod.* —*Syn.* religious, churchly, canonical, doctrinal, scriptural, patristic, apostolic, metaphysical, supernatural, theistic, deistic, scholastic, hagiographical; see also **divine** 2.—*Ant.* atheistic*, scientific, positivistic.

theology, *n.* —*Syn.* dogma, creed, theism; see **belief** 1, **faith** 2.

theorem, *n.* —*Syn.* thesis, dictum, assumption; see **doctrine** 1, **hypothesis, theory** 1.

theoretic, *mod.* —*Syn.* assumed, speculative, ideal; see **theoretical.**

theoretical, *mod.* —*Syn.* ideological, ideal, imaginative, unearthly, idealized, ideational, problematical, analytical, academic, presumed, postulated, assumed, formularized, formalistic, pedantic, codified, technical, intellectual, vague, abstract, general, conjectural, unproved, tentative, suppositional, pure, unsubstantiated, speculative, transcendental, philosophical, logical, metaphysical, contingent, instanced, open to proof, stated as a premise, in theory, on paper, in the abstract, in the realm of ideas; see also **hypothetical** 1.—*Ant.* practical*, applied, factual.

theoretically, *mod.* —*Syn.* in theory, on paper, in a sense, in idea, in a manner, in the abstract; see also **apparently, probably.**

theorist, *n.* —*Syn.* theorizer, speculator, ideologist; see **philosopher, scholar** 2, **scientist.**

theorize, *v.* —*Syn.* speculate, conjecture, hypothesize; see **guess** 1, **think** 1.

theory, *n.* **1.** [Principles]—*Syn.* postulates, data, conditions, basis, plan, provision, ideas, formularization, systemization, system, codification, code, argument, plea, scheme, foundation, method, approach, outlook, doctrine, dogma, rationale, cosmology, *Weltanschauung* (German), philosophy; see also **law** 4.
2. [Something to be proved]—*Syn.* assumption, conjecture, speculation; see **hypothesis, opinion** 1.

therapeutic, *mod.* —*Syn.* curative, healing, corrective; see **remedial.**

therapy, *n.* —*Syn.* therapeutics, remedy, healing, cure; see also **medicine** 3.
Types of therapy include the following—physical, mental, inhalation, occupational, rehabilitative, child, group, drug.

there, *mod.* —*Syn.* in that place, not here, beyond, over there, yonder, in the distance, at a distance, over yonder, just there, where I point, in that spot, at that point; see also **where** 2.
not all there (D)—*Syn.* crazy, eccentric, demented; see **insane** 1.

thereabouts, *mod.* —*Syn.* thereby, alongside, next; see **near** 1, **where** 2.

thereafter, *mod.* —*Syn.* from there on, from that day on, after that, forever after, from that day forward, consequently; see also **following, hereafter.**

thereby, *mod.* —*Syn.* by way of, how, by which; see **through** 4, **whereby.**

therefore, *conj.* and *mod.* —*Syn.* accordingly, consequently, hence, wherefore, for, since, forasmuch as, inasmuch as, for this reason, on account of, to that end, and so, on the ground, in that event, in consequence, as a result; see also **thence.**

therein, *mod.* —*Syn.* inside, inward, internally; see **there, within.**

thereupon, *mod.* —*Syn.* then, at which point, on that, thereon, suddenly, at once; see also **immediately.**

thermal, *mod.* —*Syn.* warm, tepid, thermic; see **hot** 1.

thermometer, *n.* —*Syn.* mercury, calorimeter, oral, anal, clinical thermometer, resistance thermometer, thermoelectric, thermoscope, telethermometer, thermostat, thermo-regulator; *both* (D): lollipop, temp-stick; see also **regulator.**

thermos bottle, *n.* —*Syn.* vacuum bottle, thermos flask, picnic jug; *both* (D): icy-hot, thermos; see also **bottle, container, jug.**

thesaurus, *n.* —*Syn.* lexicon, glossary, collection of words; see **dictionary.**

these, *mod.* —*Syn.* those, the indicated, the present, the aforementioned, the already stated, the referred to, hereinafter described, the previously mentioned, the well-known, the aforesaid, the above, the below; see also **certain** 6.

thesis, *n.* **1.** [A statement to be proved]—*Syn.* principle, belief, argument; see **hypothesis, opinion** 1.
2. [A learned essay, especially for advanced academic degrees]—*Syn.* dissertation, research, requirement for graduation, master's paper *or* essay; see also **exposition** 2.

Thespian, *n.* —*Syn.* player, tragedian, performer; see **actor, actress.**

the status quo, *n.* —*Syn.* prevailing condition, normal condition, mediocrity; see **average** 1, **normality** 1.

the vulgar, *n.* —*Syn.* the people, common people, the man in the street, crowd, masses, herd, mob, rabble, *hoi polloi* (Greek), pack, riffraff; *all* (D): guinea pigs, small fry, lowbrows, the other half, children of the devil; see also **people** 3.—*Ant.* aristocracy*, the elect, the elite.

they, *pron.* —*Syn.* people, men, those people, all, others, he and she, both; see also **everybody.**

thick, *mod.* **1.** [Dense]—*Syn.* compact, impervious, condensed, compressed, multitudinous, numerous, inspissated, rank, crowded, close, solid, packed, populous, profuse, populated, swarming, heaped, abundant, impenetrable, concentrated, crammed, packed together, closely packed; *all* (D): like sardines in a can, jam-packed; see also **full** 1, 3. —*Ant.* scattered*, spacious, wide-open.
2. [Deep]—*Syn.* high, in depth, third-dimensional, from front to back, edgewise; see also **deep** 2. —*Ant.* long*, wide, across.
3. [Of heavy consistency]—*Syn.* compact, heavy, viscous, viscid, dense, syrupy, ropy, coagulated, imporous, curdled, turbid, gelatinous, grumous, glutinous, gummous, gummy, grumose, opaque, vit-

rified, ossified, clotted; see also **adhesive.**—*Ant.* light*, porous, filmy.
4. [Not clear]—*Syn.* cloudy, turbid, indistinct; see **dull** 2, **muddy** 1, **obscure** 1.
5. [Stupid]—*Syn.* obtuse, ignorant, doltish; see **dull** 3.
6. [(D) Intimate]—*Syn.* cordial, familiar, fraternal; see **friendly** 1, **intimate** 1.
7. [(D) Presumptuous]—*Syn.* insolent, tactless, unbearable; see **rude** 2.
through thick and thin (D)—*Syn.* faithfully, devotedly, in good and bad times; see **loyally.**

thicken, *v.* **1.** [To become thicker]—*Syn.* coagulate, curdle, petrify, ossify, solidify, freeze, clot, set, congeal, gel, grow thick; see also **harden** 2, **stiffen** 1. —*Ant.* flow*, thaw, weaken.
2. [To make thicker]—*Syn.* reinforce, add, expand, enlarge, buttress, widen, swell; see also **harden** 1, **stiffen** 2.—*Ant.* decrease*, narrow down, slice off.

thicket, *n.*—*Syn.* bush, shrubbery, chaparral; see **brush** 4.

thickheaded, *mod.*—*Syn.* stupid, ignorant, idiotic; see **dull** 3.

thickness, *n.* **1.** [As a quality]—*Syn.* density, compactness, solidity, closeness, heaviness, stiffness, condensation, concentration, clot.—*Ant.* frailty*, thinness, slimness.
2. [As a measurement]—*Syn.* breadth, distance through, girth; see **depth** 1, **diameter, width.**

thickset, *mod.*—*Syn.* stout, stocky, stubby; see **fat** 1.

thick-skinned, *mod.*—*Syn.* callous, hardened, unfeeling; see **indifferent** 1, **obstinate.**

thief, *n.*—*Syn.* burglar, highwayman, holdup man; see **criminal, robber.**

thieve, *v.*—*Syn.* loot, rob, filch; see **steal.**

thievery, *n.*—*Syn.* burglary, robbery, pilfering; see **crime** 2, **theft.**

thievish, *mod.*—*Syn.* stealthy, furtive, cunning; see **light-fingered, secretive, sly** 1.

thigh, *n.*—*Syn.* third segment of the leg, thigh bone, femur, proximal segment, ham (D); see also **groin, leg** 1.

thimbleful, *n.*—*Syn.* trifle, pinch, dab; see **bit** 1.

thin, *mod.* **1.** [Of little thickness]—*Syn.* flimsy, slim, slight, tenuous, attenuated, diaphanous, sheer, rare, sleazy, permeable, paper-thin, wafer-sliced; see also **transparent** 1.—*Ant.* thick*, heavy, coarse.
2. [Slender]—*Syn.* slim, lean, skinny, scraggy, lank, lanky, spindly, spare, gaunt, bony, wan, rangy, skeletal, scrawny, lanky, delicate, wasted, haggard, emaciated, rawboned, shriveled, wizened, rickety, spindling, pinched, starved; see also **dainty** 1. —*Ant.* fat*, obese, heavy.
3. [Sparse]—*Syn.* scarce, insufficient, deficient; see **inadequate** 1.
4. [Having little content]—*Syn.* sketchy, slight, insubstantial, weak-kneed, vapid, weak, light, feeble, flat, diluted, thinly stretched; see also **shallow** 1, 2. —*Ant.* thick*, solid, substantal.
5. [Having little volume]—*Syn.* faint, shrill, piping, weak, rarefied, tenuous, attenuated, fragile, small, tiny, featherweight, bodiless, disembodied, ethereal, shaky; see also **light** 7.—*Ant.* thick*, heavy, dense.

thin, *v.*—*Syn.* expand, thin out, disperse, weed out, dilute, edit, delete, rarefy, reduce, attenuate; see also **decrease** 2, **weaken** 2.

thing, *n.* **1.** [An object]—*Syn.* article, object, item, lifeless object, commodity, device, gadget, material object, conversation piece, being, entity, materiality, corporeality, body, person, something, anything, everything, element, substance, piece, shape, form, figure, configuration, creature, stuff, goods, matter; *all* (D): thingumajig, gizmo, whatchamacallit, doohickey, thingumabob; see also **substance** 2.
2. [A circumstance]—*Syn.* matter, condition, situation; see **circumstance** 1.
3. [An act]—*Syn.* deed, feat, movement; see **action** 2.
4. [A characteristic]—*Syn.* quality, trait, attribute; see **characteristic.**
5. [An idea]—*Syn.* notion, opinion, impression; see **thought** 2.
6. [A pitiable person]—*Syn.* wretch, poor person, sufferer, urchin; see also **patient, refugee, tramp** 1.
7. [Belongings; *usually pl.*]—*Syn.* possessions, clothes, personals; see **property** 1.
8. [Something so vague as to be nameless]—*Syn.* affair, matter, concern, business, occurrence, anything, everything, something, stuff, point, information, subject, idea, question, indication, intimation, contrivance, word, name, shape, form, entity.
9. [Something to be done]—*Syn.* task, obligation, duty; see **job** 2.
do one's own thing (D)—*Syn.* live according to one's own principles, do what one likes, live fully; see **enjoy oneself.**
see things—*Syn.* have delusions, misperceive, suffer (from) hallucinations; see **mistake.**

things, *n.*—*Syn.* possessions, luggage, belongings; see **baggage, property** 1.

think, *v.* **1.** [To examine with the mind]—*Syn.* cogitate, ideate, muse, ponder, consider, contemplate, deliberate, stop to consider, study, reflect, imagine, conceive, examine, think twice, estimate, evaluate, appraise, resolve, ruminate, scan, confer, consult, meditate, meditate upon, take under consideration, have on one's mind, brood over, speculate, weigh, have *or* keep in mind, bear in mind; *all* (D): mull over, turn over, cudgel one's brains, sweat over, stew, bone, beat one's brains, rack one's brains, use the old bean, do some tall *or* hefty headwork, figure out, put on one's thinking cap, use one's head, pick one's steps, hammer away at, hammer out, bury oneself in; see also **analyse** 1. —*Ant.* neglect*, take for granted, accept.
2. [To believe]—*Syn.* be convinced, deem, hold; see **believe** 1.
3. [To suppose]—*Syn.* imagine, guess, presume; see **assume** 1.
4. [To form in the mind]—*Syn.* conceive, invent, create; see **imagine** 1.
5. [To remember]—*Syn.* recollect, recall, reminisce; see **remember** 1, 2.

thinkable, *mod.*—*Syn.* conceivable, within the limits, possible; see **convincing** 2, **imaginable, likely** 1.

thinker, *n.*—*Syn.* mastermind, sage, savant; see **intellectual, philosopher, scholar** 2.

thinking, *mod.* —*Syn.* rational, reasoning, reasonable, pensive, introspective, reflective, meditative, speculative, studious, deliberating, contemplative, absorbed, engrossed, intent on, ruminating, cerebrating; see also **thoughtful** 1.—*Ant.* stupid*, vacuous, irrational.
put on one's thinking cap—*Syn.* begin thinking, study, examine; see **think** 1.

thinking, *n.* —*Syn.* thought, reasoning, reason, cogitation, ideation, rationalization, contemplation, rumination, reflection, speculation, cerebration, deliberation, study, meditation, abstraction, musing, self-absorption, introspection, retrospection, intellectual perception; *both* (D): noodling, tall headwork.

think twice (about), *n.* —*Syn.* reconsider, weigh, pause, be uncertain; see also **hesitate.**

thinness, *n.* —*Syn.* slenderness, slimness, shallowness; see **lightness** 2.

thin-skinned, *mod.* —*Syn.* sensitive, touchy, moody; see **irritable.**

third, *mod.* —*Syn.* part, after the second, next but one; see **three.**

thirst, *n.* —*Syn.* dryness, need for liquid, longing, craving, cobweb throat (D); see also **appetite** 1, **desire.**

thirsty, *mod.* —*Syn.* dry, parched, arid, droughty, avid, eager, sharp-set, hankering for, burning for, craving, longing for, partial to, hungry for, keen, itching for, inclined to; *all* (D): bonedry, dry as a gourd, crazy for, wild for; see also **hungry.**—*Ant.* satisfied*, full, replete.

this, *mod.* —*Syn.* the, that, the indicated, the present, here, aforementioned, already stated.

this, *pron.* —*Syn.* the one, this one, that one, the one in question, the aforementioned one, this person, the thing indicated; see also **that.**

thistle, *n.* Thistles include the following—bull, Canada, Russian, common, Scotch, cotton, teazel, yellow, star, bur; see also **plant, weed** 1.

thither, *mod.* —*Syn.* beyond, yonder, toward; see **there.**

thong, *n.* —*Syn.* lace, string, whip; see **rope, twine.**

thorax, *n.* —*Syn.* chest, trunk, breast; see **abdomen, chest** 1.

thorn, *n.* —*Syn.* prickle, spine, brier, briar, nettle, bramble, barb, thistle; see also **point** 2, **spine** 1.

thorny, *mod.* **1.** [Thick with thorns]—*Syn.* barbed, spiny, prickly, bristly, bristled, stinging, thistly, briery, spiky, setaceous, echinate; see also **sharp** 2. —*Ant.* smooth*, soft, glabrous.
2. [Troublesome]—*Syn.* bothersome, perplexing, formidable; see **difficult** 1, 2.

thorough, *mod.* **1.** [Painstaking]—*Syn.* exact, meticulous, precise; see **accurate** 2, **careful.**
2. [Complete]—*Syn.* thoroughgoing, out-and-out, total; see **absolute** 1.

thoroughbred, *mod.* —*Syn.* full-blooded, purebred, pedigreed, papered, of full blood, of good breed; see also **registered** 2.

thoroughfare, *n.* —*Syn.* freeway, boulevard, roadway; see **highway, road** 1, **street.**

thoroughly, *mod.* —*Syn.* fully, wholly, in detail; see **completely.**

those, *mod.* —*Syn.* these, the indicated, the abovementioned, the already stated, the certain, the particular; see also **the** 1.

thou, *pron.* —*Syn.* thee, yourself, thyself; see **you.**

though, *conj.* —*Syn.* despite, even if, if; see **although, but** 1.

thought, *n.* **1.** [Mental activity]—*Syn.* speculation, reflection, deliberation, cerebration, ideation, meditation, rumination, perceiving, apprehending, seeing, consideration, reasoning, intuition, imagination, logical process, perception, insight, understanding, viewpoint, concept, brainwork, thinking, knowing, realizing, discerning, rationalizing, drawing conclusions, concluding, inferring, deducing, deriving, deduction, inducing, logic, judging, rationalization, ratiocination, judgment, argumentation, cogitation, contemplation, cognition, intellection; *all* (D): slant, brainstorm, twist, wrinkle; see also **acumen.**
2. [The result of mental activity]—*Syn.* idea, plan, view, fancy, notion, impression, image, understanding, appreciation, conception, observation, belief, feeling, opinion, guess, inference, theory, hypothesis, supposition, assumption, intuition, conjecture, deduction, postulate, premise, knowledge, evaluation, assessment, appraisal, estimate, verdict, finding, decision, determination, reflection, consideration, abstraction, conviction, tenet, presumption, intellectualization, ideation, surmise, doctrine, principle, drift, calculation, caprice, reverie, sentiment, care, worry, anxiety, uneasiness, dream.
3. [The ideas of a given time, place, people, etc.] —*Syn.* philosophy, way of life, outlook, views, principles, worldview, *Zeitgeist* (German), spirit, custom, mores.
4. [Care or attention]—*Syn.* heed, thoughtfulness, solicitude; see **attention** 1, 2, **care** 2.

thoughtful, *mod.* **1.** [Notable for thought]—*Syn.* thinking, meditative, engrossed, absorbed, rapt in, pensive, considered, seasoned, matured, studied, philosophic, contemplative, studious, cogitative, ruminative, examined, pondered, speculative, deliberative, reflective, introspective, clear-headed, level seasoned, matured, studied, philosophic, contemplative, studious, cogitative, ruminative, examined, pondered, speculative, deliberative, reflective, introspective, clear-headed, level-headed, keen, wise, well-balanced, judged, far-sighted, reasoning, rational, calculating, discerning, penetrating, politic, shrewd, careful, sensible, retrospective, intellectual; *both* (D): brainy, deep.—*Ant.* thoughtless*, unthinking, irrational.
2. [Considerate]—*Syn.* heedful, polite, courteous, solicitous, friendly, kind, kindly, unselfish, concerned, anxious, neighborly, regardful, social, cooperative, responsive, aware, sensitive, benign, indulgent, obliging, careful, attentive, gallant, chivalrous, charitable.—*Ant.* selfish*, boorish, inconsiderate.

thoughtfulness, *n.* —*Syn.* understanding, helpfulness, indulgence; see **kindness** 1.

thoughtless, *mod.* **1.** [Destitute of thought]—*Syn.* irrational, unreasoning, unreasonable, vacuous, inane, incomprehensible, witless, undiscerning, bovine, foolish, doltish, babbling, bewildered, confused, puerile, senseless, driveling, inept, dull, heavy, obtuse, feeble-minded, flighty; *all* (D): empty-headed, lame-brained, barmy, nutty, loony, rattled, sappy, dizzy; see also **stupid** 1.—*Ant.* rational*, reasoning, shrewd.

2. [Inconsiderate]—*Syn.* heedless, negligent, inattentive, careless, indiscreet, neglectful, self-centered, egocentric, selfish, asocial, antisocial, unmindful, unheeding, reckless, deaf, blind, indifferent, unconcerned, listless, apathetic, boorish, discourteous, rude, primitive, unrefined; see also **rude** 2.—*Ant.* careful*, thoughtful, unselfish.

thoughtlessness, *n.*—*Syn.* inattention, oversight, heedlessness; see **carelessness, neglect** 1.

thought (over *or* **through),** *mod.*—*Syn.* studied, thought about, revised; see **considered** 1, **investigated.**

thousand, *mod.*—*Syn.* ten hundred, millenary, thousandfold, multitudinous, myriad, numerous.

thrall, *n.*—*Syn.* bondman, serf, vassal; see **slave** 1.

thralldom, *n.*—*Syn.* servitude, subjugation, bondage; see **slavery** 1.

thrash, *v.*—*Syn.* trounce, whip, chasten; see **beat** 2, **punish.**

thread, *n.*—*Syn.* cotton, yarn, wool, lisle, filament, fiber, strand, wire, hair, gossamer, cobweb, twist, string, tape, ribbon, braid, strand; see also **cloth.**

thread, *v.* **1.** [To pass thread through a needle]—*Syn.* wire, string, run through, wind through, slip through.—*Ant.* undo*, unthread, change the thread.

2. [To Connect]—*Syn.* attach, weave together, string together; see **join** 1.

threadbare, *mod.* **1.** [Ragged]—*Syn.* shabby, seedy, frayed; see **ragged, worn** 1.

2. [Trite]—*Syn.* stale, tedious, everyday; see **common** 1, **dull** 4, **poor** 2.

threat, *n.*—*Syn.* menace, fulmination, intimidation; see **warning.**

threaten, *v.* **1.** [To warn of punishment]—*Syn.* intimidate, menace, caution, admonish, hold over, scare, torment, push around, browbeat, forewarn, bully, terrorize, abuse, bluster, fulminate, look daggers, thunder against; *all* (D): bulldoze, draw *or* pull a gun on, double the fist at; see also **frighten** 1, **abuse** 1, **warn.**—*Ant.* help*, mollify, placate.

2. [To impend]—*Syn.* endanger, be dangerous, be gathering, be in the offing, imperil, be brewing, be on the horizon, approach, come on, advance; see also **frighten** 1, **loom** 2.—*Ant.* happen*, seize, overcome.

threatened, *mod.*—*Syn.* warned, endangered, imperiled, jeopardized, in bad straits, insecure, unsafe, unprotected, vulnerable, exposed, in a crucial state, in danger, besieged, surrounded, under attack, set upon, in a bad way.—*Ant.* safe*, invulnerable, protected.

threatening, *mod.*—*Syn.* alarming, dangerous, aggressive; see **ominous, sinister, unsafe.**

three, *mod.*—*Syn.* triple, treble, threefold, third, triform, triune, tertiary, thrice, triply.

threnody, *n.*—*Syn.* dirge, requiem, lament; see **song.**

thresh, *v.* **1.** [To free grain or seed from hulls]—*Syn.* loosen, flail, tread, separate, winnow, sift, beat, garner; see **beat** 2.

2. [To chastise]—*Syn.* trounce, whip, hit; see **beat** 2, **punish.**

thresher, *n.*—*Syn.* harvest hand, harvester, pitcher, bundle-hauler, separator man, engineer, grain-shoveler; see also **laborer.**

threshing, *n.* **1.** [The act of removing grain from hulls]—*Syn.* separating, flailing, beating, treading, garnering, winnowing, sifting, harvesting; *both* (D): putting it through, combining; see also **division** 1.

2. [A beating]—*Syn.* trouncing, infliction, drubbing; see **punishment.**

threshold, *n.* **1.** [An entrance]—*Syn.* sill, doorsill, vestibule, gate, door, groundsel; see also **entrance** 1.

2. [A beginning]—*Syn.* inception, outset, start; see **origin** 1.

thrice, *mod.* **1.** [Threefold]—*Syn.* triply, threefold, trebly; see **triple.**

2. [Very]—*Syn.* greatly, highly, amply; see **very.**

thrift, *n.*—*Syn.* saving, parsimony, frugality; see **economy** 2.

thriftless, *mod.*—*Syn.* extravagant, lavish, negligent; see **wasteful.**

thrifty, *mod.*—*Syn.* saving, careful, frugal; see **economical** 1.

thrill, *n.*—*Syn.* pleasant sensation, stimulation, good feeling, refreshment, titillation, tingle, glow, flush, response, flutter, twitter, inspiration; *all* (D): kick, bang, boost, lift, wallop; see also **excitement, fun.**

thrill, *v.* **1.** [To excite]—*Syn.* animate, inspire, rouse; see **excite** 1, 2.

2. [To become excited]—*Syn.* tingle, quiver, flutter, pant, glow, vibrate, palpitate, titillate, shiver.

thrilled, *mod.*—*Syn.* animated, inspired, moved, touched, imbued, stirred, electrified, aroused; see also **excited, happy** 1.—*Ant.* indifferent*, unmoved, blasé.

thrilling, *mod.*—*Syn.* overwhelming, electrifying, exciting, exquisite, wondrous, enchanting, magnificent, breathtaking, miraculous, hair-raising, blood-tingling; see also **stimulating.**—*Ant.* common*, conventional*, ordinary.

thrive, *v.* **1.** [To grow vigorously]—*Syn.* blossom, blossom out, burgeon, wax, shoot up, flourish, mushroom, rise, bear fruit, batten, increase, radiate, shine; see also **grow.**—*Ant.* die*, wither, sicken.

2. [To prosper]—*Syn.* succeed, do well, turn out well, flourish, rise up, make one's fortune, make an auspicious start, get ahead, achieve success, advance, make progress; *all* (D): be booming, feather one's nest, get places, make it, make a go; see also **prosper.**—*Ant.* fail*, lose out, go bankrupt.

thriving, *mod.*—*Syn.* flourishing, blooming, prolific; see **growing.**

throat, *n.*—*Syn.* neck, windpipe, larynx, trachea, esophagus, jugular region, gullet, gorge, jugulum.

cut each other's throats (D)—*Syn.* ruin each other, fight, feud; see **destroy** 1.

cut one's own throat (D)—*Syn.* harm *or* damage *or* ruin oneself, cause one's own destruction, act contrary to one's best interest(s); see **commit suicide, damage** 1.

ram down someone's throat (D)—*Syn.* impose, pressure, coerce; see **force** 1.
stick in one's throat (D)—*Syn.* be difficult to say, not come easily, be disturbing; see **disturb** 2.

throaty, *mod.*—*Syn.* husky, hoarse, deep; see **hoarse.**

throb, *n.*—*Syn.* beat, pulsation, palpitation; see **beat** 2.

throb, *v.*—*Syn.* beat, pulsate, palpitate; see **beat** 3.

throne, *n.* **1.** [The seat on which a ruler sits] —*Syn.* chair of state, royal seat, dais, cathedra, divan, gaddi, guddee, masmud, masnad, raised chair; see also **chair** 1.
2. [The symbol of royal power]—*Syn.* authority, sway, dominion, royal power, sovereignty, kingship, His Royal Majesty, His Royal Highness, the Crown; see also **chair** 2, **royalty.**

throng, *n.*—*Syn.* multitude, mass, concourse; see **crowd** 1, **gathering.**

throttle, *n.*—*Syn.* starter; *both* (D); feed, gasfeed; see **accelerator.**

throttle, *v.*—*Syn.* strangle, stifle, silence; see **choke** 1.

throttled, *mod.*—*Syn.* silenced, stopped, halted; see **managed, restrained.**

through, *mod.* and *prep.* **1.** [Finished]—*Syn.* completed, over, ended; see **done** 1, **finished** 1.
2. [From one side to the other]—*Syn.* straight through, through and through, clear through (D); see **in** 2, **into, within.**
3. [During]—*Syn.* throughout, for the period of, from beginning to end; see **during.**
4. [By means of]—*Syn.* by, by way of, by reason, in virtue of, in consequence of, for, by the agency of, at the hand of, through the medium of, by dint of.
5. [Referring to continuous passage]—*Syn.* nonstop, free, unhindered, unbroken, opened, rapid, one-way; see also **consecutive** 1, **constant** 1, **regular** 3.—*Ant.* broken*, interrupted*, intermittent.

through and through, *mod.*—*Syn.* permeating, pervasive, enduring; see **penetrating** 1, **throughout.**

throughout, *mod.* and *prep.*—*Syn.* all through, during, from beginning to end, from one end to the other, everywhere, all over, in everything, in every place, up and down, from top to bottom, on all accounts, in all respects, inside and out, at full length, every bit, to the end; *all* (D): down to the ground, hide and hair, head and shoulders, from the word go, up to the brim; see also **completely.**

through thick and thin (D), *mod.*—*Syn.* in the face of adversity, in good and bad weather, in rain or shine, devotedly, loyally, constantly; see also **regularly** 1, 2.

throw, *v.* **1.** [To hurl]—*Syn.* fling, butt, bunt, pitch, fire, let go, sling, toss, heave, lob, dash, launch, chuck, bowl, cast, heave *or* hurl at; *all* (D): let fly, shy, deliver, elbow, cast off, lay across.—*Ant.* catch*, receive, grab.
2. [To send forth]—*Syn.* propel, thrust, force, project, discharge, butt, bunt, launch, put into motion, start, push into, drive, set going, impel, stick into, pur into.—*Ant.* receive*, retrieve, accept.
3. [To connect or disconnect]—*Syn.* pull a lever, turn a switch, unswitch, unhook, turn off, turn on.
4. [To force to the ground]—*Syn.* cast down, triumph over, strike down, overwhelm; *all* (D): pin, nail, flatten, buck off, pin to the mat; see also **defeat** 1, 3.—*Ant.* raise*, help up, bring on to one's feet.
5. [(D) To permit an opponent to win]—*Syn.* give up, lose the game, lose deliberately, submit, yield, surrender; *all* (D): give in, back down, chuck away, call quits, check out; see also **lose** 3.

throw away, *v.*—*Syn.* reject, refuse, turn down; see **discard.**

throwback, *n.*—*Syn.* atavism, carry-over, regression; see **remainder.**

throw cold water on, *v.*—*Syn.* thwart, belittle, minimize; see **discourage** 1.

throw down, *v.*—*Syn.* cast down, toss, let fall; see **discard, drop** 2.

throw in, *v.*—*Syn.* add, expand, give; see **increase** 1.

throw in the towel *or* **sponge** (D), *v.*—*Syn.* give up, surrender, bow to; see **yield** 1.

thrown, *mod.* **1.** [Hurled]—*Syn.* pitched, tossed, heaved, flung, sent forth, propelled, discharged, directed; see also **launched.**
2. [Beaten]—*Syn.* knocked over, sent sprawling, heaved; see **beaten** 1.

throw off (an illness), *v.*—*Syn.* get better *or* well, improve, gain strength; see **recover** 3.

throw off the track *or* **scent,** *v.*—*Syn.* misinform, abuse, trick; see **deceive.**

throw out, *v.*—*Syn.* discharge, throw away, reject; see **discard, oust.**

throw up, *v.* **1.** [To vomit]—*Syn.* spew out, disgorge, regurgitate, empty one's stomach; *both* (D): retch, barf; see also **vomit.**
2. [To quit]—*Syn.* give up, cease, terminate; see **stop** 2.
3. [To construct, usually hastily]—*Syn.* build overnight, put together, patch up, knock together; see also **build** 1.

throw together, *v.*—*Syn.* make (quickly), do in a hurry, do a rush job; see **build** 1, **manufacture.**

throw up to, *v.*—*Syn.* bring up, nag (about), taunt, mention, repeat, remind of; see also **emphasize.**

thrush, *n.* Thrushes include the following—robin, wood, hermit, dwarf hermit, olive-backed, russet-backed, willow, Wilson's, brown; see also **bird** 1.

thrust, *n.* **1.** [A jab]—*Syn.* punch, stab, poke, shove, wallop, smack, dig, nick, clout, cut; *all* (D): clip, lam, wham, whack; see also **blow** 1.
2. [An attack]—*Syn.* onset, onslaught, advance; see **attack** 1.
3. [A strong push]—*Syn.* drive, impetus, momentum, impulsion, propulsion, pressure; see also **push.**

thrust, *v.* **1.** [To jab]—*Syn.* poke, push, shove, stab, pierce, interject, stick, transfix, ram, punch, wallop; *both* (D): hang one on, elbow one's way; see also **hit** 1.—*Ant.* return*, fall back, retaliate.
2. [To attack]—*Syn.* assault, assail, push forward; see **attack** 1.

thud, *n.*—*Syn.* fall, dull sound, plop; see **noise** 1.

thug, *n.*—*Syn.* gunman, gangster, desperado, mobster, gang leader, racketeer, criminal; *all* (D): tough, mug, gorilla, hood, yegg, hoodlum; see also **robber.**

thumb, *n.*—*Syn.* pollex, first digit, preaxial digit; see **finger.**
all thumbs (D)—*Syn.* fumbling, clumsy, inept; see **awkward** 1.

under one's thumb (D)—*Syn.* under one's control, controlled, governed; see **managed.**

thump, *n.* —*Syn.* thud, knock, rap, wallop, blow, pounding, whack, slap, smack, crack; *both* (D): bop, plop; see also **noise** 1.

thump, *v.* —*Syn.* pound, knock, rap, wallop, slap, strike, whack, hit; see also **beat.**

thunder, *n.* —*Syn.* crash, peal, outburst, explosion, boom, booming, roar, rumble, clap, crack, discharge, thunderbolt, uproar, blast; see also **noise** 1.

thunder, *v.* —*Syn.* peal, boom, rumble, resound, reverberate, roll, deafen, crash, clamor, clash; see also **roar, sound** 1, **storm.**

thunderbolt, *n.* —*Syn.* explosion, crash, clap of thunder, flash, peal, boom, roll, crack, flash of lightning, thunderpeal, thunderclap, thunderstroke; see also **lightning.**

thunderous, *mod.* —*Syn.* booming, roaring, crashing; see **loud** 1, 2.

thunderstorm, *n.* —*Syn.* electric storm, squall, downpour; see **thunder, storm** 1.

thunderstruck, *mod.* —*Syn.* astonished, confounded, astounded; see **bewildered.**

thus, *mod.* —*Syn.* in this manner, so, consequently, hence, in such a way, just like that, in kind, along these lines; see also **therefore.**

thwack, *n.* —*Syn.* whack, thump, hit; see **blow** 1.

thwack, *v.* —*Syn.* whack, thrash, thump; see **hit** 1.

thwart, *v.* —*Syn.* stop, impede, frustrate; see **confuse, prevent, trammel.**

tiara, *n.* —*Syn.* coronet, diadem, circlet; see **crown** 2.

tic, *n.* —*Syn.* twitch, spasm, contraction; see **fit** 1.

tick, *n.* **1.** [A light beat]—*Syn.* clock-tick, beat, ticktock, click, light rap, slight blow, metallic sound.

2. [An insect]—*Syn.* parasite, bloodsucker, arachnid, acarida, louse, mite; see also **insect, pest** 1.

Ticks include the following—cattle, sheep, bird, wood.

3. [A mattress]—*Syn.* feather tick, straw tick, cornhusk tick, pillow, cushion; see also **bed** 1, **mattress.**

ticket, *n.* **1.** [A valid token]—*Syn.* check, certificate, notice, badge, label, voucher, stub, countercheck, rain-check, docket, tag, slip, note, card, pass, receipt, record, license, permit, passage, credential, visa, passport, document; *all* (D): paper, skull, ducat, Annie Oakley.

2. [Candidates representing a political party] —*Syn.* party list, party slate, choice, schedule, ballot; *all* (D): machine, line-up, ring, combine; see also **candidate, faction** 1, **party** 3.

that's the ticket (D)—*Syn.* that's correct, that's right, truly; see **surely.**

ticketed, *mod.* —*Syn.* ready to board, prepared, readied; see **ready** 2.

tickle, *v.* **1.** [To stimulate by a light touch]—*Syn.* rub, caress, stroke, vellicate, titillate; see also **touch** 1.

2. [To excite mentally]—*Syn.* amuse, delight, stimulate; see **excite** 1.

tickling, *n.* —*Syn.* stroking, caressing, titillation; see **touch** 2.

ticklish, *mod.* —*Syn.* sensitive, unsteady, touch; see **irritable, unstable** 2.

tidbit, *n.* —*Syn.* morsel, mouthful, bite; see **bit** 1, **delicacy** 2.

tide, *n.* —*Syn.* current, flow, flux, stream, course, sluice, undercurrent, undertow, drag, whirlpool, eddy, vortex, torrent, wave, tidal wave; see also **wave** 1, 2.

Tides of the sea include the following—low, neap, ebb, spring, full, high, flood.

tidiness, *n.* —*Syn.* neatness, spruceness, uniformity; see **cleanliness.**

tidings, *n.* —*Syn.* information, word, report; see **news** 1, 2.

tidy, *mod.* —*Syn.* orderly, trim, spruce; see **neat** 1.

tie, *n.* **1.** [A fastening]—*Syn.* band, bond, strap, bandage, brace, tackle, zipper, yoke; see also **fastener.**

2. [A necktie]—*Syn.* cravat, neckerchief, bow, four-in-hand, knot, ruff, scarf, Windsor, bolo, neckcloth, Eton tie; *all* (D): rag, rope, choker, lamb's fry; see also **necktie.**

3. [Affection]—*Syn.* bond, relation, kinship, link, affinity; see also **affection, love** 1.

4. [An equal score, or a contest having that score] —*Syn.* deadlock, draw, even game, dead heat, drawn battle, neck-and-neck contest; *all* (D): even-Steven, stalemate, level, nose finish, standoff.

5. [A railroad tie]—*Syn.* crossbeam, track support, brace, timber, toothpick (D); see also **beam** 1.

tie, *v.* **1.** [To fasten]—*Syn.* bind, make fast, attach; see **fasten** 1, **join** 1.

2. [To tie a knot in]—*Syn.* knot, make a bow, make a tie, make a knot, do up, fix a tie, make a hitch; see also **sense** 1.

3. [(D) To equal]—*Syn.* be on a par with, match, keep up with, even off, balance, parallel, break even, draw, come to a deadlock; see also **equal.**

4. [(D) To marry]—*Syn.* unite, unite in marriage, join in holy matrimony; see **marry** 1.

tied, *mod.* **1.** [Firm]—*Syn.* cinched, fixed, bound, made firm; see also **firm** 1.

2. [Even]—*Syn.* evenly matched, (running) neck and neck, in a dead heat; see **alike** 2, **equal.**

tie down, *v.* —*Syn.* cinch, fix, attach; see **fasten** 1.

tie in, *v.* —*Syn.* go with, be in relation(ship) (to), be appropriate (for); see **join** 1, **relate to.**

tie into, *v.* —*Syn.* attack, assault, fight (with); see **fight** 1, 2.

tier, *n.* —*Syn.* row, range, layer; see **line** 1.

tie up, *v.* **1.** [To fasten]—*Syn.* wrap, package, secure; see **close** 4, **enclose** 1.

2. [To obstruct]—*Syn.* hinder, stop, delay; see **hinder.**

tiff, *n.* —*Syn.* quarrel, spat, wrangle; see **fight** 1.

tiger, *n.* —*Syn.* feline, cat, tigress, tiger-cat, man-eater.

Tigers and tiger-cats include the following—Bengal *or* Royal Bengal tiger, American *or* Mexican tiger *or* jaguar, saber-toothed tiger, black tiger, red tiger, marbled tiger *or* marbled tiger-cat, clouded tiger *or* clouded tiger-cat, margay, ocelot, serval, chati, long-tailed tiger-cat *or* oceloid leopard.

tight, *mod.* **1.** [Firm]—*Syn.* taut, secure, fast, bound up, close, clasped, fixed, steady, stretched thin, established, compact, strong, stable, enduring, steadfast, unyielding, unbending, set, stuck hard, hidebound, invulnerable, snug, sturdy; see also **firm** 1. —*Ant.* loose*, tottery, shaky.

2. [Closed]—*Syn.* sealed, airtight, impenetrable, impermeable, impervious, watertight, hermetically sealed, padlocked, bolted, locked, fastened, shut tight, clamped, fixed, tied, snapped, swung to, tied up, nailed, spiked, slammed, obstructed, blocked, blind, shut, stopped up, plugged; see also **waterproof.**—*Ant.* open*, penetrable, unprotected.
3. [Close-fitting]—*Syn.* pinching, shrunken, snug, uncomfortable, cramping, skintight, short, crushing, choking, smothering, cutting.—*Ant.* loose*, ample, wide.
4. [(D) Intoxicated]—*Syn.* inebriated, drunken, tipsy; see **drunk.**
5. [(D) Stingy]—*Syn.* miserly, parsimonious, close; see **stingy.**
6. [Difficult to obtain; *said especially of money*] —*Syn.* scarce, frozen, tied up; see **rare** 2.
sit tight (D)—*Syn.* do nothing, refrain from action, stay (put); see **remain** 1.

tighten, *v.* **1.** [To make tight]—*Syn.* compress, condense, squeeze, bind, contract, strangle, constrict, crush, cramp, pinch, grip more tightly, clench, screw down, add pressure; see also **stretch** 2. —*Ant.* loosen*, relax, unloose.
2. [To become tight]—*Syn.* contract, harden, congeal, stiffen, toughen, become more disciplined *or* stricter.—*Ant.* melt, soften*, liquefy.

tightfisted, *mod.*—*Syn.* thrifty, niggardly, frugal; see **stingy.**

tight-lipped, *mod.*—*Syn.* taciturn, reticent, secretive; see **quiet** 2, **reserved** 3.

tights, *n.*—*Syn.* pantaloons, breeches, stockings; see **dress** 1, **pants** 1.

tightwad, *n.*—*Syn.* mackworm, niggard, scrimp; see **miser** 1.

tile, *n.*—*Syn.* baked clay, fired clay, tiled flooring, tiling, tilework, tile roofing, roofing tile, pantile, gutter tile, decorative tile, wall tile, plastic tile, linoleum tile, asphalt tile, vinyl tile, bathroom tile, ceramic tile, drainage tile, pipe, piping, terrazzo; see also **clay, flooring, roofing.**

till, *n.*—*Syn.* drawer, tray, box, money-box, shelf, cabinet drawer; see also **safe, vault** 2.

till, *v.*—*Syn.* cultivate, work, raise crops from; see **farm** 1.

tillable, *mod.*—*Syn.* productive, cultivable, arable; see **fertile** 1.

tiller, *n.*—*Syn.* planter, plowman, plower; see **farmer.**

tilt, *n.* **1.** [An incline]—*Syn.* slant, slope, dip, rake, drop, fall, slide; see also **inclination** 5.—*Ant.* floor*, flat land, level surface.
2. [An encounter]—*Syn.* joust, bout, conflict, contest, struggle, skirmish, collision, scrimmage, fracas, tussle, scuffle, meet; see also **attack** 1, **fight** 1.
at full tilt—*Syn.* at full speed, charging, speeding; see **moving** 1.

tilt, *v.* **1.** [To incline]—*Syn.* slant, tip, turn, set at an angle, lean, slope, rake, slouch, shift, dip, sway, make oblique, turn edgewise; see also **bend** 2. —*Ant.* straighten*, level, bring into line.
2. [To encounter]—*Syn.* charge, thrust, combat; see **fight** 2.

timber, *n.* **1.** [Standing trees]—*Syn.* wood, lumber, timberland, wood lot, grove, standing timber, virgin forest, second growth; see also **forest.**
2. [A beam]—*Syn.* rib, frame, mast, boom, tie, stringer, sill, stake, pole, club, log; see also **beam, lumber.**

timbre, *n.*—*Syn.* tone, intonation, overtone; see **pitch** 3.

time, *n.* **1.** [Duration]—*Syn.* continuance, lastingness, extent, past, present, future, infinity, spacetime; see also **today.**
Units of measuring time include the following—millisecond, second, minute, hour, day, week, month, year, term, decade, generation, lifetime, century, millennium, aeon, work period, shift; *all* (D): swing (shift), graveyard (shift), cat-eye (shift).
2. [A point in time]—*Syn.* incident, event, occurrence, occasion, time and tide, instant, term, season, tide, course, sequence, point, generation; see also **moment** 1.
3. [A period of time]—*Syn.* season, era, interval; see **age** 3.
4. [Experience]—*Syn.* background, living, participation; see **experience** 1.
5. [Leisure]—*Syn.* opportunity, spare time, free moment, ease, liberty, chance; see also **freedom** 1.
6. [Credit]—*Syn.* account, trust, terms, delayable payment; see also **credit** 4, **loan.**
7. [Circumstances; *usually plural*; *used with* the] —*Syn.* conditions, the present, nowadays, juncture; see also **circumstance** 1, **circumstances** 2.
8. [A measure of speed]—*Syn.* tempo, beat, rate, meter, rhythm, cadence, swing, accent; *both* (D): bounce, lift.
9. [A standard of measuring time]—Standards include the following—Greenwich, mean, sidereal, apparent, solar, Standard, Eastern Standard, Central Standard, Mountain Standard, Pacific Standard, Yukon Standard, Alaska Standard, daylight-saving, astronomical, nautical, apparent.
10. [A standard of measuring rhythm in music]—Musical times include the following—simple, compound, duple *or* two-part, triple *or* three-part, quadruple *or* four-part, quintuple *or* five-part, sextuple *or* six-part, mixed.

time, *v.*—*Syn.* register distance, sound a bell, clock, determine timing of, measure time; see also **measure** 1.
abreast of the times—*Syn.* up-to-date, informed, aware; see **modern** 1.
ahead of time—*Syn.* ahead of schedule, fast, earlier than expected; see **early** 2.
at one time—*Syn.* simultaneously, concurrently, at once; see **together** 2.
at the same time—*Syn.* simultaneously, concurrently, at once; see **together** 2.
at times—*Syn.* occasionally, sometimes, once in a while; see **seldom.**
behind the times—*Syn.* out of date, archaic, antediluvian; see **old-fashioned.**
behind time—*Syn.* tardy, delayed, coming later; see **late** 1.
between times—*Syn.* now and then, occasionally, sometimes; see **seldom.**
do time (D)—*Syn.* serve a prison term, go to jail, be imprisoned; see **serve time.**

for the time being—*Syn.* for the present, for now, under consideration; see **temporarily.**
from time to time—*Syn.* occasionally, sometimes, once in a while; see **frequently.**
in good time—*Syn.* at the proper time, in a short time, soon; see **quickly** 1.
in no time—*Syn.* instantly, rapidly, without delay; see **quickly** 1, **soon** 1.
in time—*Syn.* eventually, after the proper time, inevitably; see **finally** 2.
kill time—*Syn.* fill (in the) time, waste time, idle; see **wait** 1.
lose time—*Syn.* go too slow, tarry, cause a delay; see **delay** 1.
make time—*Syn.* gain time, hasten; see **hurry** 1.
make time with (D)—*Syn.* attract, lure, charm; see **seduce.**
many a time—*Syn.* often, regularly, consistently; see **frequently.**
on time—*Syn.* **1.** at the appointed time, punctually, correct; see **punctual. 2** by credit, in installments, on account; see **unpaid** 1.
out of time—*Syn.* out of pace, unreasonable, improper; see **untimely.**
pass the time of day.—*Syn.* exchange greetings, chat, converse; see **greet.**

time and again, *mod.* —*Syn.* often, many times, repeatedly; see **frequently, regularly** 1.

time-honored, *mod.* —*Syn.* reverend, eminent, noble; see **immortal** 1, **venerable** 2.

timeliness, *n.* —*Syn.* opportuneness, occasion, chance, moment, time and tide, opportunity.

timely, *mod.* —*Syn.* opportune, seasonable, in good time, fitting the times, suitable, appropriate, convenient, favorable, propitious, well-timed, modern, up-to-date, newsworthy; see also **fit** 1, 2.—*Ant.* unfavorable*, ill-timed, inappropriate.

(the) time of one's life, *n.* —*Syn.* good *or* fine *or* wonderful, etc., time, celebration, fiesta; see **event** 1, 2.

time out of mind, *mod.* —*Syn.* from time immemorial, a long time, years ago; see **old** 3, **past** 1.

timepiece, *n.* —*Syn.* timekeeper, chronometer, sundial; see **clock, watch** 1.

timeserver, *n.* —*Syn.* self-seeker, temporizer, timist; see **opportunist.**

timeserving, *mod.* —*Syn.* opportunistic, tricky, sycophantic; see **sly** 1.

timeworn, *mod.* —*Syn.* antiquated, antique, ancient; see **old** 2, 3.

timid, *mod.* **1.** [Irresolute]—*Syn.* indecisive, vacillating, compromising, wavering, capricious, fluctuating, faltering, unstable, uncertain, ambivalent, undetermined, irresponsible, shilly-shallying, apologetic, off-and-on, halfway, wayward, wobbly; *both* (D): pussyfooting, passing the buck; see also **irresolute.**—*Ant.* stern, powerful*, implacable.
2. [Cowardly]—*Syn.* fainthearted, spiritless, weak, poor-spirited, fearful, submissive, timorous, pusillanimous, shaky, apprehensive, frightened, nervous, unnerved, shamefaced, feeble, daunted, browbeaten, bullied, cowed, intimidated, shrinking, spineless, cowering, badgered; *all* (D): soft, yellow, scared spitless, chicken-livered, cold-footed; see also **cowardly** 1.—*Ant.* brave*, fearless, stouthearted.
3. [Reticent]—*Syn.* shy, withdrawn, modest; see **humble** 1.

timidity, *n.* **1.** [Fear]—*Syn.* fearfulness, cowardliness, softness; see **cowardice, fear** 2.
2. [Reserve]—*Syn.* calmness, shyness, quiet; see **reserve** 2.

tin can, *n.* —*Syn.* tin, can, tin box, hermetically sealed can, No. 1 can, No. 2 can, vacuum can; see also **container.**

tinder, *n.* —*Syn.* touchwood, splinters, kindling; see **fuel, wood** 2.

tin foil, *n.* —*Syn.* tin-foil paper, lead foil, zinc foil, candy *or* gum wrapper; *both* (D): silver paper, gold paper; see also **paper** 5.

tinge, *n.* —*Syn.* nib, shade, hint; see **trace** 1.

tingle, *v.* —*Syn.* shiver, prickle, sting, itch, creep, grow excited, get goose pimples all over (D); see also **thrill.**

tinker, *v.* —*Syn.* try to mend, play with, take apart, potter, trifle with, botch; *both* (D): mess around, monkey with; see also **repair.**

tinkle, *v.* —*Syn.* jingle, clink, chink, ring, chime, tintinnabulate, make a thin metallic sound, make a bell-like sound; see also **sound** 1.

tinkling, *mod.* —*Syn.* jingling, ringing, chiming; see **sounding.**

tinsel, *mod.* —*Syn.* tawdry, gaudy, pretentious, fake, glossy, cheap, catchpenny, alloyed, pseudo; see also **common** 1, **poor** 2.

tinsmith, *n.* —*Syn.* tinker, tinman, tinsman; see **craftsman, workman.**

tint, *n.* —*Syn.* tinge, hue, shade, color value, cast, flush, dye, tinct, taint, glow, pastel color, luminous color, pale hue, tone, tincture, dash, touch, color tone, chroma, luminosity, coloration, pigmentation, ground color, complexion; see also **color** 1. —*Ant.* whiteness*, flatness, colorlessness.

tinted, *mod.* —*Syn.* colored, shaded, dyed, tinged, painted, tinctured, washed, stained, distempered, crayoned, touched up (D).

tintinnabulation, *n.* —*Syn.* ringing, jingle, resonance; see **noise** 1.

tinware, *n.* —*Syn.* tinwork, plateware, kitchenware, pots and pans; see also **utensils.**

tiny, *mod.* —*Syn.* small, miniature, diminutive; see **little** 1.

tip, *n.* **1.** [The point]—*Syn.* apex, peak, top, summit, cap, nip, stub; see also **point** 2.—*Ant.* bottom*, middle, body.
2. [A gratuity]—*Syn.* reward, gift, compensation, fee, small change, money, lagniappe, *pourboire* (French); *all* (D): handout, grease, Boston quarter, John D., bird, turkey, lamb's tongue; see also **pay** 2.
3. [(D) A bit of information]—*Syn.* hint, clue, warning, pointer, suggestion, inkling, whisper, inside information, advice; *all* (D): a word to the wise, dope, inside wire, hot steer, in, bug, bang, buzz; see also **knowledge** 1, **news** 1.

tip, *v.* —*Syn.* slant, incline, shift; see **bend** 1, **lean** 1, **tilt** 1.

tipsy (D), *mod.* —*Syn.* intoxicated, inebriated, tight (D); see **drunk.**

tiptop, *mod.* **1.** [Topmost]—*Syn.* apical, uppermost, supreme; see **highest.**
2. [(D) Best]—*Syn.* superior, prime, choice; see **best** 1, **excellent.**

tirade, *n.* —*Syn.* harangue, diatribe, invective; see **anger, dispute** 1.

tire, *n.* —*Syn.* casing, tire and tube, one of a set *or* a pair; see also **wheel** 1.
Terms for types of tires include the following—tubeless, radial, steel radial, snow, mud, puncture-proof, recapped, low-pressure, synthetic, natural rubber, solid rubber, pneumatic, oversize, airplane, motorcycle, bicycle; *all* (D): recap, boloney, dough-nut, rubber toe, sneaker, shoe.

tire, *v.* **1.** [To become exhausted]—*Syn.* grow weary, to become fagged, break down, droop, flag, jade, pall, faint, drop, puff, sink, yawn, collapse, give out; *all* (D): wilt, go stale, poop out, burn out, crawl home on one's eyebrows; see also **weary** 2. —*Ant.* rest*, awake, relax.
2. [To make a person exhausted]—*Syn.* tax, over-tax, harass, fatigue, exhaust, overwork, strain, over-strain, overburden, depress, dispirit, pain, vex, worry, distress, deject, dishearten, unman, pros-trate, wear out; *all* (D): run a person ragged, do up *or* in, take the tuck out of; see also **weary** 1.
3. [To bore]—*Syn.* annoy, disgust, displease; see **bother** 2, **weary** 1.

tired, *mod.* —*Syn.* fatigued, weary, run-down, ex-hausted, overworked, overtaxed, wearied, worn, spent, wasted, burned out, worn-out, jaded, nar-coleptic, drooping, distressed, unmanned, drowsy, droopy, sleepy, haggard, faint, prostrated, broken-down, drained, consumed, empty, collapsing; *all* (D): all in, finished, stale, pooped out, fagged, dog-tired, dead on one's feet, pooped, done in *or* for, beat up, worn to a frazzle, played out, tuckered out, fed up; see also **bored, weak** 1, **worn** 2.—*Ant.* ac-tive*, lively, energetic.

tireless, *mod.* —*Syn.* unwearied, unwearying, untir-ing, indefatigable, unflagging, incessant, hard-working, strenuous, energetic, resolute, steadfast, persevering; see also **active** 2, **enthusiastic** 1, 3. —*Ant.* tired*, weak, listless.

tire out, *v.* **1.** [To become tired]—*Syn.* become *or* be exhausted, get tired, be overcome; see **fail** 1, **weary** 2.
2. [To make tired]—*Syn.* overcome, exhaust, wear down; see **defeat** 1, **weary** 1.

tiresome, *mod.* —*Syn.* irksome, wearying, monot-onous; see **dull** 4.

tissue, *n.* **1.** [A network]—*Syn.* web, mesh, filigree, crossing, parcel, bundle, mass, sheaf, series; see also **network** 2.
2. [Thin fabric]—*Syn.* gauze, gossamer, cobwebby material, chiffon, lace, silk, webbing, scarfing; see also **cloth, veil, web** 1.
3. [Protective layer, especially in living organisms] —*Syn.* film, membrane, intercellular substance, parenchyma, prosenchyma, adipose tissue, muscu-lar tissue, vascular tissue, fibrous tissue, connective tissue, nervous tissue; see also **muscle.**

tissue paper, *n.* —*Syn.* wrapping paper, gift wrap-pings, sanitary paper, onionskin paper, sheet, paper handkerchief; see also **paper** 5.

titan, *n.* —*Syn.* colossus, Hercules, Gargantua; see **giant** 1, 2, **monster** 1.

titanic, *mod.* —*Syn.* huge, colossal, enormous; see **large** 1.

tit for tat, *n.* —*Syn.* reprisal, retribution, requit-al; see **exchange** 2, **revenge** 1.

tithe, *n.* —*Syn.* ratable tax, assessment, levy; see **tax** 1.

titillate, *v.* —*Syn.* tickle, palpate, grapple; see **excite** 1, 2.

titillation, *n.* —*Syn.* tickling, palpation, massage; see **excitement.**

title, *n.* **1.** [A designation]—*Syn.* indication, head-ing, caption, inscription, sign, appellation; see also **name** 1.
2. [Ownership or evidence of ownership]—*Syn.* holding, right, claim, due, power, license; see also **deed,** 2, **ownership.**
3. [Mark of rank or dignity]—*Syn.* commission, decoration, medal, ribbon, coat of arms, crest, cor-don, order, authority, privilege, degree; see also **emblem.**
Titles include the following—Sir, Doctor, Mr., Mrs., Miss, Ms, Reverend, Monsignor, Father, Rabbi, Dame, King, Prince, Baron, Viscount, Earl, Marquis, Marquise, Duke, Grand Duke, Knight, Count, Sultan, Khan, Emir, Pasha, Mirza, Sahib, Effendi, Queen, Duchess, Lady, Princess, Mar-chioness, Viscountess, Countess, Monsieur, Ma-dame, Mademoiselle, Don, Doña, Herr, General, Colonel, Major, Captain, Lieutenant, Admiral, Commander, Ensign, President, Vice-President, Secretary, Speaker, Governor, Mayor, Representa-tive, Senator.

titter, *v.* —*Syn.* giggle, snicker, chuckle; see **laugh.**

tittle, *n.* —*Syn.* iota, speck, particle; see **bit** 1.

titular, *mod.* —*Syn.* nominal, in name only, epon-ymous; see **so-called.**

to, *prep.* **1.** [In the direction of]—*Syn.* toward, via, into, facing, through, directed toward, traveling to, along the line of.
2. [Indicating position]—*Syn.* over, upon, on, in front of, before.
3. [Until]—*Syn.* till, up to, extending to, stopping at; see also **until.**
4. [So that]—*Syn.* in order to, that one may, for the purpose of.
5. [Indicating degree]—*Syn.* up to, down to, as far as, in that degree, to this extent.
6. [Indicating result]—*Syn.* becoming, until, back, ending with.

toadstool, *n.* —*Syn.* fungus, fungous growth, spo-rophore, fairies'-table, frog's-stool, toad's-stool, toad's-meat; see also **mushroom, plant.**

to and fro, *mod.* —*Syn.* seesaw, zigzag, back and forth, backward(s) and forward(s), in and out, up and down, from side to side, from pillar to post, off and on, round and round, hitch and hike, forward and back, like buckets in a well.

today, *n.* —*Syn.* parasite, flatterer, fawner; see **syco-phant.**

toast, *n.* **1.** [A sentiment or person drunk to] —*Syn.* pledge, proposal, celebration, ceremony, salute, compliment, commemoration, acknowledg-ment, thanksgiving; see also **honor** 1.
Invitations for toasts include the following—here's to you, good luck, lest we forget, your health, Sir; *prosit* (German), *skoal* (Scandinavian), *salud* (Spanish), *a votre santé* (French), *lekhaim* (Yiddish);

all (D): down the hatch, here's how, mud in your eye, here's looking at you, cheers (British).
2. [Browned bread] Varieties of toast include the following—white, rye, whole-wheat, Melba, French, milk, cinnamon; see also **bread** 1.
toast, *v.* **1.** [To honor by drinking liquor]—*Syn.* drink to, pay homage to, drink to someone's health, celebrate, pledge, compliment, propose a toast, name, glorify, make special mention of; see also **drink** 2, **praise** 1.
2. [To brown bread]—*Syn.* put in a toaster, heat, dry, cook, crisp, parch.
tobacco, *n.* Forms of tobacco include the following—nicotine, cigarette, cigar, chewing tobacco, pipe tobacco, quid of tobacco, smoking tobacco, snuff; *all* (D): Lady Nicotine, coffin nails, dust, powder, cancer stick, snooze, the filthy weed, fragrant weed; see also **smoking.**
to blame, *mod.* —*Syn.* at fault, culpable, censurable; see **guilty** 2.
toboggan, *n.* —*Syn.* sledge, sleigh, bobsled; see **sled** 1, 2.
tocsin, *n.* —*Syn.* horn, siren, signal; see **alarm** 1, **warning.**
to date, *mod.* —*Syn.* until now, hereunto, so far, as yet, up to now; see also **now** 1.
today, *n.* —*Syn.* this day, the present, our time, this moment; see also **now** 1.
toddle, *v.* —*Syn.* waddle, stalk, wobble; see **walk** 1.
to-do, *n.* —*Syn.* commotion, stir, fuss; see **disorder** 2, **fight** 1.
toe, *n.* —*Syn.* digit, phalanx, front of the foot, tip of a shoe; see also **appendage** 2.
on one's toes (D)—*Syn.* alert, aware, attentive; see **careful.**
step *or* **tread on someone's toes**—*Syn.* annoy, offend, disturb; see **anger** 1.
toe the mark, *v.* —*Syn.* be good, conform, mind; see **behave** 2.
together, *mod.* **1.** [Jointly]—*Syn.* collectively, unitedly, commonly; see **mutually.**
2. [Simultaneously]—*Syn.* at the same time, concurrently, coincidentally, synchronically, contemporaneously, concomitantly, at once, in connection with, at a blow, in unison, at one jump.
togetherness (D), *n.* —*Syn.* fellow *or* family feeling, community of interest, affection; see **friendship** 1, 2, **love** 1, **society** 2.
togs (D), *n.* —*Syn.* clothing, outfit, attire; see **clothes.**
toil, *n.* —*Syn.* labor, occupation, drudgery; see **work** 2.
toil, *v.* —*Syn.* sweat, labor, slave; see **work.**
toiler, *n.* —*Syn.* worker, apprentice, workman; see **laborer.**
toilet, *n.* **1.** [Grooming one's person]—*Syn.* ablutions, dressing, morning preparations, bath, haircut, shave, shower, hairdressing, applying cosmetics; *all* (D): wash-up, tidy-up, make-up, crumb-up.
2. [A room for privacy]—*Syn.* water closet, lavatory, washroom, rest-room, men's room, women's room, powder room, gentlemen's room, ladies' room, comfort station, bathroom, bath, privy, amenity, necessarium; *all* (D): little boy's room, little girl's room, head, potty, W.C., can, altar room, chamber of commerce, poet's corner, pot, john, Chic Sale, throne room.
toilsome, *mod.* **1.** [Difficult]—*Syn.* laborious, strenuous, hard; see **difficult** 1.
2. [Dull]—*Syn.* tedious, boring, wearisome; see **dull** 4.
token, *n.* —*Syn.* mark, favor, sample; see **gift** 1.
by the same token—*Syn.* following from this, similarly, thus; see **therefore.**
in token of—*Syn.* as evidence of, by way of, as a gesture; see **representing** 1.
told, *mod.* —*Syn.* recounted, recorded, set down, reported, known, chronicled, revealed, exposed, made known, said, published, printed, announced, released, described, stated, set forth, included in the official statement, made public property, become common knowledge, related, depicted, enunciated, pronounced, given out, handed down, telegraphed, broadcast, telecast, included in a release, told in open court, confessed, admitted, well-known, discovered; see also **known** 2, **spoken.** —*Ant.* secret*, concealed, unknown.
tolerable, *mod.* **1.** [Bearable]—*Syn.* endurable, sufferable, sustainable; see **bearable.**
2. [Passable]—*Syn.* adequate, mediocre, average; see **common** 1, **poor** 2.
tolerance, *n.* **1.** [Open-mindedness]—*Syn.* lenity, concession, liberality, permission, forbearance, indulgence, mercy, compassion, license, sufference, grace, freedom of worship, understanding, sensitivity, charity, benevolence, humanity, endurance, altruism, patience, good will; see also **kindness** 1, **liberalism.**
2. [Saturation point]—*Syn.* threshold, tolerance level, end; see **limit** 2.
tolerant, *mod.* —*Syn.* understanding, receptive, sophisticated; see **liberal** 2, **patient** 1.
tolerate, *v.* **1.** [To allow]—*Syn.* permit, consent to, authorize, put up (with), stand for (D); see also **allow** 1.
2. [To endure]—*Syn.* bear, undergo, abide; see **endure** 2.
toll, *n.* **1.** [Charges]—*Syn.* duty, fee, customs, exaction, tollage; see also **price.**
2. [Loss]—*Syn.* casualties, deaths, losses; see **damage** 2.
tomahawk, *n.* —*Syn.* Indian club, hatchet, ax, war ax, stone ax, poggamoggan; see also **club** 3.
tomato, *n.* —*Syn.* tomato vine, tomato plant, tree tomato, love-apple, *pomme d'amour* (French), *tomate* (Spanish), *jitomate* (Spanish), *Lycopersicon* (Latin); see also **plant, vegetable.**
tomb, *n.* —*Syn.* vault, crypt, mausoleum; see **grave** 1, **monument** 1.
tomboy, *n.* —*Syn.* rowdy girl, hoyden; *both* (D): spitfire, tommy; see also **girl** 1.
tombstone, *n.* —*Syn.* monument, gravestone, headstone, footstone, stone, marker, cross, funerary statue.
tomcat, *n.* —*Syn.* male cat, tommy, boar cat; see **cat** 1.
tome, *n.* —*Syn.* album, portfolio, document; see **publication** 1, **writing** 2.
tomfoolery, *n.* —*Syn.* silliness, horseplay, frolic; see **fun.**

Tommy gun, *n.* —*Syn.* automatic rifle, submachine gun, machine gun; see **gun** 2, **rifle.**

tomorrow, *n.* —*Syn.* the morrow, next day in the course of time, the future, *mañana* (Spanish); see also **day** 2.

tom-tom, *n.* —*Syn.* tabla, taboret, tambourine; see **drum.**

ton, *n.* —*Syn.* twelve hundredweight, two thousand pounds, short ton, metric ton, long ton, shipping ton, displacement ton, measurement ton, freight ton; see also **weight** 1, 2.

tone, *n.* **1.** [A musical sound]—*Syn.* pitch, timbre, resonance; see **sound** 2.
2. [Quality]—*Syn.* nature, trend, temper; see **character** 1.
3. [Manner]—*Syn.* expression, condition, aspect, mode, habit; see also **mood** 1.
4. [A degree of color]—*Syn.* hue, tint, color value, blend, tinge, cast, coloration; see also **color** 1.

tone down, *v.* **1.** [To dim]—*Syn.* darken, deepen, cloud; see **shade** 2.
2. [To soften]—*Syn.* subdue, moderate, temper; see **soften** 2.

tong, *n.* —*Syn.* pincer, forcep, tweezer; see **tongs, tool** 1.

tongs, *n.* —*Syn.* pinchers, pliers, pincers, forceps, pair of tongs, sugar tongs, fire tongs, ice tongs, blacksmith's tongs; see also **utensils.**

tongue, *n.* **1.** [The movable muscle in the mouth] —*Syn.* organ of taste *or* speech, lingua, lingula; *all* (D): blabber, clacker, lapper, red rag, velvet; see also **muscle, organ** 2.
Parts of the tongue used in speech are—tip, apex, front, center, back.
2. [Speech]—*Syn.* speech, utterance, discourse; see **language** 1.
3. [Something resembling a tongue, sense 1] —*Syn.* shoe tongue, wagon pole, neap, bell clapper, peninsula, movable pin.
find one's tongue—*Syn.* recover one's ability to talk, speak (up), begin talking; see **talk** 1.
hold one's tongue—*Syn.* refrain from speaking, hold back, keep silent; see **restrain** 1.
on the tip of one's tongue—*Syn.* forgotten, not quite remembered, not readily recalled; see **abandoned** 1.

tongue-tied, *mod.* **1.** [Mute]—*Syn.* silent, speechless, aphonic; see **dumb** 1, **mute** 1.
2. [Inarticulate]—*Syn.* reticent, nervous, inarticulate; see **reserved** 3.

tonic, *n.* —*Syn.* stimulant, bracer, refresher, invigorator, medicine, conditioner, hair tonic, liver tonic, mineral water, quinine water, patent medicine; see also **drug** 2.

tonight, *n.* —*Syn.* this evening, this p.m., this night, later; see also **night** 1.

tonnage, *n.* —*Syn.* load, burden, cargo, capacity, contents.

tonsillitis, *n.* —*Syn.* inflammation, quinsy, anygdalitis; see **disease** 2.

tonsured, *mod.* —*Syn.* shaven, clipped, shorn; see **bald** 1.

too, *mod.* **1.** [Also]—*Syn.* as well, likewise, in addition, additionally, moreover, furthermore, further, besides; see also **also.**
2. [In excess]—*Syn.* excessively, over, overmuch, exceedingly, extremely, beyond measure, over and above; see also **besides.**

tool, *n.* **1.** [An implement]—*Syn.* utensil, machine, instrument, mechanism, weapon, apparatus, appliance, engine, means, contrivance, gadget (D); see also **device** 1.
Common tools include the following—can opener, hammer, knife, jack, crank, pulley, wheel, bar, crowbar, lever, sledge, winch, cam, loom, shuttle, chisel, plane, screw, brace, bit, file, saw, screwdriver, wrench, pliers, ax, hatchet, corkscrew, jimmy.
2. [One who permits himself to be used]—*Syn.* accessory, auxiliary, accomplice, hireling, dupe, intermediary, cat's-paw, medium, vehicle, agent, go-between, messenger, easy mark; *all* (D): stool pigeon, jay, hayseed, greenhorn, sucker, patsy, stooge, come-on, tuna; see also **servant.**

too much, *n.* —*Syn.* excessiveness, extravagance, fabulousness, preposterousness, overgoing, overcharge, ever so much, more than can be used, *embarras de richesse* (French), superfluity, inordinateness, vastness, prodigiousness, immensity; see also **excess** 1.—*Ant.* lack*, want, shortage.

tooth, *n.* **1.** [A dental process]—*Syn.* fang, tusk, saber-tooth, tush, ivory, snag, artificial tooth, false tooth, (edontate) (calcerous) process, bony appendage.
Human teeth include the following—incisor, canine *or* cuspid (*also* (D): eyetooth), bicuspid *or* premolar, first bicuspid, second bicuspid, molar (*also* (D): grinder), first molar, second molar, third molar *or* wisdom tooth.
2. [A toothlike *or* tooth-shaped object]—*Syn.* point, stub, projection; see **gear, peg, root.**
get *or* **sink one's teeth into** (D)—*Syn.* become occupied with, involve oneself in, be busy at; see **act** 1.
in the teeth of—*Syn.* in the face of, in conflict with, defying; see **opposing** 1.
long in the tooth (D)—*Syn.* elderly, aged, ancient; see **old** 1.
show one's teeth (D)—*Syn.* show hostility, oppose, be angry; see **threaten** 1, 2.
throw in someone's teeth (D)—*Syn.* reprimand, reproach, castigate; see **attack** 2, **censure.**

toothache, *n.* —*Syn.* pain in the tooth, aching tooth, swollen gums, absessed tooth, decayed tooth; see also **pain** 2.

tooth and nail, *mod.* —*Syn.* energetically, fervently, forcefully; see **eagerly, fiercely, vigorously.**

toothbrush, *n.* —*Syn.* electric (toothbrush), nylon *or* natural bristle toothbrush, Water Pic (trademark).

tooth-shaped, *mod.* —*Syn.* toothlike, dentoid, dentiform; see **conical, sharp** 2.

toothsome, *mod.* —*Syn.* palatable, tasty, appetizing; see **delicious** 1.

top, *mod.* **1.** [Highest]—*Syn.* topmost, uppermost, highest, on the upper end; see also **highest.**—*Ant.* bottommost, lowest*, bottom.
2. [Best]—*Syn.* prime, head, first, among the first; see also **best** 1.

top, *n.* **1.** [The uppermost portion]—*Syn.* peak, summit, crown, head, crest, tip, apex, cap, crowning point, acme, headpiece, capital, pinnacle, ze-

nith, consummation, spire, knap, finial; see also **height** 1.—*Ant.* bottom*, lower end, nadir.
2. [A cover]—*Syn.* lid, roof, ceiling; see **cover** 1.
3. [A spinning toy]—*Syn.* spinner, peg top, whipping top, musical top, whistling top, teetotum, put-and-take top, dreidel; see also **toy** 1.
4. [(D) The leader]—*Syn.* head, captain, chief, master; see also **chief** 1, **leader** 2.
blow one's top (D)—*Syn.* lose one's temper, become angry, be enraged; see **rage** 1.
off the top of one's head (D)—*Syn.* speaking offhand, chatting, casually; see **extemporaneous.**
on top—*Syn.* prosperous, thriving, superior; see **successful.**
top, *v.* **1.** [To remove the top]—*Syn.* prune, lop off, trim, cut off, decapitate, scrape off, pare down, shave off, amputate, file off, pollard, truncate, shear; see also **cut** 1.
2. [To exceed]—*Syn.* better, beat, excel, surpass, go beyond, overrun; see also **exceed.**—*Ant.* approach*, approximate, come near to.
3. [To apply topping]—*Syn.* cover, dye, roof, superimpose, spread over, hood, cloak, screen, protect, reinforce, clothe, coat; see also **paint** 2.
topcoat, *n.*—*Syn.* overcoat, spring coat, fall coat, duster, raincoat; *both* (D): raglan, reversible, topper; see also **coat** 1.
top-drawer, *mod.*—*Syn.* superior, very good, best; see **excellent.**
toper, *n.*—*Syn.* drinker, alcoholic, lush; see **drunkard.**
top hat, *n.*—*Syn.* opera hat, silk hat, beaver, high hat, topper, crush hat, gibus hat, collapsible hat; *all* (D): stovepipe hat, chimney pot, skyscraper; see also **hat.**
top-heavy, *mod.*—*Syn.* overweight, unstable, bulky, tottering, unbalanced, overloaded, cumbersome, disproportionate, overcapitalized; see also **shaky** 1.—*Ant.* balanced*, equalized, ballasted.
topic, *n.*—*Syn.* question, theme, subject, text, thesis, theorem, material, proposition, resolution, motion, argument, field of inquiry, point, point in question, matter, matter in hand, problem, moot point, affair, division, head, issue.
topical, *mod.* **1.** [Local]—*Syn.* confined, limited, insular; see **local** 1, **restricted.**
2. [Current]—*Syn.* thematic, nominal, subjective; see **modern** 1.
topless (D), *mod.*—*Syn.* almost nude, bare to the waist, exposed; see **naked** 1.
top-level, *mod.*—*Syn.* leading, superior, supreme; see **excellent, important** 1.
toplofty, *mod.*—*Syn.* haughty, pompous, arrogant; see **egotistic** 2.
topmost, *mod.*—*Syn.* uppermost, first, leading; see **highest.**
top off, *v.*—*Syn.* finish, end, bring to a conclusion; see **complete** 1.
topple, *v.*—*Syn.* tumble, plunge, go down, go over; see also **fall** 1.
top-secret, *mod.*—*Syn.* restricted, kept (very) quiet, hush-hush (D); see **secret** 1, 2.
topsy-turvy, *mod.*—*Syn.* confused, upside down, disordered, disarranged, disheveled, tangled, muddled, unhinged, out of gear, disorganized, pell-mell, disjointed, out of joint, untidy, tumultuous, riotous, dislocated, jumbled, chaotic, cluttered, littered; *both* (D): messy, cockeyed; see also **disorderly** 1.—*Ant.* orderly*, ordered, systematic.
torch, *n.*—*Syn.* beacon, light, flare, firebrand; see also **flashlight.**
carry a torch for (D)—*Syn.* pine for, miss desperately, love in vain; see **love** 1.
toreador, *n.*—*Syn.* bullfighter, picador, *torero* (Spanish); see **matador.**
torment, *n.*—*Syn.* agony, suffering, misery; see **pain** 1, 2, **torture.**
torment, *v.*—*Syn.* abuse, mistreat, torture, irritate; see also **hurt** 1.
tormentor, *n.*—*Syn.* oppressor, persecutor, tormentress; see **dictator, enemy** 1, 2, **rascal.**
torn, *mod.*—*Syn.* ripped, slit, split, severed, lacerated, mutilated, broken, rent, fractured, cracked, slashed, gashed, ruptured, snapped, sliced, burst, cleaved, wrenched, divided, pulled out, impaired, damaged, spoiled; see also **ruined** 1.—*Ant.* whole*, repaired, adjusted.
tornado, *n.*—*Syn.* hurricane, whirlwind, cyclone, typhoon, blow; see also **storm** 1, **wind** 1.
torpedo, *n.* Torpedoes include the following—aerial torpedo, submarine torpedo, jet torpedo, mechanical torpedo, radio-controlled torpedo, projectile; *all* (D): fish, whale, flying pig, egg; see also **weapon** 1.
torpid, *mod.* **1.** [Inactive]—*Syn.* dormant, motionless, inert; see **idle** 1, **latent.**
2. [Apathetic]—*Syn.* heavy, sluggish, drowsy; see **dull** 3.
torpor, *n.* **1.** [Stupor]—*Syn.* coma, dormancy, inactivity; see **stupor.**
2. [Apathy]—*Syn.* dullness, sluggishness, apathy; see **indifference** 1, **laziness.**
torque, *n.*—*Syn.* circulatory force, twist, revolving; see **energy** 3, **revolution** 1.
torrent, *n.*—*Syn.* overflow, rushing water, violent flow, deluge, downpour; see also **flood** 1, **flow.**
torrid, *mod.*—*Syn.* tropical, austral, broiling, blazing, fiery, sweltering; see also **hot** 1, **tropic** 1.
torso, *n.*—*Syn.* trunk, thorax, caudex; see **body** 3.
tortuous, *mod.* **1.** [Winding]—*Syn.* snaky, sinuous, twisting; see **crooked** 1, **winding.**
2. [Immoral]—*Syn.* deceitful, devious, perverse; see **wicked** 1, 2.
torture, *n.*—*Syn.* pain, anguish, agony, torment, tribulation, rack, crucifixion, cruciation, martyrdom, pang, dolor, ache, twinge, physical suffering, mental suffering; *both* (D): hell upon earth, bed of Procrustes; see also **cruelty.**—*Ant.* comfort*, enjoyment, delight.
torture, *v.* **1.** [To torment]—*Syn.* annoy, irritate, disturb; see **abuse** 1, **bother** 2.
2. [To injure]—*Syn.* wound, lacerate, whip; see **beat** 2, **hurt** 1.
Tory, *n.*—*Syn.* traditionalist, loyalist, cavalier; see **conservative.**
toss, *v.* **1.** [To throw easily]—*Syn.* hurl, fling, cast; see **throw** 1.
2. [To move up and down]—*Syn.* bob, buffet, stir, move restlessly, tumble, pitch, roll, heave, sway, flounder, rock, wobble, undulate, swing, rise and fall; see also **wave** 3.

toss off, *v.* —*Syn.* drink (up *or* down), swallow, gulp (down); see **drink** 1, 2.

toss-up (D), *n.* —*Syn.* deadlock, bet, draw; see **tie** 4.

tot, *n.* —*Syn.* child, infant, youngster; see **baby** 1.

total, *mod.* **1.** [Whole]—*Syn.* entire, inclusive, every; see **whole** 1.
2. [Complete]—*Syn.* utter, gross, thorough; see **absolute** 1.

total, *n.* —*Syn.* sum, entirety, result; see **whole.**

total, *v.* **1.** [To add]—*Syn.* figure, calculate, count up, ring up, tag up, sum up, add up; see also **add** 1.
2. [To amount to]—*Syn.* consist of, come to, add up to; see **amount to, equal.**

totaling, *mod.* —*Syn.* amounting to, reckoning, calculating, adding, casting, to the amount of.

totalitarian, *mod.* —*Syn.* fascistic, despotic, dictatorial; see **autocratic** 1, **tyrannical.**

totalitarianism, *n.* —*Syn.* despotism, tyranny, dictatorship; see **fascism, tyranny.**

totality, *n.* —*Syn.* everything, oneness, collectivity; see **whole.**

totally, *mod.* —*Syn.* entirely, wholly, exclusively; see **completely.**

tote (D), *v.* —*Syn.* take, haul, transport; see **carry** 1.

totem, *n.* —*Syn.* fetish, symbol, crest; see **emblem.**

to the contrary, *mod.* —*Syn.* in disagreement with, in opposition to, in contradiction of *or* to; see **against** 3, **on the contrary.**

totter, *v.* **1.** [To be near falling]—*Syn.* shake, rock, careen, lurch, quake, tremble, seesaw, teeter, dodder, crumple, sway, wobble, be loose, be weak; see also **wave** 3.
2. [To stagger]—*Syn.* stumble, falter, trip, weave, zigzag, reel, rock, roll, walk drunkenly, wobble, waver, hesitate; *both* (D): fluke, wee-waw.

touch, *n.* **1.** [The tactile sense]—*Syn.* feeling, touching, feel, perception, tactility, taction.
2. [Contact]—*Syn.* rub, stroke, pat, petting, fondling, rubbing, stroking, licking, handling, graze, scratch, brush, taste, nudge, kiss, peck, embrace, hug, cuddling, caress.
3. [(D) The act of borrowing]—*Syn.* cadging, begging, mooching (D); see **loan.**
4. [A sensation]—*Syn.* sense, impression, apprehension, impact, pressure; see also **feeling** 2.
5. [Skill]—*Syn.* knack (D), technique, finish; see **ability** 2, **method** 2, **talent** 1.
6. [A trace]—*Syn.* suggestion, scent, inkling; see **bit** 1.

touch, *v.* **1.** [To be in contact]—*Syn.* stroke, graze, rub, pat, pet, nudge, thumb, finger, paw, lick, taste, brush, kiss, glance, sweep, caress, fondle, smooth, massage, sip, partake; see also **feel** 1.
2. [To come into contact with]—*Syn.* meet, encounter, arrive at, reach, get to, come to, attain, stop at, call at, visit.—*Ant.* pass*, miss*, avoid*.
3. [To relate to]—*Syn.* involve, refer to, bear on, pertain to, regard, affect, belong to, be associated with, center upon; see also **concern** 1.
4. [To tinge]—*Syn.* tint, brush, retouch, taint, blemish, spot, color, stain.
5. [(D) To borrow from]—*Syn.* get from, obtain from, beg from; see **borrow** 1.
6. [To discuss]—*Syn.* touch on *or* upon, treat (lightly), go over; see **discuss.**

touchable, *mod.* —*Syn.* tactual, material, actual; see **real** 2, **tangible.**

touch-and-go, *mod.* **1.** [Hasty]—*Syn.* rapid, casual, superficial; see **shallow** 2.
2. [Risky]—*Syn.* ticklish, hazardous, tricky; see **dangerous** 1, 2, **uncertain** 2.

touchdown, *n.* —*Syn.* goal, score, six points; *all* (D): counter, marker, touch.

touch down, *v.* —*Syn.* alight, descend, settle; see **arrive** 1, **land** 4.

touched, *mod.* **1.** [Having been in slight contact] —*Syn.* fingered, nudged, used, brushed, handled, rubbed, stroked, rearranged, kissed, grazed, licked, tasted, fondled.
2. [Affected]—*Syn.* moved, impressed, stirred; see **affected** 1.
3. [Slightly insane]—*Syn.* odd, eccentric, peculiar, neurotic, obsessed, fanatic, queer, bizarre, unhinged, singular, flighty, moonstruck, daft, giddy; *all* (D): nutty, screwy, tetched, pixilated; see also **insane** 1.—*Ant.* sane*, sound, normal.

touching, *mod.* and *prep.* **1.** [Referring to]—*Syn.* regarding, in regard to, in reference to, reaching, as concerns, concerning; see also **about** 2.
2. [Affecting]—*Syn.* moving, pathetic, tender; see **pitiful** 1.
3. [Adjacent]—*Syn.* tangent, in contact, against; see **contiguous, near** 1, **next** 2.

touch off, *v.* **1.** [To cause to explode]—*Syn.* detonate, light the fuse, set off; see **explode** 1.
2. [To cause to start]—*Syn.* start, initiate, release; see **begin** 1, **cause** 2.

touchstone, *n.* —*Syn.* standard, test, criterion; see **proof** 1.

touch up, *v.* —*Syn.* renew, modify, rework; see **remodel, repair.**

touchy, *mod.* **1.** [Irritable]—*Syn.* ill-humored, testy, irascible; see **irritable.**
2. [Delicate]—*Syn.* harmful, hazardous, risky; see **unsafe.**

tough, *mod.* **1.** [Strong]—*Syn.* robust, wiry, mighty; see **strong** 1, 2.
2. [Cohesive]—*Syn.* solid, firm, sturdy, hard, hardened, adhesive, leathery, coherent, inseparable, molded, tight, cemented, unbreakable, in one piece, dense, closely packed.—*Ant.* weak*, fragile, brittle.
3. [Difficult to chew]—*Syn.* uncooked, half-cooked, sinewy, indigestible, inedible, fibrous, old; *both* (D): hard as nails, tough as shoe-leather; see also **raw** 1. —*Ant.* soft*, tender, overcooked.
4. [Difficult]—*Syn.* unyielding, hard, resisting, troublesome, onerous, intricate, puzzling, laborious; see also **difficult** 1, **severe** 1.—*Ant.* easy*, simple, obvious.
5. [Hardy]—*Syn.* robust, sound, capable; see **healthy** 1.
6. [(D) Rough and cruel]—*Syn.* savage, fierce, desperate, ferocious, ruffianly, uproarious, terrible, rapacious, riotous, uncontrollable, unmanageable. —*Ant.* friendly*, genial, easygoing.
7. [(D) Unfavorable]—*Syn.* bad, unfortunate, untimely; see **unfavorable** 2.
8. [(D) Excellent]—*Syn.* fine, first-class, premium; see **excellent.**

tough it out—*Syn.* persevere, persist, endure; see **endure** 1.

toupee, *n.*—*Syn.* frizz, periwig, hairpiece; see **wig.**

tour, *n.*—*Syn.* trip, voyage, travel; see **journey.**

tour, *v.*—*Syn.* voyage, vacation, take a trip; see **travel** 2.

tour de force, *n.*—*Syn.* accomplishment, attainment, stratagem; see **achievement** 2.

touring, *mod.* **1.** [Traveling]—*Syn.* journeying, vacationing, excursioning, voyaging; see also **traveling** 2.

2. [Traveling by automobile]—*Syn.* motoring, driving, riding, sight-seeing, out for a spin (D); see also **traveling** 2.

tourist, *n.*—*Syn.* sight-seer, vacationist, stranger, visitor; see also **traveler.**

tournament, *n.* **1.** [A series of athletic events] —*Syn.* meet, games, tourney, match; see also **competition** 1, 2, **sport** 3.

2. [A joust]—*Syn.* clash of arms, jousts, tourney, duel, knightly combat, test of prowess; see also **fight** 1.

tousled, *mod.*—*Syn.* disheveled, unkempt, disordered; see **dirty** 1.

tout (D), *v.*—*Syn.* praise, laud, plug (D); see **promote** 1.

tow, *v.*—*Syn.* haul, pull, drag, ferry, lug, yank, tug; see also **draw** 1.

toward, *mod.* and *prep.*—*Syn.* to, in the direction of, pointing to, via, on the way to, proceeding, moving, approaching, in relation to, close to, headed for, on the road to; see also **near** 1.

towel, *n.*—*Syn.* wiper, drier, absorbent paper, sheet, toweling, napkin, cloth, rag (D).

Towels include the following—linen, cotton, huckaback, terry, guest, face, Turkish, hand, bath, dish, tea, paper, napkin.

throw in the towel (D)—*Syn.* admit defeat, give in, surrender; see **yield** 3.

tower, *n.*—*Syn.* spire, mast, steeple, campanile, bell tower, keep, belfry, monolith, radio tower, lookout tower, skyscraper, obelisk, pillar, column, minaret, *fleche* (French), *tourelle* (French); see also **turret.**

tower, *v.*—*Syn.* look over, extend above, mount; see **overlook** 1.

to wit, *mod.*—*Syn.* namely, in particular, *videlicet* (Latin), scilicet; see also **following.**

town, *mod.*—*Syn.* civic, community, civil; see **municipal, urban** 2.

town, *n.* **1.** [In the United States, a small collection of dwellings]—*Syn.* hamlet, county seat, municipality, township, borough; *all* (D): jerkwater, hick town, falling-off place, the sticks; see also **village.**

2. [In Britain, a large municipality]—*Syn.* market town, thorp, borough; see **city.**

3. [Urban life]—*Syn.* city life, living in town; *both* (D): big time, bright lights; see also **center** 2.

4. [The people in a city, especially the prominent people]—*Syn.* townspeople, inhabitants, high life, social life, society, high circles, social register; *all* (D): upper crust, bigwigs, the cream; see also **population.**

go to town (D)—*Syn.* do well, prosper; see **succeed** 1.

town hall, *n.*—*Syn.* assembly room, courthouse, meeting hall; see **auditorium.**

town house, *n.*—*Syn.* (urban) residence, condominium; see **apartment, home** 1.

township, *n.*—*Syn.* local *or* town *or* community government, rural community, precinct; see **government** 1.

townsman, *n.*—*Syn.* inhabitant, dweller, householder; see **citizen, resident.**

town talk, *n.*—*Syn.* hearsay, scandal, grapevine (D); see **gossip** 1, **rumor** 1.

tow truck, *n.*—*Syn.* tow rig, tow *or* towing *or* service truck *or* vehicle, hoist truck; see **truck** 1.

toxic, *mod.*—*Syn.* noxious, virulent, lethal; see **deadly, poisonous.**

toxin, *n.*—*Syn.* virus, vapor, contagion; see **poison, venom** 1.

toy, *mod.*—*Syn.* childish, miniature, small, diminutive, model-sized, babylike, on a small scale, midgetlike, tiny, undersized, doll-like; see also **little** 1. —*Ant.* large*, immense, oversized.

toy, *n.* **1.** [Something designed for amusement] —*Syn.* game, plaything, pastime; see **doll, game** 1. Toys include the following—dolls, games, balls, toy weapons, blocks, puzzles, jacks, tops, skipping ropes, model cars, trains, planes, etc., bicycles, tricycles, roller skates, marbles, skateboards, hobby horses.

2. [Anything trivial]—*Syn.* foolishness, trifle, frippery, plaything, trinket, gadget, trumpery, stuff, triviality, bauble, knicknack; *all* (D): gimcrack, whimwham, gewgaw; see also **trinket.**

toy (around) (with), *v.* **1.** [(D) To flirt]—*Syn.* dally, take *or* treat lightly, fool *or* play *or* mess (around) (with) (D); see **flirt** 1, **trifle with.**

2. [To consider]—*Syn.* think about, ponder, have in mind; see **think** 1.

toyshop, *n.*—*Syn.* children's store, novelty shop, department store; see **shop, store** 1.

trace, *n.* **1.** [A very small quantity]—*Syn.* indication, fragment, dash, dab, sprinkling, tinge, nib, snick, pinch, taste, crumb, trifle, shred, drop, speck, shade, hint, shadow, nuance, iota, scintilla, particle, jot, suggestion, touch, tittle, suspicion, minimum, snippet, smidgen (D), smell, spot; see also **bit** 1.

2. [A track]—*Syn.* evidence, trail, footprint; see **mark** 1, **proof** 1, **track** 2.

trace, *v.* **1.** [To track]—*Syn.* smell out, track down, run down; see **hunt** 2, **pursue** 1, **track** 1.

2. [To discover by investigation]—*Syn.* ascertain, determine, investigate; see **discover** 1.

3. [To draw]—*Syn.* sketch, outline, copy; see **draw** 2.

traceable, *mod.*—*Syn.* derivative, detectable, identifiable, visible, verifiable, referable, ascribable, attributable, imputable, explainable, accountable; see also **obvious** 1, 2, **tangible.**

traced, *mod.* **1.** [Copied]—*Syn.* outlined, drawn, sketched, delineated, etched, impressed, imprinted, superimposed, imitated, duplicated, patterned; see also **reproduced.**

2. [Tracked]—*Syn.* followed, pursued, trailed; see **hunted, tracked.**

tracer bullet, *n.*—*Syn.* cartridge, ammunition, munition; see **bullet.**

tracery, *n.*—*Syn.* mesh, gridiron, grille; see **lattice, web** 1.

tracing, *n.*—*Syn.* imitation, reproduction, duplicate; see **copy.**

track, *n.* **1.** [A prepared way]—*Syn.* path, course, road, route, trail, lane, roadway, passage, towpath, pathway, clearing, cut, alley, avenue, walk; see also **railroad.**

Types of tracks include the following—railroad, cinder, race, turf, rail, field, trolley; monorail, third rail.

2. [Evidence left in passage]—*Syn.* footprint, trace, vestige, impression, tire track, mark, footmark, spoor, trail, imprint, remnant, record, indication, print, sign, remains, memorial, token, symbol, clue, scent, wake, monument; see also **step** 3.

keep track of—*Syn.* keep an account of, stay informed about, maintain contact with; see **track** 1.

lose track of—*Syn.* lose sight of, lose contact with, abandon; see **forget** 1.

make tracks (D)—*Syn.* run away, abandon, depart quickly; see **leave** 1.

off the track—*Syn.* deviant, variant, deviating; see **mistaken** 1.

the wrong side of the tracks (D)—*Syn.* ghetto, poor side of town, lower class neighborhood; see **slum.**

track, *v.* **1.** [To follow by evidence]—*Syn.* hunt, pursue, smell out, add up, put together, trail, follow, trace, follow the scent, follow a clue, follow footprints, draw an inference, piece together, dog; *all* (D): be hot on the trail of, tail, shadow.

2. [To dirty with tracks]—*Syn.* leave footprints, leave mud, muddy, stain, filth, soil, besmear, spatter, leave a trail of dirt, draggle; see also **dirty.**

3. [To follow in alignment]—*Syn.* move in a straight line, keep in a groove, keep in line, move in the same line, follow the track, run straight.

track down, *v.*—*Syn.* pursue, hunt (down), find; see **arrest, catch** 1, 2, **discover.**

tracked, *mod.*—*Syn.* traced, followed, trailed, hunted, dogged, chased, pursued; *both* (D): tailed, shadowed.—*Ant.* captured*, found, caught.

trackless, *mod.*—*Syn.* wild, untrodden, uninhabited; see **pathless.**

tracks, *n.* **1.** [(D) An injection scar]—*Syn.* needlemarks, punctures, injection marks; see **injection, mark** 1, **scar.**

2. [Means of passage]—*Syn.* road, way, path; see **track** 1.

3. [Evidence of passage]—*Syn.* trail, (foot)prints, marks; see **track** 2.

tracking station, *n.*—*Syn.* observatory, reporting station, check point; see **station.**

tract, *n.*—*Syn.* expanse, plot, region, stretch, piece of land, field.

tractable, *mod.* **1.** [Obedient]—*Syn.* complaisant, compliant, willing; see **docile, obedient** 1.

2. [Malleable]—*Syn.* ductile, facile, pliable; see **flexible** 1.

traction, *n.*—*Syn.* friction, adhesion, partial adherence; see **stress** 2.

tractor, *n.*—*Syn.* traction engine, farm tractor, kerosene tractor, caterpillar tractor, cat (D); see also **engine** 1.

trade, *n.* **1.** [Business]—*Syn.* commerce, sales, enterprise; see **business** 1.

2. [A craft]—*Syn.* occupation, profession, position; see **job** 1.

Common trades include the following—auto mechanic, accountant, boilermaker, baker, barber, butcher, bookbinder, bricklayer, carpenter, chef, cook, draftsman, cabinetmaker, cameraman, dressmaker, electrician, embalmer, engraver, jeweler, locksmith, metallurgist, millwright, miner, machinist, optician, operator, painter, plumber, printer, seamstress, shoemaker, tailor, textile worker, technician, toolmaker, welder.

3. [An individual business transaction]—*Syn.* deal, barter, contract; see **sale** 2.

trade, *v.* **1.** [To do business]—*Syn.* patronize, shop, purchase; see **buy** 1, **sell** 1.

2. [To give one thing for another]—*Syn.* barter, swap, give in exchange; see **exchange** 2.

trade in, —*Syn.* turn in, make part of a deal, get rid of; see **sell** 1.

trader, *n.*—*Syn.* salesman, dealer, tradesman; see **businessman, merchant.**

trade group, *n.*—*Syn.* common market, commerce, traffic; see **business** 1.

trademark, *n.*—*Syn.* label, tag, commercial stamp, manufacturer's symbol, service mark, brand, owner's initials, marks of identification.

trade on, *v.*—*Syn.* take advantage of, make use of, rely on *or* upon; see **use** 1.

tradesman, *n.*—*Syn.* storekeeper, shopkeeper, merchant, small businessman, trader, retailer; see also **businessman.**

trade union, *n.*—*Syn.* union, organized labor, guild; see **labor** 4.

trading, *n.*—*Syn.* dealing, buying, selling, exchanging, bartering, doing business, speculation, negotiating.

trading stamp, *n.*—*Syn.* certificate, token, redemption (slip); see **bond** 3, **coupon.**

tradition, *n.* **1.** [The process of preserving orally]—*Syn.* folklore, legend, fable, popular knowledge, myth, lore, wisdom of the ages; see also **story.**

2. [Cultural heritage]—*Syn.* ritual, mores, law; see **culture** 2, **custom** 2.

3. [A belief]—*Syn.* attitude, conclusion, idea; see **belief** 1, **opinion** 1.

traditional, *mod.* **1.** [Handed down orally]—*Syn.* folkloric, legendary, mythical, epical, ancestral, unwritten, balladic, told, handed down, fabulous, anecdotal, proverbial, inherited, folkloristic.

2. [Generally accepted]—*Syn.* old, acknowledged, customary, habitual, widespread, usual, widely used, popular, acceptable, established, fixed, sanctioned, universal, doctrinal, disciplinary, taken for granted, immemorial, rooted, classical, prescribed, conventional; see also **common** 1, **regular** 3.

traduce, *v.*—*Syn.* defame, libel, vilify; see **slander.**

traffic, *n.* **1.** [The flow of transport]—*Syn.* travel, passage, transportation, flux, movement, transfer, transit, ferriage, passenger service, freight shipment, truckage, cartage, influx.

2. [Dealings]—*Syn.* business, commerce, transactions, trade associations, exchange, soliciting, intercourse, familiarity, truck, interchange.

tragedian, *n.*—*Syn.* dramatist, performer, Thespian; see **actor, actress.**

tragedy, *n.* **1.** [Unhappy fate]—*Syn.* lot, bad fortune, misfortune, doom, bad end, no good end. —*Ant.* happiness*, fortune, success.
2. [A series of tragic events]—*Syn.* adversity, affliction, hardship, struggle, misadventure, curse, blight, humiliation, wreck, failure; *both* (D): one blow after another, hard knocks; see also **difficulty** 1, 2.—*Ant.* success*, prosperity, good fortune.
3. [An artistic creation climaxed by catastrophe] —*Syn.* novel, play, tragic poem, melodrama, tragic drama, Elizabethan tragedy, Greek tragedy, French classic tragedy; see also **drama** 1.—*Ant.* comedy*, satire, burlesque.

tragic, *mod.* —*Syn.* catastrophic, fateful, fatal, calamitous, disastrous, dire, ill-fated, pitiful, terrible, dreadful, awe-inspiring, deathly, deadly, unfortunate, unhappy, sad, painful, grim, appalling, crushing, heart-rending, heartbreaking, lamentable, shocking, harrowing, desolating, ill-starred, hapless, ruinous, baleful, destructive.—*Ant.* happy*, joyous, rollicking.

trail, *n.* —*Syn.* trace, way, path, tracks.

trail, *v.* **1.** [To follow]—*Syn.* track, trace, follow a scent; see **hunt** 1, 2, **pursue** 1.
2. [To lag behind]—*Syn.* fall back, loiter, tarry, linger, dawdle, be left behind, drag along; *both* (D): be out of the running, be left in the cold.—*Ant.* lead*, forge ahead, be leading.

trailer, *n.*—*Syn.* house trailer, auto home, truck trailer, auto cart; *both* (D): cracker box on wheels, bounce-along, pup; see also **home** 1.

trailer house, *n.* —*Syn.* house, mobile home, portable home; see **home** 1, **trailer.**

trailer park, *n.*—*Syn.* mobile home *or* housing area, trailer parking *or* space, trailer foundations *or* facilities; see **lot** 1.

trailing, *mod.* —*Syn.* following, behind, endmost, tracking, hunting, swept along, lagging, dawdling, falling behind, crawling, creeping; see also **losing** 1. —*Ant.* ahead*, leading, foremost.

train, *n.* **1.** [A sequence]—*Syn.* string, chain, succession; see **series.**
2. [A locomotive and attached cars]—*Syn.* transport train, passenger, freight train, local train, limited, diplomatic train, supply train, express train, excursion train, commuters' train, troop train, boat train, mail train, *rapide* (French); *all* (D): subway, underground, elevated, electric, diesel, choo-choo, gully-jumper, rattler; see also **railroad.**

train, *v.* **1.** [To drill]—*Syn.* practice, exercise, discipline; see **reach** 2.
2. [To educate]—*Syn.* instruct, tutor, enlighten; see **teach** 1.
3. [To toughen oneself]—*Syn.* prepare, inure, grow strong, get into practice, reduce, make ready, fit out, equip, qualify, bring up to standard; *both* (D): whip into shape, get a workout.—*Ant.* weaken*, break training, be unfit.
4. [To direct growth]—*Syn.* rear, lead, discipline (oneself), mold, bend, implant, guide, shape, care for, encourage, infuse, imbue, order, bring up, nurture, nurse, prune, weed; see also **raise** 1.—*Ant.* neglect*, ignore, disdain.
5. [To aim]—*Syn.* cock, level, draw a bead; see **aim** 2.

trained, *mod.* —*Syn.* prepared, qualified, cultured, initiated, skilled, informed, schooled, primed, graduated, disciplined, enlightened; see also **educated** 1.—*Ant.* inexperienced*, untrained, raw*.

trainer, *n.* —*Syn.* teacher, tutor, instructor, coach, manager, mentor, officer, master, drillmaster; *all* (D): boss, handler, pilot.

training, *mod.* —*Syn.* preliminary, educational, disciplinary, pedagogic, doctrinal, scholastic, preparatory; *both* (D): in collar, on the stocks.

training, *n.* —*Syn.* drill, practice, exercise, preparation, instruction, foundation, schooling, discipline, basic principles, groundwork, coaching, indoctrination, preliminaries; *both* (D): tune-up, build-up; see also **education.**

trait, *n.* —*Syn.* habit, manner, custom, feature, peculiarity, oddity, quality, trick, cast; see also **characteristic.**

traitor, *n.* —*Syn.* betrayer, traducer, deserter, renegade, Judas, Quisling, fifth columnist, informer, intriguer, spy, hypocrite, imposter, plotter, conspirator, turncoat, sneak, recreant, backslider; *all* (D): double-crosser, wolf in sheep's clothing, fink, rat, stool pigeon, two-timer, copperhead; see also **rebel** 1.—*Ant.* supporter*, follower, partisan.

traitorous, *mod.* **1.** [Treacherous]—*Syn.* faithless, recreant, unfaithful; see **false** 1.
2. [Treasonable]—*Syn.* seditious, disloyal, unpatriotic; see **false** 1.

trammel, *v.* —*Syn.* impede, hinder, obstruct, clog, hamper, shackle, fetter, spancel, hobble, restrain, check, encumber, cramp, retard, oppose, cumber, incommode, discommode, discompose, thwart, frustrate, circumvent, enchain, bridle, muzzle, gag, pinion, manacle, restrict, bind, tether, tie, handcuff, curb.—*Ant.* help*, aid, assist.

tramp, *n.* **1.** [A vagrant]—*Syn.* vagabond, vagrant, wanderer, bum, hobo, outcast, panhandler, hitchhiker, gypsy, loafer, unemployable; *all* (D): yegg, rail-rider, knight of the road, moocher, bo, flipper; see also **beggar** 1.
2. [Heavy footfalls]—*Syn.* trample, march, stamping, stomping, treading, gallop, pounding; *both* (D): hoofing, gallumphing; see also **step** 1, **tread.**
3. [A long walk, often in rough country]—*Syn.* hike, ramble, tour, march, turn, stroll, saunter, excursion, expedition, walking trip; *all* (D): stretch, shin, mush; see also **walk** 3.
4. [Prostitute]—*Syn.* whore, harlot, slut; see **prostitute.**

tramp, *v.* **1.** [To tread heavily]—*Syn.* march, stamp, gallop, pound, stomp, tread, trample, trip, hop, do a jig; *both* (D): hoof it, galumph around; see also **walk** 1.
2. [To wander afoot]—*Syn.* hike, stroll, ramble, tour, walk about, take a turn, go on a walking tour, explore the countryside; see also **march, walk** 1.

trample, *v.* —*Syn.* stamp on, crush, tread on, grind underfoot, injure, squash, bruise, tramp over, overwhelm; see also **defeat** 2, 3, **grind** 1.

trance, *n.* —*Syn.* coma, daze, insensibility; see **stupor.**

tranquil, *mod.* **1.** [*Said especially of people*]—*Syn.* composed, agreeable, gentle, unexcited, unexcitable, placid, amicable, peaceful, pacific, untroubled, unruffled, calm, sober, quiet, reasonable, measured,

lenient, even-tempered, smooth, gentle, poised, at ease, well-adjusted, patient, cool; see also **serene.** —*Ant.* angry*, perturbed, agitated.
2. [*Said especially of weather, nature, etc.*]—*Syn.* mild, soft, calm, temperate, moderate, low, serene, halcyon, hushed, still, whispering, murmuring, pleasing, comforting, restful, tame, sedative, soothing, even, balmy, southerly, agreeable, pastoral, paradisiacal; see also **fair** 3.

tranquilize, *v.* —*Syn.* calm, pacify, quell; see **calm down, quiet** 1, **soothe.**

tranquilizer, *n.* **1.** [Calmative medicine]—*Syn.* sleeping pill, depressant, sedative; see **drug** 2, **medicine** 2.
2. [Pacifier]—*Syn.* mitigator, moderator, temperer, assauger, alleviator, alleviative, palliative, soother, mollifier, calmative, sedative, placebo, anodyne, soporific.

tranquillity, *n.* —*Syn.* calmness, peacefulness, serenity, peace, quiet, quietude, order, law and order, quietness, composure, placidity, coolness, imperturbation.—*Ant.* disturbance*, perturbation, chaos.

transact, *v.* —*Syn.* accomplish, carry on, conclude; see **buy** 1, **negotiate** 1, **sell** 1.

transaction, *n.* —*Syn.* doing, proceeding, business, act, affair, matter, deed, action, event, step, happening, deal, sale, selling, buying, purchase, purchasing, disposal, activity, performance, execution, undertaking.

transatlantic, *mod.* —*Syn.* oceanic, transoceanic, across the Atlantic, nonstop, on the other side.

transcend, *v.* —*Syn.* rise above, transform, excel; see **exceed.**

transcendency, *n.* —*Syn.* transcendence, supremacy, primacy; see **success** 1.

transcendent, *mod.* —*Syn.* transcending, surpassing, exceeding; see **excellent, excelling.**

transcendental, *mod.* —*Syn.* transcendent, primordial, original, intuitive, intellectual, beyond grasp, unintelligible, innate, vague, obscure, fantastic.—*Ant.* clear*, evident, obvious.

transcontinental, *mod.* —*Syn.* trans-American, trans-Siberian, trans-Canadian, trans-European, cross-country, intracontinental, trans-Andean, Cape-to-Cairo.

transcribe, *v.* —*Syn.* reprint, copy, decipher; see **reproduce** 1.

transcriber, *n.* —*Syn.* copyist, copier, translator; see **scribe** 1, **secretary** 2.

transcript, *n.* —*Syn.* record, fair copy, reproduction; see **copy.**

transfer, *n.* **1.** [Ticket]—*Syn.* token, fare, check; see **ticket** 1.
2. [Recording]—*Syn.* variation, substitution, alteration; see **change** 2, **shift** 1.
3. [A document providing for a transfer, sense 2] —*Syn.* (new) orders, instructions, (new) assignment; see **command** 1, **directions.**

transfer, *v.* **1.** [To carry]—*Syn.* transport, convey, shift; see **carry** 1.
2. [To assign]—*Syn.* sell, hand over, pass the buck (D); see **assign** 1, **give** 1.

transferable, *mod.* —*Syn.* negotiable, transmittable, interchangeable, exchangeable, conveyable, assignable, consignable, movable, portable, devisable, conductible.—*Ant.* isolated*, nontransferable, fixed.

transferred, *mod.* —*Syn.* moved, removed, shifted, transported, relocated, transmitted, turned over, sent, relayed, transplanted, reassigned, transposed, restationed, conveyed, transmuted; see also **employed, shipped.**—*Ant.* fixed*, left, stationed.

transfiguration, *n.* —*Syn.* transmutation, alteration, permutation; see **reformation** 1.

transfigure, *v.* **1.** [To transform]—*Syn.* convert, transmute, modify; see **change** 1.
2. [To exalt]—*Syn.* glorify, dignify, signalize; see **idealize.**

transfix, *v.* **1.** [To fascinate]—*Syn.* captivate, bewitch, hypnotize; see **fascinate.**
2. [To impale]—*Syn.* spear, pierce, stick; see **penetrate** 1.

transform, *v.* —*Syn.* convert, mold, reconstruct; see **change** 1.

transform *or* **transformational grammar,** *n.* —*Syn.* generative grammar, new grammar, string grammar; see **grammar.**

transformation, *n.* **1.** [A change]—*Syn.* alteration, transmutation, conversion; see **change** 1, 2.
2. [A grammatical construction]—*Syn.* transform, transformed *or* transformational structure *or* construction, equivalent *or* alternative grammatical sequence *or* string; see also **adjective, adverb, clause** 2, **phrase, sentence** 2.
Transformations include the following—sentence, noun phrase, verb phrase, passive, interrogative, adjective, adverb.

transfuse, *v.* —*Syn.* inject, imbue, infuse; see **instill.**

transfusion, *n.* —*Syn.* transfer, transference, transmission, blood exchange, bleeding; see also **exchange** 1, **phlebotomy.**

transgress, *v.* —*Syn.* sin, offend, do wrong, overstep, rebel, disobey, infringe, take the law into one's own hands, break the law, entrench on, encroach upon; *both* (D): write one's own ticket, fly in the face of the law.

transgression, *n.* —*Syn.* misbehavior, trespass, infraction; see **crime** 1, **sin, violation** 1.

transgressor, *n.* —*Syn.* offender, sinner, rebel; see **criminal.**

transient, *mod.* **1.** [Temporary]—*Syn.* provisional, ephemeral, transitory; see **temporary.**
2. [In motion]—*Syn.* migrating, emigrating, vacating; see **moving** 2.

transient, *n.* —*Syn.* guest, tourist, traveler, overnight boarder, visitor.

transistor, *n.* **1.** [An electronic device]—*Syn.* electron tube, conductor, semiconductor; see **communications, electronics.**
2. [(D) Radio]—*Syn.* portable, pocket radio, battery-powered radio; see **radio** 2.

transit, *n.* **1.** [Passage]—*Syn.* transition, transference, conveyance, transportation, permeation, infiltration, penetration, osmosis.
2. [An engineer's telescope]—*Syn.* surveyor's instrument, theodolite, transit theodolite, gauge, lookstick (D); see also **telescope.**

transition, *n.* —*Syn.* shift, passage, flux, passing, development, transformation, turn, realignment; see also **change** 2.—*Ant.* stability*, constancy, durability.

transitory, *mod.* **1.** [Fleeting]—*Syn.* brief, ephemeral, short; see **fleeting.**
2. [Temporary]—*Syn.* impermanent, transient, changeable; see **temporary.**

translate, *v.* **1.** [To change into another language] —*Syn.* decode, transliterate, interpret, decipher, paraphrase, render, transpose, turn, gloss, Anglicize, do into, put in equivalent terms.
2. [To interpret]—*Syn.* explain, explicate, elucidate; see **explain, interpret** 1.
3. [To transform]—*Syn.* transmute, alter, transpose; see **change** 1.

translated, *mod.* —*Syn.* interpreted, adapted, rendered, transliterated, glossed, paraphrased, reworded, transposed, transferred, transplanted, reworked, rewritten.

translation, *n.* —*Syn.* transliteration, version, adaptation, rendition, rendering, interpretation, paraphrase, rewording, gloss, metaphrase, reading; *all* (D): pony, crib, plug, key.

translucency, *n.* —*Syn.* translucence, transparency, sheerness; see **clarity, lightness** 2.

translucent, *mod.* —*Syn.* glassy, opaque, crystalline; see **clear** 2, **transparent** 1.

transmigrate, *v.* —*Syn.* migrate, emigrate, move; see **leave** 1.

transmigration, *n.* —*Syn.* trek, pilgrimage, movement; see **emigration.**

transmission, *n.* **1.** [The act of transporting]—*Syn.* transference, conveyance, carrying, hauling, sending, transmittal, communication, transposal, deliverance, importation, exportation; see also **delivery** 2, **transportation.**
2. [The carrying of sound on radio waves]—*Syn.* conduction, passage, broadcast, telecast, simulcast, frequency, release, radiocast, hookup (D).
3. [A mechanism for adapting power]—*Syn.* gears, gear box, automatic transmission, fluid transmission, planetary transmission, syncromeshed, transmission, gears constantly enmeshed, overdrive; see also **device** 1.

transmit, *v.* **1.** [To send]—*Syn.* dispatch, forward, convey; see **send** 1, 4.
2. [To carry]—*Syn.* pass on, transfer, communicate; see **carry** 2, **send** 2.

transmitter, *n.* —*Syn.* conductor, aerial, wire; see **antenna, communications, electronics.**

transmutable, *mod.* —*Syn.* transformable, modifiable, alternative; see **changeable** 1, 2.

transmutation, *n.* **1.** [Change]—*Syn.* transfiguration, alteration, mutation; see **change** 1, **conversion** 1.
2. [Transformation]—*Syn.* metathesis, catalysis, transformation; see **change** 2.

transmute, *v.* —*Syn.* transform, convert, adapt; see **change** 1.

transparency, *n.* —*Syn.* transparence, clearness, glassiness; see **clarity.**

transparent, *mod.* **1.** [Allowing light to pass through]—*Syn.* translucent, lucid, crystalline, vitreous, pellucid, gauzy, thin, permeable, hyaline, glassy, cellophane, diaphanous; see also **clear** 2, **thin** 1.—*Ant.* dark*, black, smoky.
2. [Obvious]—*Syn.* easily seen, plain, clear, manifest, patent, understandable, clear-cut, unmistakable, apparent; see also **obvious** 1.—*Ant.* obscure*, hidden, difficult.
3. [Without hidden motives or pretense]—*Syn.* frank, open, honest, candid, clean-cut, sincere, simple, guileless, artless, ingenuous, genuine, direct, unsophisticated; see also **natural** 3.—*Ant.* sly*, crafty, shrewd.

transpire, *v.* —*Syn.* ensue, occur, befall; see **happen** 2.

transplant, *n.* —*Syn.* transplanting, transplantation, utilizing *or* introducing a donated organ, skin graft; heart *or* cardiac transplant, kidney transplant, eye transplant, etc.; see also **operation** 4.

transplant, *v.* —*Syn.* reset, reorient, transpose, remove, graft, recondition, emigrate, readapt, shift over, revamp.

transport, *n.* —*Syn.* carrier, common carrier, conveyor, mover; see also **transportation.**
Transport facilities include the following—railroad, train, transcontinental railroad, line, airline, airplane, transoceanic airline, automobile, truck, bus, steamship; cargo boat, freighter, tanker, troop ship, transport plane, liner, ferryboat, trolley car, subway, underground railroad, elevated railroad, wagon, cart, sled, bicycle.

transport, *v.* —*Syn.* convey, move, bring; see **carry** 1.

transportation, *n.* —*Syn.* conveying, conveyance, carrying, hauling, shipping, carting, moving, transferring, truckage, freightage, air lift, transference, transit, passage, ferriage, telpherage; see also **transport.**

transported, *mod.* —*Syn.* moved, conveyed, forwarded, transferred, carried, changed, shifted, impelled.

transpose, *v.* —*Syn.* interchange, reverse, transfer; see **change** 1, **exchange** 1.

transposition, *n.* —*Syn.* transposal, changing, inversion; see **change** 1, 2.

transubstantiation, *n.* —*Syn.* transformation, transmutation, mutation; see **change** 2, **conversion** 1.

transverse, *mod.* —*Syn.* crosswise, bent, intersecting; see **oblique** 1.

trap, *n.* **1.** [A device to catch game or persons] —*Syn.* net, cul-de-sac, snare, mousetrap, deadfall, spring, pit, blind, noose, trapfall, maneuver; see also **ambush.**
2. [A trick]—*Syn.* prank, practical joke, snare; see **trick** 1.

trap, *v.* —*Syn.* ensnare, seduce, fool; see **ambush, deceive.**

trapped, *mod.* —*Syn.* ambushed, cornered, at bay, with one's back to the wall (D); see also **captured** 1.

trapper, *n.* —*Syn.* hunter, huntsman, poacher, ferreter, sportsman, *voyageur* (French), game hunter.

trappings, *n.* **1.** [Trimmings]—*Syn.* adornments, trim, embellishments; see **decoration** 2.
2. [Equipment]—*Syn.* rigging, outfit, gear; see **equipment.**

trash, *n.* **1.** [Rubbish]—*Syn.* garbage, waste, refuse, dregs, filth, litter, debris, dross, oddments, sweepings, rubble, odds and ends, offal, junk, sediment, leavings, droppings; see also **excess** 4, **residue.** —*Ant.* money*, goods, riches.

2. [Persons regarded as of little account]—*Syn.* beggars, thieves, outlaws, the poor, the lower class, hobos, tramps, *hoi polloi,* (Greek), *sans culottes, canaille* (*both* French), wastrels, poor whites, sharecroppers; *all* (D): guttersnipes, varmints, good-for-nothings, white trash; see also **rascal.** —*Ant.* aristocracy*, the upper class, the wealthy.
3. [Waste matter]—*Syn.* stuff, frippery, rags, scraps, scrap, scourings, fragments, pieces, shavings, loppings, slash, rakings, slag, parings, rinsings, deads, debris, shoddy, scoria, recrement, residue; see also **sense** 1.
4. [Nonsense]—*Syn.* drivel, twaddle, prating; see **nonsense** 1.

trashing (D), *n.* —*Syn.* rioting, vandalism, wrecking; see **destruction** 1, **violence** 2.

trashy, *mod.* —*Syn.* cheap, ugly, paltry; see **useless** 1, **worthless** 1.

trauma, *n.* —*Syn.* shock, outburst, ordeal; see **confusion** 2.

travail, *n.* —*Syn.* labor, toil, drudgery; see **work** 2.

travel, *n.* **1.** [The act of journeying]—*Syn.* riding, roving, wandering, rambling, sailing, touring, biking, hiking, cruising, driving, wayfaring, going abroad, seeing the world, sight-seeing, voyaging, trekking, flying, globe-trotting, space travel, rocketing, moon shot, orbiting, manning a space station, interstellar *or* intercontinental travel, jet travel.
2. [An individual journey]—*Syn.* tour, voyage, trip; see **journey.**

travel, *v.* **1.** [To move at a regular pace]—*Syn.* cover ground, progress, go; see **move** 1.
2. [To journey]—*Syn.* tour, cruise, voyage, roam, explore, jet (to), rocket (to *or* toward), orbit, go into orbit, man *or* be in a command of a service *or* lunar, etc., module; take a jet, go by jet, migrate, trek, vacation, motor, visit, jaunt, wander, junket, adventure, quest, trip, rove, inspect, make an expedition, make a peregrination, cross the continent, cross the ocean, encircle the globe, make the grand tour, sail, see the country, go camping, go abroad, take a trip, take a train *or* boat *or* plane (for), cover, go walking *or* riding *or* bicycling, etc., make a train trip, drive, fly, sail, traverse, set out, set forth, sight-see; *both* (D): scour the country, bat around; see also **walk** 1.

traveled, *mod.* **1.** [*Said of persons*]—*Syn.* worldly, cosmopolitan, urbane, polished, seasoned, experienced, itinerant.—*Ant.* domestic*, provincial, small-town.
2. [*Said of roads*]—*Syn.* well-used, busy, operating, in use, frequented, widely known, sure, safe, well-trodden, accepted.—*Ant.* abandoned*, little-used, unexplored.

traveler, *n.* —*Syn.* voyager, adventurer, tourist, explorer, nomad, wanderer, peddler, truant, roamer, rambler, wayfarer, migrant, displaced person *or* D.P., journeyer, excursionist, junketer, sight-seer, straggler, vagabond, vagrant, hobo, tramp, gypsy, wandering Jew, gadabout, itinerant, pilgrim, rover, passenger, commuter, globe-trotter.

traveling, *mod.* **1.** [*Said of goods*]—*Syn.* passing, en route, on board, shipped, freighted, transported, moving, carried, conveyed, consigned, being hauled.
2. [*Said of people*]—*Syn.* wandering, touring, roving, on tour, vagrant, migrant, nomadic, wayfaring, itinerant, cruising, excursioning, commuting, driving, flying, ranging, sailing, riding, on vacation, migrating, voyaging; see also **moving** 2.

traveling salesman, *n.* —*Syn.* (our *or* the *or* their) representative, man in *or* covering a certain territory, traveling man; see **salesman** 2.

traverse, *v.* —*Syn.* cross over, move over, pass through; see **cross** 1.

travesty, *n.* —*Syn.* burlesque, spoof, caricature; see **parody.**

tray, *n.* —*Syn.* platter, plate, service, plate, trencher, salver, waiter, dumb-waiter, tea wagon; see also **dish** 1.

treacherous, *mod.* **1.** [Traitorous]—*Syn.* treasonable, falsehearted, unfaithful; see **false** 1.
2. [Unreliable]—*Syn.* deceptive, undependable, dangerous, risky, misleading, tricky, dissembled, untrustworthy, deceitful, false, twofaced, ensnaring, faulty, precarious, unstable, insecure, shaky, slippery, ticklish, difficult, ominous, alarming, menacing; *both* (D): dynamite, not healthy.—*Ant.* reliable*, dependable, steady.

treacherously, *mod.* —*Syn.* unscrupulously, deceitfully, faithlessly; see **falsely.**

treachery, *n.* —*Syn.* faithlessness, disloyalty, betrayal; see **dishonesty, treason.**

tread, *n.* —*Syn.* step, gait, walk, march, footsteps; see also **tramp** 2.

tread, *v.* —*Syn.* walk, step, step on; see **tramp** 1, **trample.**

treason, *n.* —*Syn.* sedition, seditiousness, disloyalty, perfidy, treachery, seditionary *or* seditious act, aid and comfort to the enemy, factious revolt; see also **crime** 2, **dishonesty, deception** 1, **revolution** 2.

treasure, *n.* —*Syn.* richness, riches, store, cache, hoard, find, abundance, reserve, nest egg, pile (D); see also **wealth** 1, 2.

treasure, *v.* —*Syn.* prize, value, appreciate, guard; see also **love** 1.

treasurer, *n.* —*Syn.* bursar, receiver, cashier, controller, comptroller, banker, paymaster, purser, curator, steward, accountant, club officer, government official, trustee; see also **accountant, teller.**

treasury, *n.* —*Syn.* repository, bank, storehouse, money exchange, central money office, exchequer, bursary, money box, strongbox, cash register, safe, depository.

treat, *n.* —*Syn.* entertainment, surprise, amusement, free passage, feast, delectable dish, source of gratification, gift; *all* (D): drinks for the crowd, setup, beano, spree.

treat, *v.* **1.** [To deal with a person or thing]—*Syn.* negotiate, manage, have to do with, have business with, behave toward, handle, make terms with, act toward, react toward, use, employ, have recourse to.—*Ant.* neglect*, ignore, have nothing to do with.
2. [To deal with a subject]—*Syn.* talk of, write of, speak of, discourse upon, arrange, manipulate, comment, interpret, explain, enlarge upon, criticize, discuss, review, approach, tackle (D).
3. [To assist toward a cure]—*Syn.* attend, administer, prescribe, dose, operate, nurse, dress, minister to, apply therapy, care for, doctor (D); see also **heal** 1.

4. [To pay for another's entertainment]—*Syn.* entertain, indulge, satisfy, amuse, divert, play host to, escort; *all* (D): set up, blow, stake to, stand to.

treatise, *n.* —*Syn.* tract, paper, monograph; see **exposition** 2.

treatment, *n.* **1.** [Usage]—*Syn.* handling, processing, dealing, approach, execution, procedure, method, manner, proceeding, way, strategy, custom, habit, employment, practice, mode, *modus operandi* (Latin); *both* (D): line, angle.

2. [Assistance toward a cure]—*Syn.* diet, operation, medical care, surgery, therapy, remedy, prescription, regimen, hospitalization, doctoring (D); see also **medicine** 2.

treaty, *n.* —*Syn.* agreement, pact, settlement, covenant, compact, cartel, convention, alliance, concordat, charter, sanction, entente, bond, understanding, arrangement, bargain, negotiation, deal (D).

tree, *n.* Trees include the following—ash, elm, oak, maple, catalpa, evergreen, birch, tulip, aspen, fir, cypress, juniper, larch *or* tamarack, pine, cedar, beech, chestnut, eucalyptus, hickory, walnut, sycamore, plane, palm, willow, locust, sequoia, redwood, poplar, acacia, cottonwood, beech, box elder, apple, cherry, peach, plum, pear, prune, banyan, baobab, bamboo, abba, calabra, betel, mahogany, ebony, bo, ironwood, bottle; see also **wood** 1.

up a tree (D)—*Syn.* cornered, in difficulty, trapped; see **in trouble** 1.

trees, *n.* —*Syn.* wood, woods, windbreak; see **forest.**

trek, *v.* —*Syn.* hike, migrate, journey; see **travel** 2.

trellis, *n.* —*Syn.* framework, arbor, grille; see **frame** 1, **lattice.**

tremble, *v.* —*Syn.* quiver, shiver, vibrate; see **shake** 1.

tremendous, *mod.* —*Syn.* huge, great, colossal; see **large** 1.

tremendously, *mod.* —*Syn.* exceedingly, amazingly, remarkably, excessively, appallingly; see also **largely** 2.

tremor, *n.* —*Syn.* trembling, shaking, shivering; see **earthquake.**

tremulous, *mod.* **1.** [Shaking]—*Syn.* trembling, quivering, palpitating; see **shaky** 1.

2. [Timid]—*Syn.* fearful, shy, timorous; see **cowardly** 1, **timid** 2.

trench, *n.* —*Syn.* rut, hollow, gully, depression, gutter, tube, furrow, drainage canal, creek, moat, dike, drain, channel, main, gorge, gulch, arroyo.

Military trenches include the following—dugout, earthwork, intrenchment, fortification, breastwork, pillbox, excavation, revetment, bunker, strong point, machine-gun nest, communication trench, front-line trench, tank-trap, foxhole; see also **defense** 2.

trenchant, *mod.* **1.** [Having a cutting edge]—*Syn.* cutting, incisive, keen, biting, pungent, severe, razor-fine; see also **sharp** 1.—*Ant.* dull*, blunt, flat.

2. [Sharp intellectually]—*Syn.* unsparing, critical, emphatic, vigorous, impressive, strong, dynamic, pointed, intense, positive, weighty, salient, significant, pithy, sententious, crushing, forcible, crisp, caustic, concise, succinct, razor-sharp, comprehensive, pregnant, neat, to the point, graphic, explicit, ponderous; see also **intelligent** 1, **profound** 2. —*Ant.* weak*, shallow, feeble.

trend, *n.* **1.** [Tendency]—*Syn.* bias, bent, leaning; see **inclination** 1.

2. [Direction]—*Syn.* course, aim, bearing; see **drift** 1.

trendsetter, *n.* —*Syn.* initiator, pacesetter, manager; see **leader** 2.

trendy (D), *mod.* —*Syn.* stylish, popular, contemporary; see **fashionable.**

trepan, *v.* —*Syn.* trick, trap, lure; see **deceive.**

trepidation, *n.* **1.** [Quaking]—*Syn.* tremor, quivering, shaking, agitation, panic.

2. [Dread]—*Syn.* shock, alarm, terror; see **fear** 1, 2.

trespass, *v.* **1.** [To transgress]—*Syn.* offend, err, displease; see **misbehave, sin, transgress.**

2. [To intrude]—*Syn.* encroach, invade, infringe; see **meddle** 1.

trespasser, *n.* **1.** [An intruder]—*Syn.* encroacher, invader, infringer; see **intruder.**

2. [An offender]—*Syn.* evildoer, misdoer, reprobate; see **criminal.**

tress, *n.* —*Syn.* shock, lock, plait; see **braid, curl, hair** 1.

trestle, *n.* —*Syn.* horse, stool, frame, support, approach.

trial, *mod.* —*Syn.* tentative, test, trial, balloon, preliminary, probationary, temporary; see also **experimental.**

trial, *n.* **1.** [An effort to learn the truth]—*Syn.* analysis, test, examination; see **experiment** 1.

2. [A case at law]—*Syn.* suit, lawsuit, fair hearing, hearing, action, case, contest, indictment, legal proceedings, claim, cross-examination, litigation, counterclaim, replevin, arraignment, prosecution, citation, court action, judicial contest, seizure, assumpsit, bill of divorce, habeas corpus, court-martial, impeachment; *all* (D): rap, try, court clash.

3. [An ordeal]—*Syn.* suffering, severe test, tribulation, affliction, trying experience, misfortune, heavy blow (D); see also **difficulty** 1, 2.

on trial—*Syn.* being tried *or* considered *or* tested *or* examined, under consideration, not yet accepted; see **on trial** 1.

trial and error (method), *n.* —*Syn.* empiricism, empirical method, by guess and by God (D); see **experiment** 1, 2, **method** 2.

triangle, *n.* Triangles include the following—equilateral, isosceles, right-angled, obtuse-angled, scalene, acute-angled.

triangular, *mod.* —*Syn.* three-cornered, three-sided, triagonal, delta-shaped, deltoid, trilateral; see also **angular** 1.

tribal, *mod.* —*Syn.* tribular, racial, kindred; see **common** 5, **group.**

tribe, *n.* —*Syn.* primitive group, ethnic group, association; see **race** 2.

Related terms include the following—society, phratry, clan, totemic unit, family, sib, sept, horde, sorory, class.

tribulation, *n.* —*Syn.* trouble, misery, sorrow; see **difficulty** 2, **grief** 1.

tribunal, *n.* —*Syn.* bench, bar, assizes; see **court** 2.

tributary, *mod.* —*Syn.* subordinate, subject, minor, accessory, small, supplementary, auxiliary, adjoining, affluent, subsidiary; see also **secondary** 1. —*Ant.* principal*, main, leading.

tributary, *n.* —*Syn.* stream, river, branch, feeder, anabranch, affluent, sidestream, offshoot.

tribute, *n.* **1.** [Recognition]—*Syn.* enconium, applause, memorial service, offering, eulogy; see also **praise** 2, **recognition** 2.

2. [Money paid a conqueror]—*Syn.* ransom, fee, levy; see **bribe.**

trice, *n.* —*Syn.* while, second, minute; see **instant, moment** 1.

trick, *n.* **1.** [A deceit]—*Syn.* wile, casuistry, fraud, deception, ruse, cheat, cover, feint, hoax, artifice, decoy, trap, stratagem, intrigue, fabrication, double-dealing, forgery, fake, illusion, invention, subterfuge, distortion, delusion, ambush, snare, blind, evasion, plot, equivocation, concealment, treachery, swindle, imposture, feigning, impersonation, dissimulation, duplicity, pretense, falsehood, falsification, perjury, disguise, conspiracy, machination, circumvention, quibble, trickery, conundrum, beguiling, chicane, chicanery, humbug, simulacrum, maneuver, sham, counterfeit; *all* (D): gyp, touch, phoney, come-on, fast one, dodge, plant, clip, sucker, deal, con game, bluff, shakedown, sell-out, con, funny business, dirty work, crooked deal, front, fakeroo, gimmick, suck-in; see also **lie** 1. —*Ant.* honesty*, truth, veracity.

2. [A prank]—*Syn.* jest, sport, practical joke; see **joke** 1.

3. [A practical method or expedient]—*Syn.* skill, facility, know-how (D); see **ability** 2, **method** 2.

4. [A round of cards]—*Syn.* deal, hand, round, shuffle.

do *or* **turn the trick** (D)—*Syn.* achieve the desired result, attain success, accomplish; see **succeed** 1.

trick, *v.* —*Syn.* dupe, outwit, fool; see **deceive.**

trickery, *n.* —*Syn.* dupery, fraud, quackery; see **deception** 1, **dishonesty.**

trickle, *v.* —*Syn.* drip, dribble, leak, seep, stream, issue, ooze, run; see also **flow** 2.

trickster, *n.* —*Syn.* fraud, confidence man, impostor; see **cheat** 1, **swindler.**

tricky, *mod.* **1.** [Sly]—*Syn.* wily, crafty, foxy; see **sly** 1.

2. [Shrewd]—*Syn.* clever, sharp, keen-witted; see **intelligent** 1.

3. [(D) Delicate or difficult]—*Syn.* complicated, intricate, critical, touchy, involved, perplexing, knotty, thorny, complex, unstable, ticklish, catchy, likely to go wrong, hanging by a thread (D); see also **difficult** 1, 2.—*Ant.* easy*, clear-cut, simple.

tricycle, *n.* —*Syn.* velocipede, three-wheeled velocipede, three-wheeled chair, three-wheeled cycle; *all* (D): trike, wheel, three-wheeler; see also **bicycle.**

tried, *mod.* —*Syn.* dependable, proved, approved, certified, used; see also **tested.**

trifle, *n.* **1.** [A small quantity]—*Syn.* particle, piece, speck; see **bit** 1.

2. [A small degree]—*Syn.* jot, eyelash, fraction; see **bit** 3.

3. [Something of little importance]—*Syn.* triviality, small matter, nothing; see **insignificance.**

trifler, *n.* —*Syn.* pretender, imposter, time waster, idler, lounger, humbug, waster, slacker, shirker, lazy person, ne'er-do-well; see also **loafer.**

trifle with, *v.* **1.** [To act without seriousness] —*Syn.* putter *or* potter, fribble, dip into, slur over, dawdle, dally, mock, play at, make fun, jest, act silly, loiter, idle about, lounge, fool around (with), indulge in horseplay; *all* (D): monkey with *or* around, fool with *or* around, mess with *or* around, doodle, string along *or* around, phutz around, horse around; see also **change** 1, **tamper.**

2. [To flirt]—*Syn.* wink at, play with *or* around, make advances; see **flirt** 1.

trifling, *mod.* —*Syn.* petty, small, insignificant; see **trivial, unimportant.**

trifling, *n.* —*Syn.* dawdling, idling, loitering; see **indifference** 1.

trill, *v.* —*Syn.* quaver, warble, wave, shake, roll, whistle, chirp, twitter, yodel; see also **sound** 1.

trim, *mod.* **1.** [Neat]—*Syn.* orderly, tidy, spruce; see **clean** 1, **neat** 1.

2. [Well-proportioned]—*Syn.* shapely, clean, well-designed, streamlined, slim, shipshape, delicate, fit, comely, well-formed, symmetrical, well-made, clean-cut, well-balanced, graceful, well-molded, harmonious, beautiful, classical, compact, smart; see also **handsome** 2.—*Ant.* disordered*, shapeless, straggly.

trim, *v.* **1.** [To cut off excess]—*Syn.* prune, shave, lop, crop, clip, shear, pare down, even up, mow, snip, plane, slice off, scrape, whittle down, carve down; see also **cut** 1.—*Ant.* increase*, lengthen, extend.

2. [To adorn]—*Syn.* ornament, embellish, beautify, betinsel, deck, beribbon, spangle, gussy up (D), emblazon, embroider; see also **decorate.**

3. [(D) To defeat]—*Syn.* whip, lick, trounce; see **defeat** 1, 3.

4. [To refuse to take a stand]—*Syn.* hedge, temporize, equivocate, dodge, vacillate, remain neutral, stand between; *all* (D): sit on a fence, shilly-shally, hem and haw; see also **hesitate, pause.**—*Ant.* oppose*, antagonize, be a partisan of.

5. [To prepare for sailing]—*Syn.* ballast, rig, outfit, hoist the sails, touch her up (D); see also **provide** 1, **sail** 1, **trim ship.**

trimmer, *n.* —*Syn.* temporizer, deceiver, sycophant; see **opportunist.**

trimming, *n.* **1.** [Ornamentation]—*Syn.* trapping, accessory, frill, embellishment, border design, embroidered hem, tassel, edging; see also **decoration** 2, **embroidery** 1.

2. [The act of cutting off excess]—*Syn.* shearing, lopping off, shaving off, making even, cutting away, clipping, snipping, mowing, nipping, cropping, shortening, pruning, paring down; see also **reducing.**—*Ant.* increasing*, extending, enlarging.

3. [(D) Defeat]—*Syn.* beating, repulse, whipping, thrashing, rebuff, upset, licking, skunking (D); see also **defeat.**—*Ant.* success*, victory, achievement.

trim one's sails (D), *v.* —*Syn.* adapt, adjust (oneself *or* one's actions), accede; see **accommodate** 2.

trim ship, *v.* —*Syn.* break out, rig, equip, outfit, ballast, put on an even keel; see also **balance** 2, **trim** 5.

trinity, *n.* **1.** [Three of a kind]—*Syn.* trio, trilogy, triplet, triplicate, threesome, triad, set of three, leash, trey.

2. [The Holy Trinity]—*Syn.* three-personed God, the God-head; Father, Son, and Holy Ghost; the

Triune God, Trinity, the Trinity in Unity, Threefold Unity, Three in One and One in Three, Trimurti; see also **God** 1, 2.

trinket, *n.* —*Syn.* plaything, toy, tinsel, frippery, knickknack, gadget, novelty, bauble; *all* (D): showpiece, dazzler, doo-dad, pretty-pretty, thingumajig; see also **jewel, jewelry, pin** 2, **ring** 2.

trio, *n.* **1.** [A combination of three]—*Syn.* trinity, triangle, triplet, triplicate, threesome, triad, set of three, leash, trey.

2. [Three musicians performing together]—*Syn.* string trio, vocal trio, swing trio (D); see **band** 4.

trip, *n.* **1.** [A journey]—*Syn.* voyage, excursion, tour; see **journey.**

2. [(D) A psychedelic experience]—*Syn.* hallucinations; *both* (D): LSD *or* heroin *or* mescaline, etc., trip, being turned on; see also **drug** 2, **indulgence** 3.

trip, *v.* **1.** [To stumble]—*Syn.* tumble, slip, lurch, slide, founder, fall, pitch, fall over, slip upon, plunge, sprawl, topple, go head over heels (D). —*Ant.* arise*, ascend, get up.

2. [To cause to stumble]—*Syn.* block, hinder, bind, tackle, overthrow, push, send headlong, kick, shove, mislead.—*Ant.* help*, pick up, give a helping hand.

3. [To step lightly]—*Syn.* skip, play, frolic; see **dance** 1, 2, **jump** 1, 3.

triple, *mod.* —*Syn.* in triplicate, by three, treble, threefold, triplex, three-ply, ternary; see also **three.**

tripod, *n.* —*Syn.* three-legged stand, holder, camera stand, tripe (D); see also **platform** 1.

tripping, *mod.* —*Syn.* nimble, spry, quick; see **agile.**

trite, *mod.* —*Syn.* hackneyed, prosaic, stereotyped; see **common** 1, **dull** 4.

triumph, *n.* **1.** [Victory]—*Syn.* conquest, mastery, achievement, ascendancy, gain, success; see also **victory** 1.

2. [Exultation]—*Syn.* jubilation, jubilee, reveling; see **celebration** 2, **joy** 3.

triumphal, *mod.* —*Syn.* ceremonial, garlanded, laurel-crowned; see **famous, honored, praised.**

triumphant, *mod.* —*Syn.* exultant, victorious, successful, lucky, winning, conquering, in the lead, triumphal, jubilant, rejoicing, dominant, laurel-crowned, champion, unbeaten, prize-winning, top-seeded, out front, triumphing, victorial, elated, in ascendancy, with flying colors.—*Ant.* beaten*, defeated, overwhelmed.

trivial, *mod.* —*Syn.* petty, trifling, small, superficial, piddling, wee, little, insignificant, frivolous, irrelevant, unimportant, nugatory, skin-deep, meaningless, mean, diminutive, slight, of no account, scanty, meager, inappreciable, microscopic, atomic, dribbling, nonessential, flimsy, inconsiderable, evanescent, vanishing, momentary, immaterial, indifferent, beside the point, minute, unessential, paltry, inferior, minor, small-minded, beggarly, useless, inconsequential, picayune, worthless, scurvy, mangy, trashy, pitiful, of little moment; *all* (D): dinky, small-town, rinky-dink, two-bit, nickle-and-dime, piffling, cutting no ice, cut and dried; see also **shallow** 2.—*Ant.* important*, great, serious*.

triviality, *n.* —*Syn.* unimportance, immateriality, paltriness; see **insignificance.**

troglodyte, *n.* —*Syn.* cave man, savage, aborigine; see **hominid.**

troll, *n.* —*Syn.* goblin, elf, sprite; see **fairy** 1.

trolley car, *n.* —*Syn.* streetcar, electric car, cable car, trackless trolley; *all* (D): trolley, electric, trolley-bus; see also **bus.**

trollop, *n.* —*Syn.* whore, streetwalker, harlot; see **prostitute.**

troop, *n.* —*Syn.* flock, collection, number, company, crowd, delegation, assemblage; see also **gathering.**

trooper, *n.* —*Syn.* cavalryman, patrolman, dragoon; see **policeman, soldier.**

troops, *n.* —*Syn.* soldiers, armed forces, rank and file, fighting men, military, regiment; see also **army** 1, **infantry.**

troopship, *n.* —*Syn.* transport, landing craft, landing ship (LS), landing ship medium (LSM), landing ship tank (LST); see also **boat, ship, transport, warship.**

trope, *n.* —*Syn.* metaphor, figure of speech, analogy; see **comparison** 2, **simile.**

trophy, *n.* —*Syn.* memorial, decoration, citation, medal, cup, crown, ribbon, memento; see also **prize.**

tropic, *mod.* **1.** [Related to the tropics]—*Syn.* tropical, equatorial, jungle, Amazonian, torrid, summer, rainy, wild, south, lush, tangled; see also **hot** 1, **wet** 2.—*Ant.* cool*, temperate, arctic.

2. [Hot]—*Syn.* thermal, torrid, burning; see **hot** 1.

tropical, *mod.* —*Syn.* hot, sultry, torrid; see **tropic** 1.

tropics, *n.* —*Syn.* torrid zone, equator, Equatorial Africa, South America, Amazon, the Congo, the Pacific Islands; see also **jungle.**

trot, *v.* —*Syn.* single-foot, jog, amble, canter, rack, ride, hurry, step lively, keep an even pace; see also **run** 2.

troth, *n.* —*Syn.* word of honor, declaration, pledge; see **promise** 1.

trot out, *v.* —*Syn.* exhibit, show, represent; see **display** 1.

(the) trots (D), *n.* —*Syn.* diarrhea, flux, looseness (of the bowels); see **disease** 1, 2, 3.

troubadour, *n.* —*Syn.* bard, musician, balladeer; see **minstrel, singer.**

trouble, *n.* **1.** [Difficulty]—*Syn.* strain, stress, struggle; see **difficulty** 1, 2.

2. [A person or thing causing trouble]—*Syn.* annoyance, difficult situation, bother, bind, hindrance, difficulty, task, puzzle, predicament, plight, problem, fear, worry, concern, inconvenience, nuisance, disturbance, calamity, catastrophe, crisis, negative function, delay, quarrel, dispute, affliction, intrusion, disquiet, irritation, trial, pain, pique, ordeal, discomfort, injury, adversity, hang-up, case, bore, gossip, problem child, pestiferous person, meddler, pest, tease, tiresome person, talkative person, inconsiderate person, intruder, troublemaker; *all* (D): fly in the ointment, monkey wrench, headache, smart aleck, buttinski, brat, holy terror, bad news, botheration, peck of trouble; see also **care** 2.—*Ant.* aid*, help, comfort*.

3. [Illness]—*Syn.* malady, ailment, affliction; see **disease** 1, 3.

4. [Civil disorder]—*Syn.* riot, turmoil, strife; see **disturbance** 2.

5. [A quarrel]—*Syn.* argument, feud, bickering; see **dispute** 1, **fight** 1.

in trouble—*Syn.* unfortunate, having trouble, in difficulty; see **in trouble.**

trouble, *v.* **1.** [To disturb]—*Syn.* disconcert, annoy, irritate; see **bother** 3, **disturb** 2.

2. [To take care]—*Syn.* be concerned with, make an effort, take pains; see **bother** 1.

troubled, *mod.* **1.** [Worried]—*Syn.* disturbed, agitated, grieved, apprehensive, pained, anxious, perplexed, afflicted, confused, puzzled, upwrought, overwrought, chagrined, bothered, harassed, vexed, plagued, teased, annoyed, concerned, uneasy, discomposed, disquieted, harried, careworn, mortified, badgered, baited, inconvenienced, put out, upset, flurried, flustered, afflicted, bored, tortured, piqued, pricked, goaded, irritated, displeased, exacerbated, tried, roused, disconcerted, pursued, fretted, chafed, galled, rubbed the wrong way, discommoded, ragged, tired, unquiet, molested, crossed, thwarted, fashed, fazed, distressed, wounded, sickened, griped, irascible, restless, irked, pestered, heckled, beset, persecuted, frightened, alarmed, terrified, scared, anguished, harrowed, tormented, provoked, stung, nettled, ruffled, fretting, perturbed, afraid, shaky, fearful, unsettled, suspicious, in turmoil, full of misgivings, shaken, careworn, dreading; *all* (D): bugged, in a quandary, between the devil and the deep blue sea, in a stew, on pins and needles, all hot and bothered, worried stiff, in a tizzy, burned up, discombobulated, miffed, peeved, all in a dither, riled, aggravated, with ants in one's pants, behind the eight ball, floored, up a tree, hung-up, up the creek without a paddle, uptight, on the anxious seat; see also **doubtful** 2.—*Ant.* calm*, at ease, settled.

2. [Pathologically disturbed]—*Syn.* schizophrenic, schizoid, psychotic, psychopathic, neurotic, psychoneurotic, paranoid; *all* (D): devoured by, hung-up, psyched-out; see also **insane** 1.

troublemaker, *n.*—*Syn.* rogue, knave, recreant; see **rascal.**

troubleshooter, *n.*—*Syn.* mediator, efficiency expert, bug-eliminator (D); see **specialist.**

troublesome, *mod.* **1.** [Causing anxiety]—*Syn.* upsetting, disquieting, alarming; see **disturbing.**

2. [Causing nuisance]—*Syn.* bothersome, inconvenient, annoying, difficult, vexing, vexatious, irritating, oppressive, repressive, distressing, upsetting, painful, dangerous, damaging.

trough, *n.*—*Syn.* dip, channel, depression between waves, hollow, cup; see also **hole** 2.

trounce, *v.* **1.** [To beat]—*Syn.* flog, pommel, thrash; see **beat** 2.

2. [To defeat]—*Syn.* conquer, beat, win, overcome; see **defeat** 1, 2, 3.

trousers, *n.*—*Syn.* slacks, breeches, knickerbockers; see **clothes, pants** 1.

trousseau, *n.*—*Syn.* bride's outfit, vesture, hope chest; see **clothes.**

trout, *n.* Trout include the following—speckled, brook, rainbow, mountain, silver, black-spotted, Dolly Varden, cutthroat, lake, salmon, steelhead, blue-backed, brown, Galway, golden, Tahoe, Rocky Mountain, Yellowstone; see also **fish.**

trowel, *n.*—*Syn.* blade, scoop, implement; see **tool** 1.

Types of trowels include the following—garden(ing), transplanting, plasterer's, mason's, pointing, bricklayer's, cement finisher's, molder's, corner, London pattern, Lowell pattern, Philadelphia pattern.

truant, *mod.* **1.** [Lazy]—*Syn.* idle, shiftless, indolent; see **lazy** 1.

2. [Errant]—*Syn.* missing, straying, playing hooky (D); see **absent.**

truant officer, *n.*—*Syn.* patrolman, officer, juvenile officer; see **policeman.**

truce, *n.*—*Syn.* armistice, peace agreement, respite, lull, amnesty, treaty of peace, terms, suspension of arms, pause, cease-fire, break, cessation; *both* (D): the olive branch, white flag; see also **peace** 1.—*Ant.* warfare*, combat, hostilities.

truck, *n.* **1.** [An automotive vehicle for hauling]—*Syn.* carriage, van, lorry, car, autotruck, automobile truck; *all* (D): buggy, semi, eighteen-wheeler, rig, crate, boat; see also **vehicle 1, wagon.**

Types of trucks include the following—delivery wagon, moving van, police van, patrol wagon, laundry truck, pickup truck, freight truck, logging truck, army truck, trailer, semitrailer, piggyback (D), piggyback truck, piggyback trailer, truck trailer, truck and trailer, truck train, cement mixer, refrigerator truck, snubnose truck, one-unit truck, freighter, garbage truck, dump truck, diesel-powered truck, chain-drive truck, amphibious truck (*also* (D): duck), half-track, mechanized landing craft (LCM), landing craft for vehicles and personnel (LCVP), landing vehicle track (LVT); (*also* (D): trac, amtrac, water buffalo, alligator).

2. [A small vehicle for moving heavy loads]—*Syn.* cart, handtruck, warehouse truck, platform truck, wagon, wheelbarrow, dumpcart, pushcart, dray, dolly, handbarrow.

3. [(D) Rubbish]—*Syn.* trivia, snippets, junk; see **trash** 3.

4. [(D) Vegetables]—*Syn.* garden varieties, summer crops, crops, potatoes, onions, carrots, greens; see also **crop, produce, vegetable.**

truck, *v.* **1.** [To send by truck]—*Syn.* ship, haul, drive, transport, cart, carry, take a load, freight; see also **send** 1.

2. [To traffic in]—*Syn.* peddle, deal in, handle; see **exchange** 1, **sell** 1.

truckle, *v.*—*Syn.* cringe, submit, cower; see **wince, yield** 1.

truck trailer, *n.*—*Syn.* van, piggyback trailer, vehicle; see **trailer, truck** 1.

truculent, *mod.* **1.** [Fierce]—*Syn.* barbarous, brutal, ferocious; see **cruel** 1, 2, **fierce** 1, **savage** 2.

2. [Rude]—*Syn.* harsh, mean, scathing; see **rude** 2.

trudge, *v.*—*Syn.* plod, step, tread; see **march, walk** 1.

true, *mod.* **1.** [Accurate]—*Syn.* precise, exact, correct; see **accurate** 1, **valid** 1.

2. [Loyal]—*Syn.* sure, dependable, sincere; see **faithful, reliable** 1, 2.

3. [Genuine]—*Syn.* authentic, actual, pure; see **genuine** 1, **real** 2, **valid** 2.

come true—*Syn.* become a fact, be actualized, come about; see **develop** 1, **happen** 2.

true-blue, *mod.* —*Syn.* loyal, staunch, dependable; see **faithful, reliable** 1.
truehearted, *mod.* —*Syn.* loyal, sincere, honest; see **faithful, reliable** 1.
truelove, *n.* —*Syn.* sweetheart, beloved, love; see **lover** 1.
true to form, *mod.* —*Syn.* usual, customary, to be expected; see **conventional** 1, **regular** 3.
true to life, *mod.* —*Syn.* true-life, realistic, revealing; see **accurate** 1, **genuine.**
truism, *n.* —*Syn.* commonplace, self-evident truth, adage; see **motto, proverb.**
trull, *n.* —*Syn.* whore, harlot, strumpet; see **prostitute.**
truly, *mod.* **1.** [Really]—*Syn.* actually, absolutely, positively; see **really** 1, **surely.**
2. [In accordance with the truth]—*Syn.* honestly, exactly, definitely, reliable, factually, correctly, unequivocally, sincerely, scrupulously, fairly, justly, validly, rightfully, righteously, punctiliously, faithfully, worthily, scientifically, unbiasedly, without bias *or* prejudice, fairly and squarely (D); see also **accurately.**—*Ant.* wrongly*, dishonestly, deceptively.
trump card (D), *n.* —*Syn.* best play, strongest means *or* device, trick; see **agent** 1, **device** 2, **strength** 1.
trumped up, *mod.* —*Syn.* falsified, concocted, magnified; see **exaggerated, false** 2.
trumpery, *n.* —*Syn.* rubbish, frivolity, bosh; see **nonsense** 1.
trumpet, *n.* —*Syn.* horn, wind instrument, bugle, cornet, brass wind; see also **musical instrument.**
trumpet call, *n.* —*Syn.* reveille, signal, blare; see **alarm** 1, **call** 4, **taps.**
trumpet-toned, *mod.* —*Syn.* strident, resounding, deafening; see **loud** 1.
trump up (D), *v.* —*Syn.* think up, devise, concoct, contrive, present fraudulent evidence, misrepresent, falsify; see also **deceive, lie** 1.
truncate, *v.* —*Syn.* lop, mangle, prune; see **trim** 1.
truncheon, *n.* —*Syn.* cudgel, bludgeon, war club; see **club** 3, **stick, weapon** 1.
trundle, *v.* —*Syn.* revolve, rotate, spin; see **turn** 1.
trunk, *n.* **1.** [A container for goods]—*Syn.* chest, case, foot locker, traveling case, baggage, luggage, suitcase; *both* (D): keister, coffin; see also **bag, container.**
2. [The torso]—*Syn.* body, soma, thorax; see **abdomen, back** 2.
3. [The stem of a tree]—*Syn.* butt, bole, block, column, stock, log; see also **stalk.**
4. [A proboscis]—*Syn.* prow, snoot, snout; see **beak, nose** 1.
truss, *n.* —*Syn.* support(er), reinforcement, supporting device; see **support** 2.
truss (up), *v.* **1.** [Support]—*Syn.* hold, bear, strengthen; see **hold** 8, **support** 1.
2. [To bind]—*Syn.* tie (up), constrict, bundle (up); see **pack** 2, **press** 1.
trust, *n.* **1.** [Reliance]—*Syn.* confidence, dependence, credence; see **faith** 1.
2. [A trusted person]—*Syn.* mainstay, guarantee, anchor, confidant, security, support, assurance, benefactor, patron, guardian, protector, savior, good angel (D).
3. [Responsibility]—*Syn.* guardianship, account, duty, liability, moment.
4. [A large company]—*Syn.* corporation, monopoly, cartel, holding company, institution; see also **business** 4, **organization** 3.
in trust—*Syn.* in another's care, held for, reserved; see **saved** 2.
trust, *v.* **1.** [To believe in]—*Syn.* swear by, believe in, place confidence in, confide in, esteem, depend upon, expect help from, presume upon, lean on, have no doubt, rest assured, be sure about, have no reservations, rely on, put faith in, give credence to, look to, count on, assume that, presume that, be persuaded by, be convinced; *all* (D): put great stock in, set great store by, bank on, take at one's word, eat up; see also **believe** 1.—*Ant.* doubt*, mistrust, disbelieve.
2. [To hope]—*Syn.* presume, take, imagine; see **assume** 1, **hope.**
3. [To place in the protection of another]—*Syn.* lend, put in safekeeping, entrust, trust to, commit, consign, commission, assign, store with, transfer, give over, place in trust of, make someone a trustee of, make someone guardian of.
4. [To give credit to]—*Syn.* advance, lend, loan, let out, grant, confer, let, patronize, aid, give financial aid to.—*Ant.* borrow*, raise money, pawn.
trusted, *mod.* —*Syn.* trustworthy, dependable, reliable, credible, trusty, tried, proved, intimate, close, faithful, loyal, true, constant, staunch, devoted, incorruptible, safe, honorable, honored, inviolable; *all* (D): on the level, kosher, A-1, regular, right, sure-fire; see also **established** 3.—*Ant.* dishonest*, questionable, unreliable.
trustee, *n.* —*Syn.* guardian, custodian, controller, lawyer, stockholder, guarantor, regent, board member, overseer, governor, appointee, administrator, member of the directorate.
trusteeship, *n.* —*Syn.* management, direction, guidance, supervision; see also **administration** 1, 2.
trustful, *mod.* —*Syn.* naive, believing, secure; see **trusting** 1.
trusting, *mod.* **1.** [Naive]—*Syn.* trustful, credulous, confiding, gullible, unsuspecting, unsuspicious, easygoing, open, candid, indulgent, obliging, well-meaning, good-natured, tenderhearted; *all* (D): green, suckerish, doughfaced, with a glass jaw; see also **naive.**—*Ant.* critical*, suspicious*, skeptical.
2. [Hopeful]—*Syn.* in hopes, expectant, confident, assured, optimistic, presuming, depending *or* counting *or* relying on *or* upon, reliant, relying; see also **hopeful** 1.
trustless, *mod.* **1.** [Unreliable]—*Syn.* treacherous, unworthy, deceitful; see **dishonest** 1, 2, **unfaithful** 1.
2. [Skeptical]—*Syn.* distrustful, cynical, doubting; see **doubtful** 2, **suspicious** 1.
trustworthiness, *n.* —*Syn.* integrity, uprightness, loyalty; see **honesty** 1, **sincerity.**
trustworthy, *mod.* —*Syn.* accurate, honest, true; see **reliable** 1.
trusty, *mod.* —*Syn.* good, superior, tried and true; see **excellent, great** 1, **reliable** 2.
trusty, *n.* —*Syn.* trusted person, trustworthy convict, prison attendant, privileged prisoner; *both* (D): psalmsinger, valet; see also **prisoner.**

truth, *n.* **1.** [Conformity to reality]—*Syn.* truthfulness, veracity, correctness, sincerity, verity, candor, openness, honesty, fidelity, frankness, revelation, exactitude, authenticity, factualism, exactness, infallibility, precision, perfection, rectitude, certainty, genuineness, accuracy, fact; *all* (D): the gospel truth, straight dope, inside track, the nitty-gritty, the facts, the case.—*Ant.* lie*, deception, falsehood.
2. [Integrity]—*Syn.* trustworthiness, honor, probity; see **honesty** 1.
in truth—*Syn.* in fact, indeed, really; see **truly** 1.

truthful, *mod.* —*Syn.* correct, frank, just; see **accurate** 1, **honest** 1.

truthfully, *mod.* —*Syn.* honestly, honorably, veraciously; see **sincerely, truly** 2.

truthfulness, *n.* —*Syn.* integrity, frankness, accuracy; see **honesty** 1, **sincerity.**

truthless, *mod.* —*Syn.* lying, deceptive, inaccurate; see **dishonest** 2, **false** 1, 2.

try, *v.* **1.** [To endeavor]—*Syn.* attempt, essay, undertake, exert (oneself), contend, strive, make an effort, risk, have a try (at), contest, wrangle, labor, work, aspire, propose, seek, try to reach, do what one can, tackle, venture, struggle for, compete for, speculate, make every effort, put oneself out, vie for, aspire to; *all* (D): attack, make a bid for, beat one's brains, bear down, shoot at *or* for, drive for, chip away at, do one's best, make a pass at, go after, go out of the way, give a workout, do all in one's power, go through fire and water, buckle down, lift a finger, break an arm, break a blood vessel, lay (oneself) out, lay to, do oneself justice, have a go at, make a go of it, go all out, leave no stone unturned, move heaven and earth, hump it, try to get figs from thistles, file a strong bid, go all lengths, go to market, knock oneself out, bunch the hits, break one's neck, bust a gut, take a crack at, give it a whirl, fight the good fight.
2. [To test]—*Syn.* assay, investigate, put to the proof; see **analyze** 1, **examine** 1, 2.
3. [To conduct a trial]—*Syn.* hear, judge, examine, adjudicate, decide, hear a case, sit in judgment, give a fair hearing.

trying, *mod.* —*Syn.* troublesome, bothersome, irritating; see **difficult** 1, 2, **severe** 2.

try on, *v.* —*Syn.* fit, have a fitting, try on for size; see **experiment** 2, **wear** 1.

try one's hand at (D), *v.* —*Syn.* attempt (for the first time), try out, make a stab at (D); see **experiment** 2, **try** 1.

tryout, *n.* —*Syn.* test, demonstration, rehearsal, hearing, audition, preliminary practice, trial, practice game; *both* (D): workout, test-up; see also **examination** 1.

try out for, *v.* —*Syn.* go out for, perform, test, compete (for), audition, experiment, probe, practice with, read for, try, give (it) a try (D); see also **rehearse** 3.

tryst, *n.* —*Syn.* rendezvous, assignation, union; see **meeting** 1.

tub, *n.* —*Syn.* keg, bucket, cask, tank, receptacle, laundry tub, bathtub, hot tub, spa, cauldron, vat, cistern, butt, firkin, tun; see also **container.**

tubby, *mod.* —*Syn.* plump, beefy, stout; see **fat** 1, **short** 1.

tube, *n.* **1.** [A pipe]—*Syn.* conduit, hose, test tube, tubing, tunnel, loom, subway; see also **pipe** 1.
2. [A metal container]—*Syn.* package, paste tube, squeeze tube; see **container.**
3. [An electronic device]—*Syn.* cell, vacuum tube, electron *or* electronic tube; see **device** 1, **machine** 1.
Terms for various electronic tubes include the following—electric eye, neon tube *or* light, fluorescent tube *or* light, radio *or* television tube, cathode ray tube, X-ray tube, photoelectric tube *or* cell, thermionic tube *or* valve, converter, gas tube, vapor tube, focus tube, high *or* low pressure tube. Scientific terms for specialized tubes include the following—Geissler tube, Crookes tube, Braun tube, traveling wave tube, negative grid electron tube, X-ray diffraction tube, grid-seal tube, disk-seal tube, grid-glow tube, glow-discharge tube, multigrid tube, multiplex tube, mercury-vapor tube, triode, thyratron, phasitron, diode, pentagrid, klystron, ignatron, magnetron, exitron.

tuberculosis, *n.* —*Syn.* lung disease, pulmonary phthisis, consumption; *all* (D): T.B., con-house disease, lung trouble; see also **disease** 2.

tuck, *n.* —*Syn.* crease, folding, pleat; see **fold** 1, 2, **plait.**

tuck in, *v.* —*Syn.* insert, put *or* squeeze in, add; see **embed** 1, **include** 2.

tuft, *n.* —*Syn.* clump, cluster, group; see **bunch** 1.

tug, *v.* —*Syn.* pull, haul, tow; see **draw** 1.

tugboat, *n.* —*Syn.* tug, towboat, tugger, tender, steam tug; see also **boat.**

tuition, *n.* —*Syn.* fee, cost, expenditure; see **charge** 1, **price.**

tumble, *v.* —*Syn.* drop, plunge, descend; see **fall** 1, **topple, trip** 1.

tumble-down, *mod.* —*Syn.* dilapidated, decrepit, rickety; see **old** 2, **shaky** 1, **unsteady** 1, **worn** 2.

tumbler, *n.* **1.** [An acrobat]—*Syn.* equilibrist, gymnast, trampolinist; see **acrobat, athlete.**
2. [A glass]—*Syn.* goblet, cup, mug; see **glass** 2.

tumbling, *mod.* —*Syn.* falling, rolling, pitching, plunging, whirling, turning in the air, falling head over heels.

tumbling, *n.* —*Syn.* acrobatics, floor exercise, mat gymnastics; see **gymnastics.**

tumefaction, *n.* —*Syn.* boil, bloating, enlargement; see **growth** 3, **swelling.**

tumid, *mod.* **1.** [Swollen]—*Syn.* bulging, distended, bloated; see **enlarged, inflated.**
2. [Pompous]—*Syn.* bombastic, sonorous, inflated; see **egotistic** 2.

tumor, *n.* —*Syn.* neoplasm, tumefaction, cyst; see **growth** 3, **swelling.**

tumult, *n.* —*Syn.* agitation, uproar, turbulence; see **confusion** 2, **disturbance** 2, **fight** 1.

tumultuous, *mod.* —*Syn.* agitated, disturbed, violent; see **turbulent.**

tun, *n.* —*Syn.* cask, tub, vessel; see **container, tank** 1.

tune, *n.* —*Syn.* melody, air, aria, song, harmony, strain, theme, piece, number, ditty, jingle, a few bars.

call the tune (D)—*Syn.* be in control, direct, manage; see **lead** 1.
change one's tune (D)—*Syn.* change one's mind, alter one's actions, be transformed; see **change** 4,
sing a different tune (D)—*Syn.* change one's mind, alter one's actions, be transformed; see **change** 4.

tune, *v.* —*Syn.* adjust the pitch, attune, put in tune, tune up, tighten the strings, use the tuning fork, set the tune; see also **harmonize** 1.

tuneful, *mod.* —*Syn.* melodious, symphonic, rhythmic; see **harmonious** 1, **musical** 1.

tune in (on) (D), *v.* —*Syn.* participate, become part of, enter into; see **join** 1, 2, **listen** 1, **receive** 1, **see** 1.

tune up (D), *v.* —*Syn.* enliven, refine, make better; see **improve** 1.

tunnel, *n.* —*Syn.* hole, burrow, underground passage, subway, tube, crawl space, crawlway, shaft, mine, pit, crosscut, drift, adit.

turban, *n.* —*Syn.* headdress, headgear, topee; see **hat.**

turbid, *mod.* —*Syn.* foul, swollen, muddy, cloudy, sedimentary, mixed, muddled, thick, impure, unsettled, roiled, unclean, filthy, smudgy, mired, befouled, grimy, messy, reeky, murky, dirty.

turbulence, *n.* —*Syn.* disorder, commotion, fracas; see **confusion** 2, **disturbance** 2, **fight** 1.

turbulent, *mod.* —*Syn.* riotous, violent, stormy, disturbed, noisy, restless, raging, howling, buffeting, thunderous, inclement, tumultuous, excited, passionate, uncontrolled, vehement, roaring, tempestuous, rampant, rowdy, lawless, disorderly, untamed, disordered, chaotic, agitated, fierce, wild, rude, rough, blustering, obstreperous, angry, storming, uproarious, clamorous, tremulous, mutinous, rebellious, destructive, hard, stern, bitter, fiery, rabid, boisterous, perturbed, foaming, shaking, demonstrative, vociferous; see also **intense.** —*Ant.* peaceful*, tranquil, at ease.

turf, *n.* —*Syn.* earth, peat, lawn; see **grass** 1, **sod.**

turgid, *mod.* **1.** [Swollen]—*Syn.* bloated, distended, puffy; see **enlarged, inflated.**
2. [Pompous]—*Syn.* bombastic, arrogant, boastful; see **egotistic** 2.

turkey, *n.* —*Syn.* turkey cock, turkey hen, bird, fowl, Thanksgiving bird, Christmas bird, gobbler, turkey gobbler, wild turkey, domestic turkey, cock of India, hen of India, *poule d'Inde* (French), *gallina de India* (Spanish), *gallo* or *gallina d'India* (Italian), *Indianische Henn* or *Huhn* (German). Turkeys include the following—bronze turkey, buff turkey, black turkey, slate turkey, white turkey, reddish brown turkey, Cambridgeshire turkey, Colorado turkey, crested turkey, Honduras turkey, Mexican turkey, native turkey, New England wild turkey, Norfolk turkey, ocellated turkey, wild turkey, brush turkey, water turkey.

turmoil, *n.* —*Syn.* agitation, turbulence, riot; see **confusion** 2, **disturbance** 2, **uproar.**

turn, *n.* **1.** [a revolution]—*Syn.* rotation, cycle, circle, round, circulation, pirouette, gyre, gyration, spin, round-about-face, roll, turning, circumrotation, spiral; see also **revolution** 1.
2. [A bend]—*Syn.* curve, winding, twist, wind, hook, shift, angle, corner, fork, branch.
3. [A turning point]—*Syn.* climax, crisis, juncture, emergency, critical period, crossing, change, new development, shift, twist.
4. [(D) A shock]—*Syn.* fright, jolt, blow; see **surprise** 2.
5. [(D) An action]—*Syn.* deed, accomplishment, service; see **aid** 1.
6. [A change in course]—*Syn.* curve, detour, deviation, corner, ground loop, stem turn, jump turn, Christiania turn (*also* (D): Christy), Telemark turn, Telemark, kick turn, inside loop, outside loop, left *or* right wing spin, tight spin, tight spiral, roll, Immelmann turn (also (D) Immelmann).
at every turn—*Syn.* in every instance, constantly, consistently; see **regularly** 1.
by turns—*Syn.* taking turns, in succession, alternately; see **progressive** 1.
call the turn—*Syn.* anticipate, predict, expect; see **fortell.**
take turns—*Syn.* do by turns, do in succession, share; see **alternate** 1.
to a turn—*Syn.* correctly, properly, to the right degree; see **perfectly** 1.

turn, *v.* **1.** [To pivot]—*Syn.* revolve, rotate, roll, spin, wheel, whirl, gyre, circulate, go around, swivel; round, twist, twirl, gyrate, ground, loop; see also **swing** 1.
2. [To reverse]—*Syn.* go back, tack, recoil, change, upset, retrace, face about, turn around, capsize, shift, alter, vary, convert, transform, invert, subvert, return, alternate.
3. [To divert]—*Syn.* deflect, veer, turn aside *or* away, sidetrack, swerve, put *or* call *or* turn off, deviate, dodge, twist, avoid, shift, switch, avert, zigzag, shy away, shunt, redirect, shunt aside *or* away, draw aside.
4. [To become]—*Syn.* grow into, change into, pass into; see **become** 1.
5. [To sour]—*Syn.* curdle, acidify, become rancid; see **ferment, sour.**
6. [To change direction]—*Syn.* swerve, swirl, swing, bend, veer, tack, round to, incline, deviate, detour, loop, curve; *all* (D): ground loop, stem turn, ramble, jump turn, kick turn, Telemark.
7. [To incline]—*Syn.* prefer, be predisposed to, favor; see **lean** 1, **tend** 2.
8. [To sprain]—*Syn.* strain, bruise, dislocate; see **hurt** 1, **wrench.**
9. [To nauseate]—*Syn.* sicken, make one sick, revolt; see **disgust.**
10. [To bend]—*Syn.* curve, twist, fold; see **bend** 1.
11. [To transform]—*Syn.* transmute, remake, transpose; see **change** 1.
12. [To make use of]—*Syn.* apply, adapt, utilize; see **use** 1.
13. [To point]—*Syn.* direct, set, train; see **aim** 2.
14. [To repel]—*Syn.* repulse, push back, throw back; see **repel** 1.

turn about, *v.* —*Syn.* turn around, pivot, reverse; see **turn** 1.

turn against, *v.* —*Syn.* revolt, disobey, defy; see **oppose** 1, 2, **rebel** 1.

turn and turn about, *mod.* —*Syn.* in turn, alternately; now one, now the other; see **equally.**

turn aside, *v.* —*Syn.* avert, deflect, divert; see **turn** 3, **veer.**

turn back, *v.* —*Syn.* retrogress, retrograde, revert; see **return** 1, 2.

turncoat, *n.* —*Syn.* betrayer, apostate, defector; see **deserter, traitor.**

turn down, *v.* **1.** [To decrease in volume, etc.] —*Syn.* hush, lower, curb; see **decrease** 2.
2. [To refuse]—*Syn.* reject, decline, rebuff; see **refuse** 1, **scorn** 2.

turned, *mod.* **1.** [Revolved]—*Syn.* spun, rounded, circled, circulated, rotated, rolled, whirled, gyrated, set going.
2. [Deflected]—*Syn.* switched, twisted, dodged, avoided, shied, away from, shifted, shunted, changed.

turn in, *v.* **1.** [To deliver]—*Syn.* hand over, transfer, give up; see **give** 1.
2. [(D) To go to bed]—*Syn.* lie down, retire, hit the hay (D); see **rest** 1.

turning, *mod.* **1.** [Bending]—*Syn.* twisting, shifting, whirling, rotating, revolving, bending, curving, shunting; see also **growing, changing.**—*Ant.* permanent*, static, fixed.
2. [Growing]—*Syn.* transforming, becoming, converting, changing; see also **growing.**

turning, *n.* —*Syn.* whirling, revolving, rotating, spinning, wheeling; see also **revolution** 1.

turning point, *n.* —*Syn.* peak, juncture, culmination; see **climax, crisis.**

turn into, *v.* **1.** [To change]—*Syn.* transform, alter, transmute; see **change** 1.
2. [To become changed]—*Syn.* be converted, transform, modify; see **change** 4.

turnip, *n.*—*Syn.* domestic turnip, rutabaga *or* Swedish turnip, turnip cabbage *or* kohlrabi, Teltow turnip, wild turnip *or* Indian turnip; see also **vegetable.**

turn loose (D), *v.* —*Syn.* liberate, emancipate, set free; see **free** 1, **release.**

turn off, *v.* **1.** [To stop the operation of]—*Syn.* stop, shut off, douse, close, shut, extinguish, shut down, turn out; *all* (D): kill the light *or* engine *or* motor, turn off the juice, log off, cut the light *or* engine *or* motor, hit the switch; see also **halt** 2.
2. [(D) To disgust]—*Syn.* repel, repulse, disinterest; see **disgust.**

turn on, *v.* **1.** [To start the operation of]—*Syn.* set going, switch on, set in motion; *all* (D): put in gear, log on, boat; see also **begin** 1.
2. [To attack]—*Syn.* strike, assail, assault; see **attack** 1, 2.
3. [(D) To take drugs]—*Syn.* take LSD, smoke marijuana; *all* (D): get high, take a trip, smoke pot, get stoned, groove, blow pot, steamroll, freak out, trip out, rock out, tune, fly, get wasted.
4. [(D) To arouse]—*Syn.* titillate, stimulate, stir up; see **excite** 1.
5. [(D) To depend on or upon]—*Syn.* hinge on, be dependent on, be based on; see **depend** 2.

turnout, *n.* **1.** [Production]—*Syn.* output, aggregate, volume; see **production** 1.
2. [A gathering]—*Syn.* assembly, attendance, group; see **gathering.**

turn out, *v.* **1.** [To stop the operation of]—*Syn.* extinguish, shut off, stop; see **turn off** 1.
2. [To dismiss]—*Syn.* discharge, evict, send away; see **dismiss** 1, 2, **oust.**
3. [To produce]—*Syn.* make, put out, build; see **manufacture** 1, **produce** 2.
4. [To get out of bed]—*Syn.* get up, rise, wake up; see **arise** 1, **wake** 2.
5. [To finish]—*Syn.* end, complete, perfect; see **achieve** 1.

turn over, *v.* **1.** [To invert]—*Syn.* overturn, reverse, subvert; see **upset** 1.
2. [To transfer]—*Syn.* hand over, give over, deliver; see **assign** 1, **give** 1.

turn over a new leaf (D), *v.* —*Syn.* get better, change for the better, make (New Year's) resolutions; see **improve** 2, **reform** 1.

turnpike, *n.* —*Syn.* toll road, freeway, roadway; see **highway.**

turn sour, *v.* —*Syn.* putrefy, rot, spoil; see **decay.**

turn the tables, *v.* —*Syn.* reverse conditions, reverse circumstances, give one his own medicine, hoist one with his own petard (D); see also **change** 1, **upset** 1.

turn to, *v.* **1.** [To rely upon]—*Syn.* confide, appeal to, depend upon; see **trust** 1.
2. [To start]—*Syn.* start to work, become interested in, take up, become engrossed in, apply oneself; see also **begin** 1.

turn to account, *v.* —*Syn.* utilize, clear, realize; see **use** 1.

turn traitor, *v.* —*Syn.* break faith, inform against, give away; see **betray** 1, **deceive.**

turn up, *v.* **1.** [To find]—*Syn.* disclose, learn, come across; see **discover** 1, **find** 1.
2. [To arrive]—*Syn.* enter, come, roll in; see **arrive** 1.
3. [To increase the volume, etc.]—*Syn.* amplify, augment, boost (D); see **increase** 1, **intensify, strengthen.**

turpentine, *n.* —*Syn.* oleoresin, terebinth extract, Chian turpentine, spirits of turpentine, oil of turpentine, thinner, paint thinner, turps (D); see also **oil.**

turpitude, *n.* —*Syn.* baseness, vileness, depravity; see **evil** 1, 2.

turquoise, *mod.* —*Syn.* blue-green, sea-green, greenish-blue, Mediterranean blue, bright blue; see also **blue** 1, **green** 1.

turret, *n.* —*Syn.* tower, revolving dome, watchtower, armored tank top, conical top, gun bulge, blister; see also **top** 1.

turtle, *n.* —*Syn.* terrapin, tortoise, chelonian, testudinate; see also **reptile.**
Turtles include the following—land, sea, sand, mud, snapping (also (D): snapper), rain, loggerhead, box, softshell *or* leatherbacked, green, hawksbill, Galapagos; mata-mata.

tusk, *n.* —*Syn.* canine (tooth), fang, incisor; see **tooth** 1.

tussle, *n.* —*Syn.* scuffle, struggle, scrap; see **fight** 1.

tutelage, *n.* **1.** [Instruction]—*Syn.* teaching, tutorship, schooling; see **education** 1.
2. [Care]—*Syn.* guardianship, charge, protection; see **custody** 1.

tutelary, *mod.* —*Syn.* protecting, guardian, advisory; see **protective.**
tutor, *n.* —*Syn.* instructor, tutorial assistant, private tutor; see **teacher** 1, 2.
tutoring, *n.* —*Syn.* coaching, training, private teaching, instruction, tutelage, guidance; see also **education** 1.
tuxedo, *n.* —*Syn.* formal suit, men's evening wear; *all* (D): tux, tuck, monkey suit, formal, straight jacket, soup-and-fish; see also **suit** 3.
T.V., *n.* —*Syn.* video; *both* (D): (boob) tube, idiot box; see **television.**
tweak, *v.* —*Syn.* twitch, squeeze, jerk; see **pinch.**
tweezers, *n.* —*Syn.* forceps, nippers, tongs; see **pincers.**
twelve, *mod.* —*Syn.* dozen, twelvefold, twelfth, duodecimo, duodecimal, uncial.
twenty, *mod.* —*Syn.* twentieth, vicenary, twentyfold, vicennial.
twice, *mod.* —*Syn.* double, doubly, once and again, over again, once over.
twig, *n.* —*Syn.* offshoot, limb, sprig; see **branch** 2.
twilight, *n.* —*Syn.* dusk, gloaming, nightfall, late afternoon, early evening, sunset, dawn, break of day, owl-light (D); see also **night** 1.
twin, *mod.* —*Syn.* identical, fellow, twofold, second, accompanying, joint, coupled, matched, copied, duplicating; see also **second, two.**—*Ant.* single*, lone, solitary.
twine, *n.* —*Syn.* binder twine, braid, cordage, cord, string, pack thread; see also **rope.**
twinge, *v.* —*Syn.* twitch, shiver, smart; see **tingle.**
twinkle, *v.* —*Syn.* shimmer, flicker, sparkle; see **shine** 1.
twinkling, *mod.* —*Syn.* sparkling, glimmering, flashing; see **bright** 1, **shimmering.**
twirl, *v.* —*Syn.* spin, rotate, twist; see **turn** 1, **whirl.**
twist, *v.* —*Syn.* wring, wrap, twine, twirl, turn around, wrap around; see also **spin** 1.
twisted, *mod.* **1.** [Crooked]—*Syn.* contorted, wrenched, bent, knotted, braided, twined, wound, wreathed, vermiculate, vermiculated, vermicular, vermiform, writhing, convolute, convoluous, twisting.—*Ant.* straight*, even, regular.
2. [Confused]—*Syn.* erroneous, perplexing, wrongheaded, awry, puzzling, unintelligible, disorganized, perverted; see also **confused** 2, **tangled, wrong** 3.—*Ant.* clear*, simple, logical.
twitch, *v.* **1.** [To pluck]—*Syn.* pull, tug, snatch, yank, clutch, grip, grab, seize, clasp, grasp; see also **jerk** 1.
2. [To jerk]—*Syn.* shiver, shudder, have a fit, kick, work, palpitate, beat, twinge, pain; see also **jerk** 1.
twitter, *v.* —*Syn.* sing, chirp, whistle, peep, cheep, coo.
two, *mod.* —*Syn.* twin, dual, binary, both, double, bifid.
two, *n.* —*Syn.* two of a kind, brace, couple; see **pair.**
in two—*Syn.* halved, divided, split; see **separated.**
put two and two together (D)—reason, sum up, reach a conclusion; see **decide.**
two-by-four (D), *mod.* —*Syn.* small, cramped, narrow; see **little** 1.
two-faced, *mod.* —*Syn.* deceitful, caviling, treacherous; see **false** 1, **hypocritical.**
twofold, *mod.* —*Syn.* twice over, duplex, double; see **two.**
tycoon, *n.* —*Syn.* executive, boss, director; see **administrator, businessman.**
tying, *mod.* —*Syn.* binding, confining, restricting, limiting, checking, curbing, restraining, shackling, cramping, strict.
type, *n.* **1.** [Kind]—*Syn.* sort, nature, character; see **kind** 2, **variety** 2.
2. [Classification]—*Syn.* standard, species, variety; see **class** 1.
3. [Representative]—*Syn.* model, sample, example, copy order; see also **representation.**
4. [Letter]—*Syn.* symbol, emblem, figure, character, sign; see also **letter** 1.
Styles of types include the following—Gothic *or* black letter, old style, new style, modern, roman, italic, script, sans serif, text, Bodoni, Cheltenham, Cloister, Cushing, Forum, Blado, Polifilo, Garamond, Goudy, Baskerville, Fournier, Times Roman, Schoolbook, Helvetica, Venezia, Granjon, Caslon, Didot, Bruce, Vale, Endeavor, Wedding, Century.
Sizes of types include the following—Excelsior *or* 3-point, Brilliant *or* 3½-point, Diamond *or* 4½-point, Pearl *or* 5-point, Agate *or* 5½-point, Nonpareil *or* 6-point, Minion *or* 7-point, Brevier *or* 8-point, Bourgeois *or* 9-point, Long Primer *or* 10-point, Small Pica *or* 11-point, Pica *or* 12-point, English *or* 14-point, Columbian *or* 16-point, Great Primer *or* 18-point.
Fonts of types include the following—standard, lightface, boldface, extrabold, cursive, open, extended, condensed, shaded, upright, expanded, wide.
type, *v.* **1.** [To use a typewriter]—*Syn.* typewrite, copy, transcribe, teletype, touch-type, hunt and peck (D).
2. [To classify]—*Syn.* categorize, normalize, standardize; see **stereotype.**
typed, *mod.* **1.** [Set down on a typewriter]—*Syn.* typewritten, copied, set up, written, transcribed; see also **printed.**
2. [Classified]—*Syn.* labeled, characterized, analyzed, symbolized, classed, prefigured, sampled, exemplified, made out to be, patterned, standardized, stylized, cast, formalized; see also **classified, marked** 1, **regulated.**
typewrite, *v.* —*Syn.* type, use a typewriter, make a typed copy, prepare a typescript, transcribe; *all* (D): massage the typewriter, play the office piano, tapwrite.
typewriter, *n.* —*Syn.* typing machine, office typewriter, portable, noiseless, electric, typewriter, electronic typewriter, word processor, ticker, teletypewriter; *all* (D): mill, office piano, typer.
typewritten, *mod.* —*Syn.* written on a typewriter, transcribed, copied, teletyped; see also **printed.**
typhoon, *n.* —*Syn.* blow, hurricane, tornado; see **storm** 1, **wind** 1.
typical, *mod.* —*Syn.* characteristic, habitual, usual, standard, representative, symbolic, normal, exemplary, illustrative, conventional, prototypical, archetypical, ideal, expected, suggestive, standardized, patterned, ordinary, average, common,

everyday, regular.—*Ant.* superior*, exceptional, extraordinary.

typify, *v.* —*Syn.* exemplify, symbolize, embody; see **mean** 1.

typing, *n.* —*Syn.* typescript, typewriting, typed copy, typewritten text, teletyping; see also **writing** 1.

typist, *n.* —*Syn.* secretary, typewriter operator, teletyper, office girl; *all* (D): key pounder, typer, typewriter, pusher.

typographic, *mod.* —*Syn.* typed, set, typographical; see **printed, written** 1.

tyrannical, *mod.* —*Syn.* dictatorial, fascistic, totalitarian, brutal, domineering, lordly; see also **absolute** 3, **autocratic** 1.

tyrannize, *v.* —*Syn.* despotize, domineer, dictate; see **dominate.**

tyranny, *n.* —*Syn.* oppression, cruelty, severity, reign of terror, despotism, absolutism; see also **autocracy, fascism.**

tyrant, *n.* —*Syn.* despot, absolute ruler, inquisitor; see **dictator.**

tyro, *n.* —*Syn.* beginner, learner, apprentice; see **amateur.**

U

ubiquitous, *mod.* —*Syn.* omnipresent, ubiquitary, all over; see **everywhere.**
ubiquity, *n.* —*Syn.* omnipresence, all-presence, everywhereness, universality, pervasion.
udder, *n.* —*Syn.* dug, pap, nipple, teat, mammilla, breast, mammary gland, milk gland.
ugliness, *n.* —*Syn.* unsightliness, homeliness, hideousness, repulsiveness, loathsomeness, unseemliness, uncomeliness, offensiveness, deformity, bad looks, ill looks, ill-favored countenance, plainness, disfigurement, monstrousness, grim aspect, foulness, horridness, inelegance, frightfulness, fearfulness, odiousness, unloveliness.—*Ant.* beauty*, fairness, attractiveness.
ugly, *mod.* **1.** [Ill-favored]—*Syn.* unsightly, loathsome, hideous, homely, repulsive, unseemly, uncomely, deformed, bad-looking, plain, disfigured, monstrous, foul, horrid, frightful, revolting, repellent, unlovely, appalling, haglike, misshapen, misbegotten, hard-featured, grisly, unprepossessing; *all* (D): horse-faced, having a face that would stop a clock, looking a mess *or* fright, looking like the devil *or* deuce, not fit to be seen.—*Ant.* handsome, beautiful*, graceful.
2. [Unpleasant]—*Syn.* nasty, nauseous, noisome, disagreeable, disgusting, odious, revolting, repellent, repulsive, sorry, vile, dirty, filthy, sordid, messy, sickening, foul; see also **unpleasant.**—*Ant.* nice*, dainty, agreeable.
3. [Dangerous]—*Syn.* pugnacious, quarrelsome, obnoxious, bellicose, rough, disagreeable, cantankerous, violent, vicious, evil, sinister, treacherous, wicked, formidable, truculent.—*Ant.* mild*, reasonable, complaisant.
ukase, *n.* —*Syn.* decree, proclamation, edict; see **judgment** 3.
ulcer, *n.* —*Syn.* boil, abscess, (focal) infection, fistula, running sore; see also **sore.**
ulcerous, *mod.* —*Syn.* ulcerative, gangrenous, cankered; see **unhealthy.**
ulterior, *mod.* **1.** [Future]—*Syn.* later, subsequent, further; see **future, last** 1.
2. [Implied]—*Syn.* undisclosed, concealed, unsaid; see **secret** 1, 3.
ultimate, *mod.* —*Syn.* final, terminal, latest; see **last** 1.
ultimately, *mod.* —*Syn.* eventually, at last, in the end, sooner or later, as a conclusion, to cap the climax, sequentially, in the sequel, after all, in consummation, at the close, at long last, in conclusion, conclusively, climactically, in due time, after a while, in after days, presently, by and by; see also **finally** 2.—*Ant.* early*, in the beginning, at present.
ultimatum, *n.* —*Syn.* demands, requirements, terms.
ultimo, *mod.* —*Syn.* last month, the past *or* previous month, a moon ago, weeks ago; see also **before** 1, **past** 1.
ultracritical, *mod.* —*Syn.* hypercritical, fussy, exigent; see **critical** 2, **severe** 1.
ultramodern, *mod.* —*Syn.* modernistic, futuristic, neoteric; see **modern** 1, 3.
ultranational, *mod.* —*Syn.* nationalistic, chauvinistic, devoted; see **patriotic.**
ultrasonic, *mod.* —*Syn.* shrill, high, supersonic, suprasonic, above 20,000 vibrations per second, too high for human ears *or* hearing.
ultraviolet, *mod.* —*Syn.* beyond violet, having wavelengths of more than 4,000 angstroms, beyond *or* out of the range of sight; see **invisible** 1, **violet.**
umbrage, *n.* —*Syn.* displeasure, offense, sense of injury; see **anger, resentment** 2.
umbrageous, *mod.* —*Syn.* dim, shaded, shadowed; see **dark** 1, **shady.**
umbrella, *n.* —*Syn.* parasol, sunshade, beach umbrella, *parapluie* (French), bumbershoot (D), brolly (British D).
umpire, *n.* —*Syn.* arbiter, arbitrator, referee, justice, moderator, mediator, negotiator, peacemaker, proprietor, compromiser, settler, inspector, assessor; *both* (D): ump, ref; see also **judge** 2.
umpteen (D), *mod.* —*Syn.* considerable, numerous, countless; see **many.**
unabbreviated, *mod.* —*Syn.* unabridged, complete, whole; see **whole** 1.
unable, *mod.* —*Syn.* incapable, powerless, weak, incompetent, unskilled, impotent, not able, inept, incapacitated, impuissant, inefficacious, helpless, unfitted, inefficient, unqualified, inadequate, ineffectual, inoperative.—*Ant.* able*, capable, effective.
unabridged, *mod.* —*Syn.* complete, total, intact; see **whole** 1.
unaccompanied, *mod.* —*Syn.* sole, solitary, deserted; see **abandoned** 1, **alone** 1.
unaccomplished, *mod.* **1.** [Unfinished]—*Syn.* incomplete, unperformed, frustrated; see **unfinished** 1.
2. [Unskilled]—*Syn.* untrained, uneducated, inexpert; see **incompetent.**
unaccountable, *mod.* —*Syn.* strange, odd, peculiar; see **mysterious** 2, **unusual** 1.
unaccounted-for, *mod.* —*Syn.* missing (in action), gone, not reporting; see **lost** 1.
unaccustomed, *mod.* **1.** [Unfamiliar]—*Syn.* strange, unknown, unusual, singular, foreign, alien, outlandish, exotic, quaint, imported, novel, bizarre,

unorthodox, different, unconventional, exceptional, suprising, altered, eccentric, variant.—*Ant.* familiar*, usual, ordinary.

2. [Unpracticed]—*Syn.* unskilled, unused, not given (to), incompetent, uninstructed, untrained, unacquainted, inexperienced, novice, ignorant, uninformed, untaught.—*Ant.* skilled, trained, experienced*.

unacquainted, *mod.*—*Syn.* ignorant, not introduced, unfamiliar, not intimate, not on speaking terms, isolated, strange, unknown, apart, aloof, secluded, withdrawn, out of touch, incommunicado.—*Ant.* friendly*, acquainted, intimate.

unadulterated, *mod.*—*Syn.* uncorrupted, unalloyed, undiluted; see **pure** 1, **untouched** 2.

unadvised, *mod.* **1.** [Careless]—*Syn.* hasty, reckless, indiscreet; see **careless** 1.

2. [Unaware]—*Syn.* uninformed, unwarned, kept in the dark (D); see **ignorant** 1.

unaffected, *mod.* **1.** [Genuine]—*Syn.* spontaneous, natural, simple, direct, straightforward, unassuming, modest, forthright, candid, frank, guileless, ingenuous, sincere, artless, plain, plainspoken.—*Ant.* ornate*, pretentious, foppish.

2. [Uninfluenced]—*Syn.* unmoved, unaltered, unchanged, untouched, unconcerned, impassive, steady; see also **calm** 1.—*Ant.* changed*, altered, modified.

unalterable, *mod.*—*Syn.* unchangeable, fixed, unavoidable; see **firm** 1, 2, **inevitable, resolute** 2.

unalterably, *mod.*—*Syn.* rigidly, unchangeably, inflexibly; see **firmly** 1, 2, **obstinately.**

unaltered, *mod.*—*Syn.* the same, not changed *or* altered, uninfluenced; see **unaffected** 2, **unchanged.**

un-American, *mod.*—*Syn.* undemocratic, fascistic, subversive; see **foreign** 1.

unanimity, *n.*—*Syn.* accord, unity, unison, concord, harmony, concordance, sympathy, congruence, conformity, correspondence, apposition, compatibility; see also **agreement** 2.—*Ant.* disagreement*, discord, dissonance.

unanimous, *mod.*—*Syn.* united, single, collective, combined, unified, concerted, harmonious, concordant, concurrent, public, popular, undivided, of one accord, agreed, common, communal, shared, universal, accepted, unquestioned, undisputed, uncontested, consonant, consistent, of a piece, with one voice, homogeneous, accordant, consensual, assenting; see also **undivided** 1.—*Ant.* different*, dissenting, irreconcilable.

unanimously, *mod.*—*Syn.* with one voice *or* one accord, harmoniously, all together, by acclamation, universally, unitedly, consensually, singly, collectively, without a dissenting voice, by common consent, by oral *or* written ballot *or* vote, in unison, co-operatively, concertedly, concurrently, popularly, commonly, undisputedly, consonantly, consistently, in agreement.—*Ant.* differently*, opposite, divergently.

unanswered, *mod.*—*Syn.* without reply, unrefuted, not responded to, unnoticed, unchallenged, unquestioned, demanding an answer, filed, in the files, ignored, unsettled, undecided, in doubt, disputed, moot, debatable, tabled, up in the air, vexed, open, pending, under consideration, undetermined; see also **uncertain** 2.—*Ant.* determined*, answered, responded to.

unapproachable, *mod.* **1.** [Distant]—*Syn.* withdrawn, hesitant, aloof; see **inaccessible, distant.**

2. [Unmatched]—*Syn.* peerless, unsurpassed, best; see **excellent, superior.**

unarm, *v.*—*Syn.* debilitate, disable, deprive of weapons; see **disarm** 1, 2, **weaken** 2.

unarmed, *mod.*—*Syn.* weaponless, defenseless, naked, harmless, undefended, disarmed, peaceable, unfortified; see also **pacific, weak** 5, 6.—*Ant.* armed*, armed to the teeth, equipped.

unasked, *mod.*—*Syn.* uninvited, not asked *or* invited, unwelcome(d); see **neglected, unpopular.**

unassailable, *mod.*—*Syn.* defended, not assailable *or* subject to attack or assault, impregnable, invulnerable; see **protected.**

unassuming, *mod.*—*Syn.* quiet, retiring, prim; see **humble** 1, **modest** 2.

unattached, *mod.*—*Syn.* independent, unbound, ungoverned; see **free** 1, 2, 3, **loose** 1.

unattended, *mod.*—*Syn.* left alone, ignored, disregarded; see **abandoned** 1, **neglected.**

unauthorized, *mod.*—*Syn.* unofficial, unapproved, unlawful; see **illegal.**

unavailing, *mod.*—*Syn.* pointless, without results, fruitless; see **futile** 1, **useless** 1.

unavoidable, *mod.*—*Syn.* inescapable, impending, sure; see **certain** 3, **inevitable.**

unaware, *mod.*—*Syn.* uninformed, unknowing, oblivious, ignorant, not cognizant, unmindful, heedless, negligent, careless, insensible, forgetful, unconcerned, blind, deaf, inattentive, without notice, deaf *or* dead to, caught napping, in a daze, not seeing the forest for the trees (D).—*Ant.* conscious*, aware, cognizant.

unawares, *mod.* **1.** [Unintentionally]—*Syn.* inadvertently, ignorantly, carelessly; see **accidentally.**

2. [Suddenly]—*Syn.* surprisingly, suddenly, abruptly; see **quickly** 1, **unexpectedly.**

unbaked, *mod.* **1.** [Uncooked]—*Syn.* underdone, green, rare; see **raw** 1.

2. [Undeveloped]—*Syn.* immature, artless, untrained; see **green** 3, **young** 2.

unbalance, *v.* **1.** [To upset]—*Syn.* capsize, overturn, tumble; see **upset** 1.

2. [To derange]—*Syn.* dement, craze, obsess; see **disturb** 2, **derange** 2.

unbalanced, *mod.* **1.** [Deranged]—*Syn.* unsound, crazy, psychotic; see **insane** 1, **troubled** 2.

2. [Unwise]—*Syn.* stupid, untrustworthy, biased; see **rash, unreliable** 1.

3. [Unsteady]—*Syn.* wobbly, shaky, treacherous; see **unstable** 1.

unbar, *v.*—*Syn.* unlock, throw open, take down the bars; see **open** 2.

unbearable, *mod.*—*Syn.* inadmissible, unacceptable, too much (D); see **intolerable.**

unbeaten, *mod.*—*Syn.* victorious, thriving, winning; see **triumphant.**

unbecoming, *mod.* **1.** [Indecent]—*Syn.* improper, salacious, unworthy; see **lewd** 1, 2.

2. [Unsuitable]—*Syn.* unsuited, unfitted, awkward; see **improper** 1.

unbelief, *n.*—*Syn.* skepticism, incredulity, agnosticism; see **doubt** 1, **uncertainty** 1.

unbelievable, *mod.* —*Syn.* beyond *or* past belief, incredible, inconceivable, staggering, unimaginable, not to be credited, dubious, doubtful, improbable, questionable, implausible, palpably false, unveracious, open to doubt, a bit thick (D); see also **false** 1, 2, 3, **unlikely.**—*Ant.* likely*, believable, probable.

unbelievably, *mod.* —*Syn.* remarkably, horribly, badly; see **strangely, terribly.**

unbeliever, *n.* —*Syn.* atheist, heretic, agnostic; see **cynic.**

unbelieving, *mod.* —*Syn.* doubting, skeptical, incredulous; see **suspicious** 1.

unbend, *v.* —*Syn.* become more natural *or* casual *or* nonchalant, be informal *or* at home, relax; see **rest** 1.

unbending, *mod.* **1.** [Rigid]—*Syn.* inflexible, crisp, stiff; see **firm** 5.
2. [Resolute]—*Syn.* firm, unyielding, stubborn; see **obstinate.**

unbiased, *mod.* —*Syn.* just, straight, impartial; see **fair** 1, **honest** 1.

unbind, *v.* **1.** [To untie]—*Syn.* unfasten, disengage, unchain; see **free** 1, **liberate** 2.
2. [To forgive]—*Syn.* release, clear, liberate; see **excuse.**

unblemished, *mod.* —*Syn.* perfect, flawless, unmarked; see **perfect** 2.

unblessed, *mod.* **1.** [Accursed]—*Syn.* unsaved, unholy, graceless; see **damned** 1, **wicked** 1.
2. [Miserable]—*Syn.* wretched, unhappy, unlucky; see **unfortunate** 2, **miserable** 1.

unblushing, *mod.* —*Syn.* shameless, brazen, forward; see **rude** 2, **lewd** 1, 2.

unborn, *mod.* —*Syn.* embryonic, incipient, expected, future, prospective, potential, latent, enwombed, in utero, anticipated, awaited.

unbosom, *v.* —*Syn.* tell, let out, vent; see **admit** 2, **confess** 3, **reveal** 1.

unbound, *mod.* —*Syn.* loose, untied, unstapled, unfastened, unwrapped, unstitched, ungirt; see also **free** 1, 2, 3.—*Ant.* bound*, stapled, tied.

unbounded, *mod.* —*Syn.* spreading, boundless, loose; see **infinite, unlimited.**

unbowed, *mod.* —*Syn.* undefeated, stubborn, resisting; see **triumphant.**

unbreakable, *mod.* —*Syn.* indestructible, durable, everlasting, perdurable, brass-bound, cast-iron, lasting, unshakable, solid, firm, unchangeable, invulnerable, incorruptible, resistant, rugged, tight, unyielding, adamantine.—*Ant.* dainty*, fragile, brittle.

unbridled, *mod.* —*Syn.* unrestrained, uncontrolled, ungoverned; see **unruly.**

unbroken, *mod.* **1.** [Whole]—*Syn.* entire, intact, unimpaired; see **whole** 2.
2. [Continuous]—*Syn.* uninterrupted, continuous, even; see **regular** 3, **smooth** 1, 2.

unbuckle, *v.* —*Syn.* unfasten, undo, unloose; see **open** 2.

unburden, *v.* **1.** [To unload]—*Syn.* dump, dispose of, relinquish; see **lighten** 1, **relieve** 2.
2. [To reveal]—*Syn.* disclose, unbosom, divulge; see **admit** 2, **confess** 3.

unbutton, *v.* —*Syn.* undo, open (up), unfasten; see **open** 2.

uncalled for, *mod.* —*Syn.* unjustified, redundant, not needed; see **superfluous, unnecessary.**

uncanny, *mod.* —*Syn.* weird, unnatural, inexplainable, supernatural, preternatural, superhuman, ghostly, mystifying, incredible, mysterious, magical, devilish; see also **magic** 1.

uncared-for, *mod.* —*Syn.* unattended, not cared for *or* looked after, loose; see **neglected.**

unceremonious, *mod.* **1.** [Informal]—*Syn.* familiar, casual, inelegant; see **careless** 1, **informal.**
2. [Abrupt]—*Syn.* curt, hurried, brief; see **rude** 1, **abrupt.**

uncertain, *mod.* **1.** [Doubtful in mind]—*Syn.* dubious, undecided, in a quandary; see **doubtful** 2.
2. [Not determined]—*Syn.* undecided, undetermined, unsettled, doubtful, changeable, unpredictable, improbable, unlikely, unfixed, unsure, indeterminate, haphazard, random, chance, casual, provisional, contingent, alterable, fluctuant, subject to change, possible, vague, conjectural, questionable, problematic, suppositional, suppositious, hypothetical, theoretical, open to question, equivocal, perplexing, debatable, dubious indefinite, unascertained, ambiguous, unresolved, debated, conjecturable, unknown, unannounced, imprecise, up in the air, in doubt, in abeyance, still in debate, on the knees of the Gods (D).

uncertainly, *mod.* —*Syn.* unreliably, illegally, confusedly; see **irregularly.**

uncertainty, *n.* **1.** [The mental state of being uncertain]—*Syn.* perplexity, doubt, puzzlement, quandary, mystification, guesswork, conjecture, indecision, ambivalence, dilemma.—*Ant.* opinion*, belief*, decision.
2. [The state of being undetermined or unknown] —*Syn.* incertitude, questionableness, contingency, obscurity, vagueness, ambiguity, equivocalness, difficulty, incoherence, intricacy, involvement, darkness, inconclusiveness, indeterminateness, improbability, unlikelihood, low probability, conjecturability; see also **doubt** 2.—*Ant.* determination*, sureness, necessity.
3. [That which is not determined or not known] —*Syn.* chance, mutability, change, unpredictability, possibility, emergence, contingency, blind spot, puzzle, enigma, question, blank, vacancy, maze, theory, risk, blind bargain, leap in the dark (D). —*Ant.* fact*, truth*, matter of record.

unchain, *v.* —*Syn.* liberate, unbind, discharge; see **free** 1.

unchangeable, *mod.* —*Syn.* fixed, unalterable, inevitable; see **firm** 1, **resolute** 2.

unchangeably, *mod.* —*Syn.* fixedly, unalterably, rigidly; see **firmly** 1, 2, **obstinately.**

unchanged, *mod.* —*Syn.* unaltered, the same, unmoved, constant, fixed, continuing, stable, permanent, eternal, durable, unvarying, invariable, consistent, persistent, firm, unvaried, resolute, perpetual, continuous, maintained, uninterrupted, fast.—*Ant.* changed*, altered, modified.

uncharitable, *mod.* —*Syn.* unforgiving, censorious, ungenerous; see **cruel** 2, **unmerciful.**

unchartered, *mod.* —*Syn.* not mapped *or* described, strange, undiscovered; see **unknown** 1, 3.

unchaste, *mod.* —*Syn.* nonvirginal, lecherous, impure; see **lewd** 2, **sensual.**

unchristian, *mod.* **1.** [Sinful]—*Syn.* irreligious, pagan, evil; see **impious** 1, **wicked** 1.
2. [Uncivil]—*Syn.* unseemly, impolite, heartless; see **ruthless** 1.

uncivil, *mod.* **1.** [Rude]—*Syn.* barbarious, crude, boorish; see **rude** 1.
2. [Ill-mannered]—*Syn.* unpolished, uncultivated, impolite; see **rude** 2.

uncivilized, *mod.* —*Syn.* barbarous, uncontrolled, barbarian; see **primitive** 3, **savage** 1, 3.

unclassified, *mod.* —*Syn.* not classified *or* ordered *or* put in order, disordered, out of order; see **confused** 2, **unknown** 1, 3.

uncle, *n.* —*Syn.* father's brother, mother's brother, elder, *avunculus* (Latin); see also **relative.**

unclean, *mod.* —*Syn.* soiled, sullied, stained, spotted, filthy, bedraggled, smeared, befouled, nasty, grimy, polluted, rank, unhealthful, defiled, impure, nonkosher, muddy, fetid, feculent, stinking, rotten, vile, decayed, contaminated, tainted, rancid, putrid, putrescent, moldy, musty, mildewed, besmirched, smirched, besmutted, smutted, besmuttered, besmeared, filmed over, bleary, dusty, sooty, smudgy, draffy, scurvy, scurfy, clogged, slimy, mucky, tarnished, murky, smudged, daubed, blurred, begrimed, spattered, bespattered, maggotty, flyblown; see also **dirty** 1, **impure** 1.—*Ant.* pure*, clean, white.

unclench, *v.* —*Syn.* unlock, release, relax; see **unfold** 1.

uncloak, *v.* **1.** [To expose]—*Syn.* tell, disclose, uncover; see **reveal** 1, **expose** 1.
2. [To undress]—*Syn.* divest, uncover, disrobe; see **undress.**

unclothe, *v.* —*Syn.* disrobe, uncover, divest; see **undress.**

uncomfortable, *mod.* **1.** [Troubled in body or mind]—*Syn.* distressed, ill at ease, uneasy, nervous, disturbed, pained, miserable, wretched, restless, fretted, annoyed, angry, in pain, smarting, suffering, discomposed, disquieted, discomfited, upset, vexed, on pins and needles, weary, tired, fatigued, exhausted, strained, worn, aching, griped, wracked, on the wrack, sore, galled, stiff, chafed, cramped, agonized, hurt, anguished.—*Ant.* quiet*, rested, happy*.
2. [Causing discomfort]—*Syn.* ill-fitting, awkward, annoying, irritating, galling, wearisome, vexatious, difficult, hard, thorny, troublesome, harsh, grievous, dolorous, bitter, excruciating, afflictive, distressing, distressful, torturing, painful, agonizing, disagreeable.—*Ant.* easy*, pleasant, grateful.

uncomfortably, *mod.* —*Syn.* distressfully, dolefully, uneasily, painfully, miserably, wretchedly, restlessly, sadly, fretfully, annoyingly, disturbingly, vexatiously, agonizingly, awkwardly, irritatingly, troublesomely, harshly, grievously, dolorously, bitterly, poignantly, sharply, keenly, excruciatingly, disagreeably, unhappily, dismally, in anguish.

uncommitted, *mod.* **1.** [Nuetral]—*Syn.* unpledged, unaffiliated, free; see **nonpartisan, neutral** 1.
2. [Reserved]—*Syn.* evasive, reticent, shy; see **withdrawn.**
3. [Withheld]—*Syn.* restrained, denied, held back; see **withheld.**

uncommon, *mod.* —*Syn.* unusual, out of the ordinary, different, extraordinary, unheard of, unique, rare, exceptional, out of the way, strange, exotic, arcane, remarkable, startling, surprising, fantastic, unaccustomed, unfamiliar, anomalous, unclassifiable, freakish, irregular, uncustomary, unconventional, unorthodox, abnormal, peculiar, odd, bizarre, eccentric, original, nondescript, prodigious, fabulous, monstrous, egregious, aberrant, curious, wonderful, unaccountable, unwonted, *outré* (French), noteworthy, queer, unparalleled, unexampled, outlandish, extreme.—*Ant.* common*, usual, ordinary.

uncommonly, *mod.* **1.** [Rarely]—*Syn.* not often, unusually, in few instances; see **infrequently, seldom.**
2. [Strangely]—*Syn.* remarkably, oddly, peculiarly; see **strangely.**

uncommunicative, *mod.* —*Syn.* reticent, silent, evasive; see **quiet** 2, **reserved** 3.

uncompromising, *mod.* —*Syn.* strong, inflexible, determined; see **fair** 1, **resolute** 2.

unconcern, *n.* —*Syn.* apathy, aloofness, coldness; see **indifference** 1.

unconcerned, *mod.* —*Syn.* indifferent, careless, feckless, heedless, apathetic, insensible, oblivious, nonchalant, insouciant, inattentive, cold, phlegmatic, impassive, supine, callous, unsympathetic, hardened, insensitive, stony, neutral, reserved, self-centered, negligent, blind, deaf, forgetful, disdainful, lukewarm, cool, lackadaisical, uninterested. —*Ant.* interested*, absorbed, attached.

unconditional, *mod.* —*Syn.* positive, definite, absolute, outright, unconstrained, without reserve, final, certain, complete, entire, whole, unrestricted, unqualified, unlimited, actual, thorough, thoroughgoing, genuine, indubitable, assured, determinate, unequivocal, full, categorical, decisive, unmistakable, clear, unquestionable.—*Ant.* restricted*, contingent, partial.

unconditionally, *mod.* —*Syn.* absolutely, thoroughly, unreservedly; see **completely.**

unconfined, *mod.* —*Syn.* loose, not confined, unrestrained; see **free** 2, 3, **unlimited.**

unconformity, *n.* —*Syn.* difference, dissent, incongruity; see **inconsistency, revolution** 2.

unconnected, *mod.* **1.** [Separate]—*Syn.* divided, detached, disconnected; see **separated.**
2. [Irrelevant]—*Syn.* impertinent, unrelated, inapplicable; see **irrelevant.**

unconscionable, *mod.* **1.** [Dishonest]—*Syn.* knavish, sneaky, criminal; see **unscrupulous.**
2. [Excessive]—*Syn.* unreasonable, too much, immoderate; see **extreme** 2.

unconscious, *mod.* **1.** [Comatose]—*Syn.* insensible, swooning, in a state of suspended animation, torid, lethargic, benumbed, inanimate, bereft of senses, senseless, insensate, drowsy, numb, inert, paralyzed, palsied, tranced, entranced, in a stupor *or* coma *or* trance, stupefied, raving, out of one's head; *both* (D): out like a light, knocked out; see also **motionless** 1.—*Ant.* conscious*, vivacious, awake.
2. [Unaware]—*Syn.* inattentive, lost, ignorant; see **careless** 1, **oblivious.**

unconscious, (*usually used with* the) *n.* —*Syn.* psyche, subliminal self, instinct, motive force; see also **memory** 1, **mind** 1.

unconsciously, *mod.* —*Syn.* abstractedly, mechanically, unthinkingly, perfunctorily, carelessly, automatically, habitually, by rote, unintentionally, inattentively, heedlessly, without reflection, negligently, disregardfully, thoughtlessly, neglectfully, hurriedly, without calculation, unguardedly. —*Ant.* deliberately*, intentionally, willfully.

unconstitutional, *mod.* —*Syn.* un-American, undemocratic, lawless; see **illegal.**

unconstitutionally, *mod.* —*Syn.* illegally, unjustly, lawlessly; see **wrongly** 1, 2.

uncontrollable, *mod.* —*Syn.* obdurate, obstinate, stubborn, ungovernable, lawless, insurgent; see also **unruly.**

uncontrolled, *mod.* —*Syn.* open, clear, free, unchecked, unhindered, boundless, ungoverned, unsuppressed, limitless, untrammeled, unbridled, unfettered, unobstructed, independent, unburdened, unbounded, unhampered, unlimited, uncurbed, unconstrained, unconfined.

unconventional, *mod.* —*Syn.* anarchistic, individual, different; see **unique** 1, **unusual** 2.

uncork, *v.* —*Syn.* open (up), unseal, remove the cork from; see **open** 2, 3, 4.

uncounted, *mod.* —*Syn.* numberless, numerous, unrecorded; see **many, unnoticed.**

uncouple, *v.* —*Syn.* sever, sunder, divorce; see **divide** 1, **separate** 2.

uncouth, *mod.* —*Syn.* ungainly, clumsy, crude; see **awkward** 1, **rude** 1, 2.

uncover, *v.* —*Syn.* unseal, uncork, unscrew, pry open, lift the lid, unstopper, dig up, reveal, tap, lay open, unclose, fish up (D); see also **open** 2.—*Ant.* close*, cover, seal up.

uncovered, *mod.* —*Syn.* exposed, conspicuous, unsafe; see **open** 4.

uncritical, *mod.* —*Syn.* imprudent, imperceptive, uninformed; see **rash.**

unction, *n.* **1.** [Ointment]—*Syn.* oil, unguent, liniment; see **salve.**
2. [Sacrament]—*Syn.* anointing, laying on of hands, blessing; see **sacrament** 1.

unctuous, *mod.* **1.** [Oily]—*Syn.* greasy, lenitive, unguent; see **oily** 1.
2. [Smooth]—*Syn.* plastic, slippery, waxy; see **oily** 2, **slippery.**
3. [Ingratiating]—*Syn.* smooth, suave, insinuating; see **affected** 2, **oily** 3.

undamaged, *mod.* —*Syn.* uninjured, unharmed, safe; see **unhurt, whole** 2.

undaunted, *mod.* —*Syn.* courageous, fearless, intrepid; see **brave** 1.

undeceive, *v.* —*Syn.* disillusion, set right, inform; see **correct** 1.

undecided, *mod.* —*Syn.* undetermined, in the middle *or* balance, unsettled, open, of two minds, ambivalent, dubious, unfinished, unconcluded, up in the air (D); see also **doubtful** 2, **uncertain** 2.

undecipherable, *mod.* —*Syn.* illegible, indistinct, impenetrable; see **obscure** 1, **vague** 2.

undefeated, *mod.* —*Syn.* unbeaten, victorious, winning; see **triumphant.**

undefended, *mod.* —*Syn.* unprotected, exposed, unguarded; see **endangered.**

undefiled, *mod.* **1.** [Sportless]—*Syn.* unsullied, unsoiled, flawless; see **clean** 1, **pure** 2.
2. [Innocent]—*Syn.* virginal, sinless, holy; see **chaste** 2, 3.

undefined, *mod.* **1.** [Infinite]—*Syn.* limitless, boundless, forever; see **endless** 1, **infinite** 1.
2. [Vague]—*Syn.* dim, unclear, indistinct; see **irregular** 4, **obscure** 1.

undemocratic, *mod.* —*Syn.* communist(ic), fascist(ic), un-American; see **autocratic** 1.

undemonstrative, *mod.* —*Syn.* restrained, reticent, distant; see **reserved** 3, **withdrawn.**

undeniable, *mod.* **1.** [Evident]—*Syn.* proven, sound, sure; see **accurate** 1, **conclusive.**
2. [Compulsory]—*Syn.* required, obligatory, binding; see **necessary** 1.

undependable, *mod.* —*Syn.* careless, unsound, inconstant; see **irresponsible, unreliable** 1.

under, *mod.* and *prep.* **1.** [Referring to physical position]—*Syn.* on the bottom of, below, on the nether side of, covered by, 'neath, concealed by, held down by, supporting, pinned beneath, on the under-side of, pressed down by, beneath.—*Ant.* above*, over, on top of.
2. [Subject to authority]—*Syn.* subordinate to, reporting to, amenable to, subjugated to, under the sway of, governed by, in the power of, obeying the dictates of, obedient to, directed by.
3. [Included within]—*Syn.* subsumed under, belonging to, corollary to, inferred from, consequent to, subsidiary to, comprised in, subsequent to, following; see also **below** 3.—*Ant.* different*, distinct from, apart.

underage, *mod.* —*Syn.* young, youthful, minor; see **juvenile** 1.

under arrest, *mod.* —*Syn.* arrested, caught, apprehended, taken into custody, seized, taken (in), handcuffed, confined, jailed, imprisoned, detained, shut up *or* penned up, put in irons, sent to prison *or* to jail; *all* (D): busted, pinched, booked, collared, nabbed, sent up the river.

underbid, *v.* —*Syn.* bargain, negotiated, outbid; see **bid** 1.

under bond, *mod.* **1.** [Responsible; *said of persons*] —*Syn.* certified, cleared, accepted; see **bonded** 1, **responsible** 1.
2. [Insured; *said of goods*]—*Syn.* certified, warranted, bonded; see **guaranteed, protected.**

underbrush, *n.* —*Syn.* thicket, brush, brushwood, boscage, jungle, (second) growth, tangle, copse, coppice, hedge, dingle, cover, wold, quick, quickset, gorse, furze, whin, spinney, scrub, bush; see also **forest.**

undercharge (for), *v.* —*Syn.* charge *or* sell for too little, cut (the) price(s), sacrifice; see **charge** 2, **sell** 1.

underclassman, *n.* —*Syn.* lowerclassman, first- *or* second-year student, novice; see **freshman, sophomore.**

underclothes, *n.* —*Syn.* nether garments, lingerie, union suit, underthings; see also **clothes, underwear.**

under construction, *mod.* —*Syn.* in production, in preparation, being built, going up.

undercover, *mod.* **1.** [Secret]—*Syn.* hidden, surreptitious, clandestine; see **secret** 3.
2. [Secretly]—*Syn.* privately, surreptitiously, stealthily; see **secretly.**

undercurrent, *n.* **1.** [Backflow]—*Syn.* cross-current, ebb tide, flow; see **undertow.**
2. [Direction]—*Syn.* trend, propensity, direction; see **inclination** 1.
3. [Indication]—*Syn.* intimation, insinuation, trace; see **hint** 1.

undercut, *v.* **1.** [To excavate]—*Syn.* undermine, hollow, gouge; see **cut** 2.
2. [To undersell]—*Syn.* undercharge, undercut, sell for less; see **sell** 1.

underdeveloped, *mod.* —*Syn.* backward, retarded, slowed down; see **little** 1, **weak** 1, 2, 3, 5.

underdog, *n.* —*Syn.* loser, underling, low man on the totem pole (D); see **failure** 2, **victim** 1.

underdone, *mod.* —*Syn.* undone, not finished, uncooked; see **rare** 5, **raw** 1.

underestimate, *v.* —*Syn.* miscalculate, miscarry, come short of, undervalue, disesteem, depreciate, underrate, disparage, do scant justice to, misprize, slight, minimize, think too little of, hold too lightly, make light of, deprecate, put down (D), set at naught.—*Ant.* exaggerate*, overestimate, overpraise.

underfed, *mod.* —*Syn.* skinny, starving, starved; see **hungry.**

under fire, *mod.* —*Syn.* in action, at the front, embattled; see **fighting.**

underfoot, *mod.* **1.** [Beneath]—*Syn.* down, at bottom, below; see **under** 1.
2. [In the way]—*Syn.* annoying, tiresome, impeding; see **disturbing.**

undergo, *v.* —*Syn.* sustain, submit to, support, experience, feel, know, be subject to, bear, meet with, endure, go through, encounter, bear up under, put up with, share, withstand.—*Ant.* avoid*, escape*, resist*.

undergone, *mod.* —*Syn.* sustained, submitted to, supported, experienced, felt, suffered, borne, met (with), known, endured, gone through, encountered, put up with, shared, seen, withstood.

undergraudate, *n.* —*Syn.* underclassman, upperclassman, freshman, sophomore, junior, senior.

underground, *mod.* **1.** [Subterranean]—*Syn.* buried, covered, subterrene, earthed over, under the sod, in the recesses of the earth, gone to earth; see also **under** 1.
2. [Secret]—*Syn.* hidden, undercover, clandestine; see **secret** 2, 3.
3. [Unconventional]—*Syn.* experimental, radical, avant-garde; see **unusual** 2.

Underground, *n.* [British]—*Syn.* subway, tube, *Métro* (French); see **subway.**

undergrowth, *n.* —*Syn.* underwood, tangle, scrub; see **brush** 4, **underbrush.**

underhanded, *mod.* —*Syn.* secret, sneaky, secretive; see **sly** 1.

underlie, *v.* —*Syn.* carry, bear, hold up; see **hold** 8.

underline, *v.* **1.** [Emphasize]—*Syn.* stress, mark, indicate; see **emphasize.**
2. [To make a line under]—*Syn.* underscore, mark, interlineate, bracket, check off, italicize.

underling, *n.* —*Syn.* subordinate, hireling, servant; see **assistant.**

undermine, *v.* **1.** [Enfeeble]—*Syn.* impair, ruin, threaten; see **weaken** 2.
2. [To excavate]—*Syn.* dig out, tunnel, hollow out; see **dig** 1.

underneath, *mod.* and *prep.* —*Syn.* beneath, 'neath (D), below, lower than, covered by; see also **under** 1.

undernourished, *mod.* —*Syn.* underfed, mistreated, afflicted with malnutrition; see **hungry.**

underpass, *n.* —*Syn.* bridge, culvert, cave; see **tunnel.**

underpinning, *n.* —*Syn.* basis, base, supporting structure(s); see **bottom** 1, **foundation** 2.

underprivileged, *mod.* —*Syn.* poor, indigent, disadvantaged, deprived, unfortunate, impoverished, needy, destitute, educationally handicapped.

underrate, *v.* —*Syn.* undervalue, discount, disparage; see **underestimate.**

underscore, *v.* —*Syn.* mark, stress, italicize; see **emphasize, underline** 2.

undersea, *mod.* —*Syn.* underwater, submarine, marine, sunken; see also **under** 1.

undersell, *v.* —*Syn.* undercut, reduce, slash, cut, undercharge, mark down; see also **sell** 1.

undershirt, *n.* —*Syn.* shirt, T-shirt, knit shirt, turtleneck, pull-over, combination shirt, skivvy (D); see also **clothes, underwear.**

underside, *n.* —*Syn.* underneath, base, root; see **bottom** 1, **foundation** 2.

undersigned, *n.* —*Syn.* person or persons named below, those signified, signers, endorsers, inditers, authors, subscribers, supporters, petitioners, covenanters, bondsmen, sanctioners, negotiators, testators, ratifiers, signatories, underwriters, notaries; see also **patron** 1.

undersized, *mod.* —*Syn.* miniature, small, tiny; see **little** 1, **minute** 1.

underskirt, *n.* —*Syn.* skirt, slip, half slip, petticoat, chemise, shimmy, bustle, hoopskirt; see also **clothes, underwear.**

understand, *v.* **1.** [To comprehend]—*Syn.* apprehend, fathom, take in, grasp, figure out, seize, take (one's meaning), identify with, know, perceive, appreciate, follow, master, conceive, be aware of, sense, recognize, grow aware, explain, interpret, cognize, see through, learn, find out, ken, see (into), catch, note, be conscious of, have cognizance of, wot, ween, realize, discern, read, distinguish, infer, deduce, induce, make out, make sense of, be apprized of, become alive to, have been around, experience, have knowledge of, be instructed in, get to the bottom of, get at the root of, penetrate, possess, be informed of, come to one's senses, see the light, make out; *all* (D): register, savvy, get, get the gist of, catch on, get the point of, dig, read between the lines, be with it, get the hand of, get the idea. —*Ant.* misunderstand*, be ignorant, go astray.
2. [To suppose]—*Syn.* guess, conjecture, surmise; see **assume** 1.
3. [To accept]—*Syn.* concede, take for granted, count on; see **agree.**

understandable, *mod.* —*Syn.* comprehensible, conceivable, appreciable, expected, to be expected, natural, normal, regular, making sense, accordant, congruous, intelligible, coherent, lucid, unambiguous, in harmony with, readable, reasonable, logical, right, customary, recognizable, justifiable, imaginable, acceptable, apprehensible, credible, on all fours with (D); see also **obvious** 2. —*Ant.* illogical*, irrational, obscure.

understandably, *mod.* —*Syn.* naturally, with good reason, sensibly; see **reasonably** 1, 2.

understanding, *mod.* —*Syn.* empathetic, kindly, generous; see **patient** 1, **sympathetic.**

understanding, *n.* **1.** [The power to understand] —*Syn.* sharpness, intelligence, comprehension; see **judgment** 1.

2. [The act of comprehending]—*Syn.* recognition, knowing, perception; see **judgment** 2, **thought** 1.

3. [That which comes from understanding, sense 2] —*Syn.* conclusion, knowledge, perception; see **belief** 1, **opinion** 1.

4. [Informal agreement]—*Syn.* meeting of minds, common view, harmony; see **agreement** 2, 3.

5. [The intellect]—*Syn.* head, brain, mentality; see **mind** 1.

understate, *v.* —*Syn.* undervalue, minimize, lessen; see **decrease** 2, **underestimate.**

understatement, *n.* —*Syn.* modest or restrained statement *or* declaration *or* estimate, etc.; belittlement, restraint, underestimate, underestimation, oversimplification, less than the truth, distortion, avoidance of overemphasis or exaggeration.

understood, *mod.* **1.** [Comprehend]—*Syn.* penetrated, realized, appreciated, known, discovered, grasped, reasoned out, rationalized, explained, experienced, discerned, distinguished, made out, learned, fathomed, searched, explored, analyzed, mastered, conned, taken to heart, dug (D).—*Ant.* unknown*, overlooked, uncomprehended.

2. [Agreed upon]—*Syn.* concerted, ratified, (reciprocally) approved, assumed, stipulated, pledged, covenanted, tacitly agreed upon, taken for granted, engaged for, settled, concluded, fixed upon, endorsed, subscribed to, accepted.

understudy, *n.* —*Syn.* alternate, double, stand-in; see **substitute.**

undertake, *v.* —*Syn.* endeavor, engage, set out, promise, try out, try, begin, commence, offer, set in motion, volunteer, initiate, commit oneself to, embark upon, venture, take upon oneself, answer for, hazard, stake, move, devote *or* pledge oneself to, shoulder, take up (for), take on *or* upon, set about, go into *or* about *or* in for, put one's hand to, have one's hands in, have in hand, launch (into *or* upon *or* forth), address oneself to, enter on *or* upon, busy oneself with; *all* (D): tackle, pitch into, fall into, buckle to, take on, take the plunge, fall to, have a try at, go for (in a big way).

undertaken, *mod.* —*Syn.* set in motion, begun, launched, embarked upon, initiated, pushed forward, ventured, started, endeavored, assumed, taken up, promised, offered, volunteered, hazarded, chanced, risked, pledged, tackled, essayed, tried, aimed at, attempted, striven for, engaged for.

undertaker, *n.* —*Syn.* mortician, funeral director, embalmer, cremator, body snatcher (D).

undertaking, *n.* —*Syn.* enterprise, attempt, endeavor, project, effort, venture, pursuit, essay, trial, experiment, hazard, emprise, move, task, job, engagement.

undertone, *n.* —*Syn.* buzz, murmur, hum; see **whisper** 1.

undertow, *n.* —*Syn.* eddy, maelstrom, whirlpool, undercurrent, indraft, vortex, reflex, surge, turbulence, riptide; see also **flow, tide.**

undervalue, *v.* —*Syn.* underrate, minimize, depreciate; see **underestimate.**

underwater, *mod.* —*Syn.* submarine, sunken, marine; see **under** 1, **undersea.**

under way, *mod.* —*Syn.* initiated, started, under construction; see **begun, undertaken.**

underwear, *n.* —*Syn.* undergarments, balbriggans, nether garments, underclothing, unmentionables, smallclothes, lingerie, intimate things, underlinen, underclothes; see also **clothes.**

Types of underwear include the following—*men:* shirt, undershirt, skivvy (D), shorts, drawers, red flannels, union suit, combination, jockey shorts, T-shirt, boxer shorts, bikini shorts, briefs, long underwear, B.V.D.'s (trademark); *women:* chemise, underskirt, camisole, slip, half slip, petticoat, girdle, panty girdle, brassiere, pettipants, garter belt, braslip, bra, panty slip, merry widow, all-in-one, corset, corselet, briefs, bodice, *cache-sexe* (French), vest, bloomer, combination, foundation garment, panty girdle, panties, panty hose, bikini, body suit, body shirt, shorts, corset cover, undervest; *all* (D): shimmy, knickers (British), snuggies; *infants:* shirt, drawers, pants, diaper, slip, rubber pants, soakers (D).

underweight, *mod.* —*Syn.* skinny, undersized, puny; see **thin** 2.

underworld, *mod.* —*Syn.* criminal, concerned with organized crime, Mafialike, gangster, mob-ruled; see also **illegal, wicked** 1.

underworld, *n.* **1.** [Hell]—*Syn.* Hades, Inferno, netherworld; see **hell** 1.

2. [Crime]—*Syn.* gangland, gangdom, rackets, organized crime, the mob, the Syndicate, the Mafia, the Cosa Nostra, the Black Hand, criminals, riffraff.

underwrite, *v.* **1.** [To subscribe]—*Syn.* sign, initial, seal; see **endorse** 2.

2. [To approve]—*Syn.* accede, consent, okay (D); see **approve** 1.

3. [To support financially]—*Syn.* finance, help, pay, support, guarantee, subsidize, endow, fund, refund, provide security *or* capital *or* financing *or* the money *or* the collateral *or* the funding (for), float stocks *or* a stock issue *or* bonds *or* a bond issue *or* bonding (for), provide subvention (for).

undesirable, *mod.* —*Syn.* objectionable, shunned, disliked, (to be) avoided, unwanted, outcast, rejected, defective, disadvantageous, inexpedient, inconvenient, incommodious, troublesome, unwished for, repellent, loathed, unsought, dreaded, annoying, insufferable, unacceptable, scorned, displeasing, disliked, distasteful, loathsome, abominable, obnoxious, unpopular, bothersome, unlikable, unwelcome, unapprovable, useless, inadmissible, unsatisfactory, disagreeable, awkward, embarrassing, unfit.—*Ant.* welcome*, proper, suitable.

undeveloped, *mod.* **1.** [Immature]—*Syn.* ignored, untaught, untrained; see **inexperienced.**

2. [Latent]—*Syn.* potential, incipient, unactualized; see **latent.**

undifferentiated, *mod.* —*Syn.* similar, not differentiated *or* distinguished, alike; see **uniform** 1, 2.

undigested, *mod.* —*Syn.* unabsorbed, unassimilated, unprocessed.

undisputed, *mod.* —*Syn.* unchallenged, uncontested, indisputable, beyond question, acknowledged, arbitrary, unquestioned, assured, tyrannous, dogmatic, authoritative, positive, final, certain, unerring, decided, indefeasible.—*Ant.* opposed*, disputed, challenged.

undistinguished, *mod.* —*Syn.* ordinary, commonplace, plain; see **common** 1, **conventional** 3, **dull** 4.

undisturbed, *mod.* —*Syn.* placid, settled, unruffled, untroubled, calm, unfretted, smooth, regular, even, uninterrupted.—*Ant.* troubled*, disturbed, vexed.

undivided, *mod.* **1.** [Unified]—*Syn.* single, united, unanimous, concerted, combined, concentrated, whole, entire, solid, complete, full, undiminished, collective.—*Ant.* separated*, different, split.

2. [Undistracted]—*Syn.* exclusive, whole, entire, full, total, complete, concentrated, vigilant, thorough, intense, wholehearted, minute, scrupulous, careful, rigid, diligent, circumspect, profound, labored, studied, particular, considerate, deliberate, detailed, continued, unflagging, intent, absorbed, engrossed, fast, fixed, steady.—*Ant.* temporary*, occasional, momentary.

undo, *v.* —*Syn.* mar, destroy, ruin, wreck, break, bring to naught, subvert, injure, overthrow, unsettle, turn topsy-turvey, upset, defeat.

undoing, *n.* **1.** [Ruin]—*Syn.* ruination, downfall, doom, reversal, destruction, misfortune, calamity, overthrow, collapse, trouble, grief, catastrophe, defeat, perdition, shipwreck, smash, wrack, subversion, discomfiture, collapse.—*Ant.* success*, accomplishment, achievement.

2. [The cause of ruin]—*Syn.* casualty, accident, mishap, misadventure, misstep, *faux pas* (French), bad hap, catastrophe, mischance, bad luck, adversity, reverse, blow, trial, affliction, visitation, stroke of fate, slip, blunder, fault, omission, difficulty, failure, error, miscalculation, trip, stumble, fumble, blunder, repulse, discouragement, death-blow, last straw, deathknell.—*Ant.* advantage*, good omen, godsend.

undone, *mod.* **1.** [Unfinished]—*Syn.* left, incomplete, unperformed; see **unfinished** 1.

2. [(D) Distraught]—*Syn.* upset, disturbed, agitated; see **troubled** 1.

3. [Ruined]—*Syn.* betrayed, destroyed, killed; see **dead** 1, **ruined** 1, 2.

undoubted, *mod.* —*Syn.* assured, sure, unquestionable, indubitable, unquestioned, irrefutable, indisputable, undisputed, unchallenged, proved, proven, established, without question, settled, fixed; see also **certain.**—*Ant.* questionable*, disputed, refuted.

undoubtedly, *mod.* —*Syn.* assuredly, without doubt, of course; see **surely, unquestionably.**

undress, *v.* —*Syn.* strip, take off one's clothes, disrobe, unclothe, dismantle, divest, become naked; *all* (D): assume the altogether, put on one's birthday suit, strip to the buff, peel, climb *or* pop *or* pile out of one's clothes.—*Ant.* dress*, put on one's clothes, attire oneself.

undue, *mod.* —*Syn.* improper, illegal, indecorous, unfair, unseemly, unjust, underhanded, sinister, forbidden, excessive, too great, unnecessary, extreme, extravagant, inordinate, unwarranted, unjustified, disproportionate, immoderate.—*Ant.* necessary*, proper, requisite.

undulant, *mod.* —*Syn.* undulating, waving, surging; see **moving** 1.

undulate, *v.* **1.** [To surge]—*Syn.* billow, wave, ripple; see **move** 1.

2. [To sway]—*Syn.* pulsate, oscillate, swing; see **wave** 3.

undulating, *mod.* —*Syn.* waving, surging, undulant; see **moving** 1.

undulation, *n.* —*Syn.* fluctuation, swaying, wave; see **sway** 1.

unduly, *mod.* —*Syn.* improperly, illegally, indecorously, unfairly, unjustly, underhandedly, excessively, extremely, extravagantly, disproportionately, immoderately; see also **unnecessarily.**—*Ant.* fairly*, rightly, moderately.

undutiful, *mod.* —*Syn.* slack, careless, disloyal; see **lazy** 1, **unfaithful** 1.

undying, *mod.* —*Syn.* everlasting, perpetual, deathless; see **eternal** 1, **immortal** 1.

unearned, *mod.* —*Syn.* won, gratis, unmerited; see **free** 4.

unearned increment, *n.* —*Syn.* profit, rise in worth *or* value, long-term capital gain(s); see **increase** 1.

unearth, *v.* **1.** [To disclose]—*Syn.* reveal, find, uncover; see **discover** 1, **learn** 1.

2. [To excavate]—*Syn.* exhume, disinter, unbury; see **dig** 1, **excavate.**

unearthly, *mod.* —*Syn.* ghoulish, frightening, ghastly, fiendish, ghostly, supernatural, preternatural, appalling, sepulchral, funereal, devilish, hair-raising, eldritch, demoniac, Satanic, eerie, spectral, uncanny, haunted, spooky (D).—*Ant.* common, familiar, homely.

uneasiness, *n.* —*Syn.* disquiet, restlessness, agitation, tumult, turmoil, restiveness, incertitude, anguish, dilemma, indecision, perturbation, apprehension, dispiritedness, anxiety, fearfulness.—*Ant.* confidence*, assurance, calm.

uneasy, *mod.* **1.** [Mentally disturbed]—*Syn.* unquiet, anxious, fearful, irascible, troubled, harassed, vexed, perturbed, alarmed, upset, afraid, apprehensive, edgy, nervous, frightened, shaky, perplexed, agitated, unsettled, suspicious, peevish, irritable, fretful, worried, anguished, in turmoil, disquieted, shaken, full of misgivings.—*Ant.* calm, collected, composed.

2. [Restless]—*Syn.* fidgety, jittery, on edge, on the *qui vive* (French), all nerves, jumpy, snappish, agitated, restive, languishing, drooping, uncomfortable, goaded, palpitant, molested, wrung, harrowed, tormented, chafed, in distress.—*Ant.* quiet*, placid, soothed.

uneconomical, *mod.* —*Syn.* extravagant, unprofitable, costly; see **expensive.**

uneducated, *mod.* —*Syn.* illiterate, unschooled, untaught; see **ignorant** 2.

unembellished, *mod.*—*Syn.* unadorned, plain, austere; see **modest** 2.

unemotional, *mod.*—*Syn.* reticent, apathetic, insensitive; see **indifferent** 1, **quiet** 2.

unemployable, *mod.*—*Syn.* useless, worthless, jobless; see **disabled.**

unemployed, *mod.*—*Syn.* out of work, laid off, at liberty, between jobs, in the bread lines, receiving charity, jobless, idle, inactive, loafing, unoccupied, without gainful employment, on the dole; *both* (D): cooling one's heels, on the shelf; see also **lazy** 1. —*Ant.* busy*, employed, at work.

unemployment, *n.*—*Syn.* work stoppage, lay-off, strike conditions; see **stopping.**

unemployment compensation, *n.*—*Syn.* (the) dole, (unemployment) benefits, (monthly) check; see **check** 1, **pay** 1, 2.

unending, *mod.*—*Syn.* interminable, everlasting, infinite, never-ending, constant, continual, eternal, ceaseless, perpetual, incessant, steady, unremitting.—*Ant.* momentary*, temporary, brief.

unendurable, *mod.*—*Syn.* excessive, unbearable, insupportable; see **extreme** 2, **intolerable.**

unenterprising, *mod.*—*Syn.* indolent, listless, tired; see **lazy, slow** 2.

unenthusiastic, *mod.*—*Syn.* distant, careless, uninterested; see **indifferent** 1, **quiet** 2.

unequal, *mod.* **1.** [Not alike]—*Syn.* odd, ill-matched, dissimilar; see **different** 1, **unlike.**
2. [One-sided]—*Syn.* uneven, unbalanced, inequitable; see **irregular** 1.

unequaled, *mod.*—*Syn.* unmatched, unrivaled, supreme; see **unique** 1.

unequally, *mod.*—*Syn.* unfairly, not evenly *or* regularly, showing favoritism; see **differently** 1, **unevenly.**

unequivocal, *mod.*—*Syn.* straightforward, clear, explicit; see **definite** 1.

unerring, *mod.*—*Syn.* faultless, errorless, impeccable, accurate, true, sure, certain, reliable, infallible, unfailing, trustworthy, exact, just, invariable, perfect.—*Ant.* wrong*, inaccurate, erring.

unessential, *mod.*—*Syn.* dispensable, minor, slight; see **irrelevant, trivial, unnecessary.**

unethical, *mod.*—*Syn.* sneaky, immoral, unfair; see **dishonest** 2, **wrong** 1.

uneven, *mod.* **1.** [Rough]—*Syn.* bumpy, rugged, jagged; see **rough** 1.
2. [Irregular]—*Syn.* notched, jagged, serrate; see **irregular** 4.
3. [Variable]—*Syn.* intermittent, spasmodic, fitful; see **irregular** 1.
4. [Odd]—*Syn.* remaining, leftover, additional; see **odd** 5.

unevenly, *mod.*—*Syn.* roughly, intermittently, irregularly, spottily, bumpily, with friction, haphazardly, wobbling, bumping, stumbling, hopping, jumpily, jumping, as if corrugated, all up and down, staggering; *all* (D); like washboard, like corduroy, like a fever chart; see also **irregularly.**

uneventful, *mod.*—*Syn.* monotonous, unexciting, quiet; see **dull** 4, 6.

unexacting, *mod.*—*Syn.* light, flexible, tolerant; see **easy** 2.

unexampled, *mod.*—*Syn.* unprecedented, new, unequaled; see **unique, unusual** 1.

unexcelled, *mod.*—*Syn.* best, superior, unrivaled; see **excellent, supreme.**

unexceptionable, *mod.*—*Syn.* irreproachable, faultless, flawless; see **perfect** 2.

unexpected, *mod.*—*Syn.* unforeseen, surprising, unlooked for, accidental, fortuitous, sudden, startling, unheralded, unpredicted, coming unaware, astonishing, staggering, stunning, electrifying, amazing, not in the cards, not on the books, past conjecture, unanticipated, not bargained for, uncontemplated, left out of calculation *or* reckoning, wonderful, prodigious, coming without previous intimation, unprepared for, instantaneous, eye-opening, like a bolt from the blue (D).—*Ant.* expected*, predicted, foreseen.

unexpectedly, *mod.*—*Syn.* surprisingly, instantaneously, suddenly, startlingly, without warning, like a bolt from the blue; see also **quickly** 1. —*Ant.* regularly*, according to prediction, as anticipated.

unexpressive, *mod.*—*Syn.* inexpressive, dull, apathetic; see **indifferent** 1, **vacant** 3.

unfading, *mod.*—*Syn.* unchanging, lasting, constant; see **permanent** 2, **perpetual** 1.

unfailing, *mod.* **1.** [Inexhaustible]—*Syn.* ceaseless, endless, infallible; see **eternal** 1, 2, **infallible.**
2. [Sure]—*Syn.* absolute, continual; see **constant** 1, **certain** 3.

unfair, *mod.* **1.** [Unjust]—*Syn.* inequitable, wrongful, wrong, unrightful, low, base, injurious, unethical, not cricket (D), bad, wicked, culpable, blamable, blameworthy, foul, illegal, improper, unsporting, shameful, cruel, shameless, dishonorable, unreasonable, discreditable, grievous, vicious, vile, undue, unlawful, petty, mean, unwarrantable, inexcusable, unjustifiable, iniquitous, immoral, injurious, criminal, forbidden, irregular.—*Ant.* fair*, proper, sporting.
2. [Not in accord with approved trade practices] —*Syn.* unethical, criminal, proscribed, cheating, discriminatory, illegal, forbidden, tricky, evasive, shady, punishable, actionable, improper.

unfairly, *mod.*—*Syn.* unjustly, unreasonably, irregularly, illegally, immorally; see also **brutally.**

unfaithful, *mod.* **1.** [Not faithful]—*Syn.* false, untrue, deceitful, foresworn, unreliable, traitorous, treasonable, perfidious, not true to, of bad faith, treacherous, untrustworthy, shifty, unreliable. —*Ant.* faithful*, constant, loyal.
2. [Having broken the marriage vow]—*Syn.* adulterous, philandering, incontinent, unchaste; see also **wicked** 1.

unfaltering, *mod.*—*Syn.* resolute, firm, steadfast; see **reliable** 1, 2.

unfamiliar, *mod.* **1.** [Unacquainted]—*Syn.* not introduced, not associated, unknown, not on speaking terms, not versed in, not in the habit of, out of contact with; see also **strange** 2.—*Ant.* friendly*, intimate, acquainted.
2. [Strange]—*Syn.* alien, outlandish, exotic, remote, foreign, unknown, novel, original, different, unusual, extraordinary, unaccustomed, unexplored, anomalous, uncommon.—*Ant.* common*, ordinary, usual.

unfashionable, *mod.*—*Syn.* outmoded, antiquated, obsolete; see **old-fashioned, unpopular.**

unfasten, *v.* —*Syn.* unsnap, untie, unlock; see **unhitch.**

unfathomable, *mod.* **1.** [Infinite]—*Syn.* boundless, unending; see **eternal** 2.
2. [Profound]—*Syn.* abstruse, unknowable, enigmatic; see **mysterious** 2.

unfavorable, *mod.* **1.** [Adverse]—*Syn.* opposed, hostile, antagonistic; see **unfriendly** 1.
2. [Not propitious]—*Syn.* inopportune, untimely, unseasonable, adverse, calamitous, unpropitious, inexpedient, bad, ill-chosen, infelicitous, ill-fated, ill-suited, ill-timed, unsuitable, improper, wrong, abortive, untoward, malapropos, inauspicious, unlucky, ill, unfortunate, regrettable, premature, tardy, late, discommodious, unfit, inadvisable, objectionable, inconvenient, disadvantageous, damaging, destructive, unseemly, ill-advised, obstructive, troublesome, embarrassing, unpromising, awkward, with a jaundiced *or* cold eye (D); see also **ominous.**

unfavorably, *mod.* —*Syn.* adversely, negatively, opposingly, oppositely, conflictingly, antagonistically, obstructively, malignantly, counteractively, contrarily, untowardly, as a deterrent, in opposition (to), in the negative, on the contrary, by contraries, by blackball(ing); *all* (D): by turning thumbs down, by dinging something, giving the red light (to); see also **against** 3.

unfeeling, *mod.* —*Syn.* heartless, inhuman, pitiless; see **cruel** 2, **ruthless** 1, 2.

unfeigned, *mod.* —*Syn.* real, sincere; see **genuine** 2.

unfilial, *mod.* —*Syn.* refractory, disobedient, insubordinate; see **rebellious** 2, 3, **unruly.**

unfilled, *mod.* **1.** [Empty]—*Syn.* vacant, void, drained; see **empty** 1.
2. [Not attended to; *said especially of orders*] —*Syn.* pending, awaiting action, delayed, held up, not dispatched, unshipped, under consideration, declined, refused; see also **unfinished** 1.

unfinished, *mod.* **1.** [Not completed]—*Syn.* uncompleted, undone, half done, imcomplete, under construction, unperformed, imperfect, unconcluded, deficient, unexecuted, unaccomplished, in preparation, in the making, not done, in the rough, sketchy, tentative, shapeless, formless, unperfected, unfulfilled, undeveloped, unassembled, defective, found wanting, cut short, immature, faulty, crude, rough.—*Ant.* done*, completed, perfected.
2. [Without a finish]—*Syn.* unpainted, unvarnished, unpolished, bare, raw, rough, crude, unprotected, uncovered, plain, undecorated, unadorned.—*Ant.* painted, varnished, enameled.

unfit, *mod.* **1.** [Incompetent]—*Syn.* unqualified, feeble, unpracticed, inexperienced, untrained, unskilled, weak, impotent, inept, clumsy, debilitated, incapacitated, badly qualified, ill-equipped, unable, unprepared, ineffective, unapt.—*Ant.* able*, fit, effective.
2. [Unsuitable]—*Syn.* improper, ill-adapted, wrong, ill-advised, unlikely, unpromising, inexpedient, inappropriate, inapplicable, inutile, useless, valueless, mistaken, incorrect, inadequate, flimsy.—*Ant.* fit*, suitable, correct.

unflagging, *mod.* —*Syn.* steady, dynamic, untiring; see **active** 2, **constant** 1.

unflappable, *mod.* —*Syn.* collected, cool, self-possessed; see **calm** 1, **deliberate** 1.

unflattering, *mod.* —*Syn.* plain, candid, blunt; see **critical** 2, **frank.**

unfledged, *mod.* **1.** [Young]—*Syn.* unfeathered, youthful, adolescent; see **young** 1.
2. [Immature]—*Syn.* undeveloped, inexperienced, raw; see **childish** 1, **young** 2.

unflinching, *mod.* —*Syn.* steadfast, constant, courageous; see **firm** 5, **resolute** 2.

unfold, *v.* **1.** [Unfurl]—*Syn.* shake out, straighten, release, display, unwind, spread out, uncurl, unwrap, unroll, give to the breeze, reel out, unbend, open, flatten, loosen, unroll, uncrease.—*Ant.* fold*, roll, lap.
2. [Reveal]—*Syn.* disclose, uncover, discover, elucidate, explain, make known, publish, expose, announce, particularize, explicate.—*Ant.* hide*, obscure, conceal.

unforeseen, *mod.* —*Syn.* surprising, abrupt, sudden; see **unexpected.**

unforgettable, *mod.* —*Syn.* notable, exceptional, extraordinary; see **impressive** 1.

unforgivable, *mod.* —*Syn.* inexcusable, unpardonable, unjustifiable, indefensible, inexpiable; see also **wrong** 1.

unforgiving, *mod.* —*Syn.* revengeful, avenging, relentless; see **cruel** 2, **ruthless** 1.

unformed, *mod.* —*Syn.* not formed, formless, incomplete; see **unfinished.**

unfortunate, *mod.* **1.** [Not promoting good fortune] —*Syn.* unpropitious, adverse, damaging; see **unfavorable** 2.
2. [Not enjoying good fortune]—*Syn.* unlucky, luckless, unhappy, hapless, afflicted, troubled, stricken, unsuccessful, without success, burdened, pained, not prosperous, ill-starred, in adverse circumstances, out of fortune, forsaken by fortune, cursed, broken, shattered, ill-fated, on the road to ruin, in a desperate plight, ruined; *all* (D): out of luck, in a bad way, jinxed, hexed, behind the eight ball, hoodooed, gone to the dogs, down on one's luck; see also **sad** 1.—*Ant.* happy*, lucky, prosperous.
3. [Not enjoying prosperity]—*Syn.* destitute, impoverished, bankrupt; see **poor** 1.

unfortunately, *mod.* **1.** [To be regretted]—*Syn.* unluckily, regrettably, unhappily, miserably, sadly, grievously, disastrously, dismally, calamitously, badly, dismayingly, sickeningly, discouragingly, catastrophically, horribly, if worst comes to worst. —*Ant.* happily*, favorably, prosperously.
2. [With ill fortune]—*Syn.* by ill hap, by chance, accidentally, predestinately, as luck would have it, by an evil chance, perversely.

unfounded, *mod.* —*Syn.* baseless, unproven, groundless; see **untrue.**

unfriendly, *mod.* **1.** [Hostile]—*Syn.* opposed, alienated, disaffected, ill-disposed, against, opposite, contrary, warlike, competitive, conflicting, antagonistic, estranged, at swords' points, at drawn daggers, inimical, at variance, at loggerheads, irreconcilable, not on speaking terms, turned against, with a chip on one's shoulder (D).—*Ant.* friendly*, intimate, approving.

2. [Lacking friendly qualities]—*Syn.* grouchy, censorious, bearish, surly, misanthropic, antisocial, uncongenial, gruff, ill-disposed, envious, uncharitable, faultfinding, combative, quarrelsome, grudging, malignant, spiteful, malicious, vengeful, resentful, hateful, captious, acrimonious, peevish, aloof, unsociable, inhospitable, crabbed, suspicious, sour; see **irritable.**—*Ant.* generous*, frank, open.

unfruitful, *mod.* —*Syn.* barren, fruitless, sterile, arid, blasted, infertile, desert, unprofitable.

unfunded, *mod.* —*Syn.* bankrupt, floating, insolvent; see **poor** 1.

unfurl, *v.* —*Syn.* unroll, unwind, loosen; see **unfold** 1.

ungainly, *mod.* —*Syn.* clumsy, gawky, inexpert; see **awkward** 1, **rude** 1.

ungentlemanly, *mod.* —*Syn.* crude, rough, uncivil; see **rude** 1.

ungodly, *mod.* **1.** [Sinful]—*Syn.* profane, godless, malevolent; see **impious** 1.

2. [Outrageous]—*Syn.* dreadful, atrocious, immoral; see **wicked** 1, 2.

ungovernable, *mod.* —*Syn.* unmanageable, wild, uncontrollable; see **rebellious** 2, 3, **unruly.**

ungracious, *mod.* —*Syn.* unpleasant, discourteous, impolite; see **rude** 1, 2.

ungraciously, *mod.* —*Syn.* unkindly, crudely, brashly; see **brutally, rudely.**

ungrammatical, *mod.* —*Syn.* inaccurate, incorrect, solecistic; see **wrong** 2.

ungrateful, *mod.* —*Syn.* thankless, unthankful, selfish, lacking in appreciation, unappreciative, grasping, demanding, self-centered, unmindful, forgetful, heedless, careless, insensible, dissatisfied, grumbling, unnatural, faultfinding, oblivious. —*Ant.* thankful*, grateful obliged.

unguarded, *mod.* —*Syn.* thoughtless, frank, careless, unwary, heedless, offhand, casual, imprudent, unwise, impulsive, ill-considered, candid, ingenuous, naive, unconscious, incautious, headlong, impolitic, spontaneous, unreflective, unpremediated. —*Ant.* deliberate*, cautious, wary.

unguent, *n.* —*Syn.* emollient, ointment, cream; see **balm** 2.

unhallowed, *mod.* **1.** [Unholy]—*Syn.* ungodly, unsanctified, unsacred; see **wicked** 2.

2. [Irreverent]—*Syn.* wicked, profane, secular; see **impious** 1.

unhandy, *mod.* **1.** [Inconvenient]—*Syn.* awkward, ill-arranged, unwieldy, ill-contrived, bothersome, clumsy, ill-adapted, cumbersome, discommodious, unfit, disadvantageous, inappropriate, unsuitable, hampering, cumbrous.—*Ant.* convenient*, manageable, commodious.

2. [Unskillful]—*Syn.* awkward, bunglesome, maladroit, clumsy, incompetent, blundering, botching, slipshod, amateur, inexpert, fumbling, inept, heavy-handed.—*Ant.* able*, accomplished, nimble.

unhappily, *mod.* —*Syn.* regrettably, lamentably, unluckily; see **badly** 1, **unfortunately.**

unhappiness, *n.* —*Syn.* sorrow, woe, sadness; see **depression** 2, **grief** 1.

unhappy, *mod.* **1.** [Sad]—*Syn.* miserable, sorrowful, wretched; see **troubled** 1.

2. [Unfortunate]—*Syn.* afflicted, troubled, in a desperate plight; see **unfortunate** 2.

unharmed, *mod.* —*Syn.* unhurt, uninjured, intact; see **safe** 1, **whole** 2.

unharmonious, *mod.* **1.** —*Syn.* discordant, shrill, unmelodious; see **harsh** 1.

2. [Opposed]—*Syn.* antagonistic, disagreeing, not in keeping (with); see **against** 3.

unharness, *v.* —*Syn.* unbuckle, unstrap, unfasten; see **unhitch.**

unhealthful, *mod.* —*Syn.* detrimental, toxic, noxious; see **dangerous** 2, **harmful.**

unhealthy, *mod.* —*Syn.* sickly, sick, in a decline, in ill health, infirm, delicate, feeble, shaky, valetudinarian, undernourished, rickety, spindling, ailing, invalid, weak, in a run-down condition, poorly (D).—*Ant.* healthy*, robust, hale.

unheard, *mod.* —*Syn.* silent, noiseless, soundless, hushed, quiet, mute, muffled, still, inaudible. —*Ant.* audible*, heard, noisy.

unheard-of, *mod.* —*Syn.* unprecedented, unique, new; see **unknown** 1, **unusual** 2.

unheeded, *mod.* —*Syn.* disregarded, neglected, overlooked, slighted, forgotten, unnoticed, abandoned, rejected, unconsidered, glossed over, slurred over, thrust aside, skimmed over, scorned, disobeyed, repudiated, put aside, winked at, ignored, uncared for, unperceived, unseen, unobserved, unnoted, unmarked, unthought of, discarded, flouted, hid under a bushel, passed by. —*Ant.* considered*, heeded, regarded.

unheralded, *mod.* —*Syn.* unsung, unnoticed, unrecognized; see **unkown** 2.

unhesitating, *mod.* —*Syn.* prompt, steadfast, immediate; see **certain** 1.

unhinge, *v.* **1.** [To detach]—*Syn.* dislodge, disjoint, disunite; see **remove** 1, **unhitch.**

2. [To upset]—*Syn.* unbalance, disorder, derange; see **disorganize.**

unhitch, *v.* —*Syn.* unhook, unfasten, disengage, detach, unloose, loosen, unbuckle, unstrap, release, unharness, uncouple, free, take out of the traces. —*Ant.* fasten*, hitch, couple.

unhoped-for, *mod.* —*Syn.* incredible, unforeseen, unexpected; see **unbelievable, unimaginable.**

unhurried, *mod.* —*Syn.* leisurely, deliberate, nonchalant; see **calm** 1, **slow** 1.

unhurt, *mod.* —*Syn.* uninjured, all right, unblemished, undamaged, intact, whole, scatheless, unharmed, unwounded, unmaimed, unbroken; see also **safe** 1.

unhygienic, *mod.* —*Syn.* unclean, unwashed, unsanitary; see **dirty** 1.

unidentifiable, *mod.* —*Syn.* unrecognizable, unperceivable, imperceptible; see **obscure** 1.

unidentified, *mod.* —*Syn.* nameless, unnamed, not known; see **anonymous, unknown** 1, 2, 3.

unidentified flying object, *n.* —*Syn.* UFO, flying saucer, spaceship, alien craft.

unification, *n.* concurrence, affinity, combination; see **alliance** 1, **union** 1.

unified, *mod.* —*Syn.* made one, united, joined, combined, concerted, synthesized, amalgamated, conjoined, incorporated, blended, identified, coalesced, federated, centralized, intertwined, consolidated, associated, cemented, coupled, allied, wedded, married, confederated, conjugated, compacted.—*Ant.* separated, distinct, disjoined.

uniform, *mod.* **1.** [Even]—*Syn.* symmetrical, regular, steady, stable, smooth, well-proportioned, normal, straight, unwarped, true, consistent, plumb.—*Ant.* crooked*, warped, askew.

2. [Alike]—*Syn.* equal, unvaried, well-matched, consonant, consistent, correspondent, mated, after the same pattern, similar, identical.—*Ant.* different*, unlike, varied.

uniform, *n.* —*Syn.* costume, suit, garb, dress, habit, attire, outfit, regimentals, dress uniform, khaki, livery; *both* (D): OD, GI; see also **clothes.**

uniformity, *n.* **1.** [Regulation]—*Syn.* steadiness, sameness, evenness; see **regularity.**

2. [Harmony]—*Syn.* unity, accord, concord; see **agreement** 2.

uniformly, *mod.* —*Syn.* without exception, with great regularity, consistently; see **evenly** 2, **regularly** 2.

unify, *v.* —*Syn.* consolidate, ally, conjoin; see **join** 1, **unite** 1.

unilateral, *mod.* —*Syn.* concerned with one side, signed by one of two factions, one-sided, unipartite, single; see also **unified.**

unilluminated, *mod.* —*Syn.* dim, black, shadowy; see **dark** 1.

unimaginable, *mod.* —*Syn.* inconceivable, incomprehensible, incredible, inapprehensible, ineffable, unbelievable, unheard of, indescribable, unthinkable, beyond comprehension, improbable; see also **impossible** 1.—*Ant.* imaginable*, conceivable, comprehensible.

unimaginative, *mod.* —*Syn.* barren, tedious, usual; see **common** 1, **dull** 7.

unimpaired, *mod.* —*Syn.* uninjured, in good shape, sound; see **perfect** 2, **whole** 2.

unimpassioned, *mod.* —*Syn.* composed, sedate, rational; see **calm** 1, **reserved** 3.

unimpeachable, *mod.* —*Syn.* blameless, irreproachable, faultless; see **innocent** 1, 2, **upright** 2.

unimpeded, *mod.* —*Syn.* unchecked, faultless, unrestrained; see **unlimited.**

unimportance, *n.* —*Syn.* immateriality, triviality, worthlessness; see **insignificance.**

unimportant, *mod.* —*Syn.* trifling, inconsiderable, slight, worthless, inconsequential, insignificant, unnecessary, immaterial, negligible, indifferent, unnecessary, beside the point, frivolous, useless, second-rate, low-ranking, of no account, of no consequence, of no moment, worthless, trivial, paltry.—*Ant.* important*, weighty, great.

unimposing, *mod.* **1.** [Unassuming]—*Syn.* kind, considerate, courteous, polite, quiet, modest, unobtrusive, humble, demure, simple, unpretentious, unassuming, unembellished; see also **reserved** 3.

2. [Tame]—*Syn.* slight, paltry, insignificant; see **dull** 4.

unimproved, *mod.* —*Syn.* ordinary, in a natural state, untutored; see **rough** 1, **wild** 1.

uninfluenced, *mod.* —*Syn.* unbiased, impartial, neutral; see **fair** 1.

uninformed, *mod.* —*Syn.* unenlightened, naive, unacquainted; see **ignorant** 1, 2, **unaware.**

uninhabitable, *mod.* —*Syn.* unfit to live in, unoccupiable, unlivable, untenantable.

uninhabited, *mod.* —*Syn.* deserted, desolate, unsettled; see **abandoned** 1, **isolated.**

uninitiated, *mod.* —*Syn.* uninformed, ignorant, inexperienced; see **naive, unaware.**

uninspired, *mod.* —*Syn.* unexcited, unmoved, unimpressed; see **indifferent** 1, **unconcerned.**

uninspiring, *mod.* —*Syn.* trite, banal, ordinary; see **common** 1, **dull** 4.

unintelligent, *mod.* —*Syn.* unlearned, untaught, uneducated; see **ignorant** 2, **stupid** 1.

unintelligible, *mod.* —*Syn.* incomprehensible, meaningless, indistinct; see **obscure** 1.

unintelligibly, *mod.* —*Syn.* indistinctly, vaguely, inaudibly; see **obscurely.**

unintentional, *mod.* —*Syn.* unthinking, involuntary, erratic; see **aimless, haphazard** 1.

unintentionally, *mod.* —*Syn.* involuntarily, incidentally, casually, accidentally, inadvertently, unthinkingly, haphazardly, without design.

uninterested, *mod.* —*Syn.* apathetic, impassive, detached; see **indifferent** 1, **unconcerned.**

uninteresting, *mod.* —*Syn.* tedious, boring, tiresome, dreary, wearisome, prosaic, pedestrian, fatiguing, monotonous, dull, drab, stale, trite, commonplace, irksome, stupid, humdrum, prosy, flat, soporific, depressing, insipid, jejune, unentertaining, uninspiring, dismal, banal; see also **dismal** 1.—*Ant.* interesting*, exciting, lively.

uninterrupted, *mod.* —*Syn.* continuous, unending, unbroken; see **consecutive** 1, **constant** 1.

uninvited, *mod.* —*Syn.* unasked, unwanted, not asked *or* invited; see **neglected, unpopular.**

uninviting, *mod.* —*Syn.* unpleasant, disagreeable, displeasing; see **offensive** 2, **unpopular.**

Union, *n.* **1.** [The United States]—*Syn.* the States, Columbia, America; *all* (D): the land of the free and the home of the brave, God's Country, the land of opportunity, the Colossus of the North; see also **America** 2, **United States.**

2. [The North in the American Civil War]—*Syn.* the Free States, Anti-Slavery States, the Northern States, Federalists; see also **north.**

union, *n.* **1.** [The act of joining]—*Syn.* unification, junction, meeting, uniting, joining, coupling, embracing, coming together, merging, fusion, mingling, concurrence, amalgam, symbiosis, commixture, amalgamation, concatenation, confluence, congregation, reconciliation, conciliation, correlation, combination, connection, annexation, linking, attachment, agglutination, coalition, conjunction, abutment, consolidation, incorporation, centralization, affiliation, confederation, copulation, coition.—*Ant.* divorce*, separation, severance.

2. [A closely knit group]—*Syn.* association, federation, society; see **organization** 3.

3. [A marriage]—*Syn.* wedlock, conjugal ties, matrimony, cohabitation, nuptial connection, match, matrimonial affiliation; *both* (D): double harness, connubial bliss.

4. [A labor union]—*Syn.* laborers, workingmen, employees; see **labor** 4.

union shop, *n.* —*Syn.* closed shop, unionized plant *or* industry *or* factory, etc.; not an open shop; see **business** 1, 4, **labor** 4.

unique, *mod.* **1.** [Existing only in one known example]—*Syn.* single, sole, peerless, matchless, incom-

parable, unprecedented, unparalleled, unequaled, novel, nonpareil, anomalous, individual, sole, *sui generis* (Latin), unexampled, lone, different, unequaled.—*Ant.* common*, frequent, many*.
2. [Rare]—*Syn.* uncommon, freakish, bizarre; see **unusual** 2.

unison, *n.*—*Syn.* concert, unity, conjunction, harmony, union, accord, agreement, co-operation, community, common consent, concord, sympathy, *rapprochement* (French), alliance, federation, league, bonds of amity, fraternity, concordance, reciprocity, fellowship.—*Ant.* opposition*, separation, discord.

unit, *n.* **1.** [A whole]—*Syn.* entirety, complement, total, totality, assemblage, assembly, system.
2. [A detail]—*Syn.* section, segment, part, fraction, piece, joint, block, square, layer, link, length, digit, member, factor.

unite, *v.* **1.** [To come together]—*Syn.* join, meet, ally, combine, solidify; harden, strengthen, condense, confederate, couple, affiliate, merge, band together, blend, mix, interpenetrate, become one, concentrate, interfuse, consolidate, entwine, intertwine, grapple, amalgamate, league, band, embody, embrace, copulate, associate, assemble, gather together, conjoin, keep together, tie in, pull together, hang together, join forces, coalesce, fuse, wed, marry, mingle, stick together, stay together.—*Ant.* divide*, separate, part.
2. [To bring together]—*Syn.* fuse, couple, blend; see **consolidate** 2, **join** 1.

united, *mod.*—*Syn.* unified, leagued, combined, affiliated, federal, confederated, integrated, amalgamated, co-operative, consolidated, concordant, concerted, congruent, associated, assembled, linked, banded, in partnership; see also **joined, organized.**—*Ant.* separated*, distinct, individual.

United Kingdom, *n.*—*Syn.* England, Scotland, Northern Ireland, Wales; the British Isles, Britain, Great Britain, the mother country; *both* (D): U.K., G.B.; see **Europe.**

United Nations, *n.*—*Syn.* UN, peace-keeping force, international society, community of nations. Divisions and functions of the United Nations include the following—General Assembly, Security Council, Economic and Social Council, Trust and Non Self-Governing Territories Trusteeship, Trusteeship Council, International Court of Justice, Secretariat.

United States, *n.*—*Syn.* America, US, United States of America, U.S.A., Columbia, the Union, these States, the States, ZI (Zone of the Interior), the land of the Stars and Stripes; *all* (D): US of A, the land of liberty, the land of the free and the home of the brave, God's country, the melting pot, the lower forty-eight (states), the outside, stateside, the mainland.

unity, *n.* **1.** [The quality of oneness]—*Syn.* homogeneity, homogeneousness, sameness, indivisibility, identity, inseparability, singleness, similarity, uniqueness, integration, uniformity, universality, all-togetherness, ensemble, wholeness; see also **whole.**—*Ant.* difference*, diversity, divorce.
2. [Union]—*Syn.* federation, confederation, compact, combination, correspondence, alliance, agreement, concord, identity of purpose, unification, aggregation; see also **organization** 3.
3. [Harmony]—*Syn.* unison, consonance, concord, agreement, consent, tuneability, accord.

universal, *mod.* **1.** [Concerning the universe]—*Syn.* cosmic, stellar, celestial, empyrean, sidereal, astronomical, cosmogonal.
2. [Worldwide]—*Syn.* tellurian, mundane, earthly, terrestrial, sublunary, terrene, human, worldly.—*Ant.* local*, restricted, district.
3. [General]—*Syn.* entire, all-embracing, prevalent, customary, usual, whole, sweeping, extensive, comprehensive, total, unlimited, limitless, endless, vast, widespread, catholic, common, regular, undisputed, accepted, unrestricted.—*Ant.* specialized*, limited, peculiar.

universality, *n.* **1.** [Generality]—*Syn.* predominance, ecumenicity, generalization; see **generality.**
2. [Entirety]—*Syn.* completeness, wholeness, totality; see **whole.**

universally, *mod.* **1.** [Concerning the universe]—*Syn.* cosmically, astronomically, celestially, zodiacally.—*Ant.* locally*, terrestrially, temporarily.
2. [Throughout the world]—*Syn.* in all climes, everywhere, from pole to pole, terrestrially, globally.—*Ant.* here*, there, occasionally.
3. [Generally]—*Syn.* entirely, prevailingly, comprehensively, customarily, extensively, totally, endlessly, unrestrictedly; see also **completely.**—*Ant.* especially*, specifically, sometimes.

universe, *n.*—*Syn.* cosmos, creation, God's handiwork, the visible world, astral system, universal frame, all created things, everything, nature, the natural world.

university, *mod.*—*Syn.* professional, advanced, graduate, college, collegiate, undergraduate, freshman, sophomore, junior, senior, learned, academic, educational.

university, *n.*—*Syn.* educational institution, institution of higher learning, multiversity, megaversity, normal school, state *or* municipal *or* provincial university; see also **academy, college, school** 1. Famous universities include the following—Paris (Sorbonne), Oxford, Cambridge, Padua, Bologna, Brussels, Halle, Zurich, Basle, Goettingen, London, Edinburgh, Dublin, Oslo, Leipzig, Vienna, Upsala, Lund, Copenhagen, Berlin, Heidelberg, Moscow, Leningrad (St. Petersburg), Kazan, Kiev, Charles (in Prague), Peking, Harvard, Yale, Princeton, Columbia, Chicago, California, Stanford, Wisconsin, Massachusetts Institute of Technology (MIT), California Institute of Technology (CIT), Melbourne.

unjust, *mod.*—*Syn.* wrong, inequitable, wrongful; see **unfair** 1.

unjustifiable, *mod.*—*Syn.* unallowable, unforgivable, unjust; see **wrong** 1.

unjustifiably, *mod.*—*Syn.* illegally, unlawfully, unrightfully; see **badly** 1, **wrongly** 2.

unjustly, *mod.*—*Syn.* brutally, cruelly, meanly; see **rudely, wrongly** 1.

unkempt, *mod.* **1.** [Dirty]—*Syn.* disorderly, unclean, untidy; see **dirty** 1.
2. [Rough]—*Syn.* unpolished, vulgar, coarse; see **crude** 1,

unkind, *mod.* —*Syn.* malignant, spiteful, mean, malicious, inhuman, inhumane, sadistic, cruel, hateful, malevolent, savage, barbarous, ruffianly; see also **rude** 1, 2.—*Ant.* kind*, benevolent, helpful.

unknown, *mod.* **1.** [Not known; *said of information*]—*Syn.* uncomprehended, unapprehended, undiscovered, untold, unexplained, unascertained, uninvestigated, unexplored, unheard of, unperceived, concealed, hidden, unrevealed.—*Ant.* known*, established, understood.
2. [Not known; *said of people*]—*Syn.* alien, unfamiliar, not introduced, unheard of, obscure, foreign, strange, unacknowledged, anonymous, unnamed, ostracized, outcast, friendless, private, retired, aloof, out of the world, rusticated, forgotten.
3. [Not known; *said of terrain*]—*Syn.* unexplored, far-off, remote, far, distant, foreign, undiscovered, exotic, hyperborean, transoceanic, transmarine, ultramontane, antipodal, at the far corners of the earth, faraway, at the uttermost ends of the earth, outlandish, unheard-of, unfrequented, untraveled, desolate, desert, unvisited, legendary, strange, Atlantean.

unladylike, *mod.* —*Syn.* unrefined, coarse, indelicate; see **rude** 1.

unlamented, *mod.* —*Syn.* unwept, unloved, unmissed; see **abandoned** 1.

unlawful, *mod.* —*Syn.* forbidden, illicit, outlawed; see **illegal.**

unlawfully, *mod.* —*Syn.* illegally, unjustly, unjustifiably; see **wrongly** 1, 2.

unlearned, *mod.* —*Syn.* unlettered, rude, boorish, uneducated, ignorant, illiterate, clownish, untutored, untaught, unread, savage, uncivilized, doltish, crass, half-taught, half-educated, uninitiated, ill-bred, unversed, uninstructed, unguided, unenlightened, benighted, dull, misguided, empty, unaccomplished, backward, superficial, pedantic, low-brow (D).—*Ant.* learned, educated, adept.

unless, *prep.* —*Syn.* saving, without the provision that, if not, except, except that, excepting that.

unlike, *mod.* —*Syn.* dissimilar, different, incongruous, contradictory, ill-assorted, hostile, opposed, inconsistent, heterogeneous, diverse, contrasted, conflicting, contrary, disparate, different as night and day, disharmonious, dissonant, discordant, like apples and oranges (D), clashing, separate, opposite, divergent, various, variant.—*Ant.* like*, similar, correspondent.

unlikelihood, *n.* —*Syn.* improbability, doubtfulness, inconceivability; see **impossibility, uncertainty** 2.

unlikely, *mod.* —*Syn.* improbable, unheard-of, incredible, implausible, not to be thought of, unbelievable, absurd, palpably false, unconvincing, not likely, scarcely possible, apparently false, contrary to expectation, inconceivable, doubtful, dubious, questionable, untoward, extraordinary, marvelous, out of the ordinary, strange.—*Ant.* likely*, probable, credible.

unlimited, *mod.* —*Syn.* infinite, limitless, boundless, unending, extensive, universal, unrestricted, unconditional, unfathomable, inexhaustible, unconfined, immense, illimitable, measureless, incalculable, interminable, without number, unfathomed, unsounded, untold, countless, numberless, incomprehensible, immeasureable, endless.

unlisted, *mod.* —*Syn.* unrecorded, unreported, not recorded *or* listed *or* reported *or* identified, etc.; see **unknown** 1, 2.

unload, *v.* —*Syn.* disburden, void, offload, discommode, discharge, dump, slough, unship, lighten, unlade, cast, unpack, unweight, relieve, remove cargo, disgorge, empty, deplane, unburden, break bulk.—*Ant.* fill*, load, pack.

unloaded, *mod.* **1.** [Removed]—*Syn.* unpacked, taken out, put away, uncrated, unwrapped.
2. [Empty]—*Syn.* void, vacated, discharged; see **empty** 1.

unlock, *v.* —*Syn.* unbar, unfasten, open the lock; see **open** 2.

unlocked, *mod.* —*Syn.* free, unbarred, unlatched; see **open** 1, 2.

unlooked-for, *mod.* —*Syn.* unanticipated, unforeseen, chance; see **unexpected.**

unloved, *mod.* —*Syn.* disliked, detested, despised; see **hated.**

unlucky, *mod.* **1.** [Unfortunate]—*Syn.* luckless, unhappy, afflicted; see **unfortunate** 2.
2. [Unpropitious]—*Syn.* ill-chosen, ill-fated, untimely; see **ominous, unfavorable** 2.

unmade, *mod.* —*Syn.* disheveled, messy, tousled; see **disorderly** 1, **unfinished** 1.

unmake, *v.* —*Syn.* ruin, depose, exterminate; see **destroy** 1.

unmanageable, *mod.* —*Syn.* uncontrollable, irrepressible, ungovernable; see **unruly.**

unmanly, *mod.* —*Syn.* weak, effeminate, womanish; see **cowardly** 1, 2, 3, **feminine** 2.

unmannerly, *mod.* —*Syn.* uncouth, discourteous, ill-mannered; see **rude** 1.

unmarried, *mod.* —*Syn.* celibate, unwed, single, virgin, maiden, bachelor, eligible, chaste, unwedded, spouseless; *all* (D): unhitched, unspliced, uncoupled, footloose and fancy-free.—*Ant.* married*, wed, wedded.

unmask, *v.* —*Syn.* pare, reveal, uncover; see **expose** 1.

unmelodious, *mod.* —*Syn.* unharmonious, dissonant, discordant; see **harsh** 1.

unmentionable, *mod.* —*Syn.* scandalous, disgraceful, ignoble; see **offensive** 2, **shameful** 1, 2.

unmerciful, *mod.* —*Syn.* merciless, pitiless, unpitying, vengeful, brutal, cruel, savage, bloodthirsty, tyrannous, monstrous, sanguine, inhumane, bestial, vindictive, ravening, cold-hearted, heartless atrocious, dead to human feeling, stony-hearted.

unmindful, *mod.* —*Syn.* forgetful, heedless, inattentive; see **careless** 1.

unmistakable, *mod.* —*Syn.* conspicuous, distinct, evident; see **clear** 1, 2, **obvious** 1.

unmitigated, *mod.* **1.** [Absolute]—*Syn.* out-and-out, clear-cut, unabridged; see **absolute** 1.
2. [Rigid]—*Syn.* thorough, austere, unbending; see **severe** 1.

unmotivated, *mod.* —*Syn.* indolent, unenterprising, nonaggressive; see **indifferent, lazy** 1.

unmoved, *mod.* **1.** [Not moved physically]—*Syn.* firm, stable, motionless, static, quiescent, solid, durable, immovable, firm as a rock, stanch, fast, moveless, statuelike, rooted, steady, immobile, unshaken, changeless, unwavering.

2. [Not moved emotionally]—*Syn.* impassive, impassible, stoic, quiet, cold, cool, calm, collected, deliberate, resolute, dispassionate, calculating, unaffected, untouched, unresponsive, unemotional, indifferent, judicious, unflinching, nerveless, cool as a cucumber (D).

unnatural, *mod.* **1.** [Contrary to nature]—*Syn.* monstrous, phenomenal, malformed, anomalous, unaccountable, abnormal, preposterous, marvelous, uncanny, wonderful, strange, incredible, sublime, Herculean, Atlantean, cyclopean, freakish, unconforming, inhuman, outrageous, unorthodox, miraculous, contrary to known laws; see also **cruel** 1, 2, **savage** 2.—*Ant.* common*, ordinary, usual.

2. [Artificial]—*Syn.* synthetic, imitation, manufactured, ersatz, concocted, make-up, fabricated, false, pseudo, fake, put-on (D), mock, spurious, phoney.—*Ant.* natural*, occurring, naturally.

unnaturally, *mod.* —*Syn.* strangely, unusually, abnormally; see **crazily.**

unnecessarily, *mod.* needlessly, causelessly, without occasion, by chance, carelessly, fortuitously, casually, haphazardly, wantonly, accidentally, unessentially, redundantly, inexpediently, uselessly, exorbitantly, superfluously, undesirably, objectionably, disadvantageously, optionally, avoidably, without cause, without reason, gratuitously; see also **foolishly.**—*Ant.* necessarily*, indispensably, unavoidably.

unnecessary, *mod.* —*Syn.* needless, causeless, fortuitous, casual, chance, haphazard, wanton, accidental, unessential, nonessential, beside the point, irrelevant, futile, extraneous, additional, redundant, useless, exorbitant, superfluous, worthless, undesirable, optional, avoidable, objectionable, disadvantageous, noncompulsory, random, dispensable, adventitious, without compulsion, uncalled for, pleonastic, gratuitous.—*Ant.* necessary*, essential, required.

unnerve, *v.* —*Syn.* unman, dishearten, discourage; see **weaken** 2, **frighten** 1.

unnoticed, *mod.* —*Syn.* unobserved, unperceived, unseen, unheeded, overlooked, inconspicuous, secret, hidden, passed by, unobtrusive, disregarded, unconsidered, unattended, neglected, unrespected, unmarked, unremembered, unscrutinized, unremarked, uncontemplated, unrecognized, slurred over, uninspected, winked at, connived at, glossed over, lost sight of, ignored, shoved into the background, undistinguished, unexamined, unwatched, unlooked at.—*Ant.* watched*, noticed, seen.

unobtrusive, *mod.* —*Syn.* modest, unassuming, meek; see **humble** 1, **reserved** 3,

unoccupied, *mod.* **1.** [Vacant]—*Syn.* uninhabited, empty, tenantless, deserted, unfurnished, void, voided, disfurnished, blank, untenanted.—*Ant.* full*, inhabited, tenanted.

2. [Idle]—*Syn.* loitering, inactive, unemployed, unengaged, at leisure, passive, lazy, quiescent, dormant, out of work.

unofficial, *mod.* —*Syn.* unconstrained, personal, casual; see **informal** 1, **private.**

unopposed, *mod.* —*Syn.* unchallenged, unrestricted, unhampered; see **free** 1, 2, 3.

unorganized, *mod.* —*Syn.* chaotic, random, disorganized; see **confused** 2, **disordered.**

unorthodox, *mod.* —*Syn.* unconventional, irregular, eccentric; see **different** 1, 2, **unusual** 2.

unpack, *v.* —*Syn.* unlade, uncrate, unwrap; see **empty** 2, **remove** 1.

unpacked, *mod.* **1.** [Not yet packed]—*Syn.* ready for packing, not wrapped, not crated, bulk, in storage.—*Ant.* packed*, wrapped, boxed.

2. [No longer packed]—*Syn.* out of its wrappings, assembled, stripped, set up; see also **removed** 1, **unloaded** 1.

unpaid, *mod.* **1.** [Owed; *said of debts*]—*Syn.* due, payable, not discharged, past due, overdue, delinquent, unsettled, unliquidated, undefrayed, outstanding.—*Ant.* paid*, discharged, defrayed.

2. [Not reimbursed; *said of creditors*]—*Syn.* due, uncompensated, unindemnified, unrewarded, defrauded, unsalaried, unfed.—*Ant.* paid*, reimbursed, indemnified.

3. [Working without salary]—*Syn.* voluntary, unsalaried, amateur, freewill, donated, contributed.

unpalatable, *mod.* —*Syn.* unsavory, disagreeable, uneatable; see **tasteless** 1.

unparalleled, *mod.* —*Syn.* unmatched, unequaled, exceptional; see **rare** 2, **single** 1, **unique** 1.

unpardonable, *mod.* —*Syn.* reprehensible, inexpiable, inexcusable; see **unforgivable.**

unperturbed, *mod.* —*Syn.* composed, tranquil, placid; see **calm** 1, 2, **undisturbed.**

unpleasant, *mod.* **1.** [Not pleasing in society] —*Syn.* disagreeable, obnoxious, boring; see **rude** 2.

2. [Not pleasing to the senses]—*Syn.* repulsive, obnoxious, abhorrent; see **offensive** 2.

unpleasantness, *n.* —*Syn.* disturbance, nuisance, bother; see **difficulty** 1, 2, **trouble** 2.

unpolished, *mod.* **1.** [Rough]—*Syn.* uneven, unlevel, unvarnished; see **raw** 2, **unfinished** 2.

2. [Vulgar]—*Syn.* rude, crude, uncouth; see **awkward** 1.

unpopular, *mod.* —*Syn.* disliked, despised, out of favor, unaccepted, abhorred, loathed, shunned, avoided, ostracized, scorned, detested, execrated, unloved, unvalued, uncared for, obnoxious; see also **offensive** 2.—*Ant.* popular*, liked, agreeable.

unprecedented, *mod.* —*Syn.* unparalleled, unique, novel, original, anomalous, abnormal, freakish, untoward, unusual, out-of-the-way, uncommon, eccentric, bizarre, odd, idiosyncratic, aberrant, prodigious, unexampled, *outré* (French), exotic, preternatural, miraculous, marvelous, outlandish, newfangled, modern, fantastic, unique; see also **single.**—*Ant.* common*, regular, everyday.

unpredictable, *mod.* —*Syn.* random, inconstant, variable; see **changeable** 1, 2, **irregular** 1.

unprejudiced, *mod.* —*Syn.* unbiased, impartial, just; see **fair** 1, **liberal** 2.

unpremeditated, *mod.* —*Syn.* hasty, unconsidered, blundering; see **rash, thoughtless** 1.

unprepared, *mod.* —*Syn.* unready, unwarned, unwary, unexpectant, surprised, taken aback, unguarded, unnotified, unadvised, unaware, unsuspecting, taken off guard; *all* (D): napping, in the dark, going off half-cocked; see also **inexperienced.**

unpretentious, *mod.* —*Syn.* simple, unassuming, prosaic; see **humble** 1.

unprincipled, *mod.* —*Syn.* unscrupulous, unethical, corrupt; see **dishonest** 2.

unproductive, *mod.* **1.** [Sterile]—*Syn.* unprolific, impotent, barren; see **sterile** 1, 2.
2. [Dry]—*Syn.* unfruitful, bare, desert; see **empty** 1.

unprofessional, *mod.* —*Syn.* improper, unethical, inadequate; see **ignorant** 2, **unsuitable.**

unprofitable, *mod.* **1.** [Producing but little financial return]—*Syn.* unthrifty, ill-requited, ill-paid, profitless, costly, expensive, unlucrative, unremunerative.—*Ant.* profitable*, gainful, productive.
2. [Useless]—*Syn.* fruitless, pointless, hopeless; see **useless** 1.

unpromising, *mod.* —*Syn.* discouraging, unfavorable, adverse; see **negative** 2, **unlikely.**

unprompted, *mod.* **1.** [Spontaneous]—*Syn.* by chance, impulsive, automatic; see **voluntary.**
2. [Unintentional]—*Syn.* unpremeditated, unconscious, involuntary; see **aimless, haphazard** 1.

unprotected, *mod.* —*Syn.* defenseless, unarmed, unguarded; see **unsafe.**

unpublished, *mod.* —*Syn.* unprinted, (still) in manuscript, manuscript, not published *or* circulated *or* distributed *or* printed *or* in print, uncirculated, undistributed; see also **unknown** 1.

unqualified, *mod.* **1.** [Absolute]—*Syn.* downright, utter, outright; see **certain** 3.
2. [Incompetent]—*Syn.* inexperienced, unprepared, incapable; see **unfit** 1.

unquestionable, *mod.* **1.** [Certain]—*Syn.* sure, obvious, clear; see **accurate** 1, **certain** 3.
2. [Faultless]—*Syn.* unexceptionable, superior, flawless; see **excellent, perfect** 2.

unquestionably, *mod.* —*Syn.* certainly, without a doubt, surely, indubitably, indisputably, definitely, reliably, absolutely, positively, incontrovertibly, indefensibly, indeed, assuredly, of course, undoubtedly, certes, undeniably, unequivocally, past a doubt, beyond doubt, beyond a shadow of a doubt, past dispute.

unquiet, *mod.* —*Syn.* agitated, disturbed, restless, stirred up, anxious, restive, nervous, ill at ease, excited, palpitant, trembling, perturbed, in commotion, in turmoil, vexed, troubled, unsettled; *all* (D): all hot and bothered, in a dither, in a tizzy, all atwitter; see also **disturbing.**

unravel, *v.* **1.** [To solve]—*Syn.* render, disclose, resolve; see **explain, interpret** 1.
2. [To untangle]—*Syn.* unwind, disengage, undo; see **free** 1.

unreadable, *mod.* —*Syn.* badly written, turgid, confused; see **dull** 3, 4, **stupid.**

unreal, *mod.* —*Syn.* visionary, delusive, deceptive, illusory, imagined, hallucinatory, ideal, dreamlike, unsubstantial, nonexistent, fanciful, misleading, fictitious, theoretical, hypothetical, fabulous, chimerical, notional, whimsical, fantastic; see also **unbelievable.**—*Ant.* genuine*, real, substantial.

unrealistic, *mod.* —*Syn.* unworkable, not sensible *or* practical *or* workable *or* applicable, etc., nonsensical; see **silly, unreliable** 1, 2.

unreasonable, *mod.* **1.** [Illogical]—*Syn.* irrational, biased, fatuous; see **illogical.**
2. [Immoderate]—*Syn.* exorbitant, extravagant, inordinate; see **extreme** 2.
3. [Senseless]—*Syn.* foolish, silly, thoughtless; see **stupid** 1, **vacant** 3.

unreasonably, *mod.* —*Syn.* illogically, irrationally, stupidly; see **foolishly.**

unrecognizable, *mod.* —*Syn.* indistinct, indefinite, undefined; see **uncertain** 2, **vague** 2.

unrefined, *mod.* —*Syn.* coarse, vulgar, boorish; see **rude** 1, 2.

unregenerate, *mod.* **1.** [Wicked]—*Syn.* sinful, carnal, profane; see **unscrupulous.**
2. [Irreligious]—*Syn.* sacrilegious, godless, atheistic; see **impious** 1.

unregulated, *mod.* —*Syn.* uncontrollable, unchecked, chaotic; see **disorderly, tangled, unlimited.**

unrelated, *mod.* —*Syn.* independent, unattached, irrelative; see **separate.**

unrelenting, *mod.* —*Syn.* cruel, merciless, pitiless; see **ruthless** 1, 2.

unreliable, *mod.* **1.** [Not reliable; *said of persons*] —*Syn.* undependable, irresponsible, unstable, wavering, deceitful, tricky, shifty, furtive, underhanded, untrue, fickle, giddy, capricious, untrustworthy, vacillating, fallible, weak, unpredictable; see also **dishonest** 1, 2.
2. [Not reliable; *said of facts and objects*]—*Syn.* deceptive, delusive, hallucinatory, plausible, specious, tricky, unsound, untrue, inaccurate, erroneous, hollow, pretended, sham, pseudo, makeshift, meretricious, misleading.

unreliably, *mod.* —*Syn.* uncertainly, shiftily, dubiously; see **irregularly, vaguely.**

unrepentant, *mod.* —*Syn.* shameless, impenitent, hardened; see **remorseless** 1.

unrequited, *mod.* —*Syn.* unthanked, unanswered, unrecompensed; see **unpaid** 2.

unreserved, *mod.* —*Syn.* boisterous, outgoing, lusty; see **loud** 2, **rude.**

unresolved, *mod.* —*Syn.* incomplete, unconcluded, unsolved; see **unfinished** 1.

unrest, *n.* **1.** [Lack of mental calm]—*Syn.* malaise, distress, discomfort, perturbation, agitation, worry, sorrow, anxiety, grief, trouble, annoyance, tension, ennui, disquiet, soul-searching, irritation, harassment, upset, vexation, chagrin, mortification, perplexity, unease, disease, stour, moodiness, disturbance, bother; *both* (D): dither, tizzy.
2. [Social or political restlessness]—*Syn.* disquiet, agitation, turmoil, strife, disturbance, turbulence, tumult, uproar, debate, contention, bickering, change, altercation, crisis, confusion, disputation, contest, controversy, quarrel, sparring, uncertainty, insurrection, suspicion, dissatisfaction.

unrestrained, *mod.* —*Syn.* unshackled, unrepressed, untrammeled; see **free** 1, 2, **unlimited.**

unrestricted, *mod.* —*Syn.* allowable, not forbidden, free; see **open** 3, **permitted.**

unrighteous, *mod.* —*Syn.* sinful, iniquitous, depraved; see **lewd** 2, **wicked** 1.

unrighteousness, *n.* —*Syn.* wickedness, immorality, sinfulness; see **blasphemy, sin.**

unripe, *mod.* **1.** [Raw]—*Syn.* green, tart, immature; see **raw** 1.
2. [Inexperienced]—*Syn.* immature, unpracticed, new; see **inexperienced.**
unrivaled, *mod.*—*Syn.* matchless, peerless, unequaled; see **unique** 1, **unusual** 1.
unroll, *v.*—*Syn.* display, uncover, present; see **expose** 1.
unruffled, *mod.*—*Syn.* collected, smooth, serene; see **calm** 1, 2, **undisturbed.**
unruly, *mod.*—*Syn.* uncontrollable, willful, headstrong, forward, forward, violent, impulsive, uncurbed, impetuous, ill-advised, rash, reckless, dashing, heedless, perverse, intractable, recalcitrant, self-assertive, refractory, rebelious, wayward, inexorable, restive, impervious, hidebound, unyielding, incorrigible, intemperate, drunken, lawless, vicious, brawling, unlicensed, rowdy, bawdy, quarrelsome, mob-minded, immovable, unwieldy, obdurate, resolute, inflexible, forceful, dogged, mulish, fanatic, irrational, unreasonable, irrepressible, high-spirited, impudent, abandoned, profligate, truculent, stubborn, obstinate, turbulent, disorderly, contumacious, self-willed, opinionated, bullheaded, ungovernable, stiff-necked, feckless; *all* (D): ornery, mean, rarin', chafing at the bit, hell-bent, skittish, dangerous.—*Ant.* docile*, tractable, responsive.
unsafe, *mod.*—*Syn.* hazardous, perilous, jeopardous, risky, threatening, treacherous, fearsome, unreliable, insecure, venturesome, lowering, unstable, fraught with peril, alarming, precarious, ticklish, giddy, dizzy, slippery, uncertain, unpromising, unprepossessing, shaky, explosive.—*Ant.* safe*, harmless, proof.
unsaid, *mod.*—*Syn.* unspoken, not spoken or expressed or uttered, etc.; unstated; see **quiet** 2, **silenced.**
unsatisfactorily, *mod.*—*Syn.* poorly, crudely, inefficiently; see **badly** 1.
unsatisfactory, *mod.*—*Syn.* disappointing, below expectation, inadequate, displeasing, undesirable, regrettable, disconcerting, disquieting, vexing, distressing, upsetting, disturbing, offensive, unacceptable, disagreeable, unwelcome, shocking, deficient; see also **poor** 2.—*Ant.* excellent*, satisfactory, gratifying.
unsavory, *mod.* **1.** [Tasteless]—*Syn.* flavorless, bland, unappetizing; see **dull** 4.
2. [Offensive]—*Syn.* disagreeable, unpleasant, revolting; see **offensive** 2.
unscathed, *mod.*—*Syn.* uninjured, unhurt, unharmed; see **safe** 1, **whole** 2.
unschooled, *mod.*—*Syn.* untrained, naive, amateur; see **ignorant** 2.
unscientific, *mod.*—*Syn.* irrational, impulsive, inconclusive; see **illogical.**
unscrew, *v.*—*Syn.* unstopper, screw out *or* off, unfasten, take out, extract, unhitch, untwist.
unscrupulous, *mod.*—*Syn.* unprincipled, unethical, immoral, base, perfidious, degraded, selfish, self-seeking, petty, dishonest, knavish, wicked, tortuous, disingenuous, slippery, Machiavellian, casuistic, improper, Jesuitic, perjured, recreant, rascally, pettifogging, shifty, underhanded, two-faced, double-faced, sly, conscienceless, arrant, venal, dishonorable, corrupt, roguish, illegitimate, illegal, unfair, unorthodox, questionable, unworthy, scandalous, disgraceful, degrading, shameless, shady (D).—*Ant.* honest*, scrupulous, fair-minded.
unscrupulously, *mod.*—*Syn.* wrongfully, cruelly, viciously; see **wrongly** 1.
unseal, *v.*—*Syn.* free, remove, crack; see **break** 1, **open** 2.
unseasonable, *mod.*—*Syn.* inappropriate, untimely, awkward; see **improper** 1, **unsuitable.**
unseat, *v.* **1.** [To unsaddle]—*Syn.* dismount, expel, get down; see **eject** 1, **remove** 1.
2. [To oust]—*Syn.* disbar, depose, replace; see **dismiss** 1, 2.
unseemly, *mod.* **1.** [In bad taste; *said of conduct*]—*Syn.* rude, improper, unbecoming, inept, ill-advised.
2. [In bad taste; *said of things*]—*Syn.* vulgar, tawdry, cheap; see **poor** 2.
unseen, *mod.*—*Syn.* imagined, imaginary, hidden, obscure, unobserved, veiled, occult, sensed, unperceived, unnoticed, unsuspected, curtained, unobtrusive, viewless, unviewed, invisible, sightless, dark, shrouded, unnoted, impalpable, imperceptible, inconspicuous, undiscovered, impenetrable, dense.
unselfish, *mod.*—*Syn.* disinterested, selfless, charitable, kind, liberal, openhanded, altruistic, large-minded, magnanimous, generous, benevolent, beneficent, indulgent, chivalrous, helpful, self-denying, self-sacrificing, loving, self-effacing, devoted, incorruptible, unbought, unbribed, unbribable.
unselfishly, *mod.*—*Syn.* openhandedly, bountifully, lavishly; see **freely** 1, 2, **generously** 1, 2.
unselfishness, *n.*—*Syn.* disinterestedness, charity, generosity, liberality, openhandedness, altruism, magnanimity, munificence, benevolence, beneficence, helpfulness, self-denial, self-sacrifice, loving-kindness, devotion, self-effcement, incorruptibility, largesse, bounty.—*Ant.* greed*, selfishness, avarice.
unsettle, *v.*—*Syn.* disrupt, displace, disarrange; see **bother** 2, 3, **disturb** 2.
unsettled, *mod.* **1.** [Undetermined]—*Syn.* undecided, unfixed, unresolved; see **uncertain** 2.
2. [Unstable]—*Syn.* confused, agitated, troubled, changing, explosive, shifting, precarious, ticklish, unpredictable, uneasy, unbalanced, perilous, complex, complicated, fluid, kinetic, active, busy, critical.—*Ant.* simple*, stable, solid.
unshaken, *mod.*—*Syn.* unmoved, unaffected, undaunted; see **firm** 1, **resolute** 2.
unsheathe, *v.*—*Syn.* open, uncover, reveal; see **remove** 1.
unsheltered, *mod.*—*Syn.* unprotected, exposed, uncovered; see **unprepared, unsafe**
unshrinking, *mod.*—*Syn.* fearless, staunch, courageous; see **brave** 1.
unsightly, *mod.*—*Syn.* hideous, deformed, homely; see **repulsive** 1, **ugly** 1.
unskilled, *mod.*—*Syn.* untrained, uneducated, amateur; see **ignorant** 2.
unskillful, *mod.*—*Syn.* maladroit, clumsy, bungling; see **awkward** 1.

unsociable, *mod.* —*Syn.* antagonistic, distant, unsocial; see **unfriendly** 1, 2.

unsolicited, *mod.* 1. [Undesirable]—*Syn.* gratuitous, undesired, unrequested; see **undesirable.**
2. [Free]—*Syn.* volunteered, offered, gratis; see **free** 4.

unsophisticated, *mod.* —*Syn.* ingenuous, innocent, simple; see **inexperienced, naive.**

unsought, *mod.* 1. [Unwanted]—*Syn.* unrequested, unsolicited, unbidden; see **undesirable.**
2. [Free]—*Syn.* volunteered, offered, gratis; see **free** 4.

unsound, *mod.* 1. [False]—*Syn.* ill-founded, erroneous, incongruous; see **false** 2, **illogical.**
2. [Insecure]—*Syn.* unreliable, unbacked, weak; see **unstable** 2.

unsparing, *mod.* 1. [Profuse]—*Syn.* lavish, liberal, plentiful; see **generous** 1, 2.
2. [Severe]—*Syn.* relentless, rigorous, merciless.

unspeakable, *mod.* —*Syn.* horrid, unutterable, abominable, horrible, fearful, inexpressible, unimaginable, dreadful, dire, shocking, appalling, frightful, frightening, alarming, preternatural, beastly, inhuman, calamitous; see also **supernatural.**

unspeakably, *mod.* —*Syn.* greatly, unbelievably, terribly; see **much** 1, 2.

unspecified, *mod.* —*Syn.* general, undefined, indefinite; see **vague** 2.

unspoiled, *mod.* —*Syn.* unblemished, spotless, faultless; see **perfect** 2, **pure** 2.

unspoken, *mod.* —*Syn.* tacit, implicit, inferred; see **implied, understood** 1.

unsportsmanlike, *mod.* —*Syn.* unfair, disgruntled, childish; see **rude** 2.

unstable, *mod.* 1. [Having a high center of gravity] —*Syn.* unsteady, wavering, unbalanced, giddy, wobbly, wiggly, weaving, shifty, precarious, top-heavy, teetering, shifting, uncertain, rattletrap, beetling, jutting, lightly balanced.—*Ant.* firm*, steady, solid.
2. [Easily disturbed]—*Syn.* variable, changeable, giddy, capricious, fluctuating, shifty, volatile, rootless, dizzy, unpredictable, uncertain, sensitive, oversensitive, thin-skinned, timid, delicate.
3. [Subject to fission]—*Syn.* fissionable, fissiparous, fractionable; see **weak** 2.

unstained, *mod.* —*Syn.* spotless, immaculate, virgin, stainless, white, unspotted, maiden, fresh, snowy, clear, pure, unblemished, unsullied, unsoiled, clean, untainted.

unsteady, *mod.* 1. [Wobbly]—*Syn.* wiggly, wavering, shaky, treacherous, unbalanced, top-heavy, leaning, ramshackle, giddy, weaving, heaving, precarious, shifting, teetering, uncertain; see also **irregular** 1.
2. [Inconstant]—*Syn.* changeable, fluctuating, vacillating, erratic, variable, uncertain, unfixed, capricious, volatile, unreliable, tricky, shifty, shaky, jerky, fluttering.

unstinted, *mod.* —*Syn.* abundant, bountiful, profuse; see **plentiful** 1, 2.

unstructured, *mod.* —*Syn.* unorganized, disorganized, unregulated; see **confused** 2, **disorderly** 1.

unstrung, *mod.* —*Syn.* unnerved, nervous, upset; see **weak** 2, 3.

unstuck, *mod.* —*Syn.* unfastened, unglued, rattling; see **loose** 1.

unstudied, *mod.* 1. [Natural]—*Syn.* instinctive, unforced, unaffected; see **spontaneous.**
2. [Unlearned]—*Syn.* unversed, untrained, untaught; see **ignorant** 2, **unaware.**

unsubstantial, *mod.* 1. [Flimsy]—*Syn.* fragile, frail, thin; see **light** 5.
2. [Unreal]—*Syn.* visionary, vaporous, imaginary; see **fantastic, unbelievable.**

unsubstantiated, *mod.* —*Syn.* unconfirmed, unattested, unsupported; see **false** 2.

unsuccessful, *mod.* —*Syn.* defeated, disappointed, frustrated, nonsuited, abortive, aborted, disastrous, unprosperous, unproductive, unfortunate, unlucky, futile, (in) vain, failing, failed, fruitless, worthless, sterile, bootless, unavailing, ineffectual, ineffective, inefficacious, immature, *manqué* (French), useless, foiled, shipwrecked, overwhelmed, overpowered, broken, overborne, ruined, destroyed, thwarted, crossed, disconcerted, dashed, circumvented, premature, inoperative, of no effect, balked, duped; *all* (D): left holding the sack, skunked, stymied, jinxed, out of luck, stuck.—*Ant.* successful*, fortunate, lucky.

unsuitable, *mod.* —*Syn.* inadequate, improper, malapropos, disagreeable, discordant, incongruous, inharmonious, incompatible, clashing, out of place, jarring, dissonant, discrepant, irrelevant, uncalled-for, dissident, inappropriate, inapt, ill-suited, unseemly, conflicting, opposite, contrary, unbecoming, unfitting, unfit, disparate, disturbing, mismatched, unapt, ill-assorted, disproportionate, divergent, mismated, unmated, inapplicable, inconformable, unassimilable, inconsistent, intrusive, infelicitious, amiss, interferring, disagreeing, uncongenial, inept, unbefitting, inapposite, inadmissible, absurd, senseless, unseasonable, unfortunate, ill-timed, unsympathetic, not in keeping, out of joint, at odds, at variance, repugnant; *both* (D): out of kilter, cockeyed.—*Ant.* fit*, suitable, proper.

unsung, *mod.* —*Syn.* slighted, disregarded, unthought of; see **neglected.**

unsure, *mod.* —*Syn.* unreliable, hesitant, doubtful; see **shaky** 1, 2, **uncertain.**

unsurpassed, *mod.* —*Syn.* unexcelled, unequaled, matchless; see **unique** 1, **unprecedented.**

unsuspected, *mod.* 1. [Undisputed]—*Syn.* trusted, uncontested, approved; see **accepted.**
2. [Unknown]—*Syn.* unconceived, unprecedented, improbable; see **unknown** 1, 2.

unsuspecting, *mod.* 1. [Gullible]—*Syn.* undoubting, confiding, credulous; see **trusting** 1.
2. [Naive]—*Syn.* innocent, inexperienced, simple; see **naive.**

unswayed, *mod.* —*Syn.* unbiased, firm, impartial; see **fair** 1, **resolute** 2.

unswerving, *mod.* —*Syn.* solid, straight, unbending; see **direct** 1.

unsymmetrical, *mod.* —*Syn.* unbalanced, unequal, askew; see **irregular** 4.

unsympathetic, *mod.* —*Syn.* unmoved, apathetic, cold; see **indifferent** 1.

unsystematic, *mod.* —*Syn.* irregular, disorderly, chaotic; see **careless** 1, **confused** 2.

untangle, *v.* —*Syn.* clear up, put in order, disentangle; see **order** 3.

untarnished, *mod.* —*Syn.* unblemished, shiny, unspotted; see **clean** 1, **pure** 2.

untaught, *mod.* **1.** [Ignorant]—*Syn.* uneducated, unlearned, unread; see **inexperienced.**
2. [Natural]—*Syn.* artless, instinctive, simple; see **spontaneous.**

untenable, *mod.* —*Syn.* unsupportable, unreasonable, unsound; see **illogical.**

unthinkable, *mod.* **1.** [Impossible]—*Syn.* inconceivable, unimaginable, improbable; see **unlikely.**
2. [Unbelievable]—*Syn.* preposterous, absurd, outlandish; see **unbelievable.**

unthinking, *mod.* **1.** [Thoughtless]—*Syn.* heedless, rude, inconsiderate; see **careless** 1.
2. [Foolish]—*Syn.* impulsive, unwise, vacant; see **rash.**

untidy, *mod.* —*Syn.* slovenly, unkempt, disorderly; see **dirty** 1.

untie, *v.* —*Syn.* unlace, unknot, loosen, unfasten; see **unhitch.**

untied, *mod.* —*Syn.* unfastened, slack, unbound; see **free** 2, 3, **loose** 1.

until, *prep.* —*Syn.* till, to, between the present and, in anticipation of, prior to, during the time preceding, down to, continuously, before the coming of, in expectation of, as far as; see also **unto.**

untimely, *mod.* —*Syn.* unseasonable, awkward, ill-timed, mistimed, inauspicious, badly timed, too early, abortive, too late, unpromising, ill-chosen, improper, unseemly, inappropriate, wrong, unfit, disagreeable, unsuited to the occasion, mistimed, intrusive, badly calculated, inopportune, out-of-date, malapropos, premature, previous (D), unpunctual, unpropitious, unlucky, unfavorable, unfortunate, inexpedient, anachronistic.—*Ant.* early*, timely, seasonable.

untiring, *mod.* —*Syn.* exhaustless, inexhaustible, powerful, unremitting, presevering, strong, unintermitted, continuing, resolute, continued, renewed, unflagging, resistless, firm, unstinted, constant, tenacious, unwearying, durable, unwearied, sedulous, steady, determined, resolute, persistent, patient, dogged, plodding, pertinacious, indefatigable, undeterred, unflinching, unfaltering, unwavering, unswerving, unresting, indomitable, unceasing, staunch, unfailing.—*Ant.* weak*, spasmodic, intermittent.

unto, *prep.* —*Syn.* to, toward, till, until, continguous to, against, up to, next to, beside, in the direction of, to the degree of, to the extreme of.

untold, *mod.* —*Syn.* uncounted, countless, unnumbered, unexpressed, many, innumerable, beyond measure, inexpressible, incalculable, undreamed of, staggering, unimaginable, multitudinous, manifold, multiple.

untouchable, *mod.* —*Syn.* taboo, forbidden, denied; see **illegal, restricted.**

untouched, *mod.* **1.** [Not harmed]—*Syn.* intact, whole, secure, unbroken, in good order, unharmed, in good condition, in a good state of preservation, safe and sound, out of danger, shipshape.
2. [Not contaminated]—*Syn.* virgin, incorrupt, clear, pure, immaculate, unstained, unblemished, spotless, sanitary, asceptic, unsullied, unsoiled, fresh.

untoward, *mod.* **1.** [Annoying]—*Syn.* irritating, vexatious, inimical; see **disturbing.**
2. [Unyielding]—*Syn.* refractory, perverse, unpliable; see **obstinate.**
3. [Improprietous]—*Syn.* unseemly, uncouth, indecorous; see **rude** 1, 2.

untrained, *mod.* —*Syn.* green, new, novice; see **ignorant** 2, **inexperienced.**

untrammeled, *mod.* —*Syn.* unhampered, unrestrained, unfettered; see **free** 2, 3.

untried, *mod.* —*Syn.* untested, uninitiated, new; see **inexperienced.**

untroubled, *mod.* —*Syn.* composed, serene, placid; see **calm** 1, 2.

untrue, *mod.* —*Syn.* false, misleading, specious, lying, hollow, deceptive, delusive, untrustworthy, deceitful, sham, fake, spurious, meretricious, incorrect, prevaricating, dissembling, wrong.

untrustworthy, *mod.* —*Syn.* guileless, conniving, deceitful; see **irresponsible, unreliable** 1, 2.

untruth, *n.* —*Syn.* falsehood, misrepresentation, evasion, lie, prevarication, distortion, deceit, canard, trick, pretense, false appearance, gull, cheat, mistake, dissimulation; *both* (D): spoof, whopper.

untruthful, *mod.* **1.** [Untrue]—*Syn.* unlikely, fake, fraudulent; see **false** 1, 2.
2. [Dishonest]—*Syn.* insincere, crooked, deceitful; see **dishonest** 1, 2.

untruthfully, *mod.* —*Syn.* untruly, dishonestly, treacherously; see **falsely, wrongly** 2.

untutored, *mod.* **1.** [Untaught]—*Syn.* unlearned, uneducated, illiterate; see **ignorant** 2.
2. [Ignorant]—*Syn.* simple, illiterate, unaware; see **naive.**

unused, *mod.* **1.** [Not used]—*Syn.* fresh, virgin, unemployed, unexhausted, remaining, good, available, usable, employable, untouched, brand-new, brank-new (Scottish), pristine.—*Ant.* old*, exhausted, worn-out.
2. [Surplus]—*Syn.* additional, remaining, superfluous; see **extra.**

unusual, *mod.* **1.** [Remarkable]—*Syn.* rare, extraordinary, strange, outstanding, great, uncommon, special, distinguished, prominent, important, noteworthy, awe-inspiring, awesome, unique, fine, unheard of, unexpected, seldom met with, surprising, superior, astonishing, amazing, prodigious, incredible, inconceivable, atypical, conspicous, exceptional, eminent, significant, memorable, renowned, refreshing, singular, fabulous, unprecedented, unparalleled, unexampled, unaccountable, stupendous, unaccustomed, wonderful, notable, superior, marvelous, striking, overpowering, electrifying, dazing, fantastic, startling, astounding, indescribable, appalling, stupefying, ineffable, *sui generis* (Latin), out of sight (D).—*Ant.* common*, familiar, customary.
2. [Different]—*Syn.* unique, extreme, uncommon, particular, exaggerated, distinctive, choice, little-known, out of the ordinary, marked, forward, unconventional, radical, exceptional, peculiar, strange, foreign, unnatural, puzzling, perplexing, confounding, disturbing, novel, advanced, startling, shocking, staggering, uncustomary, breaking

with tradition, infrequent, mysterious, mystifying, surprising, extraordinary, unparalleled, deep, profound, aberrant, singular, unorthodox, uncomfortable, not to be expected, eccentric, unbalanced, unclassifiable, unprecedented, inconsistent, individual, original, refreshing, newfangled, new, modern, recent, late, fresh, curious, unfamiliar, irregular, odd, unaccountable, alien, queer, unwonted, off-the-wall (D), quaint, freakish, bizarre, far-fetched, neurotic, exotic, outlandish, old-fashioned, out of-the-way, abnormal, irrational, monstrous, anomalous, fearful.—*Ant.* common*, ordinary, normal.

unusually, *mod.* **1.** [Not usually]—*Syn.* oddly, curiously, peculiarly; see **especially** 1, **strangely.**
2. [To a marked degree]—*Syn.* extraordinarily, remarkably, surprisingly; see **very.**

unutterable, *mod.*—*Syn.* indescribable, incredible, remarkable; see **impossible** 1, **unbelievable.**

unvarnished, *mod.*—*Syn.* plain, simple, unadorned; see **modest** 2.

unvarying, *mod.*—*Syn.* unchanging, continuing, regular; see **constant** 1.

unveil, *v.*—*Syn.* uncover, reveal, make known; see **expose** 1.

unverified, *mod.*—*Syn.* unproven, unproved, groundless; see **false** 2, **uncertain** 2.

unversed, *mod.*—*Syn.* uneducated, illiterate, unread; see **ignorant** 2, **inexperienced.**

unwanted, *mod.*—*Syn.* undesired, rejected, outcast; see **hated, unpopular.**

unwarlike, *mod.*—*Syn.* peaceful, tranquil, amiable; see **friendly** 1, **pacific.**

unwarned, *mod.*—*Syn.* unanticipative, unadvised, uninformed; see **surprised, unprepared.**

unwarranted, *mod.*—*Syn.* unjust, wrong, groundless; see **unfair** 1.

unwary, *mod.*—*Syn.* unguarded, rash, careless; see **unprepared.**

unwashed, *mod.*—*Syn.* unlaundered, unscoured, dingy, soiled, unlaved, unscrubbed; see also **dirty** 1.

unwavering, *mod.*—*Syn.* consistent, steadfast, resolute; see **regular** 3, **steady** 1.

unwelcome, *mod.*—*Syn.* uninvited, unwished for, repellent; see **undesirable, unpopular.**

unwell, *mod.*—*Syn.* ailing, ill, diseased; see **sick.**

unwholesome, *mod.*—*Syn.* unhealthful, baneful, insalubrious, toxic, poisonous, contaminated, nauseous, destructive, harmful, deleterious, pernicious, unnutritious, noxious, septic, pestilent, contagious, dangerous, lethal, venomous, envenomed, narcotic, virulent, indigestible, tainted, inedible, germ-infested, disease-ridden, rotten, putrescent, putrid, unpalatable, spoiled.—*Ant.* healthful*, wholesome, nutritious.

unwieldy, *mod.*—*Syn.* awkward, clumsy, cumbersome; see **heavy** 1.

unwilling, *mod.*—*Syn.* backward, resistant, reluctant, refractory, recalcitrant, unenthusiastic, doubtful, wayward, unready, indisposed, disinclined, averse, opposed, against, contrary, indifferent, indocile, intractable, demurring, shrinking, flinching, hesitating, shy, slack, evasive, loath, shy of, laggard, malcontent, slow, remiss, grudging, uncooperative, contrary, against the grain.—*Ant.* ready*, willing, eager.

unwillingly, *mod.*—*Syn.* grudgingly, resentfully, involuntarily, protestingly, sulkily, objecting, protesting, complaining, fighting back, under protest, without enthusiasm, with reservations *or* objections *or* complaints *or* animadversions, etc.; with the worst will in the world, kicking and squalling (D); see also **angrily.**

unwind, *v.* **1.** [To undo]—*Syn.* separate, loose, undo; see **unwrap.**
2. [To uncoil]—*Syn.* untwist, unravel, untwine; see **free** 1, **loosen** 2.
3. [To relax]—*Syn.* recline, get rid of one's tensions, calm down; see **rest** 1, 2, **relax.**

unwise, *mod.*—*Syn.* ill-considered, ill-advised, rash; see **stupid** 1.

unwisely, *mod.*—*Syn.* imprudently, inadvisedly, impulsively; see **foolishly, rashly.**

unwitting, *mod.* **1.** [Unconscious]—*Syn.* senseless, numb, comatose; see **unconscious** 1.
2. [Unintentional]—*Syn.* chance, inadvertent, accidental; see **aimless, haphazard** 1.

unwittingly, *mod.*—*Syn.* ignorantly, in ignorance, without knowledge *or* awareness; see **unconsciously.**

unwonted, *mod.* **1.** [Unusual]—*Syn.* uncommon, infrequent, rare; see **unusual** 1, 2.
2. [Uninformed]—*Syn.* unaccustomed, unacquainted, ignorant; see **unfamiliar** 1.

unworldly, *mod.*—*Syn.* spiritual, unearthly, corporeal; see **fantastic, unreal.**

unworthy, *mod.*—*Syn.* undeserving, reprehensible, dishonorable, contemptible, blamable, recreant, disreputable, irreclaimable, unbecoming, unseemly, inexcusable; see also **offensive** 2, **shameful** 2.—*Ant.* worthy*, deserving, laudable.

unwrap, *v.*—*Syn.* untie, undo, unpack, take out of wrappings, unroll, disclose, free, uncover, strip, lay bare, divest, dismantle, uncase, peel, husk, shuck, flay, expose, lay open, unclothe, denude.—*Ant.* wrap*, pack, cover*.

unwritten, *mod.* **1.** [Oral]—*Syn.* unrecorded, vocal, word-of-mouth; see **spoken.**
2. [Traditional]—*Syn.* unsaid, customary, (generally) accepted; see **traditional** 2, **understood** 2.

unwritten law, *n.*—*Syn.* tradition, oral code, (mutual) understanding; see **custom** 2.

unyielding, *mod.*—*Syn.* solid, hard, firm; see **stiff** 1.

unzip, *v.*—*Syn.* unfasten, undo, free; see **open** 3.

up, *mod.* and *prep.* **1.** [Situated above]—*Syn.* at the top of, at the crest of, at the summit of, at the apex of, nearer the top of, nearer the head of, nearer the source of.—*Ant.* down*, nearer the bottom of, farther from the head of.
2. [Moving from the earth]—*Syn.* upward, uphill, skyward, heavenward, away from the center of gravity, perpendicularly, into the air, higher, away from the earth.
3. [Expired]—*Syn.* lapsed, elapsed, run out, terminated, invalid, ended, come to a term, outdated, exhausted, finished, done.—*Ant.* continuing*, current, valid.
4. [Happening]—*Syn.* under consideration, being scrutinized, moot, live, current, pertinent, timely, relevant, pressing, urgent.
5. [Next]—*Syn.* after, in order, prospective; see **following.**

up, *v.* —*Syn.* elevate, raise up, boost; see **increase** 1, **raise** 1.
up against it (D), *mod.* —*Syn.* in trouble, badly off, facing difficulty; see **suffering, troubled.**
up and around (D), *mod.* —*Syn.* improved, improving, getting better; see **better** 3, **well** 1.
up and coming (D), *mod.* —*Syn.* industrious, prospering, alert; see **active** 2, **busy** 1.
upbraid, *v.* —*Syn.* reproach, scold, vituperate, condemn, denounce, lecture, chide, reprehend, admonish, recriminate, reprove, reprimand, castigate, tongue-lash, chastise, rebuke, revile, correct, excoriate, flay, heckle, hiss, damn, flout, deprecate, disparage, asperse, dispraise, censure, reprobate, impugn, blame, disapprove, arraign, oppugn, assail, controvert, give the lie to, expostulate, bring to book, execrate, impeach, stigmatize, brand, calumniate, rake, bark at, decry, clamor against, inveigh against, rake over the coals (D).—*Ant.* praise*, applaud, approve.
upbringing, *n.* —*Syn.* rearing, bringing up, instruction; see **childhood, training.**
upcoming, *mod.* —*Syn.* expected, future, imminent; see **forthcoming.**
update, *v.* —*Syn.* modernize, bring up to date, refresh; see **renew** 1.
up for grabs (D), *mod.* —*Syn.* ready, open to applications, not allocated; see **available, free** 4.
upgrade, *n.* —*Syn.* incline, ascent, slope; see **grade** 1, **rise** 1.
upheaval, *n.* —*Syn.* outburst, explosion, eruption; see **change** 2, **outbreak** 1.
upheld, *mod.* —*Syn.* supported, maintained, advanced; see **backed** 2.
uphill, *mod.* —*Syn.* up, toward the summit, toward the crest, skyward, ascending, climbing.—*Ant.* down*, downhill, descending.
uphold, *v.* **1.** [To hold up]—*Syn.* brace, buttress, prop; see **support** 1.
2. [To maintain]—*Syn.* confirm, sustain, back up; see **support** 2.
upholster, *v.* —*Syn.* pad, stuff, cushion, pillow, bolster, cover, drape, deck, overspread, accouter, overlay, dress.
upholstery, *n.* —*Syn.* padding, stuffing, cushioning, spring-filled cushions, pillows, filling.
up in arms, *mod.* —*Syn.* agitated, alarmed, riotous; see **aroused, excited.**
up in the air (D), *mod.* —*Syn.* undecided, confused, indecisive, uncertain, irresolute, hanging in mid-air (D).
upkeep, *n.* **1.** [Maintenance]—*Syn.* conservation, subsistence, repair; see **maintenance** 1.
2. [Cost of maintenance]—*Syn.* expense(s), outlay, expenditure; see **price.**
upland, *n.* —*Syn.* highland, hill, high ground, moor, peak, mountain, crest, summit, ridge, barrow, hogback, elevation, height, eminence, altitude, plateau, hilltop.
uplift, *n.* **1.** [Social service]—*Syn.* slum clearance, settlement work, rehabilitation, social guidance, slum improvement, social planning, social education, relief work; see also **welfare** 2.
2. [Efforts to improve the lot of mankind]—*Syn.* education, culture, enlightenment, humanitarian effort, social reform, planned economy, the Four Freedoms, social security; see also **improvement** 1.
upon, *mod.* and *prep.* **1.** [On]—*Syn.* on top of, in, attached to, visible on, against, affixed to, above, next to, located at, superimposed, above.
2. [At the time of]—*Syn.* consequent to, beginning with, at the occurrence of; see **simultaneous.**
upper, *mod.* —*Syn.* top, topmost, uppermost, above, higher, more elevated, loftier, overhead. —*Ant.* under*, lower, bottom.
upper-class, *mod.* —*Syn.* highbred, wellborn, genteel; see **noble** 3.
upper hand, *n.* —*Syn.* sway, dominion, superiority; see **advantage** 2.
uppermost, *mod.* —*Syn.* loftiest, topmost, culminating; see **highest.**
upright, *mod.* **1.** [Vertical]—*Syn.* erect, perpendicular, sky-pointing, steep, exalted, elevated, plumb, straight, upward, end up, end on, bolt upright, upended, on end.
2. [Honorable]—*Syn.* ethical, moral, virtuous, exalted, straightforward, correct, circumspect, unimpeachable, punctilious, honest, principled, fair, impartial, incorruptible, aboveboard, high-minded, manly, right.
uprising, *n.* **1.** [Revolt]—*Syn.* rebellion, riot, upheaval; see **revolution** 2.
2. [Slope]—*Syn.* ascent, upgrade, incline; see **hill.**
uproar, *n.* —*Syn.* babble, confusion, turmoil, clamor, ado, disturbance, *brouhaha,* tumult, din, racket, clatter, hubbub, fracas, hassle, clangor, jangle, bustle, commotion, strife of tongues, bickering, discord, row.
uproarious, *mod.* —*Syn.* noisy, confused, disorderly; see **loud** 2.
uproot, *v.* —*Syn.* eradicate, extract, remove, tear up by the roots, excavate, pull up, weed out, rip up.
ups and downs (D), *n.* —*Syn.* troubles, complications, uncertainties; see **difficulty** 1, 2.
upset, *mod.* —*Syn.* disconcerted, amazed, shocked; see **confused** 2, **unsettled.**
upset, *n.* —*Syn.* overthrow, destruction, reversion; see **defeat** 2, **subversion.**
upset, *v.* **1.** [To turn over]—*Syn.* overturn, upturn, subvert, turn bottom-side up, turn inside out, upend, reverse, keel over, overset, topple, tip over, turn topsy-turvy, overbalance, invert, *renverser* (French), capsize, tilt, pitch over, overthrow. —*Ant.* stand*, erect, elevate.
2. [To disturb]—*Syn.* agitate, fluster, perturb; see **bother** 2.
3. [To beat]—*Syn.* conquer, outplay, overpower; see **defeat** 1, 2, 3.
upshot, *n.* —*Syn.* conclusion, end, outcome; see **result.**
upside-down, *mod.* —*Syn.* topsy-turvy, tangled, bottom-side up, inverted, rear-end foremost, backward, the wrong way, wrong-side uppermost, *patas arriba* (Spanish); *all* (D): cart-before-the-horse, heels-over-apple-cart, heels-over-head.—*Ant.* upright*, right-side up, steady.
upstage (D), *v.* —*Syn.* draw attention from, mistreat, impose (upon); see **detract, distract.**
upstairs, *mod.* —*Syn.* in the upper story, overhead, above, up the steps; see also **upper.**

upstairs, *n.* —*Syn.* the upper story, the penthouse, the sleeping apartments, the rooms above the ground floor; see also **attic, floor** 2.

upstanding, *mod.* —*Syn.* honorable, upright, straightforward; see **honest** 1.

upstart, *n.* —*Syn.* parvenu, snob, pretender, new rich, status seeker, adventurer, opportunist, *nouveau riche, bourgeois gentilhomme* (*both* French), *or* would-be gentleman, newly rich, bourgeois, social climber, Johnny-come-lately (D).

upswing, *n.* —*Syn.* growth, boom, acceleration; see **improvement, increase** 1.

up tight (D), *mod.* **1.** [Troubled]—*Syn.* worried, concerned, apprehensive; see **troubled** 1.

2. [Cautious]—*Syn.* conventional, strict, old-fashioned; see **conservative.**

up to, *prep.* **1.** [Until]—*Syn.* before, preceding, previous; see **until.**

2. [Against]—*Syn.* contrary to, opposing, in disagreement with; see **against** 3.

3. [Dependent upon]—*Syn.* assigned to, expected of, enjoined upon, delegated to.

up-to-date, *mod.* —*Syn.* in vogue, alamode, *à la mode* (French), in fashion, up-to-the-minute, fashionable, conventional, stylish, modern, modernistic, streamlined, popular, faddish, brandnew, current, according to the prevailing taste, modish, *moderne* (French); *all* (D): the latest, trendy, in, today, with it, all the rage, styled to the minute.

up to one's ears (*or* **neck**) **in** *or* **with** (D), *mod.* —*Syn.* occupied, busy (with), absorbed (in); see **busy** 1.

uptown, *mod.* —*Syn.* in the upper parts of town, central, midtown, metropolitan, urban.

upturn, *n.* —*Syn.* upswing, upsurge, recuperation; see **improvement** 1, **recovery** 1.

upturned, *mod.* —*Syn.* tilted, tipped, upside-down, inclined, sloped, slanted, expectant, upward looking, turned up, extended; see also **oblique.**—*Ant.* bent*, pensive, downcast.

upward, *mod.* —*Syn.* up, higher, skyward, in the air, uphill, away from the earth, up the slope, on an incline, up north (D).

up with, *mod.* —*Syn.* even with, up to, equal to; see **equal.**

urban, *mod.* **1.** [Concerning city government] —*Syn.* city, metropolitan, civil; see **municipal, public** 2.

2. [Concerning city living]—*Syn.* (big) city, civic, municipal, metropolitan, megalopolitan, within the city limits, inner-city, central-city, downtown, zoned, planned, business-district, civil, nonrural, ghetto, shopping, residential, apartment-dwelling, oppidan.

urbane, *mod.* —*Syn.* suave, mannerly, courteous; see **cultured, polite** 1.

urbanity, *n.* **1.** [Courtesy]—*Syn.* civility, refinement, polish; see **courtesy** 1.

2. [Civilities]—*Syn.* amenities, decorum, courtesies; see **culture** 3, **sophistication.**

urban renewal, *n.* —*Syn.* rebuilding the inner city, modernization, bringing up to date; see **improvement** 1, 2.

urchin, *n.* —*Syn.* youngster, rogue, waif; see **child.**

urge, *v.* **1.** [To present favorably]—*Syn.* favor, further, support, speak for, propose, plead for, advance, rationalize, aid, recommend, endorse, ratify, confirm, promote, sanction, approve, commend, countenance.—*Ant.* discourage, prohibit, impede.

2. [To induce]—*Syn.* charge, beg, plead, adjure, influence, beseech, implore, ask, command, entreat, desire, request, press, inveigle, talk into, incite, move, allure, tempt, attract, influence, prompt, instigate, exhort, advise, solicit, inspire, stimulate, conjure, coax, wheedle, maneuver, draw, put up to, prevail upon.—*Ant.* restrain*, deter, discourage.

3. [To drive]—*Syn.* compel, drive, propel, impel, force, coerce, constrain, press, push, make, oblige, goad, prod, spur.—*Ant.* deny*, block, withhold.

urged, *mod.* **1.** [Supported]—*Syn.* favored, furthered, proposed, plead, advanced, aided, recommended, endorsed, ratified, confirmed, promoted, sanctioned, espoused, adopted, approved, commended, countenanced, praised; *both* (D): pushed, boosted; see also **backed** 2.—*Ant.* opposed*, prohibited, condemned.

2. [Pressed]—*Syn.* begged, charged, adjured, besought, implored, asked, commanded, entreated, desired, requested, inveigled, talked into, incited, moved, motivated, allured, lured, tempted, seduced, attracted, influenced, prompted, instigated, exhorted, advised, solicited, inspired, whipped up, stimulated, coaxed, wheedled, maneuvered, put up to, prevailed upon, compelled, obliged, propelled, driven, induced, impelled, coerced, forced, constrained.

urgency, *n.* —*Syn.* exigency, need, seriousness; see **importance** 1, **necessity** 3.

urgent, *mod.* **1.** [Of immediate importance]—*Syn.* pressing, critical, necessary, imperative, important, compelling, indispensable, momentous, wanted, required, called for, demanded, salient, chief, paramount, essential, primary, vital, principal, absorbing, all-absorbing, not to be delayed, crucial, instant, leading, capital, overruling, foremost, exigent, crying.—*Ant.* trivial*, irrelevant, untimely.

2. [Insistent]—*Syn.* compelling, hortatory, persuasive, imperious, solemn, grave, weighty, impressive, earnest, importunate, clamorous, hasty, breathless, precipitate, frantic, impetuous, imperative, convincing, beseeching, seductive, commanding, imploring, eager, zealous, anxious, moving, excited, impulsive, vigorous, enthusiastic, overpowering, masterful; see also **resolute** 2.—*Ant.* apologetic*, hesitant, diffident.

urgently, *mod.* **1.** [Critically]—*Syn.* pressingly, instantly, imperatively, necessarily, indispensably, momently, requisitely, essentially, primarily, crucially, capitally, exigently.

2. [Insistently]—*Syn.* compellingly, persuasively, imperiously, solemnly, gravely, weightily, impressively, earnestly, importunately, clamorously, hastily, breathlessly, precipitately, frantically, impetuously, convincingly, beseechingly, seductively, commandingly, imploringly, eagerly, anxious, zealously, movingly, emotionally, excitedly, impulsively, vigorously, irresistibly, enthusiastically, overpoweringly, masterfully, magisterially, compulsively.

urging, *n.* —*Syn.* begging, persuading, pleading, beseeching, imploring, inspiring, coaxing, wheedling, inducing, nagging, driving, insistence, stimulating; see also **persuasion** 1.

urinate, *v.* —*Syn.* go to the restroom *or* bathroom, have to go, micturate, excrete, use the urinal *or* bedpan, make water; *all* (D): tinkle, wizz, peepee, go to the little boy's room, take *or* have a leak, see a man about a horse.

urn, *n.* —*Syn.* vessel, jar, amphora, pot, container, cinerary *or* funerary urn.

usable, *mod.* —*Syn.* available, utilizable, employable, at hand, useful, unused, good, serviceable, applicable, ready, subservient, helpful, utile, valuable, beneficial, profitable, advantageous, fit, desirable, efficacious, instrumental, fitting, conformable, suitable, practicable, proper, practical, convenient.—*Ant.* useless*, worthless, no good.

usage, *n.* **1.** [Custom]—*Syn.* practice, wont, rule, habit, habiture, convention, way, method, mode, routine, rote, formula, acceptance, regulation, currency.

2. [Accepted language]—*Syn.* good usage, grammatical usage, approved diction; see **grammar, language** 2.

use, *n.* **1.** [The act of using]—*Syn.* practice, employment, application, usage, appliance, effecting, manner, adoption, utilization, manipulation, bringing to bear, management, handling, performance, conduct, recourse, resort, exercise, treatment, method, technique, control, resolution, realization, association.—*Ant.* neglect*, disuse, dismissal.

2. [The state of being useful]—*Syn.* utility, usefulness, usability, employment, application, value, advantage, excellence, helpfulness, convenience, suitability, expedience, aid, serviceability, merit, profit, practicability, practicality, stead, fitness, subservience, effectiveness, applicability.

use, *v.* **1.** [To make use of]—*Syn.* avail oneself of, employ, put to use, exercise, exert, put forth, utilize, apply, bring to bear, practice, play on, do with, draw on, adopt, take advantage of, make do, accept, work, put in practice, relate, make with, put to work, make shift with.—*Ant.* discard*, reject, refuse*.

2. [To make a practice of; *now used principally in the past tense*]—*Syn.* be accustomed to, practice, adapt, conform, habituate, regulate, suit, familiarize, attune.

3. [To behave toward]—*Syn.* deal with, handle, bear oneself toward; see **manage** 1.

used, *mod.* **1.** [Employed]—*Syn.* put to use, utilized, applied, adopted, adapted, accepted, put in service, practiced, turned to account.—*Ant.* discarded*, rejected, unused.

2. [Accustomed]—*Syn.* practiced, customary, suited; see **habitual** 1.

3. [Secondhand]—*Syn.* castoff, depreciated, repossessed; see **old** 2, **worn** 2.

useful, *mod.* —*Syn.* valuable, beneficial, serviceable; see **helpful** 1.

usefulness, *n.* —*Syn.* application, value, advantage, excellence, convenience, suitability, range, versatility, helpfulness, utility, usability, serviceability, merit, profitableness, practicality, practicability, fitness, propriety, adaptability; see also **use** 2.

useless, *mod.* **1.** [Unserviceable]—*Syn.* worthless, unusable, inutile, ineffectual, expendable, incompetent, of no use, ineffective, inoperative, dysfunctional, counterproductive, inefficient, unprofitable, no damn good (D).—*Ant.* efficient*, usable, operative.

2. [Futile]—*Syn.* vain, unavailing, fruitless; see **hopeless** 2.

use up, *v.* —*Syn.* consume, exhaust, squander; see **spend** 1, **waste** 1, 2.

usher, *n.* —*Syn.* conductor, guide, escort, doorman, cicerone, herald, leader, precursor, page, footboy, flunkey.

usher, *v.* —*Syn.* show in, show out, escort, receive, show around; see also **lead** 1.

ushered, *mod.* —*Syn.* escorted, led, guided, supervised, conducted, shown, attended, preceded, introduced, announced, presented, squired, heralded, directed, advanced, sponsored, brought forward.

using, *mod.* —*Syn.* employing, utilizing, applying, adopting, taking advantage of, accepting, working, practicing, manipulating, controlling, putting in service, trying out, testing, proving, wearing out.

usual, *mod.* **1.** [Ordinary]—*Syn.* general, frequent, normal; see **common** 1.

2. [Habitual]—*Syn.* wonted, accustomed, customary; see **conventional** 1.

usually, *mod.* —*Syn.* ordinarily, customarily, habitually; see **regularly** 1, 2.

usurp, *v.* —*Syn.* assume, appropriate, lay hold of; see **seize** 2.

usurpation, *n.* —*Syn.* seizure, encroachment, deposal; see **capture.**

usury, *n.* —*Syn.* robbery, exploitation, stealing; see **theft.**

utensils, *n.* [Implements; *especially for the kitchen*]—*Syn.* equipment, tools, appliances, conveniences, ware(s); see also **tool** 1.

Kitchen utensils include the following—sieve, egg beater, knife, fork, spoon, measuring cup, grater, spatula, pancake turner, can opener, egg slicer, meat grinder, butcher knife, paring knife, pastry cutter, lemon squeezer, knife sharpener, coffee grinder, blender, food processor, vegetable brush, pan scourer, frying pan, saucepan, cake pan, pie pan, roaster, bottle brush, dishpan, draining pan, sink strainer, dishmop, mixing bowl, pan lid, rolling pin, pastry board, coffee pot, bread pan, cookie sheet.

utilitarian, *mod.* —*Syn.* practical, useful, functional; see **profitable.**

utilities, *n.* —*Syn.* services, public utilities, conveniences, current necessities of modern life, household slaves.

Utilities include the following—heat, light, power, gas, water, bus, street car, telephone, electricity, garbage disposal, sewage disposal.

utility, *n.* **1.** [Usefulness]—*Syn.* use, service, advantage, convenience, benefit, serviceableness, expediency, avail, profit, favor, efficacy, efficiency, adequacy, productiveness.

2. [Utility company]—*Syn.* gas company, electricity company, water company; see **business** 4, **monopoly.**

utilize, *v.* —*Syn.* employ, appropriate, turn to account; see **use** 1.

utmost, *mod.* **1.** [Greatest]—*Syn.* ultimate, chief, entire, whole, full, unreserved, complete, unstinted, total, absolute, unlimited, unsparing, thorough, exhaustive, highest, maximum, most, top, plenary, undiminished, undivided, thoroughgoing, unmitigated, sheer, unqualified, unconditional, all-out (D).
2. [Last]—*Syn.* farthest, final, last; see **last** 1.

utopia, *n.* —*Syn.* imaginary *or* ideal place, wonderland, paradise, land of milk and honey (D); see also **heaven** 2.
Some famous utopias include the following—(the garden of) Eden, the Celestial *or* Heavenly City, Land of Beulah, the New Jerusalem, the Promised Land, (new) Canaan, Goshen, Shangri-La, (New) Atlantis, Arcadia, Happy Valley, Land of Prester John, Kingdom of Micomicon, Laputa, Cockaigne, Erewhon, Camelot, Oz, Brook Farm.

utopian, *mod.* —*Syn.* idealistic, ideological, quixotic; see **hopeful** 1, **visionary** 1.

utopian, *n.* —*Syn.* visionary, utopist, romanticist; see **idealist.**

utter, *mod.* —*Syn.* complete, total, thorough; see **absolute** 1.

utter, *v.* —*Syn.* pronounce, talk, express, come out with, articulate, voice, whisper, mutter, shout, exclaim, enunciate, air, speak, tell, declaim, phonate, disclose, declare, say, assert, affirm, asseverate, ejaculate, vocalize, proclaim, give tongue to, recite, blurt (out), let fall, announce, come out with (D).

utterance, *n.* —*Syn.* declaration, saying, phonation, assertion, announcement, pronouncement, ejaculation, vociferation, talk, speech, query, expression, sentence, declamation, statement, proclamation, recitation, asseveration, spiel, rant, jargon, response, reply, oration, peroration, set speech, delivered opinion.

uttered, *mod.* **1.** [Spoken]—*Syn.* declared, pronounced, affirmed, asserted, expressed, announced, articulated, proclaimed, declaimed, voiced, shouted, recited, rehearsed; see also **oral.** —*Ant.* withheld*, suppressed, choked in.
2. [Given forth]—*Syn.* issued, released, emitted, dispersed, broadcast, sown, delivered, propagated, given currency, circulated, disseminated, diffused, divulged, disclosed; see also **announced.**—*Ant.* withheld*, withdrawn, banned.

utterly, *mod.* —*Syn.* wholly, thoroughly, entirely; see **completely.**

uttermost, *mod.* —*Syn.* farthest, remotest, final; see **furthest, utmost** 1.

V

vacancy, *n.* **1.** [A vacated position]—*Syn.* opening, vacated post, post without an incumbent, unfilled position, unheld office, job (D).
2. [(D) A vacated residence]—*Syn.* empty house *or* room *or* apartment, lodging, quarters, tenantless house, uninhabited house, vacant house, unoccupied house, deserted house, house for rent *or* for sale.

vacant, *mod.* **1.** [Without contents]—*Syn.* devoid, void, unfilled; see **empty** 1.
2. [Without an occupant]—*Syn.* unoccupied, untenanted, tenantless, uninhabited, idle, free, deserted, abandoned, without a resident, not lived in.—*Ant.* inhabited*, occupied, tenanted.
3. [Without evidence of intelligence]—*Syn.* unintelligent, vacuous, empty-headed, foolish, giddy, inane, stupid, silly, witless, thoughtless.—*Ant.* intelligent*, witty, understanding.

vacate, *v.* **1.** [To abandon]—*Syn.* give up, quit, renounce; see **abandon** 1.
2. [To leave a residence]—*Syn.* go away, relinquish, depart; see **leave** 1.

vacation, *n.*—*Syn.* respite, rest, recreation time, intermission, recess, nonterm, holiday, leave of absence, sabbatical, time off (D).

vacationist, *n.*—*Syn.* vacationer, tourist, sightseer; see **traveler.**

vaccinate, *v.*—*Syn.* inoculate, immunize, prevent, treat, mitigate, protect, inject, shoot (D).

vaccinated, *mod.*—*Syn.* immunized, inoculated, given (hypodermic) injections, given mouth vaccine, exempted; see also **protected.**

vaccination, *n.* **1.** [The act of administering vaccine]—*Syn.* injection, hypodermic, inoculation, pricking, scratching, scarifying, spraying; *both* (D): a shot, shots; see also **treatment** 2.
2. [A result of vaccination, sense 1]—*Syn.* protection, immunization, inoculation, exemption, prevention, mitigation; see also **immunity** 2.

vacillate, *v.* **1.** [To totter]—*Syn.* waver, sway, stagger; see **reel, totter** 2.
2. [To hesitate]—*Syn.* fluctuate, dawdle, falter; see **hesitate, pause.**

vacillating, *mod.*—*Syn.* changeable, uncertain, unreliable, fickle, inconstant, unstable, mutable, fitful, irresolute, unsettled, unsteady, capricious, shifting, volatile.—*Ant.* constant*, steady, unchanging.

vacillation, *n.* **1.** [Swaying]—*Syn.* vibration, swing, fluctuation; see **sway** 1, **wave** 2.
2. [Indecision]—*Syn.* irresolution, indecision, inconstancy; see **doubt** 2, **uncertainty** 2.

vacuity, *n.* **1.** [Emptiness]—*Syn.* vacancy, nothingness, void; see **emptiness, vacuum.**
2. [Inanity]—*Syn.* nihility, disinterest, disregard; see **stupidity** 1, 2, 3.

vacuous, *mod.* **1.** [Empty]—*Syn.* void, emptied, drained; see **depleted, empty** 1.
2. [Dumb]—*Syn.* inane, blank, unreasoning; see **dull** 3, 4.

vacuum, *n.*—*Syn.* emptiness, rarefaction, void, vacuity, space, exhaustion.

vacuum cleaner, *n.*—*Syn.* vacuum (sweeper), carpet sweeper, cleaning device; see **appliance.**

vagabond, *mod.*—*Syn.* nomadic, migratory, footloose (and fancy free), wandering, roving, drifting, roaming, errant, rambling, stray, straggling, transient, tramping, moving, itinerant, peripatetic, shifting; see also **aimless, traveling** 2.

vagabond, *n.*—*Syn.* vagrant, gypsy, rover; see **tramp** 1, **traveler.**

vagary, *n.*—*Syn.* notion, caprice, whimsy; see **fancy** 3, **impulse** 2.

vagrancy, *n.*—*Syn.* itinerancy, roving, vagabondage; see **travel** 1.

vagrant, *mod.* **1.** [Having no home]—*Syn.* roaming, itinerant, nomadic; see **traveling** 2, **wandering** 1.
2. [Having no occupation]—*Syn.* begging, idling, profligate, prodigal, loafing, beachcombing, mendicant; *all* (D): panhandling, bumming, mooching.
3. [Having no fixed course]—*Syn.* wayward, capricious, erratic; see **aimless, wandering** 1.

vagrant, *n.*—*Syn.* begger, idler, loafer; see **rascal, tramp** 1.

vague, *mod.* **1.** [Not clearly expressed]—*Syn.* indefinite, unintelligible, superficial; see **obscure** 1.
2. [Not clearly understood]—*Syn.* uncertain, undetermined, unsure, doubtful, dubious, questionable, misunderstood, enigmatic, nebulous, puzzling, inexplicable, unsettled, bewildering, perplexing, problematic.—*Ant.* certain*, sure, positive.
3. [Not clearly visible]—*Syn.* dim, nebulous, dark; see **hazy** 1.

vaguely, *mod.*—*Syn.* uncertainly, unclearly, not clearly *or* certainly *or* reliably, mistily, hazily, foggily, confusedly, shiftily, unreliably, dubiously, eccentrically, unsurely, illegally, evasively, miscellaneously, unpredictably, without (clear) outlines, incapable of being fixed *or* determined *or* outlined *or* pinned down (D); see also **indefinitely** 1, **obscurely.**

vagueness, *n.*—*Syn.* ambiguity, obscurity, double entendre; see **confusion** 2, **uncertainty** 1, 2.

vain, *mod.* **1.** [Possessing unwarranted self-esteem]—*Syn.* proud, arrogant, haughty; see **egotistic** 2.
2. [Trivial]—*Syn.* frivolous, petty, insignificant; see **trivial, unimportant.**

3. [Useless]—*Syn.* worthless, unavailing, profitless; see **futile** 1, **useless** 1.

vainglorious, *mod.* —*Syn.* vain, proud, pompous; see **egotistic** 2.

vainly, *mod.* —*Syn.* in vain, uselessly, unnecessarily, fruitlessly, purposelessly, needlessly, unprofitably, bootlessly, futilely, to no purpose *or* avail, abortively; see also **hopelessly** 1, 2.

vale, *n.* —*Syn.* dell, glen, dale; see **valley.**

valediction, *n.* —*Syn.* send-off, good-by, farewell; see **departure** 1.

valedictorian, *n.* —*Syn.* first speaker, (best) student, principal speaker; see **scholar** 2, **speaker** 2.

valedictory, *mod.* —*Syn.* final, parting, terminal; see **last** 1.

valentine, *n.* —*Syn.* sentimental letter, Valentine's Day missive, St. Valentine's Day greeting, love verse; see also **card, letter** 2.

valet, *n.* —*Syn.* manservant, *valet de chambre* (French), body servant, attendant, gentleman's gentleman; see also **servant.**

valiant, *mod.* **1.** [Having a character notable for valor]—*Syn.* brave, courageous, unafraid, dauntless, valorous, undismayed, intrepid, steadfast, powerful, puissant, vigorous, stout-spirited, high-spirited, plucky, assertive, manful, manly, lion-hearted, mettlesome, aweless, undaunted, unflinching, unshrinking, self-reliant, strong-willed, indomitable, fearless, venturous, adventurous. —*Ant.* cowardly*, fearful, shy.

2. [Performed with valor]—*Syn.* heroic, great, grand, gallant, valorous, chivalrous, audacious, venturesome, noble, magnanimous, magnificent. —*Ant.* ineffective*, feeble, contemptible.

valiantly, *mod.* —*Syn.* courageously, boldly, fearlessly; see **bravely.**

valid, *mod.* **1.** [Capable of proof]—*Syn.* sound, cogent, logical, conclusive, solid, well-grounded, well-founded, tested, accurate, convincing, telling, correct, determinative, compelling, persuasive, potent, stringent, strong, ultimate, unanswerable, irrefutable.—*Ant.* wrong*, erring, misleading.

2. [Genuine]—*Syn.* true, original, factual, real, actual, pure, uncorrupted, authentic, confirmed, authoritative, trustworthy, credible, attested, efficient, efficacious, legitimate, adequate, substantial, proved *or* proven, unalloyed, unadulterated. —*Ant.* false*, fictitious, counterfeit.

validate, *v.* —*Syn.* confirm, sanction, legalize; see **approve** 1, **endorse** 1.

validity, *n.* —*Syn.* soundness, efficacy, gravity; see **originality.**

valise, *n.* —*Syn.* suitcase, grip, haversack; see **bag, baggage.**

valley, *n.* —*Syn.* vale, glen, canyon, swale, depression, hollow, trough, notch, channel, lowland, river valley, stream valley, plain, dell, *cym, col* (*both* Welsh), valley floor, coulee, dale, river bottom; see also **gap** 3, **ravine.**—*Ant.* mountain*, ridge, hilltop.

valor, *n.* —*Syn.* bravery, courage, prowess, intrepidity, boldness, gallantry, heroism, fearlessness, valiancy, chivalry, defiance, derring-do, dash, manliness, spirit, determination, hardihood, firmness; *all* (D): pluck, backbone, fight, (cast-iron) guts, grit, sand, intestinal fortitude.—*Ant.* cowardice*, fear, cowardliness.

valorous, *mod.* —*Syn.* fearless, intrepid, courageous; see **brave** 1, **chivalrous, manly.**

valuable, *mod.* **1.** [Worth money]—*Syn.* saleable, marketable, in demand, high-priced, commanding a good price, precious, costly, expensive, priceless, dear, of value, in great demand, hardly obtainable, scarce, without price, good as gold (D).—*Ant.* cheap*, unsaleable, unmarketable.

2. [Helpful]—*Syn.* important, estimable, worthy; see **helpful** 1, **relevant.**

valuation, *n.* —*Syn.* cost, appraisal, judgment; see **estimate** 1.

value, *n.* **1.** [Monetary value]—*Syn.* price, expense, cost, profit, value in exchange, equivalent, rate, amount, market price, charge, face value, assessment, appraisal.

2. [The quality of being desirable]—*Syn.* use, usefulness, utility, benefit, advantage, esteem, estimation, desirability, preference, exchangeability, marketability.

3. [Quality]—*Syn.* worth, merit, significance, consequence, goodness, condition, state, excellence, distinction, desirability, grade, finish, perfection, eminence, superiority, advantage, power, regard, importance, mark, caliber, repute.

4. [Precise signification]—*Syn.* significance, force, meaning, drift, import, sense, purpose, bearing, denotation, interpretation, implication, substance, content, connotation.

value, *v.* **1.** [To believe to be valuable]—*Syn.* esteem, prize, appreciate; see **admire** 1, **consider** 1.

2. [To set a price upon]—*Syn.* estimate, reckon, assess, appraise, fix the price of, place a value on, assay, rate, figure, compute, evaluate, judge, repute, consider, enumerate, account, charge, levy, ascertain, price.

3. [To estimate]—*Syn.* evaluate, assess, appraise; see **estimate** 1, **reckon.**

valued, *mod.* **1.** [Priced]—*Syn.* evaluated, appraised, charged; see **marked** 2.

2. [Valuable]—*Syn.* prized, treasured, esteemed; see **valuable** 1.

valueless, *mod.* —*Syn.* useless, worthless, of no value, disesteemed, unserviceable, unsaleable, not in demand.

valve, *n.* —*Syn.* flap, lid, plug; see also **device** 1, **pipe** 1.

Valves include the following—automatic, alarm, check, cutoff, side, overhead, dry-pipe, gate, lift, piston, rocking, safety, slide, throttle, sleeve, intake, exhaust, butterfly.

vamp, *v.* **1.** [To repair]—*Syn.* fix, mend, patch; see **repair.**

2. [To seduce, expecially a man]—*Syn.* make love to, beguile, attract; see **court** 1, **seduce.**

vampire, *n.* **1.** [Usurer]—*Syn.* blackmailer, thief, extortionist; see **criminal.**

2. [Flirt]—*Syn.* vamp, temptress, coquette; see **flirt.**

3. [Monster]—*Syn.* werewolf, man-beast, bloodsucker (D); see **freak** 2, **monster** 1.

van, *n.* —*Syn.* truck, small truck, delivery truck, trailer, recreational vehicle (RV), lorry (British), camper (D).

vandal, *n.* —*Syn.* despoiler, rapist, thief; see **destroyer** 1, **pirate.**

vandalism, *n.* —*Syn.* piracy, demolition, spoliation; see **destruction** 1.
vane, *n.* —*Syn.* weather vane, weathercock, wind gauge; see **device** 1.
vanguard, *n.* —*Syn.* advance guard, van, forerunners, precursors, leaders, spearhead, front, forefront, front rank, avant-garde.
vanilla, *n.* —*Syn.* vanilla extract, *Vanilla planifolia* (Latin), wild vanilla; see **flavouring.**
vanish, *v.* —*Syn.* fade (out), go away, dissolve; see **disappear.**
vanished, *mod.* —*Syn.* gone, disappeared, dissolved, faded, burned out, swallowed in the crowd (D).
vanishing, *mod.* —*Syn.* disappearing, going, fading; see **evanescent, hazy** 1.
vanity, *n.* **1.** [Personal conceit]—*Syn.* ostentation, display, show, self-love, narcissism, self-laudation, self-glorification, self-applause, pretension, vainglory, conceitedness, affection, coxcombery, foppishness, complacency, smugness.—*Ant.* modesty*, diffidence, bashfulness.
2. [Futility]—*Syn.* idleness, emptiness, uselessness; see **futility.**
3. [A toilet case]—*Syn.* vanity box, vanity roll, compact, double compact, toilet kit, powder case, make-up case.
vanity case, *n.* —*Syn.* vanity box, make-up case, toilet kit; see **compact, vanity** 3.
vanquish, *v.* —*Syn.* conquer, overcome, subdue; see **defeat** 1, 2, 3.
vanquisher, *n.* —*Syn.* conqueror, tyrant, subduer; see **victor, winner.**
vantage ground, *n.* —*Syn.* control, good position, front rank; see **influence** 2, **power** 2.
vapid, *mod.* —*Syn.* flat, insipid, boring; see **dull** 3, 4, **uninteresting.**
vapor, *n.* —*Syn.* mist, steam, condensation, smog, exhalation, breath, fog, gas, haze, smoke.
vaporization, *n.* —*Syn.* condensation, sublimation, atomization; see **evaporation.**
vaporize, *v.* —*Syn.* exhale, sublimate, volatize; see **evaporate** 1.
vaporous, *mod.* **1.** [Foggy]—*Syn.* smoggy, aerial, vapory; see **haze** 1, **misty.**
2. [Fanciful]—*Syn.* fleeting, wispy, unsubstantial; see **imaginary.**
vapors, *n.* —*Syn.* melancholy, despair, blues (D); see **depression** 2.
vapor trail, *n.* —*Syn.* contrail, wake, condensation trail; see **track** 2.
variable, *mod.* —*Syn.* inconstant, fickle, mutable, shifting, unsteady, fitful; see also **changeable** 2.
variance, *n.* —*Syn.* change, fluctuations, deviation, modification, oscillation, mutation, variety, diversity, incongruity, disagreement; see also **variation.** —*Ant.* agreement*, unity, sameness.
variant, *mod.* —*Syn.* varying, exceptional, differing; see **irregular** 1, **various.**
variant, *n.* —*Syn.* different version *or* evidence, modification, result of (normal *or* abnormal) variation, exceptional instance *or* example, irregularity; see also **exception** 2.
variation, *n.* **1.** [Change]—*Syn.* modification, alteration, mutation, diversification, deviation, shift, fluctuation, deflection, aberration, departure, variety, adaptation, curve, bend, turn, divergence, veer, digression, swerve, displacement, warping; see also **change** 1.—*Ant.* stability*, fixity, unchangeableness.
2. [Disparity]—*Syn.* inequality, difference, dissimilarity, dissimilitude, distinction, disproportion, exception, contrast, contradistinction, unconformity, irregularity, aberration, abnormality, disparity. —*Ant.* similarity*, conformity, likeness.
varied, *mod.* —*Syn.* discrete, separate, diverse; see **different** 1, 2, **mixed** 1, **various.**
variegate, *v.* —*Syn.* diversify, spatter, mottle; see **color** 1, 2.
variegated, *mod.* —*Syn.* mottled, kaleidoscopic, varicolored; see **bright** 2, **various.**
variegation, *n.* —*Syn.* diversity of color, spectrum, rainbow; see **color** 1, 2.
variety, *n.* **1.** [Quality or state of being diverse] —*Syn.* diversity, change, diversification, difference, variance, medley, mixture, mélange, potpourri, miscellany, disparateness, divergency, variation, incongruity, fluctuation, shift, change, modification, departure, heterogeneity, many-sidedness, unlikeness.
2. [Sort]—*Syn.* kind, class, division, species, genus, race, tribe, family, assortment, type, stripe, nature, kidney, ilk, character, description, rank, grade, category, classification, quality.—*Ant.* equality*, equalness, similarity.
various, *mod.* —*Syn.* different, disparate, dissimilar, diverse, diversified, diversiform, variegated, varicolored, many-sided, several, manifold, numerous, unlike, many, sundry, divers, variable, changeable, inconstant, uncertain, of any kind, all manner of, of every description, distinct; see also **multiple** 1. —*Ant.* alike*, undiversified, identical.
variously, *mod.* —*Syn.* varyingly, inconsistently, unpredictably; see **differently** 1, **unevenly.**
varlet, *n.* **1.** [An attendant]—*Syn.* aid, slave, helper; see **servant.**
2. [A scoundrel]—*Syn.* cad, knave, blackguard; see **rascal.**
varnish, *n.* Colors of varnish include the following —light oak, dark oak, golden oak, mahogany, walnut, japan black, lacquer red, gold-rust, lacquer, silver wire laquer, sheet-gold lacquer, green lacquer, brown lacquer, cream lacquer; see also **coat** 3, **cover** 2, **enamel, finish** 1.
varnish, *v.* —*Syn.* finish, paint, shellac, lacquer, wax, size, enamel, japan, surface, coat, luster, polish, gloss, adorn, refinish, glaze, gloss over.—*Ant.* expose*, remove the finish, give a natural finish.
vary, *v.* **1.** [To show changes]—*Syn.* dissent, diverge, differ, deviate, digress, swerve, depart, fluctuate, alternate, diverge *or* divaricate from, be distinguished from, range, be inconstant, mutate, be uncertain.—*Ant.* remain*, be steady, hold.
2. [To make changes]—*Syn.* convert, modify, displace; see **change** 1.
varying, *mod.* —*Syn.* diverse, differing, diverging; see **changing, different** 1.
vase, *n.* —*Syn.* vessel, urn, jar, pottery, porcelain, receptacle, flower holder, ornament.
Vases include the following—Amphora, burette, krater, lekynos, hydria, kylix, aquaemanale, oxybaphon, libation cup, funeral urn.

Styles of vases include the following—Etruscan, Greek black figure, Greek red figure, canopic, T'ang, Sung, Ming, Ch'ing (blue and white), *famille verte, famille rose* (*both* French), Samarran luster, Majolica, faience, potiche.

vassal, *n.* —*Syn.* thrall, serf, bondman; see **servant, slave** 1.

vassalage, *n.* —*Syn.* dependency, serviture, bondage; see **slavery** 1, **subjection.**

vast, *mod.* [Large]—*Syn.* huge, enormous, immense; see **broad** 1, **large** 1. **1.** [Extensive]—*Syn.* broad, far-flung, wide, spacious, expansive, spread-out, ample, far-reaching, widespread, comprehensive, detailed, all-inclusive, astronomical, prolonged, stretched out, expanded.—*Ant.* narrow*, limited, confined.

2. [Infinite]—*Syn.* boundless, limitless, forever; see **endless** 1, **eternal** 2.

vastly, *mod.* —*Syn.* greatly, much, enormously, immensely, mightily, prodigiously, extensively, tremendously, hugely; see also **largely** 2.

vastness, *n.* —*Syn.* hugeness, extent, enormity; see **expanse, size** 2.

vat, *n.* —*Syn.* vessel, cistern, tub, barrel, tank, basin, salt pit; see also **container.**

Vatican, *n.* —*Syn.* (the) Papacy, Rome, papal palace; see **Pope.**

vaudeville, *n.* —*Syn.* variety show, burlesque, skit, show, entr'acte; *both* (D): vaud, bawdeville.

vault, *n.* **1.** [A place for the dead]—*Syn.* tomb, crypt, grave, sepulcher, ossuary, catacomb, pit, tumulus, mound, barrow, cenotaph; see also **monument** 1.

2. [A place for preserving valuables]—*Syn.* safe-deposit box, strongroom, bank vault, time vault, safe, burglar-proof safe.

vault, *v.* —*Syn.* leap (over), hurdle, clear, bound, spring, jump (out), mount, pole-vault.

vaulted, *mod.* —*Syn.* domed, arched, hemispheric; see **round** 3.

vaulting, *mod.* —*Syn.* eager, opportunistic, avid; see **enthusiastic** 1, 2, 3.

vaunt, *v.* —*Syn.* swagger, brag (of), puff; see **boast** 1.

veal, *n.* —*Syn.* calf, bob veal, deaconned veal (D); see also **beef** 1, **meat.**

Cuts of veal include the following—chops, leg, loin, rack, neck, breast, chuck.

Veal dishes include the following—(breaded) veal cutlet, veal stew, calf's liver, Wiener schnitzel, veal Parmigiano, (veal) scallopini, veal bird, *tete de veau* (French).

veer, *v.* —*Syn.* swerve, deviate, depart, digress, diverge, bend, turn, divert, deflect, sheer, avert, curve.

veering, *n.* —*Syn.* deviation, variation, detour; see **change** 1, 2.

vegetable, *mod.* **1.** [Concerning flora]—*Syn.* plantlike, herblike, floral, blooming, blossoming, growing, flourishing.

2. [Without spirit]—*Syn.* dull, monotonous, stupid, passive, unthinking, stagnant, inert, humble, stationary, inactive, mild, quiet, lowly.

vegetable, *n.* —*Syn.* plant, herbaceous plant, herb, edible root.

Common vegetables include the following—*Syn.* cabbage, potato, turnip, bean, carrot, pea, celery, lettuce, parsnip, spinach, squash, tomato, pumpkin, asparagus, onion, corn, lentil, leek, garlic, radish, cucumber, artichoke, eggplant, beet, scallion, pepper, okra, kohlrabi, parsley, celtuce, chard, rhubarb, cauliflower, Brussels sprouts, broccoli, celeriac, endive, Chinese cabbage; (water) cress, chicory, kale, rutabaga.

vegetate, *v.* **1.** [To germinate]—*Syn.* sprout, bud, blossom; see **bloom, grow** 1.

2. [To stagnate]—*Syn.* hibernate, stagnate, languish; see **decay, weaken** 1.

vegetation, —*Syn.* plants, plant growth, trees, shrubs, saplings, flowers, wild flowers, grasses, herbage, herbs, pasturage, weeds, vegetables, crops; see also **nature** 2.

vehemence, *n.* —*Syn.* frenzy, fervor, impetuosity; see **intensity** 1, **violence** 2.

vehement, *mod.* —*Syn.* fierce, eager, impetuous; see **angry, intense.**

vehicle, *n.* **1.** [A conveyance]—Vehicles include the following—carriage, buggy, wagon, sleigh, cart, motor car, bus, jeep, rover, automobile, truck, station wagon, van, motorcycle, taxicab, railroad car, cab, hack, taxi.

2. [Means of expression]—*Syn.* organ, channel, agency; see **means** 1, **medium** 2.

veil, *n.* **1.** [A thin fabric]—*Syn.* scarf, kerchief, mask, gauze, film, cover, tissue; see also **web** 1.

2. [A curtain]—*Syn.* veiling, screen, mantilla, cover, shade; see also **curtain.**

3. [A light mist]—*Syn.* mist, fog, cloud, rain, haze, dimness, twilight, darkness, blur, obscurity, half-light.

vein, *n.* **1.** [A fissure]—*Syn.* cleft, aperture, opening, channel, cavity, crack, cranny, rift, chink, break, breach, slit, crevice, flaw, rupture; see also **hole** 2, 3.

2. [Ore occurring as though in a vein, sense 1] —*Syn.* lode, ledge, lead, reef, dike.

3. [A persistent quality]—*Syn.* strain, humor, mood, temper, tang, spice, dash; see also **characteristic, temperament.**

4. [A blood duct leading to the heart] Important veins include the following—jugular, pulmonary, subclavian, portal, iliac, hepatic, renal; see also **artery** 2, **vessel** 3.

5. [Anything resembling a vein, sense 4]—*Syn.* hair, thread, capillary, follicle, nerve, rib, nervure, venation.

velocity, *n.* —*Syn.* quickness, swiftness, celerity, rapidity, impetus, escape velocity, exhaust velocity; see also **speed.**

velour, *n.* —*Syn.* velvet, pile fabric, shag, mohair, plush, fur fabric, bolivia; see also **cloth.**

velvet, *mod.* —*Syn.* velvetlike, velvety, silken, shining, plushy, velourlike, fine-textured; see also **soft** 2.

velvet, *n.* Types of velvet include the following—pile velvet, cut velvet, transparent velvet, silk velvet, silk-and-cotton velvet, cotton velvet, rayon, velveteen, corduroy; see also **cloth, velour.**

venal, *mod.* —*Syn.* mercenary, dishonorable, vicious; see **corrupt** 3, **greedy** 1.

venality, *n.* —*Syn.* corruptness, sordidness, vendibility; see **dishonesty, greed.**

vend, *v.* —*Syn.* trade, peddle, auction; see **sell** 1.

vendetta, *n.* —*Syn.* squabble, quarrel, feud; see **dispute** 1, **fight** 1.
vendor, *n.* —*Syn.* vender, peddler, huckster; see **businessman, merchant.**
veneer, *n.* —*Syn.* surface, exterior, covering; see **cover** 1.
veneer, *v.* —*Syn.* overlay, cover, plate, coat, face, glue together, surface, finish.
venerable, *mod.* **1.** [Old]—*Syn.* aged, hoary, ancient; see **old** 3.
2. [Having qualities becoming to age]—*Syn.* revered, reverenced, honored, honorable, noble, august, grand, esteemed, respected, dignified, imposing, grave, serious, sage, wise, philosophical, experienced.—*Ant.* inexperienced*, callow, raw.
venerate, *v.* —*Syn.* revere, reverence, adore; see **love** 1, **worship** 2.
veneration, *n.* —*Syn.* respect, adoration, awe; see **reverence** 2, **worship** 1.
vengeance, *n.* —*Syn.* retribution, return, retaliation; see **revenge** 1.
vengeful, *mod.* —*Syn.* spiteful, revengeful, rancorous; see **vindictive** 1.
venial, *mod.* —*Syn.* excusable, pardonable, justifiable, allowable, trivial, exculpable, defensible, slight, vindicatory, warrantable, extenuatory, mild; see also **unimportant.**—*Ant.* deadly*, mortal, serious*.
Venice, *n.* —*Syn.* Bride of the Sea, Queen of the Sea, Queen of the Adriatic, *Venezia* (Italian), *Venedig* (German), *Venise* (French).
venom, *n.* **1.** [An animal poison]—*Syn.* poison, virus, toxin, bane, microbe, contagion, infection. —*Ant.* remedy*, antidote, specific.
2. [Malice]—*Syn.* virulence, ill-will, malignity; see **anger, hatred** 1, 2.
venomous, *mod.* —*Syn.* virulent, lethal, toxic; see **deadly, destructive** 2, **poisonous.**
vent, *n.* —*Syn.* ventilator, vent hole, venting hole, ventiduct, liquid-vent, vent faucet, molding, touchhole, drain, smoke hole, flue, aperture; see also **chimney.**
vent, *v.* —*Syn.* let out, drive out, discharge; see **release.**
ventilate, *v.* —*Syn.* freshen, let in fresh air, circulate fresh air, vent, air cool, air out, free, oxygenate; see also **air** 1, **cool** 2.
ventilated, *mod.* —*Syn.* aired (out), having (adequate) ventilation, not close *or* closed (up); see **airy** 1, **cool** 1, **open** 1.
ventilation, *n.* **1.** [The act of providing or changing air]—*Syn.* airing, purifying, oxygenating, freshening, opening windows, changing air, circulating air, air-conditioning.
2. [Fresh air]—*Syn.* pure air, purified air, freshened air, oxygenated air, mountain air, sea air, breeze, coolness, outside air; *both* (D): some of the outdoors, some of the climate.
ventilator, *n.* —*Syn.* cooler, air-conditioner, fan; see **vent.**
ventriloquism, *n.* —*Syn.* ventriloquy, gastriloquism, polyphonism; see **sound** 2, **speech** 2.
venture, *n.* —*Syn.* adventure, risk, hazard, peril, stake, chance, speculation, dare, experiment, trial, attempt, essay, test, gamble, undertaking, enterprise, investment; *all* (D): leap in the dark, plunge, potluck, flyer, crack, fling.
venture, *v.* —*Syn.* attempt, essay, experiment, try, try out, assay, grope, feel, speculate, gamble, stake, hazard, bet, wager, play for.
ventured, *mod.* —*Syn.* adventured, risked, hazarded, chanced, dared, experimented, tried, invested, attempted, essayed, gambled, undertaken; see also **tested.**
venturesome, *mod.* —*Syn.* risky, daring, adventurous; see **rash.**
veracious, *mod.* **1.** [Honest]—*Syn.* truthful, frank, trustworthy; see **honest** 1.
2. [True]—*Syn.* valid, genuine, true; see **accurate** 1.
veracity, *n.* **1.** [Honesty]—*Syn.* truth, truthfulness, trustworthiness, integrity, honor, honesty, ingenuousness, candor, frankness, openness, fidelity, probity, plain dealing, artlessness, sincerity, impartiality, fairness.—*Ant.* dishonesty*, falsity, insincerity.
2. [Accuracy]—*Syn.* truth, exactness, exactitude, reality, credibility, verity, actuality, correctness, trueness, conformity, verisimilitude, precision, rightness, authenticity, genuineness, veritableness, authoritativeness.—*Ant.* error*, inaccuracy, fallacy.
veranda, *n.* —*Syn.* portico, gallery, piazza, platform, porch, terrace, stoop.
verb, *n.* Verbs include the following—finite, active, neuter, passive, transitive, intransitive, auxiliary, linking, reciprocal, copulative, reflexive, strong, weak, regular, irregular, reduplicating, deponent, copula; see also **part of speech.**
verbal, *mod.* **1.** [Oral]—*Syn.* told, unwritten, lingual; see **oral, spoken.**
2. [Concerning the wording, not the content] —*Syn.* titular, verbatim, rhetorical, diplomatic, textual; see also **literal** 1, **nominal** 1.
verbal, *n.* Verbals in English include the following —infinitive, gerund, participle, gerundive, verbal noun, present participle, verbal adjective, past participle, verbal phrase, absolute *or* independent construction; see also **part of speech.**
verbally, *mod.* —*Syn.* orally, by word of mouth, person-to-person; see **literally, spoken.**
verbatim, *mod.* —*Syn.* exactly, literatim, to the letter; see **literally.**
verbiage, *n.* —*Syn.* repetition, verbosity, loquacity; see **wordiness.**
verbose, *mod.* —*Syn.* wordy, prolix, tedious, tautologous, redundant, repititious, circumlocutory, repetitive, periphrastic, abounding in tautology, diffuse, repeating, pleonastic, bombastic, involved, involuted, tortuous, loquacious, longwinded, garrulous, talkative, magniloquent, grandiloquent, rhetorical, voluble, flowery, overrhetorical, fustian, characterized by redundancy, word-mongering, farsed, stuffed; *all* (D): gabby, loudmouthed, talky, windy, big-mouthed, blabby, full of air; see also **dull** 4.—*Ant.* terse*, precise, succinct.
verbosely, *mod.* —*Syn.* bombastically, wordily, lengthily, oratorically, talkatively, expansively, redundantly, pleonastically, tirelessly, tiresomely, grandiloquently, longwindedly, episodically, maudlinly, clumsily, crudely, extravagantly, in a verbose *or* wordy *or* bombastic *or* redundant, etc., manner *or* style; not succinctly *or* economically *or* tightly

or articulately, etc.; with verbosity *or* wordiness *or* undue length *or* pleonasm, etc.; going on and on, beating around *or* about the bush (D).

verbosity, *n.* —*Syn.* circumlocution, loquacity, garrulity; see **wordiness.**

verdant, *mod.* —*Syn.* grassy, flourishing, verdurous; see **green** 2.

verdict, *n.* —*Syn.* judgment, finding, decision, answer, opinion, sentence, determination, decree, conclusion, deduction, adjudication, arbitrament.

verdure, *n.* —*Syn.* flora, greenness, herbage; see **vegetation.**

verge, *n.* —*Syn.* edge, brink, terminus; see **boundary.**

verge, *v.* —*Syn.* end, edge, touch; see **approach** 2.

verifiable, *mod.* —*Syn.* susceptible of proof, provable, correct; see **provable, valid** 1.

verification, *n.* —*Syn.* verifying, attestation, affirmation; see **confirmation** 1.

verify, *v.* —*Syn.* establish, substantiate, authenticate, prove, check, test, validate, settle, corroborate, confirm.

verifying, *n.* —*Syn.* proving, substantiating, corroborating, authenticating, validating, confirming, testing, checking; see also **confirmation** 1.

verily, *mod.* —*Syn.* certainly, unquestionably, undoubtedly, without question, in fact, beyond doubt; see also **surely.**

verisimilitude, *n.* —*Syn.* plausibility, appearance, likelihood; see **truth** 1.

veritable, *mod.* —*Syn.* authentic, true, real; see **genuine** 1.

verity, *n.* —*Syn.* truth, verisimilitude, actuality; see **reality** 1.

vermilion, *mod.* —*Syn.* vermeil, chrome-red, cinnabar, orange-vermilion, antimony, vermilion, French vermilion, Dutch vermilion, Chinese vermilion, scarlet-vermilion, orient vermilion, vermilion-red, vermilion-scarlet, vermilion-tawny; see also **red** 1.

vermin, *n.* Vermin include the following—fly, flea, louse, mite, mosquito, cockroach, bedbug, clothes moth, centipede, tick, silverfish *or* fish moth; see also **insect.**

vernacular, *mod.* **1.** [Indigenous]—*Syn.* ingrained, inherent, domesticated; see **native** 2, **natural** 1.

2. [Common]—*Syn.* vulgar, ordinary, plebian; see **common** 1.

vernacular, *n.* —*Syn.* idiom, patois, phraseology; see **dialect, language** 1.

versatile, *mod.* —*Syn.* many-sided, multifaceted, adaptable, dexterous, varied, ready, clever, handy, talented, gifted, adroit, resourceful, ingenious, accomplished; see also **able** 1, 2.

versatility, *mod.* —*Syn.* flexibility, utility, adjustability; see **adaptability, usefulness.**

verse, *n.* **1.** [Composition in poetic form]—*Syn.* poetry, metrical composition, versification, stanza, rhyme, lyric, sonnet, ode, heroic verse, dramatic poetry, blank verse, *vers libre* (French).

2. [A unit of verse, sense 1]—*Syn.* line, verse, stanza, stave, strophe, antistrophe, hemistich, distich, quatrain.

versed, *mod.* —*Syn.* skilled, trained, competent; see **learned** 2.

version, *n.* **1.** [One of various accounts]—*Syn.* report, account, varient, tale, story.

2. [A translation]—*Syn.* paraphrase, redaction, transcription; see **translation.**

vertebrae, *n.* —*Syn.* spine, spinal column, backbone, chine.

Parts of the vertebra include the following—atlas, axis, cervical, thoracic, lumbar, caudal, disk, spinous process, neural arch, anterior *and* posterior zygapophysis, transverse process, coccyx.

vertebrate, *mod.* —*Syn.* vertebral, of the *Vertebrata,* having a spinal column.

vertex, *n.* —*Syn.* peak, summit, zenith; see **top** 1.

vertical, *mod.* —*Syn.* perpendicular, plumb, upright, upward, erect, on end, cocked up, straight up.

vertiginous, *mod.* —*Syn.* whirling (about), dizzying, spinning; see **turning** 1.

vertigo, *n.* —*Syn.* dizziness, reeling, giddiness; see **disease** 3.

verve, *n.* —*Syn.* vigor, energy, liveliness; see **strength** 1.

very, *mod.* —*Syn.* extremely, exceedingly, greatly, acutely, indispensably, just so, surprisingly, astonishingly, incredibly, wonderfully, particularly, certainly, positively, exaggeratedly, emphatically, really, truly, pretty, decidedly, pressingly, notably, uncommonly, extraordinarily, prodigiously, highly, substantially, dearly, amply, vastly, extensively, noticeably, conspicuously, largely, considerably, hugely, excessively, imperatively, markedly, enormously, sizeably, materially, immensely, tremendously, superlatively, remarkably, unusually, immoderately, quite, indeed, somewhat, rather, simply, intensely, urgently, exceptionally, severely, seriously, in a great measure, to a great degree, beyond compare, on a large scale, ever so, beyond measure, by far, in the extreme, in a marked degree, to a great extent, without restraint, more or less, in part, infinitely, very much, to no small extent; *all* (D): real, right, right smart, pretty, awfully, almighty, almightily, good and, powerful, powerfully, hell of a, helluva, precious, so, to a fault, a bit of, no end; see also **much** 1.—*Ant.* hardly*, inconsiderably, scarcely.

vesicle, *n.* —*Syn.* sac, utricle, cyst; see **blister, swelling.**

vespers, *n.* —*Syn.* orison, evensong, compline; see **prayer** 2.

vessel, *n.* **1.** [A container]—*Syn.* pitcher, urn, kettle; see **container.**

2. [A ship]—*Syn.* boat, craft, bark; see **ship.**

3. [A duct; *especially for blood*]—*Syn.* blood vessel, vein, artery, capillary, canal.

vest, *n.* —*Syn.* waistcoat, jacket, garment; see **clothes.**

vestal, *mod.* —*Syn.* celibate, virginal, virtuous; see **chaste** 3, **pure** 2.

vested, *mod.* **1.** [Clothed]—*Syn.* dressed, robed, outfitted; see **clothed.**

2. [Absolute]—*Syn.* fixed, settled, complete; see **absolute** 1.

vested interests, *n.* —*Syn.* combine, cartel, combination in restraint of trade, companies (with interlocking directorates), syndicate; see also **business** 4, **monopoly.**

vestibule, *n.* —*Syn.* enclosed entrance, entry, entryway, lobby, foyer, narthex, anteroom, antechamber; see also **room** 2.

vestige, *n.* —*Syn.* trace, remains, scrap; see **remainder.**

vestments, *n.* —*Syn.* pontificatia, surplice, robe(s); see **clothes.**

vest-pocket, *mod.* —*Syn.* small, reduced, miniature; see **little** 1.

vestry, *n.* —*Syn.* church room, vestry room, robing room; see **sacristy.**

veteran, *mod.* —*Syn.* seasoned, experienced, exercised, skilled, versed, hardened, weathered, inured, steady.

veteran, *n.* **1.** [An experienced person]—*Syn.* master, expert, one long in service; *all* (D): sourdough, old hand, one of the old guard, old bird, old dog, old timer.—*Ant.* amateur*, new man, youngster.
2. [An experienced soldier]—*Syn.* ex-soldier, seasoned campaigner, member of an elite division, ex-service man, reenlisted man, old soldier; *all* (D): war horse, vet, ex-G.I.

Veteran's Day, *n.* —*Syn.* Armistice Day, Remembrance Day, November 11; see **holiday.**

veterinarian, *n.* —*Syn.* animal specialist, vet, animal doctor; see **doctor** 1.

veto, *n.* —*Syn.* interdiction, prohibition, declination, negative; see also **denial** 1, **refusal.**

veto, *v.* —*Syn.* interdict, prohibit, decline; see **deny, forbid, refuse.**

vetoed, *mod.* —*Syn.* declined, rejected, disapproved; see **no, refused.**

vex, *v.* **1.** [To trouble]—*Syn.* distress, worry, depress; see **disturb** 2.
2. [To annoy]—*Syn.* provoke, plague, irritate; see **bother** 2, 3.

vexation, *n.* **1.** [A vexed feeling]—*Syn.* uneasiness, irritation, bother; see **annoyance** 1.
2. [A cause of vexation, sense 1]—*Syn.* worry, trouble, misfortune; see **difficulty** 2.

vexatious, *mod.* —*Syn.* annoying, bothersome, irritating; see **disturbing.**

vexed, *mod.* —*Syn.* disturbed, annoyed, irritated; see **confused** 2, **troubled** 1.

via, *prep.* —*Syn.* by way of, by the route passing through, on the way to, through the medium of (D); see also **by** 2, **through** 4.

viaduct, *n.* —*Syn.* bridge, way, way over, elevated road, aquaduct, ramp.

vial, *n.* —*Syn.* flask, phial, vessel, bottle, jar.

vibrant, *mod.* **1.** [Pulsing]—*Syn.* throbbing, pulsing, quaking; see **quivering.**
2. [Active]—*Syn.* energetic, vigorous, lively; see **active** 1, 2.

vibrate, *v.* **1.** [To quiver]—*Syn.* fluctuate, flutter, waver; see **wave** 3.
2. [To sound]—*Syn.* echo, resound, reverberate; see **sound** 1.

vibration, *n.* —*Syn.* quake, wavering, vacillation, fluctuation, oscillation, quiver, shake; see also **wave** 3.

vibrato, *n.* —*Syn.* quaver, quiver, tremolo; see **vibration.**

vicar, *n.* —*Syn.* cleric, ecclesiastic, clergyman; see **minister** 1, **priest.**

vicarious, *mod.* —*Syn.* substitutional, acting, delegated; see **common** 5, **pretended.**

vice, *mod.* **1.** [Subordinate]—*Syn.* vice-admiral, vice-chairman, vice-consul, vice-dean, vice-general; see also **subordinate.**
2. [Wicked]—*Syn.* depraved, bad, pernicious; see **vicious** 1, **wicked** 1.

vice, *n.* **1.** [Depravity]—*Syn.* corruption, iniquity, wickedness; see **evil** 1.
2. [A degrading practice]—*Syn.* licentiousness, lust, lewdness, profligacy, indecency, libidinousness, sensuality, carnality.

viceroy, *n.* —*Syn.* ruler, governor, chief executive, representative, proxy.

vice versa, *mod.* —*Syn.* conversely, in reverse, the other way round, turn about, *mutatis mutandis* (Latin), about face, in opposite manner, far from it, on the contrary, in reverse English (D).

vicinity, *n.* —*Syn.* proximity, nearness, neighborhood; see **environment, region** 1.

vicious, *mod.* **1.** [Corrupt]—*Syn.* bad, debased, base, impious, profligate, demoralized, faulty, vile, foul, impure, lewd, indecent, licentious, libidinous; see also **wicked** 1, 2.—*Ant.* noble*, pure*, virtuous.
2. [Prone to cruelty]—*Syn.* wicked, evil, sinful; see **cruel** 1, 2.
3. [Not tamed]—*Syn.* wild, untamed, insubordinate; see **unruly.**

vicious circle, *n.* —*Syn.* chain of events, cause and effect, interreliant problems; see **difficulty** 1, 2, **predicament.**

viciously, *mod.* —*Syn.* cruelly, spitefully, harmfully; see **brutally, wrongly** 1, 2.

vicissitude, *n.* —*Syn.* mutability, uncertainty, alteration; see **change** 2.

victim, *n.* **1.** [One who suffers]—*Syn.* prey, sacrifice, immolation, sufferer, wretch, quarry; game, hunted, offering, scapegoat, martyr, wretch.
2. [One who is easily deceived]—*Syn.* dupe, gull, fool, cat's paw, tool, hireling, boob, gudgeon; *all* (D): sucker, (easy) mark, easy pickings, pushover, softie.

victimize, *v.* —*Syn.* cheat, swindle, dupe, trick, fool; see **deceive.**

victor, *n.* —*Syn.* winner, vanquisher, conqueror, champion, prize winner.

Victorian, *mod.* **1.** [An historical designation] —*Syn.* early Victorian, mid-Victorian, late Victorian, nineteenth-century.
2. [Conventional]—*Syn.* stuffy, strait-laced, mawkish; see **prudish.**
3. [Decorated]—*Syn.* flowery, patterned, resplendent; see **ornate** 1.

victorious, *mod.* —*Syn.* winning, triumphant, mastering; see **successful.**

victory, *n.* **1.** [The overcoming of an opponent] —*Syn.* conquest, mastery, subjugation, overcoming, overthrow, master stroke, lucky stroke, winning, gaining, defeating, subduing, destruction; *all* (D): killing, knockout, ringer, pushover; see also **triumph** 1.
2. [An instance of victory, sense 1]—*Syn.* supremacy, ascendancy, triumph, advantage, achievement, mission accomplished, success, a feather in one's cap (D).

victuals, *n.* —*Syn.* meals, fare, viands, sustenance, provisions, supplies; see also **food.**
video tape, *n.* —*Syn.* magnetic tape, video, recording; see **broadcasting, tape recorder, television.**
vie, *v.* —*Syn.* contend, strive, rival; see **compete.**
Viet Cong, *n.* —*Syn.* member of the NLF *or* Vietnamese National Liberation Front, soldier in the North Vietnamese Army, Communist, Victor Charlie (VC) (D); see also **rebel** 1, **soldier.**
view, *n.* **1.** [A sight]—*Syn.* glimpse, look, panorama, aspect, show, appearance, contour, outline, scene, picture, tableau, spectacle.
2. [A vista]—*Syn.* prospect, distance, opening, stretch, outlook, way, extended view, long view, avenue; see also **sense** 1.
3. [A picture]—*Syn.* illustration, origination, representation, composition, landscape, diorama, reproduction, design, imitation.
in view—visible, in sight, not out of sight, perceptible, perceivable; see **obvious** 1.
on view—displayed, on display, exposed; see **shown** 1;
with a view to—in order that *or* to, so that, anticipating; see **to** 4.
view, *v.* —*Syn.* observe, survey, inspect; see **see** 1.
viewer, *n.* —*Syn.* spectator, watcher, onlooker; see **observer** 1.
viewpoint, *n.* —*Syn.* point of view, perspective, standpoint, angle, slant, position, stand, aspect, light, respect, attitude, ground, point of observation, outlook.
vigil, *n.* —*Syn.* wakefulness, sleeplessness, sentry duty; see **watchfulness.**
vigilance, *n.* —*Syn.* alertness, acuity, watchfulness; see **attention** 1, 2, **diligence.**
vigilant, *mod.* —*Syn.* alert, watchful, keenly aware (of); see **careful, observant** 1, 2.
vignette, *n.* **1.** [A design]—*Syn.* sketch, engraving, headpiece; see **design** 1.
2. [A story]—*Syn.* scenario, novelette, scene; see **story.**
vigor, *n.* **1.** [Activity]—*Syn.* exercise, action, energy, motion, quickness, raciness, stalwartness, alertness, agility, nimbleness, liveliness; see also **vitality.**—*Ant.* slowness*, sluggishness, slothfulness.
2. [Force]—*Syn.* strength, vim, power, intensity, urgency, lustiness, manliness, violence, vehemence.—*Ant.* weakness*, impotence, effeminancy.
3. [Health]—*Syn.* haleness, soundness, well-being, endurance, hardiness, vitality; see also **health** 1. —*Ant.* disease*, feebleness, ill-health.
vigorous, *mod.* **1.** [Done with vigor]—*Syn.* energetic, lively, brisk; see **active** 2.
2. [Possessing vigor]—*Syn.* robust, zealous, hardy; see **healthy** 1, **strong** 1.
3. [Forceful]—*Syn.* powerful, strong, potent; see **effective, persuasive.**
vigorously, *mod.* —*Syn.* energetically, alertly, eagerly, quickly, nimbly, agilely, strenuously, resolutely, firmly, forcibly, forcefully, urgently, unfalteringly, purposefully, actively, boldly, adventurously, zealously, lustily, vibrantly, robustly, stoutly, hardily, wholeheartedly, earnestly, warmly, fervidly, passionately, sincerely, devoutly, appreciatively, with heart and soul, healthily, fearlessly, intrepidly, mightily, decidedly, by brute force, to good account, like blazes (D); see also **powerfully.**—*Ant.* calmly*, aimlessly, slowly.
vile, *mod.* —*Syn.* sordid, corrupt, debased; see **shameful** 1, 2.
vilify, *v.* —*Syn.* defame, revile, denounce; see **censure, slander.**
villa, *n.* —*Syn.* country property, suburban residence, dwelling; see **home** 1.
village, *n.* —*Syn.* hamlet, crossroads town, small town, center, thorp (British).
villain, *n.* —*Syn.* scoundrel, knave, brute; see **rascal.**
villainous, *mod.* **1.** [Depraved]—*Syn.* evil, criminal, vicious; see **wicked** 1, 2.
2. [Disagreeable]—*Syn.* detestable, objectionable, contrary; see **offensive** 2.
villainy, *n.* —*Syn.* depravity, knavery, corruptness; see **evil** 1.
vim, *n.* —*Syn.* energy, pep, power, lustiness, vigor, action, spirit.
vindicate, *v.* **1.** [To clear]—*Syn.* acquit, free, absolve; see **excuse.**
2. [To defend]—*Syn.* plead for, second, support; see **defend** 3.
3. [To justify]—*Syn.* prove, bear out, warrant; see **justify** 2.
vindication, *n.* —*Syn.* defense, acquittal, clearance, justification, proof, explanation, exoneration, exculpation, support, absolution, pardon.—*Ant.* blame*, charge, conviction.
vindictive, *mod.* —*Syn.* revengeful, retaliatory, unforgiving, implacable, vengeful, unrelenting, resentful, spiteful; see also **cruel** 1, **ruthless** 1, 2. —*Ant.* kind*, generous, forgiving.
vindictively, *mod.* —*Syn.* cruelly, vengefully, spitefully; see **brutally, wrongly** 1, 2.
vine, *n.* —*Syn.* creeper, climbing plant, creeping plant, trailing plant, stem climber, leaf climber, tendril climber; see also **plant.**
Vines include the following—grapevine, honeysuckle, trumpet vine, English ivy, Virginia creeper, poison ivy, blackberry, raspberry, briar, rambler, teaberry, dewberry, morning-glory, hopvine, bougainvillea, jasmine, pea vine, watermelon, canteloupe, cucumber, wild cucumber, gourd, pumpkin, passion flower.
vinegar, *n.* Types of vinegar include the following —(apple) cider, white, malt, beer, wine, tarragon, raspberry, beetroot, dilute, acetic acid; see also **acid.**
vineyard, *n.* —*Syn.* grapevines, vines, grapes, wine terraces, arbor, grape arbor; see also **orchard.**
vintage, *mod.* —*Syn.* selected, choice, saved; see **excellent, old** 3.
vintage, *n.* —*Syn.* crop, grapes, wine, year, a good wine.
violate, *v.* **1.** [To transgress]—*Syn.* outrage, disrupt, infringe, break, tamper (with); see also **meddle** 1.
2. [To rape]—*Syn.* dishonor, profane, defile, ravish.
violation, *n.* **1.** [Transgression]—*Syn.* infringement, infraction, negligence, misbehavior, nonobservance, violating, shattering, transgressing, (forcible) trespass, trespassing, contravention, breach, breaking, rupture, flouting; see also **crime** 1, **sin.**
2. [Rape]—*Syn.* ravishment, assault, dishonor, defilement, mistreatment, outrage, debasement, deg-

radation, pollution, invasion, subjugation, desecration, doing violence to; see also **disgrace** 2.

3. [Destruction]—*Syn.* demolition, ruin, devastation; see **destruction** 1, 2.

violence, *n.* **1.** [Violent disturbance]—*Syn.* rampage, tumult, disorder, clash, onslaught, struggle; see also **confusion** 1, **disturbance** 2, **uproar.**

2. [Violent conduct]—*Syn.* fury, force, vehemence, frenzy, brutality, savagery; see also **intensity** 1.

violent, *mod.* **1.** [Showing power]—*Syn.* strong, powerful, forceful, forcible, rough, mighty, great, potent, coercive; see also **sense** 2.—*Ant.* quiet*, peaceful, easy-going.

2. [Showing strong emotions]—*Syn.* furious, mad, savage, fierce, passionate, splitting, vehement, frenzied, demoniac, frantic, fuming, enraged, disturbed, agitated, impassioned, impetuous, urgent, maddened, aroused, inflamed, distraught, infatuated, hysterical, blue in the face (D).—*Ant.* calm*, appeased, quieted.

3. [Intense]—*Syn.* great, vehement, extreme; see **intense.**

4. [Characterized by the use of violence]—*Syn.* unnatural, unusual, destructible, murderous, homicidal, brutal, rampageous.—*Ant.* expected*, deliberate, awaited.

5. [Harsh]—*Syn.* drastic, hard, stringent; see **severe** 2.

violently, *mod.* **1.** [Characterized by violent actions]—*Syn.* destructively, forcibly, forcefully, combatively, powerfully, strongly, coercively, flagrantly, outrageously, overwhelmingly, compellingly, disturbingly, turbulently, stormily, ruinously, stubbornly, with violence, in a violent manner, abruptly, noisily, with a vengeance, like fury, rebelliously, riotously; see also **fiercely, vigorously.** —*Ant.* peacefully*, quietly, weakly.

2. [Characterized by violent emotions]—*Syn.* distractedly, furiously, angrily, vehemently, frantically, fiercely, hysterically, hilariously, passionately, urgently, madly, frenziedly, ardently, enthusiastically, impulsively.—*Ant.* mildly*, gently, undisturbedly.

violet, *mod.* —*Syn.* lavender, mauve, purplish; see **purple.**

violet, *n.* Violets include the following—purple, white, yellow, southern wood, Pacific coast wood, sweet, Parma, bird's foot, Rouen, Russian, early blue, bog blue, arrow-leaved, striped, beaked, Canada, round-leaved, hairy yellow, prairie yellow, pine, mountain; see also **flower** 2.

violin, *n.* —*Syn.* fiddle, violinette; *both* (D); crowd, crioth; see also **musical instrument.**

Violinlike instruments include the following—viol, viola, violoncello, cello, double bass, string bass, Cremona, Amati, Steiner, Klotz, Vuillaume, Forrest, Stradivarius, Guarnerius.

violinist, *n.* —*Syn.* musician, technician, virtuoso, instrumentalist, player, performer, fiddler (D).

V.I.P. (D), *n.* —*Syn.* very important person, notable, important figure; see **leader** 2, **personage** 2.

viper, *n.* Vipers include the following—adder, asp, cobra, rhinoceros viper, puff adder, tree viper, blowing viper, black viper, pit viper, rattlesnake, copperhead, water moccasin, fer-de-lance; see also **reptile, snake.**

viperous, *mod.* —*Syn.* lethal, deadly, venemous; see **poisonous.**

virago, *n.* —*Syn.* scold, vixen, ogress; see **hag, shrew.**

Virgin, *n.* —*Syn.* Madonna, Blessed Virgin Mary, Queen of Saints, Our Lady, Mother of God, Mary, the Queen of Heaven, Queen of Angels, Star of the Sea, The Virgin Mother, Immaculate Conception, Immaculate Mary; see also **saint** 2.

virgin, *mod.* **1.** [Chaste]—*Syn.* maidenly, pure, modest, virginal; see also **chaste** 2, 3.

2. [Original or natural]—*Syn.* undisturbed, fresh, new, untamed; see also **natural** 3, **original** 1, 3.

virgin, *n.* —*Syn.* maiden, unmarried woman, spinster, Madonna, *virgo intacta* (Latin).

virginity, *n.* —*Syn.* maidenhood, girlhood, spinsterhood, celibacy; see also **chastity, virtue** 1.

virile, *mod.* **1.** [Manly]—*Syn.* masculine, potent, manlike; see **male, manly.**

2. [Forceful]—*Syn.* strong, robust, forceful; see **brave** 1.

virility, *n.* —*Syn.* potency, masculinity, manliness; see **manhood** 2.

virtual, *mod.* —*Syn.* in essence, in effect, implicit, practical, in practice, in conduct, pragmatic.

virtually, *mod.* —*Syn.* for all practical purposes, practically, implicitly; see **essentially.**

virtue, *n.* **1.** [Moral excellence]—*Syn.* ideal, ethic, morality, goodness, righteousness, uprightness, ethical conduct, ethicality, good thing, respectability, rectitude, honor, honesty, candor, merit, fineness, character, excellence, value, chastity, quality, worth, kindness, innocence, generosity, trustworthiness, faithfulness, consideration; *cardinal virtues;* justice, prudence, temperance, fortitude; *theological virtues;* faith, hope, charity *or* love. —*Ant.* evil*, immorality, depravity.

2. [An individual excellence]—*Syn.* quality, characteristic, attribute, temper, way, trait, feature, accomplishment, achievement, property, distinction, capacity, power.—*Ant.* lack*, inability, incapacity.

3. [Probity in sexual conduct]—*Syn.* virginity, purity, decency; see **chastity.**

by virtue of—on (the) grounds of, because of, looking toward; see **because.**

virtuoso, *n.* —*Syn.* artiste, expert, dillettante; see **master** 3, **musician.**

virtuous, *mod.* —*Syn.* good, upright, moral; see **honest** 1, **noble** 1, 2, **worthy.**

virulent, *mod.* **1.** [Deadly]—*Syn.* destructive, venomous, injurious; see **poisonous.**

2. [Hostile]—*Syn.* antagonistic, spiteful, hateful; see **unfriendly** 1.

virus, *n.* **1.** [An infection]—*Syn.* sickness, communicability, illness; see **disease** 1, 2, **infection.**

2. [An organism]—*Syn.* micro-organism, bacillus, phage; see **germ** 3.

visa, *n.* —*Syn.* endorsement, permission, signed passport; see **permit.**

visage, *n.* —*Syn.* face, countenance, physiognomy; see **appearance** 1.

viscera, *n.* —*Syn.* intestines, entrails, bowels; see **insides.**

viscid, *mod.* —*Syn.* viscous, cohesive, sirupy; see **adhesive, thick** 3.

viscosity, *n.* —*Syn.* stickiness, viscidity, sliminess; see **coherence** 1, **thickness** 1.

vise, *n.* —*Syn.* clamp, holder, swivel vise, universal vise, carpenter's vise; see also **fastener.**

visibility, *n.* —*Syn.* perceptibility, discernibility, distinctness; see **clarity.**

visible, *mod.* —*Syn.* apparent, evident, noticeable; see **obvious** 1.

vision, *n.* **1.** [The faculty of sight]—*Syn.* sight, perception, perceiving, range of view, optics, eyesight.
2. [Understanding]—*Syn.* foresight, discernment, breadth of view, insight, penetration, intuition, divination, astuteness, keenness, foreknowledge, prescience, farsightedness; see also **acumen.**
3. [Something seen through powers of the mind] —*Syn.* imagination, poetic insight, fancy, fantasy, image, concept, conception, ideality, idea; see also **thought** 1, 2.
4. [Something seen because of an abnormality] —*Syn.* revelation, hallucination, trance, ecstasy, phantom, apparition, ghost, wraith, specter, apocalypse, nightmare, spirit, warlock; see also **fantasy** 2, **illusion** 1.

visionary, *mod.* **1.** [Impractical]—*Syn.* ideal, ideological, romantic, utopian, quixotic, in the clouds (D); see also **impractical.**—*Ant.* practical*, realistic, pragmatical.
2. [Imaginary]—*Syn.* chimerical, delusory, dreamy; see **fantastic, imaginary.**

visit, *n.* —*Syn.* social call, call, appointment, interview, formal call, talk, evening, stay, week end, holiday, visitation; see also **vacation.**

visit, *v.* **1.** [To call upon the sick]—*Syn.* call upon, bring comfort *or* cheer *or* help, minister; see **attend** 2, **encourage** 2, **nurse.**
2. [To live with for a short time]—*Syn.* stay *or* dwell with, stop with *or* by, call at *or* on *or* upon, come around, be the guest of, make a visit, sojourn awhile, revisit; see also **sense** 4.
3. [To afflict]—*Syn.* trouble, inflict, pain; see **bother** 3.
4. [To stop for business or pleasure]—*Syn.* call on *or* upon, make one's compliments to, look in on, visit with, call for, stop off, *or* in *or* over, have an appointment (with), pay a visit (to), tour, *all* (D): take in, drop in on, hit, look around, look up, be closeted with, go over to, look in, drop over, pop in, have a date; see also **sense** 2.

visitation, *n.* **1.** [An affliction]—*Syn.* calamity, trouble, adversity, misfortune, distress, pain, sorrow, sickness; see also **difficulty** 1, 2.
2. [A visit]—*Syn.* call, sojourn, temporary stay; see **visiting.**

visiting, *mod.* **1.** [On a visit]—*Syn.* staying, stopping, residing temporarily, stopping over, stopping off, wintering, summering, calling.
2. [Abroad in an official or a semiofficial capacity] —*Syn.* sojourning, calling upon, touring, inspecting, reviewing, traveling, itinerant.

visiting, *n.* —*Syn.* calling upon, staying, stopping over, sojourning, touring, viewing, reviewing, inspecting, wintering, summering, dwelling briefly.

visitor, *n.* —*Syn.* guest, caller, visitant, official inspector.

vista, *n.* —*Syn.* sight, long view, prospect; see **view** 1, 2.

visual, *mod.* —*Syn.* seen, ocular, optic, beheld, optical, imaged, perceptible, viewed, of the eye, of the vision, visible; see also **observed** 1, **obvious** 1.

visualize, *v.* —*Syn.* see in the mind's eye, imagine, envision, picture mentally, conceive, conjure *or* call up, call to mind, fancy, reflect.

vital, *mod.* **1.** [Necessary]—*Syn.* essential, contribute, indispensable, requisite; see also **necessary** 1.
2. [Alive]—*Syn.* live, animate, animated; see **alive** 1.
3. [Vigorous]—*Syn.* lively, energetic, lusty; see **active** 1, 2.

vitality, *n.* —*Syn.* life, liveliness, animation, vim, vigor, intensity, continuity, endurance, energy, spirit, ardor, audacity, spunk, fervor, verve, venturesomeness; *all* (D): pep, punch, get-up-and-go.

vitalize, *v.* —*Syn.* strengthen, energize, reanimate; see **heal** 1.

vitals, *n.* —*Syn.* organs, intestines, entrails; see **insides.**

vitamin, *n.* Types of vitamins include the following —vitamin A, vitamin B complex (vitamin B_1, vitamin B_2, vitamin B_6, vitamin B_{12}), vitamin C, vitamin D (vitamin D_1, vitamin D_2), vitamin E, vitamin H, vitamin K (vitamin K_1, vitamin K_2, vitamin K_3, vitamin K_4), vitamin P, riboflavin, lacoflavin, flavin, nicotine acid, Betalin compound, ascorbic acid, thiamin, thiamine hydrochloride, thiamine chloride, betataxin, betalin, niacinamide, niacin, calcium pantothenate, pantothenic acid, nicotinamide, pyridoxine, tocopherol; see also **medicine** 2.

vitiate, *v.* **1.** [To cancel]—*Syn.* annul, recant, delete; see **deny, revoke.**
2. [To violate]—*Syn.* spoil, debase, deprave; see **corrupt** 1.

vitreous, *mod.* —*Syn.* thin, translucent, hyaline; see **clear** 2, **transparent** 1.

vitriolic, *mod.* —*Syn.* burning, sharp, caustic; see **sarcastic.**

vituperation, *n.* —*Syn.* censure, disapproval, scolding; see **blame** 1.

vituperative, *mod.* —*Syn.* insulting, trenchant, censorious; see **critical** 2, **severe** 1.

vivacious, *mod.* —*Syn.* spirited, lively, playful; see **active** 1, 2, **happy** 1.

vivacity, *n.* —*Syn.* sprightliness, liveliness, animation; see **enthusiasm** 1, **life** 1.

viva voce, *mod.* —*Syn.* orally, vocally, articulately; see **oral.**

vivid, *mod.* **1.** [Brilliant]—*Syn.* shining, rich, glowing; see **bright** 1, 2.
2. [Distinct]—*Syn.* strong, vigorous, lucid; see **clear** 2, **definite** 2.
3. [Animated]—*Syn.* expressive, lively, expressive; see **graphic** 1, 2.

vividly, *mod.* **1.** [Clearly]—*Syn.* distinctly, strongly, sharply; see **clearly** 1, 2.
2. [With brightness and color]—*Syn.* glowingly, strikingly, flamingly; see **brightly.**

vividness, *n.* —*Syn.* sharpness, distinctness, distinction; see **clarity.**

vocabulary, *n.* —*Syn.* wordbook, dictionary, lexicon, lexis, thesaurus, stock of words, glossary, *promptorium* (Latin), scientific vocabulary, literary vocabulary, word-hoard (D); see also **diction.**

vocal, *mod.* **1.** [Verbal]—*Syn.* expressed, uttered, voiced; see **oral, spoken.**
2. [Produced by the voice; *said especially of music*] —*Syn.* full of voice, sonant, modulated, arranged for voice, sung, scored for voice, vocalized; see also **musical** 1, **singing.**

vocalist, *n.* —*Syn.* chorister, songstress, caroler; see **musician, singer.**

vocation, *n.* **1.** [The work for which one has prepared]—*Syn.* calling, mission, pursuit; see **profession** 1.
2. [The work at which one is engaged]—*Syn.* employment, trade, occupation, duty, undertaking; see also **job** 1.

vociferous, *mod.* —*Syn.* clamorous, blatant, noisy; see **loud** 1, **shrill.**

vogue, *n.* —*Syn.* fashion, style, mode, rage, trend, custom, practice, current practice, *dernier cri* (French); the thing (D); see also **fad.**

voice, *n.* **1.** [A vocal sound]—*Syn.* speech, sound, call, cry, utterance, tongue, whistle, moan, groan, song, yell, hail, howl, yowl, bark, whine, whimper, mutter, murmur, shout, bleat, bray, neigh, whinny, roar, trumpet, cluck, honk, meow, hiss, quack; see also **noise** 1.—*Ant.* silence*, dumbness, deaf-mutism.
2. [Approval or opinion]—*Syn.* decision, wish, view; see **choice** 1, **opinion** 1.
with one voice—all together, by unanimous vote, without dissent; see **unanimously.**

voice, *v.* —*Syn.* assert, cry, sound; see **talk** 1, **tell** 1.

voiced, *mod.* —*Syn.* vocal, sonant, sounded; see **oral, spoken.**

voiceless, *mod.* —*Syn.* speechless, wordless, silent; see **dumb** 1, **mute** 1.

void, *mod.* **1.** [Without force or effect]—*Syn.* barren, sterile, fruitless, meaningless, useless, invalid, vain, voided, unconfirmed, unratified, null and void, worthless, unsanctioned, set aside, avoided, forceless, unenforceable, voted out, ineffectual, ineffective, voidable.—*Ant.* valid*, in force, used.
2. [Empty]—*Syn.* unfilled, abandoned, unoccupied; see **empty** 1, **vacant** 2.

voile, *n.* —*Syn.* cotton voile, wool voile, etamine, dress material, fabric; see also **cloth.**

volatile, *mod.* **1.** [Having the qualities of a gas] —*Syn.* light, airy, imponderable, subtle, buoyant, gaseous, gasiform, vaporous, vapory, vaporizable, evaporable, effervescent, expansive, resilient, elastic.—*Ant.* heavy*, dense, solid.
2. [Having a sprightly temperament]—*Syn.* lively, light-hearted, vivacious, gay, animated, merry, flippant, teasing, playful, sprightly; see also **active** 1, 2, **happy** 1.—*Ant.* solemn*, demure, quiet.
3. [Fickle]—*Syn.* frivolous, capricious, whimsical; see **fickle** 2.

volatility, *n.* **1.** [Evaporation]—*Syn.* dryness, vaporization, volatilization; see **evaporation.**
2. [Airiness]—*Syn.* buoyancy, weightlessness, levity; see **lightness** 2.

volcano, *n.* Famous volcanoes include the following —Vesuvius, Etna, Pelee, Ararat, Kilauea, Mauna Loa, Mauna Kea, Wrangel, Krakatoa, Paricutin, Popocatepetl, Jokullo, Izalco, Quezaltenango, Conseguina, Mount Hood, Lassen Peak, Mount Shasta, Mount Baker, Mount St. Helens, Shishaldin, Erebus, Smerin, Gowong, Lamongong, Kirunga, Stromboli, Vulcano, Fujiyama, Orizaba; see also **mountain** 1.

volition, *n.* —*Syn.* wish, conation, choice, election, preference; see also **desire** 1.

volitional, *mod.* —*Syn.* willing, voluntary, free; see **optional.**

volley, *n.* —*Syn.* salvo, fusillade, round, burst, discharge, broadside, barrage, enfilade, cross fire, curtain of fire; see also **fire** 3.

voltage, *n.* —*Syn.* electric potential, potential difference, charge; see **energy** 3.

volubility, *n.* —*Syn.* fluency, loquacity, garrulity; see **eloquence** 1.

voluble, *mod.* —*Syn.* talkative, glib, loquacious; see **fluent** 2.

volume, *n.* **1.** [Quantity]—*Syn.* bulk, mass, amount; see **extent, size** 2.
2. [Contents]—*Syn.* cubical, size, dimensions; see **capacity** 1.
3. [A book]—*Syn.* printed document, tome, pamphlet; see **book** 1.
4. [Degree of sound]—*Syn.* loudness, amplification, strength; see **sound** 2.

voluminous, *mod.* **1.** [Large or extensive]—*Syn.* bulky, swelling, roomy; see **large** 1.
2. [Having many folds]—*Syn.* many-folded, coiled, convoluted, full, covering, expansive, many-layered, abundant; see also **plentiful** 2.

voluntarily, *mod.* —*Syn.* by preference, willingly, deliberately, optionally, spontaneously, freely, intentionally, at *or* by choice, of one's own choice, on one's own, in one's own sweet way, heart in hand, of one's own free will, on one's own hook, to one's heart's content, at one's discretion, on one's own initiative, with all one's heart.

voluntary, *mod.* —*Syn.* willing, willed, wished, freely, spontaneous; see also **optional.**

volunteer, *n.* —*Syn.* enlistee, enlisted man, taker; see **candidate, recruit.**

volunteer, *v.* **1.** [To make a proposal]—*Syn.* suggest, offer, bring forward; see **propose** 1.
2. [To offer one's services]—*Syn.* come forward, enlist, sign (up), submit oneself, avoid conscription, take the initiative, present *or* offer oneself, do on one's own volition *or* accord *or* account *or* of one's (own) (free) will *or* upon one's own responsibility *or* authority, take the initiative, take upon oneself, speak up, stand up and be counted; *all* (D): go in, chip in, do on one's own hook, take the bull by the horns, stand on one's own feet, take the bit between one's teeth, paddle one's own canoe, take the plunge; see also **join** 2.

volunteered, *mod.* —*Syn.* offered, proffered, signed-up; see **enlisted.**

volunteers, *n.* —*Syn.* all comers, everybody, anyone; see **recruit.**

voluptuous, *mod.* **1.** [Suited to rich satisfaction of the senses]—*Syn.* luxurious, rich, profuse, extravagant, excessive, indulgent, self-gratifying, pleasurable, self-indulgent, hedonic, hedonistic, Sybaritic, pleasure-loving, epicurian, opulent, sumptuous. —*Ant.* simple*, plain, bare.
2. [Delighting in satisfying the senses]—*Syn.* wanton, sensual, sensuous, dissipated, carnal, dissolute, licentious, lascivious, libidinous, lustful, rakish, in-

dulging, fast, lewd, salacious, bestial, erotic, ruttish, goatish.—*Ant.* severe*, ascetic, self-denying.

vomit, *v.* —*Syn.* throw up, eject, bring up, spit up, dry heave, be seasick, hurl forth, retch, ruminate, regurgitate, give forth, discharge, belch forth, spew out *or* up; *all* (D): puke, barf, toss one's cookies.

voracious, *mod.* —*Syn.* insatiable, gross, ravening; see **greedy** 1, 2.

voracity, *n.* —*Syn.* gluttony, edacity, rapacity; see **greed.**

vortex, *n.* —*Syn.* whirlpool, eddy, whirlwind, waterspout, spiral.

vote, *n.* **1.** [A ballot]—*Syn.* tally, ticket, slip of paper, ball, yes or no, rising vote, Australian ballot, secret ballot, vivavoce vote.

2. [A decision]—*Syn.* will, wish, referendum, choice, majority, unanimous vote, plebiscite; see also **election** 2.

3. [The right to vote]—*Syn.* suffrage, the franchise, manhood suffrage, universal suffrage, women's suffrage; see also **right** 1.

vote, *v.* —*Syn.* ballot, cast a vote *or* ballot, give a vote, enact, establish, determine, bring about, effect, grant, confer; *all* (D): declare, suggest, propose; see also **choose** 1, **decide.**

voted, *mod.* —*Syn.* decided, willed, chosen; see **named** 2.

vote down, *v.* —*Syn.* put down, decide against, refuse, blackball; see also **deny.**

vote for, *v.* —*Syn.* give one's vote *or* ballot to, cast a ballot for, second; see **support** 2.

vote in, *v.* —*Syn.* elect, put in, put in office; see **choose** 1.

vote out, *v.* —*Syn.* reject, remove from office, vote down; see **defeat** 1, **dismiss** 1, 2.

voter, *n.* —*Syn.* elector, balloter, registered voter, Republican *or* Democratic *or* Independent voter, member of a *or* one's constituency *or* of the electorate, part of the farm vote, labor vote, urban vote, etc.; vote caster, absentee voter, native, naturalized citizen, poll-tax payer, taxpayer, resident (voter), *vox populi(s), vox pop* (D) (*both* Latin), stay-at-home voter, straw voter, proxy (voter); *all* (D): one of the folks back home *or* at the grass-roots level *or* on the campaign trail, ballot-box stuffer, floater, fagot voter; see also **citizen.**

voting, *mod.* —*Syn.* electing, balloting, choosing, deciding; see also **electoral, selecting.**

voting, *n.* —*Syn.* balloting, taking the yeas and nays, polling, holding the election, choosing, deciding, casting votes.

votive, *mod.* —*Syn.* pledged, committed, dedicated; see **promised.**

vouch, *v.* —*Syn.* assert, avert, attest, warrant, affirm, verify, confirm, guarantee, asseverate, declare, testify, bear testimony, corroborate, protest, assure, predicate, profess, put forth, maintain, contend, depose, avow, swear, take affidavit, take a Bible oath, go bail on, kiss the Book; see also **endorse** 2.—*Ant.* deny*, repudiate, discard.

voucher, *n.* —*Syn.* declaration, affirmation, certification; see **confirmation** 1, **receipt** 2.

vow, *n.* —*Syn.* promise, affiance, pledge, solemn assertion, asseveration.

vowel, *n.* —*Syn.* vocoid, open-voiced sound, vowel sound, glide, diphthong, digraph; see also **consonant, letter** 1.

Linguistic terms referring to vowel sounds include the following—high, mid, low, front, back, rounded, unrounded, tense, slack, stressed, unstressed, nasal, nasalized, clipped, diphthongized. In English spelling, symbols to represent vowels include the following: *a, e, i, o, u, y;* in phonetics and phonemics symbols for vowels include the following ɑ, a, æ, e, ɛ, i, ɪ, ɔ, o, u, ü, ʌ, ə, ʒ.

voyage, *n.* —*Syn.* tour, trip, excursion; see **journey.**

vulcanize, *v.* —*Syn.* subject to vulcanization, treat, weld; see **harden** 1, 3, **join** 1, **repair.**

vulgar, *mod.* **1.** [Low-minded]—*Syn.* sordid, ignoble, mean, coarse, base, obscene, indecent, gross, filthy, villainous, dishonorable, unworthy, fractious, inferior, disgusting, base-minded, tasteless, common, mean-spirited, malicious, ill-tempered, sneaking, deceitful, slippery, loathsome, odious, foul-mouthed, brutish, debased, contemptible, abhorrent, profane, nasty; see also **shameful** 1, **wicked** 1.—*Ant.* noble*, high-minded, lofty.

2. [Rude in conduct]—*Syn.* crude, impolite, rough; see **rude** 1, 2.

3. [Common]—*Syn.* ordinary, familiar, popular; see **common** 1.

vulgarian, *n.* —*Syn.* parvenu, snob, boor; see **braggart.**

vulgarism, *n.* —*Syn.* slang, swearing, solecism; see **curse.**

vulgarity, *n.* —*Syn.* impudence, discourtesy, crudity; see **rudeness.**

vulnerable, *mod.* —*Syn.* woundable, exposed, assailable; see **unsafe, weak** 2, 5.

vulture, *n.* Vultures include the following—black vulture, condor, Egyptian vulture, king vulture, lammergeier, turkey buzzard; see also **bird** 1.

W

wad, *n.* **1.** [A little heap]—*Syn.* bundle, pile, mass, block, gathering, lump, tuft, clump, bunch.
2. [Soft materials used as a stopper or padding] —*Syn.* bushing, batting, backing, upholstery, plug, stop, pad, inner lining, interlining, underlining, coating, wadding, facing.
3. [(D) A considerable amount of money]—*Syn.* fortune, purse, bankroll; see **wealth** 2.

wad, *v.* —*Syn.* stuff, pad, back, cushion, stop up, reinforce, interline, underline, face, quilt, sheathe, upholster; see also **plug.**

waddle, *v.* —*Syn.* sway, wiggle, totter; see **walk** 1.

wade, *v.* —*Syn.* walk in the surf, paddle, get one's feet wet; see **swim.**

wade in, *v.* —*Syn.* start, attempt, initiate proceedings; see **tackle** 1.

wafer, *n.* —*Syn.* biscuit, hardtack, slice; see **cracker.**

waft, *v.* —*Syn.* convey, transport, transmit; see **carry.**

wag, *v.* —*Syn.* shake, waggle, swing, sway, shimmy, move from side to side.

wage, *v.* —*Syn.* conduct, make, carry on, engage in, prosecute, pursue.

wager, *n.* —*Syn.* risk, hazard, challenge; see **bet.**

wages, *n.* —*Syn.* salary, earnings, payment; see **pay** 2.

waggish, *mod.* —*Syn.* humorous, playful, jocular; see **witty.**

waggle, *v.* —*Syn.* play back and forth, sway, shimmy; see **wiggle.**

wagon, *n.* —*Syn.* wain, pushcart, buggy, truck, coach, carriage, caravan, car, covered wagon (*or* (D): prairie schooner), Conestoga wagon, cab.

waif, *n.* —*Syn.* homeless child, stray, ragamuffin; see **orphan.**

wail, *v.* —*Syn.* moan, weep, lament; see **mourn** 1.

waist, *n.* **1.** [Part of the torso]—*Syn.* waistline, middle, midriff, diaphragm, groin, waistband, waist measurement; see also **abdomen.**
2. [A garment]—*Syn.* shirt, shirtwaist, sweater, blouse, bodice, jumper, chemise, sark (D); see also **clothes.**

waistcoat, *n.* —*Syn.* vest, jacket, weskit; see **clothes.**

wait, *n.* —*Syn.* halt, interim, time wasted; see **delay** 1, **pause** 1, 2.

wait, *v.* **1.** [To await]—*Syn.* expect, anticipate, tarry, pause, wait *or* look *or* delay *or* watch *or* pray for, abide, dally, remain, idle, bide one's time, mark *or* fill time, wait *or* sit *or* stay up for, lie in wait (for), ambush; *all* (D): lie low, hole up, hang *or* stick around, cool one's heels.—*Ant.* leave*, hurry*, act.
2. [To attend at table]—*Syn.* serve, deliver, tend, act as waiter *or* waitress, arrange, set, ready, place on the table, help, portion, bus (the) dishes.
3. [To be left]—*Syn.* have left (over), be on the agenda, have to do; see **remain** 3.

waiter, *n.* —*Syn.* headwaiter, steward, attendant, footman, boy, servant, innkeeper, host, proprietor, lackey, *garçon* (French), counterman; *all* (D): tray trotter, soup juggler, soda jerk.

wait for, *v.* —*Syn.* await, expect, stay *or* sit up for; see **remain** 1, **wait** 1.

waiting, *mod.* —*Syn.* standing, languishing, in line, next in turn, expecting, hoping for, marking time, in wait, cooling one's heels (D).—*Ant.* moving*, hurrying, acting.

waiting room, *n.* —*Syn.* restroom, salon, lounge, terminal, hall, antechamber, foyer, preparation room, depot, station.

wait on, *v.* **1.** [To serve]—*Syn.* accommodate, provide, attend; see **serve** 4, **wait** 2.
2. [To result]—*Syn.* ensue, issue, arise; see **happen** 2.

waitress, *n.* —*Syn.* female attendant, servant, hostess, (counter) girl, soda dispenser, restaurant employee; *all* (D): curb hop, car hop, beanery queen, B-girl, Jennie.

wait up (for), *v.* —*Syn.* wait for, expect, stay awake; see **wait** 1, **worry** 2.

waive, *v.* —*Syn.* forgo, abandon, remove, neglect, reject, postpone, reserve, relinquish, defer, shelve, table, prorogue.

waiver, *n.* —*Syn.* relinquishment, abandonment, forgoing, reservation, refusal, rejection, disclaimer, postponement, tabling.

wake, *n.* **1.** [A track]—*Syn.* furrow, wash, following wave; see **track** 2.
2. [A funeral]—*Syn.* obsequies, funeral service(s), (last) rites; see **funeral** 1.

wake, *v.* **1.** [To waken another]—*Syn.* call, rouse, bring to life, arouse, awaken, wake up, prod, shake, nudge, break into one's slumber.
2. [To become awake]—*Syn.* get up, awake, be roused, get out of bed, open one's eyes, rise, arise, stir, stretch oneself, tumble out of bed (D).
3. [To begin to comprehend]—*Syn.* notice, see, grasp; see **understand** 1.

wakeful, *mod.* **1.** [Watchful]—*Syn.* alert, vigilant, wary; see **careful.**
2. [Restless]—*Syn.* sleepless, waking, insomnious; see **restless** 1.

wakefulness, *n.* **1.** [Watchfulness]—*Syn.* vigilance, alertness, wariness; see **attention** 1, **prudence.**
2. [Restlessness]—*Syn.* sleeplessness, somnambulism, pernoctation; see **insomnia.**

wake up, *interj.* —*Syn.* rise and shine, arise, get up, awake(n), get going *or* cracking (D).

waking, *mod.* —*Syn.* wakeful, awake, wakened, conscious, growing conscious, stirring, arising, getting up, rising, acting, sharpened, alert.—*Ant.* asleep*, sleepy, dormant.

walk, *n.* **1.** [Manner of walking]—*Syn.* gait, tread, stride; see **step** 1.
2. [Course over which one walks]—*Syn.* pavement, sidewalk, pathway, footpath, trail, track, sheepwalk, boardwalk, pier, promenade, avenue, street, road, alley, passage, dock, esplanade, platform, gangway; see also **street.**
3. [A short walking expedition]—*Syn.* stroll, ramble, turn, hike, promenade, airing, saunter, peregrination, tramp, trek, constitutional, perambulation, march, circuit, jaunt, tour.
4. [A base on balls; *in baseball*]—*Syn.* four balls; *all* (D): ticket to first, handout, Annie Oakley, pass.

walk, *v.* **1.** [To move on foot]—*Syn.* step, pace, march, tread, amble, stroll, hike, saunter, wander, ambulate, ramble, go out for an airing *or* outing, take a walk, promenade, trudge, tramp, trek, tour, take a turn, roam, rove, perambulate, meander, traipse (about), patrol, file off; *all* (D): knock about *or* around, hoof *or* jog it, toddle along, shuffle, wend one's way, bend one's steps, locomote, cruise.
2. [To cause to move on foot]—*Syn.* lead, drive, exercise, train, order a march, escort, accompany, take for a walk.
3. [To give a base on balls; *in baseball*]—*Syn.* let pass; *all* (D): give free passage, ticket to first, issue an Annie Oakley.

walk (all) over (D), *v.* —*Syn.* subdue, trample on, beat down *or* up (D); see **censure, rebuff** 1.

walk away (D), *v.* —*Syn.* vanish, depart, split (D); see **abandon** 1, 2, **leave** 1.

walker, *n.* —*Syn.* pedestrian, hiker, pilgrim, wanderer, wayfarer, trekker, rover, rambler, roamer, straggler, foot passenger, passerby, hitchhiker.

walkie-talkie, *n.* —*Syn.* portable transmitter and receiver, field radio, battery-operated two-way communication; see **radio** 2.

walking, *mod.* —*Syn.* strolling, rambling, trudging, hiking, ambulant, touring, ambling, sauntering, tramping, marching, promenading, passing, roaming, wandering, wayfaring; *both* (D): trekking, mushing.

walking papers (D), *n.* —*Syn.* discharge, dismissal, severance (pay); see **removal** 1.

walking stick, *n.* —*Syn.* cane, crutch, staff; see **stick.**

walk off, *v.* —*Syn.* depart, go one's (own) way, stalk off; see **leave** 1.

walk off *or* **out on,** *v.* —*Syn.* desert, leave, walk off from; see **abandon** 2.

walk off with (D), *v.* —*Syn.* take, appropriate, pick up; see **steal.**

walkout (D), *n.* —*Syn.* sit-down, boycott, demonstration; see **protest, strike** 1.

walk out *or* **off the job,** *v.* —*Syn.* quit, leave, go on strike; see **strike** 2.

walkover (D), *n.* —*Syn.* easy win, conquest, triumph; see **victory** 1.

walk with God, *v.* —*Syn.* live a good *or* pious *or* holy, etc., life, be good, behave oneself, obey the moral law, conform, obey, worship.

wall, *n.* **1.** [A physical barrier]—*Syn.* dam, embankment, dike, ditch, bank, levee, stockade, fence, parapet, retainer, rampart, bulwark, palisade, fort, cliff, barricade, floodgate, sluice, paling, wattle, wattling.
2. [An obstacle; *figurative*]—*Syn.* barrier, obstruction, bar, cordon, entanglement, hurdle, resistance, defense, snag, hindrance, impediment, difficulty, limitation, restriction, retardation, knot, hitch, drawback, stumbling block, check, stop, curb; *all* (D): red tape, fly in the ointment, bottleneck, red herring, detour.
3. [A side; *said of a cavity or space*]—*Syn.* flank, partition, surface, brickwork, casing, bulkhead, façade, septum, precipice, cliff, bluff, outer envelope.

wallet, *n.* —*Syn.* billfold, purse, pocketbook, notecase, card case, container, moneybag, French purse, *portemonnaie* (French); see also **folder** 2.

wallop, *v.* —*Syn.* thump, thrash, strike; see **beat** 2, **hit** 1.

wallow, *v.* —*Syn.* grovel, welter, flounder, lie in, move around *or* roll about in, bathe in, toss, immerse, be immersed in, besmirch oneself.

wall up, *v.* —*Syn.* close up, surround, wall in *or* out; see **enclose** 1.

walnut, *mod.* —*Syn.* mahogany, dark brown, reddish-brown; see **brown, red.**

walnut, *n.* —*Syn.* *Juglandaceae* (Latin), English walnut, black walnut, California walnut, butternut; *all* (D): shagbark, hickory, pecan; see also **tree.**

waltz, *n.* —*Syn.* music in three-quarter time, dance step, box step, hesitation, Viennese waltz; see also **dance** 1.

waltz, *v.* —*Syn.* box step, whirl, ballroom dance, dance in three-quarter time; see **dance** 1.

wampum (D), *n.* —*Syn.* change, cash, coins (D); see **money** 1.

wan, *mod.* —*Syn.* colorless, sickly, blanched; see **pale** 1.

wand, *n.* —*Syn.* magic stick, rod, fairy staff, scepter, baton, divining rod, caduceus.

wander, *v.* **1.** [To stroll]—*Syn.* hike, ramble, saunter; see **roam** 1, **walk** 1.
2. [To speak or think incoherently]—*Syn.* stray, shift, digress; see **ramble** 2.

wanderer, *n.* —*Syn.* adventurer, voyager, gypsy; see **explorer, traveler.**

wandering, *mod.* **1.** [Wandering in space]—*Syn.* roving, roaming, nomadic, meandering, restless, traveling, jaunting, trekking, drifting, straying, going off, strolling, ranging, prowling, ambulatory, ambulant, straggling, on the road, peripatetic, itinerant, roundabout, circuitous.—*Ant.* idle*, home-loving, sedentary.
2. [Wandering in thought]—*Syn.* discursive, digressive, disconnected; see **incoherent** 2, **incongrous** 1.

wane, *v.* —*Syn.* decline, subside, fade away; see **decrease** 1, **fade** 1.

wangle (D), *v.* —*Syn.* get, acquire, procure; see **obtain** 1.

want, *n.* **1.** [Need]—*Syn.* privation, dearth, shortage; see **lack** 2.
2. [Desire]—*Syn.* wish, craving, demand; see **desire** 1.

want, *v.* **1.** [To desire]—*Syn.* require, aspire, hanker after, have an urge for, incline toward, fancy, covet, crave, long *or* lust for, have a fondness *or* passion for, have ambition, thirst *or* hunger after, be greedy for; *both* (D): ache, have a yen *or* an itch for.
2. [To lack]—*Syn.* be deficient in, be deprived of, require; see **need.**

wanted, *mod.* —*Syn.* needed, necessary, desired, in need of, sought after, in demand, requested, asked for.—*Ant.* satisfied*, fulfilled, filled.

want in *or* **out** (D), *v.* —*Syn.* want to get *or* go in *or* out *or* leave *or* come in; anxious to go *or* come, be impatient; see **arrive** 1, **desire** 1, **leave** 1.

wanting, *mod.* **1.** [Deficient]—*Syn.* destitute, poor, in default *or* deprived *or* denuded *or* bereft *or* devoid *or* empty of, bankrupt in, cut off, lacking, short, inadequate, defective, substandard, remiss, insufficient, incomplete, missing, absent, needed, unfulfilled, on the short end (D).
2. [Desiring]—*Syn.* desirous of, covetous, longing for; see **envious** 2, **greedy** 1.

wanton, *mod.* **1.** [Unrestrained]—*Syn.* extravagant, capricious, reckless, unreserved, unfettered, free, wayward, fluctuating, changeable, whimsical, fitful, variable, fanciful, inconstant, fickle, frivolous, volatile.
2. [Lewd]—*Syn.* libidinous, lustful, licentious; see **fickle** 2, **lewd** 1, 2.
3. [Deliberately malicious]—*Syn.* unprovoked, unfair, merciless, senseless, malicious, unjustifiable, unjust, malevolent.

war, *n.* —*Syn.* fighting, hostilities, combat; see **battle** 1; **fight** 1.
Types of wars include the following—air, guerrilla, shooting, ground, sea, amphibious, three-dimensional, trench, naval, aerial, land, push-button, hot, cold, total, limited, civil, revolutionary, religious, preventive, world, offensive, defensive, biological, bacteriological, germ, chemical, atomic, nuclear, psychological, atomic-bacteriological-chemical (ABC), chemical-bacteriological-radiological (CBR); war of attrition, war to end all wars, war of nerves, campaign, crusade, Armageddon, *Blitzkrieg* (German).

war, *v.* —*Syn.* fight, battle, go to war, wage *or* make war (on *or* against), engage in combat, take the field against, contend, contest, meet in conflict, march against, attack, bombard, shell, kill, shoot, murder.

warble, *v.* —*Syn.* trill, yodel, quaver; see **sing** 1.

warbler, *n.* —*Syn.* singer, songster, songbird; see **bird** 1.
Warblers include the following—bluethroat, whitethroat, black-cap, reed, sedge, black-throated blue, chestnut-sided, yellow, hooded, worm-eating, Cape May, Dartford, grasshopper, Savi's, willow, goldcrest, yellow-throat, Cerulean; ovenbird, water thrush, redstart, wood wren.

war cry, *n.* —*Syn.* slogan, rallying cry, call to arms, rally, watchword, battle cry, war whoop (D); see also **cheer** 3.

ward, *n.* **1.** [A territorial division]—*Syn.* district, division, territory, canton, precinct, department, diocese, parish, arrondissement.
2. [A juvenile charge]—*Syn.* protégé, dependent, child, foster child, charge, orphan, godchild, adopted child.
3. [Hospital room]—*Syn.* convalescent chamber, infirmary, emergency ward; see **hospital, room** 2.

warden, *n.* —*Syn.* official, officer, overseer, superintendent, guardian, tutor, keeper, head keeper, gamekeeper, churchman, jailer, bodyguard, guard, governor, prison head; *all* (D): head screw, big bull, Father Time, deacon, Duke.

ward heeler, *n.* —*Syn.* local boss, party hack, hanger-on; see **politician** 1.

wardrobe, *n.* **1.** [A closet]—*Syn.* chest, bureau, dresser; see **closet, commode** 1.
2. [Clothing]—*Syn.* apparel, garments, vestments; see **clothes.**

wardship, *n.* —*Syn.* charge, guardianship, tutelage; see **custody** 1, **ownership.**

warehouse, *n.* —*Syn.* wholesale establishment, storehouse, stockroom, storage place, distributing center, repository, depot, shed, entrepôt, stockpile, depository, bin, elevator, storage loft; see also **barn.**

wares, *n.* —*Syn.* goods, lines, stock, products, commodities, manufactured articles, merchandise, range, stuff.

warfare, *n.* —*Syn.* military operations, hostilities, armed struggle, combat, counterinsurgency; see also **battle** 1, **war.**

war games, *n.* —*Syn.* maneuvers, military *or* naval *or* army *or* navy *or* warlike, etc., exercises, practice, simulated war of battle(s); see also **maneuver** 3.

warily, *mod.* —*Syn.* cautiously, suspiciously, vigilantly; see **carefully** 2.

wariness, *n.* —*Syn.* caution, suspicion, alertness; see **attention** 1, **care** 1.

warlike, *mod.* **1.** [Belligerent]—*Syn.* attacking, pugnacious, offensive; see **aggressive** 2.
2. [Military]—*Syn.* soldierly, bellicose, martial; see **fighting, militaristic.**
3. [Unfriendly]—*Syn.* hostile, antagonistic, contrary; see **unfriendly** 1.

warlock, *n.* —*Syn.* wizard, male witch, sorcerer; see **magician, witch.**

warlord, *n.* —*Syn.* bandit, boss, tyrant; see **ruler** 1.

warm, *mod.* **1.** [Moderately heated]—*Syn.* heated, sunny, melting, hot, mild, tepid, lukewarm, summery, temperate, clement, glowing, perspiring, sweaty, sweating, flushed; *both* (D): warmish, snug as a bug in a rug.—*Ant.* cool*, chilly, chilling.
2. [Emotional]—*Syn.* fervent, earnest, irascible, excitable, angry, amorous, emotional, passionate, heated, hot (D).
3. [Sympathetic]—*Syn.* gracious, cordial, empathetic; see **friendly** 1, **sympathetic.**

warm, *v.* —*Syn.* heat (up), warm up *or* over, put on the fire; see **cook, heat** 2.

warmly, *mod.* **1.** [Fervently]—*Syn.* passionately, emotionally, intensely; see **angrily, excitedly.**
2. [Amicably]—*Syn.* cordially, genially, affectionately; see **kindly** 2, **sympathetically.**

warmth, *n.* **1.** [Fervor]—*Syn.* fever, passion, feeling; see **emotion.**
2. [Affection]—*Syn.* friendliness, kindness, sympathy; see **affection, friendship** 2.
3. [Heat]—*Syn.* light, glow, warmness; see **heat** 1, 5, **temperature.**

warn, *v.* —*Syn.* forewarn, give notice, put on guard, give fair warning, signal, advise, prepare, alert, inform, remind, forearm, hint, prepare for the worst, offer a word of caution, admonish, counsel, exhort, enjoin, dissuade, reprove, threaten, forbid, predict, remonstrate, deprecate, prescribe, urge, recommend, prompt, suggest, advocate; *all* (D): make red lights flash, start bells ringing, cry wolf, break out a flag, tip off, give the high sign, put a bug in one's ear.

warned, *mod.*—*Syn.* informed, admonished, made aware, cautioned, advised, given warning, prepared for the worst, told, forewarned; *both* (D): tipped off, put on the lookout.

warning, *n.*—*Syn.* caution, admonition, caveat, notice, advice, alarum, forewarning, portent, omen, alert, intimation, premonition, notification, sign, alarm, indication, token, hint, lesson, information, example, distress signal(s), prediction, signal, injunction, exhortation; *all* (D): high sign, word to the wise, tip-off, SOS, handwriting on the wall.

warp, *n.*—*Syn.* lengthwise threads, skeins, ties; **fiber** 1, **loom, thread.**

warp, *v.*—*Syn.* curve, twist, pervert; see **bend** 1, 2, **distort** 3.

warrant, *n.*—*Syn.* authorization, certificate, credential, official document, summons, subpoena, security, pass, testimonial, passport, credentials, permit, license, permission, chit, verification, authentication.

warrant, *v.* **1.** [To guarantee]—*Syn.* assure, insure, vouch for; see **guarantee** 1, 2, **vouch.**

2. [To justify]—*Syn.* bear out, call for, give grounds for; see **explain, justify** 2.

3. [To authorize]—*Syn.* empower, sanction, license; see **approve** 1, **delegate** 1.

warrantable, *mod.*—*Syn.* permissible, covered, legitimate; see **lawful, legal** 1.

warranted, *mod.*—*Syn.* allowable, allowed, justified, guaranteed, certified, authorized, attested, secured, based, feasible, supported by fact.—*Ant.* false*, unwarranted, unjustified.

warranty, *n.*—*Syn.* guaranty, guarantee, written guaranty, pledge; see **guaranty** 2.

warring, *mod.*—*Syn.* at war, belligerent, battling; see **fighting.**

warrior, *n.*—*Syn.* battler, conscript, soldier, knight, fighter, hero, combatant, enlisted personnel.

warship, *n.*—*Syn.* fighting ship, armored vessel, gunboat, man-of-war, frigate, ship-of-the-line; see also **boat, ship.**

Warships include the following—battleship, cruiser, destroyer, frigate, guided-missile frigate, guided-missile destroyer, missile cruiser, attack submarine, destroyer escort, submarine, submarine chaser, aircraft carrier, escort carrier, corvette, torpedo boat, PT-boat, raider, dreadnought, superdreadnought, capital ship, flagship, landing ship, LST, LSM, LCI, LCP, LCT.

wart, *n.*—*Syn.* protuberance, spots, mole, projection, blemish, growth, bulge, tumor, wen.

war whoop, *n.*—*Syn.* shout, bellow, war cry; see **cry** 1, **yell** 1.

wary, *mod.*—*Syn.* circumspect, cautious, alert; see **careful, sly** 1.

wash, *n.* **1.** [Laundry]—*Syn.* wet wash, washing, linen, family wash, soiled clothing, clean clothes, washed clothing, rough-dry wash, flat pieces, finished laundry.

2. [The movement of water]—*Syn.* swishing, lapping, roll, swirl, rush, surging, eddy, wave, undulation, surge, heave, flow, murmur, gush, spurt.

3. [(D) A stream bed that is usually dry]—*Syn.* arroyo, gulch, canyon, gorge, ravine, valley, gap.

4. [A prepared liquid]—*Syn.* rinse, swab, coating; see **liquid.**

wash, *v.* **1.** [To bathe]—*Syn.* clean, cleanse, lave, shine, immerse, douse, soak, take a bath, (take a) shower, soap, rub the dirt off, scour, scrub, rinse, wipe, sponge, dip; *all* (D): fresh up, wash up, clean up, brush up.

2. [To launder]—*Syn.* clean, starch, scrub, put in a washing machine, boil, soap, take the grit out of, send to the laundry, scour, rinse out, soak, sozzle, drench.—*Ant.* dirty*, stain, smirch.

3. [To brush with a liquid]—*Syn.* swab, paint, whitewash, color, coat, dye, tint, stain, tinge, touch up, retouch, daub.

4. [To erode]—*Syn.* eat away, carry off, decrease, wear, wear down, remove, deteriorate.

5. [To border upon]—*Syn.* flow along, touch, lave, reach, flood, hit, run along the edge of.

6. [(D) To be convincing]—*Syn.* be plausible *or* reasonable *or* acceptable, stand up, endure examination; see **convince.**

washable, *mod.*—*Syn.* tubfast, fast, unfading, launderable, colorfast, pre-shrunk, Sanforized (trademark); *both* (D): tubbable, sudsable; see also **permanent** 2.

washed, *mod.* **1.** [Laundered]—*Syn.* cleaned, scrubbed, bleached, boiled, put through the wash, soaped.—*Ant.* dirty*, soiled, foul.

2. [Laved]—*Syn.* bathed, dipped, drenched, sponged, doused, soaked, cleansed, submerged, watered, showered.—*Ant.* dry*, scorching, desert.

washed out (D), *mod.*—*Syn.* dismissed, let go, dropped (from the program); see **discharged** 1.

washed up (D), *mod.*—*Syn.* finished, defeated, done for (D); see **ruined** 1, 2.

washer, *n.* **1.** [A flat ring]—*Syn.* disk, seat, packing, collar, lock washer, shim, patent washer; see also **part** 3.

2. [A machine for washing]—*Syn.* electric dishwasher, washing machine, laundry machine, electric washer, gasoline washer, power-driven washer; see also **appliance, machine** 1.

washing, *n.*—*Syn.* laundry, soiled clothes, dirty clothes; see **wash** 1.

Washington, *n.*—*Syn.* the Capitol, the (nation's) capital, the President, the Presidency, the White House, the Oval Office, the Congress, the Hill, the national *or* Federal government, the Supreme Court, the Pentagon, the CIA; *all* (D): the Establishment, Foggy Bottom, the mess in Washington, the Washington run-around *or* merry-go-round, on the banks of the Potomac; see also **administration** 1, 2, **city.**

washout (D), *n.*—*Syn.* disaster, disappointment, mess; see **failure** 1, 2.

wasp, *n.* Wasps include the following—common, fossorial, digging, digger, social, solitary, hunting, potter, paper, sand, wood, spider, fig, gall, cuckoo, thread-waisted; (mud) dauber, yellow jacket, hornet, *Sphex* (Latin); see also **bee** 1.

waspish, *mod.*—*Syn.* bad-tempered, snappish, crabby (D); see **irritable.**

wassail, *n.*—*Syn.* festivity, festival, crousal; see **feast.**

waste, *mod.*—*Syn.* futile, discarded, worthless, valueless, useless, empty, barren, dreary, uninhabited, desolate, profitless, superfluous, unnecessary, functionless, purposeless, pointless, unserviceable. —*Ant.* usable*, preserved, valuable.

waste, *n.* **1.** [The state of being wasted]—*Syn.* disuse, misuse, dissipation, consumption, uselessness, devastation, ruin, decay, dilapidation, loss, exhaustion, extravagance, squandering, wear and tear, wrack and ruin; see also **wear.**—*Ant.* use*, profit*, value*.
2. [Refuse]—*Syn.* rubbish, garbage, scrap; see **excess** 4, **trash** 1, 3.
3. [Unused land]—*Syn.* desert, wilds, wilderness, dustbowl, wasteland, tundra, marsh, marshland, badlands, bog, fen, moor, quagmire, swamp, wash.

waste, *v.* **1.** [To use without result]—*Syn.* dissipate, spend, consume, lose, be of no avail, come to nothing, go to waste, misuse, throw away, use up, misapply, misemploy, labor in vain; *all* (D): cast pearls before swine, send owls to Athens, carry coals to Newcastle.—*Ant.* profit*, use well, get results.
2. [To squander]—*Syn.* burn up, lavish, scatter, splurge, spend, be prodigal, indulge, abuse, empty, drain, use up, deplete, fatigue, spill, impoverish, misspend, exhaust, fritter *or* fool away, ruin, be spendthrift, divert, go through, gamble away; *all* (D): throw (money) into a well, run through, hang the expense, blow *or* scatter to the winds, blow, burn the candle at both ends.—*Ant.* save*, be thrifty, manage wisely.
3. [To be consumed gradually]—*Syn.* decay, thin out, become thin, wither, dwindle, lose weight, be diseased, run dry, run to seed, wilt, droop, decrease, disappear, drain, empty, wear, wither. —*Ant.* grow*, develop, enrich.

wasted, *mod.*—*Syn.* squandered, spent, destroyed, lost, consumed, eaten up, thrown away, shriveled, gaunt, emaciated, decayed, depleted, scattered, drained, gone for nothing, missapplied, useless, to no avail, down the drain, unappreciated, of no use, worthless.—*Ant.* preserved*, saved, useful.

wasteful, *mod.*—*Syn.* extravagant, profligate, dissipated, prodigal, liberal, immoderate, overgenerous, incontinent, thriftless, lavish, squandering, profuse, unthrifty, improvident, careless, reckless, cavalier, wild, full-handed, without stint, destructive; *all* (D): with money to burn, easy come easy go, out of bounds.—*Ant.* stingy*, miserly, tightfisted.

wastefully, *mod.*—*Syn.* extravagantly, profligately, improvidently, carelessly, wildly, immoderately, thriftlessly, recklessly, prodigally, destructively, unstintedly, incontinently, foolishly, lavishly, inconsiderately, openhandedly, imprudently, ruthlessly, profusely, overgenerously, with no thought for tomorrow, without a second thought; without restraint *or* good sense *or* consideration, etc.

waster, *n.*—*Syn.* spendthrift, prodigal, wastrel; see **beggar** 1, **loafer.**

waste time, *v.*—*Syn.* malinger, dawdle, drift; see **loaf** 1.

watch, *n.* **1.** [A portable timepiece]—*Syn.* wrist watch, pocket watch, stopwatch, chronometer, digital watch, analog watch; see also **clock.**
2. [Strict attention]—*Syn.* lookout, observation, observance, surveillance, awareness, attention, vigilance, guard, heed, watchfulness.—*Ant.* neglect*, sleepiness, apathy.
3. [A period of duty or vigilance]—*Syn.* patrol, guard duty, nightwatch, shift, vigil, picket duty, sentry duty; *all* (D): trick, dogwatch, graveyard watch.
4. [Those who keep a watch, sense 3]—*Syn.* guard, sentry, sentinel, picket, watchman, lookout, scout, spotter, observer, signalman, flagman, shore patrol (*or* (D): S.P.), military police (*or* (D): M.P.); see also **guardian** 1.

watch, *v.* **1.** [To be attentive]—*Syn.* observe, see, scrutinize, follow, attend, mark, regard, listen, wait, attend, take notice, contemplate, mind, view, pay attention, concentrate, look closely.
2. [To guard]—*Syn.* keep an eye on, keep (a) prisoner, patrol, picket, police; see also **guard** 2.

watched, *mod.*—*Syn.* guarded, spied on, followed, held under suspicion, scrutinized, observed, marked, kept under surveillance, noticed, noted, bugged (D).

watcher, *n.*—*Syn.* lookout, guard, spectator; see **watchman.**

watchful, *mod.*—*Syn.* on guard, keen, vigilant, prepared, wide-awake, careful, observant.

watchfulness, *n.*—*Syn.* vigilance, alertness, attention, caution, carefulness, wide-awakeness, wariness, readiness, awareness, promptness, circumspection, mindfulness, keenness, sharpness, acuteness, quickness, briskness, vigorousness, aliveness, animation.

watching, *mod.*—*Syn.* vigilant, wary, alert, circumspect, observant, cautious, on the lookout.

watchman, *n.*—*Syn.* day watchman, watcher, sentinel, scout, spy, ranger, observer, spotter, signalman, flagman, shore patrol, night watchman, curator, guard, detective, policeman, patrolman, sentry, keeper, caretaker, flagman, lookout; see also **guardian** 1.

watch out, *v.*—*Syn.* take care, heed, be cautious, proceed carefully, mind, go on tiptoe, take precautions, be on one's guard, make sure of, be doubly sure; *all* (D): look alive, keep an eye peeled, handle with kid gloves.

watch over, *v.*—*Syn.* protect, look after, attend to; see **guard** 2.

watchtower, *n.*—*Syn.* fire tower, lighthouse, observatory; see **lookout** 1.

watchword, *n.*—*Syn.* cue, countersign, signal; see **password, sign** 1.

water, *n.* **1.** [Water as a liquid]—*Syn.* rain, rainwater, liquid, drinking water, city water, mineral water, salt water, spa water, distilled water, limewater, H_2O, aqua pura.
2. [Water as a body]—*Syn.* spring, lake, ocean, dam, sea, puddle, pond, basin, pool, river, lagoon, reservoir, brook, stream, creek, waterfall, bayou.

water, *v.*—*Syn.* sprinkle, spray, irrigate, soak, souse, douse, wet, moisten, flood, inundate, give a (good) spraying *or* sprinkling *or* soaking *or* watering, spatter, provide moisture enough.

water bug, *n.* Water bugs include the following —skipper, skater, water beetle, walking stick, water weevil, back swimmer, giant water bug, Croton bug, gerrid, water scorpion, water mantis, water scavenger, water strider; see also **insect.**

water closet, *n.* —*Syn.* lavatory, privy, powder room; see **toilet** 2.

watercourse, *n.* **1.** [A river]—*Syn.* brook, stream, tributary; see **river.**
2. [A canal]—*Syn.* waterway, spillway, aqueduct; see **channel** 2, **trench** 1.

water down, *v.* —*Syn.* dilute, restrict, make weaker *or* less potent *or* less effective, etc.; see **weaken** 2.

watered, *mod.* **1.** [Given water]—*Syn.* sprinkled, showered, hosed, sprayed, washed, sluiced, bathed, drenched, wetted, irrigated, flooded, baptized, doused, soused, sodden, slaked, quenched; see also **wet** 1.—*Ant.* dry*, arid, thirsty.
2. [Diluted]—*Syn.* thinned, weakened, adulterated, lessened, contaminated, mixed, debased, impure, corrupt, blended, weakened, spread out, inflated, cheapened.

waterfall, *n.* —*Syn.* cataract, Niagara, fall, cascade, rapids, force fosse, watercourse, shoot; see also **water** 1, 2.

waterfowl, *n.* —*Syn.* water bird, game bird, wild game, wild duck, wild goose, brant, mallard, teal, snipe; see also **bird** 1.

waterfront, *n.* —*Syn.* wharves, embarcadero, roadstead; see **harbor** 2.

water hole, *n.* —*Syn.* (desert) well, puddle, *ojo* (Spanish); see **pool, well** 1.

water lily, *n.* Water lilies include the following— water shield, floating heart, Victoria regia *or* Royal water lily, Victoria cruziana, blue Egyptian lotus, East Indian lotus, Formosa water lily, rice-field water lily, spotted marliac, pond lily *or* yellow water lily, white water lily, golden water lily, water chinquapin *or* wankapin; see also **plant.**

water nymph, *n.* —*Syn.* sprite, mermaid, sea nymph; see **fairy** 1, **goddess.**

water power, *n.* —*Syn.* hydraulics, water works, electricity, water pressure, mechanical energy, electric power; see also **energy** 3.

waterproof, *mod.* —*Syn.* impermeable, tight, airtight, vacuum-packed, oiled, rubber-coated, watertight, insulated, impervious, hermetically sealed.

watery, *mod.* —*Syn.* moist, damp, humid, soggy, sodden, wet, thin, colorless, washed, waterlike. —*Ant.* dry*, parched, baked*.

wave, *n.* **1.** [A wall of water]—*Syn.* comber, swell, roller, heave, tidal wave, billow, tide, surge, crest, bore, tube, breaker, whitecap, curl (D).
2. [A movement suggestive of a wave]—*Syn.* surge, gush, swell, uprising, onslaught, influx, tide, flow, stream, come and go, swarm, drift, rush, crush, line after line, fluctuation.
3. [Undulating movement]—*Syn.* rocking, bending, winding, coil, curl, roll, twirl, loop, swirl, swing, sway, corkscrew, spring, lift, rippling.
4. [A line suggestive of a wave]—*Syn.* scroll, kink, convolution, meander, loop, wavy line, twist, volute, curlicue.

wave, *v.* **1.** [To flutter]—*Syn.* stream, pulse, flow, shake, fly, dance, flap, swish, swing, tremble, whirl. —*Ant.* droop, fall*, hang listless.
2. [To give an alternating movement]—*Syn.* motion, beckon, call, raise the arm, signal, greet, return a greeting, hail.
3. [To move back and forth]—*Syn.* falter, waver, oscillate, vacillate, fluctuate, pulsate, vibrate, wag, waggle, sway, lurch, bend, swing, dangle, seesaw, wobble, reel, quaver, quiver, swing from side to side, palpitate, move to and fro; see also **rock.**
4. [To undulate]—*Syn.* surge, roll, flow, wind, swell, billow, curl, twirl, swirl, coil, ripple, twist.
5. [To set hair]—*Syn.* put up, curl, set, permanent, pin (up), roll (up).

waver, *v.* —*Syn.* fluctuate, vacillate, hesitate, dilly-dally, seesaw, deliberate, reel, teeter, totter, hem and haw, pause, stagger.

wavering, *mod.* —*Syn.* vacillating, fluctuating, variable; see **changeable** 1, 2, **changing.**

wavy, *mod.* **1.** [Sinuous]—*Syn.* bumpy, crinkly, curved; see **rough** 1, **twisted.**
2. [Unsteady]—*Syn.* wavering, fluctuating, vibrating; see **changeable** 1, 2.

wax, *n.* Waxes include the following—paraffin, resin, spermaceti, oxocerite, beeswax, honeycomb, sealing wax, earwax *or* cerumen, carnauba wax, automobile wax, floor wax, furniture polish.

wax, *v.* **1.** [To increase]—*Syn.* become larger, swell, grow full; see **grow** 1.
2. [To apply wax]—*Syn.* polish, smooth, smear; see **spread** 4.

waxen, *mod.* —*Syn.* waxlike, wax-covered, pale, pallid, white, whitish, wan, sickly, blanched, unhealthy, ghostly, sallow.—*Ant.* ruddy, healthy*, robust.

waxy, *mod.* —*Syn.* slick, glistening, glassy; see **slippery, smooth** 1.

way, *n.* **1.** [Road]—*Syn.* trail, walk, byway; see **highway.**
2. [Course]—*Syn.* alternative, direction, progression, trend, tendency, distance, space, extent, bearing, orbit, approach, passage, route, gateway, entrance, access, door, gate, channel.
3. [Means]—*Syn.* method, mode, means, plan, technique, design, system, procedure, process, measure, contrivance, stroke, step, move, action, idea, outline, plot, policy, instrument.
4. [Manner]—*Syn.* form, fashion, gait, tone, guise, habit, custom, usage, behavior, style.
by the way—*Syn.* casually, by the by, as a matter of fact; see **incidentally.**
by way of—*Syn.* routed (through), detoured (through), utilizing; see **through** 4.
get out of the *or* **one's way**—*Syn.* go, remove oneself, retire; see **leave** 1, **remove** 1.
go one's (own) way—*Syn.* persevere, do what one pleases, do one's thing (D); see **choose** 1, **continue** 1, **decide.**
give way (to)—*Syn.* give preference to, permit, accede (to); see **allow** 1, **retire** 1, 3, **retreat** 1, 2.
lead the way—*Syn.* conduct, take the lead, be the leader *or* manager *or* director, etc.; see **lead** 1.
make one's way—*Syn.* progress, succeed, do well; see **advance** 1, **profit** 2, **win** 1, 4.

make way—*Syn.* draw *or* pull back, give way, withdraw; see **leave** 1, **retire** 1, 3.
on the way out—*Syn.* declining, no longer fashionable, going (out); see **old-fashioned, unpopular.**
out of the way—*Syn.* disposed of, terminated, taken out; see **away** 1, **gone** 1, 2, **remove** 1.
parting of the ways—*Syn.* break-up, agreeing to disagree, difference of opinion; see **fight** 1, **separation** 1.
see one's way (clear)—*Syn.* agree (to), be able *or* willing, be prepared to; see **can** 5.
under way—*Syn.* going, prospering, making headway; see **moving** 1.

wayfarer, *n.* —*Syn.* pilgrim, rambler, voyager; see **traveler.**

wayfaring, *mod.* —*Syn.* voyaging, rambling, vagrant; see **traveling.**

waylay, *v.* —*Syn.* wait for, assail, accost; see **ambush.**

way-out (D), *mod.* —*Syn.* very different, revolutionary, strange; see **extreme.**

way out, *n.* —*Syn.* means of escape, salvation, loophole; see **escape** 2, **exit** 1.

ways, *n.* —*Syn.* scaffolding, props, support(s), stays, frame, ground ways, bilge *or* sliding ways, launching ways, platform, framework, shores, struts.

ways and means, *n.* —*Syn.* methods, approaches, devices; see **means** 1, 2, **resources.**

wayside, *mod.* —*Syn.* roadside, side, on the road, at the curb, by *or* on the way, at the edge.

wayward, *mod.* —*Syn.* unruly, disobedient, perverse, headstrong, unmanageable, insubordinate, capricious, delinquent, incorrigible; refractory, willful, unruly, self-indulgent, changeable, recalcitrant, stubborn.—*Ant.* obedient*, stable, resolute*.

we, *pron.* —*Syn.* you and I, he and I, she and I, they and I, us.

weak, *mod.* **1.** [Lacking physical strength; *said of persons*]—*Syn.* delicate, puny, flabby, flaccid, debilitated, effeminate, frail, sickly, enervated, senile; see also **sick.**—*Ant.* strong*, healthy*, robust.
2. [Lacking physical strength; *said of things*] —*Syn.* flimsy, makeshift, brittle, unsubstantial, jerry-built, rickety, tumbledown, sleazy, shaky, unsteady, ramshackle, rotten, wobbly, tottery, top-heavy.—*Ant.* strong*, shatter-proof, sturdy.
3. [Lacking mental firmness or character]—*Syn.* weakminded, nerveless, fainthearted, irresolute, nervous, spineless, unstrung, palsied, wishy-washy, caitiff, hesitant, vacillating, frightened.—*Ant.* brave*, courageous, adventurous.
4. [Lacking in volume]—*Syn.* thin, low, soft, indistinct, feeble, faint, dim, muffled, whispered, bated, inaudible, light, stifled, dull, pale.—*Ant.* loud*, strong, forceful.
5. [Lacking in military power]—*Syn.* small, paltry, ineffectual, ineffective, inadequate, impotent, ill-equipped, insufficiently armed, limited, unorganized, undisciplined, untrained, vulnerable, exposed, assailable, unprepared.
6. [Lacking in capacity or experience]—*Syn.* unsure, raw, green, fresh, untrained, young, backward, insecure, immature, unsteady, handicapped, soft, shaky, uncertain, incomplete, untried.—*Ant.* experienced*, expert, trained*.

weaken, *v.* **1.** [To become weaker]—*Syn.* lessen, lose, decrease, relapse, soften, relax, droop, fail, wane, crumble, halt, limp, languish, fade, decline, abate, totter, tremble, flag, faint, wilt, lose spirit, become disheartened, fail in courage, slow down, break up; *both* (D): crack up, wash out.—*Ant.* revive*, strengthen*, straighten.
2. [To make weaker]—*Syn.* reduce, minimize, enervate, debilitate, exhaust, cripple, unman, emasculate, castrate, devitalize, undermine, impair, sap, enfeeble, unnerve, incapacitate, impoverish, thin, dilute; *both* (D): take the wind out of, wash up; see also **decrease** 2.—*Ant.* revive*, quicken, animate.

weakened, *mod.* —*Syn.* injured, disabled, vulnerable, weak, handicapped, feeble, unsteady, groggy, limp, open to attack.—*Ant.* fortified*, strengthened, invulnerable.

weakling, *n.* —*Syn.* puny person, feeble, creature, dotard, coward, crybaby, invertebrate, mollycoddle, milksop; *all* (D): jellyfish, sissy, jelly-bean softie, pushover, namby-pamby, puff, punk.

weak-minded, *mod.* —*Syn.* foolish, moronic, not bright; see **stupid** 1, **weak** 3.

weakness, *n.* **1.** [The state of being weak]—*Syn.* feebleness, senility, anility, delicacy, invalidity, frailty, faintness, prostration, anoxia, anoxemia, decrepitude, debility, effeminacy impotence, enervation, dizziness, femininity, infirmity.—*Ant.* strength*, good health, vitality.
2. [An instance or manner of being weak]—*Syn.* fault, failing, deficiency, defect, disturbance, lapse, vice, sore point, gap, flaw, instability, indecision, inconstancy, vulnerability.—*Ant.* virtue*, good, strength.
3. [(D) Inclination]—*Syn.* liking, tendency, bent; see **hunger, inclination** 1.

weak-willed, *mod.* —*Syn.* soft, shy, backward; see **timid** 1, 2, **weak** 3.

wealth, *n.* **1.** [Goods or services having economic utility]—*Syn.* capital, capital stock, economic resources, stock, stocks and bonds, securities, vested interests, land, property, labor power, commodities, cash, money in the bank, money, natural resources, assets; *all* (D): purse strings, dough, long green.—*Ant.* poverty*, idle resources, unemployment.
2. [Personal riches]—*Syn.* means, money, riches, substance, affluence, belongings, property, fortune, hoard, treasure, resources, revenue, cache, cash, competence, opulence, luxury, luxuriance, prosperity, pelf, abundance, money to burn (D). —*Ant.* poverty*, pauperism, straits.

wealthily, *mod.* —*Syn.* richly, extensively, opulently; see **abundantly.**

wealthy, *mod.* —*Syn.* opulent, moneyed, affluent; see **rich** 1.

wean, *v.* —*Syn.* bring up, break of, stop suckling, detach, unaccustom, reconcile to (a loss); see **remove** 1.

weapon, *n.* **1.** [An instrument for combat]—*Syn.* armament, protection, weaponry, deadly weapon, (military) hardware, sophisticated hardware, lethal weapon, defense.
Weapons include the following—club, spear, arrow, knife, catapult, bullet, dart, flechette, missile, ABM (antiballistic missile), MRV (multiple re-

entry vehicle), MIRV (multiple independently-targetable re-entry vehicle), CAM (cybernetic anthropomorphic machine), CBW (chemical and biological warfare), bomb, stick, ax, firearm, cannon, gun, musket, rifle, blackjack, whip, sword, pistol, revolver, bayonet, machine gun, warhead, airplane, tank, destroyer.

2. [A device thought of figuratively as a weapon] —*Syn.* argument, plea, evidence, influence, alibi, intimidation, threat, blackmail, scolding, sharp tongue.

wear, *n.* —*Syn.* depreciation, damage, loss, erosion, wear and tear, loss by friction, inroads of time, diminution, waste, corrosion, impairment, wearing away, dilapidation, disappearance, result of friction.—*Ant.* growth*, accretion, building up.

wear, *v.* **1.** [To use as clothing or personal ornament] —*Syn.* bear, carry, effect, put on, don, be clothed, slip *or* get *or* have on, dress in, attire, array, cover, wrap, harness, get into (D); see also **dress** 1. —*Ant.* undress*, take off, disrobe.

2. [To consume by wearing]—*Syn.* use up, use, consume, wear thin *or* out, waste, diminish, cut down, scrape off, exhaust, fatigue, weather down, impair.

3. [To be consumed by wearing]—*Syn.* fade, go to seed, decay, crumble, dwindle, shrink, decline, deteriorate, decrease, waste, become threadbare.

wear and tear, *n.* —*Syn.* depletion, wearing, effect of use; see **damage** 1, 2, **destruction** 2, **loss** 3.

wear down, *v.* **1.** [To become worn]—*Syn.* wear out, get thin(ner), get worn out; see **decrease** 1, **waste** 3.

2. [To make weary]—*Syn.* get the better of, reduce, beat; see **defeat** 1, 3, **tire** 2.

wearer, *n.* —*Syn.* mannequin, buyer, customer; see **model** 4.

weariness, *n.* —*Syn.* tiredness, exhaustion, dullness; see **fatigue, lassitude.**

wearing, *mod.* —*Syn.* tiring, exhausting, nerve-racking, jolting, hard, difficult, long, endless, discomforting, upsetting.—*Ant.* stimulating*, invigorating, bracing.

wearisome, *mod.* **1.** [Burdensome]—*Syn.* laborious, strenuous, toilsome; see **onerous.**

2. [Boring]—*Syn.* tedious, tiresome, vapid; see **dull** 4.

wear off, *v.* —*Syn.* go away, get better, decline; see **improve** 2, **stop** 2.

wear out, *v.* —*Syn.* become worn, be worthless, get thinner *or* weaker *or* softer, etc.; see **decay, waste** 1, 3.

wear out one's welcome (D), *v.* —*Syn.* stay (too long), make people tired *or* weary of one, hang around (D); see **remain** 1, **weary** 1.

wear the pants *or* **trousers** (D), *v.* —*Syn.* run things, boss (the job), domineer; see **dominate.**

weary, *mod.* —*Syn.* exhausted, fatigued, overworked; see **tired.**

weary, *v.* **1.** [To make weary]—*Syn.* annoy, vex, distress, irk, tax, strain, overwork, exhaust, fatigue, tire, tucker out (D), harass, bore, disgust, dishearten, unman, dispirit, wear out, cause ennui, leave one cold, depress, cloy, glut, jade, overstuff, burden, sicken, nauseate.—*Ant.* revive*, refresh, animate.

2. [To become weary]—*Syn.* pain, flag, be worn out, sink, droop, lose interest, fall off, tire, grow tired, drowse, doze, sicken; see also **sleep.**—*Ant.* excite, enjoy, be amused.

weary of, *mod.* —*Syn.* bored, disgusted, impatient, uninterested, disinclined, vexed, unmoved, upset, nauseated, sickened; *both* (D): bored stiff, bored to tears.—*Ant.* excited*, moved, stimulated.

weather, *n.* —*Syn.* climate, atmospheric conditions, clime (D), air conditions, drought, clear weather, sunny weather, foul weather, tempest, calm, windiness, the elements, cloudiness, heat, cold, warmth, chilliness.

weather, *v.* **1.** [To expose to the weather]—*Syn.* dry, bleach, discolor, blanch, whiten, pulverize, tan, burn, patinate, expose, harden, petrify.

2. [To pass through adversity successfully]—*Syn.* overcome, endure, become toughened, grow hardened, stand up against, bear the brunt of, acclimate oneself, grow strong through; see also **strengthen, succeed** 1.—*Ant.* fail*, be overcome, fall victim to.

weather-beaten, *mod.* —*Syn.* decayed, battered, weathered; see **decaying, old** 2, 3, **worn** 2.

weatherman, *n.* —*Syn.* weather reporter, weather prophet, weather forecaster, meteorologist, climatologist, weather bureau, weather station, newsman.

weather report, *n.* —*Syn.* weather picture, weathercast, meteorological forecast; see **forecast.**

weather vane, *n.* —*Syn.* weathercock, vane, wind gauge, wind sleeve, aerometer.

weave, *n.* —*Syn.* pattern, design, method of weaving, knitting, crocheting, darning, texture, warp and woof.

Types of weaves include the following—plain, basket, satin, twill, twining, herringbone, tapestry, Jacquard, crepe, velvet.

weave, *v.* **1.** [To construct by interlacing]—*Syn.* knit, sew, interlace, spin, twine, intertwine, crisscross, interlink, wreathe, mesh, net, knot, twill, fold, interfold, ply, reticulate, loop, splice, braid, plait, twist.

2. [To move in and out]—*Syn.* sidle through, make one's way, twist and turn, snake, zigzag, beat one's way, insinuate oneself through, wedge through; see also **curl** 1.

3. [To contrive]—*Syn.* compose, fabricate, form, make, create, body forth, manufacture, spin *or* turn out, construct, piece together.

web, *n.* **1.** [A combination of threads]—*Syn.* cobweb, lacework, netting, plait, mesh, mat, matting, wicker, weft, warp, woof.

2. [An intricate combination]—*Syn.* network, interconnection, reticulation, intermixture, entanglement, tracery, filigree, interweaving, trellis.

wed, *v.* —*Syn.* espouse, join in wedlock, give *or* take *or* receive in marriage; see **marry** 1, 2.

wedded, *mod.* —*Syn.* married, espoused, in holy matrimony; see **married.**

wedding, *n.* —*Syn.* wedlock, nuptials, matrimony; see **marriage** 1, **union** 3.

wedge, *n.* —*Syn.* spearhead, prong, entering wedge, flying column, mobile force, drive; see also **machine** 1, **tool** 1.

Devices using the principles of the wedge include the following—keystone, chock, shim, quoin, cleat, cotter.

wedlock, *n.* —*Syn.* matrimony, nuptials, espousal; see **marriage** 2, **union** 3.

wee, *mod.* —*Syn.* small, tiny, infinitesimal; see **little** 1, **minute** 1.

weed, *n.* **1.** [Wild plant]—*Syn.* noxious weed, unwanted plant, prolific plant; see **plant.**
Common weeds include the following—ragweed, nettle, wild morning-glory, pigweed, buckthorn, dandelion, lamb's quarters, buttonweed, dog fennel, plantain, quack grass, jimson weed, ironweed, wild sunflower, wild hemp, horsemint, foxtail, milkweed, wild barley, wild buckwheat, mullein, cheat grass, Russian thistle *or* tubleweed, burdock, wild carrot, Queen Anne's lace, wild parsley, tarweed, vervain, wild mustard.
2. [(D) Cigarette or cigar]—*Syn. all* (D): coffin nail, fag, joint; see **tobacco.**
3. [(D) Marijuana]—*Syn. all* (D): pot, boo, Maryjane; see **marijuana.**

week, *n.* —*Syn.* wk., seven days, six days, forty-hour week, working week, work week (D).

week after week, *mod.* —*Syn.* continually, right along, regularly; see **continuing.**

weekday, *n.* —*Syn.* working day, Mondays, Tuesdays, Wednesdays, etc.; not a Sunday *or* the Sabbath; see **day** 2.

weekend, *n.* —*Syn.* end of the week, Saturday to Monday, short vacation, English weekend, long weekend.

weekly, *mod.* —*Syn.* once every seven days; every Monday, regularly every Tuesday, etc.; once a week, occuring every week.

weep, *v.* —*Syn.* wail, moan, lament, bemoan, grieve for, blubber (D); see also **cry** 1, **mourn** 1.

weeping, *mod.* —*Syn.* crying, blubbering, sobbing, lamenting, tearful, in tears, teary-eyed, lachrymose, mourning, sorrowing, wailing, howling, moaning, shrieking; see also **sad** 1, **troubled** 1.

weepy, *mod.* —*Syn.* lachrymose, crying; see **weeping.**

weigh, *v.* **1.** [To take the weight of]—*Syn.* measure, scale, put on the scales, hold the scales, put in the balance, counterbalance, heft (D); see also **balance** 2, **measure** 1.
2. [To have weight]—*Syn.* be heavy, carry weight, be important, tell, count, show, register, press, pull, be a load, burden, tip the beams (D).
3. [To consider]—*Syn.* ponder, contemplate, balance; see **consider** 1, **estimate** 3.

weigh down, *v.* —*Syn.* push *or* pull *or* hold, etc., down; burden, oppress; see **depress** 2.

weighing, *n.* —*Syn.* measuring, estimating, considering, balancing, contemplating, evaluating, judging, deciding, thinking over.

weight, *n.* **1.** [Heaviness]—*Syn.* pressure, load, gross weight, net weight, dead weight, molecular weight, gravity, heft, burden, mass, density, adiposity, ponderousness, tonnage, ballast, substance, G-factor (D); see also **measurement** 2, **pressure** 1.—*Ant.* lightness*, buoyancy, airiness.
2. [An object used for its weight]—*Syn.* counterbalance, counterweight, counterpoise, ballast, paperweight, stone, rock, leadweight, sinker, anchor, plumb, sandbag.
3. [Importance]—*Syn.* influence, authority, sway; see **importance** 1, **power** 2.
Common weights include the following—dram, grain, ounce, pound, stone (British), hundredweight, ton, long ton, kilogram, centigram, gram, gram molecule, milligram, metric ton, metric carat, carat (grain), mole, tonneau, denier, assay ton, quintal, scruple.

weird, *mod.* —*Syn.* uncanny, ominous, eerie; see **ghastly** 1, **mysterious** 2.

weird sisters, *n.* —*Syn.* the Fates, the three witches, the Sisters Three; see **fate.**

welcome, *interj.* —*Syn.* greetings: come right in, make yourself at home, how do you do? glad to see you, won't you come in?

welcome, *mod.* **1.** [Willingly received as a guest] —*Syn.* gladly received *or* admitted, desired, appreciated, honored, esteemed, cherished.—*Ant.* undesirable*, unwelcome, unwanted.
2. [Willingly accepted]—*Syn.* desirable, agreeable, pleasant, grateful, good, pleasing, joy-bringing, delightful.—*Ant.* undesirable*, disagreeable, unpleasant.

welcome, *n.* —*Syn.* greetings, salute, salutation, a hero's welcome, handshake, (warm) reception, free entrance, entree, hospitality, friendliness, the glad hand (D).—*Ant.* rebuke*, snub, cool reception.
wear out one's welcome—*Syn.* bore (others), stay (too long), make others tired *or* weary *or* bored, etc. (with one); see **remain** 1, **weary** 1.

welcome, *v.* —*Syn.* embrace, hug, take in; see **greet.**

welcomed, *mod.* —*Syn.* received, accepted, initiated, taken in, greeted, celebrated, honored, welcome, accommodated, appreciated, hailed, entertained, coming in.—*Ant.* unpopular*, snubbed, avoided.

weld, *v.* —*Syn.* fuse, fix, combine, unite, spot-weld, seam-weld, acetylene-weld, electric-weld, resistance-weld, projection-weld; see also **join** 1.

welfare, *n.* **1.** [Personal condition]—*Syn.* health, happiness, well-being, benefit, profit, prosperity, good, good fortune, progress, state of being.
2. [Social service]—*Syn.* social work, public works, social aid, unemployment benefits, child welfare, federal aid, poverty program, social insurance, health service; see also **aid** 1, **insurance.**

well, *mod.* **1.** [In good health]—*Syn.* fine, sound, fit, trim, healthy, robust, strong, hearty, high-spirited, vigorous, hardy, hale, blooming, fresh, flourishing, rosy-cheeked, whole, in fine fettle; *all* (D): hunky-dory, corking, great, fit as a fiddle, chipper.—*Ant.* sick*, ill, infirm.
2. [Satisfactorily]—*Syn.* up to the mark, suitably, adequately, commendable, excellently, thoroughly, admirably, splendidly, favorably, famously, rightly, properly, expertly, strongly, irreproachably, ably, capably, soundly, competently.—*Ant.* badly*, poorly, unsatisfactorily.
3. [Sufficiently]—*Syn.* abundantly, adequately, completely, fully, quite, entirely, considerably, wholly, plentifully, luxuriantly, extremely.—*Ant.* hardly*, insufficiently, barely.

as well—*Syn.* in addition, additionally, along with; see **also.**

as well as—*Syn.* similarly, alike, as much *or* high *or* good, etc., as; see **equally.**

well, *n.* **1.** [A source of water]—*Syn.* spring, fountain, font, spout, geyser, wellspring, mouth, artesian well, reservoir, *cenote* (Spanish).

2. [A shaft sunk into the earth]—*Syn.* pit, hole, depression, chasm, abyss, oil well, gas well, water well.

3. [Any source]—*Syn.* beginning, derivation, fountainhead; see **origin** 3.

well-balanced, *mod.*—*Syn.* steady, sensible, well-adjusted; see **reliable** 1.

well-behaved, *mod.*—*Syn.* mannerly, courteous, civil; see **polite** 1.

well-being, *n.*—*Syn.* prosperity, happiness, fortune; see **health** 1, **welfare** 1.

well-bred, *mod.*—*Syn.* courteous, considerate, mannerly; see **polite** 1, **refined** 2.

well-defined, *mod.*—*Syn.* distinct, clear, sharp; see **definite** 2, **outlined** 1.

well-disposed (to *or* **toward),** *mod.*—*Syn.* willing, friendly, encouraging; see **favorable** 3.

well-favored, *mod.*—*Syn.* good-looking, attractive, comely; see **handsome** 2.

well-fixed (D), *mod.*—*Syn.* well-to-do, wealthy, in comfortable circumstances; see **rich** 1.

well-founded, *mod.*—*Syn.* true, probable, plausible; see **likely** 1, **reliable** 2.

well-groomed, *mod.*—*Syn.* clean, cared for, spruce; see **neat** 1.

well-informed, *mod.*—*Syn.* informed, advised, well-read; see **educated** 1, **learned** 1, 2.

well-intentioned, *mod.*—*Syn.* honorable, high-principled, good-hearted; see **moral** 1, **noble** 2, 3.

well-known, *mod.*—*Syn.* famous, reputable, recognized, renowned, eminent, illustrious, familiar, widely known, noted, acclaimed, popular, public, celebrated, in the public eye, notorious, infamous.—*Ant.* unknown*, obscure*, undiscovered.

well-nigh, *mod.*—*Syn.* practically, nearly, almost completely; see **almost, approximately.**

well-off, *mod.*—*Syn.* prosperous, well-to-do, wealthy; see **rich** 1.

well-preserved, *mod.*—*Syn.* lively, alert, in possession of one's faculties; see **active** 1, 2, **aging.**

well-rounded, *mod.*—*Syn.* well-informed, built up, having a good background; see **balanced, excellent.**

well-timed, *mod.*—*Syn.* appropriate, opportune, seasonable; see **timely.**

well-to-do, *mod.*—*Syn.* wealthy, well-off, prosperous; see **rich** 1.

Welsh, *mod.*—*Syn.* Welch, Celtic, Cymric, Old Welsh, Middle Welsh, Brythonic, Brittanic, Cornish.

welt, *n.*—*Syn.* wound, bruise, weal; see **injury** 1.

welter, *n.*—*Syn.* commotion, uproar, turmoil; see **disturbance** 2.

wench, *n.* [*Usually derogatory*]—*Syn.* maid, damsel, maiden, virgin, female, unmarried woman; *all* (D): frail, dame, babe, bimbo, bird, chick, broad, skirt, doll; see also **girl** 1, **woman** 1.

wend, *v.*—*Syn.* make one's way, saunter, stroll; see **ramble** 3, **walk** 1.

werewolf, *n.*—*Syn.* man-wolf, vampire, changeling; see **beast** 1, **monster** 1.

West, *n.* **1.** [Western Hemisphere]—*Syn.* New World, the Americas, North and South America; see **America** 1, 2.

2. [European and American Culture]—*Syn.* Occident, Western civilization, Christian society, *Abendland* (German); see also **Europe.**

3. [Western United States; *especially the cowboy and mining culture*]—*Syn.* the range, the prairies, Rocky Mountain country, Far West, Northwest, Southwest; *all* (D): where men are men, wild-and-woolly country, the wide open spaces, Cow Country, buffalo range.

west, *mod.*—*Syn.* facing west, westernly, in the west, westernmost, westerly, westward(s); see also **western** 1, 2, 3.

west, *n.*—*Syn.* occident, westward, sunset; see **direction** 1.

western, *mod.* **1.** [In or toward the west]—*Syn.* westward(s), westerly, occidental, in the west, on the west side, where the sun sets, facing west, from the east, westernly, westernmost, westbound, occidental.—*Ant.* eastern*, easterly, oriental.

2. [*Usually capital;* having characteristics of Western Civilization]—*Syn.* Grecian, Latin, Roman, American, European, Christian, Caucasian.

3. [*Sometimes capital;* having characteristics of the western part of the United States]—*Syn.* cowboy, middle-western, southwestern, far-western, in the sagebrush country, on the Western plains, in the great *or* wide open spaces, in the wild west, in the Rockies, in God's country; *both* (D): in the wild and woolly West, out where the men are men.

westward, *mod.*—*Syn.* to the west, in a westerly direction, westbound; see **western** 1.

wet, *mod.* **1.** [Covered or soaked with liquid]—*Syn.* moist, damp, soaking, soaked, drenched, soggy, muggy, dewy, watery, dank, slimy, dripping, saturated, waterlogged, sodden.—*Ant.* dry*, dried, clean*.

2. [Rainy]—*Syn.* drizzly, slushy, snowy, slippery, muddy, humid, foggy, damp, clammy, showery, stormy, drizzling, cloudy, misty.—*Ant.* clear*, sunny, cloudless.

3. [(D) Favoring or permitting liquor]—*Syn.* open, antiprohibitionist, pro-repeal, alcoholic, serving liquor.

4. [(D) Mistaken]—*Syn.* inaccurate, misled, in error; see **mistaken** 1, **wrong** 2.

wet, *v.*—*Syn.* sprinkle, dampen, splash; see **moisten.**

wetback, *n.*—*Syn.* scab labor, unskilled worker, illegally imported laborer; see **laborer, workman.**

whack, *n.*—*Syn.* stroke, thump, wham; see **blow** 1.

at *or* **in one whack**—*Syn.* suddenly, at *or* with one stroke, instantaneously; see **quickly** 1, **soon** 1.

out of whack (D)—*Syn.* out of order, not working, spoiled; see **ruined** 1, 2.

take a whack at (D)—*Syn.* attempt, endeavor, do one's best; see **try** 1.

whale, *n.* **1.** [A marine animal]—*Syn.* cetacean, leviathan, King of the Deep; see **fish.**

Whales include the following—sperm, white, right *or* Greenland, sulphur-bottom, killer, narwhal,

finback, finner, humpback, blackfish, rorqual, common rorqual, blue rorqual.
2. [(D) Something impressive]—*Syn.* a great deal, a lot, abundance, a great quantity, large amount; *all* (D): corker, whopper, helluva lot.
wham, *n.* —*Syn.* hit, knock, whack; see **blow** 1.
wharf, *n.* —*Syn.* (boat) landing, quay, pier; see **dock** 1.
what, *pron.* **1.** [An indication of a question]—*Syn.* which? what sort? what kind? what thing? what means?
2. [Something indefinite]—*Syn.* that which, whatever, something, anything, everything, whichever, anything at all.
and what not (D)—*Syn.* etc. *or* and so forth *or* etcetera, and other things (too numerous to mention), (some) more; see **anything, everything.**
what about (D), *conj.* and *prep.* —*Syn.* but what, remember, and then; see **but** 1, 2, 3.
whatever, *pron.* —*Syn.* anything, everything, no matter what, whatsoever.
what for (D), *conj.* —*Syn.* (but) why, to what end, for what purpose; see **why.**
what have you (D), *n.* —*Syn.* (other) things, (almost) anything (else), the rest; see **anything, everything.**
what if (D), *conj.* —*Syn.* but suppose, imagine, supposing; see **but** 1, 2, 3, **if.**
what it takes (D), *n.* —*Syn.* capacity, competence, aptitude; see **ability** 1, 2.
what's what (D), *n.* —*Syn.* (the) fact(s) (in the case), (the) truth, the lowdown (D); see also **answer** 1, 2, **facts.**
wheat, *n.* —*Syn.* grain, corn, staff of life, breadstuff, wheat flour.
Kinds of wheat include the following—durum *or* hard *or* macaroni, hard red spring, hard red winter, soft red winter, white; buckwheat, groats, bulgur wheat.
wheedle, *v.* —*Syn.* coax, flatter, cajole; see **beg** 1.
wheel, *n.* **1.** [A thin, circular body that turns on an axis]—*Syn.* disk, ratchet, ring, hoop, roller, roulette, caster, drum, ferris wheel, wheel trolley, flywheel, cogwheel, steering wheel, sprocket, wheel, chain wheel, water wheel, noria, sakieh.
2. [A two-wheeled vehicle]—*Syn.* bicycle, velocipede, tandem, bike (D).
3. [Machinery; *often used figuratively*]—*Syn.* motive power, dynamo, engine, apparatus, motor, engine, controlling force, instrumentality.
4. [(D) An important person]—*Syn.* personage; *both* (D): big shot, V.I.P.; see **celebrity** 2.
at the wheel—*Syn.* driving, in control, running things; see **running** 1, 2.
wheel and deal (D), *v.* —*Syn.* play fast and loose, take chances, cut corners (D); see **operate** 2, 3.
wheels (D), *n.* —*Syn.* car, vehicle, buggy (D); see **automobile.**
wheeze, *v.* —*Syn.* breathe heavily, puff, pant; see **gasp.**
whelp, *n.* —*Syn.* puppy, young animal, youngster; see **boy, youth** 3.
when, *conj.* and *mod.* **1.** [At what time?]—*Syn.* how soon? how long ago? in what period? just when? at which instant?
2. [Whenever]—*Syn.* if, at any time, at the moment that, just as soon as, in the event that, on the condition that; see also **if.**
3. [During]—*Syn.* at the same time that, immediately upon, just as, just after, at, while, meanwhile; see also **during.**
whence, *conj.* —*Syn.* from where, from what place, from what origin, wherefrom.
whenever, *conj.* —*Syn.* at any time *or* moment *or* minute *or* hour, etc.: on *or* at any occasion *or* the first opportunity, etc.; if, when, should.
where, *conj.* and *mod.* **1.** [A question as to position] —*Syn.* in what place? at which place? at what moment? whither? in what direction? toward what?
2. [An indication of position]—*Syn.* wherever, anywhere, in whatever place, at which point, in which, to which, to what end.
whereabouts, *n.* —*Syn.* location, spot, site; see **place** 3.
whereas, *conj.* —*Syn.* since, inasmuch as, insomuch as, forasmuch as, considering that, when in fact, while, while on the contrary.
whereat, *mod.* —*Syn.* at which, whereupon, following which, thereupon, after which; see also **so** 2, 3.
whereby, *mod.* —*Syn.* by which, through which, in accordance with which, with the help of which, how.
wherefore, *mod.* —*Syn.* why? for what? for which reason? therefore, so, accordingly, thereupon.
wherein, *mod.* —*Syn.* in what way? how? at which point? where? in which?
whereon, *mod.* —*Syn.* on which, at which point, thereupon, at the conclusion of which, upon which, consequently, whereupon.
wheresoever, *conj.* and *mod.* —*Syn.* at whatever place, at which place, wherever, where.
whereupon, *mod.* —*Syn.* at which point, thereupon, at the conclusion of which, whereon, upon which, consequently.
wherever, *conj.* and *mod.* —*Syn.* where, in whatever place, anywhere, in any place that, wheresoever, regardless of where, in any direction.
wherewithal, *n.* —*Syn.* resources, money, funds; see **means** 1, **savings.**
whet, *v.* —*Syn.* hone, stone, finish; see **sharpen** 1.
whether, *conj.* —*Syn.* if, either, even if, if it follows that.
whether or not, *conj.* and *mod.* **1.** [Surely]—*Syn.* in any case, certainly, positively; see **surely.**
2. [If]—*Syn.* whether, yes or no, whichever; see **if.**
whetstone, *n.* —*Syn.* grinder's stone, hone, rubstone, emery, sharpener, grindstone, oilstone, strop, grinder's wheel, carborundum wheel.
whew, *interj.* —*Syn.* well, my goodness, golly, gosh, gee whiz, dear me, goodness (gracious), for heaven's sake.
which, *conj.* —*Syn.* what, whichever, that, whatever, and that, and which.
which, *pron.* —*Syn.* what, that, one, who.
whichever, *conj.* and *mod.* —*Syn.* whatever, which, whichsoever, no matter which, whoever.
whiff, *n.* —*Syn.* scent, puff, fume; see **smell** 1, 2.
whiff, *v.* —*Syn.* inhale, sniff, scent; see **smell** 2.
while, *conj.* **1.** [As long as]—*Syn.* during, at the same time that, during the time that, whilst, throughout the time that, in the time that.

2. [Although]—*Syn.* whereas, though, even though; see **although.**

whim, *n.* —*Syn.* notion, vagary, caprice; see **fancy** 3, **inclination** 1.

whimper, *v.* —*Syn.* fuss, weep, object; see **complain** 1, **whine.**

whimsical, *mod.* —*Syn.* playful, capricious, comical; see **funny** 1.

whine, *v.* —*Syn.* sing, hum, whistle, whimper, drone, cry, mewl, moan, murmur, grumble, snivel, complain; *both* (D): gripe, beef.

whinny, *v.* —*Syn.* neigh, nicker, whicker, bray, bleat, cry.

whip, *n.* —*Syn.* switch, strap, rod, birch rod, ruler, cane, lash, scourge, knotted cord, knout, cat-o'-nine-tails, thong, blacksnake, dog whip, ox whip, bull whip, horsewhip, buggy whip, riding whip *or* crop, quirt, taws.

whip, *v.* —*Syn.* thrash, strike, scourge; see **beat** 2, **punish.**

whip hand, *n.* —*Syn.* advantage, control, domination; see **command** 2, **power** 2.

whip into shape, *v.* —*Syn.* finish, fix (up), polish (off) (D); see **complete** 1.

whipped, *mod.* **1.** [Hit]—*Syn.* lashed, scourged, strapped; see **punished.**
2. [Defeated]—*Syn.* overcome, outdone, thrashed (D); see **beaten** 1.

whipping, *n.* —*Syn.* beating, thrashing, strapping; see **mauling, punishment.**

whip up, *v.* —*Syn.* stimulate, stir (up), agitate; see **disturb** 2, **excite** 1, 2.

whir, *v.* —*Syn.* whiz, swish, vibrate; see **hum.**

whirl, *n.* **1.** [Rapid rotating motion]—*Syn.* swirl, turn, flurry, spin, gyration, reel, surge, whir; see also **revolution** 1.
2. [Confusion]—*Syn.* hurry, flutter, fluster, ferment, agitation, tempest, storm, rush, tumult, turbulence, commotion, hurly-burly, bustle, the dizzy rounds (D).

whirl, *v.* —*Syn.* turn around, rotate, spin, gyrate, wheel, swirl, twirl, revolve, gyre, turn, turn upon itself.

whirling, *mod.* —*Syn.* swirling, spinning, rotating; see **revolving** 1, **turning.**

whirlpool, *n.* —*Syn.* eddy, vortex, swirl, maelstrom, undertow, undercurrent, rapids, Scylla.

whirlwind, *n.* —*Syn.* windstorm, cyclone, tornado, twister, gale, hurricane, tempest.

whirring, *n.* —*Syn.* whizzing, humming, hissing; see **noise** 1.

whisk, *v.* —*Syn.* flit, flutter, speed; see **hurry** 1.

whisker, *n.* —*Syn.* filament, bristle, cilium; see **hair** 2.

whiskers, *n.* —*Syn.* beard, mustache, sideburns, burnsides, mutton chops, goatee, hair, face hair, imperial, Vandyke; *all* (D): alfalfa, bristles, muff, chin armor, weeds.

whiskey, *n.* —*Syn.* bourbon (whiskey), rye (whiskey), corn (whiskey), Scotch (whiskey), Irish (whiskey), Canadian (whiskey), *usquebaugh* (Scots Gaelic), *spiritus frumenti* (Latin); *all* (D): hard liquor, likker, spirits, aqua vitae, firewater, booze, sneaky pete, redeye, white lightning, rotgut, hooch, alky, corn, home-brew, moonshine, mountain dew; see also **drink** 2.

whisper, *n.* **1.** [A low, sibilant sound]—*Syn.* rustle, noise, murmur, hum, buzz, drone, undertone, hissing.
2. [A guarded utterance]—*Syn.* disclosure, divulgence, confidence, disclosure, secret, rumor, hint, secret message, underground report.

whisper, *v.* —*Syn.* speak softly, speak in a whisper, speak under one's breath, speak in an undertone, tell, talk low, speak confidentially, mutter, murmur, speak into someone's ear.—*Ant.* yell*, speak aloud, shout.

whispered, *mod.* —*Syn.* breathed, droned, muttered; see **quiet** 2.

whispering, *mod.* —*Syn.* rustling, sighing, buzzing, humming, murmuring, droning, hissing; see also **sounding.**—*Ant.* yelling*, howling, screaming.

whispering campaign, *n.* —*Syn.* slander, dirty politics, libel; see **gossip** 1.

whistle, *n.* **1.** [A shrill sound]—*Syn.* cry, shriek, howl, blast, piping, siren call, fire alarm, birdcall, signal, toot, blare; see also **noise** 1.
2. [An instrument that produces a shrill sound] —*Syn.* fife, pipe(s), steam whistle, mouth whistle, traffic whistle, siren, calliope.

whistle, *v.* **1.** [To produce a shrill blast]—*Syn.* fife, pipe, flute, trill, hiss, whiz, wheeze, shriek, howl, blare, toot, tootle; see also **sound** 1.
2. [To call with a whistle]—*Syn.* signal, summon, warn, command, flag, arrest, sound a whistle.
3. [To produce a tune by whistling]—*Syn.* warble, tootle, trill, quaver, carol, improvise.

whistling, *mod.* —*Syn.* fifing, piping, trilling, shrieking, hissing, calling, tooting, caroling, warbling.

whit, *n.* —*Syn.* jot, iota, mite; see **bit** 1, 3.

white, *mod.* **1.** [The color of fresh snow]—*Syn.* ivory, silvery, snow-white, snowy, frosted, milky, milky-white, chalky, pearly, blanched, bleached, ashen, pale, wan, albescent.—*Ant.* dark*, black, dirty.
2. [Colorless]—*Syn.* clear, transparent, clean, blank, spotless, pure, unalloyed, neutral, achromatic, achromic.—*Ant.* colored*, chromatic, mixed.
3. [Concerning the white race]—*Syn.* fair-skinned, light-complexioned, Caucasian, light-skinned, ruddy-faced; see also **European, Western** 2.—*Ant.* black*, Negro, negroid.
4. [(D) Honorable]—*Syn.* decent, splendid, kind, courageous, good-natured, considerate.
5. [Pale]—*Syn.* ashen, wan, pallid; see **pale** 1.

white-collar (D), *mod.* —*Syn.* executive, professional, business; see **administrative.**

white elephant, *n.* —*Syn.* junk, clutter, worthless *or* outmoded *or* unfashionable, etc., object; see **heirloom.**

whiten, *v.* **1.** [To become white]—*Syn.* grow hoary, blanch, turn white, turn gray, (grow) pale, be covered with snow, be silvered, change color, fade.
2. [To make white]—*Syn.* bleach, blanch, silver, paint white, whitewash, apply powder, chalk. —*Ant.* dirty*, smudge, blacken.

whiteness, *n.* —*Syn.* colorlessness, paleness, achromatism, pallidity, hoariness, snowiness.—*Ant.* darkness*, blackness, color.

white paper, *n.* —*Syn.* document, pronouncement, public *or* official statement *or* analysis *or* account; see **declaration** 2, **writing** 2.

white slave (D), *n.* —*Syn.* call girl, hustler, harlot; see **prostitute.**

whitewash, *v.* **1.** [To cover with a lime wash] —*Syn.* paint, whiten, calcimine, paint white, apply a white coating, wash.

2. [(D) To give the appearance of innocence] —*Syn.* varnish, gloss over, cover up, exonerate, vindicate, liberate, prove innocent; see also **excuse.** —*Ant.* implicate*, accuse, blame.

whither, *mod.* —*Syn.* where? in what direction? toward what place?

whittle, *v.* **1.** [To cut]—*Syn.* pare, carve, shape, fashion, shave, model, chip off.

2. [To reduce slowly]—*Syn.* lessen, diminish, shave, decrease, pare (down).

whiz (D), *n.* —*Syn.* clever person, prodigy, wonder, star, genius, gifted child, gifted person, marvel.

whiz, *v.* —*Syn.* speed, fly rapidly, dart, race, hurtle, hurry, whir, hiss, hum.

who, *pron.* —*Syn.* what, that, which, he, she, they, I, you, whoever, whichever.

whoa, *interj.* —*Syn.* stop! wait! halt! stand!

who cares? (D), *interj.* —*Syn.* never mind, no matter, it's *or* it is all the same, it makes no difference, it doesn't matter.

whoever, *pron.* —*Syn.* he who, the one who, whatever person, whatever man, no matter who.

whole, *mod.* **1.** [Entire]—*Syn.* all, every, inclusive, full, uncut, full-length, unexpurgated, undivided, unabbreviated, unabridged, integral, complete, total, aggregate, indivisible, organismic, inseparable, indissoluble, gross, undiminished, utter. —*Ant.* unfinished*, partial*, incomplete.

2. [Not broken or damaged]—*Syn.* thorough, mature, developed, unimpaired, unmarred, full, unbroken, undamaged, entire, in one piece, sound, solid, replete, untouched, without a scratch, intact, uninjured, undecayed, completed, preserved, perfect, complete, safe, in A-1 condition, shipshape, in good order, together, unified, plenary, exhaustive, conclusive, unqualified, fulfilled, accomplished, consummate; *both* (D): to the teeth, A-OK.—*Ant.* broken*, mutilated, defective.

3. [Not ill or injured]—*Syn.* hale, hearty, sound; see **healthy** 1, **well** 1.

whole, *n.* —*Syn.* unity, totality, everything, oneness, entity, entirety, collectivity, sum, unity, assemblage, aggregate, aggregation, body, lump, gross, entire stock, length and breadth, generality, mass, amount, bulk, quantity, universality, combination, complex, assembly, gross amount.—*Ant.* part*, portion, fraction.

wholehearted, *mod.* —*Syn.* sincere, earnest, candid; see **frank, hearty** 1.

wholesale, *mod.* **1.** [Dealing in large lots]—*Syn.* large-scale, discount, in the mass, quantitative, in bulk, bulk, to the retailer, by the carload, loose, in quantity, in job lots; see also **commercial** 1.—*Ant.* retail*, to the consumer, in small lots.

2. [Indiscriminate]—*Syn.* sweeping, widespread, comprehensive, extensive, complete, over-all, general, total.

wholesome, *mod.* —*Syn.* nutritive, nourishing, beneficial; see **healthful.**

whole-wheat, *mod.* —*Syn.* graham, all-wheat, all-grain, whole-grain, 100-percent-wheat.

wholly, *mod.* **1.** [Completely]—*Syn.* totally, entirely, fully; see **completely.**

2. [Exclusively]—*Syn.* solely, specifically, individually; see **only** 1.

whom, *pron.* —*Syn.* that, her, him; see **who, what** 2.

whoop, *n.* —*Syn.* hoot, shout, cry, hurrah, cheer, halloo, howl, squawk; outcry; see also **noise** 1.

whoop, *v.* —*Syn.* howl, bawl, shriek, scream, cry out, shout, bellow, jeer, boo, yell.

whooping, *mod.* —*Syn.* yelling, hooting, bawling, shouting, booing, jeering, bellowing, hollowing, hollering (D), exuberant, hilarious, gay, mad, riotous, drunken, raging.

whoop it up (D), *v.* **1.** [To raise a disturbance] —*Syn.* celebrate, riot, get drunk, get noisy; *all* (D): go on a spree *or* bat *or* toot, paint the town red, rip out.

2. [To advertise]—*Syn.* campaign for, push, propagandize.

whoops (D), *interj.* —*Syn.* oh-oh (D), sorry, oh, no; now I've *or* you've done it, etc.; see also **no.**

whopper, *n.* —*Syn.* great lie, falsehood, fabrication; see **lie** 1, **story.**

whopping (D), *mod.* —*Syn.* huge, big, mountainous; see **large** 1.

whore, *n.* —*Syn.* call girl, harlot, streetwalker; see **prostitute.**

whore, *v.* —*Syn.* engage in prostitution, prostitute oneself, solicit patrons, give oneself to hire; *all* (D): hustle, walk the pavement, cruise; see also **solicit** 3.

whorehouse, *n.* —*Syn.* house of prostitution *or* of ill fame, stews, cat house (D); see **brothel.**

whoremonger, *n.* —*Syn.* whoremaster, go-between, hustler (D); see **agent** 1, **pimp.**

whorl, *n.* —*Syn.* twirl, twist, spiral; see **coil.**

whose, *pron.* —*Syn.* to whom, belonging to what person, of the aforementioned one, from these.

why, *mod.*, *conj.* and *interrog.*—*Syn.* for what reason? how so? how? how is it that? on whose account? what is the cause that? to what end? for what purpose? on what foundation? how do you explain that? how come? (D).

whys and wherefores (D), *n.* —*Syn.* reason(s), explanation(s), cause(s); see **reason** 3.

wick, *n.* —*Syn.* thread, cord, taper, lampwick, candle end, lantern wick, candlewick; see also **candle.**

wicked, *mod.* **1.** [Morally evil]—*Syn.* sinful, immoral, unethical, corrupt, evil, base, foul, gross, dissolute, wayward, irreligious, blasphemous, profane, evil-minded, vile, bad, naughty, degenerate, depraved, incorrigible, unruly, heartless, shameless, degraded, debauched, hard, toughened, disreputable, infamous, indecent, mean, remorseless, reprobate, salacious, iniquitous, scandalous, atrocious, contemptible, nasty; *all* (D): rotten, low-down, good-for-nothing, dirty.—*Ant.* good*, virtuous, pure*.

2. [Capable of doing great damage]—*Syn.* vicious, fiendish, hellish, villainous, rascally, devilish, malevolent, plotting, conspiratorial, iniquitous, flagrant, nefarious, criminal, heinous, murderous, tricky, sinister, ignoble, monstrous, opprobrious, felonious, dangerous; *all* (D): cut-throat, ratty, slippery, crooked.—*Ant.* honest*, just, kind.

wicked, *n.*—*Syn.* dregs of society, bad, unrighteous, scum of the earth, reprobate, sons of men, children of the devil, the evil.

wickedly, *mod.*—*Syn.* sinfully, unrighteously, immorally; see **wrongfully** 1.

wickedness, *n.*—*Syn.* evil, depravity, immorality; see **blasphemy.**

wicker, *mod.*—*Syn.* straw-plaited, straw-woven, wicker-work, roped, plaited, woven, made of withes, made of osiers.

wide, *mod.* **1.** [Broad]—*Syn.* extended, spacious, deep; see **broad** 1, **extensive** 1.
2. [Loose]—*Syn.* broad, roomy, full, ample, voluminous, flowing, hanging; see also **loose** 1.
3. [Extensive]—*Syn.* large-scale, all-inclusive, universal; see **comprehensive.**
4. [Inaccurate]—*Syn.* astray, off the mark, far off; see **wrong** 2, 3.
5. [Sparse]—*Syn.* far-flung, separated, far; see **away** 1, **scattered.**

wide-awake, *mod.*—*Syn.* alert, watchful, vigilant; see **careful.**

widely, *mod.*—*Syn.* extensively, generally, publicly, nationally, internationally, universally, in many places, broadly, comprehensively.—*Ant.* locally*, in a small circle, narrowly.

widen, *v.* **1.** [To make wider]—*Syn.* add to, broaden, stretch, extend, increase, enlarge, distend, spread out, give more space, augment.—*Ant.* compress*, narrow, cramp.
2. [To become wider]—*Syn.* unfold, grow, open, stretch, grow larger, increase, swell, multiply.

wide-open, *mod.*—*Syn.* unrestricted, licentious, wild; see **lawless** 1, 2.

widespread, *mod.*—*Syn.* extensive, general, sweeping, broad, comprehensive, far-reaching, widely accepted, boundless, popular, public, unrestricted, unlimited, on a large scale, over-all.—*Ant.* secret*, obscure*, limited.

widow, *n.*—*Syn.* widow woman, relict, dowager, husbandless wife, dead man's wife; *all* (D): sod widow, grass widow, widdy, mantrap; see also **survivor, wife.**

widower, *n.*—*Syn.* surviving husband; *both* (D): grass widower, widowman; see **husband, man** 2, **survivor.**

width, *n.*—*Syn.* breadth, wideness, girth, diameter, distance across, amplitude, cross dimension, cross measurement, expanse.—*Ant.* length*, height, altitude.

wield, *v.*—*Syn.* handle, manipulate, exercise, hold high, brandish, shake, wave, swing, utilize, work, ply, operate, use, flourish.

wield power *or* **authority,** *v.*—*Syn.* dictate, rule, administer; see **manage** 1.

wiener, *n.*—*Syn.* wienerwurst, frankfurter, sausage, link; *all* (D): hot dog, dog, weenie, red-hot, foot-long; see also **meat.**

wife, *n.*—*Syn.* married woman, spouse, lady, dame, madam, matron, squaw, helpmate, helpmeet, consort, marrow, mate, housewife; *all* (D): better half, the missis, (the little) woman, wifey, ball and chain, the old lady.—*Ant.* widow*, spinster*, old maid.

take to wife—*Syn.* marry, wed, espouse; see **marry** 1.

wig, *n.*—*Syn.* periwig, peruke, postiche, artificial hair, fall, hairpiece, toupee; *both* (D): rug, piece; see also **hair** 1.

wiggle, *v.*—*Syn.* wag, waggle, wriggle, squirm, shimmy, shake, flounce, dance sensually; *both* (D): do the grinds, juggle the hips.

wigwam, *n.*—*Syn.* wickiup, tepee, lodge; see **shelter, tent.**

wild, *mod.* **1.** [Not controlled]—*Syn.* unrestrained, unmanageable, boisterous; see **disorderly** 1, **unruly.**
2. [Uncivilized]—*Syn.* barbarous, savage, undomesticated; see **primitive** 3.
3. [Not cultivated]—*Syn.* luxuriant, lush, exuberant, dense, excessive, desolate, waste, desert, weedy, untrimmed, impenetrable, uninhabited, native, natural, untouched, virgin, overgrown, uncultivated, untilled, uncared for, neglected, overrun, free, rampant.
4. [Inaccurate]—*Syn.* erratic, off, unsound; see **mistaken** 1, **wrong** 2.
5. [Stormy]—*Syn.* disturbed, raging, storming; see **turbulent.**
6. [Excited]—*Syn.* hot, eager, avid; see **excited.**
7. [Dissolute]—*Syn.* loose, licentious, profligate; see **lewd** 2.
8. [Imprudent]—*Syn.* reckless, foolish, incautious; see **careless** 1, **rash.**
run wild—*Syn.* run *or* live *or* act, etc., out of control; rage, rampage; see **escape.**

wildcat, *mod.*—*Syn.* illegal, unsound, speculative, risky, illegitimate, unsafe, unsecured, unauthorized.—*Ant.* legal*, legitimate, authorized.

wilderness, *n.*—*Syn.* primitive area, wastelands, back country, the woods, the North woods, primeval forest, uninhabited region; see also **desert, forest.**

wild-goose chase (D), *n.*—*Syn.* futile search, meaningless chase, vain inquiry, foolish *or* hopeless quest; see also **failure** 1.

wildly, *mod.* **1.** [Without restraint]—*Syn.* hastily, rashly, fiercely, violently, ferociously, uncontrollably, carelessly, quixotically, savagely, unwittingly, recklessly, confusedly, pell-mell.—*Ant.* carefully*, prudently, judiciously.
2. [With emotion]—*Syn.* heatedly, passionately, avidly; see **angrily.**

wilds, *n.*—*Syn.* uninhabited country, wasteland, wilderness, primitive country, pioneer land, bush, forest, jungle, boondocks, unexplored territory, no man's land.—*Ant.* garden*, meadow*, field*.

wile, *n.*—*Syn.* trickery, deceit, cunning, stratagem, trick, chicanery, dishonesty, plot, ruse, hoax, deception, scheming, dodge, artifice; *all* (D): bunco, humbug, flimflam, scam, monkey business, horseplay.—*Ant.* honesty*, frankness, sincerity.

will, *n.* **1.** [Desire]—*Syn.* inclination, wish, disposition, pleasure, yearning, craving, longing, hankering.—*Ant.* command*, indifference, distaste.
2. [Command]—*Syn.* order, insistence, decree; see **command** 1, **directions.**
3. [Conscious power]—*Syn.* resolution, volition, intention, will power, preference, mind, determination, self-determination, decisiveness, moral

strength, discretion, conviction, willfulness.—*Ant.* doubt*, vacillation, indecision.

4. [Testament for the disposition of property] —*Syn.* bequest, disposition, instructions, last wishes, bestowal, dispensation, last will and testament.

at will—*Syn.* whenever one wishes, at any time, *ad libitum* (Latin); see **anytime.**

will, *v.* **1.** [To exert one's will]—*Syn.* decree, order, command, demand, authorize, request, make oneself felt, decide upon, insist, direct, enjoin.

2. [To wish]—*Syn.* want, incline to, prefer; see **wish** 2.

3. [An indication of futurity]—*Syn.* shall, would, should, expect to, anticipate, look forward to, hope to, await, foresee, propose.

willful, *mod.* **1.** [Deliberate]—*Syn.* intentional, premeditated, contemplated; see **deliberate** 1.

2. [Obstinate]—*Syn.* stubborn, wayward, intractable; see **obstinate** 1.

willing, *mod.* **1.** [Zealous]—*Syn.* energetic, prompt, reliable, active, obedient, enthusiastic, responsible, agreeable, well-disposed.—*Ant.* reluctant*, grudging, stubborn.

2. [Ready to comply]—*Syn.* prepared, voluntary, ready, compliant, amenable, tractable, feeling, like, in accord with.—*Ant.* opposed*, averse, unwilling*.

willingly, *mod.* —*Syn.* gladly, readily, freely, obediently, voluntarily, with relish, at one's pleasure, on one's own account, of one's own accord, with open arms, with good cheer, without demur, freely, with pleasure, cheerfully, with all one's heart; *both* (D): at the drop of a hat, like a shot; see also **agreeably.**

willingness, *n.* —*Syn.* zeal, enthusiasm, readiness, earnestness, alacrity, eagerness, cordiality, hospitality, courteousness, compliance, good will, geniality.—*Ant.* opposition*, hostility, aversion.

will-o'-the-wisp (D), *n.* —*Syn.* passing thing, fancy, ephemera, dream, *ignis fatuus* (Latin), shadow, illusion, vision.

willow, *n.* Willows include the following—white, crack, osier, drooping, black, peach-leaved, pussy, shining, beaked, sandbar, autumn, broad-leaved, furry, silky, hoary, prairie, gray, red, yellow, arroyo, velvet, weeping, bay, goat, basket; see also **tree, wood** 2.

willowy, *mod.* —*Syn.* slender, graceful, lissome; see **thin** 2.

wilt, *v.* —*Syn.* droop, wither, weaken, flag, dry up, shrivel, fade, become flaccid, lose freshness, faint. —*Ant.* grow*, stiffen, stand*.

wily, *mod.* —*Syn.* crafty, sneaky, cunning; see **sly** 1.

win (D), *n.* —*Syn.* triumph, conquest, gain; see **success** 1, **victory** 2.

win, *v.* **1.** [To gain a victory]—*Syn.* be victorious, prevail, get the best of, come out *or* be first, conquer, overcome, overwhelm, triumph; see also **succeed** 1.

2. [To obtain]—*Syn.* get, acquire, gain; see **obtain** 1.

3. [To reach]—*Syn.* attain, accomplish, effect; see **approach** 2, 3.

4. [To convince]—*Syn.* win *or* bring, over, persuade, bring around, convert, talk into, prevail upon, sway, overcome, influence.

wince, *v.* —*Syn.* draw back, cower, cringe, flinch, quail, shrink (back), make a wry face, grimace, blench, shy, start; *both* (D): back off, chicken out.

wind, *n.* **1.** [Air in motion]—*Syn.* draft, air current, mistral, breeze, gust, gale, blast, flurry, whisk, whiff, puff, whirlwind, flutter, wafting, zephyr, trade wind, northeaster, southwester, sirocco, tempest, blow, cyclone, typhoon, twister, hurricane, sandstorm, *Fohn* (German), prevailing westerlies, stiff breeze, spanking breeze, Chinook, khamsin, Zephyrus, Boreas.

2. [(D) Fugitive information]—*Syn.* babble, report, talk; see **gossip** 1, **rumor** 1.

3. [(D) The breath]—*Syn.* respiration, inhalation, breathing; see **breath** 1.

get *or* **have wind of** (D)—*Syn.* hear of *or* about *or* from, have news of, trace; see **hear** 2.

take the wind out of one's sails (D)—*Syn.* best, get the better of, overcome; see **defeat** 1.

wind, *v.* **1.** [To wrap about]—*Syn.* coil, reel in, entwine, wreathe, shroud, fold, cover, bind, tape, bandage.

2. [To twist]—*Syn.* convolute, screw, wind up; see **bend** 2.

3. [To meander]—*Syn.* zigzag, weave, snake, twist, loop, turn, twine, ramble, swerve, deviate.

windbag, *n.* —*Syn.* talker, boaster, bore; see **braggart, gossip** 2.

windfall, *n.* —*Syn.* boon, (stoke of) luck, weal; see **blessing** 2, **surprise** 2.

winding, *mod.* —*Syn.* turning, gyrating, gyring, spiraling, twisting, snaky, serpentine, convoluted, dextrorse, dextrorsal, sinistrorse.—*Ant.* straight*, direct*, vertical*.

windmill, *n.* —*Syn.* rotating wheel, wind-driven wheel, post mill, tower mill, wind-charger, smock mill, water pump; see also **mill** 2, **pump.**

window, *n.* **1.** [An architectural opening for light and air]—*Syn.* skylight, porthole, bay window, bow window, picture window, oriel, casement, fenestration, dormer, embrasure, stained-glass, rose window, show window, bull's eye, fanlight, transom, peephole, *oeil-de-boeuf, vitrail* (*both* French).

2. [That which fills a window]—*Syn.* lattice, shutter, glass, windowpane, stained glass.

windowpane, *n.* —*Syn.* pane, square of glass, glass, glazing, window.

window shade, *n.* —*Syn.* shade, (Venetian) blind, screen, shutter, canopy, awning, jalousie, curtain.

windpipe, *n.*—*Syn.* airpipe, bronchus, trachea; see **throat.**

windshield, *n.* —*Syn.* windscreen, protection (against the wind), wrap-around; see **shield.**

wind up (D), *v.* —*Syn.* conclude, be through with, come to the end of; see **end** 1.

windy, *mod.* **1.** [Characterized by wind]—*Syn.* breezy, blustery, raw, stormy, wind-swept, airy, gusty, blowing, fresh, drafty, wind-shaken, tempestuous, boisterous.—*Ant.* calm*, quiet, still.

2. [(D) Boastful]—*Syn.* talkative, long-winded, garrulous; see **verbose.**

wine, *mod.* —*Syn.* wine-colored, maroon, dark red, grape; see also **red.**

wine, *n.* Wines include the following—fine, sparkling, still, fortified, dry, sec, brut, sweet, heavy, light, white, rosé, red, green blackberry, cherry, currant, gooseberry, dandelion; sacramental, dessert, dinner, medicinal, aperitif, cooking; California, New York State, French, varietal, vinifera, Italian, Caucasian, Chilean, etc.; *vin mousseux, vin rouge, vin rosé, vin de table* or *vin ordinaire* (all French); sherry, Tokay, port, claret, muscatel, Canary, Malaga, Burgundy, Bordeaux, Champagne, (Haut) Sauterne, Rhine wine, Riesling, Traminer, hock, Moselle, Chablis, May wine, Folle blanche, Chardonnay, zinfandel, white Chianti, red Chianti, light muscat, Catawba, Sauvignon vert, Pinot, Concord, Sauvignon blanc; see also **drink** 2.

wine and dine, *v.* —*Syn.* feast, make welcome, entertain lavishly *or* grandly *or* sumptuously, etc.; see **entertain** 2.

wing, *n.* **1.** [An organ or instrument of flight] —*Syn.* appendage, pinion, elytron, aileron, airfoil; see also **feather.**

2. [An architectural unit or extension]—*Syn.* annex, ell, addition, projection, hall, section, division, part.

3. [An organized group of aircraft]—*Syn.* flying unit, flight, flying squad, formation, air squadron; see also **unit** 1.

4. [Outer portions of a line in sports or war] —*Syn.* right wing, left wing, end of the line, end, extension, flank, side, segment.

5. [Entrance to the stage: *usually plural*]—*Syn.* offstage, backstage, behind-stage, back, flats, green room (D).

6. [(D) A pitching arm]—*Syn. all* (D): soup bone, glass arm, heave machinery; see **arm** 2.

on the wing—*Syn.* going, leaving, progressing; see **flying** 1.

take wing—*Syn.* go, depart, run (off); see **leave** 1.

take under one's wing—*Syn.* favor, help, guarantee; see **adopt** 2.

wing (D), *v.* —*Syn.* wound, injure, bring down; see **hurt** 1.

winged, *mod.* —*Syn.* alar, feathered, pteroid; see **flying** 2.

wings, *n.* —*Syn.* commission, insignia, second lieutenancy, aircorps officership.

wink, *v.* **1.** [To close one eye]—*Syn.* squint, blink, nictate, nictitate, flirt; *both* (D): make eyes at, bat the eyes.

2. [To twinkle]—*Syn.* sparkle, gleam, blink; see **flash** 1.

wink at, *v.* —*Syn.* connive, pass over, gloss over, condone, pretend not to see, excuse, permit, forgive.—*Ant.* censure*, frown upon, revile.

winking, *n.* —*Syn.* nictitating, blinking, squinting, flirting, flirtation, twinkling, sparkling, flashing.

winner, *n.* —*Syn.* victor, conqueror, prize winner, champion, winning competitor, hero, victorious *or* successful contestant, leading entrant; grand *or* national *or* Olympic champion, etc.; contest winner, medal winner, etc.; *all* (D): title-holder, champ, big boy, front runner, bell-ringer.—*Ant.* loser*, vanquished, defeated.

winning, *mod.* **1.** [Engaging]—*Syn.* attractive, charming, dazzling, courteous, agreeable, gratifying, acceptable, cute, cunning.—*Ant.* ugly*, repulsive, loathsome.

2. [Victorious]—*Syn.* champion, conquering, leading; see **triumphant.**

winnow, *v.* —*Syn.* scatter, extract, sieve; see **separate** 2, **sift** 2.

winsome, *mod.* —*Syn.* cute, engaging, entrancing; see **charming.**

winter, *n.* —*Syn.* cold season, frosty weather, wintertime, Christmastime; *all* (D): Jack Frost, King Winter, squaw winter, blackberry winter.

winter, *v.* —*Syn.* stay *or* go for the winter, vacation, hole up (D); see **dwell, live** 2.

wintry, *mod.* —*Syn.* chilly, frosty, icy, snowy, frigid, cold, bleak, raw, biting, hiemal, cutting.—*Ant.* warm*, summery, balmy.

wipe, *v.* —*Syn.* rub, clean, dry, dust, mop, clear, wash, swab, soak up, obliterate.

wipe out, *v.* **1.** [To remove]—*Syn.* erase, delete, eliminate; see **cancel** 1, **remove** 1.

2. [To exterminate]—*Syn.* slay, annihilate, eradicate; see **destroy** 1, **kill** 1.

wire, *n.* **1.** [A metal strand]—*Syn.* line, electric wire, cable, aerial, circuit, wiring, live wire, coil, conductor, filament, musical string, wire tape, wire cord.

2. [A metal net]—*Syn.* barbed wire, wire fence, wirework, wire cage, wire basket, wire cloth, wire entanglement; see also **fence** 1, 2, **net.**

3. [(D) A telegraphic message]—*Syn.* cablegram, telegram, message, night message, night letter, code message.

down to the wire (D)—*Syn.* to the (very) end, at (the) last, eventually; see **finally** 2.

get (in) under the wire (D)—*Syn.* (just) make it, succeed, (just) squeak through (D); see **arrive** 1.

pull wires—*Syn.* exert influence, go to the right people, use pull (D); see **influence, manage.**

wire, *v.* **1.** [To install wire]—*Syn.* set up a circuit, install electricity, lay wires, connect electric cables, prepare for electric(al) service; *both* (D): pipe, tie on the spiders; see also **electrify** 1.

2. [(D) To send a message by wire]—*Syn.* flash, telegraph, file; see **notify.**

wired, *mod.* —*Syn.* lined, hooked up, circuited, furnished for electricity.

wireless, *mod.* —*Syn.* radio, radioed, on the air, broadcast, beamed, shore-to-ship, ship-to-shore, short wave, transatlantic, transpacific.

wireless (British), *n.* —*Syn.* wireless set, wireless apparatus, wireless telegraphy; see **radio** 2, **telegraph.**

wire service, *n.* —*Syn.* communications system, news service, local *or* national *or* international wire(s); see **telegraph, telephone.**

wiring, *n.* **1.** [The process of installing wires] —*Syn.* electrification, electrifying, installation of wire, preparation for electric service, doing the wiring; see also **installation** 1.

2. [Installed wires]—*Syn.* wirework, electric line, cable work, cables, electric *or* electrical installations, facilities for electric power *or* light.

3. [Circuitry]—*Syn.* circuit system, filamentation, wireworks, electrical wire distribution, tubing, circuit pattern, circuiting, threading, process, route, line, path, pattern, trail.

wiry, *mod.* —*Syn.* springy, light, lean, agile, limber, supple, sinewy, strong, vibrant, strapping athletic, brawny, well-knit, energetic, muscular.

wisdom, *n.* **1.** [Intellectual power]—*Syn.* intelligence, sagacity, perspicacity; see **sanity** 1, **sense** 2.
2. [Good sense]—*Syn.* prudence, astuteness, sense, reason, clear thinking, brains, good judgment, sagacity, understanding, sanity, shrewdness, experience, practical knowledge, carefulness, vigilance, tact, balance, poise, stability, caution, solidity, hardheadedness, *savoir faire* (French), common sense; *both* (D): horse sense, savvy.—*Ant.* stupidy*, irrationality, rashness.
3. [Learning]—*Syn.* erudition, enlightment, attainment; see **knowledge** 1.

wise, *mod.* **1.** [Judicious]—*Syn.* clever, sagacious, witty; see **rational** 1, **thoughtful** 1.
2. [Shrewd]—*Syn.* calculating, cunning, crafty; see **sly** 1.
3. [Prudent]—*Syn.* tactful, sensible, wary; see **careful, discreet.**
4. [Erudite]—*Syn.* taught, scholarly, smart; see **educated** 1, **learned** 1.
5. [(D) Impudent]—*Syn.* bold, forward, offensive; see **rude** 2.

wisely, *mod.*—*Syn.* tactfully, prudently, circumspectly, sagaciously, shrewdly, judiciously, discreetly, carefully, admirably, discerningly, sagely, knowingly, reasonably, sensibly, intelligently.—*Ant.* foolishly*, stupidly, unthinkingly.

wise up (D), *v.*—*Syn.* become informed, get acquainted (with), learn one's way around (D); see **learn** 1.

wish, *n.* **1.** [Desire]—*Syn.* longing, yearning, hankering, desire, thirst, disposition.
2. [An expression of desire]—*Syn.* request, hope, intention, preference, choice, want, prayer, invocation, liking, pleasure, injunction, command, order.
3. [The object of desire]—*Syn.* goal, dream, promise; see **choice** 3, **hope** 2.

wish, *v.* **1.** [To desire]—*Syn.* covet, crave, envy; see **want** 1, **yearn.**
2. [To express a desire]—*Syn.* hope, request, entreat, prefer, want, pray for, invoke, command, order, solicit, beg, look forward to, need; see also **require** 2.
3. [To bid]—*Syn.* order, instruct, tell; see **command** 1.

wishbone, *n.*—*Syn.* furculum, breastbone, clavicle; see **bone.**

wishful, *mod.*—*Syn.* desirous, longing, eager; see **enthusiastic** 2.

wishing, *mod.*—*Syn.* hoping, yearning, desiring, craving, pining, thirsting, hungering, wanting, longing.

wishy-washy, *mod.*—*Syn.* cowardly, mediocre, feeble; see **weak** 3.

wisp, *n.*—*Syn.* tuft, cluster, shred, a few strands, lock, bit, shock, cowlick, stray lock, scolding locks.

wistful, *mod.*—*Syn.* nostalgic, melancholy, sad, longing, yearning, pensive, wishful, hopeless, half-expectant, soulful, plaintive.—*Ant.* happy*, joyous, exuberant.

wit, *n.* **1.** [Clever humor]—*Syn.* wittiness, smartness, whimsicality, jocularity, pleasantry, drollery, waggery, banter, burlesque; see also **humor** 1.
2. [An example of wit, sense 1]—*Syn.* satire, badinage, witticism, sally, whimsy, repartee, bon mot, joke, aphorism, jest, quip, epigram, pun; *both* (D): wisecrack, gag.
3. [One who possesses wit, sense 1]—*Syn.* humorist, punster, epigrammatist, comedian, banterer, clever fellow, life of the party, wag; *both* (D): wisecracker, wise guy.
at one's wits' end—*Syn.* downhearted, desperate, helpless; see **hopeless** 2, **troubled** 1.
have *or* **keep one's wits about one**—*Syn.* be ready *or* alert, take precautions, be on one's guard; see **watch out** 2.
live by one's wits—*Syn.* use sharp practices, live dangerously, take advantage (of all opportunities); see **prosper, trick.**

witch, *n.*—*Syn.* sorcerer, warlock, magician, enchantress, charmer, hag, crone.

witchcraft, *n.*—*Syn.* sorcery, magic, black magic, devil worship, black art, necromancy, witchery, divination, enchantment, spell, bewitchment, voodooism, shamanism, demonology.

with, *prep.*—*Syn.* by, in association, in the midst of, among, amidst, along with, in company with, arm in arm, hand in glove, cheek by jowl, in conjunction with, among other things, beside, alongside of, including.

withdraw, *v.* **1.** [To retire]—*Syn.* depart, draw back, take leave; see **retire** 1, 3, **retreat** 1, 2.
2. [To remove from use or circulation]—*Syn.* revoke, rescind, abolish, repeal, annul, abrogate, veto, suppress, repress, retire, stamp out, declare illegal, ban, bar, nullify, repudiate, reverse, retract, throw overboard, invalidate, quash, dissolve.—*Ant.* introduce, put on the record, establish*.
3. [To remove]—*Syn.* take *or* draw away, pull out *or* back, switch; see **eliminate** 1, **remove** 1.

withdrawal, *n.*—*Syn.* removal, retreat, retraction, resignation, alienation, abandonment, recession, revulsion, abdication, relinquishment, departure.—*Ant.* progress*, advance, appearance.

withdrawn, *mod.*—*Syn.* retired, secluded, isolated, removed, departed, cloistered, recluse, drawn back, gone into retirement, taken out, absent, retreated.—*Ant.* active*, involved, progressing.

wither, *v.*—*Syn.* shrivel, shrink, droop, wilt, decay, die, grow brown, dry up *or* out, fade, lose freshness, deteriorate, fall away.—*Ant.* revive*, reawaken, bloom.

withered, *mod.*—*Syn.* shriveled, wilted, decayed, deteriorated, shrunken, dead, browned, faded, parched, dried up, drooping, wrinkled.—*Ant.* fresh*, blooming, alive.

withering, *mod.*—*Syn.* shriveling, shrinking, wilting; see **decaying.**

withheld, *mod.*—*Syn.* concealed, held back, hidden, checked, restrained, delayed, denied, kept on leash, on ice (D).—*Ant.* free*, opened, made visible.

withhold, *v.*—*Syn.* hold back *or* out, reserve, keep; see **delay** 1, **deny.**

withholding, *mod.*—*Syn.* restraining, confining, checking, prohibiting, restricting, hindering, limiting, deterring, coercive, curbing, muzzling, bridling; see also **confining.**—*Ant.* open*, liberating, freeing.

withholding tax, *n.*—*Syn.* income tax, social security (tax), withholdings, federal tax; see also **tax** 1.

within, *mod.* and *prep.* —*Syn.* (on the) inside, indoors, in, not further than, not beyond, not over, in reach of, in a period of, not outside; see also **inside** 2.

with it (D), *mod.* —*Syn.* up to date, *au courant* (French), contemporary; see **modern** 1.

without, *mod.* and *prep.* **1.** [Outside]—*Syn.* out, outdoors, outwardly, externally, on the outside, standing outside, left out.

2. [Lacking]—*Syn.* not with, not having, in the absence of, free from, deprived of.

withstand, *v.* —*Syn.* face, confront, oppose, resist, endure, stand up to *or* against, hold out (D).

with that, *conj.* and *prep.* —*Syn.* and so, as a result, in consideration of that; see **accordingly, so** 1, 2, 3.

witness, *n.* —*Syn.* observer, onlooker, eyewitness, spectator, bystander, deponent, testifier, beholder, signatory.

witness, *v.* —*Syn.* see, observe, be a witness, be on the scene, behold, be present, testify, vouch for, stand for, look on, say under oath, depose, be on hand.

witnessed, *mod.* **1.** [Observed and attested]—*Syn.* sworn to, vouched for, alleged, borne out, validated, valid, established, verified, authenticated, substantiated, supported, upheld, endorsed, brought forward.

2. [Legally signed by a third party]—*Syn.* deposed, notarized, certified, accredited, made official, warranted, sealed, signed; see also **legal** 1.

witticism, *n.* —*Syn.* jest, quirk, quibble; see **joke** 2, **pun.**

witty, *mod.* —*Syn.* sparkling, keen, quick-witted, brilliant, whimsical, clever, bright; see also **intelligent** 1.

wizard, *n.* **1.** [A sorcerer]—*Syn.* magician, soothsayer, witch, witch doctor, necromancer, fortuneteller, astrologer, medicine man, conjurer, shaman, enchanter, hypnotist, diviner, seer, clairvoyant, palmist, augurer, medium.

2. [(D) One who works wonders]—*Syn.* wonderworker, expert, prodigy, genius, authority; *all* (D): marvel, crackerjack, seven days' wonder.

wizened, *mod.* —*Syn.* shriveled, lean, dried up; see **old** 1, **shrunken, withered.**

wobble, *v.* —*Syn.* shake, quaver, flounder, vacillate, tremble, quiver, move unsteadily (from side to side), dodder, teeter, totter, be unsteady, waver, quake, stagger, shuffle, waggle.

wobbling, *mod.* —*Syn.* shaking, quaking, trembling; see **quivering.**

wobbly, *mod.* —*Syn.* wavering, unbalanced, precarious; see **shaky** 1, **unsteady** 1.

woe, *n.* —*Syn.* sorrow, pain, misery; see **distress** 1, **grief** 1.

woebegone, *mod.* —*Syn.* despondent, depressed, dejected; see **sad** 1, **sorrowful.**

woeful, *mod.* —*Syn.* full of woe, mournful, miserable; see **pitiful** 1, **sorry** 1.

wolf, *n.* **1.** [An animal] Varieties of wolves include the following—wild dog, Eskimo dog, gray wolf, jackal, coyote, timber wolf, lobo, Japanese wolf, Indian wolf, thylacine, aardwolf; see also **animal** 2, **dog** 1.

2. [(D) A seducer]—*Syn.* Don Juan, Casanova, lothario, Lochinvar, suitor, wooer, pursuer, gallant, lady killer, lover boy (D), wild man, rapist, brute, lecher, flirt, cur, glutton, cannibal, killer, kidnapper.

woman, *n.* **1.** [An adult female]—*Syn.* lady, dame, matron, gentlewoman, maid, spinster, debutante, nymph, virgin, girl, old woman; *all* (D): chick, bird, broad, fem, doll, lolita, deb, squaw.

2. [A wife or mistress]—*Syn.* love, lover, wife; see **housewife, mistress** 2.

3. [A female servant]—*Syn.* companion, housekeeper, cleaning lady, charlady (British), washerwoman, laundress, cook, (first) maid, second maid, serving lady; see also **servant, slave** 1.

4. [Womankind]—*Syn.* feminity, fair sex, womanhood, eternal feminine, the world of women; *all* (D): the female of the species, the weaker vessel, cattle, poultry.

woman-hater, *n.* —*Syn.* misanthrope, misogyne, hater of women; see **cynic, misogynist.**

womanhood, *n.* **1.** [The state of being a woman] —*Syn.* adulthood, maturity, majority, womanliness, sexual prime, nubility, marriageable age, maidenhood, matronhood, spinsterhood, muliebrity, puberty.

2. [Womankind]—*Syn.* the fair sex, womenfolk, distaff, weaker sex, feminity, female sex, women.

womanish, *mod.* —*Syn.* womanly, effeminate, female; see **feminine** 2, **weak** 1.

womanly, *mod.* —*Syn.* effeminate, ladylike, feminine, female, gentle, modest, compassionate, wifely, sisterly, motherly, protective, womanish, weak, fair.—*Ant.* manly*, virile, masculine.

womb, *n.* —*Syn.* uterus, female cavity, prenatal chamber, organ, belly (D).

won, *mod.* —*Syn.* gained, achieved, conquered, taken, got, triumphed, overwhelmed.—*Ant.* beaten*, lost, failed.

wonder, *n.* **1.** [Amazement]—*Syn.* surprise, awe, stupefaction, admiration, wonderment, astonishment, wondering, stupor, bewilderment, perplexity, puzzlement, fascination, consternation, perturbation, confusion, shock, start, jar, jolt, incredulity.

2. [A marvel]—*Syn.* miracle, curiosity, oddity, rarity, freak, phenomenon, sensation, prodigy, act of God, portent, wonderwork, *rara avis* (Latin), spectacle, perversion, monstrous birth, prodigious event, something unnatural, the unbelievable.

wonder, *v.* **1.** [To marvel]—*Syn.* be surprised *or* startled *or* fascinated *or* amazed *or* dumbfounded *or* confounded *or* dazed *or* awestruck *or* astonished *or* agape *or* dazzled, stand *or* look aghast, be struck by, be unable to take one's eyes off, admire, gape, be taken aback, stare, be flabbergasted (D).

2. [To question]—*Syn.* be curious, query, hold in doubt; see **question** 1.

wonderful, *mod.* **1.** [Exciting wonder]—*Syn.* amazing, astonishing, incredible; see **unusual** 1, 2.

2. [Worthy of admiration]—*Syn.* fine, enjoyable, pleasing; see **excellent, pleasant** 2.

wonderfully, *mod.* —*Syn.* well, admirably, excellently, remarkably, unusually, unexpectedly, strikingly, magnificently, marvelously, beautifully, extraordinarily, amazingly, spectacularly, uncommonly, miraculously; *all* (D): famously, stunningly, first-rate, to a fare-thee-well.—*Ant.* badly*, poorly, passably.

wondering, *mod.* —*Syn.* marveling, admiring, fascinated, awed, struck, in awe, wonderstruck, guessing, pondering, speculating, flabbergasted (D).

wondrous, *mod.* —*Syn.* remarkable, unusual, extraordinary, miraculous, admirable, fascinating, awe-full, unexpected, striking, marvelous, amazing, astounding.

wont, *n.* —*Syn.* practice, manner, use; see **custom** 1, 2.

wonted, *mod.* **1.** [Usual]—*Syn.* customary, conventional, familiar; see **common** 1, **habitual** 1.
2. [Accustomed]—*Syn.* conditioned, habituated, accustomed; see **familiar** 1, **used** 1.

woo, *v.* **1.** [To make love to]—*Syn.* pay suit to, court, date, address, charm, spoon, bill and coo, make an offer, propose, seek in marriage, set one's cap for, make advances, caress, hold dear; *all* (D): carry on with, give the rush, keep company, go steady.
2. [To court, figuratively]—*Syn.* cultivate, pursue, beg, solicit, entreat, aim at, stick to, seek someone's support, toady, curry favor, turn to, seek intimacy with; *both* (D): suck up to, butter up; see also **propose** 1.

wood, *mod.* **1.** [Wooden]—*Syn.* woodlike, made of wood, hard; see **wooden** 2.
2. [Associated with the woods]—*Syn.* in the woods, wooded, woody, wood-dwelling, sylvan, woodsy, wild, shady, copselike, grovelike, arboreal, bowery, wild-grown.

wood, *n.* **1.** [A forest; *often plural*]—*Syn.* grove, woodland, copse; see **forest, timber** 1.
2. [The portion of trees within the bark]—*Syn.* log, timber, lumber, sapwood, heartwood.
Varieties of wood include the following—oak, chestnut, mahogany, sugar maple, red maple, cherry, cedar, hornbeam, walnut, hickory, butternut, hemlock, spruce, bass wood *or* linden, beech, birch, poplar, tamarack, white pine, yellow pine, gumwood, elm, cocobolo, cypress, redwood, fir, Douglas fir, ash, red oak, live oak, white oak, willow, cottonwood, lignum vitae, ebony, bamboo.
out of the woods (D)—*Syn.* out of danger, better, no longer in trouble; see **safe** 1, **saved** 1, 2.

wooded, *mod.* —*Syn.* timbered, forested, tree-covered, wild, sylvan, tree-laden, treed, reforested, woody, jungly, having cover, with enough forestation to preserve the run-off, timber-bearing, lumbering, uncut, not lumbered, not cut over *or* off, with standing timber, primeval, below the timberline, jungle covered.

wooden, *mod.* **1.** [Made of wood]—*Syn.* wood, frame, frame-built, log-built, boarded, clapboarded, plank, built of slabs; pine, oak, elm, ash, mahogany, etc.
2. [Having the characteristics of wood]—*Syn.* (in)-flammable, stiff, clumsy, resinous, temporary, hard, destructible, buoyant.

woodland, *n.* —*Syn.* wood, timberland, grove, copse, forest, timber, wilds.

woodpecker, *n.* Woodpeckers include the following—green woodpecker *or* yaffle, spotted woodpecker, red-headed woodpecker, pileated woodpecker *or* log-cock, California woodpecker, golden-winged woodpecker *or* flicker, red-shafted flicker, hairy woodpecker, downy woodpecker, North American sapsucker; see also **bird** 1.

wood(s)man, *n.* —*Syn.* forester, hunter, trapper, woodcutter, lumberjack, logger, sawyer, tree trimmer.

woodwork, *n.* —*Syn.* molding, fittings, paneling, stairway, wood finishing, doors, window frames, sashes, jambs, wood trim.

woody, *mod.* —*Syn.* woodlike, pithy, xyloid, ligneous, wooden, wooded.

wooer, *n.* —*Syn.* sweetheart, suitor, courtier; see **date** 3, **lover** 1.

woof, *n.* —*Syn.* weft, cross weave, texture; see **weave.**

wool, *n.* **1.** [Fleecy fiber, especially of sheep] —*Syn.* fleece, lamb's wool, Angora wool, Berlin *or* German wool, Shetland wool, Australian *or* Botany wool, glass wool, mineral wool; see also **fiber** 1, **fur.**
2. [Cloth made from wool]—*Syn.* tweed, flannel, gabardine, worsted, woolen, suiting, serge, broadcloth, frieze, mohair, felt, blanketing, carpeting, Botany (trademark); see also **cloth.**

woolen, *mod.* —*Syn.* made of wool, woven, worsted, wool-lined, sheepskin.

woolly, *mod.* —*Syn.* downy, fleecy, kinky, woolbearing, soft, fluffy, flocculent.

Word, *n.* —*Syn.* (the) Bible, God's Word, (the) (holy) Scripture(s), Logos, dogma, holy writings, Divine Wisdom.

word, *n.* **1.** [A unit of expression]—*Syn.* term, name, expression, designation, concept, vocable, utterance, sound, a voicing, form of speech, speech, locution, free morpheme *or* morpheme word, lexeme.
Classes of words include the following—common noun, proper noun, personal pronoun, possessive pronoun, demonstrative pronoun, relative pronoun, interrogative pronoun, indefinite pronoun, definite article, indefinite article, transitive verb, intransitive verb, descriptive adjective, quantitative adjective, participial adjective, adverb, coordinating conjunction, subordinate *or* relative conjunction, preposition, modifier, subject, predicate, loan word, root, primitive word, parent word, source word, etymon, synonym, antonym, cognative word, analogous word, derivative, slang, colloquialism, jargon, slang word, dialect word, provincialism, translation, native word, foreign word, idiom, connotative word, denotative word.
2. [Promise]—*Syn.* pledge, commitment, word of honor; see **declaration** 2, **promise.**
3. [Tidings]—*Syn.* report, news, information, advice, message, intelligence, announcement, account.
4. [A brief discourse]—*Syn.* talk, introduction, statement; see **speech** 3.
a good word—*Syn.* favorable comment, recommendation, support; see **praise** 2.
be as good as one's word—*Syn.* keep (the) faith, fulfill one's promise(s), live up to a promise *or* expectations *or* an oath, etc.; see **achieve** 1, **complete** 1.
by word of mouth—*Syn.* orally, verbally, spoken; see **oral.**
hang on someone's words—*Syn.* listen (to), adore, look up to; see **admire** 1, **listen** 1, 2.
have words with—*Syn.* argue (with), differ with *or* from, bicker; see **argue** 1, **fight** 1, 2.

in so many words—*Syn.* succinctly, cursorily, economically; see **briefly.**
man *or* **woman of his** *or* **her word**—*Syn.* honorable man *or* woman, trustworthy person, good risk; see **gentleman** 1, **lady** 2.
take at one's word—*Syn.* trust (in), have faith *or* confidence in, put one's trust in; see **believe** 1.
the word (D)—*Syn.* information, the facts (in the case), the lowdown (D); see **knowledge** 1, **truth** 1.

word-for-word, *mod.*—*Syn.* exactly, literally, verbatim; see **accurately.**

wordily, *mod.*—*Syn.* redundantly, pleonastically, bombstically; see **verbosely.**

wordiness, *n.*—*Syn.* redundance, redundancy, diffuseness, circumlocution, repetition, verbiage, verbosity, turgidity, prolixity, tautology, indirectness, periphrasis, vicious circle, flow of words, rhetoric, fullness, pleonasm, copiousness, bombast, tediousness.—*Ant.* silence*, conciseness, succinctness.

wording, *n.*—*Syn.* locution, phrasing, turn of phrase, contents, expression, style, way of putting it (D).

wordplay, *n.*—*Syn.* verbal wit, play on words, word games; see **pun.**

words, *n.* **1.** [Dispute]—*Syn.* contention, argument, wrangle; see **dispute** 1.
2. [Conversation]—*Syn.* chat, conference, communion; see **conversation, discussion** 1.

wordy, *mod.*—*Syn.* tedious, bombastic, long-winded; see **dull** 4, **verbose.**

work, *n.* **1.** [Something to be done]—*Syn.* commitment, task, obligation; see **job** 2.
2. [The doing of work, sense 1]—*Syn.* performance, endeavor, employment, production, occupation, profession, vocation, calling, practice, activity, manufacture, industry, operation, transaction, toil, labor, exertion, drudgery, functioning, stress, struggle, slavery, trial, push, attempt, effort, pains; *both* (D): elbow grease, muscle.
3. [The result of labor; *often plural*]—*Syn.* composition, feat, accomplishment, output, product, deed, act, finished article, achievement, end product, opus, opera; see also **drama** 1, **literature** 1, **movie, music** 1, **picture** 3.
4. [Occupation]—*Syn.* profession, craft, business; see **job** 1, **trade** 2.
at work—*Syn.* working, on the job, engaged; see **employed.**
give (someone) the works (D)—*Syn.* shoot, slaughter, murder; see **kill** 1.
in the works (D)—*Syn.* prepared for, budgeted, approved; see **planned, ready** 2.
make short *or* **quick work of** (D)—*Syn.* finish (off), deal with, dispose of; see **prevent, stop** 1.
out of work—*Syn.* not hired, dismissed, looking for a job; see **unemployed.**
shoot the works (D)risk *or* gamble or offer, etc., everything; go the limit, attempt; **risk, try** 1.

work, *v.* **1.** [To labor]—*Syn.* toil, slave, sweat, do a day's work *or* the chores, exert *or* apply oneself, do one's best, overexert, overwork, overstrain, get to work, work overtime *or* day and night *or* early and late, work *or* fight one's way (up), tax one's energies, pull plod, tug, chore, struggle, strive, carry on; *all* (D): do the job, punch a time clock, put in time, pour it on, not spare the horses, work one's fingers to the bone, buckle *or* bear down, work like a horse *or* a dog *or* a (galley) slave, keep at it, stay with it, put one's shoulder to the wheel, burn the candle at both ends, burn the midnight oil; see also **fight** 1.
2. [To be employed]—*Syn.* earn one's *or* a living, have *or* hold *or* occupy a position *or* job *or* post, report for work, be off the dole *or* the welfare rolls, be among the (gainfully) employed, be on the job; *all* (D): do time *or* one's stint, be working on the railroad, be a wage slave.
3. [To function]—*Syn.* go, run, serve; see **act** 1, **operate** 2.
4. [To handle successfully]—*Syn.* control, accomplish, manage; see **achieve** 1, **operate** 3.
5. [To fashion]—*Syn.* give form to, sculpture, mold; see **form** 1.
6. [To ferment]—*Syn.* sour, ripen, become worky; see **ferment.**

workable, *mod.*—*Syn.* useful, practicable, functional; see **working, usable.**

work at, *v.*—*Syn.* attempt, endeavor, do one's best; see **try** 1.

worked, *mod.*—*Syn.* fashioned, wrought, processed, treated, effected, designed, created.

worker, *n.*—*Syn.* laborer, toiler, mechanic; see **operator** 1, **workman.**

work in, *v.*—*Syn.* introduce, find a place for, squeeze in; see **include** 1.

working, *mod.* **1.** [Functioning]—*Syn.* toiling, laboring, moving, in process, in good condition, in force, in gear, in collar, in exercise, going, twitching, effective, practical, on the job, never idle, on (the) fire (D).
2. [Employed]—*Syn.* with *or* having a job, engaged, on the staff; see **employed.**

working, *n.*—*Syn.* operation, performance, functioning, fashioning, manipulation.

workings, *n.*—*Syn.* innards, mechanism, parts; see **insides, works** 1.

working with, *mod.*—*Syn.* co-operating, collaborating, assisting; see **helping.**

workman, *n.*—*Syn.* operator, mechanic, machinist, craftsman, artist, artisan, journeyman, master worker, handworker, skilled workman, white-collar worker, field workman.
Skilled workers include the following—carpenter, cabinetmaker, upholsterer, paper hanger, plasterer, bricklayer, plumber, pipefitter, coppersmith, sheet-metal worker, auto sheet-metal worker, printer, pressman, linotype operator, ship fitter, platehanger, slinger, chipper, screw machine operator, glassworker, lapping machine operator, electric-truck driver, autotruck driver, automobile mechanic, punch press operator, power sewing machine operator, addressograph operator, multigraph operator, cost accountant, clerk, file clerk, stenographer, bookkeeper, salesman, packager, darkroom operator, photographer, proofreader, railroad freight clerk, division clerk, conductor, brakeman, locomotive engineer, fireman, barber, baker, butcher, farm worker, cowboy, dairyman, waiter, waitress, laundry worker, welder, drill press operator, hydraulic press operator, automatic screw operator, jig borer operator, drill operator,

die sink operator, mason, lathe operator, gear-cutting machine operator, threading machine operator, telegrapher, teletype operator, telephone girl, radio operator, radio repairer, radio assembler, radio wirer, cigar maker, pattern builder, textile worker, tool designer, postal clerk, painter, pan coating man, galvanizer, draftsman, furrier, jewelry repairman, gold stamper, jigsaw cutter.

workmanship, *n.* —*Syn.* craftsmanship, skill, quality of work, performance, handicraft, working ability, handiwork, achievement, manufacture, execution.

work off, *v.* —*Syn.* go away, get better, disappear; see **improve** 2, **leave** 1.

work on *or* **upon** (D), *v.* —*Syn.* try to dissuade *or* encourage, use one's influence with, talk to; see **influence.**

workout, *n.* **1.** [A test]—*Syn.* tryout, drill, rehearsal; see **discipline** 1, **practice** 3.
2. [An exercise]—*Syn.* work, conditioning, gymnastics; see **discipline** 2, **drill** 3, **exercise** 1.

work out, *v.* **1.** [To solve]—*Syn.* come to terms, compromise, reach an agreement; see **agree, resolve.**
2. [To satisfy a requirement]—*Syn.* finish, do what is necessary, get something done; see **achieve** 1, **complete** 1, **satisfy** 3.

work over, *v.* **1.** [To repair]—*Syn.* fix (up), go over, redo; see **repair, repeat** 1.
2. [(D) To beat *or* punish]—*Syn.* thrash, beat up (on) (D), abuse; see **beat** 2, **punish.**

works, *n.* **1.** [Working parts]—*Syn.* cogs, wheels, gears, pistons, springs, coils, chains, rods, pulleys, wires; see also **insides.**
2. [Fortifications]—*Syn.* breastworks, earthworks, fort; see **fortification** 2, **wall** 1.
3. [(D) Punishment]—*Syn.* beating, thrashing, wallop; see **abuse** 3, **attack** 1.
4. [(D) Everything]—*Syn.* totality, entirety, the whole; see **all** 1, **everything.**

workshop, *n.* —*Syn.* plant, works, laboratory, foundry, studio, yards, establishment, mill.

work up, *v.* —*Syn.* elaborate (upon), refine, enhance; see **develop** 1, 4, **improve** 4.

work wonders, *v.* —*Syn.* revitalize, regenerate, make over; see **correct** 1, **improve** 1.

world, *n.* **1.** [The earth]—*Syn.* globe, wide world, terrestrial sphere; see **earth** 1, **planet.**
2. [The universe]—*Syn.* cosmos, nature, creation; see **universe.**
3. [A specific group]—*Syn.* realm, division, system; see **class** 1, 2.
4. [All one's surroundings]—*Syn.* environment, atmosphere, ambiance, childhood, adolescence, adulthood, experience, life, inner life, human intercourse, memory, idealization.
5. [Nonreligious affairs]—*Syn.* life of action, society, career, material pursuits, secular matters, worldly interests, business, *activa vita* (Latin), worldly distractions.
bring into the world—*Syn.* give birth (to), bear, have a baby; see **produce** 1.
for all the world—*Syn.* **1.** (D) seemingly, to all appearances, like; see **apparently. 2.** for everything and anything, no matter, what, regardless; see **anything, everything.**
in the world—*Syn.* anywhere at all, wheresoever, in the universe; see **anywhere, wherever.**
on top of the world—*Syn.* feeling fine *or* wonderful *or* happy, etc.; exuberant, successful; see **delighted, triumphant.**
out of this world—*Syn.* extraordinary, strange, remarkable; see **excellent, unusual** 1, 2.

worldly, *mod.* **1.** [Lacking spirituality or idealism] —*Syn.* mundane, earthly, ungodly, matter-of-fact, practical, secular, profane, strategic, grubbing, money-making, unprincipled, power-loving, self-centered, opportunistic, sophisticated.—*Ant.* spiritual*, religious, idealistic.
2. [Referring to life on the earth]—*Syn.* terrestrial, earthly, sublunary, mundane, telluric, human, natural, temporal.

worldly goods, *n.* —*Syn.* possessions, assets, nest egg (D); see **property** 1.

worldwide, *mod.* —*Syn.* global, universal, extensive; see **common** 5, **comprehensive.**

worm, *n.* **1.** [A small crawling animal]—*Syn.* caterpillar, grub, larva, maggot, leech, parasite, helminth.
Common worms include the following—angleworm, earthworm, threadworm, tapeworm, galleyworm, silkworm, flatworm, blindworm, roundworm, annelid worm, cutworm, army worm, cotton worm, wire worm.
2. [A debased creature]—*Syn.* wretch, hypocrite, beggar, fraud, brute, scoundrel, reprobate, snake, shyster, trickster, sneak, devil, demon, hellhound, scum, creep (D), riffraff, sharper, swindler, hoaxer.
3. [Helminthiasis; *usually plural*]—*Syn.* hookworm, intestinal worms, tapeworms; see also **infection** 1.

worm, *v.* —*Syn.* inch, insinuate oneself, sidle; see **crawl** 1, **sneak.**

wormlike, *mod.* —*Syn.* vermicular, sinuous, convoluted; see **twisted** 1.

worm out of (D), *v.* —*Syn.* evade, get out of, slip out (of); see **avoid, escape.**

worn, *mod.* **1.** [Used as clothing]—*Syn.* carried, put on, donned, displayed, exhibited, used, sported (D).
2. [Showing signs of wear]—*Syn.* frayed, threadbare, old, secondhand, ragged, shabby, impaired, used, consumed, deteriorated, torn, patched, the worse for war.—*Ant.* fresh*, new, whole.

worn-out, *mod.* —*Syn.* used (up), gone, destroyed; see **ruined** 1, 2, **useless** 1.

worried, *mod.* —*Syn.* troubled, anxious, hung up (D); see **bothered.**

worry, *n.* **1.** [The state of anxiety]—*Syn.* concern, anxiety, misery; see **care** 2, **distress** 1.
2. [A cause of worry]—*Syn.* problem, upset, disturbance; **fear** 2, **trouble** 2.

worry, *v.* **1.** [To cause worry]—*Syn.* annoy, trouble, bother, bug (D); see **depress** 2, **disturb** 2.
2. [To indulge in worry]—*Syn.* fret, chafe, grieve, take to heart, break one's heart, worry oneself, have qualms, despair, wince, agonize, writhe, suffer, turn gray with worry, be anxious, become sick with worry, stew, sweat out (D); see also **bother** 1.

worrying, *mod.* —*Syn.* pessimistic, pained, burdened, concerned, anxious, solicitous, ill at ease, disquieted, disturbed, heartsick, racking one's brains; see also **bothered.**—*Ant.* happy*, lighthearted, gay.

worrying, *n.* —*Syn.* bother, anxiety, concern; see **care** 2, **distress** 1.

worrywart (D), —*Syn.* worrier, nervous person *or* type (D), old maid (D); see **neurotic.**

worse, *mod.* —*Syn.* more evil, not so good, deteriorated; see **poor** 2.

worsen, *n.* —*Syn.* fall off, fan the flames, exacerbate; see **depress** 2.

worsened, *mod.* —*Syn.* exacerbated, depressed, lowering; see **dismal** 1.

worship, *n.* **1.** [Adoration]—*Syn.* prayer, devotion, homage, adulation, benediction, invocation, supplication, beatification, veneration, (burnt) offering, reverence, honor, Mariolatry, hagiolatry, religious ritual.

2. [A religious service]—*Syn.* Mass, vespers, devotions; see **church** 2.

worship, *v.* **1.** [To adore]—*Syn.* esteem, honor, exalt; see **admire** 1, **love** 1.

2. [To perform acts of worship]—*Syn.* sanctify, pray to, invoke, venerate, glorify, praise, exalt, offer one's prayers to, pay homage to, recite the rosary, tell one's beads, return *or* give thanks, offer thanks to, sing praises to, reverence, celebrate, adore, revere, laud, extol, magnify, chant, sing, bow down, canonize; see also **pray** 2.

worshiper, *n.* —*Syn.* churchgoer, communicant, congregant, pilgrim, supplicant, devotee, devotionalist, adorer, pietist, pious *or* devout person, celebrant, saint, priest, priestess.—*Ant.* skeptic*, atheist, agnostic.

worshipful, *mod.* —*Syn.* pious, reverent, devoted; see **religious** 2.

worst, *mod.* —*Syn.* most terrible *or* harmful *or* lethal, poorest, lowest, least, most ghastly *or* horrible *or* pitiful, least meaningful, meanest, least understanding, least effective.

worst, *n.* —*Syn.* calamity, catastrophe, ruin; see **destruction, misfortune.**

at worst—*Syn.* under the worst (possible) circumstances, unluckily, grievously; see **badly** 1, **unfortunately** 1, 2.

give one the worst of it—*Syn.* overcome, get the better of one, triumph; see **beat** 2, **defeat** 1.

if the worst comes to the worst—*Syn.* see **at worst.**

(in) the worst way—*Syn.* unluckily, disastrously, horribly; see **unfortunately.**

worst, *v.* —*Syn.* triumph over, overcome, best; see **beat** 2, **defeat** 1, 2, 3.

worsted, *n.* —*Syn.* woolens, suiting, long staple, English worsted; see also **wool** 2.

worth, *mod.* —*Syn.* deserving, meriting, equal in value to, priced at, exchangeable for, valued at, worth in the open market, pegged at, cashable for, good for, appraised at, having a face value of, reasonably estimated at, bid at, held at.

for all one is worth—*Syn.* greatly, mightily, hard; see **powerfully, vigorously.**

worth, *n.* —*Syn.* goodness, excellence, merit; see **quality** 3, **value** 1, 2, 3, 4.

worthless, *mod.* **1.** [Valueless]—*Syn.* profitless, counterproductive, barren, unprofitable, unproductive, unimportant, insignificant, counterfeit, bogus, cheap, sterile, waste, wasted, no good, trashy, inconsequential, petty, piddling, paltry, trivial, trifling, unessential, beneath notice, empty, good-for-nothing; *all* (D): no-account, junky, crowbait, not worth a damn, of no earthly use, not worth the trouble, not worth speaking of, fit for the dust hole, not able to say much for.

2. [Useless]—*Syn.* ineffective, of no use, ineffectual; see **useless** 1, **waste.**

worthlessness, *n.* —*Syn.* uselessness, impracticality, inefficiency, inadequacy, inability, ruined *or* worthless condition, lack of use *or* value, inapplicability, badness.

worthwhile, *mod.* —*Syn.* good, serviceable, useful, important, profitable, valuable, remunerative, estimable, worthy, helpful, beneficial, meritorious, excellent, rewarding, praiseworthy.

worthy, *mod.* —*Syn.* good, true, honest, honorable, reliable, trustworthy, dependable, noble, charitable, dutiful, philanthropic, virtuous, ethical, moral, pure, upright, righteous, decent, incorrupt, incorruptible, meritorious, creditable, deserving, laudable, praiseworthy, right-minded, worthy of, whole-souled, model, exemplary, sterling, sinless, stainless, blameless.—*Ant.* worthless*, bad, evil.

would-be, *mod.* —*Syn.* anticipated, assuming, supposed; see **hopeful** 1, **intended.**

wound, *mod.* —*Syn.* twisted, coiled, covered, wreathed, wrapped, twined, tired.

wound, *n.* —*Syn.* bruise, hurt, scar; see **cut** 2, **injury** 1.

wound, *v.* **1.** [To hurt the body]—*Syn.* gash, scrape, injure; see **cut** 2.

2. [To hurt the feelings]—*Syn.* trouble, upset, pain; see **bother** 3, **disturb** 2.

wounded, *mod.* —*Syn.* injured, hurt, disabled, stabbed, cut, lacerated, shot, scratched, bitten, gashed, hit, beaten, bruised, attacked; *all* (D): winged, nicked, pipped.

woven, *mod.* —*Syn.* spun, interlinked, netted, netlike, dovetailed, wreathed, sewn, intertwined, united, interlaced, interwoven, worked into.

wow (them) (D), *v.* —*Syn.* triumph, overcome, be a success; see **defeat** 1.

wraith, *n.* —*Syn.* specter, phantom, apparition; see **ghost** 1.

wrangle, *n.* —*Syn.* altercation, controversy, disagreement; see **dispute** 1, **fight** 1.

wrangle, *v.* —*Syn.* bicker, squabble, dispute; see **quarrel.**

wrap, *n.* —*Syn.* shawl, cover, blanket, fur piece, cape, jacket, coat, cloak, light outer garment.

wrap, *v.* **1.** [To twine or wind]—*Syn.* roll up, swathe, muffle, bind, fold about, encircle, coil, enclose, swaddle, bandage; see also **wind** 1.

2. [To conceal in a wrapper]—*Syn.* envelop, enwrap, protect, encase, sheathe, shroud, cover (up), shelter, clothe, cover with paper, enclose in a box. —*Ant.* unwrap*, unsheathe, open up.

wrapped, *mod.* —*Syn.* covered, sheathed, swaddled, swathed, enclosed, papered, protected, enveloped, encased, shrouded, concealed, hidden, clothed, done up.—*Ant.* open*, unwrapped, uncovered.

wrapped up in (D), *mod.*—*Syn.* in love (with), devoted (to), affectionate; see **loving.**

wrapper, *n.*—*Syn.* envelope, folder, book cover; see **cover** 2.

wrap up (D), *v.*—*Syn.* finish (off), bring to an end or a conclusion, polish off (D); see **complete** 1.

wrath, *n.*—*Syn.* fury, vengeance, madness; see **anger, rage** 2.

wrathful, *mod.*—*Syn.* furious, raging, storming; see **angry.**

wreath, *n.*—*Syn.* garland, chaplet, laurel, lei, crown, festoon, floral design, (funeral) decoration, spray, (flower) arrangement; see also **bouquet** 1.

wreck, *n.* **1.** [The act of wrecking]—*Syn.* destruction, demolition, razing, breaking up, ruination, sabotage, crash, smash, breakdown; *both* (D): crack-up, bust.

2. [Anything wrecked]—*Syn.* junk, ruins, skeleton, hulk, stubble, collapse, bones, scattered parts, rattletrap, relic, litter, pieces, shreds, waste, wreckage, debris.

3. [A shipwreck]—*Syn.* sea disaster, sinking, running aground, debacle, foundering.

4. [(D) A person in poor physical condition]—*Syn.* incurable, invalid, consumptive, nervous case, overworked person, cripple; *all* (D): mess, goner, washout, scrub, shadow, skin-and-bones, (walking) nightmare.

wreck, *v.* **1.** [To bring to ruin]—*Syn.* spoil, ruin, destroy, disfigure, mangle, smash, tear down, raze, break, split, efface, batter, torpedo, tear to pieces, put out of order, impair, injure, stave in, bash in; *all* (D): mess up, play hell with, put out of commission.—*Ant.* repair*, restore, rebuild.

2. [To shipwreck]—*Syn.* capsize, sink, founder, split on the rocks, crash on the beach, run aground, scuttle.

wreckage, *n.*—*Syn.* remains, ruins, hulk, wreck, debris, flotsam and jetsam, remnants.

wrecked, *mod.*—*Syn.* demolished, destroyed, broken (up), knocked to pieces, ruined, smashed (to bits), shipwrecked, stranded, beached, grounded, scuttled, capsized, (put) out of order, blown to bits, junked, dismantled, shattered; *all* (D): on the rocks, gone to pot, bumsquabbled, shot to hell, snafu.—*Ant.* repaired*, fixed, rebuilt.

wrecking, *mod.*—*Syn.* destroying, ruining, spoiling, smashing, breaking, splitting, shattering, undoing, battering, impairing, bashing, destructive, tearing (down).

wren, *n.* Kinds of wrens include the following—house, western house, winter, western winter, Carolina, long-billed marsh, tule marsh, cactus, cañon, rock, Nevada cañon, Berwick; see also **bird** 1.

wrench, *n.* **1.** [A violent twist]—*Syn.* jerk, strain, sprain, tug, pull, dislodgment, extrication, dislocation.

2. [A spanner] Wrenches include the following—monkey, single-head, double-head, pipe, Stillson, plumber's crescent, sparkplug, hubcap, flat, S-socket, connecting-rod, bearing; *all* (D): persuader, knuckle-buster, breakout, old Maud; see also **tool** 1.

wrench, *v.*—*Syn.* twist, pervert, bend, distort, extract, sprain, strain, pull, tug, jerk, dislodge, wrest, dislocate, yank.

wrestle, *v.*—*Syn.* grapple, struggle with, contend with, scuffle, perform in a wrestling bout; *all* (D): wrassle, tangle, grunt and growl, trade holds, tussle; see also **fight** 2.

wrestler, *n.*—*Syn.* grappler, matman, mat performer; *all* (D): rassler, bone breaker, man mountain, torso twister, tangler; see also **fighter** 1, 2.

wrestling, *n.*—*Syn.* contention, grappling, bout; see **fight** 1.

wrestling match, *n.*—*Syn.* grappling, mat game, wrestling bout; see **fight** 1, **sport** 3.

wretch, *n.*—*Syn.* scamp, rascal, villain, brute, traitor, deceiver, liar, fraud.

wretched, *mod.* **1.** [Afflicted]—*Syn.* distressed, woeful, sorrowful; see **miserable** 1, **sad** 1.

2. [Poor in quality]—*Syn.* weak, faulty, cheap; see **flimsy** 1, **poor** 2.

wretchedness, *n.*—*Syn.* misery, poverty, despondency, unhappiness, distress, grief, trouble, affliction, abjection, woe, sadness, disillusionment, depression, melancholia, dejection, discomfort, discontent, tribulation, torment, desperation, despair, desolation, bitterness; *all* (D): blue funk, dumps, blues, doldrums.—*Ant.* happiness*, joyousness, exuberance.

wriggle, *v.*—*Syn.* squirm, convulse, wiggle; see **twitch** 2.

wring, *v.*—*Syn.* press *or* squeeze out, extract, compress, twist, turn, strain, contort, bleed out, draw from.

wrinkle, *n.*—*Syn.* crease, furrow, crinkle, ridge, fold, corrugation, line, crow's foot, pucker, pleat.

wrinkle, *v.* **1.** [To form into wrinkles]—*Syn.* rumple, crease, furrow, screw up, pucker, cockle, twist, crumple, compress, crinkle.—*Ant.* straighten*, smooth out, iron.

2. [To become wrinkled]—*Syn.* grow old, shrivel up, become warped, dry up, wither lose shape; see also **wither.**

wrinkled, *mod.*—*Syn.* creased, rumpled, furrowed, puckered, warped, twisted, crumpled, cockled, crinkled, dried up, withered, unironed, unpressed, shrivelled.—*Ant.* smooth*, ironed, pressed.

writ, *n.*—*Syn.* order, decree, warrant, process, summons, replevin, command, habeas corpus.

write, *v.* **1.** [To compose in words]—*Syn.* set forth, record, formulate, draft, turn out, give a report, note down, transcribe, pen, put in writing, comment upon, go into, indite, typewrite, communicate, rewrite, produce poetry *or* plays *or* novels, do imaginative writings, correspond, scribble; see also **compose** 3.

2. [To set down in writing]—*Syn.* inscribe, sign, scrawl, address, print, letter, autograph, reproduce; *all* (D): knock *or* dash off, put in black and white, get to.

write off—*Syn.* charge off, take a loss on, recognize as a bad debt; see **lose** 2.

write up—*Syn.* expand, work up, deal at length with; see **describe, develop** 1, 4.

writer, *n.* —*Syn.* author, journalist, reporter, newspaperman, magazine writer, contributor, poet, novelist, essayist, *terzapaginista* (Italian), biographer, dramatist, playwright, librettist, scenario writer, scenarist, screenwriter, literary critic, (foreign) correspondent, feature writer, sports writer, fashion writer, shorthand writer, stenographer, anecdotist, amanuensis, ghost writer, song, writer, copyist, scribe, editor, contributing editor, war correspondent, special writer, freelance writer, representative, women's reporter; *all* (D): knight of the pen, member of the Fourth Estate, quill driver, scribbler, wordsmith, pen pusher, hack, newshound; see also **composer.**
Major writers include the following—British: Henry Fielding, Sir Walter Scott, Charlotte Brontë, George Eliot, Jane Austin, Charles Dickens, Thomas Hardy, D. H. Lawrence, James Joyce, Joseph Conrad; American: James Fenimore Cooper, Edgar Allan Poe, Ralph Waldo Emerson, Henry David Thoreau, Nathaniel Hawthorne, Herman Melville, Samuel Langhorne Clemens (Mark Twain), Henry James, Stephen Crane, Theodore Dreiser, William Faulkner, John Steinbeck, Ernest Hemingway; French: (François-Marie Arouet de) Voltaire, Jean Jacques Rosseau, Victor Hugo, Honoré de Balzac, Gustave Flaubert, Alexandre Dumas, Jules Verne, Albert Camus; Italian: Niccolo Machiavelli, Giovanni Boccaccio; German: Thomas Mann, Franz Kafka; Russian: Fyodor Dostoevsky, Leo Tolstoy, Boris Pasternak; Spanish: Miguel de Cervantes.

write-up (D), *n.* —*Syn.* press report, written description, written eulogy, laudatory account, review, publicity story; *all* (D): spread, blurb, rave, notice, build-up.

write up, *v.* —*Syn.* report, publicize, record, treat of, do a sketch of, make an account of, put into words, report on, interview, do an item for the newspapers, praise in the press; *both* (D): ballyhoo, build up; see also **interview.**

writhe, *v.* —*Syn.* contort, move painfully, squirm, distort, suffer, twist (and turn), undergo agony, turn with pain, throw a fit (D).—*Ant.* rest*, be at ease, move easily.

writhing, *mod.* —*Syn.* twisting, squirming, moving painfully, twitching, groveling, laboring, convulsed, agonized, suffering.—*Ant.* resting*, still, sleeping.

writing, *mod.* —*Syn.* corresponding with, in touch with, writing to; see **in contact with** 2.

writing, *n.* **1.** [The practice of writing]—*Syn.* transcribing, inscribing, reporting, corresponding, letter-writing, copying, typewriting, penmanship, lettering, printing, calligraphy, graphology, grammatology, grammatography, signing, autographing, stenography; see also **shorthand, typing.**
2. [Anything written]—*Syn.* literature, written matter, document, composition, article, poem, (deathless) prose, paper, theme, editorial, discourse, essay, thesis, dissertation, book, manuscript, novel, play, literary production, scenario, drama, piece, work, signature, letter, pamphlet, tract, treatise, disquisition, comment, commentary, review, recitation, certificate, record, bill; *all* (D): bit, item, piece; see also **copy.**
3. [The occupation of a writer]—*Syn.* journalism, reporting, literature, authorship, freelance writing, professional writing, auctorial pursuits, the pen, the Fourth Estate, creative writing; novel-writing, verse-writing, feature-writing, etc.; newspaper work, the writers' craft, literary artistry; *all* (D): ink-slinging, pencil-pushing, hack writing, writing for the pulps, writing for the slicks, ghost-writing.

writing desk, *n.* —*Syn.* writing table, escritoire, desk; see **table** 1.

written, *mod.* **1.** [Composed]—*Syn.* set forth, authored, penned, drawn up, reported, signed, turned out, fictionalized, arranged, rearranged, adapted, ghost-written, recorded, dictated; see also **composed** 1.
2. [Inscribed]—*Syn.* copied, scriptural, transcribed, printed, lettered, autographed, signed, put in writing, in black and white, under one's hand; see also **typed** 1.

wrong, *mod.* **1.** [Immoral]—*Syn.* evil, sinful, wicked, naughty, salacious, base, indecent, risqué, blasphemous, ungodly, amoral, dissolute, dissipated, wanton, profane, sacrilegious, depraved, corrupt, profligate; *all* (D): shady, low-down, smutty.—*Ant.* righteous*, virtuous, good.
2. [Inaccurate]—*Syn.* inexact, erroneous, sophistical, mistaken, in error, incorrect, fallacious, untrue, erring, astray, amiss, ungrounded, spurious, unsubstantial, unsound, erratic, deceiving one self, in the wrong, under an error, beside the mark, laboring under a false impression, out of line, at fault, to no purpose, not right, awry, faulty, mishandled, miscalculated, misfigured, misconstructed, misconstrued, misfashioned, mismade, altered, not precise, perverse, anachronistic, at fault in one's reckoning, wide of the mark, not according to the facts, abounding in error, badly estimated, beyond, the range of probable error; *all* (D): a mile off, all off, gummed up, crazy.—*Ant.* accurate*, correct, exact.
3. [Inappropriate]—*Syn.* unfitted, ill-fitting, disproportionate, out of focus, off balance, misplaced, awkward, gauche, ill-advised, improper, unsuitable, incongruous.—*Ant.* fit*, suitable, appropriate.
4. [Referring to a side to be kept from view] —*Syn.* reverse, back, obverse, opposite, inside.

wrong, *n.* **1.** [Injustice]—*Syn.* vice, sin, misdemeanor, crime, immorality, turpitude, indecency, transgression, misdeed, unfairness, imposition, oppression, foul play, prejudice, bias, favor, unlawful practice, villainy, delinquency, misdoing, error, miscarriage, mistake, blunder, offense, *faux pas* (French), wrongdoing, violation, tort.—*Ant.* right*, justice, fairness.
2. [An injury]—*Syn.* hurt, persecution, injustice, malevolence, cruelty, libel, abuse, harm, damage, spite, slander, false report, slight, misusage, outrage, inhumanity, over-presumption, insult, discourtesy; *all* (D): raw deal, bum steer, dirt.—*Ant.* kindness*, good deed, consideration.

wrong, *v.* —*Syn.* hurt, oppress, defame; see **abuse** 1.

wrongdoer, *n.* —*Syn.* lawbreaker, rogue, fugitive; see **criminal, sinner.**

wrongheaded, *mod.* —*Syn.* stubborn, biased, narrow; see **obstinate, prejudiced.**

wrongly, *mod.* **1.** [Unjustly]—*Syn.* unfairly, prejudicially, wrongfully, partially, badly, unjustifiably, illegally, disgracefully, sinfully, unreasonably, unlawfully, criminally, reprehensibly, inexcusably. —*Ant.* rightly*, decently, justly.
2. [Inappropriately]—*Syn.* unsuitably, improperly, awkwardly, incongruously, incorrectly, unbecomingly, indecorously, out of the question, imprudently, rashly, unnaturally, illogically, quixotically; see also **inadequately.**—*Ant.* appropriately*, tastefully, prudently.

wrought, *mod.* —*Syn.* created, manufactured, fashioned, formed, worked, processed, shaped, beaten, molded, woven, ornamented, coated, polished.

wrought-up, *mod.* —*Syn.* disturbed, anxious, agog; see **excited, tense** 1.

wrung, *mod.* —*Syn.* twisted, squeezed out, pressed, compressed, forced, dried.

wry, *mod.* —*Syn.* distorted, askew, crooked; see **twisted** 1.

X

x, *n.* —*Syn.* unknown quantity, unknown, y; see **quantity.**

Xanthippe, *n.* —*Syn.* nag, scold, virago; see **shrew.**

Xerox (trademark), *v.* —*Syn.* reproduce, make a copy of, ditto; see **copy** 2.

Xmas, *n.* —*Syn.* the Nativity, Christmas holiday, Yule; see **Christmas, holiday** 1.

X-rays, *n.* —*Syn.* Roentgen rays, radioactivity, radium emanation, actinic rays, actinism, exradio, encephalogram, ultraviolet rays, refractometry, radiant energy, cathode rays; see also **energy** 3, **ray.**

xylophone, *n.* —*Syn.* carillon, vibraphone (*or* (D): vibes), glockenspiel, marimba, gambang, *gender* (Javanese); see **musical instrument.**

Y

yacht, *n.* —*Syn.* pleasure boat, sloop, auxiliary racer, class boat, racing boat; *both* (D): sea-going taxi, single-sticker; see also **boat, ship.**

yahoo, *n.* —*Syn.* barbarian, brute, savage; see **beast** 2, **boor.**

Yale, *n.* —*Syn.* Yale University; *all* (D): old Eli, the Quad, (the) Blue, one of the Big Three, Bulldog(s); see also **university.**

yammer, *v.* —*Syn.* nag, whine, whimper; see **complain** 1.

yank, *n.* —*Syn.* twitch, jerk, wrench, flip, jiggle, tug, haul, drag; see also **pull** 1.

Yank (D), *n.* —*Syn.* American, soldier, member of the A.E.F., Yankee; *all* (D): doughboy, (GI) Joe, doughfoot.

yank, *v.* —*Syn.* pull, haul, tug, drag, jiggle, flip, wrench, twitch; see also **draw** 1, **jerk** 2.

Yankee, *mod.* **1.** [Having New England qualities] —*Syn.* homespun, individualistic, isolationist, Republican, rockbound, set, conservative, rural, clever, tricky, hard, cunning, sharp, mercantile; see also **moderate, practical.**

2. [Concerning the United States]—*Syn.* North American, Western, Occidental, westernized, Americanized; see also **American** 2.

Yankee, *n.* **1.** [A New Englander]—*Syn.* Northerner, Easterner, early settler, Abolitionist, Unionist.

2. [A person from the United States]—*Syn.* American, American citizen, North American, westerner, Occidental; *both* (D): tourist, Yank.

Yankees, *n.* —*Syn.* New York American League Baseball Club; *all* (D): Yanks, Bronx Bombers, Ruppert's Rifles, Murderers' Row; see also **baseball.**

Yanks (D), *n.* —*Syn.* American Expeditionary Force(s) *or* A.E.F., Army and Navy, Americans, American soldiers, American forces; *all* (D): doughboys, doughfeet, G.I.; see also **air force, army** 1, **marines, navy.**

yap, *v.* —*Syn.* jabber, rant, chatter; see **babble, talk** 1.

yard, *n.* **1.** [An enclosure, usually about a building] —*Syn.* court, courtyard, barnyard, backyard, corral, fold, patch, patio, terrace, play area, lawn, grass, garden, clearing, quadrangle, lot; see also **playground.**

2. [An enclosure for work]—*Syn.* brickyard, coalyard, junkyard, navy yard, dockyard, railroad yard, stockyard, lumberyard.

3. [*Often plural;* tracks for making up trains] —*Syn.* railroad yard, switchyard, railway yard, marshalling yard, terminal; *both* (D): iron harness, hump.

4. [A unit of measurement]—*Syn.* three feet, pace, step, arm-span, thirty-six inches; see also **measure** 1.

yardstick, *n.* **1.** [A rule three feet long]—*Syn.* thirty-six-inch ruler, measuring stick, molding rule, yard, yard measure; see also **ruler** 2.

2. [A unit for comparison]—*Syn.* criterion, basis for judgment, criterion, standard, gauge, norm, rule, model, pattern, test, arbitrary device; see also **measure** 2.

yarn, *n.* **1.** [Spun fiber]—*Syn.* spun wool, twist, flaxen thread, cotton fiber, rug yarn, crochet thread, knitting yarn, alpaca yarn; see also **fiber** 1, **thread.**

2. [A tale]—*Syn.* anecdote, sea story, adventure story, fictional account; see also **story.**

3. [A lie]—*Syn.* fabrication, tall story, alibi; *both* (D): fish story, cock-and-bull story; see also **lie** 1.

yaw, *v.* —*Syn.* curve, swerve, bank; see **bend** 2, **turn** 6, **veer.**

yawl, *n.* —*Syn.* vessel, sailboat, jolly-boat; see **boat, ship.**

yawn, *v.* **1.** [To open wide]—*Syn.* gape, split open, spread out, expand, give, gap, part; see also **divide** 1, **grow** 1.—*Ant.* close*, shut, come together.

2. [To give evidence of drowsiness]—*Syn.* gape, be sleepy, make a yawning sound, show weariness; see also **sleep, tire** 1.

yea, *interj.* —*Syn.* okay, aye, well; see **yes.**

yea-high (D), *mod.* —*Syn.* so *or* this high, up to here, yea-big (D); see **high** 1, **short** 1.

year, *n.* —*Syn.* twelve months, cycle, continuum of days; see **age** 3, **time** 1.

Kinds of years include the following—civil, legal, calendar, lunar, solar, astronomical, natural, sidereal, tropical, equinoctial, leap, school, fiscal.

year after year, *mod.* —*Syn.* year by year, annually; year in, year out; see **yearly.**

yearbook, *n.* —*Syn.* annual, almanac, yearly report (book), record, graduation book, class book, annual publication; see also **catalogue** 2, **journal** 1.

yearling, *n.* —*Syn.* suckling, nursling, weanling; see **animal** 2, **baby** 1.

yearly, *mod.* —*Syn.* annually, once a year, every winter, every spring, every summer, every autumn, *per annum* (Latin), year by year; see also **annual, regularly** 1.

yearn, *v.* —*Syn.* want, crave, long for, fret, chafe, ache, grieve, mourn, droop, pine, languish, be eager for, be desirous of, be ardent *or* fervent *or* passionate, wish (for), thirst *or* hunger for, aspire to, set one's heart upon; *both* (D): hanker after, have a yen for; see also **try** 1.—*Ant.* avoid*, be content, be indifferent.

yearning, *n.* —*Syn.* want, longing, craving; see **desire** 1, **wish** 1.

years, *n.* —*Syn.* agedness, oldness, senescense; see **age** 2, **senility.**

yeast, *n.* —*Syn.* leaven, zyme, ferment, barm, amylase, pepsin, diastase; see also **catalyst, enzyme, fungus.**

yeasty, *mod.* —*Syn.* foamy, lathery, bubbly; see **frothy** 1.

yegg (D), *n.* —*Syn.* felon, outlaw, safecracker; see **criminal, robber.**

yell, *n.* **1.** [A shout]—*Syn.* bellow, cry, yelp, roar, whoop, howl, screech, shriek, squeal, holler, hoot, yawp, hubbub, hullabaloo, hue and cry, protest; see also **noise** 1.

2. [Organized cheering]—*Syn.* hip-hip-hurrah, rooting, cheer, tiger (D); see also **encouragement** 2.

yell, *v.* —*Syn.* bellow, cry out, scream, shout, yelp, yap, bawl, roar, halloo, vociferate, whoop, howl, screech, shriek, shrill, squeal, squall, ululate, yammer, hoot, cheer, call, yip, give encouragement, call down, raise one's voice, yawp; *both* (D): holler, whoop it up; see also **sound** 1.

yelling, *mod.* —*Syn.* boisterous, clamorous, noisy, bawling, uproarious, turbulent, drunken, aroused, riotous, cantankerous, blatant, vociferous; see also **harsh** 1, **loud** 2.—*Ant.* quiet*, subdued, silent.

yelling, *n.* —*Syn.* cry, scream, shout, outcry, vociferation, screeching, bawling, yowling, bellowing, howling, yelping; see also **noise** 1, 2, **yell** 1, 2.

yellow, *n.* **1.** Tints and shades of yellow include the following—cream color, ivory color, old ivory, ivory-yellow, lemon color, orange-yellow, saffron, jasmine, tawny, sand, gold, sallow, buff, alizarin yellow, anilin yellow, brilliant yellow, chrome yellow, Dutch pink-yellow, Dutch yellow, gamboge yellow, golden yellow, Imperial yellow, platinum yellow, Manchester yellow *or* naphthol yellow, yellow carmine, yellow lake, yellow madder, yellow ocher; see also **color** 1, **gold** 2, **tan.**

2. [Cowardly]—*Syn.* tricky, deceitful, low, cringing, sneaking, white-livered, craven, treacherous; see also **cowardly** 1, 2, **vulgar** 1.

3. [Sensational; *said especially of some newspapers*] —*Syn.* tabloid, warmongering, chauvinistic, unethical, unprincipled; *both* (D): sexy, lowbrow; see also **exciting, lewd** 1, 2, **offensive** 2, **sensational.**

yellow, *mod.* **1.** [Having a yellowish color]—*Syn.* yellowish, golden, jaundiced-looking; see **yellow** *n.*

yelp, *v.* —*Syn.* howl, screech, hoot; see **cry** 3, **sound** 1.

yen (D), *n.* —*Syn.* longing, craving, hunger; see **desire** 1.

yeoman, *n.* **1.** [A naval clerk]—*Syn.* commissary clerk, ship's writer, officer's assistant; *all* (D): scribe, supercargo, quill driver; see also **clerk** 2, **secretary** 2.

2. [A stout fellow]—*Syn.* common man, commoner, farmer, homesteader, freeborn man, freeholder; see also **citizen, man** 2.

yes, *interj.* —*Syn.* surely, of course, certainly, good, fine, aye, true, granted, very well, *mais oui* (French), all right, O.K. *or* okay, Roger, we copy, over (to you), most assuredly, by all means, agreed, oh yes! amen, naturally, without fail, just so, good enough, even so, (in) the affirmative; *both* (D): you bet, okey-dokey.

yesterday, *mod.* —*Syn.* recently, previously, earlier; see **before** 1.

yesterday, *n.* —*Syn.* the other day, the day before, recently, last day, not long ago; see also **past** 1.

yet, *mod.* **1.** [Nevertheless]—*Syn.* notwithstanding, however, in spite of, despite, still, but, though, although, at any rate, on the other hand.

2. [Thus far]—*Syn.* until now, till, hitherto, prior to, still; see also **until.**

3. [In addition]—*Syn.* besides, additionally, further, furthermore, still further.

yield, *v.* **1.** [To surrender]—*Syn.* give up, capitulate, succumb, resign, abdicate, relinquish, quit, cede, bow, give in, come to terms, sue for peace, lay down arms, cease from, let go, submit, give oneself over, relent, admit *or* suffer defeat, forgo, humble oneself, waive; *all* (D): throw in the towel, call quits, back down, holler uncle, eat crow; see also **abandon** 1.—*Ant.* resist*, withstand, repulse.

2. [To produce]—*Syn.* bring in, return, sell for, furnish, generate, bear, bring forth, blossom, bear fruit, accrue, allow, admit; see also **bloom, produce** 1, 2.

3. [To grant]—*Syn.* accede, concur, acquiesce, allow, accept, comply, assent, concede, defer; see also **admit** 3, **agree.**

yielding, *mod.* **1.** [Producing]—*Syn.* green, fruitful, productive; see **fertile** 1, 2, **rich** 3.
2. [Flexible]—*Syn.* pliant, plastic, malleable; see **flexible** 1.
3. [In the act of giving under pressure]—*Syn.* cracking, splitting, breaking, opening, swaying, shaking, bending, creaking, budging, wavering, softening, loosening, turning, falling back; see also **soft** 2.—*Ant.* firm*, unyielding, impervious.
4. [Docile]—*Syn.* submissive, pliable, tractable; see **humble** 1, **obedient** 1.

yielding, *n.* **1.** [Submission]—*Syn.* gentleness, compliance, acquiescence; see **docility, humility.**
2. [Flexibility]—*Syn.* pliability, plasticity, pliancy; see **flexibility** 1.

yodel, *v.* —*Syn.* trill, warble, carol; see **sing** 1.

yogi, *n.* —*Syn.* mystic, fakir, anchorite; see **ascetic.**

yoke, *v.* —*Syn.* couple, link, connect, join, conjoin, harness, splice, unite, associate, bind, attach, fix, strap, buckle, bracket, hitch, lay together, tack together, secure, mate; see also **fasten** 1.—*Ant.* separate*, divorce, sever.

yolk, *n.* —*Syn.* yellow, egg-yellow, egg yolk, vitellum, yelk; see also **center** 1, **egg.**

yokel, *n.* —*Syn.* rustic, bumpkin, hayseed (D); see **boor.**

yonder, *mod.* —*Syn.* farther, away, faraway; see **distant** 1, **remote** 1.

you, *pron.* —*Syn.* yourself, you yourself, thee, thou, all of you, you too, you alone, you all (D).

young, *mod.* **1.** [In the early portion of life]—*Syn.* puerile, boyish, girlish, adolescent, juvenile, budding, juvenescent, in one's teens, childlike, youthful, pubescent, boylike, girllike, new-fledged, blooming, burgeoning, childish, half-grown, growing, blossoming, at the breast, (babe) in arms, knee high to a grasshopper (D).—*Ant.* old*, aged, senile.
2. [Inexperienced]—*Syn.* callow, green, immature, tender, raw, untutored, unlearned, junior, subordinate, inferior, unfledged, ignorant, undisciplined; *both* (D): tenderfoot, not dry behind the ears; see also **incompetence, inexperienced, naive.**—*Ant.* veteran*, expert, experienced.
3. [New]—*Syn.* fresh, modern, recent, newborn; see also **fashionable.**

youngster, *n.* —*Syn.* child, boy, girl, pupil; see **youth** 1.

you're welcome, *interj.* —*Syn.* my pleasure, forget it, think nothing of it, don't mention it, it's nothing, no problem, *de nada* (Spanish), *machts nichts* (German), *il n'y a pas de quoi* (French).

youth, *n.* **1.** [The state or quality of being young] —*Syn.* boyhood, adolescence, girlhood, childhood, early manhood *or* womanhood *or* adulthood, puberty, tender age, juvenescence, minority, youthfulness, teen age, virginity, bloom; *all* (D): teens, age of ignorance, age of indiscretion, awkward age, salad days, betweenities.—*Ant.* maturity*, old age, senility.
2. [Young people]—*Syn.* the younger generation, the rising generation, the next generation, juvenility, children, the young, college youth, working youth.
3. [A young person]—*Syn.* boy, junior, teenager, lad, youngster, stripling, minor, young man, miss, girl, maiden, fledgling, juvenile, urchin, adolescent, student; *all* (D): kid, teen, pre-teen, gosling, pup, calf; see also **child.**—*Ant.* oldster*, graybeard, dotard.

youthful, *mod.* **1.** [Possessing youth]—*Syn.* young, childlike, adolescent; see **active** 2, **juvenile** 1.
2. [Suited to youth]—*Syn.* keen, enthusiastic, zestful, vigorous, active, buoyant, lighthearted, prankish, fresh, lithe, full-blooded, full of life, full of animal spirits, limber, athletic, lightfooted, bubbling over, full of the devil (D); see also **modern** 1. —*Ant.* slow*, cautious, serious.

yowl, *n.* —*Syn.* howl, yelp, wail; see **cry** 1, **yell** 1.

yule, *n.* —*Syn.* Nativity, Christmas season, Christmastide; see **Christmas.**

Z

zany, *mod.* —*Syn.* dumb, humorous, wacky (D); see **funny** 1, **witty.**
zany, *n.* —*Syn.* comedian, simpleton, buffoon; see **clown, fool** 2.
zeal, *n.* **1.** [Enthusiasm]—*Syn.* ardor, eagerness, fervor; see **enthusiasm** 1.
2. [Industry]—*Syn.* earnestness, hustle, hustling, bustle, bustling, intensity, industry, willingness, inclination, application, determination, promptitude, dispatch, diligence, perseverance, assiduity, intentness, readiness, aptitude, enterprise, initiative; *all* (D): push, hop, what-it-takes, stick-to-itiveness; see also **attention** 2, **care** 1, **co-operation** 1.—*Ant.* idleness*, slackness, indolence.
zealot, *n.* —*Syn.* partisan, fan, bigot, fanatic, lobbyist, devotee, dogmatist, opinionist, missionary, fighter, cultist, follower, disciple, propagandist; *all* (D): plugger, bitterender, Moonie, crank, addict, bug, faddist, fiend.
zealous, *mod.* —*Syn.* fervent, devoted, ardent; see **enthusiastic** 2, 3.
zealously, *mod.* —*Syn.* with zeal, assiduously, fiercely; see **industriously, vigorously.**
zenith, *n.* —*Syn.* top, pinnacle, summit, apogee, culmination, maximum height, highest point, climax, eminence, apex, altitude, elevation, acme, tip, crest, cap, roof, peak, crown, culminating point, tiptop (D).—*Ant.* bottom*, foundation, base.
zephyr, *n.* —*Syn.* west wind, breeze, draft; see **wind** 1.
zeppelin, *n.* —*Syn.* airship, dirigible, blimp; see **balloon.**
zero, *n.* **1.** [A cipher]—*Syn.* naught, nothing, nadir, love, below freezing, the lowest point; *all* (D): goose egg, zip, zilch, duck egg, nix.
2. [Nothing]—*Syn.* nullity, oblivion, void; see **blank** 1.
zero hour (D), *n.* —*Syn.* appointed hour, target day, H-hour, now D-day; *all* (D): the time, countdown, jump-off; see also **attack** 1, **crisis.**
zest, *n.* **1.** [Relish]—*Syn.* gusto, enjoyment, pleasure, delight, good appetite, enthusiasm, cheer, delectation, satisfaction; see also **happiness** 1. —*Ant.* objection*, distaste, disgust.
2. [Savor]—*Syn.* taste, tang, piquancy, spice, bite, nip, pungency; *all* (D): punch, snap, ginger, kick, guts, body; see also **flavor** 1, **savor.**
zigzag, *mod.* —*Syn.* oblique, inclined, sloping, awry, crooked, *thrawn* (Scots), sinuous, twisted, askew, transverse, diagonal, curved, loxic, bent, crinkled, serrated, falcated, furcal, furcated, jagged, straggling, meandering, devious, erratic, rambling, oscillating, fluctuating, waggling, undulatory, vibratory, indirect, spiral, tortuous; see also **angular** 1, **irregular** 4.—*Ant.* straight*, parallel, undeviating.
zip (D), *n.* —*Syn.* energy, vigor, vim; see **strength** 1, **vim.**
zip (D), *v.* —*Syn.* run, dash, rush; see **run** 2.
zodiac, *n.* —*Syn.* celestial meridian, sign(s) of the zodiac, sky sign(s), group(s) of stars *or* planets, constellation(s); see also **constellation, planet, star** 1.
The twelve signs of the zodiac are as follows—Aquarius *or* Water Bearer, Pisces *or* Fish, Aries *or* Ram, Taurus *or* Bull, Gemini *or* Twins, Cancer *or* Crab, Leo *or* Lion, Virgo *or* Virgin, Libra *or* Scales, Scorpio *or* Scorpion, Sagittarius *or* Archer, Capricorn *or* Goat.
zone, *n.* **1.** [A band]—*Syn.* circuit, meridian, latitude; see **band** 1, **stripe.**
2. [An area]—*Syn.* region, district, territory; see **place** 3, **position** 1.
Specific zones include the following—Torrid, Frigid, Temperate, Variable, Canal, traffic, parking, danger, building, quiet, school; Tropic of Cancer, Tropic of Capricorn, Arctic Circle, Antarctic Circle.
zoned, *mod.* —*Syn.* subject to zoning ordinances, planned (for), platted; see **restricted, urban** 2.
zoning, *n.* —*Syn.* city *or* urban *or* municipal, etc., planning, controlled development; see **administration, plan** 2.
zoo, *n.* —*Syn.* menagerie, terrarium, aquarium, aviary, vivarium, zoological garden.
zoological, *mod.* —*Syn.* zoologic, mammalogical, ornithological, herpetological, ichthyological, ascidiological, echinological, conchological, entomological, arachnological, crustaceological, zoophytological, spongiological, protozoological, helminthiological; see also **alive** 1, **biological.**
zoology, *n.* —*Syn.* life science, science of organisms, biological science, natural history; see also **biology, life** 1, **natural science.**
Divisions of zoology include the following—histology, embryology, physiology, evolution, human anatomy, comparative anatomy, entomology, bacteriology, ornithology, ontogeny, genetics, cytology, ethnology, taxonomy, taxonomic zoology, systematic zoology, zoochemistry, biochemistry, ecology, paleontology, paleozoology, zootechnics, bionomics, thremmatology, embyology, helminthology, ascidiology, cetology, conchology, zoophytology, ichthyology, herpetology, mammology, mastology, therology, zoogeography, zoogamy, zoodynamics, zoopathology, zoopery, zoography.
zoom, *v.* —*Syn.* speed, rush, streak, zip, hum, soar like an airplane, climb like a homesick angel (D); see also **climb** 1, **hurry** 1, **rise** 1.

SYNONYMIES

The following paragraphs, selected and adapted from ***Webster's New World Dictionary,*** *Second College Edition, list and discriminate groups of closely related terms. Although synonyms have similar meanings, they are not always interchangeable with one another in every context. The subtle differences that distinguish such synonyms are briefly stated here, and typical examples of usage are given where they may be helpful.*

able implies power or ability to do something [*able* to make payments] but sometimes suggests special power or skill [an *able* speaker]; **capable** usually implies that only ordinary requirements are met [a *capable* machinist]; **competent** and **qualified** both imply that the necessary qualifications for something are met, but **qualified** emphasizes that certain specified requirements are complied with [a *competent* critic of modern art; a *qualified* voter]

abridgment describes a work that is shortened from a larger work, but that keeps the main contents more or less unchanged; an **abstract** is a short statement of the main contents as of a court record or a technical writing; a **summary** usually restates the main points of the matter that has gone before; a **synopsis** is a condensed, orderly treatment, as of the plot of a novel; a **digest** is a concise, systematic treatment, generally broader in scope than a synopsis

absurd means so inconsistent with what is judged as reasonable or true as to be laughable [an *absurd* hypothesis]; **ludicrous** is applied to what is so incongruous or exaggerated as to be laughable [a *ludicrous* facial expression]; **preposterous** is used to describe anything extremely absurd or ludicrous; **foolish** describes that which shows lack of good judgment or of common sense [I don't take *foolish* chances]; **ridiculous** applies to whatever causes amusement or contempt because of its extreme foolishness

adjacent things may or may not be in actual contact with each other, but they are not separated by things of the same kind [*adjacent* angles; *adjacent* buildings]; that which is **adjoining** something else touches it at some point or along some line [*adjoining* rooms]; things are **contiguous** when they touch along the whole or most of one side [*contiguous* lots]; **tangent** implies contact at a single point on a curved line or surface [a line *tangent* to a circle]

agile and **nimble** both imply quickness and lightness of movement, but **agile** stresses general skill and ease in the use of the limbs, while **nimble** suggests quick sureness in carrying out a particular act [*nimble* fingers at the keyboard]; **quick** implies speed or promptness with no indication of the degree of skill; **spry** suggests nimbleness, esp. as displayed by a vigorous, elderly person; **sprightly** suggests liveliness, gaiety, etc.

agree is the general term used to express a fitting or going together without conflict; **conform** emphasizes agreement in form or basic character [specifications must *conform* to the building code]; **accord** emphasizes fitness for each other of the things being considered together [his story does not *accord* with the facts]; **harmonize** implies a combining of different things in an orderly or pleasing arrangement [*harmonizing* colors]; **correspond** is applied to that which matches, complements, or is comparable to something else [their Foreign Office *corresponds* to our State Department]; **coincide** stresses that the things being considered are identical [their interests *coincide*]

amiable and **affable** both suggest friendliness and an easygoing temperament that make one likable, **affable** also implying a readiness to talk and be sociable; a **good-natured** person is one who tends to like others as well as to be liked by them, and is sometimes easily imposed on; **obliging** implies a ready, often cheerful, desire to be helpful [the *obliging* clerk answered my questions]; **genial** suggests cheerful sociability [our *genial* host]; **cordial** suggests sincerity and warmth [a *cordial* welcome]

appreciate implies enough understanding and judgment to see the value or to enjoy [he *appreciates* good music]; to **value** is to rate highly because of worth [I *value* your friendship]; to **prize** is to think highly of or take great satisfaction in [he *prizes* his art collection]; to **treasure** is to regard as precious and implies special care and protection; to **esteem** is to hold in high regard or respect [an *esteemed* statesman]; to **cherish** is to prize or treasure, but connotes greater affection for the thing cherished [he *cherished* his family]

argument refers to a discussion in which there is disagreement and suggests the use of reasoning and the bringing forth of facts to support or disprove a point; **dispute** basically refers to a disagreement involving debate in which there is strong feeling or anger [an international boundary *dispute*]; **controversy** suggests a disagreement that lasts a long time and has to do with a matter of some importance [the continuing *controversy* over some of Freud's theories]

avenge and **revenge** both refer to the inflicting of punishment for a wrong done, but **avenge** suggests that the motive is a wish to see justice done, whereas **revenge** implies that one wishes to get even, usually for an injury against oneself, and suggests bitter feelings of hatred and resentment

banish means to force to leave a country (not necessarily one's own) as a punishment; **exile** implies being forced to leave one's own country, either because the government has ordered it or events have made it necessary; **expatriate** suggests more strongly exile by one's own choice and often implies the getting of citizenship in another country; to **deport** is to send (an alien) out of the country, either because he entered unlawfully or because he is considered undesirable

base implies a putting of one's own interests ahead of all else, as because of greed or cowardice [*base* motives]; **mean** suggests a pettiness of character or conduct [his *mean* attempts to slander her]; **ignoble** suggests a lack of high moral qualities [to work for an *ignoble* end]; **abject** implies lowness of character and a lack of self-respect [an *abject* coward]; **sordid** suggests a depressing drabness of something mean or base [a *sordid* scheme to cheat others]; **vile** suggests disgusting foulness or wickedness [*vile* language]; **low** suggests coarseness and corruption, esp. in reference to taking unfair advantage [so *low* as to rob the poor]

beautiful is applied to that which gives the most pleasure and suggests that the thing that delights one comes close to one's ideal; **lovely** refers to that which delights by causing one to feel affection or warm admiration; **handsome** is used of that which attracts by its pleasing proportions, elegance, etc. and suggests a masculine quality; **pretty** implies daintiness or gracefulness and suggests a feminine quality; **comely** applies to persons only and suggests a wholesome attractiveness rather than great beauty; **fair** suggests beauty, esp. of complexion or features, that is fresh, bright, or perfect; **good-looking** generally equals either **handsome** or **pretty; beauteous,** a poetical synonym for **beautiful,** is now often used in a joking or belittling way

belief is the general term for the acceptance of something as true, even without being completely certain; **faith** implies complete acceptance, even without proof and, esp., of something not supported by reason; **trust** implies assurance, often based on intuition, that someone or something is reliable; **confidence** also suggests such assurance, esp. when based on reason or proof

belligerent implies a taking part in war or fighting or in warlike actions [*belligerent* nations]; **bellicose** implies a warlike nature, suggesting a readiness to fight [a *bellicose* mood]; **pugnacious** and **quarrelsome** both suggest eagerness to start a fight, but **quarrelsome** more often suggests willingness to fight for no good reason; **contentious** suggests a readiness to keep on arguing or quarreling in an annoying way

bodily refers to the human body as apart from the mind or spirit [*bodily* organs]; **physical** is often used like **bodily,** but may suggest less directly the organs or parts, etc. of the body [*physical* labor]; **corporeal** refers to the matter that makes up the body and is opposed to *spiritual* [his *corporeal* remains]; **corporal** refers to the effect of something upon the body [*corporal* punishment]; **somatic** is the word used, as in a scientific description, to refer to the body as distinct from the mind [the *somatic* differences between individuals]

bright implies in a general way the giving forth or reflecting of light, or a being filled with light [a *bright* day, star, shield, etc.]; **radiant** emphasizes the sending out of rays of light; **shining** implies a steady, continuous brightness [the *shining* sun]; **brilliant** implies strong or flashing brightness [*brilliant* sunlight, diamonds, etc.]; **luminous** is used of objects that are full of light or give off phosphorescent light; **lustrous** is used of objects whose surfaces gleam by reflected light and suggests glossiness [*lustrous* silk]

bulk, mass, and **volume** all refer to a quantity of matter or number of units making up a whole; **bulk** implies a body of great size, weight, or numbers [the lumbering *bulk* of an elephant; the *bulk* of humanity]; **mass** suggests a group or number of parts forming a single, unified body [an egg-shaped *mass;* the *mass* of workers]; **volume** implies a moving or flowing mass, often one that keeps changing [*volumes* of smoke; the *volume* of production]

calm, basically applied to the weather, suggests a lack of movement or excitement [a *calm* sea; a *calm* reply]; **tranquil** implies a deeper or more permanent peace and quiet than calm [a *tranquil* old age]; **serene** suggests a dignified tranquillity, as of a person who is at peace with himself; **placid** implies total calmness, often to the point of being dull and uninteresting [she's as *placid* as a cow]; **peaceful** suggests freedom from disorder or from a show of strong feeling [a *peaceful* gathering]

caricature refers to an imitation or drawing of a person, as in a cartoon, that exaggerates outstanding features in a comical way; **burlesque** implies the handling of a serious subject in a light and flippant way or of a trivial subject in a way that pretends to be serious; a **parody** imitates the style of a writer or of some writing very closely, but makes fun of it by using an absurd subject or a nonsensical approach; a **travesty,** on the other hand, deals with the same subject as the original but in a ridiculous style or laughable language; **satire** refers to writing in which evil, stupid, or wicked persons or institutions are ridiculed or dealt with sarcastically

cause refers to something that produces an effect or result [carelessness is often a *cause* of accidents]; **reason** implies thinking that is engaged in to explain some act or idea [she had a *reason* for laughing]; a **motive** is a thought, emotion, or desire that leads to action [the *motive* for the crime]; an **antecedent** is an event or thing that comes before, and is responsible for, a later event or thing [war always has its *antecedents*]; an **occasion** is a situation or event that allows a cause to have an effect [the court case was an *occasion* for stating a new legal principle]

cheat implies the use of dishonesty in dealing with someone, in order to get something he has; **defraud** stresses the use of deliberate deception in taking away a person's rights, property, etc. in a way that is against the law; **swindle** stresses the winning of a person's trust in order to cheat or defraud him of money, etc.; **trick** implies the use of a clever scheme or device to mislead someone, but does not necessarily suggest dishonesty; **dupe** suggests the tricking of someone who is foolish and too willing to trust others; **hoax** implies the use of a complicated scheme to dupe others, often simply in fun

childlike and **childish** are both applied to persons of any age in referring to qualities considered typical of a child, **childlike** suggesting the favorable qualities such as innocence, honesty, curiosity, zest, etc., and **childish** the unfavorable ones such as immaturity, foolishness, lack of self-control, self-centeredness, etc.

clever implies a quickness of mind or wit, as in solving a problem, in conversation, etc. [a *clever* idea; a *clever* reply]; **cunning** implies cleverness of a sly, tricky, or crafty kind [*cunning* as a fox]; **ingenious** suggests cleverness in thinking up or inventing something [an *ingenious* explanation; an *ingenious* designer]; **shrewd** suggests cleverness or sharpness in dealing with practical matters [a *shrewd* analysis; a *shrewd* bargainer]

comfort suggests any attempt to make someone less sorrowful or unhappy as by trying to cheer him up or inspire him with hope; **console** suggests the offering of help or relief to someone who has lost someone or something or has been disappointed [to *console* someone whose best friend has died]; **solace** suggests any thing or any action that makes a person less sad, depressed, bored, lonely, etc. [he *solaced* himself by playing the guitar]; **relief** suggests the easing, often just for a time, of misery or discomfort so that one can bear it more easily [to *relieve* the poor on welfare]; **soothe** implies trying to calm or lessen pain or distress [she *soothed* the child with a lullaby]

compare implies a noting of likenesses and differences and an examining of features side by side to see how they are alike or different [to *compare* Shaw with Chekov]; **contrast** implies a comparing for the express purpose of showing differences [to *contrast* city life with living in the country]

concise stresses briefness in speaking or writing so that no more words are used than are needed to express something clearly [a *concise* statement]; **terse** suggests extremely clipped and abrupt expression, as when one must be brief and to the point [the captain's *terse* command]; **laconic** implies a very brief, sometimes vague statement, as by someone who habitually says very little [the cowboy's *laconic* reply]; **succinct** indicates very brief, clear, and compact expression in which only what is essential is dealt with [a *succinct* record of the proceedings]; **pithy** suggests that what is stated in highly compressed form is important and full of meaning [a *pithy* proverb]

consent implies giving in to something proposed or requested when one has the power to do so or not [to *consent* to serve as chairman]; to **assent** is to express one's acceptance or approval of something [he *assented* to the plan favored by the others]; **agree** implies accord reached by settling differences of opinion or overcoming resistance [to *agree* on a fair price for the property]; **concur** implies agreement arrived at formally on a specific matter, often with regard to a line of action [all the doctors *concurred* in the decision to operate]; to **accede** is to yield one's assent to a proposal [he *acceded* to the union's request for arbitration]; **acquiesce** implies a giving in quietly when one may have some doubts

continual applies to that which happens again and again or goes on without stopping over a long period of time [*continual* arguments]; **continuous** applies to that which goes on without a break in either space or time [a *continuous* area of land]; **constant** stresses being steady or regular in happening or happening again and again [the *constant* beat of the heart]; **incessant** implies activity that goes on without being stopped or interrupted [*incessant* chatter]; **perpetual** applies to that which lasts or remains for an indefinitely long period of time [a *perpetual* nuisance]; **eternal** stresses an endless or timeless quality [the *eternal* truths]

copy is the broadest of the terms here referring to anything that is made to be like the original or patterned after it [a carbon *copy;* a *copy* of a designer's dress]; **reproduction** implies a close imitation of the original, often, however, with differences, as of material, size, or quality [a *reproduction* of a painting]; a **facsimile** is an exact reproduction, sometimes one differing in scale [a photostated *facsimile* of a document]; a **duplicate** is a double, or counterpart, of something, serving all the purposes of the original [all the books of a single printing are *duplicates*]; a **replica** is an exact reproduction of a work of art

criticize, in this comparison, is the general term for finding fault with or disapproving of a person or thing; **reprehend** suggests severe disapproval, usually of faults, errors, etc. rather than of people; **blame** stresses the fixing of responsibility for an error, fault, etc. [don't *blame* your laziness on the heat]; **censure** implies the expression of severe criticism or disapproval, as by a person in authority; **condemn** suggests the passing of harsh, final judgment on a person or thing considered guilty or to blame; **denounce** implies a speaking out publicly against persons or actions thought to be immoral, corrupt, evil, etc.

danger is the general word for any kind of exposure to injury, loss, etc. [the *danger* of falling on icy walks]; **peril** suggests great danger that is near at hand [flood waters put the town in *peril*]; **jeopardy** emphasizes exposure to extreme danger [reckless driving puts one's life in *jeopardy*]; **hazard** implies danger of which one may be aware but over which one has little control [the *hazards* of combat duty]; **risk** implies willingness to take a dangerous chance [he saved the day at the *risk* of his life]

deceive implies a deliberate telling of lies or acting dishonestly, usually by one who expects to gain something for himself [he was *deceived* by the salesman into paying too much for the car]; to **mislead** is to cause to follow the wrong course or do the wrong thing, although not always on purpose [*misled* by the sign into going to the wrong floor]; **beguile** implies the use of charm, tempting promises, etc. in deceiving or misleading [she *beguiled* him into believing her lies]; to **delude** is to fool someone so completely that he accepts as true or real something that is false; **betray** implies a breaking of faith while seeming to be loyal, true, or friendly

delusion implies belief in something that is contrary to fact or reality, resulting from trickery, a misunderstanding, or a mental disorder [to have *delusions* of grandeur]; **illusion** suggests or gives an appearance of something real as by copying it or making something that looks like it [movies give us the *illusion* of seeing and hearing real people]; **hallucination** gives one the impression of experiencing as though it were real something that is not actually there, as when one is drugged or has a mental disorder

dexterous implies an ability to do things with skill and precision [a *dexterous* weaver]; **adroit** adds to this the idea of cleverness, now esp. in dealing with people, ideas, etc. [they admired her *adroit* handling of an awkward situation]; **deft** suggests a nimbleness and sureness of touch [a seamstress *deft* with the needle]; **handy** suggests skill, usually without training, at a large variety of tasks [he is very *handy* around the house]

discern implies a making out of something or recognizing it clearly with the eyes or in the mind [to *discern* one's motives]; **perceive** implies a recognizing by means of any of the senses, and often, in addition, implies keen understanding or insight [to *perceive* differences in pitch; to *perceive* a change in attitude]; **distinguish** implies a perceiving clearly by sight, hearing, etc. [he *distinguished* the voices of men and women down the hall]; **observe** and **notice** both connote paying attention to some degree, and usually suggest use of the sense of sight [to *observe* an eclipse; to *notice* a sign]

disparage means to cast doubt on the worth or reputation of someone or something, often in subtle ways, as by praising with little enthusiasm or making an unfair comparison [to *disparage* a modern dramatist by comparing him with Shakespeare]; to **depreciate** is to suggest that something has less value than it is generally supposed to have; to **belittle** is to indicate, often spitefully or scornfully, one's low opinion of something's or someone's worth [always *belittling* his fellow scientist's achievements]; to **minimize** is to make seem as small as possible [a biased biographer who *minimized* his subject's faults]

distinguish implies a recognizing or setting apart from others by means of special features or characteristic qualities [to *distinguish* the Asian elephant from the African elephant]; **discriminate** suggests a distinguishing of minute or subtle differences between similar things [to *discriminate* between synonyms]; **differentiate** suggests noticing or pointing out specific differences between things by comparing them in detail [his duties as a son as *differentiated* from those as a brother]

dwarf refers to an individual that is much smaller than the usual kind and sometimes implies that the parts are deformed or not in normal proportion; **midget** refers to a very small human being who has normal form and proportions; **Pygmy,** in strict use, refers to a member of any of several small-sized African or Asian peoples, but it is sometimes used (written **pygmy**) as a synonym for **dwarf** or **midget**

ecstasy implies very strong feeling, now usually intense delight, that overpowers one's senses and lifts one into a kind of trance; **bliss** implies a state of happiness and contentment so great as to suggest the joys of heaven; **rapture** now generally suggests the intense feeling one has when something causing great joy or pleasure captures all of one's attention; **transport** implies a being carried away by any powerful feeling

eject implies generally a throwing or casting out from within [to *eject* saliva from the mouth]; **expel** suggests a driving out, as by force, specif., a forcing out of a country, organization, etc., often in disgrace [*expelled* from school]; **evict** refers to a forcing out by the use of legal means [to *evict* a tenant]; **oust** implies the getting rid of something that is not wanted, as by the use of force or the action of the law [to *oust* corrupt officials]

enormous implies a going far beyond what is normal in size, amount, or degree [an *enormous* room; *enormous* expenses]; **immense** implies size beyond the usual measurements but suggests that great size is normal for the thing described [redwoods are *immense* trees]; **huge** usually suggests a great mass or bulk [a *huge* building; *huge* profits]; **gigantic, colossal,** and **mammoth** originally implied a likeness to a *giant,* the *Colossus* of Rhodes, and an extinct elephant (the *mammoth*), and therefore these words emphasize the idea of great size, force, importance, etc., now often in an exaggerated way; **tremendous** literally suggests that which causes awe or amazement because of its great size

epicure refers to a person whose taste in food and drink is highly refined and who takes great pleasure in eating and drinking good things; a **gourmet** is one who is very fond of fine things to eat and drink, has expert knowledge about their selection and preparation, and takes pride in his ability to appreciate subtle differences in flavor and quality; **gourmand,** occasionally used to mean the same thing as **gourmet,** is more often applied to a person who has such a hearty appetite for good food that he tends to overeat

essential is applied to that which is the basic essence or fundamental nature of a thing and therefore must be present for the thing to exist, function, etc. [food is *essential* to life]; an **indispensable** person or thing cannot be done without if the specified purpose is to be achieved; **requisite** is applied to that which is required by the circumstances or for the purpose and often suggests a requirement that is demanded or insisted upon [the *requisite* skills for the job]; **necessary** implies an urgent or pressing need but not always for something that is indispensable

excessive applies to that which goes beyond what is needed, right, or usual [*excessive* demands]; **exorbitant** is applied esp. to charges, prices, etc. that are unreasonably or unfairly high [*exorbitant* profits]; **extravagant** and **immoderate** both imply excessiveness resulting from a lack of control or careful judgment [*extravagant* praise; *immoderate* smoking]; **inordinate** implies a going beyond the orderly limits of convention or good taste [his *inordinate* pride]

explain implies a making clear of something that is not known or understood [to *explain* how a machine operates]; **expound** implies an orderly and thorough explanation, often one made by a person having expert knowledge [to *expound* a theory]; **explicate** implies a scholarly analysis or explanation that is developed in detail [the *explication* of a Biblical passage]; **elucidate** implies a shedding light upon by clear and specific explanation, illustration, etc. [to *elucidate* the country's foreign policy]; to **interpret** is to bring out meanings not immediately clear, as by translation, personal insight, or special knowledge [how do you *interpret* his silence?]; **construe** suggests a particular interpretation of something that can be understood in several ways [his statement is not to be lightly *construed*]

extract implies a drawing out of something, as if by pulling [to *extract* testimony from an unwilling witness]; **educe** suggests a bringing out or evolving of something that is undeveloped [to *educe* a theory from the known facts]; **elicit** suggests difficulty or skill in drawing forth something [his jokes *elicited* laughter from the angry crowd]; **evoke** implies a calling forth, as of a mental image, by stimulating the mind or emotions [the odor *evoked* a memory of childhood]

fantastic implies a completely free use of the imagination, and suggests that which is unreal or dreamlike in a striking way [*fantastic* stage sets]; **bizarre** suggests that which is extremely strange or unusual because it is startling or unexpected [a *bizarre* combination of costumes]; **grotesque** suggests something that appears comic or frightening because it is a distortion of the real or natural [pain twisted his face into a *grotesque* mask]

fatal implies that death or disaster has occurred or will surely occur [a *fatal* disease; a *fatal* mistake]; **deadly** is applied to a thing that can and probably will cause death [a *deadly* poison]; **mortal** is applied to that which has just caused or will soon cause death [a *mortal* wound]; **lethal** is applied to that which is intended or designed to cause death [a *lethal* weapon]

flagrant applies to anything that is so clearly bad or wrong that it deserves to be criticized or condemned [a *flagrant* violation of the law]; **glaring** is used of something bad that stands out even more clearly so that it is noticed immediately [a *glaring* error in arithmetic]; **gross** implies badness or wrongness which is so extreme or disgusting that it cannot be excused or forgiven [*gross* neglect of a child]

flash implies a sudden, brief, brilliant light; **gleam** suggests a steady, narrow ray of light shining through darkness; **sparkle** implies a number of brief, bright flashes from many points of light; **glitter** implies the reflection of such bright flashes, as from metal or a jewel; **glisten** suggests the reflection of a bright light, as from a wet surface; **shimmer** refers to a soft, wavering reflection of light, as from the surface of gently moving water

frank applies to a person, remark, etc. that is free or blunt in expressing the truth or an opinion and is not held back by the usual restraints [a *frank* criticism]; **candid** implies a basic honesty that makes it impossible for one to deceive or be sly, sometimes to the point where the listener could be embarrassed [a *candid* opinion]; **open** implies a lack of secrecy and often suggests a genuine and innocent quality [her *open* admiration for him]; **outspoken** suggests a lack of restraint in offering opinions, esp. when it might be better to keep quiet

funny is the simple, general term for anything that appeals to one's sense of humor or causes laughter; **laughable** is a usually scornful term for that which is fit to be laughed at [what a *laughable* excuse!]; something that is **amusing** brings laughter or smiles by its pleasant, entertaining quality; that which is **droll** amuses one because it is quaint or strange or because of its twisted humor; **comic** is applied to that which is like a comedy in amusing one in a thoughtful way; **comical** is used of that which brings on uncontrolled laughter; **farcical** suggests a comical quality that is based on nonsense, broad humor, etc.

gaudy applies to that which is brightly colored and highly decorated but which is regarded as being in bad taste [*gaudy* furniture]; **tawdry** is used of something cheap and poorly made that is also gaudy [a *tawdry* wall hanging]; **garish** implies a glaring brightness of color and too much decoration [*garish* wallpaper]; **flashy** and **showy** imply a brightness or display that attracts attention, but **flashy** implies that it is offensive to those with more conservative tastes [a *flashy* sport coat], while **showy** does not always imply this [*showy* blossoms]

ghastly suggests the horror caused by the sight or suggestion of death [a *ghastly* smile on the dead man's face]; **grim** implies extremely disagreeable or even terrifying aspects [the *grim* life of the very poor]; **grisly** suggests an appearance or nature that causes one to be horrified [the *grisly* sights of the concentration camp]; **gruesome** suggests the fear and disgust caused by something horrible and evil [the *gruesome* details of a murder]; **macabre** implies a being concerned or fascinated with the gruesome aspects of death [a *macabre* tale]

greedy implies a desire to get or have much or more of something than is one's share or than one needs; **avaricious** stresses greed for money or riches and often suggests a being miserly; **grasping** suggests a strong eagerness for gain that shows itself in a seizing of every opportunity to get what one wants; **acquisitive** stresses the drive to keep gathering more and more wealth or possessions; **covetous** implies a strong desire for something that belongs to another person

group is the basic, general word expressing the simple idea of an assembly of persons, animals, or things without any added meaning; **herd** is applied to a group of cattle, sheep, or similar large animals feeding, living, or moving together; **flock,** to goats, sheep, or birds; **drove,** to cattle, hogs, or sheep; **pack,** to hounds or wolves; **pride,** to lions; **swarm,** to insects; **school,** to fish, porpoises, whales, etc.; **bevy,** to quails; **covey,** to partridges or quails; **flight,** to birds flying together. In extended use, **flock** connotes guidance and care, **herd, drove,** and **pack** are used as terms of contempt for people, **swarm** suggests a large mass or throng moving together, and **bevy** and **covey** are used of girls or women

happy generally suggests a feeling of great pleasure, contentment, etc. [a *happy* marriage]; **glad** more strongly implies a feeling of joy [your letter made her so *glad!*], but both **glad** and **happy** are commonly used in merely polite phrases expressing pleasure [I'm *glad,* or *happy,* to have met you]; **cheerful** implies a steady display of bright spirits, optimism, etc. [she is always *cheerful* in the morning]; **joyful** and **joyous** both imply very high spirits and rejoicing, the former generally because of a particular event [the good news made them *joyful*], and the latter usually because of a continuing situation [they were a *joyous* family]

hate implies a feeling of great dislike or a strong wish to avoid, and, with persons as the object, suggests a wish to harm them; **detest** implies extreme dislike; **despise** suggests a looking down with great contempt upon the person or thing one hates; **loathe** implies intense dislike together with extreme disgust; **abhor** implies great dislike or disgust joined with feelings of moral disapproval

hesitate implies a temporary stopping because of feeling uncertain, unwilling, or confused [he *hesitated* before entering]; **vacillate** implies a shifting back and forth in a decision, opinion, etc. [she *vacillates* in her affection]; **waver** is often applied to a holding back or hesitating after a decision has been made [do not *waver* in your determination]; **falter** suggests a pausing or slowing down, as in fear or indecision [they never *faltered* in the counterattack]

high and **tall** both refer to something which extends farther upward than is normal for its kind, and **high** also refers to something in a place far above a given level [a *high* mountain; *high* clouds], but **tall** is usually applied to people, animals, and other growing things [a *tall* woman; a *tall* tree]; **lofty** and **towering** suggest great, imposing, or very noticeable height [*lofty* peaks; a *towering* castle]

ignorant implies a lack of knowledge, either in general [an *ignorant* man] or on some particular matter [*ignorant* of the reason for their quarrel]; **illiterate** implies an inability to read or write; **unlettered** is sometimes used as a milder substitute for **illiterate,** but often implies unfamiliarity with fine literature [although a graduate engineer, he is relatively *unlettered*]; **uneducated** and **untutored** imply a lack of formal schooling [he had a brilliant, though *uneducated,* mind]

impertinent is used of speech or behavior that shows a lack of respect by not following the usual rules of politeness and good manners; **impudent** suggests bold, open, deliberate rudeness or impertinence; **insolent** implies extreme disrespect shown in speech or behavior that is deliberately insulting or filled with contempt; **saucy** suggests a light, flippant manner and improper informality in dealing with someone to whom respect should be shown

include implies a containing as part of a whole; **comprise,** in careful use, means to consist of and takes as its object the various parts that make up the whole [his library *comprises* 2,000 volumes and *includes* many first editions]; **comprehend** suggests that the object is contained within the total scope or range of the subject, sometimes by being implied [the word "beauty" *comprehends* various qualities]; **embrace** emphasizes the variety of objects comprehended [he had *embraced* a number of hobbies]; **involve** implies that an object is included because of its connection with the subject as a cause or result [acceptance of high office *involves* responsibilities]

infer suggests the arriving at a decision or opinion by reasoning from known facts or evidence [from your smile, I *infer* that you are pleased]; **deduce** stresses the use of logical and systematic reasoning in inferring something [the existence of the planet Neptune was *deduced* before its actual discovery]; **conclude** strictly implies an inference that is the final, logical result in a process of reasoning [I must, therefore, *conclude* that you are right]; **judge** stresses the careful checking and weighing of statements, arguments, etc. in reaching a conclusion; **gather** is an informal substitute for **infer** and **conclude** [I *gather* that you don't care]

instance refers to a person, thing, or event that is given as proof or support of something [the gift is an *instance* of his generosity]; **case** is applied to a happening or situation of a specified kind [a *case* of mistaken identity]; **example** is applied to something that is mentioned as typical of the members of its group [his novel is an *example* of science fiction]; **illustration** is used of an instance or example that helps to explain or make something clear [this sentence is an *illustration* of the use of a word]

intrude implies the forcing of oneself or something upon another without being asked or wanted or without having the right to do so [to *intrude* upon another's privacy]; **obtrude** suggests even more strongly that the intrusion causes an unwanted distraction or great unpleasantness [side issues keep *obtruding*]

irritate is the most general of the words here and may suggest mild impatience, continued annoyance, or a flare-up of anger [their smugness *irritates* her]; **provoke** suggests the causing of strong feelings of annoyance, resentment, or anger, often with a wish to get even [*provoked* by the insult]; **nettle** implies irritation caused as by petty, nagging remarks or actions that hurt one's pride [subtle taunts that *nettled* him]; **exasperate** implies great irritation caused by something that makes one lose one's patience or self-control [*exasperated* by the clerk's many careless mistakes]

join is the general term meaning a bringing or coming together of two or more things and may suggest direct contact, becoming a member of a group, etc.; **combine** implies a mingling together of things or a complete merging of distinct elements [to *combine* milk and water]; **unite** implies a joining or combining of things to form a single whole [the *United* States]; **connect** implies attachment by some fastening or relationship [roads *connected* by a bridge; the duties *connected* with a job]; **link** stresses firmness of a connection [*linked* together in a common cause]; **consolidate** implies a merger of distinct and separate units into a single whole for making something compact, strong, efficient, etc. [to *consolidate* one's debts]

laugh is the general word for the sounds made in expressing happiness, amusement, ridicule, etc.; **chuckle** implies the soft laughter in low tones that expresses mild amusement or inner satisfaction; **giggle** and **titter,** both often associated with children or girls, refer to a half-suppressed laugh consisting of a series of rapid, high-pitched sounds, suggesting embarrassment, silliness, etc.; **snicker** is used of a sly, half-suppressed laugh, as at another's embarrassment, confusion, etc.; **guffaw** refers to loud, hearty, coarse laughter

liberal implies tolerance of others' views as well as open-mindedness to ideas that challenge tradition, established institutions, etc.; **progressive** is the opposite of *reactionary* or *conservative* and is applied to persons who favor progress and reform in politics, education, etc. and are inclined to take direct action; **radical** is applied to those who favor fundamental or extreme change, specifically of the social structure; **left** is applied to those who are liberal or radical in their political views

liquid refers to a substance that flows readily and takes on the form of its container but stays the same in volume [water that is neither ice nor steam is a *liquid*]; **fluid** applies to any substance that flows [all liquids, gases, and viscous substances are *fluids*]

loiter implies either staying around a place without having anything to do there or moving along in a slow, rambling way [to *loiter* on street corners]; **dawdle** implies wasting time over trifles or taking more time to do something than is necessary [to *dawdle* over dinner]; **dally** suggests spending time in silly or pointless activity; **idle** suggests laziness or avoidance of work [to *idle* away the hours]

love implies intense fondness or deep devotion and may apply to various relationships or objects [sexual *love,* brotherly *love, love* of one's work, etc.]; **affection** suggests warm, tender feelings, usually not as powerful or as deep as those implied by **love** [he has no *affection* for children]; **attachment** implies connection by ties of affection, loyalty, devotion, etc. and may be felt for non-living things as well as for people [an *attachment* for an old hat]; **infatuation** implies a passion or affection that is foolish or shows poor judgment, often one that lasts only a short time [an elderly man's *infatuation* with a young girl]

lure suggests a strong force, as desire, greed, curiosity, etc., that attracts someone, often to something harmful or evil [*lured* into the plot by their false promises]; **entice** implies a clever or skillful luring [he *enticed* the squirrel to eat from his hand]; **decoy** implies the use of false appearances in luring into a trap [artificial birds are used to *decoy* wild ducks]; **beguile** suggests the use of subtle tricks in leading someone on [*beguiled* by her sweet words]; **tempt** suggests a powerful attraction that tends to overcome doubts or judgment [*tempted* by a chance for profit to invest his savings]

malice implies a deep hatred or dislike causing one to get pleasure from hurting others or seeing them suffer; **ill will** implies unfriendly feelings that lead one to wish harm, unhappiness, etc. to others; **malevolence,** a formal term for **ill will,** may also suggest that the unfriendly feelings are stronger and more evil; **spite** suggests a mean desire to get back at others by hurting or annoying them, esp. in nasty, petty ways; **rancor** implies bitter, long-lasting ill will; **malignity** suggests great malevolence that shows itself in acts of cruelty without pity

material is applied to anything that is formed of matter or substance [chairs are *material* objects]; **physical** applies either to material things known through the senses or to forces that can be measured scientifically [the *physical* world; the *physical* properties of sound]; **corporeal** applies only to material objects that have bodily form and can be touched [a house is *corporeal* property]

meaning is the general word for what is intended to be expressed or understood by something [the *meaning* of a sentence]; **sense** refers especially to any of the various meanings of a word or phrase [this word has several slang *senses*]; **import** refers to all of what is being implied by something said or done, including any subtle or hidden meanings [the full *import* of his remark came to me later]; **purport** refers to the general meaning, or main point, of something [what was the *purport* of her letter?]; **signification** is applied especially to the meaning that a certain sign, symbol, character, etc. commonly suggests to people [the *signification* of the ace of spades in fortunetelling]

memory refers to the ability or power of keeping in or bringing to mind past thoughts, images, ideas, etc. [to have a good *memory*]; **remembrance** applies to the act or process of having such events or things come to mind again [the *remembrance* of things in the past]; **recollection** implies a careful effort to remember the details of some event [his *recollection* of the campaign is not too clear]; **reminiscence** implies the thoughtful or nostalgic recollection of long-past events, usually pleasant ones, or the telling of these [he entertained us with *reminiscences* of his childhood]

mirth implies gaiety, gladness, or great amusement, esp. as expressed by laughter; **glee** implies a great, open display of joy, or it may suggest delight over another's suffering or unhappiness; **jollity** and **merriment** imply very great mirth or joy like that displayed at an especially lively and merry party or celebration; **hilarity** implies noisy and lively merriment and sometimes suggests an excessively loud display of high spirits

mix implies a combining of things so that the resulting substance is the same throughout, whether or not the separate elements can be distinguished [to *mix* paints]; **mingle** usually implies that the separate elements can be distinguished [*mingled* feelings of joy and sorrow]; **blend** implies a mixing of different varieties to produce a desired quality [a *blended* tea, whiskey, etc.] or the mingling of different elements to form a pleasing whole [a novel *blending* fact and fiction]

mood refers to a temporary state of mind and emphasizes a specified feeling [she's in a happy *mood*]; **humor** emphasizes an uncertain or unchanging quality in the mood [he wept and laughed as his *humor* moved him]; **temper** applies to a mood marked by a single, strong emotion, especially that of anger [my, he's in a nasty *temper*]

moral implies living according to accepted standards of goodness or rightness in conduct or character, especially in sexual conduct [a *moral* woman]; **ethical** implies following a carefully planned ideal code of moral principles, often the code of a particular profession [an *ethical* lawyer]; **virtuous** implies a morally excellent character concerned about justice, integrity, and, often, chastity; **righteous** implies taking a moral stand based on good or just reasons [*righteous* anger]

murmur implies a steady flow of words or sounds in a low, indistinct voice and may suggest either a contented or discontented feeling [to *murmur* a prayer]; **mutter** usually suggests angry or complaining words or sounds of this kind [to *mutter* curses]; to **mumble** is to utter words or sounds in low tones and with the mouth almost closed so that they are very hard to hear or understand [an old woman *mumbling* to herself]

naive implies a being simple and innocent in a trusting way, but sometimes suggests an almost foolish lack of worldly wisdom [his *naive* belief that all advertising is honest]; **ingenuous** suggests a childlike frankness or straightforwardness [her *ingenuous* delight in any kind of flattery]; **artless** implies the appealing open and natural quality of one who is indifferent to the effect he has on others [a simple, *artless* style of folk singing]; **unsophisticated** implies a lack of poise, worldliness, subtlety, etc. resulting from a limited experience of life [an *unsophisticated* farm boy]

need is the simple, direct word and **necessity** the more formal term referring to a lack of something that is wanted or must be had, or to the thing that is required [they are in *need* of food; food is a *necessity* for all living things]; **exigency** refers to a necessity brought about by some emergency or by specific events [the *exigencies* created by the flood]; **requisite** applies to something that cannot be done without in order to carry out some activity [a sense of rhythm is a *requisite* in a dancer]

new is applied to that which has never existed before or which has only just come into being, possession, use, etc. [a *new* coat, plan, etc.]; **fresh** is used of something so new that it still has its original appearance, quality, strength, etc. [*fresh* eggs, a *fresh* start]; **novel** implies a newness that is very strange or unusual [a *novel* idea, combination, etc.]; **modern** and **modernistic** refer to that which is associated with the present time rather than an earlier period and imply up-to-dateness, with **modernistic** sometimes being used to suggest contempt as well [*modern* dance, a *modernistic* painting]; **original** is used of that which not only is new but is also the first of its kind [an *original* plan, melody, etc.]

obscure applies to that which is unclear to the senses or to the mind either because it is concealed, veiled, or imprecisely stated or because of dullness or lack of insight in the perceiver [his motives remain *obscure*]; **vague** applies to that which is so lacking in precision or exactness that it is indistinct or unclear [a *vague* notion]; **enigmatic** and **cryptic** are used of that which baffles or bewilders, the latter word implying a deliberate intention to puzzle [his *enigmatic* behavior, a *cryptic* warning]; **ambiguous** applies to that which puzzles because it can be understood in more than one way ["The Lead Horse" is an *ambiguous* title]; **equivocal** is used of something ambiguous that is used to mislead or confuse [the politician's *equivocal* answer]

offend implies a causing displeasure or resentment in another, either on purpose or without meaning to, by hurting his feelings or by behaving in a way he considers improper [she will be *offended* if she is not invited]; **affront** implies an open and deliberate showing of disrespect or contempt [his uncalled-for criticism of their school *affronted* the graduates]; **insult** implies an affront so insolent or rude that it causes deep humiliation and resentment [to *insult* someone by calling him a liar]

ominous is used of something that seems to threaten but does not necessarily suggest that a disaster will result [his request was met by an *ominous* silence]; **portentous** is applied literally to a sign or warning, esp. of evil, but is now more often used of that which causes awe or amazement because of its wonderful or extraordinary character [the first landing on the moon was a *portentous* event]; **fateful** may imply control by or as if by fate, but is now usually applied to that which is of very important or crucial significance [a *fateful* truce conference]; **foreboding** implies a feeling that something evil or harmful will happen [a *foreboding* anxiety]

opinion is used of a conclusion or judgment which seems true or probable to one's own mind even though it may still be argued [it's my *opinion* that he'll agree]; **belief** refers to the acceptance by the mind of an idea, esp. a doctrine or dogma that others accept [religious *beliefs*]; a **view** is an opinion affected by the personal way one looks at things [she gave us her *views* on life]; a **conviction** is a strong belief about whose truth one has no doubts [I have a *conviction* of his innocence]; **sentiment** refers to an opinion that is the result of careful thought but that is influenced by emotion; **persuasion** refers to a strong belief that cannot be shaken because one wishes to believe in its truth

oppose implies attacking something that threatens or interferes with one; **resist** implies defending against something that is already actively opposed to one [one *opposes* a legislative action under consideration, one *resists* a law already passed by refusing to obey it]; **withstand** usually implies resistance that keeps the attack from being successful [can they *withstand* the heavy bombing?]

oral refers to that which is spoken, rather than written, to communicate something [an *oral* promise, request, etc.]; **verbal,** though sometimes used in the same way as **oral,** in careful discrimination refers to the use of words, either written or oral, rather than pictures, symbols, etc., to communicate an idea or feeling [a *verbal* image, portrait, etc.]

origin is applied to that from which a person or thing has its very beginning [the word "rodeo" has its *origin* in Spanish]; **source** is applied to the point or place from which something arises, comes, or develops [the sun is our *source* of energy]; **beginning** is the general term for a starting point or place [the *beginning* of a friendship]; **inception** is specifically applied to the beginning of an undertaking, organization, etc. [Smith headed the business from its *inception*]; **root** suggests an origin so deep and basic as to be the very first cause from which something stems [an error in arithmetic was the *root* of all our trouble]

pacify implies a making quiet and peaceful that which has become noisy or disorderly [to *pacify* a crying child]; **appease** suggests a pacifying by giving in to demands [to *appease* one's hunger]; **mollify** suggests a soothing of wounded feelings or calming of anger [his compliments failed to *mollify* her]; **placate** implies the changing of an unfriendly or angry attitude to a friendly or favorable one [to *placate* an offended colleague]; **propitiate** implies a calming or preventing of hostile feeling by winning the good will of a higher power [to *propitiate* a deity]; **conciliate** implies the use of arbitration, concession, persuasion, etc. in an attempt to win someone over

part is the general word for any of the components of a whole [a *part* of one's life]; **portion** often suggests a part given or assigned as a share [his *portion* of the inheritance]; a **piece** is either a part separated from the whole [a *piece* of pie] or a single unit from a collection of related things [only one *piece* missing from her set of china]; a **division** is a part formed by cutting, partitioning, classifying, etc. [the fine-arts *division* of a library]; **section** means much the same as **division** but usually suggests a smaller part [a *section* of a bookcase]; **segment** implies a part separated along natural lines of division [a *segment* of a tangerine]; a **fraction** is strictly a part contained by the whole a certain number of times without remainder, but generally it suggests a small, unimportant part [he received only a *fraction* of the benefits he was entitled to]; a **fragment** is a relatively small part separated as by breaking [a *fragment* of rock]

pay is the simple, direct word meaning to give money, etc. due for services provided, goods received, etc.; **compensate** implies a return, whether of money or something else, thought of as equal to the service given, the effort made, or the loss suffered [he could never be *compensated* for the loss of his son]; **remunerate** emphasizes the idea of payment for a service provided, but it often also implies a reward [a bumper crop *remunerated* the farmer for his labors]; to **reimburse** is to pay back what has been spent [the salesman was *reimbursed* for his traveling expenses]

perseverance implies a continuing to do something in spite of difficulties, obstacles, etc.; **persistence** may imply either steadfast perseverance that is usually admired or stubborn continuance that is usually annoying; **tenacity** and **pertinacity** both imply firmness in holding to some purpose, action, or belief, but **tenacity** suggests that such firmness is admirable, while **pertinacity** suggests a being obstinate in a way that annoys

petty is applied to that which is small, minor, unimportant, etc. compared with others of its kind, and it is often used to imply small-mindedness [*petty* cash, a *petty* grudge]; **trivial** applies to that which, because it is both petty and ordinary, has no special value [a *trivial* remark]; **trifling** applies to something so small and unimportant that it can be ignored [a *trifling* matter]; **paltry** is applied to something so small or worthless that it deserves contempt [a *paltry* wage]; **picayune** is used of a person or thing thought of as small, mean, or insignificant [a *picayune* objection]

pity implies sorrow felt for another's suffering or misfortune and sometimes suggests slight contempt as well, because the person's troubles are considered to be the result of his own weakness or inferiority [she felt *pity* for a person so ignorant]; **compassion** implies pity along with an urge to help or spare [he was moved by *compassion* and did not demand payment of the debt]; **sympathy** implies a feeling of such closeness to another that one is able to understand and even share emotionally his sorrow, etc. [he always turned to his wife for *sympathy*]

pleasant and **pleasing** are both applied to the effect of giving satisfaction or delight, but **pleasant** stresses the effect produced [a *pleasant* smile] and **pleasing,** the ability to produce such an effect [her *pleasing* ways]; **agreeable** is used of that which suits one's personal likes, mood, etc. [*agreeable* music]; **enjoyable** implies the ability to give enjoyment or pleasure [an *enjoyable* picnic]; **gratifying** implies the ability to give pleasure by satisfying one's wishes, hopes, etc. [a *gratifying* experience]

plentiful implies a large or full supply [a *plentiful* supply of books]; **abundant** implies a very plentiful or very large supply [a forest *abundant* in wild game]; **copious,** now used chiefly to refer to quantity produced, used, etc., implies a rich or continuing abundance [a *copious* harvest, discharge, etc.]; **profuse** implies a giving or pouring forth abundantly or very generously, often beyond what is needed or wanted [*profuse* in his thanks]; **ample** applies to that which is large enough to meet all demands [his savings are *ample* to see him through this crisis]

pliable and **pliant** both suggest something that can be easily bent, as a thin wooden stick, and in a more general way, a nature that gives in or adapts easily; **plastic** is used of substances, such as plaster or clay, that can be molded into various shapes which they keep after they become hard, and is also used of persons who can be easily influenced or persuaded; **ductile** suggests that which can be drawn or stretched out [copper is a *ductile* metal]; **malleable** suggests that which can be hammered, beaten, or pressed into various forms [copper is *malleable* as well as ductile]

ponder implies a weighing mentally and suggests careful consideration of a matter from all sides [to *ponder* over a problem]; **meditate** suggests quiet, deep study or thought [he *meditated* on the state of the world] or careful thinking about some plan [to *meditate* revenge]; **muse** implies a dreamlike series of thoughts [to *muse* over the past]; **ruminate** suggests turning a matter over and over in the mind [the loser *ruminated* on the cause of his defeat]

position is used of any kind of work done for salary or wages, but often only of work done by a white-collar or professional worker; **situation** now usually refers to a position that needs to be filled or to one that is desired [*situation* wanted as salesman]; **office** refers to a position that gives one authority or power, esp. in government, a corporation, etc.; a **post** is a position or office that carries important responsibilities, esp. one to which a person is appointed; **job** is now the common, basic term which can be used in place of any of the preceding terms

possible is used of anything that may exist, occur, be done, etc., depending on circumstances [a *possible* solution to a problem]; **practicable** applies to that which can easily be brought about under the existing conditions or by the means available [a *practicable* plan]; **feasible** is used of anything that is likely to be carried through to a successful conclusion and, thus, may seem worth doing [a *feasible* enterprise]

praise is the simple, basic word that refers to the expressing of approval, respect, or admiration [to *praise* a student's work]; **laud** implies great, sometimes excessive praise [the critics *lauded* the actor to the skies]; **extol** implies high, often formal praise that is meant to make the one who receives it feel proud and happy [the scientist was *extolled* for his work]; **eulogize** suggests formal praise in a speech or writing, esp. of someone who has recently died

presume implies a taking something for granted or accepting it as true, usually on the basis of probable evidence in its favor and the absence of proof against it [the man is *presumed* to be of sound mind]; **presuppose** suggests a taking something for granted without good reason [this writer *presupposes* too large a vocabulary in children]; **assume** implies the taking of something for granted as a basis for argument or action [let us *assume* his motives were good]; **postulate** implies the assuming of something as an underlying factor, often something that cannot be proved [his argument *postulates* the natural goodness of man]

previous generally implies a coming before in time or order [a *previous* meeting]; **prior** adds to this the idea of greater importance or claim as a result of being first [a *prior* obligation]; **preceding,** esp. when used with the definite article, implies a coming just before [the *preceding* night]; **antecedent** adds to the meaning of **previous** the idea of directly causing what follows [events *antecedent* to the war]; **foregoing** applies specif. to something previously said or written [the *foregoing* examples]; **former** always implies a comparison between the first and the last (called *latter*) of two persons or things just mentioned

prone, in strict use, implies a position in which one lies on one's belly [he fell *prone* upon the ground and drank from the brook]; **supine** implies a position in which one lies on one's back, and may suggest a listless feeling or passive attitude [lying *supine* on the grass and gazing lazily at the clouds]; **prostrate** implies the position of one thrown or lying flat in a prone or supine position or the state of one completely beaten, helpless, exhausted, etc. [the victim lay *prostrate* at his attacker's feet]; **recumbent** suggests a lying down or back in any position one might assume for rest or sleep [she was *recumbent* upon the couch]

punish implies making a wrongdoer suffer for his wrongdoing by paying a penalty, usually with no idea of reforming or correcting him [to *punish* a murderer by hanging him]; **discipline** suggests punishment that is intended to control the wrongdoer or to establish in him habits of self-control [to *discipline* a naughty child]; **correct** suggests punishment of a wrongdoer for the purpose of overcoming his faults [to *correct* unruly pupils]; **chastise** implies punishment, usually physical punishment, along with an attempt to correct the wrongdoer

push implies the use of force or pressure by a person or thing in contact with the object to be moved ahead, aside, etc. [to *push* a baby carriage]; **shove** implies a pushing of something so as to force it to slide along a surface, or it suggests rough handling in pushing [*shove* the box into the corner]; to **thrust** is to push with sudden, often violent force, sometimes so as to put one thing into another [he *thrust* his hand into the water]; **propel** implies a driving forward of something by a force that makes it move [the wind *propelled* the sailboat]

puzzle implies that a problem, situation, etc. is so involved or complicated that it is very hard or difficult to understand or solve; **perplex,** in addition, implies uncertainty or even worry as to what to think, say, or do; **confuse** implies a being mixed up mentally to a greater or lesser degree; **confound** implies a being so confused that one is completely frustrated or greatly astonished; **bewilder** implies such complete confusion in one's mind that one can no longer think clearly

quarrel implies a sharp disagreement full of angry words and feeling and often suggests that those arguing become unfriendly; **wrangle** suggests a noisy, fairly lengthy dispute in which each person stubbornly refuses to change his mind; **altercation** suggests a heated argument which may or may not come to blows; **squabble** implies undignified, childish arguing over a small matter; **spat** is the colloquial word for a petty quarrel and suggests a brief, angry outburst that has little lasting effect

range refers to the full extent over which something is recognizable, effective, etc. [the *range* of his knowledge]; **reach** refers to the furthest limit of effectiveness, influence, etc. [beyond the *reach* of my understanding]; **scope** is used of the area covered by a particular activity, written work, etc. having set limits [does it fall within the *scope* of this dictionary?]; **compass** suggests completeness within limits thought of as the outer edge of a circle [he did all within the *compass* of his power]; **gamut,** in this connection, refers to the full range of shades, tones, etc. within the limits of something [the full *gamut* of emotions]

rational implies the ability to reason in an orderly, carefully controlled way so as to reach conclusions logically without being swayed by emotion [Holmes's *rational* explanation of the mysterious events]; **reasonable** suggests the calm, careful use of the mind in making decisions, choices, etc. that are fair and practical [the teacher was *reasonable* in the amount of homework she required]; **sensible** implies the use of common sense based on sound judgment and practical experience [a *sensible* man who bought no more than he needed]

rebellion implies organized, armed, open resistance to the authority or government in power, and, when applied to a historical event, suggests that it failed [Shay's *Rebellion*]; **revolution** applies to a rebellion that succeeds in overthrowing an old government and establishing a new one [the American *Revolution*] or to any movement that brings about a drastic change in society [the Industrial *Revolution*]; **insurrection** suggests an outbreak that is smaller in scope and less well organized than a rebellion [the Philippine *Insurrection*]; **revolt** stresses a casting off of allegiance or a refusal to submit to established authority [a *revolt* of students against the dress code]; **mutiny** applies to a forcible revolt of soldiers or, especially, sailors against their officers [*mutiny* on the Bounty]; **uprising** is a simple, direct term for any outbreak against a government and applies specifically to a small, limited action or to the beginning of a general rebellion [local *uprisings* against the Stamp Act]

recover implies a finding or getting back something that one has lost in any manner [to *recover* stolen property, one's self-control, etc.]; **regain** emphasizes a struggle to win back something that has been taken from one [to *regain* a hill from the enemy]; **retrieve** suggests that something is beyond easy reach and requires some effort to get it back [he was determined to *retrieve* his honor]

regard usually implies a judging of someone or something according to its worth or value [the book is highly *regarded* by critics]; **respect** implies a judging to have great worth or high value, as shown by courtesy or honor [a jurist *respected* by lawyers]; **esteem,** in addition, suggests that the person or object is highly prized or desired [a friend *esteemed* for his loyalty]; **admire** suggests a feeling of enthusiastic delight in appreciating something or someone that is superior [one must *admire* such courage]

relevant implies a close, logical relationship with, and importance to, the matter being considered [*relevant* testimony]; **germane** implies such close natural connection as to be highly suitable or fitting [your memories are not really *germane* to this discussion]; **pertinent** implies an immediate and direct bearing on the matter at hand [a *pertinent* suggestion]; **apposite** applies to that which is both relevant and happily suitable or fitting [referring to an *apposite* passage in Shakespeare]; **apropos** is used of that which is right for the purpose as well as relevant [an *apropos* remark]

reliable is used of a person or thing that can be counted upon to do what is expected or required [his *reliable* assistant]; **dependable** refers to a person or thing that can be depended on, as in an emergency, and often suggests personal loyalty, levelheadedness, or steadiness [she is a *dependable* friend]; **trustworthy** applies to a person, or sometimes a thing, whose truthfulness, honesty, carefulness, etc. one has complete confidence in [a *trustworthy* source of information]; **trusty** applies to a person or thing that has in the past always been trustworthy or dependable [his *trusty* horse]

reluctant implies an unwillingness to do something, as because of dislike, uncertainty, etc. [she was *reluctant* to marry]; **disinclined** suggests a lack of desire for something, as because it fails to suit one's taste [I feel *disinclined* to argue]; **hesitant** implies a holding back from action, as because of caution, uncertainty, etc. [don't be *hesitant* about asking]; **loath** suggests a strong feeling of unwillingness [I am *loath* to depart]; **averse** suggests a deep-seated, long-lasting unwillingness [she is *averse* to borrowing money]

remark applies to a brief, more or less casual statement of opinion, etc., as in calling attention to something [a *remark* about her clothes]; an **observation** is an expression of opinion on something to which one has given special attention and thought [the warden's *observations* on prison reform]; a **comment** is a remark or observation made in explaining, criticizing, or interpreting something [*comments* on a novel]

remember implies a putting oneself in mind of something, often suggesting that the thing stays so vividly alive in the memory that one becomes conscious of it without effort [he'll *remember* this day]; **recall** and **recollect** both imply some effort to bring something back to mind, **recall,** in addition, often suggesting that one tells others what is brought back [let me *recall* what was said; to *recollect* the days of one's childhood]

replace implies a taking the place of someone or something that is now lost, gone, destroyed, worn out, etc. [we *replace* defective tubes]; **displace** suggests the forcing or driving out of a person or thing by another that replaces it [he had been *displaced* in her affections by another man]; **supersede** implies a replacing with something superior, more up-to-date, etc. [the steamship *superseded* the sailing ship]; **supplant** suggests a displacing that involves force, trickery, or an introduction of new methods [the prince had been *supplanted* by an imposter]

restrain suggests the use of strong force or authority either in preventing, or in putting down or controlling, some action [try to *restrain* your enthusiasm]; **curb, check,** and **bridle** get their meanings from the various uses of a horse's harness, **curb** implying a sudden, sharp action to bring something under control [to *curb* one's tongue], **check** implying a slowing up of action or progress [to *check* inflationary trends], and **bridle** suggesting a holding in of emotion, feelings, etc. [to *bridle* one's envy]; **inhibit,** as used in psychology, implies a holding down or keeping back of some thought or emotion [her natural warmth and affection had become *inhibited*]

ridicule implies a making fun of a person or thing by way of showing disapproval [he *ridiculed* her new hat]; **deride** suggests contempt for or a strong dislike of what is being made fun of [to *deride* another's beliefs]; **mock** suggests a ridiculing by the unkind imitation of another's mannerisms or habits [it is cruel to *mock* his lisp]; **taunt** implies insulting ridicule, esp. as shown by jeering at another and harping on something that makes him feel ashamed [they *taunted* him about his failure]

rise and **arise** both imply a coming into being, action, notice, etc., but **rise** carries an added suggestion of upward movement [empires *rise* and fall] and **arise** is often used to show a cause-and-effect relationship [accidents *arise* from carelessness]

roam implies a traveling about without a fixed goal over a large area and carries suggestions of freedom, pleasure, etc. [to *roam* about the country]; **ramble** implies an idle moving or walking about, esp. in a carefree or aimless way [we *rambled* through the woods]; **rove** suggests a wandering over a wide area, but usually implies a special purpose or activity [a *roving* reporter; *roving* bands of looters]; **range** stresses the wide area covered and sometimes suggests a search for something [hunters *ranging* the western plains]; **meander** is used of streams, paths, etc., and, less often, of people and animals, that follow a winding, seemingly aimless course

rural is the general word referring to life on the farm or in the country as distinguished from life in the city [*rural* schools]; **rustic** emphasizes the contrast between the supposed crudeness and lack of sophistication of country people and the polish and refinement of city people [*rustic* humor]; **pastoral** suggests an ideally simple sort of life as lived in the country, originally by shepherds; **bucolic,** in contrast, suggests a down-to-earth, rustic simplicity or crudeness [her *bucolic* suitor]

sarcastic implies a deliberate attempt to hurt by ridicule, mocking, sneers, etc. [a *sarcastic* reminder that work begins at 9:00 A.M.]; **ironical** or **ironic** is used of a form of sarcasm in which the meaning of what is said is directly opposite to the usual sense ["My, you're early," was his *ironical* taunt to the latecomer]; **sardonic** implies sneering or mocking bitterness in a person, or, more often, in what he says or how he looks [a *sardonic* smile]; **caustic** implies a cutting, biting, or stinging wit or sarcasm [a *caustic* tongue]

satisfy implies the fact of meeting wishes, needs, expectations, etc. fully; **content** implies a filling of needs to the degree that one is not disturbed by a desire for something more [it takes great wealth to *satisfy* him, but she is *contented* with their modest but steady income]

scream is the general word for a loud, high, piercing cry, made as in fear, pain, or anger; **shriek** suggests a sharper, more sudden or anguished cry than **scream** and is also used of loud, high-pitched, uncontrolled laughter; **screech** suggests a shrill or harsh cry that is painful or unpleasant to hear

sentimental suggests emotion of a kind that is felt in a longing or tender mood [*sentimental* music] or emotion that is exaggerated, artificial, foolish, etc. [a trashy, *sentimental* novel]; **romantic** suggests emotion stirred up by that which appeals to the imagination as it is influenced by stories of love and adventure [a *romantic* girl waiting for her knight in shining armor]; that is **mawkish** which is sentimental in a disgustingly weak, insincere, or exaggerated way [the *mawkish* lyrics of a popular love song]; that is **maudlin** which is tearfully or weakly sentimental in a foolish way [to become *maudlin* when drunk]

sharp and **keen** both apply to that which is cutting, biting, penetrating, or piercing, as because of having a very thin edge, but **sharp** may imply a harsh, disagreeable cutting quality [a *sharp* pain, tongue, etc.] and **keen,** a pleasantly biting or stimulating quality [*keen* wit, delight, etc.]; **acute** is used literally to describe an angle or end formed by lines or edges that meet in a sharp point, but may be used to suggest a very clear awareness of small differences [*acute* hearing, an *acute* intelligence] or the quality of being sharply painful to the feelings [*acute* distress]

shrewd implies a keen mind, sharp insight, and often a crafty approach in practical matters [a *shrewd* comment, businessman, etc.]; **sagacious** implies a keen insight and far-sighted judgment [a *sagacious* adviser]; **perspicacious** suggests the keen mental vision or judgment that helps one clearly to see and understand what is vague, hidden, etc. [a *perspicacious* judge of character]; **astute** implies shrewdness combined with wisdom [an *astute* politician]

silly implies ridiculous or unthinking behavior that seems to show a lack of common sense, good judgment, or seriousness [it was *silly* of you to dress so lightly]; **stupid** implies slowness in thinking or a lack of normal intelligence [he is *stupid* to believe that]; **fatuous** suggests stupidity or dullness joined with smug, mistaken satisfaction with the way things are [a *fatuous* smile]; **asinine** implies the extreme stupidity traditionally thought of as characteristic of the ass, or donkey [an *asinine* argument]

small and **little** are often used interchangeably, but **small** is preferred in referring to something of slightly less than the usual size, amount, value, importance, etc. [a *small* man, tax, matter, etc.] and **little** is more often used when no comparison is being stressed [he has his *little* faults], in expressing tenderness [his *little* sister], and in suggesting unimportance, pettiness, etc. [of *little* interest]; **diminutive** implies extreme, sometimes delicate, smallness or littleness [a *diminutive* teacup]; **minute** and the more informal **tiny** suggest that which is extremely diminutive, often to the degree that it can be noticed only by looking very closely [a *minute,* or *tiny,* difference]; **miniature** applies to a copy, model, etc. on a very small scale [*miniature* paintings]; **petite** refers specifically to a girl or woman who is small and trim in figure

sorrow refers to the deep, long-lasting mental pain caused by loss, disappointment, etc. [his secret, life-long *sorrow*]; **grief** suggests briefer, more intense mental pain resulting from a particular misfortune, disaster, etc. [her *grief* over the loss of her child]; **woe** suggests grief or misery so intense that it cannot be relieved [the war-torn nation's *woe*]

speech is the general word for a piece on some subject spoken before an audience, with or without preparation; **address** implies a formal, carefully prepared speech and usually suggests that the speaker or the speech is important [an *address* to a legislature]; **oration** suggests an eloquent, sometimes merely pompous and showy speech, esp. one delivered on some special occasion [a Fourth of July *oration*]; a **lecture** is a carefully prepared speech intended to inform or instruct the audience [a *lecture* to a college class]; **talk** suggests informality and is applied either to an unprepared speech or to an address or lecture in which the speaker purposely uses a simple, conversational approach

steep suggests a slope so sharp that it makes going up or down difficult [a *steep* hill]; **abrupt** implies a very sharp incline in a surface that breaks off suddenly from the level [an *abrupt* bank at the river's edge]; **precipitous** suggests the sudden, almost vertical drop of a precipice [*precipitous* canyon walls that few men could climb]; **sheer** indicates an incline that is straight up and down, or almost so, with a surface that is smooth and unbroken [cliffs falling *sheer* to the sea]

strong is the most general of these terms, implying power that can be used actively as well as power that resists destruction [a *strong* body, fortress, etc.]; **stout** implies ability to stand strain, pressure, wear, etc. without breaking down or giving way [a *stout* rope, heart, etc.]; **sturdy** suggests the strength of that which is solidly developed or built and thus difficult to shake, weaken, etc. [*sturdy* oaks, faith, etc.]; **tough** suggests the strength of that which is firm and resistant in quality [*tough* leather, opposition, etc.]; **stalwart** emphasizes firmness, loyalty, or reliability [a *stalwart* supporter]

stupid implies such lack of intelligence or inability to understand, learn, etc. as might be shown by one in a mental daze [a *stupid* answer]; **dull** implies a mental slowness that may be in one's makeup or may result from overfatigue, illness, etc. [the fever left him *dull* and listless]; **dense** suggests lack of sensitivity or an irritating failure to understand quickly or to react intelligently [too *dense* to take a hint]; **slow** suggests that the quickness to learn, but not necessarily the ability to learn, is below average [a pupil *slow* in his studies]

summit refers to the topmost point of a hill or similar high place or to the highest reachable level, as of achievement or rank; **peak** refers to the highest of a number of high points, as in a mountain range or in some changing action or condition [at the *peak* of his powers as a writer]; **climax** applies to the highest point in interest, force, excitement, etc. in a scale of rising values; **acme** refers to the highest possible point of perfection in the development or progress of something; **apex** suggests the highest point of a geometric figure or of a career, process, etc.; **pinnacle,** in its figurative uses, can be substituted for **summit** or **peak,** but sometimes suggests a dizzy or unsteady height [the *pinnacle* of success]; **zenith** refers to the highest point in the heavens and thus suggests fame or success reached by a spectacular rise

surprise, in this connection, implies a causing wonder because unexpected, unusual, etc. [I'm *surprised* at your concern]; **astonish** implies a surprising with something that seems unbelievable [to *astonish* with magic tricks]; **amaze** suggests an astonishing that causes confusion [*amazed* at the sudden turn of events]; **astound** suggests shocking astonishment that leaves one unable to act or think [I was *astounded* when he offered me a bribe]

talent implies a natural ability to do a certain thing and suggests that the ability has been or can be developed through training, practice, etc. [a *talent* for drawing]; **gift** suggests a special ability that is thought of as having been given, as by nature, rather than gotten through effort [a *gift* for making friends]; **aptitude** implies a special ability which makes it likely that one can do a certain kind of work easily and well [*aptitude* tests]; **faculty** implies a special ability or skill that is either natural or acquired [she has developed the *faculty* of getting along with others]; **knack** implies an ability, gained through practice or experience, to do something easily and cleverly [the *knack* of writing limericks]; **genius** may imply any great natural ability [he has a *genius* for always saying the right thing], but more often suggests an extraordinary natural power to do creative, original work in the arts or sciences [the *genius* of Leonardo da Vinci]

theory, as compared here, implies a general principle for which there is much evidence explaining how something works or comes to be [the *theory* of evolution]; **hypothesis** implies an explanation which, although there is little evidence for it, is assumed to be true, esp. as a basis for further experimenting [the nebular *hypothesis*]; **law** implies an exact principle that has been worked out by observing how certain events in nature occur over and over again under the same conditions [the *law* of the conservation of energy]

throw is the general word meaning to cause to move through the air by a rapid movement of the arm, etc.; **cast,** the preferred word in special uses [to *cast* a fishing line], generally has a more archaic or formal quality [they *cast* stones at him]; to **toss** is to throw lightly or carelessly and, usually, with an upward or sidewise motion [to *toss* a coin]; **hurl** and **fling** both imply a throwing with force or violence, but **hurl** suggests that the object thrown moves swiftly for some distance [to *hurl* a spear], while **fling** suggests that the object is thrust sharply so that it strikes a surface with considerable force [she *flung* the plate to the floor]; **pitch** implies a throwing with a definite aim or in a definite direction [to *pitch* a baseball]

transform implies a change either in outer form or inner nature, in use, etc. [she was *transformed* into a happy girl]; **transmute** suggests a change in basic nature that seems almost like a miracle [*transmuted* from a shy youth into a man about town]; **convert** implies a change in details so as to be suitable for a new use [to *convert* an attic into an apartment]; **metamorphose** suggests a surprising change produced as if by magic [a tadpole is *metamorphosed* into a frog]; **transfigure** implies a change in outward appearance which seems to make splendid or glorious [her plain features were *transfigured* with tenderness]

trite is applied to an expression or idea which has been used so often that it has lost its original freshness and force (e.g., "like a bolt from the blue"); **hackneyed** refers to expressions which through constant use have become just about meaningless (e.g., "last but not least"); **stereotyped** applies to those fixed expressions which seem almost sure to be used in certain situations (e.g., "I point with pride" in a political speech); **commonplace** is used of any obvious remark or idea that is familiar to just about everybody and is used merely as a matter of course and without any real thought (e.g., "it isn't the heat, it's the humidity")

turn, the most general word here, implies motion around, or partly around, a center or axis [a wheel *turns*]; **rotate** implies movement of a body around its own center or axis [the earth *rotates* on its axis]; **revolve** is sometimes substituted for **rotate,** but in exact use it suggests movement, usually circular or elliptical, around a center outside itself [the earth *revolves* around the sun]; **gyrate** implies movement in a spiral course, as by a tornado; **spin** and **whirl** suggest very fast and continuous rotation or revolution [a top *spins;* the leaves *whirled* about the yard]

universal is used of that which applies to every case or individual, without exception, in the class, category, etc. concerned [a *universal* practice among primitive peoples]; **general** refers to that which applies to all or nearly all of the members of a group or class [a *general* favorite among college students]; **generic** is used of that which applies to every member of a class or, specif. in biology, of a genus [a *generic* name]

use implies the putting of a thing into action or service for a given purpose, esp. its intended purpose, or, in the case of a person treated as a thing, for one's own selfish purposes [to *use* a pencil, a suggestion, etc.; he *used* his brother to advance himself]; **employ,** a more formal term, implies the putting to useful work of something not in use at that moment [to *employ* a vacant lot as a playground] and with reference to persons, suggests a providing of work and pay [he *employs* five mechanics]; **utilize** implies the putting of something to a practical or profitable use [to *utilize* by-products]

vagrant refers to a person without a fixed home who wanders about from place to place, supporting himself by begging, etc., and in legal usage refers to any person, as a prostitute or disorderly person, whose way of living may cause him to be arrested; **vagabond,** orig. implying laziness, roguishness, etc., now often suggests no more than a carefree, roaming existence; **bum, tramp,** and **hobo** are informal substitutes for **vagrant** and **vagabond,** in some senses, but **bum** specifically brings to mind a homeless drunkard who never works, **tramp,** a vagrant who lives by begging or by doing odd jobs, and **hobo,** a migratory laborer who follows seasonal work

view is the general word for that which can be seen [the *view* is cut off by the next building]; **prospect** suggests a view from a position that allows one to look out over a wide area and to a great distance [a grand *prospect* of snowy mountains and deep valleys]; **scene** suggests an attractive or dramatic view of objects, persons, etc. placed or arranged as they might be in a painting or a play [a peaceful country *scene*]; **vista** suggests a distant view seen through a long, narrow passage [at the end of the valley lay a *vista* of rolling hills and winding rivers]

wage (or **wages**) applies to money paid an employee at regular periods of time, as at hourly or piecework rates, esp. for skilled or manual labor; **salary** applies to fixed amounts usually paid monthly or twice a month, esp. to clerical or professional workers; **stipend** is a somewhat overly formal substitute for **salary,** or it is applied to a fixed payment, as an amount of money granted to a student; **fee** applies to the payment requested or given for professional services, as of a doctor, lawyer, etc.; **pay** is the general term that may be substituted for any of these words

weak, the most general of these words, implies having very little, or less than normal, physical, mental, or moral strength [a *weak* muscle, mind, character, etc.]; **feeble** is used of that which is so weak or ineffective as to be pitiable [a *feeble* old man; a *feeble* joke]; **frail** refers to that which is extremely delicate or weak, or easily broken or shattered [a *frail* body; *frail* support]; **infirm** suggests a loss of strength or soundness, as through illness or old age [his *infirm,* old grandfather]; **decrepit** implies a being broken down or worn out, as by old age or long use [a *decrepit* old horse; a *decrepit* sofa]

wise implies the ability to judge and deal with persons, situations, etc. rightly, based on a broad range of knowledge, experience, and understanding [a *wise* parent]; **sage** suggests the great wisdom of age, experience, and philosophical thought [*sage* advice]; **judicious** implies the ability to make wise decisions based on sound judgment [a *judicious* approach to a problem]; **prudent** suggests the wisdom of one who is able to recognize the most suitable or careful course of action in practical matters [a *prudent* policy]

wit refers to the ability to see contradictions, weaknesses, etc. in people and things and to make quick, sharp, often sarcastic remarks about them that delight or entertain; **humor** is applied to the ability to see and express that which is comical, or ridiculous, but suggests a kindly or sympathetic quality in the use of this ability to amuse others; **irony** refers to the humor that is implied in the difference between what is actually said and the meaning that is intended, or in the difference between appearance and reality in life

worth and **value** both refer to the amount of money or goods a thing can be exchanged for [the *worth* or *value* of the jewels]; when the terms are distinguished, **worth** refers to the basic excellence of a thing as judged by its moral or cultural qualities and the like, while **value** refers to excellence as measured by how useful, important, profitable, etc. a thing is [the true *worth* of Shakespeare's plays cannot be measured by their *value* to the commercial theater]

zealot implies great, often too great, devotion to a cause and intense activity in its support [*zealots* of reform]; **fanatic** suggests the unreasonable attitude of one who goes to any length to preserve or carry out his beliefs [an anti-smoking *fanatic*]; an **enthusiast** is one who shows a strong, eager, lively interest in an activity, cause, etc. [a sports *enthusiast*]